Philips' UNIVERSAL ATLAS

Philips'
UNIVERSAL
ATLAS

Edited by **B.M. Willett,** B.A.,
Cartographic Editor

George Philip

London—Melbourne—Milwaukee

British Library Cataloguing in Publication Data
Philips' universal atlas.— 4th ed.
1. Atlases, British
I. Universal atlas
912   G1021

ISBN
0 540 05430 5

Printed in Great Britain by
George Philip Printers Limited, London

Acknowledgment is made to the following for providing the photographs used in this atlas.
Air India, Australian Information Service, Brazilian Embassy, London, British Aircraft Corporation, British
Airways, British Leyland, British Petroleum, British Rail, British Steel Corporation, British Tourist Authority,
Central Electricity Generating Board, D. Chanter, Danish Embassy, London, Egypt Air, Fiat (England) Ltd.,
Finnish Tourist Bureau, Freightliners Ltd.,   H. Fullard,   M. H. Fullard,   Gas Council Exploration Ltd.,
Commander H. R. Hatfield/Astro Books, H. Hawes, Israeli Govt. Tourist Office, Japan Air Lines, Lufthansa,
M.A.T. Transport Ltd., Meteorological Office, London, Moroccan Tourist Office, N.A.S.A. (Space Frontiers),
National Coal Board, London,   National Maritime Museum, London,   Offshore Co.,   Pan American World
Airways, Royal Astronomical Society, London, Shell International Petroleum Co. Ltd., Swan Hunter Group,
Ltd., Swiss National Tourist Office, B. M. Willett, Woodmansterne Ltd.

Preface

The **Universal Atlas** is far more than a collection of maps of the world and contains a wealth of other information that greatly enhances its value as a work of reference. The major part of the book is the map section and the detailed index that accompanies it, but additional material includes an illustrated introduction to the evolution of the earth, world resources and economic activity, and statistics on world climates, population and economies. This material is arranged so that it can be easily consulted by the reader who wants an answer to a specific question but the presentation will also appeal to the casual browser.

The maps are arranged in continental sections, each of which is introduced by a physical and a political map of the continent as a whole, together with maps showing climate and population. These are followed by regional maps giving coverage at a larger scale. For example, all of Western Europe is covered at a scale of 1:2.5 M, while Great Britain is at a scale of 1:1 M; all of the United States is covered at scales of 1:6 M with enlargements of the East and California at 1:3 M. On a world basis, thematic maps are provided to show structure and geology, world climates and population.

The place name forms are those that are used locally. The English conventional form often appears on the map, and in the index this name is cross-referenced to the local spelling. In the case of those parts of the world that do not use a Roman script, the names have been transcribed according to the accepted systems of transcription. Chinese place names have been transcribed using the Wade-Giles system, but as the Pinyin system is increasingly used in the West a list relating Wade-Giles to Pinyin has been included at the end of the index. In the Pinyin system, to quote one example, Peking appears as Beijing.

International boundaries are drawn to show the *de facto* situation. This does not signify international recognition of that boundary but shows the limits of administration on either side of the line. The maps also show cease-fire lines which are specially labelled.

The contents page has been designed to help the reader find what he or she is looking for quickly. This not only gives a list of map titles but also includes an outline map of each continent showing the areas covered by the large-scale maps. The index will, of course, give the page number and geographic coordinates for any particular location.

In the illustrated section which precedes the maps, maps, diagrams and photographs are used to present the background to the physical, human and economic geography of the world. The data in the statistical section have all be fully revised for this edition and are a useful source of material on the economies of the principal countries of the world. The locations chosen for climatic statistics have been selected to illustrate the variety of world climates. The reader can use these figures to get some idea of what the weather will be like if they are visiting places abroad.

Contents

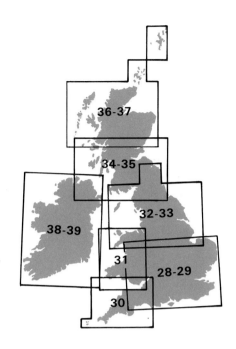

Europe

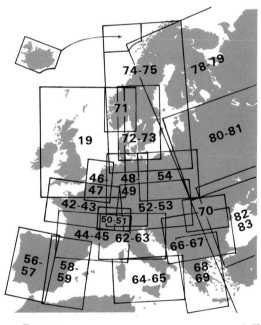

Asia

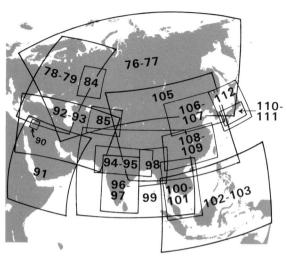

Africa

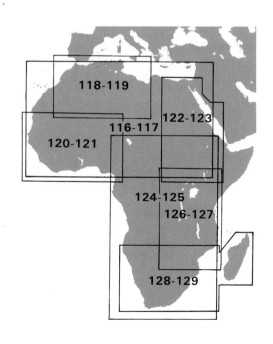

Australasia

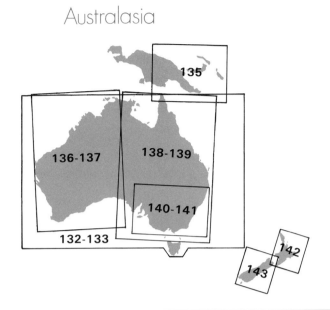

The Americas

Index

Climatic Statistics—1

These four pages give temperature and precipitation statistics for over 80 stations, which are arranged by listing the continents and the places within each continent in alphabetical order. The elevation of each station, in metres above mean sea level, is stated beneath its name. The average monthly temperature, in degrees Celsius, and the average monthly precipitation, in millimetres, are given. To the right, the average yearly rainfall, the average yearly temperature, and the annual range of temperature (the difference between the warmest and the coldest months) are also stated.

AFRICA

		Jan.	Feb.	Mar.	Apr.	May	June	July	Aug.	Sept.	Oct.	Nov.	Dec.	Year	Annual Range
Addis Ababa, Ethiopia	Precipitation	201	206	239	102	28	<3	0	<3	3	25	135	213	1 151	
2 450 m	Temperature	19	20	20	20	19	18	18	19	21	22	21	20	20	4
Cairo, Egypt	Precipitation	5	5	5	3	3	<3	0	0	<3	<3	3	5	28	
116 m	Temperature	13	15	18	21	25	28	28	28	26	24	20	15	22	15
Cape Town, South Africa	Precipitation	15	8	18	48	79	84	89	66	43	31	18	10	508	
17 m	Temperature	21	21	20	17	14	13	12	13	14	16	18	19	17	9
Casablanca, Morocco	Precipitation	53	48	56	36	23	5	0	<3	8	38	66	71	404	
50 m	Temperature	13	13	14	16	18	20	22	23	22	19	16	13	18	10
Johannesburg, South Africa	Precipitation	114	109	89	38	25	8	8	8	23	56	107	125	709	
1 665 m	Temperature	20	20	18	16	13	10	11	13	16	18	19	20	16	10
Khartoum, Sudan	Precipitation	<3	<3	<3	<3	3	8	53	71	18	5	<3	0	158	
390 m	Temperature	24	25	28	31	33	34	32	31	32	32	28	25	29	9
Kinshasa, Zaire	Precipitation	135	145	196	196	158	8	3	3	31	119	221	142	1 354	
325 m	Temperature	26	26	27	27	26	24	23	24	25	26	26	26	25	4
Lagos, Nigeria	Precipitation	28	46	102	150	269	460	279	64	140	206	69	25	1 836	
3 m	Temperature	27	28	29	28	28	26	26	25	26	26	28	28	27	4
Lusaka, Zambia	Precipitation	231	191	142	18	3	<3	<3	0	<3	10	91	150	836	
1 277 m	Temperature	21	22	21	21	19	16	16	18	22	24	23	22	21	8
Monrovia, Liberia	Precipitation	31	56	97	216	516	973	996	373	744	772	236	130	5 138	
23 m	Temperature	26	26	27	27	26	25	24	25	25	25	26	26	26	3
Nairobi, Kenya	Precipitation	38	64	125	211	158	46	15	23	31	53	109	86	958	
1 820 m	Temperature	19	19	19	19	18	16	16	16	18	19	18	18	18	3
Tananarive, Madagascar	Precipitation	300	279	178	53	18	8	8	10	18	61	135	287	1 356	
1 372 m	Temperature	21	21	21	19	18	15	14	15	17	19	21	21	19	7
Timbuktu, Mali	Precipitation	<3	<3	3	<3	5	23	79	81	38	3	<3	<3	231	
301 m	Temperature	22	24	28	32	34	35	32	30	32	31	28	23	29	13
Tunis, Tunisia	Precipitation	64	51	41	36	18	8	3	8	33	51	48	61	419	
66 m	Temperature	10	11	13	16	19	23	26	27	25	20	16	11	18	17
Walvis Bay, South Africa	Precipitation	<3	5	8	3	3	<3	<3	3	<3	<3	<3	<3	23	
7 m	Temperature	19	19	19	18	17	16	15	14	14	15	17	18	18	5

AMERICA, NORTH

		Jan.	Feb.	Mar.	Apr.	May	June	July	Aug.	Sept.	Oct.	Nov.	Dec.	Year	Annual Range
Anchorage, Alaska, U.S.A.	Precipitation	20	18	15	10	13	18	41	66	66	56	25	23	371	
40 m	Temperature	−11	−8	−5	2	7	12	14	13	9	2	−5	−11	2	25
Cheyenne, Wyo., U.S.A.	Precipitation	10	15	25	48	61	41	53	41	31	25	13	13	376	
1 871 m	Temperature	−4	−3	1	5	10	16	19	19	14	7	1	−2	7	23
Chicago, Ill., U.S.A.	Precipitation	51	51	66	71	86	89	84	81	79	66	61	51	836	
251 m	Temperature	−4	−3	2	9	14	20	23	22	19	12	5	−1	10	27
Churchill, Man., Canada	Precipitation	13	15	23	23	23	48	56	69	58	36	28	18	406	
13 m	Temperature	−28	−27	−21	−10	−1	6	12	11	5	−3	−15	−24	−8	40

	Jan.	Feb.	Mar.	Apr.	May	June	July	Aug.	Sept.	Oct.	Nov.	Dec.	Year	Annual range
Edmonton, Alta., Canada														
Precipitation	23	15	20	23	46	78	84	58	33	18	18	20	439	
676 m Temperature	−15	−11	−5	4	11	14	16	15	10	5	−4	−11	3	31
Honolulu, Hawaii, U.S.A.														
Precipitation	104	66	79	48	25	18	23	28	36	48	64	104	643	
12 m Temperature	23	18	19	20	22	24	25	26	26	24	22	19	22	8
Houston, Tex., U.S.A.														
Precipitation	89	76	84	91	119	117	99	99	104	94	89	109	1 171	
12 m Temperature	12	13	17	21	24	27	28	29	26	22	16	12	21	17
Kingston, Jamaica														
Precipitation	23	15	23	31	102	89	38	91	99	180	74	36	800	
34 m Temperature	25	25	25	26	26	28	28	28	27	27	26	26	26	3
Los Angeles, Calif., U.S.A.														
Precipitation	79	76	71	25	10	3	<3	<3	5	15	31	66	381	
95 m Temperature	13	14	14	16	17	19	21	22	21	18	16	14	17	9
Mexico City, Mexico														
Precipitation	13	5	10	20	53	119	170	152	130	51	18	8	747	
2 309 m Temperature	12	13	16	18	19	19	17	18	18	16	14	13	16	7
Miami, Fla., U.S.A.														
Precipitation	71	53	64	81	173	178	155	160	203	234	71	51	1 516	
8 m Temperature	20	20	22	23	25	27	28	28	27	25	22	21	24	8
Montreal, Que., Canada														
Precipitation	97	76	89	66	79	86	94	89	94	86	89	91	1 036	
57 m Temperature	−10	−9	−3	5	13	19	21	19	15	8	1	−7	6	31
New York, N.Y., U.S.A.														
Precipitation	94	97	91	81	81	84	107	109	86	89	76	91	1 092	
96 m Temperature	−1	−1	3	10	16	20	23	23	21	15	7	2	8	24
St. Louis, Mo., U.S.A.														
Precipitation	58	64	89	97	114	114	89	86	81	74	71	64	1 001	
173 m Temperature	0	1	7	13	19	24	26	26	22	15	8	2	14	26
San Francisco, Calif., U.S.A.														
Precipitation	119	97	79	38	18	3	<3	<3	8	25	64	112	561	
16 m Temperature	10	12	13	13	14	15	15	15	17	16	14	11	14	7
San José, Costa Rica														
Precipitation	15	5	20	46	229	241	211	241	305	300	145	41	1 798	
1 146 m Temperature	19	19	21	21	22	21	21	21	21	20	20	19	20	2
Vancouver, B.C., Canada														
Precipitation	218	147	127	84	71	64	31	43	91	147	211	224	1 458	
14 m Temperature	3	4	6	9	13	16	18	18	14	10	6	4	10	15
Washington, D.C., U.S.A.														
Precipitation	86	76	91	84	94	99	112	109	94	74	66	79	1 064	
22 m Temperature	1	2	7	12	18	23	25	24	20	14	8	3	13	24

AMERICA, SOUTH

	Jan.	Feb.	Mar.	Apr.	May	June	July	Aug.	Sept.	Oct.	Nov.	Dec.	Year	Annual range
Antofagasta, Chile														
Precipitation	0	0	0	<3	<3	3	5	3	<3	3	<3	0	13	
94 m Temperature	21	21	20	18	16	15	14	14	15	16	18	19	17	7
Buenos Aires, Argentina														
Precipitation	79	71	109	89	76	61	56	61	79	86	84	99	950	
27 m Temperature	23	23	21	17	13	9	10	11	13	15	19	22	16	14
Caracas, Venezuela														
Precipitation	23	10	15	33	79	102	109	109	107	109	94	46	836	
1 042 m Temperature	19	19	20	21	22	21	21	21	21	21	20	20	21	3
Lima, Peru														
Precipitation	3	<3	<3	<3	5	5	8	8	8	3	3	<3	41	
120 m Temperature	23	24	24	22	19	17	17	16	17	18	19	21	20	8
Manaus, Brazil														
Precipitation	249	231	262	221	170	84	58	38	46	107	142	203	1 811	
44 m Temperature	28	28	28	27	28	28	28	28	29	29	29	28	28	2
Paraná, Brazil														
Precipitation	287	236	239	102	13	<3	3	5	28	127	231	310	1 582	
260 m Temperature	23	23	23	23	23	21	21	22	24	24	24	23	23	3
Quito, Ecuador														
Precipitation	99	112	142	175	137	43	20	31	69	112	97	79	1 115	
2 879 m Temperature	15	15	15	15	15	14	14	15	15	15	15	15	15	1
Rio de Janeiro, Brazil														
Precipitation	125	122	130	107	79	53	41	43	66	79	104	137	1 082	
61 m Temperature	26	26	25	24	22	21	21	21	21	22	23	25	23	5
Santiago, Chile														
Precipitation	3	3	5	13	64	84	76	56	31	15	8	5	358	
520 m Temperature	21	20	18	15	12	9	9	10	12	15	17	19	15	12

Climatic Statistics −2

ASIA		Jan.	Feb.	Mar.	Apr.	May	June	July	Aug.	Sept.	Oct.	Nov.	Dec.	Year	Annual range
Bahrain															
	Precipitation	8	18	13	8	<3	0	0	0	0	0	18	18	81	
5 m	Temperature	17	18	21	25	29	32	33	34	31	28	24	19	26	16
Bangkok, Thailand															
	Precipitation	8	20	36	58	198	160	160	175	305	206	66	5	1 397	
2 m	Temperature	26	28	29	30	29	29	28	28	28	28	26	25	28	5
Beirut, Lebanon															
	Precipitation	191	158	94	53	18	3	<3	<3	5	51	132	185	892	
34 m	Temperature	14	14	16	18	22	24	27	28	26	24	19	16	21	14
Bombay, India															
	Precipitation	3	3	3	<3	18	485	617	340	264	64	13	3	1 809	
11 m	Temperature	24	24	26	28	30	29	27	27	27	28	27	26	27	6
Calcutta, India															
	Precipitation	10	31	36	43	140	297	325	328	252	114	20	5	1 600	
6 m	Temperature	20	22	27	30	30	30	29	29	29	28	23	19	26	11
Colombo, Sri Lanka															
	Precipitation	89	69	147	231	371	224	135	109	160	348	315	147	2 365	
7 m	Temperature	26	26	27	28	28	27	27	27	27	27	26	26	27	2
Harbin, China															
	Precipitation	5	5	10	23	43	94	112	104	46	33	8	5	488	
160 m	Temperature	−18	−15	−5	6	13	19	22	21	14	4	−6	−16	3	40
Ho Chi Minh City, Vietnam															
	Precipitation	15	3	13	43	221	330	315	269	335	269	114	56	1 984	
9 m	Temperature	26	27	29	30	29	28	28	28	27	27	27	26	28	4
Jakarta, Indonesia															
	Precipitation	300	300	211	147	114	97	64	43	66	112	142	203	1 798	
8 m	Temperature	26	26	27	27	27	27	27	27	27	27	27	26	27	1
Hong Kong															
	Precipitation	33	46	74	137	292	394	381	361	257	114	43	31	2 162	
33 m	Temperature	16	15	18	22	26	28	28	28	27	25	21	18	23	13
Kabul, Afghanistan															
	Precipitation	31	36	94	102	20	5	3	3	<3	15	20	10	338	
1 815 m	Temperature	−3	−1	6	13	18	22	25	24	20	14	7	3	12	28
Karachi, Pakistan															
	Precipitation	13	10	8	3	3	18	81	41	13	<3	3	5	196	
4 m	Temperature	19	20	24	28	30	31	30	29	28	28	24	20	26	12
New Delhi, India															
	Precipitation	23	18	13	8	13	74	180	172	117	10	3	10	640	
218 m	Temperature	14	17	23	28	33	34	31	30	29	26	20	15	25	20
Shanghai, China															
	Precipitation	48	58	84	94	94	180	147	142	130	71	51	36	1 135	
7 m	Temperature	4	5	9	14	20	24	28	28	23	19	12	7	16	24
Singapore															
	Precipitation	252	173	193	188	173	173	170	196	178	208	254	257	2 413	
10 m	Temperature	26	27	28	28	28	28	28	27	27	27	27	27	27	2
Tehran, Iran															
	Precipitation	46	38	46	36	13	3	3	3	3	8	20	31	246	
1 220 m	Temperature	2	5	9	16	21	26	30	29	25	18	12	6	17	28
Tokyo, Japan															
	Precipitation	48	74	107	135	147	165	142	152	234	208	97	56	1 565	
6 m	Temperature	3	4	7	13	17	21	25	26	23	17	11	6	14	23
Ulan Bator, Mongolia															
	Precipitation	<3	<3	3	5	10	28	76	51	23	5	5	3	208	
1 325 m	Temperature	−26	−21	−13	−1	6	14	16	14	8	−1	−13	−22	−3	42

AUSTRALIA, NEW ZEALAND and ANTARCTICA

		Jan.	Feb.	Mar.	Apr.	May	June	July	Aug.	Sept.	Oct.	Nov.	Dec.	Year	Annual range
Alice Springs, Australia															
	Precipitation	43	33	28	10	15	13	8	8	8	18	31	38	252	
579 m	Temperature	29	28	25	20	15	12	12	14	18	23	26	28	21	17
Christchurch, New Zealand															
	Precipitation	56	43	48	48	66	66	69	48	46	43	48	56	638	
10 m	Temperature	16	16	14	12	9	6	6	7	9	12	14	16	11	10
Darwin, Australia															
	Precipitation	386	312	254	97	15	3	<3	3	13	51	119	239	1 491	
30 m	Temperature	29	29	29	29	28	26	25	26	28	29	30	29	28	5
Mawson, Antarctica															
	Precipitation	11	30	20	10	44	180	4	40	3	20	0	0	362	
14 m	Temperature	0	−5	−10	−14	−15	−16	−18	−18	−19	−13	−5	−1	−11	18

		Jan.	Feb.	Mar.	Apr.	May	June	July	Aug.	Sept.	Oct.	Nov.	Dec.	Year	Annual Range
Melbourne, Australia															
	Precipitation	48	46	56	58	53	53	48	48	58	66	58	58	653	
35 m	Temperature	20	20	18	15	13	10	9	11	13	14	16	18	15	11
Perth, Australia															
	Precipitation	8	10	20	43	130	180	170	149	86	56	20	13	881	
60 m	Temperature	23	23	22	19	16	14	13	13	15	16	19	22	18	10
Sydney, Australia															
	Precipitation	89	102	127	135	127	117	117	76	73	71	73	73	1 181	
42 m	Temperature	22	22	21	18	15	13	12	13	15	18	19	21	17	10

EUROPE and U.S.S.R.

		Jan.	Feb.	Mar.	Apr.	May	June	July	Aug.	Sept.	Oct.	Nov.	Dec.	Year	Annual Range
Archangel, U.S.S.R.															
	Precipitation	31	19	25	29	42	52	62	56	63	63	47	41	530	
13 m	Temperature	−16	−14	−9	0	7	12	15	14	8	2	−4	−11	0	31
Athens, Greece															
	Precipitation	62	37	37	23	23	14	6	7	15	51	56	71	402	
107 m	Temperature	10	10	12	16	20	25	28	28	24	20	15	11	18	18
Berlin, Germany															
	Precipitation	46	40	33	42	49	65	73	69	48	49	46	43	603	
55 m	Temperature	−1	0	4	9	14	17	19	18	15	9	5	1	9	20
Istanbul, Turkey															
	Precipitation	109	92	72	46	38	34	34	30	58	81	103	119	816	
114 m	Temperature	5	6	7	11	16	20	23	23	20	16	12	8	14	18
Kazalinsk, U.S.S.R.															
	Precipitation	10	10	13	13	15	5	5	8	8	10	13	15	125	
63 m	Temperature	−12	−11	−3	6	18	23	25	23	16	8	−1	−7	7	37
Lisbon, Portugal															
	Precipitation	111	76	109	54	44	16	3	4	33	62	93	103	708	
77 m	Temperature	11	12	14	16	17	20	22	23	21	18	14	12	17	12
London, U.K.															
	Precipitation	54	40	37	37	46	45	57	59	49	57	64	48	593	
5 m	Temperature	4	5	7	9	12	16	18	17	15	11	8	5	11	14
Málaga, Spain															
	Precipitation	61	51	62	46	26	5	1	3	29	64	64	62	474	
33 m	Temperature	12	13	15	17	19	29	25	26	23	20	16	13	18	17
Moscow, U.S.S.R.															
	Precipitation	39	38	36	37	53	58	88	71	58	45	47	54	624	
156 m	Temperature	−13	−10	−4	6	13	16	18	17	12	6	−1	−7	4	31
Odessa, U.S.S.R.															
	Precipitation	57	62	30	21	34	34	42	37	37	13	35	71	473	
64 m	Temperature	−3	−1	2	9	15	20	22	22	18	12	9	1	10	25
Omsk, U.S.S.R.															
	Precipitation	15	8	8	13	31	51	51	51	28	25	18	20	318	
85 m	Temperature	−22	−19	−12	−1	10	16	18	16	10	1	−11	−18	−1	40
Palma de Mallorca, Spain															
	Precipitation	39	34	51	32	29	17	3	25	55	77	47	40	449	
10 m	Temperature	10	11	12	15	17	21	24	25	23	18	14	11	17	15
Paris, France															
	Precipitation	56	46	35	42	57	54	59	64	55	50	51	50	619	
75 m	Temperature	3	4	8	11	15	18	20	19	17	12	7	4	12	17
Rome, Italy															
	Precipitation	71	62	57	51	46	37	15	21	63	99	129	93	744	
17 m	Temperature	8	9	11	14	18	22	25	25	22	17	13	10	16	17
Shannon, Irish Republic															
	Precipitation	94	67	56	53	61	57	77	79	86	86	96	117	929	
2 m	Temperature	5	5	7	9	12	14	16	16	14	11	8	6	10	11
Stavanger, Norway															
	Precipitation	93	56	45	70	49	84	93	118	142	129	125	126	1 130	
85 m	Temperature	1	1	3	6	10	13	15	15	13	9	6	3	8	14
Stockholm, Sweden															
	Precipitation	43	30	25	31	34	45	61	76	60	48	53	48	554	
44 m	Temperature	−3	−3	−1	5	10	15	18	17	12	7	3	0	7	21
Verkhoyansk, U.S.S.R.															
	Precipitation	5	5	3	5	8	23	28	25	13	8	8	5	134	
100 m	Temperature	−50	−45	−32	−15	0	12	14	9	2	−15	−38	−48	−17	64
Warsaw, Poland															
	Precipitation	27	32	27	37	46	69	96	65	43	38	31	44	555	
110 m	Temperature	−3	−3	2	7	14	17	19	18	14	9	3	0	8	22

Population of Cities

The population figures used are from censuses or more recent estimates and are given in thousands for towns and cities over 200 000 (over 500 000 in China and 250 000 in Japan and U.S.S.R.). Where possible the population of the metropolitan areas is given e.g. Greater London, Greater New York, etc.

AFRICA

ALGERIA (1974)
Algiers 1 503
Oran 485
Constantine 350
Annaba 313
Tizi-Ouzou 224

ANGOLA (1970)
Luanda 475

CAMEROON (1976)
Douala 458
Yaoundé 314

CANARY ISLANDS (1974)
Las Palmas 328

CONGO (1975)
Brazzaville 290

EGYPT (1976)
Cairo 5 084
Alexandria 2 319
El Giza 1 247
Shubra el Kheima 394
El Mahalla el Kubra 293
Tanta 285
Port Said 263
El Mansura 258
Asyut 214
Zagazig 203

ETHIOPIA (1979)
Addis Abeba 1 210
Asmera 414

GABON (1976)
Libreville 186

GHANA (1970)
Accra 738
Kumasi 345

GUINEA (1972)
Conakry 526

IVORY COAST (1976)
Abidjan 850
Bouaké 318

KENYA (1979)
Nairobi 835
Mombasa 312

LIBYA (1973)
Tripoli 551
Benghazi 282

MADAGASCAR (1978)
Antananarivo 400

MALAWI (1977)
Blantyre 229

MALI (1976)
Bamako 404

MOROCCO (1973)
Casablanca 1 753
Rabat-Salé 596
Marrakesh 436
Fès 426
Meknès 403
Oujda 349
Kénitra 341
Tétouan 308
Safi 215
Tanger 208

MOZAMBIQUE (1970)
Maputo 384

NIGERIA (1975)
Lagos 1 477
Ibadan 847
Ogbomosho 432
Kano 399
Oshogbo 282
Ilorin 282
Abeokuta 253
Port Harcourt 242
Zaria 224
Ilesha 224
Onitsha 220
Iwo 214
Ado-Ekiti 213
Kaduna 202

SENEGAL (1976)
Dakar 799

SIERRA LEONE (1974)
Freetown 214

SOMALI REP. (1980)
Mogadishu 400

SOUTH AFRICA (1970)
Johannesburg 1 433
Cape Town 1 097
Durban 843
Pretoria 562
Port Elizabeth 469
Germiston 281

SUDAN (1973)
Khartoum 334

TANZANIA (1978)
Dar-es-Salaam 757

TUNISIA (1976)
Tunis 944
Sfax 475
Sousse 255

UGANDA (1975)
Kampala 331

ZAIRE (1974)
Kinshasa 2 008
Kananga 601
Lubumbashi 404
Mbuji Mayi 337
Kisangani 311

ZAMBIA (1980)
Lusaka 538
Kitwe 315
Ndola 282

ZIMBABWE (1978)
Harare 633
Bulawayo 366

ASIA

AFGHANISTAN (1976)
Kabul 588

BANGLADESH (1974)
Dacca 1 730
Chittagong 890
Khulna 437

BURMA (1977)
Rangoon 2 276
Mandalay 458

CAMBODIA (1973)
Phnom Penh 2 000

CHINA (1970)
Shanghai 10 820
Peking 7 570
Tientsin 4 280
Shenyang 2 800
Wuhan 2 560
Canton 2 500
Chungking 2 400
Nanking 1 750
Harbin 1 670
Luta 1 650
Sian 1 600
Lanchow 1 450
Taiyuan 1 350
Tsingtao 1 300
Chengtu 1 250
Changchun 1 200
Kunming 1 100
Tsinan 1 100
Fushun 1 080
Anshan 1 050
Chengchow 1 050
Hangchow 960
Tangshan 950
Paotow 920
Tzepo 850
Changsha 825
Shihkiachwang 800
Tsitsihar 760
Soochow 730
Kirin 720
Suchow 700
Foochow 680
Nanchang 675
Kweiyang 660
Wusih 650
Hofei 630
Hwainan 600
Penki 600
Loyang 580
Nanning 550
Huhehot 530
Sining 500
Wulumuchi 500

HONG KONG (1971)
Kowloon 2 195
Victoria 849
Tsuen Wan 272

INDIA (1971)
Calcutta 7 031
Bombay 5 971
Delhi 3 647
Madras 3 170
Hyderabad 1 796
Ahmedabad 1 742
Bangalore 1 654
Kanpur 1 275
Pune 1 135
Nagpur 930
Lucknow 749
Jaipur 615
Agra 592
Varanasi 584
Madurai 549
Indore 543
Allahabad 491
Patna 473
Surat 472
Vadodara 467
Cochin 439
Jabalpur 426
Tivandrum 410
Amritsar 408
Srinagar 403
Ludhiana 398
Sholapur 398
Gwalior 385
Hubli-Dharwar 379
Jamshedpur 357
Coimbatore 356
Mysore 356
Visakhaptnam 353
Calicut 334
Jodhpur 318
Vijaywada 317
Salem 309
Tiruchurapaili 307
Rajkot 301
Bhopal 298
Bareilly 296
Jullundur 296
Meerut 271
Guntur 270
Ajmer 263
Kolhapur 259
Algarh 252
Gorakhpur 231
Bhavnagar 225
Saharanpur 225
Chandigarh 219
Kota 213
Warangul 208
Durgapur 207
Ujjain 203
Jamnagar 200

INDONESIA (1971)
Jakarta 4 576
Surabaya 1 556
Bandung 1 202
Semarang 647
Medan 636
Palembang 583
Ujung Pandang 435
Malang 422
Surakarta 414
Yogyakarta 342
Banjarmasin 282
Pontianak 218

IRAN (1976)
Tehran 4 496
Esfahan 672
Mashhad 670
Tabriz 599
Shiraz 416
Ahvaz 329
Abadan 296
Qahremanshahr 291
Qom 247

IRAQ (1970)
Baghdad 2 969
Basra 371
Mosul 293
Kirkuk 208

ISRAEL (1977)
Tel Aviv-Jaffa 1 220
Jerusalem 376
Haifa 367

JAPAN (1980)
Tōkyō 8 349
Yokohama 2 774
Osaka 2 648
Nagoya 2 088
Kyōto 1 473
Sapporo 1 402
Kōbe 1 367
Fukuoka 1 089
Kitakyūshū 1 065
Kawasaki 1 041
Hiroshima 899
Sakai 810
Chiba 746
Sendai 665
Okayama 546
Kumamoto 526
Amagasaki 524
Higashiōsaka 522
Kagoshima 505
Hamamatsu 491
Funabashi 479
Niigata 458
Shizuoka 458
Nagasaki 447
Himeji 446
Sagamihara 439
Yokosuka 421
Kanazawa 418
Gifu 410
Nishinoyama 410
Kurashiki 404
Toyonaka 403
Matsuyama 402
Matsudo 401
Wakayama 401
Hachiōji 387
Kawaguchi 379
Utsunomiya 378
Ichikawa 364
Oita 360
Urawa 358
Omiya 354
Asahikawa 353
Hirakata 353
Fukuyama 346
Iwaki 342
Takatsuki 341
Suita 332
Nagano 324
Hakodate 320
Takamatsu 317
Toyama 305
Toyohashi 304
Kōchi 301
Fujisawa 300
Nara 298
Naha 296
Machida 295
Aomori 288
Kōriyama 286
Akita 285
Toyota 282
Yao 273
Shimonoseki 269
Maebashi 265
Miyazaki 265
Fukushima 263
Okazaki 262
Kawagoe 259
Neyagawa 256
Akashi 255
Yokkaichi 255
Ichinomiya 253
Sasebo 251

JORDAN (1977)
Amman 712
Az Zarqa 263

KOREA, NORTH (1967-70)
Pyongyang 1 500
Chongjin 265

KOREA, SOUTH (1975)
Seoul 6 879
Pusan 2 450
Taegu 1 309
Inchon 797
Kwangju 606
Taejon 506
Masan 372
Chonju 311
Seongnam 272
Utsan 253
Suweon 224

KUWAIT (1975)
Kuwait 775

LEBANON (1971)
Beirut 702

MACAU (1975)
Macau 260

MALAYSIA (1970)
Kuala Lumpur 452
Georgetown 270
Ipoh 248

MONGOLIA (1977)
Ulan Bator 400

NEPAL (1971)
Katmandu 210

PAKISTAN (1972)
Karachi 3 499
Lahore 2 165
Faisalabad 822
Hyderabad 628
Rawalpindi 615
Multan 542
Gujranwala 360
Peshawar 268
Sialkot 204
Sargodha 201

PHILIPPINES (1975)
Manila 1 438
Quezon City 995
Davao 516
Cebu 419
Caloocan 364
Iloilo 248
Pasay 241
Zamboanga 240

SAUDI ARABIA (1974)
Riyadh 667
Jedda 561
Mecca 367
Taif 205

SINGAPORE (1977)
Singapore 2 308

SRI LANKA (1981)
Colombo 1 412

SYRIA (1978)
Damascus 1 142
Aleppo 878
Homs 306
Latakia 204

TAIWAN (1973)
Taipei 3 050
Kaohsiung 1 115
Tainan 513
Taichung 497
Chilung 341
Sanchung 260
Chiai 247
Hsinchu 205

THAILAND (1977)
Bangkok 4 702

TURKEY (1980)
Istanbul 2 854
Ankara 2 204
Izmir 754
Adana 569
Bursa 466
Gaziantep 371
Konya 309
Ekisehir 326
Kayseri 273
Diyarbakir 233
Mersin 215

UNITED ARAB EMIRATES (1976)
Abu Dhabi 236
Dubai 207

VIETNAM (1973-79)
Ho Chi Minh City 3 420
Hanoi 2 571
Haiphong 1 279
Da-Nang 492
Nha-trang 216
Qui-Nhon 214
Hué 209

YEMEN, SOUTH (1977)
Aden 285

AUSTRALASIA

AUSTRALIA (1977)
Sydney 3 122
Melbourne 2 694
Brisbane 995
Adelaide 923
Perth 844
Newcastle 372
Canberra 227
Wollongong 220

NEW ZEALAND (1981)
Auckland 770
Wellington 321
Christchurch 290

EUROPE

AUSTRIA (1978)
Vienna 1 587
Graz 249
Linz 203

BELGIUM (1976)
Brussels 1 042
Antwerp 662
Liège 433
Gent 219
Charleroi 210

BULGARIA (1978)
Sofia 1 032
Plovdiv 333
Varna 279

CZECHOSLOVAKIA (1977)
Prague 1 176
Brno 363
Bratislava 350
Ostrava 317

DENMARK (1977)
Copenhagen 1 251
Århus 246

FINLAND (1979)
Helsinki 893
Tampere 243
Turku 240

FRANCE (1975)
Paris 9 863
Lyon 1 152
Marseille 1 004
Lille 929
Bordeaux 591
Toulouse 495
Nantes 438
Nice 433
Rouen 389
Grenoble 389
Toulon 379
Strasbourg 355
St-Etienne 335
Lens 313
Nancy 279
Le Havre 264
Grasse-Cannes 255
Tours 235
Clermont-Ferrand 225
Valenciennes 224
Mulhouse 219
Rennes 213
Montpellier 205
Orléans 205
Dijon 203
Douai 203

GERMANY, EAST (1977)
East Berlin 1 111
Leipzig 565
Dresden 511
Karl-Marx-Stadt 309
Magdeburg 281
Halle 233
Rostock 219
Erfurt 206

GERMANY, WEST (1978)
West Berlin 1 910
Hamburg 1 664
München 1 297
Cologne 977
Essen 658
Frankfurt am Main 631
Dortmund 613
Düsseldorf 600
Stuttgart 584
Duisburg 563
Bremen 559
Hannover 538
Bochum 406
Wuppertal 396
Bielefeld 313
Gelsenkirchen 310
Mannheim 303
Bonn 285
Karlsruhe 274
Wiesbaden 271
Münster 267
Braunschweig 263

Mönchengladbach .. 258
Kiel .. 254
Augsburg .. 245
Aachen .. 243
Oberhausen .. 231
Lübeck .. 225
Krefeld .. 224
Hagen .. 222

GREECE (1971)
Athens .. 2 101
Thessaloniki .. 557
Piraeus .. 439

HUNGARY (1980)
Budapest .. 2 060
Miskolc .. 207

IRISH REPUBLIC (1981)
Dublin .. 525

ITALY (1977)
Rome .. 2 898
Milano .. 1 706
Napoli .. 1 225
Torino .. 1 182
Genova .. 795
Palermo .. 679
Bologna .. 481
Firenze .. 464
Catánia .. 400
Bari .. 387
Venézia .. 360
Verona .. 271
Messina .. 267
Trieste .. 265
Táranto .. 245
Cágliari .. 242
Padova .. 242
Bréscia .. 215

NETHERLANDS (1978)
Rotterdam .. 1 017
Amsterdam .. 965
s'Gravenhage .. 673
Utrecht .. 472
Eindhoven .. 363
Arnhem .. 284
Heerlen-Kerkrade .. 266
Enschede-Hengelo .. 241
Haarlem .. 229
Nijmegen .. 216
Tilburg .. 212
Groningen .. 200

NORWAY (1978)
Oslo .. 645
Bergen .. 211

POLAND (1978)
Warsaw .. 1 543
Lódz .. 824
Kraków .. 719
Wroclaw .. 599
Poznań .. 538
Gdańsk .. 448
Szczecin .. 384
Katowice .. 352
Bydgoszcz .. 342
Lublin .. 295
Bytom .. 237
Gdynia .. 234
Częstochowa .. 228
Bialystok .. 210
Sosnowiec .. 208
Zabrze .. 203
Gliwice .. 201

PORTUGAL (1975)
Lisbon .. 1 612
Oporto .. 1 315

ROMANIA (1978)
Bucharest .. 1 934
Iaşi .. 279
Timişoara .. 278
Cluj .. 273
Braşov .. 268
Constanţa .. 268
Galaţi .. 253
Craiova .. 231
Ploieşti .. 206
Braila .. 200

SPAIN (1974)
Madrid .. 3 520
Barcelona .. 1 810
Valencia .. 713
Sevilla .. 569
Zaragoza .. 547
Bilbao .. 458
Malaga .. 403
Valladolid .. 275
Palma de Mallorca .. 267
Córdoba .. 250
Hospitalet .. 242
Murcia .. 241
Alicante .. 213
Granada .. 203

SWEDEN (1978)
Stockholm .. 1 380
Göteborg .. 694
Malmö .. 454

SWITZERLAND (1979)
Zürich .. 708
Basel .. 368
Genève .. 325
Berne .. 282
Lausanne .. 227

U.S.S.R. (1979)
Moscow .. 8 011
Leningrad .. 4 588
Kiyev .. 2 144
Tashkent .. 1 779
Baku .. 1 550
Kharkov .. 1 444
Gorkiy .. 1 344
Novosibirsk .. 1 312
Minsk .. 1 276
Kuybyshev .. 1 218
Sverdlovsk .. 1 211
Dnepropetrovsk .. 1 066
Tbilisi .. 1 066
Odessa .. 1 046
Chelyabinsk .. 1 031
Donetsk .. 1 021
Yerevan .. 1 019
Omsk .. 1 014
Perm .. 999
Kazan .. 993
Ufa .. 969
Rostov .. 934
Volgograd .. 929
Alma-Ata .. 910
Saratov .. 856
Riga .. 835
Krasnoyarsk .. 796
Voronezh .. 783
Zaporozhye .. 781
Lvov .. 667
Krivoy Rog .. 650
Yaroslavl .. 597
Karaganda .. 572
Krasnodar .. 560
Irkutsk .. 550
Vladivostok .. 550
Izhevsk .. 549
Novokuznetsk .. 541
Barnaul .. 533
Frunze .. 533
Khabarovsk .. 528
Tula .. 514
Kishinev .. 503
Zhdanov .. 503
Togliatti .. 502
Dushanbe .. 493
Penza .. 483
Vilnius .. 481
Samarkand .. 476
Kemerovo .. 471
Ivanovo .. 465
Ulyanovsk .. 464
Voroshilovgrad .. 463
Astrakhan .. 461
Orenburg .. 459
Ryazan .. 453
Nikolayev .. 441
Makeyevka .. 436
Tallinn .. 430
Tomsk .. 421
Kalinin .. 412
Magnitogorsk .. 406
Nizhniy Tagil .. 398
Lipetsk .. 396
Bryansk .. 394
Kirov .. 390
Arkhangelsk .. 385
Gomel .. 383
Murmansk .. 381
Groznyy .. 375
Kursk .. 375
Kaunas .. 370
Tyumen .. 359
Kaliningrad .. 355
Gorlovka .. 337
Chimkent .. 321
Kherson .. 319
Vinnitsa .. 313
Ashkhabad .. 312
Kurgan .. 310
Cheboksary .. 308
Orel .. 305
Chita .. 302
Simferopol .. 302
Naberezhnyye Chelny .. 301
Sevastopol .. 301
Ulan Ude .. 300
Vitebsk .. 297
Vladimir .. 296
Mogilev .. 290
Sochi .. 287
Semipalatinsk .. 283
Ordzhonikidze .. 279
Poltava .. 279
Taganrog .. 277
Smolensk .. 276
Ust-Kamenogorsk .. 274
Pavlodar .. 273
Tambov .. 270
Cherepovets .. 266
Prokopyevsk .. 266
Kaluga .. 265
Dzhambul .. 264
Komsomolsk-na-Amur .. 264
Saransk .. 263
Stavropol .. 258
Dzerzhinsk .. 257
Kostroma .. 255
Dneprodzerzhinsk .. 250
Makhachkala .. 250

UNITED KINGDOM (1981)
London .. 6 696
Birmingham .. 920
Glasgow .. 762
Liverpool .. 510
Sheffield .. 477
Leeds .. 449
Manchester .. 449
Edinburgh .. 419
Bristol .. 388
Belfast .. 374
Coventry .. 314
Bradford .. 281
Leicester .. 280
Cardiff .. 274
Nottingham .. 271
Hull .. 268
Wolverhampton .. 252
Stoke-on-Trent .. 252
Plymouth .. 244
Derby .. 216
Southampton .. 204

YUGOSLAVIA (1971)
Belgrade .. 775
Zagreb .. 602
Skopje .. 388
Sarajevo .. 271
Ljubljana .. 213

NORTH AMERICA

CANADA (1981)
Toronto .. 2 999
Montréal .. 2 828
Vancouver .. 1 268
Ottawa .. 718
Edmonton .. 657
Calgary .. 593
Winnipeg .. 585
Québec .. 576
Hamilton .. 542
St. Catherines .. 304
Kitchener .. 288
London .. 284
Halifax .. 278
Windsor .. 246
Victoria .. 233

COSTA RICA (1978)
San José .. 563

CUBA (1975)
Havana .. 1 861
Santiago de Cuba .. 316
Camaguey .. 222

DOMINICAN REPUBLIC (1978)
Santo Domingo .. 1 103
Santiago de los Caballeros .. 242

EL SALVADOR (1974)
San Salvador .. 366

GUATEMALA (1979)
Guatemala City .. 793

HAITI (1979)
Port-au-Prince .. 791

HONDURAS (1974)
Tegucigalpa .. 274

JAMAICA (1971)
Kingston .. 573

MEXICO (1978)
Mexico City .. 13 994
Guadalajara .. 2 343
Netzahualcóyotl .. 2 068
Monterrey .. 1 923
Puebla de Zaragoza .. 678
Ciudad Juárez .. 597
León de los Aldamas .. 590
Acapulco .. 421
Torreón .. 397
Tampico .. 375
Chihuahua .. 370
Mexicali .. 338
San Luis Potosi .. 315
Culiacán .. 302
Hermosillo .. 300
Veracruz Llave .. 295
Mérida .. 253
Aguascalientes .. 248
Saltillo .. 246
Morelia .. 239
Cuernavaca .. 227
Toluca .. 223
Durango .. 219
Reynosa .. 219
Nuevo Laredo .. 214

NICARAGUA (1974)
Managua .. 500

PANAMA (1980)
Panama .. 546

PUERTO RICO (1976)
San Juan .. 515
Bayamón .. 204

UNITED STATES (1980)
New York .. 16 065
Los Angeles .. 11 439
Chicago .. 7 697
Philadelphia .. 5 531
San Francisco .. 4 845
Detroit .. 4 605
Boston .. 3 443
Houston .. 3 086
Washington .. 3 045
Dallas .. 2 964
Cleveland .. 2 830
Miami .. 2 579
St. Louis .. 2 345
Pittsburgh .. 2 261
Baltimore .. 2 166
Minneapolis-St Paul .. 2 109
Seattle .. 2 084
Atlanta .. 2 010
San Diego .. 1 860
Cincinnati .. 1 651
Denver .. 1 615
Milwaukee .. 1 566
Tampa .. 1 550
Phoenix .. 1 512
Kansas City .. 1 322
Buffalo .. 1 241
Portland .. 1 236
New Orleans .. 1 184
Indianapolis .. 1 162
Columbus (Ohio) .. 1 089
San Antonio .. 1 070
Sacramento .. 1 011
Rochester .. 970
Salt Lake City .. 935
Providence .. 918
Memphis .. 910
Louisville .. 902
Birmingham .. 834
Oklahoma .. 830
Nashville .. 829
Dayton .. 827
Greensboro .. 823
Norfolk .. 800
Albany .. 797
Toledo .. 791
Honolulu .. 762
Jacksonville .. 736
Hartford .. 726
Orlando .. 694
Tulsa .. 679
Syracuse .. 643
Allentown .. 637
Charlotte .. 632
Richmond .. 631
Scranton .. 630
Grand Rapids .. 601
Omaha .. 566
Greenville .. 563
West Palm Beach .. 552
Austin .. 533
Tucson .. 532
Springfield (Mass.) .. 530
Youngstown .. 530
Raleigh .. 525
Flint .. 522
Fresno .. 507
Baton Rouge .. 496
El Paso .. 479
Knoxville .. 475
Lansing .. 468
Las Vegas .. 462
Albuquerque .. 449
Harrisburg .. 446
Mobile .. 440
Johnson City .. 433
Chattanooga .. 421
Charleston (S.C.) .. 416
New Haven .. 416
Wichita .. 410
Canton .. 404
Bakersfield .. 402
Columbia .. 396
Bridgeport .. 395
Little Rock .. 394
Davenport .. 383
York .. 381
Fort Wayne .. 380
Shreveport .. 377
Beaumont .. 375
Worcester .. 372
Newport News .. 364
Peoria .. 364
Lancaster .. 362
Stockton .. 347
Spokane .. 341
Des Moines .. 338
Corpus Christi .. 324
Madison .. 323
Lakeland .. 322
Augusta .. 321
Utica .. 319
Colorado Springs .. 318
Jackson .. 316
Lexington Fayette .. 316
Reading .. 313
Huntingdon .. 310
Huntsville .. 308
Evansville .. 307
Binghamton .. 301
Santa Barbara .. 298
Santa Rosa .. 292
Appleton .. 291
Salinas .. 289
Pensacola .. 284
McAllen .. 280
Erie .. 279
Kalamazoo .. 279
Rockford .. 279
South Bend .. 278
Eugene .. 273
Montgomery .. 273
Melbourne .. 270
Modesto .. 266
Duluth .. 265
Johnstown .. 264
Charleston (W.Va.) .. 261
Macon .. 252
Daytona Beach .. 251
Salem .. 250
New London .. 249
Fayetteville .. 247
Poughkeepsie .. 244
Columbus (Ga.) .. 239
Saginaw .. 227
Savannah .. 226
Waterbury .. 226
Roanoke .. 224
Lima .. 218
Provo-Orem .. 217
Killeen .. 214
Lubbock .. 212
Brownsville .. 208
Springfield (Mo.) .. 208
Fort Myers .. 204
Fort Smith .. 202
Sarasota .. 202

SOUTH AMERICA

ARGENTINA (1975)
Buenos Aires .. 8 436
Rosario .. 807
Córdoba .. 791
La Plata .. 479
Mendoza .. 471
San Miguel de Tucuman .. 366
Mar del Plata .. 300
Santa Fé .. 245
San Juan .. 218

BOLIVIA (1976)
La Paz .. 655
Santa Cruz .. 237

BRAZIL (1975)
São Paulo .. 7 199
Rio de Janeiro .. 4 858
Belo Horizonte .. 1 557
Recife .. 1 250
Salvador .. 1 237
Fortaleza .. 1 110
Pôrto Alegre .. 1 044
Nova Iguaçu .. 932
Belém .. 772
Curitiba .. 765
Brasilia .. 763
Duque de Caxias .. 537
São Gonçalo .. 534
Goiania .. 518
Santo André .. 515
Campinas .. 473
Santos .. 396
Manaus .. 389
Osasco .. 377
Niterói .. 376
São João de Meriti .. 366
Natal .. 344
Campos .. 337
São Luiz .. 330
Maceió .. 324
Guarulhos .. 311
Teresina .. 290
João Pessoa .. 288
Juiz de Fora .. 284
Londrina .. 284
São Bernardo do Campo .. 267
Jaboatao .. 259
Ribeirão Preto .. 259
Olinda .. 251
Campina Grande .. 236
Pelotas .. 232
Feira de Santana .. 227
Aracaju .. 226
Petrópolis .. 217
Sorocaba .. 208
Jundiai .. 205

CHILE (1978)
Santiago .. 3 692
Valparaiso .. 620
Concepción .. 519
Viña del Mar .. 262
Talcahuano .. 204

COLOMBIA (1973)
Bogotá .. 2 855
Medellin .. 1 159
Cali .. 990
Barranquilla .. 692
Cartagena .. 355
Bucaramanga .. 323
Cucuta .. 279
Manizales .. 232
Pereira .. 227
Ibagué .. 223

ECUADOR (1978)
Guayaquil .. 1 022
Quito .. 743

PARAGUAY (1974)
Asunción .. 565

PERU (1972)
Lima .. 3 303
Arequipa .. 302
Callao .. 297
Trujillo .. 240

URUGUAY (1975)
Montevideo .. 1 230

VENEZUELA (1976)
Caracas .. 2 576
Maracaibo .. 792
Valencia .. 439
Barquisimeto .. 430
Maracay .. 301
Barcelona-Puerto La Cruz .. 242
San Cristobal .. 241

Population of Countries

Country	Area in thousands of square km	Population in thousands	Density of population per sq. km.	Capital Population in thousands
Afghanistan	647	15 540	24	Kabul (588)
Albania	29	2 734	94	Tiranë (192)
Algeria	2 382	18 594	8	Algiers (1 503)
Angola	1 247	7 078	6	Luanda (475)
Argentina	2 767	26 863	10	Buenos Aires (8 436)
Australia	7 687	14 727	2	Canberra (227)
Austria	84	7 507	89	Vienna (1 587)
Bangladesh	144	88 656	616	Dacca (1 730)
Belgium	31	9 859	318	Brussels (1 042)
Belize	23	145	6	Belmopan (4)
Benin	113	3 567	32	Porto-Novo (104)
Bhutan	47	1 298	28	Thimphu (60)
Bolivia	1 099	5 600	5	Sucre (63) La Paz (655)
Botswana	600	819	1	Gaborone (37)
Brazil	8 512	119 099	14	Brasilia (763)
Brunei	6	213	37	Bandar Seri Begawan (37)
Bulgaria	111	8 862	80	Sofia (1 032)
Burma	677	35 289	52	Rangoon (2 276)
Burundi	28	4 512	161	Bujumbura (157)
Cambodia	181	8 872	49	Phnom Penh (2 000)
Cameroon	475	8 503	18	Yaoundé (314)
Canada	9 976	23 343	2	Ottawa (718)
Central African Rep.	623	2 370	4	Bangui (187)
Chad	1 284	4 524	4	Ndjamena (179)
Chile	757	11 104	15	Santiago (3 692)
China	9 597	982 550	102	Peking (7 570)
Colombia	1 139	27 520	24	Bogota (2 855)
Congo	342	1 537	5	Brazzaville (290)
Costa Rica	51	2 245	44	San José (563)
Cuba	115	9 833	86	Havana (1 861)
Cyprus	9	629	68	Nicosia (147)
Czechoslovakia	128	15 312	120	Prague (1 176)
Denmark	43	5 124	119	Copenhagen (1 251)
Djibouti	22	119	5	Djibouti (62)
Dominican Republic	49	5 431	111	Santo Domingo (1 103)
Ecuador	284	8 354	29	Quito (743)
Egypt	1 001	41 995	42	Cairo (5 084)
El Salvador	21	4 813	229	San Salvador (366)
Equatorial Guinea	28	363	13	Rey Malabo (37)
Ethiopia	1 222	31 065	25	Addis Abeba (1 210)
Fiji	18	631	35	Suva (118)
Finland	337	4 788	14	Helsinki (893)
France	547	53 788	98	Paris (9 863)
French Guiana	91	64	1	Cayenne (25)
Gabon	268	551	2	Libréville (186)
Gambia	11	601	55	Banjul (48)
Germany, East	108	16 737	155	East Berlin (1 111)
Germany, West	249	61 658	248	Bonn (285)
Ghana	239	11 450	48	Accra (738)
Greece	132	9 599	73	Athens (2 101)
Greenland	2 176	50	0.02	Godthåb (9)
Guatemala	109	7 262	67	Guatemala (793)
Guinea	246	5 014	20	Conakry (526)
Guinea-Bissau	36	777	22	Bissau (109)
Guyana	215	884	4	Georgetown (187)
Haiti	28	5 009	179	Port-au-Prince (791)
Honduras	112	3 691	33	Tegucigalpa (274)
Hong Kong	1	5 068	4 827	Victoria (849)
Hungary	93	10 711	115	Budapest (2 060)
Iceland	103	228	2	Reykjavik (83)
India	3 288	683 810	208	Delhi (3 647)
Indonesia	2 027	7 383	73	Jakarta (4 576)
Iran	1 648	37 447	23	Tehran (4 496)
Iraq	435	13 084	28	Baghdad (2 969)
Irish Republic	70	3 440	49	Dublin (525)
Israel	21	3 871	184	Jerusalem (376)
Italy	301	57 140	190	Rome (2 898)
Ivory Coast	322	7 973	25	Abidjan (850)
Jamaica	11	2 192	199	Kingston (573)
Japan	372	117 057	315	Tokyo (8 349)
Jordan	98	2 779	28	Amman (712)
Kenya	583	16 402	28	Nairobi (835)
Korea, North	121	17 914	148	Pyongyang (1 500)
Korea, South	98	37 449	382	Seoul (6 879)
Kuwait	18	1 356	75	Kuwait (775)
Laos	237	3 721	16	Vientiane (177)
Lebanon	10	3 161	316	Beirut (702)
Lesotho	30	1 339	45	Maseru (29)
Liberia	111	1 873	17	Monrovia (172)
Libya	1 760	2 977	2	Tripoli (551)
Luxembourg	3	364	140	Luxembourg (78)
Madagascar	587	8 742	15	Antananarivo (400)
Malawi	118	5 968	51	Lilongwe (103)
Malaysia	330	13 436	41	Kuala Lumpur (452)
Mali	1 240	6 906	6	Bamako (404)
Malta	0.3	369	1 153	Valletta (14)
Mauritania	1 031	1 634	2	Nouakchott (135)
Mauritius	2	959	480	Port Louis (141)
Mexico	1 973	71 911	36	Mexico (13 994)
Mongolia	1 565	1 595	1	Ulan Bator (400)
Morocco	447	20 242	45	Rabat (596)
Mozambique	783	12 130	15	Maputo (384)
Namibia	824	852	1	Windhoek (61)
Nepal	141	14 010	99	Katmandu (210)
Netherlands	41	14 220	347	Amsterdam (965)
New Zealand	269	3 176	12	Wellington (321)
Nicaragua	130	2 703	21	Managua (500)
Niger	1 267	5 305	4	Niamey (130)
Nigeria	924	77 082	83	Lagos (1 477)
Norway	324	4 092	13	Oslo (645)
Oman	212	891	4	Muscat (25)
Pakistan	804	82 441	103	Islamabad (77)
Panama	76	1 837	24	Panama (546)
Papua New Guinea	462	3 082	7	Port Moresby (113)
Paraguay	407	3 067	8	Asunción (565)
Peru	1 285	17 780	14	Lima (3 303)
Philippines	300	48 400	161	Manila (1 438)
Poland	313	35 815	114	Warsaw (1 543)
Portugal	92	9 933	108	Lisbon (1 612)
Puerto Rico	9	3 188	358	San Juan (515)
Romania	238	22 201	93	Bucharest (1 934)
Rwanda	26	5 046	194	Kigali (90)
Saudi Arabia	2 150	8 367	4	Riyadh (667)
Senegal	196	5 661	29	Dakar (799)
Sierra Leone	72	3 474	48	Freetown (214)
Singapore	0.6	2 391	4 122	Singapore (2 308)
Somali Republic	638	3 645	6	Mogadishu (400)
South Africa	1 221	29 285	24	Pretoria (562) Cape Town (1 097)
Spain	505	37 430	74	Madrid (3 520)
Sri Lanka	66	14 738	223	Colombo (1 412)
Sudan	2 506	18 681	8	Khartoum (334)
Surinam	163	352	2	Paramaribo (151)
Swaziland	17	547	32	Mbabane (24)
Sweden	450	8 320	18	Stockholm (1 380)
Switzerland	41	6 329	154	Berne (282)
Syria	185	8 979	49	Damascus (1 142)
Taiwan	36	17 479	486	Taipei (3 050)
Tanzania	945	17 982	19	Dar-es-Salaam (757)
Thailand	514	46 455	90	Bangkok (4 702)
Togo	56	2 699	48	Lomé (135)
Trinidad and Tobago	5	1 156	227	Port of Spain (63)
Tunisia	164	6 363	39	Tunis (944)
Turkey	781	45 218	58	Ankara (2 204)
Uganda	236	13 225	56	Kampala (331)
United Arab Emirates	84	1 040	12	Abu Dhabi (236)
U.S.S.R.	22 402	265 542	12	Moscow (8 011)
United Kingdom	245	55 945	228	London (6 696)
United States	9 363	229 805	25	Washington (3 045)
Upper Volta	274	6 908	25	Ouagadougou (169)
Uruguay	178	2 899	16	Montevideo (1 230)
Venezuela	912	13 913	15	Caracas (2 576)
Vietnam	330	52 742	160	Hanoi (2 571)
Western Samoa	3	156	55	Apia (32)
Yemen, North	195	5 926	30	Sana (448)
Yemen, South	288	1 969	7	Aden (285)
Yugoslavia	256	22 471	88	Belgrade (775)
Zaire	2 345	28 291	12	Kinshasa (2 008)
Zambia	753	5 680	8	Lusaka (538)
Zimbabwe	391	7 360	19	Harare (633)

Economic Section

Introduction

It is the aim of these statistics to present for various countries a picture of their character and position in the world in such a way that comparisons between countries may be made and a wide variety of basic questions answered.

The information includes both the sophisticated and the elementary. At all times it was thought more satisfactory to be specific about few items rather than general about many. Those chosen items are the most important within the general categories of area and demography, natural resources, industrial production and trade. The arrangement of columns corresponds to these categories. The first column is general and the rest refer to the four categories.

In case some of the terms are unfamiliar, explanations are given below in the appropriate part of the General Notes.

Table Arrangement

Country
1. Form of Government
2. Language(s).
3. Currency.
4. Average exchange rate, May 1983

Area and population
1. Area km².
2. Population and density (Estimates June 1981)
3. Birth & Death rates per 000 Average annual rate of change (1970–77).
4. Urban population, 000's. Percentage of total population.
5. Capital population, 000's

Production
1. GDP (million $) for l.a. year & annual growth rate for l.a. 5 year period; GDP per capita for l.a. year & annual growth rate for l.a. 5 year period; Industrial origin of GDP, % distribution.
2. Agricultural production, 000 tonnes.
3. Livestock, 000 head
4. Fish caught, 000 tonnes 1980.
5. Roundwood 1980, million m³.
6. Minerals mined, 000 tonnes. (Gas in teracalories).

Manufactures
1. Production/Consumption of all energy, million tonnes of coal equivalent, 1980. Electricity production, million kWh. (% Hydro-electricity, nuclear, geothermal).
2. Manufactures, 000 tonnes.
   (a) Agricultural, l.a. year.
   (b) Industrial, l.a. year.
   (Sawnwood, where given, is in 000 m³).
3. Communications: telephones & cars in use (000's), l.a. year Railways, passenger-km & tonne-km (millions). Airlines, passenger-km & tonne-km (millions). Sea cargo, loaded & unloaded 000 tonnes.

Trade
Export and Import totals, millions $.
List of major items.
Main trading partners.
Invisible trade balance. million $, 1981.
Revenue from tourism, million $, 1978
Aid given (l.a. year) or received (average 1976–8) & source, million $

General Notes

As far as possible the figures refer to 1981. When they are for different years or periods the appropriate date is mentioned in the table description shown above. For the urban and capital populations the most recent estimates or figures from the latest censuses are given; these may be 5–10 years old.

Column One
The exchange rates for the £ and U.S. $ are shown.
The C.F.A. franc is the unit of currency used throughout the African territories associated with France. (C.F.A. = Communauté Financière Africaine.)

Column Two
The area figure is for the total area of the country, including inland water bodies.
The birth and death rates are the latest figures that are available. The annual rate of change in the population is expressed as an average for the years 1975–79. The figure includes the net balance of births, deaths and migration.

Column Three
The GDP in line 1 is the Gross Domestic Product. In Communist countries the best similar measure is the NMP, the Net Material Product.

The Gross Domestic Product is a measure of a country's total production of goods and services. The figures are expressed in 'purchaser's values' which means the cost in the market of goods and services on delivery to the purchaser; that is the cost of materials, production, trade and transport charges. Imported goods and services are excluded.

The Net Material Product is not comparable to the GDP; it is the total net value of goods and production services, including taxes, in one year. Excluded are public administration, defence, personal and professional services. The conversion into dollars is based on the commercial import/export rate. The resulting figure should be used with great caution and treated as a general indicator.

The second figure is given for the GDP expressed per capita, and an annual average (over the latest available 5 year period) rate of increase is added after both. The differences between rates of increase are most illuminating.

The Industrial Origin of the GDP comes in the next line and is divided into three categories, Agriculture, Industry and Other. The percentage figures show which part of the GDP is contributed by each category.

Roundwood refers here to the forest output of wood whether for use as fuel, sawnwood or other products. The weight is without bark.

Column Four
The production and consumption of various types of energy is given as the coal equivalent. The equivalent is the conversion of the total calorific content of all energy sources into terms of the calorific value of 1 tonne of coal. The production figure is based on the home production of coal, lignite, crude petroleum, natural gas and hydro- and nuclear electricity. Imported energy sources are not included, hence the apparent discrepancy between production and consumption of energy.

Synthetic fibres refer to non-cellulosic continuous and discontinuous fibres. They include textile, glass and spun fibres. The filaments are either natural polymers or synthetic polymers. The most familiar trade names for some of these are nylon, terylene, orlon, saran etc.

Petroleum products include particular products obtained from crude petroleum and shale oil. These products are liquefied petroleum gas, naphtha motor spirit, aviation gasoline, kerosene, white spirit, jet fuel, distillate fuel oils, residual fuel oils, lubricating oils, bitumen and paraffin wax.

Vehicles refer to passenger cars and commercial vehicles and heavy trucks, but not to agricultural machinery or tractors.

Rail traffic refers to all traffic within the borders of the country, but air traffic includes domestic and international flights.

Column Five
Exports are f.o.b. and imports c.i.f.

Invisible trade concerns the provision of services to people abroad and dividends from overseas assets. The invisible trade balance is the net balance of private earnings from, and expenditure on, this exchange of non-physical ('invisible') goods. The most important activities are international banking, insurance, shipping and tourism. Government activity is not accounted for, although this may significantly alter the overall balance.

The revenue from tourism is the total income, and not a net balance.

Aid is a general term for all planned assistance to the developing countries. Aid comes from governments ('official aid') and from private organisations ('private aid'). In 1978 net total aid from the developed market economies to the developing countries was $24 535 million and the private equivalent was $40 002 million. A second distinction can be made between bilateral and multilateral aid. Bilateral aid is arranged between two governments according to their own arrangements; this method accounts for over 85% of all aid. Multilateral aid is given through institutions such as the World Bank, the E.E.C., regional institutions like the Colombo plan and other U.N. institutions.

The principal sources used in the preparation of these tables were the Yearbooks of the U.N. (Statistical, Demographic, National Accounts and International Trade), the Monthly Bulletin of Statistics of the U.N. and the Yearbooks of the F.A.O.

Abbreviations

. . .: *data not available*	c: *carats (thousand)*	m, m², m³: *metres (square, cubic) (thousand)*	hydr: *hydro-electric*	T: *thousand*
t: *tonnes*	grt: *gross registered tons (thousand)*	kWh: *kilowatt-hour*	geo: *geothermal*	nucl: *nuclear*
kg: *kilograms*	hl: *hectolitres (thousand)*	l.a.: *latest available*	M: *million*	

Country	Area and Population	Production	Manufactures	Trade

AFGHANISTAN

1. Republic
2. Pashto, Persian
3. Afghani
4. £1=99
   $1=61.64

1. 647 497 km²
2. 16 363 000; 25 per km²
3. Br 45; DR 21; AI 2.5%
4. Urb. pop.: 2 134 (14.5%)
5. Kabul 588

1. GDP $2 669 (...); $190 (...)
   Agric. 53%, Indust. 20%, Others 27%
2. Wheat 3 000   Maize 798
   Cottonseed 52   Cotton lint 28
3. Sheep 23 000   Cattle 3 980
   Goats 3 000
5. Roundwood 8
6. Coal 170   Natural Gas 23 905
   Salt 85

1. 2.72/0.97; 970 kWh (74 hydr.)
2a. Sugar 4   Sawnwood 400
    Meat 242
b. Cement 126
   Cotton woven 80
3. Telephones 31; Cars 37
   Air: 290 pass.-km; 13.9 t-km

Exports $729   Imports $924
Cotton   Food
Natural Gas   Textiles
Dried fruit   Petroleum products
Fresh fruit   Machinery
Exports to: U.S.S.R., U.K. and Pakistan
Imports from: U.S.S.R., Japan and Iran
Aid received (net): $73 from West, $164 from East

ALBANIA

1. Republic
2. Albanian
3. Lek
4. £1=10.07
   $1=6.27

1. 28 748 km²
2. 2 671 000; 90 per km²
3. BR 33; DR 8; AI 2.9%
4. Urb. pop.: 740 (34%)
5. Tirana 192

1. NMP... (9.2%); ... (6.2%)
2. Wheat 510   Maize 250
   Cottonseed 17   Cotton lint 9
3. Sheep 1 170   Goats 670
5. Roundwood 2
6. Lignite 1 020   Crude petroleum 2 800
   Chrome 390   Copper 11.5
   Nickel 8

1. 5.00/3.2; 2 450 kWh (78% hydr.)
2a. Sugar 40   Beer 144 hl
b. Cement 800   Copper 10
   Cotton woven ...   Wool, woven ...

Exports ...   Imports ...
Fuels and minerals
Exports to: India, Czechoslovakia, Poland and E. Germany
Imports from: India, Czechoslovakia, Poland and E. Germany

ALGERIA

1. Republic
2. Arabic, French
3. Algerian Dinar
4. £1=7.20
   $1=4.53

1. 2 381 741 km²
2. 19 590 000; 8 per km²
3. BR 47; DR 14; AI 3.4%
4. Urb. pop.: 8 467 (52%)
5. Algiers 1 503

1. GDP $17 931 (...); $1 001 (...)
   Agric. 8%, Indust. 39%, Others 53%
2. Wheat 1 400   Barley 750
   Grapes 462   Oranges 300
3. Sheep 12 500   Goats 2 850
4. Fish 39
5. Crude petroleum 39 528   Natural Gas 158 474
   Iron ore 1 927   Phosphates 997
                        Lead 2

1. 116.3/15.0; 6 216 kWh (5% hydr.)
2a. Wine 284   Meat 168
b. Cotton yarn 9   Cement 3 768
   Petroleum products 4 610
3. Telephones 346; Cars 400
   Rail: 1 452 pass-km; 2 016 t-km
   Air: 1 723 pass-km; 9.2 t-km
   Sea: 49 824 loaded; 13 500 unloaded

Exports $11 684   Imports $10 811
Crude petroleum   Machinery
Wine   Iron and steel
Natural Gas   Food
Exports to: France, W. Germany, U.S.A. and Italy
Imports from: France, W. Germany, Italy and U.S.A.
Aid received (net): $136 from West; $265 from East

ANGOLA

1. Republic
2. Portuguese
3. Kwanza
4. £1=49
   $1=30.31

1. 1 246 700 km²
2. 7 262 000; 6 per km²
3. BR 48; DR 23; AI 2.5%
4. Urb. pop.: 1 035 (15%)
5. Luanda 475

1. GDP $2 512 (...); $401 (...)
2. Coffee 60   Sugar cane 410
   Maize 250   Palm oil 40
3. Cattle 3 209   Goats 935
4. Fish 78
5. Roundwood 8
6. Crude petroleum 7 277   Diamonds 400 c

1. 13.12/1.03; kWh (73 hydr.)
2a. Sugar 35
b. Cement 600
   Cotton yarn 3
3. Telephones 28; Cars 75
   Rail: 418 pass-km; 5 461 t-km
   Sea: 10 044 loaded; 3 984 unloaded

Exports £1 227   Imports $625
Coffee   Machinery
Diamonds   Metals
Crude petroleum
Exports to: U.S.A., Portugal, Canada and Japan
Imports from: Portugal, W. Germany, South Africa and U.S.A.
Aid received (net): $41 from West; $76 from East

ARGENTINA

1. Republic
2. Spanish
3. Argentinian Peso
4. £1=4 106
   $1=47 213

1. 2 776 889 km²
2. 28 085 000; 10 per km²
3. BR 26; DR 9; AI 1.3%
4. Urb. pop.: 19 540 (83%)
5. Buenos Aires 8 436

1. GDP $35 227 (2.4%); $1 388 (1.0%)
   Agric. 12%, Indust. 36%, Others 52%
2. Wheat 7 900   Maize 13 500
   Linseed 598   Citrus fruits 1 418
   Wool 165   Grapes 2 700
3. Cattle 54 235   Sheep 30 000
4. Fish 384
5. Roundwood 10
6. Coal 434   Zinc 35
   Crude petroleum 25 512   Lead 34
   Natural gas 81 000   Silver 78 t

1. 51.2/49.2; 35 268 kWh (37% hydr., 6% nucl.)
2a. Meat 3 822   Wine 2 075
    Sugar 1 624
b. Cotton yarn 74   Steel 2 196
   Petroleum   Vehicles:
   products 22 190   pass. 144; comm. 29
   Cement 6 912   Iron 1 176
3. Telephones 2 404; Cars 3 000
   Rail: 12 036 pass.-km; 10 932 t-km
   Air: 6 936 pass.-km; 216 t-km
   Sea: 30 156 loaded; 10 536 unloaded

Exports $8 016   Imports $10 544
Meat   Machinery
Cereals   Iron and steel
Wool   Non-ferrous metals
Exports to: Italy, Netherlands, Brazil and U.S.A.
Imports from: U.S.A., W. Germany, Brazil and Japan
Invisible trade balance: −$4 968
Revenue from tourism: $213
Aid received (net): $29 from West

AUSTRALIA

1. Commonwealth
2. English
3. Australian Dollar
4. £1=1.75
   $1=1.03

1. 7 686 810 km²
2. 14 927 000; 2 per km²
3. BR 16; DR 7; AI 1.2%
4. Urb. pop.: 11 650 (86%)
5. Canberra 227

1. GDP $92 290 (3.0%); $6 559 (1.5%)
   Agric. 5%, Indust. 25%, Others 70%
2. Wheat 16 400   Barley 3 430
   Oats 1 530   Wool 700
   Citrus fruits 476   Other fruits 2 000
3. Sheep 133 396   Cattle 25 177
4. Fish 136
5. Roundwood 16
6. Coal 100 872   Lead 393
   Crude petroleum 18 623   Zinc 504
   Manganese 1 033   Gold 18
   Iron ore 60 480   Nickel 75
   Bauxite 25 876   Copper 223
   Silver 723t

1. 114.7/88.2; 103 200 kWh (18% hydr.)
2a. Meat 2 628   Sugar 3 450
    Sawnwood 3 314   Butter & cheese 216
b. Wool yarn 20   Cement 5 736
   Steel 7 956   Radios 38
   Petroleum   Vehicles:
   products 23 429   pass. 359; comm. 40
3. Telephones 62 663; Cars 5 799
   Rail: ...; 31 995 t-km
   Air: 24 516 pass.-km; 608 t-km
   Sea: 187 776 loaded; 26 220 unloaded

Exports $16 642   Imports $23 768
Wool   Machinery
Cereals   Vehicles
Metals   Textiles
Meat   Crude petroleum
Exports to: Japan, U.S.A. and N.Z.
Imports from: U.S.A., Japan, U.K. and W. Germany
Invisible trade balance; −$5 547
Revenue from tourism: $395
Aid given (net): $677

AUSTRIA

1. Federal Republic
2. German
3. Austrian Schilling
4. £1=26.0
   $1=16.91

1. 83 849 km²
2. 7 510 000; 90 per km²
3. BR 13; DR 12; AI 0.0%
4. Urb. pop.: 3 867 (52%)
5. Vienna 1 516

1. GDP $50 014 (3.8%); $6 660 (3.6%)
   Agric. 5%, Inust. 33%, Others 62%
2. Wheat 1 400   Barley 1 220
   Potatoes 1 200   Rye 320
                        Pears 97
3. Pigs 3 706   Cattle 2 538
5. Roundwood 14
6. Lignite 3 076   Iron ore 945
   Crude petroleum 1 344   Magnesite 1 003
   Natural gas 12 781   Antimony 601 t
   Salt 542   Lead 6

1. 9.42/31.2; 42 900 kWh (69% hydr.)
2a. Wine 2 680 hl   Sugar 490
    Sawnwood 6 782
b. Cotton yarn 18   Wool yarn 9
   Steel 5 076   Aluminium 142
   Petroleum products 7 419
3. Telephones 2 443; Cars 2 247
   Rail: 7 308 pass.-km; 10 320 t-km
   Air: 1 236 pass.-km; 17 t-km

Exports $15 845   Imports $21 048
Machinery   Machinery
Iron and steel   Food
Textiles   Textiles
Sawnwood   Vehicles
                      Chemical products
Exports to: W. Germany, Italy, Switzerland and U.K.
Imports from: W. Germany, Switzerland, Italy and France
Invisible trade balance: +$3 168
Revenue from tourism: $4 509
Aid given (net): $226

BANGLADESH

1. Republic
2. Bengali
3. Taka
4. £1=37
   $1=24.16

1. 143 998 km²
2. 89 655 000; 623 per km²
3. BR 47; DR 18; AI 2.4%
4. Urb. pop.: 8 759 (10%)
5. Dacca 1 730

1. GDP $9 376 (...); $112 (...)
   Agric. 52%, Indust. 7%, Others 41%
2. Rice 20 422   Bananas 625
   Tea 40   Jute 868
3. Cattle 35 000   Goats 11 800
4. Fish 650
5. Roundwood 10

1. 1.78/4.06; 2 400 kWh (24% hydr.)
2a. Jute 868   Sugar 155
b. Cotton yarn 46   Cement 312
3. Telephones 101; Cars 22
   Rail: 4 406 pass.-km; 739 t-km
   Sea 972 loaded; 7 500 unloaded

Exports $791   Imports $2 594
Exports to: U.S.A., Pakistan, U.S.S.R. and U.K.
Imports from: Japan, U.S.A. and U.K.
Aid received (net): $681 from West; $50 from East

For detailed table headings and notes see page 1 of this section

Country	Area and Population	Production	Manufactures	Trade

BELGIUM

1. Kingdom
2. French, Flemish, German
3. Belgian Franc
4. £1=74
   $1=46.95

Area and Population
1. 30 513 km²
2. 9 861 000; 323 per km²
3. BR 13; DR 11; AI 0.1%
4. Urb pop.: 9 286 (95%)
5. Brussels 1 042

Production
1. GDP $88 807 (3.7%), $9 025 (3.4%)
   Agric. 2%, Indust. 30%, Others 68%
2. Wheat 943 — Barley 823
   Potatoes 1 426 — Apples 131
   Pigs 5 099 — Cattle 3 116
4. Fish 46
5. Roundwood 2.7
6. Coal 6 590 — Lead 102
   Iron ore 13

Manufactures
1. 7.48/59.5; 53 640 kWh (2% hydr., 23% nucl.)
2a. Sugar 1 100 — Sawnwood 685
   b. Cotton yarn 41 — Wool yarn 79
   Steel 12 288 — Copper 418
   Coke oven coke 5 747 — Plastics 1 943
   Petroleum — Vehicles:
   products 23 663 — pass. 864; comm. 36
   Iron 9 792
3. Telephones 3 271; Cars 3 159
   Rail: 7 080 pass.-km; 751 t-km
   Air: 5 196 pass.-km; 444 t-km
   Sea: 42 804 loaded; 69 504 unloaded

Trade
Exports $55 641 (incl. Luxembourg) — Imports $62 123 (incl. Luxembourg)
Iron and steel — Machinery
Vehicles — Vehicles
Machinery — Non-ferrous metals
Non-ferrous metals — Diamonds
Textiles — Petrol
Trade is principally with:
W. Germany, France, Netherlands and U.K.
Invisible trade balance (incl. Luxembourg): + $1 596
Revenue from tourism: $1 300
Aid given (net): $2 605

BENIN

1. Republic
2. French
3. C.F.A. Franc
4. £1=554
   $1=339.82

Area and Population
1. 112 622 km²
2. 3 640 000; 32 per km²
3. BR 49; DR 19; AI 2.8%
4. Urb. pop.: 483 (14%)
5. Porto-Novo 104

Production
1. GDP $503 (2.2%); $162 (−0.5%)
   Agric. 38%, Indust. 7%, Others 55%
2. Cassava 975 — Palm oil 34
   Maize 349 — Cottonseed 15
   Groundnuts 60
3. Goats 926 — Cattle 771
4. Fish 25
5. Roundwood 3

Manufactures
1. −/0.12; 5 kWh
2a. Sawnwood 9
3. Telephones 10; Cars 14
   Rail: 133 pass.-km; 152 t-km
   Air: 139 pass.-km; 13 t-km
   Sea: 73 loaded; 982 unloaded

Trade
Exports $26 — Imports $267
Palm oil — Manufactured products
Oilseeds — Machinery
Cotton, Cocoa
Exports to: France, Netherlands and U.K.
Imports from: France, W. Germany
Netherlands and U.K.
Aid received (net): $53 from West

BOLIVIA

1. Republic
2. Spanish
3. Bolivian Peso
4. £1=67
   $1=44.0

Area and Population
1. 1 098 581 km²
2. 5 755 000; 5 per km²
3. BR 47; DR 18; AI 2.7%
4. Urb. pop.: 1 926 (42%)
5. La Paz 655, Sucre 63

Production
1. GDP $2 334 (6.0%); $477 (3.2%)
   Agric. 17%, Indust. 25%, Others 58%
2. Maize 250 — Barley 55
   Potatoes 730 — Citrus fruit 167
3. Sheep 8 750 — Goats 3 050
5. Roundwood 4
6. Antimony 13 019 — Crude petroleum 1 044
   Tin 29 — Silver 205 t
   Tungsten 3 997 t — Zinc 47
   Natural Gas 41 627 — Copper 3
   Lead 17

Manufactures
1. 5.04/1.68; 1 150 kWh (71% hydr.)
2a. Sugar 266
   b. Cement 257 — Tin 19
3. Telephones 49; Cars 35
   Rail: 398 pass.-km; 593 t-km
   Air: 960 pass.-km; 45 t-km

Trade
Exports $909 — Imports $825
Tin ore — Cars
Crude petroleum — Flour
Exports to: U.K., Argentina and U.S.A.
Imports from: U.S.A., Japan, Argentina and Brazil
Invisible trade balance: − $436
Aid received (net): $102 from West; $31 from East

BRAZIL

1. Federal Republic
2. Portuguese
3. New Cruzeiro
4. £1=647
   $1=248.82

Area and Population
1. 8 511 965 km²
2. 121 547 000; 14 per km²
3. BR 35; DR 9; AI 2.8%
4. Urb. pop.: 78 153 (64%)
5. Brasilia 1 306

Production
1. GDP $175 807 (9.2%); $1 523 (6.2%)
   Agric. 9%, Indust. 26%, Others 65%
2. Maize 21 098 — Rice 8 261
   Cassava 25 050 — Soya beans 15 000
   Bananas 6 696 — Oranges 11 399
   Cottonseed 1 206 — Tobacco 362
3. Cattle 93 000 — Pigs 35 000
4. Fish 850
5. Roundwood 217
6. Coal 4 132 — Crude petroleum 10 692
   Iron ore 44 137 — Natural Gas 28 700
   Manganese 1 000 — Asbestos 95
   Gold 4 460 kg — Tin 8
   Bauxite 6 714

Manufactures
1. 34.2/93.6; 137 388 kWh (92% hydr.)
2a. Meat 4 784 — Sugar 8 500
   Sawnwood 14 070
   b. Cotton fabric 1 076 — Iron 11 244
   Steel 13 116 — Aluminium 293
   Cement 24 864 — Radios 759
   Petroleum — Vehicles:
   products 45 987 — pass. 662; comm. 97
3. Telephones 5 525; Cars 7 500
   Rail: 11 951 pass.-km; 64 039 t-km
   Sea: 123 996 loaded; 64 068 unloaded
   Air: 10 764 pass.-km; 528 t-km

Trade
Exports $23 172 — Imports $24 007
Coffee — Machinery
Cotton — Crude petroleum
Iron ore — Cereals
Machinery — Non-ferrous metals
Exports to: U.S.A., W. Germany, Netherlands, and Japan
Imports from: U.S.A., W. Germany, Japan, Saudi Arabia and Iraq
Invisible trade balance: − $13 128
Revenue for tourism: $108
Aid received (net): $100 from West. $600 from East

BULGARIA

1. Republic
2. Bulgar
3. Lev
4. £1=1.48
   $1=0.88

Area and Population
1. 110 912 km²
2. 8 890 000; 80 per km²
3. BR 16; DR 11; AI 0.7%
4. Urb. pop.: 5 503 (62%)
5. Sofia 1 032

Production
1. NMP $15 965 (7.8%); $1 814 (7.2%)
   Agric. 18%, Indust. 51%, Others 31%
2. Wheat 4 429 — Maize 2 477
   Tobacco 133 — Grapes 1 200
3. Sheep 10 433 — Pigs 3 808
4. Fish 126
5. Roundwood 4
6. Coal 273 — Crude petroleum 243
   Lignite 28 980 — Zinc 65
   Iron ore 578 — Lead 96

Manufactures
1. 16.9/50.3; 36 960 kWh (11% hydr., 17% nucl.)
2a. Meat 650 — Sawnwood 1 466
   Wine 510 — Sugar 150
   b. Cotton yarn 85 — Iron 1 512
   Steel 2 484 — Cement 5 448
   Petroleum products 11 436
3. Telephone 1 032; Cars 480
   Rail: 6 960 pass.-km; 18 048 t-km
   Air: 555 pass.-km; 7.2 t-km
   Sea: 2 878 loaded; 19 094 unloaded

Trade
Exports $10 372 — Imports $9 650
Cigarettes — Machinery
Alcoholic drinks — Ferrous metals
Clothing — Petroleum products
The principal trade is with U.S.S.R. Then:
E. Germany
Revenue from tourism: $230
Aid given (net): $15

BURMA

1. Republic
2. Burmese
3. Kyat
4. £1=12.21
   $1=8.13

Area and Population
1. 678 033 km²
2. 36 166 000; 53 per km²
3. BR 39; DR 14; AI 2.2%
4. Urb. pop.: 5 137 (24%)
5. Rangoon 2 276

Production
1. GDP $3 563 (3.0%); $113 (0.8%)
   Agric. 46%, Indust. 11%, Others 48%
2. Rice 14 636 — Groundnuts 476
   Tobacco 55 — Jute 35
3. Cattle 8 600 — Buffaloes 1 950
4. Fish 585
5. Roundwood 26
6. Crude petroleum 1 460 — Zinc 3
   Lead 4 — Silver 25 t

Manufactures
1. 2.96/2.22; 1 080 kWh (61% hydr.)
2a. Sugar 44 — Sawnwood 415
   b. Lead 4 — Cotton yarn 13
3. Telephones 34; Cars 35
   Rail: 3 252 pass.-km; 564 t-km
   Air: 180 pass.-km; 1.4 t-km
   Sea: 732 loaded; 408 unloaded

Trade
Exports $386 — Imports $332
Sawnwood — Machinery
Rice — Textiles
Exports to: Japan, Indonesia and Vietnam
Imports from: Japan, China, W. Germany, U.K. and Singapore
Invisible trade balance: − $68
Aid received (net): $148 from West

CAMBODIA

1. Republic
2. French, Cambodian
3. Riel
4. £1=1 832
   $1=1 200

Area and Population
1. 181 035 km²
2. 8 718 000; 48 per km²
3. BR 46.0; DR 17.0; AI 2.9
4. Urb. pop.: 867 (10%)
5. Phnom Penh 2 000

Production
1. GDP $881 (...) $125 (...)
   Agric. 41%, Indust. 17%, Others 42%
2. Rice 1 160 — Maize 98
   Rubber 10 — Bananas 67
3. Cattle 956 — Pigs 223
4. Fish 21
5. Roundwood 5

Manufactures
1. −/0.13; 150 kWh
2a. Sawnwood 43
3. Telephones 71; Cars 25
   Rail: 54 pass.-km; 10 t-km
   Air: 42 pass.-km; 0.4 t-km
   Sea: 50 loaded; 583 unloaded

Trade
Exports $10 — Imports $101
Rubber — Machinery
Rice — Textiles
Cattle — Iron and Steel
Exports to: Vietnam, Hong Kong and Singapore
Imports from: France, Japan, China, Thailand and U.S.A.

CAMEROON

1. Republic
2. French, English
3. C.F.A. Franc
4. £1=554
   $1=339.82

Area and Population
1. 475 442 km²
2. 8 650 000; 18 per km²
3. BR 42; DR 19; AI 2.8%
4. Urb. pop.: 2 392 (29%)
5. Yaoundé 314

Production
1. GDP $3 309 (3.7%); $427 (1.8%)
   Agric. 31%, Indust. 12%, Others 57%
2. Coffee 105 — Groundnuts 120
   Cocoa 110 — Palm oil 80
3. Goats 2 340 — Cattle 3 200
4. Fish 69
5. Roundwood 9

Manufactures
1. 0.16/0.64; 1 346 kWh (95% hydr.)
2a. Sawnwood 494
   b. Aluminium 65
3. Telephones 22; Cars 55
   Rail: 276 pass.-km; 708 t-km
   Air: 314 pass.-km; 5.8 t-km
   Sea: 924 loaded; 2 616 unloaded

Trade
Exports $1 384 — Imports $1 602
Cocoa — Manufactured goods
Coffe — Machinery
Exports to: France, Netherlands and W. Germany
Imports from: France, W. Germany and U.S.A.
Aid received (net): $160 from West

For detailed table headings and notes see page 1 of this section

Country	Area and Population	Production	Manufactures	Trade

CANADA

1. Commonwealth
2. English, French
3. Canadian Dollar
4. £1=1.88 $1=1.23

Area and Population
1. 9 221 001 km²
2. 24 231 000; 3 per km²
3. BR 16; DR 7; AI 1.1%
4. Urb. pop.: 17 367 (76%)
5. Ottawa 718

Production
1. GDP $177 947 (4.4%); 7 572 (3.1)
   Agric. 4%, Indust. 25%, Others 71%
2. Wheat 24 519 — Barley 13 384
   Oats 3 570 — Maize 6 214
3. Cattle 12 468 — Pigs 9 585
4. Fish 1 305
5. Roundwood 161
6. Iron ore 24 367 — Crude petroleum 64 275
   Coal 25 568 — Natural Gas 655 656
   Copper 718 — Zinc 1 096
   Nickel 130 — Asbestos 1 542
   Gold 49 635 — Salt 6 222
   Lead 332

Manufactures
1. 280.0/245.2; 378 648 kWh (69% hydr., 10% nucl.)
2a. Sawnwood 41 929 — Wood pulp 19 295
   Paper 13 789 — Sugar 125
b. Iron 9 744 — Steel 15 024
   Aluminium 1 183 — Copper 465
   Radios 819 — Vehicles:
   Petroleum — pass. 803; comm. 520
   products 71 140 — Cement 9 492
3. Telephones 15283; Cars 10 367
   Rail: 2 892 pass.-km; 228 120 t-km
   Air: 31 404 pass.-km; 776 t-km
   Sea: 134 640 loaded; 67 416 unloaded

Trade
Exports $69 635 / Imports $65 622
Vehicles / Machinery
Machinery / Vehicles
Paper and cardboard / Iron and steel
Non-ferrous metals / Textiles
Wood pulp / Crude petroleum
Sawnwood / Fruit and vegetables
Crude petroleum
Wheat
Trade is principally with: U.S.A., U.K. and Japan
Invisible trade balance: −$12 383
Revenue from tourism: $1 722
Aid given (net): $2 001

CENTRAL AFRICAN REPUBLIC

1. Republic
2. French
3. Franc C.F.A.
4. £1=554 $1=364

Area and Population
1. 622 984 km²
2. 2 349 000; 4 per km²
3. BR 44; DR 23; AI 2.2%
4. Urb. pop.: 392 (27%)
5. Bangui 302

Production
1. GDP $391 (1.3%); $218 (...)
   Agric. 31%, Indust. 18%, Others 51%
2. Maize 40 — Cassava 1 021
   Bananas 144 — Coffee 17
   Groundnuts 125 — Cottonseed 14
3. Goats 873 — Cattle 1 000
5. Roundwood 3
6. Diamonds 301 c

Manufactures
1. 0.01/0.07; 64 kWh (94% hydr.)
2a. Meat 41 — Sawnwood 73
3. Telephones 5; Cars 14
   Air: 153 pass.-km; 14.6 t-km

Trade
Exports $116 / Imports $81
Diamonds / Machinery
Cotton, Coffee / Vehicles
Exports to: France, Belgium and Lux.
Imports from: France, W. Germany and Japan
Aid received (net): $43 from West

CHAD

1. Republic
2. French
3. C.F.A. Franc
4. £1=554 $1=364

Area and Population
1. 1 284 000 km²
2. 4 547 000; 4 per km²
3. BR 44; DR 24; AI 2.3%
4. Urb. pop.: 792 (18%)
5. N'Djamena 242

Production
1. GDP $665 (3.3%); $165 (1.3%)
   Agric. 41%, Indust. 13%, Others 46%
2. Millet 580 — Groundnuts 110
   Cottonseed 45 — Cotton 26
3. Cattle 3 800 — Goats 2 300
4. Fish 115
5. Roundwood 7

Manufactures
1. −/0.10; 64 kWh
2a. Meat 53
3. Telephones 7; Cars 10
   Air: 162 pass.-km; 14 t-km

Trade
Exports $59 / Imports $118
Cotton / Petroleum products
Meat / Machinery
Exports to: France, Nigeria and Cameroon
Imports from: France, Nigeria and Netherlands
Aid received (net): $86 from West, $3 from East

CHILE

1. Republic
2. Spanish
3. Chilean Peso
4. £1=110 $1=73

Area and Population
1. 756 945 km²
2. 11 294 000; 15 per km²
3. BR 32; DR 8; AI 1.6%
4. Urb. pop.: 9 006 (81%)
5. Santiago 3 853

Production
1. GDP $4 319 (0.8%); $421 (−1.0%)
   Agric. 10%, Indust. 27%, Others 63%
2. Wheat 686 — Grapes 980
   Wool 22 — Tobacco 6
3. Sheep 6 800 — Cattle 3 745
4. Fish 2 817
5. Roundwood 11
6. Coal 1 115 — Iron ore 5 952
   Crude petroleum 819 — Copper 1 081
   Natural Gas 14 108 — Moybdenum 13

Manufactures
1. 6.31/10.94; 11 880 kWh (65% hydr.)
2a. Meat 381 — Sawnwood 2 183
   Sugar 250 — Wood pulp 3 056
   Wine 585
b. Iron 684 — Steel 624
   Cotton yarn 23 — Copper 954
   Fertilizers 139 — Cement 1 584
3. Telephones 467; Cars 300
   Rail: 1 620 pass.-km; 1 728 t-km
   Air: 2 220 pass.-km; 104 t-km
   Sea: 9 947 loaded; 6 188 unloaded

Trade
Exports $3 952 / Imports $6 379
Copper / Machinery
Iron ore / Food
Fishmeal / Manufactured products
Saltpetre / Chemical products
Exports to: Japan, W. Germany, U.K., Argentina, U.S.A. and Brazil
Invisible trade balance: −$2 316
Aid received (net): $49 from West

CHINA

1. Republic
2. Chinese and others
3. Yuan
4. £1=2.99 $1=1.99

Area and Population
1. 9 561 000 km²
2. 1 007 755 000; 105 per km²
3. BR 32; DR 7; AI 1.4%
4. Urb. pop.: 188 169 (24%)
5. Peking 9 231

Production
1. GDP ... (56%); ... (3.2%)
   Agric. 48%, Indust. 42%, Others 10% (1956)
2. Rice 146 292 — Wheat 58 493
   Soya beans 13 050 — Groundnuts 3 513
   Citrus fruits 1 100 — Tobacco 872
   Tea 354 — Cotton lint 2 968
   Cottonseed 6 000
3. Pigs 310 251 — Sheep 105 200
4. Fish 4 240
5. Roundwood 224
6. Coal 618 000 — Manganese 300
   Crude petroleum 101 220 — Tungsten 11
   Iron ore 32 500 — Tin 17
   Salt 19 530 — Lead 160
   Bauxite 1 750 — Copper 150

Manufactures
1. 614.2/565.5; 306 000 kWh
2a. Meat 23 112 — Sawnwood 21 165
   Sugar 4 031
b. Iron 34 000 — Steel 35 600
   Aluminium 350 — Cement 80 000
   Cotton yarn 1 500
3. Telephones ...; Cars 50
   Rail: ...; 571 200 t-km
   Air: ...;...
   Sea: 18 200 loaded; 17 000 unloaded

Trade
Exports $22 280 / Imports $18 625
Agricultural prods. / Grain
Textiles / Cotton products
Minerals / Machinery
Crude petroleum / Primary materials
/ Petrol
Exports to: Hong Kong, U.S.S.R., Japan and Singapore
Imports from: Japan, Australia, U.S.S.R. and Canada
Aid given (net): $163

COLOMBIA

1. Republic
2. Spanish
3. Columbian Peso
4. £1=113 $1=74.54

Area and Population
1. 1 138 914 km²
2. 28 776 000; 25 per km²
3. BR 32; DR 8; AI 2.8%
4. Urb. pop.: 13 410 (60%)
5. Bogotá 2 855

Production
1. GDP $20 591 (5.7%); $803 (2.8%)
   Agric. 30%, Indust. 23%, Others 47%
2. Maize 880 — Rice 1 799
   Cassava 2 150 — Bananas 3 555
   Coffee 808 — Cottonseed 160
   Tobacco 49 — Cotton lint 87
3. Cattle 24 251 — Pigs 2 245
4. Fish 65
5. Roundwood 42
6. Coal 4 000 — Silver 3 t
   Natural gas 20 900 — Gold 8 493 kg
   Crude petroleum 6 754 — Iron ore 454

Manufactures
1. 20.5/21.2; 18 756 kWh (67% hydr.)
2a. Meat 834 — Paper 330
   Sugar 1 185 — Sawnwood 883
b. Iron 492 — Steel 264
   Petroleum products 7 148 — Cement 4 464
3. Telephones 1 410; Cars 454
   Rail: 312 pass.-km; 888 t-km
   Air: 4 212 pass.-km; 210 t-km
   Sea: 8 040 loaded; 7 272 unloaded

Trade
Exports $2 956 / Imports $5 199
Coffee / Machinery
Crude petroleum / Vehicles
Cotton / Iron and Steel
Bananas / Organic chemicals
Sugar and Honey
Exports to: U.S.A., W. Germany and Venezuela
Imports from: U.S.A., W. Germany and Venezuela
Invisible trade balance: −$397
Revenue from tourism: $295
Aid received (net): $66 from West, $290 from East

CONGO

1. Popular Republic
2. French
3. C.F.A. Franc
4. £1=554 $1=364

Area and Population
1. 342 000 km²
2. 1 578 000; 5 per km²
3. BR 45; DR 19; AI 2.6%
4. Urb. pop.: 278 (29%)
5. Brazzaville 290

Production
1. GDP $693 (...); $514 (...)
2. Cassava 530 — Palm oil 9
3. Goats 123 — Cattle 71
4. Fish 21
5. Roundwood 2
6. Gold 3 kg — Diamonds ...
   Crude petroleum 3 096

Manufactures
1. 4.23/0.34; 120 kWh (50% hydr.)
2a. Sugar 22 — Sawnwood 64
3. Telephones 13; Cars 20
   Rail: 276 pass.-km; 468 t-km
   Air: 153 pass-km; 14.6 t-km
   Sea: 2 796 loaded; 708 unloaded

Trade
Exports $510 / Imports $291
Timber / Manufactured products
/ Machinery
Exports to: France, Italy, U.S.A., Brazil and Spain
Imports from: France, U.S.A., Gabon and W. Germany
Aid received (net): $61 from West

CUBA

1. Republic
2. Spanish
3. Cuban Peso
4. £1=1.30 $1=0.86

Area and Population
1. 114 524 km²
2. 9 766 000; 85 per km²
3. BR 15; DR 6; AI 1.2%
4. Urb. pop.: 5 169 (60%)
5. Havana 1 861

Production
1. NMP $8 943 (5.4%); $943 (4.8%)
2. Rice 518 — Cassava 328
   Coffee 24 — Oranges 360
   Sugar Cane 67 000 — Tobacco 34
3. Cattle 5 900 — Pigs 1 950
4. Fish 186
5. Roundwood 1
6. Chrome 10 — Nickel 37
   Copper 3 — Crude petroleum 360

Manufactures
1. 0.42/13.1; 10 332 kWh (1.1% hydr.)
2a. Meat 284 — Sawnwood 112
   Sugar 7 359
b. Petroleum products 6 212
   Cotton, woven 156 Mm² — Cement 3 288
3. Telephones 321; Cars 80
   Rail: 1 836 pass.-km; 2 628 t-km
   Air: 816 pass.-km; 7.6 t-km
   Sea: 2 316 loaded; 2 400 unloaded

Trade
Exports $3 967 / Imports $4 509
Sugar / Machinery
Minerals / Cereals
Tobacco / Fertilizers
/ Petroleum products
Exports to: U.S.S.R., Japan and Spain
Imports from: U.S.S.R. and Japan

For detailed table headings and notes see page 1 of this section

Country	Area and Population	Production	Manufactures	Trade
CYPRUS 1. Republic 2. Greek, Turkish and English 2. Cypriot Pound 4. £1=0.78 $1=1.95	1. 9 251 km² 2. 637 000; 69 per km² 3. BR 20; DR 9; AI 0.1% 4. Urb. pop.: 270 (42%) 5. Nicosia 147	1. GDP $1 364 (0.3%); $2 200 (0.1%) Agric. 11%, Indust. 19%, Others 70% 2. Barley 101 / Potatoes 216 Grapes 213 / Oranges 123 3. Sheep 515 / Goats 360 6. Copper 5 / Asbestos 35 Chrome 7	1. —/1.20; 1 056 kWh 2a. Wine 55 / Sawnwood 60 b. Cement 1 032 3. Telephones 92; Cars 86 Air: 852 pass.-km; 18 t-km Sea: 1 572 loaded; 2 376 unloaded	Exports $562 / Imports $1 166 Vegetables / Machinery Citrus fruits / Textiles Copper / Vehicles Exports to: U.K., Saudi Arabia and Lebanon Imports from: U.K., W. Germany, Italy, Iraq and Greece Revenue from Tourism: $273
CZECHOSLOVAKIA 1. Socialist Republic 2. Czech, Slovak 3. Koruna 4. £1=16.01 $1=6.15	1. 127 869 km² 2. 15 314 000; 120 per km² 3. BR 16; DR 12; AI 0.7% 4. Urb. pop.: 9 795 (67%) 5. Prague 1 193	1. NMP $68 559 (5.1%); $4 561 (4.3%) Agric. 9%, Indust. 60%, Others 31% 2. Barley 3 500 / Wheat 5 000 Oats 400 / Potatoes 3 850 Apples 170 / Tomatoes 82 3. Pigs 7 894 / Cattle 5 002 5. Roundwood 18 6. Coal 29 150 / Silver 36 t Lignite 94 879 / Crude petroleum 84 Iron ore 558 / Antimony 480 t Natural gas 5 268	1. 66.7/99.3; 74 064 kWh (6% hydr., 6% nucl.) 2a. Meat 1 444 / Sawnwood 4 903 Sugar 870 / Butter & cheese 308 Beer 23 934 hl b. Iron 10 080 / Steel 15 264 Aluminium 32 / Plastics 913 Wool yarn 63 / Petroleum Cotton yarn 137 / products 15 107 3. Telephones 2 981; Cars 1 950 Rail: 18 048 pass.-km; 72 264 t-km Air: 1 464 pass.-km; 14 t-km	Exports $14 887 / Imports $14 650 Machinery / Machinery Manufactured goods / Petroleum Iron and steel / Non-ferrous metals Vehicles / Iron and steel Main trade is with: U.S.S.R., E. Germany, Poland and Hungary Aid given (net): $273
DENMARK 1. Kingdom 2. Danish 3. Danish Krone 4. £1=13.11 $1=8.61	1. 43 069 km² 2. 5 122 000; 119 per km² 3. BR 10; DR 11; AI 0.3% 4. Urb. pop.: 4 191 (83%) 5. Copenhagen 1 382	1. GDP $50 334 (2.8%); $9 869 (2.4%) Agric. 6%, Indust. 21%, Others 73% 2. Barley 6 010 / Oats 165 Wheat 792 / Potatoes 880 Apples 80 / Rape seed 310 3. Pigs 9 856 / Cattle 2 933 4. Fish 2 027 5. Roundwood 2 6. Crude petroleum 756	1. 0.44/26.8; 18 204 kWh 2a. Pork 995 / Beef 245 Butter & cheese 327 / Sugar 522 b. Cotton yarn 1.9 / Steel 612 Petroleum products 5 649 / Ships (grt.) 364 3. Telephones 2 907; Cars 1 428 Rail: 3 348 pass.-km; 1 272 t-km Air: 2 892 pass.-km; 132 t-km Sea: 7 068 loaded; 31 836 unloaded	Exports $15 390 / Imports $17 578 Machinery / Machinery Pork / Manufactured products Other meat / Iron and steel Fish / Textiles Exports to: Sweden, U.K. and W. Germany Imports from: W. Germany, Sweden and U.K. Invisible trade balance: −$787 Revenue from tourism: $1 120 Aid given (net): $566
ECUADOR 1. Republic 2. Spanish 3. Sucre 4. £1=124 $1=81.40	1. 283 561 km² 2. 8 644 000; 30 per km² 3. BR 42; DR 10; AI 3.6% 4. Urb. pop.: 3 485 (43%) 5. Quito 808	1. GDP $4 056 (10.5%); $574 (6.8%) Agric. 20%, Indust. 29%, Others 51% 2. Maize 246 / Rice 402 Bananas/Plantains 3 050 / Oranges 530 Cocoa 96 / Coffee 88 3. Cattle 2 366 / Sheep 2 313 4. Fish 671 5. Roundwood 6 6. Crude petroleum 10 182 / Gold 92 kg	1. 15.4/4.99; 3 155 kWh (30% hydr.) 2a. Meat 222 / Sawnwood 905 Sugar 359 b. Petroleum products 4 207 3. Telephones 240; Cars 65 Rail: 65 pass.-km; 34 t-km Air: 576 pass.-km; 8.4 t-km Sea: 9 372 loaded; 3 828 unloaded	Exports $2 481 / Imports $2 253 Bananas / Machinery Coffee / Vehicles Cocoa / Chemical products Exports to: U.S.A., Panama, Colombia and Chile Imports from: U.S.A., W. Germany and Japan Invisible trade blance: −$1 325 Aid received (net): $58 from West
EGYPT 1. Republic 2. Arabic 3. Egyptian Pound 4. £1=1.27 $1=1.21	1. 1 001 449 km² 2. 43 465 000; 43 per km² 3. BR 38; DR 10; AI 2.6% 4. Urb. pop.: 18 097 5. Cairo 5 084	1. GDP $11 450 (3.9%); $308 (1.6%) Agric. 24%, Indust. 23%, Others 53% 2. Maize 3 308 / Wheat 1 938 Rice 2 236 / Tomatoes 2 632 Oranges 895 / Dates 428 Cotton lint 500 / Cottonseed 800 3. Cattle 2 040 / Buffaloes 2 379 4. Fish 137 6. Iron ore 888 / Salt 755 Crude petroleum 31 800 / Phosphates 639	1. 48.2/20.8; 18 520 kWh (52% hydr.) 2a. Meat 449 / Sugar 679 b. Cotton yarn 245 / Iron 720 Wool yarn 10 / Steel 800 Fertilizers 357 / Cement 3 432 Petroleum products 13 630 3. Telephones 473; Cars 350 Rail: 9 300 pass.-km; 2 415 t-km Air: 3 264 pass.-km; 41 t-km Sea: 8 820 loaded; 11 496 unloaded	Exports $3 233 / Imports $8 839 Cotton, Rice / Machinery Cotton lint / Manufactured products Fruit and vegetables / Wheat, Vehicles Exports to: U.S.S.R., Italy and Netherlands Imports from: U.S.A., France, Italy, U.K. and W. Germany Invisible trade balance: −$206 Revenue from tourism: $701 Aid received (net): $1 421 from West, $36 from East
ETHIOPIA 1. Republic 2. Amharic 3. Ethiopian Birr 4. £1=3.10 $1=2.04	1. 1 221 900 km² 2. 32 158 000; 26 per km² 3. BR 50; DR 25; AI 2.6% 4. Urb. pop.: 4 225 (14%) 5. Addis-Ababa 1 277	1. GDP $2 495 (...); $91 (...) Agric. 46%, Indust. 11%, Others 43% 2. Barley 190 / Millet 190 Coffee 198 / Maize 1 100 3. Cattle 26 100 / Sheep 23 350 4. Fish 27 5. Roundwood 24 6. Gold 311 kg / Salt 80	1. 0.05/0.89; 675 kWh (71% hydr.) 2a. Sugar 165 / Sawnwood 100 b. Cotton yarn 8 / Cement 103 3. Telephones 80; Cars 40 Rail: 155 pass.-km; 208 t-km Air: 756 pass.-km; 23 t-km Sea: 378 loaded; 1 250 unloaded	Exports $418 / Imports $567 Coffee / Machinery Hides / Manufactured products Exports to: U.S.A., Djibouti and Saudi Arabia Imports from: Japan, W. Germany, Kuwait, Italy and Saudi Arabia Aid received (net): $128 from West, $46 from East
FINLAND 1. Republic 2. Finnish, Swedish 3. Markka 4. £1=8.30 $1=5.41	1. 337 009 km² 2. 4 801 000; 14 per km² 3. BR 13; DR 9; AI 0.3% 4. Urb. pop.: 2 846 (60%) 5. Helsinki 483	1. GDP $28 926 (2.9%); $6 090 (2.5%) Agric. 8%, Indust. 28%, Others 64% 2. Wheat 235 / Barley 1 080 Oats 1 008 / Potatoes 478 3. Cattle 1 766 / Pigs 1 375 4. Fish 14 5. Roundwood 47 6. Iron ore 570 / Chrome 187 Titanium 120 / Copper 38 Zinc 53 / Gold 880 kg	1. 2.62/24.6; 39 264 kWh (26% hydr., 17% nucl.) 2a. Meat 328 / Butter & cheese 148 Sawnwood 10 275 / Wood pulp 7 440 b. Paper 5 923 / Newsprint 1 556 Iron 1 968 / Steel 2 424 Cotton yarn 8 / Ships (grt) 303 Petroleum products 9 327 3. Telephones 2 127; Cars 1 170 Rail: 3 276 pass.-km; 8 388 t-km Air: 2 496 pass.-km; 56 t-km Sea: 18 420 loaded; 30 180 unloaded	Exports $14 021 / Imports $14 202 Paper and cardboard / Machinery Wood pulp / Crude petroleum Sawnwood / Petroleum products Machinery / Iron and steel Ships and boats / Textiles Clothing / Vehicles Exports to: U.K., Sweden, U.S.S.R. and W. Germany imports from: Sweden, W. Germany, U.S.S.R. and U.K. Invisible trade balance: −$904 Aid given (net): $127
FRANCE 1. Republic 2. French 3. French Franc 4. $1=11.08 $1=7.27	1. 547 026 km² 2. 53 963 000; 98 per km² 3. BR 13; DR 9; AI 0.4% 4. Urb. pop.: 38 388 (73%) 5. Paris 9 863	1. GDP $421 359 (3.7%); $7 908 (3.1%) Agric. 5%, Indust. 30%, Others 65% 2. Wheat 22 782 / Barley 10 180 Oats 1 754 / Maize 9 100 Potatoes 6 400 / Sugarbeet 31 800 Apples 1 840 / Grapes 8 800 Tomatoes 800 / Pears 435 Tobacco 46 / Wool 22 Rape seed 1 023 3. Cattle 25 553 / Pigs 11 629 Sheep 11 629 / Goats 1 241 Horses 317 4. Fish 765 5. Roundwood 30 6. Coal 18 588 / Iron ore 14 240 Crude petroleum 1 680 / Lead 19 Natural Gas 66 528 / Zinc 37 Salt 6 255 / Potash 1 969 Bauxite 1 828	1. 50.2/233.8; 260 760 kWh (27% hydr., 24% nucl.) 2a. Meat 5 506 / Butter & cheese 1 810 Wine 5 791 / Beer 21 852 hl Sugar 5 600 / Sawnwood 10 113 b. Iron 17 916 / Steel 21 264 Aluminium 605 / Cement 28 224 Plastics 2 842 / Paper 5 121 Synthetic / Petroleum fibres 202 / products 68 442 Cotton yarn 240 / Wool yarn 138 Ships (grt) 252 / Radios 3 019 Vehicles: pass. 2 953; comm. 473 3. Telephones 19 870; Cars 19 150 Rail: 55 824 pass.-km; 64 392 t-km Air: 36 504 pass.-km; 2 239 t-km Sea: 59 400 loaded; 196 200 unloaded	Export $100 497 / Imports $102 448 Machinery / Machinery Vehicles / Petrol Iron and Steel / Iron and Steel Textiles / Non-ferrous metals Wheat / Vehicles Organic chemical / Textile fibres products / Meat Non-ferrous metals / Fruits Petroleum products Petrol Wine Exports to: W. Germany, Belgium-Luxembourg, Italy and U.K. Imports from: W. Germany, Italy, Belgium-Luxembourg and U.S.A. Invisible trade balance: +$5 915 Revenue from tourism: $4 794 Aid given (net): $6 910

For detailed table headings and notes see page 1 of this section

Country	Area and Population	Production	Manufactures	Trade
FRENCH GUIANA 1. French colony 2. French 3. Franc 4. £1=11.08 　$1=7.27	1. 91 000 km² 2. 69 000; 1 per km² 3. BR 25; DR 8; AI 3.4% 4. Urb. pop.: 29 (67%) 5. Cayenne 33	2. Cassava 8　　Bananas 3 3. Pigs 7　　Cattle 6 6. Gold 100 kg	1. —/0.17; 108 kWh 2a. Sugar ...　　Sawnwood 19 3. Telephones 13; Cars 17 　Sea: 36 loaded; 228 unloaded	Exports $25　　Imports $255 Timber　　Machinery Exports to: France, U.S.A. and Japan Imports from: France, Trinidad and Tobago Aid received (net): $76 from West
GABON 1. Republic 2. French, Bantu 3. C.F.A. Franc 4. £1=554 　$1=364	1. 267 667 km² 2. 555 000; 2 per km² 3. BR 31; DR 21; AI 1.1% 4. Urb. pop.: 160 (32%) 5. Libreville 186	1. GDP $2 012 (...); $3 725 (...) 　Agric. 6%, Indust. 41%, Others 53% 2. Cassava 100　　Bananas 71 　Cocoa 4 3. Goats 90　　Sheep 100 4. Fish 27 5. Roundwood 2 6. Crude petroleum 7 656　　Gold 50 kg 　Manganese 1 175　　Uranium 1 000 t	1. 13.4/1.02; 450 kWh (78% hydr.) 2a. Sawnwood 108　　Beer 510 hl b. Petroleum products 1 174 3. Telephones 7; Cars 22 　Air: 129 pass.-km; 7.8 t-km 　Sea: 12 555 loaded; 1 382 unloaded	Exports $1 477　　Imports $532 Petrol　　Manufactured products Sawnwood　　Machinery Manganese ores　　Vehicles Export to: France, U.S.A. and Argentina Imports from: France, U.S.A. and Japan Aid received (net): $35 from West
GERMANY (East) 1. Republic 2. German 3. Ostmark 4. £1=3.60 　$1=2.43	1. 108 174 km² 2. 16 736 000; 155 per km² 3. BR 14; DR 14; AI −0.2% 4. Urb. pop.: 12 749 5. Berlin (East) 1 146	1. NMP $72 190 (4.8%); $4 034 (5.1%) 　Agric. 10%, Indust. 62%, Others 28% 2. Barley 3 800　　Rye 1 800 　Wheat 3 000　　Potatoes 10 378 　Apples 522　　Rapeseed 330 3. Pigs 12 871　　Cattle 5 722 　Sheep 2 038 4. Fish 235 5. Roundwood 9 6. Lignite 267 000　　Natural gas 28 122 　Iron ore 19　　Potash 3 422 　　　　Salt 2 741	1. 83.8/124.0; 98 796 kWh (11% nucl., 1.4% hydr.) 2a. Meat 1 919　　Butter 281 　Sugar 740　　Beer 24 000 hl 　Sawnwood 2 456 b. Cotton yarn 136　　Wool yarn 36 　Iron 2 436　　Steel 7 464 　Ships (grt) 354　　Petroleum 　Vehicles:　　products 19 000 　pass. 180; comm. 41　　Radios 1 103 　Telephones 2 956; Cars 2 533 　Rail: 23 028 pass.-km; 55 824 t-km 　Air: ...;... 　Sea: 3 504 loaded; 11 940 unloaded	Exports $19 398　　Imports 20 888 Machinery　　Machinery Vehicles　　Crude petroleum Consumer goods　　Iron ore Coal Fuels The principal trade is with: U.S.S.R., Czechoslovakia, W. Germany and Poland Aid given (net): $57
GERMANY (West) 1. Federal Republic 2. German 3. Deutschmark 4. £1=3.70 　$1=2.43	1. 248 343 km² 　(including W. Berlin) 2. 61 666 000; 248 per km² 3. BR 10; DR 12; AI 0.2% 4. Urb. pop.: 47 534 (77%) 5. Bonn 286	1. GDP $568 815 (2.4%); $9 278 (2.4%) 　Agric. 3%, Indust. 42%, Others 55% 2. Barley 8 687　　Wheat 8 314 　Rye 1 729　　Potatoes 7 800 　Apples 772　　Grapes 1 000 3. Pigs 22 553　　Cattle 15 069 4. Fish 297 5. Roundwood 33 6. Coal 88 464　　Zinc 110 　Lignite 130 620　　Natural gas 161 320 　Iron ore 515　　Crude petroleum 4 464 　Salt 15 346　　Potash 2 701	1. 160.0/352.5; 368 772 kWh (5% hydr., 11% nucl.) 2a. Meat 4 701　　Butter & cheese 1 363 　Sugar 3 600　　Sawnwood 10 604 　Wine 750　　Beer 87 919 hl b. Cotton yarn 146　　Wool yarn 60 　Iron 31 872　　Steel 42 144 　Aluminium 1 126　　Radios 4 611 　Vehicles:　　Petroleum 　pass. 3 590; comm. 312　　products 65 867 　Ships (grt) 669　　Synthetic fibres 789 3. Telephones 24 443; Cars 23 236 　Rail: 41 556 pass.-km; 62 040 t-km 　Air: 21 636 pass.-km; 1 584 t-km 　Sea: 40 332 loaded; 96 576 unloaded	Exports $176 043　　Imports $163 934 Machinery　　Machinery Vehicles　　Non-ferrous metals Iron and steel　　Crude petroleum Textiles　　Iron and steel Organic chemicals　　Textiles 　　Food Exports to: France, Netherlands, U.S.A. Belgium-Luxembourg and Italy Imports from: Netherlands, France, Belgium-Luxembourg, Italy and U.S.A. Invisible trade balance: −$119 400 Revenue from tourism: $4 806 Aid given (net): $5 934
GHANA 1. Republic 2. English 3. Cedi 4. £1=4.29 　$1=2.75	1. 238 537 km² 2. 12 063 000; 51 per km² 3. BR 48; DR 17; AI 3.5% 4. Urb. pop.: 3 017 (31%) 5. Accra 738	1. GDP $4 277 (−0.4%); $433 (−3.2%) 　Agric. 51%, Indust. 15%, Others 34% 2. Cassava 1 850　　Cocoa 230 　Groundnuts 90　　Millet 73 3. Sheep 1 700　　Goats 2 100 4. Fish 224 5. Roundwood 9 6. Bauxite 252　　Manganese 129 　Gold 10 600 kg　　Diamonds 1 950 c	1. 1.16/1.32; 4 764 kWh (99% hydr.) 2a. Sawnwood 381　　Beer 998 hl 3. Telephones 65; Cars 64 　Rail: 431 pass.-km; 305 t-km 　Air: 324 pass.-km; 3.3 t-km 　Sea: 2 433 loaded; 3 344 unloaded	Exports $1 096　　Imports $993 Cocoa　　Manufactured goods Aluminium Exports to: U.K., U.S.A., W. Germany, U.S.S.R. and Netherlands Imports from: U.S.A., U.K., W. Germany and Nigeria Invisible trade balance: −$307 Aid received (net): $84 from West
GREECE 1. Republic 2. Greek 3. Drachma 4. £1=127 　$1=83.85	1. 131 944 km² 2. 9 707 000; 74 per km² 3. BR 15; DR 9; AI 1.1% 4. Urb. pop.: 5 686 (65%) 5. Athens 3 027	1. GDP $30 040 (4.7%); $3 209 (3.9%) 　Agric. 15%, Indust. 19%, Others 66% 2. Wheat 2 750　　Potatoes 986 　Olives 1 350　　Tomatoes 1 669 　Grapes 1 603　　Tobacco 122 3. Sheep 7 920　　Goats 4 650 4. Fish 106 5. Roundwood 2 6. Iron ore 547　　Bauxite 3 185 　Lignite 27 720　　Chrome 16 　Magnesite 1 065	1. 4.80/20.5; 20 652 kWh (17% hydr.) 2a. Olive oil 280　　Wine 5 400 hl 　Butter & cheese 182 b. Cotton yarn 110　　Steel 1 000 　Cement 13 260　　Aluminium 148 　Petroleum products 14 563 3. Telephones 2 487; Cars 880 　Rail: 1 512 pass.-km; 696 t-km 　Air: 5 196 pass.-km; 76 t-km 　Sea: 21 420 loaded; 33 336 unloaded	Exports $4 292　　Imports $8 677 Tobacco　　Machinery Iron and steel　　Ships and boats Raisins　　Vehicles Aluminium　　Iron and steel Cotton　　Crude petroleum Exports to: W. Germany, Italy, France and Saudi Arabia Imports from: W. Germany, Italy and Japan Invisible trade balance: +$2 261 Revenue from tourism: $1 326
GUINEA 1. Republic 2. French 3. Syli 4. £1=34.67 　$1=22.76	1. 245 857 km² 2. 5 147 000; 21 per km² 3. BR 46; DR 21; AI 2.6% 4. Urb. pop.: 437 (11%) 5. Conakry 526	1. GDP $687 (...); $155 (...) 2. Cassava 600　　Rice 330 　Coffee 15　　Bananas 327 　Sweet potatoes 73　　Palm oil 42 3. Sheep 437　　Goats 405 5. Roundwood 3 6. Iron ore 1 000　　Bauxite 12 838 　Diamonds 80 c	1. 0.01/0.42; 500 kWh 2a. Sawnwood 90 3. Telephones 10; Cars 10 　Air: 27 pass.-km; 0.2 t-km 　Sea: 1 300 loaded; 550 unloaded	Exports $70　　Imports $100 Bauxite and aluminium　　Machinery Iron ore　　Manufactured goods Coffee　　Foods Main trade is with: Portugal and Sweden Aid received (net): $26 from West, $1 from East
HAITI 1. Republic 2. French, Creole 3. Gourde 4. £1=7.64 　$1=5.00	1. 27 750 km² 2. 5 104 000; 184 per km² 3. BR 42; DR 16; AI 1.8% 4. Urb. pop.: 1 378 (28%) 5. Port-au-Prince 863	1. GDP $1 298 (4.3%); $269 (2.6%) 　Agric. 41%, Indust. 15%, Others 44% 2. Bananas 510　　Sisal 10 　Cocoa 3　　Coffee 33 3. Pigs 2 000　　Goats 995 5. Roundwood 5 6. Bauxite 539	1. 0.03/0.27; 312 kWh (70% hydr.) 2a. Meat 58　　Sugar 52 3. Telephones 18; Cars 25 　Sea: 850 loaded; 646 unloaded	Exports $148　　Imports $266 Coffee　　Foods Bauxite　　Textiles Sugar　　Machinery Sisal　　Mineral oils Exports to: U.S.A., France and Belgium-Luxembourg Imports from: U.S.A., Neth., Antilles, Japan and Canada Aid received (net): $83 from West

For detailed table headings and notes see page 1 of this section

Country	Area and Population	Production	Manufactures	Trade

HONG KONG
- Area and Population:
  1. 1 034 km²
  2. 5 154 000; 4 985 per km²
  3. BR 17; DR 5; AI 1.9%
  4. Urb. pop.: 4 017 (96%)
  5. Victoria 849
- Political:
  1. British colony
  2. English, Chinese
  3. Hong Kong Dollar
  4. £1=10.25 $1=6.75
- Production:
  1. GDP $7 036 (8.0%); $1 699 (5.9%) Agric. 1%, Indust. 24%, Others 75%
  2. Rice 1
  3. Pigs 600   Cattle 10
  4. Fish 195
  6. Iron ore . . .
- Manufactures:
  1. –/7.27; 11 796 kWh
  2b. Cotton yarn 128   Wool yarn 6
      Woven natural silk 506 Tm²
  3. Telephones 1 251; Cars 160
     Rail: 384 pass.-km; 60 t-km
     Sea: 9 168 loaded; 26 400 unloaded
- Trade:
  Exports $21 761   Imports $24 816
  Clothing   Textiles
  Textiles   Machines
  Toys and games Diamonds
  Radios   Cotton
  Exports to: U.S.A., U.K., Japan and W. Germany
  Imports from: Japan, China, U.S.A., U.K., and Singapore
  Revenue from tourism: $786

HUNGARY
- Area and Population:
  1. 93 030 km²
  2. 10 711 000; 115 per km²
  3. BR 13; DR 14; AI 0.4%
  4. Urb. pop.: 5 679 (53%)
  5. Budapest 2 060
- Political:
  1. Republic
  2. Hungarian
  3. Forint
  4. £1=60.71 $1=41.62
- Production:
  1. NMP $56 310 (6.1%); $5 288 (5.6%) Agric. 15%, Indust. 47%, Others 38%
  2. Maize 6 500   Wheat 4 800
     Potatoes 1 600   Tobacco 15
     Apples 1 100   Grapes 850
  3. Pigs 8 330   Sheep 3 090
  4. Fish 34
  5. Roundwood 6
  6. Coal 3 065
     Lignite 22 878   Bauxite 2 914
     Natural gas 54 320   Manganese 126
                          Crude petroleum 2 028
- Manufactures:
  1. 21.3/41.2; 27 204 kWh (0.6% hydr.)
  2a. Sugar 587   Sawnwood 1 152
      Wine 550
  b. Iron 2 220   Steel 3 648
     Aluminium 74   Cotton yarn 59
     Wool yarn 13
     Petroleum products 8 193
  3. Telephones 1 143; Cars 839
     Rail: 12 372 pass.-km; 23 856 t-km
     Air: 653 pass.-km; 5.5 t-km
- Trade:
  Exports $8 712   Imports $9 128
  Machinery   Machinery
  Vehicles   Vehicles
  Fruit and vegetables   Iron and steel
  Iron and steel   Crude petroleum
  Medicinal products   Petroleum products
                        Chemical products
  Main trade is with: U.S.S.R., W. Germany, E. Germany and Czechoslovakia
  Invisible trade balance: $98
  Revenue from tourism: $415
  Aid given (net): $52

ICELAND
- Area and Population:
  1. 103 000 km²
  2. 231 000; 2 per km²
  3. BR 19; DR 7; AI 1.1%
  4. Urb. pop.: 194 (87%)
  5. Reykjavik 83
- Political:
  1. Republic
  2. Icelandic
  3. Icelandic Krona
  4. £1=32.29 $1=21.00
- Production:
  1. GDP $1 846 (4.9%); $8 392 (3.7%)
  2. Potatoes 9
  3. Sheep 797
  4. Fish 1 515
     Whaling 536
- Manufactures:
  1. 0.36/1.09; 3 228 kWh (97% hydr., 1.4% geo.)
  2a. Meat 25   Salt fish 42
  b. Aluminium 75
  3. Telephones 100; Cars 80
     Air: 1 140 pass.-km; 22 t-km
     Sea: 496 loaded; 1 279 unloaded
- Trade:
  Exports $859   Imports $980
  Fish, frozen and   Machinery
  fresh   Petroleum
  Fish, salted and   products
  smoked   Textiles
  Fish meal   Iron and Steel
  Aluminium   Paper and cardboard
  Cod liver oil
  Exports to U.S.A., U.K. and W. Germany
  Imports from: W. Germany, U.K., U.S.S.R., Denmark and Sweden

INDIA
- Area and Population:
  1. 3 268 090 km²
  2. 683 810 000; 209 per km²
  3. BR 33; DR 14; AI 2.8%
  4. Urb. pop.: 145 261 (22%)
  5. Delhi 3 647
- Political:
  1. Federal Republic
  2. Hindi, English
  3. Indian Rupee
  4. £1=15.10 $1=9.98
- Production:
  1. GDP $93 870 (3.1%); $150 (1.0%) Agric. 36%, Indust. 17%, Others 47%
  2. Wheat 36 460   Millet 10 500
     Rice 82 000   Tea 565
     Coffee 131   Tobacco 456
     Rubber 150   Jute 1 450
     Cotton lint 1 360   Cottonseed 2 720
  3. Cattle 182 000   Goats 72 144
  4. Fish 2 423
  5. Roundwood 214
  6. Coal 123 012
     Iron ore 25 953   Manganese 600
     Bauxite 1 898   Chrome 266
     Copper 26   Crude petroleum 14 916
     Zinc 31   Lead 15
- Manufactures:
  1. 100.9/126.4; 72 116 kWh (40% hydr., 3% nucl.)
  2a. Sugar 5 587   Butter & cheese 2 085
      Sawnwood 3 639
  b. Iron 9 756   Steel 10 632
     Aluminium 213   Zinc 59
     Cement 20 772   Cotton yarn 1 058
     Radios 1 919   Petroleum products 20 982
  3. Telephones 2 096; Cars 870
     Rail: 213 024 pass.-km; 156 000 t-km
     Air: 12 096 pass.-km; 449 t-km
     Sea: 36 153 loaded; 28 989 unloaded
- Trade:
  Exports $7 693   Imports $14 855
  Jute products   Machinery
  Tea   Wheat
  Iron ore   Petrol
  Iron and steel   Cotton
  Cotton goods   Iron and steel
  Exports to: U.S.A., Japan, U.S.S.R. and U.K.
  Imports from: U.S.A., U.K., Japan and W. Germany
  Revenue from tourism: $403
  Invisible trade balance: $227
  Aid received (net): $1 129 from West, $340 from East

INDONESIA
- Area and Population:
  1. 1 904 345 km²
  2. 150 520 000; 79 per km²
  3. BR 34; DR 16; AI 2.4%
  4. Urb. pop.: 23 246 (18%)
  5. Jakarta 4 576
- Political:
  1. Republic
  2. Bahasa Indonesia
  3. Rupiah
  4. £1=1 476 $1=971
- Production:
  1. GDP $44 171 (7.7%); $304 (5.1%) Agric. 31%, Indust. 28%, Others 41%
  2. Cassava 13 726   Groundnuts 855
     Rice 32 776   Copra 1 254
     Coffee 265   Tea 95
     Tobacco 85   Rubber 937
  3. Cattle 6 435   Goats 7 925
  4. Fish 1 853
  5. Roundwood 157
  6. Coal 348   Tin 35
     Bauxite 1 204   Natural gas 175 857
     Nickel 29   Crude petroleum 78 852
- Manufactures:
  1. 134.2/33.3; 7 140 kWh (36% hydr.)
  2a. Meat 452   Sawnwood 3 407
      Sugar 1 449
  b. Cement 5 256   Tin 33
     Petroleum products 23 140
  3. Telephones 347; Cars 1 400
     Rail: 4 464 pass.-km; 1 008 t-km
     Air: 5 904 pass.-km; 127 t-km
     Sea: 86 160 loaded; 18 696 unloaded
- Trade:
  Exports $22 259   Imports $13 271
  Crude petroleum   Machinery
  Petroleum products   Textiles
  Rubber   Iron and steel
  Coffee   Vehicles
  Tin   Rice
  Spices
  Exports to: Japan, Singapore, U.S.A., Trinidad and Tobago
  Imports from: U.S.A., W. Germany, Japan, and Singapore
  Aid received (net): $584 from West

IRAN
- Area and Population:
  1. 1 648 000 km²
  2. 39 320 000; 24 per km²
  3. BR 43; DR 12; AI 2.8%
  4. Urb. pop.: 17 342 (49%)
  5. Teheran 4 496
- Political:
  1. Islamic Republic
  2. Persian
  3. Rial
  4. £1=128 $1=84.90
- Production:
  1. GDP $52 835 (10.2%); $1 600 (7.4%) Agric. 9%, Indust. 48%, Others 43%
  2. Wheat 5 800   Cottonseed 175
     Rice 1 400   Cotton lint 87
     Dates 301   Tea 22
     Raisins 50   Tobacco 24
  3. Sheep 4 196   Goats 13 709
  5. Roundwood 6
  6. Natural gas 155 980   Crude petroleum 65 988
     Chrome 165   Zinc 35
     Lead 20   Salt 700
- Manufactures:
  1. 138.2/46.7; 17 150 kWh (18% hydr.)
  2a. Sugar 400
  b. Cotton yarn 65   Wool yarn 38
     Cement 6 500
     Petroleum products 27 750
  3. Telephones 829; Cars 577
     Rail: 2 981 pass.-km; 4 083 t-km
     Air: 1 608 pass.-km; 41 t-km
     Sea: 220 320 loaded; 14 532 unloaded
- Trade:
  Exports $14 279   Imports $12 247
  Crude petroleum   Machinery
  Petroleum products   Iron and steel
  Carpets   Vehicles
                   Textiles
  Exports to: U.S.S.R., W. Germany, U.S.A., Italy and Saudi Arabia
  Imports from: W. Germany, U.S.A., Japan, and U.K.
  Invisible trade balance: −$3 442
  Revenue from tourism: $224
  Aid received (net): $42 from West, $664 from East

IRAQ
- Area and Population:
  1. 434 924 km²
  2. 13 527 000; 31 per km²
  3. BR 47; DR 13; AI 3.5%
  4. Urb. pop.: 7 646 (64%)
  5. Bagdad 2 969
- Political:
  1. Republic
  2. Arabic
  3. Iraq Dinar
  4. £1=0.47 $1=0,31
- Production:
  1. GDP $18 591 (. . .); $1 561 (. . .) Agric. 7%, Indust. 63%, Others 30%
  2. Barley 600   Rice 250
     Wheat 1 100   Dates 405
     Cottonseed 11   Cotton lint 5
  3. Sheep 11 650
  6. Natural gas 14 912   Crude petroleum 44 892
- Manufactures:
  1. 195.5/7.9; 8 000 kWh (9% hydr.)
  2b. Cotton yarn 1
      Petroleum products 7 790
  3. Telephones 320; Cars 180
     Rail: 797 pass.-km; 110 t-km
     Air: 1 284 pass.-km; 50 t-km
     Sea: 35 960 loaded; 4 103 unloaded
- Trade:
  Exports $10 529   Imports $4 213
  Crude petroleum   Manufactured goods
  Dates   Machinery, Food
  Exports to: India, China and Kuwait
  Imports from: U.K., W. Germany and Japan
  Revenue from tourism: $84
  Aid received (net): $42 from West, $45 from East

IRELAND
- Area and Population:
  1. 70 283 km²
  2. 3 440 000; 48 per km²
  3. BR 19; DR 7; AI 1.5%
  4. Urb. pop.: 1 556 (52%)
  5. Dublin 525
- Political:
  1. Republic
  2. Irish, English
  3. Irish pound
  4. £1=1.17 $1=1.30
- Production:
  1. GDP $8 647 (3.4%); $2 711 (2.3%) Agric. 14%, Indust. 30%, Others 56%
  2. Barley 1 425   Wheat 320
     Potatoes 1 050   Apples 10
     Wool 9   Tomatoes 27
  3. Cattle 6 696   Sheep 1 082
  4. Fish 149
  6. Lead 29   Zinc 117
     Coal 36
- Manufactures:
  1. 1.15/10.2; 10 908 kWh (11% hydr.)
  2a. Meat 556   Sawnwood 143
      Butter & cheese 166
  b. Wool yarn 12   Petroleum
     Cotton yarn 4   products 1 951
  3. Telephones 554; Cars 682
     Rail: 1 008 pass.-km; 648 t-km
     Air: 2 184 pass.-km; 86 t-km
     Sea: 8 466 loaded; 16 379 unloaded
- Trade:
  Exports $7 787   Imports $10 603
  Cattle   Machinery
  Beef   Textiles
  Dairy products   Vehicles
  Non-ferrous metals   Iron and steel
  Machinery   Crude petroleum
  Main trade is with U.K.
  Exports to: U.S.A., France, W. Germany, Netherlands and Belgium-Lux.
  Imports from: U.S.A., W. Germany, France, Italy and Japan
  Invisible trade balance: −$394
  Revenue from tourism: $421

Country	Area and Population	Production	Manufactures	Trade

ISRAEL

Area and Population
1. 20 700 km²
2. 3 954 000; 191 per km²
3. BR 24; DR 7; AI 2.3%
4. Urb. pop.: 3 327 (88%)
5. Jerusalem 398

1. Republic
2. Hebrew, Arabic
3. Shekel
4. £1 = 60.30
   $1 = 40.60

Production
1. GDP $12 295 (5.0%); $3 332 (2.1%)
   Agric. 6%, Indust. 27%, Others 67%
2. Wheat 215   Cottonseed 152
   Oranges 920   Cotton lint 92
   Grapefruits 536   Tomatoes 268
3. Cattle 301   Sheep 230
4. Fish 26
6. Phosphates 2 216   Potash 790
   Salt 100   Crude petroleum 12

Manufactures
1. 0.22/9.16; 12 432 kWh
2a. Meat 225   Butter & cheese 60
    Wine 33 hl
b. Cotton yarn 14   Wool yarn 7
   Cement 2 304
3. Telephones 993; Cars 403
   Rail: 221 pass.-km; 636 t-km
   Air: 4 812 pass.-km; 302 t-km
   Sea: 6 024 loaded; 6 012 unloaded

Trade
Exports $5 416   Imports $7 777
  Diamonds   Machinery
  Fruit   Diamonds
  Clothing   Iron and steel
Exports to: U.S.A., W. Germany, U.K. and Hong Kong
Imports from: U.S.A., W. Germany, U.K., Netherlands and Switzerland
Invisible trade balance: −$688
Revenue from tourism: $596
Aid received (net): $780 from West

ITALY

Area and Population
1. 301 225 km²
2. 57 197 000; 190 per km²
3. BR 11; DR 10; AI 2.3%
4. Urb. pop.: 28 442 (52%)
5. Rome 2 898

1. Republic
2. Italian
3. Italian Lira
4. £1 = 2 201
   $1 = 1 445

Production
1. GDP $173 655 (2.9); $3 076 (2.1%)
   Agric. 8%, Indust. 35%, Others 57%
2. Wheat 550   Maize 7 250
   Tomatoes 4 457   Grapes 10 888
   Olives 2 800   Tobacco 123
   Oranges 1 751   Apples 1 750
   Pears 1 160   Citrus 2 695
3. Cattle 8 734   Sheep 9 277
4. Fish 445
5. Roundwood 8
6. Lignite 1 950
   Natural gas 127 837   Zinc 44
   Crude petroleum 1 464 Asbestos 144
   Iron ore 53   Bauxite 18
   Lead 21

Manufactures
1. 26.4/189.3; 185 016 kWh (26% hydr., 1.2% nucl., 1.4% geo.)
2a. Meat 3 554   Butter & cheese 670
    Sugar 2 170   Wine 7 650
    Olive 680   Sawnwood 2 717
b. Iron 12 372   Steel 24 768
   Aluminium 524   Woven silk 16
   Cotton yarn 161   Wool yarn 146
   Radios 1 540   Ships (grt) 233
   Petroleum   Vehicles:
   products 78 770   pass. 1 256; comm. 175
   Synthetic Fibres 595
3. Telephones 17 088; Cars 17 750
   Rail: 39 480 pass.-km; 16 632 t-km
   Air: 12 072 pass.-km; 492 t-km
   Sea: 35 004 loaded; 225 432 unloaded

Trade
Exports $75 215   Imports $91 022
  Machinery   Machinery
  Vehicles   Petroleum
  Textiles   Non-ferrous metals
  Clothing   Iron and steel
  Petroleum products   Textile fibres
  Shoes   Cereals
  Iron and steel   Vehicles
  Fruit   Meat
Exports to: France, W. Germany, U.S.A. and U.K.
Imports from: W. Germany, France and U.S.A.
Invisible trade balance: +$1 518
Revenue from tourism: $4 762
Aid given (net): $3 025

IVORY COAST

Area and Population
1. 322 463 km²
2. 8 298 000; 6 per km²
3. BR 48; DR 18; AI 4.2%
4. Urb. pop.: 2 174 (32%)
5. Abidjan 850

1. Republic
2. French
3. C.F.A. Franc
4. £1 = 554
   $1 = 364

Production
1. GDP $6 896 (8.6%); $906 (4.2%)
   Agric. 25%, Indust. 13%, Others 62%
2. Rice 550   Coffee 350
   Cassava 780   Cocoa 430
3. Sheep 1 200   Goats 1 250
4. Fish 77
5. Roundwood 11
6. Diamonds 48 c

Manufactures
1. 0.32/1.29; 1 836 kWh (67% hydr.)
2a. Sawnwood 670
    Petroleum products 968
3. Telephones 67; Cars 100
   Rail: 1 212 pass.-km; 600 t-km
   Air: 169 pass.-km; 13.2 t-km
   Sea: 4 356 loaded; 5 976 unloaded

Trade
Exports $2 515   Imports $2 493
  Cocoa   Machinery
  Coffee   Vehicles
Exports to: France, U.S.A., Italy and Netherlands
Imports from: France, W. Germany and U.S.A.
Invisible trade balance: −$1 285
Aid received (net): $115 from West

JAMAICA

Area and Population
1. 10 962 km²
2. 2 220 000; 203 per km²
3. BR 27; DR 6; AI 1.4%
4. Urb. pop.: 690 (37%)
5. Kingston 573

1. Commonwealth
2. English
3. Jamaica Dollar
4. £1 = 2.72
   $1 = 1.78

Production
1. GDP $2 833 (5.3%); $1 349 (3.8%)
   Agric. 9%, Indust. 32%, Others 59%
2. Bananas 118   Copra 7
   Oranges 33   Sugar cane 2 453
3. Goats 380   Cattle 300
4. Fish 10
6. Bauxite 11 606

Manufactures
1. 0.02/2.76; 2 328 kWh (5%hydr.)
2a. Meat 51   Sugar 203
b. Petroleum products 865
3. Telephones 111; Cars 60
   Rail: 83 pass.-km; 186 t-km
   Air: 1 032 pass.-km; 10.2 t-km
   Sea: 5 424 loaded; 2 628 unloaded

Trade
Exports $974   Imports $1 473
  Bauxite and alumimium Machinery
  Sugar   Textiles
  Bananas   Petroeum
Exports to: U.S.A., U.K., Canada and Norway
Imports from: U.S.A., Venezuela and U.K.
Revenue from tourism: $148
Aid received (net): $60 from West

JAPAN

Area and Population
1. 372 077 km² (incl. Ryukyu Arch.)
2. 117 645 000; 316 per km²
3. BR 13; DR 6; AI 0.9%
4. Urb. pop.: 84 967 (76%)
5. Tokyo 11 695

1. Constitutional Monarchy
2. Japanese
3. Japanese Yen
4. £1 = 364
   $1 = 238

Production
1. GDP $821 875 (5.0%); $7 153 (3.7%)
   Agric. 5%, Indust. 32%, Others 63%
2. Rice 12 824   Potatoes 3 435
   Tomatoes 1 000   Apples 847
   Pears 522   Oranges/mandarines 3 216
   Tea 103
   Tobacco 143
3. Pigs 10 065   Cattle 4 385
4. Fish 10 410
5. Roundwood 34
6. Coal 17 688   Lead 47
   Natural gas 22 944 Manganese 29
   Crude petroleum 396 Zinc 242
   Iron ore 239   Gold 3 780 kg
   Copper 52

Manufactures
1. 42.8/408.0; 521 868 kWh (15% hydr., 14% nucl.)
2a. Meat 3 022   Sugar 770
    Beer 44 210 hl   Sawnwood 37 162
    Wood pulp 9 975
b. Iron 81 684   Steel 101 676
   Aluminium 1 585   Plastics 5 911
   Cotton yarn 486   Wool yarn 113
   Woven silk 155 Mm² Newsprint 2 566
   Synthetic Fibres 1 369 Petroleum
   Vehicles: products 156 461
   pass. 6 978   Radios 18 781
   comm. 4 206   T.V. Receivers 13 927
   Ships (grt) 7 288
3. Telephones 48 646; Cars 23 659
   Rail: 316 200 pass.-km; 39 312 t-km
   Air: 32 952 pass.-km; 2 038 t-km
   Sea: 83 532 loaded; 612 720 unloaded

Trade
Exports $152 016   Imports $143 287
  Iron and steel   Crude petroleum
  Electrical machinery Machinery
  Textiles   Sawnwood
  Other machinery   Iron ore
  Vehicles   Textile fibres
  Ships and boats   Non-ferrous metals
                        Cereals
Exports to: U.S.A., S. Korea and W. Germany
Imports from: U.S.A., Australia, Saudi Arabia and Indonesia
Invisible trade balance: −$13 570
Revenue from tourism: $470
Aid given (net): $8 593

KENYA

Area and Population
1. 582 645 km²
2. 17 148 000; 29 per km²
3. BR 54; DR 14; AI 3.6%
4. Urb. pop.: 1 080 (10%)
5. Nairobi 835

1. Republic
2. Bantu, English
3. Kenyan Shilling
4. £1 = 19.64
   $1 = 12.96

Production
1. GDP $2 892 (4.6%); $216 (1.1%)
   Agric. 34%, Indust. 13%, Others 53%
2. Maize 2 250   Cottonseed 28
   Coffee 87   Tea 91
3. Cattle 11 500   Goats 4 530
4. Fish 48
5. Roundwood 27
6. Salt 20   Soda ash 153

Manufactures
1. 0.13/1.78; 1 488 kWh (71% hydr.)
2a. Sugar 440
b. Cement 1 272   Petroleum products 2 027
3. Telephones 156; Cars 198
   Rail: 8 671 pass.-km; 3 538 t-km
   (inc. Tanzania and Uganda)
   Air: 810 pass.-km; 21.9 t-km
   Sea: 1 056 loaded; 4 584 unloaded

Trade
Exports $1 172   Imports $2 068
  Coffee   Machinery
  Tea   Vehicles
  Petroleum products   Petroleum
  Pyrethrum   Iron and steel
Exports to: U.K., W. Germany and Uganda
Imports from: U.K., Japan, W. Germany, U.S.A. and Iran
Revenue from tourism: $158
Aid received (net): $189 from West

KOREA (NORTH)

Area and Population
1. 120 538 km²
2. 18 317 000; 151 per km²
3. BR 33; DR 8; AI 2.5%
4. Urb. pop.: 5 292 (37%)
5. Pyongyang 1 500

1. Republic
2. Korean
3. Won
4. £1 = 1.44
   $1 = 0.94

Production
2. Rice 4 900   Maize 2 200
   Potatoes 1 620   Tobacco 46
3. Pigs 2 100   Cattle 950
4. Fish 1 400
5. Roundwood 5
6. Coal 35 000   Zinc 130
   Lead 110   Tungsten 3.8
   Iron ore 4 525   Copper 17

Manufactures
1. 44.8/48.5; 35 000 kWh (64% hydr.)
2b. Cotton . . .   Lead 110
    Steel 4 000   Zinc 130
    Iron 3 500   Fertilizers 500
    Petroleum
    products 1 235
3. Sea: 1 300 loaded; 2 000 unloaded

Trade
Exports . . .   Imports . . .
  Minerals   Machinery
  Metal products
Main trade is with the U.S.S.R.

KOREA (SOUTH)

Area and Population
1. 98 477 km²
2. 38 723 000; 393 per km²
3. BR 25; DR 8; AI 1.8%
4. Urb. pop.: 21 441 (57%)
5. Séoul 8 367

1. Republic
2. Korean
3. Won
4. £1 = 1156
   $1 = 765

Production
1. GDP $43 942 (10.4%); $1 187 (8.4%)
   Agric. 22%, Indust. 30%, Others 48%
2. Rice 7 032   Barley 771
   Potatoes 554   Cottonseed 3
3. Pigs 2 843   Cattle 1 715
4. Fish 2 091
5. Roundwood 68
6. Coal 19 980   Gold 1 346 kg
   Iron ore 282   Tungsten 3.3

Manufactures
1. 14.8/54.3; 40 248 kWh (5% hydr., 9% nucl.)
2a. Meat 440   Sawnwood 3 043
b. Cotton yarn 245   Steel 5 892
   Radios 4 768   Iron 8 088
   Petroleum products 21 234
3. Telephones 2 387; Cars 249
   Rail: 21 240 pass.-km; 10 632 t-km
   Air: 12 180 pass.-km; 934 t-km
   Sea: 26 292 loaded; 79 020 unloaded

Trade
Exports $21 254   Imports $26 131
  Clothing   Machinery
  Plywood   Rice
  Textiles   Petrol
Exports to: U.S.A., Japan and Saudi Arabia
Imports from: Japan, U.S.A. and Saudi Arabia
Invisible trade balance: −$2 008
Revenue from tourism: $408
Aid received (net): $198 from West

Country	Area and Population	Production	Manufactures	Trade

LAOS

1. Democratic Republic
2. Laotian, French
3. Kip
4. £1=15.22
   $1=10.00

1. 236 800 km²
2. 3 811 000; 16 per km²
2. BR 44; DR 20; AI 2.4%
4. Urb. pop.: 466 (15%)
5. Vientiane 177

1. GDP $285 (...); $86 (...)
2. Rice 1 115 — Coffee 5
   Cottonseed 10 — Tobacco 5
3. Pigs 1 176 — Buffaloes 879
5. Roundwood 3
6. Tin 6

1. 0.11/0.23; 775 kWh (94% hydr.)
2a. Sawnwood 41
b. Woven silk ...
3. Telephones 7; Cars 15
   Air: 10 pass.-km; 0.1 t-km

Exports 7 — Imports 114
Sawnwood — Agricultural products
Tin — Petroleum products / Vehicles
Exports to: Thailand, Malaysia and Hong Kong
Imports from: Thailand, Japan, France and W. Germany
Aid received (net.): $40 from West, $20 from East

LEBANON

1. Republic
2. Arabic, French
3. Lebanese pound
4. £1=6.30
   $1=4.14

1. 10 400 km²
2. 2 688 000; 258 per km²
3. BR 30; DR 9; AI 2.5%
4. Urb. pop.: 1 278 (60%)
5. Beirut 702

1. GDP $3 198 (...); $1 142 (...)
   Agric. 10%, Indust. 16%, Others 74%
2. Wheat 28 — Oranges 238
   Apples 115 — Grapes 145
   Tomatoes 76 — Tobacco 5
3. Goats 380 — Sheep 280
6. Salt 35

1. 0.11/2.54; 1 800 kWh (47% hydr.)
2a. Sugar 12 — Sawnwood 33
b. Cotton yarn 5 — Petroleum products 1 795
3. Telephones 192; Cars 315
   Rail: 2 pass.-km; 42 t-km
   Air: 1 440 pass.-km; 470 t-km
   Sea: 2 004 loaded; 1 296 unloaded

Exports $436 — Imports $1701
Fruit — Machinery
Machinery — Textiles
Vegatables — Vehicles
Eggs — Petroleum products
Exports to: Saudi Arabia, Syria Libya and Kuwait
Imports from: U.S.A., W. Germany, France Italy and U.K.
Revenue from Tourism: $65
Aid received (net.): $46 from West

LIBYA

1. People's Republic
2. Arabic
3. Libyan Dinar
4. £1=0.45
   $1=0.296

1. 1 759 540 km²
2. 3 096 000; 2 per km²
3. BR 42; DR 13; AI 4.1%
4. Urb. pop.: 668 (30%)
5. Tripoli 551

1. GDP $17 421 (15.9%); $6 335 (12.1%)
   Agric. 2%, Indust. 58%, Others 40%
2. Barley 79 — Tomatoes 238
   Dates 88 — Olives 162
   Tobacco 1 — Groundnuts 13
3. Sheep 6 000 — Goats 1 500
6. Crude petroleum 55 116 — Natural gas 46 600

1. 138.3/6.50; 3 096 kWh
2a. Olive oil 16
b. Petroleum products 5 030
3. Telephones 41; Cars 400
   Air: 490 pass.-km; 6.8 t-km
   Sea: 91 536 loaded; 7 356 unloaded

Exports $22 128 — Imports $6 836
Crude petroleum — Machinery / Vehicles
Exports to: W. Germany, Italy, U.S.A. France and Spain
Imports from: Italy, U.K., W.Germany, France and Japan
Aid received (net): $10 from West

LUXEMBOURG

1. Grand Duchy
2. Luxembourgeois, French, German
3. Luxembourg Franc
4. £1=73.60
   $1=48.31

1. 2 586 km²
2. 364 000; 141 per km²
3. BR 12; DR 11; AI 0.3%
4. Urb. pop.:243 (68%)
5. Luxembourg 80

1. GDP $3 614 (2.4%); $10 040 (1.6%)
   Agric. 3%, Indust. 33%, Others 64%
2. Barley 72 — Wheat 24
   Oats 33 — Grapes 16
3. Cattle 224 — Pigs 75
6. Iron ore 125

1. 0.03/5.41; 1 212 kWh (25% hydr.)
2a. Meat 21 — Wine 97
   Beer 779 hl — Sawnwood 26
b. Iron 2 889 — Steel 3 790
3. Telephones 192; Cars 164
   Rail: 300 pass.-km; 588 t-km
   Air: 190 pass.-km; 0.3 t-km

Exports (see Belgium) — Imports (see Belgium)

MADAGASCAR

1. Republic
2. Malagasy, French
3. Malagasy Franc
4. £1=584
   $1=385

1. 587 041 km²
2. 8 955 000; 15 per km²
3. BR 45; DR 19; AI 2.6%
4. Urb. pop.: 950 (14%)
5. Antananarivo 400

1. GDP $1 744 (...); $227 (...)
   Agric. 41%, Indust. 15%, Others 44%
2. Rice 1 999 — Cassava 1 745
   Bananas 280 — Sisal 20
   Coffee 95 — Groundnuts 38
3. Cattle 10 150 — Goats 1 600
4. Fish 54
5. Roundwood 6
6. Graphite 13 — Gold 5 kg
   Chrome 50 — Titanium ...

1. 0.02/0.62; 366 kWh (30% hydr.)
2a. Sugar 112 — Sawnwood 234
b. Cotton yarn 6 — Cement 60
3. Telephones 29; Cars 57
   Rail: 276 pass.-km; 216 t-km 276
   Air: 362 pass.-km; 18.2 t-km
   Sea: 372 loaded; 984 unloaded

Exports $402 — Imports $600
Coffee — Manufactured goods
Spices — Machinery
Exports to: France, U.S.A. and Indonesia
Imports from: France, W. Germany and China
Invisible trade balance: −$243
Aid received (net.): $71 from West

MALAWI

1. Republic
2. Bantu, English
3. Kwacha
4. £1=1.64
   $1=1.12

1. 118 484 km²
2. 5 123 000; 52 per km²
3. BR 49; DR 25; AI 3.2%
4. Urb pop.: 471 (9%)
5. Lilongwe 103

1. GDP $627 (...); $119 (...)
   Agric. 49%, Indust. 11%, Others 40%
2. Maize 1 600 — Groundnuts 180
   Tea 32 — Tabacco 52
   Cottonseed 23 — Cotton lint 9
3. Goats 630 — Cattle 823
4. Fish 60
5. Roundwood 10

1. 0.05/0.29; 384 kWh (93% hydr.)
2a. Sawnwood 34 — Beer 479
3. Telephones 27; Cars 13
   Rail: 84 pass.-km; 228 t-km
   Air: 84 pass.-km; 1.2 t-km

Exports $284 — Imports $362
Tobacco — Machinery
Tea — Textiles
Groundnuts — Vehicles
Exports to: U.K., U.S.A., W. Germany and Netherlands
Imports from: U.K., Japan and South Africa
Invisible trade balance: −$159
Aid received (net.) $81 from West

MALAYSIA

1. Federation
2. Malay, Chinese, English and others
3. Ringgit
4. £1=3.52
   $1=2.30

1. 332.623 km²
2. 14 415 000; 43 per km²
3. BR 33; DR 8; AI 2.8%
4. Urb.pop.: 2 525 (29%)
5. Kuala Lumpur 452

1. GDP $8 491 (9.3%); $714 (6.6%)
   Agric. 28%, Indust. 23%, Others 49%
2. Rice 2 147 — Palm oil 2 822
   Copra 208 — Bananas 460
   Pineapple - 206 — Rubber 1 590
3. Pigs 1 188 — Cattle 430
4. Fish 737
5. Roundwood 43
6. Iron ore 295 — Tin 71
   Bauxite 701 — Tungsten 100
   Crude petroleum 13 152 — Gold 197 kg

1. 20.9/11.3; 9 540 kWh (14% hydr.)
2a. Meat 235 — Sawnwood 5 247
b. Cement 2 832
   Petroleum products 653
   Tin 70
3. Telephones 434; Cars 600
   Rail: 1 644 pass.-km; 1 128 t-km (incl. Singapore)
   Air: 4 080 pass.-km; 116 t-km
   Sea 10 512 loaded; 16 476 unloaded

Exports $12 884 — Imports $13 132
Rubber — Machinery
Tin — Crude petroleum
Sawnwood — Vehicles
Fish — Textiles
Palm oil — Rice / Iron and steel / Foods
Exports to: Singapore, Japan, U.S.A., U.K., and Netherlands
Imports from: Japan, U.K., Singapore, Australia and W. Germany
Aid received (net): $65 from West

MALI

1. Republic
2. French, Arabic
3. Mali Franc
4. £1 108
   $1=727

1. 1 240 000 km²
2. 7 150 000; 6 per km²
3. BR 43; DR 18; AI 2.7%
4. Urb. pop.: 1 077 (17%)
5. Bamako 404

1. GDP $546 (...); $94 (...)
2. Millet 980 — Rice 142
   Groundnuts 190 — Cottonseed 70
3. Sheep 6 127 — Cattle 4 422
5. Roundwood 29

1. 0.01/0.20; 110 kWh (46% hydr.)
2a. Sugar 20 — Meat 120
3. Telephones 5; Cars 20
   Rail: 156 pass.-km; 132 t-km
   Air: 73 pass.-km; 0.6 t-km

Exports $149 — Imports $354
Cattle — Manufactured goods
Fish — Machinery
Cotton — Vehicles
Exports to: France, Ivory Coast, China and U.K.
Imports from: France, Ivory Coast, China and Senegal
Aid received (net.): $112 from West, $1 from East

For detailed table headings and notes see page 1 of this section

Country	Area and Population	Production	Manufactures	Trade
MALTA 1. Commonwealth 2. Maltese, English 3. Maltese Pound 4. £1=0.65 $1=2.38	1. 316 km² 2. 366 000; 1 158 per km² 3. BR 15; DR 9; AI 1.4% 4. Urb. pop.: 296 (94%) 5. Valetta 14	1. GDP $692 (11.1%); $2 036 (11.0%) Agric. 5%, Indust. 38%, Others 57% 2. Potatoes 22 Wheat 3 Tomatoes 16 Grapes 3 3. Pigs 26 Goats 7	1. −/0.46; 552 kWh 2a. Wine 1 Wheat flour 36 3. Telephones 73; Cars 67 Air 612 pass.-km; 4.8 t-km Sea: 276 loaded; 1 380 unloaded	Exports $441 Imports $853 Clothing Foods Textiles Manufactured goods Exports to: U.K., Libya and W. Germany Imports from: U.K., Italy, W. Germany and U.S.A. Revenue from tourism: $81
MAURITANIA 1. Republic 2. Arabic, French 3. Ouguiya 4. £1=81.50 $1=53.55	1. 1 030 700 km² 2. 1 681 000; 2 per km² 3. BR 50; DR 22; AI 2.8% 4. Urb. pop.: 328 (23%) 5. Nouakchott 135	1. GDP $375 (. . .); $264 (. . .) Agric. 25%, Indust. 18%, Others 57% 2. Millet 37 Dates 14 3. Sheep 5 200 Cattle 1 200 4. Fish 34 6. Iron ore 5 593 Copper 3	1. −/0.29; 102 kWh 3. Telephones . . .; Cars 8 Air: 161 pass.-km; 14.9 t-km Sea: 7 022 loaded; 294 unloaded	Exports $259 Imports $265 Iron ore Machinery Fish Foods Exports to: France, U.K., W. Germany, Spain, Italy and Belgium Imports from: France, U.S.A., U.K. and Senegal Aid received (net); $73 from West
MEXICO 1. Federal Republic 2. Spanish 3. Mexican Peso 4. £1=226 $1=109	1. 1 972 547 km² 2. 71 193 000; 36 per km² 3. BR 38; DR 6; AI 3.6% 4. Urb. pop.: 45 796 (66%) 5. Mexico 14 750	1. GDP $81 440 (5.0%); $1 244 (1.6%) Agric. 10%, Indust. 31%, Others 59% 2. Maize 14 766 Copra 143 Bananas 1 562 Wheat 3 189 Tomatoes 1 370 Oranges 1 600 Coffee 217 Pineapples 568 Cottonseed 530 Tobacco 66 3. Cattle 31 784 Pigs 12 900 4. Fish 1 240 5. Roundwood 12 6. Crude petroleum 105 948 Lead 157 Natural gas 255 169 Zinc 212 Coal 6 756 Silver 1 655 t Iron ore 5 292 Gold 5 754 kg Copper 110 Mercury 76	1. 204.9/127.3; 73 068 kWh (25% hydr., 1.4% geo.) 2a. Meat 1 709 Sugar 2 518 Sawnwood 995 b. Iron 5 508 Steel 7 452 Aluminium 43 Radios 1 126 Cotton yarn 158 Cement 17 844 Petroleum Vehicles: products 51 477 pass. 358; comm. 172 3. Telephones 4 140; Cars 4 000 Rail: 5 244 pass.-km; 41 328 t-km Air: 14 712 pass.-km; 142 t-km Sea: 62 712 loaded; 19 032 unloaded	Exports $20 033 Imports $24 167 Cotton Machinery Sugar Vehicles Tomatoes Organic chemical Coffee products Cattle Iron and steel Machinery Paper and cardboard Petroleum products Exports to: U.S.A., Spain, Japan, W. Germany and Brazil Imports from: U.S.A., W. Germany, Japan and France Invisible trade balance: −$9 792 Revenue from tourism: $1 117 Aid received (net): $44 from West
MONGOLIA 1. People's Republic 2. Mongol 3. Tugrik 4. £1=4.79 $1=3.36	1. 1 565 000 km² 2. 1 710 000; 1 per km² 3. BR 37; DR 8; AI 3.0% 4. Urb. pop.: 836 (51%) 5. Ulan-Bator 419	1. NMP $. . . (5.3%); . . . (2.4%) 2. Wheat 240 Potatoes 55 3. Sheep 14 400 Goats 4 715 5. Roundwood 2 6. Coal 3 350 Lignite 3 087 Flourine . . . Copper 12 Molybdenum . . .	1. 1.77/2.67; 1 650 kWh 2a. Wool . . . Meat 232 Sawnwood 470 b. Cement 166 3. Telephones 38; Cars . . . Rail: 245 pass.-km; 2 738 t-km	Exports $343 Imports $506 Livestock Consumer goods Wool Machinery Meat Raw materials
MOROCCO 1. Kingdom 2. Arabic, French Spanish 3. Dirham 4. £1=9.61 $1=6.56	1. 446 550 km² 2. 20 646 000; 46 per km² 3. BR 45; DR 14; AI 3.0% 4. Urb. pop.: 7 670 (41%) 5. Rabat 596	1. GDP $10 224 (. . .); $555 (. . .) Agric. 16%, Indust. 23%, Others 61% 2. Barley 1 039 Wheat 892 Oranges 685 Grapes 210 Dates 105 Olives 350 3. Sheep 16 100 Goats 6 070 4. Fish 298 5. Roundwood 1 6. Coal 708 Cobalt 7 Iron ore 28 Lead 168 Antimony 504 Phosphates 18 562 Copper 24	1. 1.05/6.87; 4 692 kWh (32 hydr.) 2a. Meat 268 Wine 80 Olive oil 38 Sawnwood 128 Sugar 352 b. Petroleum Wool yarn 2.6 products 3 798 Cement 3 564 3. Telephones 216; Cars 425 Rail: 924 pass.-km; 3 888 t-km Air: 1 860 pass.-km; 31 t-km Sea: 20 808 loaded; 10 164 unloaded	Exports $2 249 Imports $4 185 Phosphates Machinery Oranges Manufactured goods Vegetables Exports to: France, W. Germany, Italy and Spain Imports from: France, U.S.A., W. Germany, Italy and Spain Revenue from tourism: $434 Aid received (net): $200 from West
MOZAMBIQUE 1. People's Republic 2. Portuguese, Bantu 3. Metica 4. £1=48.45 $1=29.72	1. 783 030 km² 2. 10 757 000; 14 per km² 3. BR 45; DR 19; AI 2.6% 4. Urb. pop.: 442 (6%) 5. Maputo 384	1. GDP $2 545 (. . .); $277 (. . .) 2. Cassava 2 850 Maize 200 Copra 70 Groundnuts 80 Cottonseed 37 Sisal 12 3. Cattle 1 399 Goats 335 5. Roundwood 11 6. Coal 456	1. 2.10/1.02; 14 000 kWh (97% hydr.) 2a. Sugar 185 Sawnwood 135 Beer 655 b. Petroleum products 365 3. Telephones 49; Cars 110 Rail: 396 pass.-km; 3 400 t-km Sea: 8 988 loaded; 3 540 unloaded	Exports $129 Imports $278 Cotton Machinery Cashew nuts Vehicles Sugar Iron and steel Tea Petroleum Exports to: Portugal, S. Africa, U.K. and U.S.A. Imports from: Portugal, S. Africa, W. Germany and U.K. Aid received (net): $82 from West
NAMIBIA (South West Africa) 1. Mandated Territory 2. English, African dialects 3. Rand 4. £1=1.67 $1=1.09	1. 824 292 km² 2. 1 200 000; 1 per km² 3. BR 44; DR 15; AI 2.9% 4. Urb. pop.: 200 (27%) 5. Windhoek 61	1. (incl. with South Africa) 2. Maize 30 Millet 15 3. Sheep 5 170 Cattle 3 024 4. Fish 213 5. Roundwood . . . 6. Copper 39 Zinc 37 Lead 47 Diamonds 1 898 Tin 1 Vanadium 462	2a. Meat 64 b. Copper 50 Lead 46 3. Telephones 46; Cars . . . Rail: see South Africa	Exports . . . Imports . . . (Trade included with South Africa)
NEPAL 1. Kingdom 2. Nepalese Hindu 3. Nepalese Rupee 4. £1=20.09 $1=13.20	1. 140 797 km² 2. 15 020 000; 107 per km² 3. BR 44; DR 21; AI 2.2% 4. Urb. pop.: 462 (4%) 5. Katmandu 210	1. GDP $1 452 (3.3%); $114 (0.9%) Agric. 62%, Indust. 11%, Others 27% 2. Rice 2 407 Maize 720 Wheat 477 Jute 43 3. Cattle 6 900 Goats 2 500 5. Roundwood 13	1. 0.02/0.16; 220 kWh (74% hydr.) 2a. Sugar 7 3. Telephones 9; Cars . . .	Exports $97 Imports $163 Food grains Textiles Livestock Petroleum products Jute Iron and steel Timber Machinery, Tea The main trade is with India Aid received (net.): $67 from West

For detailed table headings and notes see page 1 of this section

Country	Area and Population	Production	Manufactures	Trade

NETHERLANDS

1. Kingdom
2. Dutch
3. Gilder
4. £1 = 4.17
   $1 = 2.73

1. 33 680 km²
2. 14 246 000; 423 per km²
3. BR 13; DR 8; AI 0.7%
4. Urb. pop.: 12 368 (88%)
5. Amsterdam 958
   The Hague 673

1. GDP $118 622 (3.2%); $8 509 (2.4%)
   Agric. 5%, Indust. 30%, Others 65%
2. Barley 249   Wheat 822
   Tomatoes 400   Apples 300
   Pears 75   Potatoes 6 400
3. Pigs 10 315   Cattle 5 100
4. Fish 340
5. Roundwood 1
6. Crude petroleum 1332   Natural gas 638 825
   Salt 3 580

1. 98.0/87.8; 64 056 kWh (7% nucl.)
2a. Meat 2 020   Sugar 1 139
    (Pork 1 100)   Butter & Cheese 640
    Sawnwood 337
b. Iron 4 596   Steel 5 472
   Wool yarn 7   Cotton yarn 16
   Petroleum   Vehicles
   products 38 565   Pass. 78; comm. 12
   Plastics 2 393   Ships (grt) 183
3. Telephones 6 341; Cars 4 350
   Rail: 9 240 pass.-km; 3 312 t-km
   Air: 15 324 pass.-km; 1 100 t-km
   Sea: 74 868 loaded; 245 244 unloaded

Exports $68 756 / Imports $66 117
Machinery / Machinery
Textiles / Crude petroleum
Chemical products / Textiles
Petroleum / Vehicles
Meat / Iron and steel
Iron and steel / Clothing
Vegables / Non-ferrous metals
Exports to: West Germany, Belgium-Luxembourg, France, U.K., Italy and U.S.A.
Imports from: W. Germany, Belguim-Luxembourg, U.S.A., France, U.K. and Italy
Invisible trade balance: + $592
Revenue from tourism: 1 260
Aid given (net.): $2 528

NEW ZEALAND

1. Commonwealth
2. English
3. New Zealand Dollar
4. £1 = 2.32
   $1 = 1.52

1. 268 675 km²
2. 3 125 000; 12 per km²
3. BR 16; DR 8; AI 1.4%
4. Urb. pop.: 2 593 (83%)
5. Wellington 321

1. GDP $16 628 (...); $5 346 (...)
   Agric. 10%, Indust. 25%, Others 65%
2. Barley 187   Pears 17
   Apples 222   Wheat 368
   Tomatoes 60   Wool 385
3. Sheep 71 200   Cattle 8 581
4. Fish 98
5. Roundwood 9
6. Coal 1 944   Lignite 216
   Natural gas 10 886 Gold 218 kg
   Crude petroleum 408

1. 607/10.7; 22 704 kWh (74% hydr., 6% geo.)
2a. Meat 1 181   Butter & cheese 349
    Sawnwood 1 902   Wood pulp 1 043
    Wine 50
b. Petroleum   Vehicles:
   products 2 485   pass. 63; comm. 13
   Cement 756   Wool yarn 18
3. Telephones 1 715; Cars 1 307
   Rail: 408 pass.-km; 3 144 t-km
   Air: 5 676 pass.-km; 204 t-km
   Sea: 10 236 loaded; 9 792 unloaded

Exports $5 563 / Imports $5 684
Meat / Machinery
Wool / Textiles
Butter / Vehicles
Cheese / Iron and steel
/ Petroleum products
Exports to: U.K., Japan and Australia
Imports from: U.K., Australia, U.S.A. and Japan
Invisible trade balance: − $1 352
Revenue from tourism: $166
Aid given: (net): $73

NICARAGUA

1. Republic
2. Spanish
3. Cordoba
4. £1 = 15.22
   $1 = 10.05

1. 130 000 km²
2. 2 824 000; 22 per km²
3. BR 47; DR 12; AI 5.2%
4. Urb. pop.: 1 404 (53%)
5. Managua 608

1. GDP $1 980 (5.9%); $825 (2.4%)
   Agric. 23%, Indust. 21%, Others 56%
2. Maize 250   Rice 65
   Bananas 252   Coffee 63
   Cottonseed 115   Cotton lint 75
3. Cattle 2 401   Pigs 500
5. Roundwood 3
6. Copper 100   Gold 1 900 kg

1. 0.05/0.91; 988 kWh (40% hydr.)
2a. Sugar 193   Meat 61
    Sawnwood 402
b. Cement 161
3. Telephones 43; Cars 40
   Rail: 17 pass.-km; 10 t-km
   Air: 77 pass.-km; 1.9 t-km
   Sea: 725 loaded; 1 423 unloaded

Exports $448 / Imports $883
Cotton / Machinery
Meat / Textiles
Coffee / Iron and steel
Exports to: U.S.A., Japan, Costa Rica and W. Germany
Imports from: U.S.A., Guatemala, Costa Rica, W. Germany, Japan and Venezuela
Aid received (net): $39 from West

NIGER

1. Republic
2. Arabic, French
3. C.F.A. Franc
4. £1 = 554
   $1 = 364

1. 1 267 000 km²
2. 5 479 000; 4 per km²
3. BR 51; DR 22; AI 2.9%
4. Urb pop.: 315 (8%)
5. Niamey 130

1. GDP $699 (...); $152 (...)
   Agric. 51%, Indust. 7%, Others 42%
2. Groundnuts 100   Millet 1 117
3. Goats 7 318   Cattle 3 206
5. Roundwood 3
6. Tin 96   Uranium 3 700

1. .../0.3; 52 kWh
2a. Meat 71
3. Telephones 8; Cars 26
   Aviation: 153 pass.-km; 14.6 t-km

Exports $160 / Imports $196
Groundnuts / Manufactured goods
Exports to: France, Italy and Nigeria
Imports from: France, Ivory Coast and W. Germany
Aid received (net): $118 from West

NIGERIA

1. Federal Republic
2. English, W. African
3. Naira
4. £1 = 1.07
   $1 = 0.71

1. 923 768 km²
2. 79 680 000; 86 per km²
3. BR 50; DR 18; AI 3.2%
4. Urb. pop.: 12 535 (19%)
5. Lagos 1 477

1. GDP $47 683 (...); $682 (...)
   Agric. 26%, Indust. 38%, Others 36%
2. Cassava 11 000   Millet 3 230
   Rubber 43   Cocoa 160
   Groundnuts 580   Cottonseed 57
3. Goats 25 000   Cattle 12 500
4. Fish 480
5. Roundwood 99
6. Coal 168   Natural gas 5 167
   Tin 3   Crude petroleum 71 184

1. 153.1/11.1; 5 004 kWh (60% hydr.)
2a. Meat 813   Sugar 60
    Sawnwood 2 703
b. Petroleum products 6 465
   Cement 1 536
3. Telephones 128; Cars 400
   Rail: 785 pass.-km; 972 t-km
   Aviation: 2 304 pass.-km; 17 t-km
   Sea: 101 220 loaded; 5 000 unloaded

Exports $17 331 / Imports $10 991
Petroleum / Machinery
Cocoa / Textiles
Groundnuts / Vehicles
Tin / Iron and steel
Exports to: Bermuda, U.S.A. and Netherlands
Imports from: U.K., W. Germany, U.S.A. and Japan
Invisible trade balance: $3 944
Aid received (net): $43 from West

NORWAY

1. Kingdom
2. Norwegian
3. Norwegian Krone
4. £1 = 10.94
   $1 = 7.14

1. 324 219 km²
2. 4 100 000; 13 per km²
3. BR 13; DR 10; AI 0.4%
4. Urb. pop.: 1 779 (44%)
5. Oslo 624

1. GDP $32 275 (4.7%); $7 949 (4.1%)
   Agric. 5%, Indust. 28%, Others 67%
2. Barley 650   Apples 47
   Oats 417   Potatoes 452
3. Sheep 2 040   Cattle 983
4. Fish 2 398
5. Roundwood 8
6. Coal 312   Molybdenum ...
   Iron ore 2 644   Vanadium 460
   Copper 28   Zinc 28
   Titanium 827   Natural gas 264 634
   Crude petroleum 23 580
   Lead 3

1. 31.4/21.2; 93 516 kWh (99.4% hydr.)
2a. Butter & cheese 91   Sawnwood 2 463
    Canned fish 32   Wood pulp 1 602
    Fish meal 10
b. Iron 1 296   Steel 852
   Magnesium 39   Aluminium 638
   Paper 1 373   Wool yarn 4
   Ships (grt) 268   Petroleum products 6 525
3. Telephones 1 636; Cars 1 234
   Rail: 2 424 pass.-km; 2 880 t-km
   Air: 4 068 pass-km; 138 t-km
   Sea: 34 344 loaded; 18 324 unloaded

Exports $18 220 / Imports $15 652
Non-ferrous metals / Machinery
(mainly aluminium) / Ships and boats
Ships and boats / Vehicles
Machinery / Iron and steel
Paper and cardboard / Textiles
Fish / Non-ferrous metals
Iron and steel / Petroleum products
Exports to: U.K., Sweden, W. Germany, Denmark and U.S.A.
Imports from: Sweden, W. Germany, U.K. U.S.A. and Denmark
Invisible trade balance: − $127
Aid given (net): $575

PAKISTAN

1. Republic
2. Urdu, English
3. Pakistan Rupee
4. £1 = 19.40
   $1 = 12.91

1. 801 408 km²
2. 84 579 000; 106 per km²
3. BR 43; DR 15; AI 3.2%
4. Urb. pop.: 16 558 (26%)
5. Islamabad 77

1. GDP $12 889 (4.7%); $183 (1.9%)
   Agric. 29%, Indust. 16%, Others 55%
2. Rice 5 093   Wheat 11 340
   Dates 205   Maize 1 004
   Tobacco 67   Rapeseed 252
   Cotton lint 750   Cottonseed 1 500
3. Cattle 15 084   Sheep 28 468
4. Fish 279
5. Roundwood 18
6. Coal 1 692   Salt 620
   Natural gas 77 905 Crude petroleum 480
   Antimony 69 t   Chrome 5

1. 12.3/18.0; 17 148 kWh (64% hydr., 1 nucl.)
2a. Meat 752   Sugar 928
    Sawnwood 60   Jute 1
b. Petroleum   Cotton yarn 389
   products 3 663   Cement 3 540
3. Telephones 259; Cars 347
   Rail: 17 316 pass.-km; 8 520 t-km
   Air: 6 060 pass.-km; 254 t-km
   Sea: 3 588 loaded; 11 484 unloaded

Exports $2 880 / Imports $5 348
Textiles / Machinery
Cotton / Iron and steel
Leather / Fertilizer
Rice / Crude petroleum
/ Vehicles
Exports to: China, Japan, Iran and U.K.
Imports from: U.S.A., U.K., Japan and W. Germany
Invisible trade balance: − $545
Aid received (net): $513 from West, $226 from East

PANAMA

1. Republic
2. Spanish
3. Balboa
4. £1 = 1.53
   $1 = 1.0

1. 75 650 km²
2. 1 940 000; 26 per km²
3. BR 27; DR 6; AI 3.1%
4. Urb. pop.: 963 (51%)
5. Panama 546

1. GDP $2 043 (3.3%); $1 116 (0.2%)
   Agric. 17%, Indust. 18%, Others 65%
2. Rice 192   Bananas 1 185
   Coffee 6   Oranges 69
3. Cattle 1 525   Pigs 195
4. Fish 195
5. Roundwood 1

1. 0.10/1.22; 1 896 kWh (41% hydr.)
2a. Meat 62   Sugar 187
    Sawnwood 12
b. Petroleum products 2 239
3. Telephones 155; Cars 90
   Sea: 1 183 loaded; 3 419 unloaded

Exports $315 / Imports $1 540
Bananas / Manufactured goods
Petroleum products / Petroleum
/ Machinery
Exports to: U.S.A. and W. Germany
Imports from: U.S.A., Ecuador, Venezuela and Saudi Arabia
Invisible trade balance: + $677
Aid received (net): $35 from West

For detailed table headings and notes see page 1 of this section

Country	Area and Population	Production	Manufactures	Trade

PERU

1. Republic
2. Spanish
3. Sol
4. £1 = 1 925
   $1 = 1 253

Area and Population
1. 1 285 216 km²
2. 18 279 000; 14 per km²
3. BR 40; DR 12; AI 2.8%
4. Urb. pop.: 11 980 (67%)
5. Lima 4 279

Production
1. GDP $9 586 (3.4%); $586 (0.5%)
   Agric. 12%, Indust. 35%, Others 53%
2. Maize 587 — Rice 712
   Oranges 152 — Coffee 95
   Cottonseed 165 — Potatoes 1 627
3. Sheep 14 671 — Cattle 3 895
4. Fish 2 731
5. Roundwood 4
6. Iron ore 3 398 — Gold 1 800
   Antimony 768 — Silver 1 318 t
   Copper 328 — Zinc 497
   Lead 186 — Tungsten 549
   Molybdenum 729 — Crude petroleum 9 552

Manufactures
1. 16.1/11.0; 8 805 kWh (78% hydr.)
2a. Meat 375 — Fish Meal
    Sugar 493 — Sawnwood 585
b. Cotton yarn — Copper 274
3. Telephones 420; Cars 312
   Rail: 651 pass.-km; 612 t-km
   Air: 1 353 pass.-km; 34.8 t-km
   Sea: 10 284 loaded; 2 688 unloaded

Trade
Exports $3 364 — Imports $2 542
Copper — Machinery
Fish Meal — Chemical products
Iron ore — Wheat
Cotton — Iron and steel
Exports to: U.S.A., Japan and Italy
Imports from: U.S.A., Ecuador and Venezuela
Invisible trade balance: −$1 154
Revenue from tourism: $126
Aid received (net): $104 from West

PHILIPPINES

1. Republic
2. Tagalog, English
3. Philippine Peso
4. £1 = 14.7
   $1 = 9.84

Area and Population
1. 300 000 km²
2. 49 530 000; 165 per km²
3. BR 36; DR 9; AI 3.2%
4. Urb. pop.: 11 678 (32%)
5. Manila 1 479

Production
1. GDP $21 204 8.3%); $457 (3.3%)
   Agric. 27%, Indust. 27%, Others 46%
2. Maize 3 176 — Rice 7 720
   Bananas 4 280 — Pineapples 1 200
   Coffee 140 — Copra 2 275
   Tobacco 50
3. Pigs 7 590 — Buffaloes 2 760
4. Fish 1 558
5. Roundwood 35
6. Coal 360 — Copper 923
   Iron ore 2 — Gold 23 430 kg
   Chrome 200 — Silver 63 t

Manufactures
1. 2.69/15.3; 15 948 kWh (20% hydr., 11% geo.)
2a. Meat 762 — Sawnwood 1 529
    Salted fish 48 — Sugar 2 394
b. Plastics 63 — Petroleum
   Cotton yarn 38 — products 9 170
   Cement 4 008 — Copper 291
3. Telephones 600; Cars 400
   Rail: 252 pass.-km; 36 t-km
   Air: 6 684 pass.-km; 155 t-km
   Sea: 14 652 loaded; 19 008 unloaded

Trade
Exports $5 722 — Imports $7 946
Wood — Machinery
Sugar — Petroleum
Copra — Vehicles
Copper — Iron and steel
Exports to: U.S.A., Japan and Netherlands
Imports from: Japan, U.S.A. and Saudi Arabia
Invisible trade balance: −$543
Revenue from tourism: $356
Aid received (net): $205 from West

POLAND

1. People's Republic
2. Polish
3. Złoty
4. £1 = 127
   $1 = 86.85

Area and Population
1. 312 677 km²
2. 35 902 000; 115 per km²
3. BR 19; DR 9; AI 0.9%
4. Urb. pop.: 20 185 (58%)
5. Warsaw 1 543

Production
1. NMP $87 150 (8.1%); $2 512 (7.1%)
   Agric. 16%, Indust. 52%, Others 32%
2. Barley 3 575 — Wheat 4 203
   Rye 6 731 — Oats 2 731
   Potatoes 42 600 — Apples 800
   Tobacco 81 — Rapeseed 486
3. Pigs 18 487 — Cattle 11 801
4. Fish 640
5. Roundwood 21
6. Coal 163 020 — Nickel 2
   Lignite 35 556 — Zinc 201
   Copper 295 — Natural gas 51 189
   Lead 44 — Salt 4 393

Manufactures
1. 211.9/198.8; 115 008 kWh (2.0 hydr.)
2a. Meat 2 357 — Sawnwood 7 385
    Butter & cheese 623 — Sugar 1 872
    Salted fish 18
2b. Iron 9 348 — Steel 15 720
    Aluminium 66 — Plastics 591
    Cotton yarn 196 — Wool yarn 89
    Petroleum products 10 650 — Vehicles:
    Woven silk 1 400 Tm — pass. 240; comm. 48
    Ships (grt) 489
3. Telephones 3 095; Cars 2 270
   Rail: 48 240 pass.-km; 109 836 t-km
   Air: 2 136 pass.-km; 19 t-km
   Sea: 38 761 loaded; 27 175 unloaded

Trade
Exports $13 249 — Imports $15 475
Coal — Dairy products
Ships and boats — Iron ore
Meat — Crude petroleum
Dairy products — Cotton, Wheat
Machinery — Iron and steel
Clothing — Petroleum products
— Machinery
Main trade is with: U.S.S.R., W. Germany,
Czechoslovakia and E. Germany
Revenue from tourism: $224
Aid given (net): $103

PORTUGAL

1. Republic
2. Portuguese
3. Escudo
4. £1 = 149
   $1 = 97.35

Area and Population
1. 92 082 km²
2. 9 981 000; 108 per km²
3. BR 16; DR 10; AI 1.1%
4. Urb. pop.: 2 276 (26%)
5. Lisbon 1 612

Production
1. GDP $15 349 (4.5%); $1 577 (3.4%)
   Agric. 13%, Indust. 34%, Others 53%
2. Wheat 310 — Maize 417
   Grapes 900 — Olives 220
   Tomatoes 670 — Wool 9
3. Sheep 5 200 — Pigs 2 500
4. Fish 265
5. Roundwood 8
6. Coal 180 — Tin 269
   Iron ore 18 — Tungsten 1 392
   Copper 3 — Gold 436 kg

Manufactures
1. 1.16/11.0; 14 268 kWh (53% hydr.)
2a. Meat 461 — Sawnwood 2 230
    Canned fish 47 — Salted fish 15
    Wine 640 — Olive oil 33
b. Iron 348 — Steel 348
   Petroleum — Vehicles:
   products 7 225 — pass. 32; comm. 38
   Cotton yarn 97 — Wool yarn 14
3. Telephones 1 175; Cars 920
   Rail: 5 856 pass.-km; 996 t-km
   Air: 4 008 pass.-km; 109 t-km
   Sea: 4 500 loaded; 23 976 unloaded

Trade
Exports $4 179 — Imports $10 182
Textiles — Machinery
Clothing — Vehicles
Wine — Iron and steel
Diamonds — Cotton
Machinery — Diamonds
Fish — Cereals
Cork — Crude petroleum
Exports to: U.K., France and W. Germany
Imports from: W. Germany, U.K., U.S.A. and France
Invisible trade balance: −$41
Revenue from tourism: $600

ROMANIA

1. Socialist Republic
2. Romanian
3. Leu
4. £1 = 6.66
   $1 = 4.47

Area and Population
1. 237 500 km²
2. 22 457 000; 95 per km²
3. BR 18; DR 10; AI 1.0%
4. Urb. pop.: 10 626 (47%)
5. Bucharest 1 934

Production
1. NMP $26 450 (10.8%); $1 240 (9.8%)
   Agric. 15%, Indust. 58%, Others 27%
2. Barley 2 500 — Wheat 5 800
   Grapes 1 755 — Tomatoes 1 600
   Tobacco 39 — Sunflower seed 824
3. Sheep 15 865 — Pigs 11 542
4. Fish 174
5. Roundwood 21
6. Coal 8 196 — Lead 20
   Lignite 28 800 — Manganese 28
   Iron ore 605 — Natural gas 365 549
   Bauxite 688 — Crude petroleum 11 604

Manufactures
1. 86.9/102.3; 67 500 kWh (18% hydr.)
2a. Meat 1 824 — Sawnwood 4 690
    Sugar 640 — Butter & cheese 278
b. Iron 8 856 — Steel 13 020
   Petroleum products 22 624 — Cotton yarn 175
   Woven silk 1 00 Tm² — Wool yarn 71
   Fertilizers 2 383 — Aluminium 231
3. Telephones 1 196; Cars 235
   Rail: 22 812 pass.-km; 73 740 t-km
   Air: 1 248 pass.-km; 11.3 t-km
   Sea: 4 257 Loaded; 4 859 unloaded

Trade
Exports $12 610 — Imports $12 458
Machinery — Machinery
Consumer goods — Iron ore
Petroleum products — Coke
Cereals — Vehicles
— Iron goods
Exports to: U.S.S.R., E. Germany and W. Germany
Imports from: U.S.S.R., E. Germany and W. Germany
Aid given (net): $241

SAUDI ARABIA

1. Kingdom
2. Arabic
3. Rial
4. £1 = 5.26
   $1 = 3.45

Area and Population
1. 2 149 690 km²
2. 9 319 000; 4 per km²
3. BR 46; DR 14; AI 3.1%
4. Urb. pop.: 1 829 (23%)
5. Ar Riyād 667

Production
1. GDP $43 723 (...); $6 089 (...)
   Agric. 1%, Indust. 61%, Others 38%
2. Wheat 150 — Millet/Sorghum 112
   Dates 429 — Tomatoes 170
3. Sheep 4 000 — Goats 1 974
6. Crude petroleum 490 800 — Natural gas 90 000

Manufactures
1. 729.9/12.4; 9 000 kWh
2b. Petroleum products 23 660
    Cement 1 800
3. Telephones 185; Cars 400
   Rail: 72 pass.-km; 66 t-km
   Air: 3 546 pass.-km; 118.5 t-km
   Sea: 410 000 loaded; 9 259 unloaded

Trade
Exports $120 240 — Imports $35 244
Crude petroleum — Machinery
Petroleum products — Vehicles
— Food
Exports to: Japan, Italy, France and U.S.A.
Imports from: U.S.A., Japan and W. Germany
Invisible trade balance: −$24 618

SENEGAL

1. Republic
2. French, West African
3. C.F.A. Franc
4. £1 = 553
   $1 = 364

Area and Population
1. 196 192 km²
2. 5 811 000; 30 per km²
3. BR 55; DR 22; AI 2.6%
4. Urb. pop.: 1 149 (32%)
5. Dakar 799

Production
1. GDP $1 704 (...); $342 (...)
2. Millet 750 — Rice 120
   Bananas 2 — Groundnuts 900
3. Cattle 2 789 — Goats 890
4. Fish 359
5. Roundwood 2
6. Phosphates 1 50 — Salt 147
   Titanium ... — Zirconium ...

Manufactures
1. −/1.41; 700 kWh
2a. Sawnwood 11
b. Petroleum
   products 745 — Cement 372
3. Telephones 42; Cars 65
   Rail: 180 pass.-km; 164 t-km
   Air: 160 pass.-km; 14.7 t-km
   Sea: 3 240 loaded; 2 772 unloaded

Trade
Exports $536 — Imports $931
Groundnut oil — Food
Groundnuts — Manufactured goods
— Machinery
Main trade is with: France
Aid received (net): $149 from West

SINGAPORE

1. Republic
2. English, Chinese, Malay, Tamil
3. Singapore Dollar
4. £1 = 3.20
   $1 = 2.10

Area and Population
1. 581 km²
2. 2 443 000; 4 205 per km²
3. BR 17; DR 5; AI 1.2%
4. Urb. pop.: 2 363 (100%)
5. Singapore 2 391

Production
1. GDP $5 128 (8.6%); $2 279 (7.0%)
   Agric. 2%, Indust. 27%, Others 71%
2. Cassava 1
3. Pigs 1 166 — Cattle 9
4. Fish 16
   Granite 2 235

Manufactures
1. −/10.1; 7 440 kWh
2a. Meat 109 — Sawnwood 382
b. Manufacturing Industries ...
3. Telephones 475; Cars 208
   Rail: see Malaysia
   Air: 17 280 pass.-km; 667 t-km
   Sea: 34 236 loaded; 55 476 unloaded

Trade
Exports $20 993 — Imports $27 571
Rubber — Machinery
Petroleum products — Textiles
Machinery — Rubber
Exports to: Malaysia, U.S.A. and Japan
Imports from: Japan, Malaysia, U.S.A. and Saudi Arabia
Invisible trade balance: +$4 594
Revenue from tourism: $524
Aid received (net): $11 from West

For detailed table headings and notes see page 1 of this section

Country	Area and Population	Production	Manufactures	Trade

SOUTH AFRICA

Area and Population
1. Republic
2. English, Afrikaans
3. Rand
4. £1=1.67
   $1=1.09

1. 1 221 037 km²
2. 30 131 000; 25 per km²
3. BR 38; DR 10; AI 2.8%
4. Urb. pop.: 11 018 (48%)
5. Pretoria 562;
   Cape Town 1 097

Production
1. GDP $37 136 (3.5%); $1 296 (0.9%)
   Agric. 8%; Indust. 41%, Others 51%
2. Maize 14 645 — Wheat 2 090
   Oranges 569 — Pineapples 225
   Grapes 1 275 — Cottonseed 100
   Tobacco 34 — Wool 111
3. Sheep 31 650 — Cattle 12 200
4. Fish 640
5. Roundwood 16
6. Coal 131 184 — Manganese 5 040
   Iron 18 408 — Asbestos 249
   Copper 199 — Antimony 9 700
   Chrome 2 870 — Nickel 25
   Gold 655 728 kg — Diamonds 7 726 c

Manufactures
1. 92.4/85.4; 95 016 kWh (2.8% hydr.)
2a. Meat 1 008 — Sugar 2 050
   Wine 550 hl — Beer 22 517 hl
   Sawnwood 1 555
b. Iron 7 248 — Steel 8 940
   Copper 185 — Cotton yarn 52
   Wool yarn 21.1 — Petroleum
   Vehicles: — products 12 705
   pass. 335; comm. 31 — Cement 7 128
3. Telephones 2 320; Cars 2 400
   Rail: . . .; 96 768 t-km
   Air: 9 288 pass.-km; 334 t-km
   Sea: 47 160 loaded; 1 848 unloaded

Trade
Exports $9 618 — Imports $8 336
Diamonds — Machinery
Fruit — Vehicles
Wool — Textiles
Copper — Crude petroleum
Iron and steel — Petroleum products
Machinery — Chemical products
Cereals
Exports to: U.K., Japan, U.S.A. and W. Germany
Imports from: U.K., U.S.A., W. Germany and Japan
Invisible trade balance: −$4 323
Revenue from tourism: $321

SOUTH YEMEN

Area and Population
1. People's Republic
2. Arabic
3. South Yemen Dinar
4. £1=0.53
   $1=0.345

1. 332 910 km²
2. 1 838 000; 6 per km²
3. BR 48; DR 23; AI 1.9%
4. Urb. pop.: 529 (33%)
5. Aden 285

Production
1. GDP $242 (. . .); $147 (. . .)
   Agric. 19%, Indust. 27%, Others 54%
2. Millet 70 — Wheat 15
   Dates 43 — Cottonseed 9
3. Goats 1 350 — Sheep 980
4. Fish 75

Manufactures
1. −/0.57; 180 kWh
2b. Petroleum products 1 845
3. Telephones 9; Cars 11
   Sea: 1 426 loaded; 2 204 unloaded

Trade
Exports $248 — Imports $393
Petroleum products — Petroleum
Cotton — Cotton fabric
Cereals
Exports to: U.K., Yemen and South Africa
Imports from: Iran, Kuwait and Japan
Aid received (net): $72 from West

SPAIN

Area and Population
1. Monarchy
2. Spanish
3. Spanish Peseta
4. £1=207
   $1=135

1. 504 782 km²
2. 37 654 000; 74 per km²
3. BR 14; DR 8; AI 1.1%
4. Urb. pop.: 23 556 (64%)
5. Madrid 3 159

Production
1. GDP $133 325 (4.5%); $3 625 (3.4%)
   Agric. 9%, Indust. 28%, Others 63%
2. Barley 4 701 — Wheat 3 356
   Tomatoes 2 074 — Oranges 1 500
   Grapes 5 239 — Olives 1 348
   Cottonseed 100 — Cotton lint 65
   Tobacco 38 — Wool 21
3. Sheep 14 887 — Pigs 10 692
4. Fish 1 240
5. Roundwood 11
6. Coal 14 268 — Lead 83
   Lignite 20 676 — Tungsten 390
   Iron ore 4 206 — Mercury 1 070 t
   Copper 45 — Zinc 176
   Crude petroleum 1 380

Manufactures
1. 25.2/95.0; 110 700 kWh (28% hydr., 5% nucl.)
2a. Meat 2 538 — Sugar 1 054
   Olive oil 513 — Wine 3 331
   Sawnwood 2 050
b. Cotton yarn 94 — Wool yarn 35
   Silk fabric 252 Tm² — Copper 108
   Iron 6 528 — Steel 13 176
   Aluminium 431 — Ships (grt.) 509
   Radios 363 — Vehicles
   petroleum — pass. 862; comm. 127
   products 31 265 — Cement 28 752
3. Telephones 10 311; Cars 7 556
   Rail: 14 136 pass.-km; 12 540 t-km
   Air: 15 996 pass.-km; 455 t-km
   Sea: 48 672 loaded; 104 532 unloaded

Trade
Exports $20 337 — Imports $32 159
Machinery — Machinery
Fruits — Crude petroleum
Vegetables — Iron and steel
Footwear — Organic chemicals
Petroleum products — Maize
Textiles — Soya
Ships and boats — Sawnwood
Olive oil — Copper
Exports to: U.S.A., W. Germany, France and U.K.
Imports from: U.S.A., W. Germany, France and Saudi Arabia
Invisible trade balance: +$4 553
Revenue from tourism: $5 488

SRI LANKA

Area and Population
1. Republic
2. Sinhalese, English, Tamil
3. Sri Lanka Rupee
4. £1=34.60
   $1=22.95

1. 65 610 km²
2. 14 988 000; 228 per km²
3. BR 28; DR 6; AI 2.2%
4. Urb. pop.: 2 848 (22%)
5. Colombo 1 412

Production
1. GDP $2 379 (4.5%); $168 (2.8%)
   Agric. 34%, Indust. 14%, Others 52%
2. Rice 2 229 — Cassava 537
   Tea 210 — Copra 123
   Rubber 133 — Tobacco 8
3. Cattle 1 623 — Buffaloes 850
4. Fish 186
5. Roundwood 7
6. Graphite 9 — Salt 152
   Titanium 70

Manufactures
1. 0.18/1.54; 1 872 kWh (89% hydr.)
2a. Meat 32 — Sawnwood 26
b. Cotton yarn 8 — Petroleum
   products 1 415
3. Telephones 74; Cars 105
   Rail: 3 840 pass.-km; 196 t-km
   Air: 1 440 pass.-km; 29 t-km
   Sea: 1 188 loaded; 2 496 unloaded

Trade
Exports $1 036 — Imports $1 803
Tea — Machinery
Rubber — Rice
Copra — Sugar
Coconuts — Flour
Coconut fibre — Textiles
— Petroleum products
Exports to: U.K., Pakistan, China, and U.S.A
Imports from: Saudi Arabia, Iran and U.S.A.
Aid received (net): $217 from West, $60 from East

SUDAN

Area and Population
1. Republic
2. Arabic, Hamitic, English
3. Sudanese Pound
4. £1=2.01
   $1=0.76

1. 2 505 813 km²
2. 18 901 000; 8 per km²
3. BR 46; DR 18; AI 3.2%
4. Urb. pop.: 3 288 (20%)
5. Khartoum 334

Production
1. GDP $4 775 (. . .); $304 (. . .)
   Agric. 34%, Indust. 10%, Others 56%
2. Millet/sorghum 2 340 — Wheat 180
   Dates 119 — Groundnuts 800
   Cottonseed 187 — Cotton lint 99
3. Cattle 18 791 — Sheep 18 125
5. Roundwood 34
6. Chrome 24 — Salt 92

Manufactures
1. 0.06/1.22; 1 000 kWh (50% hydr.)
2a. Meat 427 — Sugar 235
b. Cement 140 — Petroleum
   Cotton fabrics 103 Mm² — products 988
3. Telephones 62; Cars 55
   Rail: . . .; 2 288 t-km
   Air: 552 pass.-km; 10 t-km
   Sea: 1 308 loaded; 2 220 unloaded

Trade
Exports $658 — Imports $1 529
Cotton — Machinery
Gum Arabic — Cotton fabrics
Sesame — Petrol products
Groundnuts
Exports to: Saudi Arabia, China, Japan and Italy
Imports from: U.K., W. Germany, Japan and India
Aid received (net): $170 from West, $21 from East

SWEDEN

Area and Population
1. Kingdom
2. Swedish
3. Krona
4. £1=11.41
   $1=7.47

1. 449 750 km²
2. 8 323 000; 18 per km²
3. BR 11; DR 11; AI 0.3%
4. Urb. pop.: 6 789 (83%)
5. Stockholm 1 384

Production
1. GDP $76 788 (1.6%); $9 274 (1.2%)
   Agric. 4%, Indust. 27%, Others 69%
2. Oats 1 732 — Barley 2 510
   Wheat 1 034 — Apples 92
   Potatoes 1 112 — Rapeseed 353
3. Pigs 2 800 — Cattle 1 935
4. Fish 237
5. Roundwood 53
6. Iron ore 15 093 — Lead 85
   Copper 51 — Zinc 181
   Gold 4 049 kg — Silver 169 t

Manufactures
1. 10.3/43.8; 99 960 kWh (64 hydr., 22% nucl.)
2a. Meat 545 — Butter & cheese 165
   Sugar 374 — Sawnwood 11 302
   Wood pulp 8 699
b. Iron 1 776 — Steel 3 768
   Aluminium 84 — Copper 74
   Paper 6 182 — Ships (grt) 338
   Petroleum — Vehicles:
   products 12 592 — pass. 229; comm. 60
3. Telephones 6 160; Cars 2 883
   Rail: 6 936 pass.-km; 14 592 t-km
   Air: 4 464 pass.-km; 197 t-km
   Sea: 33 420 loaded; 48 996 unloaded

Trade
Exports $28 632 — Imports $28 824
Machinery — Machinery
Iron and steel — Petroleum products
Paper and cardboard — Vehicles
Wood pulp — Textiles
Vehicles — Iron and steel
Sawnwood — Non-ferrous metals
Ships and boats — Clothing
Iron ore — Crude petroleum
Exports to: U.K., W. Germany, Denmark and Norway
Imports from: W. Germany, U.K., U.S.A. and Denmark
Invisible trade balance: −$1 941
Aid given (net): $1 250

SWITZERLAND

Area and Population
1. Federal Republic
2. German, French, Italian
3. Swiss Franc
4. £1=3.13
   $1=2.05

1. 41 288 km²
2. 6 473 000; 157 per km²
3. BR 12; DR 9; AI −0.3%
4. Urb. pop.: 3 423 (55%)
5. Bern 284

Production
1. GDP $78 669 (0.1%); $12 408 (−0.1%)
   Agric. 6%, Indust. 40%, Others 54%
2. Potatoes 1 048 — Apples 240
   Wheat 391 — Pears 55
3. Cattle 1 954 — Pigs 2 071
5. Roundwood 4
6. Salt 391

Manufactures
1. 5.8/23.7; 47 976 kWh (70% hydr., 28% nucl.)
2a. Meat 471 — Butter & cheese 160
   Wine 82 hl — Beer 3 998 hl
   Sawnwood 1 746
b. Iron 35 — Steel 784
   Aluminium 82 — Cotton yarn 42
   Petroleum — Silk fabrics 18 Mm²
   products 3 613
3. Telephones 4 292; Cars 2 247
   Rail: 9 096 pass.-km; 7 152 t-km
   Air: 11 628 pass.-km; 490 t-km

Trade
Exports $ 27 043 — Imports $30 696
Machinery — Machinery
Watches — Vehicles
Textiles — Iron and steel
Medicines — Textiles
Organic chemical — Petroleum products
products
Exports to: W. Germany, France, U.S.A., Italy and U.K.
Imports from: W. Germany, France, Italy, U.S.A. and U.K.
Invisible trade balance: +$6 934
Revenue from tourism: $2 446
Aid given (net): $3 502

For detailed table headings and notes see page 1 of this section

Country	Area and Population	Production	Manufactures	Trade
SYRIA 1. Republic 2. Arabic 3. Syrian Pound 4. £1=10.00 $1=3.95	1. 185 180 km² 2. 9 314 000; 50 per km² 3. BR 45; DR 9; AI 3.2% 4. Urb. pop.: 4 141 (48%) 5. Damascus 1 156	1. GDP $5 161 (9.8%); $702 (6.1%) Agric. 20%, Indust. 21%, Others 59% 2. Barley 1 406 — Wheat 2 086 Grapes 359 — Olives 297 Tomatoes 521 — Tobacco 17 Cottonseed 213 3. Sheep 8 800 — Goats 1 000 6. Crude petroleum 8 496 — Salt 62 Natural gas 1 864 — Phosphate 800	1. 12.9/9.4; 4 428 kWh (70% hydr.) 2a. Meat 178 — Sugar 19 Olive oil 51 b. Cement 1 812 — Petroleum Cotton, woven 355 — products 8 454 3. Telephones 212; Cars 65 Rail: 384 pass.-km; 9.4 t-km Air: 795 pass.-km; 9.4 t-km Sea: 15 612 loaded; 7 392 unloaded	Exports $2 103 — Imports $5 040 Cotton — Machinery Livestock — Iron and steel Crude petroleum — Vehicles Vegetables — Textiles Wheat — Crude petroleum Exports to: France, Italy, Greece and U.S.A. Imports from: W. Germany, Italy, France, Iraq and Romania Aid received (net): $74 from West, $131 from East
TAIWAN 1. Republic 2. Chinese 3. New Dollar 4. £1=61.15 $1=40.03	1. 35 981 km² 2. 18 135 508; 501 per km² 3. BR 26; DR 5; AI 2.1% 4. Urb. pop.: 8 211 (51%) 5. Tai-pei 3 050	1. GDP $32 337 (9.7%); $1 869 (7.7%) Agric. 11%, Indust. 46%, Others 43% 2. Rice 2 375 — Bananas 185 Groundnuts 86 — Citrus fruits 399 Pineapples 245 — Tea 25 Soya beans 16 3. Pigs 8 781 — Cattle 143 4. Fish 912 5. Roundwood 0.8 6. Coal 2 720 — Gold 1 600 kg Copper . . .	1. . . ./. . .; 40 192 kWh (12% hydr., 27% nucl.) 2a. Sugar 797 — Sawnwood 654 Meat . . . b. Steel 4 244 — Aluminium 31 Cotton yarn 157 — Radios 8 721 Petroleum products 18 367 3. Telephones 2 566; Cars 325 Rail: 7 327 pass.-km; 2 688 t-km Air: 867 pass.-km; 3 t-km Sea: 36 887 loaded; 62 440 unloaded	Exports $22 611 — Imports $21 199 Textiles — Machinery Electrical goods — Crude petroleum Timber products — Iron and steel Plastics — Chemicals Exports to: U.S.A., Japan and Hong Kong Imports from: Japan, U.S.A. and Kuwait
TANZANIA 1. Federal Republic 2. Swahili 3. Tanzanian Shilling 4. £1=14.58 $1=9.65	1. 945 087 km² 2. 18 510 000; 20 per km² 3. BR 46; DR 16; AI 2.8% 4. Urb. pop.: 2 329 (13%) 5. Dar-es-Salaam 757	1. GDP $4 564 (. . .); $254 (. . .) Agric. 44%, Indust. 10%, Others 46% 2. Maize 750 — Cassava 4 650 Bananas 1 580 — Coffee 68 Cottonseed 110 — Cotton lint 57 Tobacco 21 — Sisal 81 3. Cattle 12 673 — Goats 5 686 4. Fish 247 5. Roundwood 34 6. Gold 4 kg — Diamonds 293 c	1. 0.06/1.07; 695 kWh (75% hydr.) 2a. Meat 189 — Sawnwood 72 Sugar 124 — Beer 751 hl 3. Telephones 66; Cars 45 Rail: see Kenya Air: 37 pass.-km; 0.3 t-km Sea: 1 080 loaded; 3 180 unloaded	Exports $508 — Imports $1 226 Coffee — Machinery Cotton — Vehicles Diamonds — Textiles Sisal — Petroleum products Cashew nuts — Iron and steel Exports to: U.K., W. Germany, U.S.A. and Italy Imports from: U.K., Japan, Netherlands and W. Germany Aid received (net): $341 from West, $12 from East
THAILAND 1. Kingdom 2. Thai 3. Baht 4. £1=34.85 $1=23.00	1. 514 000 km² 2. 48 125 000; 94 per km² 3. BR 32; DR 9; AI 2.5% 4. Urb. pop.: 4 553 (13%) 5. Bangkok 4 702	1. GDP $20 030 (6.9%); $444 (4.1%) Agric. 27%, Indust. 22%, Others 51% 2. Maize 4 000 — Rice 19 000 Bananas 2 021 — Pineapples 2 000 Jute 219 — Rubber 510 Cottonseed 153 — Tobacco 87 Cassava 17 900 3. Buffaloes 6 299 — Cattle 5 062 4. Fish 1 650 5. Roundwood 38 6. Lignite 1 680 — Tungsten 3 780 Iron ore 35 — Tin 30 Antimony 3 548 — Manganese 25 Lead 41	1. 0.94/17.2; 5 336 kWh (25% hydr.) 2a. Meat 639 — Sawnwood 1 231 Sugar 1 641 b. Cotton yarn 90 — Petroleum Cement 6 288 — products 7 980 Tin 33 3. Telephones 409; Cars 271 Rail: 8 856 pass.-km; 2 808 t-km Air: 7 548 pass.-km; 282 t-km Sea: 12 456 loaded; 18 552 unloaded	Exports $7 001 — Imports $9 914 Rice — Machinery Maize — Vehicles Rubber — Iron and steel Fruit and vegetables — Crude petroleum Tin Exports to: Japan, U.S.A., Singapore, Netherlands and Indonesia Imports from: Japan, U.S.A., W. Germany and Saudi Arabia Invisible trade balance: −$660 Revenue from tourism: $400 Aid received (net): $156 from West
TOGO 1. Republic 2. Bantu, Hamitic, French 3. C.F.A. Franc 4. £1=554 $1=364	1. 56 785 km² 2. 2 705 000; 48 per km² 3. BR 48; DR 19; AI 2.6% 4. Urb. pop.: 330 (15%) 5. Lomé 135	1. GDP $626 (. . .); $266 (. . .) Agric. 28%, Indust. 12%, Others 60% 2. Cassava 470 Cocoa 15 — Coffee 9 Groundnuts 35 — Palm oil 20 3. Goats 750 — Sheep 840 5. Roundwood 1 6. Phosphates 2 927	1. −/0.25; 75 kWh (15% hydr.) 2. Food industries . . . 3. Telephones 10; Cars 20 Rail: 91 pass.-km; 38 t-km Air: 154 pass.-km; 14.7 t-km Sea: 2 796 loaded; 774 unloaded	Exports $335 — Imports $550 Cocoa — Cotton fabric Phosphates — Machinery Coffee — Food — Vehicles Exports to: France, W. Germany and Netherlands Imports from: France, W. Germany, U.K. and U.S.A. Aid received (net): $69 from West
TRINIDAD & TOBAGO 1. Commonwealth 2. English 3. Trinidad and Tobago Dollars 4. £1=3.66 $1=2.41	1. 5 128 km² 2. 1 185 000; 231 per km² 3. BR 25; DR 7; AI 0.2% 4. Urb. pop.: 460 (49%) 5. Port of Spain 66	1. GDP $2 942 (. . .); $2 638 (. . .) Agric. 3%, Indust. 51%, Others 46% 2. Rice 22 — Bananas 9 Oranges 3 Grapefruits 4 — Cocoa 2 Coffee 2 — Copra 2 3. Cattle 78 — Pigs 59 6. Natural gas 22 949 — Crude petroleum 9 780	1. 19.4/5.83; 1 836 kWh 2a. Sugar 90 — Beer 247 hl b. Petroleum products 8 262 3. Telephones 75; Cars 132 Air: 1 512 pass.-km; 18 t-km Sea: 20 832 loaded; 14 856 unloaded	Exports $3 725 — Imports $3 115 Petroleum products — Crude petroleum Petroleum — Manufactured goods Exports to: U.S.A., Netherlands and Surinam Imports from: U.S.A., U.K., Saudi Arabia and Indonesia Revenue from tourism: $91 Aid received (net): $5 from West
TUNISIA 1. Republic 2. Arabic, French 3. Dinar 4. £1=0.95 $1=0.65	1. 163 610 km² 2. 6 513 000; 40 per km² 3. BR 35; DR 11; AI 2.5% 4. Urb. pop.: 2 205 (43%) 5. Tunis 944	1. GDP $5 641 (8.5%); $934 (6.3%) Agric. 16%, Indust. 18%, Others 66% 2. Wheat 963 — Tomatoes 295 Oranges 141 — Olives 700 Grapes 141 — Dates 53 3. Sheep 4 967 — Cattle 914 4. Fish 60 5. Roundwood 2 6. Lead 6 — Crude petroleum 5 412 Iron ore 210 — Zinc 8 Phosphates 4 925 — Natural gas 4 352	1. 8.75/3.41; 2 676 kWh (0.8% hydr.) 2a. Sugar 8 — Wine 70 hl Meat 102 — Olive oil 140 b. Petroleum products 1 367 3. Telephones 158; Cars 102 Rail: 1 008 pass.-km; 1 716 t-km Air: 1 440 pass.-km; 14 t-km Sea: 4 380 loaded; 8 148 unloaded	Exports $2 189 — Imports $3 479 Petroleum — Machinery Olive oil — Wheat Phosphates — Textiles Fertilizer — Iron and steel Exports to: France, Italy, Greece and W. Germany Imports from: France, W. Germany and Italy Revenue from tourism: $415 Aid received (net): $212 from West, $16 from East
TURKEY 1. Republic 2. Turkish 3. Lira 4. £1=308 $1=205	1. 780 576 km² 2. 46 375 000; 59 per km² 3. BR 35; DR 10; AI 2.5% 4. Urb. pop.: 18 774 (45%) 5. Ankara 2 204	1. GDP $35 230 (6.9%); $873 (4.1%) Agric. 25%, Indust. 22%, Others 53% 2. Barley 5 900 — Wheat 17 040 Apples 1 479 — Oranges 723 Grapes 3 700 — Tomatoes 3 900 Cottonseed 785 — Cotton lint 488 Wool 62 — Tobacco 200 3. Sheep 48 630 — Goats 19 043 4. Fish 430 5. Roundwood 23 6. Coal 3 600 — Zinc 41 Lignite 9 504 — Crude petroleum 2 388 Iron ore 1 728 — Antimony 835 t Chrome 259 — Mercury 7 Bauxite 473 — Copper 34	1. 12.2/29.8; 20 565 kWh (42% hydr.) 2a. Meat 858 — Sawnwood 3 501 Sugar 1 300 — Wine 390 hl Olive oil 112 b. Iron 324 — Steel 1 799 Cotton yarn 166 — Wool yarn 7 Petroleum — Copper 26 products 13 986 — Cement 15 041 3. Telephones 1 379; Cars 659 Rail: 5 616 pass.-km; 5 676 t-km Air: 1 908 pass.-km; 8 t-km Sea: 6 672 loaded; 20 520 unloaded	Exports $4 721 — Imports $8 944 Cotton — Machinery Nuts — Vehicles Tobacco — Fertilizer Raisins — Crude petroleum — Iron and steel Exports to: W. Germany, U.S.A., Italy and France Imports from: W. Germany, U.S.A., Iran, Italy and France Revenue from tourism: $230 Aid received (net): $706 from West

For detailed table headings and notes see page 1 of this section

Country	Area and Population	Production	Manufactures	Trade

UGANDA

1. Republic
2. English, Bantu
3. Ugandan Shilling
4. £1=418
   $1=277

Area and Population
1. 236 036 km²
2. 13 620 000; 58 per km²
3. BR 45; DR 14; AI 3.4%
4. Urb. pop.: 747 (7%)
5. Kampala 331

Production
1. GDP $2 407 (0.1%); $208 (−3.1%)
   Agric. 53%, Indust. 10%, Others 37%
2. Cassava 1 420 · Millet/sorghum 980
   Coffee 130 · Tea 1
   Cottonseed 11 · Groundnuts 150
3. Cattle 5 500 · Goats 2 155
5. Roundwood 5
6. Tin 120 · Tungsten 139
   Copper 8

Manufactures
1. 0.08/0.37; 648 kWh (99% hydr.)
2a. Meat 142 · Sugar 5
   Sawnwood 24 · Beer 221 hl
3. Telephones 49; Cars 35
   Rail: see Kenya
   Air: 197 pass.-km; 7.4 t-km

Trade
Exports $345 · Imports $293
Coffee · Manufactured goods
Cotton · Machinery
Copper · Vehicles
Exports to: U.K., U.S.A., Spain and France
Imports from: U.K., W. Germany, Kenya and Brazil
Aid received (net): $18 from West

UNITED KINGDOM

1. Kingdom
2. English
3. English Pound
4. $1=0.623

Area and Population
1. 244 796 km²
2. 55 833 000; 228 per km²
3. BR 13; DR 12; AI −0.0%
4. Urb. pop.: 42 716 (76%)
5. London 6 696

Production
1. GDP $276 578 (2.1%); $4 955 (2.0%)
   Agric. 2%, Indust. 31%, Others 67%
2. Barley 10 149 · Wheat 8 465
   Oats 622 · Potatoes 6 400
   Apples 245 · Wool 52
3. Sheep 32 282 · Cattle 13 109
4. Fish 824
5. Roundwood 4
6. Coal 127 788 · Natural gas 359 655
   Iron ore 190 · Crude petroleum 87 036
   Tin 2 802 t · Salt 7 310
   Lead 2

Manufactures
1. 275.4/276.2; 277 716 kWh (2% hydr., 12% nucl.)
2a. Meat 2 989 · Sawnwood 1 721
   Butter & cheese 401 · Sugar 1 200
   Beer 66 418 hl
b. Iron 9 696 · Steel 10 620
   Aluminium 370 · Lead 333
   Copper 137 · Plastics 2 050
   Cotton yarn 52 · Wool yarn 183
   Synthetic fibres 552 · Silk fabric 742 Mm²
   Paper 3 791 · Radios 891
   Petroleum products 65 697 · Vehicles: pass. 955; comm. 229
   Ships (grt) 608 · Cement 12 828
3. Telephones 23 182; Cars 15 532
   Rail: 31 704 pass-km; 17 508 t-km
   Air: 50 616 pass.-km; 1 519 t-km
   Sea: 100 836 loaded; 132 540 unloaded

Trade
Exports $105 588 · Imports $100 882
Machinery · Machinery
Vehicles · Crude petroleum
Textiles · Non-ferrous metals
Diamonds · Fruit and vegetables
Non-ferrous metals · Diamonds
Iron and steel · Minerals
Alcoholic drinks · Cereals
Aircraft · Butter
· Meat
· Textiles
Exports to: U.S.A., W. Germany, France, Ireland, Belgium-Luxembourg and Netherlands
Imports from: U.S.A., W. Germany, France and Netherlands
Invisible trade balance: +$10 648
Revenue from tourism: $4 010
Aid given (net): $10 273

UNITED STATES

1. Federal Republic
2. English
3. U.S. Dollar
4. £1=1.53

Area and Population
1. 9 363 353 km²
2. 229 805 000; 25 per km²
3. BR 16; DR 9; AI 0.8%
4. Urb. pop.: 149 325 (74%)
5. Washington 3 061

Production
1. GDP $1 877 983 (3.0%); $8 612 (2.2%)
   Agric. 3%, Indust. 29%, Others 68%
2. Barley 10 414 · Oats 7 375
   Maize 208 314 · Wheat 76 026
   Oranges 9 547 · Grapefruit 2 503
   Wine 1 450 · Soya Beans 55 260
   Cottonseed 5 673 · Tobacco 929
   Rice 8 408
3. Cattle 114 321 · Pigs 64 512
4. Fish 3 635
5. Roundwood 322
6. Coal 700 908 · Nickel 10
   Iron ore 54 223 · Tungsten 4 300
   Bauxite 1 812 · Vanadium 3 875 t
   Copper 1 529 · Natural gas 4 993 616
   Gold 30 167 kg · Crude petroleum 421 308
   Lead 444 · Potash 2 052
   Molybdenum 13 · Phosphates 50 037
   Zinc 343

Manufactures
1. 2 090.4/2 369.7; 2 368 224 kWh (12% hydr., 11% nucl., 0.2 geo.)
2a. Meat 25 031 · Butter & cheese 2 514
   Sugar 5 771 · Wine 1 450
   Sawnwood 75 339 · Wood pulp 45 835
b. Cotton yarn 1 120 · Wool yarn 56
   Synthetic fibres 3 340 · Silk fabric 7 794 Mm²
   · Paper 59 131
   Copper 1 317 · Magnesium 127
   Iron 66 564 · Steel 108 876
   Aluminium 6 090 · Plastics 12 418
   Petroleum products 532 019 · Vehicles: pass. 6 238; comm. 1 690
   Radios 10 300 · Ships (grt) 558
3. Telephones 164 027; Cars 123 467
   Rail: 17 700 pass.-km; 1 341 720 t-km
   Air: 375 588 pass.-km; 10 169 t-km
   Sea: 369 132 loaded; 422 700 unloaded

Trade
Exports $228 961 · Imports $271 269
Machinery · Vehicles
Vehicles · Machinery
Aircraft · Iron and steel
Cereals · Non-ferrous metals
Chemical products · Crude petroleum
Iron and steel · Petroleum products
Non-ferrous metals · Clothing
Soya · Paper and cardboard
Metals · Textiles
Coal · Metals
Textiles
Exports to: Canada, Japan, U.K., W. Germany and Mexico
Imports from: Canada, Japan, W. Germany, U.K. and Mexico
Invisible trade balance: +$39 470
Revenue from tourism: $7 284
Aid given (net): $14 323

UPPER VOLTA

1. Republic
2. French
3. C.F.A. Franc
4. £1=554
   $1=364

Area and Population
1. 274 200 km²
2. 7 094 000; 26 per km²
3. BR 48; DR 22%; AI 2.6%
4. Urb. pop.: .... (8%)
5. Ouagadougou 169

Production
1. GDP $507 (...); $84 (...)
   Agric. 42%, Indust. 12%, Others 46%
2. Millet/sorghum 1 150 · Maize 100
   Rice 29 · Groundnuts 77
3. Cattle 2 760 · Goats 2 800
5. Roundwood 6
6. Gold ...

Manufactures
1. −/0.2; 120 kWh
2a. Meat 63
3. Telephones 8; Cars 12
   Air: 153 pass.-km; 14.6 t-km

Trade
Exports $75 · Imports $338
Livestock · Manufactured goods
Cotton · Foods
Exports to: Ivory Coast, France and China
Imports from: France, U.S.A. and Ivory Coast
Aid received (net): $116 from West

URUGUAY

1. Republic
2. Spanish
3. Uruguayan Peso
4. £1=49.67
   $1=33.88

Area and Population
1. 177 508 km²
2. 2 927 000; 16 per km²
3. BR 18; DR 10; AI 0.6%
4. Urb. pop.: 2 308 (83%)
5. Montevideo 1 230

Production
1. GDP $4 660 (1.6%); $1 612 (1.4%)
   Agric. 10%, Indust. 27%, Others 63%
2. Maize 196 · Wheat 400
   Grapes 53 · Oranges 58
   Linseed 22 · Wool 71
3. Sheep 19 980 · Cattle 10 952
4. Fish 120
5. Roundwood 2

Manufactures
1. 0.28/2.74; 3 331 kWh (68% hydr.)
2a. Meat 474 · Sawnwood 99
   Sugar 79
b. Petroleum products 1 564
3. Telephones 270; Cars 168
   Rail: 494 pass.-km; 303 t-km
   Air: 51 pass.-km; 0.2 t-km
   Sea: 430 loaded; 1 451 unloaded

Trade
Exports $1 215 · Imports $1 599
Beef · Machinery
Wool · Vehicles
Hides and skins · Crude petroleum
Exports to: W. Germany, Brazil and U.S.A.
Imports from: Argentina, Brazil, U.S.A. and Iraq
Aid received (net): $10 from West

U.S.S.R.

1. Socialist Republic
2. Russian and others
3. Rouble
4. £1=1.10
   $1=0.73

Area and Population
1. 22 402 200 km²
2. 267 697 000; 12 per km²
3. BR 19; DR 10; AI 0.9%
4. Urb. pop.: 163 586 (62%)
5. Moscow 8 099

Production
1. NMP $540 214 (5.7%); $2 086 (4.8%)
   Agric. 17%, Indust. 51%, Others 32%
2. Barley 43 000 · Wheat 88 000
   Potatoes 83 000 · Grapes 6 500
   Tomatoes 6 150 · Cottonseed 5 879
   · Tobacco 929
3. Sheep 141 573 · Cattle 115 057
4. Fish 9 412
5. Roundwood 356
6. Coal 510 000 · Tungsten 10 700 t
   Iron ore 145 202 · Zinc 1 010
   Bauxite 6 400 · Natural gas 3 879 080
   Chrome 960 · Crude petroleum 609 000
   Copper 1 140 · Phosphates 24 800
   Lead 570 · Potash 6 635
   Manganese 2 945 · Salt 14 500
   Molybdenum 17 · Asbestos 2 470
   Nickel 170 · Diamonds 9 500

Manufactures
1. 1 939.2/1 485.7; 1 325 004 kWh (14% hydr., 5% nucl.)
2a. Meat 15 367 · Sawnwood 99 600
   Butter & cheese 3 000 · Sugar 6 100
   Wine 3 200
b. Iron 107 760 · Steel 149 004
   Aluminium 2 400 · Copper 1 140
   Magnesium 70 · Paper 9 236
   Cotton yarn 1 624 · Wool yarn 426
   Synthetic fibres 1 089 · Silk fabric 45 648 Mm²
   Linen 870 · Radios 8 728
   Petroleum products 304 708 · Vehicles: pass. 1 314; comm. 874
3. Telephones 20 943; Cars 7 000
   Rail: 332 064 pass.-km; 3 507 000 t-km
   Air: 9 984 pass.-km; 318 t-km
   Sea: 150 916 loaded; 43 521 unloaded

Trade
Exports $76 449 · Imports $68 522
Machinery · Machinery
Iron and steel · Clothing
Crude petroleum · Ships
Non-ferrous metals · Iron and steel
Petroleum products · Minerals
Sawnwood · Railway rolling stock
Cotton · Shoes
Vehicles
Main trade is with: E. Germany, Poland, Czechoslovakia, Bulgaria and Hungary
Aid given (net): $3 327

For detailed table headings and notes see page 1 of this section

Country	Area and Population	Production		Manufactures		Trade	

VENEZUELA

1. Republic
2. Spanish
3. Bolivar
4. £1=6.55
   $1=4.29

1. 912 050 km^2
2. 14 313 000; 16 per km^2
3. BR 37; DR 6; AI 3.0%
4. Urb. pop.: 10 584 (76%)
5. Caracas 2 849

1. GDP $36 366 (5.8%); 2 772 (2.6%)
   Agric. 6%, Indust. 36%, Others 58%
2. Maize 415 — Bananas 1 495
   Oranges 430 — Tomatoes 180
   Cocoa 14 — Coffee 62
   Cottonseed 14 — Sesame 30
3. Cattle 10 939 — Pigs 2 287
4. Fish 172
5. Roundwood 9
6. Iron ore 10 061 — Natural gas 135 907
   Gold 865 kg — Crude petroleum 111 576
   Diamonds 763 c — Phosphates 109
   — Coal 100

1. 192.5/47.0; 31 000 kWh (47% hydr.)
2a. — Sawnwood 349
   Sugar 291
b. Iron 689 — Steel 1 824
   Cotton yarn 16 — Synthetic fibres 17
   Cement 3 426 — Vehicles:
   Petroleum — pass. 97; comm 66
   products 41 289
3. Telephones 847; Cars 1 300
   Rail: 40 pass.-km; 20 t-km
   Air: 3 528 pass.-km; 151 t-km
   Sea: 131 316 loaded; 8 568 unloaded

Exports $20 950 — Imports $10 655
Crude petroleum — Machinery
Petroleum products — Vehicles
Iron ore — Iron and steel
Coffee — Cereals
— Manufactured goods
Exports to: U.S.A., Netherlands, Antilles and Canada
Imports from: U.S.A., W. Germany and Japan
Invisible trade balance: −$3 059

VIETNAM

1. Democratic Republic
2. Vietnamese
3. Đồng
4. £1=3.83
   $1=2.18

1. 332 559 km^2
2. 54 968 000; 165 per km^2
3. BR 40; DR 14; AI 2.4%
4. Urb. pop.: 8 149 (18%)
5. Hanoi 2 571

1. Agric. 29%, Indust. 7%, Others 64%
2. Rice 12 570 — Cassava 3 400
   Groundnuts 80 — Tea 23
   Maize 540 — Tobacco 28
3. Cattle 1 450 — Buffaloes 2 200
4. Fish 1 014
5. Roundwood 64
6. Coal 5 900 — Phosphates 1 200
   Salt 375

1. 6.39/7.76; 3 900 kWh (18% hydr.)
2a. Sawnwood 520
b. Cotton yarn 10 — Cement 544
3. Telephones 47; Cars 66
   Rail: 4 043 pass.-km; 980 t-km
   Air: 390 pass.-km; 4.1 t-km
   Sea: 198 loaded; 4 875 unloaded

Exports $440 — Imports $1 210
Main trade is with U.S.S.R. and other Communist countries and Japan, France, Singapore and Hong Kong

YEMEN

1. Republic
2. Arabic
3. Riyal
4. £1=6.91
   $1=4.59

1. 195 000 km^2
2. 5 940 000; 30 per km^2
3. BR 49; DR 24; AI 2.3%
4. Urb. pop.: 331 (6%)
5. Sana 448

1. GDP 1 122 (. . .); $212 (. . .)
   Agric. 61%, Indust. 3%, Others 36%
2. Millet 70 — Wheat 70
   Coffee 4 — Cottonseed 3
3. Sheep 3 200 — Cattle 950

1. −/0.45; 75 kWh
3. Telephones 4; Cars . . .
   Sea: 25 loaded; 500 unloaded

Exports $14 — Imports $1 492
Exports to: China, S. Yemen, Italy and Saudi Arabia
Imports from: Saudi Arabia, Japan and India
Aid received (net): $42 from West

YUGOSLAVIA

1. Federal Republic
2. Croatian, Serbian
3. Yugoslavian Dinar
4. £1=115
   $1=77.66

1. 255 804 km^2
2. 22 516 000; 88 per km^2
3. BR 17; DR 9; AI 0.9%
4. Urb. pop.: 7 914 (39%)
5. Belgrade 775

1. NMP $27 637 (5.8%); $1 294 (4.8%)
   Agric. 16%, Indust. 40%, Others 44%
2. Maize 9 800 — Wheat 4 270
   Grapes 1 330 — Wool 10
   Tobacco 70
3. Sheep 7 388 — Pigs 7 869
4. Fish 58
5. Roundwood 16
6. Coal 384 — Gold 3 582 kg
   Lignite 51 864 — Lead 119
   Iron ore 1 676 — Silver 138 t
   Antimony 1 724 — Zinc 87
   Bauxite 3 252 — Chrome 2
   Copper 111 — Crude petroleum 4 380
   Natural gas 16 367

1. 28.6/45.8; 60 072 kWh (48% hydr.)
2a. Meat 1 428 — Sawnwood 4 239
   Sugar 850 — Wine 670 hl
b. Iron 3 072 — Steel 2 352
   Copper 93 — Lead 86
   Cotton yarn 118 — Wool yarn 51
   Synthetic fibres 97 — Ships (grt) 284
   Petroleum products 11 101
3. Telephones 1 556; Cars 2 417
   Rail: 10 416 pass.-km; 25 440 t-km
   Air: 2 724 pass.-km; 29 t-km
   Sea: 5 244 loaded; 23 400 unloaded

Exports $10 929 — Imports $15 757
Machinery — Machinery
Non-ferrous metals — Iron and steel
Ships and boats — Vehicles
Clothing — Textile fibres
Meat — Textiles
Textiles — Non-ferrous metals
Iron and steel — Chemical products
Shoes — Crude petroleum
Exports to: Italy, U.S.S.R. and W. Germany
Imports from: W. Germany, Italy and U.S.S.R.
Invisible trade balance: +$1 753
Revenue from tourism: $841

ZAÏRE

1. Democratic Republic
2. Kiswahili, etc.
3. Zaïre
4. £1=8.86
   $1=5.86

1. 2 345 409 km^2
2. 26 377 000; 11 per km^2
3. BR 46; DR 19; AI 2.9%
4. Urb. pop.: 7 997 (30%)
5. Kinshasa 2 008

1. GDP $3 158 (3.8%); $127 (1.0%)
   Agric. 19%, Indust. 22%, Others 59%
2. Cassava 13 000 — Maize 520
   Coffee 75 — Groundnuts 320
   Palm oil 155 — Rubber 28
   Bananas 1 790 — Cottonseed 19
3. Goats 2 722 — Cattle 1 170
4. Fish 115
5. Roundwood 10
6. Cobalt 11 — Tin 3 450 t
   Copper 505 — Zinc 76
   Manganese 21 — Diamonds 6 100 c
   Gold 1 672 kg — Tungsten 181 t
   Crude petroleum 996

1. 2.13/1.84; 4 360 kWh (99% hydr.)
2a. Sugar — Beer 4 984 hl
   Sawnwood 90
b. Copper 468 — Zinc 58
   Petroleum — Cement 475
   products 340
3. Telephones 26; Cars 40
   Rail: 467 pass.-km; 2 203 t-km
   Air: 828 pass.-km; 37 t-km
   Sea 464 loaded; 715 unloaded

Exports $662 — Imports $672
Copper — Machinery
Diamonds — Vehicles
Cobalt — Petroleum products
Coffee — Cotton fabric
Palm oil — Cereals
Exports to: Belgium-Luxembourg, U.K. and U.S.A.
Imports from: Belgium-Luxembourg, U.S.A., France and W. Germany
Aid received (net): $253 from West

ZAMBIA

1. Republic
2. English
3. Kwacha
4. £1=1.80
   $1=1.18

1. 752 614 km^2
2. 5 961 000; 8 per km^2
3. BR 49; DR 17; AI 3.2%
4. Urb. pop.: 2 280 (40%)
5. Lusaka 538

1. GDP $2 263 (3.2%); $414 (0.0%)
   Agric. 16%, Indust. 29%, Others 55%
2. Maize 1 000 — Tobacco 4
   Millet/sorghum 100 — Groundnuts 30
3. Cattle 2 151 — Goats 310
4. Fish 51
5. Roundwood 5
6. Coal 504 — Tin . . .
   Cobalt 5 — Gold 247 kg
   Copper 588 — Silver 33
   Lead 16 — Zinc 40

1. 1.61/2.77; 9 792 kWh (99% hydr.)
2a. Meat 69 — Sugar 102
   Sawnwood 42
b. Copper 572 — Zinc 42
   Lead 10 — Cement 144
3. Telephones 57; Cars 105
   Air: 552 pass.-km; 18 t-km

Exports $1 402 — Imports $1 090
Copper — Machinery
Zinc — Vehicles
Lead — Textiles
Cobalt — Iron and steel
Tobacco — Petroleum products
Exports to: Japan, U.K., W. Germany and U.S.A.
Imports from: U.K., Saudi Arabia and U.S.A.
Aid received (net): $117 from West

ZIMBABWE

1. Republic
2. English
3. Zimbabwe Dollar
4. £1=1.48
   $1=0.97

1. 390 581 km^2
2. 7 600 000; 19 per km^2
3. BR 47; DR 14; AI 3.2%
4. Urb. pop.: 1 396 (20%)
5. Harare 633

1. GDP $2 999 (3.5%); $477 (0.1%)
   Agric. 15%, Indust. 29%, Others 56%
2. Maize 2 814 — Millet/sorghum 327
   Groundnuts 239 — Tobacco 70
3. Cattle 5 000 — Goats 1 350
5. Roundwood 8
6. Coal 2 868 — Gold 11 539 kg
   Iron ore 1 092 — Nickel 15
   Chrome 300 — Tin 600
   Copper 25 — Asbestos 260

1. 3.70/4.55; 4 512 kWh (88% hydr.)
2a. Meat 146 — Sugar 390
   Sawnwood 162
b. Iron 350 — Steel 650
   Copper 25
3. Telephones 197; Cars 215
   Rail: . . .; 5 280 t-km

Exports $1 423 — Imports $1 322
Tobacco — Machinery
Asbestos — Textiles
Copper — Vehicles
Gold — Mineral fuels
Main trade with U.K., W. Germany and U.S.A.
Aid received from West

For detailed table headings and notes see page 1 of this section

Chart of the Stars

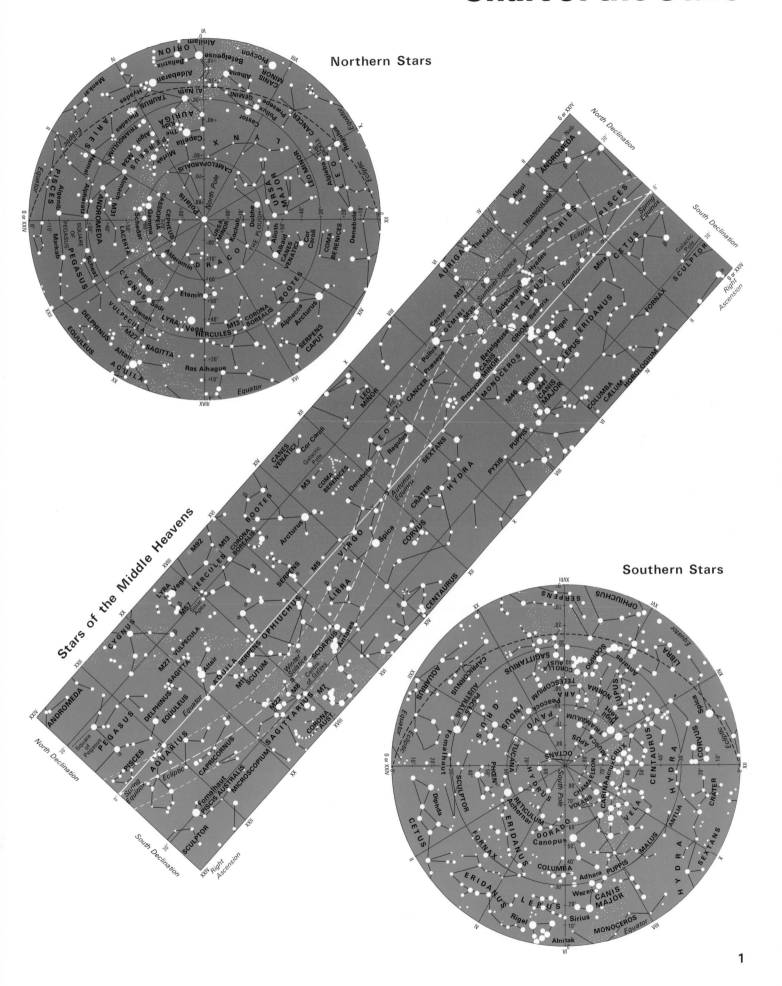

Northern Stars

Stars of the Middle Heavens

Southern Stars

1

The Solar System

The Solar System is a minute part of one of the innumerable galaxies that make up the universe. Our Galaxy is represented in the drawing to the right and The Solar System (S) lies near the plane of spiral-shaped galaxy, but 27 000 light-years from the centre. The System consists of the Sun at the centre with planets, moons, asteroids, comets, meteors, meteorites, dust and gases revolving around it. It is calculated to be at least 4 700 million years old.

The Solar System can be considered in two parts: the Inner Region planets- Mercury, Venus, Earth and Mars - all small and solid, the Outer Region planets - Jupiter, Saturn, Uranus and Neptune - all gigantic in size, and on the edge of the system the smaller Pluto.

Our galaxy

Inner region planets

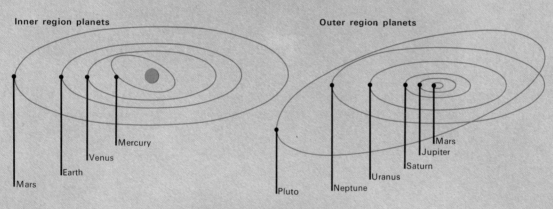

Mercury
Venus
Earth
Mars

Outer region planets

Mars
Jupiter
Saturn
Uranus
Neptune
Pluto

The planets

All planets revolve round the Sun in the same direction, and mostly in the same plane. Their orbits are shown (left) - they are not perfectly circular paths.

The table below summarizes the dimensions and movements of the Sun and planets.

The Sun

The Sun has an interior with temperatures believed to be of several million °C brought about by continuous thermo-nuclear fusions of hydrogen into helium. This immense energy is transferred by radiation into surrounding layers of gas the outer surface of which is called the chromosphere. From this "surface" with a temperature of many thousands °C "flames" (solar prominences) leap out into the diffuse corona which can best be seen at times of total eclipse (see photo right). The bright surface of the Sun, the photosphere, is calculated to have a temperature of about 6 000 °C, and when viewed through a telescope has a mottled appearance, the darker patches being called sunspots - the sites of large disturbances of the surface.

Total eclipse of the sun

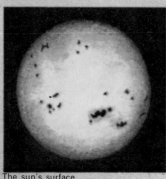
The sun's surface

	Equatorial diameter in km	Mass (earth=1)	Mean distance from sun in millions km	Mean radii of orbit (earth = 1)	Orbital inclination	Mean sidereal period (days)	Mean period of rotation on axis (days)	Number of satellites
Sun	1 392 000	332 946	—	—	—	—	25·38	—
Mercury	4 878	0·05	57·9	0·38	7°	87·9	58·6	0
Venus	12 104	0·81	108·2	0·72	3°23'	224·7	243	0
Earth	12 756	1·00	149·6	1·00	—	365·2	0·99	1
Mars	6 794	0·10	227·9	1·52	1°50'	686·9	1·02	2
Jupiter	142 800	317·9	778·3	5·20	1°18'	4332·5	0·41	14 ?
Saturn	120 000	95·1	1 427	9·53	2°29'	10759·2	0·42	11
Uranus	52 000	14·5	2 869	19·17	0°46'	30684·8	0·45	5
Neptune	48 400	17·2	4 496	30·05	1°46'	60190·5	0·67	2
Pluto	3 000 ?	0·001	5 900	39·43	17°1'	91628·6	6·38	1 ?

The Sun's diameter is 109 times greater than that of the Earth.

Distances from sun in millions km

7.9	Mercury
8.2	Venus
9.6	Earth
7.9	Mars
8.3	Jupiter
427	Saturn
869	Uranus
496	Neptune
900	Pluto

Mercury is the nearest planet to the Sun. It is composed mostly of high density metals and probably has an atmosphere of heavy inert gases.

Venus is similar in size to the Earth, and probably in composition. It is, however, much hotter and has a dense atmosphere of carbon dioxide which obscures our view of its surface.

Earth is the largest of the inner planets. It has a dense iron-nickel core surrounded by layers of silicate rock. The surface is approximately $\frac{3}{8}$ land and $\frac{5}{8}$ water, and the lower atmosphere consists of a mixture of nitrogen, oxygen and other gases supplemented by water vapour. With this atmosphere and surface temperatures usually between $-50°C$ and $+40°C$, life is possible.

Mars, smaller than the Earth, has a noticeably red appearance. Photographs taken by the Mariner probes show clearly the cratered surface and polar ice caps, probably made from frozen carbon dioxide.

The Asteroids orbit the Sun mainly between Mars and Jupiter. They consist of thousands of bodies of varying sizes with diameters ranging from yards to hundreds of miles.

Jupiter is the largest planet of the Solar System. Photographs taken by Voyager I and II have revealed an equatorial ring system and shown the distinctive Great Red Spot and rotating cloud belts in great detail.

Saturn, the second largest planet consists of hydrogen, helium and other gases. The equatorial rings are composed of small ice particles.

Uranus is extremely remote but just visible to the naked eye and has a greenish appearance. A faint equatorial ring system was discovered in 1977. The planet's axis is tilted through 98° from its orbital plane, therefore it revolves in a retrograde manner.

Neptune, yet more remote than Uranus and larger. It is composed of gases and has a bluish green appearance when seen in a telescope. As with Uranus, little detail can be observed on its surface.

Pluto. No details are known of its composition or surface. The existence of this planet was firstly surmised in a computed hypothesis, which was tested by repeated searches by large telescopes until in 1930 the planet was found. Latest evidence seems to suggest that Pluto has one satellite, provisionally named Charon.

3

The Earth

Seasons, Equinoxes and Solstices

The Earth revolves around the Sun once a year and rotates daily on its axis, which is inclined at 66½° to the orbital plane and always points into space in the same direction. At midsummer (N.) the North Pole tilts towards the Sun, six months later it points away and half way between the axis is at right angles to the direction of the Sun (right).

Earth data

Maximum distance from the Sun (Aphelion) 152 007 016 km
Minimum distance from the Sun (Perihelion) 147 000 830 km
Obliquity of the ecliptic 23° 27' 08"
Length of year - tropical (equinox to equinox) 365.24 days
Length of year - sidereal (fixed star to fixed star) 365.26 days
Length of day - mean solar day 24h 03m 56s
Length of day - mean sidereal day 23h 56m 04s

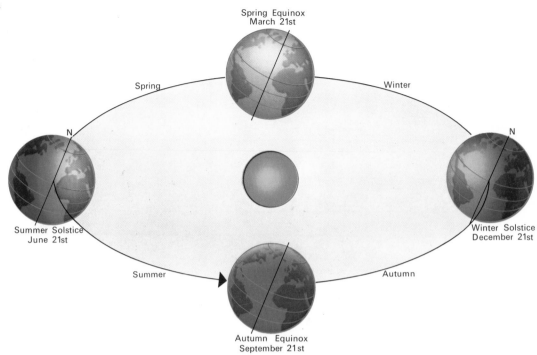

Length of day and night

At the summer solstice in the northern hemisphere, the Arctic has total daylight and the Antarctic total darkness. The opposite occurs at the winter solstice. At the equator, the length of day and night are almost equal all the year, at 30° the length of day varies from about 14 hours to 10 hours and at 50° from about 16 hours to 8 hours.

Apparent path of the Sun

The diagrams (right) illustrate the apparent path of the Sun at A the equator, B in mid latitudes say 45°N, C at the Arctic Circle 66½° and D at the North Pole where there is six months continuous daylight and six months continuous night

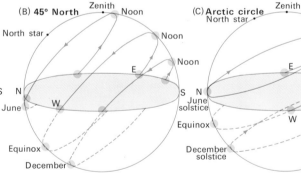

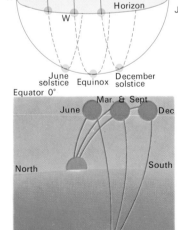

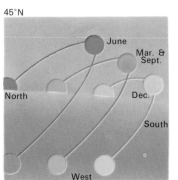

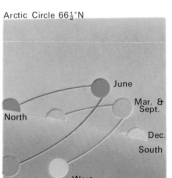

The Moon

The Moon rotates slowly making one complete turn on its axis in just over 27 days. This is the same as its period of revolution around the Earth and thus it always presents the same hemisphere ('face') to us. Surveys and photographs from space-craft have now added greatly to our knowledge of the Moon, and, for the first time, views of the hidden hemisphere.

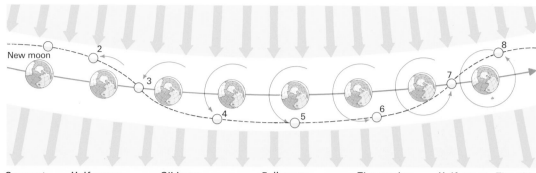

| Crescent moon(2) | Half moon, first quarter(3) | Gibbous moon (4) | Full moon (5) | The waning moon (6) | Half moon, last quarter(7) | The old moon (8) |

Phases of the Moon

The interval between one full Moon and the next is approximately 29½ days - thus there is one new Moon and one full Moon every month. The diagrams and photographs (right) show how the apparent changes in shape of the Moon from new to full arise from its changing position in relation to the Earth and both to the fixed direction of the Sun's rays.

Moon data
Distance from Earth 356 410 km
to 406 685 km
Mean diameter 3 473 km
Mass approx. $\frac{1}{81}$ of that of Earth
Surface gravity $\frac{1}{6}$ of that of Earth
Atmosphere - none, hence no clouds, no weather, no sound.
Diurnal range of temperature at the Equator +200°C

Landings on the Moon
Left are shown the landing sites of the U.S. Apollo programme.
Apollo 11 Sea of Tranquility (1°N 23°E) 1969
Apollo 12 Ocean of Storms (3°S 24°W) 1969
Apollo 14 Fra Mauro (4°S 17°W) 1971
Apollo 15 Hadley Rill (25°N 4°E) 1971
Apollo 16 Descartes (9°S 15°E) 1972
Apollo 17 Sea of Serenity (20°N 31°E) 1972

Eclipses of Sun and Moon
When the Moon passes between Sun and Earth it causes a partial eclipse of the Sun *(right 1)* if the Earth passes through the Moon's outer shadow *(P)*, or a total eclipse *(right 2)*, if the inner cone shadow crosses the Earth's surface.
In a lunar eclipse, the Earth's shadow crosses the Moon and gives either total or partial eclipses.

Tides
Ocean water moves around the Earth under the gravitational pull of the Moon, and, less strongly, that of the Sun. When solar and lunar forces pull together - near new and full Moon - high spring tides result. When solar and lunar forces are not combined - near Moon's first and third quarters - low neap tides occur.

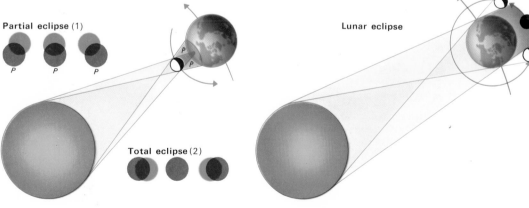

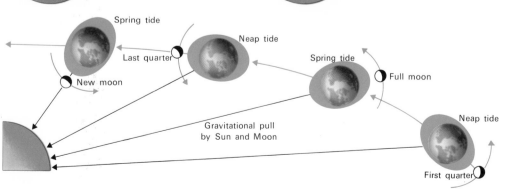

Time

Time measurement
The basic unit of time measurement is the day, one rotation of the earth on its axis. The subdivision of the day into hours and minutes is arbitrary and simply for our convenience. Our present calendar is based on the solar year of $365\frac{1}{4}$ days, the time taken for the earth to orbit the sun. A month was anciently based on the interval from new moon to new moon, approximately $29\frac{1}{2}$ days - and early calendars were entirely lunar.

Rotation of the Earth
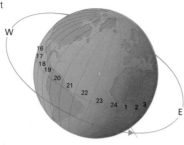

Greenwich Observatory

Prime Meridian

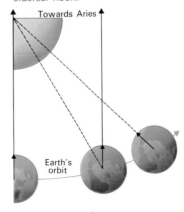

The International Date Line
When it is 12 noon at the Greenwich meridian, 180° east it is midnight of the same day while 180° west the day is only just beginning. To overcome this the International Date Line was established, approximately following the 180° meridian. Thus, for example, if one travelled eastwards from Japan (140° East) to Samoa (170° West) one would pass from Sunday night into Sunday morning.

Time zones
The world is divided into 24 time zones, each centred on meridians at 15° intervals which is the longitudinal distance the sun appears to travel every hour. The meridian running through Greenwich passes through the middle of the first zone. Successive zones to the east of Greenwich zone are ahead of Greenwich time by one hour for every 15° of longitude, while zones to the west are behind by one hour.

Night and day
As the earth rotates from west to east the sun appears to rise in the east and set in the west: when the sun is setting in Shanghai on the directly opposite side of the earth New York is just emerging into sunlight. Noon, when the sun is directly overhead, is coincident at all places on the same meridian with shadows pointing directly towards the poles.

Solar time
The time taken for the earth to complete one rotation about its own axis is constant and defines a day but the speed of the earth along its orbit around the sun is inconstant. The length of day, or 'apparent solar day', as defined by the apparent successive transits of the sun is irregular because the earth must complete more than one rotation before the sun returns to the same meridian.

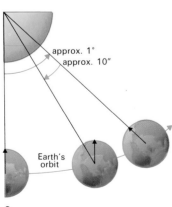
approx. 1°
approx. 10"
Earth's orbit

Sidereal time
The constant sidereal day is defined as the interval between two successive apparent transits of a star, or the first point of Aries, across the same meridian. If the sun is at the equinox and overhead at a meridian on one day, then the next day the sun will be to the east by approximately 1°; thus the sun will not cross the meridian until about 4 minutes after the sidereal noon.

Towards Aries
Earth's orbit

Astronomical clock, Delhi

Sundials
The earliest record of sundials dates back to 741 BC but they undoubtedly existed as early as 2000 BC although probably only as an upright stick or obelisk. A sundial marks the progress of the sun across the sky by casting the shadow of a central style or gnomon on the base. The base, generally made of stone, is delineated to represent the hours between sunrise and sunset.

Kendall's chronometer

Chronometers
With the increase of sea traffic in the 18th century and the need for accurate navigation clockmakers were faced with an intriguing problem. Harrison, an English carpenter, won a British award for designing a clock which was accurate at sea to one tenth of a second per day. He compensated for the effect of temperature changes by incorporating bi-metallic strips connected to thin wires and circular balance wheels.

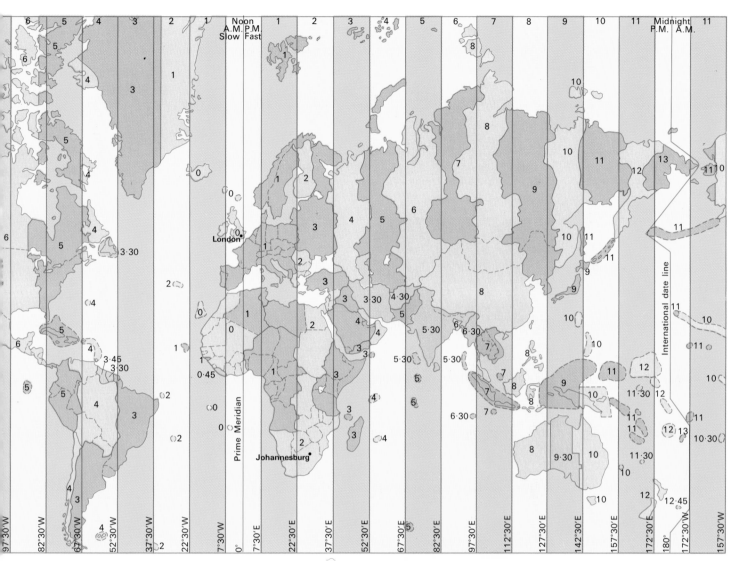

Noon A.M. P.M. Slow Fast

Midnight P.M. A.M.

London

Johannesburg

Prime Meridian

International date line

97°30'W 82°30'W 67°30'W 52°30'W 37°30'W 22°30'W 7°30'W 0° 7°30'E 22°30'E 37°30'E 52°30'E 67°30'E 82°30'E 97°30'E 112°30'E 127°30'E 142°30'E 157°30'E 172°30'E 180° 172°30'W 157°30'W

Progress of the accuracy of timekeepers

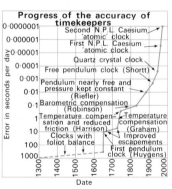

Second N.P.L. Caesium 'atomic' clock
First N.P.L. Caesium 'atomic' clock
Quartz crystal clock
Free pendulum clock (Shortt)
Pendulum nearly free and pressure kept constant (Riefler)
Barometric compensation (Robinson)
Temperature compensation and reduced friction (Harrison)
Temperature compensation (Graham)
Clocks with foliot balance
Improved escapements
First pendulum clock (Huygens)

Error in seconds per day / Date

Vibration of quartz ring

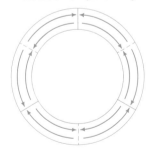

Time difference when travelling by air

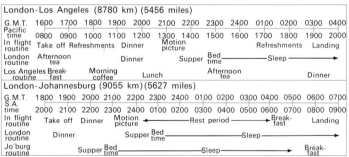

London-Los Angeles (8780 km) (5456 miles)													
G.M.T.	1600	1700	1800	1900	2000	2100	2200	2300	2400	0100	0200	0300	0400
Pacific time	0800	0900	1000	1100	1200	1300	1400	1500	1600	1700	1800	1900	2000
In flight routine	Take off	Refreshments		Dinner			Motion picture					Refreshments	Landing
London routine	Afternoon tea				Dinner		Supper		Bed time		Sleep		
Los Angeles routine	Break-fast		Morning coffee			Lunch			Afternoon tea				Dinner

London-Johannesburg (9055 km) (5627 miles)													
G.M.T.	1800	1900	2000	2100	2200	2300	2400	0100	0200	0300	0400	0500	0600	0700
S.A. time	2000	2100	2200	2300	2400	0100	0200	0300	0400	0500	0600	0700	0800	0900
In flight routine	Take off	Dinner		Motion picture			Rest period				Break-fast		Landing
London routine	Dinner			Supper	Bed time			Sleep					
Jo'burg routine			Supper	Bed time				Sleep					Break-fast

Chronographs

The invention of the chronograph by Charles Wheatstone in 1842 made it possible to record intervals of time to an accuracy of one sixtieth of a second. The simplest form of chronograph is the stop-watch. This was developed to a revolving drum and stylus and later electrical signals. A recent development is the cathode ray tube capable of recording to less than one ten-thousanth of a second.

Quartz crystal clocks

The quartz crystal clock, designed originally in America in 1929, can measure small units of time and radio frequencies. The connection between quartz clocks and the natural vibrations of atoms and molecules mean that the unchanging frequencies emitted by atoms can be used to control the oscillator which controls the quartz clock. A more recent version of the atomic clock is accurate to one second in 300 years.

International date line

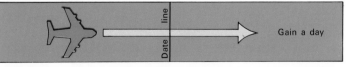

Date line — Gain a day

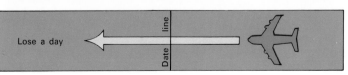

Date line — Lose a day

The Atmosphere and Clouds

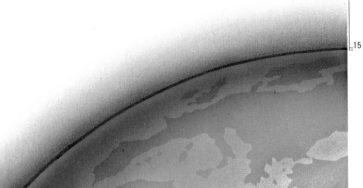

Earth's thin coating *(right)*
The atmosphere is a blanket of protective gases around the earth providing insulation against otherwise extreme alternations in temperature. The gravitational pull increases the density nearer the earth's surface so that 5/6ths of the atmospheric mass is in the first 15 kms. It is a very thin layer in comparison with the earth's diameter of 12 680 kms., like the cellulose coating on a globe.

Exosphere *(1)*
The exosphere merges with the interplanetary medium and although there is no definite boundary with the ionosphere it starts at a height of about 600 kms. The rarified air mainly consists of a small amount of atomic oxygen up to 600 kms. and equal proportions of hydrogen and helium with hydrogen predominating above 2 400 kms.

Ionosphere *(2)*
Air particles of the ionosphere are electrically charged by the sun's radiation and congregate in four main layers, D, E, F1 and F2, which can reflect radio waves. Aurorae, caused by charged particles deflected by the earth's magnetic field towards the poles, occur between 65 and 965 kms. above the earth. It is mainly in the lower ionosphere that meteors from outer space burn up as they meet increased air resistance.

Stratosphere *(3)*
A thin layer of ozone contained within the stratosphere absorbs ultra-violet light and in the process gives off heat. The temperature ranges from about -55°C at the tropopause to about -60°C in the upper part, known as the mesosphere, with a rise to about 2°C just above the ozone layer. This portion of the atmosphere is separated from the lower layer by the tropopause.

Troposphere *(4)*
The earth's weather conditions are limited to this layer which is relatively thin, extending upwards to about 8 kms. at the poles and 15 kms. at the equator. It contains about 85% of the total atmospheric mass and almost all the water vapour. Air temperature falls steadily with increased height at about 1°C for every 100 metres above sea level.

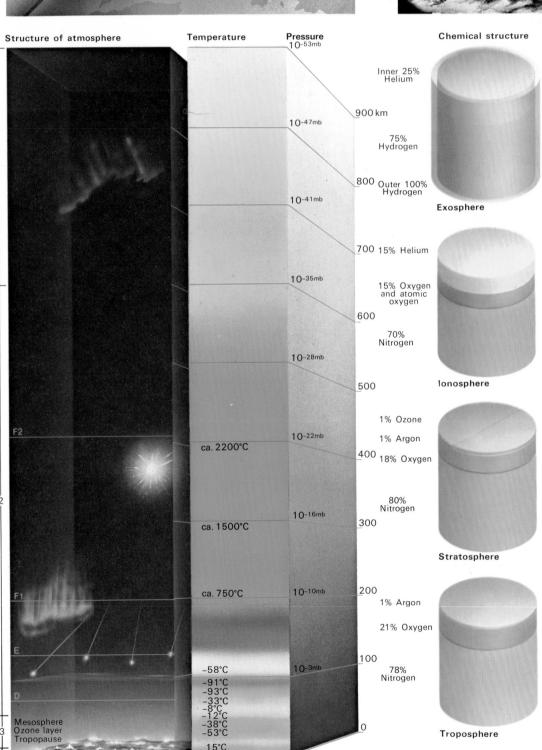

Structure of atmosphere

F2
F1
E
D
Mesosphere
Ozone layer
Tropopause

Temperature

ca. 2200°C
ca. 1500°C
ca. 750°C
-58°C
-91°C
-93°C
-33°C
-8°C
-12°C
-38°C
-53°C
15°C

Pressure

10^{-53}mb
10^{-47}mb
10^{-41}mb
10^{-35}mb
10^{-28}mb
10^{-22}mb
10^{-16}mb
10^{-10}mb
10^{-3}mb
10^{3}mb

600 km
15 km
900 km
800
700
600
500
400
300
200
100
0

Chemical structure

Inner 25% Helium
75% Hydrogen
800 Outer 100% Hydrogen
Exosphere

15% Helium
15% Oxygen and atomic oxygen
70% Nitrogen
Ionosphere

1% Ozone
1% Argon
18% Oxygen
80% Nitrogen
Stratosphere

1% Argon
21% Oxygen
78% Nitrogen
Troposphere

Pacific Ocean
Cloud patterns over the Pacific
show the paths of prevailing winds.

Circulation of the air

Circulation of the air
Owing to high temperatures in
equatorial regions the air near the
ground is heated, expands and
rises producing a low pressure
belt. It cools, causing rain, spreads
out then sinks again about latitudes
30° north and south forming high
pressure belts.

High and low pressure belts are
areas of comparative calm but
between them, blowing from high
to low pressure, are the prevailing
winds. These are deflected to the
right in the northern hemisphere
and to the left in the southern
hemisphere (Corolis effect). The
circulations appear in three distinct
belts with a seasonal movement
north and south following the
overhead sun.

Cloud types

Clouds form when damp air is
cooled, usually by rising. This
may happen in three ways: when
a wind rises to cross hills or
mountains; when a mass of air
rises over, or is pushed up by
another mass of denser air; when
local heating of the ground
causes convection currents.

Cirrus *(1)* are detached clouds
composed of microscopic ice
crystals which gleam white in the
sun resembling hair or feathers.
They are found at heights of
6 000 to 12 000 metres.

Cirrostratus *(2)* are a whitish
veil of cloud made up of ice
crystals through which the sun
can be seen often producing a
halo of bright light.

Cirrocumulus *(3)* is another
high altitude cloud formed by
turbulence between layers moving
in different directions.

Altostratus *(4)* is a grey or
bluish striated, fibrous or uniform
sheet of cloud producing light
drizzle.

Altocumulus *(5)* is a thicker
and fluffier version of cirro
cumulus, it is a white and grey
patchy sheet of cloud.

Nimbostratus *(6)* is a dark grey
layer of cloud obscuring the sun
and causing almost continuous
rain or snow.

Cumulus *(7)* are detached heaped
up, dense low clouds. The sunlit
parts are brilliant white while the
base is relatively dark and flat.

Stratus *(8)* forms dull overcast
skies associated with depressions
and occurs at low altitudes up to
1500 metres.

Cumulonimbus *(9)* are heavy
and dense clouds associated with
storms and rain. They have flat
bases and a fluffy outline
extending up to great altitudes.

High clouds

Middle clouds

Low clouds

Thousands of metres

1 Cirrus

2 Cirrostratus

3 Cirrocumulus

4 Altostratus

5 Altocumulus

6 Nimbostratus

7 Cumulus

8 Stratus

9 Cumulonimbus

Climate and Weather

All weather occurs over the earth's surface in the lowest level of the atmosphere, the troposphere. Weather has been defined as the condition of the atmosphere at any place at a specific time with respect to the various elements: temperature, sunshine, pressure, winds, clouds, fog, precipitation. Climate, on the other hand, is the average of weather elements over previous months and years.

Climate graphs *right*
Each graph typifies the kind of climatic conditions one would experience in the region to which it is related by colour to the map. The scale refers to degrees Celsius for temperature and millimetres for rainfall, shown by bars. The graphs show average observations based over long periods of time, the study of which also compares the prime factors for vegetation differences.

Development of a depression *below*
In an equilibrium front between cold and warm air masses (i) a wave disturbance develops as cold air undercuts the warm air (ii). This deflects the air flow and as the disturbance progresses a definite cyclonic circulation with warm and cold fronts is created (iii). The cold front moves more rapidly than the warm front eventually overtaking it, and occlusion occurs as the warm air is pinched out (iv).

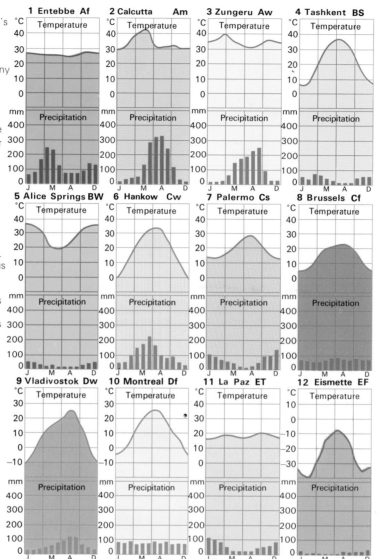

1 Entebbe Af
2 Calcutta Am
3 Zungeru Aw
4 Tashkent BS
5 Alice Springs BW
6 Hankow Cw
7 Palermo Cs
8 Brussels Cf
9 Vladivostok Dw
10 Montreal Df
11 La Paz ET
12 Eismette EF

Af Equatorial forest
Am Monsoon forest
Aw Savanna

Tropical climates

Af	Am	Aw

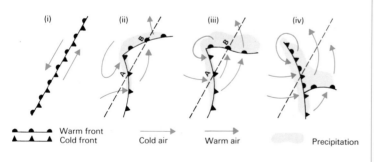

Warm front
Cold front
Cold air
Warm air
Precipitation

Frontal cloud

Precipitation

The upper diagrams show in plan view stages in the development of a depression.
The cross sections below correspond to stages (ii) to (iv).

Kinds of precipitation
Rain The condensation of water vapour on microscopic particles of dust, sulphur, soot or ice in the atmosphere forms water particles. These combine until they are heavy enough to fall as rain.

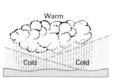

Frost Hoar, the most common type of frost, is precipitated instead of dew when water vapour changes directly into ice crystals on the surface of ground objects which have cooled below freezing point.

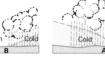

Hail Water particles, carried to a great height, freeze into ice particles which fall and become coated with fresh moisture. They are swept up again and refrozen. This may happen several times before falling as hail-stones.

Snow is the precipitation of ice in the form of flakes, or clusters, of basically hexagonal ice crystals. They are formed by the condensation of water vapour directly into ice.

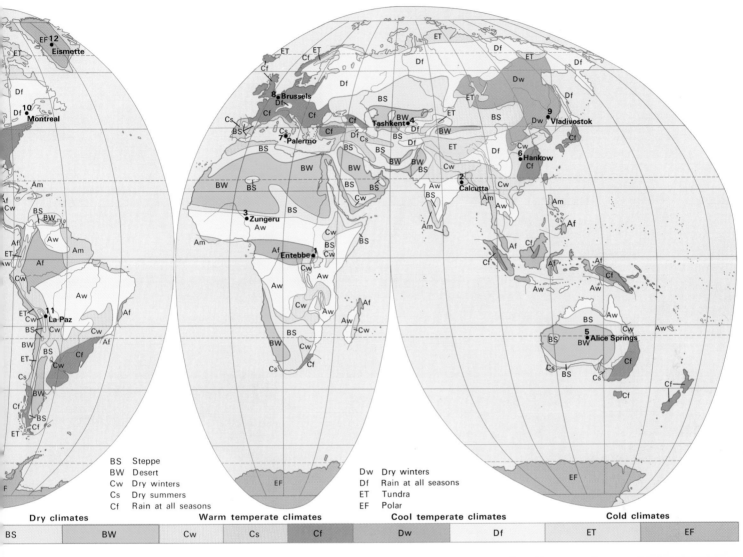

	Dry climates					Warm temperate climates		Cool temperate climates		Cold climates	

BS Steppe
BW Desert
Cw Dry winters
Cs Dry summers
Cf Rain at all seasons

Dw Dry winters
Df Rain at all seasons
ET Tundra
EF Polar

Dry climates   **Warm temperate climates**   **Cool temperate climates**   **Cold climates**

BS	BW	Cw	Cs	Cf	Dw	Df	ET	EF

Tropical storm tracks *below*

A tropical cyclone, or storm, is designated as having winds of gale force (60 kph) but less than hurricane force (120 kph). It is a homogenous air mass with upward spiralling air currents around a windless centre, or eye. An average of 65 tropical storms occur each year, over 50% of which reach hurricane force. They originate mainly during the summer over tropical oceans.

Extremes of climate & weather *right*

Tropical high temperatures and polar low temperatures combined with wind systems, altitude and unequal rainfall distribution result in the extremes of tropical rain forests, inland deserts and frozen polar wastes. Fluctuations in the limits of these extreme zones and extremes of weather result in occasional catastrophic heat-waves and drought, floods and storms, frost and snow.

Hurricane devastation

Hot desert

Tornado

Arctic dwellings

Tropical cyclone tracks
(Intense cyclones are called typhoons in the N.W. Pacific and hurricanes in the W. Atlantic)

The Earth from Space

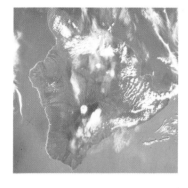

Mount Etna, Sicily *left*
Etna is at the top of the photograph, the Plain of Catania in the centre and the Mediterranean to the right. This is an infra-red photograph; vegetation shows as red, water as blue/black and urban areas as grey. The recent lava flows, as yet with no vegetation, show up as blue/black unlike the cultivated slopes which are red and red/pink.

Hawaii, Pacific Ocean *above*
This is a photograph of Hawaii, the largest of the Hawaiian Islands in the Central Pacific. North is at the top of the photograph. The snowcapped craters of the volcanoes Mauna Kea (dormant) in the north centre and Mauna Loa (active) in the south centre of the photograph can be seen. The chief town, Hilo, is on the north east coast.

River Brahmaputra, India *left*
A view looking westwards down the Brahmaputra with the Himalayas on the right and the Khasi Hills of Assam to the left.

Szechwan, China *right*
The River Tachin in the mountainous region of Szechwan, Central China. The lightish blue area in the river valley in the north east of the photograph is a village and its related cultivation.

New York, U.S.A. *left*
This infra-red photograph shows the western end of Long Island and the entrance to the Hudson River. Vegetation appears as red, water as blue/black and the metropolitan areas of New York, through the cloud cover, as grey.

The Great Barrier Reef, Australia *right*
The Great Barrier Reef and the Queensland coast from Cape Melville to Cape Flattery. The smoke from a number of forest fires can be seen in the centre of the photograph.

Eastern Himalayas, Asia
above left
A view from Apollo IX looking north-westwards over the snowcapped, sunlit mountain peaks and the head waters of the Mekong, Salween, Irrawaddy and, in the distance, with its distinctive loop, the Brahmaputra.

Atacama Desert, Chile
above right
This view looking eastwards from the Pacific over the Mejillones peninsula with the city of Antofagasta in the southern bay of that peninsula. Inland the desert and salt-pans of Atacama, and beyond, the Andes.

The Alps, Europe *right*
This vertical photograph shows the snow-covered mountains and glaciers of the Alps along the Swiss-Italian-French border. Mont Blanc and the Matterhorn are shown and, in the north, the Valley of the Rhône is seen making its sharp right-hand bend near Martigny. In the south the head waters of the Dora Baltea flow towards the Po and, in the north-west, the Lac d'Annecy can be seen.

The Evolution of the Continents

The origin of the earth is still open to much conjecture although the most widely accepted theory is that it was formed from a solar cloud consisting mainly of hydrogen. Under gravitation the cloud condensed and shrank to form our planets orbiting around the sun. Gravitation forced the lighter elements to the surface of the earth where they cooled to form a crust while the inner material remained hot and molten. Earth's first rocks formed over 3500 million years ago but since then the surface has been constantly altered.

Until comparatively recently the view that the primary units of the earth had remained essentially fixed throughout geological time was regarded as common sense, although the concept of moving continents has been traced back to references in the Bible of a break up of the land after Noah's floods. The continental drift theory was first developed by Antonio Snider in 1858 but probably the most important single advocate was Alfred Wegener who, in 1915, published evidence from geology, climatology and biology. His conclusions are very similar to those reached by current research although he was wrong about the speed of break-up.

The measurement of fossil magnetism found in rocks has probably proved the most influential evidence. While originally these drift theories were openly mocked, now they are considered standard doctrine.

The jigsaw
As knowledge of the shape and structure of the earth's surface grew, several of the early geographers noticed the great similarity in shape of the coasts bordering the Atlantic. It was this remarkable similarity which led to the first detailed geological and structural comparisons. Even more accurate fits can be made by placing the edges of the continental shelves in juxtaposition.

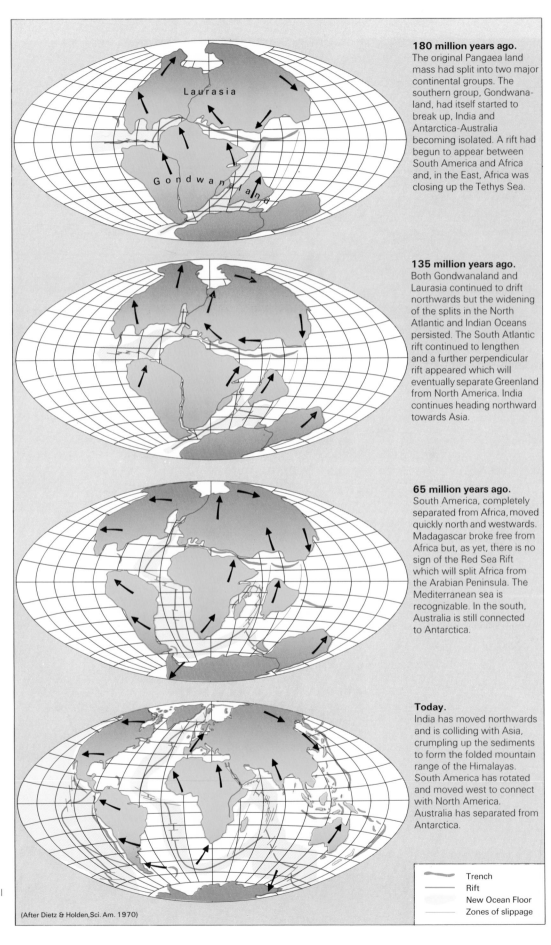

180 million years ago.
The original Pangaea land mass had split into two major continental groups. The southern group, Gondwanaland, had itself started to break up, India and Antarctica-Australia becoming isolated. A rift had begun to appear between South America and Africa and, in the East, Africa was closing up the Tethys Sea.

135 million years ago.
Both Gondwanaland and Laurasia continued to drift northwards but the widening of the splits in the North Atlantic and Indian Oceans persisted. The South Atlantic rift continued to lengthen and a further perpendicular rift appeared which will eventually separate Greenland from North America. India continues heading northward towards Asia.

65 million years ago.
South America, completely separated from Africa, moved quickly north and westwards. Madagascar broke free from Africa but, as yet, there is no sign of the Red Sea Rift which will split Africa from the Arabian Peninsula. The Mediterranean sea is recognizable. In the south, Australia is still connected to Antarctica.

Today.
India has moved northwards and is colliding with Asia, crumpling up the sediments to form the folded mountain range of the Himalayas. South America has rotated and moved west to connect with North America. Australia has separated from Antarctica.

(After Dietz & Holden, Sci. Am. 1970)

～～	Trench
—	Rift
	New Ocean Floor
	Zones of slippage

Plate tectonics

The original debate about continental drift was only a prelude to a more radical idea; plate tectonics. The basic theory is that the earth's crust is made up of a series of rigid plates which float on a soft layer of the mantle and are moved about by convection currents in the earth's interior. These plates converge and diverge along margins marked by earthquakes, volcanoes and other seismic activity. Plates diverge from mid-ocean ridges where molten lava pushes upwards and forces the plates apart at a rate of up to 30mm. a year. Converging plates form either a trench, where the oceanic plate sinks below the lighter continental rock, or mountain ranges where two continents collide. This explains the paradox that while there have always been oceans none of the present oceans contain sediments more than 150 million years old.

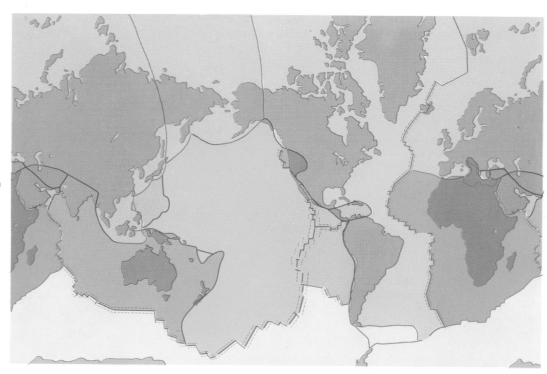

Trench boundary

The present explanation for the comparative youth of the ocean floors is that where an ocean and a continent meet the ocean plate dips under the less dense continental plate at an angle of approximately 45°. All previous crust is then ingested by downward convection currents. In the Japanese trench this occurs at a rate of about 120mm. a year.

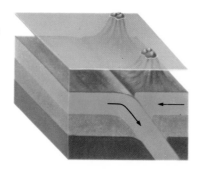

Transform fault

The recent identification of the transform, or transverse, fault proved to be one of the crucial preliminaries to the investigation of plate tectonics. They occur when two plates slip alongside each other without parting or approaching to any great extent. They complete the outline of the plates delineated by the ridges and trenches and demonstrate large scale movements of parts of the earth's surface

Ridge boundary

Ocean rises or crests are basically made up from basaltic lavas for although no gap can exist between plates, one plate can ease itself away from another. In that case hot, molten rock instantly rises from below to fill in the incipient rift and forms a ridge. These ridges trace a line almost exactly through the centre of the major oceans.

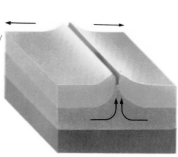

Destruction of ocean plates.

As the ocean plate sinks below the continental plate some of the sediment on its surface is scraped off and piled up on the landward side. This sediment is later incorporated in a folded mountain range which usually appears on the edge of the continent, such as the Andes. Similarly if two continents collide the sediments are squeezed up into new mountains.

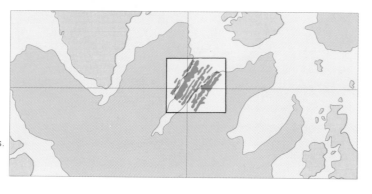

Sea floor spreading

Reversals in the earth's magnetic field have occured throughout history. As new rock emerges at the ocean ridges it cools and is magnetised in the direction of the prevailing magnetic field. By mapping the magnetic patterns either side of the ridge a symmetrical stripey pattern of alternating fields can be observed (see inset area in diagram). As the dates of the last few reversals are known the rate of spreading can be calculated.

The Unstable Earth

The earth's surface is slowly but continually being rearranged. Some changes such as erosion and deposition are extremely slow but they upset the balance which causes other more abrupt changes often originating deep within the earth's interior. The constant movements vary in intensity, often with stresses building up to a climax such as a particularly violent volcanic eruption or earthquake.

The crust *(below and right)*
The outer layer or crust of the earth consists of a comparatively low density, brittle material varying from 5 km to 50 km deep beneath the continents. This consists predominately of silica and aluminium; hence it is called 'sial'. Extending under the ocean floors and below the sial is a basaltic layer known as 'sima', consisting mainly of silica and magnesium.

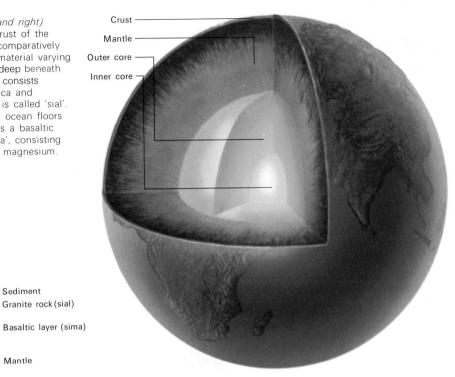

Crust
Mantle
Outer core
Inner core

Continental crust   Ocean crust

Sediment
Granite rock (sial)
Basaltic layer (sima)
Mantle

Volcanoes *(right, below and far right)*
Volcanoes occur when hot liquefied rock beneath the crust reaches the surface as lava. An accumulation of ash and cinders around a vent forms a cone. Successive layers of thin lava flows form an acid lava volcano while thick lava flows form a basic lava volcano. A caldera forms when a particularly violent eruption blows off the top of an already existing cone.

The mantle *(above)*
Immediately below the crust, at the mohorovicic discontinuity line, there is a distinct change in density and chemical properties. This is the mantle - made up of iron and magnesium silicates - with temperatures reaching 1 600 °C. The rigid upper mantle extends down to a depth of about 1 000 km below which is the more viscous lower mantle which is about 1 900 km thick.

The core *(above)*
The outer core, approximately 2 100 km thick, consists of molten iron and nickel at 2 000 °C to 5 000 °C possibly separated from the less dense mantle by an oxidised shell. About 5 000 km below the surface is the liquid transition zone, below which is the solid inner core, a sphere of 2 740 km diameter where rock is three times as dense as in the crust.

Shield volcano   **Cinder cone**   **Hornit cone**   **Caldera**

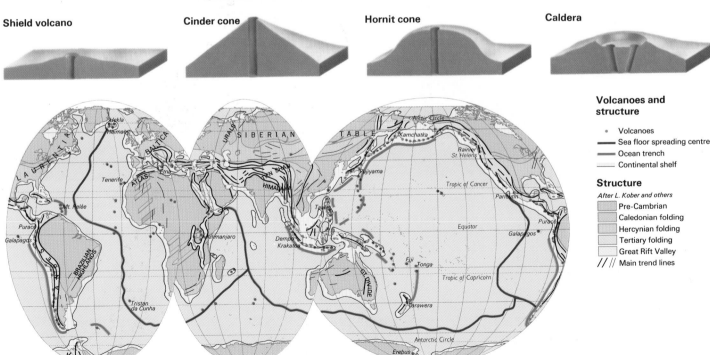

Volcanoes and structure

- Volcanoes
- Sea floor spreading centre
- Ocean trench
- Continental shelf

Structure
After L. Kober and others
- Pre-Cambrian
- Caledonian folding
- Hercynian folding
- Tertiary folding
- Great Rift Valley
- // /// Main trend lines

Major earthquakes in the last 100 years and numbers killed

Year	Location	Killed	Year	Location	Killed	Year	Location	Killed	Year	Location	Killed
1896	Japan (tsunami)	22 000	1923	Japan, Tokyo	143 000	1939/40	Turkey, Erzincan	30 000	1966	U.S.S.R., Tashkent	destroyed
1906	San Francisco	destroyed	1930	Italy, Naples	2 100	1948	Japan, Fukui	5 100	1970	N. Peru	66 800
1906	Chile, Valparaiso	22 000	1931	New Zealand, Napier	destroyed	1956	N. Afghanistan	2 000	1972	Nicaragua, Managua	7 000
1908	Italy, Messina	77 000	1931	Nicaragua, Managua	destroyed	1957	W. Iran	10 000	1974	N. Pakistan	10 000
1920	China, Kansu	180 000	1932	China, Kansu	70 000	1960	Morocco, Agadir	12 000	1976	China, Tangshan	650 000
			1935	India, Quetta	60 000	1962	N.W. Iran	10 000	1978	Iran, Tabas	11 000
			1939	Chile, Chillan	20 000	1963	Yugoslavia, Skopje	1 000	1980	Algeria, El Asnam	20 000

World distribution of earthquakes

Major earthquake zones

Areas experiencing frequent earthquakes

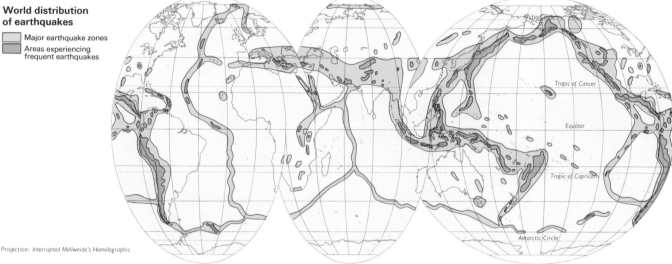

Projection: *Interrupted Mollweide's Homolographic*

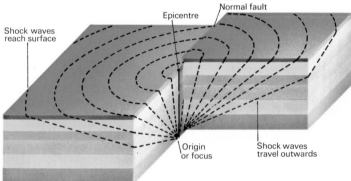

Earthquakes (right and above)

Earthquakes are a series of rapid vibrations originating from the slipping or faulting of parts of the earth's crust when stresses within build up to breaking point. They usually happen at depths varying from 8 km to 30 km. Severe earthquakes cause extensive damage when they take place in populated areas destroying structures and severing communications. Most loss of life occurs due to secondary causes i.e. falling masonry, fires or tsunami waves.

Alaskan earthquake, 1964

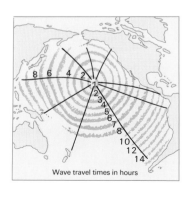

Wave travel times in hours

Tsunami waves (left)

A sudden slump in the ocean bed during an earthquake forms a trough in the water surface subsequently followed by a crest and smaller waves. A more marked change of level in the sea bed can form a crest, the start of a Tsunami which travels up to 600 km/h with waves up to 60 m high. Seismographic detectors continuously record earthquake shocks and warn of the Tsunami which may follow it.

Seismic Waves (right)

The shock waves sent out from the focus of an earthquake are of three main kinds each with distinct properties. Primary (P) waves are compressional waves which can be transmitted through both solids and liquids and therefore pass through the earth's liquid core. Secondary (S) waves are shear waves and can only pass through solids. They cannot pass through the core and are reflected at the core-mantle boundary taking a concave course back to the surface. The core also refracts the P waves causing them to alter course, and the net effect of this reflection and refraction is the production of a shadow zone at a certain distance from the epicentre, free from P and S waves. Due to their different properties P waves travel about 1,7 times faster than S waves. The third main kind of wave is a long (L) wave, a slow wave which travels along the earth's surface, its motion being either horizontal or vertical.

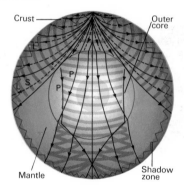

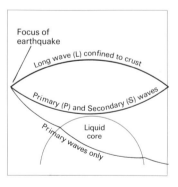

Focus of earthquake

Long wave (L) confined to crust

Primary (P) and Secondary (S) waves

Primary waves only

Liquid core

Horizontal

D M P

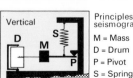

Vertical

D M S P

Principles of seismographs (left)

M = Mass
D = Drum
P = Pivot
S = Spring

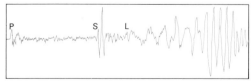

P   S   L

Seismographs are delicate instruments capable of detecting and recording vibrations due to earthquakes thousands of kilometres away. P waves cause the first tremors. S the second, and L the main shock.

The Making of Landscape

The making of landscape

The major forces which shape our land would seem to act very slowly in comparison with man's average life span but in geological terms the erosion of rock is in fact very fast. Land goes through a cycle of transformation. It is broken up by earthquakes and other earth movements, temperature changes, water, wind and ice. Rock debris is then transported by water, wind and glaciers and deposited on lowlands and on the sea floor. Here it builds up and by the pressure of its own weight is converted into new rock strata. These in turn can be uplifted either gently as plains or plateaux or more irregularly to form mountains. In either case the new higher land is eroded and the cycle recommences.

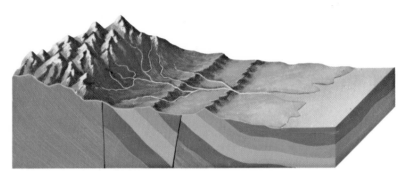

A Peneplain

Uplifted peneplain

Rivers

Rivers shape the land by three basic processes: erosion, transportation and deposition. A youthful river flows fast eroding downwards quickly to form a narrow valley (1) As it matures it deposits some debris and erodes laterally to widen the valley (2). In its last stage it meanders across a wide flat flood plain depositing fine particles of alluvium (3).

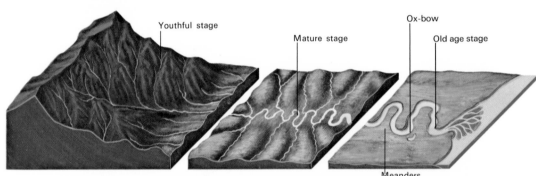

Youthful stage

Mature stage

Ox-bow

Old age stage

Meanders

Underground water

Water enters porous and permeable rocks from the surface moving downward until it reaches a layer of impermeable rock. Joints in underground rock, such as limestone, are eroded to form underground caves and caverns. When the roof of a cave collapses a gorge is formed. Surface entrances to joints are often widened to form vertical openings called swallow holes.

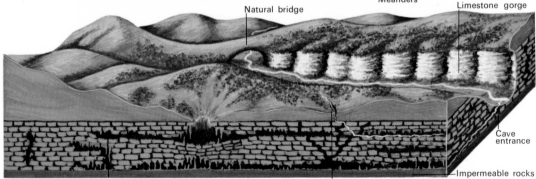

Natural bridge

Limestone gorge

Cave entrance

Impermeable rocks

Cave with stalactites and stalagmites

River disappears down swallow hole

Wind

Wind action is particularly powerful in arid and semi-arid regions where rock waste produced by weathering is used as an abrasive tool by the wind. The rate of erosion varies with the characteristics of the rock which can cause weird shapes and effects (right). Desert sand can also be accumulated by the wind to form barchan dunes (far right) which slowly travel forward, horns first.

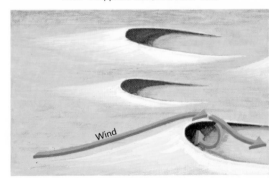

Wind

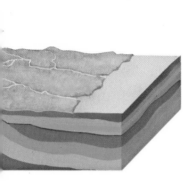

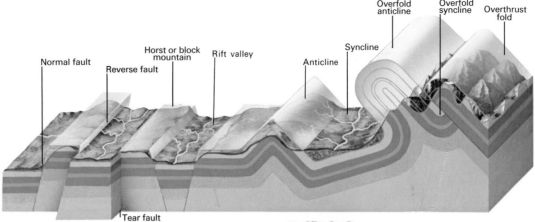

Normal fault   Reverse fault   Horst or block mountain   Rift valley   Anticline   Syncline   Overfold anticline   Overfold syncline   Overthrust fold   Tear fault

Folding and faulting

A vertical displacement in the earth's crust is called a fault or reverse fault; lateral displacement is a tear fault. An uplifted block is called a horst, the reverse of which is a rift valley. Compressed horizontal layers of sedimentary rock fold to form mountains. Those layers which bend up form an anticline, those bending down form a syncline : continued pressure forms an overfold.

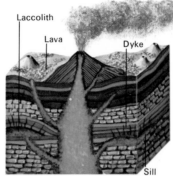

Laccolith   Lava   Dyke   Sill

Volcanic activity

When pressure on rocks below the earth's crust is released the normally semi-solid hot rock becomes liquid magma. The magma forces its way into cracks of the crust and may either reach the surface where it forms volcanoes or it may collect in the crust as sills dykes or lacoliths. When magma reaches the surface it cools to form lava.

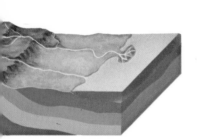

Waves

Coasts are continually changing, some retreat under wave erosion while others advance with wave deposition. These actions combined form steep cliffs and wave cut platforms. Eroded debris is in turn deposited as a terrace. As the water becomes shallower the erosive power of the waves decreases and gradually the cliff disappears. Wave action can also create other features (far right).

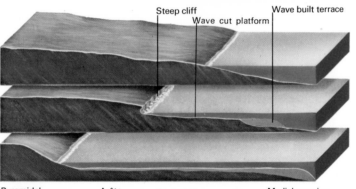

Steep cliff   Wave cut platform   Wave built terrace

Ice

These diagrams (right) show how a glaciated valley may have formed. The glacier deepens, straightens and widens the river valley whose interlocking spurs become truncated or cut off. Intervalley divides are frost shattered to form sharp aretes and pyramidal peaks. Hanging valleys mark the entry of tributary rivers and eroded rocks form medial moraine. Terminal moraine is deposited as the glacier retreats.

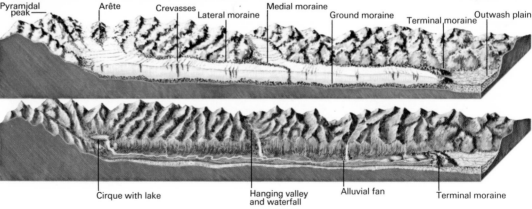

Pyramidal peak   Arête   Crevasses   Lateral moraine   Medial moraine   Ground moraine   Terminal moraine   Outwash plain

Cirque with lake   Hanging valley and waterfall   Alluvial fan   Terminal moraine

Subsidence and uplift

As the land surface is eroded it may eventually become a level plain - a peneplain, broken only by low hills, remnants of previous mountains. In turn this peneplain may be uplifted to form a plateau with steep edges. At the coast the uplifted wave platform becomes a coastal plain and in the rejuvenated rivers downward erosion once more predominates.

Rock debris forms sedimentary rock

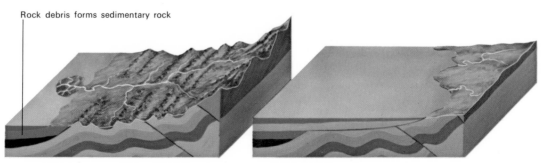

The Earth: Physical Dimensions

Its surface

Highest point on the earth's surface: Mt. Everest, Tibet - Nepal boundary   8 848 m

Lowest point on the earth's surface: The Dead Sea, Jordan   below sea level 395 m

Greatest ocean depth.: Challenger Deep, Mariana Trench   11 022 m

Average height of land   840 m

Average depth of seas and oceans   3 808 m

Dimensions

Superficial area	510 000 000 km^2
Land surface	149 000 000 km^2
Land surface as % of total area	29·2 %
Water surface	361 000 000 km^2
Water surface as % of total area	70·8 %
Equatorial circumference	40 077 km
Meridional circumference	40 009 km
Equatorial diameter	12 756·8 km
Polar diameter	12 713·8 km
Equatorial radius	6 378·4 km
Polar radius	6 356·9 km
Volume of the Earth	1 083 230 x 10^6 km^3
Mass of the Earth	5·9 x 10^{21} tonnes

The Figure of Earth

An imaginary sea-level surface is considered and called a geoid. By measuring at different places the angles from plumb lines to a fixed star there have been many determinations of the shape of parts of the geoid which is found to be an oblate spheriod with its axis along the axis of rotation of the earth. Observations from satellites have now given a new method of more accurate determinations of the figure of the earth and its local irregularities.

Land and Sea Hemispheres.

About 85% of the total land area is contained in the hemisphere centred on a point between Paris and Brussels.

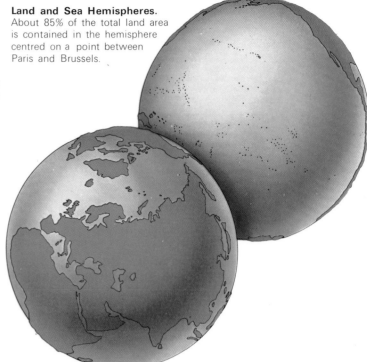

Oceans and Seas
Area in 1000 km²

Pacific Ocean	165 721	North Sea	575
Atlantic Ocean	81 660	Black Sea	448
Indian Ocean	73 442	Red Sea	440
Arctic Ocean	14 351	Baltic Sea	422
Mediterranean Sea	2 966	Persian Gulf	238
Bering Sea	2 274	St. Lawrence, Gulf of	236
Caribbean Sea	1 942	English Channel & Irish Sea	179
Mexico, Gulf of	1 813	California, Gulf of	161
Okhotsk, Sea of	1 528		
East China Sea	1 248		
Hudson Bay	1 230		
Japan, Sea of	1 049		

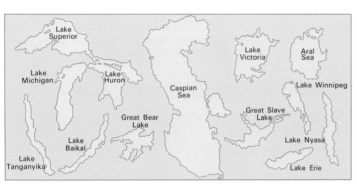

Lakes and Inland Seas
Areas in 1000 km²

Caspian Sea, Asia	424·2	Lake Ontario, N.America	19·5
Lake Superior, N.America	82·4	Lake Ladoga, Europe	18·4
Lake Victoria, Africa	69·5	Lake Balkhash, Asia	17·3
Aral Sea (Salt), Asia	63·8	Lake Maracaibo, S.America	16·3
Lake Huron, N.America	59·6	Lake Onega, Europe	9·8
Lake Michigan, N.America	58·0	Lake Eyre (Salt), Australia	9·6
Lake Tanganyika, Africa	32·9	Lake Turkana (Salt), Africa	9·1
Lake Baikal, Asia	31·5	Lake Titicaca, S.America	8·3
Great Bear Lake, N.America	31·1	Lake Nicaragua, C.America	8·0
Great Slave Lake, N.America	28·9	Lake Athabasca, N.America	7·9
Lake Nyasa, Africa	28·5	Reindeer Lake, N.America	6·3
Lake Erie, N.America	25·7	Issyk-Kul, Asia	6·2
Lake Winnipeg, N.America	24·3	Lake Torrens (Salt), Australia	6·1
Lake Chad, Africa	20·7	Koko Nor (Salt), Asia	6·0
		Lake Urmia, Asia	6·0
		Vänern. Europe	5·6

Longest rivers

	km.
Nile, Africa	6 690
Amazon, S.America	6 280
Mississipi - Missouri, N.America	6 270
Yangtze, Asia	4 990
Zaire, Africa	4 670
Amur, Asia	4 410
Hwang Ho (Yellow), Asia	4 350
Lena, Asia	4 260
Mekong, Asia	4 180
Niger, Africa	4 180
Mackenzie, N.America	4 040
Ob, Asia	4 000
Yenisei, Asia	3 800

0   1000   2000   3000   4000   5000   6000   7000

The Highest Mountains and the Greatest Depths.

Mount Everest defied the world's greatest mountaineers for 32 years and claimed the lives of many men. Not until 1920 was permission granted by the Dalai Lama to attempt the mountain, and the first successful ascent came in 1953. Since then the summit has been reached several times. The world's highest peaks have now been climbed but there are many as yet unexplored peaks in the Himalayas some of which may be over 7 600 m.

The greatest trenches are the Puerto Rico deep (9 200m.). The Tonga (10 822 m) and Mindanao (10 497 m) trenches and the Mariana Trench (11 022 m) in the Pacific. The trenches represent less than 2% of the total area of the sea-bed but are of great interest as lines of structural weakness in the Earth's crust and as areas of frequent earthquakes.

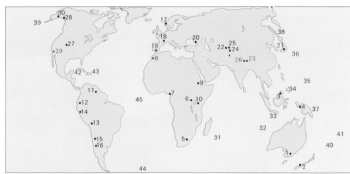

High mountains

Bathyscaphe

Waterfall

Dam

Mountain heights in metres

E. India & Oceania — Africa — South America — Europe and Asia — North America

1 Kosciusko 2 230 / 2 Mt. Cook (N.Z.) 3 764 / 3 Kinabalu 4 101 / 4 Jaya (Irian) 5 029 / 5 Mt. aux Sources 3 299 / 6 Ruwenzori 5 109 / 7 Cameroon peak 4 070 / 8 Dj. Toubkal 4 165 / 9 Ras Dashen 4 620 / 10 Kilimanjaro 5 895 / 11 Roraima 2 810 / 12 Chimborazo 6 267 / 13 Illimani 6 462 / 14 Huascaran 6 768 / 15 Ojos del Salado 6 863 / 16 Aconcagua 6 960 / 17 Galdhøpiggen 2 469 / 18 Mont Blanc 4 807 / 19 Mulhacen 3 478 / 20 Elbrus 5 633 / 21 Fujiyama 3 776 / 22 Communism peak 7 495 / 23 Everest 8 848 / 24 K2 8 611 / 25 Muztagh 7 723 / 26 Everest 8 848 / 27 Mt. Elbert 4 399 / 28 Mt. Logan 6 050 / 29 Mt. Whitney 4 418 / 30 Mt. McKinley 6 194

Ocean depths in metres

Indian Ocean — Pacific Ocean — Atlantic Ocean

31 Mauritius basin 6 400 / 32 W. Australian basin 6 459 / 33 Java trench 7 450 / 34 Mindanao trench 10 497 / 35 Mariana trench 11 022 / 36 Japan trench 10 554 / 37 Bougainville deep 9 140 / 38 Kuril trench 10 542 / 39 Aleutian trench 7 822 / 40 Kermadec trench 10 047 / 41 Tonga trench 10 822 / 42 Cayman trough 7 680 / 43 Puerto Rico trough 9 200 / 44 S. Sandwich trench 8 428 / 45 Romanche deep 7 758

Notable Waterfalls
heights in metres

Angel, Venezuela	980
Tugela, S. Africa	853
Mongefossen, Norway	774
Yosemite, California	738
Mardalsfossen, Norway	655
Cuquenan, Venezuela	610
Sutherland, N.Z.	579
Reichenbach, Switzerland	548
Wollomombi, Australia	518
Ribbon, California	491
Gavarnie, France	422
Tyssefallene, Norway	414
Krimml, Austria	370
King George VI, Guyana	366
Silver Strand, California	356
Geissbach, Switzerland	350
Staubbach, Switzerland	299
Trümmelbach, Switzerland	290
Chirombo, Zambia	268
Livingstone, Zaïre	259
King Edward VIII, Guyana	256
Gersoppa, India	253
Vettifossen Norway	250
Kalambo, Zambia	240
Kaieteur, Guyana	226
Maletsunyane, Lesotho	192
Terui, Italy	180
Kabarega, Uganda	122
Victoria, Zimbabwe-Zambia	107
Cauvery, India	97
Boyoma, Zaïre	61
Niagara, N.America	51
Schaffhausen, Switzerland	30

Notable Dams
heights in metres

Africa

Cabora Bassa, Zambezi R.	168
Akosombo Main Dam Volta R.	141
Kariba, Zambezi R.	128
Aswan High Dam, Nile R.	110

Asia

Nurek, Vakhsh R., U.S.S.R.	317
Bhakra, Sutlej R., India	226
Kurobegawa, Kurobe R., Jap.	186
Charvak, Chirchik R., U.S.S.R.	168
Okutadami, Tadami R., Jap.	157
Bratsk, Angara R., U.S.S.R.	125

Oceania

Warragamba, N.S.W., Australia	137
Eucumbene, N.S.W., Australia	116

Europe

Grande Dixence, Switz.	284
Vajont, Vajont, R., Italy	261
Mauvoisin, Drance R., Switz.	237
Contra , Verzasca R., Switz.	230
Luzzone, Brenno R., Switz.	208
Tignes, Isère R., France	180
Amir Kabir, Karadj R., U.S.S.R.	180
Vidraru, Arges R., Rom.	165
Kremasta, Acheloos R., Greece	165

North America

Mica, Columbia R., Can.	242
Oroville, Feather R.,	235
Hoover, Colorado R.,	221
Glen Canyon, Colorado R.,	216
Daniel Johnson, Can.	214
New Bullards Bar, N. Yuba R.	194
Mossyrock, Cowlitz R.,	184
Shasta, Sacramento R.,	183
W.A.C. Bennett, Canada.	183
Don Pedro, Tuolumne R.,	178
Grand Coulee, Columbia R.,	168

Central and South America

Guri, Caroni R., Venezuela.	106

Distances

Kms (distances below the diagonal are in kilometres; distances above the diagonal are in miles)

Kms	Berlin	Bombay	Buenos Aires	Cairo	Calcutta	Caracas	Chicago	Copenhagen	Darwin	Hong Kong	Honolulu	Johannesburg	Lagos	Lisbon
Berlin		3907	7400	1795	4370	5241	4402	222	8044	5440	7310	5511	3230	1436
Bombay	6288		9275	2706	1034	9024	8048	3990	4510	2683	8024	4334	4730	4982
Buenos Aires	11909	14925		7341	10268	3167	5599	7498	9130	11481	7558	5025	4919	5964
Cairo	2890	4355	11814		3541	6340	6127	1992	7216	5064	8838	3894	2432	2358
Calcutta	7033	1664	16524	5699		9609	7978	4395	3758	1653	7048	5256	5727	5639
Caracas	8435	14522	5096	10203	15464		2502	5215	11221	10166	6009	6847	4810	4044
Chicago	7084	12953	9011	3206	12839	4027		4250	9361	7783	4247	8689	5973	3992
Copenhagen	357	6422	12067	9860	7072	8392	6840		8017	5388	7088	5732	3436	1540
Darwin	12946	7257	14693	11612	6047	18059	15065	12903		2654	5369	6611	8837	9391
Hong Kong	8754	4317	18478	8150	2659	16360	12526	8671	4271		5543	6669	7360	6853
Honolulu	11764	12914	12164	14223	11343	9670	6836	11407	8640	8921		11934	10133	7821
Johannesburg	8870	6974	8088	6267	8459	11019	13984	9225	10639	10732	19206		2799	5089
Lagos	5198	7612	7916	3915	9216	7741	9612	5530	14222	11845	16308	4505		2360
Lisbon	2311	8018	9600	3794	9075	6501	6424	2478	15114	11028	12587	8191	3799	
London	928	7190	11131	3508	7961	7507	6356	952	13848	9623	11632	9071	5017	1588
Los Angeles	9311	14000	9852	12200	13120	5812	2804	9003	12695	11639	4117	16676	12414	9122
Mexico City	9732	15656	7389	12372	15280	3586	2726	9514	14631	14122	6085	14585	11071	8676
Moscow	1610	5031	13477	2902	5534	9938	8000	1561	11350	7144	11323	9161	6254	3906
Nairobi	6370	4532	10402	3536	6179	11544	12883	6706	10415	8776	17282	2927	3807	6461
New York	6385	12541	8526	9020	12747	3430	1145	6188	16047	12950	7980	12841	8477	5422
Paris	876	7010	11051	3210	7858	7625	6650	1026	13812	9630	11968	8732	4714	1454
Peking	7822	4757	19268	7544	3269	14399	10603	7202	6011	1963	8160	11710	11457	9668
Reykjavik	2385	8335	11437	5266	8687	6915	4757	2103	13892	9681	9787	10938	6718	2948
Rio de Janeiro	10025	13409	1953	9896	15073	4546	8547	10211	16011	17704	13342	7113	6035	7734
Rome	1180	6175	11151	2133	7219	8363	7739	1531	13265	9284	12916	7743	4039	1861
Singapore	9944	3914	15879	8267	2897	18359	15078	9969	3349	2599	10816	8660	11145	11886
Sydney	16096	10160	11800	14418	9138	15343	14875	16042	3150	7374	8168	11040	15519	18178
Tokyo	8924	6742	18362	9571	5141	14164	10137	8696	5431	2874	6202	13547	13480	11149
Toronto	6497	12488	9093	9233	12561	3873	700	6265	15498	12569	7465	13374	8948	5737
Wellington	18140	12370	9981	16524	11354	13122	13451	17961	5325	9427	7513	11761	16050	19575

Mexico City	Moscow	Nairobi	New York	Paris	Peking	Reykjavik	Rio de Janeiro	Rome	Singapore	Sydney	Tokyo	Toronto	Wellington	
6047	1000	3958	3967	545	4860	1482	6230	734	6179	10002	5545	4037	11272	**Berlin**
9728	3126	2816	7793	4356	2956	5179	8332	3837	2432	6313	4189	7760	7686	**Bombay**
4591	8374	6463	5298	6867	11972	7106	1214	6929	9867	7332	11410	5650	6202	**Buenos Aires**
7687	1803	2197	5605	1994	4688	3272	6149	1325	5137	8959	5947	5737	10268	**Cairo**
9494	3438	3839	7921	4883	2031	5398	9366	4486	1800	5678	3195	7805	7055	**Calcutta**
2228	6175	7173	2131	4738	8947	4297	2825	5196	11407	9534	8801	2406	8154	**Caracas**
1694	4971	8005	711	4132	6588	2956	5311	4809	9369	9243	6299	435	8358	**Chicago**
5912	970	4167	3845	638	4475	1306	6345	951	6195	9968	5403	3892	11160	**Copenhagen**
9091	7053	6472	9971	8582	3735	8632	9948	8243	2081	1957	3375	9630	3309	**Darwin**
8775	4439	5453	8047	5984	1220	6015	11001	5769	1615	4582	1786	7810	5857	**Hong Kong**
3781	7036	10739	4958	7437	5070	6081	8290	8026	6721	5075	3854	4638	4669	**Honolulu**
9063	5692	1818	7979	5426	7276	6797	4420	4811	5381	6860	8418	8310	7308	**Johannesburg**
6879	3886	2366	5268	2929	7119	4175	3750	2510	6925	9643	8376	5560	9973	**Lagos**
5391	2427	4015	3369	903	6007	1832	4805	1157	7385	11295	6928	3565	12163	**Lisbon**
5552	1552	4237	3463	212	5057	1172	5778	889	6743	10558	5942	3545	11691	**London**
1549	6070	9659	2446	5645	6251	4310	6310	6331	8776	7502	5475	2170	6719	**Los Angeles**
	6664	9207	2090	5717	7742	4635	4780	6365	10321	8058	7024	2018	6897	**Mexico City**
		3942	4666	1545	3600	2053	7184	1477	5237	9008	4651	4637	10283	**Moscow**
			7358	4029	5727	5395	5548	3350	4635	7552	6996	7570	8490	**Nairobi**
				3626	6828	2613	4832	4280	9531	9935	6741	356	8951	**New York**
					5106	1384	5708	687	6671	10539	6038	3738	11798	**Paris**
10724						4897	10773	5049	2783	5561	1304	6557	6700	**Peking**
14818	6344						6135	2048	7155	10325	5469	2600	10725	**Reykjavik**
3364	7510	11842						5725	9763	8389	11551	5180	7367	**Rio de Janeiro**
9200	2486	6485	5836						6229	10143	6127	4399	11523	**Rome**
12460	5794	9216	10988	8217						3915	3306	9350	5298	**Singapore**
7460	3304	8683	4206	2228	7882						4861	9800	1383	**Sydney**
7693	11562	8928	7777	9187	17338	9874						6410	5762	**Tokyo**
10243	2376	5391	6888	1105	8126	3297	9214						8820	**Toronto**
16610	8428	7460	15339	10737	4478	11514	15712	10025						**Wellington**
12969	14497	12153	15989	16962	8949	16617	13501	16324	6300					Miles
11304	7485	11260	10849	9718	2099	8802	18589	9861	5321	7823				
3247	7462	12183	574	6015	10552	4184	8336	7080	15047	15772	10316			
11100	16549	13664	14405	18987	10782	17260	11855	18545	8526	2226	9273	14194		

Water Resources and Vegetation

Water resources and vegetation

Fresh water is essential for life on earth and in some parts of the world it is a most precious commodity. On the other hand it is very easy for industrialised temperate states to take its existence for granted, and man's increasing demand may only be met finally by the desalination of earth's 1250 million cubic kilometres of salt water. 70% of the earth's fresh water exists as ice.

The hydrological cycle

Water is continually being absorbed into the atmosphere as vapour from oceans, lakes, rivers and vegetation transpiration. On cooling the vapour either condenses or freezes and falls as rain, hail or snow. Most precipitation falls over the sea but one quarter falls over the land of which half evaporates again soon after falling while the rest flows back into the oceans.

Distribution of water

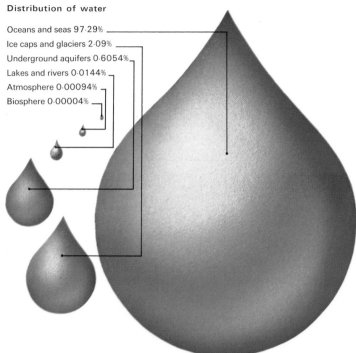

Oceans and seas 97·29%
Ice caps and glaciers 2·09%
Underground aquifers 0·6054%
Lakes and rivers 0·0144%
Atmosphere 0·00094%
Biosphere 0·00004%

Tundra

Mediterranean scrub

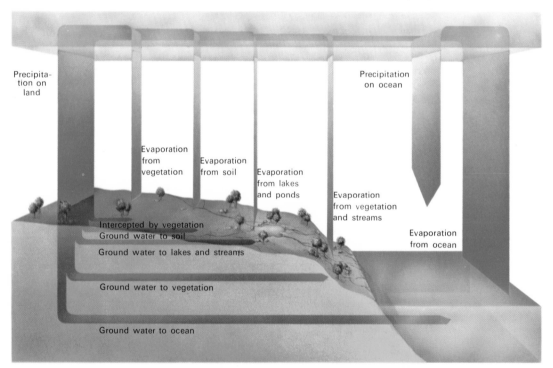

Precipitation on land

Precipitation on ocean

Evaporation from vegetation

Evaporation from soil

Evaporation from lakes and ponds

Evaporation from vegetation and streams

Evaporation from ocean

Intercepted by vegetation
Ground water to soil
Ground water to lakes and streams
Ground water to vegetation
Ground water to ocean

Domestic consumption of water

An area's level of industrialisation, climate and standard of living are all major influences in the consumption of water. On average Europe consumes 636 litres per head each day of which 180 litres is used domestically. In the U.S.A. domestic consumption is slightly higher at 270 litres per day. The graph (right) represents domestic consumption in the U.K.

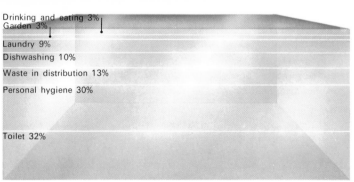

Drinking and eating 3%
Garden 3%
Laundry 9%
Dishwashing 10%
Waste in distribution 13%
Personal hygiene 30%
Toilet 32%

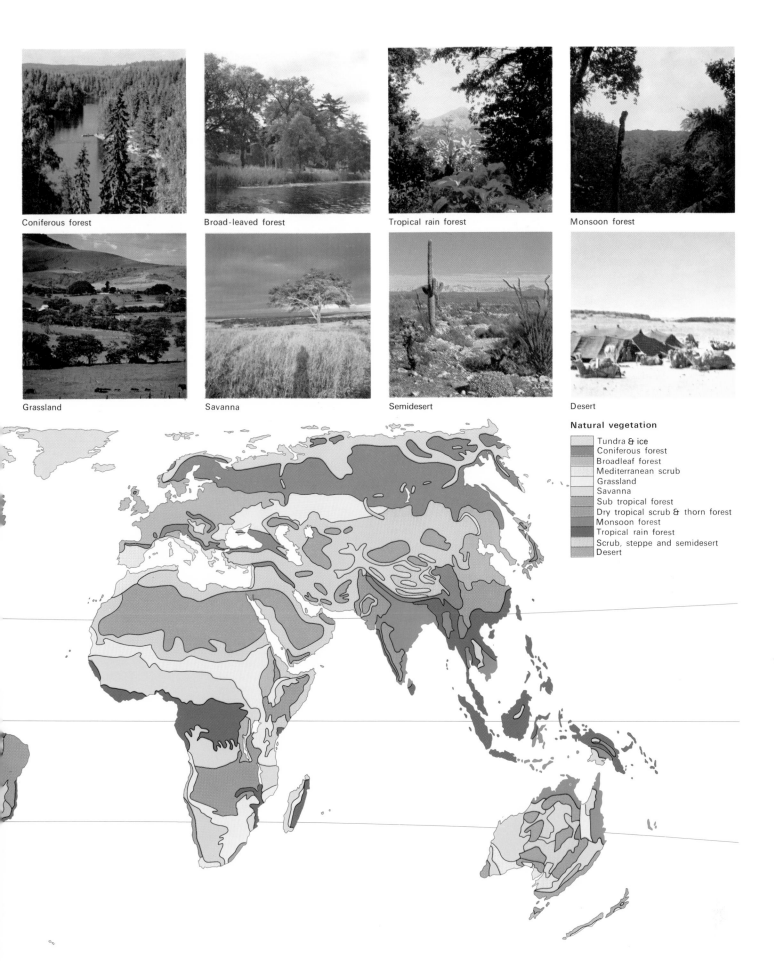

Coniferous forest

Broad-leaved forest

Tropical rain forest

Monsoon forest

Grassland

Savanna

Semidesert

Desert

Natural vegetation

Tundra & ice
Coniferous forest
Broadleaf forest
Mediterranean scrub
Grassland
Savanna
Sub tropical forest
Dry tropical scrub & thorn forest
Monsoon forest
Tropical rain forest
Scrub, steppe and semidesert
Desert

Population

Population distribution
(right and lower right)
People have always been unevenly distributed in the world. Europe has for centuries contained nearly 20% of the world's population but after the 16-19th century explorations and consequent migrations this proportion has rapidly reduced. In 1750 the Americas had 2% of the world's total: in 2000 AD they are expected to contain 16%.

The most densely populated regions are in India, China and Europe where the average density is between 100 and 200 per square km. although there are pockets of extremely high density elsewhere. In contrast Australia has only 1·5 people per square km. The countries in the lower map have been redrawn to make their areas proportional to their populations.

U.S.A.
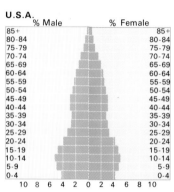

France
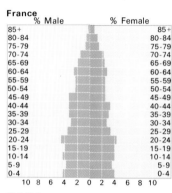

Brazil

U.S.S.R.
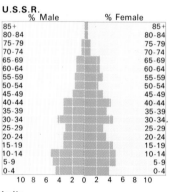

Ghana
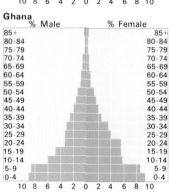

India
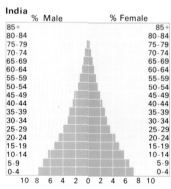

Age distribution
France shows many demographic features characteristic of European countries. Birth and death rates have declined with a moderate population growth - there are nearly as many old as young. In contrast, India and several other countries have few old and many young because of the high death rates and even higher birth rates. It is this excess that is responsible for the world's population explosion.

World population increase
Until comparatively recently there was little increase in the population of the world. About 6000 BC it is thought that there were about 200 million people and in the following 7000 years an increase of just over 100 million. In the 1800's there were about 1000 million; at present there are over 3500 million and by the year 2000 if present trends continue there would be at least 7000 million.

1650   1700   1750   1800

World population distribution

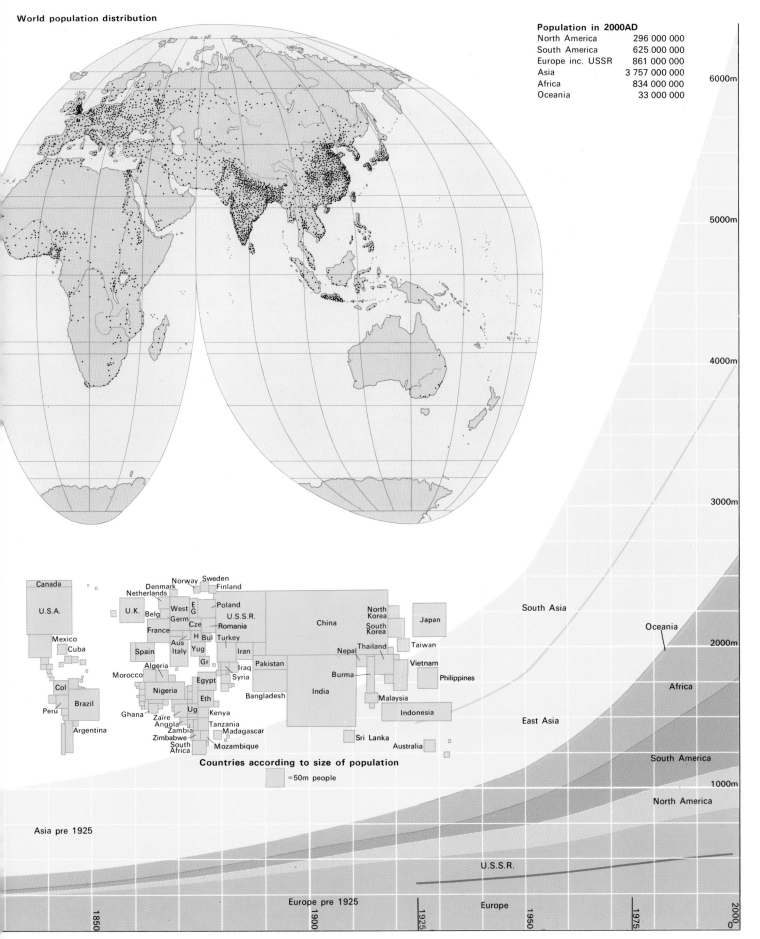

World population distribution

Population in 2000AD

North America	296 000 000
South America	625 000 000
Europe inc. USSR	861 000 000
Asia	3 757 000 000
Africa	834 000 000
Oceania	33 000 000

6000m

5000m

4000m

3000m

Canada

U.S.A.

Norway Sweden
Denmark Finland
Netherlands
U.K. West E Poland
Belg Germ G
France Cze
H Bul Romania
Aus Italy Yug Turkey
Spain Gr Iran
Algeria Iraq
Morocco Egypt Syria

Mexico
Cuba

Col

Peru Brazil

Argentina

Nigeria

Ghana
Zaïre
Angola
Zambia
Zimbabwe
South
Africa

Ug Kenya
Tanzania
Madagascar
Mozambique

Eth

U.S.S.R.

China

Nepal Thailand
Pakistan

Burma

Bangladesh India

Sri Lanka

North
Korea
South
Korea

Vietnam

Malaysia

Indonesia

Australia

Japan

Taiwan

Philippines

Countries according to size of population

=50m people

South Asia

Oceania

2000m

East Asia

Africa

South America

1000m

North America

Asia pre 1925

Europe pre 1925

U.S.S.R.

Europe

1850

1900

1925

1950

1975

2000

27

Language

Languages may be blamed partly for the division and lack of understanding between nations. While a common language binds countries together it in turn isolates them from other countries and groups. Thus beliefs, ideas and inventions remain exclusive to these groups and different cultures develop.

There are thousands of different languages and dialects spoken today. This can cause strife even within the one country, such as India, where different dialects are enough to break down the country into distinct groups.

As a result of colonization and the spread of internationally accepted languages, many countries have superimposed a completely unrelated language in order to combine isolated national groups and to facilitate international understanding, for example Spanish in South America, English in India.

Assyrian (carved)

Ancient Hebrew (painted)

Egyptian hieroglyphic (painted)

Some modern non-latin type faces

Greek
ΑΒΓΔΕΖΗΘΙΚΛΜΝΞΟΠΡΣΤΥΦΧΨΩΣ

Cyrillic
АБВГДЕЖЗИЙІКЛМНОПРСТУФХЦЧШ

Arabic
فى عام ١٨٩٧ وصل إلى إنجلترا أ نموذج

Bengali
১৮৯৭ খ্রীস্টাব্দে আধুনিক মডেলের একটি

Telugu
నిన్న న్యూయింంటికి వచ్చిన యతిథ యేమియు

Japanese
国土 の 位 置 と 地 形

Chinese
父 獨 子 出 有 之 限 地 位 司,
司 在 提 印 芬 刷 奥 業 司 上 有 能

Related languages

Certain languages showing marked similarities are thought to have developed from common parent languages for example Latin. After the retreat of the Roman Empire wherever Latin had been firmly established it remained as the new nation's language. With no unifying centre divergent development took place and Latin evolved into new languages.

Calligraphy

Writing was originally by a series of pictures, and these gradually developed in styles which were influenced by the tools generally used. Carved alphabets, such as that used by the Sumerians, tended to be angular, while those painted or written tended to be curved, as in Egyptian hieroglyphics development of which can be followed through the West Semitic, Greek and Latin alphabets to our own.

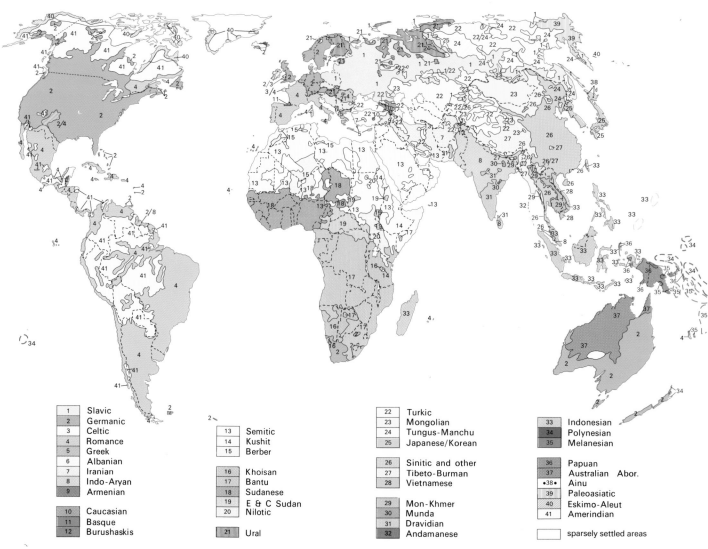

1	Slavic
2	Germanic
3	Celtic
4	Romance
5	Greek
6	Albanian
7	Iranian
8	Indo-Aryan
9	Armenian
10	Caucasian
11	Basque
12	Burushaskis

13	Semitic
14	Kushit
15	Berber
16	Khoisan
17	Bantu
18	Sudanese
19	E & C Sudan
20	Nilotic
21	Ural

22	Turkic
23	Mongolian
24	Tungus-Manchu
25	Japanese/Korean
26	Sinitic and other
27	Tibeto-Burman
28	Vietnamese
29	Mon-Khmer
30	Munda
31	Dravidian
32	Andamanese

33	Indonesian
34	Polynesian
35	Melanesian
36	Papuan
37	Australian Abor.
•38•	Ainu
39	Paleoasiatic
40	Eskimo-Aleut
41	Amerindian
	sparsely settled areas

Religion

Throughout history man has had beliefs in supernatural powers based on the forces of nature which have developed into worship of a god and some cases gods.

Hinduism honours many gods and goddesses which are all manifestations of the one divine spirit, Brahma, and incorporates beliefs such as reincarnation, worship of cattle and the caste system.

Buddhism, an offshoot of Hinduism, was founded in north east India by Gautama Buddha (563-483 BC) who taught that spiritual and moral discipline were essential to achieve supreme peace.

Confucianism is a mixture of Buddhism and Confucius' teachings which were elaborated to provide a moral basis for the political structure of Imperial China and to cover the already existing forms of ancestor worship.

Judaism dates back to c. 13th century B.C. The Jews were expelled from the Holy Land in AD70 and only reinstated in Palestine in 1948.

Islam, founded in Mecca by Muhammad (570-632 AD) spread across Asia and Africa and in its retreat left isolated pockets of adherent communities.

Christianity was founded by Jesus of Nazareth in the 1st century AD The Papal authority, established in the 4th century, was rejected by Eastern churches in the 11th century. Later several other divisions developed eg. Roman Catholicism, Protestantism.

Christian monastery

Jewish holy place

Hindu temple

Mohammedan mosque

Buddhist temple

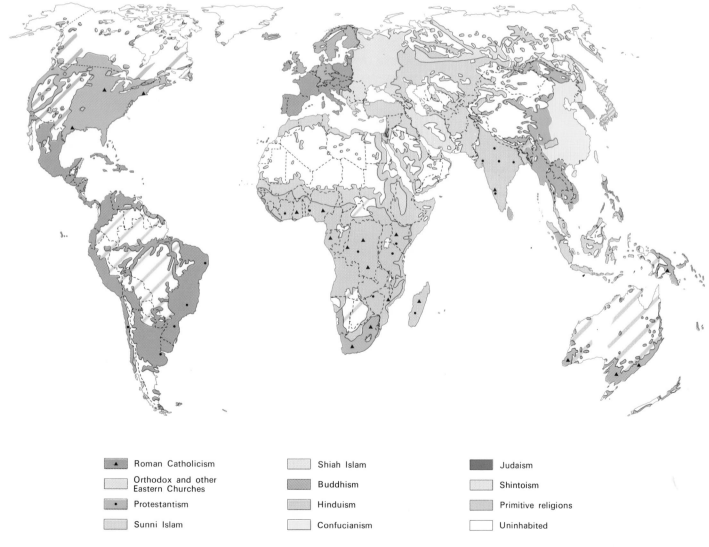

Roman Catholicism

Orthodox and other Eastern Churches

Protestantism

Sunni Islam

Shiah Islam

Buddhism

Hinduism

Confucianism

Judaism

Shintoism

Primitive religions

Uninhabited

The Growth of Cities

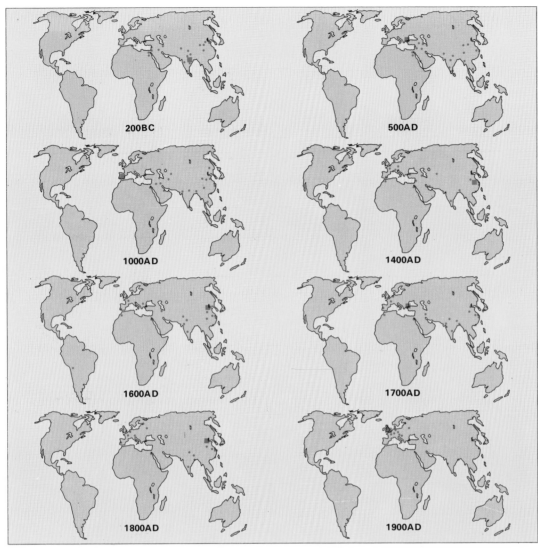

200BC

500AD

1000AD

1400AD

1600AD

1700AD

1800AD

1900AD

Sao Paulo

Increase in urbanisation
The increase in urbanisation is a result primarily of better sanitation and health resulting in the growth of population and secondarily to the movement of man off the land into industry and service occupations in the cities. Generally the most highly developed industrial nations are the most intensely urbanised although exceptions such as Norway and Switzerland show that rural industrialisation can exist.

Increase in urbanisation
The figures on the vertical columns show the urban population as a percentage of the total population for each country in the year shown.

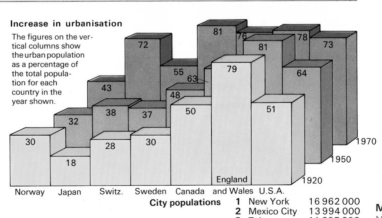

1970
1950
1920

Norway Japan Switz. Sweden Canada England U.S.A.
and Wales

Metropolitan areas
A metropolitan area can be defined as a central city linked with surrounding communities by continuous built-up areas controlled by one municipal government. With improved communications the neighbouring communities generally continue to provide the city's work-force. The graph (right) compares the total populations of the world's ten largest cities.

City populations

1	New York	16 962 000
2	Mexico City	13 994 000
3	Tokyo	11 695 000
4	Los Angeles	10 605 000
5	Shanghai	10 000 000
6	Buenos Aires	9 749 000
7	Paris	8 548 000
8	Peking	8 000 000
9	Moscow	7 909 000
10	Chicago	7 662 000

Major cities
Normally these are not only major centres of population and wealth but also of political power and trade. They are the sites of international airports and characteristically are great ports from which imported goods are distributed using the roads and railways which focus on the city. Their staple trades and industries are varied and flexible and depend on design and fashion rather than raw material production.

York

Sydney

Moscow

Tokyo

Hong Kong

Bombay

London

Cairo

Rio de Janeiro

Rome

Cities over 5 000 000 inhabitants

2 000 000-5 000 000 inhabitants

1 000 000-2 000 000 inhabitants

250 000-1 000 000 inhabitants

31

Food Resources: Vegetable

Cocoa, tea , coffee
These tropical or sub-tropical crops are grown mainly for export to the economically advanced countries. Tea and coffee are the world's principal beverages. Cocoa is used more in the manufacture of chocolate.

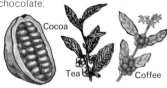
Cocoa
Tea
Coffee

Sugar beet, sugar cane
Cane Sugar - a tropical crop accounts for the bulk of the sugar entering into international trade. Beet Sugar, on the other hand, demands a temperate climate and is produced primarily for domestic consumption.

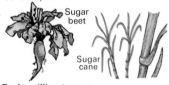
Sugar beet
Sugar cane

· Cocoa
· Tea
· Coffee

· Sugar beet
· Sugar cane

Fruit million tonnes

Italy	France	U.S.S.R.	Spain	Others	Grapes 61.7
U.S.A.	Brazil	Italy / Spain	Others		Citrus 49.9
Brazil	India	Philippines	Others		Bananas 39.3
China	Turkey	U.S.S.R.	Others		Melons 24.1
U.S.S.R.	U.S.A.	Others	Apples 31.9		

Wine

France | Italy | U.S.S.R. | Spain | Argentina | others | 1972
1975
1978
1981

0   12   24   36 million tonnes

Vegetable oilseeds and oils
Despite the increasing use of synthetic chemical products and animal and marine fats, vegetable oils extracted from these crops grow in quantity, value and importance. Food is the major use- in margarine and cooking fats.

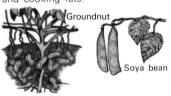
Groundnut
Soya bean

Groundnuts are also a valuable subsistence crop and the meal is used as animal feed. Soya-bean meal is a growing source of protein for humans and animals. The Mediterranean lands are the prime source of olive oil.

Rape (oil seed)
Sunflower

Cereals
Cereals include those members of the grain family with starchy edible seeds - wheat, maize, barley, oats, rye, rice, millets and sorghums.

Cereals and potatoes (not a cereal but starch-producing) are the principal source of food for our modern civilisations because of their high yield in bulk and food value per unit of land and labour required. They are also easy to store and transport, and provide food also for animals producing meat, fat, milk and eggs. Wheat is the principal bread grain of the temperate regions in which potatoes are the next most important food source. Rice is the principal cereal in the hotter. humid regions. especially in Asia. Oats, barley and maize are grown mainly for animal feed; millets and sorghums as main subsistence crops in Africa and India.

Fruit, wine
With the improvements in canning, drying and freezing, and in transport and marketing, the international trade and consumption of deciduous and soft fruits, citrus fruits and tropical fruits has greatly increased. Recent developments in the use of the peel will give added value to some of the fruit crops.

Over 80% of grapes are grown for wine and over a half in countries bordering the Mediterranean.

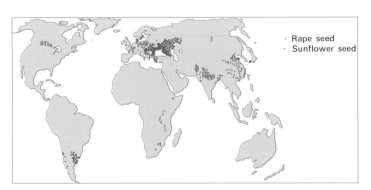
· Groundnuts
· Soya beans

· Rape seed
· Sunflower seed

Maize (or Corn)

Needs plenty of sunshine, summer rain or irrigation and frost free for 6 months. Important as animal feed and for human food in Africa, Latin America and as a vegetable and breakfast cereal.

World production 451·2 million tonnes

Barley

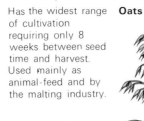

Has the widest range of cultivation requiring only 8 weeks between seed time and harvest. Used mainly as animal-feed and by the malting industry.

World production 158·7 million tonnes

Oats

Widely grown in temperate regions with the limit fixed by early autumn frosts. Mainly fed to cattle. The best quality oats are used for oatmeal, porridge and breakfast foods

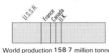

World production 43·0 million tonnes

Rice

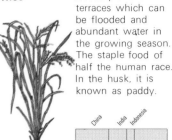

Needs plains or terraces which can be flooded and abundant water in the growing season. The staple food of half the human race. In the husk, it is known as paddy.

World production 403·2 million tonnes

Wheat

The most important grain crop in the temperate regions though it is also grown in a variety of climates e.g. in Monsoon lands as a winter crop.

World production 458·6 million tonnes

Rye

The hardiest of cereals and more resistant to cold, pests and disease than wheat. An important foodstuff in Central and E. Europe and the U.S.S.R.

World production 24·5 million tonnes

Millets

The name given to a number of related members of the grass family, of which sorghum is one of the most important. They provide nutritious grain.

World production 100·7 million tonnes

Potato

An important food crop though less nutritious weight for weight than grain crops.

World production 227·3 million tonnes

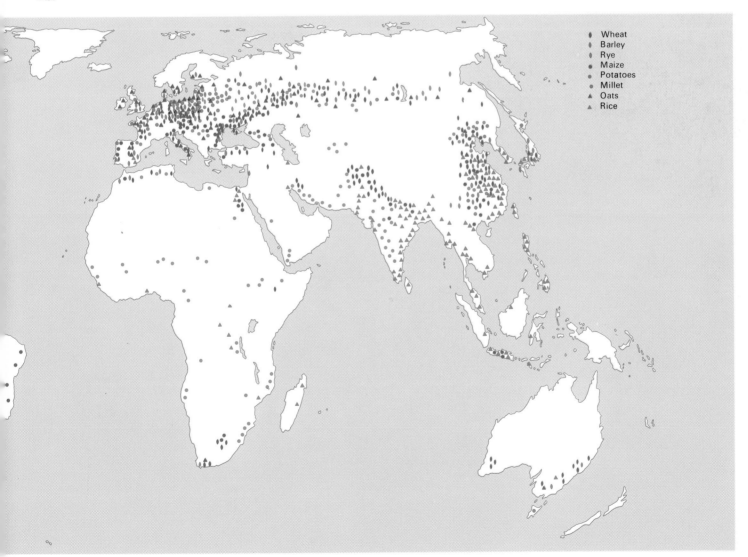

- Wheat
- Barley
- Rye
- Maize
- Potatoes
- Millet
- Oats
- Rice

Food Resources: Animal

Food resources: Animal
Meat, milk and allied foods are prime protein-providers and are also sources of essential vitamins. Meat is mainly a product of continental and savannah grasslands and the cool west coasts, particularly in Europe. Milk and cheese, eggs and fish - though found in some quantity throughout the world - are primarily a product of the temperate zones.

Beef cattle Australia, New Zealand and Argentina provide the major part of international beef exports. Western U.S.A. and Europe have considerable production of beef for their local high demand.

World production 994·0 million head

Dairy Cattle The need of herds for a rich diet and for nearby markets result in dairying being characteristic of densely-populated areas of the temperate zones-U.S.A., N.W. Europe, N.Zealand and S.E. Australia.

World production 222·1 million head

Cheese The principal producers are the U.S.A., W. Europe, U.S.S.R., and New Zealand and principal exporters Netherlands, New Zealand, Denmark and France.

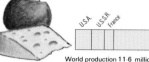
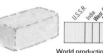
World production 11·6 million tonnes

Sheep Raised mostly for wool and meat, the skins and cheese from their milk are important products in some countries. The merino yields a fine wool and crossbreds are best for meat.

World production 1 130·8 million head

Pigs Can be reared in most climates from monsoon to cool temperate. They are abundant in China, the corn belt of the U.S.A. N.W. and C. Europe, Brazil and U.S.S.R.

World production 779·3 million head

Fish Commercial fishing requires large shoals of fish of one species within reach of markets. Freshwater fishing is also important. A rich source of protein, fish will become an increasingly valuable food source.

World production 72·4 million tonnes

Butter (includes Ghee) The biggest producers are U.S.S.R., India, France and West Germany.

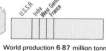
World production 6·87 million tonnes

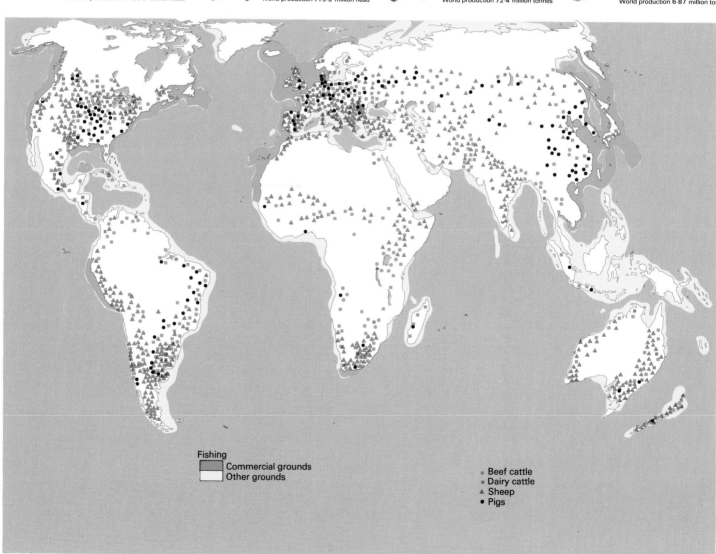

Fishing
Commercial grounds
Other grounds

■ Beef cattle
■ Dairy cattle
▲ Sheep
● Pigs

Foodstuffs fall, nutritionally, into three groups - providers of energy, protein and vitamins. Cereals and oil-seeds provide energy and second-class protein'; milk, meat and allied foods provide protein and vitamins, fruit and vegetables provide vitamins, especially Vitamin C, and some energy. To avoid malnutrition, a minimum level of these three groups of foodstuffs is required: the maps and diagrams show how unfortunately widespread are low standards of nutrition and even malnutrition.

Comparison of daily diets

Far East, Near East, Africa & Latin America

Europe, Oceania & North America

Malnutrition

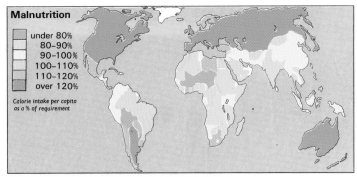

- under 80%
- 80–90%
- 90–100%
- 100–110%
- 110–120%
- over 120%

Calorie intake per capita as a % of requirement

Proportions of calories

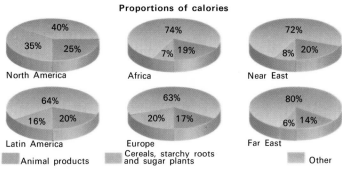

North America — 40% / 35% / 25%

Africa — 74% / 7% / 19%

Near East — 72% / 8% / 20%

Latin America — 64% / 16% / 20%

Europe — 63% / 20% / 17%

Far East — 80% / 6% / 14%

- Animal products
- Cereals, starchy roots and sugar plants
- Other

People and tractors engaged in agriculture

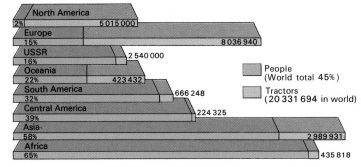

- North America — 2% — 5 015 000
- Europe — 15% — 8 036 940
- USSR — 16% — 2 540 000
- Oceania — 22% — 423 432
- South America — 32% — 666 248
- Central America — 39% — 224 325
- Asia — 58% — 2 989 931
- Africa — 65% — 435 818

- People (World total 45%)
- Tractors (20 331 694 in world)

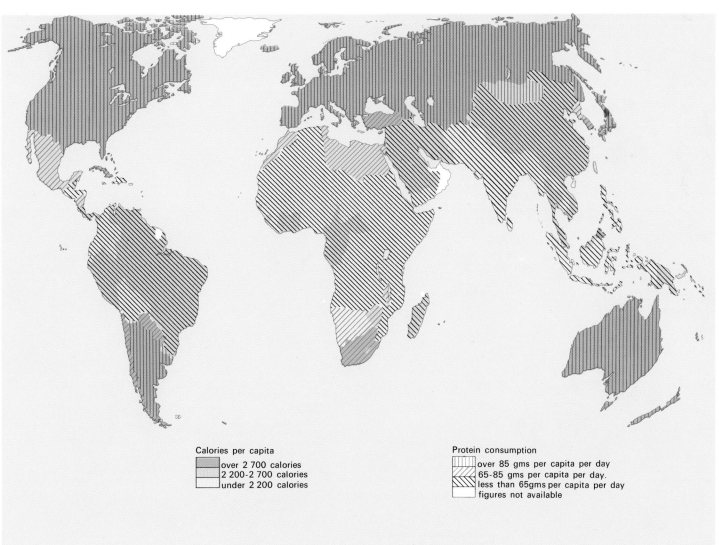

Calories per capita
- over 2 700 calories
- 2 200-2 700 calories
- under 2 200 calories

Protein consumption
- over 85 gms per capita per day
- 65-85 gms per capita per day.
- less than 65gms per capita per day
- figures not available

Mineral Resources I

Primitive man used iron for tools and vessels and its use extended gradually until iron, and later steel, became the backbone of the Modern World with the Industrial Revolution in the late 18th Century. At first, local ores were used, whereas today richer iron ores in huge deposits have been discovered and are mined on a large scale, often far away from the areas where they are used; for example, in Western Australia, Northern Sweden, Venezuela and Liberia. Iron smelting plants are today increasingly located at coastal sites, where the large ore carriers can easily discharge their cargo.

Steel is refined iron with the addition of other minerals, ferro-alloys, giving to the steel their own special properties; for example, resistance to corrosion (chromium, nickel, cobalt), hardness (tungsten, vanadium), elasticity (molybdenum), magnetic properties (cobalt), high tensile strength (manganese) and high ductility (molybdenum).

Production of Ferro-alloy metals

Molybdenum 103 118 tonnes
Chromium 4·5 million tonnes
Nickel 748 000 tonnes
Cobalt 30 800 tonnes
Tungsten 62 000 tonnes
Manganese 8·75 million tonnes
Vanadium 28 700 tonnes

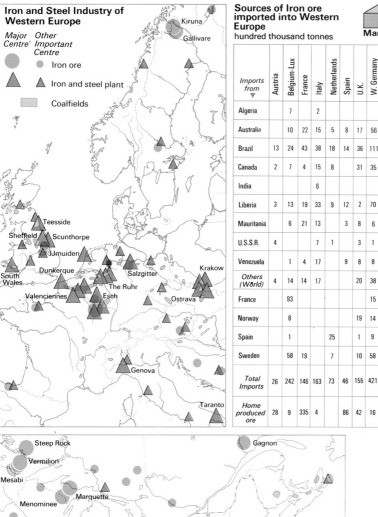

Iron and Steel Industry of Western Europe

Major Centre / Other Important Centre
- Iron ore
- Iron and steel plant
- Coalfields

Sources of Iron ore imported into Western Europe
hundred thousand tonnes

Imports from	Austria	Belgium-Lux	France	Italy	Netherlands	Spain	U.K.	W. Germany
Algeria		7		2				
Australia		10	22	15	5	8	17	56
Brazil	13	24	43	38	18	14	36	111
Canada	2	7	4	15	8		31	35
India				6				
Liberia	3	13	19	33	9	12	2	70
Mauritania		6	21	13		3	8	6
U.S.S.R.	4		7	1			3	1
Venezuela		1	4	17		9	8	8
Others (World)	4	14	14	17			20	38
France		93						15
Norway		8					19	14
Spain		1			25		1	9
Sweden		58	19		7		10	58
Total Imports	26	242	146	163	73	46	155	421
Home produced ore	28	9	335	4		86	42	16

Iron and Steel Industry of Eastern North America

Major Centre / Other Important Centre
- Iron ore
- Iron and steel plant
- Coalfields

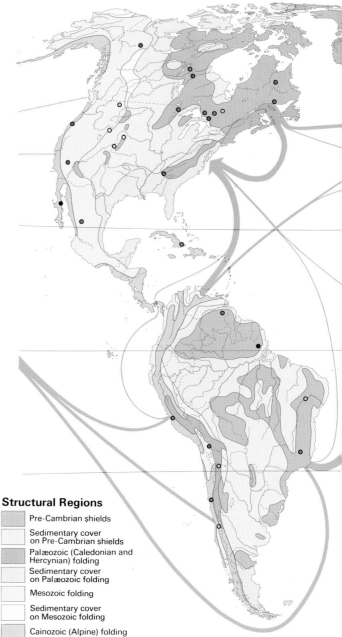

Structural Regions

- Pre-Cambrian shields
- Sedimentary cover on Pre-Cambrian shields
- Palæozoic (Caledonian and Hercynian) folding
- Sedimentary cover on Palæozoic folding
- Mesozoic folding
- Sedimentary cover on Mesozoic folding
- Cainozoic (Alpine) folding
- Sedimentary cover on Cainozoic folding

World production of Pig iron and Ferro-alloys

Total World production 531 million tonnes

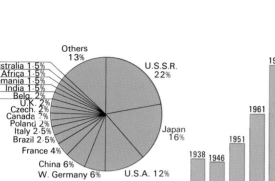

Others 13%
U.S.S.R. 22%
Japan 16%
U.S.A. 12%
W. Germany 6%
China 6%
France 4%
Brazil 2·5%
Italy 2·5%
Poland 2%
Canada 2%
Czech. 2%
U.K. 2%
Belg. 2%
India 1·5%
Romania 1·5%
S. Africa 1·5%
Australia 1·5%

Growth of World production of Pig iron and Ferro-alloys

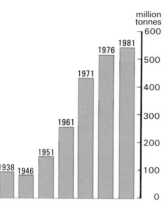

million tonnes
600
500
400
300
200
100
0

1938 1946 1951 1961 1971 1976 1981

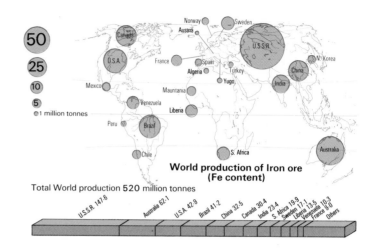

50
25
10
5
1 million tonnes

World production of Iron ore (Fe content)

Total World production 520 million tonnes

U.S.S.R. 147·6 Australia 62·1 U.S.A. 42·9 Brazil 41·2 China 32·5 Canada 30·4 India 23·4 S. Africa 19·9 Sweden 17·1 Liberia 13·5 Venezuela 10·3 France 9·0 Others

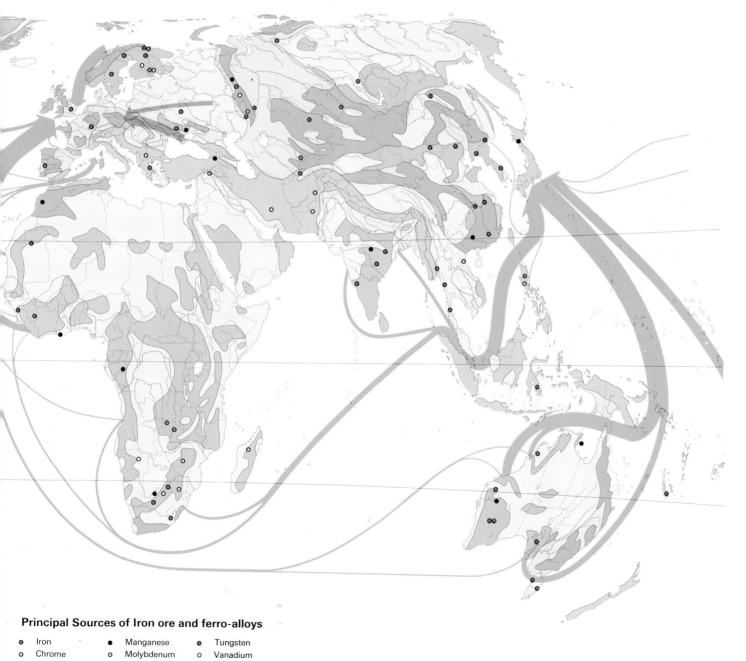

Principal Sources of Iron ore and ferro-alloys

- ● Iron
- ○ Chrome
- ◉ Cobalt
- ● Manganese
- ○ Molybdenum
- ◉ Nickel
- ● Tungsten
- ○ Vanadium
- ▬ Iron ore trade flow

Mineral Resources II

Antimony – imparts hardness when alloyed to other metals, especially lead.
Uses: type metal, pigments to paints, glass and enamels, fireproofing of textiles

World production 64 635 tonnes

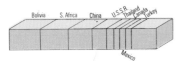

Lead – heavy, soft, malleable, acid resistant.
Uses: storage batteries, sheeting and piping, cable covering, ammunition, type metal, weights, additive to petrol.

World production 3·61 million tonnes

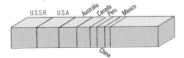

Tin – resistant to attacks by organic acids, malleable.
Uses: canning, foils, as an alloy to other metals (brass and bronze).

World production 235 200 tonnes

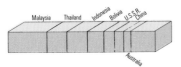

Aluminium – light, resists corrosion, good conductor.
Uses: aircraft, road and rail vehicles, domestic utensils, cables, makes highly tensile and light alloys.

World production 92·6 million tonnes (of Bauxite)

Gold – untarnishable and resistant to corrosion, highly ductile and malleable, good conductor. The pure metal is soft and it is alloyed to give it hardness.
Uses: bullion, coins, jewellery, gold-leaf, electronics.

World production 1 200 tonnes

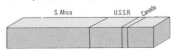

Copper – excellent conductor of electricity and heat, durable, resistant to corrosion, strong and ductile.
Uses: wire, tubing, brass (with zinc and tin), bronze (with tin), (compounds) – dyeing.

World production 7·8 million tonnes

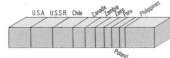

Mercury – the only liquid metal, excellent conductor of electricity
Uses: thermometers, electrical industry, gold and silver ore extraction, (compounds) – drugs, pigments, chemicals, dentistry.

World production 6 622 tonnes

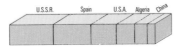

Zinc – hard metal, low corrosion factor.
Uses: brass (with copper and tin), galvanising, diecasting, medicines, paints and dyes.

World production 6·25 million tonnes

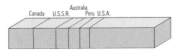

Diamonds – very hard and resistant to chemical attack, high lustre, very rare.
Uses: jewellery, cutting and abrading other materials.

World production 37·7 million carats

Silver – ductile and malleable, a soft metal and must be alloyed for use in coinage.
Uses: coins, jewellery, photography, electronics, medicines.

World production 10 422 tonnes

World consumption of non-ferrous metals

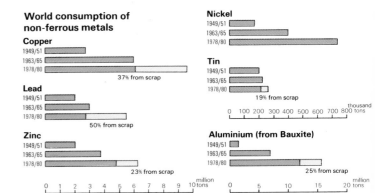

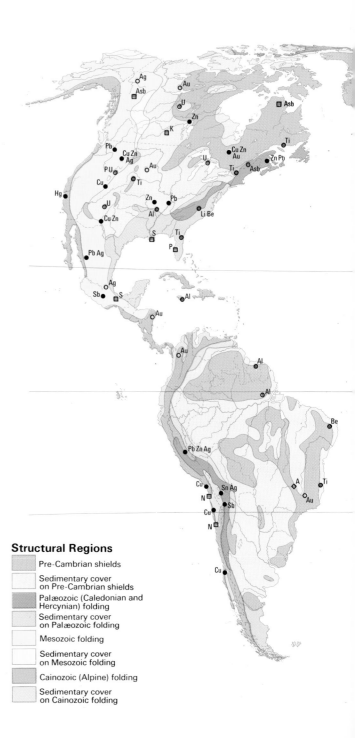

Structural Regions

- Pre-Cambrian shields
- Sedimentary cover on Pre-Cambrian shields
- Palæozoic (Caledonian and Hercynian) folding
- Sedimentary cover on Palæozoic folding
- Mesozoic folding
- Sedimentary cover on Mesozoic folding
- Cainozoic (Alpine) folding
- Sedimentary cover on Cainozoic folding

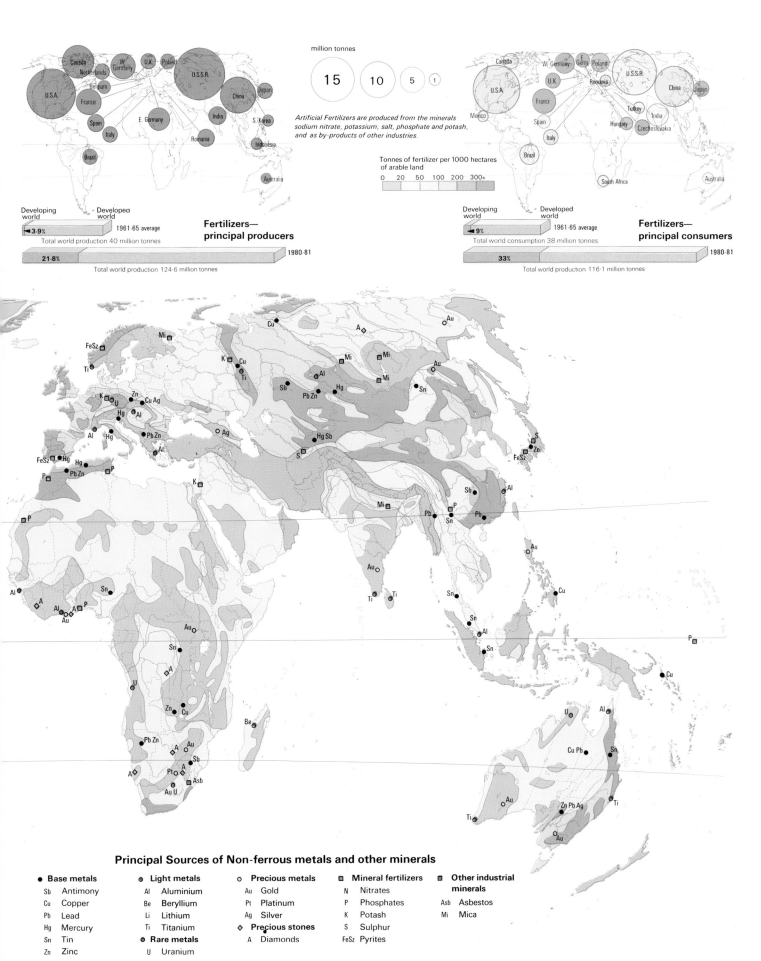

million tonnes

15 10 5 1

Artificial Fertilizers are produced from the minerals
sodium nitrate, potassium, salt, phosphate and potash,
and as by-products of other industries.

Tonnes of fertilizer per 1000 hectares
of arable land

0 20 50 100 200 300+

**Fertilizers—
principal producers**

Developing world — Developed world
◄ 3·9% 1961-65 average
Total world production 40 million tonnes

21·8% 1980-81
Total world production 124·6 million tonnes

**Fertilizers—
principal consumers**

Developing world — Developed world
◄ 9% 1961-65 average
Total world consumption 38 million tonnes

33% 1980-81
Total world production 116·1 million tonnes

Principal Sources of Non-ferrous metals and other minerals

● **Base metals**

Sb	Antimony
Cu	Copper
Pb	Lead
Hg	Mercury
Sn	Tin
Zn	Zinc

◒ **Light metals**

Al	Aluminium
Be	Beryllium
Li	Lithium
Ti	Titanium

◉ **Rare metals**

U	Uranium

○ **Precious metals**

Au	Gold
Pt	Platinum
Ag	Silver

◇ **Precious stones**

A	Diamonds

▣ **Mineral fertilizers**

N	Nitrates
P	Phosphates
K	Potash
S	Sulphur
FeSz	Pyrites

▤ **Other industrial minerals**

Asb	Asbestos
Mi	Mica

Fuel and Energy

Coal

Coal is the result of the accumulation of vegetation over millions of years. Later under pressure from overlying sediments, it is hardened through four stages: peat, lignite, bituminous coal, and finally anthracite. Once the most important source of power, coal's importance now lies in the production of electricity and as a raw material in the production of plastics, heavy chemicals and disinfectants.

20% U.S.A.
17% U.S.S.R.
13% China
7% E. Germany
6% Poland W. Germ.
3·5% U.K.
3% Czech. Australia
India S. Africa
15·5% Others

World production 3 762 million tonnes

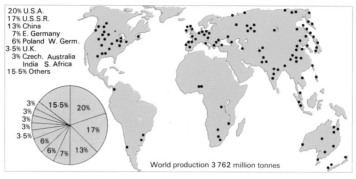

Coal mine

Oil

Oil is derived from the remains of marine animals and plants, probably as a result of pressure, heat and chemical action. It is a complex mixture of hydrocarbons which are refined to extract the various constituents. These include products such as gasolene, kerosene and heavy fuel oils. Oil is rapidly replacing coal because of easier handling and reduced pollution.

20% U.S.S.R.
16% Saudi Arabia
U.S.A.
4% Iraq Venezuela
3·5% Mexico Nigeria
3% Libya
2·5% U.K. Canada
Indonesia Iran
2% Kuwait
18% Others

World production 2 776 million tonnes

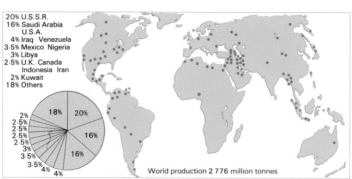

Oil derrick

Natural gas

Since the early 1960's natural gas (methane) has become one of the largest single sources of energy. By liquefaction its volume can be reduced to 1/600 of that of gas and hence is easily transported. It is often found directly above oil reserves and because it is both cheaper than coal gas and less polluting it has great potential.

37% U.S.A.
28% U.S.S.R.
5% Netherlands
Canada
2·5% U.K.
2% Romania
Indonesia Norway
1·5% Mexico
15% Others

World production 13 170 000 teracalories

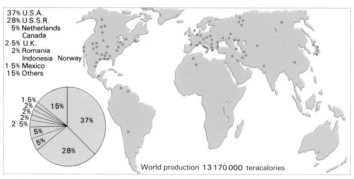

North sea gas rig

Water

Hydro-electric power stations use water to drive turbines which in turn generate electricity. The ideal site is one in which a consistently large volume of water falls a considerable height, hence sources of H.E.P. are found mainly in mountainous areas. Potential sources of hydro-electricity using waves or tides are yet to be exploited widely.

17% U.S.A.
12% U.S.S.R.
10% Canada
7% Japan
5% Brazil France
4% Norway Italy
3% Sweden Spain
Switz.
2% China
25% Others

World production 1 549 000 million kWh

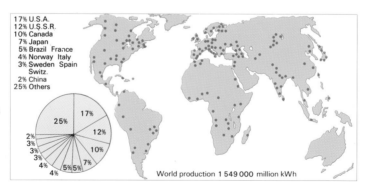

Water power

Nuclear energy

The first source of nuclear power was developed in Britain in 1956. Energy is obtained from heat generated by the reaction from splitting atoms of certain elements, of which uranium and plutonium are the most important. Although the initial installation costs are very high the actual running costs are low because of the slow consumption of fuel.

47% U.S.A.
10% Japan
7% U.S.S.R.
6% U.K. W. Germany
5% France Canada
4% Sweden
10% Others

World production 583 000 million kWh

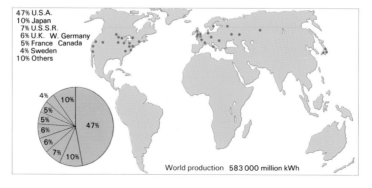

Nuclear power station

40

In a short space of time these two diagrams can change markedly; there can be a cut-back in supply owing to internal political change (Iran), or in consumption by vigorous government action (U.S.A.). The production of North Sea oil has changed the balance of oil trade in the U.K. and Norway but it is very costly to extract, relatively short-lived and is small on a world scale.

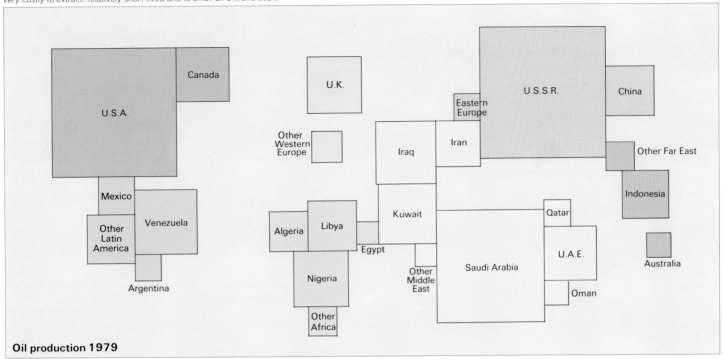

Oil production 1979

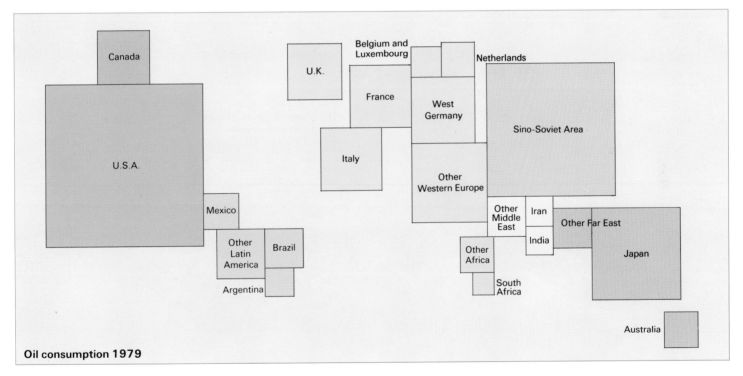

Oil consumption 1979

Oil's new super-powers *above* When countries are scaled according to their production and consumption of oil they take on new dimensions. At present, large supplies of oil are concentrated in a few countries of the Caribbean, the Middle East and North Africa, except for the vast indigenous supplies of the U.S.A. and U.S.S.R. The Middle East, with 58% of the world's reserves, produces 35% of the world's supply and yet consumes less than 3%. The U.S.A.,

despite its great production, has a deficiency of nearly 415 million tons a year, consuming 30% of the world's total. The U.S.S.R., with 11% of world reserves, produces 19% of world output and consumes 13%. Soviet production continues to grow annually although at a decreased rate since the mid-1970's. Japan, one of the largest oil importers, increased its consumption by 440% during the period 1963-73. Since then, total imports have decreased slightly.

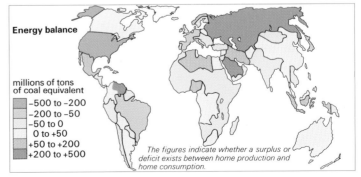

Energy balance

millions of tons of coal equivalent

-500 to -200
-200 to -50
-50 to 0
0 to +50
+50 to +200
+200 to +500

The figures indicate whether a surplus or deficit exists between home production and home consumption.

Occupations

Proportion employed in

Unclassified Agriculture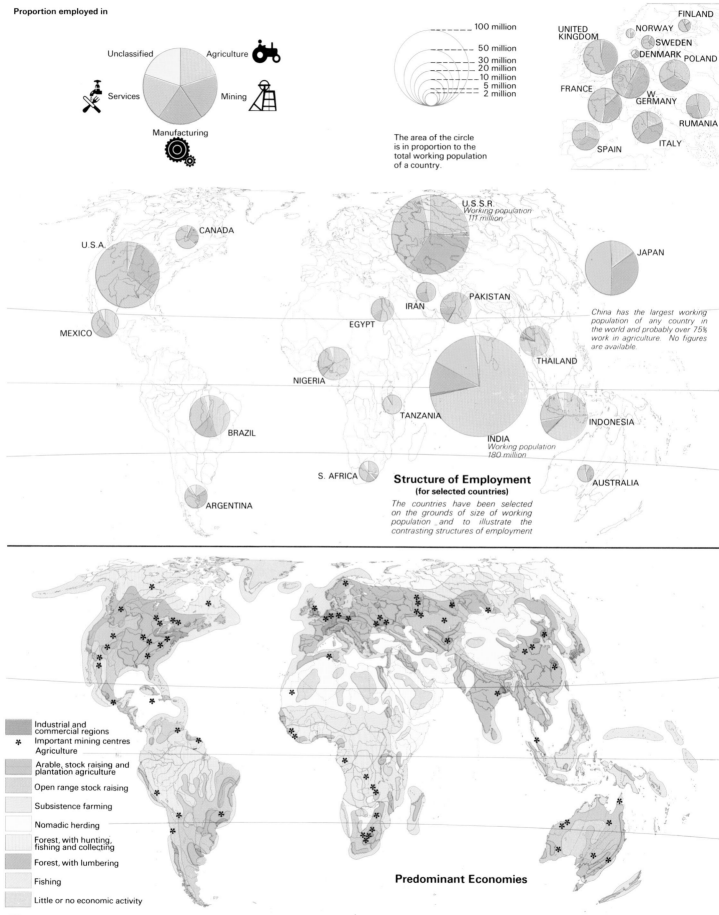

Services Mining

Manufacturing

------ 100 million
------ 50 million
------ 30 million
------ 20 million
------ 10 million
------ 5 million
------ 2 million

The area of the circle is in proportion to the total working population of a country.

FINLAND
UNITED KINGDOM NORWAY
SWEDEN
DENMARK POLAND
FRANCE W. GERMANY
RUMANIA
SPAIN ITALY

CANADA

U.S.A.

MEXICO

U.S.S.R.
Working population 111 million

JAPAN

IRAN PAKISTAN

EGYPT

China has the largest working population of any country in the world and probably over 75% work in agriculture. No figures are available.

THAILAND

NIGERIA

TANZANIA

INDONESIA

INDIA
Working population 180 million

BRAZIL

S. AFRICA

AUSTRALIA

ARGENTINA

Structure of Employment
(for selected countries)

The countries have been selected on the grounds of size of working population and to illustrate the contrasting structures of employment

Industrial and commercial regions
* Important mining centres
Agriculture
Arable, stock raising and plantation agriculture
Open range stock raising
Subsistence farming
Nomadic herding
Forest, with hunting, fishing and collecting
Forest, with lumbering
Fishing
Little or no economic activity

Predominant Economies

Industry

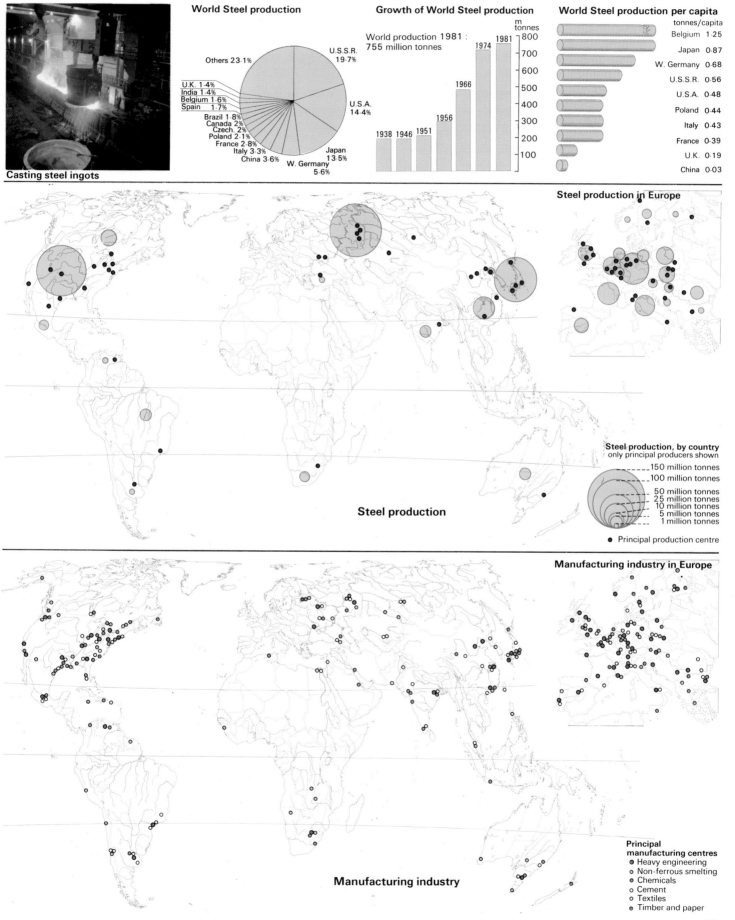

Casting steel ingots

World Steel production

- U.S.S.R. 19·7%
- U.S.A. 14·4%
- Japan 13·5%
- W. Germany 5·6%
- China 3·6%
- Italy 3·3%
- France 2·8%
- Poland 2·1%
- Czech. 2%
- Canada 2%
- Brazil 1·8%
- Spain 1·7%
- Belgium 1·6%
- India 1·4%
- U.K. 1·4%
- Others 23·1%

Growth of World Steel production

World production 1981 : 755 million tonnes

Year	m tonnes
1938	
1946	
1951	
1956	
1966	
1974	
1981	

Scale: 100–800 m tonnes

World Steel production per capita

tonnes/capita

Country	tonnes/capita
Belgium	1·25
Japan	0·87
W. Germany	0·68
U.S.S.R.	0·56
U.S.A.	0·48
Poland	0·44
Italy	0·43
France	0·39
U.K.	0·19
China	0·03

Steel production in Europe

Steel production

Steel production, by country
only principal producers shown

- 150 million tonnes
- 100 million tonnes
- 50 million tonnes
- 25 million tonnes
- 10 million tonnes
- 5 million tonnes
- 1 million tonnes

● Principal production centre

Manufacturing industry in Europe

Manufacturing industry

Principal manufacturing centres
- ● Heavy engineering
- ○ Non-ferrous smelting
- ● Chemicals
- ○ Cement
- ○ Textiles
- ● Timber and paper

43

Transport

Shipyards

Shipbuilding	tonnage launched in thousand gross registered tons
Japan 9 140	
S. Korea 1 207	
W. Germany 665	
Spain 605	
Brazil 453	
Sweden 363	
Poland 350	
U.K. 342	
Finland 311	
Denmark 306	
U.S.A. 298	
Yugoslavia 284	

• Principal shipbuilding centres

Europe

Japan

Aircraft Industry
In 1978 there were approximately 10 000 civil passenger airliners in service. This diagram shows where they were built.

U.S.A. 53%	U.S.S.R. 33%	U.K. 6% Netherlands 3% France 2%

Concorde and Boeing 747

Trade in Aircraft and Aircraft Engines

million U.S. $

	Exports			Imports	
	Aircraft	Engines		Aircraft	Engines
U.S.A.	5893	789	W. Germ.	1218	136
France	995	262	U.K.	651	543
W. Germ.	915	227	U.S.A.	604	132
U.K.	861	721	France	472	278
Canada	303		Canada	264	149
Neth.	288	836	Neth.	210	132
Italy	279	88	Japan	201	151

• Principal aircraft manufacturing centres

Motor vehicles

Production thousand units	Exports million U.S. $	Imports million U.S. $
Japan 11 184	21 601	737
U.S.A. 7 927	15 034	25 008
W. Germany 3 902	24 539	8 000
France 3 426	11 824	5 820
U.S.S.R. 2 197	1 831	1 164
Italy 1 612	5 582	4 645
Canada 1 303	9 593	11 598
U.K. 1 184	6 329	8 182
Spain 989	1 771	695

Car assembly line

Europe

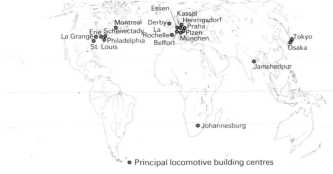
• Principal motor vehicle plants

Railway vehicles

Exports million U.S. $		Imports million U.S. $.	
Japan	496·9	Brazil	151·8
France	353·9	Mexico	95·3
W. Germany	329·3	U.S.A.	81·7
U.S.A.	306·0	S. Korea	69·6
U.K.	78·6	S. Africa	67·5
Italy	62·6	Egypt	53·0
Yugoslavia	57·5	W. Germany	52·7
Canada	48·5	Yugoslavia	52·2
S. Korea	41·7	Netherlands	48·1
Sweden	37·7	Sweden	44·4
Belg.-Lux.	27·8	U.K.	40·5
Switzerland	37·5	Belg.-Lux.	33·6
Spain	18·5	France	30·3
		Italy	30·0

Locomotive works

• Principal locomotive building centres

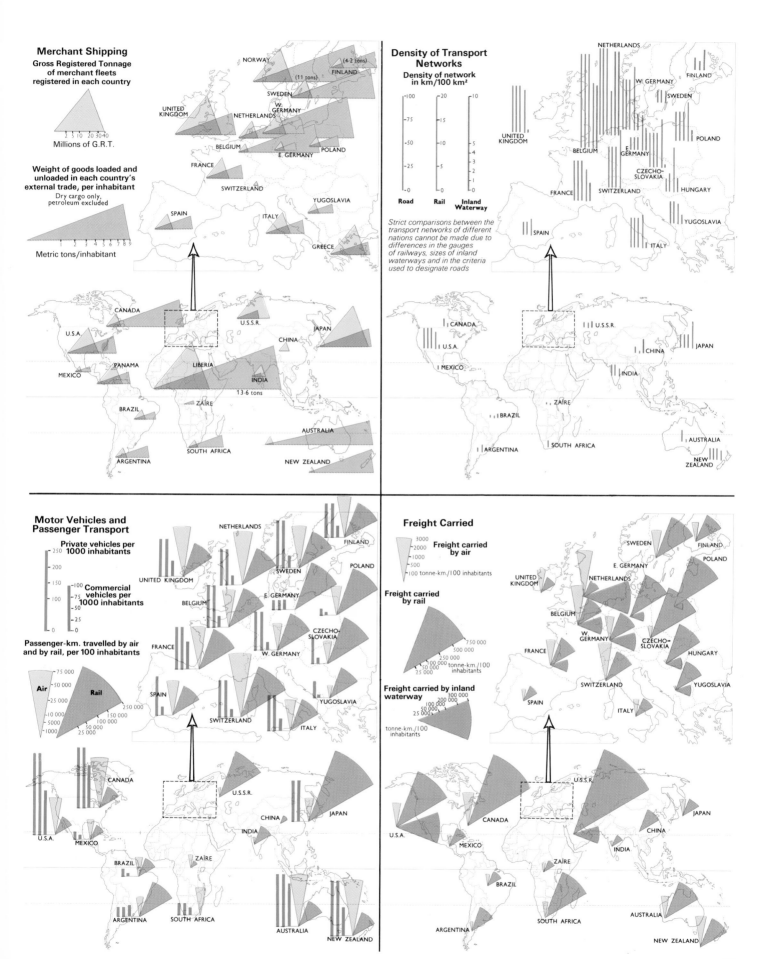

Merchant Shipping

Gross Registered Tonnage of merchant fleets registered in each country

Millions of G.R.T.

2 5 10 20 30 40

Weight of goods loaded and unloaded in each country's external trade, per inhabitant

Dry cargo only, petroleum excluded

Metric tons/inhabitant

1 2 3 4 5 6 7 8 9

Density of Transport Networks

Density of network in km/100 km²

Road   Rail   Inland Waterway

Strict comparisons between the transport networks of different nations cannot be made due to differences in the gauges of railways, sizes of inland waterways and in the criteria used to designate roads

Motor Vehicles and Passenger Transport

Private vehicles per 1000 inhabitants

Commercial vehicles per 1000 inhabitants

Passenger-km. travelled by air and by rail, per 100 inhabitants

Air   Rail

Freight Carried

Freight carried by air

3000
2000
1000
500
100 tonne-km./100 inhabitants

Freight carried by rail

750 000
500 000
250 000
100 000
50 000
25 000
tonne-km./100 inhabitants

Freight carried by inland waterway

300 000
200 000
100 000
50 000
25 000
tonne-km./100 inhabitants

45

Trade

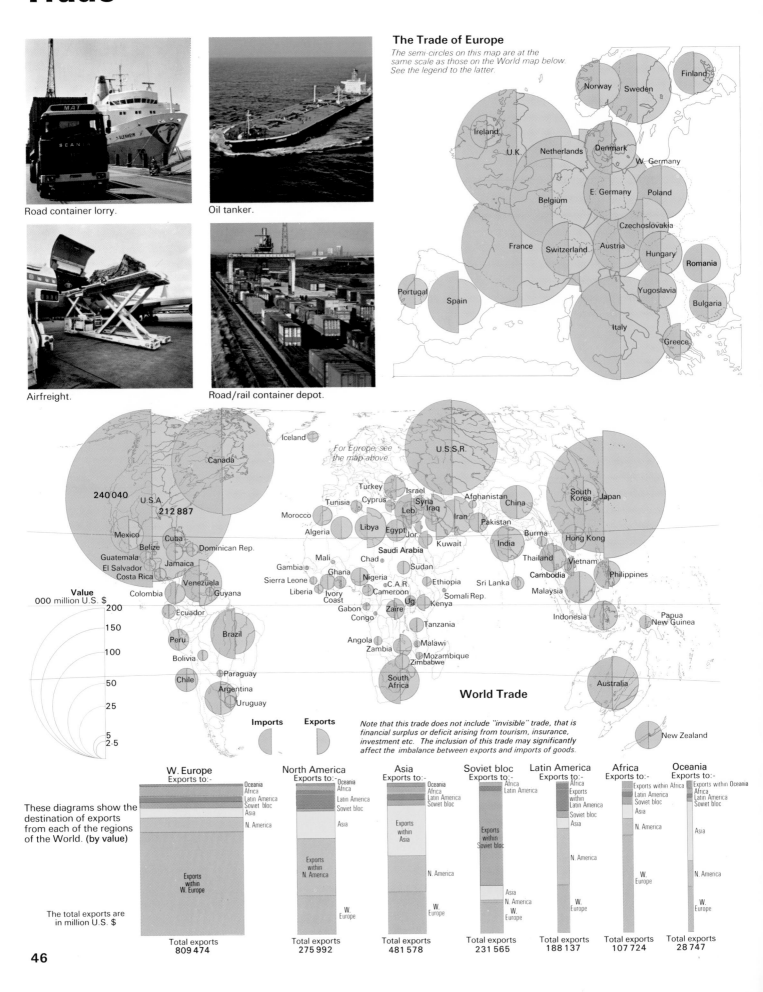

Road container lorry.

Oil tanker.

Airfreight.

Road/rail container depot.

The Trade of Europe

The semi-circles on this map are at the same scale as those on the World map below. See the legend to the latter.

Norway   Sweden   Finland

Ireland   U.K.   Netherlands   Denmark   W. Germany

Belgium   E. Germany   Poland

France   Switzerland   Austria   Czechoslovakia   Hungary   Romania

Portugal   Spain   Yugoslavia   Bulgaria

Italy   Greece

Iceland   U.S.S.R.   *For Europe, see the map above.*

Canada   240 040   U.S.A.   212 887

Turkey   Israel   Afghanistan   China   South Korea   Japan

Tunisia   Cyprus   Syria   Iraq   Iran   Pakistan

Morocco   Leb.   Egypt   Jor.   India   Burma   Hong Kong

Mexico   Cuba   Dominican Rep.   Algeria   Libya   Saudi Arabia   Kuwait   Thailand   Vietnam

Belize   Jamaica   Mali   Chad   Sudan   Sri Lanka   Cambodia   Philippines

Guatemala   El Salvador   Costa Rica   Gambia   Ghana   Nigeria   C.A.R.   Ethiopia   Malaysia

Venezuela   Guyana   Sierra Leone   Liberia   Ivory Coast   Cameroon   Somali Rep.

Colombia   Gabon   Zaire   Ug.   Kenya   Indonesia   Papua New Guinea

Ecuador   Congo   Tanzania

Peru   Brazil   Angola   Malawi   Zambia   Mozambique   Zimbabwe

Bolivia   South Africa   Australia

Paraguay   **World Trade**

Chile   Argentina   Uruguay   New Zealand

Value
000 million U.S. $
200
150
100
50
25
5
2·5

Imports   Exports

Note that this trade does not include "invisible" trade, that is financial surplus or deficit arising from tourism, insurance, investment etc. The inclusion of this trade may significantly affect the imbalance between exports and imports of goods.

W. Europe	North America	Asia	Soviet bloc	Latin America	Africa	Oceania
Exports to:-	Exports to:-	Exports to:-	Exports to:-	Exports to:-	Exports to:-	Exports to:-

W. Europe
Exports to:-
Oceania
Africa
Latin America
Soviet bloc
Asia
N. America
Exports within W. Europe

North America
Exports to:-
Oceania
Africa
Latin America
Soviet bloc
Asia
Exports within N. America
W. Europe

Asia
Exports to:-
Oceania
Africa
Latin America
Soviet bloc
Asia
Exports within Asia
N. America
W. Europe

Soviet bloc
Exports to:-
Africa
Latin America
Exports within Soviet bloc
Asia
N. America
W. Europe

Latin America
Exports to:-
Africa
Exports within Latin America
Soviet bloc
Asia
N. America
W. Europe

Africa
Exports to:-
Exports within Africa
Latin America
Soviet bloc
Asia
N. America
W. Europe

Oceania
Exports to:-
Exports within Oceania
Africa
Latin America
Soviet bloc
Asia
N. America
W. Europe

These diagrams show the destination of exports from each of the regions of the World. (by value)

The total exports are in million U.S. $

| Total exports 809 474 | Total exports 275 992 | Total exports 481 578 | Total exports 231 565 | Total exports 188 137 | Total exports 107 724 | Total exports 28 747 |

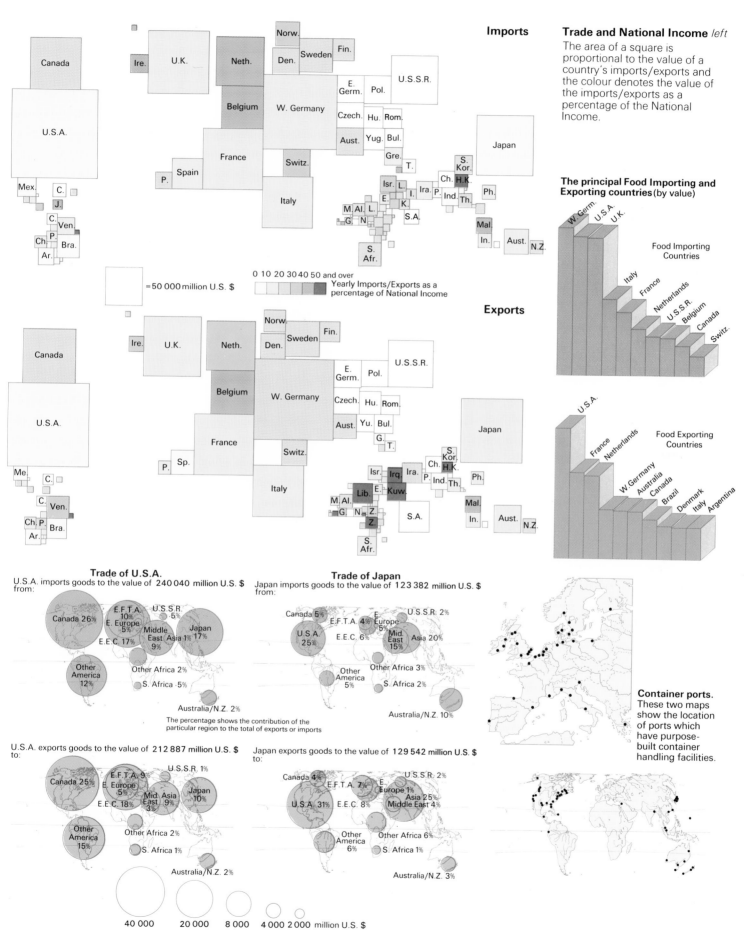

Imports

Trade and National Income *left*
The area of a square is proportional to the value of a country's imports/exports and the colour denotes the value of the imports/exports as a percentage of the National Income.

=50 000 million U.S. $

0 10 20 30 40 50 and over
Yearly Imports/Exports as a percentage of National Income

Exports

The principal Food Importing and Exporting countries (by value)

Food Importing Countries

W. Germ. / U.S.A. / U.K. / Italy / France / Netherlands / U.S.S.R. / Belgium / Canada / Switz.

Food Exporting Countries

U.S.A. / France / Netherlands / W. Germany / Australia / Canada / Brazil / Denmark / Italy / Argentina

Trade of U.S.A.
U.S.A. imports goods to the value of 240 040 million U.S. $ from:

Canada 26% / E.F.T.A. 10% / E. Europe 5% / U.S.S.R. 5% / Japan 17% / E.E.C. 17% / Middle East 9% / Asia 1% / Other America 12% / Other Africa 2% / S. Africa 5% / Australia/N.Z. 2%

The percentage shows the contribution of the particular region to the total of exports or imports

U.S.A. exports goods to the value of 212 887 million U.S. $ to:

Canada 25% / E.F.T.A. 9% / E. Europe 5% / U.S.S.R. 1% / Japan 10% / E.E.C. 18% / Mid. East 3% / Asia 9% / Other America 15% / Other Africa 2% / S. Africa 1% / Australia/N.Z. 2%

Trade of Japan
Japan imports goods to the value of 123 382 million U.S. $ from:

Canada 5% / E.F.T.A. 4% / E Europe 5% / U.S.S.R. 2% / U.S.A. 25% / E.E.C. 6% / Mid. East 15% / Asia 20% / Other America 5% / Other Africa 3% / S. Africa 2% / Australia/N.Z. 10%

Japan exports goods to the value of 129 542 million U.S. $ to:

Canada 4% / E.F.T.A. 7% / E. Europe 1% / U.S.S.R. 2% / U.S.A. 31% / E.E.C. 8% / Middle East 4% / Asia 25% / Other America 6% / Other Africa 6% / S. Africa 1% / Australia/N.Z. 3%

40 000 / 20 000 / 8 000 / 4 000 / 2 000 million U.S. $

Container ports.
These two maps show the location of ports which have purpose-built container handling facilities.

47

Wealth

The living standard of a few highly developed, urbanised, industrialised countries is a complete contrast to the conditions of the vast majority of economically undeveloped, agrarian states. It is this contrast which divides mankind into rich and poor, well fed and hungry. The developing world is still an over-whelmingly agricultural world: over 70% of all its people live off the land and yet the output from that land remains pitifully low. Many Africans, South Americans and Asians struggle with the soil but the bad years occur only too frequently and they seldom have anything left over to save. The need for foreign capital then arises.

National Income
The gap between developing and developed worlds is in fact widening eg. in 1938 the incomes for the United States and India were in the proportions of 1:15; now they are 1:53.

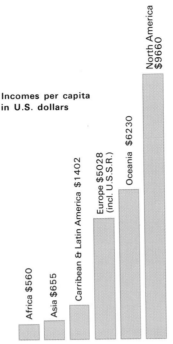

Incomes per capita in U.S. dollars

Africa $560
Asia $655
Carribean & Latin America $1402
Europe $5028 (incl. U.S.S.R.)
Oceania $6230
North America $9660

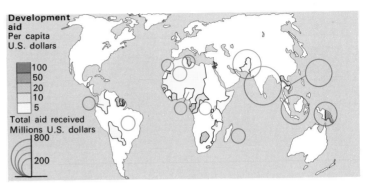

Development aid
Per capita
U.S. dollars

100
50
20
10
5

Total aid received
Millions U.S. dollars
800
200

Development aid
The provision of foreign aid, defined as assistance on con-cessional terms for promoting development, is today an accepted, though controversial aspect of the economic policies of most advanced countries towards less developed countries. Aid for development is based not merely on economic considerations but also on social, political and historical factors. The most important international committee

set up after the war was that of the U.N.; practically all aid however has been given bi-laterally direct from an industrialised country to an under-developed country. Although aid increased during the 1950's the donated proportion of industrialised countries GNP has diminished from 0.5 to 0.4%. Less developed countries share of world trade also decreased and increased population invalidated any progress made.

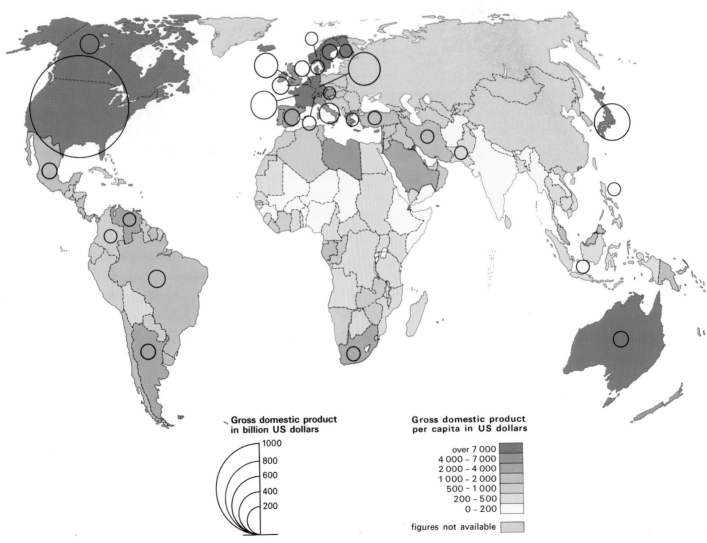

Gross domestic product in billion US dollars

1000
800
600
400
200

Gross domestic product per capita in US dollars

over 7 000
4 000 – 7 000
2 000 – 4 000
1 000 – 2 000
500 – 1 000
200 – 500
0 – 200

figures not available

SETTLEMENTS

Settlement symbols in order of size

⬓ LONDON   ◼ Stuttgart   ◉ Sevilla   ◉ Bergen   ◎ Bath   ○ *Biarritz*   ○ *Srikolayatji*

Settlement symbols and type styles vary according to
the scale of each map and indicate the importance of
towns on the map rather than specific population figures

∴ Sites of Archæological or
Historical importance

BOUNDARIES

———— International Boundaries

⸱⸱⸱ ⸱⸱⸱ ⸱⸱⸱ International Boundaries
(Undemarcated or Undefined)

⸱⸱⸱⸱⸱⸱⸱ Internal Boundaries

International boundaries show the *de facto* situation
where there are rival claims to territory

National and
Provincial Parks

COMMUNICATIONS

═══ Motorways

⌇⌇⌇ Motorways under construction

——— Principal Roads

〜 Other Roads

⊣--⊢ Road Tunnels

〜 Principal Railways

〜 Other Railways

〜⸱⸱⸱ Railways under construction

⊐--⊏ Railway Tunnels

⊃⊂ Passes

⸱⸱⸱⸱⸱ Principal Canals

⊢—⊣ Principal Oil Pipelines

_ *3386* _ Principal Shipping Routes
(Distances in Nautical Miles)

〜⸱⸱⸱ Tracks and Seasonal Roads

✿ Airports

PHYSICAL FEATURES

〜 Perennial Streams

⸱⸱⸱⸱⸱ Seasonal Streams

▲ 8848 Spot Height
in metres

⬭ Seasonal Lakes, Salt Flats

Swamps, Marshes

▼ 8050 Sea Depths.
in metres

Permanent Ice

ᵛ Wells in Desert

1134 Height of Lake Surface
Above Sea Level, in metres

Height of Land
Above Sea Level
in metres

6000 4000 3000 2000 1500 1000 400 200 0

Land Below
Sea Level

0 200 2000 4000 5000 6000 8000

Depth of Sea
in metres

Some of the maps have different contours to
highlight and clarify the principal relief features

Abbreviations of measures used   mm Millimetres   m Metres   km Kilometres   °C Degrees Celsius   mb Millibars

STRUCTURE

1 : 95 000 000

Structural Regions of the Land

- Pre-Cambrian shields
- Sedimentary cover on Pre-Cambrian shields
- Palæozoic (Caledonian and Hercynian) folding
- Sedimentary cover on Palæozoic folding
- Mesozoic folding
- Sedimentary cover on Mesozoic folding
- Cainozoic folding
- Sedimentary cover on Cainozoic folding
- Intensive Mesozoic and Cainozoic vulcanism
- Oceanic-type crust raised above sea level

Structural Regions of the Oceans

- Regions of continental-type crust
- Limit of continental shelf
- Oceanic marginal troughs
- Mid-oceanic volcanic ridges
- Rift valleys in mid-oceanic ridges
- Principal faults
- +++ Frontal line of overthrust folds

GEOLOGICAL TIME SCALE

Era	System	Orogeny	Millions of years before present
Cainozoic (Tertiary, Quaternary)	Quaternary		
	Pliocene	ALPINE FOLDING	
	Miocene		
	Oligocene		
	Eocene		50
	Paleocene	LARAMIDE FOLDING	
Mesozoic (Secondary)	Cretaceous		100
	Jurassic		150
	Triassic		200
Palæozoic (Primary) Upper	Permian		250
	Carboniferous	HERCYNIAN FOLDING	300
	Devonian		350
	Silurian	CALEDONIAN FOLDING	400
Palæozoic (Primary) Lower	Ordovician		450
	Cambrian		500
			550
Pre-Cambrian	Pre-Cambrian		600

Canadian Shield

Rocky Mountains

Appalachians

Sierra Madre

Northern Mid-A

East Pacific Ridge

Guiana Shield

Amazonian Shield

Pacific-Antarctic Ridge

40

20

20

40

VOLCANOES

Equatorial Scale 1 : 280 00

EURASIAN PLATE

AMERICAN PLATE

AFRICAN PLATE

PACIFIC PLATE

INDIAN PLATE

ANTARCTIC PLATE

Hekla
Heimaey
Azores
Vesuvius
Etna
Tenerife
Mt. Pelée
La Soufrière
Puracé
Galapagos
Cotopaxi
El Misti
Ojos del Salado
Tristan da Cunha
Mt. Cameroon
Kilimanjaro
Dempo
Krakatoa
Taal
Fujiyama
Katmai
Klyuchevski
Rainier
St. Helens
Mauna Loa
Paricutin
El Chichón
Galapagos
Ruapehu
Erebus

Projection: *Interrupted Mollweide's Homolographic*

- ● Land volcanoes active since 1700
- ○ Land volcanoes inactive since 1700
- · Submarine volcanoes
- + Geysers
- Plate boundaries
- Andesite line (boundary b sial continental crust and oceanic crust in the Pacif

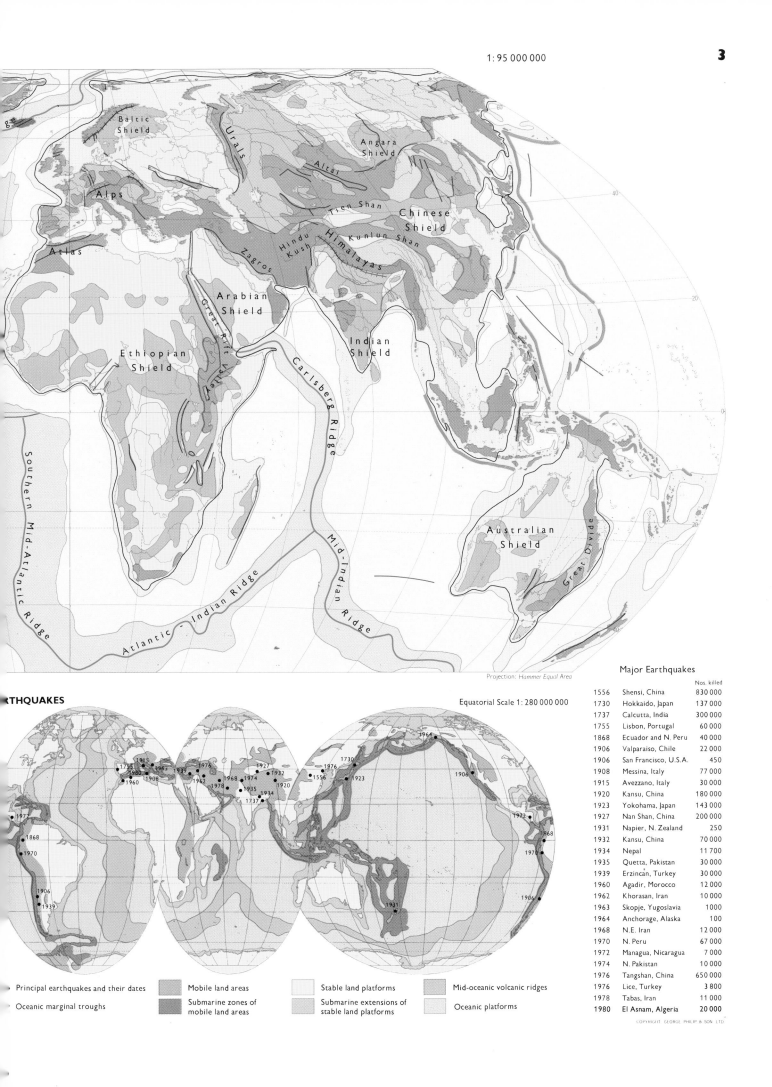

1 : 95 000 000

Baltic
Shield

Urals

Angara
Shield

Altai

Alps

Tien Shan

Chinese
Shield

Atlas

Zagros

Hindu
Kush

Himalayas

Kunlun Shan

Arabian
Shield

Great Rift

Indian
Shield

Ethiopian
Shield

Valley

Carlsberg Ridge

Southern Mid-Atlantic Ridge

Atlantic - Indian Ridge

Mid-Indian Ridge

Australian
Shield

Great Divide

Projection: *Hammer Equal Area*

Major Earthquakes

RTHQUAKES

Equatorial Scale 1 : 280 000 000

		Nos. killed
1556	Shensi, China	830 000
1730	Hokkaido, Japan	137 000
1737	Calcutta, India	300 000
1755	Lisbon, Portugal	60 000
1868	Ecuador and N. Peru	40 000
1906	Valparaiso, Chile	22 000
1906	San Francisco, U.S.A.	450
1908	Messina, Italy	77 000
1915	Avezzano, Italy	30 000
1920	Kansu, China	180 000
1923	Yokohama, Japan	143 000
1927	Nan Shan, China	200 000
1931	Napier, N. Zealand	250
1932	Kansu, China	70 000
1934	Nepal	11 700
1935	Quetta, Pakistan	30 000
1939	Erzincán, Turkey	30 000
1960	Agadir, Morocco	12 000
1962	Khorasan, Iran	10 000
1963	Skopje, Yugoslavia	1 000
1964	Anchorage, Alaska	100
1968	N.E. Iran	12 000
1970	N. Peru	67 000
1972	Managua, Nicaragua	7 000
1974	N. Pakistan	10 000
1976	Tangshan, China	650 000
1976	Lice, Turkey	3 800
1978	Tabas, Iran	11 000
1980	El Asnam, Algeria	20 000

Principal earthquakes and their dates

Oceanic marginal troughs

Mobile land areas

Submarine zones of
mobile land areas

Stable land platforms

Submarine extensions of
stable land platforms

Mid-oceanic volcanic ridges

Oceanic platforms

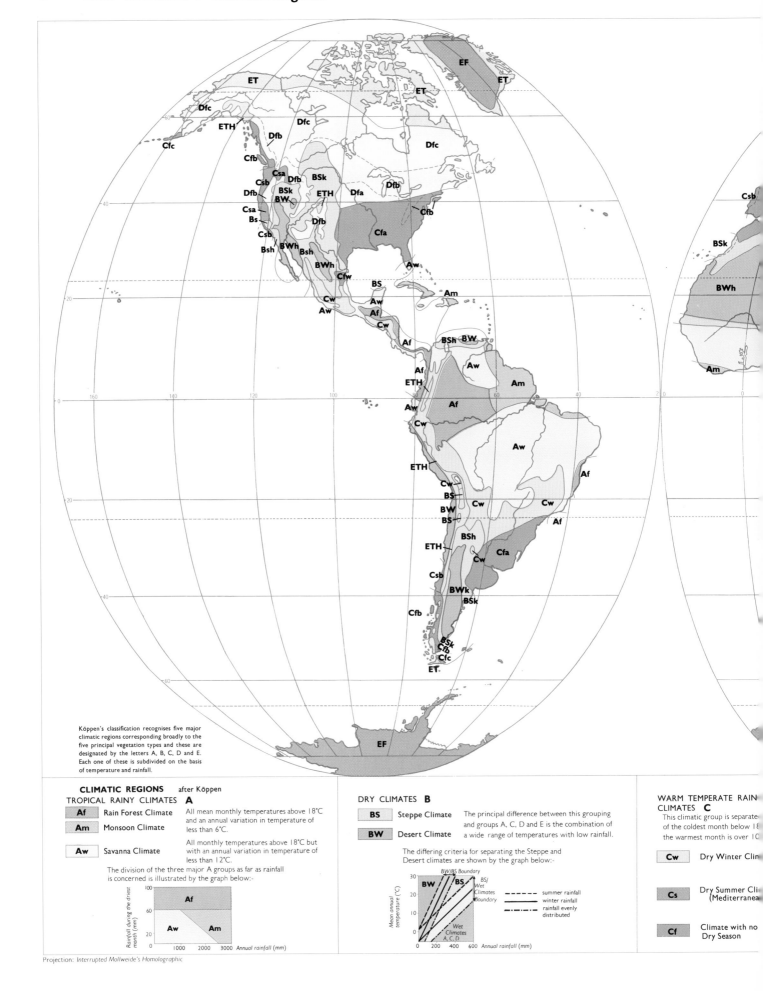

Köppen's classification recognises five major climatic regions corresponding broadly to the five principal vegetation types and these are designated by the letters A, B, C, D and E. Each one of these is subdivided on the basis of temperature and rainfall.

CLIMATIC REGIONS   after Köppen

TROPICAL RAINY CLIMATES   **A**

Af	Rain Forest Climate	All mean monthly temperatures above 18°C and an annual variation in temperature of less than 6°C.
Am	Monsoon Climate	
Aw	Savanna Climate	All monthly temperatures above 18°C but with an annual variation in temperature of less than 12°C.

The division of the three major A groups as far as rainfall is concerned is illustrated by the graph below:-

DRY CLIMATES   **B**

BS	Steppe Climate	The principal difference between this grouping and groups A, C, D and E is the combination of
BW	Desert Climate	a wide range of temperatures with low rainfall.

The differing criteria for separating the Steppe and Desert climates are shown by the graph below:-

WARM TEMPERATE RAIN CLIMATES   **C**

This climatic group is separate of the coldest month below 18 the warmest month is over 10

Cw	Dry Winter Cli
Cs	Dry Summer Cli (Mediterranea
Cf	Climate with no Dry Season

Projection: *Interrupted Mollweide's Homolographic*

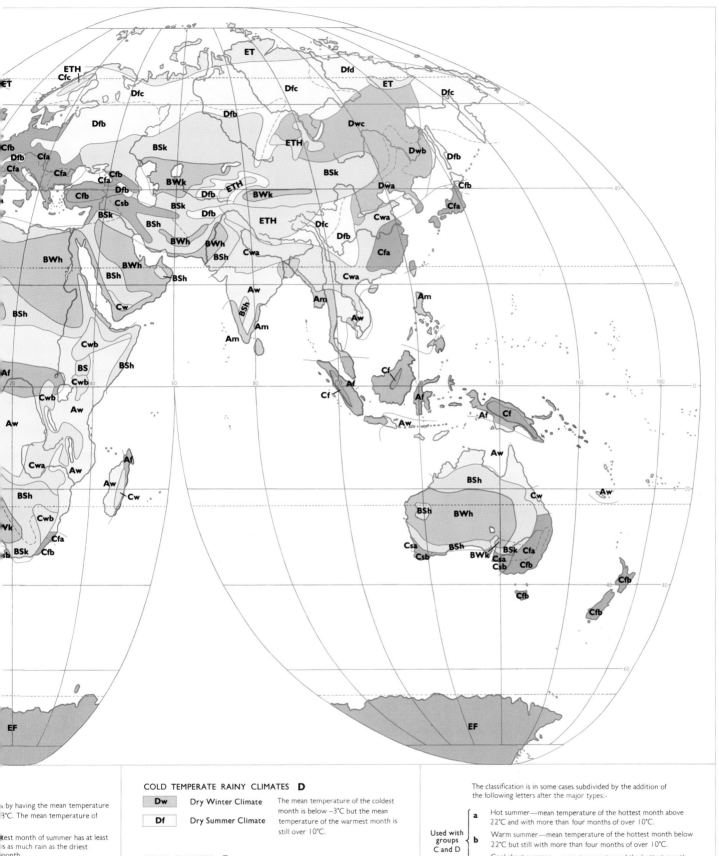

ETH
Cfc
ET
ET
Dfd
Dfc
ET
Dfc
Dfc
Dfb
Dfb
Dwc
Dfb
Cfb
Cfa
BSk
ETH
Dwb
Dfb
Dfb
Cfa
Cfa
Cfa
Cfb
BSk
BWk
Dfb
ETH
BWk
Dwa
Cfb
Csb
BSk
Dfb
Cfa
BSh
Cfa
ETH
Dfc
Cwa
BWh
BWh
Dfb
BSh
Cwa
BWh
Cfa
BSh
BSh
BWh
Cw
Cwa
Am
Am
BWh
BSh
Am
Aw
BSh
Aw
Am
Am
Cw
Cwb
Cf
BS
BSh
Cf
Af
Af
Cfa
Cwb
Af
Cf
Aw
Aw
Af
Aw
Aw
Af
Aw
Cwa
Aw
Aw
Cw
BSh
BSh
Cw
Aw
Cwb
BSh
BWh
Cfa
BSk
Cfb
Csa
BSh
BSk
Cfa
Csb
BWk
Csb
Cfb
Csa
Cfb
Cfb
EF
EF

by having the mean temperature
3°C. The mean temperature of

test month of summer has at least
s as much rain as the driest
month.

test month of winter has at least
mes as much rain as the driest
f summer The driest summer
tself has less than 30mm rainfall.

nfall throughout the year.

COLD TEMPERATE RAINY CLIMATES **D**

Dw	Dry Winter Climate	The mean temperature of the coldest month is below −3°C but the mean temperature of the warmest month is still over 10°C.
Df	Dry Summer Climate	

POLAR CLIMATES **E**

ET	Tundra Climate	The mean temperature of the warmest month is below 10°C giving permanently frozen subsoil.
	Polar Climate	The mean temperature of the warmest month is below 0°C giving permanent ice and snow.
EF		

The classification is in some cases subdivided by the addition of the following letters after the major types:-

Used with groups C and D	**a**	Hot summer—mean temperature of the hottest month above 22°C and with more than four months of over 10°C.
	b	Warm summer—mean temperature of the hottest month below 22°C but still with more than four months of over 10°C.
	c	Cool short summer —mean temperature of the hottest month below 22°C but with less than four months of over 10°C.
Used with group D	**d**	Cool short summer and cold winter—mean temperature of the hottest month below 22°C, and of the coldest month below −38°C.
Used with group B	**h**	Hot dry climate—mean annual temperature above 18°C.
	k	Cool dry climate—mean annual temperature below 18°C.
Used with group E	**H**	Polar climate due to elevation being over 1500m

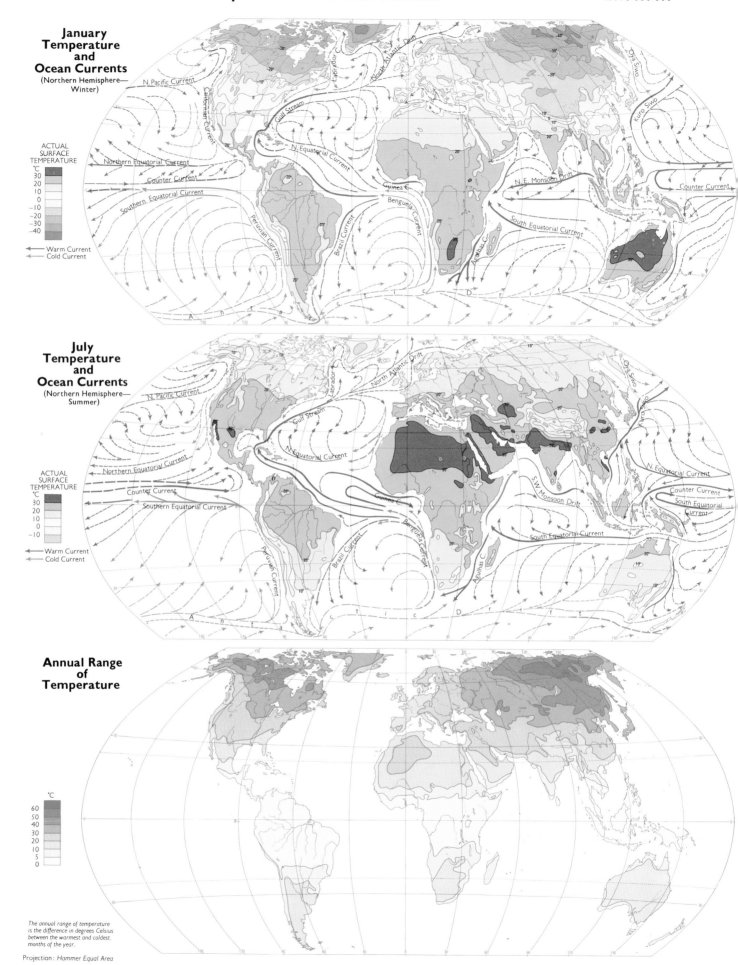

January Temperature and Ocean Currents
(Northern Hemisphere—Winter)

ACTUAL SURFACE TEMPERATURE
°C
30
20
10
0
-10
-20
-30
-40

⟵ Warm Current
⟵ Cold Current

July Temperature and Ocean Currents
(Northern Hemisphere—Summer)

ACTUAL SURFACE TEMPERATURE
°C
30
20
10
0
-10

⟵ Warm Current
⟵ Cold Current

Annual Range of Temperature

°C
60
50
40
30
20
10
5
0

The annual range of temperature is the difference in degrees Celsius between the warmest and coldest months of the year.

Projection: Hammer Equal Area

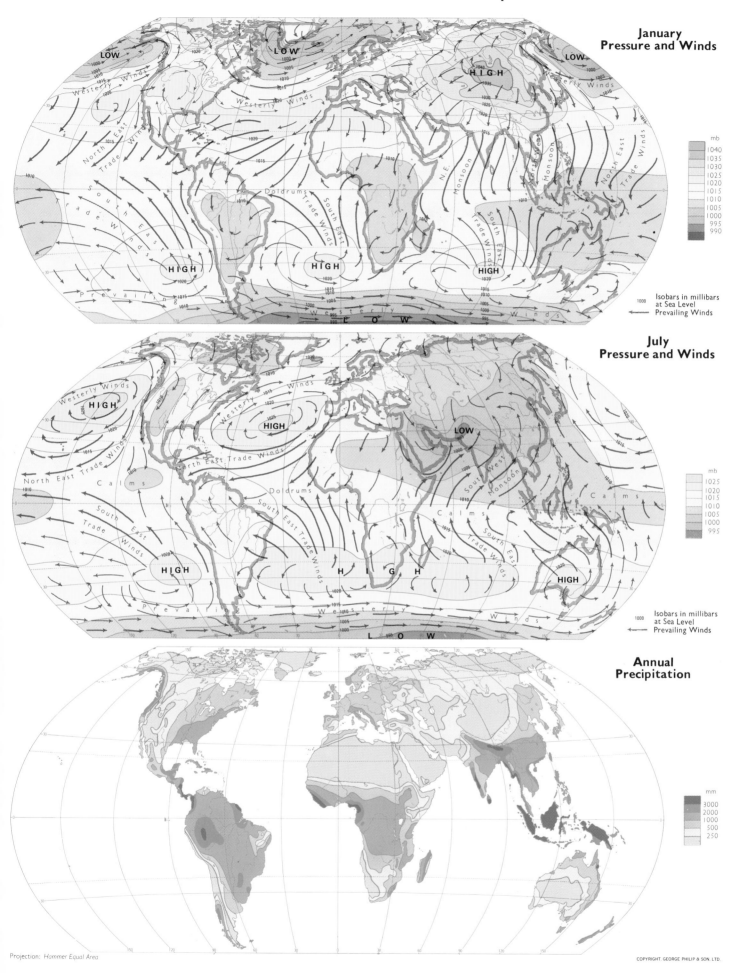

January
Pressure and Winds

July
Pressure and Winds

Annual
Precipitation

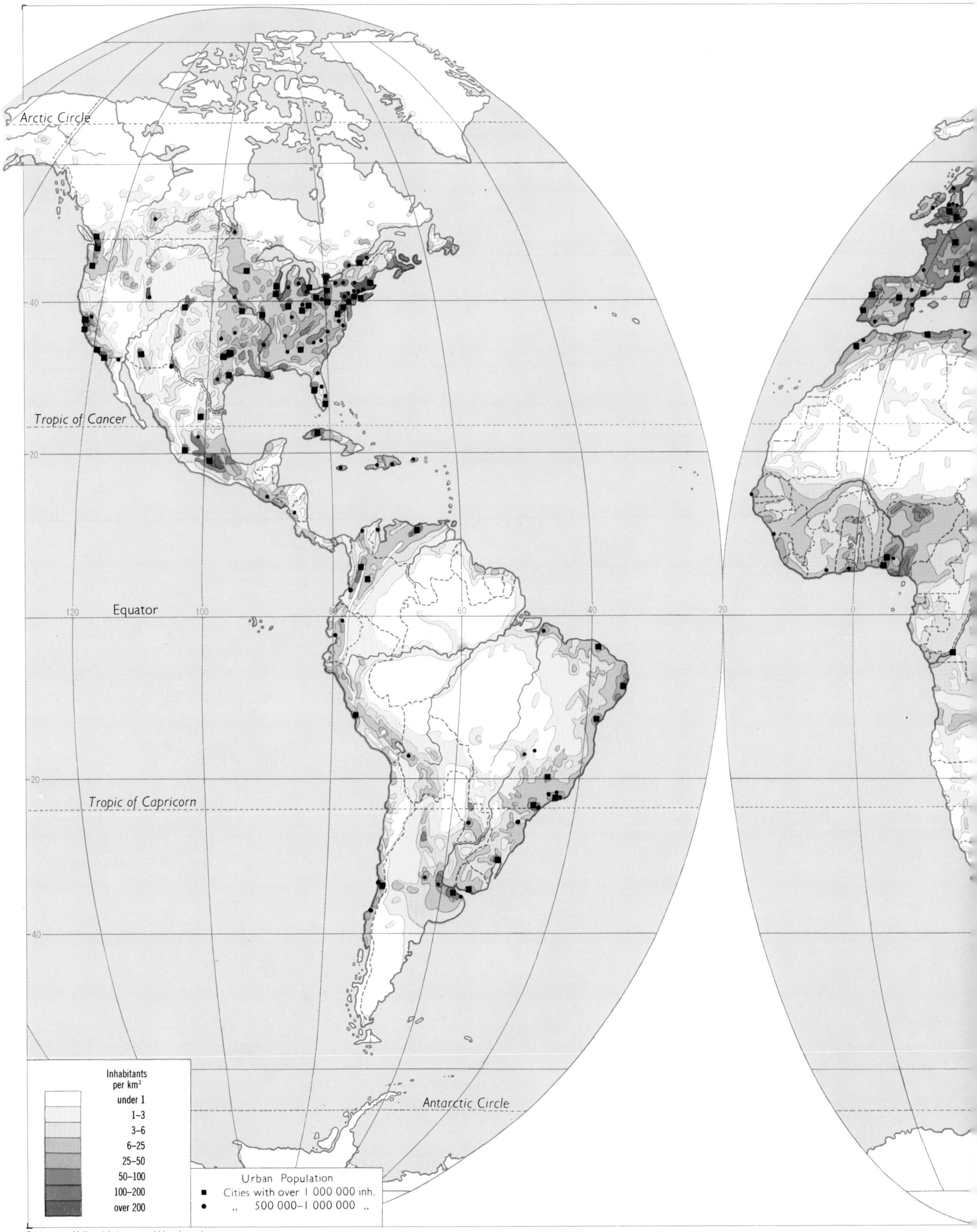
Arctic Circle
Tropic of Cancer
Equator
Tropic of Capricorn
Antarctic Circle
40
20
20
40
120
100
80
60
40
20
0
Inhabitants per km²
under 1
1–3
3–6
6–25
25–50
50–100
100–200
over 200
Urban Population
■ Cities with over 1 000 000 inh.
● ,, 500 000–1 000 000 ,,

Projection: Mollweide's Interrupted Homolographic

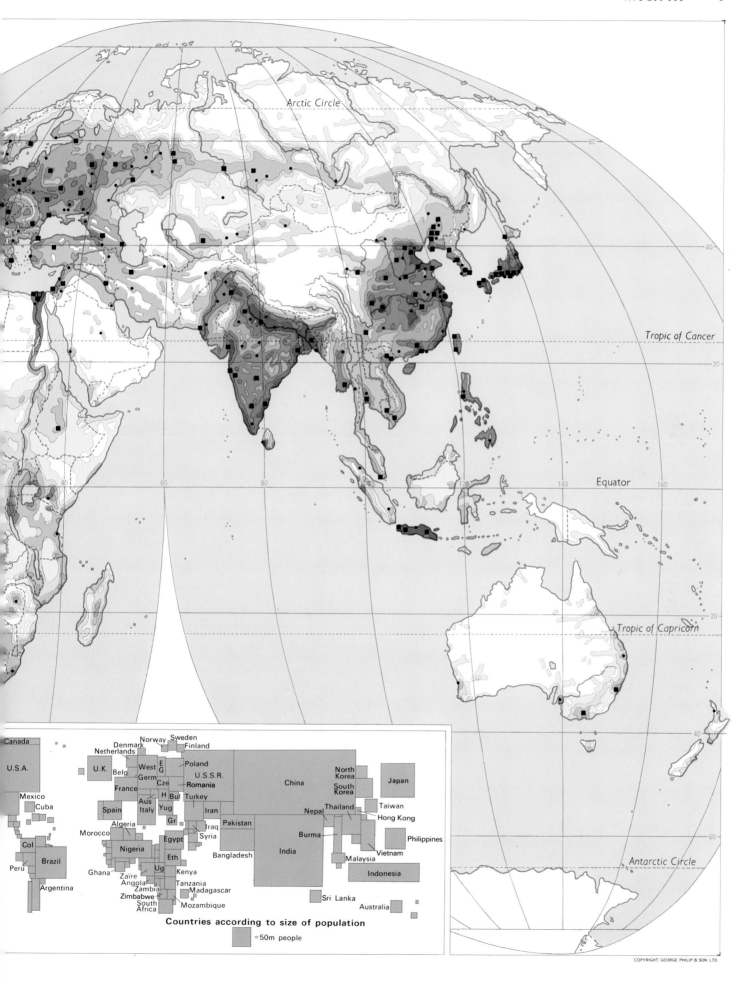

1 : 73 200 000

Arctic Circle

60

40

Tropic of Cancer

20

40   60   80   100   120   140   Equator   160

20

Tropic of Capricorn

20

40

60

Antarctic Circle

Countries according to size of population

= 50m people

Canada

U.S.A.

Mexico

Cuba

Col

Peru

Brazil

Argentina

Norway   Sweden

Denmark   Finland

Netherlands

U.K.   West   E   Poland

Belg   Germ   G

France   Cze   U.S.S.R.   China   North   Japan
                        Romania   Korea
                        Bul   Turkey   South
Spain   Aus   H   Iran   Korea   Taiwan
        Italy   Yug   Hong Kong
Algeria   Gr   Iraq   Pakistan   Nepal   Thailand
Morocco   Egypt   Syria   Burma   Philippines
Nigeria   Bangladesh   India   Vietnam
        Eth   Malaysia
Ghana   Ug   Kenya   Indonesia
    Zaïre   Tanzania
Angola   Zambia   Madagascar   Sri Lanka
Zimbabwe   Australia
South   Mozambique
Africa

Projection: *Hammer Equal Area*

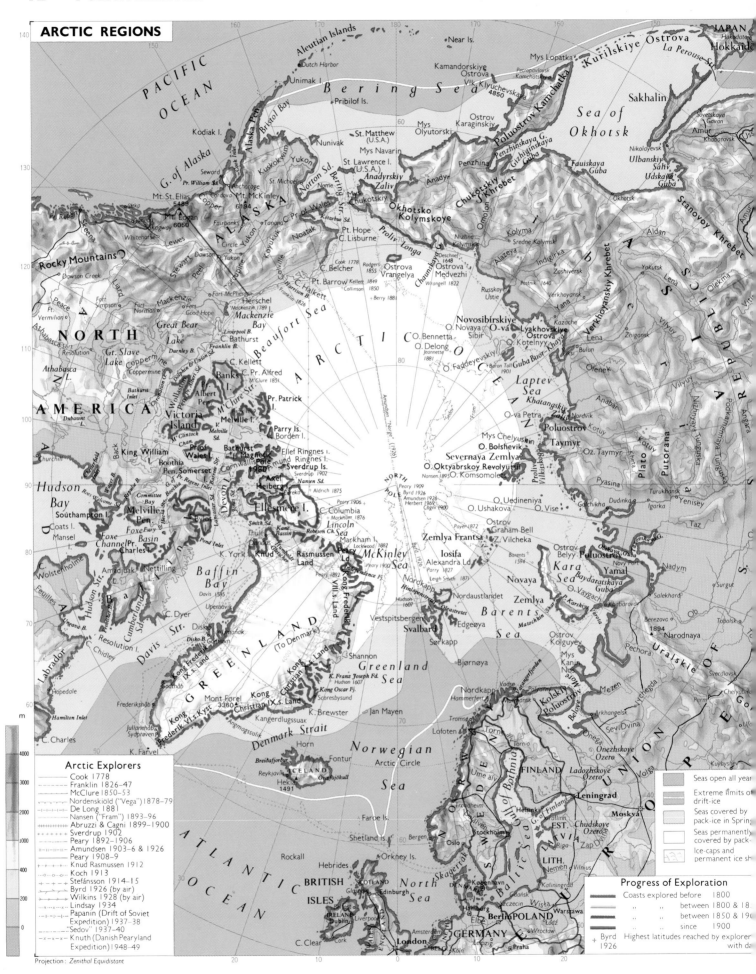

ARCTIC REGIONS

Arctic Explorers
——— Cook 1778
– – – Franklin 1826–47
········ McClure 1850–53
·–·–·– Nordenskiöld ("Vega") 1878–79
— —— De Long 1881
—·—·— Nansen ("Fram") 1893–96
++++++ Abruzzi & Cagni 1899–1900
———— Sverdrup 1902
—··—··— Peary 1892–1906
—o—o— Amundsen 1903–6 & 1926
—··—··— Peary 1908–9
—o——o— Knud Rasmussen 1912
—·o·—·o·— Koch 1913
+ + + + Stefánsson 1914–15
———— Byrd 1926 (by air)
——·——·— Wilkins 1928 (by air)
········ Lindsay 1934
—·—·—· Papanin (Drift of Soviet
           Expedition) 1937–38
———— Sedov 1937–40
—x—x—x— Knuth (Danish Pearyland
           Expedition) 1948–49

Projection: Zenithal Equidistant

Seas open all year
Extreme limits of drift-ice
Seas covered by pack-ice in Spring
Seas permanently covered by pack
Ice-caps and permanent ice sh

Progress of Exploration
———— Coasts explored before 1800
  „   „   „   between 1800 & 18
  „   „   „   between 1850 & 19
  „   „   „   since 1900
+ Byrd Highest latitudes reached by explorer
  1926   with da

ANTARCTIC REGIONS

1:35 000 000

400   0   400   800   1200 km

Sub-Glacial Limits (at Sea Level) of Polar Basins

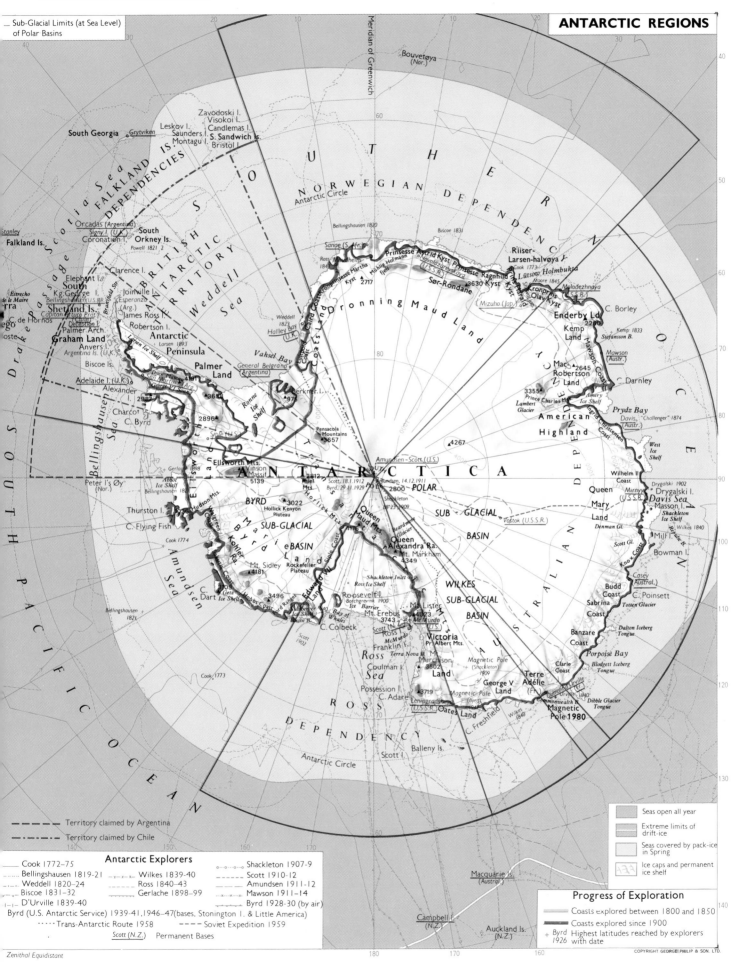

Zenithal Equidistant

--- Territory claimed by Argentina

—·— Territory claimed by Chile

Antarctic Explorers

—— Cook 1772–75	·–·– Bellingshausen 1819–21
–··– Weddell 1820–24	–·– Biscoe 1831–32
–·–· D'Urville 1839–40	

–·–· Wilkes 1839–40	—— Ross 1840–43
—— Gerlache 1898–99	

o–o–o Shackleton 1907–9
—— Scott 1910–12
—— Amundsen 1911–12
—— Mawson 1911–14
– – – Byrd 1928–30 (by air)

Byrd (U.S. Antarctic Service) 1939–41, 1946–47 (bases, Stonington I. & Little America)
····· Trans-Antarctic Route 1958   – – – Soviet Expedition 1959

· Scott (N.Z.) Permanent Bases

Seas open all year	
Extreme limits of drift-ice	
Seas covered by pack-ice in Spring	
Ice caps and permanent ice shelf	

Progress of Exploration

—— Coasts explored between 1800 and 1850

—— Coasts explored since 1900

+ Byrd 1926 Highest latitudes reached by explorers with date

COPYRIGHT GEORGE PHILIP & SON. LTD.

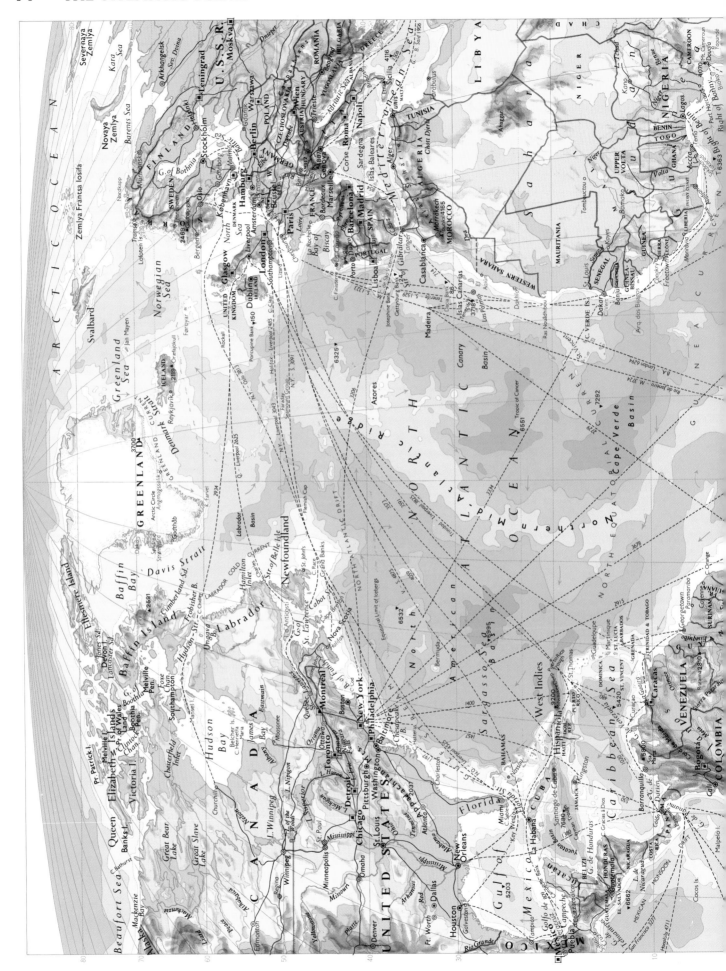

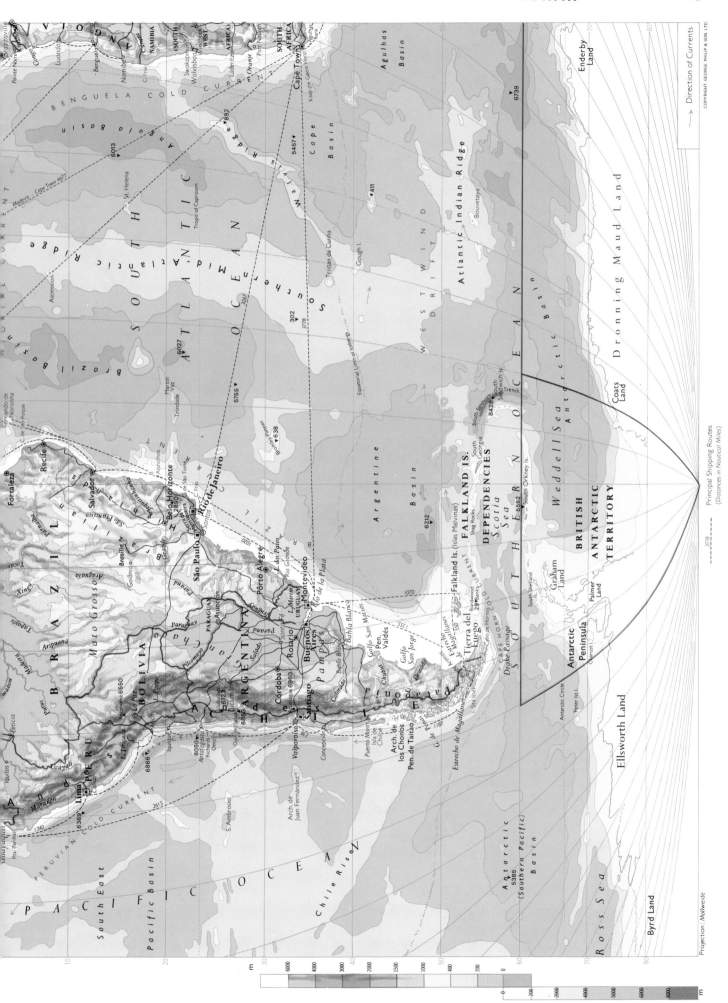

1 : 45 000 000

Projection: Mollweide

Direction of Currents

Principal Shipping Routes
(Distances in Nautical Miles)

COPYRIGHT GEORGE PHILIP & SON LTD.

1 : 20 000 000

200   0   200   400   600   800 km

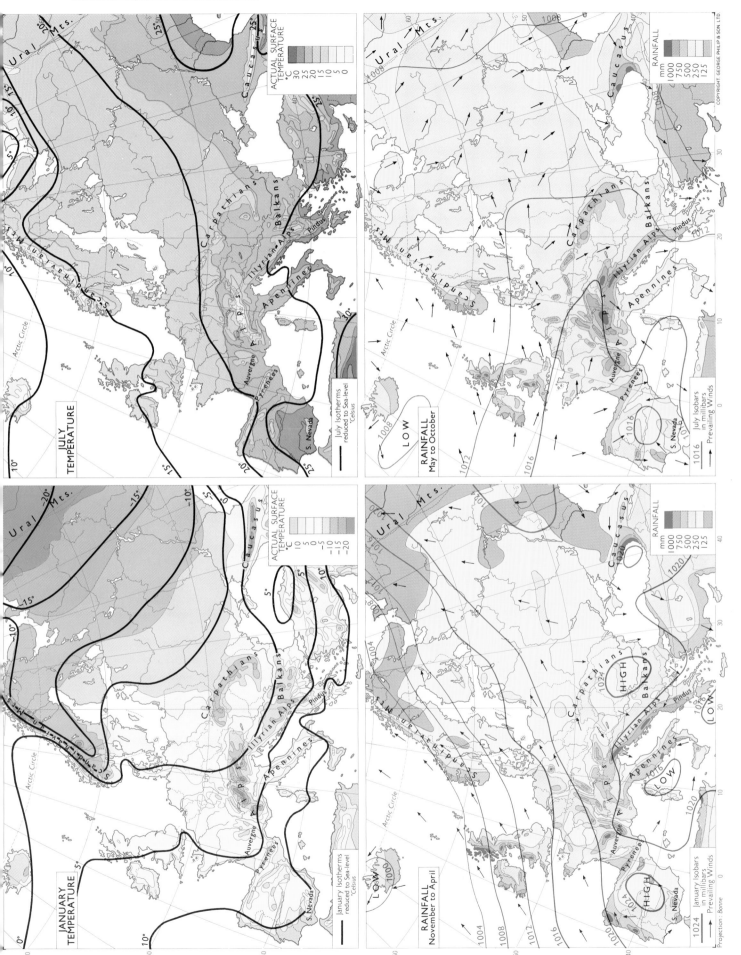

1 : 40 000 000

400   0   400   800   1200   1600 km

ACTUAL SURFACE
TEMPERATURE
°C
30
25
20
15
10
5
0

JULY
TEMPERATURE

July Isotherms
reduced to Sea-level
°Celsius

RAINFALL
mm
1000
750
500
250
125

RAINFALL
May to October

LOW

July Isobars
in millibars
Prevailing Winds

ACTUAL SURFACE
TEMPERATURE
°C
10
5
0
−5
−10
−15
−20

JANUARY
TEMPERATURE

January Isotherms
reduced to Sea-level
°Celsius

RAINFALL
mm
1000
750
500
250
125

RAINFALL
November to April

HIGH

LOW

LOW

HIGH

January Isobars
in millibars
Prevailing Winds

Projection: Bonne

COPYRIGHT GEORGE PHILIP & SON LTD

1 : 35 000 000

400   0   400   800   1200 km

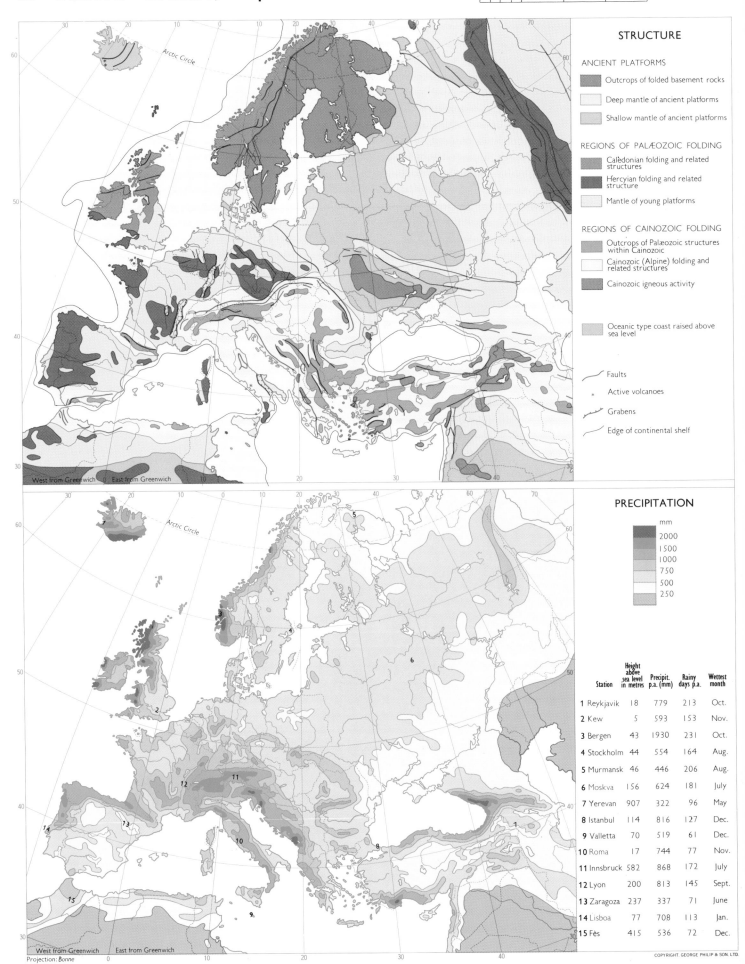

STRUCTURE

ANCIENT PLATFORMS

Outcrops of folded basement rocks

Deep mantle of ancient platforms

Shallow mantle of ancient platforms

REGIONS OF PALÆOZOIC FOLDING

Calèdonian folding and related structures

Hercyian folding and related structure

Mantle of young platforms

REGIONS OF CAINOZOIC FOLDING

Outcrops of Palæozoic structures within Cainozoic

Cainozoic (Alpine) folding and related structures

Cainozoic igneous activity

Oceanic type coast raised above sea level

Faults

Active volcanoes

Grabens

Edge of continental shelf

West from Greenwich | East from Greenwich

PRECIPITATION

	mm
	2000
	1500
	1000
	750
	500
	250

Station	Height above sea level in metres	Precipit. p.a. (mm)	Rainy days p.a.	Wettest month
1 Reykjavik	18	779	213	Oct.
2 Kew	5	593	153	Nov.
3 Bergen	43	1930	231	Oct.
4 Stockholm	44	554	164	Aug.
5 Murmansk	46	446	206	Aug.
6 Moskva	156	624	181	July
7 Yerevan	907	322	96	May
8 Istanbul	114	816	127	Dec.
9 Valletta	70	519	61	Dec.
10 Roma	17	744	77	Nov.
11 Innsbruck	582	868	172	July
12 Lyon	200	813	145	Sept.
13 Zaragoza	237	337	71	June
14 Lisboa	77	708	113	Jan.
15 Fès	415	536	72	Dec.

West from Greenwich | East from Greenwich

Projection: Bonne

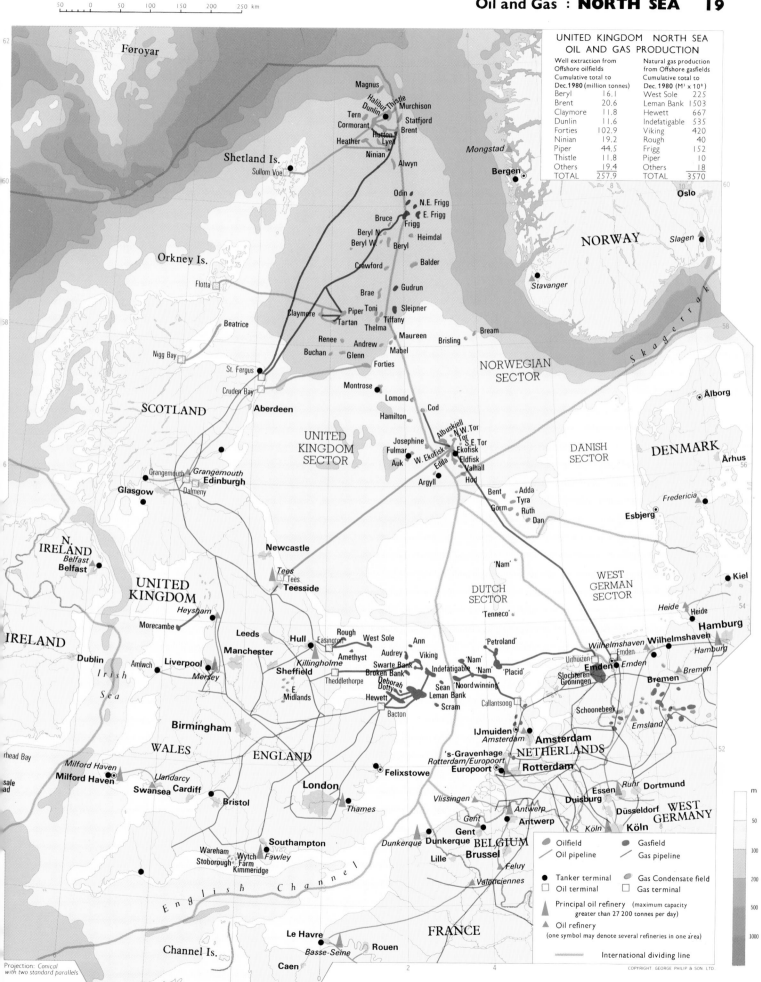

EUROPE : Density of Population

1: 20 000 000

200 0 200 400 600 800 km

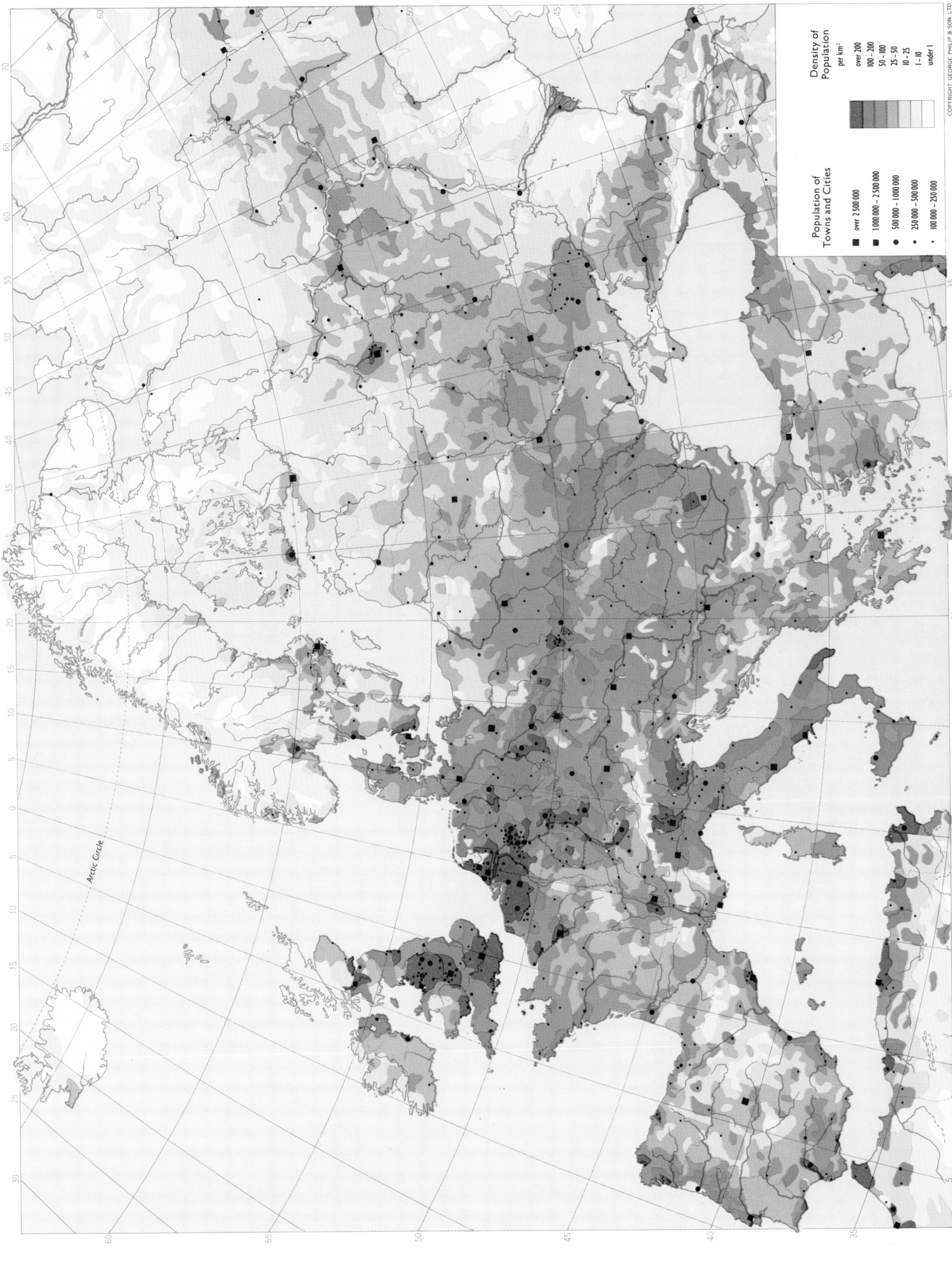
Density of Population
per km²
over 200
100 – 200
50 – 100
25 – 50
10 – 25
1 – 10
under 1
Population of Towns and Cities
over 2 500 000
1 000 000 – 2 500 000
500 000 – 1 000 000
250 000 – 500 000
100 000 – 250 000
Arctic Circle

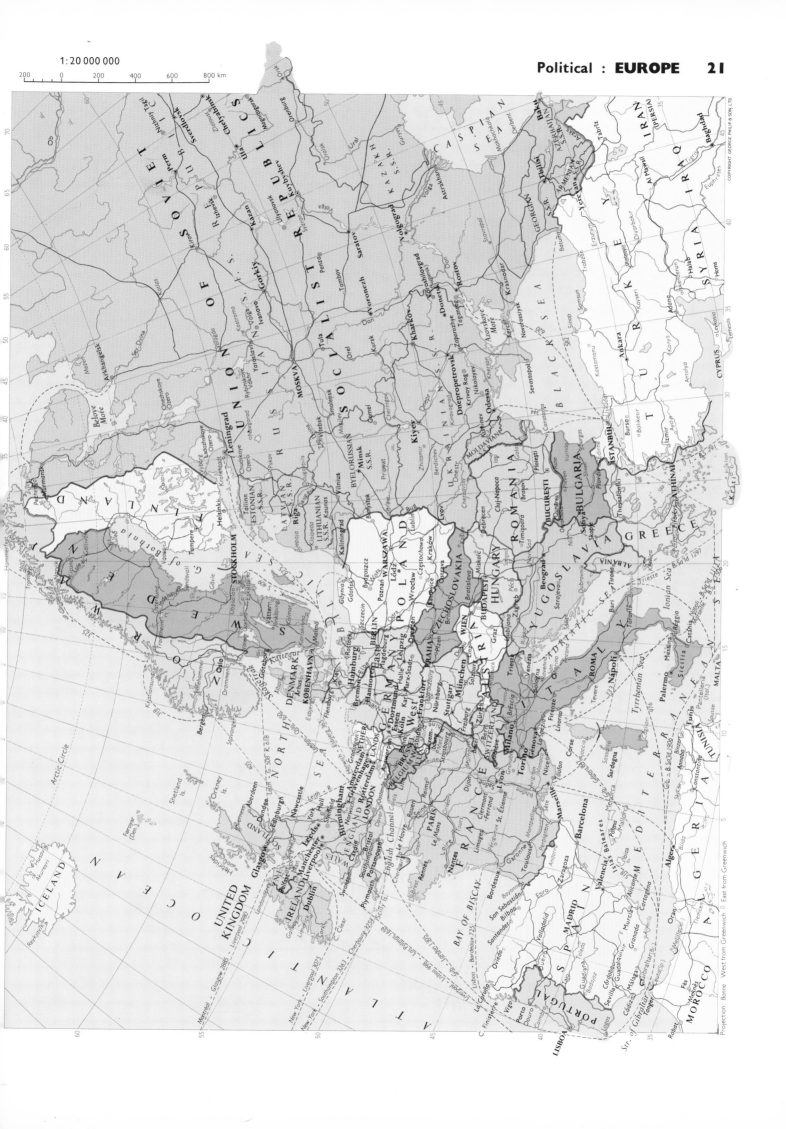

1:20 000 000

200   0   200   400   600   800 km

Projection Bonne   West from Greenwich 0 East from Greenwich

1 : 4 000 000

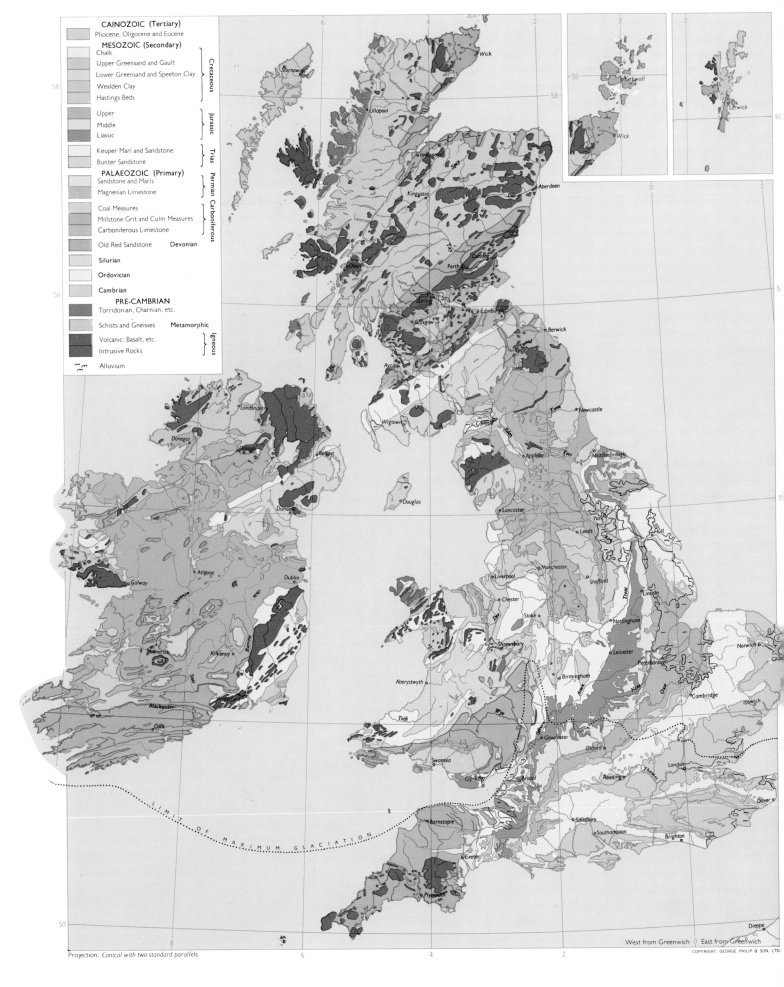

CAINOZOIC (Tertiary)
Pliocene, Oligocene and Eocene
MESOZOIC (Secondary)
Chalk
Upper Greensand and Gault
Lower Greensand and Speeton Clay
Wealden Clay
Hastings Beds

Cretaceous

Upper
Middle
Liassic

Jurassic

Keuper Marl and Sandstone
Bunter Sandstone

Trias

PALAEOZOIC (Primary)
Sandstone and Marls
Magnesian Limestone

Permian

Coal Measures
Millstone Grit and Culm Measures
Carboniferous Limestone

Carboniferous

Old Red Sandstone   Devonian

Silurian

Ordovician

Cambrian

PRE-CAMBRIAN
Torridonian, Charnian, etc.

Schists and Gneisses   Metamorphic

Volcanic: Basalt, etc.
Intrusive Rocks

Igneous

~~~ Alluvium

LIMIT OF MAXIMUM GLACIATION

Projection: Conical with two standard parallels

West from Greenwich | East from Greenwich

COPYRIGHT. GEORGE PHILIP & SON. LTD.

1 : 4 000 000

Projection: Conical with two standard parallels

COPYRIGHT. GEORGE PHILIP & SON LTD.

1 : 4 000 000

50   0   50   100   150 km

ANNUAL PRECIPITATION AND ISOBARS

ANNUAL PRECIPITATION

mm
2500
2000
1500
1250
1000
750
625
500

ANNUAL ISOBARS

1011 mb   (in Millibars)

WIND ROSES

Frequency of wind
from each direction
is indicated by the
length of each arrow

Based partly on information supplied by the Meteorological Office
and on the Climatological Atlas of the British Isles.

Projection: Conical with two standard parallels

West from Greenwich 0 East from Greenwich

COPYRIGHT. GEORGE PHILIP & SON LTD

1 : 8 500 000

50 0 50 100 150 200 250 300 km

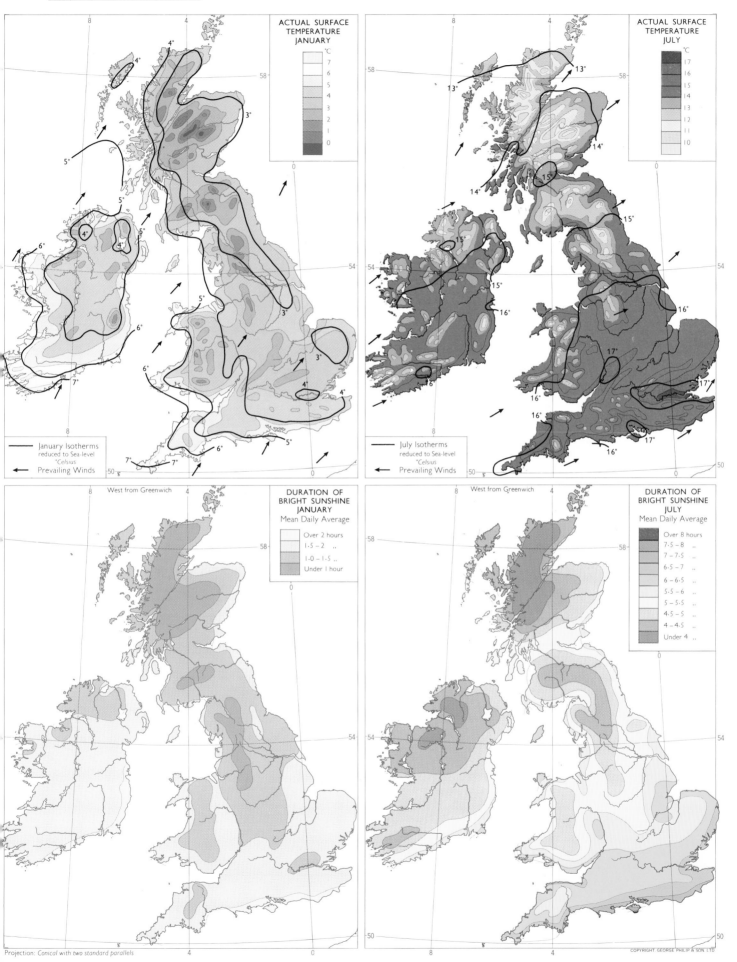

ACTUAL SURFACE
TEMPERATURE
JANUARY

°C
7
6
5
4
3
2
1
0

— January Isotherms
reduced to Sea-level
°Celsius
← Prevailing Winds

ACTUAL SURFACE
TEMPERATURE
JULY

°C
17
16
15
14
13
12
11
10

— July Isotherms
reduced to Sea-level
°Celsius
← Prevailing Winds

West from Greenwich

DURATION OF
BRIGHT SUNSHINE
JANUARY
Mean Daily Average

Over 2 hours
1·5 – 2   ..
1·0 – 1·5 ..
Under 1 hour

West from Greenwich

DURATION OF
BRIGHT SUNSHINE
JULY
Mean Daily Average

Over 8 hours
7·5 – 8   ..
7 – 7·5   ..
6·5 – 7   ..
6 – 6·5   ..
5·5 – 6   ..
5 – 5·5   ..
4·5 – 5   ..
4 – 4·5   ..
Under 4   ..

Projection: Conical with two standard parallels

COPYRIGHT GEORGE PHILIP & SON LTD

1 : 4 000 000

50   0   50   100   150 km

West from Greenwich   0   East from Greenwich
COPYRIGHT. GEORGE PHILIP & SON. LTD.

Orkney Is.
Westray
N. Ronaldsay
Sanday
ORKNEY
Mainland
Stronsay
Hoy
Kirkwall
South Ronaldsay
Thurso
Wick
CAITHNESS

Shetland Is.
Unst
Yell
Mainland
ZETLAND
Foula
Lerwick
Fair I.

Pentland Firth
Thurso
Wick
CAITHNESS
SUTHERLAND
Lairg
Golspie
Stornoway
Lewis
Harris
North Minch
North Uist
Ullapool
ROSS AND CROMARTY
Invergordon
Dingwall
Moray Firth
Elgin
Lossiemouth
Benbecula
Portree
Skye
NAIRN
MORAY
Banff
Fraserburgh
Peterhead
South Uist
Kyle of Lochalsh
Inverness
Kingussie
INVERNESS
BANFF
ABERDEEN
Barra
Rhum
Mallaig
Balmoral
KINCARDINE
Aberdeen
Eigg
Fort William
Blair Atholl
Ballater
Stonehaven
SCOTLAND
ANGUS
Coll
Ballachulish
PERTH
Forfar
Montrose
Tiree
Staffa
Iona
Oban
Firth of Lorn
Crieff
Dundee
Arbroath
Colonsay
ARGYLL
Perth
Cupar
St. Andrews
Lochgilphead
Stirling
Kinross
FIFE
Forth
CL.-Clackmannan
KIN.-Kinross
W. Loth-West Lothian
Islay
Jura
Kintyre
Helensburgh
Falkirk
Linlithgow
Kirkcaldy
Dunfermline
Dunbar
Berwick-on-Tweed
Greenock
Dumbarton
Edinburgh
Haddington
E. LOTHIAN
Paisley
Glasgow
MIDLOTHIAN
Bute
Hamilton
Motherwell
BERWICK
Duns
Campbeltown
Firth of Clyde
Kilmarnock
LANARK
PEEBLES
Galashiels
Arran
Saltcoats
Irvine
Prestwick
Ayr
Sanquhar
SELKIRK
Jedburgh
Moffat
Hawick
ROXBURGH
Alnwick
NORTH
AYR
DUMFRIES
Dumfries
NORTHUMBERLAND
SEA
Malin Hd.
Portrush
Coleraine
North Channel
WIGTOWN
KIRKCUDBRIGHT
Wigtown
Kirkcudbright
Newcastle
Tynemouth
South Shields
Tory I.
Letterkenny
Londonderry
LONDONDERRY
ANTRIM
Ballymena
Larne
Stranraer
Solway Firth
Carlisle
Gateshead
Sunderland
DONEGAL
Lifford
Ballycastle
CUMBERLAND
Durham
Hartlepool
Aran Is.
Donegal
TYRONE
Omagh
Antrim
Belfast
Mull of Galloway
Whitehaven
Appleby
DURHAM
Stockton
TEESSIDE
Middlesbrough
Whitby
NORTHERN IRELAND
ULSTER
Bangor
Newtownards
St. Bee's Hd.
WESTMORLAND
Darlington
NORTH RIDING
Errris Hd.
Donegal Bay
FERMANAGH
Enniskillen
Lower L. Erne
Lisburn
DOWN
Kendal
Northallerton
Killala Bay
Sligo
LEITRIM
Upper L. Erne
Clones
ARMAGH
Monaghan
Downpatrick
ISLE OF MAN
Windermere
Scarborough
Ballina
SLIGO
Monaghan
Dundrum
Douglas
Barrow
YORKSHIRE
Ripon
Flamborough Hd.
MAYO
Clare I.
Castlebar
ROSCOMMON
CAVAN
Cavan
Carrickmacross
Greenore
Dundalk
Morecambe Bay
Lancaster
York
EAST RIDING
Beverley
Westport
CONNACHT
Longford
LONGFORD
Ceanannus Mor
Drogheda
Blackpool
LANCASHIRE
Keighley
WEST RIDING
Leeds
Hull
Connemara
Corrib
GALWAY
Roscommon
Mullingar
MEATH
IRISH SEA
Preston
Burnley
Halifax
Bradford
Spurn Hd.
Galway
Galway Bay
Athenry
WESTMEATH
Athlone
Balbriggan
Blackburn
Bolton
Huddersfield
Wakefield
Barnsley
Scunthorpe
Doncaster
Grimsby
IRELAND
OFFALY
Tullamore
Dublin
DUBLIN
Liverpool Bay
St. Helens
Salford
Manchester
Rotherham
Sheffield
LINDSEY
Birr
Bray
Dún Laoghaire
Holyhead
Liverpool
Birkenhead
Stockport
ANGLESEY
Caernarvon
Rhyl
Flint
Chester
Macclesfield
DERBY
Chesterfield
Lincoln
CLARE
Ennis
KILDARE
LAOIS
WICKLOW
Wicklow
Caernarvon Bay
CAERNARVON
Denbigh
DENBIGH
CHESHIRE
Crewe
Wrexham
Stoke-on-Trent
Matlock
Mansfield
NOTTS
Nottingham
KESTEVEN
Boston
The Wash
Loop Hd.
Nenagh
Carlow
CARLOW
Arklow
Derby
Grantham
HOLLAND
Kings Lynn
Norwich
Thurles
Kilkenny
MERIONETH
Dolgelley
MONTGOMERY
Welshpool
STAFFORD
Stafford
Burton
LEICESTER
Leicester
Oakham
RUTLAND
PETERBOROUGH
Peterborough
NORFOLK
Gt. Yarmouth
Limerick
TIPPERARY
Tipperary
KILKENNY
Aberystwyth
Montgomery
Shrewsbury
Wolverhampton
Walsall
Lowestoft
LIMERICK
Clonmel
Carrick-on-Suir
Enniscorthy
Cardigan Bay
SHROPSHIRE
Kidderminster
Birmingham
Coventry
NORTHAMPTON
Rugby
Northampton
HUNTINGDON
CAMBS
Cambridge
Bury St. Edmunds
EAST SUFFOLK
Listowel
Tralee
Rath Luirc
WEXFORD
New Ross
Wexford
RADNOR
Llandrindod Wells
WORCESTER
Worcester
WARWICK
Leamington
Warwick
Stratford
BEDFORD
Bedford
ISLE OF ELY
WEST SUFFOLK
Ipswich
KERRY
Killarney
Mallow
Fermoy
Dungarvan
WATERFORD
Waterford
Rosslare
St. David's Hd.
Fishguard
CARDIGAN
Cardigan
BRECKNOCK
Brecon
HEREFORD
Hereford
Cheltenham
GLOUCESTER
Gloucester
OXFORD
BUCKS
Oxford
Aylesbury
Luton
HERTFORD
St. Albans
Watford
Colchester
Harwich
ESSEX
The Naze
Cahirciveen
MUNSTER
CORK
Cork
Cobh
Kinsale
Carnsore Pt.
St. George's Channel
PEMBROKE
Milford Haven
CARMARTHEN
Carmarthen
Llanelli
MONMOUTH
Monmouth
Cheltenham
Swindon
BERKS
Reading
Windsor
Kingston
LONDON
Chelmsford
Gillingham
Margate
Bandon
Blarney
Youghal
Haverfordwest
GLAMORGAN
Merthyr Tydfil
Newport
RHONDDA
Rhondda
Bristol
Bath
WILTS
SURREY
Maidstone
Canterbury
KENT
Gorey
Bantry
Mallow
Dunmanway
Milford Haven
Swansea
Port Talbot
Cardiff
Newport
Weston-super-Mare
Trowbridge
Aldershot
Guildford
Reigate
Chatham
Gillingham
Dover
Folkestone
Castletown Bere
Bristol Channel
Ilfracombe
Lundy I.
Wells
SOMERSET
Salisbury
Winchester
HANTS
Southampton
Chichester
WEST SUSSEX
EAST SUSSEX
Lewes
Hastings
Eastbourne
C. Clear
Barnstaple
Hartland Point
Taunton
Yeovil
DORSET
Dorchester
Poole
Bournemouth
Newport
Isle of Wight
Portsmouth
Worthing
Brighton
Newhaven
Bude
DEVON
Axminster
Weymouth
CORNWALL
Devonport
Torquay
Exeter
St. Austell
Camborne
Truro
Plymouth
Start Pt.
Penzance
Falmouth
ENGLISH CHANNEL
Land's End
Lizard
Isles of Scilly
Dieppe

ATLANTIC OCEAN
Outer Hebrides
Inner Hebrides

1:4 000 000

50   0   50   100   150 km

The DISTRICTS of Northern Ireland have been numbered
and can be identified by reference to this table.

1	Londonderry	14	Craigavon
2	Limavady	15	Armagh
3	Coleraine	16	Newry & Mourne
4	Ballymoney	17	Banbridge
5	Moyle	18	Down
6	Larne	19	Lisburn
7	Ballymena	20	Antrim
8	Magherafelt	21	Newtownabbey
9	Cookstown	22	Carrickfergus
10	Strabane	23	North Down
11	Omagh	24	Ards
12	Fermanagh	25	Castlereagh
13	Dungannon	26	Belfast

1 Merseyside
2 Greater Manchester
3 West Yorkshire
4 South Yorkshire
5 West Glamorgan
6 Mid Glamorgan
7 South Glamorgan

Orkney Is.   ORKNEY   Westray   N. Ronaldsay   Sanday   Stronsay   Hoy   Kirkwall   South Ronaldsay   Thurso   Wick   HIGHLAND   59   Mainland

Shetland Is.   Unst   Yell   Mainland   SHETLAND   Foula   Lerwick   60

Fair I.

ATLANTIC   OCEAN

WESTERN ISLES   Lewis   Stornoway   Harris   North Minch   North Uist   Benbecula   South Uist   Barra   St. Kilda   Flannan Is.   Outer Hebrides

Pentland Firth   Thurso   Wick   Golspie   Lairg   Ullapool   Invergordon   Dingwall   Nairn   Elgin   Lossiemouth   Moray Firth   Fraserburgh   Banff   Peterhead

HIGHLAND   GRAMPIAN   Inverness   Kingussie   Ballater   Balmoral   Aberdeen   Stonehaven

Portree   Skye   Kyle of Lochalsh   Rhum   Mallaig   Eigg   Fort William   Blair Atholl   Forfar   Montrose   Arbroath

Coll   Tiree   Mull   Staffa   Iona   Oban   Ballachulish   TAYSIDE   Crieff   Perth   Dundee   Cupar   St. Andrews

SCOTLAND   CENTRAL   FIFE   Stirling   Kirkcaldy   Dunfermline   Forth   Dunbar

Inner Hebrides   Firth of Lorn   Colonsay   Lochgilphead   Helensburgh   Greenock   Dumbarton   Edinburgh   Leith   Haddington   Berwick-on-Tweed

Jura   Islay   STRATHCLYDE   Paisley   Glasgow   LOTHIAN   Hamilton   Motherwell   Peebles   Galashiels   NORTH   SEA

Kintyre   Arran   Kilmarnock   Irvine   Ayr   BORDERS   Jedburgh   Hawick   Alnwick

Campbeltown   North Channel   Sanquhar   DUMFRIES AND GALLOWAY   Dumfries   NORTHUMBERLAND   Newcastle   Tynemouth   South Shields   TYNE & WEAR   Sunderland   Gateshead

Malin Hd.   Portrush   Stranraer   Wigtown   Kirkcudbright   Solway Firth   Carlisle   Durham   Hartlepool   CLEVELAND   Middlesbrough   Stockton   Whitby

Tory I.   Coleraine   Larne   Whitehaven   St. Bee's Hd.   CUMBRIA   Appleby   Darlington   Northallerton   Scarborough

Aran   Letterkenny   Londonderry   Ballymena   Mull of Galloway   ISLE OF MAN   Douglas   Barrow   Kendal   NORTH YORKSHIRE   Ripon   Flamborough Hd.

DONEGAL   Lifford   NORTHERN IRELAND   Belfast   Bangor   Lancaster   Morecambe Bay   York

Donegal   Omagh   ULSTER   Lisburn   Downpatrick   Dundrum   Keighley   Beverley   HUMBERSIDE

Donegal Bay   Enniskillen   Armagh   Newry   Blackpool   LANCASHIRE   Burnley   Leeds   Hull   Spurn Hd.

Erris Hd.   Killala Bay   Sligo   MONAGHAN   Clones   Preston   Blackburn   Halifax   Bradford   Wakefield   Scunthorpe   Great Grimsby

Ballina   SLIGO   CAVAN   Louth   Drogheda   IRISH SEA   Bolton   Oldham   Huddersfield   Barnsley   Doncaster   Rotherham

Achill   Castlebar   MAYO   ROSCOMMON   Longford   Cavan   An Uaimh   Liverpool   St. Helens   Salford   Manchester   Sheffield   Lincoln

CONNACHT   Roscommon   WESTMEATH   MEATH   Mullingar   Holyhead   Anglesey   Liverpool   Birkenhead   Stockport   Macclesfield   DERBY   Chesterfield   Mansfield   LINCOLN

Westport   Corrib   GALWAY   Athlone   Llandudno Bay   Rhyl   Flint   Chester   Crewe   DERBY   The Wash

Connemara   Galway   OFFALY   Tullamore   DUBLIN   Dublin   Dún Laoghaire   Bray   Caernarfon   Denbigh   CHESHIRE   Stoke-on-Trent   Derby   NOTTS   Nottingham   Boston

Galway Bay   Athenry   KILDARE   Birr   Port Laoise   Caernarfon Bay   GWYNEDD   CLWYD   Wrexham   STAFFORD   Grantham   Kings Lynn   NORFOLK   Norwich

CLARE   Ennis   LAOIS   CARLOW   WICKLOW   Wicklow   Dolgellau   Stafford   LEICESTER   Gt. Yarmouth   Lowestoft

Kilrush   Nenagh   Carlow   Arklow   Cardigan Bay   Shrewsbury   SHROPSHIRE   Welshpool   Wolverhampton   Walsall   Coventry   Leicester   Peterborough

Shannon   Listowel   LIMERICK   Thurles   Kilkenny   Aberystwyth   POWYS   Birmingham   WARWICK   NORTHAMPTON   Huntingdon   CAMBRIDGE   Cambridge   SUFFOLK   Bury St. Edmunds

M   Tralee   Limerick   TIPPERARY   KILKENNY   Cardigan   Kidderminster   Warwick   Leamington   Northampton   Wellingborough   Bedford   Ipswich

KERRY   Killarney   Tipperary   Clonmel   Carrick-on-Suir   New Ross   Wexford   DYFED   Llandrindod Wells   HEREFORD WORCESTER AND   Worcester   Stratford-on-Avon   BEDFORD   Buckingham   Huntingdon   Colchester   Harwich   The Naze

Mallow   Fermoy   WATERFORD   Waterford   St. David's Hd.   Fishguard   Cardigan   Hereford   Cheltenham   Gloucester   Monmouth   Luton   HERTFORD   Hertford   St. Albans   Watford   ESSEX   Chelmsford

MUNSTER   CORK   Dungarvan   Brecon   Carmarthen   Llanelli   Merthyr Tydfil   Rhondda   GWENT   Newport   GLOUCESTER   Swindon   BERKS   Windsor   Slough   LONDON   Southend

Killarney   Blarney   Cork   Youghal   Milford Haven   Pembroke   Swansea   Port Talbot   Cardiff   AVON   Bath   Reading   Aldershot   SURREY   Kingston   Chatham   Gillingham   Margate

C. Clear   Bandon   Kinsale   Cork Harbour   Cobh   St. George's Channel   Carnsore Pt.   Rosslare   Weston-super-Mare   Wells   Bristol   WILTS   Trowbridge   Salisbury   Winchester   Guildford   Reigate   Maidstone   KENT   Ashford   Dover   Folkestone

Bantry   Bristol Channel   Ilfracombe   SOMERSET   Taunton   Yeovil   HANTS   Southampton   Chichester   WEST SUSSEX   EAST SUSSEX   Lewes   Hastings   Eastbourne

Lundy   Barnstaple   Bude   DEVON   DORSET   Dorchester   Poole   Newport   ISLE OF WIGHT   Portsmouth   Worthing   Brighton   Newhaven

Hartland Point   Exeter   Axminster   Weymouth   Bournemouth

CORNWALL   St. Austell   Truro   Devonport   Plymouth   Torquay   Start Pt.   ENGLISH CHANNEL

Penzance   Camborne   Falmouth   Land's End   Lizard   Isles of Scilly   Dieppe

Projection : Conical with two standard parallels

West from Greenwich   East from Greenwich   COPYRIGHT. GEORGE PHILIP & SON. LTD.

1:1 000 000

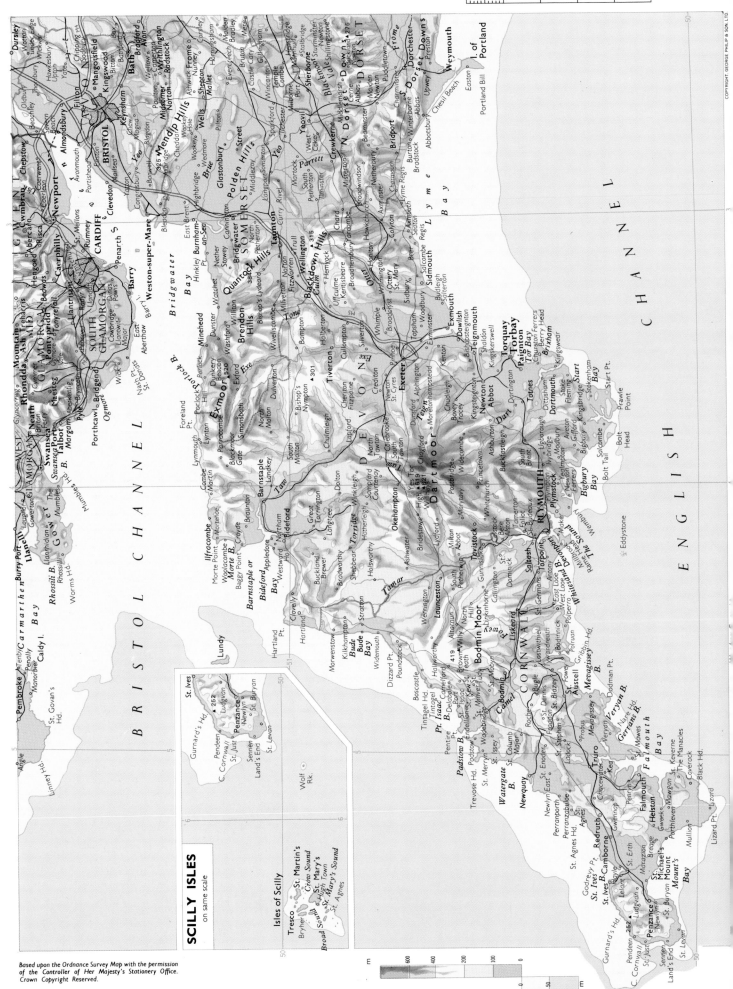

SCILLY ISLES
on same scale

Isles of Scilly

Based upon the Ordnance Survey Map with the permission of the Controller of Her Majesty's Stationery Office. Crown Copyright Reserved.

1:1 000 000

10 0 10 20 30 40 km

The Skerries
Carmel Head
Cemaes Bay
Amlwch
Wylfa Head
Llanfechell
Parys Mt.
128
Dulas B.
Moelfre
Holyhead
Holyhead B.
Holy I.
Bodedern
Valley
Gwalchmai
Llangefni
Pentraeth
Beaumaris
Red Wharf B.
Puffin I.
Conwy B.
Gt. Ormes Hd.
Llandudno
Lit. Ormes Hd.
Rhos-on-Sea
Colwyn Bay
Rhyl
Prestatyn
Newborough
Aberffraw
Malltraeth B.
Menai Str.
Waeofawr
Penmaenmawr
Deganwy
Conwy
Colwyn
Abergele
Rhuddlan
Mostyn
Holywell
Flint
LIVERPOOL
Bootle
St. Helens
Prescot
Newton le Willows
Warrington
Hoylake
Wallasey
West Kirby
Birkenhead
Bebington
MERSEYSIDE
Huyton
Garston
Widnes
Runcorn
Bromborough
Neston
Ellesmere Port
Stanley
Helsby
Frodsham
Weaverham
Northwich
Winsford

Caernarfon Bay
Penygroes
Clynnog-fawr
Nefyn
564
Llanaelhaiarn
Tudweiliog
Llanllyfni
Lleyn Peninsula
Rhiw
Aberdaron
Braich-y-pwll
Bardsey Sd.
Bardsey I.
Porth Neigwl
Abersoch
St. Tudwal's Is.
Trwyn Cilan

Bangor
Llanfairfechan
Bethesda
Carneddau
Llewelyn
1062
Caernarfon
Llanberis
Snowdon
1085
Dolwyddelan
Llanrwst
Betws-y-coed
Capel Curig
GWYNDD
Blaenau Ffestiniog
Ffestiniog
Maentwrog
Talsarnau
Porthmadog
Criccieth
Pwllheli
Llanbedrog
Harlech
Llanbedr
Barmouth
Fairbourne
Llwyngwril
Llangelynin
892
Cader Idris
Tal-y-llyn
Llanelltyd
Dolgellau
Arenig Fawr
853
Trawsfynydd
Llanuwchllyn
L. Tegid
(Bala)
Bala
Berwyn Mts.
827
Llandderfel
Corwen
Llangollen
Glyn Ceiriog
CLWYD
St. Asaph
Denbigh
Henllan
Ruthin
Mold
Buckley
Wrexham
Whitchurch
CHESHIRE
Chester
Tarporley
Nantwich
Malpas
Audlem
Market Drayton
Wem
Ellesmere
Oswestry
Whittington
Myddle
Shawbury
Shrewsbury
Wellington
The Wrekin
407

Aberdovey
(Aberdyfi)
Tywyn
Cardigan Bay
Aberystwyth
Rheidol
Devil's Bridge
Ystwyth
Borth
Talybont
752
Plynlimon
(Pumlumon)
Llanrhystyd
Llanon
New Quay
Aberaeron
Mynydd Bach
361
Tregaron
Llanarth
Llangranog
Aberporth
Cemaes Hd.
Cardigan
St. Dogmaels
Nevern
Newport
Dinas Hd.
Fishguard B.
Strumble Hd.
Goodwick
Fishguard
Mynydd Preselly
536
Letterston
Mathry
Solva
St. David's
Ramsey I.
Haverfordwest
Broad Haven
Milford Haven
Neyland
Pembroke
Tenby
Caldy I.
Manorbier
Caldy I.
St. Govan's Hd.

POWYS
Welshpool
Montgomery
Newtown
Llanidloes
Rhayader
Llandrindod Wells
Builth Wells
Knighton
Presteigne
Kington
Leominster
Hereford
HEREFORD AND WORCESTER
Weobley
Hay-on-Wye
Brecon
Black Mountains
811
Brecon Beacons
886
Abergavenny
Monmouth
Ross-on-Wye
Crickhowell
Ebbw Vale
Blaenavon
Tredegar
Merthyr Tydfil
Aberdare
Pontypool
Cwmbran
GWENT
Chepstow
Newport
Caerphilly
CARDIFF
Penarth
Barry
Pontypridd
MID GLAMORGAN
Rhondda
Bridgend
Porthcawl
SOUTH GLAMORGAN
Cowbridge
Llantwit Major
WEST GLAMORGAN
Neath
Swansea
Port Talbot
Margam
The Mumbles
Gower
Rhossili B.
Worms Hd.
Porthcawl
Llanelli
Burry Port
Pembrey
Ammanford
Carmarthen
Carmarthen Bay
Kidwelly
Laugharne
St. Clears
Whitland
Narberth
DYFED
Newcastle Emlyn
Lampeter
Llandovery
Llandeilo
Mynydd Du (Black Mtn.)
Forest Fawr
Mynydd Eppynt

BRISTOL CHANNEL

Weston-super-Mare
Bridgwater Bay
Mendip Hills
325
BRISTOL
AVON
Clevedon
Portishead
Avonmouth
Almondsbury
Filton

m
1000
800
600
400
200
100
0
50
100
m

Motorways
Motorways under construction

West from Greenwich

1:1 000 000

10   0   10   20   30   40 km

Continuation
Northwards
on same scale

NORTH

SEA

TYNE AND WEAR

NORTHUMBERLAND

BORDERS

Cheviot Hills

HADRIAN'S WALL

Newcastle-upon-Tyne

Berwick-upon-Tweed

CLEVELAND

North York
Moors

Cleveland Hills

YORKSHIRE

Vale of Pickering

Yorkshire Wolds

HUMBERSIDE

Holderness

KINGSTON-UPON-HULL

LEEDS

WEST YORKSHIRE

SOUTH YORKSHIRE

SHEFFIELD

DERBYSHIRE

NOTTINGHAM

LINCOLNSHIRE

Lincolnshire Wolds

The Wash

NORFOLK

West from Greenwich   0   East from Greenwich

COPYRIGHT. GEORGE PHILIP & SON. LTD.

Based upon the Ordnance Survey Map with the permission
of the Controller of Her Majesty's Stationery Office.
Crown Copyright Reserved.

CIB

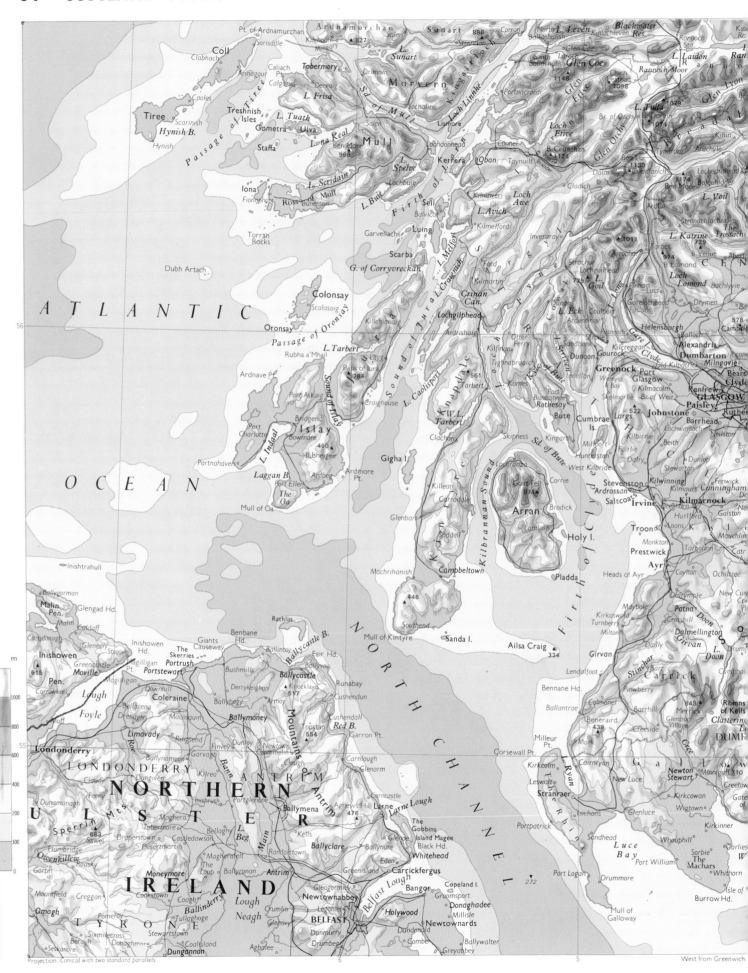

1:1 000 000

10   0   10   20   30   40 km

NORTH

SEA

Motorways

Motorways under construction

SHETLAND ISLANDS
on same scale

Hermaness
Heroldswick
Balta
Unst
Baltasound
Bluemull Sd.
Cullivoe
Uyeasound
Mu Ness
Ramna
Stacks
Whale
Firth
Fetlar
Point of Fethaland
Mid Yell
The Snap
The
Faither
North
Roe
Yell
Ronas Hill
450
Burravoe
Esha
Ness
Hillswick
Lunna Ness
St. Magnus
Bay
SHETLAND
Skaw
Taing
Out
Skerries
Muckle Roe
Brae
Voe
Whalsay
Papa
Stour
The Hàa
Papa
Sandness
S Nesting
Bay
Sd. of
Papa
Walls
Score Hd.
Vaila
Easter
Skeld
Lerwick
Gruting Voe
I. of Noss
Scalloway
Bressay
Hamnavoe
Bard Hd.
West
Burra
293
Bressay Sd.
Helli
Ness
Kettla Ness
Hoswick
Mousa
Haa
St. Ninian's I.
Scousburgh
Boddam
Fitful Hd.
B. of Quendale
Sumburgh Hd.

Butt of Lewis
Port of Ness
South Dell
Ness
Borve
Cellar Hd.
Barvas
Tolsta Hd.
North Tolsta
Carloway
Shawbost
Back
Tiumpan Hd.
Broad Bay
291
Newmarket
Portnaguiran
Great
Bernera
Uig
Callanish
Stornoway
Melbost
Eye
Peninsula
Bayble
Gallan Hd.
L.
Roag
Lewis
Chicken Hd.
Gisla
575
Lochs
Loch
Langavat
Balallan
L.
Erisort
Park
Crossbost
Cromore
Aird Brenish
Kintarvay
Gravir
Kebock Hd.
Scarp
Husinish
Husinish
Pt.
N. Harris
L. Shell
Ardvourlie
Castle
571
Beinn Mhor
759
W. L. Tarbert
Taransay
Ardhasig
L. Seaforth
Sd. of Shiant
Shiant Is.
Tarbert
WESTERN
Sd. of Taransay
Harris
Scalpay
Toe Hd.
H. L. Tarbert
Scarastavore
S. Harris
Pabbay
Leverburgh
Sd. of Pabbay
Berneray
Rodel
Renish Pt.
Rubha Hunish
Haskeir Is.
ISLES
Kilmaluag
Griminish Pt.
Sollas
Vaternish Pt.
Lochmaddy
North Uist
L. Maddy
Loch
Snizort
Uig
Rona
Sound of
Monach
Paible
Bayhead
Carinish
L. Eport
Dunvegan
Head
Stein
Waternish
Trotternish
Sound of Raasay
Monach Is.
347
Eaval
Vaternish
The Storr
719
Baleshare
Milovaig
Lepnin
Grimsay
Ronay
Dunvegan
Roskhill
Raasay
Appelcross
Forest
Gramsdale
488
Benbecula
Wiay
Bagh nam
Faoileann
Portree
Inner Sound
Kishorn
Ardivachar Pt.
L. Bee
Bracadale
Coillore
Crowlin
Is.
Carron
Howmore
South
Hecla
L. Harport
Scalpay
Rubha
Ardvule
Uist
620
B. Mhor
Fernilea
Carbost
Drynoch
Minginish
Sligachan
Kyle of
Lochalsh
L. Eynort
Cuillin
Hills
Bla Bheinn
528
Broadford
1009
Glenbrittle
Daliburgh
Lochboisdale
Rubh an
Dunain
Soay Sd.
Elgol
Glenelg
L. Boisdale
Soay
Soay
L. Scavaig
L. Eishort
Eilean
Iarmain
Teangue
Cuillin Sound
Sound of Barra
Sd. of Eriskay
Canna
Armadale
Sound of Sleat
Greian
Hd.
Eriskay
Sanday
Ardvasar
Barra
384
Kinloch
Pt. of
Sleat
Castlebay
Bruernish Pt.
Rhum
810
Mallaig
1040
Vatersay
Eigg
L. Nevis
Sandray
394
Pabbay
Sd. of Eigg
Sd. of Arisaig
Mingulay
Muck
Shona
Berneray
Barra Head
Moidart
L. Moidart
Pt. of Ardnamurchan
Kilchoan
527
Sunart
Sorisdale
Ardgour
888
Clabbach
Coll
Salen
Arinagour
Caliach
Tobermory
Drimnin
Arnagour
Calgary
Dervaig
Tiree
Treshnish
Isles
L. Frisa
Morvern
Scarinish
L. Tuath
Cleos
Hynish B.
Passage of Tiree
Lismore I.
Hynish

Inner

Hebrides

Outer

Hebrides

Little Minch

North Minch

North

Uist

Sound of Harris

Sound of Barra

Cuillin Sound

Eddrachillis
Bay
L. Inchard
L. Laxford
Handa I.
C. W
Pt. of Stoer
Drumbeg
Stoer
Rhu Coigach
Enard
Bay
Lochinver
Summer
Isles
L. Lurgainn
L. Broom
Gruinard B.
Greenstone
Pt.
Ullapool
Mellon
Charles
Aultbea
An Teallach
1062
L. na Sealga
Melvaig
L.
Ewe
Fionn
Loch
Poolewe
Longa I.
Henderson
981
Slioch
L. Gairloch
Gairloch
Talladale
Kerrysdale
L. Maree
Kinlochewe
1055
Torridon
L. Torridon
Fasagh
Shieldaig
Applecross
Coulags
Carron
Lochcarron
Stromemore
Plockton
Strome Ferry
Kyle of
Lochalsh
Dornie
Kyleakin
L. Alsh
The Saddle
1010
Glen Shiel
L. Hourn
Knoydart
L. Quoich
882
Glen Ga
L. Arkaig
Loch Morar
L. Eil
882
Kinlochmoidart
Strontian
Sunart

m
1000
800
600
400
200
100
0
m
50
100

1 : 1 000 000

10   0   10   20   30   40 km

ORKNEY ISLANDS
on same scale

Pentland Firth

Stroma
Dunnet Hd.
Holborn Hd.
Scrabster
Dunnet B.
Dounreay
THURSO
Reay
Strathy
Portskerra
Melvich
Craigtown
Dalhalvaig
Forsinain
Forsinard

Mull Hd.
Papa
Westray
Noup Hd.
Pierowall
Hollandstoun
Dennis Hd.
N. Ronaldsay
N. Ronaldsay Firth
Start Pt.
Westray
The North Sound
Berst Ness
Rapness
Overbister
Sanday
Sacquoy Hd.
Eday
Sanday Sound
Wasbister
Rousay
Papa Stronsay
Eynhallow Sd.
Brinyan
Whitehall
Brough Hd.
Twatt
Egilsay
Wyre
Stronsay
Redland
Gairsay
Lamb Hd.
L. of Harray
Dounby
Balfour
Shapinsay
Auskerry
Voy
Finstown
Wide F.
Y Firth
ORK
L. of Stenness
Kirkwall
Shapinsay Sd.
Stromness
Mull Hd.
Graemsay Sd.
Deerness
Hoy
Orphir
Deer Sd.
Gritley
Old Man of Hoy
Ward Hill
St. Mary's
Pt. of Ayre
Copinsay
Rora Hd.
477
Rose Ness
Rackwick
Scapa Flow
Burray
Lyness
Flotta
St. Margaret's Hope
Hurliness
S. Walls
Tor Ness
Swona
South Ronaldsay
Cleat
Pentland Firth
Dunnet Hd.
Stroma
Pentland Skerries
Mey
John o' Groats
Canisbay
Duncansby Hd.

Stroma
John o'
Groats
Mey
Dunnet
Canisbay
Duncansby Hd.
Sortat
Freswick
Castletown
Nybster
Halkirk
Keiss
Olgrinmore
Watten
Reiss
Noss Head
Sinclair's B.
Mybster
Staxigoe
WICK
Wick
Achavanich
Thrumster
Ulbster
Lybster
Latheron
Braemore
Dunbeath
Morven
705
Kinbrace
Berriedale
Kildonan
Ousdale
Ord of Caithness
B. Dhorain
628
Helmsdale

Whiten Hd.
Durness
L. Eriboll
Heilam
Kyle of Tongue
Tongue
Strathy Pt.
Borgie
B. Loyal
763
Loch Loyal
Ben Hope
Loch Hope
Strath Naver
Naver
Strath Halladale
Strathmore
B. Hee
L. Naver
Altnaharra
B. Klibreck
961
L. nan Clar
Loch Shin
Lairg
Morven
Shin
Torroboll
Inveran
Bonarbridge
Kincardine
Culrain
Clashmore
Dornoch
Tarbat Ness
Golspie
Embo
Fleet
L. Fleet
Brora
L. Brora
Brora
Oykel
Rosehall
Auchness
Easter Ross
Rosemarkie
B. Tharsuinn
692
Alness
Portmahomack
Balintore
Fearn
Tain
Edderton
Dornoch Firth
Kilmuir
Nigg
Balnapaling
Moray Firth
Nairn
Burghead
Branderburgh
Spey
Findochty
Portknockie
Troup Hd.
Rosehearty
Kinnairds Hd.
B. Vyvyis
1045
Invergordon
Cromarty Firth
Cromarty
Lossiemouth B.
Buckie
Cullen
Portsoy
Banff
Macduff
Fraserburgh
Inverallochy
Ross
Dingwall
Black Isle
Avoch
Campbelltown
Burghead B.
Findhorn
Hopeman
Spey Bay
Garmouth
Portgordon
Gardenstown
New Aberdour
St. Combs
Strathpeffer
Nth. Kessock
Forres
Kinloss
Lhanbryde
Fochabers
Witchburn
New Pitsligo
Rattray Hd.
Contin
Cononbridge
Beauly F.
Auldearn
Elgin
Keith
Aberchirder
Newbyth
Strichen
Crimond
Orrin Muir of Ord
Beauly
Inverness
Culloden Moor
Littlemill
Dallas
Kellas
Rothes
Fortrie
Cuminestown
Maud
Longside
St. Fergus
Strath Glass
Caledonian Canal
Nairn
Cawdor
Craigellachie
Charlestown of Aberlour
Huntly
Turriff
Old Deer
Boddam
Peterhead
The Aird
Ferness
Archiestown
Badenscoth
Deveron
Buchan
Buchan Ness
Milton
Moy
Findhorn
Dufftown
Laggan
Rhynie
Colpy
Rothienorman
Ythan
Ellon
Cruden Bay
Stray
Dores
Fort
Carn Glas-choire
659
Grantown-on-Spey
Ardwell
Insch
Tarves
Formartine
Newburgh
Foyers
Duntelchaig
Tarness
Tomatin
Dulnan Bridge
Delichrach
840
Cabrach
Lumsden
Oldmeldrum
Newmachar
Ertrogie
Carrbridge
Nethy Bridge
Tomintoul
The Buck
721
GRAMPIAN
Inverurie
Dyce
Meallfuarvonie
698
Carn na Saobhaidhe
Monadhliath Mts.
810
White Bridge
Aviemore
Boat of Garten
803
Tomnavoulin
Carn Mor
Strathdon
Don
Alford
Kemnay
Monymusk
Kintore
Balmedie
Aberdeen
Glen Moriston
Carn Ban
941
Alvie
Kincraig
Avon
Ladder Hills
Mar
Morven
872
Tarland
Lumphanan
Torphins
Ordhead
Bucksburn
Bridge of Don
Girdle Ness
Augustus
Kingussie
Cairn Gorm
1245
B. Avon
1171
Echt
Peterculter
Cults
Invergarry
Newtonmore
Ruthven
Kincraig
Spey
Dee
Ordie
Cove Bay
Laggan
Braeriach
1295
B. Macdhui
1311
Braemar
Crathie
Battater
Aboyne
Banchory
Dee
Commachmore
Creag Meagaidh
1128
Balmoral Forest
1154
Lochnagar
Mt. Keen
938
Strachan
Newtonhill
Muchalls
Dalwhinnie
Dee
Braemar
Glas Maol
1067
North Esk
Auchenblae
Stonehaven
B. Dearg
1008
Forest of Atholl
Braes of Angus
Glen Esk
Howe of the Mearns
Inverbervie
B. Alder
1143
Beinn a' Ghlo
1121
Clova
Fettercairn
Laurencekirk
Gourdon
Garry
Blair Atholl
Glen Shee
Isla
Rottal
Edzell
Johnshaven
Spean
Glen Garry
Errochty
Kirkmichael
South Esk
Marykirk
St. Cyrus
Rannoch Sta.
Kinloch Rannoch
Pitlochry
Brechin
Oykeneae
Dykehead
Montrose
L. Laidon
Tummel
Schichallion
1081
Balnaluig
Kirriemuir
Forfar
Lunan B.
Rannoch Moor
L. Rannoch
Strath Tay
Tummel
Alyth
Friockheim
Inverkeilor
L. Tulla
1029
Loch Tay
Kenmore
Aberfeldy
Dalguise
Blairgowrie
Rattray
Glamis
Marywell
B. Dorain
1074
Glen Lyon
Fearnan
B. Lawers
1214
Dunkeld
Coupar Angus
Sidlaw Hills
455
Carmyllie
Arbroath
Bankfoot
Burrelton
Muirdrum
Carnoustie
West from Greenwich
Dundee
Barry
Monifieth
Buddon Ness
Broughty Ferry

NORTH SEA

1:1 250 000

10   0   10   20   30   40   50 km

ATLANTIC

OCEAN

LEINSTER

MUNSTER

CORK

WICKLOW MOUNTAINS

WEXFORD

KILKENNY

WATERFORD

TIPPERARY

LIMERICK

CLARE

KERRY

Galway Bay

Dingle Bay

Bantry Bay

Cork Harbour

Wexford Harbour

Waterford Harbour

Dungarvan Harbour

Youghal Bay

Clonakilty Bay

Kinsale Harbour

Castlemaine Harbour

Aran Is.
(Galway)

Projection: Conical with two standard parallels

West from Greenwich

Motorways

COPYRIGHT GEORGE PHILIP & SON LTD

1000
800
600
400
200
100
0

m
50
100

1 : 4 000 000

50   0   50   100   150 km

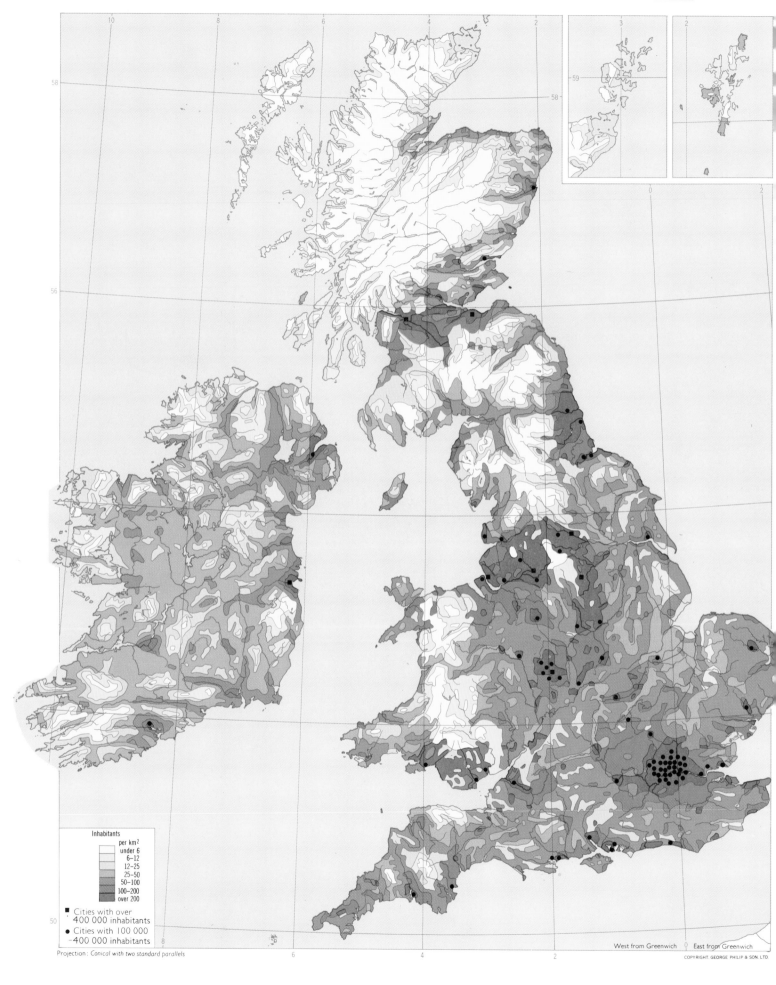

Inhabitants
per km²
under 6
6–12
12–25
25–50
50–100
100–200
over 200

■ Cities with over
400 000 inhabitants

● Cities with 100 000
–400 000 inhabitants

West from Greenwich   East from Greenwich

Projection : Conical with two standard parallels

COPYRIGHT. GEORGE. PHILIP & SON. LTD.

1:5 000 000

50 0 50 100 150 200 km

GERMANY

BELGIUM

LUX.

SWITZERLAND

ITALY

ENGLAND

SPAIN

ANDORRA

Channel Is.

CORSE

Bastia
HAUTE-
Calvi ○ CORSE
Corte 2B
Ajaccio ● CORSE-
DU-SUD 2A
Sartène

COPYRIGHT GEORGE PHILIP & SON LTD

Dunkerque
Calais ○
Boulogne- St-Omer
sur-Mer ● Béthune
Montreuil ○ Lens ○ Douai
PAS- DE- Valenciennes
CALAIS 62 Arras ● NORD 59
Abbeville ○ Cambrai ○ Avesnes-
SOMME Péronne ○ sur-Helpe
Amiens 80 Montdidier ○
Dieppe ○ Beauvais ● OISE
SEINE- Rouen ● 60 Compiègne ○ Laon ● 2
MARITIME Les Andelys ○ Senlis ○ Clermont
76 EURE PARIS Soissons ○
Le Havre Bernay ○ Evreux ● RÉGION
Caen Lisieux ○ 27 Dreux ○ Chartres ●
Bayeux ○ CALVADOS Argentan ○ Mantes- EURE-ET- Pithiviers ○
Cherbourg St-Lô ● 14 Vire ○ ORNE 61 Montagne- LOIR Orléans ●
MANCHE Avranches ○ Alençon ● au-Perche ○ 28 LOIRET 45
Coutances ○ 50 Mayenne ○ MAYENNE Nogent-le- Châteaudun ○
St-Malo ○ Fougères ○ 53 Mamers ○ Rotrou ○ Vendôme ○
St-Brieuc ● Dinan ○ ILLE-ET- Château- SARTHE 72 LOIR- Blois ●
Lannion ○ CÔTES-DU-NORD VILAINE Gontier ○ Le Mans ● ET-CHER
Guingamp ○ 22 Rennes ● 35 Laval ● La Flèche ○ 41
Morlaix ○ Segré ○ MAINE- Saumur ○ Tours ●
Brest FINISTÈRE Redon ○ Angers ● ET-LOIRE INDRE- Chinon ○
Châteaulin ○ 29 Vannes ● Châteaubriant ○ 49 ET-LOIRE
Quimper ● MORBIHAN LOIRE- Cholet ○ 37
Pontivy ○ 56 ATLANTIQUE Bressuire ○ Châtellerault ○
Lorient ○ Nazaire 44 DEUX- Parthenay ○
Nantes ● SÈVRES 79 Poitiers ●
La Roche- 79 VIENNE
sur-Yon ● Fontenay- Niort ● 86
Les Sables VENDÉE le-Comte ○
d'Olonne 85 La Rochelle ●

MOSELLE 57 Forbach Sarreguemines
Metz ● Sarrebourg Wissembourg BAS- Haguenau
Thionville ○ Château- RHIN Molsheim stein
Briey ○ Salins ○ 67
Verdun-sur- Nancy ● MEURTHE- Strasbourg ●
MEUSE Meuse Commercy ○ ET-MOSELLE Sélestat ○
55 Bar-le-Duc ● Neufchâteau ○ St-Dié ○ Ribeauvillé ○
St- Vitry-le- 54 VOSGES Colmar ●
Ste- Ménehould ○ François ○ Epinal ● 88 HAUT- Guebwiller ○
Reims ○ Châlons- Chaumont ● RHIN Mulhouse
Château- sur-Marne HAUTE- Vesoul ● Lure ○ 68 Altkirch ○
Thierry ○ MARNE Langres ○ 52 Luxeuil ○ TERR.-DE-
Meaux ○ 51 Bar-sur- SAÔNE 70 Belfort BELFORT
Provins ○ MARNE Aube ○ Besançon ● 90
SEINE-ET- Nogent-sur-Seine ○ CÔTE-D'OR Montbéliard
MARNE Troyes ● Châtillon- Dijon ● DOUBS 25
Melun ● AUBE 10 sur-Seine ○ 21 Dole ○ Pontarlier ○
ESSONNE Sens ○ Avallon ○ Beaune ○ Lons-le-Saunier ●
Montargis ○ YONNE Clamecy ○ Autun ○ Châlon- JURA 39
Auxerre ● 89 NIÈVRE Château- sur-Saône St-Claude ○
Chartres Château- 58 Chinon ○ SAÔNE-ET-LOIRE Louhans ○
Romorantin- roux 36 Nevers ● Cosne- 71 Mâcon ●
Lanthenay ○ CHER sur-Loire ○ Charolles ○ Bourg-en-Bresse ●
LOIR- Bourges ● St-Amand- Moulins ● Roanne ○ AIN 1
ET-CHER 18 Mont-Rond ○ ALLIER Villefranche-
Loches ○ Issoudun ○ 3 Vichy ○ sur-Saône ○
INDRE Châteauroux ● Montluçon ○ Thiers ○ LOIRE Lyon ●
Le Blanc ○ Montmorillon ○ La Châtre ○ Riom ○ 42 RHÔNE
Montmorillon ○ CREUSE Clermont- 69 Vienne ○
Guéret ● Aubusson ○ Ferrand ● PUY-DE-DÔME St-Étienne ●
Confolens ○ 23 Ussel ○ 63 Issoire ○ Montbrison ○
HAUTE- Bellac ○ CORRÈZE Brioude ○ Annonay ○
VIENNE Limoges ● 19 Ambert ○ Yssingeaux ○ La Tour-
87 Rochechouart ○ Tulle ● Mauriac ○ HAUTE- du-Pin ○
CHARENTE St-Jean- Brive-la- CANTAL LOIRE Belley ○
Angoulême ● d'Angély ○ Périgueux ● Gaillarde ○ 15 43 Le Puy ● HAUTE-SAVOIE
16 Nontron ○ DORDOGNE Aurillac ● St-Flour ○ Privas ● 74 Annecy ●
Cognac ○ 24 Sarlat- Figeac ○ ARDÈCHE Valence ● St-Julien-en- Thonon-
CHARENTE- Jonzac ○ la-Canéda ○ Gourdon ○ 07 Genevois ○ les-Bains
MARITIME Bergerac ○ LOT Rodez ● Die ○ DRÔME Chambéry ● Bonneville ○
17 Blaye ○ Libourne ○ 46 Cahors ● AVEYRON Mende ● 26 SAVOIE St-Jean-de-
Saintes ○ Langon ○ Marmande ○ Villefranche- 12 LOZÈRE 48 Nyons ○ 73 Maurienne ○
Rochefort ○ Bordeaux ● de-Rouergue ○ Florac ○ Gap ● Albertville ○
Lesparre- GIRONDE LOT-ET- Villeneuve- Millau ○ Le Vigan ○ Largentière ○ HAUTES- Grenoble ●
Médoc ○ 33 GARONNE sur-Lot ○ Montauban ● Albi ● Alès ○ ISÈRE Briançon ○
Dax ○ Mont-de- 47 Agen ● TARN- TARN Castres ○ GARD Lodève ○ 38 ALPES Digne ●
Bayonne ○ Marsan ● Nérac ○ ET- 81 Castelnaudary ○ Nîmes ● Montpellier ● 05 Barcelonnette ○
LANDES Condom ○ GARONNE Castres Lodève ○ HÉRAULT Grasse ○ ALPES-DE-
Oloron- 40 Mirande ○ GERS 82 Auch ● Toulouse ● 34 Béziers ○ HAUTE-PROVENCE
Ste-Marie ○ PYRÉNÉES- GERS HAUTE- Muret ○ AUDE Narbonne ○ 04 VAR Nice ●
Pau ● ATLANTIQUES 32 GARONNE Carcassonne ● Avignon ● VAUCLUSE Draguignan ○ ALPES-
64 HAUTES- St- 31 Pamiers ○ 11 Limoux ○ 84 Apt ○ 83 MARITIMES
Argelès- PYRÉNÉES Gaudens ○ ARIÈGE Foix ● Forcalquier ○ Castellane ○ 06
Gazost ○ Tarbes ● 65 St- 09 PYRÉNÉES- Aix-en- Toulon ●
Bagnères- Girons ○ ORIENTALES Arles ○ Provence ○ Marseille ●
de-Bigorre ○ Céret ○ 66 Perpignan ● BOUCHES- VAR 83
Prades ○ DU-RHÔNE 13

PARIS RÉGION
1:2 500 000

Pontoise ● VAL-D'OISE Montmorency ○
Mantes- 95 Bobigny ● SEINE-ST-
la-Jolie ○ Nanterre ● PARIS DENIS 93
St-Germain- 78 HAUTS- Nogent-s.-M. ○
en-Laye ○ Versailles ● DE- 75 Créteil ● VAL-DE-MARNE
YVELINES SEINE 94 Palaiseau ○
Rambouillet ○ Évry ● 91 Étampes ○
ESSONNE

——— Département boundary
4 Département number
⊙ Préfecture
○ Sous-préfecture

ENGLAND

Bideford
Bampton
Yeovil
Sherborne
Romsey
Eastleigh
Southampton
Fareham
Chichester
South Downs
Lewes
Battle
Hastings
Midhurst
Hayward's Heath
Rother
Tenterden
Hythe
Exeter
Dartmoor
Dorchester
Lymington
Cowes
Portsmouth
Wight
Ryde
Bognor Regis
Worthing
Brighton
Eastbourne
Bexhill
Beachy Head
Newhaven
Dungeness
Weymouth
Bournemouth
Poole
Newport
Sandown
Ventnor
Plymouth
Torquay
Paignton
Brixham
Dartmouth
Kingsbridge
Start Pt.
Lyme Bay
Portland Bill
Land's End
Lizard Pt.

English Channel

CHANNEL ISLANDS
Casquets
Alderney
Guernsey
St. Peter Port
Herm
Sark
Jersey
St. Helier
Roches Douvres
Barnouic
Les Minquiers

Cap de la Hague
Cherbourg
Pointe de Barfleur
Cap d'Antifer
Étretat
Fécamp
St-Valéry-en-Caux
Dieppe

Baie de la Seine
Le Havre
Caen
CALVADOS
Bayeux

Golfe de St-Malo
Granville
Cancale
Le Mont-St-Michel
Dinan
St-Brieuc
Rennes

Brest
Ile d'Ouessant
Mer d'Iroise
Morlaix
Quimper
CÔTES DU NORD
Lorient
Vannes
Nantes
Angers
Le Mans

Baie de Bourgneuf
Ile de Noirmoutier
Ile d'Yeu

La Roche-sur-Yon
Cholet
Poitiers
Châtellerault

Les Sables-d'Olonne
Luçon
Fontenay-le-Comte
Niort
DEUX-SÈVRES

La Rochelle
Ile de Ré
Rochefort
Ile d'Oléron
AUNIS
Saintes
Cognac
Angoulême
ANGOUMOIS
CHARENTE

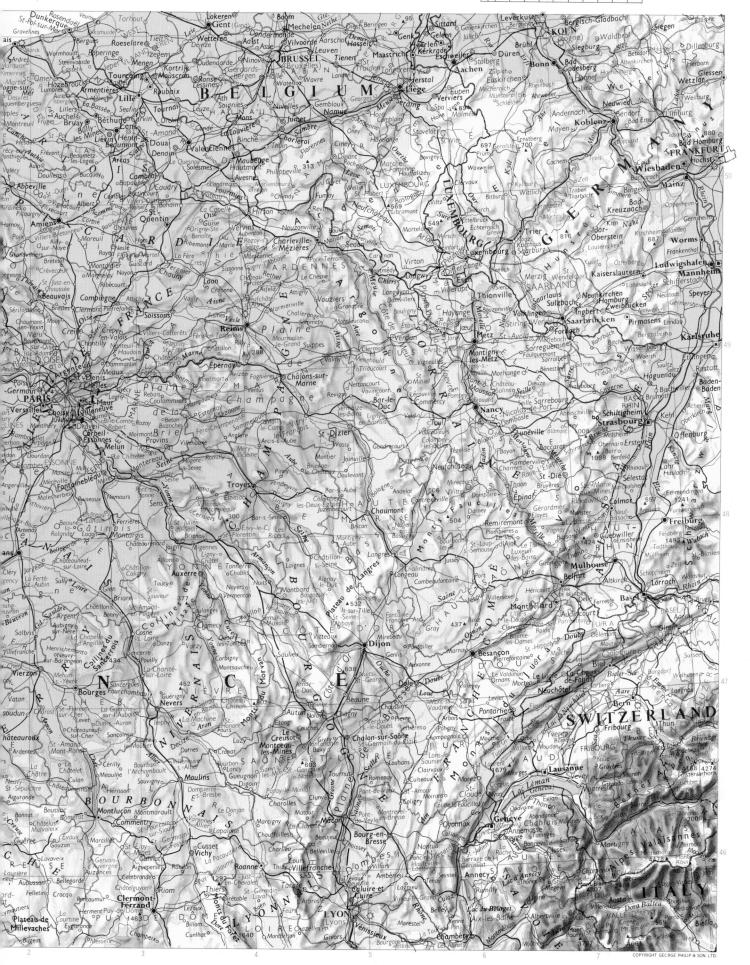

1:2 500 000

10 0 10 20 30 40 50 60 70 80 90 100 km

1 : 2 500 000

10 0 10 20 30 40 50 60 70 80 90 100 km

45

SWITZERLAND

FRANCE

ITALY

CORSICA

LIGURIAN SEA

MEDITERRANEAN SEA

Golfo di Génova

Lion

Lac Léman

LYON
St-Étienne
Grenoble
Valence
Avignon
Marseille
Toulon
Nice
MONACO
Monte-Carlo
Cannes
Antibes
Fréjus
St-Raphaël
Ste-Maxime
St-Tropez
Hyères
ILES D'HYÈRES
San Remo
Imperia (Maurizio-Oneglia)
Savona
GÉNOVA (Genova)
La Spézia
Carrara
Massa
Livorno
Bastia
Elba
Calvi
Corte
HAUTE-CORSE
CORSE DU SUD
Ajaccio
Bonifacio

Genève
Lausanne
Bern
FRIBOURG
Luzern
Schwyz
Milano (Milan)
Monza
Bergamo
Brescia
Torino
Novara
Pavia
Asti
Alessandria
Cuneo
Chambéry
Annecy
Gap

MAURES

ALPES-DE-HAUTE-PROVENCE
ALPES-MARITIMES
PROVENCE
VAUCLUSE
SAVOIE
HAUTE-SAVOIE

COPYRIGHT GEORGE PHILIP & SON LTD.

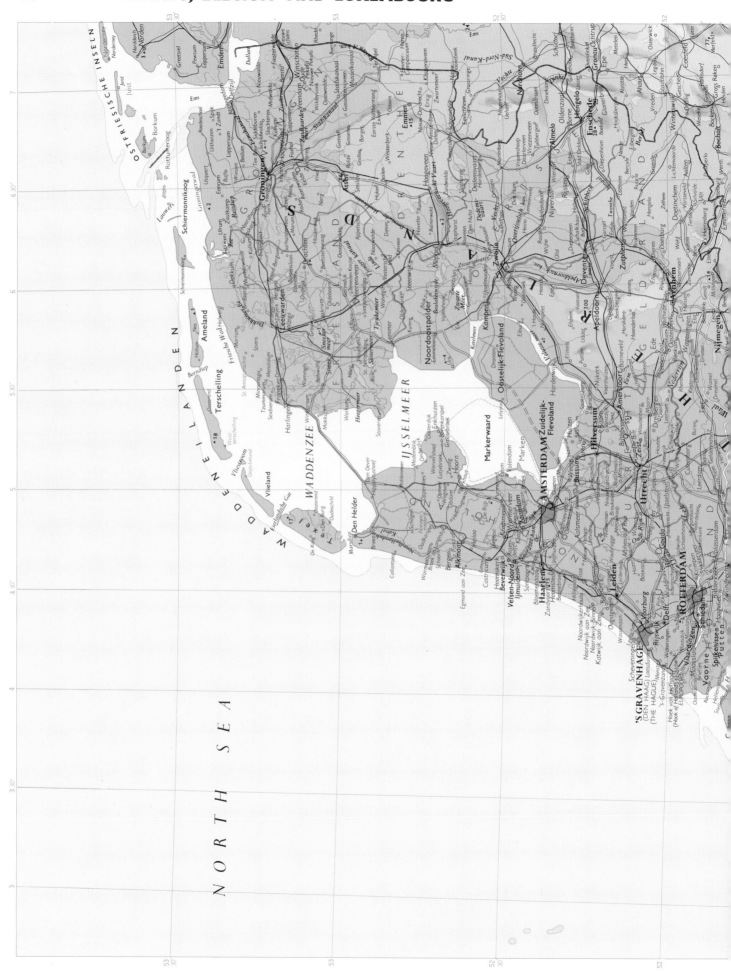

NORTH SEA

OSTFRIESISCHE INSELN

WADDEN EILANDEN

WADDENZEE

IJSSELMEER

GRONINGEN

FRIESLAND

DRENTHE

OVERIJSSEL

GELDERLAND

NOORD-HOLLAND

ZUID-HOLLAND

UTRECHT

AMSTERDAM

ROTTERDAM

'S GRAVENHAGE
(DEN HAAG)
(THE HAGUE)

Groningen

Leeuwarden

Assen

Zwolle

Emmen

Enschede

Hengelo

Apeldoorn

Deventer

Zutphen

Arnhem

Nijmegen

Amersfoort

Hilversum

Utrecht

Haarlem

Leiden

Delft

Schiedam

Den Helder

Alkmaar

Hoorn

Terschelling

Ameland

Schiermonnikoog

Vlieland

Texel

Emden

Borkum

Juist

Norderney

Noordoostpolder

Oostelijk-Flevoland

Zuidelijk-Flevoland

Markerwaard

1:1 250 000

10 5 0   10   20   30   40   50 km

Projection: Conical with two standard parallels

East from Greenwich

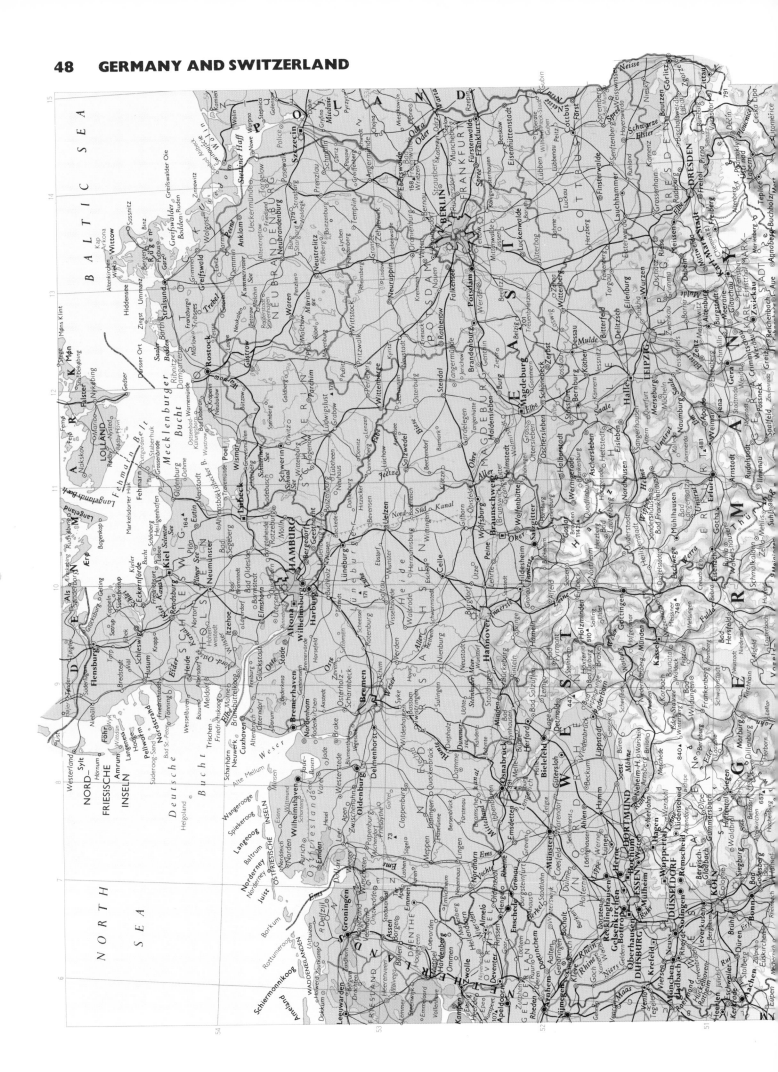

1 : 2 500 000

10 0 10 20 30 40 50 60 70 80 90 100 km

CZECHOSLOVAKIA

LUXEMBOURG

PRAHA (PRAGUE)

FRANKFURT

Wiesbaden
Mainz

Bayreuth

Nürnberg
Fürth

Regensburg

Passau

Linz

Salzburg

Innsbruck

MÜNCHEN (Munich)

Augsburg

STUTTGART

Karlsruhe

Mannheim
Heidelberg

Ulm

Neu-Ulm

Memmingen

Kempten

Bregenz

Konstanz

ST. GALLEN

ZÜRICH
Zürich

BASEL
Basel

Bern

Luzern

Freiburg

Strasbourg

Mulhouse

Belfort

SWITZERLAND

Bolzano

TRENTINO

Trento

Rovereto

VENEZIA

Udine

YUGOSLAVIA

Klagenfurt

Villach

Lausanne

Genève

Como

Bellano

COPYRIGHT GEORGE PHILIP & SON LTD

East from Greenwich

Conical with two standard parallels

m 4000 3000 2000 1500 1000 400 200 0

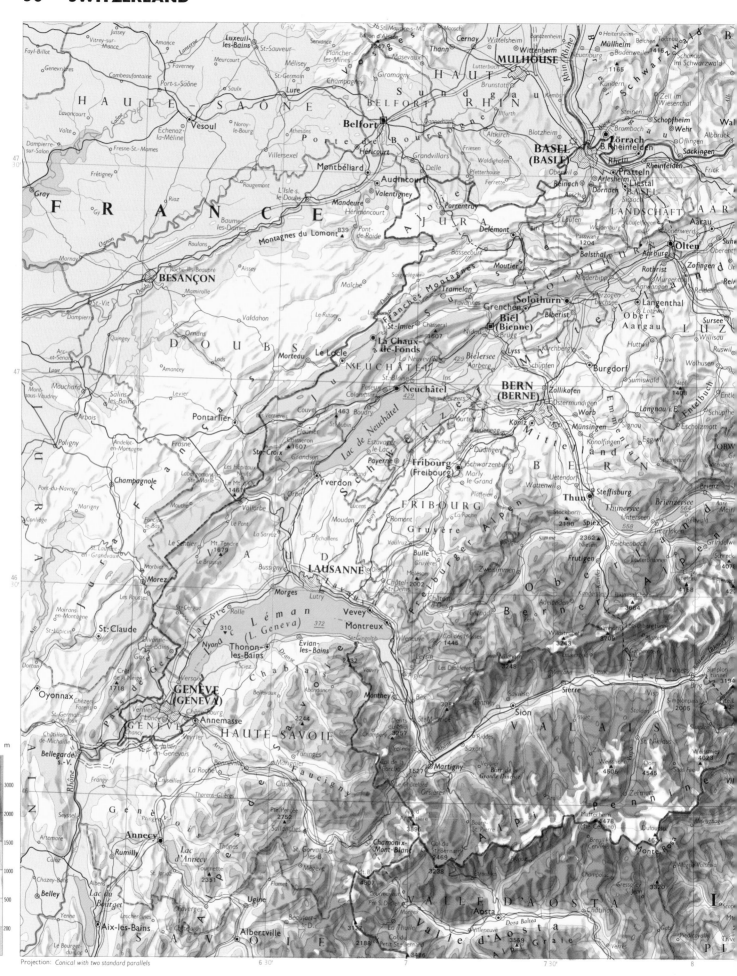

Projection: Conical with two standard parallels

1:1 000 000

10   0   10   20   30   40 km

W. GERMANY

BAYERN

SCHAFFHAUSEN

THURGAU

ZÜRICH

SCHWYZ

AUSTRIA

TIROL

VORARLBERG

LIECHTENSTEIN

Vaduz

GLARUS

GRAUBÜNDEN

National-Park

Chur

Davos

St. Moritz

TICINO

Adula-Gruppe

Bellinzona

Locarno

Lugano

Lago di Como

Sóndrio

LOMBARDIA

Como

Lecco

Varese

Verbania

BÉRGAMO

ITALY

TRENTINO

Lago di Garda

Konstanz

Lindau

Bregenz

Feldkirch

Dornbirn

St. Gallen

Winterthur

Zug

1 : 2 500 000

10 0 10 20 30 40 50 60 70 80 90 100 km

POLAND

Wrocław (Breslau)

Częstochowa

Kielce 612

Opole

KATOWICE
Bytom
Zabrze
Gliwice
Ruda Śląska
Katowice
Tychy
Rybnik

KRAKÓW

Kraków

Tarnów

TARNÓW

Rzeszów

RZESZÓW

PRZEMYSL

Przemysl

Ostrava
Frýdek-Místek

ČESKOSLOVENSKY

Olomouc

Bielsko-Biala
BIELSKO-BIALA

NOWY SĄCZ

KROSNO

Gottwaldov (Zlin)

Žilina

BESKYDY

SLOVAKIA

Trenčín

Košice

VÝCHODOSLOVENSKY

Uzhgorod
ZAKARPAT

SLOVENSKÁ SOCIALISTICKÁ REPUBLIKA

STREDOSLOVENSKÝ

Banská Bystrica

Slovenské Rudohorie
(Slovak Ore Mts.)

Mukachevo

ZÁPADOSLOVENSKÝ

Nitra

BORSOD-ABAUJ

Miskolc
Diósgyör

SZABOLCS-SZATMAR

WIEN (VIENNA)

Bratislava

Nové Zámky

Nyíregyháza

SATU-MARE

Satu Mare

Esztergom

BUDAPEST

NÓGRÁD

Salgótarján

Eger

ZEMPLÉN

Debrecen

HAJDU-BIHAR

SOPRON

Győr

GYÖR

KOMAROM

Gyöngyös

HEVES

Szolnok

SZOLNOK

Karcag

BIHAR

Oradea

Székesfehérvár

VESZPRÉM

FEJER

Kecskemét

PEST

Mezőtur

BÉKÉS

HUNGARY

Szombathely

VAS

ZALA

Veszprém

Dunaújváros

BACS- KISKUN

CSONGRÁD

Békéscsaba

Gyula

Zalaegerszeg

Balaton

Kaposvár

SOMOGY

TOLNA

Szeged

Hódmezővásárhely

Arad

ROMANIA

Nagykanizsa

Pécs

BARANYA

Baja

Subotica

Timişoara

YUGOSLAVIA

CARAȘ-SEVERIN

1 : 3 000 000

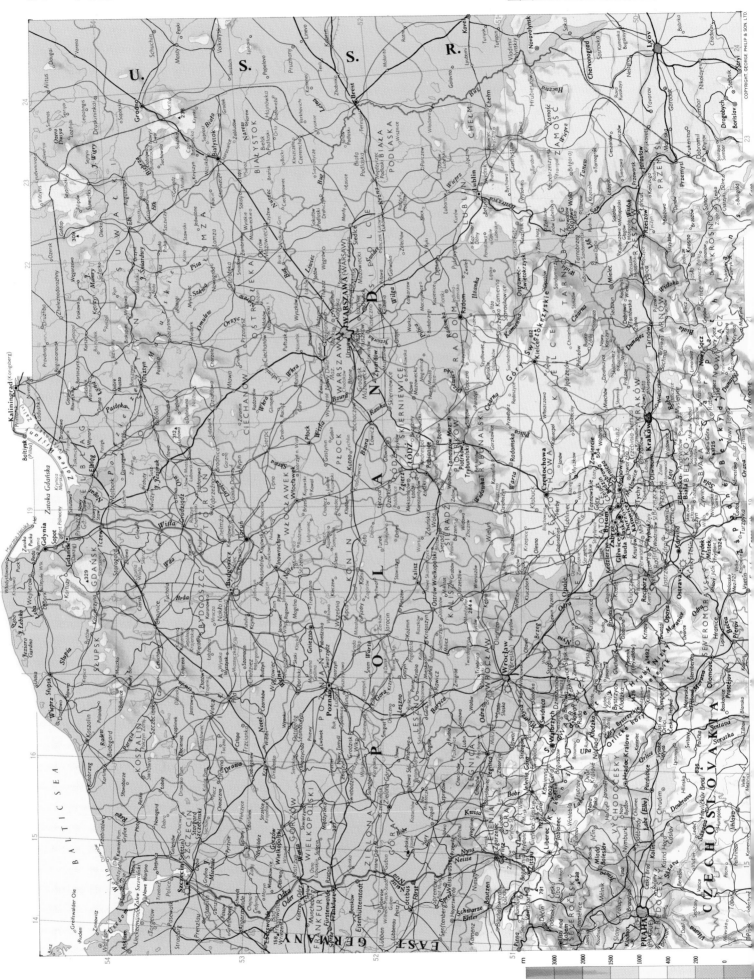

1:5 000 000

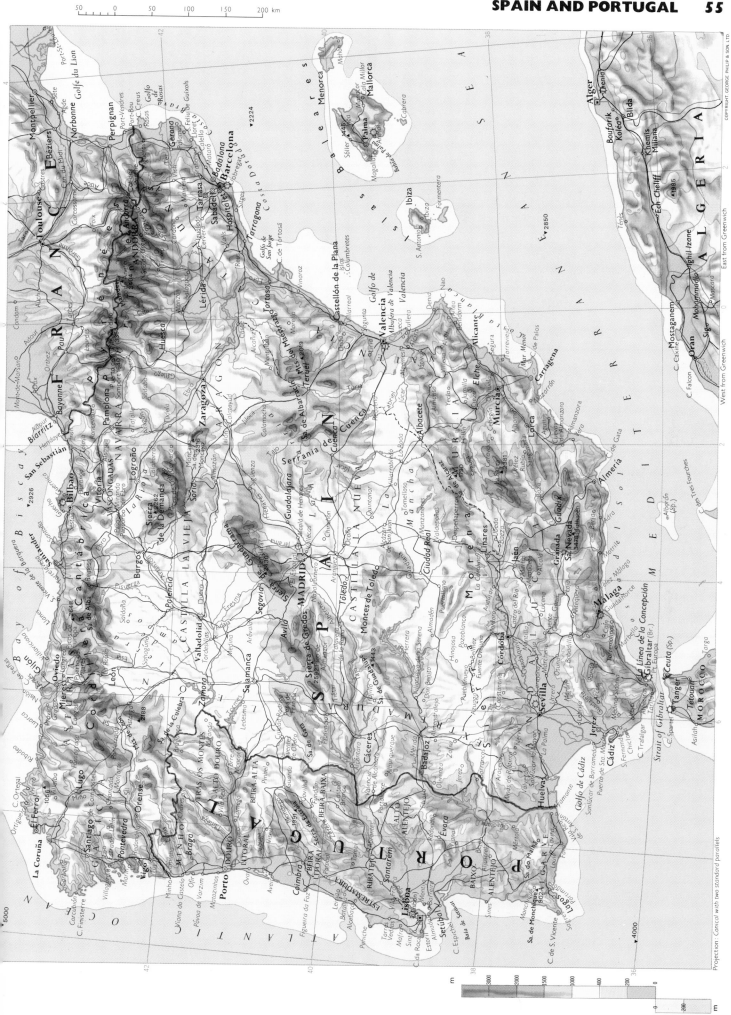

Projection : Conical with two standard parallels

1 : 2 500 000

10 0 10 20 30 40 50 60 70 80 90 100 km

MEDITERRANEAN SEA

MOROCCO

Golfo de Cádiz

Projection: Conical with two standard parallels

West from Greenwich

COPYRIGHT GEORGE PHILIP & SON LTD.

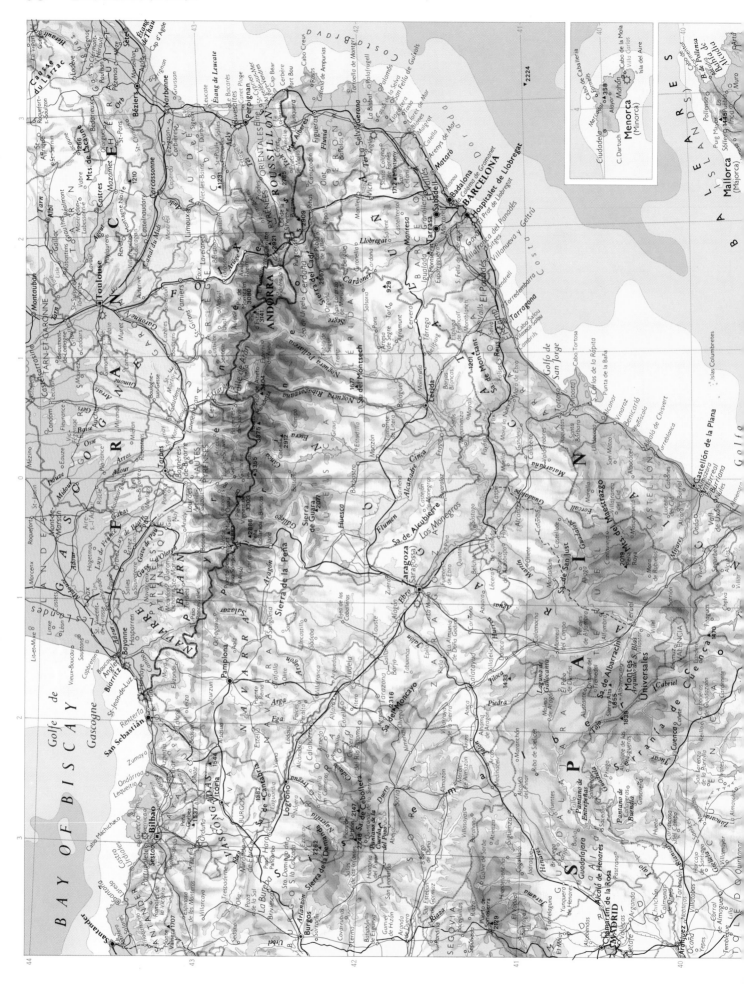

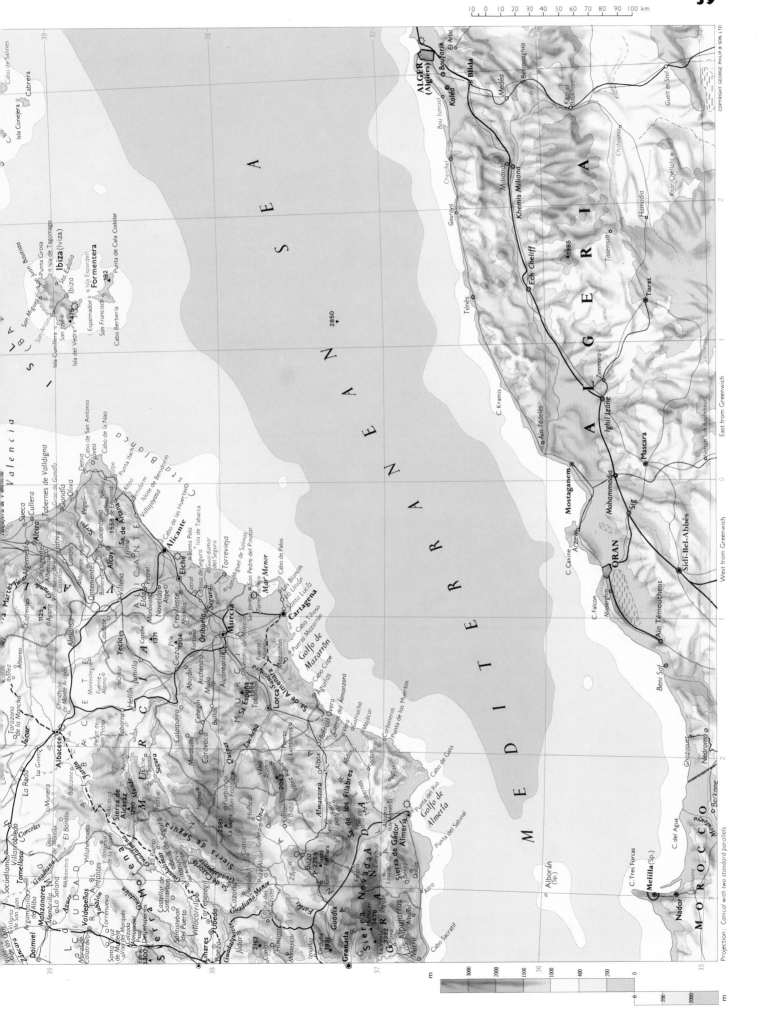

1 : 2 500 000

10 0 10 20 30 40 50 60 70 80 90 100 km

MEDITERRANEAN SEA

ALGERIA

MOROCCO

Projection: Conical with two standard parallels

East from Greenwich

West from Greenwich

ALGER (Algiers)

BouHarik   El Arba
Koléa   Blida
Cherchel   Medéa   Berrouaghia
Gouraya   Miliana
Khemis Miliana
Ténès   Ech Cheliff   1985   Tissemsilt
C. Kramis   Zemmora   Tiaret
Aïn Tédélès   Ighil Izane
Mostaganem   Mohammadia   Mascara
Arzew   Sig
C. Caxine   ORAN   Sidi-Bel-Abbès
C. Falcon   Aïn Témouchent
Masserghin
Beni Saf   Ghazaouet   Nedroma
C. Tres Forcas   Melilla (Sp.)
Nador

VALENCIA

ISLA S   BALEARES

Ibiza (Iviza)
San Antonio   Ibiza
FORMENTERA
Formentera

Alicante
Elche
Murcia
Cartagena
Granada
Sierra Nevada
Albacete

m   3000   2000   1500   1000   400   200   0
m   200   2000

LONDON
s-Gravenhage
Hoek van Holland
Rotterdam
W.
E. BER
Osnabrück
Weser
Hannover
Exmoor
Bristol
Harwich
NETH
Potsdam
Magdeburg
Spree
Münster
Braunschweig
Southampton
Brighton
Dover
Dordrecht
'z Halle
Leipzig
Dartmoor
GERMANY
Land's End
Plymouth
Portsmouth
Folkestone
Oostende
Dunkerque
Calais
Gent
Antwerpen
Mechelen
BELGIUM
Aachen
Bonn
Dortmund
Kassel
Essen
Düsseldorf
Köln
Halle
Erfurt
Thüringer
Wald
Karl-Ma
Erzgeb.
Scilly Is.
Lizard Pt.
English Channel
Boulogne
Lille
Brussel
Liège
Koblenz
Wiesbaden
Frankfurt
Plauen
Praha
Arras
Douai
Ardennes
Mainz
Würzburg
Plzeň
Cherbourg
Somme
Amiens
LUX
Trier
Darmstadt
Nürnberg
Böhmerwald
Channel Is.
Le Havre
Dieppe
St. Quentin
Verdun
Metz
Mannheim
Heidelberg
I. d'Ouessant
Jersey
St. Malo
Caen
Rouen
Reims
Marne
Châlons
Nancy
Karlsruhe
Stuttgart
Regensburg
Pte. de St-Mathieu
Brest
Alençon
Versailles
PARIS
Troyes
Épinal
Strasbourg
Ulm
Augsburg
Inn
Pte. de Penmarch
Rennes
Le Mans
Orléans
Yonne
Seine
Toul
Belfort
Freiburg
München
Salzbur
5365
Lorient
Angers
Vannes
Tours
Cher
Bourges
Dijon
Le Creusot
Besançon
Donau
Bodensee
45
Belle-Ile
St-Nazaire
Nantes
Loire
Poitiers
Vichy
Mâcon
Saône
Chalon
Bern
Zürich
LIECHT
Innsbruck
AU
Bay of Biscay
La Rochelle
Rochefort
Limoges
Mt. Dore
Clermont-
Ferrand
1886 m
St-Étienne
Lyon
Isère
Lausanne
Lac Léman
Genève
SWITZERLAND
Como
Simplonpass
Ortles
3899
TIROL
Drava
5098
C. Ortegal
Gironde
Charente
Angoulème
Auvergne
Mt. Blanc
4807
Grenoble
Torino
Bergamo
Brescia
Verona
Padova
Venezia
Gorizia
Ljublj
La Coruña
El Ferrol
Bordeaux
Périgueux
Dordogne
Lot
Cévennes
Rhône
Po
Milano
Novara
G. di
Venézia
Pula
C. Finisterre
Santander
Bilbao
San Sebastián
Biarritz
Bayonne
Adour
Garonne
Toulouse
Tarn
Nîmes
Avignon
Durance
Alessandria
Parma
Réggio
Génova
Módena
Ferrara
Santiago
Oviedo
Gijón
Picos de
Europa
León
Burgos
Pau
Pyrenees
Montpellier
Béziers
MONACO
Menton
Nice
Golfo di
Génova
La
Spézia
Firenze
Bologna
Ravenna
Folì
Rímini
ADR
Vigo
Orense
Cordillera
Cantábrica
Campos
Vitoria
Pamplona
Pico de Aneto
3404
Andorra
Sète
Cannes
Livorno
Arno
San Marino
Pontevedra
Miño
Palencia
Ebro
Narbonne
Perpignan
Marseille
Toulon
Ligurian Sea
C. Corse
Elba
Arezzo
Siena
Ancon
Porto
Duero
Valladolid
C. Creus
Golfe du Lion
Mt Cinto 2710
Bastia
Perúgia
Mte. Sabini
2914
Coimbra
Salamanca
Sa. de Guadarrama
Zaragoza
Lérida
Corse
(Corsica)
Civitavécchia
Tevere
ROMA
Ciudad
Rodrigo
Tejo
MADRID
Tajo
Guadalajara
Barcelona
Ajaccio
Olbia
Gaeta
Sa. da Estrela
Évora
PORTUGAL
Alcántara
SPAIN
Cuenca
Teruel
Tortosa
Tarragona
Ebro
Sássari
Volturno
Lisboa
Torres Vedras
Guadiana
Badajoz
La
Mancha
Jucar
Castellón
Islas Baleares
Bouches de Bonifacio
Caprera
Nápoli
Tinto
Cáceres
Toledo
Ciudad Real
Albacete
Valencia
Menorca (Minorca)
Capri
Salè
Faro
Huelva
Córdoba
Sierra
Morena
Linares
Segura
C. Nao
Ibiza
Ibiza
Palma
Mahón
Mallorca (Majorca)
Sardegna
(Sardinia)
Mt. del Gennargentu
1834
3719
Tyrrhenian Sea
Sevilla
Jaén
Granada
Guadalquivir
Murcia
Lorca
Alicante
Formentera
Cabrera
Genil
Cádiz
Jérez
Mulhacén
Sa. Nevada 3478
Almería
Cartagena
Cagliari
C. Trafalgar
Málaga
Algeciras
C. de Gata
M
E
D
I
T
E
R
Isole Éolie
(Aeolian Is.)
Str. of Gibraltar
Tanger
Gibraltar (Br.)
Ceuta (Sp.)
Alborán
(Sp.)
2887
2850
Palermo
Trápani
Isole Égadi
Larache
Tétouan
Mostaganem
Alger
Béjaïa
Skikda
Annaba
C. Bon
Bizerte
Carthage
Tunis
Marsala
Sici
Agrigento
Caltanisse
Ouezzane
Melilla (Sp.)
Oran
Chelif
Constantine
Pantelleria (It.)
Rabat
Meknès
Fes
Ghazaouet
Sidi Bel Abbès
Ech Cheliff
Chott el
Hodna
Kairouan
G. de Hammamet
Sousse
Gozo
Valletta
MALTA
MOROCCO
Moulouya
Oujda
Tlemcen
Plateaux
Tébessa
Sfax
Lampedusa
(It.)
Haut
Djelfa
Saharien
Biskra
Chott Melrhir
Iles Kerkena
3737
Aïn Sefra
ALGERIA
Chott ech Chergui
O. Djedi
Touggourt
Chott Djerid
Tozeur
Gabès
Djerba
Haut Atlas
Atlas
Figuig
Béchar
Ghardaïa
Ouargla
Hassi Messaoud
Tarâbulus
Beni Abbès
30
El Goléa
Ft. Lallemand
Jabal Nafūsah
Mizdah
Tarâbulus
L

m
4000
2000
1000
400
200
0
200
1000
2000
3000
m

1:10 000 000

100   0   100   200   300   400 km

61

Division between Greeks
and Turks in Cyprus;
Turks to the north.

SWITZERLAND

VORARLBERG

LIECHTENSTEIN

GRAUBÜNDEN

FRANCHE COMTÉ

JURA

Lyon
(Lyons)

Grenoble

Genève
(Geneva)

Lausanne

Bern
(BERNE)

Luzern

ST GALLEN

SAVOIE

HAUTE SAVOIE

DAUPHINÉ

Valence

MILANO
(Milan)

TORINO
(Turin)

Novara

Vercelli

Brescia

Bergamo

Pavia

Cremona

Piacenza

Parma

Reggio

Módena

Alessandria

Asti

Cúneo

GENOVA
(Genoa)

Savona

San Remo

Nice

MONACO

Monte Carlo

Cannes

Antibes

Toulon

MARSEILLE
(Marseilles)

Aix-en-Provence

Avignon

Arles

PROVENCE

ALPES MARITIMES

ALPES DE HAUTE PROVENCE

HAUTES ALPES

BOUCHES DU RHÔNE

Golfo di Génova

LIGURIAN SEA

La Spezia

Carrara

Massa

Lucca

Pisa

Livorno
(Leghorn)

Piombino

Elba

Arcipelago

Toscano

CORSE

(CORSICA)

HAUTE CORSE

CORSE-DU-SUD

Bastia

Ajaccio

ILES D'HYÈRES

Côte d'Azur

4000
3000
2000
1500
1000
400
200
0
200
2000
m

1 : 2 500 000

FOR CONTINUATION SEE PAGE 66

COPYRIGHT GEORGE PHILIP & SON LTD

CORSE
CORSICA

Iles Sanguinaires
G. d'Ajaccio   Tavaro
2136 Zonza
C. di Muro   Levie   Solenzara
Sartène   Propriano   Favone
G. de Valinco   Porto-Vecchio
Bonifacio   Iles Cerbicales
I. de Cavallo

Bouches de Bonifacio
Maddalena
Santa Teresa Gallura   Caprera
La Maddalena   Costa Smeralda
Asinara   Punta dello Scorno
Golfo dell'   Arzachena   Pto. Cervo
Asinara   Liscia   Golfo Aranci
Coghinas   Àggius   G. di Olbia
Porto Tórres   Témpio Pausania   Ólbia   Tavolara
Sorso   M. Limbara
Sássari   Sennori   Oschiri   1362
C. dell'Argentiera   Ósilo   L. di Coghinas   Tanaunella
Fertìlia   Ittiri   Ozieri   Posada
Alghero   Pattada   Buddusò   Siniscola
Villanova-   1259   Orune   C. Cómino
Monteleone   Bonárva   1550   Bitti
Bosa   Nùoro   Dorgali
Temo   Oliena   Golfo di
Macomer   Gennargentu   Orosei
SARDEGNA   1834   Baunei   C. di Monte Santu
C. Mannu   Sorgono   Arbatax
Cábras   SARDEGNA   Lanusei
Golfo di   Oristano   M. Arci   Làconi   Ierzu
Oristano   Arborea   812
Terralba   Mandas   Villaputzu
S. Gavino   Senorbì   Muravera
Gúspini   Monreale   Sìnnai   C. Ferrato
Arbus   Gonnosfanádiga   Dolianova   Sélargius
C. Pécora   1236   Villacidro   Sìnnai   1069
Fluminimaggiore   M. Línas   S. Vito
Iglésias   Cixerri   Siliqua   Serpentara
Portoscuso   Séstu   Quartu Sant'Elena
Carloforte   Carbonia   Cágliari
San Pietro   Santadi   1116   Golfo di
Sant'Antioco   Porto Botte   Cágliari
Sant'   Pula   C. Carbonara
Antioco   Teulada   C. Spartivento
G. di Palmas

SARDINIA

TYRRHENIAN
SEA

3719

3589

Ustica

ROMA
(Rome)   Tivoli   Subiaco
Vatican City
Fregene   Palestrina
Tevere   Valmontone   Anagni   Alatri
(Tiber)   Ferentino   Véroli
Lido di Óstia   Velletri   Cori   Ceccano   Frosinone
(Lido di Roma)   Albano   Cisterna di Latina
Prática   Lanuvio
di Mare   Aprilia   Sonnino   Priverno
Ánzio   Latina   Sezze   153
Nettuno   Pontinia   Sabáudia   Fondi   Form
Monte Circeo   Terracina
541   Gaeta
Golfo di
Zannone   Gaeta
Palmarola   Ponza   Mint
Ísole   283   Gargl
Ponziane   Mor
Ventotene

C. San Vito
Castellammare del Golfo   Favaretta
G. di Castellammare   Térrasini   PALERMO
Levanzo   Trápani   1110   Monreale   Bagheria
Ísole Égadi   Érice   Alcamo   Partinico   M.Hìmeri
Marettimo   Páceco   S. Giusepp
Favignana   Calatafími   Iato
Favignana   Salemi   Stagnone   Marineo
Marsala   Partanna   Camporeale   1613
Castelvetrano   Gibellina   Carleone   Lercara
Mazara   Bisacquino   Prizzi   Friddi
del Vallo   Campobello di Mazara   Sambuca   SIC
Belice   Menfi   di Sicília   Mussomè
Sciacca   Búrgio   Sb
Campobello di Mazara   Caltabellotta   Platani
Belice   Ribera   Racalm
Sicilian   Cattólica Eraclea   Agrigento
Channel   Siciliano   Agrigento   Favara
Porto Empédocle   Campob
Palma di Montechi

Iles de la
Galite

C. Blanc   Cani
C. Serrat   Plane
Bizerte   Zembra
(Binzert)
C. Serrat   Menzel-Bourguiba   Golfe de Tunis   C. Bon
Tabarka   Mateur   Kelibia
ALGERIA   Tébourba   TUNIS   Halq el Oued   Menzel-
El Kala   Béja   Temime
Bou Salem   Soliman   Pantelleria   Pantelleria
Medjerda   836   (It.)
TUNISIA   Nabeul   1319
Téboursouk   Zaghouan   Hammamet   MÉDITE

m
3000
2000
1500
1000
400
200
0
m
200
2000
4000
m

1 : 2 500 000

10 0 10 20 30 40 50 60 70 80 90 100 km

ADRIATIC

SEA

G. di Manfredónia

Monte Sant'Angelo

Testa del Gargano

Vieste

Manfredónia

Foggia

Barletta
Trani
Biscéglie
Molfetta
Giovinazzo

Andria
Corato
Terlizzi
Bari

Cerignola
Ascoli

Mola di Bari
Polignano a Mare
Monopoli

Minervino
Murge 686
Acquaviva
delle Fonti
Castellana Grotte
Fasano

Gioia
del Colle
Putignano
Martina
Franca
Ostuni
Céglie Messápico
Grottáglie

Altamura

Gravina
di Puglia
Laterza
Castellaneta
Mottola
Massafra

Brindisi
Francavilla Fontana
Mesagne

Matera

Ginosa
Palagiano
Táranto
Oria
Manduria

S. Pietro Vernótico
Squinzano

BASILICATA

Bernalda
Bradano
Lecce
Copertino

Golfo di
Táranto

Nardò
Galatina
Mártano
Máglie

Otranto
C. d'Otranto

Galátone
Parábita
Poggiardo

Gallípoli
Casarano
Rácale
Ugento
Tricase

Presicce

Gagliano del Capo
C. Santa Maria di Leuca

Strait of Otranto

Kérkira
(Corfu)

IONIAN

SEA

CALABRIA

Cosenza

Sila
1929

Crotone

Catanzaro

Golfo di
Sant'Eufémia

Golfo di Squillace

Vibo Valéntia

Isole Eólie o Lípari (Æolian Is.)

Strómboli

Messina

Réggio
di Cálabria

Etna
3340

Catánia

Golfo di
Catánia

Augusta

Siracusa

SICILIA

Noto

Pachino
C. Passero

MEDITERRANEAN SEA

ADRIATIC SEA

Projection: Conical with two standard parallels

East from Greenwich

1 : 2 500 000

10 0 10 20 30 40 50 60 70 80 90 100 km

69

A E G E A N   S E A

S E A   O F   C R E T E   (Sea of Candia)

I O N I A N   S E A

ATHENS (ATHÍNAI)

Khíos (Chios)

Psará

Skíros

Skópelos

Ándros

Tínos

Míkonos

Náxos

Páros

Íos

Amorgós

Astipálaia

Ikaria

K I K L Á D H E S   (C Y C L A D E S)

A R K H I P É L A G O S

Sífnos

Mílos

Kíthnos

Kéa

Kíthira (Cérigo)

Iráklion (Candia)

K R I T I   (C R E T E)

Kefallinía (Cephalonia)

Zákinthos (Zante)

Ithakí (Ithaca)

Levkás (Santa Maura)

P E L O P O N N I S O S

Korinthos (Corinth)

Corinth Canal

Spárti (Sparta)

Kalámai

Pátrai

Pírgos

A K H A Ï A

M E S S I N Í A

L A K O N Í A

A R K A D Í A

Taïyetos Óros

Párnon Óros

A T T I K Í

Khalkís (Chalcis)

Thíra

Sámos

Ródhos (Rhodes)

Kos

Kárpathos

D H O D E K Á N I S O S   (DODECANESE)

Stenón Kárpathos

Stenón Kásos

Continuation Eastwards on same scale

Projection: Conical with two standard parallels

East from Greenwich

COPYRIGHT GEORGE PHILIP & SON LTD

m 3000 2000 1500 1000 400 200 0

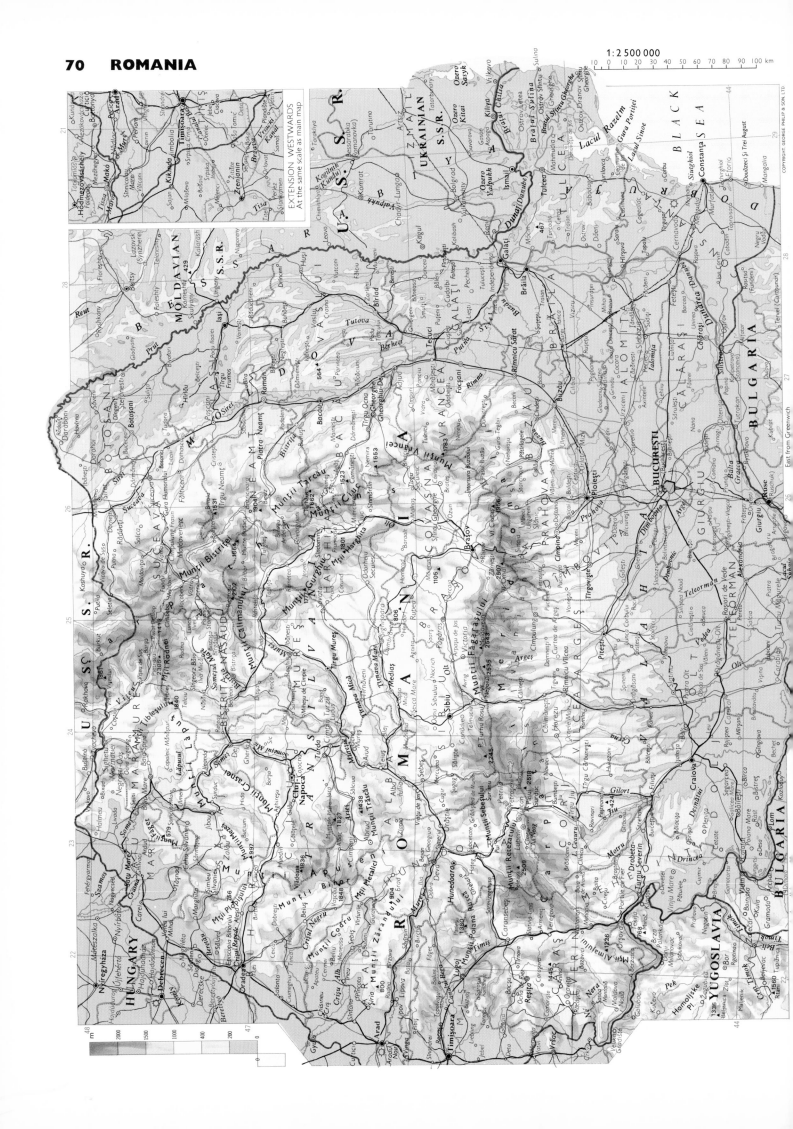

1 : 2 500 000

EXTENSION WESTWARDS
At the same scale as main map

East from Greenwich

1:2 500 000

10 0 10 20 30 40 50 60 70 80 90 100 km

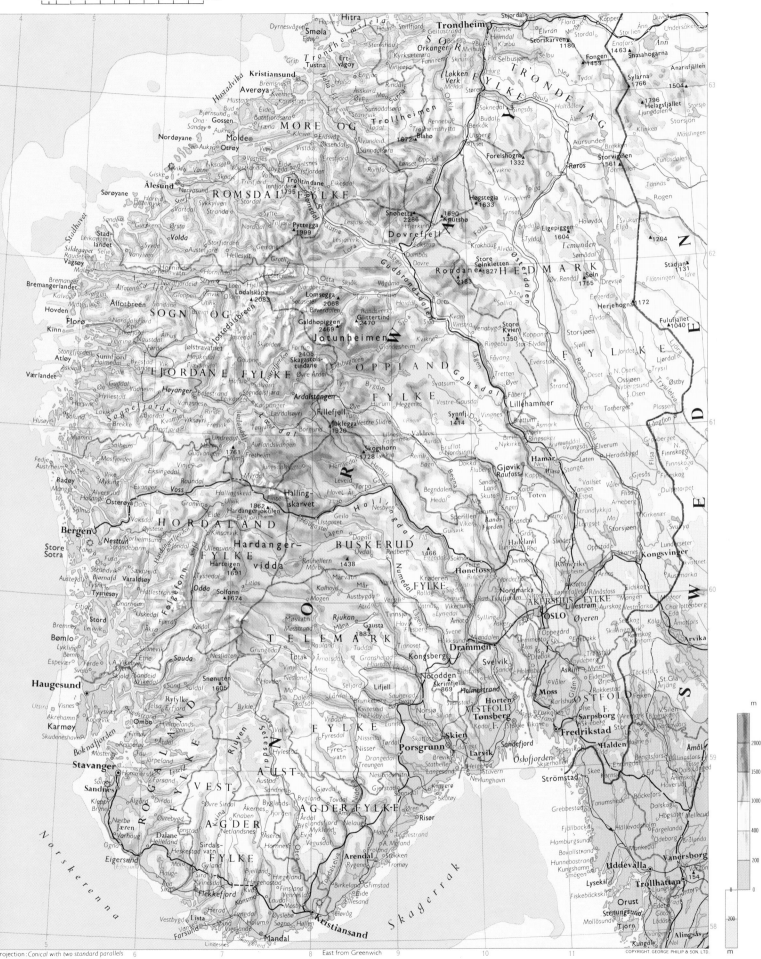

Projection : Conical with two standard parallels   East from Greenwich   COPYRIGHT. GEORGE PHILIP & SON LTD.

1:2 500 000

10 0 0 10 20 30 40 50 60 70 80 90 100 km

COPYRIGHT GEORGE PHILIP & SON LTD

POLAND

BALTIC SEA

Gotland

Visby

Öland

Bornholm

Rønne

GERMANY

Rügen

Kiel

Flensburg

Kalmar

Nybro

Karlskrona

Ronneby

Karlshamn

KALMAR LÄN

JÖNKÖPINGS LÄN

KRONOBERGS LÄN

BLEKINGE LÄN

Växjö

Ljungby

Älmhult

Hässleholm

Kristianstad

Ystad

Simrishamn

MALMÖHUS

Trelleborg

Malmö

Lund

Landskrona

Helsingborg

Helsingør

KØBENHAVN (COPENHAGEN)

Roskilde

SJÆLLAND

Næstved

Slagelse

Kalundborg

Korsør

Nyborg

Svendborg

FYN

Odense

FALSTER

LOLLAND

Maribo

Nykøbing

Esbjerg

Kolding

Haderslev

Åbenrå

Sønderborg

JYLLAND

Vejle

Herning

Silkeborg

Skanderborg

Århus

Randers

Viborg

Ålborg

Hjørring

Frederikshavn

Skagen

Norrköping

Linköping

Motala

ÖSTERGÖTLANDS LÄN

Västervik

Oskarshamn

SKARABORGS LÄN

Skövde

Falköping

Lidköping

Jönköping

Nässjö

Huskvarna

Tranås

Borås

Alingsås

Göteborg

Mölndal

Vänersborg

Trollhättan

Uddevalla

ÄLVSBORGS LÄN

HALLANDS LÄN

Halmstad

Falkenberg

Varberg

Ängelholm

Kattegat

Ålborg Bugt

Skagerrak

Tvedestrand

Arendal

Oxelösund

POLAND

Stupsk

Projection: Conical with two standard parallels

East from Greenwich

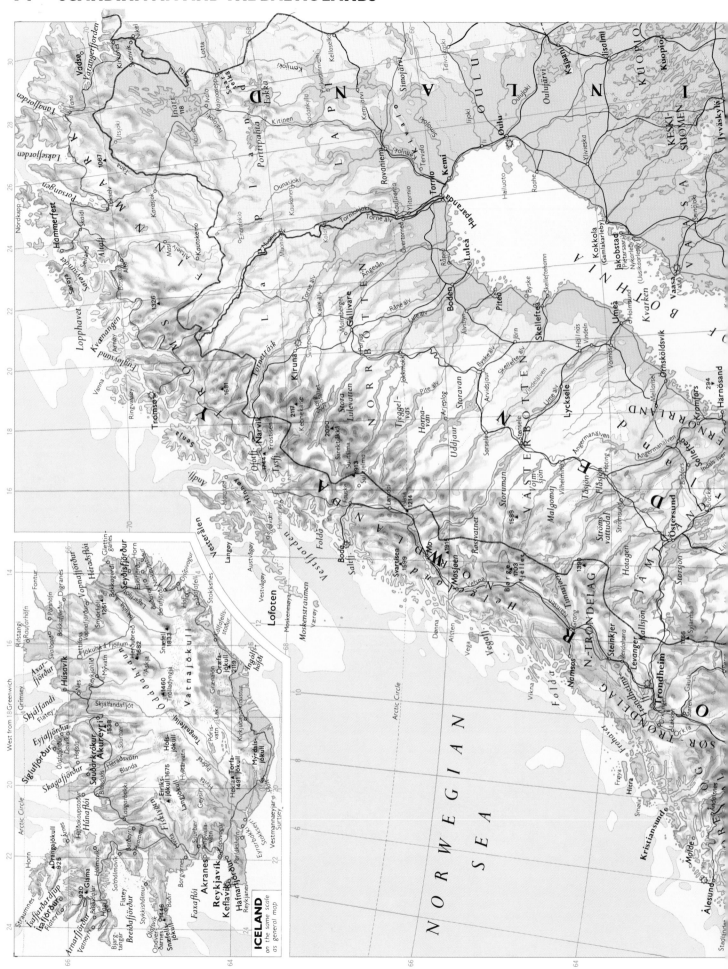

ICELAND
on the same scale
as general map

NORWEGIAN SEA

1:5 000 000

50   0   50   100   150   200 km

Heinola
Lahti
Hämeenlinna
Kotka
Lovisa
Kundo
Porvoo
HELSINKI
(Helsingfors)
Espoo
Ekenäs
Hangö (Hanko)
Rakvere
Tallinn
Haapsalu
Saaremaa (Ösel)
Kingisepp
Hiiumaa (Dago)

R.
S.
S.
F. S. R.

ESTONIAN S.S.R.
Viljandi
Valga
Valmiera
Cēsis
Riga
Rīgas Jūras Līcis (Gulf of Riga)
Pärnu
Ruhnu

Vilnius
Grodno
Białystok
Łomża
Ostrołęka

LITHUANIAN S.S.R.
Kaunas
Panevėžys
Ukmergė
Jelgava
Bauska
Šiauliai

Ventspils
Liepāja
Klaipėda
Sovetsk
Chernyakhovsk
Kaliningrad

B   A   L   T   I   C   S   E   A

Gotland
Visby
Fårö
Gotska Sandön

POLAND
Gdynia
Gdańsk
Zatoka Gdańska
Elbląg
Malbork
Grudziądz
Toruń
Bydgoszcz

Turku (Åbo)
Rauma
Pori
Uusikaupunki
Naantali

Åland (Åhvenanmaa)
Mariehamn (Maarianhamina)

STOCKHOLM
Uppsala
Västerås
Eskilstuna
Södertälje
Nyköping
Norrköping
Oxelösund
Nynäshamn
Dalarö

Söderhamn
Gävle
Sandviken
Bollnäs

Falun
Borlänge
Hedemora
Avesta
Fagersta
Sala

Örebro
Kumla
Katrineholm
Motala
Linköping
Mjölby
Skövde
Askersund

Västervik
Oskarshamn
Kalmar
Öland
Borgholm

VÄSTMANLAND
ÖSTER-GÖTLAND
KALMAR
KRONOBERG
BLEKINGE
Karlskrona
Karlshamn
Ronneby
Kristianstad
KRISTIANSTAD

Nässjö
Växjö
Vetlanda
Huskvarna
Jönköping
JÖNKÖPING
Tranås
Värnamo
Ljungby
Alvesta

Bornholm
Rønne

Szczecin (Stettin)
Kołobrzeg
Koszalin
Wolin
Świnoujście
Usedom
Rügen
Greifswald
Stralsund

Mora
Siljan
Ludvika
Vansbro

Karlstad
Filipstad
Kristinehamn
Arvika
Säffle
Åmål

Mariestad
Lidköping
Vänersborg
Trollhättan
Falköping
Ulricehamn

VÄRMLAND
ÄLVSBORG
GÖTEBORG OCH BOHUS
HALLAND
SKÅNE

Borås
Alingsås
Mölndal
GÖTEBORG
Kungsbacka

Uddevalla
Strömstad
Lysekil

Halmstad
Falkenberg
Varberg
Laholm

Helsingborg
Ängelholm
Landskrona
Helsingør
MALMÖ
København
Lund
Trelleborg
Ystad
The Sound
Simrishamn

Rostock
Wismar
Schwerin
Lübeck
Warnemünde
GERMANY
WEST
EAST

Oslo
Drammen
Kongsberg
Hønefoss
Tønsberg
Larvik
Skien
Sandefjord
Moss
Fredrikstad
Sarpsborg
Halden
Kongsvinger

BUSKERUD
TELEMARK
AUST-AGDER
VEST-AGDER
ROGALAND
HORDALAND

Arendal
Grimstad
Lillesand
Kristiansand
Mandal
Farsund
Flekkefjord
Egersund
Eigersund
Lillehammer
Hamar
Gjøvik

Bergen
Haugesund
Kopervik
Stavanger
Sandnes
Bryne

Skagerrak
Frederikshavn
Skagen
Hjørring
Ålborg
Thisted
Limfjorden
Viborg
Silkeborg
Herning
Holstebro
Randers
Århus
Horsens
Vejle
Fredericia
Kolding
Esbjerg
Ribe
Åbenrå
Flensburg

Kattegat
Anholt
Læsø
Grenen

DENMARK
Sjælland
Roskilde
Korsør
Slagelse
Næstved
Nakskov
Nykøbing
Falster
Møn

Odense
Fyn
Svendborg
Nyborg
Store Bælt
Lille Bælt
Lolland

Kiel
Kieler Bucht
Rendsburg
Neumünster
Itzehoe
Hamburg
Bremerhaven
Bremen
Oldenburg
Wilhelmshaven
Cuxhaven
Emden
Groningen
NETHERLANDS
Nordfriesische Inseln
Ostfriesische Inseln
Weser
Elbe

East from Greenwich

Projection: Conical with two standard parallels

m 2000 1500 1000 400 200 0

1:10 000 000

100   0   100   200   300   400 km

Legend box:
1 Kabardino-Balkar A.S.S.R.
2 North Ossetian A.S.S.R. (Azer.)
3 Nakhichevan A.S.S.R.
4 Chechen-Ingush A.S.S.R.
   Karagiye Depression

CASPIAN SEA

Kara Bogaz Gol

Krasnovodsk
Chelekon
Nebit Dag
Bandar-e Torkeman
Demävend 5604
Semnän
TEHRÄN
Qom
Ardekän

STEPPE S.S.R.

KAZAKHSKAYA Nizmennost'

Guryev

Fort Shevchenko
Shevchenko

Makhachkala
Derbent

DAGESTAN A.S.S.R.

KALMYK A.S.S.R.

Astrakhan'

Ergeni Vozvyshennost'

Volgograd (Stalingrad)

Volzhskiy
Leninsk

Grozny
Nalchik
Ordzhonikidze
Elbrus 5633
Kazbek 5047

GEORGIAN S.S.R.
Tbilisi
ADZHAR
Batumi

Kutaisi

ABKHAZ

Sochi
Sukhumi

CAUCASUS

AZERBAIJAN S.S.R.
Kirovabad
Baku
Alyat Pristan

ARMENIAN S.S.R.
Yerevan
Leninakan
Kirovakan
Ararat 5165

Nakhichevan

Tabriz
Ozero Sevan

Maragheh
Orümiyeh
Orümiyeh 4168

P E R S I A

Hamadän
Qahremänshahr
Baghdad
Arbil
Kirkük
I R A Q
Dijah (Tigris)
Al Mawsil
Nineveh

S Y R I A
Halab
Hamä
Homs
Dimashq (Damascus)
LEBANON
Bayrüt (Beirut)
Tarabulus (Tripoli)

Baku

Rostov
Taganrog
Makeyevka
Donetsk
Zaporozhye
Krivoy Rog
Dnepropetrovsk

KHARKOV

UKRAINIAN S.S.R.

Belgorod

Odessa
Kishinev
MOLDAVIAN S.S.R.

Nikolayev
Kherson
Sevastopol'
Simferopol'
Yalta
KRYMSKIY P-OV (Crimea)

Sea of Azov (Azovskoye More)

BLACK SEA

Novorossiysk
Krasnodar
Stavropol
Maykop
Armavir

Constanța
ROMANIA
BUCUREŞTI (Bucharest)
Brăila
Ploieşti

BULGARIA
Varna
Burgas

ISTANBUL
Marmara Denizi
Bursa
Izmit
Ankara

T U R K E Y

Anadolu Dağları

Trabzon
Erzurum
Samsun

Zonguldak
Eskişehir
Kayseri
Sivas
Malatya
Gaziantep
Adana
Konya
Antalya
CYPRUS

İzmir (Smyrna)
Ródhos
Dhodhekanisos

MEDITERRANEAN SEA

Levant

East from Greenwich

Projection: Conical with two standard parallels

Division between Greeks and Turks in Cyprus; Turks to the North.

COPYRIGHT GEORGE PHILIP & SON LTD.

m 4000 2000 1000 400 200 0 200 4000 m

1 : 5 000 000

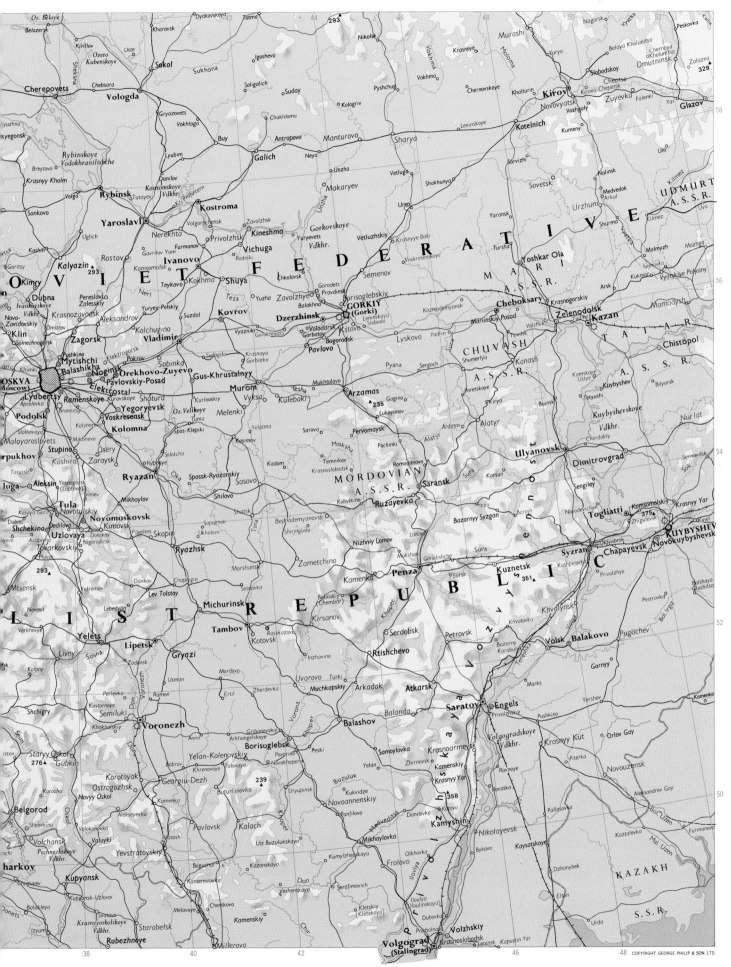

Oz. Beloye
Belozersk
Kirillov
Uste
Ozero
Kubenskoye
Sheksna
Sokol
Cherepovets
Vologda
Chebsara
Gryazovets
Vokhtoga
yegonsk
Breytovo
Rybinskoye
Vodokhranilishche
Krasnyy Kholm
Danilov
Volga
Sonkovo
Rybinsk
Tutayev
Kostromskoye
Kr. Profinterm
Vdkhr.
Goritsy
Kashin
Uglich
Yaroslavl
Nerekhta
Volgorechensk
OKimry
Kalyazin
293
Rostov
Gavrilov Yam
Dubna
Pereslavl
Zalesskiy
Yuryev-Polskiy
Ivankovskoye
Vdkhr.
Novo-
Zavidovskiy
Krasnozavodsk
Aleksandrov
Dmitrov
Kolchugino
Klin
Solnechnogorsk
Zagorsk
Pushkino
Vladimir
Istra
Mytishchi
Elektrogorsk
Pokrov
Sobinka
Khimki
Balashikha
Noginsk
Orekhovo-Zuyevo
OSKVA
Moscow)
Lyubertsy
Elektrostal
Pavlovskiy-Posad
Gus-Khrustalnyy
Aprelevka
Ramenskoye
Kurovskoye
Shatura
Podolsk
Yegoryevsk
Voskresensk
Kolomna
Stolbovaya
Kolyberovo
Bronnitsy
Mikhnevo
Maloyaroslavets
Stupino
Osery
rpukhov
Kashira
Zaraysk
Tarussa
Rybnoye
luga
Aleksin
Yesnogorsk
(Laptevo)
Ryazan
Tula
Novotulskiy
Mikhaylov
Kosaya Gora
Shchekino
Dedilovo
Novomoskovsk
Kimovsk
Shatsk
Towarkovskiy
Uzlovaya
Bogoroditsk
Pavelets
Skopin
yeva
Krupina
Plavsk
Donskoy
Ryazhsk
Mtsensk
293
Novosil
Yefremov
Dankov
Chaplygin
Lev Tolstoy
Michurinsk
Novosil
LIST
Yelets
Lebedyan
REPUBLIC
Livny
Lipetsk
Gryazi
Tambov
Rasskazovo
Kotovsk
Kolpny
Sosna
Zadonsk
Mordovo
Usman
Ertil
Shchigry
Perlevka
Ramon
Zherdevka
Uvarovo
Turki
Muchkapskiy
Arkadak
Atkarsk
Staryy Oskol
276
Gubkin
Semiluki
Voronezh
Anna
Gribanovskiy
Arkhangelskoye
Povorino
Belgorod
Khokholskiy
Korotoyak
Ostrogozhsk
Novyy Oskol
Kamenka
Georgiu-Dezh
239
Buturlinovka
Uryupinsk
Korocha
Alekseyevka
Pavlovsk
Kalach
Buzuluk
Volokonovka
Kukvidze
Novoanninskiy
Panfilovo
Volchansk
Valuyki
Rossosh
Ust Buzulukskaya
harkov
Pechnezhskoye
Vdkhr.
Kupyansk
Kantemirovka
Boguchar
Serafimovich
Chuguyev
Kupyansk-Uzlovoi
Veshenskaya
Don
Balakleya
Svatovo
Chertkovo
Kamenskiy
Izyum
Krasnoyoskolskoye
Vdkhr.
Starobelsk
Kletskiy
(Kletskaya)
Dubovka
Rubezhnoye
Chir
Millerovo
Volgograd
(Stalingrad)
Krasnoslobodsk
Volzhskiy
Kapustin Yar

Dyakovskaya
Totma
293
Nikolsk
Murashi
Peskovka
Vyatka
Kharovsk
Igoshevo
Sukhona
Soligalich
Suday
Pyshchug
Chernovskoye
Khaltutin
Kirov
Kirovo-Chepetsk
Zuyevka
Omutninsk
Slobodskoy
Cheptsa
Zalazna
329
Glazov
Vokhma
Vokhma
Krasnoye
Molona
Yurya
Belaya Kholnitsa
Chernaya
oKholnitsa
Novovyatsk
Vozhgaly
Falenki
Yar
Chukhloma
Kologriv
Leninskoye
Kotelnich
Kumeny
Uni
Sorvizhi
Nolinsk
Buy
Antropovo
Manturovo
Sharya
Medvedok
Arkul
Uva
Lyubim
Galich
Neya
Unzha
Vetluga
Yaransk
Sovetsk
Urzhum
UDMURT
A.S.S.R.
Makaryev
Shakhunya
Uren
Yaransk
Tursha
Kilmez
Mozhga
Zavolzhsk
Krasnyye Baki
Malmyzh
Kineshma
Gorkovskoye
Vdkhr.
Vetluzhskiy
Yoshkar Ola
Kukmor
Vyatskiye Polyany
Privolzhsk
Yuryevets
Voskresenskoye
Arsk
Vichuga
Rodniki
Chkalovsk
MARI
A.S.S.R.
Kazan
Krasnogorskiy
Ivanovo
Semenov
Chkolovsk
Gorodets
Pravdinsk
Borisoglebskiy
Kozmodemyansk
Cheboksary
Zelenodolsk
Mariinsky Posad
TATAR
Shuya
Teykovo
Kokhma
Yuzha
Zavolzhye
Balakhna
GORKIY
(Gorki)
Mariinskiy Posad
Tsivilsk
Mamadysh
Kovrov
Suzdal
Nerl
Dzerzhinsk
Leninskaya
Sloboda
Volodarsk
Gorbatov
Lyskovo
Yadrin
CHUVASH
A.S.S.R.
Kanash
Chistopol
Vyazniki
Gorokhovets
Bogorodsk
Pavlovo
Pyana
Sergach
Shumerlya
Kamskoye
Ustye
Kuybyshev
A. S. S. R.
Krasnaya
Gorbatka
Sudogda
Mukhtolovo
Arzamas
Gagino
Poretskoye
Kirya
Tetyushi
Biyarsk
Nurlat
Murom
Tesha
Kulebaki
235
Lukoyanov
Ardatov
Alatyr
Kuybyshevskoye
Cherdakly
Melenki
Vyksa
Yelatma
Sarova
Pervomaysk
Pochinki
Alatyr
Ulyanovsk
Dimitrovgrad
Kasimov
Tuma
Moksha
Temnikov
Romanovo
Sura
Karsun
Inza
Sernovodsk
Krasnoslobodsk
MORDOVIAN
A.S.S.R.
Saransk
Sengiley
Togliatti
375
Krasnyy Yar
Spas-Ryazanskiy
Sasovo
Kobylkino
Ruzayevka
Bazarnyy Syzgan
Novodevichye
Zhigulevsk
KUYBYSHEV
Shilovo
Sapozhok
Bednodemyanovsk
Barysh
Oktyabrsk
Novokuybyshevsk
Spensk
Shiringushi
Nizhniy Lomov
Lunino
Sura
Syzran
Chapayevsk
Privolzhye
Tsna
Sosnovka
Mokshan
Gorodishche
Kashpirovka
Balshaya
Glushitsa
Morshansk
Zametchino
Kamenka
Penza
Sursk
Kuznetsk
351
Khvalynsk
Pestravka
Zamechino
Petrovsk
Bazarny
Karabulak
Volsk
Balakovo
Pugachev
Serdobsk
Rtishchevo
Khvatovka
Balanda
Saratov
Engels
Gornyy
Balashov
Samoylovka
Marks
Volgogradskoye
Vdkhr.
Krasnyy Kut
Orlov Gay
Krasnoarmeysk
Zhirnovsk
Yelan
Kamenskiy
Rovnoye
Novouzensk
Danilovka
Krasnyy Yar
Korovo
Pallasovka
Nikolayevsk
Bykovo
Kaztalovka
Mal Uzen
Mikhaylovka
Kamyshin
Bol Uzen
Frolovo
Olkhovka
Kaysatskoye
KAZAKH
Ilovlya
Iloulinskaya
Dzhanybek
Eltin
Urda
S.S.R.

38   40   42   46   48   COPYRIGHT. GEORGE. PHILIP & SON. LTD.

1 : 5 000 000

50 0 50 100 150 200 km

50

Yelan-Kolenovskiy Pavlovka Peski Orlov Gay Chalkar Chalkar Dzhambeyty
Georgiu-Dezh Khrenovoye Talovaya Novokhopersk Samoylovka Krasnoarmeysk Zhirnovsk Krasnyy Kut Novouzensk Mergenevskiy Karsha
Bobrov Buturlinovka 239 Uryupinsk Kukvide Krasnyy Yar 358 Novatka Piterka Chapayev Ural Bazartobe
Kamenka Novoannenskiy Panfilovo Vozyshennost Volgogradskoye Aleksandrov Gay Bol. Uzen Furmanovo Antonovo
Pavlovsk Kalach Buzuluk Danilovka Vdkhr. Kotovo Kaztalovka Mal. Uzen Dzhambeyty
Rossosh Boguchar Chettkovo Medveditsa Kamyshin Nikolayevsk Dzhanybek Urda Inderborskiy
Kantemirovka Kazanskaya Serafimovich Mikhaylovka Kumylzhenskaya Bykovo Kaysatskoye El'ton Makhambet (Yamankhalinka)
Kazanskaya Don Veshenskaya Ilovlya Pallasovka Shungay Zelenyy Topol
Millerovo Don Kletskiy (Kletskaya) Frolovo Prichalnaya Volzhskiy Leninsk Kapustin Yar Vladimirovka Novobogatinskoye Guryev
Voroshilovgrad (Lugansk) Gluboky Morozovsk Surovikino Volgograd (Stalingrad) Krasnoslobodsk Akhtubinsk (Petropavlovsky) Verkhniy Baskunchak -28
Krasnodon Lenin Belaya Kalitva Chernyshkovskiy Kalach na Donu Krasnoarmeysk Volga Shungay
Krasny Luch Sverdlovsk Tsimlyanskoye Krasnodonetskaya Tsimlyansk Kotelnikovo Obilnoye Kopanovka Yenotayevka
Gukovo Shakhty Konstantinovsk Volgodonsk Dubovskoye Zavetnoye KALMYK Krasnyy Yar
Novocherkassk Ust-Donetsk Bolshaya Martynovka Zimovniki A.S.S.R. Astrakhan
Rostov Bataysk Veselovskoye Vdkhr. Manych Proletarskaya Krasnoye Kamyzyak
Azov Zernograd Mechetinskaya Remontnoye Liman Kultay
Kushchevskaya Yegorlyk Oz. Manych-Gudilo Elista (Stepnoi) Kaspiyskiy O. Kulaly Mangyshlakskiy Zaliv
Peschanokopskoye Salsk Leninsk Priyutnoye Beloye Ozero M. Tyub Karagan P-ov.
Tikhoretsk Belaya Glina Krasnogvardeyskoye Ipatovo Kalaus Kuma Storyy Biryuzyak Fort Shevchenko Mangyshlak
Korenovsk Novoaleksandrovskaya Svetlograd (Petrovskoye) Blagodarnoye Bryanskoye Shevchenko
Ust-Labinsk Izobil'nyy Prikumsk Vladimirovka O. Tyuleniy -28
Krasnodar Armavir Stavropol 831 Zelenokumsk (Vorontsovo-Aleksandrovskoye) O. Chechen
Maykop Kurgannaya K. Kuban Nevinnomyssk Kursavka Aleksandriyskaya Lopatin
Apsheronsk Labinsk Mineralnyye Vody Georgievsk Terek Kizlyar
Neftegorsk Urup Cherkessk Yessentuki Pyatigorsk Prokhladnyy Mozdok CHECHENO-
Sochi Krasnaya Polyana Teberda Kislovodsk Karachayevsk Mayskiy INGUSH Gudermes Sulak Makhachkala
Adler Matsesta Nalchik Nartkala Malgobek Groznyy A.S.S.R. Kumtorkala Kaspiysk
Gagra Elbrus 5633 KABARDINO- Elkhotovo Beslan Khasavyurt Kizil Yurt Buynaksk Izberbash Novokayakent
Gudauta Kaori BALKAR A.S.S.R. 5203 Ordzhonikidze Soyason DAGESTAN Dagestanskiye Ogni 800
Novyy Afon Tkvarcheli Kazbek 5047 Balta Tebulos 4492 Khunzakh A.S.S.R. Derbent
Sukhumi Gali Zugdidi Tsdgeri Rioni Oni Agvali Kakhib Akusha Kasumkent
Ochamchire Anaklia GEORGIA Sachkhere Tkibuli Chiatura Dusheti Tlyarata Mikhaylovka
Mikha-Tskhakaya Kutaisi Zestafoni Khashuri Tskhinvali (Stalinir) Gori Telavi Kvareli Madzhalis Khachmas
Poti Samtredia S.S.R. Borzhomi Mtskheta Lagodekhi Gurdzhaani Zakatali Samur Akhty Bazar Dyuzi 4466
Kobuleti Makharadze Khulo Tbilisi Kaspi Signakhi Alazan Sheki (Nukha) Kuba Divichi
Batumi ADZHAR A.S.S.R. Akhaltsikhe Khrami Mamueli Rustavi Citeli Ckaro Mirzaani Mingechaurskoye Vdkhr. Kutkashen Baba dag 3629 Siazan
Hopa Akhalkalaki Akstafa Iori Kura Mingechaur Agdash Shemakha Sumgait
Pazar Borcka Artvin Ardahan Childir Alaverdi Tauz Yevlakh Geokchay Mashtaga
Rize 3192 Kirovakan Kirovabad Chanlar AZERBAIJAN BAKU
Trabzon Akçaabat Surmene Ispir Narman Sarikamis Leninakan Diliran Dashkesan Mir-Bashir S.S.R. Kazi Magomed Alyata
Çakirgol 3063 Kars Artik Aragats 4090 Ozero Sevan Berda Kyurdamir Surakhany Artem
Kaçkar 3937 Oltu Digor ARMENIAN Kamo Jerter Sabirabad M. Byandovan
Bayburt Çoruh Kagizman Echmiadzin S.S.R. Yerevan Martuni Agdzhabedi Imishli Karachala

KAZAKH S.S.R. Prikaspiyskaya Nizmennost Ergeni Vozyshennost Bol'shoy Kavkaz CASPIAN SEA

COPYRIGHT GEORGE PHILIP & SON LTD.

1:5 000 000

50   0   50   100   150   200 km

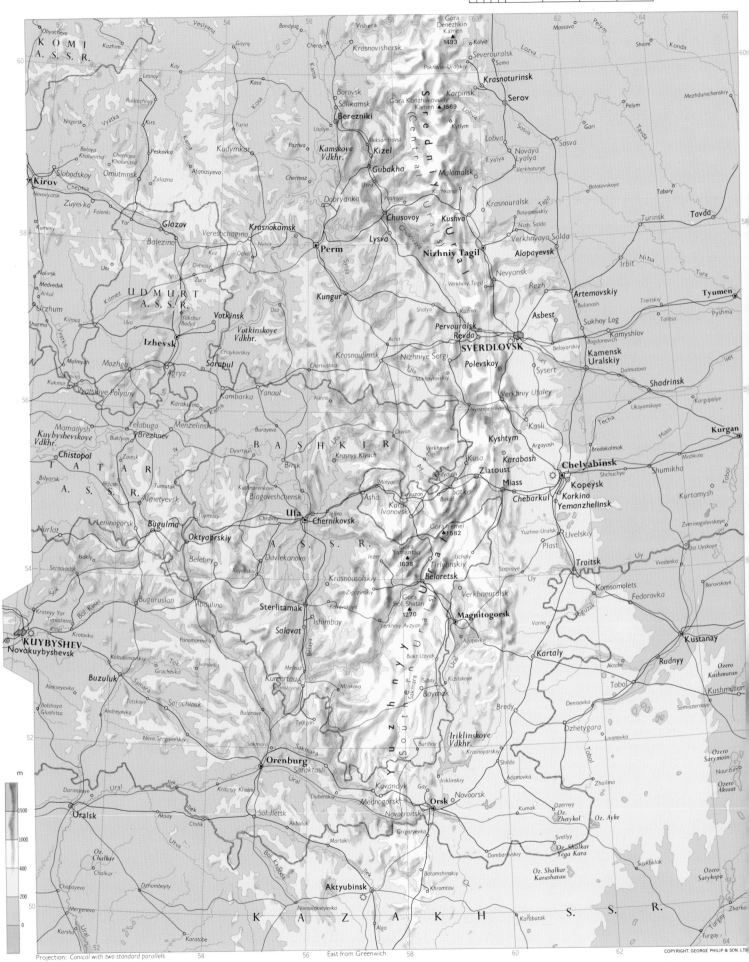

K O M I
A.S.S.R.

Obyachevo
Kazhim
Veslyana
Gayny
Bondyug
Cherdyn
Visbera
Gora
Denezhkin
Kamen
1493
Massava
Shaim
Konda

Nagorsk
Kay
Kosa
Krasnovishersk
Kalya
Lozva
Pelym
Mezhdurechenskiy

Vyatka
Kirs
Rudnichnyy
Kosa
Borovsk
Pokrovsk-Uralskiy
Severouralsk
Sama
Pelym

Slobodskoy
Omutninsk
Zalazna
Afanasyevo
Solikamsk
Berezniki
Gora Konzhakovskiy
Kamen ▲ 1569
Karpinsk
Krasnoturinsk
Sosva
Gari

Kirov
Cheptsa
Novovyatsk
Zuyevka
Falenki
Pazhva
Usolye
Kizel
Gubakha
Lobva
Lyalya
Novaya
Lyalya
Verkhoturye
Bolotskoye
Tabory

Glazov
Balezino
Vereshchagino
Krasnokamsk
Dobryanka
Chusovoy
Kushva
Nizh. Salda
Verkhnyaya Salda
Turinsk
Tavda

U D M U R T
A.S.S.R.
Kez
Ocher
Perm
Lysva
Nizhniy Tagil
Verkhniy Tagil
Nevyansk
Alapayevsk
Irbit
Nitsa

Votkinsk
Kungur
Shalya
Kuzino
Rezh
Artemovskiy
Troitskiy
Tyumen

Izhevsk
Votkinskoye
Vdkhr.
Osa
Nizhniye Sergi
Pervouralsk
Revda
Asbest
Sukhoy Log
Kamyshlov
Pyshma

Sarapul
Chaykovskiy
Krasnoufimsk
SVERDLOVSK
Polevskoy
Beloyarskiy
Bogdanovich
Talitsa

Vyatskiye Polyany
Agryz
Kambarka
Yanaul
Askino
Chernushka
Mikhaylovskiy
Verkhniy Ufaley
Sysert
Kamensk Uralskiy
Dalmatovo
Shadrinsk
Iset

Mamadysh
Kuybyshevskoye
Vdkhr.
Menzelinsk
Burayevo
B A S H K I R
Duvan
Verkhniye Kigi
Nizhnepetrovsk
Kasli
Techa
Uksyanskoye
Kargapolye

Chistopol
Brezhnev
Zainsk
Birsk
Krasnyy Klyuch
Kyshtym
Argayash
Brodokalmak
Mishkino
Kurgan

T A T A R
A. S. S. R.
Bilyarsk
Aktosh
Tumutla
Kushnarenkovo
Ay
Berdyaush
Kusa
Karabash
Miass
Chelyabinsk
Shumikha
Tobol

Almetyevsk
Blagoveshchensk
Asha
Kata
Ivanovsk
Satka
Bakal
Zlatoust
Chelyabinsk
Kopeysk
Shchuchye
Kurtamysh
Zverinogolovskoye

Leninogorsk
Tuymazy
Chishmy
Ufa
Chernikovsk
Minyar
Yuryuzan
Gora Iremel
▲ 1582
Chebarkul
Korkino
Yemanzhelinsk
Uvelskiy

Bugulma
Oktyabrskiy
Iglino
Inzer
Gora Yamantau
▲ 1638
Uchaly
Yuzhno-Uralsk
Plast
Uy
Ust Uyskoye

Belebey
Davlekanovo
Tirlyanskiy
Stepnoye
Vvedenka
Borovskoye

Murlat
Serpovatsk
Rayevskiy
Krasnousolskiy
Zigazinskiy
Beloretsk
Verkhneuralsk
Troitsk

Isaklydy
Buguruslan
Abdulino
Sterlitamak
Petrovskiy
Gora Bol. Shatan
▲ 1270
Verkhniy Avzyan
Magnitogorsk
Komsomolets
Fedorovka

Krasnyy Yar
Timashevo
Kinel
Krotovka
Ishimbay
Salavat
Bol. Kinel
Belaya
Bakr Uzyak
Agapovka
Varna
Kartaly
Kustanay

KUYBYSHEV
Novokuybyshevsk
Koltubanovskiy
Tok
Ivanovka
Grachevka
Meleuz
Mrakovo
Sibay
Kizilskoye
Ural
Magnitogorsk
Tobol
Rudnyy
Ozero
Kushmurun

Buzuluk
Samara
Sorochinsk
Bulanovo
Kumertau
Baymak
Bredy
Denisovka
Kushmurun

Alekseyevka
Bolshaya
Glushitsa
Totskoye
Andreyevka
Nova-Sergiyevskiy
Tyulgan
Iriklinskoye
Vdkhr.
Dzhetygara
Livanovka
Ozero
Sarynoin
Naurzum

Chapayevo
Sakmara
Sakmara
Buribay
Krasnoyarskiy
Shilda
Adamovka
Zhailma
Ozero
Aksuat

Mednogorsk
Orenburg
Saraktash
Kuvandyk
Gay
Iriklinskiy
Orsk
Novoorsk
Kumak
Ozernyy
Oz.
Zhetykol
Oz. Ayke

Uralsk
Ural
Ilek
Krasnyy Kholm
Dubenskiy
Novotroitsk
Ural
Grigoryevka
Oz. Shalkar
Tega Kara

Darinskoye
Aksay
Chilik
Sol Iletsk
Akbulak
Martuk
Bol. Khobda
Dombarovskiy
Oz. Shalkar
Karashatau
Suykbulak
Ozero
Sarykopa

Mergenevo
Karsha
Ural
Dzhambeyty
Karatobe
Ilek
Novoalekseyevka
Aktyubinsk
Alga
Khromtau
Karabutak
Turgay

K   A   Z   A   K   H   S.   S.   R.

m
1500
1000
400
200
50
0

East from Greenwich
COPYRIGHT. GEORGE PHILIP & SON. LTD

1:5 000 000

Projection: Conical with two standard parallels.

East from Greenwich

1:50 000 000

500   0   500   1000   1500   2000 km

m 6000 4000 2000 1200 400 200 0

200 2000 4000 6000

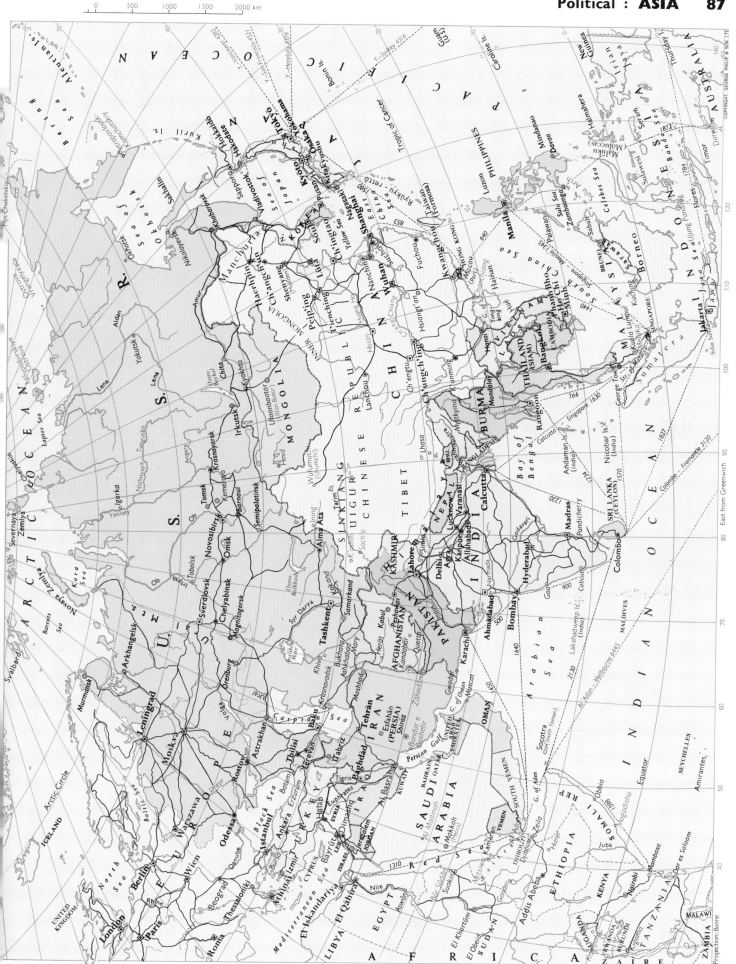

1:50 000 000

0   500   1000   1500   2000 km

COPYRIGHT. GEORGE PHILIP & SON. LTD.

Projection: Bonne

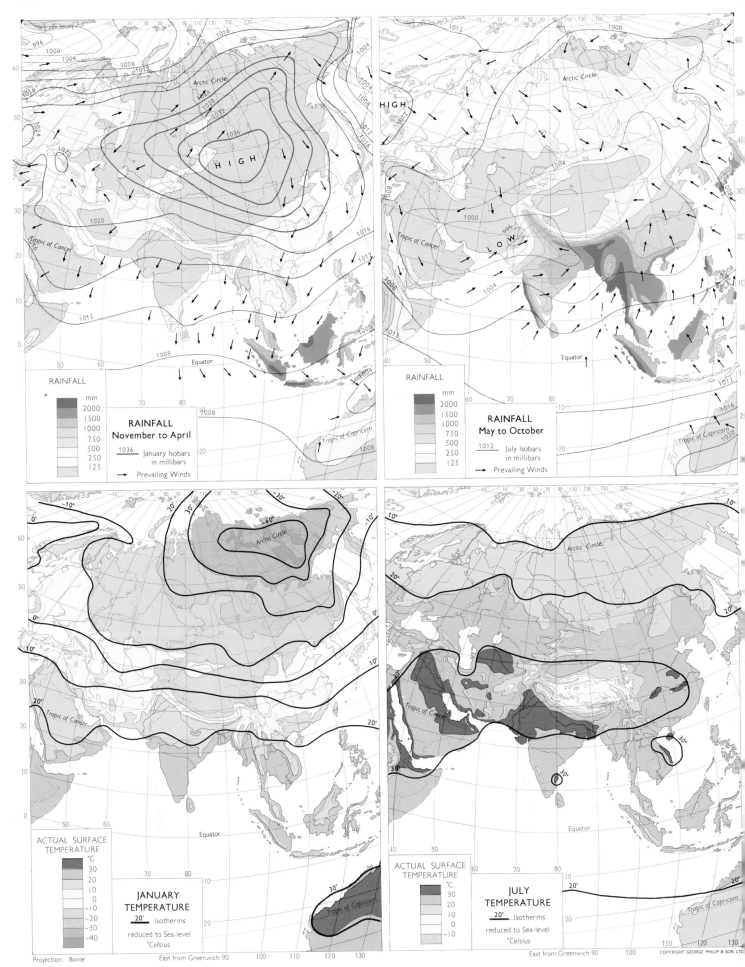

RAINFALL

	mm
	2000
	1500
	1000
	750
	500
	250
	125

**RAINFALL
November to April**

1036   January Isobars
in millibars

→   Prevailing Winds

RAINFALL

	mm
	2000
	1500
	1000
	750
	500
	250
	125

**RAINFALL
May to October**

1012   July Isobars
in millibars

→   Prevailing Winds

ACTUAL SURFACE
TEMPERATURE

	°C
	30
	20
	10
	0
	−10
	−20
	−30
	−40

**JANUARY
TEMPERATURE**

20°   Isotherms

reduced to Sea-level
°Celsius

ACTUAL SURFACE
TEMPERATURE

	°C
	30
	20
	10
	0
	−10

**JULY
TEMPERATURE**

20°   Isotherms

reduced to Sea-level
°Celsius

Projection: Bonne   East from Greenwich 90

East from Greenwich 90   COPYRIGHT. GEORGE PHILIP & SON. LTD

INDIA: MONSOONS

THEIR EVOLUTION
IS SHOWN BY
MONTHLY
CLIMATE
MAPS

RAINFALL
mm per month

mm
25
50
100
200
400

—— ISOTHERMS
*Temperature in
degrees Celsius*

—— ISOBARS
(Pressure in millibars)

← WINDS

mm
3000
2000
1000
500
250

1 : 80 000 000

East from Greenwich

Projection : Lambert's Equivalent Azimuthal

COPYRIGHT GEORGE PHILIP & SON. LTD

JANUARY

FEBRUARY

MARCH

APRIL

MAY

JUNE

JULY

AUGUST

SEPTEMBER

OCTOBER

NOVEMBER

DECEMBER

1:1 000 000

10 0 10 20 30 40 km

------- 1949–1974 Armistice lines between
Israel and the Arab States.

MEDITERRANEAN SEA

LEBANON

SYRIA

Sür
(Tyre)

Nahr al Litani
Bayt Jann
Sa'sa'
Al Majdal
BIRKET RAM
Massada
Sukatiye

Bäzüriye
Tayr Zebna
Kefar Gil'adi
Dan
Banias
Metulla
Qiryat Shemona
Qana
Tibnin
Al-Aqraba
Tall Karim
Ghabaghib

An-Naqüra
Aalma Ach Chaab
Bint Jbail
Ramot Naftali
Gonen
Under
Israeli
Occupation
Sanamen

Kefar Rosh Haniqra
Sulam Tsor
Bezet
Shomera
Sasa
Hare Meron
Tel HAZOR
Zimra
Mishmar
Al-Härrah
Namer
Izra

Nahariyya
Ben 'Ammi
N. Keziv
Kabri
Evron
Amiga
Bet Ha'Emeq
Kefar Yasif
Bet Jann
Zefat
Hazor
Rosh Pinna
Jordan
Wadi ar Ruqqad
Uassem
Mahajje

1208

'Akko
(Acre)
Majd el Kurum
Yas'in
Nahf
Rama
Amm'ad
El Agr
Khushniye
Rafid
Saham al-Jawlan

Qiryat Yam
Qiryat Bialik
Qir. Hayyim
Kafr
Manda
Maghar
Bet Netofa
Migdal
Ginnosar
Yam Kinneret
(Sea of Galilee)
Ben Gev

HAIFA
Newe Sha'anan
Qiryat Ata
Nesher
Ramat
Shefar'am
Kefar Zetim
Mizpe
Tiberias
-209
Fiq

Tirat Karmel
Kefar Hasidim
Zippori
Kafr Kanna
Lavi
Kefar Kama
Ar-Ramthä

546 ▲
Sede Ya'aqov
Yishay
Nazareth
Reina
Bet Qeshet
Yavne'el
Degania
Ash Shuna

'ATLIT
Daliyat
el Karmel
Nahalal
Migdal
Ha'Emeq
Tel Adashim
Dabburiya
Kefar Tavor
Ha Ma'a Gan

Kerem Maharal
Ramat
Ho Shofet
Yogne'am
Tabor
▲515
Mizra
Balfouriyya
Um Qeis

Dor
(Tantura)
Mishmar
Ha'Emeq
TEL
MEGIDDO
Megiddo
Afula
Kefar Yehezqel
En Harod
Yizre'el
Bet HaShitta
Nahalal

Bet Hananya
Binyamina
Or 'Aqiva
Umm el Fahm
Hare Gilboa
Bet Alfa
Newe Eitan
Tarqib
At-Tayyibah

QESARI
(CAESAREA)
N. Hadera
Karkur
Pardes Hanna
Yamun
Biqin
Bet She'an
Deir Abu Sa'id
Al Husn

Hadera
Gan Shumuel
Ya'Bud
Jenin
Qabatiya
Tirat Tsevi

Elyashiv
Jatt
Zeita
El Dotan
Emeq Dotan
Sanur
Meithalun
Tubas
1198

Netanya
Kefar Shuweika
Fara
Be'eroti
Dayr el Ghusun
Anza
Silat adh Dhahr
Burqa
Tammun
Al Mafraq

Even Yehuda
Tel Mond
Tira
Tülkarm
Anabta
Sabastiya
SAMARIA
Asira esh Shamaliya
'Ajlun
Jabal 'Ajlun
1247
Suf

Kefar Qaddum
SHECHEM
940 ▲ Eval
Talluza
Jarash
Al Madwar

Rishpon
Ra'anana
Qalqilya
Gerizim
881 Nabulus
JACOB'S WELL
Zarqa
Er Rumman

TEL ARSHAF
Herzliyya
Kefar Sava
Tell
Burqin
Bayt Furik

Ramat HaSharon
Magdiel
Under
Huwara
Awarta

Hadar Ramatayim
Rosh Ha'Ayin
Jomma'in
BaytA
Damiya
Jabal Yusha
'Ajmar

Bene
Beraq
Petah Tiqwa
Israeli
Salfit
Tahta
Qusra
1113

TEL AVIV
YAFO
(Jaffa)
Ramat
Gan
H. MIGDAL
AFEO
Sarida
Qabalan
Talfit
As Salt

Bat Yam
Or Yehuda
Kafr Ein
Lubban
SHILO
Sinjil
Sweilih

Holon
Matayim
Zaffeyim
Tirat Yehuda
Rantis
Rima

Rishon Le'Zion
Ness Ziyyona
Occupation
Bir Zeit
Silwad
Kafr Malik
Tall 'Asir
'AMMAN

N. Soreq
Nabi Rubin
Lod (Lydda)
Jifna
Baytin
Taiyiba
Auja
Wadi as Sir

Ramle
Rehovot
Na'an
Gimzo
Beit 'Ur et-Tahta
Rammun
Ramallah
Ram Allah

Qiryat 'Eqron
Giv'at
Brenner
TEL
GEZER
Bet 'Ur et-Tahta
Ein 'Arik
Betunya
Deir Dibwan

N. Lakhish
Gedera
Hazor Ashdod
Latrun
Ayalon
(Quban)
Imwas
Biddu
Ataror
El Ariha
(Jericho)
Nu'eima
Hussein
(Allenby)
Bridge

Ashdod
Gan Yavne
Qiryat Mal'akhi
Bet Shemesh
Kefar
Apu Ghosh
Mozo
JERUSALEM
(Yerushalayim, Al Quds)
Abu Dis
Kallia

Nizzanim
Abba Hillel
Negba
Zekharya
En Kerem
Tur
Ei'zariya (Bethany)
QUMRAN
Suweima

Be'eri
Toviyya
Agur
Bayt Jala
Bayt Lahm (Bethlehem)
Bayt Sahur
BURAK SULAYMAN
(SOLOMON'S POOLS)

Ashqelon
Kokhav
Mikha'el
Zohar
Adderet
Surif
Bayt Ummar
Bayt Fajjar
'Etsyon

Qiryat Gat
Gal'on
N. Guvrin
BET GUVRIN
TEL
LAKHISH
 Halhul
Sir
W. Ghar

N. Shiqma
Helez
Deror Hayil
Idna
Tarqumiyah

Beit Lahiya
Mavqi'im
Ge'a
Amazya
Düra
1020 Hebron
Bani Na'im

Jabaliya
Gaza
Nefallesim
Ruheiba

Gaza Strip

Dayral Balah
Be'eri
Bet Qama
'Yattah

Khan
Yunis
Bani Suhayla
N. Besor
N. Gerar
Melilot
Az Zahiriya
(Dhahiriya)
As-Samü'
En Gedi

Abasan
Nir Oz
Peduyyim
Gilat
Mishmar HaNegev
Mabbu'im

Mivtahim
Yesha'
Urim
Singh
Omer
N. Ze'elim
N. Ze'elim
MESADA

Kerem Shalom
Gevulot
Ze'elim
Be'er Sheva'
Neyatim
N. Be'er Shera
Arad

EGYPT

Be'er Sheva'
Nevatim

Newe Zohar

JORDAN

Irbid
Dar'ä
Zayzun
Et Turra
Ghariyat ash-Sharqiyat

(inset map, lower right):

Gaza Strip
Gaza
Ghazzah
Bet Qama
Hebron

Khan Yunis
Mishmar
Ha Negev
Be'er Sheva'
Arad

ISRAEL

Dimona
Yeroham
Sedom

Qezi'ot
SHIVTA
Oron
N. Zin

Ha Negev

Mizpe Ramon
Ramon
En Yahav

1035
Makhtesh
Ramon
Har Ramon

Lussan

EGYPT

JORDAN

1727

PETRA

N. Paran

Mikhrot
Timna

Yotvata

Girofit

Elat
Al
'Aqabah

Continuation
Southwards
1:2 500 000
0 10 20 30 km

Projection: Conical with two standard parallels

East from Greenwich

COPYRIGHT. GEORGE PHILIP & SON, LTD.

m
1000
400
200
0
200
m

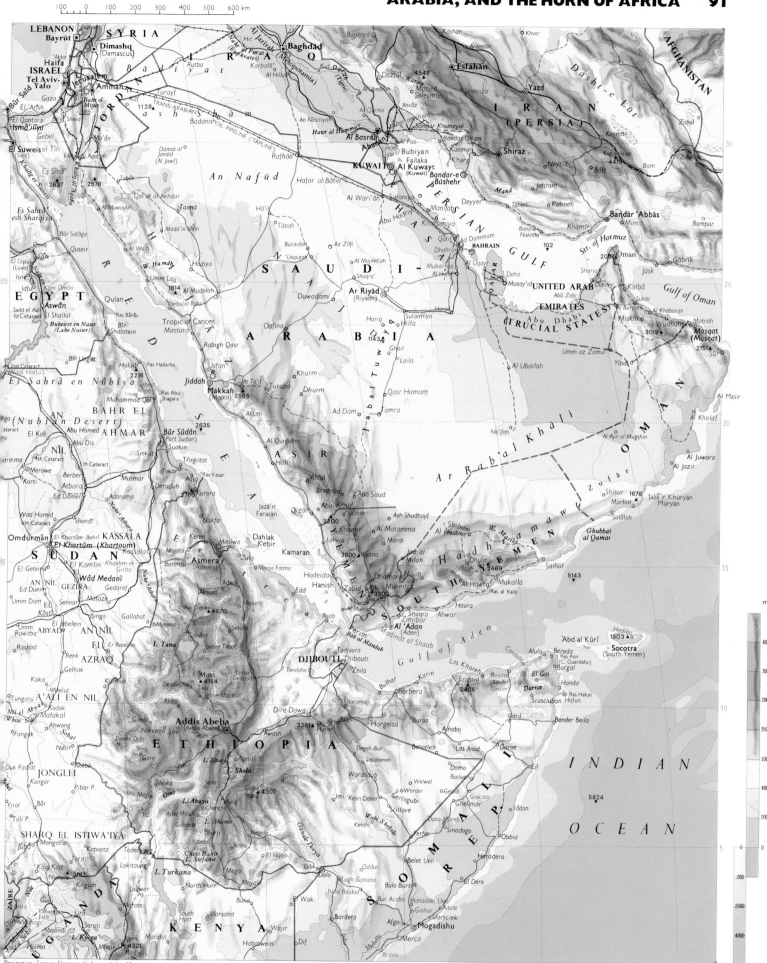

1:15 000 000

100 0 100 200 300 400 500 600 km

LEBANON
Bayrūt
SYRIA
Dimashq
(Damascus)
Haifa
Akko
ISRAEL
Tel Aviv-Yafo
Jerusalem
Amman
Gaza
Bûr Saîd
El 'Arish
Ismâ'iliya
Gebel
El Qantara
Bahr el
Miyet
JORDAN
Turayf
Ma'ān
El Suweis
(Suez)
el Tîh
Es Sînā'
2637
2578
Tabūk
Al Muwaylih
Al Akhdar

IRAQ
Hît
Al Jazirah
Nahr el Furat
(Euphrates)
Rutba
Baghdad
Karbalā'
Al Hillah
Al Kūt
Dezfûl
4548
Esfahan
Shahriza
Yazd
Kāshān
Ardestān
Khvor

IRAN
(PERSIA)
Dasht-e Lūt
Kermān
Zābol

An Nafūd

As Samāwah
An Nāsiriyah
Al Basrah
Abadan
Al Fāo
Bandar Khomeyni
Bandar Dilam
Shiraz
Neyrīz
Bām
Bampūr

KUWAIT
Al Kuwayt
(Kuwait)
Bubiyan
Failaka
Hafar al Bātin
Az Zilfi
Buraidah
'Unaizah
Al Majma'ah
Shaqrā'
Hā'il

SAUDI-

EGYPT
Aswan
1st Cataract
Buheiret en Naser
(Lake Nasser)
Es Sahra
esh Sharqiya
Qena
Qûs
El Uqsur
(Luxor)
Isna
Kôm Ombo
Idfu
Quseir
Bûr Safâga
Al Wajh
Ummi Lajj
1814
Al Madinah
Yanbu'al Bahr
Duwadami
Ar Riyād
(Riyadh)
Hariq
Sulaimiya
Hilla
Dhurm

PERSIAN GULF
BAHRAIN
102
Ad Dammam
Dhahran
Al Qatif
Al Hufūf
Doha
QATAR
Musay'id
UNITED ARAB
EMIRATES
(TRUCIAL STATES)
Abū Zabi
Abu Dhabi
Dubayy
Sharjah
Band-e
Nakhīlu
Khāmir
Lār
Bandar 'Abbās
Minab
Str. of Hormuz
2057
Oman
Jāsk
Gābrīk
Bampūr
Kalbā
Al Khābūrāh
Suhār
Miskin
3019
Masqat
(Muscat)
2151
Sūr
Al Masir
Gulf of Oman

Tropic of Cancer
ARABIA
1143
Jabal Tuwaiq
Laila
Qasr Hamam
Ghail
Umm az Zamūl
Al Ubailah
Yibal
Al Khalaf

RED SEA
Halaib
Ras Hadarba
2216
Bîr Ungat
Jiddah
Makkah
(Mecca)
2565
At Ta'if
Turaba
Khurm
Dhurm
Ad Dam
Tamra
Na'ifah
Al Jiwara
Al Jazir

AN
BAHR EL
(Nubian Desert)
El Kab
Abu Hamed
AHMAR
Bûr Sûdân
(Port Sudan)
2635
Sinkat
Suakin
Ras Abu
Shagara
Usfan
Rabigh Qasr
Mastura
Dafina
Al Lith
Al Qunfidha
Hali

Ar Rab'al Khālī

Abha
Dhahran
Abū Saud
Jaza'ir
Farasān
Qizān
3200
ASIR
Al Matamma
Marib
Ash Shudhayf
Najran
Shibam
Al Hautah
OMAN
Al Ayn al Mugshin
1678
Jazā'ir Khūryān
Mūryān
Marbat
Salālah
Shisur
W. Masila
Zufār
Ghubbat
al Qamar
5143

2nd Cataract
Wadi Halfa
Es Sahra en Nûbiya
El Kab
Abu Dis
NIL
Merowe
Berber
Atbara
Ed Dâmer
Wâd Hamid
Korti
Shendi
Musmar
Derudub
1780
Karora
Trinkitat
Tokar
Aqiq
Ras Kasar
Nakfa
Keren
Dahlak
Kebir
Mitsiwa
Zula
Omdurmân
El Khartûm Bahrî
KASSALA
El Khartûm
(Khartoum)
Kassala
Asmera
(Asmara)
Adwa
Aksum
Mekele
Mersa Fatma
3600
Sana
Dhamar
Al Mukha
Perim
Bab el Mandab
SOUTH YEMEN
Jod al
Milah
YEMEN
2469
Dhula
Nisab
Mukalla
Ras al Kalb
Saihut
Haura
Hadhramaw
Ghubbat
al Qamar
1503
Socotra
(South Yemen)
'Abd al Kūrī
Hadibu

SUDAN
El Geteina
El Kamlin
El Khartûm
GEZIRA
Wâd Medanî
AN NIL
Ed Dueim
Sennar
Mafaza
Gedaref
Barentu
Agordat
Gallabat
Metema
4620
Ras Dashan
Dabat
Gonder
Debre Tabor
Mota
4154
Talo
Debre Markos
Addis Abeba
(Addis Ababa)
Nazret
Dese
(Dessye)
Tadjoura
Tendaho
DJIBOUTI
Djibouti
Zeila
Bulhar
Berbera
Borama
Las Khareh
Erigavo
2406
Bender
Cassim
Bosaso
Candala
Bereda
(C. Asir)
Alula
Bargal
El Gal
Handa
Darror
Scusciuban
Ras Hafun
Hafun

INDIAN

Umm Dam
EL
Kôstî
Rashad
Renk
ABYAD
Umm Ruwaba
El Jebelein
Singa
Er Roseires
Gelhak
EL
AZRAQ
Kaka
Gimbi
Nekemte
Gedo
Dembi Dolo
Gore
L. Tana
L. Zwai
L. Shala
Asela
Harer
3381
Awash
Dire Dawa
Hargeisa
Burao
Degeh-Bur
Sasabeneh
Domo
Baduen
Garoe
Ajnabo
Las Anod
Welwel
Werder
Geldi
Gherlogubi
Ghelinsor
Galcaio
Iddan
Abwong
Fangak
A'ALI EN NIL
Malakal
Nasir
Sobat
ETHIOPIA
Mota
Wata
Majii
Omo
Gobu
4307
Chencha
L. Abaya
Arba Minch
Gidole
L. Shamo
Negele
Yabelo
Arero
Imi
Kebri Dehar
Wabi Shebele
Kelafo
Ferfer
Scillave
Dusa
Mareb
Sinadogo
5824
Obbia

Duk Fadiat
JONGLEI
Kongor
Pibor P.
Yirol
Bôr
Tali P.
SHARQ EL ISTIWA'IYA
Jūba
Mongalla
Kapoeta
Chew Bahir
(L. Stefanie)
L. Turkana
El Niybo
Mega
Moyale
Buna
Dolo
Lugh Ganana
Bulo Burti
El Dere
Haradera
Bardera
OCEAN

ZAIRE
Aru
Gulu
3187
Kitgum
Kaabong
Lodwar
North Horr
South Horr
Marsabit
Wajir
Habaswein
Dif
El Wak
SOMALI REP.
Bur Acaba
Mahaddei Uen
Gohar
Adale
Balet Uen
Afgoi
Iscia Baidoa
Mogadishu
Merca
Brava
Shebeli

UGANDA
L. Kyoga
Mbale
4321
Soroti
KENYA
Maralal

m
4000
3000
2000
1500
1000
400
200
0
200
2000
4000
m

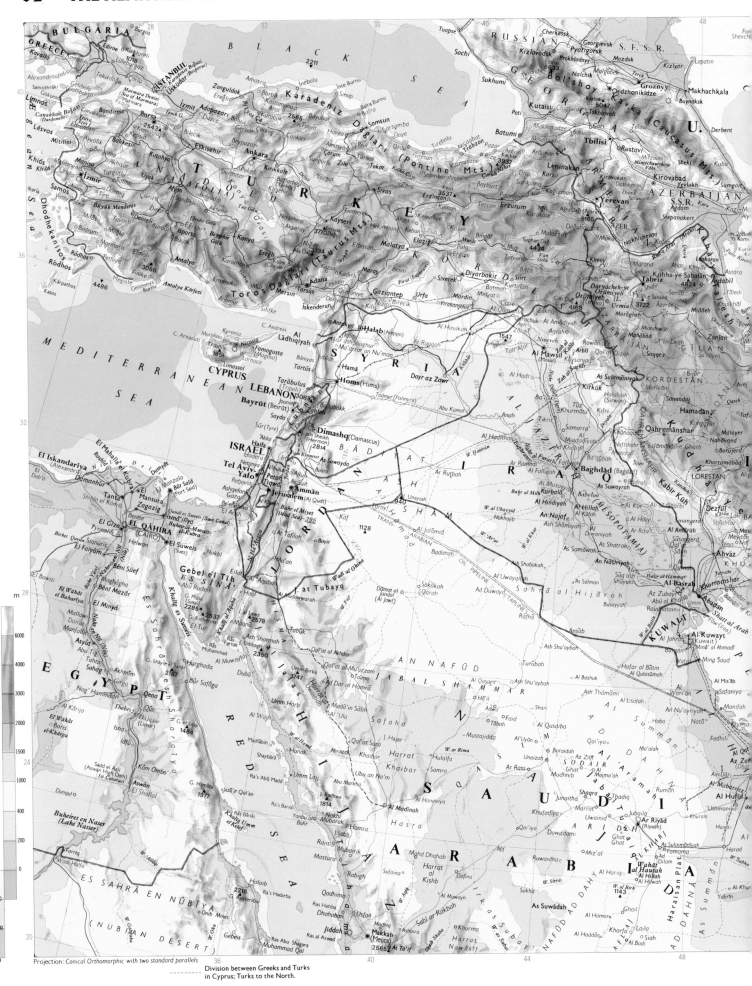

Projection: Conical Orthomorphic with two standard parallels

Division between Greeks and Turks
in Cyprus; Turks to the North.

1:10 000 000

100 0 100 200 300 400 km

KAZAKH S.S.R.

Plato Ustyurt

Kazakhskiy Zaliv

S. S. R.

KARA-KALPAKISCHE A.S.S.R.

Ozero Sudochye

Aralskoye More

PESKI KYZYLKUM   KAZAKH S.S.R.

Chimbai

Kungrod

Muynak

Nukus

Tashaus

Kungrad

U Z B E K S T A N

Turkestan

Dzhambul

Gora Manas

Tolass

Chimkent

Arys

Lenger 4488

Chatkal

Naryn

Syr Darya

Chirchik

Tashkent

Angren

Namangan

Andizhan

Osh

Kashgar (Shufu)

Leninabad

Kokand

Fergana

Margelan

KIRGIZ S.S.R.

TienShan

CHINA

Urgench

Turtkul

Khiva

Amu Darya (Oxus)

Darganata

Kattakurgan

Dzhizak

2169

Bukhara

Kogan

Samarkand

5489

TADZHIK

Dushanbe

Pik Kommunizma 7495

Pamir

Krasnovodski Poluostrov

Krasnovodsk

TURKMEN S.S.R.

Serny Zavod

Karshi

Guzar

Shakhrisyabz

Khorog

Faizabad

BADAKHSHAN

GILGIT

7190

Kerki

1880

Nebit Dag

Kizyl Arvat

Kazandzhik

KARA KUM

Chardzhou

Shirabad

Termez

Kunduz

Khanabad

TAKHAR

HINDU KUSH

Ashkhabad

Bairam Ali

Mary (Mery)

Iolotan

Andkhoi

Balkh

Mazar-i-Sharif

BALKH

FARYAB

Maimana

3494

Band-i-Turkistan

BAMIAN

Charikar

Kabul

PESHAWAR

Mohammadabad

Tedzhen

Serakhs

Herat

HERAT

Obeh

Safed Koh

Kohi-Baba 5143

WARDAK

Ghazni

PAKTIA

Islamabad

Rawalpindi

Quchan

3117

Kuh-e-Binalud

Mashhad (Meshed)

Neyshabur

Sabzevar

Kuh-e-Sorkh 3020

Torbat-e Heydariyeh

Torbat-e Jam

GHOR

URUZGAN

GHAZNI

ZABUL

Kandahar

KANDAHAR

HELMAND

Quetta

3593

DASHT-E-KAVIR (Great Salt Desert)

KHORASAN

Ferdow

Qayen

Yazdan

Birjand

Tabas

Farah

FARAH

Girishk

Registan

Dasht-i-Margo

NIMRUZ

Zabol

Chagai Hills

2462

I R A N

Kerman

Zahedan (Duzdab)

Zabol

BALUCHISTAN

P A K I S T A N

I N D I A

FARS

Shiraz

Bam

Kerman

SISTAN

Mirjaveh

Dalbandin

Makran Coast Range

KARACHI

U N I T E D   A R A B   E M I R A T E S (TRUCIAL STATES)

Abu Zabi (Abu Dhabi)

Dubayy (Dubai)

Sharjah

Oman

Masqat (Muscat)

Tropic of Cancer

A R A B I A N   S E A

Gulf of Oman

Str. of Hormuz

O M A N

Mouths of the Indus

KUTCH

Gulf of Kutch

Rann of Kutch

1:6 000 000

50   0   50   100   150   200   250 km

JAMMU AND KASHMIR
On same scale as Main Map

East from Greenwich

1:6 000 000

50   0   50   100   150   200   250 km

B A Y   O F   B E N G A L

Coromandel Coast

MADRAS

ARABIAN SEA

KARNATAKA

GOA

T A M I L

N A D U

K E R A L A

Gulf of Mannar

(Mannar)

Palk Strait

SRI LANKA
(CEYLON)

Colombo

Projection: Conical with two standard parallels

East from 80 Greenwich

m   3000   2000   1500   1000   400   200   0

m   0   200   2000   4000

1:6 000 000

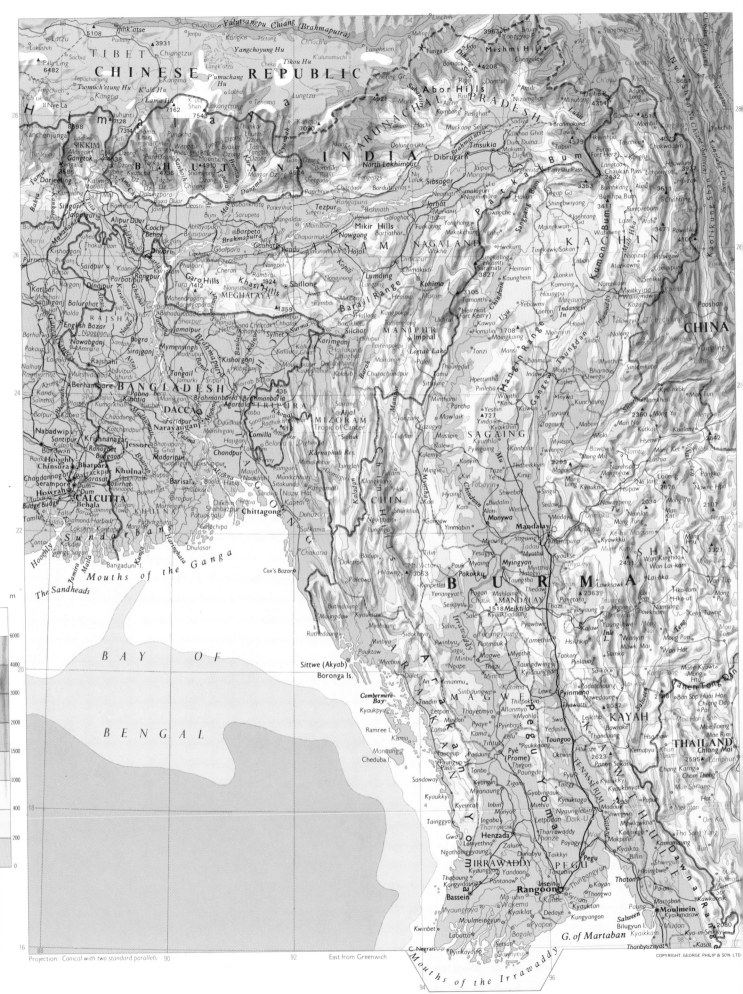

Projection: Conical with two standard parallels   East from Greenwich

1:20 000 000

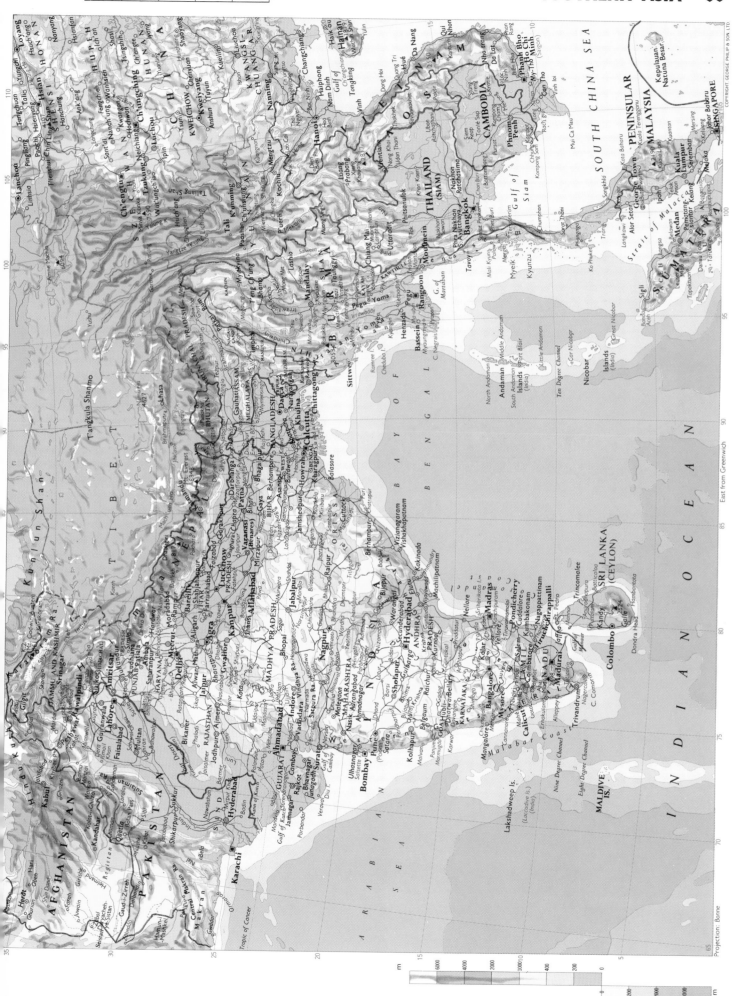

Projection: Bonne

East from Greenwich

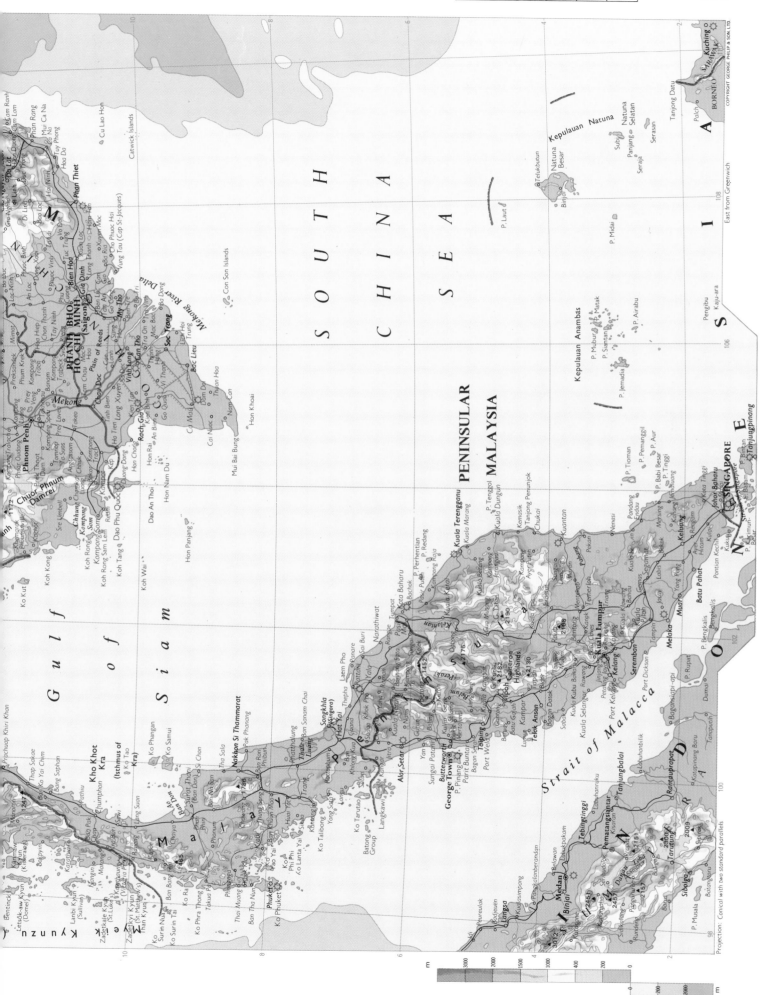

1 : 6 000 000

50   0   50   100   150   200   250 km

East from Greenwich

SOUTH

CHINA

SEA

Gulf

of

Siam

PENINSULAR
MALAYSIA

Strait of Malacca

Kepulauan Natuna

Kepulauan Anambas

BORNEO

SARAWAK

SINGAPORE

Phnom Penh

Mekong

HO CHI MINH
(Saigon)

PHANH BHO

Kuala Lumpur

Projection: Conical with two standard parallels

m
3000 2000 1500 1000 400 200 0

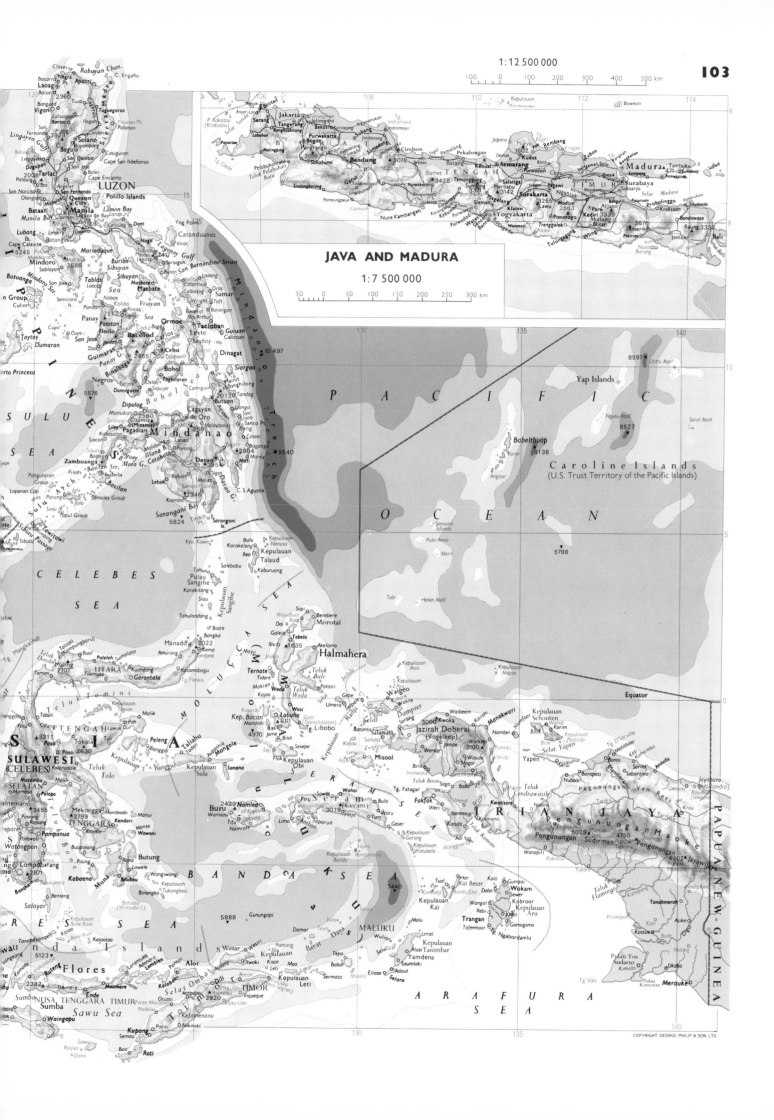

1 : 30 000 000

200   0   200   400   600   800   1000 km

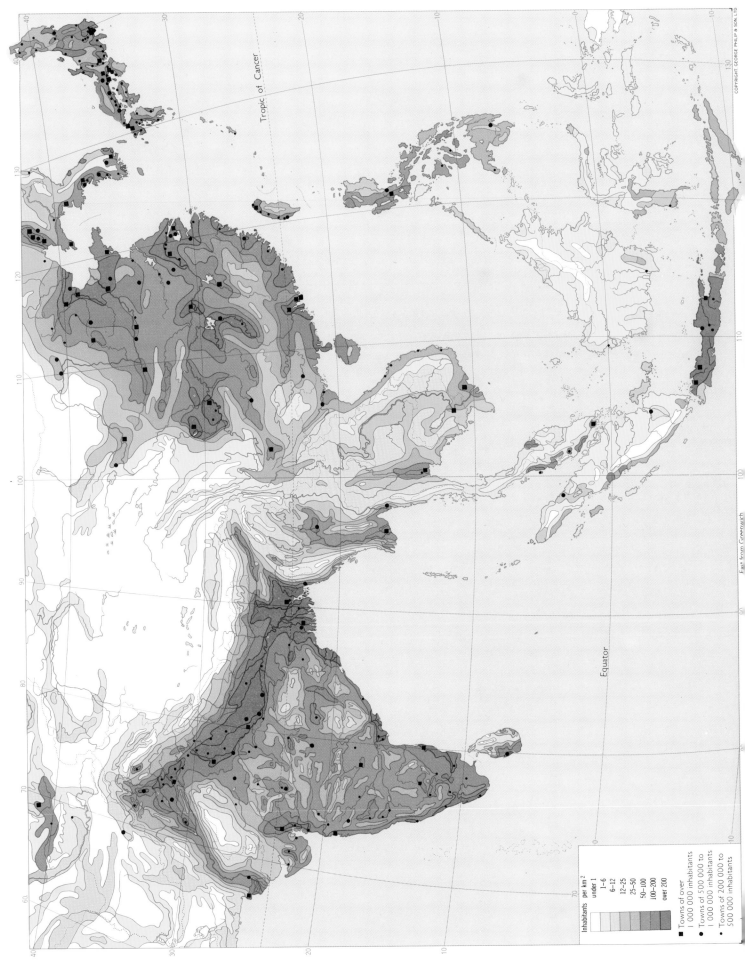

COPYRIGHT GEORGE PHILIP & SON LTD

Tropic of Cancer

Equator

East from Greenwich

Inhabitants	per km²
	under 1
	1–6
	6–12
	12–25
	25–50
	50–100
	100–200
	over 200

■ Towns of over 1 000 000 inhabitants
● Towns of 500 000 to 1 000 000 inhabitants
• Towns of 200 000 to 500 000 inhabitants

1:20 000 000

East from Greenwich

Projection: Bonne

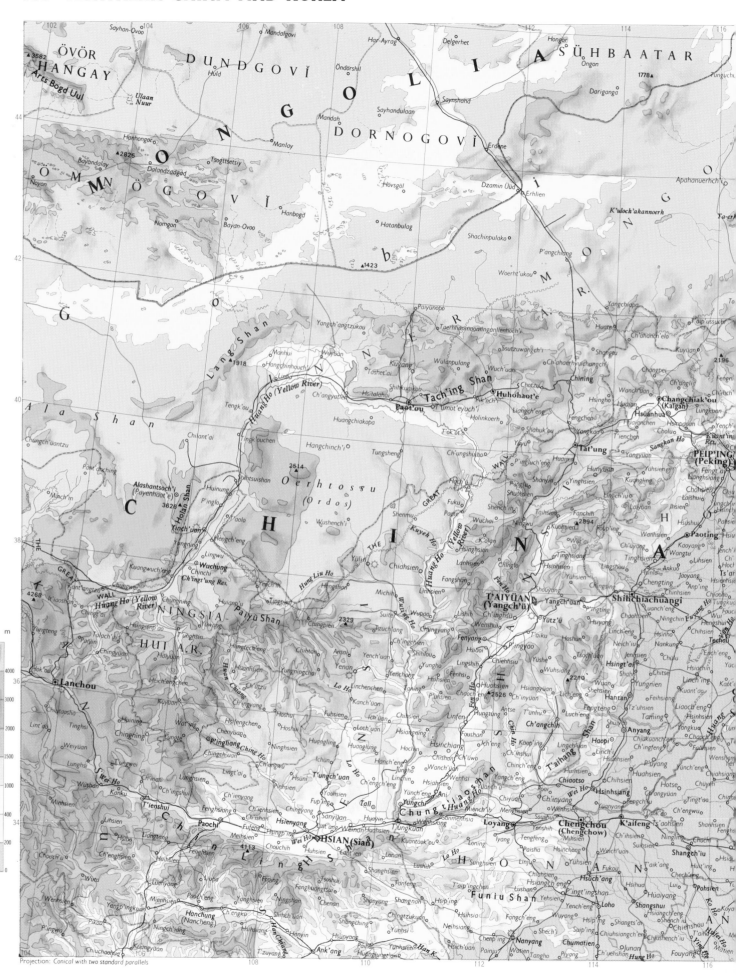

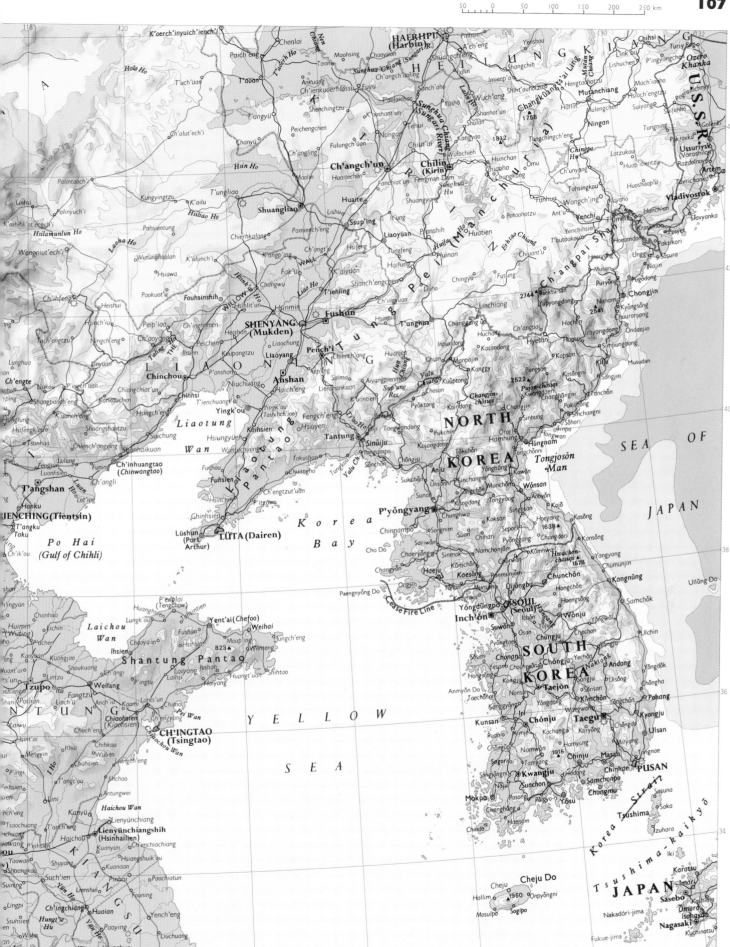

1 : 6 000 000

50   0   50   100   150   200   250 km

U. S. S. R.

HAERHPIN
(Harbin)

HEILUNGKIANG

Ozero
Khanka

Mutanchiang

Ussuriysk
(Voroshilov)

Ch'angch'un

Chilin
(Kirin)

Vladivostok

Shuangliao

Ssup'ing

Liaoyüan

Yenchi

Tumen

CHANGPAI SHAN

T'unghua

NORTH
KOREA

Chongjin

Kyŏngsŏng

SHENYANG
(Mukden)

Fushun

Pench'i

Hyesan

Kimch'aek

Hamhŭng

Hŭngnam

Chinchou

Anshan

Sinŭiju

P'yŏngyang

Wŏnsan

Tongjosŏn
Man

SEA   OF

Anju

T'angshan

Po Hai
(Gulf of Chihli)

Lüshun
(Port
Arthur)

LÜTA (Dairen)

Korea
Bay

JAPAN

TIENCHING(Tientsin)

Chinnampo

Cease Fire Line

Inch'ŏn

SEOUL
(Sŏul)

Chunch'ŏn

Kangnŭng

Ullŭng Do

Laichou
Wan

Yent'ai(Chefoo)

Weihai

Haeju

Kaesŏng

Panmunjŏm

Ŭijŏngbu

Yŏngdŭngp'o

Suwŏn

Wŏnju

SOUTH

Samch'ŏk

Shantung Pantao

KOREA

Taejŏn

Kunsan

Iri

Chŏnju

Taegu

CH'INGTAO
(Tsingtao)

YELLOW

Kwangju

Sunchon

PUSAN

Chinhae

Mokp'o

SEA

Tsushima

Korea Strait

Tsushima-kaikyō

KIANGSU

Cheju Do

JAPAN

Sasebo

Cheju

Nagasaki

COPYRIGHT. GEORGE PHILIP & SON LTD.

Projection : Conical with two standard parallels

SOUTH   CHINA   SEA

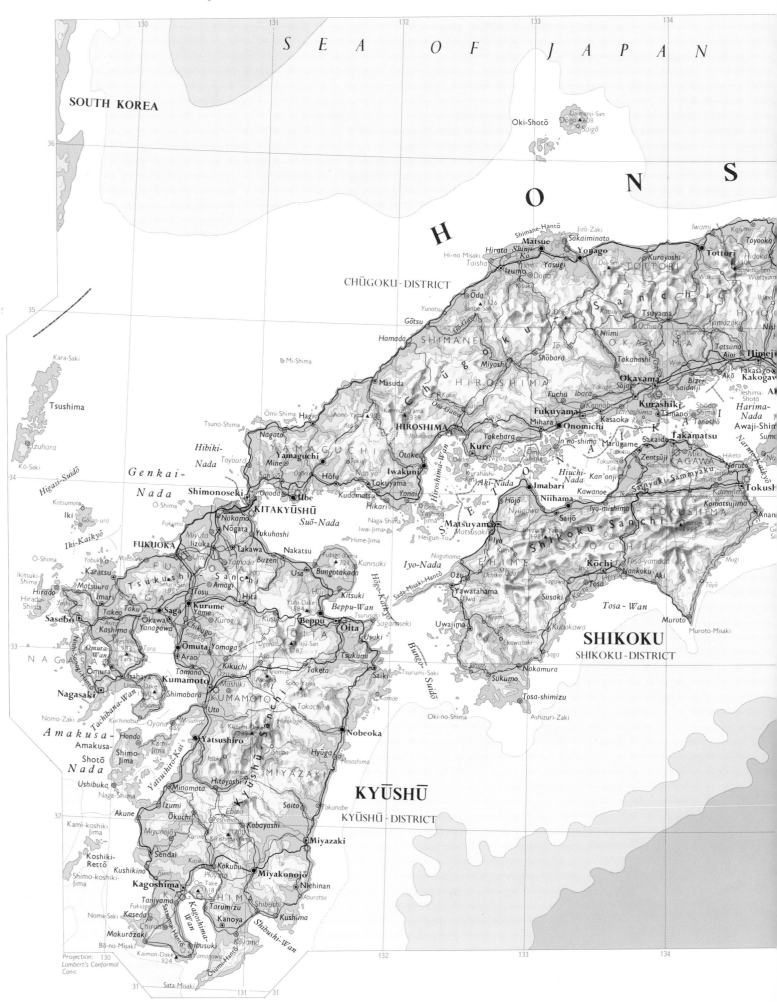

SEA OF JAPAN

SOUTH KOREA

Oki-Shotō
Daimanji-San
Dōgo ▲608
Saigō

H O N S

CHŪGOKU-DISTRICT

Shimane-Hantō
Jizō-Zaki
Iwami
Kasumi
Toyooka

Matsue
Sakaiminato
Yonago
Tottori

Hi-no Misaki
Hirata
Shinji
Kurayoshi
Hidaka

Taisha
Izumo
Yasugi
Dai-Sen
Tsuyama
Wakasa
Wadayama

Ōda
Sanbe-San ▲1126
Yamazaki
Nishi

Gōtsu
SHIMANE
Shōbara
Takahashi
Tatsuno
Aioi
Himeji

Hamada
HIROSHIMA
OKAYAMA
Takasago
Kakogawa

Masuda
Miyoshi
Fuchū
Okayama
Bizen
Saidaiji

Ōmi-Shima
Hagi
Aono Yama ▲908
Kanmuri-Yama
Shōbara
Kurashiki
Shōdo

Nagato
YAMAGUCHI
Fukuyama
Onomichi
Tamano

Tsuno-Shima
HIROSHIMA
Mihara
Takamatsu

Hibiki-Nada
Yamaguchi
Otake
Kure
Takehara
In'no-shima
Marugame
Saidai

Genkai-Nada
Mine
Hōfu
Nan'yō
Iwakuni
Zentsūji
KAGAWA

Shimonoseki
Onoda
Ube
Kudamatsu
Tokuyama
Imabari
Niihama

KITAKYŪSHŪ
Suō-Nada
Hikari
Matsuyama
Kōchi

FUKUOKA
Nōgata
Takawa
Nakatsu
EHIME

Nagasaki
Kumamoto

KYŪSHŪ
KYŪSHŪ-DISTRICT

SHIKOKU
SHIKOKU-DISTRICT

Tosa-Wan

Miyazaki

Kagoshima

Projection:
Lambert's Conformal Conic

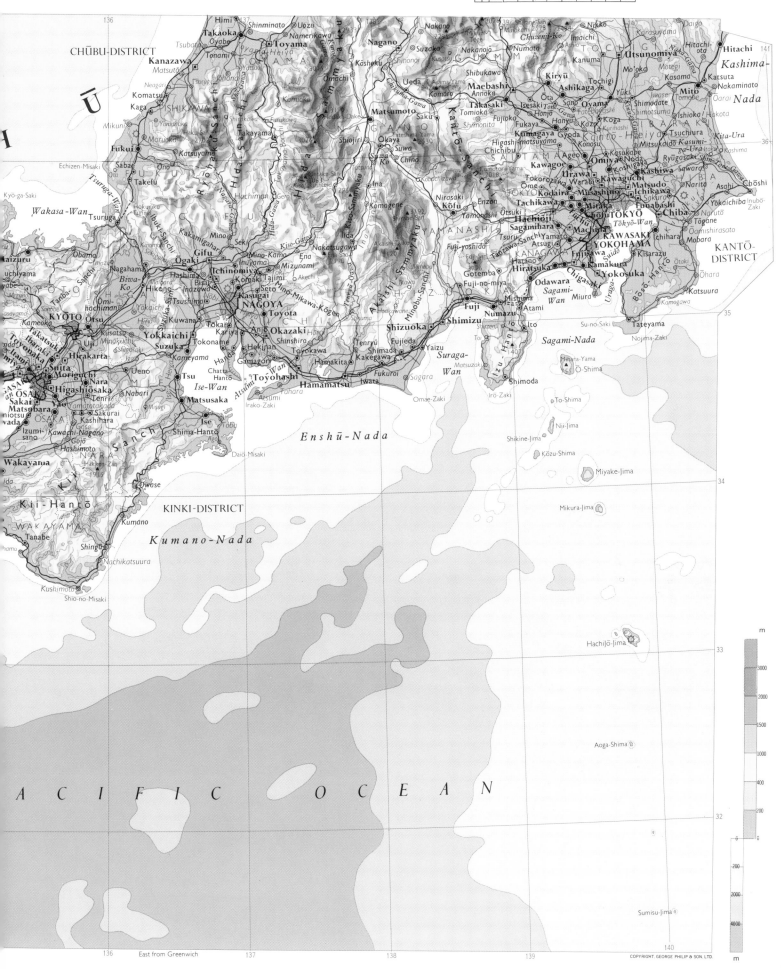

1:2 500 000

10 0 10 20 30 40 50 60 70 80 90 100 km

III

CHŪBU-DISTRICT

KINKI-DISTRICT

KANTŌ-DISTRICT

Kashima-Nada

Enshū-Nada

Kumano-Nada

Sagami-Nada

Suraga-Wan

Ise-Wan

Biwa-Ko

Wakasa-Wan

Tsuruga-Wan

Kii-Hantō

PACIFIC OCEAN

East from Greenwich

COPYRIGHT. GEORGE. PHILIP & SON. LTD.

m

3000
2000
1500
1000
400
200
0

0
200
2000
4000

m

1:7 500 000

50 0 50 100 150 200 250 300 km

CHINA

U.S.S.R.

Sikhote Alin

Turii Rog
Motaoshih
Ozero Khanka
Spassk-Dalni
Varfolomeyevka
Verkhove
Tetyukhe

Mutankiang
Ningan
Ussursk (Voroshilov)
Uglovaya
Suchan
Nakhodka

Yenki
Hunchun
Vladivostok

NORTH KOREA

Chongjin
Najin

Zaliv Petra Velikogo

Songjin
Tanchon

SEA

OF

JAPAN

Kosŏng

SOUTH KOREA

Ullung Do

Sanchŏk

Pusan

KOREA STRAIT

Tsushima-Kaikyō
Tsushima

Iki

Rebun-Tō
Rishiri-Tō
Teshio
Enbetsu
HOKKAIDŌ
Rumoi
Asahigawa
Atsuta
Otaru
Iwanai
Setana
Okushiri-Tō
Esashi

Wakkanai
Sea of Okhotsk
Otoineppu
Monbetsu
Yūbetsu
Abashiri
Kitami
Shibatsu
Nemuro
Ventoro-Kaikyō

Ishikari-Wan (Otaru-Wan)
Kamui-Misaki
Bibai
Yūbari
Sapporo
Tomakomai
Iwamisawa
Obihiro
Daisetsu 2290
Kushiro

Shiraoi
Mombetsu
Uchiura-Wan
Muroran
Urakawa
Samani

Poroshiri Dake 2052

Matsumae
Tsugaru-Kaikyō
Hakodate
Esan-Misaki
Shiriya-Zaki
Mutsu
Mutsu-Wan

Aomori
Hirosaki

Hachinohe
Kuji

Noshiro
Oga-Hanto
Odate
Towada-ko
Iwate-San 204?
Morioka
Miyako

Akita
Omono
Hanamaki
Yokote
Kamaishi

Honjō
Sakata
Tsuruoka
Mogami
Shinjo
Kogota
Ichinoseki
TŌHOKU
Ishinomaki
Shiogama
Sendai
Iwanuma

Yamagata
Yonezawa

Sado
Niigata
Shibata
Agano
Fukushima
Bandai-San

Suzu-Misaki
Nagaoka
Aizuwakamatsu
Kōriyama
Iwaki

Wajima
Kashiwazaki
Naoetsu
Tajima
Nanao
Takada
Hitachi
Takaoka
Toyama
Nagano
Maebashi Kiryū
Utsunomiya
CHUBU
Himi
Toyama-Wan
Ueda
Chichibu
Tochigi
Kaminaato

Kanazawa
Matsumoto
Takasaki
Ōmiya
Mito
Tsuchiura
Fukui
Takayama
Suwa-ko
Omiya
KANTŌ
Sawara
Ontake 3063
Shin-Tone
Urawa
Ichikawa
Chōshi
Takefu
Tsuruga
Gifu
Kōfu
Fuji-no-yama 3776
TOKYO
Maizuru
Ichinomiya
Kawaguchi
Yokohama
Yokosuka
Kyō-ga Saki
Wakasa-Wan
Hikone
Nagoya
Shimizu
Numazu
Fujisawa
Katsuura

Hi-no-Misaki
Matsue
Tottori
Toyooka
Ayabe
Ōtsu
Kuwana
Okazaki
Shizuoka
Atami
Tateyama
Izumo
CHUGOKU
Tsuyama
Kyōto
Yokkaichi
Hamamatsu
Itō
Yonago
Amagasaki
Ōsaka
Tsu
Toyohashi
Ō-Shima

Hamada
Fukuyama
Kōbe
Nara
Matsusaka
Shimada
Okayama
Akashi
Ise-Wan
Miyake-Jima
Masuda
Hokayama
Himeji
Sakai
Kishiwada
Owase
Daiō-Misaki
Nii-Jima

Hagi
Hiroshima
Onomichi
Mihara
Kurashiki
Kishiwada
Wakayama
KINKI
Miyake-Jima

Yamaguchi
Kure
Niihama
Shingū
Mikura-Jima
Tokuyama
Marugame
Takamatsu
Tokushima
Kii-Suidō

Shimonoseki
Ube
Suō-Nada
Matsuyama
Kōchi
Shio-no-Misaki
Aoga-Shima

Fukuoka
Kitakyūshū
Nakatsu
SHIKOKU
Tosa-Wan
Hachijo-Jima
Karatsu
Saga
Kurume
Beppu
Yawatahama
Muroto-Misaki
SHIKOKU

Sasebo
Ōmuta
Ōita
Uwajima
Nakamura
Ashizuri-zaki

Kashima
Aso-zan 1592
Usuki
Nobeoka
Isahaya
Kumamoto

Nagasaki
Shimabara
Yatsushiro

Shimo-Jima
Minamata
Sendai
PACIFIC

KYŪSHŪ
Miyazaki
Kobayashi
Miyakonojō

Kagoshima
Kahoya
OCEAN

Makurazaki
Shibushi-Wan

Kagoshima-Wan
Ōsumi-Kaikyō
Nishinoomote
Ōsumi-Shotō
Tane-ga-Shima
Kuchinoerabu-Jima
Yaku-Jima
Tokara-Kaikyō
Naka-no-Shima
Suwanose-Jima

Projection: Bonne
East from Greenwich

m
1500
1000
400
200
0
200
m

Ōsumi-Shotō
Kuchinoerabu-Jima
Yaku-Jima
Tokara-Kaikyō
Satsuna-Shotō
Naze
Amami Ō Shima
Setouchi
Kikai-Jima
Tokunoshima
Okinoerabu-Jima

Okinawa-Shotō
Okinawa-Jima
Ishikawa
Kerama-Shotō
Koza
Ginowan
Naha

Nansei-Shotō Trench
7507

Yaeyama-Shotō
Yonaguni-Jima
Miyako-Jima
Hirara
Ishigaki-Jima
Iriomote-Jima
Ishigaki
PACIFIC
OCEAN

RYŪKYŪ ISLANDS
Continuation southwards
in same scale

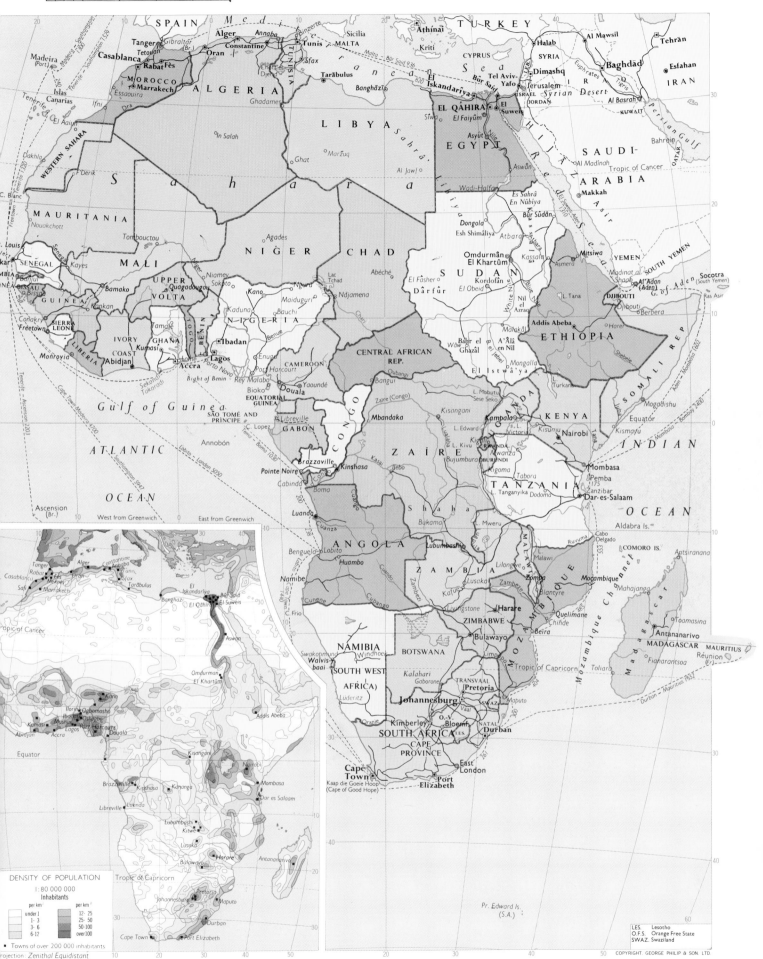

1 : 40 000 000

400 0 400 800 1200 1600 km

SPAIN
Tanger
Gibraltar (Br.)
Tetouan
Casablanca Rabat Fès
MOROCCO
Marrakech
Essaouira
Ifni
Dra
WESTERN SAHARA
Dakhla
C. Blanc
El Aaiún
Tenerife 1720
Islas Canarias
Madeira (Port.)

Alger Annaba
Constantine Binzerte
Oran Tunis MALTA
TUNISIA Sfax
Djerid Tarābulus
ALGERIA
In Salah
Ghadames
Ghat
Marzūq

LIBYA

Sicilia
Sahrā'
Al Jawf

TURKEY
Athínai
Kriti
CYPRUS

Medi   Sea
Malta Bûr Saïd 936
Banghāzī
El Iskandarîya
EL QÂHIRA El Suweis
El Faiyûm
Asyût
Nile
Aswân
Wadi-Halfa

Halab Al Mawsil
SYRIA Tehrān
Dimashq Baghdād
Tel Aviv-Yafo Esfahan
Jerusalem Syrian IRAQ
ISRAEL Desert IRAN
JORDAN Al Basrah
KUWAIT
Persian Gulf
SAUDI-
Al Madinah Tropic of Cancer
Es Sahrā' Bahrein
En Nûbiya QATAR
Bûr Sûdân **ARABIA**
Dongola Makkah
Esh Shimâliya Asir
Atbara

MAURITANIA
Nouakchott
Tombouctou
St. Louis
Senegal
Kayes
Dakar
SENEGAL
Banjul
BISSAU
GUINEA-BISSAU
Conakry
SIERRA Freetown
LEONE
Monrovia
LIBERIA

MALI
Bamako
Kankan
Agades
Niamey
Sokoto
NIGER
Kano
Maiduguri
Kaduna
Bauchi
Ouagadougou
UPPER VOLTA
Tamale
IVORY GHANA
COAST Kumasi
Abidjan Accra
Sekondi-Takoradi

Lac Tchad
CHAD
Abéché
Ndjamena
Nguru
Benue
NIGERIA
Ibadan
Lagos
Enugu
Port Harcourt
Bight of Benin
TOGO BENIN
Porto Novo

Chari
El Fâsher
DÂRFÛR
El Obeid
Kordofân
Omdurmân
El Khartûm
SUDAN
El Istwâ'ya
Bahr el Ghazâl
Wâw
CENTRAL AFRICAN
REP.
Bangui
Oubangui
Mongalla
Malâkâl
Nil
el Azraq
White Nile
Nil el
Azraq

Kassala
Asmera
Mitsiwa
L. Tana
Addis Abeba
Harer
ETHIOPIA
Shebele
A'Âla
en Nil
Mongalla

YEMEN
SOUTH YEMEN
Madînat al Shaab
Al 'Adan (Aden)
DJIBOUTI
Djibouti
Berbera
Socotra
(South Yemen)
Ras Asir
G. of Aden
SOMALI REP.

CAMEROON
Rey Malabo
Yaoundé
Douala
Bioko
EQUATORIAL GUINEA
SÃO TOMÉ AND PRÍNCIPE
C. Lopez
Libreville
GABON
Annobón
Mbandaka
CONGO
Brazzaville
Kinshasa
Pointe Noire
Boma
Cabinda
Luanda

ZAÏRE
Kisangani
Zaïre (Congo)
Lualaba
L. Mobutu Sese Seko
Kasai
Ilebo
Shaba
Bukama
Lubumbashi
Kananga

UGANDA
Kampala
L. Edward
L. Kivu
RWANDA
Kigali
Bujumbura BURUNDI
Mwanza
L. Victoria
Kigoma
Tabora
L. Tanganyika
Dodoma
TANZANIA
Dar-es-Salaam
Zanzibar
Pemba
Mombasa

KENYA
L. Turkana
Nairobi
Kisumu
Tana
Equator
Mogadishu
Kismayu

Cabo Delgado
COMORO IS.
Antsiranana

ATLANTIC

OCEAN

Ascension (Br.)
West from Greenwich
East from Greenwich

Gulf of Guinea

L. Mweru
Mbeya
L. Malawi
Lilongwe
ZAMBIA
Lusaka
Kafue
Livingstone
Benguela Lobito
ANGOLA
Huambo
Namibe
Cunene
C. Frio
Cuanza
Cuango
Kasai

Ruvuma
MALAWI
Zomba
Blantyre
Chinde
Quelimane
MOZAMBIQUE
Moçambique
Beira
Harare
ZIMBABWE
Bulawayo
Zambezi
Cubango

Mahajanga
Toamasina
Antananarivo
MADAGASCAR MAURITIUS
Réunion (Fr.)
Fianarantsoa
Toliara
Mozambique Channel

NAMIBIA
Windhoek
(SOUTH WEST
AFRICA)
Swakopmund
Walvis-baai
Lüderitz
Kalahari
BOTSWANA
Gaborone
Limpopo
TRANSVAAL
Pretoria
Johannesburg
Kimberley
O.V. Bloemf.
SWAZI.
Maputo
NATAL Durban
LES.
Orange
Vaal
SOUTH AFRICA
CAPE PROVINCE
Cape Town
Kaap die Goeie Hoop
(Cape of Good Hope)
Port Elizabeth
East London

Tropic of Capricorn

INDIAN

OCEAN

Aldabra Is.

Pr. Edward Is.
(S.A.)

LES.   Lesotho
O.F.S. Orange Free State
SWAZ.   Swaziland

COPYRIGHT. GEORGE PHILIP & SON. LTD.

DENSITY OF POPULATION
1 : 80 000 000
Inhabitants
per km²
under 1
1- 3
3- 6
6-12
per km²
12- 25
25- 50
50-100
over100
■ Towns of over 200 000 inhabitants
Projection: Zenithal Equidistant
Tropic of Cancer
Tropic of Capricorn
Equator

1:40 000 000

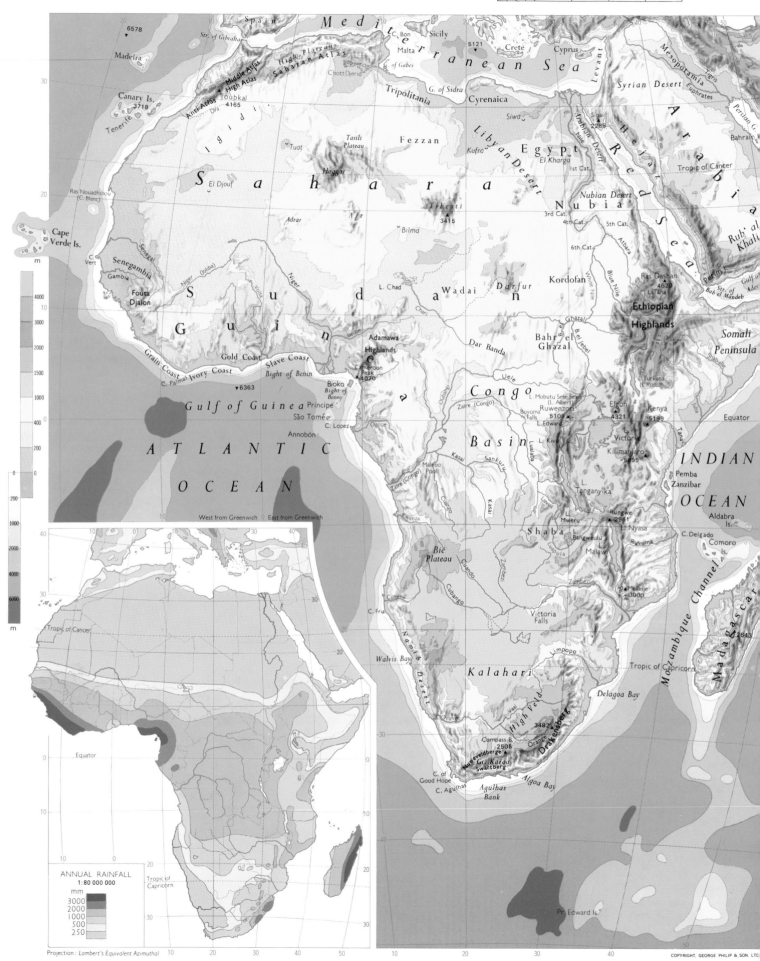

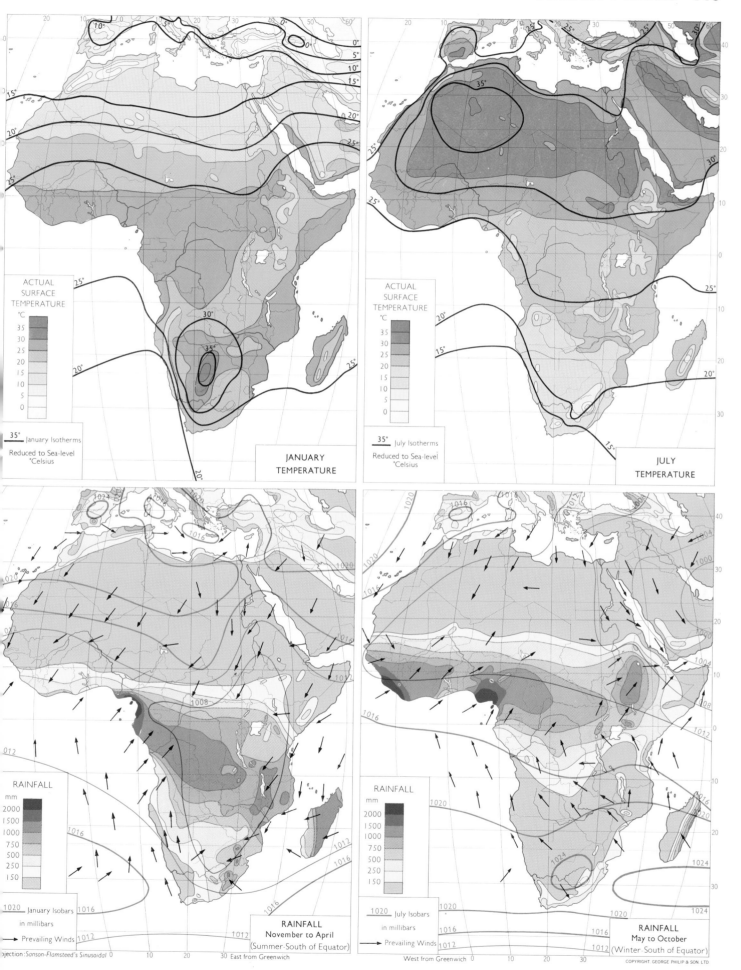

ACTUAL
SURFACE
TEMPERATURE
°C
35
30
25
20
15
10
5
0

35° January Isotherms
Reduced to Sea-level
°Celsius

JANUARY
TEMPERATURE

ACTUAL
SURFACE
TEMPERATURE
°C
35
30
25
20
15
10
5
0

35° July Isotherms
Reduced to Sea-level
°Celsius

JULY
TEMPERATURE

RAINFALL
mm
2000
1500
1000
750
500
250
150

1020 January Isobars
in millibars

Prevailing Winds

RAINFALL
November to April
(Summer-South of Equator)

RAINFALL
mm
2000
1500
1000
750
500
250
150

1020 July Isobars
in millibars

Prevailing Winds

RAINFALL
May to October
(Winter-South of Equator)

Projection:Sanson-Flamsteed's Sinusoidal   East from Greenwich

West from Greenwich

NORTH ATLANTIC

OCEAN

SPAIN

MOROCCO

WESTERN SAHARA

ALGERIA

MAURITANIA

MALI

SENEGAL

GAMBIA

GUINEA BISSAU

GUINEA

SIERRA LEONE

LIBERIA

IVORY COAST

GHANA

UPPER VOLTA

TOGO

BENIN

NIGER

NIGERIA

TUNISIA

CAMEROON

Islas Canarias (Sp.)

Madeira (Port.)

Dakar

Banjul (Bathurst)

Conakry

Freetown

Monrovia

Abidjan

Accra

Lomé

Cotonou

Lagos

Ibadan

Bamako

Ouagadougou

Niamey

Nouakchott

Casablanca

Marrakech

Rabat

Tanger

Tétouan

Fès

Meknès

Oran

Alger (Algiers)

Constantine

Tombouctou

Bight of Benin

Bioko

Projection: Sanson Flamsteed's Sinusoidal

West from Greenwich   East from Greenwich

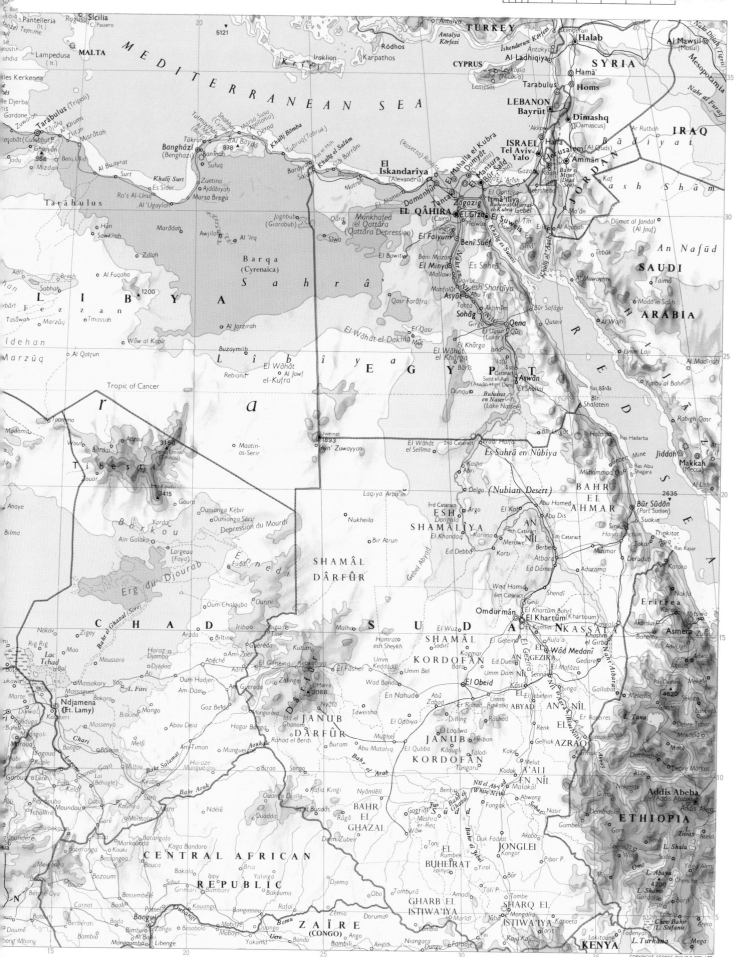

1:15 000 000

100 0 100 200 300 400 500 600 km

117

MEDITERRANEAN SEA

TURKEY

Antalya
Antalya Körfezi
İskenderun Körfezi
Halab
Al Mawsil
(Mosul)
Nahr Dijla (Tigris)
Ródhos
Karpathos
CYPRUS
Leýkosía (Nicosía)
Al Ladhiqiya
SYRIA
Hamā'
Mesopotamia
Homs
Lemesós
Tarabulus
Nahr al Furay
LEBANON
Bayrût
Dimashq
(Damascus)
IRAQ
Bādiyat
'Akka
Ar Rutbah
ISRAEL Haifa
Tel Aviv-Yafo Jerusalem
(Al Quds)
JORDAN
Amman
ash Shām
Gaza
Ma'ān
Dūmat al Jandal
(Al Jauf)

Sicilia
C. Passero
MALTA
Pantelleria
Lampedusa
5121
Iraklion
Kití

Tarâbulus (Tripoli)
Al Khums
Misrâtah
Banghâzî
(Benghazi)
Bardîyah
Marsa Susa
Apollonia
Derna
Tubruq (Tobruk)
Ra's Abu Madd

El Iskandarîya
(Alexandria)
Damanhûr
Tantâ
El Mahalla el Kubra
Dumyât
El Mansura
Bûr Sa'îd
El Qantara
Ismâ'îliya
El Suweis
Gebel
Beersheba
Al 'Aqabah
Tabūk

El Qâhira
(Cairo)
El Gîza
Helwan
El Faiyûm
Benî Suêf

SAUDI
ARABIA
An Nafûd
Taimā
Madā'in Sālih
Al Madinah

LIBYA
Tarâbulus
Surt
Ra's Al-Unuf
Marsa Brega
Ajdâbiyah

Barqa
(Cyrenaica)

Siwa
Münkhafed
el Qattâra
(Qattâra Depression)

Benî Mazâr
El Minyâ
Mallawi
Manfalût
Asyût
Sohâg
Akhmîm
Girga
Qena

Es Sahrâ'
esh Sharqîya

Bûr Safâga
Quseir

E G Y P T

Al Wajh
Umm Laj

Al 'Iraq
Awjilah
Al Jarzirah
Zillah

Sahrâ'

Qâra

El Bawiti
El Qasr
Qasr Farâfra

El Wâhât-el-Dakhla
Mût
El Wâhât
el Khârga
Bâris

Isnâ
Edfu
El Uqsur
(Luxor)

Aswân
Aswan Dam
1st
Cataract

RED
SEA

Ras Bânâs

Jiddah
Makkah
(Mecca)
Al Lith

Al Fuqaha
Tasâwah Marzûq
Idehan
Marzûq
Wâw al Kabîr
Al Qatrun

1200

Buzaymah

El Wâhât
el-Kufra
Al Jawf
Rebiana

L î b î y e

Tropic of Cancer

Uweinat
1893
Ayn' Zuwayyan

Dunqul
El Wâhât
el Selîma
2nd Cataract
Wadi Halfa
Es Sahrâ en Nûbiya

Buheiret
en Naser
(Lake Nasser)

Bîr Ungat
Halaib
Ras Hadarba

Bîr
Shalatein
Rabigh Qasr

Mine
Gebel

Muhammad Qol
Ras Abu
Shagara

At
Ta'if

Tânô Emissi
(Emi Koussi)
3150

3415
Gourp
Yardka

Maatîns-
as-Serir

Laqiya Arba'in

Delgo
(Nubian Desert)
3rd Cataract
Argo
Nukheila
Dongola
Bîr Atrun
Ed Debba
Korti
Kosha
Abri

Abu Hamed
Abu Dis
Karima
Merowe
Berber
Atbara
Ed Dâmer

BAHR
EL
AHMAR
Bûr Sûdân
(Port Sudan)
2635
Suakin
Sinkat
Haiya Junction
Musmar
Derudeb

Tókar
Aqiq
Ras Kasar

Tibesti
Zouar
Bardai
Anaye
Madama
Tûmmo

Borkou
Ain Galaka
Largeau
(Faya)
Erg du Djourab

Ennedi
Ounianga Kébir
Ounianga Sérir
Depression du Mourdi

SHAMÂL
DÂRFÛR

ESH
SHAMALÎYA

Gebel Abyad

Wâd Hamid
6th Cataract
Shendî
Geili
Omdurmân
El Khartûm Bahri
El Khartûm
(Khartoum)

Eritrea
Nakfa
Karora

CHAD
Nokov
Zigey
Mao
Rig Rig
Lac
Tchad
Bol
Massakory
Djediaba
N'Djamena
(Ft. Lamy)
Bitkine
Mongo
Bongor
Ati
L. Fitri
Moussoro
Massaguet
Haraz-Djomba
Yoo
Oum Hadjer
Am-Dam
Abéché
Adré
Oum Chalouba
Ourini
Iriba
Aoza
Guéréda
Biltine
Arada
Tine

Kutum
Malha
Kebkabiya
El Geneina
Zalingei
3088
J. Marra
Nyala
Iddi
Ghanam
Idd
GHanam
JANUB
DÂRFÛR
Mongororo
Goz Beïda
Am Guereda
Rahad el Berdi
Ghabeish
Buram
El Fasher

Umm
Keddada
Umm Bel
En Nahud

SHAMÂL
KORDOFAN
El Obeid
Wad Banda
Abu
Zabad
Er Rahad
Umm
Ruwaba

S U D A N

Hamrato
esh Sheykh
Sodiri
Ed Dueim
El Geteina

Kosti
El Dueim

El
Jebelein
Sennar
Singa
Er Raseires
Karkuj

AN
NÎL
EL
AZRAQ
Gedaref
KASSALA
Kassala
Aroma
Khashm el Girba
Adi Ugri
Barentu
Agordat
Keren
Asmera
Adwa
Aksum
Mekele
L. Tana
Gonder
Debre Tabor
Metema
ETHIOPIA
Addis Abeba
(Addis Ababa)

L. Abaya
4200
L. Shamo
Chew Bahir
(L. Stefanie)

Tûngaru
JANUB
KORDOFAN
Dilling
Rashad
Talodi
Heiban
El Lagawa
El Qubba
Kadugli
Kaka
Melut
Kodok
A'ALI
EN NÎL
Renk
Gelhak
Tungaru

Maradah

Sabha

Fezzan

Gharyân
968
Mizdah
Beni Ulid
Al Bu'ayrat
Zuetina
Es Sider
Al 'Ugaylah

Kerkenna
Gabes
Djerba
Zuwarah

Al Fuqaha

CENTRAL AFRICAN
REPUBLIC
Bangui
Bossangoa
Bozoum
Bouar
Bouca
Bria
Yalinga
Ippy
Bakala
Sibut
Bambari
Grimari
Bangassou
Djema
Rafai
Zémio
Obo
Tamburâ
Dorumo
Raga
Deim Zubeir
Wâw
Tonj
El Buheirat
Rumbek
Yirol
Bôr
JONGLEI
Kongor
Pibor P.
Akobo
Nasir
Fangak
Malakal

ZAIRE
(CONGO)
Libenge
Bomu
Uere
Bondo
Dungu
Yambio
Mboki

GHARB EL
ISTIWA'IYA
Maridi
Yambio

SHARQ EL
ISTIWA'IYA
Jûba
Kapoeta
Torit

KENYA
L. Turkana
Lokitaung
Todenyang
Mega

BAHR
EL
GHAZAL
Nyamlell
Meshra
er-Req
Gogrial
Jur
Sûdd

White Nile
Nil el Abyad
Abwong
Duk Fadiat
Kongor

EL
GEZIRA
Wâd Medanî
El Hasaheisa

AN NÎL
EL ABYAD

COPYRIGHT GEORGE PHILIP & SON LTD.

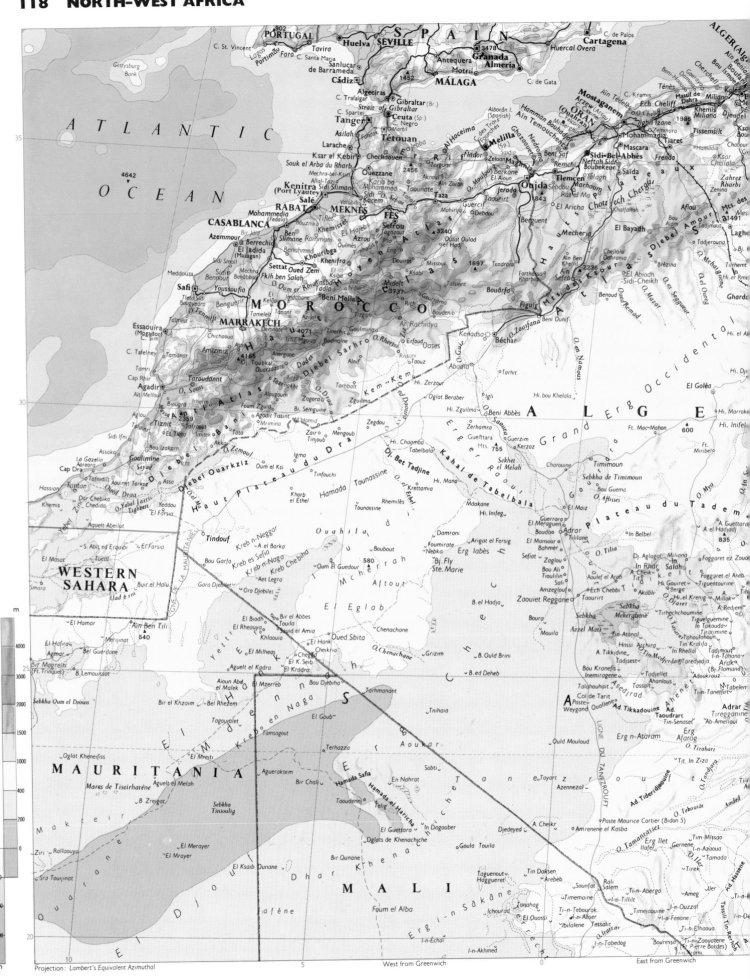

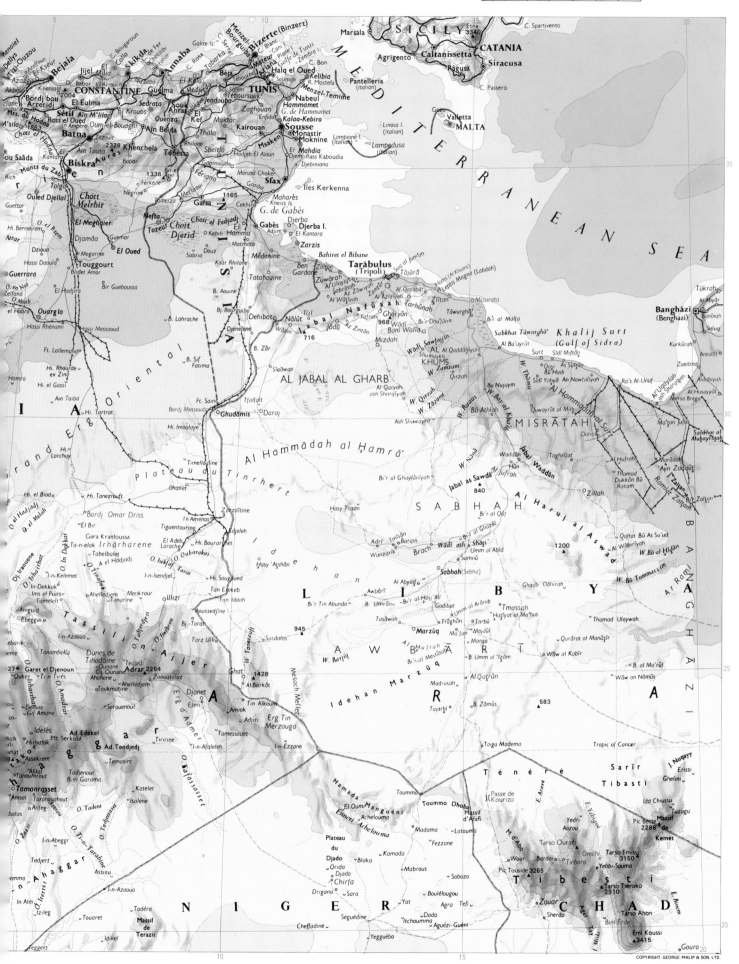

1 : 8 000 000

50 0 50 100 150 200 250 300 km

MEDITERRANEAN SEA

SICILY
Etna 3340
Marsala
Agrigento Caltanissetta CATANIA
Ragusa Siracusa
C. Spartivento
C. Passero

Pantelleria
(Italian)
Linosa I.
(Italian)
Lampedusa
(Italian)

Valletta
MALTA

Menjel
Dellys
Tizi-Ouzou
El Kseur
Azazga
Bejaia
Collo Skikda
Jijel El Milia
Annaba
C. Rosa
Tabarka
Galite Is.
Bizerte (Binzert)
Menzel
Bourguiba
Moteur Blanc
Enfidha
La Plane I.
Golfe de Tunis
Zembra I.
C. Bon
Kelibia
Nabeul
Hammamet
G. de Hammamet
Kalaa-Kebira
Sousse
Monastir
Moknine
Mahdia
Rass Kaboudia
Djebiniana

Akbkou
Bordj bou
Arreridj
El Eulma
CONSTANTINE
El Arrouch
Guelma
Souk
Ahras
Medjez
Jendouba
Béja
Medjez
Téboursouk
TUNIS
Halq el Oued
Soliman
R. Mostefa
Menzel-Temime

Setif
Ain M'lila
Ampere
Oum el-Bouaghi
Ouenza
Ain Beida
El Kef
Kef
Maktar
Thala
Zaghouan
Kairouan

Batna
Ain Touta
2328
Khenchela
Tébessa
Babor
Sbeitla
Hadjeb El Aioun
Msaken
Menzel Chaker
Djem

Biskra
Negrine
Ferkane
Fériana
Sfax
Iles Kerkenna

Ouled Djellal
Chott
Melrhir
El Meghaier
Gafsa
165
Maharès
Kneiss Is.
G. de Gabès

Nefta
Tozeur
Chott
Djerid
Kebili
Hamma
Gabès
Djerba
Djerba I.
El Kantara
Zarzis

El Oued
Douz
Sabria
Matmata
Médenine
Ben
Gardane
Bahiret el Bibane
Zaltan

Touggourt
Bidet Amar
Ksar Rhilane
Tatahouine
Zuwarah
Af'Ulaylat
Az Zawiyah
Sabratah
Tarâbulus
(Tripoli)
Tâjûra
Suq al Jum'ah
Homs (Al Khums)
Leptis Magna (Labdah)
Misrata

Ouargla
Hassi Messaoud
B. Lahrache
Dehibat
Nâlût
Tiji
Jabal Nafûsah
Yafran
968
Wâdî
Bani Walid
Gharyân
Tarhûnah
Tâwurghâ'
Bi'r al Malla

Guerrara
Zelfana
Msab
el Hobra
El Hadjira
Bir Gueboussa
Djenefene
Wazin
716
Jâdû
Al Zintan
Mizdah
Wâdî Bani Walid
Sawfajjin
Shumaykh
Al Qasabah
Bi'r Dhu'an
Sabkhat Tâwurghâ'
Al Bu'ayrat
Khalij Surt
(Gulf of Sidra)
Surt
Sîdî Miftâh

Banghâzî
(Benghazi)
Bonina

Hi. Berrekrem
Attar
O. el Rtem
Ain Taiba
Hi. Rhouïde
ex Zing
Hi. el Gassi
B. Sif
Fatima
B. Zâr
Sinawan
AL JABAL AL GHARB
Al Qaryah
ash Sharqîyah
Ash Shiwayrif
Wâdî
Zamzum
Qirzah
Sîdî Yahyâ
An Nawfaliyah
Ra's Al-Unuf
Al Uqaylah
ash Sha'âfah
Marsa Brega

IA A
Hamra
Hi. el Biod
Hi. Tanezrouft
Ohanet
Ft. Saint
Bordj Messouda
Ghudâmis
Daraj
Tiji
Timelloultine
Bi'r al Ghaylâniyah
W. Nanâ
Waddân
Jabal Waddân
Taghrîfat
Hûn
Al Hufrah
Thamad
Dukkân Bû
Ratam
Marâdah
'Ayn Zaqqûz
Râmlat
Zaltân
Bi'r Zaltân
Ma'ten Julus
Sahâbî
Mubayyiqah

IA Oriental
Grand Erg
Larchuy
Plateau du Tinrhert
Al Hammâdah al Hamrâ'
SABHAH
Jabal as Sawdâ
840
Bi'r al Qût
Zillah
Al Haruj al Aswad
1200
Qaltat Bû As Su'ûd
Al Wâbirîyah
W. Bû al Hûjah
W. Bû Tummâyil im

Hi. Tartrat
Bordj Omar Driss
Gara Kranfoussa
El Adeb
Larache
Hi. Bouraghet
Edjeleh
Tiguentourine
In Amenas
Hasy Tissan
Adri
Tmîsân
Barqin
Brach
Wâdî ash Shâti'
Wanzarik
Bi'r al Ghazâl
Umm al Abid
Samnû
Ghadîr Odhirah

Ta-n-elak
Tabelbalet
A el Hâdjadj
Ahelledjem
Hi. Sougued
Hasy 'Atshân
Awbâri
Al Hûjj 'Alî
Godduâ
Sabhah
(Sebha)

Anguid
Ebeggun
In-Dekkak
Ims el Puits
Menkrour
Tamelelt
Iulzi
Tan Ezebek
Tan Iddah
Bir Tin Abunda
Umrân
Tasâwuh
Frâghân
Tarbû
Tmassah
Hatîyat al Ma'bus
Majdûl
Thamad Ulaywah

Tassili
n'Ajjer
Tadjrédjeret
Tin-Ihou
Tarz Ulîza
Surdalas
945
Marzûq
Ma'lan
Quârat al Manâşir
B. Umm al 'Izâm

Dunes de
Tihodaïne
Tedjedi
Oj. Ounane
Adrar 2254
In-Azaoua
Ghat
1428
Al Barkât
W. Batjîl
Al Hûjrah
Bi'r al Mastûtin
Marga
B. al Ma'rûf
Wâw al Kabir

27 Garet el Djenoun
Ouket Tin Tirès
Ahohene
Toukmatine
Ahelledjem
Djanet
Eleri
Tin Alkoum
Idehan Marzûq
Madrusah
Al Qatrûn
583
Wâw an Nâmûs

Irharharene
Iherir
Tiririne
Amikor
Adjiri
Erg Tin
Merzouga
In-Ezzane
Tajerhi
B. Zâmûs
Taiga Madema
Tropic of Cancer

Ahaggar
Idelès
Mt. Serkoûf
Ad. Edekel
Ad. Tendjedj
Temasint
Ténéré
Sarîr
Tibesti
J. Nuqayy
Erissi
Ghelini

Tamanrasset
Tarâhaouhout
B. el Garama
Katelet
Isalene
Hamada
Toummo
Passe de
Kourizo
E. Arave
E. Xibughé
Yedri
Aozou
Idd Chiussu
Tuzugbi

Amsel
Arifeg
O. Tadent
El Oum
Manguéni
Achelouma
Toummo
Dhoba
Massif
d'Afafi
Madama
Latouma
M. d'Aozou
Tarso Ourari
Omchi
Tarso Emissi
3150
Yebbi-Sauma
Massif de
Kemet
Pic Bette
2286

n. Ahaggar
Tadjenout
Assiou
Plateau
du
Djado
Blaka
Orida
Djado
Chirfa
Kamada
Mabrous
Fezzane
Sobazo
Pic Touside 3265
Wour
Bardaï
Tieboro
Tibesti
Tarso Tieroko
2910

In Abeggr
In Azaoua
Tedjert
Drigana
Sara
Yat
Boulélougou
Agra Tefi
Zouar
Sherda
Tibesti
CHAD
Tarso Ahon
Bini Erde
Emi Koussi
3415
Gouro

NIGER
Touaret
Tadéra
Massif de
Terazit
Cheffadine
Séguédine
Dada
Itchoumma
Aguézi-Guéni
Yeggueba

COPYRIGHT. GEORGE PHILIP & SON, LTD

Projection: Lambert's Equivalent Azimuthal

Gambia and Senegal have agreed to the amalgamation of their economies and armies. This new confederation is known as Senegambia.

West from

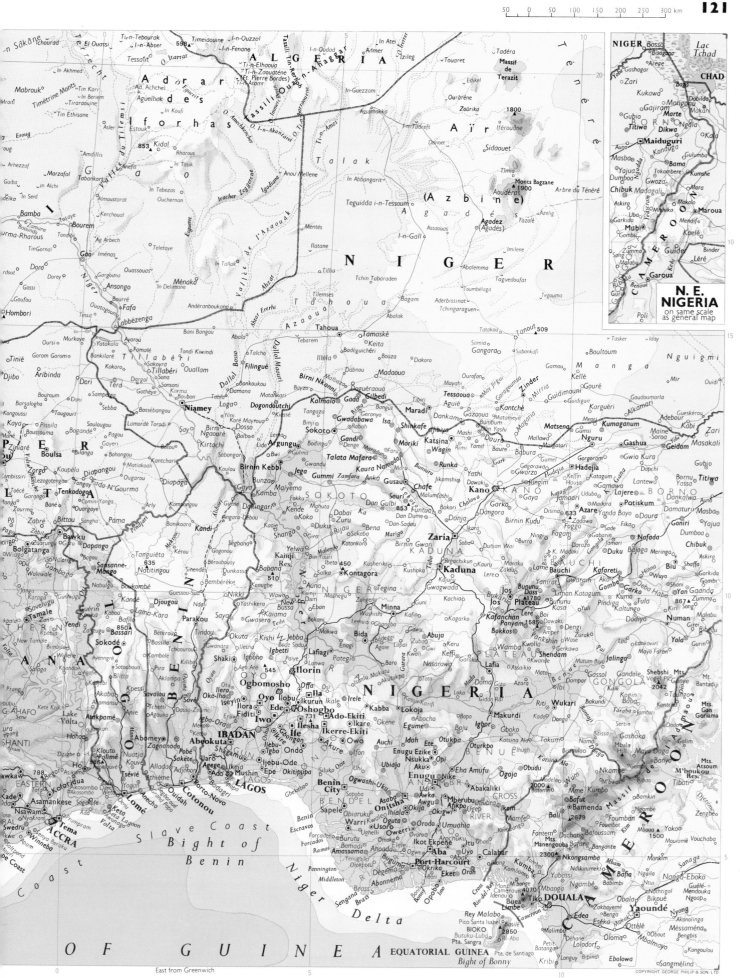

1:8 000 000

50 0 50 100 150 200 250 300 km

NIGER

ALGERIA

Adrar des Iforhas

Tassili-n-Ahaggar

Aïr (Azbine)

Agadez (Agadès)

Talak

Massif de Terazit

NIGER

MALI

Gao

Niamey

Sokoto

Maradi

Zinder

KANO

Kano

Kaduna

Zaria

NIGERIA

BENIN

TOGO

GHANA

Tamale

Accra

Lomé

Cotonou

Porto-Novo

LAGOS

IBADAN

Abeokuta

Ilorin

Ogbomosho

Oyo

Benin City

Onitsha

Enugu

Port-Harcourt

Calabar

DOUALA

Yaoundé

CAMEROON

EQUATORIAL GUINEA

Bight of Benin

Bight of Bonny

Slave Coast

Niger Delta

OF GUINEA

BORNO

CHAD

NIGER Bosso

Lac Tchad

Maiduguri

Maroua

Garoua

CAMEROON

N. E. NIGERIA
on same scale
as general map

East from Greenwich

THE NILE DELTA
1:4 000 000

YEMEN

Hodeida

Farasān Kebir

Nora

Dahlak Kebir

Mitsiwa

Asmera (Asmara)

Keren

DJIBOUTI

Djibouti

Dire Dawa

E T H I O P I A

ADDIS ABEBA (Addis Ababa)

Dese

L. Tana

Gonder

Aksum

G O J A M

S H E W A

A R U S I

W E L E G A

I L U B A B O R

Gore

K E F A

G E M U G O F A

S I D A M O

L. Turkana (L. Rudolf)

S O M A L I
REP.

K E N Y A

KASSALA

Kassala

Gedaref

Khashm el Girba

S U D A N

Omdurman

El Khartûm Bahri

El Khartûm (Khartoum)

Wad Medani

Shendi

Ed Dueim

El Kôsti

A N N I L

Singa

El Obeid

K O R D O F Â N

SHAMÂL KORDOFÂN

JANUB KORDOFÂN

Dilling

Jebalan Nubah (Nuba Mts.)

En Nahud

Abu Zabad

D A R F U R

SHAMÂL DARFUR

JANUB DARFUR

El Fasher

A ' Â L Î N Î L

Malakâl

Nâ S H A R Q

B A H R E L G H A Z A L

Wâw

I S T I W Â I Y A

Juba

C E N T R A L
A F R I C A N
R E P U B L I C

Z A Ï R E (C O N G O)

U G A N D A

NORTHERN

m
4000 3000 2000 1500 1000 400 200 0

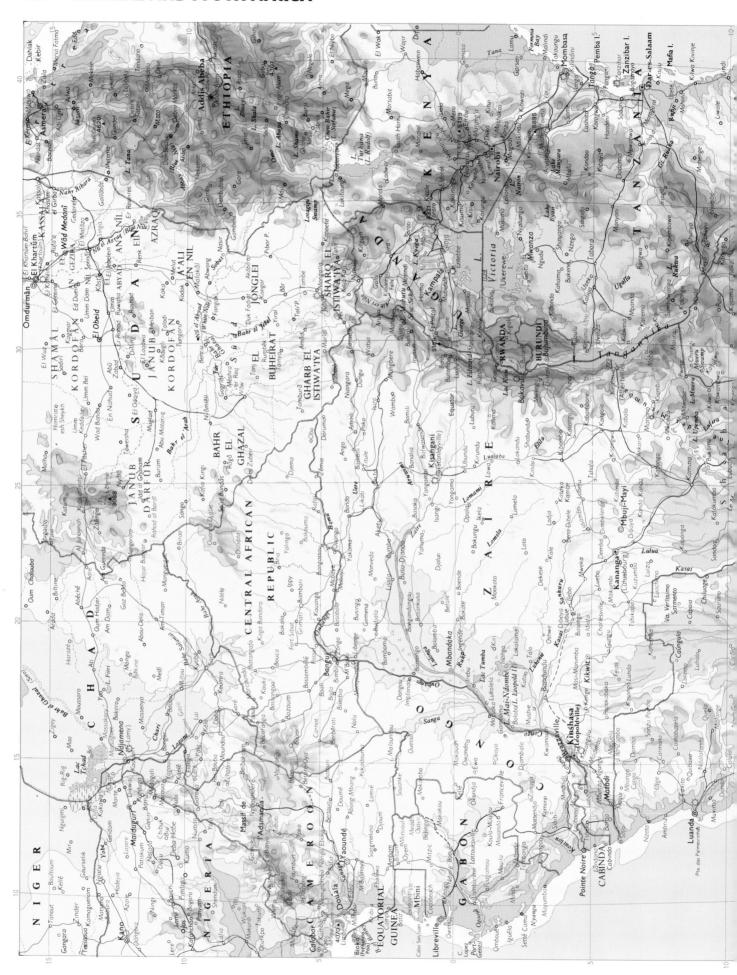

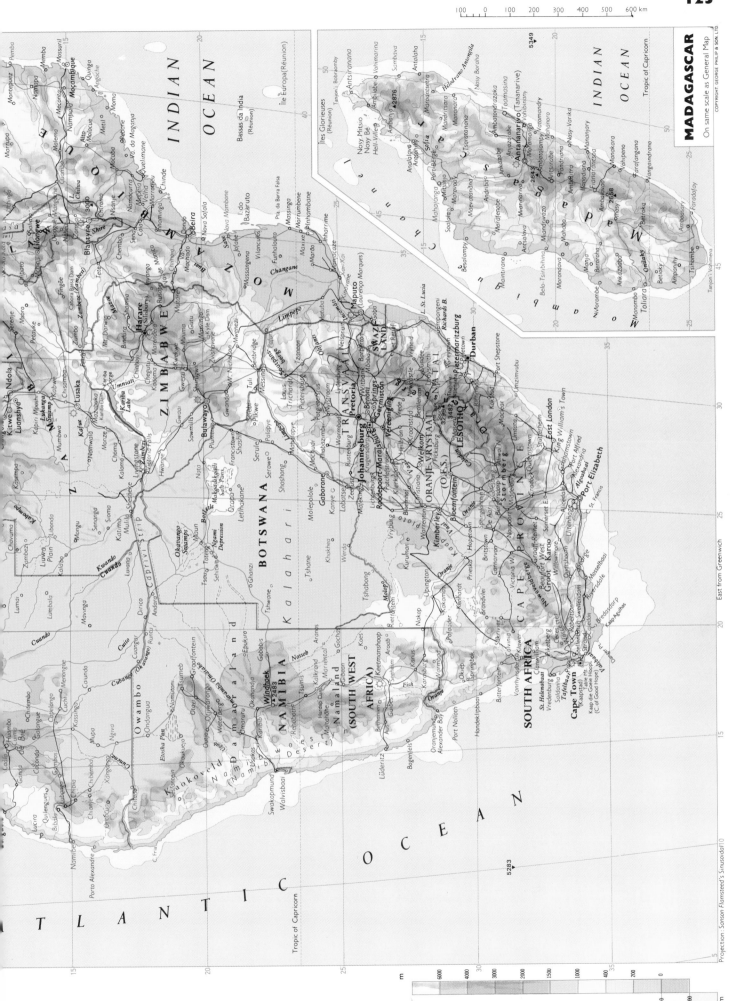

1:15 000 000

100   0   100   200   300   400   500   600 km

MADAGASCAR
On same scale as General Map

COPYRIGHT GEORGE PHILIP & SON LTD.

INDIAN

OCEAN

INDIAN

OCEAN

Tropic of Capricorn

East from Greenwich

Projection: Samson Flamsteed's Sinusoidal

ATLANTIC   OCEAN

Tropic of Capricorn

ZAMBIA

ZIMBABWE

MOZAMBIQUE

BOTSWANA

NAMIBIA
(SOUTH WEST
AFRICA)

SOUTH AFRICA

TRANSVAAL

SWAZILAND

NATAL

LESOTHO

ORANJE-VRYSTAAT
(O.F.S.)

CAPE PROVINCE

Kalahari

Namib Desert

Harare

Bulawayo

Lusaka

Windhoek

Gaborone

Johannesburg

Pretoria

Durban

Bloemfontein

Kimberley

Cape Town

Port Elizabeth

East London

Antananarivo
(Tananarive)

m   6000 4000 3000 2000 1500 1000 400 200 0

m   200

SOMALI REP.

ETHIOPIA

SIDAMO

GEMU-GOFA

KENYA

UGANDA

SUDAN

TANZANIA

RWANDA

BURUNDI

CENTRAL AFRICAN REPUBLIC

ZAIRE

ORIENTAL

KASAI

Victoria Lake

L. Turkana (L. Rudolf)

L. Albert

L. Kyoga

L. Edward

L. Kivu

L. Tanganyika

L. Mobutu

NAIROBI

MOMBASA

DAR ES SALAAM

Zanzibar

Pemba I.

Kampala

Entebbe

Jinja

Kisangani

Bukavu

Kindu

Tabora

Dodoma

Arusha

COAST

EASTERN

NORTH EASTERN

TANA RIVER

SERENGETI Plain

GREAT RIFT VALLEY

Equator

1:8 000 000

50   0   50   100   150   200   250   300 km

I N D I A N

O C E A N

A N G O L A

ZAMBIA

MALAWI

MOZAMBIQUE

ZIMBABWE

BOTSWANA

TRANSVAL

Projection: Lambert's Equivalent Azimuthal

East from Greenwich

COPYRIGHT GEORGE PHILIP & SON LTD

m   6000 4000 3000 2000 1500 1000 400 200

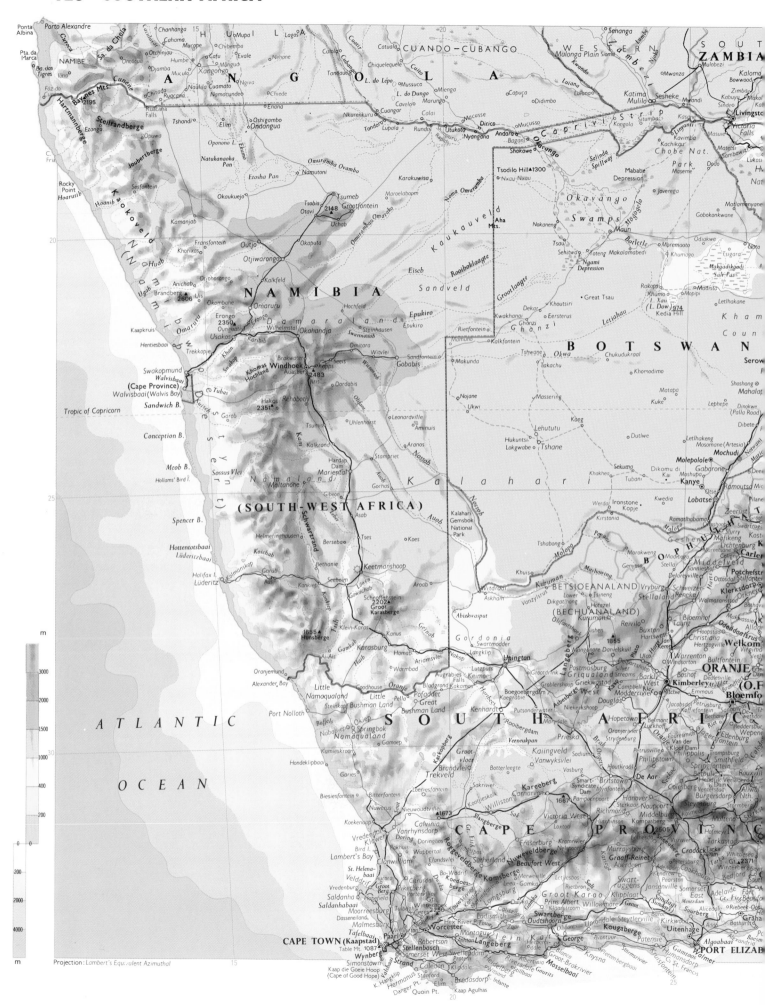

ANGOLA

CUANDO-CUBANGO

WESTERN

ZAMBIA

NAMIBIA

(SOUTH-WEST AFRICA)

BOTSWANA

Cap
Caprivi Strip

Okavango Swamps

Kalahari

Etosha Pan

Kaukauveld Mts.

Sandveld

Kalahari Gemsbok National Park

Namib Desert

Windhoek

Tropic of Capricorn

ATLANTIC

OCEAN

SOUTH AFRICA

CAPE PROVINCE

Great Karoo

BOPHUTHATSWANA

BETSJOEANALAND
(BECHUANALAND)

ORANJE
(O.F.S.)

Bloemfontein

Kimberley

Gordonia

Griqualand West

Bushman Land

Little Namaqualand

Great Namaqualand

Klein Karoo

CAPE TOWN (Kaapstad)

Kaap die Goeie Hoop
(Cape of Good Hope)

PORT ELIZABETH

Projection: Lambert's Equivalent Azimuthal

m
3000
2000
1500
1000
400
200
0
200
2000
4000
m

1 : 8 000 000

50   0   50   100   150   200   250   300 km

MALAWI

ZAMBÉZ

MOZAMBIQUE

CHANNEL

MOZAMBIQUE

M O Z A M B I Q U E   C H A N N E L

IMBABWE

ZIMBABWE

MASHONALAND NORTH

HARARE (Salisbury)

MATABELELAND

SOUTH

Beira

VENDA

PRETORIA

HANNESBURG

Springs

SWAZILAND

MAPUTO

Maputo (Lourenço Marques)

NATAL

PIETERMARITZBURG

DURBAN

ZULULAND

Lake St. Lucia

Richards Bay

INDIAN

OCEAN

London

East from Greenwich

Antsiranana

Mahajanga

ANTANANARIVO

Antsirabe

Toamasina

Morondava

Toliara

FIANARANTSOA

Tropic of Capricorn

Faradofay

M A D A G A S C A R

MADAGASCAR

On same scale as General Map

COPYRIGHT GEORGE PHILIP & SON. LTD.

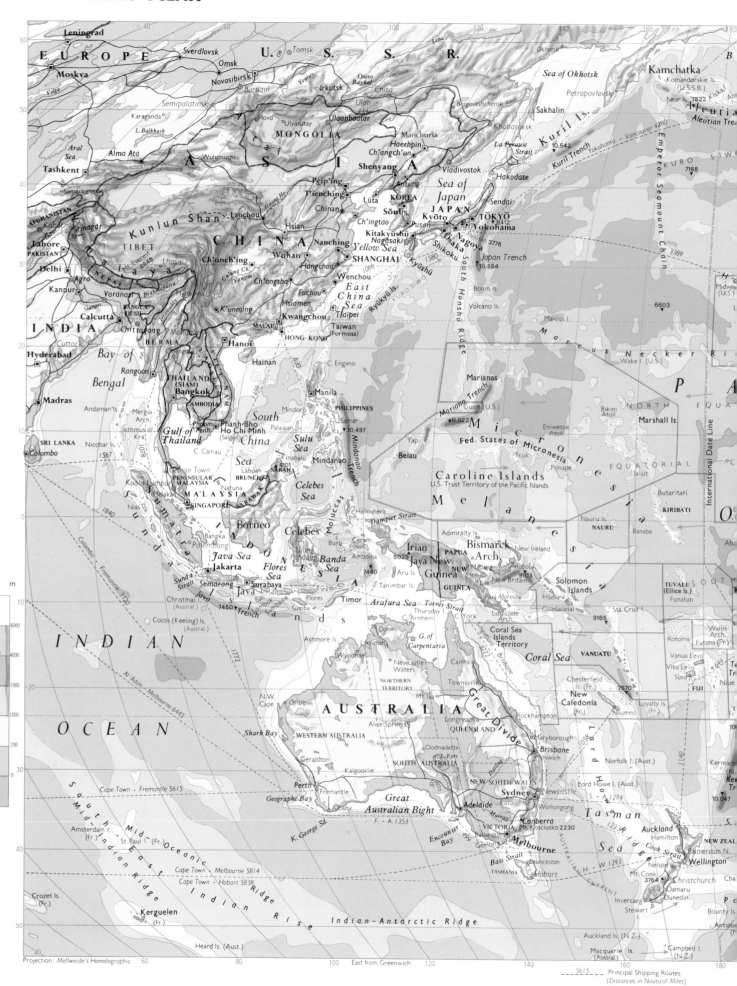

Projection: Mollweide's Homolographic   East from Greenwich

_ _ _ _ 5615 _ _ _ _ Principal Shipping Routes
(Distances in Nautical Miles)

ALASKA
6050
Gulf of Alaska
Prince of Wales I.
Sitka
Juneau
Prince Rupert
Kitimat
Queen Charlotte Is.

GREENLAND
C. Farewell

BRITISH
ISLES

R O C K Y
Dawson Creek
Churchill
Lynn Lake
Belcher Is.
Hudson Bay

C A N A D A
Scheffervile
Hamilton Inlet

NORTH

Edmonton
Prince Albert
Saskatoon
L. Winnipeg
James Bay
Labrador
Strait of Belle Isle

NORTH AMERICA
Vancouver
Victoria
Medicine Hat
Regina
Winnipeg
St. Lawrence
Québec
G. of St. Lawrence
Newfoundland

Vancouver I.
Seattle
Tacoma
Portland
Spokane
Helena
Butte
Boise
Bismarck
Missouri
Duluth
L. Superior
Sault Ste Marie
St. Paul
Montréal
Ottawa
Toronto
Fredericton
Pr. Edward I.
C. Breton I.
Saint John
Sable I.
Southampton 3091

Anticosti
C. Race

ATLANTIC

C. Blanco
Mountains
Cheyenne
Des Moines
Milwaukee
CHICAGO
Michigan
Huron
Detroit
L. Erie
Pittsburgh
Buffalo
Boston
C. Sable

Sacramento
Oakland
San Francisco
4418
Salt Lake City
Denver
Kansas
UNITED STATES
St. Louis
Indianapolis
Cincinnati
Appalachian Mts.
Baltimore
Washington
NEW YORK
Philadelphia

OCEAN

Mendocino Séascarp
C. Mendocino

Los Angeles
San Diego
Santa Fé
Oklahoma
Little Rock
Memphis
Atlanta
Richmond
Norfolk
C. Hatteras

New York - Recife 3678

Murray Seascarp
2091
CALIFORNIAN CURRENT

El Paso
Ciudad Juárez
Austin
Dallas
Houston
San Antonio
Galveston
Mobile
New Orleans
Savannah
Jacksonville

Bermuda (U.K.)
Panamá - Liverpool 4530

Guadalupe
6225
Pto. Eugenia
Sierra Madre
Torreón
Monterrey
Tampico
Gulf of Mexico
Tampa
Miami
Florida Strait
BAHAMAS

Tropic of Cancer
Clarion Fracture Zone
C. S. Lucas
Gulf of California
San Luis Potosí
Mérida
Yucatan Channel
CUBA
La Habana

Hawaiian Is. (U.S.A.)
Ridge
Honolulu
Oahu
Hawaii
I. (U.S.)

Revilla Gigedo Is. (Mexico)
Aguascalientes
Guadalajara
México
Veracruz
Puebla
5700
7680
JAMAICA
Kingston
HAITI
DOM. REP.
9200
Santo Domingo
PUERTO RICO
St. Thomas (U.S.)
Virgin Is.
West Indies
Hispaniola
Leeward Is.

I F I C
CURRENT

Acapulco
3277
GUATEMALA
Guatemala 3662
HONDURAS
Tegucigalpa
BELIZE
Caribbean Sea
Guadeloupe (Fr.)
Martinique (Fr.)
BARBADOS

Palmyra Is. (U.S.)
Teraina
Tabuaeran
Kirimati

Clipperton Fracture Zone
Clipperton I. (Fr.)
3606
4711
SALVADOR
NICARAGUA
Managua
CENTRAL AMERICA
Barranquilla
Curaçao (Ne.)
Windward Is.
TRINIDAD & TOBAGO

Jarvis I. (U.S.)
E A N

CURRENT
Malden I.
Starbuck I.

Equator
Galápagos (Ecuador)
COSTA RICA
San José
PANAMA
Panamá Canal
Maracaibo
Caracas
VENEZUELA

Tongareva
Penrhyn Is.
Manihiki
Suwarrow Is. (Suvorov)

Vostok I.
Flint I.
Caroline I.

Marquesas Is. (Fr.)

Cocos I.
835
Medellín
Bogotá
Cali
COLOMBIA

Tahiti - Panamá 4570
C. S.Francisco
Quito
ECUADOR
Chimborazo 6267
Guayaquil
Cuenca
Iquitos
Manaus
Amazon

Cook Islands
1303
Society Is. (Fr.)
Windward Is.
Tahiti (Fr.)
Tuamotu Archipelago (Fr.)

C. Pariñas
Chiclayo
Trujillo
Lobos I.
706
BRAZIL
SOUTH

Manuae
French Polynesia

Auckland - Panamá 6510
East Pacific Ridge
6369
Callao
PERU
Lima
AMERICA

Rarotonga
Austral
Seamount Chain

Cúzco
L. Titicaca
Illampu & Ancohuma 6550
La Paz
BOLIVIA

Tubuai Is. (Austral Is.) (Fr.)
Rapa Iti (Fr.)
Pitcairn I. (U.K.)
Ducie I. (U.K.)

Southeast Pacific Basin

Arequipa
16866
Peru
Iquique
Chile
PERUVIAN CURRENT

Tropic of Capricorn
Sala-y-Gomez (Chile)
San Félix (Chile)
San Ambrosio (Chile)

8050
Antofagasta
Trench
Salta
Tucumán
Asunción
PARAGUAY
Corrientes

Easter Is. (Chile)
Pto. Alegre

eastern

Arch. de Juan Fernández (Chile)
Alejandro Selkirk
Robinson Crusoe
Aconcagua 6960
Valparaíso
Santiago
Córdoba
Rosario
URUGUAY
Santa Fé
Paysandú

Concepción
Buenos Aires
La Plata
Montevideo
Río de la Plata
ARGENTINA
Mar del Plata

Chile Rise
P.A. - Valparaíso 1414
1355 1295
G. of San Matías
SOUTH

Chonos Arch.
Neuquén
Buenos Aires
Montevideo
ATLANTIC

Basin
Pacific-Antarctic Ridge
WEST WIND DRIFT
Pacific-Antarctic Basin
G. of Penas
Wellington
CAPE HORN CURRENT
Patagonia
P.A. -
P. Deseado
Sta. Cruz
G. of San Jorge
Argentine Basin
6212
OCEAN

Punta Arenas
Str. of Magellan
Tierra del Fuego
C. Horn
Falkland Is. (U.K.)
Stanley
South Georgia

COPYRIGHT. GEORGE PHILIP & SON. LTD.

Projection: *Bonne*   East from Greenwich

1:14 000 000

100   0   100   200   300   400   500   600 km

Thursday I. Banks I. C. York
Prince of Wales I. Newcastle B.
Wessel
Is. English Co. Is.
C. Wilberforce
Melville B.
m B. Gove
C. Arnhem
P. Bradshaw
Caledon B.
Blue Mud B. C. Grey
Myangula
Groote Eylandt
C. Beatrice
Limmen Bight
Maria I.
Sir Edward Pellew Group
Vanderlin I.
Arthur Borroloola
Mornington C. van
Diemen
Wellesley Is.
Bentinck I.
Burketown
Normanton

Endeavour Str.
Shelburne B.
P. Musgrave
Cape C. Grenville
Wenlock Temple B.
Duifken Pt. C. Weymouth
Albatross B. Weipa C. Direction
York
Archer Holroyd
Peninsula
Coen
C. Keer-Weer

Gulf of
Carpentaria

Coleman
Normanby
Laura C. Flattery
C. Bedford
Cooktown
Mitchell Mossman
Chillagoe Mareeba Trinity Bay
Cairns C. Grafton
Atherton Bartle Frere 1612
Innisfail

Croydon Einasleigh
Newcastle Forsyth
Gilbert Ravenshoe
Norman Ingham
Hinchinbrook I.
Palm Is.
Halifax B.
Townsville
C. Cleveland
C. Bowling Green

CORAL

SEA

ISLANDS

CORAL SEA

TERRITORY

Misima I.
Louisiade
Archipelago
Rossel I.
Tagula I.
San Cristobal
Rennell

Lihou Rfs.
& Cays.

Burketown
Normanton
Gregory Ra.

Dobbyn
Carnoweal
Austral Downs
Mount Isa
Mary Kathleen
Cloncurry
Julia Cr.
Richmond
Hughenden
Pentland
Charters
Towers
Dalrymple Hill
Bowen
Proserpine
Whitsunday I.
Cumberland Is.

P A C I F I C

Chesterfield Is.
Avon Is.

TABLELAND
Leichhardt
BARKLY
Kajabbi
Selwyn Range
Duchess
Urandangi Dajarra
Selwyn

QUEENSLAND

Winton Muttaburra
Boulia

Longreach
Ilfracombe Barcaldine
Aramac
Clermont
Blackall Alpha
Jundah Emerald
Yaraka Springsure

Mackay
Netherdale
Collinsville
Denham Ra.
Peak Ra.
Drummond Ra.
Blair Athol
Sarina

Broad Sd.
Palmerston

C. Townshend
Townshend I.
Swain
Rfs.
Saumarez Rf.
Bird I.
Bellona Rfs.

Bedourie
Birdsville
Windorah

Gt.
Desert
Hanson

Macumba
Warburton
L. Yamma
Yamma

L. Machattie
Eyre Cr.

Adavale
Augathella
Charleville
Quilpie
Bulloo
Thargomindah

CAPRICORN
Mt. Morgan
Rockhampton
Keppel B.
C. Capricorn
P. Curtis
Gladstone Bustard Head
Biloela
Theodore Monto Burnett
Childers Bundaberg
Gayndah Hervey Sandy C.
Maryborough Bay
Wondai Fraser I.

Tropic of Capricorn

Cato I.

L. Eyre
(North) –52
L. Gregory
L. Eyre (South)
L. Blanche

Cooper Creek

Streaky Cr.

Tibooburra

Grey Range
Yaraka
Mitchell
Warrego
Ra.
Expedition Ra.
Dawson
Roma
Condamine

Gympie
Nambour
Bribie I.
Moreton I.
N. Stradbroke I.
Brisbane
Southport
Sutherland
C. Byron
Ballina
Clarence

TRALIA
Leigh Creek
Copley
Flinders Ranges
L. Frome
L. Callabonna

BALONNE
Dirranbandi
Goondiwindi
St. George
Moonie
Toowoomba

Warwick
Stanthorpe
Mt. Barney
Macintyre
Gwydir
Moree
Warialda
Inverell
Tenterfield
New England Range
Armidale
Grafton
Mountain
Coffs Harbour

Woomera
Pimba
St. Mary's Pk.
1089
Hawker
NEW
SOUTH

Bourke
Walgett
Narrabri
Liverpool
Plains
Barwon

Macleay
Kempsey
Port Macquarie

Pt. Stephens

Spencer
Gulf
C. Yorke Pen.
G. St.
Vincent
Adelaide
Spencer
Alexandrina
Backstairs Pass
Kangaroo I.
Encounter

WALES

Cobar
Nyngan
Dubbo
Mudgee
Wellington
Parkes
Forbes
Orange
Bathurst
Cowra
Young
Lithgow
Cessnock
Newcastle
Singleton
Muswellbrook
Sugarloaf Pt.

Wimmera

VICTORIA

Ararat
Ballarat
Geelong

MELBOURNE

TASMAN

SEA

King I.
Bass Strait

Hunter I.
C. Grim
Devonport
Burnie

TASMANIA

Hobart
P. Davey

Lord Howe I.

COPYRIGHT GEORGE PHILIP & SON LTD

1:60 000 000

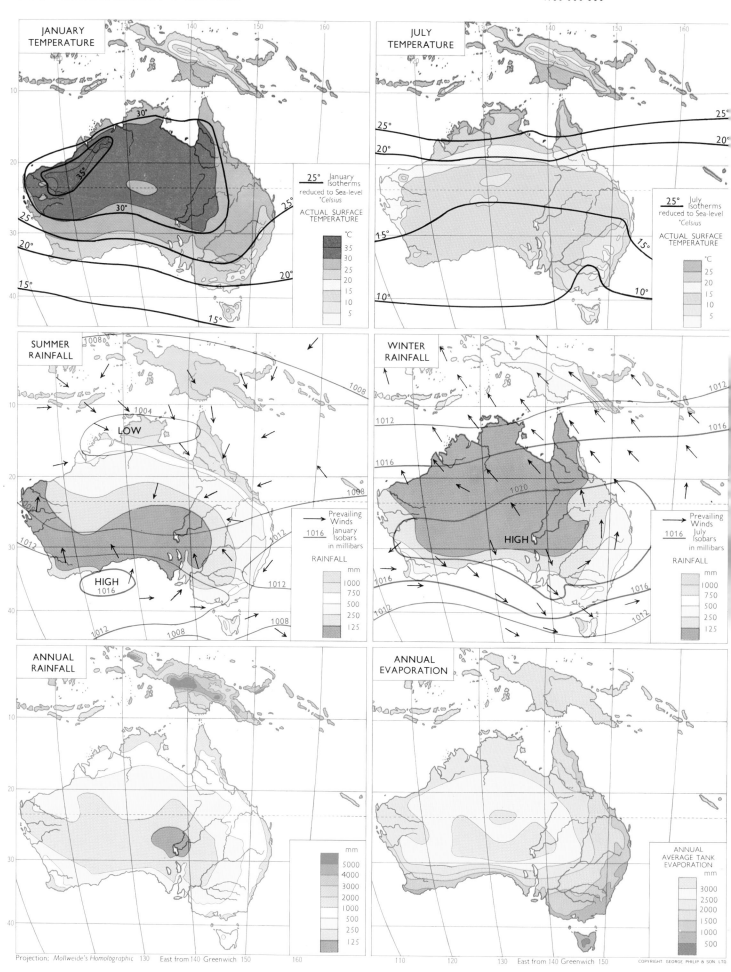

JANUARY TEMPERATURE

25° January Isotherms reduced to Sea-level °Celsius

ACTUAL SURFACE TEMPERATURE
°C
35
30
25
20
15
10
5

JULY TEMPERATURE

25° July Isotherms reduced to Sea-level °Celsius

ACTUAL SURFACE TEMPERATURE
°C
25
20
15
10
5

SUMMER RAINFALL

LOW

HIGH
1016

→ Prevailing Winds January Isobars
1016 in millibars

RAINFALL
mm
1000
750
500
250
125

WINTER RAINFALL

HIGH

→ Prevailing Winds July Isobars
1016 in millibars

RAINFALL
mm
1000
750
500
250
125

ANNUAL RAINFALL

mm
5000
4000
3000
2000
1000
500
250
125

ANNUAL EVAPORATION

ANNUAL AVERAGE TANK EVAPORATION
mm
3000
2500
2000
1500
1000
500

Projection: *Mollweide's Homolographic*   130   East from 140 Greenwich 150   160

110   120   130   East from 140 Greenwich 150

COPYRIGHT GEORGE PHILIP & SON LTD

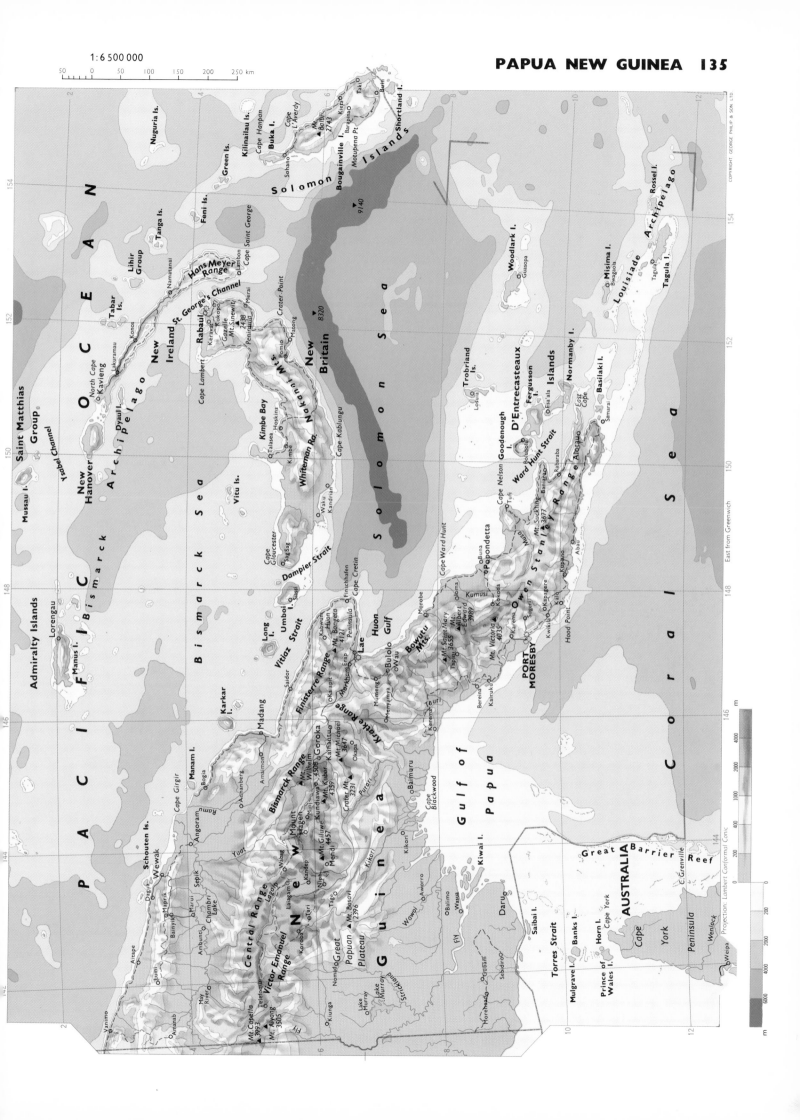

1:6 500 000

50   0   50   100 150 200 250 km

COPYRIGHT GEORGE PHILIP & SON LTD.

P A C I F I C   O C E A N

Nuguria Is.

Kilinailau Is.
Green Is.
Cape Hanpan
Buka I.
Cape L'Averdy
Mt. Balbi
2743
Takt
Bum
Kieta
Barapina
Buin
Sohano
Bougainville I.
Motupena Pt.
Shortland I.

S o l o m o n   I s l a n d s

9140

Feni Is.
Tanga Is.
Lihir Group
Tabar Is.
Namatanai
Cape Saint George
Lemkon
Merai
Crater Point

S o l o m o n   S e a

Woodlark I.
Guasopa
Misima I.
Bwagaoia
Rossel I.
Louisiade Archipelago
Tagula
Tagula I.

Saint Matthias Group
Mussau I.
Ysabel Channel
North Cape
Kavieng
Takuramau
Konos
New Hanover
Dyaull
St. George's Channel
Hans Meyer Range
Kokopo
Gazelle Peninsula
Mt. Sinewit
2438
Rabaul
Keravat
Ponio
Matong
8320
New Britain
Nakanai Mts.
Whiteman Ra.
Hoskins
Kimbe Bay
Talasea
Kimbe
Cape Kablungu

A r c h i p e l a g o

B i s m a r c k

B i s m a r c k   S e a

Cape Lambert

Vitu Is.
Waku
Kandrian

Trobriand Is.
Losuia
Kiriwina
Fergusson
Dobu
Esa'ala
Normanby I.
Basilaki I.
East Cape
Samarai

D'Entrecasteaux Islands
Goodenough I.
Ward Hunt Strait
Rabaraba

Admiralty Islands
Lorengau
Manus I.

Cape Gloucester
Pag Sag
Dampier Strait
Long I.
Umboi I.
Vitiaz Strait
Saidor
Sialt
Finschhafen
Cape Cretin
Huon Peninsula
Mt. Bangeta
4121
Kabwum
Huon
Morobe
Cape Ward Hunt
Buna
Popondetta
Kumusi
Kokoda
Mt. Albert Edward
3989
Mt. Victoria
4035
Karema
Kwikila
Kapogere
Kupiano
Kalo
Hood Point

Owen Stanley Range
Mt. Suckling
3677

Karkar I.
Madang
Manam I.
Bogia
Adnanberg
Amaimon
Finisterre Range
Goroka
Kaiapit
Mt. Michael
3647
Okapa
Kratke Range
Lae
Bulolo
Wau
Bowutu Mts.
Mt. Saint Mary
3655
Tapini 3655
Mumeng
Chimbumaya
Kerema
Abau

Cape Girgir
Schouten Is.
Wewak
Angoram
Yuat
Ramu
Mount Hagen
Mt. Wilhelm
4508
Mt. Giluwe
4357
Kundiawa
Mt. Kubor
4339
Crater Mt.
3231
Kainantu
Okari
Goari
Purari

Central Range
Bismarck Range

Aitape
Vanimo
Lumi
Amanab
May River
Mt. Capella
3993
Mt. Aiyang
3505
Telefomin
Victor Emanuel Range
Mt. Bosavi
2396
Great Papuan Plateau
Kikori I.
Kikori

N e w   G u i n e a

Cape Nelson
Tufi

G u l f   o f   P a p u a

Cape Blackwood
Baimuru

Kiwai I.
Daru
Saibai I.
Fly
Lake Murray
Strickland
Kiunga
Nomad
Balimo
Morehead
Sebidiro

Torres Strait
Mulgrave I.
Banks I.
Horn I.
Prince of Wales I.
Cape York
C. Grenville
Great Barrier Reef
Cape York Peninsula
Weipa
Wenlock

A U S T R A L I A

C o r a l   S e a

East from Greenwich
Projection: Lambert Conformal Conic

m
4000
2000
1000
400
200
0
200
2000
4000
6000
m

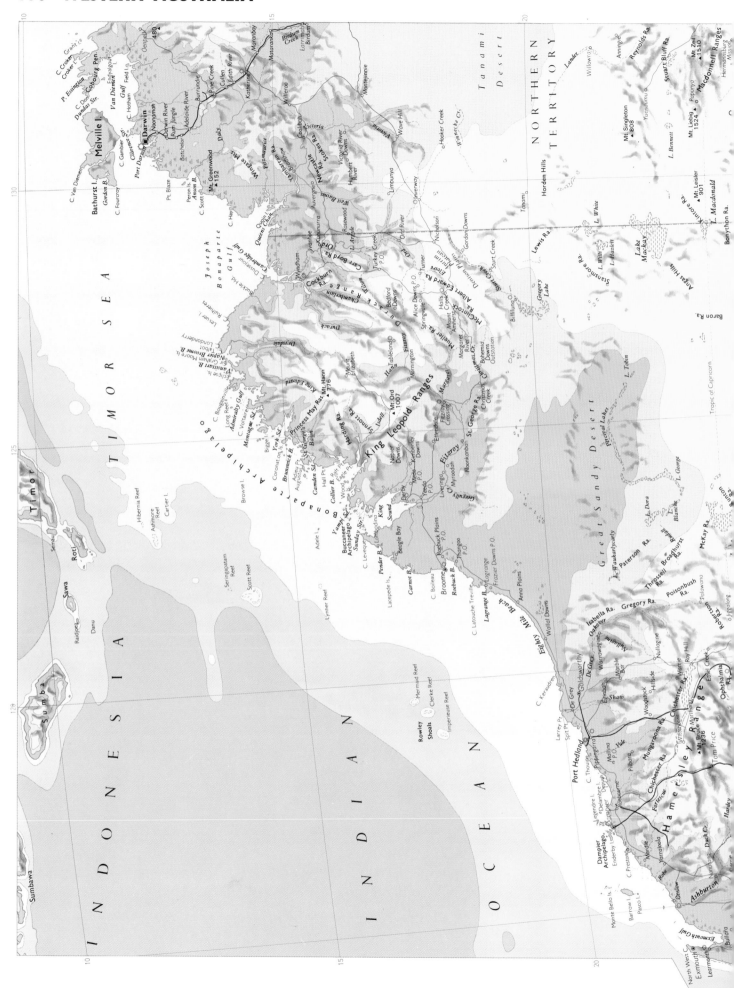

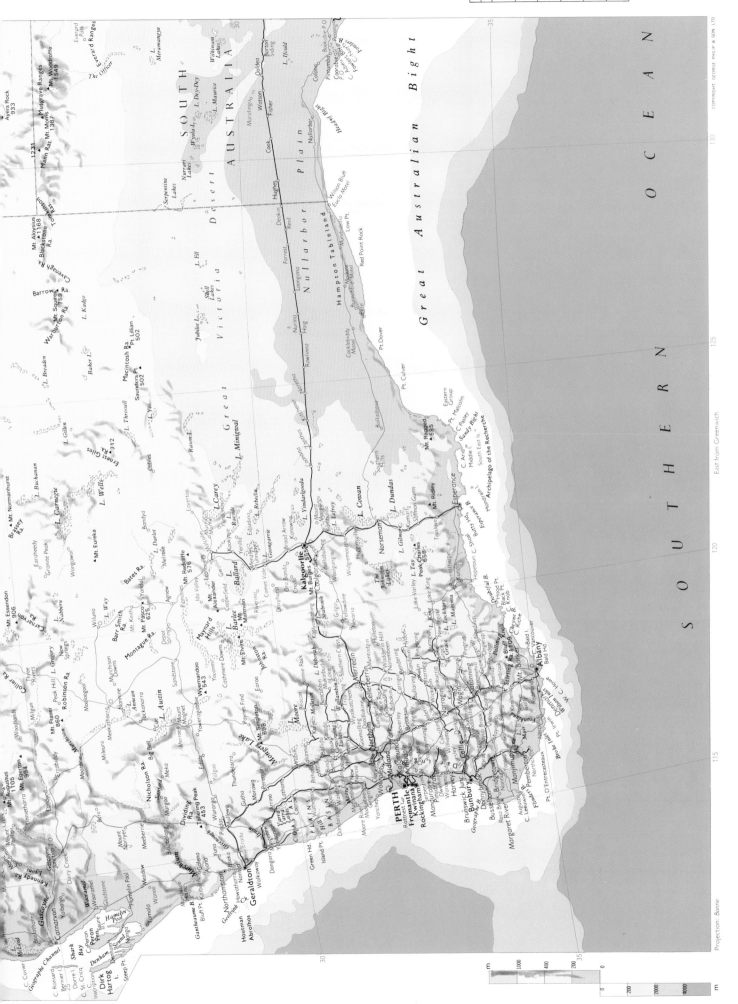

1 : 8 000 000

50   0   50   100   150   200   250   300 km

S O U T H

A U S T R A L I A

Great Australian Bight

S O U T H E R N   O C E A N

Great Victoria Desert

Gibson Desert

Nullarbor Plain

Hampton Tableland

Archipelago of the Recherche

Everard Ranges
Ayers Rock 933
The Olifier
L. Merumangye
Mt. Woodroffe 1549
Musgrave Ranges
Mt. Morris 1387
Mann Ras. 1168
1231
Wilkinson Lakes
L. Dey-Dey
L. Maurice
Wynda L.
Nurrari Lakes
Serpentine Lakes
L. Kadgo
Shell Lakes

Mt. Aloysius 1168
Mt. Blackstone
Cavenagh Ra.
Tomkinson Ra.

Barrow Ra.
Mt. Squires 759
Warburton Ra.
L. Breaden
L. Baker I.
L. Hopkins
L. Throssell
Macintosh Ra.
Pt. Lilian 502
Saunders Pt. 502
L. Yeo

Jubilee L.
Shell Lakes
Rason L.
Cables

Ernest Giles Ra. 112
L. Wells
L. Carnegie
L. Buchanan
Brassey Ra.
L. Carnegie

Oldea
Barton Siding
Colona
Pinumba
Bookche P.O.
Coorabie
Fowlers B.
Murlingo
Watson
Fisher
Cook
Hughes
Deakin
Reid
Forrest
Nurina
Loongana
Haig
Cocklebiddy Motel
Madura Motel
Mundrabilla
Eucla Motel
Balladonia
Pt. Dover
Pt. Culver
Pt. Malcolm
Wilson Bluff
Low Pt.
Red Point Rock
Eyre
C. Pasley
Eastern Group
Middle I.
C. Arid
Sandy Bight
C. Le Grand
South East Is.

Kalgoorlie 555
Coolgardie
Boulder
Widgiemooltha
Norseman
L. Cowan
L. Dundas
L. Lefroy
Mt. Ridley
Mt. Ragged 585
Esperance
Esperance B.

L. Carey
Laverton
Mt. Margaret
Mt. Morgans
Leonora
Gwalia
Menzies
Broad Arrow
Bardoc
Kanowna
Bulong
Kookynie
Yerilla
Niagara
Goongarrie

L. Minigwal
L. Rebecca
L. Yindarlgooda
Mt. Burges
Comet Vale

Mt. Redcliffe 576
Mt. Alexander
Copperfield
Ballard
L. Barlee
Mt. Manmon
Riverina
Bullabulling
Seabrook
Yellowdine
Nucoria
Southern Cross

Ballard
Mt. Keith
Mt. Pasco 625
Mt. Elvire
Johnston Ra.
Bates Ra.
Mt. Eureka
Mt. Way
Wanarn
Agnew
Yundamindera

Montague Ra.
Barr Smith Ra.
Wiluna
Nabberu
Depot Springs
Cashmere Downs
Sandstone
Yuinmery
Diemals
Bullfinch

Carnarvon Ra. 906
Mt. Essendon
Robinson Ra.
Peak Hill
New Springs
Meekatharra
Nannine
L. Way

Collier Ra.
Three Rivers
Murchison Downs
Moorarie
Mileura
Big Bell
Cue
Mt. Magnet
Paynes Find

Mt. Augustus 1105
Mt. Gould
Mt. Padbury
Mt. Fraser 860
L. Austin
Austin
Tuckanarra
Mt. Gibson
Mt. Singleton 698

Gascoyne R.
Kennedy Ra.
Mullewa
Mt. Murphy
Mt. Narryer
Yalgoo
Morawa
Perenjori
Lake Moore

Carnarvon
Gladstone
Wooramel
Woodleigh
Byro
Meeberrie
Murgoo
Dividing Peak 453
Talering Peak
Bunjil

Shark Bay
Denham
Hamelin Pool
Hamelin Pool
Overlander
Wooramel
Yaringa
Murchison R.
Northampton
Geraldton
Greenough
Walkaway
Dongara
Mingenew
Three Springs
Coorow
Moora

Dirk Hartog I.
C. Cuvier
C. Ronsard
Bernier I.
Dorre I.
C. St. Cricq
Inscription Pt.
Steep Pt.
Denham Sound
Peron Peninsula
Geographe Channel
Gantheaume B.
Bluff Pt.
Green Hd.
Island Pt.

Houtman Abrolhos

PERTH
Fremantle
Rottnest I.
Midland
Armadale
Mandurah
Pinjarra
Rockingham
Kwinana
Bunbury
Busselton
C. Naturaliste
Geographe B.
Margaret River
Augusta
C. Leeuwin
Cape to Cape
Pt. D'Entrecasteaux

Northam
York
Beverley
Brookton
Narrogin
Wagin
Katanning
Gnowangerup
Kojonup
Bridgetown
Manjimup
Pemberton
Mt. Barker
Cranbrook
Mt. Manypeaks
Albany
King George Sound
Stirling Ra.
Bluff Knoll 1109
Torbay
W. C. Howe
Frankland R.
Broke Inlet

Moora
Dowerin
Wongan Hills
Goomalling
Kellerberrin
Merredin
Southern Cross
Corrigin
Narembeen
Hyden
Lake King
L. Grace
Newdegate
Ravensthorpe
Hopetoun
C. Riche

L. Johnston
L. Lefroy
Peak Charles 658
L. King
L. Tay
Mt. Gilmore
Israelite B.

m
1000
400
200
0
200
2000
4000
m

East from Greenwich

Projection: Bonne

COPYRIGHT GEORGE PHILIP & SON, LTD.

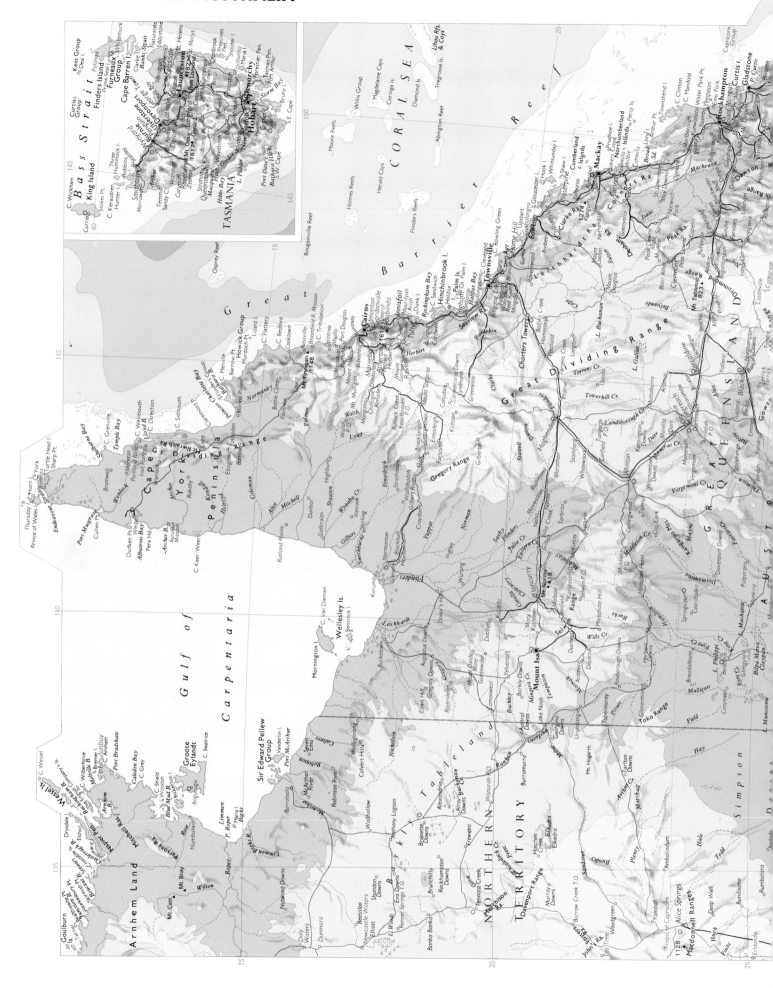

1:8 000 000

50   0   50   100   150   200   250   300 km

TASMAN

SEA

QUEENSLAND

NEW SOUTH WALES

BRISBANE

SYDNEY

CANBERRA
COMMONWEALTH TERR.

VICTORIA

MELBOURNE

SOUTH AUSTRALIA

ADELAIDE

Bass Strait

King Island

Flinders Island

Furneaux Group

Cape Barren I.

Clarke I.
Banks Strait

East from Greenwich

Projection: Bonne

COPYRIGHT GEORGE PHILIP & SON, LTD.

m   1500   1000   400   200   0
0   200   2000   4000   m

Parakylia · Benbonyathe 1058 · Lake Frome · Caradoc · Peri Lake

Leigh Creek · Copley · Broughams Gate · Packsaddle · White Cliffs · Nimba

Mt. Deception 682 ▲ · Beltana · Koonawarra · Glen Gowrie

L. Younghusband · L. Hanson · Koolymilka P.O. · Nilpena · McDougalls Well · Sturts Meadows · Grassmere · Menamurtee · Kalkaroo

L. Hart · Arcoona · Parachilna · Frome Downs · Mulga Valley · Wilangee · Langidoon · Wilcannia · Wol.

Wirraminna · Pimba · Woomera · St. Mary Pk. 1165 · Wilpena Cr. · Benagerie · Mooleulooloo · Silverton · Stephens Creek · Cawkers Well · Volo · Goonalga · Poo L.

Island Lagoon · Pernatty Lagoon · Cotabena · Hawker · Siccus · Glenorchy · Boolcoomata · Wahratta · Broken Hill · Darling

Lake Gairdner · L. Macfarlane · Hesso · Gordon · Mount Victor · Mingary · Cockburn · Menindee L. · Menindee · Talyawalka (Ana branch) · Teryaweyna L. · Ba

32 · Mt. Ive · Mt. Brown 965 ▲ · Quorn · Olary · Mannahill · Mutooroo · Leonora Downs · Cawndilla L. · Mount Manara

Port Augusta West · Carrieton · Eurelia · Yunta · Netley Gap · Tandou L. · Boolaboolka L. · N · E

Siam · Port Augusta · Wilmington · Orroroo · Paratoo · Nackara · Kimberley · Gum Lake · Darnick · Beilpajah

Buckleboo · Lake Gilles · Iron Knob · 969 · Mt. Remarkable · Booleroo Centre · Black Rock · Peterborough · Quondong · Oakbank · L. Popilta · Popio L. · Traveller's Lake · Tartna Point · Gyp

Kimba · Iron Baron · Laura · Jamestown · Terowie · Braemar · Morganville · Belmore · Burtundy · Manfred · Clare

Darke Peak · Pondooma · Whyalla · Port Pirie · Gladstone · Hallett · Mt. Bryan 934 · Canopus · Bulpunga · Arumpo · Magenta

Cowell · Crystal Brook · Gulnare · Spalding · Gluepot · L. Victoria · Hatfield P.O.

Rudall · Port Broughton · Brinkworth · Burra · Lethero

Wallaroo · Snowtown · Blyth · Clare · Farrell Flat · L. Victoria · Wentworth

34 · Arno Bay · Bute · Robertstown · Morgan · Renmark · Murray · Merbein · Mildura · Pitarpunga L. · Murrumbidgee · Oxley

Ungarra · Kadina · Bowmans · Balaklava · Point Pass · Waikerie · Holder · Barmera · Berri · Yamba · Nangiloc · Red Cliffs · Bidura

Moonta · Owen · Hamley Bridge · Kapunda · Eudunda · Maggea · Yinkanie · Loxton · Morkalla · Werrimull · Benanee · Balranald

Koppio · Tumby Bay · Maitland · Port Wakefield · Mallala · Nuriootpa · Tanunda · Angaston · Sedan · Swan Reach · Wanbi · Veitch · Taplan · Hattah · Annuello · Kooloonong · Perekerten · Moula

Poonindie · Ardrossan · Port Victoria · Truro · Holder · Kunlara · Alawoona · Meribah · Nowingi · Robinvale · Natya · Piangil · Niemur

Port Lincoln · Minlaton · Salisbury · Elizabeth · Woodside · Sanderston · Copeville · Kalyan · Sandalwood · Walpeup · Ouyen · Kulwin · Nyah West · Wako

C. Donington · THISTLE I. · Corny Pt. · Port Adelaide · ADELAIDE · Mannum · Peebinga · Cowangie · Tutye · Pier Millan · Speed · Swan Hill

West Pt. · GAMBIER IS. · Carribee · St. · Glenelg · Brighton · Mt. Barker · Murray Bridge · Karoonda · Marama · Pinnaroo · Patchewollock · L. Tyrrell · Waitchie · Ultima

C. Spencer · Marion Bay · Edithburgh · Willunga · McLaren Vale · Strathalbyn · Tailem Bend · Peake · Lameroo · Yarto · Berriwillock · Meatian

Investigator · Normanville · Finniss · Milang · Cooke Plains · Geranium · Culgoa · Quambatook · Tragowel

Western River · Kingscote · Victor Harbour · Goolwa · L. Alexandrina · L. Yumali · Coonalpyn · L. Albacutya · Rainbow · Birchip · Avoca · Cohu

C. Borda · Pennershaw · Cape Jervis · Encounter Bay · Albert · Meningie · Culburra · Tintinara · Keith · Lake Hindmarsh · Yaapeet · Wycheproof · Mincha

KANGAROO I. · D'Estrees Bay · Backstairs Passage · Yanac · Jeparit · Brim · Charlton · Mitiamo

Vivonne · The Cooring · Salt Creek · Keith · Bordertown · Diapur · Nhill · Antwerp · Warracknabeal · Litchfield · Korong Vale

C. du Couedic · Vivonne Bay · G. Gantheaume · Younghusband Peninsula · Wolseley · Kaniva · Dimboola · Minyip · Murtoa · Donald · Wedderburn · Inglewood · Bridgewa

36 · Lacepede Bay · Frances · Goroke · Natimuk · WIMMERA · Cope Cope · St. Arnaud · Eaglehawk

Kingston S.E. · C. Jaffa · Reedy Creek · Kybybolite · Morea (Carpolac) · Jallumba · Toolondo · Deep Lead · Bolangum · Maryborough · Castlemaine · Talbot · Kyne

Naracoorte · Glenorchy · Wimmera · Horsham · The Grampians · Stawell · Ararat · Dunolly · Maldon · Daylesford · Creswick

Glenroy · Balmoral · Glenelg · Mt. William 1167 · Maroona · Beaufort · Clunes · Waubra · BALLA

Beachport · L. George · Kalangadoo · Penola · Englefield · Cavendish · Willaura · Minerva · Scarsdale · Elaine

Rivoli B. · Millicent · Nangwarry · Casterton · Coleraine · Dartmoor · Branxholme · Penshurst · Dunkeld · Skipton · Cressy · Inverleigh

L. Bonney · Mount Gambier · Condah · Macarthur · Mortlake · Derrinallum · Yarrowee

38 · C. Northumberland · Port MacDonnell · Heywood · Camperdown · Alvie · Winchelsea · Quee

Discovery Bay · Portland · Koroit · Terang · Cobden · Colac · Aireys · Lorne

C. Bridgewater · Portland Bay · Port Fairy · Allansford · Timboon · Forrest

C. Nelson · WARRNAMBOOL · Port Campbell · Lavers Hill · Apollo Bay · C. Otway

GEELONG · VIC

m
2000
1500
1000
400
200
0
0
200
2000
4000
m

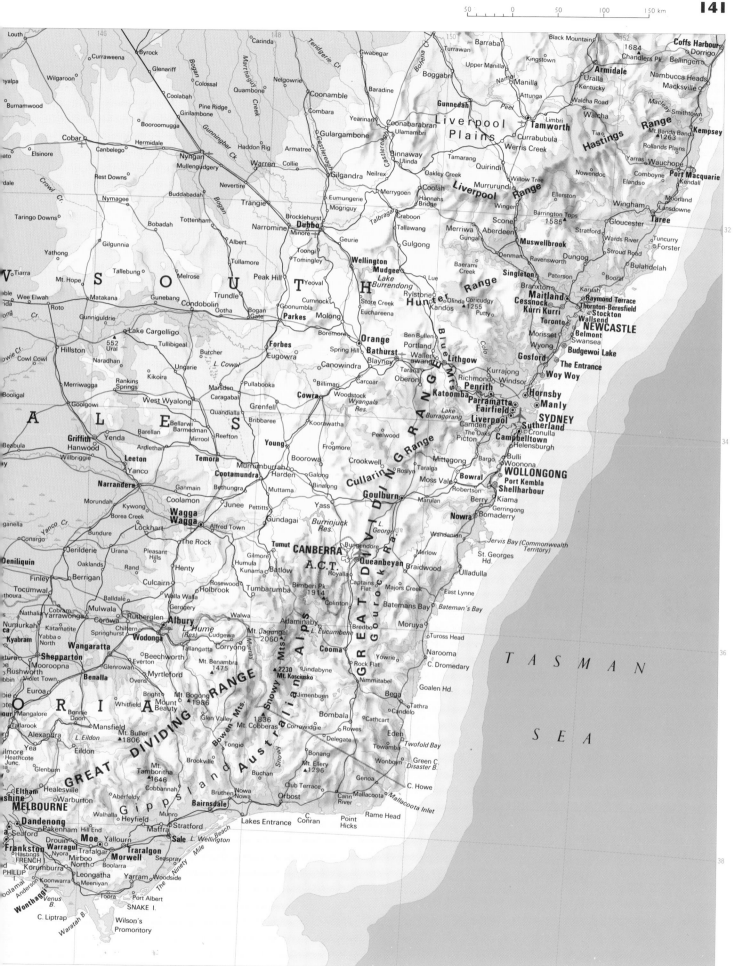

1:4 000 000

141

COPYRIGHT GEORGE PHILIP & SON LTD

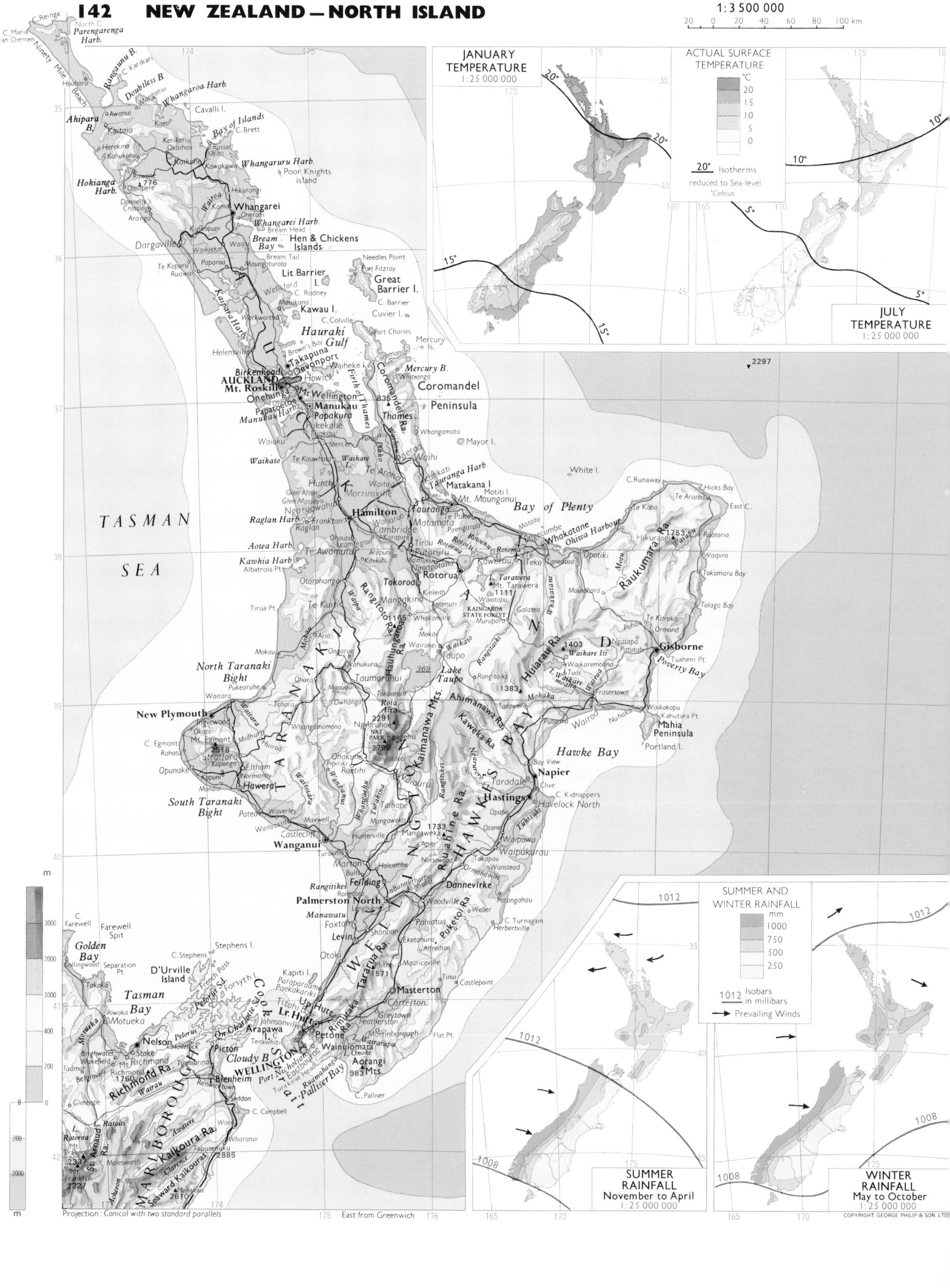

1:3 500 000

20   0   20   40   60   80   100 km

JANUARY
TEMPERATURE
1:25 000 000

ACTUAL SURFACE
TEMPERATURE
°C
20
15
10
5
0

20° Isotherms
reduced to Sea-level
°Celsius

JULY
TEMPERATURE
1:25 000 000

SUMMER AND
WINTER RAINFALL
mm
1000
750
500
250

1012 Isobars
in millibars
→ Prevailing Winds

SUMMER
RAINFALL
November to April
1:25 000 000

WINTER
RAINFALL
May to October
1:25 000 000

COPYRIGHT GEORGE PHILIP & SON LTD.

TASMAN SEA

Projection: Conical with two standard parallels   East from Greenwich

m
3000
2000
1000
400
200
0
200
2000
m

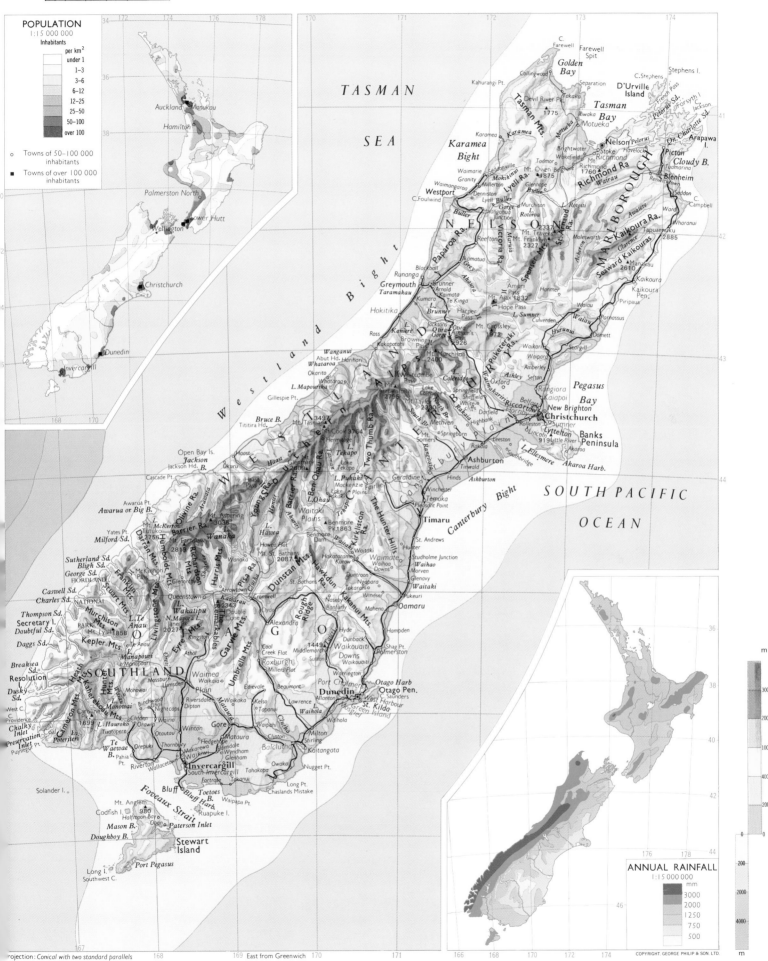

1:3 500 000

20 0 20 40 60 80 100 km

POPULATION
1:15 000 000

Inhabitants
per km²

under 1
1-3
3-6
6-12
12-25
25-50
50-100
over 100

o Towns of 50-100 000 inhabitants

■ Towns of over 100 000 inhabitants

Auckland Manukau
Hamilton

Palmerston North

Lower Hutt
Wellington

Christchurch

Dunedin

Invercargill

TASMAN

SEA

Karamea
Bight

Golden
Bay

Tasman
Bay

D'Urville
Island

Picton
Cloudy B.

NELSON

MARLBOROUGH

Westport

Greymouth

Hokitika

Westland Bight

WESTLAND

SOUTHERN ALPS

Mt Cook 3764

CANTERBURY

Christchurch
Lyttelton

Banks
Peninsula

Pegasus
Bay

Timaru

Canterbury Bight

SOUTH PACIFIC

OCEAN

Oamaru

SOUTHLAND

OTAGO

Queenstown

Dunedin

Invercargill
South Invercargill

Gore

Bluff

Foveaux Strait

Stewart
Island

Projection: Conical with two standard parallels

East from Greenwich

ANNUAL RAINFALL
1:15 000 000
mm

3000
2000
1250
750
500

COPYRIGHT. GEORGE PHILIP & SON. LTD.

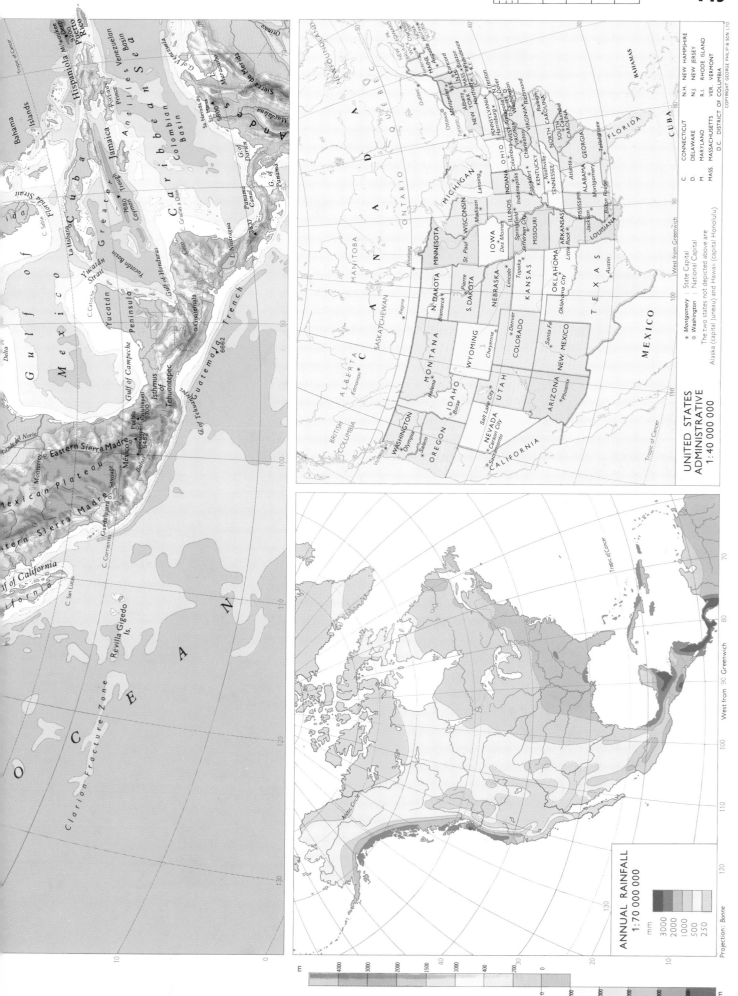

1:30 000 000

200 0 200 400 600 800 1000 km

UNITED STATES
ADMINISTRATIVE 1:40 000 000

ANNUAL RAINFALL
1:70 000 000

1 : 70 000 000

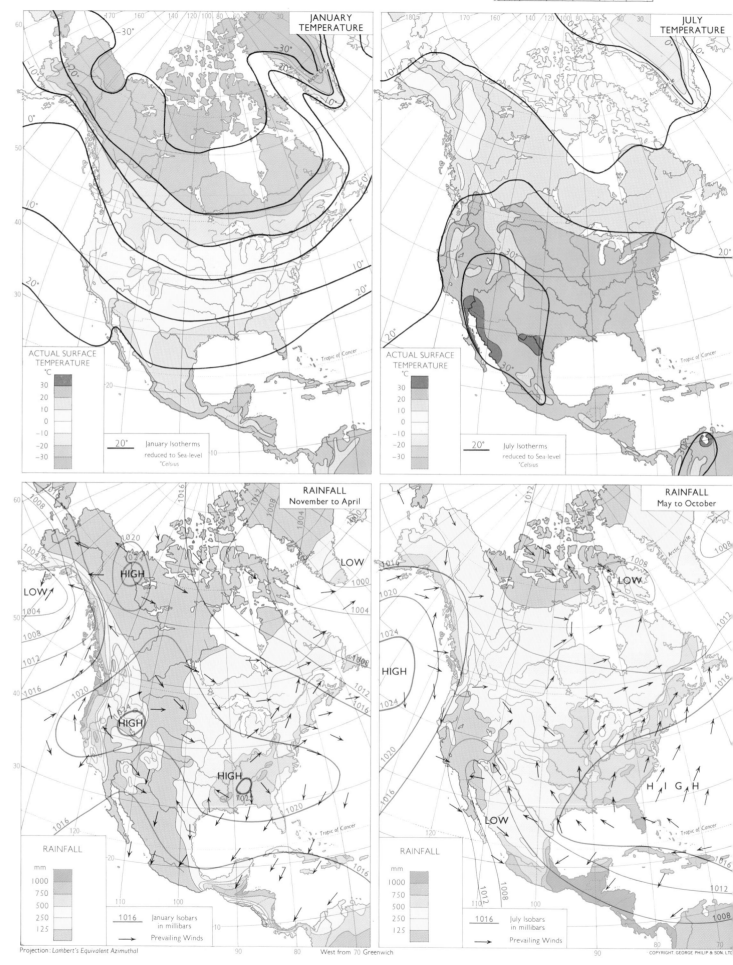

JANUARY
TEMPERATURE

ACTUAL SURFACE
TEMPERATURE
°C

	30
	20
	10
	0
	-10
	-20
	-30

20°   January Isotherms
reduced to Sea-level
°Celsius

JULY
TEMPERATURE

ACTUAL SURFACE
TEMPERATURE
°C

	30
	20
	10
	0
	-10
	-20
	-30

20°   July Isotherms
reduced to Sea-level
°Celsius

RAINFALL
November to April

RAINFALL

mm

	1000
	750
	500
	250
	125

1016   January Isobars
in millibars
→   Prevailing Winds

RAINFALL
May to October

RAINFALL

mm

	1000
	750
	500
	250
	125

1016   July Isobars
in millibars
→   Prevailing Winds

Projection : Lambert's Equivalent Azimuthal

West from 70 Greenwich

COPYRIGHT GEORGE PHILIP & SON, LTD.

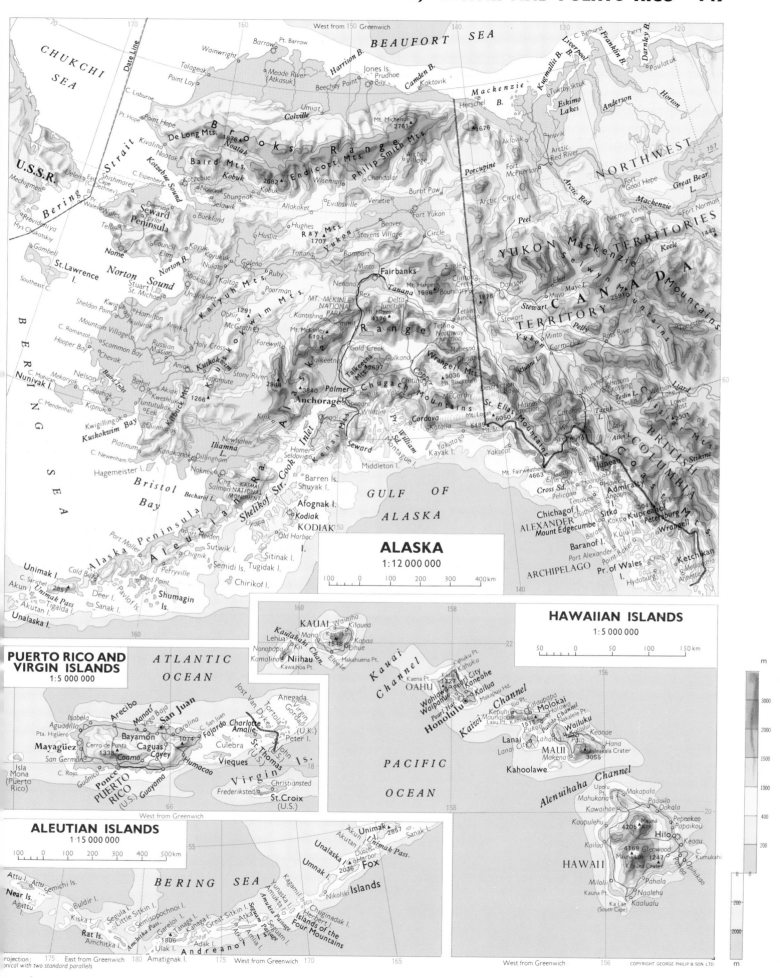

m
3000
2000
1500
1000
400
200
0
200
2000
m

Projection: Bonne

1:15 000 000

100   0   100   200   300   400   500   600 km

von Island
ancaster Sound

Baffin Bay

GREENLAND

ATLANTIC

Davis Strait

Hudson Strait

Ungava Bay

Hudson Bay

NEW

COAST OF LABRADOR

QUEBEC

NEWFOUNDLAND

St. John's

James Bay

Gulf of
St. Lawrence

ST-PIERRE et MIQUELON (Fr)

PR. EDWARD I.

NEW BRUNSWICK

NOVA SCOTIA

Halifax

MONTRÉAL

Québec

MAINE

Saint John

OCEAN

Ottawa

VERMONT

NEW HAMPSHIRE

MASS.

Boston

TORONTO

London

Buffalo

NEW YORK

CONN.

Providence

DETROIT

Cleveland

PENNSYLVANIA

NEW JERSEY

NEW YORK

West from Greenwich   COPYRIGHT. GEORGE PHILIP & SON. LTD.

1:7 000 000

50 0 50 100 150 200 250 300 km

COAST OF NEWFOUNDLAND

LABRADOR

QUEBEC

NEWFOUNDLAND

Smallwood Reservoir

L. Melville

Mealy Mts.

Happy Valley

Goose Bay

Churchill Falls

Labrador City
Wabush

Str. of Belle Isle
Belle I.

St. Anthony

Corner Brook

Deer Lake

Grand Falls

Gander

St. John's
Avalon Peninsula

Conception B.

GULF OF ST. LAWRENCE

Î. d'Anticosti

Sept-Îles
Port-Cartier

Baie-Comeau

Gaspé
Pén. de Gaspé
Mts. Chic-Chocs

Rimouski
Matane
Mont-Joli

Rivière-du-Loup

Edmundston

Îs. de la Madeleine (Quebec)

Cabot Strait

SAINT-PIERRE ET MIQUELON (Fr.)

St. Pierre
Miquelon

Channel-Port aux Basques

PRINCE EDWARD ISLAND

Summerside
Charlottetown

Cape Breton Island

Sydney
Glace Bay
New Waterford
Sydney Mines
N. Sydney
Louisbourg

NEW BRUNSWICK

Fredericton
Saint John
Moncton
Bathurst
Campbellton
Chatham
Newcastle
Grand Falls

NOVA SCOTIA

Truro
New Glasgow
Stellarton
Amherst
Antigonish
Mulgrave
Canso

Dartmouth
Halifax
Lunenburg
Bridgewater
Liverpool
Shelburne
Yarmouth
Digby
Annapolis Royal

Bay of Fundy

Sable I. (Nova Scotia)

MAINE

Bangor
Augusta
Waterville
Lewiston
Auburn
Portland
Brunswick
Bath
Rumford
Berlin
Bethel

Old Town
Brewer
Calais
Eastport

BOSTON
Brockton
Manchester
Nashua
Portsmouth
Dover
Concord
Lawrence
Haverhill
Gloucester
Lynn

ATLANTIC OCEAN

West from Greenwich

COPYRIGHT. GEORGE PHILIP & SON, LTD.

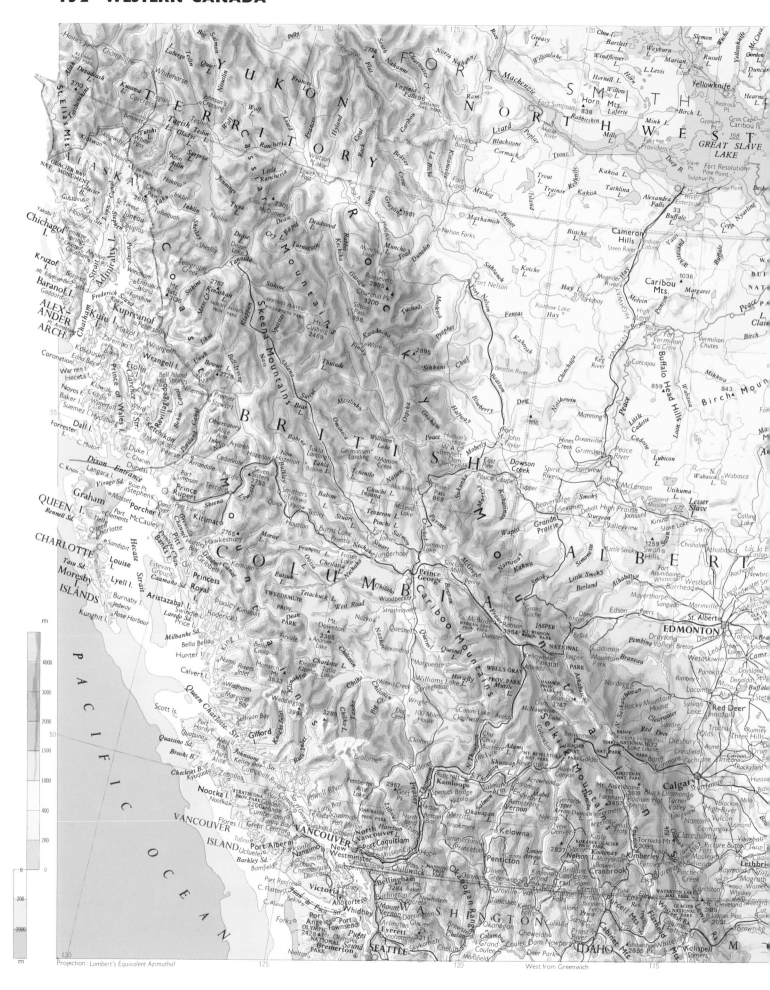

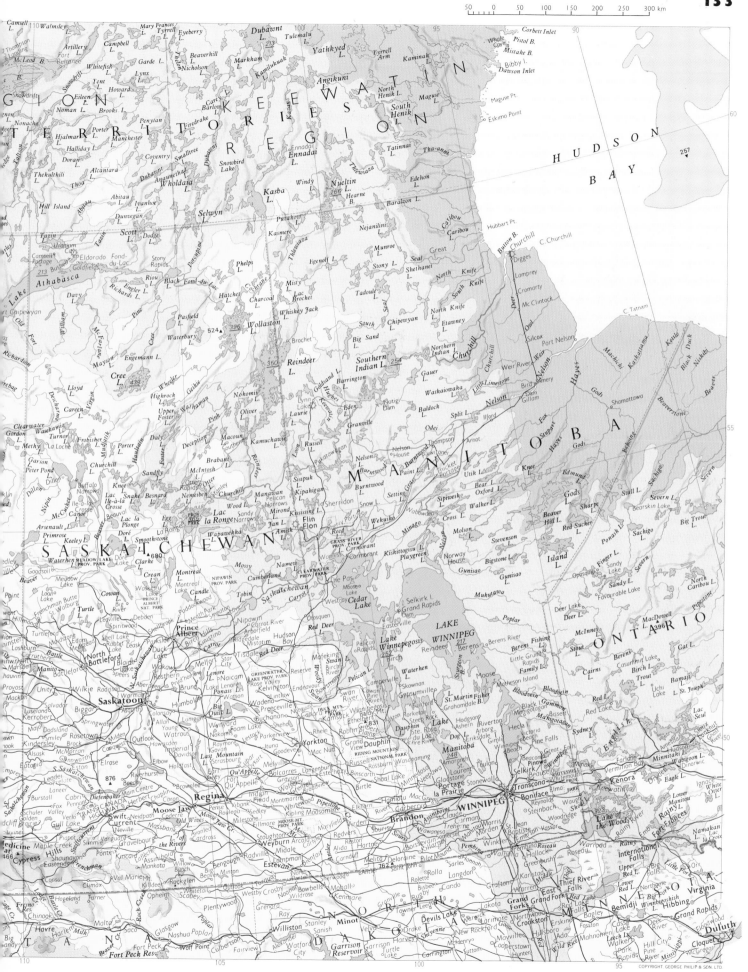

1 : 7 000 000

50 0 50 100 150 200 250 300 km

HUDSON

BAY

KEEWATIN

TERRITORIES   REGION

Hubbart Pt.

C. Churchill

Churchill

Port Nelson

MANITOBA

SASKATCHEWAN

ONTARIO

Lake Athabasca

Reindeer L.

Southern Indian L.

Cree L.

Lac la Ronge

Flin Flon

Lake Winnipeg

Lake Winnipegosis

Cedar Lake

Prince Albert

North Battleford

Saskatoon

Regina

Moose Jaw

Swift Current

Medicine Hat

Cypress

Dauphin

Brandon

WINNIPEG

St. Boniface

Transcona

Portage la Prairie

Selkirk

Kenora

Lake of the Woods

Fort Frances

International Falls

Grand Forks

Thief River Falls

Duluth

MONTANA

NORTH DAKOTA

MINNESOTA

Fort Peck Res.

Garrison Reservoir

Devils Lake

Minot

Williston

COPYRIGHT GEORGE PHILIP & SON. LTD.

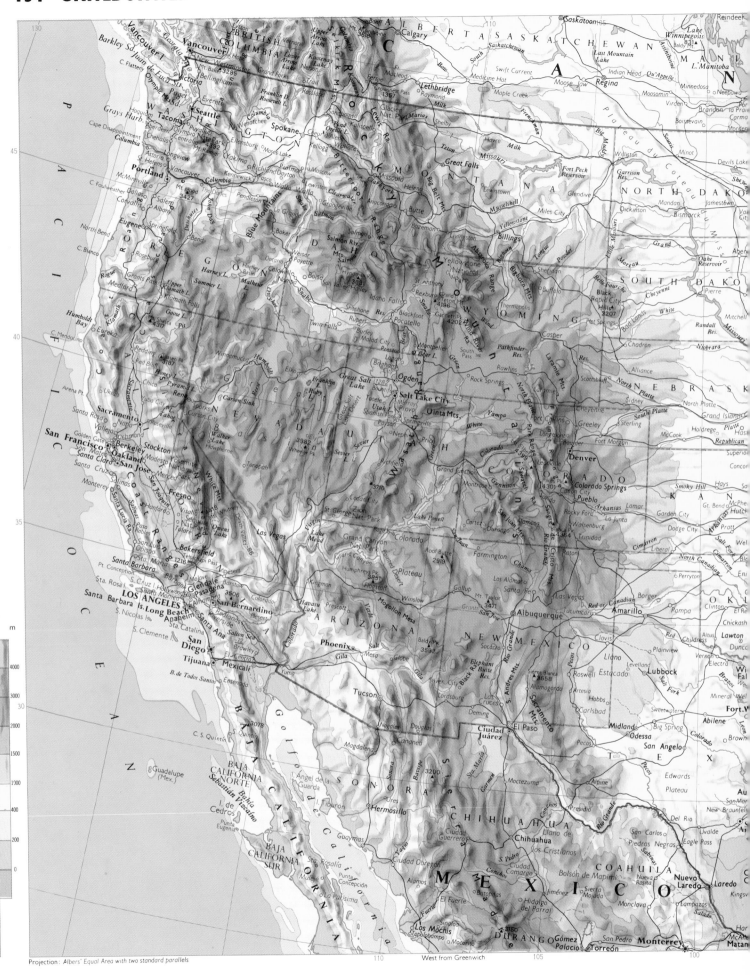

Projection: Albers' Equal Area with two standard parallels

West from Greenwich

100   0   100   200   300   400   500 km

COPYRIGHT. GEORGE PHILIP & SON. LTD

LAKE SUPERIOR
LAKE HURON
LAKE ONTARIO
LAKE ERIE
Georgian Bay
ONTARIO
QUEBEC
CANADA
MICHIGAN
WISCONSIN
ILLINOIS
INDIANA
OHIO
KENTUCKY
WEST VIRGINIA
VIRGINIA
PENNSYLVANIA
NEW YORK
NEW JERSEY
MARYLAND
DELAWARE
MASS.
NEW HAMPSHIRE
VERMONT
D.C.
CHICAGO
MILWAUKEE
DETROIT
TOLEDO
CLEVELAND
PITTSBURGH
BUFFALO
TORONTO
MONTREAL
OTTAWA
BOSTON
NEW YORK
PHILADELPHIA
BALTIMORE
WASHINGTON
CINCINNATI
INDIANAPOLIS
COLUMBUS
AKRON

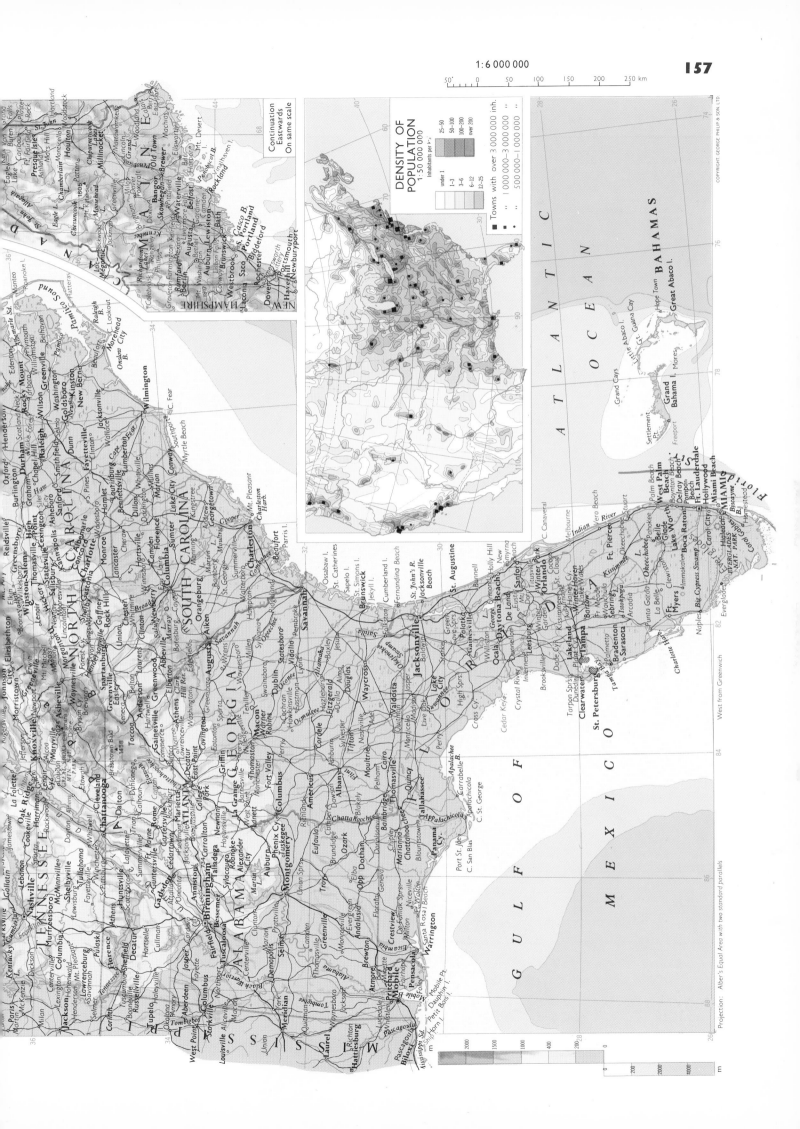

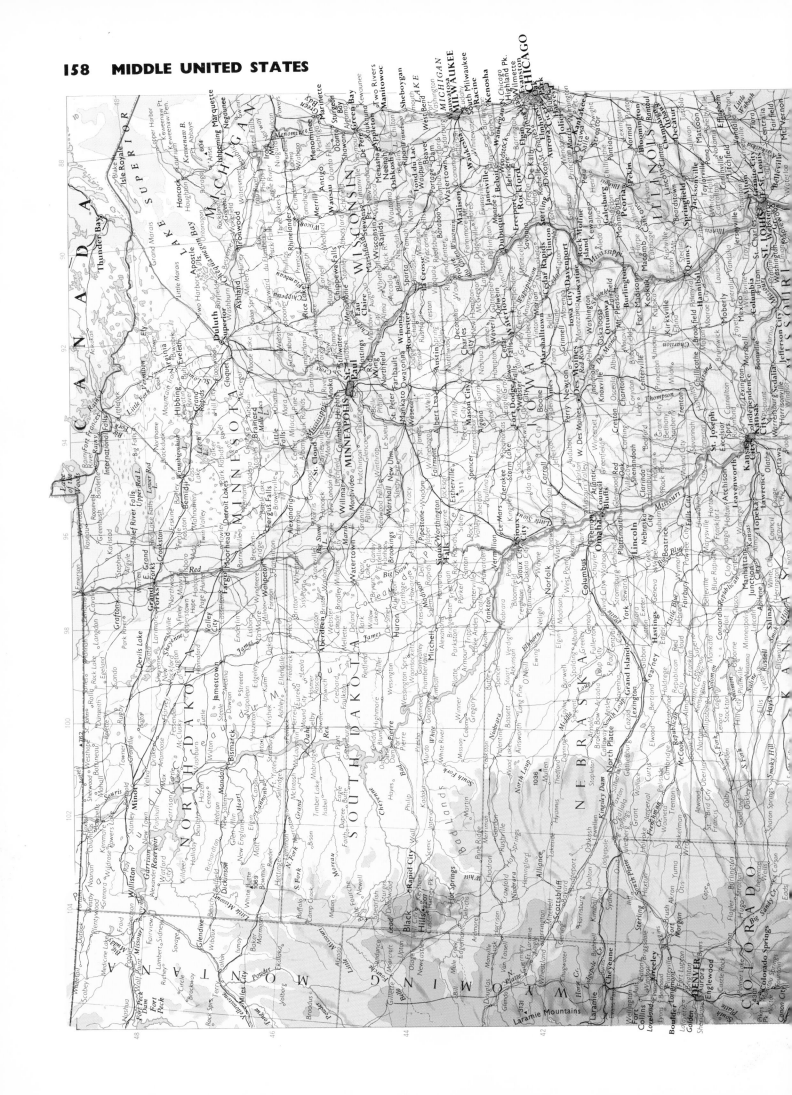

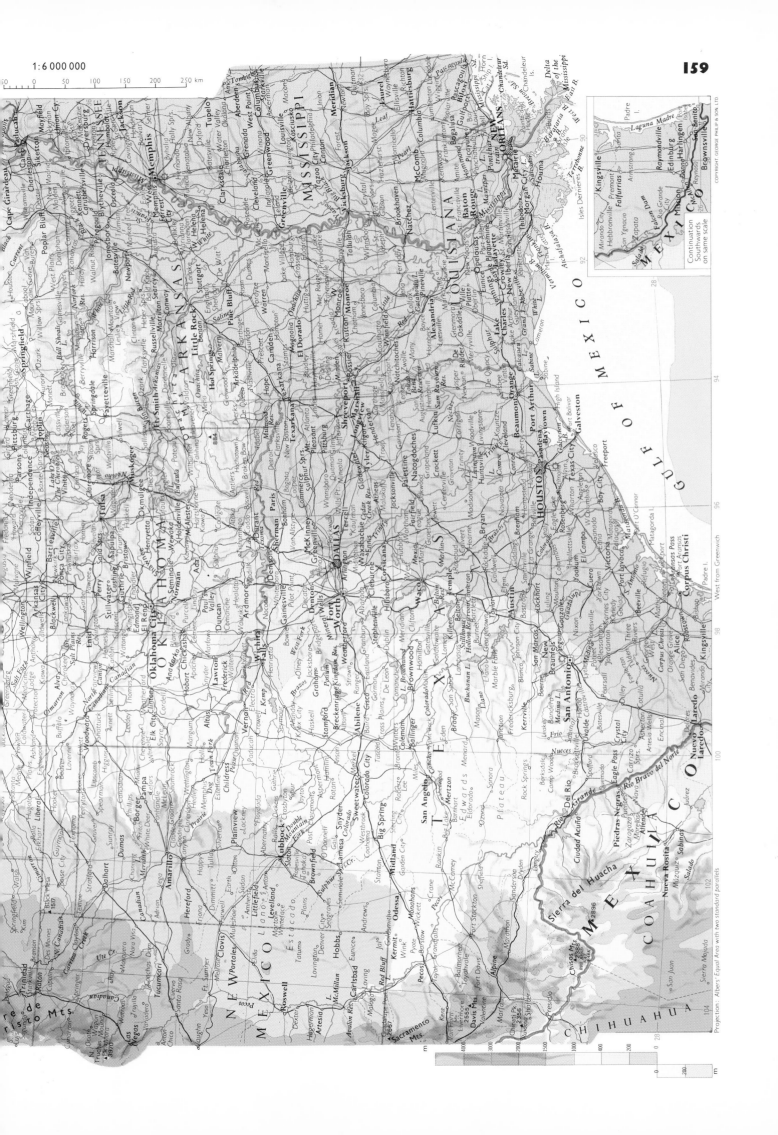

1:6 000 000

50   0   50   100   150   200   250 km

GULF OF MEXICO

TENNESSEE

MISSISSIPPI

ARKANSAS

LOUISIANA

OKLAHOMA

TEXAS

NEW MEXICO

MEXICO

COAHUILA

CHIHUAHUA

Laguna Madre

Continuation
Southwards
on same scale

Projection : Albers' Equal Area with two standard parallels

West from Greenwich

COPYRIGHT GEORGE PHILIP & SON LTD.

1:6 000 000

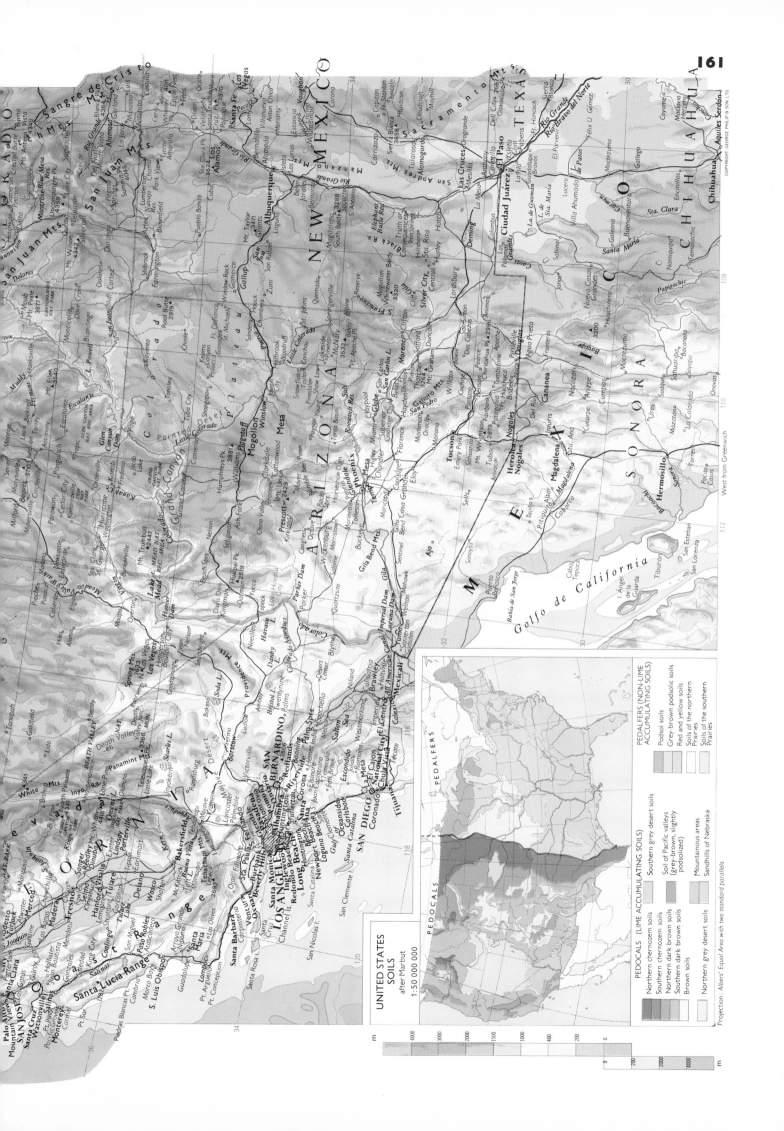

**UNITED STATES
SOILS**

after Marbut

1:50 000 000

PEDOCALS (LIME ACCUMULATING SOILS)

- Northern chernozem soils
- Southern chernozem soils
- Northern dark brown soils
- Southern dark brown soils
- Brown soils
- Northern grey desert soils
- Southern grey desert soils
- Soil of Pacific valleys (grey-brown, slightly podsolized)
- Mountainous areas
- Sandhills of Nebraska

PEDALFERS (NON-LIME ACCUMULATING SOILS)

- Podsol soils
- Grey-brown podsolic soils
- Red and yellow soils
- Soils of the northern Prairies
- Soils of the southern Prairies

Projection: Albers' Equal Area with two standard parallels

West from Greenwich

COPYRIGHT GEORGE PHILIP & SON, LTD

1:3 000 000

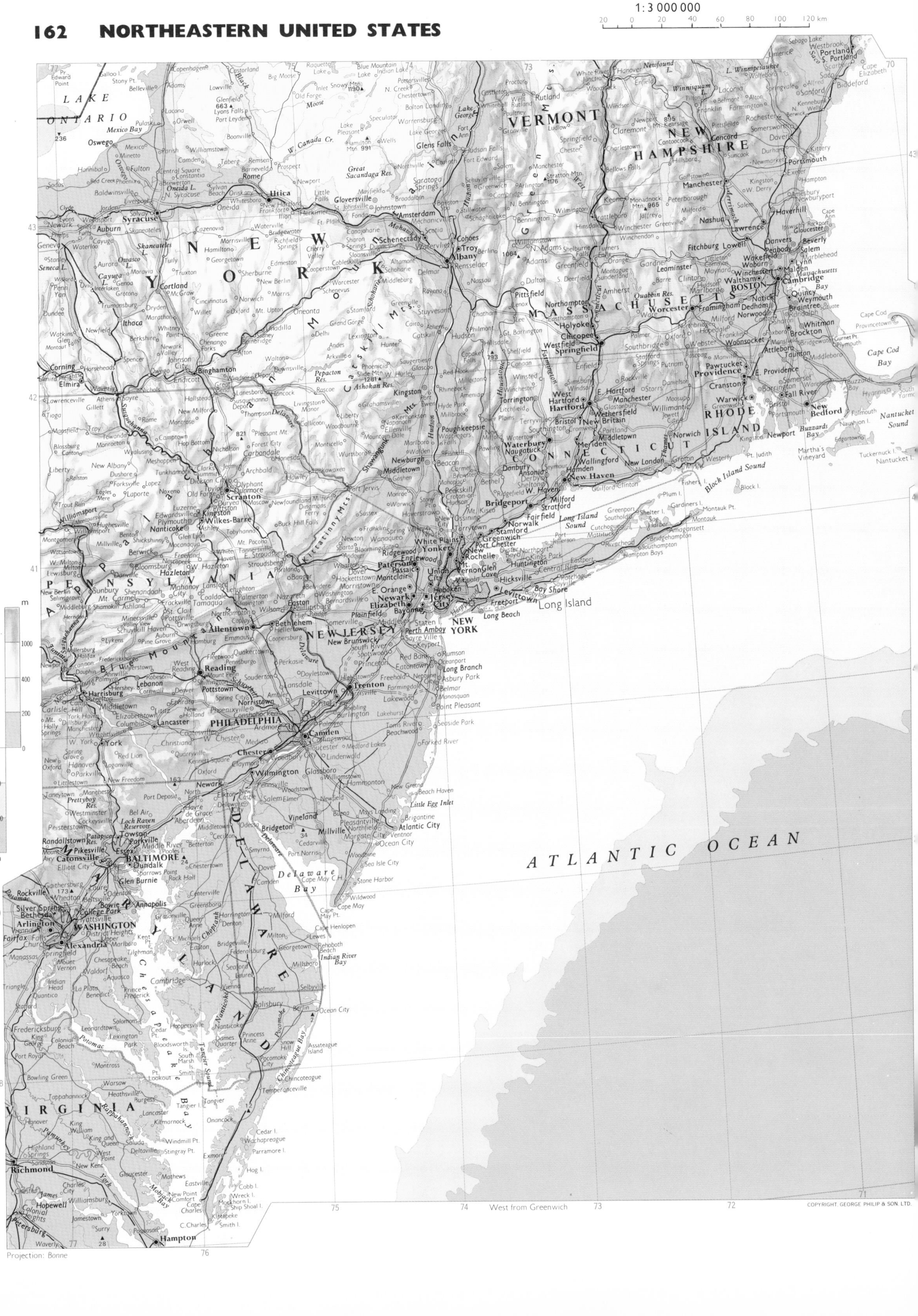

20 0 20 40 60 80 100 120 km

LAKE ONTARIO

VERMONT

NEW HAMPSHIRE

NEW YORK

MASSACHUSETTS

CONNECTICUT

RHODE ISLAND

PENNSYLVANIA

NEW JERSEY

NEW YORK

Long Island

ATLANTIC OCEAN

DELAWARE

MARYLAND

VIRGINIA

Chesapeake Bay

Delaware Bay

WASHINGTON

BALTIMORE

PHILADELPHIA

BOSTON

Long Island Sound

Block Island Sound

West from Greenwich

COPYRIGHT GEORGE PHILIP & SON LTD.

Projection: Bonne

1:3 000 000

20 0 20 40 60 80 100 120 140 km

NEVADA

PACIFIC

OCEAN

SAN FRANCISCO

Sacramento

Stockton

Modesto

Fresno

Bakersfield

LOS ANGELES

San Diego

Tijuana

YOSEMITE NATIONAL PARK

DEATH VALLEY

NATIONAL MONUMENT

SEQUOIA NAT. PARK

KINGS CANYON MEMORIAL PARK

Santa Barbara

Ventura

Oxnard

Long Beach

Anaheim

Santa Ana

San Bernardino

Riverside

Palm Springs

Salton Sea

JOSHUA TREE NAT. MON.

ANZA BORREGO DESERT STATE PARK

Mojave Desert

Santa Barbara Channel

San Pedro Channel

Channel Islands

Monterey Bay

projection: Bonne   West from Greenwich   COPYRIGHT
GEORGE PHILIP & SON, LTD.

m
4000
3000
2000
1500
1000
400
200
0
200
2000
m

PACIFIC

OCEAN

REFERENCE TO NUMBERS

1	Federal District	5	México
2	Aguascalientes	6	Morelos
3	Guanajuato	7	Querétaro
4	Hidalgo	8	Tlaxcala

Projection: Bi-polar oblique Conical Orthomorphic

West from Greenwich

m

4000
3000
2000
1500
1000
400
200
0
200
2000
4000

m

GULF OF MEXICO

Projection: Bi-polar oblique Conical Orthomorphic

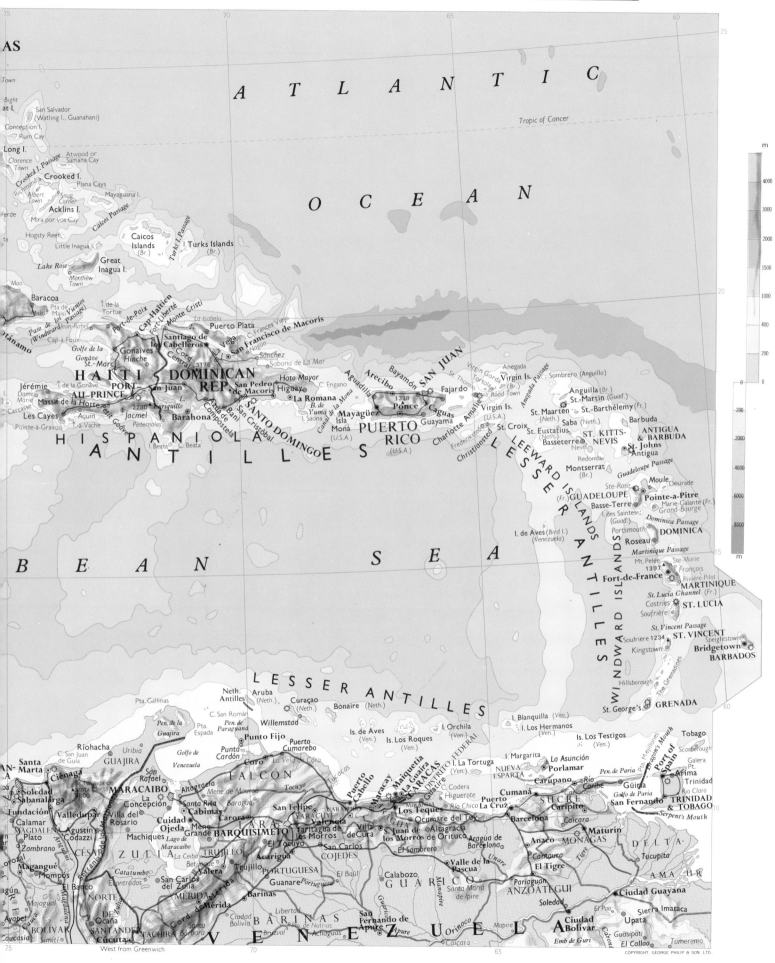

1 : 8 000 000

50   0   50   100   150   200   250   300 km

AS

Town

Bight
at I.

Long I.
Clarence
Town
Crooked I. Passage   **Crooked I.**
Richmond
Albert   *Snug*   Plana Cays
Town   *Corner*   Mayaguana I.
verde   Mira por vos Cay
Acklins I.

Hogsty Reef
Little Inagua I.   **Caicos**
Lake Rose   **Islands**   Turks I. Passage   **Turks Islands**
Matthew   **Great**   *(Br.)*   *(Br.)*
Town   **Inagua I.**

Baracoa
Pta. de los   I. de la
Maisí   Tortue   Monte Cristi
tánamo   *Paso de los Vientos*   Port-de-Paix   **Cap-Haïtien**   La Isabela
(Windward Passage)   Jean-Rabel   Fort-Liberté   *C. Frances Viejo*
Cap-à-Foux   Port-Liberté   Puerto Plata
Golfe de la   **Gonaïves**   **Santiago de**   La Vega   San Francisco de Macorís
Gonâve   Hinche   **los Cabelleros**   *Cord.*   *Nagua*
St-Marc   *Central*   3175   Sánchez
HAITI   **DOMINICAN**   Sabana de La Mar
Jérémie   I. de la Gonâve   PORT-   San Juan   **REP.**   Hato Mayor
Dame-   **AU-PRINCE**   San Pedro   C. Engano
Marie   2280   Enriquillo   *Azua de*   **de Macorís**   Higüey
Carcasse   Massif de la Hotte   L.   Compostela   B. de
Les Cayes   *Aquin*   Jacmel   **Barahona**   Yuma
Pointe-à-Gravois   La-Vache   Pedernales   *San Cristóbal*   **SANTO DOMINGO**
I. Beata   C. Beata

HISPANIOLA

ANTILLES

1 : 30 000 000

200   0   200   400   600   800   1000 km

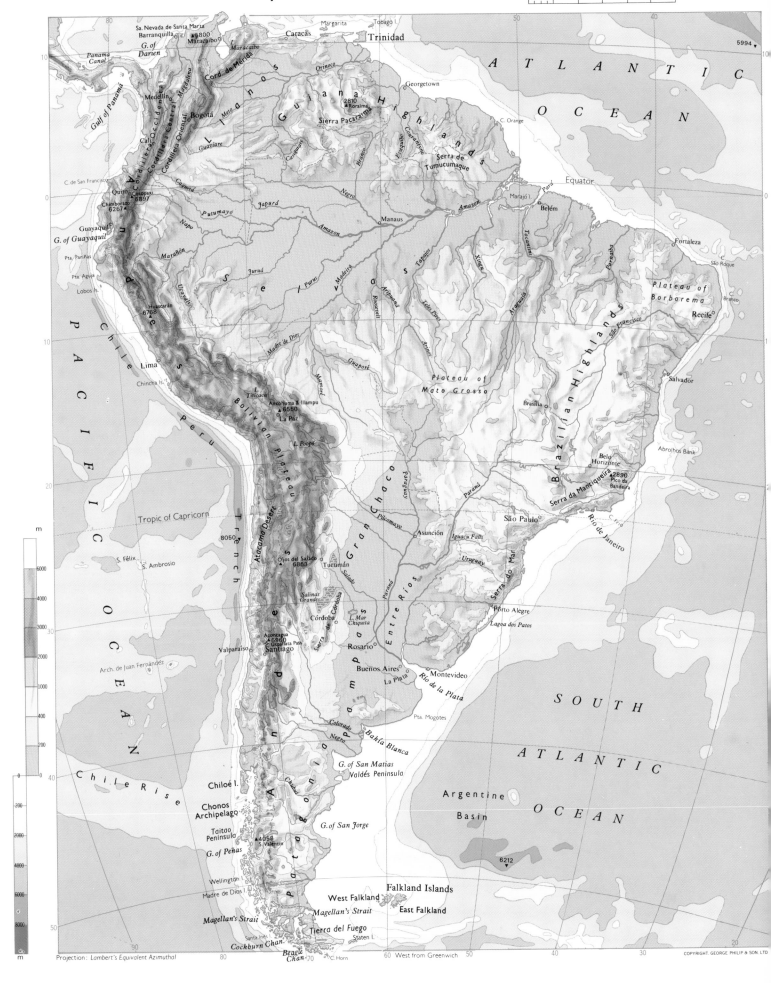

Sa. Nevada de Santa Marta
Barranquilla ● ▲5800
Maracaibo ●
G. of Darién
Panama Canal
Medellín ●
Cord. de Mérida
Caracas
Margarita
Tobago I.
Trinidad
ATLANTIC
OCEAN
5994 ▾
Bogotá ●
Cali ●
Cordillera Occidental
Cordillera Central
Cordillera Oriental
Magdalena
Llanos
Orinoco
Meta
Guaviare
Guiana Highlands
Georgetown
Sierra Pacaraima
▲2810 Roraima
Serra de Tumucumaque
C. Orange
C. de San Francisco
Quito ● Cotopaxi 5897
Chimborazo 6267 ▲
Napo
Putumayo
Japurá
Caquetá
Negro
Branco
Essequibo
Corentijne
Courantyne
Equator
Pará
Amazon
Manaus
Marajó I.
Belém
Guayaquil ●
G. of Guayaquil
Pta. Pariñas
Pta. Aguja
Marañón
Jurúa
Purus
Amazon
Madeira
Aripuaná
Roosevelt
Tapajós
Xingu
Tocantins
Araguaia
Parnaíba
Fortaleza
São Roque
Lobos Is.
Ucayali
Madre de Dios
Teles Pires
Plateau of Borborema
Branco
Recife
Huascarán 6768 ▲
Andes
Selvas
Guaporé
Aripuaná
Javari
São Francisco
Salvador
Lima ●
Chincha Is.
L. Titicaca
Ancohuma & Illampu 6550 ▲
La Paz ●
L. Poopó
Bolivian Plateau
Mamoré
Guaporé
Plateau of Mato Grosso
Brasília ●
Brazilian Highlands
Abrolhos Bank
PACIFIC
Chile
Peru
Trench
Tropic of Capricorn
Atacama Desert
8050
Ojos del Salado 6863
Tucumán ●
Salado
Gran Chaco
Pilcomayo
Bermejo
Paraguay
Paraná
Asunción ●
Belo Horizonte ●
▲2890 Pico da Bandeira
Serra da Mantiqueira
São Paulo ●
Rio de Janeiro
Caru
S. Félix
S. Ambrosio
Salinas Grandes
Córdoba ●
L. Mar Chiquita
Sierra de Córdoba
Iguaçu Falls
Uruguay
Paraná
Entre Ríos
Sierra do Mar
Pôrto Alegre ●
Lagoa dos Patos
OCEAN
Arch. de Juan Fernández
Aconcagua 6960 ▲
Uspallata Pass
Valparaíso ●
Santiago ●
Rosario ●
Buenos Aires ●
Pampas
La Plata ●
Montevideo ●
Rio de la Plata
Pta. Mogotes
SOUTH
ATLANTIC
Chile Rise
Colorado
Bahía Blanca
Negro
G. of San Matías
Valdés Peninsula
Argentine
Basin
OCEAN
Chiloé I.
Chubut
G. of San Jorge
Chonos Archipelago
Taitao Peninsula
S. Valentín 4058 ▲
G. of Peñas
Patagonia
Andes
6212
Wellington I.
Madre de Dios I.
Falkland Islands
West Falkland
East Falkland
Magellan's Strait
Magellan's Strait
Tierra del Fuego
Santa Inés I.
Staten I.
Cockburn Chan.
Beagle Chan.
C. Horn

m
6000
4000
3000
2000
1000
400
200
0
200
2000
4000
6000
8000
m

Projection : Lambert's Equivalent Azimuthal   80   70   60   West from Greenwich   50   40   COPYRIGHT. GEORGE PHILIP & SON. LTD

1:80 000 000

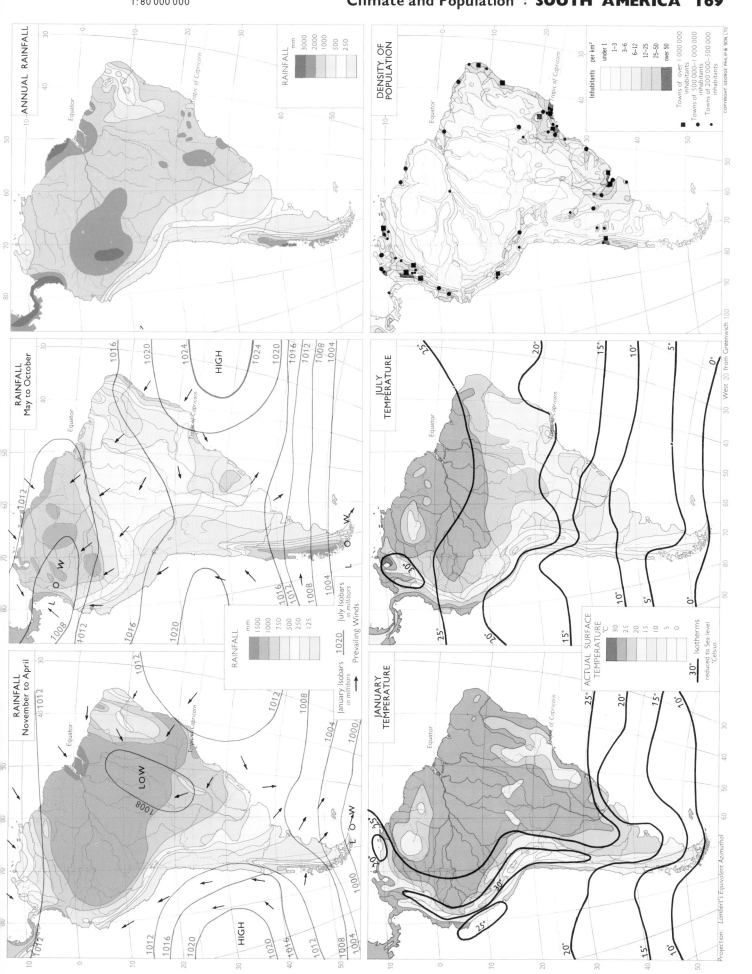

ANNUAL RAINFALL

RAINFALL mm
3000
2000
1000
500
250

DENSITY OF POPULATION

Inhabitants per km²
under 1
1–3
3–6
6–12
12–25
25–50
over 50

Towns of over 1 000 000 inhabitants
Towns of 500 000–1 000 000 inhabitants
Towns of 200 000–500 000 inhabitants

COPYRIGHT GEORGE PHILIP & SON LTD

RAINFALL May to October

HIGH

RAINFALL mm
1500
1000
750
500
250
125

1020 July Isobars in millibars
January Isobars in millibars
Prevailing Winds

RAINFALL November to April

LOW

HIGH

JULY TEMPERATURE

JANUARY TEMPERATURE

ACTUAL SURFACE TEMPERATURE °C
30
25
20
15
10
5
0

Isotherms reduced to Sea-level
Celsius

Projection: Lambert's Equivalent Azimuthal

West 20 from Greenwich 100

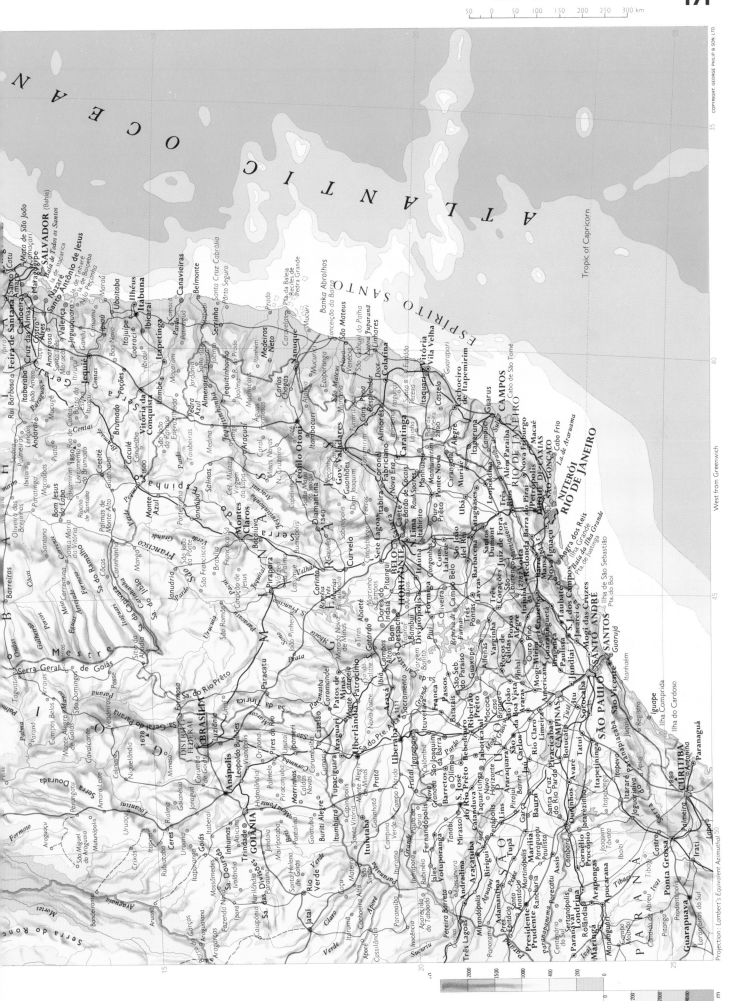

1:8 000 000

50 0 50 100 150 200 250 300 km

ATLANTIC OCEAN

Tropic of Capricorn

ESPÍRITO SANTO

SALVADOR (Bahia)

B R A Z I L

M I N A S

G E R A I S

BRASÍLIA

GOIÂNIA

BELO HORIZONTE

RIO DE JANEIRO

NITERÓI

SÃO PAULO

SANTO ANDRÉ

SANTOS

CAMPINAS

CURITIBA

P A R A N Á

S Ã O   P A U L O

West from Greenwich

Projection: Lambert's Equivalent Azimuthal 50

COPYRIGHT GEORGE PHILIP & SON LTD

m

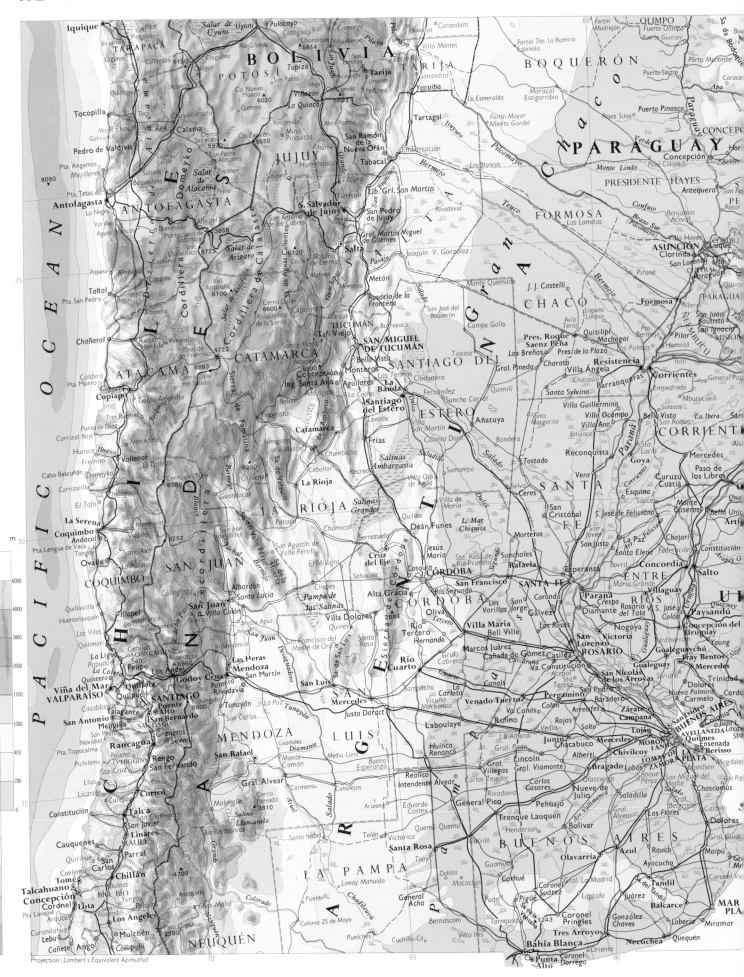

Projection: Lambert's Equivalent Azimuthal

1:8 000 000

50 0 50 100 150 200 250 300 km

173

GROSSO

DO SUL

Três Lagoas · Andradina · Mirassol · S. José
Olímpia · Passos · BELO
do Rio Prêto · HORIZONTE
N. Lima
Itabirito
Congonhas
Cons.
Lafaiete
Vitória
Itaquari
Vila
Velha
Guaraparí

Xavantina · Mirandópolis · Catanduva · Batatais · São Seb. · Oliveira
Araçatuba · Taquaritinga · Ribeirão · do Paraíso · Campo Belo · Ouro
Prêto · Ponte Nova
Panorama · Biguri · Penápolis · Jaboticabal · Prêto · Guaxupé · Represa de · Três · São João · Uba · Carangola
Furnas · Pontes · del Rei · Castelo
Cachoeiro
de Itapemirim

Adamantina · Lins · Casa · Mococa · Alfenas · Lavras · Barbacena · Cataguases
São · Santa Anastácio · Tupã · Branca · Varginha · Santos · Itaperuna
Martinópolis · Araraquara · São João · Poços de · Corações · Dumont · Juiz de Fora · Leopoldina · Guarus
Presidente · Marília · Bauru · da Boa Vista · Caldas · Pouso · São · Três · Além Paraíba · Paraíba do Sul
Prudente · Rancharia · Paraguaçu · Araras · Pinhal · Alegre · Lourenço · Rios · CAMPOS
Paulista · Rio Claro · Limeira · Ouro Pino · Itajubá · 2787 · Volta · RIO DE JANEIRO
Paranavaí · Assis · Santa Cruz · Piracicaba · Americana · Mogi-Mirim · Serra · Redonda · Barra do Piraí · Nova Friburgo
Sertanópolis · do Rio Pardo · CAMPINAS · Guaratinguetá · Barra · Petrópolis · Macaé
Ourinhos · Avaré · Jundiaí · Bragança · Mansa · Nova Iguaçu · DUQUE DE CAXIAS
Londrina · Cornélio · Jacarèzinho · Botucatu · Itu · S.J. dos Campos · Jacareí · SÃO GONÇALO
Maringá · Procópio · Tatui · Sorocaba · Angra dos Reis · NITERÓI
Apucarana · Arapongas · Itapetininga · SÃO PAULO · SANTO ANDRÉ · RIO DE JANEIRO · Cabo Frio
La. de Araruama

Cruzeiro · Itararé · Paranapiacaba · São Vicente · Ilha de São Sebastião
do Oeste · PARANÁ · Jaguariaíva · Guarujá · Pta. do Boi
Guaíra · Apial · Registro
Cândido de Abreu · Iguape
BRAZIL · Ilha Comprida
Pto. Mendes · Ponta Grossa · Prudentópolis · Ilha do Cardoso

Pitanga · 1889 · CURITIBA
Cascavel · Palmeira · Antonina
Foz do Iguaçu · Irati · Lapa · Paranaguá
Iguaçu Falls · União da · Guaratuba
Vitória · Rio Negro · São Francisco do Sul
Mafra · Joinvile
Pto. União · Caçador · Itajaí
Blumenau
1340 · Brusque
Chapecó · SANTA CATARINA · Rio do Sul
Joaçaba · Campos Novos
Erechim · Lajes · Ilha de Santa Catarina
Florianópolis
1808
Caràzinho · Passo Fundo
Vacaria · Tubarão · Laguna
Cruz Alta · Criciúma · Cabo Santa Marta Grande
Bento Gonçalves · Araranguá
Caxias do Sul

RIO GRANDE
Santa Maria · Santa Cruz · Nôvo Hamburgo
do Sul · Montenegro · Taquará
São
Cachoeira do Sul · Rio Pardo · Leopoldo · Osorio
PÔRTO ALEGRE
DO SUL
Santana do · São
Livramento · Gabriel · Sa. Encantadas
Dom Pedrito · Caçapava · Camaquã
do Sul · Camaquã
Bagé · Sa. do Canguçu
Pelotas · Lagoa dos Patos
Mostardas

AY

Melo · Rio Grande
Jaguarão
Rio Branco · Lagoa Mirim · Lagoa Mangueira
Sta. Clara
de Olimar
Treinta y Tres · Santa Vitória do Palmar
José Batlle
y Ordóñez
Aigua · Castillos
Minas · Rocha
San Carlos
Maldonado

EVIDEO

A T L A N T I C

O C E A N

Tropic of Capricorn

25

30

35

5304

55   West from Greenwich   50   45   40

Projection: Sanson-Flamsteed's Sinusoidal

1 : 16 000 000

200 100   0   200   400   600 km

ATLANTIC OCEAN

Curaçao (Neth.)   BARBADOS
Barranquilla   G. La Guaira   TRINIDAD
Maracaibo   Caracas   & TOBAGO
Panamá   Barquisimeto
Medellín   VENEZUELA   Georgetown
Bogotá   G.   GUIANA   Paramaribo   FR.
COLOMBIA   Casiquiare   SURINAM   Cayenne
Quito   Belém
ECUADOR   Equator
Guayaquil   Manaus
Chiclayo   Marañón   BRAZIL   Fortaleza
Trujillo   João Pessoa
PERU   Natal   Recife
Callao   Lima   Cuzco   Paulistano
BOLIVIA   La Paz   Brasília
Arequipa   Cochabamba   Belo
Mollendo   Sucre   Corumbá   Horizonte
Iquique   PARAGUAY   São Paulo   Rio de
Antofagasta   Asunción   Curitiba   Janeiro
Tropic of Capricorn   Niterói
            Tucumán
Valparaíso   Córdoba   ARGENTINA   Rio Grande do Sul   Pôrto Alegre
Santiago   Mendoza   Rosário   URUGUAY
Concepción   Buenos   Montevideo
Temuco   Aires   La Plata
            Bahía
            Blanca
Puerto   Chubut   G. San
Montt   Matías
        Patagonia   G. San Jorge
    Punta   Strecho de
    Arenas   Magallanes   Falkland Is.
    C. Froward   Tierra del Fuego   (Br.)
        C. de Hornos

POLITICAL

1 : 80 000 000

COPYRIGHT. GEORGE PHILIP & SON, LTD.

1:16 000 000

INDEX

The number printed in bold type against each index entry indicates the map page where the feature will be found. The geographical coordinates which follow the name are sometimes only approximate but are close enough for the place name to be located.

An open square □ signifies that the name refers to an administrative subdivision of a country while a solid square ■ follows the name of a country. (□) follows the old county names of the U.K.

The alphabetical order of names composed of two or more words is governed primarily by the first word and then by the second. This rule applies even if the second word is a description or its abbreviation, R.,L.,I. for example. Names composed of a proper name (Gibraltar) and a description (Strait of) are positioned alphabetically by the proper name. If the same place name occurs twice or more times in the index and all are in the same country, each is followed by the name of the administrative subdivision in which it is located. The names are placed in the alphabetical order of the subdivisions. If the same place name occurs twice or more in the index and the places are in different countries they will be followed by their country names, the latter governing the alphabetical order. In a mixture of these situations the primary order is fixed by the alphabetical sequence of the countries and the secondary order by that of the country subdivisions.

A. C. T. – Australian Capital Territory
A. R. – Autonomous Region
A. S. S. R. – Autonomous Soviet Socialist Republic
Afghan. – Afghanistan
Afr. – Africa
Ala. – Alabama
Alas. – Alaska
Alg. – Algeria
Alta. – Alberta
Amer. – America
And. P. – Andhra Pradesh
Ang. – Angola
Arch. – Archipelago
Arg. – Argentina
Ariz. – Arizona
Ark. – Arkansas
Atl. Oc. – Atlantic Ocean
Austral. – Australia
B. – Baie, Bahía, Bay, Bucht, Bugt
B.A. – Buenos Aires
B.C. – British Columbia
Bangla. – Bangladesh
Barr. – Barrage
Bay. – Bayern
Belg. – Belgium
Berks. – Berkshire
Bol. – Bolshoi
Bots. – Botswana
Br. – British
Bri. – Bridge
Bt. – Bight
Bucks. – Buckinghamshire
Bulg. – Bulgaria
C. – Cabo, Cap, Cape
C. Prov. – Cape Province
Calif. – California
Camb. – Cambodia
Cambs. – Cambridgeshire
Can. – Canada
Cat. – Cataract, Cataracta
Cent. – Central
Chan. – Channel
Co. – Country
Colomb. – Colombia
Colo. – Colorado
Conn. – Connecticut
Cord. – Cordillera
Cr.. – Creek
Cumb. – Cumbria
Czech. – Czechoslovakia
D.C. – District of Columbia
Del. – Delaware
Dep. – Dependency
Derby. – Derbyshire
Des. – Desert
Dist. – District
Dj. – Djebel
Dumf. & Gall. – Dumfries and Galloway
E. – East
Eng. – England
Fed. – Federal, Federation
Fla. – Florida

For. – Forest
Fr. – France, French
Fs. – Falls
Ft. – Fort
G. – Golf, Golfo, Gulf, Guba
Ga. – Georgia
Germ. – Germany
Glam. – Glamorgan
Glos. – Gloucestershire
Gr. – Grande, Great, Greater, Group
H.K. – Hong Kong
H.P. – Himachal Pradesh
Hants. – Hampshire
Harb. – Harbor, Harbour
Hd. – Head
Here. & Worcs. – Hereford and Worcester
Herts. – Hertfordshire
Holl. – Holland
Hung. – Hungary
I.o.M. – Isle of Man
I. of W. – Isle of Wight
I.(s). – Île, Ilha, Insel, Isla, Island
Id. – Idaho
Ill. – Illinois
Ind. – Indiana
Ind. Oc. – Indian Ocean
J. – Jabal, Jabel, Jazira
Junc. – Junction
K. – Kap, Kapp
K. – Kuala
Kal. – Kalmyk A.S.S.R.
Kans. – Kansas
Kpl. – Kapell
Ky. – Kentucky
L. – Lac, Lacul, Lago, Lagoa, Lake, Limni, Loch, Lough
La. – Lousiana
Lancs. – Lancashire
Leb. – Lebanon
Leics. – Leicestershire
Lim. – Limerick
Lincs. – Lincolnshire
Lit. – Little
Lr. – Lower
Lt. Ho. – Light House
Mad. P. – Madhya Pradesh
Madag. – Madagascar
Malay. – Malaysia
Man. – Manitoba
Manch. – Manchester
Maran. – Maranhão
Mass. – Massachusetts
Md. – Maryland
Me. – Maine
Mend. – Mendoza
Mer. – Méridionale
Mich. – Michigan
Mid. – Middle
Minn. – Minnesota
Miss. – Mississippi
Mo. – Missouri
Mong. – Mongolia
Mont. – Montana

Moroc. – Morocco
Mozam. – Mozambique
Mt.(e). – Mont, Monte, Monti, Montaña, Mountain
Mys. – Mysore
N. – North, Northern, Nouveau
N.B. – New Brunswick
N.C. – North Carolina
N.D. – North Dakota
N.H. – New Hampshire
N.I. – North Island
N.J. – New Jersey
N. Mex. – New Mexico
N.S. – Nova Scotia
N.S.W. – New South Wales
N.T. – Northern Territory
N.W.T. – North West Territory
N.Y. – New York
N.Z. – New Zealand
Nat. – National
Nat Park. – National Park
Nebr. – Nebraska
Neth. – Netherlands
Nev. – Nevada
Newf. – Newfoundland
Nic. – Nicaragua
Northants. – Northamptonshire
Northumb. – Northumberland
Notts. – Nottinghamshire
O. – Oued, ouadi
O.F.S. – Orange Free State
Okla. – Oklahoma
Ont. – Ontario
Or. – Orientale
Oreg. – Oregon
Os. – Ostrov
Oxon. – Oxfordshire
Oz. – Ozero
P. – Pass, Passo, Pasul, Pulau
P.E.I. – Prince Edward Island
P.N.G. – Papua New Guinea
P.O. – Post Office
P. Rico. – Puerto Rico
Pa. – Pennsylvania
Pac. Oc. – Pacific Ocean
Pak. – Pakistan
Pass. – Passage
Pen. – Peninsula, Peninsule
Phil. – Philippines
Pk. – Park, Peak
Plat. – Plateau
P-ov. – Poluostrov
Port. – Portugal, Portuguese
Prom. – Promontory
Prov. – Province, Provincial
Pt. – Point
Pta. – Ponta, Punta
Pte. – Pointe
Qué. – Québec
Queens. – Queensland
R. – Rio, River
R.I. – Rhode Island
R.S.F.S.R. – Russian Soviet Federal Socialist Republic
Ra.(s). – Range(s)
Raj. – Rajasthan

Reg. – Region
Rep. – Republic
Res. – Reserve, Reservoir
Rhld. – Pfz. – Rheinland – Pfalz
S. – San, South
S. Afr. – South Africa
S. Austral. – South Australia
S.D. – South Dakota
S.-Holst. – Schleswig-Holstein
S.I. – South Island
S. Leone – Sierra Leone
S.S.R. – Soviet Socialist Republic
S.-U. – Sinkiang-Uighur
Sa. – Serra, Sierra
Sard. – Sardinia
Sask. – Saskatchewan
Scot. – Scotland
Sd. – Sound
Sept. – Septentrionale
Sib. – Siberia
Som. – Somerset
Span. – Spanish
Sprs. – Springs
St. – Saint
Sta. – Santa, Station
Staffs. – Staffordshire
Ste. – Sainte
Sto. – Santo
Str. – Strait, Stretto
Switz. – Switzerland
T.O. – Telegraph Office
Tas. – Tasmania
Tenn. – Tennessee
Terr. – Territory
Tex. – Texas
Tg. – Tanjung
Thai. – Thailand
Tipp. – Tipperary
Trans. – Transvaal
U.K. – United Kingdom
U.S.A. – United States of America
U.S.S.R. – Union of Soviet Socialist Republics
Ukr. – Ukraine
Ut.P. – Uttar Pradesh
Utd. – United
Va. – Virginia
Vdkhr. – Vodokhranilishche
Venez. – Venezuela
Vic. – Victoria
Viet. – Vietnam
Vol. – Volcano
Vt. – Vermont
W. – Wadi, West
W.A. – Western Australia
W. Isles – Western Isles
Wash. – Washington
Wilts. – Wiltshire
Wis. – Wisconsin
Wlkp. – Wielkopolski
Wyo. – Wyoming
Yorks. – Yorkshire
Yug. – Yugoslavia
Zimb. – Zimbabwe

Please refer to the table at the end of the index for recent placename changes in Angola, Iran, Madagascar, Mozambique, Vietnam and Zimbabwe. There is also a table giving the Pin Yin equivalents of the modified Wade–Giles nameforms for the principal Chinese placenames which appear in this Atlas.

A

Name	Ref & Coordinates
Aabenraa-Sønderborg Amt □	73 55 0N 9 30 E
Aachen	48 50 47N 6 4 E
Aadorf	15 47 30N 8 55 E
Aaiun	116 27 9N 13 12W
Aal	73 55 39N 8 18 E
Aâlâ en Nîl □	123 8 50N 29 55 E
Aalen	49 48 49N 10 6 E
Aalma ech Chaab	90 33 7N 35 9 E
Aalsmeer	46 52 17N 4 43 E
Aalsö	73 56 23N 10 52 E
Aalst, Belg.	47 50 56N 4 2 E
Aalst, Neth.	152 50 57N 4 20 E
Aalten	46 51 56N 6 35 E
Aalter	47 51 5N 3 28 E
Aarau	50 47 23N 8 4 E
Aarburg	50 47 2N 7 16 E
Aardenburg	47 51 16N 3 28 E
Aare, R.	50 47 33N 8 14 E
Aareavaara	74 67 27N 23 29 E
Aargau □	50 47 26N 8 10 E
Aarhus Amt □	73 56 15N 10 15 E
Aarle	47 51 30N 5 38 E
Aarschot	47 50 59N 4 49 E
Aarsele	47 51 0N 3 26 E
Aartrijke	47 51 7N 3 6 E
Aarwangen	50 47 15N 7 46 E
Aasleagh	38 53 37N 9 40W
Aastrup	73 55 34N 8 49 E
Aba, Congo	126 3 58N 30 17 E
Aba, Nigeria	121 5 10N 7 19 E
Âbâ, Jazîrat	123 13 30N 32 31 E
Abadan	92 30 22N 48 20 E
Abade, Ethiopia	123 9 22N 38 12 E
Abade, Iran	93 31 8N 52 40 E
Abadin	56 43 21N 7 29W
Abadla	118 31 2N 2 45W
Abaeté	171 19 9 S 45 27W
Abaeté, R.	171 18 2 S 45 12W
Abaetetuba	170 1 40 S 48 50W
Abai	173 25 58 S 55 54W
Abak	121 4 58N 7 50 E
Abakaliki	121 6 22N 8 2 E
Abakan	77 53 40N 91 10 E
Abal Nam	122 25 20N 38 37 E
Abalemma	121 16 12N 7 50 E
Aballetuba	170 1 40 S 51 15W
Abanilla	59 38 12N 1 3W
Abano Terme	63 45 22N 11 46 E
Abarán	59 38 12N 1 23W
Abarqu	93 31 10N 53 20 E
Abasan	90 31 19N 34 21 E
Abasberes	123 11 33N 35 23 E
Abashiri	112 44 0N 144 15 E
Abashiri-Wan	112 44 0N 144 30 E
Abau	135 10 11 S 148 46 E
Abaújszántó	53 48 16N 21 12 E
Abaya L.	123 6 30N 37 50 E
Abbadia San Salvatore	63 42 53N 11 40 E
Abbay, R., (Nîl el Azraq)	123 10 17N 35 22 E
Abbaye, Pt.	156 46 58N 88 4w
Abbetorp	73 56 57N 16 8 E
Abbeville, France	43 50 6N 1 49 E
Abbeville, La., U.S.A.	159 30 0N 92 7w
Abbeville, S.C., U.S.A.	157 34 12N 82 21w
Abbey	39 53 7N 8 25w
Abbey Town	32 54 50N 3 18w
Abbeydorney	39 52 21N 9 40w
Abbeyfeale	39 52 23N 9 20w
Abbeyleix	39 52 55N 7 20w
Abbeyside	39 52 5N 7 36w
Abbiategrasso	62 45 23N 8 55 E
Abbieglassie	139 27 15 S 147 28 E
Abbotabad	94 34 10N 73 15 E
Abbots Bromley	28 52 50N 1 52w
Abbots Langley	29 51 43N 0 25w
Abbotsbury	28 50 40N 2 36w
Abbotsford, Can.	152 49 0N 122 10w
Abbotsford, U.S.A.	158 44 55N 90 20w
Abcoude	46 52 17N 4 59 E
'Abd al Kuri	91 12 5N 52 20 E
Abdulino	84 53 42N 53 40 E
Abe, L.	123 11 8N 41 47 E
Abéché	117 13 50N 20 35 E
Abejar	58 41 48N 2 47W
Abekr	123 12 45N 28 50 E
Abêlessa	118 22 58N 4 47 E
Abelti	123 8 10N 37 30 E
Abengourou	120 6 42N 3 27W
Åbenrå	73 55 3N 9 25 E
Abeokuta	121 7 3N 3 19 E
Aber	126 2 12N 32 25 E
Aber-soch	31 52 50N 4 31W
Aberaeron	31 52 15N 4 16W
Aberayron = Aberaeron	31 52 15N 4 16W
Abercarn	31 51 39N 3 9W
Aberchirder	37 57 34N 2 40W
Abercorn	139 25 12 S 151 5 E
Abercorn = Mbala	127 8 46 S 31 17 E
Abercrave	31 51 48N 3 42W
Aberdare	31 51 43N 3 27W
Aberdare Ra.	126 0 15 S 36 50 E
Aberdaron	31 52 48N 4 41W
Aberdeen, Austral.	141 32 9 S 150 56 E
Aberdeen, Can.	153 52 20N 106 8W
Aberdeen, S. Afr.	128 32 28 S 24 2 E
Aberdeen, U.K.	37 57 9N 2 6W
Aberdeen, Md., U.S.A.	162 39 30N 76 14W
Aberdeen, S.D., U.S.A.	158 45 30N 98 30W
Aberdeen, Wash., U.S.A.	160 47 0N 123 50W
Aberdeen (□)	26 57 18N 2 30W
Aberdour	35 56 2N 3 18W
Aberdovey	31 52 33N 4 3W
Aberdulais	31 51 41N 3 46W
Aberfeldy, Austral.	141 37 42 S 146 22 E
Aberfeldy, U.K.	37 56 37N 3 50W
Aberffraw	31 53 11N 4 28W
Aberfoyle	34 56 10N 4 23W
Abergaria-a-Velha	56 40 41N 8 32W
Abergavenny	31 51 49N 3 1W
Abergele	31 53 17N 3 35W
Abergwili	31 51 52N 4 18W
Abergynolwyn	31 52 39N 3 58W
Aberkenfig	31 51 33N 3 36W
Aberlady	35 56 0N 2 51W
Abernathy	159 33 49N 101 49W
Abernethy	35 56 19N 3 18W
Aberporth	31 52 8N 4 32W
Abersychan	31 51 44N 3 3W
Abertillery	31 51 44N 3 9W
Aberystwyth	31 52 25N 4 6W
Abha	122 18 0N 42 34 E
Abhayapuri	98 26 24N 90 38 E
Abidiya	122 18 18N 34 3 E
Abidjan	120 5 26N 3 58W
Abilene, Kans., U.S.A.	158 39 0N 97 16W
Abilene, Texas, U.S.A.	159 32 22N 99 40W
Abingdon, U.K.	28 51 40N 1 17W
Abingdon, Ill., U.S.A.	158 40 53N 90 23W
Abingdon, Va., U.S.A.	157 36 46N 81 56W
Abington	35 55 30N 3 42W
Abington Reef	138 18 0 S 149 35 E
Abitan L.	153 60 27N 107 15W
Abitan, R.	153 59 53N 109 3W
Abitibi L.	150 48 40N 79 40W
Abiy Adi	123 13 39N 39 3 E
Abkhaz A.S.S.R. □	83 43 0N 41 0 E
Abkit	77 64 10N 157 10 E
Abnûb	122 27 18N 31 4 E
Åbo = Turku	75 60 27N 22 14 E
Abo, Massif d'	119 21 41N 16 8 E
Abocho	121 7 35N 6 56 E
Abohar	94 30 10N 74 10 E
Aboisso	120 5 30N 3 5W
Abomey	121 7 10N 2 5 E
Abondance	45 46 18N 6 42 E
Abong Mbang	124 4 0N 13 8 E
Abonnema	121 4 41N 6 49 E
Abony	53 47 12N 20 3 E
Aboso	120 5 23N 1 57W
Abou Deïa	117 11 20N 19 20 E
Aboyne	37 57 4N 2 48W
Abqaiq	92 26 0N 49 45 E
Abra Pampa	172 22 43 S 65 42W
Abrantes	57 39 24N 8 7W
Abraveses	56 40 41N 7 55 E
Abreojos, Pta.	164 26 50N 113 40W
Abreschviller	43 48 39N 7 6 E
Abrets, Les	45 45 32N 5 35 E
Abri, Esh Shimâliya, Sudan	123 20 50N 30 27 E
Abri, Kordofân, Sudan	123 11 40N 30 21 E
Abrolhos, Arquipélago dos	171 18 0 S 38 30W
Abrolhos, banka	171 18 0 S 38 0W
Abrud	70 46 19N 23 5 E
Abruzzi □	63 42 15N 14 0 E
Absaroka Ra.	160 44 40N 110 0W
Abū al Khasib	92 30 25N 48 0 E
Abū 'Ali	92 27 20N 49 27 E
Abu Arish	91 16 53N 42 48 E
Abû Ballas	122 24 26N 27 36 E
Abu Deleiq	123 15 57N 33 48 E
Abū Dhabī	93 24 28N 54 36 E
Abū Dis	90 31 47N 35 16 E
Abu Dis	122 19 12N 33 38 E
Abu Dom	123 16 18N 32 25 E
Abū Gabra	123 11 2N 26 50 E
Abû Ghôsh	90 31 48N 35 6 E
Abū Gubeiha	123 11 30N 31 15 E
Abu Habl, W.	123 12 37N 31 0 E
Abu Hamed	122 19 32N 33 13 E
Abū Haraz, Esh Shimâliya, Sudan	122 19 8N 32 18 E
Abû Haraz, Nîl el Azraq, Sudan	123 14 35N 34 30 E
Abû Higar	123 12 50N 33 59 E
Abu Kamal	92 34 30N 41 0 E
Abu Markha	92 25 4N 38 22 E
Abu Qîr	122 31 18N 30 0 E
Abu Qireiya	122 24 5N 35 28 E
Abu Qurqas	122 28 1N 30 44 E
Abu Salama	122 27 10N 35 51 E
Abu Simbel	122 22 18N 31 40 E
Abu Tig	122 27 4N 31 15 E
Abu Tiga	123 12 47N 34 12 E
Abû Zabad	123 12 25N 29 10 E
Abu Zenîma	122 29 0N 33 15 E
Abuja	121 9 16N 7 2 E
Abunã	174 9 40 S 65 20W
Abunã, R.	174 9 41 S 65 20W
Aburatsu	110 31 34N 131 24 E
Aburo, Mt.	126 2 4N 30 53 E
Abut Hd.	143 43 7 S 170 15 E
Abwong	123 9 2N 32 14 E
Åby	73 58 40N 16 10 E
Aby, Lagune	120 5 15N 3 14W
Acacías	174 3 59N 73 46W
Acajutla	166 13 36N 89 50W
Acámbaro	164 20 0N 100 40W
Acaponeta	164 22 30N 105 20W
Acapulco de Juárez	165 16 51N 99 56W
Acarai, Serra	175 1 50N 57 50W
Acaraú	170 2 53 S 40 7W
Acari	170 6 31 S 36 38W
Acarigua	174 9 33N 69 12W
Acatlan	165 18 10N 98 3W
Acayucán	165 17 59N 94 58W
Accéglio	62 44 28N 6 59 E
Accomac	156 37 43N 75 40W
Accra	121 5 35N 0 6W
Accrington	32 53 46N 2 22W
Acebal	172 33 20 S 60 50W
Aceh □	102 4 0N 97 30 E
Acerenza	65 40 50N 15 58 E
Acerra	65 40 57N 14 22 E
Aceuchal	57 38 39N 6 30W
Achaguas	174 7 46N 68 14W
Achak Gomba	99 33 30N 96 25 E
Achalpur	96 21 22N 77 32 E
Achavanich	37 58 22N 3 25W
Achel	47 51 15N 5 29 E
A'ch'eng	107 45 33N 127 0 E
Achenkirch	52 47 32N 11 45 E
Achensee	52 47 26N 11 45 E
Acher	94 23 10N 72 32 E
Achern	49 48 37N 8 5 E
Acheron, R.	143 42 16 S 173 4 E
Achill	38 53 56N 9 55W
Achill Hd.	38 53 59N 10 15W
Achill I.	38 53 58N 10 5W
Achill Sd.	38 53 53N 9 55W
Achillbeg I.	38 53 51N 9 58W
Achim	48 53 1N 9 2 E
Achimota	121 5 35N 0 15W
Achinsk	77 56 20N 90 20 E
Achisay	85 43 35N 68 53 E
Achit	84 56 48N 57 54 E
Achnasheen	36 57 35N 5 5W
Achnashellach	36 57 28N 5 20W
Achol	123 6 35N 31 32 E
A'Chralaig, Mt.	36 57 11N 5 10W
Acireale	65 37 37N 15 9 E
Ackerman	159 33 20N 89 8W
Acklin's I.	167 22 30N 74 0W
Acland, Mt.	133 24 50 S 148 20 E
Aclare	38 54 4N 8 54W
Acle	29 52 38N 1 32 E
Acme	152 51 33N 113 30W
Aconcagua	172 32 50 S 70 0W
Aconcagua □	172 32 15 S 70 30W
Aconcagua, Cerro	172 32 39 S 70 0W
Aconquija, Mt.	172 27 0 S 66 0W
Acopiara	170 6 6 S 39 27W
Açores, Is. dos	14 38 44N 29 0W
Acquapendente	63 42 45N 11 50 E
Acquasanta	63 42 46N 13 24 E
Acquaviva delle Fonti	65 40 53N 16 50 E
Acqui	62 44 40N 8 28 E
Acre = 'Akko	90 32 35N 35 4 E
Acre □	174 9 1 S 71 0W
Acre, R.	174 10 45 S 68 25W
Acri	65 39 29N 16 23 E
Acs	53 47 42N 18 0 E
Acton Burnell	28 52 37N 2 41W
Açu	170 5 34 S 36 54W
Ad Dam	91 20 33N 44 45 E
Ad Dammam	92 26 20N 50 5 E
Ad Dar al Hamra	92 27 20N 37 45 E
Ad Dawhah	93 25 15N 51 35 E
Ad Dilam	92 23 55N 47 10 E
Ada, Ethiopia	123 8 48N 38 51 E
Ada, Ghana	121 5 44N 0 40 E
Ada, Minn., U.S.A.	158 47 20N 96 30W
Ada, Okla., U.S.A.	159 34 50N 96 45W
Ada, Yugo.	66 45 49N 20 9 E
Adair C.	12 71 50N 71 0W
Adaja, R.	56 41 15N 4 50W
Adale	91 2 58N 46 27 E
Adalslinden	72 63 27N 16 55 E
Adam	93 22 15N 57 28 E
Adamantina	171 21 42 S 51 4W
Adamaoua, Massif de l'	121 7 20N 12 20 E
Adamawa Highlands = Adamaoua	121 7 20N 12 20 E
Adamello, Mt.	62 46 10N 10 34 E
Adami Tulu	123 7 53N 38 41 E
Adaminaby	141 36 0 S 148 45 E
Adamovka	84 51 32N 59 56 E
Adams, Mass., U.S.A.	162 42 38N 73 8W
Adams, N.Y., U.S.A.	162 43 50N 76 3W
Adams, Wis., U.S.A.	158 43 59N 89 50W
Adam's Bridge	97 9 15N 79 40 E
Adams L.	152 51 10N 119 40W
Adams Mt.	160 46 10N 121 28W
Adam's Peak	97 6 55N 80 45 E
Adamuz	57 38 2N 4 32W
Adana	92 37 0N 35 16 E
Adanero	56 40 56N 4 36W
Adapazari	92 40 48N 30 25 E
Adarama	123 17 10N 34 52 E
Adare	39 52 34N 8 48W
Adare, C.	13 71 0 S 171 0 E
Adavale	139 25 52 S 144 32 E
Adayio	123 14 29N 40 50 E
Adda, R.	62 45 25N 9 30 E
Addis Ababa = Addis Abeba	123 9 2N 38 42 E
Addis Abeba	123 9 2N 38 42 E
Addis Alem	123 9 0N 38 17 E
Addlestone	29 51 22N 0 30W
Addo	128 33 32 S 25 44 E
Addu Atoll	87 0 30 S 73 0 E
Adebour	121 13 17N 11 50 E
Adel	157 31 10N 83 28W
Adelaide, Austral.	140 34 52 S 138 30 E
Adelaide, Bahamas	166 25 0N 77 31W
Adelaide I.	13 67 15 S 68 30W
Adelaide Pen.	148 68 15N 97 30W
Adelaide River	136 13 15 S 131 7 E
Adelanto	163 34 35N 117 22W
Adelboden	50 46 29N 7 33 E
Adele, I.	136 15 32 S 123 9 E
Adélie, Terre	13 67 0 S 140 0 E
Ademuz	58 40 5N 1 13W
Aden	91 12 50N 45 0 E
Aden, G. of	91 13 0N 50 0 E
Adendorp	128 33 25 S 24 30 E
Adhoi	94 23 26N 70 32 E
Adi	103 4 15 S 133 30 E
Adi Daro	123 14 20N 38 14 E
Adi Keyih	123 14 51N 39 22 E
Adi Kwala	123 14 38N 38 48 E
Adi Ugri	123 14 58N 38 48 E
Adieu, C.	137 32 0 S 132 10 E
Adieu Pt.	136 15 14 S 124 35 E
Adigala	123 10 24N 42 15 E
Adige, R.	63 45 9N 11 25 E
Adigrat	123 14 20N 39 26 E
Adilabad	96 19 33N 78 35 E
Adin	160 41 10N 121 0W
Adin Khel	93 32 45N 68 5 E
Adinkerke	47 51 5N 2 36 E
Adirampattinam	97 10 28N 79 20 E
Adirondack Mts.	156 44 0N 74 15W
Adis Dera	123 10 12N 38 46 E
Adjohon	121 6 41N 2 32 E
Adjud	70 46 7N 27 10 E
Adjumani	126 3 20N 31 50 E
Adlavik Is.	151 55 2N 58 45W
Adler	83 43 28N 39 52 E
Adliswil	51 47 19N 8 32 E
Admer	119 20 21N 5 27 E
Admer, Erg d'	119 24 0N 9 5 E
Admiralty B.	13 62 0 S 59 0W
Admiralty G.	136 14 20 S 125 55 E
Admiralty I.	147 57 40N 134 35W
Admiralty Inlet	160 48 0N 122 40W
Admiralty Is.	135 2 0 S 147 0 E
Admiralty Ra.	13 72 0 S 164 0 E
Ado	121 6 36N 2 56 E
Ado Ekiti	121 7 38N 5 12 E
Adok	123 8 10N 30 20 E
Adola	123 11 14N 41 44 E
Adonara	103 8 15 S 123 5 E
Adoni	97 15 33N 77 18W
Adony	53 47 6N 18 52 E
Adour, R.	44 43 32N 1 32W
Adra, India	95 23 30N 86 42 E
Adra, Spain	59 36 43N 3 3W
Adraj	91 20 1N 51 0 E
Adrano	65 37 40N 14 49 E
Adrar	118 27 51N 0 11W
Adrar des Iforhas	121 19 40N 1 40 E
Adrasman	85 40 38N 69 58 E
Adré	117 13 40N 22 20 E
Adri	119 27 32N 13 2 E
Adria	63 45 4N 12 3 E
Adrian, Mich., U.S.A.	156 41 55N 84 0W
Adrian, Tex., U.S.A.	159 35 19N 102 37W
Adriatic Sea	60 43 0N 16 0 E
Adrigole	39 51 44N 9 42W
Adua	103 1 45 S 129 50 E
Aduku	126 2 03N 32 45 E
Adula	51 46 30N 9 3 E
Adung Long	98 28 7N 97 42 E
Adur	97 9 8N 76 40 E
Adwa, Ethiopia	123 14 15N 38 52 E
Adwa, Si Arab.	92 27 15N 42 35 E
Adwick le Street	33 53 35N 1 12W
Adzhar A.S.S.R. □	83 42 0N 42 0 E
Adzopé	120 6 7N 3 49W
Æbelø I.	73 55 39N 10 10 E
Æbeloft	73 56 12N 10 41 E
Æbeltoft Vig. B.	73 56 9N 10 35 E
Ægean Is.	61 38 0N 25 0 E
Ægean Sea	61 37 0N 25 0 E
Aenemuiden	47 51 30N 3 40 E
Ænes	71 60 5N 6 8 E
Æolian Is. = Eólie, I.	65 38 40N 15 7 E
Aerhchin Shanmo	105 38 0N 88 0 E
Aerhshan	105 47 9N 119 59 E
Aerht'ai Shan	105 48 0N 90 0 E
Æro	73 54 53N 10 20 E
Ærø	73 54 52N 10 25 E
Ærøskøbing	73 54 53N 10 24 E
Aesch	50 47 28N 7 36 E
Aëtós	69 37 15N 21 50 E
Afafi, Massif d'	119 22 11N 14 48 E
Afanasyevo	84 58 52N 53 15 E
Afándou	69 36 18N 28 12 E
Afarag, Erg	118 23 50N 2 47 E
Afdera, Mt.	123 13 16N 41 5 E
Affreville = Khemis Miliania	118 36 11N 2 14 E
Affric, L.	36 57 15N 5 5W
Affric, R.	37 57 15N 5 40W
Afghanistan ■	93 33 0N 65 0 E
Afgoi	91 2 7N 44 59 E
Afif	92 23 53N 42 56 E
Afikpo	121 5 53N 7 54 E
Aflisses, O.	118 28 30N 0 50 E
Aflou	118 34 7N 2 3 E
Afodo	123 10 18N 34 49 E
Afogados da Ingàzeira	170 7 45 S 37 39W
Afognak I.	147 58 10N 152 50W

Afragola	65	40 54N	14 15 E
Africa	114	10 0N	20 0 E
Afton	162	42 14N	75 31W
Aftout	118	26 50N	3 45W
Afuá	170	0 15 S	50 10W
Afula	90	32 37N	35 17 E
Afyon Karahisar	92	38 20N	30 15 E
Agadès	121	16 58N	7 59 E
Agadir	118	30 28N	9 35W
Agadir Tissint	118	29 57N	7 16W
Agano, R.	112	37 50N	139 30 E
Agapa	77	71 27N	89 15 E
Agapovka	84	53 18N	59 8 E
Agar	94	23 40N	76 2 E
Agaro	123	7 50N	36 38 E
Agartala	98	23 50N	91 23 E
Agassiz	152	49 14N	121 46W
Agat	123	15 38N	38 16 E
Agattu I.	147	52 25N	172 30 E
Agbelouvé	121	6 35N	1 14 E
Agboville	120	5 55N	4 15W
Agdam	83	40 0N	46 58 E
Agdash	83	40 44N	47 22 E
Agde	44	43 19N	3 28 E
Agde, C. d'	44	43 16N	3 28 E
Agdz	118	30 47N	6 30W
Agen	44	44 12N	0 38 E
Ageo	111	35 58N	139 36 E
Ager Tay	119	20 0N	17 41 E
Agersø	73	55 13N	11 12 E
Agger	73	56 47N	8 13 E
Aggersborg	73	57 0N	9 16 E
Aggius	64	40 56N	9 4 E
Aghalee	38	54 32N	6 17W
Aghavannagh	39	52 55N	6 25W
Aghern	39	52 5N	8 10W
Aghil Mts.	93	36 0N	77 0 E
Aghil Pass	93	36 15N	76 35 E
Aginskoye	77	51 6N	114 32 E
Agira	65	37 40N	14 30 E
Aglou	118	29 50N	9 50W
Agly, R.	44	42 46N	3 3 E
Agna Branca	170	7 57 S	47 19W
Agnes	137	28 0 S	120 30 E
Agnew	137	28 1 S	120 30 E
Agnews Hill	38	54 51N	5 55W
Agnibilékrou	120	7 10N	3 11W
Agnita	70	45 59N	24 40 E
Agnone	65	41 49N	14 20 E
Ago	111	33 36N	135 29 E
Agofie	121	8 27N	0 15 E
Agogna, R.	62	45 8N	8 42 E
Agogo, Ghana	121	6 50N	1 1W
Agogo, Sudan	123	7 50N	28 45 E
Agon	42	49 2N	1 34W
Agön	72	61 33N	17 25 E
Agön I.	72	61 34N	17 23 E
Agordo	63	46 18N	12 2 E
Agout, R.	44	43 47N	1 41 E
Agra	94	27 17N	77 58 E
Agrado	174	2 15N	75 46W
Agramunt	58	41 48N	1 6 E
Agreda	58	41 51N	1 55W
Agri	73	56 14N	10 32 E
Ağri Daği	92	39 50N	44 15 E
Agri, R.	65	40 17N	16 15 E
Agrigento	64	37 19N	13 33 E
Agrinion	69	38 37N	21 27 E
Agrøpoli	65	40 23N	14 59 E
Agryz	84	56 33N	53 2 E
Agua Caliente, Mexico	164	26 30N	108 20W
Agua Caliente, U.S.A.	163	32 29N	116 59W
Agua Caliente Springs	163	32 56N	116 19W
Agua Clara	175	20 25 S	52 45W
Agua Prieta	164	31 20N	109 32W
Aguadas	174	5 40N	75 38W
Aguadilla	147	18 27N	67 10W
Aguadulce	166	8 15N	80 32W
Aguanaval, R.	164	23 45N	103 10W
Aguanga	163	33 27N	116 51W
Aguanus, R.	151	50 13N	62 5W
Aguapeí, R.	171	21 0 S	51 0W
Aguapey, R.	172	29 7 S	56 36W
Aguaray Guazú, R.	172	24 47 S	57 19W
Aguarico, R.	174	0 0	77 30W
Aguas Blancas	172	24 15 S	69 55W
Aguas Calientes, Sierra de	172	25 26 S	67 27W
Águas Formosas	171	17 5 S	40 57W
Aguas, R.	58	41 20N	0 30W
Aguascalientes	164	22 0N	102 12W
Aguascalientes □	164	22 0N	102 20W
Agudo	57	38 59N	4 52W
Agueda	56	40 34N	8 27W
Agueda, R.	56	40 45N	6 37W
Aguelt el Kadra	118	25 3N	7 6W
Agueni N'Ikko	118	32 29N	5 47W
Aguié	121	13 31N	7 46 E
Aguilafuente	56	41 13N	4 7W
Aguilar	57	37 31N	4 40W
Aguilar de Campóo	56	42 47N	4 15W
Aguilares	172	27 26 S	65 35W
Aguilas	59	37 23N	1 35W
Aguja, C. de la	174	11 18N	74 12W
Aguja, Pta.	174	6 0 S	81 0W
Agulaa	123	13 40N	39 40 E
Agulhas, Kaap	128	34 52 S	20 0 E
Agung	102	8 20 S	115 28 E
Agur, Israel	90	31 42N	34 55 E
Agur, Uganda	126	2 28N	32 55 E
Aguš	70	46 28N	26 15 E
Agusan, R.	103	9 20N	125 50 E
Agvali	83	42 36N	46 8 E
Aha Mts.	128	19 45 S	21 0 E
Ahaggar	119	23 0N	6 30 E
Ahamansu	121	7 38N	0 35 E
Ahar	92	38 35N	47 0 E
Ahascragh	38	53 24N	8 20W
Ahaura	143	42 20 S	171 32 E
Ahaura, R.	143	42 21 S	171 34 E
Ahaus	48	52 4N	7 1 E
Ahelledjem	119	26 37N	6 58 E
Ahimanawa Ra.	130	39 5 S	176 30 E
Ahipara B.	142	35 5 S	173 5 E
Ahiri	96	19 30N	80 0 E
Ahlen	48	51 45N	7 52 E
Ahmad Wal	94	29 18N	65 58 E
Ahmadabad (Ahmedabad)	94	23 0N	72 40 E
Ahmadnagar (Ahmednagar)	96	19 7N	74 46 E
Ahmadpur	94	29 12N	71 10 E
Ahmar Mts.	123	9 20N	41 15 E
Ahoada	121	5 8N	6 36 E
Ahoghill	38	54 52N	6 23W
Ahome	164	25 55N	109 11W
Ahr, R.	48	50 25N	6 52 E
Ahrensbök	48	54 0N	10 34 E
Ahrweiler	48	50 31N	7 3 E
Ahsã, Wahatāal	92	25 50N	49 0 E
Ahuachapán	166	13 54N	89 52W
Ahuriri, R.	143	44 31 S	170 12 E
Åhus	73	55 56N	14 18 E
Ahväz	92	31 20N	48 40 E
Ahvenanmaa	75	60 15N	20 0 E
Ahzar	121	15 30N	3 20 E
Aibaq	93	36 15N	68 5 E
Aichach	49	48 28N	11 9 E
Aichi-ken □	111	35 0N	137 15 E
Aidone	65	37 26N	14 26 E
Aiello Cálabro	65	39 6N	16 12 E
Aigle	50	46 18N	6 58 E
Aignay-le-Duc	43	47 40N	4 43 E
Aigre	44	45 54N	0 1 E
Aigua	173	34 13 S	54 46W
Aigueperse	44	46 3N	3 13 E
Aigues-Mortes	45	43 35N	4 12 E
Aiguilles	45	44 47N	6 51 E
Aiguillon	44	44 18N	0 21 E
Aiguillon, L'	44	46 20N	1 16W
Aigurande	44	46 27N	1 49 E
Aihui	105	50 16N	127 28 E
Aija	174	9 50 S	77 45W
Aijal	98	23 40N	92 44 E
Aiken	157	33 34N	81 50W
Ailao Shan	108	24 0N	101 30 E
Aillant-sur-Tholon	43	47 52N	3 20 E
Aillik	151	55 11N	59 18W
Ailly-sur-Noye	43	49 45N	2 20 E
Ailsa Craig, I.	34	55 15N	5 7W
Aim	77	59 0N	133 55 E
Aimere	103	8 45 S	121 3 E
Aimogasta	172	28 33 S	66 50W
Aimorés	171	19 30 S	41 4W
Aimorés, Serra dos	171	17 50 S	40 30W
Ain □	45	46 5N	5 20 E
Ain Banaiyah	93	23 0N	51 0 E
Aïn-Beïda	119	35 50N	7 35 E
Ain ben Khellil	118	33 15N	0 49W
Ain Ben Tili	118	25 59N	9 27W
Aïn Benian	118	36 48N	2 55 E
'Ain Dalla	122	27 20N	27 23 E
Ain Dar	92	25 55N	49 10 E
Ain el Mafki	122	27 30N	28 15 E
Ain Girba	122	29 20N	25 14 E
Aïn M'lila	119	36 2N	6 35 E
Ain Qeiqab	122	29 42N	24 55 E
Ain, R.	45	45 52N	5 11 E
Aïn Rich	118	34 38N	24 55 E
Aïn-Sefra	118	32 47N	0 37W
Aïn Sheikh Murzúk	122	26 47N	27 45 E
Ain Sukhna	122	29 32N	32 20 E
Aïn Tédelès	118	36 0N	0 21 E
Aïn-Témouchent	118	35 16N	1 8W
Aïn Touta	119	35 26N	5 54 E
Ain Zeitûn	122	29 10N	25 48 E
Aïn Zorah	118	34 37N	3 32W
Ainabo	91	9 0N	46 25 E
Ainazi	80	57 50N	24 24 E
Aine Galakka	117	18 10N	18 30 E
Aínos Óros	69	38 10N	20 35 E
Ainsdale	32	53 37N	3 2W
Ainsworth	158	42 33N	99 52W
Aioi	110	34 48N	134 28 E
Aion	77	69 50N	169 0 E
Aipe	174	3 13N	75 15W
Aïr	121	18 30N	8 0 E
Airaines	43	49 58N	1 55 E
Aird Brenish, C.	36	58 8N	7 8W
Aird, The, dist.	37	57 26N	4 30W
Airdrie	35	55 53N	3 57W
Aire	43	50 37N	2 22 E
Aire, Isla del	58	39 48N	4 16 E
Aire, R.	33	53 42N	0 54W
Aire-sur-l'Adour	44	43 42N	0 15W
Aireys Inlet	140	38 29 S	144 5 E
Airolo	51	46 32N	8 37 E
Airvault	42	46 50N	0 8W
Aisgill	32	54 23N	2 21W
Aishihik	147	61 40N	137 46W
Aisne □	43	49 42N	3 40 E
Aisne, R.	43	49 26N	2 50 E
Aït Melloul	118	30 25N	9 29W
Aitana, Sierra de	59	38 35N	0 24W
Aitape	135	3 11 S	142 22 E
Aith	37	59 8N	2 38W
Aitkin	158	46 32N	93 43W
Aitolía Kai Akarnanía □	69	38 45N	21 18 E
Aitolikón	69	38 26N	21 21 E
Aitoska Planina	67	42 45N	27 30 E
Aiuaba	170	6 38 S	40 7W
Aiud	70	46 19N	23 44 E
Aix-en-Provence	45	43 32N	5 27 E
Aix-la-Chapelle = Aachen	48	50 47N	6 4 E
Aix-les-Bains	45	45 41N	5 53 E
Aix-les-Thermes	44	42 43N	1 51 E
Aix-sur-Vienne	44	45 48N	1 8 E
Aiyang, Mt.	135	5 10 S	141 20 E
Aiyangpienmen	107	40 55N	124 30 E
Aiyansh	152	55 17N	129 2W
Aíyina	69	37 45N	23 26 E
Aíyinion	68	40 28N	22 28 E
Aíyion	69	38 15N	22 5 E
Aizenay	42	46 44N	1 38W
Aizpute	80	56 43N	21 40 E
Aizuwakamatsu	112	37 30N	139 56 E
Ajaccio	45	41 55N	8 40 E
Ajaccio, G. d'	45	41 52N	8 40 E
Ajalpán	165	18 22N	97 15W
Ajana	137	27 56 S	114 35 E
Ajanta Ra.	96	20 28N	75 50 E
Ajax, Mt.	143	42 35 S	172 5 E
Ajdabiyah	119	30 54N	20 4 E
Ajdīr, Raïs	119	33 4N	11 44 E
Ajdovščina	63	45 54N	13 54 E
Ajibar	123	10 35N	38 36 E
'Ajlun	90	32 18N	35 47 E
Ajman	93	25 25N	55 30 E
Ajmer	94	26 28N	74 37 E
Ajo	161	32 18N	112 54W
Ajoie	50	47 22N	7 0 E
Ajok	123	9 15N	28 28 E
Ajua	120	4 50N	1 55W
Ak Dağ	92	36 30N	30 0 E
Akaba	121	8 10N	1 2 E
Akabli	118	26 49N	1 31 E
Akaishi-Dake	111	35 27N	138 9 E
Akaishi-Sammyaku	111	35 25N	138 10 E
Akaki Beseka	123	8 55N	38 45 E
Akala	123	15 39N	36 13 E
Akaroa	143	43 49 S	172 59 E
Akaroa Harb.	131	43 54 S	172 59 E
Akasha	122	21 10N	30 32 E
Akashi	110	34 45N	135 0 E
Akbou	119	36 31N	4 31 E
Akbulak	84	51 1N	55 37 E
Akdala	85	45 2N	74 35 E
Akechi	111	35 18N	137 23 E
Akegbe	121	6 17N	7 28 E
Akelamo	103	1 35N	129 40 E
Akershus Fylke □	71	60 10N	11 15 E
Akeru, R.	96	17 25N	80 0 E
Aketi	124	2 38N	23 47 E
Akhaïa □	69	38 5N	21 45 E
Akhalkalaki	83	41 27N	43 25 E
Akhaltsikhe	83	41 40N	43 0 E
Akharnaí	69	38 5N	23 44 E
Akhelóös, R.	69	39 5N	21 25 E
Akhendriá	69	34 58N	25 16 E
Akhéron, R.	68	39 31N	20 29 E
Akhisar	92	38 56N	27 48 E
Akhladhókambos	69	37 31N	22 35 E
Akhmîm	122	26 31N	31 47 E
Akhnur	95	32 52N	74 45 E
Akhtopol	67	42 6N	27 56 E
Akhtubinsk (Petropavlovskiy)	83	48 27N	46 7 E
Akhty	83	41 30N	47 45 E
Akhtyrka	80	50 25N	35 0 E
Aki	110	33 30N	133 54 E
Aki-Nada	110	34 5N	132 40 E
Akiak	147	60 50N	161 12W
Akimiski I.	150	52 50N	81 30W
Akimovka	82	46 44N	35 0 E
Akincilar	69	37 57N	27 25 E
Akinum	138	6 15 S	149 30 E
Åkirkeby	73	55 4N	14 55 E
Akita	112	39 45N	140 0 E
Akita-ken □	112	39 40N	140 30 E
Akjoujt	120	19 45N	14 15W
Akka	118	29 28N	8 9W
'Akko	90	32 35N	35 4 E
Akkol, Kazakh, U.S.S.R.	85	45 0N	75 39 E
Akkol, Kazakh, U.S.S.R.	85	43 36N	70 45 E
Akköy	69	37 30N	27 18 E
Akkrum	46	53 3N	5 50 E
Aklampa	121	8 15N	2 10 E
Aklavik, Can.	147	68 12N	135 0W
Aklavik, N.W.T., Can.	147	68 12N	135 0W
Akmuz	85	41 15N	76 10 E
Aknoul	118	34 40N	3 55W
Akô	110	34 45N	134 24 E
Ako	121	10 19N	10 48 E
Akobo, R.	123	7 10N	34 25 E
Akola	96	20 42N	77 2 E
Akonolinga	121	3 50N	12 18 E
Akordat	123	15 30N	37 40 E
Akosombo Dam	121	6 20N	0 5 E
Ak'osu	105	41 15N	80 14 E
Akot, India	96	21 10N	77 10 E
Akot, Sudan	123	6 31N	30 9 E
Akpatok I.	149	60 25N	68 8W
Akranes	74	64 19N	22 6W
Åkrehamn	71	59 16N	5 10 E
Akreïjit	120	18 19N	9 11W
Akrítas Venétiko, Ákra	69	36 43N	21 54 E
Akron, Colo., U.S.A.	158	40 13N	103 15W
Akron, Ohio, U.S.A.	156	41 7N	81 31W
Akrotíri, Ákra	68	40 26N	25 27W
Aksai Chih, L.	95	35 15N	79 55 E
Aksaray	92	38 25N	34 2 E
Aksarka	76	66 31N	67 50 E
Aksehir	92	38 18N	31 30 E
Aksenovo Zilovskoye	77	53 20N	117 40 E
Aksuat, Ozero	84	51 32N	64 34 E
Aksum	123	14 5N	38 40 E
Aktash, R.S.F.S.R., U.S.S.R.	84	52 2N	52 7 E
Aktash, Uzbek S.S.R., U.S.S.R.	85	39 55N	65 55 E
Aktobe	84	52 55N	62 22 E
Aktogay	85	44 25N	76 44 E
Aktyubinsk	79	50 17N	57 10 E
Aktyuz	85	42 54N	76 7 E
Aku	121	6 40N	7 18 E
Akulurak	147	62 40N	164 35W
Akun I.	147	54 15N	165 30W
Akune	110	32 1N	130 12 E
Akure	121	7 15N	5 5 E
Akureyri	74	65 40N	18 6W
Akusha	83	42 18N	47 30 E
Akutan I.	147	53 30N	166 0W
Akzhar	85	43 8N	71 37 E
Al Abyār	119	32 9N	20 29 E
Al Amadiyah	92	37 5N	43 30 E
Al Amārah	92	31 55N	47 15 E
Al Aqabah	92	29 37N	35 0 E
Al Ashkhara	93	21 50N	59 30 E
Al Ayn al Mugshin	91	19 35N	54 40 E
Al 'Azīzīyah	119	32 30N	13 1 E
Al Badi	92	22 0N	46 35 E
Al Barah	90	31 55N	35 12 E
Al Barkāt	119	24 56N	10 14 E
Al Basrah	92	30 30N	47 50 E
Al Baydā	117	32 30N	21 40 E
Al Bu'ayrāt	119	31 24N	15 44 E
Al Buqay'ah	90	32 15N	35 30 E
Al Dīwaniyah	92	32 0N	45 0 E
Al Fallujah	92	33 20N	43 55 E
Al Fāw	92	30 0N	48 30 E
Al Hadithan	92	34 0N	41 13 E
Al Hamad	92	31 30N	39 30 E
Al Hamar	92	22 23N	46 6 E
Al Hariq	92	23 29N	46 27 E
Al Hasakah	92	36 35N	40 45 E
Al Hauta	91	16 5N	48 20 E
Al Havy	92	32 5N	46 5 E
Al Hillah, Iraq	92	32 30N	44 25 E
Al Hillah, Si Arab.	92	23 35N	46 50 E
Al Hilwah	92	23 24N	46 48 E
Al Hindiya	92	32 30N	44 10 E
Al Hoceïma	118	35 8N	3 58W
Al Hufrah, Awbārī, Libya	119	25 32N	14 1 E
Al Hufrah, Misrātah, Libya	119	29 5N	18 3 E
Al Hufuf	92	25 25N	49 45 E
Al Husayyāt	119	30 24N	20 37 E
Al Husn	90	32 29N	35 52 E
Al Irq	117	29 5N	21 35 E
Al Ittihad = Madinat al Shaab	91	12 50N	45 0 E
Al Jahrah	92	29 25N	47 40 E
Al Jalāmid	92	31 20N	39 45 E
Al Jarzirah	117	26 10N	21 20 E
Al Jawf	117	24 10N	23 24 E
Al Jazir	91	18 30N	56 31 E
Al Jubail	92	27 0N	49 50 E
Al Juwara	91	19 0N	57 13 E
Al Khābūrah	93	23 57N	57 5 E
Al Khalih	90	31 32N	35 6 E
Al Khums (Homs)	119	32 40N	14 17 E
Al Kut	92	32 30N	46 0 E
Al Kuwayt	92	29 20N	48 0 E
Al Ladhiqiyah	92	35 30N	35 45 E
Al Lith	122	20 9N	40 15 E
Al Madīnah	92	24 35N	39 52 E
Al-Mafraq	90	32 17N	36 14 E
Al Majma'ah	92	25 57N	45 22 E
Al Manamah	93	26 10N	50 30 E
Al Marj	117	32 25N	20 30 E
Al Masīrah	91	20 25N	58 50 E
Al Mawsil	92	36 15N	43 5 E
Al Miqdadiyah	92	34 0N	45 0 E
Al Mubarraz	92	25 30N	49 40 E
Al Muharraq	93	26 15N	50 40 E
Al Mukha	91	13 18N	43 15 E
Al Musayyib	92	32 40N	44 25 E
Al Muwaylih	92	27 40N	35 30 E
Al Qaddāhīyah	119	31 15N	15 9 E
Al Qamishli	92	37 10N	41 10 E
Al Qaryah ash Sharqīyah	119	30 28N	13 40 E
Al Qasabāt	119	32 39N	14 1 E
Al Qatif	92	26 35N	50 0 E
Al Qatrun	119	24 56N	15 3 E
Al Quaisūmah	92	28 10N	46 20 E
Al Quds	90	31 47N	35 10 E
Al Qunfidha	122	19 3N	41 4 E
Al Quraiyat	93	23 17N	58 53 E
Al Qurnah	92	31 1N	47 25 E
Al 'Ula	92	26 35N	38 0 E
Al Uqaylah	119	30 12N	19 10 E
Al Uqayr	92	25 40N	50 15 E
Al' Uwayqilah	92	30 30N	42 10 E
Al 'Uyūn	92	26 30N	43 50 E
Al Wajh	122	26 10N	36 30 E
Al Wakrah	93	25 10N	51 40 E

Al Warīah 92 27 50N 47 30 E
Al Wātīyah 119 32 28N 11 57 E
Ala, Italy 62 45 46N 11 0 E
Ala, Sweden 72 61 13N 17 9 E
Ala Shan 105 40 0N 104 0 E
Alabama □ 157 31 0N 87 0W
Alabama, R. 157 31 30N 87 35W
Alaçati 69 38 16N 26 23 E
Alaejos 56 41 18N 5 13W
Alagna Valsésia 62 45 51N 7 56 E
Alagôa Grande 170 7 3 S 35 35W
Alagôas □ 170 9 0 S 36 0W
Alagoinhas 171 12 0 S 38 20W
Alagón 58 41 46N 1 12W
Alagón, R. 56 39 50N 6 50W
Alajuela 166 10 2N 84 8W
Alakamisy 129 21 19 S 47 14 E
Alakurtti 78 67 0N 30 30 E
Alam Ajaib 122 25 55N 27 14 E
Alameda, Spain 57 37 12N 4 39W
Alameda, Calif., U.S.A. 163 37 46N 122 15W
Alameda, N. Mex., U.S.A. 161 35 10N 106 43W
Alameda, S.D., U.S.A. 160 43 2N 112 30W
Alamitos, Sierra de los 164 26 30N 102 20W
Alamo 161 37 21N 115 10W
Alamogordo 161 32 59N 106 0W
Alamos 164 27 0N 109 0W
Alamosa 161 37 30N 106 0W
Åland 75 60 15N 20 0 E
Aland 96 17 36N 76 35 E
Ålandroal 57 38 41N 7 24W
Ålands hav 75 60 10N 19 30 E
Alange, Presa de 57 38 45N 6 18W
Alangouassou 120 7 30N 4 34W
Alanis 57 38 3N 5 43W
Alanya 92 36 38N 32 0 E
Alaotra, L. 129 17 30 S 48 30 E
Alapayevsk 84 57 52N 61 42 E
Alar del Rey 56 42 38N 4 20W
Alaraz 56 40 45N 5 17W
Alaşehir 79 38 23N 28 30 E
Alashantsoch'i 106 38 59N 105 45 E
Alaska □ 147 65 0N 150 0W
Alaska, G. of 147 58 0N 145 0W
Alaska Highway 152 60 0N 130 0W
Alaska Pen. 147 56 0N 160 0W
Alaska Range 147 62 50N 151 0W
Alássio 62 44 1N 8 10 E
Alatri 64 41 44N 13 21 E
Alatyr 81 54 45N 46 35 E
Alatyr, R. 81 54 45N 45 30 E
Alausí 174 2 0 S 78 50W
Álava □ 58 42 48N 2 28W
Alava, C. 160 48 10N 124 40W
Alaverdi 83 41 2N 44 37 E
Alawoona 140 34 45 S 140 30 E
Alaykel 85 40 15N 74 25 E
Alayor 58 39 57N 4 8 E
Alayskiy Khrebet 85 39 45N 72 0 E
Alazan, R. 83 41 25N 46 35 E
Alba 62 44 41N 8 1 E
Alba □ 70 46 10N 23 30 E
Alba de Tormes 56 40 50N 5 30W
Alba-Iulia 70 46 8N 23 39 E
Albac 70 46 28N 23 1 E
Albacete 59 39 0N 1 50W
Albacete □ 59 38 50N 2 0W
Albacutya, L. 140 35 45 S 141 58 E
Ålbæk 73 57 36N 10 25 E
Ålbæk Bugt 73 57 35N 10 40 E
Albaida 59 38 51N 0 31W
Albalate de las Nogueras 58 40 22N 2 18W
Albalate del Arzobispo 58 41 6N 0 31W
Albania ■ 68 41 0N 20 0 E
Albano Laziale 64 41 44N 12 40 E
Albany, Austral. 137 35 1 S 117 58 E
Albany, Ga., U.S.A. 157 31 40N 84 10W
Albany, Minn., U.S.A. 158 45 37N 94 38W
Albany, N.Y., U.S.A. 162 42 29N 73 47W
Albany, Oreg., U.S.A. 160 44 41N 123 0W
Albany, Tex., U.S.A. 159 32 45N 99 20W
Albany, R. 150 52 17N 81 31W
Albardón 172 31 20 S 68 30W
Albarracín 58 40 25N 1 26W
Albarracín, Sierra de 58 40 30N 1 30W
Albatross B. 138 12 45 S 141 30 E
Albatross Pt. 142 38 7 S 174 44 E
Albegna, R. 63 42 40N 11 28 E
Albemarle 157 35 27N 80 15W
Albemarle Sd. 157 36 0N 76 30W
Albenga 62 44 3N 8 12 E
Alberche, R. 56 40 10N 4 30W
Alberdi 172 26 14 S 58 20W
Alberes, Mts. 58 42 28N 2 56 E
Alberga 139 27 12 S 135 28 E
Alberga, R. 136 26 50 S 133 40 E
Alberique 59 39 7N 0 30W
Alberni 152 49 20N 124 50W
Albersdorf 48 54 8N 9 19 E
Albert, Austral. 141 32 22 S 147 30 E
Albert, Can. 151 45 51N 64 38W
Albert, France 43 50 0N 2 38 E
Albert Canyon 152 51 8N 117 41W
Albert Edward, Mt. 135 8 26 S 147 24 E
Albert Edward Ra. 136 18 17 S 127 57 E
Albert L., Austral. 140 35 30 S 139 10 E
Albert L., U.S.A. 160 42 40N 120 8W
Albert Lea 158 43 32N 93 20W
Albert, L. = Mobutu Sese Seko, L. 126 1 30N 31 0 E
Albert Nile, R. 126 3 16N 31 38 E

Albert Town 167 22 37N 74 33 E
Alberta □ 152 54 40N 115 0W
Alberti 172 35 1 S 60 16W
Albertinia 128 34 11 S 21 34 E
Albertirsa 53 47 14N 19 37 E
Albertkanaal 47 51 14N 4 26 E
Alberton 151 46 50N 64 0W
Albertville 45 45 40N 6 22 E
Albertville = Kalemie 126 5 55 S 29 9 E
Albi 44 43 56N 2 9 E
Albia 158 41 0N 92 50W
Albina 175 5 37N 54 15W
Albina, Pta. 128 15 52 S 11 44 E
Albino 62 45 47N 9 48 E
Albion, Idaho, U.S.A. 160 42 21N 113 37W
Albion, Mich., U.S.A. 156 42 15N 84 45W
Albion, Nebr., U.S.A. 158 41 47N 98 0W
Ablasserdam 46 51 52N 4 40 E
Abocácer 58 40 21N 0 1 E
Alböke 73 56 57N 16 47 E
Alborán, I. 57 35 57N 3 0W
Alborea 59 39 17N 1 24W
Ålborg 73 57 2N 9 54 E
Ålborg Bugt 73 56 50N 10 35 E
Alborz, Reshteh-Ye Kūkhā-Ye 93 36 0N 52 0 E
Albox 59 37 23N 2 8W
Albreda 152 52 35N 119 10W
Albrighton 28 52 38N 2 17W
Albuera, La 57 38 45N 6 49W
Albufeira 57 37 5N 8 15W
Albula, R. 51 46 38N 9 30 E
Albuñol 59 36 48N 3 11W
Albuquerque 161 35 5N 106 47W
Albuquerque, Cayos de 166 12 10N 81 50W
Alburno, Mte. 65 40 32N 15 20 E
Alburquerque 57 39 15N 6 59W
Albury 141 36 3 S 146 56 E
Albuskjell, oilfield 19 56 40N 3 0 E
Alby 72 62 30N 15 28 E
Alcácer do Sal 57 38 22N 8 33W
Alcalá de Chisvert 58 40 19N 0 13 E
Alcalá de Guadaira 57 37 20N 5 50W
Alcalá de Henares 58 40 28N 3 22W
Alcalá de los Gazules 57 36 29N 5 43W
Alcalá la Real 57 37 27N 3 57W
Alcamo 64 37 59N 12 55 E
Alcanadre 58 42 24N 2 7W
Alcanadre, R. 58 41 43N 0 12W
Alcanar 58 40 33N 0 28 E
Alcanede 57 39 25N 8 49W
Alcanena 57 39 27N 8 40W
Alcañices 57 41 41N 6 21W
Alcañiz 58 41 2N 0 8W
Alcântara 170 2 20 S 44 30W
Alcántara 57 39 41N 6 57W
Alcantara L. 153 60 57N 108 9W
Alcantarilla 59 37 59N 1 12W
Alcaracejos 57 38 24N 4 58W
Alcaraz 59 38 40N 2 29W
Alcaraz, Sierra de 59 38 40N 2 20W
AlcáRovas 57 38 23N 8 9W
Alcarria, La 58 40 31N 2 45W
Alcaudete 57 37 35N 4 5W
Alcázar de San Juan 59 39 24N 3 12W
Alcester 28 52 13N 1 52W
Alcira 59 39 9N 0 30W
Alcoa 157 35 50N 84 0W
Alcobaça, Brazil 171 17 30 S 39 13W
Alcobaça, Port. 57 39 32N 9 0W
Alcobendas 58 40 32N 3 38W
Alcolea del Pinar 58 41 2N 2 28W
Alcora 58 40 5N 0 14W
Alcoutim 57 37 25N 7 28W
Alcova 160 42 37N 106 52W
Alcoy 59 38 43N 0 30W
Alcubierre, Sierra de 58 41 45N 0 22W
Alcublas 58 39 48N 0 43W
Alcudia 58 39 51N 3 9 E
Alcudia, Bahía de 58 39 45N 3 14 E
Alcudia, Sierra de la 57 38 34N 4 30W
Aldama 165 22 25N 98 4W
Aldan 77 58 40N 125 30 E
Aldan, R. 77 62 30N 135 10 E
Aldborough 33 54 6N 1 21W
Aldbourne 28 51 28N 1 38W
Aldbrough 33 53 50N 0 7W
Aldeburgh 29 52 9N 1 35 E
Aldeia Nova 57 37 55N 7 24W
Alden I. 71 61 19N 4 45 E
Alder 160 45 27N 112 3W
Alder Pk. 163 35 53N 121 22W
Alderbury 28 51 4N 1 45W
Alderley Edge 32 53 18N 2 15W
Aldermaston 28 51 23N 1 9W
Alderney, I. 42 49 42N 2 12W
Aldershot 29 51 15N 0 43W
Aldersyde 152 50 40N 113 53W
Aldingham 32 54 8N 3 3W
Aledo 158 41 10N 90 50W
Alefa 123 11 55N 36 55 E
Aleg 120 17 3N 13 55W
Alegre 173 20 50 S 41 30W
Alegrete 173 29 40 S 56 0W
Aleisk 76 52 40N 83 0 E
Alejandro Selkirk, I. 131 33 50 S 80 15W
Aleksandriya, U.S.S.R. 79 50 45N 26 25 E
Aleksandriya, U.S.S.R. 82 48 42N 33 3 E
Aleksandrov 81 56 23N 38 44 E
Aleksandrov Gay. 81 50 15N 48 35 E
Aleksandrovac 66 44 28N 21 13 E

Aleksandrovka 82 48 55N 32 20 E
Aleksandrovo 67 43 14N 24 51 E
Aleksandrovsk 84 59 9N 57 33 E
Aleksandrovsk-Sakhaliniskiy 77 50 50N 142 20 E
Aleksandrovskiy Zavod 77 50 40N 117 50 E
Aleksandrovskoye 76 60 35N 77 50 E
Aleksandrów Kujawski 54 52 53N 18 43 E
Aleksandrów Łódzki 54 51 49N 19 17 E
Alekseyevka, R.S.F.S.R., U.S.S.R. 81 50 43N 38 40 E
Alekseyevka, R.S.F.S.R., U.S.S.R. 84 52 35N 51 17 E
Aleksin 81 54 31N 37 9 E
Aleksinac 66 43 31N 21 42 E
Além Paraíba 173 21 52 S 42 41W
Alemania, Argent. 172 25 40 S 65 30W
Alemania, Chile 172 25 10 S 69 55W
Ålen 71 62 51N 11 17 E
Alençon 42 48 27N 0 4 E
Alentejo, Alto- 55 39 0N 7 40W
Alentejo, Baixo- 55 38 0N 8 30W
Alenuihaha Chan. 147 20 25N 156 0W
Aleppo 92 36 10N 37 15 E
Alert B. 152 50 30N 127 35W
Aléria 45 42 5N 9 26 E
Alès 45 44 9N 4 5 E
Aleşd 70 47 3N 22 22 E
Alessándria 62 44 54N 8 37 E
Alestrup 73 56 42N 9 29 E
Ålesund 71 62 28N 6 12 E
Alet 123 8 14N 29 2 E
Alet-les-Bains 44 43 0N 2 14 E
Aletschgletscher 50 46 28N 8 2 E
Aletschhorn 50 46 28N 8 0 E
Aleutian Is. 147 52 0N 175 0W
Aleutian Ra. 147 55 0N 155 0W
Alexander 158 47 51N 103 40W
Alexander Arch. 147 57 0N 135 0W
Alexander B. 128 28 36 S 16 33 E
Alexander City 157 32 58N 85 57W
Alexander I. 13 69 0 S 70 0W
Alexander, Mt. 137 28 58 S 120 16 E
Alexandra, Austral. 141 37 8 S 145 40 E
Alexandra, N.Z. 143 45 14 S 169 25 E
Alexandra Falls 152 60 29N 116 18W
Alexandria, Brazil 171 6 25 S 38 1W
Alexandria, B.C., Can. 152 52 35N 122 27W
Alexandria, Ont., Can. 150 45 19N 74 38W
Alexandria, Rumania 70 43 57N 25 24 E
Alexandria, S. Afr. 128 33 38 S 26 28 E
Alexandria, U.K. 34 55 59N 4 40W
Alexandria, Ind., U.S.A. 156 40 18N 85 40W
Alexandria, La., U.S.A. 159 31 20N 92 30W
Alexandria, Minn., U.S.A. 158 45 50N 95 20W
Alexandria, S.D., U.S.A. 158 43 40N 97 45W
Alexandria, Va., U.S.A. 162 38 47N 77 1W
Alexandria = El Iskandarīya 122 31 0N 30 0 E
Alexandria Bay 156 44 20N 75 52W
Alexandrina, L. 140 35 25 S 139 10 E
Alexandroúpolis 68 40 50N 25 54 E
Alexis Creek 152 52 10N 123 20W
Alexis, R. 151 52 33N 56 8W
Alfambra 58 40 33N 1 5W
Alfândega da Fé 56 41 20N 6 59W
Alfaro 58 42 10N 1 50W
Alfatar 67 43 59N 27 13 E
Alfeld 48 52 0N 9 49 E
Alfenas 173 21 40 S 44 0W
Alfiós, R. 69 37 36N 21 54 E
Alfonsine 63 44 30N 12 1 E
Alford, Grampian, U.K. 37 57 13N 2 42W
Alford, Lincs., U.K. 33 53 16N 0 10 E
Alfred 162 43 28N 70 40W
Alfred Town 141 35 8 S 147 30 E
Alfredton 142 40 41 S 175 54 E
Alfreton 33 53 6N 1 22W
Alfriston 29 50 48N 0 10 E
Alfta 72 61 21N 16 4 E
Alftanes 74 64 29N 22 10W
Alga 84 49 53N 57 20 E
Algaba, La 57 37 27N 6 1W
Algar 57 36 40N 5 39W
Ålgård 71 58 46N 5 53 E
Ålgård 71 58 46N 5 53 E
Algarinejo 57 37 19N 4 9W
Algarve 57 37 15N 8 10W
Algeciras 57 36 9N 5 28W
Algemesí 59 39 11N 0 27W
Alger 118 36 42N 3 8 E
Algeria ■ 118 35 10N 3 11 E
Alghero 64 40 34N 8 20 E
Algiers = Alger 118 36 42N 3 8 E
Algoabaai 128 33 50 S 25 45 E
Algodonales 57 36 54N 5 24W
Algodor, R. 56 39 51N 3 48W
Algoma, Mich., U.S.A. 156 44 35N 87 27W
Algoma, Oreg., U.S.A. 160 42 25N 121 54W
Algonquin Prov. Pk. 150 45 50N 78 30W
Alhama de Almería 59 36 57N 2 34W
Alhama de Aragón 58 41 18N 1 54W
Alhama de Granada 57 37 0N 3 59W
Alhama de Murcia 59 37 51N 1 25W
Alhambra, Spain 59 38 54N 3 4W
Alhambra, U.S.A. 163 34 8N 118 10W
Alhaurín el Grande 57 36 39N 4 41W
Alhucemas = Al-Hoceïma 118 35 8N 3 58W
Ali al Gharbi 92 32 30N 46 45 E

Ali Bayramly 83 39 43N 48 52 E
Ali Khel 94 33 56N 69 35 E
Ali Sabieh 123 11 10N 42 44 E
Ália 64 37 47N 13 42 E
Aliabad 93 28 10N 57 35 E
Aliaga 58 40 40N 0 42W
Aliakmon, R. 68 40 10N 22 0 E
Alibag 96 18 38N 72 56 E
Alibo 123 9 52N 37 5 E
Alibunar 66 45 5N 20 57 E
Alicante 59 38 23N 0 30W
Alicante □ 59 38 30N 0 37W
Alice, S. Afr. 128 32 48 S 26 55 E
Alice, U.S.A. 159 27 47N 98 1W
Alice Arm 152 55 29N 129 31W
Alice Downs 136 17 45 S 127 56 E
Alice, Punta dell' 65 39 23N 17 10 E
Alice, R., Queens., Austral. 138 15 35 S 142 20 E
Alice, R., Queens., Austral. 138 24 2 S 144 50 E
Alice Springs 138 23 40 S 135 50 E
Alicedale 128 33 15 S 26 4 E
Aliceville 157 33 9N 88 10W
Alick Cr. 138 20 35 S 142 10 E
Alicudi, I. 65 38 33N 14 20 E
Alida 153 49 25N 101 55W
Aligarh, India 93 27 55N 78 10 E
Aligarh, Raj., India 94 25 55N 76 15 E
Aligarh, Ut. P., India 94 27 55N 78 10 E
Aligudarz 92 33 25N 49 45 E
Alijó 56 41 16N 7 27W
Alimena 65 37 42N 14 4 E
Alimnia 69 36 16N 27 43 E
Aling Kangri 99 31 45N 84 45 E
Alingaabro 73 56 56N 10 32 E
Alingsås 73 57 56N 12 31 E
Alipore 95 22 32N 88 24 E
Alipur 94 29 25N 70 55 E
Alipur Duar 98 26 30N 89 35 E
Aliquippa 156 40 38N 80 18W
Aliste, R. 56 41 48N 6 14W
Alivérion 69 38 24N 24 2 E
Aliwal North 128 30 45 S 26 45 E
Alix 152 52 24N 113 11W
Aljezur 57 37 18N 8 49W
Aljustrel 57 37 55N 8 10W
Alkamari 121 13 27N 11 10 E
Alken 47 50 53N 5 18 E
Alkhalaf 91 20 30N 58 13 E
Alkmaar 46 52 37N 4 45 E
All American Canal 161 32 45N 115 0W
Allada 121 6 41N 2 9 E
Allah Dad 94 25 38N 67 34 E
Allahabad 95 25 25N 81 58 E
Allakaket 147 66 30N 152 45W
Allakh Yun 77 60 50N 137 5 E
Allal Razi 118 34 30N 6 39W
Allan 153 51 53N 106 4W
Allanche 44 45 14N 2 57 E
Allanmyo 98 19 16N 95 17 E
Allanridge 128 27 45 S 26 40 E
Allansford 140 38 26 S 142 39 E
Allanton 143 45 55 S 170 15 E
Allanwater 150 50 14N 90 10W
Allaqi, Wadi 122 22 15N 34 55 E
Allard Lake 151 50 40N 63 10W
Allariz 56 42 11N 7 50W
Allassac 44 45 15N 1 29 E
Alle 47 49 51N 4 58 E
Allegan 156 42 32N 85 52W
Allegheny Mts. 156 38 0N 80 0W
Allegheny, R. 156 41 14N 79 50W
Allègre 44 45 12N 3 41 E
Allen, Bog of 39 53 15N 7 0W
Allen, L. 38 54 30N 8 5W
Allen R. 35 54 53N 2 13W
Allenby (Hussein) Bridge 90 31 53N 35 33 E
Allendale 35 54 55N 2 15W
Allende 164 28 20N 100 50W
Allenheads 35 54 49N 2 12W
Allentown 162 40 36N 75 30W
Allentsteig 52 48 41N 15 20 E
Allenwood 39 53 16N 6 53W
Alleppey 97 9 30N 76 28 E
Alleröd 73 55 54N 12 19 E
Alleur 47 50 39N 5 31 E
Allevard 45 45 24N 6 5 E
Alliance, Nebr., U.S.A. 158 42 10N 102 50W
Alliance, Ohio, U.S.A. 156 40 53N 81 7W
Allier □ 44 46 25N 3 0 E
Allier, R. 43 46 57N 3 4 E
Alligator Cr., Queens., Austral. 138 21 20 S 149 12 E
Alligator Cr., Queens., Austral. 138 19 23 S 146 58 E
Allihies 39 51 39N 10 4W
Allingåbrl 73 56 28N 10 20 E
Allingåbro 73 56 28N 10 20 E
Allinge 73 55 17N 14 50 E
Alliston 150 44 9N 79 52W
Alloa 35 56 7N 3 49W
Allonby 32 54 45N 3 27W
Allos 45 44 15N 6 38 E
Alma, Can. 151 48 35N 71 40W
Alma, Kans., U.S.A. 158 39 1N 96 22W
Alma, Mich., U.S.A. 156 43 25N 84 40W
Alma, Nebr., U.S.A. 158 40 10N 99 25W
Alma, Wis., U.S.A. 158 44 19N 91 54W
Alma Ata 85 43 15N 76 57 E
Almada 57 38 40N 9 9W
Almaden 138 17 22 S 144 40 E

Almadén Amungen

Almadén	57	38 49N	4 52W
Almagro	57	38 50N	3 45W
Almalyk	85	40 50N	69 35E
Almanor, L.	160	40 15N	121 11W
Almansa	59	38 51N	1 5W
Almanza	56	42 39N	5 3W
Almanzor, Pico de	56	40 15N	5 18W
Almanzora, R.	59	37 22N	2 21W
Almarcha, La	58	39 41N	2 24W
Almas	171	11 33S	47 9W
Almaş, Mţii	70	44 49N	22 12E
Almazán	58	41 30N	2 30W
Almazora	58	39 57N	0 3W
Almeirim, Brazil	175	1 30S	52 0W
Almeirim, Port.	57	39 12N	8 37W
Almelo	46	52 22N	6 42E
Almenar	58	41 43N	2 12W
Almenara, Brazil	171	16 11S	40 42W
Almenara, Spain	58	39 46N	0 14W
Almenara, Sierra de	59	37 34N	1 32W
Almendralejo	57	38 41N	6 26W
Almería	59	36 52N	2 32W
Almería □	59	37 20N	2 20W
Almería, G. de	59	36 41N	2 28W
Almetyevsk	84	54 53N	52 20E
Almhult	73	56 32N	14 10E
Almirante	166	9 10N	82 30W
Almiropótamos	69	38 16N	24 11E
Almirós	69	39 11N	22 45E
Almodôvar	57	37 31N	8 2W
Almodóvar del Campo	57	38 43N	4 10W
Almogia	57	36 50N	4 32W
Almonaster la Real	57	37 52N	6 48W
Almond R.	35	56 27N	3 27W
Almondsbury	28	51 33N	2 34W
Almonte, R.	57	39 41N	6 12W
Almora	95	29 38N	79 4E
Almoradi	59	38 7N	0 46W
Almorox	56	40 14N	4 24W
Almoustarat	121	17 35N	0 8E
Älmult	73	56 33N	14 8E
Almuñécar	57	36 43N	3 41W
Almunia, La de Doña Godina	58	41 29N	1 23W
Almvik	73	57 49N	16 30E
Aln, R.	35	55 24N	1 35W
Alness	37	57 41N	4 15W
Alness R.	37	57 45N	4 20W
Alnif	118	31 10N	5 8W
Alnmouth	35	55 24N	1 37W
Alnön I.	72	62 26N	17 33E
Alnwick	35	55 25N	1 42W
Aloi	126	2 16N	33 10E
Alon	98	22 12N	95 5E
Alonsa	153	50 50N	99 0W
Alor, I.	103	8 15S	124 30E
Alor Setar	101	6 7N	100 22E
Alora	57	36 49N	4 46W
Alosno	57	37 33N	7 7W
Alot'ai	105	47 52N	88 7E
Alotau	135	10 16S	150 30E
Alougoum	118	30 17N	6 56W
Aloysius Mt.	137	26 0S	128 38E
Alpaugh	163	35 53N	119 29W
Alpedrinha	56	40 6N	7 27W
Alpena	156	45 6N	83 24W
Alpercatas, R.	170	6 2S	44 19W
Alpes-de-Haute-Provence □	45	44 8N	6 10E
Alpes-Maritimes □	45	43 55N	7 10E
Alpes Valaisannes	50	46 4N	7 30E
Alpha	138	23 39S	146 37E
Alphen	47	51 29N	4 58E
Alphen aan den Rijn	46	52 7N	4 40E
Alphington	30	50 41N	3 32W
Alpi Apuan	62	44 7N	10 14E
Alpi Craie	43	45 40N	7 0E
Alpi Lepontine	51	46 22N	8 27E
Alpi Orobie	62	46 7N	10 0E
Alpi Retiche	51	46 45N	10 0E
Alpiarça	57	39 15N	8 35W
Alpine, Ariz., U.S.A.	161	33 57N	109 4W
Alpine, Calif., U.S.A.	163	32 50N	116 46W
Alpine, Tex., U.S.A.	159	30 35N	103 35W
Alpnach	51	46 57N	8 17E
Alrewas	28	52 43N	1 44W
Alrø	73	55 52N	10 5E
Alroy Downs	138	19 20S	136 5E
Als	73	56 46N	10 18E
Alsace	43	48 15N	7 25E
Alsager	32	53 7N	2 20W
Alsask	153	51 21N	109 59W
Alsásua	58	42 54N	2 10W
Alseda	73	57 27N	15 20E
Alsen	72	63 23N	13 56E
Alsfeld	48	50 44N	9 19E
Alsh, L.	36	57 15N	5 39W
Alsónémedi	53	47 34N	19 15E
Alsten	74	65 58N	12 40E
Alston	32	54 48N	2 26W
Alta	74	69 57N	23 10E
Alta Gracia	172	31 40S	64 30W
Alta Lake	152	50 10N	123 0W
Alta, Sierra	58	40 31N	1 30W
Alta Sierra	163	35 42N	118 33W
Altaelva	74	69 46N	23 45E
Altafjorden	74	70 5N	23 5E
Altagracia	174	10 45N	71 30W
Altai = Aerht'ai Shan	105	48 0N	90 0E
Altamaha, R.	157	31 50N	82 0W
Altamira, Brazil	175	3 0S	52 10W
Altamira, Chile	172	25 47S	69 51W
Altamira, Colomb.	174	2 3N	75 47W
Altamira, Mexico	165	22 24N	97 55W
Altamira, Cuevas de	56	43 20N	4 5W
Altamont	162	42 43N	74 3W
Altamura	65	40 50N	16 33E
Altanbulag	54	50 19N	106 30E
Altar	164	30 40N	111 50W
Altarnun	30	50 35N	4 30W
Altata	164	24 30N	108 0W
Altavista	156	37 9N	79 22W
Altdorf	51	46 52N	8 36E
Altea	59	38 38N	0 2W
Altenberg	48	50 46N	13 47E
Altenbruch	48	53 48N	8 44E
Altenburg	48	50 59N	12 28E
Altenkirchen	48	50 41N	7 38E
Altenmarkt	52	47 43N	14 39E
Alter do Châo	57	39 12N	7 40W
Altkirch	43	47 37N	7 15E
Altnaharra	37	58 17N	4 27W
Alto Adige = Trentino-Alto Adige	62	46 5N	11 0E
Alto Araguaia	175	17 15S	53 20W
Alto Chindio	127	16 19S	35 25E
Alto Cuchumatanes	164	15 30N	91 10W
Alto del Inca	172	24 10S	68 10W
Alto Ligonha	127	15 30S	38 11E
Alto Molocue	127	15 50S	37 35E
Alto Paraná □	173	25 0S	54 50W
Alto Parnaíba	170	9 6S	45 57W
Alto Santo	170	5 31S	38 15W
Alto Turi	170	2 54S	45 38W
Alto Uruguay, R.	173	27 0S	53 30W
Alton, U.K.	29	51 8N	0 59W
Alton, Ill., U.S.A.	158	38 55N	90 5W
Alton, N.H., U.S.A.	162	43 27N	71 13W
Alton Downs	139	26 7S	138 57E
Altona	48	53 32N	9 56E
Altoona	156	40 32N	78 24W
Altopáscio	62	43 50N	10 40E
Altos	170	5 3S	42 28W
Altrincham	32	53 25N	2 21W
Altstätten	51	47 22N	9 33E
Alturas	160	41 36N	120 37W
Altus	159	34 30N	99 25W
Alucra	83	40 22N	38 47E
Aluksône	80	57 24N	27 3E
Alula	91	11 50N	50 45E
Alupka	82	44 23N	34 2E
Alushta	82	44 40N	34 25E
Alusi	103	7 35S	131 40E
Alustante	58	40 36N	1 40W
Alva, U.K.	35	56 9N	3 49W
Alva, U.S.A.	159	36 50N	98 50W
Alvaiázere	56	39 49N	8 23W
Alvangen	73	58 0N	12 7E
Älvängen	73	57 58N	12 8E
Alvarado, Mexico	165	18 40N	95 50W
Alvarado, U.S.A.	159	32 25N	97 15W
Alvaro Obregón, Presa	164	27 55N	109 52W
Alvastra	73	58 20N	14 44E
Alvdal	71	62 6N	10 37E
Alvear	172	29 5S	56 30W
Alvechurch	28	52 22N	1 58W
Alverca	57	38 56N	9 1W
Alveringen	47	51 1N	2 43E
Alvesta	73	56 54N	14 35E
Älvho	72	61 30N	14 45E
Alvie, Austral.	140	38 14S	143 30E
Alvie, U.K.	37	57 10N	3 50W
Alvin	159	29 23N	95 12W
Alvito	57	38 15N	8 0W
Älvkarleby	75	60 32N	17 40E
Alvra, Pic d'	51	46 35N	9 50E
Alvros	72	62 3N	14 38E
Älvsborgs län □	73	58 30N	12 30E
Älvsby	74	65 42N	20 52E
Älvsbyn	74	65 40N	20 0E
Alvsered	73	57 14N	12 51E
Alwar	94	27 38N	76 34E
Alwaye	97	10 8N	76 24E
Alwinton	35	55 20N	2 7W
Alwyn, oilfield	19	60 30N	1 45E
Alyangula	133	13 55S	136 30E
Alyaskitovyy	77	64 45N	141 30E
Alyata	83	39 58N	49 25E
Alyth	37	56 38N	3 15W
Alzada	158	45 3N	104 22W
Alzano Lombardo	62	45 44N	9 43E
Alzette, R.	47	49 45N	6 6E
Alzey	49	49 48N	8 4E
Am-Dam	117	12 40N	20 35E
Am Djeress	117	16 15N	22 50E
Am Guereda	117	12 53N	21 14E
Am Timan	117	11 0N	20 10E
Am-Zoer	124	14 13N	21 23E
Amadeus, L.	137	24 54S	131 0E
Amadi, Congo	126	3 40N	26 40E
Amadi, Sudan	123	5 29N	30 25E
Amadi, Zaïre	126	3 40N	26 40E
Amadia	92	37 6N	43 30E
Amadjuak	149	64 0N	72 39W
Amadjuak L.	149	65 0N	71 8W
Amadora	57	38 45N	9 13W
Amaga	174	6 3N	75 42W
Amagansett	162	40 58N	72 8W
Amagasaki	111	34 42N	135 20E
Amager	73	55 37N	12 35E
Amagi	110	33 25N	130 39E
Amagunze	121	6 20N	7 40E
Amaimon	135	5 12S	145 30E
Amakusa-Nada	110	32 35N	130 5E
Amakusa-Shotō	110	32 15N	130 10E
Amål	72	59 2N	12 40E
Åmål	72	59 3N	12 42E
Amalapuram	96	16 35N	81 55E
Amalfi, Colomb.	174	6 55N	75 4W
Amalfi, Italy	65	40 39N	14 34E
Amaliás	69	37 47N	21 22E
Amalner	96	21 5N	75 5E
Amambaí	173	23 5S	55 13W
Amambaí, R.	173	23 22S	53 56W
Amambay □	173	23 0S	56 0W
Amambay, Cordillera de	173	20 30S	56 0W
Amami-O-Shima	112	28 0N	129 0E
Amanab	135	3 40S	141 14E
Amandola	63	42 59N	13 21E
Amanfrom	121	7 20N	0 25E
Amangeldy	76	50 10N	65 10E
Amantea	65	39 8N	16 3E
Amapá	170	2 5N	50 50W
Amapá □	170	1 40N	52 0W
Amar Gedid	123	14 27N	25 13E
Amara, Iraq	92	31 57N	47 12E
Amara, Sudan	123	10 25N	34 10E
Amarante, Brazil	170	6 14S	42 50W
Amarante, Port.	56	41 16N	8 5W
Amarante do Maranhão	170	5 36S	46 45W
Amaranth	153	50 36N	98 43W
Amarapura	98	21 54N	96 3E
Amaravati, R.	97	10 50N	77 42E
Amaravati = Amraoti	96	20 55N	77 45E
Amareleja	57	38 12N	7 13W
Amargosa	171	13 2S	39 36W
Amargosa, R.	163	36 14N	116 51W
Amargosa Ra., mts	163	36 25N	116 40W
Amarillo	159	35 14N	101 46W
Amaro Leite	171	13 58S	49 9W
Amaro, Mt.	63	42 5N	14 6E
Amarpur, India	99	23 30N	91 45E
Amarpur, Bihar, India	95	25 5N	87 0E
Amarpur, Tripura, India	99	23 30N	91 45E
Amasra	92	41 45N	32 30E
Amassama	121	5 1N	6 2E
Amasya	92	40 40N	35 50E
Amatignak I.	147	51 19N	179 10W
Amatikulu	129	29 3S	31 33E
Amatitlán	166	14 29N	90 38W
Amatrice	63	42 38N	13 16E
Amay	47	50 33N	5 19E
Amazon, R.	175	2 0S	53 30W
Amazonas □, Brazil	174	4 20S	64 0W
Amazonas □, Colomb.	174	1 0S	72 0W
Amazonas □, Venez.	174	3 30N	66 0W
Amazonas, R.	175	2 0S	53 30W
Ambad	96	19 38N	75 50E
Ambahakily	129	21 36S	43 41E
Ambala	94	30 23N	76 56E
Ambalangoda	97	6 15N	80 5E
Ambalapuzha	97	9 25N	76 25E
Ambalavao	129	21 50S	46 56E
Ambalindum	138	23 23S	134 40E
Ambam	124	2 20N	11 15E
Ambanifilao	129	12 48S	49 47E
Ambanja	129	13 40S	48 27E
Ambararata	129	13 41S	48 27E
Ambarchik	77	69 40N	162 20E
Ambarijeby	129	14 56S	47 41E
Ambarnath	96	19 12N	73 22E
Ambaro, B. d'	129	13 23S	48 38E
Ambasamudram	97	8 43N	77 25E
Ambato	174	1 5S	78 42W
Ambato-Boéni	129	16 28S	46 43E
Ambato, Sierra de	172	28 25N	66 10W
Ambatolampy	129	19 20S	47 35E
Ambatondrazaka	129	17 55S	48 28E
Ambatosoratra	129	17 37S	48 31E
Ambenja	129	15 17S	46 58E
Ambeno	103	9 20S	124 30E
Amberg	49	49 25N	11 52E
Ambergris Cay	165	18 0N	88 0W
Ambérieu-en-Bugey	45	45 57N	5 20E
Amberley	143	43 9S	172 44E
Ambert	44	45 33N	3 44E
Ambevongo	129	15 25S	42 26E
Ambia	129	16 11S	45 33E
Ambidédi	120	14 35N	11 47W
Ambikapur	95	23 15N	83 15E
Ambikol	122	21 20N	30 50E
Ambilobé	125	13 10S	49 3E
Ambinanindrano	129	20 5S	48 23E
Ambjörnarp	73	57 25N	13 17E
Amble	35	55 20N	1 36W
Ambler	162	40 9N	75 13W
Ambleside	32	54 26N	2 58W
Amblève	47	50 21N	6 10E
Amblève, R.	47	50 25N	5 45E
Ambo, Begemdir & Simen, Ethiopia	123	12 20N	37 30E
Ambo, Shewa, Ethiopia	123	9 0N	37 48E
Ambo, Peru	174	10 5S	76 10W
Ambodifototra	129	16 59S	49 52E
Ambodilazana	129	18 6S	49 10E
Ambohimahasoa	129	21 7S	47 13E
Ambohimanga du Sud	129	20 52S	47 36E
Ambon	103	3 35S	128 20E
Ambongao, Cones d'	129	17 0S	45 0E
Amboseli L.	126	2 40S	37 10E
Ambositra	129	20 31S	47 25E
Amboy	163	34 33N	115 51W
Ambre, C. d'	129	12 40S	49 10E
Ambre, Mt. d'	125	12 30S	49 10E
Ambriz	124	7 48S	13 8E
Ambrizete	124	7 10S	12 52E
Ambunti	135	4 13S	142 52E
Ambut	97	12 48N	78 43E
Amby	139	26 30S	148 11E
Amchitka I.	147	51 30N	179 0W
Amchitka P.	147	51 30N	179 0W
Amderma	76	69 45N	61 30E
Ameca	164	20 30N	104 0W
Ameca, R.	164	20 40N	105 15W
Amecameca	165	19 10N	98 57W
Ameland	46	53 27N	5 45E
Amélia	63	42 34N	12 25E
Amèlie-les-Bains-Palalda	44	42 29N	2 41E
Amen	77	68 45N	180 0E
Amendolaro	65	39 58N	16 34E
Amenia	162	41 51N	73 33W
America	47	51 27N	5 59E
American Falls	160	42 46N	112 56W
American Falls Res.	160	43 0N	112 50W
American Highland	13	73 0S	75 0E
Americana	173	22 45S	47 20W
Americus	157	32 0N	84 10W
Amersfoort, Neth.	46	52 9N	5 23E
Amersfoort, S. Afr.	129	26 59S	29 53E
Amersham	29	51 40N	0 38W
Amery, Austral.	137	31 9S	117 5E
Amery, Can.	153	56 34N	94 3W
Ames	158	42 0N	93 40W
Amesbury, U.K.	28	51 10N	1 46W
Amesbury, U.S.A.	162	42 50N	70 52W
Amesdale	153	50 2N	92 55W
Ameson	150	49 50N	84 35W
Amethyst, gasfield	19	53 38N	0 40E
Amfíklia	69	38 38N	22 35E
Amfilokhía	69	38 52N	21 9E
Amfípolis	68	40 48N	23 52E
Ámfissa	69	38 32N	22 22E
Amga, R.	77	61 0N	132 0E
Amgu	77	45 45N	137 15E
Amherst, Burma	99	16 2N	97 20E
Amherst, Can.	151	45 48N	64 8W
Amherst, Mass., U.S.A.	162	42 21N	72 30W
Amherst, Tex., U.S.A.	159	34 0N	102 24W
Amherst, Mt.	136	18 11S	126 59E
Amherstburg	150	42 6N	83 6W
Amiata Mte.	63	42 54N	11 40E
Amiens	43	49 54N	2 16E
Amigdhalokefáli	69	35 23N	23 30E
Amili	98	28 25N	95 52E
Amîndaion	68	40 42N	21 42E
Amirante Is.	11	6 0S	53 0E
Amisk L.	153	54 35N	102 15W
Amistati, Presa	164	29 24N	101 0W
Amite	159	30 47N	90 31W
Åmli	71	58 45N	8 32E
Amlia I.	147	52 5N	173 30W
Amlwch	31	53 24N	4 21W
Amm Adam	123	16 20N	36 1E
'Ammān	90	32 0N	35 52E
Ammanford	31	51 48N	4 0W
Ammerån	72	63 9N	16 13E
Ammerån	72	63 9N	16 13E
Ammersee	49	48 0N	11 7E
Ammerzoden	46	51 45N	5 13E
Ammi'ad	90	32 55N	35 32E
Amnat Charoen	100	15 51N	104 38E
Amne Machin	105	34 30N	100 0E
Amnéville	43	49 16N	6 9E
Amo Chiang, R.	108	22 56N	101 47E
Amorebieta	58	43 13N	2 44W
Amorgós	69	36 50N	25 57E
Amory	57	33 59N	88 30W
Amos	150	48 35N	78 5W
Åmot	71	59 54N	9 54E
Åmot	71	59 34N	8 0E
Åmotsdal	71	59 37N	8 26E
Amour, Djebel	118	33 42N	1 37E
Amoy = Hsiamen	109	24 25N	118 4E
Amozoc	165	19 2N	98 3W
Ampang	101	3 8N	101 45E
Ampanihy	129	24 40S	44 45E
Amparihy Est.	129	23 57S	47 20E
Ampasindava, B. d'	129	13 40S	48 15E
Ampasindava, Presqu'ile d'	129	13 42S	47 55W
Amper	121	9 25N	9 40E
Ampère	119	35 44N	5 27E
Ampleforth	33	54 13N	1 8W
Ampombiantambo	129	12 42S	48 57E
Amposta	58	40 43N	0 34E
Ampotaka	129	25 3S	44 41E
Ampoza	129	22 20S	44 44E
Ampthill	29	52 3N	0 30W
Amqa	90	32 59N	35 10E
Amqui	151	48 28N	67 27W
Amraoti	96	20 55N	77 45E
Amreli	94	21 35N	71 17E
Amrenene el Kasba	118	22 10N	0 30E
Amriswil	51	47 33N	9 18E
Amritsar	94	31 35N	74 57E
Amroha	95	28 53N	78 30E
Amrum	48	54 37N	8 21E
Amsel	119	22 47N	5 29E
Amsterdam, Neth.	46	52 23N	4 54E
Amsterdam, U.S.A.	162	42 58N	74 10W
Amsterdam, I.	11	37 30S	77 30E
Amstetten	52	48 7N	14 51E
Amu Darya, R.	76	37 50N	65 0E
Amuay	174	11 50N	70 10W
Amukta I.	147	52 29N	171 20W
Amund Ringnes I.	12	78 20N	96 25W
Amundsen Gulf	148	71 0N	124 0W
Amundsen Sea	13	72 0S	115 0W
Amungen	72	61 10N	15 40E

Amuntai **Anza**

Amuntai **102** 2 28 S 115 25 E
Amur, R. **77** 53 30N 122 30 E
Amurang **103** 1 5N 124 40 E
Amuri Pass **143** 42 31 S 172 11 E
Amurrio **58** 43 3N 3 0W
Amurzet **77** 47 50N 131 5 E
Amusco **56** 42 10N 4 28W
Amvrakikós Kólpos **69** 39 0N 20 55 E
Amvrosiyvka **83** 47 43N 38 30 E
Amzeglouf **118** 26 50N 0 1 E
An **98** 22 29N 96 54 E
An Bien **101** 9 45N 105 0 E
An Geata Mór, (Binghamstown) **38** 54 13N 10 0W
An Hoa **100** 15 30N 108 20 E
An Loc **101** 11 40N 106 50 E
An Nafud **92** 28 15N 41 0 E
An Najaf **92** 32 3N 44 15 E
An-Nâqûrah **90** 33 7N 35 8 E
An Nasiriyah **92** 31 0N 46 15 E
An Nawfaliyah **119** 30 54N 17 58 E
An Nhon (Binh Dinh) **100** 13 55N 109 7 E
An Nîl □ **123** 17 30N 33 0 E
An Nîl el Abyad □ **123** 14 0N 32 15 E
An Nu'ayriyah **92** 27 30N 48 30 E
An Teallach, Mt. **36** 57 49N 5 18W
An Thoi, Dao **101** 9 58N 104 0 E
An Tuc **100** 13 57N 108 39 E
An Uaimh **38** 53 39N 6 40W
Åna-Sira **71** 58 17N 6 25 E
Anabta **90** 32 19N 35 7 E
Anabuki **110** 34 2N 134 11 E
Anaco **174** 9 27N 64 28W
Anaconda **160** 46 7N 113 0W
Anacortes **160** 48 30N 122 40W
Anadarko **159** 35 4N 98 15W
Anadia, Brazil **170** 9 42 S 36 18W
Anadia, Port. **56** 40 26N 8 27W
Anadolu **92** 38 0N 29 0 E
Anadyr **77** 64 35N 177 20 E
Anadyr, R. **77** 66 50N 171 0 E
Anadyrskiy Zaliv **77** 64 0N 180 0 E
Anáfi **69** 36 22N 25 48 E
Anafópoulo **69** 36 17N 25 50 E
Anagni **64** 41 44N 13 8 E
Anah **92** 34 25N 42 0 E
Anaheim **163** 33 50N 118 0W
Anahim Lake **152** 52 28N 125 18W
Anáhuac **164** 27 14N 100 9W
Anai Mudi, Mt. **97** 10 12N 77 20 E
Anaimalai Hills **97** 10 20N 76 40 E
Anajás **170** 0 59 S 49 57W
Anajatuba **170** 3 16 S 44 37W
Anakapalle **96** 17 42N 83 06 E
Anakie **138** 23 32 S 147 45 E
Anaklia **83** 42 22N 41 35 E
Analalava **129** 14 35 S 48 0 E
Analapasy **129** 25 11 S 46 40 E
Anam **121** 6 19N 6 41 E
Anambar, R. **94** 30 10N 68 50 E
Anambas, Kepulauan **102** 3 20N 106 30 E
Anamoose **158** 47 55N 100 7W
Anamosa **158** 42 7N 91 17W
Anamur **92** 36 8N 32 58 E
Anan **110** 33 54N 134 40 E
Anand **94** 22 32N 72 59 E
Anandpur **96** 21 16N 86 13 E
Anánes **69** 36 33N 24 9 E
Anantapur **97** 14 39N 77 42 E
Anantnag **95** 33 45N 75 10 E
Ananyev **82** 47 44N 29 57 E
Anapa **82** 44 55N 37 25 E
Anápolis **171** 16 15 S 48 50W
Anar **93** 30 55N 55 13 E
Anarak **93** 33 25N 53 40 E
Anatolia = Anadolu **92** 38 0N 29 0 E
Anatone **160** 46 9N 117 4W
Añatuya **172** 28 20 S 62 50W
Anaunethad L. **153** 60 55N 104 25W
Anaye **117** 19 15N 12 50 E
Anbyŏn **107** 39 1N 127 35 E
Ancaster **33** 52 59N 0 32W
Ancenis **42** 47 21N 1 10W
Anch'i **109** 25 3N 118 13 E
Anch'ing **109** 30 37N 117 0 E
Anch'iu **107** 36 25N 119 10 E
Ancholme, R. **33** 53 42N 0 32W
Anchorage **147** 61 10N 149 50W
Ancião **56** 39 56N 8 27W
Ancohuma, Nevada **174** 16 0 S 68 50W
Ancon **164** 8 57N 79 33W
Ancón **174** 11 50 S 77 10W
Ancona **63** 43 37N 13 30 E
Ancrum **35** 55 31N 2 35W
Ancud **176** 42 0 S 73 50W
Ancud, G. de **176** 42 0 S 73 0W
Andacollo, Argent. **172** 37 10 S 70 42W
Andacollo, Chile **172** 30 15 S 71 10W
Andado **138** 25 25 S 135 15 E
Andalgalá **172** 27 40 S 66 30W
Åndalsnes **71** 62 35N 7 43 E
Andalucía **57** 37 35N 5 0W
Andalusia **157** 31 51N 86 30W
Andalusia = Andalucía **57** 37 35N 5 0W
Andaman Is. **101** 12 30N 92 30 E
Andaman Sea **101** 13 0N 96 0 E
Andaman Str. **101** 12 15N 92 20 E
Andara **128** 18 2 S 21 9 E
Andaraí **171** 12 48 S 41 20W
Andeer **51** 46 36N 9 26 E
Andelfingen **51** 47 36N 8 41 E
Andelot **43** 46 51N 5 56 E
Andelys, Les **42** 49 15N 1 25 E
Andenne **47** 50 30N 5 5 E
Andéranboukane **121** 15 26N 3 2 E
Anderlecht **47** 50 50N 4 19 E
Anderlues **47** 50 25N 4 16 E
Andermatt **51** 46 38N 8 35 E
Andernach **48** 50 24N 7 25 E
Andernos **44** 44 44N 1 6W
Anderslöv **73** 55 26N 13 19 E
Anderson, Austral. **141** 38 32 S 145 27 E
Anderson, Calif., U.S.A. **160** 40 30N 122 19W
Anderson, Ind., U.S.A. **156** 40 5N 85 40W
Anderson, Mo., U.S.A. **159** 36 43N 94 29W
Anderson, S.C., U.S.A. **157** 34 32N 82 40W
Anderson, Mt. **129** 25 5 S 30 42 E
Anderson, R. **147** 69 42N 129 0W
Anderstorp **73** 57 19N 13 39 E
Andes **162** 42 12N 74 47W
Andes, mts. **174** 20 0 S 68 0W
Andfjorden **74** 69 10N 16 20 E
Andhra, L. **96** 18 30N 73 32 E
Andhra Pradesh □ **97** 15 0N 80 0 E
Andikíthira **69** 35 52N 23 15 E
Andímilos **69** 36 47N 24 12 E
Andíparos **69** 37 0N 25 3 E
Andípaxoi **69** 39 9N 20 13 E
Andípsara **69** 38 30N 25 29 E
Andizhan **76** 41 10N 72 0 E
Andkhui **93** 36 52N 65 8 E
Andoharano **129** 22 58 S 43 45 E
Andol **96** 17 51N 78 4 E
Andong **107** 36 40N 128 43 E
Andorra ■ **58** 42 30N 1 30 E
Andorra La Vella **58** 42 31N 1 32 E
Andover, U.K. **28** 51 13N 1 29W
Andover, U.S.A. **162** 40 59N 74 44W
Andradina **171** 20 54 S 51 23W
Andrahary, Mt. **129** 13 37 S 49 17 E
Andraitx **58** 39 35N 2 25 E
Andramasina **129** 19 11 S 47 35 E
Andrano-Velona **129** 18 10 S 46 52 E
Andranopasy **129** 21 17 S 43 44 E
Andreanof Is. **147** 51 0N 178 0W
Andreapol **80** 56 40N 32 17 E
Andreas **32** 54 23N 4 25W
Andrespol **54** 51 45N 19 34 E
Andrew, oilfield **19** 58 4N 1 24 E
Andrews, S.C., U.S.A. **157** 33 29N 79 30W
Andrews, Tex., U.S.A. **159** 32 18N 102 33W
Andreyevka **84** 52 19N 51 55 E
Ándria **65** 41 13N 16 17 E
Andrian **65** 46 30N 11 13 E
Andriba **129** 17 30 S 46 58 E
Andrijevica **66** 42 45N 19 48 E
Andrítsaina **69** 37 29N 21 52 E
Androka **129** 24 58 S 44 2 E
Ándros **69** 37 50N 24 50 E
Andros I. **166** 24 30N 78 0W
Andros Town **166** 24 43N 77 47W
Andrychów **54** 49 51N 19 18 E
Andújar **57** 38 3N 4 5W
Aneby **73** 57 48N 14 49 E
Anécho **121** 6 12N 1 34 E
Anegada I. **147** 18 45N 64 20W
Anergane **118** 31 4N 7 14W
Aneto, Pico de **58** 42 37N 0 40 E
Anfeg **119** 22 29N 5 58 E
Anfu **109** 27 23N 114 37 E
Ang Thong **100** 14 35N 100 31 E
Anga **77** 60 35N 132 0 E
Angamos, Punta **172** 23 1 S 70 32W
Anganch'i **98** 47 9N 123 48 E
Angara, R. **77** 58 30N 97 0 E
Angarsk **77** 52 30N 104 0 E
Angas Downs **137** 24 49 S 132 14 E
Angas Ra. **137** 23 0 S 127 50 E
Angaston **140** 34 30 S 139 8 E
Ånge **72** 62 31N 15 35 E
Ångebo **72** 61 58N 16 22 E
Angel de la Guarda, I. **164** 29 30N 113 30W
Ängelholm **73** 56 15N 12 58 E
Angellala **139** 26 24 S 146 54 E
Angels Camp **163** 38 8N 120 30W
Ångelsberg **72** 59 58N 16 0 E
Angenong **99** 31 57N 94 10 E
Anger, R. **123** 9 30N 36 35 E
Angereb **123** 13 11N 37 7 E
Angereb, R. **123** 14 0N 36 0 E
Ångermanälven **72** 62 40N 18 0 E
Angermünde **48** 53 1N 14 0 E
Angers **42** 47 30N 0 35W
Angerville **43** 48 19N 2 0 E
Ängesån **74** 66 50N 22 15 E
Anghiari **63** 43 32N 12 3 E
Angical **171** 12 0 S 44 42W
Angical do Piauí **171** 6 5 S 42 44W
Angikuni L. **153** 62 0N 100 0W
Angkor **100** 13 22N 103 50 E
Angle **31** 51 40N 5 3W
Anglem Mt. **143** 46 45 S 167 53 E
Anglés **58** 41 57N 2 38 E
Anglesey (□) **26** 53 17N 4 20W
Anglesey, I. **31** 53 17N 4 20W
Anglet **44** 43 29N 1 31W
Angleton **159** 29 12N 95 23W
Angleur **47** 50 36N 5 35 E
Anglure **43** 48 35N 3 50 E
Angmagssalik **12** 65 40N 37 20W
Angmering **29** 50 48N 0 28W
Ango **126** 4 10N 26 5 E
Angoche **127** 16 8 S 40 0 E
Angoche, I. **127** 16 20 S 39 50 E
Angol **172** 37 56 S 72 45W
Angola **156** 41 40N 85 0W
Angola ■ **125** 12 0 S 18 0 E
Angoon **147** 57 40N 134 40W
Angoram **135** 4 4 S 144 4 E
Angoulême **44** 45 39N 0 10 E
Angoumois **44** 45 30N 0 25 E
Angra dos Reis **173** 23 0 S 44 10W
Angra-Juntas **128** 27 39 S 15 31 E
Angran **76** 80 59N 69 3 E
Angren **85** 41 1N 70 12 E
Angtassom **101** 11 1N 104 41 E
Angu **126** 3 25N 24 28 E
Anguilla ■ **167** 18 14N 63 5W
Angurugu **138** 14 0 S 136 25 E
Angus (□) **26** 56 45N 2 55W
Angus, Braes of **37** 56 51N 3 0W
Anhanduí, R. **173** 21 46 S 52 9W
Anhée **47** 50 18N 4 53 E
Anholt **73** 56 42N 11 33 E
Anhsi **105** 40 30N 96 0 E
Anhsiang **109** 29 24N 112 9 E
Anhua, Hunan, China **109** 28 22N 111 10 E
Anhua, Kwangsi-Chuang, China **108** 25 10N 108 21 E
Anhwei □ **109** 33 15N 116 50 E
Ani, Kiangsi, China **109** 28 50N 115 32 E
Ani, Shansi, China **106** 35 3N 111 2 E
Aniak **147** 61 58N 159 50W
Anicuns **171** 16 28 S 49 58W
Ánidhros **69** 36 38N 25 43 E
Anié **121** 7 42N 1 8 E
Animas **161** 31 58N 108 58W
Ånimskog **73** 58 53N 12 35 E
Anin **101** 15 36N 97 50 E
Anivorano **129** 18 44 S 48 58 E
Anjangaon **96** 21 10N 77 20 E
Anjar **94** 23 6N 70 10 E
Anjen **109** 26 42N 113 19 E
Anjiabé **129** 12 7 S 49 20 E
Anjidiv I. **97** 14 40N 74 10 E
Anjō **111** 34 57N 137 5 E
Anjou **42** 47 20N 0 15W
Anjozorobe **129** 18 22 S 47 52 E
Anju **107** 39 36N 125 40 E
Anka **121** 12 13N 5 58 E
Ank'ang **108** 32 38N 109 5 E
Ankara **92** 40 0N 32 54 E
Ankaramena **129** 21 57 S 46 39 E
Ankazoabo **129** 22 18 S 44 31 E
Ankazobé **129** 18 20 S 47 10 E
Ankazotokana **129** 21 20 S 48 9 E
Ankisabé **129** 19 17 S 46 29 E
Anklesvar **96** 21 38N 73 3 E
Ankober **123** 9 35N 39 40 E
Ankoro **126** 6 45 S 26 55 E
Ankuang **107** 45 19N 123 40 E
Ankuo **106** 38 25N 115 19 E
Anlu **109** 31 12N 113 38 E
Anlung **108** 25 6N 106 31 E
Anmyŏn Do **107** 36 25N 126 25 E
Ånn **72** 63 19N 12 34 E
Ann Arbor **156** 42 17N 83 45W
Ann C., Antarct. **13** 66 30 S 50 30 E
Ann C., U.S.A. **162** 42 39N 70 37W
Ann, gasfield **19** 53 40N 2 5 E
Ånn L. **72** 63 15N 12 35 E
Anna, U.S.A. **159** 37 28N 89 10W
Anna, U.S.S.R. **81** 51 38N 40 23 E
Anna Branch, R. **139** 34 2 S 141 50 E
Anna Plains **136** 19 17 S 121 37 E
Annaba **119** 36 50N 7 46 E
Annaberg-Buchholz **48** 50 34N 12 58 E
Annagassan **38** 53 53N 6 20W
Annagh Hd. **38** 54 15N 10 5W
Annaka **111** 36 19N 138 54 E
Annalee, R. **38** 54 3N 7 15W
Annalong **38** 54 7N 5 55W
Annam = Trung-Phan **101** 16 30N 107 30 E
Annamitique, Chaîne **100** 17 0N 106 0 E
Annan **35** 55 0N 3 17W
Annan, R. **35** 54 58N 3 18W
Annanberg **135** 4 52 S 144 42 E
Annandale **35** 55 10N 3 25W
Annapolis **162** 39 0N 76 30W
Annapolis Royal **151** 44 44N 65 32W
Annapurna **95** 28 34N 83 50 E
Annascaul **39** 52 10N 10 3W
Anne, oilfield **19** 55 24N 5 7 E
Annean, L. **137** 26 54 S 118 14 E
Anneberg **73** 57 32N 12 6 E
Annecy **45** 45 55N 6 8 E
Annecy, L. d' **45** 45 52N 6 10 E
Annemasse **45** 46 12N 6 16 E
Annestown **39** 52 8N 7 18W
Annette **147** 55 2N 131 35W
Annfield Plain **33** 54 52N 1 45W
Annie Peak **137** 33 53 S 119 59 E
Anning **108** 24 58N 102 30 E
Anningie **136** 21 50 S 133 7 E
Anniston **157** 33 45N 85 50W
Annobón **114** 1 35 S 3 35 E
Annonay **45** 45 15N 4 40 E
Annonciation, L' **150** 46 25N 74 55W
Annot **45** 43 58N 6 38 E
Annotto Bay **166** 18 17N 77 3W
Annuello **140** 34 53 S 142 55 E
Annville **162** 40 18N 76 32W
Áno Arkhánai **69** 35 16N 25 11 E
Áno Porróia **68** 41 17N 23 2 E
Áno Viánnos **69** 35 2N 25 21 E
Anoka **158** 45 10N 93 26W
Anorotsangana **129** 13 56 S 47 55 E
Anp'ing, Hopei, China **106** 38 13N 115 31 E
Anp'ing, Liaoning, China **107** 41 10N 123 30 E
Ans **47** 50 39N 5 32 E
Ansai **106** 36 54N 109 10 E
Ansbach **49** 49 17N 10 34 E
Anse au Loup, L' **151** 51 32N 56 50W
Anse, L' **150** 46 47N 88 28W
Anseba, R. **123** 16 15N 37 45 E
Anserma **174** 5 13N 75 48W
Anseroeul **47** 50 43N 3 32 E
Anshan **107** 41 3N 122 58 E
Anshun **105** 26 2N 105 57 E
Ansley **158** 41 19N 99 24W
Ansó **58** 42 51N 0 48W
Anson **159** 32 46N 99 54W
Anson B. **136** 13 20 S 130 6 E
Ansongo **121** 15 25N 0 35 E
Ansonia **162** 41 21N 73 6W
Ansonville **150** 48 46N 80 43W
Anstey **28** 52 41N 1 14W
Anstey Hill **109** 34 51 S 138 44 E
Anstruther **35** 56 14N 2 40W
Ansudu **103** 2 11 S 139 22 E
Antabamba **174** 14 40 S 73 0W
Antakya **92** 36 14N 36 10 E
Antalaha **129** 14 57 S 50 20 E
Antalya **92** 36 52N 30 45 E
Antalya Körfezi **92** 36 15N 31 30 E
Antananrivo **125** 18 55 S 47 35 E
Antanimbaribé **129** 21 30 S 44 48 E
Antarctic Pen. **13** 67 0 S 60 0W
Antarctica **125** 90 0 S 0 0
Antela, Laguna **56** 42 7N 7 40W
Antelope **127** 21 2 S 28 31 E
Anten **73** 58 5N 12 22 E
Antenor Navarro **170** 6 44 S 38 27W
Antequera, Parag. **172** 24 8 S 57 7W
Antequera, Spain **57** 37 5N 4 33W
Antero Mt. **161** 38 45N 106 43W
Anthemoús **68** 40 31N 23 15 E
Anthony, Kans., U.S.A. **159** 37 8N 98 2W
Anthony, N. Mex., U.S.A. **161** 32 1N 106 37W
Anthony Lagoon **138** 18 0 S 135 30 E
Anti Atlas, Mts. **118** 30 30N 6 30W
Antibes **45** 43 34N 7 6 E
Antibes, C. d' **45** 43 31N 7 7 E
Anticosti, Í. de **151** 49 30N 63 0W
Antifer, C. d' **42** 49 41N 0 10 E
Antigo **158** 45 8N 89 5W
Antigonish **151** 45 38N 61 58W
Antigua **166** 14 34N 90 41W
Antigua Bahama, Canal de la **166** 22 10N 77 30W
Antigua, I. **167** 17 0N 61 50W
Antilla **166** 20 40N 75 50W
Antimony **161** 38 7N 112 0W
Antioch **163** 38 7N 121 45W
Antioquia **174** 6 40N 75 55W
Antioquia □ **174** 7 0N 75 30W
Antipodes Is. **130** 49 45 S 178 40 E
Antler **158** 48 58N 101 18W
Antler, R. **153** 49 8N 101 0W
Antlers **159** 34 15N 95 35W
Antofagasta **172** 23 50 S 70 30W
Antofagasta □ **172** 24 0 S 69 0W
Antofagasta de la Sierra **172** 26 5 S 67 20W
Antofallá **172** 25 30 S 68 5W
Antofalla, Salar de **172** 25 40 S 67 45W
Antoing **47** 50 34N 3 27 E
Anton **159** 33 49N 102 5W
Anton Chico **161** 35 12N 105 5W
Antongil, B. d' **129** 15 30 S 49 50 E
Antonibe **129** 15 7 S 47 24 E
Antonibe, Presqu'île d' **129** 15 30 S 49 50 E
Antonina **173** 25 26 S 48 42W
Antonito **161** 37 4N 106 1W
Antonovo **83** 49 25N 51 42 E
Antony **30** 50 22N 4 13W
Antrain **42** 48 28N 1 30W
Antrim **38** 54 43N 6 13W
Antrim □ **38** 54 42N 6 20W
Antrim Co. **38** 54 58N 6 20W
Antrim, Mts. of **38** 54 57N 6 8W
Antrim Plateau **136** 18 8 S 128 20 E
Antrodoco **63** 42 25N 13 4 E
Antropovo **81** 58 26N 42 51 E
Antsalova **129** 18 40 S 44 37 E
Antse **106** 36 15N 112 15 E
Antsirabé **129** 19 55 S 47 2 E
Antsohihy **129** 14 50 S 47 50 E
Ant'u **107** 43 6N 128 54 E
Antung **107** 40 10N 124 18 E
Antungwei **107** 35 10N 119 20 E
Antwerp **140** 36 17 S 142 4 E
Antwerp = Antwerpen **47** 51 13N 4 25 E
Antwerpen **47** 51 13N 4 25 E
Antwerpen □ **47** 51 15N 4 40 E
Antz'u **106** 39 31N 116 41 E
Anupgarh **94** 29 10N 73 10 E
Anuradhapura **97** 8 22N 80 28 E
Anvaing **47** 50 41N 3 34 E
Anvers = Antwerp(en) **47** 51 13N 4 25 E
Anvers I. **13** 64 30 S 63 40W
Anvik **147** 62 37N 160 20W
Anxious B. **139** 33 24 S 134 45 E
Anyama **120** 5 30N 4 3W
Anyang **106** 36 7N 114 26 E
Anyer-Lor **103** 6 6 S 105 56 E
Anyüan **109** 25 9N 115 21 E
Anza, Jordan **90** 32 22N 35 12 E
Anza, U.S.A. **163** 33 35N 116 39W

Anza Borrego Desert State Park

Arizpe

Anza Borrego Desert State Park 163 33 0N 116 26W
Anzhero-Sudzhensk 76 56 10N 83 40E
Anzio 64 41 28N 12 37E
Aoga-Shima 111 32 28N 139 46E
Aoiz 58 42 46N 1 22W
Aomori 112 40 45N 140 45E
Aomori-ken □ 112 40 45N 140 40E
Aonla 95 28 16N 79 11E
Aono-Yama 110 34 28N 131 48E
Aorangi Mts. 142 41 49S 175 22E
Aoreora 118 28 51N 10 53W
Aosta 62 45 43N 7 20E
Aoudéras 121 17 45N 8 20E
Aouinet Torkoz 118 28 31N 9 46W
Aoukar □ 118 23 50N 2 45W
Aouker 120 23 48N 4 0W
Aoulef el Arab 118 26 55N 1 2E
Aoullouz 118 30 44N 8 1W
Apa 108 32 55N 101 40E
Apa, R. 172 22 6S 58 2W
Apache, Ariz., U.S.A. 161 31 46N 109 6W
Apache, Okla., U.S.A. 159 34 53N 98 22W
Apahanuerhch'i 106 43 58N 116 2E
Apalachee B. 157 30 0N 84 0W
Apalachicola 157 29 40N 85 0W
Apalachicola, R. 157 30 0N 85 0W
Apapa 121 6 25N 3 25E
Apaporis, R. 174 0 30S 70 30W
Aparecida do Taboado 171 20 5S 51 5W
Aparri 103 18 22N 121 38E
Aparurén 174 5 6N 62 8W
Apateu 70 46 36N 21 47E
Apatin 66 45 40N 19 0E
Apatzingán 164 19 0N 102 20W
Apeldoorn 46 52 13N 5 57E
Apeldoornsch Kanal 46 52 29N 6 5E
Apen 48 53 12N 7 47E
Apenam 102 8 35S 116 13E
Apennines 16 44 20N 10 20E
Apia 174 5 5N 75 58W
Apiacás, Serra dos 174 9 50S 57 0W
Apiaí 174 24 31S 48 50W
Apinajé 171 11 31S 48 18W
Apiti 142 39 58S 175 54E
Apizaco 165 19 26N 98 9W
Aplahové 121 6 56N 1 41E
Aplao 174 16 0S 72 40W
Apo, Mt. 103 6 53N 125 14E
Apodi 170 5 39S 37 48W
Apolda 48 51 1N 11 30E
Apollo Bay 140 38 45S 143 40E
Apollonia, Greece 69 36 58N 24 43E
Apollonia, Libya 117 32 52N 21 59E
Apolo 174 14 30S 68 30W
Aporé, R. 171 19 27S 50 57W
Aporema 170 1 14N 50 49W
Apostle Is. 158 46 50N 90 30W
Apóstoles 173 28 0S 56 0W
Apostolovo 82 47 39N 33 39E
Apoteri 174 4 2N 58 32W
Appalachian Mts. 156 38 0N 80 0W
Appelscha 46 52 57N 6 21E
Appeninni 65 41 0N 15 0E
Appeninno Ligure 62 44 30N 9 0E
Appenzell 51 47 20N 9 25E
Appenzell-Ausser Rhoden □ 51 47 23N 9 23E
Appenzell-Inner Rhoden □ 51 47 20N 9 25E
Appiano 63 46 27N 11 17E
Appingedam 46 53 19N 6 51E
Apple Valley 163 34 30N 117 11W
Appleby 32 54 35N 2 29W
Applecross 36 57 26N 5 50W
Applecross For. 36 57 27N 5 40W
Appledore, Devon, U.K. 30 51 3N 4 12W
Appledore, Kent, U.K. 29 51 2N 0 47E
Appleton 156 44 17N 88 25W
Approuague 170 4 20N 52 0W
Apreivka 81 55 33N 37 4E
Apricena 65 41 47N 15 25E
Aprigliano 65 39 17N 16 19E
Aprília 64 41 38N 12 38E
Apsheronsk 83 44 28N 39 42E
Apsley Str. 136 11 35S 130 28E
Apt 45 43 53N 5 24E
Apucarana 173 23 55S 51 33W
Apulia = Puglia 65 41 0N 16 30E
Apure □ 174 7 10N 68 50W
Apure, R. 174 8 0N 69 20W
Apurimac, R. 174 12 10S 73 30W
Apurito, R. 174 7 50N 67 0W
Apuseni, Munţii 70 46 30N 22 45E
Aq Chah 93 37 0N 66 5E
'Aqaba 122 29 31N 35 0E
'Aqaba, Khalîj al 92 28 15N 33 20E
Aqîq 122 18 14N 38 12E
Aqîq, Khalîg 122 18 20N 38 10E
'Aqraba 90 32 9N 35 20E
'Aqrah 92 36 46N 43 45E
Aquanish 151 50 14N 62 2W
Aquasco 162 38 35N 76 43W
Aquidaba 171 10 17S 37 2W
Aquidauana 175 20 30S 55 50W
Aquila, L' 63 42 21N 13 24E
Aquiles Serdán 164 28 37N 105 54W
Aquin 167 18 16N 73 24W
Ar Ramadi 92 33 25N 43 20E
Ar-Ramthā 90 32 34N 36 0E
Ar Rass 92 25 50N 43 40E
Ar Rifai 92 31 50N 46 10E
Ar Riyād 92 24 41N 46 42E
Ar Rub 'al Khālī 91 21 0N 51 0E
Ar Rutbah 92 33 0N 40 15E
Arab, Khalîg el 122 30 55N 29 0E
Arab, Shott al 92 30 0N 48 31E
Araba 121 13 7N 5 0E
Arabatskaya Strelka 82 45 40N 35 0E
Arabba 63 46 30N 11 51E
Arabelo 174 4 55N 64 13W
Arabia 86 25 0N 45 0E
Arabian Desert 122 28 0N 32 20E
Arabian Sea 86 16 0N 65 0E
Aracajú 170 10 55S 37 4W
Aracataca 174 10 38N 74 9W
Aracati 170 4 30S 37 44W
Araçatuba 173 21 10S 50 30W
Aracena 57 37 53N 6 38W
Aracruz 171 19 49S 40 16W
Araçuaí 171 16 52S 42 4W
Araçuaí, R. 171 16 46S 42 2W
Arad 66 46 10N 21 20E
Arada 117 15 0N 20 20E
Aradu Nou 66 46 8N 21 20E
Arafura Sea 103 10 0S 135 0E
Aragats 83 40 30N 44 15E
Aragón 58 41 25N 1 0W
Aragón, R. 58 42 35N 0 50W
Aragona 64 37 24N 13 36E
Aragua □ 174 10 0N 67 10W
Aragua de Barcelona 174 9 28N 64 49W
Araguacema 170 8 50S 49 20W
Araguaçu 171 12 49S 49 51W
Araguaia, R. 170 7 0S 49 15W
Araguaína 170 7 12S 48 12W
Araguari 171 18 38S 48 11W
Araguari, R. 170 1 0N 51 40W
Araguatins 170 5 38S 48 7W
Araioses 170 2 53S 41 55W
Arak 118 25 20N 3 45E
Arāk 92 34 0N 49 40E
Arakan □ 98 19 0N 94 15E
Arakan Coast 99 19 0N 94 0E
Arakan Yoma 98 20 0N 94 30E
Arákhova 69 38 28N 22 35E
Araks, R. = Aras, Rud-e 92 39 10N 47 10E
Aral Sea = Aralskoye More 76 44 30N 60 0E
Aralsk 76 46 50N 61 20E
Aralskoye More 76 44 30N 60 0E
Aramac 138 22 58S 145 14E
Arambagh 95 22 53N 87 48E
Aramû, Mţii de 70 47 10N 22 30E
Aran Fawddwy, Mt. 31 52 48N 3 40W
Aran, I. 38 55 0N 8 30W
Aran Is. 39 53 5N 9 42W
Aranci 64 41 5N 3 40W
Aranci, Golfo 64 41 0N 9 35E
Aranda de Duero 58 41 39N 3 42W
Arandelovac 66 44 18N 20 37E
Aranga 142 35 44S 173 40E
Aranjuez 56 40 1N 3 40W
Aranos 125 24 9S 19 7E
Aransas Pass 159 28 0N 97 9W
Aranyaprathet 101 13 41N 102 30E
Aranzazu 174 5 16N 75 30W
Arao 110 32 59N 130 25E
Araouane 120 18 55N 3 30W
Arapahoe 158 40 22N 99 53W
Arapari 170 5 34S 49 15W
Arapawa I. 131 41 13S 174 20E
Arapey Grande, R. 172 30 55S 57 49W
Arapiraca 170 9 45S 36 39W
Arapkir 92 39 5N 38 30E
Arapongas 173 23 29S 51 28W
Arapuni 130 38 3S 175 37E
Araranguá 173 29 0S 49 30W
Araraquara 171 21 50S 48 0W
Araras 173 5 15S 60 35W
Ararás, Serra dos 173 25 0S 53 10W
Ararat, Austral. 140 37 16S 143 0E
Ararat, Turkey 92 39 50N 44 15E
Ararat, Mt. = Ağri Daği 92 39 50N 44 15E
Arari 170 3 28S 44 47W
Araria 95 26 9N 87 33E
Araripe 171 7 12S 40 8W
Araripe, Chapada do 170 7 20S 40 30W
Araripina 170 7 33S 40 34W
Araro 123 4 41N 38 50E
Araruama, Lagoa de 173 22 53S 42 12W
Araruna 170 6 52S 35 44W
Aras 71 59 42N 10 31E
Aras, Rud-e 92 39 10N 47 10E
Araticu 170 1 58S 49 51W
Arauca 174 7 0N 70 40W
Arauca □ 174 6 40N 71 0W
Arauca, R. 174 7 30N 69 0W
Arauco 172 37 16S 73 25W
Arauco □ 172 37 40S 73 25W
Araújos 171 19 56S 45 14W
Arauquita 174 7 2N 71 25W
Araure 174 9 34N 69 13W
Arawa 123 9 57N 41 58E
Arawhata 143 43 59S 168 38E
Arawhata, R. 143 44 0S 168 40E
Araxá 171 19 35S 46 55W
Araya, Pen. de 174 10 40N 64 0W
Arba 123 9 0N 40 20E
Arba Jahan 126 2 5N 39 2E
Arba, L' 118 36 40N 3 9E
Arba Minch 123 6 0N 37 30E
Arbah, Wadi al 90 30 30N 35 5E
Arbatax 64 39 57N 9 42E
Arbedo 51 46 12N 9 3E
Arbeláez 174 4 17N 74 26W
Arbīl 92 36 15N 44 5E
Arboga 72 59 24N 15 52E
Arbois 43 46 55N 5 46E
Arbon 51 47 31N 9 26E
Arbore 123 5 3N 36 50E
Arborea 64 39 46N 8 34E
Arborfield 153 53 6N 103 39W
Arborg 153 50 54N 97 13W
Arbrå 72 61 28N 16 22E
Arbresle, L' 45 45 50N 4 26E
Arbroath 37 56 34N 2 35W
Arbuckle 160 39 3N 122 2W
Arbus 64 39 30N 8 33E
Arbuzinka 82 47 52N 31 25E
Arc 43 47 28N 5 34E
Arcachon 44 44 40N 1 10W
Arcachon, Bassin d' 44 44 42N 1 10W
Arcadia, Fla., U.S.A. 157 27 20N 81 50W
Arcadia, La., U.S.A. 159 32 34N 92 53W
Arcadia, Nebr., U.S.A. 158 41 29N 99 4W
Arcadia, Wis., U.S.A. 158 44 13N 91 29W
Arcata 160 40 55N 124 4W
Arcévia 63 43 29N 12 58E
Archangel = Arkhangelsk 78 64 40N 41 0E
Archar 66 43 50N 22 54E
Archbald 162 41 30N 75 31W
Archena 59 38 9N 1 16W
Archer B. 138 13 20S 141 30E
Archer, R. 138 13 25S 142 50E
Archers Post 126 0 35N 37 35E
Archidona 57 37 6N 4 22W
Archiestown 37 57 28N 3 20W
Arci, Monte 64 39 47N 8 44E
Arcidosso 63 42 51N 11 30E
Arcila = Asilah 118 35 29N 6 0W
Arcis-sur-Aube 43 48 32N 4 10E
Arckaringa 139 27 56S 134 45E
Arckaringa Cr. 139 28 10S 135 22E
Arco, Italy 62 45 55N 10 54E
Arco, U.S.A. 160 43 45N 113 16W
Arcola 153 49 40N 102 30W
Arcoona 140 31 2S 137 1E
Arcos, Brazil 171 20 17S 45 32W
Arcos, Spain 58 41 12N 2 16W
Arcos de los Frontera 57 36 45N 5 49W
Arcot 97 12 53N 79 20E
Arcoverde 170 8 25S 37 4W
Arctic Ocean 12 78 0N 160 0W
Arctic Red, R. 147 66 0N 132 0W
Arctic Red River 147 67 15N 134 0W
Arctic Village 147 68 5N 145 45W
Arda, R., Bulg. 67 41 40N 25 40E
Arda, R., Italy 62 44 53N 9 52E
Ardabil 92 38 15N 48 18E
Ardagh 39 52 30N 9 5W
Ardakan 93 30 20N 52 5E
Ardal 71 59 9N 6 13E
Ardales 57 36 53N 4 51W
Ardalstangen 71 61 14N 7 43E
Ardara 38 54 47N 8 25W
Ardatov 81 54 51N 46 15E
Ardavasar 36 57 3N 5 54E
Ardbeg 34 55 38N 6 6W
Ardcath 38 53 36N 6 21W
Ardcharnich 36 57 52N 5 5W
Ardchyle 34 56 26N 4 24W
Ardèche □ 45 44 42N 4 16E
Ardee 38 53 51N 6 32W
Arden Stby. 73 56 46N 9 52E
Ardennes 47 49 30N 5 10E
Ardennes □ 43 49 35N 4 40E
Ardentes 43 46 45N 1 50E
Ardentinny 34 56 3N 4 56E
Arderin, Mt. 39 53 3N 7 40W
Ardestan 93 33 20N 52 25E
Ardfert 39 52 20N 9 49W
Ardfinnan 39 52 20N 7 53W
Ardglass 38 54 16N 5 38W
Ardgour 36 56 45N 5 25W
Ardgroom 39 51 44N 9 53W
Ardhas, R. 68 41 36N 26 25E
Ardhasig 36 57 55N 6 51W
Ardhéa 68 40 58N 22 3E
Ardila, R. 57 38 10N 7 20W
Ardingly 29 51 3N 0 3W
Ardino 67 41 34N 25 9E
Ardivachar Pt. 36 57 23N 7 25W
Ardkearagh 39 51 48N 10 11W
Ardkeen 38 54 27N 5 31W
Ardlethan 141 34 22S 146 53E
Ardlui 34 56 19N 4 43W
Ardmore, Austral. 138 21 39S 139 11E
Ardmore, Okla., U.S.A. 159 34 10N 97 5W
Ardmore, Pa., U.S.A. 162 39 58N 75 18W
Ardmore, S.D., U.S.A. 158 43 0N 103 40W
Ardmore Hd. 39 51 58N 7 43W
Ardmore Pt. 34 55 40N 6 0W
Ardnacrusha 39 52 43N 8 38W
Ardnamurchan, Pen. 36 56 43N 6 0W
Ardnamurchan Pt. 36 56 44N 6 14W
Ardnaree 38 54 6N 9 8W
Ardnave Pt. 34 55 54N 6 20W
Ardooie 47 50 59N 3 13E
Ardore Marina 65 38 11N 16 10E
Ardrahan 39 53 10N 8 48W
Ardres 43 50 50N 2 0E
Ardrishaig 34 56 0N 5 27W
Ardrossan, Austral. 140 34 26S 137 53E
Ardrossan, U.K. 34 55 39N 4 50W
Ards □ 38 54 35N 5 30W
Ards Pen. 38 54 30N 5 25W
Ardud 70 47 37N 22 52E
Ardunac 83 41 8N 42 5E
Ardvoulie Castle 36 58 0N 6 45W
Ardwell 37 57 20N 3 5W
Åre 72 63 22N 13 15E
Arecibo 147 18 29N 66 42W
Areia Branca 170 5 0S 37 0W
Aremark 71 59 15N 11 42E
Arena de la Ventana, Punta 164 24 4N 109 52W
Arenales, Cerro 176 47 5S 73 40W
Arenas 56 43 17N 4 50W
Arenas de San Pedro 56 40 12N 5 5W
Arenas, Pta. 174 10 20N 62 39W
Arendal 71 58 28N 8 46E
Arendonk 47 51 19N 5 5E
Arendsee 48 52 52N 11 27E
Arenig Fach, Mt. 31 52 55N 3 45E
Arenig Fawr, Mt. 31 52 56N 3 45W
Arenys de Mar 58 41 35N 2 33E
Arenzano 62 44 24N 8 40E
Areópolis 69 36 40N 22 22E
Arequipa 174 16 20S 71 30W
Arero 123 4 41N 38 50E
Arês 171 6 11S 35 9W
Arès 44 44 47N 1 8W
Arévalo 56 41 3N 4 43W
Arezzo 63 43 28N 11 50E
Arga, R. 58 42 30N 1 50W
Argalasti 68 39 13N 23 13E
Argamasilla de Alba 59 39 8N 3 5W
Arganda 58 40 19N 3 26W
Arganil 56 40 13N 8 3W
Argayash 84 55 29N 60 52E
Argelès-Gazost 44 43 0N 0 6W
Argelès-sur-Mer 44 42 34N 3 1E
Argent-sur-Sauldre 43 47 33N 2 25E
Argenta, Can. 152 50 20N 116 55W
Argenta, Italy 63 44 37N 11 50E
Argentan 42 48 45N 0 1W
Argentário, Mte. 63 42 23N 11 11E
Argentat 44 45 6N 1 56E
Argentera 62 44 23N 6 58E
Argenteuil 43 48 57N 2 14E
Argentia 151 47 18N 53 58W
Argentiera, C. dell' 64 40 44N 8 8E
Argentière, Aiguilles d' 50 45 58N 7 2E
Argentina 174 0 34N 74 17W
Argentina ■ 176 35 0S 66 0W
Argentino, L. 176 50 10S 73 0W
Argenton-sur-Creuse 44 46 36N 1 30E
Argentré 42 48 5N 0 40W
Argeş □ 70 45 0N 24 45E
Argeş, R. 70 44 30N 25 50E
Arghandab, R. 94 32 15N 66 23E
Argo 122 19 28N 30 30E
Argo, I. 122 19 28N 30 30E
Argolikós Kólpos 69 37 20N 22 52E
Argolís □ 69 37 38N 22 50E
Argonne 43 49 0N 5 20E
Árgos 69 37 40N 22 43E
Árgos Orestikón 68 40 27N 21 26E
Argostólion 69 38 12N 20 33E
Arguedas 58 42 11N 1 36W
Arguello, Pt. 163 34 34N 120 40W
Argun, R. 77 53 20N 121 28E
Argungu 121 12 40N 4 31E
Argus Pk. 163 35 52N 117 26W
Argyle 158 48 23N 96 49W
Argyle Downs 136 16 17S 128 47E
Argyle, L. 136 16 20S 128 40E
Argyll (□) 26 56 18N 5 15W
Argyll, Dist. 34 56 14N 5 10W
Argyll, oilfield 19 56 8N 3 5E
Argyrádhes 68 39 27N 19 58E
Århus 73 56 8N 10 11E
Aria 142 38 33S 175 0E
Ariamsvlei 128 28 9S 19 51E
Ariana 119 36 52N 10 12E
Ariano Irpino 65 41 10N 15 4E
Ariano nel Polèsine 63 44 56N 12 5E
Aribinda 121 14 17N 0 52W
Arica, Chile 174 18 32S 70 20W
Arica, Colomb. 174 2 0S 71 50W
Arica, Peru 174 1 30S 75 30W
Arid, C. 137 34 1S 123 10E
Arida 111 33 29N 135 44E
Ariège □ 44 42 56N 1 30E
Ariège, R. 44 42 56N 1 25E
Arieş, R. 70 46 24N 23 20E
Arilje 66 43 44N 20 7E
Arima 167 10 38N 61 17W
Arinagour 34 56 38N 6 31W
Arinos, R. 174 11 15S 57 0W
Ario de Rosales 164 19 12N 101 42W
Aripuanã 174 9 25S 60 30W
Aripuanã, R. 174 7 30S 60 25W
Ariquemes 174 9 55S 63 6W
Arisaig 36 56 55N 5 50W
Arisaig, Sd. of 36 56 50N 5 50W
Arîsh, W. el 122 30 25N 34 52E
Arismendi 174 8 29N 68 22W
Arissa 123 11 10N 41 35E
Aristazabal, I. 152 52 40N 129 10W
Arita 110 33 11N 129 54E
Arivaca 161 31 37N 111 25W
Arivonimamo 129 19 1S 47 11E
Ariyalur 97 11 8N 79 8E
Ariza 58 41 19N 2 3W
Arizaro, Salar de 172 24 40S 67 50W
Arizona 172 35 45S 65 25W
Arizona □ 161 34 20N 111 30W
Arizpe 164 30 20N 110 11W

Arjang Atalaia

Arjang	72	59 24N	12 9 E
Arjäng	72	59 24N	12 8 E
Arjeplog	74	66 3N	18 2 E
Arjona, Colomb.	174	10 14N	75 22W
Arjona, Spain	57	37 56N	4 4W
Arjuno	103	7 49 S	112 19 E
Arka	77	60 15N	142 0 E
Arkadak	81	51 58N	43 19 E
Arkadelphia	159	34 5N	93 0W
Arkadhia □	69	37 30N	22 20 E
Arkaig, L.	36	56 58N	5 10W
Arkansas □	159	35 0N	92 30W
Arkansas City	159	37 4N	97 3W
Arkansas, R.	159	35 20N	93 30W
Arkathos, R.	68	39 20N	21 4 E
Arkhángelos	69	36 13N	28 7 E
Arkhangelsk	78	64 40N	41 0 E
Arkhangelskoye	81	51 32N	40 58 E
Arkiko	123	15 33N	39 30 E
Arkle R.	32	54 25N	2 0W
Arklow	39	52 48N	6 10W
Arklow Hd.	39	52 46N	6 10W
Arkoi	69	37 24N	26 44 E
Arkona, Kap	48	54 41N	13 26 E
Arkonam	97	13 7N	79 43 E
Arkösund	73	58 29N	16 56 E
Arkoúdhi	69	38 33N	20 43 E
Arkticheskiy, Mys	77	81 10N	95 0 E
Arkul	84	57 17N	50 3 E
Arkville	162	42 9N	74 37W
Arlanc	44	45 25N	3 42 E
Arlanza, R.	56	42 6N	4 0W
Arlanzón, R.	56	42 12N	4 0W
Arlberg Pass	49	49 9N	10 12 E
Arlee	160	47 10N	114 4W
Arles	45	43 41N	4 40 E
Arlesheim	50	47 30N	7 37 E
Arless	39	52 53N	7 1W
Arlington, S. Afr.	129	28 1 S	27 53 E
Arlington, Oreg., U.S.A.	160	45 48N	120 6W
Arlington, S.D., U.S.A.	158	44 25N	97 4W
Arlington, Va., U.S.A.	162	38 52N	77 5W
Arlington, Vt., U.S.A.	162	43 5N	73 9W
Arlington, Wash., U.S.A.	160	48 11N	122 4W
Arlon	47	49 42N	5 49 E
Arlöv	73	55 38N	13 5 E
Arly	121	11 35N	1 28 E
Armadale, Austral.	137	32 12 S	116 0 E
Armadale, Lothian, U.K.	35	55 54N	3 42W
Armadale, Skye, U.K.	36	57 24N	5 54W
Armagh, Can.	137	46 41N	70 32W
Armagh, U.K.	38	54 22N	6 40W
Armagh □	38	54 18N	6 37W
Armagh Co.	38	54 16N	6 35W
Armagnac	44	43 44N	0 10 E
Armançon, R.	43	47 51N	4 7 E
Armavir	83	45 2N	41 7 E
Armenia	174	4 35N	75 45W
Armenian S.S.R. □	83	40 0N	41 0 E
Armeniş	70	45 13N	22 17 E
Armentières	43	50 40N	2 50 E
Armero	174	4 58N	74 54W
Armidale	141	30 30 S	151 40 E
Armour	158	43 20N	98 25W
Armoy	38	55 8N	6 20W
Arms	150	49 34N	86 3W
Armstead	160	45 0N	112 56W
Armstrong, B.C., Can.	152	50 25N	119 10W
Armstrong, Ont., Can.	150	50 18N	89 4W
Armstrong, U.S.A.	159	26 59N	90 48W
Armstrong Cr.	136	16 35 S	131 40 E
Armur	96	18 48N	78 16 E
Arnaia	68	40 30N	23 40 E
Arnarfjörður	74	65 48N	23 40W
Arnay-le-Duc	43	47 10N	4 27 E
Arnedillo	58	42 13N	2 14W
Arnedo	58	42 12N	2 5W
Arnes	74	66 1N	21 31W
Årnes	71	60 7N	11 28 E
Arnett	159	36 9N	99 44W
Arney	38	54 17N	7 41W
Arnhem	46	51 58N	5 55 E
Arnhem B.	138	12 20 S	136 10 E
Arnhem, C.	138	12 20 S	137 0 E
Arnhem Ld.	138	13 10 S	135 0 E
Arni	97	12 43N	79 19 E
Arnissa	68	40 47N	21 49 E
Arno Bay	140	33 54 S	136 34 E
Arno, R.	62	43 44N	10 20 E
Arnold, N.Z.	143	42 29 S	171 25 E
Arnold, U.K.	33	53 0N	1 8W
Arnold, Calif., U.S.A.	163	38 15N	120 20W
Arnold, Nebr., U.S.A.	158	41 29N	100 10W
Arnoldstein	52	46 33N	13 43 E
Arnot	153	55 46N	96 41W
Arnøy	74	70 9N	20 40 E
Arnprior	150	45 26N	76 21W
Arnsberg	48	51 25N	8 10 E
Arnside	32	54 12N	2 49W
Arnstadt	48	50 50N	10 56 E
Aroa	174	10 26N	68 54W
Aroab	125	26 41 S	19 39 E
Aroánia Óri	69	37 56N	22 12 E
Aroche	57	37 56N	6 57W
Aroeiras	170	7 31 S	35 41W
Arolla	50	46 2N	7 29 E
Arolsen	48	51 23N	9 1 E
Arona	62	45 45N	8 32 E
Arosa	51	46 47N	9 41 E
Arosa, Ría de	56	42 28N	8 57W
Arpajon, Cantal, France	44	44 54N	2 28 E
Arpajon, Seine et Oise, France	43	48 37N	2 12 E
Arpino	64	41 40N	13 35 E
Arra Mts.	39	52 50N	8 22W
Arrabury	139	26 45 S	141 0 E
Arrah	95	25 35N	84 32 E
Arraias	171	12 56 S	46 57W
Arraias, R.	170	7 30 S	49 20W
Arraiolos	57	38 44N	7 59W
Arran, I.	34	55 34N	5 12W
Arrandale	152	54 57N	130 0W
Arras	43	50 17N	2 46 E
Arreau	44	42 54N	0 22 E
Arrecife	116	28 59N	13 40W
Arrecifes	172	34 06 S	60 9W
Arrée, Mts. d'	42	48 26N	3 55W
Arriaga, Chiapas, Mexico	165	16 15N	93 52W
Arriaga, San Luís de Potosi, Mexico	164	21 55N	101 23W
Arrild	73	55 8N	8 58 E
Arrilalah P.O.	138	23 43 S	143 54 E
Arrino	137	29 30 S	115 40 E
Arrochar	34	56 12N	4 45W
Arrojado, R.	171	13 24 S	44 20W
Arromanches-les-Bains	42	49 20N	0 38W
Arronches	57	39 8N	7 16W
Arrou	42	48 6N	1 8 E
Arrow L.	38	54 3N	8 20W
Arrow Rock Res.	160	43 45N	115 50W
Arrowhead	152	50 40N	117 55W
Arrowhead, L.	163	34 16N	117 10W
Arrowsmith, Mt.	143	30 7N	141 38 E
Arrowtown	143	44 57 S	168 50 E
Arroyo de la Luz	57	39 30N	6 38W
Arroyo Grande	163	35 9N	120 32W
Års	73	56 48N	9 30 E
Ars	44	46 13N	1 30W
Ars-sur-Moselle	43	49 5N	6 4 E
Arsenault L.	153	53 6N	108 32W
Arsiero	63	45 49N	11 22 E
Arsikere	97	13 15N	76 15 E
Arsk	81	56 10N	49 50 E
Årskogen	72	62 8N	17 20 E
Árta	69	39 8N	21 2 E
Artá	58	39 40N	3 20 E
Árta □	68	39 15N	26 0 E
Arteaga	164	18 50N	102 20W
Arteijo	56	43 19N	8 29W
Artem,Os.	83	40 28N	50 20 E
Artémou	120	15 38N	12 16W
Artemovsk	82	48 35N	37 55 E
Artemovski	83	54 45N	93 35 E
Artemovskiy	84	57 21N	61 54 E
Artenay	43	48 5N	1 50 E
Artern	48	51 22N	11 18 E
Artesa de Segre	58	41 54N	1 3 E
Artesia	159	32 55N	104 25W
Artesia Wells	159	28 17N	99 18W
Artesian	158	44 2N	97 54W
Arth	51	47 4N	8 31 E
Arthez-de-Béarn	44	43 29N	0 38W
Arthington	120	6 35N	10 45W
Arthur Cr.	138	22 30 S	136 25 E
Arthur Pt.	138	22 7 S	150 3 E
Arthur, R.	138	41 2 S	144 40 E
Arthur's Pass	143	42 54 S	171 35 E
Arthur's Town	167	24 38N	75 42W
Arthurstown	39	52 15N	6 58W
Artigas	172	30 20 S	56 30W
Artigavan	38	54 51N	7 24W
Artik	83	40 38N	44 50 E
Artillery L.	153	63 9N	107 52W
Artois	43	50 20N	2 30 E
Artotína	69	38 42N	22 2 E
Artvin	92	41 14N	41 44 E
Aru, Kepulauan	103	6 0 S	134 30 E
Arua	126	3 1N	30 58 E
Aruanã	171	15 0 S	51 10W
Aruba I.	167	12 30N	70 0W
Arudy	44	43 7N	0 28W
Arumpo	140	33 48 S	142 55 E
Arun, R.	95	27 30N	87 15 E
Arun R.	29	50 48N	0 33W
Arunachal Pradesh □	98	28 0N	95 0 E
Arundel	29	50 52N	0 32W
Aruppukottai	97	9 31N	78 8 E
Arusha	126	3 20 S	36 40 E
Arusha □	126	4 0 S	36 30 E
Arusha Chini	126	3 32 S	37 20 E
Arusi □	123	7 45N	39 00 E
Aruvi	97	8 48N	79 53 E
Aruwimi, R.	126	1 30N	25 0 E
Arva	38	53 57N	7 35W
Arvada	160	44 43N	106 6W
Arvaklu	97	8 20N	79 58 E
Arvayheer	105	46 15N	102 48 E
Arve, R.	45	46 11N	6 8 E
Arvi	96	20 59N	78 16 E
Arvida	151	48 25N	71 14W
Arvidsjaur	74	65 35N	19 10 E
Arvika	72	59 40N	12 36 E
Arvin	163	35 12N	118 50W
Arys	85	42 26N	68 48 E
Arys, R.	85	42 45N	68 15 E
Arzachena	64	41 5N	9 27 E
Arzamas	81	55 27N	43 55 E
Arzew	118	35 50N	0 23W
Arzgir	83	45 18N	44 23 E
Arzignano	63	45 30N	11 20 E
As	47	51 1N	5 35 E
Aš	52	50 13N	12 12 E
As Salt	90	32 2N	35 43 E
As Samawah	92	31 15N	45 15 E
As-Samū	90	31 24N	35 4 E
As Sulaimānīyah	92	35 35N	45 29 E
As Sulṭon	119	31 4N	17 8 E
As Suwaih	93	22 10N	59 33 E
As Suwayda	92	32 40N	36 30 E
As Suwayrah	92	32 55N	45 0 E
Asab	128	25 30 S	18 0 E
Asaba	121	6 12N	6 38 E
Asadabad	92	34 50N	48 10 E
Asafo	120	6 20N	2 40W
Asahi	111	35 43N	140 39 E
Asahi-Gawa, R.	110	34 36N	133 58 E
Asahikawa	112	43 45N	142 30 E
Asale, L.	123	14 0N	40 20 E
Asama-Yama	111	36 24N	138 31 E
Asamankese	121	5 50N	0 40W
Asankrangwa	120	5 45N	2 30W
Asansol	95	23 40N	87 1 E
Åsarna	72	62 40N	14 20 E
Åsarna	72	62 39N	14 22 E
Asbe Teferi	123	9 4N	40 49 E
Asbesberge	128	29 0 S	23 0 E
Asbest	84	57 0N	61 30 E
Asbestos	151	45 47N	71 58W
Asbury Park	162	40 15N	74 1W
Ascensión	164	31 6N	107 59W
Ascensión, B. de la	165	19 50N	87 20W
Ascension, I.	15	8 0 S	14 15W
Aschach	49	48 23N	14 0 E
Aschaffenburg	49	49 58N	9 8 E
Aschendorf	48	53 2N	7 22 E
Aschersleben	48	51 45N	11 28 E
Asciano	63	43 14N	11 32 E
Áscoli Piceno	63	42 51N	13 34 E
Áscoli Satriano	65	41 11N	15 32 E
Ascona	51	46 9N	8 46 E
Ascope	174	7 46 S	79 8W
Ascot	29	51 24N	0 41W
Ascotán	172	21 45 S	68 17W
Aseb	123	13 0N	42 40 E
Åseda	73	57 10N	15 20 E
Åseda	73	57 10N	15 20 E
Asedjrad	118	24 51N	1 29 E
Asela	123	8 0N	39 0 E
Asenovgrad	67	42 1N	24 51 E
Åseral	71	58 37N	7 25 E
Åseral	71	58 38N	7 26 E
Asfeld	43	49 27N	4 5 E
Asfordby	29	52 45N	0 57W
Asfûn el Matâ'na	122	25 26N	32 30 E
Åsgårdstrand	71	59 22N	10 27 E
Ash	29	51 17N	1 16 E
Ash Fork	161	35 14N	112 32W
Ash Grove	159	37 21N	93 36W
Ash Shām,Bādiyat	92	31 30N	40 0 E
Ash Shāmīyah	92	31 55N	44 35 E
Ash Shatrah	92	31 30N	46 10 E
Ash Shuna	90	32 32N	35 34 E
Asha	84	55 0N	57 16 E
Ashaira	122	21 40N	40 40 E
Ashanti	121	7 30N	2 0W
Ashau	100	16 6N	107 22 E
Ashbourne, Ireland	38	53 31N	6 24W
Ashbourne, U.K.	33	53 2N	1 44W
Ashburn	157	31 42N	83 40W
Ashburton, N.Z.	143	43 53 S	171 48 E
Ashburton, U.K.	30	50 31N	3 45W
Ashburton Downs	136	23 25 S	117 4 E
Ashburton, R., Austral.	136	21 40 S	114 56 E
Ashburton, R., N.Z.	131	44 2 S	171 50 E
Ashby-de-la-Zouch	28	52 45N	1 29W
Ashchurch	28	52 0N	2 7W
Ashcroft	152	50 40N	121 20W
Ashdod	90	31 49N	34 35 E
Ashdot Ya'aqov	90	32 39N	35 35 E
Ashdown Forest	29	51 4N	0 2 E
Asheboro	157	35 43N	79 46W
Asherton	159	28 25N	99 43W
Asheville	157	35 39N	82 30W
Asheweig, R.	150	54 17N	87 12W
Ashford, Austral.	139	29 15 S	151 3 E
Ashford, Derby., U.K.	33	53 13N	1 43W
Ashford, Kent, U.K.	29	51 8N	0 53 E
Ashford, U.S.A.	160	46 45N	122 2W
Ashikaga	111	36 28N	139 29 E
Ashington	35	55 12N	1 35W
Ashio	111	36 38N	139 27 E
Ashizuri-Zaki	110	32 35N	132 50 E
Ashkarkot	94	33 3N	67 58 E
Ashkhabad	85	38 0N	57 50 E
Ashland, Kans., U.S.A.	159	37 13N	99 43W
Ashland, Ky., U.S.A.	156	38 25N	82 40W
Ashland, Me., U.S.A.	151	46 34N	68 26W
Ashland, Mont., U.S.A.	160	45 41N	106 12W
Ashland, Nebr., U.S.A.	158	41 5N	96 27W
Ashland, Ohio, U.S.A.	156	40 52N	82 20W
Ashland, Oreg., U.S.A.	160	42 10N	122 38W
Ashland, Pa., U.S.A.	162	40 45N	76 22W
Ashland, Va., U.S.A.	156	37 46N	77 30W
Ashland, Wis., U.S.A.	158	46 40N	90 52W
Ashley, N.D., U.S.A.	158	46 3N	99 23W
Ashley, Pa., U.S.A.	162	41 14N	75 53W
Ashmont	152	54 7N	111 29W
Ashmore Is.	136	12 14 S	123 50 E
Ashmore Reef	136	12 14 S	123 5 E
Ashmûn	122	30 18N	30 55 E
Ashokan Res.	162	41 56N	74 13W
Ashquelon	90	31 42N	34 55 E
Ashtabula	156	41 52N	80 50W
Ashti	96	18 50N	75 15 E
Ashton, S. Afr.	128	33 50 S	20 5 E
Ashton, U.S.A.	160	44 6N	111 30W
Ashton-in-Makerfield	32	53 29N	2 39W
Ashton-u.-Lyne	32	53 30N	2 8 E
Ashuanipi, L.	151	52 45N	66 15W
Ashurst	142	40 16 S	175 45 E
Ashurstwood	29	51 6N	0 2 E
Ashwater	30	50 43N	4 18W
Ashwick	28	51 13N	2 31W
Asia	86	45 0N	75 0 E
Asia, Kepulauan	103	1 0N	131 13 E
Asiago	63	45 52N	11 30 E
Asifabad	96	19 30N	79 24 E
Asilah	118	35 29N	6 0W
Asinara	64	41 5N	8 15 E
Asinara, G. dell'	64	41 0N	8 30 E
Asinara I.	64	41 5N	8 15 E
Asino	76	57 0N	86 0 E
Asir	91	18 40N	42 30 E
Asir, Ras	91	11 55N	51 10 E
Aska	96	19 37N	84 42 E
Askeaton	39	52 37N	8 58W
Asker	71	59 50N	10 26 E
Askersund	73	58 53N	14 55 E
Askim	71	59 35N	11 10 E
Askino	84	56 5N	56 34 E
Askja	74	65 3N	16 48W
Åskloster	73	57 13N	12 11 E
Askrigg	32	54 19N	2 6W
Asl	122	29 33N	32 44 E
Aslackby	33	52 53N	0 23W
Asmar	93	35 10N	71 27 E
Asmera (Asmara)	123	15 19N	38 55 E
Asnæs	73	55 40N	11 0 E
Åsnen	73	56 35N	15 45 E
Åsnes	71	60 37N	11 59 E
Asni	118	31 17N	7 58W
Aso	110	33 0N	130 42 E
Aso-Zan	110	32 53N	131 6 E
Asoa	126	4 35N	25 48 E
Asola	62	45 12N	10 25 E
Asotin	60	46 14N	117 2W
Aspatria	32	54 45N	3 20W
Aspe	59	38 20N	0 40W
Aspen	161	39 12N	106 56W
Aspermont	159	33 11N	100 15W
Aspiring, Mt.	143	44 23 S	168 46 E
Aspres	45	44 32N	5 44 E
Aspur	94	23 58N	74 7 E
Asquith	153	52 8N	107 13W
Assa	118	28 35N	9 6W
Assaba, Massif de l'	120	16 10N	11 45W
Assam □	98	25 45N	92 30 E
Assamakka	121	19 21N	5 38 E
Assateague I.	162	38 5N	75 6W
Asse	47	50 54N	4 6 E
Assebroek	47	51 11N	3 17 E
Assekrem	119	23 16N	5 49 E
Assémini	64	39 18N	9 0 E
Assen	46	53 0N	6 35 E
Assendelft	46	52 29N	4 45 E
Assenede	47	51 14N	3 46 E
Assens, Odense, Denmark	73	56 41N	10 3 E
Assens, Randers, Denmark	73	55 16N	9 55 E
Assesse	47	50 22N	5 2 E
Assiniboia	153	49 40N	105 59W
Assiniboine, R.	153	49 53N	97 8W
Assinica L.	150	50 30N	75 20W
Assinie	120	5 9N	3 17W
Assis	173	22 40 S	50 20W
Assisi	63	43 4N	12 36 E
Ássos	69	38 22N	20 33 E
Assynt	36	58 25N	5 10W
Assynt, L.	36	58 25N	5 15W
Astakidha	69	35 53N	26 50 E
Astalfort	44	44 4N	0 40 E
Astara	79	38 30N	48 50 E
Astee	39	52 33N	9 36W
Asten	47	51 24N	5 45 E
Asti	62	44 54N	8 11 E
Astillero	56	43 24N	3 49W
Astipálaia	69	36 32N	26 22 E
Aston, C.	149	70 10N	67 40W
Aston Clinton	29	51 48N	0 44W
Astorga	56	42 29N	6 8W
Astoria	160	46 16N	123 50W
Åstorp	73	56 6N	12 55 E
Astrakhan	83	46 25N	48 5 E
Astudillo	56	42 12N	4 22W
Asturias	56	43 15N	6 0W
Astwood Bank	28	52 15N	1 55W
Asunción	172	25 21 S	57 30W
Asunción, La	174	11 2N	63 53W
Åsunden	73	57 47N	13 18 E
Asutri	123	15 25N	35 45 E
Aswa, R.	126	2 30N	33 5 E
Aswad,Rasal	122	21 20N	39 0 E
Aswân	122	24 4N	32 57 E
Aswân High Dam = Sadd el Aali	122	24 5N	32 54 E
Asyût	122	27 11N	31 4 E
Asyûti, Wadi	122	27 18N	31 20 E
Aszód	53	47 39N	19 28 E
At Tafilah	92	30 45N	35 30 E
At Ta'if	122	21 5N	40 27 E
Atacama	172	25 40 S	67 40W
Atacama □	172	27 30 S	70 0W
Atacama, Desierto de	176	24 0 S	69 20W
Atacama, Salar de	172	24 0 S	68 20W
Ataco	174	3 35N	75 23W
Atakor	119	23 27N	5 31 E
Atakpamé	121	7 31N	1 13 E
Atalaia	114	9 25 S	36 0W

Atalándi **Ayutla**

Atalándi	**69**	38 39N	22 58 E
Atalaya	**174**	10 45 S	73 50W
Ataléia	**171**	18 3 S	41 6W
Atami	**111**	35 0N	139 55 E
Atankawng	**98**	25 50N	97 47 E
Atar	**116**	20 30N	13 5W
Atara	**77**	63 10N	129 10 E
Ataram, Erg d'	**118**	23 57N	2 0 E
Atarfe	**57**	37 13N	3 40W
Atascadero	**163**	35 32N	120 44W
Atasu	**76**	48 30N	71 0 E
Atauro	**103**	8 10 S	125 30 E
Atbara	**122**	17 42N	33 59 E
Atbara, R.	**122**	17 40N	33 56 E
Atbashi	**85**	41 10N	75 48 E
Atbashi, Khrebet	**85**	40 50N	75 30 E
Atchafalaya B.	**159**	29 30N	91 20W
Atchison	**158**	39 40N	95 0W
Atebubu	**121**	7 47N	1 0W
Ateca	**58**	41 20N	1 49W
Aterno, R.	**63**	42 18N	13 45 E
Atesine, Alpi	**62**	46 55N	11 30 E
Atessa	**63**	42 5N	14 27 E
Ath	**47**	50 38N	3 47 E
Ath Thamami	**92**	27 45N	35 30 E
Athabasca	**152**	54 45N	113 20W
Athabasca, L.	**153**	59 15N	109 15W
Athabasca, R.	**153**	58 40N	110 50W
Athboy	**38**	53 37N	6 55W
Athea	**39**	52 27N	9 18W
Athenry	**39**	53 18N	8 45W
Athens, Ala., U.S.A.	**157**	34 49N	86 58W
Athens, Ga., U.S.A.	**157**	33 56N	83 24W
Athens, N.Y., U.S.A.	**162**	42 15N	73 48W
Athens, Ohio, U.S.A.	**156**	39 52N	82 6W
Athens, Pa., U.S.A.	**162**	41 57N	76 36W
Athens, Tex., U.S.A.	**159**	32 11N	95 48W
Athens = Athínai	**69**	37 58N	23 46 E
Atherstone	**28**	52 35N	1 32W
Atherton, Austral.	**138**	17 17 S	145 30 E
Atherton, U.K.	**32**	53 32N	2 30W
Athiéme	**121**	6 37N	1 40 E
Athínai	**69**	37 58N	23 46 E
Athleague	**38**	53 34N	8 17W
Athlone	**38**	53 26N	7 57W
Athni	**96**	16 44N	75 6 E
Athol	**143**	45 30 S	168 35 E
Atholl, Forest of	**37**	56 51N	3 50W
Atholville	**151**	47 59N	66 43W
Áthos, Mt.	**68**	40 9N	24 22 E
Athus	**47**	49 34N	5 50 E
Athy	**39**	53 0N	7 0W
Ati	**123**	13 5N	29 2 E
Atiak	**126**	3 12N	32 2 E
Atiamuri	**142**	38 24 S	176 5 E
Atico	**174**	16 14 S	73 40W
Atienza	**58**	41 12N	2 52W
Atikokan	**150**	48 45N	91 37W
Atikonak L.	**151**	52 40N	64 32W
Atka, U.S.A.	**147**	52 5N	174 40W
Atka, U.S.S.R.	**77**	60 50N	151 48 E
Atkarsk	**81**	51 55N	45 2 E
Atkasuk (Meade River)	**147**	70 30N	157 20W
Atkinson	**158**	42 35N	98 59W
Atlanta, Ga., U.S.A.	**157**	33 50N	84 24W
Atlanta, Tex., U.S.A.	**159**	33 7N	94 8W
Atlantic	**158**	41 25N	95 0W
Atlantic City	**162**	39 25N	74 25W
Atlantic Ocean	**14**	0 0	20 0W
Atlántico □	**174**	10 45N	75 0W
Atlas, Great, Mts.	**114**	33 0N	5 0W
Atlin	**147**	59 31N	133 41W
Atlin Lake	**147**	59 26N	133 45W
'Atlit	**90**	32 42N	34 56 E
Atløy	**71**	61 21N	4 58 E
Atmakur	**97**	14 37N	79 40 E
Atmore	**157**	31 2N	87 30W
Atnarko	**152**	52 25N	126 0W
Atō	**110**	34 25N	131 40 E
Atoka	**159**	34 22N	96 10W
Átokos	**69**	38 28N	20 49 E
Atolia	**163**	35 19N	117 37W
Atotonilco el Alto	**164**	20 20N	98 40W
Atouguia	**57**	39 20N	9 20W
Atoyac, R.	**165**	16 30N	97 31W
Åtrafors	**73**	57 02N	12 40 E
Atrak, R.	**93**	37 50N	57 0 E
Åtran	**73**	57 7N	12 57 E
Atrato, R.	**174**	6 40N	77 0W
Atrauli	**94**	28 2N	78 20 E
Atri	**63**	42 35N	14 0 E
Atsbi	**122**	13 52N	39 50 E
Atsumi	**111**	34 35N	137 4 E
Atsumi-Wan	**111**	34 44N	137 13 E
Atsuta	**112**	43 24N	141 26 E
Attalla	**157**	34 2N	86 5W
Attawapiskat	**150**	52 56N	82 24W
Attawapiskat, L.	**150**	52 18N	87 54W
Attawapiskat, R.	**150**	52 57N	82 18W
Attendorn	**48**	51 8N	7 54 E
Attersee	**52**	47 55N	13 31 E
Attert	**47**	49 45N	5 47 E
Attica	**156**	40 20N	87 15W
Attichy	**43**	49 25N	3 3 E
Attigny	**43**	49 28N	4 35 E
Attikamagen L.	**151**	55 0N	66 30W
Attikí Kai Arkhipélagos □	**69**	38 10N	23 40 E
Attil	**90**	32 23N	35 4 E
Attleboro	**162**	41 56N	71 18W
Attleborough	**29**	52 32N	1 1 E
Attock	**94**	33 52N	72 20 E
Attopeu	**100**	14 48N	106 50 E
Attu	**147**	52 55N	173 10W
Attunga	**141**	30 55 S	150 50 E
Attur	**97**	11 35N	78 30 E
Attymon	**39**	53 20N	8 37W
Atuel, R.	**172**	36 17 S	66 50W
Atvidaberg	**73**	58 12N	16 0 E
Atwater	**163**	37 21N	120 37W
Atwood	**158**	39 52N	101 3W
Au Sable Pt.	**150**	46 0N	86 0W
Au Sable, R.	**156**	44 25N	83 20W
Aubagne	**45**	43 17N	5 37 E
Aubange	**47**	49 34N	5 48 E
Aubarede Pt.	**103**	17 15N	122 20 E
Aube □	**43**	48 15N	4 0 E
Aubel	**47**	50 42N	5 51 E
Aubenas	**45**	44 37N	4 24 E
Aubenton	**43**	49 50N	4 12 E
Auberry	**163**	37 7N	119 29W
Aubigny-sur-Nère	**43**	47 30N	2 24 E
Aubin	**44**	44 33N	2 15 E
Aubrac, Mts. d'	**44**	44 38N	2 58 E
Auburn, Ala., U.S.A.	**157**	32 37N	85 30W
Auburn, Calif., U.S.A.	**160**	38 50N	121 4W
Auburn, Ind., U.S.A.	**156**	41 20N	85 0W
Auburn, Nebr., U.S.A.	**158**	40 25N	95 50W
Auburn, N.Y., U.S.A.	**162**	42 57N	76 39W
Auburn, Penn., U.S.A.	**162**	40 36N	76 6W
Auburn Range	**139**	25 15 S	150 30 E
Auburndale	**157**	28 5N	81 45W
Aubusson	**44**	45 57N	2 11 E
Auch	**44**	43 39N	0 36 E
Auchel	**43**	50 30N	2 29 E
Auchenblae	**37**	56 54N	2 26W
Auchencairn	**35**	54 51N	3 52W
Auchi	**121**	7 6N	6 13 E
Auchinleck	**34**	55 28N	4 18W
Auchness	**37**	58 0N	4 36W
Auchterarder	**35**	56 18N	3 43W
Auchterderran	**35**	56 8N	3 16W
Auchtermuchty	**35**	56 18N	3 15W
Auchtertyre	**36**	57 17N	5 35W
Auckland	**142**	36 52 S	174 46 E
Auckland □	**142**	38 35 S	177 0 E
Auckland Is.	**142**	51 0 S	166 0 E
Aude □	**44**	43 8N	2 28 E
Aude, R.	**44**	44 13N	3 15 E
Auden	**150**	50 14N	87 53W
Auderghem	**47**	50 49N	4 26 E
Auderville	**42**	49 43N	1 57W
Audierne	**42**	48 1N	4 34W
Audincourt	**43**	47 30N	6 50 E
Audlem	**32**	52 59N	2 31W
Audo Ra.	**123**	6 20N	41 50 E
Audrey, gasfield	**19**	53 35N	2 0 E
Audubon	**158**	41 43N	94 56W
Aue	**48**	50 34N	12 43 E
Auerbach	**48**	50 30N	12 25 E
Auffay	**42**	49 43N	1 07 E
Augathella	**139**	25 48 S	146 35 E
Augher	**38**	54 25N	7 10W
Aughnacloy	**38**	54 25N	6 58W
Aughrim, Clare, Ireland	**39**	53 0N	8 57W
Aughrim, Galway, Ireland	**39**	53 18N	8 19W
Aughrim, Wicklow, Ireland	**39**	52 52N	6 20W
Aughrus More	**38**	53 34N	10 10W
Augrabies Falls	**128**	28 35 S	20 20 E
Augsburg	**49**	48 22N	10 54 E
Augusta, Italy	**65**	37 14N	15 12 E
Augusta, Ark., U.S.A.	**159**	35 17N	91 25W
Augusta, Ga., U.S.A.	**157**	33 29N	81 59W
Augusta, Kans., U.S.A.	**159**	37 40N	97 0W
Augusta, Me., U.S.A.	**151**	44 20N	69 46 E
Augusta, Mont., U.S.A.	**160**	47 30N	112 29W
Augusta, Wis., U.S.A.	**158**	44 41N	91 8W
Augustenborg	**73**	54 57N	9 53 E
Augustine	**159**	31 30N	94 37W
Augusto Cardosa	**127**	12 40 S	34 50 E
Augustów	**54**	53 51N	23 00 E
Augustus Downs	**138**	18 35 S	139 55 E
Augustus I.	**136**	15 20 S	124 30 E
Augustus, Mt.	**137**	24 20 S	116 50 E
Auk, oilfield	**19**	56 25N	2 15 E
Aukan	**123**	15 29N	40 50 E
Aukum	**163**	38 34N	120 43W
Auld, L.	**136**	22 32 S	123 44 E
Auldearn	**37**	57 34N	3 50W
Aulla	**62**	44 12N	9 57 E
Aulnay	**44**	46 2N	0 22W
Aulne, R.	**42**	48 17N	4 16W
Ault	**158**	40 40N	104 42W
Ault-Onival	**42**	50 5N	1 29 E
Aultbea	**36**	57 50N	5 36W
Aulus-les-Bains	**44**	42 49N	1 19 E
Aumale	**43**	49 46N	1 46 E
Aumont-Aubrac	**44**	44 43N	3 17 E
Auna	**121**	10 9N	4 42 E
Aundh	**96**	17 33N	74 23 E
Aunis	**44**	46 0N	0 50W
Auponhia	**103**	1 58 S	125 27 E
Aups	**45**	43 37N	6 15 E
Aur, P.	**101**	2 35N	104 10 E
Aura	**98**	26 59N	97 57 E
Aurahorten, Mt.	**71**	59 15N	6 53 E
Auraiya	**95**	26 28N	79 33 E
Aurangabad, Bihar, India	**95**	24 45N	84 18 E
Aurangabad, Maharashtra, India	**96**	19 50N	75 23 E
Auray	**42**	47 40N	3 0W
Aurès	**119**	35 8N	6 30 E
Aurich	**48**	53 28N	7 30 E
Aurilândia	**171**	16 44 S	50 28W
Aurillac	**44**	44 55N	2 26 E
Aurlandsvangen	**71**	60 55N	7 12 E
Auronza	**63**	46 33N	12 27 E
Aurora, Brazil	**171**	6 57 S	38 58W
Aurora, S. Afr.	**128**	32 40 S	18 29 E
Aurora, Colo., U.S.A.	**158**	39 44N	104 55W
Aurora, Ill., U.S.A.	**156**	41 42N	88 12W
Aurora, Mo., U.S.A.	**159**	36 58N	93 42W
Aurora, Nebr., U.S.A.	**158**	40 55N	98 0W
Aurora, N.Y., U.S.A.	**162**	42 45N	76 42W
Aurskog	**71**	59 55N	11 26 E
Aurukun Mission	**138**	13 20 S	141 45 E
Aus	**128**	26 35 S	16 12 E
Auskerry I.	**37**	59 2N	2 35W
Aust-Agder fylke □	**75**	58 55N	7 40 E
Austad	**71**	58 58N	7 37 E
Austerlitz = Slavikov	**53**	49 10N	16 52 E
Austevoll	**71**	60 5N	5 13 E
Austin, Austral.	**137**	27 40 S	117 50 E
Austin, Minn., U.S.A.	**158**	43 37N	92 59W
Austin, Nev., U.S.A.	**160**	39 30N	117 1W
Austin, Tex., U.S.A.	**159**	30 20N	97 45W
Austin, L.	**137**	27 40 S	118 0 E
Austral Downs	**138**	20 30 S	137 45 E
Austral Is. = Tubuai, Îles	**143**	25 0 S	150 0 E
Australia ■	**133**	23 0 S	135 0 E
Australian Alps	**141**	36 30 S	148 8 E
Australian Cap. Terr.	**139**	35 15 S	149 8 E
Australian Dependency	**13**	73 0 S	90 0 E
Austria ■	**52**	47 0N	14 0 E
Austvågøy	**74**	68 20N	14 40 E
Autelbas	**47**	49 39N	5 52 E
Auterive	**44**	43 21N	1 29 E
Authie, R.	**43**	50 22N	1 38 E
Autlan	**164**	19 40N	104 30W
Autun	**43**	46 58N	4 17 E
Auvelais	**47**	50 27N	4 38 E
Auvergne, Austral.	**136**	15 39 S	130 1 E
Auvergne, France	**44**	45 20N	3 0 E
Auxerre	**43**	47 48N	3 32 E
Auxi-le-Château	**43**	50 15N	2 8 E
Auxonne	**43**	47 10N	5 20 E
Auzances	**44**	46 2N	2 30 E
Avaldsnes	**71**	59 21N	5 20 E
Avallon	**43**	47 30N	3 53 E
Avalon	**163**	33 21N	118 20W
Avalon Pen.	**151**	47 30N	53 20W
Avalon Res.	**159**	32 30N	104 30W
Avanigadda	**97**	16 0N	80 56 E
Avaré	**173**	23 4 S	48 58W
Ávas	**68**	40 57N	25 56 E
Avawata Mts.	**163**	35 30N	116 20W
Avebury	**28**	51 25N	1 52W
Aveh	**92**	35 40N	49 15 E
Aveiro, Brazil	**175**	3 10 S	55 5W
Aveiro, Port.	**56**	40 37N	8 38W
Aveiro □	**56**	40 40N	8 35W
Avelgem	**47**	50 47N	3 27 E
Avellaneda	**172**	34 50 S	58 10W
Avellino	**65**	40 54N	14 46 E
Avenal	**163**	36 0N	120 8W
Avenchen	**50**	46 53N	7 2 E
Averøya	**71**	63 0N	7 35 E
Aversa	**65**	40 58N	14 11 E
Avery	**160**	47 22N	115 56W
Aves, Islas de	**174**	12 0N	67 40W
Avesnes-sur-Helpe	**43**	50 8N	3 55 E
Avesta	**72**	60 9N	16 10 E
Aveton Gifford	**30**	50 17N	3 51W
Aveyron □	**44**	44 22N	2 45 E
Avezzano	**63**	42 2N	13 24 E
Avgó	**69**	35 33N	25 37 E
Aviá Terai	**172**	26 45 S	60 50W
Aviano	**63**	46 3N	12 35 E
Avich, L.	**34**	56 17N	5 25W
Aviemore	**37**	57 11N	3 50W
Avigliana	**62**	45 7N	7 13 E
Avigliano	**65**	40 44N	15 41 E
Avignon	**45**	43 57N	4 50 E
Ávila	**56**	40 39N	4 43W
Ávila □	**56**	40 30N	5 0W
Avila Beach	**163**	35 11N	120 44W
Ávila, Sierra de	**56**	40 40N	5 0W
Avilés	**56**	43 35N	5.57W
Avionárion	**69**	38 31N	24 8 E
Avisio, R.	**63**	46 14N	11 18 E
Aviz	**57**	39 4N	7 53W
Avize	**43**	48 59N	4 0 E
Avoca, Austral.	**139**	37 5 S	143 26 E
Avoca, Ireland	**39**	52 52N	6 13W
Avoca, R., Austral.	**140**	35 40 S	143 43 E
Avoca, R., Ireland	**39**	52 48N	6 10W
Avoch	**37**	57 34N	4 10W
Avola, Can.	**152**	51 45N	119 19W
Avola, Italy	**65**	36 56N	15 7 E
Avon	**158**	43 0N	98 3W
Avon □	**28**	51 30N	2 40W
Avon Downs	**133**	19 58 S	137 25 E
Avon Is.	**133**	19 37 S	158 17 E
Avon, R., Austral.	**137**	31 40 S	116 7 E
Avon, R., Avon, U.K.	**28**	51 30N	2 43W
Avon, R., Grampian, U.K.	**37**	57 25N	3 25W
Avon, R., Hants., U.K.	**28**	50 44N	1 45W
Avon, R., Warwick, U.K.	**28**	52 0N	2 9W
Avondale, N.Z.	**142**	36 54 S	174 42 E
Avondale, Rhod.	**127**	17 43 S	30 58 E
Avonlea	**153**	50 0N	105 0W
Avonmouth	**28**	51 30N	2 42W
Avranches	**42**	48 40N	1 20W
Avrig	**70**	45 43N	24 21 E
Avrillé	**44**	46 28N	1 28W
Avtovac	**66**	43 9N	18 35 E
Avu Meru □	**126**	3 20 S	36 50 E
Awag el Baqar	**123**	10 10N	33 10 E
Awaji	**111**	34 32N	135 1 E
Awaji-Shima	**110**	34 30N	134 50 E
Awali	**93**	26 0N	50 30 E
Awantipur	**95**	33 55N	75 3 E
Awanui	**142**	35 4 S	173 17 E
Awarja, R.	**96**	18 0N	76 15 E
Awarta	**90**	32 10N	35 17 E
Awarua Pt.	**143**	44 15 S	168 5 E
Awasa, L.	**123**	7 0N	38 30 E
Awash	**123**	9 1N	40 10 E
Awash, R.	**123**	11 30N	42 0 E
Awaso	**120**	6 15N	2 22W
Awatere, R.	**143**	41 37 S	174 10 E
Awbarī	**119**	26 46N	12 57 E
Awe, L.	**34**	56 15N	5 15W
Aweil	**123**	8 42N	27 20 E
Awgu	**121**	6 4N	7 24 E
Awjilah	**117**	29 8N	21 7 E
Aworro	**135**	7 43 S	143 11 E
Ax-les-Thermes	**44**	42 44N	1 50 E
Axarfjörður	**74**	66 15N	16 45W
Axbridge	**28**	51 17N	2 50W
Axe Edge	**32**	53 14N	2 2W
Axe R.	**28**	51 17N	2 52W
Axel	**47**	51 16N	3 55 E
Axel Heiberg I.	**12**	80 0N	90 0W
Axelfors	**73**	57 26N	13 7 E
Axholme, Isle of	**33**	53 30N	1 10 E
Axim	**120**	4 51N	2 15W
Axintele	**70**	44 37N	26 47 E
Axiós, R.	**68**	40 57N	22 35 E
Axmarsbruk	**72**	61 3N	17 10 E
Axminster	**30**	50 47N	3 1W
Axmouth	**30**	50 43N	3 2W
Axstedt	**48**	53 26N	8 43 E
Axvall	**73**	58 23N	13 34 E
Ay	**43**	49 3N	4 0 E
Ay, R.	**84**	56 8N	57 40 E
Ayabaca	**174**	4 40 S	79 53W
Ayabe	**111**	35 20N	135 20 E
Ayacucho, Argent.	**172**	37 5 S	58 20W
Ayacucho, Peru	**174**	13 0 S	74 0W
Ayaguz	**76**	48 10N	80 0 E
Ayakkuduk	**85**	41 12N	65 12 E
Ayakok'umu Hu	**105**	37 30N	89 20 E
Ayakudi	**97**	10 57N	77 6 E
Ayamonte	**57**	37 12N	7 24W
Ayan	**77**	56 30N	138 16 E
Ayancık	**82**	41 57N	34 18 E
Ayapel	**174**	8 19N	75 9W
Ayapel, Sa. de	**174**	7 45N	75 30W
Ayaş	**82**	40 10N	32 14 E
Ayaviri	**174**	14 50 S	70 35W
Aydın □	**92**	37 40N	27 40 E
Aye	**47**	50 14N	5 18 E
Ayenngré	**121**	8 40N	1 1 E
Ayer Hitam	**101**	1 55N	103 11 E
Ayeritam	**101**	5 24N	100 15 E
Ayers Rock	**136**	25 23 S	131 5 E
Ayiá	**68**	39 43N	22 45 E
Áyia Anna	**69**	38 52N	23 24 E
Ayía Marína, Kásos, Greece	**69**	35 27N	26 53 E
Ayía Marína, Leros, Greece	**69**	37 11N	26 48 E
Ayía Paraskeví	**68**	39 14N	26 16 E
Ayía Rouméli	**69**	35 14N	23 58 E
Ayiássos	**69**	39 5N	26 23 E
Áyios Andréas	**69**	37 21N	22 45 E
Áyios Evstrátios	**68**	39 34N	24 58 E
Áyios Ioánnis, Ákra	**69**	35 20N	25 40 E
Áyios Kírikos	**69**	37 34N	26 17 E
Áyios Matthaíos	**68**	39 30N	19 47 E
Áyios Míron	**69**	35 15N	25 1 E
Áyios Nikólaos	**69**	35 11N	25 41 E
Áyios Pétros	**69**	38 38N	20 33 E
Áyios Yeóryios	**69**	37 28N	23 57 E
Aykathonísi	**69**	37 28N	27 0 E
Ayke, Ozero	**84**	51 57N	61 36 E
Aylesbury	**29**	51 48N	0 49W
Aylesford	**29**	51 18N	0 29 E
Aylmer L.	**148**	64 0N	108 30W
Aylsham	**29**	52 48N	1 16 E
Ayn Zālah	**92**	36 45N	42 35 E
'Ayn Zaqqūt	**119**	29 0N	19 30 E
Ayna	**59**	38 34N	2 3W
Aynho	**28**	51 59N	1 15W
Ayni	**85**	39 23N	68 32 E
Ayolas	**172**	27 10 S	56 59W
Ayom	**123**	7 49N	28 23 E
Ayon, Ostrov	**77**	69 50N	169 0 E
Ayora	**59**	39 3N	1 3W
Ayr, Austral.	**138**	19 35 S	147 25 E
Ayr, U.K.	**34**	55 28N	4 37W
Ayr (□)	**26**	55 25N	4 25W
Ayr, Heads of	**34**	55 25N	4 43W
Ayr, R.	**34**	55 29N	4 40W
Ayre, Pt. of	**37**	58 55N	2 43W
Ayre, Pt. of I.o.M.	**32**	54 27N	4 21W
Aysgarth	**32**	54 18N	2 0W
Aysha	**123**	10 50N	42 23 E
Ayton	**138**	15 45 S	145 25 E
Ayton, Borders, U.K.	**35**	55 51N	2 6W
Ayton, N. Yorks., U.K.	**33**	54 15N	0 29W
Aytos	**67**	42 47N	27 16 E
Aytoska Planina	**67**	42 45N	27 30 E
Ayu, Kepulauan	**103**	0 35N	131 5 E
Ayutla, Guat.	**166**	14 40N	92 10W

Ayutla Balasore

Ayutla, Mexico 165 16 58N 99 17W
Ayutthaya = Phra Nakhon Si A. 101 14 25N 100 30 E
Ayvalık 92 39 20N 26 46 E
Aywaille 47 50 28N 5 40 E
Az Zahiriya 90 31 25N 34 58 E
Az Zahran 92 26 10N 50 7 E
Az-Zarqā 90 32 5N 36 4 E
Az Zāwiyah 119 32 52N 12 56 E
Az-Zilfī 92 26 12N 44 52 E
Az Zintān 119 31 59N 12 9 E
Az Zubayr 92 30 20N 47 50 E
Azambuja 57 39 4N 8 51W
Azamgarh 95 26 35N 83 13 E
Azaouak, Vallée de l' 121 15 50N 3 20 E
Azārbāijān □ 92 37 0N 44 30 E
Azare 121 11 55N 10 10 E
Azay-le-Rideau 42 47 16N 0 30 E
Azazga 119 36 48N 4 22 E
Azbine = Aïr 121 18 0N 8 0 E
Azeffoun 119 36 51N 4 26 E
Azemmour 118 33 14N 9 20W
Azerbaijan S.S.R. □ 83 40 20N 48 0 E
Azezo 123 12 28N 37 15 E
Azilal,Beni Mallal 118 32 0N 6 30W
Azimganj 95 24 14N 84 16 E
Aznalcóllar 57 37 32N 6 17W
Azogues 174 2 35 S 78 0W
Azor 90 32 2N 34 48 E
Azores, Is. 14 38 44N 29 0W
Azov 83 47 3N 39 25 E
Azov Sea = Azovskoye More 82 46 0N 36 30 E
Azovskoye More 82 46 0N 36 30 E
Azovy 76 64 55N 64 35 E
Azpeitia 58 43 12N 2 19W
Azrou 118 33 28N 5 19W
Aztec 161 36 54N 108 0W
Azúa de Compostela 167 18 25N 70 44W
Azuaga 57 38 16N 5 39W
Azuara 58 41 15N 0 53W
Azuara, R. 58 41 12N 0 55W
Azúcar, Presa del 165 26 0N 99 5W
Azuer, R. 57 38 50N 3 15W
Azuero, Pen. de 166 7 30N 80 30W
Azul 172 36 42 S 59 43W
Azusa 163 34 8N 117 52W
Azzaba 119 36 48N 7 6 E
Azzano Décimo 63 45 53N 12 46 E

B

B. Curri 68 42 22N 20 5 E
Ba Don 100 17 45N 106 26 E
Ba Dong 101 9 40N 106 33 E
Ba Ngoi = Cam Lam 101 11 50N 109 10 E
Ba, R. 56 13 5N 109 0 E
Ba Tri 101 10 2N 106 36 E
Baa 103 10 50 S 123 0 E
Baamonde 56 43 7N 7 44W
Baar 51 47 12N 8 32 E
Baarle Nassau 47 51 27N 4 56 E
Baarlo 47 51 20N 6 6 E
Baarn 46 52 12N 5 17 E
Bāb el Māndeb 91 12 35N 43 25 E
Baba Burnu 68 39 29N 26 2 E
Baba dag 83 41 0N 48 55 E
Baba, Mt. 67 42 44N 23 59 E
Babaçulândia 170 7 13 S 47 46W
Babadag 70 44 53N 28 44 E
Babaeski 67 41 26N 27 6 E
Babahoyo 174 1 40 S 79 30W
Babakin 137 32 7 S 118 1 E
Babana 121 10 31N 3 46 E
Babar, Alg. 119 35 10N 7 6 E
Babar, Pak. 94 31 7N 69 32 E
Babar, I. 103 8 0 S 129 30 E
Babarkach 94 29 45N 68 0 E
Babayevo 81 59 24N 35 55 E
Babb 160 48 56N 113 27W
Babbitt 163 38 32N 118 39W
Babenhausen 49 49 57N 8 56 E
Babi Besar, P. 101 2 25N 103 59 E
Babia Gora 54 49 38N 19 38 E
Babile 123 9 16N 42 11 E
Babinda 138 17 20 S 145 56 E
Babine 152 55 20N 126 35W
Babine L. 152 54 48N 126 0W
Babine, R. 152 55 45N 127 44W
Babo 103 2 30 S 133 30 E
Babócsa 53 46 2N 17 21 E
Babol 93 36 40N 52 50 E
Babol Sar 93 36 45N 52 45 E
Baboma 126 2 30N 28 10 E
Baborówo Kietrz 53 50 7N 18 1 E
Baboua 124 5 49N 14 58 E
Babuna, mts. 66 41 30N 21 40 E
Babura 121 12 51N 8 59 E
Babusar Pass 95 35 12N 73 59 E
Babushkin 81 55 45N 37 40 E
Babušnica 66 43 7N 22 27 E
Babylon, Iraq 92 32 40N 44 30 E
Babylon, U.S.A. 162 40 42N 73 20W
Bač 66 45 29N 19 17 E
Bac Can 100 22 08N 105 49 E
Bac Giang 100 21 16N 106 11 E
Bac Kan 101 22 5N 105 50 E
Bac Lieu = Vinh Loi 101 9 17N 105 43 E
Bac Ninh 100 21 13N 106 4 E
Bac Phan 100 22 0N 105 0 E
Bac Quang 100 22 30N 104 48 E
Bacabal 170 4 15N 44 45W
Bacalar 165 18 12N 87 53W
Bacan,Pulau 103 0 50 S 127 30 E
Bacarès, Le 44 42 47N 3 3 E
Bacarra 103 18 15N 120 37 E
Baccarat 43 48 28N 6 42 E
Bacchus Marsh 140 37 43 S 144 27 E
Bacerac 164 30 18N 108 50W
Bach Long Vi,Dao 100 20 10N 107 40 E
Bachaquero 174 9 56N 71 8W
Bacharach 49 50 3N 7 46 E
Bachclina 76 57 45N 67 20 E
Bachok 101 6 4N 102 25 E
Bachuma 123 6 31N 36 1 E
Bačina 66 43 42N 21 23 E
Back 36 58 17N 6 20W
Back, R. 148 65 10N 104 0W
Bačka Palanka 66 45 17N 19 27 E
Bačka Topola 66 45 49N 19 39 E
Bäckefors 73 58 48N 12 9 E
Bački Petrovac 66 45 29N 19 32 E
Backnang 49 48 57N 9 26 E
Backstairs Passage 133 35 40 S 138 5 E
Bacolod 103 10 40N 122 57 E
Bacqueville 42 49 47N 1 0 E
Bacs-Kiskun □ 53 46 43N 19 30 E
Bácsalmás 53 46 8N 19 17 E
Bacton 29 52 50N 1 29 E
Bacuit 103 11 20N 119 20 E
Bacup 32 53 42N 2 12W
Bacǔu 70 46 35N 26 55 E
Bacǔu □ 70 46 30N 26 45 E
Bad Aussee 52 47 43N 13 45 E
Bad Axe 150 43 48N 82 59W
Bad Bergzabem 49 49 6N 8 0 E
Bad Bramstedt 48 53 56N 9 53 E
Bad Doberan 48 54 6N 11 55 E
Bad Driburg 48 51 44N 9 0 E
Bad Ems 49 50 22N 7 44 E
Bad Frankenhausen 48 51 21N 11 3 E
Bad Freienwalde 52 52 46N 14 2 E
Bad Godesberg 48 50 41N 7 4 E
Bad Hersfeld 48 50 52N 9 42 E
Bad Hofgastein 52 47 17N 13 6 E
Bad Homburg 49 50 17N 8 33 E
Bad Honnef 48 50 39N 7 13 E
Bad Ischl 52 47 44N 13 38 E
Bad Kissingen 49 50 11N 10 5 E
Bad Kreuznach 49 49 47N 7 47 E
Bad Lands 158 43 40N 102 10W
Bad Lauterberg 48 51 38N 10 29 E
Bad Leonfelden 52 48 31N 14 18 E
Bad Lippspringe 48 51 47N 8 46 E
Bad Mergentheim 49 49 29N 9 47 E
Bad Münstereifel 48 50 33N 6 46 E
Bad Nauheim 49 50 24N 8 45 E
Bad Oeynhausen 48 52 16N 8 45 E
Bad Oldesloe 48 53 56N 10 17 E
Bad Orb 49 50 16N 9 21 E
Bad Pyrmont 48 51 59N 9 5 E
Bad, R. 158 44 10N 100 50W
Bad Ragaz 51 47 0N 9 30 E
Bad St. Peter 48 54 23N 8 32 E
Bad Salzuflen 48 52 8N 8 44 E
Bad Segeberg 48 53 58N 10 16 E
Bad Tölz 49 47 43N 11 34 E
Bad Waldsee 49 47 56N 9 46 E
Bad Wildungen 48 51 7N 9 10 E
Bad Wimpfen 49 49 12N 9 10 E
Bad Windsheim 49 49 29N 10 25 E
Badagara 97 11 35N 75 40 E
Badagri 121 6 25N 2 55 E
Badajoz 57 38 50N 6 59W
Badajoz □ 57 38 40N 6 30W
Badakhshan □ 93 36 30N 71 0 E
Badalona 58 41 26N 2 15 E
Badalzai 94 29 50N 65 35 E
Badampahar 96 22 10N 86 10 E
Badanah 92 30 58N 41 30 E
Badas 102 4 33N 114 25 E
Badas, Kepulauan 102 0 45N 107 5 E
Baddo, R. 93 28 15N 65 0 E
Bade 103 7 10 S 139 35 E
Baden, Austria 53 48 1N 16 13 E
Baden, Switz. 51 47 28N 8 18 E
Baden-Baden 49 48 45N 8 15 E
Baden Park 140 32 8 S 144 12 E
Baden-Württemberg □ 49 48 40N 9 0 E
Badenoch 37 58 16N 4 5W
Badenscoth 37 57 27N 2 30W
Badeso 123 9 58N 40 52 E
Badgastein 52 47 7N 13 9 E
Badger, Can. 151 49 0N 56 4W
Badger, U.S.A. 163 36 38N 119 1W
Badghis □ 93 35 0N 63 0 E
Badgom 95 34 1N 74 45 E
Badhoevedorp 46 52 20N 4 47 E
Badia Polesine 63 45 6N 11 30 E
Badin 94 24 38N 68 54 E
Badnera 96 20 48N 77 44 E
Badogo 120 11 2N 8 13W
Badrinath 95 30 45N 79 30 E
Baduen 91 7 15N 47 40 E
Badulla 97 7 1N 81 7 E
Badupi 98 21 36N 93 27 E
Bække 73 55 35N 9 6 E
Baena 57 37 37N 4 20W
Baerami Creek 141 32 27 S 150 27 E
Baetas 174 6 5 S 62 15W
Baexem 47 51 13N 5 53 E
Baeza, Ecuador 174 0 25 S 77 45W
Baeza, Spain 59 37 57N 3 25W
Bafa 93 31 40N 55 25 E
Bafa Gölü 69 37 30N 27 29 E
Bafatá 120 12 8N 15 20W
Baffin Bay 12 72 0N 64 0W
Baffin I. 149 68 0N 75 0W
Bafia 121 4 40N 11 10 E
Bafilo 121 9 22N 1 22 E
Bafing, R. 120 11 40N 10 45W
Baflo 46 53 22N 6 31 E
Bafoulabé 120 13 50N 10 55W
Bafq 93 31 40N 55 20 E
Bafra 82 41 34N 35 54 E
Baft 93 29 15N 56 38 E
Bafut 121 6 6N 10 2 E
Bafwakwandji 126 1 12N 26 52 E
Bafwasende 126 1 3N 27 5 E
Bagalkot 96 16 10N 75 40 E
Bagamoyo 126 6 28 S 38 55 E
Bagamoyo □ 126 6 20 S 38 30 E
Bagan Datok 101 3 59N 100 47 E
Bagan Serai 101 5 1N 100 32 E
Bagan Siapiapi 102 2 12N 100 50 E
Baganga 103 7 34N 126 33 E
Bagasra 94 21 59N 71 77 E
Bagawi 123 12 20N 34 18 E
Bagdad 163 34 35N 115 53W
Bagdarin 77 54 26N 113 36 E
Bagé 173 31 20 S 54 15W
Bagenalstown = Muine Bheag 39 52 42N 6 57W
Baggs 160 41 8N 107 46W
Baggy Pt. 30 51 11N 4 12W
Bagh 95 33 59N 73 45 E
Bagh nam Faoileann, B. 36 57 22N 7 13W
Baghdād 92 33 20N 44 30 E
Bagherhat 98 22 40N 89 47 E
Bagheria 64 38 5N 13 30 E
Baghin 93 30 12N 56 45 E
Baghlan 93 36 12N 69 0 E
Baghlan □ 93 36 0N 68 30 E
Baginbun Hd. 39 52 10N 6 50W
Bagley 158 47 30N 95 22W
Bagnacavallo 63 44 25N 11 58 E
Bagnara Cálabra 65 38 16N 15 49 E
Bagnères-de-Bigorre 44 43 5N 0 9 E
Bagnères-de-Luchon 44 42 47N 0 38 E
Bagni di Lucca 62 44 1N 10 37 E
Bagno di Romagna 63 43 50N 11 59 E
Bagnoles-de-l'Orne 42 48 32N 0 25W
Bagnolo Mella 62 45 27N 10 14 E
Bagnols-les-Bains 44 44 30N 3 40 E
Bagnols-sur-Cèze 45 44 10N 4 36 E
Bagnorégio 63 42 38N 12 7 E
Bagolino 62 45 49N 10 28 E
Bagotville 151 48 22N 70 54W
Bagrdan 66 44 5N 21 11 E
Bagshot 29 51 22N 0 41W
Baguio 103 16 26N 120 34 E
Bahabón de Esgueva 58 41 52N 3 43W
Bahadurabad 98 25 11N 89 44 E
Bahadurgarh 94 28 40N 76 57 E
Bahama, Canal Viejo de 166 22 10N 77 30W
Bahama Is. 167 24 40N 74 0W
Bahamas ■ 167 24 0N 74 0W
Bahariya,El Wâhât el 122 28 0N 28 50 E
Bahau 101 2 48N 102 26 E
Bahawalnagar 94 30 0N 73 15 E
Bahawalpur 94 29 37N 71 40 E
Bahawalpur □ 94 29 5N 71 3 E
Baheri 95 28 45N 79 34 E
Baheta 123 13 27N 42 10 E
Bahi 126 5 58 S 35 21 E
Bahi Swamp 126 6 10 S 35 0 E
Bahia = Salvador 171 13 0 S 38 30W
Bahia □ 171 12 0N 42 0W
Bahía Blanca 172 38 35 S 62 13W
Bahía de Caráquez 174 0 40 S 80 27W
Bahía Honda 166 22 54N 83 10W
Bahía, Islas de la 166 16 45N 86 15W
Bahía Laura 176 48 10 S 66 30W
Bahía Negra 174 20 5 S 58 5W
Bahir Dar Giyorgis 123 11 33N 37 25 E
Bahmer 118 27 32N 0 10W
Bahönye 53 46 25N 17 28 E
Bahr Aouk 124 9 20N 20 40 E
Bahr Dar 123 11 37N 37 10 E
Bahr el Abiad 123 9 30N 31 40 E
Bahr el Ahmer □ 122 20 0N 35 0 E
Bahr el Arab 123 9 50N 27 10 E
Bahr el Azraq 123 10 30N 35 0 E
Bahr el Ghazâl □ 123 7 0N 28 0 E
Bahr el Ghazâl, R. 123 9 0N 30 0 E
Bahr el Jebel 123 7 30N 30 30 E
Bahr Salamat 124 10 0N 19 0 E
Bahr Yûsef 122 28 25N 30 35 E
Bahra 92 21 25N 39 32 E
Bahra el Burullus 122 31 28N 30 48 E
Bahra el Manzala 122 31 28N 32 01 E
Bahraich 95 27 38N 81 50 E
Bahrain ■ 93 26 0N 50 35 E
Bahramabad 93 30 28N 56 2 E
Bahu Kalat 93 25 50N 61 20 E
Bai 120 13 35N 3 28W
Bai Bung, Mui 101 8 38N 104 44 E
Bai Duc 100 18 3N 105 49 E
Bai Thuong 100 19 54N 105 23 E
Baia-Mare 70 47 40N 23 17 E
Baia-Sprie 70 47 41N 23 43W
Baião 170 2 40 S 49 40W
Baïbokoum 117 7 40N 14 45 E
Baidoa 91 3 8N 43 30 E
Baie Comeau 151 49 12N 68 10W
Baie de l'Abri 151 50 3N 67 0W
Baie Johan Beetz 151 50 18N 62 50W
Baie St. Paul 151 47 28N 70 32W
Baie Trinité 151 49 25N 67 20W
Baie Verte 151 49 55N 56 12W
Baignes 44 45 28N 0 25W
Baigneux-les-Juifs 43 47 31N 4 39 E
Ba'ījī 92 35 0N 43 30 E
Baikal, L. 77 53 0N 108 0 E
Bailadila, Mt. 96 18 43N 81 15 E
Baildon 33 53 52N 1 46W
Baile Atha Cliath = Dublin 39 53 20N 6 18W
Bailei 123 6 44N 40 18 E
Bailén 57 38 8N 3 48W
Baileux 47 50 2N 4 23 E
Bailhongal 97 15 55N 74 53 E
Bailique, Ilha 170 1 2N 49 58W
Bailleul 43 50 44N 2 41 E
Baillieborough 38 53 55N 7 0W
Baimuru 135 7 35 S 144 51 E
Bain-de-Bretagne 42 47 50N 1 40W
Bainbridge, U.K. 32 54 18N 2 7W
Bainbridge, Ga., U.S.A. 157 30 53N 84 34W
Bainbridge, N.Y., U.S.A. 162 42 17N 75 29W
Baing 103 10 14 S 120 34 E
Bainville 158 48 8N 104 10W
Bainyik 135 3 40 S 143 4 E
Baird 159 32 25N 99 25W
Baird Inlet 147 64 49N 164 18W
Baird Mts. 147 67 10N 160 15W
Bairnsdale 141 37 48 S 147 36 E
Baissa 121 7 14N 10 38 E
Baitadi 95 29 35N 80 25 E
Baixa Grande 171 11 57 S 40 11W
Baiyuda 122 17 35N 32 07 E
Baja 53 46 12N 18 59 E
Baja California 164 32 10N 115 12W
Baja, Pta. 164 29 50N 116 0W
Bajah, Wadi 122 23 14N 39 20 E
Bajana 94 23 7N 71 49 E
Bajimba 139 29 22 S 152 0 E
Bajimba, Mt. 139 29 17 S 152 6 E
Bajina Bašta 66 43 58N 19 35 E
Bajitpur 95 24 13N 91 0 E
Bajmok 66 45 57N 19 24 E
Bajo Boquete 167 8 49N 82 27W
Bajoga 121 10 57N 11 20 E
Bajool 138 23 40 S 150 35 E
Bak 53 46 43N 16 51 E
Bakal 84 54 56N 58 48 E
Bakala 117 6 15N 20 20 E
Bakanas 85 44 50N 76 15 E
Bakar 63 45 18N 14 32 E
Bakel, Neth. 47 51 30N 5 45 E
Bakel, Senegal 120 14 56N 12 20W
Baker, Calif., U.S.A. 163 35 16N 116 8W
Baker, Mont., U.S.A. 158 46 22N 104 12W
Baker, Nev., U.S.A. 160 38 59N 114 7W
Baker, Oreg., U.S.A. 160 44 50N 117 55W
Baker Is. 130 0 10N 176 35 E
Baker, L., Austral. 137 26 54 S 126 5 E
Baker, L., Can. 148 64 0N 96 0W
Baker Lake 148 64 20N 96 3W
Baker Mt. 160 48 50N 121 49W
Baker's Dozen Is. 150 56 45N 78 45W
Bakersfield 163 35 25N 119 0W
Bakewell 33 53 13N 1 40W
Bakhchisaray 82 44 40N 33 45 E
Bakhmach 80 51 10N 32 45 E
Bakhtiari □ 92 32 0N 49 0 E
Bakia 123 5 18N 25 45 E
Bakinskikh Komissarov 92 39 20N 49 15 E
Bakırköy 67 40 59N 28 53 E
Bakkafjörðr 74 66 2N 14 48W
Bakkagerði 74 65 31N 13 49W
Bakke 71 58 25N 6 39 E
Bakony Forest = Bakony Hegység 53 47 10N 17 30 E
Bakony Hegység 53 47 10N 17 30 E
Bakony, R. 53 47 35N 17 54 E
Bakori 121 11 34N 7 25 E
Bakouma 117 5 40N 22 56 E
Bakov 52 50 27N 14 55 E
Bakpakty 85 44 35N 76 40 E
Bakr Uzyak 84 52 59N 58 38 E
Baku 83 40 25N 49 45 E
Bakwanga = Mbuji Mayi 124 6 9 S 23 40 E
Bal'a 90 32 20N 35 6 E
Bala, L. = Tegid, L. 31 52 53N 3 38W
Balabac I. 102 8 0N 117 0 E
Balabac, Selat 102 7 53N 117 5 E
Balabagh 94 34 25N 70 12 E
Balabakk 92 34 0N 36 10 E
Balabalangan, Kepulauan 102 2 20 S 117 30 E
Balaghat 96 21 49N 80 12 E
Balaghat Ra. 96 18 50N 76 30 E
Balaguer 58 41 50N 0 50 E
Balakhna 81 56 35N 43 32 E
Balaklava, Austral. 140 34 7 S 138 22 E
Balaklava, U.S.S.R. 82 44 30N 33 30 E
Balakleya 82 49 28N 36 55 E
Balakovo 81 52 4N 47 55 E
Balallan 36 58 5N 6 35W
Balancán 165 17 48N 91 32W
Balanda 81 51 30N 44 40 E
Balangir 96 20 43N 83 35 E
Balapur 96 21 22N 76 45 E
Balashikha 81 55 49N 37 59 E
Balashov 81 51 30N 43 10 E
Balasinor 94 22 57N 73 23 E
Balasore 96 21 35N 87 3 E

Balassagyarmat **Bangor**

Balassagyarmat	53	48 4N	19 15 E
Balât	122	25 36N	29 19 E
Balaton	53	46 50N	17 40 E
Balatonfüred	53	46 58N	17 54 E
Balatonszentgyörgy	53	46 41N	17 19 E
Balazote	59	38 54N	2 09W
Balbeggie	35	56 26N	3 19W
Balbi, Mt.	135	5 55S	154 58 E
Balblair	37	57 39N	4 11W
Balboa	166	9 0N	79 30W
Balbriggan	38	53 35N	6 10W
Balcarce	172	38 0S	58 10W
Balcarres	153	50 50N	103 35W
Balchik	67	43 28N	28 11 E
Balclutha	143	46 15S	169 45 E
Bald Hd.	137	35 6S	118 1 E
Bald Hill, W. Australia, Austral.	137	31 36S	116 13 E
Bald Hill, W. Australia, Austral.	137	24 55S	119 57 E
Bald I.	137	34 57S	118 27 E
Bald Knob	159	35 20N	91 35W
Baldegger-See	51	47 12N	8 17 E
Balder, oilfield	19	59 10N	2 20 E
Balderton	33	53 3N	0 46W
Baldock	29	51 59N	0 11W
Baldock L.	153	56 33N	97 57W
Baldoyle	38	53 24N	6 10W
Baldwin, Fla., U.S.A.	156	30 15N	82 10W
Baldwin, Mich., U.S.A.	156	43 54N	85 53W
Baldwinsville	162	43 10N	76 19W
Bale	63	45 4N	13 46 E
Baleares □	58	39 30N	3 0 E
Baleares, Islas	58	39 30N	3 0 E
Balearic Is. = Baleares, Islas	58	39 30N	3 0 E
Baleia, Ponta da	171	17 40S	39 7W
Balen	47	51 10N	5 10 E
Baler	103	15 46N	121 34 E
Balerna	51	45 52N	9 0 E
Baleshare I.	36	57 30N	7 21W
Balezino	84	58 2N	53 6 E
Balfate	166	15 48N	86 25W
Balfe's Creek	138	20 12S	145 55 E
Balfour, S. Afr.	129	26 38S	28 35 E
Balfour, U.K.	37	59 2N	2 54W
Balfour Downs	137	22 45S	120 50 E
Balfouriyya	90	32 38N	35 18 E
Balfron	34	56 4N	4 20W
Bali	121	5 54N	10 0 E
Bali □	102	8 20S	115 0 E
Bali, I.	102	8 20S	115 0 E
Bali, Selat	103	8 30S	114 35 E
Baligród	54	49 20N	22 17 E
Balikesir	92	39 35N	27 58 E
Balikpapan	102	1 10S	116 55 E
Balimbing	103	5 10N	120 3 E
Balimo	135	8 6S	142 57 E
Baling	101	5 41N	100 55 E
Balintore	37	57 45N	3 55W
Balipara	99	26 50N	92 45 E
Balit	95	36 15N	74 40 E
Baliza	175	16 0S	52 20W
Balk	46	52 54N	5 35 E
Balkan Mts. = Stara Planina	67	43 15N	23 0 E
Balkan Pen.	16	42 0N	22 0 E
Balkh = Wazirabad	93	36 44N	66 47 E
Balkh □	93	36 30N	67 0 E
Balkhash	76	46 50N	74 50 E
Balkhash, Ozero	76	40 0N	74 50 E
Balla, Ireland	38	53 48N	9 7W
Balla, Pak.	99	24 10N	91 35 E
Ballachulish	36	56 40N	5 10W
Balladonia	137	32 27S	123 51 E
Ballagan Pt.	38	54 0N	6 6W
Ballaghaderreen	38	53 55N	8 35W
Ballantrae	34	55 6N	5 0W
Ballara	140	32 19S	140 45 E
Ballarat	139	37 33S	143 50 E
Ballard, L.	137	29 20S	120 10 E
Ballarpur	96	19 50N	79 23 E
Ballater	37	57 2N	3 2W
Ballaugh	32	54 20N	4 32W
Balldale	141	36 20N	146 33 E
Ballenas, Canal de las	164	29 10N	113 45W
Balleni	70	45 48N	27 51 E
Balleny Is.	13	66 30S	163 0 E
Ballia	95	25 46N	84 12 E
Ballickmoyler	39	52 54N	7 2W
Ballidu	137	30 35S	116 45 E
Ballina, Austral.	139	28 50S	153 31 E
Ballina, Mayo, Ireland	38	54 7N	9 10W
Ballina, Tipp., Ireland	39	52 49N	8 27W
Ballinagar	39	53 15N	7 21W
Ballinagh = Bellananagh	38	53 55N	7 25W
Ballinalack	38	53 38N	7 28W
Ballinalea	39	53 0N	6 8W
Ballinalee	38	53 46N	7 40W
Ballinamallard	38	54 30N	7 36W
Ballinameen	38	53 54N	8 19W
Ballinamore	38	54 3N	7 48W
Ballinamore Bridge	38	53 30N	8 24W
Ballinascarty	39	51 40N	8 52W
Ballinasloe	39	53 20N	8 12W
Ballincollig	39	51 52N	8 35W
Ballindaggin	39	52 33N	6 43W
Ballinderry	38	53 2N	8 13W
Ballinderry R.	38	54 40N	6 32W
Ballindine	38	53 40N	8 57W
Ballineen	39	51 43N	8 57W
Balling	73	56 38N	8 51 E
Ballingarry, Lim., Ireland	39	53 1N	8 3W
Ballingarry, Tipp., Ireland	39	52 29N	8 50W
Ballingarry, Tipp., Ireland	39	52 35N	7 32W
Ballingeary	39	51 51N	9 13W
Ballinger	159	31 45N	99 58W
Ballinhassig	39	51 48N	8 33W
Ballinlough	38	53 45N	8 39W
Ballinluig	37	56 40N	3 40W
Ballinrobe	38	53 36N	9 13W
Ballinskelligs	39	51 50N	10 17W
Ballinskelligs B.	39	51 46N	10 11W
Ballintober	38	53 43N	8 25W
Ballintoy	38	55 13N	6 20W
Ballintra	38	54 35N	8 9W
Ballinunty	39	52 36N	7 40W
Ballinure	39	52 34N	7 46W
Ballivian	172	22 41S	62 10W
Ballivor	38	53 32N	6 50W
Ballo Pt.	79	8 55N	13 18W
Balloch	34	56 0N	4 35W
Ballon	39	48 10N	0 16 E
Ballston Spa	162	43 0N	73 51W
Ballybay	38	54 8N	6 52W
Ballybofey	38	54 48N	7 47W
Ballyboghil	38	53 32N	6 16W
Ballybogy	38	55 8N	6 33W
Ballybunion	39	52 30N	9 40W
Ballycanew	39	52 37N	6 18W
Ballycarney	39	52 35N	6 44W
Ballycastle	38	55 12N	6 15W
Ballycastle B.	38	55 12N	6 15W
Ballyclare, Ireland	38	53 40N	8 0W
Ballyclare, U.K.	38	54 46N	6 0W
Ballyclerahan	39	52 25N	7 48W
Ballycolla	39	52 53N	7 27W
Ballyconneely	38	53 27N	10 5W
Ballyconneely B.	38	53 23N	10 8W
Ballyconnell	38	54 7N	7 35W
Ballycotton	39	51 50N	8 0W
Ballycroy	38	54 2N	9 49W
Ballydavid	39	53 12N	8 28W
Ballydavid Hd.	39	52 15N	10 20W
Ballydehob	39	51 34N	9 28W
Ballydonegan	39	51 37N	10 12W
Ballydonegan B.	39	51 38N	10 6W
Ballyduff, Kerry, Ireland	39	52 27N	9 40W
Ballyduff, Waterford, Ireland	39	52 9N	8 2W
Ballyforan	38	53 29N	8 18W
Ballygar	38	53 33N	8 20W
Ballygarrett	39	52 34N	6 15W
Ballygawley	38	54 27N	7 2W
Ballyglass	38	53 45N	9 9W
Ballygorman	38	55 23N	7 20W
Ballyhahill	39	52 33N	9 13W
Ballyhaise	38	54 3N	7 20W
Ballyhalbert	38	54 30N	5 28W
Ballyhaunis	38	53 47N	8 47W
Ballyheige I.	39	52 22N	9 51W
Ballyhoura Hills	39	52 18N	8 33W
Ballyjamesduff	38	53 52N	7 11W
Ballylanders	39	52 25N	8 21W
Ballylaneen	39	52 10N	7 25W
Ballylongford	39	52 34N	9 30W
Ballylooby	39	52 20N	7 59W
Ballylynan	39	52 57N	7 02W
Ballymacoda	39	51 53N	7 56W
Ballymagorry	38	54 52N	7 26W
Ballymahon	38	53 35N	7 45W
Ballymena	38	54 53N	6 18W
Ballymena □	38	54 53N	6 18W
Ballymoe	38	53 41N	8 28W
Ballymoney	38	55 5N	6 30W
Ballymoney □	38	55 5N	6 23W
Ballymore	39	53 30N	7 40W
Ballymore Eustace	39	53 8N	6 38W
Ballymote	38	54 5N	8 30W
Ballymurphy	39	52 33N	6 52W
Ballymurray	38	53 36N	8 8W
Ballynabola	39	52 21N	6 50W
Ballynacally	39	52 42N	9 7W
Ballynacargy	38	53 35N	7 32W
Ballynacorra	39	51 53N	8 10W
Ballynagore	38	53 24N	7 29W
Ballynahinch	38	54 24N	5 55W
Ballynahown	38	53 21N	7 52W
Ballynameen	38	54 58N	6 41W
Ballynamona	39	52 5N	8 39W
Ballynure	38	54 47N	5 59W
Ballyquintin, Pt.	38	54 20N	5 30W
Ballyragget	39	52 47N	7 20W
Ballyroan	39	52 57N	7 20W
Ballyronan	38	54 43N	6 32W
Ballyroney	38	54 17N	6 8W
Ballysadare	38	54 12N	8 30W
Ballyshannon	38	54 30N	8 10W
Ballyvaughan	39	53 7N	9 10W
Ballyvourney	39	51 57N	9 10W
Ballyvoy	38	55 11N	6 11W
Ballywalter	38	54 33N	5 30W
Ballywilliam	39	52 27N	6 52W
Balmaceda	176	46 0S	71 50W
Balmaclellan	35	55 6N	4 5W
Balmazújváros	53	47 37N	21 21 E
Balmedie	37	57 14N	2 4W
Balmhorn	50	46 26N	7 42 E
Balmoral	140	37 15S	141 48 E
Balmoral For.	37	57 0N	3 15W
Balmorhea	159	31 2N	103 41W
Balnapaling	37	57 42N	4 2W
Balonne, R.	139	28 47S	147 56 E
Balovale	125	13 30S	23 15 E
Balquhidder	34	56 22N	4 22W
Balrampur	95	27 30N	82 20 E
Balranald	140	34 38S	143 33 E
Balş	70	44 22N	24 5 E
Balsas	165	18 0N	99 40W
Balsas, R., Goias, Brazil	170	9 0S	48 0W
Balsas, R., Maranhão, Brazil	170	7 15S	44 35W
Balsas, R., Mexico	164	18 30N	101 20W
Bålsta	72	59 35N	17 30 E
Balsthal	50	47 19N	7 41 E
Balta, Rumania	70	44 54N	22 38 E
Balta, U.S.A.	158	48 12N	100 7W
Balta, U.S.S.R.	82	48 2N	29 45 E
Balta, I.	36	60 44N	0 49W
Baltanás	56	41 56N	4 15W
Baltasound	36	60 47N	0 53W
Baltic Sea	75	56 0N	20 0 E
Baltiisk	75	54 38N	19 55 E
Baltim	122	31 35N	31 10 E
Baltimore, Ireland	39	51 29N	9 22W
Baltimore, U.S.A.	162	39 18N	76 37W
Baltinglass	39	52 57N	6 42W
Baltrum	48	53 43N	7 25 E
Baluchistan □	93	27 30N	65 0 E
Balurghat	95	25 15N	88 44 E
Balvicar	34	56 17N	5 38W
Balygychan	77	63 56N	154 12 E
Bam	93	29 7N	58 14 E
Bam La	99	29 25N	98 35 E
Bama	121	11 33N	13 33 E
Bamako	120	12 34N	7 55W
Bamba	121	17 5N	1 0W
Bambari	117	5 40N	20 35 E
Bambaroo	107	18 50S	146 11 E
Bamberg, Ger.	49	49 54N	10 53 E
Bamberg, U.S.A.	157	33 19N	81 1W
Bambesi	123	9 45N	34 40 E
Bambey	120	14 42N	16 28W
Bambili	126	3 40N	26 0 E
Bamboo	138	14 34S	143 20 E
Bambouti	126	5 25N	27 12 E
Bambuí	171	20 1S	45 58W
Bamburgh	35	55 36N	1 42W
Bamenda	121	5 57N	10 11 E
Bamfield	152	48 45N	125 10W
Bamford	33	53 21N	1 41W
Bamian □	93	35 0N	67 0 E
Bamkin	121	6 3N	11 27 E
Bampton, Devon, U.K.	30	50 59N	3 29W
Bampton, Oxon., U.K.	28	51 44N	1 33W
Bampur	93	27 15N	60 21 E
Bampur, R.	93	27 20N	59 30 E
Ban Aranyaprathet	100	13 41N	102 30 E
Ban Ban	100	19 31N	103 15 E
Ban Bang Hin	101	9 32N	98 35 E
Ban Bua Chum	100	15 11N	101 12 E
Ban Bua Yai	100	15 33N	102 26 E
Ban Chiang Klang	100	19 15N	100 55 E
Ban Chik	100	17 15N	102 22 E
Ban Choho	100	15 2N	102 9 E
Ban Dan Lan Hoi	100	17 0N	99 35 E
Ban Don	100	12 53N	107 48 E
Ban Don = Surat Thani	101	9 8N	99 20 E
Ban Don, Go	101	9 20N	99 25 E
Ban Dong	100	19 14N	100 3 E
Ban Hong	100	18 18N	98 50 E
Ban Houei Sai	101	20 22N	100 32 E
Ban Kaeng	100	17 29N	100 7 E
Ban Kantang	101	7 25N	99 31 E
Ban Keun	100	18 22N	102 35 E
Ban Khai	100	12 46N	101 18 E
Ban Khe Bo	101	19 10N	104 39 E
Ban Kheun	100	20 13N	101 7 E
Ban Khlong Kua	101	6 57N	100 8 E
Ban Khuan Mao	101	7 50N	99 37 E
Ban Khun Yuam	100	18 49N	97 57 E
Ban Ko Yai Chim	101	11 17N	99 26 E
Ban Kok	100	16 40N	103 40 E
Ban Laem	100	13 13N	99 59 E
Ban Lao Ngam	100	15 28N	106 10 E
Ban Le Kathe	100	15 49N	98 53 E
Ban Mae Chedi	100	19 11N	99 31 E
Ban Mae Laeng	100	20 1N	99 17 E
Ban Mae Sariang	100	18 0N	97 56 E
Ban Me Thuot	100	12 40N	108 3 E
Ban Mi	100	15 3N	100 32 E
Ban Muong Mo	100	19 4N	103 58 E
Ban Na Mo	100	17 7N	105 40 E
Ban Na San	101	8 33N	99 52 E
Ban Na Tong	100	20 56N	101 47 E
Ban Nam Bac	100	20 38N	102 20 E
Ban Nam Ma	100	22 2N	101 37 E
Ban Ngang	100	15 59N	106 11 E
Ban Nong Bok	100	17 5N	104 48 E
Ban Nong Boua	100	15 40N	106 33 E
Ban Nong Pling	100	15 40N	100 10 E
Ban Pak Chan	101	10 32N	98 51 E
Ban Phai	100	16 4N	102 44 E
Ban Pong	100	13 50N	99 55 E
Ban Ron Phibun	101	8 9N	99 51 E
Ban Sanam Chai	101	7 33N	100 25 E
Ban Sangkha	100	14 37N	103 52 E
Ban Tak	100	17 2N	99 4 E
Ban Tako	100	14 5N	102 40 E
Ban Takua Pa	101	8 55N	98 25 E
Ban Tha Dua	100	17 59N	98 39 E
Ban Tha Li	100	17 37N	101 25 E
Ban Tha Nun	101	8 12N	98 18 E
Ban Thahine	100	14 12N	105 33 E
Ban Thateng	101	15 25N	106 27 E
Ban Xien Kok	100	20 54N	100 39 E
Ban Yen Nhan	100	20 57N	106 2 E
Baña, La, Punta de	58	40 33N	0 40 E
Banadar Daryay Oman □	93	25 30N	56 0 E
Banadia	174	6 54N	71 49W
Banagher	39	53 12N	8 0W
Banalia	126	1 32N	25 5 E
Banam	101	11 20N	105 17 E
Banamba	120	13 29N	7 22W
Banana	138	24 28S	150 8 E
Bananal, I. do	171	11 30S	50 30W
Banaras = Varanasi	95	25 22N	83 8 E
Banas, R., Gujarat, India	94	24 25N	72 30 E
Banas, R., Madhya Pradesh, India	95	24 15N	81 30 E
Bânâs, Ras.	122	23 57N	35 50 E
Banat □	66	45 45N	21 15 E
Banbridge	38	54 21N	6 17W
Banbridge □	38	54 21N	6 16W
Banbury	28	52 4N	1 21W
Banchory	37	57 3N	2 30W
Bancroft	150	45 3N	77 51W
Bancroft = Chililabombwe	127	12 18S	27 43 E
Band	67	46 30N	24 25 E
Band-i-Turkistan, Ra.	93	35 2N	64 0 E
Banda	95	25 30N	80 26 E
Banda Aceh	102	5 35N	95 20 E
Banda Banda, Mt.	141	31 10S	152 28 E
Banda Elat	103	5 40S	133 5 E
Banda, Kepulauan	103	4 37S	129 50 E
Banda, La	172	27 45S	64 10W
Banda, Punta	164	31 47N	116 50W
Banda Sea	103	6 0S	130 0 E
Bandama, R.	120	6 32N	5 30W
Bandanwara	94	26 9N	74 38 E
Bandar = Masulipatnam	97	16 12N	81 12 E
Bandar 'Abbâs	93	27 15N	56 15 E
Bandar-e Bûshehr	93	28 55N	50 55 E
Bandar-e Chārak	93	26 45N	54 20 E
Bandar-e Deylam	92	30 5N	50 10 E
Bandar-e Lengeh	93	26 35N	54 58 E
Bandar-e Ma'shur	92	30 35N	49 10 E
Bandar-e-Nakhīlu	93	26 58N	53 30 E
Bandar-e-Pahlavi	92	37 30N	49 30 E
Bandar-e Rīg	93	29 30N	50 45 E
Bandar-e Shah	93	37 0N	54 10 E
Bandar-e-Shahpur	92	30 30N	49 5 E
Bandar Maharani = Muar	101	2 3N	102 34 E
Bandar Penggaram = Batu Pahat	101	1 50N	102 56 E
Bandar Seri Begawan	102	4 52N	115 0 E
Bandawe	127	11 58S	34 5 E
Bande, Belg.	47	50 10N	5 25 E
Bande, Spain	56	42 3N	7 58W
Bandeira, Pico da	173	20 26S	41 47W
Bandeirante	171	13 41S	50 48W
Bandera, Argent.	172	28 55S	62 20W
Bandera, U.S.A.	159	29 45N	99 3W
Banderas, Bahía de	164	20 40N	105 30W
Bandi-San	112	37 36N	140 4 E
Bandia, R.	96	19 30N	80 25 E
Bandiagara	120	14 12N	3 29W
Bandirma	92	40 20N	28 0 E
Bandon	39	51 44N	8 45W
Bandon, R.	39	51 40N	8 11W
Bandula	127	19 0S	33 7 E
Bandundu	124	3 15S	17 22 E
Bandung	103	6 36S	107 48 E
Bandya	137	27 40S	122 5 E
Bañeres	59	38 44N	0 38W
Banes	167	21 0N	75 42W
Bañeza, La	56	42 17N	5 54W
Banff, Can.	152	51 10N	115 34W
Banff, U.K.	37	57 40N	2 32W
Banff Nat. Park	152	51 30N	116 15W
Banfora	120	10 40N	4 40W
Bang Fai, R.	100	16 57N	104 45 E
Bang Hieng, R.	100	16 24N	105 40 E
Bang Krathum	100	16 34N	100 18 E
Bang Lamung	100	13 3N	100 56 E
Bang Mun Nak	100	16 2N	100 23 E
Bang Pa In	100	14 14N	100 35 E
Bang Rakam	100	16 45N	100 7 E
Bang Saphan	101	11 14N	99 28 E
Bangala Dam	127	21 7S	31 25 E
Bangalore	97	12 59N	77 40 E
Bangangte	121	5 8N	10 32 E
Bangaon	95	23 0N	88 47 E
Bangassou	124	4 55N	23 55 E
Bangeta, Mt.	135	6 21S	147 3 E
Banggai	103	1 40S	123 30 E
Banggi, P.	102	7 50N	117 0 E
Banghāzī	119	32 11N	20 3 E
Bangil	103	7 36S	112 50 E
Bangjang	123	11 23N	32 41 E
Bangka, Pulau, Celebes, Indon.	103	1 50N	125 5 E
Bangka, Pulau, Sumatera, Indon.	102	2 0S	105 50 E
Bangka, Selat	102	3 30S	105 30 E
Bangkalan	103	7 2S	112 46 E
Bangkinang	102	0 18N	100 5 E
Bangko	102	2 5S	102 9 E
Bangkok	100	13 45N	100 31 E
Bangladesh ■	98	24 0N	90 0 E
Bangolo	120	7 1N	7 29W
Bangor, Me., U.S.A.	151	44 48N	68 42W

Bangor **Bassevelde**

Bangor, Pa., U.S.A. **162** 40 51N 75 13W
Bangor, N.I., U.K. **38** 54 40N 5 40W
Bangor, Wales, U.K. **31** 53 13N 4 9W
Bangued **103** 17 40N 120 37 E
Bangui **124** 4 23N 18 35 E
Banguru **126** 0 30N 27 10 E
Bangweulu, L. **127** 11 0 S 30 0 E
Bangweulu Swamp **127** 11 20 S 30 15 E
Banham **29** 52 27N 1 3 E
Bani **167** 18 16N 70 22W
Bani Bangou **121** 15 3N 2 42 E
Bani, Djebel **118** 29 16N 8 0W
Bani Na'im **90** 31 31N 35 10 E
Bani, R. **120** 12 40N 6 30W
Bani Suhayla **90** 31 21N 34 19 E
Bania **120** 9 4N 3 6W
Baniara **135** 9 44 S 149 54 E
Banihal Pass **95** 33 30N 75 12 E
Banīnah **119** 32 0N 20 12 E
Baniyas **92** 35 10N 36 0 E
Banja Luka **66** 44 49N 17 26 E
Banjak, Kepulauan **102** 2 10N 97 10 E
Banjar **103** 7 24 S 108 30 E
Banjarmasin **102** 3 20 S 114 35 E
Banjarnegara **103** 7 24 S 109 42 E
Banjul **120** 13 28N 16 40W
Banka Banka **138** 18 50 S 134 0 E
Bankend **35** 55 2N 3 31W
Bankeryd **73** 57 53N 14 6 E
Banket **127** 17 27 S 30 19 E
Bankfoot **35** 56 30N 3 31W
Bankhead **37** 57 11N 2 10W
Bankilaré **121** 14 35N 0 44 E
Bankipore **95** 25 35N 85 10 E
Banks I., B.C., Can. **152** 53 20N 130 0W
Banks I., N. W. Terr., Can. **12** 73 15N 121 30W
Banks I., P.N.G. **135** 10 10 S 142 15 E
Banks Peninsula **143** 43 45 S 173 15 E
Banks Str. **138** 40 40 S 148 10 E
Bankura **95** 23 11N 87 18 E
Bankya **66** 42 43N 23 8 E
Bann R., Down, U.K. **38** 54 30N 6 31W
Bann R., Londonderry, U.K. **38** 55 10N 6 34W
Bannalec **42** 47 57N 3 42W
Bannang Sata **101** 6 16N 101 16 E
Bannerton **140** 34 42 S 142 47 E
Banning, Can. **150** 48 44N 91 56W
Banning, U.S.A. **163** 33 58N 116 58W
Banningville = Bandundu **124** 3 15 S 17 22 E
Bannockburn, Zimb. **127** 20 17 S 29 48 E
Bannockburn, U.K. **35** 56 5N 3 55W
Bannow **39** 52 12N 6 50W
Bannow B. **39** 52 13N 6 48W
Bannu **93** 33 0N 70 18 E
Bañolas **58** 42 16N 2 44 E
Banon **45** 44 2N 5 38 E
Baños de la Encina **57** 38 10N 3 46W
Baños de Molgas **56** 42 15N 7 40W
Bánovce **53** 48 44N 18 16 E
Banská Bystrica **53** 48 46N 19 14 E
Banská Stiavnica **53** 48 25N 18 55 E
Bansko **67** 41 52N 23 28 E
Banswara **94** 23 32N 74 24 E
Bantama **121** 7 48N 0 42W
Bante **121** 8 25N 1 53 E
Banteer **39** 52 8N 8 53W
Banten **103** 6 5 S 106 8 E
Bantry **39** 51 40N 9 28W
Bantry, B. **39** 51 35N 9 50W
Bantul **103** 7 55 S 110 19 E
Bantva **94** 21 29N 70 12 E
Bantval **97** 12 55N 75 0 E
Banu **93** 35 35N 69 5 E
Banwell **28** 51 19N 2 51W
Banya **67** 42 33N 24 50 E
Banyo **121** 6 52N 11 45 E
Banyuls **44** 42 29N 3 8 E
Banyumas **103** 7 32 S 109 18 E
Banyuwangi **103** 8 13 S 114 21 E
Banzare Coast **13** 66 30 S 125 0 E
Banzyville = Mobayi **124** 4 15N 21 8 E
Bao Ha **100** 22 11N 104 21 E
Bao Lac **100** 22 57N 105 40 E
Bao Loc **101** 11 32N 107 48 E
Bap **94** 27 23N 72 18 E
Bapatla **97** 15 55N 80 30 E
Bapaume **43** 50 7N 2 50 E
Bâqa el Gharbiya **90** 32 25N 35 2 E
Baqūbah **92** 33 45N 44 50 E
Baquedano **172** 23 20 S 69 52W
Bar, U.S.S.R. **82** 49 4N 27 40 E
Bar, Yugo. **66** 42 8N 19 8 E
Bar Harbor **151** 44 15N 68 20W
Bar-le-Duc **43** 48 47N 5 10 E
Bar-sur-Aube **43** 48 14N 4 40 E
Bar-sur-Seine **43** 48 7N 4 20 E
Barabai **102** 2 32 S 115 34 E
Barabinsk **76** 55 20N 78 20 E
Baraboo **158** 43 28N 89 46W
Baracoa **167** 20 20N 74 30W
Baradero **172** 33 52 S 59 29W
Baradine **141** 30 56 S 149 4 E
Baraga **158** 46 49N 88 29W
Barahona, Dom. Rep. **167** 18 13N 71 7W
Barahona, Spain **58** 41 17N 2 39W
Barail Range **99** 25 15N 93 20 E
Barakhola **99** 25 0N 92 45 E
Barakot **95** 21 33N 84 59 E
Barakula **139** 26 30 S 150 33 E
Baralaba **138** 24 13 S 149 50 E
Baralzon L. **153** 60 0N 98 3W
Baramati **96** 18 11N 74 33 E
Baramba **96** 20 25N 85 23 E
Barameiya **122** 18 32N 36 38 E
Baramula **95** 34 15N 74 20 E
Baran **94** 25 9N 76 40 E
Baranoa **174** 10 48N 74 55W
Baranof I. **147** 57 0N 135 10W
Baranovichi **80** 53 10N 26 0 E
Baranów Sandomierski **54** 50 29N 21 30 E
Baranya □ **53** 46 0N 18 15 E
Barão de Cocais **171** 19 56 S 43 28W
Barão de Grajaú **170** 6 45 S 43 1W
Barão de Melgaço **174** 11 50 S 60 45W
Baraolt **70** 46 5N 25 34 E
Barapasi **103** 2 15 S 137 5 E
Barapina **135** 6 21 S 155 25 E
Barasat **95** 22 46N 88 31 E
Barasoli **123** 13 38N 42 0W
Barat Daya, Kepuluan **103** 7 30 S 128 0 E
Barataria B. **159** 29 15N 89 45W
Baraut **94** 29 13N 77 7 E
Baraya **174** 3 10N 75 4W
Barbacena **173** 21 15 S 43 56W
Barbacoas, Colomb. **174** 1 45N 78 0W
Barbacoas, Venez. **174** 9 29N 66 58W
Barbados ■ **167** 13 0N 59 30W
Barbalha **170** 7 19 S 39 17W
Barban **63** 45 0N 14 4 E
Barbastro **58** 42 2N 0 5 E
Barbate **57** 36 13N 5 56W
Barberton, S. Afr. **129** 25 42 S 31 2 E
Barberton, U.S.A. **156** 41 0N 81 40W
Barbigha **95** 25 21N 85 47 E
Barbourville **157** 36 57N 83 52W
Barbuda I. **167** 17 30N 61 40W
Barca d'Alva **56** 41 0N 7 0W
Barca, La **164** 20 20N 102 40W
Barcaldine **138** 23 33 S 145 13 E
Barcarrota **57** 38 31N 6 51W
Barce = Al Marj **117** 32 25N 20 40 E
Barcellona Pozzo di Gotto **65** 38 8N 15 15 E
Barcelona, Spain **58** 41 21N 2 10 E
Barcelona, Venez. **174** 10 10N 64 40W
Barcelona □ **58** 41 30N 2 0 E
Barcelonette **45** 44 23N 6 40 E
Barcelos **174** 1 0 S 63 0W
Barcin **54** 52 52N 17 55 E
Barcoo, R. **138** 28 29 S 137 46 E
Barcs **53** 45 58N 17 28 E
Barczewo **54** 53 50N 20 42 E
Bard, Hd. **36** 60 6N 1 5W
Barda **83** 40 25N 47 10 E
Bardai **119** 21 25N 17 0 E
Bardas Blancas **172** 35 49 S 69 45W
Bardejov **53** 49 18N 21 15 E
Bardera **91** 2 20N 42 27 E
Bardi **62** 44 38N 9 43 E
Bardiyah **117** 31 45N 25 0 E
Bardney **33** 53 13N 0 19W
Bardo **54** 50 31N 16 42 E
Bardoc **137** 30 18 S 121 12 E
Bardoli **96** 21 12N 73 5 E
Bardsey, I. **31** 52 46N 4 47W
Bardsey Sound **31** 52 47N 4 46W
Bardstown **156** 37 50N 85 29W
Bareilly **95** 28 22N 79 27 E
Barellan **141** 34 16 S 146 24 E
Barengapara **98** 25 14N 90 14 E
Barentin **42** 49 33N 0 58 E
Barenton **42** 48 38N 0 50W
Barents Sea **12** 73 0N 39 0 E
Barentu **123** 15 2N 37 35 E
Barfleur **42** 49 40N 1 17W
Barford **28** 52 15N 1 35W
Barga **62** 44 5N 10 30 E
Bargal **91** 11 25N 51 0 E
Bargara **138** 24 50 S 152 25 E
Barge **62** 44 43N 7 19 E
Barge, La **160** 41 12N 110 4W
Bargnop **123** 9 32N 28 25 E
Bargo **141** 34 18 S 150 35 E
Bargoed **31** 51 42N 3 22W
Bargteheide **48** 53 42N 10 13 E
Barguzin **77** 53 37N 109 37 E
Barh **95** 25 29N 85 46 E
Barhaj **95** 26 18N 83 44 E
Barham **29** 51 12N 1 10 E
Barhi **95** 24 15N 85 25 E
Bari, India **94** 26 39N 77 39 E
Bari, Italy **65** 41 6N 16 52 E
Bari Doab **94** 30 20N 73 0 E
Baria = Phuoc Le **101** 10 39N 107 19 E
Bariadi □ **126** 2 45 S 34 40 E
Barika **118** 35 23N 5 22 E
Barinas **174** 8 36N 70 15W
Barinas □ **174** 8 10N 69 50W
Baring C. **148** 70 0N 117 30W
Baringo **126** 0 47N 36 16 E
Baringo □ **126** 0 55N 36 0 E
Baringo, L. **126** 0 47N 36 16 E
Barinitas **174** 8 45N 70 25W
Baripada **96** 21 57N 86 45 E
Bariri **171** 22 4 S 48 44W
Bârîs **122** 24 42N 30 31 E
Barisal **98** 22 30N 90 20 E
Barisan, Bukit **102** 3 30 S 102 15 E
Barito, R. **102** 2 50 S 114 50 E
Barjac **45** 44 20N 4 22 E
Barjols **45** 43 34N 6 2 E
Barjūji, W. **119** 25 26N 12 12 E
Bark L. **150** 46 58N 82 25W
Barka **122** 17 30N 37 34 E
Barkah **93** 23 40N 58 0 E
Barker, Mt. **139** 35 4 S 138 55 E
Barking **29** 51 31N 0 10 E
Barkley Sound **152** 48 50N 125 10W
Barkly Downs **138** 20 30 S 138 30 E
Barkly East **129** 30 58 S 27 33 E
Barkly Tableland **138** 19 50 S 138 40 E
Barkly West **128** 28 5 S 24 31 E
Barkol, Wadi **122** 17 40N 32 0 E
Barksdale **159** 29 47N 100 2W
Barlborough **33** 53 17N 1 17W
Barlby **33** 53 48N 1 3W
Barlee, L. **137** 29 15 S 119 30 E
Barlee, Mt. **137** 24 35 S 128 10 E
Barlee Ra. **137** 23 30 S 116 0 E
Barlett **163** 36 29N 118 2W
Barletta **65** 41 20N 16 17 E
Barlinek **54** 53 0N 15 15 E
Barlingbo **73** 57 35N 18 27 E
Barlow L. **153** 62 00N 103 0W
Barmby Moor **33** 53 55N 0 47W
Barmedman **141** 34 9 S 147 21 E
Barmer **94** 25 45N 71 20 E
Barmera **140** 34 15 S 140 28 E
Barmoor **35** 55 38N 2 0W
Barmouth **31** 52 44N 4 3W
Barmstedt **48** 53 47N 9 46 E
Barna **39** 53 14N 9 10W
Barnaderg **38** 53 29N 8 43W
Barnagar **94** 23 7N 75 19 E
Barnard Castle **32** 54 33N 1 55W
Barnato **141** 31 38 S 145 0 E
Barnaul **76** 53 20N 83 40 E
Barnby Moor **33** 53 21N 1 0W
Barne Inlet **13** 80 15 S 160 0 E
Barnes **141** 36 2 S 144 47 E
Barnesville **157** 33 6N 84 9W
Barnet **29** 51 37N 0 15W
Barnetby le Wold **33** 53 34N 0 24W
Barneveld, Neth. **96** 52 7N 5 36 E
Barneveld, U.S.A. **162** 43 16N 75 14W
Barneville **42** 49 23N 1 46W
Barney, Mt. **133** 28 17 S 152 44 E
Barngo **138** 25 3 S 147 20 E
Barnhart **159** 31 10N 101 8W
Barnoldswick **32** 53 55N 2 11W
Barnsley **33** 53 33N 1 29W
Barnstaple **30** 51 5N 4 3W
Barnstaple B. **30** 51 5N 4 25W
Barnsville **158** 46 43N 96 28W
Baro **121** 8 35N 6 18 E
Baro, R. **123** 8 25N 33 40 E
Baroda **94** 25 29N 76 35 E
Baroda = Vadodara, India **93** 22 20N 73 10 E
Baroda = Vadodara, Gujarat, India **94** 22 20N 73 10 E
Baron Ra. **136** 23 30 S 127 45 E
Barpali **96** 21 11N 83 35 E
Barpathar **98** 26 17N 93 53 E
Barpeta **95** 26 20N 91 10 E
Barqa **117** 27 0N 20 0 E
Barqin **119** 27 33N 13 34 E
Barques, Pte. aux **156** 44 5N 82 55W
Barquinha **57** 39 28N 8 25W
Barquisimeto **174** 9 58N 69 13W
Barr, France **43** 48 25N 7 28 E
Barr, U.K. **34** 55 13N 4 44W
Barr Smith Ra. **137** 27 10 S 120 15 E
Barra, Brazil **170** 11 5 S 43 10W
Barra, Gambia **120** 13 21N 16 36W
Barra da Estiva **171** 13 38 S 41 19W
Barra de Navidad **164** 19 12N 104 41W
Barra do Corda **170** 5 30 S 45 10W
Barra do Mendes **171** 11 43 S 42 4W
Barra do Pirai **173** 22 30 S 43 50W
Barra Falsa, Pta. da **129** 22 58 S 35 37 E
Barra Hd. **36** 56 47N 7 40W
Barra, I. **36** 57 0N 7 30W
Barra Mansa **173** 22 35 S 44 12W
Barra, Sd. of **36** 57 4N 7 25W
Barraba **141** 30 21 S 150 35 E
Barrackpur **95** 22 44N 88 30 E
Barrafranca **65** 37 22N 14 10 E
Barranca, Lima, Peru **174** 10 45 S 77 50W
Barranca, Loreto, Peru **174** 4 50 S 76 50W
Barrancabermeja **174** 7 0N 73 50W
Barrancas, Colomb. **174** 10 57N 72 50W
Barrancas, Venez. **174** 8 55N 62 5W
Barrancos **57** 38 10N 6 58W
Barranqueras **172** 27 30 S 59 0W
Barranquilla, Atlántico, Colomb. **174** 11 0N 74 50W
Barranquilla, Vaupés, Colomb. **174** 1 39N 72 19W
Barras, Brazil **170** 4 15 S 42 18W
Barras, Colomb. **174** 1 45 S 73 13W
Barraute **150** 48 26N 77 38W
Barre, U.S.A. **156** 44 15N 72 30W
Barre, U.S.A. **162** 42 26N 72 6W
Barreal **172** 31 33 S 69 28W
Barreiras **171** 12 8 S 45 0W
Barreirinhas **170** 2 30 S 42 50W
Barreiro **57** 38 40N 9 6W
Barreiros **170** 8 49 S 35 12W
Barrême **45** 43 57N 6 23 E
Barren I. **101** 12 17N 95 50 E
Barren Is., Madag. **129** 18 25 S 43 40 E
Barren Is., U.S.A. **147** 58 45N 152 0W
Barren Junc. **139** 30 5 S 149 0 E
Barretos **171** 20 30 S 48 35W
Barrhead, Can. **152** 54 10N 114 24W
Barrhead, U.K. **34** 55 48N 4 23W
Barrhill **34** 55 7N 4 46W
Barrie **150** 44 24N 79 40W
Barrier, C. **142** 36 25 S 175 32 E
Barrier Ra., Austral. **140** 31 0 S 141 30 E
Barrier Ra., N.Z. **143** 44 5 S 169 42 E
Barrier Rf., Gt. **138** 19 0 S 149 0 E
Barrière **152** 51 12N 120 7W
Barrington, Austral. **133** 31 58 S 151 55 E
Barrington, Ill., U.S.A. **156** 42 8N 88 5W
Barrington, R.I., U.S.A. **162** 41 43N 71 20W
Barrington L. **153** 56 55N 100 15W
Barrington Tops. **141** 32 6 S 151 28 E
Barringun **139** 29 1 S 145 41 E
Barrow **147** 71 16N 156 50W
Barrow Creek T.O. **138** 21 30 S 133 55 E
Barrow I. **136** 20 45 S 115 20 E
Barrow-in-Furness **32** 54 8N 3 15W
Barrow Pt. **138** 14 20 S 144 40 E
Barrow, Pt. **147** 71 22N 156 30W
Barrow, R. **39** 52 10N 6 57W
Barrow Ra. **137** 26 0 S 127 40 E
Barrow Strait **12** 74 20N 95 0W
Barrow upon Humber **33** 53 41N 0 22W
Barrowford **32** 53 51N 2 14W
Barruecopardo **56** 41 4N 6 40W
Barruelo **56** 42 54N 4 17W
Barry, S. Glam., U.K. **31** 51 23N 3 19W
Barry, Tayside, U.K. **35** 56 29N 2 45W
Barry I. **31** 51 23N 3 17W
Barry's Bay **150** 45 29N 77 41W
Barry's Pt. **39** 51 36N 8 40W
Barsalogho **121** 13 25N 1 3W
Barsat **95** 36 10N 72 45 E
Barsi **96** 18 10N 75 50 E
Barsø **73** 55 7N 9 33 E
Barsoi **99** 25 48N 87 57 E
Barstow, Calif., U.S.A. **163** 34 58N 117 2W
Barstow, Tex., U.S.A. **170** 31 30N 103 25W
Barthélemy, Col **100** 19 26N 104 6 E
Bartica **174** 6 25N 58 40W
Bartle Frere, Mt. **138** 17 27 S 145 50 E
Bartlesville **159** 36 50N 95 58W
Bartlett **159** 30 46N 97 30W
Bartlett, L. **152** 63 5N 118 20W
Bartolomeu Dias **127** 21 10 S 35 8 E
Barton **33** 54 28N 1 38W
Barton Siding **137** 30 31 S 132 39 E
Barton-upon-Humber **33** 53 41N 0 27W
Bartoszyce **54** 54 15N 20 55 E
Bartow **157** 27 53N 81 49W
Barú, I. de **174** 10 15N 75 35W
Baruth **48** 52 3N 13 31 E
Barvas **36** 58 21N 6 31W
Barvaux **47** 50 21N 5 29 E
Barvenkovo **82** 48 57N 37 0 E
Barwani **94** 22 2N 74 57 E
Barwell **28** 52 35N 1 22W
Barysh **81** 49 2N 25 18 E
Bas-Rhin □ **43** 48 40N 7 30 E
Bašaid **66** 45 38N 20 25 E
Basa'idu **93** 26 35N 55 20 E
Basal **94** 33 33N 72 13 E
Basalt **163** 38 0N 118 15W
Basankusa **124** 1 5N 19 50 E
Basawa **94** 34 15N 70 50 E
Bascharage **47** 49 34N 5 55 E
Bascuñán, Cabo **172** 28 52 S 71 35W
Basècles **47** 50 32N 3 39 E
Basel (Basle) **50** 47 35N 7 35 E
Basel Landschaft □ **50** 47 26N 7 45 E
Basel-Stadt □ **50** 47 35N 7 35 E
Basento, R. **65** 40 35N 16 10 E
Bashi Channel **105** 21 15N 122 0 E
Bashkir A.S.S.R. □ **84** 54 0N 57 0 E
Basilaki, I. **135** 10 35 S 151 0 E
Basilan, Selat **103** 6 50N 122 0 E
Basilanl, I. **103** 6 35N 122 0 E
Basildon **29** 51 34N 0 29 E
Basilicata □ **65** 40 30N 16 0 E
Basim **96** 20 3N 77 0 E
Basin **160** 44 22N 108 2W
Basing **28** 51 16N 1 3W
Basingstoke **28** 51 15N 1 5W
Basirhat **98** 22 40N 88 54 E
Baskatong Res. **150** 46 46N 75 50W
Baskerville C. **136** 17 10 S 122 15 E
Basle = Basel **50** 47 35N 7 35 E
Basmat **96** 19 15N 77 12 E
Basoda **94** 23 52N 77 54 E
Basodino **51** 46 25N 8 28 E
Basoka **126** 1 16N 23 40 E
Basongo **124** 4 15 S 20 20 E
Basque Provinces = Vascongadas **58** 42 50N 2 45W
Basra = Al Basrah **92** 30 30N 47 50 E
Bass Rock **35** 56 5N 2 40W
Bass Strait **138** 39 15 S 146 30 E
Bassano, del Grappa **63** 45 45N 11 45 E
Bassari **121** 9 19N 0 57 E
Bassas da India **125** 22 0 S 39 0 E
Basse **120** 13 13N 14 15W
Basse-Terre, I. **167** 16 0N 61 40W
Bassecourt **50** 47 20N 7 15 E
Bassée, La **43** 50 31N 2 49 E
Bassein, Burma **98** 16 30N 94 30 E
Bassein, India **96** 19 26N 72 48 E
Bassein Myit **99** 16 45N 94 30 E
Bassenthwaite, L. **32** 54 40N 3 14W
Basseterre **167** 17 17N 62 43W
Bassett, Nebr., U.S.A. **158** 42 37N 99 30W
Bassett, Va., U.S.A. **157** 36 48N 79 59W
Bassevelde **47** 51 15N 3 41 E

Bassi	94	30 44N	76 21 E
Bassigny	43	48 0N	5 10 E
Bassikounou	120	15 55N	6 1W
Bassilly	47	50 40N	3 56 E
Bassum	48	52 50N	8 42 E
Båstad	73	56 25N	12 51 E
Båstad	73	56 25N	12 51 E
Bastak	93	27 15N	54 25 E
Bastar	96	19 25N	81 40 E
Basti	95	26 52N	82 55 E
Bastia	45	42 40N	9 30 E
Bastia Umbra	63	43 4N	12 34 E
Bastide, La	44	44 35N	3 55 E
Bastogne	47	50 1N	5 43 E
Baston	29	52 43N	0 19W
Bastrop	159	30 5N	97 22W
Basuto	128	19 50 S	26 25 E
Basutoland = Lesotho	129	29 0 S	28 0 E
Basyanovskiy	84	58 19N	60 44 E
Bat Yam	90	32 2N	34 44 E
Bata, Eq. Guin.	124	1 57N	9 50 E
Bata, Rumania	70	46 1N	22 4 E
Bataan	103	14 40N	120 25 E
Bataan Pen.	103	14 38N	120 30 E
Batabanó	166	22 40N	82 20W
Batabanó, G. de	167	22 30N	82 30W
Batac	103	18 3N	120 34 E
Batagoy	77	67 38N	134 38 E
Batak	67	41 57N	24 12 E
Batalha	57	39 40N	8 50W
Batama	126	0 58N	26 33 E
Batamay	77	63 30N	129 15 E
Batamshinskiy	84	50 36N	58 16 E
Batang	103	6 55 S	109 40 E
Batangafo	117	7 25N	18 20 E
Batangas	103	13 35N	121 10 E
Batanta, I.	103	0 55N	130 40 E
Bataszék	66	46 10N	18 44 E
Batatais	173	20 54 S	47 37W
Batavia	156	43 0N	78 10W
Bataysk	83	47 3N	39 45 E
Batchelor	136	13 4 S	131 1 E
Bateman's B.	141	35 40 S	150 12 E
Batemans Bay	141	35 44 S	150 11 E
Bates Ra.	137	27 25 S	121 0 E
Batesburg	157	33 54N	81 32W
Batesville, Ark., U.S.A.	159	35 48N	91 40W
Batesville, Miss., U.S.A.	159	34 17N	89 58W
Batesville, Tex., U.S.A.	159	28 59N	99 38W
Batetski	80	58 47N	30 16 E
Bath, U.K.	28	51 22N	2 22W
Bath, Maine, U.S.A.	151	43 50N	69 49W
Bath, N.Y., U.S.A.	156	42 20N	77 17W
Batheay	101	11 59N	104 57 E
Bathford	28	51 23N	2 18W
Bathgate	35	55 54N	3 38W
Bâthie, La	46	45 37N	6 28 E
Bathmen	46	52 15N	6 29 E
Bathurst, Austral.	141	33 25 S	149 31 E
Bathurst, Can.	151	47 37N	65 43W
Bathurst B.	138	14 16 S	144 25 E
Bathurst C.	147	70 30N	128 30W
Bathurst, C.	147	70 34N	128 0W
Bathurst, Gambia = Banjul	120	13 28N	16 40W
Bathurst Harb.	138	43 15 S	146 10 E
Bathurst I., Austral.	136	11 30 S	130 10 E
Bathurst I., Can.	12	76 30N	130 10W
Bathurst Inlet	148	66 50N	108 1W
Batie	120	9 53N	2 53W
Batley	33	53 43N	1 38W
Batlow	141	35 31 S	148 9 E
Batman	92	37 55N	41 5 E
Batna	119	35 34N	6 15 E
Batoka	127	16 45 S	27 15 E
Baton Rouge	159	30 30N	91 5W
Batong, Ko	101	6 32N	99 12 E
Batopilas	164	27 45N	107 45W
Batouri	124	4 30N	14 25 E
Battambang	100	13 7N	103 12 E
Batticaloa	97	7 43N	81 45 E
Battice	47	50 39N	5 50 E
Battipáglia	65	40 38N	15 0 E
Battir	90	31 44N	35 8 E
Battle, Can.	153	52 58N	110 52W
Battle, U.K.	29	50 55N	0 30 E
Battle Camp	138	15 20 S	144 40 E
Battle Creek	156	42 20N	85 36W
Battle Harbour	151	52 16N	55 35W
Battle Lake	158	46 20N	95 43W
Battle Mountain	160	40 45N	117 0W
Battle, R.	153	52 43N	108 15W
Battlefields	127	18 37 S	29 47 E
Battleford	153	52 45N	108 15W
Battonya	53	46 16N	21 3 E
Batu Caves	101	3 15N	101 40 E
Batu Gajah	101	4 28N	101 3 E
Batu, Kepulauan	102	0 30 S	98 25 E
Batu, Mt.	123	6 55N	39 45 E
Batu Pahat	101	1 50N	102 56 E
Batuata, P.	103	6 30 S	122 20 E
Batulaki	103	5 40N	125 30 E
Batumi	83	41 30N	41 30 E
Baturadja	102	4 11 S	104 15 E
Baturité	170	4 28 S	38 45W
Baturité, Serra de	170	4 25 S	39 0W
Baubau	103	5 25 S	123 50 E
Bauchi	121	10 22N	9 48 E
Bauchi □	121	10 10N	10 0 E
Baud	42	47 52N	3 1W
Baudette	158	48 46N	94 35W
Baudouinville = Moba	126	7 0 S	29 48 E
Baudour	47	50 29N	3 50 E
Bauer, C.	139	32 44 S	134 4 E
Baugé	42	47 31N	0 8W
Bauhinia Downs	138	24 35 S	149 18 E
Baule, La	42	47 18N	2 23W
Bauma	51	47 3N	8 53 E
Baume les Dames	43	47 22N	6 22 E
Baunei	64	40 2N	9 41 E
Bauru	173	22 10 S	49 0W
Baús	175	18 22 S	52 47W
Bauska	80	56 25N	25 15 E
Bautzen	48	51 11N	14 25 E
Baux, Les	45	43 45N	4 51 E
BavaniŠte	66	44 49N	20 53 E
Bavaria = Bayern	49	49 7N	11 30 E
Båven	72	59 35N	17 30 E
Bavispe, R.	164	29 30N	109 11W
Bawdsey	29	52 1N	1 27 E
Bawdwin	98	23 5N	97 50 E
Bawean	102	5 46 S	112 35 E
Bawku	121	11 3N	0 19W
Bawlake	98	19 11N	97 21 E
Bawnboy	38	54 8N	7 40W
Bawtry	33	53 25N	1 1W
Baxley	157	31 43N	82 23W
Baxter Springs	159	37 3N	94 45W
Bay Bulls	151	47 19N	52 50W
Bay City, Mich., U.S.A.	156	43 35N	83 51W
Bay City, Oreg., U.S.A.	160	45 45N	123 58W
Bay City, Tex., U.S.A.	159	28 59N	95 55W
Bay de Verde	151	48 5N	52 54W
Bay, Laguna de	103	14 20N	121 11 E
Bay of Islands	142	35 15 S	174 6 E
Bay St. Louis	159	30 18N	89 22W
Bay Shore	162	40 44N	73 15W
Bay Springs	159	31 58N	89 18W
Bay View	142	39 25 S	176 50 E
Baya	127	11 53 S	27 25 E
Bayamo	166	20 20N	76 40W
Bayamón	147	18 24N	66 10W
Bayan Kara Shan	99	34 0N	98 0 E
Bayan-Ovoo	106	47 47N	112 5 E
Bayana	94	26 55N	77 18 E
Bayanaul	76	50 45N	75 45 E
Bayandalay	106	43 30N	103 29 E
Bayanga	124	2 53N	16 19 E
Bayanhongor	105	46 8N	100 43 E
Bayard	158	41 48N	103 17W
Baybay	103	10 40N	124 55 E
Bayble	36	58 12N	6 13W
Bayburt	92	40 15N	40 20 E
Bayerischer Wald	49	49 0N	13 0 E
Bayern □	49	49 7N	11 30 E
Bayeux	42	49 17N	0 42W
Bayfield	158	46 50N	90 48W
Bayir	92	30 45N	36 55 E
Baykadam	85	43 48N	69 58 E
Baykal, Oz.	77	53 0N	108 0 E
Baykit	77	61 50N	95 50 E
Baykonur	76	47 48N	65 50 E
Baymak	84	52 36N	58 19 E
Baynes Mts.	128	17 15 S	13 0 E
Bayombong	103	16 30N	121 10 E
Bayon	43	48 30N	6 20 E
Bayona	56	42 6N	8 52W
Bayonne, France	44	43 30N	1 28W
Bayonne, U.S.A.	162	40 41N	74 7W
Bayovar	174	5 50 S	81 0W
Baypore, R.	97	11 10N	75 47 E
Bayram-Ali	76	37 37N	62 10 E
Bayreuth	49	49 56N	11 35 E
Bayrischzell	49	47 39N	12 1 E
Bayrūt	92	33 53N	35 31 E
Baysun	85	38 12N	67 12 E
Bayt Aula	90	31 37N	35 2 E
Bayt Fajjar	90	31 38N	35 9 E
Bayt Fūrīk	90	32 11N	35 20 E
Bayt Jala	90	31 43N	35 11 E
Bayt Lahm	90	31 43N	35 12 E
Bayt Rīma	90	32 2N	35 6 E
Bayt Sāhūr	90	31 42N	35 13 E
Bayt Ummar	90	31 38N	35 7 E
Bayta at Tahtā	90	32 9N	35 18 E
Baytin	90	31 56N	35 14 E
Baytown	159	29 42N	94 57W
Bayzhansay	85	43 14N	69 54 E
Bayzo	121	13 52N	4 35 E
Baza	59	37 30N	2 47W
Bazar Dyuzi	83	41 12N	48 10 E
Bazarny Karabulak	81	52 30N	46 20 E
Bazarnyy Syzgan	81	53 45N	46 40 E
Bazartobe	83	49 26N	51 45 E
Bazaruto, I. do	129	21 40 S	35 28 E
Bazas	44	44 27N	0 13W
Bazuriye	90	33 15N	35 16 E
Beabula	141	34 26 S	145 9 E
Beach	158	46 57N	104 0W
Beach Haven	162	39 34N	74 14W
Beachley	28	51 37N	2 39W
Beachport	140	37 29 S	140 0 E
Beachwood	162	39 55N	74 8W
Beachy Head	29	50 44N	0 16 E
Beacon, Austral.	137	30 26 S	117 52 E
Beacon, U.S.A.	162	41 32N	73 58W
Beaconia	153	50 25N	96 31W
Beaconsfield, Austral.	133	41 11 S	146 48 E
Beaconsfield, U.K.	29	51 36N	0 39W
Beadnell	35	55 33N	1 38W
Beagle Bay	136	16 32 S	122 54 E
Beagle, Canal	176	55 0 S	68 30W
Bealanana	129	14 33N	48 44 E
Bealey	143	43 2 S	171 36 E
Beaminster	28	50 48N	2 44W
Bear I.	39	51 38N	9 50W
Bear I. Nor.	12	74 30N	19 0 E
Bear L., B.C., Can.	152	56 10N	126 52W
Bear L., Man., Can.	153	55 8N	96 0W
Bear L., U.S.A.	160	42 0N	111 20W
Bearcreek	160	45 11N	109 6W
Beardmore	150	49 36N	87 57W
Beardmore Glacier	13	84 30 S	170 0 E
Beardstown	158	40 0N	90 25W
Bearn	44	43 28N	0 36W
Bearpaw Mt.	160	48 15N	109 55W
Bearsden	34	55 55N	4 21W
Bearskin Lake	150	53 58N	91 2W
Bearsted	29	51 15N	0 35 E
Beas de Segura	59	38 15N	2 53W
Beasain	58	43 3N	2 11W
Beata, C.	167	17 40N	71 30W
Beata, I.	167	17 34N	71 31W
Beatrice, Zimb.	127	18 15 S	30 55 E
Beatrice, U.S.A.	158	40 20N	96 40W
Beatrice, C.	138	14 20 S	136 55 E
Beatrice, oilfield	19	58 7N	3 6W
Beattock	35	55 19N	3 27W
Beatton, R.	152	56 15N	120 45W
Beatton River	152	57 26N	121 20W
Beatty	163	36 58N	116 46W
Beaucaire	45	43 48N	4 39 E
Beauce, Plaines de	43	48 10N	2 0 E
Beauceville	151	46 13N	70 46W
Beaudesert	139	27 59 S	153 0 E
Beaufort, Austral.	140	37 25 S	143 25 E
Beaufort, Malay.	102	5 30N	115 40 E
Beaufort, N.C., U.S.A.	157	34 45N	76 40W
Beaufort, S.C., U.S.A.	157	32 25N	80 40W
Beaufort Sea	12	72 0N	140 0W
Beaufort-West	128	32 18 S	22 36 E
Beaugency	43	47 47N	1 38 E
Beauharnois	150	45 20N	73 52W
Beaujeu	45	46 10N	4 35 E
Beaujolais	45	46 0N	4 25 E
Beaulieu, Loiret, France	44	47 31N	2 49 E
Beaulieu, Vendée, France	45	46 41N	1 37W
Beaulieu, U.K.	28	50 49N	1 27W
Beaulieu, R.	152	62 3N	113 11W
Beauly	37	57 29N	4 27W
Beauly Firth	37	57 30N	4 20W
Beauly, R.	37	57 26N	4 28W
Beaumaris	31	53 16N	4 7W
Beaumetz-les-Loges	43	50 15N	2 40 E
Beaumont, Belg.	47	50 15N	4 14 E
Beaumont, France	44	44 45N	0 46 E
Beaumont, N.Z.	143	45 50 S	169 33 E
Beaumont, Calif., U.S.A.	163	33 56N	116 58W
Beaumont, Tex., U.S.A.	159	30 5N	94 8W
Beaumont-le-Roger	42	49 4N	0 47 E
Beaumont-sur-Oise	43	49 9N	2 17 E
Beaune	43	47 2N	4 50 E
Beaune-la-Rolande	43	48 4N	2 25 E
Beauraing	47	50 7N	4 57 E
Beausejour	153	50 5N	96 35 E
Beausset, Le	45	43 10N	5 46 E
Beauvais	43	49 25N	2 8 E
Beauval	153	55 9N	107 37W
Beauvoir, Deux Sèvres, France	44	46 12N	0 30W
Beauvoir, Vendée, France	42	46 55N	2 1W
Beaver, Alaska, U.S.A.	147	66 20N	147 30W
Beaver, Okla., U.S.A.	159	36 52N	100 31W
Beaver, Utah, U.S.A.	161	38 20N	112 45W
Beaver City	158	40 13N	99 50W
Beaver Dam	158	43 28N	88 50W
Beaver Falls	156	40 44N	80 20W
Beaver Hill L.	153	54 16N	94 59W
Beaver I.	150	45 40N	85 31W
Beaver, R.	152	59 52N	124 20W
Beaver, R	150	55 55N	87 48W
Beaver, R.	153	55 26N	107 45W
Beaverhill L., Man., Can.	153	54 5N	94 50W
Beaverhill L., N.W.T., Can.	153	63 2N	111 22W
Beaverhill L., Alb.	152	53 27N	112 32W
Beaverlodge	152	55 11N	119 29W
Beavermouth	152	51 32N	117 23W
Beaverstone, R.	150	54 59N	89 25W
Beawar	94	26 3N	74 18 E
Bebedouro	173	21 0 S	48 25W
Bebington	32	53 23N	3 1W
Beboa	129	17 22 S	44 33 E
Bebra	48	50 59N	9 48 E
Beccles	29	52 27N	1 33 E
Bečej	66	45 36N	20 3 E
Beceni	70	45 23N	26 48 E
Becerreá	56	42 51N	7 10W
Béchar	118	31 38N	2 18 E
Becharof L.	147	58 0N	156 30W
Bechuanaland = Botswana	125	23 0 S	24 0 E
Bechyně	52	49 17N	14 29 E
Beckermet	32	54 26N	3 31W
Beckfoot	32	54 50N	3 25W
Beckingham	33	53 24N	0 49W
Beckley	156	37 50N	81 8W
Bécon	42	47 30N	0 50W
Bečva, R.	53	49 31N	17 40 E
Bedale	33	54 18N	1 35W
Bédar	59	37 11N	1 59W
Bédarieux	44	43 37N	3 10 E
Bédarrides	45	44 2N	4 54 E
Beddone, Mt.	138	25 50 S	134 20 E
Bedele	123	8 31N	35 44 E
Bedel, Pereval	85	41 26N	78 26 E
Bederkesa	48	53 37N	8 50 E
Bedford, Can.	150	45 7N	72 59W
Bedford, S. Afr.	128	32 40 S	26 10 E
Bedford, U.K.	29	52 8N	0 29W
Bedford, Ind., U.S.A.	156	38 50N	86 30W
Bedford, Iowa, U.S.A.	158	40 40N	94 41W
Bedford, Ohio, U.S.A.	156	41 23N	81 32W
Bedford, Va., U.S.A.	156	37 25N	79 30W
Bedford □	29	52 4N	0 28W
Bedford, C.	138	15 14 S	145 21 E
Bedford Downs	136	17 19 S	127 20 E
Bedford Level	29	52 25N	0 5 E
Bedków	54	51 36N	19 44 E
Bedlington	35	55 8N	1 35W
Bednesti	152	53 50N	123 10W
Bednja, R.	63	46 12N	16 25 E
Bednodemyanovsk	81	53 55N	43 15 E
Bedourie	138	24 30 S	139 30 E
Bedretto	51	46 31N	8 31 E
Bedum	47	53 18N	6 36 E
Bedwas	31	51 36N	3 10W
Bedworth	28	52 28N	1 29W
Bedzin	54	50 19N	19 7 E
Bee L.	36	57 22N	7 21W
Beebyn	137	27 0 S	117 48 E
Beech Grove	156	39 40N	86 2W
Beechey Point	147	70 27N	149 18W
Beechworth	141	36 22 S	146 43 E
Beechy	153	50 53N	107 24W
Beeford	33	53 58N	0 18W
Beek, Gelderland, Neth.	46	51 55N	6 11 E
Beek, Limburg, Neth.	47	50 57N	5 48 E
Beek, Noord Brabant, Neth.	47	51 32N	5 38 E
Beekbergen	46	52 10N	5 58 E
Beelitz	48	52 14N	12 58 E
Beemem	47	51 9N	3 21 E
Beenleigh	139	27 43 S	153 10 E
Beer	30	50 41N	3 5W
Be'er Sheva'	90	31 15N	34 48 E
Be'er Sheva', N.	90	31 12N	34 40 E
Be'er Toviyyao	90	31 44N	34 42 E
Be'eri	90	31 25N	34 30 E
Be'erotayim	90	32 19N	34 59 E
Beersheba = Be'er Sheva'	90	31 15N	34 48 E
Beerta	46	53 11N	7 6 E
Beerze, R.	46	51 39N	5 20 E
Beesd	46	51 53N	5 11 E
Beesel	47	51 16N	6 2 E
Beeskow	48	52 9N	14 14 E
Beeston	33	52 55N	1 11W
Beetaloo	138	17 15 S	133 50 E
Beetsterzwaag	46	53 4N	6 5 E
Beetzendorf	48	52 42N	11 6 E
Beeville	159	28 27N	97 44W
Befale	124	0 25N	20 45 E
Befandriana	125	21 55 S	44 0 E
Befotaka, Diégo-Suarez, Madag.	129	14 30 S	48 0 E
Befotaka, Fianarantsoa, Madag.	129	23 49 S	47 0 E
Beg, L.	38	54 48N	6 28W
Bega	141	36 41 S	149 51 E
Bega, Canalul	66	45 37N	20 46 E
Begelly	31	51 45N	4 44W
• Begemdir & Simen □	123	13 55N	37 30 E
Begna	71	60 41N	9 42 E
Begonte	56	43 10N	7 40W
Begu-Sarai	95	25 24N	86 9 E
Beguildy	31	52 25N	3 11W
Béhagle = Lai	117	9 25N	16 30 E
Behara	125	24 55 S	46 20 E
Behbehan	92	30 30N	50 15 E
Behror	94	27 51N	76 20 E
Behshahr	93	36 45N	53 35 E
Beida (Al Bayda)	117	32 30N	21 40 E
Beighton	33	53 21N	1 21W
Beilen	46	52 52N	6 27 E
Beilngries	49	49 1N	11 27 E
Beilpajah	140	32 54 S	143 52 E
Beilul	123	13 2N	42 20 E
Beinn a' Ghlo, Mt.	37	56 51N	3 42W
Beinn Mhor, Mt.	36	57 59N	6 39W
Beira	127	19 50 S	34 52 E
Beira-Alta	55	40 35N	7 35W
Beira-Baixa	55	40 2N	7 30W
Beira-Litoral	55	40 5N	8 30W
Beirut = Bayrūt	92	33 53N	35 31 E
Beit Bridge	127	14 58 S	30 15 E
Beit Hanum	90	31 32N	34 32 E
Beit Lahiya	90	31 32N	34 30 E
Beit 'Ur et Tahta	90	31 54N	35 5 E
Beit Yosef	90	32 34N	35 33 E
Beitbridge	127	22 12 S	30 0 E
Beith	34	55 45N	4 38W
Beituniya	90	31 54N	35 10 E
Beiuş	70	46 40N	22 21 E
Beja	57	38 2N	7 53W
Béja	119	36 43N	9 12 E
Beja □	57	37 55N	7 55W
Béjaïa	119	36 42N	5 2 E
Béjar	56	40 23N	5 46W
Bejestan	93	34 30N	58 5 E
Bekabad	85	40 13N	69 14 E
Bekasi	103	6 20 S	107 0 E
Békés	53	46 47N	21 9 E
Békés □	53	46 45N	21 0 E
Békéscsaba	53	46 40N	21 10 E
Bekily	129	24 13 S	45 19 E
Bekkevoort	47	50 57N	4 58 E
Bekkjarvik	71	60 1N	5 13 E

*Renamed Gonder

Bekoji **Berghem**

Bekoji 123 7 40N 38 20E
Bekok 101 2 20N 103 7E
Bekopaka 129 19 9S 44 45E
Bekwai 121 6 30N 1 34W
Bel Air 162 39 32N 76 21W
Bela, India 95 25 50N 82 0E
Bela, Pak. 94 26 12N 66 20E
Bela Crkva 66 44 55N 21 27E
Bela Palanka 66 43 13N 22 17E
Bela Vista, Brazil 173 22 12S 56 20W
Bela Vista, Mozam. 129 26 10S 32 44E
Bélâbre 44 46 34N 1 8E
Belaia, Mt. 123 11 25N 36 8E
Belalcázar 57 38 35N 5 10W
Belanovica 66 44 15N 20 23E
Belavenona 129 24 50S 47 4E
Belawan 102 3 33N 98 32E
Belaya Glina 83 46 5N 40 48E
Belaya Kalitva 83 48 13N 40 50E
Belaya Kholunitsa 84 58 41N 50 13E
Belaya, R. 84 55 54N 53 33E
Belaya Tserkov 80 49 45N 30 10E
Belbroughton 28 52 23N 2 5W
Belceşti 70 47 19N 27 7E
Bełchatów 54 51 21N 19 22E
Belcher, C. 12 75 0N 160 0W
Belcher Is. 150 56 15N 78 45W
Belchite 58 41 18N 0 43W
Belclare 38 53 29N 8 55W
Belcoo 38 54 18N 7 52W
Belderg 38 54 18N 9 33W
Beldringe 73 55 28N 10 21E
Belebey 84 54 7N 54 7E
Belém de São Francisco 170 8 46S 38 58W
Belém (Pará) 170 1 20S 48 30W
Belén, Argent. 172 27 40S 67 5W
Belén, Colomb. 174 1 26N 75 56W
Belén, Parag. 172 23 30S 57 6W
Belen 161 34 40N 106 50W
Belene 67 43 39N 25 10E
Bélesta 44 42 55N 1 56E
Belet Uen 91 4 30N 45 5E
Belev 81 53 50N 36 5E
Belfast, N.Z. 143 43 27S 172 39E
Belfast, S. Afr. 129 25 42S 30 2E
Belfast, U.K. 38 54 35N 5 56W
Belfast, U.S.A. 151 44 30N 69 0W
Belfast □ 38 54 35N 5 56W
Belfast, L. 38 54 40N 5 50W
Belfeld 47 51 18N 6 6E
Belfeoram 151 47 32N 55 30W
Belfield 158 46 54N 103 11W
Belford 35 55 36N 1 50W
Belfort 43 47 38N 6 50E
Belfort □ 43 47 38N 6 52E
Belfry 160 45 10N 109 2W
Belgaum 97 15 55N 74 35E
Belgioioso 62 45 9N 9 21E
Belgium ■ 47 51 30N 5 0E
Belgooly 138 51 44N 8 30W
Belgorod 82 50 35N 36 35E
Belgorod Dnestrovskiy 82 46 11N 30 23E
Belgrade 160 45 50N 111 10W
Belgrade = Beograd 66 44 50N 20 37E
Belgrove 143 41 27S 172 59E
Belhaven 157 35 34N 76 35W
Beli 121 7 52N 10 58E
Beli Drim, R. 66 42 25N 20 34E
Beli Manastir 66 45 45N 18 36E
Beli Timok, R. 66 43 39N 22 14E
Belice, R. 64 37 44N 12 58E
Belinga 124 1 10N 13 2E
Belingwe 127 20 29S 29 57E
Belingwe, N., mt. 127 20 37S 29 55E
Belinsky (Chembar) 81 53 0N 43 25E
Belinţ 66 45 48N 21 54E
Belinyu 102 1 35S 105 50E
Beliton, Is. 102 3 10S 107 50E
Belitung, I. 102 3 10S 107 50E
Beliu 70 46 30N 22 0E
Belize ■ 165 17 0N 88 30W
Belize City 165 17 25N 88 0W
Beljanica 66 44 08N 21 43E
Bell 151 53 50N 53 10E
Bell Bay 138 41 6S 146 53E
Bell I. 151 50 46N 55 35W
Bell Irving, R. 152 56 12N 129 5W
Bell Peninsula 149 63 50N 82 0W
Bell, R. 150 49 48N 77 38W
Bell Rock = Inchcape Rock 35 56 26N 2 24W
Bell Ville 172 32 40S 62 40W
Bella Bella 152 52 10N 128 10W
Bella Coola 152 52 25N 126 40W
Bella Unión 172 30 15S 57 40W
Bella Vista, Corrientes, Argent. 172 28 33S 59 0W
Bella Vista, Tucuman, Argent. 172 27 10S 65 25W
Bella Yella 120 7 24N 10 9W
Bellacorick 38 54 8N 9 35W
Bellaghy 38 54 50N 6 31W
Bellágio 62 45 59N 9 15E
Bellaire 156 40 1N 80 46W
Bellananagh 38 53 55N 7 25W
Bellarena 38 55 7N 6 57W
Bellarwi 141 34 6S 147 13E
Bellary 97 15 10N 76 56E
Bellata 139 29 53S 149 46E
Bellavary 38 53 54N 9 9W
Belle Fourche 158 44 43N 103 52W
Belle Fourche, R. 158 44 25N 105 0W
Belle Glade 157 26 43N 80 38W
Belle Ile 42 47 20N 3 10W
Belle Isle 151 51 57N 55 25W
Belle-Isle-en-Terre 42 48 33N 3 23W
Belle Isle, Str. of 151 51 30N 56 30W
Belle, La 157 26 45N 81 22W
Belle Plaine, Iowa, U.S.A. 158 41 51N 92 18W
Belle Plaine, Minn., U.S.A. 158 44 35N 93 48W
Belledonne 45 45 11N 6 0E
Belledune 151 47 55N 65 50W
Belleek 38 54 30N 8 6W
Bellefontaine 156 40 20N 83 45W
Bellefonte 156 40 56N 77 45W
Bellegarde, Ain, France 45 46 4N 5 49E
Bellegarde, Creuse, France 43 45 59N 2 19E
Bellegarde, Loiret, France 43 48 0N 2 26E
Belleoram 151 47 31N 55 25W
Belleville, Can. 150 44 10N 77 23W
Belleville, Rhône, France 45 46 7N 4 45E
Belleville, Vendée, France 42 46 48N 1 28W
Belleville, Ill., U.S.A. 158 38 30N 90 0W
Belleville, Kans., U.S.A. 158 39 51N 97 38W
Belleville, N.Y., U.S.A. 162 43 46N 76 10W
Bellevue, Can. 152 49 35N 114 22W
Bellevue, U.S.A. 160 43 25N 144 23W
Belley 45 45 46N 5 41E
Bellin (Payne Bay) 149 60 0N 70 0W
Bellingen 141 30 25S 152 50E
Bellingham, U.K. 35 55 09N 2 16W
Bellingham, U.S.A. 160 48 45N 122 27W
Bellingshausen Sea 13 66 0S 80 0W
Bellinzona 51 46 11N 9 1E
Bello 174 6 20N 75 33W
Bellona Reefs 133 21 26S 159 0E
Bellows Falls 162 43 10N 72 30W
Bellpat 94 29 0N 68 5E
Bellpuig 58 41 37N 1 1E
Belluno 63 46 8N 12 6E
Bellville 159 29 58N 96 18W
Belmar 162 40 10N 74 2W
Bélmez 57 38 17N 5 17W
Belmont, Austral. 141 33 4S 151 42E
Belmont, U.S.A. 162 43 27N 71 29W
Belmonte, Brazil 171 16 0S 39 0W
Belmonte, Port. 56 40 21N 7 20W
Belmonte, Spain 58 39 34N 2 43W
Belmopan 165 17 18N 88 30W
Belmore 140 33 34S 141 13E
Belmullet 38 54 13N 9 58W
Belo Horizonte 171 19 55S 43 56W
Belo Jardim 170 8 20S 36 26W
Belo-sur-Mer 129 20 42S 44 33E
Belo-sur-Tsiribihana 129 19 40S 43 30E
Belogorsk, R.S.F.S.R., U.S.S.R. 77 51 0N 128 20E
Belogorsk, Ukraine, U.S.S.R. 82 45 3N 34 35E
Belogradchik 66 43 37N 22 40E
Belogradets 67 43 22N 27 18E
Beloha 129 25 10S 45 3E
Beloit, Kans., U.S.A. 158 39 32N 98 9W
Beloit, Wis., U.S.A. 158 42 35N 89 0W
Belokholunitskiy 81 58 55N 50 43E
Belomorsk 78 64 35N 34 30E
Belonia 98 23 15N 91 30E
Belopolye 80 51 14N 34 20E
Beloretsk 84 53 58N 58 24E
Belovo 76 54 30N 86 0E
Beloyarskiy 84 56 45N 61 24E
Beloye More 78 66 0N 38 0E
Beloye, Oz. 78 60 10N 37 35E
Beloye Ozero 83 45 15N 46 50E
Belozersk 81 60 0N 37 30E
Belpasso 65 37 37N 15 0E
Belper 33 53 2N 1 29W
Belsay 35 55 6N 1 53W
Belsele 47 51 9N 4 6E
Belsito 64 37 50N 13 47E
Beltana 140 30 48S 138 25E
Belterra 175 2 45S 55 0W
Beltinci 63 46 37N 16 20E
Belton, Humberside, U.K. 33 53 33N 0 49W
Belton, Norfolk, U.K. 29 52 35N 1 39E
Belton, S.C., U.S.A. 157 34 31N 82 39W
Belton, Tex., U.S.A. 159 31 4N 97 30W
Beltra, Mayo, Ireland 38 53 57N 9 24W
Beltra, Sligo, Ireland 38 54 12N 8 36W
Beltra L. 38 53 56N 9 28W
Beltsy 82 47 48N 28 0E
Belturbet 38 54 6N 7 28W
Belukha 76 49 50N 86 50E
Beluran 102 5 48N 117 35E
Beluša 53 49 5N 18 27E
Belušió 66 43 50N 21 10E
Belvedere Marittimo 65 39 37N 15 52E
Belvès 44 44 46N 1 0E
Belvidere, Ill., U.S.A. 158 42 15N 88 55W
Belvidere, N.J., U.S.A. 162 40 48N 75 5W
Belville 38 54 40N 9 22W
Belvis de la Jara 57 39 45N 4 57W
Belyando, R. 138 21 38S 146 50E
Belyj Jar 76 58 26N 84 39E
Belyy 80 55 48N 32 51E
Belyy, Ostrov 76 73 30N 71 0E
Belyye Vody 85 42 25N 69 50E
Belz 80 50 23N 24 1E
Belzig 48 52 8N 12 36E
Belzoni 159 33 12N 90 30W
Bemaraha, Plat. du 129 18 40S 44 45E
Bemarivo, Majunga, Madag. 129 17 6S 44 31E
Bemarivo, Tuléar, Madag. 129 21 45S 44 45E
Bemarivo, R. 129 21 45S 44 45E
Bemavo 129 21 33S 45 25E
Bembéréke 121 10 11N 2 43E
Bembesi 127 20 0S 28 58E
Bembesi, R. 127 20 0S 28 58E
Bembézar, R. 57 38 0N 5 20W
Bembridge 28 50 41N 1 4W
Bemidji 158 47 30N 94 50W
Bemmel 46 51 54N 5 54E
Ben Alder 37 55 59N 4 30W
Ben Avon 37 57 6N 3 28W
Ben Bheigeir, Mt. 34 55 43N 6 6W
Ben Bullen 141 33 12S 150 2E
Ben Chonzine 35 56 27N 4 0W
Ben Cruachan, Mt. 34 56 26N 5 8W
Ben Dearg 37 57 47N 4 58W
Ben Dearg, mt. 37 56 54N 3 49W
Ben Dhorain 37 58 7N 3 50W
Ben Dorian 34 56 30N 4 42W
Ben Gardane 119 33 11N 11 11E
Ben Hee 37 58 16N 4 43W
Ben Hope, mt. 37 58 24N 4 36W
Ben Klibreck 37 58 14N 4 25W
Ben Lawers, mt. 37 56 33N 4 13W
Ben Lomond, mt. 139 30 1S 151 43E
Ben Lomond mt. 138 41 38S 147 42E
Ben Lomond, mt. 34 56 12N 4 39W
Ben Loyal 37 58 25N 4 25W
Ben Luc 101 10 39N 106 29E
Ben Lui, mt. 34 56 24N 4 50W
Ben Macdhui 37 57 4N 3 40W
Ben Mhor 36 57 16N 7 21W
Ben More, Mull, U.K. 34 56 26N 6 2W
Ben More, Perth, U.K. 34 56 23N 4 31W
Ben More Assynt 37 58 7N 4 51W
Ben Nevis, mt., N.Z. 143 45 15S 169 0E
Ben Nevis, mt., U.K. 36 56 48N 5 0W
Ben Ohau Ra. 143 44 1S 170 4E
Ben Quang 100 17 3N 106 55E
Ben Stack 36 58 20N 4 58W
Ben Tharsiunn 37 57 47N 4 20W
Ben Venue 34 56 13N 4 28W
Ben Vorlich 34 56 22N 4 15W
Ben Wyvis, mt. 37 57 40N 4 35W
Bena 121 11 20N 5 50E
Bena Dibele 124 4 4S 22 50E
Benagalbón 57 36 45N 4 15W
Benagerie 140 31 25S 140 22E
Benahmed 118 33 4N 7 9W
Benalla 141 36 30S 146 0E
Benambra, Mt. 141 36 31S 147 34E
Benamejí 57 37 16N 4 33W
Benanee 140 34 31S 142 52E
Benares = Varanasi 95 25 22N 83 8E
Benavente, Port. 57 38 59N 8 49W
Benavente, Spain 56 42 2N 5 43W
Benavides, Spain 56 42 30N 5 54W
Benavides, U.S.A. 159 27 35N 98 28W
Benbane Hd. 38 55 15N 6 30W
Benbaun, Mt. 38 53 30N 9 50W
Benbecula, I. 36 57 26N 7 21W
Benbonyathe, Mt. 140 30 25S 139 11E
Benburb 38 54 25N 6 42W
Bencubbin 137 30 48S 117 52E
Bend 160 44 2N 121 15W
Bendel □ 121 6 0N 6 0E
Bender Beila 91 9 30N 50 48E
Bender Cassim 91 11 12N 49 18E
Bendering 137 32 23S 118 18E
Bendery 82 46 50N 29 50E
Bendigo 140 36 40S 144 15E
Beneden Knijpe 46 52 58N 5 59E
Benedick 162 38 31N 76 41W
Beneditinos 170 5 27S 42 22W
Benedito Leite 170 7 13S 44 34W
Benei Beraq 129 32 5N 34 50E
Bénéna 120 13 9N 4 17W
Beneraird, Mt. 34 55 4N 4 57W
Benešöv 52 49 46N 14 41E
Bénestroff 43 48 54N 6 45E
Benet 44 46 22N 0 35W
Benevento 65 41 7N 14 45E
Benfeld 43 48 22N 7 34E
Beng Lovea 100 12 36N 105 34E
Benga 127 16 11S 33 40E
Bengal, Bay of 99 15 0N 90 0E
Bengawan Solo 103 7 5S 112 25E
Benghazi = Banghāzī 119 32 11N 20 3E
Bengkalis 102 1 30N 102 10E
Bengkulu 102 3 50S 102 12E
Bengkulu □ 102 3 48S 102 16E
Bengough 153 49 25N 105 10W
Benguela 125 12 37S 13 25E
Benguerir 118 32 16N 7 56W
Benguérua, Î. 129 21 58S 35 28E
Benha 122 30 26N 31 8E
Beni 126 0 30N 29 27E
Beni Abbès 118 30 5N 2 5W
Beni Haoua 118 36 30N 1 30E
Benî Mazâr 122 28 32N 30 44E
Beni Mellal 118 32 21N 6 21W
Beni Ounif 118 32 0N 1 10W
Beni, R. 174 10 30S 66 0W
Beni Saf 118 35 17N 1 15W
Benî Suêf 122 29 5N 31 6E
Beniah L. 152 63 23N 112 17W
Benicarló 58 40 23N 0 23E
Benicia 163 38 3N 122 9W
Benidorm 59 38 33N 0 9W
Benidorm, Islote de 59 38 31N 0 9W
Benin ■ 121 10 0N 2 0E
Benin, Bight of 121 5 0N 3 0E
Benin City 121 6 20N 5 31E
Benington 33 52 59N 0 5E
Benisa 59 38 43N 0 03E
Benjamin Aceval 172 24 58S 57 34W
Benjamin Constant 174 4 40S 70 15W
Benjamin Hill 164 30 10N 111 10W
Benkelman 158 40 7N 101 32W
Benlidi 138 24 35S 144 50E
Benmore Pk. 143 44 25S 170 8E
Bennane Hd. 34 55 9N 5 2W
Bennebroek 46 52 19N 4 36E
Bennekom 46 52 0N 5 41E
Bennett 147 59 56N 134 53W
Bennettsbridge 39 52 36N 7 12W
Bennettsville 157 34 38N 79 39W
Bennington 162 42 52N 73 12W
Benoa 102 8 50S 115 20E
Bénodet 42 47 53N 4 7W
Benoni 129 26 11S 28 18E
Benoud 118 32 20N 0 16E
Benque Viejo 165 17 5N 89 8W
Bensheim 49 49 40N 8 38E
Benson, U.K. 28 51 37N 1 6W
Benson, U.S.A. 161 31 59N 110 19W
Bent 93 26 20N 59 25E
Benteng 103 6 10S 120 30E
Bentinck I. 138 17 3S 139 35E
Bentiu 123 9 10N 29 55E
Bentley, Hants., U.K. 29 51 12N 0 52W
Bentley, S. Yorks, U.K. 33 53 33N 1 9W
Bento Gonçalves 173 29 10S 51 31W
Benton, Ark., U.S.A. 159 34 30N 92 35W
Benton, Calif., U.S.A. 163 37 48N 118 32W
Benton, Ill., U.S.A. 158 38 0N 88 55W
Benton, Pa., U.S.A. 162 41 12N 76 23W
Benton Harbor 156 42 10N 86 28W
Bentong 101 3 31N 101 55E
Bentu Liben 123 8 32N 38 21E
Benue □ 121 7 30N 7 30E
Benue Plateau □ 121 8 0N 8 30E
Benue, R. 121 7 50N 6 30E
Benwee Hd. 38 54 20N 9 50W
Beo 103 4 25N 126 50E
Beograd 66 44 50N 20 37E
Beowawe 160 40 45N 117 0W
Beppu 110 33 15N 131 30E
Beppu-Wan 110 33 18N 131 34E
Ber Dagan 90 32 1N 34 49E
Bera 98 24 5N 89 37E
Beragh 38 54 34N 7 10W
Berakit 123 14 38N 39 29E
Berati 68 40 43N 19 59E
Berber 122 18 0N 34 0E
Berbéra 117 10 33N 16 35E
Berbera 91 10 30N 45 2E
Berbérati 124 4 15N 15 40E
Berberia, Cabo 59 38 39N 1 24E
Berbice, R. 174 5 20N 58 10W
Berceto 62 44 30N 10 0E
Berchtesgaden 49 47 37N 13 1E
Berck-sur-Mer 43 50 25N 1 36E
Berdichev 82 49 57N 28 30E
Berdsk 76 54 47N 83 2E
Berdyansk 82 46 45N 36 50E
Berdyaush 84 55 9N 59 9E
Bere Alston 30 50 29N 4 11W
Bere Regis 28 50 45N 2 13W
Berea 156 37 35N 84 18W
Berebere 103 2 25N 128 45E
Bereda 91 11 45N 51 0E
Bereina 135 8 39S 146 30E
Berekum 120 7 29N 2 34W
Berenice 122 24 2N 35 25E
Berens I. 153 52 18N 97 18W
Berens, R. 153 51 21N 97 0W
Berens River 153 52 25N 97 0W
Berestechko 80 50 22N 25 5E
Bereşti 70 46 6N 27 50E
Berettyo, R. 53 47 32N 21 47E
Berettyóújfalu 53 47 13N 21 33E
Beretŭu, R. 70 47 30N 22 7E
Berevo 129 19 44S 44 58E
Berevo-sur-Ranobe 129 17 14S 44 17E
Bereza 80 52 31N 24 51E
Berezhany 80 49 26N 24 58E
Berezina, R. 80 54 10N 28 10E
Berezna 80 51 35N 30 46E
Berezniki 84 59 24N 56 46E
Berezovka 82 47 25N 30 55E
Berezovo 76 64 0N 65 0E
Berg 71 59 10N 11 18E
Berga, Spain 58 42 6N 1 48E
Berga, Kalmar, Sweden 73 57 14N 16 3E
Berga, Kronoberg, Sweden 73 56 55N 14 0E
Bergama 92 39 8N 27 15E
Bergambacht 46 51 56N 4 48E
Bérgamo 62 45 42N 9 40E
Bergantiños 56 43 20N 8 40W
Bergedorf 48 53 28N 10 12E
Bergeijk 47 51 19N 5 21E
Bergen, Ger. 48 54 24N 13 26E
Bergen, Norway 71 60 23N 5 20E
Bergen-Binnen 46 52 40N 4 43E
Bergen-op-Zoom 47 51 30N 4 18E
Bergerac 44 44 51N 0 30E
Bergheim 48 50 57N 6 38E
Berghem 46 51 46N 5 33E

Bergisch-Gladbach Billesdon

Bergisch-Gladbach 48 50 59N 7 9E
Bergkvara 73 56 23N 16 5E
Bergschenhoek 46 51 59N 4 30E
Bergsjö 72 61 59N 17 3E
Berguent 118 34 1N 2 0W
Bergues 43 50 58N 2 24E
Bergum 46 53 13N 5 59E
Bergvik 72 61 16N 16 50E
Berhala, Selat 102 1 0S 104 15E
Berhampore 95 24 2N 88 27E
Berhampur 96 19 15N 84 54E
Berheci, R. 70 46 7N 27 19E
Berhungra 139 34 46S 147 52E
Bering Sea 130 58 0N 167 0E
Bering Str. 147 66 0N 170 0W
Beringarra 137 26 0S 116 55E
Beringen, Belg. 47 51 3N 5 14E
Beringen, Switz. 51 47 38N 8 34E
Beringovskiy 77 63 3N 179 19E
Berislav 82 46 50N 33 30E
Berisso 172 34 40S 58 0W
Berja 59 36 50N 2 56W
Berkane 118 34 52N 2 20W
Berkel, R. 46 52 8N 6 12E
Berkeley 163 37 52N 122 20W
Berkeley Springs 156 39 38N 78 12W
Berkhamsted 29 51 45N 0 33W
Berkhout 46 52 38N 4 59E
Berkner I. 13 79 30S 50 0W
Berkovitsa 67 43 16N 23 8E
Berkshire 162 42 19N 76 11W
Berkshire □ 28 51 30N 1 20W
Berkshire Downs 28 51 30N 1 30W
Berkyk 71 62 50N 9 59E
Berlaar 47 51 7N 4 39E
Berland, R. 152 54 0N 116 50W
Berlanga 57 38 17N 5 50W
Berlave 47 51 2N 4 0E
Berleburg 48 51 3N 8 22E
Berlenga, I. 75 39 25N 9 30W
Berlick 47 51 22N 6 9E
Berlin, Ger. 48 52 32N 13 24E
Berlin, Md., U.S.A. 162 38 19N 75 12W
Berlin, N.H., U.S.A. 156 44 29N 71 10W
Berlin, N.Y., U.S.A. 162 42 42N 73 23W
Berlin, E. □ 48 52 30N 13 30E
Berlin, W. □ 48 52 30N 13 20E
Bermeja, Sierra 57 36 45N 5 11W
Bermejo, R., Formosa, Argent. 172 26 30S 58 50W
Bermejo, R., San Juan, Argent. 172 30 0S 68 0W
Bermeo 58 43 25N 2 47W
Bermillo de Sayago 56 41 22N 6 8W
Bermuda, I. 10 32 45N 65 0W
Bern (Berne) 50 46 57N 7 28E
Bern (Berne) □ 50 46 45N 7 40E
Bernalda 65 40 24N 16 44E
Bernalillo 161 35 17N 106 37W
Bernam, R. 101 3 45N 101 5E
Bernardo de Irigoyen 173 26 15S 53 40W
Bernardsville 162 40 43N 74 34W
Bernasconi 172 37 55S 63 44W
Bernau 49 47 53N 12 20E
Bernay 42 49 5N 0 35E
Berndorf 52 47 59N 16 1E
Berne = Bern 50 46 57N 7 28E
Berner Alpen 50 46 27N 7 35E
Berneray, I. 36 56 47N 7 38W
Bernese Oberland = Oberland 50 46 27N 7 35E
Bernier I. 137 24 50S 113 12E
Bernina Pass 51 46 22N 9 54E
Bernina, Piz 51 46 20N 9 54E
Bernissart 47 50 28N 3 39E
Beroroha 125 21 40S 45 10E
Béroubouey 121 10 34N 2 46E
Beroun 52 49 57N 14 5E
Berounka, R. 52 50 0N 13 47E
Berovo 66 41 42N 22 51E
Berrahal 119 36 54N 7 33E
Berre 45 43 28N 5 11E
Berre, Étang de 45 43 27N 5 5E
Berrechid 118 33 18N 7 36W
Berri 140 34 14S 140 35E
Berriedale 37 58 12N 3 30W
Berriew 31 52 36N 3 12W
Berrigan 141 35 38S 145 49E
Berrouaghia 118 36 10N 2 53E
Berrwillock 140 35 36S 142 59E
Berry, Austral. 141 34 46S 150 43E
Berry, France 43 47 0N 2 0E
Berry Hd. 30 50 24N 3 29W
Berry Is. 166 25 40N 77 50W
Berryville 159 36 23N 93 35W
Bersenbrück 48 52 33N 7 56E
Berst Ness 37 59 16N 3 0W
Berthaund 158 40 21N 105 5W
Berthier Is. 136 14 29S 124 59E
Berthold 158 48 19N 101 45W
Bertincourt 43 50 5N 2 58E
Bertoua 124 4 30N 13 45E
Bertraghboy, B. 38 53 22N 9 54W
Bertrand 158 40 35N 99 38W
Bertrange 47 49 37N 6 3E
Bertrix 47 49 51N 5 15E
Beruas 101 4 30N 100 47E
Berufjörður 74 64 48N 14 29W
Berur Hayil 90 31 34N 34 38E
Berwick 162 41 4N 76 17W
Berwick (□) 26 55 46N 2 30W
Berwick-upon-Tweed 35 55 47N 2 0W
Berwyn Mts. 31 52 54N 3 26W
Beryl N., oilfield 19 59 37N 1 30E
Beryl, oilfield 19 59 28N 1 30E
Beryl W., oilfield 19 59 32N 1 20E
Berzasca 66 44 39N 21 58E
Berzence 53 46 12N 17 11E
Besal 95 35 4N 73 56E
Besalampy 129 16 43S 44 29E
Besançon 43 47 9N 6 0E
Besar 102 2 40S 116 0E
Beserah 101 3 50N 103 21E
Beshenkovichi 80 55 2N 29 29E
Beška 66 45 8N 20 6E
Beskids, Mts. 53 49 35N 18 40E
Beslan 83 43 22N 44 28E
Besna Kobila 66 42 31N 22 10E
Besnard L. 153 55 25N 106 0W
Beşparmak Daği 69 37 32N 27 30E
Bessarabiya 70 46 20N 29 0E
Bessarabka 82 46 21N 28 51E
Bessbrook 38 54 12N 6 25W
Bessèges 45 44 18N 4 8E
Bessemer 158 46 27N 90 0W
Bessin 42 49 21N 1 0W
Bessines-sur-Gartempe 42 46 6N 1 22E
Best 47 51 31N 5 23E
Bet Alfa 90 32 31N 35 25E
Bet Guvrin 90 31 37N 34 54E
Bet Hashitta 90 32 31N 35 27E
Bet Ha'tmeq 90 32 58N 35 8E
Bet Qeshet 90 32 41N 35 21E
Bet She'an 90 32 30N 35 30E
Bet Tadjine, Djebel 118 29 0N 3 30W
Bet Yosef 90 32 34N 35 33E
Betafo 129 19 50S 46 51E
Betanzos 56 43 15N 8 12W
Bétaré-Oya 124 5 40N 14 5E
Betekom 47 50 59N 4 47E
Bétera 58 39 35N 0 28W
Bethal 129 26 27S 29 28E
Bethanien 125 26 31S 17 8E
Bethany, S. Afr. 128 29 34S 25 59E
Bethany, U.S.A. 158 40 18N 94 0W
Bethany = Eizarilya 90 31 47N 35 15E
Bethel, U.S.A. 147 60 50N 161 50W
Bethel, Conn., U.S.A. 162 41 22N 73 25W
Bethesda, U.K. 31 53 11N 4 3W
Bethesda, U.S.A. 162 38 59N 77 6W
Bethlehem, S. Afr. 129 28 14S 28 18E
Bethlehem, U.S.A. 162 40 39N 75 24W
Bethlehem = Bayt Lahm 90 31 43N 35 12E
Bethulie 128 30 30S 25 59E
Béthune 43 50 30N 2 38E
Béthune, R. 42 49 56N 1 5E
Bethungra 141 34 45S 147 51E
Betijoque 174 9 23N 70 44W
Betim 171 19 58S 44 13W
Betioky 129 23 48S 44 20E
Beton Bazoches 43 48 42N 3 15E
Betong 101 5 45N 101 5E
Betoota 138 25 40S 140 42E
Betroka 129 23 16S 46 0E
Betsiamites 151 48 56N 68 40W
Betsiamites, R. 151 48 56N 68 40W
Betsiboka, R. 129 17 0S 47 0E
Betsjoeanaland 128 26 30S 22 30E
Bettembourg 47 49 31N 6 6E
Betterton 162 39 52N 76 4W
Betteshanger 29 51 14N 1 20E
Bettiah 95 26 48N 84 33E
Bettles 147 66 54N 150 50W
Bèttola 62 44 46N 9 35E
Bettws Bledrws 31 52 9N 4 2W
Bettyhill 37 58 31N 4 12W
Betul 96 21 48N 77 59E
Betung 102 2 0S 103 10E
Betws-y-Coed 31 53 4N 3 49W
Beuca 70 44 14N 24 56E
Beuil 45 44 6N 7 0E
Beulah, Can. 153 50 16N 101 02W
Beulah, U.S.A. 158 47 18N 101 47W
Beuvronne, La 46 48 59N 2 41E
Bevensen 48 53 5N 10 34E
Beveren 47 51 12N 4 16E
Beverley, Austral. 137 32 9S 116 56E
Beverley, U.K. 33 53 52N 0 26W
Beverlo 47 51 7N 5 13E
Beverly, Can. 152 53 36N 113 21W
Beverly, Mass., U.S.A. 162 42 32N 70 50W
Beverly, Wash., U.S.A. 160 46 55N 119 59W
Beverly Hills 163 34 4N 118 29W
Beverwijk 46 52 28N 4 38E
Bewdley 28 52 23N 2 19W
Bex 50 46 15N 7 0E
Bexhill 29 50 51N 0 29E
Bexley 29 51 26N 0 10E
Beyin 120 5 1N 2 41W
Beykoz 67 41 8N 29 7E
Beyla 120 8 30N 8 38W
Beynat 44 45 8N 1 44E
Beyneu 76 45 10N 55 3E
Beypazaı 92 40 10N 31 48E
Beyşehir Gölü 92 37 40N 31 45E
Bezdan 66 45 28N 18 57E
Bezerros 171 8 14S 35 45W
Bezet 90 33 4N 35 8E
Bezhitsa 80 53 19N 34 17E
Béziers 44 43 20N 3 12E
Bezwada = Vijayawada 97 16 31N 80 39E
Bhachau 93 23 20N 70 16E
Bhadarwah 95 32 58N 75 46E
Bhadra, R. 97 13 0N 76 0E
Bhadrakh 96 21 10N 86 30E
Bhadravati 97 13 49N 76 15E
Bhagalpur 95 25 10N 87 0E
Bhairab 98 22 51N 89 34E
Bhairab Bazar 98 24 4N 90 58E
Bhaisa 96 19 10N 77 58E
Bhakkar 94 31 40N 71 5E
Bhakra Dam 95 31 30N 76 45E
Bhamo 98 24 15N 97 15E
Bhamragarh 96 19 30N 80 40E
Bhandara 96 21 5N 79 42E
Bhanrer Ra. 94 23 40N 79 45E
Bharat = India 93 24 0N 78 0E
Bharatpur 94 27 15N 77 30E
Bharuch 96 21 47N 73 0E
Bhatghar L. 96 18 10N 73 48E
Bhatiapara Ghat 98 23 13N 89 42E
Bhatkal 97 13 58N 74 35E
Bhatpara 95 22 50N 88 25E
Bhattiprolu 97 16 7N 80 45E
Bhaun 94 32 55N 72 40E
Bhaunagar = Bhavnagar 94 21 45N 72 10E
Bhavani 97 11 27N 77 43E
Bhavani, R. 97 11 30N 77 15E
Bhavnagar 94 21 45N 72 10E
Bhawanipatna 96 19 55N 83 30E
Bhera 94 32 29N 72 57E
Bhilsa = Vidisha 94 23 28N 77 53E
Bhilwara 94 25 25N 74 38E
Bhima, R. 96 17 20N 76 30E
Bhimber 95 32 59N 74 3E
Bhimvaram 96 16 30N 81 30E
Bhind 96 26 30N 78 46E
Bhir 96 19 4N 75 58E
Bhiwandi 96 19 15N 73 0E
Bhiwani 94 28 50N 76 9E
Bhola 98 22 45N 90 35E
Bhongir 96 17 30N 78 56E
Bhopal 94 23 20N 77 53E
Bhor 96 18 12N 73 53E
Bhubaneswar 96 20 15N 85 50E
Bhuj 94 23 15N 69 49E
Bhumibol Dam 100 17 15N 98 58E
Bhusaval 96 21 15N 69 49E
Bhutan ■ 98 27 25N 89 50E
Biafra, B. of = Bonny, Bight of 121 3 30N 9 20E
Biak 103 1 0S 136 0E
Biała 54 50 24N 17 40E
Biała Piska 54 53 37N 22 5E
Biała Podlaska 54 52 4N 23 6E
Biała Podlaska □ 54 52 0N 23 0E
Biała, R. 54 49 46N 20 53E
Białogard 54 54 2N 15 58E
Biały Bór 54 53 53N 16 51E
Białystok 54 53 10N 23 10E
Białystok □ 54 53 9N 23 10E
Biancavilla 65 37 39N 14 50E
Biano Plateau = Manika Plateau 127 9 55S 26 24E
Biaro 103 2 5N 125 26E
Biarritz 44 43 29N 1 33W
Biasca 51 46 22N 8 58E
Biba 122 28 55N 31 0E
Bibaï 112 43 19N 141 52E
Bibby I. 153 61 55N 93 0W
Biberach 49 48 5N 9 49E
Biberist 50 47 11N 7 34E
Bibey, R. 56 42 24N 7 13W
Bibiani 120 6 30N 2 8W
Bibile 97 7 10N 81 25E
Biboohra 138 16 56S 145 25E
Bibungwa 126 2 40S 28 15E
Bibury 28 51 46N 1 50W
Bic 151 48 20N 68 41W
Bicaj 68 42 0N 20 25E
Bicaz 70 46 53N 26 5E
Biccari 65 41 23N 15 12E
Bicester 28 51 53N 1 9W
Biche, La, R. 152 59 57N 123 50W
Bichena 123 10 28N 38 10E
Bickerton I. 138 13 45S 136 10E
Bicknell, Ind., U.S.A. 156 38 50N 87 20W
Bicknell, Utah, U.S.A. 161 38 16N 111 35W
Bicsad 70 47 56N 23 28E
Bicton 28 52 43N 2 47W
Bida 121 9 3N 5 58E
Bidar 96 17 55N 77 35E
Biddeford 151 43 30N 70 28W
Biddenden 29 51 7N 0 40E
Biddu 90 31 50N 35 8E
Biddulph 32 53 8N 2 11W
Biddwara 123 5 11N 38 34E
Biddya 90 32 7N 35 4E
Bideford 30 51 1N 4 13W
Bideford Bay 30 51 5N 4 20W
Bidford on Avon 28 52 9N 1 53W
Bidor 101 4 6N 101 15E
Bidura 140 34 10S 143 21E
Bié 125 12 22S 16 55E
Bié Plateau 125 12 0S 16 0E
Bieber 160 41 4N 121 6W
Biel (Bienne) 50 47 8N 7 14E
Bielawa 54 50 43N 16 37E
Bielé Karpaty 53 49 5N 18 0E
Bielefeld 48 52 2N 8 31E
Bielersee 50 47 6N 7 5E
Biella 62 45 33N 8 3E
Bielsk Podlaski 54 52 47N 23 12E
Bielsko-Biała 54 49 50N 19 8E
Bielsko-Biała □ 54 49 45N 19 15E
Bien Hoa 101 10 57N 106 49E
Bienfait 153 49 10N 102 50W
Bienne = Biel 50 47 8N 7 14E
Bienvenida 57 38 18N 6 12W
Bienville, L. 150 55 5N 72 40W
Biescas 58 42 37N 0 20W
Biesiesfontein 128 30 57S 17 58E
Bietigheim 49 48 57N 9 8E
Bievre 47 49 57N 5 1E
Biferno, R. 65 41 40N 14 38E
Big B. 151 55 43N 60 35W
Big Bear City 163 34 16N 116 51W
Big Bear L. 163 34 15N 116 56W
Big Beaver 153 49 10N 105 10W
Big Beaver House 150 52 59N 89 50W
Big Bell 137 27 21S 117 40E
Big Belt Mts. 160 46 50N 111 30W
Big Bend 129 26 50S 32 2E
Big Bend Nat. Park 159 29 15N 103 15W
Big Black, R. 159 32 35N 90 30W
Big Blue, R. 158 40 20N 96 40W
Big Cr. 152 51 42N 122 41W
Big Creek 163 37 11N 119 14W
Big Cypress Swamp 157 26 12N 81 10W
Big Delta 147 64 15N 145 0W
Big Falls 158 48 11N 93 48W
Big Horn 160 46 11N 107 25W
Big Horn Mts. = Bighorn Mts. 160 44 30N 107 30W
Big Horn R. 160 45 30N 108 10W
Big Lake 159 31 12N 101 25W
Big Moose 162 43 49N 74 58W
Big Muddy, R. 158 48 25N 104 45W
Big Pine 163 37 12N 118 17W
Big Piney 160 42 32N 110 3W
Big Quill L. 153 51 55N 105 22W
Big, R. 151 54 50N 58 55W
Big Rapids 156 43 42N 85 27W
Big River 153 53 50N 107 0W
Big Sable Pt. 156 44 5N 86 30W
Big Salmon 147 61 50N 136 0W
Big Sand L. 153 57 45N 99 45W
Big Sandy 160 48 12N 110 9W
Big Sandy Cr. 158 38 52N 103 11W
Big Sioux, R. 158 44 20N 96 53W
Big Smoky Valley 163 38 30N 117 15W
Big Snowy Mt. 160 46 50N 109 15W
Big Spring 159 32 10N 101 25W
Big Springs 158 41 4N 102 3W
Big Stone City 158 45 20N 96 30W
Big Stone Gap 157 36 52N 82 45W
Big Stone L. 158 44 25N 96 35W
Big Sur 163 36 15N 121 48W
Big Trout L. 150 53 40N 90 0W
Biganos 44 44 39N 0 59W
Bigbury 30 50 17N 3 52W
Bigbury B. 30 50 18N 3 58W
Bigerymunal, Mt. 137 27 25S 120 40E
Bigfork 160 48 3N 114 2W
Biggar 153 52 4N 108 0W
Bigge I. 136 14 35S 125 10E
Biggenden 139 25 31S 152 4E
Biggleswade 29 52 6N 0 16W
Bighorn Mts. 160 44 30N 107 30W
Bignona 120 12 52N 16 23W
Bigorre 44 43 5N 0 2E
Bigstone L. 153 53 42N 95 44W
Bigtimber 160 45 53N 110 0W
Bigwa 126 7 10S 39 10E
Bihaó 63 44 49N 15 57E
Bihar 95 25 5N 85 40E
Bihar □ 95 25 0N 86 0E
Biharamulo 126 2 25S 31 25E
Biharamulo □ 126 2 30S 31 20E
Biharkeresztes 53 47 8N 21 44E
Bihé Plateau 125 12 0S 16 0E
Bihor □ 70 47 0N 22 10E
Bihor, Munţii 70 46 29N 22 47E
Bijagós, Arquipélago dos 120 11 15N 16 10W
Bijaipur 94 26 2N 77 36E
Bijapur, Mad. P., India 96 18 50N 80 50E
Bijapur, Mysore, India 96 16 50N 75 55E
Bijar 92 35 52N 47 35E
Bijeljina 66 44 46N 19 17E
Bijni 98 26 30N 90 40E
Bijnor 94 29 27N 78 11E
Bikaner 94 28 2N 73 18E
Bikapur 95 26 30N 82 7E
Bikin 77 46 50N 134 20E
Bikini, atoll 130 12 0N 167 30E
Bikoro 124 0 48S 18 15E
Bikoué 121 5 55S 11 50E
Bilād Banī Bū 'Ali 93 22 0N 59 20E
Bilara 94 26 14N 73 53E
Bilaspara 98 26 13N 90 14E
Bilaspur, India 99 22 2N 82 15E
Bilaspur, Mad. P., India 95 22 2N 82 15E
Bilaspur, Punjab, India 94 31 19N 76 50E
Bilauk Taungdan 100 13 0N 99 0E
Bilbao 58 43 16N 2 56W
Bilbor 70 47 18N 25 30E
Bildudalur 74 65 41N 23 36W
Bilecik 92 40 5N 30 5E
Bileóa 66 42 53N 18 27E
Bilibino 77 68 3N 166 20E
Bilibiza 127 12 30S 40 20E
Bilin 98 17 14N 97 15E
Bilir 77 65 40N 131 20E
Bilishti 68 40 37N 20 59E
Bill 158 43 18N 105 18W
Billa 121 8 55N 12 15E
Billabalong 137 27 25S 115 49E
Billericay 29 51 38N 0 25E
Billesdon 29 52 38N 0 56W

Billiluna Blenheim

Billiluna 136 19 37 S 127 41 E
Billimari 71 33 41 S 148 37 E
Billingham 33 54 36N 1 18W
Billinghay 33 53 5N 0 17W
Billings 160 45 43N 108 29W
Billingsfors 72 58 59N 12 15 E
Billingshurst 29 51 2N 0 28W
Billom 44 45 43N 3 20 E
Bilma 117 18 50N 13 30 E
Bilo Gora 66 45 53N 17 15 E
Biloela 138 24 24 S 150 31 E
Biloxi 159 30 30N 89 0W
Bilpa Morea Claypan 138 25 0 S 140 0 E
Bilston 28 52 34N 2 5W
Bilthoven 46 52 8N 5 12 E
Biltine 117 14 40N 20 50 E
Bilugyun 98 16 24N 97 32 E
Bilyana 138 18 5 S 145 50 E
Bilyarsk 84 54 58N 50 22 E
Bilzen 47 50 52N 5 31 E
Bima 103 8 22 S 118 49 E
Bimban 122 24 24N 32 54 E
Bimberi Peak, mt. 141 35 44 S 148 51 E
Bimbila 121 8 54N 0 5 E
Bimbo 124 4 15N 18 33 E
Bina-Etawah 94 24 13N 78 14 E
Binačka Morava, R. 66 42 30N 19 35 E
Binalbagan 103 10 12N 122 50 E
Binalong 141 34 40 S 148 39 E
Binatang 102 2 10N 111 40 E
Binbrook 33 53 26N 0 9W
Binche 47 50 26N 4 10 E
Binda 139 27 52 S 147 21 E
Bindi Bindi 137 30 37 S 116 22 E
Bindle 139 27 40 S 148 45 E
Bindura 127 17 18 S 31 18 E
Bingara, N.S.W., Austral. 139 29 52 S 150 36 E
Bingara, Queens., Austral. 139 28 10 S 144 37 E
Bingen 49 49 57N 7 53 E
Bingerville 120 5 18N 3 49W
Bingham, U.K. 33 52 57N 0 55W
Bingham, U.S.A. 151 45 5N 69 50W
Bingham Canyon 160 40 31N 112 10W
Binghamton 38 42 9N 75 54W
Bingley 32 53 51N 1 50W
Bingöl 92 39 20N 41 0 E
Binh Dinh = An Nhon 100 13 55N 109 7 E
Binh Khe 100 13 57N 108 51 E
Binh Son 100 15 20N 108 40 E
Binjai 102 3 50N 98 30 E
Binnaway 141 31 28 S 149 24 E
Binongko 103 5 55 S 123 55 E
Binscarth 153 50 37N 101 17W
Bint 93 26 22N 59 25 E
Bint Jaibail 90 33 8N 35 25 E
Bintan 102 1 0N 104 0 E
Bintulu 102 3 10N 113 0 E
Binyamina 90 32 32N 34 56 E
Binza 123 5 25N 28 40 E
Binzert = Bizerte 119 37 15N 9 50 E
Bio-Bío □ 172 37 35 S 72 0W
Bio Culma 123 7 20N 42 15 E
Biograd 63 43 56N 15 29 E
Biokovo 66 43 23N 17 0 E
Biougra 118 30 15N 9 14W
Biq'at Bet Netofa 90 32 49N 35 22 E
Bir 93 19 0N 75 54 E
Bîr Abû Hashim 122 23 42N 34 6 E
Bîr Abû M'nqar 122 26 33N 27 33 E
Bîr Adal Deib 122 22 35N 36 10 E
Bir al Malfa 119 31 58N 15 18 E
Bîr 'Asal 122 25 55N 34 20 E
Bir Autrun 117 18 15N 26 40 E
Bîr Dhu'fân 119 31 59N 14 32 E
Bîr Diqnash 122 31 3N 25 23 E
Bir el Abbes 118 26 7N 6 9W
Bir-el-Ater 119 34 46N 8 3 E
Bîr el Basur 122 29 51N 25 49 E
Bîr el Gellaz 122 30 50N 26 40 E
Bîr el Shaqqa 122 30 54N 25 1 E
Bîr Fuad 122 30 35N 26 28 E
Bîr Haimur 122 22 45N 33 40 E
Bîr Kanayis 122 24 59N 33 15 E
Bîr Kerawein 122 27 10N 28 25 E
Bir Lemouissat 118 25 0N 10 32W
Bîr Maql 122 23 7N 33 40 E
Bîr Misaha 122 22 13N 27 59 E
Bir Mogreïn, (Fort Trinquet) 116 25 10N 11 25W
Bîr Murr 122 23 28N 30 10 E
Bîr Nabala 90 31 52N 35 12 E
Bîr Nakheila 122 24 1N 30 50 E
Bîr Qâtrani 122 30 55N 26 10 E
Bîr Ranga 122 24 25N 35 15 E
Bir Ras 123 12 0N 44 0 E
Bîr Sahara 122 22 54N 28 40 E
Bîr Seiyâla 122 25 10N 34 50 E
Bir Semguine 118 30 1N 5 39W
Bîr Shalatein 122 23 5N 35 25 E
Bîr Shebb 122 22 25N 29 40 E
Bîr Shût 122 23 50N 35 15 E
Bîr Terfawi 122 22 57N 28 55 E
Bîr Umm Qubûr 122 24 35N 34 2 E
Bîr Ungât 122 22 8N 33 48 E
Bîr Za'farâna 122 29 10N 32 40 E
Bîr Zāmus 119 24 16N 15 6 E
Bîr Zeidûn 122 25 45N 34 40 E
Bir Zeit 90 31 59N 35 11 E
Bira 103 2 3 S 132 2 E
Bîra 70 47 2N 27 3 E
Biramfero 120 11 40N 9 10W
Birao 117 10 20N 22 40 E
Birawa 126 2 20 S 28 48 E
Bîrca 70 43 59N 23 36 E
Birch 29 51 50N 0 54 E
Birch Hills 153 52 59N 105 25W
Birch I. 153 52 26N 99 54W
Birch L., N.W.T., Can. 152 62 4N 116 33W
Birch L., Ont., Can. 150 51 23N 92 18W
Birch L., U.S.A. 150 47 48N 91 43W
Birch Mts. 152 57 30N 113 10W
Birch River 153 52 24N 101 6W
Birchington 29 51 22N 1 18 E
Birchip 140 35 56 S 142 55 E
Birchiş 70 45 58N 22 0 E
Birchwood 143 45 55 S 167 53 E
Bird 153 56 30N 94 13W
Bird City 158 39 48N 101 33W
Bird I., Austral. 133 22 10 S 155 28 E
Bird I., S. Afr. 128 32 3 S 18 17 E
Birdaard 46 53 18N 5 53 E
Birdhip 139 35 52 S 142 50 E
Birdlip 28 51 50N 2 7W
Birdsville 138 25 51 S 139 20 E
Birdum 136 15 39 S 133 13 E
Birecik 92 37 0N 38 0 E
Bireuen 102 5 14N 96 39 E
Birhan 123 10 45N 37 55 E
Birifo 120 13 30N 14 0 E
Birigui 173 21 18 S 50 16W
Birimgan 138 22 41 S 147 25 E
Birjand 93 32 57N 59 10 E
Birk 122 18 8N 41 30 E
Birka 122 22 11N 40 38 E
Birkdale 32 53 38N 3 2W
Birkenhead, N.Z. 142 36 49 S 174 46 E
Birkenhead, U.K. 32 53 24N 3 1W
Birket Qârûn 122 29 30N 30 40 E
Birkfeld 52 47 21N 15 45 E
Birkhadem 118 36 43N 3 3 E
Birlad 70 46 15N 27 38 E
Birmingham, U.K. 28 52 30N 1 55W
Birmingham, U.S.A. 157 33 31N 86 50W
Birmitrapur 96 22 30N 84 10 E
Birni Ngaouré 121 13 5N 2 51 E
Birni Nkonni 121 13 55N 5 15 E
Birnin Gwari 121 11 0N 6 45 E
Birnin Kebbi 121 12 32N 4 12 E
Birnin Kudu 121 11 30N 9 29 E
Birobidzhan 77 48 50N 132 50 E
Birqin 90 32 23N 35 15 E
Birr 39 53 7N 7 55W
Birrie, R. 139 29 43 S 146 37 E
Birs, R. 50 47 24N 7 32 E
Birsilpur 94 28 11N 72 58 E
Birsk 84 55 25N 55 30 E
Birtin 70 46 59N 22 31 E
Birtle 153 50 30N 101 5W
Birtley, Northumberland, U.K. 35 55 5N 2 12W
Birtley, Tyne & Wear, U.K. 35 54 53N 1 34W
Birur 93 13 30N 75 55 E
Biryuchiy, Ostrov 82 46 10N 35 0 E
Birzai 80 56 11N 24 45 E
Bîrzava 70 46 7N 21 59 E
Bisa 103 1 10 S 127 40 E
Bisáccia 65 41 0N 15 20 E
Bisacquino 64 37 42N 13 13 E
Bisai 111 35 16N 136 44 E
Bisalpur 95 28 14N 79 48 E
Bisbal, La 58 41 58N 3 2 E
Bisbee 161 31 30N 110 0W
Biscay, B. of 14 45 0N 2 0W
Biscayne B. 157 25 40N 80 12W
Biscéglie 65 41 14N 16 30 E
Bischofshofen 52 47 26N 13 14 E
Bischofswerda 48 51 8N 14 11 E
Bischofszell 51 47 29N 9 15 E
Bischwiller 43 48 41N 7 50 E
Biscoe I. 13 66 0 S 67 0W
Biscostasing 150 47 18N 82 9W
Biscucuy 174 9 22N 69 59W
Biševo, I. 63 42 57N 16 3 E
Bisha 123 15 30N 37 31 E
Bisha, Wadi 122 20 30N 43 0 E
Bishop, Calif., U.S.A. 163 37 20N 118 26W
Bishop, Tex., U.S.A. 159 27 35N 97 49W
Bishop Auckland 33 54 40N 1 40W
Bishop's Castle 28 52 29N 3 0W
Bishop's Cleeve 28 51 56N 2 3W
Bishop's Falls 151 49 2N 55 30W
Bishop's Frome 28 52 8N 2 29W
Bishops Lydeard 28 51 4N 3 12W
Bishop's Nympton 30 50 58N 3 44W
Bishop's Stortford 29 51 52N 0 11 E
Bishop's Waltham 28 50 57N 1 13W
Bishopsteignton 30 50 32N 3 32W
Bishopstoke 28 50 58N 1 19W
Bisignano 65 39 30N 16 17 E
Bisina, L. 126 1 38N 33 56 E
Biskra 119 34 50N 5 44 E
Biskupiec 54 53 53N 20 58 E
Bislig 103 8 15N 126 27 E
Bismarck 158 46 49N 100 49W
Bismarck Arch. 135 2 30 S 150 0 E
Bismarck Ra. 135 5 35 S 145 0 E
Bismarck Sea 135 4 10 S 146 50 E
Bismark 48 52 39N 11 31 E
Biso 126 1 44N 31 26 E
Bison 158 45 34N 102 28W
Bispfors 74 63 1N 16 39 E
Bispgarden 72 63 2N 16 40 E
Bissagos = Bijagós 120 11 15N 16 10W
Bissau 120 11 45N 15 45W
Bissett 153 51 2N 95 41W
Bissikrima 120 10 50N 10 58W
Bistcho L. 152 59 45N 118 50W
Bistreţu 70 43 54N 23 23 E
Bistrica = Ilirska Bistrica 63 45 34N 14 14 E
Bistriţa 70 47 9N 24 35 E
Bistriţa Năsăud □ 70 47 15N 24 30 E
Bistriţa, R. 70 47 10N 24 30 E
Bistriţei, Munţii 70 47 15N 25 40 E
Biswan 95 27 29N 81 2 E
Bisztynek 54 54 8N 20 53 E
Bitam 124 2 5N 11 25 E
Bitche 43 48 58N 7 25 E
Bitkine 124 11 59N 18 13 E
Bitlis 92 38 20N 42 3 E
Bitola (Bitolj) 66 41 5N 21 21 E
Bitonto 65 41 7N 16 40 E
Bitter Creek 160 41 39N 108 36W
Bitter L., Gt. 122 30 15N 32 40 E
Bitter L. = Buheirat-Murrat el Kubra 122 30 15N 32 40 E
Bitterfeld 48 51 36N 12 20 E
Bitterfontein 128 31 0 S 18 32 E
Bitteroot, R. 160 46 30N 114 20W
Bitterroot Range 160 46 0N 114 20W
Bitterwater 163 36 23N 121 0W
Bitti 64 40 29N 9 20 E
Bitton 28 51 25N 2 27W
Bittou 121 11 17N 0 18W
Bitumount 152 57 26N 112 40W
Biu 121 10 40N 12 3 E
Bivolari 70 47 31N 27 27 E
Bîvolu 70 47 16N 25 58 E
Biwa-Ko 111 35 15N 135 45 E
Biwabik 158 47 33N 92 19W
Biylikol, Ozero 85 43 5N 70 45 E
Biysk 76 52 40N 85 0 E
Bizana 129 30 50 S 29 52 E
Bizen 110 34 43N 134 8 E
Bizerte (Binzert) 119 37 15N 9 50 E
Bjandovan, Mys 83 39 45N 49 28 E
Bjargtangar 74 65 30N 24 30W
Bjärka-Säby 73 58 16N 15 44 E
Bjarnanes 74 64 20N 15 6W
Bjelasica 66 42 50N 19 40 E
Bjelo Polje 66 43 1N 19 45 E
Bjelovar 66 45 56N 16 49 E
Bjerringbro 73 56 23N 9 39 E
Björbo 72 60 27N 14 44 E
Björkhamre 72 61 24N 16 25 E
Björkhult 73 57 50N 15 40 E
Björneborg 72 59 14N 14 16 E
Bjuv 73 56 5N 12 55 E
Bla Bheinn 36 57 14N 6 7W
Blaby 28 52 34N 1 10W
Blace 66 43 18N 21 17 E
Blachownia 54 50 49N 18 56 E
Black Combe, mt. 32 54 16N 3 20W
Black Diamond 152 50 45N 114 14W
Black Esk R. 35 55 14N 3 13W
Black Forest = Schwarzwald 49 48 0N 8 0 E
Black Hd., Ireland 39 53 9N 9 18W
Black Hd., Antrim, U.K. 38 54 56N 5 42W
Black Hd., Cornwall, U.K. 30 50 1N 5 6W
Black Hills 158 44 0N 103 50W
Black I. 153 51 12N 96 30W
Black Island Sd. 162 41 10N 71 45W
Black Isle, Reg. 37 57 35N 4 15W
Black L., Can. 153 59 12N 105 15W
Black L., U.S.A. 156 45 28N 84 15W
Black Mesa, Mt. 159 36 57N 102 55W
Black Mt. = Mynydd Du 31 51 45N 3 45W
Black Mountain 141 30 18 S 151 39 E
Black Mts. 31 51 52N 3 5W
Black Pt. 137 34 30 S 119 25 E
Black R. 38 53 54N 7 42W
Black, R., Ark., U.S.A. 159 36 15N 90 45W
Black, R., N.Y., U.S.A. 162 43 59N 76 40W
Black, R., Wis., U.S.A. 158 44 18N 90 52W
Black, R., Vietnam = Da, R. 100 21 15N 105 20 E
Black Range, Mts. 161 33 30N 107 55W
Black River 166 18 0N 77 50W
Black Rock 140 32 50 S 138 44 E
Black Sea 21 43 30N 35 0 E
Black Volta, R. 120 9 0N 2 40W
Black Warrior, R. 157 33 0N 87 45W
Blackall 138 24 25 S 145 45 E
Blackball 143 42 22 S 171 26 E
Blackbull 138 17 55 S 141 45 E
Blackburn 32 53 44N 2 30W
Blackburn, Mt. 147 61 5N 142 3W
Blackbutt 139 26 51 S 152 6 E
Blackdown Hills 28 50 57N 3 15W
Blackduck 158 47 43N 94 32W
Blackfoot 160 43 13N 112 12W
Blackfoot, R. 160 47 0N 113 35W
Blackford 35 56 15N 3 48W
Blackie 152 50 36N 113 37W
Blackmoor Gate 30 51 9N 3 55W
Blackmoor Vale 28 50 54N 2 28W
Blackpool 32 53 48N 3 3W
Blackridge 138 22 35 S 147 35 E
Blackrock 39 53 18N 6 11W
Blacks Harbour 151 45 3N 66 49W
Blacksburg 156 37 17N 80 23W
Blacksod B. 38 54 6N 10 0W
Blacksod Pt. 38 54 7N 10 5W
Blackstairs Mt. 39 52 33N 6 50W
Blackstone 156 37 6N 78 0W
Blackstone, R. 152 61 5N 122 55W
Blackstone Ra. 137 26 00 S 129 00 E
Blackville 151 46 44N 65 50W
Blackwater, Austral. 138 23 35 S 148 53 E
Blackwater, Can. 152 53 20N 123 0W
Blackwater, Ireland 39 52 26N 6 20W
Blackwater Cr. 139 25 56 S 144 30 E
Blackwater, R., Limerick, Ireland 39 51 55N 7 50W
Blackwater, R., Meath, Ireland 38 53 40N 6 40W
Blackwater, R., Essex, U.K. 29 51 44N 0 53 E
Blackwater, R., Ulster, U.K. 38 54 31N 6 35W
Blackwater Res. 37 56 42N 4 45W
Blackwell 159 36 55N 97 20W
Blackwells Corner 163 35 37N 119 47W
Blackwood 35 55 40N 3 56W
Blackwood, C. 135 7 49 S 144 31 E
Bladel 47 51 22N 5 13 E
Bladinge 73 56 52N 14 29 E
Blädinge 73 56 52N 14 29 E
Blaenau Ffestiniog 31 53 0N 3 57W
Blaenavon 31 51 46N 3 5W
Blagaj 66 43 16N 17 55 E
Blagdon 28 51 19N 2 42W
Blagnac 44 43 38N 1 24 E
Blagodarnoye 83 45 7N 43 37 E
Blagoevgrad (Gorna Dzhumayo) 66 42 2N 23 5 E
Blagoveshchensk, Amur, U.S.S.R. 77 50 20N 127 30 E
Blagoveshchensk, Urals, U.S.S.R. 84 55 1N 55 59 E
Blagoveshchenskoye 85 43 18N 74 12 E
Blaina 31 51 46N 3 10W
Blaine 160 48 59N 122 43W
Blaine Lake 153 52 51N 106 52W
Blainville 43 48 33N 6 23 E
Blair 158 41 38N 96 10W
Blair Athol 138 22 42 S 147 31 E
Blair Atholl 37 56 46N 3 50W
Blairgowrie 37 56 36N 3 20W
Blairmore 152 49 40N 114 25W
Blaj 70 46 10N 23 57 E
Blake Pt. 158 48 12N 88 27W
Blakely 157 31 22N 85 0W
Blakeney, Glos., U.K. 28 51 45N 2 29W
Blakeney, Norfolk, U.K. 29 52 57N 1 1 E
Blâmont 43 48 35N 6 50 E
Blanc, C., Maurit. 116 20 50N 17 0W
Blanc, C., Tunisia 119 37 15N 9 56 E
Blanc, Le 44 46 37N 1 3 E
Blanc, Mont 45 45 48N 6 50 E
Blanc Sablon 151 51 24N 57 8W
Blanca, Bahía 176 39 10 S 61 30W
Blanca Peak 161 37 35N 105 29W
Blanchard 159 35 8N 97 40W
Blanche, C. 139 33 1 S 134 9 E
Blanche L., S. Austral., Austral. 139 29 15 S 139 40 E
Blanche L., W. Austral., Austral. 136 22 25 S 123 17 E
Blanco, S. Afr. 128 33 55 S 22 23 E
Blanco, U.S.A. 159 30 7N 98 30W
Blanco, C., C. Rica 166 9 34N 85 8W
Blanco, C., Peru 174 4 10 S 81 10W
Blanco, C., Spain 59 39 21N 2 51 E
Blanco, C., U.S.A. 160 42 50N 124 40W
Blanco, R. 172 31 54 S 69 42W
Blanda 74 65 20N 19 40W
Blandford Forum 28 50 52N 2 10W
Blanding 161 37 35N 109 30W
Blanes 58 41 40N 2 48 E
Blangy 43 49 14N 0 17 E
Blanice, R. 52 49 10N 14 5 E
Blankenberge 47 51 20N 3 9 E
Blankenburg 48 51 46N 10 56 E
Blanquefort 44 44 55N 0 38W
Blanquilla, La 174 11 51N 64 37W
Blanquillo 173 32 53 S 55 37W
Blansko 53 49 22N 16 40 E
Blantyre 127 15 45 S 35 0 E
Blaricum 46 52 16N 5 14 E
Blarney 39 51 57N 8 35W
Blaski 54 51 38N 18 30 E
Blatná 52 49 25N 13 52 E
Blatnitsa 67 43 41N 28 32 E
Blatten 50 46 16N 8 0 E
Blåvands Huk 75 55 33N 8 4 E
Blaydon 35 54 58N 1 47W
Blaye 44 45 8N 0 40W
Blaye-les-Mines 44 44 1N 2 8 E
Blayney 141 33 32 S 149 14 E
Blaze, Pt. 136 12 56 S 130 11 E
Blazowa 54 49 53N 22 7 E
Bleadon 28 51 18N 2 57W
Blean 29 51 18N 1 3 E
Bleasdale Moors 32 53 57N 2 40W
Bleckede 48 53 18N 10 43 E
Bled 63 46 27N 14 7 E
Blednaya, Gora 76 65 50N 65 30 E
Bléharis 47 50 31N 3 25 E
Bleiburg 52 46 35N 14 49 E
Blejeşti 70 44 19N 25 27 E
Bleking län □ 73 56 20N 15 20 E
Blenheim 143 41 38 S 174 5 E

Bléone, R **Booral**

Bléone, R.	**45**	44 5N	6 0E
Bletchingdon	**28**	51 51N	1 16W
Bletchley	**29**	51 59N	0 44W
Bleymard, Le	**44**	44 30N	3 42E
Blidet Amor	**119**	32 59N	5 58E
Blidö	**72**	59 37N	18 53E
Blidsberg	**73**	57 56N	13 30E
Bligh Sound	**143**	44 47S	167 32E
Blind River	**150**	46 10N	82 58W
Blinishti	**68**	41 52N	19 58E
Blinnenhorn	**51**	46 26N	8 19E
Blisworth	**29**	52 11N	0 56W
Blitar	**103**	8 5S	112 11E
Blitta	**121**	8 23N	1 6E
Block I.	**162**	41 11N	71 35W
Blockley	**28**	52 1N	1 45W
Bloemendaal	**46**	52 24N	4 39E
Bloemfontein	**128**	29 6S	26 14E
Bloemhof	**128**	27 38S	25 32E
Blofield	**29**	52 38N	1 25E
Blois	**42**	47 35N	1 20E
Blokziji	**46**	52 43N	5 58E
Blomskog	**72**	59 16N	12 2E
Blonduös	**74**	65 40N	20 12W
Bloodsworth Is.	**162**	38 9N	76 3W
Bloodvein, R.	**153**	51 47N	96 43W
Bloody Foreland	**38**	55 10N	8 18W
Bloomer	**158**	45 8N	91 30W
Bloomfield, Iowa, U.S.A.	**158**	40 44N	92 26W
Bloomfield, N. Mexico, U.S.A.	**161**	36 46N	107 59W
Bloomfield, Nebr., U.S.A.	**158**	42 38N	97 15W
Bloomfield R.	**138**	15 56S	145 22E
Bloomingdale	**162**	41 33N	74 26W
Bloomington, Ill., U.S.A.	**158**	40 49N	89 0W
Bloomington, Ind., U.S.A.	**156**	39 10N	86 30W
Bloomsburg	**162**	41 0N	76 30W
Blora	**103**	6 57S	111 25E
Blossburg	**162**	41 40N	77 4W
Blouberg	**129**	23 8S	29 0E
Blountstown	**157**	30 28N	85 5W
Bloxham	**28**	52 1N	1 22W
Bludenz	**52**	47 10N	9 50E
Blue I.	**156**	41 40N	87 40W
Blue Lake	**160**	40 53N	124 0W
Blue Mesa Res.	**161**	38 30N	107 15W
Blue Mountain Lake	**162**	43 52N	74 30W
Blue Mountain Peak	**167**	18 0N	76 40W
Blue Mts., Austral.	**133**	33 40S	150 0E
Blue Mts., Jamaica	**167**	18 0N	76 40W
Blue Mts., Ore., U.S.A.	**160**	45 15N	119 0W
Blue Mts., Pa., U.S.A.	**156**	40 30N	76 0W
Blue Mud B.	**138**	13 30S	136 0E
Blue Nile = Nîl el Azraq	**123**	12 30N	34 30E
Blue Nile □ = An Nîl el Azraq □	**123**	12 30N	34 30E
Blue Nile, R. = Nîl el Azraq	**123**	10 30N	35 0E
Blue Ridge, Mts.	**157**	36 30N	80 15W
Blue Stack Mts.	**38**	54 46N	8 5W
Blueberry, R.	**152**	56 45N	120 49W
Bluefield	**156**	37 18N	81 14W
Bluefields	**166**	12 0N	83 50W
Bluemull Sd.	**36**	60 45N	1 0W
Blueskin B.	**143**	45 44S	170 38E
Bluff, Austral.	**138**	23 35S	149 4E
Bluff, N.Z.	**143**	46 37S	168 20E
Bluff, U.S.A.	**147**	64 50N	147 15W
Bluff Downs	**138**	19 37S	145 30E
Bluff Harbour	**143**	46 36S	168 21E
Bluff Knoll, Mt.	**137**	34 24S	118 15E
Bluff Pt.	**137**	27 50S	114 5E
Bluffton	**156**	40 43N	85 9W
Blumenau	**173**	27 0S	49 0W
Blumenthal	**48**	53 5N	12 20E
Blümisalphorn	**50**	46 30N	7 47E
Blundeston	**29**	52 33N	1 42E
Blunt	**158**	44 32N	100 0W
Bly	**160**	42 23N	121 0W
Blyberg	**72**	61 9N	14 11E
Blyth, Austral.	**140**	33 49S	138 28E
Blyth, Northumberland, U.K.	**35**	55 8N	1 32W
Blyth, Notts., U.K.	**33**	53 22N	1 2W
Blyth Bridge	**35**	55 41N	3 22W
Blyth, R.	**35**	55 8N	1 30W
Blythburgh	**29**	52 19N	1 36E
Blythe	**161**	33 40N	114 33W
Blyton	**33**	53 25N	0 42W
Bo, Norway	**71**	59 25N	9 3E
Bo, S. Leone	**120**	7 55N	11 50W
Bo Duc	**101**	11 58N	106 50E
Bō-no-Misaki	**110**	31 15N	130 13E
Boa I.	**38**	54 30N	7 50W
Boa Nova	**171**	14 22S	40 10W
Boa Viagem	**170**	5 7S	39 44W
Boa Vista	**174**	2 48N	60 30W
Boaco	**166**	12 29N	85 35W
Boal	**56**	43 25N	6 49W
Boat of Garten	**37**	57 15N	3 45W
Boatman	**139**	27 16S	146 55E
Bobadah	**141**	32 19S	146 41E
Bobbili	**96**	18 35N	83 30E
Bóbbio	**62**	44 47N	9 22E
Bobcaygeon	**150**	44 33N	78 33W
Böblingen	**57**	48 41N	9 1E
Bobo-Dioulasso	**120**	11 8N	4 13W
Boboc	**67**	45 13N	26 59E
Bobolice	**54**	53 58N	16 37E
Boboshevo	**66**	42 9N	23 0E
Bobov Dol	**66**	42 20N	23 0E
Bóbr, R.	**54**	51 50N	15 15E
Bobrinets	**82**	48 4N	32 5E
Bobrov	**81**	51 5N	40 2E
Bobruysk	**80**	53 10N	29 15E
Bobures	**174**	9 15N	71 11W
Boca de Uracoa	**174**	9 8N	62 20W
Bôca do Acre	**174**	8 50S	67 27W
Bocage	**41**	49 0N	1 0W
Bocaiúva	**171**	17 7S	43 49W
Bocanda	**120**	7 5N	4 31W
Bocaranga	**117**	7 0N	15 35E
Bocas del Dragon	**174**	11 0N	61 50W
Bocas del Toro	**166**	9 15N	82 20W
Bocdam	**36**	59 55N	1 16W
Boceguillas	**58**	41 20N	3 39W
Bochnia	**54**	49 58N	20 27E
Bocholt, Belg.	**47**	51 10N	5 35E
Bocholt, Ger.	**48**	51 50N	6 35E
Bochov	**52**	50 9N	13 3E
Bochum	**48**	51 28N	7 12E
Bockenem	**48**	52 1N	10 8E
Bocoyna	**164**	27 52N	107 35W
Bocq, R.	**47**	50 20N	4 55E
Boçsa Montanŭ	**66**	45 21N	21 47E
Boda	**124**	4 19N	17 26E
Böda	**73**	57 15N	17 3E
Boda	**74**	57 15N	17 0E
Bodaybo	**77**	57 50N	114 0E
Boddam	**37**	57 28N	1 46W
Boddington	**137**	32 50S	116 30E
Bodedern	**31**	53 17N	4 29W
Bodegraven	**46**	52 5N	4 46E
Boden	**74**	65 50N	21 42E
Bodenham	**28**	52 9N	2 41W
Bodensee	**51**	47 35N	9 25E
Bodenteich	**48**	52 49N	10 41E
Boderg, L.	**38**	53 52N	8 0W
Bodhan	**96**	18 40N	77 55E
Bodiam	**29**	51 1N	0 33E
Bodinayakkanur	**97**	10 2N	77 10E
Bodinga	**121**	12 58N	5 10E
Bodinnick	**30**	50 20N	4 37W
Bodio	**51**	46 23N	8 55E
Bodmin	**30**	50 28N	4 44W
Bodmin Moor	**30**	50 33N	4 36W
Bodø	**74**	67 17N	14 24E
Bodrog, R.	**53**	48 15N	21 35E
Bodrum	**92**	37 5N	27 30E
Bódva, R.	**53**	48 19N	20 45E
Bodyke	**39**	52 53N	8 38W
Boechout	**47**	51 10N	4 30E
Boegoebergdam	**128**	29 7S	22 9E
Boekelo	**46**	52 12N	6 49E
Boelenslaan	**46**	53 10N	6 10E
Boën	**45**	45 44N	4 0E
Boende	**124**	0 24S	21 12E
Boerne	**159**	29 48N	98 41W
Boertange	**46**	53 1N	7 12E
Boezinge	**47**	50 54N	2 52E
Boffa	**120**	10 16N	14 3W
Bofin L.	**38**	53 51N	7 55W
Bofors	**72**	59 19N	14 34E
Bogale	**98**	21 16N	92 24E
Bogalusa	**159**	30 50N	89 55W
Bogan Gate	**141**	33 7S	147 49E
Bogan, R.	**141**	32 45S	148 8E
Bogantungan	**138**	23 41S	147 17E
Bogata	**159**	33 26N	95 10W
Bogatió	**66**	44 51N	19 30E
Bogdan, Mt.	**67**	42 37N	24 20E
Bogdanovitch	**84**	56 47N	62 1E
Bogenfels	**125**	27 25S	15 25E
Bogense	**73**	55 34N	10 5E
Boggabilla	**139**	28 36S	150 24E
Boggabri	**141**	30 45S	150 0E
Boggeragh Mts.	**39**	52 2N	8 55W
Boghari = Ksar el Boukhari	**118**	35 51N	2 52E
Bogia	**135**	4 9S	145 0E
Bognor Regis	**29**	50 47N	0 40W
Bogø	**73**	54 55N	12 2E
Bogo	**103**	11 3N	124 0E
Bogodukhov	**80**	50 9N	35 33E
Bogong, Mt.	**141**	36 47S	147 17E
Bogor	**103**	6 36S	106 48E
Bogoro	**121**	9 37N	9 29E
Bogoroditsk	**81**	53 47N	38 8E
Bogorodsk	**81**	56 4N	43 30E
Bogorodskoye	**77**	52 22N	140 30E
Bogoso	**120**	5 38N	2 3W
Bogotá	**174**	4 34N	74 0W
Bogotol	**76**	56 15N	89 50E
Bogra	**98**	24 51N	89 22E
Boguchany	**77**	58 40N	97 30E
Boguchar	**83**	49 55N	40 32E
Bogué	**120**	16 45N	14 10W
Boguslav	**82**	49 47N	30 53E
Boguszów Lubawka	**54**	50 43N	15 56E
Bohain	**43**	49 59N	3 28E
Bohemia	**52**	50 0N	14 0E
Bohemia Downs	**136**	18 53S	126 14E
Bohemian Forest = Böhmerwald	**49**	49 30N	12 40E
Bohena Cr.	**139**	30 17S	149 42E
Boheraphuca	**39**	53 1N	7 45W
Bohinjska Bistrica	**63**	46 17N	14 1E
Böhmerwald	**49**	49 30N	12 40E
Bohmte	**48**	52 24N	8 20E
Bohola	**38**	53 54N	9 4W
Boholl, I.	**103**	9 50N	124 10E
Bohotleh	**91**	8 20N	46 25E
Boi	**121**	9 35N	9 27E
Boi, Pta. de	**173**	23 55S	45 15W
Boiano	**65**	41 28N	14 29E
Boiestown	**151**	46 27N	66 26W
Boigu I.	**138**	9 15S	143 30E
Boileau, C.	**136**	17 40S	122 7E
Boipeba, I. de	**171**	13 39S	38 55W
Bois, Les	**50**	47 11N	6 50E
Bois, R.	**171**	18 35S	50 2W
Boischot	**47**	51 3N	4 47E
Boisdale L.	**36**	57 9N	7 19W
Boise	**160**	43 43N	116 9W
Boise City	**159**	36 45N	102 30W
Boissevain	**153**	49 15N	100 0W
Boite, R.	**63**	46 24N	12 13E
Boitzenburg	**48**	55 16N	13 36E
Boizenburg	**48**	53 22N	10 42E
Bojador C.	**116**	26 0N	14 30W
Bojanow	**54**	51 43N	16 42E
Bøjden	**73**	55 6N	10 7E
Bojnurd	**93**	37 30N	57 20E
Bojonegoro	**103**	7 11S	111 54E
Boju	**121**	7 22N	7 55E
Boka	**66**	45 22N	20 52E
Boka Kotorska	**66**	42 23N	18 32E
Bokala	**120**	8 31N	4 33W
Boké	**120**	10 56N	14 17W
Bokhara, R.	**139**	29 55S	146 42E
Bokkos	**121**	9 17N	9 1E
Boknafjorden	**71**	59 14N	5 40E
Bokombayevskoye	**85**	47 7N	77 0E
Bokoro	**117**	12 25N	17 14E
Bokote	**124**	0 12S	21 8E
Bokpyin	**101**	11 18N	98 42E
Boksitogorsk	**80**	59 32N	33 56E
Bokungu	**124**	0 35S	22 50E
Bol, Chad	**124**	13 30N	15 0E
Bol, Yugo.	**63**	43 18N	16 38E
Bolama	**120**	11 30N	15 30W
Bolan Pass	**93**	29 50N	67 20E
Bolangum	**140**	36 42S	142 54E
Bolaños, R.	**164**	22 0N	104 10W
Bolbec	**42**	49 30N	0 30E
Bolchereche	**76**	56 4N	74 45E
Boldeşti	**70**	45 3N	26 2E
Bole	**123**	6 36N	37 20E
Bolekhov	**80**	49 0N	24 0E
Bolesławiec	**54**	51 17N	15 37E
Bolgary	**78**	55 3N	48 50E
Bolgatanga	**121**	10 44N	0 53W
Bolgrad	**82**	45 40N	28 32E
Boli	**123**	6 2N	28 48E
Bolinao C.	**103**	16 30N	119 55E
Bolívar, Argent.	**172**	36 15S	60 53W
Bolívar, Antioquía, Colomb.	**174**	5 50N	76 1W
Bolívar, Cauca, Colomb.	**174**	2 0N	77 0W
Bolivar, Mo., U.S.A.	**159**	37 38N	93 22W
Bolivar, Tenn., U.S.A.	**159**	35 14N	89 0W
Bolívar □	**174**	9 0N	74 40W
Bolivia ■	**174**	17 6S	64 0W
Boljevac	**66**	43 51N	21 58E
Bolkhov	**81**	53 25N	36 0E
Bollène	**45**	44 18N	4 45E
Bollington	**32**	53 18N	2 8W
Bollnäs	**72**	61 21N	16 24E
Bollon	**139**	28 2S	147 29E
Bollstabruk	**72**	63 1N	17 40E
Bollullos	**57**	37 19N	6 32W
Bolmen	**73**	56 55N	13 40E
Bolney	**29**	50 59N	0 11W
Bolo Silase	**123**	8 51N	39 27E
Bolobo	**124**	2 6S	16 20E
Bologna	**63**	44 30N	11 20E
Bologne	**43**	48 10N	5 8E
Bologoye	**80**	57 55N	34 0E
Bolomba	**124**	0 35N	19 0E
Bolonchenticul	**165**	20 0N	89 49W
Bolong	**103**	6 6N	122 16E
Bolotovskoye	**84**	58 31N	62 28E
Boloven, Cao Nguyen	**100**	15 10N	106 30E
Bolpur	**95**	23 40N	87 45E
Bolsena	**63**	42 40N	11 58E
Bolsena, L. di	**63**	42 35N	11 55E
Bolshaya Glushitsa	**81**	52 24N	50 29E
Bolshaya Khobda, R.	**84**	50 50N	54 53E
Bolshaya Kinel, R.	**84**	53 14N	50 30E
Bolshaya Lepetrikha	**82**	47 11N	33 57E
Bolshaya Martynovka	**83**	47 12N	41 46E
Bolshaya Shatan, Gora	**84**	53 37N	58 3E
Bolshevik, Ostrov	**77**	78 30N	102 0E
Bolshezemelskaya Tundra	**78**	67 0N	56 0E
Bolshoi Kavkas	**83**	42 50N	44 0E
Bolshoi Tuters, O.	**80**	59 44N	26 57E
Bolshoy Atlym	**76**	62 25N	66 50E
Bolshoy Tokmak	**82**	47 16N	35 42E
Bol'soj T'uters, O.	**80**	59 44N	26 57E
Bolsover	**33**	53 14N	1 18W
Bolsward	**46**	53 3N	5 32E
Bolt Head	**30**	50 13N	3 48W
Bolt Tail	**30**	50 13N	3 55W
Boltaña	**58**	42 28N	0 4E
Boltigen	**50**	46 38N	7 24E
Bolton	**32**	53 35N	2 26W
Bolton Abbey	**32**	53 59N	1 53W
Bolton by Bowland	**32**	53 56N	2 21W
Bolton Landing	**162**	43 32N	73 35W
Bolton le Sands	**32**	54 7N	2 49W
Bolton-on-Dearne	**33**	53 31N	1 19W
Bolu	**92**	40 45N	31 35E
Bolubolu	**135**	9 21S	150 20E
Bolus Hd.	**39**	51 48N	10 20W
Bolvadin	**92**	38 45N	31 57E
Bolzano (Bozen)	**63**	46 30N	11 20E
Bom Conselho	**170**	9 42S	37 26W
Bom Despacho	**171**	19 43S	45 15W
Bom Jardim	**171**	7 47S	35 35W
Bom Jesus	**170**	9 4S	44 22W
Bom Jesus da Gurguéia, Serra	**170**	9 0S	43 0W
Bom Jesus da Lapa	**171**	13 15S	43 25W
Boma	**124**	5 50S	13 4E
Bomaderry	**141**	34 52S	150 37E
Bōmba, Khalīj	**117**	32 20N	23 15E
Bomba, La	**164**	31 53N	115 2W
Bombala	**141**	36 56S	149 15E
Bombarral	**57**	39 15N	9 9W
Bombay	**96**	18 55N	72 50E
Bomboma	**124**	2 25N	18 55E
Bombombwa	**126**	2 18N	19 3E
Bomi Hills	**120**	7 1N	10 38E
Bomili	**126**	1 45N	27 5E
Bomokandi, R.	**126**	3 10N	28 15E
Bomongo	**124**	1 27N	18 21E
Bomu, R.	**124**	4 40N	23 30E
Bon C.	**119**	37 1N	11 2E
Bon Sar Pa	**100**	12 24N	107 35E
Bonaduz	**15**	46 49N	9 25E
Bonaire, I.	**167**	12 10N	68 15W
Bonang	**141**	37 11S	148 41E
Bonanza	**166**	13 54N	84 35W
Bonaparte Archipelago	**136**	14 0S	124 30E
Boñar	**56**	42 52N	5 19W
Bonarbridge	**37**	57 53N	4 20W
Bonäset	**72**	63 16N	18 45E
Bonaventure	**151**	48 5N	65 32W
Bonavista	**151**	48 40N	53 5W
Bonavista, C.	**151**	48 42N	53 5W
Bonchester Bri.	**35**	55 23N	2 36W
Bonchurch	**28**	50 36N	1 11W
Bondeno	**63**	44 53N	11 22E
Bondo	**124**	3 55N	23 53E
Bondoukoro	**120**	9 51N	4 25W
Bondoukou	**120**	8 2N	2 47W
Bondowoso	**120**	7 56S	113 49E
Bondyug	**84**	60 29N	55 56E
Bone Rate, I.	**103**	7 25S	121 5E
Bone Rate, Kepulauan	**103**	6 30S	121 10E
Bone, Teluk	**103**	4 10S	120 50E
Bonefro	**65**	41 42N	14 55E
Bo'ness	**35**	56 0N	3 38W
Bong Son = Hoai Nhon	**100**	14 26N	109 1E
Bongandanga	**124**	1 24N	21 3E
Bonge	**123**	6 5N	37 16E
Bongor	**117**	10 35N	15 20E
Bongouanou	**120**	6 42N	4 15W
Bonham	**159**	33 30N	96 10W
Bonherden	**47**	51 1N	4 32E
Bonifacio	**45**	41 24N	9 10E
Bonifacio, Bouches de	**64**	41 12N	9 15E
Bonin Is.	**130**	27 0N	142 0E
Bonito de Santa Fé	**171**	7 19S	38 31W
Bonn	**48**	50 43N	7 6E
Bonnat	**44**	46 20N	1 53E
Bonne B.	**151**	40 31N	58 0W
Bonne Espérance, I.	**151**	51 24N	57 40W
Bonne Terre	**159**	37 55N	90 38W
Bonners Ferry	**160**	48 38N	116 21W
Bonnert	**47**	49 43N	5 49E
Bonnétable	**42**	48 11N	0 25E
Bonneuil Matours	**42**	46 41N	0 34E
Bonneville	**45**	46 5N	6 24E
Bonney, L.	**140**	37 50S	140 20E
Bonnie Doon	**141**	37 2S	145 53E
Bonnie Rock	**137**	30 29S	118 22E
Bonny, France	**43**	47 34N	2 50E
Bonny, Nigeria	**121**	4 25N	7 13E
Bonny, Bight of	**121**	3 30N	9 20E
Bonny, R.	**121**	4 20N	7 14E
Bonnyrigg	**35**	55 52N	3 8W
Bonnyville	**153**	54 20N	110 45W
Bonoi	**103**	1 45S	137 41E
Bonorva	**64**	40 25N	8 47E
Bonsall	**163**	33 16N	117 14W
Bontang	**102**	0 10N	117 30E
Bonthain	**103**	5 34S	119 56E
Bonthe	**120**	7 30N	12 33W
Bonyeri	**120**	5 1N	2 46W
Bonyhád	**53**	46 18N	18 32E
Bonython Ra.	**136**	23 40S	128 45E
Boogardie	**137**	28 2S	117 45E
Bookabie P.O.	**137**	31 50S	132 41E
Booker	**159**	36 29N	100 30W
Boolaboolka, L.	**140**	32 38S	143 10E
Boolarra	**141**	38 20S	146 20E
Boolathanna	**137**	21 40S	113 41E
Boolcoomata	**140**	31 57S	140 33E
Booleroo Centre	**140**	32 53S	138 21E
Booligal	**141**	33 58S	144 53E
Booloo Downs	**137**	23 52S	119 33E
Boom	**47**	51 6N	4 20E
Boonah	**139**	27 58S	152 41E
Boondall	**108**	27 20S	153 4E
Boone, Iowa, U.S.A.	**158**	42 5N	93 53W
Boone, N.C., U.S.A.	**157**	36 14N	81 43W
Booneville, Ark., U.S.A.	**159**	35 10N	93 54W
Booneville, Miss., U.S.A.	**157**	34 39N	88 34W
Boongoondoo	**138**	22 55S	145 55E
Boonville, Ind., U.S.A.	**156**	38 3N	87 13W
Boonville, Mo., U.S.A.	**158**	38 57N	92 45W
Boonville, N.Y., U.S.A.	**162**	43 31N	75 20W
Booral	**141**	32 30S	151 56E

Boorindal Bramminge

Boorindal 139 30 22 S 146 11 E
Booroomugga 141 31 17 S 146 27 E
Boorowa 141 34 28 S 148 44 E
Boot 32 54 24 N 3 18 W
Boothia, Gulf of 149 71 0 N 91 0 W
Boothia Pen. 148 71 0 N 94 0 W
Bootle, Cumb., U.K. 32 54 17 N 3 24 W
Bootle, Merseysude, U.K. 32 53 28 N 3 1 W
Booué 124 0 5 S 11 55 E
Bopeechee 139 29 36 S 137 22 E
Bophuthatswana □ 126 26 0 S 26 0 E
Bopo 79 7 33 N 7 50 E
Boppard 49 50 13 N 7 36 E
Boquete 166 8 46 N 82 27 W
Boquillas 164 29 17 N 102 53 W
Bor 52 49 41 N 12 45 E
Bôr 123 6 10 N 31 40 E
Bor, Sweden 73 57 9 N 14 10 E
Bor, Yugo. 66 44 8 N 22 7 E
Borah, Mt. 160 44 19 N 113 46 W
Borang 123 4 50 N 30 59 E
Borås 73 57 43 N 12 56 E
Borås 73 57 43 N 12 56 E
Borazjan 93 29 22 N 51 10 E
Borba, Brazil 174 4 12 S 59 34 W
Borba, Port. 57 38 50 N 7 26 W
Borborema, Planalto da 170 7 0 S 37 0 W
Borçka 83 41 25 N 41 41 E
Borculo 46 52 7 N 6 31 E
Borda, C. 140 35 45 S 136 34 E
Bordeaux 44 44 50 N 0 36 W
Borden, Austral. 137 34 3 S 118 12 E
Borden, Can. 151 46 18 N 63 47 W
Borden I. 12 78 30 N 111 30 W
Borders □ 35 55 45 N 2 50 W
Bordertown 140 36 19 S 140 45 E
Borðeyri 74 65 12 N 21 6 W
Bordighera 62 43 47 N 7 40 E
Bordj bou Arridj 119 36 4 N 4 45 E
Bordj Djeneiene 119 31 47 N 10 3 E
Bordj el Hobra 119 32 9 N 4 51 E
Bordj Fly Ste. Marie 118 27 19 N 2 32 W
Bordj-in-Eker 119 24 9 N 5 3 E
Bordj Ménaiel 119 36 46 N 3 43 E
Bordj Nili 118 33 28 N 3 2 E
Bordj Zelfana 119 32 27 N 4 15 E
Bordoba 85 39 31 N 73 16 E
Bordon Camp 29 51 6 N 0 52 W
Borea Creek 141 35 5 S 146 35 E
Borehamwood 29 51 40 N 0 15 W
Borek Wlkp. 54 51 54 N 17 11 E
Boreland 35 55 12 N 3 16 W
Boremore 141 33 15 S 149 0 E
Borensberg 73 58 34 N 15 17 E
Borgarnes 74 64 32 N 21 55 W
Borgefjellet 74 65 20 N 13 45 E
Borger, Neth. 46 52 54 N 6 33 E
Borger, U.S.A. 159 35 40 N 101 20 W
Borgerhout 47 51 12 N 4 28 E
Borghamn 73 58 23 N 14 41 E
Borgholm 73 56 52 N 16 39 E
Bórgia 65 38 50 N 16 30 E
Borgie R. 37 58 28 N 4 20 W
Borgo San Dalmazzo 62 44 19 N 7 29 E
Borgo San Lorenzo 63 43 57 N 11 21 E
Borgo Val di Taro 62 44 29 N 9 47 E
Borgomanero 62 45 41 N 8 28 E
Borgonovo Val Tidone 62 45 1 N 9 28 E
Borgorose 63 42 12 N 13 14 E
Borgosésia 62 45 43 N 8 17 E
Borgvattnet 72 63 26 N 15 48 E
Borhaug 71 58 6 N 6 33 E
Borikhane 100 18 33 N 103 43 E
Borisoglebsk 81 51 27 N 42 5 E
Borisoglebskiy 81 56 28 N 43 59 E
Borisov 80 54 17 N 28 28 E
Borisovka 85 43 15 N 68 10 E
Borisovo-Sudskoye 81 59 58 N 35 57 E
Borispol 80 50 21 N 30 59 E
Borja, Peru 174 4 20 S 77 40 W
Borja, Spain 58 41 48 N 1 34 W
Borjas Blancas 58 41 31 N 0 52 E
Borkou 117 18 15 N 18 50 E
Borlänge 72 60 29 N 15 26 E
Borley, C. 13 66 15 S 52 30 E
Bormida, R. 62 44 35 N 8 10 E
Bórmio 62 46 28 N 10 22 E
Born 47 51 2 N 5 49 E
Borna 48 51 8 N 12 31 E
Borndiep, Str. 46 53 27 N 5 35 E
Borne 46 52 18 N 6 46 E
Bornem 47 51 6 N 4 14 E
Borneo, I. 102 1 0 N 115 0 E
Bornholm, I. 73 55 10 N 15 0 E
Bornholmsgattet 73 55 15 N 14 20 E
Borno □ 121 12 30 N 12 30 E
Bornos 57 36 48 N 5 42 W
Bornu Yassa 121 12 14 N 12 25 E
Borodino 80 55 31 N 35 40 E
Borogontsy 77 62 42 N 131 8 E
Boromo 120 11 45 N 2 58 W
Boron 163 35 0 N 117 39 W
Boronga Is. 98 19 58 N 93 6 E
Borongan 103 11 37 N 125 26 E
Bororen 138 24 13 S 151 33 E
Borotangba Mts. 123 6 30 N 25 0 E
Boroughbridge 33 54 6 N 1 23 W
Borovan 67 43 27 N 23 45 E
Borovichi 80 58 25 N 33 55 E
Borovsk, Moscow, U.S.S.R. 81 55 12 N 36 24 E
Borovsk, Urals, U.S.S.R. 84 59 43 N 56 40 E
Borovskoye 84 53 48 N 64 12 E
Borradaile, Mt. 136 12 5 S 132 51 E
Borrby 73 55 27 N 14 10 E
Borrego Springs 163 33 15 N 116 23 W
Borriol 58 40 4 N 0 4 W
Borris 39 32 36 N 6 57 W
Borris-in-Ossory 39 52 57 N 7 40 W
Borrisokane 39 53 0 N 8 8 W
Borrisoleigh 39 52 48 N 7 58 W
Borroloola 138 16 4 S 136 17 E
Borrowdale 32 54 31 N 3 10 W
Borsa 70 47 41 N 24 50 E
Borsod-Abaúj-Zemplén □ 53 48 20 N 21 0 E
Borssele 47 51 26 N 3 45 E
Bort-les-Orgues 44 45 24 N 2 29 E
Borth 31 52 29 N 4 3 W
Borujerd 92 33 55 N 48 50 E
Borve 36 58 25 N 6 28 W
Borzhomi 83 41 48 N 43 28 E
Borzna 80 51 18 N 32 26 E
Borzya 77 50 24 N 116 31 E
Bos. Dubica 63 45 10 N 16 50 E
Bos. Gradiška 66 45 10 N 17 15 E
Bos. Grahovo 63 44 12 N 16 26 E
Bos. Kostajnica 63 45 11 N 16 33 E
Bos. Krupa 63 44 53 N 16 10 E
Bos. Novi 63 45 2 N 16 22 E
Bos. Petrovac 63 44 35 N 16 21 E
Bos. Samac 66 45 3 N 18 29 E
Bosa 64 40 17 N 8 32 E
Bosaga 85 37 33 N 65 41 E
Bosanska Brod 66 45 10 N 18 0 E
Bosanski Novi 63 45 2 N 16 22 E
Bosavi, Mt. 135 6 30 S 142 49 E
Bosbury 28 52 5 N 2 27 W
Boscastle 30 50 42 N 4 42 W
Boscotrecase 65 40 46 N 14 28 E
Bosham 29 50 50 N 0 51 W
Boshoek 128 25 30 S 27 9 E
Boshof 128 28 31 S 25 13 E
Boshrūyeh 93 33 50 N 57 30 E
Bosilegrad 66 42 30 N 22 27 E
Boskoop 46 52 4 N 4 40 E
Boskovice 53 49 29 N 16 40 E
Bosna i Hercegovina □ 66 44 0 N 18 0 E
Bosna, R. 66 44 50 N 18 10 E
Bosnia = Bosna 66 44 0 N 18 0 E
Bosnik 103 1 5 S 136 10 E
Bōsō-Hantō 111 35 20 N 140 20 E
Bosobolo 124 4 15 N 19 50 E
Bosporus = Karadeniz Boğazı 92 41 10 N 29 10 E
Bossangoa 117 6 35 N 17 30 E
Bossekop 74 69 57 N 23 15 E
Bossembélé 117 5 25 N 17 40 E
Bossier City 159 32 28 N 93 38 W
Bosso 121 13 43 N 13 19 E
Bossut C. 136 18 42 S 121 35 E
Boston, U.K. 33 52 59 N 0 2 W
Boston, U.S.A. 162 42 20 N 71 0 W
Boston Bar 152 49 52 N 121 22 W
Bosut, R. 66 45 5 N 19 2 E
Boswell, Can. 152 49 28 N 116 45 W
Boswell, U.S.A. 159 34 1 N 95 30 W
Botad 94 22 15 N 71 40 E
Botany Bay 139 34 0 S 151 14 E
Botene 100 17 35 N 101 12 E
Botevgrad 67 42 55 N 23 47 E
Bothaville 128 27 23 S 26 34 E
Bothel 32 54 43 N 3 16 W
Bothnia, G. of 74 63 0 N 21 0 E
Bothwell 138 42 20 S 147 1 E
Boticas 56 41 41 N 7 40 W
Botletle R. 128 20 10 S 24 10 E
Botoroaga 70 44 8 N 25 32 E
Botoşani 70 47 42 N 26 41 E
Botoşani □ 70 47 50 N 26 50 E
Botro 120 7 51 N 5 19 W
Botswana ■ 125 22 0 S 24 0 E
Bottesford 33 52 57 N 0 48 W
Bottineau 158 48 49 N 100 25 W
Bottrop 48 51 34 N 6 59 E
Botucatu 173 22 55 S 48 30 W
Botwood 151 49 6 N 55 23 W
Bou Alam 118 33 50 N 1 26 E
Bou Ali 118 27 11 N 0 4 W
Bou Djébéha 120 18 25 N 2 45 W
Bou Garfa 118 27 4 N 7 59 W
Bou Guema 118 28 49 N 0 19 E
Bou Iblane, Djebel 118 33 50 N 4 0 W
Bou Ismail 118 36 38 N 2 42 E
Bou Izakarn 118 29 12 N 6 46 W
Bou Kahil, Djebel 118 34 22 N 9 23 E
Bou Saâda 119 35 11 N 4 9 E
Bou Salem 119 36 45 N 9 2 E
Bouaké 120 7 40 N 5 2 W
Bouar 124 6 0 N 15 40 E
Bouârfa 118 32 32 N 1 58 E
Bouca 117 6 45 N 18 25 E
Boucau 44 43 32 N 1 29 W
Boucaut B. 138 12 0 S 134 25 E
Bouches-du-Rhône □ 45 43 37 N 5 2 E
Bouda 118 27 50 N 0 27 W
Boudenib 118 31 59 N 3 31 W
Boudry 50 46 57 N 6 50 E
Boufarik 118 36 34 N 2 58 E
Bougainville C. 136 13 57 S 126 4 E
Bougainville I. 135 6 0 S 155 0 E
Bougainville Reef 138 15 30 S 147 5 E
Bougaroun, C. 119 37 6 N 6 30 E
Bougie = Bêjaïa 119 36 42 N 5 2 E
Bougouni 120 11 30 N 7 20 W
Bouillon 47 49 44 N 5 3 E
Bouïra 119 36 20 N 3 59 E
Boujad 118 32 46 N 6 24 W
Bouladuff 39 52 42 N 7 55 W
Boulder, Austral. 132 30 46 S 121 30 E
Boulder, Colo., U.S.A. 158 40 3 N 105 10 W
Boulder, Mont., U.S.A. 160 46 14 N 112 4 W
Boulder City 161 36 0 N 114 50 W
Boulder Creek 163 37 7 N 122 7 W
Boulder Dam = Hoover Dam 161 36 0 N 114 45 W
Bouleau, Lac au 150 47 40 N 77 35 W
Boulhaut 118 33 30 N 7 1 W
Boulia 138 22 52 S 139 51 E
Bouligny 43 49 17 N 5 45 E
Boulogne, R. 42 46 50 N 1 25 W
Boulogne-sur-Gesse 44 43 18 N 0 38 E
Boulogne-sur-Mer 43 50 42 N 1 36 E
Boulsa 121 12 39 N 0 34 W
Boultoum 121 14 45 N 10 25 E
Boumalne 118 31 25 N 6 0 W
Boun Neua 100 21 38 N 101 54 E
Boun Tai 100 21 23 N 101 58 E
Bouna 120 9 10 N 3 0 W
Boundary 147 64 11 N 141 2 W
Boundary Pk. 163 37 51 N 118 21 W
Boundiali 120 9 30 N 6 20 W
Bountiful 160 40 57 N 111 58 W
Bounty I. 130 46 0 S 180 0 E
Bour Khaya 77 71 50 N 133 10 E
Bourbon-l'Archambault 44 46 36 N 3 4 E
Bourbon-Lancy 44 46 37 N 3 45 E
Bourbonnais 44 46 28 N 3 0 E
Bourbonne 43 47 59 N 5 45 E
Bourem 121 17 0 N 0 24 W
Bourg 44 45 3 N 0 34 W
Bourg-Argental 45 45 18 N 4 32 E
Bourg-de-Péage 45 45 2 N 5 3 E
Bourg-en-Bresse 45 46 13 N 5 12 E
Bourg-St.-Andéol 45 44 23 N 4 39 E
Bourg-St.-Maurice 45 45 35 N 6 46 E
Bourg-St.-Pierre 50 45 57 N 7 12 E
Bourganeuf 44 45 57 N 1 45 E
Bourges 43 47 9 N 2 25 E
Bourget, L. du 45 45 44 N 5 52 E
Bourgneuf 42 47 2 N 1 58 W
Bourgneuf, B. de 42 47 3 N 2 10 W
Bourgneuf, Le 42 48 10 N 0 59 W
Bourgogne 43 47 0 N 4 30 E
Bourgoin-Jallieu 45 45 36 N 5 17 E
Bourke 139 30 8 S 145 55 E
Bourlamaque 150 48 5 N 77 56 W
Bourne 29 52 46 N 0 22 W
Bournemouth 28 50 43 N 1 53 W
Bourriot-Bergonce 44 44 7 N 0 14 W
Bourton-on-the-Water 28 51 53 N 1 45 W
Bouscat, Le 44 44 53 N 0 32 W
Boussac 44 46 22 N 2 13 E
Boussens 44 43 12 N 0 58 E
Bousso 117 10 34 N 16 52 E
Boussu 47 50 26 N 3 48 E
Bouthillier, Le 151 47 47 N 64 55 W
Boutilimit 120 17 45 N 14 40 W
Bouvet I. 15 55 0 S 3 30 E
Bouznika 118 33 46 N 7 6 W
Bouzonville 43 49 17 N 6 32 E
Bova Marina 65 37 59 N 15 56 E
Bovalino Marina 65 38 9 N 16 10 E
Bovec 63 46 20 N 13 33 E
Bovenkarspel 46 52 41 N 5 14 E
Bóves 62 44 19 N 7 29 E
Boves 62 44 19 N 7 33 E
Bovey Tracey 30 50 36 N 3 40 W
Bovigny 47 50 12 N 5 55 E
Bovill 160 46 58 N 116 27 W
Bovino 65 41 15 N 15 20 E
Bow Island 152 49 50 N 111 23 W
Bow, R. 152 51 10 N 115 0 W
Bowbells 158 48 47 N 102 19 W
Bowdle 158 45 30 N 100 2 W
Bowelling 137 33 25 S 116 30 E
Bowen 138 20 0 S 148 16 E
Bowen Mts. 141 37 0 S 148 0 E
Bowen, R. 138 20 24 S 147 20 E
Bowes 32 54 31 N 1 59 W
Bowie, U.S.A. 162 39 0 N 76 47 W
Bowie, Ariz., U.S.A. 161 32 15 N 109 30 W
Bowie, Tex., U.S.A. 159 33 33 N 97 50 W
Bowland, Forest of 32 54 0 N 2 30 W
Bowling Green, Ky., U.S.A. 156 37 0 N 86 25 W
Bowling Green, Ohio, U.S.A. 156 41 22 N 83 40 W
Bowling Green, Va., U.S.A. 162 38 3 N 77 21 W
Bowling Green, C. 138 19 19 S 147 25 E
Bowman 158 46 12 N 103 21 W
Bowman, I. 13 65 0 S 104 0 E
Bowmans 140 34 10 S 138 17 E
Bowmanville 150 43 55 N 78 41 W
Bowmore 34 55 45 N 6 18 W
Bowness, Can. 152 50 55 N 114 25 W
Bowness, Solway, U.K. 32 54 57 N 3 13 W
Bowness, Windermere, U.K. 32 54 22 N 2 56 W
Bowral 141 34 26 S 150 27 E
Bowraville 139 30 37 S 152 52 E
Bowron, R. 152 54 3 N 121 50 W
Bowser L. 152 56 30 N 129 30 W
Bowsman 153 52 14 N 101 12 W
Bowutu Mts. 135 7 45 S 147 10 E
Bowwood 127 17 5 S 26 20 E
Box 28 51 24 N 2 16 W
Box Hill 29 51 16 N 0 16 W
Boxelder Creek 160 47 20 N 108 30 W
Boxholm 73 58 12 N 15 3 E
Boxley 29 51 17 N 0 34 E
Boxmeer 47 51 38 N 5 56 E
Boxtel 47 51 36 N 5 9 E
Boyabat 82 41 28 N 34 42 E
Boyacá □ 174 5 30 N 72 30 W
Boyanup 137 33 30 S 115 40 E
Boyce 159 31 25 N 92 39 W
Boyd L. 150 61 30 N 103 20 W
Boyer, R. 152 58 27 N 115 57 W
Boyle 38 53 58 N 8 19 W
Boyne City 156 45 13 N 85 1 W
Boyne, R. 38 53 40 N 6 34 W
Boynton Beach 157 26 31 N 80 3 W
Boyoma, Chutes 124 0 12 N 25 25 E
Boyup Brook 137 33 50 S 116 23 E
Bozburun 69 36 43 N 28 8 E
Bozcaada 68 39 49 N 26 3 E
Bozeat 29 52 14 N 0 41 W
Bozeman 160 45 40 N 111 0 W
Bozepole Wlk. 54 54 33 N 17 56 E
Bozevac 66 44 32 N 21 24 E
Bozouls 44 44 28 N 2 43 E
Bozoum 117 6 25 N 16 35 E
Bozovici 70 44 56 N 22 1 E
Bra 62 44 41 N 7 50 E
Brabant □ 47 50 46 N 4 30 E
Brabant L. 153 54 18 N 108 5 W
Brabrand 73 56 9 N 10 7 E
BraC 63 43 20 N 16 40 E
Bracadale 36 57 22 N 6 24 W
Bracadale, L. 36 57 20 N 6 30 W
Bracciano 63 42 6 N 12 10 E
Bracciano, L. di 63 42 8 N 12 11 E
Bracebridge 150 45 2 N 79 19 W
Bracebridge Heath 33 53 13 N 0 32 W
Brach 119 27 31 N 14 20 E
Bracieux 43 47 30 N 1 30 E
Bräcke 72 62 45 N 15 26 E
Brackettville 159 29 21 N 100 20 W
Brackley 28 52 3 N 1 9 W
Bracknell 29 51 24 N 0 45 W
Braco 35 56 16 N 3 55 W
Brad 70 46 10 N 22 50 E
Brădano, R. 65 40 41 N 16 20 E
Bradda Hd. 32 54 6 N 4 46 W
Bradenton 157 27 25 N 82 35 W
Bradford, U.K. 33 53 47 N 1 45 W
Bradford, Pa., U.S.A. 156 41 58 N 78 41 W
Bradford, Vt., U.S.A. 162 43 59 N 72 9 W
Bradford-on-Avon 28 51 20 N 2 15 W
Brading 28 50 41 N 1 9 W
Bradley, Ark., U.S.A. 159 33 7 N 93 39 W
Bradley, Calif., U.S.A. 163 35 52 N 120 48 W
Bradley, S.D., U.S.A. 158 45 10 N 97 40 W
Bradley Institute 127 17 7 S 31 25 E
Bradore Bay 151 51 27 N 57 18 W
Bradshaw 136 15 21 S 130 16 E
Bradwell-on-Sea 29 51 44 N 0 55 E
Bradworthy 30 50 54 N 4 22 W
Brady 159 31 8 N 99 25 W
Brae 36 60 23 N 1 20 W
Brae, oilfield 19 58 45 N 1 18 E
Brædstrup 73 55 58 N 9 37 E
Braemar, Queens., Austral. 139 25 35 S 152 20 E
Braemar, S. Austral., Austral. 140 33 12 S 139 35 E
Braemar, U.K. 37 57 2 N 3 20 W
Braemar, dist. 37 57 2 N 3 20 W
Braemore, Grampian, U.K. 37 58 16 N 3 33 W
Braemore, Highland, U.K. 36 57 45 N 5 2 W
Braeriach Mt. 37 57 4 N 3 44 W
Braga 56 41 35 N 8 25 W
Braga □ 56 41 30 N 8 30 W
Bragado 172 35 2 S 60 27 W
Bragança, Brazil 170 1 0 S 47 2 W
Bragança, Port. 56 41 48 N 6 50 W
Bragança □ 56 41 30 N 6 45 W
Bragança Paulista 173 22 55 S 46 32 W
Brahmanbaria 98 23 50 N 91 15 E
Brahmani, R. 96 21 0 N 85 15 E
Brahmaputra, R. 98 26 30 N 93 30 E
Brahmaur 93 32 28 N 76 32 E
Braich-y-Pwll 31 52 47 N 4 46 W
Braidwood 141 35 27 S 149 49 E
Brailsford 33 52 58 N 1 35 W
Braine-l'Alleud 47 50 42 N 4 23 E
Braine-le-Comte 47 50 37 N 4 8 E
Brainerd 158 46 20 N 94 10 W
Braintree, U.K. 29 51 53 N 0 34 E
Braintree, U.S.A. 162 42 11 N 71 0 W
Braithwaite Pt. 138 12 5 S 133 50 E
Brak, R. 128 29 50 S 23 10 E
Brake 48 53 19 N 8 30 E
Brakel 46 51 49 N 5 5 E
Brakne-Hoby 73 56 12 N 15 8 E
Bräkne-Hoby 73 56 14 N 15 6 E
Brakpan 129 26 13 S 28 20 E
Brakwater 128 22 28 S 17 3 E
Brålanda 73 58 12 N 12 21 E
Brålanda 73 58 34 N 12 21 E
Brăila 70 45 19 N 27 59 E
Brăila □ 70 45 5 N 27 30 E
Bralorne 152 50 50 N 123 15 W
Bramford 29 52 5 N 1 6 E
Bramminge 73 55 28 N 8 42 E

Bramon **Brøttum**

Bramon 72 62 14N 17 40 E
Brampton, Can. 150 43 45N 79 45W
Brampton, Cambs., U.K. 29 52 19N 0 13W
Brampton, Cumb., U.K. 32 54 56N 2 43W
Bramsche 48 52 25N 7 58 E
Bramshott 29 51 5N 0 47W
Bramwell 138 12 8 S 142 37 E
Brancaster 29 52 58N 0 40 E
Branco, Cabo 170 7 9 S 34 47W
Branco, R. 174 0 0 61 15W
Brande 73 55 57N 9 8 E
Brandenburg 48 52 24N 12 33 E
Brander, Pass of 34 56 25N 5 10W
Branderburgh 37 57 43N 3 17W
Brandfort 128 28 40 S 26 30 E
Brandon, Can. 153 49 50N 99 57W
Brandon, Durham, U.K. 33 54 46N 1 37W
Brandon, Suffolk, U.K. 29 52 27N 0 37 E
Brandon, U.S.A. 156 43 48N 73 4W
Brandon, U.S.A. 162 44 2N 73 5W
Brandon B. 39 52 17N 10 8W
Brandon, Mt. 39 52 15N 10 15W
Brandon Pt. 39 52 18N 10 10W
Brandsen 172 35 10 S 58 15W
Brandval 71 60 19N 12 1 E
Brandvlei 128 30 25 S 20 30 E
Brandýs 52 50 10N 14 40 E
Branford 162 41 15N 72 48W
Braniewo 54 54 25N 19 50 E
Brännarp 73 56 46N 12 38 E
Bransby 139 28 10 S 142 0 E
Bransfield Str. 13 63 0 S 59 0W
Branson, Colo., U.S.A. 159 37 4N 103 53W
Branson, Mo., U.S.A. 159 36 40N 93 18W
Branston 33 53 13N 0 28W
Brantford 150 43 15N 80 15W
Brantôme 44 45 22N 0 39 E
Branxholme 140 37 52 S 141 49 E
Branxton 141 32 38 S 151 21 E
Branzi 62 46 0N 9 46 E
Bras d'or, L. 151 45 50N 60 50W
Brasiléia 174 11 0 S 68 45W
Brasília 171 15 47 S 47 55 E
Braslav 80 55 38N 27 0 E
Braslovče 63 46 21N 15 3 E
Braşov 70 45 38N 25 35 E
Braşov □ 70 45 45N 25 15 E
Brass 121 4 35N 6 14 E
Brass, R. 121 4 15N 6 13 E
Brasschaat 47 51 19N 4 27 E
Brassey, Barisan 102 5 0N 117 15 E
Brassey Ra. 137 25 8 S 122 15 E
Brasstown Bald, Mt. 157 34 54N 83 45W
Brassus, Le 50 46 35N 6 13 E
Brasted 29 51 16N 0 8 E
Bratislava 53 48 10N 17 7 E
Bratsk 77 56 10N 101 30 E
Bratteborg 73 57 37N 14 4 E
Brattleboro 162 42 53N 72 37W
Brattvær 71 63 25N 7 48 E
Braţul Chilia, R. 70 45 25N 29 20 E
Braţul Sfîntu Gheorghe, R. 70 45 0N 29 20 E
Braţul Sulina, R. 70 45 10N 29 20 E
Bratunac 66 44 13N 19 21 E
Braunau 52 48 15N 13 3 E
Braunschweig 48 52 17N 10 28 E
Braunton 30 51 6N 4 9W
Brava 91 1 20N 44 8 E
Bråviken 72 58 38N 16 32 E
Bravo del Norte, R. 164 30 30N 105 0W
Brawley 163 32 58N 115 30W
Bray, France 43 49 15N 1 40 E
Bray, Ireland 39 53 12N 6 6W
Bray, U.K. 29 51 30N 0 42W
Bray Hd. 39 51 52N 10 26W
Bray, Mt. 138 14 0N 134 30 E
Bray-sur-Seine 43 48 25N 3 14 E
Brazeau, R. 152 52 55N 115 14W
Brazil 156 39 30N 87 8W
Brazil ■ 174 5 0N 20 0W
Brazilian Highlands 170 18 0 S 46 30W
Brazo Sur, R. 172 25 30 S 58 0W
Brazos, R. 159 30 30N 96 20W
Brazzaville 124 4 9 S 15 12 E
Brčko 66 44 54N 18 46 E
Breadalbane, Austral. 138 23 50 S 139 35 E
Breadalbane, U.K. 34 56 30N 4 15W
Breaden, L. 137 25 51 S 125 28 E
Breage 30 50 6N 5 17W
Breaksea Sd. 143 45 35 S 166 35 E
Bream Bay 142 35 56 S 174 28 E
Bream Head 142 35 51 S 174 36 E
Bream Tail 142 36 3 S 174 36 E
Breamish, R. 35 55 30N 1 55W
Breas 172 25 29 S 70 24W
Brebes 103 6 52 S 109 3 E
Brechin 37 56 44N 2 40W
Brecht 47 51 21N 4 38 E
Breckenridge, Colo., U.S.A. 160 39 30N 106 2W
Breckenridge, Minn., U.S.A. 158 46 20N 96 36W
Breckenridge, Tex., U.S.A. 159 32 48N 98 55W
Breckland 23 52 30N 0 40 E
Brecknock (□) 26 51 58N 3 25W
Břeclav 53 48 46N 16 53 E
Brecon 31 51 57N 3 23W
Brecon Beacons 31 51 53N 3 27W
Breda 47 51 35N 4 45 E
Bredaryd 73 57 10N 13 45 E
Bredasdorp 128 34 33 S 20 2 E
Bredbo 141 35 58 S 149 10 E
Brede 29 50 56N 0 37 E
Bredene 47 51 14N 2 59 E
Bredon Hill 28 52 3N 2 2W
Bredy 84 52 26N 60 21 E
Bree 47 51 8N 5 35 E
Breezand 46 52 53N 4 49 E
Bregalnica, R. 66 41 50N 22 20 E
Bregenz 52 47 30N 9 45 E
Bregning 73 56 8N 8 30 E
Bréhal 42 48 53N 1 30W
Bréhat, I. de 42 48 51N 3 0W
Breiðafjörður 74 65 15N 23 15W
Breil 45 43 56N 7 31 E
Breisach 49 48 2N 7 37 E
Brejinho de Nazaré 170 11 1 S 48 34W
Brejo 170 3 41 S 42 47W
Brekke 71 61 1N 5 26 E
Bremangerlandet 71 61 51N 5 0 E
Bremangerpollen 71 61 51N 5 0 E
Bremen 48 53 4N 8 47 E
Bremen □ 48 53 6N 8 46 E
Bremer I. 138 12 5 S 136 45 E
Bremerhaven 48 53 34N 8 35 E
Bremerton 160 47 30N 122 38W
Bremervörde 48 53 28N 9 10 E
Bremgarten 51 47 21N 8 21 E
Bremnes 71 59 47N 5 8 E
Bremsnes 71 63 6N 7 40 E
Brendon Hills 28 51 6N 3 25W
Brenes 57 37 32N 5 54W
Brenham 159 30 5N 96 27W
Brenner Pass 52 47 0N 11 30 E
Breno 62 45 57N 10 20 E
Brent, Can. 150 46 2N 78 29W
Brent, U.K. 29 51 33N 0 18W
Brent, oil and gasfield 19 61 0N 1 45 E
Brenta, R. 63 45 11N 12 18 E
Brentwood, U.K. 29 51 37N 0 19W
Brentwood, U.S.A. 163 37 55N 121 42W
Bréscia 62 45 33N 10 13 E
Breskens 47 51 23N 3 33 E
Breslau = Wrocław. 54 51 5N 17 5 E
Bresle, R. 43 50 4N 1 21 E
Bresles 43 49 25N 2 13 E
Bressanone 63 46 43N 11 40 E
Bressay 36 60 10N 1 6W
Bressay I. 36 60 10N 1 5W
Bressay Sd. 36 60 8N 1 10W
Bresse, La 43 48 0N 6 53 E
Bresse, Plaine de 43 46 20N 5 10 E
Bressuire 42 46 51N 0 30W
Brest, France 42 48 24N 4 31W
Brest, U.S.S.R. 80 52 10N 23 40 E
Bretagne 42 48 0N 3 0W
Bretçu 70 46 7N 26 18 E
Breteuil 43 49 38N 2 18 E
Breton 152 53 7N 114 28W
Breton Sd. 159 29 40N 89 12W
Brett, C. 142 35 10 S 174 20 E
Bretten 49 49 2N 8 43 E
Bretuil 42 48 50N 0 53 E
Breukelen 46 52 10N 5 0 E
Brevard 157 35 19N 82 42W
Breves 170 1 40 S 50 29W
Brevik 71 59 4N 9 42 E
Brewarrina 139 30 0 S 146 51 E
Brewer 151 44 43N 68 50W
Brewer, Mt. 163 36 44N 118 28W
Brewerton 162 43 14N 76 9W
Brewood 28 52 41N 2 10W
Brewster, N.Y., U.S.A. 162 41 23N 73 37W
Brewster, Wash., U.S.A. 160 48 10N 119 51W
Brewster, Kap 12 70 7N 22 0W
Brewton 157 31 9N 87 2W
Breyten 129 26 16 S 30 0 E
Breytovo 81 58 18N 37 50 E
Brézina 118 33 4N 1 14 E
Březnice 52 49 32N 13 57 E
Breznik 66 42 44N 22 50 E
Brezno 53 48 50N 19 40 E
Bria 117 6 30N 21 58 E
Briançon 45 44 54N 6 39 E
Briare 43 47 38N 2 45 E
Bribbaree 141 34 10 S 147 51 E
Bribie I. 139 27 0 S 152 58 E
Brickaville 129 18 49 S 49 4 E
Bricon 43 48 5N 5 0 E
Bricquebec 42 49 29N 1 39W
Bride 32 54 24N 4 23W
Bridestowe 30 50 41N 4 7W
Bridge 29 51 14N 1 8 E
Bridge of Allan 35 56 9N 3 57W
Bridge of Don 37 57 10N 2 8W
Bridge of Earn 35 56 20N 3 25W
Bridge of Orchy 34 56 29N 4 48W
Bridge of Weir 34 55 51N 4 35W
Bridge, R. 152 50 50N 122 40W
Bridgehampton 162 40 56N 72 18W
Bridgend, Islay, U.K. 34 55 46N 6 15W
Bridgend, Mid Glam., U.K. 31 51 30N 3 35W
Bridgeport, Calif., U.S.A. 163 38 14N 119 15W
Bridgeport, Conn., U.S.A. 162 41 12N 73 12W
Bridgeport, Nebr., U.S.A. 158 41 42N 103 10W
Bridgeport, Tex., U.S.A. 159 33 15N 97 45W
Bridger 160 45 20N 108 58W
Bridgeton 162 39 29N 75 10W
Bridgetown, Austral. 137 33 58 S 116 7 E
Bridgetown, Barbados 167 13 0N 59 30W
Bridgetown, Can. 151 44 55N 65 18W
Bridgetown, Ireland 39 52 13N 6 33W
Bridgeville 162 38 45N 75 36W
Bridgewater, Austral. 140 36 36 S 143 59 E
Bridgewater, Can. 151 44 25N 64 31W
Bridgewater, Mass., U.S.A. 162 41 59N 70 56W
Bridgewater, N.Y., U.S.A. 162 42 58N 75 15W
Bridgewater, S.D., U.S.A. 158 43 34N 97 29W
Bridgewater, C. 140 38 23 S 141 23 E
Bridgnorth 28 52 33N 2 25W
Bridgwater 28 51 7N 3 0W
Bridgwater B. 28 51 15N 3 15W
Bridlington 33 54 6N 0 11W
Bridlington B. 33 54 4N 0 10W
Bridport, Austral. 138 40 59 S 147 23 E
Bridport, U.K. 28 50 43N 2 45W
Brie-Comte-Robert 43 48 40N 2 35 E
Brie, Plaine de 43 48 35N 3 10 E
Briec 42 48 6N 4 0W
Brielle 46 51 54N 4 10 E
Brienne-le-Château 43 48 24N 4 30 E
Brienon 43 48 0N 3 35 E
Brienz 50 46 46N 8 2 E
Brienzersee 50 46 44N 7 53 E
Brierfield 32 53 49N 2 15W
Brierley Hill 28 52 29N 2 7W
Briey 43 49 14N 5 57 E
Brig 50 46 18N 7 59 E
Brigantine 162 39 24N 74 22W
Brigg 33 53 33N 0 30W
Briggsdale 158 40 40N 104 20W
Brigham City 160 41 30N 112 1W
Brighouse 33 53 42N 1 47W
Brighstone 29 50 38N 1 36W
Bright 141 36 42 S 146 56 E
Brightlingsea 29 51 49N 1 1 E
Brighton, Austral. 140 35 5 S 138 30 E
Brighton, Can. 150 44 2N 77 44W
Brighton, U.K. 29 50 50N 0 9W
Brighton, U.S.A. 158 39 59N 104 50W
Brightstone 28 50 38N 1 23W
Brightwater 143 41 22 S 173 9 E
Brignogan-Plage 42 48 40N 4 20W
Brignoles 45 43 25N 6 5 E
Brigstock 29 52 27N 0 38W
Brihuega 58 40 45N 2 52W
Brikama 120 13 15N 16 45W
Brill 28 51 49N 1 3W
Brilliant 152 49 19N 117 38W
Brilon 48 51 23N 8 32 E
Brim 140 36 3 S 142 27 E
Brimfield 28 52 18N 2 42W
Bríndisi 65 40 39N 17 55 E
Brinkley 159 34 55N 91 15W
Brinklow 28 52 25N 1 22W
Brinkworth, Austral. 140 33 42 S 138 26 E
Brinkworth, U.K. 28 51 33N 1 59W
Brinyan 37 59 8N 3 0W
Brion I. 151 47 46N 61 26W
Brionne 42 49 11N 0 43 E
Brionski, I. 63 44 55N 13 45 E
Brioude 44 45 18N 3 23 E
Briouze 42 48 42N 0 23W
Brisbane 139 27 25 S 153 2 E
Brisbane, R. 139 27 24 S 153 9 E
Brisignella 63 44 14N 11 46 E
Bristol, U.K. 28 51 26N 2 35W
Bristol, Conn., U.S.A. 162 41 44N 72 57W
Bristol, Pa., U.S.A. 162 40 6N 74 52W
Bristol, R.I., U.S.A. 162 41 40N 71 15W
Bristol, S.D., U.S.A. 158 45 25N 97 43W
Bristol B. 147 58 0N 160 0W
Bristol Channel 30 51 18N 4 30W
Bristol I. 13 58 45 S 28 0W
Bristol L. 161 34 23N 116 0W
Briston 29 52 52N 1 4 E
Bristow 159 35 5N 96 28W
British Antarctic Territory 13 66 0 S 45 0W
British Columbia □ 152 55 0N 125 15W
British Guiana = Guyana 174 5 0N 59 0W
British Honduras = Belize 165 17 0N 88 30W
British Isles 16 55 0N 4 0W
Briton Ferry 31 51 37N 3 50W
Brits 129 25 37 S 27 48 E
Britstown 128 30 37 S 23 30 E
Britt 150 45 46N 80 34W
Brittany = Bretagne 42 48 0N 3 0W
Brittas 39 53 14N 6 29W
Brittatorp 73 57 3N 14 58 E
Britton 158 45 50N 97 47W
Brive-la-Gaillarde 44 45 10N 1 32 E
Briviesca 58 42 32N 3 19W
Brixham 30 50 24N 3 31W
Brixton 138 23 32 S 144 57 E
Brixworth 29 52 20N 0 54W
Brize Norton 28 51 46N 1 35W
Brlik, U.S.S.R. 76 44 0N 74 5 E
Brlik, Kazakh S.S.R., U.S.S.R. 85 44 5N 73 31 E
Brlik, Kazakh S.S.R., U.S.S.R. 85 43 40N 73 49 E
Brno 53 49 10N 16 35 E
Bro 72 59 13N 13 2 E
Broach = Bharuch 96 21 47N 73 0 E
Broad Arrow 137 30 23 S 121 15 E
Broad B. 36 58 14N 6 16W
Broad Chalke 28 51 2N 1 54W
Broad Clyst 30 50 46N 3 27W
Broad Haven, Ireland 38 54 20N 9 55W
Broad Haven, U.K. 31 51 46N 5 6W
Broad Law, Mt. 35 55 30N 3 22W
Broad, R. 157 34 30N 81 26W
Broad Sd., Austral. 138 22 0 S 149 45 E
Broad Sd., U.K. 30 49 56N 6 19W
Broadalbin 162 43 3N 74 12W
Broadford, Austral. 141 37 14 S 145 4 E
Broadford, Clare, Ireland 39 52 48N 8 38W
Broadford, Limerick, Ireland 39 52 21N 8 59W
Broadford, U.K. 36 57 14N 5 55W
Broadhembury 30 50 49N 3 16W
Broadhurst Ra. 136 22 30 S 122 30 E
Broads, The 29 52 45N 1 30 E
Broadsound Ra. 133 22 50 S 149 30 E
Broadstairs 29 51 21N 1 28 E
Broadus 158 45 28N 105 27W
Broadview 153 50 22N 102 35W
Broadway, Ireland 39 52 13N 6 23W
Broadway, U.K. 28 52 2N 1 51W
Broadwindsor 28 50 49N 2 49W
Broager 73 54 53N 9 40 E
Broaryd 73 57 7N 13 15 E
Brochet, Man., Can. 153 57 53N 101 40W
Brochet, Manitoba, Can. 153 57 55N 101 40W
Brochet, Québec, Can. 150 47 12N 72 42W
Brochet, L. 153 58 36N 101 35W
Brock 153 51 26N 108 43W
Brocken 48 51 48N 10 40 E
Brockenhurst 28 50 49N 1 34W
Brocklehurst 141 32 9 S 148 38 E
Brockman Mt. 137 22 25 S 117 15 E
Brockville 150 44 35N 75 41W
Brockway 158 47 18N 105 46W
Brockworth 28 51 51N 2 9W
Brod 66 41 35N 21 17 E
Brodarevo 66 43 14N 19 44 E
Brodeur Pen. 149 72 30N 88 10W
Brodick 34 55 34N 5 9W
Brodnica 54 53 15N 19 25 E
Brodokalmak 84 55 35N 62 6 E
Brody 80 50 5N 25 10 E
Broechem 47 51 11N 4 38 E
Broek 46 52 26N 5 0 E
Broek op Langedijk 46 52 41N 4 49 E
Brogan 160 44 14N 117 32W
Broglie 42 49 0N 0 30 E
Brok 54 52 43N 21 52 E
Broke Inlet 137 34 55 S 116 25 E
Broken Bank, gasfield 19 53 20N 2 4 E
Broken Bow, Nebr., U.S.A. 158 41 25N 99 35W
Broken Bow, Okla., U.S.A. 159 34 2N 94 43W
Broken Hill 140 31 58 S 141 29 E
Broken Hill = Kabwe 127 14 27 S 28 28 E
Brokind 73 58 13N 15 42 E
Bromborough 32 53 20N 3 0W
Bromham 28 51 23N 2 3W
Bromhead 153 49 18N 103 40W
Bromley 29 51 20N 0 5 E
Bromölla 73 56 5N 14 28 E
Brompton 33 54 22N 1 25W
Bromsgrove 28 52 20N 2 3W
Bromyard 28 52 12N 2 30W
Brønderslev 73 57 16N 9 57 E
Brong Ahafo 120 7 50N 2 0 E
Bronkhorstspruit 129 25 46 S 28 45 E
Bronnitsy 81 55 27N 38 10 E
Bronte, Italy 65 37 48N 14 49 E
Bronte, U.S.A. 159 31 54N 100 18W
Bronte Park 138 42 8 S 146 30 E
Brookeborough 38 54 19N 7 23W
Brookfield 158 39 50N 93 4W
Brookhaven 159 31 40N 90 25W
Brookings, Oreg., U.S.A. 160 42 4N 124 10W
Brookings, S.D., U.S.A. 158 44 20N 96 45W
Brooklands 138 18 5 S 144 0 E
Brookmere 152 49 52N 120 53W
Brooks 152 50 35N 111 55W
Brooks B. 152 50 15N 127 55W
Brooks L. 153 61 55N 106 35W
Brooks Ra. 147 68 40N 147 0W
Brooksville 157 28 32N 82 21W
Brookton 137 32 22 S 116 57 E
Brookville 156 39 25N 85 0W
Brooloo 139 26 30 S 152 43 E
Broom, L. 36 57 55N 5 15W
Broome 136 18 0 S 122 15 E
Broomehill 137 31 51 S 117 39 E
Broomfield 28 51 46N 0 28 E
Broomhill 35 55 19N 1 36W
Broons 42 48 20N 2 16W
Brora 37 58 0N 3 50W
Brora L. 37 58 3N 3 58W
Brora, R. 37 58 4N 3 52W
Brosarp 73 55 44N 14 8 E
Brösarp 73 55 43N 14 6 E
Broseley 28 52 36N 2 30W
Brosna, R. 39 53 8N 8 0W
Broşteni 70 47 14N 25 43 E
Brotas de Macaúbas 171 12 0 S 42 38W
Brothers 160 43 56N 120 39W
Brothertoft 33 53 0N 0 5W
Brotton 33 54 34N 0 55W
Brøttum 71 61 2N 10 34 E

Brough **Bura**

Brough, Cumbria, U.K. 32 54 32N 2 19W
Brough, Humberside, U.K. 33 53 44N 0 35W
Brough Hd. 37 59 8N 3 20W
Broughams Gate 140 30 51S 140 59E
Broughshane 38 54 54N 6 12W
Broughton, Austral. 138 20 10S 146 20E
Broughton, Borders, U.K. 35 55 37N 3 25W
Broughton, Humberside, U.K. 33 53 33N 0 36W
Broughton, Northampton, U.K. 29 52 22N 0 45W
Broughton, Yorkshire, U.K. 33 54 26N 1 8W
Broughton-in-Furness 32 54 17N 3 12W
Broughty Ferry 35 56 29N 2 50W
Broumov 53 50 35N 16 20E
Brouwershaven 46 51 45N 3 55E
Brouwershavensche Gat 46 51 46N 3 50E
Brovary 80 50 34N 30 48E
Brovst 73 57 6N 9 31E
Browerville 158 46 3N 94 50W
Brown, Mt. 140 32 30S 138 0E
Brown, Pt. 139 32 32S 133 50E
Brown Willy, Mt. 30 50 35N 4 34W
Brownfield 159 33 10N 102 15W
Browngrove 38 53 33N 8 49W
Brownhills 28 52 38N 1 57W
Browning 160 48 35N 113 10W
Brownlee 153 50 43N 106 1W
Browns Bay 142 36 40S 174 40E
Brownstown Hd. 39 52 8N 7 8W
Brownsville, Oreg., U.S.A. 160 44 29N 123 0W
Brownsville, Tenn., U.S.A. 159 35 35N 89 15W
Brownsville, Tex., U.S.A. 159 25 56N 97 25W
Brownwood 159 31 45N 99 0W
Brownwood, L. 159 31 51N 98 35W
Browse I. 136 14 7S 123 33E
Broxburn 35 55 56N 3 23W
Broye, R. 50 46 52N 6 58E
Brozas 57 39 37N 6 47W
Bruas 101 4 31N 100 46E
Bruay-en-Artois 43 50 29N 2 33E
Bruce Bay 143 43 35S 169 42E
Bruce, gasfield 19 59 45N 1 32E
Bruce Mines 150 46 20N 83 45W
Bruce, Mt. 136 22 37S 118 8E
Bruce Rock 137 31 52S 118 8E
Bruchsal 49 49 9N 8 39E
Bruck a.d. Leitha 53 48 1N 16 47E
Bruck a.d. Mur 52 47 24N 15 16E
Brückenau 49 50 17N 9 48E
Brŭdiceni 70 45 3N 23 4E
Brue, R. 28 51 10N 2 59W
Bruernish Pt. 36 57 0N 7 22W
Bruff 39 52 29N 8 35W
Brugelette 47 50 35N 3 52E
Bruges = Brugge 47 51 13N 3 13E
Brugg 50 47 29N 8 11E
Brugge 47 51 13N 3 13E
Brühl 48 50 49N 6 51E
Bruinisse 47 51 40N 4 5E
Brûlé 152 53 15N 117 58W
Brûlon 42 47 58N 0 15W
Brûly 47 49 58N 4 32E
Brumado 171 14 14S 41 40W
Brumado, R. 171 14 13S 41 40W
Brumath 43 48 43N 7 40E
Brummen 46 52 5N 6 10E
Brumunddal 71 60 53N 10 56E
Brunchilly 138 18 50S 134 30E
Brundidge 157 31 43N 85 45W
Bruneau 160 42 57N 115 55W
Bruneau, R. 160 42 45N 115 50W
Brunei = Bandar Seri Begawan 102 4 52N 115 0E
Brunei ■ 102 4 50N 115 0E
Brunette Downs 138 18 40S 135 55E
Brunflo 72 63 5N 14 50E
Brunico 63 46 50N 11 55E
Brünig, Col de 50 46 46N 8 8E
Brunkeberg 71 59 26N 8 28E
Brunna 72 59 52N 17 25E
Brunnen 51 46 59N 8 37E
Brunner 143 42 27S 171 20E
Brunner, L. 143 42 27S 171 20E
Brunnsvik 72 60 12N 15 8E
Bruno 153 52 20N 105 30W
Brunsberg 72 59 38N 12 52E
Brunsbüttelkoog 48 53 52N 9 13E
Brunssum 47 50 57N 5 59E
Brunswick, Ga., U.S.A. 157 31 10N 81 30W
Brunswick, Md., U.S.A. 156 39 20N 77 38W
Brunswick, Me., U.S.A. 151 43 53N 69 50W
Brunswick, Mo., U.S.A. 158 39 26N 93 10W
Brunswick = Braunschweig 48 52 17N 10 28E
Brunswick B. 136 15 15S 124 50E
Brunswick Junction 137 33 15S 115 50E
Brunswick, Pen. de 176 53 30S 71 30W
Bruntál 53 50 0N 17 27E
Brunton 35 55 2N 2 6W
Bruny I. 138 43 20S 147 15E
Bruree 39 52 25N 8 40W
Brus Laguna 166 15 47N 84 35W
Brusartsi 66 43 40N 23 5E
Brush 158 40 17N 103 33W
Brusio 51 46 14N 10 8E
Brusque 173 27 5S 49 0W
Brussel 47 50 51N 4 21E
Brussels = Bruxelles 47 50 51N 4 21E
Brustem 47 50 48N 5 14E
Bruthen 141 37 42S 147 50E
Bruton 28 51 6N 2 28W
Bruvik 71 60 29N 5 40E
Bruxelles 47 50 51N 4 21E
Bruyères 43 48 10N 6 40E
Brwinow 54 52 9N 20 40E
Bryagovo 67 41 58N 25 8E
Bryan, Ohio, U.S.A. 156 41 30N 84 30W
Bryan, Texas, U.S.A. 159 30 40N 96 27W
Bryan, Mt. 140 33 30S 139 0E
Bryansk 80 53 13N 34 25E
Bryanskoye 83 44 9N 47 10E
Bryant 58 44 39N 97 26W
Bryggja 71 61 56N 5 27E
Bryher I. 30 49 57N 6 21W
Brymbo 31 53 4N 3 5W
Brynamman 31 51 49N 3 52W
Bryncethin 31 51 33N 3 34W
Bryne 71 58 44N 5 38E
Brynmawr 31 51 48N 3 11W
Bryrup 73 56 2N 9 30E
Bryson City 157 35 28N 83 25W
Bryte 163 38 35N 121 33W
Brza Palanka 66 44 28N 22 37E
Brzava, R. 66 45 21N 20 45E
Brzeg 54 50 52N 17 30E
Brzeg Dln 54 51 16N 16 41E
Brzesko 54 49 59N 20 34E
Brześć Kujawski 54 52 36N 18 55E
Brzeszcze 54 49 59N 19 10E
Brzeziny 54 51 49N 19 42E
Brzozów 54 49 41N 22 3E
Bu Athiah 119 30 1N 15 30E
Bu Craa 116 26 45N 17 2E
Buapinang 103 4 40S 121 30E
Buayan 103 5 3N 125 28E
Buba 120 11 40N 14 59W
Bubanza 126 3 6S 29 23E
Bucaramanga 174 7 0N 73 0W
Buccaneer Arch. 136 16 7S 123 20E
Bucchiánico 63 42 20N 14 10E
Bucecea 70 47 47N 26 28E
Bŭceşti 70 46 50N 27 11E
Buchach 80 49 5N 25 25E
Buchan, Austral. 141 37 30S 148 12E
Buchan, U.K. 37 57 32N 2 8W
Buchan Ness 37 57 29N 1 48W
Buchan, oilfield 19 57 55N 0 0
Buchanan, Can. 153 51 40N 102 45W
Buchanan, Liberia 120 5 57N 10 2W
Buchanan Cr. 138 17 10S 138 6E
Buchanan, L., Queens., Austral. 138 21 35S 145 52E
Buchanan, L., W. Australia, Austral. 137 25 33S 123 2E
Buchanan, L., U.S.A. 159 30 50N 98 25W
Buchans 151 49 50N 56 52W
Bucharest = Bucureşti 70 44 27N 26 10E
Buchholz 48 53 19N 9 51E
Buchloe 49 48 3N 10 45E
Buchlyvie 34 56 7N 4 20W
Buchon, Pt. 163 35 15N 120 54W
Buchs 51 47 10N 9 28E
Buck Hill Falls 162 41 11N 75 16W
Buck, The, mt. 37 57 19N 3 0W
Buckden 29 52 17N 0 16W
Bückeburg 48 52 16N 9 2E
Buckeye 161 33 28N 112 40W
Buckfastleigh 30 50 28N 3 47W
Buckhannon 156 39 2N 80 10W
Buckhaven 35 56 10N 3 2W
Buckie 37 57 40N 2 58W
Buckingham, Can. 150 45 37N 75 24W
Buckingham, U.K. 29 52 0N 0 59W
Buckingham □ 29 51 50N 0 55W
Buckingham B. 138 12 10S 135 40E
Buckingham Can. 97 14 0N 80 5E
Buckinguy 139 31 3S 147 30E
Buckland 147 66 0N 161 5W
Buckland Brewer 30 50 56N 4 14W
Buckle Hd. 136 14 26S 127 52E
Buckleboo 140 32 54S 136 12E
Buckley, U.K. 31 53 10N 3 5W
Buckley, U.S.A. 160 47 10N 122 2W
Bucklin 159 37 37N 99 40W
Bucksburn 37 57 10N 2 10W
Bucquoy 43 50 9N 2 43E
Buctouche 151 46 30N 64 45W
Bucureşti 70 44 27N 26 10E
Bucyrus 156 40 48N 83 0W
Budacul, Munte 41 47 5N 25 40E
Budafok 53 47 26N 19 2E
Budalin 98 22 20N 95 10E
Budapest 53 47 29N 19 5E
Budaun 95 28 5N 79 10E
Budd Coast 13 67 0S 112 0E
Buddabadah 141 31 56S 147 14E
Buddon Ness 35 56 29N 2 42W
Buddusò 64 40 35N 9 18E
Bude 30 50 49N 4 33W
Bude Bay 30 50 50N 4 40W
Budel 47 51 17N 5 34E
Budeşti 70 44 13N 26 30E
Budge Budge 95 22 30N 88 25E
Budgewoi Lake 141 33 13S 151 34E
Budia 58 40 38N 2 46W
Búdir 74 64 49N 23 23W
Budjala 124 2 50N 19 40E
Budle B. 35 55 37N 1 45W
Budleigh Salterton 30 50 37N 3 19W
Búdrio 63 44 31N 11 31E
Budva 66 42 17N 18 50E
Budzyn 54 52 54N 16 59E
Buea 121 4 10N 9 9E
Buellton 163 34 37N 120 12W
Buena 162 39 31N 74 56W
Buena Vista, Colo., U.S.A. 161 38 56N 106 6W
Buena Vista, Va., U.S.A. 156 37 47N 79 23W
Buena Vista L. 163 35 15N 119 21W
Buenaventura 164 29 50N 107 30W
Buenaventura, B. de 174 3 48N 77 17W
Buendía, Pantano de 58 40 25N 2 43W
Buenópolis 171 17 54S 44 11W
Buenos Aires, Argent. 172 34 30S 58 20W
Buenos Aires, Colomb. 174 1 36N 73 18W
Buenos Aires, C. Rica 166 9 10N 83 20W
Buenos Aires □ 172 36 30S 60 0W
Buenos Aires, Lago 176 46 35S 72 30W
Buesaco 174 1 23N 77 9W
Buffalo, Can. 153 50 49N 110 42W
Buffalo, Mo., U.S.A. 159 37 40N 93 5W
Buffalo, Okla., U.S.A. 159 36 55N 99 42W
Buffalo, S.D., U.S.A. 159 45 39N 103 31W
Buffalo, Wyo., U.S.A. 160 44 25N 106 50W
Buffalo Center 147 64 2N 145 50W
Buffalo Head Hills 152 57 25N 115 55W
Buffalo L. 152 52 27N 112 54W
Buffalo Narrows 153 55 51N 108 29W
Buffalo, R. 152 57 50N 117 1W
Buffels, R. 129 29 36S 17 15E
Buford 157 34 5N 84 0W
Bug, R., Poland 54 51 20N 23 40E
Bug, R., U.S.S.R. 82 48 0N 31 0E
Buga 174 4 0N 77 0W
Buganda □ 126 0 0N 31 30E
Buganga 126 0 25N 32 0E
Bugeat 44 45 36N 1 55E
Buggenhout 47 51 1N 4 12E
Buggs I. L. 157 36 20N 78 30W
Buglawton 32 53 12N 2 11W
Bugle 30 50 23N 4 46W
Bugojno 66 44 2N 17 25E
Bugsuk, I. 102 8 15N 117 15E
Bugue, Le 44 44 55N 0 56E
Bugulma 84 54 33N 52 48E
Buguma 121 4 42N 6 55E
Bugun Shara 105 49 0N 104 0E
Buguruslan 84 53 39N 52 26E
Buheirat-Murrat-el-Kubra 122 30 15N 32 40E
Buhl, Idaho, U.S.A. 160 42 35N 114 54W
Buhl, Minn., U.S.A. 158 47 30N 92 46W
Buhŭeşti 70 46 47N 27 32E
Buhuşi 70 46 41N 26 45E
Buick 159 37 8N 91 2W
Bŭicoi 70 45 3N 25 52E
Buie L. 34 56 20N 5 55W
Bŭileşti 70 44 01N 23 20E
Builth Wells 31 52 10N 3 26W
Buina Qara 93 36 20N 67 0E
Buinsk 81 55 0N 48 18E
Buíque 170 8 37S 37 9W
Buis-les-Baronnies 45 44 17N 5 16E
Buit, L. 151 50 59N 63 13W
Buitenpost 46 53 15N 6 9E
Buitrago 56 41 0N 3 38W
Bujalance 57 37 54N 4 23W
Buján 56 42 59N 8 36W
Bujaraloz 58 41 29N 0 10W
Buje 63 45 24N 13 39E
Buji 135 9 8S 142 11E
Bujnurd 93 37 35N 57 15E
Bujumbura (Usumbura) 126 3 16S 29 18E
Bük 53 47 22N 16 45E
Buk 54 52 21N 16 17E
Buka I. 135 5 10S 154 35E
Bukachacha 77 52 55N 116 50E
Bukama 127 9 10S 25 50E
Bukandula 126 0 13N 31 50E
Bukavu 126 2 20S 28 52E
Bukene 126 4 15S 32 48E
Bukhara 85 39 48N 64 25E
Bukima 126 1 50S 33 25E
Bukit Mertajam 101 5 22N 100 28E
Bukittinggi 102 0 20S 100 20E
Bukkapatnam 97 14 14N 77 46E
Buklyan 84 55 42N 52 10E
Bukoba 126 1 20S 31 49E
Bukoba □ 126 1 30S 32 0E
Bukowno 54 50 17N 19 35E
Bukrale 123 4 32N 42 0E
Bukuru 121 9 42N 8 48E
Bukuya 126 0 40N 31 52E
Bula 120 12 7N 15 43W
Bülach 51 47 31N 8 32E
Bulahdelah 141 32 23S 152 13E
Bulan 103 12 40N 123 52E
Bulanash 84 57 16N 62 0E
Bulandshahr 94 28 28N 77 58E
Bulanovo 84 52 27N 55 10E
Bulantai 99 36 33N 92 18E
Bûlâq 122 25 10N 30 38E
Bulawayo 127 20 7S 28 32E
Buldana 96 20 30N 76 18E
Buldir I. 147 52 20N 175 55E
Bulford 28 51 11N 1 45W
Bulgan 105 48 45N 103 34E
Bulgaria ■ 67 42 35N 25 30E
Bulgroo 138 25 47S 143 58E
Bulgunnia 139 30 10S 134 53E
Bulhar 91 10 25N 44 30E
Buli, Teluk 103 1 5N 128 25E
Buliluyan, C. 102 8 20N 117 15E
Bulki 123 6 11N 36 31E
Bulkington 163 52 29N 1 25W
Bulkley, R. 152 55 15N 127 40W
Bulkur 77 71 50N 126 30E
Bull Shoals L. 159 36 40N 93 5W
Bullabulling 137 31 1S 120 32E
Bullange 47 50 24N 6 15E
Bullaque, R. 57 39 20N 4 13W
Bullara 136 22 40S 114 3E
Bullaring 137 32 30S 117 45E
Bullas 59 38 2N 1 40W
Bulle 50 46 37N 7 3E
Buller Gorge 143 41 40S 172 10E
Buller, Mt. 141 37 10S 146 28E
Buller, R. 143 41 44S 171 36E
Bullfinch 137 30 58S 119 3E
Bulli 141 34 15S 150 57E
Bullock Cr. 138 17 51S 143 45E
Bulloo Downs, Queens., Austral. 139 28 31S 142 57E
Bulloo Downs, W.A., Austral. 137 24 0S 119 32E
Bulloo L. 139 28 43S 142 25E
Bulloo, R. 139 28 43S 142 30E
Bulls 142 40 10S 175 24E
Bully-les-Mines 43 50 27N 2 44E
Bulnes 172 36 42S 72 19W
Bulo Burti 91 3 50N 45 33E
Bulolo 135 7 10S 146 40E
Bulpunga 140 33 47S 141 45E
Bulqiza 68 40 30N 20 21E
Bulsar 96 20 40N 72 58E
Bultfontein 128 28 18S 26 10E
Bulu Karakelong 103 4 35N 126 50E
Buluan 103 9 0N 125 30E
Bŭlŭciţa 70 44 23N 23 8E
Bulukumba 103 5 33S 120 11E
Bulun 77 70 37N 127 30E
Bulwell 33 53 1N 1 12W
Bumba 124 2 13N 22 30E
Bumbiri I. 126 1 40S 31 55E
Bumble Bee 161 34 8N 112 18W
Bumbum 121 14 10N 8 10E
Bumhkang 98 26 51N 97 40E
Bumhpa Bum 98 26 51N 97 14E
Bumi, R. 127 17 30S 28 30E
Bumtang, R. 98 26 56N 90 53E
Buna, Kenya 124 2 58N 39 30E
Buna, P.N.G. 135 8 42S 148 27E
Bunaiyin 92 23 10N 51 8E
Bunaw 39 51 47N 9 50W
Bunazi 126 1 3S 31 23E
Bunbeg 38 55 4N 8 18W
Bunbury 132 33 20S 115 35E
Bunclody 39 52 40N 6 40W
Buncrana 38 55 8N 7 28W
Bundaberg 139 24 54S 152 22E
Bünde 48 52 11N 8 33E
Bundey, R. 138 21 46S 135 37E
Bundi 94 25 30N 75 35E
Bundooma 138 24 54S 134 16E
Bundoran 38 54 24N 8 17W
Bundukia 123 5 14N 30 55E
Bundure 141 35 10S 146 1E
Bŭneasa 70 45 56N 27 55E
Bunessan 34 56 18N 6 15W
Bung Kan 100 18 23N 103 37E
Bungay 29 52 27N 1 26E
Bungendore 141 35 14S 149 30E
Bungil Cr. 138 27 5S 149 5E
Bungō-Suidō 110 33 0N 132 15E
Bungoma 126 0 34N 34 34E
Bungotakada 110 33 35N 131 25E
Bungu 126 7 35S 39 0E
Bunguran N. Is. 102 4 45N 108 0E
Bunia 126 1 35N 30 20E
Bunji 95 35 45N 74 40E
Bunju 102 3 35N 117 50E
Bunker Hill 163 39 15N 117 8W
Bunkerville 161 36 47N 114 6W
Bunkie 159 31 1N 92 12W
Bunmahon 39 52 8N 7 22W
Bunnanaddan 38 54 3N 8 35W
Bunnell 157 29 28N 81 12W
Bunnik 46 52 4N 5 12E
Bunnyconnellan 38 54 7N 9 1W
Bunnythorpe 142 40 16S 175 39E
Buñol 59 39 25N 0 47W
Bunsbeek 47 50 50N 4 56E
Bunschoten 46 52 14N 5 22E
Buntingford 29 51 57N 0 1W
Buntok 102 1 40S 114 58E
Bununu 121 9 51N 9 32E
Bununu Doss 121 10 6N 9 25E
Bunwell 29 52 30N 1 9E
Bunyoro □ = Western □ 126 1 45N 31 30E
Bunza 121 12 8N 4 0E
Búoareyri 74 65 2N 14 13W
Buol 103 1 15N 121 32E
Buon Brieng 100 13 9N 108 12E
Buong Long 100 13 44N 106 59E
Buorkhaya, Mys 77 71 50N 133 10E
Buqbuq 122 31 29N 25 29E
Buqei'a 90 32 58N 35 20E
Bur Acaba 91 3 12N 44 20E
Bûr Fuad 122 31 15N 32 20E
Bûr Safâga 122 26 43N 33 57E
Bûr Sa'îd 122 31 16N 32 18E
Bûr Sûdân 122 19 32N 37 9E
Bûr Taufiq 122 29 54N 32 32E
Bura 126 1 4S 39 58E

Buraidah **Caithness, Ord of, C**

Buraidah 92 26 20N 44 8 E
Buraimī, Al Wāhāt al 93 24 15N 55 43 E
Burak Sulayman 90 31 42N 35 7 E
Burama 91 9 55N 43 7 E
Burao 91 9 32N 45 32 E
Buras 159 29 20N 89 33W
Burayevo 84 55 50N 55 24 E
Burbage, Derby, U.K. 32 53 15N 1 55W
Burbage, Leics., U.K. 28 52 31N 1 20W
Burbage, Wilts., U.K. 28 51 21N 1 40W
Burbank 163 34 9N 118 23W
Burcher 141 33 30 S 147 16 E
Burdekin, R. 138 19 38 S 147 25 E
Burdett 152 49 50N 111 32W
Burdur 92 37 45N 30 22 E
Burdwan 95 23 16N 87 54 E
Bure 123 10 40N 37 4 E
Bure, R. 29 52 38N 1 45 E
Bureba, La 58 42 36N 3 24W
Buren 46 51 55N 5 20 E
Burfell 74 64 5N 20 56W
Burford 28 51 48N 1 38W
Burg, Magdeburg, Ger. 48 52 16N 11 50 E
Burg, Schleswig-Holstein, Ger. 48 54 25N 11 10 E
Burg el Arab 122 30 54N 29 32 E
Burg et Tuyur 122 20 55N 27 56 E
Burgan 92 29 0N 47 57 E
Burgas 67 42 33N 27 29 E
Burgaski Zaliv 67 42 30N 27 39 E
Burgdorf, Ger. 48 52 27N 10 0 E
Burgdorf, Switz. 50 47 3N 7 37 E
Burgenland □ 53 47 20N 16 20 E
Burgeo 151 47 37N 57 38W
Burgersdorp 128 31 0 S 26 20 E
Burges, Mt. 137 30 50 S 121 5 E
Burgess 162 37 53N 76 21W
Burgess Hill 29 50 57N 0 7W
Burgh-le-Marsh 33 53 10N 0 15 E
Burghclere 28 51 19N 1 20W
Burghead 37 57 42N 3 30W
Burghead B. 37 57 40N 3 33W
Bùrgio 64 37 35N 13 18 E
Bürglen 51 46 53N 8 40 E
Burglengenfeld 49 49 11N 12 2 E
Burgo de Osma 58 41 35N 3 4W
Burgohondo 56 40 26N 4 47W
Burgos 58 42 21N 3 41W
Burgos □ 58 42 21N 3 42W
Burgstädt 48 50 55N 12 49 E
Burgsteinfurt 48 52 9N 7 23 E
Burgsvik 73 57 3N 18 19 E
Burguillos del Cerro 57 38 23N 6 35W
Burgundy = Bourgogne 43 47 0N 4 30 E
Burhanpur 96 21 18N 76 20 E
Burhou Rocks 42 49 45N 2 15W
Buri Pen. 123 15 25N 39 55 E
Burias, I. 103 12 55N 123 5 E
Buribay 84 51 57N 58 10 E
Burica, Punta 166 8 3N 82 51W
Burigi, L. 126 2 2 S 31 22 E
Burin, Can. 151 47 1N 55 14W
Burin, Jordan 90 32 11N 35 15 E
Buriram 100 15 0N 103 0 E
Buriti Alegre 171 18 9 S 49 3W
Buriti Bravo 170 5 50 S 43 50W
Buriti dos Lopes 170 3 10 S 41 52W
Burji 123 5 29N 37 51 E
Burkburnett 159 34 7N 98 35W
Burke 160 47 31N 115 56W
Burke, R. 138 23 12 S 139 33 E
Burketown 138 17 45 S 139 33 E
Burk's Falls 150 45 37N 79 24W
Burley, Hants, U.K. 28 50 49N 1 41W
Burley, N. Yorks., U.K. 33 53 55N 1 46W
Burley, U.S.A. 160 42 37N 113 55W
Burlingame 163 37 35N 122 21W
Burlington, Colo., U.S.A. 158 39 21N 102 18W
Burlington, Iowa, U.S.A. 158 40 50N 91 5W
Burlington, Kans., U.S.A. 158 38 15N 95 47W
Burlington, N.C., U.S.A. 157 36 7N 79 27W
Burlington, N.J., U.S.A. 162 40 5N 74 50W
Burlington, Wash., U.S.A. 160 48 29N 122 19W
Burlington, Wis., U.S.A. 156 42 41N 88 18W
Burlyu-Tyube 76 46 30N 79 10 E
Burma ■ 98 21 0N 96 30 E
Burnabbie 137 32 7 S 126 21 E
Burnaby I. 152 52 25N 131 19W
Burnamwood 141 31 7 S 144 53 E
Burnet 159 30 45N 98 11W
Burnett, R. 133 24 45 S 152 23 E
Burney 160 40 56N 121 41W
Burnfoot 38 55 4N 7 15W
Burngup 137 33 2 S 118 42 E
Burnham, Essex, U.K. 29 51 37N 0 50 E
Burnham, Somerset, U.K. 28 51 14N 3 0W
Burnham Market 29 52 57N 0 43 E
Burnie 138 41 4 S 145 56 E
Burnley 32 53 47N 2 15W
Burnmouth 35 55 50N 2 4W
Burnoye 85 42 36N 70 47 E
Burns, Oreg., U.S.A. 160 43 40N 119 4W
Burns, Wyo., U.S.A. 158 41 13N 104 18W
Burns Lake 152 54 20N 125 45W
Burnside, L. 137 25 25 S 123 0 E
Burnt Paw 147 67 2N 142 43W
Burntisland 35 56 4N 3 14W
Burntwood L. 153 55 22N 100 26W
Burntwood, R. 153 56 8N 96 34W
Burqa 90 32 18N 35 11 E
Burra 140 33 40 S 138 55 E
Burragorang, L. 141 33 52 S 150 37 E
Burramurra 138 20 25N 137 15 E
Burravoe 36 60 30N 1 3W
Burray I. 37 58 50N 2 54W
Burreli 68 41 36N 20 1 E
Burrelton 35 56 30N 3 16W
Burren 39 53 9N 9 5W
Burren Junction 139 30 7 S 148 59 E
Burrendong Dam 139 32 39 S 149 6 E
Burrendong Res. 141 32 45 S 149 10 E
Burriana 58 39 50N 0 4W
Burrinjuck Res. 141 35 0 S 148 36 E
Burro, Serranías del 164 29 0N 102 0W
Burrow Hd. 34 54 40N 4 23W
Burrundie 136 13 32 S 131 42 E
Burruyacú 172 26 30 S 64 40W
Burry Port 31 51 41N 4 17W
Bursa 92 40 15N 29 5 E
Burseryd 73 57 12N 13 17 E
Burstall 153 50 39N 109 54W
Burstwick 33 53 43N 0 6W
Burton 32 54 10N 2 43W
Burton Agnes 33 54 4N 0 18W
Burton Bradstock 28 50 41N 2 43W
Burton Fleming 33 54 8N 0 20W
Burton L. 150 54 45N 78 20W
Burton Latimer 29 52 23N 0 41W
Burton upon Stather 33 53 39N 0 41W
Burton-upon-Trent 28 52 48N 1 39W
Burtonport 38 54 59N 8 26W
Burtundy 140 33 45 S 142 15 E
Burtville 137 28 42 S 122 33 E
Buru, I. 103 3 30 S 126 30 E
Burufu 120 10 25N 2 50W
Burujird 92 33 58N 48 41 E
Burullus, Bahra el 122 31 25N 31 0 E
Burunday 85 43 20N 76 51 E
Burundi ■ 126 3 15 S 30 0 E
Burung 102 0 21N 108 25 E
Bururi 126 3 57 S 29 37 E
Burutu 121 5 20N 5 29 E
Burwash 29 50 59N 0 24 E
Burwash Landing 147 61 21N 139 0W
Burwell, U.K. 29 52 17N 0 20 E
Burwell, U.S.A. 158 41 49N 99 8W
Bury 32 53 36N 2 19W
Bury St. Edmunds 29 52 15N 0 42 E
Buryat A.S.S.R. □ 77 53 0N 110 0 E
Burzenin 54 51 28N 18 47 E
Busalla 62 44 34N 8 58 E
Busango Swamp 127 14 15 S 25 45 E
Busayyah 92 30 0N 46 10 E
Busby 152 53 55N 114 0W
Bushati 68 41 58N 19 34 E
Bushell 153 59 31N 108 45W
Bushenyi 126 0 35 S 30 10 E
Bushey 29 51 38N 0 20W
Bushman Land 128 29 30 S 19 30 E
Bushmills 38 55 14N 6 32W
Bushnell, Ill., U.S.A. 158 40 32N 90 30W
Bushnell, Nebr., U.S.A. 158 41 18N 103 50W
Busia □ 126 0 25N 34 6 E
Busie 120 10 29N 2 22W
Businga 124 3 16N 20 59 E
Buskerud fylke □ 75 60 13N 9 0 E
Busko Zdrój 54 50 28N 20 42 E
Busovača 66 44 6N 17 53 E
Busra 92 32 30N 36 25 E
Bussa 121 10 11N 4 32 E
Bussang 43 47 50N 6 50 E
Busselton 137 33 42 S 115 15 E
Bussigny 50 46 33N 6 33 E
Bussum 46 52 16N 5 10 E
Bustard Hd. 133 24 0 S 151 48 E
Busto Arsizio 62 45 40N 8 50 E
Busto, C. 56 43 34N 6 28W
Busu-Djanoa 124 1 50N 21 5 E
Busuangal, I. 103 12 10N 120 0 E
Büsum 48 54 7N 8 50 E
Buta 126 2 50N 24 53 E
Butare 126 2 31 S 29 52 E
Bute 140 33 51 S 138 2 E
Bute (□) 26 55 40N 5 10W
Bute, I. 34 55 48N 5 2W
Bute Inlet 152 50 40N 124 53W
Bute, Kyles of 34 55 55N 5 10W
Bute, Sd. of 34 55 43N 5 8W
Butemba 126 1 9N 31 37 E
Butembo 126 0 9N 29 18 E
Butera 65 37 10N 14 10 E
Bütgenbach 47 50 26N 6 12 E
Buthidaung 98 20 52N 92 32 E
Butiaba 126 1 50N 31 20 E
Butler 158 38 17N 94 18W
Bütschwil 51 47 23N 9 5 E
Butte, Mont., U.S.A. 160 46 0N 112 31W
Butte, Nebr., U.S.A. 158 42 56N 98 54W
Butterfield, Mt. 137 24 45 S 128 7 E
Buttermere 32 54 32N 3 17W
Butterworth 101 5 24N 100 23 E
Buttevant 39 52 14N 8 40 E
Buttfield, Mt. 137 24 45 S 128 9 E
Button B. 153 58 45N 94 23W
Buttonwillow 163 35 24N 119 28W
Butty Hd. 137 33 54 S 121 39 E
Butuan 103 8 57N 125 33 E
Butuku-Luba 121 3 29N 8 33 E
Butung, I. 103 5 0 S 122 45 E
Buturlinovka 81 50 50N 40 35 E
Butzbach 48 50 24N 8 40 E
Buxar 95 25 34N 83 58 E
Buxton, S. Afr. 128 27 38 S 24 42 E
Buxton, U.K. 32 53 16N 1 54W
Buxy 43 46 44N 4 40 E
Buyaga 77 59 50N 127 0 E
Buynaksk 83 42 36N 47 42 E
Buyr Nuur 105 47 50N 117 42 E
Büyük çekmece 67 41 2N 28 35 E
Büyük Kemikli Burun 68 40 20N 26 15 E
Büyük Menderes, R. 79 37 45N 27 40 E
Buzançais 42 46 54N 1 25 E
Buzau, Pasul 70 45 35N 26 12 E
Buzaymah 117 24 35N 22 0 E
Buzen 110 33 35N 131 5 E
Buzet 63 45 24N 13 58 E
Buzi, R. 127 19 52 S 34 30 E
Buziaş 66 45 38N 21 36 E
Buzuluk 84 52 48N 52 12 E
Buzuluk, R. 81 50 50N 52 12 E
Buzŭu 70 45 10N 26 50 E
Buzŭu □ 70 45 20N 26 30 E
Buzŭu, R. 70 45 10N 27 20 E
Buzzards Bay 162 41 45N 70 38W
Bwagaoia 135 10 40 S 152 52 E
Bwana Mkubwe 127 13 8 S 28 38 E
Byala, Ruse, Bulg. 67 43 28N 25 44 E
Byala, Varna, Bulg. 67 42 53N 27 55 E
Byala Slatina 67 43 26N 23 55 E
Byandovan, Mys 83 39 45N 49 28 E
Bychawa 54 51 1N 22 36 E
Byczyha 54 51 7N 18 12 E
Bydgoszcz 54 53 10N 18 0 E
Bydgoszcz □ 54 53 16N 17 33 E
Byelorussian S.S.R. □ 80 53 30N 27 0 E
Byers 158 39 46N 104 13W
Byfield 28 52 10N 1 15W
Bygland 71 58 50N 7 48 E
Byglandsfjord 71 58 40N 7 50 E
Byglandsfjorden 71 58 44N 7 50 E
Byhalia 159 34 53N 89 41W
Bykhov 80 53 31N 30 14 E
Bykle 71 59 20N 7 22 E
Bykovo 83 49 50N 45 25 E
Bylas 161 33 11N 110 9W
Bylchau 31 53 9N 3 32W
Bylderup 73 54 57N 9 6 E
Bylot I. 149 73 13N 78 34W
Byrd Land = Marie Byrd Land 13 79 30 S 125 0W
Byrd Sub-Glacial Basin 13 82 0 S 120 0W
Byro 137 26 5 S 116 11 E
Byrock 141 30 40 S 146 27 E
Byron B. 151 54 42N 57 40W
Byron, C. 133 28 38 S 153 40W
Byrranga, Gory 77 75 0N 100 0 E
Byrum 73 57 16N 11 0 E
Byske 74 64 57N 21 11 E
Byske, R. 74 65 20N 20 0 E
Bystrovka 85 42 47N 75 42 E
Bystrzyca Kłodzka 54 50 19N 16 39 E
Byten 80 52 50N 25 27 E
Bytom 54 50 25N 19 0 E
Bytom Ordz. 54 51 44N 15 48 E
Bytów 54 54 10N 17 30 E
Byumba 126 1 35 S 30 4 E
Byvalla 72 61 22N 16 27 E
Bzéma 117 24 50N 22 20 E
Bzenec 53 48 58N 17 18 E

C

Ca Mau = Quan Long 101 9 7N 105 8 E
Ca Mau, Mui = Bai Bung 101 8 35N 104 42 E
Ca Na 101 11 20N 108 54 E
Ca, R. 100 18 45N 105 45 E
Caacupé 172 25 23N 57 5W
Caamano Sd. 152 52 55N 129 25W
Caatingas 170 7 0 S 52 30W
Caazapá 172 26 8 S 56 19W
Caazapá □ 173 26 10 S 56 0W
Caballería, Cabo de 58 40 5N 4 5 E
Cabañaquinta 56 43 10N 5 38W
Cabanatuan 103 15 30N 121 5 E
Cabanes 58 40 9N 0 2 E
Cabano 151 47 40N 68 56 E
Cabazon 163 33 55N 116 47W
Cabbage Tree Hd. 108 27 20 S 153 5 E
Cabedelo 170 7 0 S 34 50W
Cabeza del Buey 57 38 44N 5 13W
Cabildo 172 32 30 S 71 5W
Cabimas 174 10 30N 71 25W
Cabinda 124 5 40 S 12 11 E
Cabinda □ 124 5 0 S 12 30 E
Cabinet Mts. 160 48 0N 115 30W
Cables 137 27 55 S 123 25 E
Cableskill 162 42 39N 74 30W
Cabo Blanco 176 47 56 S 65 47W
Cabo Delgado □ 127 10 35 S 40 35 E
Cabo Frio 173 22 51 S 42 3W
Cabo Pantoja 174 1 0 S 75 10W
Cabonga Reservoir 150 47 20N 76 40W
Cabool 159 37 10N 92 8W
Caboolture 139 27 5 S 152 58 E
Cabora Bassa Dam 127 15 20 S 32 50 E
Caborca (Heroica) 164 30 40N 112 10W
Cabot Strait 151 47 15N 59 40W
Cabra 57 37 30N 4 28W
Cabra del Santo Cristo 59 37 42N 3 16W
Cabrach 37 57 20N 3 0W
Cabras 64 39 57N 8 30 E
Cabrera, I. 59 39 6N 2 59 E
Cabrera, Sierra 56 42 12N 6 40W
Cabri 153 50 35N 108 25W
Cabriel, R. 59 39 20N 1 20W
Cabruta 174 7 50N 66 10W
Caburan 103 6 3N 125 45 E
Cabuyaro 174 4 18N 72 49W
Cacabelos 56 42 36N 6 44W
Čačak 66 43 54N 20 20 E
Cáceres, Brazil 174 16 5 S 57 40W
Cáceres, Colomb. 174 7 35N 75 20W
Cáceres, Spain 57 39 26N 6 23W
Cáceres □ 57 39 45N 6 0W
Cache B. 150 46 26N 80 1W
Cache Bay 150 46 22N 80 0W
Cachepo 57 37 20N 7 49W
Cacheu 120 12 14N 16 8W
Cachi 172 25 5 S 66 10W
Cachimbo, Serra do 175 9 30 S 55 0W
Cáchira 174 7 21N 73 17W
Cachoeira 171 12 30 S 39 0W
Cachoeira Alta 171 18 48 S 50 58W
Cachoeira de Itapemirim 173 20 51 S 41 7W
Cachoeira do Sul 173 30 3 S 52 53W
Cachoeiro do Arari 170 1 1 S 48 58W
Cachopo 57 37 20N 7 49W
Cacolo 124 10 9 S 19 21 E
Caconda 125 13 48 S 15 8 E
Caçu 171 18 37 S 51 4W
Caculé 171 14 30 S 42 13W
Cadamstown 39 53 7N 7 39W
Cadarga 139 26 8 S 150 58 E
Cadaux 137 30 48 S 117 15 E
Čadca 53 49 26N 18 45 E
Caddo 159 34 8N 96 18W
Cadenazzo 51 46 9N 8 57 E
Cader Idris 31 52 43N 3 56W
Cadereyta Jiménez 165 25 40N 100 0W
Cadí, Sierra del 58 42 17N 1 42 E
Cadibarrawirracanna, L. 139 28 52 S 135 27 E
Cadillac, Can. 150 48 14N 78 23W
Cadillac, France 44 44 38N 0 20W
Cadillac, U.S.A. 156 44 16N 85 25W
Cadiz 103 11 30N 123 15 E
Cádiz 57 36 30N 6 20W
Cádiz □ 57 36 36N 5 45W
Cádiz, G. de 57 36 40N 7 0W
Cadomin 152 53 2N 117 20W
Cadotte, R. 152 56 43N 117 10W
Cadours 44 43 44N 1 2 E
Cadoux 137 30 46 S 117 7 E
Caen 42 49 10N 0 22W
Caenby Corner 33 53 23N 0 32W
Caergwrle 29 53 6N 3 3W
Caerhun 31 53 14N 3 50W
Caerleon 31 51 37N 2 57W
Caernarfon 31 53 8N 4 17W
Caernarfon B. 31 53 4N 4 40W
Caernarvon = Caernarfon 31 53 8N 4 17W
Caernarvon (□) 26 53 8N 4 17W
Caerphilly 31 51 34N 3 13W
Caersws 31 52 32N 3 27W
Caerwent 31 51 37N 2 47W
Cæsarea = Qesari 90 32 30N 34 53 E
Caeté 171 20 0 S 43 40W
Caetité 171 13 50 S 42 50W
Cafayate 172 26 2 S 66 0W
Cafu 128 16 30 S 15 8 E
Cagayan de Oro 103 8 30N 124 40 E
Cagayan, R. 103 18 25N 121 42 E
Cagli 63 43 32N 12 38 E
Cágliari 64 39 15N 9 6 E
Cágliari, G. di 64 39 8N 9 10 E
Cagnano Varano 65 41 49N 15 47 E
Cagnes-sur-Mer 45 43 40N 7 9 E
Caguas 147 18 14N 66 4W
Caha Mts. 39 51 45N 9 40W
Caher I. 38 53 44N 10 1W
Caherconlish 39 52 36N 8 30W
Cahermore 39 51 35N 10 2W
Cahir 39 52 23N 7 56W
Cahirciveen 39 51 57N 10 13W
Cahore Pt. 39 52 34N 6 11W
Cahors 44 44 27N 1 27 E
Cahuapanas 174 5 15 S 77 0W
Cai Ban, Dao 100 21 10N 107 27 E
Cai Nuoc 101 8 56N 105 1 E
Caianda 127 11 29 S 23 31 E
Caibarién 166 22 30N 79 30W
Caicara 174 7 38N 66 10W
Caicó 170 6 20 S 37 0W
Caicos Is. 167 21 40N 71 40W
Caicos Passage 167 22 45N 72 45W
Caihaique 176 45 30 S 71 45W
Caird Coast 13 75 0 S 25 0W
Cairn Gorm 37 57 7N 3 40W
Cairn Table 35 55 30N 4 0W
Cairngorm Mts. 37 57 6N 3 42W
Cairnryan 34 54 59N 5 0W
Cairns 138 16 57 S 145 45 E
Cairo, Ga., U.S.A. 157 30 52N 84 12W
Cairo, Illinois, U.S.A. 159 37 0N 89 10W
Cairo, N.Y., U.S.A. 162 42 18N 74 0W
Cairo = El Qâhira 122 30 1N 31 14 E
Cairo Montenotte 62 44 23N 8 16 E
Caister-on-Sea 29 52 38N 1 43 E
Caistor 33 53 29N 0 20W
Caithness (□) 26 58 25N 3 25W
Caithness, Ord of, C. 37 58 35N 3 37W

Caiundo   Canton

Caiundo 125 15 50S 17 52E
Caiza 174 20 2S 65 40W
Cajamarca 174 7 5S 78 28W
Cajapió 170 2 58S 44 48W
Cajarc 44 44 29N 1 50E
Cajàzeiros 170 7 0S 38 30W
Čajetina 66 43 47N 19 42E
Čajniče 66 43 34N 19 5E
Çakirgöl 83 40 33N 39 40E
Cala 57 37 59N 6 21W
Cala Cadolar 59 38 38N 1 35E
Cala, R. 57 37 50N 6 8W
Calabar 121 4 57N 8 20E
Calabozo 174 9 0N 67 20W
Calábria □ 65 39 24N 16 30E
Calaburras, Pta. de 57 36 30N 4 38W
Calaceite 58 41 1N 0 11E
Calafat 70 43 58N 22 59E
Calafate 176 50 25S 72 25W
Calahorra 58 42 18N 1 59W
Calais, France 43 50 57N 1 56E
Calais, U.S.A. 151 45 5N 67 20W
Calais, Pas de 160 50 57N 1 20E
Calalaste, Sierra de 172 25 0S 67 0W
Calama, Brazil 174 8 0S 62 50W
Calama, Chile 172 22 30S 68 55W
Calamar, Bolívar, Colomb. 174 10 15N 74 55W
Calamar, Vaupés, Colomb. 174 1 58N 72 32W
Calamian Group 103 11 50N 119 55E
Calamocha 58 40 50N 1 17W
Calanaque 174 0 5S 64 0W
Calañas 57 37 40N 6 53W
Calanda 58 40 56N 0 15W
Calang 102 4 30N 95 43E
Calangiánus 64 40 56N 9 12E
Calapan 103 13 25N 121 7E
Calasparra 59 38 14N 1 41W
Calatafimi 64 37 56N 12 50E
Calatayud 58 41 20N 1 40W
Calauag 103 13 55N 122 15E
Calavà, C. 65 38 11N 14 55E
Calavite, Cape 103 13 26N 120 10E
Calbe 48 51 57N 11 47E
Calca 174 13 10S 72 0W
Calci 62 43 44N 10 31E
Calcidica = Khalkidhiki □ 170 40 25N 23 40E
Calcutta 95 22 36N 88 24E
Caldaro 63 46 23N 11 15E
Caldas □ 174 5 15N 75 30W
Caldas da Rainha 57 39 24N 9 8W
Caldas de Reyes 56 42 36N 8 39W
Caldas Novas 171 17 45S 48 38W
Caldbeck 32 54 45N 3 3W
Calder Bridge 32 54 27N 3 31W
Calder Hall 32 54 26N 3 31W
Calder, R. 33 53 44N 1 21W
Caldera 172 27 5S 70 55W
Caldew R. 32 54 54N 2 59W
Caldiran 92 39 7N 44 0E
Caldwell, Idaho, U.S.A. 160 43 45N 116 42W
Caldwell, Kans., U.S.A. 159 37 5N 97 37W
Caldwell, Texas, U.S.A. 159 30 30N 96 42W
Caldy I. 31 51 38N 4 42W
Caledon, S. Afr. 128 34 14S 19 26E
Caledon, U.K. 38 54 22N 6 50W
Caledon B. 138 12 45S 137 0E
Caledon, R. 128 30 0S 26 46E
Caledonian Can. 37 56 50N 5 6W
Calella 58 41 37N 2 40E
Calemba 128 16 0S 15 38E
Calera, La 172 32 50S 71 10W
Calexico 161 32 40N 115 33W
Calf of Man 32 54 4N 4 48W
Calgary, Can. 152 51 0N 114 10W
Calgary, U.K. 34 56 34N 6 17W
Calhoun 157 34 30N 84 55W
Cali 174 3 25N 76 35W
Caliach Pt. 34 56 37N 6 20W
Calicoan, I. 103 10 59N 125 50E
Calicut 93 11 15N 75 43E
Calicut, (Kozhikode) 97 11 15N 75 43E
Caliente 161 37 43N 114 34W
California 158 38 37N 92 30W
California □ 160 37 25N 120 0W
California, Baja 164 32 10N 115 12W
California, Baja, T.N. □ 164 30 0N 115 0W
California, Baja, T.S. □ 164 25 50N 111 50W
California City 163 35 7N 117 57W
California, Golfo de 164 27 0N 111 0W
California Hot Springs 163 35 51N 118 41W
California, Lr. = California, Baja 164 25 50N 111 50W
Calilegua 172 23 45S 64 42W
Călimăneşti 70 45 14N 24 20E
Calingasta 172 31 15S 69 30W
Calipatria 161 33 8N 115 30W
Calistoga 160 38 36N 122 32W
Calitri 65 40 54N 15 25E
Calkini 165 20 21N 90 3W
Callabonna, L. 139 29 40S 140 5E
Callac 42 48 25N 3 27W
Callafo 91 6 48N 43 47E
Callan 39 52 33N 7 25W
Callanish 36 58 12N 6 43W
Callantsoog 46 52 50N 4 42E
Callao 174 12 0S 77 0W
Callaway 158 41 20N 99 56W
Calles 165 23 2N 98 42W
Callicoon 162 41 46N 75 3W
Callide 138 24 18S 150 28E
Calling Lake 152 55 15N 113 12W
Callington 30 56 30N 4 19W
Calliope 138 24 0S 151 16E
Callosa de Ensarriá. 59 38 40N 0 8W
Callosa de Segura 59 38 1N 0 53W
Callow 38 53 58N 9 2W
Calne 28 51 26N 2 0W
Calola 128 16 25S 17 48E
Calore, R. 65 41 8N 14 45E
Caloundra 139 26 45S 153 10E
Calpe 59 38 39N 0 3E
Calshot 28 50 49N 1 18W
Calstock, Can. 150 49 47N 84 9W
Calstock, U.K. 30 50 30N 4 13W
Caltabellotta 64 37 36N 13 11E
Caltagirone 65 37 13N 14 30E
Caltanissetta 65 37 30N 14 3E
Caluire-et-Cuire 45 45 49N 4 51E
Calulo 124 10 1S 14 56E
Calumbo 124 9 0S 13 20E
Caluso 62 45 18N 7 52E
Calvados □ 42 49 5N 0 15W
Calvert 159 30 59N 96 50W
Calvert Hills 138 17 15S 137 20E
Calvert I. 152 51 30N 128 0W
Calvert, R. 138 16 17S 137 44E
Calvert Ra. 136 24 0S 122 30E
Calvillo 164 21 51N 102 43W
Calvinia 128 31 28S 19 45E
Calwa 163 36 42N 119 46W
Calzada Almuradiel 59 38 32N 3 28W
Calzada de Calatrava 57 38 42N 3 46W
Cam Lam 101 11 54N 109 10E
Cam Pha 100 21 1N 107 18E
Cam, R. 29 52 21N 0 16E
Cam Ranh 101 11 54N 109 12E
Cam Xuyen 100 18 15N 106 0E
Camabatela 124 8 20S 15 26E
Camacã 171 15 24S 39 30W
Camaçari 171 12 41S 38 18W
Camacho 164 24 25N 102 18W
Camaguán 174 8 6N 67 36W
Camagüey 166 21 20N 78 0W
Camaiore 62 43 57N 10 18E
Camamu 171 13 57S 39 7W
Camaná 174 16 30S 72 50W
Camaquã, R. 173 30 50S 52 50W
Camaret 42 48 16N 4 37W
Camargo 174 20 38S 65 15E
Camargue 45 43 34N 4 34E
Camarillo 163 34 13N 119 2W
Camariñas 56 43 8N 9 12W
Camarón, C. 166 16 0N 85 0W
Camarones, Argent. 176 44 50S 65 40W
Camarones, Chile 174 19 0S 69 58W
Camas 160 45 35N 122 24W
Camas Valley 160 43 0N 123 46W
Cambados 56 42 31N 8 49W
Cambará 173 23 2S 50 5W
Cambay 94 22 23N 72 33E
Cambay, G. of 94 20 45N 72 30E
Camberley 29 51 20N 0 44W
Cambil 59 37 40N 3 33W
Cambo 35 55 9N 1 57W
Cambo-les-Bains 44 43 22N 1 23W
Cambodia ■ 100 12 15N 105 0E
Camborne 30 50 13N 5 18W
Cambrai 43 50 11N 3 14E
Cambria 163 35 44N 121 6W
Cambrian Mts. 31 52 25N 3 52W
Cambridge, Can. 150 43 23N 80 15W
Cambridge, Jamaica 166 18 18N 77 54W
Cambridge, N.Z. 142 37 54S 175 29E
Cambridge, U.K. 29 52 13N 0 8E
Cambridge, Idaho, U.S.A. 160 44 36N 116 52W
Cambridge, Mass., U.S.A. 162 42 20N 71 8W
Cambridge, Md., U.S.A. 162 38 33N 76 2W
Cambridge, Minn., U.S.A. 158 45 34N 93 15W
Cambridge, Nebr., U.S.A. 158 40 20N 100 12W
Cambridge, N.Y., U.S.A. 162 43 2N 73 22W
Cambridge, Ohio, U.S.A. 156 40 1N 81 22W
Cambridge Bay 148 69 10N 105 0W
Cambridge Gulf 136 14 45S 128 0E
Cambridgeshire □ 29 52 12N 0 7E
Cambrils 58 41 8N 1 3E
Cambuci 173 21 35S 41 55W
Camden, Austral. 141 34 1S 150 43E
Camden, U.K. 29 51 33N 0 10W
Camden, Ala., U.S.A. 157 31 59N 87 15W
Camden, Ark., U.S.A. 159 33 30N 92 50W
Camden, Del., U.S.A. 162 39 7N 75 33W
Camden, Me., U.S.A. 151 44 14N 69 6W
Camden, N.J., U.S.A. 162 39 57N 75 1W
Camden, N.Y., U.S.A. 162 43 20N 75 45W
Camden, S.C., U.S.A. 157 34 17N 80 34W
Camden, B. 147 71 0N 145 0W
Camden Sound 136 15 27S 124 25E
Camel R. 30 50 28N 4 49W
Camelford 30 50 37N 4 41W
Camembert 42 48 53N 0 10E
Cámeri 62 45 30N 8 40E
Camerino 63 43 10N 13 4E
Cameron, Ariz., U.S.A. 161 35 55N 111 31W
Cameron, La., U.S.A. 159 29 50N 93 18W
Cameron, Mo., U.S.A. 158 39 42N 94 14W
Cameron, Tex., U.S.A. 159 30 53N 97 0W
Cameron Falls 150 49 8N 88 19W
Cameron Highlands 101 4 27N 101 22E
Cameron Hills 152 59 48N 118 0W
Cameron Mts. 143 46 1S 167 0E
Cameroon ■ 124 3 30N 12 30E
Camerota 65 40 2N 15 21E
Cameroun, Mt. 121 4 45N 8 55E
Cameroun, R. 121 4 0N 9 35E
Camerton 28 51 18N 2 27W
Cametá 170 2 0S 49 30W
Caminha 56 41 50N 8 50W
Camino 163 38 47N 120 40W
Camira Creek 139 29 15S 152 58E
Camiranga 170 1 48S 46 17W
Cammachmore 37 57 2N 2 9W
Camocim 170 2 55S 40 50W
Camogli 62 44 21N 9 9E
Camolin 39 52 37N 6 26W
Camooweal 138 19 56S 138 7E
Camopi, R. 175 3 12N 52 17W
Camp Crook 158 45 36N 103 59W
Camp Hill 162 40 15N 76 56W
Camp Nelson 163 36 8N 118 39W
Camp Wood 159 29 47N 100 0W
Campagna 65 40 40N 15 5E
Campana 172 34 10S 58 55W
Campana, I. 176 48 20S 75 10W
Campanario 57 38 52N 5 36W
Campania □ 65 40 50N 14 45E
Campbell 163 37 17N 121 57W
Campbell, C. 143 41 47S 174 18E
Campbell I. 142 52 30S 169 0E
Campbell L. 153 63 14N 106 55W
Campbell River 152 50 5N 125 20W
Campbell Town 138 41 52S 147 30E
Campbellpur 94 33 46N 72 20E
Campbellsville 156 37 23N 85 12W
Campbellton, Alta., Can. 152 53 32N 113 15W
Campbellton, N.B., Can. 151 47 57N 66 43W
Campbelltown, Austral. 141 34 4S 150 49E
Campbelltown, U.K. 37 57 34N 4 2W
Campbeltown 34 55 25N 5 36W
Campeche 165 19 50N 90 32W
Campeche □ 165 19 50N 90 32W
Campeche, Golfo de 165 19 30N 93 0W
Camperdown 140 38 14S 143 9E
Camperville 153 51 59N 100 9W
Campi Salentina 65 40 22N 18 2E
Campidano 64 39 30N 8 40E
Campillo de Altobuey 58 39 36N 1 49W
Campillo de Llerena 57 38 30N 5 50W
Campillos 57 37 4N 4 51W
Campina Grande 170 7 20S 35 47W
Campiña, La 57 37 45N 4 45W
Campina Verde 171 19 31S 49 28W
Campinas 173 22 50S 47 0W
Campine 47 51 8N 5 20E
Campinho 170 14 30S 39 10W
Campli 63 42 44N 13 40E
Campo 124 2 15N 9 58E
Campo Beló 171 21 0S 45 30W
Campo de Criptana 59 39 25N 3 7W
Campo de Gibraltar 57 36 15N 5 25W
Campo Flórido 171 19 47S 48 35W
Campo Formoso 170 10 30S 40 20W
Campo Grande 175 20 25S 54 40W
Campo Maior, Brazil 170 4 50S 42 12W
Campo Maior, Port. 57 38 59N 7 7W
Campo Mourão 171 24 3S 52 22W
Campo Tencia 51 46 26N 8 43E
Campo Túres 63 46 53N 11 55E
Campoalegre 174 2 41N 75 20W
Campobasso 65 41 34N 14 40E
Campobello di Licata 64 37 16N 13 55E
Campobello di Mazara 64 37 38N 12 45E
Campofelice 64 37 54N 13 53E
Camporeale 64 37 53N 13 3E
Campos 173 21 50S 41 20W
Campos Altos 171 19 41S 46 10W
Campos Belos 171 13 10S 46 45W
Campos del Puerto 59 39 26N 3 1E
Campos Novos 173 27 21S 51 20W
Campos Sales 170 7 4S 40 23W
Camprodón 58 42 19N 2 23E
Campsie Fells 23 56 2N 4 20W
Camptown 162 41 44N 76 14W
Campuya, R. 174 1 10S 74 0W
Camrose, Can. 152 53 0N 112 50W
Camrose, U.K. 31 51 50N 5 2W
Camsall L. 153 72 32N 106 47W
Camsell Portage 153 59 37N 109 15W
Camurra 139 29 21S 149 52E
Can Gio 101 10 25N 106 58E
Can Tho 101 10 2N 105 46E
Canada ■ 148 60 0N 100 0W
Cañada de Gómez 73 32 55S 61 30W
Canadian 159 35 56N 100 25W
Canadian, R. 159 36 0N 98 45W
Canairiktok, R. 151 54 30N 62 30W
Canajoharie 162 42 54N 74 35W
Çanakkale 68 40 8N 26 30E
Çanakkale Boğazi 68 40 0N 26 0E
Canal de l'Est 43 48 45N 5 35E
Canal Flats 152 50 10N 115 48W
Canal latéral à la Garonne 44 44 25N 0 15E
Canalejas 172 35 15S 66 34W
Canals 172 33 35S 62 40W
Canáls 59 38 58N 0 35W
Canandaigua 156 42 55N 77 18W
Cananea 164 31 0N 110 20W
Canarias, Islas 116 29 30N 17 0W
Canarreos, Arch. de los 166 21 35N 81 40W
Canary Is. = Canarias, Islas 116 29 30N 17 0W
Canastra, Serra da 171 20 0S 46 20W
Canatlán 164 24 31N 104 47W
Canaveral, C. 157 28 28N 80 31W
Cañaveras 58 40 27N 2 14W
Canavieiras 171 15 39S 39 0W
Canbelego 141 31 32S 146 18E
Canberra 141 35 15S 149 8E
Canby, Calif., U.S.A. 160 41 26N 120 58W
Canby, Minn., U.S.A. 158 44 44N 96 15W
Canby, Oregon, U.S.A. 160 45 24N 122 45W
Cancale 42 48 40N 1 50W
Candala 91 11 30N 49 58E
Candas 56 43 35N 5 45W
Candé 42 47 34N 1 0W
Candea = Iráklion 69 35 20N 25 12E
Candela 65 41 8N 15 31E
Candelaria 173 27 29S 55 44W
Candelaria, Pta. de la 56 43 45N 8 0W
Candeleda 56 40 10N 5 14W
Candelo 141 36 47S 149 43E
Candia = Iráklion 69 35 20N 25 12E
Cândido de Abreu 171 24 35S 51 20W
Cândido Mendes 170 1 27S 45 43W
Candle L. 153 53 50N 105 18W
Cando 158 48 30N 99 14W
Canea = Khaniá 69 35 30N 24 4E
Canela 170 10 15S 48 25W
Canelli 62 44 44N 8 18E
Canelones 172 34 32S 56 10W
Canet-Plage 44 42 41N 3 2E
Cañete, Chile 172 37 50S 73 30W
Cañete, Cuba 167 20 36N 74 43W
Cañete, Peru 174 13 0S 76 30W
Cañete, Spain 58 40 3N 1 54W
Cañete de las Torres 57 37 53N 4 19W
Canfranc 58 42 42N 0 31W
Cangamba 125 13 40S 19 54E
Cangas 56 42 16N 8 47W
Cangas de Narcea 56 43 10N 6 32W
Cangas de Onís 56 43 21N 5 8W
Canguaretama 170 6 20S 35 5W
Canguçu 173 31 22S 52 43W
Canhotinho 171 8 53S 36 12W
Cani, Is. 119 36 21N 10 5E
Canicado 125 24 2S 33 2E
Canicatti 64 37 21N 13 50E
Canicattini 65 37 1N 15 3E
Canim, L. 152 51 45N 120 50W
Canim Lake 152 51 17N 120 54W
Canindé 170 4 22S 39 19W
Canindé, R. 170 6 15S 42 52W
Canipaan 102 8 33N 117 15E
Canisbay 37 58 38N 3 6W
Canisp Mt. 36 58 8N 5 5W
Cañitas 164 23 36N 102 43W
Cañiza, La 56 42 13N 8 16W
Cañizal 56 41 20N 5 22W
Canjáyar 59 37 1N 2 44W
Cankırı 92 40 40N 33 30E
Cankuzo 126 3 10S 30 31E
Canlaon, Mt. 103 9 27N 118 25E
Canmore 152 51 7N 115 18W
Cann River 141 37 35S 149 7E
Canna I. 36 57 3N 6 33W
Canna, Sd. of 36 57 1N 6 30W
Cannanore 97 11 53N 75 27E
Cannes 45 43 32N 7 0E
Cannich 37 57 20N 4 48W
Canning Basin 136 19 50S 124 0E
Canning Town 95 22 23N 88 40E
Cannington 28 51 8N 3 4W
Cannock 28 52 42N 2 2W
Cannock Chase, hills 23 52 43N 2 0W
Cannon Ball, R. 158 46 20N 101 20W
Cannondale, Mt. 138 25 13S 148 57E
Caño Colorado 174 2 18N 68 22W
Canoe L. 153 55 10N 108 15W
Canol 147 65 15N 126 50W
Canon City 158 39 30N 105 20W
Canonbie 35 55 4N 2 58W
Canopus 140 33 29S 140 42E
Canora 153 51 40N 102 30W
Canosa di Púglia 65 41 13N 16 4E
Canourgue, Le 44 44 26N 3 13E
Canowindra 141 33 35S 148 38E
Canso 151 45 20N 61 0W
Cantabria, Sierra de 58 42 40N 2 30W
Cantabrian Mts. = Cantábrica 56 43 0N 5 10W
Cantábrica, Cordillera 56 43 0N 5 10W
Cantal □ 44 45 4N 2 45E
Cantanhede 56 40 20N 8 36W
Cantaura 174 9 19N 64 21W
Çantavieja 58 40 31N 0 25W
Čantavir 66 45 55N 19 46E
Canterbury, Austral. 138 25 23S 141 53E
Canterbury, U.K. 29 51 17N 1 5E
Canterbury □ 143 43 45S 171 19E
Canterbury Bight 143 44 16S 171 55E
Canterbury Plains 143 43 55S 171 22E
Cantil 163 35 18N 117 58W
Cantillana 57 37 36N 5 50W
Canto do Buriti 170 8 7S 42 58W
Canton, Ga., U.S.A. 157 34 13N 84 29W
Canton, Ill., U.S.A. 158 40 32N 90 0W
Canton, Mass., U.S.A. 162 42 9N 71 9W
Canton, Miss., U.S.A. 159 32 40N 90 1W
Canton, Mo., U.S.A. 158 40 10N 91 33W
Canton, Ohio, U.S.A. 156 40 47N 81 22W
Canton, Okla., U.S.A. 159 36 5N 98 36W

Canton, Pa., U.S.A. 162 41 39N 76 51W
Canton, S.D., U.S.A. 158 43 20N 96 35W
Canton = Kuangchou 109 23 10N 113 10E
*Canton I. 130 2 30S 172 0W
Canton L. 159 36 12N 98 40W
Cantù 62 45 44N 9 8E
Canudos 174 7 13S 58 5W
Canulloit 161 31 58N 106 36W
Canutama 174 6 30S 64 20W
Canvey 29 51 32N 0 35E
Canyon, Can. 147 47 25N 84 36W
Canyon, Texas, U.S.A. 159 35 0N 101 57W
Canyon, Wyo., U.S.A. 160 44 43N 110 36W
Canyonlands Nat. Park 161 38 25N 109 30W
Canyonville 160 42 55N 123 14W
Canzo 62 45 54N 9 18E
Cao Bang 100 22 40N 106 15E
Cao Lanh 101 10 27N 105 38E
Caoles 34 56 32N 6 43W
Caolisport, Loch 34 55 54N 5 40W
Cáorle 63 45 36N 12 51E
Cap-aux-Meules 151 47 23N 61 52W
Cap Chat 151 49 6N 66 40W
Cap-de-la-Madeleine 150 46 22N 72 31W
Cap Haïtien 167 19 40N 72 20W
Cap St.-Jacques = Vung Tau 101 10 21N 107 4E
Capa Stilo 65 38 25N 16 25E
Capáccio 65 40 26N 15 4E
Capaia 124 8 27S 20 13E
Capanaparo, R. 174 7 0N 67 30W
Capanema 170 1 12S 47 11W
Caparo, R. 174 7 30N 70 30W
Capatárida 174 11 11N 70 37W
Capbreton 44 43 39N 1 26W
Capdenac 44 44 34N 2 5E
Cape Barren I. 138 40 25S 148 15E
Cape Breton Highlands Nat. Park 151 46 50N 60 40W
Cape Breton I. 151 46 0N 60 30W
Cape Charles 162 37 15N 75 59W
Cape Coast 121 5 5N 1 15W
Cape Cod B. 162 41 50N 70 18W
Cape Dorset 149 64 14N 76 32W
Cape Dyer 149 66 40N 61 22W
Cape Fear, R. 157 34 30N 78 25W
Cape Girardeau 159 37 20N 89 30W
Cape Jervis 140 35 40S 138 5E
Cape May 162 39 1N 74 53W
Cape May C.H. 162 39 5N 74 50W
Cape May Pt. 162 38 56N 74 56W
Cape Montague 151 46 5N 62 25W
Cape Palmas 120 4 25N 7 49W
Cape Preston 136 20 51S 116 12E
Cape Province □ 128 32 0S 23 0E
Cape, R. 138 20 37S 147 1E
Cape Tormentine 151 46 8N 63 47W
Cape Town (Kaapstad) 128 33 55S 18 22E
Cape Verde Is. 14 17 10N 25 20W
Cape York Peninsula 138 33 34S 115 33E
Capel 29 51 8N 0 18W
Capel Curig 31 53 6N 3 55W
Capela 170 10 30S 37 0W
Capela de Campo 170 4 40S 41 55W
Capelinha 171 17 42S 42 31W
Capella 138 23 2S 148 1E
Capella, G. 138 4 45S 140 50E
Capella, Mt. 135 5 4S 141 8E
Capelle, La 43 49 59N 3 50E
Capendu 44 43 11N 2 31E
Capernaum = Kefar Nahum 90 32 54N 35 32E
Capestang 44 43 20N 3 2E
Capim 170 1 41S 47 47W
Capim, R. 170 3 0S 48 0W
Capinópolis 171 18 41S 49 35W
Capitan 161 33 40N 105 41W
Capitola 163 36 59N 121 57W
Capivara, Serra da 171 14 35S 45 0W
Capizzi 65 37 50N 14 26E
Čapljina 66 43 35N 17 43E
Capoche, R. 127 15 0S 32 45E
Cappamore 39 52 38N 8 20W
Cappoquin 39 52 9N 7 46W
Capraia, I. 62 43 2N 9 50E
Caprarola 63 42 21N 12 11E
Capreol 150 46 43N 80 56W
Caprera, I. 64 41 12N 9 28E
Capri, I. 65 40 34N 14 15E
Capricorn, C. 133 23 30S 151 13E
Capricorn Group 138 23 30S 151 55E
Capricorn Ra. 136 23 20S 117 0E
Caprino Veronese 62 45 37N 10 47E
Caprivi Strip 128 18 0S 23 0E
Captainganj 95 26 55N 83 45E
Captain's Flat 141 35 35S 149 27E
Captieux 44 44 18N 0 16W
Cápua 65 41 7N 14 15E
Capulin 159 36 48N 103 59W
Caquetá □ 174 1 0N 74 0W
Caquetá, R. 174 1 0N 76 20W
Cáqueza 174 4 25N 73 57W
Carabobo 174 10 10N 68 5W
Caracal 70 44 8N 24 22E
Caracaraí 174 1 50N 61 8W
Caracas 174 10 30N 66 55W
Caracol, Piauí, Brazil 170 9 15S 43 45W
Caracol, Rondonia, Brazil 174 9 15S 64 20W
Caradoc 140 30 35S 143 5E
Caragabal 141 33 49S 147 45E
Caragh L. 39 52 3N 9 50W
Caráglio 62 44 25N 7 25E
*Renamed Abariringa

Caraí 171 17 12S 41 42W
Carajás, Serra dos 170 6 0S 51 30W
Caramanta 174 5 33N 75 38W
Carangola 173 20 50S 42 5W
Carani 137 30 57S 116 28E
Caransebeş 70 45 28N 22 18E
Carapelle, R. 65 41 20N 15 35E
Caraş Severin □ 66 45 10N 22 10E
Caraşova 66 45 11N 21 51E
Caratasca, Laguna 166 15 30N 83 40W
Caratec 42 48 40N 3 55W
Caratinga 171 19 50S 42 10W
Caratunk 151 45 13N 69 55W
Caraúbas 170 7 43S 36 31W
Caravaca 59 38 8N 1 52W
Caravággio 62 45 30N 9 39E
Caravelas 171 17 45S 39 15W
Caraveli 174 15 45S 73 25W
Caràzinho 173 28 0S 53 0W
Carballino 56 42 26N 8 5W
Carballo 56 43 13N 8 41W
Carberry 153 49 50N 99 25W
Carbia 56 42 48N 8 14W
Carbó 164 29 42N 110 58W
Carbon 152 51 30N 113 9W
Carbonara, C. 64 39 8N 9 30E
Carbondale, Colo, U.S.A. 160 39 30N 107 10W
Carbondale, Ill., U.S.A. 159 37 45N 89 10W
Carbondale, Pa., U.S.A. 162 41 37N 75 30W
Carbonear 151 47 42N 53 13W
Carboneras 59 37 0N 1 53W
Carboneras de Guadazaón 58 39 54N 1 50W
Carbonia 64 39 10N 8 30E
Carbost 36 57 19N 6 21W
Carbury 38 53 22N 6 58W
Carcabuey 57 37 27N 4 17W
Carcagente 59 39 8N 0 28W
Carcajou 152 57 47N 117 6W
Carcasse, C. 167 18 30N 74 28W
Carcassonne 44 43 13N 2 20E
Carche 59 38 26N 1 9W
Carcoar 141 33 36S 149 8E
Carcross 147 60 13N 134 45W
Cardabia 136 23 2S 113 55E
Cardamom Hills 97 9 30N 77 15E
Cárdenas, Cuba 166 23 0N 81 30W
Cárdenas, San Luis Potosí, Mexico 166 22 0N 99 41W
Cárdenas, Tabasco, Mexico 165 17 59N 93 21W
Cardenete 58 39 46N 1 41W
Cardiff 31 51 28N 3 11W
Cardiff-by-the-Sea 163 33 1N 117 17W
Cardigan 31 52 6N 4 41W
Cardigan (□) 26 52 6N 4 41W
Cardigan B. 31 52 30N 4 30W
Cardington 29 52 7N 0 23W
Cardón 174 11 37N 70 14W
Cardona, Spain 58 41 56N 1 40E
Cardona, Uruguay 172 33 53S 57 18W
Cardoner, R. 58 42 0N 1 33E
Cardross 153 49 50N 105 40W
Cardston 152 49 15N 113 20W
Cardwell 138 18 14S 146 2E
Careen L. 153 57 0N 108 11W
Carei 70 47 40N 22 29E
Carentan 42 49 19N 1 15W
Carey, Idaho, U.S.A. 160 43 19N 113 58W
Carey, Ohio, U.S.A. 156 40 58N 83 22W
Carey, L. 137 29 0S 122 15E
Carey L. 153 62 12N 102 55W
Careysburg 120 6 34N 10 30W
Cargados Garajos, Is. 11 17 0S 59 0E
Cargelligo, L. 139 33 17S 146 24E
Cargèse 45 42 7N 8 35E
Carhaix-Plouguer 42 48 18N 3 36W
Carhué 172 37 10S 62 50W
Cariacica 171 20 16S 40 25W
Cariaco 174 10 29N 63 33W
Caribaná, Pta. 174 8 37N 76 52W
Caribbean Sea 167 15 0N 75 0W
Cariboo Mts. 152 53 0N 121 0W
Caribou, Can. 153 53 15N 121 55W
Caribou, U.S.A. 151 46 55N 68 0W
Caribou I. 150 47 22N 85 49W
Caribou Is. 152 61 55N 113 15W
Caribou L., Man., Can. 153 59 21N 96 10W
Caribou L., Ont., Can. 150 50 25N 89 5W
Caribou Mts. 152 59 12N 115 40W
Caribou, R., Man., Can. 153 59 20N 94 44W
Caribou, R., N.W.T., Can. 152 61 27N 125 45W
Carichic 164 27 56N 107 3W
Carignan 43 49 38N 5 10E
Carignano 62 44 55N 7 40E
Carillo 164 26 50N 103 55W
Carinda 141 30 28S 147 41E
Cariñena 58 41 20N 1 13W
Carinhanha 171 14 15S 44 0W
Carinhanha, R. 171 14 20S 43 47W
Carini 64 38 9N 13 10E
Carinish 36 57 31N 7 20W
Carinola 64 41 11N 13 58E
Carinthia □ = Kärnten 52 46 52N 13 30E
Caripito 174 10 8N 63 6W
Caririacu 171 7 2S 39 17W
Carisbrooke 28 50 42N 1 19W
Caritianas 174 9 20S 63 0W
Cark 32 54 11N 2 59W
Carlentini 65 37 15N 15 2E
Carleton Place 150 45 8N 76 9W

Carleton Rode 29 52 30N 1 6E
Carletonville 128 26 23S 27 22E
Carlin 160 40 50N 116 5W
Carlingford 38 54 3N 6 10W
Carlingford, L. 38 54 0N 6 5W
Carlinville 158 39 20N 89 55W
Carlisle, U.K. 32 54 54N 2 55W
Carlisle, U.S.A. 162 40 12N 77 10W
Carlitte, Pic 44 42 35N 1 43E
Carloforte 64 39 10N 8 18E
Carlops 35 55 47N 3 20W
Carlos Casares 172 35 53S 61 20W
Carlos Chagas 171 17 43S 40 45W
Carlos Tejedor 172 35 25S 62 25W
Carlota, La 172 33 30S 63 20W
Carlow 39 52 50N 6 58W
Carlow □ 39 52 43N 6 50W
Carloway 36 58 17N 6 48W
Carlsbad, Calif., U.S.A. 163 33 11N 117 25W
Carlsbad, N. Mex., U.S.A. 159 32 20N 104 7W
Carlton 33 52 58N 1 6W
Carlton Colville 29 52 27N 1 41E
Carlton Miniott 33 54 13N 1 22W
Carluke 35 55 44N 3 50W
Carlyle, Can. 153 49 40N 102 20W
Carlyle, U.S.A. 158 38 38N 89 23W
Carmacks 147 62 5N 136 16W
Carmagnola 62 44 50N 7 42E
Carman 153 49 30N 98 0W
Carmangay 152 50 10N 113 10W
Carmanville 151 49 23N 54 19W
Carmarthen 31 51 52N 4 20W
Carmarthen (□) 26 53 40N 4 18W
Carmarthen B. 31 51 40N 4 30W
Carmaux 44 44 3N 2 10E
Carmel, Calif., U.S.A. 163 36 38N 121 55W
Carmel, N.Y., U.S.A. 162 41 25N 73 38W
Carmel Hd. 31 53 24N 4 34W
Carmel Mt. 90 32 45N 35 3E
Carmel Valley 163 36 29N 121 43W
Carmelo 172 34 0S 58 10W
Carmen, Colomb. 174 9 43N 75 8W
Carmen, Parag. 173 27 13S 56 12W
Carmen de Patagones 176 40 50S 63 0W
Carmen, I. 164 26 0N 111 20W
Carmen, R. 164 30 42N 106 29W
Cármenes 56 42 58N 5 34W
Carmensa 172 35 15S 67 40W
Carmi 156 38 6N 88 10W
Carmichael 163 38 38N 121 19W
Carmila 138 21 55S 149 24E
Carmo do Paranaiba 171 18 59S 46 21W
Carmona 57 37 28N 5 42W
Carmyllie 37 56 36N 2 41W
Carn Ban 37 57 6N 4 15W
Carn Eige 36 57 17N 5 9W
Carn Glas Chorie 37 57 20N 3 50W
Carn Mor 37 57 14N 3 13W
Carn na Saobhaidh 37 57 12N 4 20W
Carna 39 53 20N 9 50W
Carnarvon, Queens., Austral. 138 24 48S 147 45E
Carnarvon, W. Austral., Austral. 137 24 51S 113 42E
Carnarvon, S. Afr. 128 30 56S 22 8E
Carnarvon Ra., Queensland, Austral. 138 25 15S 148 30E
Carnarvon Ra., W.A., Austral. 137 25 0S 120 45E
Carnaxide 57 38 43N 9 14W
Carncastle 38 54 55N 5 52W
Carndonagh 38 55 15N 7 16W
Carnduff 153 49 10N 101 50W
Carnedd Llewelyn, Mt. 31 53 9N 3 58W
Carnegie, L. 137 26 5S 122 30E
Carnew 39 52 43N 6 30W
Carney 38 54 20N 8 30W
Carnforth 32 54 8N 2 47W
Carnic Alps = Karnische Alpen 63 46 34N 12 50E
Carnlough 38 55 0N 6 0W
Carno 31 52 34N 3 31W
Carnon 44 43 32N 3 59E
Carnot 124 4 59N 15 56E
Carnot B. 136 17 20S 121 30E
Carnoustie 35 56 30N 2 41W
Carnsore Pt. 39 52 10N 6 20W
Carnwath 35 55 42N 3 38W
Caro 156 43 29N 83 27W
Carolina, Brazil 170 7 10S 47 30W
Carolina, S. Afr. 129 26 5S 30 6E
Carolina, La 57 38 17N 3 38W
Caroline I. 131 9 15S 150 3W
Caroline Is. 130 8 0N 150 0E
Caroline Pk. 143 45 57S 167 15E
Carolside 152 51 20N 111 40W
Caron 153 50 30N 105 50W
Caroni, R. 174 6 0N 62 40W
Carora 174 10 11N 70 5W
Carovigno 65 40 42N 17 40E
Carpathians, Mts. 53 49 40N 19 30E
Carpaţii Meridionali 70 45 30N 25 0E
Carpenédolo 62 45 22N 10 25E
Carpentaria Downs 138 18 44S 144 20E
Carpentaria, G. of 133 14 0S 139 0E
Carpentras 45 44 3N 5 2E
Carpi 62 44 47N 10 52E
Carpina 170 7 51S 35 15W
Carpino 65 41 50N 15 51E
Carpinteria 163 34 25N 119 31W
Carpio 56 41 13N 5 7W
Carpolac = Morea 140 36 45S 141 18E

Carr Boyd Ra. 136 16 15S 128 35E
Carra L. 38 53 41N 9 12W
Carrabelle 157 29 52N 84 40W
Carracastle 38 53 57N 8 42W
Carradale 34 55 35N 5 30W
Carraipia 174 11 16N 72 22W
Carrara 62 44 5N 10 7E
Carrascosa del Campo 58 40 2N 2 45W
Carrauntohill, Mt. 39 52 0N 9 49W
Carraweena 139 29 10S 140 0E
Carrbridge 37 57 17N 3 50W
Carriacou, I. 167 12 30N 61 28W
Carribee 140 35 7S 136 57E
Carrick 38 54 40N 8 39W
Carrick, dist. 34 55 12N 4 38W
Carrick-on-Shannon 38 53 57N 8 7W
Carrick-on-Suir 39 52 22N 7 30W
Carrick Ra. 143 45 15S 169 8E
Carrickart 38 55 10N 7 47W
Carrickbeg 39 52 20N 7 25W
Carrickboy 38 53 36N 7 40W
Carrickfergus 38 54 43N 5 50W
Carrickfergus □ 38 54 43N 5 49W
Carrickmacross 38 54 0N 6 43W
Carrieton 140 32 25S 138 31E
Carrigaholt 39 52 37N 9 42W
Carrigahorig 39 53 4N 8 10W
Carrigaline 39 51 49N 8 22W
Carrigallen 38 53 59N 7 40W
Carrigan Hd. 38 54 38N 8 40W
Carrignavar 39 52 0N 8 29W
Carrigtwohill 39 51 55N 8 15W
Carrington 158 47 30N 99 7W
Carrión de los Condes 56 42 20N 4 37W
Carrión, R. 56 42 42N 4 47W
Carrizal 174 12 1N 72 11W
Carrizal Bajo 172 28 5S 71 20W
Carrizalillo 172 29 0S 71 30W
Carrizo Cr. 159 36 30N 103 40W
Carrizo Springs 159 28 28N 99 50W
Carrizozo 161 33 40N 105 57W
Carroll 158 42 2N 94 55W
Carrollton, Ga., U.S.A. 157 33 36N 85 5W
Carrollton, Ill., U.S.A. 158 39 20N 90 25W
Carrollton, Ky., U.S.A. 156 38 40N 85 10W
Carrollton, Mo., U.S.A. 158 39 19N 93 24W
Carron L. 36 57 22N 5 35W
Carron R., U.K. 36 57 30N 5 30W
Carron R., U.K. 37 57 51N 4 21W
Carrot, R. 153 53 50N 101 17W
Carrot River 153 53 17N 103 35W
Carrouges 42 48 34N 0 10W
Carrowkeel 38 55 7N 7 12W
Carrowmore L. 38 54 12N 9 48W
Carruthers 153 52 52N 109 16W
Carryduff 38 54 32N 5 52W
Çarşamba 92 41 15N 36 45E
Carsoli 63 42 7N 13 3E
Carson 158 46 27N 101 29W
Carson City 160 39 12N 119 46W
Carson Sink 160 39 50N 118 40W
Carsonville 156 43 25N 82 39W
Carsphairn 34 55 13N 4 15W
Carstairs 35 55 42N 3 41W
Cartagena, Colomb. 174 10 25N 75 33W
Cartagena, Spain 59 37 38N 0 59W
Cartago, Colomb. 174 4 45N 75 55W
Cartago, C. Rica 166 9 50N 84 0W
Cartaret 42 49 23N 1 47W
Cartaxo 57 39 10N 8 47W
Cartaya 57 37 16N 7 9W
Cartersville 157 34 11N 84 48W
Carterton 142 41 2S 175 31E
Carthage, Ark., U.S.A. 159 34 4N 92 32W
Carthage, Ill., U.S.A. 158 40 25N 91 10W
Carthage, Mo., U.S.A. 159 37 10N 94 20W
Carthage, N.Y., U.S.A. 156 43 59N 75 37W
Carthage, S.D., U.S.A. 158 44 14N 97 38W
Carthage, Texas, U.S.A. 159 32 8N 94 20W
Cartier I. 136 12 31S 123 29E
Cartmel 32 54 13N 2 57W
Cartwright 151 53 41N 56 58W
Caruaru 170 8 15S 35 55W
Carúpano 174 10 45N 63 15W
Carutapera 170 1 13S 46 1W
Caruthersville 159 36 10N 89 40W
Carvarzere 63 45 8N 12 7E
Carvin 43 50 30N 2 57E
Carvoeiro 174 1 30S 61 59W
Carvoeiro, Cabo 57 39 21N 9 24W
Casa Agapito 174 2 3N 73 58W
Casa Branca, Brazil 171 21 46S 47 4W
Casa Branca, Port. 57 38 29N 8 12W
Casa Grande 161 32 53N 111 51W
Casa Nova 170 9 10S 41 5W
Casablanca, Chile 172 33 20S 71 25W
Casablanca, Moroc. 118 33 36N 7 36W
Casacalenda 65 41 45N 14 50E
Casalbordino 63 42 10N 14 34E
Casale Monferrato 62 45 8N 8 28E
Casalmaggiore 62 44 59N 10 25E
Casalpusterlengo 62 45 10N 9 40E
Casamance, R. 120 12 54N 15 0W
Casamássima 65 40 58N 16 55E
Casanare, R. 174 6 30N 71 20W
Casarano 65 40 0N 18 10E
Casares 57 36 27N 5 16W
Casas Grandes 164 30 22N 108 0W
Casas IbáPez 59 39 17N 1 30W
Casasimarro 59 39 22N 2 3W
Casatejada 56 39 54N 5 40W
Casavieja 56 40 17N 4 46W
Cascade, Idaho, U.S.A. 160 44 30N 116 2W

Cascade

Cepin

Cascade, Mont., U.S.A.	160	47 16N	111 46W
Cascade Locks	160	45 44N	121 54W
Cascade Pt.	143	44 1S	168 20E
Cascade Ra.	160	45 0N	121 30W
Cascais	57	38 41N	9 25W
Cascina	62	43 40N	10 32E
Caselle Torinese	62	45 12N	7 39E
Caserta	65	41 5N	14 20E
Cashel	39	52 31N	7 53W
Cashla B.	39	53 12N	9 37W
Cashmere	160	47 31N	120 30W
Cashmere Downs	137	28 57S	119 35E
Casigua	174	11 2N	71 1W
Casiguran	103	16 15N	122 15E
Casilda	172	33 10S	61 10W
Casimcea	70	44 45N	28 23E
Casino	139	28 52S	153 3E
Casiquiare, R.	174	2 45N	66 20W
Caslan	152	54 38N	112 31W
Casma	174	9 30S	78 20W
Casmalia	163	34 50N	120 32W
Casola Valsenio	63	44 12N	11 40E
Cásoli	63	42 7N	14 18E
Caspe	58	41 14N	0 1W
Casper	160	42 52N	106 27W
Caspian Sea	79	43 0N	50 0E
Casquets	42	49 46N	2 15W
Cass City	156	43 34N	83 15W
Cass Lake	158	47 23N	94 38W
Cassá de la Selva	58	41 53N	2 52E
Cassano Iónio	65	39 47N	16 20E
Cassel	43	50 48N	2 30E
Casselton	158	47 0N	97 15W
Cássia	171	20 36S	46 56W
Cassiar	152	59 16N	129 40W
Cassiar Mts.	152	59 30N	130 30W
Cassils	152	50 29N	112 15W
Cassinga	125	15 5S	16 23E
Cassino	64	41 30N	13 50E
Cassiporé, C.	170	3 50N	51 5W
Cassis	45	43 14N	5 32E
Cassville	159	36 45N	93 59W
Cástagneto Carducci	62	43 9N	10 36E
Castaic	163	34 30N	118 38W
Castanhal	170	1 18S	47 55W
Castanheiro	174	0 17S	65 38W
Casteau	47	50 32N	4 2E
Castéggio	62	45 1N	9 8E
Castejón de Monegros	58	41 37N	0 15W
Castel di Sangro	65	41 41N	14 5E
Castel San Giovanni	62	45 4N	9 25E
Castel San Pietro	63	44 23N	11 30E
Castelbuono	65	37 56N	14 4E
Casteldelfino	62	44 35N	7 4E
Castelfiorentino	62	43 36N	10 58E
Castelfranco Emília	62	44 37N	11 2E
Castelfranco Veneto	63	45 40N	11 56E
Casteljaloux	44	44 19N	0 6E
Castellabate	65	40 18N	14 55E
Castellammare del Golfo	64	38 2N	12 53E
Castellammare di Stábia	65	40 47N	14 29E
Castellammare, G. di	64	38 5N	12 55E
Castellamonte	62	45 23N	7 42E
Castellana Grotte	65	40 53N	17 10E
Castellane	45	43 50N	6 31E
Castellaneta	65	40 40N	16 57E
Castellar de Santisteban	59	38 16N	3 8W
Castelleone	62	45 19N	9 47E
Castelli	172	36 7S	57 47W
Castelló de Ampurias	58	42 15N	3 4E
Castellón □	58	40 15N	0 5W
Castellón de la Plana	58	39 58N	0 3W
Castellote	58	40 48N	0 15W
Castelltersol	58	41 45N	2 8E
Castelmáuro	65	41 50N	14 40E
Castelnau-de-Médoc	44	45 2N	0 48W
Castelnaudary	44	43 20N	1 58E
Castelnovo ne' Monti	62	44 27N	10 26E
Castelnuovo di Val di Cécina	62	43 12N	10 54E
Castelo	173	20 53S	41 42E
Castelo Branco	56	39 50N	7 31W
Castelo Branco □	56	39 52N	7 45W
Castelo de Paiva	56	41 2N	8 16W
Castelo de Vide	57	39 25N	7 27W
Castelo do Piauí	170	5 20S	41 33W
Castelsarrasin	44	44 2N	1 7E
Casteltérmini	64	37 32N	13 38E
Castelvetrano	64	37 40N	12 46E
Casterton	140	37 30S	141 30E
Castets	44	43 52N	1 6W
Castiglione del Lago	63	43 7N	12 3E
Castiglione della Pescáia	62	42 46N	10 53E
Castiglione della Stiviere	62	45 23N	10 30E
Castiglione Fiorentino	63	43 20N	11 55E
Castilblanco	57	39 17N	5 5W
Castilla La Nueva	57	39 45N	3 20W
Castilla La Vieja	56	41 55N	4 0W
Castilla, Playa de	57	37 0N	6 33W
Castille = Castilla	56	40 0N	3 30W
Castilletes	174	11 51N	71 19W
Castillón	164	28 20N	103 38W
Castillon-en-Couserans	44	42 56N	1 1E
Castillon-la-Bataille	44	44 51N	0 2W
Castillonès	44	44 39N	0 37E
Castillos	173	34 12S	53 52W
Castle Acre	29	52 42N	0 42W
Castle Cary	28	51 5N	2 32W
Castle Dale	160	39 11N	111 1W
Castle Donington	28	52 50N	1 20W
Castle Douglas	35	54 57N	3 57W
Castle Eden	54	54 45N	1 20W
Castle Point	142	40 54N	176 15E
Castle Rock, Colo., U.S.A.	158	39 26N	104 50W
Castle Rock, Wash., U.S.A.	160	46 20N	122 58W
Castlebar	38	53 52N	9 17W
Castlebay	36	56 57N	7 30W
Castlebellingham	38	53 53N	6 22W
Castleblakeney	38	53 26N	8 28W
Castleblayney	38	54 7N	6 44W
Castlebridge	39	52 23N	6 28W
Castlecliff	142	39 57S	174 59E
Castlecomer	39	52 49N	7 13W
Castleconnell	39	52 44N	8 30W
Castledawson	38	54 47N	6 35W
Castlederg	38	54 43N	7 35W
Castledermot	39	52 55N	6 50W
Castlefinn	38	54 47N	7 35W
Castleford	33	53 43N	1 21W
Castlegar	152	49 20N	117 40W
Castlegate	160	39 45N	110 57W
Castlegregory	39	52 16N	10 0W
Castlehill	38	51 1N	9 49W
Castleisland	39	52 14N	9 28W
Castlemaine, Austral.	140	37 2S	144 12E
Castlemaine, Ireland	39	52 10N	9 42W
Castlemaine Harb.	39	52 8N	9 50W
Castlemartyr	39	51 54N	8 3W
Castlepollard	38	53 40N	7 20W
Castlereagh	38	53 47N	8 30W
Castlereagh □	38	54 33N	5 33W
Castlereagh B.	138	12 10S	135 10E
Castlereagh, R.	141	30 12S	147 32E
Castleside	32	54 50N	1 52W
Castleton, Derby., U.K.	33	53 20N	1 47W
Castleton, N. Yorks., U.K.	33	54 27N	0 57W
Castleton, U.S.A.	162	43 37N	73 11W
Castletown, Geoghegan, Ireland	38	53 27N	7 30W
Castletown, Laois, Ireland	38	52 58N	7 31W
Castletown, Meath, Ireland	39	53 47N	6 41W
Castletown, I. of Man	32	54 4N	4 40W
Castletown, U.K.	37	58 35N	3 22W
Castletown Bearhaven	39	51 40N	9 54W
Castletownroche	39	52 10N	8 28W
Castletownshend	39	51 31N	9 11W
Castlevale	138	24 30S	146 48E
Castlewellan	38	54 16N	5 57W
Castor	152	52 15N	111 50W
Castorland	162	43 53N	75 31W
Castres	44	43 37N	2 13E
Castricum	46	52 33N	4 40E
Castries	167	14 0N	60 50W
Castril	59	37 48N	2 46W
Castro, Brazil	173	24 45S	50 0W
Castro, Chile	176	42 30S	73 50W
Castro Alves	171	12 46S	39 26W
Castro del Río	57	37 41N	4 29W
Castro Marim	57	37 13N	7 26W
Castro Urdiales	58	43 23N	3 19W
Castro Verde	57	37 41N	8 4W
Castrojeriz	56	42 17N	4 9W
Castropol	56	43 32N	7 0W
Castroreale	65	38 5N	15 15E
Castrovillari	65	39 49N	16 11E
Castroville, Calif., U.S.A.	163	36 46N	121 45W
Castroville, Tex, U.S.A.	159	29 20N	98 53W
Castuera	57	38 43N	5 37W
Casummit L.	150	51 29N	92 22W
Cat Ba	100	20 50N	107 0E
Cat I., Bahamas	167	24 30N	75 30W
Cat I., U.S.A.	159	30 15N	89 7W
Cat L.	150	51 40N	91 50W
Čata	53	47 58N	18 38E
Catacamas	166	14 54N	85 56W
Catacaos	174	5 20S	80 45W
Cataguases	173	21 23S	42 39W
Catahoula L.	159	31 30N	92 5W
Catalão	171	18 10S	47 57W
Çatalca	92	41 9N	28 28E
Catalina	151	48 31N	53 4W
Catalonia = Cataluña	58	41 40N	1 15E
Cataluña	58	41 40N	1 15E
Catamarca	172	28 30S	65 50W
Catamarca □	172	28 30S	65 50W
Catanduanas, Is.	103	13 50N	124 20E
Catanduva	173	21 5S	48 58W
Catánia	65	37 31N	15 4E
Catánia, G. di	65	37 25N	15 8E
Catanzaro	65	38 54N	16 38E
Catarman	103	12 28N	124 1E
Catastrophe C.	136	34 59S	136 0E
Catcleugh	35	55 19N	2 22W
Cateau, Le	43	50 6N	3 30E
Cateel	103	7 47N	126 24E
Catende	170	8 40S	35 43W
Caterham	29	51 16N	0 4W
Cathcart, Austral.	141	36 2S	149 24E
Cathcart, S. Afr.	128	32 18S	27 10E
Catine	41	46 30N	0 15W
Catio	120	11 17N	15 15W
Catismiña	174	4 5N	63 52W
Catita	170	9 31S	43 1W
Catlettsburg	156	38 23N	82 38W
Cato I.	133	23 15S	155 32E
Catoche, C.	165	21 40N	87 0W
Catolé	171	7 19S	36 1W
Catolé do Rocha	170	6 21S	37 45W
Caton	32	54 5N	2 41W
Catonsville	162	39 16N	76 44W
Catral	59	38 10N	0 47W
Catria, Mt.	63	43 28N	12 42E
Catrimani	174	0 27N	61 41W
Catrine	34	55 30N	4 20W
Catsfield	29	50 53N	0 28E
Catskill	162	42 14N	73 52W
Catskill Mts.	162	42 15N	74 15W
Catt, Mt.	138	13 49S	134 23E
Catterick	33	54 23N	1 38W
Cattólica	63	43 58N	12 43E
Cattólica Eraclea	64	37 27N	13 24E
Catton	35	54 56N	2 16W
Catu	171	12 21S	38 23W
Catuala	128	16 25S	19 2E
Catur	127	13 45S	35 30E
Catwick Is.	101	10 0N	109 0E
Cauca □	174	2 30N	76 50W
Cauca, R.	174	7 25N	75 30W
Caucasia	174	8 0N	75 12W
Caucasus Mts. = Bolshoi Kavkas	83	42 50N	44 0E
Caucaia	170	3 40S	38 35W
Caudebec-en-Caux	42	49 30N	0 42E
Caudete	59	38 42N	1 2W
Caudry	43	50 7N	3 22E
Caulkerbush	35	54 54N	3 40W
Caulnes	42	48 18N	2 10W
Caulónia	65	38 23N	16 25E
Caungula	124	8 15S	18 50E
Cáuquenes	172	36 0S	72 30W
Caura, R.	174	6 20N	64 30W
Cauresi, R.	127	17 40S	33 10E
Causapscal	151	48 19N	67 12W
Causeway	39	52 25N	9 45W
Caussade	44	44 10N	1 33E
Cauterets	44	42 52N	0 8W
Cauvery, R.	93	12 0N	77 45E
Caux	42	49 38N	0 35E
Cava dei Tirreni	65	40 42N	14 42E
Cávado, R.	56	41 37N	8 15W
Cavaillon	45	43 50N	5 2E
Cavalaire-sur-Mer	45	43 10N	6 33E
Cavalcante	171	13 48S	47 30W
Cavalerie, La	44	44 0N	3 10E
Cavalese	63	46 17N	11 29E
Cavalier	158	48 50N	97 39W
Cavalli Is.	142	35 0S	173 58E
Cavallo, I.	45	41 22N	9 16E
Cavally, R.	120	5 0N	7 40W
Cavan	38	54 0N	7 22W
Cavan □	38	53 58N	7 10W
Cavanagh Ra.	137	26 10S	122 50E
Cavárzere	63	45 8N	12 6E
Cave City	156	37 13N	85 57W
Cavenagh Range	137	26 12S	127 55E
Cavendish	140	37 31S	142 2E
Cavers	150	48 55N	87 41W
Caviana, Ilha	170	0 15N	50 0W
Cavite	103	14 20N	120 55E
Cavour	62	44 47N	7 22E
Cavtat	66	42 35N	18 13E
Cawdor	37	57 31N	3 56W
Cawkers Well	140	31 41S	142 57E
Cawndilla, L.	140	32 30S	142 15E
Cawnpore = Kanpur	95	26 35N	80 20E
Cawood	33	53 50N	1 7W
Cawston	29	52 47N	1 10E
Caxias	174	5 0S	43 27W
Caxias do Sul	173	29 10S	51 10W
Caxine, C.	118	35 56N	0 27W
Caxito	124	8 30S	13 30E
Cay Sal Bank	166	23 45N	80 0W
Cayambe	174	0 3N	78 22W
Cayce	157	33 59N	81 2W
Cayenne	175	5 0N	52 18W
Cayes, Les	167	18 15N	73 46W
Cayeux-sur-Mer.	43	50 10N	1 30E
Cayey	147	18 7N	66 10W
Caylus	44	44 15N	1 47E
Cayman Brac, I.	166	19 43N	79 49W
Cayman Is.	166	19 40N	79 50W
Cayo	165	17 10N	89 0W
Cayo Romano, I.	167	22 0N	73 30W
Cayuga	162	42 28N	76 30W
Cayuga L.	162	42 45N	76 45W
Cazalla de la Sierra	57	37 56N	5 45W
Cazaux et de Sanguinet, Étang de	44	44 29N	1 10W
Cazenovia	162	42 56N	75 51W
Cazères	44	43 13N	1 5E
Čazin	63	44 57N	15 57E
Čazma	63	45 45N	16 39E
Cazombo	125	12 0S	22 48E
Cazorla, Spain	59	37 55N	3 2W
Cazorla, Venez.	174	8 1N	67 0W
Cazorla, Sierra de	59	38 5N	2 55W
Cea, R.	56	42 40N	5 5W
Ceamurlia de Jos	67	44 43N	28 47E
Ceanannas Mor	38	53 42N	6 53W
Ceará = Fortaleza	170	3 35S	38 35W
Ceará □	170	5 0S	40 0W
Ceará Mirim	170	5 38S	35 25W
Ceauru, L.	70	44 58N	23 11E
Cebaco, I.	166	7 33N	81 9W
Cebollar	172	29 10S	66 35W
Cebollera, Sierra de	58	42 0N	2 30W
Cebreros	56	40 27N	4 28W
Cebú	103	10 18N	123 54E
Cebú, I.	103	10 15N	123 40E
Ceccano	64	41 34N	13 18E
Cece	53	46 46N	18 39E
Cechi	120	6 15N	4 25W
Cecil Plains	139	27 30S	151 11E
Cecilton	162	39 24N	75 52W
Cécina	62	43 19N	10 33E
Cécina, R.	62	43 19N	10 40E
Ceclavin	56	39 50N	6 45W
Cedar City	161	37 41N	113 3W
Cedar Creek Res.	159	32 15N	96 0W
Cedar Falls	158	42 39N	92 29W
Cedar I.	162	37 35N	75 32W
Cedar Key	157	29 9N	83 5W
Cedar L.	153	53 20N	100 10W
Cedar Pt.	162	38 18N	76 25W
Cedar, R.	158	41 50N	91 20W
Cedar Rapids	158	42 0N	91 38W
Cedarburg	156	43 18N	87 55W
Cedartown	157	34 1N	85 15W
Cedarvale	152	55 1N	128 22W
Cedarville	160	41 37N	120 13W
Cedeira	56	43 39N	8 2W
Cedral	164	23 50N	100 42W
Cedrino, R.	64	40 8N	9 25E
Cedro	170	6 34S	39 3W
Cedros, I. de	164	28 10N	115 20W
Ceduna	139	32 7S	133 46E
Cedynia	54	52 53N	14 12E
Ceepeecee	152	49 52N	126 42W
Cefalù	65	38 3N	14 1E
Cega, R.	56	41 17N	4 10W
Cegléd	53	47 11N	19 47E
Céglie Messápico	65	40 39N	17 31E
Cehegín	59	38 6N	1 48W
Cehu-Silvaniei	70	47 24N	23 9E
Ceiba, La	166	15 40N	86 50W
Ceica	70	46 53N	22 10E
Ceira, R.	56	40 15N	7 55W
Cekhira	119	34 20N	10 5E
Celano	63	42 6N	13 30E
Celanova	56	42 9N	7 58W
Celaya	164	20 31N	100 37W
Celbridge	39	53 20N	6 33W
Celebes I. = Sulawesi	103	2 0S	120 0E
Celebes Sea	103	3 0N	123 0E
Celga	123	12 38N	37 3E
Celina	156	40 32N	84 31W
Čelić	66	44 43N	18 47E
Celje	63	46 16N	15 18E
Cellar Hd.	36	58 25N	6 10W
Celldömölk	53	47 16N	17 10E
Celle	48	52 37N	10 4E
Celles	47	50 42N	3 28E
Celorica da Beira	56	40 38N	7 24W
Cemaes Bay	31	53 24N	4 27W
Cemaes Hd.	31	52 7N	4 44W
Cement	159	34 56N	98 8W
Čemerno	66	43 26N	20 26E
Cemmaes Road	31	52 39N	3 41W
Cenarth	31	52 3N	4 32W
Cenis, Col du Mt.	45	45 15N	6 55E
Ceno, R.	62	44 40N	9 52E
Cenon	44	44 50N	0 33W
Centallo	62	44 30N	7 35E
Centenário do Sul	171	22 48S	51 57W
Center, N.D., U.S.A.	158	47 9N	101 17W
Center, Texas, U.S.A.	159	31 50N	94 10W
Centerfield	160	39 9N	111 56W
Centerville, Ala., U.S.A.	157	32 55N	87 7W
Centerville, Calif., U.S.A.	163	36 44N	119 30W
Centerville, Iowa, U.S.A.	158	40 45N	92 57W
Centerville, Miss., U.S.A.	159	31 10N	91 3W
Centerville, S.D., U.S.A.	158	43 10N	96 58W
Centerville, Tenn., U.S.A.	157	35 46N	87 29W
Centerville, Tex., U.S.A.	159	31 15N	95 56W
Cento	63	44 43N	11 16E
Central	170	11 8S	42 8W
Central □, Kenya	126	0 30S	33 30E
Central □, Malawi	126	13 30S	33 30E
Central □, U.K.	34	56 0N	4 30W
Central □, Zambia	127	14 25S	28 50E
Central African Republic ■	124	7 0N	20 0E
Central Auckland □	142	37 30S	175 30E
Central City, Ky., U.S.A.	156	37 20N	87 7W
Central City, Nebr., U.S.A.	158	41 8N	98 0W
Central, Cordillera, C. Rica	166	10 10N	84 5W
Central, Cordillera, Dom. Rep.	167	19 15N	71 0W
Central I., L. Turkana	126	3 30N	36 0E
Central Islip	162	40 49N	73 13W
Central Makran Range	93	26 30N	64 15E
Central Patricia	150	51 30N	90 9W
Central Ra.	135	5 0S	143 0E
Central Russian Uplands	16	54 0N	36 0E
Central Siberian Plateau	77	65 0N	105 0E
Central Square	162	43 17N	76 9W
Centralia, Ill., U.S.A.	158	38 32N	89 5W
Centralia, Mo., U.S.A.	158	39 12N	92 6W
Centralia, Wash., U.S.A.	160	46 46N	122 59W
Centúripe	65	37 37N	14 41E
Cephalonia = Kefallinia	69	38 28N	20 30E
Cepin	66	45 32N	18 34E

Ceprano

Château d'Oex

Ceprano **64** 41 33N 13 30 E
Ceptura **70** 45 1N 26 21 E
Ceram I. = Seram I. **103** 3 10 S 129 0 E
Ceram Sea **103** 2 30 S 128 30 E
Cerbère **44** 42 26N 3 10 E
Cerbicales, Îles **45** 41 33N 9 22 E
Cerbu **70** 44 46N 24 46 E
Cercal **57** 37 48N 8 40W
Cercemaggiore **65** 41 27N 14 43 E
Cerdaña **58** 42 22N 1 35 E
Cerdedo **56** 42 33N 8 23W
Cerea **63** 45 12N 11 13 E
Ceres, Argent. **172** 29 55 S 61 55W
Ceres, Brazil **171** 15 17 S 49 35W
Ceres, Italy **62** 45 19N 7 22 E
Ceres, S. Afr. **128** 33 21 S 19 18 E
Ceres, U.K. **35** 56 18N 2 57W
Ceres, U.S.A. **163** 37 35N 120 57W
Céret **44** 42 30N 2 42 E
Ceretė **174** 8 53N 75 48W
Cerfontaine **47** 50 11N 4 26 E
Cerignola **65** 41 17N 15 53 E
Cerigo = Kíthira **69** 36 9N 23 0 E
Cérilly **44** 46 37N 2 50 E
Cerisiers **43** 48 8N 3 30 E
Cerizay **42** 46 50N 0 40W
Çerkeş **92** 40 40N 32 58 E
Cerknica **63** 45 48N 14 21 E
Çermerno **66** 43 35N 20 25 E
Cerna **70** 44 4N 28 17 E
Cerna, R. **70** 44 45N 24 0 E
Cernavodŭ **70** 44 22N 28 3 E
Cernay **43** 47 44N 7 10 E
Cerne Abbas **28** 50 49N 2 29W
Cernik **66** 45 17N 17 22 E
Cerralvo, I. **164** 24 20N 109 45 E
Cerreto Sannita **65** 41 17N 14 34 E
Cerrig-y-druidion **31** 53 2N 3 34W
Cerritos **164** 22 20N 100 20W
Cerro **161** 36 47N 105 36W
Cêrro Corá **171** 6 3 S 36 21W
Cerro de Punta, Mt. **147** 18 10N 67 0W
Certaldo **62** 43 32N 11 2 E
Cervaro, R. **65** 41 21N 15 30 E
Cervera **58** 41 40N 1 16 E
Cervera de Pisuerga **56** 42 51N 4 30W
Cervera del Río Alhama **58** 42 2N 1 58W
Cérvia **63** 44 15N 12 20 E
Cervignano del Friuli **63** 45 49N 13 20 E
Cervinara **65** 41 2N 14 36 E
Cervo **56** 43 40N 7 24W
Cervoine **45** 42 20N 9 29 E
Cesanâtico **63** 44 12N 12 22 E
César □ **174** 9 0N 73 30W
Cesaro **65** 37 50N 14 38 E
Cesena **63** 44 9N 12 14 E
Cesenático **63** 44 12N 12 22 E
Cësis **80** 57 17N 25 28 E
Česká Třebová **53** 49 54N 16 27 E
Česke Budějovice **52** 48 55N 14 25 E
České Velenice **52** 48 45N 15 1 E
Českézemě **52** 50 0N 14 0 E
Ceskomoravská Vrchovina **52** 49 20N 15 45 E
Český Brod **52** 50 4N 14 52 E
Čéský Krumlov **52** 48 43N 14 21 E
Český Těšin **53** 49 45N 18 39 E
Çeşme **69** 38 20N 26 23 E
Cess, R. **120** 5 25N 9 35W
Cessnock **141** 32 50 S 151 21 E
Cestos, R. **120** 5 30N 9 30W
Cetate **70** 44 7N 23 2 E
Cetina, R. **63** 43 50N 16 30 E
Cetinje **66** 42 23N 18 59 E
Cetraro **65** 39 30N 15 56 E
Ceuta **118** 35 52N 5 18W
Ceva **62** 44 23N 8 0 E
Cévennes, mts. **44** 44 10N 3 50 E
Ceylon = Sri Lanka ■ **97** 7 30N 80 50 E
Cha-am **100** 12 48N 99 58 E
Cha Pa **100** 22 21N 103 50 E
Chaam **47** 51 30N 4 52 E
Chabeuil **45** 44 54N 5 1 E
Chabjuwardoo B. **137** 23 0 S 113 30 E
Chablais **45** 46 20N 6 36 E
Chablis **43** 47 47N 3 48 E
Chabounia **118** 35 30N 2 38 E
Chacabuco **172** 34 40 S 60 27W
Chacewater **30** 50 15N 5 8W
Chachapoyas **174** 6 15 S 77 50W
Chachoengsao **100** 13 42N 101 5 E
Chachran **93** 28 55N 70 30 E
Chachro **94** 25 5N 70 15 E
Chaco □ **172** 25 0 S 61 0W
Chaco Austral **176** 27 30 S 61 40W
Chaco Boreal **172** 22 30 S 60 10W
Chaco Central **176** 24 0 S 61 0W
Chad ■ **117** 12 30N 17 15 E
Chadan **77** 51 17N 91 35 E
Chadileuvú, R. **172** 37 0 S 65 55W
Chadiza **127** 14 10 S 33 34 E
Chadron **158** 42 50N 103 0W
Chadyr-Lunga **82** 46 3N 28 51 E
Chae Hom **100** 18 43N 99 35 E
Chaem, R. **100** 18 11N 98 38 E
Chaeryŏng **107** 38 24N 125 36 E
Chafurray **174** 3 10N 73 14W
Chagai **93** 29 30N 63 0 E
Chagai Hills **93** 29 30N 63 0 E
Chagda **77** 58 45N 130 30 E
Chagford **30** 50 40N 3 50W
Chagny **43** 46 57N 4 45 E
Chagoda **80** 59 10N 35 25 E
Chagos Arch. **86** 6 0 S 72 0 E
Chãh Bahãr **93** 25 20N 60 40 E
Ch'ahaerhyuichungch'i **106** 41 18N 112 48 E
Ch'ahanch'elo **106** 41 41N 114 15 E
Chahar Buriak **93** 30 15N 62 0 E
Chãhr-e Babak **93** 30 10N 55 20 E
Chahsikiang **105** 32 32N 79 41 E
Chahtung **98** 26 41N 98 10 E
Chai-nat **100** 15 11N 100 8 E
Chaibasa **99** 22 42N 85 49 E
Chaillé-les-Marais **44** 46 25N 1 2W
Chaise Dieu, La **44** 45 20N 3 40 E
Chaiya **101** 9 23N 99 14 E
Chaiyaphum **100** 15 48N 102 2 E
Chaize-le-Vicomté, La **42** 46 40N 1 18W
Chaj Doab **94** 32 0N 73 0 E
Chajari **172** 30 42N 58 0W
Chakaria **98** 21 45N 92 5 E
Chake Chake **126** 5 15 S 39 45 E
Chakhansur **93** 31 10N 62 0 E
Chaklashi **94** 22 40N 72 52 E
Chakonipau, L. **151** 56 18N 68 30W
Chakradharpur **95** 22 45N 85 40 E
Chakwadam **98** 27 29N 98 31 E
Chakwal **94** 32 50N 72 45 E
Chala **174** 15 48 S 74 20W
Chalais **44** 45 16N 0 3 E
Chalakudi **97** 10 18N 76 20 E
Chalcatongo **165** 17 4N 97 34W
Chalchihuites **164** 23 29N 103 53W
Chalcis = Khalkís **69** 38 27N 23 42 E
Chale **28** 50 35N 1 19W
Chaleur B. **151** 47 55N 65 30W
Chalfant **163** 37 32N 118 21W
Chalfont St. Peter **29** 51 36N 0 33W
Chalhuanca **174** 14 15 S 73 5W
Ch'aling **109** 26 47N 113 45 E
Chaling Hu **105** 34 55N 98 0 E
Chalisgaon **96** 20 30N 75 10 E
Chalkar **83** 50 35N 51 52 E
Chalkar Oz. **83** 50 33N 51 45 E
Chalky Inlet **143** 46 3 S 166 31 E
Challans **42** 46 50N 1 52W
Challapata **174** 19 0 S 66 50W
Challerange **43** 49 18N 4 46 E
Challis **160** 44 32N 114 25W
Chalna **95** 22 36N 89 35 E
Chalon-sur-Saône **43** 46 48N 4 50 E
Chalonnes **42** 47 20N 0 45W
Châlons-sur-Marne **43** 48 58N 4 20 E
Châlus **44** 45 39N 0 58 E
Cham, Ger. **49** 49 12N 12 40 E
Cham, Switz. **51** 47 11N 8 28 E
Cham, Cu Lao **100** 15 57N 108 30 E
Chama, R. **127** 36 57N 106 37W
Chaman **93** 30 58N 66 25 E
Chamarajanagar-Ramasamudram **97** 11 52N 76 52 E
Chamartín de la Rosa **58** 40 28N 3 40W
Chamba, India **94** 32 35N 76 10 E
Chamba, Tanz. **125** 11 37 S 37 0 E
Chambal, R. **94** 26 0N 76 55 E
Chamberlain, Austral. **136** 15 58 S 127 54 E
Chamberlain, U.S.A. **158** 43 50N 99 21W
Chambers **161** 35 13N 109 30W
Chambersburg **156** 39 53N 77 41W
Chambéry **45** 45 34N 5 55 E
Chambeshi **127** 12 39 S 28 1 E
Chambeshi, R. **124** 10 20 S 31 58 E
Chambois **42** 48 48N 0 6 E
Chambon-Feugerolles, Le **45** 45 24N 4 18 E
Châmbon, Le **45** 45 35N 4 26 E
Chambord **151** 48 25N 72 6W
Chamboulive **44** 45 26N 1 42 E
Chambri L. **135** 4 15 S 143 10 E
Chamela **164** 19 32N 105 5W
Chamical **172** 30 22 S 66 27W
Chamkar Luong **101** 11 0N 103 45 E
Chamonix **45** 45 55N 6 51 E
Champa **95** 22 2N 82 43 E
Champagne, Can. **152** 60 49N 136 30W
Champagne, France **43** 49 0N 4 40 E
Champagnole **43** 46 45N 5 55 E
Champaign **156** 40 8N 88 14W
Champassak **100** 14 53N 105 52 E
Champaubert **43** 48 50N 3 45 E
Champdeniers **44** 46 29N 0 25W
Champeix **44** 45 37N 3 8 E
Champerico **166** 14 18N 91 55W
Champier **50** 45 27N 5 17 E
Champion B. **137** 28 44 S 114 36 E
Champlain **151** 46 27N 72 24W
Champotón **165** 19 20N 90 50W
Chamusca **57** 39 21N 8 29W
Chana **101** 6 55N 100 44 E
Chañaral **172** 26 15 S 70 50W
Chanasma **94** 23 44N 72 5 E
Chanca, R. **57** 37 49N 7 15W
Chanchiang **109** 21 15N 110 20 E
Chancy **50** 46 8N 6 0 E
Chanda **96** 19 57N 79 25 E
Chandalar **147** 67 30N 148 35W
Chandausi **95** 28 27N 78 49 E
Chandeleur Is. **59** 29 45N 88 53W
Chandeleur Sd. **159** 29 58N 88 40W
Chandernagore **95** 22 52N 88 24 E
Chandigarh **94** 30 30N 76 58 E
Chandler, Can. **151** 48 18N 64 46W
Chandler, Ariz., U.S.A. **161** 33 20N 111 56W
Chandler, Okla., U.S.A. **159** 35 43N 97 20W
Chandler's Ford **28** 50 59N 1 23W
Chandlers Peak **141** 30 24 S 152 10 E
Chandmani **105** 45 20N 97 59 E
Chandpur, Bangla. **98** 22 8N 90 55 E
Chandpur, India **94** 29 8N 78 19 E
Chang **94** 26 59N 68 30 E
Ch'ang Chiang, R. **109** 31 40N 121 50 E
Chang, Ko **101** 12 0N 102 23 E
Changa **95** 33 53N 77 35 E
Changanacheri **97** 9 25N 76 31 E
Changane, R. **125** 23 30 S 33 50 E
Ch'anganpao **108** 26 9N 109 42 E
Changchiak'ou **106** 40 50N 114 53 E
Ch'angchiang **100** 19 19N 108 43 E
Ch'angchih **106** 36 11N 113 6 E
Ch'angchou **109** 31 47N 119 58 E
Changchou **109** 24 31N 117 40 E
Ch'angch'un **107** 43 58N 125 19 E
Ch'angch'unling **107** 45 22N 125 28 E
Changdori **107** 38 30N 127 40 E
Ch'angfeng **109** 32 27N 117 9 E
Changhsing **109** 31 0N 119 56 E
Ch'anghua **109** 30 10N 119 15 E
Changhua **109** 24 2N 120 30 E
Changhŭng **107** 34 41N 126 52 E
Changhŭngni **107** 40 24N 128 19 E
Ch'angi **107** 36 51N 119 23 E
Changjin **107** 40 23N 127 15 E
Changjin-chŏsuji **107** 40 30N 127 15 E
Changkuangts'ai Ling **107** 45 50N 128 50 E
Changli **107** 39 40N 119 19 E
Ch'angling **107** 44 16N 123 57 E
Ch'anglo, Fukien, China **109** 25 58N 119 31 E
Ch'anglo, Fukien, China **109** 26 40N 117 20 E
Ch'anglo, Kwangtung, China **109** 24 4N 115 37 E
Changlun **101** 6 25N 100 26 E
Changming **108** 31 44N 104 44 E
Ch'angning, Hunan, China **109** 26 25N 112 15 E
Ch'angning, Szechwan, China **108** 28 38N 104 57 E
Ch'angning, Yunnan, China **108** 24 50N 99 36 E
Ch'angpai **107** 41 26N 128 0 E
Ch'angpai Shan **107** 42 25N 129 0 E
Changpei **106** 41 7N 114 51 E
Ch'angp'ing **106** 40 12N 116 12 E
Changp'ing **109** 25 18N 117 24 E
Changpu **109** 24 2N 117 31 E
Ch'angsha **109** 28 15N 113 0 E
Ch'angshan **109** 28 57N 118 31 E
Ch'angshou **108** 29 50N 107 2 E
Ch'angshu **109** 31 33N 120 45 E
Ch'angshun **108** 25 59N 106 25 E
Ch'angt'ai **109** 24 34N 117 50 E
Ch'angte **109** 29 5N 111 42 E
Ch'angt'ing **109** 25 52N 116 20 E
Ch'angt'u **107** 42 47N 124 0 E
Ch'angtu **108** 31 10N 97 14 E
Ch'angt'u Shan **109** 30 15N 122 20 E
Ch'angwu **106** 35 9N 107 42 E
Changwu **107** 42 24N 122 30 E
Ch'angyang **109** 30 28N 111 9 E
Ch'angyatien **106** 40 40N 108 46 E
Changyeh **105** 38 56N 100 37 E
Changyŏn **107** 38 15N 125 6 E
Ch'angyüan **106** 35 17N 114 50 E
Chanhanga **128** 16 0 S 14 8 E
Chanhua **107** 37 42N 118 8 E
Chani **108** 25 36N 103 49 E
Channapatna **97** 12 40N 77 15 E
Channel Is. **42** 49 30N 2 40W
Channel Islands **163** 33 30N 119 0W
Channing, Mich., U.S.A. **156** 46 9N 88 1W
Channing, Tex., U.S.A. **159** 35 45N 102 20W
Chantada **56** 42 36N 7 46W
Chanthaburi **100** 12 38N 102 12 E
Chantilly **43** 49 12N 2 29 E
Chantonnay **42** 46 40N 1 3W
Chantrey Inlet **148** 67 48N 96 20W
Chanute **159** 37 45N 85 25W
Chanyü **107** 44 39N 122 45 E
Chanza, R. **57** 37 49N 7 15W
Ch'ao Hu **109** 31 40N 117 30 E
Chao Phraya Lowlands **100** 15 30N 100 0 E
Chao Phraya, R. **100** 13 32N 100 36 E
Ch'aoan **109** 23 41N 116 33 E
Chaoan **109** 23 47N 117 5 E
Chaoch'eng, Shansi, China **106** 36 26N 111 43 E
Chaoch'eng, Shantung, China **106** 36 3N 115 35 E
Chaochiao **108** 28 1N 102 49 E
Chaoch'ing **109** 23 7N 112 24 E
Chaohsien **106** 37 45N 114 46 E
Ch'aohsien **109** 31 41N 117 49 E
Chaop'ing **109** 24 1N 110 59 E
Chaot'ung **108** 27 19N 103 42 E
Ch'aoyang, Kwangtung, China **109** 23 10N 116 30 E
Ch'aoyang, Liaoning, China **107** 41 46N 120 16 E
Chaoyüan, Heilungkiang, China **107** 45 30N 125 8 E
Chaoyüan, Shantung, China **107** 37 22N 120 24 E
Chap Kuduk **76** 48 45N 55 5 E
Chapala **127** 15 50 S 37 35 E
Chapala, Lago de **164** 20 10N 103 20W
Chaparmukh **98** 26 12N 92 31 E
Chapayevo **83** 50 25N 51 10 E
Chapayevsk **81** 53 0N 49 40 E
Chapecó **173** 27 14 S 52 41W
Chapel-en-le-Frith **32** 53 19N 1 54W
Chapel Hill **157** 35 53N 79 3W
Chapelle-d'Angillon, La **43** 47 21N 2 25 E
Chapelle Glain, La **42** 47 38N 1 11W
Chapeyevo **84** 50 12N 51 10 E
Chapleau **150** 47 50N 83 24W
Chaplin **153** 50 28N 106 40W
Chaplino **82** 48 8N 36 15 E
Chaplygin **81** 53 15N 39 55 E
Chapra **95** 25 48N 84 50 E
Char **116** 21 40N 12 45W
Chara **77** 56 54N 118 12 E
Charadai **172** 27 35 S 60 0W
Charagua **174** 19 45 S 63 10W
Charak **93** 26 46N 54 18 E
Charalá **174** 6 17N 73 10W
Charaña **174** 17 30 S 69 35W
Charapita **174** 0 37 S 74 21W
Charata **172** 27 13 S 61 14W
Charcas **164** 23 10N 101 20W
Charcoal L. **153** 58 49N 102 22W
Charcot I. **13** 70 0 S 75 0W
Chard, Can. **153** 55 55N 111 10W
Chard, U.K. **28** 50 52N 2 59W
Chardara **76** 41 16N 67 59 E
Chardara, Step **85** 42 20N 68 0 E
Charduar **98** 26 51N 92 46 E
Chardzhou **85** 39 6N 63 34 E
Charente-Maritime □ **44** 45 50N 0 35W
Charente □ **44** 45 50N 0 16W
Charente, R. **44** 45 41N 0 30W
Charentsavan **83** 40 35N 44 41 E
Chârib, G. **122** 28 6N 32 54 E
Charikar **93** 35 0N 69 10 E
Charing **29** 51 12N 0 49 E
Charité, La **43** 47 10N 3 0 E
Chariton R. **158** 39 19N 92 58W
Charkhari **95** 25 24N 79 45 E
Charkhi Dadri **94** 28 37N 76 17 E
Charlbury **28** 51 52N 1 29W
Charlemont **38** 54 26N 6 40W
Charleroi **47** 50 24N 4 27 E
Charles, C. **162** 37 10N 75 52W
Charles City, Iowa, U.S.A. **158** 43 2N 92 41W
Charles City, Va., U.S.A. **162** 37 20N 77 4W
Charles L. **153** 59 50N 110 33W
Charles, Pk. **137** 32 53 S 121 8 E
Charles Town **156** 39 20N 77 50W
Charleston, Miss., U.S.A. **159** 34 2N 90 3W
Charleston, Mo., U.S.A. **159** 36 52N 89 20W
Charleston, S.C., U.S.A. **157** 32 47N 79 56W
Charleston, W. Va., U.S.A. **157** 38 24N 81 36W
Charlestown, Ireland **38** 53 58N 8 48W
Charlestown, S. Afr. **129** 27 26 S 29 53 E
Charlestown, Ind., U.S.A. **156** 38 29N 85 40W
Charlestown, N.H., U.S.A. **162** 43 14N 72 24W
Charlestown of Aberlour **37** 57 27N 3 13W
Charlesville **124** 5 27 S 20 59 E
Charleville **139** 26 24 S 146 15 E
Charleville-Mézières **43** 49 44N 4 40 E
Charleville = Rath Luirc **39** 52 21N 8 40W
Charlevoix **156** 45 19N 85 14W
Charlieu **45** 46 10N 4 10 E
Charlotte, Mich., U.S.A. **156** 42 36N 84 48W
Charlotte, N.C., U.S.A. **157** 35 16N 80 46W
Charlotte Amalie **147** 18 22N 64 56W
Charlotte Harb. **157** 26 45N 82 10W
Charlotte Waters **136** 25 56N 134 54 E
Charlottenberg **72** 59 54N 12 17 E
Charlottesville **156** 38 1N 78 30W
Charlottetown **151** 46 14N 63 8W
Charlton, Austral. **140** 36 16 S 143 24 E
Charlton, U.S.A. **158** 40 59N 93 20W
Charlton I. **150** 52 0N 79 20W
Charlton Kings **28** 51 52N 2 3W
Charlwood **29** 51 8N 0 12W
Charmes **43** 48 22N 6 17 E
Charminster **28** 50 43N 2 28W
Charmouth **28** 50 45N 2 54W
Charnwood Forest **23** 52 43N 1 18W
Charny **151** 46 43N 71 15W
Charolles **45** 46 27N 4 16 E
Charost **43** 47 0N 2 7 E
Charouïne **118** 29 0N 0 15W
Charre **127** 17 19 S 35 10 E
Charroux **44** 46 9N 0 25 E
Charsadda **94** 34 7N 71 45 E
Charters Towers **138** 20 5 S 146 13 E
Chartham **29** 51 14N 1 1 E
Chartre, La **42** 47 42N 0 34 E
Chartres **42** 48 29N 1 30 E
Chascomús **172** 35 30 S 58 0W
Chasefu **127** 11 55N 32 58 E
Chaslands Mistake **143** 46 38 S 169 22 E
Chasseneuil-sur-Bonnieure **44** 45 52N 0 29 E
Chata **94** 27 42N 77 30 E
Châtaigneraie, La **42** 46 38N 0 45W
Chatal Balkan = Udvoy Balkan **67** 42 50N 26 50 E
Château-Chinon **43** 47 4N 3 56 E
Château d'Oex **50** 46 28N 7 8 E

Château-du-Loir Ch'iench'engchen

Château-du-Loir 42 47 40N 0 25 E
Château Gontier 42 47 50N 0 42W
Château-la-Vallière 42 47 30N 0 20 E
Château-Landon 43 48 8N 2 40 E
Château, Le 44 45 52N 1 12W
Château Porcien 43 49 31N 4 13 E
Château Renault 42 47 36N 0 56 E
Château-Salins 43 48 50N 6 30 E
Château-Thierry 43 49 3N 3 20 E
Châteaubourg 43 48 7N 1 25W
Châteaubriant 42 47 43N 1 23W
Châteaudun 42 48 3N 1 20 E
Châteaugiron 42 48 3N 1 30W
Châteaulin 42 48 11N 4 8W
Châteaumeillant 44 46 35N 2 12 E
Châteauneuf 42 48 35N 1 15 E
Châteauneuf-du-Faou 42 48 11N 3 50W
Châteauneuf-sur-Charente 44 45 36N 0 3W
Châteauneuf-sur-Cher 43 46 52N 2 18 E
Châteauneuf-sur-Loire 43 47 52N 2 13 E
Châteaurenard 45 43 53N 4 51 E
Châteauroux 43 46 50N 1 40 E
Châtel-Guyon 44 45 55N 3 4 E
Châtel St. Denis 50 46 32N 6 54 E
Châtelaillon-Plage 44 46 5N 1 5W
Châtelard, Le 50 46 4N 6 57 E
Châtelaudren 42 48 33N 2 59W
Chatelet 47 50 24N 4 32 E
Châtelet, Le, Cher, France 44 46 40N 2 20 E
Châtelet, Le, Seine et Marne, France 43 48 30N 2 47 E
Châtellerault 42 46 50N 0 30 E
Châtelus-Malvaleix 44 46 18N 2 1 E
Chatham, N.B., Can. 151 47 2N 65 28W
Chatham, Ont., Can. 150 42 24N 82 11W
Chatham, U.K. 29 51 22N 0 32 E
Chatham, Alaska, U.S.A. 147 57 30N 135 0W
Chatham, La., U.S.A. 159 32 22N 92 26W
Chatham, N.Y., U.S.A. 162 42 21N 73 32W
Chatham Is. 130 44 0S 176 40W
Chatham Str. 152 57 0N 134 40W
Châtillon, Loiret, France 43 47 36N 2 44 E
Châtillon, Marne, France 43 49 5N 3 43 E
Chatillon 62 45 45N 7 40 E
Châtillon-Coligny 43 47 50N 2 51 E
Châtillon-en-Bazois 43 47 3N 3 39 E
Châtillon-en-Diois 45 44 41N 5 29 E
Châtillon-sur-Seine 43 47 50N 4 33 E
Châtillon-sur-Sèvre 42 46 56N 0 45W
Chatkal, R. 85 41 38N 70 1 E
Chatkalskiy Khrebet 85 41 30N 70 45 E
Chatmohar 95 24 15N 89 26 E
Chatra 95 24 12N 84 56 E
Chatrapur 96 19 22N 85 2 E
Châtre, La 44 46 35N 1 59 E
Chatsworth 127 19 32S 30 46 E
Chatta-Hantō 111 34 45N 136 55 E
Chattahoochee 157 30 43N 84 51W
Chattanooga 157 35 2N 85 17W
Chatteris 29 52 27N 0 3 E
Chatton 35 55 34N 1 55W
Chaturat 100 15 34N 101 51 E
Chatyrkel, Ozero 85 40 40N 75 18 E
Chatyrtash 85 40 55N 76 25 E
Chau Phu 101 10 42N 105 7 E
Chaudes-Aigues 44 44 51N 3 1 E
Chauffailes 44 46 13N 4 20 E
Chauk 98 20 53N 94 49 E
Chaukan La 99 27 0N 97 15 E
Chaukan Pass 98 27 8N 97 10 E
Chaulnes 43 49 48N 2 47 E
Chaumont 43 48 7N 5 8 E
Chaumont-en-Vexin 43 49 16N 1 53 E
Chaumont-sur-Loire 42 47 29N 1 11 E
Chaunay 44 46 13N 0 9 E
Chauny 43 49 37N 3 12 E
Chausey, Îs. 42 48 52N 1 49W
Chaussin 43 46 59N 5 22 E
Chauvin 153 52 45N 110 10W
Chaux de Fonds, La 50 47 7N 6 50 E
Chaves, Brazil 170 0 15S 49 55W
Chaves, Port. 56 41 45N 7 32W
Chavuma 125 13 10S 22 55 E
Chawang 101 8 25N 99 30 E
Ch'aya 108 30 35N 98 3 E
Chayan 85 43 5N 69 25 E
Chayek 85 41 55N 74 30 E
Chaykovskiy 84 56 47N 54 9 E
Chazelles-sur-Lyon 45 45 39N 4 22 E
Cheadle, Gr. Manchester, U.K. 32 53 23N 2 14W
Cheadle, Staffs., U.K. 32 52 59N 1 59W
Cheadle Hulme 32 53 22N 2 12W
Cheb (Eger) 52 50 9N 12 20 E
Chebarkul 84 55 0N 60 25 E
Cheboksary 81 56 8N 47 30 E
Cheboygan 156 45 38N 84 29W
Chebsara 81 59 10N 38 45 E
Chech, Erg 118 25 0N 2 15W
Chechaouen 118 35 9N 5 15W
Chechen 83 43 59N 47 40 E
Chech'eng 106 34 4N 115 13 E
Checheno-Ingush, A.S.S.R. □ 83 43 30N 45 29 E
Chechon 107 37 8N 128 12 E
Checiny 54 50 46N 20 37 E
Checleset B. 152 50 5N 127 35W
Checotah 159 35 31N 95 30W
Chedabucto B. 151 45 25N 61 8W
Cheddar 28 51 16N 2 47W
Cheddleton 32 53 5N 2 2W
Cheduba I. 98 18 45N 93 40 E
Cheepie 139 26 43S 144 59 E
Ch'eerhch'en Ho, R. 105 39 30N 88 15 E
Chef-Boutonne 44 46 7N 0 4W
Chefoo = Yent'ai 107 37 30N 121 12 E
Chefornak 147 60 10N 164 15W
Chegdomyn 77 51 7N 132 52 E
Chegga 118 25 15N 5 40W
Chehalis 160 46 44N 122 59W
Cheju 107 33 28N 126 30 E
Cheju Do 107 33 29N 126 34 E
Chejung 109 27 13N 119 52 E
Chekalin 81 54 10N 36 10 E
Chekao 109 31 46N 117 45 E
Chekiang □ 109 29 30N 120 0 E
Chela, Sa. da 128 16 20S 13 20 E
Chelan, Can. 153 52 38N 103 22 E
Chelan, U.S.A. 160 47 49N 120 0W
Chelan, L. 152 48 5N 120 30W
Cheleken 76 39 26N 53 7 E
Chelforó 176 39 0S 66 40W
Chéliff, O. 118 36 0N 0 8 E
Chelkar 76 47 40N 59 32 E
Chelkar Tengiz, Solonchak 76 48 0N 62 30 E
Chellala Dahrania 118 33 2N 0 1 E
Chelles 43 48 52N 2 33 E
Chełm 54 51 8N 23 30 E
Chełm □ 54 51 15N 23 30 E
Chelmarsh 28 52 29N 2 25W
Chełmek 54 50 6N 19 16 E
Chelmer, R. 29 51 45N 0 42 E
Chełmno 54 53 20N 18 30 E
Chelmsford 29 51 44N 0 29 E
Chełmza 54 53 10N 18 39 E
Chelsea, Austral. 141 38 5S 145 8 E
Chelsea, Okla., U.S.A. 159 36 35N 95 25W
Chelsea, Vermont, U.S.A. 162 43 59N 72 27W
Cheltenham 28 51 55N 2 5W
Chelva 58 39 45N 1 0W
Chelyabinsk 84 55 10N 61 24 E
Chelyuskin, C. 86 77 30N 103 0 E
Chemainus 152 48 55N 123 48W
Chemikovsk 78 56 31N 58 11 E
Chemillé 42 47 14N 0 45W
Chemnitz = Karl-Marx-Stadt 48 50 50N 12 55 E
Chemor 101 4 44N 101 6 E
Chemult 160 43 14N 121 54W
Chen, Gora 77 65 10N 141 20 E
Chenab, R. 94 30 40N 73 30 E
Chenachane, O. 118 25 30N 3 30W
Chenan 106 33 16N 109 1 E
Chenango Forks 162 42 15N 75 51W
Chencha 123 6 15N 37 32 E
Ch'ench'i 109 28 1N 110 13 E
Ch'enchiachiang 107 34 25N 119 50 E
Chenchiang 109 32 12N 119 27 E
Chenchieh 108 23 15N 107 9 E
Chênée 47 50 37N 5 37 E
Cheney 160 47 38N 117 34W
Chenfeng 108 25 25N 105 51 E
Chengan 108 28 30N 107 30 E
Ch'engch'eng 106 35 6N 109 52 E
Ch'engchiang 108 24 40N 102 55 E
Chengchou 106 34 38N 113 43 E
Chengchow = Chengchou 106 34 38N 113 43 E
Chengelee 98 28 47N 96 16 E
Chengho 109 27 25N 118 46 E
Ch'enghsi Hu 109 32 22N 116 12 E
Ch'enghsien, Chekiang, China 109 29 30N 120 48 E
Ch'enghsien, Kansu, China 106 33 42N 105 36 E
Ch'engk'ou 108 31 58N 108 48 E
Ch'engku 106 33 9N 107 22 E
Ch'engkung 108 24 53N 102 45 E
Ch'engmai 100 19 44N 109 59 E
Ch'engpu 109 26 12N 110 5 E
Ch'engte 107 41 0N 117 58 E
Chengting 106 38 8N 114 37 E
Ch'engtu 108 30 45N 104 0 E
Ch'engtung Hu 109 32 17N 116 23 E
Ch'engtzut'uan 107 39 30N 122 30 E
Ch'engwu 106 35 0N 115 56 E
Ch'engyang 107 36 20N 120 16 E
Chengyang 109 32 36N 114 23 E
Chengyangkuan 109 32 29N 116 37 E
Chenhai 109 29 57N 121 42 E
Ch'enhsien 109 25 48N 113 2 E
Chenhsiung 108 27 27N 104 50 E
Chenhsü 108 27 6N 120 16 E
Chenkán 165 19 8N 90 58W
Chenk'ang 108 24 4N 99 18 E
Chenlai 107 45 52N 123 12 E
Chenning 108 25 57N 105 51 E
Chenp'ing 106 33 2N 112 14 E
Ch'enp'ing 108 31 52N 109 31 E
Chenyüan, Kansu, China 106 35 59N 107 2 E
Chenyüan, Kweichow, China 108 27 0N 108 20 E
Cheo Reo = Hau Bon 101 13 25N 108 28 E
Cheom Ksan 100 14 13N 104 56 E
Chepelare 67 41 44N 24 40 E
Chepén 174 7 10S 79 15W
Chepes 172 31 20S 66 35W
Chepo 166 9 10N 79 6W
Chepstow 31 51 38N 2 40W
Cheptsa, R. 81 58 36N 50 4 E
Cheptulil, Mt. 126 1 25N 35 35 E
Chequamegon B. 158 46 40N 90 30W
Chequeche 127 14 13S 38 30 E
Cher □ 43 47 10N 2 30 E
Chér, R. 43 47 10N 2 10 E
Cheran 98 25 45N 90 44 E
Cherasco 62 44 39N 7 50 E
Cheratte 47 50 40N 5 41 E
Cheraw 157 34 42N 79 54W
Cherbourg 42 49 39N 1 40W
Cherchell 118 36 35N 2 12 E
Cherdakly 81 54 25N 48 50 E
Cherdyn 84 60 24N 56 29 E
Cheremkhovo 77 53 32N 102 40 E
Cherepanovo 76 54 15N 83 30 E
Cherepovets 81 59 5N 37 55 E
Chergui, Chott Ech 118 34 10N 0 25 E
Cheri 121 13 26N 11 21 E
Cherikov 80 53 32N 31 20 E
Cheriton 28 51 3N 1 9W
Cheriton Fitzpaine 30 50 51N 3 38W
Cherkessk 83 44 25N 42 10 E
Cherlak 76 54 15N 74 55 E
Chermoz 84 58 46N 56 10 E
Chernak 85 43 24N 68 2 E
Chernaya Kholunitsa 84 58 51N 51 52 E
Cherni, Mt. 67 42 35N 23 18 E
Chernigov 80 51 28N 31 20 E
Chernikovsk 84 54 48N 56 8 E
Chernobyl 80 51 13N 30 15 E
Chernogorsk 77 54 5N 91 10 E
Chernomorskoye 82 45 31N 32 46 E
Chernovskoye 81 58 48N 47 20 E
Chernovtsy 82 48 0N 26 0 E
Chernoye 77 70 30N 89 10 E
Chernushka 84 56 29N 56 3 E
Chernyakhovsk 80 54 29N 21 48 E
Chernyshevskiy 77 62 40N 112 30 E
Chernyshkovskiy 83 48 30N 42 28 E
Cherokee, Iowa, U.S.A. 158 42 40N 95 30W
Cherokee, Okla., U.S.A. 159 36 45N 98 25W
Cherokees, L. of the 159 36 50N 95 12W
Cherquenco 176 38 35S 72 0W
Cherrapunji 99 25 17N 91 47 E
Cherry Creek 160 39 50N 114 58W
Cherry Valley, U.S.A. 162 42 48N 74 45W
Cherry Valley, U.S.A. 163 33 59N 116 57W
Cherryvale 159 37 20N 95 33W
Cherskiy 77 68 45N 161 18 E
Cherskogo Khrebet 77 65 0N 143 0 E
Chertkovo 83 49 25N 40 19 E
Chertsey 29 51 23N 0 30W
Cherven 80 53 45N 28 13 E
Cherven-Bryag 67 43 17N 24 7 E
Cherwell, R. 28 51 46N 1 18W
Chesapeake Bay 162 38 0N 76 12W
Chesapeake Beach 162 38 41N 76 32W
Chesha B. = Cheshskaya G. 78 67 20N 47 0 E
Chesham 29 51 42N 0 36W
Cheshire □ 32 53 14N 2 30W
Cheshunt 29 51 42N 0 1W
Chesil Beach 23 50 37N 2 33W
Cheslatta L. 152 53 49N 125 20W
Chesne, Le 43 49 30N 4 45 E
Cheste 59 39 30N 0 41W
Chester, U.K. 32 53 12N 2 53W
Chester, Calif., U.S.A. 160 40 22N 121 22W
Chester, Ill., U.S.A. 158 37 58N 89 50W
Chester, Mont., U.S.A. 160 48 31N 111 0W
Chester, Pa., U.S.A. 162 39 54N 75 20W
Chester, S.C., U.S.A. 157 34 44N 81 13W
Chester, Va., U.S.A. 162 37 21N 77 27W
Chester, Vt., U.S.A. 162 43 16N 72 36W
Chester-le-Street 33 54 53N 1 34W
Chesterfield, Can. 148 63 0N 91 0W
Chesterfield, U.K. 33 53 14N 1 26W
Chesterfield, U.S.A. 162 37 23N 77 31W
Chesterfield I. 129 16 20S 43 58 E
Chesterfield, Îles 133 19 52S 158 15 E
Chesterfield Inlet 148 63 30N 90 45W
Chesterton Range 138 25 30S 147 27 E
Chestertown 162 39 13N 76 4W
Chesuncook L. 151 46 0N 69 10W
Chetaibi 119 37 1N 7 20 E
Cheticamp 151 46 37N 60 59W
Chetumal 165 18 30N 88 20W
Chetumal, Bahía de 165 18 40N 88 10W
Chetwynd 152 55 45N 121 45W
Chevanceaux 44 45 18N 0 14W
Cheviot Hills 35 55 20N 2 30W
Cheviot Ra. 138 25 20S 143 45 E
Cheviot, The 35 55 29N 2 8W
Chew Bahir 123 4 40N 30 50 E
Chew Magna 28 51 21N 2 37W
Chewelah 160 48 17N 117 43W
Cheyenne, Okla., U.S.A. 159 35 40N 99 40W
Cheyenne, Wyo., U.S.A. 158 41 9N 104 49W
Cheyenne, R. 158 44 50N 101 0W
Cheyenne Wells 158 38 51N 102 23W
Cheylard, Le 45 44 55N 4 25 E
Cheyne B. 137 34 35S 118 50 E
Chhabra 94 24 40N 76 54 E
Chhang 102 12 15N 104 14 E
Chhatak 95 25 5N 91 37 E
Chhatarpur 95 24 55N 79 43 E
Chhep 100 13 45N 105 24 E
Chhindwara 95 22 2N 78 59 E
Chhlong 101 12 15N 105 58 E
Chhuk 101 10 46N 104 8 E
Chi, R. 100 15 11N 104 43 E
Chiaho 109 25 33N 112 15 E
Chiahsiang 106 35 25N 116 21 E
Chiahsien, Hensi, China 106 38 6N 110 28 E
Chiahsien, Honan, China 106 33 58N 113 13 E
Chiahsing 109 30 45N 120 43 E
Chiai 109 23 29N 120 25 E
Chiali 109 23 10N 120 11 E
Chialing Chiang, R. 108 30 2N 106 19 E
Chiamussu 105 46 50N 130 21 E
Chian, Kiangsi, China 109 27 8N 115 0 E
Chian, Kirin, China 107 41 6N 126 10 E
Chiang Dao 100 19 22N 98 58 E
Chiang Kham 100 19 32N 100 18 E
Chiang Khan 100 17 52N 101 36 E
Chiang Khong 100 20 17N 100 24 E
Chiang Mai 100 18 47N 98 59 E
Chiang Saen 100 20 16N 100 5 E
Chiangch'eng 108 22 36N 101 50 E
Chiangchiat'un 107 40 54N 120 36 E
Chiangching 108 29 13N 106 15 E
Chiangchun 109 23 5N 120 5 E
Chianghua 109 25 2N 111 45 E
Chiangk'ou 108 27 42N 108 50 E
Chiangling 109 30 21N 112 5 E
Chiangmen 109 22 37N 113 3 E
Chiangpei 108 29 47N 106 29 E
Chiangp'ing 108 21 36N 108 8 E
Chiangshan 109 28 45N 118 37 E
Chiangta 108 31 28N 99 12 E
Chiangti 108 27 1N 103 37 E
Chiangyin 109 31 50N 120 18 E
Chiangyü 108 31 47N 104 45 E
Chiangyung 109 25 16N 111 20 E
Chianie 125 15 35S 13 40 E
Ch'iaochia 108 26 57N 103 3 E
Chiaochou Wan 107 36 10N 120 15 E
Chiaoho, Hopei, China 106 38 1N 116 17 E
Chiaoho, Kirin, China 107 43 42N 127 19 E
Chiaohsien 107 36 20N 120 0 E
Chiaoling 109 24 40N 117 10 E
Chiaotso 106 35 17N 113 18 E
Chiapa de Corzo 165 16 42N 93 0W
Chiapa, R. 165 16 42N 93 0W
Chiapas □ 165 17 0N 92 45W
Chiaramonte Gulfi 65 37 1N 14 41 E
Chiaravalle 63 38 41N 16 24 E
Chiaravalle Centrale 65 38 41N 16 25 E
Chiari 62 45 31N 9 55 E
Chiashan 109 32 37N 118 8 E
Chiasso 51 45 50N 9 0 E
Chiating 109 31 21N 121 15 E
Chiautla 165 18 18N 98 34W
Chiávari 62 44 20N 9 20 E
Chiavenna 62 46 18N 9 23 E
Chiawang 107 34 30N 117 22 E
Chiayü 109 29 59N 113 54 E
Chiba 111 35 30N 140 7 E
Chiba-ken □ 111 35 30N 140 20 E
Chibabava 129 20 25S 33 35 E
Chibemba 125 15 48S 14 8 E
Chibougamau 150 49 56N 74 24W
Chibougamau L. 150 49 50N 74 20W
Chibougamau, R. 150 49 50N 75 40W
Chibuk 121 10 52N 12 50 E
Chibuto 129 24 40S 33 33 E
Chic-Chocs, Mts. 151 48 55N 66 0W
Chic-Chocs, Parc Prov. des 151 48 55N 66 20W
Chicacole = Srikakulam 97 18 14N 84 4 E
Chicago 156 41 53N 87 40W
Chicago Heights 156 41 29N 87 37W
Chicago North 156 42 20N 87 50W
Chichagof I. 152 58 0N 136 0W
Chichaoua 118 31 32N 8 44W
Chichén Itzá 165 20 40N 88 32W
Chichester 29 50 50N 0 47W
Chichester Ra. 136 21 35S 117 45 E
Chich'i 109 30 4N 118 34 E
Ch'ichiang 108 29 0N 106 40 E
Chichibu 111 36 5N 139 10 E
Ch'ich'ihaerh 105 47 22N 123 57 E
Chichiriviche 174 10 56N 68 16W
Ch'ich'un 109 30 14N 115 25 E
Chickasha 159 35 0N 98 0W
Chicken Hd. 31 58 10N 6 15W
Chiclana de la Frontera 57 36 26N 6 9W
Chiclayo 174 6 42S 79 50W
Chico 160 39 45N 121 54W
Chico, R., Chubut, Argent. 160 44 0S 67 0W
Chico, R., Santa Cruz, Argent. 176 49 30S 69 30W
Chicoa 125 15 35S 32 20 E
Chicomo 129 24 31S 34 6 E
Chicontepec 165 20 58N 98 10W
Chicopee 162 42 6N 72 37W
Chicoutimi 151 48 28N 71 5W
Chidambaram 97 11 20N 79 45 E
Chiddingfold 29 51 6N 0 37W
Chidenguele 129 24 55S 34 2 E
Chidley C. 149 60 23N 64 26W
Chiehshiu 106 37 0N 111 55 E
Ch'iehmo 105 38 8N 85 32 E
Chiehshou 106 33 20N 115 24 E
Chiehyang 109 23 37N 116 19 E
Chiem Hoa 100 22 12N 105 17 E
Chiemsee 49 47 53N 12 27 E
Chiench'ang 107 41 16N 124 28 E
Chiench'angying 107 40 8N 118 50 E
Ch'iench'engchen 108 27 12N 109 50 E

Ch'ienchiang Chomen Swamp

Ch'ienchiang, Hupeh, China 109 30 25N 112 51 E
Ch'ienchiang, Kwangsi-Chuang, China 108 23 40N 108 58 E
Ch'ienchiang, Szechwan, China 108 29 31N 108 46 E
Chiench'uan 108 26 28N 99 52 E
Chiengi 124 8 45S 29 10 E
Chienho 108 26 39N 108 35 E
Ch'ienhsi 108 27 3N 106 0 E
Ch'ienhsien 106 34 30N 108 10 E
Chienko 108 32 0N 105 23 E
Chienli 109 29 49N 112 53 E
Chienou 109 27 5N 118 20 E
Ch'ienshan, Anhwei, China 109 30 41N 116 35 E
Ch'ienshan, Kiangsi, China 109 28 18N 117 40 E
Chienshih 108 30 40N 109 43 E
Chienshui 108 23 37N 102 49 E
Chiente 109 29 29N 119 16 E
Chienti, R. 63 43 15N 13 30 E
Chienwei 108 29 13N 103 56 E
Chienyang 109 27 21N 118 5 E
Ch'ienyang, Hunan, China 109 27 18N 110 10 E
Ch'ienyang, Kansu, China 106 34 35N 107 2 E
Chienyang 108 30 24N 104 33 E
Chierhkalang 107 43 6N 122 54 E
Chieri 62 45 0N 7 50 E
Chiese, R. 62 45 45N 10 35 E
Chieti 63 42 22N 14 10 E
Chièvres 47 50 35N 3 48 E
Chigasaki 111 35 19N 139 24 E
Chignecto B. 151 45 48N 64 40W
Chignik 147 56 15N 158 27W
Chigorodó 174 7 41N 76 42W
Chiguana 172 21 0S 67 50W
Chihari 107 38 40N 126 30 E
Ch'ihch'i 109 21 59N 112 58 E
Chihchiang, Hunan, China 108 27 27N 109 41 E
Chihchiang, Hupei, China 109 30 19N 111 30 E
Chihchin 108 26 42N 105 45 E
Ch'ihfeng 107 42 18N 118 57 E
Chihkou 107 35 55N 119 13 E
Chihli, G. of = Po Hai 107 38 40N 119 0 E
Ch'ihshui 108 29 29N 105 38 E
Ch'ihshui Ho, R. 108 28 53N 105 48 E
Chihsi 107 45 20N 130 55 E
Ch'ihsien 106 34 33N 114 47 E
Chihsien, Honan, China 106 35 25N 114 5 E
Chihsien, Hopei, China 106 37 34N 115 34 E
Chihsien, Shansi, China 106 36 8N 110 39 E
Chihtan 106 36 56N 108 47 E
Chihte 109 30 9N 117 0 E
Chihuahua 164 28 40N 106 3W
Chihuahua □ 164 28 40N 106 3W
Chihuatlán 164 19 14N 104 35W
Chiili 85 44 20N 66 15 E
Chik Ballapur 97 13 25N 77 45 E
Chikawawa 127 16 2S 34 50 E
Chikhli 96 20 20N 76 18 E
Chikmagalur 97 13 15N 75 45 E
Chikodi 96 16 26N 74 38 E
Chikonde 127 12 16S 31 38 E
Ch'ik'ou 107 38 37N 117 35 E
Chikugo 110 33 14N 130 28 E
Chikuma-Gawa, R. 111 36 59N 138 35 E
Chilac 165 18 20N 97 24W
Chilako, R. 152 53 53N 122 57W
Chilam Chavki 95 35 5N 75 5 E
Chilanga 127 15 33S 28 16 E
Chilant'ai 106 39 45N 105 45 E
Chilapa 165 17 40N 99 20W
Chilas 95 35 25N 74 5 E
Chilaw 93 7 30N 79 50 E
Chilcotin, R. 152 51 44N 122 23W
Childers 139 25 15S 152 17 E
Childress 159 34 30N 100 50W
Chile ■ 176 35 0S 71 15W
Chilecito 172 29 0S 67 40W
Chilete 174 7 10S 78 50W
Chilham 29 51 15N 0 59 E
Chilik, Kazakh S.S.R., U.S.S.R. 84 51 7N 53 55 E
Chilik, Kirgiz S.S.R., U.S.S.R. 85 43 33N 78 17 E
Chililabombwe (Bancroft) 125 12 18S 27 43 E
Chilin 105 43 53N 126 38 E
Ch'ilin Hu 105 31 50N 89 0 E
Chilka L. 96 19 40N 85 25 E
Chilko, L. 152 52 60N 124 10W
Chilko, R. 152 52 6N 124 9W
Chillagoe 138 17 14S 144 33 E
Chillán 172 36 40S 72 10W
Chillicothe, Ill., U.S.A. 158 40 55N 89 32W
Chillicothe, Mo., U.S.A. 158 39 45N 93 30W
Chillicothe, Ohio, U.S.A. 156 39 53N 82 58W
Chilliwack 152 49 10N 122 0W
Chilo 94 27 12N 73 32 E
Chiloane, Î. 129 20 40S 34 55 E
Chiloé, I. de 176 42 50S 73 45W
Chilpancingo 165 17 30N 99 40W
Chiltern 141 36 10S 146 36 E
Chiltern Hills 29 51 44N 0 42W
Chilton 156 44 1N 88 12W
Chiluage 124 9 15S 21 42 E
Chilubula 127 10 14S 30 51 E
Chilumba 127 10 28S 34 12 E
Chilung 109 25 3N 121 45 E
Chilwa, L. (Shirwa) 127 15 15S 35 40 E
Chimacum 160 48 1N 122 53W
Chimaltitán 164 21 46N 103 50W
Chimán 166 8 45N 78 40W
Chimay 47 50 3N 4 20 E
Chimbay 76 42 57N 59 47 E
Chimborazo 174 1 20S 78 55W
Chimbote 174 9 0S 78 35W
Ch'imen 109 29 56N 117 47 E
Chimion 85 40 15N 71 32 E
Chimishliya 70 46 34N 28 44 E
Chimkent 85 42 18N 69 36 E
Chimo 107 36 23N 120 27 E
Chimpembe 127 9 31S 29 33 E
Chin □ 98 22 0N 93 0 E
Chin Chiang, R. 109 28 23N 115 48 E
Chin Hills 98 22 30N 93 30 E
Chin Ho, R. 106 35 2N 113 25 E
Chin Ling Shan 106 34 0N 107 0 E
Ch'in Shui, R. 109 26 13N 115 15 E
China 164 25 40N 99 20W
China ■ 105 30 0N 110 0 E
China Lake 163 35 44N 117 37W
Chinacates 164 25 0N 105 14W
Chinacota 174 7 37N 72 36W
Ch'inan 106 34 50N 105 35 E
Chinan 106 36 32N 117 0 E
Chinandega 166 12 30N 87 0W
Chinati Pk. 159 30 0N 104 25W
Chincha Alta 174 13 20S 76 0W
Chinch'eng 106 35 30N 112 50 E
Chinchi 106 37 57N 106 6 E
Chinch'i 109 27 54N 116 44 E
Chinchiang, Fukien, China 109 24 54N 118 35 E
Chinchiang, Kiangsi, China 109 29 44N 115 59 E
Chinchiang, Yunnan, China 108 26 14N 100 34 E
Chinchilla 139 26 45S 150 38 E
Chinchilla de Monte Aragón 59 38 53N 1 40W
Chinchón 58 40 9N 3 26W
Chinchorro, Banco 165 18 35N 87 20W
Ch'inchou 108 21 58N 108 35 E
Chinchou 107 41 8N 121 6 E
Chinch'uan 108 31 30N 101 55 E
Chincoteague 162 37 58N 75 21W
Chincoteague B. 162 38 5N 75 8W
Chinde 127 18 45S 36 30 E
Chindo 107 34 28N 126 15 E
Chindwin, R. 98 21 26N 95 15 E
Chineni 95 33 2N 75 15 E
Ch'ing Chiang, R. 109 29 51N 112 22 E
Ch'ing Hai 105 37 0N 100 20 E
Ching Ho, R. 106 34 29N 109 5 E
Ching Shan 109 31 40N 111 30 E
Chinga 127 15 13S 38 35 E
Chingan 109 28 52N 115 22 E
Ch'ingchen 108 26 32N 106 30 E
Ch'ingch'eng 107 37 11N 117 42 E
Chingchiang 109 32 2N 120 16 E
Ch'ingchiang, Kiangsi, China 109 28 5N 115 30 E
Ch'ingchiang, Kiangsu, China 107 33 33N 119 4 E
Ch'ingchien 106 37 12N 110 6 E
Chingch'uan 106 35 15N 107 22 E
Ch'ingfeng 106 35 54N 115 7 E
Chinghai 106 38 56N 116 55 E
Ch'inghomen 107 41 45N 121 25 E
Chinghsi 108 23 8N 106 25 E
Ch'inghsien 106 38 35N 116 48 E
Chinghsien 109 30 42N 118 23 E
Ch'inghsü 106 37 40N 112 20 E
Chinghung 108 22 0N 100 49 E
Chingi Chiang, R. 108 29 32N 103 44 E
Chingku 108 23 28N 100 42 E
Chingleput 97 12 42N 79 58 E
Ch'ingliu 109 26 12N 116 48 E
Chinglo 106 38 24N 111 54 E
Ch'inglung 108 25 48N 105 14 E
Chingmen 109 30 58N 112 6 E
Chingning, Chekiang, China 109 27 58N 119 38 E
Chingning, Kansu, China 106 35 30N 105 45 E
Chingola 127 12 31S 27 53 E
Chingole 127 13 4S 34 17 E
Chingpien 106 37 24N 108 36 E
Chingpo Hu 107 43 50N 128 50 E
Ch'ingp'u 109 31 9N 121 6 E
Chingshan 109 31 2N 113 3 E
Chingshih 109 29 40N 111 50 E
Ch'ingshui 106 34 44N 106 2 E
Chingsing 106 38 5N 114 8 E
Chingt'ai 106 37 10N 104 8 E
Ch'ingtao 107 36 5N 120 25 E
Chingte 109 30 19N 118 31 E
Chingtechen 109 29 19N 117 15 E
Ch'ingt'ien 109 28 9N 120 17 E
Chingtung 108 24 22N 100 50 E
Chingtzukuan 106 33 13N 111 2 E
Chinguar 125 12 18S 16 45 E
Chinguetti 116 20 25N 12 15W
Chingune 129 20 33S 35 0 E
Ch'ingyang 105 36 5N 107 40 E
Chingyang 106 34 32N 108 52 E
Ch'ingyang, Anhwei, China 109 30 38N 117 50 E
Ch'ingyang, Ningsia Hui, China 106 36 5N 107 40 E
Chingyü 107 42 22N 126 45 E
Chingyüan 106 36 35N 104 40 E
Ch'ingyüan, Chekiang, China 109 27 37N 119 3 E
Ch'ingyüan, Kwangtung, China 109 23 42N 112 58 E
Ch'ingyüan, Liaoning, China 107 42 6N 124 55 E
Ch'ingyün 107 37 53N 117 23 E
Chinhae 107 35 9N 128 40 E
Chinhanguanine 129 25 21S 32 30 E
Chinhsi 107 40 49N 120 55 E
Chinhsiang 106 35 5N 116 18 E
Chinhsien, Hopei, China 106 38 2N 115 2 E
Chinhsien, Kiangsi, China 109 28 22N 116 14 E
Chinhsien, Liaoning, China 107 39 6N 121 3 E
Chinhua 109 29 9N 119 41 E
Ch'inhuangtao 107 39 57N 119 40 E
Chining, Inner Mongolia, China 106 41 2N 113 8 E
Chining, Shantung, China 106 35 19N 116 36 E
Chiniot 94 31 45N 73 0 E
Chinipas 164 27 22N 108 32W
Chinju 107 35 12N 128 2 E
Chink'ou 109 30 20N 114 7 E
Chinle 161 36 14N 109 38W
Chinmen 109 24 27N 118 21 E
Chinmen Tao, I. 109 24 25N 118 25 E
Chinnamanur 97 9 50N 77 16 E
Chinnampo 107 38 52N 125 28 E
Chinning 108 24 40N 102 35 E
Chinnur 96 18 57N 79 43 E
Chino, Japan 111 35 59N 138 9 E
Chino, U.S.A. 163 34 1N 117 41W
Chino Valley 161 34 54N 112 28W
Chinon 42 47 10N 0 15 E
Chinook, Can. 153 51 28N 110 59W
Chinook, U.S.A. 160 48 35N 109 19W
Chinp'ing, Kweichow, China 108 26 40N 109 7 E
Chinp'ing, Yunnan, China 108 22 46N 103 15 E
Chinsali 124 10 30S 32 2 E
Chinsha 108 27 29N 106 15 E
Chinsha Chiang, R. = Yangtze Chiang, R. 108 27 30N 99 30 E
Chinshan 109 30 3N 121 13 E
Ch'inshui 106 35 41N 112 11 E
Chintamani 97 13 26N 78 3 E
Chint'an 109 31 45N 119 35 E
Chint'ang 108 30 51N 104 27 E
Chinwangtao = Ch'inhuangtao 107 39 57N 119 40 E
Ch'inyang 106 35 5N 112 55 E
Ch'inyüan 106 36 31N 112 15 E
Chióggia 63 45 13N 12 15 E
Chíos = Khíos 69 38 27N 26 9 E
Chip Lake 152 53 35N 115 35W
Chipai L. 150 52 56N 87 53W
Chipata (Ft . Jameson) 127 13 38S 32 28 E
Chipewyan L. 153 58 0N 98 27W
Chipinga 127 20 13S 32 36 E
Chipiona 57 36 44N 6 26W
Chipley 157 30 45N 85 32W
Chiplun 96 17 31N 73 34 E
Chipman 151 46 6N 65 53W
Chipoka 127 13 57S 34 28 E
Chiporovtsi 66 43 24N 22 52 E
Chippenham 28 51 27N 2 7W
Chippewa Falls 158 44 55N 91 22W
Chippewa, R. 158 44 45N 91 55W
Chipping Campden 28 52 4N 1 48W
Chipping Norton 28 51 56N 1 32W
Chipping Ongar 29 51 43N 0 15 E
Chipping Sodbury 28 51 31N 2 23W
Chiquian 174 10 10S 77 0W
Chiquimula 166 14 51N 89 37W
Chiquinquirá 174 5 37N 73 50W
Chir, R. 83 48 45N 42 10 E
Chirala 97 15 50N 80 20 E
Chiramba 127 16 55S 34 39 E
Chiran 110 31 22N 130 27 E
Chiras 93 35 14N 65 40 E
Chirawa 94 28 14N 75 42 E
Chirayinkil 97 8 41N 76 49 E
Chirbury 28 52 35N 3 6W
Chirchik 85 41 29N 69 35 E
Chirfa 117 20 55N 12 14 E
Chiricahua Pk. 161 31 53N 109 14W
Chirikof I. 147 55 50N 155 40W
Chiriquí, Golfo de 166 8 0N 82 10W
Chiriquí, Lago de 166 9 10N 82 0W
Chiriquí, Vol. 166 8 55N 82 35W
Chirivira Falls 127 21 10S 32 12 E
Chirk 31 52 57N 3 4W
Chirmiri 99 23 15N 82 20 E
Chirnogi 70 44 7N 26 32 E
Chirnside 35 55 47N 2 11W
Chiromo 125 16 30S 35 7 E
Chirpan 67 42 10N 25 19 E
Chirripó Grande, cerro 166 9 29N 83 29W
Chisamba 127 14 55S 28 20 E
Chisapani Garhi 99 27 30N 84 2 E
Ch'ishan 106 34 28N 107 35 E
Chishan 106 35 36N 110 59 E
Ch'ishan 109 22 44N 120 31 E
Chishmy 84 54 35N 55 23 E
Chisholm 152 54 55N 114 10W
Chishou 108 28 12N 109 43 E
Chishui 109 27 14N 115 10 E
Chisimba Falls 127 10 12S 30 56 E
Chisineu Criş 66 46 32N 21 37 E
Chisledon 28 51 30N 1 44W
Chisone, R. 62 45 0N 7 5 E
Chisos Mts. 159 29 20N 103 15W
Chistian Mandi 94 29 50N 72 55 E
Chistopol 81 55 25N 50 38 E
Chita, Colomb. 174 6 11N 72 28W
Chita, U.S.S.R. 77 52 0N 113 25 E
Chitado 125 17 10S 14 8 E
Ch'it'ai 105 44 1N 89 28 E
Chitapur 96 17 10N 76 50 E
Chitembo 125 13 30S 16 50 E
Chitina 147 61 30N 144 30W
Chitinghsilin 105 32 51N 92 28 E
Chitipa 127 9 41S 33 19 E
Chitokoloki 125 13 43S 23 4 E
Chitorgarh 94 24 52N 74 43 E
Chitrakot 96 19 20N 81 40 E
Chitral 93 35 50N 71 56 E
Chitravati, R. 97 14 30N 78 0 E
Chitré 167 7 59N 80 27W
Chitse 106 36 54N 114 52 E
Chittagong 98 22 19N 91 55 E
Chittagong □ 98 24 5N 91 25 E
Chittoor 97 13 15N 79 5 E
Chittur 97 10 40N 76 45 E
Chitu 123 8 38N 37 58 E
Ch'itung, Hunan, China 109 26 47N 112 7 E
Ch'itung, Kiangsu, China 109 31 49N 121 40 E
Chiuant'u 107 42 33N 128 19 E
Chiuchaohua 108 32 20N 105 45 E
Chiuch'engch'i 108 27 10N 108 42 E
Chiuchiang, Kiangsi, China 109 29 43N 115 55 E
Chiuchiang, Kwangtung, China 109 22 50N 112 50 E
Chiuch'uan 105 39 46N 98 34 E
Chiuhsiangch'eng 109 33 13N 114 50 E
Chiukuanch'eng 106 35 50N 115 22 E
Chiuling Shan 109 28 50N 114 20 E
Chiuliuch'eng 108 24 32N 109 15 E
Chiulung 108 28 59N 101 32 E
Ch'iungchou Haihsia 100 20 10N 110 15 E
Ch'iunghai 100 19 15N 110 26 E
Chiunglai 108 30 25N 103 30 E
Chiunglai Shan 108 31 20N 102 50 E
Ch'iungshan 100 19 51N 110 26 E
Chiuningkang 109 26 48N 114 6 E
Ch'iupei 108 24 3N 104 12 E
Chiushench'iu 106 33 10N 115 8 E
Chiushengch'i 108 27 31N 109 12 E
Chiusi 63 43 1N 11 58 E
Chiut'ai 107 44 10N 125 49 E
Chiutaosha 106 35 39N 103 45 E
Chiuwuch'ing 106 39 23N 116 53 E
Chiva 59 39 27N 0 41W
Chivasso 62 45 10N 7 52 E
Chivilcoy 172 35 0S 60 0W
Chiwanda 127 11 23S 34 55 E
Chiwefwe 127 13 37S 29 31 E
Chiyang 107 37 0N 117 13 E
Ch'iyang 109 20 35N 111 52 E
Chiyüan 106 35 5N 112 39 E
Chiyün 109 28 35N 120 2 E
Chizera 127 13 10S 25 0 E
Chkalov = Orenburg 78 52 0N 55 5 E
Chkolovsk 81 56 50N 43 10 E
Chlumec 52 50 9N 15 29 E
Chmielnik 54 50 37N 20 43 E
Cho Bo 100 20 46N 105 10 E
Cho Do 107 38 30N 124 40 E
Cho Phuoc 101 10 26N 107 18 E
Choba 126 2 30N 38 5 E
Chobe National Park 128 21 30S 25 0 E
Chobe, R. 128 18 10S 24 10 E
Chobol 121 11 53N 13 1 E
Chochiwŏn 107 36 37N 127 18 E
Chocianów 54 51 35N 15 33 E
Chociwel 54 53 29N 15 21 E
Chocó □ 174 6 0N 77 0W
Chocontá 174 5 9N 73 41W
Chodaków 54 52 16N 20 18 E
Chodavaram 96 17 40N 82 50 E
Chodecz 54 52 56N 19 2 E
Chodziez 54 52 58N 17 0 E
Choele Choel 176 39 11S 65 40W
Chōfu 111 35 39N 139 33 E
Chohsien 106 39 30N 116 0 E
Choiseul I. 130 7 0S 156 40 E
Choisy-le-Roi 43 48 45N 2 24 E
Choix 164 26 40N 108 10W
Chojna 54 52 58N 14 25 E
Chojnice 54 53 42N 17 40 E
Chojnów 54 51 25N 15 58 E
Choke Mts. 123 11 18N 37 15 E
Chokurdakh 77 70 38N 147 55 E
Cholame 163 35 44N 120 18W
Cholet 42 47 4N 0 52W
Chollerton 35 55 4N 2 7W
Cholpon-Ata 85 42 40N 77 6 E
Cholsey 28 51 34N 1 10W
Cholu 106 40 19N 115 5 E
Choluteca 166 13 20N 87 14W
Choluteca, R. 166 13 5N 87 20W
Chom Bung 100 13 37N 99 36 E
Chom Thong 100 18 25N 98 41 E
Choma 127 16 48S 26 59 E
Chomen Swamp 123 9 20N 37 10 E

Chomu Clee Hills

Chomu 94 27 15N 75 40 E
Chomutov 52 50 28N 13 23 E
Chon Buri 100 13 22N 100 59 E
Chon Thanh 101 11 24N 106 36 E
Chŏnan 107 36 48N 127 9 E
Chonburi 101 13 21N 101 1 E
Chone 174 0 40 S 80 0W
Chong Kai 100 13 57N 103 35 E
Chong Mek 100 15 10N 105 27 E
Chŏngdo 107 35 38N 128 42 E
Chŏngha 107 36 12N 129 21 E
Chŏngjin 107 41 47N 129 50 E
Chŏngju 107 39 40N 125 5 E
Chŏngułp 107 35 35N 126 50 E
Chŏnju 107 35 50N 127 4 E
Chonos, Arch. de los 176 45 0 S 75 0W
Chopda 96 21 20N 75 15 E
Chopim, R. 173 25 35 S 53 5W
Choptank, R. 162 38 41N 76 0W
Chorbat La 95 34 42N 76 37 E
Chorley 32 53 39N 2 39W
Chormet el Melah 119 30 11N 16 29 E
Chorolque, Cerro 172 20 59 S 66 5W
Choroszcz 54 53 10N 22 59 E
Chortkov 80 49 2N 25 46 E
Chorul Tso 95 32 30N 82 30 E
Chŏrwŏn 107 38 15N 127 10 E
Chorzele 54 53 15N 21 2 E
Chorzów 54 50 18N 19 0 E
Chos-Malal 172 37 15 S 70 5W
Chosan 107 40 50N 125 47 E
Choshi 111 35 45N 140 45 E
Choszczno 54 53 7N 15 25 E
Choteau 160 47 50N 112 10W
Chotila 94 22 30N 71 15 E
Chotzu 106 40 52N 112 33 E
Chou Shan 109 30 2N 122 6 E
Chouchih 106 34 8N 108 14 E
Chouch'ü 106 33 46N 104 18 E
Chouning 109 27 15N 119 13 E
Chouts'un 107 36 48N 117 52 E
Ch'ouyang 108 23 14N 104 35 E
Chowchilla 163 37 11N 120 12W
Chowkham 98 20 52N 97 28 E
Choybalsan 105 48 4N 114 30 E
Christchurch, N.Z. 143 43 33 S 172 47 E
Christchurch, U.K. 28 50 44N 1 47W
Christiana, S. Afr. 128 27 52 S 25 8 E
Christiana, U.S.A. 162 39 40N 75 40W
Christiansfeld 73 55 21N 9 29 E
Christiansö, I. 73 55 19N 15 12 E
Christiansted 147 17 45N 64 42W
Christie B. 153 62 32N 111 10W
Christina, R. 153 56 40N 111 3W
Christmas Cr. 136 18 53 S 125 55 E
Christmas Creek 136 18 29 S 125 23 E
Christmas I., Ind. Oc. 142 10 0 S 105 40 E
Christmas I., Pac. Oc. 131 1 58N 157 27W
Christopher L. 137 24 49 S 127 42 E
Chrudim 52 49 58N 15 43 E
Chrzanów 54 50 10N 19 21 E
Chtimba 127 10 35 S 34 13 E
Chu 85 43 36N 73 42 E
Ch'u Chiang, R. 108 30 2N 106 19 E
Chu Chua 152 51 22N 120 10W
Chu Lai 100 15 28N 108 45 E
Chu, R., U.S.S.R. 85 45 0N 67 44 E
Chu, R., Viet. 100 19 53N 105 45 E
Chuadanga 98 23 38N 88 51 E
Ch'üanchou, Fukien, China 109 24 56N 118 35 E
Ch'üanchou, Kwangsi-Chuang, China 109 25 59N 111 4 E
Chuangho 107 39 42N 123 0 E
Chüannan 109 24 50N 114 40 E
Chūbu □ 112 36 45N 137 30 E
Chubut, R. 176 43 0 S 70 0W
Chuch'eng 107 36 0N 119 16 E
Chuch'i 108 32 19N 109 52 E
Chuchi, Chekiang, China 109 29 43N 120 14 E
Chuchi, Honan, China 106 34 27N 115 39 E
Chuchi L. 152 55 12N 124 30W
Ch'uching 108 25 34N 103 45 E
Chuchou 109 27 50N 113 10 E
Chudleigh 30 50 35N 3 36W
Chudovo 80 59 10N 31 30 E
Chudskoye, Oz. 80 58 13N 27 30 E
Ch'üehshan 109 32 48N 114 1 E
Chugach Mts. 147 62 0N 146 0W
Chugiak 147 61 7N 149 10W
Chuginadak I. 147 52 50N 169 45W
Chūgoku □ 110 35 0N 133 0 E
Chūgoku-Sanchi 110 35 0N 133 0 E
Chuguyev 82 49 55N 36 45 E
Chugwater 158 41 48N 104 47W
Chuhai 109 22 17N 113 34 E
Chühsien 107 35 35N 118 49 E
Ch'uhsien, China 109 28 57N 118 58 E
Ch'uhsien, China 109 32 18N 118 18 E
Chuhsien 105 28 57N 118 58 E
Ch'ühsien 108 30 51N 107 1 E
Ch'uhsiung 108 25 2N 101 32 E
Chüjung 109 31 56N 119 10 E
Chukai 101 4 13N 103 25 E
Chukhloma 81 58 45N 42 40 E
Chūko 111 36 44N 139 27 E
Chukotskiy Khrebet 77 68 0N 175 0 E
Chukotskiy, Mys 77 66 10N 169 3 E
Chukotskoye More 77 68 0N 175 0W
Chula Vista 163 32 39N 117 8W
Chulak-Kurgan 85 43 46N 69 9 E
Chülu 106 37 13N 115 1 E
Chulucanas 174 5 0 S 80 0W
Chum Phae 100 16 32N 102 6 E
Chum Saeng 100 15 55N 100 15 E
Chumar 95 32 40N 78 35 E
Chumatien 109 33 0N 114 4 E
Chumbicha 172 29 0 S 66 10W
Chumerna 67 42 45N 25 55 E
Chumikan 77 54 40N 135 10 E
Chumphon 101 10 35N 99 14 E
Chumuare 127 14 31 S 31 50 E
Chumunjin 107 37 55N 127 44 E
Chunchŏn 107 37 58N 127 44 E
Chunga 127 15 0 S 26 2 E
Ch'ungan 109 27 45N 118 0 E
Ch'ungch'ing, Szechwan, China 108 29 30N 106 30 E
Ch'ungch'ing, Szechwan, China 108 30 27N 103 43 E
Chungch'üantzu 106 39 22N 102 42 E
Chunggang ŭp 107 41 48N 126 48 E
Chunghsiang 109 31 10N 112 35 E
Chunghsien 108 30 17N 108 4 E
Chunghwa 107 38 52N 125 47 E
Ch'ungi 109 25 42N 114 19 E
Ch'ungjen 109 27 44N 116 2 E
Chungju 107 36 58N 127 58 E
Chungkang 107 43 42N 127 37 E
Chungking = Ch'ungch'ing 108 29 30N 106 30 E
Ch'ungli 106 40 5N 115 12 E
Chungli 109 24 57N 121 13 E
Ch'ungming 109 31 27N 121 24 E
Ch'ungming Tao, I. 109 31 35N 121 40 E
Chungmu 107 34 50N 128 20 E
Chungning 106 35 22N 105 40 E
Chungshan, Kwangsi-Chuang, China 109 24 30N 111 17 E
Chungshan, Kwangtung, China 109 22 31N 113 20 E
Ch'ungshuiho 106 39 54N 111 34 E
Ch'ungte 109 30 32N 120 26 E
Chungt'iaoshan 106 35 0N 111 30 E
Chungtien 108 27 51N 99 42 E
Ch'ungtso 108 22 20N 107 20 E
Chungtu 108 24 41N 109 42 E
Chungwei 106 37 35N 105 10 E
Chungyang 106 37 24N 111 10 E
Chungyang Shanmo 109 23 10N 121 0 E
Chungyüan 100 19 9N 110 28 E
Chünhsien 109 32 40N 111 15 E
Chunian 94 31 10N 74 0 E
Chunya 127 8 30 S 33 27 E
Chunya □ 126 7 48 S 33 0 E
Ch'unyang 107 43 42N 129 26 E
Chuquibamba 174 15 47N 72 44W
Chuquicamata 172 22 15 S 69 0W
Chuquisaca □ 172 23 30 S 63 30W
Chur 51 46 52N 9 32 E
Churachandpur 98 24 20N 93 40 E
Church Hill 38 55 0N 7 53W
Church House 152 50 20N 125 10W
Church Stretton 28 52 32N 2 49W
Churchdown 28 51 53N 2 9W
Churchill 153 58 47N 94 11W
Churchill, C. 153 58 46N 93 12W
Churchill Falls 151 53 36N 64 19W
Churchill L. 153 55 55N 108 20W
Churchill Pk. 152 58 10N 125 10W
Churchill, R., Man., Can. 153 58 47N 94 12W
Churchill, R., Newf., Can. 151 53 19N 60 10W
Churchill, R., Sask., Can. 153 58 47N 94 12W
Churchtown 39 52 12N 6 20W
Churfisten 51 47 8N 9 17 E
Churston Ferrers 30 50 23N 3 32W
Churu 94 28 20N 75 0 E
Churuguaro 174 10 49N 69 32W
Churwalden 51 46 47N 9 33 E
Chusan 109 32 13N 110 24 E
Chushul 95 33 40N 78 40 E
Chusovaya, R. 84 58 18N 56 22 E
Chusovoy 84 58 15N 57 40 E
Chust 85 41 0N 71 13 E
Ch'ützu 106 36 24N 107 27 E
Chuuronjang 107 41 35N 129 40 E
Chuvash A.S.S.R.□ 81 55 30N 48 0 E
Chuwassu 108 28 48N 97 27 E
Ch'üwu 106 35 35N 111 23 E
Ch'üyang 106 38 37N 114 41 E
Chüyeh 106 35 23N 116 6 E
Ciacova 66 45 35N 21 10 E
Cicero 156 41 48N 87 48W
Cicero Dantas 170 10 36 S 38 23W
Cidacos, R. 58 42 15N 2 10W
Cide 82 41 40N 32 50 E
Ciechanów 54 52 52N 20 38 E
Ciechanów □ 54 53 0N 20 30 E
Ciechocinek 54 52 53N 18 45 E
Ciego de Avila 166 21 50N 78 50W
Ciénaga 174 11 1N 74 15W
Ciénaga de Oro 174 8 53N 75 37W
Cienfuegos 166 22 10N 80 30W
Cieplice Slaskie Zdrój 54 50 50N 15 40 E
Cierp 44 42 55N 0 40 E
Cíes, Islas 56 42 12N 8 55W
Cieszyn 54 49 45N 18 35 E
Cieza 59 38 17N 1 23W
Cifuentes 58 40 47N 2 37W
Ciha Pa. 101 22 20N 103 47 E
Cijara, Pantano de 57 39 18N 4 52W
Cijulang 103 7 42 S 108 27 E
Cikampek 103 6 23 S 107 28 E
Cilacap 103 7 43 S 109 0 E
Cıldır 83 41 10N 43 20 E
Cilgerran 31 52 4N 4 39W
Cilician Gates P. 92 37 20N 34 52 E
Cilician Taurus 92 36 40N 34 0 E
Cilnicu 70 44 54N 23 4 E
Cimarron, Kans., U.S.A. 159 37 50N 100 20W
Cimarron, N. Mex., U.S.A. 159 36 30N 104 52W
Cimarron, R. 159 37 10N 102 10W
Cîmpia Turzii 70 46 34N 23 53 E
Cîmpina 70 45 10N 25 45 E
Cîmpulung, Argeş, Rumania 70 45 17N 25 3 E
Cîmpulung, Suceava, Rumania 70 47 32N 25 30 E
Cîmpuri 67 46 0N 26 50 E
Cinca, R. 58 42 20N 0 9 E
Cincer 66 43 55N 17 5 E
Cinch, R. 157 36 0N 84 15W
Cincinnati 156 39 10N 84 26W
Cincinnatus 162 42 33N 75 54W
Cinderford 28 51 49N 2 30W
Cîndeşti 70 45 15N 26 42 E
Ciney 47 50 18N 5 5 E
Cinigiano 63 42 53N 11 23 E
Cinogli 63 43 23N 13 10 E
Cinto, Mt. 45 42 24N 8 54 E
Cioranii 70 44 45N 26 25 E
Çiotat, La 45 43 12N 5 36 E
Čiovo 63 43 30N 16 17 E
Cipó 171 11 6 S 38 31W
Circle, Alaska, U.S.A. 147 65 50N 144 10W
Circle, Montana, U.S.A. 158 47 26N 105 35W
Circleville, Ohio, U.S.A. 156 39 35N 82 57W
Circleville, Utah, U.S.A. 161 38 12N 112 24W
Cirebon 103 6 45 S 108 32 E
Cirencester 28 51 43N 1 59W
Cireşu 70 44 47N 22 31 E
Cirey-sur-Vezouze 43 48 35N 6 57 E
Ciriè 62 45 14N 7 35 E
Cirò 65 39 23N 17 3 E
Cisco 159 32 25N 99 0W
Cislău 70 45 14N 26 33 E
Cisna 54 49 12N 22 20 E
Cisneros 174 6 33N 75 4W
Cisnădie 70 45 42N 24 9 E
Cisterna di Latina 64 41 35N 12 50 E
Cisternino 65 40 45N 17 26 E
Cité de Cansado 116 20 51N 17 0W
Citega (Kitega) 126 3 30 S 29 58 E
Citeli-Ckaro 83 41 33N 46 0 E
Citlaltépetl, mt. 165 19 0N 97 20W
Citrusdal 128 32 35 S 19 0 E
Città della Pieve 63 42 57N 12 0 E
Città di Castello 63 43 27N 12 14 E
Città Sant' Angelo 63 42 32N 14 5 E
Cittadella 63 45 39N 11 48 E
Cittaducale 63 42 24N 12 58 E
Cittanova 65 38 22N 16 0 E
Ciucaş, mt. 70 45 31N 25 56 E
Ciudad Acuña 164 29 20N 101 10W
Ciudad Altamirano 164 18 20N 100 40W
Ciudad Bolívar 174 8 5N 63 30W
Ciudad Camargo 164 27 41N 105 10W
Ciudad de Valles 165 22 0N 98 30W
Ciudad del Carmen 165 18 20N 97 50W
Ciudad Delicias = Delicias 164 28 10N 105 30W
Ciudad Guerrero 164 28 33N 107 28W
Ciudad Guzmán 164 19 40N 103 30W
Ciudad Juárez 164 31 40N 106 28W
Ciudad Madero 165 22 19N 97 50W
Ciudad Mante 165 22 50N 99 0W
Ciudad Obregón 164 27 28N 109 59W
Ciudad Piar 174 7 27N 63 19W
Ciudad Real 57 38 59N 3 55W
Ciudad Real □ 57 38 50N 4 0W
Ciudad Rodrigo 56 40 35N 6 32W
Ciudad Trujillo = Sto. Domingo 167 18 30N 70 0W
Ciudad Victoria 165 23 41N 99 9W
Ciudadela 58 40 0N 3 50 E
Ciulniţa 70 44 26N 27 22 E
Civa, B. 82 41 20N 36 40 E
Cividale del Friuli 63 46 6N 13 25 E
Civita Castellana 63 42 18N 12 24 E
Civitanova Marche 63 43 18N 13 41 E
Civitavécchia 63 42 6N 11 46 E
Civitella del Tronto 63 42 48N 13 40 E
Civray 44 46 10N 0 17 E
Çivril 92 38 20N 29 55 E
Cixerri, R. 64 39 45N 8 40 E
Cizre 92 37 19N 42 10 E
Clabach 34 56 38N 6 36W
Clabby 38 54 24N 7 22W
Clach Leathad 34 56 36N 7 52W
Clachan, N. Uist., U.K. 36 57 33N 7 20W
Clachan, Strathclyde, U.K. 34 55 45N 5 35W
Clackline 137 31 40 S 116 32 E
Clackmannan 35 56 10N 3 50W
Clackmannan (□) 26 56 10N 3 47W
Clacton-on-Sea 29 51 47N 1 10 E
Cladich 34 56 21N 5 5W
Claire, L. 152 58 35N 112 5W
Clairemont 159 33 9N 100 44W
Clairvaux-les-Laes 45 46 35N 5 45 E
Clamecy 43 47 28N 3 30 E
Clane 39 53 18N 6 40W
Clanfield 29 50 56N 1 0W
Clanton 157 32 48N 86 36W
Clanwilliam 128 32 11 S 18 52 E
Clar, L. nan 37 58 17N 4 8W
Clara 39 53 20N 7 38W
Clara, R. 138 19 8 S 142 30 E
Claraville 163 35 24N 118 20W
Clare, N.S.W., Austral. 140 33 24 S 143 54 E
Clare, S. Austral., Austral. 140 33 50 S 138 37 E
Clare, N. Ireland, U.K. 38 54 25N 6 19W
Clare, Suffolk, U.K. 29 52 5N 0 36 E
Clare, U.S.A. 156 43 47N 84 45W
Clare □ 39 52 20N 7 38W
Clare I. 38 53 48N 10 0W
Clare, R. 38 53 20N 9 0W
Clarecastle 39 52 50N 8 58W
Clareen 39 53 4N 7 49W
Claregalaway 39 53 20N 8 57W
Claremont 162 43 23N 72 20W
Claremont Pt. 138 14 1 S 143 41 E
Claremore 159 36 20N 95 20W
Claremorris 38 53 45N 9 0W
Clarence I. 13 61 30 S 53 50W
Clarence, I. 176 54 0 S 72 0W
Clarence, R., Austral. 139 29 25 S 153 22 E
Clarence, R., N.Z. 143 42 10 S 173 56 E
Clarence Str., Austral. 136 12 0 S 131 0 E
Clarence Str., U.S.A. 152 55 40N 132 10W
Clarence Town 167 23 6N 74 59W
Clarendon, Ark., U.S.A. 159 34 41N 91 20W
Clarendon, Tex., U.S.A. 159 34 58N 100 54W
Clarenville 151 48 10N 54 1W
Claresholm 152 50 0N 113 45W
Clarie Coast 13 67 0 S 135 0 E
Clarinbridge 39 53 13N 8 55W
Clarinda 158 40 45N 95 0W
Clarion 158 42 41N 93 46W
Clark 158 44 55N 97 45W
Clark Fork 160 48 9N 116 9W
Clark Fork, R. 160 48 0N 115 40W
Clark Hill Res. 157 33 45N 82 20W
Clarkdale 161 34 53N 112 3W
Clarke City 151 50 12N 66 38W
Clarke, I. 138 40 32 S 148 10 E
Clarke L. 153 54 24N 106 54W
Clarke Ra. 138 20 45 S 148 20 E
Clarks Fork, R. 160 45 0N 109 30W
Clark's Harbour 151 43 25N 65 38W
Clarks Station 163 38 8N 116 42W
Clarks Summit 162 41 31N 75 44W
Clarksburg 156 39 18N 80 21W
Clarksdale 159 34 12N 90 33W
Clarkston 160 46 28N 117 2W
Clarksville, Ark., U.S.A. 159 35 29N 93 27W
Clarksville, Tenn., U.S.A. 157 36 32N 87 20W
Clarksville, Tex., U.S.A. 159 33 37N 94 59W
Claro, R. 171 19 8 S 50 40W
Clashmore 37 57 53N 4 8W
Clatskanie 160 46 9N 123 12W
Clatteringshaws L. 34 55 3N 4 17W
Claude 159 35 8N 101 22W
Claudio 171 20 26 S 44 46W
Claudy 38 54 55N 7 10W
Claunie L. 36 57 8N 5 6W
Claveria 103 18 37N 121 15 E
Claverley 28 52 32N 2 19W
Clay 163 38 17N 121 10W
Clay Center 158 39 27N 97 9W
Clay Cross 33 53 11N 1 26W
Clay Hd. 32 54 13N 4 23W
Claydon 29 52 6N 1 7 E
Clayette, La 45 46 17N 4 19 E
Claymont 162 39 48N 75 28W
Claymore, oilfield 19 58 30N 0 15W
Claypool 161 33 27N 110 55W
Clayton, Idaho, U.S.A. 160 44 12N 114 31W
Clayton, N. Mex., U.S.A. 159 36 30N 103 10W
Cle Elum 160 47 15N 120 57W
Cleady 39 51 53N 9 32W
Clear C. 39 51 26N 9 30W
Clear I. 39 51 26N 9 30W
Clear Lake, Calif., U.S.A. 160 39 5N 122 47W
Clear Lake, S.D., U.S.A. 158 44 48N 96 41W
Clear Lake, Wash., U.S.A. 160 48 27N 122 15W
Clear Lake Res. 160 41 55N 121 10W
Clearfield, Pa., U.S.A. 156 41 0N 78 27W
Clearfield, Utah, U.S.A. 160 41 10N 112 0W
Clearmont 160 44 43N 106 29W
Clearwater, Can. 152 51 38N 120 2W
Clearwater, U.S.A. 157 27 58N 82 45W
Clearwater Cr. 152 61 36N 125 30W
Clearwater L. 150 56 10N 75 0W
Clearwater, Mts. 160 46 20N 115 30W
Clearwater Prov. Park 153 54 0N 101 0W
Clearwater, R., Alta., Can. 152 52 22N 114 57W
Clearwater, R., Alta., Can. 153 56 44N 111 23W
Clearwater, R., B.C., Can. 152 51 38N 120 3W
Cleat 37 58 45N 2 56W
Cleator Moor 32 54 30N 3 32W
Cleburne 159 32 18N 97 25W
Cleddau R. 31 51 46N 4 44W
Clee Hills 23 52 26N 2 35W

Cleethorpes **Columbia**

Cleethorpes **33** 53 33N 0 2W
Cleeve Cloud **28** 51 56N 2 0W
Cleggan **38** 53 33N 10 7W
Clelles **45** 44 50N 5 38E
Clemency **47** 49 35N 5 53E
Clent **28** 52 25N 2 6W
Cleobury Mortimer **28** 52 23N 2 28W
Clerke Reef **136** 17 22S 119 20E
Clerks Rocks **13** 56 0S 36 30W
Clermont **133** 22 49S 147 39E
Clermont-en-Argonne **43** 49 5N 5 4E
Clermont-Ferrand **44** 45 46N 3 4E
Clermont-l'Hérault **44** 43 38N 3 26E
Clerval **43** 47 25N 6 30E
Cléry-Saint-André **43** 47 50N 1 46E
Cles **62** 46 21N 11 4E
Clevedon **28** 51 26N 2 52W
Cleveland, Austral. **139** 27 30S 153 15E
Cleveland, Miss., U.S.A. **159** 33 43N 90 43W
Cleveland, Ohio, U.S.A. **156** 41 28N 81 43W
Cleveland, Okla., U.S.A. **159** 36 21N 96 33W
Cleveland, Tenn., U.S.A. **157** 35 9N 84 52W
Cleveland, Tex., U.S.A. **159** 30 18N 95 0W
Cleveland □ **33** 54 35N 1 8E
Cleveland, C. **138** 19 11S 147 1E
Cleveland Hills **33** 54 25N 1 11W
Clevelândia **173** 26 24S 52 23W
Clevvaux **47** 50 4N 6 2E
Clew Bay **38** 53 54N 9 50W
Clewiston **157** 26 44N 80 50W
Cley **29** 52 57N 1 3E
Clifden, Ireland **38** 53 30N 10 2W
Clifden, N.Z. **143** 46 1S 167 42E
Clifden B. **38** 53 29N 10 5W
Cliff **161** 33 0N 108 44W
Cliffe **29** 51 27N 0 31E
Cliffony **38** 54 25N 8 28W
Clifford **28** 52 6N 3 6W
Clift Sound **36** 60 4N 1 17W
Clifton, Austral. **139** 27 59S 151 53E
Clifton, Ariz., U.S.A. **161** 33 8N 109 23W
Clifton, Tex., U.S.A. **159** 31 46N 97 35W
Clifton Forge **156** 37 49N 79 51W
Climax **153** 49 10N 108 20W
Clingmans Dome **157** 35 35N 83 30W
Clint **161** 31 37N 106 11W
Clinton, B.C., Can. **152** 51 6N 121 35W
Clinton, Ont., Can. **150** 43 37N 81 32W
Clinton, N.Z. **143** 46 12S 169 23E
Clinton, Ark., U.S.A. **159** 35 37N 92 30W
Clinton, Conn., U.S.A. **162** 41 17N 72 32W
Clinton, Ill., U.S.A. **158** 40 8N 89 0W
Clinton, Ind., U.S.A. **156** 39 40N 87 22W
Clinton, Iowa, U.S.A. **158** 41 50N 90 12W
Clinton, Mass., U.S.A. **162** 42 26N 71 40W
Clinton, Mo., U.S.A. **158** 38 20N 93 46W
Clinton, N.C., U.S.A. **157** 35 5N 78 15W
Clinton, Okla., U.S.A. **159** 35 30N 99 0W
Clinton, S.C., U.S.A. **157** 34 30N 81 54W
Clinton, Tenn., U.S.A. **157** 36 6N 84 10W
Clinton C. **138** 22 30S 150 45E
Clinton Colden L. **148** 64 58N 107 27W
Clintonville **158** 44 35N 88 46W
Clipperton, I. **143** 10 18N 109 13W
Clipston **29** 52 26N 0 58W
Clisson **42** 47 5N 1 16W
Clitheroe **32** 53 52N 2 23W
Clive **142** 39 36S 176 58E
Clive L. **152** 63 13N 118 54W
Cloates, Pt. **136** 22 43S 113 40E
Clocolan **129** 28 55S 27 34E
Clodomira **172** 27 35S 64 14W
Clogh **39** 52 51N 7 11W
Cloghan, Donegal, Ireland **38** 54 50N 7 56W
Cloghan, Offaly, Ireland **39** 53 13N 7 53W
Cloghan, W'meath, Ireland **38** 53 33N 7 15W
Clogheen **39** 52 17N 8 0W
Clogher **38** 54 25N 7 10W
Clogher Hd. **38** 53 48N 6 15W
Cloghjordan **39** 52 57N 8 2W
Cloghran **38** 53 26N 6 14W
Clonakilty **39** 51 37N 8 53W
Clonakilty B. **39** 51 33N 8 50W
Clonbur **38** 53 32N 9 21W
Cloncurry, Austral. **138** 20 40S 140 28E
Cloncurry, Ireland **38** 53 26N 6 47W
Cloncurry, R. **138** 18 37S 140 40E
Clondalkin **39** 53 20N 6 25W
Clonee **38** 53 25N 6 28W
Cloneen **39** 52 28N 7 36W
Clones **38** 54 10N 7 13W
Clonkeen **39** 51 59N 9 20W
Clonmany **38** 55 16N 7 24W
Clonmel **39** 52 22N 7 42W
Clonmore **39** 52 49N 6 35W
Clonroche **39** 52 27N 6 42W
Clontarf **38** 53 22N 6 10W
Cloonakool **38** 54 6N 8 47W
Cloone **38** 53 57N 7 47W
Cloonfad **38** 53 41N 8 45W
Cloppenburg **48** 52 50N 8 3E
Cloquet **158** 46 40N 92 30W
Clorinda **172** 25 16S 57 45W
Closeburn **35** 55 13N 3 45W
Cloud Peak **160** 44 30N 107 10W
Cloudcroft **161** 33 0N 105 48W
Cloudy B. **143** 41 25S 174 10E
Clough, Ballymena, U.K. **38** 54 58N 6 16W
Clough, Down, U.K. **38** 54 18N 5 50W
Cloughton **33** 54 20N 0 27W
Clova **37** 56 50N 3 4W
Clovelly **30** 51 0N 4 25W
Cloverdale **160** 38 49N 123 0W
Clovis, Calif., U.S.A. **163** 36 54N 119 45W
Clovis, N. Mex., U.S.A. **159** 34 20N 103 10W
Clowne **33** 53 18N 1 16W
Cloyne **39** 51 52N 8 7W
Club Terrace **141** 37 35S 148 58E
Cluj-Napoca **70** 46 47N 23 38E
Cluj □ **70** 46 45N 23 30E
Clun **28** 52 26N 3 2W
Clun Forest **28** 52 27N 3 7W
Clunbury **28** 52 25N 2 55W
Clunes, Austral. **140** 37 20S 143 45E
Clunes, U.K. **36** 56 57N 4 58W
Cluny **45** 46 26N 4 38E
Cluses **45** 46 5N 6 35E
Clusone **62** 45 54N 9 58E
Clutha, R. **143** 46 20S 169 49E
Clwyd □ **31** 53 5N 3 20W
Clwyd, R. **31** 53 12N 3 30W
Clwydian Ra. **31** 53 10N 3 15W
Clydach **31** 51 42N 3 54W
Clyde, Austral. **139** 28 48S 143 40E.
Clyde, Can. **149** 70 30N 68 30W
Clyde, N.Z. **143** 45 12S 169 20E
Clyde, Firth of **34** 55 20N 5 0W
Clyde, R. **34** 55 46N 4 58W
Clydebank **34** 55 54N 4 25W
Clydesdale **35** 55 42N 3 50W
Clynnog-fawr **31** 53 2N 4 22W
Côa, R. **56** 40 45N 7 0W
Coachella **163** 33 44N 116 13W
Coachella Canal **163** 32 43N 114 57W
Coachford **39** 51 54N 8 48W
Coachman's Cove **151** 50 6N 56 20W
Coagh **38** 54 39N 6 37W
Coahoma **159** 32 17N 101 20W
Coahuayana, R. **164** 18 41N 103 45W
Coahuayutla **164** 18 19N 101 42W
Coahuila □ **164** 27 0N 112 30W
Coal Creek Flat **143** 45 27S 169 19E
Coal I. **143** 46 8S 166 40E
Coal, R. **152** 59 39N 126 57W
Coalane **127** 17 48S 37 2E
Coalbrookdale **28** 52 38N 2 30W
Coalburn **35** 55 35N 3 55W
Coalcomán **164** 18 40N 103 10W
Coaldale, Can. **152** 49 45N 112 35W
Coaldale, U.S.A. **163** 38 2N 117 55W
Coaldale, Pa., U.S.A. **162** 40 50N 75 54W
Coalgate **159** 34 35N 96 13W
Coalinga **163** 36 10N 120 21W
Coalisland **38** 54 33N 6 42W
Coalspur **152** 53 15N 117 0W
Coalville, U.K. **28** 52 43N 1 21W
Coalville, U.S.A. **160** 40 58N 111 24W
Coamo **147** 18 5N 66 22W
Coaraci **171** 14 38S 39 32W
Coari **174** 4 8S 63 7W
Coast □ **126** 2 40S 39 45E
Coast Mts. **152** 52 0N 126 0W
Coast Range **163** 40 0N 124 0W
Coastal Plains Basin **137** 30 10S 115 30E
Coatbridge **35** 55 52N 4 2W
Coatepec **165** 19 27N 96 58W
Coatepeque **166** 14 46N 91 55W
Coatesville **162** 39 59N 75 30W
Coaticook **151** 45 10N 71 46W
Coats I. **149** 62 30N 83 0W
Coats Land **13** 77 0S 25 0W
Coatzacoalcos **165** 18 7N 94 35W
Cobadin **70** 44 5N 28 13E
Cobalt **150** 47 25N 79 42W
Cobán **166** 15 30N 90 21W
Cobar **141** 31 27S 145 48E
Cobb I. **162** 37 17N 75 42W
Cobbannah **141** 37 37S 147 12E
Cobberas, Mt. **141** 36 53S 148 12E
Cobden **140** 38 20S 143 3E
Cóbh **39** 51 50N 8 18W
Cobija **174** 11 0S 68 50W
Cobourg **150** 43 58N 78 10W
Cobourg Pen. **136** 11 20S 132 15E
Cobram **141** 35 54S 145 40E
Cobre **160** 41 6N 114 25W
Cóbué **125** 12 0S 34 58E
Coburg **49** 50 15N 10 58E
Coca **56** 41 13N 4 32W
Coca, R. **174** 0 25S 77 5W
Cocal **170** 3 28S 41 34W
Cocanada = Kakinada **96** 16 55N 82 20E
Cocentaina **59** 38 45N 0 27W
Cocha, La **172** 27 50S 65 40W
Cochabamba **174** 17 15S 66 20W
Coche, I. **174** 10 47N 63 56W
Cochem **49** 50 8N 7 7E
Cochemane **127** 17 0S 32 54E
Cochilha Grande de Albardão **173** 28 30S 51 30W
Cochin **97** 9 55N 76 22E
Cochin China **101** 10 30N 106 0E
Cochin China = Nam-Phan **101** 10 30N 106 0E
Cochise **161** 32 6N 109 58W
Cochran **157** 32 25N 83 23W
Cochrane, Alta., Can. **152** 51 11N 114 30W
Cochrane, Ont., Can. **150** 49 0N 81 0W
Cochrane, L. **176** 47 10S 72 0W
Cochrane, R. **153** 57 53N 101 34W
Cockatoo I. **136** 16 6S 123 37E
Cockburn **140** 32 5S 141 0E
Cockburn, Canal **176** 54 30S 72 0W
Cockburn, C. **136** 11 20S 132 52E
Cockburn I. **150** 45 55N 83 22W
Cockburn Ra. **136** 15 46S 128 0E
Cockburnspath **35** 55 56N 2 23W
Cockenzie **35** 55 58N 2 59W
Cockerham **32** 53 58N 2 49W
Cockermouth **32** 54 40N 3 22W
Cockeysville **162** 39 29N 76 39W
Cockfield **29** 52 8N 0 47E
Cocklebiddy **137** 32 0S 126 3E
Coco Chan. **101** 13 50N 93 25E
Coco Is. **101** 14 0N 93 12E
Coco, Pta. **174** 2 58N 77 43W
Coco, R. (Wanks) **166** 14 10N 85 0W
Cocoa **157** 28 22N 80 40W
Cocobeach **124** 0 59N 9 34E
Cocoli, R. **120** 12 0N 14 0W
Cocora **70** 44 45N 27 3E
Côcos **171** 14 10S 44 33W
Cocos (Keeling) Is. **11** 12 12S 96 54E
Côcos, R. **171** 12 44S 44 48W
Cod, C. **162** 42 8N 70 10W
Cod, gasfield **19** 57 8N 2 35E
Codajás **174** 3 40S 62 0W
Coddenham **29** 52 8N 1 8E
Codera, C. **174** 10 35N 66 4W
Coderre **153** 50 11N 106 31W
Codigoro **63** 44 50N 12 5E
Codó **170** 4 30S 43 55W
Codogno **62** 45 10N 9 42E
Codróipo **63** 45 57N 13 0E
Codru, Munţii **70** 46 30N 22 15E
Cods Hd. **39** 51 40N 10 7W
Cody **160** 44 35N 109 0W
Coe Hill **150** 44 52N 77 50W
Coelemu **172** 36 30S 72 48W
Coelho Neto **170** 4 15S 43 0W
Coen **138** 13 52S 143 12E
Coesfeld **48** 51 56N 7 10E
Coeur d'Alene **160** 47 45N 116 51W
Coevorden **46** 52 40N 6 44E
Coffeyville **159** 37 0N 95 40W
Coffin B. Pen. **136** 34 20S 135 10E
Coffs Harbour **141** 30 16S 153 5E
Cofre de Perote, Cerro **165** 19 30N 97 10W
Cofrentes **59** 39 13N 1 5W
Cogealac **70** 44 36N 28 36E
Coggeshall **29** 51 53N 0 41E
Coghinas, R. **64** 40 55N 8 48E
Cognac **44** 45 41N 0 20W
Cogne **62** 45 37N 7 21E
Cogolludo **58** 40 59N 3 10W
Cohagen **160** 47 2N 106 45W
Cohoes **162** 42 47N 73 42W
Cohuna **140** 35 45S 144 15E
Coiba I. **166** 7 30N 81 40W
Coig, R. **176** 51 0S 70 20W
Coigach, dist. **36** 58 0N 5 10W
Coillore **36** 57 21N 6 23W
Coimbatore **97** 11 2N 76 59E
Coimbra **56** 40 15N 8 27W
Coimbra □ **56** 40 12N 8 25W
Coin **57** 36 40N 4 48W
Cojedes □ **174** 9 20N 68 20W
Cojimies **174** 0 20N 80 0W
Cojocna **70** 46 45N 23 50E
Cojutepequé **166** 13 41N 88 54W
Čoka **66** 45 57N 20 12E
Cokeville **160** 42 4N 111 0W
Col di Tenda **62** 44 7N 7 36E
Colaba Pt. **96** 18 54N 72 47E
Colac **140** 38 21S 143 35E
Colachel **97** 8 10N 77 15E
Colares **57** 38 48N 9 30W
Colatina **171** 19 32S 40 37W
Colbinabbin **141** 36 38S 144 48E
Colby, U.K. **32** 54 6N 4 42W
Colby, U.S.A. **158** 39 27N 101 2W
Colchagua □ **172** 34 30S 71 0W
Colchester **29** 51 54N 0 55E
Cold Fell **32** 54 54N 2 40W
Coldingham **35** 55 53N 2 10W
Coldstream **35** 55 39N 2 14W
Coldwater **159** 37 18N 99 24W
Coldwell **150** 48 45N 86 30W
Colebrook **138** 42 31S 147 12E
Colebrooke **30** 50 45N 3 44W
Coleford **28** 51 46N 2 38W
Coleman, Can. **152** 49 40N 114 30W
Coleman, U.S.A. **159** 31 52N 99 30W
Coleman, R. **138** 15 6S 141 38E
Colenso **129** 28 44S 29 50E
Coleraine, Austral. **140** 37 36S 141 40E
Coleraine, U.K. **38** 55 8N 6 40E
Coleraine □ **38** 55 8N 6 40E
Coleridge, L. **143** 43 17S 171 30E
Coleroon, R. **97** 11 0N 79 0E
Colesberg **128** 30 45S 25 5E
Coleshill **28** 52 30N 1 42W
Coleville **163** 38 44N 119 30W
Colfax, La., U.S.A. **159** 31 35N 92 39W
Colfax, Wash., U.S.A. **160** 46 57N 117 28W
Colgrave Sd. **36** 60 35N 1 0W
Colhué Huapi, L. **176** 45 30S 69 0W
Cólico **62** 46 8N 9 22E
Coligny **128** 46 24N 5 21E
Colima **164** 19 10N 103 40W
Colima □ **164** 19 10N 103 40W
Colima, Nevado de **164** 19 30N 103 40W
Colina **172** 33 13S 70 45W
Colina do Norte **120** 12 28N 15 0W
Colinas, Goiás, Brazil **171** 14 15S 48 2W
Colinas, Maranhão, Brazil **170** 6 0S 44 10W
Colinton, Austral. **141** 35 50S 149 10E
Colinton, U.K. **35** 55 54N 3 17W
Coll, I. **34** 56 40N 6 35W
Collaguasi **172** 21 5S 68 45W
Collarada, Peña **58** 42 43N 0 29W
Collarenebri **139** 29 33S 148 36E
Collbran **161** 39 16N 107 58W
Colle Salvetti **62** 43 34N 10 27E
Colle Sannita **65** 41 22N 14 48E
Colléchio **62** 44 23N 10 10E
Colleen Bawn **127** 21 0S 29 12E
College Park, Ga., U.S.A. **157** 33 42N 84 27W
College Park, Md., U.S.A. **162** 39 0N 76 55W
Collette **151** 46 40N 65 30W
Collie, N.S.W., Austral. **141** 31 41S 148 18E
Collie, W. Austral., Austral. **137** 33 22S 116 8E
Collier B. **136** 16 10S 124 15E
Collier Law Pk. **32** 54 47N 1 59W
Collier Ra. **137** 24 45S 119 10E
Collin **35** 55 4N 3 30W
Colline Metallifere **62** 43 10N 11 0E
Collingbourne **28** 51 16N 1 39W
Collingswood **162** 39 55N 75 4W
Collingwood, Austral. **138** 22 20S 142 31E
Collingwood, Can. **150** 44 29N 80 13W
Collingwood, N.Z. **143** 40 25S 172 40E
Collingwood B. **138** 9 30S 149 30E
Collins **150** 50 17N 89 27W
Collinsville **138** 20 30S 147 56E
Collipulli **172** 37 55S 72 30W
Collison Ra. **136** 14 49S 127 25E
Collo **119** 36 58N 6 37E
Collon **38** 53 46N 6 29W
Collonges **45** 46 9N 5 52E
Collooney **38** 54 11N 8 28W
Colmar **43** 48 5N 7 20E
Colmars **45** 44 11N 6 39E
Colmenar **57** 36 54N 4 20W
Colmenar de Oreja **58** 40 6N 3 25W
Colmenar Viejo **56** 40 39N 3 47W
Colmor **159** 36 18N 104 36W
Colne **32** 53 51N 2 11W
Colne, R., Essex, U.K. **29** 51 55N 0 50E
Colne, R., Herts., U.K. **29** 51 36N 0 30W
Colnett, Cabo **164** 31 0N 116 20W
Colo, R. **141** 33 25S 150 52E
Cologna Véneta **63** 45 19N 11 21E
Colomb-Béchar = Béchar **118** 31 38N 2 18E
Colombey-les-Belles **43** 48 32N 5 54E
Colombey-les-deux Églises **43** 48 20N 4 50E
Colômbia **171** 20 10S 48 40W
Colombia **174** 3 24N 79 49W
Colombia ■ **174** 3 45N 73 0W
Colombier **50** 46 58N 6 53E
Colombo **97** 6 56N 79 58E
Colombus, Kans., U.S.A. **159** 37 15N 94 30W
Colombus, Nebr., U.S.A. **158** 41 30N 97 25W
Colombus, N.Mex., U.S.A. **161** 31 54N 107 43W
Colome **158** 43 20N 99 44W
Colón, Argent. **172** 32 12S 58 30W
Colón, Cuba **166** 22 42N 80 54W
Colón, Panama **166** 9 20N 80 0W
Colonel Hill **167** 22 50N 74 21W
Colonella **63** 42 52N 13 50E
Colonia del Sacramento **173** 34 25S 57 50W
Colonia Dora **172** 28 34S 62 59W
Colonia Las Heras **176** 46 30S 69 0W
Colonia Sarmiento **176** 45 30S 68 15W
Colonial Hts. **162** 37 15N 77 25W
Colonne, C. delle **65** 39 2N 17 11E
Colonsay **153** 51 59N 105 52W
Colonsay, I. **34** 56 4N 6 12W
Colorado □ **154** 37 40N 106 0W
Colorado Aqueduct **161** 34 17N 114 10W
Colorado City **159** 32 25N 100 50W
Colorado Desert **154** 34 20N 116 0W
Colorado Plateau **161** 36 40N 110 30W
Colorado, R., Argent. **172** 37 30S 69 0W
Colorado, R., Ariz., U.S.A. **161** 33 30N 114 30W
Colorado, R., Calif., U.S.A. **161** 34 0N 114 33W
Colorado, R., Tex., U.S.A. **159** 29 40N 96 30W
Colorado Springs **158** 38 55N 104 50W
Colorno **62** 44 55N 10 21E
Colossal **141** 30 52S 147 3E
Colotepec **165** 15 47N 97 3W
Colotlán **164** 22 6N 103 16W
Colpy **37** 57 23N 2 35W
Colsterworth **29** 52 48N 0 37W
Coltishall **29** 52 44N 1 21E
Colton, Calif., U.S.A. **163** 34 4N 117 20W
Colton, Wash., U.S.A. **160** 46 41N 117 6W
Columbia, La., U.S.A. **159** 32 7N 92 5W
Columbia, Miss., U.S.A. **158** 31 16N 89 50W
Columbia, Mo., U.S.A. **158** 38 58N 92 20W
Columbia, Pa., U.S.A. **162** 40 2N 76 30W
Columbia, S.C., U.S.A. **157** 34 0N 81 0W

Columbia Coroaci

Columbia, Tenn., U.S.A. 157 35 40N 87 0W
Columbia, C. 12 83 0N 70 0W
Columbia City 156 41 8N 85 30W
Columbia, District of □ 156 38 55N 77 0W
Columbia Falls 160 48 25N 114 16W
Columbia Heights 158 45 5N 93 10W
Columbia, Mt. 152 52 8N 117 20W
Columbia Basin 160 47 30N 118 30W
Columbia, R. 160 45 49N 120 0W
Columbretes, Is. 58 39 50N 0 50 E
Columbus, Ga., U.S.A. 157 32 30N 84 58W
Columbus, Ind., U.S.A. 156 39 14N 85 55W
Columbus, Miss., U.S.A. 157 33 30N 88 26W
Columbus, Mont., U.S.A. 160 45 45N 109 14W
Columbus, N.D., U.S.A. 158 48 52N 102 48W
Columbus, Ohio, U.S.A. 156 39 57N 83 1W
Columbus, Tex., U.S.A. 159 29 42N 96 33W
Columbus, Wis., U.S.A. 158 43 20N 89 2W
Colunda 125 12 7 S 23 36 E
Colunga 56 43 29N 5 16W
Colusa 160 39 15N 122 1W
Colville 160 48 33N 117 54W
Colville, C. 142 36 29 S 175 21 E
Colville, R. 147 69 15N 152 0W
Colwell 35 55 4N 2 4W
Colwich 28 52 48N 1 58W
Colwyn 31 53 17N 3 43W
Colwyn Bay 31 53 17N 3 44W
Colyton 30 50 44N 3 4W
Comácchio 63 44 41N 12 10 E
Comalcalco 165 18 16N 93 13W
Comallo 176 41 0 S 70 5W
Comana 70 44 10N 26 10 E
Comanche, Okla., U.S.A. 159 34 27N 97 58W
Comanche, Tex., U.S.A. 159 31 55N 98 35W
Comăneşti 70 46 25N 26 26 E
Comayagua 166 14 25N 87 37W
Combahee, R. 157 32 45N 80 50W
Combara 141 31 10 S 148 22 E
Combe Martin 30 51 12N 4 2W
Combeaufontaine 43 47 38N 5 54 E
Comber 38 54 33N 5 45W
Combermere Bay 98 19 37N 93 34 E
Comblain 47 50 29N 5 35 E
Combles 43 50 0N 2 50 E
Combourg 42 48 25N 1 46W
Comboyne 141 31 34 S 152 34 E
Combronde 44 45 58N 3 5 E
Comeragh Mts. 39 52 17N 7 35W
Comercinho 171 16 19 S 41 47W
Comet 138 23 36 S 148 38 E
Comet Vale 137 29 55 S 121 4 E
Comilla 98 23 28N 91 10 E
Comines 47 50 46N 3 0 E
Comino, C. 64 40 28N 9 47 E
Cómiso 65 36 57N 14 35 E
Comitán 165 16 18N 92 9W
Commentry 44 46 20N 2 46 E
Commerce, Ga., U.S.A. 157 34 10N 83 25W
Commerce, Tex., U.S.A. 159 33 15N 95 50W
Commercy 43 48 40N 5 34 E
Committee B. 149 68 30N 86 30W
Commonwealth B. 13 67 0 S 144 0 E
Commoron Cr., R. 139 28 22 S 150 8 E
Communism Pk. = Kommunizma, Pk. 93 38 40N 72 20 E
Como 62 45 48N 9 5 E
Como, L. di 62 46 5N 9 17 E
Comodoro Rivadavia 176 45 50 S 67 40W
Comores, Arch. des 11 10 0 S 50 0 E
Comores, Is. 11 12 10 S 44 15 E
Comorin, C. 97 8 3N 77 40 E
Comorişte 70 45 10N 21 35 E
Comoro Is. 11 12 10 S 44 15 E
Comox 152 49 42N 124 55W
Compiègne 43 49 24N 2 50 E
Compíglia Maríttima 62 43 4N 10 37 E
Comporta 57 38 22N 8 46W
Compostela 164 21 15N 104 53W
Comprida, I. 173 24 50 S 47 42W
Compton, U.K. 28 51 2N 1 19W
Compton, U.S.A. 163 33 54N 118 13W
Compton Downs 139 30 28 S 146 30 E
Comrie 35 56 22N 4 0W
Con Cuong 100 19 2N 104 54 E
Côn Dao 101 8 45N 106 45 E
Con Son, Is. 101 8 41N 106 37 E
Conakry 120 9 29N 13 49W
Conara Junction 138 41 50 S 147 26 E
Conargo 141 35 16 S 145 10 E
Conatlán 164 24 30N 104 42W
Concarneau 42 47 52N 3 56W
Conceiçáo, Brazil 170 7 33 S 38 31W
Conceiçáo, Mozam. 127 18 47 S 36 7 E
Conceiçáo da Barra 171 18 35 S 39 45W
Conceiçáo do Araguaia 170 8 0 S 49 2W
Conceiçáo do Canindé 170 7 54 S 41 34W
Conceiçáo do Mato Dentro 171 19 1 S 43 25W
Concepcián 165 18 15N 90 5W
Concepción, Argent. 172 27 20 S 65 35W
Concepción, Boliv. 174 15 50 S 61 40W
Concepción, Chile 172 36 50 S 73 0W
Concepción, Colomb. 174 0 5N 75 37W
Concepción, Parag. 172 23 30 S 57 20W
Concepción, Venez. 174 10 48N 71 46W
Concepción □ 172 37 0 S 72 30W
Concepcion, C. 154 34 30N 120 34W
Concepción del Oro 164 24 40N 101 30W
Concepción del Uruguay 172 32 35 S 58 20W
Concepción, L. 174 17 20 S 61 10W
Concepción, La = Ri-Aba 121 3 28N 84 0 E
Concepción, Punta 164 26 55N 111 50W
Concepción, R. 164 30 32N 113 2W
Conception B. 128 23 55 S 14 22 E
Conception I. 167 23 52N 75 9W
Conception, Pt. 163 34 27N 120 28W
Concession 127 17 27 S 30 56 E
Conchas Dam 159 35 25N 104 10W
Conche 151 50 48N 55 58W
Conches-en-Ouche 50 48 58N 0 58 E
Concho 161 34 32N 109 43W
Concho, R. 159 31 30N 100 8W
Conchos, R., Chihnahua, Mexico 164 29 20N 105 0W
Conchos, R., Tamaulipas, Mexico 165 25 0N 97 32W
Concon 172 32 56 S 71 33W
Concord, Calif., U.S.A. 163 37 59N 122 2W
Concord, N.C., U.S.A. 157 35 28N 80 35W
Concord, N.H., U.S.A. 162 43 12N 71 30W
Concórdia, Argent. 172 31 20 S 58 2W
Concórdia, Brazil 174 4 36 S 66 36W
Concordia, Colomb. 174 2 39N 72 47W
Concordia, Mexico 164 23 18N 106 2W
Concordia, U.S.A. 158 39 35N 97 40W
Concordia, La 165 16 8N 92 38W
Concots 44 44 26N 1 40 E
Concrete 160 48 35N 121 49W
Condah 140 37 57 S 141 44 E
Condamine, R. 133 27 7 S 149 48 E
Condat 44 45 21N 2 46 E
Conde 171 11 49 S 37 37W
Condé 43 50 26N 3 34 E
Conde 158 45 13N 98 5W
Condé-sur-Noireau 42 48 51N 0 33W
Condeúba 171 15 0 S 42 0W
Condobolin 141 33 4 S 147 6 E
Condom 44 43 57N 0 22 E
Condon 160 45 15N 120 8W
Condove 62 45 8N 7 19 E
Condover 28 52 39N 2 46W
Conegliano 63 45 53N 12 18 E
Conejera, I. 59 39 11N 2 58 E
Conejos 164 26 14N 103 53W
Conflans-en-Jarnisy 43 49 10N 5 52 E
Confolens 44 46 2N 0 40 E
Confuso, R. 172 24 10 S 59 0W
Congleton 32 53 10N 2 12W
Congo 170 7 48 S 36 40W
Congo ■ 124 1 0 S 16 0 E
Congo Basin 114 0 10 S 24 30 E
Congo, Democratic Rep. of = Zaïre ■ 124 3 0 S 22 0 E
Congo (Kinshasa) ■ = Zaïre ■ 124 1 0 S 16 0 E
Congo, R. = Zaïre, R. 124 1 30N 28 0 E
Congonhas 173 20 30 S 43 52W
Congresbury 28 51 20N 2 49W
Congress 161 34 11N 112 56W
Congucu 113 31 25 S 52 30W
Conil 57 36 17N 6 10W
Coningsby 33 53 7N 0 9W
Conisbrough 33 53 29N 1 12W
Coniston, Can. 150 46 29N 80 51W
Coniston, U.K. 32 54 22N 3 6W
Coniston Water 32 54 20N 3 5W
Conjeevaram = Kancheepuram 97 12 52N 79 45 E
Conjuboy 138 18 35 S 144 45 E
Conklin 153 55 38N 111 5W
Conlea 139 30 7 S 144 35 E
Conn, L. 38 54 3N 9 15W
Conna 39 52 5N 8 8W
Connacht 38 53 23N 8 40W
Connah's Quay 31 53 13N 3 6W
Conneaut 156 41 55N 80 32W
Connecticut □ 162 41 40N 72 40W
Connecticut, R. 162 41 17N 72 21W
Connel 34 56 27N 5 24W
Connel Park 34 55 22N 4 15W
Connell 160 46 45N 118 58W
Connemara 38 53 29N 9 45W
Conner, La 160 48 22N 122 27W
Connersville 156 39 40N 85 10W
Connonagh 39 51 35N 9 8W
Connor, Mt. 136 14 34 S 126 4 E
Connors Ra. 138 21 40 S 149 10 E
Conoble 141 32 55 S 144 42 E
Cononaco, R. 174 1 20 S 76 30W
Conquest 153 51 32N 107 14W
Conquet, Le 42 48 21N 4 46W
Conrad 160 48 11N 112 0W
Conran, C. 141 37 49 S 148 44 E
Conroe 159 30 15N 95 28W
Conselheiro Lafaiete 173 20 40 S 43 48W
Conselheiro Pena 171 19 10 S 41 30W
Consett 32 54 52N 1 50W
Conshohocken 162 40 5N 75 18W
Consort 153 52 1N 110 46W
Constance = Konstanz 49 47 39N 9 10 E
Constance, L. = Bodensee 51 47 35N 9 25 E
Constanța 70 44 14N 28 38 E
Constanța □ 70 44 15N 28 15 E
Constantia 162 43 15N 76 1W
Constantina 57 37 51N 5 40W
Constantine 119 36 25N 6 42 E
Constitución, Chile 172 35 20 S 72 30W
Constitución, Uruguay 172 31 0 S 58 10W
Consuegra 57 39 28N 3 43W
Consul 153 49 20N 109 30W
Contact 160 41 50N 114 56W
Contai 95 21 54N 87 55 E
Contamana 174 7 10 S 74 55W
Contarina 63 45 2N 12 13 E
Contas, R. 171 13 5 S 41 53W
Contes 45 43 49N 7 19 E
Conthey 50 46 14N 7 28 E
Contin 37 57 34N 4 35W
Contoocook 162 43 13N 71 45W
Contra Costa 129 25 9 S 33 30 E
Contres 43 47 24N 1 26 E
Contrexéville 43 48 6N 5 53 E
Convención 174 8 28N 73 21W
Conversano 65 40 57N 17 8 E
Convoy 38 54 52N 7 40W
Conway, Ark., U.S.A. 159 35 5N 92 30W
Conway, N.H., U.S.A. 162 43 58N 71 8W
Conway, S.C., U.S.A. 157 33 49N 79 2W
Conway = Conwy 31 53 17N 3 50W
Conway, L. 139 28 17 S 135 35 E
Conwy 31 53 17N 3 50W
Conwy Bay 31 53 17N 3 57W
Conwy, R. 31 53 18N 3 50W
Coober Pedy 136 29 1 S 134 43 E
Coobina 137 23 22 S 120 10 E
Cooch Behar 98 26 22N 89 29 E
Cook, Austral. 137 30 37 S 130 25 E
Cook, U.S.A. 158 47 49N 92 39W
Cook, Bahía 176 55 10 S 70 0W
Cook Inlet 147 59 0N 151 0W
Cook Is. 131 20 0 S 160 0W
Cook, Mount 143 43 36 S 170 9 E
Cook Strait 143 41 15 S 174 29 E
Cooke Plains 140 35 23 S 139 34 E
Cookeville 157 36 12N 85 30W
Cookham 29 51 33N 0 42W
Cookhouse 128 32 44 S 25 47 E
Cookstown 38 54 40N 6 43W
Cookstown □ 38 54 40N 6 43W
Cooktown 138 15 30 S 145 16 E
Coolabah 141 31 1 S 146 43 E
Cooladdi 139 26 37 S 145 23 E
Coolah 141 31 48 S 149 41 E
Coolamon 141 34 46 S 147 8 E
Coolaney 38 54 10N 8 36W
Coolangatta 139 28 11 S 153 29 E
Coole 38 53 42N 7 23W
Coolgardie 137 30 55 S 121 8 E
Coolgreany 39 52 46N 6 14W
Coolibah 136 15 33 S 130 56 E
Coolidge 161 33 1N 111 35W
Coolidge Dam 161 33 10N 110 30W
Coolmore 38 54 33N 8 12W
Cooma 141 36 12 S 149 8 E
Coomacarrea Mts. 39 51 59N 10 0W
Coonabarabran 141 31 14 S 149 18 E
Coonalpyn 140 35 43 S 139 52 E
Coonamble 141 30 56 S 148 27 E
Coonana 137 31 0 S 123 0 E
Coondapoor 97 13 42N 74 40 E
Coongie 139 27 9 S 140 8 E
Coongoola 139 27 43 S 145 47 E
Cooninie, L. 139 26 4 S 139 59 E
Coonoor 97 11 10N 76 45 E
Cooper 159 33 20N 95 40W
Cooper Cr. 139 28 29 S 137 46 E
Cooper, R. 157 33 0N 79 55W
Coopersburg 162 40 31N 75 23W
Cooperstown, N.D., U.S.A. 158 47 30N 98 14W
Cooperstown, New York, U.S.A. 162 42 42N 74 57W
Coorabie P.O. 137 31 54 S 132 18 E
Coorabulka 138 23 41 S 140 20 E
Coorong, The 133 35 50 S 139 20 E
Coorow 137 29 53 S 116 2 E
Cooroy 139 26 22 S 152 54 E
Coos Bay 160 43 26N 124 7W
Cootamundra 141 34 36 S 148 1 E
Cootehill 38 54 5N 7 5W
Cooyar 139 26 59 S 151 51 E
Cooyeana 138 24 29 S 138 45 E
Copahué, Paso 172 37 49 S 71 8W
Copainalá 165 17 8N 93 11W
Copake Falls 162 42 7N 73 31W
Copán 166 14 50N 89 9W
Cope 158 39 44N 102 50W
Cope, Cabo 59 37 26N 1 28W
Cope Cope 140 36 27 S 143 5 E
Copeland I. 38 54 38N 5 33W
Copenhagen 162 43 54N 75 41W
Copenhagen = København 73 55 41N 12 34 E
Copertino 65 40 17N 18 2W
Copeville 140 34 47 S 139 51 E
Copiapó 172 27 15 S 70 20 E
Copiapó, R. 172 27 19 S 70 56W
Copinsay I. 37 58 54N 2 40W
Coplay 162 40 44N 75 29W
Copley 140 30 24 S 138 26 E
Copp L. 152 60 14N 114 40W
Copparo 63 44 52N 11 49 E
Copper Center 147 62 10N 145 25W
Copper Cliff 150 46 28N 81 4W
Copper Harbor 156 47 31N 87 55W
Copper Mountain 152 49 20N 120 30W
Copper Queen 127 17 29 S 29 18 E
Copper R. 147 61 30N 144 30W
Copperbelt □ 127 13 15N 27 30 E
Copperfield 137 29 1 S 120 26 E
Coppermine 148 67 50N 115 5W
Coppermine, R. 148 67 49N 115 4W
Copperopolis 163 37 58N 120 38W
Cöppingen 49 48 42N 9 40 E
Copythorne 28 50 56N 1 34W
Coquet, I. 35 55 21N 1 30W
Coquet, R. 35 55 18N 1 45W
Coquilhatville = Mbandaka 124 0 1N 18 18 E
Coquille 160 43 15N 124 6W
Coquimbo 172 30 0 S 71 20W
Coquimbo □ 172 31 0 S 71 0W
Cora, oilfield 19 55 45N 4 45 E
Corabia 70 43 48N 24 30 E
Coraçáo de Jesus 171 11 39 S 39 56W
Coracora 174 15 5 S 73 45W
Coradi, Is. 65 40 27N 71 10 E
Coral Harbour 149 64 8N 83 10W
Coral Rapids 150 50 20N 81 40W
Coral Sea 142 15 0 S 150 0 E
Coral Sea Islands Terr. 133 20 0 S 155 0 E
Corato 65 41 12N 16 22 E
Corbeil-Essonnes 43 48 36N 2 26 E
Corbie 43 49 54N 2 30 E
Corbières, mts. 44 42 55N 2 35 E
Corbigny 43 47 16N 3 40 E
Corbin 156 37 0N 84 3W
Corbion 47 49 48N 5 0 E
Corbones, R. 57 37 25N 5 35W
Corbridge 35 54 58N 2 0W
Corby, Lincs., U.K. 29 52 49N 0 31W
Corby, Northants., U.K. 29 52 29N 0 41W
Corcoles, R. 59 39 12N 2 40W
Corcoran 163 36 6N 119 35W
Corcubión 56 42 56N 9 12W
Cord. de Caravaya 174 14 0 S 70 30W
Cordele 157 31 55N 83 49W
Cordell 159 35 18N 99 0W
Cordenons 63 45 59N 12 42 E
Cordes 44 44 5N 1 57 E
Cordillera Oriental 174 5 0N 74 0W
Cordisburgo 171 19 7 S 44 21W
Córdoba 172 31 20 S 64 10W
Córdoba 164 26 20N 103 20W
Córdoba, Mexico 165 18 50N 97 0W
Córdoba, Spain 57 37 50N 4 50W
Córdoba □, Argent. 172 31 22 S 64 15W
Córdoba □, Colomb. 174 8 20N 75 40W
Córdoba □, Spain 57 38 5N 5 0W
Córdoba, Sierra de 172 31 10 S 64 25W
Cordon 103 16 42N 121 32 E
Cordova, Ala., U.S.A. 157 33 45N 87 12W
Cordova, Alaska, U.S.A. 147 60 36N 145 45W
Corella 58 42 7N 1 48W
Corella, R. 138 19 34 S 140 47 E
Coremas 170 7 1 S 37 58W
Corfe Castle 28 50 58N 2 3W
Corfe Mullen 28 50 45N 2 0W
Corfield 138 21 40 S 143 21 E
Corfu = Kerkira 68 39 38N 19 50 E
Corgo 56 42 56N 7 25W
Cori 64 41 39N 12 53 E
Coria 56 40 0N 6 33W
Coricudgy, Mt. 141 32 51 S 150 24 E
Corigliano Cálabro 65 39 36N 16 31 E
Coringa Is. 138 16 58 S 149 58 E
Corinna 138 41 35 S 145 10 E
Corinth, Miss., U.S.A. 157 34 54N 88 30W
Corinth, N.Y., U.S.A. 162 43 15N 73 50W
Corinth = Korinthos 69 37 56N 22 55 E
Corinth Canal 69 37 48N 23 0 E
Corinth, G. of = Korinthiakós 69 38 16N 22 30 E
Corinto, Brazil 171 18 20 S 44 30W
Corinto, Nic. 166 12 30N 87 10W
Corj □ 70 45 5N 23 25 E
Cork 39 51 54N 8 30W
Cork □ 39 51 50N 8 50W
Cork Harbour 39 51 46N 8 16W
Corlay 42 48 20N 3 5W
Corleone 64 37 48N 13 16 E
Corleto Perticara 65 40 23N 16 2 E
Çorlu 67 41 11N 27 49 E
Cormack L. 152 60 56N 121 37W
Cormóns 63 45 58N 13 29 E
Cormorant 153 54 14N 100 35W
Cormorant L. 153 54 15N 100 50W
Cormorant, oilfield 19 61 0N 1 10 E
Corn Hill, Mt. 38 53 48N 7 43W
Corn Is. 167 12 0N 83 0W
Cornelio 164 29 55N 111 8W
Cornélio Procópio 173 23 7 S 50 40W
Cornell 158 45 10N 91 8W
Corner Brook 151 48 57N 57 58W
Corner Inlet 133 38 45 S 146 20 E
Cornforth 33 54 42N 1 28W
Corniglio 62 44 29N 10 5 E
Corning, Ark., U.S.A. 159 36 27N 90 34W
Corning, Calif., U.S.A. 160 39 56N 122 9W
Corning, Iowa, U.S.A. 158 40 57N 94 40W
Corning, N.Y., U.S.A. 162 42 10N 77 3W
Cornwall, Austral. 138 41 33 S 148 7 E
Cornwall, Can. 150 45 2N 74 44W
Cornwall, U.S.A. 162 40 17N 76 25W
Cornwall □ 30 50 26N 4 40W
Cornwall, C. 30 50 8N 5 42W
Cornwallis I. 12 75 8N 95 0W
Corny Pt. 140 34 55 S 137 0 E
Coro 174 11 25N 69 41W
Coroaci 171 18 35 S 42 17W

Coroatá Crooksville

Coroatá 170 4 20S 44 0W
Corocoro 174 17 15S 69 19W
Corofin 39 53 27N 8 50W
Coroico 174 16 0S 67 50W
Coromandel, Brazil 171 18 28S 47 13W
Coromandel, N.Z. 142 36 45S 175 31E
Coromandel Coast 97 12 30N 81 0E
Coromandel Pen. 142 37 0S 175 45E
Coromandel Ra. 142 37 0S 175 40E
Coromorant, L. 153 54 20N 100 50W
Corona, Austral. 139 31 16S 141 24E
Corona, Calif., U.S.A. 163 33 49N 117 36W
Corona, N. Mex., U.S.A. 161 34 15N 105 32W
Coronada B. 166 9 0N 83 40W
Coronado 163 32 45N 117 9W
Coronado, Bahia de 166 9 0N 83 40W
Coronation 152 52 5N 111 27W
Coronation Gulf 148 68 25N 112 0W
Coronation I., Antarct. 13 60 45S 46 0W
Coronation I., U.S.A. 152 55 52N 134 20W
Coronation Is. 136 14 57S 124 55E
Coronda 172 31 58S 60 56W
Coronel 172 37 0S 73 10W
Coronel Bogado 172 27 11S 56 18W
Coronel Dorrego 172 38 40S 61 10W
Coronel Fabriciano 171 19 31S 42 38W
Coronel Murta 171 16 37S 42 11W
Coronel Oviedo 172 25 24S 56 30W
Coronel Pringles 172 38 0S 61 30W
Coronel Suárez 172 37 30S 62 0W
Coronel Vidal 172 37 28S 57 45W
Coronie 170 5 55N 56 25W
Corovoda 68 40 31N 20 14E
Corowa 141 35 58S 146 21E
Corozal, Belize 165 18 30N 88 30W
Corozal, Colomb. 174 9 19N 75 18W
Corpach 36 56 50N 5 9W
Corps 45 44 50N 5 56E
Corpus 173 27 10S 55 30W
Corpus Christi 159 27 50N 97 28W
Corpus Christi L. 159 28 5N 97 54W
Corque 174 18 10S 67 50W
Corral de Almaguer 58 39 45N 3 10W
Corran 36 56 44N 5 14W
Corrandibby Ra. 137 26 0S 115 20E
Corraun Pen. 38 53 58N 10 15W
Corrégio 62 44 46N 10 47E
Corrente 170 10 27S 45 10W
Corrente, R. 170 13 8S 43 28W
Correntes, C. das 129 24 6S 35 34E
Correntina 171 13 20S 44 39W
Corrèze □ 44 45 20N 1 45E
Corrib, L. 38 53 25N 9 10W
Corrie 34 55 39N 5 10W
Corrientes 172 27 30S 58 45W
Corrientes □ 172 28 0S 57 0W
Corrientes, C., Colomb. 174 5 30N 77 34W
Corrientes, C., Cuba 166 21 43N 84 30W
Corrientes, C., Mexico 164 20 25N 105 42W
Corrientes, R., Argent. 172 30 21S 59 33W
Corrientes, R., Colomb. 174 3 15S 75 58W
Corrigan 159 31 0N 94 48W
Corrigin 137 32 20S 117 53E
Corringham 33 53 25N 0 42W
Corris 31 52 41N 3 49W
Corrowidgie 141 36 56S 148 50E
Corry 156 41 55N 79 39W
Corryong 141 36 12S 147 53E
Corryvrecken, G. of 34 56 10N 5 44W
Corse, C. 45 43 1N 9 25E
Corse-du-Sud □ 45 41 45N 9 0E
Corse, I 45 42 0N 9 0E
Corsewall Pt. 34 55 0N 5 10W
Corsham 28 51 25N 2 11W
Corsica = Corse 45 42 0N 9 0E
Corsicana 159 32 5N 96 30W
Corsley 28 51 12N 2 14W
Corsock 35 55 54N 3 56W
Corté 45 42 19N 9 11E
Corte do Pinto 57 37 42N 7 29W
Cortegana 57 37 52N 6 49W
Cortez 161 37 24N 108 35W
Cortina d'Ampezzo 63 46 32N 12 9E
Cortland 162 42 35N 76 11W
Corton 29 52 31N 1 46E
Cortona 63 43 16N 12 0E
Coruche 57 38 57N 8 30W
Çorum 92 40 30N 35 5E
Corumbá, Goias, Brazil 171 16 0S 48 50W
Corumbá, Mato Grosso, Brazil 174 19 0S 57 30W
Corumbá R. 171 17 25S 48 30W
Corumbaíba 171 18 9S 48 34W
Coruña □ 56 43 0N 8 37E
Coruña, La 56 43 20N 8 25W
Coruña, La □ 56 43 10N 8 30W
Corund 70 46 30N 25 13E
Corunna = La Coruña 56 43 20N 8 25W
Coruripe 171 10 5S 36 10W
Corvallis 160 44 36N 123 15W
Corve, R. 28 52 22N 2 43W
Corvette, L. de la 150 53 25N 73 55W
Corwen 31 52 59N 3 23W
Corydon 158 40 42N 93 22W
Cosalá 164 24 28N 106 40W
Cosamaloapán 165 18 23N 95 50W
Coseley 28 52 33N 2 6W
Cosenza 65 39 17N 16 14E
Coşereni 70 44 38N 26 35E
Cosham 28 50 51N 1 3W
Coshocton 156 40 17N 81 51W
Cosne-s.-Loire 43 47 24N 2 54E
Coso Junction 163 36 3N 117 57W
Coso Pk. 163 36 13N 117 44W
Cospeito 56 43 12N 7 34W
Cosquín 172 31 15S 64 30W
Cossato 62 45 34N 8 10E
Cossé-le-Vivien 42 47 57N 0 54W
Costa Azul 50 43 25N 6 50E
Costa Blanca 59 38 25N 0 10W
Costa Brava 58 41 30N 3 0E
Costa del Sol 57 36 30N 4 30W
Costa Dorada 58 40 45N 1 15E
Costa Mesa 163 33 39N 117 55W
Costa Rica 164 31 20N 112 40W
Costa Rica ■ 166 10 0N 84 0W
Costa Smeralda 64 41 5N 9 35E
Costelloe 39 53 20N 9 33W
Costessey 29 52 40N 1 11E
Costigliole d'Asti 62 44 48N 8 11E
Costilla 161 37 0N 105 30W
Coştiui 70 47 53N 24 2E
Cosumnes, R. 163 38 14N 121 25W
Coswig 48 51 52N 12 31E
Cotabato 103 7 14N 124 15E
Cotabena 140 31 42S 138 11E
Cotagaita 172 20 45S 65 30W
Côte d'Azur 45 43 25N 6 50E
Côte d'Or 43 47 10N 4 50E
Côte d'Or □ 43 47 30N 4 50E
Côte, La 50 46 25N 6 15E
Côte-St. André, La 45 45 24N 5 15E
Coteau des Prairies 158 44 30N 97 0W
Coteau du Missouri, Plat. du 154 47 0N 101 0W
Cotegipe 171 12 2S 44 15W
Cotentin 42 49 30N 1 30W
Côtes de Meuse 43 49 15N 5 22E
Côtes-du-Nord □ 42 48 25N 2 40W
Cotherstone 32 54 34N 1 59W
Cotiella 58 42 31N 0 19E
Cotina, R. 66 43 36N 19 9E
Cotonou 121 6 20N 2 25E
Cotopaxi, Vol. 174 0 30S 78 30W
Cotronei 65 39 9N 16 27E
Cotswold Hills 28 51 42N 2 10W
Cottage Grove 160 43 48N 123 2W
Cottbus 48 51 44N 14 20E
Cottbus □ 48 51 43N 13 30E
Cottenham 29 52 18N 0 8E
Cottingham 36 53 47N 0 23W
Cottonwood, Can. 152 53 5N 121 50W
Cottonwood, U.S.A. 161 34 48N 112 1W
Coubre, Pte. de la 44 45 42N 1 15W
Couches 43 46 53N 4 30E
Couço 57 38 59N 8 17W
Coudersport 156 41 45N 78 1W
Couedic, C. du 140 36 5S 136 40E
Couëron 42 47 13N 1 44W
Coueson, R. 42 48 20N 1 15W
Couhé-Vérac 44 46 18N 0 12E
Couillet 47 50 23N 4 28E
Coulags 36 57 26N 5 24W
Coulanges, Deux Sèvres, France 44 46 58N 0 35W
Coulanges, Yonne, France 43 47 30N 3 30E
Coulee City 160 47 44N 119 12W
Coulman I. 13 73 35S 170 0E
Coulommiers 43 48 50N 3 3E
Coulonge, R. 150 45 52N 76 46W
Coulport 34 56 3N 4 53W
Coulterville 163 37 42N 120 12W
Council 147 64 55N 163 45W
Council Bluffs 158 41 20N 95 50W
Council Grove 158 38 41N 96 30W
Coupar Angus 35 56 33N 3 17W
Courantyne, R. 174 5 0N 57 45W
Courçon 44 46 15N 0 50W
Cours 45 46 7N 4 19E
Courseulles 42 49 20N 0 29W
Court-St.-Etienne 47 50 38N 4 34E
Courtenay 152 49 45N 125 0W
Courtine, La 44 45 43N 2 16E
Courtland 163 38 20N 121 34W
Courtmacsherry 39 51 38N 8 43W
Courtmacsherry B. 39 51 37N 8 37W
Courtown 39 52 39N 6 14W
Courtrai = Kortrijk 47 50 50N 3 17E
Courville 42 48 28N 1 15E
Coutances 42 49 3N 1 28W
Couterne 42 48 30N 0 25W
Coutras 44 45 3N 0 8W
Coutts 152 49 0N 111 57W
Couvet 50 46 57N 6 38E
Couvin 47 50 3N 4 29E
Covarrubias 58 42 4N 3 31W
Covasna 70 45 50N 26 10E
Covasna □ 70 45 50N 26 0E
Cove Bay 37 57 5N 2 5W
Coventry 28 52 25N 1 31W
Coventry L. 153 61 15N 106 15W
Cover R. 32 54 14N 1 45W
Coverack 30 50 2N 5 6W
Covilhã 56 40 17N 7 31W
Covina 163 34 5N 117 52W
Covington, Ga., U.S.A. 157 33 36N 83 50W
Covington, Ky., U.S.A. 156 39 5N 84 30W
Covington, Okla., U.S.A. 159 36 21N 97 36W
Covington, Tenn., U.S.A. 159 35 34N 89 39W
Cowal Creek Settlement 138 10 54S 142 20E
Cowal, dist. 34 56 5N 5 8W
Cowal, L. 141 33 40S 147 25E
Cowan 153 52 5N 100 45W
Cowan, L. 137 31 45S 121 45E
Cowan L. 153 54 0N 107 15W
Cowangie 140 35 12S 141 26E
Coward Springs 139 29 24S 136 48E
Cowarie 139 27 45S 138 15E
Cowarna 137 30 55S 122 40E
Cowbridge 31 51 28N 3 28W
Cowcowing Lakes 137 30 55S 117 20E
Cowdenbeath 35 56 7N 3 20W
Cowell 140 33 39S 136 56E
Cowes 28 50 45N 1 18W
Cowfold 29 50 58N 0 16W
Cowl Cowl 141 33 36S 145 18E
Cowley 28 51 43N 1 12W
Cowpen 35 55 8N 1 34W
Cowra 141 33 49S 148 42E
Coxim 175 18 30S 54 55W
Cox's Bazar 98 21 26N 91 59E
Cox's Cove 151 49 7N 58 5W
Coyame 164 29 28N 105 6W
Coylton 34 55 26N 4 31W
Coyuca de Benítez 165 17 1N 100 8W
Coyuca de Catalán 164 18 58N 100 41W
Cozad 158 40 55N 99 57W
Cozie, Alpi 62 44 50N 6 59E
Cozumel 165 20 31N 86 55W
Cozumel, Isla de 165 20 30N 86 40W
Craanford 39 52 40N 6 23W
Craboon 141 32 3S 149 30E
Cracow 139 25 17S 150 17E
Cradock 128 32 8S 25 36E
Craggie 37 57 25N 4 6W
Craig, Alaska, U.S.A. 147 55 30N 133 5W
Craig, Colo., U.S.A. 160 40 32N 107 44W
Craigavon = Portadown 38 54 27N 6 26W
Craigavon = Lurgan 38 54 28N 6 20W
Craigellachie 37 57 29N 3 9W
Craighouse 34 55 50N 5 58W
Craigmore 127 20 28S 32 30E
Craignish, L. 34 56 11N 5 32W
Craigtown 37 58 30N 3 53W
Crail 35 56 16N 2 38W
Crailsheim 49 49 7N 10 5E
Craiova 70 44 21N 23 48E
Cramlington 35 55 5N 1 36W
Crampel 117 7 8N 19 81E
Cramsie 138 23 20S 144 15E
Cranberry Portage 153 54 35N 101 23W
Cranborne 28 50 55N 1 55W
Cranborne Chase 29 50 56N 2 6W
Cranbrook, Tas., Austral. 138 42 0S 148 5E
Cranbrook, W. Austral., Austral. 137 34 18S 117 33E
Cranbrook, Can. 152 49 30N 115 46W
Cranbrook, U.K. 29 51 6N 0 33E
Crandon 158 45 32N 88 52W
Crane, Oregon, U.S.A. 160 43 21N 118 39W
Crane, Texas, U.S.A. 159 31 26N 102 27W
Cranfield Pt. 38 54 1N 6 3W
Cranleigh 29 51 8N 0 29W
Cranshaws 35 55 51N 2 30W
Cranston 162 41 47N 71 27W
Cranwell 33 53 4N 0 29W
Craon 42 47 50N 0 58W
Craonne 43 49 27N 3 46E
Crasna 70 46 32N 27 51E
Crasna, R. 70 47 44N 27 35E
Crater Lake 160 42 55N 122 3W
Crater Mt. 135 6 37S 145 7E
Crater Pt. 135 5 25S 152 9E
Crateús 170 5 10S 40 50W
Crathie 37 57 3N 3 12W
Crati, R. 65 39 41N 16 30E
Crato, Brazil 171 7 10S 39 25W
Crato, Port. 57 39 16N 7 39W
Crau 45 43 32N 4 40E
Craughwell 39 53 15N 8 44W
Craven Arms 28 52 27N 2 49W
Crawford, U.K. 35 55 28N 3 40W
Crawford, U.S.A. 158 42 40N 103 25W
Crawford, oilfield 19 59 7N 1 30E
Crawfordsville 156 40 2N 86 51W
Crawley 29 51 7N 0 10W
Cray 31 51 55N 3 38W
Crazy Mts. 160 46 14N 110 30W
Creag Meagaidh, mt. 37 56 57N 4 38W
Crean L. 153 54 5N 106 9W
Crèche, La 44 46 23N 0 19W
Crécy-en-Brie 43 48 50N 2 53E
Crécy-en-Ponthieu 43 50 15N 1 53E
Crécy-sur-Serre 43 49 40N 3 32E
Credenhill 28 52 6N 2 49W
Crediton 30 50 47N 3 39W
Credo 137 30 28S 120 45E
Cree L. 153 57 30N 106 30W
Cree, R., Can. 153 58 57N 105 47W
Cree, R., U.K. 34 54 51N 4 24W
Creede 161 37 56N 106 59W
Creegh 39 52 45N 9 25W
Creel 164 27 45N 107 38W
Creeside 34 55 4N 4 41W
Creeslough 38 55 8N 7 55W
Creetown 34 54 54N 4 23W
Creeves 39 52 33N 9 3W
Creggan 38 54 39N 7 0W
Cregganbaun 38 53 42N 9 48W
Creighton 158 42 30N 97 52W
Creil 43 49 15N 2 34E
Crema 62 45 21N 9 40E
Cremona 62 45 8N 10 2E
Crepaja 66 45 1N 20 38E
Crépy 43 49 37N 3 32E
Crépy-en-Valois 43 49 14N 2 54E
Cres 63 44 58N 14 25E
Cresbard 158 45 13N 98 57W
Crescent, Okla., U.S.A. 159 35 38N 97 36W
Crescent, Oreg., U.S.A. 160 43 30N 121 37W
Crescent City 160 41 45N 124 12W
Crescentino 62 45 11N 8 7E
Crespino 63 44 59N 11 51E
Crespo 172 32 2S 60 19W
Cressman 150 47 40N 72 55W
Cressy 140 38 2S 143 40E
Crest 45 44 44N 5 2E
Crested Butte 161 38 57N 107 0W
Crestline 163 34 14N 117 18W
Creston, Can. 152 49 10N 116 31W
Creston, Calif., U.S.A. 163 35 32N 120 33W
Creston, Iowa, U.S.A. 158 41 0N 94 20W
Creston, Wash., U.S.A. 160 47 47N 118 36W
Creston, Wyo., U.S.A. 160 41 46N 107 50W
Crestone 161 35 2N 106 0W
Crestview, Calif., U.S.A. 163 37 46N 118 58W
Crestview, Fla., U.S.A. 157 30 45N 86 35W
Creswick 140 37 25S 143 51E
Crete 158 40 38N 96 58W
Crete = Kriti 69 35 15N 25 0E
Crete, La, Can. 152 58 10N 116 29W
Crete, La, Alta., Can. 152 58 11N 116 24W
Crete, Sea of 69 26 0N 25 0E
Cretin, C. 135 6 40S 147 53E
Creus, C. 58 42 20N 3 19E
Creuse □ 44 46 0N 2 0E
Creuse, R. 44 47 0N 0 34E
Creusot, Le 43 46 50N 4 24E
Creuzburg 48 51 3N 10 15E
Crevalcore 63 44 41N 11 10E
Crèvecœur-le-Grand 43 49 37N 2 5E
Crevillente 59 38 12N 0 48W
Crewe 32 53 6N 2 28W
Crewkerne 28 50 53N 2 48W
Crianlarich 34 56 24N 4 37W
Crib Point 139 38 22S 145 13E
Criccieth 31 52 55N 4 15W
Criciúma 173 28 40S 49 23W
Crick 28 52 22N 1 9W
Crickhowell 31 51 52N 3 8W
Cricklade 28 51 38N 1 50W
Crieff 35 56 22N 3 50W
Criffell Mt. 35 54 56N 3 38W
Crikvenica 63 45 11N 14 40E
Crillon, Mt. 152 58 39N 137 14W
Crimea = Krymskaya 82 45 0N 34 0E
Crimmitschau 48 50 48N 12 23E
Crimond 37 57 35N 1 53W
Crinan Canal 34 56 4N 5 30W
Crinkill 39 53 5N 7 55E
Cristalândia 170 10 36S 49 11W
Cristeşti 70 47 15N 26 33E
Cristino Castro 170 8 49S 44 13W
Crişul Alb, R. 66 46 25N 21 40E
Crişul Negru, R. 70 46 38N 22 26E
Crişul Repede, R. 70 47 20N 22 25E
Crivitz 48 53 35N 11 39E
Crixás 171 14 27S 49 58W
Crna Gora □ 66 42 40N 19 20E
Crna Trava 66 42 49N 22 19E
Crni Drim, R. 66 41 17N 20 40E
Crni Timok, R. 66 43 53N 22 0E
Crnoljeva Planina 66 42 20N 21 0E
Črnomeij 63 45 33N 15 10E
Croagh Patrick, mt. 38 53 46N 9 40W
Croatia = Hrvatska 63 45 20N 16 0E
Crocker, Barisan 102 5 0N 116 30E
Crocketford 35 55 3N 3 49W
Crockets Town 38 54 8N 9 7W
Crockett 159 31 20N 95 30W
Crocodile Is. 138 11 43S 135 8E
Crocodile, R. 129 25 30S 31 15E
Crocq 44 45 52N 2 21E
Croghan 38 53 55N 8 13W
Croglin 32 54 50N 2 37W
Crohy Hd. 38 54 55N 8 28W
Croisic, Le 42 47 18N 2 30W
Croisic, Pte. du. 42 47 19N 2 31W
Croix, La, L. 150 48 20N 92 15W
Croker, C. 136 10 58S 132 35E
Croker, I. 136 11 12N 132 32E
Crolly 38 55 2N 8 16W
Cromalt Hills 36 58 0N 5 2W
Cromarty, Can. 153 58 3N 94 9W
Cromarty, U.K. 37 57 40N 4 2W
Cromarty Firth 37 57 40N 4 15W
Cromdale, Hills of 37 57 20N 3 28W
Cromer 29 52 56N 1 18E
Cromore 36 58 6N 6 23W
Cromwell, N.Z. 143 45 3S 169 14E
Cromwell, U.S.A. 162 41 36N 72 39W
Cronat 43 46 43N 3 40E
Crondall 29 51 13N 0 51W
Cronulla 141 34 3S 151 8E
Crook 33 54 43N 1 45W
Crooked I. 167 22 50N 74 10W
Crooked Island Passage 167 23 0N 74 30W
Crooked, R., Can. 152 54 10N 122 35W
Crooked, R., U.S.A. 160 44 30N 121 0W
Crooklands 32 54 16N 2 43W
Crookston, Minn., U.S.A. 158 47 50N 96 40W
Crookston, Nebr., U.S.A. 158 42 56N 100 45W
Crookstown 39 51 50N 8 50W
Crooksville 156 39 45N 82 8W

Crookwell Dalandzadgad

Crookwell 141 34 28 S 149 24 E
Croom 39 52 32N 8 43W
Crosby, Cumb., U.K. 32 54 45N 3 25W
Crosby, Merseyside, U.K. 32 53 30N 3 2W
Crosby, Minn., U.S.A. 158 46 28N 93 57W
Crosby, N.D., U.S.A. 153 48 55N 103 18W
Crosby Ravensworth 32 54 34N 2 35W
Crosbyton 159 33 37N 101 12W
Cross City 157 29 35N 83 5W
Cross Fell 32 54 44N 2 29W
Cross L. 153 54 45N 97 30W
Cross Plains 159 32 8N 99 7W
Cross, R. 121 4 46N 8 20 E
Cross River □ 121 6 0N 8 0 E
Cross Sound 147 58 20N 136 30W
Crossakiel 38 53 43N 7 2W
Crossbost 36 58 8N 6 27W
Crossdoney 38 53 57N 7 27W
Crosse, La, Kans., U.S.A. 158 38 33N 99 20W
Crosse, La, Wis., U.S.A. 158 43 48N 91 13W
Crossett 159 33 10N 91 57W
Crossfarnoge Pt. 39 52 10N 6 37W
Crossfield 152 51 25N 114 0W
Crossgar 38 54 22N 5 46W
Crosshaven 39 51 48N 8 19W
Crosshill 34 55 19N 4 39W
Crossley, Mt. 143 42 50 S 172 5 E
Crossmaglen 38 54 5N 6 37W
Crossmolina 38 54 6N 9 21W
Croton-on-Hudson 162 41 12N 73 55W
Crotone 65 39 5N 17 6 E
Crouch, R. 29 51 37N 0 53 E
Crow Agency 160 45 40N 107 30W
Crow Hd. 39 51 34N 10 9W
Crow, R. 152 59 41N 124 20W
Crow Sound 30 49 56N 6 16W
Crowborough 29 51 3N 0 9 E
Crowell 159 33 59N 99 45W
Crowl Creek 141 32 0 S 145 30 E
Crowland 29 52 41N 0 10W
Crowle 33 53 36N 0 49W
Crowley 159 30 15N 92 20W
Crowley, L. 163 37 53N 118 42W
Crowlin Is. 36 57 20N 5 50W
Crown Point 156 41 24N 87 23W
Crows Landing 163 37 23N 121 6W
Crows Nest 139 27 16 S 152 4 E
Crowsnest Pass 152 49 40N 114 40W
Croyde 30 51 7N 4 13W
Croydon, Austral. 138 18 13 S 142 14 E
Croydon, U.K. 29 51 18N 0 5W
Crozet, Île 11 46 27 S 52 0 E
Crozon 42 48 15N 4 30W
Cruces, Pta. 174 6 39N 77 32W
Cruden Bay 37 57 25N 1 50W
Crudgington 28 52 46N 2 33W
Crumlin 38 54 38N 6 12W
Crummer Peaks 138 6 40 S 144 0 E
Crummock Water L. 32 54 33N 3 18W
Crusheen 39 52 57N 8 52W
Cruz, C. 166 19 50N 77 50W
Cruz das Almas 171 12 40 S 39 6W
Cruz de Malta 170 8 15 S 40 20W
Cruz del Eje 172 30 45 S 64 50W
Cruz, La, Colomb. 174 1 35N 76 58W
Cruz, La, C. Rica 166 11 4N 85 39W
Cruz, La, Mexico 164 23 55N 106 54W
Cruzeiro 173 22 50 S 45 0W
Cruzeiro do Oeste 173 23 46 S 53 4W
Cruzeiro do Sul 174 7 35 S 72 35W
Cry L. 152 58 45N 128 5W
Cryfow Sl. 54 51 2N 15 24 E
Crymmych 31 51 59N 4 40W
Crystal Brook 140 33 21 S 138 12 E
Crystal City, Mo., U.S.A. 158 38 15N 90 23W
Crystal City, Tex., U.S.A. 159 28 40N 99 50W
Crystal Falls 156 46 9N 88 11W
Crystal River 157 28 54N 82 35W
Crystal Springs 159 31 59N 90 25W
Čáslav 52 49 54N 15 22 E
Csongrád 53 46 43N 20 12 E
Csongrád □ 53 46 32N 20 15 E
Csorna 53 47 38N 17 18 E
Csurgo 53 46 16N 17 9 E
Ctesiphon 92 33 9N 44 35 E
Cu Lao Hon 101 10 54N 108 18 E
Cua Rao 100 19 16N 104 27 E
Cuácua, R. 127 18 0 S 36 0 E
Cuamato 128 17 2 S 15 7 E
Cuamba = Nova Preixo 127 14 45 S 36 22 E
Cuando 128 16 25 S 22 2 E
Cuando Cubango □ 128 16 25 S 20 0 E
Cuando, R. 125 14 0 S 19 30 E
Cuangar 128 17 28 S 14 40 E
Cuango 124 6 15 S 16 35 E
Cuarto, R. 172 33 25 S 63 2W
Cuatrociénegas de Carranza 164 26 59N 102 5W
Cuauhtémoc 164 28 25N 106 52W
Cuba, Port. 57 38 10N 7 54W
Cuba, U.S.A. 161 36 0N 107 0W
Cuba ■ 166 22 0N 79 0W
Cuballing 137 32 50 S 117 10 E
Cubango, R. 128 16 15 S 17 45 E
Cuchi 125 14 37 S 17 10 E
Cuchumatanes, Sierra de los 166 15 35N 91 25W
Cuckfield 29 51 0N 0 8W
Cucurpe 164 30 20N 110 43W
Cucurrupí 174 4 23N 76 56W
Cúcuta 174 7 54N 72 31W
Cudahy 156 42 54N 87 50W
Cudalbi 70 45 46N 27 41 E
Cuddalore 97 11 46N 79 45 E
Cuddapah 97 14 30N 78 47 E
Cuddapan, L. 138 25 45 S 141 26 E
Cudgewa 141 36 10 S 147 42 E
Cudillero 56 43 33N 6 9W
Cudworth 33 53 35N 1 25W
Cue 137 27 25 S 117 54 E
Cuéllar 56 41 23N 4 21W
Cuenca, Ecuador 174 2 50 S 79 9W
Cuenca, Spain 58 40 5N 2 10W
Cuenca □ 58 40 0N 2 0W
Cuenca, Serranía de 58 39 55N 1 50W
Cuencamé 164 24 53N 103 41W
Cuerda del Pozo, Pantano de la 58 41 51N 2 44W
Cuernavaca 165 18 50N 99 20W
Cuero 159 29 5N 97 17W
Cuers 45 43 14N 6 5 E
Cuervo 159 35 5N 104 25W
Cuesmes 47 50 26N 3 56 E
Cuevas de Altamira 56 43 20N 4 5W
Cuevas del Almanzora 59 37 18N 1 58W
Cuevo 174 20 25N 63 30W
Cugir 70 43 48N 23 25 E
Cugno 123 6 14N 42 31 E
Cuhimbre 174 0 10 S 75 23W
Cuiabá 175 15 30 S 56 0W
Cuiabá, R. 175 16 50 S 56 30W
Cuidad Bolivar 174 8 21N 70 34W
Cuilcagh, Mt. 38 54 12N 7 50W
Cuilco 166 15 24N 91 58W
Cuillin Hills 36 57 14N 6 15W
Cuillin Sd. 36 57 4N 6 20W
Cuima 125 13 0 S 15 45 E
Cuiseaux 45 46 30N 5 22 E
Cuité 170 6 29 S 36 9W
Cuito, R. 128 16 50 S 19 30 E
Cuitzeo, L. 164 19 55N 101 5W
Cujmir 70 44 13N 22 57 E
Culan 44 46 34N 2 20 E
Cŭlaraşi 43 44 14N 27 23 E
Culbertson 158 48 9N 104 30W
Culburra 140 35 50 S 139 58 E
Culcairn 141 35 41 S 147 3 E
Culdaff 38 55 17N 7 10W
Culebra, I. 147 18 19N 65 17W
Culebra, Sierra de la 56 41 55N 6 20W
Culemborg 46 51 58N 5 14 E
Culgoa 140 35 44 S 143 6 E
Culgoa, R. 139 29 56 S 146 20 E
Culiacán 164 24 50N 107 40W
Culiacán, R. 164 24 30N 107 42W
Cŭlimani, Munţii 70 47 12N 25 0 E
Cŭlineşti 70 45 21N 24 18 E
Culion, I. 103 11 54N 120 1 E
Cúllar de Baza 59 37 35N 2 34W
Cullarin Range 141 34 30 S 149 30 E
Cullaville 38 54 4N 6 40W
Cullen, Austral. 136 13 58 S 131 54 E
Cullen, U.K. 37 57 45N 2 50W
Cullen Pt. 138 11 57 S 141 54 E
Cullera 59 39 9N 0 17W
Cullin L. 38 53 58N 9 12W
Cullivoe 36 60 43N 1 0W
Cullman 157 34 13N 86 50W
Culloden Moor 37 57 29N 4 7W
Cullompton 30 50 52N 3 23W
Cullyhanna 38 54 8N 6 35W
Culm, R. 30 50 46N 3 31W
Culoz 45 45 47N 5 46 E
Culpataro 140 33 40 S 144 22 E
Culpeper 156 38 29N 77 59W
Culrain 37 57 55N 4 25W
Culross 35 56 4N 3 38W
Cults 37 57 8N 2 10W
Culuene, R. 175 12 15 S 53 10W
Culvain Mt. 36 56 55N 5 19W
Culver, Pt. 137 32 54 S 124 43 E
Culverden 143 42 47 S 172 49 E
Cumali 69 36 42N 27 28 E
Cumaná 174 10 30N 64 5W
Cumari 171 18 16 S 48 11W
Cumberland, Can. 152 49 40N 125 0W
Cumberland, Md., U.S.A. 156 39 40N 78 43W
Cumberland, Wis., U.S.A. 158 45 32N 92 3W
Cumberland (□) 26 54 44N 2 55W
Cumberland I. 157 30 52N 81 30W
Cumberland Is. 138 20 35 S 149 10 E
Cumberland L. 153 54 3N 102 18W
Cumberland Pen. 149 67 0N 64 0W
Cumberland Plat. 157 36 0N 84 30W
Cumberland, R. 157 36 15N 87 0W
Cumberland Sd. 149 65 30N 66 0W
Cumborah 139 29 40 S 147 45 E
Cumbrae Is. 34 55 46N 4 54W
Cumbres Mayores 57 38 4N 6 39W
Cumbria □ 32 54 35N 2 55W
Cumbrian Mts. 32 54 30N 3 0W
Cumbum 97 15 40N 79 10 E
Cuminestown 37 57 32N 2 17W
Cummerower See 48 53 47N 12 52 E
Cummertrees 35 55 0N 3 20W
Cummings Mtn. 163 35 2N 118 34W
Cummins 139 34 16 S 135 43 E
Cumnock, Austral. 141 32 59 S 148 46 E
Cumnock, U.K. 34 55 27N 4 18W
Cumnor 28 51 44N 1 20W
Cumpas 164 30 0N 109 48W
Cumuruxatiba 171 17 6 S 39 13W
Cumwhinton 32 54 51N 2 49W
Cuñaré 174 0 49N 72 32W
Cuncumén 172 31 53 S 70 38W
Cunderdin 137 31 37 S 117 12 E
Cundinamarca □ 174 5 0N 74 0W
Cunene, R. 128 17 0 S 15 0 E
Cúneo 62 44 23N 7 31 E
Cunillera, I. 59 38 59N 1 13 E
Cunlhat 44 45 38N 3 32 E
Cunnamulla 139 28 2 S 145 38 E
Cunninghame, Reg. 34 55 38N 4 35W
Cuorgnè 62 45 23N 7 39 E
Cupar, Can. 153 50 57N 104 10W
Cupar, U.K. 35 56 20N 3 0W
Cupica 174 6 50N 77 30W
Cupica, Golfo de 174 6 25N 77 30W
Ćuprija 66 43 57N 21 26 E
Curaçá 170 8 59 S 39 54W
Curaçao, I. 167 12 10N 69 0W
Curanilahue 172 37 29 S 73 28W
Curaray, R. 174 1 30 S 75 30W
Curatabaca 174 6 19N 62 51W
Curbarado 174 7 3N 76 54W
Curbur 137 26 28 S 115 55 E
Cure, La 50 46 28N 6 4 E
Curepto 172 35 8 S 72 1W
Curiapo 174 8 33N 61 5W
Curicó 172 34 55 S 71 20W
Curicó □ 172 34 50 S 71 15W
Curimatá 170 10 2 S 44 17W
Curiplaya 174 0 16N 74 52W
Curitiba 173 25 20 S 49 10W
Curlew Mts. 38 54 0N 8 20W
Curoca Norte 128 16 15 S 12 58 E
Currabubula 141 31 16 S 150 44 E
Curracunya 139 28 29 S 144 9 E
Curraglass 39 52 5N 8 4W
Currais Novos 170 6 13 S 36 30W
Curralinho 170 1 35 S 49 30W
Curran, L. = Terewah, L. 139 29 50 S 147 24 E
Currane L. 39 51 50N 10 8W
Currant 160 38 51N 115 32W
Curranyalpa 141 30 53 S 144 39 E
Curraweena 141 30 47 S 145 54 E
Currawilla 138 25 10 S 141 20 E
Current, R. 159 37 15N 91 10W
Currie, Austral. 138 39 56 S 143 53 E
Currie, U.K. 35 55 53N 3 17W
Currie, U.S.A. 160 40 16N 114 45W
Currie, Mt. 129 30 29 S 29 21 E
Currituck Sd. 157 36 20N 75 50W
Curry Rivel 28 51 2N 2 52W
Curryglass 39 51 40N 9 50W
Curtea-de-Argeş 70 45 12N 24 42 E
Curtis, Spain 56 43 7N 8 4W
Curtis, U.S.A. 158 40 41N 100 32W
Curtis, I. 138 23 35 S 151 10 E
Curtis, Pt. 138 23 53 S 151 21 E
Curuá, I. 170 0 48N 50 10W
Curuapanema, R. 175 7 0 S 54 30W
Curuçá 170 0 35 S 47 50W
Curuguaty 173 24 19 S 55 49W
Curupira, Serra 174 1 25N 64 30W
Cururupu 170 1 50 S 44 50W
Curuzú Cuatiá 172 29 50 S 58 5W
Curvelo 171 18 45 S 44 27W
Curyo 140 35 50 S 142 47 E
Cushendall 38 55 5N 6 3W
Cushendun 38 55 8N 6 3W
Cushina 39 53 11N 7 10W
Cushing, Mt. 152 57 35N 126 57W
Cusihuiriáchic 164 28 10N 106 50W
Cussabat 119 32 39N 14 1 E
Cusset 44 46 8N 3 28 E
Custer 158 43 45N 103 38W
Cut Bank 160 48 40N 112 15W
Cutchogue 162 41 1N 72 30W
Cuthbert 157 31 47N 84 47W
Cutler 163 36 31N 119 17W
Cutra L. 39 53 2N 8 48W
Cutro 65 39 1N 16 58 E
Cuttaburra, R. 139 29 43 S 144 22 E
Cuttack 96 20 25N 85 57 E
Cuvier, C. 137 23 14 S 113 22 E
Cuvier I. 142 36 27 S 175 50 E
Cuxhaven 48 53 51N 8 41 E
Cuyabeno 174 0 16 S 75 53W
Cuyahoga Falls 156 41 8N 81 30W
Cuyo 103 10 50N 121 5 E
Cuyuni, R. 175 7 0N 59 30W
Cuzco 174 13 32 S 72 0W
Cuzco, Mt. 174 20 0 S 66 50W
Čŭzŭneşti 70 44 36N 27 3 E
Čvrsnica, Mt. 66 43 36N 17 35 E
Cwmbran 31 51 39N 3 0W
Cwrt 31 52 35N 3 55W
Cyangugu 126 2 29 S 28 54 E
Cybinka 54 52 12N 14 46 E
Cyclades = Kikladhes 69 37 20N 24 30 E
Cygnet 138 43 8 S 147 1 E
Cymmer 31 51 37N 3 38W
Cynthiana 156 38 23N 84 10W
Cynwyl Elfed 31 51 55N 4 22W
Cypress Hills 153 49 40N 109 30W
Cyprus ■ 92 35 0N 33 0 E
Cyrenaica □ 117 27 0N 20 0 E
Cyrene 117 32 39N 21 18 E
Czaplinek 54 53 34N 16 14 E
Czar 153 52 27N 110 50W
Czarne 54 53 42N 16 58 E
Czarnków 54 52 55N 16 38 E
Czechoslovakia ■ 53 49 0N 17 0 E
Czechowice-Dziedzice 54 49 54N 18 59 E
Czeladz 54 50 16N 19 2 E
Czempin 54 52 9N 16 33 E
Czersk 54 53 46N 17 58 E
Czerwiensk 54 52 1N 15 13 E
Czerwionka 54 50 7N 18 37 E
Częstochowa 54 50 49N 19 7 E
Częstochowa □ 54 50 45N 19 0 E
Czlopa 54 53 6N 16 6 E
Człuchów 54 53 41N 17 22 E

D

Da Lat 101 11 56N 108 25 E
Da Nang 100 16 4N 108 13 E
Da, R. 100 21 15N 105 20 E
Daarlerveen 46 52 26N 6 34 E
Dab'a, Ras el 122 31 3N 28 31 E
Dabai 121 11 25N 5 15 E
Dabajuro 174 11 2N 70 40W
Dabakala 120 8 15N 4 20W
Dabatou 120 11 50N 9 20W
Dabburiya 90 32 42N 35 22 E
Daberas 128 25 27 S 18 30 E
Dabhoi 94 22 10N 73 20 E
Dabie 54 53 27N 14 45 E
Dabola 120 10 50N 11 5W
Dabong 101 5 23N 103 1 E
Dabou 120 5 20N 4 23W
Daboya 121 9 30N 1 20W
Dabra Berhan 123 9 42N 39 15 E
Dabra Sina 123 9 51N 39 45 E
Dabra Tabor 123 11 50N 37 58 E
Dabra Zabit 123 11 48N 38 30 E
Dabrowa Górnicza 54 50 15N 19 10 E
Dabrowa Tarnówska 54 50 10N 20 59 E
Dabrówno 54 53 27N 20 2 E
Dabus, R. 123 10 12N 35 0 E
Dacca 98 23 43N 90 26 E
Dacca □ 98 24 0N 90 25 E
Dachau 49 48 16N 11 27 E
Dadanawa 174 3 0N 59 30W
Daday 82 41 28N 33 35 E
Daddato 123 12 24N 42 45 E
Dade City 157 28 20N 82 12W
Dadiya 121 9 35N 11 24 E
Dadra and Nagar Haveli □ 96 20 5N 73 0 E
Dadri = Charkhi Dadri 94 28 37N 76 17 E
Dadu 94 26 45N 67 45 E
Daer R. 35 55 23N 3 39W
Daet 103 14 2N 122 55 E
Dagaio 123 6 8N 40 40 E
Dagana 120 16 30N 15 20W
Dagash 122 19 19N 33 25 E
Dagestan, A.S.S.R. □ 83 42 30N 47 0 E
Daggett 163 34 43N 116 52W
Daggs Sd. 143 45 23 S 166 45 E
Daghfeli 122 19 18N 32 40 E
Daghirie 123 11 40N 41 50 E
Dagö = Hiiumaa 80 58 50N 22 45 E
Dagoreti 126 1 18 S 36 4 E
Dagua 135 3 27 S 143 20 E
Dagupan 103 16 3N 120 20 E
Dahab 122 28 30N 34 31 E
Dahlak Kebir 123 15 50N 40 10 E
Dahlenburg 48 53 11N 10 43 E
Dahlonega 157 34 35N 83 59W
Dahme 48 51 51N 13 25 E
Daho 121 10 28N 11 18 E
Dahomey ■ = Benin ■ 121 8 0N 2 0 E
Dahra 120 15 22N 15 30W
Dahra, Massif de 118 36 7N 1 21 E
Dai Hao 100 18 1N 106 25 E
Dai-Sen 110 35 22N 133 32 E
Daigo 111 36 46N 140 21 E
Dailly 34 55 16N 4 44W
Daimanji-San 110 36 14N 133 20 E
Daimiel 59 39 5N 3 35W
Daintree 138 16 20 S 145 20 E
Daiō-Misaki 111 34 15N 136 45 E
Dairen = Lüta 107 38 55N 121 40 E
Dairût 122 27 34N 30 43 E
Dairymple 34 55 24N 4 36W
Daisetsu-Zan 112 43 30N 142 57 E
Daitari 96 21 10N 85 46 E
Daitō 110 35 19N 132 58 E
Dajarra 138 21 42 S 139 30 E
Dak Dam 100 12 20N 107 21 E
Dak Nhe 100 15 28N 107 48 E
Dak Pek 100 15 4N 107 44 E
Dak Song 101 12 19N 107 35 E
Dak Sui 100 14 55N 107 43 E
Dakala 121 14 27N 2 27 E
Dakar 120 14 34N 17 29W
Dakhla 116 23 50N 15 53W
Dakhla, El Wâhât el- 122 25 30N 28 50 E
Dakhovskaya 83 44 13N 40 13 E
Dakingari 121 11 37N 4 1 E
Dakor 94 22 45N 73 11 E
Dakoro 121 14 31N 6 46 E
Dakota City 158 42 27N 96 28W
Dakota, North 158 47 30N 100 0W
Đakovica 66 42 22N 20 26 E
Dakovo 66 45 19N 18 24 E
Dakra 120 15 22N 15 30W
Dalaba 120 10 42N 12 15W
Dalälven, L. 72 61 27N 17 15 E
Dalandzadgad 106 43 27N 104 30 E

Dalarö Degeh-Bur

Dalarö 75 59 8N 18 24 E
Dalat 101 12 3N 108 32 E
Dalbandin 93 29 0N 4 23 E
Dalbeattie 35 54 55N 3 50W
Dalbosjön, L. 73 58 40N 12 45 E
Dalby, Austral. 139 27 10 S 151 17 E
Dalby, Sweden 73 55 42N 13 22 E
Dale, Sogn og Fjordane, Norway 71 61 27N 7 28 E
Dale, Sogn og Fjordane, Norway 71 61 22N 5 23 E
Dale, U.K. 31 51 42N 5 11W
Dalen, Neth. 46 52 42N 6 46 E
Dalen, Norway 71 59 26N 8 0 E
Dalet 98 19 59N 93 51 E
Daletme 98 21 36N 92 46 E
Dalfsen 46 52 31N 6 16 E
Dalga 122 27 39N 30 41 E
Dalgaranger, Mt. 137 27 50 S 117 5 E
Dalhalvaig 37 58 28N 3 53W
Dalhart 159 36 0N 102 30W
Dalhousie, Can. 151 48 0N 66 26W
Dalhousie, India 94 32 38N 76 0 E
Daliburgh 36 57 10N 7 23W
Dalj 174 45 28N 18 58 E
Dalkeith 35 55 54N 3 5W
Dalkey 39 53 16N 6 7W
Dall I. 152 54 59N 133 25W
Dallarnil 139 25 19 S 152 2 E
Dallas, U.K. 37 57 33N 3 32W
Dallas, Oregon, U.S.A. 160 45 0N 123 15W
Dallas, Texas, U.S.A. 159 32 50N 96 50W
Dallol 123 14 14N 40 17 E
Dalmacija 66 43 20N 17 0 E
Dalmally 34 56 25N 5 0W
Dalmatia = Dalmacija 66 43 20N 17 0 E
Dalmatovo 84 56 16N 62 56 E
Dalmellington 34 55 20N 4 25W
Dalneretchensk 77 45 50N 133 40 E
Daloa 120 7 0N 6 30W
Dalry 34 55 44N 4 42W
Dalrymple, Mt. 133 21 1 S 148 39 E
Dalsjöfors 73 57 46N 18 5 E
Dalskog 73 58 44N 12 18 E
Dalton, Can. 150 48 11N 84 1W
Dalton, Cumbria, U.K. 33 54 9N 3 11W
Dalton, Dumfries, U.K. 35 55 3N 3 22W
Dalton, N. Yorks., U.K. 33 54 28N 1 32W
Dalton, Ga., U.S.A. 103 34 45N 85 0W
Dalton, Mass., U.S.A. 162 42 28N 73 11W
Dalton, Nebr., U.S.A. 158 41 27N 103 0W
Dalton Post 152 66 42N 137 0W
Daltonganj 95 24 0N 84 4 E
Dalvík 74 65 58N 18 32W
Dalwhinnie 37 56 56N 4 14W
Daly City 163 37 42N 122 28W
Daly L. 153 56 32N 105 39W
Daly, R. 136 13 21 S 130 18 E
Daly Waters 138 16 15 S 133 24 E
Dalystown 38 53 26N 7 23W
Dam 170 4 45N 55 0W
Dam Doi 101 8 59N 105 12 E
Dam Gillan 153 56 20N 94 40W
Dam Ha 100 21 21N 107 36 E
Dama, Wadi 122 27 12N 35 50 E
Daman 96 20 25N 72 57 E
Daman □ 96 20 25N 72 58 E
Damanhûr 122 31 0N 30 30 E
Damar, I. 103 7 15 S 128 30 E
Damaraland 128 21 0 S 17 0 E
Damascus = Dimashq 92 33 30N 36 18 E
Damaturu 121 11 45N 11 55 E
Damāvand 93 36 0N 52 0 E
Damāvand, Qolleh-ye 93 35 45N 52 10 E
Damba, Angola 124 6 44 S 15 29 E
Damba, Ethiopia 123 15 10N 38 47 E
Dâmbovnic, R. 70 44 28N 25 18 E
Dame Marie 167 18 36N 74 26W
Damerham 28 50 57N 1 52W
Dames Quarter 162 38 11N 75 54W
Damghan 93 36 10N 54 17 E
Damietta = Dumyât 122 31 24N 31 48 E
Damin 93 27 30N 60 40 E
Damiya 90 32 6N 35 34 E
Damman 92 26 25N 50 2 E
Dammarie 43 48 20N 1 30 E
Dammartin 43 49 3N 2 41 E
Dammastock 51 46 38N 8 24 E
Damme 48 52 32N 8 12 E
Damodar, R. 95 23 17N 87 35 E
Damoh 95 23 50N 79 28 E
Dampier 136 20 41 S 116 42 E
Dampier Arch. 136 20 38 S 116 32 E
Dampier Downs 136 18 24 S 123 5 E
Dampier, Selat 103 0 40 S 131 0 E
Dampier Str. 135 5 50 S 148 0 E
Damrei, Chuor Phnum 101 12 30N 103 0 E
Damville 42 48 51N 1 5 E
Damvillers 43 49 20N 5 21 E
Dan Chadi 121 12 47N 5 17 E
Dan Dume 121 11 28N 7 8 E
Dan Gora 121 11 30N 8 7 E
Dan Gulbi 121 11 40N 6 15 E
Dan, oilfield 19 55 30N 5 10 E
Dan Sadau 121 11 25N 6 20 E
Dana 103 11 0 S 122 52 E
Dana, Lac 150 50 53N 77 20W
Dana, Mt 163 37 54N 119 12W
Danakil Depression 123 12 45N 41 0 E
Danao 103 10 31N 124 1 E
Danbury 162 41 23N 73 29W
Danby L. 161 34 17N 115 0W
Dand 94 31 28N 65 32 E
Dandaragan 137 30 40 S 115 40 E
Dandeldhura 95 29 20N 80 35 E
Dandeli 93 15 5N 74 30 E
Dandenong 141 38 0 S 145 15 E
Dandkandi 98 23 32N 90 43 E
Danforth 151 45 39N 67 57W
Dang Raek 101 14 40N 104 0 E
Dangara 85 38 6N 69 22 E
*Danger Is. 131 10 53 S 165 49W
Danger Pt. 128 34 40 S 19 17 E
Dangla 123 11 18N 36 56 E
Dangora 121 11 30N 8 7 E
Dangrek, Phnom 100 14 15N 105 0 E
Daniel 160 42 56N 110 2W
Daniel's Harbour 151 50 13N 57 35W
Danielskull 128 28 11 S 23 33 E
Danielson 162 41 50N 71 52W
Danilov 81 58 16N 40 13 E
Danilovgrad 66 42 38N 19 9 E
Danilovka 81 50 25N 44 12 E
Danissa 126 3 15N 40 58 E
Danja 121 11 29N 7 30 E
Dankalwa 121 11 52N 12 12 E
Dankama 121 13 20N 7 44 E
Dankhar Gompa 93 32 10N 78 10 E
Dankov 81 53 20N 39 5 E
Danlí 166 14 4N 86 35W
Dannemora 75 60 12N 17 51 E
Dannenberg 48 53 7N 11 4 E
Dannevirke 142 40 12 S 176 8 E
Dannhauser 129 28 0 S 30 3 E
Dansalan 103 8 2N 124 30 E
Dansville 156 42 32N 77 41W
Dantan 95 21 57N 87 20 E
Danube, R. 53 45 0N 28 20W
Danubyo 98 17 15N 95 35 E
Danvers 162 42 34N 70 55 E
Danville, Ill., U.S.A. 156 40 10N 87 40W
Danville, Ky., U.S.A. 156 37 40N 84 45W
Danville, Pa., U.S.A. 162 40 58N 76 37W
Danville, Va., U.S.A. 157 36 40N 79 20W
Danzig = Gdansk 54 54 22N 18 40 E
Dão 103 10 30N 122 6 E
Dão, R. 56 40 28N 8 0W
Daosa 94 26 52N 76 20 E
Daoud = Aïn Beida 119 35 50N 7 29 E
Daoulas 42 48 22N 4 17W
Dapango 121 10 55N 0 16 E
Dar al Hamra, Ad 92 27 22N 37 43 E
Dar es Salaam 126 6 50 S 39 12 E
Dar'á 90 32 36N 36 7 E
Darab 93 28 50N 54 30 E
Darabani 70 48 10N 26 39 E
Daraj 119 30 10N 10 28 E
Daraut Kurgan 85 39 33N 72 11 E
Daravica 66 42 32N 20 8 E
Daraw 121 24 22N 32 51 E
Darazo 121 11 1N 10 24W
Darband 94 34 30N 72 50 E
Darbhanga 95 26 15N 86 8 E
Darby 160 46 2N 114 7W
D'Arcy 152 50 35N 122 30W
Darda 66 45 40N 18 41 E
Dardanelle 163 38 2N 119 50W
Dardanelles = Canakkale Boğlazi 92 40 0N 26 20 E
Dardenelle 159 35 12N 93 9W
Darent, R. 29 51 22N 0 12 E
Darfield 143 43 29 S 172 7 E
Darfo 62 45 43N 10 11 E
Dargai 94 34 25N 71 45 E
Dargan Ata 76 40 40N 62 20 E
Dargaville 142 35 57 S 173 52 E
Darharala 120 8 23N 4 20W
Dari 123 5 48N 30 26 E
Darién, G. del 174 9 0N 77 0W
Darién, Serranía del 174 8 30N 77 30W
Dariganga 106 45 5N 113 45 E
Darinskoye 84 51 20N 51 44 E
Darjeeling 95 27 3N 88 18 E
Dark Cove 151 48 47N 54 13W
Darkan 137 33 20 S 116 43 E
Darke Peak 140 33 27 S 136 12 E
Darkot Pass 95 36 45N 73 26 E
Darlaston 28 52 35N 2 1W
Darling Downs 139 28 30 S 152 0 E
Darling, R. 140 34 4 S 141 54 E
Darling Ra. 137 32 30 S 116 0 E
Darlington, U.K. 33 54 33N 1 33W
Darlington, S.C., U.S.A. 157 34 18N 79 50W
Darlington, Wis., U.S.A. 158 42 43N 90 7W
Darlot, L. 137 27 48 S 121 35 E
Darłowo 54 54 25N 16 25 E
Darmstadt 49 49 51N 8 40 E
Darnall 129 29 23 S 31 18 E
Darnétal 42 49 25N 1 10 E
Darney 43 48 5N 6 0 E
Darnick 140 32 48 S 143 38 E
Darnley B. 147 69 30N 123 30W
Darnley, C. 13 68 0 S 69 0 E
Daroca 58 41 9N 1 25W
Darr 138 23 13 S 144 7 E
Darr, R. 138 23 39 S 143 50 E
Darragh 39 52 47N 9 7W
Darran Mts. 143 44 37 S 167 59 E
Darrington 160 48 14N 121 37W
Darror, R. 91 10 30N 50 0 E
Darsana 98 23 35N 88 48 E
Darsi 97 15 46N 79 44 E
Darsser Ort 48 54 27N 12 30 E
Dart, R., N.Z. 143 44 20 S 168 20 E
Dart, R., U.K. 30 50 24N 3 36W
*Renamed Pukapuka

Dartford 29 51 26N 0 15 E
Dartington 30 50 26N 3 42W
Dartmoor, Austral. 140 37 56N 141 19 E
Dartmoor, U.K. 30 50 36N 4 0W
Dartmouth, Austral. 138 23 31 S 144 44 E
Dartmouth, Can. 151 44 40N 63 30W
Dartmouth, U.K. 30 50 21N 3 35W
Dartmouth, L. 139 26 4 S 145 18 E
Darton 33 53 36N 1 32W
Dartuch, C. 58 39 55N 3 49 E
Daru, P.N.G. 135 9 3 S 143 13 E
Daru, S. Leone 120 8 0N 10 52W
Darvel 34 55 37N 4 20W
Darvel Bay 103 4 50N 118 20 E
Darwen 32 53 42N 2 29W
Darwha 96 20 15N 77 45 E
Darwin, Austral. 136 12 25 S 130 51 E
Darwin, U.S.A. 163 36 15N 117 35W
Darwin, Mt. 127 16 45 S 31 33 E
Darwin River 136 12 50 S 130 58 E
Daryacheh-ye-Sistan 93 31 0N 61 0 E
Daryapur 96 20 55N 77 20 E
Dase 123 14 53N 37 15 E
Dashato, R. 123 7 25N 42 40 E
Dashkesan 83 40 40N 46 0 E
Dasht-e Kavīr 93 34 30N 55 0 E
Dasht-e Lut 93 31 30N 58 0 E
Dasht-i-Khash 93 32 0N 62 0 E
Dasht-i-Margo 93 30 40N 62 30 E
Dasht-i-Nawar 94 33 52N 68 0 E
Dasht, R. 93 25 40N 62 20 E
Daska 94 32 20N 74 20 E
Dassa-Zoume 121 7 46N 2 14 E
Dasseneiland 128 33 37 S 18 3 E
Datça 69 36 46N 27 40 E
Datia 95 25 39N 78 27 E
Dattapur 96 20 45N 78 15 E
Daugava 80 57 0N 24 0 E
Daugavpils 80 55 53N 26 32 E
Daulat Yar 93 34 30N 65 45 E
Daulatabad 96 19 57N 75 15 E
Daun 49 50 5N 6 53 E
Dauphin, Can. 153 51 9N 100 5W
Dauphin, U.S.A. 162 40 22N 76 56W
Dauphin I. 157 30 16N 88 10W
Dauphin L. 153 51 20N 99 45W
Dauphiné 45 45 15N 5 25 E
Dauqa 122 19 30N 41 0 E
Daura, Kano, Nigeria 121 13 2N 8 21 E
Daura, N.-E., Nigeria 121 11 31N 11 24 E
Davadi 120 14 10N 16 3W
Davangere 97 14 25N 75 50 E
Davao 103 7 0N 125 40 E
Davao, G. of 103 6 30N 125 48 E
Davar Panab 93 27 25N 62 15 E
Dave 74 52 55N 1 50W
Davenport, Calif., U.S.A. 163 37 1N 122 12W
Davenport, Iowa, U.S.A. 158 41 30N 90 40W
Davenport, Wash., U.S.A. 160 47 40N 118 5W
Davenport Downs 138 24 8 S 141 7 E
Davenport Ra. 138 20 28 S 134 0 E
Daventry 28 52 16N 1 10W
David 166 8 30N 82 30W
David City 158 41 18N 97 10W
David Gorodok 80 52 4N 27 8 E
Davidson 153 51 16N 105 59W
Davik 71 61 53N 5 33 E
Davis 163 38 33N 121 45W
Davis Dam 161 35 11N 114 35W
Davis Inlet 151 55 50N 60 45W
Davis Mts. 159 30 42N 104 15W
Davis Str. 149 65 0N 58 0W
Davlekanovo 84 54 13N 55 3 E
Davos 51 46 48N 9 49 E
Davy L. 153 58 53N 108 18W
Davyhurst 137 30 2 S 120 40 E
Dawa, R. 123 5 0N 39 5 E
Dawaki, Jos, Nigeria 121 9 25N 9 33 E
Dawaki, Kano, Nigeria 121 12 5N 8 23 E
Dawayima 90 31 33N 34 55 E
Dawes Ra. 138 24 40 S 150 40 E
Dawley 28 52 40N 2 29W
Dawlish 30 50 34N 3 28W
Dawna Range 98 16 30N 98 30 E
Dawnyein 98 15 54N 95 36 E
Dawros Hd. 38 54 48N 8 32W
Dawson, Can. 147 64 10N 139 30W
Dawson, Ga., U.S.A. 157 31 45N 84 28W
Dawson, N.D., U.S.A. 158 46 56N 99 45W
Dawson Creek 152 55 45N 120 15W
Dawson, I. 176 53 50 S 70 50W
Dawson Inlet 153 61 50N 93 25W
Dawson, R. 133 23 25 S 150 10 E
Dawson Range 138 24 30 S 149 48 E
Dawson's 127 17 0 S 30 57 E
Daylesford 140 37 21 S 144 9 E
Dayr al-Ghusūn 90 32 21N 35 4 E
Dayr az Zawr 92 35 20N 40 5 E
Daysland 152 52 50N 112 20W
Dayton, Ohio, U.S.A. 156 39 45N 84 10W
Dayton, Tenn., U.S.A. 157 35 30N 85 1W
Dayton, Wash., U.S.A. 160 46 20N 118 0W
Daytona Beach 157 29 14N 81 0W
Dayville 160 44 33N 119 37W
De Aar 128 30 39 S 24 0 E
De Bilt 46 52 6N 5 11 E
De Funiak Springs 157 30 42N 86 10W
De Grey 136 20 12 S 119 12 E
De Grey, R. 136 20 0 S 119 13 E
De Kalb 158 41 55N 88 45W
De Koog 46 53 6N 4 46 E
De Land 157 29 1N 81 19W
De Leon 159 32 9N 98 35W
De Long Mts. 147 68 10N 163 0W
De Long, Ostrova 77 76 40N 149 20 E
De Panne 47 51 6N 2 34 E
De Pere 156 44 28N 88 1W
De Queen 159 34 3N 94 24W
De Quincy 159 30 30N 93 27W
De Ridder 159 30 48N 93 15W
De Rijp 46 52 33N 4 51 E
De Smet 158 44 25N 97 35W
De Tour Village 156 45 49N 83 56W
De Witt 159 34 19N 91 20W
Dead Sea = Miyet, Bahr el 92 31 30N 35 30 E
Deadwood 58 44 25N 103 43W
Deadwood L. 152 59 10N 128 30W
Deaf Adder Cr. 136 13 0 S 132 47 E
Deakin 137 30 46 S 129 58 E
Deal 29 51 13N 1 25 E
Dealesville 128 28 41 S 25 44 E
Dean, Forest of 28 51 50N 2 35W
Deán Funes 172 30 20 S 64 20W
Dearborn 150 42 18N 83 15W
Dearham 32 54 43N 3 28W
Dease L. 152 58 40N 130 5W
Dease Lake 152 58 25N 130 6W
Dease, R. 152 59 56N 128 32W
Death Valley 163 36 27N 116 52W
Death Valley Junc. 163 36 21N 116 30W
Death Valley Nat. Monument 163 36 30N 117 0W
Deauville 42 49 23N 0 2 E
Deba Habe 121 10 14N 11 20 E
Debaltsevo 82 48 22N 38 26 E
Debar 66 41 21N 20 37 E
Debba 123 14 20N 41 18 E
Debden 153 53 30N 106 50W
Debdou 118 33 59N 3 0W
Debeeti 128 23 45 S 26 32 E
Deben, R. 29 52 4N 1 19 E
Debenham 29 52 14N 1 10 E
Debessy 84 57 39N 53 49 E
Dębica 54 50 2N 21 25 E
Deblin 54 51 34N 21 50 E
Debo, L. 120 15 14N 3 57W
Debolt 152 55 12N 118 1W
Deborah, gasfield 19 53 4N 1 50 E
Deborah, L. 137 30 45 S 119 0 E
Debrc 66 44 38N 19 53 E
Debre Birhan 123 9 41N 39 31 E
Debre Markos 123 10 20N 37 40 E
Debre May 123 11 20N 37 25 E
Debre Sina 123 9 51N 39 50 E
Debre Tabor 123 11 50N 38 26 E
Debrecen 53 47 33N 21 42 E
Dečani 66 42 30N 20 10 E
Decatur, Ala., U.S.A. 157 34 35N 87 0W
Decatur, Ga., U.S.A. 157 33 47N 84 17W
Decatur, Ill., U.S.A. 158 39 50N 89 0W
Decatur, Ind., U.S.A. 156 40 52N 85 28W
Decatur, Texas, U.S.A. 159 33 15N 97 35W
Decazeville 44 44 34N 2 15 E
Deccan 97 14 0N 77 0 E
Deception I. 13 63 0 S 60 15W
Deception L. 153 56 33N 104 13W
Deception, Mt. 140 30 42 S 138 16 E
Decize 43 46 50N 3 28 E
Decollatura 65 39 2N 16 21 E
Decorah 158 43 20N 91 50W
Deda 70 46 56N 24 50 E
Dedaye 98 16 24N 95 53 E
Deddington 28 51 58N 1 19W
Dedemsvaart 46 52 36N 6 28 E
Dedham 162 42 14N 71 10W
Dedilovo 81 53 59N 37 50 E
Dédougou 120 12 30N 3 35W
Deduru Oya 97 7 32N 81 45 E
Dedza 127 14 20 S 34 20 E
Dee, R., Eng.-Wales, U.K. 31 53 15N 3 7W
Dee, R., Scot., U.K. 37 57 4N 2 7W
Deel R. 38 53 35N 7 9W
Deelish 39 51 41N 9 18W
Deep B. 152 61 15N 116 35W
Deep Lead 140 37 0 S 142 43 E
Deep Well 138 24 20 S 134 0 E
Deepdale 136 26 22 S 114 20 E
Deeping Fen 29 52 45N 0 15W
Deeping, St. Nicholas 29 52 44N 0 11W
Deepwater 139 29 25 S 151 51 E
Deer I. 147 54 55N 162 20W
Deer Lake, Newf., Can. 151 49 11N 57 27W
Deer Lake, Ontario, Can. 153 52 36N 94 20W
Deer Lodge 160 46 25N 112 40W
Deer Park 160 47 55N 117 21W
Deer, R. 153 58 23N 94 13W
Deer River 158 47 21N 93 44W
Deer Sound 37 58 58N 2 50W
Deeral 138 17 14 S 145 55 E
Deerdepoort 128 24 37 S 26 27 E
Deering 147 66 5N 162 50W
Deerlijk 47 50 51N 3 22 E
Deerness 37 58 57N 2 44W
Deesa 94 24 18N 72 10 E
Deferiet 162 44 2N 75 41W
Defiance 156 41 20N 84 20W
Deganwy 31 53 18N 3 49W
Deganya 90 32 43N 35 34 E
Degebe, R. 57 38 21N 7 37W
Degeh-Bur 91 8 11N 43 31 E

Degema Dieuze

Degema 121 4 50N 6 48 E
Degerfors 74 64 16N 19 46 E
Degersfor 73 59 20N 14 28 E
Degersheim 51 47 23N 9 12 E
Degersiö 72 63 13N 18 3 E
Deggendorf 49 48 49N 12 59 E
Degloor 96 18 34N 77 33 E
Deh Bīd 93 30 39N 53 11 E
Deh Kheyr 93 28 45N 54 40 E
Deh Titan 93 33 45N 63 50 E
Dehibat 119 32 0N 10 47 E
Dehiwala 97 6 50N 79 51 E
Dehkhvareqan 92 37 50N 45 55 E
Dehra Dun 94 30 20N 78 4 E
Dehri 95 24 50N 84 15 E
Deinze 47 50 59N 3 32 E
Deir Abu Sa'id 90 32 30N 38 42 E
Deir Dibwan 90 31 55N 35 15 E
Dej 70 47 10N 23 52 E
Deje 72 59 35N 13 29 E
Dekar 128 18 30 S 23 10 E
Dekemhare 123 15 6N 39 0 E
Dekese 124 3 24 S 21 24 E
Dekhkanabad 85 38 21N 66 30 E
Del Mar 163 32 58N 117 16W
Del Norte 161 37 47N 106 27W
Del Rey, Rio 121 4 30N 8 48 E
Del Rio, Mexico 164 29 22N 100 54W
Del Rio, U.S.A. 159 29 15N 100 50W
Delabole 30 50 37N 4 45W
Delagoa B. 129 25 50 S 32 45 E
Delagua 159 32 35N 104 40W
Delai 122 17 21N 36 6 E
Delambre I. 136 20 27 S 117 4 E
Delano 163 35 48N 119 13W
Delareyville 128 26 41 S 25 26 E
Delavan 158 42 40N 88 39W
Delaware 156 40 20N 83 0W
Delaware □ 162 39 0N 75 40W
Delaware B. 162 38 50N 75 0W
Delaware City 162 39 34N 75 36W
Delaware, R. 162 39 20N 75 25W
Delčevo 66 41 58N 22 46 E
Delchirach 37 57 23N 3 20W
Delegate 141 37 4 S 148 56 E
Delémont 50 47 22N 7 20 E
Delft 46 52 1N 4 22 E
Delft I. 97 9 30N 79 40 E
Delfzijl 46 53 20N 6 55 E
Delgado, C. 127 10 45 S 40 40 E
Delgerhet 106 45 50N 110 30 E
Delgo 122 20 6N 30 40 E
Delhi, India 94 28 38N 77 17 E
Delhi, U.S.A. 162 42 17N 74 56W
Deli Jovan 66 44 13N 22 9 E
Delia 152 51 38N 112 23W
Delice, R. 92 39 45N 34 15 E
Delicias 164 28 10N 105 30W
Delicias, Laguna 164 28 7N 105 40W
Delimiro Gouveia 170 9 23 S 37 59W
Delitzsch 48 51 32N 12 22 E
Dell City 161 31 58N 105 19W
Dell Rapids 158 43 53N 96 44W
Delle 43 47 30N 7 2 E
Dellys 119 36 50N 3 57 E
Delmar, Del., U.S.A. 162 38 27N 75 34W
Delmar, N.Y., U.S.A. 162 42 5N 73 50W
Delmenhorst 48 53 3N 8 37 E
Delmiro 170 9 24 S 38 6W
Delnice 63 45 23N 14 50 E
Deloraine, Austral. 138 41 30 S 146 40 E
Deloraine, Can. 153 49 15N 100 29W
Delorme, L. 151 54 31N 69 52W
Delovo 66 44 55N 20 52 E
Delphi 156 40 37N 86 40W
Delphos 156 40 51N 84 17W
Delportshoop 128 28 22 S 24 20 E
Delray Beach 157 26 27N 80 4W
Delsbo 72 61 48N 16 32 E
Delta, Colo., U.S.A. 161 38 44N 108 5W
Delta, Utah, U.S.A. 160 39 21N 112 29W
Delta Amacuro □ 174 8 30N 61 30W
Deltaville 162 37 33N 76 20W
Delungra 139 29 39 S 150 51 E
Delvin 38 53 37N 7 8W
Delvina 68 39 59N 20 4 E
Delvinákion 68 39 57N 20 32 E
Demak 103 6 50 S 110 40 E
Demanda, Sierra de la 58 42 15N 3 0W
Demba 124 5 28 S 22 15 E
Dembecha 123 10 32N 37 30 E
Dembi 123 8 5N 36 25 E
Dembia 126 3 33N 25 48 E
Dembidolo 123 8 34N 34 50 E
Demchok 93 32 40N 79 29 E
Demer, R. 47 51 0N 5 8 E
Demerais, L. 150 47 35N 77 0W
Demerara, R. 174 7 0N 58 0W
Demidov 80 55 10N 31 30 E
Deming 161 32 10N 107 50W
Demini, R. 174 0 46N 62 56W
Demmin 48 53 54N 13 2 E
Demmit 152 55 20N 119 50W
Demnate 118 31 44N 6 59W
Demonte 62 44 18N 7 18 E
Demopolis 157 32 30N 87 48W
Dempo, Mt. 102 4 10 S 103 15 E
Demyansk 80 57 30N 32 27 E
Den Bemmel 46 51 43N 4 26 E
Den Burg 46 53 3N 4 47 E
Den Chai 100 17 59N 100 4 E
Den Dungen 47 51 41N 5 22 E
Den Haag = 's Gravenhage 46 52 7N 4 17 E
Den Ham 46 52 28N 6 30 E
Den Helder 46 52 57N 4 45 E
Den Hulst 46 52 36N 6 16 E
Den Oever 46 52 56N 5 2 E
Denain 43 50 20N 3 22 E
Denair 163 37 32N 120 48W
Denau 85 38 16N 67 54 E
Denbigh 31 53 12N 3 26W
Denbigh (□) 26 53 8N 3 30W
Denby Dale 33 53 35N 1 40W
Denchin 99 31 35N 95 15 E
Dendang 102 3 7 S 107 56 E
Dender, R. 47 51 2N 4 6 E
Denderhoutem 47 50 53N 4 2 E
Denderleeuw 47 50 54N 4 5 E
Dendermonde 47 51 2N 4 5 E
Deneba 123 9 47N 39 10 E
Denekamp 46 52 22N 7 1 E
Denezhkin Kamen, Gora 84 60 25N 59 32 E
Denge 121 12 52N 5 21 E
Dengi 121 9 25N 9 55 E
Denham 137 25 56 S 113 31 E
Denham Ra. 138 21 55 S 147 46 E
Denham Sd. 137 25 45 S 113 15 E
Denholm 153 52 40N 108 0W
Denia 59 38 49N 0 8 E
Denial B. 139 32 14 S 133 32 E
Deniliquin 141 35 30 S 144 58 E
Denison, Iowa, U.S.A. 158 42 0N 95 18W
Denison, Texas, U.S.A. 159 33 50N 96 40W
Denison Plains 136 18 35 S 128 0 E
Denison Range 136 28 30 S 136 5 E
Denisovka 84 52 28N 61 46 E
Denizli 92 37 42N 29 2 E
Denkez Iyesus 123 12 27N 37 43 E
Denman 141 32 24 S 150 42 E
Denmark 137 34 59 S 117 18 E
Denmark ■ 73 55 30N 9 0 E
Denmark Str. 14 66 0N 30 0W
Dennis Hd. 37 59 23N 2 26W
Denniston 143 41 45 S 171 49 E
Denny 35 56 1N 3 55W
Denpasar 102 8 45 S 115 5 E
Dent 32 54 17N 2 28W
Denton, E. Sussex, U.K. 29 50 48N 0 5 E
Denton, Gr. Manchester, U.K. 32 53 26N 2 10W
Denton, Lincs., U.K. 33 52 52N 0 42W
Denton, Md., U.S.A. 162 38 53N 75 50W
Denton, Mont., U.S.A. 160 47 25N 109 56W
Denton, Texas, U.S.A. 159 33 12N 97 10W
D'Entrecasteaux, C. 137 34 50 S 115 59 E
D'Entrecasteaux Is. 135 9 0 S 151 0 E
D'Entrecasteaux Pt. 137 34 50 S 115 57 E
Dents du Midi 50 46 10N 6 56 E
Denu 121 6 4N 1 8 E
Denver, Colo., U.S.A. 158 39 45N 105 0W
Denver, Pa., U.S.A. 162 40 14N 76 8W
Denver City 159 32 58N 102 48W
Deoband 94 29 42N 77 43 E
Deobhog 96 19 53N 82 44 E
Deogarh 96 21 32N 84 45 E
Deoghar 95 24 30N 86 59 E
Deolali 96 19 50N 73 50 E
Deoli 94 25 50N 75 50 E
Deoria 95 26 31N 83 48 E
Deosai, Mts. 95 35 40N 75 0 E
Deposit 162 42 5N 75 23W
Depot Spring 137 27 55 S 120 3 E
Depuch I. 136 20 35 S 117 44 E
Deputatskiy 77 69 18N 139 54 E
Dera Ghazi Khan 94 30 5N 70 43 E
Dera Ismail Khan 94 31 50N 70 50 E
Dera Ismail Khan □ 94 32 30N 70 0 E
Derati Wells 126 3 52N 36 37 E
Derbent 74 42 5N 48 15 E
Derby, Austral. 136 17 18 S 123 38 E
Derby, U.K. 33 52 55N 1 28W
Derby, U.S.A. 162 41 20N 73 5W
Derby □ 33 52 55N 1 28W
Derecske 53 47 20N 21 33 E
Derg, L. 39 53 0N 8 20W
Derg, R. 38 54 42N 7 26W
Dergachi 81 50 3N 36 3 E
Dergaon 99 26 45N 94 0 E
Dermantsi 67 43 8N 24 17 E
Derna 117 32 40N 22 35 E
Dernieres Isles 159 29 0N 90 45W
Derriana, L. 39 51 54N 10 1W
Derrinallum 140 37 57 S 143 15 E
Derry R. 39 52 43N 6 35W
Derrybrien 39 53 4N 8 38W
Derrygonnelly 38 54 25N 7 50W
Derrygrogan 39 53 19N 7 23W
Derrykeighan 38 55 8N 6 30W
Derrylin 38 54 12N 7 34W
Derry = Londonderry 38 55 0N 7 19W
Derrynasaggart Mts. 39 51 58N 9 15W
Derryrush 38 53 23N 9 40W
Derryveagh Mts. 38 55 0N 8 40W
Derudub 122 17 31N 36 7 E
Dervaig 34 56 35N 6 13W
Derval 42 47 40N 1 41W
Dervéni 69 38 8N 22 25 E
Derwent 153 53 41N 110 58W
Derwent, R., Derby, U.K. 33 52 53N 1 17W
Derwent, R., N. Yorks., U.K. 33 53 45N 0 57W
Derwent, R., Tyne & Wear, U.K. 35 54 58N 1 40W
Derwentwater, L. 32 53 34N 3 9W
Des Moines, Iowa, U.S.A. 158 41 35N 93 37W
Des Moines, N. Mex., U.S.A. 159 36 50N 103 51W
Des Moines, R. 158 40 23N 91 25W
Desaguadero, R., Argent. 172 33 28 S 67 15W
Desaguadero, R., Boliv. 174 17 30 S 68 0W
Desborough 29 52 27N 0 50W
Deschaillons 151 46 32N 72 7W
Descharme, R. 153 56 51N 109 13W
Deschutes, R. 160 45 30N 121 0W
Dese 123 11 5N 39 40 E
Deseado, R. 176 40 0 S 69 0W
Desemboque 164 30 30N 112 27W
Desenzano del Gardo 62 45 28N 10 32 E
Desert Center 161 33 45N 115 27W
Desert Hot Springs 163 33 58N 116 30W
Desertmartin 38 54 47N 6 40W
Desford 28 52 38N 1 19W
Désirade, I. 167 16 18N 61 3W
Deskenatlata L. 152 60 55N 112 3W
Desna, R. 80 52 0N 33 15 E
Desnǔtui, R. 70 44 15N 23 27 E
Desolación, I. 176 53 0 S 74 0W
Despeñaperros, Paso 59 38 24N 3 30W
Despotovac 66 44 6N 21 30 E
Dessa 121 14 44N 1 6 E
Dessau 48 51 49N 12 15 E
Dessel 47 51 15N 5 7 E
Dessye = Dese 123 11 5N 39 40 E
D'Estress B. 140 35 55 S 137 45 E
Desuri 94 25 18N 73 35 E
Desvrès 43 50 40N 1 48 E
Det Udom 100 14 54N 105 5 E
Detinjá, R. 66 43 51N 19 45 E
Detmold 48 51 55N 8 50 E
Detour Pt. 156 45 37N 86 35W
Detroit, Mich., U.S.A. 150 42 13N 83 22W
Detroit, Tex., U.S.A. 159 33 40N 95 10W
Detroit Lakes 158 46 50N 95 50W
Dett 127 18 32 S 26 57 E
Dettifoss 74 65 49N 16 24W
Děčin 52 50 47N 14 12 E
Deurne, Belg. 47 51 12N 4 24 E
Deurne, Neth. 47 51 27N 5 49 E
Deutsche Bucht 48 54 10N 7 51 E
Deutschlandsberg 52 46 49N 15 14 E
Deux-Acren, Les 47 50 44N 3 51 E
Deux-Sèvres □ 42 46 35N 0 20W
Deva 70 45 53N 22 55 E
Devakottai 97 9 55N 78 45 E
Devaprayag 95 30 13N 78 35 E
Dévaványa 53 47 2N 20 59 E
Deveci Daği 82 40 10N 36 0 E
Devecser 53 47 6N 17 26 E
Deventer 46 52 15N 6 10 E
Deveron, R. 37 57 40N 2 31W
Devesel 70 44 28N 22 41 E
Devgad, I. 97 14 48N 74 5 E
Devil R., Pk. 143 40 56 S 172 37 E
Devils Bridge 31 52 23N 3 50W
Devils Den 163 35 46N 119 58W
Devils Lake 158 48 5N 98 50W
Devils Paw, mt. 152 58 47N 134 0W
Devils Pt. 97 9 26N 80 6 E
Devilsbit Mt. 39 52 50N 7 58W
Devin 67 41 44N 24 24 E
Devizes 28 51 21N 2 0W
Devnya 67 43 13N 27 33 E
Devolli, R. 68 40 57N 20 15 E
Devon 152 53 24N 113 44W
Devon I. 12 75 47N 88 0W
Devonport, Austral. 138 41 10 S 146 22 E
Devonport, N.Z. 142 36 49 S 174 49 E
Devonport, U.K. 30 50 23N 4 11W
Devonshire □ 30 50 50N 3 40W
Dewas 94 22 59N 76 3 E
Dewetsdorp 128 29 33 S 26 39 E
Dewgad Baria 94 22 40N 73 55 E
Dewsbury 33 53 42N 1 38W
Dexter, Mo., U.S.A. 159 36 50N 90 0W
Dexter, N. Mex., U.S.A. 159 33 15N 104 25W
Dey-Dey, L. 137 29 12 S 131 4 E
Deyhuk 93 33 15N 104 25W
Deyyer 93 27 55N 51 55 E
Dezadeash L. 152 60 28N 136 58W
Dezfūl 92 32 20N 48 30 E
Dezh Shahpur 92 35 30N 46 25 E
Dezhneva, Mys 77 66 10N 169 3 E
Dhaba 92 27 25N 35 40 E
Dháfni 69 37 48N 22 1 E
Dhahaban 122 21 58N 39 3 E
Dhahiriya = Qz Zahiriya 90 31 25N 34 58 E
Dhahran 92 26 9N 50 10 E
Dhama Dzong 99 28 15N 91 15 E
Dhamási 68 39 43N 22 11 E
Dhampur 95 29 19N 78 33 E
Dhamtari 96 20 42N 81 35 E
Dhanbad 95 23 50N 86 30 E
Dhangarhi 99 28 55N 80 40 E
Dhankuta 95 26 55N 87 20 E
Dhanora 96 20 20N 80 22 E
Dhar 94 22 35N 75 26 E
Dharampur, Mad. P., India 94 22 13N 75 18 E
Dharampur, Maharashtra, India 96 20 32N 73 17 E
Dharapuram 97 10 45N 77 34 E
Dharmapuri 97 12 10N 78 10 E
Dharmavaram 97 14 29N 77 44 E
Dharmsala, (Dharamsala) 94 32 16N 73 23 E
Dhaulagiri Mt. 95 28 45N 83 45 E
Dhebar, L. 94 24 10N 74 0 E
Dhenkanal 96 20 45N 85 35 E
Dhenoúsa 69 37 8N 25 48 E
Dhesfina 69 38 25N 22 31 E
Dheskáti 68 39 55N 21 49 E
Dhespotikó 69 36 57N 24 58 E
Dhidhimótikhon 68 41 22N 26 29 E
Dhikti, Mt. 69 35 8N 25 29 E
Dhilianáta 69 38 15N 20 34 E
Dhílos 69 37 23N 25 15 E
Dhimitsána 69 37 36N 22 3 E
Dhirfis, Mt. 69 38 40N 23 54 E
Dhodhekánisos 69 36 35N 27 0 E
Dhofar 91 17 0N 54 10 E
Dhokós 69 37 20N 23 20 E
Dholiana 68 39 54N 20 32 E
Dholka 94 22 44N 72 29 E
Dholpur 94 26 45N 77 59 E
Dhomokós 69 39 10N 22 18 E
Dhond 96 18 26N 74 40 E
Dhoraji 94 21 45N 70 37 E
Dhoxáthon 68 41 9N 24 16 E
Dhragonisi 69 37 27N 25 29 E
Dhrangadhra 94 22 59N 71 31 E
Dhriopós 69 37 35N 24 35 E
Dhrol 94 22 40N 70 25 E
Dhubaibah 93 23 25N 54 35 E
Dhubri 98 26 2N 90 2 E
Dhulasar 98 21 52N 90 14 E
Dhulia 96 20 58N 74 50 E
Dhupdhara 98 25 58N 91 4 E
Dhurm 122 20 18N 42 53 E
Di Linh 101 11 35N 108 4 E
Di Linh, Cao Nguyen 101 11 30N 108 0 E
Dia, I. 69 35 26N 25 13 E
Diable, Mt. 163 37 53N 121 56W
Diablerets, Les 50 46 22N 7 10 E
Diablo Range 163 37 0N 121 5W
Diafarabé 120 14 17N 4 57W
Diala 120 13 59N 10 0W
Dialakoro 120 12 18N 7 54W
Diallassagou 120 13 47N 3 41W
Diamante 172 32 5 S 60 40W
Diamante, R. 172 34 31 S 66 56W
Diamantina 171 18 5 S 43 40W
Diamantina, R. 138 22 25 S 142 20 E
Diamantino 175 14 30 S 56 30W
Diamond Harbour 95 22 11N 88 14 E
Diamond Is. 138 17 25 S 151 5 E
Diamond Mts. 160 40 0N 115 58W
Diamond Springs 163 38 42N 120 49W
Diamondville 160 41 51N 110 30W
Diano Marina 62 43 55N 8 3 E
Dianópolis 171 11 38 S 46 50W
Dianra 120 8 45N 6 14W
Diaole, Î. du. 170 5 15N 52 45W
Diapaga 121 12 5N 1 46 E
Diapangou 121 12 5N 0 10 E
Diapur 140 36 19 S 141 29 E
Diariguila 120 10 35N 10 2W
Dibai (Dubai) 93 25 15N 55 20 E
Dibaya 124 6 20 S 22 0 E
Dibaya Lubue 124 4 12 S 19 54 E
Dibba 93 25 45N 56 16 E
Dibbi 123 4 10N 41 52 E
Dibden 28 50 53N 1 24W
Dibega 92 35 50N 43 46 E
Dibër 68 41 38N 20 15 E
Dibete 128 23 45 S 26 32 E
Dibi 123 4 10N 41 52 E
Dibrugarh 98 27 29N 94 55 E
Dibulla 174 11 17N 73 19W
Dickinson 158 46 50N 102 40W
Dickson 157 36 5N 87 22W
Dickson City 162 41 29N 75 40W
Dicomano 63 43 53 S 11 30 E
Didam 46 51 57N 6 8 E
Didcot 28 51 36N 1 14W
Didesa, W. 123 9 40N 35 50 E
Didiéni 120 14 5N 7 50W
Didsbury 152 51 35N 114 10W
Didwana 94 27 17N 74 25 E
Die 45 44 47N 5 22 E
Diébougou 120 11 0N 3 15W
Diefenbaker L. 153 51 0N 106 55W
Diego Garcia, I. 11 9 50 S 75 0 E
Diégo Suarez 129 12 25 S 49 20 E
Diekirch 47 49 52N 6 10 E
Diélette 42 49 33N 1 52W
Diéma 120 14 32N 9 3W
Diemen 46 52 21N 4 58 E
Diemering 120 12 29N 16 47W
Dien Ban 100 15 53N 108 16 E
Diên Biên Phu 100 21 20N 103 0 E
Dien Khanh 101 12 15N 109 6 E
Diepenheim 46 52 12N 6 33 E
Diepenveen 46 52 18N 6 9 E
Diepholz 48 52 37N 8 22 E
Diepoldsau 51 47 23N 9 40 E
Dieppe 42 49 54N 1 4 E
Dieren 46 52 3N 6 6 E
Dierks 159 34 9N 94 0W
Diessen 47 51 29N 5 10 E
Diessenhofen 51 47 42N 8 46 E
Diest 47 50 58N 5 4 E
Dietikon 51 47 24N 8 24 E
Dieulefit 45 44 32N 5 4 E
Dieuze 43 48 30N 6 40 E

Diever **Donskoy**

Diever	**46**	52 51N	6 19E
Diffa	**121**	13 34N	12 33E
Differdange	**47**	49 81N	5 54E
Dig	**94**	27 28N	77 20E
Digba	**126**	4 25N	25 42E
Digboi	**98**	27 23N	95 38E
Digby	**151**	44 41N	65 50W
Digges	**153**	58 40N	94 0W
Digges Is.	**149**	62 40N	77 50W
Digges Lamprey	**153**	58 33N	94 8W
Dighinala	**98**	23 15N	92 5E
Dighton	**158**	38 30N	100 26W
Digne	**45**	44 5N	6 12E
Digoin	**44**	46 29N	3 58E
Digos	**103**	6 45N	125 20E
Digranes	**74**	66 4N	14 44E
Digras	**96**	20 6N	77 45E
Dihang, R.	**99**	27 30N	96 30E
Dijlah	**92**	37 0N	42 30E
Dijle, R.	**47**	50 58N	4 41E
Dijon	**43**	47 20N	5 0E
Dikala	**123**	4 45N	31 28E
Dikhal	**123**	11 8N	42 20E
Dikomu di Kai, Mt.	**128**	24 51S	24 36E
Diksmuide	**47**	51 2N	2 52E
Dikson	**76**	73 40N	80 5E
Dikumbiya	**123**	14 45N	37 30E
Dikwa	**121**	12 4N	13 30E
Dila	**123**	6 14N	38 22E
Dilam	**92**	23 55N	47 10E
Dilbeek	**47**	50 51N	4 17E
Dili	**103**	8 39S	125 34E
Dilizhan	**83**	41 46N	44 57E
Dillenburg	**48**	50 44N	8 17E
Dilley	**159**	28 40N	99 12W
Dilling	**123**	12 3N	29 35E
Dillingen	**49**	49 22N	6 42E
Dillingham	**147**	59 5N	158 30W
Dillon, Can.	**153**	55 56N	108 56W
Dillon, Mont., U.S.A.	**160**	45 9N	112 36W
Dillon, S.C., U.S.A.	**157**	34 26N	79 20W
Dillon, R.	**153**	55 56N	108 56W
Dillsburg	**162**	40 7N	77 2W
Dilolo	**14**	10 28S	22 18E
Dilsen	**47**	51 2N	5 44E
Dilston	**138**	41 22S	147 10E
Dima	**123**	6 19N	36 15E
Dimapur	**98**	25 54N	93 45E
Dimas	**164**	23 43N	106 47W
Dimashq	**92**	33 30N	36 18E
Dimbelenge	**124**	4 30N	23 0E
Dimbokro	**120**	6 45N	4 30W
Dimboola	**140**	36 28S	142 0E
Dîmbovița □	**70**	45 0N	25 30E
Dîmbovita, R.	**70**	44 40N	26 0E
Dimbulah	**138**	17 2S	145 4E
Dimitriya Lapteva, Proliv	**77**	73 0N	140 0E
Dimitrovgrad, Bulg.	**67**	42 5N	25 35E
Dimitrovgrad, U.S.S.R.	**81**	54 25N	49 33E
Dimitrovgrad, Yugo.	**66**	43 0N	22 48E
Dimmitt	**159**	34 36N	102 16W
Dimo	**123**	5 19N	29 10E
Dimona	**90**	31 2N	35 1E
Dimovo	**66**	43 43N	22 50E
Dinagat I.	**103**	10 10N	125 40E
Dinajpur	**98**	25 33N	88 43E
Dinan	**42**	48 28N	2 2W
Dinant	**47**	50 16N	4 55E
Dinapore	**95**	25 38N	85 5E
Dinar	**92**	38 5N	30 15E
Dinard	**42**	48 38N	2 6W
Dinaric Alps	**16**	44 0N	17 30E
Dinas Hd.	**31**	52 2N	4 56W
Dinas Mawddwy	**31**	52 44N	3 41W
Dinas Powis	**31**	51 25N	3 14W
Dinder, Nahr ed	**123**	12 32N	35 0E
Dindi, R.	**96**	16 24N	78 15E
Dindigul	**97**	10 25N	78 0E
Dingelstädt	**48**	51 19N	10 19E
Dingila	**126**	3 25N	26 25E
Dingle	**39**	52 9N	10 17W
Dingle B.	**39**	52 3N	10 20W
Dingle Harbour	**39**	52 7N	10 12W
Dingmans Ferry	**162**	41 13N	74 55W
Dingo	**138**	23 38S	149 19E
Dingolfing	**49**	48 38N	12 30E
Dinguiraye	**120**	11 30N	10 35W
Dingwall	**37**	57 36N	4 26W
Dingyadi	**121**	13 0N	0 53E
Dinh Lap	**100**	21 33N	107 6E
Dinh, Mui	**101**	11 22N	109 1E
Dinhata	**98**	26 8N	89 27E
Dinkel	**46**	52 30N	6 58E
Dinokwe (Palla Road)	**128**	23 29S	26 37E
Dinosaur National Monument	**160**	40 30N	108 45W
Dinslaken	**47**	51 34N	6 41E
Dintel, R.	**47**	51 39N	4 22E
Dinuba	**163**	36 37N	119 22W
Dinxperlo	**46**	51 52N	6 30E
Dio	**73**	56 37N	14 15E
Diosgyör	**53**	48 7N	20 43E
Diosig	**70**	47 18N	22 2E
Dioundiou	**121**	12 37N	3 33E
Diourbel	**120**	14 39N	16 12W
Diphu Pass	**98**	28 9N	97 20E
Diplo	**94**	24 25N	69 35E
Dipolog	**103**	8 36N	123 20E
Dipşa	**70**	46 58N	24 27E
Dipton	**143**	45 54S	168 22E
Dir	**93**	35 08N	71 59E
Diré	**120**	15 20N	3 25W
Dire Dawa	**123**	9 35N	41 45E
Direction, C.	**138**	12 51S	143 32E
Diriamba	**166**	11 51N	86 19W
Dirico	**125**	17 50S	20 42E
Dirk Hartog I.	**137**	25 50S	113 5E
Dirranbandi	**139**	28 33S	148 17E
Disa	**123**	12 5N	34 15E
Disappointment, C.	**160**	46 20N	124 0W
Disappointment L.	**136**	23 20S	122 40E
Disaster B.	**141**	37 15S	150 0E
Discovery	**148**	63 0N	115 0W
Discovery B.	**140**	38 10S	140 40E
Disentis	**51**	46 42N	8 50E
Dishna	**122**	26 9N	32 32E
Disina	**121**	11 35N	9 50E
Disko	**12**	69 45N	53 30W
Disko Bugt	**12**	69 10N	52 0W
Disna	**80**	55 32N	28 11E
Disna, R.	**80**	55 20N	27 30E
Dison	**47**	50 37N	5 51E
Diss	**29**	52 23N	1 6E
Disteghil Sar	**95**	36 20N	75 5E
Distington	**32**	54 35N	3 33W
District Heights	**162**	38 51N	76 53W
District of Columbia □	**162**	38 55N	77 0W
Distrito Federal □, Brazil	**171**	15 45S	47 45W
Distrito Federal □, Venez.	**174**	10 30N	66 55W
Disûq	**122**	31 8N	30 35E
Ditchingham	**29**	52 28N	1 26E
Ditchling & Beacon	**29**	50 59N	0 7W
Ditinn	**120**	10 53N	12 11W
Dittisham	**30**	50 22N	3 36W
Ditton Priors	**28**	52 30N	2 33W
Diu, I.	**94**	20 45N	70 58E
Diver	**150**	46 44N	79 30W
Dives	**42**	49 18N	0 8W
Dives, R.	**42**	49 18N	0 7W
Divi Pt.	**97**	15 59N	81 9E
Divichi	**83**	41 15N	48 57E
Divide	**160**	45 48N	112 47W
Dividing Ra.	**137**	27 45S	116 0E
Divinopólis	**171**	20 10S	44 54W
Divisões, Serra dos	**171**	17 0S	51 0W
Divnoye	**83**	45 55N	43 27E
Divo	**120**	5 48N	5 15W
Diwal Kol	**94**	34 23N	67 52E
Dixie	**160**	45 37N	115 27W
Dixon, Calif., U.S.A.	**163**	38 27N	121 49W
Dixon, Ill., U.S.A.	**158**	41 50N	89 30W
Dixon, Mont., U.S.A.	**160**	47 19N	114 25W
Dixon, N. Mex., U.S.A.	**161**	36 15N	105 57W
Dixon Entrance	**153**	54 30N	132 0W
Dixonville	**152**	56 32N	117 40W
Diyarbakir	**92**	37 55N	40 18E
Dizzard Pt.	**30**	50 46N	4 38W
Djabotaoure	**121**	8 35N	0 58E
Djado	**119**	21 4N	12 14E
Djado, Plateau du	**119**	21 29N	12 21E
Djakarta = Jakarta	**103**	6 9S	106 49E
Djakovo	**66**	45 19N	18 24E
Djamâa	**119**	33 32N	5 59E
Djamba	**128**	16 45S	13 58E
Djambala	**124**	2 20S	14 30E
Djanet	**119**	24 35N	9 32E
Djang	**121**	5 30N	10 5E
Djaul I.	**135**	2 58S	150 57E
Djawa = Jawa	**103**	7 0S	110 0E
Djebiniana	**119**	35 1N	11 0E
Djelfa	**118**	34 40N	3 15E
Djema	**126**	6 9N	25 15E
Djeneïene	**119**	31 45N	10 9E
Djenné	**120**	14 0N	4 30W
Djenoun, Garet el	**119**	25 4N	5 31E
Djerba	**119**	33 52N	10 51E
Djerba, Île de	**119**	33 56N	11 0E
Djerid, Chott	**119**	33 42N	8 30E
Djibo	**121**	14 15N	1 35W
Djibouti	**123**	11 30N	43 5E
Djibouti ■	**123**	11 30N	42 15E
Djidjelli	**119**	36 52N	5 50E
Djirlange	**101**	11 44N	108 15E
Djofra	**119**	28 59N	15 47E
Djolu	**124**	0 45N	22 5E
Djorf el Youdi	**118**	32 14N	9 8W
Djougou	**121**	9 40N	1 45E
Djoum	**124**	2 41N	12 35E
Djourab, Erg du	**117**	16 40N	18 50E
Djugu	**126**	1 55N	30 35E
Djúpivogur	**74**	64 39N	14 17W
Djursholm	**72**	59 25N	18 6E
Djursland	**73**	56 27N	10 45E
Dmitriev-Lgovskiy	**80**	52 10N	35 0E
Dmitriya Lapteva, Proliv	**77**	73 0N	140 0E
Dmitrov	**81**	56 25N	37 32E
Dmitrovsk Orlovskiy	**80**	52 29N	35 10E
Dneiper, R. = Dnepr	**80**	52 29N	35 10E
Dnepr, R.	**82**	50 0N	31 0E
Dneprodzerzhinsk	**82**	48 32N	34 30E
Dneprodzerzhinskoye Vdkhr.	**77**	49 0N	34 0E
Dnepropetrovsk	**82**	48 30N	35 0E
Dneprorudnoye	**82**	47 21N	34 58E
Dnestr, R.	**82**	48 30N	26 30E
Dnestrovski = Belgorod	**82**	50 35N	36 35E
Dniester = Dnestr	**82**	48 30N	26 30E
Dno	**80**	57 50N	29 58E
Doan Hung	**100**	21 38N	105 10E
Doba	**117**	8 40N	16 50E
Dobané	**126**	6 20N	24 39E
Dobbiaco	**63**	46 44N	12 13E
Dobbyn	**138**	19 44S	139 59E
Dobczyce	**54**	49 52N	20 25E
Döbeln	**48**	51 7N	13 10E
Doberai, Jazirah	**103**	1 25S	133 0E
Dobiegniew	**54**	52 59N	15 45E
Doblas	**172**	37 5S	64 0W
Dobo	**103**	5 45S	134 15E
Doboj	**66**	44 46N	18 6E
Dobra, Poland	**54**	53 34N	15 20E
Dobra, Dîmbovița, Rumania	**67**	44 52N	25 40E
Dobra, Hunedoara, Rumania	**70**	45 54N	22 36E
Dobre Miasto	**54**	53 58N	20 26E
Dobrinishta	**67**	41 49N	23 34E
Dobriš	**52**	49 46N	14 10E
Dobrodzien	**54**	50 45N	18 25E
Dobrogea	**70**	44 30N	28 15E
Dobruja = Dobrogea	**70**	44 30N	28 15E
Dobrush	**80**	52 28N	30 35E
Dobryanka	**84**	58 27N	56 25E
Dobrzyn n. Wisła	**54**	52 39N	19 22E
Dobtong	**123**	6 25N	31 40E
Doc, Mui	**100**	17 58N	106 30E
Doce, R.	**171**	19 37S	39 49W
Docking	**29**	52 55N	0 39E
Doda	**95**	33 10N	75 34E
Döda Fallet	**72**	63 4N	16 35E
Doddington	**29**	52 29N	0 3E
Dodecanese = Dhodhekánisos	**69**	36 35N	27 0E
Dodewaard	**46**	51 55N	5 39E
Dodge Center	**158**	44 1N	92 57W
Dodge City	**159**	37 42N	100 0W
Dodge L.	**153**	59 50N	105 36W
Dodgeville	**158**	42 55N	90 8W
Dodman Pt.	**30**	50 13N	4 49W
Dodo	**123**	5 10N	29 57E
Dodola	**123**	6 59N	39 11E
Dodoma	**126**	6 8S	35 45E
Dodoma □	**126**	6 0S	36 0E
Dodsland	**153**	51 50N	108 45W
Dodson	**160**	48 23N	108 4W
Doesburg	**46**	52 1N	6 9E
Doetinchem	**46**	51 59N	6 18E
Doftana	**70**	45 17N	25 45E
Dog Creek	**152**	51 35N	122 14W
Dog L., Man., Can.	**152**	51 2N	98 31W
Dog L., Ont., Can.	**150**	48 12N	89 16W
Dog, R.	**152**	57 50N	94 40W
Doganbey	**69**	37 40N	27 10E
Dogi	**93**	32 20N	62 50E
Dogliani	**62**	44 35N	7 55E
Dōgo	**110**	36 15N	133 16E
Dōgo-San	**110**	35 2N	133 13E
Dògondoutchi	**121**	13 38N	4 2E
Dogoraoua	**121**	14 0N	5 31E
Dogran	**94**	31 48N	73 35E
Dohad	**94**	22 50N	74 15E
Dohazari	**99**	22 10N	92 5E
Doheny	**150**	47 4N	72 35W
Doherty	**150**	46 58N	79 44W
Doi, I.	**103**	2 21N	127 49E
Doi Luang	**101**	18 20N	101 30E
Doi Saket	**100**	18 52N	99 9E
Doig, R., Alta., Can.	**152**	56 57N	120 0W
Doig, R., B.C., Can.	**152**	56 25N	120 40W
Dois Irmãos, Serra	**171**	8 30S	41 5W
Dokka	**71**	60 49N	10 7E
Dokka, R.	**71**	61 7N	10 0E
Dokkum	**46**	53 20N	5 59E
Dokkumer Ee, R.	**46**	53 18N	5 52E
Dokri Mohenjodaro	**94**	27 25N	68 7E
Dol	**42**	48 34N	1 47W
Dolak, Pulau = Kolepom, P.	**103**	8 0S	138 30E
Doland	**158**	44 55N	98 5W
Dolbeau	**151**	48 53N	72 18W
Dôle	**43**	47 7N	5 31E
Doleib, W.	**123**	10 30N	33 15E
Dolgarrog	**31**	53 11N	3 50W
Dolgellau	**31**	52 44N	3 53W
Dolgelly = Dolgellau	**31**	52 44N	3 53W
Dolginovo	**80**	54 39N	27 29E
Dolianovo	**64**	39 23N	9 11E
Dolinskaya	**82**	48 16N	32 36E
Dolisie	**124**	4 0S	13 10E
Dolj □	**70**	44 10N	23 30E
Dolla	**39**	52 47N	8 12W
Dollar	**35**	56 9N	3 41W
Dollart	**46**	53 20N	7 10E
Dolna Banya	**67**	42 18N	23 44E
Dolni Dubnik	**67**	43 24N	24 26E
Dolo	**63**	45 25N	12 4E
Dolo Bay	**123**	4 11N	42 3E
Dolomites = Dolomiti	**63**	46 30N	11 40E
Dolomiti	**63**	46 30N	11 40E
Dolores, Argent.	**172**	36 20S	57 40W
Dolores, Mexico	**164**	28 53N	108 27W
Dolores, Uruguay	**172**	33 34S	58 15W
Dolores, Colo., U.S.A.	**161**	37 30N	108 30W
Dolores, Tex., U.S.A.	**159**	27 40N	99 38W
Dolores, R.	**159**	38 30N	108 55W
Đolovo	**66**	44 55N	20 52E
Dolphin and Union Str.	**148**	69 5N	114 45W
Dolphin C.	**176**	51 10S	50 0W
Dolphinton	**35**	55 42N	3 28W
Dolsk	**54**	51 59N	17 3E
Dolton	**30**	50 53N	4 2W
Dolwyddelan	**31**	53 3N	3 53W
Dom	**50**	46 6N	7 50E
Dom Joaquim	**171**	18 57S	43 16W
Dom Pedrito	**173**	31 0S	54 40W
Dom Pedro	**170**	4 29S	44 27W
Doma	**121**	8 25N	8 18E
Domasi	**127**	15 22S	35 10E
Domat Ems	**51**	46 50N	9 27E
Domazlice	**52**	49 28N	13 0E
Dombarovskiy	**84**	50 46N	59 32E
Dombås	**71**	62 6N	9 4E
Dombasle	**43**	49 8N	5 10E
Dombe Grande	**125**	12 56S	13 8E
Dombes	**45**	46 3N	5 0E
Dombóvár	**53**	46 21N	18 9E
Dombrád	**53**	48 13N	21 54E
Domburg	**47**	51 34N	3 30E
Domel, I = Letsok-aw-kyun	**101**	11 30N	98 25E
Domérat	**44**	46 21N	2 32E
Domett	**143**	42 53S	173 12E
Domeyko	**172**	29 0S	71 30W
Domeyko, Cordillera	**172**	24 30S	69 0W
Domfront	**42**	48 37N	0 40W
Dominador	**172**	24 21S	69 20W
Dominica I.	**167**	15 20N	61 20W
Dominica Passage	**167**	15 10N	61 20W
Dominican Rep. ■	**167**	19 0N	70 30W
Dömitz	**48**	53 9N	11 13E
Domme	**44**	44 48N	1 12E
Dommel, R.	**47**	51 30N	5 20E
Dommerby	**73**	56 33N	9 5E
Domo	**91**	7 50N	47 10E
Domodossóla	**62**	46 6N	8 19E
Dompaire	**43**	48 14N	6 14E
Dompierre	**44**	46 31N	3 41E
Dompin	**120**	5 10N	2 5W
Domrémy	**43**	48 26N	5 40E
Domsjö	**72**	63 16N	18 41E
Domville, Mt.	**139**	28 1S	151 15E
Domvraina	**69**	38 15N	22 59E
Domzale	**63**	46 9N	3 6E
Don Benito	**57**	38 53N	5 51W
Don, C.	**136**	11 18S	131 46E
Don Duong	**101**	11 51N	108 35E
Don Martín, Presa de	**164**	27 30N	100 50W
Don Pedro Res.	**163**	37 43N	120 24W
Don, R., India	**97**	16 40N	75 55W
Don, R., Eng., U.K.	**33**	53 41N	0 51W
Don, R., Scot., U.K.	**37**	57 14N	2 5W
Don, R., U.S.S.R.	**83**	49 35N	41 40E
Dona Ana	**127**	17 25S	35 17E
Donabate	**38**	53 30N	6 9W
Donadea	**38**	53 20N	6 45W
Donaghadee	**38**	54 38N	5 32W
Donaghmore, Ireland	**39**	52 54N	7 37W
Donaghmore, U.K.	**38**	54 33N	6 50W
Donald	**140**	36 23S	143 0E
Donalda	**152**	52 35N	112 34W
Donaldsonville	**159**	30 2N	91 50W
Donalsonville	**157**	31 3N	84 52W
Donard	**39**	53 1N	6 37W
Donau-Kanal	**49**	49 1N	11 27E
Donau, R.	**53**	47 55N	17 20E
Donaueschingen	**49**	47 57N	8 30E
Donawitz	**52**	47 22N	15 4E
Doncaster	**33**	53 31N	1 9W
Dondo, Angola	**74**	9 45S	14 25E
Dondo, Mozam.	**127**	19 33S	34 46E
Dondo, Teluk	**103**	0 29N	120 45E
Dondra Head	**97**	5 55N	80 40E
Donegal	**38**	54 39N	8 8W
Donegal □	**38**	54 53N	8 0W
Donegal B.	**38**	54 30N	8 35W
Donegal Har.	**38**	54 35N	8 15W
Donegal Pt.	**39**	52 44N	9 38W
Doneraile	**39**	52 13N	8 37W
Donets, R.	**81**	48 50N	38 45E
Donetsk	**82**	48 0N	37 45E
Dong	**121**	9 20N	12 15E
Dong Ba Thin	**101**	12 8N	109 13E
Dong Dang	**100**	21 4N	106 57E
Dong Giam	**100**	19 15N	105 31E
Dong Ha	**100**	16 49N	107 8E
Dong Hene	**100**	16 16N	105 18E
Dong Hoi	**100**	17 29N	106 36E
Dong Khe	**100**	22 26N	106 27E
Dong Van	**100**	23 16N	105 22E
Dong Xoai	**101**	11 32N	106 55E
Donga	**121**	7 45N	10 2E
Dongara	**137**	29 14S	114 57E
Dongargarh	**96**	21 10N	80 40E
Dongen	**47**	51 38N	4 56E
Donges	**42**	47 18N	2 4W
Donggala	**103**	0 30S	119 40E
Dongola	**122**	19 9N	30 22E
Dongou	**124**	2 0N	18 5E
Donhead	**28**	51 1N	2 8W
Donington	**33**	52 54N	0 12W
Donington, C.	**140**	34 45S	136 0E
Doniphan	**159**	36 40N	90 50W
Donja Stubica	**63**	45 59N	16 0E
Donji Dušnik	**66**	43 12N	22 5E
Donji Miholjac	**66**	45 45N	18 10E
Donji Milanovac	**66**	44 28N	22 6E
Donji Vakuf	**66**	44 8N	17 24E
Donjon, Le	**44**	46 22N	3 48E
Dønna	**74**	66 6N	12 30E
Donna	**74**	66 6N	12 30E
Donna	**159**	26 12N	98 2W
Donna Nook, Pt.	**33**	53 29N	0 9E
Donnaconna	**151**	46 41N	71 41W
Donnelly's Crossing	**142**	35 42S	173 38E
Donnybrook	**137**	33 34S	115 48E
Donor's Hills	**138**	18 42S	140 33E
Donoughmore	**39**	52 0N	8 42W
Donskoy	**81**	53 55N	38 15W

Donya Lendava **Duncan Town**

Donya Lendava	63	46 35N	16 25 E
Donzère	45	44 28N	4 43 E
Donzy	43	47 20N	3 6 E
Dooagh	38	53 59N	10 7W
Doochary	38	54 54N	8 10W
Doodlakine	137	31 34 S	117 51 E
Dooega Hd.	38	53 54N	10 3W
Doon L.	34	55 15N	4 22W
Doon, R.	34	55 26N	4 41W
Doonbeg	39	52 44N	9 31W
Doonbeg R.	39	52 42N	9 20W
Doorn	46	52 2N	5 20 E
Dor (Tantura)	90	32 37N	34 55 E
Dora Báltea, R.	62	45 42N	7 25 E
Dora, L.	136	22 0 S	123 0 E
Dora Riparia, R.	62	45 7N	7 24 E
Dorada, La	174	5 30N	74 40W
Dorading	123	8 30N	33 5 E
Doran L.	153	61 13N	108 6W
Dorat, Le	44	46 14N	1 5 E
Dörby	73	56 20N	16 12 E
Dorchester, Dorset, U.K.	28	50 42N	2 28W
Dorchester, Oxon., U.K.	28	51 38N	1 10W
Dorchester, C.	149	65 27N	77 27W
Dordogne □	44	45 5N	0 40 E
Dordogne, R.	44	45 2N	0 36W
Dordrecht, Neth.	46	51 48N	4 39 E
Dordrecht, S. Afr.	128	31 20 S	27 3 E
Doré L.	153	54 46N	107 17W
Doré Lake	153	54 38N	107 54W
Dore, Mt.	44	45 32N	2 50 E
Dore, R.	44	45 59N	3 28 E
Dores	37	57 22N	4 20W
Dores do Indaiá	171	19 27 S	45 36W
Dorfen	49	48 16N	12 10 E
Dorgali	64	40 18N	9 35 E
Dori	121	14 3N	0 2W
Doring, R.	128	32 30 S	19 30 E
Dorion	150	45 23N	74 3W
Dorking	29	51 14N	0 20W
Dormaa-Ahenkro	120	7 15N	2 52W
Dormo, Ras	123	13 14N	42 35 E
Dornach	50	47 29N	7 37 E
Dornberg	63	45 45N	13 50 E
Dornbirn	52	47 25N	9 45 E
Dornes	43	46 48N	3 18 E
Dornie	36	57 17N	5 30W
Dornoch	37	57 52N	4 0W
Dornoch, Firth of	37	57 52N	4 0W
Dornogovi □	106	44 0N	110 0 E
Doro	121	16 9N	0 51W
Dorog	53	47 42N	18 45 E
Dorogobuzh	80	54 50N	33 10 E
Dorohoi	70	47 56N	26 30 E
Döröö Nuur	105	47 40N	93 30 E
Dorre I.	137	25 13 S	113 12 E
Dorrigo	141	30 20 S	152 44 E
Dorris	160	41 59N	121 58W
Dorset □	28	50 48N	2 25W
Dorsten	48	51 40N	6 55 E
Dorstone	28	52 4N	3 0W
Dortmund	48	51 32N	7 28 E
Dörtyol	92	36 52N	36 12 E
Dorum	48	53 40N	8 33 E
Doruma	126	4 42N	27 33 E
Dorya, W.	123	5 15N	41 30 E
Dos Bahías, C.	176	44 58 S	65 32W
Dos Cabezas	161	32 1N	109 37W
Dos Hermanas	57	37 16N	5 55W
Dos Palos	163	36 59N	120 37W
Dosara	121	12 20N	6 5 E
Doshi	93	35 35N	68 50 E
Dosso	121	13 0N	3 13 E
Döstrup	73	56 41N	9 42 E
Dot	152	50 12N	121 25W
Dothan	157	31 10N	85 25W
Dottignies	47	50 44N	3 19 E
Dotty, gasfield	19	53 3N	1 48 E
Douai	43	50 21N	3 4 E
Douala	121	4 0N	9 45 E
Douarnenez	42	48 6N	4 21W
Double Island Pt.	139	25 56 S	153 11 E
Doubrava, R.	52	49 40N	15 30 E
Doubs □	43	47 10N	6 20 E
Doubs, R.	43	46 53N	5 1 E
Doubtful B.	137	34 15 S	119 28 E
Doubtful Sd.	143	45 20 S	166 49 E
Doubtless B.	142	34 55 S	173 26 E
Doucet	150	48 15N	76 35W
Doudeville	42	49 43N	0 47 E
Doué	42	47 11N	0 20W
Douentza	120	14 58N	2 48W
Douglas, S. Afr.	128	29 4 S	23 46 E
Douglas, U.K.	32	54 9N	4 29W
Douglas, U.K.	35	55 33N	3 50W
Douglas, Alaska, U.S.A.	147	58 23N	134 32W
Douglas, Ariz., U.S.A.	161	31 21N	109 30W
Douglas, Ga., U.S.A.	157	31 32N	82 52W
Douglas, Wyo., U.S.A.	158	42 45N	105 20W
Douglas Hd.	32	54 9N	4 28W
Douglastown	151	48 46N	64 24W
Douglasville	157	33 46N	84 43W
Douirat	118	33 2N	4 11W
Doukáton, Ákra	69	38 34N	20 30 E
Doulevant	43	48 22N	4 53 E
Doullens	43	50 10N	2 20 E
Doulus Hd.	39	51 57N	10 19W
Doumé	124	4 15N	13 25 E
Douna	120	12 40N	6 0W
Dounby	37	59 4N	3 13W
Doune	35	56 12N	4 3W
Dounreay	37	58 40N	3 28W
Dour	47	50 24N	3 46 E
Dourada, Serra	171	13 10 S	48 45W
Dourados	173	22 9 S	54 50W
Dourados, R.	173	21 58 S	54 18W
Dourdan	43	48 30N	2 0 E
Douro Litoral □	55	41 10N	8 20W
Douro, R.	56	41 1N	8 16W
Douŭzeci Si Trei August	70	43 50N	28 40 E
Douvaine	45	46 19N	6 16 E
Douz	119	33 25N	9 0 E
Dove	32	52 51N	1 36W
Dove Brook	151	53 40N	57 40W
Dove Creek	161	37 53N	108 59W
Dove Dale	33	53 10N	1 47W
Dove, R.	33	54 20N	0 55W
Dover, Austral.	138	43 18 S	147 2 E
Dover, U.K.	29	51 7N	1 19 E
Dover, Del., U.S.A.	162	39 10N	75 31W
Dover, N.H., U.S.A.	162	43 5N	70 51W
Dover, N.J., U.S.A.	162	40 53N	74 34W
Dover, Ohio, U.S.A.	156	40 32N	81 30W
Dover-Foxcroft	151	45 14N	69 14W
Dover Plains	162	41 43N	73 35W
Dover, Pt.	137	32 32 S	125 32 E
Dover, Str. of	16	51 0N	1 30 E
Doveridge	32	52 54N	1 49 E
Dovey, R.	31	52 32N	4 0W
Dovre	71	62 0N	9 15 E
Dovrefjell	71	62 15N	9 33 E
Dowa	127	13 38 S	33 58 E
Dowagiac	156	42 0N	86 8W
Dowlatabad	93	28 20N	50 40 E
Down □	38	54 20N	5 50W
Down, Co.	38	54 20N	6 0W
Downey	160	42 29N	112 3W
Downham	29	52 26N	0 15 E
Downham Market	29	52 36N	0 22 E
Downhill	38	55 10N	6 48W
Downieville	160	39 34N	120 50W
Downpatrick	38	54 20N	5 43W
Downpatrick Hd.	38	54 20N	9 21W
Downs Division	139	27 10 S	150 44 E
Downs, The	38	53 30N	7 15W
Downsville	162	42 5N	74 60W
Downton	28	51 0N	1 44W
Dowra	38	54 11N	8 2W
Doylestown	162	40 21N	75 10W
Doyung	99	33 40N	99 25 E
Dra, Cap	118	28 58N	11 0W
Draa, O.	118	30 29N	6 1W
Drachten	46	53 7N	6 5 E
Drăgănești	70	44 9N	24 32 E
Drăgănești-Viașca	70	44 5N	25 33 E
Dragaš	66	42 5N	20 35 E
Drăgăsani	70	44 39N	24 17 E
Dragina	66	44 30N	19 25 E
Dragocvet	66	44 0N	21 15 E
Dragonera, I.	58	39 35N	2 19 E
Dragon's Mouth	174	11 0N	61 50W
Dragovistica, (Berivol)	66	42 22N	22 39 E
Draguignan	45	43 30N	6 27 E
Drain	160	43 45N	123 17W
Drake, Austral.	139	28 55 S	152 25 E
Drake, U.S.A.	158	47 56N	100 31W
Drake Passage	13	58 0 S	68 0W
Drakensberg	129	31 0 S	25 0 E
Dráma	68	41 9N	24 10 E
Dráma □	68	41 10N	24 0 E
Drammen	71	59 42N	10 12 E
Drangajökull	74	66 9N	22 15W
Drangan	39	52 32N	7 36W
Drangedal	71	59 6N	9 3 E
Dranov, Ostrov	70	44 55N	29 30 E
Draperstown	38	54 48N	6 47 E
Dras	95	34 25N	75 48 E
Drau, R.	52	47 46N	13 33 E
Drava, R.	66	45 50N	18 0W
Draveil	43	48 41N	2 25 E
Dravograd	63	46 36N	15 5 E
Drawa, R.	54	53 6N	15 56 E
Drawno	54	53 13N	15 46 E
Drawsko Pom	54	53 35N	15 50 E
Drayton Valley	152	53 25N	114 58W
Dreghorn	34	55 36N	4 30W
Dreibergen	46	52 3N	5 17 E
Drejö	73	54 58N	10 25 E
Dren	66	43 8N	20 44 E
Drenagh	38	55 3N	6 55W
Drenthe □	54	52 52N	6 40 E
Drentsche Hoofdvaart	46	52 39N	6 4 E
Dresden	48	51 2N	13 45 E
Dresden □	48	51 12N	14 0 E
Dreumel	47	51 51N	5 26 E
Dreux	42	48 44N	1 23 E
Drezdenko	54	52 50N	15 49 E
Driel	46	51 57N	5 49 E
Driffield	33	54 0N	0 25W
Driftwood	150	49 8N	81 23 E
Drigana	119	20 51N	12 17 E
Driggs	160	43 50N	111 8W
Drimnin	36	56 36N	6 0W
Drimoleague	39	51 40N	9 15W
Drin-i-zi, R.	68	41 37N	20 28 E
Drina, R.	66	44 30N	19 10 E
Drincea, R.	70	44 20N	22 55 E
Drînceni	70	46 49N	28 10 E
Drini, R.	68	42 20N	20 0 E
Drinjača, R.	66	44 20N	19 0 E
Driva	71	62 33N	9 38 E
Driva, R.	71	62 34N	9 33 E
Drivstua	71	62 26N	9 37 E
Drniš	63	43 51N	16 10 E
Drøbak	71	59 39N	10 39 E
Dröbak	75	59 39N	10 48 E
Drobbakk	71	59 39N	10 39 E
Drobin	54	52 42N	19 58 E
Drogheda	38	53 45N	6 20W
Drogichin	80	52 15N	25 8 E
Drogobych	80	49 20N	23 30 E
Droichead Nua	39	53 11N	6 50W
Droitwich	28	52 16N	2 10W
Dromahair	38	54 13N	8 18W
Dromara	38	54 21N	6 1W
Dromard	38	54 14N	8 40W
Drôme □	45	44 38N	5 15 E
Drôme, R.	45	44 46N	4 46 E
Dromedary, C.	141	36 17 S	150 10 E
Dromiskin	38	53 56N	6 25W
Dromod	38	53 52N	7 55W
Dromore, Down, U.K.	38	54 24N	6 10W
Dromore, Tyrone, U.K.	38	54 31N	7 28W
Dromore West	38	54 15N	8 50W
Dronero	62	44 29N	7 22 E
Dronfield, Austral.	138	21 12 S	140 3 E
Dronfield, U.K.	33	53 18N	1 29W
Dronninglund	73	57 10N	10 19 E
Dronrijp	46	53 11N	5 39 E
Drosendorf	52	48 52N	15 37 E
Drouin	141	38 10 S	145 53 E
Drouzhba	67	43 22N	28 0 E
Drum	38	54 6N	7 9W
Drumbeg, N. Ire., U.K.	38	54 33N	6 0W
Drumbeg, Scot., U.K.	36	58 15N	5 12W
Drumcard	38	54 14N	7 42W
Drumcliffe	38	54 20N	8 30W
Drumcondra	38	53 50N	6 40W
Drumheller	152	51 25N	112 40W
Drumjohn	34	55 14N	4 15W
Drumkeerin	38	54 10N	8 8W
Drumlish	38	53 50N	7 47W
Drummond	160	46 46N	113 4W
Drummond I.	150	46 0N	83 40W
Drummond Pt.	139	34 9 S	135 16 E
Drummond Ra.	138	23 45 S	147 10 E
Drummondville	150	45 55N	72 25W
Drummore	34	54 41N	4 53W
Drumquin	38	54 38N	7 30W
Drumright	159	35 59N	96 38W
Drumshanbo	38	54 2N	8 4W
Drumsna	38	53 57N	8 0W
Drunen	47	51 41N	5 8 E
Druridge B.	35	55 16N	1 32W
Druskinankaj	80	54 3N	23 58 E
Drut, R.	80	52 32N	30 0 E
Druten	46	51 53N	5 36 E
Druya	80	55 45N	27 15 E
Druzhina	77	68 14N	145 18 E
Drvar	63	44 21N	16 2 E
Drvenik	63	43 27N	16 3 E
Dry Tortugas	166	24 38N	82 55W
Dryanovo	67	42 59N	25 28 E
Dryden, Can.	153	49 50N	92 50W
Dryden, N.Y., U.S.A.	162	42 30N	76 18W
Dryden, Tex., U.S.A.	159	30 3N	102 3W
Drygalski I.	13	66 0 S	92 0 E
Drygarn Fawr	31	52 13N	3 39W
Drymen	70	56 4N	4 28W
Drynoch	36	57 17N	6 18W
Drysdale I.	138	11 41 S	136 0 E
Drysdale, R.	136	13 59 S	126 51 E
Dschang	121	5 32N	10 3 E
Du	121	10 26N	1 34W
Du Bois	156	41 8N	78 46W
Du Quoin	158	38 0N	89 10W
Duanesburg	162	42 45N	74 11W
Duaringa	138	23 42 S	149 42 E
Dúba	92	27 10N	35 40 E
Dubai = Dubayy	93	25 18N	55 20 E
Dubawnt, L.	153	63 4N	101 42W
Dubawnt, R.	153	64 33N	100 6W
Dubayy	93	25 18N	55 20 E
Dubbeldam	46	51 47N	4 43 E
Dubbo	141	32 11 S	148 35 E
Dubele	126	2 56N	29 35 E
Dübendorf	51	47 24N	8 37 E
Dubenskiy	84	51 27N	56 38 E
Dubh Artach	34	56 8N	6 40W
Dubica	63	45 17N	16 48 E
Dublin, Ireland	38	53 20N	6 18W
Dublin, Ga., U.S.A.	157	32 30N	83 0W
Dublin, Tex., U.S.A.	159	32 0N	98 20W
Dublin □	38	53 24N	6 20W
Dublin, B.	39	53 24N	6 20W
Dubna	81	54 8N	36 52 E
Dubno	80	50 25N	25 45 E
Dubois	160	44 7N	112 9W
Dubossary	82	47 15N	29 10 E
Dubossasy Vdkhr.	82	47 30N	29 0 E
Dubovka	83	49 5N	44 50 E
Dubovskoye	83	47 28N	42 40 E
Dubrajpur	95	23 48N	87 25 E
Dubrêkah	120	9 46N	13 31W
Dubrovitsa	80	51 31N	26 35 E
Dubrovnik	66	42 39N	18 6 E
Dubrovskoye	77	58 55N	111 0 E
Dubuque	158	42 30N	90 41W
Duchesne	160	40 14N	110 22W
Duchess	138	21 20 S	139 50 E
Ducie I.	131	24 47 S	124 40W
Duck Cr., N.S.W., Austral.	139	31 4 S	147 6 E
Duck Cr., W. Australia, Austral.	136	22 37 S	116 53 E
Duck Lake	153	52 50N	106 16W
Duck, Mt.	153	51 27N	100 35W
Duck Mt. Prov. Parks	153	51 45N	101 0W
Duckwall Mtn.	163	37 58N	120 7W
Duddington	29	52 36N	0 32W
Duddon R.	32	54 12N	3 15W
Düdelange	47	49 29N	6 5 E
Duderstadt	48	51 30N	10 15 E
Dudhi	99	24 15N	83 10 E
Dudhnai	98	25 59N	90 47 E
Düdingen	50	46 52N	7 12 E
Dudinka	77	69 30N	86 0 E
Dudley	28	52 30N	2 5W
Dudna, R.	96	19 36N	76 20 E
Dueñas	56	41 52N	4 33W
Dŭeni	70	44 51N	28 10 E
Dueodde	73	54 59N	15 4 E
Dueré	171	11 20 S	49 17W
Duero, R.	56	41 37N	4 25W
Duff Is.	142	9 0 S	167 0 E
Duffel	47	51 6N	4 30 E
Duffield	33	52 59N	1 30W
Dufftown	37	57 26N	3 9W
Dufourspitz	50	45 56N	7 52 E
Dugi, I.	63	44 0N	15 0 E
Dugo Selo	63	45 51N	16 18 E
Duhak	93	33 20N	57 30 E
Duifken Pt.	138	12 33 S	141 38 E
Duisburg	48	51 27N	6 42 E
Duitama	174	5 50N	73 2W
Duiveland	47	51 38N	4 0 E
Duiwelskloof	129	23 42 S	30 10 E
Dukana	126	3 59N	37 20 E
Dukati	68	40 16N	19 32 E
Duke I.	152	54 50N	131 20W
Dukhan	93	25 25N	50 50 E
Dukhovshchina	80	55 15N	32 27 E
Duki	93	30 14N	68 25 E
Dukla	54	49 30N	21 35 E
Duku, North-Eastern, Nigeria	121	10 43N	10 43 E
Duku, North-Western, Nigeria	121	11 11N	4 55 E
Dulas B.	31	53 22N	4 16W
Dulawan	103	7 5N	124 20 E
Dulce, Golfo	166	8 40N	83 20W
Dulce, R.	172	29 30 S	63 0W
Duleek	38	53 40N	6 24W
Dŭlgopol	67	43 3N	27 22 E
Dullewala	94	31 50N	71 25 E
Dülmen	48	51 49N	7 18 E
Dulnain Bridge	37	57 19N	3 40W
Dulovo	67	43 48N	27 9 E
Dululu	138	23 48 S	150 15 E
Duluth	158	46 48N	92 10W
Dulverton	28	51 2N	3 33W
Dum Dum	95	22 39N	88 26 E
Dum Duma	99	27 40N	95 40 E
Dumaguete	103	9 17N	123 15 E
Dumai	102	1 35N	101 20 E
Dumaran I.	103	10 33N	119 50 E
Dumaring	103	1 46N	118 10 E
Dumas, Ark., U.S.A.	159	33 52N	91 30W
Dumas, Okla., U.S.A.	159	35 50N	101 58W
Dūmat al Jandal	92	29 55N	39 40 E
Dumba I.	71	61 43N	4 50 E
Dumbarton	34	55 58N	4 35W
Dumbleyung	137	33 17 S	117 42 E
Dumbrăveni	70	46 14N	24 34 E
Dumfries	35	55 4N	3 37W
Dumfries & Galloway □	35	54 30N	4 0W
Dumfries (□)	26	55 0N	3 30W
Dŭmienesti	70	46 44N	27 1 E
Dumka	95	24 0N	87 22 E
Dumoine L.	150	46 55N	77 55W
Dumoine, R.	150	46 13N	77 51W
Dumraon	95	25 33N	84 8 E
Dumyât	122	31 24N	31 48 E
Dumyât, Masabb	122	31 28N	32 0 E
Dun Laoghaire, (Dunleary)	39	53 17N	6 9W
Dun-le-Palestel	44	46 18N	1 39 E
Dun-sur-Auron	43	46 53N	2 33 E
Duna, R.	53	45 51N	18 48 E
Dunaff Hd.	38	55 18N	7 30W
Dunaföldvár	53	46 50N	18 57 E
Dunai, R.	53	47 50N	18 52 E
Dunaj, R.	67	45 17N	29 32 E
Dunajec, R.	54	50 12N	20 52 E
Dunajska Streda	53	48 0N	17 37 E
Dunamanagh	38	54 53N	7 20W
Dunans	34	56 4N	5 9W
Dunany Pt.	38	53 51N	6 15W
Dunapatai	53	46 39N	19 4 E
Dunaszekcsö	53	46 22N	18 45 E
Dunaújváros	53	47 0N	18 57 E
Dunav, R.	66	45 0N	20 21 E
Dunavtsi	66	43 57N	22 53 E
Dunback	143	45 23 S	170 36 E
Dunbar, Austral.	138	16 0 S	142 22 E
Dunbar, U.K.	35	56 0N	2 32W
Dunbarton (□)	26	56 4N	4 42W
Dunbeath	37	58 15N	3 25W
Dunblane	35	56 10N	3 58W
Dunboyne	38	53 25N	6 30W
Duncan, Can.	152	48 45N	123 40W
Duncan, Ariz., U.S.A.	161	32 46N	109 6W
Duncan, Okla., U.S.A.	159	34 25N	98 0W
Duncan L.	152	62 51N	113 58W
Duncan, L., Brit. Col., Can.	150	50 20N	117 0W
Duncan, L., Qué., Can.	152	53 29N	77 58W
Duncan Pass.	101	11 0N	92 30 E
Duncan Town	166	22 15N	75 45W

Duncansby **Ecoporanga**

Duncansby 37 58 37N 3 3W
Duncansby Head 37 58 39N 3 0W
Dunchurch 28 52 21N 1 19W
Duncormick 39 53 14N 6 40W
Dundalk, Ireland 38 53 55N 6 45W
Dundalk, U.S.A. 162 39 15N 76 31W
Dundalk, B. 38 53 55N 6 15W
Dundas 150 43 17N 79 59W
Dundas I. 152 54 30N 130 50W
Dundas, L. 137 32 35S 121 50E
Dundas Str. 136 11 15S 131 35E
Dundee, S. Afr. 129 28 11S 30 15E
Dundee, U.K. 35 56 29N 3 0W
Dundee, U.S.A. 162 42 32N 76 59W
Dundgovi □ 106 45 10N 106 0E
Dundo 124 7 23S 20 48E
Dundonald 38 54 37N 5 50W
Dundoo 139 27 40S 144 37E
Dundrennan 35 54 49N 3 56W
Dundrum, Ireland 39 53 17N 6 15W
Dundrum, U.K. 38 54 17N 5 50W
Dundwara 95 27 48N 79 9E
Dunedin, N.Z. 143 45 50S 170 33E
Dunedin, U.S.A. 157 28 1N 82 45W
Dunedin, R. 152 59 30N 124 5W
Dunfanaghy 38 55 10N 7 59W
Dunfermline 35 56 5N 3 28W
Dungannon 38 54 30N 6 47W
Dungannon □ 38 54 30N 6 55W
Dungarpur 94 23 52N 73 45E
Dungarvan 39 52 6N 7 40W
Dungarvan Harb. 39 52 5N 7 35W
Dungas 121 13 4N 9 20E
Dungavel 35 55 37N 4 7W
Dungbura La 99 34 41N 93 18E
Dungeness 29 50 54N 0 59E
Dungiven 38 54 55N 6 56W
Dunglow 38 54 57N 8 20W
Dungo, L. do 128 17 15S 19 0E
Dungog 141 32 22S 151 40E
Dungourney 39 51 58N 8 5W
Dungu 124 2 32N 28 22E
Dungunâb 122 21 10N 37 9E
Dungunâb, Khalîg 122 21 5N 37 12E
Dunhinda Falls 97 7 5N 81 6E
Dunières 45 45 13N 4 20E
Dunk I. 138 17 59S 146 14E
Dunkeld, Austral. 140 37 40S 142 22E
Dunkeld, U.K. 37 56 34N 3 36W
Dunkerque 43 51 2N 2 20E
Dunkery Beacon 28 51 15N 3 37W
Dunkineely 38 54 38N 8 22W
Dunkirk 156 42 30N 79 18W
Dunkirk = Dunkerque 43 51 2N 2 20E
Dunkuj 123 11 15N 33 0E
Dunkur 123 11 58N 35 58E
Dunkwa, Central, Ghana 120 6 0N 1 47W
Dunkwa, Central, Ghana 121 5 30N 1 0W
Dunlap 158 41 50N 95 30W
Dunlavin 39 53 3N 6 40W
Dunleary = Dun Laoghaire 39 53 17N 6 8W
Dunleer 38 53 50N 6 23W
Dunlin, oilfield 19 61 12N 1 40E
Dunloe, Gap of 39 52 2N 9 40W
Dunlop 34 55 43N 4 32W
Dunloy 38 55 1N 6 25W
Dunmanus B. 39 51 31N 9 50W
Dunmanway 39 51 43N 9 8W
Dunmara 138 16 42S 133 25E
Dunmod 105 47 45N 106 58E
Dunmore, Ireland 38 53 37N 8 44W
Dunmore, U.S.A. 162 41 27N 75 38W
Dunmore East 39 52 9N 7 0W
Dunmore Town 166 25 30N 76 39W
Dunmurry 38 54 33N 6 0W
Dunn 157 35 18N 78 36W
Dunnellon 157 29 4N 82 28W
Dunnet 37 58 37N 3 20W
Dunnet B. 37 58 37N 3 23W
Dunnet Hd. 37 58 38N 3 22W
Dunning, U.K. 35 56 18N 3 37W
Dunning, U.S.A. 158 41 52N 100 4W
Dunolly 140 36 51S 143 44E
Dunoon 34 55 57N 4 56W
Dunqul 122 23 40N 31 10E
Duns 35 55 47N 2 20W
Dunscore 35 55 8N 3 48W
Dunseith 158 48 49N 100 2W
Dunsford 30 50 41N 3 40W
Dunshaughlin 38 53 31N 6 32W
Dunsmuir 160 41 0N 122 10W
Dunstable 29 51 53N 0 31W
Dunstan Mts. 143 44 53S 169 35E
Dunster, Can. 152 53 8N 119 50W
Dunster, U.K. 28 51 11N 3 28W
Dunston 28 52 46N 2 7W
Duntelchaig, L. 37 57 20N 4 18W
Dunton Green 29 51 17N 0 11E
Duntroon 143 44 51S 170 40E
Dunûrea, R. 70 45 0N 29 40E
Dunvegan 36 57 26N 6 35W
Dunvegan Hd. 36 57 30N 6 42W
Dunvegan L. 153 60 8N 107 10W
Duong Dong 101 10 13N 103 58E
Dupree 158 45 4N 101 35W
Dupuyer 160 48 11N 112 31W
Duque de Caxias 173 22 45S 43 19W
Dura 90 31 31N 35 1E
Durack 136 15 33S 127 52E
Durack Ra. 136 16 50S 127 40E
Durance, R. 45 43 55N 4 45E
Durand 156 42 54N 83 58W
Durango, Mexico 164 24 3N 104 39W
Durango, Spain 58 43 13N 2 40W
Durango, U.S.A. 161 37 10N 107 50W
Durango □ 164 25 0N 105 0W
Duranillin 137 33 30S 116 45E
Durant 159 34 0N 96 25W
Duratón, R. 56 41 27N 4 0W
Durazno 172 33 25S 56 38W
Durazzo = Durrësi 68 41 19N 19 28E
Durban, France 44 43 0N 2 49W
Durban, S. Afr. 129 29 49S 31 1E
Dúrcal 57 37 0N 3 34W
Đurdevac 66 46 2N 17 3E
Düren 48 50 48N 6 30E
Durg 96 21 15N 81 22E
Durgapur 95 23 30N 87 9E
Durham, Can. 150 44 10N 80 49W
Durham, U.K. 33 54 47N 1 34W
Durham, N.C., U.S.A. 157 36 0N 78 55W
Durham, N.H., U.S.A. 162 43 8N 70 56W
Durham □ 32 54 42N 1 45W
Durham Downs 139 26 6S 149 3E
Durlstone Hd. 28 50 35N 1 58W
Durmitor Mt. 66 43 18N 19 0E
Dûrmûneşti 70 46 21N 26 33E
Durness 37 58 34N 4 45W
Durness, Kyle of 37 58 35N 4 55W
Durrandella 138 24 3S 146 35E
Durrësi 68 41 19N 19 28E
Durrie 138 25 40S 140 15E
Durrington 28 51 12N 1 47W
Durrow 39 53 20N 7 31W
Durrus 39 51 37N 9 32W
Dursey Hd. 39 51 34N 10 41W
Dursey I. 39 51 36N 10 12W
Dursley 28 51 41N 2 21W
Durtal 42 47 40N 0 18W
Duru 126 4 20N 28 50E
Durup 73 56 45N 8 57E
D'Urville Island 143 40 50S 173 55E
Duryea 162 41 20N 75 45W
Dusa Mareb 91 5 40N 46 33E
Dûsh 122 24 35N 30 41E
Dushak 76 37 20N 60 10E
Dushanbe 85 38 33N 68 48E
Dusheti 83 42 0N 44 55E
Dushore 162 41 31N 76 24W
Dusky Sd. 143 45 47S 166 30E
Dussejour, C. 136 14 45S 128 13E
Düsseldorf 48 51 15N 6 46E
Dussen 46 51 44N 4 59E
Duszniki Zdrój 54 51 26N 16 22E
Dutch Harbour 147 53 54N 166 35W
Dutlhe 128 23 58S 23 46E
Dutsan Wai 121 10 50N 8 10E
Dutton, R. 138 20 44S 143 10E
Duvan 84 55 42N 57 54E
Duved 72 63 24N 12 55E
Duvno 66 43 42N 17 13E
Duwadami 92 24 35N 44 15E
Duzdab = Zāhedān 93 29 30N 60 50E
Dve Mogili 67 43 47N 25 55E
Dvina, Sev. 78 56 30N 24 0E
Dvina, Zap. 80 61 40N 45 30E
Dvinsk = Daugavpils 80 55 33N 26 32E
Dvinskaya Guba 78 65 0N 39 0E
Dvor 63 45 4N 16 22E
Dvorce 53 49 50N 17 34E
Dvur Králové 52 50 27N 15 50E
Dwarka 94 22 18N 69 8E
Dwellingup 137 32 43S 116 4E
Dwight 156 41 5N 88 25W
Dyakovskoya 81 60 5N 41 12E
Dyatkovo 80 53 48N 34 27E
Dyaul, I. 138 3 0S 150 55E
Dyce 37 57 12N 2 11W
Dyer 163 37 40N 118 5W
Dyer, C. 149 67 0N 61 0W
Dyerbeldzhin 85 41 13N 74 54E
Dyersburg 159 36 2N 89 20W
Dyfed □ 31 52 0N 4 30W
Dyje, R. 53 48 50N 16 45E
Dyke Acland Bay 138 8 45S 148 45E
Dykehead 37 56 43N 3 0W
Dyle, R. 47 50 58N 4 41E
Dymchurch 29 51 2N 1 0E
Dymock 28 51 58N 2 27W
Dynevor Downs 139 28 10S 144 20E
Dynów 54 49 50N 22 11E
Dypvag 71 79 40N 9 8E
Dyrnes 71 63 25N 7 52E
Dysart, Can. 153 50 57N 104 2W
Dysart, U.K. 35 56 8N 3 8W
Dysjön 72 62 38N 15 31E
Dyulgeri 67 42 18N 27 23E
Dyurtyuli 84 55 9N 54 4E
Dzambeyty 83 50 15N 52 30E
Dzaudzhikau = Ordzhonikidze 83 43 0N 44 35E
Dzerzhinsk 80 53 40N 27 7E
Dzhailma 76 51 30N 61 50E
Dzhalal-Abad 84 40 56N 73 0E
Dzhalinda 77 53 40N 124 0E
Dzhambeyty 84 50 16N 52 35E
Dzhambul 85 42 54N 71 22E
Dzhambul, Gora 85 44 54N 73 0E
Dzhankoi 82 45 40N 34 30E
Dzhanybek 83 49 25N 46 50E
Dzhardzhan 77 68 10N 123 5E
Dzharkurgan 85 37 31N 67 25E
Dzhelinde 77 70 0N 114 20E
Dzherzhinsk 80 53 48N 27 19E
Dzhetygara 84 52 11N 61 12E
Dzhetym, Khrebet 85 41 30N 77 0E
Dzhezkazgan 76 47 10N 67 40E
Dzhizak 85 40 6N 67 50E
Dzhugdzur, Khrebet 77 57 30N 138 0E
Dzhuma 85 39 42N 66 40E
Dzhumgoltau, Khrebet 85 42 15N 74 30E
Dzhungarskiye Vorota 76 45 0N 82 0E
Dzhvari 83 42 42N 42 4E
Działdowo 54 53 15N 20 15E
Działoszyce 54 50 22N 20 20E
Działoszyn 54 51 6N 18 50E
Dzibilchaltún 165 21 5N 89 36W
Dzierzgon 54 53 58N 19 20E
Dzierzoniow 54 50 45N 16 39E
Dzilam de Bravo 165 21 24N 88 53W
Dzioua 119 33 14N 5 14E
Dziwnów 54 54 2N 14 45E
Dzungaria 105 44 10N 88 0E
Dzungarian Gates = Dzhungarskiye V. 105 45 0N 82 0E

E

Eabamet, L. 150 51 30N 87 46W
Eads 158 38 30N 102 46W
Eagle, Alaska, U.S.A. 147 64 44N 141 29W
Eagle, Colo., U.S.A. 160 39 45N 106 55W
Eagle Butt 158 45 1N 101 12W
Eagle Grove 158 42 37N 93 53W
Eagle L., Calif., U.S.A. 160 40 35N 120 50W
Eagle L., Me., U.S.A. 151 46 23N 69 22W
Eagle Lake 159 29 35N 96 21W
Eagle Nest 161 36 33N 105 13W
Eagle Pass 159 28 45N 100 35W
Eagle Pk. 163 38 10N 119 25W
Eagle Pt. 136 16 11S 124 23E
Eagle, R. 151 53 36N 57 26W
Eagle River 158 45 55N 89 17W
Eaglehawk 140 36 43S 144 16E
Eagles Mere 162 41 25N 76 33W
Eaglesfield 35 55 3N 3 12W
Eagleshan 34 55 44N 4 18W
Eakring 33 53 9N 0 59W
Ealing 29 51 30N 0 19W
Earaheedy 137 25 34S 121 29E
Earby 32 53 55N 2 8W
Eardisland 28 52 14N 2 50W
Eardisley 28 52 8N 3 0W
Earith 29 52 21N 0 1E
Earl Grey 153 50 57N 104 43W
Earl Shilton 28 52 35N 1 20W
Earl Soham 29 52 14N 1 15E
Earle 159 35 18N 90 26W
Earlimart 163 35 53N 119 16W
Earls Barton 29 52 16N 0 44W
Earl's Colne 29 51 56N 0 43E
Earlsferry 35 56 11N 2 50W
Earlston 35 55 39N 2 40W
Earn, L. 34 56 23N 4 14W
Earn, R. 35 56 20N 3 19W
Earnslaw, Mt. 143 44 32S 168 27E
Earoo 137 29 34S 118 22E
Earsdon 35 55 4N 1 30W
Earth 159 34 18N 102 30W
Easebourne 29 51 0N 0 42W
Easington, Durham, U.K. 33 54 50N 1 24W
Easington, Yorks., U.K. 33 54 40N 0 7W
Easington Colliery 33 54 49N 1 19W
Easingwold 33 54 8N 1 11W
Easky 38 54 17N 8 58W
Easley 157 34 52N 82 35W
East Aberthaw 31 51 23N 3 23W
East Anglian Hts. 29 52 10N 0 17E
East Angus 151 45 30N 71 40W
East, B. 159 29 2N 89 16W
East Barming 29 51 15N 0 29E
East Bathurst 151 47 35N 65 40W
East Bengal 99 24 0N 90 0E
East Bergholt 29 51 58N 1 2E
East Beskids, mts. 53 49 30N 18 45E
East Brent 28 51 14N 2 55W
East C., N.Z. 142 37 42S 178 35E
East C., P.N.G. 135 10 13S 150 53E
East Chicago 156 41 40N 87 30W
East China Sea 105 30 5N 126 0E
East Coulee 152 51 23N 112 27W
East Cowes 28 50 45N 1 17W
East Dereham 29 52 40N 0 57E
East Falkland 176 51 30S 58 30W
East Fen 33 53 4N 0 5E
East Florenceville 151 46 26N 67 36W
East Grand Forks 158 47 55N 97 5W
East Greenwich 162 41 40N 71 27W
East Grinstead 29 51 8N 0 1W
East Harling 29 52 26N 0 55E
East Hartford 162 41 46N 72 39W
East Helena 160 46 37N 111 58W
East Ilsley 28 51 33N 1 15W
East Indies 102 0 0 120 0E
East Jordan 156 45 10N 85 7W
East Kilbride 35 55 46N 4 10W
East Kirkby 33 53 5N 1 15W
East Lansing 156 42 44N 84 37W
East Linton 35 56 0N 2 40W
East Liverpool 156 40 39N 80 35W
East London 129 33 0S 27 55E
East Looe 30 50 22N 4 28W
East Los Angeles 163 34 1N 118 9W
East Lynne 141 35 35S 150 16E
East Main (Eastmain) 151 52 20N 78 30W
East Markham 33 53 15N 0 53W
East Midlands, oilfield 19 53 20N 0 45W
East Moor 33 53 15N 1 30W
East, Mt. 137 29 0S 122 30E
East Orange 162 40 46N 74 13W
East P. 151 46 27N 61 58W
East Pakistan = Bangladesh 99 24 0N 90 0E
East Pine 152 55 48N 120 5W
East Point 157 33 40N 84 28W
East Providence 162 41 49N 71 23W
East Retford 33 53 19N 0 55W
East St. Louis 158 38 36N 90 10W
East Schelde, R. 47 51 38N 3 40E
E. Siberian Sea 77 73 0N 160 0E
East Stroudsburg 162 41 0N 75 11W
East Sussex □ 29 50 55N 0 20E
East Tawas 156 44 17N 83 31W
East Toorale 139 30 27S 145 28E
East Walker, R. 163 38 52N 119 10W
East Wemyss 35 56 8N 3 5W
East Woodhay 28 51 21N 1 26W
Eastbourne, N.Z. 142 41 19S 174 55E
Eastbourne, U.K. 29 50 46N 0 18E
Eastchurch 29 51 23N 0 53E
Eastend 153 49 32N 108 50W
Easter Islands 143 27 0S 109 0W
Easter Ross, dist. 37 57 50N 4 35W
Easter Skeld 36 60 12N 1 27W
Eastern □ 126 0 0S 38 30E
Eastern Cr. 138 20 40S 141 35E
Eastern Ghats 97 15 0N 80 0E
Eastern Group, Is. 137 33 30S 124 30E
Eastern Province □ 120 8 15N 11 0W
Easterville 153 53 8N 99 49W
Easthampton 162 42 16N 72 40W
Eastland 159 32 26N 98 45W
Eastleigh 28 50 58N 1 21W
Eastmain (East Main) 150 52 20N 78 30W
Eastmain, R. 150 52 27N 72 26W
Eastman 157 32 13N 83 41W
Eastnor 28 52 2N 2 22W
Easton, Dorset, U.K. 28 50 32N 2 27W
Easton, Northants., U.K. 29 52 37N 0 31W
Easton, Somerset, U.K. 28 51 28N 2 42W
Easton, Md., U.S.A. 162 38 47N 76 7W
Easton, Pa., U.S.A. 162 40 41N 75 15W
Easton, Wash., U.S.A. 160 47 14N 121 8W
Eastport, Maine, U.S.A. 151 44 57N 67 0W
Eastport, N.Y., U.S.A. 162 40 50N 72 44W
Eastry 29 51 15N 1 19E
Eastview 150 45 27N 75 40W
Eastville 162 37 21N 75 57W
Eastwood 33 53 2N 1 17W
Eaton, U.K. 29 52 52N 0 46W
Eaton, U.S.A. 158 40 35N 104 42W
Eaton, L. 136 22 55S 130 57E
Eaton Socon 29 52 13N 0 18W
Eatonia 153 51 13N 109 25W
Eatonton 157 33 22N 83 24W
Eatontown 162 40 18N 74 7W
Eau Claire, S.C., U.S.A. 157 34 5N 81 2W
Eau Claire, Wis., U.S.A. 158 44 46N 91 30W
Eauze 44 43 53N 0 7E
Eaval, Mt. 36 57 33N 7 12W
Ebagoola 138 14 15S 143 12E
Eban 121 9 40N 4 50E
Ebberston 33 54 14N 0 35W
Ebbw Vale 31 51 47N 3 12W
Ebeggui 119 26 2N 6 0E
Ebeltoft 75 56 12N 10 41E
Ebensee 52 47 48N 13 46E
Eberbach 49 49 27N 8 59E
Eberswalde 48 52 49N 13 50E
Ebikon 51 47 5N 8 21E
Ebingen 49 48 13N 9 1E
Ebino 110 32 2N 130 48E
Ebnat-Kappel 51 47 16N 9 7E
Eboli 65 40 39N 15 2E
Ebolowa 121 2 55N 11 10E
Ebony 128 22 6S 15 15E
Ébrié, Lagune 120 5 12N 4 40W
Ebro, Pantano del 56 43 0N 3 58W
Ebro, R. 58 41 49N 1 5W
Ebstorf 48 53 2N 10 23E
Ecaussines-d'Enghien 47 50 35N 4 11E
Ecclefechan 35 55 3N 3 18W
Eccleshall 28 52 52N 2 14W
Eceabat 68 40 11N 26 21E
Éceuillé 42 47 10N 1 19E
Ech Chebbi 118 26 41N 0 29E
Echallens 50 46 38N 6 38E
Echaneni 77 27 33S 32 6E
Echelles, Les 45 45 27N 5 45E
Echizen-Misaki 111 35 59N 135 57E
Echmiadzin 83 40 12N 44 19E
Echo Bay, N.W.T., Can. 148 66 10N 117 40W
Echo Bay, Ont., Can. 150 46 29N 84 4W
Echoing, R. 153 55 51N 92 5W
Echt, Neth. 47 51 7N 5 52E
Echt, U.K. 37 57 8N 2 26W
Echternach 47 49 49N 6 3E
Echuca 141 36 3S 144 46E
Ecija 57 37 30N 5 10W
Eck L. 34 56 5N 5 0W
Eckernförde 48 54 26N 9 50E
Eckington 33 53 19N 1 21W
Eclipse Is. 136 13 54S 126 19E
Ecommoy 42 47 50N 0 17E
Ecoporanga 171 18 23S 40 50W

Écos **Eldorado**

Écos	43	49 9N	1 35 E
Écouché	42	48 42N	0 10W
Ecuador ■	174	2 0 S	78 0W
Ed	73	58 55N	11 55 E
Ed Dabbura	122	17 40N	34 15 E
Ed Damer	122	17 27N	34 0 E
Ed Debba	122	18 0N	30 51 E
Ed-Déffa	122	30 40N	26 30 E
Ed Deim	123	10 10N	28 20 E
Ed Dueim	123	14 0N	32 10 E
Ed Dzong	99	32 11N	90 12 E
Edah	137	28 16 S	117 10 E
Edam, Can.	153	53 11N	108 46W
Edam, Neth.	46	52 31N	5 3 E
Edapally	97	11 19N	78 3 E
Eday, I.	37	59 11N	2 47W
Eday Sd.	37	59 12N	2 45W
Edd	123	14 0N	41 30 E
Edda, oilfield	19	56 25N	3 15 E
Edderton	37	57 50N	4 10W
Eddrachillis B.	36	58 16N	5 10W
Eddystone	30	50 11N	4 16W
Eddystone Pt.	138	40 59 S	148 20 E
Ede, Neth.	46	52 4N	5 40 E
Ede, Nigeria	121	7 45N	4 29 E
Ede, Sweden	72	62 10N	16 50 E
Édea	121	3 51N	10 9 E
Edegem	47	51 10N	4 27 E
Edehon L.	153	60 25N	97 15W
Edekel, Adrar	119	23 56N	6 47 E
Eden, Austral.	141	37 3 S	149 55 E
Eden, U.K.	38	54 44N	5 47W
Eden, Tex., U.S.A.	159	31 16N	99 50W
Eden, Wyo., U.S.A.	160	42 2N	109 27W
Eden L.	153	56 38N	100 15W
Eden, R.	32	54 57N	3 2W
Edenbridge	29	51 12N	0 4 E
Edenburg	128	29 43 S	25 58 E
Edendale	143	46 19 S	168 48 E
Edenderry	39	53 21N	7 3W
Edenton	157	36 5N	76 36W
Edenville	129	27 37 S	27 34 E
Ederny	38	54 32N	7 40W
Edgar	158	40 25N	98 0W
Edgartown	162	41 22N	70 28W
Edge Hill	28	52 7N	1 28W
Edge I.	12	77 45N	22 30 E
Edgecumbe	142	37 59 S	176 47 E
Edgefield	157	33 43N	81 59W
Edgeley	158	46 27N	98 41W
Edgemont	158	43 15N	103 53W
Edgeøya	12	77 45N	22 30 E
Edgeworthstown = Mostrim	38	53 42N	7 36W
Edhessa	68	40 48N	22 5 E
Edievale	143	45 49 S	169 22 E
Edina, Liberia	120	6 0N	10 19W
Edina, U.S.A.	158	40 6N	92 10W
Edinburg	159	26 22N	98 10W
Edinburgh	35	55 57N	3 12W
Edington	28	51 17N	2 6W
Edirne	67	41 40N	26 45 E
Edison	163	35 21N	118 52W
Edithburgh	140	35 5 S	137 43 E
Edjeleh	119	28 25N	9 40 E
Edjudina	137	29 48 S	122 23 E
Edmeston	162	42 42N	75 15W
Edmond	159	35 37N	97 30W
Edmondbyers	32	54 50N	1 59W
Edmonds	160	47 47N	122 22W
Edmonton, Austral.	138	17 2 S	145 46 E
Edmonton, Can.	152	53 30N	113 30W
Edmund L.	153	54 45N	93 17W
Edmundston	151	47 23N	68 20W
Edna	159	29 0N	96 40W
Edna Bay	152	55 55N	133 40W
Edolo	62	46 10N	10 21 E
Edouard, L.	126	0 25 S	29 40 E
Edremit	92	39 40N	27 0 E
Edsbyn	72	61 23N	15 49 E
Edsel Ford Ra.	13	77 0 S	143 0W
Edsele	72	63 25N	16 32 E
Edson	152	53 40N	116 28W
Eduardo Castex	172	35 50 S	64 25W
Edward I.	150	48 22N	88 37W
Edward, L. (Idi Amin Dada, L.)	126	0 25 S	29 40 E
Edward, R.	140	35 0 S	143 30 E
Edward VII Pen.	13	80 0 S	160 0W
Edwards	163	34 55N	117 51W
Edwards Plat.	159	30 30N	101 5W
Edwardsville	162	41 15N	75 56W
Edzell	37	56 49N	2 40W
Edzo	152	62 49N	116 4W
Eefde	46	52 10N	6 13 E
Eek	147	60 10N	162 0W
Eekloo	47	51 11N	3 33 E
Eelde	46	53 8N	6 34 E
Eem, R.	46	52 16N	5 20 E
Eems Kanaal	46	53 18N	6 46 E
Eems, R.	46	53 26N	6 57 E
Eenrum	46	53 22N	6 28 E
Eernegem	47	51 8N	3 2 E
Eerste Valthermond	46	52 53N	6 58 E
Eersterivier	128	34 0 S	18 45 E
Efate, I. (Vate)	46	17 40 S	168 25 E
Eferding	52	48 18N	14 1 E
Eferi	119	24 30N	9 28 E
Effingham	156	39 8N	88 30W
Effiums	121	6 35N	8 0 E
Effretikon	51	47 25N	8 42 E
Efiduasi	121	6 45N	1 25W
Eforie Sud	70	44 1N	28 37 E
Ega, R.	58	42 32N	1 58W
Égadi, Ísole	64	37 55N	12 10 E
Eganville	150	45 32N	77 5W
Egeland	158	48 42N	99 6W
Egenolf L.	153	59 3N	100 0W
Eger	53	47 53N	20 27 E
Eger, R.	53	47 43N	20 32 E
Egersund = Eigersund	75	58 26N	6 1 E
Egerton, Mt.	137	24 42 S	117 44 E
Egg L.	153	55 5N	105 30W
Eggenburg	52	48 38N	15 50 E
Eggiwil	50	46 52N	7 47 E
Egham	29	51 25N	0 33W
Egilsay I.	37	59 10N	2 56W
Eginbah	136	20 53 S	119 47 E
Egletons	44	45 24N	2 3 E
Eglisau	51	47 35N	8 31 E
Egmond-aan-Zee	46	52 37N	4 38 E
Egmont, C.	142	39 16 S	173 45 E
Egmont, Mt.	142	39 17 S	174 5 E
Egogi Bad	123	13 10N	41 30 E
Egremont	32	54 28N	3 33W
Eğridir Gölü	92	37 53N	30 50 E
Egton	33	54 27N	0 45W
Egtved	73	55 38N	9 18 E
Egua	174	5 5N	68 0W
Éguas, R.	171	13 26 S	44 14W
Egume	121	7 30N	7 14 E
Éguzon	44	46 27N	1 33 E
Egvekinot	77	66 19N	179 50W
Egyek	53	47 39N	20 52 E
Egypt ■	122	28 0N	31 0 E
Eha Amufu	121	6 30N	7 40 E
Ehime-ken □	110	33 30N	132 40 E
Ehingen	49	48 16N	9 43 E
Ehrwald	52	47 24N	10 56 E
Eibar	58	43 11N	2 28W
Eibergen	46	52 6N	6 39 E
Eichstätt	49	48 53N	11 12 E
Eidanger	71	59 7N	9 43 E
Eide	71	60 31N	6 44 E
Eider, R.	48	54 15N	8 50 E
Eidsberg	71	59 32N	11 16 E
Eidsfoss	71	59 36N	10 2 E
Eidsvold	139	25 25 S	151 12 E
Eidsvoll	75	60 19N	11 14 E
Eifel	49	50 10N	6 45 E
Eiffel Flats	127	18 20 S	30 0 E
Eigersund	71	58 26N	6 1 E
Eigg, I.	36	56 54N	6 10W
Eigg, Sd. of	36	56 52N	6 15W
Eighty Mile Beach	136	19 30 S	120 40 E
Eil	91	8 0N	49 50 E
Eil, L.	36	56 50N	5 15W
Eilat	90	29 30N	34 56 E
Eildon	141	37 14 S	145 55 E
Eildon, L.	139	37 10 S	146 0 E
Eileen L.	153	62 16N	107 37W
Eilenburg	48	51 28N	12 38 E
Ein 'Arik	90	31 54N	35 8 E
Ein el Luweiqa	123	14 5N	33 50 E
Einasleigh	138	18 32 S	144 5 E
Einasleigh, R.	138	17 30 S	142 17 E
Einbeck	48	51 48N	9 50 E
Eindhoven	47	51 26N	5 30 E
Einsiedeln	51	47 7N	8 46 E
Eiríksjökull	74	64 46N	20 24W
Eirlandsche Gat	46	53 12N	4 54 E
Eirunepé	174	6 35 S	70 0W
Eisden	47	50 59N	5 42 E
Eisenach	48	50 58N	10 18 E
Eisenberg	48	50 59N	11 50 E
Eisenerz	52	47 32N	15 54 E
Eisenhüttenstadt	48	52 9N	14 41 E
Eisenkappel	52	46 29N	14 36 E
Eisenstadt	53	47 51N	16 31 E
Eiserfeld	47	50 50N	8 0 E
Eisfeld	49	50 25N	10 54 E
Eishort, L.	36	57 9N	6 0W
Eisleben	48	51 31N	11 31 E
Eizariya (Bethany)	90	31 47N	35 15 E
Ejby	73	55 25N	9 56 E
Eje, Sierra del	56	42 24N	6 54W
Ejea de los Caballeros	58	42 7N	1 9W
Ejido	174	8 33N	71 14W
Ejura	121	7 25N	1 25 E
Ejutla	165	16 34N	96 44W
Ekalaka	158	45 55N	104 30 E
Ekawasaki	110	33 13N	132 46 E
Ekeryd	73	57 37N	14 6 E
Eket	121	4 38N	7 56W
Eketahuna	142	40 38 S	175 43 E
Ekhinos	68	41 16N	25 1W
Ekibastuz	76	51 40N	75 22 E
Ekimchan	77	53 0N	133 0W
Ekofisk, oilfield	19	56 35N	3 0 E
Ekofisk, W., oilfield	19	56 35N	3 5 E
Ekoli	126	0 23 S	24 13 E
Ekoln, I.	72	59 45N	17 40 E
Eksjö	73	57 40N	14 58W
Ekwan Pt.	150	53 16N	82 7W
Ekwan, R.	150	53 12N	82 15W
El Abiodh	118	32 53N	0 31 E
El Aïoun	118	34 33N	2 30W
El 'Aiyat	122	29 36N	31 15 E
El Alamein	122	30 48N	28 58 E
El Aqaba	90	29 31N	35 0 E
El Arahal	57	37 15N	5 33W
El Araq	122	28 40N	26 20 E
El Arba	118	36 28N	3 12 E
El Arba du Rharb	118	34 50N	5 59W
El Aricha	118	34 13N	1 16W
El Arîhā	90	31 52N	35 27 E
El Arish	138	17 49 S	146 1 E
El 'Arîsh	122	31 8N	33 50 E
El Arnaud	119	36 7N	5 49 E
El Arrouch	119	36 37N	6 53 E
*El Asnam	118	36 10N	1 20 E
El Astillero	56	43 24N	3 49W
El Badâri	122	27 4N	31 25 E
El Bahrein	122	28 30N	26 25 E
El Ballâs	122	26 2N	32 43 E
El Balyana	122	26 10N	32 3 E
El Baqeir	122	18 40N	33 40 E
El Barco de Ávila	56	40 21N	5 31W
El Barco de Valdeorras	56	42 23N	7 0W
El Bauga	122	18 18N	33 52 E
El Baúl	174	8 57N	68 17W
El Bawiti	122	28 25N	28 45 E
El Bayadh	118	33 40N	1 1 E
El Bierzo	56	42 45N	6 30W
El Biodh	118	26 0N	6 32W
El Bluff	166	11 59N	83 40W
El Bonillo	59	38 57N	2 35W
El Cajon	163	32 49N	117 0W
El Callao	174	7 25N	61 50W
El Camp	58	41 5N	1 10 E
El Campo	159	29 10N	96 20W
El Carmen	174	1 16N	66 52W
El Castillo	57	37 41N	6 19W
El Centro	161	32 50N	115 40W
El Cerro, Boliv.	174	17 30 S	61 40W
El Cerro, Spain	57	37 45N	6 57W
El Cocuy	174	6 25N	72 27W
El Coronil	57	37 5N	5 38W
El Cuy	176	39 55 S	68 25W
El Cuyo	165	21 30N	87 40W
El Dab'a	122	31 0N	28 27 E
El Dátil	164	30 7N	112 15W
El Deir	122	25 25N	32 20 E
El Dere	91	3 50N	47 8 E
El Díaz	165	21 1N	87 17W
El Dificul	174	9 51N	74 14W
El Díos	164	20 40N	87 20W
El Diviso	174	1 22N	78 14W
El Djouf	120	20 0N	11 30 E
El Dorado, Colomb.	174	1 11N	71 52W
El Dorado, Ark., U.S.A.	159	33 10N	92 40W
El Dorado, Kans., U.S.A.	159	37 55N	96 56W
El Dorado, Venez.	174	6 55N	61 30W
El Dorado Springs	159	37 54N	93 59W
El Eglab	118	26 20N	4 30W
El Escorial	56	40 35N	4 7W
El Faiyûm	122	29 19N	30 50 E
El Fâsher	123	13 33N	25 26 E
El Fashn	122	28 50N	30 54 E
El Ferrol	56	43 29N	3 14W
El Fifi	123	10 4N	25 0 E
El Fuerte	164	26 30N	108 40W
El Gal	91	10 58N	50 20 E
El Gebir	123	13 40N	29 40 E
El Gedida	122	25 40N	28 30 E
El Geneina	117	13 27N	22 45 E
El Geteina	123	14 50N	32 27 E
El Gezira	123	14 0N	33 0 E
El Gezira □	123	15 0N	33 0 E
El Gîza	122	30 0N	31 10 E
El Goléa	118	30 30N	2 50 E
El Guettar	119	34 5N	4 38 E
El Hadjire	119	32 36N	5 30 E
El Hagiz	123	15 15N	35 50 E
El Hajeb	118	33 41N	5 23W
El Hammâm	122	30 52N	29 25 E
El Hank, Alg.	118	25 38N	5 29W
El Hank, Maurit.	118	24 37N	7 0W
El Haql	122	29 15N	34 59 E
El Hawata	123	13 25N	34 42 E
El Heiz	122	27 50N	28 40 E
El 'Idisât	122	25 30N	32 35 E
El Iskandarîya	122	31 0N	30 0 E
El Istwâ'ya □	123	5 0N	30 0 E
El Jadida	118	33 16N	9 31W
El Jorf Lasfar, C.	118	33 5N	8 54W
El Kab	122	19 27N	32 46 E
El Kala	119	36 50N	8 30 E
El Kamlin	123	15 3N	33 11 E
El Kantara, Alg.	119	35 14N	5 45 E
El Kantara, Tunisia	119	33 45N	10 58 E
El Karaba	122	18 32N	33 41 E
El Kef	119	36 12N	8 47 E
El Kelâa des Srarhna	118	32 4N	7 27W
El Khandaq	122	18 30N	30 30 E
El Khârga	122	25 30N	30 33 E
El Khartûm	123	15 31N	32 35 E
El Khartûm Bahrî	123	15 40N	32 31 E
El-Khroubs	119	36 10N	6 55 E
El Khureiba	122	28 3N	35 10 E
El Kseur	119	36 46N	4 49 E
El Ksiba	118	32 45N	6 1W
El Kuntilla	122	30 1N	34 45 E
El Ladhiqiya	92	35 20N	35 30 E
El Laqeita	122	25 50N	33 15 E
El Leiya	123	16 15N	35 28 E
El Mafâza	123	13 38N	34 30 E
El Mahalla el Kubra	122	31 0N	31 0 E
El Mahârîq	122	25 35N	30 35 E
El Maiz	118	28 19N	0 9W
El-Maks el-Bahari	122	24 30N	30 40 E
El Manshâh	122	26 26N	31 50 E
El Mansour	118	27 47N	0 14W
El Mansûra	122	31 0N	31 19 E
El Mantico	174	7 27N	62 32W
El Manzala	122	31 10N	31 50 E
El Marâgha	122	26 35N	31 10 E
El Masid	123	15 15N	33 0 E
El Matariya	122	31 15N	32 0 E
El Meghaier	119	33 55N	5 58 E
El Melfa	119	31 58N	15 18 E
El Meraguen	118	28 0N	0 7W
El Metemma	123	16 50N	33 10 E
El Miamo	174	7 39N	61 46W
El Milagro	172	30 59 S	65 59W
El Milheas	118	25 27N	6 57W
El Milia	119	36 51N	6 13 E
El Minyâ	122	28 7N	30 33 E
El Molar	58	40 42N	3 45W
El Monte	163	34 4N	118 2W
El Mreyye	120	18 0N	6 0W
El Obeid	123	13 8N	30 10 E
El Oro = Sta. María del Oro	164	25 50N	105 20W
El Oro de Hidalgo	165	19 48N	100 8W
El Oued	119	33 20N	6 58 E
El Ouig	120	19 31N	0 27 E
El Palmar	174	7 58N	61 53W
El Palmito, Presa	164	25 40N	105 3W
El Panadés	58	41 10N	1 30 E
El Pao	174	9 38N	68 8W
El Pardo	56	40 31N	3 47W
El Paso	161	31 50N	106 30W
El Paso Robles	163	35 38N	120 41W
El Pedernoso	59	39 29N	2 45W
El Pedroso	57	37 51N	5 45W
El Pilar	174	10 32N	63 9W
El Pobo de Dueñas	58	40 46N	1 39W
El Portal	163	37 44N	119 49W
El Porvenir, Mexico	164	31 15N	105 51W
El Porvenir, Venez.	174	4 42N	71 19W
El Prat de Llobregat	58	41 18N	2 3 E
El Progreso	166	15 26N	87 51W
El Provencío	59	39 23N	2 35W
El Pueblito	164	29 3N	105 4W
El Qahîra	122	30 1N	31 14 E
El Qantara	122	30 51N	32 20 E
El Qasr	122	25 44N	28 42 E
El Qubba	123	11 10N	27 5 E
El Quseima	122	30 40N	34 15 E
El Qusîya	122	27 29N	30 44 E
El Râshda	122	25 36N	28 57 E
El Reno	159	35 30N	98 0W
El Rheauya	118	25 52N	6 30W
El Ribero	56	42 30N	8 30W
El Rîdisiya	122	24 56N	32 51 E
El Rio	163	34 14N	119 10W
El Ronquillo	57	37 44N	6 10W
El Rubio	57	37 22N	5 0W
El Saff	122	29 34N	31 16 E
El Salado	174	8 56N	73 55W
El Salto	164	23 47N	105 22W
El Salvador ■	166	13 50N	89 0W
El Sancejo	57	37 4N	5 6W
El Sauce	166	13 0N	86 40W
El Shallal	122	24 0N	32 53 E
El Suweis	122	29 58N	32 31 E
El Temblador	174	8 59N	62 44W
El Thamad	122	29 40N	34 28 E
El Tigre	174	8 55N	64 15W
El Tocuyo	174	9 47N	69 48W
El Tofo	172	29 22 S	71 18W
El Tránsito	172	28 52 S	70 17W
El Tûr	122	28 14N	33 36 E
El Turbio	176	51 30 S	72 40W
El Uqsur	122	25 41N	32 38 E
El Vado	58	41 2N	3 18W
El Vallés	58	41 35N	2 20 E
El Vigía	174	8 38N	71 39W
El Wak	124	2 49N	40 56 E
El Waqf	122	25 45N	32 15 E
El Wâsta	122	29 19N	31 12 E
El Weguet	123	5 28N	42 17 E
Ela	123	12 50N	42 20 E
Elafónisos	69	36 29N	22 56 E
Elaine	140	37 44 S	144 2 E
Elamanchili = Yellamanchilli	96	17 26N	82 50 E
Elan R.	31	52 17N	3 40W
Elan Village	31	52 18N	3 34W
Elands	141	31 37 S	152 20 E
Elandsvlei	128	32 19 S	19 31 E
Élassa	69	35 18N	26 21 E
Elassón	68	39 53N	22 12 E
Elat	103	5 40 S	133 5 E
Elateia	69	38 37N	22 46 E
Elâziğ	92	38 37N	39 22 E
Elba	157	31 27N	86 4W
Elba, I.	62	42 48N	10 15 E
Elbasani	68	41 9N	20 9 E
Elbasani-Berati	68	40 58N	20 0 E
Elbe, R.	48	53 15N	10 7 E
Elbert, Mt.	161	39 12N	106 36W
Elberta	156	44 35N	86 14W
Elberton	157	34 7N	82 51W
Elbeuf	42	49 17N	1 2 E
Elbląg □	54	54 15N	19 30 E
Elblag (Elbing)	54	54 10N	19 25 E
Elbow	153	51 7N	106 35W
Elbrus, Mt.	83	43 30N	42 30 E
Elburg	46	52 26N	5 50 E
Elburz Mts. = Alborz	93	36 0N	52 0 E
Elche	59	38 15N	0 42W
Elche de la Sierra	59	38 27N	2 3W
Elcho I.	138	11 55 S	135 45 E
Elda	59	38 29N	0 47W
Eldfisk, oilfield	19	56 25N	3 30 E
Eldon, Iowa, U.S.A.	97	40 50N	92 12W
Eldon, Mo., U.S.A.	158	38 20N	92 38W
Eldora	158	42 20N	93 5W
Eldorado, Argent.	173	26 28 S	54 43W

*Renamed Ech Cheliff

Eldorado Ermelo

Eldorado, Ont., Can. 97 44 40N 77 32W
Eldorado, Sask., Can. 153 59 35N 108 30W
Eldorado, Mexico 164 24 0N 107 30W
Eldorado, Ill., U.S.A. 156 37 50N 88 25W
Eldorado, Tex., U.S.A. 159 30 52N 100 35W
Eldoret 126 0 30N 35 25E
Electra 159 34 0N 99 0W
Eleele 147 21 54N 159 35W
Elefantes, R. 129 24 0S 32 30E
Elektrogorsk 81 55 56N 38 50E
Elektrostal 81 55 41N 38 32E
Elele 121 5 5N 6 50E
Elena 67 42 55N 25 53E
Elephant Butte Res. 161 33 45N 107 30W
Elephant I. 13 61 0S 55 0W
Elephant Pass 97 9 35N 80 25E
Elesbão Veloso 170 6 13S 42 8W
Eleshnitsa 67 41 52N 23 36E
Eleuthera I. 166 25 0N 76 20W
Elevsís 69 38 4N 23 26E
Elevtheroúpolis 68 40 52N 24 20E
Elfin Cove 147 58 11N 136 20W
Elgåhogna, Mt. 72 62 7N 12 7E
Elgepiggen 71 62 10N 11 21E
Elgeyo-Marakwet □ 126 0 45N 35 30E
Elgg 51 47 29N 8 52E
Elgin, Can. 151 45 48N 65 10W
Elgin, U.K. 37 57 39N 3 20W
Elgin, Ill., U.S.A. 156 42 0N 88 20W
Elgin, N.D., U.S.A. 158 46 24N 101 46W
Elgin, Nebr., U.S.A. 158 41 58N 98 3W
Elgin, Nev., U.S.A. 161 37 27N 114 36W
Elgin, Oreg., U.S.A. 160 45 37N 118 0W
Elgin, Texas, U.S.A. 159 30 21N 97 22W
Elgol 36 57 9N 6 6W
Elgon, Mt. 126 1 10N 34 30E
Elham 29 51 9N 1 7E
Eliase 103 8 10S 130 55E
Elida 159 33 56N 103 41W
Elie 153 49 48N 97 52W
Elie de Beaumont, Mt. 143 43 30S 170 20E
Elikón, Mt. 69 38 18N 22 45E
Elim 147 64 35N 162 20W
Elin Pelin 126 42 40N 23 38E
Elisabethville = Lubumbashi 127 11 32S 27 38E
Eliseu Martins 170 8 13S 43 42W
Elishaw 35 55 16N 2 14W
Elista 83 46 16N 44 14E
Elit 123 15 10N 37 0E
Elizabeth, Austral. 140 34 42S 138 41E
Elizabeth, U.S.A. 162 40 37N 74 12W
Elizabeth City 157 36 18N 76 16W
Elizabetha 126 1 3N 23 37E
Elizabethton 157 36 20N 82 13W
Elizabethtown, Ky., U.S.A. 156 37 40N 85 54W
Elizabethtown, Pa., U.S.A. 162 40 8N 76 36W
Elizondo 58 43 12N 1 30W
Elk City 159 35 25N 99 25W
Elk Grove 163 38 25N 121 22W
Elk Island Nat. Park 152 53 47N 112 59W
Elk Lake 150 47 40N 80 25W
Elk Point 153 53 54N 110 55W
Elk River, Idaho, U.S.A. 160 46 50N 116 8W
Elk River, Minn., U.S.A. 158 45 17N 93 34W
Elkedra 138 21 9S 135 26E
Elkedra, R. 138 21 8S 136 22E
Elkhart, Ind., U.S.A. 156 41 42N 85 55W
Elkhart, Kans., U.S.A. 159 37 3N 101 54W
Elkhorn 153 49 59N 101 14W
Elkhorn, R. 158 42 0N 98 15W
Elkhotovo 83 43 19N 44 15E
Elkhovo 67 42 10N 26 40E
Elkin 157 36 17N 80 50W
Elkins 156 38 53N 79 53W
Elko, Can. 152 49 20N 115 10W
Elko, U.S.A. 160 40 40N 115 50W
Elkton 162 39 36N 75 50W
Ell, L. 137 29 13S 127 46E
Elland 33 53 41N 1 49W
Ellecom 46 52 2N 6 6E
Ellef Ringnes I. 12 78 30N 102 2W
Ellen, Mt. 161 38 4N 110 56W
Ellen R. 32 54 44N 3 24W
Ellendale, Austral. 136 17 56S 124 48E
Ellendale, U.S.A. 158 46 3N 98 30W
Ellensburg 160 47 0N 120 30W
Ellenville 162 41 42N 74 23W
Eller Beck Bri. 33 54 23N 0 40W
Ellerston 141 31 49S 151 20E
Ellery, Mt. 141 37 28S 148 40E
Ellesmere 32 52 55N 2 53W
Ellesmere I. 12 79 30N 80 0W
Ellesmere, L. 131 43 46S 172 27E
Ellesmere Port 32 53 17N 2 55W
Ellesworth Land 13 74 0S 85 0W
Ellezelles 47 50 44N 3 42E
Ellice Is. 130 8 0S 176 0E
Ellicott City 162 39 16N 76 48W
Ellington 35 55 14N 1 34W
Ellinwood 158 38 27N 98 37W
Elliot, Austral. 138 17 33S 133 32E
Elliot, S. Afr. 129 31 22S 27 48E
Elliot Lake 150 46 35N 82 35W
Ellis 158 39 0N 99 39W
Ellisville 157 31 38N 89 12W
Ellon 37 57 21N 2 5W
Ellore = Eluru 96 16 48N 81 8E
Ells, R. 152 57 18N 111 40W
Ellsworth 158 38 47N 98 15W
Ellsworth Land 13 76 0S 89 0W
Ellwangen 49 48 57N 10 9E
Ellwood City 156 40 52N 80 19W
Elm 51 46 54N 9 10E
Elma, Can. 153 49 52N 95 55W
Elma, U.S.A. 160 47 0N 123 30E
Elmer 162 39 36N 75 10W
Elmhurst 156 41 52N 87 58W
Elmina 121 5 5N 1 21W
Elmira, Can. 151 46 30N 61 59W
Elmira, U.S.A. 162 42 8N 76 49W
Elmira Heights 162 42 8N 76 50W
Elmore, Austral. 140 36 30S 144 37E
Elmore, U.S.A. 163 33 7N 115 49W
Elmshorn 48 53 44N 9 40E
Elmswell 29 52 14N 0 53E
Elorza 174 7 3N 69 31W
Eloy 161 32 46N 111 46W
Éloyes 43 48 6N 6 36E
Elphin, Ireland 38 53 50N 8 11W
Elphin, U.K. 36 58 4N 5 3W
Elphinstone 138 21 30S 148 17E
Elrose 153 51 12N 108 0W
Elsas 150 48 32N 82 55W
Elsinore, Austral. 141 31 35S 145 11E
Elsinore, Cal., U.S.A. 163 33 40N 117 15W
Elsinore, Utah, U.S.A. 161 38 40N 112 2W
Elsinore = Helsingor 73 56 2N 12 35E
Elspe 48 51 10N 8 1E
Elspeet 46 52 17N 5 48E
Elst 46 51 55N 5 51E
Elsterwerda 48 51 27N 13 32E
Elstree 29 51 38N 0 16W
Elten 46 51 52N 6 9E
Eltham, Austral. 141 37 43S 145 12E
Eltham, N.Z. 142 39 26S 174 19E
Elton 83 49 5N 46 52E
Eluru 96 16 48N 81 8E
Elvas 57 38 50N 7 17W
Elven 42 47 44N 2 36W
Elverum 71 60 53N 11 34E
Elvire, Mt. 137 21 52S 116 50E
Elvire, R. 136 17 51S 128 11E
Elvo, R. 62 45 32N 8 14E
Elvran 71 63 24N 11 3E
Elwood, Ind., U.S.A. 156 40 20N 85 50W
Elwood, Nebr., U.S.A. 158 40 38N 99 51W
Ely, U.K. 29 52 24N 0 16E
Ely, Minn., U.S.A. 158 47 54N 91 52W
Ely, Nev., U.S.A. 160 39 10N 114 50W
Elyashiv 90 32 23N 34 55E
Elyria 156 41 22N 82 8W
Emådalen 72 61 20N 14 44E
Emaiygi, R. 80 58 30N 26 30E
Emba 76 48 50N 58 8E
Embarcación 172 23 10S 64 0W
Embarras Portage 153 58 27N 111 28W
Embleton 35 55 30N 1 38W
Embo 37 57 55N 4 0W
Embóna 69 36 13N 27 51E
Embrach 51 47 30N 8 36E
Embrun 45 44 34N 6 30E
Embu 126 0 32S 37 38E
Embu □ 126 0 30S 37 35E
Emden 48 53 22N 7 12E
Emeq Hula 90 33 5N 35 8E
'Emeq Yizre'el 90 32 35N 35 12E
Emerald 138 23 32S 148 10E
Emerson 153 49 0N 97 10W
Emery 161 38 59N 111 17W
Emery Park 161 32 10N 110 59W
Emi Koussi, Mt. 117 20 0N 18 55E
Emilia-Romagna □ 62 44 33N 10 40E
Emilius, Mt. 62 45 41N 7 23E
Eminabad 94 32 2N 74 8E
Emine 67 42 40N 27 56E
Emlichheim 48 52 37N 6 51E
Emly 39 52 28N 8 20W
Emmaboda 73 56 37N 15 32E
Emmaus 162 40 32N 75 30W
Emme, R. 50 47 0N 7 42E
Emmeloord 46 52 44N 5 46E
Emmen, Neth. 47 52 48N 6 57E
Emmen, Switz. 51 47 4N 8 17E
Emmendingen 49 48 7N 7 51E
Emmental 50 47 0N 7 35E
Emmer-Compascum 46 52 49N 7 2E
Emmerich 48 51 50N 6 12E
Emmet 138 24 45S 144 30E
Emmetsburg 158 43 3N 94 40W
Emmett 160 43 51N 116 33W
Emőd 53 47 57N 20 47E
Emona 67 42 43N 27 53E
Empalme 164 28 1N 110 49W
Empangeni 129 28 50S 31 52E
Empedrado 172 28 0S 58 46W
Empoli 62 43 43N 10 57E
Emporia, Kans., U.S.A. 158 38 25N 96 16W
Emporia, Va., U.S.A. 157 36 41N 77 32W
Emporium 156 41 30N 78 17W
Empress 153 50 57N 110 0W
Emptinne 47 50 19N 5 8E
Ems, R. 48 52 37N 7 16E
Emsdetten 48 52 11N 7 31E
Emsworth 29 50 51N 0 56E
Emu 140 36 44S 143 26E
Emu Park 138 23 13S 150 50E
Emu Ra. 136 23 0S 122 0E
Emyvale 38 54 20N 6 57W
En Gedi 90 31 28N 35 25E
En Harod 90 32 33N 35 22E
'En Kerem 90 31 47N 35 6E
En Nahud 123 12 45N 28 25E
en Namous, O. 118 31 15N 0 10W
Ena 111 35 25N 137 25E
Ena-San 111 35 26N 137 36E
Enafors 72 63 17N 12 20E
Enambú 174 1 1N 70 17W
Enana 128 17 30S 16 23E
Enånger 72 61 30N 17 9E
Enard B. 36 58 5N 5 20W
Enbetsu 112 44 44N 141 47E
Encantadas, Serra 173 30 40S 53 0W
Encanto, Cape 103 20 20N 121 40E
Encarnación 173 27 15S 56 0W
Encarnación de Diaz 164 21 30N 102 20W
Ench'eng 106 37 9N 116 16E
Enchi 120 5 53N 2 48W
Encinal 159 28 3N 99 25W
Encinillas 164 33 3N 117 17W
Encinitas 163 33 3N 117 17W
Encino 161 34 46N 106 16W
Encounter B. 140 35 45S 138 45E
Encruzilhada 171 15 31S 40 54W
Endau 101 2 40N 103 38E
Endau, R. 101 2 30N 103 30E
Ende 103 8 45S 121 30E
Endeavour 153 52 10N 102 39W
Endeavour Str. 138 10 45S 142 0E
Endelave 73 55 46N 10 18E
Enderbury I. 131 3 8S 171 5W
Enderby, Can. 152 50 35N 119 10W
Enderby, U.K. 28 52 35N 1 15W
Enderby I. 136 20 35S 116 30E
Enderby Land 13 66 0S 53 0E
Enderlin 158 46 45N 97 41W
Endicott, N.Y., U.S.A. 162 42 6N 76 2W
Endicott, Wash., U.S.A. 160 47 0N 117 45W
Endicott Mts. 147 68 0N 152 30W
Endröd 53 46 55N 20 47E
Endyalgout I. 136 11 40S 132 35E
Enebakk 71 59 46N 11 9E
Enez 68 40 45N 26 5E
Enfida 119 36 6N 10 28E
Enfield, U.K. 29 51 39N 0 4W
Enfield, U.S.A. 162 43 34N 71 57W
Engadin 51 46 45N 10 10E
Engadine, Lower = Engiadina Bassa 51 46 51N 10 18E
Engadine, Upper = Engiadin 'Ota 51 46 38N 10 0E
Engano, C. 167 18 30N 68 20W
Engaño, C. 103 18 35N 122 23E
Engeddi 90 31 28N 35 25E
Engelberg 51 46 48N 8 26E
Engels 81 51 28N 46 6E
Engemann L. 153 55 55N 106 55W
Enger 71 60 35N 10 20E
Enggano, I. 102 5 20S 102 40E
Enghien 47 50 37N 4 2E
Engiadin 'Ota 51 46 38N 10 0E
Engiadina Bassa 51 46 51N 10 18E
Engkilili 102 1 3N 111 42E
England 159 34 30N 91 58W
England □ 27 53 0N 2 0W
Englee 151 50 45N 56 5W
Englefield 140 37 21S 141 48E
Englehart 150 47 49N 79 52W
Engler L. 153 59 8N 106 52W
Englewood, Colo., U.S.A. 158 39 40N 105 0W
Englewood, Kans., U.S.A. 159 37 7N 99 59W
Englewood, N.J., U.S.A. 162 40 54N 73 59W
English Bazar 95 24 58N 88 21E
English Channel 42 50 0N 2 0W
English Company Is. 133 12 0S 137 0E
English, R. 153 50 30N 93 50W
English River 150 49 20N 91 0W
Enid 159 36 26N 97 52W
Enipévs, R. 68 39 22N 22 17E
Eniwetok 131 11 30N 152 16E
Enjil 118 33 12N 4 32W
Enkeldoorn 127 19 2S 30 52E
Enkhuizen 46 52 42N 5 17E
Enköping 72 59 37N 17 4E
Enlo 108 24 0N 107 7E
Enna 65 37 34N 14 15E
Ennadai 153 61 8N 100 53W
Ennadai L. 153 61 0N 101 0W
Ennedi 117 17 15N 22 0E
Ennell L. 38 53 29N 7 25W
Ennerdale Water 32 54 32N 3 24W
Enngonia 139 29 21S 145 50E
Enningdal 71 58 59N 11 33E
Ennis, Ireland 39 52 51N 8 59W
Ennis, Mont., U.S.A. 160 45 27N 111 48W
Ennis, Texas, U.S.A. 159 32 15N 96 40W
Enniscorthy 39 52 30N 6 35W
Enniskean 39 51 44N 8 56W
Enniskerry 39 53 12N 6 10W
Enniskillen 38 54 20N 7 40W
Ennistimon 39 52 56N 9 18W
Enns 52 48 12N 14 28E
Enns, R. 52 48 8N 14 27E
Enoggera Range 108 27 26S 152 56E
Enoggera Res. 109 27 27S 152 55E
Enontekiö 74 68 23N 23 37E
Enp'ing 109 22 11N 112 18E
Enriquillo, L. 167 18 20N 72 5W
Ens 46 52 38N 5 50E
Enschede 46 52 13N 6 53E
Ensenada, Argent. 172 34 55S 57 55W
Ensenada, Mexico 164 31 50N 116 50W
Enshih 108 30 18N 109 27E
Enshū-Nada 111 34 27N 137 38E
Ensisheim 43 47 50N 7 20E
Enstone 28 51 55N 1 25W
Entebbe 126 0 4N 32 28E
Enter 46 52 17N 6 35E
Enterprise, Can. 152 60 47N 115 45W
Enterprise, Oreg., U.S.A. 160 45 30N 117 11W
Enterprise, Utah, U.S.A. 161 37 37N 113 36W
Entlebuch 50 46 59N 8 4E
Entrance 152 53 25N 117 50W
Entre Ríos, Boliv. 172 21 30S 64 25W
Entre Ríos, Mozam. 127 14 57S 37 20E
Entre Ríos □ 172 30 30S 58 30W
Entre Rios, Bahia 171 11 56S 38 5W
Entrecasteaux, Pt. d' 137 34 50S 115 56E
Entrepeñas, Pantano de 58 40 34N 2 42W
Entwistle 152 53 30N 115 0W
Enugu 121 6 30N 7 30E
Enugu Ezike 121 7 0N 7 29E
Enumclaw 160 47 12N 122 0W
Envermeu 42 49 53N 1 15E
Envigado 174 6 10N 75 35W
Enza, R. 62 44 33N 10 22E
Enzan 111 35 42N 138 44E
Eólie o Lípari, Is. 65 38 30N 14 50E
Epa 138 8 28S 146 52E
Epanomí 68 40 25N 22 59E
Epe, Neth. 47 52 21N 5 59E
Epe, Nigeria 121 6 36N 3 59E
Épernay 43 49 3N 3 56E
Épernon 43 48 35N 1 40E
Ephesus 92 38 0N 27 30E
Ephraim 160 39 30N 111 37W
Ephrata, Pa., U.S.A. 162 40 11N 76 11W
Ephrata, Wash., U.S.A. 160 47 28N 119 32W
Epila 58 41 36N 1 17W
Épinac-les-Mines 43 46 59N 4 31E
Épinal 43 48 19N 6 27E
Episcopia Bihorului 70 47 12N 21 55E
Epitálion 69 37 37N 21 30E
Eport L. 36 57 33N 7 10W
Epping 29 51 42N 0 8E
Epping Forest 29 51 40N 0 5E
Epsom 29 51 19N 0 16W
Epukiro 125 21 30S 19 0E
Epworth 33 53 30N 0 50W
Equatorial Guinea ■ 124 2 0S 78 0W
Équeurdreville-Hainneville 42 49 40N 1 40W
Er Rahad 123 12 45N 30 32E
Er Rif 118 35 1N 4 1W
Er Roseires 123 11 55N 34 30E
Er Rumman 90 32 9N 35 48E
Eradu 137 28 40S 115 2E
Erandol 96 20 56N 75 20E
Erap 135 6 37S 146 51E
Erāwadī Myit, R. = Irrawaddy, R. 98 19 30N 95 15E
Erba, Italy 62 45 49N 9 12E
Erba, Sudan 122 19 5N 36 40E
Ercha 77 69 45N 147 20E
Erciyas Daği 92 38 30N 35 30E
Erdene 106 44 30N 111 10E
Erding 49 48 18N 11 55E
Erebus, Mt. 13 77 35S 167 0E
Erechim 173 27 35S 52 15W
Ereğli 92 41 15N 31 30E
Erei, Monti 65 37 20N 14 20E
Erembodegem 47 50 56N 4 4E
Eresma, R. 56 41 13N 4 30W
Eressós 69 39 11N 25 57E
Erewadi Myitwanya 99 15 30N 95 0E
Erfenis Dam 128 28 30S 26 50E
Erfjord 71 59 20N 6 14E
Erfoud 118 31 30N 4 15W
Erfurt 48 50 58N 11 2E
Erfurt □ 48 51 10N 10 30E
Ergani 92 38 26N 39 49E
Erğene, R. 67 41 20N 27 0E
Ergeni Vozyshennost 83 47 0N 44 0E
Erhlien 106 43 42N 112 2E
Erhlin 109 23 54N 120 22E
Erhtao Chiang, R. 107 42 35N 128 10E
Erhyüan 108 26 7N 99 57E
Eria, R. 56 42 10N 6 8W
Eriba 123 16 40N 36 10E
Eriboll, L. 37 58 28N 4 41W
Erica 46 52 43N 6 56E
Érice 64 38 4N 12 34E
Ericht, L. 37 56 50N 4 25W
Erie 156 42 10N 80 7W
Erigavo 91 10 35N 47 35E
Erikoúsa 68 39 55N 19 14E
Eriksdale 153 50 52N 98 7W
Erikslund 72 62 31N 15 54E
Erímanthos 69 37 57N 21 50E
Erimo-misaki 112 41 50N 143 15E
Eriskay I. 36 57 4N 7 18W
Eriskay, Sd. of 36 57 5N 7 20W
Erisort L. 36 58 5N 6 30W
Eriswil 50 47 5N 7 46E
Erith 152 53 25N 116 46W
Erithraí 69 38 13N 23 20E
Eritrea □ 123 14 0N 41 0E
Erjas, R. 56 39 45N 6 52W
Erker, L. 79 59 51N 18 29E
Erlangen 49 49 35N 11 0E
Erldunda 138 25 14S 133 12E
Ermelo, Neth. 46 52 35N 5 35E
Ermelo, S. Afr. 129 26 31S 29 59E

Ermenak Fairmount

Ermenak 92 36 44N 33 0E
Ermióni 69 37 23N 23 15E
Ermoúpolis = Siros 69 37 28N 24 57E
Ernakulam 97 9 59N 76 19E
Erne, Lough 38 54 26N 7 46W
Erne, R. 38 54 30N 8 16W
Ernée 42 48 18N 0 56W
Ernest Giles Ra. 137 27 0S 123 45E
Erode 97 11 24N 77 45E
Eromanga 139 26 40S 143 11E
Erongo 128 21 39S 15 58E
Erongoberg 128 21 45S 15 32E
Erp 47 51 36N 5 37E
Erquelinnes 47 50 19N 4 8E
Erquy 42 48 38N 2 29W
Erquy, Cap d' 42 48 39N 2 29W
Err, Piz d' 51 46 34N 9 43E
Errabiddy 137 25 25S 117 5E
Erramala Hills 97 15 30N 78 15E
Errer, R. 123 42 35N 8 40E
Errigal, Mt. 38 55 2N 8 8W
Errill 39 52 52N 7 40W
Erris Hd. 38 54 19N 10 0W
Errochty, L. 37 56 45N 4 10W
Errogie 37 57 16N 4 23W
Errol 35 56 24N 3 13W
Erseka 68 40 22N 20 40E
Erskine 158 47 37N 96 0W
Erstein 43 48 25N 7 38E
Erstfeld 51 46 50N 8 38E
Ertil 81 51 55N 40 50E
Ertvågøy 71 63 12N 8 25E
Ertvelde 47 51 11N 3 45E
Erundu 128 20 39S 16 26E
Eruwa 121 7 33N 3 26E
Ervalla 72 59 28N 15 16E
Ervy-le-Châtel 43 48 2N 3 55E
Erwin 157 36 10N 82 28W
Erzgebirge 48 50 25N 13 0E
Erzin 77 50 15N 95 10E
Erzincan 92 39 46N 39 30E
Erzurum 92 39 57N 41 15E
Es Sahrâ' Esh Sharqîya 122 26 0N 33 30E
Es Sider 119 30 50N 18 21E
Es Sînâ' 122 29 0N 34 0E
Es Souk 121 18 48N 1 2E
Es Sûkî 123 13 20N 34 58E
Esa'ala 135 9 45S 150 49E
Esambo 126 3 48S 23 30E
Esan-misaki 112 41 40N 141 10E
Esbjerg 73 55 29N 8 29E
Escada 170 8 22S 35 14W
Escalante 161 37 47N 111 37W
Escalante, R. 161 37 45N 111 0W
Escalón 164 26 40N 104 20W
Escalona 56 40 9N 4 29W
Escambia, R. 157 30 45N 87 15W
Escanaba 156 45 44N 87 5W
Escant, R. 47 51 2N 3 45E
Esch-sur-Alzette 47 49 32N 6 0E
Eschallens 50 46 39N 6 38E
Eschede 48 52 44N 10 13E
Escholzmatt 50 46 55N 7 56E
Eschwege 48 51 10N 10 3E
Eschweiler 48 50 49N 6 14E
Escondida, La 164 24 6N 99 55W
Escondido 163 33 9N 117 4W
Escrick 33 53 53N 1 3W
Escuinapa 164 22 50N 105 50W
Escuintla 166 14 20N 90 48W
Escuminac 151 48 0N 67 0W
Escutillas = Ceba 174 6 33N 70 24W
Eséka 121 3 41N 10 44E
Esens 48 53 40N 7 35E
Esera, R. 58 42 24N 0 22E
Esfahan □ 93 33 0N 53 0E
Esgueva, R. 56 41 46N 4 14W
Esh Sham = Dimashq 92 33 30N 36 18E
Esh Shamâlîya □ 122 19 0N 31 0E
Esha Ness 36 60 30N 1 36W
Eshowe 129 28 50S 31 30E
Eshta' ol 90 31 47N 35 0E
Esiama 120 4 48N 2 25W
Esino, R. 63 43 28N 13 8E
Esk R. 32 54 23N 3 21W
Esk, R., Dumfries, U.K. 35 54 58N 3 4W
Esk, R., N. Yorks., U.K. 33 54 27N 0 36W
Eskdale 35 55 12N 3 4W
Eskifjördur 74 65 3N 13 55W
Eskilstuna 72 59 22N 16 32E
Eskimo Ls. 147 69 15N 132 17W
Eskimo Pt. 153 61 10N 94 3W
Eskişehir 92 39 50N 30 35E
Esla, R. 56 41 45N 5 50W
Eslöv 73 55 50N 13 20E
Esmeralda, La 172 22 16S 62 33W
Esmeraldas 174 1 0N 79 40W
Esneux 47 50 32N 5 33E
Espa 71 60 35N 11 15E
Espada, Pta. 174 12 5N 71 7W
Espalion 44 44 32N 2 47E
Espalmador, I. 59 38 48N 1 26E
Espanola 150 46 15N 81 46W
Espardell, I. del 59 38 47N 1 25E
Esparraguera 58 41 33N 1 52E
Esparta 166 9 59N 84 40W
Espejo 57 37 40N 4 34W
Espenberg, C. 147 66 35N 163 40W
Esperança 170 7 1S 35 51W
Esperance 137 33 45S 121 55E
Esperance B. 137 33 48S 121 55E
Esperantinópolis 170 4 53S 44 53W
Esperanza 172 31 29S 61 3W
Esperanza, La, Argent. 172 24 9S 64 52W
Esperanza, La, Boliv. 174 14 20S 62 0W
Esperanza, La, Cuba 166 22 46N 83 44W
Esperanza, La, Hond. 166 14 15N 88 10W
Espéraza 44 42 56N 2 14E
Espevær Lt. Ho. 71 59 35N 5 7E
Espichel, C. 57 38 22N 9 16W
Espiel 57 38 11N 5 1W
Espigão, Serra do 173 26 35S 50 30W
Espinal 174 4 9N 74 53W
Espinazo, Sierra del = Espinhaço, Serra do 171 17 30S 43 30W
Espinhaço, Serra do 171 17 30S 43 30W
Espinho 56 41 1N 8 38W
Espinilho, Serra do 173 28 30S 55 0W
Espino 174 8 34N 66 1W
Espinosa de los Monteros 56 43 5N 3 34W
Espírito Santo □ 171 20 0S 40 45W
Espíritu Santo, B. del 165 19 15N 79 40W
Espíritu Santo, I. 164 24 30N 110 23W
Espita 165 21 1N 88 19W
Esplanada 171 11 47S 37 57W
Espluga de Francolí 58 41 24N 1 7E
Espuña, Sierra de 59 37 51N 1 35W
Espungabera 129 20 29S 32 45E
Esquel 176 42 40S 71 20W
Esquimalt 148 48 30N 123 23W
Esquina 172 30 0S 59 30W
Essaouira (Mogador) 118 31 32N 9 42W
Essarts, Les 42 46 47N 1 12W
Essebie 126 2 58N 30 40E
Essen, Belg. 47 51 28N 4 28E
Essen, Ger. 48 51 28N 6 59E
Essendon, Mt. 137 25 0S 120 30E
Essequibo, R. 174 5 45N 58 50W
Essex 162 39 18N 76 29W
Essex □ 29 51 48N 0 30E
Esslingen 49 48 43N 9 19E
Essonne □ 43 48 30N 2 20E
Essvik 72 62 18N 17 24E
Estadilla 58 42 4N 0 16E
Estados, I. de los 176 54 40S 64 30W
Estagel 44 42 47N 2 40E
Estância 170 11 16S 37 26W
Estancia 161 34 50N 106 1W
Estarreja 56 40 45N 8 35W
Estats, P. d' 44 42 40N 1 40E
Estavayer le Lac 50 46 51N 6 51E
Estcourt 129 28 58S 29 53E
Este 63 45 12N 11 40E
Esteban 56 43 33N 6 5W
Estelí 166 13 9N 86 22W
Estella 58 42 40N 2 0W
Estelline, S.D., U.S.A. 158 44 39N 96 52W
Estelline, Texas, U.S.A. 159 34 35N 100 27W
Estena, R. 57 39 23N 4 44W
Estepa 57 37 17N 4 52W
Estepona 57 36 24N 5 7W
Esterhazy 153 50 37N 102 5W
Esternay 43 48 44N 3 33E
Esterri de Aneu 58 42 38N 1 5E
Estevan 153 49 10N 102 59W
Estevan Group 152 53 3N 129 38W
Estherville 158 43 25N 94 50W
Estissac 43 48 16N 3 48E
Eston, Can. 153 51 8N 108 40W
Eston, U.K. 33 54 33N 1 6W
Estonian S.S.R. □ 80 48 30N 25 30E
Estoril 57 38 42N 9 23W
Estrada, La 56 42 43N 8 27W
Estrêla, Serra da 56 40 10N 7 45W
Estrella 59 38 25N 3 35W
Estremadura 57 39 0N 9 0W
Estremoz 57 38 51N 7 39W
Estrondo, Serra do 170 7 20S 48 0W
Esztergom 53 47 47N 18 44E
Et Tieta 118 29 37N 9 15W
Et Turra 90 32 39N 35 39E
Étables-sur-Mer 42 48 38N 2 51W
Etah 95 27 35N 78 40E
Etain 43 49 13N 5 38E
Etalle 47 49 40N 5 36E
Etamamu 151 50 18N 59 59W
Étampes 43 48 26N 2 10E
Etang 43 46 52N 4 10E
Etanga 128 17 55S 13 00E
Étaples 43 50 30N 1 39E
Etawah 95 26 48N 79 6E
Etawah, R. 157 34 20N 84 15W
Etawney L. 153 57 50N 96 50W
Etchingham 29 51 0N 0 27E
Eteh 121 7 2N 7 28E
Etelia 121 19 10N 0 55E
Ethe 47 49 35N 5 35E
Ethel Creek 136 22 55S 120 11E
Ethel, Oued el 118 28 31N 3 37W
Ethelbert 153 51 32N 100 25W
Ethiopia ■ 91 8 0N 40 0E
Ethiopian Highlands 114 10 0N 37 0E
Etive, L. 34 56 30N 5 12W
Etna, Mt. 65 37 45N 15 0E
Etne 71 59 40N 5 56E
Etoile 127 11 33S 27 30E
Etolin I. 152 56 5N 132 20W
Eton 29 51 29N 0 37W
Etoshapan 128 18 40S 16 30E
Etowah 157 35 20N 84 30W
Étrépagny 42 49 18N 1 36E
Étretat 42 49 42N 0 12E
Etroits, Les 151 47 24N 68 54W
Etropole 68 43 50N 24 0E
Ettelbrüch 47 49 50N 6 5E
Ettelbruck 47 49 51N 6 5E
Etten 47 51 34N 4 38E
Ettington 28 52 8N 1 38W
Ettlingen 49 48 58N 8 25E
Ettrick Forest 35 55 30N 3 0W
Ettrick Water 35 55 31N 2 55W
Etuku 126 3 42S 25 45E
Etzatlán 164 20 48N 104 5W
Etzna 165 19 35N 90 15W
Eu 42 50 3N 1 26E
Euboea = Évvoia 69 38 40N 23 40E
Euchareena 141 32 57S 149 6E
Eucla Basin 137 31 19S 126 9E
Euclid 156 41 32N 81 31W
Euclides da Cunha 170 10 31S 39 1W
Eucumbene, L. 141 36 2S 148 40E
Eudora 159 33 5N 91 17W
Eudunda 140 34 12S 139 7E
Eufaula, Ala., U.S.A. 157 31 55N 85 11W
Eufaula, Okla., U.S.A. 159 35 20N 95 33W
Eufaula, L. 159 35 15N 95 28W
Eugene 160 44 0N 123 8W
Eugenia, Punta 164 27 50N 115 5W
Eugowra 141 33 22S 148 24E
Eulo 139 28 10S 145 3E
Eumungerie 141 31 56N 148 36E
Eunice, La., U.S.A. 159 30 35N 92 28W
Eunice, N. Mex., U.S.A. 159 32 30N 103 10W
Eupen 47 50 37N 6 3E
Euphrates = Furat, Nahr al 92 33 30N 43 0E
Eure □ 42 49 6N 1 0E
Eure-et-Loir □ 42 48 22N 1 30E
Eureka, Can. 12 80 0N 85 56W
Eureka, Calif., U.S.A. 160 40 50N 124 0W
Eureka, Kans., U.S.A. 159 37 50N 96 20W
Eureka, Mont., U.S.A. 160 48 53N 115 6W
Eureka, Nev., U.S.A. 160 39 32N 116 2W
Eureka, S.D., U.S.A. 158 45 49N 99 38W
Eureka, Utah, U.S.A. 160 40 0N 112 0W
Eureka, Mt. 137 26 35S 121 35E
Eurelia 140 32 33S 138 35E
Euroa 141 36 44S 145 35E
Europa, Île 125 22 20S 40 22E
Europa, Picos de 56 43 10N 5 0W
Europa Pt. 55 36 2N 6 32W
Europa Pt. = Europa, Pta. de 57 36 3N 5 21W
Europa, Pta. de 57 36 3N 5 21W
Europe 16 20 0N 20 0E
Europoort 46 51 57N 4 10E
Euskirchen 48 50 40N 6 45E
Eustis 157 28 54N 81 36W
Eutin 48 54 7N 10 38E
Eutsuk L. 152 53 20N 126 45W
Euxton 32 53 41N 2 42W
Eva Downs 138 18 1S 134 52E
Eval, Mt. 90 32 15N 35 15E
Evanger 71 60 39N 6 7E
Evans 158 40 25N 104 43W
Evans Head 139 29 7S 153 27E
Evans L. 150 50 50N 77 0W
Evans P. 158 41 0N 105 35W
Evanston, Ill., U.S.A. 156 42 0N 87 40W
Evanston, Wy., U.S.A. 160 41 10N 111 0W
Evansville, Ind., U.S.A. 156 38 0N 87 35W
Evansville, Wis., U.S.A. 158 42 47N 89 18W
Evanton 37 57 40N 4 20W
Evato 129 20 37S 47 10E
Évaux-les-Bains 44 46 12N 2 29E
Eveleth 158 47 35N 92 40W
Even Yahuda 90 32 16N 34 53E
Evensk 77 61 57N 159 14E
Evenstad 71 61 25N 11 7E
Everard, C. 141 37 49S 149 17E
Everard, L. 139 31 30S 135 0E
Everard Ras. 137 27 5S 132 28E
Evercreech 28 51 8N 2 30W
Everdale 141 31 52S 144 46E
Evere 47 50 52N 4 25E
Everest, Mt. 95 28 5N 86 58E
Everett 160 48 0N 122 10W
Evergem 47 51 7N 3 43E
Everglades 157 26 0N 80 30W
Evergreen 157 31 28N 86 55W
Everöd 73 55 53N 14 5E
Everson 160 48 57N 122 22W
Everton 141 36 25S 146 33E
Evesham 28 52 6N 1 57W
Evian-les-Bains 45 46 24N 6 35E
Evinayong 124 1 50N 10 35E
Évinos, R. 69 38 27N 21 40E
Evisa 45 42 15N 8 48E
Évora 57 38 33N 7 57W
Évora □ 57 38 33N 7 50W
Évreux 42 49 0N 1 8E
Évritania □ 69 39 5N 21 30E
Évron 42 48 23N 1 58W
Évros □ 68 41 10N 26 0E
Evrótas, R. 69 36 50N 22 40E
Évvoia 69 38 30N 24 0E
Évvoia □ 69 38 40N 23 40E
Ewe, L. 36 57 49N 5 38W
Ewell 29 51 20N 0 15W
Ewhurst 29 51 9N 0 25W
Ewing 158 42 18N 98 22W
Ewo 124 0 48S 14 45E
Exaltación 174 13 10S 65 20W
Excelsior 139 33 6S 149 59W
Excelsior Springs 158 39 20N 94 10W
Excideuil 44 45 20N 1 4E
Exe, R. 30 50 38N 3 27W
Exeter, U.K. 30 50 43N 3 31W
Exeter, Calif., U.S.A. 163 36 17N 119 9W
Exeter, Nebr., U.S.A. 158 40 43N 97 30W
Exeter, N.H., U.S.A. 162 43 0N 70 58W
Exford 28 51 8N 3 39W
Exloo 46 52 53N 6 52E
Exmes 42 48 45N 0 10E
Exminster 30 50 40N 3 29W
Exmoor 30 51 10N 3 59W
Exmore 162 37 32N 75 50W
Exmouth, Austral. 136 22 6S 114 0E
Exmouth, U.K. 30 50 37N 3 26W
Exmouth G. 136 22 15S 114 15E
Expedition Range 138 24 30S 149 12E
Exton 29 52 42N 0 38W
Extremadura 57 39 30N 6 5W
Exu 171 7 31S 39 43W
Exuma Sound 166 24 30N 76 20W
Eyam 33 53 17N 1 40W
Eyasi, L. 126 3 30S 35 0E
Eyawaddi Myit 98 15 50N 95 6E
Eye, Camb., U.K. 29 52 36N 0 11W
Eye, Norfolk, U.K. 29 52 19N 1 9E
Eye Pen. 36 58 13N 6 10W
Eyeberry L. 153 63 8N 104 43W
Eyemouth 35 55 53N 2 5W
Eygurande 44 45 40N 2 26E
Eyhatten 47 50 43N 6 1E
Eyisen 82 41 0N 36 50E
Eyjafjorður 74 66 15N 18 30W
Eymet 44 44 40N 0 25E
Eymoutiers 44 45 40N 1 45E
Eynhallow Sd. 37 59 8N 3 7W
Eynort, L. 36 57 13N 7 18W
Eynsham 28 51 47N 1 21W
Eyrarbakki 74 63 52N 21 9W
Eyre 137 32 15S 126 18E
Eyre Cr. 138 26 40S 139 0E
Eyre, L. 133 29 30S 137 26E
Eyre L., (North) 139 28 30S 137 20E
Eyre L., (South) 139 29 18S 137 25E
Eyre Mts. 143 45 25S 168 25E
Eyre Pen. 139 33 30S 137 17E
Eyrecourt 39 53 12N 8 8W
Ez Zeidab 122 17 25N 33 55E
Ez Zergoun, W. 118 32 45N 2 25E
Ezcaray 58 42 19N 3 0W
Ezine 68 39 48N 26 12E

F

Fabens 161 31 30N 106 8W
Fåborg 73 55 6N 10 15E
Fabriano 63 43 20N 12 52E
Fabrizia 43 38 29N 16 19E
Făcăeni 70 44 32N 27 53E
Facatativá 174 4 49N 74 22W
Facture 44 44 39N 0 58W
Fada 117 17 13N 21 34E
Fada-n-Gourma 121 12 10N 0 30E
Fadd 53 46 28N 18 49E
Faddeyevski, Ostrov 77 76 0N 150 0E
Fadhili 92 26 55N 49 10E
Fadlab 122 17 42N 34 2E
Faenza 63 44 17N 11 53E
Fafa 121 15 22N 0 48E
Fafe 56 41 27N 8 11W
Fagam 121 11 1N 10 1E
Fågelsjö 72 61 50N 14 35E
Fagerhult 73 57 8N 15 40E
Fagernes 71 60 59N 9 14E
Fagersta 72 60 1N 15 46E
Fåglavik 73 58 6N 13 6E
Fagnano Castello 65 39 31N 16 4E
Fagnano, L. 176 54 30S 68 0W
Fagnières 43 48 58N 4 20E
Fahral 93 29 0N 59 0E
Fahūd 93 22 18N 56 28E
Faid 92 27 1N 42 52E
Faido 51 46 29N 8 48E
Fair, C. 138 12 24S 143 16E
Fair Hd. 38 55 14N 6 10W
Fair Isle 23 59 30N 1 40W
Fair Oaks 163 38 39N 121 16W
Fairbank 161 31 44N 110 12W
Fairbanks 147 64 59N 147 40W
Fairbourne 31 52 42N 4 3W
Fairbury 158 40 5N 97 5W
Fairfax, Okla., U.S.A. 159 36 37N 96 45W
Fairfax, Va., U.S.A. 162 38 51N 77 18W
Fairfield, Austral. 141 33 53S 150 57E
Fairfield, Ala., U.S.A. 157 33 30N 87 0W
Fairfield, Calif., U.S.A. 163 38 14N 122 1W
Fairfield, Conn., U.S.A. 162 41 8N 73 16W
Fairfield, Idaho, U.S.A. 160 43 27N 114 52W
Fairfield, Ill., U.S.A. 156 38 20N 88 20W
Fairfield, Iowa, U.S.A. 158 41 0N 91 58W
Fairfield, Mont., U.S.A. 160 47 40N 112 0W
Fairfield, Texas, U.S.A. 159 31 40N 96 0W
Fairford, Can. 153 51 37N 98 38W
Fairford, U.K. 28 51 42N 1 48W
Fairhope 157 30 35N 87 50W
Fairlie, N.Z. 143 44 5S 170 49E
Fairlie, U.K. 34 55 44N 4 52W
Fairlight 29 50 53N 0 40E
Fairmead 163 37 5N 120 10W
Fairmont, Minn., U.S.A. 158 43 37N 94 30W
Fairmont, W. Va., U.S.A. 156 39 29N 80 10W
Fairmont Hot Springs 152 50 20N 115 56W
Fairmount 163 34 45N 118 26W

Fairplay **Field**

Fairplay	**161**	39 9N	107 0W
Fairport	**156**	43 8N	77 29W
Fairview, Austral.	**138**	15 31S	144 17E
Fairview, Can.	**152**	56 5N	118 25W
Fairview, N. Dak., U.S.A.	**158**	47 49N	104 7W
Fairview, Okla., U.S.A.	**159**	36 19N	98 30W
Fairview, Utah, U.S.A.	**160**	39 50N	111 0W
Fairweather, Mt.	**147**	58 55N	137 45W
Faith	**158**	45 2N	102 4W
Faither, The, C.	**36**	60 34N	1 30W
Faizabad, Afghan.	**93**	37 7N	70 33E
Faizabad, India	**95**	26 45N	82 10E
Faizpur	**96**	21 14N	75 49E
Fajardo	**147**	18 20N	65 39W
Fakenham	**29**	52 50N	0 51E
Fakfak	**103**	3 0S	132 15E
Fakiya	**170**	42 10N	27 4E
Fakobli	**120**	7 23N	7 23W
Fakse	**73**	55 15N	12 8E
Fakse B.	**73**	55 11N	12 15E
Fakse Ladeplads	**73**	55 16N	12 9E
Fak'u	**107**	42 31N	123 26E
Falaise	**42**	48 54N	0 12W
Falaise, Mui	**100**	19 6N	105 45E
Falakrón Óros	**68**	41 15N	23 58E
Falam	**98**	23 0N	93 45E
Falcarragh	**38**	55 8N	8 8W
Falces	**58**	42 24N	1 48W
Falcón □	**174**	11 0N	69 50W
Falcon, C.	**118**	35 50N	0 50W
Falcón Dam	**159**	26 50N	99 20W
Falconara Marittima	**63**	43 37N	13 23E
Faldingworth	**33**	53 21N	0 22W
Faléa	**120**	12 16N	11 17W
Falelatai	**84**	13 55S	171 59W
Falenki	**84**	58 22N	51 35E
Faleshty	**82**	47 32N	27 44E
Falfurrias	**159**	27 8N	98 8W
Falher	**152**	55 44N	117 15W
Falkenberg, Ger.	**48**	51 34N	13 13E
Falkenberg, Sweden	**73**	56 54N	12 30E
Falkensee	**48**	52 35N	13 6E
Falkenstein	**48**	50 27N	12 24E
Falkirk	**35**	56 0N	3 47W
Falkland	**35**	56 15N	3 13W
Falkland Is.	**176**	51 30S	59 0W
Falkland Is. Dep.	**13**	57 0S	40 0W
Falkland Sd.	**176**	52 0S	60 0W
Falkonéra	**69**	36 50N	23 52E
Falköping	**73**	58 12N	13 33E
Fall Brook	**161**	33 25N	117 12W
Fall River	**162**	41 45N	71 5W
Fall River Mills	**160**	41 1N	121 30W
Fallbrook	**163**	33 23N	117 15W
Fallmore	**38**	54 6N	10 5W
Fallon, Mont., U.S.A.	**158**	46 52N	105 8W
Fallon, Nev., U.S.A.	**160**	39 31N	118 51W
Falls Church	**162**	38 53N	77 11W
Falls City, Nebr., U.S.A.	**158**	40 0N	95 40W
Falls City, Oreg., U.S.A.	**160**	44 54N	123 29W
Falmey	**121**	12 36N	2 51E
Falmouth, Jamaica	**166**	18 30N	77 40W
Falmouth, U.K.	**30**	50 9N	5 5W
Falmouth, Ky., U.S.A.	**156**	38 40N	84 20W
Falmouth, Mass., U.S.A.	**162**	41 34N	70 38W
Falmouth B.	**30**	50 7N	5 3E
False B.	**128**	34 15S	18 40E
False Divi Pt.	**97**	15 35N	80 50E
Falset	**58**	41 7N	0 50E
Falso, C.	**166**	15 12N	83 21W
Falster	**73**	54 45N	11 55E
Falsterbo	**73**	55 23N	12 50E
Falsterbokanalen	**73**	55 25N	12 56E
Falstone	**35**	55 10N	2 26W
Faluja	**90**	31 48N	31 37E
Falun	**72**	60 37N	15 37E
Famagusta	**92**	35 8N	33 55E
Famaka	**123**	11 24N	34 52E
Famatina, Sierra, de	**172**	29 5S	68 0W
Family L.	**153**	51 54N	95 27W
Famoso	**163**	35 37N	119 12W
Fampotabe	**129**	15 56S	50 8E
Fan i Madh, R.	**68**	41 56N	20 16E
Fana, Mali	**120**	13 0N	6 56W
Fana, Norway	**71**	60 16N	5 20E
Fanad Hd.	**38**	55 17N	7 40W
Fanambana	**129**	13 34S	50 0E
Fanárion	**68**	39 24N	21 47E
Fanch'ang	**109**	31 2N	118 13E
Fanchiat'un	**107**	43 42N	125 5E
Fanchih	**106**	39 14N	113 19E
Fandriana	**129**	20 14S	47 21E
Fang	**100**	19 55N	99 13E
Fangch'eng, Honan, China	**106**	33 16N	112 59E
Fangch'eng, Kwangsi-Chuang, China	**108**	21 46N	108 21E
Fanghsien	**109**	32 0N	111 0E
Fangliao	**109**	22 22N	130 35E
Fangshan	**106**	38 0N	111 16E
Fangtzu	**107**	36 39N	119 15E
Fannich, L.	**36**	57 40N	5 0W
•Fanning I.	**131**	3 51N	159 22W
Fanny Bay	**152**	49 27N	124 48W
Fanø	**73**	55 25N	8 25E
Fano	**63**	43 50N	13 0E
Fanø, I.	**73**	55 25N	8 25E
Fanshaw	**152**	57 11N	133 30W
Fao (Al Fāw)	**92**	30 0N	48 30E
Faqirwali	**94**	29 27N	73 0E

*Renamed Tubuaeran

Fara in Sabina	**63**	42 13N	12 44E
Farab	**85**	39 9N	63 36E
Faraday Seamount Group	**14**	50 0N	27 0W
Faradje	**126**	3 50N	29 45E
Farafangana	**129**	22 49S	47 50E
Farâfra, El Wâhât el-	**122**	27 15N	28 20E
Farah	**93**	32 20N	62 7E
Farah □	**93**	32 25N	62 10E
Farahalana	**129**	14 26S	50 10E
Faraid, Gebel	**122**	23 33N	35 19E
Faraid Hd.	**37**	58 35N	4 48W
Faramana	**120**	11 56N	4 45W
Faranah	**120**	10 3N	10 45W
Farasān, Jazā'ir	**91**	16 45N	41 55E
Farasan Kebir	**91**	16 40N	42 0E
Faratsiho	**129**	19 24S	46 57E
Fardes, R.	**59**	37 25N	3 10W
Fareham	**28**	50 52N	1 11W
Farewell	**147**	62 30N	154 0W
Farewell, C.	**143**	40 29S	172 43E
Farewell C. = Farvel, K.	**12**	59 48N	43 55W
Farewell Spit	**143**	40 35S	173 0E
Farfán	**174**	0 16N	76 41W
Fargo	**158**	47 0N	97 0W
Faria, R.	**90**	32 12N	35 27E
Faribault	**158**	44 15N	93 19W
Faridkot	**94**	30 44N	74 45E
Faridpur, Bangla.	**98**	23 15N	90 0E
Faridpur, India	**95**	18 14N	79 34E
Farila	**72**	61 48N	15 50E
Färila	**72**	61 48N	15 50E
Farim	**120**	12 27N	15 17W
Farimān	**93**	35 40N	60 0E
Farina	**139**	30 3S	138 15E
Faringdon	**28**	51 39N	1 34W
Faringe	**72**	59 55N	18 7E
Farinha, R.	**170**	6 15S	47 30W
Färjestaden	**73**	56 38N	16 25E
Farmakonisi	**69**	37 17N	27 8E
Farmerville	**159**	32 48N	92 23W
Farmingdale	**162**	40 12N	74 10W
Farmington, Calif., U.S.A.	**163**	37 56N	121 0W
Farmington, N. Mex., U.S.A.	**161**	36 45N	108 28W
Farmington, N.H., U.S.A.	**162**	43 25N	71 3W
Farmington, Utah, U.S.A.	**160**	41 0N	111 58W
Farmington, R.	**162**	41 51N	72 38W
Farmville	**156**	37 19N	78 22W
Farnborough	**29**	51 17N	0 46W
Farne Is.	**35**	55 38N	1 37W
Farnham	**29**	51 13N	0 49W
Farnham, Mt.	**152**	45 20N	72 55W
Farnworth	**32**	53 33N	2 24W
Faro, Brazil	**175**	2 0S	56 45W
Faro, Port.	**57**	37 2N	7 55W
Fårö	**75**	58 0N	19 10E
Faro □	**57**	37 12N	8 10W
Faroe Is.	**16**	62 0N	7 0W
Farquhar, C.	**137**	23 38S	113 36E
Farquhar, Mt.	**136**	22 18S	116 53E
Farr	**37**	57 21N	4 13W
Farranfore	**39**	52 10N	9 32W
Farrars, Cr.	**138**	25 35S	140 43E
Farrashband	**93**	28 57N	52 5E
Farrell	**156**	41 13N	80 29W
Farrell Flat	**140**	33 48S	138 48E
Farrukhabad	**95**	27 30N	79 32E
Fars □	**93**	29 30N	55 0E
Fársala	**68**	39 17N	22 23E
Farsø	**73**	56 46N	9 19E
Farsö	**73**	56 48N	9 20E
Farstrup	**73**	56 59N	9 28E
Farsund	**71**	58 5N	6 55E
Fartura, Serra da	**173**	26 21S	52 52W
Faru	**121**	12 48N	6 12E
Farum	**73**	55 49N	12 21E
Farvel, Kap	**12**	59 48N	43 55W
Farwell	**159**	34 25N	103 0W
Faryab	**93**	28 7N	57 14E
Fasa	**93**	29 0N	53 32E
Fasag	**36**	57 33N	5 32W
Fasano	**65**	40 50N	17 20E
Fashoda	**123**	9 50N	32 2E
Faskari	**79**	11 42N	6 58E
Faslane	**34**	56 3N	4 49W
Fastnet Rock	**39**	51 22N	9 37W
Fastov	**80**	50 7N	29 57E
Fatehgarh	**95**	27 25N	79 35E
Fatehpur, Raj., India	**94**	28 0N	75 4E
Fatehpur, Ut. P., India	**95**	27 8N	81 7E
Fatick	**120**	14 19N	16 27W
Fatima	**151**	47 24N	61 53W
Fátima	**57**	39 37N	8 39W
Fatoya	**120**	11 37N	9 10W
Faucilles, Monts	**43**	48 5N	5 50E
Fauldhouse	**35**	55 50N	3 44W
Faulkton	**158**	45 4N	99 8W
Faulquemont	**43**	49 3N	6 36E
Fauquemberques	**43**	50 36N	2 5E
Faure I.	**137**	25 52S	113 50E
Fauresmith	**128**	29 44S	25 17E
Fauske	**74**	67 17N	15 25E
Fauvillers	**47**	49 51N	5 40E
Faux-Cap	**129**	25 33S	45 32E
Favara	**64**	37 19N	13 39E
Faversham	**29**	51 18N	0 54E
Favignana	**64**	37 56N	12 18E
Favone	**45**	41 47N	9 26E

Favourable Lake	**150**	52 50N	93 39W
Fawley	**28**	50 49N	1 20W
Fawn, R.	**150**	52 22N	88 20W
Fawnskin	**163**	34 16N	116 56W
Faxaflói	**74**	64 29N	23 0W
Faxälven	**72**	63 13N	17 13E
Faya = Largeau	**117**	17 58N	19 6E
Fayence	**45**	43 38N	6 42E
Fayette, Ala., U.S.A.	**157**	33 40N	87 50W
Fayette, La., U.S.A.	**156**	40 22N	86 52W
Fayette, Mo., U.S.A.	**158**	39 10N	92 40W
Fayetteville, Ark., U.S.A.	**159**	36 0N	94 5W
Fayetteville, N.C., U.S.A.	**157**	35 0N	78 58W
Fayetteville, Tenn., U.S.A.	**157**	35 0N	86 30W
Fayón	**58**	41 15N	0 20E
Fazeley	**28**	52 36N	1 42W
Fazenda Nova	**171**	16 11S	50 48W
Fazilka	**94**	30 27N	74 2E
Fazilpur	**94**	29 18N	70 29E
F'Derik	**116**	22 40N	12 45W
Fé, La	**166**	22 2N	84 15W
Feakle	**39**	52 56N	8 41W
Feale, R.	**39**	52 26N	9 28W
Fear, C.	**157**	33 45N	78 0W
Fearn	**37**	57 47N	4 0W
Fearnan	**37**	56 34N	4 6W
Feather, R.	**160**	39 30N	121 20W
Featherston	**142**	41 6S	175 20E
Featherstone	**127**	18 42S	30 55E
Fécamp	**42**	49 45N	0 22E
Fedala = Mohammeda	**118**	33 44N	7 21W
Fedamore	**39**	52 33N	8 36W
Federación	**172**	31 0S	57 55W
Federalsburg	**162**	38 42N	75 47W
Fedjadj, Chott el	**119**	33 52N	9 14E
Fedje	**71**	60 47N	4 43E
Fedorovka	**84**	53 38N	62 42E
Feeagh L.	**38**	53 56N	9 35W
Feeny	**38**	54 54N	7 0W
Fehérgyarmat	**53**	48 0N	22 30E
Fehmarn	**48**	54 26N	11 10E
Fehmarn Bælt	**73**	54 35N	11 20E
Feihsiang	**106**	36 32N	114 47E
Feihsien	**107**	35 12N	118 0E
Feilding	**142**	40 13S	175 35E
•Feira	**65**	15 35S	30 16E
Feira de Santana	**171**	12 15S	38 57W
Fejér □	**53**	47 9N	18 30E
Fejø	**73**	54 55N	11 30E
Felanitx	**59**	39 27N	3 7E
Feldbach	**52**	46 57N	15 52E
Feldberg	**48**	53 20N	13 26E
Feldberg, mt.	**49**	47 51N	7 58E
Feldis	**51**	46 48N	9 26E
Feldkirch	**52**	47 15N	9 37E
Feldkirchen	**52**	46 44N	14 6E
Felhit	**123**	16 40N	38 1E
Felipe Carrillo Puerto	**165**	19 38N	88 3W
Felixlândia	**171**	18 47S	44 55W
Felixstowe	**29**	51 58N	1 22W
Felletin	**44**	45 53N	2 11E
Felpham	**29**	50 47N	0 38W
Felton, U.K.	**35**	55 18N	1 42W
Felton, U.S.A.	**163**	37 3N	122 4W
Feltre	**63**	46 1N	11 55E
Feltwell	**29**	52 29N	0 32E
Femø	**73**	54 58N	11 53E
Femunden	**71**	62 10N	11 53E
Fen Ho, R.	**106**	35 36N	110 42E
Fench'ing	**108**	24 35N	99 54E
Fénérive	**129**	17 22S	49 25E
Fenerwa	**123**	13 5N	39 3E
Fengári	**68**	40 25N	25 32E
Fengchen	**106**	40 30N	113 0E
Fengch'eng, Kiangsi, China	**109**	28 10N	115 43E
Fengch'eng, Liaoning, China	**107**	40 30N	124 2E
Fengchieh	**108**	31 3N	109 28E
Fengch'iu	**106**	35 2N	114 24E
Fenghsiang	**106**	34 26N	107 18E
Fenghsien, Kiangsu, China	**106**	34 42N	116 34E
Fenghsien, Shanghai, China	**109**	30 55N	121 27E
Fenghsien, Shensi, China	**106**	33 56N	106 41E
Fenghsin	**109**	28 42N	115 23E
Fenghua	**109**	29 40N	121 24E
Fenghuang	**108**	27 58N	109 19E
Fenghuangtsui	**106**	33 30N	109 27E
Fengi	**108**	25 35N	100 20E
Fengjun	**107**	39 51N	118 8E
Fengk'ai	**109**	23 26N	111 30E
Fengkang	**108**	27 58N	107 47E
Fengloho	**109**	31 29N	112 29E
Fengning	**106**	41 12N	116 32E
Fengshan, Hopei, China	**107**	41 13N	117 6E
Fengshan, Kwangsi-Chuang, China	**108**	24 32N	107 3E
Fengt'ai, Anhwei, China	**109**	32 44N	116 43E
Fengt'ai, Peip'ing, China	**106**	39 51N	116 17E
Fengteng	**106**	36 25N	114 14E
Fengtu	**108**	29 58N	107 59E
Fengyuang	**109**	32 52N	117 32E
Fenhsi	**106**	36 38N	111 31E
Feni	**109**	27 48N	114 41E
Feni Is.	**135**	4 0S	153 40E
Fenit	**39**	52 17N	9 51W

*Renamed Luangwa

Fennagh	**39**	52 42N	6 50W
Fennimore	**158**	42 58N	90 41W
Fenny	**98**	22 55N	91 32E
Fenny Bentley	**33**	53 4N	1 43W
Fenny Compton	**28**	52 9N	1 20W
Fenny Stratford	**29**	51 59N	0 42W
Feno, C. de	**45**	41 58N	8 33E
Fenoarivo	**129**	18 26S	46 34E
Fens, The	**29**	52 45N	0 2E
Fenton, Can.	**153**	53 0N	105 35W
Fenton, U.S.A.	**156**	42 47N	83 44W
Fenwick	**34**	55 38N	4 25W
Fenyang	**106**	37 19N	111 46E
Feodosiya	**82**	45 2N	35 28E
Fer, C. de	**119**	37 3N	7 10E
Ferbane	**39**	53 17N	7 50W
Ferdows	**93**	33 58N	58 2E
Fère-Champenoise	**43**	48 45N	4 0E
Fère-en-Tardenois	**43**	49 10N	3 30E
Fère, La	**43**	49 40N	3 20E
Ferentino	**64**	41 42N	13 14E
Ferfer	**91**	5 18N	45 20E
Fergana	**85**	40 23N	71 46E
Ferganskaya Dolina	**85**	40 50N	71 30E
Ferganskiy Khrebet	**85**	41 0N	73 50E
Fergus	**150**	43 43N	80 24W
Fergus Falls	**158**	46 25N	96 0W
Fergus, R.	**39**	52 45N	9 0W
Ferguson	**150**	47 50N	73 30W
Fergusson I.	**135**	9 30S	150 45E
Fériana	**119**	34 59N	8 33E
Feričanci	**66**	45 32N	18 0E
Ferkane	**119**	34 37N	7 26E
Ferkéssédougou	**120**	9 35N	5 6W
Ferlach	**52**	46 32N	14 18E
Ferland	**150**	50 19N	88 27W
Ferlo, Vallée du	**120**	15 15N	14 15W
Fermanagh (□)	**38**	54 21N	7 40W
Fermo	**63**	43 10N	13 42E
Fermoselle	**56**	41 19N	6 27W
Fermoy	**39**	52 4N	8 18W
Fernagh	**38**	54 2N	7 51W
Fernan Nuñ,z	**57**	37 40N	4 44W
Fernández	**172**	27 55S	63 50W
Fernandina	**157**	30 40N	81 30W
Fernando de Noronha, I.	**170**	4 0S	33 10W
Fernando do Noronho □	**170**	4 0S	33 10W
Fernando Póo = Bioko	**113**	3 30N	8 40E
Fernandópolis	**171**	20 16S	50 14W
Ferndale, Calif., U.S.A.	**160**	40 37N	124 12W
Ferndale, Wash., U.S.A.	**160**	48 51N	122 41W
Ferness	**37**	57 28N	3 44W
Fernhurst	**29**	51 3N	0 43W
Fernie	**152**	49 30N	115 5W
Fernilea	**36**	57 18N	6 24W
Fernlees	**138**	23 51S	148 7E
Fernley	**160**	39 42N	119 20W
Feroke	**97**	11 9N	75 46E
Ferozepore	**94**	30 55N	74 40E
Férrai	**68**	40 53N	26 10E
Ferrandina	**65**	40 30N	16 28E
Ferrara	**63**	44 50N	11 36E
Ferrato, C.	**64**	39 18N	9 39E
Ferreira do Alentejo	**57**	38 4N	8 6W
Ferreñafe	**174**	6 35S	79 50W
Ferret, C.	**44**	44 38N	1 15W
Ferrette	**43**	47 30N	7 20E
Ferriday	**159**	31 35N	91 33W
Ferrières	**43**	48 5N	2 48E
Ferriete	**62**	44 40N	9 30E
Ferrol	**56**	43 29N	8 15W
Ferron	**160**	39 3N	111 3W
Ferros	**171**	19 14S	43 2W
Ferryhill	**33**	54 42N	1 32W
Ferryland	**151**	47 2N	52 53W
Ferté Bernard, La	**42**	48 10N	0 40E
Ferté, La	**43**	48 57N	3 6E
Ferté-Mace, La	**42**	48 35N	0 21W
Ferté-St. Aubin, La	**43**	47 42N	1 57E
Ferté-Vidame, La	**42**	48 37N	0 53E
Fertile	**158**	47 37N	96 18W
Fertília	**64**	40 37N	8 13E
Fertöszentmiklós	**53**	47 35N	16 53E
Fès	**118**	34 0N	5 0W
Feschaux	**47**	50 9N	4 54E
Feshi	**124**	6 0S	18 10E
Fessenden	**158**	47 42N	99 44W
Fet	**71**	59 57N	11 12E
Feteşti	**70**	44 22N	27 51E
Fethaland, Pt.	**36**	60 39N	1 20W
Fethard	**39**	52 29N	7 42W
Fethiye	**92**	36 36N	29 10E
Fetlar, I.	**36**	60 36N	0 52W
Fettercairn	**37**	56 50N	2 33W
Feuerthalen	**51**	47 32N	8 38E
Feurs	**45**	45 45N	4 13E
Fezzan	**117**	27 0N	15 0E
Ffestiniog	**31**	52 58N	3 56W
Fforest Fawr, mt.	**31**	51 52N	3 35W
Fiambalá	**172**	27 45S	67 37W
Fianarantsoa	**125**	21 20S	46 45E
Fianarantsoa □	**129**	19 30S	47 0E
Fianga	**117**	9 55N	15 20E
Fibiş	**66**	45 57N	21 26E
Fichot, I.	**151**	51 12N	55 40W
Fichtelgebirge	**49**	50 10N	12 0E
Ficksburg	**129**	28 51S	27 53E
Fiddown	**39**	52 20N	7 20W
Fidenza	**62**	44 51N	10 3E
Field	**150**	46 31N	80 1W

Field I **Fort Garland**

Field I.	136	12 5S	132 23E
Field, R.	138	23 48S	138 0E
Fields Finds	137	29 0S	117 10E
Fierenana	129	18 29S	48 24E
Fiéri	68	40 43N	19 33E
Fiesch	50	46 25N	8 12E
Fife □	35	56 13N	3 2W
Fife Ness	35	56 17N	2 35W
Fifth Cataract	123	18 15N	33 50E
Figeac	44	44 37N	2 2E
Figline Valdarno	63	43 37N	11 28E
Figtree	127	20 22S	28 20E
Figueira da Foz	56	40 7N	8 54W
Figueiró dos Vinhos	56	39 55N	8 16W
Figueras	58	42 18N	2 58E
Figuig	118	32 5N	1 11W
Fihaonana	129	18 36S	47 12E
Fiherenana, R.	129	22 50S	44 0E
Fiji ■	142	17 20S	179 0E
Fiji Is.	130	17 20S	179 0E
Fik	90	32 46N	35 41E
Fika	121	11 15N	11 13E
Filabres, Sierra de los	59	37 13N	2 20W
Filadélfia, Brazil	170	7 21S	47 30W
Filadélfia, Italy	65	38 47N	16 17E
Filadelfia	172	22 25S	60 0W
Fil'akovo	53	48 17N	19 50E
Filby	29	52 40N	1 39E
Filchner Ice Shelf	13	78 0S	60 0W
Filer	160	42 30N	114 35W
Filey	33	54 13N	0 18W
Filey B.	33	54 12N	0 15W
Filiaşi	70	44 32N	23 31E
Filiátes	68	39 38N	20 16E
Filiatrá	69	37 9N	21 35E
Filicudi, I.	65	38 35N	14 33E
Filiourí, R.	68	41 15N	25 40E
Filipstad	72	59 43N	14 9E
Filisur	51	46 41N	9 40E
Fillmore, Can.	153	49 50N	103 25W
Fillmore, U.S.A.	163	34 23N	118 58W
Filottrano	63	43 28N	13 20E
Filton	28	51 29N	2 34E
Filyos	82	41 34N	32 4E
Filyos çayi	92	41 35N	32 10E
Finale Ligure	62	44 10N	8 21E
Finale nell' Emília	63	44 50N	11 18E
Fiñana	59	37 10N	2 50W
Fincham	29	52 38N	0 30E
Findhorn	37	57 39N	3 36W
Findhorn, R.	37	57 38N	3 38W
Findlay	156	41 0N	83 41W
Findon	29	50 53N	0 24W
Finea	38	53 46N	7 23W
Finedon	29	52 20N	0 40W
Finger L.	153	53 9N	93 30W
Fingest	29	51 35N	0 52W
Finglas	38	53 22N	6 18W
Fingõe	127	15 12S	31 50E
Finike	92	36 21N	30 10E
Finistère □	42	48 20N	4 0W
Finisterre	56	42 54N	9 16W
Finisterre, C.	56	42 50N	9 19W
Finisterre Ra.	135	6 0S	146 30E
Finke	138	25 34S	134 35E
Finke, R.	138	24 54S	134 16E
Finland ■	78	70 0N	27 0E
Finland, G. of	78	60 0N	26 0E
Finlay, R.	152	55 50N	125 10W
Finley, Austral.	141	35 38S	145 35E
Finley, U.S.A.	158	47 35N	97 50W
Finn, R.	38	54 50N	7 55W
Finnart	34	56 7N	4 48W
Finnigan, Mt.	138	15 49S	145 17E
Finniss	140	35 24S	138 48E
Finniss, C.	139	33 38S	134 51E
Finnmark fylke □	74	69 30N	25 0E
Finschhafen	135	6 33S	147 50E
Finse	71	60 36N	7 30E
Finspång	73	58 45N	15 43E
Finsta	72	59 45N	18 34E
Finsteraarhorn	50	46 31N	8 10E
Finsterwalde	48	51 37N	13 42E
Finsterwolde	46	53 12N	7 6E
Finstown	37	59 0N	3 8W
Fintona	38	54 30N	7 20W
Fintown	38	54 52N	8 8W
Finucanel I.	132	20 19S	118 30E
Finvoy	38	55 0N	6 29W
Fionn L.	36	57 46N	5 30W
Fionnphort	34	56 19N	6 23W
Fiora, R.	63	42 25N	11 35E
Fiordland National Park	143	45 0S	167 50E
Fiorenzuola d'Arda	62	44 56N	9 54E
Fiq	90	32 46N	35 41E
Fire River	150	48 47N	83 36W
Firebag, R.	153	57 45N	111 21W
Firebaugh	163	36 52N	120 27W
Firedrake L.	153	61 25N	104 30W
Firenze	63	43 47N	11 15E
Firkessédougou	120	9 35N	5 6W
Firmi	44	44 32N	2 19E
Firminy	45	45 23N	4 18E
Firoz Kohi	93	34 45N	63 0E
Firozabad	95	27 10N	78 25E
First Cataract	122	24 1N	32 51E
Firūzābād	93	28 52N	52 35E
Firuzkuh	93	35 50N	52 40E
Firvale	152	52 27N	126 13W
Fish, R.	128	27 40S	17 30E
Fisher	137	30 30S	131 0E
Fisher B.	153	51 35N	97 13W
Fishguard	31	51 59N	4 59W
Fishguard B.	31	52 2N	4 58W
Fishing L.	153	52 10N	95 24W
Fishkill	162	41 32N	73 53W
Fishtoft	33	52 27N	0 2E
Fishtown	120	4 24N	7 45E
Fiskivötn	74	64 50N	20 45W
Fiskum	71	59 42N	9 46E
Fismes	43	49 20N	3 40E
Fister	71	59 10N	6 5E
Fitchburg	162	42 35N	71 47W
Fitero	58	42 4N	1 52W
Fitful Hd.	36	59 54N	1 20W
Fitjar	71	59 55N	5 17E
Fitri, L.	124	12 50N	17 28E
Fitz Roy	176	47 10S	67 0W
Fitzgerald, Can.	152	59 51N	111 36W
Fitzgerald, U.S.A.	157	31 45N	83 10W
Fitzmaurice, R.	136	14 50S	129 50E
Fitzpatrick	150	47 29N	72 46W
Fitzroy Crossing	136	18 9S	125 38E
Fitzroy, R., Queens., Austral.	138	23 32S	150 52E
Fitzroy, R., W. Australia, Austral.	136	17 25S	124 0E
Fiume = Rijeka	63	45 20N	14 21E
Fiumefreddo Brúzio	65	39 14N	16 4E
Five Alley	39	53 9N	7 51W
Five Points	163	36 26N	120 6W
Fivemiletown	38	54 23N	7 20W
Fizi	126	4 17S	28 55E
Fjæra	71	59 52N	6 22E
Fjaere	71	58 23N	8 36E
Fjellerup	73	56 29N	10 34E
Fjerritslev	73	57 5N	9 15E
Fkih ben Salah	118	32 45N	6 45W
Fla	71	60 25N	9 26E
Flå	71	63 13N	10 18E
Flagler	158	39 20N	103 4W
Flagstaff	161	35 10N	111 40W
Flagstone	152	49 4N	115 10W
Flaherty, I.	150	56 15N	79 15W
Flåm	75	60 52N	7 14E
Flambeau, R.	158	45 40N	90 50W
Flamborough	33	54 7N	0 7W
Flamborough Hd.	33	54 8N	0 4W
Flaming Gorge Dam	160	40 50N	109 25W
Flaming Gorge L.	160	41 15N	109 30W
Flamingo, Teluk	103	5 30S	138 0E
Flanders = Flandres	47	51 10N	3 15E
Flandre Occidental □	47	51 0N	3 0E
Flandre Orientale □	47	51 0N	4 0E
Flandreau	158	44 5N	96 38W
Flandres, Plaines des	47	51 10N	3 15E
Flannan Is.	23	58 9N	7 52W
Flaren L.	73	57 2N	14 5E
Flåsjön	74	64 5N	15 50E
Flat, R.	152	61 51N	128 0W
Flat River	159	37 50N	90 30W
Flatey, Barðastrandarsýsla, Iceland	74	66 10N	17 52W
Flatey, Suður-þingeyjarsýsla, Iceland	74	65 22N	22 56W
Flathead L.	160	47 50N	114 0W
Flattery, C., Austral.	138	14 58S	145 21E
Flattery, C., U.S.A.	160	48 21N	124 43W
Flavy-le-Martel	43	49 43N	3 12E
Flawil	51	47 26N	9 11E
Flaxton	158	48 52N	102 24W
Flèche, La	42	47 42N	0 5W
Fleeming, C.	136	11 15S	131 21E
Fleet	29	51 16N	0 50W
Fleetwood, U.K.	32	53 55N	3 1W
Fleetwood, U.S.A.	162	40 27N	75 49W
Flekkefjord	71	58 18N	6 39E
Flémalle	47	50 36N	5 28E
Flensborg Fjord	73	54 50N	9 40E
Flensburg	48	54 46N	9 28E
Flers	42	48 47N	0 33W
Flesberg	71	59 51N	9 22E
Fletton	29	52 34N	0 13W
Fleurance	44	43 52N	0 40E
Fleurier	50	46 54N	6 35E
Fleurus	47	50 29N	4 32E
Flickerbäcken	72	61 47N	12 34E
Flims	51	46 50N	9 17E
Flin Flon	153	54 46N	101 53W
Flinders B.	137	34 19S	115 9E
Flinders Group, Is.	138	14 11S	144 15E
Flinders I.	138	40 0S	148 0E
Flinders, R.	138	17 36S	140 36E
Flinders Ranges	140	31 30S	138 30E
Flinders Reefs	138	17 37S	148 31E
Flint	156	43 5N	83 19W
Flint (□)	26	53 15N	3 12W
Flint, I.	131	11 26S	151 48W
Flint, R.	157	31 20N	84 10W
Flinton	139	27 55S	149 32E
Fliseryd	73	57 6N	16 15E
Flitwick	29	51 59N	0 30W
Flix	58	41 14N	0 32E
Flixecourt	43	50 0N	2 5E
Flobecq	47	50 44N	3 45E
Floda	72	60 30N	14 53E
Flodden	35	55 37N	2 8W
Floodwood	158	46 55N	92 55W
Flora, N. Tröndelag, Norway	71	63 27N	11 22E
Flora, Sogn & Fjordane, Norway	71	61 35N	5 1E
Flora, U.S.A.	156	38 40N	88 30W
Florac	44	44 20N	3 37E
Florala	157	31 0N	86 20W
Florânia	170	6 8S	36 49W
Floreffe	47	50 26N	4 46E
Florence, Ala., U.S.A.	157	34 50N	87 50W
Florence, Ariz., U.S.A.	161	33 0N	111 25W
Florence, Colo., U.S.A.	158	38 26N	105 0W
Florence, Oreg., U.S.A.	160	44 0N	124 3W
Florence, S.C., U.S.A.	157	34 5N	79 50W
Florence = Firenze	63	43 47N	11 15E
Florence, L.	139	28 53S	138 9E
Florennes	47	50 15N	4 35E
Florensac	44	43 23N	3 28E
Florenville	47	49 40N	5 19E
Flores, Azores	16	39 13N	31 13W
Flores, Brazil	170	7 51S	37 59W
Flores, Guat.	166	16 50N	89 40W
Flores I.	152	49 20N	126 10W
Flores, I.	103	8 35S	121 0E
Flores Sea	102	6 30S	124 0E
Floresta	170	9 46S	37 26W
Floresville	159	29 10N	98 10W
Floriano	170	6 50S	43 0W
Florianópolis	173	27 30S	48 30W
Florida, Cuba	166	21 32N	78 14W
Florida, Uruguay	173	34 7S	56 10W
Florida □	157	28 30N	82 0W
Florida B.	167	25 0N	81 20W
Florida Keys	167	25 0N	80 40W
Florida, Strait of	167	25 0N	80 0W
Florídia	65	37 6N	15 9E
Flórina	68	40 48N	21 26E
Flórina □	68	40 45N	21 20E
Florningen	72	61 50N	12 16E
Florø	71	61 35N	5 1E
Flosta	71	58 32N	8 56E
Flower's Cove	151	51 14N	56 46W
Floydada	159	33 58N	101 18W
Flüela Pass	51	46 45N	9 57E
Fluk	103	1 42S	127 38E
Flumen, R.	58	41 50N	0 25W
Flumendosa, R.	64	39 30N	9 25E
Fluminimaggiore	64	39 25N	8 30E
Flums	51	47 6N	9 21E
Flushing = Vlissingen	47	51 26N	3 34E
Fluvià, R.	58	42 12N	3 7E
Fly, R.	135	8 25S	143 0E
Foam Lake	153	51 40N	103 32W
Foča	66	43 31N	18 47E
Focşani	70	45 41N	27 15E
Fofo Fofo	138	8 9S	147 6E
Foggaret el Arab	118	27 3N	2 59E
Foggaret ez Zoua	118	27 20N	3 0E
Fóggia	65	41 28N	15 31E
Foggo	121	11 21N	9 57E
Foglia, R.	63	43 50N	12 32E
Fogo	151	49 43N	54 17W
Fogo I.	151	49 40N	54 5W
Fohnsdorf	52	47 12N	14 40E
Föhr	48	54 40N	8 30E
Foia, Cerro da	57	37 19N	8 10W
Foix	44	42 58N	1 38E
Fojnica	66	43 59N	17 51E
Fokang	109	23 52N	113 31E
Fokino	80	53 30N	34 10E
Fokís □	69	38 30N	22 15E
Fokstua	71	62 8N	9 16E
Folda, Nord-Trøndelag, Norway	74	64 41N	10 50E
Folda, Nordland, Norway	74	67 38N	14 50E
Földeák	53	46 19N	20 30E
Folette, La	157	36 23N	84 9W
Foley	128	30 25N	87 40W
Foleyet	150	48 15N	82 25W
Folgefonni	71	60 23N	6 34E
Foligno	63	42 58N	12 40E
Folkestone	29	51 5N	1 11E
Folkston	157	30 55N	82 0W
Follett	159	36 30N	100 12W
Follónica	62	42 55N	10 45E
Folsom	160	38 41N	121 7W
Fond-du-Lac	153	59 19N	107 12W
Fond du lac	158	43 46N	88 26W
Fond-du-Lac, R.	153	59 17N	106 0W
Fondak	118	35 34N	5 35W
Fondi	64	41 21N	13 25E
Fonfría	56	41 37N	6 9W
Fongen	71	63 11N	11 38E
Fonni	64	40 5N	9 16E
Fonsagrada	56	43 8N	7 4W
Fonseca, G. de	166	13 10N	87 40W
Fontaine-Française	43	47 32N	5 21E
Fontainebleau	43	48 24N	2 40E
Fontas, R.	152	58 14N	121 48W
Fonte Boa	174	2 25S	66 0W
Fontem	121	5 32N	9 52E
Fontenay-le-Comte	44	46 28N	0 48W
Fontenelle	151	48 54N	64 33W
Fontur	74	66 23N	14 32W
Fonyód	53	46 44N	17 33E
Foochow = Fuchou	109	26 5N	119 18E
Foping	106	33 22N	108 19E
Foppiano	62	46 21N	8 24E
Föra	73	57 1N	16 51E
Forbach	43	49 10N	6 52E
Forbes	141	33 22S	148 0E
Forbesganj	95	26 17N	87 18E
Forcados	121	5 26N	5 26E
Forcados, R.	121	5 25N	5 20E
Forcall, R.	58	40 40N	0 12W
Forcalquier	45	43 58N	5 47E
Forchheim	49	49 42N	11 4E
Forclaz, Col de la	50	46 3N	7 1E
Ford City	163	35 9N	119 27W
Førde	71	61 27N	5 53E
Fordingbridge	28	50 56N	1 48W
Fordongianus	44	40 0N	8 50E
Fords Bridge	139	29 41S	145 29E
Fordyce	159	33 50N	92 20W
Forécariah	120	9 20N	13 10W
Forel	12	66 52N	36 55W
Foremost	152	49 26N	111 25W
Forenza	65	40 50N	15 50E
Forest, Belg.	47	50 49N	4 20E
Forest, U.S.A.	159	32 21N	89 27W
Forest City, Ark., U.S.A.	159	35 0N	90 50W
Forest City, Iowa, U.S.A.	158	43 12N	93 39W
Forest City, N.C., U.S.A.	157	35 23N	81 50W
Forest Grove	160	45 31N	123 4W
Forest Lawn	152	51 4N	114 0W
Forest Row	29	51 6N	0 3E
Forestburg	152	52 35N	112 1W
Forestier Pen.	138	43 0S	148 0E
Forestville, Can.	151	48 48N	69 20W
Forestville, U.S.A.	156	44 41N	87 29W
Forez, Mts. du	44	45 40N	3 50E
Forfar	37	56 40N	2 53W
Forges-les-Eaux	43	49 37N	1 30E
Forget	150	49 40N	102 50W
Forked River	162	39 50N	74 12W
Forks	160	47 56N	124 23W
Forksville	162	41 29N	76 35W
Forli	63	44 14N	12 2E
Forman	158	46 9N	97 43W
Formazza	62	46 23N	8 26E
Formby Pt.	32	53 33N	3 7W
Formentera, I.	59	38 40N	1 30E
Formentor, C. de	58	39 58N	3 13E
Fórmia	64	41 15N	13 34E
Formiga	171	20 27S	45 25W
Formigine	62	44 37N	10 51E
Formiguères	44	42 37N	2 5E
Formosa, Argent.	172	26 15S	58 10W
Formosa, Brazil	171	15 32S	47 20W
Formosa = Taiwan ■	109	24 0N	121 0E
Formosa □	172	26 5S	58 10W
Formosa Bay	126	2 40S	40 20E
Formosa Strait	109	24 40N	120 0E
Formoso, R.	171	10 34S	49 56W
Fornaes, C.	73	56 27N	10 58E
Fornells	58	40 4N	4 4E
Fornos de Algodres	56	40 38N	7 32W
Fornovo di Taro	62	44 42N	10 7E
Forres	37	57 37N	3 38W
Forrest, Vic., Austral.	140	38 22S	143 40E
Forrest, W. Australia, Austral.	137	30 51S	128 6E
Forrest Lakes	137	29 12S	128 46E
Forrest, Mt.	137	24 48S	127 45E
Forrières	47	50 8N	5 17E
Fors, Jämtland, Sweden	72	63 0N	16 40E
Fors, Kopparberg, Sweden	72	60 14N	16 20E
Forsa	72	61 44N	16 55E
Forsand	71	58 54N	6 5E
Forsayth	138	18 33S	143 34E
Forsbacka	72	60 39N	16 54E
Forse	72	63 8N	17 1E
Forserum	73	57 42N	14 30E
Forshaga	72	59 33N	13 29E
Forshem	73	58 38N	13 30E
Forsmo	72	63 16N	17 11E
Forst	48	51 43N	14 37E
Forster	141	32 12S	152 31E
Forsyth, Ga., U.S.A.	157	33 4N	83 55W
Forsyth, Mont., U.S.A.	160	46 14N	106 37W
Forsyth I.	143	40 58S	174 5E
Fort Albany	150	52 15N	81 35W
Fort Ann	162	43 25N	73 30W
Fort Apache	161	33 50N	110 0W
Fort Archambault = Sarh	117	9 5N	18 23E
Fort Assiniboine	152	54 20N	114 45W
Fort Augustus	37	57 9N	4 40W
Fort Babine	152	55 22N	126 37W
Fort Beaufort	128	32 46S	26 40E
Fort Benton	160	47 50N	110 40W
Fort Bragg	160	39 28N	123 50W
Fort Bretonnet = Bousso	117	10 34N	16 52E
Fort Bridger	160	41 22N	110 20W
Fort Charlet = Djanet	121	24 35N	9 32E
Fort Chimo	149	58 6N	68 25W
Fort Chipewyan	153	58 42N	111 8W
Fort Collins	158	40 30N	105 4W
Fort Coulonge	150	45 50N	76 45W
Fort Crampel = Kaga Bandoro	117	7 8N	19 18E
Fort-Dauphin	129	25 2S	47 0E
Fort Davis	159	30 38N	103 53W
Fort-de-France	167	14 36N	61 2W
Fort de Polignac = Illizi	119	26 31N	8 32E
Fort de Possel = Possel	124	5 5N	19 10E
Fort Defiance	161	35 47N	109 4W
Fort Dodge	158	42 29N	94 10W
Fort Flatters = Bordj Omar Driss	119	27 10N	6 40E
Fort Foureau = Kousseri	117	12 0N	14 55E
Fort Frances	153	48 35N	93 25W
Fort Franklin	148	65 30N	123 45W
Fort Garland	161	37 28N	105 30W

Fort George **Frýdek-Místek**

Fort George	**151**	53 50N	79 0W
Fort George, R.	**150**	53 50N	77 0W
Fort Good-Hope	**147**	66 14N	128 40W
Fort Gouraud = F'Dérik	**116**	22 40N	12 45W
Fort Grahame	**152**	56 30N	124 35W
Fort Hancock	**161**	31 19N	105 56W
Fort Hauchuca	**161**	31 32N	110 30W
Fort Hertz (Putao)	**99**	27 28N	97 30E
Fort Hope	**150**	51 30N	88 10W
Fort Irwin	**163**	35 16N	116 34W
Fort Jameson = Chipata	**127**	13 38S	32 38E
Fort Johnston	**127**	14 25S	35 16E
Fort Kent	**151**	47 12N	68 30W
Fort Klamath	**160**	42 45N	122 0W
Fort Lallemand	**119**	31 13N	6 17E
Fort-Lamy = Ndjamena	**117**	12 4N	15 8E
Fort Lapperrine = Tamanrasset	**119**	22 56N	5 30E
Fort Laramie	**158**	42 15N	104 30W
Fort Lauderdale	**157**	26 10N	80 5W
Fort Liard	**152**	60 20N	123 30W
Fort Liberté	**167**	19 42N	71 51W
Fort Lupton	**158**	40 8N	104 48W
Fort Mackay	**152**	57 12N	111 41W
Fort McKenzie	**151**	57 20N	69 0W
Fort Macleod	**152**	49 45N	113 30W
Fort MacMahon	**118**	29 51N	1 45E
Fort McMurray	**152**	56 44N	111 23W
Fort McPherson	**147**	67 30N	134 55W
Fort Madison	**158**	40 39N	91 20W
Fort Meade	**157**	27 45N	81 45W
Fort Miribel	**118**	29 31N	2 55E
Fort Morgan	**158**	40 10N	103 50W
Fort Myers	**157**	26 30N	82 0W
Fort Nelson	**152**	58 50N	122 38W
Fort Nelson, R.	**152**	59 32N	124 0W
Fort Norman	**147**	64 57N	125 30W
Fort Pacot (Chirfa)	**119**	20 55N	12 14E
Fort Payne	**157**	34 25N	85 44W
Fort Peck	**160**	47 1N	105 30W
Fort Peck Dam	**160**	48 0N	106 20W
Fort Peck Res.	**160**	47 40N	107 0W
Fort Pierce	**158**	27 29N	80 19W
Fort Pierre	**158**	44 25N	100 25W
Fort Pierre Bordes	**118**	20 0N	2 55E
Fort Portal	**126**	0 40N	30 20E
Fort Providence	**152**	61 21N	117 40W
Fort Qu'Appelle	**153**	50 45N	103 50W
Fort Randall	**147**	55 10N	162 48W
Fort Reliance	**153**	63 0N	109 20W
Fort Resolution	**152**	61 10N	113 40W
Fort Rixon	**127**	20 2S	29 17E
Fort Roseberry = Mansa	**127**	11 10S	28 50E
Fort Rupert (Rupert House)	**150**	51 30N	78 40W
Fort Saint	**119**	30 13N	9 31E
Fort St. James	**152**	54 30N	124 10W
Fort St. John	**152**	56 15N	120 50W
Fort Sandeman	**94**	31 20N	69 25E
Fort Saskatchewan	**152**	53 40N	113 15W
Fort Scott	**159**	38 0N	94 40W
Fort Selkirk	**147**	62 43N	137 22W
Fort Severn	**150**	56 0N	87 40W
Fort Shevchenko	**83**	44 30N	50 10W
Fort Sibut = Sibut	**117**	5 52N	19 10E
Fort Simpson	**152**	61 45N	121 23W
Fort Smith, Can.	**152**	60 0N	111 51W
Fort Smith, U.S.A.	**159**	35 25N	94 25W
Fort Stanton	**161**	33 33N	105 36W
Fort Stockton	**159**	30 48N	103 2W
Fort Sumner	**159**	34 24N	104 8W
Fort Thomas	**161**	33 2N	109 59W
Fort Trinquet = Bir Mogrein	**116**	25 10N	11 25W
Fort Valley	**157**	32 33N	83 52W
Fort Vermilion	**152**	58 24N	116 0W
Fort Victoria	**127**	20 8S	30 55E
Ft. Walton Beach	**157**	30 25N	86 40W
Fort Wayne	**156**	41 5N	85 10W
Fort William	**36**	56 48N	5 8W
Fort William = Thunder Bay	**150**	48 20N	89 10W
Fort Worth	**159**	32 45N	97 25W
Fort Yates	**158**	46 8N	100 38W
Fort Yukon	**147**	66 35N	145 12W
Fortaleza	**170**	3 35S	38 35W
Forte Coimbra	**174**	19 55S	57 48W
Forte Rocadas	**125**	16 38S	15 22E
Forteau	**151**	51 28N	57 1W
Fortescue	**136**	21 4S	116 4E
Fortescue, R.	**136**	21 20S	116 5E
Forth, Firth of	**35**	56 5N	2 55W
Forthassa Rharbia	**118**	32 52N	1 11W
Forties, oilfield	**19**	57 40N	1 0E
Fortin Corrales	**174**	22 21S	60 35W
Fortín Guachalla	**174**	22 22S	62 23W
Fortín Rojas Silva	**172**	22 40S	59 3W
Fortín Siracuas	**174**	21 3S	61 46W
Fortín Teniente Montania	**172**	22 1S	59 45W
Fortore, R.	**63**	41 40N	15 0E
Fortrose	**143**	46 38S	168 45E
Fortuna, Spain	**59**	38 11N	1 7W
Fortuna, Cal., U.S.A.	**160**	48 38N	124 8W
Fortuna, N.D., U.S.A.	**158**	48 55N	103 48W
Fortune Bay	**151**	47 30N	55 22W
Forty Mile	**147**	64 20N	140 30W
Forūr	**93**	26 20N	54 30E
Fos	**62**	43 20N	4 57E
Fos do Jordão	**174**	9 30S	72 14W
Fos-sur-Mer	**45**	43 26N	4 56E
Foshan	**109**	23 4N	113 5E
Fossacesia	**63**	42 15N	14 30E
Fossano	**62**	44 39N	7 40E
Fosses-la-Ville	**47**	50 24N	4 41E
Fossil	**160**	45 0N	120 9W
Fossilbrook	**138**	17 47S	144 29E
Fossombrone	**63**	43 41N	12 49E
Fosston	**158**	47 33N	95 39W
Foster, R.	**153**	55 47N	105 49W
Fosters Ra.	**138**	21 35S	133 48E
Fostoria	**156**	41 8N	83 25W
Fou Chiang, R.	**108**	30 3N	106 21E
Fouch'eng	**106**	37 52N	116 8E
Fougamou	**124**	1 38S	11 39E
Fougères	**42**	48 21N	1 14W
Fouhsinshih	**107**	42 13N	121 51E
Foul Pt.	**97**	8 35N	81 25E
Foula, I.	**23**	60 10N	2 5W
Fouling	**108**	29 40N	107 20E
Foulpointe	**129**	17 41S	49 31E
Foum el Alba	**118**	20 45N	3 0W
Foum el Kreneg	**118**	29 0N	0 58W
Foum Tatahouine	**119**	32 57N	10 29E
Foum Zguid	**118**	30 2N	6 59W
Foumban	**121**	5 45N	10 50E
Foundiougne	**120**	14 5N	16 32W
Founing	**107**	33 47N	119 48E
Fountain, Colo., U.S.A.	**158**	38 42N	104 40W
Fountain, Utah, U.S.A.	**160**	39 41N	111 50W
Fountain Springs	**163**	35 54N	118 51W
Foup'ing	**106**	38 55N	114 13E
Four Mts., Is. of the	**147**	52 0N	170 30W
Fourchambault	**43**	47 0N	3 3E
Fourchu	**151**	45 43N	60 17W
Fourcroy, C.	**136**	11 45S	130 2E
Fourmies	**43**	50 1N	4 2E
Fournás	**69**	39 3N	21 52E
Foúrnoi	**69**	37 36N	26 32E
Fours	**43**	46 50N	3 42E
Foushan	**106**	35 58N	111 51E
Fouta Djalon	**120**	11 20N	12 10W
Foux, Cap-à-	**167**	19 43N	73 27W
Fouyang	**109**	32 55N	115 52E
Foveaux Str.	**143**	46 42S	168 10E
Fowler, Calif., U.S.A.	**163**	36 41N	119 41W
Fowler, Colo., U.S.A.	**158**	38 10N	104 0W
Fowler, Kans., U.S.A.	**159**	37 28N	100 7W
Fowlers B.	**137**	31 59S	132 34E
Fowlers Bay	**137**	32 0S	132 29E
Fowlerton	**159**	28 26N	98 50W
Fox Is.	**147**	52 30N	166 0W
Fox, R.	**153**	56 3N	93 18W
Fox Valley	**153**	50 30N	109 25W
Foxboro	**162**	42 4N	71 16W
Foxe Basin	**149**	68 30N	77 0W
Foxe Channel	**149**	66 0N	80 0W
Foxe Pen.	**149**	65 0N	76 0W
Foxen, L.	**72**	59 25N	11 55E
Foxhol	**46**	53 10N	6 43E
Foxpark	**160**	41 4N	106 6W
Foxton	**142**	40 29S	175 18E
Foyle, Lough	**38**	55 6N	7 8W
Foynes	**38**	52 30N	9 5W
Foz	**56**	43 33N	7 20W
Foz do Cunene	**128**	17 15S	11 55E
Foz do Gregório	**174**	6 47S	71 0W
Foz do Iguaçu	**173**	25 30S	54 30W
Frackville	**162**	40 46N	76 15W
Fraga	**58**	41 32N	0 21E
Fraire	**47**	50 16N	4 31E
Frameries	**47**	50 24N	3 54E
Framlingham	**29**	52 14N	1 20E
Franca	**171**	20 25S	47 30W
Francavilla al Mare	**63**	42 25N	14 16E
Francavilla Fontana	**65**	40 32N	17 35E
France ■	**41**	47 0N	3 0E
Frances	**140**	36 41S	140 55E
Frances Creek	**136**	13 25S	132 3E
Frances L.	**152**	61 23N	129 30W
Frances, R.	**152**	60 16N	129 10W
Francés Viejo, C.	**167**	19 40N	70 0W
Franceville	**124**	1 40S	13 32E
Franche Comté □	**43**	46 30N	5 50E
Franches Montagnes	**50**	47 10N	7 0E
Francis-Garnier	**118**	36 30N	1 30E
Francis Harbour	**151**	52 34N	55 44W
Francisco I. Madero, Coahuila, Mexico	**164**	25 48N	103 18W
Francisco I. Madero, Durango, Mexico	**164**	24 32N	104 22W
Francisco Sá	**171**	16 28S	43 30W
Francistown	**125**	21 7S	27 33E
Francofonte	**65**	37 13N	14 50E
François	**151**	47 35N	56 45W
Francois L.	**152**	54 0N	125 30W
François, Le	**167**	14 38N	60 57W
Francorchamps	**47**	50 27N	5 57E
Franeker	**46**	53 12N	5 33E
Frankado	**123**	12 30N	43 12E
Frankenberg	**48**	51 3N	8 47E
Frankenthal	**49**	49 32N	8 21E
Frankford = Kilcormac	**39**	53 10N	7 43W
Frankfort, Ind., U.S.A.	**156**	40 20N	86 33W
Frankfort, Kans., U.S.A.	**158**	39 42N	96 26W
Frankfort, Ky., U.S.A.	**156**	38 12N	84 52W
Frankfort, Mich., U.S.A.	**156**	44 38N	86 14W
Frankfort, N.Y., U.S.A.	**162**	43 2N	75 4W
Frankfurt □	**48**	52 30N	14 0E
Frankfurt am Main	**49**	50 7N	8 40E
Frankfurt an der Oder	**48**	52 50N	14 31E
Fränkische Alb	**49**	49 20N	11 30E
Fränkische Saale	**49**	50 7N	9 49E
Fränkische Saale, R.	**49**	50 7N	9 49E
Fränkische Schweiz	**49**	49 45N	11 10E
Frankland, R.	**137**	35 0S	116 48E
Franklin, Ky., U.S.A.	**157**	36 40N	86 30W
Franklin, La., U.S.A.	**159**	29 45N	91 30W
Franklin, Mass., U.S.A.	**162**	42 4N	71 23W
Franklin, Nebr., U.S.A.	**158**	40 9N	98 55W
Franklin, N.H., U.S.A.	**162**	43 28N	71 39W
Franklin, N.J., U.S.A.	**162**	41 9N	74 38W
Franklin, Pa., U.S.A.	**156**	41 22N	79 45W
Franklin, Tenn., U.S.A.	**157**	35 54N	86 53W
Franklin, Va., U.S.A.	**157**	36 40N	76 58W
Franklin, W. Va., U.S.A.	**156**	38 38N	79 21W
•Franklin □	**149**	71 0N	99 0W
Franklin B.	**147**	69 45N	126 0W
Franklin D. Roosevelt L.	**160**	48 30N	118 16W
Franklin I.	**13**	76 10S	168 30E
Franklin, L.	**160**	40 20N	115 26W
Franklin Mts., Can.	**148**	66 0N	125 0W
Franklin Mts., N.Z.	**143**	44 55S	167 45E
Franklin Str.	**148**	72 0N	96 0W
Franklinton	**159**	30 53N	90 10W
Franklyn Mt.	**143**	42 4S	172 42E
Franks Peak	**160**	43 50N	109 5W
Frankston	**141**	38 8S	145 8E
Frankton Junc.	**142**	37 47S	175 16E
Fränsta	**72**	62 30N	16 11E
Frant	**29**	51 5N	0 17E
Frantsa Josifa, Zemlya	**76**	76 0N	62 0E
Franz	**150**	48 25N	84 30W
Franz Josef Fd.	**12**	73 20N	22 0E
Franz Josef Land = Frantsa Josifa	**76**	76 0N	62 0E
Franzburg	**48**	54 9N	12 52E
Frascati	**64**	41 48N	12 41E
Fraser I.	**139**	25 15S	153 10E
Fraser L.	**152**	54 0N	124 50W
Fraser, Mt.	**137**	25 35S	118 20E
Fraser, R., B.C., Can.	**152**	49 7N	123 11W
Fraser, R., Newf., Can.	**151**	56 39N	63 10W
Fraserburg	**128**	31 55S	21 30E
Fraserburgh	**37**	57 41N	2 0W
Fraserdale	**150**	49 55N	81 37W
Frasertown	**142**	38 58S	177 28E
Frashëri	**68**	40 23N	20 26E
Frasne	**43**	46 50N	6 10E
Frater	**150**	47 20N	84 25W
Frauenfeld	**51**	47 34N	8 54E
Fray Bentos	**172**	33 10S	58 15W
Frazier Downs P.O.	**136**	18 48S	121 42E
Frechilla	**56**	42 8N	4 50W
Fredericia	**73**	55 34N	9 45E
Frederick, Md., U.S.A.	**162**	39 25N	77 23W
Frederick, Okla., U.S.A.	**159**	34 22N	99 0W
Frederick, S.D., U.S.A.	**158**	45 55N	98 29W
Frederick Reef	**133**	20 58S	154 23E
Frederick Sd.	**153**	57 10N	134 0W
Fredericksburg, Tex., U.S.A.	**159**	30 17N	98 55W
Fredericksburg, Va., U.S.A.	**162**	38 16N	77 29W
Frederickstown	**159**	37 35N	90 15W
Fredericton	**151**	45 57N	66 40W
Fredericton Junc.	**151**	45 41N	66 40W
Frederiksberg	**72**	60 12N	14 25E
Frederiksborg Amt □	**73**	55 50N	12 10E
Frederikshåb	**12**	62 0N	49 30W
Frederikshavn	**73**	57 28N	10 31E
Frederikssund	**73**	55 50N	12 3E
Frederiksted	**147**	17 43N	64 53W
Fredonia, Ariz., U.S.A.	**161**	36 59N	112 36W
Fredonia, Kans., U.S.A.	**159**	37 34N	95 50W
Fredonia, N.Y., U.S.A.	**156**	42 26N	79 20W
Fredrikstad	**71**	59 13N	10 57E
Freehold	**162**	40 15N	74 18W
Freel Pk.	**163**	38 52N	119 53W
Freeland	**162**	41 3N	75 48W
Freeling, Mt.	**136**	22 35S	133 06E
Freels, C.	**151**	49 15N	53 30W
Freeman, Calif., U.S.A.	**163**	35 35N	117 53W
Freeman, S.D., U.S.A.	**158**	43 25N	97 20W
Freeport, Bahamas	**167**	25 45N	88 30E
Freeport, Can.	**151**	44 15N	66 20W
Freeport, Ill., U.S.A.	**158**	42 18N	89 40W
Freeport, N.Y., U.S.A.	**162**	40 39N	73 35W
Freeport, Tex., U.S.A.	**159**	28 55N	95 22W
Freetown	**120**	8 30N	13 10W
Freevater Forest	**37**	57 51N	4 45W
Fregenal de la Sierra	**57**	38 10N	6 39W
Fregene	**64**	41 50N	12 12E
Fregeneda, La	**56**	40 58N	6 54W
Fréhel C.	**42**	48 40N	2 20W
Freiberg	**48**	50 55N	13 20E
Freibourg = Fribourg	**50**	46 49N	7 9E
Freiburg, Baden, Ger.	**49**	48 0N	7 52E
Freiburg, Sachsen, Ger.	**48**	53 49N	9 17E
Freiburger Alpen	**50**	46 37N	7 10E
Freire	**176**	39 0S	72 50W
Freirina	**172**	28 30S	70 27W
Freising	**49**	48 24N	11 47E
Freistadt	**52**	48 30N	14 30E
Freital	**48**	51 0N	13 40E
Fréjus	**45**	43 25N	6 44E
Fremantle	**137**	32 1S	115 47E
Fremont, Calif., U.S.A.	**163**	37 32N	122 57W
Fremont, Mich., U.S.A.	**156**	43 29N	85 59W
Fremont, Nebr., U.S.A.	**158**	41 30N	96 30W
Fremont, Ohio, U.S.A.	**156**	41 20N	83 5W
Fremont, L.	**160**	43 0N	109 50W
Fremont, R.	**161**	38 15N	110 20W
French Camp	**163**	37 53N	121 16W
French Cr.	**156**	41 30N	80 2W
French Guiana ■	**175**	4 0N	53 0W
French I.	**141**	38 20S	145 22E
French Terr. of Afars & Issas □ = Djibouti	**123**	11 30N	42 15E
Frenchglen	**160**	42 56N	119 0W
Frenchman Butte	**153**	53 36N	109 36W
Frenchman Creek, R.	**158**	40 34N	101 35W
Frenchman, R.	**160**	49 25N	108 20W
Frenchpark	**38**	53 53N	8 25W
Frenda	**118**	35 2N	1 1E
Fresco, R.	**175**	7 15S	51 30W
Freshfield, C.	**13**	68 25S	151 10E
Freshford	**39**	52 45N	7 25W
Freshwater	**28**	50 42N	1 31W
Fresnillo	**164**	23 10N	103 0W
Fresno	**163**	36 47N	119 50W
Fresno Alhandiga	**56**	40 42N	5 37W
Fresno Res.	**160**	48 47N	110 0W
Freswick	**37**	58 35N	3 5W
Freuchie	**35**	56 14N	3 8W
Freudenstadt	**49**	48 27N	8 25E
Freux	**47**	49 59N	5 27E
Frévent	**43**	50 15N	2 17E
Frew, R.	**138**	20 0S	135 38E
Frewena	**138**	19 50S	135 50E
Freycinet, C.	**137**	34 9S	115 0E
Freycinet Pen.	**138**	42 10S	148 25E
Fria	**120**	10 27N	13 32W
Fria, La	**174**	8 13N	72 15W
Friant	**163**	36 59N	119 43W
Frías	**172**	28 40S	65 5W
Fribourg	**50**	46 49N	7 9E
Fribourg □	**50**	45 40N	7 0E
Frick	**50**	47 31N	8 1E
Fridafors	**73**	56 25N	14 39E
Fridaythorpe	**33**	54 2N	0 40W
Friedberg, Bayern, Ger.	**49**	48 21N	10 59E
Friedberg, Hessen, Ger.	**10**	50 19N	8 45E
Friedland	**49**	53 40N	13 33E
Friedrichshafen	**49**	47 39N	9 29E
Friedrichskoog	**48**	54 1N	8 52E
Friedrichsort	**48**	54 24N	10 11E
Friedrichstadt	**48**	54 23N	9 6E
Friendly (Tonga) Is.	**130**	19 50S	174 30W
Friesach	**52**	46 57N	14 24E
Friesack	**48**	52 43N	12 35E
Friesche Wad	**46**	53 22N	5 44E
Friesland □	**46**	53 5N	5 50E
Friesoythe	**48**	53 1N	7 51E
Frigate, L.	**150**	53 15N	74 45W
Frigg E., gasfield	**19**	59 50N	2 20E
Frigg, gasfield	**19**	59 50N	2 15E
Frigg N.E., gasfield	**19**	60 0N	2 17E
Frillesås	**73**	57 20N	12 12E
Frimley	**29**	51 18N	0 43W
Frinnaryd	**73**	57 55N	14 50E
Frinton-on-Sea	**29**	51 50N	1 16E
Frio, C.	**128**	18 0S	12 0E
Frio, R.	**159**	29 40N	99 40W
Friockheim	**37**	56 39N	2 40W
Friona	**159**	34 40N	102 42W
Frisa, Loch	**34**	56 34N	6 5W
Frisian Is.	**48**	53 30N	6 0E
Fristad	**73**	57 50N	13 0E
Fritch	**159**	35 40N	101 35W
Fritsla	**73**	57 33N	12 47E
Fritzlar	**48**	51 8N	9 19E
Friuli-Venezia-Giulia □	**63**	46 0N	13 0E
Frizington	**32**	54 33N	3 30W
Frobisher B.	**149**	63 0N	67 0W
Frobisher L.	**153**	56 20N	108 15W
Frobisher Sd.	**149**	62 30N	66 0W
Frodsham	**32**	53 17N	2 45W
Frogmore	**141**	34 15S	148 52E
Frohavet	**74**	64 5N	9 35E
Froid	**158**	48 20N	104 29W
Froid-Chapelle	**47**	50 9N	4 19E
Frolovo	**83**	49 45N	43 30E
Fromberg	**160**	45 19N	108 58W
Frombork	**54**	54 21N	19 41E
Frome	**28**	51 16N	2 17W
Frome Downs	**140**	31 13S	139 46E
Frome, L.	**140**	30 45S	139 45E
Frome, R.	**28**	50 44N	2 5W
Fromentine	**42**	46 53N	2 9W
Frómista	**56**	42 16N	4 25W
Front Range	**160**	40 0N	105 10W
Front Royal	**156**	38 55N	78 10W
Fronteira	**57**	39 3N	7 39W
Fronteiras	**170**	7 5S	40 37W
Frontera	**165**	18 30N	92 40W
Frontignan	**44**	43 27N	3 45E
Frosinone	**64**	41 38N	13 20E
Frosolone	**65**	41 34N	14 27E
Frostburg	**156**	39 43N	78 57W
Frostisen	**74**	68 14N	17 10E
Frouard	**43**	48 47N	6 8E
Frövi	**72**	59 28N	15 24E
Frower Pt.	**39**	51 40N	8 30W
Froya	**71**	63 43N	8 40E
Frøya	**71**	63 43N	8 40E
Fröya I.	**74**	63 45N	8 45E
Fruges	**43**	50 30N	2 8E
Frumoasa	**70**	46 28N	25 48E
Frunze	**85**	42 54N	74 36E
Fruška Gora	**66**	45 7N	19 30E
Frutal	**171**	20 0S	49 0W
Frutigen	**50**	46 35N	7 38E
Frýdek-Místek	**53**	49 40N	18 20E

*Now part of Central Arctic and Baffin

Frýdlant Garibaldi Prov. Park

Frýdlant, Severočeský, Czech. 52 50 56N 15 9 E
Frýdlant, Severomoravsky, Czech. 53 49 35N 18 20 E
Fryvaldov = Jesenik 53 50 0N 17 8 E
Fthiótis □ 69 38 50N 22 25 E
Fu 72 60 57N 14 44 E
Fuan 109 27 9N 119 38 E
Fucécchio 62 43 44N 10 51 E
Fuch'ing 109 25 43N 119 22 E
Fuchou, Fukien, China 109 26 5N 119 18 E
Fuchou, Liaoning, China 107 39 45N 121 45 E
Fuchū 110 34 34N 133 14 E
Fūchū 111 35 40N 139 29 E
Fuch'üan 108 26 42N 107 33 E
Fuch'uan 109 24 50N 111 16 E
Fucino, L. 44 42 0N 13 30 E
Fuencaliente 57 38 25N 4 18W
Fuengirola 57 36 32N 4 41W
Fuente-Alamo 59 38 44N 1 24W
Fuente de Cantos 57 38 15N 6 18W
Fuente de San Esteban, La 56 40 49N 6 15W
Fuente del Maestre 57 38 31N 6 28W
Fuente el Fresno 57 39 14N 3 46W
Fuente Ovejuna 57 38 15N 5 25W
Fuentes de Andalucía 57 37 28N 5 20W
Fuentes de Ebro 58 41 31N 0 38W
Fuentes de León 57 38 5N 6 32W
Fuentes de Oñoro 56 40 33N 6 52W
Fuentesaúco 56 41 15N 5 30W
Fuerte Olimpo 172 21 0 S 58 0W
Fuerte, R. 164 26 0N 109 0W
Fuerteventura, I. 116 28 30N 14 0W
Fuertey 38 53 37N 8 16W
Fufeng 106 34 20N 107 51 E
Fûget 70 45 52N 22 10 E
Fûget, Munţii 70 45 50N 22 9 E
Fugløysund 74 70 15N 20 20 E
Fûgûraş 70 45 48N 24 58 E
Fûgûraş, Munţii 70 45 40N 24 40 E
Fuhai 105 47 6N 87 23 E
Fuhsien, Liaoning, China 107 39 38N 122 0 E
Fuhsien, Shensi, China 106 36 2N 109 20 E
Fuhsingchen 108 22 47N 101 5 E
Fujaira 93 25 7N 56 18 E
Fuji 111 35 9N 138 39 E
Fuji-no-miya 111 35 20N 138 40 E
Fuji-San 111 35 22N 138 44 E
Fuji-yoshida 111 35 50N 138 46 E
Fujieda 111 34 52N 138 16 E
Fujioka 111 36 15N 139 5 E
Fujisawa 111 35 22N 139 29 E
Fukien □ 109 26 0N 117 30 E
Fukou 106 34 3N 114 27 E
Fuku 106 39 2N 111 3 E
Fukuchiyama 111 35 25N 135 9 E
Fukui 111 36 0N 136 10 E
Fukui-ken □ 111 36 0N 136 12 E
Fukuma 110 33 46N 130 28 E
Fukung 108 26 58N 98 54 E
Fukuoka 110 33 30N 130 30 E
Fukuoka-ken □ 110 33 30N 131 0 E
Fukuroi 111 34 45N 137 55 E
Fukushima 112 37 30N 140 15 E
Fukushima-ken □ 112 37 30N 140 15 E
Fukuyama 110 34 35N 133 20 E
Fûlciu 70 46 17N 28 7 E
Fulda 48 50 32N 9 41 E
Fullerton, Calif., U.S.A. 163 33 52N 117 58W
Fullerton, Nebr., U.S.A. 158 41 25N 98 0W
Fulmar, oilfield 19 56 30N 2 8 E
Fülöpszállás 53 46 49N 19 16 E
Fûlticeni 70 47 21N 26 20W
Fulton, Mo., U.S.A. 158 38 50N 91 55W
Fulton, N.Y., U.S.A. 162 43 20N 76 22W
Fuluälven 72 61 18N 13 4 E
Fulufjället 72 61 32N 12 41 E
Fulungch'üan 107 44 24N 124 37 E
Fülüpszállás 53 46 49N 19 16 E
Fumay 43 50 0N 4 40 E
Fumbusi 121 10 25N 1 20W
Fumel 44 44 30N 0 58 E
Fumin 108 25 14N 102 29 E
Funabashi 111 35 45N 140 0 E
Funafuti, I. 130 8 30 S 179 0 E
Funchal 116 32 45N 16 55W
Fundación 174 10 31N 74 11W
Fundão, Brazil 171 19 55 S 40 24W
Fundão, Port. 56 40 8N 7 30W
Fundu 127 14 58 S 30 14 E
Fundy, B. of 151 45 0N 56 0W
Funes 174 1 0N 77 28W
Funing, Hopei, China 107 39 54N 119 12 E
Funing, Yunnan, China 108 23 37N 105 36 E
Funiu Shan 106 33 40N 112 30 E
Funsi 120 10 21N 1 54W
Funtua 121 11 30N 7 18 E
Fupien 108 31 18N 102 27 E
Fup'ing 106 34 47N 109 7 E
Fur 73 56 50N 9 0 E
Furat, Nahr al 92 33 30N 43 0 E
Furbero 165 20 22N 97 31W
Furka Pass 51 46 34N 8 35 E
Furmanov 81 57 25N 41 3 E
Furmanovka 85 44 17N 72 57 E
Furmanovo 83 49 42N 49 25 E
Furnas, Reprêsa de 173 20 50 S 45 0W
Furneaux Group 138 40 10 S 147 50 E
Furness, Pen. 32 54 12N 3 10W
Fürstenau 48 52 32N 7 40 E
Fürstenfeld 52 47 3N 16 3 E
Fürstenfeldbruck 49 48 10N 11 15 E
Fürstenwalde 48 52 20N 14 3 E
Fürth 49 49 29N 11 0 E
Fürth i. Wald 49 49 19N 12 51 E
Furtwangen 49 48 3N 8 14 E
Furudal 72 61 10N 15 11 E
Furukawa 111 36 14N 137 11 E
Furusund 72 59 40N 18 55 E
Fury and Hecla Str. 149 69 56N 84 0W
Fusa 71 60 12N 5 37 E
Fusagasugá 174 4 21N 74 22W
Fuscaldo 65 39 25N 16 1 E
Fushan 107 37 30N 121 5 E
Fushë Arrëzi 68 42 4N 20 2 E
Fushun, Liaoning, China 107 41 50N 123 55 E
Fushun, Szechwan, China 108 29 13N 105 0 E
Fush'un Chiang, R. 109 30 5N 120 5 E
Fusio 51 46 27N 8 40 E
Füssen 49 47 35N 10 43 E
Fusui 108 22 35N 107 58 E
Fusung 107 42 15N 127 20 E
Futago-Yama 110 33 35N 131 36 E
Futing 109 27 15N 120 10 E
Futuk 121 9 45N 10 56 E
Futuna I. 130 14 25 S 178 20 E
Fûurei 70 45 6N 27 19 E
Fuwa 122 31 12N 30 33 E
Fuyang 109 30 5N 119 56 E
Fuyang Ho, R. 106 38 14N 116 5 E
Fuyü 107 45 10N 124 50 E
Fuyüan 105 47 40N 132 30 E
Füzesgyarmat 53 47 6N 21 14 E
Fwaka 125 12 5 S 29 25 E
Fylde 32 53 50N 2 58W
Fylingdales Moor 33 54 22N 0 32W
Fyn 73 55 20N 10 30 E
Fyne, L. 34 56 0N 5 20W
Fyns Amt □ 73 55 15N 10 30 E
Fynshav 73 54 59N 9 59 E
Fyresvatn 71 59 6N 8 10 E
Fyvie 37 57 26N 2 24W

G

Gaanda 121 10 10N 12 27 E
Gaba 123 6 20N 35 7 E
Gaba Tula 82 0 20N 38 35 E
Gabah, C. 91 8 0N 50 0 E
Gabarin 121 11 8N 10 27 E
Gabbs 163 38 52N 117 55W
Gabela 124 11 0 S 14 37 E
Gaberones = Gaborone 128 24 37 S 25 57 E
Gabès 119 33 53N 10 2 E
Gabès, Golfe de 119 34 0N 10 30 E
Gabgaba, W. 122 22 10N 33 5 E
Gabin 54 52 23N 19 41 E
Gabon ■ 124 0 10 S 10 0 E
Gaborone 128 24 37 S 25 57 E
Gabrovo 67 42 52N 25 27 E
Gacé 42 48 49N 0 20 E
Gach Saran 93 30 15N 50 45 E
Gacko 66 43 10N 18 33 E
Gada 121 13 38N 5 36 E
Gadag 97 15 30N 75 45 E
Gadamai 123 17 11N 36 10 E
Gadap 94 25 5N 67 28 E
Gadarwara 95 22 50N 78 50 E
Gäddede 74 64 30N 14 15 E
Gadebusch 48 53 41N 11 6 E
Gadein 123 8 10N 28 45 E
Gadhada 94 22 0N 71 35 E
Gadmen 51 46 45N 8 16 E
Gádor, Sierra de 59 36 57N 2 45W
Gadsden, Ala., U.S.A. 157 34 1N 86 0W
Gadsden, Ariz., U.S.A. 161 32 35N 114 47W
Gadwal 96 16 10N 77 50 E
Gaerwen 31 53 13N 4 17W
Gaeta 64 41 12N 13 35 E
Gaeta, G. di 64 41 0N 13 25 E
Gaffney 157 35 10N 81 31W
Gafsa 119 34 24N 8 51 E
Gagarin (Gzhatsk) 80 55 30N 35 0 E
Gagetown 151 45 46N 66 29W
Gagino 81 55 15N 45 10 E
Gagliano del Capo 65 39 50N 18 23 E
Gagnef 72 60 36N 15 5 E
Gagnoa 120 6 4N 5 55W
Gagnon 151 51 50N 68 5W
Gagnon, L. 153 62 3N 110 27W
Gagra 83 43 20N 40 10 E
Gah 44 43 12N 0 27W
Gahini 126 1 50 S 30 30 E
Gahmar 95 25 27N 83 55 E
Gaibandha 98 25 20N 89 36 E
Gaïdhouronísi 69 34 53N 25 41 E
Gail 159 32 48N 101 25W
Gail, R. 52 46 37N 13 15 E
Gaillac 44 43 54N 1 54 E
Gaillon 42 49 10N 1 20 E
Gaima 135 8 9 S 142 59 E
Gainesville, Fla., U.S.A. 157 29 38N 82 20W
Gainesville, Ga., U.S.A. 157 34 17N 83 47W
Gainesville, Mo., U.S.A. 159 36 35N 92 26W
Gainesville, Tex., U.S.A. 159 33 40N 97 10W
Gainford 33 54 34N 1 44W
Gainsborough 33 53 23N 0 46W
Gairdner L. 140 31 30 S 136 0 E
Gairloch 36 57 42N 5 40W
Gairloch L. 36 57 43N 5 45W
Gairlochy 36 56 55N 5 0W
Gairsay, I. 37 59 4N 2 59W
Gais 51 47 22N 9 27 E
Gaithersburg 162 39 9N 77 12W
Gaj 66 45 28N 17 3 E
Gajale 121 11 25N 8 10 E
Gajiram 121 12 29N 13 9 E
Gakuch 95 36 7N 73 45 E
Gal Oya Res. 97 8 5N 80 55 E
Galachipa 98 22 8N 90 26 E
Galadi 121 13 5N 6 20 E
Galán, Cerro 172 25 55 S 66 52W
Galana, R. 126 3 0 S 39 10 E
Galangue 125 13 48 S 16 3 E
Galanta 53 48 11N 17 45 E
Galápagos, Is. 131 0 0 89 0W
Galas, R. 101 4 55N 101 57 E
Galashiels 35 55 37N 2 50W
Galatás 69 37 30N 23 26 E
Galatea 142 38 24 S 176 45 E
Galaţi 70 45 27N 28 2 E
Galaţi □ 70 45 45N 27 30 E
Galatina 65 40 10N 18 10 E
Galátone 65 40 8N 18 3 E
Galax 157 36 42N 80 57W
Galaxídhion 69 38 22N 22 23 E
Galbally 39 52 24N 8 17W
Galbraith 138 16 25 S 141 30 E
Galdhøpiggen 71 61 38N 8 18 E
Galeana 164 24 50N 100 4W
Galela 103 1 50N 127 55 E
Galena, Austral. 137 27 48 S 114 42 E
Galena, U.S.A. 147 64 42N 157 0W
Galeota Point 167 10 8N 61 0W
Galera 59 37 45N 2 33W
Galera, Pta. de la 174 10 48N 75 16W
Galesburg 158 40 57N 90 23W
Galey R. 39 52 30N 9 23W
Galgate 32 53 59N 2 47W
Galheirão, R. 171 12 23 S 45 5W
Galheiros 171 13 18 S 46 25W
Galicea Mare 70 44 4N 23 19 E
Galich, R.S.F.S.R., U.S.S.R. 81 58 23N 42 18 E
Galich, Uk., U.S.S.R. 80 49 10N 24 40 E
Galiche 67 43 34N 23 50 E
Galicia 56 42 43N 8 0W
Galijp 46 53 10N 5 58 E
Galilee = Hagalil 90 32 53N 35 18 E
Galilee, L. 138 22 20 S 145 50 E
Galite, Is. de la 119 37 30N 8 59 E
Galivro Mts. 161 32 40N 110 30W
Gallan Hd. 36 58 14N 7 0W
Gallarate 62 45 40N 8 48 E
Gallatin 157 36 24N 86 27W
Galle 97 6 5N 80 10 E
Gallego 164 29 49N 106 22W
Gállego, R. 58 42 23N 0 30W
Gallegos, R. 176 51 50 S 71 0W
Galley Hd. 39 51 32N 8 56W
Galliate 62 45 27N 8 44 E
Gallinas, Pta. 174 12 28N 71 40W
Gallipoli 65 40 8N 18 0 E
Gallipoli = Gelibolu 68 40 28N 26 43 E
Gallipolis 156 38 50N 82 10W
Gällivare 74 67 9N 20 40 E
Gällö 72 62 56N 15 15 E
Gallo, C. di 64 38 13N 13 19 E
Gallocanta, Laguna de 58 40 58N 1 30W
Galloway 34 55 0N 4 25W
Galloway, Mull of 34 54 38N 4 50W
Gallup 161 35 30N 108 54W
Gallur 58 41 52N 1 19W
Gallyaaral 85 40 2N 67 35 E
Galmi 121 13 58N 5 41 E
Gal'on 90 31 38N 34 51 E
Galong 141 34 37 S 148 34 E
Galoya 93 8 10N 80 55 E
Galston 34 55 36N 4 22W
Galt, Can. 150 43 21N 80 19W
Galt, U.S.A. 163 38 15N 121 18W
Galtström 72 62 10N 17 30 E
Galtür 52 46 58N 10 11 E
Galty Mts. 39 52 22N 8 10W
Galtymore, Mt. 39 52 22N 8 12W
Galva 158 41 10N 90 0W
Galve de Sorbe 58 41 13N 3 10W
Galveston 159 29 15N 94 48W
Galveston B. 159 29 30N 94 50W
Gálvez, Argent. 172 32 0 S 61 20W
Gálvez, Spain 57 39 42N 4 16W
Galway 39 53 16N 9 4W
Galway □ 38 53 16N 9 3W
Galway B. 39 53 10N 9 20W
Gam, R. 100 21 55N 105 12 E
Gamagōri 111 34 50N 137 14 E
Gamare, L. 123 11 32N 41 40 E
Gamarra 174 8 20N 73 45W
Gamawa 121 12 10N 10 31 E
Gambaga 121 10 30N 0 28W
Gambat 94 27 17N 68 26 E
Gambela 123 8 14N 34 38 E
Gambell 147 63 55N 171 50W
Gambia ■ 120 13 25N 16 0W
Gambia, R. 120 13 20N 15 45W
Gambier, C. 136 11 56 S 130 57 E
Gambier Is. 140 35 3 S 136 30 E
Gamboli 94 29 53N 68 24 E
Gamboma 124 1 55 S 15 52 E
Gamboola 138 16 29 S 143 43 E
Gameleira 170 7 50 S 50 0W
Gamerco 161 35 33N 108 56W
Gamleby 73 57 54N 16 20W
Gamlingay 29 52 9N 0 11W
Gammelgarn 171 57 24N 18 49 E
Gammon, R. 153 51 24N 95 44W
Gamōda-Saki 110 33 50N 134 45 E
Gan (Addu Atoll) 87 0 10 S 71 10 E
Gan Shemu'el 90 32 28N 34 56 E
Gan Yavne 90 31 48N 34 42 E
Ganado, Ariz., U.S.A. 161 35 46N 109 41W
Ganado, Tex., U.S.A. 159 29 4N 96 31W
Gananoque 150 44 20N 76 10W
Ganaveh 93 29 35N 50 35 E
Gand 47 51 2N 3 37 E
Gandak, R. 95 27 0N 84 8 E
Gandava 94 28 32N 67 32 E
Gander 151 48 18N 54 29W
Gander L. 151 48 58N 54 35W
Ganderowe Falls 127 17 20 S 29 10 E
Gandesa 58 41 3N 0 26 E
Gand = Gent 47 51 2N 3 37 E
Gandhi Sagar 94 24 40N 75 40 E
Gandi 121 12 55N 5 49 E
Gandia 59 38 58N 0 9W
Gandino 62 45 50N 9 52 E
Gandole 121 8 28N 11 35 E
Gandu 171 13 45 S 39 30W
Ganedidalem = Gani 103 0 48 S 128 14 E
Ganetti 122 18 0N 31 10 E
Ganga, Mouths of the 95 21 30N 90 0 E
Ganga, R. 95 25 0N 88 0 E
Ganganagar 94 29 56N 73 56 E
Gangapur 94 26 32N 76 37 E
Gangara 121 14 35N 8 40 E
Gangavati 97 15 30N 76 36 E
Gangaw 98 22 5N 94 15 E
Ganges 44 43 56N 3 42 E
Ganges = Ganga, R. 95 25 0N 88 0 E
Gangoh 94 29 46N 77 18 E
Gangtok 98 27 20N 88 37 E
Ganj 95 27 45N 78 47 E
Ganmain 141 34 47 S 147 1 E
Gannat 44 46 7N 3 11 E
Gannett Pk. 160 43 15N 109 47W
Gannvalley 158 44 3N 98 57W
Ganserdorf 53 48 20N 16 43 E
Ganta (Gompa) 120 7 15N 8 59W
Gantheaume B. 137 27 40 S 114 10 E
Gantheaume, C. 140 36 4 S 137 25 E
Gantsevichi 80 52 42N 26 30 E
Ganyushkino 83 46 35N 49 20 E
Ganzi 123 4 30N 31 15 E
Gao □ 121 18 0N 1 0 E
Gao Bang 101 22 37N 106 18 E
Gaoua 120 10 20N 3 8W
Gaoual 120 11 45N 13 25W
Gaouz 118 31 52N 4 20W
Gap 45 44 33N 6 5 E
Gar Dzong 93 32 20N 79 55 E
Gara, L. 38 53 57N 8 26W
Garachiné 166 8 0N 78 12W
Garanhuns 170 8 50 S 36 30W
Garawe 120 4 35N 8 0W
Garba Tula 126 0 30N 38 32 E
Garber 159 36 30N 97 36W
Garberville 160 40 11N 123 50W
Garboldisham 29 52 24N 0 57 E
Garça 171 22 14 S 49 37W
Garças, R. 170 8 43 S 39 41W
Gard □ 45 44 2N 4 10 E
Garda, L. di 62 45 40N 10 40 E
Gardanne 45 43 27N 5 27 E
Garde L. 153 62 50N 106 13W
Gardelegen 48 52 32N 11 21 E
Garden City, Kans., U.S.A. 159 38 0N 100 45W
Garden City, Tex., U.S.A. 159 31 52N 101 28W
Garden Grove 163 33 47N 117 55W
Gardenstown 37 57 40N 2 20W
Gardez 94 33 31N 68 59 E
Gardhiki 69 38 50N 21 55 E
Gardian 117 15 45N 19 40 E
Gardiner, Can. 150 49 19N 81 2W
Gardiner, Mont., U.S.A. 160 45 3N 110 53W
Gardiner, New Mexico, U.S.A. 159 36 55N 104 29W
Gardiners I. 162 41 4N 72 5W
Gardner 162 42 35N 72 0W
Gardner Canal 152 53 27N 128 8W
Gardnerville 160 38 59N 119 47W
Gardo 91 9 18N 49 20 E
Gare, L. 34 56 1N 4 50W
Garelochhead 34 56 7N 4 50W
Gareloi I. 147 51 49N 178 50W
Garešnica 66 45 36N 16 56 E
Garéssio 62 44 12N 8 1 E
Garey 163 34 53N 120 19W
Garfield, Utah, U.S.A. 160 40 45N 112 15W
Garfield, Wash., U.S.A. 160 47 3N 117 8W
Garforth 33 53 48N 1 22W
Gargaliánoi 69 37 4N 21 38 E
Gargano, Mte. 65 41 43N 15 43 E
Gargans, Mt. 44 45 37N 1 39 E
Gargantua, C. 150 47 35N 85 0W
Gargoune 121 15 56N 0 13 E
Gargrave 32 53 58N 2 7W
Garhshankar 94 31 13N 76 11 E
Gari 84 59 26N 62 21 E
Garibaldi 152 49 56N 123 15W
Garibaldi Prov. Park 152 49 50N 122 40W

Garies **Ghent**

Garies **125** 30 32 S 17 59 E
Garigliano, R. **64** 41 13N 13 44 E
Garissa **126** 0 25 S 39 40 E
Garissa □ **126** 0 20 S 40 0 E
Garkida **121** 10 27N 12 36 E
Garko **121** 11 45N 8 53 E
Garland **160** 41 47N 112 10W
Garlasco **62** 45 11N 8 55 E
Garlieston **34** 54 47N 4 22W
Garm **85** 39 0N 70 20 E
Garmab **94** 32 50N 65 30 E
Garmisch-Partenkirchen **49** 47 30N 11 5 E
Garmo **126** 61 51N 8 48 E
Garmouth **37** 57 40N 3 8W
Garmsar **93** 35 20N 52 25 E
Garner **158** 43 4N 93 37W
Garnett **158** 38 18N 95 12W
Garo Hills **95** 25 30N 90 30 E
Garoe **91** 8 35N 48 40 E
Garoke **139** 36 45 S 141 30 E
Garona, R. **58** 42 55N 0 45 E
Garonne, R. **44** 45 2N 0 36W
Garoua (Garwa) **121** 9 19N 13 21 E
Garraway **120** 4 35N 8 0W
Garrel **48** 52 58N 7 59 E
Garrigues **44** 43 40N 3 30 E
Garrison, Ireland **38** 54 25N 8 5W
Garrison, Mont., U.S.A. **160** 46 37N 112 56W
Garrison, N.D., U.S.A. **158** 31 50N 94 28W
Garrison, Tex., U.S.A. **159** 47 39N 101 27W
Garrison Res. **158** 47 30N 102 0W
Garron Pt. **38** 55 3N 6 0W
Garrovillas **57** 39 40N 6 33W
Garrucha **59** 37 11N 1 49W
Garry L., Can. **148** 65 58N 100 18W
Garry L., U.K. **37** 57 5N 4 52W
Garry, R. **37** 56 47N 3 47W
Garsdale Head **32** 54 19N 2 19W
Garsen **124** 2 20 S 40 5 E
Garson L., Alta., Can. **153** 56 19N 110 2W
Garson L., Sask., Can. **153** 56 20N 110 1W
Garstang **32** 53 53N 2 47W
Garston **32** 53 21N 2 55W
Gartempe, R. **44** 46 47N 0 49 E
Gartok **93** 31 59N 80 30 E
Gartz **48** 54 17N 13 21 E
Garu, Ghana **121** 10 55N 0 20W
Garu, Nigeria **121** 13 35N 5 25 E
Garub **128** 26 37 S 16 0 E
Garupá **170** 1 25 S 51 35W
Garut **103** 7 14 S 107 53 E
Garvagh **38** 55 0N 6 41W
Garvaghey **38** 54 29N 7 8W
Garvald **35** 55 55N 2 39W
Garvão **57** 37 42N 8 21W
Garvellachs, Is. **34** 56 14N 5 48W
Garvie Mts. **143** 45 30 S 168 50 E
Garwa **95** 24 11N 83 47 E
Garwolin **54** 51 55N 21 38 E
Gary **156** 41 35N 87 20W
Garzón **174** 2 10N 75 40W
Gasan Kuli **76** 37 40N 54 20 E
Gascogne **44** 43 45N 0 20 E
Gascogne, G. de **58** 44 0N 2 0W
Gascony = Gascogne **44** 43 45N 0 20 E
Gascoyne Junc. Teleg. Off. **137** 25 2 S 115 17 E
Gascoyne, R. **137** 24 52 S 113 37 E
Gascueña **58** 40 18N 2 31W
Gash, W. **123** 15 0N 37 15 E
Gashaka **121** 7 20N 11 29 E
Gasherbrum **95** 35 40N 76 40 E
Gashua **121** 12 54N 11 0 E
Gasmata **138** 6 15 S 150 30 E
Gaspé **151** 48 52N 64 30W
Gaspé, C. **151** 48 48N 64 7W
Gaspé Pass. **151** 49 10N 64 0W
Gaspé Pen. **151** 48 45N 65 40W
Gaspésie, Parc Prov. de la **151** 48 55N 65 50W
Gaspesian Prov. Park **151** 49 0N 66 45W
Gassaway **156** 38 42N 80 43W
Gasselte **46** 52 58N 6 48 E
Gasselternijveen **46** 52 59N 6 51 E
Gássino Torinese **62** 45 8N 7 50 E
Gassol **121** 8 34N 10 25 E
Gastonia **157** 35 17N 81 10W
Gastoúni **69** 37 51N 21 15 E
Gastoúri **68** 39 34N 19 54 E
Gastre **176** 42 10 S 69 15W
Gata, C. de **59** 36 41N 2 13W
Gata, Sierra de **56** 40 20N 6 20W
Gataga, R. **152** 58 35N 126 59W
Gatchina **80** 59 35N 30 0 E
Gatehouse of Fleet **34** 54 53N 4 10W
Gateshead **35** 54 57N 1 37W
Gatesville **159** 31 29N 97 45W
Gaths **127** 26 2 S 30 32 E
Gatico **172** 22 40 S 70 20W
Gatinais **43** 48 5N 2 40 E
Gâtine, Hauteurs de **44** 46 35N 0 45W
Gatineau, Parc de la **150** 45 20N 76 0W
Gatineau, R. **150** 45 27N 75 42W
Gatley **32** 53 25N 2 15W
Gatooma **125** 18 20 S 29 52 E
Gattinara **62** 45 37N 8 22 E
Gatun, L. **166** 9 7N 79 56W
Gaucín **57** 36 31N 5 19W
Gaud-i-Zirreh **93** 29 45N 62 0 E
Gauer L. **153** 57 0N 97 50W
Gauhati **98** 26 10N 91 45 E
Gauja, R. **80** 57 10N 24 45 E
Gaula, R. **71** 62 57N 11 0 E
Gaurain-Ramecroix **47** 50 36N 3 30 E
Gaurdak **85** 37 50N 66 4 E
Gaussberg, Mt. **13** 66 45 S 89 0 E
Gausta **71** 59 50N 8 37 E
Gausta, Mt. **75** 59 48N 8 40 E
Gavá **58** 41 18N 2 0 E
Gavarnie **44** 42 44N 0 3W
Gavater **93** 25 10N 61 23 E
Gavdhopoúla **69** 34 56N 24 0 E
Gávdhos **69** 34 50N 24 5 E
Gavere **47** 50 55N 3 40 E
Gavião **57** 39 28N 7 50W
Gaviota **163** 34 29N 120 13W
Gavle **72** 60 41N 17 13 E
Gävle **72** 60 40N 17 9 E
Gävleborgs Lan □ **72** 61 20N 16 15 E
Gavorrano **62** 42 55N 10 55 E
Gavray **42** 49 55N 1 20W
Gavrilov Yam **81** 57 10N 39 37 E
Gávrion **69** 37 54N 24 44 E
Gawachab **128** 27 4 S 17 55 E
Gawai **98** 27 56N 97 40 E
Gawilgarh Hills **96** 21 15N 76 45 E
Gawler **140** 34 30 S 138 42 E
Gawler Ranges **136** 32 30 S 135 45 E
Gawthwaite **32** 54 16N 3 6W
Gay **84** 51 27N 58 27 E
Gaya, India **95** 24 47N 85 4 E
Gaya, Niger **121** 11 58N 3 28 E
Gaya, Nigeria **121** 11 57N 9 0 E
Gaylord **156** 45 1N 84 35W
Gayndah **139** 25 35 S 151 39 E
Gayny **84** 60 18N 54 19 E
Gaysin **82** 48 57N 28 25 E
Gayton **29** 52 45N 0 35 E
Gayvoron **82** 48 22N 29 45 E
Gaywood **29** 52 46N 0 26 E
Gaza **90** 31 30N 34 28 E
Gaza □ **129** 23 10 S 32 45 E
Gaza Strip **90** 31 29N 34 25 E
Gazaoua **121** 13 32N 7 55 E
Gazelle Pen. **135** 4 40 S 152 0 E
Gazi **126** 1 3N 24 30 E
Gaziantep **92** 37 6N 37 23 E
Gbanga **120** 7 19N 9 13W
Gbekebo **121** 6 26N 4 48 E
Gboko **121** 7 17N 9 4 E
Gbongan **121** 7 28N 4 20 E
Gcuwa **129** 32 20 S 28 11 E
Gdansk **54** 54 22N 18 40 E
Gdansk □ **54** 54 10N 18 30 E
Gdanska, Zatoka **54** 54 30N 19 20 E
Gdov **80** 58 40N 27 55 E
Gdynia **54** 54 35N 18 33 E
Geashill **39** 53 14N 7 20W
Gebe, I. **103** 0 5N 129 25 E
Gebeit Mine **122** 21 3N 36 29 E
Gecoa **123** 7 30N 35 18 E
Gedaref **123** 14 2N 35 28 E
Gedera **90** 31 49N 34 46 E
Gedinne **47** 49 59N 4 56 E
Gedney **29** 52 47N 0 5W
Gedo **123** 9 2N 37 25 E
Gèdre **44** 42 47N 0 2 E
Gedser **73** 54 35N 11 55 E
Gedser Odde, C. **73** 54 30N 12 5 E
Geel **47** 51 10N 4 59 E
Geelong **140** 38 10 S 144 22 E
Geelvink Chan. **137** 28 30 S 114 0 E
Geer, R. **47** 50 51N 5 42 E
Geestenseth **48** 53 31N 8 51 E
Geesthacht **48** 53 25N 10 20 E
Geffen **46** 51 44N 5 28 E
Geh **126** 26 10N 60 0 E
Geia **90** 31 38N 34 37 E
Geidam **121** 12 57N 11 57 E
Geikie, R. **153** 57 45N 103 52W
Geilenkirchen **48** 50 58N 6 8 E
Geili **123** 16 1N 32 37 E
Geilo **71** 60 32N 8 14 E
Geinica **53** 48 51N 20 55 E
Geisingen **49** 47 55N 8 37 E
Geita **126** 2 48 S 32 12 E
Geita □ **126** 2 50 S 32 10 E
Gel, R. **123** 7 5N 29 10 E
Gel River **123** 7 5N 29 10 E
Gela, Golfo di **65** 37 0N 14 8 E
Geladi **91** 6 59N 46 30 E
Gelderland □ **46** 52 5N 6 10 E
Geldermalsen **46** 51 53N 5 17 E
Geldern **48** 51 32N 6 18 E
Geldrop **47** 51 25N 5 32 E
Geleen **47** 50 57N 5 49 E
Gelehun **120** 8 20N 11 40W
Gelendzhik **82** 44 33N 38 17 E
Gelibolu **68** 40 28N 26 43 E
Gelnhausen **49** 50 12N 9 12 E
Gelsenkirchen **48** 51 30N 7 5 E
Gelting **48** 54 43N 9 53 E
Gemas **101** 2 37N 102 36 E
Gembloux **47** 50 34N 4 43 E
Gembu **121** 8 58N 12 31 E
Gemena **124** 3 20N 19 40 E
Gemerek **92** 39 15N 36 10 E
Gemert **47** 51 33N 5 41 E
Gemiston **128** 26 15 S 28 10 E
Gemlik **92** 40 28N 29 13 E
Gemmi **50** 46 25N 7 37 E
Gemona del Friuli **63** 46 16N 13 7 E
Gemsa **122** 27 39N 33 35 E
Gemu-Gofa □ **123** 5 40N 36 40 E
Gemünden **49** 50 3N 9 43 E
Genale **123** 6 0N 39 30 E
Genappe **47** 50 37N 4 27 E
Gençay **44** 46 23N 0 23 E
Gendringen **46** 51 52N 6 21 E
Gendt **46** 51 53N 5 59 E
Geneina, Gebel **122** 29 2N 33 55 E
Genemuiden **46** 52 38N 6 2 E
General Acha **172** 37 20 S 64 38W
General Alvear, B. A., Argent. **172** 36 0 S 60 0W
General Alvear, Mend., Argent. **172** 35 0 S 67 40W
General Artigas **172** 26 52 S 56 16W
General Belgrano **172** 36 0 S 58 30W
General Cabrera **172** 32 53 S 63 58W
General Cepeda **164** 25 23N 101 27W
General Guido **172** 36 40 S 57 50W
General Juan Madariaga **172** 37 0 S 57 0W
General La Madrid **172** 37 30 S 61 10W
General MacArthur **103** 11 18N 125 28 E
General Martin Mignuel de Güemes **172** 24 50 S 65 0W
General Paz **172** 27 45 S 57 36W
General Paz, L. **176** 44 0 S 72 0W
General Pico **172** 35 45 S 63 50W
General Pinedo **172** 27 15 S 61 30W
General Pinto **172** 34 45 S 61 50W
General Roca **176** 30 0 S 67 40W
General Sampaio **170** 4 2 S 39 29W
General Santos **103** 6 12N 125 14 E
General Toshevo **67** 43 42N 28 6 E
General Treviño **165** 26 14N 99 29W
General Trías **164** 28 21N 106 22W
General Viamonte **172** 35 1 S 61 3W
General Villegas **172** 35 0 S 63 0W
Generoso, Mte. **51** 45 56N 9 2 E
Genesee **160** 46 31N 116 59W
Genesee, R. **156** 41 35N 78 0W
Geneseo, Ill., U.S.A. **158** 41 25N 90 10W
Geneseo, Kans., U.S.A. **158** 38 32N 98 8W
Geneva, Ala., U.S.A. **157** 31 2N 85 52W
Geneva, Nebr., U.S.A. **158** 40 35N 97 35W
Geneva, N.Y., U.S.A. **162** 42 53N 77 0W
Geneva, Ohio, U.S.A. **156** 41 49N 80 58W
Geneva = Genève **50** 46 12N 6 9 E
Geneva, L. **156** 42 38N 88 30W
Geneva, L. = Léman, Lac **50** 46 26N 6 30 E
Genève **50** 46 12N 6 9 E
Genève □ **50** 46 10N 6 10 E
Gengenbach **49** 48 25N 8 0 E
Genichesk **82** 46 12N 34 50 E
Genil, R. **57** 37 12N 3 50W
Génissiat, Barrage de **45** 46 1N 5 48 E
Genk **47** 50 58N 5 32 E
Genkai-Nada **110** 34 0N 130 0 E
Genlis **43** 47 15N 5 12 E
Gennargentu, Mt. del **64** 40 0N 9 10 E
Gennep **47** 51 41N 5 59 E
Gennes **42** 47 20N 0 17W
Genoa, Austral. **141** 37 29 S 149 35 E
Genoa, Nebr., U.S.A. **158** 41 31N 97 44W
Genoa, N.Y., U.S.A. **162** 42 40N 76 32W
Genoa = Génova **62** 44 24N 8 57 E
Génova **62** 44 24N 8 56 E
Génova, Golfo di **62** 44 0N 9 0 E
Gent **47** 51 2N 3 37 E
Gentbrugge **47** 51 3N 3 47 E
Genteng **103** 7 25 S 106 23 E
Genthin **48** 52 24N 12 10 E
Gentio do Ouro **170** 11 25 S 42 30W
Geographe B. **137** 33 30 S 113 20 E
Geographe Chan. **137** 24 30 S 113 0 E
Geokchay **83** 40 42N 47 43 E
George, Can. **151** 46 12N 62 32W
George, S. Afr. **128** 33 58 S 22 29 E
George, L., New South Wales, Austral. **141** 35 10 S 149 25 E
George, L., S. Austral., Austral. **140** 37 25 S 140 0 E
George, L., W. A., Austral. **137** 22 45 S 123 40 E
George, L., Uganda **126** 0 5N 30 10 E
George, L., Fla., U.S.A. **157** 29 15N 81 35W
George, L., N.Y., U.S.A. **162** 43 30N 73 30W
George, Mt. **137** 25 17 S 119 0 E
George, R. **151** 58 49N 66 10W
George River = Port Nouveau **149** 58 30N 65 50W
George Sound **143** 44 52 S 167 25 E
George Town, Austral. **138** 41 5 S 146 49 E
George Town, Bahamas **166** 23 33N 75 47W
George Town, Malay. **101** 5 25N 100 19 E
George V Coast **13** 67 0 S 148 0 E
George West **159** 28 18N 98 5W
Georgetown, Austral. **133** 18 17 S 143 33 E
Georgetown, Ont., Can. **150** 43 40N 80 0W
Georgetown, P.E.I., Can. **151** 46 13N 62 24W
Georgetown, Cay. Is. **166** 19 20N 81 24W
Georgetown, Gambia **120** 13 30N 14 47W
Georgetown, Guyana **174** 6 50N 58 12W
Georgetown, Colo., U.S.A. **160** 39 46N 105 49W
Georgetown, Del., U.S.A. **162** 38 42N 75 23W
Georgetown, N.Y., U.S.A. **162** 42 46N 75 44W
Georgetown, Ohio, U.S.A. **156** 38 50N 83 50W
Georgetown, S.C., U.S.A. **157** 33 22N 79 15W
Georgetown, Tex., U.S.A. **159** 30 45N 98 10W
Georgi Dimitrov **67** 42 15N 23 54 E
Georgia □ **156** 32 0N 82 0W
Georgia, Str. of **152** 49 25N 124 0W
Georgian B. **150** 45 15N 81 0W
Georgian S.S.R. □ **83** 41 0N 45 0 E
Georgievsk **83** 44 12N 43 28 E
Georgina Downs **138** 21 10 S 137 40 E
Georgina, R. **138** 23 30 S 139 47 E
Georgiu-Dezh **81** 51 3N 39 20 E
Georgiyevka **85** 43 3N 74 43 E
Gera **48** 50 53N 12 5 E
Gera □ **48** 50 45N 11 30 E
Geraardsbergen **47** 50 45N 3 53 E
Geral de Goias, Serra **171** 12 0 S 46 0W
Geral do Paranã Serra **171** 15 0 S 47 0W
Geral, Serra, Bahia, Brazil **171** 14 0 S 41 0W
Geral, Serra, Goiás, Brazil **170** 11 15 S 46 30W
Geral, Serra, Santa Catarina, Brazil **173** 26 25 S 50 0W
Geraldine, N.Z. **143** 44 5 S 171 15 E
Geraldine, U.S.A. **160** 47 45N 110 18W
Geraldton, Austral. **137** 28 48 S 114 32 E
Geraldton, Can. **150** 49 44N 86 59W
Geranium **140** 35 23 S 140 11 E
Gerardmer **43** 48 3N 6 50 E
Gerdine, Mt. **147** 61 32N 152 30W
Gerede **82** 40 45N 32 10 E
Gérgal **59** 37 7N 2 31W
Geriban **91** 7 10N 48 55 E
Gerik **101** 5 25N 100 8 E
Gering **158** 41 51N 103 40W
Gerizim **90** 32 13N 35 15 E
Gerlach **160** 40 43N 119 27W
Gerlachovka, Mt. **53** 49 11N 20 7 E
Gerlafingen **50** 47 10N 7 34 E
Gerlev **73** 56 36N 10 9 E
Gerlogubi **91** 6 53N 45 3 E
German Planina **66** 42 33N 22 0 E
Germansen Landing **152** 55 43N 124 40W
Germany, East ■ **48** 52 0N 12 0 E
Germany, West ■ **48** 52 0N 9 0 E
Germersheim **49** 49 13N 8 0 E
Germiston **125** 26 11 S 28 10 E
Gernsheim **49** 49 44N 8 29 E
Gero **111** 35 48N 137 14 E
Gerogery **141** 35 50 S 147 1 E
Gerolstein **49** 50 12N 6 24 E
Gerona **58** 41 58N 2 46 E
Gerona □ **58** 42 11N 2 30 E
Gérouville **47** 49 37N 5 26 E
Gerrans B. **30** 50 12N 4 57W
Gerrard **152** 50 30N 117 17W
Gerrards Cross **29** 51 35N 0 32W
Gerrild **73** 56 30N 10 50 E
Gerringong **141** 34 46 S 150 47 E
Gers □ **44** 43 35N 0 38 E
Gersau **51** 47 0N 8 32 E
Gersoppa Falls **97** 14 12N 74 46 E
Gerufa **128** 19 8 S 26 0 E
Gerze **92** 41 45N 35 10 E
Geseke **48** 51 38N 8 29 E
Geser **103** 3 50N 130 35 E
Gesso, R. **62** 44 21N 7 20 E
Gesves **47** 50 24N 5 4 E
Getafe **56** 40 18N 3 44W
Gethsémani **151** 50 13N 60 40W
Gettysburg, Pa., U.S.A. **156** 39 47N 77 18W
Gettysburg, S.D., U.S.A. **158** 45 3N 99 56W
Getz Ice Shelf **13** 75 0 S 130 0W
Geul, R. **47** 50 53N 5 43 E
Geurie **141** 32 22 S 148 50 E
Gevaudan **44** 44 40N 3 40 E
Gevgelija **66** 41 9N 22 30 E
Gévora, R. **57** 38 53N 6 57W
Gex **45** 46 21N 6 3 E
Geyikli **68** 39 50N 26 12 E
Geyser **160** 47 17N 110 30W
Geysir **74** 64 19N 20 18W
Geyve **82** 40 32N 30 18 E
Ghaghara, R. **95** 26 0N 84 20 E
Ghail **92** 21 40N 46 20 E
Ghalla, Wadi el **123** 12 0N 28 58 E
Ghana ■ **121** 6 0N 1 0W
Ghandhi Dam **93** 24 30N 75 35 E
Ghansor **95** 22 39N 80 1 E
Ghanzi **128** 21 50 S 21 45 E
Ghanzi □ **128** 21 50 S 21 45 E
Gharbîya, Es Sahrâ el **122** 27 40N 26 30 E
Ghard Abû Muharik **122** 26 50N 30 0 E
Ghardaïa **118** 32 31N 3 37 E
Gharyān **119** 32 10N 13 0 E
Ghât **119** 24 59N 10 19 E
Ghat Ghat **92** 26 0N 45 5 E
Ghatal **95** 22 40N 87 46 E
Ghatampur **95** 26 8N 80 13 E
Ghatprabha, R. **96** 16 15N 75 20 E
Ghazal, Bahr el **117** 15 0N 17 0 E
Ghazaouet **118** 35 8N 1 50W
Ghaziabad **94** 28 42N 77 35 E
Ghazipur **95** 25 38N 83 35 E
Ghazni **94** 33 30N 68 17 E
Ghazni □ **93** 33 0N 68 0 E
Ghedi **62** 45 24N 10 16 E
Ghelari **70** 45 42N 22 45 E
Ghelinsor **91** 6 35N 46 55 E
Ghent = Gand **47** 51 4N 3 43 E

Gheorghe Gheorghiu-Dej 70 46 17N 26 47 E
Gheorgheni 70 46 43N 25 41 E
Ghergani 70 44 37N 25 37 E
Gherla 70 47 0N 23 57 E
Ghilarza 64 40 8N 8 50 E
Ghisonaccia 45 42 1N 9 26 E
Ghizao 94 33 30N 65 59 E
Ghizar, R. 95 36 10N 73 4 E
Ghod, R. 96 18 40N 74 15 E
Ghorat □ 93 34 0N 64 20 E
Ghost River, Can. 150 51 0N 91 27W
Ghost River, Ont., Can. 150 51 25N 83 20W
Ghot Ogrein 122 31 10N 25 20 E
Ghotaru 94 27 20N 70 1 E
Ghotki 94 28 5N 69 30 E
Ghudāmis 119 30 11N 9 29 E
Ghugri 95 22 39N 80 41 E
Ghugus 96 20 0N 79 0 E
Ghulam Mohammad Barrage 94 25 30N 67 0 E
Ghuriān 93 34 17N 61 25 E
Gia Dinh 101 10 49N 106 42 E
Gia Lai = Pleiku 101 14 3N 108 0 E
Gia Nghia 101 12 0N 107 42 E
Gia Ngoc 100 14 50N 108 58 E
Gia Vuc 100 14 42N 108 34 E
Giamda Dzong 99 30 3N 93 2 E
Giannutri, I. 62 42 16N 11 5 E
Giant Forest 163 36 36N 118 43W
Giant Mts. = Krkonose 52 50 50N 16 10 E
Giant's Causeway 38 55 15N 6 30W
Giarabub = Jaghbub 117 29 42N 24 38 E
Giarre 65 37 44N 15 10 E
Giaveno 62 45 3N 7 20 E
Gibara 166 21 0N 76 20W
Gibbon 158 40 49N 98 45W
Gibe, R. 123 6 25N 36 10 E
Gibellina 64 37 48N 13 0 E
Gibeon 128 25 7s 17 45 E
Gibraléon 57 37 23N 6 58W
Gibraltar 57 36 7N 5 22W
Gibraltar Pt. 33 53 6N 0 20 E
Gibraltar, Str. of 57 35 55N 5 40W
Gibson Des. 136 24 0s 126 0 E
Gibsons 152 49 24N 123 32W
Gida. G. 12 72 30N 77 0 E
Giddalur 97 15 20N 78 57 E
Gidde 123 5 40N 37 25 E
Giddings 159 30 11N 96 58W
Gide 123 9 52N 35 5 E
Gien 43 47 40N 2 36 E
Giessen 48 50 34N 8 40 E
Gieten 46 53 0N 6 46 E
Gif-sur-Yvette 46 48 42N 2 8 E
Gifatin, Geziret 122 27 10N 33 50 E
Gifford 35 55 54N 2 45W
Gifford Creek 137 24 3s 116 16 E
Gifhorn 48 52 29N 10 32 E
Gifu 111 35 30N 136 45 E
Gifu-ken □ 111 36 0N 137 0 E
Gigant 83 46 28N 41 30 E
Giganta, Sa. de la 164 25 30N 111 30W
Gigen 67 43 40N 24 28 E
Giggleswick 32 54 5N 2 19W
Gigha, I. 39 55 42N 5 45W
Giglio, I. 62 42 20N 10 52 E
Gignac 44 43 39N 3 32 E
Gigüela, R. 58 39 47N 3 0W
Gijón 56 43 32N 5 42W
Gil I. 152 53 12N 129 15W
Gila Bend 161 33 0N 112 46W
Gila Bend Mts. 161 33 15N 113 0W
Gila, R. 161 33 5N 108 40W
Gilau 138 5 38s 149 3 E
Gilbedi 121 13 40N 5 45 E
*Gilbert Is. 130 1 0s 176 0 E
Gilbert Plains 153 51 9N 100 28W
Gilbert, R. 138 16 35N 141 15 E
Gilbert River 138 18 9s 142 52 E
Gilberton 138 19 16s 143 35 E
Gilbués 170 9 50s 45 21W
Gilford 38 54 23N 6 20W
Gilford I. 152 50 40N 126 30W
Gilgai 137 31 15s 119 56 E
Gilgandra 141 31 43s 148 39 E
Gilgil 126 0 30s 36 20 E
Gilgit 95 35 50N 74 15 E
Gilgit, R. 95 35 50N 74 25 E
Gilgunnia 141 32 26s 146 2 E
Giligulgul 139 26 26s 150 0 E
Gilima 126 3 53N 28 15 E
Giljeva Planina 66 43 9N 20 0 E
Gill L. 38 54 15N 8 25W
Gillam 153 56 20N 94 40W
Gilleleje 73 56 8N 12 19 E
Gillen, L. 137 26 11s 124 38 E
Gilles, L. 140 32 50s 136 45 E
Gillespie Pt. 143 43 24s 169 49 E
Gillett 162 41 57N 76 48W
Gillette 158 44 20N 105 38W
Gilliat 138 20 40s 141 28 E
Gillingham, Dorset, U.K. 28 51 2N 2 15W
Gillingham, Kent, U.K. 29 51 23N 0 34 E
Gilmer 159 32 44N 94 55W
Gilmore 141 35 14s 148 12 E
Gilmore, L. 137 32 29s 121 37 E
Gilmour 137 44 48N 77 37W
Gilo 123 7 35N 34 30 E
Gilo, R. 161 33 5N 108 40 E
Gilort, R. 70 44 38N 23 32 E
Gilroy 163 37 1N 121 37W
* Renamed Kiribati

Gilsland 32 55 0N 2 34W
Gilũu 70 46 45N 23 23W
Giluwe, Mt. 135 6 8s 143 52 E
Gilwern 31 51 49N 3 5W
Gilze 47 51 32N 4 57 E
Gimåfors 72 62 40N 16 25 E
Gimbi 123 9 3N 35 42 E
Gimigliano 65 38 53N 16 32 E
Gimli 153 50 40N 97 10W
Gimmi 123 9 0N 37 20 E
Gimo 72 60 11N 18 12 E
Gimont 44 43 38N 0 52 E
Gimzo 90 31 56N 34 56 E
Gin Ganga 97 6 5N 80 7 E
Gin Gin 139 25 0s 151 44 E
Gînâh 122 25 21N 30 30 E
Gindie 138 23 44s 148 8 E
Gineta, La 59 39 8N 2 1W
Gingin 137 31 22s 115 54 E
Gîngiova 70 43 54N 23 50 E
Ginir 123 7 12N 40 40 E
Ginosa 65 40 35N 16 45 E
Ginowan 112 26 15N 127 47 E
Ginzo de Limia 56 42 3N 7 47W
Giohar 91 2 20N 45 15 E
Gióia del Colle 65 40 49N 16 55 E
Gióia, G. di 65 38 30N 15 50 E
Gióia Táuro 65 38 26N 15 53 E
Gioiosa Iónica 65 38 20N 16 19 E
Gióna, Óros 69 38 38N 22 14 E
Giong, Teluk 103 4 50N 118 20 E
Giovi, P. dei 62 44 30N 8 55 E
Giovinazzo 65 41 10N 16 40 E
Gippsland 133 37 45s 147 15 E
Gir Hills 94 21 0N 71 0 E
Girab 94 26 2N 70 38 E
Giralla 136 22 31s 114 15 E
Giraltovce 53 49 7N 21 32 E
Girard 159 37 30N 94 50W
Girardot 174 4 18N 74 48W
Girdle Ness 37 57 9N 2 2W
Giresun 92 40 45N 38 30 E
Girga 122 26 17N 31 55 E
Girgir, C. 135 3 50s 144 35 E
Giridih 95 24 10N 86 21 E
Girifalco 65 38 49N 16 25 E
Girilambone 141 31 16s 146 57 E
Girishk 93 31 47N 64 24 E
Giro 121 11 7N 4 42 E
Giromagny 43 47 44N 6 50 E
Gironde □ 44 44 45N 0 30W
Gironde, R. 44 45 27N 0 53W
Gironella 58 42 2N 1 53 E
Giru 138 19 30s 147 5 E
Girvan 34 55 15N 4 50W
Girvan R. 34 55 18N 4 51W
Gisborne 142 38 39s 178 5 E
Gisburn 32 53 56N 2 16W
Gisenyi 126 1 41s 29 30 E
Giske 71 62 30N 6 3 E
Gisla 36 58 7N 6 53W
Gislaved 73 57 19N 13 32 E
Gisors 43 49 15N 1 40 E
Gissarskiy, Khrebet 85 39 0N 69 0 E
Gistel 47 51 9N 2 59 E
Giswil 50 46 50N 8 11 E
Gitega (Kitega) 126 3 26s 29 56 E
Gits 47 51 0N 3 6 E
Giubiasco 51 46 11N 9 1 E
Giugliano in Campania 65 40 55N 14 12 E
Giuliana 63 42 45N 13 58 E
Giulianova 63 42 45N 13 58 E
Giurgeni 70 44 45N 27 38 E
Giurgiu 70 43 52N 25 57 E
Giv'at Brenner 90 31 52N 34 47 E
Give 73 55 51N 9 13 E
Givet 43 50 8N 4 49 E
Givors 45 45 35N 4 45 E
Givry, Belg. 47 50 23N 4 2 E
Givry, France 43 46 41N 4 46 E
Giza (El Giza) 122 30 1N 31 11 E
Gizhduvan 85 40 6N 64 41 E
Gizhiga 77 62 0N 150 27 E
Gizhiginskaya, Guba 77 61 0N 158 0 E
Gizycko 54 54 2N 21 48 E
Gizzeria 65 38 57N 16 10 E
Gjegjan 68 41 58N 20 3 E
Gjerpen 71 59 15N 9 33 E
Gjerstad 71 58 54N 9 0 E
Gjiri-i-Vlorës 68 40 29N 19 27 E
Gjirokastër 68 40 7N 20 16 E
Gjoa Haven 148 68 20N 96 0W
Gjøvdal 71 58 52N 8 19 E
Gjøvik 71 60 47N 10 43 E
Glace Bay 151 46 11N 59 58W
Glacier B. 152 58 30N 136 10W
Glacier Nat. Park 152 51 15N 117 30W
Glacier National Park 160 48 35N 113 40W
Glacier Peak Mt. 160 48 7N 121 7W
Gladewater 159 32 30N 94 58W
Gladstone, Queens., Austral. 74 23 52s 151 16 E
Gladstone, S.A., Austral. 140 33 15s 138 22 E
Gladstone, W. Australia, Austral. 137 25 57s 114 17 E
Gladstone, Can. 153 50 13N 98 57W
Gladstone, U.S.A. 156 45 52N 87 1W
Gladwin 156 43 59N 84 29W
Gladys L. 152 59 50N 133 0W
Glafsfjorden 72 59 30N 12 45 E
Głagów Małapolski 53 50 10N 21 56 E
Gláma 74 65 48N 23 0W
Gláma, R. 71 60 30N 12 8 E

Glamis 37 56 37N 3 0W
Glamorgan (□) 26 51 37N 3 35W
Glamorgan, Vale of 23 50 45N 3 15W
Glan, Phil. 103 5 45N 125 20 E
Glan, Sweden 73 58 37N 16 0 E
Glanaman 31 51 48N 3 56W
Glanaruddery Mts. 39 52 20N 9 27W
Glandore 39 51 33N 9 7W
Glandore Harb. 39 51 33N 9 8W
Glanerbrug 46 52 13N 6 58 E
Glanton 35 55 25N 1 54W
Glanworth 39 52 10N 8 25W
Glarner Alpen 51 46 50N 9 0 E
Glärnisch 51 47 0N 9 0 E
Glarus 51 47 3N 9 4 E
Glarus □ 51 47 0N 9 5 E
Glas Maol 37 56 52N 3 20W
Glasco, Kans., U.S.A. 158 39 25N 97 50W
Glasco, N.Y., U.S.A. 162 42 3N 73 57W
Glasgow, U.K. 34 55 52N 4 14W
Glasgow, Ky., U.S.A. 156 37 2N 85 55W
Glasgow, Mont., U.S.A. 160 48 12N 106 35W
Glasnevin 38 53 22N 6 18W
Glassboro 162 39 42N 75 7W
Glasslough 38 54 20N 6 53W
Glastonbury, U.K. 28 51 9N 2 42W
Glastonbury, U.S.A. 162 41 42N 72 27W
Glatt, R. 51 47 28N 8 32 E
Glattfelden 51 47 33N 8 30 E
Glauchau 48 50 50N 12 33 E
Glazov 81 58 9N 52 40 E
Glbovo 67 42 1N 24 43 E
Gleichen 152 50 50N 113 0W
Gleisdorf 52 47 6N 15 44 E
Glemsford 29 52 6N 0 41 E
Glen Affric 36 57 15N 5 0W
Glen Afton 142 37 46s 175 4 E
Glen Almond 35 56 28N 3 50W
Glen B. 38 54 43N 8 45W
Glen Burnie 162 39 10N 76 37W
Glen Canyon Dam 161 37 0N 111 25W
Glen Canyon Nat. Recreation Area 161 37 30N 111 0W
Glen Coe 23 56 40N 5 0W
Glen Cove 162 40 51N 73 37W
Glen Esk 37 56 53N 2 50W
Glen Etive 34 56 37N 5 0W
Glen Florrie 136 22 55s 115 59 E
Glen Garry, Inv., U.K. 36 57 3N 5 7W
Glen Garry, Per., U.K. 37 56 47N 4 5W
Glen Gowrie 140 31 4s 143 10 E
Glen Helen 32 54 14N 4 35W
Glen Innes 139 29 40s 151 39 E
Glen Lyon, U.K. 37 56 35N 4 20W
Glen Lyon, U.S.A. 162 41 10N 76 7W
Glen Massey 142 37 38s 175 2 E
Glen Mor 36 57 10N 4 58W
Glen Moriston 36 57 10N 4 58W
Glen Orchy 34 56 27N 4 52W
Glen Orrin 37 57 30N 4 45W
Glen Oykel 37 58 5N 4 50W
Glen, R. 29 52 50N 0 7W
Glen Shee 37 56 45N 3 25W
Glen Shiel 36 57 8N 5 20W
Glen Spean 36 56 53N 4 40W
Glen Trool Lodge 34 55 5N 4 30W
Glen Ullin 158 46 48N 101 46W
Glen Valley 141 36 54s 147 28 E
Glenade 38 54 22N 8 17W
Glenamoy 38 54 14N 9 40W
Glénans, Is. de 42 47 42N 4 0W
Glenariff 141 30 50s 146 33 E
Glenarm 38 54 58N 5 58W
Glenart Castle 39 52 48N 6 12W
Glenavy, N.Z. 143 44 54s 171 7 E
Glenavy, U.K. 38 54 36N 6 12W
Glenbarr 34 55 34N 5 40W
Glenbeigh 39 52 3N 9 57W
Glenbrittle 36 57 13N 6 18W
Glenbrook 142 33 46s 150 37 E
Glenburn 141 37 31s 145 27 E
Glencoe, S. Afr. 129 28 11s 30 11 E
Glencoe, U.S.A. 158 44 45N 94 10W
Glencolumbkille 38 54 43N 8 41W
Glendale, Can. 150 46 45N 84 2W
Glendale, Zimb. 127 17 22s 31 5 E
Glendale, Ariz., U.S.A. 161 33 40N 112 8W
Glendale, Calif., U.S.A. 163 34 7N 118 18W
Glendale, Oreg., U.S.A. 160 42 44N 123 29W
Glendive 158 47 7N 104 40W
Glendo 158 42 30N 105 0W
Glendora 163 34 8N 117 52W
Gleneagles 35 56 16N 3 44W
Glenealy 39 52 59N 6 10W
Gleneely 38 52 14N 7 8W
Glenelg, Austral. 140 34 58s 138 31 E
Glenelg, U.K. 36 57 13N 5 37W
Glenelg, R. 140 38 4s 140 59 E
Glenfarne 38 54 17N 8 0W
Glenfield 162 43 43N 75 24W
Glenfinnan 36 56 52N 5 28W
Glengad Hd. 38 55 19N 7 11W
Glengariff 39 51 45N 9 33W
Glengormley 38 54 41N 5 57W
Glengyle 138 24 48s 139 37 E
Glenham 143 46 26s 168 52 E
Glenhope 143 41 40s 172 39 E
Glenisland 38 53 59N 9 26W
Glenkens, The 34 55 10N 4 15W
Glenluce 34 54 53N 4 50W
Glenmary, Mt. 143 44 0s 169 55 E
Glenmaye 32 54 11N 4 42W
Glenmora 159 31 1N 92 34W

Glenmorgan 139 27 14s 149 42 E
Glenn, oilfield 19 57 55N 0 15 E
Glennagevlagh 38 53 36N 9 41W
Glennamaddy 38 53 37N 8 33W
Glenn's Ferry 160 43 0N 115 15W
Glenoe 38 54 47N 5 50W
Glenorchy, S. Austral., Austral. 140 31 55s 139 46 E
Glenorchy, Tas., Austral. 138 42 49s 147 18 E
Glenorchy, Vic., Austral. 140 36 55s 142 41 E
Glenore 138 17 50s 141 12 E
Glenormiston 138 22 55s 138 50 E
Glenreagh 139 30 2s 153 1 E
Glenrock 160 42 53N 105 55W
Glenrothes 35 56 12N 3 11W
Glenrowan 141 36 29s 146 13 E
Glenroy, S. Australia, Austral. 140 37 13s 140 48 E
Glenroy, W. Australia, Austral. 136 17 16s 126 14 E
Glenroy, S. Afr. 132 26 23s 28 17 E
Glens Falls 162 43 19N 73 39W
Glentane 38 53 25N 8 30W
Glenties 38 54 48N 8 18W
Glenville 156 38 56N 80 50W
Glenwood, Alta., Can. 152 49 21N 113 31W
Glenwood, Newf., Can. 151 49 0N 54 47W
Glenwood, Ark., U.S.A. 159 34 20N 93 30W
Glenwood, Hawaii, U.S.A. 147 19 29N 155 10W
Glenwood, Iowa, U.S.A. 158 41 7N 95 41W
Glenwood, Minn., U.S.A. 158 45 38N 95 21W
Glenwood Sprs. 160 39 39N 107 15W
Gletsch 51 46 34N 8 22 E
Glettinganes 74 65 30N 13 37W
Glin 39 52 34N 9 17W
Glina 63 45 20N 16 6 E
Glinojeck 54 52 49N 20 21 E
Glinsk 39 53 23N 9 49W
Glittertind 71 61 40N 8 32 E
Gliwice (Gleiwitz) 54 50 22N 18 41 E
Globe 161 33 25N 110 53W
Glodeanu-Siliştea 70 44 50N 26 48 E
Glödnitz 52 46 53N 14 7 E
Glodyany 70 47 45N 27 31 E
Gloggnitz 52 47 41N 15 56 E
Głogów 54 51 37N 16 5 E
Głogowek 54 50 21N 17 53 E
Gloria, La 174 8 37N 73 48W
Glorieuses, Îs. 129 11 30s 47 20 E
Glossop 32 53 27N 1 56W
Gloucester, Austral. 141 32 0s 151 59 E
Gloucester, U.K. 28 51 52N 2 15W
Gloucester, U.S.A. 162 42 38N 70 39W
Gloucester, Va., U.S.A. 162 37 25N 76 32W
Gloucester, C. 135 5 26s 148 21 E
Gloucester City 162 39 54N 75 8W
Gloucester, I. 138 20 0s 148 30 E
Gloucestershire □ 28 51 44N 2 10W
Gloversville 162 43 5N 74 18W
Glovertown 151 48 40N 54 03W
Głubczyce 54 50 13N 17 52 E
Glubokiy 83 48 35N 40 25 E
Glubokoye 80 55 10N 27 45 E
Głuchołazy 54 50 19N 17 24 E
Glücksburg 48 54 48N 9 34 E
Glückstadt 48 53 46N 9 28 E
Gluepot 140 33 45s 140 0 E
Glukhov 80 51 40N 33 50 E
Glussk 80 52 53N 28 41 E
Głó wno 54 51 59N 19 42 E
Glyn-ceiriog 31 52 56N 3 12W
Glyn Neath 31 51 45N 3 37W
Glyncorrwg 31 51 40N 3 39W
Glyngøre 73 56 46N 8 52 E
Glynn 39 52 29N 6 55W
Gmünd, Kärnten, Austria 52 46 54N 13 31 E
Gmünd, Niederösterreich, Austria 52 48 45N 15 0 E
Gmunden 52 47 55N 13 48 E
Gnarp 72 62 3N 17 16 E
Gnesta 72 59 3N 17 17 E
Gniew 54 53 50N 18 50 E
Gniewkowo 54 52 54N 18 25 E
Gniezno 54 52 30N 17 35 E
Gnoien 48 53 58N 12 41 E
Gnopp 123 8 47N 29 50 E
Gnosall 28 52 48N 2 15W
Gnosjö 73 57 22N 13 43 E
Gnowangerup 137 33 58s 117 59 E
Go Cong 101 10 22N 106 40 E
Gô-no-ura 110 33 44N 129 40 E
Goa 97 15 33N 73 59 E
Goa □ 97 15 33N 73 59 E
Goageb 128 26 49s 17 15 E
Goalen Hd. 141 36 33s 150 4 E
Goalpara 98 26 10N 90 40 E
Goalundo 95 23 50N 89 47 E
Goaso 120 6 48N 2 30W
Goat Fell 34 55 37N 5 11W
Goba, Ethiopia 123 7 1N 39 59 E
Goba, Mozam. 129 26 15s 32 13 E
Gobabis 128 22 16s 19 0 E
Gobi, desert 105 44 0N 111 0 E
Gobichettipalayam 97 11 31N 77 21 E
Gobō 111 33 53N 135 10 E
Gobo 123 5 40N 30 10 E

Goch Grand Bassa

Goch 48 51 40N 6 9E
Gochas 125 24 59S 19 25E
Godalming 29 51 12N 0 37W
Godavari Point 96 17 0N 82 20E
Godavari, R. 96 19 5N 79 0E
Godbout 151 49 20N 67 38W
Godda 95 24 50N 87 20E
Goddua 119 26 26N 14 19E
Godech 66 43 1N 23 4E
Godegård 73 58 43N 15 8E
Goderich 150 43 45N 81 41W
Goderville 42 49 38N 0 22E
Godhavn 12 69 15N 53 38W
Godhra 94 22 49N 73 40E
Godmanchester 29 52 19N 0 11W
Gödöllö 53 47 38N 19 25E
Godoy Cruz 172 32 56S 68 52W
Godrevy Pt. 30 50 15N 5 24W
Gods L. 153 54 40N 94 15W
Gods, R. 153 56 22N 92 51W
Godshill 28 50 38N 1 13W
Godstone 29 51 15N 0 3W
Godthåb 12 64 10N 51 46W
Godwin Austen (K2) 93 36 0N 77 0E
Goeie Hoop, Kaap die 128 34 24S 18 30E
Goeland, L. 150 49 50N 76 48W
Goeree 46 51 50N 4 0E
Goes 47 51 30N 3 55E
Goffstown 162 43 1N 71 36W
Gogama 150 47 35N 81 43W
Gogango 138 23 40S 150 2E
Gogebic, L. 158 46 30N 89 34W
Gogha 94 21 32N 72 9E
Gogolin 54 50 30N 18 0E
Gogra, R. = Ghaghara 99 26 0N 84 20E
Gogriâl 123 8 30N 28 0E
Goiana 170 7 33S 34 59W
Goiandira 171 11 46S 46 40W
Goianésia 171 15 18S 49 7W
Goiânia 171 16 35S 49 20W
Goiás 171 15 55S 50 10W
Goiás □ 170 12 10S 48 0W
Goiatuba 171 18 1S 49 23W
Goil L. 34 56 8N 4 52W
Goirle 47 51 31N 5 4E
Góis 56 40 10N 8 6W
Goisern 52 47 38N 13 38E
Gojam □ 123 10 55N 36 30E
Gojeb, W. 123 7 12N 36 40E
Gojō 111 34 21N 135 42E
Gojra 94 31 10N 72 40E
Gokak 97 16 11N 74 52E
Gokarannath 95 27 57N 80 39E
Gokarn 97 14 33N 74 17E
Gökçeada 68 40 10N 26 0E
Gokteik 99 22 26N 97 0E
Gokurt 94 29 47N 67 26E
Gøl 73 57 4N 9 42E
Gola 95 28 3N 80 32E
Gola I. 38 55 4N 8 20W
Golaghat 98 26 30N 94 0E
Golakganj 95 26 8N 89 52E
Golaya Pristen 82 46 29N 32 23E
Golchikha 12 71 45N 84 0E
Golconda 160 40 58N 117 32W
Gold Beach 160 42 25N 124 25W
Gold Coast, Austral. 139 28 0S 153 25E
Gold Coast, W. Afr. 121 4 0N 1 40W
Gold Creek 147 62 45N 149 45W
Gold Hill 160 42 28N 123 2W
Gold Point 163 37 21N 117 21W
Gold River 152 49 40N 126 10E
Goldach 51 47 28N 9 28E
Goldau 51 47 3N 8 33E
Goldberg 48 53 34N 12 6E
Golden, Can. 152 51 20N 117 0W
Golden, Ireland 39 52 30N 8 0W
Golden, U.S.A. 158 39 42N 105 30W
Golden Bay 143 40 40S 172 50E
Golden Gate 160 37 54N 122 30W
Golden Hinde, mt. 152 49 40N 125 44W
Golden Prairie 153 50 13N 109 37W
Golden Rock 97 10 45N 78 48E
Golden Vale 39 52 33N 8 17W
Goldendale 160 45 53N 120 48W
Goldfield 163 37 45N 117 13W
Goldfields 153 59 28N 108 29W
Goldpines 153 50 45N 93 05W
Goldsand L. 153 57 2N 101 8W
Goldsboro 157 35 24N 77 59W
Goldsmith 159 32 0N 102 40W
Goldsworthy 136 20 21S 119 30E
Goldsworthy, Mt. 136 20 23S 119 31E
Goldthwaite 159 31 25N 98 32W
Goleen 39 51 30N 9 43W
Golegã 57 39 24N 8 29W
Goleniów 54 53 35N 14 50E
Goleta 163 34 27N 119 50W
Golfito 166 8 41N 83 5W
Golfo degli Aranci 65 41 0N 9 38E
Goliad 159 28 40N 97 22W
Golija 66 43 22N 20 15E
Golija, Mts. 66 43 5N 18 45E
Golina 54 52 15N 18 4E
Golo, R. 45 42 31N 9 32E
Golovanesvsk 82 48 25N 30 30E
Gölpazari 82 40 17N 30 17E
Golra 94 33 37N 72 56E
Golspie 37 57 58N 3 58W
Golub Dobrzyn 54 53 7N 19 2E
Golubac 66 44 38N 21 38E
Golyama Kamchiya, R. 67 43 2N 27 18E
Goma, Ethiopia 123 8 29N 36 53E
Goma, Rwanda 126 2 11S 29 18E
Goma, Zaîre 126 1 37S 29 10E
Gomare 128 19 25S 22 8E
Gomati, R. 95 26 30N 81 50E
Gombari 126 2 45N 29 3E
Gombe 121 10 19N 11 2E
Gombe, R. 126 4 30S 32 50E
Gombi 121 10 12N 12 45E
Gomel 80 52 28N 31 0E
Gomera, I. 116 28 10N 17 5W
Gometra I. 34 56 30N 6 18W
Gómez Palacio 164 25 40N 104 40W
Gommern 48 52 54N 11 47E
Gomogomo 103 6 25S 134 53E
Gomoh 99 23 52N 86 10E
Gomotartsi 66 44 6N 22 57E
Goms 50 46 30N 8 15E
Gonābād 93 34 15N 58 45E
Gonaïves 167 19 20N 72 50W
Gonâve, G. de la 167 19 29N 72 42W
Gonâve, I. de la 167 18 45N 73 0W
Gönc 53 48 28N 21 14E
Gonda 95 27 9N 81 58E
Gondab-e Kāvūs 93 37 20N 55 25E
Gondal 94 21 58N 70 52E
Gonder 123 12 23N 37 30E
Gondia 96 21 30N 80 10E
Gondola 127 19 4S 33 37E
Gondomar, Port. 56 41 10N 8 35W
Gondomar, Spain 56 42 7N 8 45W
Gondrecourt-le-Château 43 48 26N 5 30E
Gongola □ 121 8 0N 12 0E
Gongola, R. 121 10 30N 10 22E
Goniadz 54 53 30N 22 44E
Goniri 121 11 30N 12 15E
Gonnesa 64 39 17N 8 27E
Gonno-Altaysk 76 51 50N 86 5E
Gonnos 68 39 52N 22 29E
Gonnosfanadiga 64 39 30N 8 39E
Gonzales, Calif., U.S.A. 163 36 35N 121 30W
Gonzales, Tex., U.S.A. 159 29 30N 97 30W
González Chaves 172 38 02S 60 05W
Good Hope, C. of = Goeie Hoop 128 34 24S 18 30E
Goode 139 31 58S 133 45E
Goodenough I. 135 9 20S 150 15E
Gooderham 150 44 54N 78 21W
Goodeve 153 51 4N 103 10W
Gooding 160 43 0N 114 50W
Goodland 158 39 22N 101 44W
Goodnight 159 35 4N 101 13W
Goodooga 139 29 1S 147 28E
Goodrich 28 51 52N 2 38W
Goodsoil 153 54 24N 109 13W
Goodsprings 161 35 51N 115 30W
Goodwick 31 52 0N 5 0W
Goodwin, Mt. 136 14 13S 129 32E
Goodwood 29 50 53N 0 44W
Goole 33 53 42N 0 52W
Goolgowi 141 33 58S 145 41E
Goolwa 140 35 30S 138 47E
Goomalling 137 31 15S 116 42E
Goombalie 139 29 59S 145 26E
Goonalga 140 31 45S 143 37E
Goonda 127 19 48S 33 57E
Goondiwindi 139 28 30S 150 21E
Goongarrie 137 30 2S 121 8E
Goonumbla 141 32 59S 148 11E
Goonyella 138 21 47S 147 58E
Goor 46 52 13N 6 33E
Gooray 139 28 25S 150 2E
Goose Bay 151 53 15N 60 20W
Goose L. 160 42 0N 120 30W
Goose R. 151 53 20N 60 35W
Goothinga 138 17 36S 140 50E
Gooty 97 15 7N 77 41E
Gop 93 22 5N 69 50E
Gopalganj, Bangla. 98 23 1N 89 50E
Gopalganj, India 95 26 28N 84 30E
Goppenstein 50 46 23N 7 46E
Göppingen 49 48 42N 9 40E
Gor 59 37 23N 2 58W
Góra 54 51 40N 16 31E
Gorakhpur 95 26 47N 83 32E
Gorbatov 81 56 12N 43 2E
Gorbea, Peña 58 43 1N 2 50W
Gorda 163 35 53N 121 26W
Gorda, Punta 166 14 10N 83 10W
Gordon, Austral. 140 32 7S 138 20E
Gordon, U.K. 35 55 41N 2 32W
Gordon, U.S.A. 158 42 49N 102 6W
Gordon B. 136 11 35S 130 10E
Gordon Downs 136 18 48S 128 40E
Gordon L., Alta., Can. 153 56 30N 110 25W
Gordon L., N.W.T., Can. 152 63 5N 113 11W
Gordon, R. 138 42 27S 145 30E
Gordon River 137 34 10S 117 15E
Gordonia 128 28 13S 21 10E
Gordonvale 138 17 5S 145 50E
Gore 139 28 17S 151 30E
Goré 117 7 59N 16 49E
Gore, Ethiopia 123 8 12N 35 32E
Gore, N.Z. 143 46 5S 168 58E
Gore B. 150 45 57N 82 28W
Gorebridge 35 55 51N 3 2W
Goresbridge 39 52 38N 7 0W
Gorey 39 52 41N 6 18W
Gorgan 93 36 55N 54 30E
Gorge, The 138 18 27S 145 30E
Gorgona, I. 174 3 0N 78 10W
Gorgona I. 62 43 27N 9 52E
Gorgora 123 12 15N 37 17E
Gori 83 42 0N 44 7E
Gorinchem 46 51 50N 4 59E
Goring, Oxon, U.K. 28 51 31N 1 8W
Goring, Sussex, U.K. 29 50 49N 0 26W
Gorinhatã 171 19 15S 49 45W
Goritsy 81 57 4N 36 43E
Gorízia 63 45 56N 13 37E
Gorka 54 51 39N 16 58E
Gorki = Gorkiy 81 56 20N 44 0E
Gorkiy 81 57 20N 44 0E
Gorkovskoye Vdkhr. 81 57 2N 43 4E
Gorleston 29 52 35N 1 44E
Gorlev 73 55 30N 11 15E
Gorlice 54 49 35N 21 11E
Görlitz 54 51 10N 14 59E
Gorlovka 81 48 25N 37 58E
Gorman, Calif., U.S.A. 163 34 47N 118 51W
Gorman, Tex., U.S.A. 159 32 15N 98 43W
Gorna Oryakhovitsa 67 43 7N 25 40E
Gorna Radgona 63 46 40N 16 2E
Gornja Tuzla 66 44 35N 18 46E
Gornji Grad 63 46 20N 14 52E
Gornji Milanovac 66 44 00N 20 29E
Gornji Vafuk 66 43 57N 17 34E
Gorno Ablanovo 67 43 37N 25 43E
Gorno Filinskoye 76 60 5N 70 0E
Gornyy 81 51 50N 48 30E
Gorodenka 82 48 41N 25 29E
Gorodets 81 56 38N 43 28E
Gorodische 81 53 13N 45 40E
Gorodnitsa 80 50 46N 27 26E
Gorodnya 80 51 55N 31 33E
Gorodok, Byelorussia, U.S.S.R. 80 55 30N 30 3E
Gorodok, Ukraine, U.S.S.R. 80 49 46N 23 32E
Goroka 135 6 7S 145 25E
Goroke 140 36 43S 141 29E
Gorokhov 80 50 15N 24 45E
Gorokhovets 81 56 13N 42 39E
Gorom Gorom 121 14 26N 0 14W
Goromonzi 127 17 52S 31 22E
Gorong, Kepulauan 103 4 5S 131 15E
Gorongosa, Sa. da 127 18 27S 32 2E
Gorongose, R. 129 20 40S 34 30E
Gorontalo 103 0 35N 123 13E
Goronyo 121 13 29N 5 39E
Gorredijk 46 53 0N 6 3E
Gorron 42 48 25N 0 50W
Gorseinon 31 51 40N 4 2W
Gorssel 46 52 12N 6 12E
Gort 39 53 4N 8 50W
Gortin 38 54 43N 7 13W
Gorumahisani 96 22 20N 86 24E
Gorumna I. 39 53 15N 9 44W
Gorzkowice 54 51 13N 19 36E
Gorzno 54 53 12N 19 38E
Gorzów Slaski 54 51 3N 18 22E
Gorzów Wielkopolski 54 52 43N 15 15E
Gorzów Wielkopolski □ 54 52 45N 15 30E
Gosainthan, Mt. 99 28 20N 85 45E
Gosberton 33 52 52N 0 10W
Göschenen 51 46 40N 8 36E
Gōse 111 34 27N 135 44E
Gosford 141 33 23N 151 18E
Gosforth 32 54 24N 3 27W
Goshen, S. Afr. 128 25 50S 25 0E
Goshen, Calif., U.S.A. 163 36 21N 119 25W
Goshen, Ind., U.S.A. 156 41 36N 85 46W
Goshen, N.Y., U.S.A. 162 41 23N 74 21W
Goslar 48 51 55N 10 23E
Gospič 63 44 35N 15 23E
Gosport 28 50 48N 1 8W
Gossa, I. 71 62 52N 6 50E
Gossau 51 47 25N 9 15E
Gosse, R. 138 19 32S 134 37E
Gostivar 66 41 48N 20 57E
Gostyn 54 51 50N 17 3E
Gostynin 54 52 26N 19 29E
Göta 73 58 6N 12 10E
Göta älv 73 57 42N 11 54E
Göta Kanal 73 58 35N 14 15E
Götaland, reg. 73 58 0N 14 0E
Göteborg 73 57 43N 11 59E
Göteborg & Bohus □ 75 58 20N 11 50E
Gotemba 111 35 18N 138 56E
Götene 73 58 32N 13 30E
Gotha 48 50 56N 10 42E
Gothenburg 158 40 58N 100 8W
Gothenburg = Göteborg 73 57 43N 11 59E
Gotse Delchev (Nevrokop) 67 41 43N 23 46E
Gotska Sandön 75 58 24N 19 15E
Gōtsu 110 35 0N 132 14E
Göttingen 48 51 31N 9 55E
Gottwaldov (Zlin) 53 49 14N 17 40E
Gouda 46 52 1N 4 42E
Goudhurst 29 51 7N 0 28E
Goudiry 120 14 15N 12 45E
Gough I. 15 40 10S 9 45W
Gouin Res. 150 48 35N 74 40W
Gouitafla 120 7 30N 5 53W
Goula Touila 118 21 50N 1 57E
Goulburn 141 34 44S 149 44E
Goulburn Is. 138 11 40S 133 20E
Gould, mt. 137 25 46S 117 18E
Goulia 120 10 1N 7 11W
Goulimine 118 28 50N 10 0W
Goulmima 118 31 41N 4 57W
Gouménissa 68 40 56N 22 37E
Goumeur 119 20 40N 18 30E
Goundam 135 16 25N 3 45W
Gounou-Gaya 124 9 38N 15 31E
Goúra 69 37 56N 22 20E
Gourara 118 29 0N 0 30E
Gouraya 118 36 31N 1 56E
Gourdon, France 44 44 44N 1 23E
Gourdon, U.K. 37 56 50N 2 15W
Gouré 121 14 0N 10 10E
Gourits, R. 128 34 15S 21 45E
Gourma Rharous 121 16 55N 2 5W
Gournay-en-Bray 43 49 29N 1 44E
Gouro 117 19 30N 19 30E
Gourock 34 55 58N 4 49W
Gourock Ra. 141 36 0S 149 25E
Gourselik 121 13 31N 10 52E
Goursi 120 12 42N 2 37W
Gouvêa 171 18 27S 43 44W
Gouzon 44 46 12N 2 14E
Govan 153 51 20N 105 0W
Gove 133 12 25S 136 55E
Goverla 82 49 9N 24 30E
Governador Valadares 171 18 15S 41 57W
Governor's Harbour 166 25 10N 76 14W
Gowan 138 25 0S 145 0E
Gowanda 156 42 29N 78 58W
Gower, The 31 51 35N 4 10W
Gowerton 31 51 38N 4 2W
Gowna, L. 38 53 52N 7 35W
Gowran 39 52 38N 7 5W
Goya 172 29 10S 59 10W
Goyder's Lagoon 139 27 3S 139 58E
Goyllarisquizga 174 10 19S 76 31W
Goz Beîda 117 12 20N 21 30E
Goz Regeb 123 16 3N 35 33E
Gozdnica 54 51 28N 15 4E
Gozo (Ghaudex) 60 36 0N 14 13E
Graaff-Reinet 128 32 13S 24 32E
Graasten 73 54 57N 9 34E
Grabow 48 53 17N 11 31E
Grabów 54 51 31N 18 7E
Grabs 51 47 11N 9 27E
Gračac 63 44 18N 15 57E
Gračanica 66 44 43N 18 18E
Graçay 43 47 10N 1 50E
Grace 160 42 38N 111 46W
Grace, L., (North) 137 33 10S 118 20E
Grace, L., (South) 137 33 15S 118 25E
Graceville 158 45 36N 96 23W
Grachevka 84 52 55N 52 52E
Gracias a Dios, C. 166 15 0N 83 20W
Gradačac 66 44 52N 18 26E
Gradaús 170 7 43S 51 11W
Gradaús, Serra dos 170 8 0S 50 45W
Gradeska Planina 66 41 30N 22 15E
Gradets 67 42 46N 26 30E
Gradignan 66 44 47N 0 36W
Gradnitsa 67 42 57N 24 58E
Grado, Italy 63 45 40N 13 20E
Grado, Spain 56 43 23N 6 4W
Gradule 139 28 32S 149 15E
Grady 159 34 52N 103 15W
Graeca, Lacul 70 44 5N 26 10E
Graemsay I. 37 58 56N 3 17W
Graénalon, L. 74 64 10N 17 20W
Grafham Water 29 52 18N 0 17W
Grafton, Austral. 139 29 38S 152 58E
Grafton, U.S.A. 158 48 30N 97 25W
Grafton, C. 133 16 51S 146 0E
Gragnano 65 40 42N 14 30E
Graham, Can. 150 49 20N 90 30W
Graham, N.C., U.S.A. 157 36 5N 79 22W
Graham, Tex., U.S.A. 159 33 7N 98 38W
Graham Bell, Os. 76 80 5N 70 0E
Graham I. 152 53 40N 132 30W
Graham Land 13 65 0S 64 0W
Graham Mt. 161 32 46N 109 58W
Graham, R. 152 56 31N 122 17W
Grahamdale 153 51 23N 98 30W
Grahamstown 128 33 19S 26 31E
Grahamsville 162 41 51N 74 33W
Grahovo 66 42 40N 18 4E
Graïba 119 34 30N 10 13E
Graide 47 49 58N 5 4E
Graigue 39 52 51N 6 56W
Graiguenamanagh 39 52 32N 6 58W
Grain Coast 120 4 20N 10 0W
Grainthorpe 33 53 27N 0 5E
Graivoron 80 50 29N 35 39E
Grajaú 170 5 50S 46 30W
Grajaú, R. 170 3 41S 44 48W
Grajewo 54 53 39N 22 30E
Gramada 66 43 49N 22 39E
Gramat 44 44 48N 1 43E
Gramisdale 36 57 29N 7 18W
Grammichele 65 37 12N 14 37E
Grampian □ 37 57 0N 3 0W
Grampians, Mts. 140 37 0S 142 20E
Gran Canaria 116 27 55N 15 35W
Gran Chaco 156 25 0S 61 0W
Gran Paradiso 62 49 33N 7 17E
Gran Sabana, La 174 5 30N 61 30W
Gran Sasso d'Italia, Mt. 44 42 25N 13 30E
Granada, Nic. 166 11 58N 86 0W
Granada, Spain 59 37 10N 3 35W
Granada, U.S.A. 158 38 5N 102 13W
Granada □ 57 37 5N 4 30W
Granard 38 53 47N 7 30W
Granbo 72 61 16N 16 33E
Granbury 159 32 28N 97 48W
Granby 150 45 25N 72 45W
Grand Bahama I. 166 26 40N 78 30W
Grand Bank 151 47 6N 55 48W
Grand Bassa 120 6 0N 10 2W

Grand Bassam **Grillby**

Grand Bassam **120** 5 10N 3 49W
Grand Bérébу **120** 4 38N 6 55W
Grand-Bourg **167** 15 53N 61 19W
Grand Canal **39** 53 15N 8 10W
Grand Canyon National Park **161** 36 15N 112 20W
Grand Cayman **166** 19 20N 81 20W
Grand Cess **120** 4 40N 8 12W
Grand 'Combe, La **45** 44 13N 4 2E
Grand Coulee **160** 47 48N 119 1W
Grand Coulee Dam **160** 48 0N 118 50W
Grand Erg Occidental **118** 30 20N 1 0E
Grand Erg Oriental **119** 30 0N 6 30E
Grand Falls **151** 47 2N 67 46W
Grand Forks, Can. **152** 49 0N 118 30W
Grand Forks, U.S.A. **158** 48 0N 97 3W
Grand-Fougeray **42** 47 43N 1 44W
Grand Fougeray, Le **42** 47 44N 1 43W
Grand Haven **156** 43 3N 86 13W
Grand I. **150** 46 30N 86 40W
Grand Island **158** 40 59N 98 25W
Grand Isle **159** 29 15N 89 58W
Grand Junction **161** 39 0N 108 30W
Grand L., N.B., Can. **151** 45 57N 66 7W
Grand L., Newf., Can. **151** 48 45N 57 45W
Grand L., Newf., Can. **151** 53 40N 60 30W
Grand L., Newf., Can. **151** 49 0N 57 30W
Grand L., U.S.A. **159** 29 55N 92 45W
Grand Lac **150** 47 35N 77 35W
Grand Lahou **120** 5 10N 5 0W
Grand Lake **160** 40 20N 105 54W
Grand-Leez **47** 50 35N 4 45E
Grand Lieu, Lac de **42** 47 6N 1 40W
Grand Manan I. **151** 44 45N 66 52W
Grand Marais, Can. **158** 47 45N 90 25W
Grand Marais, U.S.A. **156** 46 39N 85 59W
Grand Mère **150** 46 36N 72 40W
Grand Motte, La **45** 48 35N 1 4E
Grand Popo **121** 6 15N 1 44E
Grand Portage **150** 47 58N 89 41W
Grand Pressigny, Le **42** 46 55N 0 48E
Grand, R., Mo., U.S.A. **160** 39 23N 93 27W
Grand, R., S.D., U.S.A. **160** 45 45N 101 30W
Grand Rapids, Can. **153** 53 12N 99 19W
Grand Rapids, Mich., U.S.A. **156** 42 57N 85 40W
Grand Rapids, Minn., U.S.A. **158** 47 19N 93 29W
Grand St.-Bernard, Col. du **50** 45 53N 7 11E
Grand Teton **160** 43 45N 110 57W
Grand Valley **160** 39 30N 108 2W
Grand View **153** 51 11N 100 51W
Grandas de Salime **56** 43 13N 6 53W
Grande **170** 11 30S 44 30W
Grande, B. **176** 50 30S 68 20W
Grande Baie **151** 48 19N 70 52W
Grande Cache **152** 53 53N 119 8W
Grande, Coxilha **173** 28 18S 51 30W
Grande de Santiago, R. **164** 21 20N 105 50W
Grande Dixence, Barr. de la **50** 46 5N 7 23E
Grande-Entrée **151** 47 30N 61 40W
Grande, I. **171** 23 9S 44 14W
Grande, La **160** 45 15N 118 0W
Grande Prairie **152** 55 15N 118 50W
Grande, R., Jujuy, Argent. **172** 23 9S 65 52W
Grande, R., Mendoza, Argent. **172** 36 52S 69 45W
Grande R. **174** 18 35S 63 0W
Grande, R., Brazil **171** 20 0S 50 0W
Grande, R., Spain **59** 39 6N 0 48W
Grande, R., U.S.A. **159** 29 20N 100 40W
Grande Rivière **151** 48 26N 64 30W
Grande, Serra, Goiás, Brazil **170** 11 15S 46 30W
Grande, Serra, Maranhao, Brazil **170** 4 30S 41 20W
Grande, Serra, Piauí, Brazil **170** 8 0S 45 0W
Grande Vallée **151** 49 14N 65 8W
Grandes Bergeronnes **151** 48 16N 69 35W
Grandfalls **159** 31 21N 102 51W
Grandglise **47** 50 30N 3 42E
Grandoe Mines **152** 56 29N 129 54W
Grândola **57** 38 12N 8 35W
Grandpré **43** 49 20N 4 50E
Grandson **50** 46 49N 6 39E
Grandview, Can. **153** 51 10N 100 42W
Grandview, U.S.A. **160** 46 13N 119 58W
Grandvilliers **43** 49 40N 1 57E
Graneros **172** 34 5S 70 45W
Graney L. **39** 53 0N 8 40W
Grange **38** 54 24N 8 32W
Grange, La, Austral. **136** 18 45S 121 43E
Grange, La, U.S.A. **163** 37 42N 120 27W
Grange, La, Ga., U.S.A. **157** 33 4N 85 0W
Grange, La, Ky., U.S.A. **156** 38 20N 85 20W
Grange, La, Tex., U.S.A. **159** 29 54N 96 52W
Grange-over-Sands **32** 54 12N 2 55W
Grangemouth **35** 56 1N 3 43W
Granger **160** 46 25N 120 5W
Grangesberg **72** 60 6N 15 1E
Grängesberg **72** 60 6N 15 1E
Grangetown **33** 54 36N 1 7W
Grangeville **160** 45 57N 116 4W
Granite City **158** 38 45N 90 3W
Granite Falls **158** 44 45N 95 35W
Granite Mtn. **163** 33 5N 116 28W
Granite Peak **137** 25 40S 121 20E
Granite Pk., mt. **160** 45 8N 109 52W
Granitnyy, Pik **85** 39 32N 70 20E
Granity **143** 41 39S 171 51E
Granja **170** 3 17S 40 50W
Granja de Moreruela **56** 41 48N 5 44W
Granja de Torrehermosa **57** 38 19N 5 35W
Gränna **73** 58 1N 14 28E
Granollers **58** 41 39N 2 18E
Gransee **48** 53 0N 13 10E
Grant, Can. **150** 50 6N 86 18W
Grant, U.S.A. **158** 40 53N 101 42W
Grant City **158** 40 30N 94 25W
Grant, I. **136** 11 10S 132 52E
Grant, Mt. **163** 38 34N 118 48W
Grant Range Mts. **161** 38 30N 115 30W
Grantham **33** 52 55N 0 39W
Grantown-on-Spey **37** 57 19N 3 36W
Grants **161** 35 14N 107 57W
Grant's Pass **160** 42 30N 123 22W
Grantsburg **158** 45 46N 92 44W
Grantshouse **35** 55 53N 2 17W
Grantsville **160** 40 35N 112 32W
Granville, France **42** 48 50N 1 35W
Granville, U.K. **38** 54 30N 6 47W
Granville, N.D., U.S.A. **158** 48 18N 100 48W
Granville, N.Y., U.S.A. **162** 43 24N 73 16W
Granville L. **153** 56 18N 100 30W
Grao de Gandía **59** 39 0N 0 27W
Grapeland **159** 31 30N 95 25W
Gras, L. de **148** 64 30N 110 30W
Graskop **129** 24 56S 30 49E
Gräsmark **72** 59 58N 12 44E
Grasmere, Austral. **139** 35 1S 117 45E
Grasmere, U.K. **32** 54 28N 3 2W
Gräsö **72** 60 21N 18 28E
Graso **72** 60 28N 18 35E
Grasonville **162** 38 57N 76 13W
Grass, R. **153** 56 3N 96 33W
Grass Range **160** 47 0N 109 0W
Grass River Prov. Park **153** 54 40N 100 50W
Grass Valley, Calif., U.S.A. **160** 39 18N 121 0W
Grass Valley, Oreg., U.S.A. **160** 45 28N 120 48W
Grassano **65** 40 38N 16 17E
Grasse **45** 43 38N 6 56E
Grassington **32** 54 5N 2 0W
Grassmere **140** 31 24S 142 38E
Grate's Cove **151** 48 8N 53 0W
Graubünden (Grisons) □ **51** 46 45N 9 30E
Graulhet **44** 43 45N 1 58E
Graus **58** 42 11N 0 20E
Gravatá **170** 6 59S 35 29W
Grave **46** 51 46N 5 44E
Grave, Pte. de **44** 45 34N 1 4W
's-Graveland **46** 52 15N 5 7E
Gravelbourg **153** 49 50N 106 35W
Gravelines **43** 51 0N 2 10E
's-Gravendeel **46** 51 47N 4 37E
's-Gravenhage **46** 52 7N 4 17E
's-Gravenpolder **47** 51 28N 3 54E
's-Gravensance **46** 52 0N 4 9E
Graversfors **73** 58 42N 16 8E
Gravesend, Austral. **139** 29 35S 150 20E
Gravesend, U.K. **29** 51 25N 0 22E
Gravina di Púglia **65** 40 48N 16 25E
Gravir **36** 58 2N 6 25W
Gravois, Pointe-à **167** 16 15N 73 45W
Gravone, R. **45** 42 3N 8 54E
Grävsnäs **73** 58 5N 12 29E
Gray **43** 47 27N 5 35E
Grayling **156** 44 40N 84 42W
Grayling, R. **152** 59 21N 125 0W
Grayrigg **32** 54 22N 2 40W
Grays Harbor **160** 46 55N 124 8W
Grays L. **160** 43 8N 111 30W
Grays Thurrock **29** 51 28N 0 23E
Grayson **153** 50 45N 102 40W
Grayvoron **80** 50 29N 35 39E
Graz **52** 47 4N 15 27E
Grazalema **57** 36 46N 5 23W
Grdelica **66** 42 55N 22 3E
Greasy L. **152** 62 55N 122 12W
Great Abaco I. **166** 26 15N 77 10W
Great Australia Basin **133** 26 0S 140 0E
Great Australian Bight **137** 33 30S 130 0E
Great Ayton **33** 54 29N 1 8W
Great Baddow **29** 51 43N 0 31E
Great Bahama Bank **166** 23 15N 78 0W
Great Barrier I. **142** 36 11S 175 25E
Great Barrier Reef **138** 19 0S 149 0E
Great Barrington **162** 42 11N 73 22W
Great Basin **154** 40 0N 116 30W
Great Bear L. **148** 65 0N 120 0W
Great Bear, R. **148** 65 0N 124 0W
Great Belt **73** 55 20N 11 0E
Great Bena **162** 41 57N 75 45W
Great Bend **158** 38 25N 98 55W
Great Bentley **29** 51 51N 1 5E
Great Bernera, I. **137** 58 15N 6 50W
Great Bitter Lake **122** 30 15N 32 40E
Great Blasket, I. **39** 52 5N 10 30W
Great Britain **16** 54 0N 2 15W
Great Bushman Land **128** 29 20S 19 20E
Great Central **152** 49 20N 125 10W
Great Chesterford **29** 52 4N 0 11E
Great Clifton **32** 54 39N 3 29W
Great Coco I. **101** 14 10N 93 25E
Great Divide **141** 23 0S 146 0E
Great Dunmow **29** 51 52N 0 22E
Great Exuma I. **166** 23 30N 75 50W
Great Falls, Can. **153** 50 27N 96 1W
Great Falls, U.S.A. **160** 47 27N 111 12W
Great Fish R., S. Afr. **128** 33 28S 27 5E
Great Fish R., S. Afr. **128** 31 30S 20 16E
Great Gonerby **33** 52 56N 0 40W
Great Guana Cay **166** 24 0N 76 20W
Great Hanish **123** 13 40N 43 0E
Great Harbour Deep **151** 50 35N 56 25W
Great Harwood **32** 52 41N 2 49W
Great I., Can. **153** 58 53N 96 35W
Great I., Ireland **39** 51 52N 8 15W
Great Inagua I. **167** 21 0N 73 20W
Gt. Indian Desert = Thar Desert **94** 28 0N 72 0E
Great Jarvis **151** 47 39N 57 12W
Great Karoo = Groot Karoo **128** 32 30S 23 0E
Great Lake **138** 41 50S 146 30E
Great Lakes **153** 44 0N 82 0W
Great Malvern **28** 52 7N 2 19W
Great Massingham **29** 52 47N 0 41E
Great Missenden **29** 51 42N 0 42W
Gt. Namaqualand = Groot Namakwaland **128** 26 0S 18 0E
Great Orme's Head **31** 53 20N 3 52W
Great Ouse, R. **29** 52 20N 0 8E
Great Palm I. **138** 18 45S 146 40E
Great Papuan Plateau **135** 6 30S 142 25E
Great Plains **50** 45 0N 100 0W
Great Ruaha, R. **126** 7 30S 35 0E
Great Salt Lake **160** 41 0N 112 30W
Great Salt Lake Desert **160** 40 20N 113 50W
Great Salt Plains Res. **159** 36 40N 98 15W
Great Sandy Desert **136** 21 0S 124 0E
Great Sandy I. = Fraser I. **139** 25 15S 153 0E
Great Scarcies, R. **120** 9 30N 12 40W
Great Shefford **28** 51 29N 1 27W
Great Shelford **29** 52 9N 0 9E
Great Shunner Fell **32** 54 22N 2 16W
Great Sitkin I. **147** 52 0N 176 10W
Great Slave L. **152** 61 23N 115 38W
Great Stour, R. **29** 51 21N 1 15E
Gt. Sugar Loaf, mt. **39** 53 10N 6 10W
Great Torrington **30** 50 57N 4 9W
Gt. Victoria Des. **137** 29 30S 126 30E
Great Wall **106** 38 30N 109 30E
Gt. Waltham **29** 51 47N 0 29E
Great Whale, R. **150** 55 20N 75 30W
Great Whernside, mt. **147** 54 9N 1 59W
Great Winterhoek, mt. **128** 33 07S 19 10E
Great Wyrley **28** 52 40N 2 1W
Great Yarmouth **29** 52 40N 1 45E
Great Yeldham **29** 52 1N 0 33E
Greater Antilles **167** 17 40N 74 0W
Greater Manchester □ **32** 53 30N 2 15W
Greatham **33** 54 38N 1 14W
Grebbestad **73** 58 42N 11 15E
Grebenka **80** 50 9N 32 22E
Greco, Mt. **64** 41 48N 14 0E
Gredos, Sierra de **56** 40 20N 5 0W
Greece ■ **68** 40 0N 23 0E
Greeley, Colo., U.S.A. **158** 40 30N 104 40W
Greeley, Nebr., U.S.A. **158** 41 36N 98 32W
Green B. **156** 45 0N 87 30W
Green Bay **156** 44 30N 88 0W
Green C. **141** 37 13S 150 1E
Green Cove Springs **157** 29 59N 81 40W
Green Hammerton **33** 54 2N 1 17W
Green Hd. **137** 30 5S 114 56E
Green Is. **135** 4 35S 154 10E
Green Island **143** 45 55S 170 26E
Green Lowther, Mt. **35** 55 22N 3 44W
Green R., Ky., U.S.A. **156** 37 54N 87 30W
Green R., Utah, U.S.A. **161** 39 0N 110 6W
Green R., Wyo., U.S.A. **160** 43 2N 110 2W
Green R., Wyo., U.S.A. **160** 41 44N 109 28W
Greenbush **158** 48 46N 96 10W
Greencastle, U.K. **38** 54 2N 6 5W
Greencastle, U.S.A. **156** 39 40N 86 48W
Greene **162** 42 20N 75 45W
Greenfield, Calif., U.S.A. **163** 35 15N 119 0W
Greenfield, Calif., U.S.A. **163** 36 19N 121 15W
Greenfield, Ind., U.S.A. **156** 39 47N 85 51W
Greenfield, Iowa, U.S.A. **158** 41 18N 94 28W
Greenfield, Mass., U.S.A. **162** 42 38N 72 38W
Greenfield, Miss., U.S.A. **159** 37 28N 93 50W
Greenhead **35** 54 58N 2 31W
Greening **150** 48 10N 74 55W
Greenisland **38** 54 42N 5 50W
Greenland **12** 66 0N 45 0W
Greenland Sea **12** 73 0N 10 0W
Greenlaw **35** 55 42N 2 28W
Greenock **34** 55 57N 4 46W
Greenodd **32** 54 14N 3 3W
Greenore **38** 54 2N 6 8W
Greenore Pt. **39** 52 15N 6 20W
Greenough, R. **137** 28 54S 115 36E
Greenport **162** 41 5N 72 23W
Greensboro, Ga., U.S.A. **157** 33 34N 83 12W
Greensboro, Md., U.S.A. **162** 38 59N 75 48W
Greensboro, N.C., U.S.A. **157** 36 7N 79 46W
Greensburg, Ind., U.S.A. **156** 39 20N 85 30W
Greensburg, Kans., U.S.A. **159** 37 38N 99 20W
Greensburg, Pa., U.S.A. **156** 40 18N 79 31W
Greenstone Pt. **36** 57 55N 5 38W
Greenville, Liberia **120** 5 7N 9 6W
Greenville, Ala., U.S.A. **157** 31 50N 86 37W
Greenville, Calif., U.S.A. **160** 40 8N 121 0W
Greenville, Ill., U.S.A. **158** 38 53N 89 22W
Greenville, Me., U.S.A. **151** 45 30N 69 32W
Greenville, Mich., U.S.A. **156** 43 12N 85 14W
Greenville, Miss., U.S.A. **159** 33 25N 91 0W
Greenville, N.C., U.S.A. **157** 35 37N 77 26W
Greenville, N.H., U.S.A. **162** 42 46N 71 49W
Greenville, N.Y., U.S.A. **162** 42 25N 74 1W
Greenville, Ohio, U.S.A. **156** 40 5N 84 38W
Greenville, Pa., U.S.A. **156** 41 23N 80 22W
Greenville, S.C., U.S.A. **157** 34 54N 82 24W
Greenville, Tenn., U.S.A. **157** 36 13N 82 51W
Greenville, Tex., U.S.A. **159** 33 5N 96 5W
Greenwater Lake Prov. Park **153** 52 32N 103 30W
Greenway **31** 51 56N 4 49W
Greenwich, U.K. **29** 51 28N 0 0
Greenwich, Conn., U.S.A. **162** 41 1N 73 38W
Greenwich, N.Y., U.S.A. **162** 43 2N 73 36W
Greenwood, Can. **152** 49 10N 118 40W
Greenwood, Miss., U.S.A. **159** 33 30N 90 4W
Greenwood, S.C., U.S.A. **157** 34 13N 82 13W
Greenwood, Mt. **136** 13 48S 130 4E
Gregory **158** 43 14N 99 20W
Gregory Downs **138** 18 35S 138 45E
Gregory, L. **139** 28 55S 139 0E
Gregory L. **136** 20 5S 127 0E
Gregory, L. **137** 25 38S 119 58E
Gregory Lake **136** 20 10S 127 30E
Gregory, R. **138** 17 53S 139 17E
Gregory Ra., Queens., Austral. **138** 19 30S 143 40E
Gregory Ra., W. Austral., Austral. **136** 21 20S 121 12E
Greian Hd. **36** 57 1N 7 30W
Greiffenberg **48** 53 6N 13 57E
Greifswald **48** 54 6N 13 23E
Greifswalder Bodden **48** 54 12N 13 35E
Greifswalder Oie **48** 54 15N 13 55E
Grein **52** 48 14N 14 51E
Greiner Wald **52** 48 30N 15 0E
Greiz **48** 50 39N 12 12E
Gremikha **78** 67 50N 39 40E
Grenå **73** 56 25N 10 53E
Grenada **159** 33 45N 89 50W
Grenada I. ■ **167** 12 10N 61 40W
Grenade **44** 43 47N 1 17E
Grenadines **167** 12 40N 61 20W
Grenchen **50** 47 12N 7 24E
Grenen **73** 57 44N 10 40E
Grenfell, Austral. **141** 33 52S 148 8E
Grenfell, Can. **153** 50 30N 102 56W
Grenoble **45** 45 12N 5 42E
Grenora **158** 48 38N 103 54W
Grenville, C. **138** 12 0S 143 13E
Grenville Chan. **152** 53 40N 129 46W
Gréoux-les-Bains **45** 43 55N 5 52E
Gresham **160** 45 30N 122 31W
Gresik **103** 9 13S 112 38E
Gressoney St. Jean **62** 45 49N 7 47E
Greta **32** 54 9N 2 36W
Greta R. **32** 54 36N 3 5W
Gretna, U.K. **35** 54 59N 3 4W
Gretna, U.S.A. **159** 30 0N 90 2W
Gretna Green **35** 55 0N 3 3W
Gretton **29** 52 33N 0 40W
Grevelingen Krammer **46** 51 44N 4 0E
Greven **48** 52 7N 7 36E
Grevená **68** 40 4N 21 25E
Grevená □ **68** 40 2N 21 25E
Grevenbroich **48** 51 6N 6 32E
Grevenmacher **47** 49 41N 6 26E
Grevesmühlen **48** 53 51N 11 10E
Grevie **73** 56 22N 12 46E
Grevinge **73** 55 48N 11 34E
Grey, C. **138** 13 0S 136 35E
Grey, R. **143** 42 27S 171 12E
Grey Range **133** 27 0S 143 30E
Grey Res. **151** 48 20N 56 30W
Greyabbey **38** 54 32N 5 35W
Greybull **160** 44 30N 108 3W
Greystone **32** 54 39N 2 52W
Greystones **39** 53 9N 6 4W
Greytown, N.Z. **142** 41 5S 175 29E
Greytown, S. Afr. **129** 29 1S 30 36E
Gribanovskiy **81** 51 28N 41 50E
Gribbell I. **152** 53 23N 129 0W
Gribbin Head **30** 50 18N 4 41W
Gridley **160** 39 27N 121 47W
Griekwastad **128** 28 49S 23 15E
Griffin **157** 33 17N 84 14W
Griffith **141** 34 18S 146 2E
Griffith Mine **153** 50 47N 93 25W
Grigoryevka **84** 50 48N 58 18E
Grijalva, R. **164** 16 20N 92 20W
Grijpskerk **46** 53 16N 6 18E
Grillby **72** 59 38N 17 15E

Grim, C.	**133**	40 45 S	144 45 E
Grimaïlov	**80**	49 20 N	26 5 E
Grimari	**117**	5 43 N	20 0 E
Grimbergen	**47**	50 56 N	4 22 E
Grimeton	**73**	57 6 N	12 25 E
Griminish Pt.	**36**	57 40 N	7 30 W
Grimma	**48**	51 14 N	12 44 E
Grimmen	**48**	54 6 N	13 2 E
Grimsay I.	**36**	57 29 N	7 12 W
Grimsby	**33**	53 35 N	0 5 W
Grimsel Pass	**51**	46 34 N	8 23 E
Grimsey	**74**	66 33 N	18 0 W
Grimshaw	**152**	56 10 N	117 40 W
Grimstad	**71**	58 22 N	8 35 E
Grindelwald	**50**	46 38 N	8 2 E
Grindsted	**73**	55 46 N	8 55 E
Grindstone Island	**151**	47 25 N	62 0 W
Grindu	**70**	44 44 N	26 50 E
Grinduşul, Mt.	**70**	46 40 N	26 7 E
Griñón	**56**	40 13 N	3 51 W
Grinnell	**158**	41 45 N	92 43 W
Grip	**71**	63 16 N	7 37 E
Griqualand East	**129**	30 30 S	29 0 E
Griqualand West	**128**	28 40 S	23 30 E
Griquet	**151**	51 30 N	55 35 W
Grisolles	**44**	43 49 N	1 19 E
Grisons □	**49**	46 40 N	9 30 E
Grisslehamm	**72**	60 5 N	18 49 E
Grita, La	**174**	8 8 N	71 59 W
Gritley	**37**	58 56 N	2 45 W
Grivegnée	**47**	50 37 N	5 36 E
Griz Nez	**43**	50 50 N	1 35 E
Grizebeck	**32**	54 16 N	3 10 W
Grmeč Planina	**63**	44 43 N	16 16 E
Groais I.	**151**	50 55 N	55 35 W
Groblersdal	**129**	25 15 S	29 25 E
Grobming	**52**	47 27 N	13 54 E
Grocka	**66**	44 40 N	20 42 E
Grodek	**80**	52 46 N	23 38 E
Grodkow	**54**	50 43 N	17 40 E
Grodno	**80**	53 42 N	23 52 E
Grodzisk Mazowiecki	**54**	52 7 N	20 37 E
Grodzisk Wlkp.	**54**	52 15 N	16 22 E
Grodzyanka	**80**	53 31 N	28 42 E
Groenlo	**46**	52 2 N	6 37 E
Groesbeck	**159**	31 32 N	96 34 W
Groesbeek	**46**	51 47 N	5 58 E
Groix	**42**	47 38 N	3 29 W
Groix, I. de	**42**	47 38 N	3 28 W
Grójec	**54**	51 50 N	20 58 E
Grolloo	**46**	52 56 N	6 41 E
Gronau	**48**	52 13 N	7 2 E
Grong	**74**	64 25 N	12 8 E
Groningen	**46**	53 15 N	6 35 E
Groningen □	**46**	53 16 N	6 40 E
Groninger Wad	**46**	53 27 N	6 30 E
Grönskåra	**73**	57 5 N	15 43 E
Gronsveld	**47**	50 49 N	5 44 E
Groom	**159**	35 12 N	100 59 W
Groomsport	**38**	54 41 N	5 37 W
Groot Berg, R.	**128**	32 50 S	18 20 E
Groot-Brakrivier	**128**	34 2 S	22 18 E
Groot Karoo	**128**	32 35 S	23 0 E
Groot Namakwaland = Namaland	**128**	26 0 S	18 0 E
Groot, R.	**128**	33 10 S	23 35 E
Groote Eylandt	**138**	14 0 S	136 50 E
Grootebroek	**46**	52 41 N	5 13 E
Grootfontein	**128**	19 31 S	18 6 E
Grootlaagte, R.	**128**	21 10 S	21 20 E
Gros C.	**152**	61 59 N	113 32 W
Grosa, Punta	**59**	39 6 N	1 36 E
Grósio	**62**	46 18 N	10 17 E
Grosne, R.	**45**	46 30 N	4 40 E
Gross Glockner	**52**	47 5 N	12 40 E
Gross Ottersleben	**48**	52 5 N	11 33 E
Grossa, Pta.	**170**	1 20 N	50 0 W
Grossenbrode	**48**	54 21 N	11 4 E
Grossenhain	**48**	51 17 N	13 32 E
Grosseto	**62**	42 45 N	11 7 E
Grossgerungs	**52**	48 34 N	14 57 E
Grosswater B.	**151**	54 20 N	57 40 W
Grote Gette, R.	**47**	50 51 N	5 6 E
Grote Nete, R.	**47**	51 8 N	4 34 E
Groton, U.S.A.	**162**	41 22 N	72 12 W
Groton, U.S.A.	**162**	42 36 N	76 22 W
Grottaglie	**65**	40 32 N	17 25 E
Grottaminarda	**65**	41 5 N	15 4 E
Grouard Mission	**152**	55 33 N	116 9 W
Grouin, Pointe du	**42**	48 43 N	1 51 W
Groundhog, R.	**150**	48 45 N	82 20 W
Grouse Creek	**160**	41 51 N	113 57 W
Grouw	**46**	53 5 N	5 51 E
Groveland	**163**	37 50 N	120 14 W
Grovelsjön	**72**	62 6 N	12 16 E
Grover City	**163**	35 7 N	120 37 W
Groveton	**159**	31 5 N	95 4 W
Groznjan	**63**	45 22 N	13 43 E
Groznyy	**83**	43 20 N	45 45 E
Grubbenvorst	**47**	51 25 N	6 9 E
Grubišno Polje	**66**	45 44 N	17 12 E
Grudusk	**54**	53 3 N	20 38 E
Grudziadz	**54**	53 30 N	18 47 E
Gruinard B.	**36**	57 56 N	5 35 W
Gruissan	**44**	43 8 N	3 7 E
Grumo Áppula	**65**	41 2 N	16 43 E
Grums	**72**	59 22 N	13 5 E
Grünau	**125**	27 45 S	18 26 E
Grünberg	**48**	50 37 N	8 55 E
Grundy Center	**158**	42 22 N	92 45 W
Grungedal	**71**	59 44 N	7 43 E
Gruting Voe	**36**	60 12 N	1 32 W
Gruver	**159**	36 19 N	101 20 W
Gruyères	**50**	46 35 N	7 4 E
Gruza	**66**	43 54 N	20 46 E
Gryazi	**81**	52 30 N	39 58 E
Gryazovets	**81**	58 50 N	40 20 E
Grybów	**54**	49 36 N	20 55 E
Grycksbo	**72**	60 40 N	15 29 E
Gryfice	**54**	53 55 N	15 13 E
Gryfino	**54**	53 16 N	14 29 E
Grytgöl	**73**	58 49 N	15 33 E
Grythyttan	**72**	59 41 N	14 32 E
Grytviken	**13**	53 50 S	37 10 W
Gstaad	**50**	46 28 N	7 18 E
Gua	**99**	22 18 N	85 20 E
Gua Musang	**101**	4 53 N	101 58 E
Guacanayabo, Golfo de	**166**	20 40 N	77 20 W
Guacara	**174**	10 14 N	67 53 W
Guachipas	**172**	25 40 S	65 30 W
Guachiria, R.	**174**	5 30 N	71 30 W
Guadajoz, R.	**57**	37 50 N	4 51 W
Guadalajara, Mexico	**164**	20 40 N	103 20 W
Guadalajara, Spain	**58**	40 37 N	3 12 W
Guadalajara □	**58**	40 47 N	3 0 W
Guadalcanal	**57**	38 5 N	5 52 W
Guadalcanal, I.	**130**	9 32 S	160 12 E
Guadalén, R.	**59**	38 30 N	3 7 W
Guadales	**172**	34 30 S	67 55 W
Guadalete, R.	**57**	36 45 N	5 47 W
Guadalhorce, R.	**57**	36 50 N	4 42 W
Guadalimar, R.	**59**	38 10 N	2 53 W
Guadalmena, R.	**59**	38 31 N	2 50 W
Guadalmez, R.	**57**	38 33 N	4 42 W
Guadalope, R.	**58**	41 0 N	0 13 W
Guadalquivir, R.	**57**	38 0 N	4 0 W
Guadalupe, Brazil	**170**	6 44 S	43 47 W
Guadalupe, Spain	**57**	39 27 N	5 17 W
Guadalupe, U.S.A.	**163**	34 59 N	120 33 W
Guadalupe Bravos	**164**	31 20 N	106 10 W
Guadalupe de los Reyes	**164**	25 23 N	104 15 W
Guadalupe I.	**131**	29 0 N	118 50 W
Guadalupe Pk.	**161**	31 50 N	105 30 W
Guadalupe, R.	**159**	29 25 N	97 30 W
Guadalupe, Sierra de	**55**	39 28 N	5 30 W
Guadalupe y Calvo	**164**	26 6 N	106 58 W
Guadarrama, Sierra de	**56**	41 0 N	4 0 W
Guadeloupe, I.	**167**	16 20 N	61 40 W
Guadeloupe Passage	**167**	16 50 N	68 15 W
Guadiamar, R.	**57**	37 9 N	6 20 W
Guadiana Menor, R.	**59**	37 45 N	3 7 W
Guadiana, R.	**57**	37 45 N	7 35 W
Guadiaro, R.	**57**	36 39 N	5 17 W
Guadiato, R.	**57**	37 55 N	4 53 W
Guadiela, R.	**58**	40 30 N	2 23 W
Guadix	**59**	37 18 N	3 11 W
Guafo, Boca del	**176**	43 35 S	74 0 W
Guaina	**174**	5 9 N	63 36 W
Guainía □	**174**	2 30 N	69 00 W
Guaíra	**173**	24 5 S	54 10 W
Guaira, La	**174**	10 36 N	66 56 W
Guaitecas, Islas	**176**	44 0 S	74 30 W
Guajará-Mirim	**174**	10 50 S	65 20 W
Guajira, La □	**174**	11 30 N	72 30 W
Guajira, Pen. de la	**167**	12 0 N	72 0 W
Gualan	**166**	15 8 N	89 22 W
Gualdo Tadino	**63**	43 14 N	12 46 E
Gualeguay	**172**	33 10 S	59 20 W
Gualeguaychú	**172**	33 3 S	58 31 W
Guam I.	**130**	13 27 N	144 45 E
Guamá	**170**	1 37 S	47 29 W
Guama	**174**	10 16 N	68 49 W
Guamá, R.	**170**	1 29 S	48 30 W
Guamareyes	**174**	0 30 S	73 0 W
Guaminí	**172**	37 1 S	62 28 W
Guampí, Sierra de	**174**	6 0 N	65 35 W
Guamuchil	**164**	25 25 N	108 3 W
Guanabacoa	**166**	23 8 N	82 18 W
Guanabara □	**173**	23 0 S	43 25 W
Guanacaste	**166**	10 40 N	85 30 W
Guanacaste, Cordillera del	**166**	10 40 N	85 4 W
Guanacevío	**164**	25 40 N	106 0 W
Guanajay	**166**	22 56 N	82 42 W
Guanajuato	**164**	21 0 N	101 20 W
Guanajuato □	**164**	20 40 N	101 20 W
Guanambi	**171**	14 13 S	42 47 W
Guanare	**174**	8 42 N	69 12 W
Guanare, R.	**174**	8 50 N	68 50 W
Guandacol	**172**	29 30 S	68 40 W
Guane	**166**	22 10 N	84 0 W
Guanhães	**171**	18 47 S	42 57 W
Guanica	**147**	17 58 N	66 55 W
Guanipa, R.	**174**	9 20 N	63 30 W
Guanta	**174**	10 14 N	64 36 W
Guantánamo	**167**	20 10 N	75 20 W
Guapí	**174**	2 36 N	77 54 W
Guápiles	**166**	10 10 N	83 46 W
Guaporé	**173**	12 0 S	64 0 W
Guaporé, R.	**174**	13 0 S	63 0 W
Guaqui	**174**	16 41 S	68 54 W
Guara, Sierra de	**58**	42 19 N	0 15 W
Guarabira	**170**	6 51 S	35 29 W
Guarapari	**173**	20 40 S	40 30 W
Guarapuava	**171**	25 20 S	51 30 W
Guaratinguetá	**173**	22 49 S	45 9 W
Guaratuba	**173**	25 53 S	48 38 W
Guard Bridge	**35**	56 21 N	2 52 W
Guarda	**56**	40 32 N	7 20 W
Guarda □	**56**	40 40 N	7 20 W
Guardafui, C. = Asir, Ras	**91**	11 55 N	51 10 E
Guardamar del Segura	**59**	38 5 N	0 39 W
Guardavalle	**65**	38 31 N	16 30 E
Guardia, La	**56**	41 56 N	8 52 W
Guardiagrele	**63**	42 11 N	14 11 E
Guardo	**56**	42 47 N	4 50 W
Guareña	**57**	38 51 N	6 6 W
Guareña, R.	**56**	41 25 N	5 25 W
Guaria □	**172**	25 45 N	56 30 W
Guárico □	**174**	8 40 N	66 35 W
Guarujá	**173**	24 2 S	46 25 W
Guarus	**173**	21 30 S	41 20 W
Guasave	**164**	25 34 N	108 27 W
Guasdualito	**174**	7 15 N	70 44 W
Guasipati	**174**	7 28 N	61 54 W
Guasopa	**135**	9 12 S	152 56 E
Guastalla	**62**	44 55 N	10 40 E
Guatemala	**166**	14 40 N	90 30 W
Guatemala ■	**166**	15 40 N	90 30 W
Guatire	**174**	10 28 N	66 32 W
Guaviare, R.	**174**	3 30 N	71 0 W
Guaxupé	**173**	21 10 S	47 5 W
Guayabal	**174**	4 43 N	71 37 W
Guayama	**147**	17 59 N	66 7 W
Guayaquil	**174**	2 15 S	79 52 W
Guayaquil, Golfo de	**174**	3 10 S	81 0 W
Guaymallen	**172**	32 50 S	68 45 W
Guaymas	**164**	27 50 N	111 0 W
Guba, Ethiopia	**123**	4 52 N	39 18 E
Guba, Zaïre	**127**	10 38 S	26 27 E
Gubakha	**84**	58 52 N	57 36 E
Gubam	**135**	8 39 S	141 53 E
Gúbbio	**63**	43 20 N	12 34 E
Gubio	**121**	12 30 N	12 42 E
Gubkin	**81**	51 17 N	37 32 E
Guča	**66**	43 46 N	20 15 E
Guchil	**101**	5 35 N	102 10 E
Gudalur	**97**	11 30 N	76 29 E
Gudata	**83**	43 7 N	40 32 E
Gudbrandsdal	**75**	61 33 N	10 0 E
Guddu Barrage	**93**	28 30 N	69 50 E
Gudenå	**73**	56 27 N	9 40 E
Gudermes	**83**	43 24 N	46 20 E
Gudhjem	**73**	55 12 N	14 58 E
Gudiña, La	**56**	42 4 N	7 8 W
Gudivada	**96**	16 30 N	81 15 E
Gudiyatam	**97**	12 57 N	78 55 E
Gudmundra	**72**	62 56 N	17 47 E
Gudrun, gasfield	**19**	58 50 N	1 48 E
Gudur	**97**	14 12 N	79 55 E
Guebwiller	**43**	47 55 N	7 12 E
Guecho	**58**	43 21 N	2 59 W
Guéckédou	**120**	8 40 N	10 5 W
Guelma	**119**	36 25 N	7 29 E
Guelph	**150**	43 35 N	80 20 W
Guelt es Stel	**118**	35 12 N	3 1 E
Guelttara	**118**	29 23 N	2 10 W
Guemar	**119**	33 30 N	6 57 E
Guéméné-Penfao	**42**	47 38 N	1 50 W
Guéméné-sur-Scorff	**42**	48 4 N	3 13 W
Güemes	**172**	24 50 S	65 0 W
Guéné	**121**	11 44 N	3 16 E
Guer	**42**	47 54 N	2 8 W
Guérande	**42**	47 20 N	2 26 W
Guerche, La	**42**	47 57 N	1 16 W
Guerche-sur-l'Aubois, La	**43**	46 58 N	2 56 E
Guercif	**118**	34 14 N	3 21 W
Guéréda	**124**	14 31 N	22 5 E
Guéret	**44**	46 11 N	1 51 E
Guérigny	**43**	47 6 N	3 10 E
Guernica	**58**	43 19 N	2 40 W
Guernsey	**158**	42 19 N	104 45 W
Guernsey I.	**42**	49 30 N	2 35 W
Guerrara, Oasis, Alg.	**119**	32 51 N	4 35 E
Guerrara, Saoura, Alg.	**118**	28 5 N	0 8 W
Guerrero □	**165**	17 30 N	100 0 W
Guerzim	**118**	29 45 N	1 47 W
Güeşti	**70**	44 48 N	25 19 E
Guestling Green	**29**	50 53 N	0 40 E
Gueugnon	**45**	45 36 N	4 3 E
Gueydan	**159**	30 3 N	92 30 W
Guezendi = Ghesendor	**119**	21 14 N	18 14 E
Guglia, P. dal	**51**	46 28 N	9 45 E
Guglionesi	**63**	51 55 N	14 54 E
Guhra	**93**	27 36 N	56 8 E
Guia Lopes da Laguna	**173**	21 26 S	56 7 W
Guiana Highlands	**174**	5 0 N	60 0 W
Guibes	**128**	26 41 S	16 49 E
Guider	**121**	9 55 N	13 59 E
Guidimouni	**121**	13 42 N	9 31 E
Guiglo	**120**	6 45 N	7 30 W
Guija	**125**	34 35 S	33 15 E
Guijo de Coria	**56**	40 6 N	6 28 W
Guildford	**29**	51 14 N	0 34 W
Guilford, Conn., U.S.A.	**162**	41 15 N	72 40 W
Guilford, Me., U.S.A.	**151**	45 12 N	69 25 W
Guillaumes	**45**	44 5 N	6 52 E
Guillestre	**45**	44 39 N	6 40 E
Guilsfield	**31**	52 42 N	3 9 W
Guilvinec	**42**	47 48 N	4 17 W
Guimarães, Braz.	**170**	2 9 S	44 35 W
Guimarães, Port.	**56**	41 28 N	8 24 W
Guimaras I.	**103**	10 35 N	122 37 E
Guinea ■	**120**	10 20 N	10 0 W
Guinea Bissau ■	**120**	12 0 N	15 0 W
Guinea, Gulf of	**121**	3 0 N	2 30 E
Guinea, Port. = Guinea Bissau	**120**	12 0 N	15 0 W
Güines	**166**	22 50 N	82 0 W
Guingamp	**42**	48 34 N	3 10 W
Guipavas	**42**	48 26 N	4 29 W
Guipúzcoa □	**58**	43 12 N	2 15 W
Guir, O.	**118**	39 29 N	2 58 W
Guirgo	**121**	11 48 N	1 21 W
Güiria	**174**	10 32 N	62 18 W
Guisborough	**33**	54 32 N	1 2 W
Guiscard	**43**	49 40 N	3 0 E
Guise	**43**	49 52 N	3 35 E
Guitiriz	**56**	43 11 N	7 50 W
Guivan	**103**	11 5 N	125 55 E
Gujan-Mestras	**44**	44 38 N	1 4 W
Gujar Khan	**84**	33 15 N	73 21 E
Gujarat □	**94**	23 20 N	71 0 E
Gujranwala	**94**	32 10 N	74 12 E
Gujrat	**94**	32 40 N	74 2 E
Gukhothae	**101**	17 2 N	99 50 E
Gukovo	**83**	48 1 N	39 58 E
Gulak	**121**	10 50 N	13 30 E
Gulargambone	**141**	31 20 S	148 30 E
Gulbahar	**93**	35 5 N	69 10 E
Gulbarga	**96**	17 20 N	76 50 E
Gulbene	**80**	57 8 N	26 52 E
Gulcha	**85**	40 19 N	73 26 E
Guldborg Sd.	**73**	54 39 N	11 50 E
Guledgud	**97**	16 3 N	75 48 E
Gulf Basin	**136**	15 20 S	129 0 E
Gulfport	**159**	30 28 N	89 3 W
Gulgong	**141**	32 20 S	149 30 E
Gulistan, Pak.	**94**	30 36 N	66 35 E
Gulistan, U.S.S.R.	**85**	40 29 N	68 46 E
Gulkana	**147**	62 15 N	145 48 W
Gull Lake	**153**	50 10 N	108 29 W
Gullane	**35**	56 2 N	2 50 W
Gullegem	**47**	50 51 N	3 13 E
Gullringen	**73**	57 48 N	15 44 E
Güllük	**69**	37 12 N	27 36 E
Gulma	**121**	12 40 N	4 23 E
Gulmarg	**95**	34 3 N	74 25 E
Gulnam	**123**	6 55 N	29 30 E
Gulnare	**140**	33 27 S	138 27 E
Gulpaigan	**92**	33 26 N	50 20 E
Gulpen	**47**	50 49 N	5 53 E
Gülpinar	**68**	39 32 N	26 10 E
Gulshad	**76**	46 45 N	74 25 E
Gulsvik	**71**	60 24 N	9 38 E
Gulu	**126**	2 48 N	32 17 E
Gulwe	**126**	6 30 S	36 25 E
Gulyaypole	**82**	47 45 N	36 21 E
Gum Lake	**140**	32 42 S	143 9 E
Gumal, R.	**94**	32 5 N	70 5 E
Gumbaz	**94**	30 2 N	69 0 E
Gumel	**121**	12 39 N	9 22 E
Gumiel de Hizán	**58**	41 46 N	3 41 W
Gumlu	**138**	19 53 S	147 41 E
Gumma-ken □	**111**	36 30 N	138 20 E
Gummersbach	**48**	51 2 N	7 32 E
Gummi	**121**	12 4 N	5 9 E
Gümüşane	**92**	40 30 N	39 30 E
Gümüşhaciköy	**82**	40 50 N	35 18 E
Gumzai	**103**	5 28 S	134 42 E
Guna	**94**	24 40 N	77 19 E
Guna Mt.	**123**	11 50 N	37 40 E
Gundagai	**141**	35 3 S	148 6 E
Gundih	**103**	7 10 S	110 56 E
Gundlakamma, R.	**97**	15 30 N	80 15 E
Gunebang	**141**	33 5 S	146 38 E
Gungal	**141**	32 17 S	150 32 E
Gungi	**123**	10 20 N	38 3 E
Gungu	**124**	5 43 S	19 20 E
Gunisao L.	**153**	53 33 N	96 15 W
Gunisao, R.	**153**	53 56 N	97 53 W
Gunnedah	**141**	30 59 S	150 15 E
Gunniguldrie	**141**	33 12 S	146 8 E
Gunningbar Cr.	**141**	31 14 S	147 6 E
Gunnison, Colo., U.S.A.	**161**	38 32 N	106 56 W
Gunnison, Utah, U.S.A.	**160**	39 11 N	111 48 W
Gunnison, R.	**161**	38 50 N	108 30 W
Gunnworth	**153**	51 20 N	108 9 W
Guntakal	**97**	15 11 N	77 27 E
Guntersville	**157**	34 18 N	86 16 W
Guntong	**101**	4 36 N	101 3 E
Guntur	**96**	16 23 N	80 30 E
Gunungapi	**103**	6 45 S	126 30 E
Gunungsitoli	**102**	1 15 N	97 30 E
Gunungsugih	**102**	4 58 S	105 7 E
Gunupur	**96**	19 5 N	83 50 E
Gunworth	**153**	51 20 N	108 10 W
Gunza	**124**	10 50 S	13 50 E
Gunzenhausen	**49**	49 6 N	10 45 E
Gupis	**95**	36 15 N	73 20 E
Gura	**94**	25 12 N	71 39 E
Gura Humorului	**70**	47 35 N	25 53 E
Gura Teghii	**70**	45 30 N	26 25 E
Gurage, mt.	**123**	8 20 N	38 20 E
Gurchan	**92**	34 55 N	49 25 E
Gurdaspur	**94**	32 5 N	75 25 E
Gurdon	**159**	33 55 N	93 10 W
Gurdzhaani	**83**	41 43 N	45 52 E
Gurgan	**93**	36 51 N	54 25 E
Gurgaon	**94**	28 33 N	77 10 E
Gurghiu, Munţii	**70**	46 41 N	25 15 E
Gurguéia, R.	**170**	6 50 S	43 24 W
Guria	**62**	44 30 N	9 0 E
Gurk, R.	**52**	46 48 N	14 20 E
Gurkha	**95**	28 5 N	84 40 E
Gurla Mandhata	**95**	30 30 N	81 10 E
Gurley	**139**	29 45 S	149 48 E
Gurnard's Head	**30**	50 12 N	5 37 W
Gurnet Pt.	**162**	42 1 N	70 34 W
Gurrumbah	**138**	17 30 S	144 55 E
Gurun	**101**	5 49 N	100 27 E
Gürün	**92**	38 41 N	37 22 E
Gurupá	**175**	1 20 S	51 45 W
Gurupá, I. Grande de	**175**	1 0 S	51 45 W
Gurupi	**171**	11 43 S	49 4 W
Gurupi, R.	**170**	3 20 S	47 20 W
Gurupi, Serra do	**170**	5 0 S	47 30 W
Guryev	**83**	47 5 N	52 0 E
Gus	**126**	3 2 N	36 57 E

Gus-Khrsutalnyy Han Chiang, R

Gus-Khrsutalnyy 81 55 42N 40 35 E
Gusau 121 12 18N 6 31 E
Gusev 80 54 35N 22 20 E
Gushiago 121 9 55N 0 15W
Gusinje 66 42 35N 19 50 E
Gúspini 64 39 32N 8 38 E
Gusselby 72 59 38N 15 14 E
Güssing 53 47 3N 16 20 E
Gustanj 63 46 36N 14 49 E
Gustavus 147 58 25N 135 58W
Gustine 163 37 21N 121 0W
Güstrow 48 53 47N 12 12 E
Gusum 73 58 16N 16 30 E
Gŭtaia 70 45 26N 21 30 E
Gütersloh 48 51 54N 8 25 E
Gutha 137 28 58 S 115 55 E
Guthalungra 138 19 52 S 147 50 E
Guthrie 159 35 55N 97 30W
Guttannen 51 46 38N 8 18 E
Guttenberg 158 42 46N 91 10W
Guyana ■ 174 5 0N 59 0W
Guyenne 44 44 30N 0 40 E
Guyman 159 36 45N 101 30W
Guyra 139 30 15 S 151 40 E
Guzar 85 38 36N 66 15 E
Guzmán, Laguna de 164 31 25N 107 25W
Gwa 98 17 30N 94 40 E
Gwaai 127 19 15 S 27 45 E
Gwabegar 141 30 31 S 149 0 E
Gwadabawa 121 13 20N 5 15 E
Gwādar 93 25 10N 62 18 E
Gwagwada 121 10 15N 7 15 E
Gwalchmai 31 53 16N 4 23W
Gwalia 137 28 54 S 121 20 E
Gwalior 94 26 12N 78 10 E
Gwanara 121 18 55N 3 10 E
Gwanda 127 20 55 S 29 0 E
Gwandu 121 12 30N 4 41 E
Gwane 126 4 45N 25 48 E
Gwaram 121 11 15N 9 51 E
Gwarzo 121 12 20N 8 55 E
Gwasero 121 9 30N 8 30 E
Gwaun-Cae-Gurwen 31 51 46N 3 51W
Gweebarra B. 38 54 52N 8 21W
Gweedore 38 55 4N 8 15W
Gweek 30 50 6N 5 12W
Gwelo 125 19 28 S 29 45 E
Gwennap 30 50 12N 5 9W
Gwent □ 31 51 45N 2 55W
Gweta 128 20 12 S 25 17 E
Gwi 121 9 0N 7 10 E
Gwinn 156 46 15N 87 29W
Gwio Kura 121 12 40N 11 2 E
Gwolu 120 10 58N 1 59W
Gwoza 121 11 12N 13 40 E
Gwyddelwern 31 53 2N 3 23W
Gwydir, R. 139 29 27 S 149 48 E
Gwynedd □ 31 53 0N 4 0W
Gya La 95 28 45N 84 45 E
Gyangtse 99 28 50N 89 33 E
Gydanskiy P-ov. 76 70 0N 78 0 E
Gyland 71 58 24N 6 45 E
Gympie 139 26 11 S 152 38 E
Gyobingauk 98 18 13N 95 39 E
Gyoda 111 36 10N 139 30 E
Gyoma 53 46 56N 20 58 E
Gyöngyös 53 47 48N 20 15 E
Györ 53 47 41N 17 40 E
Györ-Sopron □ 53 47 40N 17 20 E
Gypsum Palace 140 32 37 S 144 9 E
Gypsum Pt. 152 61 53N 114 35W
Gypsumville 153 51 45N 98 40W
Gyttorp 72 59 31N 14 58 E
Gyula 53 46 38N 21 17 E
Gzhatsk = Gagarin 80 55 30N 35 0 E

H

Ha Coi 100 21 26N 107 46 E
Ha Dong 100 20 58N 105 46 E
Ha Giang 100 22 50N 104 59 E
Ha Nam = Phu-Ly 100 20 35N 105 50 E
Ha Tien 101 10 23N 104 29 E
Ha Tinh 100 18 20N 105 54 E
Ha Trung 100 20 0N 105 50 E
Haa, The 36 60 20N 1 0 E
Haacht 47 50 59N 4 37 E
Haag 49 48 11N 12 12 E
Haaksbergen 46 52 9N 6 45 E
Haaltert 47 50 55N 4 1 E
Haamstede 47 51 42N 3 45 E
Haapamäki 74 62 18N 24 28 E
Haapsalu 80 58 56N 23 30 E
Haarby 73 55 13N 10 8 E
Haarlem 46 52 23N 4 39 E
Haast 143 43 51 S 169 1 E
Haast P. 143 44 6 S 169 21 E
Haast, R. 143 43 50 S 169 2 E
Haastrecht 46 52 0N 4 47 E
Hab Nadi Chauki 94 25 0N 66 50 E
Hab, R. 93 25 15N 67 8 E
Haba 92 27 10N 47 0 E
Habana, La 166 23 8N 82 22W
Habaswein 126 1 2N 39 30 E
Habay 152 58 50N 118 44W
Habay-la-Neuve 47 49 44N 5 38 E
Habiganj 98 24 24N 91 30 E
Hablingbo 73 57 12N 18 16 E
Habo 73 57 55N 14 6 E
Haccourt 47 50 44N 5 40 E
Hachenburg 48 50 40N 7 49 E
Hachijō-Jima 111 33 5N 139 45 E
Hachinohe 112 40 30N 141 29 E
Hachiōji 111 35 30N 139 30 E
Hachŏn 107 40 29N 129 2 E
Hachy 47 49 42N 5 41 E
Hacketstown 39 52 52N 6 35W
Hackett 152 52 9N 112 28W
Hackettstown 162 40 51N 74 50W
Hackney 29 51 33N 0 2W
Hackthorpe 32 54 37N 2 42W
Hadali 94 32 16N 72 11 E
Hadarba, Ras 122 22 4N 36 51 E
Hadd, Ras al 93 22 35N 59 50 E
Haddenham 29 51 46N 0 56W
Haddington 35 55 57N 2 48W
Haddon Rig 141 31 27 S 147 52 E
Hadeija 121 12 30N 10 5 E
Hadeija, R. 121 12 20N 9 30W
Haden 139 27 13 S 151 54 E
Hadera 90 32 27N 34 55 E
Haderslev 73 55 15N 9 30 E
Hadhra 122 20 10N 41 5 E
Hadhramaut = Hadramawt 91 15 30N 49 30 E
Hadibu 91 12 35N 54 2 E
Hadjeb el Aïoun 119 35 21N 9 32 E
Hadleigh 29 52 3N 0 58 E
Hadley 28 52 42N 2 28W
Hadlow 29 51 12N 0 20 E
Hadong 107 35 5N 127 44 E
Hadramawt 91 15 30N 49 30 E
Hadrians Wall 35 55 0N 2 30W
Hadsten 73 56 19N 10 3 E
Hadsund 73 56 44N 10 8 E
Haeju 107 38 3N 125 45 E
Haenam 107 34 34N 126 15 E
Haerhpin 107 45 45N 126 45 E
Hafar al Batin 92 28 25N 46 50 E
Hafizabad 94 32 5N 73 40 E
Haflong 98 25 10N 93 5 E
Hafnarfjörður 74 64 4N 21 57W
Haft-Gel 92 31 30N 49 32 E
Hafun 91 10 25N 51 16 E
Hafun, Ras 91 10 29N 51 20 E
Hagalil 90 32 53N 35 18 E
Hagar Banga 117 10 40N 22 45 E
Hagari, R. 97 14 0N 76 45 E
Hagemeister I. 147 58 42N 161 0W
Hagen 48 51 21N 7 29 E
Hagenow 48 53 25N 11 10 E
Hagerman 159 33 5N 104 22W
Hagerstown 156 39 39N 77 46W
Hagetmau 44 43 39N 0 37W
Hagfors 72 60 3N 13 45 E
Häggenås 72 63 24N 14 55 E
Hagi, Iceland 74 65 28N 23 25W
Hagi, Japan 110 34 30N 131 30 E
Hagion Evstratios 68 39 30N 25 0 E
Hagion Óros 68 40 37N 24 6 E
Hags Hd. 39 52 57N 9 30W
Hague, C. de la 42 49 44N 1 56W
Hague, The = s'-Gravenhage 47 52 7N 4 17 E
Haguenau 43 48 49N 7 47 E
Hai □ 126 3 10 S 37 10 E
Hai Duong 100 20 56N 106 19 E
Haian, Kiangsu, China 109 32 37N 120 33 E
Haian, Kwangtung, China 109 20 18N 110 11 E
Haich'eng, Fukien, China 109 24 24N 117 51 E
Haich'eng, Liaoning, China 107 40 52N 122 45 E
Haichou 107 34 34N 119 6 E
Haichou Wan 107 35 0N 119 30 E
Haidar Khel 94 33 58N 68 38 E
Haifa 90 32 46N 35 0 E
Haifeng 109 22 59N 115 21 E
Haig 137 30 55 S 126 10 E
Haiger 48 50 44N 8 12 E
Haik'ang 109 20 56N 110 4 E
Haik'ou 100 20 5N 110 20 E
Hā'il 92 27 28N 42 2 E
Hailaerh 105 49 12N 119 42 E
Hailakandi 98 24 42N 92 34 E
Hailey 160 43 30N 114 15W
Haileybury 150 47 30N 79 38W
Hailin 107 44 32N 129 24 E
Hailing Tao 109 21 37N 111 65 E
Hailsham 29 50 52N 0 17 E
Hailun 105 47 27N 126 56 E
Hailung 107 42 30N 125 40 E
Hailuoto 74 65 3N 24 45 E
Haimen, Chekiang, China 109 28 39N 121 25 E
Haimen, Kwangtung, China 109 23 15N 116 35 E
Hainan 100 19 0N 110 0 E
Hainan Str. = Ch'iungcho Haihsia 100 20 10N 110 15 E
Hainaut □ 47 50 30N 4 0 E
Hainburg 53 48 9N 16 56 E
Haines, Alaska, U.S.A. 147 59 20N 135 36W
Haines, Oreg., U.S.A. 160 44 51N 117 59W
Haines City 157 28 6N 81 35W
Haines Junction 147 60 45N 137 30W
Hainfeld 52 48 3N 15 48 E
Haining 109 30 23N 120 30 E
Hainton 33 53 21N 0 13W
Haiphong 100 20 47N 106 35 E
Hait'an Tao 109 25 35N 119 45 E
Haiti ■ 167 19 0N 72 30W
Haiya Junc. 122 18 20N 36 40 E
Haiyang 107 36 45N 121 15 E
Haiyen 109 30 28N 120 57 E
Haiyüan, Kwangsi-Chuang, China 108 22 6N 107 25 E
Haiyüan, Ningsia Hui, China 106 36 32N 105 40 E
Haja 103 3 19 S 129 37 E
Hajdú-Bihar □ 53 47 30N 21 30 E
Hajdúböszörmény 53 47 40N 21 30 E
Hajdúdurog 53 47 48N 21 30 E
Hajdúhadház 53 47 40N 21 40 E
Hajdúnánás 53 47 50N 21 26 E
Hajdúsámson 53 47 37N 21 42 E
Hajdúszobaszló 53 47 27N 21 22 E
Haji Langar 93 35 50N 79 20 E
Hajiganj 98 23 15N 90 50 E
Hajipur 95 25 45N 85 20 E
Hajr 93 24 0N 56 34 E
Haka 98 22 39N 93 37 E
Hakansson, Mts. 127 8 40 S 25 45 E
Hakantorp 73 58 18N 12 55 E
Håkantorp 73 58 18N 12 55 E
Hakataramea 143 44 30 S 170 30 E
Hakataramea, R. 143 44 35 S 170 40 E
Hakken-Zan 111 34 10N 135 54 E
Hakodate 112 41 45N 140 44 E
Hakota 111 36 5N 140 30 E
Haku-San 111 36 9N 136 46 E
Hakun 98 26 46N 95 42 E
Hala 93 25 43N 68 20 E
Hala Hu 105 38 15N 97 40 E
Halab = Aleppo 92 36 10N 37 15 E
Halabjah 92 35 10N 45 58 E
Halaib 122 22 5N 36 30 E
Halanzy 47 49 33N 5 44 E
Halawa 147 21 9N 156 47W
Halbe 122 19 40N 42 15 E
Halberstadt 48 51 53N 11 2 E
Halberton 30 50 55N 3 24W
Halcombe 142 40 8 S 175 30 E
Halcyon, Mt. 103 13 0N 121 30 E
Halden 72 59 7N 11 23 E
Haldensleben 48 52 17N 11 30 E
Haldia 99 22 5N 88 3 E
Haldwani 95 29 25N 79 30 E
Hale 32 53 24N 2 21W
Hale, R. 138 24 56 S 135 53 E
Haleakala Crater 147 20 43N 156 12W
Halen 47 50 57N 5 6 E
Halesowen 28 52 27N 2 2W
Halesworth 29 52 21N 1 30 E
Haleyville 157 34 15N 87 40W
Half Assini 120 5 1N 2 50W
Halfmoon B. 143 46 50 S 168 5 E
Halfway 160 44 56N 117 8W
Halfway, R. 152 56 12N 121 32W
Halhul 90 31 35N 35 7 E
Hali 122 18 40N 41 15 E
Haliburton 150 45 3N 78 30W
Halibut, oilfield 19 61 20N 1 36 E
Halifax, Austral. 138 18 32 S 146 22 E
Halifax, Can. 151 44 38N 63 35W
Halifax, U.K. 32 53 43N 1 51W
Halifax, U.S.A. 162 40 25N 76 55W
Halifax B. 138 18 50 S 147 0 E
Halifax I. 128 26 38 S 15 4 E
Halil, R. 93 27 40N 58 30 E
Halkirk 37 58 30N 3 30W
Hall 52 47 17N 11 30 E
Hall Land 12 81 20N 60 0W
Hall Pt. 136 15 40 S 124 23 E
Hallabro 73 56 22N 15 5 E
Halland 73 56 55N 12 50 E
Hallands län □ 73 56 50N 12 50 E
Hallands Väderö 73 56 27N 12 34 E
Hallandsås 73 56 22N 13 0 E
Halle, Belg. 47 50 44N 4 13W
Halle, Nordrhein-Westfalen, Ger. 48 52 4N 8 20 E
Halle, Sachsen-Anhalt, Ger. 48 51 29N 12 0 E
Halle □ 48 51 28N 11 58 E
Hällefors 72 59 47N 14 31 E
Hallein 52 47 40N 13 5 E
Hällekis 73 58 38N 13 27 E
Hallett 140 33 25 S 138 55 E
Hallettsville 159 29 28N 96 57W
Hallevadsholm 73 58 37N 11 33 E
Hällevadsholm 73 58 35N 11 33 E
Halley Bay 13 75 31 S 26 36W
Hallia, R. 96 16 55N 79 10 E
Halliday 158 47 20N 102 25W
Halliday L. 153 61 21N 108 56W
Hallim 107 33 24N 126 15 E
Hallingdal, R. 75 60 34N 9 12 E
Hallingskeid 71 60 40N 7 17 E
Hällnäs 74 64 19N 19 36 E
Hallock 153 48 47N 97 57W
Hallow 28 52 14N 2 15W
Hall's Creek 136 18 16 S 127 46 E
Hallsberg 72 59 5N 15 7 E
Hallstahammar 72 59 38N 16 15 E
Hallstatt 52 47 33N 13 38 E
Hallstavik 72 60 5N 18 37 E
Hallstead 162 41 56N 75 45W
Hallwiler See 50 47 16N 8 12 E
Hallworthy 30 50 38N 4 34W
Halmahera, I. 103 0 40N 128 0 E
Halmeu 70 47 57N 23 2 E
Halmstad 73 56 41N 12 52 E
Halq el Oued 119 36 53N 10 10 E
Hals 73 56 59N 10 18 E
Halsa 71 63 3N 8 14 E
Halsafjorden 71 63 5N 8 10 E
Hälsingborg = Helsingborg 73 56 3N 12 42 E
Halstad 158 47 21N 96 41W
Halstead 29 51 59N 0 39 E
Haltdalen 71 62 56N 11 8 E
Haltern 48 51 44N 7 10 E
Haltwhistle 35 54 58N 2 27W
Ham 128 49 44N 3 3 E
Ham Tan 101 10 40N 107 45 E
Ham Yen 100 22 4N 105 3 E
Hamã 92 35 5N 36 40 E
Hamab 128 28 7 S 19 16 E
Hamad 123 15 20N 33 32 E
Hamada 110 34 50N 132 10 E
Hamadān 92 34 52N 48 32 E
Hamadān □ 92 35 0N 49 0 E
Hamadh 122 24 55N 39 3 E
Hamadia 118 35 28N 1 57 E
Hamakita 111 34 45N 137 47 E
Hamale 120 10 56N 2 45W
Hamamatsu 111 34 45N 137 45 E
Hamar 71 60 48N 11 7 E
Hamar Koke 123 51 5N 36 45 E
Hamarøy 74 68 5N 15 38 E
Hamâta, Gebel 122 24 17N 35 0 E
Hambantota 93 6 10N 81 10 E
Hamber Prov. Park 152 52 20N 118 0W
Hambledon 28 50 56N 1 6W
Hambleton Hills 33 54 17N 1 12W
Hamburg, Ger. 48 53 32N 9 59 E
Hamburg, Ark., U.S.A. 159 33 15N 91 47W
Hamburg, Iowa, U.S.A. 158 40 37N 95 38W
Hamburg, Pa., U.S.A. 162 40 33N 76 0W
Hamburg □ 48 53 30N 10 0 E
Hamden 162 41 21N 72 56W
Hame 75 61 30N 24 0 E
Hämeen Lääni 75 61 24N 24 10 E
Hämeenlinna 75 61 0N 24 28 E
Hamelin Pool 137 26 22 S 114 20 E
Hamelin Pool Bay 137 26 10 S 114 5 E
Hameln 48 52 7N 9 24 E
Hamersley 136 22 20 S 117 37 E
Hamersley Ra. 136 22 0 S 117 45 E
Hamhung 107 40 0N 127 30 E
Hami 105 42 47N 93 32 E
Hamilton, Austral. 140 37 45 S 142 2 E
Hamilton, Can. 150 43 20N 79 50W
Hamilton, N.Z. 142 37 47 S 175 19 E
Hamilton, U.K. 35 55 47N 4 2W
Hamilton, Alas., U.S.A. 147 62 55N 164 0W
Hamilton, Mont., U.S.A. 160 46 20N 114 6W
Hamilton, N.Y., U.S.A. 162 42 49N 75 31W
Hamilton, Ohio, U.S.A. 156 39 20N 84 35W
Hamilton, Tex., U.S.A. 159 31 40N 98 5W
Hamilton Downs 106 21 25 S 142 23 E
Hamilton, gasfield 19 56 54N 2 13 E
Hamilton Hotel 138 22 45 S 140 40 E
Hamilton Inlet 151 54 0N 57 30W
Hamilton Mt. 162 43 25N 74 22W
Hamilton, R., Queens., Austral. 138 23 30 S 139 47 E
Hamilton, R., S. Austral., Austral. 136 26 40 S 134 20 E
Hamiota 153 50 11N 100 38W
Hamlet 157 34 56N 79 40W
Hamley Bridge 140 34 17 S 138 35 E
Hamlin 159 32 58N 100 8W
Hamm 48 51 40N 7 58 E
Hammam bou Hadjar 118 35 23N 0 58W
Hammamet 119 36 24N 10 38 E
Hammamet, G. de 119 36 10N 10 48 E
Hammarö, I. 72 59 20N 13 30 E
Hammarstrand 72 63 7N 16 20 E
Hamme 47 51 6N 4 8 E
Hamme-Mille 47 50 47N 4 43 E
Hammel 73 56 16N 9 52 E
Hammelburg 49 50 7N 9 54 E
Hammenton 156 39 40N 74 47W
Hammeren 73 55 18N 14 47 E
Hammerfest 74 70 39N 23 41 E
Hammersmith 29 51 30N 0 15W
Hammond, Ind., U.S.A. 156 41 40N 87 30W
Hammond, La., U.S.A. 159 30 32N 90 30W
Hammonton 162 39 38N 74 48W
Hamnavoe 36 60 25N 1 5W
Hamneda 73 56 41N 13 51 E
Hamoir 47 50 25N 5 32 E
Hamont 47 51 15N 5 32 E
Hampden 143 45 18 S 170 50 E
Hampshire □ 28 51 3N 1 20W
Hampshire Downs 28 51 10N 1 10W
Hampton, Ark., U.S.A. 159 33 35N 92 29W
Hampton, Iowa, U.S.A. 158 42 42N 93 12W
Hampton, N.H., U.S.A. 162 42 56N 70 48W
Hampton, S.C., U.S.A. 157 32 52N 81 2W
Hampton, Va., U.S.A. 162 37 4N 76 18W
Hampton Bays 162 40 53N 72 31W
Hampton Harbour 136 20 30 S 116 30 E
Hampton in Arden 28 52 26N 1 42W
Hampton Tableland 137 32 0N 127 0 E
Hamra 92 24 2N 38 55 E
Hamrange 72 60 59N 17 5 E
Hamrat esh Sheykh 123 14 45N 27 55 E
Hamre 71 60 33N 5 20 E
Hamun Helmand 93 31 15N 61 15 E
Hamun-i-Lora, Pak. 93 29 38N 64 58 E
Hamun-i-Lora, Pak. 93 29 38N 64 58 E
Hamun-i-Mashkel 93 28 30N 63 0 E
Hamyang 107 35 32N 127 42 E
Han Chiang, R., Hupeh, China 109 30 35N 114 15 E

Han Chiang, R Hawzen

Han Chiang, R., Kwangtung, China 109 23 30N 116 48 E
Hana 147 20 45N 155 59W
Hanak 122 25 32N 37 0 E
Hanamaki 112 39 23N 141 7 E
Hanang □ 126 4 10 S 35 40 E
Hanang, mt. 126 4 30 S 35 25 E
Hanau 49 50 8N 8 56 E
Hanbogd 106 43 11N 107 10 E
Hanch'eng 106 35 30N 110 30 E
Hanchiang 109 25 29N 119 5 E
Hanch'uan 109 30 39N 113 46 E
Hanchuang 107 34 36N 117 22 E
Hanchung 106 33 10N 107 2 E
Hancock, Mich., U.S.A. 158 47 10N 88 35W
Hancock, Minn., U.S.A. 158 45 26N 95 46W
Hancock, Pa., U.S.A. 162 41 57N 75 19W
Handa, Japan 111 34 53N 137 0 E
Handa, Somalia 91 10 37N 51 2 E
Handa I. 36 58 23N 5 10W
Handen 72 59 12N 18 12 E
Handeni 124 5 25 S 38 2 E
Handeni □ 126 5 30 S 38 0 E
Handlová 155 48 45N 18 35 E
Handub 122 19 15N 37 25 E
Handwara 95 34 21N 74 20 E
Handzame 47 51 2N 3 0 E
Hanegev 90 30 50N 35 0 E
Haney 152 49 12N 122 40W
Hanford 163 36 25N 119 39W
Hang Chat 100 18 20N 99 21 E
Hang Dong 100 18 41N 98 55 E
Hangang, R. 107 37 50N 126 30 E
Hangayn Nuruu 105 47 30N 100 0 E
Hangchinch'i 106 39 54N 108 56 E
Hangchinhouch'i 106 41 55N 107 15 E
Hangchou 109 30 15N 120 8 E
Hangchou Wan 109 30 30N 121 30 E
Hanger 73 57 6N 13 58 E
Hangklip, K. 128 34 26 S 18 48 E
Hangö (Hanko) 75 59 59N 22 57 E
Hanhongor 106 43 55N 104 28 E
Hanish J. 91 13 45N 42 46 E
Hanita 90 33 5N 35 10 E
Hankinson 158 46 9N 96 58W
Hanko = Hangö 75 59 59N 22 57 E
Hank'ou 109 30 40N 114 18 E
Hankow = Hank'ou 109 30 40N 114 18 E
Hanksville 161 38 19N 110 45W
Hanku 107 39 16N 117 50 E
Hanle 95 32 42N 79 4 E
Hanmer 143 42 32 S 172 50 E
Hann, Mt. 136 16 0 S 126 0 E
Hann, R. 136 17 26 S 126 17 E
Hanna 152 51 40N 111 54W
Hannaford 158 47 23N 98 18W
Hannah 158 48 58N 98 42W
Hannah B. 150 51 40N 80 0W
Hannahs Bridge 141 31 55 S 149 41 E
Hannibal, Mo., U.S.A. 158 39 42N 91 22W
Hannibal, N.Y., U.S.A. 162 43 19N 76 35W
Hannik 122 18 12N 32 20 E
Hanningfield Water 29 51 40N 0 30 E
Hannover 48 52 23N 9 43 E
Hannut 47 50 40N 5 4 E
Hanö 73 56 0N 14 50 E
Hanö, I. 73 56 2N 14 50 E
Hanöbukten 73 55 35N 14 30 E
Hanoi 100 21 5N 105 55 E
Hanover, S. Afr. 128 31 4 S 24 29 E
Hanover, N.H., U.S.A. 162 43 43N 72 17W
Hanover, Pa., U.S.A. 162 39 46N 76 59W
Hanover, Va., U.S.A. 162 37 46N 77 22W
Hanover = Hannover 48 52 23N 9 43 E
Hanover, I. 176 51 0 S 74 50W
Hanpan, C. 135 5 0 S 154 35 E
Hans Meyer Ra. 135 4 20 S 152 55 E
Hansholm 73 57 8N 8 38 E
Hanshou 109 28 55N 111 58 E
Hansi 94 29 10N 75 57 E
Hansjö 72 61 10N 14 40 E
Hanson, L. 140 31 0 S 136 15 E
Hanson Range 136 27 0 S 136 30 E
Hansted 73 57 8N 8 36 E
Hantan 105 36 42N 114 30 E
Hante 47 50 19N 4 11 E
Hanton 106 36 42N 114 30 E
Hanwood 141 34 26 S 146 3 E
Hanyang 109 30 35N 114 0 E
Hanyin 108 32 53N 108 37 E
Hanyū 111 36 10N 139 32 E
Hanyüan 108 29 21N 102 43 E
Haoch'ing 108 26 34N 100 12 E
Haokang 105 47 25N 132 8 E
Haopi 106 35 57N 114 13 E
Haparanda 74 65 52N 24 8 E
Hapert 47 51 22N 5 15 E
Happy 159 34 47N 101 50W
Happy Camp 160 41 52N 123 30W
Happy Valley 151 53 15N 60 20W
Hapsu 107 41 13N 128 51 E
Hapur 94 28 45N 77 45 E
Haql 92 29 10N 35 0 E
Har 103 5 16 S 133 14 E
Har-Ayrag 106 45 47N 109 16 E
Har Tuv 90 31 46N 35 0 E
Har Us Nuur 105 48 0N 92 10 E
Har Yehuda 90 31 35N 34 57 E
Harad 92 24 15N 49 0 E
Haradera 91 4 33N 47 38 E
Haradh 92 24 15N 49 0 E
Haramsøya 71 62 39N 6 12 E
Haran 92 36 48N 39 0 E
Harat 123 16 5N 39 26 E
Haraze 117 14 20N 19 12 E
Haraze-Mangueigne 117 7 22N 17 3 E
Harbin = Haerhpin 107 45 45N 126 45 E
Harboør 73 56 38N 8 10 E
Harbor Beach 156 43 50N 82 38W
Harbor Springs 156 45 28N 85 0W
Harbour Breton 151 47 29N 55 50W
Harbour Deep 151 50 25N 56 30W
Harbour Grace 151 47 40N 53 22W
Harburg 48 53 27N 9 58 E
Hårby 73 55 13N 10 7 E
Harcourt 138 24 17 S 149 55 E
Harda 94 22 27N 77 5 E
Hardangerfjorden. 71 60 15N 6 0 E
Hardangerjøkulen 71 60 30N 7 0 E
Hardangervidda 71 60 20N 7 20 E
Hardap Dam 128 24 32 S 17 50 E
Hardegarijp 46 53 13N 5 57 E
Harden 141 34 32 S 148 24 E
Hardenberg 46 52 34N 6 37 E
Harderwijk 46 52 21N 5 38 E
Hardey, R. 136 22 45 S 116 8 E
Hardin 160 45 50N 107 35W
Harding 129 30 22 S 29 55 E
Harding Ra. 136 16 17 S 124 55 E
Hardisty 152 52 40N 111 18W
Hardman 160 45 12N 119 49W
Hardoi 95 27 26N 80 15 E
Hardwar 94 29 58N 78 16 E
Hardy 159 36 20N 91 30W
Hardy, Pen. 176 55 30 S 68 20W
Hare B. 151 51 15N 55 45W
Hare Gilboa 90 32 31N 35 25 E
Hare Meron 90 32 59N 35 24 E
Harelbeke 47 50 52N 3 20 E
Haren, Ger. 48 52 47N 7 18 E
Haren, Neth. 46 53 11N 6 36 E
Harer 123 9 20N 42 8 E
Harer □ 123 7 12N 42 0 E
Hareto 123 9 23N 37 6 E
Harfleur 42 49 30N 0 10 E
Hargeisa 91 9 30N 44 2 E
Hargshamn 72 60 12N 18 30 E
Hari, R., Afghan. 93 34 20N 64 30 E
Hari, R., Indon. 102 1 10 S 101 50 E
Haricha, Hamada el 118 22 40N 3 15W
Harihar 97 14 32N 75 44 E
Harim, J. al 60 26 0N 56 10 E
Harima-Nada 110 34 30N 134 35 E
Haringey 29 51 35N 0 7W
Haringhata, R. 98 22 0N 89 58 E
Haringvliet 46 51 48N 4 10 E
Haripad 97 9 14N 76 28 E
Harirūd 93 35 0N 61 0 E
Harkat 122 20 25N 39 40 E
Harlan, Iowa, U.S.A. 158 41 37N 95 20W
Harlan, Tenn., U.S.A. 157 36 58N 83 20W
Harlech 31 52 52N 4 7W
Harlem 160 48 29N 108 39W
Harleston 29 52 25N 1 18 E
Harlingen, Neth. 46 53 11N 5 25 E
Harlingen, U.S.A. 159 26 30N 97 50W
Harlow 29 51 47N 0 9 E
Harlowton 160 46 30N 109 54W
Harmånger 72 61 55N 17 20 E
Harmil 123 16 30N 40 10 E
Harney Basin 160 43 30N 119 0W
Harney L. 160 43 0N 119 0W
Harney Pk. 158 43 52N 103 33W
Härnön 72 62 36N 18 0 E
Harnösand 72 62 38N 18 5 E
Haro 58 42 35N 2 55W
Haro, C. 164 27 50N 110 55W
Haroldswick 36 60 48N 0 50W
Håroy 73 55 13N 10 8 E
Harp L. 151 55 5N 61 50W
Harpe, La 158 40 30N 91 0W
Harpenden 29 51 48N 0 20W
Harpenhalli 97 14 47N 76 2 E
Harper 120 4 25N 7 43 E
Harper Mt. 147 64 15N 143 57W
Harplinge 73 56 45N 12 45 E
Harport L. 36 57 20N 6 20W
Harput 92 38 48N 39 15 E
Harrand 94 29 28N 70 3 E
Harrat al Kishb 92 22 30N 40 15 E
Harrat al Umuirid 92 26 50N 38 0 E
Harrat Khaibar 122 25 45N 40 0 E
Harrat Nawāsif 122 21 30N 42 0 E
Harray, L. of 37 59 0N 3 15W
Harricana, R. 150 50 30N 79 10W
Harrietsham 29 51 15N 0 41 E
Harriman 157 36 0N 84 35W
Harrington, U.K. 32 54 37N 3 55W
Harrington, U.S.A. 162 38 56N 75 35W
Harrington Harbour 151 50 31N 59 30W
Harris 36 57 50N 6 55W
Harris L. 136 31 10 S 135 10 E
Harris Mts. 143 44 49 S 168 49 E
Harris, Sd. of 36 57 44N 7 6W
Harrisburg, Ill., U.S.A. 159 37 42N 88 30W
Harrisburg, Nebr., U.S.A. 158 41 36N 103 46W
Harrisburg, Oreg., U.S.A. 160 44 25N 123 10W
Harrisburg, Pa., U.S.A. 162 40 18N 76 52W
Harrismith 129 28 15 S 29 8 E
Harrison, Ark., U.S.A. 159 36 10N 93 4W
Harrison, Idaho, U.S.A. 160 47 30N 116 51W
Harrison, Nebr., U.S.A. 158 42 42N 103 52W
Harrison B. 147 70 25N 151 0W
Harrison, C. 151 55 0N 58 0W
Harrison L. 152 49 33N 121 50W
Harrisonburg 156 38 28N 78 52W
Harrisonville 158 38 45N 93 45W
Harriston 150 43 57N 80 53W
Harrisville 150 44 40N 83 19W
Harrogate 33 53 59N 1 32W
Harrow 29 51 35N 0 15W
Harry, L. 139 29 23 S 138 19 E
Harsefeld 48 53 26N 9 31 E
Harskamp 46 52 8N 5 46 E
Harstad 74 68 48N 16 30 E
Hart 156 43 42N 86 21W
Hart, L. 140 31 10 S 136 25 E
Hartbees, R. 128 29 8 S 20 48 E
Hartberg 52 47 17N 15 58 E
Harteigen, Mt. 71 60 11N 7 5 E
Hartest 29 52 7N 0 41 E
Hartford, Conn., U.S.A. 162 41 47N 72 41W
Hartford, Ky., U.S.A. 156 37 26N 86 50W
Hartford, S.D., U.S.A. 158 43 40N 96 58W
Hartford, Wis., U.S.A. 158 43 18N 88 25W
Hartford City 156 40 22N 85 20W
Harthill 35 55 52N 3 45W
Hartland, Can. 151 46 20N 67 32W
Hartland, U.K. 30 50 59N 4 29W
Hartland Pt. 30 51 2N 4 32W
Hartlebury 28 52 20N 2 13W
Hartlepool 33 54 42N 1 11W
Hartley, Zimb. 127 18 10 S 30 7 E
Hartley, U.K. 35 55 5N 1 27W
Hartley Bay 152 53 25N 129 15W
Hartmannberge 128 17 0 S 13 0 E
Hartney 153 49 30N 100 35W
Hartpury 28 51 55N 2 18W
Hartselle 157 34 25N 86 55W
Hartshorne 159 34 51N 95 30W
Hartsville 157 34 23N 80 2W
Hartwell 157 34 21N 82 52W
Harunabad 94 29 35N 73 2 E
Harur 97 12 3N 78 29 E
Harvard, Mt. 161 39 0N 106 5W
Harvey, Austral. 137 33 5 S 115 54 E
Harvey, Ill., U.S.A. 156 41 40N 87 50W
Harvey, N.D., U.S.A. 158 47 50N 99 58W
Harwell 28 51 40N 1 17W
Harwich 29 51 56N 1 18 E
Harwood 33 53 54N 1 30W
Haryana □ 94 29 0N 76 10 E
Harz 48 51 40N 10 40 E
Harzé 47 50 27N 5 40 E
Harzgerode 48 51 38N 11 8 E
Hasa 92 26 0N 49 0 E
Hasaheisa 123 14 25N 33 20 E
Hasani 122 25 0N 37 8 E
Hasanpur 94 28 51N 78 9 E
Haselünne 48 52 40N 7 30 E
Hasharon 90 32 12N 34 49 E
Hashefela 90 31 30N 34 43 E
Hashima 111 35 20N 136 40 E
Hashimoto 111 34 19N 135 37 E
Hasjö 72 63 2N 16 20 E
Håsjö 72 63 1N 16 5 E
Haskell, Kans., U.S.A. 159 35 51N 95 40W
Haskell, Tex., U.S.A. 159 33 10N 99 45W
Haskier Is. 36 57 42N 7 40W
Haslach 49 48 16N 8 7 E
Hasle 73 55 11N 14 44 E
Haslemere 29 51 5N 0 41W
Haslev 73 55 18N 11 57 E
Haslingden 32 53 43N 2 20W
Hasparren 44 43 24N 1 18W
Hassan 92 13 0N 76 5 E
Hasselt, Belg. 47 50 56N 5 21 E
Hasselt, Neth. 46 52 36N 6 6 E
Hassene, Ad. 118 21 0N 4 0 E
Hassfurt 49 50 2N 10 30 E
Hassi Berrekrem 119 33 45N 5 16 E
Hassi Daoula 119 33 4N 5 38 E
Hassi el Biod 119 28 30N 6 0 E
Hassi el Heïda 74 29 34N 0 14W
Hassi Inifel 118 29 50N 3 41 E
Hassi Marroket 119 30 10N 3 0 E
Hassi Messaoud 119 31 43N 6 8 E
Hassi Taguenza 172 29 8N 0 23W
Hassi Zerzour 118 30 51N 3 56W
Hässleby 73 57 37N 15 30 E
Hässleholmen 73 56 9N 13 45 E
Hastière-Lavaux 47 50 13N 4 49 E
Hastigrow 37 58 32N 3 15W
Hastings, Austral. 141 38 18 S 145 12 E
Hastings, N.Z. 142 39 39 S 176 52 E
Hastings, U.K. 29 50 51N 0 36 E
Hastings, Mich., U.S.A. 156 42 40N 82 20W
Hastings, Minn., U.S.A. 158 44 41N 92 51W
Hastings, Nebr., U.S.A. 158 40 34N 98 22W
Hastings Ra. 141 31 15 S 152 14 E
Hästveda 73 56 17N 13 55 E
Hat Nhao 101 14 46N 106 32 E
Hat Yai 101 7 1N 100 27 E
Hatanbulag 106 43 8N 109 14 E
Hatano 111 35 22N 139 14 E
Hatch 161 32 45N 107 8W
Hatches Creek 138 20 56 S 135 12 E
Hatchet L. 153 58 36N 103 40W
Haţeg 70 45 36N 22 55 E
Haţeg, Mţii 70 45 25N 23 0 E
Hatert 46 51 49N 5 50 E
Hatfield 29 51 46N 0 11W
Hatfield Broad Oak 29 51 48N 0 16 E
Hatfield Post Office 140 33 54 S 143 49 E
Hatgal 105 50 26N 100 9 E
Hatherleigh 30 50 49N 4 4W
Hathersage 33 53 20N 1 39W
Hathras 94 27 36N 78 6 E
Hatia 99 22 30N 91 5 E
Hato de Corozal 174 6 11N 71 45W
Hato Mayor 167 18 46N 69 15W
Hattah 140 34 48 S 142 17 E
Hattem 46 52 28N 6 4 E
Hatteras, C. 157 35 10N 75 30W
Hattiesburg 159 31 20N 89 20W
Hatton, Can. 153 50 2N 109 50W
Hatton, U.K. 37 57 24N 1 57W
Hatvan 53 47 40N 19 45 E
Hau Bon (Cheo Reo) 100 13 25N 108 28 E
Hau Duc 100 15 20N 108 13 E
Hauchinango 164 20 12N 97 45W
Haug 71 60 23N 10 26 E
Haugastøl 71 60 30N 7 50 E
Haugesund 71 59 23N 5 13 E
Haugh of Urr 35 55 0N 3 51W
Haughangaroa Ra. 142 38 42 S 175 40 E
Haughley 29 52 13N 0 59 E
Haukelisæter 71 59 51N 7 9 E
Haulerwijk 46 53 4N 6 20 E
Haultain, R. 153 55 51N 106 46W
Haungpa 98 25 29N 96 7 E
Haura 91 13 50N 47 35 E
Hauraki Gulf 142 36 35 S 175 5 E
Hausruck 52 48 6N 13 30 E
Haut Atlas 118 32 0N 7 0W
Haut-Rhin □ 43 48 0N 7 15 E
Haut Zaïre □ 126 2 20N 26 0 E
Hauta Oasis 92 23 40N 47 0 E
Hautah, Wahāt al 92 23 40N 47 0 E
Haute-Corse □ 45 42 30N 9 30 E
Haute-Garonne □ 44 43 28N 1 30 E
Haute-Loire □ 44 45 5N 3 50 E
Haute-Marne □ 43 48 10N 5 20 E
Haute-Saône □ 43 47 45N 6 10 E
Haute-Savoie □ 45 46 0N 6 20 E
Haute-Vienne □ 44 45 50N 1 10 E
Hauterive 151 49 10N 68 16W
Hautes-Alpes □ 45 44 42N 6 20 E
Hautes Fagnes 47 50 34N 6 6 E
Hautes-Pyrénées □ 44 43 0N 0 10 E
Hauteville-Lompnes 45 45 59N 5 35 E
Hautmont 43 50 15N 3 55 E
Hautrage 47 50 29N 3 46 E
Hauts-de-Seine □ 43 48 52N 2 15 E
Hauts Plateaux 118 34 14N 1 0 E
Hauxley 35 55 21N 1 35W
Havana 158 40 19N 90 3W
Havana = La Habana 166 23 8N 82 22W
Havant 29 50 51N 0 59W
Havasu, L. 161 34 18N 114 8W
Havdhem 73 57 10N 18 20 E
Havelange 47 50 23N 5 15 E
Havelian 94 34 2N 73 10 E
Havelock, N.B., Can. 151 46 2N 65 24W
Havelock, Ont., Can. 150 44 26N 77 53W
Havelock, N.Z. 143 41 17 S 173 48 E
Havelock I. 101 11 55N 93 2 E
Havelte 46 52 46N 6 14 E
Haverfordwest 31 51 48N 4 59W
Haverhill, U.K. 29 52 6N 0 27 E
Haverhill, U.S.A. 162 42 50N 71 2W
Haveri 97 14 53N 75 24 E
Haverigg 32 54 12N 3 16W
Havering 29 51 33N 0 20 E
Haverstraw 162 41 12N 73 58W
Håverud 73 58 50N 12 28 E
Havîrna 70 48 4N 26 43 E
Havlíčkuv Brod 52 49 36N 15 33 E
Havnby 73 55 5N 8 34 E
Havre 160 48 40N 109 34W
Havre-Aubert 151 47 12N 62 0W
Havre de Grace 162 39 33N 76 6W
Havre, Le 42 49 30N 0 5 E
Havre St. Pierre 151 50 18N 63 33W
Havza 92 41 0N 35 35 E
Haw, R. 157 37 43N 80 52W
Hawaii □ 147 20 30N 157 0W
Hawaii I. 147 20 0N 155 0W
Hawaiian Is. 147 20 30N 156 0W
Hawarden, Can. 153 51 25N 106 36W
Hawarden, U.K. 31 53 11N 3 2W
Hawarden, U.S.A. 158 43 2N 96 28W
Hawea Flat 143 44 40 S 169 19 E
Hawea Lake 143 44 28 S 169 19 E
Hawera 142 39 35 S 174 19 E
Hawes 32 54 18N 2 12W
Hawes Water, L. 32 54 32N 2 48W
Hawick 35 55 25N 2 48W
Hawk Junction 150 48 30N 84 38W
Hawkchurch 30 50 47N 2 56W
Hawkdun Ra. 143 44 53 S 170 5 E
Hawke B. 142 39 25 S 177 20 E
Hawker 28 31 59 S 138 22 E
Hawke's Bay □ 142 39 45 S 176 35 E
Hawke's Harbour 151 53 2N 55 50W
Hawkesbury 150 45 35N 74 40W
Hawkesbury I. 152 53 37N 129 3W
Hawkesbury Pt. 138 11 55 S 134 5 E
Hawkesbury River 133 33 50 S 151 44W
Hawkesbury Upton 28 51 34N 2 19W
Hawkhurst 29 51 2N 0 31 E
Hawkinsville 157 32 17N 83 30W
Hawkshead 32 54 23N 3 0W
Hawkwood 139 25 45 S 150 50 E
Hawley, Minn., U.S.A. 158 46 58N 96 20W
Hawley, Pa., U.S.A. 162 41 28N 75 11W
Haworth 32 53 50N 1 57W
Hawsker 33 54 27N 0 34W
Hawthorne 163 38 31N 118 37W
Hawzen 123 13 58N 39 28 E

Haxby Higashiōsaka

Haxby 33 54 1N 1 4W
Haxtun 158 40 40N 102 39W
Hay, Austral. 141 34 30S 144 51E
Hay, U.K. 31 52 4N 3 9W
Hay, C. 136 14 5S 129 29E
Hay L. 152 58 50N 118 50W
Hay Lakes 152 53 12N 113 2W
Hay, R., Austral. 138 24 10S 137 20E
Hay, R., Can. 152 60 0N 116 56W
Hay River 152 60 51N 115 44W
Hay Springs 158 42 40N 102 38W
Hayange 43 49 20N 6 2E
Hayato 110 31 40N 130 43E
Hayburn Wyke 33 54 22N 0 28W
Haycock 147 65 10N 161 20W
Hayden, Ariz., U.S.A. 161 33 2N 110 54W
Hayden, Wyo., U.S.A. 160 40 30N 107 22W
Haydenville 162 42 22N 72 42W
Haydon 138 18 0S 141 30E
Haydon Bridge 35 54 58N 2 15W
Haye Descartes, La 42 46 58N 0 42E
Haye-du-Puits, La 42 49 17N 1 33W
Hayes 158 44 22N 101 1W
Hayes Pen. 12 75 30N 65 0W
Hayes, R. 153 57 3N 92 12W
Hayle 30 50 12N 5 25W
Haymana 92 39 30N 32 35E
Haynesville 159 33 0N 93 7W
Hays, Can. 152 50 6N 111 48W
Hays, U.S.A. 158 38 55N 99 25W
Hayton 32 54 55N 2 45W
Hayward, Calif., U.S.A. 163 37 40N 122 5W
Hayward, Wis., U.S.A. 158 46 2N 91 30W
Hayward's Heath 29 51 0N 0 5W
Hazard 156 37 18N 83 10W
Hazaribagh 95 23 58N 85 26E
Hazaribagh Road 95 24 12N 85 57E
Hazebrouck 43 50 42N 2 31E
Hazelton, Can. 152 55 20N 127 42W
Hazelton, U.S.A. 158 46 30N 100 15W
Hazen 160 39 37N 119 2W
Hazerswoude 46 52 5N 4 36E
Hazlehurst 157 31 50N 82 35W
Hazleton 156 40 58N 76 0W
Hazlett, L. 136 21 30S 128 48E
Hazrat Imam 93 37 15N 68 50E
Heacham 29 52 55N 0 30E
Head of Bight 137 31 30S 131 25E
Headcorn 29 51 10N 0 39E
Headford 38 53 28N 9 6W
Headington 28 51 46N 1 13W
Headlands 127 18 15S 32 2E
Healdsburg 160 38 33N 122 51W
Healdton 159 34 16N 97 31W
Healesville 141 37 35S 145 30E
Heanor 33 53 1N 1 20W
Heard I. 11 53 0S 74 0E
Hearne 159 30 54N 96 35W
Hearne B. 153 60 10N 99 10W
Hearne L. 152 62 20N 113 10W
Hearst 150 49 40N 83 41W
Heart, R. 158 46 40N 101 30W
Heart's Content 151 47 54N 53 27W
Heath Mts. 143 45 39S 167 9E
Heath Pt. 151 49 8N 61 40W
Heath Steele 151 47 17N 66 5W
Heathcote 141 36 56S 144 45E
Heather, oilfield 19 60 55N 0 50E
Heathfield 29 50 58N 0 18E
Heathsville 162 37 55N 76 28W
Heavener 159 34 54N 94 36W
Hebbronville 159 27 20N 98 40W
Hebburn 35 54 59N 1 30W
Hebden Bridge 32 53 45N 2 0W
Hebel 139 28 58S 147 47E
Heber Springs 159 35 29N 91 39W
Hebgen, L. 160 44 50N 111 15W
Hebrides, U.K. 36 57 30N 7 0W
Hebrides, Inner Is., U.K. 36 57 20N 6 40W
Hebrides, Outer Is., U.K. 36 57 50N 7 25W
Hebron, Can. 149 58 12N 62 38W
Hebron, N.D., U.S.A. 158 46 56N 102 2W
Hebron, Nebr., U.S.A. 158 40 15N 97 33W
Hebron (Al Khalil) 90 31 32N 35 6E
Heby 72 59 56N 16 53E
Hecate Str. 152 53 10N 130 30W
Hechingen 49 48 20N 8 58E
Hechtel 47 51 8N 5 22E
Heckington 33 52 59N 0 17W
Hecla 158 45 56N 98 8W
Hecla I. 153 51 10N 96 43W
Hecla Mt. 36 57 18N 7 15W
Heddal 71 59 36N 9 20E
Heddon 35 55 0N 1 47W
Hédé 42 48 18N 1 49W
Hede 72 62 23N 13 30E
Hedemora 72 60 18N 15 58E
Hedgehope 143 46 12S 168 34E
Hedley 159 34 53N 100 39W
Hedmark □ 75 61 17N 11 40E
Hedmark fylke □ 71 61 17N 11 40E
Hednesford 28 52 43N 2 0W
Hedon 33 53 44N 0 11W
Hedrum 71 59 7N 10 5E
Heeg 46 52 58N 5 37E
Heegermeer 46 52 56N 5 32E
Heemskerk 46 52 31N 4 40E
Heemstede 46 52 22N 4 37E
Heer 47 50 50N 5 43E
Heerde 46 52 24N 6 2E
's Heerenburg 46 51 53N 6 16E
's Heerenloo 46 52 19N 5 36E
Heerenveen 46 52 57N 5 55E
Heerhugowaard 46 52 40N 4 51E
Heerlen 47 50 55N 6 0E
Heerlerheide 47 50 54N 5 58E
Heers 47 50 45N 5 18E
Heesch 46 51 44N 5 32E
Heestert 47 50 47N 3 25E
Heeze 47 51 23N 5 35E
Hegyalja, Mts. 53 48 25N 21 25E
Heich'engchen 106 36 16N 106 19E
Heide 48 54 10N 9 7E
Heide, oilfield 19 54 5N 9 5E
Heidelberg, Ger. 49 49 23N 8 41E
Heidelberg, C. Prov., S. Afr. 128 34 6S 20 59E
Heidelberg, Trans., S. Afr. 129 26 30S 28 23E
Heidenheim 49 48 40N 10 10E
Heigun-To 110 33 47N 132 14E
Heikant 47 51 15N 4 1E
Heilam 37 58 31N 4 40W
Heilbron 129 27 16S 27 59E
Heilbronn 49 49 8N 9 13E
Heiligenblut 52 47 2N 12 51E
Heiligenhafen 48 54 21N 10 58E
Heiligenstadt 48 51 22N 10 9E
Heilungkiang □ 46 48 0N 128 0E
Heim 71 63 26N 9 5E
Heimdal, gasfield 19 59 35N 2 15E
Heino 46 52 26N 6 14E
Heinola 75 61 13N 26 24E
Heinsburg 153 53 50N 110 30W
Heinsch 47 49 42N 5 44E
Heinsun 98 25 52N 95 35E
Heinze Is. 101 14 25N 97 45E
Heirnkut 98 25 14N 94 44E
Heishan 107 41 40N 122 3E
Heishui, Liaoning, China 107 42 6N 119 22E
Heishui, Szechwan, China 108 32 15N 103 0E
Heist 47 51 20N 3 15E
Heist-op-den-Berg 47 51 5N 4 44E
Heistad 71 59 35N 9 40E
Hejaz = Hijāz 92 26 0N 37 30E
Hekelegem 47 50 55N 4 7E
Hekimhan 92 38 50N 38 0E
Hekinan 111 34 52N 137 0E
Hekla 74 63 56N 19 35W
Hel 54 54 38N 18 50E
Helagsfjället 72 62 54N 12 25E
Helchteren 47 51 4N 5 22E
Helden 47 51 19N 6 0E
Helechosa 57 39 22N 4 53W
Helena, Ark., U.S.A. 159 34 30N 90 35W
Helena, Mont., U.S.A. 160 46 40N 112 0W
Helendale 163 34 45N 117 19W
Helensburgh, Austral. 141 34 11S 151 1E
Helensburgh, U.K. 34 56 0N 4 44W
Helensville 142 36 41S 174 29E
Helets 90 31 36N 34 39E
Helgasjön 73 57 0N 14 50E
Helgeland 74 66 20N 13 30E
Helgeroa 71 59 0N 9 45E
Helgoland, I. 48 54 10N 7 51E
Helgum 72 63 25N 16 50E
Heligoland = Helgoland 48 54 10N 7 51E
Heliopolis 122 30 6N 31 17E
Hell-Ville 129 13 25S 48 16E
Hellebæk 73 56 4N 12 32E
Helleland 71 58 33N 6 7E
Hellendoorn 46 52 24N 6 27E
Hellertown 162 40 35N 75 21W
Hellevoetsluis 46 51 50N 4 8E
Helli Ness 36 60 3N 1 10W
Hellick Kenyon Plateau 13 82 0S 110 0W
Hellifield 32 54 0N 2 13W
Hellin 59 38 31N 1 40W
Hellum 73 57 16N 10 10E
Helmand □ 93 31 20N 64 0E
Helmand, R. 94 34 0N 67 0E
Helmond 47 51 29N 5 41E
Helmsdale 37 58 7N 3 40W
Helmsley 33 54 15N 1 2W
Helmstedt 48 52 16N 11 0E
Helnæs 73 55 9N 10 0E
Helper 160 39 44N 110 56W
Helperby 33 54 8N 1 20W
Helsby 32 53 16N 2 47W
Helsingborg 73 56 3N 12 42E
Helsinge 73 56 2N 12 12E
Helsingfors = Helsinki 75 60 15N 25 3E
Helsingør 73 56 2N 12 35E
Helsinki (Helsingfors) 75 60 15N 25 3E
Helston 30 50 7N 5 17W
Helvick Hd. 39 52 3N 7 33W
Helvoirt 47 51 38N 5 14E
Helwân 122 29 50N 31 20E
Hem 71 59 26N 10 0E
Hemavati, R. 97 12 50N 67 0E
Hemel Hempstead 29 51 45N 0 28W
Hemet 163 33 45N 116 59W
Hemingford 158 42 21N 103 4W
Hemphill 159 31 21N 93 49W
Hempstead 159 30 5N 96 5W
Hempton 29 52 50N 0 49E
Hemse 73 57 15N 18 22E
Hemsö, I. 72 62 43N 18 5E
Hemsön 72 62 42N 18 5E
Hemsworth 33 53 37N 1 21W
Hemyock 30 50 55N 1 13W
Hen & Chicken Is. 142 35 58S 174 45E
Henares, R. 58 40 55N 3 0W
Hendaye 44 43 23N 1 47W
Henderson, Argent. 172 36 18S 61 43W
Henderson, U.K. 36 57 42N 5 47W
Henderson, Ky., U.S.A. 156 37 50N 87 38W
Henderson, Nev., U.S.A. 161 36 2N 115 0W
Henderson, Pa., U.S.A. 157 35 25N 88 40W
Henderson, Tex., U.S.A. 159 32 5N 94 49W
Hendersonville 157 35 21N 82 28W
Hendon 139 28 5S 151 50E
Hendorf 70 46 4N 24 5E
Henfield 29 50 56N 0 17W
Hengch'eng 106 38 26N 106 26E
Hengelo, Gelderland, Neth. 46 52 3N 6 19E
Hengelo, Overijssel, Neth. 46 52 16N 6 48E
Hengfeng 109 28 25N 117 35E
Henghsien 108 22 36N 109 16E
Hengoed 31 51 39N 3 14W
Hengshan, Hunan, China 109 27 15N 112 51E
Hengshan, Shansi, China 106 37 56N 108 53E
Hengshui 106 37 43N 115 42E
Hengtaohotze 107 44 55N 129 3E
Hengyang 109 26 51N 112 30E
Hengyanghsien 109 26 58N 112 21E
Hénin-Beaumont 43 50 25N 2 58E
Henley 29 51 32N 0 53W
Henley-in-Arden 28 52 18N 1 47W
Henllan 31 53 13N 3 29W
Henlopen, C. 162 38 48N 75 5W
Henlow 29 51 2N 0 18W
Hennan, L. 72 62 3N 15 55E
Henne 73 55 44N 8 11E
Hennebont 42 47 49N 3 19W
Hennenman 128 27 59S 27 1E
Hennessy 159 36 8N 97 53W
Hennigsdorf 48 52 38N 13 13E
Henribourg 153 53 25N 105 38W
Henrichemont 43 47 20N 2 21E
Henrietta 159 33 50N 98 15W
Henrietta Maria C. 150 55 9N 82 20W
Henry 158 41 5N 89 20W
Henryetta 159 35 2N 96 0W
Henstridge 28 50 59N 2 24W
Hentiyn Nuruu 105 48 30N 108 30E
Henty 141 35 30N 147 0E
Henzada 98 17 38N 95 35E
Heppner 160 45 27N 119 34W
Herad 71 58 8N 6 47E
Héraðsflói 74 65 42N 14 12W
Héraðsvötn 74 65 25N 19 5W
Herald Cays 138 16 58S 149 9E
Herât 93 34 20N 62 7E
Herât □ 93 35 0N 62 0E
Hérault □ 44 43 34N 3 15E
Hérault, R. 44 43 20N 3 32E
Herbert 153 50 30N 107 10W
Herbert Downs 138 23 7S 139 9E
Herbert I. 147 52 49N 170 10W
Herbert, R. 138 18 31S 146 17E
Herberton 138 17 28S 145 25E
Herbertstown 39 52 32N 8 29W
Herbiers, Les 42 46 52N 1 0W
Herbignac 42 47 27N 2 18W
Herborn 48 50 40N 8 19E
Herby 54 50 45N 18 50E
Hercegnovi 66 42 30N 18 33E
Herðubreið 74 65 11N 16 21W
Herdla 71 60 34N 4 56E
Hereford, U.K. 28 52 4N 2 42W
Hereford, U.S.A. 159 34 50N 102 28W
Hereford and Worcester □ 28 52 10N 2 30W
Herefordshire □ 26 52 15N 2 50W
Herefoss 71 58 32N 8 32E
Herekino 142 35 18S 173 11E
Herent 47 50 54N 4 40E
Herentals 47 51 12N 4 51E
Herenthout 47 51 8N 4 45E
Herfølge 73 55 26N 12 9E
Herford 48 52 7N 8 40E
Héricourt 43 47 32N 6 55E
Herington 158 38 43N 97 0W
Herisau 51 47 22N 9 17E
Hérisson 44 46 32N 2 42E
Herjehogna 75 61 43N 12 7E
Herk, R. 47 50 56N 5 12E
Herkenbosch 47 51 9N 6 4E
Herkimer 162 43 0N 74 59W
Herm I. 42 49 30N 2 28W
Herma Ness 36 60 50N 0 54W
Hermagor 52 46 38N 13 23E
Herman 158 45 51N 96 8W
Hermandez 163 36 24N 120 46W
Hermann 158 38 40N 91 25W
Hermannsburg 48 52 49N 10 6E
Hermannsburg Mission 136 23 57S 132 45E
Hermanus 128 34 27S 19 12E
Herment 44 45 45N 2 24E
Hermidale 141 31 30S 146 42E
Hermiston 160 45 50N 119 16W
Hermitage 143 43 44S 170 5E
Hermitage B. 151 47 33N 56 10W
Hermite, Is. 176 55 50S 68 0W
Hermon, Mt. = Sheikh, J. ash 92 33 20N 36 0E
Hermosillo 164 29 10N 111 0W
Hernad, R. 53 48 20N 21 15E
Hernandarias 173 25 20S 54 40W
Hernando, Argent. 172 32 28S 63 40W
Hernando, U.S.A. 159 34 50N 89 59W
Herndon 162 40 43N 76 51W
Herne, Belg. 47 50 44N 4 2E
Herne, Ger. 48 51 33N 7 12E
Herne Bay 29 51 22N 1 8E
Herne Hill 137 31 45S 116 5E
Herning 73 56 8N 8 58E
Heroica Nogales 164 31 14N 110 56W
Heron Bay 150 48 40N 85 25W
Heröy 71 62 18N 5 45E
Herreid 158 45 53N 100 5W
's Herrenbroek 46 52 32N 6 1E
Herrera 57 39 12N 4 50W
Herrera de Alcántar 57 39 39N 7 25W
Herrera de Pisuerga 56 42 35N 4 20W
Herrera del Duque 57 39 10N 5 3W
Herrero, Punta 165 19 17N 87 27W
Herrick 138 41 5S 147 55E
Herrin 159 37 50N 89 0W
Herrljunga 73 58 5N 13 1E
Hersbruck 49 49 30N 11 25E
Herschel I. 147 69 35N 139 5W
Herseaux 47 50 43N 3 15E
Herselt 47 51 3N 4 53E
Herserange 47 49 30N 5 48E
Hershey 162 40 17N 76 39W
Herstal 47 50 40N 5 38E
Herstmonceux 29 50 53N 0 21E
Hersvik 71 61 10N 4 53E
Hertford 29 51 47N 0 4W
Hertford □ 29 51 51N 0 5W
's Hertogenbosch 47 51 42N 5 18E
Hertzogville 128 28 9S 25 30E
Hervás 56 40 16N 5 52W
Herve 47 50 38N 5 48E
Hervey B. 133 25 0S 152 52E
• Hervey Is. 131 19 30S 159 0W
Hervey Junction 150 46 50N 72 29W
Herwijnen 46 51 50N 5 7E
Herzberg, Cottbus, Ger. 48 51 40N 13 13E
Herzberg, Niedersachsen, Ger. 48 51 38N 10 20E
Herzele 47 50 53N 3 53E
Herzliyya 90*32 10N 34 50E
Herzogenbuchsee 50 47 11N 7 42E
Herzogenburg 52 48 17N 15 41E
Hesdin 43 50 21N 2 0E
Hesel 48 53 18N 7 36E
Heskestad 71 58 28N 6 22E
Hesperange 47 49 35N 6 10E
Hesperia 163 34 25N 117 18W
Hesse = Hessen 48 50 57N 9 20E
Hessen □ 48 50 57N 9 20E
Hessle 33 53 44N 0 28E
Hetch Hetchy Aqueduct 163 37 36N 121 25W
Heteren 46 51 58N 5 46E
Hethersett 29 52 35N 1 10E
Hettinger 158 46 8N 102 38W
Hetton-le-Hole 35 54 49N 1 26W
Hettstedt 48 51 39N 11 30E
Heugem 47 50 49N 5 42E
Heule 47 50 51N 3 15E
Heusden, Belg. 47 51 2N 5 17E
Heusden, Neth. 46 51 44N 5 8E
Hève, C. de la 42 49 30N 0 5E
Heverlee 47 50 52N 4 42E
Heves □ 53 47 50N 20 0E
Hevron, N. 90 31 28N 34 52E
Hewett, C. 149 70 16N 67 45W
Hewett, gasfield 19 53 5N 1 50E
Hex River 128 33 30S 19 35E
Hexham 35 54 58N 2 7W
Heybridge 29 51 44N 0 42E
Heyfield 141 37 59S 146 47E
Heysham 32 54 5N 2 53W
Heytesbury 28 51 11N 2 7W
Heythuysen 47 51 15N 5 55E
Heywood, Austral. 140 38 8S 141 37E
Heywood, U.K. 32 53 36N 2 13W
Hi-no-Misaki 110 35 26N 132 38E
Hi Vista 163 34 44N 117 46W
Hiamen 109 31 52N 121 15E
Hiawatha, Kans., U.S.A. 158 39 55N 95 33W
Hiawatha, Utah, U.S.A. 160 39 37N 111 1W
Hibbing 158 47 30N 93 0W
Hibbs B. 138 42 35S 145 15E
Hibbs, Pt. 138 42 38S 145 15E
Hibernia Reef 136 12 0S 123 23E
Hibiki-Nada 110 34 0N 130 0E
Hickman 159 36 35N 89 8W
Hickory 157 35 46N 81 17W
Hicks Bay 142 37 34S 178 21E
Hicksville 162 40 46N 73 30W
Hida-Gawa 70 47 10N 23 9E
Hida-Gawa, R. 111 35 26N 137 3E
Hida-Sammyaku 111 36 30N 137 40E
Hida-Sanchi 111 36 10N 137 0E
Hidaka 110 35 30N 134 44E
Hidalgo □ 164 20 30N 99 10W
Hidalgo del Parral 164 26 58N 105 40W
Hidalgo, Presa M. 164 26 30N 108 35W
Hiddensee 48 54 30N 13 6E
Hidrolândia 171 17 0S 49 15W
Hieflau 52 47 36N 14 46E
Hiendelaencina 58 41 5N 3 0W
Hierro I. 116 27 57N 17 56E
Higashi-matsuyama 111 36 2N 139 25E
Higashiōsaka 111 34 40N 135 37E

*Renamed Manuae

Higasi-Suidō

Hong Kong ■

Higasi-Suidō 110 34 0N 129 30 E
Higgins 159 36 9N 100 1W
Higginsville 137 31 42S 121 38 E
Higgs I. L. 157 36 20N 78 30W
High Atlas = Haut Atlas 118 32 30N 5 0W
High Bentham 32 54 8N 2 31W
High Borrow Bri. 32 54 26N 2 43W
High Bridge 162 40 40N 74 54W
High Ercall 28 52 46N 2 37W
High Hesket 32 54 47N 2 49W
High I. 151 56 40N 61 10W
High Island 159 29 32N 94 22W
High Level 152 58 31N 117 8W
High Pike, mt. 32 54 43N 3 4W
High Point 157 35 57N 79 58W
High Prairie 152 55 30N 116 30W
High River 152 50 30N 113 50W
High Springs 157 29 50N 82 40W
High Tatra 53 49 30N 20 00 E
High Veld = Hoëveld 129 26 30S 30 0 E
High Willhays, hill 30 50 41N 3 59W
High Wycombe 29 51 37N 0 45W
Higham Ferrers 29 52 18N 0 36W
Highbank 138 47 34S 171 45 E
Highbridge 28 51 13N 2 59W
Highbury 138 16 25S 143 9 E
Highclere 28 51 20N 1 22W
Highland □ 36 57 30N 5 0W
Highland Pk. 156 42 10N 87 50W
Highland Springs 162 37 33N 77 20W
Highley 28 52 25N 2 23W
Highmore 158 44 35N 99 26W
Highrock L. 153 57 5N 105 32W
Hightae 35 55 5N 3 27W
Hightstown 162 40 16N 74 31W
Highworth 28 51 38N 1 42W
Higley 161 33 27N 111 46W
Higüay 167 18 37N 68 42W
Higüero, Pta. 147 18 22N 67 16W
Hiiumaa 80 58 50N 22 45 E
Híjar 58 41 10N 0 27W
Hijāz 91 26 0N 37 30 E
Hiji 110 33 22N 131 32 E
Hijken 46 52 54N 6 30 E
Hikari 110 33 58N 131 58 E
Hiketa 110 34 13N 134 24 E
Hiko 161 37 30N 115 13W
Hikone 111 35 15N 136 10 E
Hikurangi, East Court 142 37 55S 178 4 E
Hikurangi, Mt. 142 37 55S 178 4 E
Hilawng 98 21 23N 93 48 E
Hildburghhausen 49 50 24N 10 43 E
Hildesheim 48 52 9N 9 55 E
Hilgay 29 52 34N 0 23 E
Hill 150 45 40N 74 45W
Hill City, Idaho, U.S.A. 160 43 20N 115 2W
Hill City, Kans., U.S.A. 158 39 25N 99 51W
Hill City, Minn., U.S.A. 158 46 57N 93 35W
Hill City, S.D., U.S.A. 158 43 58N 103 35W
Hill End 141 38 1S 146 9 E
Hill Island L. 153 60 30N 109 50W
Hill, R. 137 30 23S 115 3 E
Hilla, Iraq 92 32 30N 44 27 E
Hilla, Si Arab. 92 23 35N 46 50 E
Hillared 73 57 37N 13 10 E
Hillegom 46 52 18N 4 35 E
Hillerød 73 55 56N 12 19 E
Hillerstorp 73 57 20N 13 52 E
Hilli 98 25 17N 89 1 E
Hillingdon 29 51 33N 0 29W
Hillman 156 45 5N 83 52W
Hillmond 153 53 26N 109 41W
Hillsboro, Kans., U.S.A. 158 38 28N 97 10W
Hillsboro, N. Mex., U.S.A. 161 33 0N 107 35W
Hillsboro, N. Mex., U.S.A. 161 33 0N 107 35W
Hillsboro, N.D., U.S.A. 158 47 23N 97 9W
Hillsboro, N.H., U.S.A. 156 43 8N 71 56W
Hillsboro, Oreg., U.S.A. 160 45 31N 123 0W
Hillsboro, Tex., U.S.A. 159 32 0N 97 10W
Hillsborough, U.K. 38 54 28N 6 6W
Hillsborough, W. Indies 167 12 28N 61 28W
Hillsdale, Mich., U.S.A. 156 41 55N 84 40W
Hillsdale, N.Y., U.S.A. 162 42 11N 73 30W
Hillside 136 21 45S 119 23 E
Hillsport 150 49 27N 85 34W
Hillston 141 33 30S 145 31 E
Hillswick 36 60 29N 1 28W
Hilltown 38 54 12N 6 8W
Hilo 147 19 44N 155 5W
Hilonghilong, mt. 103 9 10N 125 45 E
Hilpsford Pt. 32 54 4N 3 12W
Hilvarenbeek 47 51 29N 5 8 E
Hilversum 46 52 14N 5 10 E
Himachal Pradesh □ 94 31 30N 77 0 E
Himalaya 99 29 0N 84 0 E
Himara 68 40 8N 19 43 E
Himatnagar 93 23 37N 72 57 E
Hime-Jima 110 33 43N 131 40 E
Himeji 110 34 50N 134 40 E
Himi 111 36 50N 137 0 E
Himmerland 73 56 45N 9 30 E
Hims = Homs 92 34 40N 36 45 E
Hinako, Kepulauan 102 0 50N 97 20 E
Hinche 167 19 9N 72 1W
Hinchinbrook I. 138 18 20S 146 15 E
Hinckley, U.K. 28 52 33N 1 21W
Hinckley, U.S.A. 160 39 18N 112 41W
Hindås 73 57 42N 12 27 E
Hindaun 94 26 44N 77 5 E
Hinde Rapids (Hells Gate) 126 5 25S 27 3 E
Hinderwell 33 54 32N 0 45W
Hindhead 29 51 6N 0 42W
Hindley 32 53 32N 2 35W
Hindmarsh L. 140 36 5S 141 55 E
Hindol 95 20 40N 85 10 E
Hinds 143 43 59S 171 36 E
Hindsholm 73 55 30N 10 40 E
Hindu Bagh 94 30 56N 67 57 E
Hindu Kush 93 36 0N 71 0 E
Hindubagh 93 30 56N 67 57 E
Hindupur 97 13 49N 77 32 E
Hines Creek 152 56 20N 118 40W
Hinganghat 96 20 30N 78 59 E
Hingeon 47 50 32N 4 59 E
Hingham, U.K. 29 52 35N 0 59 E
Hingham, U.S.A. 160 48 40N 110 29W
Hingol, R. 93 25 30N 65 30 E
Hingoli 96 19 41N 77 15 E
Hinkley Pt. 28 50 59N 3 32W
Hinlopenstretet 12 79 35N 18 40 E
Hinna 121 10 25N 11 28 E
Hinnøy 74 68 40N 16 28 E
Hino 111 35 0N 136 15 E
Hinojosa 55 38 30N 5 17W
Hinojosa del Duque 57 38 30N 5 17W
Hinokage 110 32 39N 131 24 E
Hinsdale 160 48 26N 107 2W
Hinstock 28 52 50N 2 28W
Hinterrhein, R. 51 46 40N 9 25 E
Hinton, Can. 152 53 26N 117 34W
Hinton, U.S.A. 156 37 40N 80 51W
Hinwil 51 47 18N 8 51 E
Hippolytushoef 46 52 54N 4 58 E
Hirado 110 33 22N 129 33 E
Hirado-Shima 110 33 20N 129 30 E
Hirakarta 111 34 48N 135 40 E
Hirakud 96 21 32N 83 51 E
Hirakud Dam 96 21 32N 83 45 E
Hirara 112 24 48N 125 17 E
Hirata 110 35 24N 132 49 E
Hiratsuka 111 35 19N 139 21 E
Hirhafok 119 23 49N 5 45 E
Hirlůu 70 47 23N 27 0 E
Hiromi 110 33 13N 132 36 E
Hirosaki 112 40 34N 140 28 E
Hiroshima 110 34 30N 132 30 E
Hiroshima-ken □ 112 34 50N 133 0 E
Hiroshima-Wan 110 34 5N 132 20 E
Hirsoholmene 73 57 30N 10 36 E
Hirson 43 49 55N 4 4 E
Hîrşova 70 44 40N 27 59 E
Hirtshals 73 57 36N 9 57 E
Hirwaun 31 51 43N 3 30W
Hisoy 71 58 26N 8 44 E
Hispaniola, I. 165 19 0N 71 0W
Hissar 94 29 12N 75 45 E
Histon 29 52 15N 0 6 E
Hita 110 33 20N 130 58 E
Hitachi 111 36 36N 140 39 E
Hitachiota 111 36 30N 140 30 E
Hitchin 29 51 57N 0 16W
Hitoyoshi 110 32 13N 130 45 E
Hitra 71 63 30N 8 45 E
Hitzacker 48 53 9N 11 1 E
Hiuchi-Nada 110 34 5N 133 20 E
Hjalmar L. 153 61 33N 109 25W
Hjälmare Kanal 72 59 20N 15 59 E
Hjälmaren 72 59 18N 15 40 E
Hjartdal 71 59 37N 8 41 E
Hjärtsäter 73 58 35N 12 3 E
Hjerkinn 71 62 13N 9 33 E
Hjerpsted 73 55 2N 8 39 E
Hjo 73 58 22N 4 17 E
Hjørring 73 57 29N 9 59 E
Hjorted 73 57 37N 16 19 E
Hjortkvarn 73 58 54N 15 26 E
Hko-ut 98 21 40N 97 46 E
Hkyenhpa 98 27 43N 97 25 E
Hlaingbwe 98 17 8N 97 50 E
Hlinsko 52 49 45N 15 54 E
Hlohovec 53 48 26N 17 49 E
Hlwaze 98 18 54N 96 37 E
Ho 121 6 37N 0 27 E
Ho Chi Minh, Phanh Bho 101 10 58N 106 40 E
Ho Thuong 100 19 32N 105 48 E
Hoa Binh 100 20 50N 105 20 E
Hoa Da (Phan Ri) 100 11 16N 108 40 E
Hoa Hiep 101 11 34N 105 51 E
Hoadley 152 52 45N 114 30W
Hoai Nhon (Bon Son) 100 14 28N 109 1 E
Hoare B. 149 65 17N 62 55W
Hobart, Austral. 138 42 50S 147 21 E
Hobart, U.S.A. 159 35 0N 99 5W
Hobbs 159 32 40N 103 3W
Hobjærg 73 56 19N 9 32 E
Hobo 174 2 35N 75 30W
Hoboken, Belg. 47 51 11N 4 21 E
Hoboken, U.S.A. 162 40 45N 74 4W
Hobro 73 56 39N 9 46 E
Hobscheid 47 49 42N 5 57 E
Hoburg C. 73 56 54N 18 8 E
Hoburgen 73 56 55N 18 7 E
Hochang 108 27 8N 104 45 E
Hochatown 159 34 11N 94 39W
Hochdorf 51 47 10N 8 17 E
Hochiang 108 28 48N 105 48 E
Hochien 106 38 26N 116 5 E
Hoch'ih 108 24 43N 108 2 E
Hoching 106 35 37N 110 43 E
Hoch'iu 109 32 21N 116 13 E
Höchst 49 50 6N 8 33 E
Hoch'ü 106 39 26N 111 8 E
Hoch'uan 108 30 2N 106 18 E
Hockenheim 49 49 18N 8 33 E
Hod, oilfield 19 56 10N 3 25 E
Hodaka-Dake 111 36 17N 137 39 E
Hodde 73 55 42N 8 39 E
Hodder R. 32 53 57N 2 27W
Hoddesdon 29 51 45N 0 1W
Hodeïda 91 14 50N 43 0 E
Hodge, R. 33 54 14N 0 55W
Hodgson 153 51 13N 97 36W
Hódmezóvásárhely 53 46 28N 20 22 E
Hodna, Chott el 119 35 30N 5 0 E
Hodonín 53 48 50N 17 0 E
Hodsager 73 56 19N 8 51 E
Hoeamdong 107 42 30N 130 16 E
Hoëdic, I. 42 47 21N 2 52W
Hoegaarden 47 50 47N 4 53 E
Hoek van Holland 46 52 0N 4 7 E
Hoeksche Waard 46 51 46N 4 25 E
Hoenderloo 46 52 7N 5 52 E
Hoengsŏng 107 37 29N 127 59 E
Hoensbroek 47 50 55N 5 55 E
Hoeryong 107 42 30N 129 58 E
Hoeselt 47 50 51N 5 29 E
Hoëveld 129 26 30S 30 0 E
Hoeven 47 51 35N 4 35 E
Hoeyang 107 38 43N 127 36 E
Hof, Ger. 49 50 18N 11 55 E
Hof, Iceland 74 64 33N 14 40W
Höfðakaupstaður 74 65 50N 20 19W
Hofei 109 31 52N 117 15 E
Hoff 32 54 34N 2 31W
Hofgeismar 48 51 29N 9 23 E
Hofors 72 60 35N 16 15 E
Hofsjökull 74 64 49N 18 48W
Hofsós 74 65 53N 19 26W
Hōfu 110 34 3N 131 34 E
Hofuf 92 25 20N 49 40 E
Hög-Gia, Mt. 71 62 23N 10 7 E
Hog I. 162 37 26N 75 42W
Hogan Group 139 39 13S 147 1 E
Höganäs 73 56 13N 12 34 E
Hogansville 157 33 14N 84 50W
Hogarth, Mt. 138 21 50S 137 0 E
Hogeland 160 48 51N 108 40W
Högen 72 61 47N 14 11 E
Hogenaki Falls 97 12 6N 77 50 E
Högfors, Örebro, Sweden 72 59 58N 15 3 E
Högfors, Västmanlands, Sweden 72 60 2N 16 3 E
Hoggar = Ahaggar 119 23 0N 6 30 E
Hōgo-Kaikyo 110 33 20N 131 58 E
Hog's Back, hill 29 51 13N 0 40W
Hogs Hd. 39 51 46N 10 13W
Högsäter 73 58 38N 12 5 E
Högsby 73 57 10N 16 1 E
Högsjo 72 59 4N 15 44 E
Hogsthorpe 33 53 13N 0 19 E
Hogsty Reef 167 21 41N 73 48W
Hohe Rhön 49 50 24N 9 58 E
Hohe Tauern 52 47 11N 12 40 E
Hohenau 53 48 36N 16 55 E
Hohenems 52 47 22N 9 42 E
Hohenstein Ernstthal 48 50 48N 12 43 E
Hohenwald 157 35 35N 87 30W
Hohenwestedt 48 54 6N 9 40 E
Hohoe 121 7 8N 0 32 E
Hohsi 108 24 9N 102 38 E
Hohsien, Anhwei, China 109 31 43N 118 22 E
Hohsien, Kwangsi-Chuang, China 109 24 25N 111 31 E
Hohsüeh 109 30 2N 112 25 E
Hôi An 100 15 30N 108 19 E
Hoi Xuan 100 20 25N 105 9 E
Hoisington 158 38 33N 98 50W
Højer 73 54 58N 8 42 E
Hōjō 110 33 58N 132 46 E
Hok 73 57 31N 14 16 E
Hokensås 73 58 0N 14 5 E
Hökensås 73 58 0N 14 5 E
Hökerum 73 57 51N 13 16 E
Hokianga Harbour 142 35 31S 173 22 E
Hokitika 143 42 42S 171 0 E
Hokkaidō 112 43 30N 143 0 E
Hokkaidō □ 112 43 30N 143 0 E
Hokksund 71 59 44N 9 59 E
Hok'ou, Kansu, China 106 36 9N 103 29 E
Hok'ou, Kwantang, China 109 23 13N 112 45 E
Hok'ou, Yunnan, China 108 22 39N 103 57 E
Hokow 101 22 39N 103 57 E
Hol-Hol. 123 11 20N 42 50 E
Holan Shan 106 38 50N 105 50 E
Holbæk 73 55 43N 11 43 E
Holbeach 29 52 48N 0 1 E
Holbeach Marsh 29 52 52N 0 5 E
Holborn Hd. 37 58 37N 3 30W
Holbrook, Austral. 141 35 42S 147 18 E
Holbrook, U.S.A. 161 35 0N 110 0W
Holden 152 53 13N 112 11W
Holden Fillmore 160 39 0N 112 26W
Holdenville 159 35 5N 96 25W
Holder 140 34 21S 140 0 E
Holderness 33 53 45N 0 5W
Holdfast 153 50 58N 105 25W
Holdrege 153 40 25N 99 30W
Hole 71 60 6N 10 12 E
Hole-Narsipur 97 12 48N 76 16 E
Holešov 53 49 20N 17 35 E
Holguín 166 20 50N 76 20W
Holinkoerh 106 40 23N 111 53 E
Holíč 53 48 49N 17 10 E
Holkham 29 52 57N 0 48 E
Holla, Mt. 123 7 5N 36 35 E
Hollabrunn 52 48 34N 16 5 E
Hollams Bird I. 128 24 40S 14 30 E
Holland 156 42 47N 86 7W
Holland Fen 33 53 0N 0 8W
Holland-on-Sea 29 51 48N 1 12 E
Hollandia = Jajapura 103 2 28S 140 38 E
Hollands Bird I. 128 24 40S 14 30 E
Hollandsch Diep 47 51 41N 4 30 E
Hollandsch IJssel, R. 46 51 55N 4 34 E
Hollandstoun 37 59 22N 2 25W
Höllen 71 58 6N 7 49 E
Holleton 137 31 55S 119 0 E
Hollidaysburg 156 40 26N 78 25W
Hollis 159 34 45N 99 55W
Hollister 161 36 51N 121 24W
Hollum 46 53 26N 5 38 E
Holly 158 38 7N 102 7W
Holly Hill 157 29 15N 81 3W
Holly Springs 159 34 45N 89 25W
Hollymount 38 53 40N 9 7W
Hollywood, Ireland 39 53 6N 6 35W
Hollywood, Calif., U.S.A. 154 34 7N 118 25W
Hollywood, Fla., U.S.A. 157 26 0N 80 9W
Holm 72 62 40N 16 40 E
Holman Island 148 71 0N 118 0W
Hólmavík 74 65 42N 21 40W
Holme, Humberside,, U.K. 33 53 50N 0 48W
Holme, N. Yorks., U.K. 32 53 34N 1 50W
Holmedal 71 59 46N 5 50 E
Holmedal, Fjordane 71 61 22N 5 11 E
Holmegil 72 59 10N 11 44 E
Holmes Chapel 32 53 13N 2 21W
Holmes Reefs 138 16 27S 148 0 E
Holmestrand 71 59 31N 10 14 E
Holmfirth 33 53 34N 1 48W
Holmsbu 71 59 32N 10 27 E
Holmsjön 72 62 26N 15 20 E
Holmsland Klit 73 56 0N 8 5 E
Holmsund 74 63 41N 20 20 E
Holmwood 29 51 12N 0 19W
Hölö 72 59 3N 17 36 E
Holo Ho, R. 107 44 54N 122 22 E
Holod 70 46 49N 22 8 E
Holon 90 32 2N 34 47 E
Holroyd, R. 138 14 10S 141 36 E
Holsen 71 61 25N 6 8 E
Holstebro 73 56 22N 8 37 E
Holsworthy 30 50 48N 4 21W
Holt, Iceland 74 63 33N 19 48W
Holt, Clwyd, U.K. 31 53 4N 2 52W
Holt, Norfolk, U.K. 29 52 55N 1 4 E
Holte 73 55 50N 12 29 E
Holten 46 52 17N 6 26 E
Holton Harbour 151 54 31N 57 12W
Holton le Clay 33 53 29N 0 3W
Holtville 161 32 50N 115 27W
Holum 71 58 6N 7 32 E
Holwerd 46 53 22N 5 54 E
Holy Cross 147 62 10N 159 52W
Holy I., England, U.K. 35 55 42N 1 48W
Holy I., Scotland, U.K. 34 55 31N 5 4W
Holy I., Wales, U.K. 31 53 17N 4 37W
Holyhead 31 53 18N 4 38W
Holyhead B. 31 53 20N 4 35W
Holyoke, Mass., U.S.A. 162 42 14N 72 37W
Holyoke, Nebr., U.S.A. 158 40 39N 102 18W
Holyrood 151 47 27N 53 8W
Holywell 31 53 16N 3 14W
Holywood 38 54 38N 5 50W
Holzminden 48 51 49N 9 31 E
Homa Bay 126 0 36S 34 22 E
Homa Bay □ 126 0 50S 34 30 E
Homalin 98 24 55N 95 0 E
Homberg 48 51 2N 9 20 E
Hombori 121 15 20N 1 38W
Homburg 49 49 19N 7 21 E
Home B. 149 68 40N 67 10W
Home Hill 138 19 43S 147 25 E
Homedale 160 43 42N 116 59W
Homer, Alaska, U.S.A. 147 59 40N 151 35W
Homer, La., U.S.A. 159 32 50N 93 4W
Homestead, Austral. 138 20 20S 145 40 E
Homestead, U.S.A. 157 25 29N 80 27W
Hominy 159 36 26N 96 24W
Homnabad 96 17 45N 77 5 E
Homoine 129 23 55S 35 8 E
Homorod 70 46 5N 25 15 E
Homs = Al Khums 119 32 40N 14 17 E
Homs (Hims) 92 34 40N 36 45 E
Hon Chong 101 10 16N 104 38 E
Hon Me 100 19 23N 105 56 E
Honan □ 106 34 10N 113 10 E
Honbetsu 112 43 7N 143 37 E
Honda 174 5 12N 74 45W
Hondeklipbaai 125 30 19S 17 17 E
Hondo, Japan 110 32 27N 130 12 E
Hondo, U.S.A. 159 29 22N 99 6W
Hondo, R. 165 18 25N 88 21W
Honduras ■ 166 14 40N 86 30W
Honduras, Golfo de 166 16 50N 87 0W
Hönefoss 71 60 10N 10 12 E
Honey L. 160 40 13N 120 14W
Honfleur 42 49 25N 0 13 E
Hōng 73 55 30N 11 14 E
Hong Gai 100 20 57N 107 5 E
Hong Kong ■ 109 22 11N 114 14 E

Hong, R Hsiushui

Hong, R. 100 20 17N 106 34 E
Hongchŏn 107 37 44N 127 53 E
Hongha, R. 101 22 0N 104 0 E
Hongor 106 45 56N 112 50 E
Hongsa 100 19 43N 101 20 E
Hongsŏng 107 36 37N 126 38 E
Honguedo, Détroit d' 151 49 15N 64 0W
Hongwon 107 40 0N 127 56 E
Honiara 142 9 30S 160 0 E
Honington 33 52 58N 0 35W
Honiton 30 50 48N 3 11W
Honjo, Akita, Japan 112 39 23N 140 3 E
Honjo, Gumma, Japan 111 36 14N 139 11 E
Honkawane 111 35 5N 138 5 E
Honkorâb, Ras 122 24 35N 35 10 E
Honolulu 147 21 19N 157 52W
Honshū 112 36 0N 138 0 E
Hontoria del Pinar 58 41 50N 3 10W
Hoo 29 51 25N 0 33 E
Hood Mt. 160 45 15N 122 0W
Hood, Pt. 137 34 23S 119 34 E
Hood Pt. 135 10 4S 147 45 E
Hood River 160 45 45N 121 37W
Hoodsport 160 47 24N 123 7W
Hooge 48 54 31N 8 36 E
Hoogerheide 47 51 26N 4 20 E
Hoogeveen 46 52 44N 6 30 E
Hoogeveensche Vaart 46 52 42N 6 12 E
Hoogezand 46 53 11N 6 45 E
Hooghly-Chinsura 95 22 53N 88 27 E
Hooghly, R. 95 21 59N 88 10 E
Hoogkerk 46 53 13N 6 30 E
Hooglede 47 50 59N 3 5 E
Hoogstraten 47 51 24N 4 46 E
Hoogvliet 46 51 52N 4 21 E
Hook 29 51 17N 0 55W
Hook Hd. 39 52 8N 6 57W
Hook I. 138 20 4S 149 0 E
Hook of Holland = Hoek v. Holland 47 52 0N 4 7 E
Hooker 159 36 55N 101 10W
Hooker Cr. 136 18 23S 130 50 E
Hoonah 147 58 15N 135 30W
Hooper Bay 147 61 30N 166 10W
Hoopersville 162 38 16N 76 11W
Hoopeston 156 40 30N 87 40W
Hoopstad 128 27 50S 25 55 E
Höör 73 55 55N 13 33 E
Hoorn 46 52 38N 5 4 E
Hoover Dam 161 36 0N 114 45W
Hop Bottom 162 41 41N 75 47W
Hopà 83 41 28N 41 30 E
Hope, Can. 152 49 25N 121 25 E
Hope, U.K. 31 53 7N 3 2W
Hope, Ark., U.S.A. 159 33 40N 93 30W
Hope, N.D., U.S.A. 158 47 21N 97 42W
Hope Bay 13 65 0S 55 0W
Hope, L. 139 28 24S 139 18 E
Hope L. 37 58 24N 4 38W
Hope Pt. 147 68 20N 166 50W
Hope Town 157 26 30N 76 30W
Hopedale, Can. 151 55 28N 60 13W
Hopedale, U.S.A. 162 42 8N 71 33W
Hopefield 128 33 3S 18 22 E
Hopei □ 107 39 25N 116 45 E
Hopelchén 165 19 46N 89 50W
Hopeman 37 57 42N 3 26W
Hopen 71 63 27N 8 2 E
Hopetoun 137 33 57S 120 7 E
Hopetown, Austral. 140 35 42S 142 22 E
Hopetown, S. Afr. 128 29 34S 24 3 E
Hopewell 162 37 18N 77 17W
Hopien-Ts'un 108 27 40N 101 55 E
Hopin 98 21 14N 96 53 E
Hop'ing 109 24 26N 114 56 E
Hopkins 158 40 31N 94 45W
Hopkins, L. 136 24 15S 128 35 E
Hopkinsville 157 36 52N 87 26W
Hopland 160 39 0N 123 7W
Hopo 108 31 24N 99 0 E
Hoptrup 73 55 11N 9 28 E
Hop'u 108 21 41N 109 10 E
Hoquiam 160 46 50N 123 55W
Hōrai 111 34 58N 137 32 E
Horazdovice 52 49 19N 13 42 E
Hörby 73 55 50N 13 44 E
Horcajo de Santiago 58 39 50N 3 1W
Hordaland fylke □ 71 60 25N 6 15 E
Horden 33 54 45N 1 17W
Hordern Hills 136 20 40S 130 20 E
Hordio 91 10 36N 51 8 E
Horezu 70 45 6N 24 0 E
Horgen 51 47 15N 8 35 E
Horgoš 66 46 10N 20 0 E
Horice 52 50 21N 15 39 E
Horley 29 51 10N 0 10W
Horlick Mts. 13 84 0S 102 0W
Hormoz 93 27 35N 55 0 E
Hormuz, I. 93 27 8N 56 28 E
Hormuz Str. 93 26 30N 56 30 E
Horn, Austria 52 48 39N 15 40 E
Horn, Isafjarðarsýsla, Iceland 74 66 28N 22 28W
Horn, Suður-Múlasýsla, Iceland 74 65 10N 13 31W
Horn, Neth. 47 51 12N 5 57 E
Horn, Cape = Hornos, C. de 176 55 50S 67 30W
Horn Head 38 55 13N 8 0W
Horn I., Austral. 138 10 37S 142 17 E
Horn I., P.N.G. 135 10 35S 142 20 E
Horn, I. 157 30 17N 88 40W
Horn Mts. 152 62 15N 119 15W
Horn, R. 152 61 30N 118 1W
Hornachuelos 57 37 50N 5 14W
Hornavan 74 66 15N 17 30 E
Hornbæk, Frederiksborg, Denmark 73 56 5N 12 26 E
Hornbæk, Viborg, Denmark 73 56 28N 9 58 E
Hornbeck 159 31 22N 93 20W
Hornbrook 160 41 58N 122 37W
Hornburg 48 52 2N 10 36 E
Hornby 143 43 33S 172 33 E
Horncastle 33 53 13N 0 8W
Horndal 72 60 18N 16 23 E
Horndean 29 50 56N 1 5W
Hornell 156 42 23N 77 41W
Hornell L. 152 62 20N 119 25W
Hornepayne 150 49 14N 84 48W
Hornindal 71 61 58N 6 30 E
Horningsham 28 51 11N 2 16W
Hornitos 163 37 30N 120 14W
Hornnes 71 58 34N 7 45 E
Hornos, Cabo de 176 55 50S 67 30 E
Hornoy 43 49 50N 1 54 E
Hornsberg, Jamtland, Sweden 72 63 14N 14 40 E
Hornsberg, Kronobergs, Sweden 72 56 37N 13 47 E
Hornsby 141 33 42S 151 2 E
Hornsea 33 53 55N 0 10W
Hornslandet Pen. 72 61 35N 17 37 E
Hornslet 73 56 18N 10 19 E
Hornu 47 50 26N 3 50 E
Hörnum 73 54 44N 8 18 E
Horovice 52 49 48N 13 53 E
Horqueta 172 23 15S 56 55W
Horra, La 56 41 44N 3 53W
Horred 73 57 22N 12 28 E
Horse Cr. 158 41 33N 104 45W
Horse Is. 151 50 15N 55 50W
Horsefly L. 152 52 25N 121 0W
Horseheads 162 42 10N 76 49W
Horseleap 38 53 25N 7 34W
Horsens 73 55 52N 9 51 E
Horsens Fjord 73 55 50N 10 0 E
Horseshoe 137 25 27S 118 31 E
Horseshoe Dam 161 33 45N 111 35W
Horsforth 33 53 50N 1 39W
Horsham, Austral. 140 36 44S 142 13 E
Horsham, U.K. 29 51 4N 0 20W
Horsham St. Faith 29 52 41N 1 15 E
Horsovsky Tyn 52 49 31N 12 58 E
Horst 47 51 27N 6 3 E
Horsted Keynes 29 51 2N 0 1W
Horten 71 59 25N 10 32 E
Hortobágy, R. 53 47 30N 21 6 E
Horton 158 39 42N 95 30W
Horton-in-Ribblesdale 32 54 9N 2 19W
Horton, R. 147 69 56N 126 52W
Hörvik 73 56 2N 14 45 E
Horw 51 47 1N 8 19 E
Horwich 32 53 37N 2 33W
Horwood, L. 150 48 10N 82 20W
Hosaina 123 7 30N 37 47 E
Hosdurga 97 13 40N 76 17 E
Hose, Pegunungan 102 2 5N 114 6 E
Hoshan 109 31 24N 116 20 E
Hoshangabad 94 22 45N 77 45 E
Hoshiarpur 94 31 30N 75 58 E
Hoshui 106 36 0N 107 59 E
Hoshun 106 37 19N 113 34 E
Hosingen 47 50 1N 6 6 E
Hoskins 135 5 29S 150 27 E
Hosmer 158 45 36N 99 29W
Hososhima 110 32 26N 131 40 E
Hospental 51 46 37N 8 34 E
Hospet 97 15 15N 76 20 E
Hospital 39 52 30N 8 28W
Hospitalet de Llobregat 58 41 21N 2 6 E
Hospitalet, L' 44 42 36N 1 47 E
Hoste, I. 176 55 0S 69 0W
Hostens 44 44 30N 0 40W
Hoswick 36 60 0N 1 15W
Hot 100 18 8N 98 29 E
Hot Creek Ra. 160 39 0N 116 0W
Hot Springs, Ark, U.S.A. 159 34 30N 93 0W
Hot Springs, S.D., U.S.A. 158 43 25N 103 30W
Hotagen, L. 74 63 50N 14 30 E
Hotazel 128 27 17S 23 00 E
Hotchkiss 161 38 55N 107 47W
Hotham, C. 136 12 2S 131 18 E
Hot'ien 105 37 7N 79 55 E
Hoting 74 64 8N 16 15 E
Hotolishti 68 41 10N 20 25 E
Hotse 106 35 14N 115 27 E
Hotte, Massif de la 167 18 30N 73 45W
Hottentotsbaai 128 26 8S 14 59 E
Hotton 47 50 16N 5 26 E
Houat, I. 42 47 24N 2 58W
Houck 161 35 15N 109 15W
Houdan 43 48 48N 1 35 E
Houdeng-Goegnies 47 50 29N 4 10 E
Houei Sai 100 20 18N 100 26 E
Houffalize 47 50 8N 5 48 E
Houghton 158 47 9N 88 39W
Houghton L. 156 44 20N 84 40W
Houghton-le-Spring 35 54 51N 1 28W
Houghton Regis 29 51 54N 0 32W
Houhora 142 34 49S 173 9 E
Houille, R. 47 50 8N 4 50 E
Houlton 151 46 5N 68 0W
Houma 159 29 35N 90 50W
Houmt Souk = Djerba 119 33 53N 10 37 E
Houndé 120 11 34N 3 31W
Hounslow 29 51 29N 0 20W
Hourn L. 36 57 7N 5 35W
Hourtin 44 45 11N 1 4W
Housatonic, R. 162 41 10N 73 7W
Houston, Can. 152 54 25N 126 30W
Houston, Mo., U.S.A. 159 37 20N 92 0W
Houston, Tex., U.S.A. 159 29 50N 95 20W
Houten 46 52 2N 5 10 E
Houthalen 47 51 2N 5 23 E
Houthem 47 50 48N 2 57 E
Houthulst 47 50 59N 2 57 E
Houtman Abrolhos 137 28 43S 113 48 E
Houyet 47 50 11N 5 1 E
Hova 73 58 53N 14 14 E
Høvag 71 58 10N 8 15 E
Hövåg 71 58 10N 8 16 E
Hovd 105 48 1N 91 39 E
Hovden 71 59 33N 7 22 E
Hove 29 50 50N 0 10W
Hoveton 29 52 45N 1 23 E
Hovingham 33 54 10N 0 59W
Hovmantorp 73 56 47N 15 7 E
Hövsgöl 106 43 37N 109 39 E
Hovsta 72 59 22N 15 15 E
Howakil 123 15 10N 40 16 E
Howar, W., (Shau) 123 17 0N 25 30 E
Howard, Austral. 139 25 16S 152 32 E
Howard, Kans., U.S.A. 159 37 30N 96 16W
Howard, S.D., U.S.A. 158 44 2N 97 30W
Howard I. 138 12 10S 135 24 E
Howard L. 153 62 15N 105 57W
Howatharra 137 28 29S 114 33 E
Howden 33 53 45N 0 52W
Howe 160 43 48N 113 0W
Howe, C. 141 37 30S 150 0 E
Howell 156 42 38N 84 0W
Howick, N.Z. 142 36 54S 174 48 E
Howick, S. Afr. 129 29 28S 30 14 E
Howick Group 138 14 20S 145 30 E
Howitt, L. 139 27 40S 138 40 E
Howley 151 49 12N 57 2W
Howmore 36 57 18N 7 23W
Howrah 95 22 37N 88 27 E
Howth 38 53 23N 6 3W
Howth Hd. 38 53 21N 6 0W
Hoxne 29 52 22N 1 11 E
Höxter 48 51 45N 9 26 E
Hoy I. 37 58 50N 3 15W
Hoy Sd. 37 58 57N 3 20W
Hoya 48 52 47N 9 10 E
Høyanger 71 61 25N 6 50 E
Höydalsmo 71 59 30N 8 15 E
Hoyerswerda 48 51 26N 14 14 E
Hoylake 32 53 24N 3 11W
Höyland 71 58 50N 5 43 E
Hoyleton 140 34 2S 138 34 E
Hoyos 56 40 9N 6 45W
Hoyüan 109 23 50N 114 40 E
Hpawlum 98 27 12N 98 12 E
Hpettintha 98 24 14N 95 23 E
Hpizow 98 26 57N 98 24 E
Hpungan Pass 99 27 30N 96 55 E
Hrádec Králové 52 50 15N 15 50 E
Hrádek 53 48 46N 16 16 E
Hranice 53 49 34N 17 45 E
Hron, R. 53 48 0N 18 4 E
Hrubieszów 54 50 49N 23 51 E
Hrubý Nizký Jeseník 53 50 7N 17 10 E
Hrvatska 63 45 20N 16 0 E
Hsenwi 98 23 22N 97 55 E
Hsi Chiang, R. 109 22 20N 113 20 E
Hsiach'engtzu, Heilungkiang, China 107 44 41N 130 27 E
Hsiach'engtzu, Schechwan, China 108 29 24N 101 46 E
Hsiachiang 109 27 33N 115 10 E
Hsiaching 106 36 57N 115 59 E
Hsiach'uan Shan 109 21 40N 112 37 E
Hsiahsien 106 35 12N 111 11 E
Hsiai 106 34 17N 116 11 E
Hsiakuan 108 25 39N 100 9 E
Hsiamen 109 24 30N 118 7 E
Hsian 106 34 17N 109 0 E
Hsiang Chiang, R. 109 29 30N 113 10 E
Hsiangch'eng, Honan, China 106 33 50N 113 29 E
Hsiangch'eng, Honan, China 106 33 13N 114 50 E
Hsiangch'eng, Szechwan, China 108 29 0N 99 46 E
Hsiangchou 108 23 58N 109 41 E
Hsiangfan 109 32 7N 112 9 E
Hsianghsiang 109 27 46N 112 30 E
Hsiangning 106 36 1N 110 47 E
Hsiangshan 109 29 18N 121 37 E
Hsiangshuik'ou 107 34 12N 119 34 E
Hsiangt'an 109 27 55N 112 52 E
Hsiangtu 108 23 14N 106 57 E
Hsiangyang 109 32 2N 112 6 E
Hsiangyin 109 28 40N 112 53 E
Hsiangyüan 106 36 32N 113 2 E
Hsiangyün 108 25 29N 100 35 E
Hsiaochin 108 31 1N 102 23 E
Hsiaofeng 109 30 36N 119 33 E
Hsiaohsien 106 34 2N 116 56 E
Hsiaohsinganling Shanmo 105 48 45N 127 0 E
Hsiaoi 106 37 7N 111 46 E
Hsiaokan 109 30 57N 113 53 E
Hsiaoshan 109 30 10N 120 15 E
Hsiaot'ai Shan 107 36 18N 116 38 E
Hsiap'u 109 26 58N 119 57 E
Hsiawa 107 42 38N 120 31 E
Hsich'ang 108 27 50N 102 18 E
Hsichieht'o 108 30 24N 108 13 E
Hsich'uan 109 33 0N 111 24 E
Hsich'ung 108 31 0N 105 48 E
Hsiehch'eng 107 34 48N 117 15 E
Hsiehmaho 109 31 38N 111 12 E
Hsienchü 109 28 51N 120 44 E
Hsienfeng 108 29 40N 109 7 E
Hsienhsien 106 38 2N 116 12 E
Hsienning 109 29 51N 114 15 E
Hsienshui Ho, R. 108 30 5N 101 5 E
Hsienyang 106 34 22N 108 48 E
Hsienyu 109 25 24N 118 40 E
Hsifei Ho, R. 109 32 38N 116 39 E
Hsifeng, Kweichow, China 108 27 5N 106 42 E
Hsifeng, Liaoning, China 107 42 44N 124 42 E
Hsifengchen 106 35 40N 107 42 E
Hsifengk'ou 107 40 24N 118 19 E
Hsiho 106 34 2N 105 12 E
Hsihsia, Honan, China 106 33 30N 111 30 E
Hsihsia, Shantung, China 107 37 25N 120 48 E
Hsihsiang 108 33 1N 107 40 E
Hsihsien, Honan, China 109 32 24N 114 52 E
Hsihsien, Shensi, China 106 36 41N 110 56 E
Hsihua 106 33 47N 114 31 E
Hsilamunlun Ho, R. 107 43 24N 123 42 E
Hsiliao Ho, R. 107 43 24N 123 42 E
Hsilin 108 24 30N 105 3 E
Hsin Chiang, R. 109 28 50N 116 40 E
Hsin Ho, R. 107 43 33N 123 31 E
Hsinchan 107 43 52N 127 20 E
Hsinch'ang 109 29 30N 120 54 E
Hsincheng 106 34 25N 113 46 E
Hsinch'eng, Hopei, China 106 39 15N 115 59 E
Hsinch'eng, Kwangsi-Chuang, China 108 24 4N 108 40 E
Hsinchiang 106 35 40N 111 15 E
Hsinchien 108 23 58N 102 47 E
Hsinchin 107 39 25N 121 59 E
Hsinching 108 30 25N 103 49 E
Hsinchi'u 107 41 53N 119 40 E
Hsinchou 109 30 52N 114 48 E
Hsinchu 109 24 48N 120 58 E
Hsinfeng, Kiangsi, China 109 25 27N 114 58 E
Hsinfeng, Kiangsi, China 109 26 7N 116 11 E
Hsinfeng, Kwangtung, China 109 24 4N 114 12 E
Hsingan 109 25 39N 110 39 E
Hsingch'eng 107 40 40N 120 48 E
Hsingho 106 40 52N 113 58 E
Hsinghsien 106 38 31N 111 4 E
Hsinghua 107 32 55N 119 52 E
Hsinghua Wan 109 25 20N 119 20 E
Hsingi 108 25 5N 104 55 E
Hsinging 109 26 25N 110 44 E
Hsingjen 108 25 25N 105 13 E
Hsingjenp'ao 106 37 0N 105 0 E
Hsingkuo 109 26 26N 115 16 E
Hsinglung 107 40 29N 117 32 E
Hsingning 109 24 8N 115 43 E
Hsingp'ing 108 34 18N 108 26 E
Hsingshan 109 31 10N 110 51 E
Hsingt'ai 106 37 5N 114 38 E
Hsingyeh 108 22 45N 109 52 E
Hsinhailien = Lienyünchiangshih 107 34 37N 119 13 E
Hsinhsiang 106 35 15N 113 54 E
Hsinhsien, Shansi, China 106 38 24N 112 47 E
Hsinhsien, Shantung, China 106 36 15N 115 40 E
Hsinhsing 109 22 45N 112 11 E
Hsinhua 109 27 43N 111 18 E
Hsinhui 109 22 32N 113 0 E
Hsini 109 22 12N 110 53 E
Hsining 105 36 37N 101 46 E
Hsink'ai Ho, R. 107 41 10N 122 5 E
Hsinkan 109 27 45N 115 21 E
Hsinkao Shan 109 23 25N 120 52 E
Hsinlit'un 107 42 2N 122 19 E
Hsinlo 106 38 15N 114 40 E
Hsinmin 107 42 0N 122 52 E
Hsinpaoan 106 40 27N 115 23 E
Hsinpin 107 41 43N 125 2 E
Hsinp'ing 108 24 6N 101 58 E
Hsinshao 109 27 20N 111 26 E
Hsint'ai 107 35 54N 117 44 E
Hsint'ien 109 25 56N 112 13 E
Hsints'ai 109 32 44N 114 59 E
Hsinyang 109 30 10N 114 6 E
Hsinyeh 109 37 31N 112 21 E
Hsinyü 109 27 48N 114 56 E
Hsipaw 98 22 37N 97 18 E
Hsip'ing, Honan, China 106 33 34N 110 45 E
Hsip'ing, Honan, China 106 33 23N 114 2 E
Hsishni 109 30 27N 115 13 E
Hsitalahai 106 40 38N 109 38 E
Hsiu Shui, R. 109 29 13N 116 0 E
Hsiujen 109 24 26N 110 14 E
Hsiunghsien 106 38 59N 116 11 E
Hsiungyüeh 107 40 12N 122 12 E
Hsiuning 109 29 51N 118 15 E
Hsiushan 108 28 25N 108 59 E
Hsiushui 109 29 2N 114 34 E

Hsiuwen **Ibara**

Hsiuwen	**108**	26 52N	106 35 E
Hsiuyen	**107**	40 19N	123 15 E
Hsiyang	**106**	37 27N	113 46 E
Hsüanch'eng	**109**	30 54N	118 41 E
Hsüanen	**108**	29 59N	109 24 E
Hsüanhan	**108**	31 25N	107 38 E
Hsüanhua	**106**	40 38N	115 5 E
Hsüanwei	**108**	26 13N	104 5 E
Hsüch'ang	**106**	34 1N	113 53 E
Hsüchou	**107**	34 15N	117 10 E
Hsüehfeng Shan	**109**	27 0N	110 30 E
Hsüehweng Shan	**109**	24 24N	121 12 E
Hsun Chiang, R.	**109**	23 30N	111 30 E
Hsünhsien	**106**	35 40N	114 32 E
Hsüni	**106**	35 6N	108 20 E
Hsüntien	**108**	25 33N	103 15 E
Hsünwu	**109**	24 57N	115 28 E
Hsünyang	**108**	32 48N	109 27 E
Hsüp'u	**109**	27 56N	110 36 E
Hsüshui	**106**	39 1N	115 39 E
Hsüwen	**109**	20 20N	110 9 E
Hsüyung	**108**	28 6N	105 21 E
Htawgaw	**98**	25 57N	98 23 E
Hua Hin	**100**	12 34N	99 58 E
Huaan	**109**	25 1N	117 33 E
Huachacalla	**164**	18 45 S	68 17W
Huachinera	**164**	30 9N	108 55W
Huachipato	**172**	36 45 S	73 09W
Huacho	**174**	11 10 S	77 35W
Huachón	**174**	10 35 S	76 0W
Huachou	**109**	21 38N	110 35 E
Huacrachuco	**174**	8 35 S	76 50W
Huahsien, Honan, China	**106**	35 33N	114 34 E
Huahsien, Shensi, China	**106**	34 31N	109 46 E
Huai Yot	**101**	7 45N	99 37 E
Huaiachen	**106**	40 33N	114 30 E
Huaian, Hopei, China	**106**	40 33N	114 30 E
Huaian, Kiangsu, China	**107**	33 31N	119 8 E
Huaichi	**109**	24 0N	112 8 E
Huaihua	**109**	27 34N	109 56 E
Huaijen	**106**	39 50N	113 7 E
Huaijou	**106**	40 20N	116 37 E
Huainan	**109**	32 39N	117 2 E
Huaining	**109**	30 21N	116 42 E
Huaite	**107**	43 30N	124 50 E
Huaitechen	**107**	43 52N	124 45 E
Huaiyang	**106**	33 50N	115 2 E
Huaiyüan, Anhwei, China	**109**	32 58N	117 13 E
Huaiyüan, Kwangsi-Chuang, China	**108**	24 36N	108 27 E
Huajuapan	**165**	17 50N	98 0W
Huajung	**109**	29 34N	112 34 E
Hualien	**109**	24 0N	121 30 E
Huallaga, R.	**174**	5 30 S	76 10W
Hualpai Pk.	**161**	35 8N	113 58W
Huan Chiang, R.	**106**	36 4N	107 40 E
Huancabamba	**174**	5 10 S	79 15W
Huancané	**174**	15 10 S	69 50W
Huancapi	**174**	13 25 S	74 0W
Huancavelica	**174**	12 50 S	75 5W
Huancayo	**174**	12 5 S	75 0W
Huanchiang	**108**	24 50N	108 15 E
Huang Ho, R.	**107**	36 50N	118 20 E
Huangchiakopa	**106**	40 20N	109 18 E
Huangch'uan	**109**	32 8N	115 4 E
Huanghsien, Hunen, China	**108**	27 22N	109 10 E
Huanghsien, Shantung, China	**107**	37 38N	120 30 E
Huangkang	**109**	30 27N	114 50 E
Huanglienp'u	**108**	25 32N	99 44 E
Huangling	**106**	35 36N	109 17 E
Huangliu	**105**	18 20N	108 50 E
Huanglung	**106**	35 37N	109 58 E
Huanglungt'an	**109**	32 38N	110 33 E
Huangmei	**109**	30 4N	115 56 E
Huangshih	**109**	30 10N	115 2 E
Huangt'uan	**107**	36 55N	121 41 E
Huangyang	**109**	26 37N	111 42 E
Huangyen	**109**	28 37N	121 12 E
Huanhsien	**106**	36 32N	107 10 E
Huaning	**108**	24 12N	102 55 E
Huanjen	**107**	41 16N	125 21 E
Huanp'ing	**108**	26 54N	107 55 E
Huant'ai	**107**	36 57N	118 5 E
Huánuco	**174**	9 55 S	76 15W
Huap'ing	**108**	26 37N	101 13 E
Huap'itientzu	**107**	43 30N	130 2 E
Huaraz	**174**	9 30 S	77 32W
Huarmey	**174**	10 5 S	78 5W
Huasamota	**164**	22 30N	104 30W
Huascarán	**174**	9 0 S	77 30W
Huasco	**172**	28 24 S	71 15W
Huasco, R.	**172**	28 27 S	71 13W
Huasna	**163**	35 6N	120 24W
Huatabampo	**164**	26 50N	109 50W
Huate	**106**	41 57N	114 4 E
Huatien	**107**	42 58N	126 50 E
Huauchinango	**165**	20 11N	98 3W
Huautla	**164**	18 20N	96 50W
Huautla de Jiménez	**165**	18 8N	96 51W
Huay Namota	**164**	21 56N	104 30W
Huayin	**106**	34 36N	110 2 E
Huayllay	**174**	11 03 S	76 21W
Huayüan	**108**	28 30N	109 25 E
Hubbard	**159**	31 50N	96 50W
Hubbart Pt.	**153**	59 21N	94 41W
Hubli-Dharwar	**97**	15 22N	75 15 E
Huchang	**107**	41 25N	127 2 E
Huchuetenango	**164**	15 25N	91 30W
Hückelhoven-Ratheim	**48**	51 6N	6 3 E
Hucknall	**33**	53 3N	1 12W
Huddersfield	**33**	53 38N	1 49W
Hudi	**122**	17 43N	34 28 E
Hudiksvall	**72**	61 43N	17 10 E
Hudson, Can.	**153**	50 6N	92 09W
Hudson, Mich., U.S.A.	**156**	41 50N	84 20W
Hudson, N.H., U.S.A.	**162**	42 46N	71 26W
Hudson, N.Y., U.S.A.	**162**	42 15N	73 46W
Hudson, Wis., U.S.A.	**158**	44 57N	92 45W
Hudson, Wyo., U.S.A.	**160**	42 54N	108 37W
Hudson B.	**153**	59 0N	91 0W
Hudson Bay, Can.	**149**	60 0N	86 0W
Hudson Bay, Sask., Can.	**153**	52 51N	102 23W
Hudson Falls	**162**	43 18N	73 34W
Hudson, R.	**162**	40 42N	74 2W
Hudson Str.	**148**	62 0N	70 0W
Hudson's Hope	**152**	56 0N	121 54W
Hué	**100**	16 30N	107 35 E
Huebra, R.	**56**	40 54N	6 28W
Huedin	**70**	46 52N	23 2 E
Huehuetenango	**166**	15 20N	91 28W
Huejúcar	**164**	22 21N	103 13W
Huelgoat	**42**	48 22N	3 46W
Huelma	**59**	37 39N	3 28W
Huelva	**57**	37 18N	6 57W
Huelva □	**57**	37 40N	7 0W
Huelva, R.	**57**	37 46N	6 15W
Huentelauquén	**172**	31 38 S	71 33W
Huércal Overa	**59**	37 23N	1 57W
Huerta, Sa. de la	**172**	31 10 S	67 30W
Huertas, C. de las	**59**	38 21N	0 24W
Huerva, R.	**58**	41 13N	1 15W
Huesca	**58**	42 8N	0 25W
Huesca □	**58**	42 20N	0 1 E
Huéscar	**59**	37 44N	2 35W
Huétamo	**164**	18 36N	100 54W
Huete	**58**	40 10N	2 43W
Hugh, R.	**138**	25 1 S	134 10 E
Hugh Town	**30**	49 55N	6 19W
Hughenden	**138**	20 52 S	144 10 E
Hughes, Austral.	**137**	30 42 S	129 31 E
Hughes, U.S.A.	**147**	66 0N	154 20W
Hughesville	**162**	41 14N	76 44W
Hugo, Colo., U.S.A.	**158**	39 12N	103 27W
Hugo, Okla., U.S.A.	**159**	34 0N	95 30W
Hugoton	**159**	37 18N	101 22W
Huhehot = Huhohaot'e	**106**	40 50N	110 39 E
Huhohaot'e	**106**	40 50N	110 39 E
Huhsien	**106**	34 8N	108 34 E
Huian	**109**	25 4N	118 47 E
Huianp'u	**106**	37 30N	106 40 E
Huiarau Ra.	**142**	38 45 S	176 55 E
Huich'ang	**109**	25 32N	115 45 E
Huichapán	**165**	20 24N	99 40W
Huichou	**109**	23 5N	114 24 E
Huifa Ho, R.	**107**	43 6N	126 53 E
Huihsien, Honan, China	**106**	35 32N	113 54 E
Huihsien, Kansu, China	**106**	33 46N	106 6 E
Huila	**128**	15 30 S	15 0 E
Huila □	**174**	2 30N	75 45W
Huila, Nevado del	**174**	3 0N	76 0W
Huilai	**109**	23 4N	116 18 E
Huili	**108**	26 39N	102 11 E
Huimin	**107**	37 29N	117 29 E
Huinan	**107**	42 40N	126 5 E
Huinca Renancó	**172**	34 51 S	64 22W
Huining	**106**	35 41N	105 8 E
Huinung	**106**	39 0N	106 45 E
Huiroa	**142**	39 15 S	174 30 E
Huise	**47**	50 54N	3 36 E
Huishui	**108**	26 8N	106 35 E
Huissen	**46**	51 57N	5 57 E
Huiting	**106**	34 6N	116 4 E
Huitse	**108**	26 22N	103 15 E
Huit'ung	**108**	26 56N	109 36 E
Huixtla	**165**	15 9N	92 28W
Huiya	**92**	24 40N	49 15 E
Huizen	**46**	52 18N	5 14 E
Hukawng Valley	**99**	26 30N	96 30 E
Hukou	**109**	29 45N	116 13 E
Hukuma	**123**	14 55N	36 2 E
Hukuntsi	**128**	23 58 S	21 45 E
Hula	**123**	6 33N	38 30 E
Hulaifa	**92**	25 58N	41 0 E
Hulan	**105**	46 0N	126 44 E
Huld	**106**	45 5N	105 30 E
Hûlda	**90**	31 50N	34 51 E
Hull, Can.	**150**	45 20N	75 40W
Hull, U.K.	**33**	53 45N	0 20W
Hullavington	**28**	51 31N	2 9W
Hulme End	**32**	53 8N	1 51W
Hulst	**47**	51 17N	4 2 E
Hultsfred	**73**	57 30N	15 52 E
Hulun Ch'ih	**105**	49 1N	117 32 E
Humacao	**147**	18 9N	65 50W
Humahuaca	**172**	23 10 S	65 25W
Humaitá	**174**	7 35 S	62 40W
Humaita	**172**	27 2 S	58 31W
Humansdorp	**128**	34 2 S	24 46 E
Humber, Mouth of	**33**	53 32N	0 8 E
Humber, R.	**33**	53 40N	0 10W
Humberside □	**33**	53 50N	0 30W
Humbert River	**136**	16 30 S	130 45 E
Humble	**159**	29 59N	95 10W
Humboldt, Can.	**153**	52 15N	105 9W
Humboldt, Iowa, U.S.A.	**158**	42 42N	94 15W
Humboldt, Tenn., U.S.A.	**157**	35 50N	88 55W
Humboldt Gletscher	**12**	79 30N	62 0W
Humboldt, R.	**160**	40 55N	116 0W
Humbolt Mts.	**143**	44 30 S	168 15 E
Hume	**163**	36 48N	118 54W
Hume, L.	**141**	36 0 S	147 0 E
Humenné	**53**	48 55N	21 50 E
Humphreys, Mt.	**163**	37 17N	118 40W
Humphreys Pk.	**161**	35 24N	111 38W
Humpolec	**52**	49 31N	15 20 E
Humshaugh	**35**	55 3N	2 8W
Humula	**141**	35 30 S	147 46 E
Hün	**119**	29 2N	16 0 E
Hun Chiang, R.	**107**	40 52N	125 42 E
Huna Floi	**74**	65 50N	20 50W
Hunan □	**109**	27 30N	111 30 E
Hunch'un	**107**	42 52N	130 21 E
Hundested	**73**	55 58N	11 52 E
Hundred House	**31**	52 11N	3 17W
Hundred Mile House	**152**	51 38N	121 18W
Hundshögen, mt.	**72**	62 57N	13 46 E
Hunedoara	**70**	45 40N	22 50 E
Hunedoara □	**70**	45 45N	22 54 E
Hünfeld	**48**	50 40N	9 47 E
Hung Chiang, R.	**108**	27 7N	109 57 E
Hung Ho, R.	**109**	32 24N	115 32 E
Hung Liu Ho, R.	**106**	38 3N	109 10 E
Hung Yen	**100**	20 39N	106 4 E
Hungan	**109**	31 18N	114 33 E
Hungary ■	**53**	47 20N	19 20 E
Hungary, Plain of	**16**	47 0N	20 0 E
Hungchiang	**109**	27 0N	110 0 E
Hungerford, Austral.	**139**	28 58 S	144 24 E
Hungerford, U.K.	**28**	51 25N	1 30W
Hunghai Wan	**109**	22 45N	115 15 E
Hunghu	**109**	29 49N	113 30 E
Hüngnam	**107**	39 55N	127 45 E
Hungshui Ho, R.	**108**	23 24N	110 12 E
Hungtech'eng	**106**	36 48N	107 6 E
Hungt'ou Hsü	**109**	22 4N	121 25 E
Hungt'se Hu	**107**	33 15N	118 45 E
Hungtung	**106**	36 15N	111 37 E
Hungya	**108**	29 56N	103 25 E
Hungyüan	**108**	32 46N	102 42 E
Huni Valley	**120**	5 33N	1 56W
Hunmanby	**33**	54 12N	0 19W
Hunsberge	**128**	27 58 S	17 5 E
Hunsrück, mts.	**49**	50 0N	7 30 E
Hunstanton	**29**	52 57N	0 30 E
Hunsur	**97**	12 16N	76 16 E
Hunte, R.	**48**	52 47N	8 28 E
Hunter, N.Z.	**143**	44 36 S	171 2 E
Hunter, N.D., U.S.A.	**158**	47 12N	97 17W
Hunter, N.Y., U.S.A.	**162**	42 13N	74 13W
Hunter Hills, The	**143**	44 26 S	170 46 E
Hunter, I.	**138**	40 30 S	144 54 E
Hunter I.	**152**	51 55N	128 0W
Hunter Mts.	**143**	45 43 S	167 25 E
Hunter, R.	**143**	44 21 S	169 27 E
Hunter Ra.	**141**	32 45 S	150 15 E
Hunters Road	**127**	19 9 S	29 49 E
Hunterston	**34**	55 43N	4 55W
Hunterton	**139**	26 12 S	148 30 E
Hunterville	**142**	39 56 S	175 35 E
Huntingburg	**156**	38 20N	86 58W
Huntingdon, Can.	**150**	45 10N	74 10W
Huntingdon, U.K.	**29**	52 20N	0 11W
Huntingdon, N.Y., U.S.A.	**162**	40 52N	73 25W
Huntingdon, Pa., U.S.A.	**156**	40 28N	78 1W
Huntingdon & Peterborough (□)	**26**	52 23N	0 10W
Huntingdon I.	**151**	53 48N	56 45W
Huntington, U.K.	**33**	54 0N	1 4W
Huntington, Id., U.S.A.	**160**	44 22N	117 21W
Huntington, Ind., U.S.A.	**156**	40 52N	85 30W
Huntington, Ut., U.S.A.	**160**	39 24N	111 1W
Huntington, W. Va., U.S.A.	**156**	38 20N	82 30W
Huntington Beach	**163**	33 40N	118 0W
Huntington Park	**161**	34 58N	118 15W
Huntly, N.Z.	**142**	37 34 S	175 11 E
Huntly, U.K.	**37**	57 27N	2 48W
Huntsville, Can.	**150**	45 20N	79 14W
Huntsville, Ala., U.S.A.	**157**	34 45N	86 35W
Huntsville, Tex., U.S.A.	**159**	30 50N	95 35W
Hunyani Dams.	**127**	18 0 S	31 10 E
Hunyani, R.	**127**	18 0 S	31 10 E
Hunyüan	**106**	39 44N	113 42 E
Hunza, R.	**95**	36 24N	75 50 E
Huohsien	**106**	36 38N	111 43 E
Huon, G.	**135**	7 0 S	147 30 E
Huon Pen.	**135**	6 20 S	147 30 E
Huong Hoa	**100**	16 37N	106 45 E
Huong Khe	**100**	18 13N	105 41 E
Huonville	**138**	43 0 S	147 5 E
Huoshaop'u	**107**	43 23N	130 26 E
Hupei □	**109**	31 5N	113 5 E
Hurbanovo	**53**	47 51N	18 11 E
Hurezani	**70**	44 49N	23 40 E
Hurghada	**122**	27 15N	33 50 E
Hŭrghita □	**70**	46 30N	25 30 E
Hŭrghita Mţii	**70**	46 25N	25 35 E
Hurley, N. Mex., U.S.A.	**161**	32 45N	108 7W
Hurley, Wis., U.S.A.	**158**	46 26N	90 10W
Hurlford	**34**	55 35N	4 29W
Hurliness	**37**	58 47N	3 15W
Hurlock	**162**	38 38N	75 52W
Huron, Calif., U.S.A.	**163**	36 12N	120 6W
Huron, S.D., U.S.A.	**158**	44 30N	98 20W
Hurricane	**161**	37 10N	113 12W
Hursley	**28**	51 1N	1 23W
Hurso	**123**	9 35N	41 33 E
Hurstbourne Tarrant	**28**	51 17N	1 27W
Hurstpierpoint	**29**	50 56N	0 11W
Hurum, Buskerud, Norway	**71**	59 36N	10 23 E
Hurum, Oppland, Norway	**71**	61 9N	8 46 E
Hurunui, R.	**143**	42 54 S	173 18 E
Hurup	**73**	56 46N	8 25 E
Husaby	**73**	58 35N	13 25 E
Húsavík	**74**	66 3N	17 21W
Husband's Bosworth	**28**	52 27N	1 3W
Husi	**70**	46 41N	28 7 E
Husinish Pt.	**36**	57 59N	7 6W
Huskvarna	**73**	57 47N	14 15 E
Huslia	**147**	65 40N	156 30W
Husøy	**71**	61 3N	4 44 E
Hussar	**152**	51 3N	112 41W
Hussein (Allenby) Br.	**90**	31 53N	35 33 E
Hustopéce	**53**	48 57N	16 43 E
Husum, Ger.	**48**	54 27N	9 3 E
Husum, Sweden	**72**	63 21N	19 12 E
Hutchinson, Kans., U.S.A.	**159**	38 3N	97 59W
Hutchinson, Minn, U.S.A.	**158**	44 50N	94 22W
Huttenberg	**52**	46 56N	14 33 E
Hüttental	**47**	50 53N	8 1 E
Huttig	**159**	33 5N	92 10W
Hutton, Mt.	**139**	25 51 S	148 20 E
Hutton, oilfield	**19**	61 0N	1 30 E
Hutton Ra.	**137**	24 45 S	124 30 E
Huttwil	**50**	47 7N	7 50 E
Huwarā	**90**	32 9N	35 15 E
Huwun	**123**	4 23N	40 6 E
Huy	**47**	50 31N	5 15 E
Huyton	**32**	53 25N	2 52W
Hvaler	**71**	59 4N	11 1 E
Hvammsfjörður	**74**	65 4N	22 5W
Hvammur	**74**	65 13N	21 49W
Hvar	**63**	43 10N	16 45 E
Hvar, I.	**63**	43 11N	16 28 E
Hvarski Kanal	**63**	43 15N	16 35 E
Hvítá, Arnessýsla, Iceland	**74**	64 0N	20 58W
Hvítá, Mýrasýsla, Iceland	**74**	64 40N	21 5W
Hvitárvatn	**74**	63 37N	19 50W
Hvitsten	**71**	59 35N	10 42 E
Hwachon-chŏsuji	**107**	38 5N	127 50 E
Hwang Ho = Huang Ho, R.	**107**	36 50N	118 20 E
Hwekum	**98**	26 7N	95 22 E
Hyannis, Mass., U.S.A.	**162**	41 39N	70 17W
Hyannis, Nebr., U.S.A.	**158**	41 60N	101 45W
Hyargas Nuur	**105**	49 12N	93 34 E
Hyattsville	**162**	38 59N	76 55W
Hybo	**72**	61 49N	16 15 E
Hydaburg	**147**	55 15N	132 45W
Hyde, N.Z.	**143**	45 18 S	170 16 E
Hyde, U.K.	**32**	53 26N	2 6W
Hyde Park	**162**	41 47N	73 56W
Hyden	**137**	32 24 S	118 46 E
Hyderabad, India	**96**	17 10N	78 29 E
Hyderabad, Pak.	**94**	25 23N	68 36 E
Hyderabad □	**94**	25 3N	68 24 E
Hyères	**45**	43 8N	6 9 E
Hyères, Is. d'	**45**	43 0N	6 28 E
Hyesan	**107**	41 20N	128 10 E
Hyland Post	**139**	57 40N	128 10W
Hyland, R.	**152**	59 52N	128 12W
Hylestad	**71**	59 6N	7 29 E
Hyllested	**71**	56 17N	10 46 E
Hyltebruk	**73**	56 59N	13 15 E
Hymia	**95**	33 40N	78 2 E
Hyndman Pk.	**160**	44 4N	114 0W
Hynish	**34**	56 27N	6 54W
Hynish B.	**34**	56 29N	6 40W
Hyōgo-ken □	**110**	35 15N	135 0 E
Hyrum	**160**	41 35N	111 56W
Hysham	**160**	46 21N	107 11W
Hythe	**29**	51 4N	1 5 E
Hyūga	**110**	32 25N	131 35 E
Hyvinkä	**75**	60 38N	24 50 E

I

I Ho, R.	**107**	34 10N	118 4 E
I-n-Azaoua	**119**	20 45N	7 31 E
I-n-Échaïe	**118**	20 10N	2 5W
I-n-Gall	**121**	6 51N	7 1 E
I-n-Tabedog	**118**	19 54N	1 3 E
Iabès, Erg	**118**	27 30N	2 2W
Iaco, R.	**174**	10 25 S	70 30W
Iaçu	**171**	12 45 S	40 13W
Iakora	**129**	23 6 S	46 40 E
Ialomiţa □	**70**	44 30N	27 30 E
Ianca	**70**	45 6N	27 29 E
Iar Connacht	**39**	53 20N	9 20W
Iara	**70**	46 31N	23 35 E
Iaşi □	**70**	47 20N	27 0 E
Iaşi (Jassy)	**70**	47 10N	27 40 E
Iauaretê	**174**	0 30N	69 5W
Iaucdjovac, (Port Harrison)	**149**	58 25N	78 15W
Iba	**103**	15 22N	120 0 E
Ibadan	**121**	7 22N	3 58 E
Ibagué	**174**	4 27N	73 14W
Ibaiti	**171**	23 50 S	50 10W
Iballja	**68**	42 12N	20 0 E
Ibar, R.	**66**	43 15N	20 40 E
Ibara	**110**	34 36N	133 28 E

Ibaraki-ken □ Inhambane

Ibaraki-ken □ 111 36 10N 140 10 E
Ibararaki 111 34 49N 135 34 E
Ibarra 174 0 21N 78 7W
Ibba 123 4 49N 29 2 E
Ibba, Bahr el 123 5 30N 28 55 E
Ibbenbüren 48 52 16N 7 41 E
Ibembo 126 2 35N 23 35 E
Ibera, Laguna 172 28 30 S 57 9W
Iberian Peninsula 16 40 0N 5 0W
Iberville 150 45 19N 73 17W
Iberville, Lac d' 150 55 55N 73 15W
Ibi 121 8 15N 9 50 E
Ibiá 171 19 30 S 46 30W
Ibicaraí 171 14 51 S 39 36W
Ibicuí 171 14 51 S 39 59W
Ibicuy 172 33 55 S 59 10W
Ibioapaba, Serra da 170 20 14 S 40 25W
Ibipetuba 171 11 0 S 44 32W
Ibiracu 171 19 50 S 40 30W
Ibitiara 171 12 39 S 42 13W
Ibiza 59 38 54N 1 26 E
Ibiza, I. 59 39 0N 1 30 E
Iblei, Monti 65 37 15N 14 45 E
Ibo 127 12 22 S 40 32 E
Ibonma 103 3 22 S 133 31 E
Ibotirama 171 12 13 S 43 12W
Ibriktepe 68 41 2N 26 33 E
Ibshawâi 122 29 21N 30 40 E
Ibstock 28 52 42N 1 23W
Ibu 103 1 35N 127 25 E
Ibuki-Sanchi 111 35 25N 136 34 E
Ibǔneşti 70 46 45N 24 50 E
Iburg 48 52 10N 8 3 E
Ibusuki 110 31 12N 130 32 E
Ibwe Munyama 127 16 5 S 28 31 E
Ica 174 14 0 S 75 30W
Ica, R. 174 2 55 s 69 0W
Icabarú 174 4 20N 61 45W
Içana 174 1 21N 69 0W
Icatu 170 2 46 S 44 4W
Iceland, I. ■ 74 65 0N 19 0W
Icha 77 55 30N 156 0 E
Ichang 109 25 25N 112 55 E
Ich'ang 109 30 40N 111 20 E
Ichchapuram 96 19 10N 84 40 E
Icheng 109 32 16N 119 12 E
Ich'eng, Hupeh, China 109 31 43N 112 12 E
Ich'eng, Shansi, China 106 35 42N 111 40 E
Ichihara 111 35 28N 140 5 E
Ichikawa 111 35 44N 139 55 E
Ichilo, R. 174 16 30 S 64 45W
Ichinomiya, Gifu, Japan 111 35 18N 136 48 E
Ichinomiya, Kumamoto, Japan 110 32 58N 131 5 E
Ichinoseki 112 38 55N 141 8 E
Ichŏn 107 37 17N 127 27 E
Icht 118 29 6N 8 54W
Ichtegem 47 51 5N 3 1 E
Ich'uan 106 36 4N 110 6 E
Ich'un 105 47 42N 128 54 E
Ichün 106 35 23N 109 7 E
Ich'un, Heilungkiang, China 105 47 42N 128 54 E
Ich'un, Kiangsi, China 109 27 47N 114 22 E
Icó 170 6 24 S 38 51W
Icoraci 170 1 18 S 48 28W
Icy C. 12 70 25N 162 0W
Icy Str. 153 58 20N 135 30W
Ida Grove 158 42 20N 95 25W
Ida Valley 137 28 42 S 120 29 E
Idabel 159 33 53N 94 50W
Idaga Hamus 123 14 13N 39 35 E
Idah 121 6 10N 6 40 E
Idaho □ 160 44 10N 114 0W
Idaho City 160 43 50N 115 52W
Idaho Falls 160 43 30N 112 10W
Idaho Springs 160 39 49N 105 30W
Idanha-a-Nova 56 39 50N 7 15W
Idanre 121 7 8N 5 5 E
Idar-Oberstein 49 49 43N 7 19 E
Idd el Ghanam 117 11 30N 24 25 E
Iddan 91 6 10N 49 5 E
Idehan 119 27 10N 11 30 E
Idehan Marzūq 119 24 50N 13 51 E
Idelès 119 23 58N 5 53 E
Idfû 122 25 0N 32 49 E
Idhi Oros 69 35 15N 24 45 E
Idhra 69 37 20N 23 28 E
Idi 102 4 55N 97 45 E
Idi Amin Dada, L. 93 0 25 S 29 40 E
Idiofa 124 4 55 S 19 42 E
Idkerberget 72 60 22N 15 15 E
Idle 33 53 50N 1 45W
Idle, R. 33 53 27N 0 49W
Idmiston 28 51 8N 1 43W
Idna 90 31 34N 34 58 E
Idria 163 36 25N 120 41W
Idrija 63 46 0N 14 5 E
Idritsa 80 56 25N 28 57 E
Idstein 49 50 13N 8 17 E
Idsworth 29 50 56N 0 56W
Idutywa 125 32 8 S 28 18 E
Ieper 47 50 51N 2 53 E
Ierápetra 69 35 0N 25 44 E
Ierissós 68 40 22N 23 52 E
Ierissóu Kólpos 68 40 27N 23 57 E
Ierzu 64 39 48N 9 32 E
Ieshima-Shotō 110 34 40N 134 32 E
Iesi 63 43 32N 13 12 E
Ifach, Punta 59 38 38N 0 5 E
Ifanadiana 129 21 29 S 47 39 E
Ife 121 7 30N 4 31 E
Iférouâne 121 19 5N 8 35 E
Ifni 118 29 25N 10 10W
Ifon 121 6 58N 5 40 E
Iga 111 34 45N 136 10 E
Iganga 126 0 30N 33 28 E
Igarapava 171 20 3 S 47 47W
Igarapé Açu 170 1 4 S 47 33W
Igarapé-Mirim 170 1 59 S 48 58W
Igarka 77 67 30N 87 20 E
Igatimi 173 24 5 S 55 30W
Igatpuri 96 19 40N 73 35 E
Igbetti 121 8 44N 4 8 E
Igbo-Ora 121 7 10N 3 15 E
Igboho 121 8 40N 3 50 E
Iggesund 72 61 39N 17 10 E
Igherm 118 30 7N 8 18W
Ighil Izane 118 35 44N 0 31 E
Iglene 118 22 57N 4 58 E
Iglésias 64 39 19N 8 27 E
Igli 118 30 25N 2 12W
Iglino 84 54 50N 56 26 E
Igloolik Island 149 69 20N 81 30W
Igma 118 29 9N 6 11W
Igma, Gebel el 122 28 55N 34 0 E
Ignace 150 49 30N 91 40W
Igoshevo 81 59 25N 42 35 E
Igoumenitsa 68 39 32N 20 18 E
Igra 84 57 33N 53 7 E
Iguaçu, Cat. del 173 25 41N 54 26W
Iguaçu, R. 173 25 30 S 53 10W
Iguala 165 18 20N 99 40W
Igualada 58 41 37N 1 37 E
Iguape 171 24 43 S 47 33W
Iguape, R. 173 24 40 S 48 0W
Iguassu = Iguaçu 173 25 41N 54 26W
Iguatu 170 6 20 S 39 18W
Iguéla 124 2 0 S 9 16 E
Igumale 121 6 47N 7 55 E
Igunga □ 126 4 20 S 33 45 E
Ihiala 121 5 40N 6 55 E
Ihosy 129 22 24 S 46 8 E
Ihotry, L. 129 21 56 S 43 41 E
Ihsien, Anwhei, China 109 29 53N 117 57E
Ihsien, Hopeh, China 106 39 21N 115 29E
Ihsien, Liaoning, China 107 41 34N 121 15E
Ihsien, Shantung, China 107 37 11N 119 55E
Ihuang 109 27 32N 115 57 E
Ii 74 65 15N 25 30 E
Iida 111 35 35N 138 0 E
Iiey 138 18 53 S 141 12 E
Iijoki 74 65 20N 26 15 E
Iisalmi 74 63 32N 27 10 E
Iizuka 110 33 38N 130 42 E
Ijebu-Igbo 121 6 56N 4 1 E
Ijebu-Ode 121 6 47N 3 52 E
IJmuiden 46 52 28N 4 35 E
IJssel, R. 46 52 35N 5 50 E
IJsselmeer 46 52 45N 5 20 E
IJsselmuiden 46 52 34N 5 57 E
IJsselstein 46 52 1N 5 2 E
Ijuí, R. 173 27 58 S 55 20W
Ijüin 110 31 37N 130 24 E
IJzendijke 47 51 19N 3 37 E
IJzer, R. 47 51 9N 2 44 E
Ik, R. 84 55 55N 52 36 E
Ikamatua 41 42 15 S 171 41 E
Ikare 121 7 18N 5 40 E
Ikaria, I. 69 37 35N 26 10 E
Ikast 73 56 8N 9 10 E
Ikawa 111 35 13N 138 15 E
Ikeda 111 34 1N 133 48 E
Ikeja 121 6 28N 3 45 E
Ikela 124 1 0S 23 35 E
Ikerre 121 7 25N 5 19 E
Ikhtiman 67 42 27N 23 48 E
Iki 110 33 45N 129 42 E
Iki-Kaikyō 110 33 40N 129 45 E
Ikimba L. 126 1 30 S 31 20 E
Ikire 121 7 10N 4 15 E
Ikirun 121 7 54N 4 40 E
Ikitsuki-Shima 110 33 23N 129 26 E
Ikole 121 7 40N 5 37 E
Ikom 121 6 0N 8 42 E
Ikopa, R. 129 17 45 S 46 40 E
Ikot Ekpene 121 5 12N 7 40 E
Ikungu 126 1 33 S 33 42 E
Ikuno 110 35 10N 134 48 E
Ila 121 8 0N 4 51 E
Ilam 95 26 58N 87 58 E
Ilan, China 105 46 14N 129 33 E
Ilan, Taiwan 109 24 45N 121 44 E
Ilanskiy 77 56 14N 96 3 E
Ilanz 51 46 46N 9 12 E
Ilaomita, R. 47 44 47N 27 0 E
Ilaro Agege 121 6 53N 3 3 E
Ilayangudi 97 9 34N 78 37 E
Ilbilbie 138 21 45 S 149 20 E
Ilchester 28 51 0N 2 41W
Ile-à-la Crosse 153 55 27N 107 53W
Ile-à-la-Crosse, Lac 153 55 40N 107 45W
Île Bouchard, L' 42 47 7N 0 26 E
Île de France □ 43 49 0N 2 20 E
Ilebo 124 4 17 S 20 47 E
Ileje □ 127 9 30 S 33 25 E
Ilek 84 51 32N 53 21 E
Ilek, R. 84 51 30N 53 22 E
Ilen R. 39 51 38N 9 19W
Ilero 121 8 0N 3 20 E
Ilesha, West-Central, Nigeria 121 7 37N 4 40 E
Ilesha, Western, Nigeria 121 8 57N 3 28E
Ilford 153 56 4N 95 35W
Ilfov □ 70 44 20N 26 0 E
Ilfracombe, Austral. 138 23 30 S 144 30 E
Ilfracombe, U.K. 30 51 13N 4 8W
Ilha Grande, Baia da 171 23 9S 44 30W
Ílhavo 56 40 33N 8 43W
Ilheus 171 14 49 S 39 2W
Ili 85 45 53N 77 10 E
Ilia 70 45 57N 22 40 E
Ilia □ 69 37 45N 21 35 E
Iliamna L. 147 59 35N 155 30W
Iliang, Yunnan, China 108 24 54N 103 9E
Iliang, Yunnan, China 108 27 35N 104 1E
Ilich 85 40 50N 68 27 E
Ilico 172 34 50 S 72 20W
Iliff 158 40 50N 103 3W
Iliki 69 38 24N 23 15 E
Ilio Pt. 147 21 13N 157 16W
Iliodhrómia 68 39 12N 23 50 E
Ilion 162 43 0N 75 3W
Ilirska Bistrica 63 45 34N 14 14 E
Iliysk 76 44 10N 77 20 E
Ilkal 97 15 57N 76 8 E
Ilkeston 33 52 59N 1 19W
Ilkley 21 53 56N 1 49W
Illana B. 103 7 35N 123 45 E
Illapel 172 32 0 S 71 10W
'Illar 90 32 23N 35 7 E
Ille 44 42 40N 2 37 E
Ille-et-Vilaine □ 42 48 10N 1 30W
Iller, R. 49 47 53N 10 10 E
Illescás 56 40 8N 3 51W
Illig 91 7 47N 49 45 E
Illimani, Mte. 174 16 30 S 67 50W
Illinois □ 155 40 15N 89 30W
Illinois, R. 155 40 10N 90 20W
Illizi 119 26 31N 8 32 E
Illora 57 37 17N 3 53W
Ilmen, Oz. 80 58 15N 31 10 E
Ilmenau 48 50 41N 10 55 E
Ilminster 28 50 55N 2 56W
Ilo 174 17 40 S 71 20W
Ilobu 121 7 45N 4 25 E
Ilohuli Shan 105 51 20N 124 20 E
Iloilo 103 10 45N 122 33 E
Ilok 66 45 15N 19 20 E
Ilora 121 7 45N 3 50 E
Ilorin 121 8 30N 4 35 E
Ilovatka 81 50 30N 46 50 E
Ilovlya 83 49 15N 44 2 E
Ilovlya, R. 83 49 38N 44 20 E
Iłowa 54 51 30N 15 10 E
Ilubabor □ 123 7 25N 35 0 E
Ilukste 80 55 55N 26 20 E
Ilung 108 31 34N 106 24 E
Ilva Micá 70 47 17N 24 40 E
Ilwaki 103 7 55 S 126 30 E
Ilyichevsk 82 46 10N 30 35 E
Imabari 110 34 4N 133 0 E
Imadahane 118 32 8N 7 0W
Imaichi 111 36 6N 139 16 E
Imaloto, R. 129 23 10 S 45 15 E
Iman = Dalneretchensk 77 45 50N 133 40 E
Imari 110 33 15N 129 52 E
Imasa 122 18 0N 36 12 E
Imathía □ 68 40 30N 22 15 E
Imbâbah 122 30 5N 31 12 E
Imbler 160 45 31N 118 0W
Imbros = Imroz 68 40 10N 26 0 E
Imen 108 24 40N 102 9 E
Imeni Panfilova 85 43 23N 77 7 E
Imeni Poliny Osipenko 77 55 25N 136 29 E
Imeri, Serra 174 0 50N 65 25W
Imerimandroso 129 17 26 S 48 35 E
Imi (Hinna) 123 6 35N 42 30 E
Imi n'Tanoute 118 31 13N 8 51 E
Imienp'o 107 45 0N 128 16 E
Imishly 83 39 49N 48 4 E
Imiteg 118 29 43N 8 10W
Imlay 160 40 45N 118 9W
Immingham 33 53 37N 0 12W
Immokalee 157 26 25N 81 20W
Imo □ 121 5 15N 7 20 E
Imola 63 44 20N 11 42 E
Imotski 66 43 27N 17 21 E
Imperatriz 170 5 30 S 47 29W
Impéria 62 43 52N 8 0 E
Imperial, Can. 153 51 21N 105 28W
Imperial, Calif., U.S.A. 161 32 52N 115 34W
Imperial, Nebr., U.S.A. 158 40 38N 101 39W
Imperial Beach 163 32 35N 117 8W
Imperial Dam 161 32 50N 114 30W
Imperial Valley 163 32 55N 115 30W
Imperieuse Reef 136 17 36 S 118 50 E
Impfondo 124 1 40N 18 0 E
Imphal 98 24 48N 93 56 E
Imphy 43 46 56N 3 15 E
Imroz = Gökçeada 68 40 10N 26 0 E
Imst 52 47 15N 10 44 E
Imuruan B. 103 10 40N 119 10 E
In Belbel 118 27 55N 1 12 E
In Delimane 121 15 52N 1 31 E
In-Gall 121 16 51N 7 1 E
In Rhar 118 27 10N 1 59 E
In Salah 118 27 10N 2 32 E
In Tallak 121 16 19N 3 15 E
Ina 111 35 50N 138 0 E
Ina-Bonchi 111 35 45N 137 58 E
Inagh 39 52 53N 9 11W
Inajá 170 8 54 S 37 49W
Inangahua Junc. 143 41 52 S 171 59 E
Inanwatan 103 2 10 S 132 5 E
Iñapari 174 11 0 S 69 40W
Inari 74 68 54N 27 5 E
Inari, L. 74 69 0N 28 0 E
Inazawa 111 35 15N 136 47 E
Inca 58 39 43N 2 54 E
Incaguasi 172 29 12 S 71 5W
Ince 32 53 32N 2 38W
İnce Burnu 92 42 2N 35 0 E
Inch 39 52 42N 8 8W
Inch Br. 39 52 49N 9 6W
Inchard, Loch 36 58 28N 5 2W
Inchcape Rock 35 56 26N 2 24W
Inchigeelagh 39 51 50N 9 8W
Inchini 123 8 55N 37 37 E
Inchkeith, I. 35 56 2N 3 8W
Inchnadamph 36 58 9N 5 0W
Inch'ŏn 107 37 27N 126 40 E
Inchture 35 56 26N 3 8W
Incio 56 42 39N 7 21W
Incomáti, R. 129 25 15 S 32 35 E
Incudine, Mte. l' 45 41 50N 9 12 E
Inda Silase 123 14 10N 38 15 E
Indaal L. 34 55 44N 6 20W
Indalsälven 72 62 36N 17 30 E
Indaw 98 24 15N 96 5 E
Indbir 123 8 7N 37 52 E
Indefatigable, gasfield 19 53 20N 2 40 E
Independence, Calif., U.S.A. 163 36 51N 118 7W
Independence, Iowa, U.S.A. 158 42 27N 91 52W
Independence, Kans., U.S.A. 159 37 10N 95 50W
Independence, Mo., U.S.A. 158 39 3N 94 25W
Independence, Oreg., U.S.A. 160 44 53N 123 6W
Independence Fjord 12 82 10N 29 0W
Independence Mts. 160 41 30N 116 2W
Independência 170 5 23 S 40 19W
Independencia, La 165 16 31N 91 47W
Independenţa 70 45 25N 27 42 E
Inderborskly 83 48 30N 51 42 E
India ■ 87 20 0N 80 0 E
Indian Cabins 152 59 52N 117 2W
Indian Harbour 151 54 27N 57 13W
Indian Head 153 50 30N 103 35W
Indian House L. 151 56 30N 64 30W
Indian Lake 162 43 47N 74 16W
Indian Ocean 11 5 0 S 75 0 E
Indian River B. 162 38 36N 75 4W
Indiana 156 40 38N 79 9W
Indiana □ 156 40 0N 86 0W
Indianapolis 156 39 42N 86 10W
Indianola, Iowa, U.S.A. 158 41 20N 93 38W
Indianola, Miss., U.S.A. 159 33 27N 90 40W
Indianópolis 171 19 2 S 47 55 E
Indiapora 171 19 57 S 50 17W
Indiaroba 171 11 32 S 37 31W
Indiga 78 67 50N 48 50 E
Indigirka, R. 77 69 0N 147 0 E
Indija 66 45 6N 20 7 E
Indio 163 33 46N 116 15W
Indonesia ■ 102 5 0 S 115 0 E
Indore 94 22 42N 75 53 E
Indramaju 103 6 21 S 108 20 E
Indramaju, Tg. 103 6 20 S 108 20 E
Indravati, R. 96 19 0N 81 15 E
Indre □ 43 47 12N 1 39 E
Indre-et-Loire □ 42 47 12N 0 40 E
Indre, R. 42 47 2N 1 8 E
Indre Söndeled 71 58 46N 9 5 E
Indus, Mouth of the 94 24 00N 68 00 E
Indus, R. 94 28 40N 70 10 E
İnebolu 92 41 55N 33 40E
Infante, Kaap 128 34 27 S 20 51 E
Infantes 59 38 43N 3 1W
Infiernillo, Presa del 164 18 9N 102 0W
Infiesto 56 43 21N 5 21W
Ingá 171 7 17 S 35 36W
Ingatestone 29 51 40N 0 23W
Ingelmunster 47 50 56N 3 16 E
Ingende 124 0 12 S 18 57 E
Ingenio Santa Ana 172 27 25 S 65 40W
Ingesvang 73 56 10N 9 20 E
Ingham 138 18 43 S 146 10 E
Ingichka 85 39 47N 65 58 E
Ingleborough, mt. 32 54 11N 2 23W
Inglefield Land 143 78 30N 70 0W
Ingleton 32 54 9N 2 29W
Inglewood, Queensland, Austral. 139 28 25 S 151 8 E
Inglewood, Vic., Austral. 140 36 29 S 143 53 E
Inglewood, N.Z. 142 39 9 S 174 14 E
Inglewood, U.S.A. 163 33 58N 118 21W
Ingoldmells, Pt. 33 53 11N 0 21 E
Ingólfshöfði 74 63 48N 16 39W
Ingolstadt 49 48 45N 11 26 E
Ingomar 160 46 43N 107 37W
Ingonish 151 46 42N 60 18W
Ingore 120 12 24N 15 48W
Ingul, R. 82 47 30N 32 15 E
Ingulec 82 47 42N 33 4 E
Ingulets, R. 82 47 20N 33 20 E
Inguri, R. 83 42 58N 42 17 E
Inhaca, I. 129 26 1 S 32 57 E
Inhafenga 129 20 36 S 33 47 E
Inhambane 125 23 54 S 35 30 E

Inhambane □ **Itaueira**

Inhambane □	129	22 30 S	34 20 E
Inhambupe	171	11 47 S	38 21 W
Inhaminga	127	18 26 S	35 0 E
Inharrime	129	24 30 S	35 0 E
Inharrime, R.	129	24 30 S	35 0 E
Inhassoro	127	21 50 S	35 15 E
Inhuma	170	6 40 S	41 42 W
Inhumas	171	16 22 S	49 30 W
Iniesta	59	39 27 N	1 45 W
Ining, Kwangsi-Chuang, China	109	25 8 N	109 57 E
Ining, Sinkiang-Uigur, China	105	43 54 N	81 21 E
Inírida, R.	174	3 0 N	68 40 W
Inishark	38	53 36 N	10 17 W
Inishark I.	38	53 38 N	10 17 W
Inishbofin I., Donegal, Ireland	38	55 10 N	8 10 W
Inishbofin I., Galway, Ireland	38	53 35 N	10 12 W
Inisheer	39	53 3 N	9 32 W
Inishfree B.	38	55 4 N	8 20 W
Inishkea Is.	38	54 8 N	10 10 W
Inishmaan I.	39	53 5 N	9 35 W
Inishmore, I.	39	53 8 N	9 45 W
Inishmurray I.	38	54 26 N	8 40 W
Inishowen Hd.	38	55 14 N	6 56 W
Inishowen, Pen.	38	55 14 N	7 15 W
Inishrush	38	54 52 N	6 32 W
Inishtooskert I.	39	52 10 N	10 35 W
Inishturk I.	38	53 42 N	10 8 W
Inishvickillane	39	52 3 N	10 37 W
Inistioge	39	52 30 N	7 5 W
Injune	139	25 46 S	148 32 E
Inkberrow	28	52 13 N	1 59 W
Inklin	152	58 56 N	133 5 W
Inklin, R.	152	58 50 N	133 10 W
Inkom	160	42 51 N	112 7 W
Inkpen Beacon	28	51 22 N	1 28 W
Inle Aing	98	20 30 N	96 58 E
Inn, R.	49	48 35 N	13 28 E
Innamincka	139	27 44 S	140 46 E
Innellan	34	55 54 N	4 58 W
Inner Mongolia □	106	44 50 N	117 40 E
Inner Sound	36	57 30 N	5 55 W
Innerleithen	35	55 37 N	3 4 W
Innertkirchen	50	46 43 N	8 14 E
Innetalling I.	150	56 0 N	79 0 W
Innfield	38	53 25 N	6 50 W
Inniscrone	38	54 13 N	69 0 W
Innisfail, Austral.	138	17 33 S	146 5 E
Innisfail, Can.	152	52 0 N	113 57 W
Innishannon	39	51 45 N	8 40 W
Inniskeen	38	54 0 N	6 35 W
In'no-shima	110	34 19 N	133 10 E
Innsbruck	52	47 16 N	11 23 E
Ino	110	33 33 N	133 26 E
Inocência	171	19 47 S	51 48 W
Inongo	124	1 35 S	18 30 E
Inosu	174	12 22 N	71 38 W
Inoucdjouac (Port Harrison)	149	58 27 N	78 6 W
Inowrocław	54	52 50 N	18 20 E
Inpundong	107	41 25 N	126 34 E
Inquisivi	174	16 50 S	66 45 W
Ins	50	47 1 N	7 7 E
Insch	37	57 20 N	2 39 W
Inscription, C.	137	25 29 S	112 59 E
Insein	98	17 15 N	96 0 E
Însurăţei	70	44 50 N	27 40 E
Intendente Alvear	172	35 12 S	63 32 W
Interior	158	43 46 N	101 59 W
Interlaken, Switz.	50	46 41 N	7 50 E
Interlaken, U.S.A.	162	42 37 N	76 43 W
International Falls	158	48 36 N	93 25 W
Interview I.	101	12 55 N	92 42 E
Inthanon, Mt.	101	18 35 N	98 29 E
Intiyaco	172	28 50 S	60 0 W
Intragna	51	46 11 N	8 42 E
Inubō-Zaki	111	35 42 N	140 52 E
Inútil, B.	176	53 30 S	70 15 W
Inuvik	147	68 16 N	133 40 W
Inuyama	111	35 23 N	136 56 E
Inver B.	38	54 35 N	8 28 W
Inverallochy	37	57 40 N	1 56 W
Inveran, Ireland	39	53 14 N	9 28 W
Inveran, U.K.	37	57 58 N	4 26 W
Inveraray	34	56 13 N	5 5 W
Inverbervie	37	56 50 N	2 17 W
Invercargill	143	46 24 S	168 24 E
Inverell	139	29 45 S	151 8 E
Invergarry	37	57 5 N	4 48 W
Invergordon	37	57 41 N	4 10 W
Invergowrie	35	56 29 N	3 5 W
Inverie	36	57 2 N	5 40 W
Inverkeilor	37	56 38 N	2 33 W
Inverkeithing	35	56 2 N	3 24 W
Inverleigh	140	38 6 S	144 3 E
Invermere	152	50 30 N	116 2 W
Invermoriston	37	57 13 N	4 38 W
Inverness, Can.	151	46 15 N	61 19 W
Inverness, U.K.	37	57 29 N	4 12 W
Inverness, U.S.A.	157	28 50 N	82 20 W
Inverness (□)	26	57 6 N	4 40 W
Invershiel	36	57 13 N	5 25 W
Inverurie	37	57 15 N	2 21 W
Inverway	136	17 50 S	129 38 E
Investigator Group	136	34 45 S	134 20 E
Investigator Str.	140	35 30 S	137 0 E
Inyanga	127	18 12 S	32 40 E
Inyangahi, mt.	127	18 20 S	32 20 E
Inyantue	127	18 30 S	26 40 E
Inyazura	127	18 40 S	31 40 E
Inyo Range	161	37 0 N	118 0 W
Inyokern	163	35 37 N	117 54 W
Inywa	98	22 4 N	94 44 E
Inza	81	53 55 N	46 25 E
Inzell	49	47 48 N	12 15 E
Inzer	84	54 14 N	57 34 E
Inzhavino	81	52 22 N	42 23 E
Ioánnina (Janinà) □	68	39 39 N	20 57 E
Iōhen	110	32 58 N	132 32 E
Iola	159	38 0 N	95 20 W
Ioma	135	8 19 S	147 52 E
Ion Corvin	70	44 7 N	27 50 E
Iona I.	34	56 20 N	6 25 W
Ionava	80	55 8 N	24 12 E
Ione, Calif., U.S.A.	163	38 20 N	121 0 W
Ione, Wash., U.S.A.	160	48 44 N	117 29 W
Ionia	156	42 59 N	85 7 W
Ionian Is. = Ionioi Nisoi	69	38 40 N	20 0 E
Ionian Sea	61	37 30 N	17 30 E
Iónioi Nísoi	69	38 40 N	20 8 E
Ioniškis	80	56 13 N	23 35 E
Iori, R.	83	41 12 N	46 10 E
Íos, I.	69	36 41 N	25 20 E
Iowa □	158	42 18 N	93 30 W
Iowa City	158	41 40 N	91 35 W
Iowa Falls	158	42 30 N	93 15 W
Ipala	126	4 30 S	33 5 E
Ipameri	171	17 44 S	48 9 W
Ipanema	75	9 48 S	41 45 W
Ipáti	69	38 52 N	22 14 E
Ipatovo	83	45 45 N	42 50 E
Ipel, R.	53	48 10 N	19 35 E
Ipiales	174	0 50 N	77 37 W
Ipiaú	171	14 8 S	39 44 W
Ipin	108	28 48 N	104 33 E
Ipinlang	108	25 5 N	101 58 E
Ipirá	171	12 10 S	39 44 W
Ipiros □	68	39 30 N	20 30 E
Ipixuna	174	7 0 S	71 40 W
Ipoh	101	4 35 N	101 5 E
Iporá	171	16 28 S	51 7 W
Ippy	117	6 5 N	21 7 E
Ipsárion Óros	68	40 40 N	24 40 E
Ipswich, Austral.	139	27 35 S	152 46 E
Ipswich, U.K.	29	52 4 N	1 9 E
Ipswich, N.H., U.S.A.	162	42 40 N	70 50 W
Ipswich, S.D., U.S.A.	158	45 28 N	99 20 W
Ipu	170	4 23 S	40 44 W
Ipueiras	170	4 33 S	40 43 W
Ipupiara	171	11 49 S	42 37 W
Iput, R.	80	53 0 N	32 10 E
Iquique	174	20 19 S	70 5 W
Iquitos	174	3 45 S	73 10 W
Iracoubo	175	5 30 N	53 10 W
Iráklia, I.	69	36 50 N	25 28 E
Iráklion	69	35 20 N	25 12 E
Iráklion □	69	35 10 N	25 10 E
Irako-Zaki	111	34 35 N	137 1 E
Irala	173	25 55 S	54 35 W
Iramba □	126	4 30 S	34 30 E
Iran ■	93	33 0 N	53 0 E
Iran, Pegunungan	102	2 20 N	114 50 E
Iran, Plateau of	43	33 00 N	55 0 E
Iranamadu Tank	97	9 23 N	80 29 E
Iranshahr	93	27 75 N	60 40 E
Irapa	174	10 34 N	62 35 W
Irapuato	164	20 40 N	101 40 W
Iraq ■	92	33 0 N	44 0 E
Irarrar, W.	118	20 10 N	1 30 E
Irati	173	25 25 S	50 38 W
Irbid	90	32 35 N	35 48 E
Irbit	84	57 41 N	63 3 E
Irchester	29	52 17 N	0 40 W
Irebu	124	0 40 S	17 55 E
Irecê	170	11 18 S	41 52 W
Iregua, R.	58	42 22 N	2 24 E
Ireland ■	38	53 0 N	8 0 W
Ireland's Eye	38	53 25 N	6 4 W
Irele	121	7 40 N	5 40 E
Iremel, Gora	84	54 33 N	58 50 E
Iret	77	60 10 N	154 5 E
Irgiz, Bol.	81	52 10 N	49 10 E
Irharharene	119	27 37 N	7 30 E
Irharrhar, O.	119	27 30 N	6 0 E
Irhyangdong	107	41 15 N	129 30 E
Iri	107	35 59 N	127 0 E
Irian Jaya □	103	4 0 S	137 0 E
Iriba	124	15 7 N	22 15 E
Irié	120	8 15 N	9 10 W
Iriklinskiy	84	51 39 N	58 38 E
Iringa	126	7 48 S	35 43 E
Iringa □, Tanz.	126	7 48 S	35 43 E
Iringa □, Tanz.	127	9 0 S	35 0 E
Irinjalakuda	97	10 21 N	76 14 E
Iriomote-Jima	112	24 19 N	123 48 E
Iriona	166	15 57 N	85 11 W
Irish Sea	32	54 0 N	5 0 W
Irish Town	93	40 55 S	145 9 E
Irkeshtam	85	39 41 N	73 55 E
Irkutsk	77	52 10 N	104 20 E
Irlam	32	53 26 N	2 27 W
Irma	153	52 55 N	111 14 W
Irmak	92	39 58 N	33 25 E
Irō-Zaki	111	34 36 N	138 51 E
Iroise	42	48 15 N	4 45 W
Iron Baron	140	33 3 S	137 11 E
Iron Gate = Porţile de Fier	70	44 42 N	22 30 E
Iron Knob	140	32 46 S	137 8 E
Iron, L.	38	53 37 N	7 34 W
Iron Mountain	156	45 49 N	88 4 W
Iron River	158	46 6 N	88 40 W
Ironbridge	28	52 38 N	2 29 W
Ironhurst	138	18 5 S	143 28 E
Ironstone Kopje, Mt.	128	25 17 S	24 5 E
Ironton, Mo., U.S.A.	159	37 40 N	90 40 W
Ironton, Ohio, U.S.A.	156	38 35 N	82 40 W
Ironwood	158	46 30 N	90 10 W
Iroquois Falls	150	48 46 N	80 41 W
Irpen	80	50 30 N	30 8 E
Irrara Cr.	139	29 35 S	145 31 E
Irrawaddy	98	17 0 N	95 0 E
Irrawaddy □	98	17 0 N	95 0 E
Irrawaddy, R.	98	15 50 N	95 6 E
Irsina	65	40 45 N	16 15 E
Irt R.	32	54 24 N	3 25 W
Irthing R.	35	54 25 N	2 48 W
Irthlingborough	29	52 20 N	0 37 W
Irtysh, R.	76	53 36 N	75 30 E
Irumu	126	1 32 N	29 53 E
Irún	58	43 20 N	1 52 W
Irurzun	58	42 55 N	1 50 W
Irvine, Can.	153	49 57 N	110 16 W
Irvine, U.K.	34	55 37 N	4 40 W
Irvine, U.S.A.	156	37 42 N	83 58 W
Irvinestown	38	54 28 N	7 38 W
Irwin, Pt.	137	35 5 S	116 55 E
Irwin, R.	137	29 15 S	114 54 E
Irymple	140	34 14 S	142 8 E
Is-sur-Tille	43	47 30 N	5 10 E
Isa	121	13 14 N	6 24 E
Isaac, R.	138	22 55 S	149 20 E
Isabel	158	45 27 N	101 22 W
Isabela, Dom. Rep.	167	19 58 N	71 2 W
Isabela, Pto Rico	147	18 30 N	67 01 W
Isabela, Cord.	166	13 30 N	85 25 W
Isabela, I.	164	21 51 N	105 55 W
Isabella Ra.	136	21 0 S	121 4 E
Ísafjarðardjúp	74	66 10 N	23 0 W
Ísafjörður	74	66 5 N	23 9 W
Isagarh	94	24 48 N	77 51 E
Isahaya	110	32 52 N	130 2 E
Isaka	126	3 56 S	32 59 E
Isakly	84	54 8 N	51 32 E
Isangi	124	0 52 N	24 10 E
Isar, R.	49	48 40 N	12 30 E
Isarco, R.	63	46 40 N	11 35 E
Ísari	69	37 22 N	22 0 E
Isbergues	43	50 36 N	2 24 E
Isbiceni	70	43 45 N	24 40 E
Ischia, I.	64	40 45 N	13 51 E
Iscuandé	174	2 28 N	77 59 W
Isdell, R.	136	16 27 S	124 51 E
Ise	111	34 25 N	136 45 E
Ise-Heiya	111	34 40 N	136 30 E
Ise-Wan	111	34 43 N	136 43 E
Isefjord	73	55 53 N	11 50 E
Iseltwald	50	46 43 N	7 58 E
Isenthal	51	46 55 N	8 34 E
Iseo	62	45 40 N	10 3 E
Iseo, L. di	62	45 45 N	10 3 E
Iseramagazi	126	4 37 S	32 10 E
Isère □	45	45 15 N	5 40 E
Isère, R.	44	45 15 N	5 30 E
Iserlohn	48	51 22 N	7 40 E
Isèrnia	65	41 35 N	14 12 E
Isesaki	111	36 19 N	139 12 E
Iset, R.	84	56 36 N	66 24 E
Iseyin	121	8 0 N	3 36 E
Isfara	85	40 7 N	70 38 E
Ishan	108	24 30 N	108 41 E
Ishara	121	6 40 N	3 40 E
Ishigaki	112	24 20 N	124 10 E
Ishikari-Wan	112	43 20 N	141 20 E
Ishikawa	112	26 25 N	127 48 E
Ishikawa-ken □	111	36 30 N	136 30 E
Ishim	76	56 10 N	69 18 E
Ishim, R.	76	57 45 N	71 10 E
Ishimbay	84	53 28 N	56 2 E
Ishinomaki	112	38 32 N	141 20 E
Ishioka	111	36 11 N	140 16 E
Ishizuchi-Yama	110	33 45 N	133 6 E
Ishkashim	85	36 44 N	71 37 E
Ishkuman	95	36 30 N	73 50 E
Ishmi	68	41 33 N	19 34 E
Ishpeming	156	46 30 N	87 40 W
Ishua	121	7 15 N	5 50 E
Ishui	107	35 50 N	118 32 E
Ishurdi	98	24 9 N	89 3 E
Isigny-sur-Mer	42	49 19 N	1 6 W
Işik	82	40 40 N	32 35 E
Isil Kul	76	54 55 N	71 16 E
Isili	44	39 45 N	9 6 E
Isiolo	126	0 24 N	37 33 E
Isipingo	129	30 00 S	30 57 E
Isipingo Beach	129	30 00 S	30 57 E
Isiro	126	2 53 N	27 58 E
Iskander	85	41 36 N	69 41 E
İskenderun	92	36 32 N	36 10 E
İskilip	82	40 50 N	34 20 E
Iskut, R.	152	56 45 N	131 49 W
Iskyr, R.	67	43 35 N	24 20 E
Isla Cristina	57	37 13 N	7 17 W
Isla, La	174	6 51 N	76 56 W
Isla, R.	37	56 32 N	3 20 W
Islamabad	94	33 40 N	73 0 E
Islamkot	94	24 42 N	70 13 E
Islampur	96	17 2 N	72 9 E
Island Falls, Can.	150	49 35 N	81 20 W
Island Falls, U.S.A.	151	46 0 N	68 25 W
Island L.	153	53 47 N	94 25 W
Island Lagoon	140	31 30 S	136 40 E
Island Pt.	137	30 20 S	115 1 E
Island Pond	156	44 50 N	71 50 W
Island, R.	152	60 25 N	121 12 W
Islands, B. of, Can.	151	49 11 N	58 15 W
Islands, B. of, N.Z.	142	35 20 S	174 20 E
Islay, I.	34	55 46 N	6 10 W
Islay Sound	34	55 45 N	6 5 W
Isle-Adam, L'	43	49 6 N	2 14 E
Isle aux Morts	151	47 35 N	59 0 W
Isle-Jourdain, L', Gers, France	44	43 36 N	1 5 E
Isle-Jourdain, L', Vienne, France	42	46 13 N	0 31 E
Isle, L', Tarn, France	44	43 52 N	1 49 E
Isle, L', Vaucluse, France	45	43 55 N	5 3 E
Isle of Whithorn	34	54 42 N	4 22 W
Isle of Wight □	28	50 40 N	1 20 W
Isle Ornsay	36	57 9 N	5 50 W
Isle Royale	158	48 0 N	88 50 W
Isle-sur-la-Sorgue, L'	45	43 55 N	5 2 E
Isle-sur-le-Doubs, L'	43	47 26 N	6 34 E
Isle Vista	163	34 27 N	119 52 W
Isleham	29	52 21 N	0 24 E
Islet, L'	151	47 4 N	70 23 W
Isleta	161	34 58 N	106 46 W
Isleton	163	38 10 N	121 37 W
Islip	28	51 49 N	1 12 W
Ismail	82	45 22 N	28 46 E
Ismâ'ilîya	122	30 37 N	32 18 E
Ismay	158	46 33 N	104 44 W
Isna	122	25 17 N	32 30 E
Isogstalo	95	34 15 N	78 46 E
Isola del Liri	64	41 39 N	13 32 E
Isola della Scala	62	45 16 N	11 0 E
Isola di Capo Rizzuto	65	38 56 N	17 5 E
Isparta	92	37 47 N	30 30 E
Isperikh	67	43 43 N	26 50 E
Íspica	65	36 47 N	14 53 E
Israel ■	90	32 0 N	34 50 E
Isseka	137	28 22 S	114 35 E
Issia	120	6 33 N	6 33 W
Issoire	44	45 32 N	3 15 E
Issoudun	43	46 57 N	2 0 E
Issyk-Kul, Ozero	85	42 25 N	77 15 E
İstanbul	92	41 0 N	29 0 E
Istmina	174	5 10 N	76 39 W
Istok	66	42 45 N	20 24 E
Istokpoga, L.	157	27 22 N	81 14 W
Istra, U.S.S.R.	81	55 55 N	36 50 E
Istra, Yugo.	63	45 10 N	14 0 E
Istranca Dağlari	67	41 48 N	27 30 E
Istres	45	43 31 N	4 59 E
Istria = Istra	63	45 10 N	14 0 E
Itá	172	25 29 N	57 21 W
Itabaiana, Paraíba, Brazil	170	7 18 S	35 19 W
Itabaiana, Sergipe, Brazil	170	10 41 S	37 26 W
Itabaianinha	170	11 16 S	37 47 W
Itaberaba	171	12 32 S	40 18 W
Itaberaí	171	16 2 S	49 48 W
Itabira	171	19 37 S	43 13 W
Itabirito	173	20 15 S	43 48 W
Itabuna	171	14 48 S	39 16 W
Itacaiunas, R.	170	5 21 S	49 8 W
Itacajá	170	8 19 S	47 46 W
Itaete	171	13 0 S	41 5 W
Itaguaçu	171	19 48 S	40 51 W
Itaguari, R.	171	14 11 S	44 40 W
Itaguatins	170	5 47 S	47 29 W
Itaim, R.	170	7 2 S	42 2 W
Itainópolis	170	7 24 S	41 31 W
Itaituba	175	4 10 S	55 50 W
Itajaí	173	27 0 S	48 45 W
Itajubá	173	22 24 S	45 30 W
Itajuípe	171	14 41 S	39 22 W
Itaka	127	8 50 S	32 49 E
Itako	111	35 56 N	140 33 E
Italy ■	60	42 0 N	13 0 E
Itamataré	170	2 16 S	46 24 W
Itambacuri	171	18 1 S	41 42 W
Itambé	171	15 15 S	40 37 W
Itambe, mt.	170	18 30 S	43 15 W
Itampolo	129	24 41 S	43 57 E
Itanhaém	121	24 9 S	46 47 W
Itanhém	171	17 9 S	40 20 W
Itano	110	34 1 N	134 28 E
Itapaci	171	14 57 S	49 34 W
Itapagé	170	3 41 S	39 34 W
Itaparica, I. de	171	12 54 S	38 42 W
Itapebi	171	15 56 S	39 32 W
Itapecerica	171	20 28 S	45 7 W
Itapecuru-Mirim	170	3 24 S	44 20 W
Itapecuru, R.	170	3 20 S	44 15 W
Itaperuna	171	21 10 S	42 0 W
Itapetinga	171	15 15 S	40 15 W
Itapetininga	173	23 36 S	48 7 W
Itapeva	173	23 59 S	48 59 W
Itapicuru	170	10 50 S	38 40 W
Itapicuru, R.	170	5 40 S	44 30 W
Itapipoca	170	3 30 S	39 35 W
Itapiúna	170	4 33 S	38 57 W
Itaporanga	171	7 18 S	38 10 W
Itapuá □	173	26 40 S	55 40 W
Itapuranga	171	15 35 S	49 59 W
Itaquari	173	20 12 S	40 25 W
Itaquatiana	174	2 58 S	58 30 W
Itaquí	172	29 0 S	56 30 W
Itararé	173	24 6 S	49 23 W
Itarsi	94	22 36 N	77 51 E
Itarumã	171	18 42 S	51 25 W
Itatí	172	27 16 S	58 15 W
Itatira	170	4 30 S	39 37 W
Itatuba	174	5 40 S	63 20 W
Itaueira	170	7 36 S	43 2 W

Itaueira, R Jedrzejów

Itaueira, R.	170	6 41 S	42 55 W
Itaúna	171	20 4 S	44 34 W
Itchen, R.	28	50 57 N	1 20 W
Itéa	69	38 25 N	22 25 E
Ithaca	162	42 25 N	76 30 W
Ithaca = Itháki	69	38 25 N	20 43 E
Itháki, I.	69	38 25 N	20 40 E
Ithon R.	31	52 16 N	3 23 W
It'iaoshan	106	37 10 N	104 2 E
Itinga	171	16 36 S	41 47 W
Itiruçu	171	13 31 S	40 9 W
Itiúba	171	10 43 S	39 51 W
Ito	111	34 58 N	139 5 E
Itonamas, R.	174	13 0 S	64 25 W
Itsa	122	29 15 N	30 40 E
Itsukaichi	110	34 22 N	132 8 E
Itsuki	110	32 24 N	130 50 E
Itteville	46	48 31 N	2 21 E
Ittiri	64	40 38 N	8 32 E
Itu, Brazil	173	23 10 S	47 15 W
Itu, Hupeh, China	109	30 24 N	111 26 E
Itu, Shantung, China	107	36 41 N	118 28 E
Itu, Nigeria	121	5 10 N	7 58 E
Ituaçu	171	13 50 S	41 18 W
Ituango	174	7 4 N	75 45 W
Ituiutaba	171	19 0 S	49 25 W
Itumbiara	171	18 20 S	49 10 W
Ituna	153	51 10 N	103 30 W
It'ung	107	43 20 N	125 17 E
Itunge Port	127	9 40 S	33 55 E
Itupiranga	170	5 9 S	49 20 W
Iturama	171	19 44 S	50 11 W
Iturbe	172	23 0 S	65 25 W
Ituri, R.	126	1 45 N	26 45 E
Iturup, Ostrov	77	45 0 N	148 0 E
Ituverava	171	20 20 S	47 47 W
Ituyuro, R.	172	22 40 S	63 50 W
Itzehoe	48	53 56 N	9 31 E
Ivalo	74	68 38 N	27 35 E
Ivalojoki	74	68 30 N	27 0 E
Ivanaj	68	42 17 N	19 25 E
Ivanhoe, N.S.W., Austral.	140	32 56 S	144 20 E
Ivanhoe, N.T., Austral.	136	15 41 S	128 41 E
Ivanhoe, U.S.A.	163	36 23 N	119 13 W
Ivanhoe L.	153	60 25 N	106 30 W
Ivanić Grad	63	45 41 N	16 25 E
Ivanjica	66	43 35 N	20 12 E
Ivanjscie	63	46 12 N	16 13 E
Ivankovskoye Vdkhr.	81	56 48 N	36 55 E
Ivano-Frankovsk, (Stanislav)	80	49 0 N	24 40 E
Ivanovka	84	52 34 N	53 23 E
Ivanovo, Byelorussia, U.S.S.R.	80	52 7 N	25 29 E
Ivanovo, R.S.F.S.R., U.S.S.R.	81	57 5 N	41 0 E
Ivato	129	20 37 S	47 10 E
Ivaylovgrad	67	41 32 N	26 8 E
Ivinghoe	29	51 50 N	0 38 W
Ivinheima, R.	173	21 48 S	54 15 W
Iviza = Ibiza	59	39 0 N	1 30 E
Ivohibe	129	22 31 S	46 57 E
Ivolândia	171	16 34 S	50 51 W
Ivory Coast ■	120	7 30 N	5 0 W
Ivösjön	73	56 8 N	14 25 E
Ivrea	62	45 30 N	7 52 E
Ivugivik, (N.D. d'Ivugivic)	149	62 24 N	77 55 W
Ivybridge	30	50 24 N	3 56 W
Iwahig	102	8 35 N	117 32 E
Iwai-Jima	110	33 47 N	131 58 E
Iwaki	112	37 3 N	140 55 E
Iwakuni	110	34 15 N	132 8 E
Iwami	110	35 32 N	134 15 E
Iwamisawa	112	43 12 N	141 46 E
Iwanai	112	42 58 N	140 30 E
Iwanuma	112	38 7 N	140 58 E
Iwase	110	36 21 N	140 6 E
Iwata	111	34 49 N	137 59 E
Iwate-ken □	112	39 30 N	141 30 E
Iwate-San	112	39 51 N	141 0 E
Iwo	121	7 39 N	4 9 E
Iwonicz-Zdroj	54	49 37 N	21 47 E
Ixiamas	174	13 50 S	68 5 W
Ixopo	129	30 11 S	30 5 E
Ixtepec	165	16 40 N	95 10 W
Ixtlán de Juárez	165	17 23 N	96 28 W
Ixtlán del Rio	164	21 5 N	104 28 W
Ixworth	29	52 18 N	0 50 E
Iyang, Honan, China	106	34 9 N	112 25 E
Iyang, Hunan, China	109	28 36 N	112 20 E
Iyang, Kiangsi, China	109	28 23 N	117 25 E
Iyo	110	33 45 N	132 45 E
Iyo-mishima	110	33 58 N	133 30 E
Iyo-Nada	110	33 40 N	132 20 E
Izabal, L.	166	15 30 N	89 10 W
Izamal	165	20 56 N	89 1 W
Izberbash	83	42 35 N	47 45 E
Izbica Kujawski	54	52 25 N	18 30 E
Izegem	47	50 55 N	3 12 E
Izgrev	67	43 36 N	26 58 E
Izh, R.	84	55 58 N	52 38 E
Izhevsk	84	56 51 N	53 14 E
Izmail	82	45 22 N	28 46 E
Izmir (Smyrna)	79	38 25 N	27 8 E
Izmit	92	40 45 N	29 50 E
Izola	63	45 32 N	13 39 E
Izu-Hantō	111	34 45 N	139 0 E
Izuhara	110	34 12 N	129 17 E
Izumi	110	32 5 N	130 22 E
Izumiotsu	111	34 30 N	135 24 E
Izumisano	111	34 40 N	135 43 E
Izumo	110	35 20 N	132 55 E
Izyaslav	80	50 5 N	25 50 E
Izyum	82	49 12 N	37 28 E
J			
Jaba	123	6 20 N	35 7 E
Jaba'	90	32 20 N	35 13 E
Jabaliya	90	31 32 N	34 27 E
Jabalón, R.	59	38 45 N	3 35 W
Jabalpur	95	23 9 N	79 58 E
Jablah	92	35 20 N	36 0 E
Jablanac	63	44 42 N	14 56 E
Jablonec	52	50 43 N	15 10 E
Jablonica	53	48 37 N	17 26 E
Jabłonowo	54	53 23 N	19 10 E
Jaboatão	170	8 7 S	35 1 W
Jaboticabal	173	21 15 S	48 17 W
Jabukovac	66	44 22 N	22 21 E
Jaburu	174	5 30 S	64 0 W
Jaca	58	42 35 N	0 33 W
Jacala	165	21 1 N	99 11 W
Jacaré, R.	170	10 3 S	42 13 W
Jacarei	173	23 20 S	46 0 W
Jacarèzinho	173	23 5 S	50 0 W
Jáchal	172	30 5 S	69 0 W
Jáchymov	52	50 22 N	12 55 E
Jacinto	171	16 10 S	40 17 W
Jack Lane B.	151	55 45 N	60 35 W
Jackfish	150	48 45 N	87 0 W
Jackman	151	45 35 N	70 17 W
Jacksboro	159	33 14 N	98 15 W
Jackson, Austral.	139	26 39 S	149 39 E
Jackson, Ala., U.S.A.	157	31 32 N	87 53 W
Jackson, Calif., U.S.A.	159	37 25 N	89 42 W
Jackson, Ill., U.S.A.	163	38 25 N	120 47 W
Jackson, Ky., U.S.A.	156	37 35 N	83 22 W
Jackson, Mich., U.S.A.	156	42 18 N	84 25 W
Jackson, Minn., U.S.A.	158	43 35 N	95 30 W
Jackson, Miss., U.S.A.	159	32 20 N	90 10 W
Jackson, Ohio, U.S.A.	156	39 0 N	82 40 W
Jackson, Tenn., U.S.A.	157	35 40 N	88 50 W
Jackson, Wyo., U.S.A.	160	43 30 N	110 49 W
Jackson Bay, Can.	152	50 32 N	125 57 W
Jackson Bay, N.Z.	143	43 58 S	168 42 E
Jackson, C.	143	40 59 S	174 20 E
Jackson, L.	160	43 55 N	110 40 W
Jacksons	143	42 46 S	171 32 E
Jacksonville, Ala., U.S.A.	157	33 49 N	85 45 W
Jacksonville, Calif., U.S.A.	163	37 52 N	120 24 W
Jacksonville, Fla., U.S.A.	157	30 15 N	81 38 W
Jacksonville, Ill., U.S.A.	158	39 42 N	90 15 W
Jacksonville, N.C., U.S.A.	157	34 50 N	77 29 W
Jacksonville, Oreg., U.S.A.	160	42 13 N	122 56 W
Jacksonville, Tex., U.S.A.	159	31 58 N	95 12 W
Jacksonville Beach	157	30 19 N	81 26 W
Jacmel	167	18 20 N	72 40 W
Jacob Lake	161	36 45 N	112 12 W
Jacobabad	94	28 20 N	68 29 E
Jacobeni	70	47 25 N	25 20 E
Jacobina	170	11 11 S	40 30 W
Jacob's Well	90	32 13 N	35 13 E
Jacques Cartier, Mt.	151	48 57 N	66 0 W
Jacques Cartier Pass	151	49 50 N	62 30 W
Jacqueville	120	5 12 N	4 25 W
Jacui, R.	173	30 2 S	51 15 W
Jacuipe, R.	171	12 30 S	39 5 W
Jacundá, R.	170	1 57 S	50 26 W
Jade	48	53 22 N	8 14 E
Jadebusen, B.	48	53 30 N	8 15 E
Jadoigne	47	50 43 N	4 52 E
Jadotville = Likasi	127	10 55 S	26 48 E
Jadovnik	66	43 20 N	19 45 E
Jadraque	58	40 55 N	2 55 W
Jādū	119	32 0 N	12 0 E
Jaén, Peru	174	5 25 S	78 40 W
Jaén, Spain	57	37 44 N	3 43 W
Jaén □	57	37 50 N	3 30 W
Jafène	118	20 35 N	5 30 W
Jaffa = Tel Aviv-Yafo	90	32 4 N	34 48 E
Jaffa, C.	140	36 58 S	139 40 E
Jaffna	97	9 45 N	80 2 E
Jaffrey	162	42 50 N	72 4 W
Jagadhri	94	30 10 N	77 20 E
Jagadishpur	95	25 30 N	84 21 E
Jagdalpur	96	19 3 N	82 6 E
Jagersfontein	128	29 44 S	25 27 E
Jaghbub	117	29 42 N	24 38 E
Jagraon	93	30 50 N	75 25 E
Jagst, R.	49	49 13 N	10 0 E
Jagtial	96	18 50 N	79 0 E
Jaguaquara	171	13 32 S	39 58 W
Jaguariaíva	173	24 10 S	49 50 W
Jaguaribe	170	5 53 S	38 37 W
Jaguaribe, R.	170	6 0 S	38 35 W
Jaguaruana	170	4 50 S	37 47 W
Jagüey	166	22 35 N	81 7 W
Jagungal, Mt.	141	36 8 S	148 22 E
Jahangirabad	94	28 19 N	78 4 E
Jahrom	92	28 30 N	53 31 E
Jaicós	170	7 21 S	41 8 W
Jainti	98	26 45 N	89 40 E
Jaintiapur	98	25 8 N	92 7 E
Jaipur	94	27 0 N	76 10 E
Jajarm	93	37 5 N	56 20 E
Jajce	66	44 19 N	17 17 E
Jajere	121	11 58 N	11 25 E
Jajpur	96	20 53 N	86 22 E
Jakarta	103	6 9 S	106 49 E
Jakobstad (Pietarsaari)	74	63 40 N	22 43 E
Jakupica	66	41 45 N	21 22 E
Jal	159	32 8 N	103 8 W
Jala	93	27 30 N	62 40 E
Jalalabad, Afghan.	94	34 30 N	70 29 E
Jalalabad, India	95	26 41 N	79 42 E
Jalalpur Jattan	94	32 38 N	74 19 E
Jalama	163	34 29 N	120 29 W
Jalapa, Guat.	166	14 45 N	89 59 W
Jalapa, Mexico	165	19 30 N	96 50 W
Jalas, Jabal al	92	27 30 N	36 30 E
Jalaun	95	26 8 N	79 25 E
Jales	171	20 16 S	50 33 W
Jaleswar	95	26 38 N	85 48 E
Jalgaon, Maharashtra, India	96	21 2 N	76 31 E
Jalgaon, Maharashtra, India	96	21 0 N	75 42 E
Jalhay	47	50 33 N	5 58 E
Jalingo	121	8 55 N	11 25 E
Jalisco □	164	20 0 N	104 0 W
Jalkot	95	35 20 N	73 24 E
Jallas, R.	56	42 57 N	9 0 W
Jallumba	140	36 55 N	141 57 E
Jalna	96	19 48 N	75 57 E
Jalón, R.	58	41 20 N	1 40 W
Jalpa	164	21 38 N	102 58 W
Jalpaiguri	98	26 32 N	88 46 E
Jalq	93	27 35 N	62 33 E
Jaluit I.	130	6 0 N	169 30 E
Jamaari	121	11 44 N	9 53 E
Jamaica, I. ■	166	18 10 N	77 30 W
Jamalpur, Bangla.	98	24 52 N	90 2 E
Jamalpur, India	95	25 18 N	86 28 E
Jamalpurganj	95	23 2 N	88 1 E
Jamanxim, R.	175	6 30 S	55 50 W
Jambe	103	1 15 S	132 10 E
Jambes	47	50 27 N	4 52 E
Jambi	102	1 38 S	103 30 E
Jambusar	94	22 3 N	72 51 E
Jamdena, I. = Yamdena	103	7 45 S	131 20 E
James B.	150	53 30 N	80 0 W
James, R., Dak., U.S.A.	158	44 50 N	98 0 W
James, R., Va., U.S.A.	162	37 0 N	76 27 W
James Ranges	136	24 10 S	132 0 E
James Ross I.	13	63 58 S	50 94 W
Jamestown, Austral.	140	33 10 S	138 32 E
Jamestown, S. Afr.	128	31 6 S	26 45 E
Jamestown, Ky., U.S.A.	156	37 0 N	85 5 W
Jamestown, N.D., U.S.A.	158	47 0 N	98 30 W
Jamestown, N.Y., U.S.A.	156	42 5 N	79 18 W
Jamestown, Tenn., U.S.A.	157	36 25 N	85 0 W
Jamestown, Va., U.S.A.	162	37 12 N	76 46 W
Jamiltepec	165	16 17 N	97 49 W
Jamkhandi	97	16 30 N	75 15 E
Jamma'in	90	32 8 N	35 12 E
Jammalamadugu	97	14 51 N	78 25 E
Jammerbugt	73	57 15 N	9 20 E
Jammu	94	32 43 N	74 54 E
Jammu & Kashmir □	95	34 25 N	77 0 E
Jamnagar	94	22 30 N	70 0 E
Jamner	96	20 45 N	75 45 E
Jamoigne	47	49 41 N	5 24 E
Jampur	94	29 39 N	70 32 E
Jamrud	94	34 2 N	71 24 E
Jamshedpur	95	22 44 N	86 20 E
Jamtara	95	23 59 N	86 41 E
Jämtlands län □	72	62 40 N	13 50 E
Jamuna, R.	98	23 51 N	89 45 E
Jamurki	98	24 9 N	90 2 E
Jan Kemp	128	27 55 S	24 51 E
Jan L.	153	54 56 N	102 55 W
Jan Mayen Is.	12	71 0 N	11 0 W
Janaúba	171	15 48 S	43 19 W
Janaucu, I.	170	0 30 N	50 10 W
Jand	94	33 30 N	72 0 E
Janda, Laguna de la	57	36 15 N	5 45 W
Jandaia	171	17 6 S	50 7 W
Jandaq	92	34 3 N	54 22 E
Jandola	94	32 20 N	70 9 E
Jandowae	139	26 45 S	151 7 E
Jandrain-Jandrenouilles	47	50 40 N	4 58 E
Jándula, R.	57	38 25 N	3 55 W
Jane Pk.	142	45 15 S	168 20 E
Janesville	158	42 39 N	89 1 W
Janga	121	10 5 N	1 0 W
Jangaon	96	17 44 N	79 5 E
Janhtang Ga	98	26 32 N	96 38 E
Jani Khel	93	32 45 N	68 25 E
Janja	66	44 40 N	19 17 E
Janjevo	66	42 35 N	21 19 E
Janjina	66	42 58 N	17 25 E
Janos	164	30 45 N	108 10 W
Jánoshalma	53	46 18 N	19 21 E
Jánosháza	53	47 8 N	17 12 E
Jánossomorja	53	47 47 N	17 11 E
Janów	54	50 43 N	22 30 E
Janów Lubelski	54	50 48 N	22 23 E
Janów Podlaski	54	52 11 N	23 11 E
Janowiec Wlkp.	54	52 45 N	17 30 E
Januária	171	15 25 S	44 25 W
Janub Dârfûr □	123	11 0 N	25 0 E
Janub Kordofân □	123	12 0 N	30 0 E
Janville	43	48 10 N	1 50 E
Janzé	42	47 55 N	1 28 W
Jaop'ing	109	23 43 N	117 0 E
Jaora	94	23 40 N	75 10 E
Jaoyang	106	38 14 N	115 44 E
Japan ■	112	36 0 N	136 0 E
Japan, Sea of	112	40 0 N	135 0 E
Japan Trench	142	28 0 N	145 0 E
Japara	103	6 30 S	110 40 E
Japen, I. = Yapen	103	1 50 S	136 0 E
Japero	103	4 59 S	137 11 E
Japurá	174	1 48 S	66 30 W
Japurá, R.	174	3 8 S	64 46 W
Jaque	174	7 27 N	78 15 W
Jaques Cartier, Détroit de	151	50 0 N	63 30 W
Jara, La	161	37 16 N	106 0 W
Jaraguá	171	15 45 S	49 20 W
Jaraicejo	57	39 40 N	5 49 W
Jaraiz	56	40 4 N	5 45 W
Jarales	161	34 44 N	106 51 W
Jarama, R.	58	40 50 N	3 20 W
Jarandilla	56	40 8 N	5 39 W
Jaranwala	94	31 15 N	73 20 E
Jarash	90	32 17 N	35 54 E
Järbo	72	60 42 N	16 38 E
Jarbridge	160	41 56 N	115 27 W
Jardim	172	21 28 S	56 9 W
Jardín, R.	59	38 50 N	2 10 W
Jardines de la Reina, Is.	166	20 50 N	78 50 W
Jargalant = Hovd	105	48 1 N	91 38 E
Jargeau	43	47 50 N	2 7 E
Jarmen	48	53 56 N	13 20 E
Järna, Kopp., Sweden	72	60 33 N	14 26 E
Järna, Stockholm, Sweden	72	59 7 N	17 35 E
Jarnac	44	45 40 N	0 11 W
Jarny	43	49 9 N	5 53 E
Jarocin	54	51 59 N	17 29 E
Jaroměř	52	50 22 N	15 52 E
Jarosław	54	50 2 N	22 42 E
Järpås	73	58 23 N	12 57 E
Järpås	73	58 23 N	12 57 E
Järpen	72	63 21 N	13 26 E
Jarrahdale	137	32 24 S	116 5 E
Jarres, Plaine des	100	19 27 N	103 10 E
Jarrow	35	54 58 N	1 28 W
Jarso	123	5 15 N	37 30 E
Järved	72	63 16 N	18 43 E
Jarvis I.	131	0 15 S	159 55 W
Jarvornik	53	50 23 N	17 2 E
Jarwa	95	27 45 N	82 30 E
Jaša Tomió	66	45 26 N	20 50 E
Jasien	54	51 46 N	15 0 E
Jasin	101	2 20 N	102 26 E
Jāsk	93	25 38 N	57 45 E
Jasło	54	49 45 N	21 30 E
Jasper, Can.	152	52 55 N	118 5 W
Jasper, Ala., U.S.A.	157	33 48 N	87 16 W
Jasper, Ark., U.S.A.	97	36 0 N	93 10 W
Jasper, Fla., U.S.A.	157	30 31 N	82 58 W
Jasper, La., U.S.A.	159	30 59 N	93 58 W
Jasper, S.D., U.S.A.	158	43 52 N	96 22 W
Jasper Nat. Park	152	52 50 N	118 8 W
Jasper Place	152	53 33 N	113 25 W
Jastrebarsko	63	45 41 N	15 39 E
Jastrowie	54	53 26 N	16 49 E
Jastrzebie Zdroj	54	49 57 N	18 35 E
Jászapáti	53	47 32 N	20 10 E
Jászárokszállás	53	47 39 N	20 1 E
Jászberény	53	47 30 N	19 55 E
Jászkiser	53	47 27 N	20 20 E
Jászladány	53	47 23 N	20 18 E
Jataí	171	17 50 S	51 45 W
Jati	94	24 27 N	68 19 E
Jatibarang	103	6 28 S	108 18 E
Jatinegara	103	6 13 S	106 52 E
Játiva	59	39 0 N	0 32 W
Jatobal	170	4 35 S	49 33 W
Jatt	90	32 24 N	35 2 E
Jaú	173	22 10 S	48 30 W
Jau al Milah	91	15 15 N	45 40 E
Jauche	47	50 41 N	4 57 E
Jauja	174	11 45 S	75 30 W
Jaunelgava	80	56 35 N	25 0 E
Jaunpur	95	25 46 N	82 44 E
Java = Jawa	103	7 0 S	110 0 E
Java Sea	102	4 35 S	107 15 E
Javadi Hills	97	12 40 N	78 40 E
Jávea	59	38 48 N	0 10 E
Javhlant = Ulyasutay	105	47 45 N	96 49 E
Javla	96	17 18 N	75 9 E
Javron	42	48 25 N	0 25 W
Jawa	103	7 0 S	110 0 E
Jawor	54	51 4 N	16 11 E
Jaworzno	54	50 13 N	19 22 E
Jay	159	33 17 N	94 46 W
Jayawijaya, Pengunungan	103	7 0 S	139 0 E
Jaydot	153	49 15 N	110 15 W
Jaynagar	99	26 43 N	86 9 E
Jayton	159	33 17 N	100 35 W
Jazminal	164	24 56 N	101 25 W
Jean	161	35 47 N	115 20 W
Jean Marie River	152	61 32 N	120 38 W
Jean Rabel	167	19 50 N	73 30 W
Jeanerette	159	29 52 N	91 38 W
Jebba, Moroc.	118	35 11 N	4 43 W
Jebba, Nigeria	121	9 9 N	4 48 E
Jebel	66	40 35 N	21 15 E
Jebel Aulia	123	15 10 N	32 31 E
Jebel Qerri	123	16 16 N	32 50 E
Jedburgh	35	55 28 N	2 33 W
Jedlicze	54	49 43 N	21 40 E
Jedlnia-Letnisko	54	51 25 N	21 19 E
Jedrzejów	54	50 35 N	20 15 E

Jedway **Kaboudia, Rass**

Jedway **152** 52 17N 131 14W
Jeetze, R. **48** 52 58N 11 6 E
Jefferson, Iowa, U.S.A. **158** 42 3N 94 25W
Jefferson, Tex., U.S.A. **159** 32 45N 94 23W
Jefferson, Wis., U.S.A. **158** 43 0N 88 49W
Jefferson City **157** 36 8N 83 30W
Jefferson, Mt., Calif., U.S.A. **163** 38 51N 117 0W
Jefferson, Mt., Oreg., U.S.A. **160** 44 45N 121 50W
Jeffersonville **156** 38 20N 85 42W
Jega **121** 12 15N 4 23 E
Jekabpils **80** 56 29N 25 57 E
Jelenia Góra **54** 50 50N 15 45 E
Jelenia Góra □ **54** 51 0N 15 30 E
Jelgava **80** 56 41N 22 49 E
Jelica **66** 43 50N 20 17 E
Jelli **123** 5 25N 31 45 E
Jellicoe **150** 49 40N 87 30W
Jelšava **53** 48 37N 20 15 E
Jemaja **103** 3 5N 105 45 E
Jemaluang **101** 2 16N 103 52 E
Jemappes **47** 50 27N 3 54 E
Jember **103** 8 11 S 113 41 E
Jembongan, I. **102** 6 45N 117 20 E
Jemmapes = Azzaba **119** 36 48N 7 6 E
Jemnice **52** 49 1N 15 34 E
Jena, Ger. **48** 50 56N 11 33 E
Jena, U.S.A. **159** 31 41N 92 7W
Jench'iu **106** 38 43N 116 5 E
Jendouba **119** 36 29N 8 47 E
Jenhochieh **108** 26 29N 101 45 E
Jenhsien **106** 37 8N 114 37 E
Jenhua **109** 25 5N 113 45 E
Jenhuai **108** 27 53N 106 17 E
Jenin **90** 32 28N 35 18 E
Jenkins **156** 37 13N 82 41W
Jennings **159** 30 10N 92 45W
Jennings, R. **152** 59 38N 132 5W
Jenny **73** 57 47N 16 35 E
Jeparit **140** 36 8 S 142 1 E
Jequié **171** 13 51 S 40 5W
Jequitaí, R. **171** 17 4 S 44 50W
Jequitinhonha **171** 16 30 S 41 0W
Jequitinhonha, R. **171** 15 51 S 38 53W
Jerada **118** 34 40N 2 10W
Jerantut **101** 3 56N 102 22 E
Jérémie **167** 18 40N 74 10W
Jeremoabo **170** 10 4 S 38 21W
Jerez de García Salinas **164** 22 39N 103 0W
Jerez de la Frontera **57** 36 41N 6 7W
Jerez de los Caballeros **57** 38 20N 6 45W
Jerez, Punta **165** 22 58N 97 40W
Jericho **138** 23 38 S 146 6 E
Jericho = El Arīhā **90** 31 52N 35 27 E
Jerichow **48** 52 30N 12 2 E
Jerilderie **141** 35 20 S 145 41 E
Jermyn **162** 41 31N 75 31W
Jerome **161** 34 50N 112 0W
Jersey City **162** 40 41N 74 8W
Jersey, I. **42** 49 13N 2 7W
Jersey Shore **156** 41 17N 77 18W
Jerseyville **158** 39 5N 90 20W
Jerumenha **171** 7 5 S 43 30W
Jerusalem **90** 31 47N 35 10 E
Jervaulx **33** 54 19N 1 41W
Jervis B. **141** 35 8 S 150 46 E
Jervis, C. **139** 35 38 S 138 6 E
Jesenice **63** 46 28N 14 3 E
Jesenik **53** 50 0N 17 8 E
Jeseník (Frývaldov) **53** 50 15N 17 11 E
Jesenske **53** 48 20N 20 10 E
Jesselton = Kota Kinabalu **102** 6 0N 116 12 E
Jessnitz **48** 51 42N 12 19 E
Jessore **98** 23 10N 89 10 E
Jesup **157** 31 30N 82 0W
Jesús Carranza **165** 17 28N 95 1W
Jesús María **172** 30 59 S 64 5W
Jetmore **159** 38 10N 99 57W
Jetpur **94** 21 45N 70 10 E
Jette **47** 50 53N 4 20 E
Jevnaker **71** 60 15N 10 26 E
Jewett **159** 31 20N 96 8W
Jewett City **162** 41 36N 72 0W
Jeypore **96** 18 50N 82 38 E
Jeziorany **54** 53 58N 20 46 E
J.F. Rodrigues **170** 2 55 S 50 20W
Jhajjar **94** 28 37N 76 14 E
Jhal Jhao **93** 26 20N 65 35 E
Jhalakati **98** 22 39N 90 12 E
Jhalawar **94** 24 35N 76 10 E
Jhang Maghiana **94** 31 15N 72 15 E
Jhansi **95** 25 30N 78 36 E
Jharia **95** 23 45N 86 18 E
Jharsaguda **99** 21 50N 84 5 E
Jharsuguda **96** 21 50N 84 5 E
Jhelum **94** 33 0N 73 45 E
Jhelum, R. **95** 31 50N 72 10 E
Jhunjhunu **94** 28 10N 75 20 E
Jiangshan **95** 28 45N 118 37 E
Jibão, Serra do **171** 14 48 S 45 0W
Jibiya **121** 13 5N 7 12 E
Jibou **70** 47 15N 23 17 E
Jicin **52** 50 25N 15 20 E
Jicarón, I. **166** 7 10N 81 50W
Jiddah **92** 21 29N 39 16 E
Jido **99** 29 2N 94 58 E
Jifna **90** 31 58N 35 13 E
Jiggalong **136** 23 24 S 120 47 E
Jihk'atse **107** 29 15N 88 53 E
Jihlava **52** 49 28N 15 35 E
Jihočeský □ **52** 49 8N 14 35 E
Jihomoravský □ **53** 49 5N 16 30 E
Jiht'u **105** 33 27N 79 42 E
Jijiga **91** 9 20N 42 50 E
Jijona **59** 38 34N 0 30W
Jikamshi **121** 12 12N 7 45 E
Jiloca, R. **58** 41 0N 1 20W
Jílové **52** 49 52N 14 29 E
Jim Jim Cr. **136** 12 50 S 132 32 E
Jima **123** 7 40N 36 55 E
Jimbolia **66** 45 47N 20 57 E
Jimena de la Frontera **57** 36 27N 5 24W
Jimenbuen **141** 36 42 S 148 53 E
Jiménez **164** 27 10N 105 0W
Jind **94** 29 19N 76 16 E
Jindabyne **141** 36 25 S 148 35 E
Jindrichuv Hradeç **52** 49 10N 15 2 E
Jinja **126** 0 25N 33 12 E
Jinjang **101** 3 13N 101 39 E
Jinjini **120** 7 20N 3 42W
Jinnah Barrage **93** 32 58N 71 33 E
Jinotega **166** 13 6N 85 59W
Jinotepe **166** 11 50N 86 10W
Jiparaná (Machado), R. **174** 8 45 S 62 20W
Jipijapa **174** 1 0 S 80 40W
Jiquilpán **164** 19 57N 102 42W
Jisresh Shughur **92** 35 49N 36 18 E
Jitarning **137** 32 48 S 117 57 E
Jitra **101** 6 16N 100 25 E
Jiu, R. **70** 44 50N 23 20 E
Jiuchin **109** 25 53N 116 0 E
Jiuli **108** 24 6N 97 54 E
Jizera, R. **52** 50 21N 14 48 E
Jizl Wadi **122** 26 30N 38 0 E
Jizō-zaki **110** 35 34N 133 20 E
Joaçaba **173** 27 5 S 51 31W
Joaima **171** 16 39 S 41 2W
João **170** 2 46 S 50 59W
João Amaro **171** 12 46 S 40 22W
João Câmara **170** 5 32 S 35 48W
João de Almeida **125** 15 10 S 13 50 E
João Pessoa **170** 7 10 S 34 52W
João Pinheiro **171** 17 45 S 46 10W
Joaquim Távora **171** 23 30 S 49 58W
Joaquín V. González **172** 25 10 S 64 0W
Jobourg, Nez de **42** 49 41N 1 57W
Joch'iang **105** 39 2N 88 0 E
Jódar **59** 37 50N 3 21W
Jodhpur **94** 26 23N 73 2 E
Joe Batt's Arm **151** 49 44N 54 10W
Joensuu **78** 62 37N 29 49 E
Joeuf **43** 49 12N 6 1 E
Jofane **125** 21 15 S 34 18 E
Joggins **151** 45 42N 64 27W
Jogjakarta = Yogyakarta **103** 7 49 S 110 22 E
Jōhana **111** 36 37N 136 57 E
Johannesburg, S. Afr. **129** 26 10 S 28 8 E
Johannesburg, U.S.A. **163** 35 22N 117 38W
Johannisnäs **72** 62 45N 16 15 E
Johansfors, Halland, Sweden **73** 56 50N 12 58 E
Johansfors, Kronoberg, Sweden **73** 56 42N 15 32 E
John Days, R. **160** 45 0N 120 0W
John o' Groats **37** 58 39N 3 3W
Johnshaven **37** 56 48N 2 20W
Johnson **159** 37 35N 101 48W
Johnson City, N.Y., U.S.A. **162** 42 7N 75 57W
Johnson City, Tenn., U.S.A. **157** 36 18N 82 21W
Johnson City, Tex., U.S.A. **159** 30 15N 98 24W
Johnson Cy. **156** 42 9N 67 0W
Johnson Ra. **137** 29 40 S 119 15 E
Johnsondale **163** 35 58N 118 32W
Johnsons Crossing **152** 60 29N 133 18W
Johnsonville **142** 41 13 S 174 48 E
Johnston **31** 51 45N 5 5W
Johnston Falls = Mambilima Falls **127** 10 31 S 28 45 E
Johnston I. **131** 17 10N 169 8 E
Johnston Lakes **137** 32 20 S 120 45 E
Johnston Ra. **137** 29 40 S 119 20 E
Johnstone **34** 55 50N 4 31W
Johnstone Str. **152** 50 28N 126 0W
Johnstown, Ireland **39** 52 46N 7 34W
Johnstown, N.Y., U.S.A. **162** 43 1N 74 20W
Johnstown, Pa., U.S.A. **156** 40 19N 78 53W
Johnstown Bridge **38** 53 23N 6 53W
Johor □ **101** 2 5N 103 20 E
Johor Baharu **101** 1 28N 103 46 E
Johor, S. **101** 1 45N 103 47 E
Joigny **43** 48 0N 3 20 E
Joinvile **173** 26 15 S 48 55 E
Joinville **43** 48 27N 5 10 E
Joinville I. **13** 63 15N 55 30W
Jojutla **165** 18 37N 99 11W
Jokkmokk **74** 66 35N 19 50 E
Jökulsá á Brú **74** 65 40N 16 16W
Jökulsá Fjöllum **74** 65 30N 16 15W
Jökulsa R. **74** 65 30N 16 15W
Jolan **163** 35 58N 121 9W
Joliet **156** 41 30N 88 0W
Joliette **150** 46 3N 73 24W
Jolo I. **103** 6 0N 121 0 E
Jome, I. **103** 1 16 S 127 30 E
Jönåker **73** 58 44N 16 40 E
Jönaker **73** 58 44N 16 43 E
Jones C. **150** 54 33N 79 35W
Jones Sound **12** 76 0N 89 0W
Jonesboro, Ark., U.S.A. **159** 35 50N 90 45W
Jonesboro, Ill., U.S.A. **159** 37 26N 89 18W
Jonesboro, La., U.S.A. **159** 32 15N 92 41W
Jonesport **151** 44 32N 67 38W
Jönköping **73** 57 45N 14 10 E
Jönköpings län □ **75** 57 30N 14 30 E
Jonquière **151** 48 27N 71 14W
Jonsberg **73** 58 30N 16 48 E
Jonsered **73** 57 45N 12 10 E
Jonzac **44** 45 27N 0 28W
Joplin **159** 37 0N 94 25W
Jordan, Phil. **103** 10 41N 122 38 E
Jordan, Mont., U.S.A. **160** 47 25N 106 58W
Jordan, N.Y., U.S.A. **162** 43 4N 76 29W
Jordan ■ **92** 31 0N 36 0 E
Jordan, R. **90** 32 10N 35 32 E
Jordan Valley **160** 43 0N 117 2W
Jordânia **171** 15 45 S 40 11W
Jordanów **54** 49 41N 19 49 E
Jorhat **98** 26 45N 94 20 E
Jörn **74** 65 4N 20 1 E
Jørpeland **71** 59 3N 6 1 E
Jorquera, R. **172** 28 3 S 69 58W
Jos **121** 9 53N 8 51 E
Jošanička Banja **66** 43 24N 20 47 E
José Batlle y OrdóPez **173** 33 20 S 55 10W
Josefow **54** 52 10N 21 11 E
Joseni **70** 47 42N 25 29 E
Joseph **160** 45 27N 117 13W
Joseph Bonaparte G. **136** 14 35 S 128 50 E
Joseph City **161** 35 0N 110 16W
Joseph, Lac **151** 52 45N 65 18W
Josephine, oilfield **19** 58 35N 2 45 E
Joshua Tree **163** 34 8N 116 19W
Joshua Tree Nat. Mon. **163** 33 56N 116 5W
Josselin **42** 47 57N 2 33W
Jostedal **71** 61 35N 7 15 E
Jostedalsbre, Mt. **71** 61 45N 7 0 E
Jotunheimen **71** 61 35N 8 25 E
Jounieh **92** 33 59N 35 30 E
Jourdanton **159** 28 54N 98 32W
Journe **46** 52 58N 5 48 E
Joussard **152** 55 22N 115 57W
Joux, Lac de **50** 46 39N 6 18 E
Jouzjan □ **93** 36 10N 66 0 E
Jovellanos **166** 22 40N 81 10W
Jowai **98** 25 26N 92 12 E
Joyce's Country, dist. **38** 53 32N 9 30W
Joyeuse **45** 44 29N 4 16 E
Jozini Dam **129** 27 27 S 32 7 E
Ju Shui, R. **109** 28 36N 116 4 E
Juan Aldama **164** 24 20N 103 23W
Juan Bautista **161** 36 55N 121 33W
Juan Bautista Alberdi **172** 34 26 S 61 48W
Juan de Fuca Str. **160** 48 15N 124 0W
Juan de Nova, I. **129** 17 3 S 42 45 E
Juan Fernández, Arch. de **131** 33 50 S 80 0W
Juan José Castelli **172** 25 57 S 60 37W
Juan L. Lacaze **172** 34 26 S 57 25W
Juárez, Argent. **172** 37 40 S 59 43W
Juárez, Mexico **164** 27 37N 100 44W
Juárez, Sierra de **164** 32 0N 116 0W
Juatinga, Ponta de **171** 23 17 S 44 30W
Juàzeiro **170** 9 30 S 40 30W
Juàzeiro do Norte **170** 7 10 S 39 18W
Jûbâ **123** 4 57N 31 35 E
Juba, R. **91** 1 30N 42 35 E
Jubaila **92** 24 55N 46 25 E
Jûbâl **122** 27 30N 34 0 E
Jubbulpore = Jabalpur **95** 23 9N 79 58 E
Jübek **48** 54 31N 9 24 E
Jubga **83** 44 19N 38 48 E
Jubilee L. **137** 29 0 S 126 50 E
Juby, C. **116** 28 0N 12 59W
Júcar, R. **58** 40 8N 2 13W
Júcaro **166** 21 37N 78 51W
Juch'eng **109** 25 32N 113 39 E
Juchitán **165** 16 27N 95 5W
Judaea = Yehuda **90** 31 35N 34 57 E
Judenburg **52** 47 12N 14 38 E
Judith Gap **160** 46 48N 109 46W
Judith Pt. **162** 41 20N 71 30W
Judith, R. **160** 47 30N 109 30W
Juian **109** 27 45N 120 38 E
Juich'ang **109** 29 40N 115 39 E
Juigalpa **166** 12 6N 85 26W
Juillac **44** 45 20N 1 19 E
Juist, I. **48** 53 40N 7 0 E
Juiz de Fora **171** 21 43 S 43 19W
Jujuy **172** 24 10 S 65 25W
Jujuy □ **172** 23 20 S 65 40W
Jukao **109** 32 24N 120 35 E
Julesberg **158** 41 0N 102 20W
Juli **174** 16 10 S 69 25W
Julia Cr. **138** 20 0 S 141 11 E
Julia Creek **138** 20 39 S 141 44 E
Juliaca **174** 15 25 S 70 10W
Julian **163** 33 4N 116 38W
Julian Alps = Julijske Alpe **63** 46 15N 14 1 E
Julianakanaal **47** 51 6N 5 52 E
Julianehåb **12** 60 43N 46 0W
Julianstown **38** 53 40N 6 16W
Jülich **48** 50 55N 6 20 E
Julier P. **51** 46 28N 9 32 E
Julijske Alpe **63** 46 15N 14 1 E
Julimes **164** 28 25N 105 27W
Jullundur **94** 31 20N 75 40 E
Jumbo **127** 17 30 S 30 58 E
Jumento, Cayos **167** 23 0N 75 40 E
Jumet **47** 50 27N 4 25 E
Jumilla **59** 38 28N 1 19W
Jumla **95** 29 15N 82 13 E
Jumna, R. = Yamuna **94** 27 0N 78 30 E
Junagadh **94** 21 30N 70 30 E
Junan **109** 32 58N 114 31 E
Junction, Tex., U.S.A. **159** 30 29N 99 48W
Junction, Utah, U.S.A. **161** 38 10N 112 15W
Junction B. **138** 11 52 S 133 55 E
Junction City, Kans., U.S.A. **158** 39 4N 96 55W
Junction City, Oreg., U.S.A. **160** 44 20N 123 12W
Jundah **138** 24 46 S 143 2 E
Jundiaí **173** 23 10 S 47 0W
Juneau **147** 58 26N 134 30W
Junee **141** 34 53 S 147 35 E
Jung Chiang, R. **108** 23 25N 110 0 E
Jungan **108** 25 14N 109 23 E
Jungch'ang **108** 29 27N 105 33 E
Jungch'eng **107** 37 9N 122 23 E
Jungchiang **108** 25 56N 108 31 E
Jungching **108** 29 49N 102 55 E
Jungfrau **50** 46 32N 7 58 E
Jungho **106** 35 21N 110 32 E
Junghsien, Kwangsi-Chuang, China **109** 22 52N 110 33 E
Junghsien, Szechwan, China **108** 29 29N 104 22 E
Junglinster **47** 49 43N 6 15 E
Jungshahi **94** 24 52N 67 44 E
Jungshui **108** 24 14N 109 23 E
Juniata, R. **162** 40 30N 77 40W
Junín **172** 34 33 S 60 57W
Junín de los Andes **176** 39 45 S 71 0W
Junnar **96** 19 12N 73 58 E
Junquera, La **58** 42 25N 2 53 E
Junta, La **159** 38 0N 103 30W
Juntura **160** 43 44N 119 4W
Juparanã, Lagoa **171** 19 35 S 40 18W
Jupiter, R. **151** 49 29N 63 37W
Juquiá **171** 24 19 S 47 38W
Jur, Nahr el **123** 8 45N 29 0 E
Jura **43** 46 35N 6 5 E
Jura □ **43** 46 47N 5 45 E
Jura, I. **34** 56 0N 5 50W
Jura, Paps of, mts. **34** 55 55N 6 0W
Jura, Sd. of **34** 55 57N 5 45W
Jura Suisse **50** 47 10N 7 0 E
Jurado **174** 7 7N 77 46W
Jurby Hd. **32** 54 23N 4 31W
Jurien B. **132** 30 17 S 115 0 E
Jurilovca **70** 44 46N 28 52W
Jurm **93** 36 50N 70 45 E
Juruá, R. **174** 2 30 S 66 0W
Juruena, R. **174** 7 20 S 58 3W
Juruti **175** 2 9 S 56 4W
Jushan **107** 36 54N 121 30 E
Jussey **43** 47 50N 5 55 E
Justo Daract **172** 33 52 S 65 12W
Jüterbog **48** 51 59N 13 6 E
Juticalpa **166** 14 40N 85 50W
Jutland **16** 56 0N 8 0 E
Jutphaas **46** 52 2N 5 6 E
Jutung **109** 32 19N 121 14 E
Juvigny-sous-Andaine **42** 48 32N 0 30W
Juvisy **43** 48 43N 2 23 E
Juwain **93** 31 45N 61 30 E
Juyüan **109** 24 46N 113 16 E
Juzennecourt **43** 48 10N 5 0 E
Jye-kundo **99** 33 0N 96 50 E
Jylhama **74** 64 34N 26 40 E
Jylland **73** 56 15N 9 20 E
Jylland (Jutland) **73** 56 25N 9 30 E
Jyväskylä **74** 62 14N 25 44 E

K

K. Sedili Besar **101** 1 55N 104 5 E
K2, Mt. **95** 36 0N 77 0 E
Ka Lae (South C.) **147** 18 55N 155 41W
Kaaia, Mt. **147** 21 31N 158 9W
Kaap die Goeie Hoop **128** 34 24 S 18 30 E
Kaap Plato **128** 28 30 S 24 0 E
Kaapkruis **128** 21 43 S 14 0 E
Kaapstad = Cape Town **125** 33 56 S 18 27 E
Kaatsheuvel **47** 51 39N 5 2 E
Kabaena, I. **103** 5 15 S 122 0 E
Kabala **120** 9 38N 11 37W
Kabale **126** 1 15 S 30 0 E
Kabalo **126** 6 0 S 27 0 E
Kabambare **126** 4 41 S 27 39 E
Kabango **127** 8 35 S 28 30 E
Kabanjahe **102** 8 2N 98 27 E
Kabara **120** 16 40N 2 50W
Kabardinka **82** 44 40N 37 57 E
Kabardino-Balkar, A.S.S.R. □ **83** 43 30N 43 30 E
Kabarega Falls **126** 2 15N 31 38 E
Kabasalan **103** 7 47N 122 44 E
Kabba **121** 7 57N 6 3 E
Kabe **110** 34 31N 132 31 E
Kabi **121** 13 30N 12 35 E
Kabin Buri **100** 13 57N 101 43 E
Kabinakagami L. **150** 48 54N 84 25W
Kabinda **126** 6 23 S 24 28 E
Kablungu, C. **135** 6 20 S 150 1 E
Kabna **122** 19 6N 32 40 E
Kabompo **127** 13 30 S 24 14 E
Kabompo, R. **127** 13 50 S 24 10 E
Kabondo **127** 8 58 S 25 40 E
Kabongo **126** 7 22 S 25 33 E
Kabou **121** 9 28N 0 55 E
Kaboudia, Rass **119** 35 13N 11 10 E

Kabra	138	23 25S	150 25E
Kabūd Gonbad	93	37 5N	59 45E
Kabuiri	121	11 30N	13 30E
Kabul	94	34 28N	69 18E
Kabul □	93	34 0N	68 30E
Kabul, R.	94	34 30N	69 13E
Kabunga	126	1 38S	28 3E
Kaburuang	103	3 50N	126 30E
Kabushiya	123	16 54N	33 41E
Kabwe	127	14 30S	28 29E
Kabwum	135	6 11S	147 15E
Kačanik	66	42 13N	21 12E
Kachanovo	80	57 25N	27 38E
Kachebera	127	13 56S	32 50E
Kachin □	98	26 0N	97 0E
Kachira, Lake	126	0 40S	31 0E
Kachiry	76	53 10N	75 50E
Kachisi	123	9 40N	37 57E
Kachkanar	84	58 42N	59 33E
Kachot	101	11 30N	103 3E
Kaçkar	83	40 45N	41 30E
Kadaingti	98	17 37N	97 32E
Kadan Kyun, I.	101	12 30N	98 20E
Kadanai, R.	94	32 0N	66 10E
Kadarkút	53	46 13N	17 39E
Kadayanallur	97	9 3N	77 22E
Kaddi	121	13 40N	5 40E
Kade	121	6 7N	0 56W
Kadgo, L.	137	25 30S	125 30E
Kadi	94	23 18N	72 23E
Kadina	140	34 0S	137 43E
Kadiri	97	14 12N	78 13E
* Kadiyevka	83	48 35N	38 30E
Kadoka	158	43 50N	101 31W
Kadom	81	54 37N	42 24E
Kaduna	121	10 30N	7 21E
Kaduna □	121	11 0N	7 30E
Kaduna, R.	121	10 5N	8 10E
Kadyoha	120	8 58N	5 53W
Kadzhi-Say	85	42 8N	77 10E
Kaedi	120	16 9N	13 28W
Kaelé	121	10 15N	14 15E
Kaena Pt.	147	21 35N	158 17W
Kaeng Khoï	100	14 35N	101 0E
Kaeo	142	35 6S	173 49E
Kaerh, China	105	31 45N	80 22E
Kaerh, Sudan	123	5 35N	31 20E
Kaesŏng	107	37 58N	126 35E
Kaf	92	31 25N	37 20E
Kafakumba	124	9 38S	23 46E
Kafan	79	39 18N	46 15E
Kafanchan	121	9 40N	8 20E
Kafareti	121	10 25N	11 12E
Kaffrine	120	14 8N	15 36W
Kafia Kingi	117	9 20N	24 25E
Kafinda	127	12 32S	30 20E
Kafirévs, Ákra	69	38 9N	24 8E
Kafiristan	93	35 0N	70 30E
Kafr Ana	70	32 2N	34 48E
Kafr 'Ein	90	32 3N	35 7E
Kafr el Dauwâr	122	31 8N	30 8E
Kafr Kama	90	32 44N	35 26E
Kafr Kannā	90	32 45N	35 20E
Kafr Malik	90	32 0N	35 18E
Kafr Mandā	90	32 49N	35 15E
Kafr Quaddum	90	32 14N	35 7E
Kafr Ra'i	90	32 23N	35 9E
Kafr Sir	90	33 19N	35 23E
Kafr Yasif	90	32 58N	35 10E
Kafue	127	15 46S	28 9E
Kafue Flats	127	15 32S	27 0E
Kafue Gorge	127	16 0S	28 0E
Kafue Hook	127	14 58S	26 0E
Kafue Nat. Park	65	15 30S	25 40E
Kafue, R.	125	15 30S	26 0E
Kafulwe	127	9 0S	29 1E
Kaga, Afghan.	94	34 14N	70 10E
Kaga, Japan	111	36 16N	136 15E
Kagamil I.	147	53 0N	169 40W
Kagan	85	39 43N	64 33E
Kagawa-ken □	110	34 15N	134 0E
Kagera R.	126	1 15S	31 20E
Kagoshima	110	31 36N	130 40E
Kagoshima-ken □	110	30 0N	130 0E
Kagoshima-Wan	110	31 0N	130 40E
Kagul	82	45 50N	28 15E
Kahajan, R.	102	2 10S	114 0E
Kahama	126	4 8S	32 30E
Kahama □	126	3 40S	32 0E
Kahang	101	2 12N	103 32E
Kahe	126	3 30S	37 25E
Kahemba	124	7 18S	18 55E
Kaherekoua Mts.	143	45 45S	167 15E
Kahniah, R.	152	58 15N	120 55W
Kahnuj	93	27 55N	57 40E
Kahoka	158	40 25N	91 42W
Kahoolawe, I.	147	20 33N	156 35W
Kahuku & Pt.	147	21 41N	157 57W
Kahulai	147	20 54N	156 28W
Kahurangi, Pt.	143	40 50S	172 10E
Kahuta	94	33 35N	73 24E
Kai Kai	128	19 52S	21 15E
Kai, Kepulauan	103	5 55S	132 45W
Kaiama	121	9 36N	4 1E
Kaiapit	135	6 18S	146 18E
Kaiapoi	143	42 24S	172 40E
Kaibara	111	35 8N	135 5E
K'aichien	109	23 45N	111 47E
K'aifeng	106	34 50N	114 27E
Kaihsien	107	40 25N	122 25E
K'aihsien	108	31 12N	108 25E
K'aihua	109	29 9N	118 24E
Kaiingveld	128	30 0S	22 0E
Kaikohe	142	35 25S	173 49E
Kaikoura	143	42 25S	173 43E
Kaikoura Pen.	143	42 25S	173 43E
Kaikoura Ra.	143	41 59S	173 41E
Kailahun	120	8 18N	10 39W
Kailashahar	98	25 19N	92 0E
Kaili	108	26 32N	107 57E
K'ailu	107	43 35N	121 12E
Kailua	147	19 39N	156 0W
Kaimana	103	3 30S	133 45E
Kaimanawa Mts.	142	39 15S	175 56E
Kaimata	143	42 34S	171 28E
Kaimganj	95	27 33N	79 24E
Kaimon-Dake	110	31 11N	130 32E
Kaimur Hill	95	24 30N	82 0E
Kainan	110	34 9N	135 12E
Kainantu	135	6 18S	145 52E
Kaingaroa Forest	142	38 30S	176 30E
Kainji Res.	121	10 1N	4 40E
Kaipara Harb.	142	36 25S	174 14E
K'aip'ing	109	22 31N	112 32E
Kaipokok B.	151	54 54N	59 47W
Kairana	94	29 33N	77 15E
Kairiru, I.	138	3 20S	143 20E
Kaironi	103	0 47S	133 40E
Kairouan	119	35 45N	10 5E
Kairuku	135	8 51S	146 35E
Kaiserslautern	49	49 30N	7 43E
Kaitaia	142	35 8S	173 17E
Kaitangata	143	46 17S	169 51E
Kaithal	94	29 48N	76 26E
Kaitu, R.	94	33 20N	70 20E
Kaiwi Channel	147	21 13N	157 30W
K'aiyang	108	27 4N	106 55E
K'aiyüan, Liaoning, China	107	42 33N	124 4E
K'aiyüan, Yunnan, China	108	23 47N	103 10E
Kaiyuh Mts.	147	63 40N	159 0W
Kajaani	74	64 17N	27 46E
Kajabbi	138	20 0S	140 1E
Kajan, R.	102	2 40N	116 40E
Kajang	101	2 59N	101 48E
Kajeli	103	3 20S	127 10E
Kajiado	126	1 53S	36 48E
Kajiki	110	31 44N	130 40E
Kajo Kaji	123	3 58N	31 40E
Kajoa, I.	103	0 1N	127 28E
Kajuagung	102	3 8S	104 46E
Kakabeka Falls	150	48 24N	89 37W
Kakamas	125	28 45S	20 33E
Kakamega	126	0 20N	34 46E
Kakamega □	126	0 20N	34 46E
Kakamigahara	111	35 28N	136 48E
Kakanj	66	44 9N	18 7E
Kakanui Mts.	143	45 10S	170 30E
Kakapotahi	143	43 0S	170 45E
Kake, Japan	110	34 36N	132 19E
Kake, U.S.A.	147	57 0N	134 0W
Kakegawa	111	34 45N	138 1E
Kakhib	83	42 28N	46 34E
Kakhovskoye Vdkhr.	82	47 5N	34 16E
Kakia	125	24 48S	23 22E
Kakinada = Cocanada	99	16 50N	82 11E
Kakinada (Cocanada)	96	16 50N	82 11E
Kakisa L.	152	60 56N	117 43W
Kakisa, R.	152	61 3N	117 10W
Kakogawa	110	34 46N	134 51E
Kaktovik	147	70 8N	143 50W
Kakwa, R.	152	54 37N	118 28W
Kala	121	12 2N	14 40E
Kala Oya.	97	8 15N	80 0E
Kala Shank'ou	95	35 42N	78 20E
Kalaa-Kebira	119	35 59N	10 32E
Kalabagh	94	33 0N	71 28E
Kalabáka	68	39 42N	21 39E
Kalabo	125	14 58S	22 33E
Kalach	81	50 22N	41 0E
Kaladan, R.	99	21 30N	92 45E
Kalahari, Des.	128	24 0S	22 0E
Kalahari Gemsbok Nat. Pk.	128	26 0S	20 30E
Kalahasti	97	13 45N	79 44E
Kalai-Khumb	85	38 28N	70 46E
Kalaja e Turrës	68	41 10N	19 28E
Kalakamati	129	20 40S	27 25E
Kalakan	77	55 15N	116 45E
K'alak'unlun Shank'ou	95	35 33N	77 46E
Kalam	95	35 34N	72 30E
Kalama, U.S.A.	160	46 0N	122 55W
Kalama, Zaïre	126	2 52S	28 35E
Kalamariá	68	40 33N	22 55E
Kalamata	69	37 3N	22 10E
Kalamazoo	156	42 20N	85 35W
Kalamazoo, R.	156	42 40N	86 12W
Kalamb	96	18 3N	74 48E
Kalambo Falls	127	8 37S	31 35E
Kálamos, I.	69	38 37N	20 55E
Kalamoti	69	38 15N	26 4E
Kalamunda	137	32 0S	116 0E
Kalangadoo	140	37 34S	140 41E
Kalannie	137	30 22S	117 5E
Kalao, I.	103	7 21S	121 0E
Kalaotoa, I.	103	7 20S	121 50E
Kälarne	72	62 59N	16 8E
Kalárovo	53	47 54N	18 0E
Kalasin	100	16 26N	103 30E
Kalat	93	29 8N	66 31E
Kalat □	93	27 0N	64 30E
Kalat-i-Ghilzai	93	32 15N	66 58E
Kálathos (Calato)	69	36 9N	28 8E
Kalaupapa	147	21 12N	156 59W
Kalaus, R.	83	45 40N	43 30E
Kalávrita	69	38 3N	22 8E
Kalaw	98	20 37N	96 35E
Kalba	120	9 30N	2 42W
Kalbarri	137	27 40S	114 10E
Kaldhovd	71	60 5N	8 20E
Kalecik	82	40 4N	33 26E
Kalegauk Kyun	99	15 33N	97 35E
Kalehe	126	2 6S	28 50E
Kalema	126	1 12S	31 55E
Kalemie	124	5 55S	29 9E
Kalemyo	98	23 11N	94 4E
Kalety	54	50 35N	18 52E
Kalewa	98	22 41N	95 32E
Kálfafellsstaður	74	64 11N	15 53W
Kalgan = Changchiak'ou	106	40 50N	114 53E
Kalgoorlie	137	30 40S	121 22E
Kaliakra, Nos	67	43 21N	28 30E
Kalianda	102	5 50S	105 45E
Kalibo	103	11 43N	122 22E
Kaliganj Town	98	23 25N	89 8E
Kalima	126	2 33S	26 32E
Kalimantan Barat □	102	0 0	110 30E
Kalimantan Selatan □	102	4 10S	115 30E
Kalimantan Tengah □	102	2 0S	113 30E
Kalimantan Timor □	102	1 30N	116 30E
Kálimnos, I.	69	37 0N	27 0E
Kalimpong	95	27 4N	88 35E
Kalinadi, R.	97	14 50N	74 20E
Kalinin	81	56 55N	35 55E
Kaliningrad	80	54 42N	20 32E
Kalinino	83	45 12N	38 59E
Kalininskoye	85	42 50N	73 49E
Kalinkovichi	80	52 12N	29 20E
Kalinovik	66	43 31N	18 29E
Kalipetrovo (Starčevo)	67	44 5N	27 14E
Kaliro	126	0 56N	33 30E
Kalirrákhi	68	40 40N	24 35E
Kalispell	160	48 10N	114 22W
Kalisz	54	51 45N	18 8E
Kalisz □	54	51 30N	18 0E
Kalisz Pom	54	53 17N	15 55E
Kaliua	126	5 5S	31 48E
Kaliveli Tank	97	12 5N	79 50E
Kalix R.	74	67 0N	22 0E
Kalka	94	30 56N	76 57E
Kalkaroo	140	31 12S	143 54E
Kalkaska	150	44 44N	85 11W
Kalkfeld	128	20 57S	16 14E
Kalkfontein	128	22 4S	20 57E
Kalkfontein Dam	128	29 30S	24 15E
Kalkrand	128	24 1S	17 35E
Kall L.	72	63 35N	13 10E
Kallakurichi	97	11 44N	79 1E
Kållandsö	73	58 40N	13 5E
Källby	73	58 30N	13 8E
Kallia	86	31 46N	35 30E
Kallidaikurichi	97	8 38N	77 31E
Kallinge	73	56 15N	15 18E
Kallithéa	69	37 55N	23 41E
Kallmeti	68	41 51N	19 41E
Kalloní, Kólpos	69	39 10N	26 10E
Kallsjön	74	63 38N	13 0E
Kalltorp	73	58 23N	13 20E
Kalmalo	121	13 40N	5 20E
Kalmar	73	56 40N	16 20E
Kalmar län □	73	57 25N	16 15E
Kalmar sund	73	56 40N	16 25E
Kalmthout	47	51 23N	4 29E
Kalmyk A.S.S.R. □	83	46 5N	46 1E
Kalmykovo	83	49 0N	51 35E
Kalna	95	23 13N	88 25E
Kalo	135	10 1S	147 48E
Kalocsa	53	46 32N	19 0E
Kalofer	67	42 37N	24 59E
Kalol, Gujarat, India	94	23 15N	72 33E
Kalol, Gujarat, India	94	22 37N	73 31E
Kalola	127	10 0S	28 0E
Kalolímnos	69	37 4N	27 8E
Kalomo	127	17 0S	26 30E
Kaloneróń	69	37 20N	21 38E
Kalpi	95	26 8N	79 47E
Kalrayan Hills	97	11 45N	78 40E
Kalsubai, Mt.	96	17 35N	73 45E
Kaltbrunn	51	47 13N	9 2E
Kaltungo	121	9 48N	11 19E
Kalu	94	25 5N	67 39E
Kaluga	81	54 35N	36 10E
Kalulushi	127	12 50S	28 3E
Kalundborg	73	55 41N	11 5E
Kalush	80	42 9N	24 12E
Kałuszyn	54	52 13N	21 52E
Kalutara	97	6 35N	80 0E
Kalwaria	54	49 53N	19 41E
Kalya	84	60 15N	59 59E
Kalyan, Austral.	140	34 55S	139 49E
Kalyan, India	96	20 30N	74 3E
Kalyani	174	17 53N	76 59E
Kalyazin	81	57 15N	37 45E
Kam Keut	101	18 20N	104 48E
Kama, Burma	98	22 10N	95 10E
Kama, Zaïre	126	3 30S	27 5E
Kama, R.	84	60 0N	53 0E
Kamachumu	126	1 37S	31 37E
Kamae	110	32 48N	131 56E
Kamaguenam	121	13 36N	10 30E
Kamaing	98	24 26N	94 55E
Kamaishi	112	39 20N	142 0E
Kamakura	111	35 19N	139 33E
Kamalia	94	30 44N	72 42E
Kamalino	147	21 50N	160 14W
Kamamaung	98	17 21N	97 40E
Kamango	126	0 40N	29 52E
Kamapanda	127	12 5S	24 0E
Kamaran	91	15 28N	42 35E
Kamashi	85	38 51N	65 23E
Kamativi	127	18 15S	0 27E
Kamba	121	11 50N	3 45E
Kambalda	137	31 10S	121 37E
Kambam	97	9 45N	77 16E
Kambar	94	27 37N	68 1E
Kambarka	84	56 15N	54 11E
Kambia	120	9 3N	12 53W
Kambolé	127	8 47S	30 48E
Kambove	127	10 51S	26 33E
Kamchatka, P-ov.	77	57 0N	160 0E
Kamde	138	8 0S	140 58E
Kamen	76	53 50N	81 30E
Kamen Kashirskiy	80	51 39N	24 56E
Kamenica	66	44 25N	19 40E
Kamenice	52	49 18N	15 2E
Kamenjak, Rt.	63	44 47N	13 55E
Kamenka, R.S.F.S.R., U.S.S.R.	78	65 58N	44 0E
Kamenka, R.S.F.S.R., U.S.S.R.	81	50 47N	39 20E
Kamenka Bugskaya	80	50 8N	24 16E
Kamenka Dneprovskaya	82	47 29N	34 14E
Kamensk	76	56 25N	62 45E
Kamensk Shakhtinskiy	83	48 23N	40 20E
Kamensk-Uralskiy	84	56 25N	62 2E
Kamenskiy	81	50 48N	45 25E
Kamenskoye	77	62 45N	165 30E
Kamenyak	67	43 24N	26 57E
Kamenz	48	51 17N	14 7E
Kameoka	111	35 0N	135 35E
Kames	34	55 53N	5 15W
Kameyama	111	34 51N	126 27E
Kami	68	42 17N	20 18E
Kami-Jima	110	32 27N	130 20E
Kami-koshiki-Jima	110	31 50N	129 52E
Kamiah	160	46 12N	116 2W
Kamien Krajenskie	54	53 32N	17 32E
Kamien Pomorski	54	53 57N	14 43E
Kamiensk	54	51 12N	19 29E
Kamiita	110	34 6N	134 22E
Kamilonísion	69	35 50N	26 15E
Kamilukuak, L.	153	62 22N	101 40W
Kamina	127	8 45S	25 0E
Kaminak L.	153	62 10N	95 0W
Kamioka	111	36 25N	137 15E
Kamituga Mungombe	126	3 2S	28 10E
Kamiyaku	112	30 25N	130 30E
Kamloops	152	50 40N	120 20W
Kamo	143	35 42S	174 20E
Kamogawa	111	35 5N	140 5E
Kamoke	94	32 4N	74 4E
Kamono	124	3 10S	13 20E
Kamp, R.	52	48 35N	15 26E
Kampala	126	0 20N	32 30E
Kampar	101	4 18N	101 9E
Kampar, R.	102	0 30N	102 0E
Kampen	46	52 33N	5 53E
Kamperland	47	51 34N	3 43E
Kamphaeng Phet	100	16 28N	99 30E
Kampolombo, L.	127	11 30S	29 35E
Kampong Ayer Puteh	101	4 15N	103 10E
Kampong Jerangau	101	4 50N	103 10E
Kampong Raja	101	5 45N	102 35E
Kampong Sedili Besar	101	1 56N	104 8E
Kampong To	101	6 3N	101 13E
Kampot	101	10 36N	104 10E
Kamptee	94	21 9N	79 19E
Kampti	120	10 7N	3 25W
Kampuchea ■ = Cambodia	100	12 15N	105 0E
Kamrau, Teluk	103	3 30S	133 45E
Kamsack	153	51 34N	101 54W
Kamskove Ustye	81	55 10N	49 20E
Kamskoye Vdkhr.	78	58 0N	56 0E
Kamuchawie L.	153	56 18N	101 59W
Kamui-Misaki	112	45 3N	142 30E
Kamyshin	81	50 10N	45 30E
Kamyshlov	84	56 50N	62 43E
Kamyzyak	83	46 4N	48 10E
Kan	98	20 53N	93 49E
Kan Chiang, R.	109	29 45N	116 10E
Kanaaupscow	150	54 2N	76 30W
Kanab	161	37 3N	112 29W
Kanab Creek	161	37 0N	112 40W
Kanaga I.	147	51 45N	177 22W
Kanagawa-ken □	111	35 20N	139 20E
Kanairiktok, R.	151	55 2N	60 18W
Kanakanak	147	59 0N	158 58W
Kanakapura	97	12 33N	77 28E
Kanália	68	39 30N	22 53E
Kananga	124	5 55S	22 18E
Kanarraville	161	37 34N	113 12W
Kanash	81	55 48N	47 32E
Kanawha, R.	156	39 40N	82 0W
Kanayis, Ras el	122	31 30N	28 5E
Kanazawa	111	36 30N	136 38E
Kanbalu	98	17 55N	85 24E
Kanchanaburi	100	14 8N	99 31E
Kanchenjunga, Mt.	95	27 50N	88 10E
Kanchipuram (Conjeeveram)	97	12 52N	79 45E
Kanchou	109	25 51N	114 59E
Kanch'üan	106	36 19N	109 19E
Kanda Kanda	124	6 52S	23 48E
Kandagach	79	49 20N	57 15E
Kandahar	94	31 32N	65 30E
Kandahar □	94	31 0N	65 0E
Kandalaksha	78	67 9N	32 30E
Kandalakshkiyzaliv	78	66 0N	35 0E

* Renamed Stakhanov

Kandalu **Kástron**

Kandalu 93 29 55N 63 20E
Kandangan 102 2 50S 115 20E
Kandanos 69 35 19N 23 44E
Kandé 121 9 57N 1 53E
Kandep 135 5 54S 143 32E
Kander, R. 50 46 33N 7 38E
Kandersteg 50 46 30N 7 40E
Kandewu 127 14 1S 26 16E
Kandhíla 69 37 46N 22 22E
Kandhkot 94 28 16N 69 8E
Kandhla 94 29 18N 77 19E
Kandi, Benin 121 11 7N 2 55E
Kandi, India 95 23 58N 88 5E
Kandinduna 127 13 58S 24 19E
Kandira 92 41 5N 30 10E
Kandla 94 23 0N 70 10E
Kandos 141 32 45S 149 58E
Kandrach 93 25 30N 65 30E
Kandrian 135 6 14S 149 37E
Kandukur 95 15 12N 79 57E
Kandy 97 7 18N 80 43E
Kane 156 41 39N 78 53W
Kane Bassin 12 79 30N 68 0W
Kanel 120 13 18N 14 35W
Kaneohe 147 21 25N 157 48W
Kanevskaya 83 46 3N 39 3E
Kanfanar 63 45 7N 13 50E
Kang 93 30 55N 61 55E
Kangaba 120 11 56N 8 25W
Kangar 101 6 27N 100 12E
Kangaroo I. 140 35 45S 137 0E
Kangaroo Mts. 138 23 25S 142 0E
Kangavar 92 34 40N 48 0E
Kangean, Kepulauan 102 6 55S 115 23E
Kangerdlugsuaé 12 68 10N 32 20W
Kanggye 107 41 0N 126 35E
Kanggyŏng 107 36 10N 126 0E
Kanghwa 107 37 45N 126 30E
K'angkang 108 32 46N 101 3E
Kangnŭng 107 37 45N 128 54E
Kango 124 0 11N 10 5E
K'angp'ing 107 43 45N 123 20E
Kangpokpi 98 25 8N 93 58E
K'angting 108 30 2N 102 0E
Kangtissu Shan 95 31 0N 82 0E
Kangto, Mt. 99 27 50N 92 35E
Kangyao 107 44 15N 126 40E
Kangyidaung 98 16 56N 94 54E
Kanhangad 97 12 21N 74 58E
Kanheri 96 19 13N 72 50E
Kani, China 99 29 25N 95 25E
Kani, Ivory C. 120 8 29N 6 36W
Kaniama 126 7 30S 24 12E
Kaniapiskau L. 151 54 10N 69 55W
Kaniapiskau, R. 151 57 40N 69 30E
Kanibadam 85 40 17N 70 25E
Kanin Nos, Mys 78 68 45N 43 20E
Kanin, P-ov. 78 68 0N 45 0E
Kanina 68 40 23N 19 30E
Kaniva 140 36 22S 141 18E
Kanjiza 66 46 3N 20 4E
Kanjut Sar 95 36 15N 75 25E
Kankakee 156 41 6N 87 50W
Kankakee, R. 156 41 13N 87 0W
Kankan 120 10 30N 9 15W
Kanker 96 20 10N 81 40E
Kankouchen 107 40 30N 119 27E
Kanku 106 34 45N 105 12E
Kankunskiy 77 57 37N 126 8E
Kanmuri-Yama 110 34 30N 132 4E
Kannabe 110 34 32N 133 23E
Kannapolis 157 35 32N 80 37W
Kannauj 95 27 3N 79 26E
Kannod 93 22 45N 76 40E
Kano 121 12 2N 8 30E
Kano □ 121 12 30N 9 0E
Kan'onji 110 34 7N 133 39E
Kanoroba 120 9 7N 6 8W
Kanowit 102 2 14N 112 20E
Kanowna 137 30 32S 121 31E
Kanoya 110 31 25N 130 50E
Kanózuga 54 49 58N 22 25E
Kanpetlet 98 21 10N 93 59E
Kanpur 95 26 35N 80 20E
Kansas □ 158 38 40N 98 0W
Kansas City, Kans., U.S.A. 158 39 0N 94 40W
Kansas City, Mo., U.S.A. 158 39 3N 94 30W
Kansas, R. 158 39 15N 96 20W
Kansenia 127 10 20S 26 0E
Kansk 77 56 20N 95 37E
Kansŏng 107 38 24N 128 30E
Kansu □ 105 35 30N 104 30E
Kant 85 42 53N 74 51E
Kant'angtzu 106 37 28N 104 33E
Kantché 121 13 31N 8 30E
Kantemirovka 83 49 43N 39 55E
Kantharalak 100 14 39N 104 39E
Kantishna 147 63 31N 151 5W
Kantō □ 111 36 0N 140 0E
Kantō-Heiya 111 36 0N 139 30E
Kantō-Sanchi 111 35 50N 138 50E
Kantu-long 98 19 57N 97 36E
Kanturk 39 52 10N 8 55W
Kantzu 108 31 37N 100 0E
Kanuma 111 36 44N 139 42E
Kanus 128 27 50S 18 39E
Kanye 128 25 0S 25 28E
Kanyu 128 20 7S 24 37E
Kanyü 107 34 53N 119 9E
Kanzene 127 10 30S 25 12E
Kanzi, Ras 126 7 1S 39 33E
Kaoan 109 28 25N 115 22E
Kaochou 109 21 55N 110 52E
Kaohofu 109 30 43N 116 49E
Kaohsien 108 28 21N 104 31E
Kaohsiung 109 22 35N 120 16E
Kaok'eng 109 27 39N 114 4E
Kaoko Otavi 125 18 12S 13 45E
Kaokoveld 128 19 0S 13 0E
Kaolack 120 14 5N 16 8W
Kaolan Shan 109 21 55N 113 15E
Kaolikung Shan 108 26 0N 98 55E
Kaomi 107 36 25N 119 45E
Kaopao Hu 109 32 50N 119 15E
Kaop'ing 106 35 48N 112 55E
K'aoshant'un 107 44 25N 124 27E
Kaot'ang 106 36 51N 116 13E
Kaoyang 106 38 42N 115 47E
Kaoyu 109 32 46N 119 32E
Kaoyüan 107 37 7N 118 0E
Kapaa 147 22 5N 159 19W
Kapadvanj 94 23 5N 73 0E
Kapagere 135 9 46S 147 42E
Kapanga 124 8 30S 22 40E
Kapanovka 83 47 28N 46 50E
Kapata 127 14 16S 26 15E
Kapellen 47 51 19N 4 25E
Kapello, Ákra 69 36 9N 23 3E
Kapema 127 10 45S 28 22E
Kapfenberg 52 47 26N 15 18E
Kapiri Mposhi 127 13 59S 28 43E
Kapiskau 150 52 50N 82 1W
Kapiskau, R. 150 52 47N 81 55W
Kapit 102 2 0N 113 5E
Kapiti I. 142 40 50S 174 56E
Kaplice 52 48 42N 14 30E
Kapoe 101 9 34N 98 32E
Kapoeta 123 4 50N 33 35E
Kápolnásnyék 53 47 16N 18 41E
Kaponga 143 39 29S 174 9E
Kapos, R. 53 46 30N 18 20E
Kaposvár 53 46 25N 17 47E
Kappeln 48 54 37N 9 56E
Kapps 128 22 32S 17 18E
Kaprije 63 43 42N 15 43E
Kaprijke 47 51 13N 3 38E
Kapsan 107 41 4N 128 19E
Kapsukas 80 54 33N 23 19E
Kapuas Hulu, Pegunungan 102 1 30N 113 30E
Kapuas, R. 102 0 20N 111 40E
Kapuka 127 10 30S 32 55E
Kapulo 127 8 18S 29 15E
Kapunda 140 34 20S 138 56E
Kapurthala 94 31 23N 75 25E
Kapuskasing 150 49 25N 82 30W
Kapuskasing, R. 150 49 49N 82 0W
Kapustin Yar 83 48 37N 45 40E
Kaputar, Mt. 139 30 15S 150 10E
Kaputir 126 2 5N 35 28E
Kapuvár 53 47 36N 17 1E
Kara, Turkey 69 38 29N 26 19E
Kara, U.S.S.R. 76 69 10N 65 25E
Kara Bogaz Gol, Zaliv 76 41 0N 53 30E
Kara Burun 69 38 41N 26 28E
Kara, I. 69 36 58N 27 30E
Kara Kalpak A.S.S.R. □ 76 43 0N 60 0E
Kara Kum 76 39 30N 60 0E
Kara-Saki 110 34 41N 129 30E
Kara Sea 76 75 0N 70 0E
Kara Su 85 40 44N 72 53E
Kara, Wadi 122 20 40N 42 0E
Karabash 84 55 29N 60 14E
Karabekaul 85 38 30N 64 8E
Karabük 82 41 10N 32 30E
Karabulak 85 44 54N 78 30E
Karaburuni 68 40 25N 19 20E
Karabutak 84 49 59N 60 14E
Karachala 83 39 45N 48 53E
Karachayevsk 83 43 50N 42 0E
Karachev 80 53 10N 35 5E
Karachi 94 24 53N 67 0E
Karachi □ 94 25 30N 67 0E
Karad 96 17 15N 74 10E
Karadeniz Boğazı 92 41 10N 29 5E
Karadeniz Dağlari 92 41 30N 35 0E
Karaga 121 9 58N 0 28W
Karagajly 76 49 26N 76 0E
Karaganda 76 49 50N 73 0E
Karaginskiy, Ostrov 77 58 45N 164 0E
Karagwe □ 126 2 0S 31 0E
Karaikal 97 10 59N 79 50E
Karaikkudi 97 10 0N 78 45E
Karaitivu I. 97 9 45N 79 52E
Karaj 93 35 4N 51 0E
Karak, Jordan 90 31 14N 35 40E
Karak, Malay. 101 3 25N 102 2E
Karakas 76 48 20N 83 30E
Karakitang 103 3 14N 125 28E
Karakobis 128 22 3S 20 37E
Karakoram 95 35 20N 76 0E
Karakoram P. = K'alak'unlun Shank'ou 95 35 33N 77 46E
Karakoram Pass 93 35 20N 78 0E
Karakul, Tadzhik, S.S.R., U.S.S.R. 85 39 2N 73 33E
Karakul, Uzbek S.S.R., U.S.S.R. 85 39 22N 63 50E
Karakuldzha 85 40 39N 73 26E
Karakulino 84 56 1N 53 43E
Karalon 77 57 5N 115 50E
Karaman 92 37 14N 33 13E
Karambu 102 3 53S 116 6E
Karamea 143 41 14S 172 6E
Karamea Bight 143 41 22S 171 40E
Karamea, R. 143 41 13S 172 26E
Karamet Niyaz 85 37 45N 64 34E
Karamoja □ 126 3 0N 34 15E
Karamsad 94 22 35N 72 50E
Karanganjar 103 7 38S 109 37E
Karanja 96 20 29N 77 31E
Karapoit 142 37 53S 175 32E
Karaşar 82 40 21N 31 55E
Karasburg 128 28 0S 18 44E
Karasino 76 66 50N 86 50E
Karasjok 74 69 27N 25 30E
Karasuk 76 53 44N 78 2E
Karasuk □ 126 2 12N 35 15E
Karasuyama 111 36 39N 140 9E
Karatau 85 43 10N 70 28E
Karatau, Khrebet 85 43 30N 69 30E
Karativu, I. 97 8 22N 79 52E
Karatiya 90 31 39N 34 43E
Karatobe 84 49 44N 53 30E
Karatoya, R. 98 24 7N 89 36E
Karaturuk 85 43 35N 78 0E
Karaul-Bazar 85 39 30N 64 48E
Karauli 94 26 30N 77 4E
Karavasta 68 40 53N 19 28E
Karawa 124 3 18N 20 17E
Karawanken 52 46 30N 14 40E
Karazhal 76 48 2N 70 49E
Karbala 92 32 47N 44 3E
Kårböle 72 61 59N 15 22E
Karcag 53 47 19N 21 1E
Karcha, R. 95 34 15N 75 57E
Kärda 73 57 10N 13 49E
Kardeljevo 66 43 2N 17 27E
Kardhámila 69 38 35N 26 5E
Kardhítsa 68 39 23N 21 54E
Kardhítsa □ 68 39 15N 21 50E
Kärdla 80 58 50N 22 40E
Kareeberge 128 30 50S 22 0E
Kareima 122 18 30N 31 49E
Karelian A.S.S.R. □ 78 65 30N 32 30E
Karema, P.N.G. 135 9 12S 147 18E
Karema, Tanz. 126 6 49S 30 24E
Karen 101 12 49N 92 53E
Karganrud 92 37 55N 49 0E
Kargapolye 84 55 57N 64 24E
Kargasok 76 59 3N 80 53E
Kargat 76 55 10N 80 15E
Kargı 82 41 11N 34 30E
Kargil 95 34 32N 76 12E
Kargowa 54 52 5N 15 51E
Karguéri 121 13 36N 10 30E
Kariai 69 40 14N 24 19E
Kariba 127 16 28S 28 36E
Kariba Dam 125 16 30S 28 35E
Kariba Gorge 127 16 30S 28 35E
Kariba Lake 127 16 40S 28 25E
Karibib 128 21 0S 15 56E
Karikal 97 10 59N 79 50E
Karikkale 92 39 55N 33 30E
Karimata, Kepulauan 102 1 40S 109 0E
Karimata, Selat 102 2 0S 108 20E
Karimnagar 96 18 26N 79 10E
Karimundjawa, Kepulauan 102 5 50S 110 30E
Karin 91 10 50N 45 52E
Káristos 69 38 1N 24 29E
Karitane 51 45 38S 170 39E
Kariya 111 34 58N 137 1E
Karkal 97 13 15N 74 56E
Karkar I. 135 4 40S 146 0E
Karkinitskiy Zaliv 82 45 36N 32 35E
Karkur 90 32 29N 34 57E
Karkur Tohl 122 22 5N 25 5E
Karl Libknekht 80 51 40N 35 45E
Karl-Marx-Stadt 48 50 50N 12 55E
Karl-Marx-Stadt □ 48 50 45N 13 0E
Karla, L = Voiviis, Limni 68 39 35N 22 45E
Karlino 54 54 3N 15 53E
Karlobag 63 44 32N 15 5E
Karlovac 63 45 31N 15 36E
Karlovka 82 49 29N 35 8E
Karlovy Vary 52 50 13N 12 51E
Karlsborg 73 58 33N 14 33E
Karlshamn 73 56 10N 14 51E
Karlskoga 72 59 22N 14 33E
Karlskrona 73 56 10N 15 35E
Karlsruhe 49 49 3N 8 23E
Karlstad, Sweden 72 59 23N 13 30E
Karlstad, U.S.A. 158 48 38N 96 30W
Karmøy 71 59 15N 5 15E
Karnal 94 29 42N 77 2E
Karnali, R. 95 29 0N 82 0E
Karnaphuli Res. 98 22 40N 92 20E
Karnataka □ 97 13 15N 77 0E
Karnes City 159 28 53N 97 53W
Karni 120 10 45N 2 40W
Karnische Alpen 52 46 36N 13 0E
Karnobat 67 42 40N 27 0E
Kärnten □ 52 46 52N 13 30E
Karo 120 12 16N 2 22W
Karoi 127 16 48S 29 45E
Karonga 127 9 57S 33 55E
Karoonda 140 35 1S 139 59E
Karos, Is. 69 36 54N 25 40E
Karousâdhes 68 39 47N 19 45E
Karpalund 73 56 4N 14 5E
Kárpathos, I. 69 35 37N 27 10E
Kárpathos, Stenón 69 36 0N 27 30E
Karpinsk 84 59 45N 60 1E
Karpogory 78 63 59N 44 27E
Karrebaek 73 55 12N 11 39E
Kars 92 40 40N 43 5E
Karsakpay 76 47 55N 66 40E
Karsha 83 49 45N 51 35E
Karshi 85 38 53N 65 48E
Karsun 81 54 14N 46 57E
Kartál Óros 68 41 15N 25 13E
Kartaly 84 53 3N 60 40E
Kartapur 94 31 27N 75 32E
Kartuzy 54 54 22N 18 10E
Karuah 141 32 37S 151 56E
Karufa 103 3 50S 133 20E
Karumba 138 17 31S 140 50E
Karumo 126 2 25S 32 50E
Karumwa 126 3 12S 32 38E
Karungu 126 0 50S 34 10E
Karunjie 136 16 18S 127 12E
Karup 73 56 19N 9 10E
Karur 97 10 59N 78 2E
Karviná 53 49 53N 18 25E
Karwar 93 14 55N 74 13E
Karwi 95 25 12N 80 57E
Kas Kong 101 11 27N 102 12E
Kasache 127 13 25S 34 20E
Kasai 110 34 55N 134 52E
Kasai Occidental □ 127 6 30S 22 30E
Kasai Oriental □ 126 5 0S 24 30E
Kasai, R. 124 8 20S 22 0E
Kasaji 127 10 25S 23 27E
Kasama, Japan 111 36 23N 140 16E
Kasama, Zambia 127 10 16S 31 9E
Kasandong 107 41 18N 126 55E
Kasane 128 17 34S 24 50E
Kasanga 127 8 30S 31 10E
Kasangulu 124 4 15S 15 15E
Kasaoka 110 34 30N 133 30E
Kasaragod 97 12 30N 74 58E
Kasat 98 15 56N 98 13E
Kasba 98 25 51N 87 37E
Kasba L. 153 60 20N 102 10W
Kasba Tadla 118 32 36N 6 17W
Kaschmar 93 35 16N 58 26E
Kaseberga 73 55 24N 14 8E
Kaseda 110 31 25N 130 19E
Kasempa 127 13 30S 25 44E
Kasenga 127 10 20S 28 45E
Kasese 126 0 13N 30 3E
Kasewa 127 14 28S 28 53E
Kasganj 95 27 48N 78 42E
Kashabowie 150 48 40N 90 26W
Kashan 93 34 5N 51 30E
Kashgar = K'oshin 105 39 29N 75 58E
Kashihara 111 34 35N 135 37E
Kashima, Ibaraki, Japan 111 35 58N 140 38E
Kashima, Saga, Japan 110 33 7N 130 6E
Kashima-Nada 111 36 0N 140 45E
Kashimbo 127 11 12S 26 19E
Kashin 81 57 20N 37 36E
Kashipur, Orissa, India 96 19 16N 83 3E
Kashipur, Ut. P., India 95 29 15N 79 0E
Kashira 81 54 45N 38 10E
Kashiwa 111 35 52N 139 59E
Kashiwazaki 112 37 22N 138 33E
Kashkasu 85 39 54N 72 44E
Kashmir □ 95 32 44N 74 54E
Kashmor 94 28 28N 69 32E
Kashpirovka 81 53 0N 48 30E
Kashum Tso 99 34 45N 86 0E
Kashun Noerh 105 42 25N 101 0E
Kasimov 81 54 55N 41 20E
Kasing 126 6 15S 26 58E
Kaskaskia, R. 157 37 58N 89 57W
Kaskattama, R. 153 57 3N 90 4W
Kaskelan 85 43 20N 76 35E
Kaskinen (Kaskö) 74 62 22N 21 15E
Kaskö (Kaskinen) 74 62 22N 21 15E
Kasli 84 55 53N 60 46E
Kaslo 152 49 55N 117 0W
Kasmere L. 153 59 34N 101 10W
Kasonawedjo 127 1 50S 137 41E
Kasongo 126 4 30S 26 33E
Kasongo Lunda 124 6 35S 17 0E
Kásos, I. 69 35 20N 26 55E
Kásos, Stenón 69 35 30N 26 30E
Kaspi 83 41 54N 44 17E
Kaspiysk 83 42 45N 47 40E
Kaspiyskiy 83 45 22N 47 23E
Kassab ed Doleib 123 13 30N 33 35E
Kassaba 122 22 40N 29 55E
Kassala 123 15 23N 36 26E
Kassala □ 123 15 20N 36 26E
Kassan 85 39 2N 65 35E
Kassandra 68 40 0N 23 30E
Kassansay 85 41 15N 71 31E
Kassel 48 51 19N 9 32E
Kassinger 122 18 46N 31 51E
Kassiopi 80 39 48N 19 55E
Kassue 103 6 58S 139 21E
Kastamonu 92 41 25N 33 43E
Kastav 63 45 22N 14 20E
Kastélli 69 35 29N 23 38E
Kastéllion 69 35 12N 25 20E
Kastellorizon = Megiste 61 36 8N 29 34E
Kastellou, Ákra 69 35 30N 27 15E
Kasterlee 47 51 15N 4 59E
Kastlösa 73 56 26N 16 25E
Kastó, I. 69 38 35N 20 55E
Kastóri 69 37 10N 22 17E
Kastoria 68 40 30N 21 15E
Kastoría □ 68 40 30N 21 15E
Kastorías 68 40 30N 21 20E
Kastornoye 81 51 55N 38 2E
Kástron 68 39 53N 25 8E

Kastrosikiá **Kerman**

Kastrosikiá 69 39 6N 20 36 E
Kasugai 111 35 12N 136 59 E
Kasukabe 111 35 58N 139 49 E
Kasulu 126 4 37 S 30 5 E
Kasulu □ 126 4 37 S 30 5 E
Kasumi 110 35 38N 134 38 E
Kasumiga-Ura 111 36 0N 140 25 E
Kasumkent 83 41 47N 48 15 E
Kasungu 127 13 0 S 33 29 E
Kasur 94 31 5N 74 25 E
Kata 77 58 46N 102 40 E
Kataba 127 16 10 S 25 10 E
Katako Kombe 126 3 25 S 24 20 E
Katákolon 69 37 38N 21 19 E
Katale 126 4 52 S 31 7 E
Katalla 147 60 10N 144 35W
Katama 123 9 35N 38 36 E
Katamatite 141 36 6 S 145 41 E
Katanda 126 0 55 S 29 21 E
Katanga = Shaba 126 8 0 S 25 0 E
Katanghan □ 93 36 0N 69 0 E
Katangi 96 21 56N 79 50 E
Katangli 77 51 42N 143 14 E
Katanich 123 6 0N 33 40 E
Katanning 132 33 40 S 117 33 E
Katastári 69 37 50N 20 45 E
Katav Ivanovsk 84 54 45N 58 12 E
Katavi Swamps 126 6 50 S 31 10 E
Katerini 68 40 18N 22 37 E
Katesbridge 38 54 18N 6 8W
Katha 99 24 10N 96 30 E
Katherina, Gebel 122 28 30N 33 57 E
Katherine 136 14 27 S 132 20 E
Kathiawar, dist. 93 22 20N 71 0 E
Kathua 95 32 23N 75 30 E
Kati 120 12 41N 8 4W
Katiet 102 2 21 S 99 44 E
Katihar 95 25 34N 87 36 E
Katima Mulilo 125 17 28 S 24 13 E
Katima Mulilo Rapids 128 17 28 S 24 13 E
Katimbira 127 12 40 S 34 0 E
Katiola 120 8 10N 5 10W
Katkopberg 128 30 0 S 20 0 E
Katlanovo 66 41 52N 21 40 E
Katmai Nat. Monument 147 58 30N 155 0W
Katmai, vol. 147 58 20N 154 59W
Katmandu 95 27 45N 85 12 E
Kato Akhaïa 69 38 8N 21 33 E
Kato Stazros 68 40 39N 23 43 E
Katol 96 21 17N 78 38 E
Katompi 124 6 2 S 26 23 E
Katonga, R. 126 0 15N 31 50 E
Katoomba 141 33 41 S 150 19 E
Katowice 54 50 17N 19 5 E
Katowice □ 53 50 15N 19 0 E
Katrine L. 34 56 15N 4 30W
Katrineholm 72 59 9N 16 12 E
Katsepe 129 15 45 S 46 15 E
Katsina 121 7 10N 9 20 E
Katsina Ala, R. 121 6 52N 9 40 E
Katsumoto 110 33 51N 129 42 E
Katsuta 111 36 25N 140 31 E
Katsuura 111 35 15N 140 20 E
Katsuyama 111 36 3N 136 30 E
Kattakurgan 85 39 55N 66 15 E
Kattawaz 93 32 48N 68 23 E
Kattawaz-Urgun □ 93 32 10N 62 20 E
Kattegat 73 57 0N 11 20 E
Katumba 126 7 40 S 25 10 E
Katungu 126 2 55 S 40 3 E
Katwa 95 23 30N 89 25 E
Katwijk-aan-Zee 46 52 12N 4 24 E
Katy 54 51 2N 16 45 E
Kau Tao 101 10 6N 99 48 E
Kauai Chan. 147 21 45N 158 50W
Kauai, I. 147 19 30N 155 30W
Kaufakha 90 31 29N 34 40 E
Kaufbeuren 49 47 42N 10 37 E
Kaufman 159 32 35N 96 20W
Kaukauna 156 44 20N 88 13W
Kaukauveld 128 20 0 S 20 15 E
Kaukonen 74 67 31N 24 53 E
Kaulille 47 51 11N 5 31 E
Kauliranta 74 66 27N 23 41 E
Kaunas 80 54 54N 23 54 E
Kaunghein 98 25 41N 95 26 E
Kaupulehu 147 19 43N 155 53W
Kaura Namoda 121 12 37N 6 33 E
Kautokeino 74 69 0N 23 4 E
Kavacha 77 60 16N 169 51 E
Kavadarci 66 41 26N 22 3 E
Kavaja 68 41 11N 19 33 E
Kavali 97 14 55N 80 1 E
Kavälla 68 40 57N 24 28 E
Kavälla □ 68 41 05N 24 30 E
Kavälla Kólpos 68 40 50N 24 25 E
Kavanayén 174 5 38N 61 48W
Kavarna 67 43 26N 28 22 E
Kavieng 135 2 36 S 150 51 E
Kavkaz, Bolshoi 83 42 50N 44 0 E
Kavousi 69 35 7N 25 51 E
Kaw = Caux 175 4 30N 52 15W
Kawa 123 13 42N 32 34 E
Kawachi-Nagano 111 34 28N 135 31 E
Kawagoe 111 35 55N 139 29 E
Kawaguchi 111 35 52N 138 45 E
Kawaihae 147 20 3N 155 50W
Kawaihoa Pt. 147 21 47N 160 12W
Kawaikini, Mt. 147 22 0N 159 30W
Kawakawa 142 35 23 S 174 6 E
Kawama 127 9 30 S 28 30 E
Kawambwa 127 9 48 S 29 3 E
Kawanoe 110 34 1N 133 34 E
Kawarau 143 45 3 S 169 0 E
Kawardha 95 22 0N 81 17 E
Kawasaki 111 35 35N 138 42 E
Kawau I. 142 36 25 S 174 52 E
Kawene 150 48 45N 91 15W
Kawerau 142 38 7 S 176 42 E
Kawhia Harbour 142 38 5 S 174 51 E
Kawick Peak 163 37 58N 116 57W
Kawkareik 98 16 33N 98 14 E
Kawlin 98 23 47N 95 41 E
Kawnro 99 22 48N 99 8 E
Kawthaung 101 10 5N 98 36 E
Kawthoolei □ = Kawthuk 98 18 0N 97 30 E
Kawthuk □ 98 18 0N 97 30 E
Kawya 98 16 40N 97 50 E
Kay 84 59 57N 52 59 E
Kaya 121 13 25N 1 10W
Kayah □ 98 19 15N 97 15 E
Kayaho 107 43 5N 129 46 E
Kayak I. 147 60 0N 144 30W
Kayan 98 16 54N 96 34 E
Kayangulam 97 9 10N 76 33 E
Kaycee 160 43 45N 106 46W
Kayenta 161 36 46N 110 15W
Kayes 120 14 25N 11 30W
Kayima 120 8 54N 11 15W
Kayl 47 49 29N 6 2 E
Kayomba 127 13 11 S 24 2 E
Kayoro 121 11 0N 1 28W
Kayrakkumskoye Vdkhr. 85 40 20N 70 0 E
Kayrunnera 139 30 40 S 142 30 E
Kaysatskoye 83 49 47N 46 49 E
Kayseri 92 38 45N 35 30 E
Kaysville 160 41 2N 111 58W
Kazachinskoye 77 56 16N 107 36 E
Kazachye 77 70 52N 135 58 E
Kazakh S.S.R. □ 85 50 0N 58 0 E
Kazakhstan 84 51 11N 53 0 E
Kazan 81 55 48N 49 3 E
Kazan, R. 153 64 2N 95 30W
Kazanluk 67 42 38N 25 35 E
Kazanskaya 83 49 50N 40 30 E
Kazarman 85 41 24N 73 59 E
Kazatin 82 49 45N 28 50 E
Kazerun 93 29 38N 51 40 E
Kazhim 84 60 21N 51 33 E
Kazi Magomed 83 40 3N 49 0 E
Kazimierza Wielki 54 50 15N 20 30 E
Kazincbarcika 53 48 17N 20 36 E
Kazo 111 36 7N 139 36 E
Kaztalovka 83 49 47N 48 43 E
Kazu 98 25 27N 97 46 E
Kazumba 124 6 25 S 22 5 E
Kazvin 92 36 15N 50 0 E
Kazym, R. 76 63 40N 68 30 E
Kcynia 54 53 0N 17 30 E
Ké 120 13 58N 5 18W
Ke-hsi Mansam 98 21 56N 97 50 E
Ke-Macina 120 14 5N 5 20W
Kéa 69 37 35N 24 22 E
Kea 30 50 13N 5 4W
Kéa, I. 69 37 30N 24 22 E
Keaau 147 19 37N 155 3W
Keady 38 54 15N 6 42W
Keal, Loch na 34 56 30N 6 5W
Kealkill 39 51 45N 9 20W
Keams Canyon 161 35 53N 110 9W
Keanae 147 20 52N 156 9W
Kearney 158 40 45N 99 3W
Kearsage, Mt. 162 43 25N 71 51W
Keban 92 38 50N 38 50 E
Kebele 123 12 52N 40 40 E
Kebi 120 9 18N 6 37W
Kebili 119 33 47N 9 0 E
Kebkabiya 117 13 50N 24 0 E
Kebnekaise, mt. 74 67 54N 18 33 E
Kebock Hd. 36 58 1N 6 20W
Kebri Dehar 91 6 45N 44 17 E
Kebumen 103 7 42 S 109 40 E
Kecel 53 46 31N 19 16 E
Kechika, R. 152 59 41N 127 12W
Kecskemét 53 46 57N 19 35 E
Kedada 123 5 30N 35 58 E
Kedah □ 101 5 50N 100 40 E
Kedainiai 80 55 15N 23 57 E
Kedgwick 151 47 40N 67 20W
Kedia Hill 128 21 28 S 24 37 E
Kediri 103 7 51 S 112 1 E
Kédougou 120 12 35N 12 10W
Kedzierzyn 54 50 20N 18 12 E
Keefers 152 50 0N 121 40W
Keel 38 53 59N 10 2W
Keelby 33 53 34N 0 15W
Keele 32 53 0N 2 17W
Keele, R. 147 64 15N 127 0W
Keeler 163 36 29N 117 52W
Keeley L. 153 54 54N 108 8W
Keeling Is. = Cocos Is. 142 12 12 S 96 54 E
Keelung = Chilung 109 25 3N 121 45 E
Keen, Mt. 37 56 58N 2 54W
Keenagh 38 53 36N 7 50W
Keene, Calif., U.S.A. 163 35 13N 118 33W
Keene, N.H., U.S.A. 162 42 57N 72 17W
Keeper, Mt. 39 52 46N 8 17W
Keer-Weer, C. 138 14 0 S 141 32 E
Keerbergen 47 51 1N 4 38 E
Keeten Mastgat 47 51 36N 4 0 E
Keetmanshoop 128 26 35 S 18 8 E
Keewatin 158 47 23N 93 0W
Keewatin □ 153 63 20N 94 40W
Keewatin, R. 153 56 29N 100 46W
Kefa □ 123 6 55N 36 30 E
Kefallinía, I. 69 38 28N 20 30 E
Kefamenanu 103 9 28 S 124 38 E
Kefar Ata 90 32 48N 35 7 E
Kefar Etsyon 90 31 39N 35 7 E
Kefar Hasidim 90 32 47N 35 5 E
Kefar Hittim B. 90 32 48N 35 27 E
Kefar Nahum 90 32 54N 35 22 E
Kefar Sava 90 32 11N 34 54 E
Kefar Szold 90 33 11N 35 34 E
Kefar Vitkin 90 32 22N 34 53 E
Kefar Yehezqel 90 32 34N 35 22 E
Kefar Yona 90 32 20N 34 54 E
Kefar Zekharya 90 31 43N 34 57 E
Keffi 121 8 55N 7 43 E
Keflavík 74 64 2N 22 35W
Keg River 152 57 54N 117 7W
Kegalla 97 7 15N 80 21 E
Kegashka 151 50 14N 61 18W
Kegworth 28 52 50N 1 17W
Kehl 49 48 34N 7 50 E
Keighley 32 53 52N 1 54W
Keimaneigh, P. of 39 51 49N 9 17W
Keimoes 128 28 41 S 21 0 E
Keiss 37 58 33N 3 6W
Keïta 121 14 46N 5 56 E
Keith, Austral. 140 36 0 S 140 20 E
Keith, U.K. 37 57 33N 2 58W
Keith Arm 148 65 20N 122 15W
Kekaygyr 85 40 42N 75 32 E
Kekri 94 26 0N 75 10 E
Kël 77 69 30N 124 10 E
Kelamet 123 16 0N 38 20 E
Kelang 101 3 2N 101 26 E
Kelani Ganga, R. 97 6 58N 79 50 E
Kelantan □ 101 5 10N 102 0 E
Kelantan, R. 101 6 13N 102 14 E
Këlcyra 68 40 22N 20 12 E
Keld 32 54 24N 2 11W
Keles, R. 85 41 1N 68 37 E
Kelheim 49 48 58N 11 57 E
Kelibia 119 36 50N 11 3 E
Kellas 37 57 33N 3 23W
Kellé, Congo 124 0 8 S 14 38 E
Kellé, Niger 121 14 18N 10 10 E
Keller 160 48 2N 118 44W
Kellerberrin 137 31 36 S 117 38 E
Kellett C. 12 72 0N 126 0W
Kellogg 160 47 30N 116 5W
Kelloselkä 74 66 56N 28 53 E
Kells, Ireland 39 52 33N 7 18W
Kells, U.K. 38 54 48N 6 13W
Kells = Ceanannas Mor 38 53 42N 6 53W
Kells, Rhinns of 34 55 9N 4 22W
Kelmentsy 80 48 30N 26 50 E
Kélo 124 9 10N 15 45 E
Kelowna 152 49 50N 119 25W
Kelsale 29 52 15N 1 30 E
Kelsall 32 53 14N 2 44W
Kelsey Bay 152 50 25N 126 0W
Kelso, N.Z. 143 45 54 S 169 15 E
Kelso, U.K. 35 55 36N 2 27W
Kelso, U.S.A. 160 46 10N 122 57W
Keltemashat 85 42 25N 70 8 E
Keluang 101 2 3N 103 18 E
Kelvedon 29 51 50N 0 43 E
Kelvington 153 52 10N 103 30W
Kem 78 65 0N 34 38 E
Kem-Kem 118 30 40N 4 30W
Kem, R. 78 64 45N 32 20 E
Kema 103 1 22N 125 8 E
Kemah 92 39 32N 39 5 E
Kemano 152 53 35N 128 0W
Kemapyu 98 18 49N 97 19 E
Kemasik 101 4 25N 103 25 E
Kembolcha 123 11 29N 39 42 E
Kemenets-Podolskiy 82 48 40N 26 30 E
Kemerovo 76 55 20N 85 50 E
Kemi 74 65 44N 24 34 E
Kemi älv = Kemijoki 74 65 47N 24 32 E
Kemijärvi 74 66 43N 27 22 E
Kemijoki 74 65 47N 24 32 E
Kemmel 47 50 47N 2 50 E
Kemmerer 160 41 52N 110 30W
Kemnay 37 57 14N 2 28W
Kemp Coast 13 69 0 S 55 0 E
Kemp L. 159 33 45N 99 15W
Kempsey, Austral. 141 31 1 S 152 50 E
Kempsey, U.K. 28 52 8N 2 11W
Kempston 29 52 7N 0 30W
Kempt, L. 150 47 25N 74 22W
Kempten 49 47 42N 10 18 E
Kemptville 150 45 0N 75 38W
Ken L. 35 55 0N 4 8W
Kenadsa 118 31 48N 2 26W
Kenai 147 60 35N 151 20W
Kenai Mts. 147 60 0N 150 0W
Kendal, Indon. 103 6 56 S 110 14 E
Kendal, U.K. 32 54 19N 2 44W
Kendall 141 31 35 S 152 44 E
Kendall, R. 138 14 4 S 141 35 E
Kendallville 156 41 25N 85 15W
Kendari 103 3 50 S 122 30 E
Kendawangan 102 2 32 S 110 17 E
Kende 121 11 30N 4 12 E
Kendenup 137 34 30 S 117 38 E
Kendrapara 96 20 35N 86 30 E
Kendrick 160 46 43N 116 41W
Kendrikí Kai Dhitikí Makedhonia □ 68 40 30N 22 0 E
Kene Thao 100 17 44N 101 25 E
Kenema 120 7 50N 11 14W
Keng Kok 100 16 26N 105 12 E
Keng Tawng 98 20 45N 98 18 E
Keng Tung, Burma 99 21 0N 99 30 E
Keng Tung, Burma 99 21 0N 99 30 E
Kenge 124 4 50 S 16 55 E
Kengeja 126 5 26 S 39 45 E
Kengma 108 23 34N 99 24 E
Kenhardt 128 29 19 S 21 12 E
Kenilworth 28 52 22N 1 35W
Kenimekh 85 40 16N 65 7 E
Kéninkoumou 120 15 17N 12 18W
Kénitra (Port Lyautey) 118 34 15N 6 40W
Kenmare, Ireland 39 51 52N 9 35W
Kenmare, U.S.A. 158 48 40N 102 4W
Kenmare, R. 39 51 40N 10 0W
Kenmore 37 56 35N 4 0W
Kenn Reef 133 21 12 S 155 46 E
Kennebec 158 43 56N 99 54W
Kennedy 127 18 52 S 27 10 E
Kennedy, C. = Canaveral, C. 157 28 28N 80 31W
Kennedy, Mt. 148 60 19N 139 0W
Kennedy Ra. 137 24 45 S 115 10 E
Kennedy Taungdeik 99 23 35N 94 4 E
Kennet, R. 28 51 24N 1 7W
Kenneth Ra. 137 23 50 S 117 8 E
Kennett 159 36 7N 90 0W
Kennett Square 162 39 51N 75 43W
Kennewick 160 46 11N 119 2W
Kenninghall 29 52 26N 1 0 E
Kénogami 151 48 25N 71 15W
Kenogami, R. 150 51 6N 84 28W
Kenora 153 49 50N 94 35W
Kenosha 156 42 33N 87 48W
Kensington, Can. 151 46 28N 63 34W
Kensington, U.S.A. 158 39 48N 99 2W
Kensington Downs 138 22 31 S 144 19 E
Kent, Ohio, U.S.A. 156 41 8N 81 20W
Kent, Oreg., U.S.A. 160 45 11N 120 45W
Kent, Tex., U.S.A. 159 31 5N 104 12W
Kent □ 29 51 12N 0 40 E
Kent Gr. 138 39 30 S 147 20 E
Kent Pen. 148 68 30N 107 0W
Kent Pt. 162 38 50N 76 22W
Kent, Vale of 23 51 12N 0 30 E
Kentau 85 43 32N 68 36 E
Kentdale 137 34 54 S 117 3 E
Kentisbeare 30 50 51N 3 18W
Kentland 156 40 45N 87 25W
Kenton, U.K. 30 50 37N 3 28W
Kenton, U.S.A. 156 40 40N 83 35W
Kentucky 141 30 45 S 151 28 E
Kentucky □ 156 37 20N 85 0W
Kentucky Dam 156 37 2N 88 15W
Kentucky L. 157 36 0N 88 0W
Kentucky, R. 156 38 41N 85 11W
Kentville 151 45 6N 64 29W
Kentwood 159 31 0N 90 30W
Kenya ■ 126 2 20N 38 0 E
Kenya, Mt. 126 0 10 S 37 18 E
Keo Nena, Deo 100 18 23N 105 10 E
Keokuk 158 40 25N 91 24W
Kep, Camb. 101 10 29N 104 19 E
Kep, Viet. 100 21 24N 106 16 E
Kep-i-Gjuhëzës 68 40 28N 19 15 E
Kep-i-Palit 68 41 25N 19 21 E
Kep-i-Rodonit 68 41 32N 19 30 E
Kepi 103 6 32 S 139 19 E
Kepice 54 54 16N 16 51 E
Kepler Mts. 143 45 25 S 167 20 E
Kepno 54 51 18N 17 58 E
Keppel B. 133 23 21 S 150 55 E
Kepsut 92 39 40N 28 15 E
Kepuhi 147 22 13N 159 21W
Kepulauan, R. 103 5 30 S 139 0 E
Kepulauan Sunda, Ketjil Barat □ 102 8 50 S 117 30 E
Kepulauan Sunda, Ketjil Timor □ 103 9 30 S 122 0 E
Kerala □ 97 11 0N 76 15 E
Kerama-Shotō 112 26 12N 127 22 E
Keran 95 34 35N 73 59 E
Kerang 140 35 40 S 143 55 E
Keratéa 69 37 48N 23 58 E
Keraudren, C., Tas., Austral. 136 40 22 S 144 47 E
Keraudren, C., W. Austral., Austral. 138 19 58 S 119 45 E
Keravat 135 4 17 S 152 2 E
Keray 93 26 15N 57 30 E
Kerch 82 45 20N 36 20 E
Kerchinskiy Proliv 82 45 10N 36 30 E
Kerchoual 121 17 20N 0 20 E
Kerem Maharal 90 32 39N 34 59 E
Kerema 135 7 58 S 145 50 E
Keren 123 15 45N 38 28 E
Kerewan 120 13 35N 16 10W
Kerguelen I. 11 48 15 S 69 10 E
Kerhonkson 162 41 46N 74 11W
Keri 69 37 40N 20 49 E
Keri Kera 123 12 21N 32 37 E
Kericho 126 0 22 S 35 15 E
Kericho □ 126 0 30 S 35 15 E
Kerikeri 143 35 12 S 173 59 E
Kerinci 102 2 5 S 101 0 E
Kerkdriel 46 51 47N 5 20 E
Kerkenna, Iles 119 34 48N 11 1 E
Kerki 85 37 50N 65 12 E
Kérkira 68 39 38N 19 50 E
Kerkrade 47 50 53N 6 4 E
Kerma 122 19 33N 30 32 E
Kermadec Is. 130 31 8 S 175 16W
Kermān 93 30 15N 57 1 E
Kerman 163 36 43N 120 4W

Kermān □ Killavullen

Kermān □ 93 30 0N 57 0E
Kermanshah 92 34 23N 47 0E
Kermanshah □ 92 34 0N 46 30E
Kerme Körfezi 69 36 55N 27 50E
Kermen 67 42 30N 26 16E
Kermit 159 31 56N 103 3W
Kern, R. 163 35 16N 119 18W
Kerns 51 46 54N 8 17E
Kernville 163 35 45N 118 26W
Keroh 101 5 43N 101 1E
Kerr, Pt. 142 34 25S 173 5E
Kerrera I. 34 56 24N 5 32W
Kerrobert 157 52 0N 109 11W
Kerrville 159 30 1N 99 8W
Kerry 31 52 28N 3 16W
Kerry □ 39 52 7N 9 35W
Kerry Hd. 39 52 26N 9 56W
Kerrysdale 36 57 41N 5 39W
Kersa 123 9 28N 41 48E
Kerstinbo 72 60 16N 16 58E
Kerteminde 73 55 28N 10 39E
Kertosono 103 7 38S 112 9E
Keru 123 15 40N 37 5E
Kerulen, R. 105 48 48N 117 0E
Kerzaz 118 29 29N 1 25W
Kerzers 50 46 59N 7 12E
Kesagami L. 150 50 23N 80 15W
Kesagami, R. 150 51 4N 79 45W
Kesan 68 41 49N 26 38E
Kesch, Piz 51 46 38N 9 53E
Kesh 38 54 31N 7 43W
Keski Suomen □ 74 62 45N 25 15E
Kessel, Belg. 47 51 8N 4 38E
Kessel, Neth. 47 51 17N 6 3E
Kessel-Lo 47 50 53N 4 43E
Kessingland 29 52 25N 1 41E
Kestell 129 28 17S 28 42E
Kestenga 78 66 0N 31 50E
Kesteren 46 51 56N 5 34E
Keswick 32 54 35N 3 9W
Keszthely 53 46 50N 17 15E
Keta 121 5 49N 1 0E
Ketapang 102 1 55S 110 0E
Ketchikan 147 55 25N 131 40W
Ketchum 160 43 50N 114 27W
Kete Krachi 121 7 55N 0 1W
Ketef, Khalîg Umm el 122 23 40N 35 35E
Ketelmeer 46 52 36N 5 46E
Keti Bandar 94 24 8N 67 27E
Ketri 94 28 1N 75 50E
Ketrzyn 54 54 7N 21 22E
Kettering 29 52 24N 0 44W
Kettla, Ness 36 60 3N 1 20W
Kettle Falls 160 48 41N 118 2W
Kettle Ness 33 54 32N 0 41W
Kettle, R. 153 56 23N 94 34W
Kettleman City 163 36 1N 119 58W
Kettlewell 32 54 8N 2 2W
Kety 54 49 51N 19 16E
Kevin 160 48 45N 111 58W
Kewanee 158 41 18N 90 0W
Kewaunee 156 44 27N 87 30W
Keweenaw B. 156 46 56N 88 23W
Keweenaw Pen. 156 47 30N 88 0W
Keweenaw Pt. 156 47 26N 87 40W
Kexby 33 53 21N 0 41W
Key Harbour 150 45 50N 80 45W
Key, L. 38 54 0N 8 15W
Key West 166 24 40N 82 0W
Keyingham 33 53 42N 0 7W
Keyling Inlet 136 14 50S 129 40E
Keymer 29 50 55N 0 5W
Keynsham 28 51 25N 2 30W
Keynshamburg 127 19 15S 29 40E
Keyport 162 40 26N 74 12W
Keyser 156 39 26N 79 0W
Keystone, S.D., U.S.A. 158 43 54N 103 27W
Keystone, W. Va., U.S.A. 156 37 30N 81 30W
Keyworth 28 52 52N 1 8W
Kez 84 57 55N 53 46E
Kezhma 77 59 15N 100 57E
Kezmarok 53 49 10N 20 28E
Khabarovo 76 69 30N 60 30E
Khabarovsk 77 48 20N 135 0E
Khachmas 83 41 31N 48 42E
Khachraud 94 23 25N 75 20E
Khadari, W. el 123 10 35N 26 16E
Khadro 94 26 11N 68 50E
Khadyzhensk 83 44 26N 39 32E
Khadzhilyangar 95 35 45N 79 20E
Khagaria 95 25 18N 86 32E
Khaibar 92 25 38N 39 28E
Khaibor 122 25 49N 39 16E
Khaipur, Bahawalpur, Pak. 94 29 34N 72 17E
Khaipur, Hyderabad, Pak. 94 27 32N 68 49E
Khair 94 27 57N 77 46E
Khairabad 95 27 33N 80 47E
Khairagarh 95 21 27N 81 2E
Khairpur 93 27 32N 68 49E
Khairpur □ 94 23 30N 69 8E
Khakhea 125 24 48S 23 22E
Khalach 85 38 4N 64 52E
Khalfallah 118 34 33N 0 16E
Khalij-e-Fars □ 93 28 20N 51 45E
Khalilabad 95 26 48N 83 5E
Khálki 68 39 36N 22 30E
Khálki, I. 69 36 15N 27 35E
Khalkidhiki □ 68 40 25N 23 20E
Khalkís 69 38 27N 23 42E
Khalmer-Sede = Tazovskiy 76 67 30N 78 30E
Khalmer Yu 76 67 58N 65 1E
Khalturin 81 58 40N 48 50E
Kham Kent 100 18 15N 104 43E
Khamaria 96 23 10N 80 52E
Khama's Country 128 21 45S 26 30E
Khamba Dzong 99 28 25N 88 30W
Khambhalia 94 22 14N 69 41E
Khamgaon 96 20 42N 76 37E
Khammam 96 17 11N 80 6E
Khān Yūnis 90 31 21N 34 18E
Khan Yunus 90 31 21N 34 18E
Khanabad, Afghan. 93 36 45N 69 5E
Khanabad, U.S.S.R. 85 40 59N 70 38E
Khānaqīn 92 34 23N 45 25E
Khandrá 69 35 3N 26 8E
Khandwa 96 21 49N 76 22E
Khandyga 77 62 30N 134 50E
Khanewal 94 30 20N 71 55E
Khanga Sidi Nadji 119 34 50N 6 50E
Khanh Duong 100 12 44N 108 44E
*Khanh Hung 101 9 36N 105 58E
Khaniá 69 35 30N 24 4E
Khaniá □ 69 35 0N 24 0E
Khanion Kólpos 69 35 33N 23 55E
Khanka, Oz. 76 45 0N 132 30E
Khanna 94 30 42N 76 16E
Khanpur 94 28 42N 70 35E
Khantau 85 44 13N 73 48E
Khanty-Mansiysk 76 61 0N 69 0E
Khapalu 95 35 10N 76 20E
Kharagpur 95 22 20N 87 25E
Kharaij 122 21 25N 41 0E
Kharan Kalat 93 28 34N 65 21E
Kharanaq 93 32 20N 54 45E
Kharda 96 18 40N 75 40E
Khardung La 95 34 20N 77 43E
Kharfa 92 22 0N 46 35E
Kharg, Jazireh 92 29 15N 50 28E
Khârga, El Wâhât el 122 25 0N 30 0E
Khargon, India 95 21 45N 75 35E
Khargon, India 96 21 45N 75 40E
Kharit, Wadi el 122 24 5N 34 10E
Kharkov 82 49 58N 36 20E
Kharmanli 67 41 55N 25 55E
Kharovsk 81 59 56N 40 13E
Kharsaniya 92 27 10N 49 10E
Khartoum = El Khartûm 123 15 31N 32 35E
Khartoum □ 123 16 0N 33 0E
Khasab 93 26 14N 56 15E
Khasavyurt 83 43 30N 46 40E
Khasebake 128 20 42S 24 29E
Khash 93 28 15N 61 5E
Khashm el Girba 123 14 59N 35 58E
Khasi Hills 98 25 30N 91 30E
Khaskovo 67 41 56N 25 30E
Khatanga 77 72 0N 102 20E
Khatanga, Zaliv 12 66 0N 112 0E
Khatauli 94 29 17N 77 43E
Khatyrchi 85 40 2N 65 58E
Khatyrka 77 62 3N 175 15E
Khavar □ 92 37 20N 46 0E
Khavast 85 40 10N 68 49E
Khawa 122 29 45N 40 25E
Khaydarken 85 39 57N 71 20E
Khazzân Jabal el Awliyâ 123 15 24N 32 20E
Khe Bo 100 19 8N 104 41E
Khe Long 100 21 29N 104 46E
Khed, Maharashtra, India 96 18 51N 73 56E
Khed, Maharashtra, India 96 17 43N 73 27E
Khed Brahma 93 24 7N 73 5E
Khekra 94 28 52N 77 20E
Khemarak Phouminville 101 11 37N 102 59E
Khemis Miliana 118 36 11N 2 14E
Khemisset 118 33 50N 6 1W
Khemmarat 100 16 10N 105 15E
Khenchela 119 35 28N 7 11E
Khenifra 118 32 58N 5 46W
Khenmarak Phouminville 102 11 40N 102 58E
Kherrata 119 36 27N 5 13E
Kherson 82 46 35N 32 35E
Khersónisos Akrotíri 69 35 30N 24 10E
Khetinsiring 99 32 54N 92 50E
Khiliomódhion 69 37 48N 22 51E
Khilok 77 51 30N 110 45E
Khimki 81 55 50N 37 20E
Khingan, mts. 86 47 0N 119 30E
Khios 69 38 27N 26 9E
Khisar-Momina Banya 67 42 30N 24 44E
Khiuma = Hiiumaa 80 58 50N 22 45E
Khiva 76 41 30N 60 18E
Khiyav 92 38 30N 47 45E
Khlaouia 118 25 50N 6 32W
Khlong Khlung 100 16 12N 99 43E
Khlong, R. 101 15 30N 98 50E
Khmelnitsky 82 49 23N 27 0E
Khmer Republic ■ = Cambodia 100 12 15N 105 0E
Khoai, Hon 101 8 26N 104 50E
Khodzhent 85 40 14N 69 37E
Khoi 92 38 40N 45 0E
Khojak P. 93 30 55N 66 30E
Khok Kloi 101 8 17N 98 19E
Khok Pho 101 6 43N 101 6E
Khokholskiy 81 51 35N 38 50E
Kholm 80 57 10N 31 15E

*Renamed Soc Trang

Kholmsk 77 35 5N 139 48E
Khomas Hochland 128 22 40S 16 0E
Khomayn 92 33 40N 50 7E
Khomo 128 21 7S 24 35E
Khon Kaen 100 16 30N 102 47E
Khong, Camb. 101 13 55N 105 56E
Khong, Laos 100 14 7N 105 51E
Khong, R., Laos 101 15 0N 106 50E
Khong, R., Thai. 101 17 45N 104 20E
Khong Sedone 100 15 34N 105 49E
Khonh Hung (Soc Trang) 101 9 37N 105 50E
Khonu 77 66 30N 143 25E
Khoper, R. 81 52 0N 43 20E
Khor el 'Atash 123 13 20N 34 15E
Khóra 69 37 3N 21 42E
Khóra Sfákion 69 35 15N 24 9E
Khorasan □ 93 34 0N 58 0E
Khorat = Nakhon Ratchasima 100 14 59N 102 12E
Khorat, Cao Nguyen 100 15 30N 102 50E
Khorat Plat. 101 15 30N 102 50E
Khorb el Ethel 118 28 44N 6 11W
Khorog 85 37 30N 71 36E
Khorol 82 49 48N 33 15E
Khorramabad 92 33 30N 48 25E
Khorramshahr 92 30 29N 48 15E
Khota Kota 127 12 55S 34 15E
Khotan = Hot'ien 105 37 7N 79 55E
Khotin 82 48 31N 26 27E
Khouribga 118 32 58N 6 50W
Khowai 98 24 5N 91 40E
Khoyniki 80 51 54N 29 55E
Khrami, R. 83 41 30N 44 30E
Khrenovoye 81 51 4N 40 6E
Khristianá, I. 69 36 14N 25 13E
Khromtau 84 50 17N 58 27E
Khtapodhiá, I. 69 37 24N 25 34E
Khu Khan 100 14 42N 104 12E
Khufaifiya 92 24 50N 44 35E
Khugiani 94 31 28N 66 14E
Khulna 98 22 45N 89 34E
Khulna □ 98 22 45N 89 35E
Khulo 83 41 33N 42 19E
Khunzakh 83 42 35N 46 42E
Khur 93 32 55N 58 18E
Khurai 94 24 3N 78 23E
Khurais 92 24 55N 48 5E
Khurja 94 28 15N 77 58E
Khurma 92 21 58N 42 3E
Khūryān Mūryān, Jazā 'ir 91 17 30N 55 58E
Khush 93 32 55N 62 10E
Khushab 94 32 20N 72 20E
Khuzdar 94 27 52N 66 30E
Khuzestan □ 92 31 0N 50 0E
Khvalynsk 81 52 30N 48 2E
Khvatovka 81 52 24N 46 32E
Khvor 93 33 45N 55 0E
Khvormuj 93 28 40N 51 30E
Khvoy 92 38 35N 45 0E
Khvoynaya 80 58 49N 34 28E
Khwaja Muhammad 93 36 0N 70 0E
Khyber Pass 94 34 10N 71 8E
Kiabukwa 127 8 40S 24 48E
Kiadho, R. 96 19 50N 76 55E
Kiama 141 34 40S 150 50E
Kiamba 126 6 0N 124 40E
Kiambi 126 7 15S 28 0E
Kiambu 126 1 8S 36 50E
Kiangsi □ 109 27 20N 115 40E
Kiangsu □ 109 33 0N 119 50E
Kiania 129 20 18S 47 8E
Kiaohsien = Chiaohsien 107 36 20N 120 0E
Kibæk 73 56 2N 8 51E
Kibanga Port 126 0 10S 32 58E
Kibangou 124 3 18S 12 22E
Kibara 126 2 8S 33 30E
Kibara, Mts. 126 8 25S 27 10E
Kibombo 126 3 57S 25 53E
Kibondo 126 3 35S 30 45E
Kibondo □ 126 4 0S 30 55E
Kibumbu 126 3 32S 29 45E
Kibungu 126 2 10S 30 32E
Kibuye, Burundi 126 3 39S 29 59E
Kibuye, Rwanda 126 2 3S 29 21E
Kibwesa 126 6 30S 29 58E
Kibwezi 124 2 27S 37 57E
Kibworth Beauchamp 29 52 33N 0 59W
Kičevo 66 41 34N 20 59E
Kichiga 77 59 50N 163 5E
Kicking Horse Pass 152 51 27N 116 25W
Kidal 121 17 50N 1 22E
Kidderminster 28 52 24N 2 13W
Kidete 126 6 25S 37 17E
Kidira 120 14 28N 12 13W
Kidlington 28 51 49N 1 18W
Kidnappers, C. 142 39 38S 177 5E
Kidsgrove 32 53 6N 2 15W
Kidston 138 18 52S 144 8E
Kidstones 32 54 15N 2 2W
Kidugalle 126 6 49S 38 15E
Kidwelly 31 51 44N 4 20W
Kiel 48 54 16N 10 8E
Kiel Canal = Nord-Ostee-Kanal 48 54 15N 9 40E
Kielce 54 50 58N 20 42E
Kielce □ 54 51 0N 20 40E
Kielder 35 55 14N 2 35W
Kieldrecht 47 51 17N 4 11E
Kieler Bucht 48 54 30N 10 30E
Kien Binh 101 9 55N 105 19E
Kien Hung 101 9 43N 105 17E
Kien Tan 101 10 7N 105 17E
Kienchwan 99 26 30N 99 45E
Kienge 127 10 30S 27 30E
Kiessé 121 13 29N 4 1E
Kieta 135 6 12S 155 36E
Kiev = Kiyev 80 50 30N 30 28E
Kiffa 120 16 50N 11 15W
Kifisiá 69 38 4N 23 49E
Kifissós, R. 69 38 30N 23 0E
Kifri 92 34 45N 45 0E
Kigali 126 1 5S 30 4E
Kigarama 126 1 1S 31 50E
Kigoma □ 126 5 0S 30 0E
Kigoma-Ujiji 126 5 30S 30 0E
Kigomasha, Ras 126 4 58S 38 58E
Kihee 139 27 23S 142 37E
Kihikihi 142 38 2S 175 22E
Kii-Hantō 111 34 0N 135 45E
Kii-Sanchi 111 34 20N 136 0E
Kijik 147 60 20N 154 20W
Kikai-Jima 112 28 19N 129 58E
Kikinda 66 45 50N 20 30E
Kikládhes □ 69 37 0N 25 0E
Kikládhes, Is. 69 37 20N 24 30E
Kikoira 141 33 59S 146 40E
Kikori 135 7 13S 144 15E
Kikori, R. 135 7 5S 144 0E
Kikuchi 110 32 59N 130 47E
Kikwit 124 5 5S 18 45E
Kil 72 59 30N 13 20E
Kilafors 72 61 14N 16 36E
Kilakarai 97 9 12N 78 47E
Kilauea 147 22 13N 159 25W
Kilauea Crater 147 19 24N 155 17W
Kilbaha 39 52 35N 9 51W
Kilbeggan 38 53 22N 7 30W
Kilbeheny 39 52 18N 8 13W
Kilbennan 38 53 33N 8 54W
Kilbirnie 34 55 46N 4 42W
Kilbrannan Sd. 34 55 40N 5 23W
Kilbride 39 52 56N 6 5W
Kilbrien 39 52 12N 7 40W
Kilbrittain 39 51 40N 8 42W
Kilbuck Mts. 147 60 30N 160 0W
Kilchberg 51 47 18N 8 33E
Kilchoan 36 56 42N 6 8W
Kilcock 38 53 24N 6 40W
Kilcoe 39 51 33N 9 26W
Kilcogan 39 53 13N 8 52W
Kilconnell 39 53 20N 8 25W
Kilcoo 38 54 14N 6 1W
Kilcormac 39 53 11N 7 44W
Kilcoy 139 26 59S 152 30E
Kilcreggan 34 55 59N 4 50W
Kilcrohane 39 51 35N 9 44W
Kilcullen 39 53 8N 6 45W
Kilcurry 38 54 3N 6 26W
Kildare 39 53 10N 6 50W
Kildare □ 39 53 10N 6 50W
Kildavin 39 52 41N 6 42W
Kildemo 39 52 37N 8 50W
Kildonan 37 58 10N 3 50W
Kildorrery 39 52 15N 8 25W
Kilembe 126 0 15N 30 3E
Kilfenora 39 53 0N 9 13W
Kilfinan 34 55 57N 5 19W
Kilfinnane 39 52 21N 8 30W
Kilgarvan 39 51 54N 9 28W
Kilgore 159 32 22N 94 40W
Kilham 33 54 4N 0 22W
Kilian Qurghan 93 36 52N 78 3E
Kilifi 126 3 40S 39 48E
Kilifi □ 126 3 30S 39 40E
Kilimanjaro □ 126 4 0S 38 0E
Kilimanjaro, Mt. 126 3 7S 37 20E
Kilinailau, Is. 135 4 45S 155 20E
Kilindini 126 4 4S 39 40E
Kilis 92 36 50N 37 10E
Kiliya 82 45 28N 29 16E
Kilju 107 40 57N 129 25E
Kilkea 39 52 57N 6 55W
Kilkee 39 52 41N 9 40W
Kilkeel 38 54 4N 6 0W
Kilkelly 38 53 53N 8 50W
Kilkenny 39 52 40N 7 17W
Kilkenny □ 39 52 35N 7 15W
Kilkerrin 38 52 32N 8 36W
Kilkhampton 30 50 53N 4 30W
Kilkieran 39 53 20N 9 45W
Kilkieran B. 38 53 18N 9 45W
Kilkis 68 40 58N 22 57E
Kilkís □ 68 41 5N 22 50E
Kilkishen 39 52 49N 8 45W
Kilknock 38 53 42N 8 53W
Kill 39 52 11N 7 20W
Killadoon 38 53 44N 9 53W
Killadysert 39 52 40N 9 7W
Killala 38 54 13N 9 12W
Killala B. 38 54 20N 9 12W
Killaloe 39 52 48N 8 28W
Killam 152 52 47N 111 51W
Killane 39 53 20N 7 6W
Killard, Pt. 38 54 18N 5 31W
Killare 38 53 28N 7 34W
Killarney, Man., Can. 150 49 10N 99 40W
Killarney, Ont., Can. 153 45 55N 81 30W
Killarney, Ireland 39 52 2N 9 30W
Killarney, L's. of 39 52 0N 9 30W
Killary Harb. 38 53 38N 9 52W
Killashandra 38 54 1N 7 32W
Killashee 38 53 40N 7 52W
Killavally 38 53 22N 7 29W
Killavullen 39 52 8N 8 32W

Killchianaig **Kíthnos**

Killchianaig 34 56 2N 5 48W
Killdeer, Can. 153 49 6N 106 22W
Killdeer, U.S.A. 158 47 26N 102 48W
Killeagh 39 51 56N 8 0W
Killean 34 55 38N 5 40W
Killeen 159 31 7N 97 45W
Killeenleigh 39 51 58N 8 49W
Killeigh 39 53 14N 7 27W
Killenaule 39 52 35N 7 40W
Killianspick 39 52 21N 7 18W
Killiecrankie P. 37 56 44N 3 46W
Killimor 39 53 10N 8 17W
Killin 34 56 28N 4 20W
Killiney 39 53 15N 6 8W
Killingdal 71 62 47N 11 26 E
Killinghall 33 54 1N 1 33W
Killíni 69 37 55N 21 8 E
Killíni, Mts. 69 37 54N 22 25 E
Killinick 39 52 15N 6 29W
Killorglin 39 52 6N 9 48W
Killough 38 54 16N 5 40W
Killtullagh 39 53 17N 8 37W
Killucan 38 53 30N 7 10W
Killurin 39 52 23N 6 35W
Killybegs 38 54 38N 8 26W
Killyleagh 38 54 24N 5 40W
Kilmacolm 34 55 54N 4 39W
Kilmacthomas 39 52 13N 7 27W
Kilmaganny 39 52 26N 7 20W
Kilmaine 38 53 33N 9 10W
Kilmaley 39 52 50N 9 11W
Kilmallock 39 52 22N 8 35W
Kilmaluag 36 57 40N 6 18W
Kilmanagh 39 52 38N 7 28W
Kilmarnock, U.K. 34 55 36N 4 30W
Kilmarnock, U.S.A. 162 37 43N 76 23W
Kilmartin 34 56 8N 5 29W
Kilmaurs 34 55 37N 4 33W
Kilmeaden 39 52 15N 7 15W
Kilmeedy 39 52 25N 8 55W
Kilmelford 34 56 16N 5 30W
Kilmez 84 56 58N 50 55 E
Kilmez, R. 84 56 58N 50 28 E
Kilmichael 39 51 49N 9 4W
Kilmichael Pt. 39 52 44N 6 8W
Kilmihill 39 52 44N 9 18W
Kilmore, Austral. 141 37 25 S 144 53 E
Kilmore, Ireland 39 52 12N 6 35W
Kilmore Quay 39 52 10N 6 36W
Kilmuir 37 57 44N 4 7W
Kilmurry 39 52 47N 9 30W
Kilmurvy 39 53 9N 9 46W
Kilnaleck 38 53 52N 7 21W
Kilninver 34 56 20N 5 30W
Kilombero □ 127 8 0 S 37 0 E
Kilondo 127 9 45 S 34 20 E
Kilosa 126 6 48 S 37 0 E
Kilosa □ 126 6 48 S 37 0 E
Kilpatrick 39 51 46N 8 42W
Kilrea 38 54 58N 6 34W
Kilrenny 35 56 15N 2 40W
Kilronan 39 53 8N 9 40W
Kilrush 39 52 39N 9 30W
Kilsby 28 52 20N 1 11W
Kilsheelan 39 52 23N 7 37W
Kilsmo 72 59 6N 15 35 E
Kilsyth 35 55 58N 4 3W
Kiltamagh 38 53 52N 9 0W
Kiltealy 39 52 34N 6 45W
Kiltegan 39 52 53N 6 35W
Kiltoom 38 53 30N 8 0W
Kilwa □ 127 9 0 S 39 0 E
Kilwa Kisiwani 127 8 58 S 39 32 E
Kilwa Kivinje 127 8 45 S 39 25 E
Kilwa Masoko 127 8 55 S 39 30 E
Kilwinning 34 55 40N 4 41W
Kilworth 39 52 10N 8 15W
Kilworth, mts. 39 52 10N 8 15W
Kim 159 37 18N 103 20W
Kimamba 126 6 45 S 37 10 E
Kimba 140 33 8 S 136 23 E
Kimball, Nebr., U.S.A. 158 41 17N 103 20W
Kimball, S.D., U.S.A. 158 43 47N 98 57W
Kimbe 135 5 33 S 150 11 E
Kimbe B. 135 5 15 S 150 30 E
Kimberley, N.S.W., Austral. 140 32 50 S 141 4 E
Kimberley, W. Australia, Austral. 136 16 20 S 127 0 E
Kimberley, Can. 152 49 40N 115 59W
Kimberley, S. Afr. 128 28 43 S 24 46 E
Kimberley, dist. 132 16 20 S 127 0 E
Kimberley Downs 136 17 24 S 124 22 E
Kimberly 160 42 33N 114 25W
Kimbolton 29 52 17N 0 23W
Kimchŏn 107 36 11N 128 4 E
Kími 69 38 38N 24 6 E
Kimje 107 35 48N 126 45 E
Kimmeridge, oilfield 19 50 36N 2 6W
Kimolos 69 36 48N 24 37 E
Kimolos, I. 69 36 48N 24 35 E
Kimovsk 81 54 0N 38 29 E
Kimparana 120 12 48N 5 0W
Kimry 81 56 55N 37 15 E
Kimsquit 152 52 45N 126 57W
Kimstad 73 58 35N 15 58 E
Kinabalu, mt. 102 6 0N 116 0 E
Kinaros, I. 69 36 59N 26 15 E
Kinaskan L. 152 57 38N 130 8W
Kinawley 38 54 14N 7 40W
Kinbrace 37 58 16N 3 56W
Kincaid 153 49 40N 107 0W
Kincardine, Can. 150 44 10N 81 40W
Kincardine, Fife, U.K. 35 56 4N 3 43W
Kincardine, Highland, U.K. 37 57 52N 4 20W
Kincardine (□) 26 56 56N 2 28W
Kincraig 37 57 8N 3 57W
Kindersley 153 51 30N 109 10W
Kindia 120 10 0N 12 52W
Kindu 126 2 55 S 25 50 E
Kinel 84 53 15N 50 40 E
Kineshma 81 57 30N 42 5 E
Kinesi 126 1 25 S 33 50 E
Kineton 28 52 10N 1 30W
King and Queen 162 37 42N 76 50W
King City 163 36 11N 121 8W
King Cr. 138 24 35 S 139 30 E
King Edward, R. 136 14 14 S 126 35 E
King Frederick VI Land 12 63 0N 43 0W
King Frederick VIII Land 12 77 30N 25 0W
King George 162 38 15N 77 10W
King George B. 176 51 30 S 60 30W
King George I. 13 60 0 S 60 0W
King George Is. 149 53 40N 80 30W
King George Sd. 132 35 5 S 118 0 E
King I., Austral. 138 39 50 S 144 0 E
King I., Can. 152 52 10N 127 40W
King I. = Kadah Kyun 101 12 30N 98 20 E
King, L. 137 33 10 S 119 35 E
King Leopold Ranges 136 17 20 S 124 20 E
King, Mt. 138 25 10 S 147 30 E
King Sd. 136 16 50 S 123 20 E
King William I. 148 69 10N 97 25W
King William, L. 50 42 14 S 146 15 E
King William's Town 128 32 51 S 27 22 E
Kingairloch, dist. 36 56 37N 5 30W
Kingaroy 139 26 32 S 151 51 E
Kingarrow 38 54 55N 8 5W
Kingarth 34 55 45N 5 2W
Kingfisher 159 35 50N 97 55W
Kinghorn 35 56 4N 3 10W
Kingisepp 80 59 25N 28 40 E
Kingisepp (Kuressaare) 80 58 15N 22 15 E
Kingman, Ariz., U.S.A. 161 35 12N 114 2W
Kingman, Kans., U.S.A. 159 37 41N 96 9W
Kings B. 12 78 0N 15 0 E
Kings Canyon National Park 163 37 0N 118 35W
King's Lynn 29 52 45N 0 25 E
Kings Mountain 157 35 13N 81 20W
Kings Park 162 40 53N 73 16W
King's Peak 160 40 46N 110 27W
King's, R. 39 52 32N 7 12W
Kings, R. 163 36 10N 119 50W
King's Sutton 28 52 1N 1 16W
King's Worthy 28 51 6N 1 18W
Kingsbarns 35 56 18N 2 40W
Kingsbridge 30 50 17N 3 46W
Kingsburg 163 36 35N 119 36W
Kingsbury 28 52 33N 1 41W
Kingscote 140 35 33 S 137 31 E
Kingscourt 38 53 55N 6 48W
Kingskerswell 30 50 30N 3 34W
Kingsland 28 52 15N 2 49W
Kingsley 158 42 37N 95 58W
Kingsley Dam 158 41 20N 101 40W
Kingsport 157 36 33N 82 36W
Kingsteignton 30 50 32N 3 35W
Kingston, Can. 150 44 14N 76 30W
Kingston, Jamaica 166 18 0N 76 50W
Kingston, N.Z. 143 45 20 S 168 43 E
Kingston, U.K. 28 51 23N 1 40W
Kingston, N.Y., U.S.A. 162 41 55N 74 0W
Kingston, Pa., U.S.A. 162 41 19N 75 58W
Kingston, R.I., U.S.A. 162 41 29N 71 30W
Kingston South East 140 36 51 S 139 55 E
Kingston-upon-Thames 29 51 23N 0 20W
Kingstown, Austral. 141 30 29 S 151 6 E
Kingstown, St. Vinc. 167 13 10N 61 10W
Kingstree 157 33 40N 79 48W
Kingsville, Can. 150 42 2N 82 45W
Kingsville, U.S.A. 159 27 30N 97 53W
Kingswear 30 50 21N 3 33W
Kingswood 28 51 26N 2 31W
Kington 28 52 12N 3 2W
Kingtung 99 24 30N 100 50 E
Kingussie 37 47 5N 4 2W
Kinistino 153 52 57N 105 2W
Kinkala 124 4 18 S 14 49 E
Kinki □ 111 35 0N 135 30 E
Kinleith 142 38 20 S 175 56 E
Kinloch, N.Z. 143 44 51 S 168 20 E
Kinloch, L. More, U.K. 37 58 17N 4 50W
Kinloch, Rhum, U.K. 36 57 0N 6 18W
Kinloch Rannoch 37 56 41N 4 12W
Kinlochbervie 36 58 28N 5 5W
Kinlochewe 36 57 37N 5 20W
Kinlochiel 36 56 52N 5 20W
Kinlochleven 36 56 42N 4 59W
Kinlochmoidart 36 56 47N 5 43W
Kinloss 37 57 38N 3 28W
Kinlough 38 54 27N 8 16W
Kinn 71 61 34N 4 45 E
Kinna 73 57 32N 12 42 E
Kinnaird 152 49 17N 117 39W
Kinnaird's Hd. 37 57 40N 2 0W
Kinnared 73 57 2N 13 7 E
Kinnegad 38 53 28N 7 8W
Kinneret 90 32 44N 35 34 E
Kinneret, Yam 90 32 45N 35 35 E
Kinneviken, B. 73 58 38N 18 20 E
Kinnitty 39 53 6N 7 44W
Kino 164 28 45N 111 59W
Kinoje, R. 150 52 8N 81 25W
Kinomoto 111 35 30N 136 13 E
Kinoni, C. Afr. 123 5 40N 26 10 E
Kinoni, Uganda 126 0 41 S 30 28 E
Kinping 101 22 56N 103 15 E
Kinrooi 47 51 9N 5 45 E
Kinross 35 56 13N 3 25W
Kinross (□) 26 56 13N 3 25W
Kinsale 39 51 42N 8 31W
Kinsale Harbour 39 51 40N 8 30W
Kinsale Head, gasfield 19 51 20N 8 0W
Kinsale Old Hd. 39 51 37N 8 32W
Kinsarvik 71 60 22N 6 43 E
Kinshasa 124 4 20 S 15 15 E
Kinsley 159 37 57N 99 30W
Kinston 157 35 18N 77 35W
Kintampo 121 8 5N 1 41W
Kintap 102 3 51 S 115 13 E
Kintaravay 36 58 4N 6 42W
Kintore 37 57 14N 2 20W
Kintore Ra. 137 23 15 S 128 47 E
Kintyre, Mull of 34 55 17N 5 4W
Kintyre, pen. 34 55 30N 5 35W
Kinu 98 22 46N 95 37 E
Kinu-Gawa, R. 111 35 36N 139 57 E
Kinushseo, R. 150 55 15N 83 45W
Kinuso 152 55 25N 115 25W
Kinvara 39 53 8N 8 57W
Kinyangiri 126 4 35 S 34 37 E
Kióni 69 38 27N 20 41 E
Kiosk 150 46 6N 78 53W
Kiowa, Kans., U.S.A. 159 37 3N 98 30W
Kiowa, Okla., U.S.A. 159 34 45N 95 50W
Kipahigan L. 153 55 20N 101 55W
Kipanga 126 6 15 S 35 20 E
Kiparissía 69 37 15N 21 40 E
Kiparissiakós Kólpos 69 37 25N 21 25 E
Kipawa Res. Prov. Park 150 47 0N 78 30W
Kipembawe 124 7 38 S 33 27 E
Kipengere Ra. 127 9 12 S 34 15 E
Kipili 126 7 28 S 30 32 E
Kipini 126 2 30 S 40 32 E
Kipling 153 50 6N 102 38W
Kipnuk 147 59 55N 164 7W
Kippen 34 56 8N 4 12W
Kippure, Mt. 39 53 11N 6 23W
Kipushi 127 11 48 S 27 12 E
Kir 124 1 29 S 19 25 E
Kirandul 96 18 33N 81 10 E
Kiratpur 94 29 32N 78 12 E
Kirchberg 50 47 5N 7 35 E
Kirchhain 48 50 49N 8 54 E
Kirchheim 49 48 38N 9 20 E
Kirchheim Bolanden 49 49 40N 8 0 E
Kirchschlag 53 47 30N 16 19 E
Kircubbin 38 54 30N 5 33W
Kirensk 77 57 50N 107 55 E
Kirgiz S.S.R. □ 85 42 0N 75 0 E
Kirgiziya Steppe 79 50 0N 55 0 E
Kiri 124 1 29 S 19 25 E
Kiriburu 96 22 0N 85 0 E
Kirikkale 92 39 51N 33 32 E
Kirikopuni 142 35 50 S 174 1 E
Kirillov 81 59 51N 38 14 E
Kirin □ 107 43 50N 125 45 E
Kirindi, R. 97 6 15N 81 20 E
Kirishi 80 51 28N 31 59 E
Kirishima-Yama 110 31 58N 130 55 E
Kiriwina Is. = Trobriand Is. 138 8 40 S 151 0 E
Kirk Michael 32 54 17N 4 35W
Kirkbean 35 54 56N 3 35W
Kirkbride 32 54 54N 3 13W
Kirkburton 33 53 36N 1 42W
Kirkby 32 53 29N 2 54W
Kirkby-in-Ashfield 33 53 6N 1 15W
Kirkby Lonsdale 32 54 13N 2 36W
Kirkby Malzeard 33 54 10N 1 38W
Kirkby Moorside 33 54 16N 0 56W
Kirkby Steven 32 54 27N 2 23W
Kirkby Thore 32 54 38N 2 34W
Kirkcaldy 35 56 7N 3 10W
Kirkcolm 34 54 59N 5 4W
Kirkconnel 35 55 23N 4 0W
Kirkcowan 34 54 53N 4 38W
Kirkcudbright 35 54 50N 4 3W
Kirkcudbright (□) 26 55 4N 4 0W
Kirkcudbright B. 35 54 46N 4 0W
Kirkeby 73 55 7N 8 33 E
Kirkee 96 18 34N 73 56 E
Kirkenær 71 60 27N 12 3 E
Kirkenes 74 69 40N 30 5 E
Kirkham 32 53 47N 2 52W
Kirkinner 34 54 59N 4 28W
Kirkintilloch 35 55 57N 4 10W
Kirkjubæjarklaustur 74 63 47N 18 4W
Kirkland, Ariz., U.S.A. 161 34 29N 112 46W
Kirkland, Wash., U.S.A. 160 47 40N 122 10W
Kirkland Lake 150 48 9N 80 2W
Kirklareli 67 41 44N 27 15 E
Kirkliston 35 55 55N 3 27W
Kirkliston Ra. 143 44 25 S 170 34 E
Kirkmichael 37 56 43N 3 31W
Kirkoswald 32 54 46N 2 41W
Kirkoswold 34 55 19N 4 48W
Kirkstone P. 32 54 29N 2 55W
Kirksville 158 40 8N 92 35W
Kirkuk 92 35 30N 44 21 E
Kirkwall 37 58 59N 2 59W
Kirkwhelpington 35 55 9N 2 0W
Kirkwood 128 33 22 S 25 15 E
Kirlampudi 96 17 12N 82 12 E
Kirn 49 49 46N 7 29 E
Kirov, R.S.F.S.R., U.S.S.R. 81 54 3N 34 12 E
Kirov, R.S.F.S.R., U.S.S.R. 84 58 35N 49 40 E
Kirovabad 83 40 45N 46 10 E
Kirovakan 83 41 0N 44 0 E
Kirovo 85 40 26N 70 36 E
Kirovo-Chepetsk 81 58 28N 50 0 E
Kirovograd 82 48 35N 32 20 E
Kirovsk, R.S.F.S.R., U.S.S.R. 78 67 48N 33 50 E
Kirovsk, Ukraine, U.S.S.R. 83 48 35N 38 30 E
Kirovski 83 45 51N 48 11 E
Kirovskiy 85 44 52N 78 12 E
Kirovskoye 85 42 39N 71 35 E
Kirriemuir, Can. 153 51 56N 110 20W
Kirriemuir, U.K. 37 56 41N 3 0W
Kirs 84 59 21N 52 14 E
Kirsanov 81 52 35N 42 40 E
Kirşehir 92 39 14N 34 5 E
Kirstonia 128 25 30 S 23 45 E
Kirtachi 121 12 52N 2 30 E
Kirthar Range 93 27 0N 67 0 E
Kirtling 29 52 11N 0 27 E
Kirtlington 28 51 54N 1 9W
Kirton 39 52 56N 0 3W
Kirton-in-Lindsey 33 53 29N 0 35W
Kiruna 74 67 52N 20 15 E
Kirundu 124 0 50 S 25 35 E
Kirup 137 33 40 S 115 50 E
Kiryū 111 36 24N 139 20 E
Kiryu 81 55 5N 46 45 E
Kirzhach 81 56 12N 38 50 E
Kisa 73 58 0N 15 39 E
Kisaga 126 4 30 S 34 23 E
Kisalaya 166 14 40N 84 3W
Kisámou, Kólpos 69 35 30N 23 38 E
Kisanga 126 2 30N 26 35 E
Kisangani 126 0 35N 25 15 E
Kisar, I. 103 8 5 S 127 10 E
Kisaran 102 2 47N 99 29 E
Kisarawe 126 6 53 S 39 0 E
Kisarawe □ 126 7 3 S 39 0 E
Kisarazu 111 35 23N 139 55 E
Kisbér 53 47 30N 18 0 E
Kiselevsk 76 54 5N 86 6 E
Kishanganga, R. 95 34 50N 74 15 E
Kishanganj 95 26 3N 88 14 E
Kishangarh 94 27 50N 70 30 E
Kishi 121 9 1N 3 45 E
Kishinev 82 47 0N 28 50 E
Kishinoi 82 47 1N 28 50 E
Kishiwada 111 34 28N 135 22 E
Kishkeam 39 52 15N 9 12 E
Kishon 90 32 33N 35 12 E
Kishorganj 98 24 26N 90 40 E
Kishorn L. 36 57 22N 5 40W
Kishtwar 95 33 20N 75 48 E
Kisii 126 0 40 S 34 45 E
Kisii □ 126 0 40 S 34 45 E
Kisiju 124 7 23 S 39 19 E
Kısır, Dağ 83 41 0N 43 5 E
Kisizi 126 1 0 S 29 58 E
Kiska I. 147 52 0N 177 30 E
Kiskatinaw, R. 152 56 8N 120 10W
Kiskittogisu L. 153 54 13N 98 20W
Kiskomárom = Zalakomár 53 46 33N 17 10 E
Kiskörös 53 46 37N 19 20 E
Kiskundorozsma 53 46 16N 20 5 E
Kiskunfelégyháza 53 46 42N 19 53 E
Kiskunhalas 53 46 28N 19 37 E
Kiskunmajsa 53 46 30N 19 48 E
Kislovodsk 83 43 50N 42 45 E
Kismayu 113 0 20 S 42 30 E
Kiso-Gawa, R. 111 35 2N 136 45 E
Kiso-Sammyaku 111 35 30N 137 45 E
Kisofukushima 111 35 52N 137 43 E
Kisoro 126 1 17 S 29 48 E
Kispest 53 47 27N 19 9 E
Kissidougou 120 9 5N 10 0W
Kissimmee 157 28 18N 81 22W
Kissimmee, R. 157 27 20N 81 0W
Kississing L. 153 55 10N 100 47W
Kistanje 63 43 58N 15 55 E
Kisterenye 53 48 3N 19 50 E
Kisújszállás 53 47 12N 20 50 E
Kisuki 110 35 17N 132 54 E
Kisumu 126 0 3 S 34 45 E
Kisvárda 53 48 14N 22 4 E
Kiswani 126 4 5 S 37 57 E
Kiswere 127 9 27 S 39 30 E
Kit Carson 158 38 48N 102 45W
Kita 120 13 5N 9 25W
Kita-Ura 111 36 0N 140 34 E
Kitab 85 39 7N 66 52 E
Kitakami, R. 112 38 25N 141 19 E
Kitakyūshū 110 33 50N 130 50 E
Kitale 126 1 0N 35 12 E
Kitami 112 43 48N 143 54 E
Kitangiri, L. 126 4 5 S 34 20 E
Kitano-Kaikyō 110 34 17N 134 58 E
Kitaya 127 10 38 S 40 8 E
Kitchener, Austral. 137 30 55 S 124 8 E
Kitchener, Can. 150 43 27N 80 29W
Kitchigami, R. 150 50 35N 78 5W
Kitega = Citega 126 3 30 S 29 58 E
Kiteto □ 126 5 0 S 37 0 E
Kitgum Matidi 126 3 17N 32 52 E
Kíthira 69 36 9N 23 0 E
Kíthira, I. 69 36 15N 23 0 E
Kíthnos 69 37 26N 24 27 E

Kíthnos, I.	69	37 25N	24 25 E
Kitimat	152	54 3N	128 38W
Kitinen, R.	74	67 34N	26 40 E
Kitiyab	123	17 13N	33 35 E
Kitros	68	40 22N	22 34 E
Kitsuki	110	33 35N	131 37 E
Kittakittaooloo, L.	139	28 3 S	138 14 E
Kittanning	156	40 49N	79 30W
Kittatinny Mts.	162	41 0N	75 0W
Kittery	162	43 7N	70 42W
Kitui	126	1 17 S	38 0 E
Kitui □	126	1 30 S	38 25 E
Kitwe	127	12 54 S	28 7 E
Kitzbühel	52	47 27N	12 24 E
Kitzingen	49	49 44N	10 9 E
Kivalina	147	67 45N	164 40W
Kivalo	74	66 18N	26 0 E
Kivarli	94	24 33N	72 46 E
Kivotós	68	40 13N	21 26 E
Kivu □	126	3 10 S	27 0 E
Kivu, L.	126	1 48 S	29 0 E
Kiwai I.	135	8 35 S	143 30 E
Kiyev	80	50 30N	30 28 E
Kiyevskoye Vdkhr.	80	51 0N	30 0 E
Kizel	84	59 3N	57 40 E
Kiziguru	126	1 46 S	30 23 E
Kizil Jilga	95	35 26N	79 50 E
Kizil Kiya	76	40 20N	72 35 E
Kızılcahaman	82	40 30N	32 30 E
Kızılırmak	83	39 15N	36 0 E
Kizilskoye	84	52 44N	58 54 E
Kizimkazi	126	6 28 S	39 30 E
Kizlyar	83	43 51N	46 40 E
Kizyl-Arvat	76	38 58N	56 15 E
Kjellerup	73	56 17N	9 25 E
Klabat, Teluk	102	1 30 S	105 40 E
Kladanj	66	44 14N	18 42 E
Kladnica	66	43 23N	20 2 E
Kladno	52	50 10N	14 7 E
Kladovo	66	44 36N	22 33 E
Klaeng	100	12 47N	101 39 E
Klagenfurt	52	46 38N	14 20 E
Klagerup	73	55 36N	13 17 E
Klagshamn	73	55 32N	12 53 E
Klagstorp	73	55 22N	13 23 E
Klaipeda	80	55 43N	21 10 E
Klakring	73	55 42N	9 59 E
Klamath Falls	160	42 20N	121 50W
Klamath Mts.	160	41 20N	123 0W
Klamath, R.	160	41 40N	123 30W
Klang = Kelang	101	3 1N	101 33 E
Klangklang	98	22 41N	93 26 E
Klanjec	63	46 3N	15 45 E
Klappan, R.	152	58 0N	129 43W
Klarälven	72	60 32N	13 15 E
Klaten	103	7 43 S	110 36 E
Klatovy	52	49 23N	13 18 E
Klawak	152	55 35N	133 0W
Klawer	128	31 44 S	18 36 E
Klazienaveen	46	52 44N	7 0 E
Kłecko	54	52 38N	17 25 E
Kleczew	54	52 22N	18 9 E
Kleena Kleene	152	52 0N	124 50W
Klein	160	46 26N	108 31W
Klein-Karas	128	27 33 S	18 7 E
Klein Karoo	128	33 45 S	21 30 E
Kleine Gette, R.	47	50 51N	5 6 E
Kleine Nete, R.	47	51 12N	4 46 E
KlekovaCa, mt.	63	44 25N	16 32 E
Klemtu	152	52 35N	128 55W
Klenovec, Czech.	53	48 36N	19 54 E
Klenovec, Yugo.	66	31 32N	20 49 E
Klepp	71	59 48N	5 36 E
Klerksdorp	128	26 51 S	26 38 E
Kletnya	80	53 30N	33 2 E
Kletsk	80	53 5N	26 45 E
Kletskiy	83	49 20N	43 0 E
Kleve	48	51 46N	6 10 E
Klickitat	160	45 50N	12 10W
Klimovichi	80	53 36N	32 0 E
Klin	81	56 28N	36 48 E
Klinaklini, R.	152	51 21N	125 40W
Klinte	73	53 35N	10 12 E
Klintehamn	73	57 22N	18 12 E
Klintsey	80	52 50N	32 10 E
Klipplaat	128	33 0 S	24 22 E
Klisura	67	42 40N	24 28 E
Klitmøller	73	57 3N	8 30 E
Kljajióevo	66	45 45N	19 17 E
Ključ	63	44 32N	16 48 E
Kłobuck	54	50 55N	19 5 E
Kłodzko	54	50 28N	16 38 E
Kloetinge	47	51 30N	3 56 E
Klondike	147	64 0N	139 26W
Kloosterzande	47	51 22N	4 1 E
Klosi	68	41 28N	20 10 E
Klosterneuburg	53	48 18N	16 19 E
Klosters	51	46 52N	9 52 E
Kloten, Sweden	72	59 54N	15 19 E
Kloten, Switz.	51	47 27N	8 35 E
Klötze	48	52 38N	11 9 E
Klouto	121	6 57N	0 44 E
Klovborg	73	55 56N	9 30 E
Klövsjöfj, mt.	72	62 36N	13 57 E
Kluane, L.	147	61 15N	138 40W
Kluang = Keluang	101	1 59N	103 20 E
Kluczbork	54	50 58N	18 12 E
Klundert	47	51 40N	4 32 E
Klyuchevskaya, Guba	83	55 50N	160 30 E
Kmelnitski	80	49 23N	27 0 E
Knapdale, dist.	34	55 55N	5 30W
Knaresborough	33	54 1N	1 29W
Knebworth	29	51 52N	0 11W
Knee L., Man., Can.	153	55 3N	94 45W
Knee L., Sask., Can.	153	55 51N	107 0W
Knesselare	47	51 9N	3 26 E
Knezha	67	43 30N	23 56 E
Knic	66	43 53N	20 45 E
Knight Inlet	152	50 45N	125 40W
Knighton	31	52 21N	3 2W
Knights Ferry	163	37 50N	120 40W
Knight's Landing	160	38 50N	121 43W
Knin	63	44 1N	16 17 E
Knittelfeld	52	47 13N	14 51 E
Knjazevac	66	43 35N	22 18 E
Knob, C.	137	34 32 S	119 16 E
Knock	38	53 48N	8 55W
Knockananna	39	52 52N	6 34W
Knockhoy Mt.	39	51 49N	9 27W
Knocklayd Mt.	38	55 10N	6 15W
Knocklofty	39	52 20N	7 49W
Knockmahon	39	52 8N	7 21W
Knockmealdown Mts.	39	52 16N	8 0W
Knocknaskagh Mt.	39	52 7N	8 25W
Knokke	47	51 20N	3 17 E
Knott End	32	53 55N	3 0W
Knottingley	33	53 42N	1 15W
Knowle	28	52 23N	1 43W
Knox	156	41 18N	86 36W
Knox, C.	152	54 11N	133 5W
Knox City	159	33 26N	99 38W
Knox Coast	13	66 30 S	108 0 E
Knoxville, Iowa, U.S.A.	158	41 20N	93 5W
Knoxville, Pa., U.S.A.	157	41 57N	77 26W
Knoxville, Tenn., U.S.A.	157	35 58N	83 57W
Knoydart, dist.	36	57 3N	5 33W
Knurów	54	50 13N	18 38 E
Knutsford	32	53 18N	2 22W
Knutshø	71	62 18N	9 41 E
Knysna	128	34 2 S	23 2 E
Knyszyn	54	53 20N	22 56 E
Ko Chang	101	12 0N	102 20 E
Ko Ho, R.	109	32 58N	117 13 E
Ko Kha	100	18 11N	99 24 E
Ko Kut	101	11 40N	102 32 E
Ko Phangan	101	9 45N	100 10 E
Ko Phra Thong	101	9 6N	98 15 E
Kō-Saki	110	34 5N	129 13 E
Ko Samui	101	9 30N	100 0 E
Koartac (Notre Dame de Koartac)	149	61 5N	69 36 E
Koba, Aru, Indon.	103	6 37 S	134 37 E
Koba, Bangka, Indon.	102	2 26 S	106 14 E
Kobarid	63	46 15N	13 30 E
Kobayashi	110	31 56N	130 59 E
Kōbe	111	34 45N	135 10 E
Kobelyaki	82	49 11N	34 9 E
København	73	55 41N	12 34 E
Koblenz, Ger.	49	50 21N	7 36 E
Koblenz, Switz.	50	47 37N	8 14 E
Kobo	123	12 2N	39 56 E
Kobrin	80	52 15N	24 22 E
Kobroor, Kepulauan	103	6 10 S	134 30 E
Kobuchizawa	111	35 52N	138 19 E
Kobuk	147	66 55N	157 0W
Kobuk, R.	147	66 55N	157 0W
Kobuleti	83	41 55N	41 45 E
Kobylin	54	51 43N	17 12 E
Kobyłka	54	52 21N	21 10 E
Kobylkino	81	54 8N	43 46 E
Kobylnik	80	54 58N	26 39 E
Kočani	66	41 55N	22 25 E
Koçarli	69	37 45N	27 43 E
Koceljevo	66	44 28N	19 50 E
Kočevje	63	45 39N	14 50 E
Kochang	107	35 41N	127 55 E
Kochas	95	25 15N	83 56 E
Kōchi	110	33 30N	133 35 E
Kōchi-Heiya	110	33 28N	133 30 E
Kōchi-ken □	110	33 40N	133 30 E
Kochiu	108	23 25N	103 7 E
Kochkor-Ata	85	41 1N	72 29 E
Kochkorka	85	42 13N	75 46 E
Kodaikanai	97	10 13N	77 32 E
Kodaira	111	35 44N	139 29 E
Koddiyar Bay	97	8 33N	81 15 E
Kodiak	147	57 30N	152 45W
Kodiak I.	147	57 30N	152 45W
Kodiang	101	6 21N	100 18 E
Kodinar	94	20 46N	70 46 E
Kodori, R.	83	43 0N	41 40 E
Koekelare	47	51 5N	2 59 E
K'oerch'inyuich-'iench'i	107	46 5N	122 5 E
Koerhmu	105	36 22N	94 55 E
Koersel	47	51 3N	5 17 E
Koes	125	26 0 S	19 15 E
Köflach	13	47 4N	15 4 E
Koforidua	121	6 3N	0 17W
Kōfu	111	35 40N	138 30 E
Koga	111	36 11N	139 43 E
Kogaluk, R.	151	56 12N	61 44W
Kogan	139	27 2 S	150 40 E
Kogin Baba	121	7 55N	11 35 E
Kogizman	92	40 5N	43 10 E
Kogon	121	11 20N	14 32W
Kogota	112	38 33N	141 3 E
Koh-i-Bab, mts.	93	34 30N	67 0 E
Koh-i-Khurd	94	33 30N	65 59 E
Koh-i-Mazar	94	32 30N	66 25 E
Kohat	94	33 40N	71 29 E
Kohima	98	25 35N	94 10 E
Kohler Ra.	13	77 0N	110 0W
Kohtla-Järve	80	59 20N	27 20 E
Kohukohu	142	36 31 S	173 38 E
Koindong	107	40 28N	126 18 E
Kojabuti	103	2 36 S	140 37 E
Kojetin	53	49 21N	17 20 E
Kojima	110	34 20N	133 38 E
Kōjo	110	34 33N	133 55 E
Kojŏ	107	38 58N	127 58 E
Kojonup	137	33 48 S	117 10 E
Kok Yangak	85	41 2N	73 12 E
Koka	122	20 5N	30 35 E
Kokand	85	40 30N	70 57 E
Kokanee Glacier Prov. Park	152	49 47N	117 10W
Kokas	103	2 42 S	132 26 E
Kokava	53	48 35N	19 50 E
Kokchetav	76	53 20N	69 10 E
Kokemäenjoki	75	61 32N	21 44 E
Kokemäenjoki = Kumo älv	75	61 32N	21 44 E
Kokhma	81	56 55N	41 18 E
Kokkola (Gamlakarleby)	74	63 50N	23 8 E
Koko, Mid-Western, Nigeria	121	6 5N	5 28 E
Koko, North-Western, Nigeria	121	11 28N	4 29 E
Koko Kyunzu	101	14 10N	93 25 E
Koko-Nor = Ch'ing Hai	105	37 0N	100 20 E
Koko Shili	99	35 20N	91 0 E
Kokoda	135	8 54 S	147 47 E
Kokolopozo	120	5 8N	6 5W
Kokomo	156	40 30N	86 6W
Kokopo	135	4 22 S	152 19 E
Kokoro	121	14 12N	0 55 E
Kokoura	77	71 35N	144 50 E
Koksan	107	38 46N	126 40 E
Koksengir, Gora	85	44 21N	65 6 E
Koksoak, R.	149	54 5N	64 10W
Kokstad	125	30 32 S	29 29 E
Kokubu	110	31 44N	130 46 E
Kola	78	68 45N	33 8 E
Kola, I.	103	5 35 S	134 30 E
Kola Pen. = Kolskiy P-ov.	78	67 30N	38 0 E
Kolagede	103	7 54 S	110 26 E
Kolahoi	95	34 12N	75 22 E
Kolahun	120	8 15N	10 4W
Kolaka	103	4 3 S	121 46 E
K'olamai	105	45 30N	84 55 E
K'olan	106	38 43N	111 32 E
Kolar	97	13 12N	78 15 E
Kolar Gold Fields	97	12 58N	78 16 E
Kolari	74	67 20N	23 48 E
Kolarovgrad	67	43 27N	26 42 E
Kolarovo	53	47 56N	18 0 E
Kolašin	66	42 50N	19 31 E
Kolayat	93	27 50N	72 50 E
Kolby	73	55 49N	10 33 E
Kolby Kås	73	55 48N	10 32 E
Kolchugino	81	56 17N	39 22 E
Kolda	120	12 55N	14 50W
Koldewey I.	12	77 0N	18 0W
Kolding	73	55 30N	9 29 E
Kole	124	3 16 S	22 42 E
Koléa	118	36 38N	2 46 E
*Kolepom, Pulau	103	8 0 S	138 30 E
Kölfors	72	62 9N	16 30 E
Kolguyev, Ostrov	78	69 20N	48 30 E
Kolham	46	53 11N	6 44 E
Kolhapur	96	16 43N	74 15 E
Kolia	120	9 46N	6 28W
Kolín	52	50 2N	15 9 E
Kolind	73	56 21N	10 34 E
Kölleda	48	51 11N	11 14 E
Kollegal	97	12 9N	77 9 E
Kolleru L.	96	16 40N	81 10 E
Kollum	46	53 17N	6 10 E
Kolmanskop	128	26 45 S	15 14 E
Köln	48	50 56N	6 58 E
Koło	54	52 14N	18 40 E
Kołobrzeg	54	54 10N	15 35 E
Kologriv	81	58 48N	44 25 E
Kolokani	120	13 35N	7 45W
Kolomna	81	55 8N	38 45 E
Kolomyya	82	48 31N	25 2 E
Kolondiéba	120	11 5N	6 54W
Kolonodale	103	2 3 S	121 25 E
Kolosib	98	24 15N	92 45 E
Kolpashevo	76	58 20N	83 5 E
Kolpino	80	59 44N	30 39 E
Kolpny	81	52 12N	37 10 E
Kolskiy Poluostrov	78	67 30N	38 0 E
Kolskiy Zaliv	78	69 23N	34 0 E
Koltubanovskiy	84	52 57N	52 2 E
Kolubara, R.	66	44 35N	20 15 E
Kolumna	54	51 36N	19 14 E
Koluszki	54	51 45N	19 46 E
Kolwezi	124	10 40 S	25 25 E
Kolyberovo	81	55 15N	38 40 E
Kolyma, R.	77	64 40N	153 0 E
Kolymskoye, Okhotsko	77	63 0N	157 0 E
Kôm Ombo	122	24 25N	32 52 E
Komagene	111	35 44N	137 58 E
Komaki	111	35 17N	136 55 E
Komandorskiye Ostrava	77	55 0N	167 0 E
Komárno	53	47 49N	18 5 E
Komárom	53	47 43N	18 7 E
Komárom □	53	47 35N	18 20 E
Komarovo	80	58 38N	33 40 E
Komatsu	111	36 25 S	136 30 E
Komatsukima	110	34 0N	134 35 E
Kombissiri	121	12 4N	1 20W
Kombori	120	13 26N	3 56W
Kombóti	69	39 6N	21 5 E
Komen	63	45 49N	13 45 E
Komenda	121	5 4N	1 28W
Komi, A.S.S.R. □	84	64 0N	55 0 E
Komiza	63	43 3N	16 11 E
Komló	53	46 15N	18 16 E
Kommamur Canal	97	16 0N	80 25 E
Kommunarsk	83	48 30N	38 45 E
Kommunizma, Pik	85	39 0N	72 2 E
Komnes	71	59 30N	9 55 E
Komodo	103	8 37 S	119 20 E
Komoé	120	5 12N	3 44W
Komono	124	3 15 S	13 20 E
Komoran, Pulau	103	8 18 S	138 45 E
Komoro	111	36 19N	138 26 E
Komorze	54	62 8N	17 38 E
Komotiri	68	41 9N	25 26 E
Kompong Bang	101	12 24N	104 40 E
Kompong Cham	101	11 54N	105 30 E
Kompong Chhnang	101	12 20N	104 35 E
Kompong Chikreng	100	13 5N	104 18 E
Kompong Kleang	101	13 6N	104 8 E
Kompong Luong	101	11 49N	104 48 E
Kompong Pranak	101	13 35N	104 55 E
Kompong Som	101	10 38N	103 30 E
Kompong Som, Chhung	101	10 50N	103 32 E
Kompong Speu	101	11 26N	104 32 E
Kompong Sralao	100	14 5N	105 46 E
Kompong Thom	100	12 35N	104 51 E
Kompong Trabeck, Camb.	100	13 6N	105 14 E
Kompong Trabeck, Camb.	101	11 9N	105 28 E
Kompong Trach, Camb.	101	11 25N	105 48 E
Kompong Trach, Camb.	118	10 34N	104 28 E
Kompong Tralach	101	11 54N	104 47 E
Komrat	82	46 18N	28 40 E
Komsberge	128	32 40 S	20 45 E
Komsomolabad	85	38 50N	69 55 E
Komsomolets	84	53 45N	62 2 E
Komsomolets, Ostrov	77	80 30N	95 0 E
Komsomolsk, R.S.F.S.R., U.S.S.R.	77	50 30N	137 0 E
Komsomolsk, Turkmen S.S.R., U.S.S.R.	85	39 2N	63 36 E
Komsomolskiy	81	53 30N	49 40 E
Kona, Niger	121	13 33N	8 3 E
Kona, Nigeria	121	8 58N	11 15 E
Konakovo	81	56 52N	36 45 E
Konam Dzong	99	29 5N	93 0 E
Konawa	159	34 59N	96 46W
Kondagaon	96	19 35N	81 35 E
Konde	126	4 57 S	39 45 E
Kondiá	68	39 52N	25 10 E
Kondinin	137	32 34 S	118 8 E
Kondoa	126	4 55 S	35 50 E
Kondoa □	126	5 0 S	36 0 E
Kondratyevo	77	57 30N	98 30 E
Konduga	121	11 35N	13 26 E
Kong	120	8 54N	4 36W
Kong Christian IX.s Land	12	68 0N	36 0W
Kong Christian X.s Land	12	74 0N	29 0W
Kong Frederik VIII.s Land	12	78 30N	26 0W
Kong Frederik VI.s Kyst	12	63 0N	43 0W
Kong, Koh	101	11 20N	103 0 E
Kong Oscar Fjord	12	72 20N	24 0W
Kong, R.	100	13 32N	105 58 E
Konga	73	56 30N	15 6 E
Kongeå	73	55 24N	8 39 E
Kongju	107	36 30N	127 0 E
Konglu	98	27 13N	97 57 E
Kongolo	126	5 22 S	27 0 E
Kongoussi	121	13 19N	1 32W
Kongsberg	71	59 39N	9 39 E
Kongsvinger	71	60 12N	12 2 E
Kongsvoll	71	62 20N	9 36 E
Kongwa	126	6 11 S	36 26 E
Koni	127	10 40 S	27 11 E
Koni, Mts.	127	10 36 S	27 10 E
Koniecpol	54	50 46N	19 40 E
Königsberg = Kaliningrad	80	54 42N	20 32 E
Königslutter	48	52 14N	10 50 E
Königswusterhausen	48	52 19N	13 38 E
Konin	54	52 12N	18 15 E
Konin □	54	52 15N	18 30 E
Konispol	68	39 42N	20 10 E
Kónitsa	68	40 5N	20 48 E
Köniz	50	46 56N	7 25 E
Konjic	66	43 42N	17 58 E
Konjice	63	46 20N	15 28 E
Konkouré, R.	120	10 30N	13 40W
Könnern	48	51 40N	11 45 E
Konnur	96	16 14N	74 49 E
Kono	120	8 30N	11 5W
Konoğlu	82	40 35N	31 50 E
Konolfingen	50	46 54N	7 38 E
Konongo	121	6 40N	1 15W
Konos	135	3 10 S	151 44 E
Konosha	78	61 0N	40 5 E
Kōnosu	111	36 3N	139 31 E
Konotop	80	51 12N	33 7 E
Konskaya, R.	82	47 30N	35 0 E
Konskie	54	51 15N	20 23 E
Konsmo	71	58 16N	7 23 E
Konstantinovka	82	48 32N	37 39 E
Konstantinovski, R.S.F.S.R., U.S.S.R.	81	57 45N	39 35 E

*Renamed Yos Sudarso, Pulau

CIB

Konstantinovski **Krokom**

Konstantinovski, R.S.F.S.R., U.S.S.R. 83 47 33N 41 10 E
Konstantynów Łódzki 54 51 45N 19 20 E
Konstanz 49 47 39N 9 10 E
Kontagora 121 10 23N 5 27 E
Kontich 47 51 8N 4 26 E
Kontum 100 14 24N 108 0 E
Kontum, Plat. du 100 14 30N 108 0 E
Konya 92 37 52N 32 35 E
Konyin 98 22 58N 94 42 E
Konz Karthaus 49 49 41N 6 36 E
Konza 124 1 45 S 37 0 E
Konzhakovskiy Kamen, Gora 84 59 38N 59 8 E
Koog 12 52 27N 4 49 E
Kookynie 137 29 17 S 121 22 E
Koolan I. 136 16 0 S 123 45 E
Kooline 136 22 57 S 116 20 E
Kooloonong 140 34 48 S 143 10 E
Koolyanobbing 137 30 48 S 119 36 E
Koolymilka P.O. 140 30 58 S 136 32 E
Koondrook 140 35 33 S 144 8 E
Koorawatha 141 34 2 S 148 33 E
Koorda 137 30 48 S 117 35 E
Kooskia 160 46 9N 115 59W
Koostatak 153 51 26N 97 26W
Kootenai, R. 160 48 30N 115 30W
Kootenay L. 153 49 45N 117 0W
Kootenay Nat. Park 152 51 0N 116 0W
Kootingal 173 31 1 S 151 3 E
Kopa 85 43 31N 75 50 E
Kopaonik Planina 66 43 10N 21 0 E
Kopargaon 96 19 51N 74 28 E
Kópavogur 74 64 6N 21 55W
Koper 63 45 31N 13 44 E
Kopervik 71 59 17N 5 17 E
Kopeysk 84 55 7N 61 37 E
Kopi 139 33 24 S 135 40 E
Köping 72 59 31N 16 3 E
Kopiste 63 42 48N 16 42 E
Kopliku 68 42 15N 19 25 E
Köpmanholmen 72 63 10N 18 35 E
Köpmannebro 73 58 45N 12 30 E
Koppal 97 15 23N 76 5 E
Koppang 71 61 34N 11 3 E
Kopparberg 75 59 52N 15 0 E
Kopparbergs län □ 147 61 20N 14 15 E
Koppeh Dāgh 93 38 0N 58 0 E
Kopperå 71 63 24N 11 50 E
Kopperå 71 63 24N 11 52 E
Koppio 140 34 26 S 135 51 E
Koppom 72 59 43N 12 10 E
Koprivlen 67 41 36N 23 53 E
Koprivnica 63 46 12N 16 45 E
Koprivshtitsa 67 42 40N 24 19 E
Kopychintsy 80 49 7N 25 58 E
Korab, mt. 66 41 44N 20 40 E
Korakiána 68 39 42N 19 45 E
Koraput 96 18 50N 82 40 E
Korba 95 22 20N 82 45 E
Korbach 48 51 17N 8 50 E
Korbu, G. 101 4 41N 101 18 E
Korça 68 40 37N 20 50 E
Korça □ 68 40 40N 20 50 E
Korčula 63 42 57N 17 8 E
Korčula, I. 63 42 57N 17 0 E
Korčulanski Kanal 63 43 3N 16 40 E
Kordestān □ 92 36 0N 47 0 E
Korea 107 40 0N 127 0 E
Korea Bay 107 39 0N 124 0 E
Korea, South ■ 107 36 0N 128 0 E
Korea Strait 107 34 0N 129 30 E
Koregaon 96 17 40N 74 10 E
Korenevo 80 51 27N 34 55 E
Korenovsk 83 45 12N 39 22 E
Korets 80 50 40N 27 5 E
Korgus 122 19 16N 33 48 E
Korhogo 120 9 29N 5 28W
Koribundu 120 7 41N 11 46W
Koridina 139 29 42 S 143 25 E
Korim 103 0 58 S 136 10 E
Korinthía □ 69 37 50N 22 35 E
Korinthiakós Kólpos 69 38 16N 22 30 E
Kórinthos 69 37 56N 22 55 E
Korioumé 120 16 35N 3 0W
Kōriyama 112 37 24N 140 23 E
Korkino 84 54 54N 61 23 E
Körmend 53 47 5N 16 35 E
Kornat, I. 63 43 50N 15 20 E
Korneshty 82 47 21N 28 1 E
Korneuburg 53 48 20N 16 20 E
Korning 73 56 30N 9 44 E
Kornsjø 71 58 57N 11 39 E
Kornstad 71 62 59N 7 27 E
Koro, Ivory C. 120 8 32N 7 30W
Koro, Mali 120 14 1N 2 58W
Koroba 135 5 44 S 142 47 E
Korocha 81 50 55N 37 30 E
Korogwe 124 5 5 S 38 25 E
Korogwe □ 126 5 0 S 38 20 E
Koroit 140 38 18 S 142 24 E
Korong Vale 140 36 22 S 143 45 E
Koróni 69 36 48N 21 57 E
Korónia, Limni 68 40 47N 23 37 E
Koronis 69 37 12N 25 35 E
Koronowo 54 53 19N 17 55 E
Koror 103 7 20N 134 28 E
Körös, R. 53 46 45N 20 20 E
Köröstarcsa 53 46 53N 21 3 E
Korosten 80 50 57N 28 25 E
Korotoyak 81 51 1N 39 2 E
Korraraika, B. de 129 17 45 S 43 57 E
Korsakov 77 46 30N 142 42 E
Korshavn 71 58 2N 7 0 E
Korshunovo 77 58 37N 110 10 E
Korsör 73 55 20N 11 9 E
Korsze 54 54 11N 21 9 E
Kortemark 47 51 2N 3 3 E
Kortessem 47 50 52N 5 23 E
Korti 122 18 0N 31 40 E
Kortrijk 47 50 50N 3 17 E
Korumburra 141 38 26 S 145 50 E
Korwai 94 24 7N 78 5 E
Koryakskiy Khrebet 77 61 0N 171 0 E
Koryŏng 107 35 44N 128 15 E
Kos 69 36 52N 27 19 E
Kos, I. 69 36 50N 27 15 E
Kosa, Ethiopia 123 7 50N 36 50 E
Kosa, U.S.S.R. 84 59 56N 55 0 E
Kosa, R. 84 60 11N 55 10 E
Kosaya Gora 81 54 10N 37 30 E
Koschagy 79 46 40N 54 0 E
Kosciusko 159 33 3N 89 34W
Kosciusko, I. 152 56 0N 133 40W
Kosciusko, Mt. 141 36 27 S 148 16 E
Kösély, R. 53 47 25N 21 30 E
Kosgi 96 16 58N 77 43 E
Kosha 122 20 50N 30 30 E
Koshigaya 111 35 54N 139 48 E
K'oshih 105 39 29N 75 58 E
K'oshihk'ot'engch'i 107 43 17N 117 24 E
Koshiki-Rettō 110 31 45N 129 49 E
Kōshoku 111 36 38N 138 6 E
Koshtëbë 85 41 5N 74 15 E
Kosi 94 27 48N 77 29 E
Kosi-meer 129 27 0 S 32 50 E
Košice 53 48 42N 21 15 E
Kosjerič 66 44 0N 19 55 E
Koslan 78 63 28N 48 52 E
Kosŏng 107 38 48N 128 24 E
Kosovska-Mitrovica 66 42 54N 20 52 E
Kosścian 54 52 5N 16 40 E
Kosścierzyna 54 54 8N 17 59 E
Kosso 120 5 3N 5 47W
Kostajnica 63 45 17N 16 30 E
Kostanjevica 63 45 51N 15 27 E
Kostelec 53 50 14N 16 35 E
Kostenets 67 42 15N 23 52 E
Koster 128 25 52 S 26 54 E
Kôstî 123 13 8N 32 43 E
Kostolac 66 44 43N 21 15 E
Kostroma 81 57 50N 41 58 E
Kostromskoye Vdkhr. 81 57 52N 40 49 E
Kostrzyn 54 52 24N 17 14 E
Kostyukovichi 80 53 10N 32 4 E
Koszalin 54 54 12N 16 8 E
Koszalin □ 54 54 10N 16 10 E
Kőszeg 53 47 23N 16 33 E
Kot Adu 94 30 30N 71 0 E
Kot Moman 94 32 13N 73 0 E
Kota 94 25 14N 75 49 E
Kota Baharu 101 6 7N 102 14 E
Kota Kinabalu 102 6 0N 116 12 E
Kota-Kota = Khota Kota 127 12 55 S 34 15 E
Kota Tinggi 101 1 44N 103 53 E
Kotaagung 102 5 38 S 104 29 E
Kotabaru 102 3 20 S 116 20 E
Kotabumi 102 4 49 S 104 46 E
Kotamobagu 103 0 57N 124 31 E
Kotaneelee, R. 152 60 11N 123 42W
Kotawaringin 102 2 28 S 111 27 E
Kotchandpur 98 23 24N 89 1 E
Kotcho L. 152 59 7N 121 12W
Kotel 67 42 52N 26 26 E
Kotelnich 81 58 20N 48 10 E
Kotelnikovo 83 47 45N 43 15 E
Kotelnyy, Ostrov 77 75 10N 139 0 E
Kothagudam 96 17 30N 80 40 E
Kothapet 96 19 21N 79 28 E
Köthen 48 51 44N 11 59 E
Kothi 95 24 45N 80 40 E
Kotiro 94 26 17N 67 13 E
Kotka 75 60 28N 26 58 E
Kotlas 78 61 15N 47 0 E
Kotlenska Planina 67 42 56N 26 30 E
Kotli 94 33 30N 73 55 E
Kotmul 95 35 32N 75 10 E
Kotohira 110 34 11N 133 49 E
Kotonkoro 121 11 3N 5 58 E
Kotor 66 42 25N 18 47 E
Kotor Varoš 66 44 38N 17 22 E
Kotoriba 63 46 23N 16 48 E
Kotovo 81 50 22N 44 45 E
Kotovsk 82 47 55N 29 35 E
Kotputli 94 27 43N 76 12 E
Kotri 94 25 22N 68 22 E
Kotri, R. 96 19 45N 80 35 E
Kótronas 69 36 38N 22 29 E
Kötschach-Mauthen 52 46 41N 13 1 E
Kottayam 97 9 35N 76 33 E
Kottur 97 10 34N 76 56 E
Kotturu 93 14 45N 76 10 E
Kotuy, R. 77 70 30N 103 0 E
Kotzebue 147 66 50N 162 40W
Kotzebue Sd. 147 66 30N 164 0W
Kouango 124 5 0N 20 10 E
Koudekerke 47 51 29N 3 33 E
Koudougou 120 12 10N 2 20W
Koufonísi, I. 69 34 56N 26 8 E
Koufonísia, I. 69 36 57N 25 35 E
Kougaberge 128 33 48 S 24 20 E
Kouibli 120 7 15N 7 14W
Kouilou, R. 124 4 10 S 12 5 E
Kouki 124 7 22N 17 3 E
Koula Moutou 124 1 15 S 12 25 E
Koulen 100 13 50N 104 40 E
Koulikoro 120 12 40N 7 50W
Koumala 138 21 38 S 149 15 E
Koumankoun 120 11 58N 6 6W
Koumbia, Guin. 120 11 54N 13 40W
Koumbia, Upp. Vol. 120 11 10N 3 50W
Koumboum 120 10 25N 13 0W
Koumpenntoum 120 13 59N 14 34W
Koumra 117 8 50N 17 35 E
Koumradskiy 76 47 20N 75 0 E
Koundara 120 12 29N 13 18W
Kountze 159 30 20N 94 22W
Koupangtzu 107 41 22N 121 46 E
Koupéla 121 12 11N 0 21 E
Kourizo, Passe de 119 22 28N 15 27 E
Kouroussa 120 10 45N 9 45W
Koussané 120 14 53N 11 14W
Kousseri 117 12 0N 14 55 E
Koutiala 120 12 25N 5 35W
Kouto 120 9 53N 6 25W
Kouvé 121 6 25N 0 59 E
KovaCica 66 45 5N 20 38 E
Kovel 80 51 10N 24 20 E
Kovilpatti 97 9 10N 77 50 E
Kovin 66 44 44N 20 59 E
Kovrov 81 56 25N 41 25 E
Kovur, Andhra Pradesh, India 96 17 3N 81 39 E
Kovur, Andhra Pradesh, India 97 14 30N 80 1 E
Kowal 54 52 32N 19 7 E
Kowalewo Pomorskie 54 53 10N 18 52 E
Kowkash 150 50 20N 87 20W
Kowloon 109 22 20N 114 15 E
Kowŏn 107 39 26N 127 14 E
Kōyama 110 31 20N 130 56 E
Koyan, Pegunungan 102 3 15N 114 30 E
Koyang 106 33 31N 116 11 E
Koytash 85 40 11N 67 19 E
Koyuk 147 64 55N 161 20W
Koyukuk, R. 147 65 45N 156 30W
Koyulhisar 82 40 20N 37 52 E
Koza 112 26 19N 127 46 E
Kozan 92 37 35N 35 50 E
Kozàni 68 40 19N 21 47 E
Kozàni □ 68 40 18N 21 45 E
Kozara, Mts. 63 45 0N 17 0 E
Kozarac 63 44 58N 16 48 E
Kozelsk 80 54 2N 35 38 E
Kozhikode = Calicut 97 11 15N 75 43 E
Kozhva 78 65 10N 57 0 E
Koziegłowy 54 50 37N 19 8 E
Kozje 63 46 5N 15 35 E
Kozle 54 50 20N 18 8 E
Kozlodui 67 43 45N 23 42 E
Kozlovets 67 43 30N 25 20 E
Kozmin 54 51 48N 17 27 E
Kōzu-Shima 111 34 13N 139 10 E
Kozuchów 54 51 45N 15 31 E
Kpabia 121 9 10N 0 20W
Kpandae 121 8 30N 0 2W
Kpandu 121 7 2N 0 18 E
Kpessi 121 8 4N 1 16 E
Kra Buri 101 10 22N 98 46 E
Kra, Isthmus of = Kra, Kho Khot 101 10 15N 99 30 E
Kra, Kho Khot 101 10 15N 99 30 E
Krabbendijke 47 51 26N 4 7 E
Krabi 101 8 4N 98 55 E
Kragan 103 6 43 S 111 38 E
Kragerø 71 58 52N 9 25 E
Kragujevac 66 44 2N 20 56 E
Krajenka 54 53 18N 16 59 E
Krakatau = Rakata, Pulau 102 6 10 S 105 20 E
Krakor 100 12 32N 104 12 E
Kraków 54 50 4N 19 57 E
Kraków □ 53 50 0N 20 0 E
Kraksaan 103 7 43 S 113 23 E
Kråksmala 73 57 2N 15 20 E
Kråkstad 71 59 40N 10 50 E
Kråkstad 71 59 39N 10 55 E
Kralanh 100 13 35N 103 25 E
Králiky 53 50 6N 16 45 E
Kraljevo 66 43 44N 20 41 E
Kralovice 52 49 59N 13 29 E
Královsky Chlmec 53 48 27N 22 0 E
Kralupy 52 50 13N 14 20 E
Kramatorsk 82 48 50N 37 30 E
Kramer 161 35 0N 117 38W
Kramfors 72 62 55N 17 48 E
Kramis, C. 118 36 26N 0 45 E
Krångede 72 63 9N 16 10 E
Krångede 72 63 9N 16 6 E
Kraniá 68 39 53N 21 18 E
Kranidhion 69 37 20N 23 10 E
Kranj 63 46 16N 14 22 E
Kranjska Gora 63 46 29N 13 48 E
Kranzberg 128 21 59 S 15 37 E
Krapina 63 46 10N 15 52 E
Krapina, R. 63 46 0N 15 55 E
Krapivna 81 53 58N 37 10 E
Krapkowice 54 50 29N 17 56 E
Kras Polyana 83 43 40N 40 25 E
Krashyy Klyuch 84 55 23N 56 39 E
Kraskino 77 42 44N 130 48 E
Krâslava 80 55 52N 27 12 E
Kraslice 52 50 19N 12 31 E
Krasnaya Gorbatka 81 55 52N 41 45 E
Krasnik Fabryezny 54 50 58N 22 11 E
Krasnoarmeisk 82 48 18N 37 11 E
Krasnoarmeysk, R.S.F.S.R., U.S.S.R. 81 50 32N 45 50 E
Krasnoarmeysk, R.S.F.S.R., U.S.S.R. 83 48 30N 44 25 E
Krasnodar 83 45 5N 38 50 E
Krasnodonetskaya 83 48 5N 40 50 E
Krasnog Dardeiskoye 82 45 32N 34 16 E
Krasnogorskiy 81 56 10N 48 28 E
Krasnograd 82 49 27N 35 27 E
Krasnogvardeysk 85 39 46N 67 16 E
Krasnogvardeyskoye 83 45 52N 41 33 E
Krasnoïarsk 77 56 8N 93 0 E
Krasnokamsk 84 58 4N 55 48 E
Krasnokutsk 80 50 10N 34 50 E
Krasnoperekopsk 82 46 0N 33 54 E
Krasnoselkupsk 76 65 20N 82 10 E
Krasnoslobodsk 83 48 42N 44 33 E
Krasnoturinsk 84 59 46N 60 12 E
Krasnoufimsk 84 56 57N 57 46 E
Krasnouralsk 84 58 21N 60 3 E
Krasnousolskiy 84 53 54N 56 27 E
Krasnovishersk 84 60 23N 57 3 E
Krasnovodsk 79 40 0N 52 52 E
Krasnoyarsk 77 56 8N 93 0 E
Krasnoyarskiy 84 51 58N 59 55 E
Krasnoye, Kal., U.S.S.R. 83 46 16N 45 0 E
Krasnoye, R.S.F.S.R., U.S.S.R. 81 59 15N 47 40 E
Krasnoye, Ukr., U.S.S.R. 80 49 56N 24 42 E
Krasnozavodsk 81 56 38N 38 16 E
Krasny Liman 82 48 58N 37 50 E
Krasny Sulin 83 47 52N 40 8 E
Krasnystaw 54 50 57N 23 5 E
Krasnyy 80 49 56N 24 42 E
Krasnyy Kholm, R.S.F.S.R., U.S.S.R. 81 58 10N 37 10 E
Krasnyy Kholm, R.S.F.S.R., U.S.S.R. 84 51 35N 54 9 E
Krasnyy Kut 81 50 50N 47 0 E
Krasnyy Luch 83 48 13N 39 0 E
Krasnyy Yar, Kal., U.S.S.R. 83 46 43N 48 23 E
Krasnyy Yar, R.S.F.S.R., U.S.S.R. 81 50 42N 44 45 E
Krasnyy Yar, R.S.F.S.R., U.S.S.R. 81 53 30N 50 22 E
Krasnyyoskolskoye, Vdkhr. 82 49 30N 37 30 E
Kraśnik 54 50 55N 22 5 E
Kraszna, R. 53 48 0N 22 20 E
Kratie 100 12 32N 106 10 E
Kratke Ra. 135 6 45 S 146 0 E
Kratovo 66 42 6N 22 10 E
Kravanh, Chuor Phnum 101 12 0N 103 32 E
Krawang 103 6 19N 107 18 E
Krefeld 48 51 20N 6 22 E
Kremaston, Límni 69 38 52N 21 30 E
Kremenchug 82 49 5N 33 25 E
Kremenchugskoye Vdkhr. 82 49 20N 32 30 E
Kremenets 82 50 8N 25 43 E
Kremenica 66 40 55N 21 25 E
Kremennaya 82 49 1N 38 10 E
Kremikovtsi 67 42 46N 23 28 E
Kremmen 48 52 45N 13 1 E
Kremmling 160 40 10N 106 30W
Kremnica 53 48 45N 18 50 E
Krems 52 48 25N 15 36 E
Kremsmünster 52 48 3N 14 8 E
Kretinga 80 55 53N 21 15 E
Krettamia 118 28 47N 3 27W
Krettsy 80 58 15N 32 30 E
Kreuzlingen 51 47 38N 9 10 E
Kribi 121 2 57N 9 56 E
Krichem 67 46 16N 24 28 E
Krichev 80 53 45N 31 50 E
Kriens 51 47 2N 8 17 E
Krim, mt. 63 45 53N 14 30 E
Krimpen 46 51 55N 4 34 E
Krionéri 69 38 20N 21 35 E
Krishna, R. 96 16 30N 77 0 E
Krishnagiri 97 12 32N 78 16 E
Krishnanagar 95 23 24N 88 33 E
Krishnaraja Sagara 97 12 20N 76 30 E
Kristianopel 73 56 12N 16 0 E
Kristiansand 71 58 9N 8 1 E
Kristianstad 73 56 2N 14 9 E
Kristianstad □ 75 56 15N 14 0 E
Kristiansund 71 63 7N 7 45 E
Kristiinankaupunki 74 62 16N 21 21 E
Kristinehamn 72 59 18N 14 13 E
Kristinestad 74 62 16N 21 21 E
Kríti, I. 69 35 15N 25 0 E
Kritsá 69 35 10N 25 41 E
Kriva Palanka 66 42 11N 22 19 E
Kriva, R. 66 42 12N 22 18 E
Krivaja, R. 66 44 15N 18 22 E
Krivelj 66 44 8N 22 5 E
Krivoy Rog 82 47 51N 33 20 E
Krizevci 63 46 3N 16 32 E
Krk 63 45 5N 14 36 E
Krk, I. 63 45 8N 14 40 E
Krka, R. 63 45 50N 15 30 E
Krkonoše 52 50 50N 16 10 E
Krnov 53 50 5N 17 40 E
Krobia 54 51 47N 16 59 E
Kročehlavy 52 50 8N 14 9 E
Kroeng Krai 101 14 55N 98 30 E
Krokawo 54 54 47N 18 9 E
Krokeai 69 36 53N 22 32 E
Kroken, Norway 71 58 57N 9 8 E
Kroken, Sweden 71 59 2N 11 23 E
Krokom 72 63 20N 14 30 E

Krolevets **Kuybyshevskoye Vdkhr**

Krolevets 80 51 35N 33 20 E
Kroměříz 53 49 18N 17 21 E
Krommenie 46 52 30N 4 46 E
Krompachy 53 48 54N 20 52 E
Kromy 80 52 40N 35 48 E
Kronobergs län □ 73 56 45N 14 30 E
Kronprins Harald Kyst 13 70 0S 35 1 E
Kronprins Olav Kyst 13 69 0S 42 0 E
Kronprinsesse Märtha Kyst 13 73 30S 10 0W
Kronshtadt 80 60 5N 29 35 E
Kroonstad 125 27 43S 27 19 E
Kröpelin 48 54 4N 11 48 E
Kropotkin 77 45 25N 40 35 E
Kropp 48 54 24N 9 32 E
Krósniewice 54 52 15N 19 11 E
Krosno 54 49 35N 21 56 E
Krośno □ 54 49 30N 22 0 E
Krosno Odrz 54 52 3N 15 7 E
Krościenko 54 49 29N 20 25 E
Krotoszyn 54 51 42N 17 23 E
Krotovka 84 53 18N 51 10 E
Krraba 68 41 13N 20 0 E
Krško 63 45 57N 15 30 E
Krstača, mt. 66 42 57N 20 8 E
Kruger Nat. Pk. 129 24 0S 31 40 E
Krugersdorp 129 26 5S 27 46 E
Kruidfontein 128 32 48S 21 59 E
Kruiningen 47 51 27N 4 2 E
Kruis, Kaap 128 21 55S 13 57 E
Kruishoutem 47 50 54N 3 32 E
Kruisland 47 51 34N 4 25 E
Kruja 68 41 32N 19 46 E
Krulevshchina 80 55 5N 27 45 E
Kruma 68 42 37N 20 28 E
Krumovgrad 67 41 29N 25 38 E
Krung Thep=Bangkok 100 13 45N 100 35 E
Krupanj 66 44 25N 19 22 E
Krupina 53 48 22N 19 5 E
Krupinica, R. 53 48 15N 19 5 E
Kruševac 66 43 35N 21 28 E
Krušovo 66 41 23N 21 19 E
Kruszwica 54 52 40N 18 20 E
Kruzof I. 152 57 10N 135 40W
Krylbo 72 60 7N 16 15 E
Krymsk Abinsk 82 44 50N 38 0 E
Krymskaya 82 45 0N 34 0 E
Krynica 54 49 25N 20 57 E
Krynica Morska 54 54 23N 19 28 E
Krynki 54 53 17N 23 43 E
Kryulyany 70 47 12N 29 9 E
Krzepice 54 50 58N 18 50 E
Krzeszowice 54 50 8N 19 37 E
Krzywin 54 51 58N 16 50 E
Krzyz 54 52 52N 16 0 E
Ksabi, Alg. 118 29 8N 0 58W
Ksabi, Moroc. 118 32 51N 4 13W
Ksar Chellala 118 35 13N 2 19 E
Ksar el Boukhari 118 35 51N 2 52 E
Ksar el Kebir 118 35 0N 6 0W
*Ksar es Souk 118 31 58N 4 20W
Ksar Rhilane 119 33 0N 9 39 E
Ksiba 118 32 46N 6 0W
Ksour, Mts. des 118 32 45N 0 30W
Kstovo 81 56 12N 44 13 E
Kuachou 109 32 14N 119 24 E
Kuala 102 2 46N 105 47 E
Kuala Berang 101 5 5N 103 1 E
Kuala Dungun 101 4 45N 103 25 E
Kuala Kangsar 101 4 46N 100 56 E
Kuala Kerai 101 5 30N 102 12 E
Kuala Klawang 101 2 56N 102 5 E
Kuala Kubu Baharu 101 3 34N 101 39 E
Kuala Lipis 101 4 10N 102 3 E
Kuala Lumpur 101 3 9N 101 41 E
Kuala Marang 101 5 12N 103 13 E
Kuala Nerang 101 6 16N 100 37 E
Kuala Pilah 101 2 45N 102 15 E
Kuala Rompin 101 2 49N 103 29 E
Kuala Selangor 101 3 20N 101 15 E
Kuala Terengganu 101 5 20N 103 8 E
Kuala Trengganu 101 5 20N 103 8 E
Kualakahi Chan 147 22 2N 159 53W
Kualakapuas 102 2 55S 114 20 E
Kualakurun 102 1 10S 113 50 E
Kualapembuang, Indon. 102 3 14S 112 38 E
Kualapembuang, Indon. 102 2 52S 111 45 E
Kuanaan 107 34 8N 119 24 E
Kuanch'eng 107 40 39N 118 32 E
Kuandang 103 0 56N 123 1 E
Kuangan 108 30 30N 106 35 E
Kuangch'ang 109 26 50N 116 15 E
Kuangchou 109 23 12N 113 12 E
Kuangfeng 109 28 26N 118 12 E
Kuanghan 108 30 56N 104 15 E
Kuanghua 109 32 22N 111 43 E
Kuangjao 107 37 5N 118 25 E
Kuangling 106 39 47N 114 10 E
Kuangnan 108 24 3N 105 3 E
Kuangning 109 23 40N 112 23 E
Kuangshi 109 29 55N 115 25 E
Kuangshun 108 26 5N 106 16 E
Kuangte 109 30 54N 119 26 E
Kuangtse 109 27 30N 117 24 E
Kuangwuch'eng 106 37 49N 108 51 E
Kuangyüan 108 32 22N 105 50 E
Kuanhsien 108 31 0N 103 40 E
Kuanling 108 25 55N 105 35 E
Kuanp'ing 109 31 39N 110 16 E
Kuantan 101 3 49N 103 20 E
Kuant'ao 106 36 31N 115 16 E
Kuantaok'ou 106 34 18N 111 1 E
K'uantien 107 40 47N 124 43 E
Kuanyang 109 25 29N 111 9 E
Kuanyün 107 34 17N 119 15 E
Kuaram 123 12 25N 39 30 E
Kuba 83 41 21N 48 32 E
Kubak 93 27 10N 63 10 E
Kuban, R. 82 45 5N 38 0 E
Kubenskoye, Oz. 81 59 40N 39 25 E
Kuberle 83 47 0N 42 20 E
Kubokawa 110 33 12N 133 8 E
Kubor 135 6 10S 144 44 E
Kubrat 67 43 49N 26 31 E
Kučevo 66 44 30N 21 40 E
Kucha Gompa 95 34 25N 76 56 E
Kuchaman 94 27 13N 74 47 E
Kuch'ang 108 24 58N 102 45 E
Kuchang 109 28 37N 109 56 E
K'uche K'uerhlo 105 41 43N 82 54 E
Kuchenspitze 49 47 3N 10 14 E
Kuchiang 109 27 11N 114 47 E
Kuching 102 1 33N 110 25 E
Kuchinoerabu-Jima 112 30 28N 130 11 E
Kuchinotsu 110 32 36N 130 11 E
Kuçove = Qytet Stalin 68 40 47N 19 57 E
Kud, R. 94 26 30N 66 12 E
Kuda 93 23 10N 71 15 E
Kudalier, R. 96 18 20N 78 40 E
Kudamatsu 110 34 0N 131 52 E
Kudara 85 38 25N 72 39 E
Kudat 102 6 55N 116 55 E
Kudremukh, Mt. 97 13 15N 75 20 E
Kuduarra Well 136 20 38S 126 20 E
Kudus 103 6 48S 110 51 E
Kudymkar 84 59 1N 54 39 E
Kuei Chiang, R. 109 23 33N 111 18 E
Kueich'i 109 28 17N 117 11 E
Kueich'ih 109 30 42N 117 30 E
Kueichu 108 26 25N 106 40 E
Kueihsien 108 23 6N 109 36 E
Kueilin 109 25 20N 110 18 E
Kueip'ing 108 23 24N 110 5 E
Kueiting 108 26 30N 107 17 E
Kueitung 109 26 12N 114 0 E
Kueiyang, Hunan, China 109 25 44N 112 43 E
Kueiyang, Kweichow, China 108 26 35N 106 43 E
K'uerhlo 105 41 44N 86 9 E
Kufra, El Wâhât el 117 24 17N 23 15 E
Kufrinja 90 32 20N 35 41 E
Kufstein 52 47 35N 12 11 E
Kugmallit B. 147 29 0N 134 0W
Kugong, I. 150 56 18N 79 50W
Kūh-e-Alijuq 93 31 30N 51 41 E
Kūh-e-Dinar 93 30 10N 51 0 E
Kūh-e-Hazaran 93 29 35N 57 20 E
Kūh-e-Jebel Barez 93 29 0N 58 0 E
Kūh-e-Sorkh 93 35 30N 58 45 E
Kūh-e-Taftan 93 28 40N 61 0 E
Kūhak 93 27 12N 63 10 E
Kūhha-ye-Bashakerd 93 26 45N 59 0 E
Kūhha-ye Sabalān 93 38 15N 47 45 E
Kuhnsdorf 52 46 37N 14 38 E
Kuhpayeh 93 32 44N 52 20 E
Kui Buri 101 12 3N 99 52 E
Kuinre 46 52 47N 5 51 E
Kuiseb, R. 125 23 40S 15 30 E
Kuiu I. 147 56 40N 134 15W
Kujangdong 107 39 57N 126 1 E
Kuji 112 40 11N 141 46 E
Kujū-San 110 33 5N 131 15 E
Kujukuri-Heiya 111 35 45N 140 30 E
Kukavica, mt. 66 42 48N 21 57 E
Kukawa 121 12 58N 13 27 E
Kukerin 137 33 13S 118 0 E
Kukësi 68 42 5N 20 20 E
Kukësi □ 68 42 25N 20 15 E
Kukko 123 8 26N 41 35 E
Kukmor 84 56 11N 50 54 E
Kukup 101 1 20N 103 27 E
K'uk'ushihli Shanmo 105 35 20N 91 0 E
Kukvidze 81 50 40N 43 15 E
Kula, Bulg. 66 43 52N 22 36 E
Kula, Yugo. 66 45 37N 19 32 E
Kulai 101 1 44N 103 35 E
Kulal, Mt. 126 2 42N 36 57 E
Kulaly, O. 83 45 0N 50 0 E
Kulanak 85 41 22N 75 30 E
Kulasekharapattanam 97 8 20N 78 0 E
Kuldiga 80 56 58N 21 59 E
Kuldja = Ining 105 43 54N 81 21 E
Kuldu 123 12 50N 28 30 E
Kulebaki 81 55 22N 42 25 E
Kulen Vakuf 63 44 35N 16 2 E
Kulgam 95 33 36N 75 2 E
Kuli 83 42 2N 46 12 E
Kulim 101 5 22N 100 34 E
Kulin 137 32 40S 118 2 E
Kulja 137 30 28S 117 18 E
Küllük 69 37 12N 27 36 E
Kulm 158 46 22N 98 58W
K'uloch'akonnoerh 106 43 25N 114 50 E
Kulsary 76 46 59N 54 1 E
Kultay 83 45 5N 51 40 E
Kulti 95 23 43N 86 50 E
Kulu 93 37 12N 115 2 E
Kulumadau 138 9 15S 152 50 E
K'ulunch'i 107 42 44N 121 44 E
Kulunda 76 52 45N 79 15 E
Kulungar 94 34 0N 69 2 E
Kulwin 140 35 0S 142 42 E
Kulyab 85 37 55N 69 50 E
Kum Tekei 76 43 10N 79 30 E
Kuma 110 33 39N 132 54 E
Kuma, R. 83 44 55N 45 57 E
Kumaganum 121 13 8N 10 38 E
Kumagaya 111 36 9N 139 22 E
Kumak 84 51 10N 60 8 E
Kumamoto 110 32 45N 130 45 E
Kumamoto-ken □ 110 32 30N 130 40 E
Kumano 111 33 54N 136 5 E
Kumano-Nada 111 33 47N 136 20 E
Kumanovo 66 42 9N 21 42 E
Kumara 143 42 37S 171 12 E
Kumarkhali 98 23 51N 89 15 E
Kumarl 137 32 47S 121 33 E
Kumasi 120 6 41N 1 38W
Kumba 121 4 36N 9 24 E
Kumbakonam 97 10 58N 79 25 E
Kumbarilla 139 27 15S 150 55 E
Kumbo 121 6 15N 10 36 E
Kumbukkan Oya 97 6 35N 81 40 E
Kŭmchŏn 107 38 10N 126 29 E
Kumdok 95 33 32N 78 10 E
Kumeny 81 58 10N 49 47 E
Kŭmhwa 107 38 17N 127 28 E
Kumi 126 1 30N 33 58 E
Kumkale 68 40 30N 26 13 E
Kumla 72 59 8N 15 10 E
Kumo 121 10 1N 11 12 E
Kumon Bum 98 26 30N 97 15 E
Kumotori-Yama 111 35 51N 138 57 E
Kumta 97 14 29N 74 32 E
Kumtorkala 83 43 2N 46 50 E
Kumukahi, C. 147 19 31N 154 49W
Kumusi, R. 135 8 16S 148 13 E
Kumylzhenskaya 83 49 51N 42 38 E
Kunágota 53 46 26N 21 3 E
Kunama 141 35 35S 148 4 E
Kunar 93 34 30N 71 3 E
Kunashir, Ostrov 77 44 0N 146 0 E
Kunch 95 26 0N 79 10 E
Kunda 80 59 30N 26 34 E
Kundiawa 135 6 2S 145 1 E
Kundip 137 33 42S 120 10 E
Kundla 94 21 21N 71 25 E
Kunduz 93 36 50N 68 50 E
Kunduz □ 93 36 50N 68 50 E
Kunene, R. 128 17 15S 13 40 E
Kungala 139 29 58S 153 7 E
Kungälv 73 57 53N 11 59 E
Kungan 109 30 4N 112 12 E
Kungch'eng 109 24 50N 110 49 E
K'ungch'iao Ho 105 41 48N 86 47 E
Kŭngdong 107 39 9N 126 5 E
Kungey Alatau, Khrebet 85 42 50N 77 0 E
Kunghit I. 152 52 6N 131 3W
Kungho 105 36 28N 100 45 E
Kungka 108 28 44N 100 22 E
Kungkuan 108 21 50N 109 33 E
Kungrad 76 43 6N 58 54 E
Kungsbacka 73 57 30N 12 5 E
Kungshan 108 27 41N 98 37 E
Kungt'an 108 28 49N 108 38 E
Kungur 84 57 25N 56 57 E
Kungurri 138 21 3S 148 46 E
Kungyangon 98 16 27N 96 1 E
Kungyingtzu 107 43 38N 121 0 E
Kunhar, R. 95 35 0N 73 40 E
Kunhegyes 53 47 22N 20 36 E
Kunimi-Dake 110 32 33N 131 1 E
Kuningan 103 6 59S 108 29 E
Kunisaki 110 33 33N 131 45 E
Kunlara 140 34 54S 139 55 E
Kunlong 98 23 20N 98 50 E
Kunlun Shan 105 36 0N 86 30 E
Kunmadaras 53 47 28N 20 45 E
K'unming 108 25 5N 102 40 E
Kunnamkulam 97 10 38N 76 7 E
Kunrade 47 50 53N 5 57 E
Kunsan 107 35 59N 126 45 E
K'unshan 109 31 22N 121 0 E
Kunszentmárton 53 46 50N 20 20 E
Kununurra 136 15 40S 128 39 E
Kunwarara 138 22 55S 150 9 E
Kuohsien 106 38 57N 112 46 E
Kuopio 74 62 53N 27 35 E
Kuopion Lääni □ 74 63 25N 27 10 E
Kupa, R. 63 45 30N 16 10 E
Kupang 103 10 19S 123 39 E
Kupeik'ou 107 40 42N 117 9 E
Kupiano 135 10 4S 148 14 E
Kupreanof I. 147 56 50N 133 30W
Kupres 66 44 1N 17 15 E
Kupyansk 82 49 45N 37 35 E
Kupyansk-Uzlovoi 82 49 52N 37 34 E
Kur, R. 98 26 50N 91 0 E
Kura, R. 83 40 20N 47 30 E
Kurahashi-Jima 110 34 8N 132 31 E
Kuranda 138 16 48S 145 35 E
Kurandvad 96 16 45N 74 39 E
Kurashiki 110 34 40N 133 50 E
Kurayoshi 110 35 26N 133 50 E
Kurday 85 43 21N 74 59 E
Kurdistan, reg. 92 37 30N 42 0 E
Kurduvadi 96 18 8N 75 29 E
Kure 110 34 14N 132 32 E
Kuressaare = Kingisepp 80 58 15N 22 15 E
Kurgaldzhino 76 50 35N 70 20 E
Kurgan, R.S.F.S.R., U.S.S.R. 77 64 5N 172 50W
Kurgan, R.S.F.S.R., U.S.S.R. 84 55 26N 65 18 E
Kurgan-Tyube 85 37 50N 68 47 E
Kuria Muria I = Khyryān Muryān J. 91 17 30N 55 58 E
Kurichchi 97 11 36N 77 35 E
Kuridala 138 21 16S 140 29 E
Kurigram 98 25 49N 89 39 E
Kurihashi 111 36 8N 139 42 E
Kuril Trench 142 44 0N 153 0 E
Kurilskiye Ostrova 77 45 0N 150 0 E
Kuring Kuru 128 17 42S 18 32 E
Kuringen 47 50 56N 5 18 E
Kurino 110 31 57N 130 43 E
KüRKkkuyu 68 39 35N 26 27 E
Kurkur 122 23 50N 32 0 E
Kurkûrah 119 31 30N 20 1 E
Kurla 96 19 5N 72 52 E
Kurlovski 81 55 25N 40 40 E
Kurma 123 13 55N 24 40 E
Kurmuk 123 10 33N 34 21 E
Kurnalpi 137 30 29S 122 16 E
Kurnool 97 15 45N 78 0 E
Kurobe-Gawe, R. 111 36 55N 137 25 E
Kurogi 110 33 12N 130 40 E
Kurovskoye 81 55 35N 38 55 E
Kurow 143 44 4S 170 29 E
Kurrajong, N.S.W., Austral. 141 33 33S 150 42 E
Kurrajong, W.A., Austral. 137 28 39S 120 59 E
Kurram, R. 94 33 30N 70 15 E
Kurri Kurri 141 32 50S 151 28 E
Kuršenai 80 56 1N 23 3 E
Kurseong 95 26 56N 88 18 E
Kursk 81 51 42N 36 11 E
Kuršumlija 66 43 9N 21 19 E
Kuršumlijska Banja 66 43 3N 21 11 E
Kurtalon 92 37 55N 41 40 E
Kurtamysh 84 54 55N 64 27 E
Kurty, R. 85 44 16N 76 42 E
Kuru (Chel), Bahr el 123 8 10N 26 50 E
Kuruman 128 27 28S 23 28 E
Kurume 110 33 15N 130 30 E
Kurunegala 97 7 30N 80 18 E
Kurya 77 61 15N 108 10 E
Kusa 84 55 20N 59 29 E
Kuşadası 69 37 52N 27 15 E
Kuşadası Körfezı 69 37 56N 27 0 E
Kusatsu, Gumma, Japan 111 36 37N 138 36 E
Kusatsu, Shiga, Japan 111 34 58N 136 5 E
Kusawa L. 152 60 20N 136 13W
Kusel 49 49 31N 7 25 E
Kushchevskaya 83 46 33N 39 35 E
Kushikino 110 31 44N 130 16 E
Kushima 110 31 29N 131 14 E
Kushimoto 111 33 28N 135 47 E
Kushin 109 32 12N 115 48 E
Kushiro 112 43 0N 144 25 E
Kushiro, R. 112 42 59N 144 23 E
Kushk 93 34 55N 62 30 E
Kushka 76 35 20N 62 18 E
Kushmurun 84 52 27N 64 36 E
Kushmurun, Ozero 84 52 40N 64 48 E
Kushnarenkovo 84 55 6N 55 22 E
Kushol 95 33 40N 76 36 E
Kushrabat 85 40 18N 66 32 E
Kushtia 98 23 55N 89 5 E
Kushum, R. 83 50 40N 50 20 E
Kushva 84 58 18N 59 45 E
Kuskokwim Bay 147 59 50N 162 56W
Kuskokwim Mts. 147 63 0N 156 0W
Kuskokwim, R. 147 61 48N 157 0W
Küsnacht 51 47 19N 8 15 E
Kussa 123 4 9N 38 58 E
Küssnacht 51 47 5N 8 26 E
Kustanay 84 53 10N 63 35 E
Kusu 110 33 16N 131 9 E
Kusung 108 28 25N 105 12 E
Kut, Ko 101 11 40N 102 35 E
Kutá Horq 52 49 57N 15 16 E
Kutahya 92 39 30N 30 2 E
Kutaisi 83 42 19N 42 40 E
Kutaradja = Banda Aceh 102 5 35N 95 20 E
Kutatjane 102 3 45N 97 50 E
Kutch, G. of 94 22 50N 69 15 E
Kutch, Rann of 94 24 0N 70 0 E
Kut'ien 109 26 36N 118 48 E
Kutina 63 45 29N 16 48 E
Kutiyana 94 21 36N 70 2 E
Kutjevo 66 45 23N 17 55 E
Kutkai 98 23 27N 97 56 E
Kutkashen 83 40 58N 47 47 E
Kutná Hora 52 49 57N 15 16 E
Kutno 54 52 15N 19 23 E
Kuttabul 138 21 5S 148 48 E
Kutu 124 2 40S 18 11 E
Kutum 123 14 20N 24 10 E
Kúty 53 48 40N 17 3 E
Kuŭptong 107 40 45N 126 1 E
Kuurne 47 50 51N 3 18 E
Kuvandyk 84 51 28N 57 21 E
Kuvasay 85 40 18N 71 59 E
Kuvshinovo 80 57 2N 34 11 E
Kuwait = Al Kuwayt 92 29 30N 47 30 E
Kuwait ■ 92 29 30N 47 30 E
Kuwana 111 35 0N 136 43 E
Kuyang 106 41 8N 110 1 E
Kuybyshev 81 55 27N 78 19 E
Kuybyshevo, Ukraine S.S.R., U.S.S.R. 82 47 25N 36 40 E
Kuybyshevo, Uzbek S.S.R., U.S.S.R. 85 40 20N 71 15 E
Kuybyshevskiy 85 37 52N 68 44 E
Kuybyshevskoye Vdkhr. 81 55 2N 49 30 E

*Renamed Ar Rachidya,

Kuyeh Ho, R
Lambay I

Kuyeh Ho, R. 106 38 30N 110 44 E
Kuylyuk 85 41 14N 69 17 E
Kuyto, Oz. 78 64 40N 31 0 E
Kuyüan, Hopeh, China 106 41 34N 115 38 E
Kuyüan, Ningsia Hui, China 106 36 1N 106 17 E
Kuzhithura 97 8 18N 77 11 E
Kuzino 84 57 1N 59 27 E
Kuzmin 66 45 2N 19 25 E
Kuznetsk 81 53 12N 46 40 E
Kuzomen 78 66 22N 36 50 E
Kvænangen 74 69 55N 21 15 E
Kvam 71 61 40N 9 42 E
Kvamsøy 71 61 7N 6 28 E
Kvarken 74 63 30N 21 0 E
Kvarner 63 44 50N 14 10 E
Kvarnerič 63 44 43N 14 37 E
Kvarnsveden 72 60 32N 15 25 E
Kvarntorp 72 59 8N 15 17 E
Kvås 71 58 16N 7 14 E
Kvernes 71 63 1N 7 44 E
Kvillsfors 73 57 24N 15 29 E
Kvina, R. 71 58 43N 6 52 E
Kvinesdal 71 58 18N 6 59 E
Kviteseid 71 59 24N 8 29 E
Kwabhaca 129 30 51 S 29 0 E
Kwadacha, R. 152 57 28N 125 38W
Kwakhanai 128 21 39 S 21 16 E
Kwakoegron 175 5 25N 55 25W
Kwale, Kenya 126 4 15 S 39 31 E
Kwale, Nigeria 121 6 18N 5 28 E
Kwale □ 126 4 15 S 39 10 E
Kwamouth 124 3 9 S 16 20 E
Kwando, R. 128 16 48 S 22 45 E
Kwangdaeri 107 40 31N 127 32 E
Kwangju 107 35 9N 126 54 E
Kwangsi-Chuang A.R. □ 109 24 0N 109 0 E
Kwangtung □ 109 23 45N 114 0 E
Kwara □ 121 8 0N 5 0 E
Kwaraga 128 20 26 S 24 32 E
Kwataboahegan, R. 150 51 9N 80 50W
Kwatisore 103 3 7 S 139 59 E
Kweichow □ 108 27 20N 107 0 E
Kweiyang = Kueiyang 108 26 35N 106 43 E
Kwethluk 147 60 45N 161 34W
Kwidzyn 54 54 45N 18 58 E
Kwigillingok 147 59 50N 163 10W
Kwiguk 147 63 45N 164 35W
Kwikila 135 9 49 S 147 38 E
Kwimba □ 126 3 0 S 33 0 E
Kwinana 137 32 15 S 115 47 E
Kwitaba 126 3 56 S 29 39 E
Kya-in-Seikkyi 98 16 2N 98 8 E
Kyabe 117 9 30N 19 0 E
Kyabra Cr. 139 25 36 S 142 55 E
Kyabram 139 36 19 S 145 4 E
Kyaiklat 98 16 46N 96 52 E
Kyaikmaraw 98 16 23N 97 44 E
Kyaikthin 98 23 32N 95 40 E
Kyaikto 100 17 20N 97 3 E
Kyakhta 77 50 30N 106 25 E
Kyangin 98 18 20N 95 20 E
Kyaring Tso 99 31 5N 88 25 E
Kyaukhnyat 98 18 15N 97 31 E
Kyaukpadaung 99 20 52N 95 8 E
Kyaukpyu 99 19 28N 93 30 E
Kyaukse 98 21 36N 96 10 E
Kyauktaw 98 21 16N 96 44 E
Kyawkku 98 21 48N 96 56 E
Kyburz 163 38 47N 120 18W
Kybybolite 140 36 53 S 140 55 E
Kyegegwa 126 0 30N 31 0 E
Kyeintali 98 18 0N 94 29 E
Kyela □ 127 9 45 S 34 0 E
Kyenjojo 126 0 40N 30 37 E
Kyidaunggan 98 19 53N 96 12 E
Kyle Dam 127 20 15 S 31 0 E
Kyle, dist. 34 55 32N 4 25W
Kyle of Lochalsh 36 57 17N 5 43W
Kyleakin 36 57 16N 5 44W
Kyneton 140 37 10 S 144 29 E
Kynuna 138 21 37 S 141 55 E
Kyō-ga-Saki 111 35 45N 135 15 E
Kyoga, L. 126 1 35N 33 0 E
Kyogle 139 28 40 S 153 0 E
Kyongju 107 35 51N 129 14 E
Kyongpyaw 99 17 12N 95 10 E
Kyŏngsŏng 107 41 35N 129 36 E
Kyōto 111 35 0N 135 45 E
Kyōto-fu □ 111 35 15N 135 30 E
Kyrínia 92 35 20N 33 20 E
Kyritz 48 52 57N 12 25 E
Kyrkebyn 72 59 18N 13 3 E
Kyrping 71 59 45N 6 5 E
Kyshtym 84 55 42N 60 34 E
Kystatyam 77 67 20N 123 10 E
Kytalktakh 77 65 30N 123 40 E
Kytlym 84 59 30N 59 12 E
Kyu-hkok 98 24 4N 98 4 E
Kyulyunken 77 64 10N 137 5 E
Kyunhla 98 23 25N 95 15 E
Kyuquot 152 50 3N 127 25W
Kyuquot Sd. 83 50 0N 127 25W
Kyurdamir 83 40 25N 48 3 E
Kyūshū 110 33 0N 131 0 E
Kyūshū □ 110 33 0N 131 0 E
Kyūshū-Sanchi 110 32 45N 131 40 E
Kyustendil 66 42 25N 22 41 E
Kyusyur 77 70 39N 127 15 E
Kywong 141 34 58 S 146 44 E
Kyzyl 77 51 50N 94 30 E
Kyzyl-Kiya 85 40 16N 72 8 E
Kyzyl Orda 85 44 56N 65 30 E
Kyzyl Rabat 76 37 45N 74 55 E
Kyzylkum 84 42 30N 65 0 E
Kyzylsu, R. 85 39 11N 72 2 E
Kzyl-orda 85 44 48N 65 28 E

L

Laa 53 48 43N 16 23 E
Laage 48 53 55N 12 21 E
Laasphe 48 50 56N 8 23 E
Laau Pt. 147 21 57N 159 40W
Laba, R. 83 45 0N 40 30 E
Laban, Burma 98 25 52N 96 40 E
Laban, Ireland 39 53 8N 8 50W
Labasheeda 39 52 37N 9 15W
Labastide 44 43 28N 2 39 E
Labastide-Murat 44 44 39N 1 33 E
Labbézenga 121 15 2N 0 48 E
Labdah = Leptis Magna 119 32 40N 14 12 E
Labé 120 11 24N 12 16W
Labe, R. 52 50 3N 15 20 E
Laberec, R. 53 21 57N 49 7 E
Laberge, L. 152 61 11N 135 12W
Labin 63 45 5N 14 8 E
Labinsk 83 44 40N 40 48W
Labis 101 2 22N 103 2 E
Labiszyn 54 52 57N 17 54 E
Laboa 103 8 6 S 122 50 E
Laboe 48 54 25N 10 13 E
Labouheyre 44 44 13N 0 55W
Laboulaye 172 34 10 S 63 30W
Labrador City 151 52 57N 66 55W
Labrador, Coast of ■ 149 53 20N 61 0W
Labranzagrande 174 5 33N 72 34W
Lábrea 174 7 15 S 64 51W
Labrède 44 44 41N 0 32W
Labuan, I. 102 5 15N 115 38W
Labuha 103 0 30 S 127 30 E
Labuhan 103 6 26 S 105 50 E
Labuhanbajo 103 8 28 S 120 1 E
Labuissière 47 50 19N 4 11 E
Labuk, Telok 102 6 10N 117 50 E
Labutta 98 16 9N 94 46 E
Labytnangi 78 66 29N 66 40 E
Lac Allard 151 50 33N 63 24W
Lac Bouchette 151 48 16N 72 11W
Lac du Flambeau 158 46 1N 89 51W
Lac Édouard 151 47 40N 72 16W
Lac la Biche 152 54 45N 111 58W
Lac-Mégantic 151 45 35N 70 53W
Lac Seul 153 50 28N 92 0W
Lac Thien 100 12 25N 108 11 E
Lacanau, Étang de 44 44 58N 1 7W
Lacanau Médoc 44 44 59N 1 5W
Lacantum, R. 165 16 36N 90 40W
Lacara, R. 57 39 7N 6 25W
Lacaune 44 43 43N 2 40 E
Lacaune, Mts. de 44 43 43N 2 50 E
Laccadive Is. = Lakshadweep Is. 86 10 0N 72 30 E
Laceby 33 53 32N 0 10W
Lacepede B. 140 36 40 S 139 40 E
Lacepede Is. 136 16 55 S 122 0 E
Lacerdónia 127 18 3 S 35 35 E
Lachen, Sikkim 98 47 12N 8 51 E
Lachen, Switz. 51 47 12N 8 51 E
Lachi 94 33 25N 71 20 E
Lachine 150 45 30N 73 40W
Lachlan 139 42 50 S 147 3 E
Lachlan, R. 140 34 22 S 143 55 E
Lachmangarh 94 27 50N 75 4 E
Lachute 150 45 39N 74 21 E
Lackagh Hills 38 54 14N 8 0W
Lackawanna 156 42 49N 78 50W
Lackawaxen 162 41 29N 74 59W
Lacock 28 51 24N 2 8W
Lacombe 152 52 30N 113 44W
Lacona 162 43 37N 76 5W
Láconi 64 39 54N 9 4 E
Laconia 162 43 32N 71 30W
Lacq 44 43 25N 0 35W
Lacrosse 160 46 51N 117 58W
Ladainha 171 17 39 S 41 44W
Ladakh Ra. 95 34 0N 78 0 E
Ladder Hills 37 57 14N 3 13W
Ladhar Bheinn 36 57 5N 5 37W
Ladhon, R. 69 37 40N 21 50 E
Lâdik 82 40 57N 35 58 E
Ladismith 128 33 28 S 21 15 E
Lādiz 93 28 55N 61 15 E
Ladnun 94 27 38N 74 25 E
Ladock 30 50 19N 4 58W
Ladoga, L. = Ladozhskoye Oz. 78 61 15N 30 30 E
Ladon 43 48 0N 2 30 E
Ladozhskoye Ozero 76 61 15N 30 30 E
Ladrone Is. = Mariana Is. 130 17 0N 145 0 E
Lady Babbie 127 18 30 S 29 20 E
Lady Beatrix L. 150 5 20N 76 50W
Lady Edith Lagoon 136 20 36 S 126 47 E
Lady Grey 128 30 43 S 27 13 E
Ladybank 35 56 16N 3 8W
Ladybrand 128 29 9 S 27 29 E
Lady's I. Lake 39 52 12N 6 23W
Ladysmith, Can. 152 49 0N 123 49W
Ladysmith, S. Afr. 129 28 32 S 29 46 E
Ladysmith, U.S.A. 158 45 27N 91 4W
Lae 135 6 40 S 147 2 E
Laem Ngop 101 12 10N 102 26 E
Laem Pho 101 6 55N 101 19 E
Læsø 73 57 15N 10 53 E
Læsø Rende 73 57 20N 10 45 E
Lafayette, Colo., U.S.A. 158 40 0N 105 2W
Lafayette, Ga., U.S.A. 157 34 44N 85 15W
Lafayette, La., U.S.A. 159 30 18N 92 0W
Lafayette, Tenn., U.S.A. 157 36 35N 86 0W
Laferté 150 48 37N 78 48W
Laferte, R. 152 61 53N 117 44W
Laffan's Bridge 39 52 36N 7 45W
Lafia 121 8 30N 8 34 E
Lafiagi 121 8 52N 5 20 E
Lafleche 153 49 45N 106 40W
Lafon 123 5 5N 32 29 E
Laforest 150 47 4N 81 12W
Laforsen 72 61 56N 15 3 E
Lagaip, R. 135 5 4 S 141 52 E
Lagan 73 56 32N 12 58 E
Lagan, R. 38 54 35N 5 55W
Lagarfljót 74 65 40N 14 18W
Lagarto 170 10 54 S 37 41W
Lagarto, Serra do 173 23 0 S 57 15W
Lage, Ger. 48 52 0N 8 47 E
Lage, Spain 56 43 13N 9 0W
Lage-Mierde 47 51 25N 5 9 E
Lågen 71 61 29N 10 2 E
Lågen, R. 75 61 30N 10 20 E
Lägerdorf 48 53 53N 9 35 E
Lagg 34 56 57N 5 50W
Laggan, Grampian, U.K. 37 57 24N 3 6W
Laggan, Highland, U.K. 37 57 3N 4 48W
Laggan B. 34 55 40N 6 20W
Laggan L. 37 56 57N 4 30W
Laggers Pt. 139 30 52 S 153 4 E
Laghman □ 93 34 20N 70 0 E
Laghouat 118 33 50N 2 59 E
Laghy 38 54 37N 8 7W
Lagnieu 45 45 55N 5 20 E
Lagny 43 48 52N 2 40 E
Lago 65 39 9N 16 8 E
Lagôa 57 37 8N 8 27W
Lagoaça 56 41 11N 6 44W
Lagodekhi 83 41 50N 46 22 E
Lagónegro 65 40 8N 15 45 E
Lagonoy Gulf 103 13 50N 123 50 E
Lagos, Nigeria 121 6 25N 3 27 E
Lagos, Port. 57 37 5N 8 41W
Lagos de Moreno 164 21 21N 101 55W
Lagrange 136 14 13 S 125 46 E
Lagrange B. 136 18 38 S 121 42 E
Laguardia 58 42 33N 2 35W
Laguépie 44 44 8N 1 57 E
Laguna, Brazil 173 28 30 S 48 50W
Laguna, U.S.A. 161 35 3N 107 28W
Laguna Beach 163 33 31N 117 52W
Laguna Dam 161 32 55N 114 30W
Laguna de la Janda 57 36 15N 5 45W
Laguna Limpia 172 26 32 S 59 45W
Laguna Madre 165 27 0N 97 20W
Laguna Veneta 63 45 23N 12 25 E
Lagunas, Chile 172 21 0 S 69 45W
Lagunas, Peru 174 5 10 S 75 35W
Lagunillas 174 10 8N 71 16W
Lahad Datu 103 5 0N 118 30 E
Lahaina 147 20 52N 156 41W
Lahan Sai 100 14 25N 102 52 E
Lahanam 100 16 16N 105 16 E
Lahardaun 38 54 2N 9 20W
Laharpur 95 27 43N 80 56 E
Lahat 102 3 45 S 103 30 E
Lahe 98 19 18N 93 36 E
Lahewa 102 1 22N 97 12 E
Lahijan 93 37 10N 50 6 E
Lahn, R. 48 50 52N 8 35 E
Laholm 73 56 30N 13 2 E
Laholmsbukten 73 56 30N 12 45 E
Lahontan Res. 160 39 28N 118 58W
Lahore 94 31 32N 74 22 E
Lahore □ 94 31 55N 74 5 E
Lahpongsel 98 27 7N 98 25 E
Lahr 49 48 20N 7 52 E
Lahti 75 60 58N 25 40 E
Lai (Béhagle) 117 9 25N 16 30 E
Lai Chau 100 22 5N 103 3 E
Lai-hka 98 21 16N 97 40 E
Laiagam 135 5 33 S 143 30 E
Laian 109 32 27N 118 25 E
Laichou Wan 107 37 30N 119 30 E
Laidley 139 27 39 S 152 20 E
Laidon L. 37 56 40N 4 40W
Laifeng 108 29 31N 109 18 E
Laigle 42 48 46N 0 38 E
Laignes 43 47 50N 4 20 E
Laihsi 107 36 51N 120 30 E
Laikipia □ 126 0 30N 36 30 E
Laila 92 22 10N 46 40 E
Laillahue, Mt. 174 17 0 S 69 30W
Laingsburg 128 33 9 S 20 52 E
Laipin 108 23 42N 109 16 E
Lairg 37 58 1N 4 24W
Lais 102 3 35 S 102 0 E
Laishui 106 39 23N 115 42 E
Laiwu 107 36 12N 117 38 E
Laiyang 107 36 58N 120 41 E
Laiyüan 106 39 19N 114 41 E
Laja, R. 164 20 55N 100 46W
Lajes, Rio Grande d. N., Brazil 170 5 41 S 36 14W
Lajes, Sta. Catarina, Brazil 173 27 48 S 50 20W
Lajinha 171 20 9 S 41 37W
Lajkovac 66 44 27N 20 14 E
Lajosmizse 53 47 3N 19 32 E
Lak Sao 100 18 11N 104 59 E
Laka Chih 95 30 40N 81 10 E
Lakaband 94 31 2N 69 15 E
Lakar 103 8 15 S 128 17 E
Lake Alpine 163 38 29N 120 0W
Lake Andes 158 43 10N 98 32W
Lake Anse 156 46 42N 88 25W
Lake Arthur 159 30 8N 92 40W
Lake Brown 137 30 56 S 118 20 E
Lake Cargelligo 141 33 15 S 146 22 E
Lake Charles 159 31 10N 93 10W
Lake City, Colo, U.S.A. 161 38 3N 107 27W
Lake City, Fla., U.S.A. 157 30 10N 82 40W
Lake City, Iowa, U.S.A. 158 42 12N 94 42W
Lake City, Mich., U.S.A. 156 44 20N 85 10W
Lake City, Minn., U.S.A. 158 44 28N 92 21W
Lake City, S.C., U.S.A. 157 33 40N 79 44W
Lake Coleridge 143 43 17 S 171 30 E
Lake District 23 54 30N 3 10W
Lake George 162 43 25N 73 43W
Lake Grace 137 33 7 S 118 28 E
Lake Harbour 149 62 30N 69 50W
Lake Havasu City 161 34 25N 114 29W
Lake Hughes 163 34 41N 118 26W
Lake Isabella 163 35 38N 118 28W
Lake King 137 33 5 S 119 45 E
Lake Lenore 153 52 24N 104 59W
Lake Louise 152 51 30N 116 10W
Lake Mason 137 27 30 S 119 30 E
Lake Mead Nat. Rec. Area 161 36 0N 114 30W
Lake Mills 158 43 23N 93 33W
Lake Murray 135 6 48 S 141 29 E
Lake Nash 138 20 57 S 138 0 E
Lake of the Woods 155 49 0N 95 0W
Lake Pleasant 162 43 28N 74 25W
Lake Providence 159 32 49N 91 12W
Lake River 150 54 22N 82 31W
Lake Superior Prov. Park 150 47 45N 84 45W
Lake Tekapo 143 43 55 S 170 30 E
Lake Traverse 150 45 56N 78 4W
Lake Varley 137 32 48 S 119 30 E
Lake Village 159 33 20N 91 19W
Lake Wales 157 27 55N 81 32W
Lake Worth 157 26 36N 80 3W
Lakefield 150 44 25N 78 16W
Lakehurst 162 40 1N 74 19W
Lakeland 157 28 0N 82 0W
Lakenheath 29 52 25N 0 30 E
Lakes Entrance 141 37 50 S 148 0 E
Lakeside, Ariz., U.S.A. 161 34 12N 109 59W
Lakeside, Calif., U.S.A. 163 32 52N 116 55W
Lakeside, Nebr., U.S.A. 158 42 5N 102 24W
Lakeview, N.Y., U.S.A. 156 42 43N 78 57W
Lakeview, Oreg., U.S.A. 160 42 15N 120 22W
Lakewood, Calif., U.S.A. 163 33 51N 118 8W
Lakewood, N.J., U.S.A. 162 40 5N 74 13W
Lakhaniá 69 35 58N 27 54 E
Lákhi 69 35 24N 23 27 E
Lakhimpur 95 27 14N 94 7 E
Lakhipur, Assam, India 98 24 48N 93 0 E
Lakhipur, Assam, India 98 26 2N 90 18 E
Lakhonpheng 100 15 54N 105 34 E
Lakhpat 94 23 48N 68 47 E
Laki 74 64 4N 18 14W
Lakin 159 37 58N 101 18W
Lakitusaki, R. 150 54 21N 82 25W
Lakki 93 32 38N 70 50 E
Lakonía □ 69 36 55N 22 30 E
Lakonikós Kólpos 69 36 40N 22 40 E
Lakor, I. 103 8 15 S 128 17 E
Lakota, Ivory C. 120 5 50N 5 30W
Lakota, U.S.A. 158 48 0N 98 22W
Laksefjorden 74 70 45N 26 50 E
Lakselv 74 70 2N 24 56 E
Lakselvbukt 74 69 26N 19 40 E
Lakshadweep Is. 86 10 0N 72 30 E
Laksham 98 23 14N 91 8 E
Lakshmi Kantapur 95 22 5N 88 20 E
Lakshmipur 98 22 38N 88 16 E
Lakuramau 135 2 54 S 151 15 E
Lala Ghat 99 24 30N 92 40 E
Lala Musa 94 32 40N 73 57 E
Lalago 126 3 28 S 33 58 E
Lalapanzi 127 19 20 S 30 15 E
Lalganj 95 25 52N 85 13 E
Lalibala 123 12 8N 39 10 E
Lalin 107 45 14N 126 52 E
Lalín 56 42 40N 8 5W
Lalin Ho, R. 107 45 28N 125 43 E
Lalinde 44 44 50N 0 44 E
Lalitapur 99 26 36N 85 32 E
Lalitpur 95 24 42N 78 28 E
Lam 100 21 21N 106 31 E
Lam Pao Res. 100 16 50N 103 15 E
Lama Kara 121 9 30N 1 15 E
Lamaing 99 15 25N 97 53 E
Lamaipum 98 25 40N 97 57 E
Lamar, Colo., U.S.A. 158 38 9N 102 35W
Lamar, Mo., U.S.A. 159 37 30N 94 20W
Lamas 174 6 28 S 76 31W
Lamastre 45 44 59N 4 35 E
Lamaya 108 29 50N 99 56 E
Lamb Hd. 37 59 5N 2 32W
Lambach 52 48 6N 13 51 E
Lamballe 42 48 29N 2 31W
Lambaréné 124 0 20 S 10 12 E
Lambay I. 38 53 30N 6 0W

Lambayeque □ **Lawrenceville**

Lambayeque □	**174**	6 45 S	80 0 W
Lamberhurst	**29**	51 5 N	0 21 E
Lambert	**158**	47 44 N	104 39 W
Lambert, C.	**135**	4 11 S	151 31 E
Lambert Land	**12**	79 12 N	20 30 W
Lambesc	**45**	43 39 N	5 16 E
Lambeth	**29**	51 27 N	0 7 W
Lambi Kyun, (Sullivan I.)	**101**	10 50 N	98 20 E
Lámbia	**69**	37 52 N	21 53 E
Lambley	**35**	54 56 N	2 30 W
Lambon	**135**	4 45 S	152 48 E
Lambourn	**28**	51 31 N	1 31 W
Lambro, R.	**62**	45 18 N	9 20 E
Lambs Hd.	**39**	51 44 N	10 10 W
Lame	**121**	10 27 N	9 12 E
Lame Deer	**160**	45 45 N	106 40 W
Lamego	**56**	41 5 N	7 52 W
Lameque	**151**	47 45 N	64 38 W
Lameroo	**140**	35 19 S	140 33 E
Lamesa	**159**	32 45 N	101 57 W
Lamhult	**73**	57 12 N	14 36 E
Lamía	**69**	38 55 N	22 41 E
*Lamitan	**103**	6 40 N	122 10 E
Lammermuir	**35**	55 50 N	2 25 W
Lammermuir Hills	**35**	55 50 N	2 40 W
Lamoille	**160**	40 47 N	115 31 W
Lamon Bay	**103**	14 30 N	122 20 E
Lamont, Can.	**152**	53 46 N	112 50 W
Lamont, U.S.A.	**163**	35 15 N	118 55 W
Lampa	**174**	15 10 S	70 30 W
Lampang	**100**	18 18 N	99 31 E
Lampasas	**159**	31 5 N	98 10 W
Lampaul	**42**	48 28 N	5 7 W
Lampazos de Naranjo	**164**	27 2 N	100 32 W
Lampedusa, I.	**60**	35 36 N	12 40 E
Lampeter	**31**	52 6 N	4 6 W
Lampione, I.	**119**	35 33 N	12 20 E
Lampman	**153**	49 25 N	102 50 W
Lamprechtshausen	**52**	48 0 N	12 58 E
Lampung	**102**	1 48 S	115 0 E
Lamu, Burma	**98**	19 14 N	94 10 E
Lamu, Kenya	**126**	2 10 S	40 55 E
Lamy	**161**	35 30 N	105 58 W
Lan Tsan Kiang (Mekong)	**87**	18 0 N	104 15 E
Lanai City	**147**	20 50 N	156 56 W
Lanai I.	**147**	20 50 N	156 55 W
Lanak La	**95**	34 27 N	79 32 E
Lanaken	**47**	50 53 N	5 39 E
Lanak'o Shank'ou = Lanak La	**95**	34 27 N	79 32 E
Lanao, L.	**103**	7 52 N	124 15 E
Lanark	**35**	55 40 N	3 48 W
Lanark (□)	**26**	55 37 N	3 50 W
Lancashire □	**32**	53 40 N	2 30 W
Lancaster, Can.	**151**	45 17 N	66 10 W
Lancaster, U.K.	**32**	54 3 N	2 48 W
Lancaster, Calif., U.S.A.	**163**	34 47 N	118 8 W
Lancaster, Ky., U.S.A.	**156**	37 40 N	84 40 W
Lancaster, Pa., U.S.A.	**162**	40 4 N	76 19 W
Lancaster, S.C., U.S.A.	**157**	34 45 N	80 47 W
Lancaster, Va., U.S.A.	**162**	37 46 N	76 28 W
Lancaster, Wis., U.S.A.	**158**	42 48 N	90 43 W
Lancaster Sd.	**12**	74 13 N	84 0 W
Lancer	**153**	50 48 N	108 53 W
Lanchester	**33**	54 50 N	1 44 W
Lanch'i	**109**	29 11 N	119 30 E
Lanchou	**106**	36 5 N	103 55 E
Lanciano	**63**	42 15 N	14 22 E
Lancing	**29**	50 49 N	0 19 W
Łancut	**54**	50 10 N	22 20 E
Lancy	**50**	46 12 N	6 8 E
Lândana	**124**	5 11 S	12 5 E
Landau	**49**	49 12 N	8 7 E
Landeck	**52**	47 9 N	10 34 E
Landen	**47**	50 45 N	5 3 E
Lander, Austral.	**136**	20 25 S	132 0 E
Lander, U.S.A.	**160**	42 50 N	108 49 W
Landerneau	**42**	48 28 N	4 17 W
Landeryd	**73**	57 7 N	13 15 E
Landes □	**44**	43 57 N	0 48 W
Landes, Les	**44**	44 20 N	1 0 W
Landete	**58**	39 56 N	1 25 W
Landi Kotal	**94**	34 7 N	71 6 E
Landivisiau	**42**	48 31 N	4 6 W
Landkey	**30**	51 2 N	4 0 W
Landor	**137**	25 10 S	117 0 E
Landquart	**51**	46 58 N	9 32 E
Landquart, R.	**51**	46 50 N	9 47 E
Landrecies	**43**	50 7 N	3 40 E
Land's End, Can.	**12**	76 10 N	123 0 W
Land's End, U.K.	**30**	50 4 N	5 43 W
Landsberg	**49**	48 3 N	10 52 E
Landsborough Cr.	**138**	22 28 S	144 35 E
Landsbro	**73**	57 24 N	14 56 E
Landschaft	**50**	47 28 N	7 40 E
Landshut	**48**	48 31 N	12 10 E
Landskrona	**73**	56 53 N	12 50 E
Landvetter	**73**	57 41 N	12 17 E
Lane	**73**	58 25 N	12 3 E
Laneffe	**47**	50 17 N	4 35 E
Lanesboro	**162**	41 57 N	75 34 W
Lanesborough	**38**	53 40 N	8 0 W
Lanett	**157**	33 0 N	85 15 W
Lang Bay	**152**	49 17 N	124 21 W
Lang Qua	**100**	22 16 N	104 27 E
Lang Shan	**106**	41 0 N	106 20 E
Lang Suan	**101**	9 57 N	99 4 E
Langaa	**73**	56 23 N	9 51 E
Lángadhás	**68**	40 46 N	23 2 E
Langádhia	**69**	37 43 N	22 1 E
Långan	**72**	63 19 N	14 44 E
Langara I.	**152**	54 14 N	133 1 W
Langavat L.	**36**	58 4 N	6 48 W
Langchen Khambah (Sutlej)	**95**	31 25 N	80 0 E
Langch'i	**109**	31 10 N	119 10 E
Langchung	**108**	31 31 N	105 58 E
Langdon	**158**	48 47 N	98 24 W
Langdorp	**47**	50 59 N	4 52 E
Langeac	**44**	45 7 N	3 29 E
Langeb, R.	**122**	17 28 N	36 50 E
Langeberge, C. Prov., S. Afr.	**128**	28 15 S	22 33 E
Langeberge, C. Prov., S. Afr.	**128**	33 55 S	21 20 E
Langeland	**73**	54 56 N	10 48 E
Langelands Bælt	**73**	54 55 N	10 56 E
Langemark	**47**	50 55 N	2 55 E
Langen	**49**	53 36 N	8 36 E
Langenburg	**153**	50 51 N	101 43 W
Langeness	**48**	54 34 N	8 35 E
Langenlois	**52**	48 29 N	15 40 E
Langensalza	**48**	51 6 N	10 40 E
Langenthal	**50**	47 13 N	7 47 E
Langeoog	**48**	53 44 N	7 33 E
Langeskov	**73**	55 22 N	10 35 E
Langesund	**71**	59 0 N	9 45 E
Langhem	**73**	57 36 N	13 14 E
Länghem	**73**	57 36 N	13 14 E
Langhirano	**62**	44 39 N	10 16 E
Langholm	**35**	55 9 N	2 59 W
Langidoon	**140**	31 36 S	142 2 E
Langjökull	**74**	64 39 N	20 12 W
Langkawi I.	**101**	6 20 N	99 45 E
Langkawi, P.	**101**	6 25 N	99 45 E
Langkon	**102**	6 30 N	116 40 E
Langk'ouhsü	**109**	26 8 N	115 10 E
Langlade, Can.	**150**	48 14 N	76 10 W
Langlade, St. P. & M.	**151**	46 50 N	56 20 W
Langlo	**139**	26 26 S	146 5 E
Langlois	**160**	42 54 N	124 26 W
Langnau	**50**	46 56 N	7 47 E
Langness	**32**	54 3 N	4 37 W
Langogne	**44**	44 43 N	3 50 E
Langon	**44**	44 33 N	0 16 W
Langøya	**74**	68 45 N	15 10 E
Langport	**28**	51 2 N	2 51 W
Langres	**43**	47 52 N	5 20 E
Langres, Plateau de	**43**	47 45 N	5 20 E
Langsa	**102**	4 30 N	97 57 E
Långsele	**72**	63 12 N	17 4 E
Långshyttan	**72**	60 27 N	16 2 E
Langson	**100**	21 52 N	106 42 E
Langstrothdale Chase	**32**	54 14 N	2 13 W
Langtai	**108**	26 6 N	105 20 E
Langtao	**98**	27 15 N	97 34 E
Langting	**98**	25 31 N	93 7 E
Langtoft	**29**	52 42 N	0 19 W
Langtree	**30**	50 55 N	4 11 W
Langtry	**159**	29 50 N	101 33 W
Langu	**101**	6 53 N	99 47 E
Languedoc □	**44**	43 58 N	3 22 E
Langwies	**51**	46 50 N	9 44 E
Lanhsien	**106**	38 17 N	111 38 E
Lanigan	**153**	51 51 N	105 2 W
Lank'ao	**106**	34 50 N	114 49 E
Lanna	**72**	59 16 N	14 56 E
Lannemezan	**44**	43 8 N	0 23 E
Lannercost	**138**	18 35 S	146 0 E
Lannilis	**42**	48 35 N	4 32 W
Lannion	**42**	48 46 N	3 29 W
Lanouaille	**44**	45 24 N	1 9 E
Lanp'ing	**108**	26 25 N	99 24 E
Lansdale	**162**	40 14 N	75 18 W
Lansdowne	**141**	31 48 S	152 30 E
Lansdowne House	**150**	52 14 N	87 53 W
Lansford	**162**	40 48 N	75 55 W
Lanshan	**109**	25 18 N	112 6 E
Lansing	**156**	42 47 N	84 32 W
Lanslebourg-Mont-Cenis	**45**	45 17 N	6 52 E
Lanta Yai, Ko	**101**	7 35 N	99 3 E
Lant'ien	**106**	34 3 N	109 20 E
Lants'ang	**108**	22 40 N	99 58 E
Lants'ang Chiang, R.	**108**	30 0 N	98 0 E
Lantsien	**99**	32 4 N	96 6 E
Lants'un	**107**	36 24 N	120 10 E
Lantuna	**103**	8 19 S	124 8 E
Lanus	**172**	34 44 S	58 27 W
Lanusei	**64**	39 53 N	9 31 E
Lanzarote, I.	**116**	29 0 N	13 40 W
Lanzo Torinese	**62**	45 16 N	7 29 E
Lao Bao	**100**	16 35 N	106 30 E
Lao Cai	**100**	22 30 N	103 57 E
Lao, R.	**65**	39 45 N	15 45 E
Laoag	**103**	18 7 N	120 34 E
Laoang	**103**	12 32 N	125 8 E
Laoha Ho, R.	**107**	43 24 N	120 39 E
Laois □	**39**	53 0 N	7 20 W
Laon	**43**	49 33 N	3 35 E
Laona	**156**	45 32 N	88 41 W
Laos ■	**100**	17 45 N	105 0 E
Lapa	**173**	25 46 S	49 44 W
Lapalisse	**44**	46 15 N	3 44 E
Laparan Cap, I.	**103**	6 0 N	120 0 E
Lapeer	**156**	43 3 N	83 20 W
Lapford	**30**	50 52 N	3 49 W
Lapi □	**74**	67 0 N	27 0 E
Lapland = Lappland	**74**	68 7 N	24 0 E
Laporte	**162**	41 27 N	76 30 W
Lapovo	**66**	44 10 N	21 2 E
Lappland	**74**	68 7 N	24 0 E
Laprida	**172**	37 34 S	60 45 W
Laptev Sea	**77**	76 0 N	125 0 E
Lapush	**160**	47 56 N	124 33 W
Lăpusu, R.	**70**	47 25 N	23 40 E
Lar	**93**	27 40 N	54 14 E
Lara	**140**	38 2 S	144 26 E
Lara □	**174**	10 10 N	69 50 W
Larabanga	**120**	9 16 N	1 56 W
Laracha	**56**	43 15 N	8 35 W
Larache	**118**	35 10 N	6 5 W
Laragh	**39**	53 0 N	6 20 W
Laragne-Montéglin	**45**	44 18 N	5 49 E
Laramie	**158**	41 15 N	105 29 W
Laramie Mts.	**158**	42 0 N	105 30 W
Laranjeiras	**170**	10 48 S	37 10 W
Laranjeiras do Sul	**173**	25 23 S	52 23 W
Larantuka	**103**	8 5 S	122 55 E
Larap	**103**	14 18 N	122 39 E
Larat, I.	**103**	7 0 S	132 0 E
Larbert	**35**	56 2 N	3 50 W
Lärbro	**73**	57 47 N	18 50 E
Larch, R.	**149**	57 30 N	71 0 W
Lårdal	**71**	59 20 N	8 25 E
Lårdal	**71**	59 25 N	8 10 E
Larde	**127**	16 28 S	39 43 E
Larder Lake	**150**	48 5 N	79 40 W
Lárdhos, Ákra	**69**	36 4 N	28 10 E
Laredo, Spain	**58**	43 26 N	3 28 W
Laredo, U.S.A.	**159**	27 34 N	99 29 W
Laredo Sd.	**152**	52 30 N	128 53 W
Laren	**46**	52 16 N	5 14 E
Largeau (Faya)	**117**	17 58 N	19 6 E
Largentière	**45**	44 34 N	4 18 E
Largs	**34**	55 48 N	4 51 W
Lari	**62**	43 34 N	10 35 E
Lariang	**103**	1 35 S	119 25 E
Larimore	**158**	47 55 N	97 35 W
Larino	**65**	41 48 N	14 54 E
Lárisa	**68**	39 38 N	22 28 E
Lárisa □	**68**	39 39 N	22 24 E
Larkana	**94**	27 32 N	68 2 E
Larkollen	**71**	59 20 N	10 41 E
Larnaca	**92**	35 0 N	33 35 E
Lárnax	**92**	35 0 N	33 35 E
Larne	**38**	54 52 N	5 50 W
Larne L.	**38**	54 52 N	5 50 W
Larned	**158**	38 15 N	99 10 W
Laroch	**36**	56 40 N	5 9 W
Larochette	**47**	49 47 N	6 13 E
Laroquebrou	**44**	44 58 N	2 12 E
Larrey, Pt.	**136**	19 55 S	119 7 E
Larrimah	**136**	15 35 S	133 12 E
Larsen Ice Shelf	**13**	67 0 S	62 0 W
Larteh	**121**	5 50 N	0 5 W
Laru	**126**	2 54 N	24 25 E
Larvik	**71**	59 4 N	10 0 E
Laryak	**76**	61 15 N	80 0 E
Larzac, Causse du	**44**	44 0 N	3 17 E
Las Animas	**159**	38 8 N	103 18 W
Las Anod	**91**	8 26 N	47 19 E
Las Blancos	**59**	37 38 N	0 49 W
Las Bonitas	**174**	7 50 N	65 40 W
Las Brenās	**172**	27 5 S	61 7 W
Las Cabezas de San Juan	**57**	37 0 N	5 58 W
Las Cruces	**161**	32 25 N	106 50 W
Las Flores	**172**	36 0 S	59 0 W
Las Heras, Mendoza, Argent.	**173**	32 51 S	68 49 W
Las Heras, Santa Cruz, Argent.	**176**	46 30 S	69 0 W
Las Huertas, Cabo de	**59**	38 22 N	0 24 W
Las Khoreh	**91**	11 4 N	48 20 E
Las Lajas	**176**	38 30 S	70 25 W
Las Lajitas	**174**	6 55 N	65 39 W
Las Lomitas	**172**	24 35 S	60 50 W
Las Marismas	**57**	37 5 N	6 20 W
Las Mercedes	**174**	9 7 N	66 24 W
Las Navas de la Concepción	**57**	37 56 N	5 30 W
Las Navas de Tolosa	**57**	38 18 N	3 38 W
Las Palmas, Argent.	**172**	27 8 S	58 45 W
Las Palmas, Canary Is.	**116**	28 10 N	15 28 W
Las Palmas □	**116**	28 10 N	15 28 W
Las Piedras	**173**	34 35 S	56 20 W
Las Plumas	**176**	43 40 S	67 15 W
Las Rosas	**172**	32 30 S	61 40 W
Las Tablas	**166**	7 49 N	80 14 W
Las Termas	**172**	27 29 S	64 52 W
Las Tres Marías, Is.	**164**	20 12 N	106 30 W
Las Varillas	**172**	32 0 S	62 50 W
Las Vegas, Nev., U.S.A.	**161**	36 10 N	115 5 W
Las Vegas, N.M., U.S.A.	**161**	35 35 N	105 10 W
Lascano	**173**	33 35 S	54 18 W
Lascaux	**44**	45 5 N	1 10 E
Lashburn	**153**	53 10 N	109 40 W
Lashio	**98**	22 56 N	97 45 E
Lashkar	**94**	26 10 N	78 10 E
Łasin	**54**	53 30 N	19 2 E
Lasithi □	**69**	35 5 N	25 50 E
Lask	**54**	51 34 N	19 8 E
Laskill	**33**	54 19 N	1 6 W
Laško	**63**	46 10 N	15 16 E
Lassance	**171**	17 54 S	44 34 W
Lassay	**42**	48 27 N	0 30 W
Lassen, Pk.	**160**	40 20 N	121 0 W
Lasswade	**35**	55 53 N	3 8 W
Last Mountain L.	**153**	51 5 N	105 14 W
Lastoursville	**124**	0 55 S	12 38 E
Lastovo	**63**	42 46 N	16 55 E
Lastovo, I.	**63**	42 46 N	16 55 E
Lastovski Kanal	**63**	42 50 N	17 0 E
Lat Yao	**100**	15 45 N	99 48 E
Latacunga	**174**	0 50 S	78 35 W
Latakia = Al Ladhiqiya	**92**	35 30 N	35 45 E
Latchford	**150**	47 20 N	79 50 W
Laterza	**65**	40 38 N	16 47 E
Latham	**137**	29 44 S	116 20 E
Lathen	**48**	52 51 N	7 21 E
Latheron	**37**	58 17 N	3 20 W
Lathrop Wells	**163**	36 39 N	116 24 W
Latiano	**65**	40 33 N	17 43 E
Latina	**64**	41 26 N	12 53 E
Latisana	**63**	45 47 N	13 1 E
Latium = Lazio	**63**	42 0 N	12 30 E
Laton	**163**	36 26 N	119 41 W
Latorica, R.	**53**	48 31 N	22 0 E
Latouche	**147**	60 0 N	148 0 W
Latouche Treville, C.	**136**	18 27 S	121 49 E
Latrobe	**138**	38 8 S	146 44 E
Latrobe, Mt.	**139**	39 0 S	146 23 E
Latrónico	**65**	40 5 N	16 0 E
Latrun	**90**	31 50 N	34 58 E
Latur	**96**	18 25 N	76 40 E
Latvia, S.S.R. □	**80**	56 50 N	24 0 E
Latzu	**105**	29 10 N	87 45 E
Lauchhammer	**48**	51 35 N	13 40 E
Laudal	**71**	58 15 N	7 30 E
Lauder	**35**	55 43 N	2 45 W
Lauderdale	**35**	55 43 N	2 44 W
Lauenburg	**48**	53 23 N	10 33 E
Läufelfingen	**50**	47 24 N	7 52 E
Laufen	**50**	47 25 N	7 30 E
Laugarbakki	**74**	65 20 N	20 55 W
Laugharne	**31**	51 45 N	4 28 W
Laujar	**59**	37 0 N	2 54 W
Launceston, Austral.	**138**	41 24 S	147 8 E
Launceston, U.K.	**30**	50 38 N	4 21 W
Laune, R.	**39**	52 5 N	9 40 W
Launglon Bok	**101**	13 50 N	97 54 E
Laupheim	**49**	48 13 N	9 53 E
Laura, Queens., Austral.	**133**	15 32 S	144 32 E
Laura, S.A., Austral.	**140**	33 10 S	138 18 E
Lauragh	**39**	51 46 N	9 46 W
Laureana di Borrello	**65**	38 28 N	16 5 E
Laurel, Del., U.S.A.	**162**	38 33 N	75 34 W
Laurel, Md., U.S.A.	**162**	39 6 N	76 51 W
Laurel, Miss., U.S.A.	**159**	31 50 N	89 0 W
Laurel, Mont., U.S.A.	**160**	45 46 N	108 49 W
Laurencekirk	**37**	56 50 N	2 30 W
Laurencetown	**39**	53 14 N	8 11 W
Laurens	**157**	34 32 N	82 2 W
Laurentian Plat.	**151**	52 0 N	70 0 W
Laurentides, Parc Prov. des	**151**	47 45 N	71 15 W
Lauria	**65**	40 3 N	15 50 E
Laurie I.	**13**	60 0 S	46 0 W
Laurie L.	**153**	56 35 N	101 57 W
Laurieston	**35**	54 57 N	4 2 W
Laurinburg	**157**	34 50 N	79 25 W
Laurium	**156**	47 14 N	88 26 W
Lausanne	**50**	46 32 N	6 38 E
Laut Kecil, Kepulauan	**102**	4 45 S	115 40 E
Laut, Kepulauan	**102**	4 45 N	108 0 E
Lauterbach	**48**	50 39 N	9 23 E
Lauterbrunnen	**50**	46 36 N	7 55 E
Lauterecken	**49**	49 38 N	7 35 E
Lauwe	**47**	50 47 N	3 12 E
Lauwers	**46**	53 32 N	6 23 E
Lauwers Zee	**46**	53 21 N	6 13 E
Lauzon	**151**	46 48 N	71 10 W
Lava Hot Springs	**160**	42 38 N	112 1 W
Lavadores	**56**	42 14 N	8 41 W
Lavagna	**62**	44 18 N	9 22 E
Laval	**42**	48 4 N	0 48 W
Lavalle	**172**	28 15 S	65 15 W
Lavandou, Le	**45**	43 8 N	6 22 E
Lâvara	**68**	41 19 N	26 22 E
Lavardac	**44**	44 12 N	0 20 E
Lavaur	**44**	43 42 N	1 49 E
Lavaux	**50**	46 30 N	6 45 E
Lavaveix	**44**	46 5 N	2 8 E
Lavelanet	**44**	42 57 N	1 51 E
Lavello	**65**	41 4 N	15 47 E
Lavendon	**29**	52 11 N	0 39 W
Lavenham	**29**	52 7 N	0 48 E
Laverendrye Prov. Park	**150**	46 15 N	17 15 W
Laverne	**159**	36 43 N	99 58 W
Lavers Hill	**140**	38 40 S	143 25 E
Laverton	**137**	28 44 S	122 29 E
Lavi	**90**	32 47 N	35 25 E
Lavik	**71**	61 6 N	5 25 E
Lávkos	**69**	39 9 N	23 14 E
Lavos	**56**	40 6 N	8 49 W
Lavras	**173**	21 20 S	45 0 W
Lavre	**57**	38 46 N	8 22 W
Lavrentiya	**77**	65 35 N	171 0 W
Lávrion	**69**	37 40 N	24 4 E
Lavumisa	**129**	27 20 S	31 55 E
Lawas	**102**	4 55 N	115 40 E
Lawele	**103**	5 16 S	123 3 E
Lawers	**35**	56 31 N	4 9 W
Lawksawk	**98**	21 15 N	96 52 E
Lawn Hill	**138**	18 36 S	138 33 E
Lawng Pit	**99**	26 45 N	98 35 E
Lawra	**120**	10 39 N	2 51 W
Lawrence, Austral.	**173**	29 30 S	153 8 E
Lawrence, Kans., U.S.A.	**158**	39 0 N	95 10 W
Lawrence, Mass., U.S.A.	**162**	42 40 N	71 9 W
Lawrenceburg, Ind., U.S.A.	**156**	39 5 N	84 50 W
Lawrenceburg, Tenn., U.S.A.	**157**	35 12 N	87 19 W
Lawrenceville, Ga., U.S.A.	**157**	33 55 N	83 59 W

*Renamed Isabela

Lawrenceville **Lexington**

Lawrenceville, Pa., U.S.A. 162 42 0N 77 8W
Laws 163 37 24N 118 20W
Lawton 159 34 33N 98 25W
Lawu Mt. 103 7 40S 111 13E
Laxa 72 59 0N 14 37E
Laxey 32 54 15N 4 23W
Laxfield 29 52 18N 1 23E
Laxford, L. 36 58 25N 5 10W
Laxmeshwar 97 15 9N 75 28E
Laysan I. 143 25 30N 167 0W
Laytonville 160 39 44N 123 29W
Laytown 38 53 40N 6 15W
Laza 98 26 30N 97 38E
Lazarevac 66 44 23N 20 17E
Lazio □ 63 42 10N 12 30E
Lazonby 32 54 45N 2 42W
Łazy 54 50 27N 19 24E
Łbzenica 54 53 18N 17 15E
Lea 33 53 22N 0 45W
Lea, R. 29 51 40N 0 3W
Leach 101 12 21N 103 46E
Lead 158 44 20N 103 40W
Leadenham 33 53 5N 0 33W
Leader 153 50 50N 109 30W
Leadhills 35 55 25N 3 47W
Leadville 161 39 17N 106 23W
Leaf, R., Can. 149 58 47N 70 4W
Leaf, R., U.S.A. 159 31 45N 89 20W
Leakey 159 29 45N 99 45W
Leaksville 157 36 30N 79 49W
Lealui 125 15 10S 23 2E
Leamington, Can. 150 42 3N 82 36W
Leamington, N.Z. 130 37 55S 175 29E
Leamington, U.K. 28 52 18N 1 32W
Leamington, U.S.A. 160 39 37N 112 17W
Leandro Norte Alem 173 27 34S 55 15W
Leane L. 39 52 2N 9 32W
Leaoto, Mt. 70 45 20N 25 20E
Leap 39 51 34N 9 11W
Learmonth 136 22 40S 114 10E
Leask 153 53 5N 106 45W
Leatherhead 29 51 18N 0 20W
Leavenworth, Mo., U.S.A. 158 39 25N 95 0W
Leavenworth, Wash., U.S.A. 160 47 44N 120 37W
Łeba 54 54 45N 17 32E
Lebak 103 6 32N 124 5E
Lebane 66 42 56N 21 44E
Lebanon, Ind., U.S.A. 156 40 3N 86 55W
Lebanon, Kans., U.S.A. 158 39 50N 98 35W
Lebanon, Ky., U.S.A. 156 37 35N 85 15W
Lebanon, Mo., U.S.A. 159 37 40N 92 40W
Lebanon, Oreg., U.S.A. 160 44 31N 122 57W
Lebanon, Pa., U.S.A. 162 40 20N 76 28W
Lebanon, Tenn., U.S.A. 157 36 15N 86 20W
Lebanon ■ 92 34 0N 36 0E
Lebbeke 47 51 0N 4 8E
Lebec 163 34 36N 118 59W
Lebedin 80 50 35N 34 30E
Lebedyan 81 53 0N 39 10E
Lebomboberge 129 24 30S 32 0E
Łebork 54 54 33N 17 46E
Lebrija 57 36 53N 6 5W
Lebu 172 37 40S 73 47W
Lecce 65 40 20N 18 10E
Lecco 62 45 50N 9 27E
Lecco, L. di. 62 45 51N 9 22E
Lécera 58 41 13N 0 43W
Lech 52 47 13N 10 9E
Lech, R. 49 48 45N 10 45E
Lechlade 28 51 42N 1 40W
Lechtaler Alpen 52 47 15N 10 30E
Lectoure 44 43 56N 0 38E
Łeczyca 54 52 5N 19 45E
Ledbury 28 52 3N 2 25W
Lede 47 50 58N 3 59E
Ledeberg 47 51 2N 3 45E
Ledec 52 49 41N 15 18E
Ledesma 56 41 6N 5 59W
Leduc 152 53 20N 113 30W
Ledyczek 54 53 33N 16 59E
Lee, U.K. 28 50 47N 1 11W
Lee, U.S.A. 160 40 35N 115 36W
Lee Vining 163 37 58N 119 7W
Leech L. 158 47 9N 94 23W
Leedey 159 35 53N 99 24W
Leeds, U.K. 33 53 48N 1 34W
Leeds, U.S.A. 157 33 32N 86 30W
Leek, Neth. 46 53 10N 6 24E
Leek, U.K. 32 53 7N 2 2W
Leende 47 51 21N 5 33E
Leer 48 53 13N 7 29E
Leerdam 46 51 54N 5 6E
Leersum 46 52 0N 5 26E
Leesburg 157 28 47N 81 52W
Leeston 143 43 45S 172 19E
Leesville 159 31 12N 93 15W
Leeton 141 34 23S 146 23E
Leeuwarden 46 53 15N 5 48E
Leeuwin, C. 137 34 20S 115 9E
Leeward Is. 167 16 30N 63 30W
Lefors 159 35 30N 100 50W
Lefroy, L. 137 31 21S 121 40E
Legal 152 53 55N 113 45W
Legendre I. 136 20 22S 116 55E
Leghorn = Livorno 62 43 32N 10 18E
Legion 127 21 25S 28 30E
Legionowo 54 52 25N 20 50E
Léglise 47 49 48N 5 32E
Legnago 63 45 10N 11 19E
Legnano 62 45 35N 8 55E
Legnica 54 51 12N 16 10E
Legnica □ 54 51 30N 16 0E
Legoniel 38 54 38N 6 0W
Legrad 63 46 17N 16 51E
Legume 139 28 20S 152 12E
Leh 95 34 15N 77 35E
Lehi 160 40 20N 112 0W
Lehighton 162 40 50N 75 44W
Lehinch 39 52 56N 9 21E
Lehliu 70 44 29N 26 20E
Lehrte 48 52 22N 9 58E
Lehua, I. 147 22 1N 160 6W
Lehututu 128 23 54S 21 55E
Lei Shui, R. 109 26 56N 112 39E
Leiah 94 30 58N 70 58E
Leibnitz 52 46 47N 15 34E
Leicester 28 52 39N 1 9W
Leicester □ 28 52 40N 1 10W
Leichhardt, R. 133 17 50S 139 49E
Leichhardt Ra. 138 20 46S 147 40E
Leichou Chiang, R. 109 20 52N 110 10E
Leichou Pantao 108 20 40N 110 10E
Leiden 46 52 9N 4 30E
Leiderdorp 46 52 9N 4 32E
Leidschendam 46 52 5N 4 24E
Leie, R. 47 51 2N 3 45E
Leigh, Gr. Manch., U.K. 32 53 29N 2 31W
Leigh, Here. & Worcs., U.K. 28 52 10N 2 21W
Leigh Creek 140 30 28S 138 24E
Leighlinbridge 39 52 45N 7 2W
Leighton Buzzard 29 51 55N 0 39W
Leignon 47 50 16N 5 7E
Leiktho 98 19 13N 96 35E
Leinster, Mt. 39 52 38N 6 47W
Leinster, prov. 39 53 0N 7 10W
Leintwardine 28 52 22N 2 51W
Leipo 108 28 15N 103 34E
Leipzig 48 51 20N 12 23E
Leipzig □ 48 51 20N 12 30E
Leiria 57 39 46N 8 53W
Leiria □ 57 39 46N 8 53W
Leisler, Mt. 136 23 23S 129 30E
Leiston 29 52 13N 1 35E
Leith 35 55 59N 3 10W
Leith Hill 29 51 10N 0 23W
Leitha, R. 53 47 57N 17 5E
Leitholm 35 55 42N 2 16W
Leitrim 38 54 0N 8 5W
Leitrim □ 38 54 8N 8 0W
Leiyang 109 26 24N 112 51E
Leiza 58 43 5N 1 55W
Lek, R. 46 51 54N 4 38E
Lekáni 68 41 10N 24 35E
Leke 47 51 6N 2 54E
Lekhainá 69 37 57N 21 16E
Lekkerkerk 46 51 54N 4 41E
Leknice 61 51 34N 14 45E
Leksula 103 3 46S 126 31E
Leland 159 33 25N 90 52W
Leland Lakes 153 60 0N 110 59W
Lelant 30 50 11N 5 26W
Leleque 176 42 15S 71 0W
Lelu 98 19 4N 95 30E
Lelystad 46 52 30N 5 25E
Lema 121 12 58N 4 13E
Lemagrut, mt. 123 3 9S 35 22E
Leman Bank, gasfield 19 53 5N 2 20E
Léman, Lac 50 46 26N 6 30E
Lemelerveld 46 52 26N 6 20E
Lemera 126 3 0S 28 55E
Lemery 103 13 58N 120 56E
Lemesós 92 34 42N 33 1E
Lemgo 48 52 2N 8 52E
Lemhi Ra. 160 44 30N 113 30W
Lemmer 46 52 51N 5 43E
Lemmon 158 45 59N 102 10W
Lemon Grove 163 32 45N 117 2W
Lemoore 163 36 23N 119 46W
Lempdes 44 45 22N 3 17E
Lemvig 73 56 33N 8 20E
Lemyethna 98 21 10N 95 52E
Lena, R. 77 64 30N 127 0E
Lenadoon Pt. 38 54 19N 9 3W
Lencloître 42 46 50N 0 20E
Lençóis 171 12 35S 41 43W
Lendalfoot 34 55 12N 4 55W
Lendelede 47 50 53N 3 16E
Lendinara 63 45 4N 11 37E
Lene L. 38 53 40N 7 12W
Lengau de Vaca, Punta 172 30 14S 71 38W
Lenger 85 42 12N 69 54E
Lengerich 48 52 12N 7 50E
Lenggong 101 5 6N 100 58E
Lengyeltóti 53 46 40N 17 40E
Lenham 29 51 14N 0 44E
Lenhovda 73 57 0N 15 16E
Lenia 123 4 10N 37 25E
Lenin 83 48 20N 40 56E
Lenina, Pik 85 39 20N 72 55E
Leninabad 85 40 17N 69 37E
Leninakan 83 41 0N 42 50E
Leningrad 80 59 55N 30 20E
Leninogorsk, Kazakh S.S.R., U.S.S.R. 76 50 20N 83 30E
Leninogorsk, R.S.F.S.R., U.S.S.R. 84 54 36N 52 30E
Leninpol 85 42 29N 71 55E
Leninsk, R.S.F.S.R., U.S.S.R. 83 48 40N 45 15E
Leninsk, Uzbek S.S.R., U.S.S.R. 85 40 38N 72 15E
Leninsk-Kuznetskiy 76 55 10N 86 10E
Leninskaya 81 56 7N 44 29E
Leninskoye, R.S.F.S.R., U.S.S.R. 77 47 56N 132 38E
Leninskoye, R.S.F.S.R., U.S.S.R. 81 58 23N 47 3E
Leninskoye, Uzbek S.S.R., U.S.S.R. 85 41 45N 69 23E
Lenk 50 46 27N 7 28E
Lenkoran 79 39 45N 48 50E
Lenmalu 103 1 58S 130 0E
Lennard, R. 136 17 22S 124 20E
Lennox Hills 34 56 3N 4 12W
Lennoxtown 34 55 58N 4 14W
Leno 62 45 24N 10 14E
Lenoir 157 35 55N 81 36W
Lenoir City 157 35 40N 84 20W
Lenora 158 39 39N 100 1W
Lenore L. 153 52 30N 104 59W
Lenox 162 42 20N 73 18W
Lens, Belg. 47 50 33N 3 54E
Lens, France 43 50 26N 2 50E
Lens St. Remy 47 50 39N 5 7E
Lensk (Mukhtuya) 77 60 48N 114 55E
Lenskoye 82 45 3N 34 1E
Lent 46 51 52N 5 52E
Lentini 65 37 18N 15 0E
Lenwood 163 34 53N 117 7W
Lenzburg 50 47 23N 8 11E
Lenzen 48 53 6N 11 26E
Lenzerheide 51 46 44N 9 34E
Léo 120 11 3N 2 2W
Leoben 52 47 22N 15 5E
Leola 158 45 47N 98 58W
Leominster, U.K. 28 52 15N 2 43W
Leominster, U.S.A. 162 42 32N 71 45W
Léon 44 43 53N 1 18W
León, Mexico 164 21 7N 101 30W
León, Nic. 166 12 20N 86 51W
León, Spain 56 42 38N 5 34W
Leon 158 40 40N 93 40W
León □ 56 42 40N 5 55W
León, Montañas de 56 42 30N 6 18W
Leonardtown 162 38 19N 76 39W
Leonel, Mte. 50 46 15N 8 5E
Leonforte 65 37 39N 14 22E
Leongatha 141 38 30S 145 58E
Leonídhion 69 37 9N 22 52E
Leonora 137 28 49S 121 19E
Leonora Downs 140 32 29S 142 5E
Léopold II, Lac = Mai-Ndombe 124 2 0S 18 0E
Leopoldina 173 21 28S 42 40W
Leopoldo Bulhões 171 16 37S 48 46W
Leopoldsburg 47 51 7N 5 13E
Léopoldville = Kinshasa 124 4 20S 15 15E
Leoti 158 38 31N 101 19W
Leoville 153 53 39N 107 33W
Lépa, L. do 128 17 0S 19 0E
Lepe 57 37 15N 7 12W
Lepel 80 54 50N 28 40E
Lephin 36 57 26N 6 43W
Lepikha 77 64 45N 125 55E
Lépo, L. do 128 17 0S 19 0E
Lepontine Alps 62 46 22N 8 27E
Lepsény 53 47 0N 18 15E
Leptis Magna 119 32 40N 14 12E
Lequeitio 58 43 20N 2 32W
Lerbäck 72 58 56N 15 2E
Lercara Friddi 64 37 42N 13 36E
Lerdo 164 25 32N 103 32W
Léré 124 9 39N 14 13E
Lere 121 9 43N 9 18E
Leribe 129 28 51S 28 3E
Lérici 62 44 4N 9 48E
Lérida 58 41 37N 0 39E
Lérida □ 58 42 6N 1 0E
Lérins, Is. de 45 43 31N 7 3E
Lerma 56 42 0N 3 47W
Léros, I. 69 37 10N 26 50E
Lérouville 43 48 50N 5 30E
Lerrig 39 52 22N 9 47W
Lerwick 36 60 10N 1 10W
Les 70 46 58N 21 50E
Lesbos, I. = Lésvos 69 39 0N 26 20E
Lesbury 35 55 25N 1 37W
Lésina, L. di 63 41 53N 15 25E
Lesja 71 62 7N 8 51E
Lesjaverk 71 62 12N 8 34E
Lesko 54 49 30N 22 23E
Leskov, I. 13 56 0S 28 0W
Leskovac 68 43 0N 21 58E
Leskovec 68 40 10N 20 34E
Leslie, U.K. 35 56 12N 3 12W
Leslie, U.S.A. 159 35 50N 92 35W
Lesmahagow 35 55 38N 3 55W
Lesna 54 51 0N 15 15E
Lesneven 42 48 35N 4 20W
Lesniča 66 44 39N 19 20E
Lesnoy 84 59 47N 52 9E
Lesnoye 80 58 15N 35 31E
Lesotho ■ 129 29 40S 28 0E
Lesozavodsk 77 45 30N 133 20E
Lesparre-Médoc 44 45 18N 0 57W
Lessay 42 49 14N 1 30W
Lesse, R. 47 50 15N 4 54E
Lesser Antilles 167 12 30N 61 0W
Lesser Slave L. 152 55 30N 115 25W
Lessines 47 50 42N 3 50E
Lestock 153 51 19N 103 59W
Lesuer I. 136 13 50S 127 17E
Lesuma 128 17 58S 25 12E
Lésvos, I. 69 39 0N 26 20E
Leswalt 34 54 56N 5 6W
Leszno 54 51 50N 16 30E
Leszno □ 54 51 45N 16 30E
Letchworth 29 51 58N 0 13W
Letea, Ostrov 70 45 18N 29 20E
Lethbridge 152 49 45N 112 45W
Lethero 140 33 33S 142 30E
Lethlhakeng 128 24 0S 24 59E
Leti 103 8 10S 127 40E
Leti, Kepulauan 103 8 10S 128 0E
Letiahau, R. 128 21 40S 23 30E
Leticia 174 4 0S 70 0W
Letpadan 98 17 45N 96 0E
Letpan 98 19 28N 93 52E
Letsôk-aw-Kyun (Domel I.) 101 11 30N 98 25E
Letterbreen 38 54 18N 7 43W
Letterfrack 38 53 33N 9 58W
Letterkenny 38 54 57N 7 42W
Lettermacaward 38 54 51N 8 18W
Lettermore I. 39 53 18N 9 40W
Lettermullan 39 53 15N 9 44W
Letterston 31 51 56N 5 0W
Lettoch 37 57 22N 3 30W
Leu 70 44 10N 24 0E
Leucadia 163 33 4N 117 18W
Leucate 44 42 56N 3 3E
Leucate, Étang de 44 42 50N 3 0E
Leuchars 35 56 23N 2 53W
Leuk 50 46 19N 7 37E
Leukerbad 50 46 24N 7 36E
Leupegem 47 50 50N 3 36E
Leuser, G. 102 4 0N 96 51E
Leutkirch 49 47 49N 10 1E
Leuven (Louvain) 47 50 52N 4 42E
Leuze, Hainaut, Belg. 47 50 36N 3 37E
Leuze, Namur, Belg. 47 50 33N 4 54E
Lev Tolstoy 81 53 13N 39 29E
Levádhia 69 38 27N 22 54E
Levan 160 39 37N 111 32W
Levanger 74 63 45N 11 19E
Levani 68 40 40N 19 28E
Lévanto 62 44 10N 9 37E
Levanzo, I. 64 38 0N 12 19E
Levelland 159 33 38N 102 17W
Leven, Fife, U.K. 35 56 12N 3 0W
Leven, Humb., U.K. 33 53 54N 0 18W
Leven, Banc du 129 12 30S 47 45E
Leven, L. 35 56 12N 3 22W
Leven R. 33 54 27N 1 15W
Levens 45 43 50N 7 12E
Leveque C. 136 16 20S 123 0E
Leverano 65 40 16N 18 0E
Leverburgh 36 57 46N 7 0W
Leverkusen 48 51 2N 6 59E
Levet 43 46 56N 2 22E
Levice 53 48 13N 18 35E
Levick, Mt. 13 75 0S 164 0E
Levico 63 46 0N 11 18E
Levie 45 41 40N 9 7E
Levier 43 46 58N 6 8E
Levin 142 40 37S 175 18E
Levis 151 46 48N 71 9W
Levis, L. 152 62 37N 117 58W
Levítha, I. 69 37 0N 26 28E
Levittown, N.Y., U.S.A. 162 40 41N 73 31W
Levittown, Pa., U.S.A. 162 40 10N 74 51W
Levka 67 41 52N 26 15E
Lévka, Mt. 69 35 18N 24 3E
Levkás 69 38 48N 20 43E
Levkás, I. 69 38 40N 20 43E
Levkimmi 68 39 25N 20 3E
Levkôsia = Nicosia 92 35 10N 33 25E
Levoča 53 48 59N 20 35E
Levroux 43 47 0N 1 38E
Levski 67 43 21N 25 10E
Levskigrad 67 42 38N 24 47E
Lewe 98 19 38N 96 7E
Lewellen 158 41 22N 102 5W
Lewes, U.K. 29 50 53N 0 2E
Lewes, U.S.A. 156 38 45N 75 8W
Lewes, L. 148 60 30N 134 20W
Lewin Brzeski 54 50 45N 17 37E
Lewis, Butt of 36 58 30N 6 12W
Lewis, I. 36 58 10N 6 40W
Lewis, R. 160 48 0N 113 15W
Lewis Ra. 136 20 3S 128 50E
Lewisburg, Pa., U.S.A. 162 40 57N 76 57W
Lewisburg, Tenn., U.S.A. 157 35 29N 86 46W
Lewisham 29 51 27N 0 1W
Lewisporte 151 49 15N 55 3W
Lewiston, U.K. 37 57 19N 4 30W
Lewiston, Idaho, U.S.A. 160 45 58N 117 0W
Lewiston, Utah, U.S.A. 160 42 0N 111 56W
Lewistown, Mont., U.S.A. 160 47 0N 109 25W
Lewistown, Pa., U.S.A. 156 40 37N 77 33W
Lexington, Ill., U.S.A. 158 40 37N 88 47W
Lexington, Ky., U.S.A. 156 38 6N 84 30W
Lexington, Md., U.S.A. 162 38 16N 76 27W
Lexington, Miss., U.S.A. 159 33 8N 90 2W
Lexington, Mo., U.S.A. 158 39 7N 93 55W
Lexington, N.C., U.S.A. 157 35 50N 80 13W
Lexington, Nebr., U.S.A. 158 40 48N 99 45W
Lexington, N.Y., U.S.A. 162 42 15N 74 22W
Lexington, Oreg., U.S.A. 160 45 29N 119 46W

Lexington **Litija**

Lexington, Tenn., U.S.A. **157** 35 38N 88 25W
Leyburn **33** 54 19N 1 50W
Leyland **32** 53 41N 2 42W
Leysdown on Sea **29** 51 23N 0 57 E
Leysin **50** 46 21N 7 0 E
Leyte, I. **103** 11 0N 125 0 E
Lezay **44** 46 17N 0 0 E
Lèze, R. **44** 43 28N 1 25 E
Lezha **68** 41 47N 19 42 E
Lézignan-Corbières **44** 43 13N 2 43 E
Lezoux **44** 45 49N 3 21 E
Lgov **80** 51 42N 35 10 E
Lhanbryde **37** 57 38N 3 12W
Lhariguo **99** 30 29N 93 4 E
Lhasa **105** 29 39N 91 6 E
Lhokseumawe **102** 5 20N 97 10 E
Lhuntsi Dzong **98** 27 39N 91 10 E
Li, Finland **74** 65 20N 25 20 E
Li, Thai. **100** 17 48N 98 57 E
Li Shui, R. **109** 29 24N 112 1 E
Liádhoi, I. **69** 36 50N 26 11 E
Liang Liang **103** 5 58N 121 30 E
Liang Shan **108** 23 42N 99 48 E
Lianga **103** 8 38N 126 6 E
Liangch'eng, Inner Mongolia, China **106** 40 26N 112 14 E
Liangch'eng, Shantung, China **107** 35 35N 119 32 E
Lianghok'ou **108** 29 10N 108 44 E
Lianghsiang **106** 39 44N 116 8 E
Liangp'ing **108** 30 41N 107 49 E
Liangpran, Gunong **102** 1 0N 114 23 E
Liangtang **106** 33 56N 106 12 E
Liao Ho, R. **107** 40 39N 122 12 E
Liaoch'eng **106** 36 26N 115 58 E
Liaochung **107** 41 30N 122 42 E
Liaoning □ **107** 41 15N 122 0 E
Liaotung Pantao **107** 40 0N 122 22 E
Liaotung Wan **107** 40 30N 121 30 E
Liaoyang **107** 41 17N 123 11 E
Liaoyüan **107** 42 55N 125 10 E
Liapádhes **68** 39 42N 19 40 E
Liard, R. **152** 61 51N 121 18W
Liari **94** 25 37N 66 30 E
Libau = Liepaja **80** 56 30N 21 0 E
Libby **160** 48 20N 115 10W
Libenge **124** 3 40N 18 55 E
Liberal, Kans., U.S.A. **159** 37 4N 101 0W
Liberal, Mo., U.S.A. **159** 37 35N 94 30W
Liberec **52** 50 47N 15 7 E
Liberia **166** 10 40N 85 30W
Liberia ■ **120** 6 30N 9 30W
Libertad **174** 8 20N 69 37W
Libertad, La **166** 16 47N 90 7W
Liberty, Mo., U.S.A. **158** 39 15N 94 24W
Liberty, N.Y., U.S.A. **162** 41 48N 74 45W
Liberty, Pa., U.S.A. **162** 41 34N 77 6W
Liberty, Tex., U.S.A. **159** 30 5N 94 50W
Libiaz **53** 50 7N 19 21 E
Libin **47** 49 59N 5 15 E
Libiya, Sahrâ' **114** 27 35N 25 0 E
Libohava **68** 40 3N 20 10 E
Libourne **44** 44 55N 0 14W
Libramont **47** 49 55N 5 23 E
Librazhdi **68** 41 12N 20 22 E
Libreville **124** 0 25N 9 26 E
Libya ■ **117** 28 30N 17 30 E
Libyan Plateau = Ed-Déffa **122** 30 40N 26 30 E
Licantén **172** 34 55 S 72 0W
Licata **64** 37 6N 13 55 E
Lich'eng **106** 36 59N 113 31 E
Lichfield **28** 52 40N 1 50W
Lichiang **108** 26 54N 100 12 E
Lichin **107** 37 32N 118 20 E
Lichtaart **47** 51 13N 4 55 E
Lichtenburg **128** 26 8 S 26 8 E
Lichtenfels **49** 50 7N 11 4 E
Lichtenvoorde **46** 51 59N 6 34 E
Lichtervelde **47** 51 2N 3 9 E
Lich'uan, Hupeh, China **109** 30 18N 108 51 E
Lich'uan, Kiangsi, China **109** 27 14N 116 51 E
Licosa, Punta **65** 40 15N 14 53 E
Lida, U.S.A. **163** 37 30N 117 30W
Lida, U.S.S.R. **80** 53 53N 25 15 E
Lidhult **73** 56 50N 13 27 E
Lidingö **73** 59 22N 18 8 E
Lidköping **73** 58 31N 13 14 E
Lido, Italy **63** 45 25N 12 23 E
Lido, Niger **121** 12 54N 3 44 E
Lido di Ostia **64** 41 44N 12 14 E
Lidzbark **54** 53 15N 19 49 E
Lidzbark Warminski **54** 54 7N 20 34 E
Liebenwalde **48** 52 51N 13 23 E
Lieberose **48** 51 59N 14 18 E
Liebling **66** 45 36N 21 20 E
Liechtenstein ■ **49** 47 8N 9 35 E
Liederkerke **47** 50 52N 4 5 E
Liège **47** 50 38N 5 35 E
Liège □ **47** 50 32N 5 35 E
Liegnitz = Legnica **54** 51 12N 16 10 E
Liempde **47** 51 35N 5 23 E
Lienart **126** 3 3N 25 31 E
Lienartville **126** 3 3N 25 31 E
Liench'eng **109** 25 47N 116 48 E
Lienchiang, Fukien, China **109** 26 11N 119 32 E
Lienchiang, Kwangtung, China **109** 21 36N 110 16 E
Lienhsien **109** 24 50N 112 23 E
Lienp'ing **109** 24 22N 114 30 E
Lienshan, Kwangtung, China **109** 24 37N 112 2 E
Lienshan, Yunnan, China **108** 24 48N 97 54 E
Lienshankuan **107** 40 58N 123 46 E
Lienshui **107** 33 46N 119 18 E
Lienyüan **109** 27 41N 111 40 E
Lienyünchiang **107** 34 47N 119 30 E
Lienyünchiangshih **107** 34 37N 119 13 E
Lienz **52** 46 50N 12 46 E
Liepāja **80** 56 30N 21 0 E
Lier **47** 51 7N 4 34 E
Lierneux **47** 50 17N 5 47 E
Lieshout **47** 51 31N 5 36 E
Lieşta **70** 45 38N 27 34 E
Liestal **50** 47 29N 7 44 E
Lieşti **70** 45 38N 27 34 E
Liévin **43** 50 24N 2 47 E
Lièvre, R. **150** 45 31N 75 26W
Liezen **52** 47 34N 14 15 E
Liffey, R. **39** 53 21N 6 20W
Lifford **38** 54 50N 7 30W
Liffré **42** 48 12N 1 30W
Lifjell **71** 59 27N 8 45 E
Lightning Ridge **139** 29 22 S 148 0 E
Lignano **63** 45 42N 13 8 E
Ligny-er-Barrois **43** 48 36N 5 20 E
Ligny-le-Châtel **43** 47 54N 3 45 E
Ligoúrion **69** 37 37N 23 2 E
Ligua, La **172** 32 30 S 71 16W
Liguria □ **62** 44 30N 9 0 E
Ligurian Sea **62** 43 20N 9 0 E
Lihir Group **135** 3 0 S 152 35 E
Lihou Reefs and Cays **138** 17 25 S 151 40 E
Lihsien, Hopeh, China **106** 38 29N 115 34 E
Lihsien, Hunan, China **109** 29 38N 111 45 E
Lihsien, Kansu, China **106** 34 11N 105 2 E
Lihsien, Szechwan, China **108** 31 28N 103 17 E
Lihue **147** 21 59N 159 24W
Lihwa **99** 30 4N 100 18 E
Likasi **127** 10 55 S 26 48 E
Likati **124** 3 20N 24 0 E
Likhoslavl **80** 57 12N 35 30 E
Likhovski **83** 48 10N 40 10 E
Likoma I. **127** 12 3 S 34 45 E
Likumburu **127** 9 43 S 35 8 E
Liling **109** 27 40N 113 30 E
Lill **47** 51 15N 4 50 E
Lille **43** 50 38N 3 3 E
Lille Bælt **73** 55 30N 9 45 E
Lillebonne **42** 49 30N 0 32 E
Lillehammer **71** 61 8N 10 30 E
Lillers **43** 50 35N 2 28 E
Lillesand **71** 58 15N 8 23 E
Lillestrøm **71** 59 58N 11 5 E
Lillian Point, Mt. **137** 27 40 S 126 6 E
Lillo **58** 39 45N 3 20W
Lillooet, R. **152** 49 15N 121 57W
Lilongwe **127** 14 0 S 33 48 E
Liloy **103** 8 4N 122 39 E
Lilun **108** 28 3N 100 27 E
Lim, R. **66** 43 0N 19 40 E
Lima, Indon. **103** 3 37 S 128 4 E
Lima, Peru **174** 12 0 S 77 0W
Lima, Sweden **72** 60 55N 13 20 E
Lima, Mont., U.S.A. **160** 44 41N 112 38W
Lima, Ohio, U.S.A. **156** 40 42N 84 5W
Lima, R. **56** 41 50N 8 18W
Limanowa **54** 49 42N 20 22 E
Limassol **92** 34 42N 33 1 E
Limavady **38** 55 3N 6 58W
Limavady □ **38** 55 0N 6 55W
Limay Mahuida **172** 37 10 S 66 45W
Limay, R. **176** 39 40 S 69 45W
Limbang **102** 4 42N 115 6 E
Limbara, Monti **64** 40 50N 9 10 E
Limbdi **94** 22 34N 71 51 E
Limbourg **47** 50 37N 5 56 E
Limbourg □ **47** 51 2N 5 25 E
Limbri **141** 31 3 S 151 5 E
Limbunya **136** 17 14 S 129 50 E
Limburg **49** 50 22N 8 4 E
Limburg □ **47** 51 20N 5 55 E
Limedsforsen **72** 60 52N 13 25 E
Limeira **173** 22 35 S 47 28W
Limenária **68** 40 38N 24 32 E
Limerick **39** 52 40N 8 38W
Limerick □ **39** 52 30N 8 50W
Limerick Junction **39** 52 30N 8 12W
Limestone, R. **153** 56 31N 94 7W
Limfjorden **73** 56 55N 9 0 E
Limia, R. **56** 41 55N 8 8W
Limmared **73** 57 34N 13 20 E
Limmat, R. **51** 47 26N 8 20 E
Limmen **46** 52 34N 4 42 E
Limmen Bight **138** 14 40 S 135 35 E
Limmen Bight R. **138** 15 7 S 135 44 E
Límni **69** 38 43N 23 18 E
Límnos, I. **68** 39 50N 25 5 E
Limoeiro **170** 7 52 S 25 27W
Limoeiro do Norte **170** 5 5 S 38 0W
Limoges **44** 45 50N 1 15 E
Limón **167** 10 0N 83 2W
Limon **158** 39 18N 103 38W
Limone **62** 44 12N 7 32 E
Limousin **44** 46 0N 1 0 E
Limousin, Plateau de **44** 46 0N 1 0 E
Limoux **44** 43 4N 2 12 E
Limpopo, R. **129** 23 15 S 32 5 E
Limpsfield **29** 51 15N 0 1 E
Limu Ling, mts. **100** 19 0N 109 20 E
Limuru **126** 1 2 S 36 35 E
Lin **68** 41 4N 20 38 E
Linan **109** 30 13N 119 40 E
Linares **172** 35 50 S 71 40W
Linàres **174** 1 23N 77 31W
Linares, Mexico **165** 24 50N 99 40W
Linares, Spain **59** 38 10N 3 40W
Linares □ **172** 36 0 S 71 0W
Línas Mte. **64** 39 25N 8 38 E
Linchenchen **106** 36 28N 110 0 E
Linch'eng **106** 37 26N 114 34 E
Linch'i **106** 35 46N 113 53 E
Linchiang **107** 41 50N 126 55 E
Linchin **106** 35 6N 110 33 E
Linch'ing **106** 36 56N 115 45 E
Linch'ü **107** 36 30N 118 32 E
Linch'uan **109** 28 0N 116 20 E
Lincluden **35** 55 5N 3 40W
Lincoln, Argent. **172** 34 55N 61 30W
Lincoln, N.Z. **143** 43 38 S 172 30 E
Lincoln, U.K. **33** 53 14N 0 32W
Lincoln, Ill., U.S.A. **158** 40 10N 89 20W
Lincoln, Kans., U.S.A. **158** 39 6N 98 9W
Lincoln, Maine, U.S.A. **151** 45 27N 68 29W
Lincoln, N. Mex., U.S.A. **161** 33 30N 105 26W
Lincoln, Nebr., U.S.A. **158** 40 50N 96 42W
Lincoln, N.H., U.S.A. **162** 44 3N 71 40W
Lincoln □ **33** 53 14N 0 32W
Lincoln Sea **12** 84 0N 55 0W
Lincoln Wolds **33** 53 20N 0 5W
Lincolnton **157** 35 30N 81 15W
Lind, Austral. **138** 18 58 S 144 30 E
Lind, U.S.A. **160** 47 0N 118 33W
Lindale **32** 54 14N 2 54W
Lindås **71** 60 44N 5 10 E
Lindås, Norway **71** 60 44N 5 9 E
Lindås, Sweden **73** 56 38N 15 35 E
Lindau **49** 47 33N 9 41 E
Linde **46** 52 50N 6 57 E
Linden, Guyana **174** 6 0N 58 10W
Linden, Calif., U.S.A. **163** 38 1N 121 5W
Linden, Tex., U.S.A. **159** 33 0N 94 20W
Lindenheuvel **47** 50 59N 5 48 E
Lindenwold **162** 39 49N 72 59W
Linderöd **73** 55 56N 13 47 E
Linderödsåsen **73** 55 53N 13 53 E
Lindesberg **72** 59 36N 15 15 E
Lindesnes **71** 57 58N 7 3 E
Lindfield **29** 51 2N 0 5W
Lindi **127** 9 58 S 39 38 E
Lindi □ **127** 9 40 S 38 30 E
Lindi, R. **126** 1 25N 25 50 E
Lindoso **56** 41 52N 8 11W
Lindow **48** 52 58N 12 58 E
Lindsay, Can. **150** 44 22N 78 43W
Lindsay, Calif., U.S.A. **163** 36 14N 119 6W
Lindsay, Okla., U.S.A. **159** 34 51N 97 37W
Lindsborg **158** 38 35N 97 40W
Linea de la Concepciōn, La **55** 36 15N 5 23W
Linea de la Concepción, La **57** 36 15N 5 23W
Linfen **106** 36 5N 111 32 E
Lingakok **99** 29 55N 87 38 E
Lingayer **103** 16 1N 120 14 E
Lingayer G. **103** 16 10N 120 15 E
Lingch'iu **106** 39 28N 114 10 E
Lingch'uan, Kwangsi Chuang, China **109** 25 25N 110 20 E
Lingch'uan, Shansi, China **106** 35 46N 113 26 E
Lingen **48** 52 32N 7 21 E
Lingfield **29** 51 11N 0 1W
Lingga, Kepulauan **102** 0 10 S 104 30 E
Linghed **72** 60 48N 15 55 E
Linghsien, Hunan, China **109** 26 26N 113 45 E
Linghsien, Shantung, China **106** 37 21N 116 34 E
Lingle **158** 42 10N 104 18W
Lingling **109** 26 13N 111 37 E
Lingpi **107** 33 33N 117 33 E
Lingshan **108** 22 26N 109 17 E
Lingshih **106** 36 51N 111 47 E
Lingshou **106** 38 18N 114 22 E
Lingshui **100** 18 27N 110 0 E
Lingt'ai **106** 35 4N 107 37 E
Linguéré **120** 15 25N 15 5W
Lingwu **106** 38 5N 106 20 E
Lingyün **108** 24 24N 106 31 E
Linh Cam **100** 18 31N 105 31 E
Linhai **109** 28 51N 121 7 E
Linhares **171** 19 25 s 40 4W
Linho **106** 40 50N 107 30 E
Linhsi **107** 43 37N 118 8 E
Linhsia **105** 35 36N 103 5 E
Linhsiang **109** 29 29N 113 30 E
Linhsien **106** 37 57N 110 57 E
Lini **107** 35 5N 118 20 E
Linju **106** 34 14N 112 45 E
Link **68** 41 4N 20 38 E
Linkao **100** 19 56N 109 42 E
Linkinhorne **30** 50 31N 4 22W
Linköping **73** 58 28N 15 36 E
Link'ou **107** 45 18N 130 15 E
Linli **109** 29 27N 111 39 E
Linlithgow **35** 55 58N 3 38W
Linn, Mt. **160** 40 0N 123 0W
Linney Head **31** 51 37N 5 4W
Linnhe, L. **34** 56 36N 5 25W
Linosa **119** 35 51N 12 50 E
Lins **173** 21 40 S 49 44W
Linshui **108** 30 18N 106 55 E
Linslade **29** 51 55N 0 40W
Lint'ao **106** 35 20N 104 0 E
Linth, R. **49** 46 54N 9 0 E
Linthal **51** 46 54N 9 0 E
Lintlaw **153** 52 4N 103 14W
Linton, Can. **151** 47 15N 72 16W
Linton, U.K. **29** 52 6N 0 19 E
Linton, Ind., U.S.A. **156** 39 0N 87 10W
Linton, N. Dak., U.S.A. **158** 46 21N 100 12W
Lints'ang **108** 23 54N 100 0 E
Lint'ung **106** 34 24N 109 13 E
Linville **139** 26 50 S 152 11 E
Linwu **109** 25 17N 112 33 E
Linxe **44** 43 56N 1 13W
Linyanti, R. **128** 18 10 S 24 10 E
Linyüan **107** 41 18N 119 15 E
Linz, Austria **52** 48 18N 14 18 E
Linz, Ger. **48** 50 33N 7 18 E
Lion-d'Angers, Le **42** 47 37N 0 43W
Lion, G. du **44** 43 0N 4 0 E
Lioni **65** 40 52N 15 10 E
Lion's Den **127** 17 15 S 30 5 E
Lion's Head **150** 44 58N 81 15W
Liozno **80** 55 0N 30 50 E
Lipali **127** 15 50 S 35 50 E
Lipari **65** 38 26N 14 58 E
Lipari, Is. **65** 38 40N 15 0 E
Lipetsk **81** 52 45N 39 35 E
Lipiany **54** 53 2N 14 58 E
Lip'ing **108** 26 16N 109 8 E
Lipkany **82** 48 14N 26 25 E
Lipljan **66** 42 31N 21 7 E
Lipnik **53** 49 32N 17 36 E
Lipno **54** 52 49N 19 15 E
Lipo **108** 25 25N 107 53 E
Lipova **66** 46 8N 21 42 E
Lipovets **82** 49 12N 29 1 E
Lippstadt **48** 51 40N 8 19 E
Lipsco **54** 51 10N 21 36 E
Lipscomb **159** 36 16N 100 28W
Lipsko **54** 51 9N 21 40 E
Lipsói, I. **69** 37 19N 26 50 E
Liptovsky Svaty Milkula **53** 49 6N 19 35 E
Liptrap C. **141** 38 50 S 145 55 E
Lip'u **109** 24 30N 110 23 E
Lira **126** 2 17N 32 57 E
Liri, R. **64** 41 25N 13 45 E
Liria **58** 39 37N 0 35W
Lisala **124** 2 12N 21 38 E
Lisbellaw **38** 54 20N 7 32W
Lisboa **57** 38 42N 9 10W
Lisboa □ **57** 39 0N 9 12W
Lisbon **158** 46 30N 97 46W
Lisbon = Lisboa **57** 38 42N 9 10W
Lisburn **38** 54 30N 6 9W
Lisburne, C. **147** 68 50N 166 0W
Liscannor **39** 52 57N 9 24W
Liscannor, B. **39** 52 57N 9 24W
Liscarroll **39** 52 15N 8 44W
Liscia, R. **64** 41 5N 9 17 E
Liscomb **151** 45 2N 62 0W
Lisdoonvarna **39** 53 2N 9 18W
Lishe Ho, R. **108** 24 18N 101 32 E
Lishih **106** 37 30N 111 7 E
Lishu **107** 43 20N 124 37 E
Lishuchen **107** 45 5N 130 40 E
Lishui, Chekiang, China **109** 28 27N 119 54 E
Lishui, Kiangsu, China **109** 31 38N 119 2 E
Lisianski I. **130** 25 30N 174 0W
Lisieux **42** 49 10N 0 12 E
Lisischansk **83** 48 55N 38 30 E
Liskeard **30** 50 27N 4 29W
Lismore, N.S.W., Austral. **139** 28 44 S 153 21 E
Lismore, Vic., Austral. **133** 37 58 S 143 21 E
Lismore, Ireland **39** 52 8N 7 58W
Lismore I. **34** 56 30N 5 30W
Lisnacree **38** 54 4N 6 5W
Lisnaskea **38** 54 15N 7 27W
Liss **29** 51 3N 0 53W
Lissatinning Bri. **39** 51 55N 10 1W
Lisse **46** 52 16N 4 33 E
Lisselton **39** 52 30N 9 34W
Lissycasey **39** 52 44N 9 12W
List **48** 55 1N 8 26 E
Lista, Norway **71** 58 7N 6 39 E
Lista, Sweden **75** 59 19N 16 16 E
Lister, Mt. **13** 78 0 S 162 0 E
Liston **139** 28 39 S 152 6 E
Listowel, Can. **150** 43 44N 80 58W
Listowel, Ireland **39** 52 27N 9 30W
Listowel Dns. **139** 25 10 S 145 12 E
Lit-et-Mixe **44** 44 2N 1 15W
Lit'ang, Kwangsi-Chuang, China **108** 23 11N 109 5 E
Lit'ang, Szechwan, China **108** 30 4N 100 18 E
Litang **103** 5 27N 118 31 E
Lit'ang Ho, R. **108** 28 5N 101 28 E
Litcham **29** 52 43N 0 49 E
Litchfield, Austral. **140** 36 18 S 142 52 E
Litchfield, Conn., U.S.A. **162** 41 44N 73 12W
Litchfield, Ill., U.S.A. **158** 39 10N 89 40W
Litchfield, Minn., U.S.A. **158** 45 5N 95 0W
Liteni **70** 47 32N 26 32 E
Litherland **32** 53 29N 3 0W
Lithgow **141** 33 25 S 150 8 E
Lithínon, Ákra **69** 34 55N 24 44 E
Lithuania S.S.R. □ **80** 55 30N 24 0 E
Litija **63** 46 3N 14 50 E

Lititz **Londonderry**

Lititz	162	40 9N	76 18W
Litókhoron	68	40 8N	22 34 E
Litomĕrice	52	50 33N	14 10 E
Litomysi	53	49 52N	16 20 E
Litschau	52	48 58N	15 4 E
Little Abaco I.	157	26 50N	77 30W
Little Aden	91	12 41N	45 6 E
Little America	13	79 0N	160 0W
Little Andaman I.	101	10 40N	92 15 E
Little Barrier I.	142	36 12 S	175 8 E
Little Belt	72	55 8N	9 55 E
Little Belt Mts.	160	46 50N	111 0W
Little Blue, R.	158	40 18N	97 45W
Little Bushman Land	128	29 10 S	18 10 E
Little Cadotte, R.	152	56 41N	117 6W
Little Cayman, I.	166	19 41N	80 3W
Little Churchill, R.	153	57 30N	95 22W
Little Coco I.	101	14 0N	93 15 E
Little Colorado, R.	161	36 0N	111 31W
Little Current	150	45 55N	82 0W
Little Current, R.	150	50 57N	84 36W
Little Egg Inlet	162	39 30N	74 20W
Little Falls, Minn., U.S.A.	158	45 58N	94 19W
Little Falls, N.Y., U.S.A.	162	43 3N	74 50W
Lit. Grand Rapids	153	52 0N	95 29W
Lit. Humbaldt, R.	160	41 20N	117 27W
Lit. Inagua I.	167	21 40N	73 50W
Little Lake	163	35 58N	117 58W
Little Longlac	150	49 42N	86 58W
Little Marais	158	47 24N	91 8W
Little Mecatiná I.	151	50 30N	59 25W
Little Minch	36	57 35N	6 45W
Lit. Miquelon I.	151	46 45N	56 25W
Lit. Missouri R.	158	46 40N	103 50W
Little Namaqualand	128	29 0 S	17 9 E
Little Ormes Hd.	31	53 19N	3 47W
Little Ouse, R.	29	52 25N	0 50 E
Little Para, R.	109	34 47 S	138 25 E
Little Rann of Kutch	94	23 25N	71 25 E
Little Red, R.	159	35 40N	92 15W
Little River	143	43 45 S	172 49 E
Little Rock	159	34 41N	92 10W
Little Ruaha, R.	126	7 50 S	35 30 E
Little Sable Pt.	156	43 40N	86 32W
Little Scarcies, R.	125	9 30N	12 25W
Little Sioux, R.	147	42 20N	95 55W
Little Smoky	152	54 44N	117 11W
Little Smoky River	152	55 40N	117 38W
Little Snake, R.	160	40 45N	108 15W
Little Wabash, R.	156	38 40N	88 20W
Little Walsingham	29	52 53N	0 51 E
Little Whale, R.	150	55 50N	75 0W
Littleborough	32	53 38N	2 8W
Littlefield	159	33 57N	102 17W
Littlefork	158	48 24N	93 35W
Littlehampton, Austral.	109	35 3 S	138 52 E
Littlehampton, U.K.	29	50 48N	0 32W
Littlemill	37	57 31N	3 49W
Littleport	29	52 27N	0 18 E
Littlestone-on-Sea	29	50 59N	0 59 E
Littlestown	162	39 45N	77 3W
Littleton Common	162	42 32N	71 28W
Litu	108	28 24N	101 16 E
Liuan	109	31 45N	116 30 E
Liuch'eng	108	24 39N	109 14 E
Liuchou	108	24 15N	109 22 E
Liuchuang	107	33 9N	120 18 E
Liuheng Tao	109	29 43N	122 8 E
Liuho, Kiangsu, China	109	32 20N	118 51 E
Liuho, Kirin, China	107	42 16N	125 42 E
Liukou	107	40 57N	118 18 E
Liuli	127	11 3 S	34 38 E
Liupa	106	33 40N	107 0 E
Liuwa Plain	125	14 20 S	22 30 E
Liuyang	109	28 9N	113 38 E
Livada	70	47 52N	23 5 E
Livadherón	68	40 2N	21 57 E
Livanovka	84	52 6N	61 59 E
Livarot	42	49 0N	0 9 E
Live Oak	157	30 17N	83 0W
Liveringa	136	18 3 S	124 10 E
Livermore	163	37 41N	121 47W
Livermore, Mt.	159	30 45N	104 8W
Liverpool, Austral.	141	33 54 S	150 58 E
Liverpool, Can.	151	44 5N	64 41W
Liverpool, U.K.	32	53 25N	3 0W
Liverpool, U.S.A.	162	43 6N	76 13W
Liverpool Bay, Can.	147	70 0N	128 0W
Liverpool Bay, U.K.	23	53 30N	3 20W
Liverpool Plains	141	31 15 S	150 15 E
Liverpool Ra.	141	31 50 S	150 30 E
Livingston, Guat.	166	15 50N	88 50W
Livingston, U.K.	45	55 52N	3 33W
Livingston, Calif., U.S.A.	163	37 23N	120 43W
Livingston, Mont., U.S.A.	160	45 40N	110 40W
Livingstone	159	30 44N	94 54W
Livingstone Falls	126	5 25 S	13 35 E
Livingstone I.	13	63 0 S	60 15W
Livingstone (Maramba)	127	17 46 S	25 52 E
Livingstone Memorial	127	12 20 S	30 18 E
Livingstone Mts., N.Z.	143	45 15 S	168 9 E
Livingstone Mts., Tanz.	127	9 40 S	34 20 E
Livingstonia	127	10 38 S	34 5 E
Livno	66	43 50N	17 0 E
Livny	81	52 30N	37 30 E
Livorno	62	43 32N	10 18 E
Livramento	173	30 55 S	55 30W
Livramento do Brumado	171	13 39 S	41 50W
Livron-sur-Drôme	45	44 46N	4 51 E
Liwale	127	9 48 S	37 58 E
Liwale □	127	9 0 S	38 0 E
Liwale Chini	127	9 40 S	38 0 E
Lixnaw	39	52 24N	9 37W
Lixoúrion	69	38 14N	20 24 E
Liyang	109	31 22N	119 30 E
Lizard	30	49 58N	5 10W
Lizard I.	138	14 42 S	145 30 E
Lizard Pt.	30	49 57N	5 11W
Lizarda	170	9 36 S	46 41W
Lizzano	65	40 23N	17 25 E
Ljig	66	44 13N	20 18 E
Ljubija	63	44 55N	16 35 E
Ljubinje	66	42 58N	18 5 E
Ljubljana	63	46 4N	14 33 E
Ljubno	63	46 25N	14 46 E
Ljubovija	66	44 11N	19 22 E
Ljubuški	66	43 12N	17 34 E
Ljung	73	58 1N	13 3 E
Ljungan	72	62 18N	17 23 E
Ljungan, R.	74	62 30N	14 30 E
Ljungaverk	72	62 30N	16 5 E
Ljungby	73	56 49N	13 55 E
Ljusdal	72	61 46N	16 3 E
Ljusnan	72	61 12N	17 8 E
Ljusnan, R.	75	62 0N	15 20 E
Ljusne	72	61 13N	17 7 E
Ljutomer	63	46 31N	16 11 E
Lki	67	41 28N	23 43 E
Llagostera	58	41 50N	2 54 E
Llanaber	31	52 45N	4 5W
Llanaelhaiarn	31	52 59N	4 24W
Llanafan-fawr	31	52 12N	3 29W
Llanarmon Dyffryn Ceiriog	31	52 53N	3 15W
Llanarth	31	52 12N	4 19W
Llanarthney	31	51 51N	4 9W
Llanbedr	31	52 40N	4 7W
Llanbedrog	31	52 52N	4 29W
Llanberis	31	53 7N	4 7W
Llanbister	31	52 22N	3 19W
Llanbrynmair	31	52 36N	3 19W
Llancanelo, Salina	172	35 40 S	69 8W
Llandaff	31	51 29N	3 13W
Llanddewi-Brefi	31	52 11N	3 57W
Llandilo	31	51 45N	4 0W
Llandogo	31	51 44N	2 40W
Llandovery	31	51 59N	3 49W
Llandrillo	31	52 56N	3 27W
Llandrindod Wells	31	52 15N	3 23W
Llandudno	31	53 19N	3 51W
Llandybie	31	51 49N	4 0W
Llandyfriog	31	52 2N	4 26W
Llandygwydd	31	52 3N	4 33W
Llandyrnog	31	53 10N	3 19W
Llandyssul	31	52 3N	4 20W
Llanelli	31	51 41N	4 11W
Llanelltyd	31	52 45N	3 54W
Llanenddwyn	31	52 48N	4 7W
Llanerchymedd	31	53 20N	4 22W
Llanes	56	43 25N	4 50W
Llanfaelog	31	53 13N	4 29W
Llanfair Caereinion	31	52 39N	3 20W
Llanfair Talhaiarn	31	53 13N	3 37W
Llanfairfechan	31	53 15N	3 58W
Llanfechell	31	52 23N	4 25W
Llanfyllin	31	52 47N	3 17W
Llangadog	31	51 56N	3 53W
Llangefni	31	53 15N	4 20W
Llangelynin	31	52 39N	4 7W
Llangennech	31	51 41N	4 10W
Llangerniew	31	53 12N	3 41W
Llangollen	31	52 58N	3 10W
Llangranog	31	52 11N	4 29W
Llangurig	31	52 25N	3 36W
Llangynog	31	52 50N	3 24W
Llanharan	31	51 32N	3 28W
Llanidloes	31	52 28N	3 31W
Llanilar	31	52 22N	4 2W
Llanllyfni	31	53 2N	4 18W
Llannor	31	52 55N	4 25W
Llano Estacado	154	34 0N	103 0W
Llano R.	159	30 50N	99 0W
Llanon	31	52 17N	4 9W
Llanos	174	3 25N	71 35W
Llanpumpsaint	31	51 56N	4 19W
Llanrhaedr-ym-Mochnant	31	52 50N	3 18W
Llanrhidian	31	51 36N	4 11W
Llanrhystyd	31	52 19N	4 9W
Llanrwst	31	53 8N	3 49W
Llansannan	31	53 10N	3 35W
Llansawel	31	52 0N	4 1W
Llanstephan	31	51 46N	4 24W
Llanthony	31	51 57N	3 2W
Llantrisant	31	51 33N	3 22W
Llanuwchllyn	31	52 52N	3 41W
Llanvihangel Crucorney	31	51 53N	2 58W
Llanwenog	31	52 6N	4 11W
Llanwrda	31	51 58N	3 52W
Llanwrtyd Wells	31	52 6N	3 39W
Llanyblodwel	28	52 47N	3 8W
Llanybyther	31	52 4N	4 10W
Llanymynech	28	52 48N	3 6W
Llanystymdwy	31	52 56N	4 17W
Llera	165	23 19N	99 1W
Llerena	57	38 17N	6 0W
Llethr Mt.	31	52 47N	3 58W
Lleyn Peninsula	31	52 55N	4 35W
Llico	172	34 46 S	72 5W
Llobregat, R.	58	41 19N	2 9 E
Lloret de Mar	58	41 41N	2 53 E
Lloyd B.	138	12 45 S	143 27 E
Lloyd Barrage	95	27 46N	68 50 E
Lloyd L.	153	57 22N	108 57W
Lloydminster	153	53 20N	110 0W
Lluchmayor	59	39 29N	2 53 E
Llullaillaco, volcán	172	24 30 S	68 30W
Llwyngwril	31	52 41N	4 6W
Llyswen	31	52 2N	3 18W
Lo	47	50 59N	2 45 E
Lo Ho, Honan, China	106	34 48N	113 4 E
Lo Ho, Shensi, China	106	34 41N	110 6 E
Lo, R.	100	21 18N	105 25 E
Loa	161	38 18N	111 46W
Loa, R.	172	21 30 S	70 0W
Loan	109	27 24N	115 49 E
Loanhead	35	55 53N	3 10W
Loano	62	44 8N	8 14 E
Loans	34	55 33N	4 39W
Lobatse	125	25 12 S	25 40 E
Löbau	48	51 5N	14 42 E
Lobaye, R.	128	4 30N	17 0 E
Lobbes	47	50 21N	4 16 E
Lobenstein	48	50 25N	11 39 E
Lobería	172	38 10 S	58 40W
Łobez	54	53 38N	15 39 E
Lobito	125	12 18 S	13 35 E
Lobón, Canal de	57	38 50N	6 55W
Lobos	172	35 2 S	59 0W
Lobos, I.	164	21 27N	97 13W
Lobos, Is.	168	6 35 S	80 45W
Lobstick L.	151	54 0N	65 12W
Lobva	84	59 10N	60 30 E
Lobva, R.	84	59 8N	60 48 E
Loc Binh	100	21 46N	106 54 E
Loc Ninh	101	11 50N	106 34 E
Locarno	51	46 10N	8 47 E
Loch Raven Res.	162	39 26N	76 33W
Lochaber	36	56 55N	5 0W
Lochailort	36	56 53N	5 40W
Lochaline	36	56 32N	5 47W
Loch'ang	109	25 10N	113 20 E
Lochans	34	54 52N	5 1W
Lochboisdale	36	57 10N	7 20W
Lochbuie	34	56 21N	5 52W
Lochcarron	36	57 25N	5 30W
Lochdonhead	34	56 27N	5 40W
Loche L., La	153	56 40N	109 30W
Loche, La	153	56 29N	109 26W
Lochearnhead	34	56 24N	4 19W
Lochem	46	52 9N	6 26 E
Loch'eng	108	24 47N	108 54 E
Loches	42	47 7N	1 0 E
Lochgelly	35	56 7N	3 18W
Lochgilphead	34	56 2N	5 37W
Lochgoilhead	34	56 10N	4 54W
Lochiang	108	31 21N	104 28 E
Lochih	108	30 18N	105 0 E
Loch'ing	109	28 8N	120 57 E
Loch'ing Wan	109	28 4N	121 5 E
Lochinver	36	58 9N	5 15W
Lochlaggan Hotel	37	56 59N	4 25W
Lochmaben	35	55 8N	3 27W
Lochmaddy	36	57 36N	7 10W
Lochnagar, Queens., Austral.	138	24 34 S	144 52 E
Lochnagar, Queens., Austral.	138	23 33 S	145 38 E
Lochnagar, Mt.	37	56 57N	3 14W
Łochow	54	52 33N	21 42 E
Lochranza	34	55 42N	5 18W
Lochs Park, Reg.	36	58 7N	6 33W
Loch'uan	106	35 48N	109 35 E
Lochwinnoch	34	55 47N	4 39W
Lochy, L.	37	56 58N	4 55W
Lochy, R.	36	56 52N	5 3W
Lock	139	33 34 S	135 46 E
Lock Haven	156	41 7N	77 31W
Lockeford	163	38 10N	121 9W
Lockeport	151	43 47N	65 4W
Lockerbie	35	55 7N	3 21W
Lockhart, Austral.	141	35 14 S	146 40 E
Lockhart, U.S.A.	159	29 55N	97 40W
Lockhart, L.	137	33 15 S	119 3 E
Lockington	140	36 16 S	144 34 E
Lockport	156	43 12N	78 42W
Locle, Le	50	47 3N	6 44 E
Locminé	42	47 54N	2 51W
Locri	65	38 14N	16 14 E
Locronan	42	48 7N	4 15W
Loctudy	42	47 50N	4 12W
Lod	90	31 57N	34 54 E
Lodalskåpa	71	61 47N	7 13 E
Loddon	29	52 32N	1 29 E
Lodève	44	43 44N	3 19 E
Lodge Grass	160	45 21N	107 27W
Lodgepole	158	41 12N	102 40W
Lodgepole Cr.	158	41 20N	104 30W
Lodhran	94	29 32N	71 30 E
Lodi, Italy	62	45 19N	9 30 E
Lodi, U.S.A.	163	38 12N	121 16W
Lodja	124	3 30 S	23 23 E
Lodji	103	1 38 S	127 28 E
Lodosa	58	42 25N	2 4W
Lodose	73	58 5N	12 10 E
Lödöse	73	58 2N	12 9 E
Lodwar	126	3 10N	35 40 E
Łodz	54	51 45N	19 27 E
Łodz □	54	51 45N	19 27 E
Loengo	126	4 48 S	26 30 E
Lofer	52	47 35N	12 41 E
Lofoten	74	68 10N	13 0 E
Lofoten Is.	74	68 30N	15 0 E
Lofsen	72	62 7N	13 57 E
Loftahammar	73	57 54N	16 41 E
Loftsdalen	72	62 10N	13 20 E
Loftus	33	54 33N	0 52W
Lofty Ra.	136	24 15 S	119 30 E
Loga	121	13 37N	3 14 E
Logan, Kans., U.S.A.	158	39 23N	99 35W
Logan, Ohio, U.S.A.	156	39 25N	82 22 E
Logan, Utah, U.S.A.	160	41 45N	111 50W
Logan, Mt.	147	60 41N	140 22W
Logan Pass	152	48 41N	113 44W
Logansport	156	31 58N	93 58W
Loganville	162	39 51N	76 42W
Logo	123	5 20N	30 18 E
Logo Dergo	123	6 10N	29 18 E
Logroño	58	42 28N	2 32W
• Logroño □	58	42 28N	2 27W
Logrosán	57	39 20N	5 32W
Løgstør	73	56 58N	9 14 E
Lohardaga	95	23 27N	84 45 E
Loheia	91	15 45N	42 40 E
Lohja	75	60 12N	24 5 E
Loho	106	33 33N	114 5 E
Lohr	49	50 0N	9 35 E
Loikaw	98	19 40N	97 17 E
Loimaa	75	60 50N	23 5 E
Loir-et-Cher □	43	47 40N	1 20 E
Loire □	45	45 40N	4 5 E
Loire-Atlantique □	42	47 25N	1 40W
Loire, R.	42	47 16N	2 10W
Loiret □	43	47 58N	2 10 E
Loitz	48	53 58N	13 8 E
Loja, Ecuador	174	3 59 S	79 16W
Loja, Spain	57	37 10N	4 10W
Lojung	108	24 27N	109 36 E
Loka	123	4 13N	31 0 E
Lokandu	124	2 30 S	25 45 E
Løken	71	59 48N	11 29 E
Lokerane	128	24 54 S	24 42 E
Lokeren	47	51 6N	3 59 E
Lokhvitsa	80	50 25N	33 18 E
Lokichokio	126	4 19N	34 13 E
Lokitaung	124	4 12N	35 48 E
Lokka	74	67 49N	27 45 E
Løkken, Denmark	73	57 22N	9 41 E
Løkken, Norway	71	63 8N	9 45 E
Loknya	80	56 49N	30 4 E
Lokobo	123	4 20N	30 30 E
Lokoja	121	7 47N	6 45 E
Lokolama	124	2 35 S	19 50 E
Loktung	100	18 41N	109 5 E
Lokuti	123	4 21N	33 15 E
Lokwei	100	19 12N	110 30 E
Lol	123	5 28N	29 36 E
Lol, R.	123	9 0N	28 10 E
Lola	120	7 52N	8 29W
Lolibai, Gebel	123	3 50N	33 50 E
Lolimi	123	4 35N	34 0 E
Loliondo	124	2 2 S	35 39 E
Lolland	73	54 45N	11 30 E
Lollar	48	50 39N	8 43 E
Lolo	160	46 50N	114 8W
Lolodorf	121	3 16N	10 49 E
Lolungchung	126	30 43N	96 7 E
Lom	67	43 48N	23 20 E
Lom Kao	100	16 53N	101 14 E
Lom, R.	66	43 45N	23 7 E
Lom Sak	100	16 47N	101 15 E
Loma	160	47 59N	110 29W
Loma Linda	163	34 3N	117 16W
Lomami, R.	126	1 0 S	24 40 E
Lomas de Zamóra	172	34 45 S	58 25W
Lombadria	136	16 31 S	122 54 E
Lombard	160	46 7N	111 28W
Lombardia □	62	45 35N	9 45 E
Lombardy = Lombardia	62	45 35N	9 45 E
Lombez	44	43 29N	0 55 E
Lomblen, I.	103	8 30 S	123 32 E
Lombok, I.	102	8 35 S	116 20 E
Lomé	121	6 9N	1 20 E
Lomela	124	2 5 S	23 52 E
Lomela, R.	124	1 30 S	22 50 E
Lomello	62	45 11N	8 46 E
Lometa	159	31 15N	98 25W
Lomie	124	3 13N	13 38 E
Loming	123	4 27N	33 40W
Lomma	73	55 43N	13 6 E
Lomme, R.	47	50 8N	5 10 E
Lommel	47	51 14N	5 19 E
Lomond	152	50 24N	112 36W
Lomond, gasfield	19	57 18N	1 12 E
Lomond, L.	34	56 8N	4 38W
Lomond, mt.	139	30 0 S	151 45 E
Lomphat	101	13 30N	106 59 E
Lompobatang, mt.	103	5 24 S	119 56 E
Lompoc	163	34 41N	120 32W
Lomsegga	71	61 49N	8 21 E
Łomza	54	53 10N	22 2 E
Łomza □	54	53 0N	22 30 E
Lonan	106	34 6N	110 10 E
Lonavla	96	18 46N	73 29 E
Loncoche	176	39 20 S	72 50W
Londa	97	15 30N	74 30 E
Londe, La	45	43 8N	6 14 E
Londerzeel	47	51 0N	4 19 E
Londiani	126	0 10 S	35 33 E
Londinières	42	49 50N	1 25 E
London, Can.	150	43 0N	81 15W
London, U.K.	29	51 30N	0 5W
London, Ky., U.S.A.	156	37 11N	84 5W
London, Ohio, U.S.A.	156	39 54N	83 28W
London □	29	51 30N	0 5W
Londonderry	38	55 0N	7 20W

*Renamed La Rioja

Londonderry, C **Lugano, L. di**

Londonderry, C. **136** 13 45 S 126 55 E
Londonderry, Co. **38** 55 0N 7 20W
Londonderry, I. **176** 55 0 S 71 0W
Londrina **173** 23 0 S 51 10W
Lone Pine **163** 36 35N 118 2W
Long Beach, Calif., U.S.A. **163** 33 46N 118 12W
Long Beach, N.Y., U.S.A. **162** 40 35N 73 40W
Long Beach, Wash., U.S.A. **160** 46 20N 124 1W
Long Bennington **33** 52 59N 0 45W
Long Branch **162** 40 19N 74 0W
Long Clawson **29** 52 51N 0 56W
Long Crendon **29** 51 47N 1 0W
Long Eaton **33** 52 54N 1 16W
Long Gully **109** 35 1 S 138 40 E
Long I., Austral. **138** 22 8 S 149 53 E
Long I., Bahamas **167** 23 20N 75 10W
Long I., Can. **150** 44 23N 66 19W
Long I., Ireland **39** 51 30N 9 35W
Long I., P.N.G. **135** 5 20 S 147 5 E
Long I., U.S.A. **162** 40 50N 73 20W
Long I. Sd. **162** 41 10N 73 0W
Long Itchington **28** 52 16N 1 24W
Long L. **150** 49 30N 86 50W
Long, L. **34** 56 4N 4 50W
Long L. **162** 43 57N 74 25W
Long Melford **29** 52 5N 0 44 E
Long Mt. **31** 52 38N 3 7W
Long Mynd **23** 52 35N 2 50W
Long Pine **158** 43 33N 99 50W
Long Pocket **138** 18 30 S 146 0 E
Long Pt., Can. **151** 48 47N 58 46W
Long Pt., N.Z. **143** 46 34 S 169 36 E
Long Preston **32** 54 0N 2 16W
Long Ra. **151** 49 30N 57 30W
Long Range Mts **151** 48 0N 58 30W
Long Reef **136** 13 55 S 125 45 E
Long Str. **12** 70 0N 175 0 E
Long Sutton **29** 52 47N 0 9 E
Long Thanh **101** 10 47N 106 57 E
Long Xuyen **101** 10 19N 105 28 E
Longá **69** 36 53N 21 55 E
Longa I. **36** 57 45N 5 50W
Longarone **63** 46 15N 12 18 E
Longburn **142** 40 23 S 175 35 E
Longdam **99** 28 12N 98 16 E
Longeau **43** 47 47N 5 20 E
Longford, Austral. **138** 41 32 S 147 3 E
Longford, Ireland **38** 53 43N 7 50W
Longford, U.K. **28** 51 53N 2 14W
Longford □ **38** 53 42N 7 45W
Longforgan **35** 56 28N 3 8W
Longframlington **35** 55 18N 1 47W
Longhawan **102** 2 15N 114 55 E
Longhorsley **35** 55 15N 1 46W
Longhoughton **35** 55 26N 1 38W
Longido **126** 2 43 S 36 35 E
Longiram **102** 0 5 S 115 45 E
Longkin **98** 25 39N 96 22 E
Longlac **150** 49 45N 86 25W
Longlier **47** 49 52N 5 27 E
Longling **99** 24 42N 98 58 E
Longmont **158** 40 10N 105 4W
Longnawan **102** 21 50N 114 55 E
Longobucco **65** 39 27N 16 37 E
Longone, R. **117** 10 0N 15 40 E
Longreach **138** 23 28 S 144 14 E
Longridge **32** 53 50N 2 37W
Long's Peak **160** 40 20N 105 50W
Longside **37** 57 30N 1 57W
Longton, Austral. **138** 21 0 S 145 55 E
Longton, Lancs., U.K. **32** 53 43N 2 48W
Longton, Stafford, U.K. **32** 53 00N 2 8W
Longtown **32** 55 1N 2 59W
Longué **42** 47 22N 0 8W
Longueau **42** 49 52N 2 22 E
Longuyon **43** 49 27N 5 35 E
Longview, Can. **152** 50 32N 114 10W
Longview, Tex., U.S.A. **159** 32 30N 94 45W
Longview, Wash., U.S.A. **160** 46 9N 122 58W
Longvilly **47** 50 2N 5 50 E
Longwy **43** 49 30N 5 45 E
Lonigo **63** 45 23N 11 22 E
Loning **106** 34 28N 111 42 E
Löningen **48** 54 43N 7 44 E
Lonja, R. **63** 45 30N 16 40 E
Lonkor Tso **95** 32 40N 83 15 E
Lonoke **159** 34 48N 91 57W
Lonouaille **44** 46 30N 1 35 E
Lons-le-Saunier **43** 46 40N 5 31 E
Lønsdal **74** 66 46N 15 26 E
Lønstrup **73** 57 29N 9 47 E
Looc **103** 12 20N 112 5 E
Lookout, C., Can. **150** 55 18N 83 56W
Lookout, C., U.S.A. **157** 34 30N 76 30W
Lookout, Pt. **162** 38 2N 76 21W
Loolmalasin, mt. **126** 3 0 S 35 53 E
Loomis **153** 49 15N 108 45W
Loon L. **153** 44 50N 77 15W
Loon Lake **153** 54 2N 109 10W
Loon-op-Zand **47** 51 38N 5 5 E
Loon, R., Alta., Can. **152** 57 8N 115 3W
Loon, R., Man., Can. **153** 55 53N 101 59W
Loongana **137** 30 52 S 127 5 E
Loop Hd. **39** 52 34N 9 55W
Loosduinen **46** 52 3N 4 14 E
Lop Buri **100** 14 48N 100 37 E
Lop Nor **105** 40 20N 90 10 E
Lopare **66** 44 39N 18 46 E
Lopatin **83** 43 50N 47 35 E
Lopatina, G. **77** 50 0N 143 30 E
Lopaye **123** 6 37N 33 40 E
Lopera **57** 37 56N 4 14W
Lopez **162** 41 27N 76 20W
Lopez C. **124** 0 47 S 8 40 E
Lop'ing, Kiangsi, China **109** 28 57N 117 5 E
Lop'ing, Yunnan, China **108** 24 56N 104 20 E
Lopodi **123** 5 5N 33 15 E
Loppem **47** 51 9N 3 12 E
Loppersum **46** 53 20N 6 44 E
Lopphavet **74** 70 27N 21 15 E
Lora Cr. **139** 28 10 S 135 22 E
Lora del Río **57** 37 39N 5 33W
Lora, La **56** 42 45N 4 0W
Lora, R. **93** 32 0N 67 15 E
Lorain **156** 41 20N 82 5W
Loralai **94** 30 29N 68 30 E
Lorca **59** 37 41N 1 42W
Lord Howe I. **130** 31 33 S 159 6 E
Lordsburg **161** 32 15N 108 45W
Lorengau **135** 2 1 S 147 15 E
Loreto, Brazil **170** 7 5 S 45 30W
Loreto, Italy **63** 43 26N 13 36 E
Loreto, Mexico **164** 26 1N 111 21W
Loreto Aprutina **63** 42 24N 13 59 E
Lorgues **45** 43 28N 6 22 E
Lorica **174** 9 14N 75 49W
Lorient **42** 47 45N 3 23W
Lorne, Austral. **140** 38 33 S 143 59 E
Lorne, U.K. **34** 56 26N 5 10W
Lorne, Firth of **34** 56 20N 5 40W
Lörrach **49** 47 36N 7 38 E
Lorraine **43** 49 0N 6 0 E
Lorrainville **150** 47 21N 79 23W
Los Alamos, Calif., U.S.A. **163** 34 44N 120 17W
Los Alamos, N. Mex., U.S.A. **161** 35 57N 106 17W
Los Altos **163** 37 23N 122 7W
Los Andes **172** 32 50 S 70 40W
Los Ángeles **172** 37 28 S 72 23W
Los Angeles **163** 34 0N 118 10W
Los Angeles Aqueduct **163** 35 25N 118 0W
Los Banos **163** 37 8N 120 56W
Los Barrios **57** 36 11N 5 30W
Los Blancos, Argent. **172** 23 45 S 62 30W
Los Blancos, Spain **59** 37 38N 0 49W
Los Gatos **163** 37 15N 121 59W
Los, Îles de **120** 9 30N 13 50W
Los Lamentos **164** 30 36N 105 50W
Los Lunas **161** 34 55N 106 47W
Los Mochis **164** 25 45N 109 5W
Los Monegros **58** 41 29N 0 3W
Los Muertos, Punta de **59** 36 57N 1 54W
Los Olivos **163** 34 40N 120 7W
Los Palacios **166** 22 35N 83 15W
Los Palacios y Villafranca **57** 37 10N 5 55W
Los Reyes **164** 19 21N 99 7W
Los Roques, Is. **167** 11 50N 66 45W
Los Santos de Maimona **57** 38 37N 6 22W
Los Testigos, Is. **174** 11 23N 63 6W
Los Vilos **172** 32 0 S 71 30W
Los Yébenes **57** 39 36N 3 55W
Loshan, Honan, China **109** 32 12N 114 32 E
Loshan, Szechwan, China **108** 29 34N 103 44 E
Loshkalakh **77** 62 45N 147 20 E
Lošinj, I. **63** 44 55N 14 45 E
Losser **46** 52 16N 7 1 E
Lossiemouth **37** 57 43N 3 17W
Lostwithiel **30** 50 24N 4 41W
Losuia **135** 8 30 S 151 4 E
Lot □ **44** 44 39N 1 40 E
Lot-et-Garonne □ **44** 44 22N 0 30 E
Lot, R. **44** 44 18N 0 20 E
Lota, Austral. **108** 27 28 S 153 11 E
Lota, Chile **172** 37 5 S 73 10W
Løten **71** 60 51N 11 21 E
Lothian, (□) **26** 55 55N 3 35W
Lothiers **43** 46 42N 1 33 E
Lotien **108** 25 29N 106 39 E
Lot'ien **109** 30 47N 115 20 E
Lot'ing **107** 39 26N 118 56 E
Loting **109** 22 46N 111 34 E
Lötschberg **49** 46 25N 7 53 E
Lotschbergtunnel **50** 46 26N 7 43 E
Lottefors **72** 61 25N 16 24 E
Lotung, China **100** 18 44N 109 9 E
Lotung, Taiwan **109** 24 41N 121 46 E
Lotz'u **108** 25 19N 102 18 E
Lotzukou **107** 43 44N 130 20 E
Lotzwil **50** 47 12N 7 48 E
Loudéac **42** 48 11N 2 47W
Loudon **157** 35 41N 84 22W
Loudun **42** 47 0N 0 5 E
Loué **42** 47 59N 0 9W
Loue, R. **42** 47 4N 6 10 E
Louga **120** 15 45N 16 5W
Loughborough **28** 52 46N 1 11W
Loughbrickland **38** 54 19N 6 19W
Loughmore **39** 52 45N 7 50W
Loughor **31** 51 39N 4 5W
Loughrea **39** 53 11N 8 33W
Loughros More, B. **38** 54 48N 8 30W
Louhans **45** 46 38N 5 12 E
Louis Gentil **118** 32 16N 8 31W
Louis Trichardt **125** 23 0 S 29 55 E
Louis XIV, Pte. **150** 54 37N 79 45W
Louisa **156** 38 5N 82 40W
Louisbourg **151** 45 55N 60 0W
Louisbourg Nat. Historic Park **151** 45 58N 60 20W
Louisburgh **38** 53 46N 9 49W
Louise I. **152** 52 55N 131 40W
Louiseville **150** 46 20N 73 0W
Louisiade Arch. **135** 11 10 S 153 0 E
Louisiana **158** 39 25N 91 0W
Louisiana □ **159** 30 50N 92 0W
Louisville, Ky., U.S.A. **156** 38 15N 85 45W
Louisville, Miss., U.S.A. **159** 33 7N 89 3W
Loulay **44** 46 3N 0 30W
Loulé **57** 37 9N 8 0W
Lount L. **153** 50 10N 94 20W
Louny **52** 50 20N 13 48 E
Loup City **158** 41 19N 98 57W
Loupe, La **42** 48 29N 1 1 E
Lourdes **44** 43 6N 0 3W
Lourdes-de-Blanc-Sablon **151** 51 24N 57 12W
Lourenço-Marques, B. de **129** 25 50 S 32 45 E
Lourenço-Marques = Maputo **129** 25 58 S 32 32 E
Loures **57** 38 50N 9 9W
Lourinhã **57** 39 14N 9 17W
Louroux Béconnais, Le **42** 47 30N 0 55W
Lousã **56** 40 7N 8 14W
Louth, Austral. **141** 30 30 S 145 8 E
Louth, Ireland **38** 53 47N 6 33W
Louth, U.K. **33** 53 23N 0 0W
Louth □ **38** 53 55N 6 30W
Louti **109** 27 45N 111 58 E
Loutrá Aidhipsoú **69** 38 54N 23 2 E
Loutráki **69** 38 0N 22 57 E
Louveigné **47** 50 32N 5 42 E
Louvière, La **47** 50 27N 4 10 E
Louviers **42** 49 12N 1 10 E
Lovat, R. **80** 56 30N 31 20 E
Love **153** 53 29N 104 10W
Loveland **158** 40 27N 105 4W
Lovell **160** 44 51N 108 20W
Lovelock **160** 40 17N 118 25W
Lóvere **62** 45 50N 10 4 E
Loviisa = Lovisa **75** 60 31N 26 20 E
Loving **159** 32 17N 104 4W
Lovington **159** 33 0N 103 20W
Lovios **56** 41 55N 8 4W
Lovisa (Loviisa) **75** 60 28N 26 12 E
Lovosice **52** 50 30N 14 2 E
Lovran **63** 45 18N 14 15 E
Lovrin **66** 45 58N 20 48 E
Lövstabukten **72** 60 35N 17 45 E
Low Pt. **137** 32 25 S 127 25 E
Low Rocky Pt. **133** 42 59 S 145 29 E
Lowa **124** 1 25 S 25 47 E
Lowa, R. **126** 1 15 S 27 40 E
Lowell **162** 42 38N 71 19W
Lower Arrow L. **152** 49 40N 118 5W
Lower Austria = Niederösterreich **52** 48 25N 15 40 E
Lower Beeding **29** 51 2N 0 15W
Lower Hermitage **109** 34 49 S 138 46 E
Lower Hutt **142** 41 10 S 174 55 E
Lower L. **160** 41 17N 120 3W
Lower Lake **160** 38 56N 122 36W
Lower Neguac **151** 47 20N 65 10W
Lower Post **152** 59 58N 128 30W
Lower Sackville **151** 44 45N 63 43W
Lower Saxony = Niedersachsen **48** 52 45N 9 0 E
Lower Seal, L. **150** 56 30N 74 23W
Lower Woolgar **138** 19 47 S 143 27 E
Lowes Water L. **32** 54 35N 3 23W
Lowestoft **29** 52 29N 1 44 E
Lowick **35** 55 38N 1 57W
Łowicz **54** 52 6N 19 55 E
Lowther Hills **35** 55 20N 3 40W
Lowville **162** 43 48N 75 30W
Loxton **140** 34 28 S 140 31 E
Loyal L. **37** 58 24N 4 20W
Loyalty Is. **130** 21 0 S 167 30 E
Loyang **106** 34 41N 112 28 E
Loyauté, Îles **130** 21 0 S 167 30 E
Loyeh **108** 24 48N 106 34 E
Loyev **80** 57 7N 30 40 E
Loyoro **126** 3 22N 34 14 E
Loyüan **109** 26 30N 119 33 E
Loz **63** 45 43N 14 14 E
Lozère □ **44** 44 35N 3 30 E
Loznica **66** 44 32N 19 14 E
Lozovaya **82** 49 0N 36 27 E
Lozva, R. **84** 59 36N 62 20 E
Lu **98** 45 0N 8 29 E
Lü-Tao **109** 22 47N 121 20 E
Luabo **147** 18 30 S 36 10 E
Luacano **124** 11 15 S 21 37 E
Lualaba, R. **126** 5 45 S 26 50 E
Luampa **127** 15 4 S 24 20 E
Luan **103** 6 10N 124 25 E
Luan Chau **100** 21 38N 103 24 E
Luan Ho, R. **107** 39 25N 119 15 E
Luanch'eng **106** 37 53N 114 39 E
Luanda **124** 8 58 S 13 9 E
Luang Doi **100** 18 30N 101 0 E
Luang Prabang **100** 19 45N 102 10 E
Luang Thale **101** 7 30N 100 15 E
Luangwa, R. **125** 14 25 S 30 25 E
Luangwa Val. **127** 13 30 S 31 30 E
Luanho **107** 40 56N 117 42 E
Luanhsien **107** 39 45N 118 44 E
Luanping **107** 40 56N 117 42 E
Luanshya **127** 13 3 S 28 28 E
Luapula □ **127** 11 0 S 29 0 E
Luapula, R. **127** 12 0 S 28 50 E
Luarca **56** 43 32N 6 32W
Luashi **127** 10 50 S 23 36 E
Lubalo **124** 9 10 S 19 15 E
Luban **54** 51 5N 15 15 E
Lubana, Osero **80** 56 45N 27 0 E
Lubang Is. **103** 13 50N 120 12 E
Lubartów **54** 51 28N 22 42 E
Lubawa **54** 53 30N 19 48 E
Lubban **90** 32 9N 35 14 E
Lubbeek **47** 50 54N 4 50 E
Lübben **48** 51 56N 13 54 E
Lübbenau **48** 51 49N 13 59 E
Lubbock **159** 33 40N 102 0W
Lubcroy **37** 57 58N 4 47W
Lübeck **48** 53 52N 10 41 E
Lübecker Bucht **48** 54 3N 11 0 E
Lubefu **126** 4 47 S 24 27 E
Lubefu, R. **126** 4 47 S 24 27 E
Lubero = Luofu **126** 0 1 S 29 15 E
Lubicon L. **152** 56 23N 115 56W
Lubien Kujawski **54** 52 23N 19 9 E
Lubin **54** 51 24N 16 11 E
Lublin **54** 51 12N 22 38 E
Lublin □ **54** 51 5N 22 30 E
Lubliniec **54** 50 43N 18 45 E
Lubny **80** 50 3N 32 58 E
Lubok Antu **102** 1 3N 111 50 E
Lubon **54** 52 21N 16 51 E
Lubongola **126** 2 35 S 27 50 E
Lubotin **53** 49 17N 20 53 E
Lubraniec **54** 52 33N 18 50 E
Lubsko **54** 51 45N 14 57 E
Lübtheen **48** 53 18N 11 4 E
Lubuagan **103** 17 21N 121 10 E
Lubudi **124** 6 50 S 21 20 E
Lubudi, R. **127** 9 30 S 25 0 E
Lubuhanbilik **102** 2 33N 100 14 E
Lubuk Linggau **102** 3 15 S 102 55 E
Lubuk Sikaping **102** 0 10N 100 15 E
Lubumbashi **127** 11 32 S 27 28 E
Lubunda **126** 5 12 S 26 41 E
Lubungu **127** 14 35 S 26 24 E
Lubutu **126** 0 45 S 26 30 E
Luc An Chau **100** 22 6N 104 43 E
Luc-en-Diois **45** 44 36N 5 28 E
Luc, Le **45** 43 23N 6 21 E
Lucan **38** 53 21N 6 27W
Lucania, Mt. **147** 60 48N 141 25W
Lucca **62** 43 50N 10 30 E
Luccens **50** 46 43N 6 51 E
Luce Bay **138** 54 45N 4 48W
Lucea **166** 18 25N 78 10W
Lucedale **157** 30 55N 88 34W
Lucena, Phil. **103** 13 56N 121 37 E
Lucena, Spain **57** 37 27N 4 31W
Lucena del Cid **58** 40 9N 0 17W
Lučenec **53** 48 18N 19 42 E
Lucera **65** 41 30N 15 20 E
Lucerne = Luzern **51** 47 3N 8 18 E
Lucerne Valley **163** 34 27N 116 57W
Lucero **164** 30 49N 106 30W
Luchai **108** 24 33N 109 48 E
Luchena, R. **59** 37 50N 2 0W
Luch'eng **106** 36 18N 113 15 E
Lucheringo, R. **127** 12 0 S 36 5 E
Luch'i **109** 28 17N 110 10 E
Luchiang, China **109** 31 14N 117 17 E
Luchiang, Taiwan **109** 24 1N 120 22 E
Luchou **108** 28 53N 105 22 E
Lüchow **48** 52 58N 11 8 E
Luch'uan **109** 22 20N 110 14 E
Lucindale **93** 36 59 S 140 23 E
Lucira **125** 14 0 S 12 35 E
Luckau **48** 51 50N 13 43 E
Luckenwalde **48** 52 5N 13 11 E
Lucknow **95** 26 50N 81 0 E
Lucomagno, Paso del **51** 46 34N 8 49 E
Luçon **44** 46 28N 1 10W
Luda Kamchiya, R. **67** 42 50N 27 0 E
Ludbreg **63** 46 15N 16 38 E
Lüdenscheid **48** 51 13N 7 37 E
Lüderitz **128** 26 41 S 15 8 E
Ludewa □ **127** 10 0 S 34 50 E
Ludgershall **28** 51 15N 1 38W
Ludgvan **30** 50 9N 5 30W
Ludhiana **94** 30 57N 75 56 E
Lüdinghausen **48** 51 46N 7 28 E
Ludington **156** 43 58N 86 27W
Ludlow, U.K. **28** 52 23N 2 42W
Ludlow, Calif., U.S.A. **163** 34 43N 116 10W
Ludlow, Vt., U.S.A. **162** 43 25N 72 40W
Luduş **70** 46 29N 24 5 E
Ludvika **72** 60 8N 15 14 E
Ludwigsburg **49** 48 53N 9 11 E
Ludwigshafen **49** 49 27N 8 27 E
Ludwigslust **48** 53 19N 11 28 E
Ludza **80** 56 32N 27 43 E
Lue **141** 32 38 S 149 50 E
Luebo **124** 5 21 S 21 17 E
Lüehyang **106** 33 20N 106 3 E
Lueki **126** 3 20 S 25 48 E
Luena, Zaîre **127** 9 28 S 25 43 E
Luena, Zambia **127** 10 40 S 30 25 E
Luepa **174** 5 43N 61 31W
Lufeng, Kwangtung, China **109** 23 2N 115 37 E
Lufeng, Yunnan, China **108** 25 10N 102 5 E
Lufira R. **124** 9 30 S 27 0 E
Lufkin **159** 31 25N 94 40W
Lufupa **127** 10 37 S 24 50 E
Luga **80** 58 40N 29 55 E
Luga, R. **80** 59 5N 28 30 E
Lugano **51** 46 0N 8 57 E
Lugano, L. di **51** 46 0N 9 0 E

Lugansk McIlwraith Ra

Lugansk = Voroshilovgrad 83 48 35N 39 29 E
Lugard's Falls 126 3 6S 38 41 E
Lugela 127 16 25S 36 43 E
Lugenda, R. 127 12 35S 36 50 E
Lugh Ganana 91 3 48N 42 40 E
Lugnaquilla, Mt. 39 52 48N 6 28W
Lugnvik 72 62 56N 17 55 E
Lugo, Italy 63 44 25N 11 53 E
Lugo, Spain 56 43 2N 7 35W
Lugo □ 56 43 0N 7 30W
Lugoj 66 45 42N 21 57 E
Lugones 56 43 26N 5 50W
Lugovoy 76 43 0N 72 20 E
Lugovoye 85 42 55N 72 43 E
Lugwardine 28 52 4N 2 38W
Luhe, R. 48 53 7N 10 0 E
Luhsi, Yunan, China 108 24 31N 103 46 E
Luhsi, Yunnan, China 108 24 27N 98 36 E
Luhuo 108 31 24N 100 41 E
Lui 106 33 52N 115 28 E
Luiana 125 17 25S 22 30E
Luichart L. 37 57 36N 4 43W
Luichow Pen. = Leichou Pantao 108 20 40N 110 5 E
Luing I. 34 56 15N 5 40W
Luino 62 46 0N 8 42 E
Luís 164 26 36N 109 11W
Luís Correia 170 3 0S 41 35W
Luís Gomes 171 6 25S 38 23W
Luís Gonçalves 170 5 37S 50 25W
Luisa 124 7 40S 22 30 E
Luiza 124 7 40S 22 30 E
Luizi 126 6 0S 27 25 E
Luján 172 34 45S 59 5W
Lukanga Swamp 127 14 30S 27 40 E
Lukenie, R. 124 3 0S 18 50 E
Lukhisaral 95 27 11N 86 5 E
Lukolela 124 1 10S 17 12 E
Lukosi 127 18 30S 26 30 E
Lukovit 67 43 13N 24 11 E
Lukoyanov 81 55 2N 44 20 E
Lukuhu 108 27 46N 100 50 E
Lukulu 125 14 35S 23 25 E
Lula 126 0 30N 25 10 E
Lule, R. 74 65 35N 22 10 E
Luleå 74 65 35N 22 10 E
Lüleburgaz 67 41 23N 27 28 E
Luliang 108 25 3N 103 39 E
Luling 159 29 45N 97 40W
Lulonga, R. 124 1 0N 19 0 E
Lulua, R. 124 6 30S 22 50 E
Luluabourg = Kananga 124 5 55S 22 18 E
Lulung 107 39 55N 118 57 E
Lumai 125 13 20S 21 25 E
Lumajang 103 8 8S 113 16 E
Lumbala, Angola 125 12 36S 22 30 E
Lumbala, Angola 125 14 18S 21 18 E
Lumberton, Miss., U.S.A. 159 31 4N 89 28W
Lumberton, N. Mex., U.S.A. 161 36 58N 106 57W
Lumberton, N.C., U.S.A. 157 34 37N 78 59W
Lumbres 43 50 40N 2 5 E
Lumbwa 126 0 12S 35 28 E
Lumby 152 50 10N 118 50W
Lumding 98 25 46N 93 10 E
Lumege 125 11 45S 20 50 E
Lumeyen 123 4 55N 33 28 E
Lumi 135 3 30S 142 2 E
Lummen 47 50 59N 5 12 E
Lumphanan 37 57 8N 2 41W
Lumsden, N.Z. 143 45 44S 168 27 E
Lumsden, U.K. 37 57 16N 2 51W
Lumut 101 4 13N 100 37 E
Lumut, Tg. 102 3 50S 105 58 E
Lunan 108 24 47N 103 16 E
Lunan B. 37 56 40N 2 25W
Lunavada 94 23 8N 73 37 E
Lunca 70 47 22N 25 1 E
Lund, Norway 74 68 42N 18 9 E
Lund, Sweden 73 55 41N 13 12 E
Lund, U.S.A. 160 38 53N 115 0W
Lunda 124 9 40S 20 12 E
Lundazi 125 12 20S 33 7 E
Lunde 71 59 17N 9 5 E
Lunderskov 73 55 29N 9 19 E
Lundi, R. 127 21 15S 31 25 E
Lundu 102 1 40N 109 50 E
Lundy, I. 30 51 10N 4 41W
Lune, R. 32 54 0N 2 51W
Lüneburg 48 53 15N 10 23 E
Lüneburg Heath = Lüneburger Heide 48 53 0N 10 0 E
Lüneburger Heide 48 53 0N 10 0 E
Lunel 45 43 39N 4 9 E
Lünen 48 51 36N 7 31 E
Lunenburg 151 44 22N 64 18W
Lunéville 43 48 36N 6 30 E
Lung Chiang, R. 108 24 30N 109 15 E
Lunga, R. 127 13 0S 26 33 E
Lungan 108 23 11N 107 41 E
Lungch'ang 108 29 20N 105 19 E
Lungch'ih 108 29 25N 103 24 E
Lungchou 108 22 24N 106 50 E
Lungch'üan 109 28 5N 119 7 E
Lungch'uan, Kwangtung, China 109 24 6N 115 15 E
Lungch'uan, Yunnan, China 108 24 16N 97 58 E
Lungern 50 46 48N 8 10 E
Lungholt 74 63 35N 18 10 E
Lunghsi 106 35 3N 104 38 E
Lunghsien 106 34 47N 107 0 E
Lunghua 107 41 18N 117 42 E
Lunghui 109 27 18N 110 52 E
Lungi Airport 120 8 40N 16 47 E
Lungk'ou 107 37 42N 120 21 E
Lungkuan 106 40 45N 115 43 E
Lungkukang 108 32 18N 99 7 E
Lungleh 98 22 55N 92 45 E
Lungli 108 26 27N 106 58 E
Lunglin 108 24 43N 105 26 E
Lungling 108 24 38N 98 35 E
Lungmen 109 23 44N 114 15 E
Lungming 108 23 4N 107 14 E
Lungnan 109 24 54N 114 47 E
Lungngo 98 21 57N 93 36 E
Lungshan 108 29 27N 109 23 E
Lungsheng 109 25 48N 110 0 E
Lungte 106 35 38N 106 6 E
Lungyen 109 25 9N 117 0 E
Lungyu 109 29 2N 119 10 E
Luni 94 26 0N 73 6 E
Luni, R. 94 25 40N 72 20 E
Luninets 80 52 15N 27 0 E
Luning 163 38 30N 118 10W
Lunino 81 53 35N 45 6 E
Lunna Ness 36 60 27N 1 4W
Lunner 71 60 19N 10 35 E
Lunsemfwa Falls 127 14 30S 29 6 E
Lunsemfwa, R. 127 14 50S 30 10 E
Lunteren 46 52 5N 5 38 E
Luofu 126 0 1S 29 15 E
Luozi 124 4 54S 14 0 E
Lupeni 70 45 21N 23 13 E
Łupków 53 49 15N 22 4 E
Lupundu 127 14 18S 26 45 E
Luque, Parag. 172 25 19S 57 25W
Luque, Spain 57 37 35N 4 16W
Luray 156 38 39N 78 26W
Lure 43 47 40N 6 30 E
Luremo 124 8 30S 17 50 E
Lurgainn L. 36 58 1N 5 15W
Lurgan 38 54 28N 6 20W
Luristan 92 33 20N 47 0 E
Lusaka 127 15 28S 28 16 E
Lusambo 126 4 58S 23 28 E
Luseland 153 52 5N 109 24W
Lushan, Honan, China 106 33 45N 113 10 E
Lushan, Kweichow, China 108 26 33N 107 58 E
Lushan, Szechwan, China 108 30 10N 102 59 E
Lushih 106 34 4N 110 2 E
Lushnja 68 40 55N 19 41 E
Lushoto 126 4 47S 38 20 E
Lushoto □ 126 4 45S 38 20 E
Lushui 108 25 51N 98 55 E
Lüshun 107 38 48N 121 16 E
Lusignan 44 46 26N 0 8 E
Lusigny-sur-Barse 43 48 16N 4 15 E
Lusk, Ireland 38 53 32N 6 10W
Lusk, U.S.A. 158 42 47N 104 27W
Luss 34 56 6N 4 40W
Lussac-les-Châteaux 44 46 24N 0 43 E
Lussanvira 171 20 42S 51 7W
Lüta 107 38 55N 121 40 E
Luti 108 7 14S 157 0 E
Luting 108 29 56N 102 12 E
Luton 29 51 53N 0 24W
Lutong 102 4 30N 114 0 E
Lutry 50 46 31N 6 42 E
Lutsk 80 50 50N 25 15 E
Lutterworth 28 52 28N 1 12W
Luverne 158 43 35N 96 12W
Luvua 127 8 48S 25 17 E
Luwegu, R. 127 9 30S 36 20 E
Luwingu, Mt. 124 10 15S 30 2 E
Luwuk 103 10 0S 122 40 E
Luxembourg 47 49 37N 6 9 E
Luxembourg □ 47 49 58N 5 30 E
Luxembourg ■ 47 50 0N 6 0 E
Luxeuil-les-Bains 43 47 49N 6 24 E
Luxor = El Uqsur 122 25 41N 32 38 E
Luy de Béarn, R. 44 43 39N 0 48W
Luy de France, R. 44 43 39N 0 48W
Luy, R. 44 43 39N 1 9W
Luyksgestel 47 51 17N 5 20 E
Luz, Brazil 171 19 48S 45 40W
Luz, France 44 42 53N 0 1 E
Luzern 51 47 3N 8 18 E
Luzern □ 50 47 2N 7 55 E
Luzerne 162 41 17N 75 54W
Luziânia 171 16 20S 48 0W
Luzilândia 170 3 28S 42 22W
Luzon, I. 103 16 0N 121 0 E
Luzy 43 46 47N 3 58 E
Luzzi 65 39 28N 16 17 E
Lvov 80 49 40N 24 0 E
Lwówek 54 52 28N 16 10 E
Lwówek Śląski 54 51 7N 15 38 E
Lyakhovichi 80 53 2N 26 32 E
Lyakhovskiye, Ostrova 77 73 40N 141 0 E
Lyaki 83 40 34N 47 22 E
Lyall Mt. 142 45 16S 167 32 E
* Lyallpur 94 31 30N 73 5 E
Lyalya, R. 84 59 9N 61 29 E
Lyaskovets 67 43 6N 25 44 E
Lybster 37 58 18N 3 16W
Lychen 48 53 13N 13 20 E
Lyckeby 73 56 12N 15 37 E
Lycksele 74 64 38N 18 40 E
Lydd 29 50 57N 0 56 E
Lydda = Lod 90 31 57N 34 54 E
*Renamed Faisalabad
Lydenburg 129 25 10S 30 29 E
Lydford 30 50 38N 4 7W
Lydham 28 52 31N 2 59W
Lyell 143 41 48S 172 4 E
Lyell I. 152 52 40N 131 35W
Lyell, oilfield 19 60 55N 1 12 E
Lyell Range 143 41 38S 172 20 E
Lygnern 73 57 30N 12 15 E
Lykens 162 40 34N 76 42W
Lykling 71 59 42N 5 12 E
Lyman 160 41 24N 110 15W
Lyme Bay 23 50 36N 2 55W
Lyme Regis 30 50 44N 2 57W
Lyminge 29 51 7N 1 6 E
Lymington 28 50 46N 1 32W
Lymm 32 53 23N 2 30W
Lympne 29 51 4N 1 2 E
Lynchburg 156 37 23N 79 10W
Lynd, R. 138 16 28S 143 18 E
Lynd Ra. 139 25 30S 149 20 E
Lynden 160 48 56N 122 32W
Lyndhurst, N.S.W., Austral. 138 33 41S 149 2 E
Lyndhurst, Queens., Austral. 138 19 12S 144 20 E
Lyndhurst, S. Australia, Austral. 139 30 15S 138 18 E
Lyndhurst, U.K. 28 50 53N 1 33W
Lyndon, R. 137 23 29S 114 6 E
Lyneham 28 51 30N 1 57W
Lyngdal, Agder, Norway 71 58 8N 7 7 E
Lyngdal, Buskerud, Norway 71 59 54N 9 32 E
Lynher Reef 136 15 27S 121 55 E
Lynmouth 30 51 14N 3 50W
Lynn 162 42 28N 70 57W
Lynn Canal 152 58 50N 135 20W
Lynn L. 153 56 30N 101 40W
Lynn Lake 153 56 51N 101 3W
Lynton 30 51 14N 3 50W
Lyntupy 80 55 4N 26 23 E
Lynx L. 153 62 25N 106 15W
Lyø 73 55 3N 10 9 E
Lyon 45 45 46N 4 50 E
Lyonnais 45 45 45N 4 15 E
Lyons, Colo., U.S.A. 158 40 17N 105 15W
Lyons, Ga., U.S.A. 157 32 10N 82 15W
Lyons, Kans., U.S.A. 158 38 24N 98 13W
Lyons, N.Y., U.S.A. 162 43 3N 77 0W
Lyons = Lyon 45 45 46N 4 50 E
Lyons Falls 162 43 37N 75 22W
Lyons, R. 137 25 2S 115 9 E
Lyrestad 73 58 48N 14 4 E
Lysá 52 50 11N 14 51 E
Lysekil 73 58 17N 11 26 E
Lyskovo 81 56 0N 45 3 E
Lyss 50 47 4N 7 19 E
Lysva 84 58 07N 57 49 E
Lysvik 72 60 1N 13 9 E
Lytchett Minster 28 50 44N 2 3W
Lytham St. Anne's 32 53 45N 2 58W
Lythe 33 54 30N 0 40W
Lytle 159 29 14N 98 46W
Lyttelton 143 43 35S 172 44 E
Lytton 152 50 13N 121 31W
Lyuban 80 59 16N 31 18 E
Lyubim 81 58 20N 40 50 E
Lyubimets 67 41 50N 26 5 E
Lyuboml 81 51 10N 24 2 E
Lyubotin 82 50 0N 36 4 E
Lyubytino 80 58 50N 33 16 E
Lyudinovo 80 53 52N 34 28 E

M

Ma, R. 100 19 47N 105 56 E
Ma'ad 90 32 37N 35 36 E
Maam Cross 38 53 28N 9 32W
Maamba 128 17 17S 26 28 E
Ma'an 92 30 12N 35 44 E
Maanshan 109 31 40N 118 30 E
Maarheeze 47 51 19N 5 36 E
Maarianhamina 75 60 5N 19 55 E
Maarn 47 52 3N 5 22 E
Maarssen 46 52 9N 5 2 E
Maartensdijk 46 52 9N 5 10 E
Maas 38 54 49N 8 21W
Maas, R. 47 51 48N 4 55 E
Maasbracht 47 51 9N 5 54 E
Maasbree 47 51 22N 6 3 E
Maasdan 46 51 48N 4 34 E
Maasdijk 46 51 58N 4 13 E
Maaseik 47 51 6N 5 45 E
Maasin 102 10 5N 124 55 E
Maasland 46 51 57N 4 16 E
Maasniel 47 51 12N 6 1 E
Maassluis 47 51 56N 4 16 E
Maastricht 47 50 50N 5 40 E
Maatin-es-Sarra 117 21 45N 22 0 E
Maave 129 21 4S 34 47 E
Mabein 98 23 29N 96 37 E
Mabel L. 152 50 35N 118 43W
Mabel, oilfield 19 58 6N 1 36 E
Mabenge 126 4 15N 24 12 E
Mablethorpe 33 53 21N 0 14 E
Mabrouk 121 19 29N 1 15W
Mabton 127 46 13N 120 1W
Mac Bac 101 9 46N 106 7 E
Mc Grath 147 62 58N 155 40W
Macachin 172 37 10S 63 43W
Macadam Ra. 136 14 40S 129 50 E
Macaé 173 22 20S 41 55W
Macaguane 174 6 35N 71 43W
Macaíba 170 5 15S 35 21W
Macajuba 171 12 9S 40 22W
McAlester 159 34 57N 95 40W
Macamic 150 48 45N 79 0W
Macão 57 39 35N 7 59W
Macao = Macau ■ 109 22 16N 113 35 E
Macapá 175 0 5N 51 10W
Macarani 171 15 33S 40 24W
Macarena, Serranía de la 174 2 45N 73 55W
Macarthur 140 38 5S 142 0 E
McArthur, R. 136 16 45S 136 0 E
McArthur River 138 16 27S 137 7 E
Macau 170 5 0S 36 40W
Macau ■ 109 22 16N 113 35 E
Macaúbas 171 13 2S 42 42W
McBride 152 53 20N 120 10W
McCamey 159 31 8N 102 15W
McCammon 160 42 41N 112 11W
McCarthy 147 61 25N 143 0W
McCauley I. 152 53 40N 130 15W
Macclesfield 32 53 16N 2 9W
McClintock 153 57 50N 94 10W
McClintock Chan. 148 72 0N 102 0W
McClintock Ra., Mts. 136 18 44S 127 38 E
McCloud 160 41 14N 122 5W
McCluer Gulf 103 2 20S 133 0 E
McCluer I. 136 11 5S 133 0 E
McClure, L. 163 37 35N 120 16W
McClusky 158 47 30N 100 31W
McComb 159 31 20N 90 30W
McConnell Creek 152 56 53N 126 30W
McCook 158 40 15N 100 35W
McCulloch 152 49 45N 119 15W
McCusker, R. 153 55 32N 108 39W
McDame 152 59 44N 128 59W
McDermitt 160 42 0N 117 45W
McDonald I. 11 54 0S 73 0 E
Macdonald L. 137 23 30S 129 0 E
Macdonald Ra. 136 15 35S 124 50 E
Macdonnell Ranges 136 23 40S 133 0 E
McDouall Peak 139 29 51S 134 55 E
Macdougall L. 148 66 00N 98 27W
McDougalls Well 140 31 8S 141 15 E
MacDowell L. 150 52 15N 92 45W
Macduff 37 57 40N 2 30W
Mace 150 48 55N 80 0W
Maceda 56 42 16N 7 39W
Macedo da Cavaleiros 124 11 25S 16 45 E
Macedo de Cavaleiros 56 41 31N 6 57W
Macedonia = Makedonija 66 41 53N 21 40 E
Macedonia = Makhedonia 68 40 39N 22 0 E
Maceió 170 9 40S 35 41W
Maceira 57 39 41N 8 55W
Macenta 120 8 35N 9 20W
Macerata 63 43 19N 13 28 E
McFarland 163 35 41N 119 14W
Macfarlane, L. 140 32 0S 136 40 E
McFarlane, R. 153 59 12N 107 58W
McGehee 159 33 40N 91 25W
McGill 160 39 27N 114 50W
Macgillycuddy's Reeks, mts. 39 52 2N 9 45W
McGraw 162 42 35N 76 4W
MacGregor 153 49 57N 98 48W
McGregor, Iowa, U.S.A. 158 42 58N 91 15W
McGregor, Minn., U.S.A. 158 46 37N 93 17W
McGregor, R. 152 55 10N 122 0W
McGregor Ra. 139 27 0S 142 45 E
Mach 93 29 50N 67 20 E
Machacalis 171 17 5S 40 45W
Machachi 174 0 30S 78 15W
Machado, R. = Jiparana 174 8 45S 62 20W
Machagai 172 26 56S 60 2W
Machakos 126 1 30S 37 15 E
Machakos □ 126 1 30S 37 15 E
Machala 174 3 10S 79 50W
Machanga 129 20 59S 35 0 E
Machar Marshes 123 9 28N 33 21 E
Machattie, L. 138 24 50S 139 48 E
Machava 129 25 54S 32 28 E
Machece 127 19 15S 35 32 E
Machecoul 42 47 0N 1 49W
Machelen 47 50 55N 4 26 E
Mach'eng 109 31 11N 115 2 E
Mcherrah 118 27 0N 4 30W
Machevna 77 61 20N 172 20 E
Machezo, mt. 57 39 21N 4 20W
Machiang 108 26 30N 107 35 E
Mach'iaoho 107 44 41N 130 32 E
Machias 151 44 40N 67 34W
Machichaco, Cabo 58 43 28N 2 47W
Machichi, R. 153 57 3N 92 6W
Machida 111 35 28N 139 23 E
Machilipatnam 99 16 12N 81 12 E
Machilipatnam = Masulipatnam 96 16 12N 131 15 E
Machine, La 43 46 54N 3 27 E
Mchinja 127 9 44S 39 45 E
Mchinji 127 13 47S 32 58 E
Machiques 174 10 4N 72 34W
Machrihanish 34 55 25N 5 42W
Machupicchu 174 13 8S 72 30W
Machynlleth 31 52 36N 3 51W
•Macias Nguema Biyoga 113 3 30N 8 40 E
McIlwraith Ra. 138 13 50S 143 20 E
•Renamed Bioko

Macina **Makgobistad**

Macina 120 14 40N 4 50W
Macina, Canal de 120 13 50N 5 40W
McIntosh 158 45 57N 101 20W
McIntosh L. 153 55 11N 104 41W
MacIntosh Range, Mts. 137 24 45S 121 33E
Macintyre, R. 139 28 37S 149 40E
Macizo Galaico 56 42 30N 7 30W
Mackay, Austral. 138 21 8S 149 11E
Mackay, U.S.A. 160 43 58N 113 37W
Mackay, L. 136 22 30S 129 0E
Mackay, R. 152 57 10N 111 38W
McKay Ra. 137 23 0S 122 30E
McKeesport 156 40 21N 79 50W
Mackenzie 152 55 20N 123 05W
McKenzie 157 36 10N 88 31W
Mackenzie Bay 147 69 0N 137 30W
Mackenzie City = Linden 174 6 0N 58 10W
Mackenzie Highway 152 58 0N 117 15W
Mackenzie Mts. 147 64 0N 128 0W
Mackenzie Plains 143 44 10S 170 25W
Mackenzie, R., Austral. 138 23 38S 149 46E
Mackenzie, R., Can. 148 69 10N 134 20W
McKenzie, R. 160 44 2N 122 30W
•Mackenzie, Terr. 149 61 30N 144 30W
McKerrow L. 143 44 25S 168 5E
Mackinaw City 156 45 47N 84 44W
McKinlay 138 21 16S 141 18E
McKinlay, R. 138 20 50S 141 28E
McKinley, Mt. 147 63 10N 151 0W
McKinley Sea 12 84 0N 10 0W
McKinney 159 33 10N 96 40W
Mackinnon Road 126 3 40S 39 1E
Mackintosh Ra. 137 27 39S 125 32E
McKittrick 163 35 18N 119 39W
Mackmyra 72 60 40N 17 3E
Macksville 141 30 40S 152 56E
McLaren Vale 140 35 13S 138 31E
McLaughlin 158 45 50N 100 50W
Maclean 139 29 26S 153 16E
McLean 159 35 15N 100 35W
McLeansboro 158 38 5N 88 30W
Maclear 129 31 2S 28 23E
Macleay, R. 141 30 56S 153 0E
McLennan 152 55 42N 116 50W
MacLeod, B. 152 62 53N 110 0W
McLeod L. 137 24 9S 113 47E
McLeod, L. 137 24 50S 114 0E
MacLeod Lake 152 54 58N 123 0W
McIlwraith Ra., Mts. 138 13 43S 143 23E
McLoughlin, Mt. 160 42 30N 122 30W
McLure 152 51 2N 120 13W
McMillan L. 159 32 40N 104 20W
McMinnville, Oreg., U.S.A. 160 45 16N 123 11W
McMinnville, Tenn., U.S.A. 157 35 43N 85 45W
McMorran 153 51 19N 108 42W
McMurdo Sd. 13 77 0S 170 0E
McMurray = Fort McMurray 152 56 45N 111 27W
McNary 161 34 4N 109 53W
McNaughton L. 152 52 0N 118 10W
Macnean L. 38 54 19N 7 52W
MacNutt 153 51 5N 101 36W
Macodoene 129 23 32S 35 5E
Macomb 158 40 25N 90 40W
Macomer 64 40 16N 8 48E
Mâcon 45 46 19N 4 50E
Macon, Ga., U.S.A. 157 32 50N 83 37W
Macon, Miss., U.S.A. 157 33 7N 88 31W
Macon, Mo., U.S.A. 158 39 40N 92 26W
Macondo 125 12 37S 23 46E
Macosquink 38 55 5N 6 43W
Macossa 127 17 55S 33 56E
Macoun L. 153 56 32N 103 50W
Macovane 129 21 30S 35 0E
McPherson 158 38 25N 97 40W
McPherson Pk. 163 34 53N 119 53W
Macpherson Ra. 139 28 15S 153 15E
Macquarie Harbour 138 42 15S 145 15E
Macquarie Is. 130 50 0S 160 0E
Macquarie, R. 139 30 50S 147 30E
McRae, Mt. 136 22 17S 117 35E
MacRobertson Coast 13 68 30S 63 0E
Macroom 39 51 54N 8 57W
McSwyne's B. 38 54 37N 8 25W
Macu 174 0 25N 69 15W
Macugnaga 62 45 57N 7 58E
Macuirima 127 19 14S 35 5E
Macuiza 127 8 7S 34 29E
Macujer 174 0 24N 73 0W
Macumba, R. 133 27 11S 136 0E
Macuse 127 17 45S 37 17E
Macuspana 165 17 46N 92 36W
Macusse 128 17 48S 20 23E
Mácuzari, Presa 164 27 10N 109 10W
Macuze 127 17 45S 37 17E
Madā 'in Sālih 122 26 51N 37 58E
Madagali 121 10 56N 13 33E
Madagascar ■ 129 20 0S 47 0E
Madagascar, I. 129 20 0S 47 0E
Madam 120 7 58N 3 32W
Madama 119 22 0N 14 0E
Madame I. 151 45 30N 60 58W
Madanapalle 97 13 33N 78 34E
Madang 135 5 12S 145 49E
Madaoua 121 14 5N 6 27E
Madara 121 11 45N 10 35E
Madaripur 98 23 2N 90 15E
Madauk 98 17 56N 96 52E
Madawaska 150 45 30N 77 55W
Madawaska, R. 150 45 27N 76 21W
*Now part of Fort Smith □

Madaya 98 22 20N 96 10E
Madbar 123 6 17N 30 45E
Maddalena, I. 64 41 15N 9 23E
Maddalena, La 64 41 13N 9 25E
Maddaloni 65 41 4N 14 23E
Maddy, L. 36 57 36N 7 8W
Made 47 51 41N 4 49E
Madebele 123 12 30N 41 10E
Madeira, Is. 116 32 50N 17 0W
Madeira, R. 174 5 30S 61 20W
Madeleine, Is. de la 151 47 30N 61 40W
Madeley 28 52 38N 2 28W
Madely 32 52 59N 2 20W
Madenda 127 13 42S 35 1W
Madera 163 37 0N 120 1W
Madha 96 18 0N 75 55E
Madhubani 95 26 21N 86 7E
Madhumati, R. 98 22 53N 89 52E
Madhupur 126 24 18N 86 37E
Madhya Pradesh □ 94 21 50N 81 0E
Madi Opei 126 3 47N 33 5E
Madill 159 34 5N 96 49W
Madimba, Mozam. 127 4 58S 15 6E
Madimba, Zaïre 124 5 0S 15 0E
Madinat al Shaab 91 12 50N 45 0E
Madingou 124 4 10S 13 33E
Madirovalo 129 16 26S 46 32E
Madison, Fla., U.S.A. 157 30 29N 83 26W
Madison, Ind., U.S.A. 156 38 42N 85 20W
Madison, Nebr., U.S.A. 158 41 53N 97 25W
Madison, S.D., U.S.A. 158 44 0N 97 8W
Madison, Wis., U.S.A. 158 43 5N 89 25W
Madison City 158 43 5N 93 10W
Madison Junc. 160 44 42N 110 56W
Madison, R. 160 45 0N 111 48W
Madisonville 156 37 42N 87 30W
Madista 128 21 15S 25 6E
Madiun 103 7 38S 111 32E
Madol 123 9 3N 27 45E
Madona 80 56 53N 26 5E
Madonie, Le, Mts. 64 37 50N 13 50E
Madoonga 174 26 56S 117 35E
Madras, India 97 13 8N 80 19E
Madras, U.S.A. 160 44 40N 121 10W
Madras = Tamil Nadu □ 97 11 0N 77 0E
Madre de Dios, I. 176 50 20N 75 10W
Madre de Dios, R. 174 11 30S 67 30W
Madre del Sur, Sierra 165 17 30N 100 0W
Madre, Laguna 165 25 0N 97 30W
Madre Occidental, Sierra 164 27 0N 107 0W
Madre Oriental, Sierra 164 25 0N 100 0W
Madre, Sierra, Mexico 165 16 0N 93 0W
Madre, Sierra, Phil. 103 17 0N 122 0E
Madri 94 24 16N 73 32E
Madrid 56 40 25N 3 45W
Madrid □ 56 40 30N 3 45W
Madridejos 57 39 28N 3 33W
Madrigal de las Altas Torres 56 41 5N 5 0W
Madrona, Sierra 57 38 27N 4 16W
Madroñera 57 39 26N 5 42W
Madu 123 14 37N 26 4E
Madura Motel 137 31 55S 127 0E
Madura, Selat 103 7 30S 113 20E
Madurai 97 9 55N 78 10E
Madurantakam 97 12 30N 79 50E
Madurta 109 35 1S 138 44E
Maduru Oya 97 7 40N 81 7E
Madzhalis 83 42 9N 47 47E
Mae Chan 100 20 9N 99 52E
Mae Hong Son 100 19 16N 98 8E
Mae Khlong, R. 100 13 24N 100 0E
Mae Phrik 100 17 27N 99 7E
Mae Ramat 100 16 58N 98 31E
Mae Rim 100 18 54N 98 57E
Mae Sot 100 16 43N 98 34E
Mae Suai 100 19 39N 99 33E
Mae Tha 100 18 28N 99 8E
Maebaru 110 33 33N 130 12E
Maebashi 111 36 24N 139 4E
Maella 58 41 8N 0 7E
Maentwrog 31 52 57N 4 0W
Maerhk'ang 108 31 51N 102 28E
Mâeruş 70 45 53N 25 31E
Maesteg 31 51 36N 3 40W
Maestra, Sierra 166 20 15N 77 0W
Maestrazgo, Mts. del 58 40 30N 0 25W
Maevatanana 125 16 56N 46 49E
Ma'fan 119 25 56N 14 56E
Mafeking, Can. 153 52 40N 101 10W
•Mafeking, S. Afr. 128 25 50S 25 38E
Maféré 120 5 30N 3 2W
Mafeteng 128 29 51S 27 15E
Maffe 47 50 21N 5 19E
Maffra 141 37 53S 146 58E
Mafia □ 126 7 50S 39 30E
Mafia I. 126 7 45S 39 50E
Mafou 109 31 34N 115 15E
Mafra, Brazil 173 26 10N 50 0W
Mafra, Port. 57 38 55N 9 20W
Mafungabusi Plateau 127 18 30S 29 8E
Magadan 77 59 30N 151 0E
Magadi 126 1 54S 36 19E
Magadi, L. 126 1 54S 36 19E
Magaliesburg 129 26 1S 27 32E
Magallanes, Estrecho de 176 52 30S 75 0W
Magangué 174 9 14N 74 45W
Magaria 121 13 4N 9 5W
Magburaka 120 8 47N 12 0W
Magdal 90 32 51N 35 30E
*Renamed Mafikeng

Magdalen Is. = Madeleine, Is. de la 151 47 30N 61 40W
Magdalena, Argent. 172 35 5S 57 30W
Magdalena, Boliv. 174 13 13S 63 57W
Magdalena, Mexico 164 30 50N 112 0W
Magdalena, U.S.A. 161 34 10N 107 20W
Magdalena □ 174 10 0N 74 0W
Magdalena, B. 164 24 30N 112 10W
Magdalena, I. 164 24 40N 112 15W
Magdalena, Llano de la 164 25 0N 111 30W
Magdalena, mt. 102 4 25N 117 55E
Magdalena, R., Colomb. 174 8 30N 74 0W
Magdalena, R., Mexico 164 30 50N 112 0W
Magdeburg 48 52 8N 11 36E
Magdeburg □ 48 52 20N 11 40E
Magdelaine Cays 138 16 33S 150 18E
Magdiel 90 32 10N 34 54E
Magdub 123 13 42N 25 5E
Magee 159 31 53N 89 45W
Magee, I. 38 54 48N 5 44W
Magelang 103 7 29S 110 13E
Magellan's Str. 176 52 30S 75 0W
Magellan's Str. = Magallanes, Est. de 176 52 30S 75 0W
Magenta, Austral. 140 33 51S 143 34E
Magenta, Italy 62 45 28N 8 53E
Magenta, L. 137 33 30S 119 10E
Maggea 140 34 28S 140 2E
Maggia 51 46 15N 8 42E
Maggia, R. 51 46 18N 8 36E
Maggiorasca, Mt. 62 44 33N 9 29E
Maggiore, L. 62 46 0N 8 35E
Maghama 120 15 32N 12 57W
Maghar 90 32 54N 35 24E
Maghera 38 54 51N 6 40W
Magherafelt 38 54 44N 6 37W
Maghnia 118 34 50N 1 43W
Maghull 32 53 31N 2 56W
Magilligan 38 55 10N 6 53W
Magilligan Pt. 38 55 10N 6 58W
Magione 63 43 10N 12 12E
Maglaj 66 44 33N 18 7E
Magliano in Toscana 63 42 36N 11 18E
Máglie 65 40 8N 18 17E
Magnac-Laval 44 46 13N 1 11E
Magnetic Pole, 1976, (South) 13 68 48S 139 30E
Magnetic Pole, 1976(North) 12 76 12N 100 12W
Magnisía □ 69 39 24N 22 46E
Magnitogorsk 84 53 27N 59 4E
Magnolia, Ark., U.S.A. 159 33 18N 93 12W
Magnolia, Miss., U.S.A. 159 31 8N 90 28W
Magnor 71 59 56N 12 15E
Magnus, oilfield 19 61 40N 1 20E
Magny-en-Vexin 43 49 9N 1 47E
Màgoé 127 15 45S 31 42E
Magog 151 45 18N 72 9W
Magoro 126 1 45N 34 12E
Magosta = Famagusta 92 35 8N 33 55E
Magoye 127 16 1S 27 30E
Magpie L. 151 51 0N 64 40W
Magrath 152 49 25N 112 50W
Magro, R. 59 39 20N 0 45W
Magruder Mt. 163 37 25N 117 33W
Magrur, W. 123 16 5N 26 30E
Magu □ 126 2 45S 33 15E
Maguarinho, C. 170 0 15S 48 30W
Maguire's Bri. 38 54 18N 7 28W
Maguse L. 153 61 40N 95 10W
Maguse Pt. 153 61 20N 93 50W
Maguse River 153 61 20N 94 25W
Magwe 98 20 10N 95 0E
Maha Sarakham 100 16 12N 103 16E
Mahābād 92 36 50N 45 45E
Mahabaleshwar 96 17 58N 73 50E
Mahabarat Lekh 95 28 30N 82 0E
Mahabo 129 20 23S 44 40E
Mahad 96 18 6N 73 29E
Mahadeo Hills 94 22 20N 78 30E
Mahadeopur 96 18 48N 80 0E
Mahagi 126 2 20N 31 0E
Mahajamba, B. de la 129 15 24S 47 5E
Mahajamba, R. 129 17 0S 47 30E
Mahajan 94 28 48N 73 56E
Mahajilo, R. 129 19 30S 46 0E
Mahakam, R. 102 1 0N 114 40E
Mahalapye 128 23 1S 26 51E
Mahalla el Kubra 122 31 10N 31 0E
Mahallāt 93 33 55N 50 30E
Mahanadi R. 96 20 33N 85 0E
Mahanagh 38 53 31N 8 42W
Mahanoro 129 19 54S 48 48E
Mahanoy City 162 40 48N 76 10W
Maharashtra □ 96 19 30N 75 30E
Maharès 119 34 32N 10 29E
Mahari Mts. 126 6 20S 30 0E
Mahasolo 129 19 7S 46 22E
Mahaweli Ganga 97 8 0N 81 10E
Mahaxay 100 17 22N 105 48E
Mahboobabad 96 17 42N 80 2E
Mahbubnagar 96 16 45N 77 59E
Mahd Dhahab 92 25 55N 45 30E
Mahdia 119 35 28N 11 0E
Mahé 97 11 42N 75 34E
Mahe 95 33 10N 78 32E
Mahendra Giri, mt. 97 8 20N 77 30E
Mahendraganj 98 25 20N 89 45E
Mahenge 127 8 45S 36 35E
Maheno 143 45 10S 170 50E
Mahia Pen. 142 39 9S 177 55E
Mahirija 118 34 0N 3 16W

Mahlaing 98 21 6N 95 39E
Mahmiya 123 17 5N 33 50E
Mahmud Kot 94 30 16N 71 0E
Mahmudia 70 45 5N 29 5E
Mahnomen 158 47 22N 95 57W
Mahoba 95 25 15N 79 55E
Mahón 58 39 50N 4 18E
Mahone Bay 151 44 30N 64 20W
Mahopac 162 41 22N 73 45W
Mahsü 108 30 31N 100 19E
Mahukona 147 20 11N 155 52W
Mahuta 121 11 32N 4 58E
Mai-Ndombe, L. 124 2 0S 18 0E
Mai-Sai 100 20 20N 99 55E
Maibara 111 35 19N 136 17E
Maîche 43 47 16N 6 48E
Maicuru, R. 175 1 0S 54 30W
Máida 65 38 51N 16 21E
Maidan Khula 94 33 36N 69 50E
Maiden Bradley 28 51 9N 2 18W
Maiden Newton 28 50 46N 2 35W
Maidenhead 29 51 31N 0 42W
Maidi 123 16 20N 42 45E
Maidstone, Can. 153 53 5N 109 20W
Maidstone, U.K. 29 51 16N 0 31E
Maiduguri 121 12 0N 13 20E
Maignelay 43 49 32N 2 30E
Maigualida, Sierra 174 5 30N 65 10W
Maijdi 98 22 48N 91 10E
Maikala Ra. 96 22 0N 81 0E
Mailly-le-Camp 43 48 41N 4 12E
Mailsi 94 29 48N 72 15E
Maimana 93 35 53N 64 38E
Main Barrier Ra. 133 31 10S 141 20E
Main Centre 153 50 35N 107 21W
Main Coast Ra. 138 16 22S 145 10E
Main, R., Ger. 49 50 13N 11 0E
Main, R., U.K. 38 54 49N 6 20W
Mainburg 49 48 37N 11 49E
Maindargi 96 17 33N 74 21E
Maine 42 48 0N 0 0E
Maine □ 151 45 20N 69 0W
Maine-et-Loire □ 42 47 31N 0 30W
Maine, R. 39 52 10N 9 40W
Maïne-Soroa 121 13 13N 12 2E
Maingkwan 98 26 15N 96 45E
Mainit, L. 103 9 31N 125 30E
Mainkaing 98 24 48N 95 16E
Mainland, I., Orkneys, U.K. 37 59 0N 3 10W
Mainland, I., Shetlands, U.K. 36 60 15N 1 22W
Mainpuri 95 27 18N 79 4E
Maintenon 43 48 35N 1 35E
Maintirano 129 18 3S 44 1E
Mainvault 47 50 39N 3 43E
Mainz 49 50 0N 8 17E
Maipú 172 37 0S 58 0W
Maipures 174 5 11N 67 49W
Maiquetía 174 10 36N 66 57W
Maira, R. 62 44 29N 7 15E
Mairabari 98 26 30N 92 30E
Mairipotaba 171 17 18S 49 28W
Maisí 167 20 17N 74 9W
Maisi, C. 167 20 10N 74 10W
Maisse 43 48 24N 2 21E
Maissin 47 49 58N 5 10E
Maitland, N.S.W., Austral. 141 32 44S 151 36E
Maitland, S. Australia, Austral. 140 34 23S 137 40E
Maitland, L. 137 27 11S 121 3E
Maiyema 121 12 5N 4 25E
Maíz, Islas del 166 12 15N 83 4W
Maizuru 111 35 25N 135 22E
Majagual 174 8 33N 74 38W
Majalengka 103 6 55S 108 14E
Majd el Kurum 90 32 56N 35 15E
Majene 103 3 27S 118 57E
Majevica Planina 66 44 45N 18 50E
Maji 123 6 20N 35 30E
Major 153 51 52N 109 37W
Majorca, I. = Mallorca, I. 58 39 30N 3 0E
Majors Creek 141 35 33S 149 45E
Majunga 125 15 40S 46 25E
Majunga □ 129 17 0S 47 0E
Maka 120 13 40N 14 10W
Makak 121 3 36N 11 0E
Makale 103 3 6S 119 51E
Makamba 126 4 8S 29 49E
Makamik 150 48 45N 79 0W
Makapuu Hd. 147 21 19N 157 39W
Makarewa 143 46 20S 168 21E
Makari 124 12 35N 14 28E
Makarikari = Makgadikgadi 128 20 40S 25 45E
Makarovo 77 57 40N 107 45E
Makarska 66 43 20N 17 2E
Makaryev 81 57 52N 43 50E
Makasar = Ujung Pandang 103 5 10S 119 20E
Makasar, Selat 103 1 0S 118 20E
Makat 76 47 39N 53 19E
Makedhonía □ 68 40 39N 22 0E
Makedonija □ 66 41 53N 21 40E
Makena 147 20 39N 156 27W
Makeni 120 8 55N 12 5W
Maker 30 50 20N 4 10W
Makeyevka 82 48 0N 38 0E
Makgadikgadi 128 20 40S 25 45E
Makgadikgadi Salt Pans 128 20 40S 25 45E
Makgobistad 128 25 45S 25 12E

Makhachkala **Manitou I**

Name	Page	Lat.	Long.
Makhachkala	83	43 0N	47 15 E
Makharadze	83	41 55N	42 2 E
Makian, I.	103	0 12N	127 20 E
†Makin, I.	130	3 30N	174 0 E
Makindu	124	2 7 S	37 40 E
Makinsk	76	52 37N	70 26 E
Makkah	122	21 30N	39 54 E
Makkovik	151	55 0N	59 10W
Makkum	46	53 3N	5 25 E
Maklakovo	77	58 16N	92 29 E
Makó	53	46 14N	20 33 E
Makokou	124	0 40N	12 50 E
Makongo	126	3 15N	26 17 E
Makoro	126	3 10N	29 59 E
Makoua	124	0 5 S	15 50 E
Maków Podhal	54	49 43N	19 45 E
Makrá, I.	69	36 15N	25 54 E
Makrai	93	22 2N	77 0 E
Makran	93	26 13N	61 30 E
Makran Coast Range	93	25 40N	4 0 E
Makrana	94	27 2N	74 46 E
Mákri	68	40 52N	25 40 E
Maksimkin Yar	76	58 58N	86 50 E
Maktar	119	35 48N	9 12 E
Mākū	92	39 15N	44 31 E
Makuan	108	23 2N	104 24 E
Makum	98	27 30N	95 23 E
Makumbe	128	20 15 S	24 26 E
Makumbi	124	5 50 S	20 43 E
Makunda	128	22 30 S	20 7 E
Makurazaki	110	31 15N	130 20 E
Makurdi	120	7 43N	8 28 E
Makwassie	128	27 17 S	26 0 E
Mal	98	26 51N	86 45 E
Mal B.	39	52 50N	9 30W
Mal-i-Gjalicës së Lumës	68	42 2N	20 25 E
Mal i Gribës	68	40 17N	9 45 E
Mal i Nemërçkës	68	40 15N	20 15 E
Mal i Tomorit	68	40 42N	20 11 E
Mala Kapela	63	44 45N	15 30 E
Mala, Pta.	166	7 28N	80 2W
Malabang	103	7 36N	124 3 E
Malabar Coast	97	11 0N	75 0 E
Malacca = Melaka	101	2 15N	102 15 E
Malacca, Str. of	101	3 0N	101 0 E
Malacky	53	48 27N	17 0 E
Malad City	160	41 10N	112 20 E
Maladetta, Mt.	59	42 40N	0 30 E
Malafaburi	123	10 37N	40 30 E
Málaga, Colomb.	174	6 42N	72 44W
Málaga, Spain	57	36 43N	4 23W
Malaga	159	32 12N	104 2W
Málaga □	57	36 38N	4 58W
Malagarasi	126	5 5 S	30 50 E
Malagarasi, R.	126	3 50 S	30 30 E
Malagasy Rep. ■ = Madagascar ■	129	20 0 S	47 0 E
Malagón	57	39 11N	3 52W
Malagón, R.	57	37 40N	7 20W
Malahide	38	53 26N	6 10W
Malaimbandy	129	20 20 S	45 36 E
Malakâl	123	9 33N	31 50 E
Malakand	94	34 40N	71 55 E
Malakoff	159	32 10N	95 55W
Malakwa	152	50 55N	118 50W
Malamyzh	77	50 0N	136 50 E
Malang	103	7 59 S	112 35 E
Malanje	124	9 30 S	16 17 E
Mälaren	72	59 30N	17 10 E
Malargüe	172	35 40 S	69 30W
Malartic	150	48 9N	78 9W
Malatya	92	38 25N	38 20 E
Malawi ■	127	13 0 S	34 0 E
Malawi, L. (Lago Niassa)	127	12 30 S	34 30 E
Malay Pen.	101	7 25N	100 0 E
• Malaya □	101	4 0N	102 0 E
Malaya Belözerka	82	47 12N	34 56 E
Malaya Vishera	80	58 55N	32 25 E
Malaybalay	103	8 5N	125 15 E
Malayer	92	34 19N	48 51 E
Malaysia ■	102	5 0N	110 0 E
• Malaysia, Western □	101	5 0N	102 0 E
Malazgirt	92	39 10N	42 33 E
Malbaie, La	151	47 40N	70 10W
Malbon	138	21 5 S	140 17 E
Malbooma	139	30 41 S	134 11 E
Malbork	54	54 3N	19 10 E
Malca Dube	123	6 40N	41 52 E
Malchin	48	53 43N	12 44 E
Malchow	48	53 29N	12 25 E
Malcolm	137	28 51 S	121 25 E
Malcolm, Pt., S. Australia, Austral.	109	34 52 S	138 29 E
Malcolm, Pt., W. Australia, Austral.	137	33 48 S	123 45 E
Malczyce	54	51 14N	16 29 E
Maldegem	47	51 14N	3 26 E
Malden, Mass., U.S.A.	162	42 26N	71 5W
Malden, Mo., U.S.A.	159	36 35N	90 0W
Malden I.	143	4 3 S	155 1W
Maldive Is. ■	86	2 0N	73 0W
Maldon, Austral.	140	37 0 S	144 6 E
Maldon, U.K.	29	51 43N	0 41 E
Maldonado	173	35 0 S	55 0W
Maldonado, Punta	165	16 19N	98 35W
Malé	62	46 20N	10 55 E
Malé Karpaty	53	48 30N	17 20 E
Maléa, Ákra	69	36 28N	23 7 E
Malegaon	96	20 30N	74 30 E
Malei	127	17 12 S	36 58 E
Malela	126	4 22 S	26 8 E
Malenge	127	12 40 S	26 42 E
Målerås	73	56 54N	15 34 E
Malerkotla	94	30 32N	75 58 E
Máles	69	36 6N	25 35 E
Malesherbes	43	48 15N	2 24 E
Maleske Planina	66	41 38N	23 7 E
Malestroit	42	47 49N	2 25W
Malfa	65	38 35N	14 50 E
Malgobek	83	43 30N	44 52 E
Malgomaj L.	74	64 40N	16 30 E
Malgrat	58	41 39N	2 46 E
Malham Tarn	32	54 6N	2 11W
Malhão, Sa. do	55	37 25N	8 0W
Malheur L.	160	43 19N	118 42W
Malheur, R.	160	43 55N	117 55W
Mali	120	12 10N	12 20W
Mali ■	121	15 0N	10 0W
Mali H Ka R.	98	25 42N	97 30 E
Mali Kanal	66	45 36N	19 24 E
Mali Kyun, I.	101	13 0N	98 20 E
Mali, R.	99	26 20N	97 40 E
Malibu	163	34 2N	118 41W
Malih, Nahr al	90	32 20N	35 29 E
Malik	103	0 39 S	123 16 E
Malili	103	2 42 S	121 23 E
Malimba, Mts.	126	7 30 S	29 30 E
Malin, Ireland	38	55 18N	7 16W
Malin, U.S.S.R.	80	50 46N	29 15 E
Malin Hd.	38	55 18N	7 16W
Malin Pen.	38	55 20N	7 17W
Malinau	102	3 35N	116 30 E
Malindi	126	3 12 S	40 5 E
Maling, Mt.	103	1 0N	121 0 E
Malingping	103	6 45 S	106 2 E
Malinyi	127	8 56 S	36 0 E
Maliqi	68	40 45N	20 48 E
Malita	103	6 19N	125 39 E
Malkapur, Maharashtra, India	96	16 57N	74 0W
Malkapur, Maharashtra, India	96	20 53N	76 17 E
Małkinia Grn.	54	52 42N	21 58 E
Malko Turnovo	67	41 59N	27 31 E
Mallacoota	141	37 40 S	149 40 E
Mallacoota Inlet	141	37 40 S	149 40 E
Mallaha	90	33 6N	35 35 E
Mallaig	36	57 0N	5 50W
Mallala	140	34 26 S	138 30 E
Mallawan	95	27 4N	80 12 E
Mallawi	122	27 44N	30 44 E
Mallemort	45	43 44N	5 11 E
Málles Venosta	62	46 42N	10 32 E
Mállia	69	35 17N	25 27 E
Mallina P.O.	136	20 53 S	118 2 E
Mallorca, I.	58	39 30N	3 0 E
Mallow	39	52 8N	8 40W
Malltraeth B.	31	53 7N	4 30W
Mallwyd	31	52 43N	3 41W
Malmbäck	73	57 34N	14 28 E
Malmberget	74	67 11N	20 40 E
Malmèdy	47	50 25N	6 2 E
Malmesbury, S. Afr.	128	33 28 S	18 41 E
Malmesbury, U.K.	28	51 35N	2 5W
Malmö	75	55 36N	12 59 E
Malmöhus län □	73	55 45N	13 30 E
Malmslätt	73	58 27N	15 33 E
Malmyzh	84	56 31N	50 41 E
Malmyzh Mozhga	81	56 35N	50 30 E
Malnaş	70	46 2N	25 49 E
Malo Konare	67	42 12N	24 24 E
Maloarkhangelsk	81	52 28N	36 30 E
Maloja	51	46 25N	9 35 E
Maloja Pass	51	46 23N	9 42 E
Malolos	103	14 50N	121 2 E
Malomalsk	84	58 45N	59 53 E
Malombe L.	127	14 40 S	35 15 E
Malomir	67	42 16N	26 30 E
Malone	156	44 50N	74 19W
Malorad	67	43 28N	23 41 E
Malorita	80	51 41N	24 3 E
Maloyaroslovets	81	55 2N	36 20 E
Malozemelskaya Tundra	78	67 0N	50 0 E
Malpartida	57	39 26N	6 30W
Malpas	32	53 3N	2 47W
Malpelo I.	174	4 3N	80 35W
Malpica	56	43 19N	8 50W
Malprabha, R.	97	15 40N	74 50 E
Malta, Brazil	170	6 54 S	37 31W
Malta, Idaho, U.S.A.	160	42 15N	113 50W
Malta, Mont., U.S.A.	160	48 20N	107 55W
Malta ■	64	35 50N	14 0 E
Maltahöhe	125	24 55 S	17 0 E
Maltby	33	53 25N	1 12W
Malters	50	47 3N	8 11 E
Malton	33	54 9N	0 48W
Maluku □	103	3 0 S	128 0 E
Maluku, Kepulauan	103	3 0 S	128 0 E
Malumfashi	121	11 48N	7 39 E
Malung, China	108	25 18N	103 20 E
Malung, Sweden	72	60 42N	13 44 E
Malvalli	97	12 28N	77 8 E
Malvan	97	16 2N	73 30 E
Malvern, U.K.	28	52 7N	2 19W
Malvern, U.S.A.	159	34 22N	92 50W
Malvern Hills	28	52 0N	2 19W
Malvern Wells	28	52 4N	2 19W
Malvérnia	129	22 6 S	31 42 E
Malvik	71	63 25N	10 40 E
Malvinas Is. = Falkland Is.	174	51 30 S	59 0W
Malya	126	3 5 S	33 38 E
Malybay	85	43 30N	78 25 E
Mama	77	58 18N	112 54 E
Mamadysh	81	55 44N	51 23 E
Mamaia	70	44 18N	28 37 E
Mamaku	142	38 5 S	176 8 E
Mamanguape	170	6 50 S	35 4W
Mamasa	103	2 55 S	119 20 E
Mambasa	126	1 22N	29 3 E
Mamberamo, R.	103	2 0 S	137 50 E
Mambilima Falls	127	10 31 S	28 45 E
Mambirima	127	11 25 S	27 33 E
Mambo	126	4 52 S	38 22 E
Mambrui	126	3 5 S	40 5 E
Mameigwess L.	150	52 35N	87 50W
Mamer	47	49 38N	6 2 E
Mamers	42	48 21N	0 22 E
Mamfe	121	5 50N	9 15 E
Mammamattawa	150	50 25N	84 23W
Mámmola	65	38 23N	16 13 E
Mammoth	161	32 46N	110 43W
Mamoré, R.	175	9 55 S	65 20W
Mamou	120	10 15N	12 0W
Mampatá	120	11 54N	14 53W
Mampawah	102	0 30N	109 5 E
Mampong	121	7 6N	1 26W
Mamuju	103	2 50 S	118 50 E
Man	120	7 30N	7 40W
Man, I. of	32	54 15N	4 30W
Man Na	98	23 27N	97 19 E
Man O' War Peak	151	56 58N	61 40W
Man, R.	96	17 20N	75 0 E
Man Tun	98	23 2N	98 38 E
Mana, Fr. Gui.	175	5 45N	53 55W
Mana, U.S.A.	147	22 3N	159 45W
Mana, R.	123	6 20N	40 41 E
Måna, R.	71	59 55N	8 50 E
Manaar, Gulf of	97	8 30N	79 0 E
Manacacias, R.	174	4 23N	72 4W
Manacapuru	174	3 10 S	60 50W
Manacles, The	30	50 3N	5 5W
Manacor	58	39 32N	3 12 E
Manage	47	50 31N	4 15 E
Managua	166	12 0N	86 20W
Managua, L.	166	12 20N	86 30W
Manaia	142	39 33 S	174 8 E
Manakana	129	13 45 S	50 4 E
Manakara	129	22 8 S	48 1 E
Manakau Mt.	143	42 15 S	173 42 E
Manam I.	135	4 5 S	145 0 E
Manamāh, Al	93	26 11N	50 35 E
Manambao, R.	129	17 35 S	44 45 E
Manambato	129	13 43 S	49 7 E
Manambolo, R.	129	19 20 S	45 0 E
Manambolosy	129	16 2 S	49 40 E
Mananara	129	16 10 S	49 30 E
Mananara, R.	129	23 25 S	48 10 E
Mananjary	129	21 13 S	48 20 E
Manantenina	129	24 17 S	47 19 E
Manaos = Manaus	174	3 0 S	60 0W
Manapouri	143	45 34 S	167 39 E
Manapouri, L.	143	45 32 S	167 32 E
Manar, R.	96	18 50N	77 20 E
Manas, Gora	85	42 22N	71 2 E
Manas, R.	99	26 12N	90 40 E
Manasarowar, L.	105	30 45N	81 20 E
Manasarowar L.	105	30 45N	81 20 E
Manasir	93	24 30N	51 10 E
Manaslu, Mt.	95	28 33N	84 33 E
Manasquan	162	40 7N	74 3W
Manassa	161	37 12N	105 58W
Manassas	162	38 45N	77 28W
Manassu	105	44 18N	86 13 E
Manati	147	18 26N	66 29W
Manaung Kyun	98	18 45N	93 40 E
Manaus	174	3 0 S	60 0W
Manawan L.	153	55 24N	103 14W
Manawatu, R.	142	40 28 S	175 12 E
Manay	103	7 17N	126 33 E
Manby	33	53 22N	0 6 E
Mancelona	156	44 54N	85 5W
Mancha, La	59	39 10N	2 54W
Mancha Real	57	37 48N	3 39W
Manchaster, L.	108	27 29 S	152 46 E
Manche □	42	49 10N	1 20W
Manchester, U.K.	32	53 30N	2 15W
Manchester, Conn., U.S.A.	162	41 47N	72 30W
Manchester, Ga., U.S.A.	157	32 53N	84 32W
Manchester, Iowa, U.S.A.	158	42 28N	91 27W
Manchester, Ky., U.S.A.	156	38 40N	83 45W
Manchester, N.H., U.S.A.	162	42 58N	71 29W
Manchester, Pa., U.S.A.	162	40 4N	76 43W
Manchester, Vt., U.S.A.	162	43 10N	73 5W
Manchester L.	153	61 28N	107 29W
Manchouli	105	49 46N	117 24 E
Manchuria = Tung Pei	107	44 0N	126 0 E
Manciano	63	42 35N	11 30 E
Mancifa	123	6 53N	41 50 E
Mand, R.	93	28 20N	52 30 E
Manda, Chunya, Tanz.	127	6 51 S	32 29 E
Manda, Jombe, Tanz.	127	10 30 S	34 40 E
Mandabé	125	21 0 S	44 55 E
Mandaguari	173	23 32 S	51 42W
Mandah	106	44 27N	108 20 E
Mandal	71	58 2N	7 25 E
Mandalay	99	22 0N	96 10 E
Mandalay = Mandale	98	22 0N	96 10 E
Mandale	99	22 0N	96 10 E
Mandalgovi	106	45 45N	106 20 E
Mandali	92	33 52N	45 28 E
Mandalya Körfezi	69	37 15N	27 20 E
Mandan	158	46 50N	101 0W
Mandapeta	96	16 47N	81 56 E
Mandar, Teluk	103	3 35 S	119 4 E
Mandas	64	39 40N	9 8 E
Mandasaur	93	24 3N	75 8 E
Mandasor (Mandsaur)	94	24 3N	75 8 E
Mandawai (Katingan), R.	102	1 30 S	113 0 E
Mandelieu-la-Napoule	45	43 34N	6 57 E
Mandera	126	3 55N	41 42 E
Mandera □	126	3 30N	41 0 E
Manderfeld	47	50 20N	6 20 E
Mandi, India	94	31 39N	76 58 E
Mandi, Zambia	127	14 30 S	23 45 E
Mandimba	125	14 20 S	35 40 E
Mandioli	103	0 40 S	127 20 E
Mandla	95	22 39N	80 30 E
Mandø	73	55 18N	8 33 E
Mandoto	129	19 34 S	46 17 E
Mandoúdhion	69	38 48N	23 29 E
Mandra	94	33 23N	73 12 E
Mandráki	69	36 36N	27 11 E
Mandrase, R.	129	25 10 S	46 30 E
Mandritsara	129	15 50 S	48 49 E
Mandsaur (Mandasor)	94	24 3N	75 8 E
Mandurah	137	32 36 S	115 48 E
Mandúria	65	40 25N	17 38 E
Mandvi	96	22 51N	69 22 E
Mandya	97	12 30N	77 0 E
Mandzai	94	30 55N	67 6 E
Mané	121	12 59N	1 21W
Manea	29	52 29N	0 10 E
Maner, R.	97	18 30N	79 40 E
Maneroo	138	23 22 S	143 53 E
Maneroo Cr.	138	23 21 S	143 53 E
Manfalût	122	27 20N	30 52 E
Manfred	140	33 19 S	143 45 E
Manfredónia	65	41 40N	15 55 E
Manfredónia, G. di	65	41 30N	16 10 E
Manga, Brazil	171	14 46 S	43 56W
Manga, Upp. Vol.	121	11 40N	1 4W
Mangabeiras, Chapada das	170	10 0 S	46 30W
Mangahan	142	40 26 S	175 48 E
Mangalagiri	96	16 26N	80 36 E
Mangaldai	98	26 26N	92 2 E
Mangalia	70	43 50N	28 35 E
Mangalore, Austral.	141	36 56 S	145 10 E
Mangalore, India	97	12 55N	74 47 E
Manganeses	56	41 45N	5 43W
Mangaon	96	18 15N	73 20 E
Manger	71	60 38N	5 3W
Mangerton Mt.	39	51 59N	9 30W
Manggar	102	2 50 S	108 10 E
Manggawitu	103	4 8 S	133 32 E
Mangin Range	98	24 15N	95 45 E
Mangla Dam	95	33 32N	73 50 E
Manglaur	94	29 44N	77 49 E
Mangoche	125	14 25 S	35 16 E
Mangoky, R.	129	21 55 S	44 40 E
Mangole I.	103	1 50 S	125 55 E
Mangombe	126	1 20 S	26 48 E
Mangonui	142	35 1 S	173 32 E
Mangotsfield	28	51 29N	2 29W
Mangualde	56	40 38N	7 48W
Mangueigne	117	10 40N	21 5 E
Mangueira, Lagoa da	173	33 0 S	52 50W
Manguéni, Hamada	119	22 47N	12 56 E
Mangum	159	34 50N	99 30W
Mangyai	105	37 50N	91 38 E
Mangyshlak P-ov.	83	43 40N	52 30 E
Manhattan, Kans., U.S.A.	158	39 10N	96 40W
Manhattan, Nev., U.S.A.	163	38 31N	117 3W
Manhiça	129	25 23 S	32 49 E
Manhuaçu	171	20 15 S	42 2W
Manhui	106	41 1N	107 14 E
Manhumirim	171	20 22 S	41 57W
Mani	99	34 52N	87 11 E
Maní	174	4 49N	72 17W
Mania, R.	129	19 55 S	46 10 E
Maniago	63	46 11N	12 40 E
Manica	127	18 58 S	32 59 E
Manica e Sofala □	129	19 10 S	33 45 E
Manicaland □	127	19 10 S	32 30 E
Manicoré	174	6 0 S	61 10W
Manicouagan L.	151	51 25N	68 15W
Manicouagan, R.	151	49 30N	68 30W
Manifah	92	27 30N	49 0 E
Manifold	138	22 41 S	150 40 E
Manigotagan	153	51 6N	96 8W
Manigotagan L.	153	50 52N	95 37W
Manihiki I.	131	10 24 S	161 1W
Manika, Plat. de	127	10 0 S	25 5 E
Manikganj	98	23 52N	90 0 E
Manila, Phil.	103	14 40N	121 3 E
Manila, U.S.A.	160	41 0N	109 44W
Manila B.	103	14 0N	120 0 E
Manilla	141	30 45 S	150 43 E
Manimpé	120	14 11N	5 28W
Maningory	129	17 9 S	49 30 E
Manipur □	98	24 30N	94 0 E
Manipur, R.	98	23 45N	93 40 E
Manisa	92	38 38N	27 30 E
Manistee	156	44 15N	86 20W
Manistee, R.	156	44 15N	86 21W
Manistique	156	45 59N	86 18W
Manito L.	153	52 43N	109 43W
Manitoba □	153	55 30N	97 0W
Manitoba, L.	153	51 0N	98 45W
Manitou	153	49 15N	98 32W
Manitou I.	150	47 22N	87 30W

* Renamed Peninsular Malaysia
† Renamed Butaritari

Manitou Is — Marosakoa

Manitou Is.	156	45 8N	86 0W
Manitou L., Ont., Can.	153	49 15N	93 0W
Manitou L., Qué., Can.	151	50 55N	65 17W
Manitoulin I.	150	45 40N	82 30W
Manitowaning	150	45 46N	81 49W
Manitowoc	156	44 8N	87 40W
Manizales	174	5 5N	75 32W
Manja	129	21 26S	44 20E
Manjacaze	125	24 45S	34 0E
Manjakandriana	129	18 55S	47 47E
Manjeri	97	11 7N	76 11E
Manjhand	94	25 50N	68 10E
Manjil	92	36 46N	49 30E
Manjimup	137	34 15S	116 6E
Manjra, R.	96	18 20N	77 20E
Mankaiana	129	26 38S	31 6E
Mankato, Kans., U.S.A.	158	39 49N	98 11W
Mankato, Minn., U.S.A.	158	44 8N	93 59W
Mankono	120	8 10N	6 10W
Mankota	153	49 25N	107 5W
Manlay	106	44 9N	106 50E
Manlleu	58	42 2N	2 17E
Manly, N.S.W., Austral.	141	33 48S	151 17E
Manly, Queens., Austral.	108	27 27S	153 11E
Manmad	96	20 18N	74 28E
Mann Ranges, Mts.	137	26 6S	130 5E
Manna	102	4 25S	102 55E
Mannahill	140	32 25S	140 0E
Mannar	97	9 1N	79 54E
Mannar, G. of	97	8 30N	79 0E
Mannar I.	97	9 5N	79 45E
Mannargudi	97	10 45N	79 32E
Männedorf	51	47 15N	8 43E
Mannheim	49	49 28N	8 29E
Manning, Can.	152	56 53N	117 39W
Manning, U.S.A.	157	33 40N	80 9W
Manning Prov. Park	152	49 5N	120 45W
Mannington	156	39 35N	80 25W
Manningtree	29	51 56N	1 3E
Mannu, C.	64	40 2N	8 24E
Mannu, R.	64	39 35N	8 56E
Mannum	140	34 57S	139 12E
Mano	120	8 3N	12 12W
Manokwari	103	0 54S	134 0E
Manolás	69	38 4N	21 21E
Manombo	129	22 57S	43 28E
Manono	124	7 15S	27 25E
Manorbier	31	51 38N	4 48W
Manorhamilton	38	54 19N	8 11W
Manosque	45	43 49N	5 47E
Manouane L.	151	50 45N	70 45W
Manpojin	107	41 6N	126 24E
Manresa	58	41 48N	1 50E
Mans, Le	42	48 0N	0 10E
Mansa, Gujarat, India	94	23 27N	72 45E
Mansa, Punjab, India	94	30 0N	75 27E
Mansa, Zambia	127	11 13S	28 55E
Mansel I.	149	62 0N	79 50W
Mansenra	94	34 20N	73 11E
Mansfield, Austral.	141	37 4S	146 6E
Mansfield, U.K.	33	53 8N	1 12W
Mansfield, La., U.S.A.	159	32 2N	93 40W
Mansfield, Mass., U.S.A.	162	42 2N	71 12W
Mansfield, Ohio, U.S.A.	156	40 45N	82 30W
Mansfield, Pa., U.S.A.	162	41 48N	77 4W
Mansfield, Wash., U.S.A.	160	47 51N	119 44W
Mansfield Woodhouse	33	53 11N	1 11W
Mansi	98	24 40N	95 44E
Mansidão	170	10 43S	44 2W
Mansilla de las Mulas	56	42 30N	5 25W
Mansle	44	45 52N	0 9E
Manso, R.	171	14 0S	52 0W
Mansôa	120	12 0N	15 20W
Manson Cr.	152	55 37N	124 25W
Mansoura, Djebel	119	36 1N	4 31E
Manta	174	1 0S	80 40W
Mantalingajan, Mt.	102	8 55N	117 45E
Mantare	126	2 42S	33 13E
Manteca	163	37 50N	121 12W
Mantecal	174	7 34N	69 17W
Mantekomu Hu	99	34 40N	89 0E
Mantena	171	18 47S	40 59W
Manteo	157	35 55N	75 41W
Mantes-la-Jolie	43	49 0N	1 41E
Manthani	96	18 40N	79 35E
Manthelan	42	47 9N	0 47E
Manti	160	39 23N	111 32W
Mantiqueira, Serra da	173	22 0S	44 0W
Manton, U.K.	29	52 37N	0 41W
Manton, U.S.A.	156	44 23N	85 25W
Mantorp	73	58 21N	15 20E
Mántova	62	45 10N	10 47E
Mänttä	74	62 0N	24 40E
Mantua = Mántova	62	45 10N	10 47E
Mantung	140	34 35S	140 3E
Manturova	81	58 10N	44 30E
Manu	174	12 10S	71 0W
Manucan	103	8 14N	123 3E
Manuel Alves Grande, R.	170	7 27S	47 35W
Manuel Alves, R.	171	11 19S	48 28W
Manui I.	103	3 35S	123 5E
Manukau	142	37 1S	174 55E
Manukau Harbour	142	37 3S	174 45E
Manunui	142	38 54S	175 21E
Manus I.	135	2 0S	147 0E
Manvi	97	15 57N	76 59E
Manville, R.I., U.S.A.	162	41 58N	71 28W
Manville, Wyo., U.S.A.	158	42 48N	104 36W
Manwath	96	19 19N	76 32E
Many	159	31 36N	93 28W
Manyane	128	23 21S	21 42E
Manyara L.	126	3 40S	35 50E
Manych-Gudilo, Oz.	83	46 24N	42 38E
Manych, R.	83	47 0N	41 15E
Manyonga, R.	126	4 5S	34 0E
Manyoni	126	5 45S	34 55E
Manyoni □	126	6 30S	34 30E
Manzai	94	32 20N	70 15E
Manzala, Bahra el	122	31 10N	31 56E
Manzanares	59	39 0N	3 22W
Manzaneda, Cabeza de	56	42 12N	7 15W
Manzanillo, Cuba	166	20 20N	77 10W
Manzanillo, Mexico	164	19 0N	104 20W
Manzanillo, Pta.	166	9 30N	79 40W
Manzano Mts.	161	34 30N	106 45W
Manzini	129	26 30S	31 25E
Mao	117	14 4N	15 19E
Maohsing	107	45 31N	124 32E
Maoke, Pengunungan	102	3 40S	137 30E
Maolin	107	43 55N	123 25E
Maoming	109	21 39N	110 54E
Maopi T'ou	109	21 56N	120 43E
Maoping	109	30 51N	110 54E
Maowen	108	31 41N	103 52E
Mapastepec	165	15 26N	92 54W
Mapia, Kepulauan	103	0 50N	134 20E
Mapien	108	28 48N	103 39E
Mapimí	164	25 50N	103 31W
Mapimí, Bolsón de	164	27 30N	103 15W
Map'ing	109	31 36N	113 33E
Mapinga	126	6 40S	39 12E
Mapinhane	129	22 20S	35 0E
Maple Creek	153	49 55N	109 29W
Mapleton	160	44 4N	123 58W
Maplewood	158	38 33N	90 18W
Mappinga	109	34 58S	138 52E
Maprik	135	3 44S	143 3E
Mapuca	97	15 36N	73 46E
Mapuera, R.	174	0 30S	58 25W
Maputo	129	25 58S	32 32E
Maqnā	92	28 25N	34 50E
Maquela do Zombo	124	6 0S	15 15E
Maquinchao	176	41 15S	68 50W
Maquoketa	158	42 4N	90 40W
Mar Chiquita, L.	172	30 40S	62 50W
Mar del Plata	172	38 0S	57 30W
Mar Menor, L.	59	37 40N	0 45W
Mar, Reg.	37	57 11N	2 53W
Mar, Serra do	173	25 30S	49 0W
Mara, Bangla.	98	28 11N	94 7E
Mara, Tanz.	126	1 30S	34 32E
Mara □, Tanz.	126	1 45S	34 20E
Mara □, Tanz.	126	1 30S	34 32E
Maraã	174	1 43S	65 25W
Marabá	170	5 20S	49 5W
Maracá, I. de	170	2 10N	50 30W
Maracaibo	174	10 40N	71 37W
Maracaibo, Lago de	174	9 40N	71 30W
Maracaju	173	21 38S	55 9W
Maracanã	170	0 46S	47 27W
Maracás	171	13 26S	40 27W
Maracay	174	10 15N	67 36W
Marādah	119	29 4N	19 4E
Maradi	121	13 35N	8 10E
Maradun	121	12 35N	6 18E
Marāgheh	92	37 30N	46 12E
Maragogipe	171	12 46S	38 55W
Marajó, B. de	170	1 0S	48 30W
Marajó, Ilha de	170	1 0S	49 30W
Maralal	124	1 0N	36 38E
Maralinga	137	29 45S	131 15E
Marama	140	35 10S	140 10E
Marampa	120	8 45N	10 28W
Maramureş □	70	47 45N	24 0E
Maran	101	3 35N	102 45E
Marana	161	32 30N	111 9W
Maranboy	136	14 40S	132 40E
Maranchón	58	41 6N	2 15W
Marand	92	38 30N	45 45E
Marandellas	127	18 5S	31 42E
Maranguape	170	3 55S	38 50W
Maranhão = São Luis	170	2 31S	44 16W
Maranhão □	170	5 0S	46 0W
Marañ ó n, R.	174	4 50S	75 35W
Marano, L. di	63	45 42N	13 13E
Maranoa R.	139	27 50S	148 37E
Maraş	92	37 37N	36 53E
Mărăşeşti	70	45 52N	27 5E
Maratea	65	39 59N	15 43E
Marateca	57	38 34N	8 40W
Marathókambos	69	37 43N	26 42E
Marathon, Austral.	138	20 51S	143 32E
Marathon, Can.	150	48 44N	86 23W
Marathón	69	38 11N	23 58E
Marathon, N.Y., U.S.A.	162	42 25N	76 3W
Marathon, Tex., U.S.A.	159	30 15N	103 15W
Maratua, I.	103	2 10N	118 35E
Maraú	171	14 6S	39 0W
Marazion	30	50 8N	5 29W
Marbat	91	17 0N	54 45E
Marbella	57	36 30N	4 57W
Marble Bar	136	21 9S	119 44E
Marble Falls	159	30 30N	98 15W
Marblehead	162	42 29N	70 51W
Marburg	48	50 49N	8 44E
Marby	72	63 7N	14 18E
Marcal, R.	53	47 21N	17 15E
Marcali	53	46 35N	17 25E
Marcaria	62	45 7N	10 34E
March	29	52 33N	0 5E
Marchand = Rommani	118	33 20N	6 40W
Marché	44	46 0N	1 20E
Marche □	63	43 22N	13 10E
Marche-en-Famenne	47	50 14N	5 19E
Marchena	57	37 18N	5 23W
Marches = Marche	63	43 22N	13 10E
Marciana Marina	62	42 44N	10 12E
Marcianise	65	41 3N	14 16E
Marcigny	45	46 17N	4 2E
Marcillac-Vallon	44	44 29N	2 27E
Marcillat	44	46 12N	2 38E
Marcinelle	47	50 24N	4 26E
Marck	43	50 57N	1 57E
Marckolsheim	43	48 10N	7 30E
Marcos Juárez	172	32 42S	62 5W
Marcus I.	130	24 0N	153 45E
Mardan	94	34 20N	72 0E
Marden	28	52 7N	2 42W
Mardie	136	21 12S	115 59E
Mardin	92	37 20N	40 36E
Marechal Deodoro	170	9 43S	35 54W
Maree L.	36	57 40N	5 30W
Mareeba	138	16 59S	145 28E
Mareham le Fen	33	53 7N	0 3W
Marek	103	4 41S	120 24E
Marek = Stanke Dimitrov	66	42 27N	23 9E
Maremma	62	42 45N	11 15E
Maréna	120	14 0N	7 30W
Marenberg	63	46 38N	15 13E
Marengo	158	41 42N	92 5W
Marennes	126	45 49N	1 5W
Marenyi	126	4 22S	39 8E
Marerano	129	21 23S	44 52E
Maréttimo, I.	64	37 58N	12 5E
Mareuil-sur-Lay	44	46 32N	1 14W
Marfa	159	30 15N	104 0W
Marfleet	33	53 45N	0 15W
Margable	123	12 54N	42 38E
Margam	31	51 33N	3 45W
Marganets	82	47 40N	34 40E
Margao	97	14 12N	73 58E
Margaree Harbour	151	46 26N	61 8W
Margaret Bay	152	51 20N	127 20W
Margaret L.	152	58 56N	115 25W
Margaret, R.	136	12 57S	131 16E
Margaret River	137	33 57S	115 7E
Margarita, Isla de	174	11 0N	64 0W
Margarítion	68	39 22N	20 26E
Margate, S. Afr.	129	30 50S	30 20E
Margate, U.K.	29	51 23N	1 24E
Margate City	162	39 20N	74 31W
Margelan	85	40 27N	71 42E
Margeride, Mts. de la	44	44 43N	3 38E
Margherita	98	27 16N	95 40E
Margherita di Savola	65	41 25N	16 5E
Marghita	70	47 22N	22 22E
Margonin	54	52 58N	17 5E
Margreten	50	47 49N	5 49E
Marguerite	152	52 30N	122 25W
Marhoum	118	34 27N	0 11W
Mari, A.S.S.R. □	81	56 30N	48 0E
María Elena	172	22 18S	69 40W
María Grande	172	31 45S	59 55W
Maria, I.	138	14 52S	135 45E
Maria I.	138	42 35S	148 0E
Maria van Diemen, C.	142	34 29S	172 40E
Mariager	73	56 40N	10 0E
Mariager Fjord	73	56 42N	10 19E
Mariakani	126	3 50S	39 27E
Marian L.	152	63 0N	116 15W
Mariana	171	20 23S	43 25W
Mariana Is.	130	17 0N	145 0E
Mariana Trench	130	13 0N	145 0W
Marianao	166	23 8N	82 24W
Mariani	98	26 39N	94 19E
Marianna, Ark., U.S.A.	159	34 48N	90 48W
Marianna, Fla., U.S.A.	157	30 45N	85 15W
Mariannelund	73	57 37N	15 35E
Mariánské Lázně	52	49 57N	12 41E
Marias, R.	160	48 26N	111 40W
Mariato, Punta	166	7 12N	80 52W
Mariazell	52	47 47N	15 19E
Marib	91	15 25N	45 20E
Maribo	73	54 48N	11 30E
Maribor	63	46 36N	15 40E
Marico, R.	128	24 25S	26 30E
Maricopa, Ariz., U.S.A.	161	33 5N	112 2W
Maricopa, Calif., U.S.A.	163	35 7N	119 27W
Marîdî	123	4 55N	29 25E
Marîdî, W.	123	5 25N	29 21E
Marie Galante, I.	167	15 56N	61 16W
Mariecourt	149	61 30N	72 0W
Mariefred	72	59 15N	17 12E
Mariehamn (Maarianhamina)	75	60 5N	19 57E
Marienberg, Ger.	48	50 40N	13 10E
Marienberg, Neth.	47	52 30N	6 35E
Marienberg, P.N.G.	138	3 54S	144 10E
Marienbourg	47	50 6N	4 31E
Mariental	128	24 36S	18 0E
Mariestad	73	58 43N	13 50E
Marietta, Ga., U.S.A.	157	34 0N	84 30W
Marietta, Ohio, U.S.A.	156	39 27N	81 27W
Marignane	45	43 25N	5 13E
Mariinsk	76	56 10N	87 20E
Mariinskiy Posad	81	56 10N	47 45E
Marília	173	22 0S	50 0W
Marillana	136	22 37S	119 24E
Marín	56	42 23N	8 42W
Marina	163	36 41N	121 48W
Marina di Cirò	65	39 22N	17 8E
Mariña, La	56	43 30N	7 40W
Marina Plains	138	14 37S	143 57E
Marinduque, I.	103	13 25N	122 0E
Marine City	156	42 45N	82 29W
Marinel, Le	127	10 25S	25 17E
Marineo	64	37 57N	13 23E
Marinette, Ariz., U.S.A.	161	33 41N	112 16W
Marinette, Wis., U.S.A.	156	45 4N	87 40W
Maringá	173	23 35S	51 50W
Marinha Grande	57	39 45N	8 56W
Marino	109	35 3S	138 31E
Marino Rocks	109	35 3S	138 31E
Marion, Austral.	109	34 59S	138 33E
Marion, Ala., U.S.A.	157	32 33N	87 20W
Marion, Ill., U.S.A.	159	37 45N	88 55W
Marion, Ind., U.S.A.	156	40 35N	85 40W
Marion, Iowa, U.S.A.	158	42 2N	91 36W
Marion, Kans., U.S.A.	158	38 25N	97 2W
Marion, Mich., U.S.A.	156	44 7N	85 8W
Marion, N.C., U.S.A.	157	35 42N	82 0W
Marion, Ohio, U.S.A.	156	40 38N	83 8W
Marion, S.C., U.S.A.	157	34 11N	79 22W
Marion, Va., U.S.A.	157	36 51N	81 29W
Marion Bay	140	35 12S	136 59E
Marion, L.	157	33 30N	80 15W
Marion Reef	138	19 10S	152 17E
Maripa	174	7 26N	65 9W
Mariposa	163	37 31N	119 59W
Mariscal Estigarribia	172	22 3S	60 40W
Maritime Alps = Alpes Maritimes	62	44 10N	7 10E
Maritsa	67	42 1N	25 50E
Maritsá	69	36 22N	28 10E
Maritsa, R.	67	42 15N	24 0E
Mariyampole = Kapsukas	80	54 33N	23 19E
Marjan	93	32 5N	68 20E
Mark	34	55 2N	5 1W
Marka	122	18 14N	41 19E
Markapur	97	15 44N	79 19E
Markaryd	73	56 28N	13 35E
Marke	47	50 48N	3 14E
Marked Tree	159	35 35N	90 24W
Markelo	46	52 14N	6 30E
Markelsdorfer Huk	48	54 33N	11 0E
Marken	46	52 26N	5 12E
Markerwaard	46	52 33N	5 15E
Market Bosworth	28	52 37N	1 24W
Market Deeping	29	52 40N	0 20W
Market Drayton	32	52 55N	2 30W
Market Harborough	29	52 29N	0 55W
Market Lavington	28	51 17N	1 59W
Market Rasen	33	53 24N	0 20W
Market Weighton	33	53 52N	0 40W
Markethill	38	54 18N	6 31W
Markfield	28	52 42N	1 18W
Markham I.	12	84 0N	0 45W
Markham L.	153	62 30N	102 35W
Markham Mts.	13	83 0S	164 0E
Markham, R.	135	6 41S	147 2E
Marki	54	52 20N	21 2E
Markinch	35	56 12N	3 9W
Markleeville	163	38 42N	119 47W
Markoupoulon	69	37 53N	23 57E
Markovac	66	44 14N	21 7E
Markovo	77	64 40N	169 40E
Markoye	121	14 39N	0 2E
Marks	81	51 45N	46 50E
Marks Tey	29	51 53N	0 48E
Marksville	159	31 10N	92 2W
Markt Schwaben	49	48 14N	11 49E
Marktredwitz	49	50 1N	12 2E
Marlboro, Can.	152	53 30N	116 50W
Marlboro, U.S.A.	162	42 19N	71 33W
Marlboro, N.Y., U.S.A.	162	41 36N	73 58W
Marlborough, Austral.	138	22 46S	149 52E
Marlborough, U.K.	28	51 26N	1 44W
Marlborough □	143	41 45S	173 33E
Marlborough Downs	28	51 25N	1 55W
Marle	43	49 43N	3 47E
Marlin	159	31 25N	96 50W
Marlow, Austral.	141	35 17S	149 55E
Marlow, Ger.	48	54 8N	12 34E
Marlow, U.K.	29	51 34N	0 47W
Marlow, U.S.A.	159	34 40N	97 58W
Marly-le-Grand	50	46 47N	7 10E
Marmagao	97	15 25N	73 56E
Marmande	44	44 30N	0 10E
Marmara denizi	82	40 45N	28 15E
Marmara, I.	82	40 35N	27 38E
Marmara, Sea of = Marmara denizi	92	40 45N	28 15E
Marmaris	92	36 50N	28 14E
Marmarth	158	46 21N	103 52W
Marmion L.	150	48 55N	91 30W
Marmion Mt.	137	29 16S	119 50E
Marmolada, Mte.	63	46 25N	11 55E
Marmolejo	57	38 3N	4 13W
Marmora	150	44 28N	77 41W
Marnay	43	47 20N	5 48E
Marne	48	53 57N	9 1E
Marne □	43	49 0N	4 10E
Marne, R.	43	48 53N	4 25E
Marnhull	28	50 58N	2 20W
Maro	124	8 30N	19 0E
Maroa	174	2 43N	67 33W
Maroala	129	15 23S	47 59E
Maroantsetra	129	15 26S	49 44E
Marocco ■	129	32 0N	5 50W
Maromandia	129	14 13S	48 5E
Maroni, R.	175	4 0N	52 0W
Marónia	68	40 53N	25 24E
Maroochydore	139	26 29S	153 5E
Maroona	140	37 27S	142 54E
Maros, R.	53	46 25N	20 20E
Marosakoa	129	15 26S	46 38E

Marostica Maya, R

Marostica 63 45 44N 11 40 E
Maroua 121 10 40N 14 20 E
Marovoay 129 16 6S 46 39 E
Marple 32 53 23N 2 5W
Marquard 128 28 40S 27 28 E
Marqueira 57 38 41N 9 9W
Marquesas Is. = Marquises 131 9 30S 140 0W
Marquette 156 46 30N 87 21W
Marquise 43 50 50N 1 40 E
Marquises, Is. 131 9 30S 140 0W
Marra 139 31 12S 144 10 E
Marra, Gebet 123 7 20N 27 35 E
Marradi 63 44 5N 11 37 E
Marrakech 118 31 40N 8 0W
Marrat 92 25 0N 45 35 E
Marrawah 138 40 55S 144 42 E
Marrecas, Serra das 170 9 0S 41 0W
Marree 139 29 39S 138 1 E
Marrimane 129 22 58S 33 34 E
Marromeu 125 18 40S 36 25 E
Marroqui, Punta 56 36 0N 5 37W
Marrowie Creek 141 33 23S 145 40 E
Marrubane 127 18 0S 37 0 E
Marrum 46 53 19N 5 48 E
Marrupa 127 13 8S 37 30 E
Mars, Le 158 43 0N 96 0W
Marsa Susa (Apollonia) 117 32 52N 21 59 E
Marsabit 126 2 18N 38 0 E
Marsabit □ 126 2 45N 37 45 E
Marsala 64 37 48N 12 25 E
Marsciano 63 42 54N 12 20 E
Marsden 141 33 47N 147 32 E
Marsdiep 46 52 58N 4 46 E
Marseillan 44 43 23N 3 31 E
Marseille 45 43 18N 5 23 E
Marseilles = Marseille 45 43 18N 5 23 E
Marsh I. 159 29 35N 91 50W
Marshall, Liberia 120 6 8N 10 22W
Marshall, Ark., U.S.A. 159 35 58N 92 40W
Marshall, Mich., U.S.A. 156 42 17N 84 59W
Marshall, Minn., U.S.A. 158 44 25N 95 45W
Marshall, Mo., U.S.A. 158 39 8N 93 15W
Marshall, Tex., U.S.A. 159 32 29N 94 20W
Marshall Is. 130 9 0N 171 0 E
Marshall, R. 138 22 59S 136 59 E
Marshalltown 158 42 0N 93 0W
Marshfield, U.K. 28 51 27N 2 18W
Marshfield, Mo., U.S.A. 159 37 20N 92 58W
Marshfield, Wis., U.S.A. 158 44 42N 90 10W
Mársico Nuovo 65 40 26N 15 43 E
Marske by the sea 33 54 35N 1 0W
Märsta 72 59 37N 17 52 E
Marstal 73 54 51N 10 30 E
Marston Moor 33 53 58N 1 17W
Marstrand 73 57 53N 11 35 E
Mart 159 31 34N 96 51W
Marta, R. 63 42 18N 11 47 E
Martaban 98 16 30N 97 35 E
Martaban, G. of 98 15 40N 96 30 E
Martano 65 40 14N 18 18 E
Martapura 102 3 22S 114 56 E
Marte 121 12 23N 13 46 E
Martebo 73 57 45N 18 30 E
Martelange 47 49 49N 5 43 E
Martés, Sierra 59 39 20N 1 0W
Marthaguy Creek 141 30 50S 147 45 E
Martham 29 52 42N 1 38 E
Martha's Vineyard 162 41 25N 70 35W
Martigné Ferchaud 42 47 50N 1 20W
Martigny 50 46 6N 7 3 E
Martigues 45 43 24N 5 4 E
Martil 118 35 36N 5 15W
Martin, Czech. 53 49 6N 18 48 E
Martin, S.D., U.S.A. 158 43 11N 101 45W
Martin, Tenn., U.S.A. 159 36 23N 88 51W
Martin, L. 157 32 45N 85 50W
Martin, R. 58 41 2N 0 43W
Martina 51 46 53N 10 28 E
Martina Franca 65 40 42N 17 20 E
Martinborough 142 41 14S 175 29 E
Martinez 163 38 1N 122 8W
Martinho Campos 171 19 20S 45 13W
Martinique, I. 167 14 40N 61 0W
Martinique Passage 167 15 15N 61 0W
Martinon 69 38 25N 23 15 E
Martinópolis 173 22 11S 51 12W
Martins 171 6 5S 37 55W
Martinsberg 52 48 22N 15 9 E
Martinsburg 156 39 30N 77 57W
Martinsville, Ind., U.S.A. 156 39 29N 86 23W
Martinsville, Va., U.S.A. 157 36 41N 79 52W
Martley 28 52 14N 2 22W
Martock 28 50 58N 2 47W
Marton 142 40 4S 175 23 E
Martorell 58 41 28N 1 56 E
Martos 57 37 44N 3 58W
Martre, La, L. 148 63 8N 117 16W
Martre, La, R. 148 63 0N 118 0W
Martuk 84 50 46N 56 31 E
Martuni 83 40 9N 45 10 E
Maru 121 12 22N 6 22 E
Marudi 102 4 10N 114 25 E
Maruf 93 31 30N 67 0 E
Marugame 110 34 15N 133 55 E
Maruggio 65 40 20N 17 33 E
Marui 135 4 4S 143 2 E
Maruim 170 10 45S 37 5W
Marulan 141 34 43S 150 3 E
Marum 46 53 9N 6 16 E
Marunga 128 17 20S 20 2 E
Marungu, Mts. 126 7 30S 30 0 E
Maruoka 111 36 9N 136 16 E
Marvejols 44 44 33N 3 19 E
Marvine Mt. 161 38 44N 111 40W
Marwar 94 25 43N 73 45 E
Mary 76 37 40N 61 50 E
Mary Frances L. 153 63 19N 106 13W
Mary Kathleen 138 20 35S 139 48 E
Maryborough, Queens., Austral. 139 25 31S 152 37 E
Maryborough, Vic., Austral. 140 37 0S 143 44 E
Maryets 81 56 17N 49 47 E
Maryfield 153 49 50N 101 35W
Marykirk 37 56 47N 2 30W
Maryland □ 156 39 10N 76 40W
Maryland Jc. 127 12 45S 30 31 E
Maryport 32 54 43N 3 30W
Mary's Harbour 151 52 18N 55 51W
Marystown 151 47 10N 55 10W
Marysvale 161 38 25N 112 17W
Marysville, Can. 152 49 35N 116 0W
Marysville, Calif., U.S.A. 160 39 14N 121 40W
Marysville, Kans., U.S.A. 158 39 50N 96 38W
Marysville, Ohio, U.S.A. 156 40 15N 83 20W
Marytavy 30 50 34N 4 6W
Maryvale 139 28 4S 152 12 E
Maryville 157 35 50N 84 0W
Marywell 37 56 35N 2 31W
Marzo, Punta 174 6 50N 77 42W
Marzuq 119 25 53N 14 10 E
Masada = Mesada 90 31 20N 35 19 E
Masafa 127 13 50S 27 30 E
Masai 101 1 29N 103 55 E
Masai Steppe 126 4 30S 36 30 E
Masaka 126 0 21S 31 45 E
Masakali 121 13 2N 12 32 E
Masalima, Kepulauan 102 5 10S 116 50 E
Masamba 103 2 30S 120 15 E
Masan 107 35 11N 128 32 E
Masanasa 59 39 25N 0 25W
Masandam, Ras 93 26 30N 56 30 E
Masasi 127 10 45S 38 52 E
Masasi □ 127 10 45S 38 50 E
Masaya 166 12 0N 86 7W
Masba 121 10 35N 13 1 E
Mascara 118 35 26N 0 6 E
Mascota 164 20 30N 104 50W
Masela 103 8 9S 129 51 E
Maseme 147 18 46S 25 3 E
Maseru 128 29 18S 27 30 E
Mashaba 127 20 2S 30 29 E
Mashabih 92 25 35N 36 30 E
Masham 33 54 15N 1 40W
Mashan 108 23 44N 108 14 E
Masherbrum, mt. 95 35 38N 76 18 E
Mashhad 93 36 20N 59 35 E
Mashi 121 13 0N 7 54 E
Mashiki 110 32 51N 130 53 E
Mashki Chah 93 29 5N 62 30 E
Mashkode 150 47 2N 84 7W
Mashonaland, North, □ 127 16 30S 30 0 E
Mashonaland, South, □ 127 18 0S 31 30 E
Mashtagi 83 40 35N 50 0 E
Masi 74 69 26N 23 50 E
Masi-Manimba 124 4 40S 18 5 E
Masindi 126 1 40N 31 43 E
Masindi Port 126 1 43N 32 2 E
Masirah 91 20 25N 58 50 E
Masisea 174 8 35S 74 15W
Masisi 126 1 23S 28 49 E
Masjed Solyman 92 31 55N 49 25 E
Mask, L. 38 53 36N 9 24W
Maski 97 15 56N 76 46 E
Maslen Nos 67 42 18N 27 48 E
Maslinica 63 43 24N 16 13 E
Masnou 58 41 28N 2 20 E
Masoala, C. 129 15 59S 50 13 E
Masoarivo 129 19 3S 44 19 E
Masohi 103 3 2S 128 15 E
Masomeloka 129 20 17S 48 37 E
Mason, Nev., U.S.A. 163 38 56N 119 8W
Mason, S.D., U.S.A. 158 45 12N 103 27W
Mason, Tex., U.S.A. 159 30 45N 99 15W
Mason B. 143 46 55S 167 45 E
Mason City 160 48 0N 119 0W
Masqat 93 23 37N 58 36 E
Massa 62 44 2N 10 7 E
Massa Marittima 62 43 3N 10 52 E
Massa, O. 118 30 0N 9 30W
Massachusetts □ 162 42 25N 72 0W
Massachusetts B. 162 42 30N 70 0W
Massada 90 33 12N 35 45 E
Massafra 65 40 35N 17 8 E
Massaguet 117 12 28N 15 26 E
Massakory 117 13 0N 15 49 E
Massangena 129 21 34S 33 0 E
Massapê 170 3 31S 40 19W
Massarosa 62 43 53N 10 17 E
Massat 44 42 53N 1 21 E
Massava 84 60 40N 62 6 E
Massawa = Mitsiwa 123 15 35N 39 25 E
Massena 156 44 52N 74 55W
Massenya 117 11 30N 16 25 E
Masset 152 54 0N 132 0W
Massiac 44 45 15N 3 11 E
Massif Central 44 45 30N 2 21 E
Massillon 156 40 47N 81 30W
Massinga 125 23 15S 35 22 E
Massingir 129 23 46S 32 4 E
Mässlingen 98 62 42N 12 48 E
Massman 138 16 25S 145 25 E
Masson I. 13 66 10S 93 20 E
Mastaba 122 20 52N 39 30 E
Mastanli = Momchilgrad 21 41 33N 25 23 E
Masterton 142 40 56S 175 39 E
Mástikho, Ákra 68 38 10N 26 2 E
Mastuj 95 36 20N 72 36 E
Mastung 93 29 50N 66 42 E
Mastura 122 23 7N 38 52 E
Masuda 110 34 40N 131 51 E
Masulipatam 96 16 12N 81 12 E
Maswa □ 126 1 20S 34 0 E
Mat, R. 68 41 40N 20 0 E
Mata de São João 171 12 31S 38 17W
Matabeleland North □ 127 20 0S 28 0 E
Matabeleland South □ 127 19 0S 29 0 E
Mataboor 103 1 41S 138 3 E
Matachel, R. 57 38 32N 6 0W
Matachewan 150 47 56N 80 39W
Matad 105 47 12N 115 29 E
Matadi 124 5 52S 13 31 E
Matador 153 50 49N 107 56W
Matagalpa 166 13 10N 85 40W
Matagami 150 49 45N 77 34W
Matagami, L. 150 49 50N 77 40W
Matagorda 159 28 43N 96 0W
Matagorda, B. 159 28 30N 96 15W
Matagorda I. 159 28 10N 96 40W
Matak, P. 101 3 18N 106 16 E
Matakana 141 32 59S 145 54 E
Matale 97 7 30N 80 44 E
Matam 120 15 34N 13 17W
Matamata 142 37 48S 175 47 E
Matameye 121 13 26N 8 28 E
Matamoros, Campeche, Mexico 165 25 53N 97 30W
Matamoros, Coahuila, Mexico 164 25 45N 103 1W
Matamoros, Puebla, Mexico 165 18 2N 98 17W
Matamoros, Tamaulipas, Mexico 165 25 50N 97 30W
Matana, D. 103 2 30S 121 25 E
Matandu, R. 127 8 35S 39 40 E
Matane 151 48 50N 67 33W
Mat'ang, Szechwan, China 108 31 54N 102 55 E
Mat'ang, Yunnan, China 108 23 30N 104 4 E
Matankari 121 13 46N 4 1 E
Matanuska 148 61 38N 149 0W
Matanzá 174 7 22N 73 2W
Matanzas 166 23 0N 81 40W
Matapá, Ákra 69 36 22N 22 27 E
Matapedia 151 48 0N 66 59W
Matara 97 5 58N 80 30 E
Mataram 102 8 41S 116 10 E
Matarani 174 16 50S 72 10W
Mataranka 136 14 55S 133 4 E
Mataró 58 41 32N 2 29 E
Matarraña, R. 58 40 55N 0 8 E
Mataruška Banja 66 43 40N 20 45 E
Matata 142 37 54S 176 48 E
Matatiele 129 30 20S 28 49 E
Mataura 143 46 11S 168 51 E
Mataura, R. 143 45 49S 168 44 E
Matehuala 164 23 40N 100 50W
Mateira 171 18 54S 50 30W
Mateke Hills 127 21 48S 31 0 E
Matélica 63 43 15N 13 0 E
Matera 65 40 40N 16 37 E
Mátészalka 53 47 58N 22 20 E
Matetsi 127 18 12S 26 0 E
Mateur 119 37 0N 9 48 E
Mateyev Kurgan 83 47 35N 38 47 E
Matfors 72 62 21N 17 2 E
Matha 44 45 52N 0 20W
Matheson I. 153 51 45N 96 56W
Mathews 162 37 26N 76 19W
Mathias Pass 143 43 7S 171 6 E
Mathis 159 28 4N 97 48W
Mathoura 141 35 50S 144 55 E
Mathry 31 51 56N 5 6W
Mathura 94 27 30N 77 48 E
Mati 103 6 55N 126 15 E
Mati, R. 68 41 40N 20 0 E
Matías Romero 165 16 53N 95 2W
Matibane 127 14 49S 40 45 E
Matien 109 32 55N 116 26 E
Matlock 33 53 8N 1 32W
Matmata 119 33 30N 9 59 E
Matna 123 13 49N 35 10 E
Mato Grosso □ 175 14 0S 55 0W
Mato Grosso, Planalto do 174 15 0S 54 0W
Mato Verde 171 15 23S 42 52W
Matochkin Shar 76 73 10N 56 40 E
Matong 135 5 36S 151 50 E
Matopo Hills 127 20 36S 28 20 E
Matopos 127 20 20S 28 29 E
Matour 45 46 19N 4 29 E
Matozinhos 56 41 11N 8 42W
Matrah 93 23 37N 58 30 E
Matrûh 122 31 19N 27 9 E
Matsang Tsangpo (Brahmaputra), R. 99 29 25N 88 0 E
Matsena 121 13 5N 10 5 E
Matsesta 83 43 34N 39 44 E
Matsu Tao 109 26 9N 119 56 E
Matsubara 111 34 33N 135 34 E
Matsudo 111 35 47N 139 54 E
Matsue 110 35 25N 133 10 E
Matsumae 112 41 26N 140 7 E
Matsumoto 111 36 15N 138 0 E
Matsusaka 111 34 34N 136 32 E
Matsutō 111 36 31N 136 34 E
Matsuura 110 33 20N 129 49 E
Matsuyama 110 33 45N 132 45 E
Mattagami, R. 150 50 43N 81 29W
Mattancheri 97 9 50N 76 15 E
Mattawa 150 46 20N 78 45W
Mattawamkeag 151 45 30N 68 30W
Matterhorn, mt. 50 45 58N 7 39 E
Mattersburg 53 47 44N 16 24 E
Matthew Town 167 20 57N 73 40W
Matthew's Ridge 174 7 37N 60 10W
Mattice 150 49 40N 83 20W
Mattituck 162 40 58N 72 32W
Mattmar 72 63 18N 13 54 E
Mattoon 156 39 30N 88 20W
Matua 102 2 58S 110 52 E
Matuba 129 24 28S 32 49 E
Matucana 174 11 55S 76 15W
Matun 94 33 22N 69 58 E
Maturín 174 9 45N 63 11W
Matutina 171 19 13S 45 58W
Matzuzaki 111 34 43N 138 50 E
Mau-é-ele 129 24 18S 34 2 E
Mau Escarpment 126 0 40S 36 0 E
Mau Ranipur 95 25 16N 79 8 E
Mauagami, R. 150 49 30N 82 0W
Maubeuge 43 50 17N 3 57 E
Maubourguet 44 43 29N 0 1 E
Mauchline 34 55 31N 4 23W
Maud 37 57 30N 2 8W
Maud, Pt. 137 23 6S 113 45 E
Maude 140 34 29S 144 18 E
Maudheim 13 71 5S 11 0W
Maudin Sun 99 16 0N 94 30 E
Maués 174 3 20S 57 45W
Mauganj 99 24 50N 81 55 E
Maughold 32 54 18N 4 17W
Maughold Hd. 32 54 18N 4 17W
Maui I. 147 20 45N 156 20 E
Maulamyaing 99 16 30N 97 40 E
Maule □ 172 36 5S 72 30W
Mauleon 44 43 14N 0 54W
Maulvibazar 98 24 29N 91 42 E
Maum 38 53 31N 9 35W
Maumee 156 41 35N 83 40W
Maumee, R. 156 41 42N 83 28W
Maumere 103 8 38S 122 13 E
Maumturk Mts. 38 53 32N 9 42W
Maun 128 20 0S 23 26 E
Mauna Kea, Mt. 147 19 50N 155 28W
Mauna Loa, Mt. 147 19 50N 155 28W
Maunath Bhanjan 95 25 56N 83 33 E
Maungaturoto 142 36 6S 174 23 E
Maungdow 98 21 14N 94 5 E
Maungmagan Is. 99 14 0S 97 48 E
Maungmagan Kyunzu 101 14 0N 97 48 E
Maupin 160 45 12N 121 9W
Maure-de-Bretagne 42 47 53N 2 0W
Maureen, oilfield 19 58 5N 1 45 E
Maurepas L. 159 30 18N 90 35W
Maures, mts. 45 43 15N 6 15 E
Mauriac 44 45 13N 2 19 E
Maurice L. 137 29 30S 131 0 E
Mauriceville 142 40 45S 175 35 E
Maurienne 45 45 15N 6 20 E
Mauritania ■ 116 20 50N 10 0W
Mauritius ■ 11 20 0S 57 0 E
Mauron 42 48 9N 2 18W
Maurs 44 44 43N 2 12 E
Maurthe, R. 43 48 47N 6 9 E
Mauston 158 43 48N 90 5W
Mauterndorf 52 47 9N 13 40 E
Mauvezin 44 43 44N 0 53 E
Mauzé-sur le Mignon 44 46 12N 0 41W
Mavelikara 97 9 14N 76 32 E
Mavinga 125 15 50S 20 10 E
Mavli 94 24 45N 73 55 E
Mavqi'im 90 31 38N 34 32 E
Mavrova 68 40 26N 19 32 E
Mavuradonha Mts. 127 16 30S 31 30 E
Mawa 126 2 45N 26 33 E
Mawana 94 29 6N 77 58 E
Mawand 94 29 33N 68 38 E
Mawer 153 50 46N 106 22W
Mawgan 30 50 4N 5 10W
Mawkmai 98 20 14N 97 50 E
Mawlaik 98 23 40N 94 26 E
Mawlawkho 98 17 50N 97 38 E
Mawson Base 13 67 30S 65 0 E
Max 158 47 50N 101 20W
Maxcanú 165 20 40N 90 10W
Maxhamish L. 152 59 50N 123 17W
Maxixe 129 23 54S 35 17 E
Maxwellheugh 35 55 35N 2 23W
Maxwelltown 142 39 51S 174 49 E
Maxwelton, Queens., Austral. 138 15 45S 142 30 E
Maxwelton, Queens., Austral. 138 20 43S 142 41 E
May Downs 138 22 38S 148 55 E
May, I. of 35 56 11N 2 32W
May Nefalis 123 15 0N 38 12 E
May Pen 166 17 58N 77 15W
May River 135 4 19S 141 58 E
Maya 58 43 12N 1 29W
Maya Gudo, Mt. 123 7 30N 37 8 E
Maya Mts. 165 16 30N 89 0W
Maya, R. 77 58 20N 135 0 E

Mayaguana Island Menglien

Mayaguana Island 167 21 30N 72 44W
Mayagüez 147 18 12N 67 9W
Mayahi 121 13 58N 7 40E
Mayals 58 41 22N 0 30E
Mayang 108 27 53N 109 48E
Mayanup 137 33 58S 116 25E
Mayapán 165 20 38N 89 27W
Mayarf 167 20 40N 75 39W
Mayarí 167 20 40N 75 41W
Mayavaram = Mayuram 97 11 3N 79 42E
Maybell 160 40 30N 108 4W
Maybole 34 55 21N 4 41W
Maychew 123 12 50N 39 42E
Maydena 138 42 45S 146 39E
Maydos 68 40 13N 26 20E
Mayen 49 50 18N 7 10E
Mayenne 42 48 20N 0 38W
Mayenne □ 42 48 10N 0 40W
Mayer 161 34 28N 112 17W
Mayerthorpe 152 53 57N 115 8W
Mayfield, Derby., U.K. 33 53 1N 1 47W
Mayfield, E. Sussex, U.K. 29 51 1N 0 17E
Mayfield, Ky., U.S.A. 157 36 45N 88 40W
Mayfield, N.Y., U.S.A. 162 43 6N 74 16W
Mayhill 161 32 58N 105 30W
Maykop 83 44 35N 40 25E
Mayli-Say 85 41 17N 72 24E
Maymyo 100 22 2N 96 28E
Maynard 162 42 30N 71 33W
Maynard Hills 137 28 35S 119 50E
Mayne, Le, L. 151 57 5N 68 30W
Mayne, R. 138 23 40S 142 10E
Maynooth, Can. 150 45 14N 77 56W
Maynooth, Ireland 38 53 22N 6 38W
Mayo 147 63 38N 135 57W
Mayo □ 139 53 47N 9 7W
Mayo Bridge 38 54 11N 6 13W
Mayo L. 147 63 45N 135 0W
Mayo, R. 164 26 45N 109 47W
Mayon, Mt. 103 13 15N 123 42E
Mayor I. 142 37 16S 176 17E
Mayorga 56 42 10N 5 16W
Mays Landing 162 39 27N 74 44W
Mayskiy 83 43 47N 43 59E
Mayson L. 153 57 55N 107 10W
Maysville 156 38 43N 84 16W
Mayu, I. 103 1 30N 126 30E
Mayuram 97 11 3N 79 42E
Mayville 158 47 30N 97 23W
Mayya 77 61 44N 130 18E
Mazabuka 127 15 52S 27 44E
Mazagán = El Jadida 118 33 11N 8 17W
Mazagão 175 0 20S 51 50W
Mazama 152 49 43N 120 8W
Mazamet 44 43 30N 2 20E
Mazán 174 3 15S 73 0W
Mazapil 164 24 38N 101 34W
Mazar-i-Sharif 93 36 41N 67 0E
Mazar, O. 118 32 0N 1 38E
Mazara del Vallo 64 37 40N 12 34E
Mazarredo 176 47 10S 66 50W
Mazarrón 59 37 38N 1 19W
Mazarrón, Golfo de 59 37 27N 1 19W
Mazaruni, R. 174 6 15N 60 0W
Mazatán 164 29 0N 110 8W
Mazatenango 166 14 35N 91 30W
Mazatlán 164 23 10N 106 30W
Mâzhãn 93 32 30N 59 0E
Mazheikyai 80 56 20N 22 20E
Mazinãn 93 36 25N 56 48E
Mazoe 127 17 28S 30 58E
Mazoe R. 125 16 45S 32 30E
Mazoi 127 16 42S 33 7E
Mazrûb 123 14 0N 29 20E
Mazurian Lakes = Mazurski, Pojezierze 54 53 50N 21 0E
Mazurski, Pojezierze 54 53 50N 21 0E
Mazzarino 65 37 19N 14 12E
Mbaba 120 14 59N 16 44W
Mbabane 129 26 18S 31 6E
Mbagne 120 16 6N 14 47W
M'bahiakro 120 7 33N 4 19W
M'Baiki 124 3 53N 18 1E
Mbala 127 8 46S 31 17E
Mbale 126 1 8N 34 12E
Mbalmayo 121 3 33N 11 33E
Mbamba Bay 127 11 13S 34 49E
Mbandaka 124 0 1S 18 18E
Mbanga 121 4 30N 9 33E
Mbanza Congo 124 6 18S 14 16E
Mbanza Ngungu 124 5 12S 14 53E
Mbarara 126 0 35S 30 25E
Mbatto 120 6 28N 4 22W
Mbenkuru, R. 127 9 25S 39 50E
Mberubu 121 6 10N 7 38E
Mbesuma 127 10 0S 32 2E
Mbeya 127 8 54S 33 29E
Mbeya □ 126 8 15S 33 30E
Mbia 123 6 15N 29 18E
Mbimbi 127 13 25S 23 2E
Mbinga 127 10 50S 35 0E
Mbinga □ 127 10 50S 35 0E
Mbini □ 124 1 30N 10 0E
Mbiti 123 5 42N 28 3E
Mboki 123 5 19N 25 58E
Mboro 120 15 9N 16 54W
Mboune 120 14 42N 13 34W
Mbour 120 14 22N 16 54W
Mbout 120 16 1N 12 38W
Mbozi □ 127 9 0S 32 50E
Mbuji-Mayi 126 6 9S 23 40E
Mbulu 124 3 45S 35 30E
Mbulu □ 126 3 52S 35 33E
Mbumbi 128 18 26S 19 59E
Mburucuyá 172 28 1S 58 14W
M'chounech 119 34 57N 6 1E
M'Clure Str., Can. 10 75 0N 118 0W
M'Clure Str., Can. 12 74 0N 120 0W
Mdennah 118 24 37N 6 0W
Mead L. 161 36 1N 114 44W
Meade, Can. 150 49 26N 83 51W
Meade, U.S.A. 159 37 18N 100 25W
Meadow 137 26 35S 114 40E
Meadow Lake 153 54 10N 108 26W
Meadow Lake Prov. Park 153 54 27N 109 0W
Meadville 156 41 39N 80 9W
Meaford 150 44 36N 80 35W
Mealfuarvonie, Mt. 37 57 15N 4 34W
Mealhada 56 40 22N 8 27W
Mealsgate 32 54 46N 3 14W
Mealy Mts. 151 53 10N 60 0W
Meander, R. = Menderes, Büyük 92 37 45N 27 40E
Meander River 152 59 2N 117 42W
Meare's, C. 160 45 37N 124 0W
Mearim, R. 170 3 4S 44 35W
Mearns, Howe of the 37 56 52N 2 26W
Measham 28 52 43N 1 30W
Meath □ 38 53 32N 6 40W
Meath Park 153 53 27N 105 22W
Meatian 140 35 34S 143 21E
Meaulne 44 46 36N 2 28E
Meaux 43 48 58N 2 50E
Mecanhelas 127 15 12S 35 54E
Mecca 163 33 37N 116 3W
Mecca = Makkah 122 21 30N 39 54E
Mechanicsburg 162 40 12N 77 0W
Mechanicville 162 42 54N 73 41W
Mechara 123 8 36N 40 20E
Mechelen, Anvers, Belg. 47 51 2N 4 29E
Mechelen, Limbourg, Belg. 47 50 58N 5 41E
Méchéria 118 33 35N 0 18W
Mechernich 48 50 35N 6 39E
Mechetinskaya 83 46 45N 40 32E
Mecidiye 68 40 38N 26 32E
Mecitözü 82 40 32N 35 25E
Mecklenburg B. 48 54 20N 11 40E
Meconta 127 14 59S 39 50E
Meda 56 40 57N 7 18W
Meda P.O. 136 17 22S 123 59E
Meda, R. 136 17 20S 124 30E
Medaguine 118 33 41N 3 26E
Medak 96 18 1N 78 15E
Medan 102 3 40N 98 38E
Medanosa, Pta. 176 48 0S 66 0W
Medawachchiya 97 8 30N 80 30E
Meddouza, cap 118 32 33N 9 9W
Médéa 118 36 12N 2 50E
Mededa 66 43 44N 19 15E
Medeiros Neto 171 17 20S 40 14W
Medel, Pic 51 46 37N 8 55E
Medellín 174 6 15N 75 35W
Medemblik 46 52 46N 5 8E
Meder 123 14 42N 40 44E
Mederdra 120 17 0N 15 38W
Medford, Oreg., U.S.A. 160 42 20N 122 52W
Medford, Wis., U.S.A. 158 45 9N 90 21W
Medford Lakes 162 39 52N 74 48W
Medgidia 70 44 15N 28 19E
Medi 123 5 4N 30 42E
Media 162 39 55N 75 23W
Media Agua 172 31 58S 68 25W
Media Luna 172 34 45S 66 44W
Mediaş 70 46 9N 24 22E
Medical Lake 160 47 41N 117 42W
Medicina 63 44 29N 11 38E
Medicine Bow 160 41 56N 106 11W
Medicine Hat 153 50 0N 110 45W
Medicine Lake 158 48 30N 104 30W
Medicine Lodge 159 37 20N 98 37W
Medina, Brazil 171 16 15S 41 29W
Medina, Colomb. 174 4 30N 73 21W
Medina, N.D., U.S.A. 158 46 57N 99 20W
Medina, N.Y., U.S.A. 156 43 15N 78 27W
Medina, Ohio, U.S.A. 156 41 9N 81 50W
Medina = Al Madīnah 92 24 35N 39 52E
Medina de Ríoseco 56 41 53N 5 3W
Medina del Campo 56 41 18N 4 55W
Medina L. 159 29 35N 98 58W
Medina, R. 159 29 10N 98 20W
Medina-Sidonia 57 36 28N 5 57W
Medinaceli 58 41 12N 2 30W
Mediterranean Sea 60 35 0N 15 0E
Medjerda, O. 119 36 35N 8 30E
Medkovets 67 43 37N 23 10E
Medley 153 54 25N 110 16W
Mednogorsk 84 51 24N 57 37E
Médoc 44 45 10N 0 56W
Medstead, Can. 153 53 19N 108 5W
Medstead, U.K. 28 51 7N 1 4W
Medulin 63 44 49N 13 55E
Medveda 66 42 50N 21 32E
Medveditsa, R. 81 50 30N 44 0E
Medvedok 81 57 20N 50 1E
Medvezhi, Ostrava 77 71 0N 161 0E
Medvezhyegorsk 78 63 0N 34 25E
Medway, R. 29 51 12N 0 23E
Medyn 81 54 59N 35 56E
Medzev 53 48 43N 20 55E
Medzilaborce 53 49 17N 21 52E
Meeandh 108 27 26S 153 6E
Meeberrie 137 26 57S 116 0E
Meekatharra 137 26 32S 118 29E
Meeker 160 40 1N 107 58W
Meelpaeg L. 151 48 18N 56 35W
Meeniyan 141 38 35S 146 0E
Meer 47 51 27N 4 45E
Meerane 48 50 51N 12 30E
Meerbeke 47 50 50N 4 3E
Meerle 47 51 29N 4 48E
Meerssen 47 50 53N 5 50E
Meerut 94 29 1N 77 50E
Meeteetsa 160 44 10N 108 56W
Meeuwen 47 51 6N 5 31E
Mega 123 3 57N 38 30E
Megálo Khorío 69 36 27N 27 24E
Megálo Petalí, I. 69 38 0N 24 15E
Megalópolis 69 37 25N 22 7E
Meganísi, I. 69 38 39N 20 48E
Mégantic 151 45 36N 70 56W
Mégara 69 37 58N 23 22E
Megarine 119 33 14N 6 2E
Megdhova, R. 69 39 10N 21 45E
Megen 46 51 49N 5 34E
Mégève 45 45 51N 6 37E
Meghalaya □ 98 25 50N 91 0E
Meghalayap 99 25 40N 89 55E
Meghezez, Mt. 123 9 18N 39 26E
Meghna, R. 98 23 45N 90 40E
Megiddo 90 32 36N 35 11E
Mégiscane, L. 150 48 35N 75 55W
Megiste 61 36 8N 29 34E
Mehadia 70 44 56N 22 23E
Mehaigne, R. 47 50 32N 5 13E
Mehaïguene, O. 118 32 20N 2 45E
Meharry, Mt. 132 22 59S 118 35E
Mehedinti □ 70 44 40N 22 45E
Meheisa 122 19 38N 32 57E
Mehndawal 95 26 58N 83 5E
Mehsana 94 23 39N 72 26E
Mehun-sur-Yèvre 43 47 10N 2 13E
Mei Chiang, R. 109 24 24N 116 35E
Meia Ponte, R. 171 18 32S 49 36W
Meichuan 109 30 9N 115 33E
Meidrim 31 51 51N 4 3W
Meiganga 124 6 20N 14 10E
Meigh 38 54 8N 6 22W
Meihsien, Kwangtung, China 109 24 18N 116 7E
Meihsien, Shensi, China 106 34 16N 107 42E
Meijel 47 51 21N 5 53E
Meiktila 98 21 0N 96 0E
Meilen 51 47 16N 8 39E
Meiningen 48 50 32N 10 25E
Meio, R. 171 13 36S 49 7W
Meira, Sierra de 56 43 15N 7 15W
Meiringen 50 46 43N 8 12E
Meishan 108 30 3N 103 51E
Meissen 48 51 10N 13 29E
Meit'an 108 27 48N 107 28E
Meithalun 90 32 21N 35 16E
Méjean 44 44 15N 3 30E
Mejillones 172 23 10S 70 30W
Meka 137 27 25S 116 48E
Mekambo 124 1 2N 14 5E
Mekdela 123 11 24N 39 10E
Mekhtar 93 30 30N 69 15E
Meklong = Samut Songkhram 101 13 24N 100 1E
Meknès 118 33 57N 5 33W
Meko 121 7 27N 2 52E
Mekong, R. 101 18 0N 104 15E
Mekongga 103 3 50S 121 30E
Mekoryok 147 60 20N 166 20W
Melagiri Hills 97 12 20N 77 30E
Melah, Sebkhet el 118 29 20N 1 30W
Melaka 101 2 15N 102 15E
Melaka □ 101 2 20N 102 15E
Melalap 102 5 10N 116 5E
Mélambes 69 35 8N 24 40E
Melanesia 130 4 0S 155 0E
Melapalaiyam 97 8 39N 77 44E
Melbost 36 58 12N 6 20W
Melbourn 29 52 5N 0 1E
Melbourne, Austral. 141 37 50S 145 0E
Melbourne, U.K. 28 52 50N 1 25W
Melbourne, U.S.A. 157 28 13N 80 14W
Melcésine 62 45 46N 10 48E
Melchor Múzquiz 164 27 50N 101 40W
Melchor Ocampo (San Pedro Ocampo) 164 24 52N 101 40W
Méldola 63 44 7N 12 3E
Meldorf 48 54 5N 9 5E
Mêle-sur-Sarthe, Le 42 48 31N 0 22E
Melegnano 62 45 21N 9 20E
Melekess = Dimitrovgrad 81 54 25N 49 33E
Melenci 66 45 32N 20 20E
Melenki 81 55 20N 41 37E
Meleuz 84 52 58N 55 55E
Melfi, Chad 117 11 0N 17 59E
Melfi, Italy 65 41 0N 15 40E
Melfort, Can. 153 52 50N 104 37W
Melfort, Zimb. 127 18 0S 31 25E
Melfort, Loch 34 56 13N 5 33W
Melgaço 56 42 7N 8 15W
Melgar de Fernamental 56 42 27N 4 17W
Melhus 71 63 17N 10 18E
Melick 47 51 10N 6 1E
Melide 51 45 57N 8 57E
Meligalá 69 37 15N 21 59E
Melilla 118 35 21N 2 57W
Melilot 42 31 22N 34 37E
Melipilla 172 33 42S 71 15W
Mélissa Óros 69 37 32N 26 4E
Melita 153 49 15N 101 5W
Mélito di Porto Salvo 65 37 55N 15 47E
Melitopol 82 46 50N 35 22E
Melk 52 48 13N 15 20E
Melksham 28 51 22N 2 9W
Mellan-Fryken 72 59 45N 13 10E
Mellansel 74 63 25N 18 17E
Melle, Belg. 47 51 0N 3 49E
Melle, France 44 46 14N 0 10W
Melle, Ger. 48 52 12N 8 20E
Mellégue, O. 119 36 32N 8 51E
Mellen 158 46 19N 90 36W
Mellerud 73 58 41N 12 28E
Mellette 158 45 11N 98 29W
Mellid 56 42 55N 8 1W
Mellish Reef 133 17 25S 155 50E
Mellit 123 14 15N 25 40E
Mellon Charles 36 57 52N 5 37W
Melmerby 32 54 44N 2 35W
Melnik 67 40 58N 23 25E
Mělník 52 50 22N 14 23E
Melo 173 32 20S 54 10W
Melolo 103 9 53S 120 40E
Melones Res. 163 37 57N 120 31W
Melouprey 100 13 48N 105 16E
Melovoye 83 49 25N 40 5E
Melrhir, Chott 119 34 25N 6 24E
Melrose, N.S.W., Austral. 141 32 42S 146 57E
Melrose, W. Australia, Austral. 137 27 50S 121 15E
Melrose, U.K. 35 55 35N 2 44W
Melrose, U.S.A. 159 34 27N 103 33W
Mels 51 47 3N 9 25E
Melsele 47 51 13N 4 17E
Melsonby 33 54 28N 1 41W
Melstone 160 46 45N 108 0W
Melsungen 48 51 8N 9 34E
Melton 29 52 51N 1 1E
Melton Constable 29 52 52N 1 1E
Melton Mowbray 29 52 46N 0 52W
Melun 43 48 32N 2 39E
Melunga 128 17 15S 16 22E
Melur 97 10 2N 78 23E
Melut 123 10 30N 32 20E
Melvaig 36 57 48N 5 49W
Melvich 37 58 33N 3 55W
Melville 153 50 55N 102 50W
Melville B. 138 12 0S 136 45E
Melville, C. 138 14 11S 144 30E
Melville I., Austral. 136 11 30S 131 0E
Melville I., Can. 12 75 30N 111 0W
Melville, L., Newf., Can. 151 53 45N 59 40W
Melville, L., Newf., Can. 151 59 30N 53 40W
Melville Pen. 149 68 0N 84 0W
Melvin L. 38 54 26N 8 10W
Melvin, R. 152 59 11N 117 31W
Mélykút 53 46 11N 19 25E
Memaliaj 68 40 25N 19 58E
Memba 127 14 11S 40 30E
Memboro 103 9 30S 119 30E
Membrilla 59 38 59N 3 21W
Memel 129 27 38S 29 36E
Memel = Klaipeda 80 55 43N 21 10E
Memmingen 49 47 59N 10 12E
Memphis, Tenn., U.S.A. 159 35 7N 90 0W
Memphis, Tex., U.S.A. 159 34 45N 100 30W
Mena 159 34 40N 94 15W
Menai Bridge 31 53 14N 4 11W
Menai Strait 31 53 7N 4 20W
Ménaka 121 15 59N 2 18E
Menaldum 46 53 13N 5 40E
Menamurtee 140 31 25S 143 11E
Menarandra, R. 129 25 0S 44 50E
Menard 159 30 57N 99 58W
Menasha 156 44 13N 88 27W
Menate 102 0 12S 112 47E
Mendawai, R. 102 1 30S 113 0E
Mende 44 44 31N 3 30E
Mendebo Mts. 123 7 0N 39 22E
Mendenhall, C. 147 59 44N 166 10W
Menderes, R. 92 37 25N 28 45E
Mendez 165 25 7N 98 34W
Mendhar 95 33 35N 74 10E
Mendi, Ethiopia 123 9 47N 35 4E
Mendi, P.N.G. 135 6 11S 143 47E
Mendip Hills 28 51 17N 2 40W
Mendlesham 29 52 15N 1 4E
Mendocino 160 39 26N 123 50W
Mendong Gompa 99 31 16N 85 11E
Mendota, Calif., U.S.A. 163 36 46N 120 24W
Mendota, Ill., U.S.A. 158 41 35N 89 5W
Mendoza 172 32 50S 68 52W
Mendoza □ 172 33 0S 69 0W
Mendrisio 51 45 52N 8 59E
Mene Grande 174 9 49N 70 56W
Menemen 92 38 18N 27 10E
Menen 47 50 47N 3 7E
Menfi 64 37 36N 12 57E
Meng-pan 99 23 5N 100 19E
Meng-so 101 22 33N 99 31E
Meng-wang 99 22 17N 100 32E
Meng Wang 101 22 18N 100 31E
Mengch'eng 106 33 17N 116 34E
Mengeš 63 46 24N 14 35E
Menggala 102 4 20S 105 15E
Menghai 108 21 58N 100 28E
Menghsien 106 34 54N 112 47E
Mengíbar 57 37 58N 3 48W
Mengla 108 21 28N 101 35E
Menglien 108 22 21N 99 36E

Mengoub Mikołajki

Mengoub 118 29 49N 5 26W
Mengpolo 108 24 24N 99 14E
Mengshan 109 24 12N 110 31E
Mengting 108 23 33N 98 5E
Mengtz = Mengtzu 108 23 25N 103 20E
Mengtzu 108 23 25N 103 20E
Mengyin 107 35 40N 117 55E
Menihek L. 151 54 0N 67 0W
Menin 47 50 47N 3 7E
Menindee 140 32 20N 142 25E
Menindee, L. 140 32 20N 142 25E
Meningie 140 35 43S 139 20E
Menkúng 99 28 38N 98 24E
Menlo Park 163 37 27N 122 12W
Menominee 156 45 9N 87 39W
Menominee, R. 156 45 30N 87 50W
Menomonie 158 44 50N 91 54W
Menor, Mar 59 37 43N 0 48W
Menorca, I. 58 40 0N 4 0E
Mentawai, Kepulauan 102 2 0S 99 0E
Mentekab 101 3 29N 102 21E
Menton 45 43 50N 7 29E
Menyamya 135 7 10S 145 59E
Menzel-Bourguiba 119 39 9N 9 49E
Menzel Chaker 119 35 0N 10 26E
Menzelinsk 84 55 53N 53 1E
Menzies 137 29 40S 120 58E
Me'ona (Tarshiha) 90 33 1N 35 15E
Meoqui 164 28 17N 105 29W
Mepaco 127 15 57S 30 48E
Meppel 47 52 42N 6 12E
Meppen 48 52 41N 7 20E
Mequinenza 58 41 22N 0 17E
Mer Rouge 159 32 47N 91 48W
Merabéllou, Kólpos 69 35 10N 25 50E
Merai 135 4 52S 152 19E
Merak 103 5 55S 106 1E
Meramangye, L. 137 28 25S 132 13E
Merano (Meran) 63 46 40N 11 10E
Merate 62 45 42N 9 23E
Merauke 103 8 29S 140 24E
Merbabu, Mt. 103 7 30S 110 40E
Merbein 140 34 10S 142 2E
Merca 91 1 48N 44 50E
Mercadal 58 39 59N 4 5E
Mercara 97 12 30N 75 45E
Mercato Saraceno 63 43 57N 12 11E
Merced 163 37 18N 120 30W
Merced Pk. 163 37 36N 119 24W
Merced, R. 163 37 21N 120 58W
Mercedes, Buenos Aires, Argent. 172 34 40S 59 30W
Mercedes, Corrientes, Argent. 172 29 10S 58 5W
Mercedes, San Luis, Argent. 172 33 5S 65 21W
Mercedes, Uruguay 172 33 12S 58 0W
Merceditas 172 28 20S 70 35W
Mercer 142 37 16S 175 5E
Merchtem 47 50 58N 4 14E
Mercy C. 149 65 0N 62 30W
Merdrignac 42 48 11N 2 27W
Mere, Belg. 47 50 55N 3 58E
Mere, U.K. 28 51 5N 2 16W
Meredith C. 176 52 15S 60 40W
Meredith, L. 159 35 30N 101 35W
Merei 70 45 7N 26 43E
Merelbeke 47 51 0N 3 45E
Méréville 43 48 20N 2 5E
Merewa 123 7 40N 36 54E
Mergenevo 84 49 56N 51 18E
Mergenevskiy 83 49 59N 51 15E
Mergui 101 12 30N 98 35E
Mergui Arch. = Myeik Kyunzu 101 11 30N 97 30E
Meribah 140 34 43S 140 51E
Mérida, Mexico 165 20 50N 89 40W
Mérida, Spain 57 38 55N 6 25W
Mérida, Venez. 174 8 36N 71 8W
Mérida □ 174 8 30N 71 10W
Mérida, Cord. de 174 9 0N 71 0W
Meriden, U.K. 28 52 27N 1 36W
Meriden, U.S.A. 162 41 33N 72 47W
Meridian, Idaho, U.S.A. 160 43 41N 116 25W
Meridian, Miss., U.S.A. 157 32 20N 88 42W
Meridian, Tex., U.S.A. 159 31 55N 97 37W
Mering 49 48 15N 11 0E
Merioneth (□) 26 52 49N 3 55W
Merirumã 175 1 15N 54 50W
Merke 85 42 52N 73 11E
Merkel 159 32 30N 100 0W
Merkem 47 50 57N 2 51E
Merksem 47 51 16N 4 25E
Merksplas 47 51 22N 4 52E
Merlebach 43 49 5N 6 52E
Merlerault, Le 42 48 41N 0 16E
Mermaid Mt. 108 27 29S 152 49E
Mermaid Reef 136 17 6S 119 36E
Mern 73 55 3N 12 3E
Merowe 122 18 29N 31 46E
Merredin 137 31 28S 118 18E
Merrick, Mt. 34 55 8N 4 30W
Merrill, Oregon, U.S.A. 160 42 2N 121 37W
Merrill, Wis., U.S.A. 158 45 11N 89 41W
Merrimack, R. 162 42 49N 70 49W
Merritt 152 50 10N 120 45W
Merriwa 141 32 6S 150 22E
Merriwagga 141 33 47S 145 43E
Merroe 137 27 53S 117 50E
Merry I. 150 55 29N 77 31W
Merrygoen 141 31 51S 149 12E
Merryville 159 30 47N 93 31W
Mersa Fatma 123 14 57N 40 17E
Mersch 47 49 44N 6 7E
Merse, dist. 35 55 40N 2 30W
Mersea I. 29 51 48N 0 55E
Merseburg 48 51 20N 12 0E
Mersey, R. 32 53 20N 2 56W
Merseyside □ 32 53 25N 2 55W
Mersin 92 36 51N 34 36E
Mersing 101 2 25N 103 50E
Merta 94 26 39N 74 4E
Mertert 47 49 43N 6 29E
Merthyr Tydfil 31 51 45N 3 23W
Mértola 57 37 40N 7 40E
Merton 29 51 25N 0 13W
Mertzig 47 49 51N 6 1E
Mertzon 159 31 17N 100 48W
Méru 43 49 13N 2 8E
Meru 126 0 3N 37 40E
Meru □ 126 0 3N 37 46E
Meru, mt. 126 3 15S 36 46E
Merville 43 50 38N 2 38E
Méry-sur-Seine 43 48 31N 3 54E
Merzifon 82 40 53N 35 32E
Merzig 49 49 26N 6 37E
Merzouga, Erg Tin 119 24 0N 11 4E
Mesa 161 33 20N 111 56W
Mesa, La, Colomb. 174 4 38N 74 28W
Mesa, La, Calif., U.S.A. 163 32 48N 117 5W
Mesa, La, N. Mex., U.S.A. 161 32 6N 106 48W
Mesach Mellet 119 24 30N 11 30E
Mesada 90 31 20N 35 19E
Mesagne 65 40 34N 17 48E
Mesaras, Kólpos 69 35 6N 24 47E
Meschede 48 51 20N 8 17E
Mesfinto 123 13 30N 37 22E
Mesgouez, L. 150 51 20N 75 0W
Meshchovsk 80 54 22N 35 17E
Meshed = Mashhad 93 36 20N 59 35E
Meshoppen 162 41 36N 76 3W
Mesick 156 44 24N 85 42W
Mesilinka, R. 152 56 6N 124 30W
Mesilla 161 32 20N 107 0W
Meslay-du-Maine 42 47 58N 0 33W
Mesocco 51 46 23N 9 12E
Mesolóngion 69 38 27N 21 28E
Mesopotamia, reg. 92 33 30N 44 0E
Mesoraca 65 39 5N 16 47E
Mésou Volímais 69 37 53N 27 35E
Mess Cr. 152 57 55N 131 14W
Messac 42 47 49N 1 50W
Messad 118 34 8N 3 30E
Méssaména 121 3 48N 12 49E
Messancy 47 49 36N 5 49E
Messeix 44 45 37N 2 33E
Messina, Italy 65 38 10N 15 32E
Messina, S. Afr. 129 22 20S 30 12E
Messina, Str. di 65 38 5N 15 35E
Messini 69 37 4N 22 1E
Messínia □ 69 37 10N 22 0E
Messiniakós, Kólpos 69 36 45N 22 5E
Mestá, Ákra 69 38 16N 25 53E
Mesta, R. 67 41 30N 24 0E
Mestanza 57 38 35N 4 4W
Město Teplá 52 49 59N 12 52E
Mestre 63 45 30N 12 13E
Mestre, Espigão 171 12 30S 46 10W
Městys Zelezná Ruda 52 49 8N 13 15E
Meta □ 174 3 30N 73 0W
Meta, R. 174 6 20N 68 5W
Metagama 150 47 0N 81 55W
Metaline Falls 160 48 52N 117 22W
Metán 172 25 30S 65 0W
Metauro, R. 63 43 45N 12 59E
Metchosin 152 48 15N 123 37W
Metehara 123 8 58N 39 57E
Metema 123 12 56N 36 13E
Metengobalame 127 14 49S 34 30E
Méthana 69 37 35N 23 23E
Metheringham 33 53 9N 0 22W
Methlick 37 57 26N 2 13W
Methóni 69 36 49N 21 42E
Methuen, Mt. 136 15 54S 124 44E
Methven, N.Z. 143 43 38S 171 40E
Methven, U.K. 35 56 25N 3 35W
Methwin, Mt. 137 25 3S 120 45E
Methwold 29 52 30N 0 33E
Methy L. 153 56 28N 109 30W
Metil 125 16 24S 39 0E
Metkovets 67 43 37N 23 10E
Metković 66 43 6N 17 39E
Metlakatla 147 55 10N 131 33W
Metlaoui 119 34 24N 8 24E
Metlika 63 45 40N 15 20E
Metowra 139 25 3S 146 15E
Metropolis 159 37 10N 88 47W
Métsovon 68 39 48N 21 12E
Mettet 47 50 19N 4 41E
Mettuppalaiyam 97 11 18N 76 59E
Mettur 97 11 48N 77 47E
Mettur Dam 95 11 45N 77 45E
Metulla 90 33 17N 35 34E
Metz 43 49 8N 6 10E
Meulaboh 102 4 11N 96 3E
Meulan 43 49 0N 1 52E
Meung-sur-Loire 43 47 50N 1 40E
Meureudu 102 5 19N 96 10E
Meurthe-et-Moselle □ 43 48 52N 6 0E
Meuse □ 43 49 8N 5 25E
Meuse, R. 47 50 45N 5 41E
Meuselwitz 48 51 3N 12 18E
Mevagissey 30 50 16N 4 48W
Mevagissey Bay 30 50 15N 4 40W
Mexborough 33 53 29N 1 18W
Mexia 159 31 38N 96 32W
Mexiana, I. 170 0 0 49 30W
Mexicali 164 32 40N 115 30W
México 165 19 20N 99 10W
Mexico, Me., U.S.A. 156 44 35N 70 30W
Mexico, Mo., U.S.A. 158 39 10N 91 55W
Mexico, N.Y., U.S.A. 162 43 28N 76 18W
Mexico ■ 164 20 0N 100 0W
México □ 164 19 20N 99 10W
Mexico, G. of 165 25 0N 90 0W
Mey 37 58 38N 3 14W
Meyenburg 48 53 19N 12 15E
Meymac 44 45 32N 2 10E
Meyrargues 45 43 38N 5 32E
Meyrueis 44 44 12N 3 27E
Meyssac 44 45 3N 1 40E
Mezdra 67 43 12N 23 35E
Mèze 44 43 27N 3 36E
Mezen 78 65 50N 44 20E
Mezha, R. 80 55 50N 31 45E
Mezhdurechenskiy 84 59 36N 65 56E
Mezidon 42 49 5N 0 1W
Mézières 43 49 45N 4 42E
Mézilhac 45 44 49N 4 21E
Mézin 44 44 4N 0 16E
Mezöberény 53 46 49N 21 3E
Mezöfalva 53 46 55N 18 49E
Mezöhegyes 53 46 19N 20 49E
Mezökövácsháza 53 46 25N 20 57E
Mezökövesd 53 47 49N 20 35E
Mézos 44 44 5N 1 10W
Mezötúr 53 47 0N 20 41E
Mezquital 164 23 29N 104 23W
Mezzolombardo 62 46 13N 11 5E
Mgeta 127 8 22S 38 6E
Mglin 80 53 2N 32 50E
Mhlaba Hills 127 18 30S 30 30E
Mhow 94 22 33N 75 50E
Mi-Shima 110 34 46N 131 9E
Miahuatlán 165 16 21N 96 36W
Miajadas 57 39 9N 5 54W
Mialar 94 26 15N 70 20E
Miallo 138 16 28S 145 22E
Miami, Ariz., U.S.A. 161 33 25N 111 0W
Miami, Fla., U.S.A. 157 25 52N 80 15W
Miami, Tex., U.S.A. 159 35 44N 100 38W
Miami Beach 157 25 49N 80 6W
Miami, R. 156 39 20N 84 40W
Miamisburg 156 39 40N 84 11W
Miandowāb 92 37 0N 46 5E
Miandrivazo 125 19 50S 45 56E
Miāneh 92 37 30N 47 40E
Mianwali 94 32 38N 71 28E
Miaoli 109 24 34N 120 48E
Miarinarivo 129 18 57S 46 55E
Miass 84 54 59N 60 6E
Miass, R. 84 56 6N 64 30E
Miasteczko Kraj 54 53 7N 17 1E
Miastko 54 54 0N 16 58E
Mica Dam 152 52 5N 118 32W
Mica Res. 152 51 55N 118 00W
Michael, Mt. 135 6 27S 145 22E
Michalovce 29 48 44N 21 54E
Micheldever 28 51 7N 1 17W
Michelson, Mt. 147 69 20N 144 20W
Michelstadt 49 49 40N 9 0E
Michigan □ 155 44 40N 85 40W
Michigan City 156 41 42N 86 56W
Michigan, L. 156 44 0N 87 0W
Michih 106 37 49N 110 7E
Michikamau L. 151 54 0N 64 0W
Michipicoten 150 47 55N 84 55W
Michipicoten I. 150 47 40N 85 50W
Michoacan □ 164 19 0N 102 0W
Michurin 67 42 9N 27 51E
Michurinsk 81 52 58N 40 27E
Mickle Fell 32 54 38N 2 16W
Mickleover 33 52 55N 1 32W
Mickleton, Oxon., U.K. 28 52 5N 1 45W
Mickleton, Yorks., U.K. 32 54 36N 2 3W
Miclere 138 22 34S 147 32E
Micronesia 130 17 0N 160 0E
Micǔsasa 70 46 7N 24 7E
Mid Calder 35 55 53N 3 23W
Mid Glamorgan □ 31 51 40N 3 25W
Mid Yell 36 60 36N 1 5W
Midai, P. 101 3 0N 107 47E
Midale 153 49 25N 103 20W
Midas 160 41 14N 116 56W
Middagsfjället 72 63 27N 12 19E
Middelbeers 47 51 28N 5 15E
Middelburg, Neth. 47 51 30N 3 36E
Middelburg, C. Prov., S. Afr. 128 31 30S 25 0E
Middelburg, Trans., S. Afr. 129 25 49N 29 28E
Middelfart 73 55 30N 9 43E
Middelharnis 46 51 46N 4 10E
Middelkerke 47 51 11N 2 49E
Middelrode 47 51 41N 5 26E
Middelveld 128 29 45S 22 30E
Middle Alkali L. 160 41 30N 120 3W
Middle Andaman I. 101 12 30N 92 30E
Middle Brook 151 48 40N 54 20W
Middle I. 137 28 55S 113 55E
Middle River 162 39 19N 76 25W
Middle Zoy 28 51 5N 2 54W
Middleboro 162 41 49N 70 55W
Middleburg, N.Y., U.S.A. 162 42 36N 74 19W
Middleburg, Pa., U.S.A. 162 40 47N 77 3W
Middlebury 162 44 0N 73 9W
Middleham 33 54 17N 1 49W
Middlemarch 143 45 30S 170 9E
Middlemarsh 28 50 51N 2 29W
Middleport 156 39 0N 82 5W
Middlesbrough 33 54 35N 1 14W
Middlesex, Belize 165 17 2N 88 31W
Middlesex, U.S.A. 162 40 36N 74 30W
Middleton, Can. 151 44 57N 65 4W
Middleton, Gr. Manchester, U.K. 32 53 33N 2 12W
Middleton, Norfolk, U.K. 29 52 43N 0 29E
Middleton Cheney 28 52 4N 1 17W
Middleton Cr. 138 22 35S 141 51E
Middleton I. 147 59 30N 146 28W
Middleton-in-Teesdale 32 54 38N 2 5W
Middleton in the Wolds 33 53 56N 0 35W
Middleton P.O. 138 22 22S 141 32E
Middletown, U.K. 38 54 18N 6 50W
Middletown, Conn., U.S.A. 162 41 37N 72 40W
Middletown, Del., U.S.A. 162 39 30N 84 21W
Middletown, N.Y., U.S.A. 162 41 28N 74 28W
Middletown, Pa., U.S.A. 162 40 12N 76 44W
Middlewich 32 53 12N 2 28W
Midelt 118 32 46N 4 44W
Midhurst, N.Z. 142 39 17S 174 18E
Midhurst, U.K. 29 50 59N 0 44W
Midi, Canal du 44 43 45N 1 21E
Midi d'Ossau 58 42 50N 0 25W
Midland, Austral. 137 31 54S 115 59E
Midland, Can. 150 44 45N 79 50W
Midland, Mich., U.S.A. 156 43 37N 84 17W
Midland, Tex., U.S.A. 159 32 0N 102 3W
Midland Junc. 137 31 50S 115 58E
Midlands □ 127 19 40S 29 0E
Midleton 39 51 52N 8 12W
Midlothian, Austral. 138 17 10S 141 12E
Midlothian, U.S.A. 159 32 30N 97 0W
Midlothian (□) 26 55 45N 3 15W
Midnapore 95 22 25N 87 21E
Midongy du Sud 129 23 35S 47 1E
Midongy, Massif de 129 23 30S 47 0E
Midskog 73 58 56N 14 5E
Midsomer Norton 28 51 17N 2 29W
Midvale 160 40 39N 111 58W
Midway Is. 130 28 13N 177 22W
Midwest 160 43 27N 106 11W
Midwolda 46 53 12N 6 52E
Midzur 66 43 24N 22 40E
Mie-ken □ 111 34 30N 136 10E
Miechów 54 50 21N 20 5E
Miedzyborz 54 51 39N 17 24E
Miedzychód 54 52 35N 15 53E
Miedzylesie 54 50 41N 16 40E
Miedzyrzec Podlaski 54 51 58N 22 45E
Miedzyrzecz 54 52 26N 15 35E
Miedzyzdroje 54 53 56N 14 26E
Miejska Górka 54 51 39N 16 58E
Miélan 44 43 27N 0 19E
Mielelek 138 6 1S 148 58E
Mienchʼih 106 34 48N 111 40E
Mienchu 108 31 22N 104 7E
Mienga 128 17 12S 19 48E
Mienhsien 106 33 11N 106 36E
Mienning 108 28 30N 102 10E
Mienyang, Hupei, China 109 30 10N 113 20E
Mienyang, Szechwan, China 108 31 28N 104 46E
Miercurea Ciuc 70 46 21N 25 48E
Mieres 56 43 18N 5 48W
Mierlo 47 51 27N 5 37E
Mieso 123 9 15N 40 43E
Mieszkowice 54 52 47N 14 30E
Migdal 90 32 51N 35 30E
Migdal Afeq 90 32 5N 34 58E
Migennes 43 47 58N 3 31E
Migliarino 63 44 54N 11 56E
Miguel Alemán, Presa 165 18 15N 96 40W
Miguel Alves 170 4 11S 42 55W
Miguel Calmon 170 11 26S 40 36W
Mihara 110 34 24N 133 5E
Mihara-Yama 111 34 43N 139 23E
Mihsien 106 34 31N 113 22E
Mii 108 26 50N 102 3E
Mijares, R. 58 40 15N 0 50W
Mijas 57 36 36N 4 40W
Mijdrecht 46 52 13N 4 52E
Mijilu 121 10 22N 13 19E
Mikese 126 6 48S 37 55E
Mikha Tskhakaya 83 42 15N 42 7E
Mikhailovgrad 67 43 27N 23 16E
Mikhailovka 82 47 16N 35 27E
Mikhaylov 81 54 20N 39 0E
Mikhaylovka, Azerbaijan, U.S.S.R. 83 41 31N 48 52E
Mikhaylovka, R.S.F.S.R., U.S.S.R. 81 50 3N 43 5E
Mikhaylovski 84 56 27N 59 7E
Mikhnevo 81 55 4N 37 59E
Miki, Hyōgō, Japan 110 34 48N 134 59E
Miki, Kagawa, Japan 110 34 12N 134 7E
Mikinai 69 37 43N 22 46E
Mikindani 127 10 15S 40 2E
Mikkeli 75 61 43N 27 25E
Mikkeli □ 74 62 0N 28 0E
Mikkelin Lääni □ 74 61 56N 28 0E
Mikkwa, R. 152 58 25N 114 46W
Mikniya 123 17 0N 33 45E
Mikołajki 54 53 49N 21 37E

Mikoł Mjømna

Mikołów 53 50 10N 18 50 E
Míkonos, I. 69 37 30N 25 25 E
Mikrón Dhérion 68 41 19N 26 6 E
Mikulov 53 48 48N 16 39 E
Mikumi 126 7 26 S 37 9 E
Mikun 78 62 20N 50 0 E
Mikuni 111 36 13N 136 9 E
Mikuni-Tōge 111 36 50N 138 40 E
Mikura-Jima 111 33 52N 139 36 E
Mila 119 36 27N 6 16 E
Milaca 158 45 45N 93 40W
Milagro 174 2 0 S 79 30W
Milan, Mo., U.S.A. 158 40 10N 93 5W
Milan, Tenn., U.S.A. 157 35 55N 88 45W
Milan = Milano 62 45 28N 9 10 E
Milang, S. Australia, Austral. 139 32 2 S 139 10 E
Milang, S. Australia, Austral. 140 35 24 S 138 58 E
Milange 127 16 3 S 35 45 E
Milano 62 45 28N 9 10 E
Milâs 92 37 20N 27 50 E
Milazzo 65 38 13N 15 13 E
Milbank 158 45 17N 96 38W
Milborne Port 28 50 58N 2 28W
Milden 153 51 29N 107 32W
Mildenhall 29 52 20N 0 30 E
Mildura 140 34 13 S 142 9 E
Miléai 68 39 20N 23 9 E
Miles, Austral. 139 26 40 S 150 23 E
Miles, U.S.A. 159 31 39N 100 11W
Miles City 158 46 30N 105 50W
Milestone 153 49 59N 104 31W
Mileto 65 38 37N 16 3 E
Miletto, Mte. 65 41 26N 14 23 E
Mileurà 137 26 22 S 117 20 E
Milevsko 52 49 27N 14 21 E
Milford, Ireland 39 52 20N 8 52W
Milford, Conn., U.S.A. 162 41 13N 73 4W
Milford, Del., U.S.A. 162 38 52N 75 27W
Milford, Mass., U.S.A. 162 42 8N 71 30W
Milford, N.H., U.S.A. 162 42 50N 71 39W
Milford, Pa., U.S.A. 162 41 20N 74 47W
Milford, Utah, U.S.A. 161 38 20N 113 0W
Milford Haven 31 51 43N 5 2W
Milford Haven, B. 31 51 40N 5 10W
Milford on Sea 28 50 44N 1 36W
Milford Sd. 143 44 34 S 167 47 E
Milgun 137 25 6 S 118 18 E
Milh, Ras el 117 32 0N 24 55 E
Miliana, Aïn Salah, Alg. 118 27 20N 2 32 E
Miliana, Médéa, Alg. 118 36 12N 2 15 E
Milicz 54 51 31N 17 19 E
Miling 137 30 30 S 116 17 E
Militello in Val di Catánia 65 37 16N 14 46 E
Milk, R. 160 48 40N 107 15W
Milk River 152 49 10N 112 5W
Mill 47 51 41N 5 48 E
Mill City 160 44 45N 122 28W
Mill, I. 13 66 0 S 101 30 E
Mill Valley 163 37 54N 122 32W
Millau 44 44 8N 3 4 E
Millbrook, U.K. 30 50 19N 4 12W
Millbrook, U.S.A. 162 41 47N 73 42W
Millbrook Res. 109 34 50 S 138 49 E
Mille Lacs, L. 158 46 10N 93 30W
Mille Lacs, L. des 150 48 45N 90 35W
Milledgeville 157 33 7N 83 15W
Millen 157 32 50N 81 57W
Miller 158 44 35N 98 59W
Millerovo 83 48 57N 40 28 E
Miller's Flat 143 45 39 S 169 23 E
Millersburg 162 40 32N 76 58W
Millerton, N.Z. 143 41 39 S 171 54 E
Millerton, U.S.A. 162 41 57N 73 32W
Millerton, L. 163 37 0N 119 42W
Milleur Pt. 34 55 2N 5 5W
Millevaches, Plat. de 44 45 45N 2 0 E
Millicent 140 37 34 S 140 21 E
Millingen 46 51 52N 6 2 E
Millinocket 151 45 45N 68 45W
Millisle 38 54 38N 5 33W
Millmerran 139 27 53 S 151 16 E
Millom 32 54 13N 3 16W
Millport 34 55 45N 4 55W
Mills L. 152 61 30N 118 20W
Millsboro 162 38 36N 75 17W
Millstreet 39 52 4N 9 5W
Milltown, Galway, Ireland 38 53 37N 8 54W
Milltown, Kerry, Ireland 39 52 9N 9 42W
Milltown, U.K. 37 57 33N 4 48W
Milltown Malbay 39 52 51N 9 25W
Millville, N.J., U.S.A. 162 39 22N 75 0W
Millville, Pa., U.S.A. 162 41 7N 76 32W
Millwood Res. 159 33 45N 94 0W
Milly 43 48 24N 2 20 E
Milly Milly 137 26 4 S 116 43 E
Milna 63 43 20N 16 28 E
Milnathort 35 56 14N 3 25W
Milne Inlet 149 72 30N 80 0W
Milne, R. 138 21 10 S 137 33 E
Milngavie 34 55 57N 4 20W
Milnor 158 46 19N 97 29W
Milnthorpe 32 54 14N 2 47W
Milo, Can. 152 50 34N 112 53W
Milo, China 108 24 28N 103 23 E
Mililii 147 22 8N 159 42W
Mílos 69 36 44N 24 25 E
Mílos, I. 69 36 44N 24 25 E
Milo evo 66 45 42N 20 20 E
Miłoslaw 54 52 12N 17 32 E
Milovaig 36 57 27N 6 45W
Milparinka P.O. 139 29 46 S 141 57 E
Miltenberg 49 49 41N 9 13 E
Milton, N.Z. 143 46 7 S 169 59 E
Milton, Dumf. & Gall., U.K. 34 55 18N 4 50W
Milton, Hants., U.K. 28 50 45N 1 40W
Milton, Northants, U.K. 29 52 12N 0 55W
Milton, Calif., U.S.A. 163 38 3N 120 51W
Milton, Del., U.S.A. 162 38 47N 75 19W
Milton, Fla., U.S.A. 157 30 38N 87 0W
Milton, Pa., U.S.A. 162 41 0N 76 53W
Milton Abbot 30 50 35N 4 16W
Milton-Freewater 160 45 57N 118 24W
Milton Keynes 29 52 3N 0 42W
Milverton 28 51 2N 3 15W
Milwaukee 156 43 9N 87 58W
Milwaukie 160 45 27N 122 39W
Mim 120 6 57N 2 33W
Mimizan 44 44 12N 1 13W
Mimon 52 50 38N 14 43 E
Mimoso 171 15 10 S 48 5W
Min Chiang, R., China 105 28 48N 104 33 E
Min Chiang, R., Fukien, China 109 26 5N 119 37 E
Min Chiang, R., Szechwan, China 108 28 48N 104 33 E
Min-Kush 85 41 4N 74 28 E
Mina 161 38 21N 118 9W
Mina Pirquitas 172 22 40 S 66 40W
Mina Saud 92 28 45N 48 20 E
Minā'al Ahmadī 92 29 5N 48 10 E
Mīnāb 93 27 10N 57 1 E
Minago, R. 153 54 33N 98 13W
Minakami 111 36 49N 138 59 E
Minaki 153 50 0N 94 40W
Minakuchi 111 34 58N 136 10 E
Minamata 110 32 10N 130 30 E
Minamitane 112 30 25N 130 54 E
Minas Basin 151 45 20N 64 12W
Minas de Rio Tinto 57 37 42N 6 22W
Minas de San Quintín 57 38 49N 4 23W
Minas Gerais □ 171 18 50 S 46 0W
Minas Novas 171 17 15 S 42 36W
Minas, Sierra de las 166 15 9N 89 31W
Minatitlán 165 17 58N 94 35W
Minbu 98 20 10N 95 0 E
Minbya 98 20 22N 93 16 E
Mincha 140 36 1 S 144 6 E
Minch'in 106 38 42N 103 11 E
Minch'ing 109 26 13N 118 51 E
Minchinhampton 28 51 42N 2 10W
Mincio, R. 62 45 8N 10 55 E
Mindanao, I. 103 8 0N 125 0 E
*Mindanao Sea 103 9 0N 124 0 E
Mindanao Trench 103 8 0N 128 0 E
Mindelheim 49 48 4N 10 30 E
Minden, Ger. 48 52 18N 8 54 E
Minden, U.S.A. 159 32 40N 93 20W
Mindiptana 103 5 45 S 140 22 E
Mindon 98 19 21N 94 44 E
Mindoro, I. 103 13 0N 121 0 E
Mindoro Strait 103 12 30N 120 30 E
Mindouli 124 4 12 S 14 28 E
Mine 110 34 12N 131 7 E
Mine Hd. 39 52 0N 7 37W
Minehead 28 51 12N 3 29W
Mineola, N.Y., U.S.A. 162 40 45N 73 38W
Mineola, Tex., U.S.A. 159 32 40N 95 30W
Minera 31 53 3N 3 7W
Mineral King 163 36 27N 118 36W
Mineral Wells 159 32 50N 98 5W
Mineralnyye Vody 83 44 18N 43 15 E
Minersville, Pa., U.S.A. 162 40 40N 76 17W
Minersville, Utah, U.S.A. 161 38 14N 112 58W
Minervino Murge 65 41 6N 16 4 E
Minette 157 30 54N 87 43W
Minetto 162 43 24N 76 28W
Mingan 151 50 20N 64 0W
Mingary, Austral. 140 32 8 S 140 45 E
Mingary, U.K. 36 56 42N 6 5W
Mingch'i 109 26 24N 117 12 E
Mingchiang 109 32 28N 114 8 E
Mingechaur 83 40 52N 47 0 E
Mingechaurskoye Vdkhr. 83 40 56N 47 20 E
Mingela 138 19 52 S 146 38 E
Mingenew 137 29 12 S 115 21 E
Mingera Cr. 138 20 38 S 138 10 E
Mingin 98 22 50N 94 30 E
Minginish, Dist. 36 57 14N 6 15W
Minglanilla 58 39 34N 1 38W
Mingulay I. 36 56 50N 7 40W
Minho □ 55 41 25N 8 20W
Minho, R. 55 41 58N 8 40W
Minhou 109 26 0N 119 18 E
Minhow = Fuchou 109 26 5N 119 18 E
Minhsien 106 34 26N 104 2 E
Minidoka 160 42 47N 113 34W
Minigwal L. 137 29 31 S 123 14 E
Minilya 137 23 55 S 114 0 E
Minilya, R. 137 23 45 S 114 0 E
Mininera 140 37 37 S 142 58 E
Minióevo 66 43 42N 22 18 E
Minipi, L. 151 52 25N 60 45W
Minj 135 5 54 S 144 30 E
Mink L. 152 61 54N 117 40W
Minlaton 140 34 45 S 137 35 E
Minna 121 9 37N 6 30 E
*Renamed Bohol Sea
Minneapolis, Kans., U.S.A. 158 39 11N 97 40W
Minneapolis, Minn., U.S.A. 158 44 58N 93 20W
Minnesota □ 158 46 40N 94 0W
Minnesund 71 60 23N 11 14 E
Minnie Creek 137 24 3 S 115 42 E
Minnigaff 34 54 58N 4 30W
Minnitaki L. 150 49 47N 91 5W
Mino 111 35 32N 136 55 E
Mino-Kamo 111 35 23N 137 2 E
Mino-Mikawa-Kōgen 111 35 10N 137 30 E
Miño, R. 56 41 58N 8 40W
Minobu 111 35 22N 138 26 E
Minobu-Sanchi 111 35 14N 138 20 E
Minorca = Menorca 58 40 0N 4 0 E
Minore 141 32 14 S 148 27 E
Minot 158 48 10N 101 15W
Minquiers, Les 42 48 58N 2 8W
Minsen 48 53 43N 7 58 E
Minsk 80 53 52N 27 30 E
Minsk Mazowiecki 54 52 10N 21 33 E
Minster 29 51 20N 1 20 E
Minster-on-Sea 29 51 25N 0 50 E
Minsterley 28 52 38N 2 56W
Mintaka Pass 93 37 0N 74 58 E
Minthami 98 23 55N 94 16 E
Mintlaw 37 57 32N 1 59W
Minto 147 64 55N 149 20W
Minto L. 150 48 0N 84 45W
Minton 153 49 10N 104 35W
Minturn 160 39 45N 106 25W
Minturno 64 41 15N 13 43 E
Minûf 122 30 26N 30 52 E
Minusinsk 77 53 50N 91 20 E
Minutang 98 28 15N 96 30 E
Minvoul 124 2 9N 12 8 E
Minya Konka 108 29 34N 101 53 E
Minyar 84 55 4N 57 33 E
Minyip 140 36 29 S 142 36 E
Mionica 66 44 14N 20 6 E
Mios Num, I. 103 1 30 S 135 10 E
Miquelon 151 47 3N 56 20W
Miquelon, St. Pierre et, □ 151 47 8N 56 24W
Mir-Bashir 83 40 11N 46 58 E
Mira, Italy 63 45 26N 12 9 E
Mira, Port. 56 40 26N 8 44W
Mira, R. 57 37 30N 8 30W
Mirabella Eclano 65 41 3N 14 59 E
Miracema do Norte 170 9 33 S 48 24W
Mirador 170 6 22 S 44 22W
Miraflores 164 23 21N 109 45W
Miraj 96 16 50N 74 45 E
Miram 138 21 15 S 148 55 E
Miram Shah 94 33 0N 70 0 E
Miramar, Argent. 172 38 15 S 57 50W
Miramar, Mozam. 129 23 50 S 35 35 E
Miramas 45 43 33N 4 59 E
Mirambeau 44 45 23N 0 35W
Miramichi B. 151 47 15N 65 0W
Miramont-de-Guyenne 44 44 37N 0 21 E
Miranda 175 20 10 S 56 15W
Miranda de Ebro 58 42 41N 2 57W
Miranda do Corvo 56 40 6N 8 20W
Miranda do Douro 56 41 30N 6 16W
Mirando City 159 27 28N 98 59W
Mirandola 62 44 53N 11 2 E
Mirandópolis 173 21 9 S 51 6W
Mirango 127 13 32 S 34 58 E
Mirano 63 45 29N 12 6 E
Miraporvos, I. 167 22 9N 74 30W
Mirassol 173 20 46 S 49 28W
Mirboo North 141 38 24 S 146 10 E
Mirear, I. 122 23 15N 35 41 E
Mirebeau, Côte d'Or, France 43 47 25N 5 20 E
Mirebeau, Vienne, France 42 46 49N 0 10 E
Mirecourt 43 48 20N 6 10 E
Mirgorod 80 49 58N 33 50 E
Miri 102 4 18N 114 0 E
Miriam Vale 138 24 20 S 151 33 E
Mirim, Lagoa 173 32 45 S 52 50W
Mirimire 174 11 10N 68 43W
Mirny 13 66 0 S 95 0 E
Mirnyy 77 62 33N 113 53 E
Mirond L. 153 55 6N 102 47W
Mirosławiec 54 53 20N 16 5 E
Mirpur 95 33 15N 73 50 E
Mirpur Bibiwari 94 28 33N 67 44 E
Mirpur Khas 94 25 30N 69 0 E
Mirpur Sakro 94 24 33N 67 41 E
Mirrool 141 34 19 S 147 10 E
Mirror 152 52 30N 113 7W
Mîrsani 70 44 1N 23 59 E
Mirsk 54 50 58N 15 23 E
Miryang 107 35 31N 128 44 E
Mirzaani 83 41 24N 46 5 E
Mirzapur 95 25 10N 82 45 E
Misantla 165 19 56N 96 50W
Miscou I. 151 47 57N 64 31W
Misery, Mt. 108 34 52 S 138 48 E
Mish'ab, Ra'as al 92 28 15N 48 43 E
Mishan 105 45 31N 132 2 E
Mishawaka 156 41 40N 86 8W
Mishbih, Gebel 122 22 48N 34 38 E
Mishima 111 35 10N 138 52 E
Mishkino 84 55 20N 63 55 E
Mishmar Aiyalon 90 31 52N 34 57 E
Mishmar Ha' Emeq 90 32 37N 35 7 E
Mishmar Ha Negev 90 31 22N 34 48 E
Mishmar Ha Yarden 90 33 0N 35 56 E
Mishmi Hills 98 29 0N 96 0 E
Misilmeri 64 38 2N 13 25 E
Misima I. 135 10 40 S 152 45 E
Misión, La 164 32 5N 116 50W
Misiones □, Argent. 173 27 0 S 55 0W
Misiones □, Parag. 172 27 0 S 56 0W
Miskin 93 23 44N 56 52 E
Miskitos, Cayos 166 14 26N 82 50W
Miskolc 53 48 7N 20 50 E
Misoke 126 0 42 S 28 2 E
Misoöl, I. 103 2 0 S 130 0 E
Misrātah 119 32 18N 15 3 E
Missanabie 150 48 20N 84 6W
Missão Velha 170 7 15 S 39 10W
Misserghin 118 35 44N 0 49W
Missinaibi L. 150 48 23N 83 40W
Missinaibi, R. 150 50 30N 82 40W
Mission, S.D., U.S.A. 158 43 21N 100 36W
Mission, Tex., U.S.A. 159 26 15N 98 30W
Mission City 152 49 10N 122 15W
Missisa L. 150 52 20N 85 7W
Mississagi 150 46 15N 83 9W
Mississippi, R. 159 35 30N 90 0W
Mississippi Sd. 159 30 25N 89 0W
Missoula 160 47 0N 114 0W
Missouri □ 158 38 25N 92 30W
Missouri, Little, R. 160 46 0N 111 35W
Missouri, R. 158 40 20N 95 40W
Mistake B. 153 62 8N 93 0W
Mistassini L. 150 51 0N 73 40W
Mistassini, R. 151 48 42N 72 20W
Mistastin L. 151 55 57N 63 20W
Mistatim 153 52 52N 103 22W
Mistelbach 53 48 34N 16 34 E
Misterbianco 65 37 32N 15 0 E
Misterton, Notts., U.K. 33 53 27N 0 49W
Misterton, Som., U.K. 28 50 51N 2 46W
Mistretta 65 37 56N 14 20 E
Misty L. 153 58 53N 101 40W
Misugi 111 34 31N 136 16 E
Misumi 110 32 37N 130 27 E
Mît Ghamr 122 30 42N 31 12 E
Mitaka 111 35 40N 139 33 E
Mitan 85 40 0N 66 35 E
Mitatib 123 15 59N 36 12 E
Mitchel Troy 31 51 46N 2 45W
Mitcheldean 28 51 51N 2 29W
Mitchell, Austral. 139 26 29 S 147 58 E
Mitchell, Ind., U.S.A. 156 38 42N 86 25W
Mitchell, Nebr., U.S.A. 158 41 58N 103 45W
Mitchell, Oreg., U.S.A. 160 44 31N 120 8W
Mitchell, S.D., U.S.A. 158 43 40N 98 0W
Mitchell, Mt. 157 35 40N 82 20W
Mitchell, R. 138 15 12 S 141 35 E
Mitchelstown 39 52 16N 8 18W
Mitchelton 108 27 25 S 152 59 E
Mitha Tiwana 94 32 13N 72 6 E
Míthimna 68 39 20N 26 12 E
Mitiamo 140 36 12 S 144 15 E
Mitilíni 69 39 6N 26 35 E
Mitilíni = Lesvos 68 39 0N 26 20 E
Mitilinoi 69 37 42N 26 56 E
Mitla 165 16 55N 96 24W
Mito 111 36 20N 140 30 E
Mitsinjo 129 16 1 S 45 52 E
Mitsiwa 123 15 35N 39 25 E
Mitsiwa Channel 123 15 30N 40 0 E
Mitsukaidō 111 36 1N 139 59 E
Mittagong 141 34 28 S 150 29 E
Mittelland 50 46 50N 7 23 E
Mittelland Kanal 48 52 23N 7 45 E
Mittenwalde 48 52 16N 13 33 E
Mittweida 48 50 59N 13 0 E
Mitu 108 25 21N 100 32 E
Mitú 174 1 8N 70 3W
Mituas 174 3 52N 68 49W
Mitumba 126 7 8 S 31 2 E
Mitumba, Chaîne des 126 10 0 S 26 20 E
Mitwaba 127 8 2N 27 17 E
Mityana 126 0 23N 32 2 E
Mitzick 124 0 45N 11 40 E
Miura 111 35 12N 139 40 E
Mius, R. 83 47 30N 39 0 E
Mixteco, R. 165 18 11N 98 30W
Miyagi-Ken □ 112 38 15N 140 45 E
Miyâh, W. el 122 25 10N 33 30 E
Miyake-Jima 111 34 0N 139 30 E
Miyako 112 39 40N 141 75 E
Miyako-Jima 112 24 45N 125 20 E
Miyakonojō 110 31 32N 131 5 E
Miyanojō 110 31 54N 130 27 E
Miyanoura-Dake 112 30 20N 130 26 E
Miyata 110 33 49N 130 42 E
Miyazaki 110 31 56N 131 30 E
Miyazaki-ken □ 110 32 0N 131 30 E
Miyazu 110 35 35N 135 10 E
Miyet, Bahr el 92 31 30N 35 30 E
Miyoshi 110 34 48N 132 51 E
Miyün 106 40 20N 116 49 E
Mizamis = Ozamiz 103 8 15N 123 50 E
Mizdah 119 31 30N 13 0 E
Mizen Hd., Cork, Ireland 39 51 27N 9 50W
Mizen Hd., Wick., Ireland 39 52 52N 6 4W
Mizil 70 44 59N 26 29 E
Mizoram □ 98 23 0N 92 40 E
Mizuho 111 35 6N 135 17 E
Mizunami 111 35 22N 137 15 E
Mjöbäck 73 57 28N 12 53 E
Mjölby 73 58 20N 15 10 E
Mjømna 71 60 55N 4 55 E

Mjörn Montcornet

Mjörn 73 57 55N 12 25 E
Mjøsa 71 60 40N 11 0 E
Mkata 126 5 45 S 38 20 E
Mkokotoni 126 5 55 S 39 15 E
Mkomazi 126 4 40 S 38 7 E
Mkulwe 127 8 37 S 32 20 E
Mkumbi, Ras 126 7 38 S 39 55 E
Mkushi 127 14 25 S 29 15 E
Mkushi River 127 13 40 S 29 30 E
Mkuze, R. 129 27 45 S 32 30 E
Mkwaya 126 6 17 S 35 40 E
Mladá Boleslav 52 50 27N 14 53 E
Mladenovac 66 44 28N 20 44 E
Mlala Hills 126 6 50 S 31 40 E
Mlange 127 16 2 S 35 33 E
Mlava, R. 66 44 35N 21 18 E
Mława 54 53 9N 20 25 E
Mlinište 63 44 15N 16 50 E
Mljet, I. 66 42 43N 17 30 E
Młynary 54 54 12N 19 46 E
Mme 121 6 18N 10 14 E
Mo, Hordaland, Norway 71 60 49N 5 48 E
Mo, Telemark, Norway 71 59 28N 7 50 E
Mo, Sweden 72 61 19N 16 47 E
Mo i Rana 74 66 15N 14 7 E
Moa, I. 103 8 0 S 128 0 E
Moa, R. 120 7 0N 11 40W
Moab 161 38 40N 109 35W
Moabi 124 2 24 S 10 59 E
Moalie Park 139 29 42 S 143 3 E
Moaña 56 42 18N 8 43W
Moanda 124 1 28 S 13 21 E
Moapo 161 36 45N 114 37W
Moate 39 53 25N 7 43W
Moba 126 7 0 S 29 48 E
Mobara 111 35 25N 140 18 E
Mobaye 124 4 25N 21 5 E
Mobayi 124 4 15N 21 8 E
Moberley 158 39 25N 92 25W
Moberly, R. 152 56 12N 120 55W
Mobert 150 48 41N 85 40W
Mobile 157 30 41N 88 3W
Mobile B. 157 30 30N 88 0W
Mobile, Pt. 157 30 15N 88 0W
Mobjack B. 162 37 16N 76 22W
Möborg 73 56 24N 8 21 E
Mobridge 158 45 40N 100 28W
Mobutu Sese Seko, L. 126 1 30N 31 0 E
Moc Chav 100 20 50N 104 38 E
Moc Hoa 101 10 46N 105 56 E
Mocabe Kasari 127 9 58 S 26 12 E
Mocajuba 170 2 35 S 49 30W
Moçambique 127 15 3 S 40 42 E
Moçambique □ 127 14 45 S 38 30 E
Mocanaqua 162 41 9N 76 8W
Mochiang 108 23 25N 101 44 E
Mochiara Grove 128 20 43 S 21 50 E
Mochudi 128 24 27 S 26 7 E
Mocimboa da Praia 127 11 25 S 40 20 E
Mociu 70 46 46N 24 3 E
Möckeln 73 56 40N 14 15 E
Mockhorn I. 162 37 10N 75 52W
Moclips 160 47 14N 124 10W
Moçâmedes □ 128 16 35 S 12 30 E
Mocoa 174 1 15N 76 45W
Mococa 173 21 28 S 47 0W
Mocorito 164 25 20N 108 0W
Moctezuma 164 30 12N 106 26W
Moctezuma, R. 165 21 59N 98 34W
Mocuba 125 16 54 S 37 25 E
Moda 98 24 22N 96 29 E
Modane 45 45 12N 6 40 E
Modasa 94 23 30N 73 21 E
Modave 47 50 27N 5 18 E
Modbury, Austral. 109 34 50 S 138 41 E
Modbury, U.K. 30 50 21N 3 53W
Modder, R. 128 28 50 S 24 50 E
Modderrivier 128 29 2 S 24 38 E
Módena 62 44 39N 10 55 E
Modena 161 37 55N 113 56W
Modesto 163 37 43N 121 0W
Módica 65 36 52N 14 45 E
Modigliana 63 44 9N 11 48 E
Modjokerto 103 7 29 S 112 25 E
Modlin 54 52 24N 20 41 E
Mödling 53 48 5N 16 17 E
Modo 123 5 31N 30 33 E
Modra 53 48 19N 17 20 E
Modreeny 39 52 57N 8 6W
Modriča 66 44 57N 18 17 E
Moe 141 38 12 S 146 19 E
Moebase 127 17 3 S 38 41 E
Moei, R. 101 17 25N 98 10 E
Moëlan-s-Mer 42 47 49N 3 38W
Moelfre 31 53 21N 4 15W
Moengo 175 5 45N 54 20W
Moergestel 47 51 33N 5 11 E
Moësa, R. 51 46 12N 9 10 E
Moffat 35 55 20N 3 27W
Moga 94 30 48N 75 8 E
Mogadiscio = Mogadishu 91 2 2N 45 25 E
Mogadishu 91 2 2N 45 25 E
Mogador = Essaouira 118 31 32N 9 42W
Mogadouro 56 41 22N 6 47W
Mogami-gawa, R. 112 38 45N 140 0 E
Mogaung 98 25 20N 97 0 E
Møgeltønder 73 54 57N 8 48 E
Mogente 59 38 52N 0 45W
Moggil 108 27 34 S 152 52 E
Mogho 123 4 54N 40 16 E
Mogi das Cruzes 173 23 45 S 46 20W
Mogi-Guaçu, R. 173 20 53 S 48 10W
Mogi-Mirim 173 22 20 S 47 0W
Mogielnica 54 51 42N 20 41 E
Mogilev 80 53 55N 30 18 E
Mogilev Podolskiy 82 48 20N 27 40 E
Mogilno 54 52 39N 17 55 E
Mogincual 125 15 35 S 40 25 E
Mogliano Veneto 63 45 33N 12 15 E
Mogocha 77 53 40N 119 50 E
Mogoi 103 1 55 S 133 10 E
Mogok 98 23 0N 96 40 E
Mogollon 161 33 25N 108 55W
Mogollon Mesa 161 43 40N 111 0W
Mogriguy 141 32 3 S 148 40 E
Moguer 57 37 15N 6 52W
Mogumber 137 31 2 S 116 3 E
Mohács 53 45 58N 18 41 E
Mohaka, R. 142 39 7 S 177 12 E
Mohall 158 48 46N 101 30W
Mohammadābād 93 37 30N 59 5 E
Mohammedia 118 33 44N 7 21W
Mohave Desert 161 35 0N 117 30W
Mohawk 161 32 45N 113 50W
Mohawk, R. 162 42 47N 73 42W
Moheda 73 57 1N 14 35 E
Mohembo 125 18 15 S 21 43 E
Moher, Cliffs of 39 52 58N 9 30W
Mohican, C. 147 60 10N 167 30W
Mohill 38 53 57N 7 52W
Möhne, R. 48 51 29N 8 10 E
Mohnyin 98 24 47N 96 22 E
Moholm 73 58 37N 14 5 E
Mohon 43 49 45N 4 44 E
Mohoro 126 8 6 S 39 8 E
Moia 123 5 3N 28 2 E
Moidart, L. 36 56 47N 5 40W
Moinabad 96 17 44N 77 16 E
Moineşti 70 46 28N 26 21 E
Mointy 76 47 40N 73 45 E
Moira 38 54 28N 6 16W
Moirais 69 35 4N 24 56 E
Moirans 45 45 20N 5 33 E
Moirans-en-Montagne 45 46 26N 5 43 E
Moisäkula 80 58 3N 24 38 E
Moisie 151 50 7N 66 1W
Moisie, R. 151 50 6N 66 5W
Moissac 44 44 7N 1 5 E
Moita 57 38 38N 8 58W
Mojácar 59 37 6N 1 55W
Mojados 56 41 26N 4 40W
Mojave 163 35 8N 118 8W
Mojave Desert 163 35 0N 116 30W
Mojo, Boliv. 172 21 48 S 65 33W
Mojo, Ethiopia 123 8 35N 39 5 E
Mojo, I. 102 8 10 S 117 40 E
Moju, R. 170 1 40 S 48 25W
Mokai 142 38 32 S 175 56 E
Mokambo 127 12 25 S 28 20 E
Mokameh 95 25 24N 85 55 E
Mokau, R. 142 38 35 S 174 55 E
Mokelumne Hill 163 38 18N 120 43W
Mokelumne, R. 163 38 23N 121 25W
Mokhós 69 35 16N 25 27 E
Mokhotlong 126 29 22 S 29 2 E
Mokihinui 143 41 33 S 171 58 E
Moknine 119 35 35N 10 58 E
Mokokchung 99 26 15N 94 30 E
Mokpalin 98 17 26N 96 53 E
Mokpo 107 34 50N 126 30 E
Mokra Gora 66 42 50N 20 30 E
Mokronog 63 45 57N 15 9 E
Moksha, R. 81 54 45N 43 40 E
Mokshan 81 52 25N 44 35 E
Mokta Spera 120 16 38N 9 6W
Moktama Kwe 99 15 40N 96 30 E
Mol 47 51 11N 5 5 E
Mola, C. de la 58 39 53N 4 20 E
Mola di Bari 65 41 3N 17 5 E
Moland 71 59 11N 8 6 E
Moláoi 69 36 49N 22 56 E
Molat, I. 63 44 15N 14 50 E
Molchanovo 76 57 40N 83 50 E
Mold 31 53 10N 3 10W
Moldava nad Bodvou 53 48 38N 21 0 E
Moldavia = Moldova 70 46 30N 27 0 E
Moldavian S.S.R.□ 82 47 0N 28 0 E
Molde 71 62 45N 7 9 E
Moldotau, Khrebet 85 41 35N 75 0 E
Moldova 70 46 30N 27 0 E
Moldova Nouŭ 70 44 45N 21 41 E
Moldoveanu, mt. 67 45 36N 24 45 E
Mole Creek 138 41 32 S 146 24 E
Mole, R. 29 51 13N 0 15W
Molepolole 125 24 28 S 25 28 E
Moléson 50 46 33N 7 1 E
Molesworth 143 42 5 S 173 16 E
Molfetta 65 41 12N 16 35 E
Molina de Aragón 58 40 46N 1 52W
Moline 158 41 30N 90 30W
Molinella 63 44 38N 11 40 E
Molinos 172 25 28 S 66 15W
Moliro 126 8 12 S 30 30 E
Molise □ 63 41 45N 14 30 E
Moliterno 65 40 14N 15 50 E
Mollahat 98 22 56N 89 48 E
Mölle 73 56 17N 12 31 E
Molledo 56 43 8N 4 6W
Mollendo 174 17 0 S 72 0W
Mollerin, L. 137 30 30 S 117 35 E
Mollerusa 58 41 37N 0 54 E
Mollina 57 37 8N 4 38W
Mölln 48 53 37N 10 41 E
Mollösund 73 58 4N 11 30 E
Mölltorp 73 58 30N 14 26 E
Mölndal 73 57 40N 12 3 E
Mölnlycke 73 57 40N 12 8 E
Molo 98 23 22N 96 53 E
Molochansk 82 47 15N 35 23 E
Molochaya, R. 82 47 0N 35 30 E
Molodechno 80 54 20N 26 50 E
Molokai, I. 147 21 8N 157 0W
Moloma, R. 81 59 0N 48 15 E
Molong 141 33 5 S 148 54 E
Molopo, R. 125 25 40 S 24 30 E
Mólos 69 38 47N 22 37 E
Molotov, Mys 77 81 10N 95 0 E
Moloundou 124 2 8N 15 15 E
Molsheim 43 48 33N 7 29 E
Molson L. 153 54 22N 95 32W
Molteno 128 31 22 S 26 22 E
Molu, I. 103 6 45 S 131 40 E
Molucca Sea 103 4 0 S 124 0 E
Moluccas = Maluku, Is. 103 1 0 S 127 0 E
Molusi 128 20 21 S 24 29 E
Moma, Mozam. 127 16 47 S 39 4 E
Moma, Zaïre 126 1 35 S 23 52 E
Momanga 128 18 7 S 21 41 E
Momba 140 30 58 S 143 30 E
Mombaça 170 15 43 S 48 43W
Mombasa 126 4 2 S 39 43 E
Mombetsu, Hokkaido, Japan 112 42 27N 142 4 E
Mombetsu, Hokkaido, Japan 112 44 21N 143 22 E
Mombuey 56 42 3N 6 20W
Momchilgrad 67 41 33N 25 23 E
Momi 126 1 42 S 27 0 E
Momignies 47 50 2N 4 10 E
Mompós 174 9 14N 74 26W
Møn 73 54 57N 12 15 E
Mon, R. 99 20 25N 94 30 E
Mona, Canal de la 167 18 30N 67 45W
Mona, I. 167 18 5N 67 54W
Mona Passage 167 18 0N 67 40W
Mona, Punta, C. Rica 166 9 37N 82 36W
Mona, Punta, Spain 57 36 43N 3 45W
Monach Is. 36 57 32N 7 40W
Monach, Sd. of 36 57 34N 7 26W
Monaco ■ 44 43 46N 7 23 E
Monadhliath Mts. 37 57 10N 4 4W
Monadnock Mt. 162 42 52N 72 7W
Monagas □ 174 9 20N 63 0W
Monaghan 38 54 15N 6 58W
Monaghan □ 38 54 10N 7 0W
Monahans 159 31 35N 102 50W
Monapo 127 14 50 S 40 12 E
Monar For. 36 57 27N 5 10W
Monar L. 36 57 26N 5 8W
Monarch Mt. 152 51 55N 125 57W
Monasterevan 39 53 10N 7 5W
Monastier-sur-Gazeille, Le 44 44 57N 3 59 E
Monastir 119 35 50N 10 49 E
Monastyriska 80 49 8N 25 14 E
Monavullagh Mts. 39 52 14N 7 35W
Moncada 58 39 30N 0 24W
Moncalieri 62 45 0N 7 40 E
Moncalvo 62 45 3N 8 15 E
Moncarapacho 57 37 5N 7 46W
Moncayo, Sierra del 58 41 48N 1 50W
Mönchengladbach 48 51 12N 6 23 E
Monchique 57 37 19N 8 38W
Monchique, Sa. de, 55 37 18N 8 39W
Monclova 164 26 50N 101 30W
Monção 56 42 4N 8 27W
Moncontant 42 46 43N 0 36W
Moncontour 42 48 22N 2 38W
Moncton 151 46 7N 64 51W
Mondego, Cabo 56 40 11N 8 54W
Mondego, R. 56 40 28N 8 0W
Mondeodo 103 3 21 S 122 9 E
Mondolfo 63 43 45N 13 8 E
Mondoñedo 56 43 25N 7 23W
Mondoví 62 44 23N 7 56 E
Mondovi 158 44 37N 91 40W
Mondragon 45 44 13N 4 44 E
Mondragone 64 41 8N 13 52 E
Mondrain I. 137 34 9 S 122 14 E
Monduli □ 126 3 0 S 36 0 E
Monemvasía 69 36 41N 23 3 E
Monessen 156 40 9N 79 50W
Monesterio 57 38 6N 6 15W
Monestier-de-Clermont 45 44 55N 5 38 E
Monet 150 48 10N 75 40W
Monêtier-les-Bains, Le 45 44 58N 6 30 E
Monett 159 36 55N 93 56W
Moneygall 39 52 54N 7 59W
Moneymore 38 54 42N 6 40W
Monfalcone 63 45 49N 13 32 E
Monflanquin 44 44 32N 0 47 E
Monforte 57 39 6N 7 25W
Monforte de Lemos 56 42 31N 7 33W
Mong Cai 101 21 27N 107 54 E
Möng Hsu 99 21 54N 98 30 E
Mong Hta 98 19 50N 98 35 E
Mong Ket 98 23 8N 98 22 E
Möng Kung 98 21 35N 97 35 E
Mong Kyawt 98 19 56N 98 45 E
Mong Lang 101 20 29N 97 52 E
Möng Nai 98 20 32N 97 55 E
Möng Pai 98 19 40N 97 15 E
Mong Pawk 99 22 4N 99 16 E
Mong Ping 98 21 22N 99 2 E
Mong Pu 98 20 55N 98 44 E
Mong Ton 98 20 25N 98 45 E
Mong Tung 98 22 2N 97 41 E
Mong Wa 99 21 26N 100 27 E
Mong Yai 98 22 28N 98 3 E
Mongalla 123 5 8N 31 55 E
Monger, L. 137 29 25 S 117 5 E
Monghyr 95 25 23N 86 30 E
Mongla 98 22 8N 89 35 E
Mongngaw 98 22 47N 96 59 E
Mongo 117 12 14N 18 43 E
Mongolia ■ 105 47 0N 103 0 E
Mongonu 121 12 40N 13 32 E
Mongororo 124 12 22N 22 26 E
Mongoumba 124 3 33N 18 40 E
Mongpang 101 23 5N 100 25 E
Mongu 125 15 16 S 23 12 E
Mongua 128 16 43 S 15 20 E
Moniaive 35 55 11N 3 55W
Monifieth 35 56 30N 2 48W
Monistral-St.-Loire 45 45 17N 4 11 E
Monitor, Pk. 163 38 52N 116 35W
Monitor, Ra. 163 38 30N 116 45W
Monivea 38 53 22N 8 42W
Monk 153 47 7N 69 59W
Monkey Bay 127 14 7 S 35 1 E
Monkey River 165 16 22N 88 29W
Monki 54 53 23N 22 48 E
Monkira 138 24 46 S 140 30 E
Monkoto 124 1 38 S 20 35 E
Monmouth, U.K. 31 51 48N 2 43W
Monmouth, U.S.A. 158 40 50N 90 40W
Monmouth (□) 26 51 34N 3 5W
Monnow R. 28 51 54N 2 48W
Mono, L. 163 38 0N 119 9W
Mono, Punta del 166 12 0N 83 30W
Monolith 163 35 7N 118 22W
Monópoli 65 40 57N 17 18 E
Monor 53 47 21N 19 27 E
Monóvar 59 38 28N 0 53W
Monowai 143 45 53 S 167 25 E
Monowai, L. 143 45 53 S 167 25 E
Monreal del Campo 58 40 47N 1 20W
Monreale 64 38 6N 13 16 E
Monroe, La., U.S.A. 159 32 32N 92 4W
Monroe, Mich., U.S.A. 156 41 55N 83 26W
Monroe, N.C., U.S.A. 157 35 2N 80 37W
Monroe, Utah, U.S.A. 161 38 45N 111 39W
Monroe, Wis., U.S.A. 158 42 38N 89 40W
Monroe City 158 39 40N 91 40W
Monroeton 162 41 43N 76 29W
Monroeville 157 31 33N 87 15W
Monrovia, Liberia 120 6 18N 10 47W
Monrovia, U.S.A. 161 34 7N 118 1W
Mons 47 50 27N 3 58 E
Møns Klint 73 54 57N 12 33 E
Monsaraz 57 38 28N 7 22W
Monse 103 4 0 S 123 10 E
Monségur 44 44 38N 0 4 E
Monsélice 63 43 13N 11 45 E
Monster 46 52 1N 4 10 E
Mont-aux-Sources 129 28 44 S 28 52 E
Mont-de-Marsin 44 43 54N 0 31W
Mont d'Or, Tunnel 43 46 45N 6 18 E
Mont-Dore, Le 44 45 35N 2 50 E
Mont Joli 151 48 37N 68 10W
Mont Laurier 150 46 35N 75 30W
Mont Luis 151 42 31N 2 6 E
Mont St. Michel 42 48 40N 1 30W
Mont-sur-Marchienne 47 50 23N 4 24 E
Mont Tremblant Prov. Park 150 46 30N 74 30W
Montabaur 48 50 26N 7 49 E
Montacute 109 34 53 S 138 45 E
Montagnac 44 43 29N 3 28 E
Montagnana 63 45 13N 11 29 E
Montagu 128 33 45 S 20 8 E
Montagu, I. 164 58 30 S 26 15W
Montague, Can. 151 46 10N 62 39W
Montague, Calif., U.S.A. 160 41 47N 122 30W
Montague, Mass., U.S.A. 162 42 31N 72 33W
Montague, I. 164 31 40N 144 46W
Montague I. 147 60 0N 147 0W
Montague Ra. 137 29 15 S 119 30 E
Montague Sd. 136 14 28 S 125 20 E
Montaigu 42 46 59N 1 18W
Montalbán 58 40 50N 0 45W
Montalbano di Elicona 65 38 1N 15 0 E
Montalbano Iónico 65 40 17N 16 33 E
Montalbo 58 39 53N 2 42W
Montalcino 63 43 4N 11 30 E
Montalegre 56 41 49N 7 47W
Montalto di Castro 63 42 20N 11 36 E
Montalto Uffugo 65 39 25N 16 9 E
Montalvo 163 34 15N 119 12W
Montamarta 56 41 39N 5 49W
Montaña 174 6 0 S 73 0W
Montana 50 46 19N 7 29 E
Montana □ 154 47 0N 110 0W
Montánchez 57 39 15N 6 8W
Montañita 174 1 30N 75 28W
Montargis 43 48 0N 2 43 E
Montauban 44 44 0N 1 21 E
Montauk 162 41 3N 71 57W
Montauk Pt. 162 41 4N 71 52W
Montbard 43 47 38N 4 20 E
Montbéliard 43 47 31N 6 48 E
Montblanch 58 41 23N 1 4 E
Montbrison 45 45 36N 4 3 E
Montçalm, Pic de 44 42 40N 1 25 E
Montceau-les-Mines 43 46 40N 4 23 E
Montchanin 62 46 47N 4 30 E
Montclair 162 40 53N 74 49W
Montcornet 43 49 40N 4 0 E

Montcuq **Morvan, Mts. du**

Montcuq 44 44 21N 1 13 E
Montdidier 43 49 38N 2 35 E
Monte Albán 165 17 2N 96 45W
Monte Alegre 175 2 0S 54 0W
Monte Alegre de Goiás 171 13 14S 47 10W
Monte Alegre de Minas 171 18 52S 48 52W
Monte Azul 171 15 9S 42 53W
Monte Bello Is. 136 20 30S 115 45 E
Monte Carlo 45 43 46N 7 23 E
Monte Carmelo 171 18 43S 47 29W
Monte Caseros 172 30 10S 57 50W
Monte Comán 172 34 40S 68 0W
Monte Cristi 167 19 52N 71 39W
Monte Libano 16 8 5N 75 29W
Monte Lindo, R. 172 25 30S 58 40W
Monte Quemado 172 25 53S 62 41W
Monte Redondo 56 39 53N 8 50W
Monte San Savino 63 43 20N 11 42 E
Monte Sant' Angelo 65 41 42N 15 59 E
Monte Santo, C. di 64 40 5N 9 42 E
Monte Visto 161 37 40N 106 8W
Monteagudo 173 27 14S 54 8W
Montealegre 59 38 48N 1 17W
Montebello 150 45 40N 74 55W
Montebelluna 63 45 47N 12 3 E
Montebourg 42 49 30N 1 20W
Montecastrilli 63 42 40N 12 30 E
Montecatini Terme 62 43 55N 10 48 E
Montecito 163 34 26N 119 40W
Montecristi 174 1 0S 80 40W
Montecristo, I. 62 42 20N 10 20 E
Montefalco 63 42 53N 12 38 E
Montefiascone 63 42 31N 12 2 E
Montefrío 57 37 20N 3 39W
Montegnée 47 50 38N 5 31 E
Montego B. 166 18 30N 78 0W
Montegranaro 63 43 13N 13 38 E
Monteiro 170 7 22S 37 38W
Monteith 140 35 11S 139 23 E
Montejicar 59 37 33N 3 30W
Montejinnie 136 16 40S 131 45 E
Montekomu Hu 99 34 40N 89 0 E
Montelibano 174 8 5N 75 29W
Montélimar 45 44 33N 4 45 E
Montella 65 40 50N 15 0 E
Montellano 57 36 59N 5 36W
Montello 158 43 49N 89 21W
Montelupo Fiorentino 62 43 44N 11 2 E
Montemór-o-Novo 57 38 40N 8 12W
Montemór-o-Velho 56 40 11N 8 40W
Montemorelos 165 25 11N 99 42W
Montendre 44 45 16N 0 26W
Montenegro 173 29 39S 51 29W
Montenegro □ 66 42 40N 19 20 E
Montenero di Bisaccia 63 42 0N 14 47 E
Montepuez 127 13 8S 38 59 E
Montepuez, R. 127 12 40S 40 15 E
Montepulciano 63 43 5N 11 46 E
Montereale 63 42 31N 13 13 E
Montereau 43 48 22N 2 57 E
Monterey 163 36 35N 121 57W
Monterey, B. 163 36 50N 121 55W
Montería 174 8 46N 75 53W
Monteros 172 27 11S 65 30W
Monterotondo 63 42 3N 12 36 E
Monterrey 164 25 40N 100 30W
Montes Altos 170 5 50S 47 4W
Montes Claros 171 16 30S 43 50W
Montes de Toledo 57 39 35N 4 30W
Montesano 160 47 0N 123 39W
Montesárchio 65 41 5N 14 37 E
Montescaglioso 65 40 34N 16 40 E
Montesilvano 63 42 30N 14 8 E
Montevarchi 63 43 30N 11 32 E
Monteverde 124 8 45S 16 45 E
Montevideo 173 34 50S 56 11W
Montezuma 158 41 32N 92 35W
Montfaucon, Haute-Loire, France 45 45 11N 4 20 E
Montfaucon, Meuse, France 43 49 16N 5 8 E
Montfort 47 51 7N 5 58 E
Montfort-l'Amaury 43 48 47N 1 49 E
Montfort-sur-Meu 42 48 8N 1 58W
Montgenèvre 45 44 56N 6 42 E
Montgomery, U.K. 31 52 34N 3 9W
Montgomery, Ala., U.S.A. 157 32 20N 86 20W
Montgomery, Pa., U.S.A. 162 41 10N 76 53W
Montgomery, W. Va., U.S.A. 156 38 9N 81 21W
Montgomery = Sahiwal 94 30 45N 73 8 E
Montgomery (□) 26 52 34N 3 9W
Montgomery Pass 163 37 58N 118 20W
Montguyon 44 45 12N 0 12W
Monthey 50 46 15N 6 56 E
Monticelli d'Ongina 62 45 3N 9 56 E
Monticello, Ark., U.S.A. 159 33 40N 91 48W
Monticello, Fla., U.S.A. 157 30 35N 83 50W
Monticello, Ind., U.S.A. 156 40 40N 86 45W
Monticello, Iowa, U.S.A. 158 42 18N 91 18W
Monticello, Ky., U.S.A. 157 36 52N 84 50W
Monticello, Minn., U.S.A. 158 45 17N 93 52W
Monticello, Miss., U.S.A. 159 31 35N 90 8W
Monticello, N.Y., U.S.A. 162 41 37N 74 42W
Monticello, Utah, U.S.A. 161 37 55N 109 27W
Montichiari 62 45 28N 10 29 E
Montieri 43 48 30N 4 45 E
Montignac 44 45 4N 1 10 E
Montignies-sur-Sambre 47 50 24N 4 29 E
Montigny-les-Metz 43 49 7N 6 10 E
Montigny-sur-Aube 43 47 57N 4 45 E
Montijo 57 38 52N 6 39W
Montijo, Presa de 57 38 55N 6 26W
Montilla 57 37 36N 4 40W
Montivideo 158 44 55N 95 40W
Montlhéry 43 48 39N 2 15 E
Montluçon 44 46 22N 2 36 E
Montmagny 151 46 58N 70 34W
Montmarault 53 46 11N 2 54 E
Montmartre 153 50 14N 103 27W
Montmédy 43 49 30N 5 20 E
Montmélian 45 45 30N 6 4 E
Montmirail 43 48 51N 3 30 E
Montmoreau-St.-Cybard 44 45 23N 0 8 E
Montmorency 151 46 53N 71 11W
Montmorillon 44 46 26N 0 50 E
Montmort 43 48 55N 3 49 E
Monto 138 24 52S 151 12 E
Montório al Vomano 63 42 35N 13 38 E
Montoro 57 38 1N 4 27W
Montour Falls 162 42 20N 76 51W
Montpelier, Idaho, U.S.A. 160 42 15N 111 29W
Montpelier, Ohio, U.S.A. 156 41 34N 84 40W
Montpelier, Vt., U.S.A. 156 44 15N 72 38W
Montpellier 44 43 37N 3 52 E
Montpezat-de-Quercy 44 44 15N 1 30 E
Montpon-Ménestrol 44 45 2N 0 11 E
Montréal, Can. 150 45 31N 73 34W
Montréal, France 44 43 13N 2 8 E
Montréal L. 153 54 20N 105 45W
Montreal Lake 153 54 3N 105 46W
Montredon-Labessonnié 44 43 45N 2 18 E
Montréjeau 44 43 6N 0 35 E
Montrésor 42 47 10N 1 10 E
Montreuil 43 50 27N 1 45 E
Montreuil-Bellay 42 47 8N 0 9W
Montreux 50 46 26N 6 55 E
Montrevault 42 47 17N 1 2W
Montrevel-en-Bresse 45 46 21N 5 8 E
Montrichard 42 47 20N 1 10 E
Montrose, U.K. 37 56 43N 2 28W
Montrose, Col., U.S.A. 161 38 30N 107 52W
Montrose, Pa., U.S.A. 162 41 50N 75 55W
Montrose, oilfield 19 57 20N 1 35 E
Montross 162 38 6N 76 50W
Monts, Pte des 151 49 27N 67 12W
Montsalvy 44 44 41N 2 30 E
Montsant, Sierra de 58 41 17N 0 1 E
Montsauche 43 47 13N 4 0 E
Montsech, Sierra del 58 42 0N 0 45 E
Montseny 58 42 29N 1 2 E
Montserrat, I. 167 16 40N 62 10W
Montserrat, mt. 58 41 36N 1 49 E
Montuenga 56 41 3N 4 38W
Montuiri 58 39 34N 2 59 E
Monveda 124 2 52N 21 30 E
Monymusk 37 57 13N 2 32W
Mônyo 98 17 59N 95 30 E
Mônywa 98 22 7N 95 11 E
Monza 62 45 35N 9 15 E
Monze 127 16 17S 27 29 E
Monze, C. 94 24 47N 66 37 E
Monzón 58 41 52N 0 10 E
Mook 46 51 46N 5 54 E
Mo'oka 111 36 26N 140 1 E
Moolawatana 139 29 55S 139 45 E
Mooleulooloo 140 31 36S 140 32 E
Mooliabeenee 137 31 20S 116 2 E
Mooloogool 137 26 2S 119 5 E
Moomin, Cr. 139 29 44S 149 20 E
Moonah, R. 138 22 3S 138 33 E
Moonbeam 150 49 20N 82 10W
Mooncoin 39 52 18N 7 17W
Moonie 139 27 46S 150 20 E
Moonie, R. 139 27 45S 150 0 E
Moonta 140 34 6S 137 32 E
Moora 137 30 37S 115 58 E
Mooraberree 138 25 13S 140 54 E
Moorarie 137 25 56S 117 35 E
Moorcroft 158 44 17N 104 58W
Moore, L. 137 29 50S 117 35 E
Moore, R. 137 31 22S 115 30 E
Moore Reefs 138 16 0S 149 5 E
Moore River Native Settlement 137 31 1S 115 56 E
Moorebank 47 33 56S 150 56 E
Moorefield 156 39 5N 78 59W
Mooresville 157 35 36N 80 45W
Moorfoot Hills 35 55 44N 3 8W
Moorhead 158 47 0N 97 0W
Moorland 141 31 46S 152 38 E
Mooroopna 141 36 25S 145 22 E
Moorpark 163 34 17N 118 53W
Moorreesburg 128 33 6S 18 38 E
Moorslede 47 50 54N 3 4 E
Moosburg 49 48 28N 11 57 E
Moose Factory 150 51 20N 80 40W
Moose I. 153 51 42N 97 10W
Moose Jaw 153 50 24N 105 30W
Moose Jaw R. 153 50 34N 105 18W
Moose Lake, Can. 153 53 43N 100 20W
Moose Lake, U.S.A. 158 46 27N 92 48W
Moose Mountain Cr. 153 49 13N 102 12W
Moose Mtn. Prov. Park 153 49 48N 102 25W
Moose, R. 150 51 20N 80 25W
Moose River 150 50 48N 81 17W
Moosehead L. 151 45 40N 69 40W
Moosomin 153 50 9N 101 40W
Moosonee 150 51 17N 80 39W
Moosup 162 41 44N 71 52W
Mopeia 125 17 30S 35 40 E
Mopipi 128 21 6S 24 55 E
Mopoi 123 5 6N 26 54 E
Moppin 139 29 12S 146 45 E
Mopti 120 14 30N 4 0W
Moqatta 123 14 38N 35 50 E
Moquegua 174 17 15S 70 46W
Mór 53 47 25N 18 12 E
Móra 57 38 55N 8 10W
Mora, Sweden 72 61 2N 14 38 E
Mora, Minn., U.S.A. 158 45 52N 93 19W
Mora, N. Mex., U.S.A. 161 35 58N 105 21W
Mora de Ebro 58 41 6N 0 38 E
Mora de Rubielos 58 40 15N 0 45W
Mora la Nueva 58 41 7N 0 39 E
Morača, R. 66 42 40N 19 20 E
Morada Nova 170 5 7S 38 23W
Morada Nova de Minas 171 18 37S 45 22W
Moradabad 94 28 50N 78 50 E
Morafenobe 129 17 50S 44 53 E
Morag 54 53 55N 19 56 E
Moral de Calatrava 59 38 51N 3 33W
Moraleja 56 40 6N 6 43W
Morales 174 2 45N 76 38W
Moramanga 125 18 56S 48 12 E
Moran, Kans., U.S.A. 159 37 53N 94 35W
Moran, Wyo., U.S.A. 160 43 53N 110 37W
Morano Cálabro 65 39 51N 16 8 E
Morant Cays 166 17 22N 76 0W
Morant Pt. 166 17 55N 76 12W
Morar 36 56 58N 5 49W
Morar L. 36 56 57N 5 40W
Moratalla 59 38 14N 1 49W
Moratuwa 97 6 45N 79 55 E
Morava, R. 53 49 50N 16 50 E
Moravatio 164 19 51N 100 25W
Moravia, Iowa, U.S.A. 158 40 50N 92 50W
Moravia, N.Y., U.S.A. 162 42 43N 76 25W
Moravian Hts. = Ceskemoravská V. 52 49 30N 15 40 E
Moravica, R. 66 43 40N 20 8 E
Moravice, R. 53 49 50N 17 43 E
Moravița 66 45 17N 21 14 E
Moravska Trebová 53 49 45N 16 40 E
Moravské Budějovice 52 49 4N 15 49 E
Morawa 137 29 13S 116 0 E
Morawhanna 174 8 30N 59 40W
Moray (□) 26 57 32N 3 25W
Moray Firth 37 57 50N 3 30W
Morbach 49 49 48N 7 7 E
Morbegno 62 46 8N 9 34 E
Morbihan □ 42 47 55N 2 50W
Morcenx 44 44 0N 0 55W
Mordelles 42 48 5N 1 52W
Morden 153 49 15N 98 10W
Mordovian S.S.R.□ 81 54 20N 44 30 E
Mordovo 81 52 13N 40 50 E
More L. 37 58 18N 4 52W
Møre og Romsdal □ 71 63 0N 9 0 E
Morea 140 36 45S 141 18 E
Moreau, R. 158 45 15N 102 45W
Morebattle 35 55 30N 2 20W
Morecambe 32 54 5N 2 52W
Morecambe B. 32 54 7N 3 0W
Morecambe, gasfield 19 53 57N 3 40W
Moree 139 29 28S 149 54 E
Morehead, P.N.G. 135 8 41S 141 41 E
Morehead, U.S.A. 156 38 12N 83 22W
Morehead City 157 34 46N 76 44W
Moreira 174 0 34S 63 26W
Morelia 164 19 40N 101 11W
Morella, Austral. 138 23 0S 143 47 E
Morella, Spain 58 40 35N 0 2 E
Morelos 164 26 42N 107 40W
Morelos □ 165 18 40N 99 10W
Morena, Sierra 57 38 20N 4 0W
Morenci 161 33 7N 109 20W
Moreni 70 44 59N 25 36 E
Moreno 171 8 7S 35 6W
Mores, I. 157 26 15N 77 35W
Moresby I. 152 52 30N 131 40W
Morestel 45 45 40N 5 28 E
Moret 43 48 22N 2 48 E
Moreton B. 133 27 10S 153 10 E
Moreton, I. 139 27 10S 153 25 E
Moreton-in-Marsh 28 51 59N 1 42W
Moreton Telegraph Office 138 12 22S 142 30 E
Moretonhampstead 30 50 39N 3 45W
Moreuil 43 49 46N 2 30 E
Morez 45 46 31N 6 2 E
Morgan, Austral. 140 34 0S 139 35 E
Morgan, U.S.A. 160 41 3N 111 44W
Morgan City 159 29 40N 91 15W
Morgan Hill 163 37 8N 121 39W
Morganfield 156 37 40N 87 55W
Morganton 157 35 46N 81 48W
Morgantown 156 39 39N 79 58W
Morganville, Queens., Austral. 139 25 10S 152 0 E
Morganville, S. Australia, Austral. 140 33 10S 140 32 E
Morgat 42 48 15N 4 32 E
Morgenzon 129 26 45S 29 36 E
Morges 50 46 31N 6 29 E
Morhange 43 48 55N 6 38 E
Mori 62 45 51N 10 59 E
Morialmée 47 50 17N 4 30 E
Morialta Falls Reserve 109 34 54S 138 43 E
Moriarty 161 35 3N 106 2W
Morice L. 152 53 50N 127 40W
Morichal 174 2 10N 70 34W
Morichal Largo, R. 174 8 55N 63 0W
Moriguchi 111 34 44N 135 34 E
Moriki 121 12 52N 6 30 E
Morinville 152 53 49N 113 41W
Morioka 112 39 45N 141 8 E
Moris 164 28 8N 108 32W
Morisset 141 33 6S 151 30 E
Morkalla 140 34 23S 141 10 E
Morlaàs 44 43 21N 0 18W
Morlaix 42 48 36N 3 52W
Morlanwelz 47 50 28N 4 15 E
Morley 33 53 45N 1 36W
Mormanno 65 39 53N 15 59 E
Mormant 43 48 37N 2 52 E
Morney 139 25 22S 141 23 E
Morningside 108 27 28S 153 4 E
Mornington, Victoria, Austral. 141 38 15S 145 5 E
Mornington, W. Australia, Austral. 136 17 31S 126 6 E
Mornington, Ireland 38 53 42N 6 17W
Mornington I. 138 16 30S 139 30 E
Mornington, I. 176 49 50S 75 30W
Mórnos, R. 69 38 30N 22 0 E
Moro 123 10 50N 30 9 E
Moro G. 103 6 30N 123 0 E
Morobe 135 7 49S 147 38 E
Morocco ■ 118 32 0N 5 50W
Morococha 174 11 40S 76 5W
Morogoro 126 6 50S 37 40 E
Morogoro □ 126 8 0S 37 0 E
Morokweng 125 26 12S 23 45 E
Moroleón 164 20 8N 101 32W
Morombé 129 21 45S 43 22 E
Moron 172 34 39S 58 37W
Morón 166 22 0N 78 30W
Morón de Almazán 58 41 29N 2 27W
Morón de la Frontera 57 37 6N 5 28W
Morondava 129 20 17S 44 17 E
Morondo 120 8 57N 6 47W
Morongo Valley 163 34 3N 116 37W
Moronou 120 6 16N 4 59W
Morotai, I. 103 2 10N 128 30 E
Moroto 124 2 28N 34 42 E
Moroto Summit, Mt. 126 2 30N 34 43 E
Morozov (Bratan), mt. 67 42 30N 25 10 E
Morozovsk 83 48 25N 41 50 E
Morpeth 35 55 11N 1 41W
Morrelganj 98 22 28N 89 51 E
Morrilton 159 35 10N 92 45W
Morrinhos, Ceara, Brazil 170 3 14S 40 7W
Morrinhos, Minas Gerais, Brazil 171 17 45S 49 10W
Morrinsville 142 37 40S 175 32 E
Morris, Can. 153 49 25N 97 22W
Morris, Ill., U.S.A. 156 41 20N 88 20W
Morris, Minn., U.S.A. 158 45 33N 95 56W
Morris, N.Y., U.S.A. 162 42 33N 75 15W
Morris, Mt. 137 26 9S 131 4 E
Morrisburg 150 44 55N 75 7W
Morrison 158 41 47N 90 0W
Morristown, Ariz., U.S.A. 161 33 54N 112 45W
Morristown, N.J., U.S.A. 162 40 48N 74 30W
Morristown, S.D., U.S.A. 158 45 57N 101 44W
Morristown, Tenn., U.S.A. 157 36 18N 83 20W
Morrisville, N.Y., U.S.A. 162 42 54N 75 39W
Morrisville, Pa., U.S.A. 162 40 13N 74 47W
Morro Agudo 171 20 44S 48 4W
Morro Bay 163 35 27N 120 54W
Morro do Chapéu 171 11 33S 41 9W
Morro, Pta. 172 27 6S 71 0W
Morros 170 2 52S 44 3W
Morrosquillo, Golfo de 167 9 35N 75 40W
Morrum 73 56 12N 14 45 E
Morrumbene 125 23 31S 35 16 E
Mors 73 56 50N 8 45 E
Morshank 81 53 28N 41 50 E
Mörsil 72 63 19N 13 40 E
Mortagne, Charente Maritime, France 44 45 28N 0 49W
Mortagne, Orne, France 42 48 30N 0 32 E
Mortagne, Vendée, France 42 46 59N 0 57W
Mortagne-au-Perche 42 48 31N 0 33 E
Mortagne, R. 43 48 30N 6 30 E
Mortain 42 48 40N 0 57W
Mortara 62 45 15N 8 43 E
Morte Bay 30 51 10N 4 13W
Morte Pt. 30 51 13N 4 14W
Morteau 43 47 3N 6 35 E
Mortehoe 30 51 12N 4 12W
Morteros 172 30 50S 62 0W
Mortes, R. das 171 11 45S 50 44W
Mortimer's Cross 28 52 17N 2 50W
Mortlake 140 38 5S 142 50 E
Morton, Tex., U.S.A. 159 33 39N 102 49W
Morton, Wash., U.S.A. 160 46 33N 122 17W
Morton Fen 29 52 45N 0 23W
Mortsel 47 51 11N 4 27 E
Morundah 141 34 57S 146 19 E
Moruya 141 35 58N 150 3 E
Morvan, Mts. du 43 47 5N 4 0 E

Morven Mukden

Morven, Austral. 139 26 22S 147 5E
Morven, N.Z. 143 44 50S 171 6E
Morven, dist. 34 56 38N 5 44W
Morven, mt., Grampian, U.K. 37 57 8N 3 1W
Morven, mt., Highland, U.K. 37 58 15N 3 40W
Morvern 36 56 38N 5 44W
Morwell 141 38 10S 146 22E
Moryn 54 52 51N 14 22E
Mosalsk 80 54 30N 34 55E
Mosbach 49 49 21N 9 9E
Mosciano Sant' Ángelo 63 42 42N 13 52E
Moscos Is. 101 14 0N 97 30E
Moscow, Idaho, U.S.A. 160 46 45N 116 59W
Moscow, Pa., U.S.A. 162 41 20N 75 31W
Moscow = Moskva 81 55 45N 37 35E
Mosel, R. 49 50 22N 7 36E
Moselle □ 43 48 59N 6 33E
Moselle, R. 47 50 22N 7 36E
Moses Lake 160 47 16N 119 17W
Mosgiel 143 45 53S 170 21E
Moshi 126 3 22S 37 18E
Moshi □ 126 3 22S 37 18E
Moshupa 128 24 46S 25 29E
Mósina 54 52 15N 16 50E
Mosjøen 74 65 51N 13 12E
Moskenesøya 74 67 58N 13 0E
Moskenstraumen 74 67 47N 13 0E
Moskva 81 55 45N 37 35E
Moskva, R. 81 55 5N 38 51E
Moslavačka Gora 63 45 40N 16 37E
Mošóenice 63 45 17N 14 16E
Mosomane (Artesia) 128 24 2S 26 19E
Mosonmagyaróvár 53 47 52N 17 18E
Mo orin 66 45 19N 20 4E
Mospino 82 47 52N 38 0E
Mosquera 174 2 35N 78 30W
Mosquero 159 35 48N 103 57W
Mosqueruela 58 40 21N 0 27W
Mosquitia 166 15 20N 84 10W
Mosquitos, Golfo de los 166 9 15N 81 10W
Moss 71 59 27N 10 40E
Moss Vale 141 34 32S 150 25E
Mossaka 124 1 15S 16 45E
Mossâmedes, Angola 125 15 7S 12 11E
Mossâmedes, Brazil 171 16 7S 50 11W
Mossbank 153 49 56N 105 56W
Mossburn 143 45 41S 168 15E
Mosselbaai 128 34 11S 22 8E
Mossendjo 124 2 55S 12 42E
Mosses, Col des 50 46 25N 7 7E
Mossgiel 140 33 15S 144 30E
Mossley 32 53 31N 2 1W
Mossman 138 16 28S 145 23E
Mossoró 170 5 10S 37 15W
Mossuril 127 14 58S 40 42E
Mossy, R. 153 54 5N 102 58W
Most 52 50 31N 13 38E
Mostar 66 43 22N 17 50E
Mostardas 173 31 2S 50 51W
Mostefa, Rass 119 36 55N 11 3E
Mosterøy 71 59 5N 5 37E
Mostiska 80 49 48N 23 4E
Mostrim 38 53 42N 7 38W
Mosty 80 53 27N 24 38E
Mostyn 31 53 18N 3 14W
Mosul = Al Mawsil 92 36 20N 43 5E
Mosulpo 107 33 20N 126 17E
Mosvatn, L. 71 59 52N 8 5E
Mota del Cuervo 58 39 30N 2 52W
Mota del Marqués 56 41 38N 5 11W
Motagua, R. 166 15 44N 88 14W
Motala 73 58 32N 15 1E
Motcombe 28 51 1N 2 12W
Motegi 111 36 32N 140 11E
Mothe-Achard, La 42 46 37N 1 40W
Motherwell 35 55 48N 4 0W
Motihari 95 26 37N 85 1E
Motilla del Palancar 58 39 34N 1 55W
Motnik 63 46 14N 14 54E
Motocurunya 174 4 24N 64 5W
Motovun 63 45 20N 13 50E
Motozintea de Mendoza 165 15 21N 92 14W
Motril 59 36 44N 3 37W
Motrul, R. 70 44 44N 22 59E
Mott 158 46 25N 102 14W
Motte-Chalançon, La 45 44 30N 5 21E
Motte, La 45 44 20N 6 3E
Mottisfont 28 51 22N 1 32W
Mottola 65 40 38N 17 0E
Motueka 143 41 7S 173 1E
Motul 165 21 0N 89 20W
Motupena Pt. 135 6 30S 155 10E
Mouchalagane, R. 151 50 56N 68 41W
Moúdhros 68 39 50N 25 18E
Moudjeria 120 17 50N 12 15W
Moudon 50 46 40N 6 49E
Mouila 124 1 50S 11 0E
Moulamein 140 35 3S 144 1E
Moule, Le 167 16 20N 61 22W
Moulins 44 46 35N 3 19E
Moulmein 98 16 30N 97 40E
Moulmeingyun 98 16 23N 95 16E
Moulouya, O. 118 35 8N 2 22W
Moulton, U.K. 29 52 17N 0 51W
Moulton, U.S.A. 159 29 35N 97 8W
Moultrie 157 31 11N 83 47W
Moultrie, L. 157 33 25N 80 10W
Mound City, Mo., U.S.A. 158 40 2N 95 25W
Mound City, S.D., U.S.A. 158 45 46N 100 3W
Moúnda, Ákra 69 38 5N 20 45E
Moundou 117 8 40N 16 10E
Moundsville 156 39 53N 80 43W
Moung 100 12 46N 103 27E
Mount Airy 162 36 31N 80 37W
Mount Amherst 136 18 24S 126 58E
Mount Angel 160 45 4N 122 46W
Mount Augustus 137 24 20S 116 56E
Mount Barker, S.A., Austral. 140 35 5S 138 52E
Mount Barker, W.A., Austral. 137 34 38S 117 40E
Mount Barker Junc. 109 35 1S 138 52E
Mount Beauty 141 36 47S 147 10E
Mount Bellew Bridge 38 53 28N 8 30W
Mount Buckley 138 20 6S 148 0E
Mount Carmel, Ill., U.S.A. 156 38 20N 87 48W
Mount Carmel, Pa., U.S.A. 162 40 46N 76 25W
Mount Clemens 150 42 35N 82 50W
Mount Coolon 138 21 25S 147 25E
Mount Cootatha Park 108 27 29S 152 57E
Mount Crosby 108 27 32S 152 48E
Mount Darwin 125 16 47S 31 38E
Mount Desert I. 151 44 25N 68 25W
Mount Dora 157 28 49N 81 32W
Mount Douglas 138 21 35S 146 50E
Mount Edgecumbe 147 57 8N 135 22W
Mount Elizabeth 136 16 0S 125 50E
Mount Enid 136 21 42S 116 26E
Mount Forest 150 43 59N 80 43W
Mount Fox 138 18 45S 145 45E
Mount Gambier 140 37 50S 140 46E
Mount Garnet 138 17 37S 145 6E
Mount Goldsworthy 132 20 25S 119 39E
Mount Gravatt 108 27 32S 153 5E
Mount Hagen 135 5 52S 144 16E
Mount Hope, N.S.W., Austral. 141 32 51S 145 51E
Mount Hope, S.A., Austral. 139 34 7S 135 23E
Mount Hope, U.S.A. 156 37 52N 81 9W
Mount Horeb 158 43 0N 89 42W
Mount Howitt 139 26 31S 142 16E
Mount Isa 138 20 42S 139 26E
Mount Ive 140 32 25S 136 5E
Mount Keith 137 27 15S 120 30E
Mount Kisco 162 41 12N 73 44W
Mount Laguna 163 32 52N 116 25W
Mount Larcom 138 23 48S 150 59E
Mount Lavinia 93 6 50N 79 50E
Mount Lofty Ra. 133 34 35S 139 5E
Mount McKinley Nat. Pk. 147 64 0N 150 0W
Mount Magnet 137 28 2S 117 47E
Mount Manara 140 32 29S 143 58E
Mount Margaret 139 26 54S 143 21E
Mount Maunganui 142 37 40S 176 14E
Mount Monger 137 31 0S 122 0E
Mount Morgan 138 23 40S 150 25E
Mount Morris 156 42 43N 77 50W
Mount Mulligan 138 16 45S 144 47E
Mount Narryer 137 26 30S 115 55E
Mount Newman 136 23 18S 119 45E
Mount Nicholas 137 22 54S 120 27E
Mount Oxide 138 19 30S 139 29E
Mount Pearl 151 47 31N 52 47W
Mount Penn 162 40 20N 75 54W
Mount Perry 139 25 13S 151 42E
Mount Phillips 137 24 25S 116 15E
Mount Pleasant, Iowa, U.S.A. 158 41 0N 91 35W
Mount Pleasant, Mich., U.S.A. 156 43 35N 84 47W
Mount Pleasant, S.C., U.S.A. 157 32 45N 79 48W
Mount Pleasant, Tenn., U.S.A. 157 35 31N 87 11W
Mount Pleasant, Tex., U.S.A. 159 33 5N 95 0W
Mount Pleasant, Ut., U.S.A. 160 39 40N 111 29W
Mount Pocono 162 41 8N 75 21W
Mount Rainier Nat. Park. 160 46 50N 121 43W
Mount Revelstoke Nat. Park 152 51 5N 118 30W
Mount Robson 152 52 56N 119 15W
Mount Robson Prov. Park 152 53 0N 119 0W
Mount Samson 108 27 18S 152 51E
Mount Sandiman 137 24 25S 115 30E
Mount Shasta 160 41 20N 122 18W
Mount Somers 143 43 45S 171 27E
Mount Sterling, Ill., U.S.A. 158 40 0N 90 40W
Mount Sterling, Ky., U.S.A. 158 38 0N 84 0W
Mount Surprise 138 18 10S 144 17E
Mount Talbot 38 53 31N 8 18W
Mount Tom Price 137 22 50S 117 40E
Mount Upton 162 42 26N 75 23W
Mount Vernon, Austral. 137 24 15S 118 15E
Mount Vernon, D.C., U.S.A. 162 38 47N 77 10W
Mount Vernon, Ill., U.S.A. 162 38 17N 88 57W
Mount Vernon, Ind., U.S.A. 158 38 17N 88 57W
Mount Vernon, N.Y., U.S.A. 156 40 57N 73 49W
Mount Vernon, Ohio, U.S.A. 156 40 20N 82 30W
Mount Vernon, Wash., U.S.A. 160 48 27N 122 18W
Mount Victor 140 32 11S 139 44E
Mount Whaleback 132 23 18S 119 44E
Mount Willoughby 139 27 58S 134 8E
Mountain Ash 31 51 42N 3 22W
Mountain Center 163 33 42N 116 44W
Mountain City, Nev., U.S.A. 160 41 54N 116 0W
Mountain City, Tenn., U.S.A. 157 36 30N 81 50W
Mountain Dale 162 41 41N 74 32W
Mountain Grove 159 37 5N 92 20W
Mountain Home, Ark., U.S.A. 159 36 20N 92 25W
Mountain Home, Idaho, U.S.A. 160 43 11N 115 45W
Mountain Iron 158 47 30N 92 87W
Mountain Park. 152 52 50N 117 15W
Mountain View, Ark., U.S.A. 159 35 52N 92 10W
Mountain View, Calif., U.S.A. 161 37 26N 122 5W
Mountain Village 147 62 10N 163 50W
Mountainair 161 34 35N 106 15W
Mountcharles 38 54 37N 8 12W
Mountfield 38 54 34N 7 10W
Mountmellick 39 53 7N 7 20W
Mountnorris 38 54 15N 6 29W
Mountnorris B. 136 11 25S 132 45E
Mountrath 39 53 0N 7 30W
Mounts Bay 30 50 3N 5 27W
Mountsorrel 28 52 43N 1 9W
Mountvernon 152 48 25N 122 20W
Mouping 107 37 24N 121 35E
Moura, Austral. 138 24 35S 149 58E
Moura, Brazil 174 1 25S 61 45W
Moura, Port. 57 38 7N 7 30W
Mourão 57 38 22N 7 22W
Mourdi, Depression du 117 18 10N 23 0E
Mourdiah 120 14 35N 7 25W
Moure, La 158 46 27N 98 17W
Mourenx 44 43 23N 0 36W
Mouri 121 5 6N 1 14W
Mourilyan 138 17 35S 146 3E
Mourmelon-le-Grand 43 49 8N 4 22E
Mourne Mts. 38 54 10N 6 0W
Mourne, R. 38 54 45N 7 39W
Mouroubra 137 29 42S 117 52E
Mourzouq 119 25 53N 14 10W
Mousa I. 36 60 0N 1 10W
Mouscron 47 50 45N 3 12E
Moussoro 117 13 50N 16 35E
Mouthe 43 46 44N 6 12E
Moutier 50 47 16N 7 21E
Moutiers 45 45 29N 6 31E
Mouting 108 25 22N 101 32E
Moutong 103 0 28N 121 13E
Mouy 43 49 18N 2 20E
Mouzáki 68 39 25N 21 37E
Movas 164 28 10N 109 25W
Moville 38 55 11N 7 3W
Moxhe 47 50 38N 5 5E
Moxotó, R. 170 9 19S 38 14W
Moy, Inverness, U.K. 37 57 22N 4 3W
Moy, Ulster, U.K. 38 54 27N 6 40W
Moy, R. 38 54 5N 8 50W
Moyagee 137 27 48S 117 48E
Moyahua 164 21 16N 103 10W
Moyale, Ethiopia 123 3 34N 39 4E
Moyale, Kenya 126 3 30N 39 0E
Moyamba 120 8 15N 12 30W
Moyasta 39 52 40N 9 31W
Moycullen 39 53 20N 9 10W
Moyie 152 49 17N 115 50W
Moyle □ 38 55 10N 6 15W
Moylett 38 53 57N 7 7W
Moynalty 38 53 48N 6 52W
Moyne 39 52 45N 7 43W
Moyobamba 174 6 0S 77 0W
Moyvalley 38 53 26N 6 55W
Moza 90 31 48N 35 8E
Mozambique = Moçambique 125 15 3S 40 42E
Mozambique ■ 129 19 0S 35 0E
Mozambique Chan. 129 20 0S 39 0E
Mozdok 83 43 45N 44 48E
Mozhaisk 81 55 30N 36 2E
Mozhga 84 56 26N 52 15E
Mozirje 63 46 22N 14 58E
Mozua 126 3 57N 24 2E
Mozyr 80 52 0N 29 15E
Mpanda 126 6 23S 31 40E
Mpanda □ 126 6 23S 31 40E
Mpésoba 120 12 31N 5 39W
Mpika 127 11 51S 31 25E
Mpraeso 121 6 50N 0 50W
Mpulungu 127 8 51S 31 5E
Mpwapwa 124 6 30S 36 30E
Mpwapwa □ 126 6 30S 36 20E
Mragowo 54 53 57N 21 18E
Mrakovo 84 52 43N 56 38E
Mramor 66 43 20N 21 45E
Mrhaïer 119 33 55N 5 58E
Mrimina 118 29 50N 7 9W
Mrkonjió Grad 66 44 26N 17 4E
Mrkopalj 63 45 21N 14 52E
Mrocza 54 53 16N 17 35E
Msab, Oued en 119 32 35N 5 20E
Msaken 119 35 49N 10 33E
M'Salu, R. 127 12 25S 39 15E
Msambansovu, mt. 127 15 50S 30 3E
M'sila 119 35 46N 4 30E
Msoro 125 13 35S 31 50E
Msta, R. 80 58 30N 33 30E
Mstislavl 80 54 0N 31 50E
Mszana Dolna 54 49 41N 20 5E
Mszczonów 54 51 58N 20 33E
Mtama 127 10 17S 39 21E
Mtilikwe, R. 127 21 0S 31 12E
Mtsensk 81 53 25N 36 30E
Mtskheta 83 41 52N 44 45E
Mtwara 124 10 20S 40 20E
Mtwara □ 126 1 0S 39 0E
Mtwara-Mikindani 127 10 20S 40 20E
Mu Gia, Deo 100 17 40N 105 47E
Mu Ness 36 60 41N 0 50W
Mu, R. 98 21 56N 95 38E
Muaná 170 1 25S 49 15W
Muanda 124 6 0S 12 20E
Muang Chiang Rai 100 19 52N 99 50E
Muang Kalasin 101 16 26N 103 30E
Muang Lampang 101 18 16N 99 32E
Muang Lamphun 100 18 40N 98 53E
Muang Nan 101 18 52N 100 42E
Muang Phetchabun 101 16 23N 101 12E
Muang Phichit 101 16 29N 100 21E
Muang Ubon 101 15 15N 104 50E
Muang Yasothon 101 15 50N 104 10E
Muar 101 2 3N 102 34E
Muar, R. 101 2 15N 102 48E
Muarabungo 102 1 40S 101 10E
Muaradjuloi 102 0 12S 114 3E
Muaraenim 102 3 40S 103 50E
Muarakaman 102 0 2S 116 45E
Muaratebo 102 1 30S 102 26E
Muaratembesi 102 1 42S 103 2E
Muaratewe 102 0 50S 115 0E
Mubairik 92 23 22N 39 8E
Mubarakpur 95 26 12N 83 24E
Mubende 126 0 33N 31 22E
Mubi 121 10 18N 13 16E
Mubur, P. 101 3 20N 106 12E
Mucajaí, Serra do 174 2 23N 61 10W
Much Dewchurch 28 51 58N 2 45W
Much Marcle 28 51 59N 2 27W
Much Wenlock 28 52 36N 2 34W
Muchalls 37 57 2N 2 10W
Mücheln 48 51 18N 11 49E
Muchinga Mts. 127 11 30S 31 30E
Muchkapskiy 81 51 52N 42 28E
Mŭcin 70 45 16N 28 8E
Muck, I. 36 56 50N 6 15W
Muckadilla 139 26 35S 148 23E
Muckle Roe I. 36 60 22N 1 22W
Muckross Hd. 38 54 37N 8 35W
Mucubela 129 16 53S 37 49E
Mucugê 171 13 5S 37 49E
Mucuri 171 18 0S 40 0W
Mucurici 171 18 6S 40 31W
Mud I. 108 27 20S 153 14E
Mud L. 160 40 15N 120 15W
Mudanya 82 40 25N 28 50E
Mùddy, R. 161 38 30N 110 55W
Mudgee 141 32 32S 149 31E
Mudhnib 92 25 50N 44 18E
Mudjatik, R. 153 56 1N 107 36W
Mudon 98 16 15N 97 44E
Muecate 127 14 55S 39 34E
Muêda 127 11 36S 39 28E
Muela, La 58 41 36N 1 7W
Mueller Ra., Mts. 136 18 18S 126 46E
Muerto, Mar 165 16 10N 94 10W
Muff 38 55 4N 7 16W
Mufindi □ 127 8 30S 35 20E
Mufou Shan 109 29 15N 114 20E
Mufulira 127 12 32S 28 15E
Mufumbiro Range 126 1 25S 29 30E
Mugardos 56 43 27N 8 15W
Muge 57 39 3N 8 40W
Muge, R. 57 39 15N 8 18W
Múggia 63 45 36N 13 47E
Mugi 110 33 40N 134 25E
Mugia 56 43 3N 9 17W
Mugila, Mts. 126 7 0S 28 50E
Muğla 92 37 15N 28 28E
Múglizh 67 42 37N 25 32E
Mugu 95 29 45N 82 30E
Muhammad Qol 122 20 53N 37 9E
Muhammad Râs 122 27 50N 34 0E
Muhammadabad 95 26 4N 83 25E
Muharraqa = Sa'ad 90 31 28N 34 33E
Muhesi, R. 126 6 40S 35 5E
Muheza □ 126 5 0S 39 0E
Mühldorf 49 48 14N 12 23E
Mühlhausen 48 51 12N 10 29E
Mühlig-Hofmann-fjella 13 72 30S 5 0E
Muhutwe 126 1 35S 31 45E
Mui Bai Bung 101 8 35N 104 42E
Mui Ron 101 18 7N 106 27E
Muiden 46 52 20N 5 4E
Muine Bheag 39 52 42N 6 59W
Muiños 56 41 58N 7 59W
Muir, L. 137 34 30S 116 40E
Muir of Ord 37 57 30N 4 35W
Muirdrum 35 56 31N 2 40W
Muirkirk 35 55 31N 4 6W
Muja 123 12 2N 39 30E
Mukachevo 80 48 27N 22 45E
Mukah 102 2 55N 112 5E
Mukalla 91 14 33N 49 2E
Mukawwa, Geziret 122 23 55N 35 53E
Mukdahan 100 16 32N 104 43E
Mukden = Shenyang 107 41 48N 123 27E

Mukeiras Nabari

Mukeiras 91 13 59N 45 52E
Mukhtolovo 81 55 29N 43 15E
Mukinbudin 137 30 55S 118 5E
Mukombwe 127 15 48S 26 32E
Mukomuko 102 2 20S 101 10E
Mukomwenze 126 6 49S 27 15E
Mukry 85 37 54N 65 12E
Muktsar 94 30 30N 74 30E
Muktsar Bhatinda 94 30 15N 74 57E
Mukur 94 32 50N 67 50E
Mukutawa, R. 153 53 10N 97 24W
Mukwela 127 17 0S 26 40E
Mula 59 38 3N 1 33W
Mula, R. 96 19 16N 74 20E
Mulanay 103 13 30N 122 30E
Mulange 126 3 40S 27 10E
Mulatas, Arch. de las 166 6 51N 78 31W
Mulchén 172 37 45S 72 20W
Mulde, R. 48 50 55N 12 42E
Mule Creek 158 43 19N 104 8W
Muleba 126 1 50S 31 37E
Muleba □ 126 2 0S 31 30E
Mulegé 164 26 53N 112 1W
Mulegns 51 46 32N 9 38E
Mulengchen 107 44 32N 130 14E
Muleshoe 159 34 17N 102 42W
Mulga Valley 140 31 8S 141 3E
Mulgathing 139 30 15S 134 0E
Mulgrave 151 45 38N 61 31W
Mulgrave I. 135 10 5S 142 10E
Mulhacén 59 37 4N 3 20W
Mülheim 48 51 26N 6 53W
Mulhouse 43 47 40N 7 20E
Muli, China 99 28 21N 100 40E
Muli, China 108 27 50N 101 15E
Mull Head 37 59 23N 2 53W
Mull I. 34 56 27N 6 0W
Mull, Ross of, dist. 34 56 20N 6 15W
Mull, Sound of 34 56 30N 5 50W
Mullagh 39 53 13N 8 25W
Mullaghareirk Mts. 39 52 20N 9 10W
Mullaittvu 97 9 15N 80 55E
Mullardoch L. 36 57 30N 5 0W
Mullen 158 42 5N 101 0W
Mullengudgery 141 31 43S 147 29E
Mullens 156 37 34N 81 22W
Muller, Pegunungan 102 0 30N 113 30E
Muller Ra. 138 5 30S 143 0E
Mullet Pen. 38 54 10N 10 2W
Mullewa 137 28 29S 115 30E
Mullheim 49 47 48N 7 37E
Mulligan, R. 138 26 40S 139 0E
Mullin 159 31 33N 98 38W
Mullinahone 39 52 30N 7 31W
Mullinavat 39 52 23N 7 10W
Mullingar 38 53 31N 7 20W
Mullins 157 34 12N 79 15W
Mullion 30 50 1N 5 15W
Mullsjö 73 57 56N 13 55E
Mullumbimby 139 28 30S 153 30E
Mulobezi 127 16 45S 25 7E
Mulrany 38 53 54N 9 47W
Mulroy B. 38 55 15N 7 45W
Mulshi L. 96 18 30N 73 20E
Multai 96 21 39N 78 15E
Multan 94 30 15N 71 30E
Multan □ 94 30 29N 72 29E
Multrå 72 63 10N 17 24E
Mulumbe, Mts. 127 8 40S 27 30E
Mulungushi Dam 127 14 48S 28 48E
Mulvane 159 37 30N 97 15W
Mulwad 122 18 45N 30 39E
Mulwala 141 35 59S 146 0E
Mumbles 31 51 34N 4 0W
Mumbles Hd. 31 51 33N 4 0W
Mumbwa 125 15 0S 27 0E
Mumeng 135 7 1S 146 37E
Mumra 83 45 45N 47 41E
Mun 101 15 17N 103 0E
Mun, R. 100 15 19N 105 30E
Muna, I. 103 5 0S 122 30E
Muna Sotuta 165 20 29N 89 43W
Munawwar 95 32 47N 74 27E
Münchberg 49 50 11N 11 48E
Müncheberg 48 52 30N 14 9E
München 49 48 8N 11 33E
Munchen-Gladbach = Mönchengladbach 48 51 12N 6 23E
Muncho Lake 152 59 0N 125 50W
Munchŏn 107 39 14N 127 19E
Münchwilen 51 47 38N 8 59E
Muncie 156 40 10N 85 20W
Mundakayam 97 9 30N 76 32E
Mundala, Puncak 103 4 30S 141 0E
Mundare 152 53 35N 112 20W
Munday 159 33 26N 99 39W
Münden 48 51 25N 9 42E
Mundesley 29 52 53N 1 24E
Mundiwindi 136 23 47S 120 9E
Mundo Novo 171 11 50S 40 29W
Mundo, R. 59 38 30N 2 15W
Mundra 94 22 54N 69 26E
Mundrabilla 137 31 52S 127 51E
Munera 59 39 2N 2 29W
Muneru, R. 96 16 45N 80 3E
Mungallala 139 26 25S 147 34E
Mungallala Cr. 139 28 53S 147 5E
Mungana 138 17 8S 144 27E
Mungaoli 94 24 24N 78 7E
Mungari 127 17 12S 33 42E
Mungbere 124 2 36N 28 28E
Mungindi 139 28 58S 149 1E
Munhango 125 12 10S 18 38E
Munhango R. 125 11 30S 19 30E
Munich = München 49 48 8N 11 35E
Munising 156 46 25N 86 39W
Munjiye 122 18 47N 41 20W
Munka-Ljungby 73 56 16N 12 58E
Munkedal 73 58 28N 11 40E
Munkfors 72 59 50N 13 30E
Muñoz Gamero, Pen. 176 52 30S 73 5E
Munro 141 37 56S 147 11E
Munroe L. 153 59 13N 98 35W
Munsan 107 37 51N 126 48E
Munshiganj 98 23 33N 90 32E
Münsingen 50 46 52N 7 32E
Munster 43 48 2N 7 8E
Münster, Niedersachsen, Ger. 48 52 59N 10 5E
Münster, Nordrhein-Westfalen, Ger. 48 51 58N 7 37E
Münster, Switz. 51 46 30N 8 17E
Munster □ 39 52 20N 8 40W
Muntadgin 137 31 45S 118 33E
Muntele Mare 70 46 30N 23 12E
Muntok 102 2 5S 105 10E
Muon Pak Beng 101 19 51N 101 4E
Muong Beng 100 20 23N 101 46E
Muong Boum 100 22 24N 102 49E
Muong Er 100 20 49N 104 1E
Muong Hai 100 21 3N 101 49E
Muong Hiem 100 20 5N 103 22E
Muong Houn 100 20 8N 101 23E
Muong Hung 100 20 56N 103 53E
Muong Kau 100 15 6N 105 47E
Muong Khao 100 19 47N 103 29E
Muong Khoua 100 21 5N 102 31E
Muong La 101 20 52N 102 5E
Muong Liep 100 18 29N 101 40E
Muong May 100 14 49N 106 56E
Muong Ngeun 100 20 36N 101 3E
Muong Ngoi 100 20 43N 102 41E
Muong Nhie 100 22 12N 102 28E
Muong Nong 100 16 22N 106 30E
Muong Ou Tay 100 22 7N 101 48E
Muong Oua 100 18 18N 101 20E
Muong Pak Bang 100 19 54N 101 8E
Muong Penn 100 20 13N 103 52E
Muong Phalane 100 16 39N 105 34E
Muong Phieng 100 19 6N 101 32E
Muong Phine 100 16 32N 106 2E
Muong Sai 100 20 42N 101 59E
Muong Saiapoun 100 18 24N 101 31E
Muong Sen 100 19 24N 104 8E
Muong Sing 100 21 11N 101 9E
Muong Son 100 20 27N 103 19E
Muong Soui 100 19 33N 102 52E
Muong Va 100 21 53N 102 19E
Muong Xia 100 20 19N 104 50E
Muonio 74 67 57N 23 40E
Muonio älv 74 67 48N 23 25E
Muotathal 51 46 58N 8 46E
Muotohora 142 38 18S 177 40E
Mupa 125 16 5S 15 50E
Muqaddam, Wadi 123 17 0N 32 0E
Mur-de-Bretagne 42 48 12N 3 0W
Mur, R. 52 47 7N 13 55E
Mura, R. 63 46 37N 16 9E
Murallón, Cuerro 176 49 55S 73 30W
Muralto 51 46 11N 8 49E
Muranda 126 1 52S 29 20E
Murang'a 126 0 45S 37 9E
Murashi 81 59 30N 49 0E
Murat 44 45 7N 2 53E
Murau 52 47 6N 14 10E
Muravera 64 39 25N 9 35E
Murça 56 41 24N 7 28W
Murchison 143 41 49S 172 21E
Murchison Downs 137 26 45S 118 55E
Murchison Falls = Kabarega Falls 126 2 15N 31 38E
Murchison House 137 27 39S 114 14E
Murchison Mts. 143 45 13S 167 23E
Murchison, oilfield 19 61 25N 1 40E
Murchison, R. 137 26 45S 116 15E
Murchison Ra. 138 20 0S 134 10E
Murchison Rapids 127 15 55S 34 35E
Murcia 59 38 2N 1 10W
Murcia □ 59 37 50N 1 30W
Murdo 158 43 56N 100 43W
Murdoch Pt. 138 14 37S 144 55E
Murdock Hill 109 34 59S 138 55E
Mure, La 45 44 55N 5 48E
Mureş □ 70 46 45N 24 40E
Mureşul, R. 70 46 15N 20 13E
Muret 44 43 30N 1 20E
Murfatlar 70 44 10N 28 26E
Murfreesboro 157 35 50N 86 21W
Murg 51 47 8N 9 13E
Murgab 85 38 10N 73 59E
Murgeni 70 46 12N 28 1E
Murgenthal 50 47 16N 7 50E
Murgon 139 26 15S 151 54E
Murgoo 137 27 24S 116 28E
Muri 51 47 17N 8 21E
Muriaé 173 21 8S 42 23W
Murias de Paredes 56 42 52N 6 19W
Murici 170 9 19S 35 56W
Muriel Mine 127 17 14S 30 40E
Muritiba 171 12 55S 39 15W
Murits see 48 53 25N 12 40E
Murjo Mt. 103 6 36S 110 53E
Murka 126 3 27S 38 0E
Murmansk 78 68 57N 33 10E
Murmerwoude 46 53 18N 6 0E
Murnau 49 47 40N 11 11E
Muro, France 45 42 34N 8 54E
Muro, Spain 58 39 45N 3 3E
Muro, C. di 45 41 44N 8 37E
Muro Lucano 65 40 45N 15 30E
Murom 81 55 35N 42 3E
Muroran 112 42 25N 141 0E
Muros 56 42 45N 9 5W
Muros y de Noya, Ria de 56 42 45N 9 0W
Muroto 110 33 18N 134 9E
Muroto-Misaki 110 33 15N 134 10E
Murowana Gosślina 54 52 35N 17 0E
Murphy 160 43 11N 116 33W
Murphys 163 38 8N 120 28W
Murphysboro 159 37 50N 89 20W
Murrat 122 18 51N 29 33E
Murray, Ky., U.S.A. 157 36 40N 88 20W
Murray, Utah, U.S.A. 160 40 41N 111 58W
Murray Bridge 140 35 6S 139 14E
Murray Downs 138 21 4S 134 40E
Murray Harb. 151 46 0N 62 28W
Murray, L., P.N.G. 135 7 0S 141 35E
Murray, L., U.S.A. 157 34 8N 81 30W
Murray, R., S. Australia, Austral. 140 35 20S 139 22E
Murray, R., W. Australia, Austral. 133 32 33S 115 45E
Murray, R., Can. 152 56 11N 120 45W
Murraysburg 128 31 58S 23 47E
Murree 94 33 56N 73 28E
Murrieta 163 33 33N 117 13W
Murrin Murrin 137 28 50S 121 45E
Murrough 39 53 7N 9 18W
Murrumbidgee, R. 140 34 40S 143 0E
Murrumburrah 141 34 32S 148 22E
Murrurundi 141 31 42S 150 51E
Murshid 122 21 40N 31 10E
Murshidabad 95 24 11N 88 19E
Murska Sobota 63 46 39N 16 12E
Murtazapur 96 20 40N 77 25E
Murten 50 46 56N 6 7E
Murten-see 50 46 56N 7 4E
Murtle L. 152 52 8N 119 38W
Murtoa 140 36 35S 142 28E
Murton 33 54 51N 1 22W
Murtosa 56 40 44N 8 40W
Muru 123 6 36N 29 16E
Murungu 126 4 12S 31 10E
Murupara 142 38 28S 176 42E
Murwara 95 23 46N 80 28E
Murwillumbah 139 28 18S 153 27E
Mürz, R. 52 47 30N 15 25E
Mürzzuschlag 52 47 36N 15 41E
Muş 92 38 45N 41 30E
Musa, Gebel (Sinai) 122 28 32N 33 59E
Musa Khel 94 30 29N 69 52E
Musa Qala (Musa Kala) 93 32 20N 64 50E
Musa, R. 135 9 3S 148 55E
Musaffargarh 93 30 10N 71 10E
Musairik, Wadi 122 19 30N 43 10E
Musala, I. 102 1 41N 98 28E
Musalla, mt. 67 42 13N 23 37E
Musan 107 42 12N 129 12E
Musangu 127 10 28S 23 55E
Musasa 126 3 25S 31 30E
Musashino 111 35 42N 139 34E
Muscat = Masqat 93 23 37N 58 36E
Muscat & Oman = Oman 91 23 0N 58 0E
Muscatine 158 41 25N 91 5W
Musel 56 43 34N 5 42W
Musetula 127 14 28S 24 1E
Musgrave Ras. 137 26 0S 132 0E
Mushie 124 2 56S 17 4E
Mushin 121 6 32N 3 21E
Musi, R., India 96 17 10N 79 25E
Musi, R., Indon. 102 2 55S 103 40E
Muskeg, R. 152 60 20N 123 20W
Muskegon 156 43 15N 86 17W
Muskegon Hts. 156 43 12N 86 17W
Muskegon, R. 156 43 25N 86 0W
Muskogee 159 35 50N 95 25W
Muskwa, R. 152 58 47N 122 48W
Musmar 122 18 6N 35 40E
Musofu 127 13 30S 29 0E
Musoma 126 1 30S 33 48E
Musoma □ 126 1 50S 34 30E
Musquaro, L. 151 50 38N 61 5W
Musquodoboit Harbour 151 44 50N 63 9W
Mussau I. 135 1 30S 149 40E
Musselburgh 35 55 57N 3 3W
Musselkanaal 46 52 57N 7 0E
Musselshell, R. 160 46 30N 108 15W
Mussidan 44 45 2N 0 22E
Mussomeli 64 37 35N 13 43E
Musson 47 49 33N 5 42E
Mussooree 94 30 27N 78 6E
Mussuco 128 17 2S 19 3E
Mustafa Kemalpaşa 92 40 3N 28 25E
Mustajidda 92 26 30N 41 50E
Mustang 95 29 10N 83 55E
Mustapha, C. 119 36 55N 11 3E
Musters, L. 176 45 20S 69 25W
Musudan 107 40 50N 129 43E
Muswellbrook 141 32 16S 150 56E
Muszyna 53 49 22N 20 55E
Mût 122 25 28N 28 58E
Mut 92 36 40N 33 28E
Mutan Chiang, R. 107 46 18N 129 31E
Mutanchiang 107 44 40N 129 35E
Mutanda, Mozam. 129 21 0S 33 34E
Mutanda, Zambia 127 12 15S 26 13E
Muthill 35 56 20N 3 50W
Mutis 174 1 4N 77 25W
Mutooroo 140 32 26S 140 55E
Mutshatsha 127 10 35S 24 20E
Mutsu-Wan 112 41 5N 140 55E
Muttaburra 138 22 38S 144 29E
Muttama 141 34 46S 148 8E
Mutton Bay 151 50 50N 59 2W
Mutton I. 39 52 50N 9 31W
Mutuáli 127 14 55S 37 0E
Mutung 108 29 35N 106 51E
Mutunópolis 171 13 40S 49 15W
Muvatupusha 97 9 53N 76 35E
Muxima 124 9 25S 13 52E
Muy, Le 45 43 28N 6 34E
Muy Muy 166 12 39N 85 36W
Muya 77 56 27N 115 39E
Muyaga 126 3 14S 30 33E
Muyunkum, Peski 85 44 12N 71 0E
Muzaffarabad 95 34 25N 73 30E
Muzaffargarh 94 30 5N 71 14E
Muzaffarnagar 94 29 26N 77 40E
Muzaffarpur 95 26 7N 85 32E
Muzhi 76 65 25N 64 40E
Muzillac 42 47 35N 2 30W
Muzkol, Khrebet 85 38 22N 73 20E
Muzo 174 5 32N 74 6W
Muzon C. 152 54 40N 132 40W
Mvôlô 123 6 10N 29 53E
Mwadui 126 3 35S 33 40E
Mwandi Mission 127 17 30S 24 51E
Mwango 126 6 48S 24 12E
Mwanza, Katanga, Congo 126 7 55S 26 43E
Mwanza, Kwango, Congo 127 5 29S 17 43E
Mwanza, Malawi 126 16 58S 24 28E
Mwanza, Tanz. 126 2 30S 32 58E
Mwanza □ 126 2 0S 33 0E
Mwaya 126 9 32S 33 55E
Mweelrea, Mt. 38 53 37N 9 48W
Mweka 124 4 50S 21 40E
Mwenga 126 3 1S 28 21E
Mwepo 127 11 50S 26 10E
Mweru, L. 127 9 0S 29 0E
Mweza Range 127 21 0S 30 0E
Mwimbi 127 8 38S 31 39E
Mwinilunga 127 11 43S 24 25E
Mwinilunga, Mt. 127 11 43S 24 25E
My Tho 101 10 29N 106 23E
Mya, O. 119 30 46N 4 44E
Myadh 124 1 16N 13 10E
Myanaung 98 18 25N 95 10E
Myaungmya 98 16 30N 95 0E
Mybster 37 58 27N 3 24W
Myddfai 31 51 59N 3 47W
Myddle 28 52 49N 2 47W
Myerstown 162 40 22N 76 18W
Myingyan 98 21 30N 95 30E
Myitkyina 98 25 30N 97 26E
Myittha, R. 98 16 15N 94 34E
Myjava 53 48 41N 17 37E
Mylor 109 35 3S 138 46E
Mymensingh 98 24 45N 90 24E
Myndmere 158 46 23N 97 7W
Mynydd Bach, Hills 31 52 16N 4 6W
Mynydd Eppynt, Mts. 31 52 4N 3 30W
Mynydd Prescelly, mt. 31 51 57N 4 48W
Mynzhilgi, Gora 85 43 48N 68 51E
Myogi 101 21 24N 96 28E
Myrdal 71 60 43N 7 10E
Mýrdalsjökull 74 63 40N 19 6W
Myrrhee 136 36 46S 146 17E
Myrtle Beach 157 33 43N 78 50W
Myrtle Creek 160 43 0N 123 19W
Myrtle Point 160 43 0N 124 4W
Myrtleford 141 36 34S 146 44E
Myrtletown 108 27 23S 153 8E
Mysen 71 59 33N 11 20E
Myslenice 54 49 51N 19 57E
Myslibórz 54 52 55N 14 50E
Mysłowice 54 50 15N 19 12E
Mysore 97 12 17N 76 41E
Mysore □ = Karnataka 142 13 15N 77 0E
Mystic 162 41 21N 71 58W
Mystishchi 81 55 50N 37 50E
Myszkow 54 50 45N 19 22E
Mythen 51 47 2N 8 42E
Myton 160 40 10N 110 2W
Mývatn 74 65 36N 17 0W
Mze, R. 52 49 47N 12 50E
Mzimba 127 11 48S 33 33E
Mzuzu 127 11 30S 33 55E

N

N' Dioum 120 16 31N 14 39W
Na-lang 98 22 42N 97 33E
Na Noi 100 18 19N 100 43E
Na Phao 100 17 35N 105 44E
Na Sam 100 22 3N 106 37E
Na San 100 21 12N 104 2E
Naaldwijk 46 51 59N 4 13E
Naalehu 147 19 4N 155 35W
Na'am 123 9 42N 28 27E
Na'an 90 31 53N 34 52E
Naantali 75 60 29N 22 2E
Naarden 46 52 18N 5 9E
Naas 39 53 12N 6 40W
Nababeep 128 29 36S 17 46E
Nabadwip 95 23 34N 88 20E
Nabari 111 34 37N 136 5E

Nabas Nashville

Nabas	103	11 47N	122 6E
Nabberu, L.	137	25 30S	120 30E
•Naberezhnyye Chelny	84	55 42N	52 19E
Nabesna	147	62 33N	143 10W
Nabeul	119	36 30N	10 51E
Nabha	94	30 26N	76 14E
Nabi Rubin	90	31 56N	34 44E
Nabire	103	3 15S	136 27E
Nabisar	94	25 8N	69 40E
Nabispi, R.	151	50 14N	62 13W
Nabiswera	126	1 27N	32 15E
Nablus = Nābulus	90	32 14N	35 15E
Naboomspruit	129	24 32S	28 40E
Nābulus	90	32 14N	35 15E
Nabúri	127	16 53S	38 59E
Nacala-Velha	127	14 32S	40 34E
Nacaome	166	13 31N	87 30W
Nacaroa	127	14 22S	39 56E
Naches	160	46 48N	120 49W
Nachikatsuura	111	33 33N	135 58E
Nachingwea	127	10 49S	38 49E
Nachingwea □	127	10 30S	38 30E
Nachna	94	27 34N	71 41E
Náchod	53	50 25N	16 8E
Nacimento Res.	163	35 46N	120 53W
Nacka	72	59 17N	18 12E
Nackara	140	32 48S	139 12E
Naco, Mexico	164	31 20N	109 56W
Naco, U.S.A.	161	31 24N	109 58W
Nacogdoches	159	31 33N	95 30W
Nácori Chico	164	29 39N	109 1W
Nacozari	164	30 30N	109 50W
Nadi	122	18 40N	33 41E
Nadiad	94	22 41N	72 56E
Nador	118	35 14N	2 58W
Nadushan	93	32 2N	53 35E
Nadvornaya	80	48 40N	24 35E
Nadym	76	63 35N	72 42E
Nadym, R.	76	65 30N	73 0E
Nærbø	71	58 40N	5 39E
Næstved	73	55 13N	11 44E
Nafada	121	11 8N	11 20E
Näfels	51	47 6N	9 4E
Nafferton	33	54 1N	0 24W
Naft Shāh	92	34 0N	45 30E
Nafūd ad Dahy	92	22 0N	45 0E
Nafūsah, Jabal	119	32 12N	12 30E
Nag Hammâdi	122	26 2N	32 18E
Naga	103	13 38N	123 15E
Naga Hills	99	26 0N	94 30E
Naga, Kreb en	118	24 12N	6 0W
Naga-Shima, Kagoshima, Japan	110	32 10N	130 9E
Naga-Shima, Yamaguchi, Japan	110	33 55N	132 5E
Nagagami, R.	150	49 40N	84 40W
Nagahama, Ehime, Japan	111	33 36N	132 29E
Nagahama, Shiga, Japan	111	35 23N	136 16E
Nagai Parkar	94	24 28N	70 46E
Nagaland □	98	26 0N	94 30E
Nagambie	141	36 47S	145 10E
Nagano	111	36 40N	138 10E
Nagano-ken □	111	36 15N	138 0E
Nagaoka	112	37 27N	138 50E
Nagappattinam	97	10 46N	79 51E
Nagar Parkar	93	24 30N	70 35E
Nagara-Gawa, R.	111	35 1N	136 43E
Nagari Hills	97	15 30N	79 45E
Nagarjuna Sagar	96	16 35N	79 17E
Nagasaki	110	32 47N	129 50E
Nagasaki-ken □	110	32 50N	129 40E
Nagato	110	34 19N	131 5E
Nagaur	94	27 15N	73 45E
Nagbhir	96	20 34N	79 42E
Nagchu Dzong	99	31 22N	91 54E
Nagercoil	97	8 12N	77 33E
Nagina	95	29 30N	78 30E
Nagineh	93	34 20N	57 15E
Nagold	49	48 38N	8 40E
Nagoorin	138	24 17S	151 15E
Nagorsk	81	59 18N	50 48E
Nagorum	126	4 1N	34 33E
Nagoya	111	35 10N	136 50E
Nagpur	96	21 8N	79 10E
Nagrong	99	32 46N	84 16E
Nagua	167	19 23N	69 50W
Nagyatád	53	46 14N	17 22E
Nagyecsed	53	47 53N	22 24E
Nagykanizsa	53	46 28N	17 0E
Nagykörös	53	46 55N	19 48E
Nagyléta	53	47 23N	21 55E
Naha	112	26 13N	127 42E
Nahalal	90	32 41N	35 12E
Nahanni Butte	152	61 2N	123 20W
Nahanni Nat. Pk.	152	61 15N	125 0W
Naharayim	90	32 28N	35 33E
Nahariyya	90	33 1N	35 5E
Nahāvand	92	34 10N	48 30E
Nahe, R.	49	49 48N	7 33E
Nahf	90	32 56N	35 18E
Nahîya, Wadi	122	27 37N	32 0E
Nahlin	152	58 55N	131 38W
Nahud	122	18 12N	41 40E
Naiapu	70	44 12N	25 47E
Naicá	164	27 53N	105 31W
Naicam	153	52 30N	104 30W
Na'ifah	91	19 59N	50 46E
Naila	49	50 19N	11 43E
Nailsea	28	51 25N	2 44W
Nailsworth	28	51 41N	2 12W
Nain	151	56 34N	61 40W
Na'in	93	32 54N	53 0E
Naini Tal	95	29 23N	79 30E
Nainpur	93	22 30N	80 10E
Naintré	42	46 46N	0 29E
Naira, I.	103	4 28S	130 0E
Nairn	37	57 35N	3 54W
Nairn (□)	26	57 28N	3 52W
Nairn R.	37	57 32N	3 58W
Nairobi	126	1 17S	36 48E
Naivasha	126	0 40S	36 30E
Naivasha □	126	0 40S	36 30E
Naivasha L.	126	0 48S	36 20E
Najac	44	44 14N	1 58E
Najafābād	93	32 40N	51 15E
Najd	92	26 30N	42 0E
Nájera	58	42 26N	2 48W
Najerilla, R.	58	42 15N	2 45W
Najibabad	94	29 40N	78 20E
Najin	107	42 12N	130 15E
Naju	107	35 3N	126 43E
Naka-Gawa, R.	111	36 20N	140 36E
Naka-no-Shima	112	29 51N	129 46E
Nakalagba	126	2 50N	27 58E
Nakama	110	33 56N	130 43E
Nakaminato	111	36 21N	140 36E
Nakamura	110	33 0N	133 0E
Nakanai Mts.	135	5 40S	151 0E
Nakano	111	36 45N	138 22E
Nakanojō	111	36 35N	138 51E
Nakatane	112	30 31N	130 57E
Nakatsu	110	33 40N	131 15E
Nakatsugawa	111	35 29N	137 30E
Nakelele Pt.	147	21 2N	156 35W
Nakfa	123	16 40N	38 25E
Nakhichevan, A.S.S.R. □	79	39 14N	45 30E
Nakhl	122	29 55N	33 43E
Nakhl Mubarak	92	24 10N	38 10E
Nakhodka	77	43 10N	132 45E
Nakhon Nayok	100	14 12N	101 13E
Nakhon Pathom	100	13 49N	100 3E
Nakhon Phanom	100	17 23N	104 43E
Nakhon Ratchasima (Khorat)	100	14 59N	102 12E
Nakhon Sawan	100	15 35N	100 10E
Nakhon Si Thammarat	100	8 29N	100 0E
Nakhon Thai	100	17 17N	100 50E
Nakina, B.C., Can.	152	59 12N	132 52W
Nakina, Ont., Can.	150	50 10N	86 40W
Nakło n. Noteoja	54	53 9N	17 38E
Naknek	147	58 45N	157 0W
Nakodar	94	31 8N	75 31E
Nakomis	127	39 19N	89 19W
Nakskov	73	54 50N	11 8E
Näkten	72	62 48N	14 38E
Naktong, R.	107	35 7N	128 57E
Nakur	94	30 2N	77 32E
Nakuru	126	0 15S	35 5E
Nakuru □	126	0 15S	35 5E
Nakuru, L.	126	0 23S	36 5E
Nakusp	152	50 20N	117 45W
Nal, R.	94	27 0N	65 50E
Nalchik	83	43 30N	43 33E
Nälden	72	63 21N	14 14E
Näldsjön	72	63 25N	14 15E
Nalerigu	121	10 35N	0 25W
Nalgonda	96	17 6N	79 15E
Nalhati	95	24 17N	87 52E
Nalinnes	47	50 19N	4 27E
Nallamalai Hills	97	15 30N	78 50E
Nalón, R.	56	43 35N	6 10W
Nālūt	119	31 54N	11 0E
Nam Can	101	8 46N	104 59E
Nam Dinh	100	20 25N	106 5E
Nam Du, Hon	101	9 41N	104 21E
'Nam', gasfields	19	53 17N	3 36E
Nam Ngum	100	18 35N	102 34E
'Nam', oilfield	19	54 50N	4 40E
Nam-Phan	101	10 30N	106 0E
Nam Phong	100	16 42N	102 52E
Nam Tha	100	20 58N	101 30E
Nam Tok	100	14 14N	99 4E
Nam Tso = Namu Hu	105	30 45N	90 30E
Namacurra	125	17 30S	36 50E
Namakkal	97	11 13N	78 13E
Namaland, Africa	128	26 0S	18 0E
Namaland, S. Afr.	128	30 0S	18 0E
Namangan	85	41 0N	71 40E
Namapa	127	13 43S	39 50E
Namasagali	126	1 2N	33 0E
Namatanai	135	3 40S	152 29E
Nambala	120	14 1N	5 58W
Namber	103	1 2S	134 57E
Nambour	139	26 32S	152 58E
Nambucca Heads	141	30 37S	153 0E
Namcha Barwa	105	29 40N	95 10E
Namche Bazar	95	27 51N	86 47E
Namchonjŏm	107	38 15N	126 26E
Namêche	47	50 28N	5 0E
Namecund	127	14 54S	37 37E
Nameh	102	2 34N	116 21E
Nameponda	127	15 50S	39 50E
Namerikawa	111	36 46N	137 20E
Námestovo	53	49 24N	19 25E
Nametil	127	15 40S	39 15E
Náměšt nad Oslavou	53	49 12N	16 10E
Namew L.	153	54 14N	101 56W
Namhsan	98	22 48N	97 42E
Nami	101	6 2N	100 46E
Namib Desert = Namib Woestyn	128	22 30S	15 0E
Namib-Woestyn	128	22 30S	15 0E
Namibia □	128	22 0S	18 9E
Namiquipa	164	29 15N	107 25W
Namja Pass	95	30 0N	82 25E
Namkhan	98	23 50N	97 41E
Namlea	103	3 10S	127 5E
Namoi, R.	141	30 12S	149 30E
Namous, O.	118	30 44N	0 18W
Nampa	160	43 40N	116 40W
Nampula	127	15 6S	39 7E
Namrole	103	3 46S	126 46E
Namsen	74	64 27N	11 42E
Namsen, R.	74	64 40N	12 45E
Namsos	74	64 28N	11 0E
Namtu	98	23 5N	97 28E
Namtumbo	127	10 30S	36 4E
Namu	152	51 52N	127 41W
Namu Hu	105	30 45N	90 30E
Namur	47	50 27N	4 52E
Namur □	47	50 17N	5 0E
Namutoni	128	18 49S	16 55E
Namwala	127	15 44S	26 30E
Namwŏn	107	35 23N	127 23E
Namysłow	54	51 6N	17 42E
Nan	100	18 48N	100 46E
Nan Ling	109	25 0N	112 30E
Nan, R.	100	15 42N	100 9E
Nan Shan	105	38 30N	99 0E
Nana	70	44 17N	26 34E
Nãnã, W.	119	30 0N	15 24E
Nanaimo	152	49 10N	124 0W
Nanam	107	41 44N	129 40E
Nan'an	109	24 58N	118 23E
Nanango	139	26 40S	152 0E
Nanao	109	23 26N	117 1E
Nanch'ang	109	28 40N	115 50E
Nanchang, Fukien, China	109	24 26N	117 18E
Nanchang, Hupei, China	109	31 47N	111 42E
Nanch'eng	109	27 33N	116 35E
Nancheng = Hanchung	106	33 10N	107 2E
Nanchiang	108	32 21N	106 50E
Nanchiao	108	22 2N	100 15E
Nanchien	106	25 5N	100 30E
Nanching	109	32 3N	118 47E
Nanchishan Liehtao	108	27 28N	121 4E
Nanch'uan	108	29 7N	107 16E
Nanch'ung	108	30 50N	106 4E
Nancy	43	48 42N	6 12E
Nanda Devi, Mt.	95	30 30N	80 30E
Nandan	110	34 10N	134 42E
Nander	96	19 10N	77 20E
Nandewar Ra.	139	30 15S	150 35E
Nandi □	126	0 15N	35 0E
Nandikotkur	97	15 52N	78 18E
Nandura	96	20 52N	76 25E
Nandurbar	96	21 20N	74 15E
Nandyal	97	15 30N	78 30E
Nanfeng	109	27 10N	116 24E
Nanga	137	26 7S	113 45E
Nanga Eboko	121	4 41N	12 22E
Nanga Parbat, mt.	95	35 10N	74 35E
Nangade	127	11 5S	39 36E
Nangapinoh	102	0 20S	111 14E
Nangarhar □	93	34 20N	70 0E
Nangatajap	102	1 32S	110 34E
Nangeya Mts.	126	3 30N	33 30E
Nangis	43	48 33N	3 0E
Nangodi	121	10 58N	0 42W
Nangola	120	12 41N	6 35W
Nangwarry	140	37 33S	140 48E
Nanhsien	109	29 22N	112 25E
Nanhsiung	109	25 10N	114 18E
Nanhua	108	25 10N	101 20E
Nanhui	109	31 3N	121 46E
Nani Hu	109	31 10N	118 55E
Nanjangud	97	12 6N	76 43E
Nanjeko	127	5 31S	23 30E
Nanjirinji	127	9 41S	39 5E
Nankana Sahib	94	31 27N	73 38E
Nank'ang	109	25 38N	114 45E
Nanking = Nanching	109	32 5N	118 45E
Nankoku	110	33 29N	133 38E
Nankung	106	37 22N	115 20E
Nanling	109	30 56N	118 19E
Nannine	137	26 51S	118 18E
Nanning	108	22 48N	108 20E
Nannup	137	33 59S	115 48E
Nanpa	108	32 13N	104 51E
Nanp'an Chiang, R.	108	25 0N	106 11E
Nanpara	95	27 52N	81 33E
Nanp'i	106	38 4N	116 34E
Nanp'ing, Fukien, China	109	26 38N	118 10E
Nanp'ing, Hupeh, China	109	29 55N	112 2E
Nanpu	108	31 19N	106 2E
Nanripe	127	13 52S	38 52E
Nansei-Shotō	112	26 0N	128 0E
Nansen Sd.	12	81 0N	91 0W
Nansio	126	2 3S	33 4E
Nanson	137	28 35S	114 45E
Nant	44	44 1N	3 18E
Nantes	42	47 12N	1 33W
Nanteuil-le-Haudouin	43	49 9N	2 48E
Nantiat	44	46 1N	1 11E
Nanticoke	162	41 12N	76 1W
Nanticoke, R.	162	38 16N	75 56W
Nanton, Can.	152	50 21N	113 46W
Nanton, China	108	24 59N	107 32E
Nantua	45	46 10N	5 35E
Nantucket	162	41 17N	70 6W
Nantucket I.	155	41 16N	70 3W
Nantucket Sd.	162	41 30N	70 15W
Nant'ung	109	32 0N	120 55E
Nantwich	32	53 5N	2 31W
Nanuque	171	17 50S	40 21W
Nanutarra	136	22 32S	115 30E
Nanyang	106	33 0N	112 32E
Nan'yō	110	34 3N	131 49E
Nanyüan	106	39 48N	116 24E
Nanyuki	126	0 2N	37 4E
Nao, C. de la	59	38 44N	0 14E
Nao Chou Tao	109	20 55N	110 35E
Nao, La, Cabo de	59	38 44N	0 14E
Naococane L.	151	52 50N	70 45W
Naogaon	98	24 52N	88 52E
Napa	163	38 18N	122 17W
Napa, R.	163	38 10N	122 19W
Napamute	147	61 30N	158 45W
Napanee	150	44 15N	77 0W
Napanoch	162	41 44N	74 2W
Nape	100	18 18N	105 6E
Nape Pass = Keo Neua, Deo	100	18 23N	105 10E
Napf	50	47 1N	7 56E
Napiéolédougou	120	9 18N	5 35W
Napier	142	39 30S	176 56E
Napier Broome B.	136	14 2S	126 37E
Napier Downs	136	17 11S	124 36E
Napier Pen.	138	12 4S	135 43E
Naples	157	26 10N	81 45W
Naples = Nápoli	65	40 50N	14 5E
Nap'o	108	23 44N	106 49E
Napo □	174	0 30S	77 0W
Napo, R.	174	3 5S	73 0W
Napoleon, N. Dak., U.S.A.	158	46 32N	99 49W
Napoleon, Ohio, U.S.A.	156	41 24N	84 7W
Nápoli	65	40 50N	14 5E
Nápoli, G. di	65	40 40N	14 10E
Napopo	126	4 15N	28 0E
Napoule, La	45	43 31N	6 56E
Nappa	32	53 58N	2 14W
Nappa Merrie	139	27 36S	141 7E
Naqâda	122	25 53N	32 42E
Nara, Japan	111	34 40N	135 49E
Nara, Mali	120	15 25N	7 20W
Nara, Canal	94	26 0N	69 20E
Nara-ken □	111	34 30N	136 0E
Nara Visa	159	35 39N	103 10W
Naracoorte	140	36 58S	140 45E
Naradhan	141	33 34S	146 17E
Narasapur	96	16 26N	81 50E
Narasaropet	96	16 14N	80 4E
Narathiwat	101	6 40N	101 55E
Narayanganj	98	23 31N	90 33E
Narayanpet	96	16 45N	77 30E
Narberth	31	51 48N	4 45W
Narbonne	44	43 11N	3 0E
Narborough	28	52 34N	1 12W
Narcea, R.	56	43 15N	6 30W
Nardò	65	40 10N	18 0E
Nare Head	30	50 12N	4 55W
Narembeen	137	32 7S	118 17E
Naretha	137	31 0S	124 45E
Nari, R.	94	29 10N	67 50E
Narin	93	36 5N	69 0E
Narinda, B. de	129	14 55S	47 30E
Narino □	174	1 30N	78 0W
Narita	111	35 47N	140 19E
Narmada, R.	94	22 40N	77 30E
Narnaul	94	28 5N	76 11E
Narni	63	42 30N	12 30E
Naro, Ghana	120	10 22N	2 27W
Naro, Italy	64	37 18N	13 48E
Naro Fominsk	81	55 23N	36 32E
Narodnaya, G.	78	65 5N	60 0E
Narok	126	1 20S	33 30E
Narok □	126	1 20S	33 30E
Narón	56	43 32N	8 9W
Narooma	141	36 14S	150 4E
Narowal	94	32 6N	74 52E
Narrabri	139	30 19S	149 46E
Narran, R.	139	28 37S	148 12E
Narrandera	141	34 42S	146 31E
Narraway, R.	152	55 44N	119 55W
Narrogin	137	32 58S	117 14E
Narromine	141	32 12S	148 12E
Narrows, str.	36	57 20N	6 5W
Narsampet	96	17 57N	79 58E
Narsinghpur	95	22 54N	79 14E
Naruto	110	34 11N	134 37E
Narutō	111	35 36N	140 25E
Naruto-Kaikyō	110	34 14N	134 39E
Narva	80	59 10N	28 5E
Narva, R.	80	59 10N	27 50E
Narvik	74	68 28N	17 26E
Narvskoye Vdkhr.	80	59 10N	28 5E
Narwana	94	29 39N	76 6E
Naryan-Mar	78	68 0N	53 0E
Naryilco	139	28 37S	141 53E
Narym	76	59 0N	81 58E
Narymskoye	76	49 10N	84 15E
Naryn	85	41 26N	75 58E
Naryn, R.	85	40 52N	71 36E
Nasa	74	66 29N	15 23E
Nasa, mt.	74	66 32N	15 23E
Nasarawa	121	8 32N	7 41E
Naseby, N.Z.	143	45 1S	170 10E
Naseby, U.K.	29	52 24N	0 59W
Naser, Buheirat en	122	23 0N	32 30E
Nash Pt.	31	51 24N	3 34W
Nashua, Iowa, U.S.A.	158	42 55N	92 34W
Nashua, Mont., U.S.A.	160	48 10N	106 25W
Nashua, N.H., U.S.A.	162	42 50N	71 25W
Nashville, Ark., U.S.A.	159	33 56N	93 50W

*Renamed Brezhnev

Nashville **Nevillé-Pont-Pierre**

Nashville, Ga., U.S.A. **157** 31 13N 83 15W
Nashville, Tenn., U.S.A. **157** 36 12N 86 46W
Našice **66** 45 32N 18 4E
Nasielsk **54** 52 35N 20 50E
Nasik **96** 20 2N 73 50E
Nasirabad, Bangla. **95** 24 42N 90 30E
Nasirabad, India **94** 26 15N 74 45E
Nasirabad, Pak. **96** 28 25N 68 25E
Naskaupi, R. **151** 53 47N 60 51W
Naso **65** 38 8N 14 46E
Nass, R. **152** 55 0N 129 40W
Nassau, Bahamas **166** 25 0N 77 30W
Nassau, U.S.A. **162** 42 30N 73 34W
Nassau, Bahía **176** 55 20S 68 0W
Nasser City = Kôm Ombo **122** 24 25N 32 52E
Nasser, L. = Naser, Buheiret en **122** 23 0N 32 30E
Nassian **120** 7 58N 2 57W
Nässjö **73** 57 38N 14 45E
Nastopoka Is. **150** 57 0N 77 0W
Näsum **73** 56 10N 14 29E
Näsviken **72** 61 46N 16 52E
Nata, Bots. **128** 20 7S 26 4E
Nata, China **100** 19 37N 109 17E
Nata, Si Arab. **92** 27 15N 48 35E
Nata, Tanz. **125** 2 0S 34 25E
Natagaima **174** 3 37N 75 6W
Natal, Brazil **170** 5 47S 35 13W
Natal, Can. **152** 49 43N 114 51W
Natal, Indon. **102** 0 35N 99 0E
Natal □ **129** 28 30S 30 30E
Natalinci **66** 44 15N 20 49E
Natanz **93** 33 30N 51 55E
Natashquan **151** 50 14N 61 46W
Natashquan Pt. **151** 50 8N 61 40W
Natashquan, R. **151** 50 7N 61 50W
Natchez **159** 31 35N 91 25W
Natchitoches **159** 31 47N 93 4W
Naters **50** 46 19N 8 0E
Nathalia **141** 36 1S 145 7E
Nathdwara **94** 24 55N 73 50E
Natick **162** 42 16N 71 19W
Natih **93** 22 25N 56 30E
Natimuk **140** 36 42S 142 0E
Nation, R. **152** 55 30N 123 32W
National City **163** 32 45N 117 7W
National Mills **153** 52 52N 101 40W
Natitingou **121** 10 20N 1 26E
Natividad, I. de **164** 27 50N 115 10W
Natkyizin **101** 14 57N 97 59E
Natogyi **98** 21 25N 95 39E
Natoma **158** 39 14N 99 0W
Natron L. **126** 2 20S 36 0E
Natrûn, W. el. **122** 30 25N 30 0E
Natuna Besar, Kepulauan **101** 4 0N 108 15E
Natuna Selatan, Kepulauan **101** 2 45N 109 0E
Naturaliste, C. **132** 33 32S 115 0E
Naturaliste C. **138** 40 50S 148 15E
Naturaliste Channel **137** 25 20S 113 0E
Natya **140** 34 57S 143 13E
Nau **85** 40 9N 69 22E
Nau-Nau **128** 18 57S 21 4E
Nau Qala **94** 34 5N 68 5E
Naubinway **150** 46 7N 85 27W
Naucelle **44** 44 13N 2 20E
Nauders **52** 46 54N 10 30E
Nauen **48** 52 36N 12 52E
Naujoji Vilnia **80** 54 48N 25 27E
Naumburg **48** 51 10N 11 48E
Nauru I. **130** 0 25N 166 0E
Naurzum **84** 51 32N 64 34E
Naushahra **93** 34 0N 72 0E
Nauta **174** 4 20S 73 35W
Nautanwa **99** 27 20N 83 25E
Nautla **165** 20 20N 96 50W
Nava **164** 28 25N 100 46W
Nava del Rey **56** 41 22N 5 6W
Navacerrada, Puerto de **56** 40 47N 4 0W
Navahermosa **57** 39 41N 4 28W
Navalcarnero **56** 40 17N 4 5W
Navalmoral de la Mata **56** 39 52N 5 16W
Navalvillar de Pela **57** 39 9N 5 24W
Navan = An Uaimh **38** 53 39N 6 40W
Navarino, I. **176** 55 0S 67 30W
Navarra □ **58** 42 40N 1 40W
Navarre **44** 43 15N 1 20E
Navarreux **44** 43 20N 0 47W
Navasota **159** 30 20N 96 5W
Navassa I. **167** 18 30N 75 0W
Nave **62** 45 35N 10 17E
Navenby **33** 53 7N 0 32W
Naver L. **37** 58 18N 4 20W
Naver, R. **37** 58 34N 4 15W
Navia **56** 43 24N 6 42W
Navia de Suarna **56** 42 58N 6 59W
Navia, R. **56** 43 15N 6 50W
Navidad **172** 33 57S 71 50W
Navlya **80** 52 53N 34 15E
Navoi **85** 40 9N 65 22E
Navojoa **164** 27 0N 109 30W
Navolato **164** 24 47N 107 42W
Navolok **78** 62 33N 39 57E
Návpaktos **69** 38 23N 21 42E
Návplion **69** 37 33N 22 50E
Navrongo **121** 10 57N 0 58W
Navsari **96** 20 57N 72 59E
Nawa Kot **94** 28 21N 71 24E
Nawabganj **98** 24 35N 81 14E
Nawabganj, Bara Banki **95** 26 56N 81 14E
Nawabganj, Bareilly **95** 28 32N 79 40E
Nawabshah **94** 26 15N 68 25E
Nawada **95** 24 50N 85 25E
Nawakot **95** 28 0N 85 10E
Nawalgarh **96** 27 50N 75 15E
Nawansnahr **95** 32 33N 74 48E
Nawapara **95** 20 52N 82 33E
Nawi **122** 18 32N 30 50E
Nawng Hpa **98** 21 52N 97 52E
Náxos **69** 37 8N 25 25E
Náxos, I. **69** 37 5N 25 30E
Nay **44** 43 10N 0 18W
Nay Band **93** 27 20N 52 40E
Naya **174** 3 13N 77 22W
Naya, R. **174** 3 13N 77 22W
Nayakhan **77** 62 10N 159 0E
Nayarit □ **164** 22 0N 105 0W
Nayé **120** 14 28N 12 12W
Nayung **108** 26 50N 105 17E
Nazaré, Bahia, Brazil **171** 13 0S 39 0W
Nazaré, Goiás, Brazil **170** 6 23S 47 40W
Nazaré, Port. **57** 39 36N 9 4W
Nazaré Antônio de Jesus **171** 13 2S 39 0W
Nazaré da Mata **171** 7 44S 35 14W
Nazareth, Israel **90** 32 42N 35 17E
Nazareth, U.S.A. **162** 40 44N 75 19W
Nazas **164** 25 10N 104 0W
Nazas, R. **164** 25 20N 104 4W
Naze **112** 28 22N 129 27E
Naze, The **29** 51 43N 1 19E
Nazeret **123** 8 45N 39 15E
Nazir Hat **98** 22 35N 91 55E
Nazko **152** 53 1N 123 37W
Nazko, R. **152** 53 7N 123 34W
Nchacoongo **129** 24 20S 35 9E
Nchanga **127** 12 30S 27 49E
Ncheu **127** 14 50S 34 37E
Ndala **126** 4 45S 33 23E
Ndali **121** 9 50N 2 46E
Ndareda **126** 4 12S 35 30E
Ndélé **117** 8 25N 20 36E
Ndendeé **124** 2 29S 10 46E
Ndjamena **117** 12 4N 15 8E
Ndjolé **124** 0 10S 10 45E
Ndola **127** 13 0S 28 34E
Ndoto Mts. **126** 2 0N 37 0E
Ndrhamcha, Sebkra de **120** 18 30N 15 55W
Nduguti **126** 4 18S 34 41E
NE Frt. Agency = Arun. Pradesh □ **98** 28 0N 95 0E
Nea **71** 63 15N 11 0E
Néa Epidhavros **69** 37 40N 23 7E
Néa Filippiás **68** 39 12N 20 53W
Néa Kallikrátiá **68** 40 21N 23 1E
Néa Vissi **68** 41 34N 26 33E
Neagari **111** 36 26N 136 25E
Neagh, Lough **38** 54 35N 6 25W
Neah Bay **160** 48 25N 124 40W
Neale L. **137** 24 15S 130 0E
Neamarrói **127** 15 58S 36 50E
Neamţ □ **70** 47 0N 26 20E
Neápolis, Kozan, Greece **68** 40 20N 21 24E
Neápolis, Kriti, Greece **69** 35 15N 25 36E
Neápolis, Lakonia, Greece **69** 36 27N 23 8E
Near Is. **147** 53 0N 172 0W
Neath **31** 51 39N 3 49W
Neath, R. **23** 51 46N 3 35W
Nebbou **121** 11 9N 1 51W
Nebine Cr. **139** 29 7S 146 56E
Nebo **138** 21 42S 148 42E
Nebolchy **81** 59 12N 32 58E
Nebraska □ **158** 41 30N 100 0W
Nebraska City **158** 40 40N 95 52W
Necedah **158** 44 2N 90 7W
Nechako, R. **152** 53 30N 122 44W
Neches, R. **159** 31 80N 94 20W
Neckar, R. **49** 48 43N 9 15E
Necochea **172** 38 30S 58 50W
Nectar Brook **140** 32 43S 137 57E
Nedelišće **63** 46 23N 16 22E
Neder Rijn, R. **46** 51 57N 6 2E
Nederbrakel **47** 50 48N 3 46E
Nederlandsöy I. **71** 62 20N 5 35E
Nederweert **47** 51 17N 5 45E
Nedha, R. **69** 37 25N 21 45E
Nedroma **118** 35 1N 1 45W
Nedstrand **71** 59 21N 5 49E
Neede **46** 52 8N 6 37E
Needham Market **29** 52 9N 1 2E
Needilup **137** 33 55S 118 45E
Needles **161** 34 50N 114 35W
Needles, Pt. **142** 36 3S 175 25E
Needles, The **28** 50 48N 1 19W
Ñeembucú □ **172** 27 0S 58 0W
Neemuch (Nimach) **94** 24 30N 74 50E
Neenah **156** 44 10N 88 30W
Neepawa **153** 50 20N 99 30W
Neer **47** 51 16N 5 59E
Neerheylissem **47** 51 5N 5 42E
Neeroeteren **47** 50 44N 4 58E
Neerpelt **47** 51 13N 5 26E
Nefta **119** 33 53N 7 58E
Neftah Sidi Boubekeur **118** 35 1N 0 4E
Neftegorsk **83** 44 25N 39 45E
Neftenbach **51** 47 32N 8 41E
Neftyannye Kamni **79** 40 20N 50 55E
Nefyn **31** 52 57N 4 29W
Negapatam = Nagappattinam **97** 10 46N 79 38E
Negaunee **156** 46 30N 87 36W
Negba **90** 31 40N 34 41E
Negele **123** 5 20N 39 30E
Negeri Sembilan □ **101** 2 50N 102 10E
Negev = Hanegev **90** 30 50N 35 0E
Negolu **70** 45 48N 24 32E
Negombo **97** 7 12N 79 50E
Negotin **66** 44 16N 22 37E
Negotino **66** 41 29N 22 9E
Negra, La **172** 23 46S 70 18W
Negra, Peña **56** 42 11N 6 30W
Negra Pt. **103** 18 40N 120 50E
Negrais C. **98** 16 0N 94 30E
Negreira **56** 42 54N 8 45W
Negreşti **70** 46 50N 27 30E
Négrine **119** 34 30N 7 30E
Negro, C. **118** 35 40N 5 11W
Negro, R., Argent. **176** 40 0S 64 0W
Negro, R., Brazil **174** 0 25S 64 0W
Negro, R., Uruguay **173** 32 30S 55 30W
Negros, I. **103** 10 0N 123 0E
Negru Vodă **70** 43 47N 28 21E
Nehbandān **93** 31 35N 60 5E
Neheim-Hüsten **48** 51 27N 7 58E
Nehoiaşu **70** 45 24N 26 20E
Neichiang **108** 29 35N 105 0E
Neich'iu **106** 37 17N 114 31E
Neidpath **153** 50 12N 107 20W
Neihart **160** 47 0N 110 52W
Neihsiang **106** 33 3N 111 53E
Neilrex **141** 31 44S 149 20E
Neilston **34** 55 47N 4 27W
Neilton **160** 47 24N 123 59W
Neira de Jusá **56** 42 53N 7 14W
Neisse, R. **48** 51 0N 15 0E
Neiva **174** 2 56N 75 18W
Nejanilini L. **153** 59 33N 97 48W
Nejo **123** 9 30N 35 28E
Nekemte **123** 9 4N 36 30E
Nêkheb **122** 25 10N 33 0E
Neksø **73** 55 4N 15 8E
Nelas **56** 40 32N 7 52W
Nelaug **71** 58 39N 8 40E
Nelgowrie **141** 30 54S 148 7E
Nelia **138** 20 39S 142 12E
Nelidovo **80** 56 13N 32 49E
Neligh **158** 42 11N 98 2W
Nelkan **77** 57 50N 136 15E
Nellikuppam **97** 11 46N 79 43E
Nellore **97** 14 27N 79 59E
Nelma **77** 47 30N 139 0E
Nelson, Can. **152** 49 30N 117 20W
Nelson, N.Z. **143** 41 18S 173 16E
Nelson, U.K. **32** 53 50N 2 14W
Nelson, Ariz., U.S.A. **161** 35 35N 113 24W
Nelson, Nev., U.S.A. **161** 35 46N 114 55W
Nelson □ **143** 42 11S 172 15E
Nelson, C., Austral. **140** 38 26S 141 32E
Nelson, C., P.N.G. **135** 9 0S 149 20E
Nelson, Estrecho **176** 51 30S 75 0W
Nelson Forks **152** 59 30N 124 0W
Nelson House **153** 55 47N 98 51W
Nelson I. **147** 60 40N 164 40W
Nelson L. **153** 55 48N 100 7W
Nelson, R. **153** 54 33N 98 2W
Nelspruit **126** 25 29S 30 59E
Néma **120** 16 40N 7 15W
Neman (Nemunas), R. **80** 53 30N 25 10E
Neméa **69** 37 49N 22 40E
Nemegos **150** 47 40N 83 15W
Nemeiben L. **153** 55 20N 105 20W
Nemira, Mt. **70** 46 17N 26 19E
Nemiscau **150** 49 30N 111 15W
Nemours **43** 48 16N 2 40E
Nemunas, R. **80** 55 25N 21 10E
Nemuro **112** 43 20N 145 35E
Nemuro-Kaikyō **112** 43 30N 145 30E
Nemuy **77** 55 40N 135 55E
Nenagh **39** 52 52N 8 11W
Nenana **147** 64 30N 149 0W
Nenasi **101** 3 9N 103 23E
Nenchiang **105** 49 11N 125 13E
Nene, R. **29** 52 38N 0 7E
Neno **127** 15 25S 34 40E
Nenusa, Kepulauan **103** 4 45N 127 1E
Neodesha **159** 37 30N 95 37W
Néon Petritsi **68** 41 16N 23 15E
Neópolis **170** 10 18S 36 35W
Neosho **159** 36 56N 94 28W
Neosho, R. **159** 35 59N 95 10W
Nepal ■ **95** 28 0N 84 30E
Nepalganj **95** 28 0N 81 40E
Nephi **160** 39 43N 111 52W
Nephin Beg Ra. **38** 54 0N 9 40W
Nephin, Mt. **38** 54 1N 9 21W
Nepomuk **52** 49 29N 13 35E
Neptune City **162** 40 13N 74 4W
Néra, R. **66** 44 52N 21 45E
Nerac **44** 44 19N 0 20E
Nerchinsk **77** 52 0N 116 39E
Nerchinskiy Zavod **77** 51 10N 119 30E
Nereju **70** 45 43N 26 43E
Nerekhta **81** 57 26N 40 38E
Neret L. **151** 54 45N 70 44W
Neretva, R. **66** 43 30N 17 50E
Neretvanski **66** 43 7N 17 10E
Neringa **80** 55 21N 21 5E
Nerja **57** 36 43N 3 55W
Nerl, R. **81** 56 30N 40 30E
Nerokoúrou **69** 35 29N 24 3E
Nerpio **59** 38 11N 2 16W
Nerva **57** 37 42N 6 30W
Nes, Iceland **74** 65 53N 17 24W
Nes, Neth. **46** 53 26N 5 47E
Nes Ziyyona **90** 31 56N 34 48W
Nesbyen **71** 60 34N 9 6E
Nescopeck **162** 41 3N 76 12W
Nesebyr **67** 42 41N 27 46E
Nesflaten **71** 59 38N 6 48E
Neskaupstaður **74** 65 9N 13 42W
Nesland **71** 59 31N 7 59E
Neslandsvatn **71** 58 57N 9 10E
Nesle **43** 49 45N 2 53E
Nesodden **71** 59 48N 10 40E
Ness, dist. **36** 58 27N 6 20W
Ness, Loch **37** 57 15N 4 30W
Nesslau **51** 47 14N 9 13E
Neston **32** 53 17N 3 3W
Nestórion Óros **68** 40 24N 21 16E
Néstos, R. **68** 41 20N 24 35E
Nesttun **71** 60 19N 5 21E
Nesvizh **80** 53 14N 26 38E
Netanya **90** 32 20N 34 51E
Nèthe, R. **47** 51 5N 4 55E
Netherdale **138** 21 10S 148 33E
Netherlands ■ **47** 52 0N 5 30E
Netherlands Guiana = Surinam **170** 4 0N 56 0W
Nethy Bridge **37** 57 15N 3 40W
Netley **28** 50 53N 1 21W
Netley Gap **28** 32 43S 139 59E
Netley Marsh **28** 50 55N 1 32W
Neto, R. **65** 39 10N 16 58E
Netrakong **98** 24 53N 90 47E
Nettancourt **43** 48 51N 4 57E
Nettilling L. **149** 66 30N 71 0W
Nettlebed **29** 51 34N 0 54W
Nettleham **33** 53 15N 0 28W
Nettuno **64** 41 29N 12 40E
Netzahualcoyotl, Presa **165** 17 10N 93 30W
Neu-Isenburg **49** 50 3N 8 42E
Neu Ulm **49** 48 23N 10 2E
Neubrandenburg **48** 53 33N 13 17E
Neubrandenburg □ **48** 53 30N 13 20E
Neubukow **48** 54 1N 11 40E
Neuburg **49** 48 43N 11 11E
Neuchâtel **50** 47 0N 6 55E
Neuchâtel □ **50** 47 0N 6 55E
Neuchâtel, Lac de **50** 46 53N 6 50E
Neudau **52** 47 11N 16 6E
Neuenegg **50** 46 54N 7 18E
Neuenhaus **48** 52 30N 6 55E
Neuf-Brisach **43** 48 0N 7 30E
Neufchâteau, Belg. **47** 49 50N 5 25E
Neufchâteau, France **43** 48 21N 5 40E
Neufchâtel **43** 49 43N 1 30E
Neufchâtel-sur-Aisne **43** 49 26N 4 0E
Neuhaus **48** 53 16N 10 54E
Neuhausen **51** 47 41N 8 37E
Neuilly-St. Front **43** 49 10N 3 15E
Neukalen **49** 53 49N 12 48E
Neumarkt **49** 49 16N 11 28E
Neumünster **48** 54 4N 9 58E
Neung-sur-Beuvron **43** 47 30N 1 50E
Neunkirchen, Austria **52** 47 43N 16 4E
Neunkirchen, Ger. **49** 49 23N 7 6E
Neuquén **176** 38 0S 68 0E
Neuquén □ **172** 38 0S 69 50W
Neuruppin **48** 52 56N 12 48E
Neuse, R. **157** 35 5N 77 40W
Neusiedl **53** 47 57N 16 50E
Neusiedler See **53** 47 50N 16 47E
Neuss **48** 51 12N 6 39E
Neussargues-Moissac **44** 45 9N 3 1E
Neustadt, Bay., Ger. **49** 49 42N 12 10E
Neustadt, Bay., Ger. **49** 48 48N 11 47E
Neustadt, Bay., Ger. **49** 49 34N 10 37E
Neustadt, Bay., Ger. **49** 50 23N 11 0W
Neustadt, Gera, Ger. **48** 50 45N 11 43E
Neustadt, Hessen, Ger. **48** 50 51N 9 9E
Neustadt, Niedersachsen, Ger. **48** 52 30N 9 30E
Neustadt, Potsdam, Ger. **48** 52 50N 12 27E
Neustadt, Rhld-Pfz., Ger. **49** 49 21N 8 10E
Neustadt, S.-Holst., Ger. **48** 54 6N 10 49E
Neustrelitz **48** 53 22N 13 4E
Neuveville, La **50** 47 4N 7 6E
Neuvic **44** 45 23N 2 16E
Neuville, Belg. **95** 50 11N 4 32E
Neuville, France **43** 45 52N 4 51E
Neuville-aux-Bois **43** 48 4N 2 3E
Neuvy-St.-Sépulchure **44** 46 35N 1 48E
Neuvy-sur-Barangeon **43** 47 20N 2 15E
Neuwerk, I. **48** 53 55N 8 30E
Neuwied **48** 50 26N 7 29E
Neva, R. **78** 59 50N 30 30E
Nevada **159** 37 20N 94 40W
Nevada □ **160** 39 20N 117 0W
Nevada City **163** 39 20N 121 0W
Nevada de Sta. Marta, Sa. **174** 10 55N 73 50W
Nevada, Sierra, Spain **59** 37 3N 3 15W
Nevada, Sierra, U.S.A. **160** 39 0N 120 30W
Nevado, Cerro **172** 35 30S 68 20W
Nevado de Colima, Mt. **164** 19 35N 103 45W
Nevanka **77** 56 45N 98 55E
Nevasa **94** 19 34N 75 0E
Nevel **80** 56 0N 29 55E
Nevele **47** 51 3N 3 28E
Nevern **31** 52 2N 4 49W
Nevers **43** 47 0N 3 9E
Nevertire **141** 31 50S 147 44E
Neville **153** 49 58N 107 39W
Nevillé-Pont-Pierre **42** 47 33N 0 33E

Nevinnomyssk — Nîl el Abyad, Bahr

Nevinnomyssk 83 44 40N 42 0E
Nevis I. 167 17 0N 62 30W
Nevis, L. 36 57 0N 5 43W
Nevlunghavn 71 58 58N 9 53E
Nevoria 137 31 25S 119 25E
Nevrokop = Gotse Delchev 67 41 43N 23 46E
Nevşehir 92 38 33N 34 40E
Nevyansk 84 57 30N 60 13E
New Abbey 35 54 59N 3 38W
New Aberdour 37 57 39N 2 12W
New Adawso 121 6 50N 0 2W
New Albany, Ind., U.S.A. 156 38 20N 85 50W
New Albany, Miss., U.S.A. 159 34 30N 89 0W
New Albany, Pa., U.S.A. 162 41 35N 76 28W
New Alresford 28 51 6N 1 10W
New Amsterdam 174 6 15N 57 30W
New Angledool 139 29 10S 147 55E
New Bedford 162 41 40N 70 52W
New Berlin, N.Y., U.S.A. 162 42 38N 75 20W
New Berlin, Pa., U.S.A. 162 40 50N 76 57W
New Bern 157 35 8N 77 3W
New Birmingham 39 52 36N 7 38W
New Boston 159 33 27N 94 21W
New Braunfels 159 29 43N 98 9W
New Brighton, N.Z. 143 43 29S 172 43E
New Brighton, U.K. 32 53 27N 3 2W
New Britain 162 41 41N 72 47W
New Britain, I. 135 5 50S 150 20E
New Brunswick 162 40 30N 74 28W
New Brunswick □ 151 46 50N 66 30W
New Buildings 38 54 57N 7 21W
New Bussa 121 9 53N 4 31E
New Byrd 13 80 0S 120 0W
New Caledonia, I. 130 21 0S 165 0E
New Castile = Castilla La Neuva 57 39 45N 3 20W
New Castle, Del., U.S.A. 162 39 40N 75 34W
New Castle, Ind., U.S.A. 156 39 55N 85 23W
New Castle, Pa., U.S.A. 156 41 0N 80 20W
New Chapel Cross 39 51 51N 10 12W
New City 162 41 8N 74 0W
New Cumnock 34 55 24N 4 13W
New Cuyama 163 34 57N 119 38W
New Deer 37 57 30N 2 10W
New Delhi 94 28 37N 77 13E
New Denver 152 50 0N 117 25W
New England 158 46 36N 102 47W
New England Ra. 139 30 20S 151 45E
New Forest 28 50 53N 1 40W
New Freedom 162 39 44N 76 42W
New Galloway 35 55 4N 4 10W
New Glasgow 151 45 35N 62 36W
New Gretna 162 39 35N 74 28W
New Guinea, I. 135 4 0S 136 0E
New Hampshire □ 156 43 40N 71 40W
New Hampton 158 43 2N 92 20W
New Hanover 129 29 22S 30 31E
New Hanover I. 135 2 30S 150 10E
New Hartford 162 43 4N 75 18W
New Haven 162 41 20N 72 54W
New Hazelton 152 55 20N 127 30W
*New Hebrides, Is. 130 15 0S 168 0E
New Holland, U.K. 33 53 42N 0 22W
New Holland, U.S.A. 162 40 6N 76 5W
New Iberia 159 30 2N 91 54W
New Inn 39 53 5N 7 10W
New Ireland, I. 135 3 20S 151 50E
New Jersey □ 162 39 50N 74 10W
New Kensington 156 40 36N 79 43W
New Kent 162 37 31N 76 59W
New Lexington 156 39 40N 82 15W
New Liskeard 150 47 31N 79 41W
New London, Conn., U.S.A. 162 41 23N 72 8W
New London, Minn., U.S.A. 158 45 17N 94 55W
New London, Wis., U.S.A. 158 44 23N 88 43W
New Luce 34 54 57N 4 50W
New Madrid 159 36 40N 89 30W
New Meadows 160 45 0N 116 10W
New Mexico □ 154 34 30N 106 0W
New Milford, Conn., U.S.A. 162 41 35N 73 25W
New Milford, Pa., U.S.A. 162 41 50N 75 45W
New Mills 32 53 22N 2 0W
New Norcia 137 30 57S 116 13E
New Norfolk 138 42 46S 147 2E
New Orleans 159 30 0N 90 5W
New Oxford 162 39 52N 77 4W
New Philadelphia 156 40 29N 81 25W
New Pitsligo 37 57 35N 2 11W
New Plymouth, Bahamas 166 26 56N 77 20W
New Plymouth, N.Z. 142 39 4S 174 5E
New Point Comfort 162 37 18N 76 15W
New Providence I. 166 25 0N 77 30W
New Quay 31 52 13N 4 21W
New Radnor 31 52 15N 3 10W
New Richmond 158 45 6N 92 34W
New Roads 159 30 43N 91 30W
New Rockford 158 47 44N 99 7W
New Romney 29 50 59N 0 57E
New Ross 39 52 24N 6 58W
New Rossington 33 53 30N 1 4W
New Salem 158 46 51N 101 25W
New Siberian Is. = Novosibirskiye Os. 77 75 0N 140 0E
New Smyrna Beach 157 29 0N 80 50W
New South Wales □ 139 33 0S 146 0E
New Springs 137 25 49S 120 1E
New Tamale 121 9 10N 1 10W
New Tredegar 31 51 43N 3 15W
New Ulm 158 44 15N 94 30W
New Waterford 151 46 13N 60 4W
New Westminster 152 49 10N 122 52W
New York □ 156 42 40N 76 0W
New York City 162 40 45N 74 0W
New Zealand ■ 143 40 0S 176 0E
Newala 127 10 58S 39 10E
Newala □ 127 10 46S 39 20E
Newark, U.K. 33 53 6N 0 48W
Newark, Del., U.S.A. 162 39 42N 75 45W
Newark, N.J., U.S.A. 162 40 41N 74 12W
Newark, N.Y., U.S.A. 162 43 2N 77 10W
Newark, Ohio, U.S.A. 156 40 5N 82 30W
Newark Valley 162 42 14N 76 11W
Newberg 160 45 22N 123 0W
Newberry 156 46 20N 85 32W
Newberry Springs 163 34 50N 116 41W
Newbiggin-by-the-Sea 35 55 12N 1 31W
Newbigging 35 55 42N 3 33W
Newbliss 38 54 10N 7 8W
Newborough 31 53 10N 4 22W
Newbridge, Kildare, Ireland 39 53 11N 6 50W
Newbridge, Limerick, Ireland 38 52 33N 9 0W
Newbridge-on-Wye 31 52 13N 3 27W
Newbrook 152 54 24N 112 57W
Newburgh, Fife, U.K. 35 56 21N 3 15W
Newburgh, Grampian, U.K. 37 57 19N 2 0W
Newburgh, U.S.A. 162 41 30N 74 1W
Newburn 35 54 57N 1 45W
Newbury 28 51 24N 1 19W
Newburyport 162 42 48N 70 50W
Newby Bridge 32 54 16N 2 59W
Newbyth 37 57 35N 2 17W
Newcastle, Austral. 141 33 0S 151 40E
Newcastle, Can. 151 47 1N 65 38W
Newcastle, Ireland 39 53 5N 6 4W
Newcastle, S. Afr. 125 27 45S 29 58E
Newcastle, U.K. 38 54 13N 5 54W
Newcastle, U.S.A. 158 43 50N 104 12W
Newcastle Emlyn 31 52 2N 4 29W
Newcastle Ra. 136 15 45S 130 15E
Newcastle-under-Lyme 32 53 2N 2 15W
Newcastle-upon-Tyne 35 54 59N 1 37W
Newcastle Waters 136 17 30S 133 28E
Newcastle West 38 52 27N 9 3W
Newcastleton 35 55 10N 2 50W
Newchurch 31 52 9N 3 10W
Newdegate 137 33 6S 119 0E
Newe Etan 90 32 30N 35 32E
Newe Sha'anan 90 32 47N 34 59E
Newe Zohar 90 31 9N 35 21E
Newell 158 44 48N 103 25W
Newenham, C. 147 58 40N 162 15W
Newent 28 51 56N 2 24W
Newfield, N.J., U.S.A. 162 39 33N 75 1W
Newfield, N.Y., U.S.A. 162 42 18N 76 33W
Newfound L. 162 43 40N 71 47W
Newfoundland 151 48 30N 56 0W
Newfoundland □ 151 48 28N 56 0W
Newhalem 152 48 41N 121 16W
Newhalen 147 59 40N 155 0W
Newhall 163 34 23N 118 32W
Newham 29 51 31N 0 2E
Newhaven 29 50 47N 0 4E
Newington, N. Kent, U.K. 29 51 21N 0 40E
Newington, S. Kent, U.K. 29 51 5N 1 8E
Newinn 39 52 28N 7 54W
Newkirk 159 36 52N 97 3W
Newlyn 30 50 6N 5 33W
Newlyn East 30 50 22N 5 3W
Newmachar 37 57 16N 2 11W
Newman 163 37 19N 121 1W
Newman, Mt. 137 23 20S 119 34E
Newmarket, Ireland 39 52 13N 9 0W
Newmarket, Lewis, U.K. 36 58 14N 6 24W
Newmarket, Suffolk, U.K. 29 52 15N 0 23E
Newmarket, U.S.A. 162 43 4N 70 57W
Newmarket-on-Fergus 39 52 46N 8 54W
Newmill 37 57 34N 2 58W
Newmills 38 54 56N 7 49W
Newmilns 34 55 36N 4 20W
Newnan 157 33 22N 84 48W
Newnes 139 33 9S 150 16E
Newnham 28 51 48N 2 27W
Newport, Essex, U.K. 29 51 58N 0 13E
Newport, Gwent, U.K. 31 51 35N 3 0W
Newport, I. of W., U.K. 28 50 42N 1 18W
Newport, Salop, U.K. 28 52 47N 2 22W
Newport, Ark., U.S.A. 159 35 38N 91 15W
Newport, Ky., U.S.A. 156 39 5N 84 23W
Newport, N.H., U.S.A. 162 43 23N 72 8W
Newport, Oreg., U.S.A. 160 44 41N 124 2W
Newport, R.I., U.S.A. 162 41 30N 71 19W
Newport, Tenn., U.S.A. 157 35 39N 83 12W
Newport, Wash., U.S.A. 160 48 11N 117 2W
Newport B. 38 53 52N 9 38W
Newport Beach 163 33 40N 117 58W
Newport News 162 37 2N 76 54W
Newport on Tay 35 56 27N 2 56W
Newport Pagnell 29 52 5N 0 42W
Newquay 30 50 24N 5 6W
Newry 38 54 10N 6 20W
Newry & Mourne □ 38 54 10N 6 15W
Newton, Iowa, U.S.A. 158 41 40N 93 3W
Newton, Kans., U.S.A. 159 38 2N 97 30W
Newton, Mass., U.S.A. 156 42 21N 71 10W
Newton, N.C., U.S.A. 157 35 42N 81 10W
Newton, N.J., U.S.A. 162 41 3N 74 46W
Newton, Texas, U.S.A. 159 30 54N 93 42W
Newton Abbot 30 50 32N 3 37W
Newton Arlosh 32 54 53N 3 15W
Newton-Aycliffe 33 54 36N 1 33W
Newton Boyd 139 29 45S 152 16E
Newton Ferrers 30 50 19N 4 3W
Newton le Willows 32 53 28N 3 27W
Newton St. Cyres 30 50 46N 3 35W
Newton Stewart 34 54 57N 4 30W
Newtonabbey □ 38 54 45N 6 0W
Newtongrange 35 55 52N 3 4W
Newtonhill 37 57 1N 20 52E
Newtonmore 37 57 4N 4 7W
Newtown, Ireland 39 52 20N 8 47W
Newtown, Scot, U.K. 35 55 34N 2 38W
Newtown, Wales, U.K. 31 52 31N 3 19W
Newtown Crommelin 38 54 59N 6 13W
Newtown Cunningham 38 55 0N 7 32W
Newtown Forbes 38 53 46N 7 50W
Newtown Gore 38 54 3N 7 41W
Newtown Hamilton 38 54 12N 6 35W
Newtownabbey 38 54 40N 5 55W
Newtownards 38 54 37N 5 40W
Newtownbutler 38 54 12N 7 22W
Newtownmount-kennedy 39 53 5N 6 7W
Newtownstewart 38 54 43N 7 22W
Nexon 48 45 41N 1 10E
Neya 81 58 21N 43 49E
Neyland 31 51 43N 4 58W
Neyrīz 93 29 15N 54 55E
Neyshābūr 93 36 10N 58 20E
Neyyattinkara 97 8 26N 77 5E
Nezhin 80 51 5N 31 55E
Nezperce 160 46 13N 116 15W
Ngabang 102 0 30N 109 55E
Ngaiphaipi 98 22 14N 93 15E
Ngambé 121 5 48N 11 29E
Ngami Depression 128 20 30S 22 46E
Ngamo 127 19 3S 27 25E
Ngandjuk 103 7 32S 111 55E
Ngao 100 18 46N 99 59E
Ngaoundéré 124 7 15N 13 35E
Ngapara 143 44 57S 170 46E
Ngara 126 2 29S 30 40E
Ngara □ 126 2 29S 30 40E
Ngaruawahia 142 37 42S 175 11E
Ngatapa 142 38 32S 177 45E
Ngathainggyaung 98 17 24N 95 5E
Ngauruhoe, Mt. 142 39 13S 175 45E
Ngawi 103 7 24S 111 26E
Ngetera 121 12 40S 12 46E
Ngha Lo 101 21 33N 104 28E
Nghia Lo 100 21 33N 104 28E
Ngoma 127 13 8S 33 45E
Ngomahura 127 20 33S 30 57E
Ngomba 127 8 20S 32 53E
Ngonye Falls 128 16 35S 23 30E
Ngop 123 6 17N 30 9E
Ngorkou 120 15 40N 3 41W
Ngorongoro 126 3 11S 35 32E
Ngozi 126 2 54S 29 50E
Ngudu 126 2 58S 33 25E
N'Guigmi 117 14 20N 13 20E
Nguna, I. 100 17 26S 168 21E
Ngunga 126 3 37S 33 37E
Ngungu 143 6 15N 28 16E
Ngunguru 94 35 37S 174 30E
Nguru 121 12 56N 10 29E
Nguru Mts. 126 6 0S 37 30E
Nguyen Binh 100 22 39N 105 56E
Ngwenya 129 26 5S 31 7E
Nha Trang 101 12 16N 109 10E
Nhacoongo 129 24 18S 35 14E
Nhangutazi, Lago 129 24 0S 34 30E
Nhill 140 36 18S 141 40E
Nho Quan 100 20 18N 105 45E
Nhulunbuy 138 12 10S 136 45E
Nia-nia 126 1 30N 27 40E
Niafounké 120 16 0N 4 5W
Niagara 156 45 45N 88 0W
Niagara Falls, Can. 150 43 7N 79 5W
Niagara Falls, N. Amer. 150 43 5N 79 5W
Niah 102 3 58N 113 46E
Niamey 121 13 27N 2 6E
Nianforando 120 9 37N 10 36W
Nianfors 72 61 36N 16 46E
Niangara 126 3 50N 27 50E
Niantic 162 41 19N 72 12W
Nias, I. 102 1 0N 97 40E
Niassa □ 127 13 30S 36 0E
Niassa, Lago 127 12 30S 34 30E
Nibbiano 62 44 54N 9 20E
Nibe 73 56 59N 9 38E
Nibong Tebal 101 5 10N 100 29E
Nicaragua ■ 166 11 40N 85 30W
Nicaragua, Lago de 166 12 50N 85 30W
Nicastro 65 39 0N 16 18E
Nice 45 43 42N 7 14E
Niceville 157 30 30N 86 30W
Nichinan 110 31 38N 131 23E
Nicholas, Chan. 166 23 30N 80 30W
Nicholasville 156 37 54N 84 31W
Nichols 162 42 1N 76 22W
Nicholson, Austral. 136 18 2S 128 54E
Nicholson, Can. 150 47 58N 83 47W
Nicholson, U.S.A. 162 41 37N 75 47W
Nicholson, R. 138 17 31S 139 36E
Nicholson Ra. 137 27 15S 116 30E
Nicobar Is. 86 9 0N 93 0E
Nicoclí 174 8 26N 76 48W
Nicola 152 50 8N 120 40W
Nicolet 150 46 17N 72 35W
Nicolls Town 166 25 8N 78 0W
Nicosia, Cyprus 92 35 10N 33 25E
Nicosia, Italy 65 37 45N 14 22E
Nicótera 65 38 33N 15 57E
Nicoya 166 10 9N 85 27W
Nicoya, Golfo de 166 10 0N 85 0W
Nicoya, Pen. de 166 9 45N 85 40W
Nidau 50 47 7N 7 15E
Nidd, R. 33 54 1N 1 32W
Nidda 48 50 24N 9 2E
Nidda, R. 49 50 25N 9 2E
Nidderdale 33 54 5N 1 46W
Nidzica 54 53 25N 20 28E
Niebüll 48 54 47N 8 49E
Niederaula 48 50 48N 9 37E
Niederbipp 50 47 16N 7 42E
Niederbronn 43 48 57N 7 39E
Niedere Tauern 93 47 18N 14 0E
Niedermarsberg 48 51 28N 8 52E
Niederösterreich □ 52 48 25N 15 40E
Niedersachsen □ 48 54 45N 9 0E
Niel 47 51 7N 4 20E
Niellé 120 10 5N 5 38W
Niemba 126 5 58S 28 24E
Niemcza 54 50 42N 16 47E
Niemodlin 54 50 38N 17 38E
Niemur 140 35 17S 144 9E
Nienburg 48 52 38N 9 15E
Nienchʼingtʼangkula Shan 105 30 10N 90 0E
Niepołomice 54 50 3N 20 13E
Niesen 50 46 38N 7 39E
Niesky 48 51 18N 14 48E
Nieszawa 54 52 52N 18 42E
Nieuw Amsterdam 46 52 43N 6 52E
Nieuw Beijerland 46 51 49N 4 20E
Nieuw-Buinen 46 52 58N 6 56E
Nieuw-Dordrecht 46 52 45N 6 59E
Nieuw Hellevoet 46 51 51N 4 8E
Nieuw Loosdrecht 46 52 12N 5 8E
Nieuw Nickerie 175 6 0N 57 10W
Nieuw-Schoonebeek 46 52 39N 7 0E
Nieuw-Vassemeer 47 51 34N 4 12E
Nieuw-Vennep 46 52 16N 4 38E
Nieuw-Weerdinge 46 52 51N 6 59E
Nieuwe-Niedorp 46 52 44N 4 54E
Nieuwe-Pekela 46 53 5N 6 58E
Nieuwe-Schans 46 53 11N 7 12E
Nieuwe-Tonge 47 51 43N 4 10E
Nieuwendijk 46 51 46N 4 55E
Nieuwerkerken 47 50 52N 5 12E
Nieuwkoop 46 52 9N 4 48E
Nieuwleusen 46 52 34N 6 17E
Nieuwnamen 47 51 18N 4 9E
Nieuwolda 46 53 15N 6 58E
Nieuwpoort 47 51 8N 2 45E
Nieuwveen 46 52 12N 4 46E
Nieves 56 42 7N 8 26W
Nièvre □ 43 47 10N 5 40E
Nigata 110 34 13N 132 39E
Nigde 92 38 0N 34 40E
Nigel 129 26 27S 28 25E
Niger □ 121 10 0N 5 0E
Niger ■ 121 13 30N 10 0E
Niger, R. 121 10 0N 4 40E
Nigeria ■ 121 8 30N 8 0E
Nigg B. 37 57 41N 4 5W
Nightcaps 143 45 57S 168 14E
Nigrita 68 40 56N 23 29E
Nihtaur 94 29 27N 78 23E
Nii-Jima 111 34 20N 139 15E
Niigata 112 37 58N 139 0E
Niigata-ken □ 112 37 15N 138 45E
Niihama 110 33 55N 133 10E
Niihau, I. 147 21 55N 160 10W
Niimi 110 34 59N 133 28E
Nijar 59 36 53N 2 15W
Nijkerk 46 52 13N 5 30E
Nijlen 47 51 10N 4 40E
Nijmegen 47 51 50N 5 52E
Nijverdal 46 52 22N 6 28E
Nike 121 6 26N 7 29E
Nikel 74 69 30N 30 5E
Nikiniki 103 9 40S 124 30E
Nikitas 68 40 17N 23 34E
Nikki 121 9 58N 3 21E
Nikkō 111 36 45N 139 35E
Nikolayev 82 46 58N 32 7E
Nikolayevsk-na-Amur 77 53 40N 140 50E
Nikolayevski 81 50 10N 45 35E
Nikolsk 81 59 30N 45 28E
Nikolski 147 53 0N 168 50W
Nikolskoye, Amur, U.S.S.R. 77 47 50N 131 5E
Nikolskoye, Kamandorskiye, U.S.S.R. 77 55 12N 166 0E
Nikopol, Bulg. 67 43 43N 24 54E
Nikopol, U.S.S.R. 82 47 35N 34 25E
Niksar 82 40 31N 37 2E
Nīkshah 93 26 15N 60 10E
Nik ió 66 42 50N 18 57E
Nîl el Abyad, Bahr 123 9 30N 31 40E

* Renamed Vanuatu

Nîl el Azraq □	**123**	12 30N	34 30 E
Nîl el Azraq, Bahr	**123**	10 30N	35 0 E
Nîl, Nahr el	**122**	27 30N	30 30 E
Nila	**103**	8 24 S	120 29 E
Niland	**161**	33 16N	115 30W
Nile □	**126**	2 0N	31 30 E
Nile Delta	**122**	31 40N	31 0 E
Nile, R. = Nîl, Nahr el	**122**	27 30N	30 30 E
Niles	**156**	41 8N	80 40W
Nilgiri Hills	**97**	11 30N	76 30 E
Nilo Peçanha	**171**	13 37 S	39 6W
Nilpena	**140**	30 58 S	138 20 E
Nimach = Neemuch	**94**	24 30N	74 50 E
Nimar	**96**	21 49N	76 22 E
Nimba, Mt.	**120**	7 39N	8 30W
Nimbahera	**94**	24 37N	74 45 E
Nîmes	**45**	43 50N	4 23 E
Nimfaion, Ákra	**68**	40 5N	24 20 E
Nimingarra	**132**	20 31 S	119 55 E
Nimmitabel	**141**	36 29 S	149 15 E
Nimneryskiy	**77**	58 0N	125 10 E
Nimule	**123**	3 32N	32 3 E
Nimy	**47**	50 28N	3 57 E
Nin	**63**	44 16N	15 12 E
Nindigully	**139**	28 21 S	148 50 E
Ninemile	**152**	56 0N	130 7W
Ninemilehouse	**39**	52 28N	7 29W
Ninety Mile Beach	**130**	34 45 S	173 0 E
Ninety Mile Beach, The	**133**	38 15 S	147 24 E
Nineveh	**92**	36 25N	43 10 E
Ninfield	**29**	50 53N	0 26 E
Ningaloo	**136**	22 41 S	113 41 E
Ningan	**107**	44 23N	129 26 E
Ningch'eng	**107**	41 34N	119 20 E
Ningch'iang	**106**	32 49N	106 13 E
Ningchin	**106**	37 37N	114 55 E
Ningching Shan	**108**	31 45N	97 15 E
Ninghai	**109**	29 18N	121 25 E
Ninghsiang	**109**	28 15N	112 30 E
Ninghsien	**106**	35 35N	107 58 E
Ninghua	**109**	26 14N	116 36 E
Ningkang	**109**	26 45N	113 58 E
Ningkuo	**109**	30 38N	118 58 E
Ninglang	**108**	27 19N	100 53 E
Ningling	**106**	34 27N	115 19 E
Ningming	**108**	22 12N	107 5 E
Ningnan	**108**	27 7N	102 42 E
Ningpo	**109**	29 53N	121 33 E
Ningshan	**106**	33 12N	108 29 E
Ningsia Hui A.R. □	**106**	37 45N	106 0 E
Ningte	**109**	26 45N	120 0 E
Ningtsin	**99**	29 44N	98 28 E
Ningtu	**109**	26 22N	115 48 E
Ningwu	**106**	29 2N	112 15 E
Ningyang, Fukien, China	**109**	25 44N	117 8 E
Ningyang, Shantung, China	**106**	35 46N	116 47 E
Ningyüan	**109**	25 36N	111 54 E
Ninh Binh	**100**	20 15N	105 55 E
Ninh Giang	**100**	20 44N	106 24 E
Ninh Hoa	**100**	12 30N	109 7 E
Ninh Ma	**100**	12 48N	109 21 E
Ninian, oilfield	**19**	60 42N	1 30 E
Ninove	**47**	50 51N	4 2 E
Nioaque	**173**	21 5 S	55 50W
Niobrara	**158**	42 48N	97 59W
Niobrara R.	**158**	42 30N	103 0W
Nioki	**124**	2 47 S	17 40 E
Niono	**120**	14 15N	6 0W
Nioro	**120**	15 30N	9 30W
Nioro du Rip	**120**	13 40N	15 50W
Nioro du Sahel	**120**	15 30N	9 30W
Niort	**44**	46 19N	0 29W
Niou	**121**	12 42N	2 1W
Nipa	**135**	6 9 S	143 29 E
Nipan	**138**	24 45 S	150 0 E
Nipani	**96**	16 20N	74 25 E
Nipawin	**153**	53 20N	104 0W
Nipawin Prov. Park	**153**	54 0N	104 37W
Nipigon	**150**	49 0N	88 17W
Nipigon, L.	**150**	49 50N	88 30W
Nipin, R.	**153**	55 46N	109 2W
Nipishish L.	**151**	54 12N	60 45W
Nipissing L.	**150**	46 20N	80 0W
Nipomo	**163**	35 4N	120 29W
Niquelândia	**171**	14 33 S	48 23W
Nira, R.	**96**	18 5N	74 25 E
Nirasaki	**111**	35 42N	138 27 E
Nirmal	**96**	19 3N	78 20 E
Nirmali	**95**	26 20N	86 35 E
Niš	**66**	43 19N	21 58 E
Nisa	**57**	39 30N	7 41W
Nisab	**91**	14 25N	46 29 E
Nišava, R.	**66**	43 20N	22 10 E
Niscemi	**65**	37 8N	14 21 E
Nishi-Sonogi-Hantō	**110**	32 55N	129 45 E
Nishinomiya	**111**	34 45N	135 20 E
Nishinoomote	**112**	30 43N	130 59 E
Nishio	**111**	34 52N	137 3 E
Nishiwaki	**110**	34 59N	134 48 E
Nísiros, I.	**69**	36 35N	27 12 E
Niskibi, R.	**150**	56 29N	88 9W
Nisko	**54**	50 35N	22 7 E
Nispen	**47**	51 29N	4 28 E
Nisporeny	**70**	47 4N	28 10 E
Nissafors	**73**	57 25N	13 37 E
Nissan	**73**	56 40N	12 51 E
Nissan I.	**138**	4 30 S	154 10 E
Nissedal	**71**	59 10N	8 30 E
Nisser	**71**	59 7N	8 28 E
Nissum Fjord	**73**	56 20N	8 11 E
Nistelrode	**47**	51 42N	5 34 E
Nisutlin, R.	**152**	60 14N	132 34W
Nitchequon	**151**	53 10N	70 58W
Niterói	**173**	22 52 S	43 0W
Nith, R.	**35**	55 20N	3 5W
Nithsdale	**35**	55 14N	3 50W
Niton	**28**	50 35N	1 14W
Nitra	**53**	48 19N	18 4 E
Nitra, R.	**53**	48 30N	18 7 E
Nitsa, R.	**84**	57 29N	64 33 E
Nittedal	**71**	60 1N	10 57 E
Niuchieh	**108**	27 47N	104 16 E
Niuchuang	**107**	40 58N	122 38 E
Niue I. (Savage I.)	**130**	19 2 S	169 54W
Niulan Chiang, R.	**108**	27 24N	103 9 E
Niut, Mt.	**102**	0 55N	109 30 E
Nivelles	**47**	50 35N	4 20 E
Nivernais	**43**	47 0N	3 40 E
Nixon, Nev., U.S.A.	**160**	39 54N	119 22W
Nixon, Tex., U.S.A.	**159**	29 17N	97 45W
Nizam Sagar	**96**	18 10N	77 58 E
Nizamabad	**96**	18 45N	78 7 E
Nizamghat	**98**	28 20N	95 45 E
Nizhanaya Tunguska	**77**	64 20N	93 0 E
Nizhiye Sergi	**84**	56 40N	59 18 E
Nizhne Kolymsk	**77**	68 40N	160 55 E
Nizhne-Vartovskoye	**76**	60 56N	76 38 E
Nizhneangarsk	**77**	56 0N	109 30 E
Nizhnegorskiy	**82**	45 27N	34 38 E
Nizhneudinsk	**77**	55 0N	99 20 E
Nizhniy Lomov	**81**	53 34N	43 38 E
Nizhniy Novgorod = Gorkiy	**81**	56 20N	44 0 E
Nizhniy Pyandzh	**85**	37 12N	68 35 E
Nizhniy Tagil	**84**	57 55N	59 57 E
Nizhny Salda	**84**	58 8N	60 42 E
Nizké Tatry	**53**	48 55N	20 0 E
Nizza Monferrato	**62**	44 46N	8 22 E
Njakwa	**127**	11 1 S	33 56 E
Njinjo	**127**	8 34 S	38 44 E
Njombe	**124**	9 20 S	34 50 E
Njombe □	**127**	9 20 S	34 49 E
Njombe, R.	**126**	7 15 S	34 30 E
Nkambe	**121**	6 35N	10 40 E
Nkana	**127**	13 0 S	28 8 E
Nkawkaw	**121**	6 36N	0 49W
Nkhata Bay	**124**	11 33 S	34 16 E
Nkhota Kota	**127**	12 56 S	34 15 E
Nkongsamba	**121**	4 55N	9 55 E
Nkunka	**127**	14 57 S	25 58 E
Nkwanta	**120**	6 10N	2 10W
Nmai Pit, R.	**99**	25 30N	98 0 E
Nmai, R.	**99**	25 30N	98 0 E
Nmaushahra	**95**	33 11N	74 15 E
Nnewi	**121**	6 0N	6 59 E
Noakhali = Maijdi	**98**	22 50N	90 45 E
Noatak	**147**	67 32N	163 10W
Noatak, R.	**147**	68 0N	161 0W
Nobber	**38**	53 49N	6 45W
Nobeoka	**110**	32 36N	131 41 E
Nōbi-Heiya	**111**	35 15N	136 45 E
Noblejas	**58**	39 58N	3 26W
Noblesville	**156**	40 1N	85 59W
Noce, R.	**62**	46 22N	11 0 E
Nocera Inferiore	**65**	40 45N	14 37 E
Nocera Terinese	**65**	39 2N	16 9 E
Nocera Umbra	**63**	43 8N	12 47 E
Nochixtlán	**165**	17 28N	97 14W
Noci	**65**	40 47N	17 7 E
Nockatunga	**139**	27 42 S	142 42 E
Nocona	**159**	33 48N	97 45W
Nocrich	**70**	45 55N	24 26 E
Noda, Japan	**111**	35 56N	139 52 E
Noda, U.S.S.R.	**77**	47 30N	142 5 E
Noel	**159**	36 36N	94 29W
Nogales, Mexico	**164**	31 36N	94 29W
Nogales, U.S.A.	**161**	31 33N	115 50W
Nōgata	**110**	33 48N	130 54 E
Nogent-en-Bassigny	**43**	48 0N	5 20 E
Nogent-le-Rotrou	**42**	48 20N	0 50 E
Nogent-sur-Seine	**43**	48 30N	3 30 E
Noggerup	**137**	33 32 S	116 5 E
Noginsk, Moskva, U.S.S.R.	**81**	55 50N	38 25 E
Noginsk, Sib., U.S.S.R.	**77**	64 30N	90 50 E
Nogoa, R.	**138**	23 33 S	148 32 E
Nogoyá	**172**	32 24 S	59 48W
Nógrád □	**53**	48 0N	19 30 E
Nogueira de Ramuin	**56**	42 21N	7 43W
Noguera Pallaresa, R.	**58**	42 15N	1 0 E
Noguera Ribagorzana, R.	**58**	42 15N	0 45 E
Nohar	**94**	29 11N	74 49 E
Noi, R.	**101**	14 50N	100 15 E
Noire, Mts.	**42**	48 11N	3 40W
Noirétable	**44**	45 48N	3 46 E
Noirmoutier	**42**	47 0N	2 15W
Noirmoutier, Î. de	**42**	46 58N	2 10W
Nojane	**128**	23 15 S	20 14 E
Nojima-Zaki	**111**	34 54N	139 53 E
Nok Kundi	**93**	28 50N	62 45 E
Nokaneng	**128**	19 47 S	22 17 E
Nokhtuysk	**77**	60 0N	117 45 E
Nokomis	**153**	51 35N	105 0W
Nokomis L.	**153**	57 0N	103 0W
Nokou	**124**	14 35N	14 47 E
Nol	**73**	57 56N	12 5 E
Nola, C. Afr. Emp.	**124**	3 35N	16 10 E
Nola, Italy	**65**	40 54N	14 29 E
Nolay	**43**	46 58N	4 35 E
Nolby	**72**	62 17N	17 26 E
Noli, C. di	**62**	44 12N	8 26 E
Nolinsk	**84**	57 28N	49 57 E
Noma Omuramba, R.	**128**	19 6 S	20 30 E
Noma-Saki	**110**	31 25N	130 7 E
Nomad	**135**	6 19 S	142 13 E
Noman L.	**153**	62 15N	108 55W
Nombre de Dios	**166**	9 34N	79 28W
Nome	**147**	64 30N	165 30W
Nomo-Zaki	**110**	32 35N	129 44 E
Nonacho L.	**153**	61 57N	109 28W
Nonancourt	**42**	48 47N	1 11 E
Nonant-le-Pin	**42**	48 42N	0 12 E
Nonda	**138**	20 40 S	142 28 E
Nong Chang	**100**	15 23N	99 51 E
Nong Het	**100**	19 29N	103 59 E
Nong Khae	**101**	14 29N	100 53 E
Nong Khai	**100**	17 50N	102 46 E
Nonoava	**164**	27 22N	106 38W
Nonopapa	**147**	21 50N	160 15W
Nonthaburi	**100**	13 51N	100 34 E
Nontron	**44**	45 31N	0 40 E
Noonamah	**136**	12 40 S	131 4 E
Noonan	**158**	48 51N	102 59W
Noondoo	**139**	28 35 S	148 30 E
Noonkanbah	**102**	18 30 S	124 50 E
Noord-Bergum	**46**	53 14N	6 1 E
Noord Brabant □	**47**	51 40N	5 0 E
Noord Holland □	**46**	52 30N	4 45 E
Noordbeveland	**47**	51 45N	3 50 E
Noordeloos	**46**	51 55N	4 56 E
Noordhollandsch Kanaal	**46**	52 55N	4 48 E
Noordhorn	**46**	53 16N	6 24 E
Noordoostpolder	**46**	52 45N	5 45 E
Noordwijk aan Zee	**46**	52 14N	4 26 E
Noordwijk-Binnen	**46**	52 14N	4 27 E
Noordwijkerhout	**46**	52 16N	4 30 E
'Noordwinning', gasfield	**19**	53 13N	3 10 E
Noordzee Kanaal	**46**	52 28N	4 35 E
Noorvik	**147**	66 50N	161 14W
Noorwolde	**46**	52 54N	6 8 E
Nootka	**152**	49 38N	126 38W
Nootka I.	**152**	49 40N	126 50W
Noqui	**124**	5 55 S	13 30 E
Nora, Ethiopia	**123**	16 6N	40 4 E
Nora, Sweden	**72**	59 32N	15 2 E
Noranda	**150**	48 20N	79 0W
Norberg	**72**	60 4N	15 56 E
Norbottens län □	**74**	66 58N	20 0 E
Nórcia	**63**	42 50N	13 5 E
Norco	**163**	33 56N	117 33W
Nord □	**43**	50 15N	3 30 E
Nord-Ostee Kanal	**48**	54 5N	9 15 E
Nord-Süd Kanal	**48**	53 0N	10 32 E
Nord-Trondelag Fylke □	**74**	64 20N	12 0 E
Nordagutu	**71**	59 25N	9 20 E
Nordaustlandet	**12**	79 55N	23 0 E
Nordborg	**73**	55 5N	9 50 E
Nordby, Fanø, Denmark	**73**	55 27N	8 24 E
Nordby, Samsø, Denmark	**73**	55 58N	10 32 E
Norddal	**71**	62 15N	7 14 E
Norddalsfjord kpl.	**71**	61 39N	5 23 E
Norddeich	**48**	53 37N	7 10 E
Nordegg	**152**	52 29N	116 5W
Nordelph	**29**	52 34N	0 18 E
Norden	**48**	53 35N	7 12 E
Nordenham	**48**	53 29N	8 28 E
Norderhov	**71**	60 7N	10 17 E
Norderney	**48**	53 42N	7 9 E
Norderney, I.	**48**	53 42N	7 15 E
Nordfjord	**71**	61 55N	5 30 E
Nordfriesische Inseln	**48**	54 40N	8 20 E
Nordhausen	**48**	51 29N	10 47 E
Nordhorn	**48**	52 27N	7 4 E
Nordjyllands Amt □	**73**	57 0N	10 0 E
Nordkapp, Norway	**74**	71 10N	25 44 E
Nordkapp, Svalb.	**12**	80 31N	20 0 E
Nordkinn	**16**	71 3N	28 0 E
Nordland Fylke □	**74**	65 40N	13 0 E
Nördlingen	**49**	48 50N	10 30 E
Nordrhein-Westfalen □	**48**	51 45N	7 30 E
Nordstrand, I.	**48**	54 27N	8 50 E
Nordvik	**77**	73 40N	110 57 E
Nore	**71**	60 10N	9 0 E
Nore R.	**39**	52 40N	7 20W
Noreena Cr.	**136**	22 20 S	120 25 E
Norefjell	**71**	60 16N	9 29 E
Norembega	**150**	48 59N	80 43W
Noresund	**71**	60 11N	9 37 E
Norfolk, Nebr., U.S.A.	**158**	42 3N	97 25W
Norfolk, Va., U.S.A.	**156**	36 52N	76 15W
Norfolk □	**29**	52 39N	1 0 E
Norfolk Broads	**29**	52 30N	1 15 E
Norfolk I.	**130**	28 58 S	168 3 E
Norfork Res.	**159**	36 25N	92 0W
Norg	**46**	53 4N	6 28 E
Norham	**35**	55 44N	2 9W
Norilsk	**77**	69 20N	88 0 E
Norley	**139**	27 45 S	143 48 E
Normal	**158**	40 30N	89 0W
Norman	**159**	35 12N	97 30W
Norman, R.	**138**	19 20 S	142 35 E
Norman Wells	**147**	65 17N	126 45W
Normanby	**142**	39 32 S	174 18 E
Normanby I.	**135**	10 55 S	151 5 E
Normanby, R.	**138**	14 23 S	144 10 E
Normandie	**42**	48 45N	0 10 E
Normandie, Collines de	**42**	48 55N	0 45W
Normandin	**150**	48 49N	72 31W
Normandy = Normandie	**42**	48 45N	0 10 E
Normanhurst, Mt.	**137**	25 13 S	122 30 E
Normanton, Austral.	**138**	17 40 S	141 10 E
Normanton, U.K.	**33**	53 41N	1 26W
Normanville	**140**	35 27 S	138 18 E
Norna, Mt.	**138**	20 55 S	140 42 E
Nornalup	**137**	35 0 S	116 48 E
Ñorquay	**153**	51 53N	102 5W
Ñorquinco	**176**	41 51 S	70 55W
Norrahammar	**73**	57 43N	14 7 E
Norrbottens län □	**74**	66 50N	18 0 E
Norrby	**74**	64 55N	18 15 E
Nørre Åby	**73**	55 27N	9 52 E
Nørre Nebel	**73**	55 47N	8 17 E
Nørresundby	**73**	57 5N	9 52 E
Norris	**160**	45 40N	111 48W
Norristown	**162**	40 9N	75 15W
Norrköping	**73**	58 37N	16 11 E
Norrland □	**74**	66 50N	18 0 E
Norrtälje	**72**	59 46N	18 42 E
Norseman	**137**	32 8 S	121 43 E
Norsholm	**73**	58 31N	15 59 E
Norsk	**77**	52 30N	130 0 E
Norte de Santander □	**174**	8 0N	73 0W
North Adams	**162**	42 42N	73 6W
North America	**50**	40 0N	70 0W
North Andaman I.	**101**	13 15N	92 40 E
North Atlantic Ocean	**14**	30 0N	50 0W
North Ballachulish	**36**	56 42N	5 9W
North Battleford	**153**	52 50N	108 17W
North Bay	**150**	46 20N	79 30W
North Belcher Is.	**150**	56 50N	79 50W
North Bend, Can.	**152**	49 50N	121 35W
North Bend, U.S.A.	**160**	43 28N	124 7W
North Bennington	**162**	42 56N	73 15W
North Berwick, U.K.	**35**	56 4N	2 44W
North Berwick, U.S.A.	**162**	43 18N	70 43W
North Br., Ashburton R.	**143**	43 30 S	171 30 E
North Buganda □	**126**	1 0N	32 0 E
North Canadian, R.	**159**	36 48N	103 0W
North C., Antarct.	**13**	71 0N	166 0 E
North C., Can.	**151**	47 2N	60 20W
North, Cape	**151**	47 2N	60 25W
North C., N.Z.	**142**	34 23 S	173 4 E
North C., P.N.G.	**135**	2 32 S	150 50 E
North C., Spitsbergen	**12**	80 40N	20 0 E
North Caribou L.	**150**	52 50N	90 40W
North Carolina □	**157**	35 30N	80 0W
North Cerney	**28**	51 45N	1 58W
North Channel, Br. Is.	**34**	55 0N	5 30W
North Channel, Can.	**150**	46 0N	83 0W
North Chicago	**156**	42 19N	87 50W
North Collingham	**33**	53 8N	0 46W
North Dakota □	**158**	47 30N	100 0W
North Dandalup	**137**	32 30 S	116 2 E
N. Dorset Downs	**28**	50 50N	2 30W
North Down □	**38**	54 40N	5 45W
North Downs	**29**	51 17N	0 30W
North East	**162**	39 36N	75 56W
North Eastern □	**126**	1 30N	40 0 E
North Esk, R.	**37**	56 44N	2 25W
North European Plain	**16**	55 0N	20 0 E
N. Foreland, Pt.	**29**	51 22N	1 28 E
North Fork	**163**	37 14N	119 29W
N. Frisian Is. = Nordfr'sche Inseln	**48**	54 50N	8 20 E
N. Harris, dist.	**36**	58 0N	6 55W
North Henik L.	**153**	61 45N	97 40W
North Hill	**30**	50 33N	4 26W
North Horr	**126**	3 20N	37 8 E
North Hykeham	**33**	53 10N	0 35W
North I., Kenya	**126**	4 5N	36 5 E
North I., N.Z.	**143**	38 0 S	175 0 E
North Kamloops	**152**	50 40N	120 25W
North Kessock	**37**	57 30N	4 15W
North Knife L., Can.	**153**	58 0N	97 0W
North Knife L., Man., Can.	**153**	58 5N	97 5W
North Knife, R.	**153**	58 53N	94 45W
North Koel, R.	**95**	23 50N	84 5 E
North Korea ■	**105**	40 0N	127 0 E
N. Lakhimpur	**99**	27 15N	94 10 E
N. Las Vegas	**161**	36 15N	115 6W
North Mara □	**126**	1 20 S	34 20 E
North Minch	**36**	58 5N	5 55W
North Molton	**30**	51 3N	3 48W
North Nahanni, R.	**152**	62 15N	123 20W
North Ossetian A.S.S.R. □	**83**	43 30N	44 30 E
North Palisade	**163**	37 6N	118 32W
North Petherton	**28**	51 6N	3 1W
North Platte	**158**	41 10N	100 50W
North Platte, R.	**160**	42 50N	106 50W
North Pt., Austral.	**108**	27 23 S	153 14 E
North Pt., Can.	**151**	47 5N	65 0W
North Pole	**12**	90 0N	0 0 E
North Portal	**153**	49 0N	102 33W
North Powder	**160**	45 2N	117 59W
North Queensferry	**35**	56 1N	3 22W
North Riding (□)	**26**	54 22N	1 30W
North Roe, dist.	**36**	60 40N	1 22W
North Ronaldsay, I.	**37**	59 20N	2 30W
North Sea	**19**	56 0N	4 0 E
North Sentinel, I.	**101**	11 35N	92 15 E
North Somercotes	**33**	53 28N	0 9 E
North Sound	**39**	53 10N	9 48W
North Sound, The	**37**	59 18N	2 45W
North Sporades = Voríai Sporádhes	**69**	39 0N	24 10 E
North Stradbroke I.	**133**	27 35 S	153 28 E
North Sunderland	**35**	55 35N	1 40W
North Sydney	**151**	46 12N	60 21W
North Syracuse	**162**	43 8N	76 7W
N. Taranaki Bt.	**82**	38 45 S	174 20 E

North Tawton
Nyirbátor

North Tawton **30** 50 48N 3 55W
North Thompson, R. **152** 50 40N 120 20W
North Thoresby **33** 53 27N 0 3W
North Tidworth **28** 51 14N 1 40W
North Tolsta **36** 58 21N 6 13W
N. Tonawanda **156** 43 5N 78 50W
N. Truchas Pk. **161** 36 0N 105 30W
North Twin I. **150** 53 20N 80 0W
North Tyne, R. **35** 54 59N 2 7W
North Uist I. **36** 57 40N 7 15W
North Vancouver **152** 49 25N 123 20W
North Vermilion **152** 58 25N 116 0W
North Vernon **156** 39 0N 85 35W
North Vietnam ■ **100** 22 0N 105 0E
North Wabasca L. **152** 56 0N 113 55W
North Walsham **29** 52 49N 1 22E
North West C. **136** 21 45S 114 9E
North West Highlands **36** 57 35N 5 2W
North West River **151** 53 30N 60 10W
North Western □ **127** 13 30S 25 30E
North York Moors **33** 54 25N 0 50W
North Yorkshire □ **33** 54 15N 1 25W
Northallerton **33** 54 20N 1 26W
Northam, Austral. **132** 31 35S 116 42E
Northam, S. Afr. **137** 24 55S 27 15E
Northam, U.K. **30** 51 2N 4 13W
Northampton, Austral. **137** 28 21S 114 33E
Northampton, U.K. **29** 52 14N 0 54W
Northampton, Mass., U.S.A. **162** 42 22N 72 39W
Northampton, Pa., U.S.A. **162** 40 38N 75 24W
Northampton □ **29** 52 16N 0 55W
Northampton Downs **138** 24 35S 145 48E
Northbridge **162** 42 12N 71 40W
Northcliffe **137** 34 39S 116 7E
N.E. Land **12** 80 0N 24 0E
N.E. Providence Chan. **166** 26 0N 76 0W
Northeast Providence Channel **166** 26 0N 76 0W
Northeim **48** 51 42N 10 0E
Northern □, Malawi **127** 11 0S 34 0E
Northern □, Uganda **126** 3 5N 32 30E
Northern □, Zambia **127** 10 30S 31 0E
Northern Circars **96** 17 30N 82 30E
Northern Indian L. **153** 57 20N 97 20W
Northern Ireland □ **38** 54 45N 7 0W
Northern Light, L. **150** 48 15N 90 39W
Northern Province □ **120** 9 0S 11 30W
Northern Territory □ **136** 16 0S 133 0E
Northfield, Minn., U.S.A. **158** 44 37N 93 10W
Northfield, N.J., U.S.A. **162** 39 22N 74 33W
Northfleet **29** 51 26N 0 20E
Northiam **29** 50 59N 0 39E
Northland □ **143** 35 30S 173 30E
Northleach **28** 51 49N 1 50W
Northome **158** 47 53N 94 15W
Northop **31** 53 13N 3 8W
Northport, Ala., U.S.A. **157** 33 15N 87 35W
Northport, Mich., U.S.A. **156** 45 8N 85 39W
Northport, N.Y., U.S.A. **162** 40 53N 73 20W
Northport, Wash., U.S.A. **160** 48 55N 117 48W
Northrepps **29** 52 53N 1 20E
Northumberland □ **35** 55 12N 2 0W
Northumberland, C. **140** 38 5S 140 40E
Northumberland Is. **138** 21 30S 149 50E
Northumberland Str. **151** 46 20N 64 0W
Northville **162** 43 13N 74 11W
Northway Junction **147** 63 0N 141 55W
N.W. Providence Chan. **166** 26 0N 78 0W
Northwest Terr. **148** 65 0N 100 0W
N.W.Basin **137** 25 45S 115 0E
Northwich **32** 53 16N 2 30W
Northwold **29** 52 33N 0 37E
Northwood, Iowa, U.S.A. **158** 43 27N 93 12W
Northwood, N.D., U.S.A. **158** 47 44N 97 30W
Norton, Rhod. **127** 17 52S 30 40E
Norton, N. Yorks., U.K. **33** 54 9N 0 48W
Norton, Suffolk, U.K. **29** 52 15N 0 52E
Norton, U.S.A. **158** 39 50N 100 0W
Norton B. **147** 64 40N 162 0W
Norton Fitzwarren **28** 51 1N 3 10W
Norton Sd. **147** 64 0N 165 0W
Norton Summit **109** 34 56S 138 43E
Nortorf **48** 54 14N 9 47E
Norwalk, Calif., U.S.A. **163** 33 54N 118 5W
Norwalk, Conn., U.S.A. **162** 41 9N 73 25W
Norwalk, Ohio, U.S.A. **156** 41 13N 82 38W
Norway **156** 45 46N 87 57W
Norway ■ **74** 67 0N 11 0E
Norway House **153** 53 59N 97 50W
Norwegian Dependency **13** 66 0N 15 0E
Norwegian Sea **14** 66 0N 1 0E
Norwich, U.K. **29** 52 38N 1 17E
Norwich, Conn., U.S.A. **162** 41 33N 72 5W
Norwich, N.Y., U.S.A. **162** 42 32N 75 30W
Norwood, Austral. **109** 34 56S 138 39E
Norwood, U.S.A. **162** 42 10N 71 10W
Noshiro **112** 40 12N 140 0E
Noshiro, R. **112** 40 15N 140 15E
Nosok **76** 70 10N 82 20E
Nosovka **80** 50 50N 31 30E
Nosratābād **93** 29 55N 60 0E
Noss Hd. **37** 58 29N 3 4W
Noss, I. of **36** 60 8N 1 1W
Nossa Senhora da Glória **170** 10 14S 37 25W
Nossa Senhora das Dores **170** 10 29S 37 13W
Nossebro **73** 58 12N 12 43E
Nossob **128** 22 15S 17 48E
Nossob, R. **128** 25 15S 20 30E
Nosy Bé, I. **125** 13 25S 48 15E
Nosy Mitsio, I. **125** 12 54S 48 36E
Nosy Varika **125** 20 35S 48 32E
Notigi Dam **153** 56 40N 99 10W
Notikewin **152** 56 55N 117 50W
Notikewin, R. **152** 56 59N 117 38W
Notios Evvoïkós Kólpos **69** 38 20N 24 0E
Noto **65** 36 52N 15 4E
Notò, G. di **65** 36 50N 15 10E
Notodden **71** 59 35N 9 17E
Notre Dame **151** 46 18N 64 46W
Notre Dame B. **151** 49 45N 55 30W
Notre Dame de Koartac **149** 60 55N 69 40W
Notre Dame d'Ivugivic **149** 62 20N 78 0W
Nottaway, R. **150** 51 22N 78 55W
Nøtterøy **71** 59 14N 10 24E
Nottingham **33** 52 57N 1 10W
Nottingham □ **33** 53 10N 1 0W
Nottoway, R. **156** 37 0N 77 45W
Notwani, R. **128** 24 14S 26 20E
Nouadhibou **116** 21 0N 17 0W
Nouakchott **120** 18 20N 15 50W
Nouméa **130** 22 17S 166 30E
Noup Hd. **37** 59 20N 3 2W
Noupoort **128** 31 10S 24 57E
Nouveau Comptoir (Paint Hills) **150** 53 0N 78 49W
Nouvelle Calédonie **142** 21 0S 165 0E
Nouzonville **43** 49 48N 4 44E
Nova-Annenskiy **81** 50 32N 42 39E
Nová Bana **53** 48 28N 18 39E
Nová Bystrice **52** 49 2N 15 8E
Nova Chaves **124** 10 50S 21 15E
Nova Cruz **170** 6 28S 35 25W
Nova Era **171** 19 45S 43 3W
Nova Esperança **173** 23 8S 52 13W
Nova Friburgo **173** 22 10S 42 30W
Nova Gaia **124** 10 10S 17 35E
Nova Gradiška **66** 45 17N 17 28E
Nova Granada **171** 20 30S 49 20W
Nova Iguaçu **173** 22 45S 43 28W
Nova Iorque **170** 7 0S 44 5W
Nova Lamego **120** 12 19N 14 11W
Nova Lima **173** 19 59S 43 51W
Nova Lisboa = Huambo **125** 12 42S 15 54E
Nova Lusitânia **127** 19 50S 34 34E
Nova Mambone **129** 21 0S 35 3E
Nova Mesto **63** 45 47N 15 12E
Nova Paka **52** 50 29N 15 30E
Nova Ponte **171** 19 8S 47 41W
Nova Preixo **127** 14 45S 36 22E
Nova Scotia □ **151** 45 10N 63 0W
Nova Sofala **129** 20 7S 34 48E
Nova Varoš **66** 43 29N 19 48E
Nova Venécia **171** 18 45S 40 24W
Nova Zagora **67** 42 32N 25 59E
Novaci, Rumania **70** 45 10N 23 42E
Novaci, Yugo. **66** 41 5N 21 29E
Novaleksandrovskaya **83** 45 29N 41 17E
Novalorque **171** 6 48S 44 0W
Novara **62** 45 27N 8 36E
Novato **163** 38 6N 122 35W
Novaya Kakhovka **82** 46 42N 33 27E
Novaya Ladoga **78** 60 7N 32 16E
Novaya Lyalya **84** 58 50N 60 35E
Novaya Sibir, O. **77** 75 10N 150 0E
Novaya Zemlya **76** 75 0N 56 0E
Novelda **59** 38 24N 0 45W
Novellara **62** 44 50N 10 43E
Noventa Vicentina **63** 45 18N 11 30E
Novgorod **80** 58 30N 31 25E
Novgorod Severskiy **80** 52 2N 33 10E
Novgorod Volynski **80** 50 38N 27 47E
Novi Bečej. **66** 45 36N 20 10E
Novi Grad **63** 45 19N 13 33E
Novi Knezeva **66** 46 4N 20 8E
Novi Krichim **67** 42 22N 24 31E
Novi Ligure **62** 44 45N 8 47E
Novi-Pazar **67** 43 25N 27 15E
Novi Pazar **66** 43 12N 20 28E
Novi Sad **66** 45 18N 19 52E
Novi Vinodolski **63** 45 10N 14 48E
Novigrad **63** 44 10N 15 32E
Noville **47** 50 4N 5 46E
Novo Acôrdo **170** 13 10S 46 48W
Nôvo Cruzeiro **171** 17 29S 41 53W
Novo Freixo **127** 14 49S 36 30E
Nôvo Hamburgo **173** 29 37S 51 7W
Novo Horizonte **171** 21 25S 49 10W
Novo Luso **103** 4 3S 126 6E
Novo Redondo **124** 11 10S 13 48E
Novo Selo **66** 44 11N 22 47E
Novo-Sergiyevskiy **84** 52 5N 53 38E
Novo-Zavidovskiy **81** 56 32N 36 29E
Novoalekseyevka **84** 50 8N 55 39E
Novoataysk **76** 53 30N 84 0E
Novoazovsk **82** 47 15N 38 4E
Novobelitsa **80** 52 27N 31 2E
Novobogatinskoye **83** 47 26N 51 17E
Novocherkassk **83** 47 27N 40 5E
Novodevichye **81** 53 37N 48 58E
Novograd Volynskiy **80** 50 40N 27 35E
Novogrudok **80** 53 40N 25 50E
Novokayakent **83** 42 45N 42 52E
Novokazalinsk **76** 45 40N 61 40E
Novokhopersk **81** 51 5N 41 50E
Novokuybyshevsk **84** 53 7N 49 58E
Novokuznetsk **76** 54 0N 87 10E
Novomirgorod **82** 48 57N 31 33E
Novomoskovsk, R.S.F.S.R., U.S.S.R. **81** 54 5N 38 15E
Novomoskovsk, Ukrainian S.S.R., U.S.S.R. **81** 48 33N 35 17E
Novoorsk **84** 51 21N 59 2E
Novopolotsk **80** 55 38N 28 37E
Novorossiysk **82** 44 43N 37 52E
Novorzhev **80** 57 3N 29 25E
Novoselitsa **82** 48 14N 26 15E
Novoshakhtinsk **83** 47 39N 39 58E
Novosibirsk **76** 55 0N 83 5E
Novosibirskiye Ostrava **77** 75 0N 140 0E
Novosil **81** 52 58N 36 58E
Novosokolniki **80** 56 33N 28 42E
Novotroitsk **84** 51 10N 58 15E
Novotroitskoye **85** 43 42N 73 46E
Novotulskiy **81** 54 10N 37 36E
Novoukrainka **82** 48 25N 31 30E
Novouzensk **81** 50 32N 48 17E
Novovolynsk **80** 50 45N 24 4E
Novovyatsk **84** 58 24N 49 45E
Novozybkov **80** 52 30N 32 0E
Novska **66** 45 19N 17 0E
Novy Bug **82** 47 34N 34 29E
Nový Bydzov **52** 50 14N 15 29E
Novy Dwór Mazowiecki **54** 52 26N 20 44E
Nový Jičín **53** 49 15N 18 0E
Novyy Oskol **81** 50 44N 37 55E
Novyy Port **76** 67 40N 72 30E
Novyye Aneny **70** 46 51N 29 13E
Now Shahr **93** 36 40N 51 40E
Nowa Deba **54** 50 26N 21 41E
Nowa Nowa **141** 37 44S 148 3E
Nowa Skalmierzyce **54** 51 43N 18 0E
Nowa Sól **54** 51 48N 15 44E
Nowe **54** 53 41N 18 44E
Nowe Miasteczko **54** 51 42N 15 42E
Nowe Miasto **54** 51 38N 20 34E
Nowe Miasto Lubawskie **54** 53 27N 19 33E
Nowe Warpno **54** 53 42N 14 18E
Nowen Hill **39** 51 42N 9 15W
Nowendoc **141** 31 32S 151 44E
Nowgong **98** 26 20N 92 50E
Nowingi **140** 34 33S 142 15E
Nowogard **54** 53 41N 15 10E
Nowogród **54** 53 14N 21 53E
Nowra **141** 34 53S 150 35E
Nowthanna Mt. **137** 27 0S 118 40E
Nowy Dwór **54** 53 40N 23 0E
Nowy Korczyn **54** 50 19N 20 48E
Nowy Sącz **54** 49 40N 20 41E
Nowy Sącz □ **54** 49 30N 20 30E
Nowy Staw **54** 54 13N 19 2E
Nowy Targ **53** 49 30N 20 2E
Nowy Tomysśl **54** 52 19N 16 10E
Noxen **162** 41 25N 76 4W
Noxon **160** 48 0N 115 54W
Noya **56** 42 48N 8 53W
Noyant **42** 47 30N 0 6E
Noyers **43** 47 40N 4 0E
Noyes, I. **152** 55 30N 133 40W
Noyon **43** 49 34N 3 0E
Nriquinha **125** 16 0S 21 25E
Nsa, O. en **119** 32 23N 5 20E
Nsanje **127** 16 55S 35 12E
Nsawam **121** 5 50N 0 24W
Nsomba **127** 10 45S 29 59E
Nsopzup **98** 25 51N 97 30E
Nsukka **121** 7 0N 7 50E
Nuanetsi **125** 21 15S 30 48E
Nuanetsi, R. **127** 21 10S 31 20E
Nuatja **121** 7 0N 1 10E
Nuba Mts. = Nubāh, Jibālan **123** 12 0N 31 0E
Nubāh, Jibālan **123** 12 0N 31 0E
Nûbîya, Es Sahrâ En **122** 21 30N 33 30E
Ñuble □ **172** 37 0S 72 0W
Nuboai **103** 2 10S 136 30E
Nubra, R. **95** 34 50N 77 25E
Nudgee **108** 27 22S 153 5E
Nudgee Beach **108** 27 21S 153 6E
Nădlac **66** 46 10N 20 50E
Nudo Ausangate, Mt. **174** 13 45S 71 10W
Nudo de Vilcanota **174** 14 30S 70 0W
Nueces, R. **159** 28 18N 98 39W
Nueltin L. **153** 60 30N 99 30W
Nuenen **47** 51 29N 5 33E
Nueva Antioquia **174** 6 5N 69 26W
Nueva Casas Grandes **164** 30 25N 107 55W
Nueva Esparta □ **174** 11 0N 64 0W
Nueva Gerona **166** 21 53N 82 49W
Nueva Imperial **176** 38 45S 72 58W
Nueva Palmira **172** 33 52S 58 20W
Nueva Rosita **164** 28 0N 101 20W
Nueva San Salvador **166** 13 40N 89 25W
Nuéve de Julio **172** 35 30S 61 0W
Nuevitas **166** 21 30N 77 20W
Nuevo, Golfo **176** 43 0S 64 30W
Nuevo Guerrero **165** 26 34N 99 15W
Nuevo Laredo **165** 27 30N 99 40W
Nuevo León □ **164** 25 0N 100 0W
Nuevo Rocafuerte **174** 0 55S 76 50W
Nugget Pt. **143** 46 27S 169 50E
Nugrus Gebel **122** 24 58N 39 34E
Nuhaka **142** 39 3S 177 45E
Nuhurowa, I. **103** 5 30S 132 45E
Nuits **43** 47 10N 4 56E
Nuits-St.-Georges **43** 47 10N 4 56E
Nukey Bluff, Mt. **132** 32 32S 135 40E
Nukheila (Merga) **122** 19 1N 26 21E
Nukus **76** 42 20N 59 40E
Nuland **46** 51 44N 5 26E
Nulato **147** 64 40N 158 10W
Nules **58** 39 51N 0 9W
Nullagine **136** 21 53S 120 6E
Nullagine, R. **136** 21 20S 120 20E
Nullarbor **137** 31 28S 130 55E
Nullarbor Plain **137** 30 45S 129 0E
Numalla, L. **139** 28 43S 144 20E
Numan **121** 9 29N 12 3E
Numansdorp **46** 51 43N 4 26E
Numata **111** 36 45N 139 4E
Numatinna, W. **123** 6 38N 27 15E
Numazu **111** 35 7N 138 51E
Numbulwar **138** 14 15S 135 45E
Numfoor, I. **103** 1 0S 134 50E
Numurkah **141** 36 0S 145 26E
Nun, R. **105** 47 30N 124 40E
Nunaksaluk, I. **151** 55 49N 60 20W
Nundah **108** 27 24S 152 54E
Nuneaton **28** 52 32N 1 29W
Nungo **127** 13 23S 37 43E
Nungwe **126** 2 48S 32 2E
Nunivak I. **147** 60 0N 166 0W
Nunkun, Mt. **95** 33 57N 76 8E
Nunney **28** 51 13N 2 20W
Nunspeet **46** 52 21N 5 45E
Nuoro **64** 40 20N 9 20E
Nŭousa **68** 40 42N 22 9E
Nuqayy, Jabal **119** 23 11N 19 30E
Nuquí **174** 5 42N 77 17W
Nurata **85** 40 33N 65 41E
Nuratau, Khrebet **85** 40 40N 66 30E
Nure, R. **62** 44 40N 9 32E
Nuremburg = Nürnberg **49** 49 26N 11 5E
Nuri **164** 28 2N 109 22W
Nurina **137** 30 44S 126 23E
Nuriootpa **140** 34 27S 139 0E
Nurlat **84** 54 29N 50 45E
Nürnberg **49** 49 26N 11 5E
Nurrari Lakes **137** 29 1S 130 5E
Nurri **64** 39 43N 9 13E
Nusa Barung **103** 8 22S 113 20E
Nusa Kambangan **103** 7 47S 109 0E
Nusa Tenggara □ **102** 7 30S 117 0E
Nusa Tenggara Barat **102** 8 50S 117 30E
Nusa Tenggara Timur **103** 9 30S 122 0E
Nushki **94** 29 35N 65 65E
Nŭsŭud **70** 47 19N 24 29E
Nutak **149** 57 28N 61 52W
Nuth **47** 50 55N 5 53E
Nutwood Downs **138** 15 49S 134 10E
Nuwaiba **122** 28 58N 34 40E
Nuwakot **95** 28 10N 83 55E
Nuwara Eliya **97** 6 58N 80 55E
Nuwefontein **128** 28 1S 19 6E
Nuweveldberge **128** 32 10S 21 45E
Nuyts Arch. **139** 32 12S 133 20E
Nuyts, C. **137** 32 2S 132 21E
Nuyts, Pt. **132** 35 4S 116 38E
Nuzvid **96** 16 47N 80 53E
NW Tor, oilfield **19** 56 42N 3 13E
Nyaake (Webo) **120** 4 52N 7 37W
Nyabing **137** 33 30S 118 7E
Nyack **162** 41 5N 73 57W
Nyadal **72** 62 48N 17 59E
Nyagyn **76** 62 8N 63 36E
Nyah West **140** 35 11S 143 21E
Nyahanga **126** 2 20S 33 37E
Nyahua **126** 5 25S 33 23E
Nyahururu **126** 0 2N 36 27E
Nyahururu Falls **126** 0 2N 36 27E
Nyakanazi **126** 3 2S 31 10E
Nyakasu **126** 3 58S 30 6E
Nyakrom **121** 5 40N 0 50W
Nyâlâ **123** 12 2N 24 58E
Nyamandhlovu **127** 19 55S 28 16E
Nyambiti **126** 2 48S 33 27E
Nyamwaga **126** 1 27S 34 33E
Nyandekwa **126** 3 57S 32 32E
Nyanga, L. **137** 29 57S 126 10E
Nyangana **128** 18 0S 20 40E
Nyanguge **126** 2 30S 33 12E
Nyangwena **127** 15 18S 28 45E
Nyanji **127** 14 25S 31 46E
Nyankpala **121** 9 21N 0 58W
Nyanza, Burundi **126** 4 21S 29 36E
Nyanza, Rwanda **126** 2 20S 29 42E
Nyanza □ **126** 0 10S 34 15E
Nyarling, R. **152** 60 41N 113 23W
Nyasa, L. = Malawi, L. **127** 12 0S 34 30E
Nyaunglebin **98** 17 52N 96 42E
Nyazepetrovsk **84** 56 3N 59 36E
Nyazwidzi, R. **127** 19 35S 32 0E
Nyborg **73** 55 18N 10 47E
Nybro **73** 56 44N 15 55E
Nybster **37** 58 34N 3 6W
Nyda **76** 66 40N 73 10E
Nyenchen Tanglha Shan **99** 30 30N 95 0E
Nyeri **126** 0 23S 36 56E
Nyeri □ **126** 0 25S 56 55E
Nyerol **123** 8 41N 32 1E
Nyhem **72** 62 54N 15 37E
Nyiel **123** 6 9N 31 4E
Nyika Plat. **127** 10 30S 36 0E
Nyilumba **127** 10 30S 40 22E
Nyinahin **120** 6 43N 2 3W
Nyirbátor **53** 47 49N 22 9E

Nyíregyháza Oldmeldrum

Nyíregyháza 53 48 0N 21 47 E
Nykarleby (Uusikaarlepyy) 74 63 32N 22 31 E
Nykobing 73 54 56N 11 52 E
Nykøbing, Falster, Denmark 73 54 56N 11 52 E
Nykøbing, Mors, Denmark 73 56 48N 8 51 E
Nykøbing, Sjælland, Denmark 73 55 55N 11 40 E
Nyköbing 73 56 49N 8 50 E
Nyköping 73 58 45N 17 0 E
Nykroppa 72 59 37N 14 18 E
Nykvarn 72 59 11N 17 25 E
Nyland 72 63 1N 17 45 E
Nylstroom 129 24 42 S 28 22 E
Nymagee 141 32 7 S 146 20 E
Nymburk 52 50 10N 15 1 E
Nymindegab 73 55 50N 8 12 E
Nynäshamn 72 58 54N 17 57 E
Nyngan 141 31 30 S 147 8 E
Nyon 50 46 23N 6 14 E
Nyons 45 44 22N 5 10 E
Nyora 141 38 20 S 145 41 E
Nyord 73 55 4N 12 13 E
Nysa 54 50 40N 17 22 E
Nysa, R. 54 52 4N 14 46 E
Nyssa 160 43 56N 117 2W
Nysted 73 54 40N 11 44 E
Nytva 84 57 56N 55 20 E
Nyūgawa 110 33 56N 133 5 E
Nyunzu 126 5 57 S 27 58 E
Nyurba 77 63 17N 118 20 E
Nzega 126 4 10 S 33 12 E
Nzega □ 126 4 10 S 33 10 E
N'Zérékoré 120 7 49N 8 48W
Nzilo, Chutes de 127 10 18 S 25 27 E
Nzubuka 126 4 45 S 32 50 E

O

O-Shima, Fukuoka, Japan 110 33 54N 130 25 E
O-Shima, Nagasaki, Japan 110 33 29N 129 33 E
O-Shima, Shizuoka, Japan 111 34 44N 139 24 E
Oa, Mull of 34 55 35N 6 20W
Oa, The, Pen. 34 55 36N 6 17W
Oacoma 158 43 50N 99 26W
Oadby 28 52 37N 1 7W
Oahe 158 44 33N 100 29W
Oahe Dam 158 44 28N 100 25W
Oahe Res 158 45 30N 100 15W
Oahu I. 147 21 30N 158 0W
Oak Creek 160 40 15N 106 59W
Oak Harb. 160 48 20N 122 38W
Oak Lake 153 49 45N 100 45W
Oak Park 156 41 55N 87 45W
Oak Ridge 157 36 1N 84 5W
Oak View 163 34 24N 119 18W
Oakbank, S. Australia, Austral. 109 34 59 S 138 51 E
Oakbank, S. Australia, Austral. 140 33 4 S 140 33 E
Oakdale, Calif., U.S.A. 163 37 49N 120 56W
Oakdale, La., U.S.A. 159 30 50N 92 38W
Oakengates 28 52 42N 2 29W
Oakes 158 46 14N 98 4W
Oakesdale 160 47 11N 117 9W
Oakey 139 27 25 S 151 43 E
Oakham 29 52 40N 0 43W
Oakhill 156 38 0N 81 7W
Oakhurst 163 37 19N 119 40W
Oakland 163 37 50N 122 18W
Oakland City 156 38 20N 87 20W
Oaklands, N.S.W., Austral. 141 35 34 S 146 10 E
Oaklands, S. Australia, Austral. 109 35 1 S 138 32 E
Oakley 160 42 14N 113 55W
Oakley Creek 141 31 37 S 149 46 E
Oakover, R. 136 20 43 S 120 33 E
Oakridge 160 43 47N 122 31W
Oakwood 159 31 35N 95 47W
Oamaru 143 45 5 S 170 59 E
Oamishirasato 111 35 23N 140 18 E
Oarai 111 36 21N 140 40 E
Oasis, Calif., U.S.A. 163 33 28N 116 6W
Oasis, Nev., U.S.A. 163 37 29N 117 55W
Oates Coast 13 69 0 S 160 0 E
Oatman 161 35 1N 114 19W
Oaxaca 165 17 2N 96 40W
Oaxaca □ 165 17 0N 97 0W
Ob, R. 76 62 40N 66 0E
Oba 150 49 4N 84 7W
Obala 121 4 9N 11 32 E
Obama, Eukui, Japan 111 35 30N 135 45 E
Obama, Nagasaki, Japan 110 32 43N 130 13 E
Oban, N.Z. 143 46 55 S 168 10 E
Oban, U.K. 34 56 25N 5 30W
Obatogamau L. 150 49 34N 74 26W
Obbia 91 5 25N 48 30 E
Obdam 46 52 41N 4 55 E
Obed 152 53 30N 117 10W
Obeh 93 34 28N 63 10 E
Ober-Aagau 50 47 10N 7 45 E
Obera 173 27 21 S 55 2W
Oberalppass 51 46 39N 8 35 E
Oberalpstock 51 46 45N 8 47 E
Oberammergau 49 47 35N 11 3 E
Oberdrauburg 52 46 44N 12 58 E
Oberengadin 51 46 35N 9 55 E
Oberentfelden 50 47 21N 8 2 E
Oberhausen 48 51 28N 6 50 E
Oberkirch 49 48 31N 8 5 E
Oberland 50 46 30N 7 30 E
Oberlin, Kans., U.S.A. 158 39 52N 100 31W
Oberlin, La., U.S.A. 159 30 42N 92 42W
Obernai 43 48 28N 7 30 E
Oberndorf 49 48 17N 8 35 E
Oberon 141 33 45 S 149 52 E
Oberösterreich □ 52 48 10N 14 0 E
Oberpfalzer Wald 49 49 30N 12 25 E
Oberseebach 51 48 53N 7 58 E
Obersiggenthal 51 47 29N 8 18 E
Oberstdorf 49 47 25N 10 16 E
Oberwil 50 47 32N 7 33 E
Obi, Kepulauan 103 1 30 S 127 30 E
Obiaruku 121 5 51N 6 9 E
Óbidos, Brazil 175 1 50 S 55 30W
Óbidos, Port. 57 39 19N 9 10W
Obihiro 112 42 25N 143 12 E
Obilnoye 83 47 32N 44 30 E
Öbisfelde 48 52 27N 10 57 E
Objat 44 45 16N 1 24 E
Obluchye 77 49 10N 130 50 E
Obninsk 81 55 8N 36 13 E
Obo, C. Afr. Emp. 123 5 20N 26 32 E
Obo, Ethiopia 123 3 34N 38 52 E
Oboa, Mt. 126 1 45N 34 45 E
Obock 123 12 0N 43 20 E
Oborniki 54 52 39N 16 59 E
Oborniki Śl. 54 51 17N 16 53 E
Obot 123 4 32N 37 13 E
Obout 121 3 28N 11 47 E
Oboyan 81 51 20N 36 28 E
Obrenovac 66 44 40N 20 11 E
O'Briensbridge 39 52 46N 8 30W
Obrovac 63 44 11N 15 41 E
Observatory Inlet 152 55 25N 129 45W
Obshchi Syrt 16 52 0N 53 0 E
Obskaya Guba 76 70 0N 73 0 E
Obuasi 121 6 17N 1 40W
Obubra 121 6 8N 8 20 E
Obyachevo 84 60 20N 49 37 E
Obzor 67 42 50N 27 52 E
Ocala 157 29 11N 82 5W
Ocampo 164 28 9N 108 8W
Ocaña 58 39 55N 3 30W
Ocanomowoc 158 43 7N 88 30W
Ocate 159 36 12N 104 59W
Occidental, Cordillera 174 5 0N 76 0W
Ocean City, Md., U.S.A. 162 38 20N 75 5W
Ocean City, N.J., U.S.A. 162 39 18N 74 34W
Ocean Falls 152 52 25N 127 40W
Ocean I. 130 0 45 S 169 50 E
Ocean Park 160 46 30N 124 2W
Oceanlake 160 45 0N 124 0W
Oceano 163 35 6N 120 37W
Oceanside 163 33 13N 117 26W
Ochagavia 58 42 55N 1 5W
Ochakov 82 46 35N 31 30 E
Ochamchire 83 42 46N 41 32 E
Ochamps 47 49 56N 5 16 E
Och'eng 109 30 20N 114 51 E
Ocher 84 57 53N 54 42 E
Ochiai 110 35 1N 133 45 E
Ochil Hills 35 56 14N 3 40W
Ochiltree 34 55 26N 4 23W
Ochre River 153 51 4N 99 47W
Ochsenfurt 49 49 38N 10 3 E
Ocilla 157 31 35N 83 12W
Ockelbo 72 60 54N 16 45 E
Ocmulgee, R. 157 32 0N 83 19W
Ocna Mureş 70 46 23N 23 49 E
Ocna-Sibiului 70 45 52N 24 2 E
Ocnele Mari 70 45 8N 24 18 E
Oconee, R. 157 32 30N 82 55W
Oconto 156 44 52N 87 53W
Oconto Falls 156 44 52N 88 10W
Ocós 166 14 31N 92 11W
Ocosingo 165 18 4N 92 15W
Ocotal 166 13 41N 86 41W
Ocotlán 164 20 21N 102 42W
Ocquier 47 50 24N 5 24 E
Ocreza, R. 56 39 50N 7 35W
Öcsa 53 47 17N 19 15 E
Octave 161 34 10N 112 43W
Octeville 42 49 38N 1 40W
Octyabrskoy Revolyutsii, Os. 77 79 30N 97 0 E
Ocumare del Tuy 174 10 7N 66 46W
Ocussi 103 9 20 S 124 30 E
Oda, Ghana 121 5 50N 1 5W
Oda, Ehime, Japan 110 33 36N 132 53 E
Oda, Shimane, Japan 110 35 11N 132 30 E
Ödåkra 73 56 9N 12 45 E
Ödåkra 73 56 7N 12 45 E
Odanakumadona 128 20 55 S 24 46 E
Ódáoahraun 74 65 5N 17 0W
Odate 112 40 16N 140 34 E
Odawara 111 35 20N 139 6 E
Odda 71 60 3N 6 35 E
Odder 73 55 58N 10 10 E
Oddobo 123 12 21N 42 6 E
Oddur 91 4 0N 43 35 E
Ödeborg 73 58 32N 11 58 E
Odei, R. 153 56 6N 96 54W
Odemira 57 37 35N 8 40W
Ödemiş 92 38 15N 28 0 E
Odense 73 55 22N 10 23 E
Odenton 162 39 5N 76 42W
Odenwald 48 49 18N 9 0 E
Oder, R. 48 53 0N 14 12 E
Oderzo 63 45 47N 12 29 E
Odessa, Del., U.S.A. 162 39 27N 75 40W
Odessa, Tex., U.S.A. 159 31 51N 102 23W
Odessa, Wash., U.S.A. 160 47 25N 118 35W
Odessa, U.S.S.R. 82 46 30N 30 45 E
Odiel, R. 57 37 30N 6 55W
Odienné 120 9 30N 7 34W
Odiham 29 51 16N 0 56W
Odin, gasfield 19 60 5N 2 10 E
Odoben 121 5 38N 0 56W
Odobeşti 70 45 43N 27 4 E
Odolanów 54 51 34N 17 40 E
O'Donnell 159 33 0N 101 48W
Odoorn 46 52 51N 6 51 E
Odorheiul Secuiesc 70 46 21N 25 21 E
Odoyevo 81 53 56N 36 42 E
Odra, R., Czech. 53 49 43N 17 47 E
Odra, R., Poland 54 52 40N 14 28 E
Odra, R., Spain 56 42 30N 4 15W
Odzaci 66 45 30N 19 17 E
Odzak 66 45 3N 18 18 E
Odzi 125 19 0 S 32 20 E
Oedelem 47 51 10N 3 21 E
Oegstgeest 46 52 11N 4 29 E
Oeiras, Brazil 170 7 0 S 42 8W
Oeiras, Port. 57 38 41N 9 18W
Oelrichs 158 43 11N 103 14W
Oelsnitz 48 50 24N 12 11 E
Oenpelli 136 12 20 S 133 4 E
Oensingen 50 47 17N 7 43 E
Oerhtossu, reg. 106 39 20N 108 30 E
Ofanto, R. 65 41 8N 15 50 E
Ofen Pass 51 46 37N 10 17 E
Offa 121 8 13N 4 42 E
Offaly □ 39 53 15N 7 30W
Offenbach 49 50 6N 8 46 E
Offenbeek 47 51 17N 6 5 E
Offenburg 126 48 27N 7 56 E
Offerdal 72 63 28N 14 0 E
Offida 63 42 56N 13 40 E
Offranville 42 49 52N 1 0 E
Ofidhousa, I. 69 36 33N 26 8 E
Ofotfjorden 74 68 27N 16 40 E
Oga-Hantō 111 39 58N 139 59 E
Ogahalla 150 50 6N 85 51W
Ogaki 111 35 21N 136 37 E
Ogallala 158 41 12N 101 40W
Ogbomosho 121 8 1N 3 29 E
Ogden, Iowa, U.S.A. 158 42 3N 94 0W
Ogden, Utah, U.S.A. 160 41 13N 112 1W
Ogdensburg 156 44 40N 75 27W
Ogeechee, R. 157 32 30N 81 32W
Oglio, R. 62 45 15N 10 15 E
Ogmore 138 22 37 S 149 35 E
Ogmore, R. 31 51 29N 3 37W
Ogmore Vale 30 51 35N 3 32W
Ogna 71 58 31N 5 48 E
Ognon, R. 43 47 43N 6 32 E
Ogoja 121 6 38N 8 39 E
Ogoki 150 51 35N 86 0W
Ogoki L. 150 50 50N 87 10W
Ogoki, R. 150 51 38N 85 57W
Ogoki Res. 150 50 45N 88 15W
Ogooué, R. 124 1 0 S 10 0 E
Ogori 110 34 6N 131 24 E
Ogosta, R. 67 43 35N 23 35 E
Ogowe, R. = Ogooué, R. 124 1 0 S 10 0 E
Ograzden 66 41 30N 22 50 E
Ogrein 122 17 55N 34 50 E
Ogulin 63 45 16N 15 16 E
Ogun □ 121 7 0N 3 0 E
Oguni 110 33 4N 131 2 E
Oguta 121 5 44N 6 44 E
Ogwashi-Uku 121 6 15N 6 30 E
Ogwe 121 5 0N 7 14 E
Ohai 143 44 55 S 168 0 E
Ohakune 142 39 24 S 175 24 E
Ohara 111 35 15N 140 23 E
Ohau, L. 143 44 15 S 169 53 E
Ohaupo 142 37 56 S 175 20 E
Ohey 47 50 26N 5 8 E
O'Higgins □ 172 34 15 S 71 1W
Ohio □ 156 40 20N 83 0W
Ohio, R. 156 38 0N 86 0W
Ohiwa Harbour 142 37 59 S 177 10 E
Ohre, R. 52 50 10N 12 30 E
Ohrid 66 41 8N 20 52 E
Ohridsko, Jezero 66 41 8N 20 52 E
Ohrigstad 129 24 41 S 30 36 E
Öhringen 49 49 11N 9 31 E
Oi Ho 108 28 37N 98 16 E
Oignies 47 50 28N 3 0 E
Oil City 156 41 26N 79 40W
Oildale 163 35 25N 119 1W
Oilgate 39 52 25N 6 30W
Oinousa, I. 69 38 33N 26 14 E
Oirschot 47 51 30N 5 18 E
Oise □ 43 49 28N 2 30 E
Oise, R. 43 49 53N 3 50 E
Oisterwijk 47 51 35N 5 12 E
Oita 110 33 14N 131 36 E
Oita-ken □ 110 33 15N 131 30 E
Oiticica 170 5 3 S 41 5W
Ojai 163 34 28N 119 16W
Ojinaga 164 29 34N 104 25W
Ojocaliente 164 30 25N 106 30W
Ojos del Salado 172 27 0 S 68 40W
Oka, R. 81 56 20N 43 59 E
Okahandja 128 22 0 S 16 59 E
Okahukura 142 38 48N 175 14 E
Okaihau 142 35 19 S 173 36 E
Okakune 142 39 26 S 175 24 E
Okanagan L. 152 50 0N 119 30W
Okanogan 160 48 22N 119 35W
Okanogan, R. 160 48 40N 119 24W
Okány 53 46 52N 21 21 E
Okapa 135 6 38 S 145 39 E
Okaputa 128 20 5 S 17 0 E
Okara 94 30 50N 73 25 E
Okarito 143 43 15 S 170 9 E
Okato 142 39 12 S 173 53 E
Okaukuejo 125 19 10 S 16 0 E
Okavango, R. = Cubango, R. 125 16 15 S 18 0 E
Okavango Swamp 128 19 30 S 23 0 E
Okawa 110 33 9N 130 21 E
Okaya 111 36 0N 138 10 E
Okayama 110 34 40N 133 54 E
Okayama-ken □ 110 35 0N 133 50 E
Okazaki 111 34 57N 137 10 E
Oke-Iho 121 8 1N 3 18 E
Okeechobee 157 27 16N 80 46W
Okeechobee L. 157 27 0N 80 50W
Okefenokee Swamp 157 30 50N 82 15W
Okehampton 30 50 44N 4 1W
Okene 121 7 32N 6 11 E
Oker, R. 48 52 7N 10 34 E
Okha 77 53 40N 143 0 E
Ókhi Óros 69 38 5N 24 25 E
Okhotsk 77 59 20N 143 10 E
Okhotsk, Sea of 77 55 0N 145 0 E
Okhotskiy Perevoz 77 61 52N 135 35 E
Okhotsko Kolymskoy 77 63 0N 157 0 E
Oki-no-Shima 110 32 44N 132 33 E
Oki-Shotō 110 36 15N 133 15 E
Okiep 128 29 39 S 17 53 E
Okigwi 121 5 52N 7 20 E
Okija 121 5 54N 6 55 E
Okinawa-Jima 112 26 32N 128 0 E
Okinawa-Shotō 112 27 0N 128 0 E
Okinoerabu-Jima 112 27 21N 128 33 E
Okitipupa 121 6 31N 4 50 E
Oklahoma □ 159 35 20N 97 30W
Oklahoma City 159 35 25N 97 30W
Okmulgee 159 35 38N 96 0W
Oknitsa 82 48 25N 27 20 E
Okolo 126 2 37N 31 8 E
Okondeka 128 21 38 S 15 37 E
Okondja 124 0 35 S 13 45 E
Okonek 54 53 32N 16 51 E
Okrika 121 4 47N 7 4 E
Oksby 73 55 33N 8 8 E
Oktyabr 85 43 41N 77 12 E
Oktyabrskiy 84 54 28N 53 28 E
Okuchi 110 32 4N 130 37 E
Okulovka 80 58 19N 33 28 E
Okuru 143 43 55 S 168 55 E
Okushiri-Tō 112 42 15N 139 30 E
Okuta 121 9 14N 3 12 E
Okwa, R. 128 22 25 S 22 30 E
Okwoga 121 7 3N 7 42 E
Ola 159 35 2N 93 10W
Ólafsfjörður 74 66 4N 18 39W
Ólafsvík 74 64 53N 23 43W
Olancha 163 36 15N 118 1W
Olancha Pk. 163 36 15N 118 7W
Olanchito 167 15 30N 86 30W
Öland 73 56 45N 16 50 E
Olargues 44 43 34N 2 53 E
Olary 140 32 18 S 140 19 E
Olascoaga 172 35 15 S 60 39W
Olathe 158 38 50N 94 50W
Olavarría 172 36 55 S 60 20W
Oława 54 50 57N 17 20 E
Ölbia 64 40 55N 9 30 E
Ölbia, G. di 64 40 55N 9 35 E
Old Bahama Chan. 166 22 10N 77 30W
Old Baldy Pk = San Antonio, Mt. 163 34 17N 117 38W
Old Castile = Castilla la Vieja 56 41 55N 4 0W
Old Castle 38 53 46N 7 10W
Old Cork 138 22 57 S 142 0 E
Old Dale 163 34 8N 115 47W
Old Deer 37 57 30N 2 3W
Old Dongola 122 18 11N 30 44 E
Old Factory 150 52 36N 78 43W
Old Forge, N.J., U.S.A. 162 43 43N 74 58W
Old Forge, N.Y., U.S.A. 162 43 43N 74 58W
Old Forge, Pa., U.S.A. 162 41 20N 75 46W
Old Fort, R. 153 58 36N 110 24W
Old Harbor 147 57 12N 153 22W
Old Kilpatrick 34 55 56N 4 34W
Old Leake 33 53 2N 0 6 E
Old Leighlin 39 52 46N 7 2W
Old Man of Hoy 37 58 53N 3 25W
Old Point Comfort 162 37 0N 76 20W
Old Radnor 31 52 14N 3 7W
Old Serenje 127 13 7 S 30 45 E
Old Shinyanga 126 3 33 S 33 27 E
Old Town 151 45 0N 68 50W
Old Wives L. 153 50 5N 106 0W
Oldbury 28 52 30N 2 0W
Oldeani 126 3 22 S 35 35 E
Oldenburg, Niedersachsen, Ger. 48 53 10N 8 10 E
Oldenburg, S.-Holst, Ger. 48 54 16N 10 53 E
Oldenzaal 46 52 19N 6 53 E
Oldham 32 53 33N 2 8W
Oldman, R. 152 49 57N 111 42W
Oldmeldrum 37 57 20N 2 19W

Olds Örken, L

Olds 152 51 50N 114 10W
Olean 156 42 8N 78 25W
Oléggio 62 45 36N 8 38 E
Oleiros 56 39 56N 7 56W
Olekma, R. 77 58 0N 121 30 E
Olekminsk 77 60 40N 120 30 E
Olema 163 38 3N 122 47W
Olen 47 51 9N 4 52 E
Olenek 77 68 20N 112 30 E
Olenek, R. 77 71 0N 123 50 E
Olenino 80 56 15N 33 20 E
Oléron, I. d' 44 45 55N 1 15W
Olesno 54 50 51N 18 26 E
Oleśnica 54 51 13N 17 22 E
Olevsk 80 51 18N 27 39 E
Olga 77 43 50N 135 0 E
Olga, L. 150 49 47N 77 15W
Olga, Mt. 137 25 20S 130 40 E
Olgastretet 12 78 35N 25 0 E
Ølgod 73 55 49N 8 36 E
Olgrinmole 37 58 29N 3 33W
Olhão 57 37 3N 7 48W
Olib 63 44 23N 14 44 E
Olib, I. 63 44 23N 14 44 E
Oliena 64 40 18N 9 22 E
Oliete 58 41 1N 0 41W
Olifants, R. 125 24 5S 31 20 E
Olifantshoek 128 27 57S 22 42 E
Ólimbos 69 35 44N 27 11 E
Ólimbos, Óros 68 40 6N 22 23 E
Olímpia 173 20 44S 48 54W
Olimpo□ 172 20 30S 58 45W
Olinda 170 8 1S 34 51W
Olindiná 170 11 22S 38 21W
Oling Hu 105 34 52N 97 30 E
Olite 58 42 29N 1 40W
Oliva, Argent. 172 32 0S 63 38W
Oliva, Spain 59 38 58N 0 15W
Oliva de la Frontera 57 38 17N 6 54W
Oliva, Punta del 56 43 37N 5 28W
Olivares 58 39 46N 2 20W
Oliveira, Bahia, Brazil 171 12 23S 38 35W
Oliveira, Minas Gerais, Brazil 171 20 50S 44 50W
Oliveira de Azemeis 56 40 49N 8 29W
Oliveira dos Brejinhos 171 12 19S 42 54W
Olivença 127 11 47S 35 13 E
Olivenza 57 38 41N 7 9W
Oliver 152 49 20N 119 30W
Oliver L. 153 56 56N 103 22W
Olivine Ra. 143 44 15S 168 30 E
Olivone 51 46 32N 8 57 E
Olkhovka 83 49 48N 44 32 E
Olkusz 54 50 18N 19 33 E
Ollagüe 172 21 15S 68 10W
Ollerton 33 53 12N 1 1W
Olloy 47 50 5N 4 36 E
Olmedo 56 41 20N 4 43W
Olmos, L. 172 33 25S 63 19W
Olney, U.K. 29 52 9N 0 42W
Olney, Ill., U.S.A. 156 38 40N 88 0W
Olney, Tex., U.S.A. 159 33 25N 98 45W
Olofström 73 56 17N 14 32 E
Oloma 121 3 29N 11 19 E
Olomane, R. 151 50 14N 60 37W
Olomouc 53 49 38N 17 12 E
Olonets 78 61 10N 33 0 E
Olongapo 103 14 50N 120 18 E
Oloron-Ste.-Marie 44 43 11N 0 38W
Olot 58 42 11N 2 30 E
Olovo 66 44 8N 18 35 E
Olovyannaya 77 50 50N 115 10 E
Olpe 48 51 2N 7 50 E
Olsene 47 50 58N 3 28 E
Olshanka 82 48 16N 30 58 E
Olst 46 52 20N 6 7 E
Olsztyn 54 53 48N 20 29 E
Olsztyn□ 54 54 0N 21 0 E
Olsztynek 54 53 34N 20 19 E
Olt□ 70 44 20N 24 30 E
Olt, R. 70 43 50N 24 40 E
Olten 50 47 21N 7 53 E
Oltenita 70 44 7N 26 42 E
Olton 159 34 16N 102 7W
Oltu 92 40 35N 41 50 E
Oluanpi 109 21 54N 120 51 E
Oluego 58 41 47N 2 0W
Olvera 57 36 55N 5 18W
Olympia, Greece 69 37 39N 21 39 E
Olympia, U.S.A. 160 47 0N 122 58W
Olympic Mts. 160 47 50N 123 45W
Olympic Nat. Park 160 47 48N 123 30W
Olympus, Mt. 160 47 52N 123 40W
Olympus, Mt. = Olimbos, Oros 68 40 6N 22 23 E
Olyphant 162 41 28N 75 37W
Om Hajer 123 14 20N 36 41 E
Om Koï 100 17 48N 98 22 E
Omachi 111 36 30N 137 50 E
Omae-Zaki 111 34 36N 138 14 E
Omagh 38 54 36N 7 20W
Omagh□ 38 54 35N 7 15W
Omaha 158 41 15N 96 0W
Omak 160 48 24N 119 31W
Oman■ 92 23 0N 58 0 E
Oman, G. of 93 24 30N 58 30 E
Omaruru 128 21 26S 16 0 E
Omaruru, R. 128 21 44S 14 30 E
Omate 174 16 45S 71 0W
Ombai, Selat 103 8 30S 124 50 E
Ombersley 28 52 17N 2 12W
Ombo 71 59 18N 6 0 E
Ombombo 128 18 43S 13 57 E
Omboué 124 1 35S 9 15 E
Ombrone, R. 62 42 48N 11 15 E
Omchi 119 21 22N 17 53 E
Omdraai 128 20 5S 21 56 E
Omdurmân 121 15 40N 32 28 E
Ome 111 35 47N 139 15 E
Omegna 62 45 52N 8 23 E
Omeonga 126 3 40S 24 22 E
Ometepe, Isla de 166 11 32N 85 35W
Ometepec 165 16 39N 98 23W
Omez 90 32 22N 35 0 E
Omi-Shima, Ehime, Japan 110 34 15N 133 0 E
Omi-Shima, Yamaguchi, Japan 110 34 15N 131 9 E
Omihachiman 111 35 7N 136 3 E
Omineca, R. 152 56 3N 124 16W
Omiš 63 43 28N 16 40 E
Omisalj 63 45 13N 14 32 E
Omitara 128 22 16S 18 2 E
Ōmiya 111 35 54N 139 38 E
Omme 73 55 56N 8 32 E
Ommen 46 52 31N 6 26 E
Ömnöovi□ 106 43 15N 104 0 E
Omono, R. 112 39 46N 140 3 E
Omsk 76 55 0N 73 38 E
Omsukchan 77 62 32N 155 48 E
Omul, Mt. 70 45 27N 25 29 E
Omura 110 33 8N 130 0 E
Omura-Wan 110 32 57N 129 52 E
Omuramba, R. 125 19 10S 19 20 E
Omurtag 67 43 8N 26 26 E
Ōmuta 110 33 0N 130 26 E
Omutninsk 84 58 45N 52 4 E
On 47 50 11N 5 18 E
On-Take 110 31 35N 130 39 E
Oña 58 42 43N 3 25W
Onaga 158 39 32N 96 12W
Onalaska 158 43 53N 91 14W
Onamia 158 46 4N 93 38W
Onancock 162 37 42N 75 49W
Onang 103 3 2S 118 55 E
Onaping L. 150 47 3N 81 30W
Onarheim 71 59 57N 5 35 E
Oñate 58 43 3N 2 25W
Onavas 164 28 28N 109 30W
Onawa 158 42 2N 96 2W
Onaway 156 45 21N 84 11W
Oncesti 70 43 56N 25 52 E
Onchan 32 54 11N 4 27W
Oncocua 128 16 30S 13 40 E
Onda 58 39 55N 0 17W
Ondaejin 107 41 34N 129 40 E
Ondangua 128 17 57S 16 4 E
Ondárroa 58 43 19N 2 25W
Ondas, R. 171 12 8S 45 0W
Ondava, R. 53 48 50N 21 40 E
Onderdijk 46 52 45N 5 8 E
Ondo, Japan 110 24 11N 132 32 E
Ondo, Nigeria 121 7 4N 4 47 E
Ondo□ 121 7 0N 5 0 E
Ondombo 128 21 3S 16 5 E
Öndörhaan 105 47 19N 110 39 E
Ondörshil 106 45 33N 108 5 E
Ondverdarnes 74 64 52N 24 0W
One Tree Hill 109 34 43S 138 46 E
Onega 78 64 0N 38 10 E
Onega, G. of = Onezhskaya G. 78 64 30N 37 0 E
Onega, L. = Onezhskoye Oz. 78 62 0N 35 30 E
Onega, R. 78 63 0N 39 0 E
Onehunga 142 36 55N 174 30 E
Oneida 162 43 5N 75 40W
Oneida L. 162 43 12N 76 0W
O'Neill 158 42 30N 98 38W
Onekotan, Ostrov 77 49 59N 154 0 E
Onema 126 4 35S 24 30 E
Oneonta, Ala., U.S.A. 157 33 58N 86 29W
Oneonta, N.Y., U.S.A. 162 42 26N 75 5W
Onerahi 142 35 45S 174 22 E
Onezhskaya Guba 78 64 30N 37 0 E
Onezhskoye Ozero 78 62 0N 35 30 E
Ongarue 142 38 42S 175 19 E
Ongerup 137 33 58S 118 28 E
Ongjin 107 37 56N 125 21 E
Ongkharak 100 14 8N 101 1 E
Ongoka 126 1 20S 26 0 E
Ongole 97 15 33N 80 2 E
Ongon 106 45 41N 113 5 E
Onhaye 47 50 15N 4 50 E
Oni 83 42 33N 43 26 E
Onida 158 44 42N 100 5W
Onilahy, R. 129 23 30S 44 0 E
Onitsha 121 6 6N 6 42 E
Onkaparinga, R. 109 35 2S 138 47 E
Onmaka 98 22 17N 96 41 E
Onny, R. 28 52 30N 2 50W
Ono, Japan 110 34 51N 134 56 E
Ono, Japan 111 35 59N 136 29 E
Onoda 110 33 59N 131 11 E
Onomichi 110 34 25N 133 12 E
Onpyŏngni 107 33 25N 126 55 E
Ons, Islas de 56 42 23N 8 55W
Onsala 73 57 26N 12 0 E
Onslow 136 21 40S 115 0 E
Onslow B. 157 34 10N 77 0W
Onstwedde 46 52 2N 7 4 E
Ontake-San 111 35 53N 137 29 E
Ontaneda 56 43 12N 3 57W
Ontario, Calif., U.S.A. 163 34 2N 117 40W
Ontario, Oreg., U.S.A. 160 44 1N 117 1W
Ontario□ 150 52 0N 88 10W
Ontario, L. 150 43 40N 78 0W
Onteniente 59 38 50N 0 35W
Ontonagon 158 46 52N 89 19W
Ontur 59 38 38N 1 29W
Onyx 163 35 41N 118 14W
Oodnadatta 139 27 33S 135 30 E
Ooglaamie 12 72 1N 157 0W
Ookala 147 20 1N 155 17W
Ooldea 137 30 27S 131 50 E
Ooltgensplaat 47 51 41N 4 21 E
Oona River 152 53 57N 130 16W
Oordegem 47 50 58N 3 54 E
Oorindi 138 20 40S 141 1 E
Oost-Vlaanderen□ 47 51 5N 3 50 E
Oost-Vlieland 46 53 18N 5 4 E
Oostakker 47 51 6N 3 46 E
Oostburg 47 51 19N 3 30 E
Oostduinkerke 47 51 7N 2 41 E
Oostelijk-Flevoland 46 52 31N 5 38 E
Oostende 47 51 15N 2 50 E
Oosterbeek 46 51 59N 5 51 E
Oosterdijk 46 52 44N 5 14 E
Oosterend, Frise, Neth. 46 53 24N 5 23 E
Oosterend, Holl. Sept., Neth. 46 53 5N 4 52 E
Oosterhout, Brabank, Neth. 47 51 39N 4 52 E
Oosterhout, Gueldre, Neth. 46 51 53N 5 50 E
Oosterschelde 47 51 33N 4 0 E
Oosterwolde 46 53 0N 6 17 E
Oosterzele 47 50 57N 3 48 E
Oostkamp 47 51 9N 3 14 E
Oostmalle 47 51 18N 4 44 E
Oostrozebekke 47 50 55N 3 21 E
Oostvleteven 47 50 56N 2 45 E
Oostvoorne 46 51 55N 4 5 E
Oostzaan 46 52 26N 4 52 E
Ootacamund 97 11 30N 76 44 E
Ootha 141 33 6S 147 29 E
Ootmarsum 46 52 24N 6 54 E
Ootsa L. 152 53 50N 126 20W
Ootsi 128 25 2S 25 45 E
Opaka 67 43 28N 26 10 E
Opala, U.S.S.R. 77 52 15N 156 15 E
Opala, Zaïre 124 1 11S 24 45 E
Opalenica 54 52 18N 16 24 E
Opalton 138 23 15S 142 46 E
Opan 67 42 13N 25 41 E
Opanake 97 6 35N 80 40 E
Opapa 142 39 47S 176 42 E
Opasatika 150 49 30N 82 50W
Opasquia 153 53 16N 93 34W
Opatija 63 45 21N 14 17 E
Opatów 54 50 50N 21 27 E
Opava 53 49 57N 17 58 E
Opawica, L. 150 49 35N 75 55W
Opeinde 46 53 8N 6 4 E
Opelousas 159 30 35N 92 0W
Opémisca L. 150 50 0N 75 0W
Open Bay Is. 143 43 51S 168 51 E
Opglabbeek 47 51 3N 5 35 E
Opheim 160 48 52N 106 30W
Ophir, U.K. 147 58 56N 3 11W
Ophir, U.S.A. 147 63 10N 156 40W
Ophthalmia Ra. 136 23 15S 119 30 E
Opi 121 6 36N 7 28 E
Opien 108 29 15N 103 24 E
Opinaca L. 150 52 39N 76 20W
Opinaca, R. 150 52 15N 78 2W
Opioo 47 51 37N 5 54 E
Opiskotish, L. 151 53 10N 67 50W
Opmeer 46 52 42N 4 57 E
Opobo 121 4 35N 7 34 E
Opochka 80 56 42N 28 45 E
Opoczno 54 51 22N 20 18 E
Opole 54 50 42N 17 58 E
Opole□ 54 50 40N 17 56 E
Oporto = Porto 56 41 8N 8 40W
Opotiki 142 38 1S 177 19 E
Opp 157 31 19N 86 13W
Oppegård 71 59 48N 10 48 E
Oppenheim 49 49 50N 8 22 E
Opperdoes 46 52 45N 5 4 E
Oppido Mamertina 65 38 16N 15 59 E
Oppland fylke□ 71 61 15N 9 30 E
Oppstad 71 60 17N 11 40 E
Opua 142 35 19S 174 9 E
Opunake 142 39 26S 173 52 E
Opuzen 66 43 1N 17 34 E
Or Yehuda 90 32 2N 34 50 E
Ora 63 46 20N 11 19 E
Ora Banda 137 30 20S 121 0 E
Oracle 161 32 45N 110 46W
Oradea 70 47 2N 21 58 E
Öræfajökull 74 64 2N 16 39W
Orahovac 66 42 24N 20 40 E
Orahovica 66 45 35N 17 52 E
Orai 95 25 58N 79 30 E
Oraison 45 43 55N 5 55 E
Oran, Alg. 118 35 37N 0 39W
Oran, Argent. 172 23 10S 64 20W
Oran, Ireland 38 53 40N 8 20W
Orange, Austral. 141 33 15S 149 7 E
Orange, France 45 44 8N 4 47 E
Orange, Calif., U.S.A. 163 33 47N 117 51W
Orange, Mass., U.S.A. 162 42 35N 72 15W
Orange, Tex., U.S.A. 159 30 0N 93 40W
Orange, Va., U.S.A. 156 38 17N 78 5W
Orange, C. 175 4 20N 51 30W
Orange Cove 163 36 38N 119 19W
Orange Free State = Oranje Vrystaat 128 28 30S 27 0 E
Orange Free State□ 128 28 30S 27 0 E
Orange Grove 159 27 57N 97 57W
Orange, R. = Oranje, R. 128 28 30S 18 0 E
Orange Walk 165 18 6N 88 33W
Orangeburg 157 33 27N 80 53W
Orangerie B. 138 10 30S 149 30 E
Orangeville 150 43 55N 80 5W
Oranienburg 48 52 45N 13 15 E
Oranje, R. 128 28 30S 18 0 E
Oranje Vrystaat□ 128 28 30S 27 0 E
Oranjemund (Orange Mouth) 128 28 32S 16 29 E
Oranmore 39 53 16N 8 57W
Orapa 128 21 13S 25 25 E
Oras 103 12 9N 125 22 E
Orašje 66 45 1N 18 42 E
Oraşul Stalin = Braşov 70 45 7N 25 39 E
Orava, R. 53 49 24N 19 20 E
Oraviţa 66 45 6N 21 43 E
Orb, R. 44 43 28N 3 5 E
Orba, R. 62 44 45N 8 40 E
Ørbæk 73 55 17N 10 39 E
Orbe 50 46 43N 6 32 E
Orbec 42 49 1N 0 23 E
Orbetello 63 42 26N 11 11 E
Órbigo, R. 56 42 40N 5 45W
Orbost 141 37 40S 148 29 E
Örbyhus 72 60 15N 17 43 E
Orbyhus 72 60 13N 17 43 E
Orce 59 37 44N 2 28W
Orce, R. 59 37 45N 2 30W
Orchies 43 50 28N 3 14 E
Orchila, Isla 167 11 48N 66 10W
Orco, R. 62 45 20N 7 45 E
Orcutt 163 34 52N 120 27W
Ord 136 17 23S 128 51 E
Ord, Mt. 136 17 20S 125 34 E
Ord, R. 136 15 33S 128 35 E
Ordenes 56 43 5N 8 29W
Orderville 161 37 18N 112 43W
Ordhead 37 57 10N 2 31W
Ordie 37 57 6N 2 54W
Ordos (Oerhtossu) 106 39 0N 108 0 E
Ordu 92 40 57N 37 53 E
Orduña 58 42 58N 2 58W
Orduña, Mte. 59 37 20N 3 30W
Ordway 158 38 15N 103 42W
Ordzhonikidze, R.S.F.S.R., U.S.S.R. 83 43 0N 44 35 E
Ordzhonikidze, Ukraine S.S.R., U.S.S.R. 82 47 32N 34 3 E
Ordzhonikidze, Uzbek S.S.R., U.S.S.R. 85 41 21N 69 22 E
Ordzhonikidzeabad 85 38 34N 69 1 E
Ore, Sweden 72 61 8N 15 10 E
Ore, Zaïre 126 3 17N 29 30 E
Ore Mts. = Erzgebirge 49 50 25N 13 0 E
Örebic 66 43 0N 17 11 E
Örebro 72 59 20N 15 18 E
Örebro län□ 72 59 27N 15 0 E
Oregon 158 42 1N 89 20W
Oregon□ 160 44 0N 120 0W
Oregon City 160 45 21N 122 35W
Öregrund 72 60 21N 18 30 E
Öregrundsgrepen 72 60 25N 18 15 E
Orekhov 82 47 30N 35 32 E
Orekhovo-Zuyevo 81 55 50N 38 55 E
Orel 81 52 57N 36 3 E
Orel, R. 82 49 5N 35 25 E
Orellana, Canal de 57 39 2N 6 0W
Orellana la Vieja 57 39 1N 5 32W
Orellana, Pantano de 57 39 5N 5 10W
Orem 160 40 27N 111 45W
Oren 69 37 3N 27 57 E
Orenburg 84 51 45N 55 6 E
Orense 56 42 19N 7 55W
Orense□ 56 42 15N 7 30W
Orepuki 143 46 19S 167 46 E
Orestiás 68 41 30N 26 33 E
Øresund 73 55 45N 12 45 E
Oreti, R. 143 45 39S 168 14 E
Orford 29 52 6N 1 31 E
Orford Ness 29 52 6N 1 31 E
Organá 58 42 13N 1 20 E
Orgaz 57 39 39N 3 53W
Orgeyev 82 47 9N 29 10 E
Orgon 45 43 47N 5 3 E
Orhon Gol, R. 105 50 21N 106 5 E
Oria 65 40 30N 17 38 E
Orient 139 28 7S 143 3 E
Orient Bay 150 49 20N 88 10W
Oriente 172 38 44S 60 37W
Origny 43 49 50N 3 30 E
Origny-Ste.-Benoîte 43 49 50N 3 30 E
Orihuela 59 38 7N 0 55W
Orihuela del Tremedal 58 40 33N 1 39W
Oriku 68 40 20N 19 30 E
Orinoco, Delta del 167 8 30N 61 0W
Orinoco, R. 174 5 45N 67 40W
Orion 153 49 28N 110 49W
Oriskany 162 43 9N 75 20W
Orissa□ 96 21 0N 85 0 E
Oristano 64 39 54N 8 35 E
Oristano, Golfo di 64 39 50N 8 22 E
Orizaba 165 18 50N 97 10W
Orizare 67 42 44N 27 39 E
Orizona 171 17 3S 48 18W
Ørje 71 59 29N 11 39 E
Orjen, mt. 66 42 35N 18 34 E
Orjiva 59 36 53N 3 24W
Orkanger 71 63 18N 9 52 E
Orkelljunga 73 56 17N 13 17 E
Örken, L. 73 57 11N 15 0 E

Örkény Owen

Örkény 53 47 9N 19 26E
Orkla 71 63 18N 9 51E
Orkla, R. 74 63 18N 9 51E
Orkney 128 26 42S 26 40E
Orkney □ 37 59 0N 3 0W
Orkney Is. 37 59 0N 3 0W
Orland 160 39 46N 122 12W
Orlando 157 28 30N 81 25W
Orlando, C.d' 65 38 10N 14 43E
Orléanais 43 48 0N 2 0E
Orléans 43 47 54N 1 52E
Orleans, I. d' 156 46 54N 70 58W
Orlice, R. 52 50 5N 16 10E
Orlické Hory 53 50 15N 16 30E
Orlov 53 49 17N 20 51E
Orlov Gay 81 51 4N 48 19E
Orlovat 66 45 14N 20 33E
Ormara 93 25 16N 64 33E
Ormea 62 44 9N 7 54E
Ormesby St. Margaret 29 52 39N 1 42E
Ormília 68 40 16N 23 33E
Ormoc 103 11 0N 124 37E
Ormond, N.Z. 142 38 33S 177 56E
Ormond, U.S.A. 157 29 13N 81 5W
Ormondville 142 40 5S 176 19E
Ormoz 63 46 25N 16 10E
Ormskirk 32 53 35N 2 53W
Ornans 43 47 7N 6 10E
Orne □ 42 48 40N 0 0E
Orneta 54 54 8N 20 9E
Ørnhøj 73 56 13N 8 34E
Ornö 72 59 4N 18 24E
Örnsköldsvik 72 63 17N 18 40E
Oro Grande 163 34 36N 117 20W
Oro, R. 164 26 8N 105 58W
Orocué 174 4 48N 71 20W
Orodo 121 5 34N 7 4E
Orogrande 161 32 20N 106 4W
Orol 56 43 34N 7 39W
Oromocto 151 45 54N 66 29W
Oron, Israel 90 30 55N 35 1E
Oron, Nigeria 121 4 48N 8 14E
Oron, Switz. 50 46 34N 6 50E
Oron, R. 77 69 21N 95 43E
Oronsay I. 34 56 0N 6 14W
Oronsay, Pass of 34 56 0N 6 10W
Oropesa 56 39 57N 5 10W
Oroquieta 103 8 32N 123 44E
Orori 107 40 1N 127 27E
Orós 170 6 15S 38 55W
Orosei, G. di 64 40 15N 9 40E
Orosháza 53 46 32N 20 42E
Orotukan 77 62 16N 151 42E
Oroville, Calif., U.S.A. 160 39 31N 121 30W
Oroville, Wash., U.S.A. 160 48 58N 119 30W
Orowia 143 46 1S 167 50E
Orphir 37 58 56N 3 8W
Orrefors 73 56 50N 15 45E
Orroroo 140 32 43S 138 38E
Orsa 72 61 7N 14 37E
Orsara di Puglia 65 41 17N 15 16E
Orsasjön 72 61 7N 14 37E
Orsha 80 54 30N 30 25E
Orsières 50 46 2N 7 9E
Orsk 84 51 12N 58 34E
Ørslev 73 55 23N 11 56E
Orsogna 63 42 13N 14 17E
Orşova 70 44 41N 22 25E
Ørsted 73 56 30N 10 20E
Orta, L. d' 62 45 48N 8 21E
Orta Nova 65 41 20N 15 40E
Orte 63 42 28N 12 23E
Ortegal, C. 56 43 43N 7 52W
Orthez 44 43 29N 0 48W
Ortho 47 50 8N 5 37E
Ortigueira 56 43 40N 7 50W
Ortles, mt. 62 46 31N 10 33E
Orto, Tokay 85 42 20N 76 1E
Ortón, R. 174 10 50S 67 0W
Orton Tebay 32 54 28N 2 35W
Ortona 63 42 21N 14 24E
Orune 64 40 25N 9 20E
Oruro 174 18 0S 67 19W
Orust 73 58 10N 11 40E
Orŭştie 70 45 50N 23 10E
Oruzgan 94 32 30N 66 35E
Orvault 42 47 17N 1 38E
Orvieto 63 42 43N 12 8E
Orwell 162 43 35N 75 60W
Orwell, R. 29 52 2N 1 12E
Orwigsburg 162 40 38N 76 6W
Oryakhovo 66 43 40N 23 57E
Orzinuovi 62 45 24N 9 55E
Orzysz 54 53 50N 21 58E
Os 71 60 9N 5 30E
Osa 84 57 17N 55 26E
Osa, Pen. de 166 8 0N 84 0W
Osage, Iowa, U.S.A. 158 43 15N 92 50W
Osage, Wyo., U.S.A. 158 43 59N 104 25W
Osage City 158 38 43N 95 51W
Osage, R. 158 38 15N 92 30W
Ōsaka 111 34 30N 135 30E
Osaka-fu □ 111 34 40N 135 30E
Osaka-Wan 111 34 30N 135 18E
Osan 107 37 11N 127 4E
Osawatomie 158 38 30N 94 55W
Osborne 158 39 30N 98 45W
Osby 73 56 23N 13 59E
Osceola, Ark., U.S.A. 159 35 40N 90 0W
Osceola, Iowa, U.S.A. 158 41 0N 93 20W
Oschatz 48 51 17N 13 8E
Oschersleben 48 52 2N 11 13E
Oschiri 64 40 43N 9 7E
Osečina 66 44 23N 19 34E
Ösel = Saaremaa 80 58 30N 22 30W
Osenovka 66 70 40N 120 50E
Osëry 81 54 52N 38 28E
Osh 85 40 37N 72 49E
Oshan 108 24 11N 102 24E
Oshawa 150 43 50N 78 45W
Oshikango 128 17 9S 16 10E
Oshima 110 33 11N 132 24E
Oshkosh, Nebr., U.S.A. 156 41 27N 102 20W
Oshkosh, Wis., U.S.A. 156 44 3N 88 35W
Oshmyany 80 54 26N 25 58E
Oshogbo 121 7 48N 4 37E
Oshwe 124 3 25S 19 28E
Osica de Jos 70 44 14N 24 20E
Osieczna 54 51 55N 16 40E
Osijek 66 45 34N 18 41E
Osilo 64 40 45N 8 41E
Osimo 63 43 40N 13 30E
Osintorf 80 54 34N 30 31E
Osipovichi 80 53 25N 28 33E
Oskaloosa 158 41 18N 92 40W
Oskarshamn 73 57 15N 16 27E
Oskelaneo 150 48 5N 75 15W
Oskol, R. 81 50 20N 38 0E
Oslo 71 59 55N 10 45E
Oslob 103 9 31N 123 26E
Oslofjorden 71 59 20N 10 35E
Osmanabad 96 18 5N 76 10E
Osmancık 82 40 45N 34 47E
Osmand Ra. 136 17 10S 128 45E
Osmaniye 92 37 5N 36 10E
Osmo 72 58 58N 17 55E
Osmotherley 33 54 22N 1 18W
Osnabrück 48 52 16N 8 2E
Osobláha 53 50 17N 17 44E
Osolo 71 59 53N 10 52E
Osona 128 22 3S 16 59E
Osorio 173 29 53S 50 17W
Osorno, Chile 176 40 25S 73 0W
Osorno, Spain 56 42 24N 4 22W
Osorno, Vol. 176 41 0N 72 30W
Osoyoos 152 49 0N 119 30W
Ospika, R. 152 56 20N 124 0W
Osprey Reef 138 13 52S 146 36E
Oss 46 51 46N 5 32E
Ossa de Montiel 59 38 58N 2 45W
Ossa, Mt. 138 41 52S 146 3E
Ossa, Oros 68 39 47N 22 42E
Ossabaw I. 157 31 45N 81 8W
Ossendrecht 47 51 24N 4 20E
Ossett 33 53 40N 1 35W
Ossining 162 41 9N 73 50W
Ossipee 162 43 41N 71 9W
Osśno Lubuskie 54 52 28N 14 51E
Ossokmanuan L. 151 53 25N 65 0W
Ossora 77 59 20N 163 13E
Oświęcim 54 50 2N 19 11E
Ostashkov 80 57 4N 33 2E
Oste, R. 48 53 30N 9 12E
Ostend = Oostende 47 51 15N 2 50E
Oster 80 50 57N 30 46E
Osterburg 48 52 47N 11 44E
Österby 72 60 13N 17 55E
Österbymo 73 57 49N 15 15E
Österdalälven 72 61 30N 13 45E
Östergötlands Län □ 72 58 35N 15 45E
Osterholz-Scharmbeck 48 53 14N 8 48E
Østerild 73 57 3N 8 50E
Østerild 73 57 2N 8 51E
Österkorsberga 73 57 18N 15 6E
Ostermundigen 50 46 58N 7 30E
Osterøya 71 60 32N 5 30E
Östersund 72 63 10N 14 38E
Østfold fylke □ 71 59 25N 11 25E
Ostfriesische Inseln 48 53 45N 7 15E
Ostia Lido (Lido di Roma) 64 41 43N 12 17E
Ostiglia 63 45 4N 11 9E
Ostrava 53 49 51N 18 18E
Ostrgrog 54 52 37N 16 33E
Ostróda 54 53 42N 19 58E
Ostrog 80 50 20N 26 30E
Ostrogozhsk 81 50 55N 39 7E
Ostrołeka 54 53 4N 21 38E
Ostrołeka □ 54 53 0N 21 30E
Ostrov, Bulg. 67 43 40N 24 9E
Ostrov, Rumania 70 44 6N 27 24E
Ostrov, U.S.S.R. 80 57 25N 28 20E
Ostrów Mazowiecka 54 52 50N 21 51E
Ostrów Wielkopolski 54 51 36N 17 44E
Ostrowiec-Swietokrzyski 54 50 55N 21 22E
Ostrozac 66 43 43N 17 49E
Ostrzeszów 54 51 25N 17 52E
Ostseebad-Kühlungsborn 48 54 10N 11 40E
Östsinni 71 60 53N 10 3E
Ostuni 65 40 44N 17 34E
Osum, R. 67 43 35N 25 0E
Osumi-Hanto 110 31 20N 130 55E
Osumi-Kaikyō 112 30 55N 130 50E
Osumi, R. 68 40 40N 20 10E
Osumi-Shoto 112 30 30N 130 40E
Osuna 57 37 14N 5 8W
Oswaldtwistle 32 53 43N 2 27W
Oswego 162 43 29N 76 30W
Oswestry 28 52 52N 3 3W
Ota, Japan 111 35 11N 136 38E
Ota, Japan 111 36 18N 139 22E
Ota-Gawa 110 34 21N 132 18E
Otago □ 143 45 20S 169 20E
Otago Harb. 143 45 47S 170 42E
Otago Pen. 143 45 48S 170 45E
Otahuhu 142 36 56S 174 51E
Otake 110 34 12N 132 13E
Otaki, Japan 111 35 17N 140 15E
Otaki, N.Z. 142 40 45S 175 10E
Otane 142 39 54S 176 39E
Otar 85 43 32N 75 12E
Otaru 112 43 10N 141 0E
Otaru-Wan 112 43 25N 141 1E
Otautau 143 46 9S 168 1E
Otava, R. 52 49 16N 13 32E
Otavalo 174 0 20N 78 20W
Otavi 128 19 40S 17 24E
Otchinjau 128 16 30S 13 56E
Otelec 66 45 36N 20 50E
Otero de Rey 56 43 6N 7 36W
Othello 160 46 53N 119 8W
Othonoí, I. 68 39 52N 19 22E
Othris, Mt. 69 39 4N 22 42E
Otira 143 42 49S 171 35E
Otira Gorge 143 42 53S 171 33E
Otis 158 40 12N 102 58W
Otjiwarongo 128 20 30S 16 33E
Otley 33 53 54N 1 41W
Otmuchow 54 50 28N 17 10E
Otočac 63 44 53N 15 12E
Otoineppu 112 44 44N 142 16E
Otorohanga 142 38 12S 175 14E
Otoskwin, R. 150 52 13N 88 6W
Otosquen 153 53 17N 102 1W
Otoyo 110 33 43N 133 45E
Otra 71 58 8N 8 1E
Otranto 65 40 9N 18 28E
Otranto, C.d' 65 40 7N 18 30E
Otranto, Str. of 65 40 15N 18 40E
Otrøy 71 62 43N 6 50E
Otsuki 111 35 36N 138 57E
Otta 71 61 46N 9 32E
Ottapalam 97 10 46N 76 23E
Ottawa, Can. 150 45 27N 75 42W
Ottawa, Ill., U.S.A. 156 41 20N 88 55W
Ottawa, Kans., U.S.A. 158 38 40N 95 10W
Ottawa Is. 149 59 35N 80 16W
Ottawa, R. 150 47 45N 78 35W
Ottélé 121 3 38N 11 19E
Ottenby 73 56 15N 16 24E
Otter L. 153 55 35N 104 39W
Otter R. 30 50 47N 3 12W
Otter Rapids, Ont., Can. 150 50 11N 81 39W
Otter Rapids, Sask., Can. 153 55 38N 104 44W
Otterburn 35 55 14N 2 12W
Otterndorf 48 53 47N 8 52E
Otteröy, I. 71 62 45N 6 50E
Ottersheim 52 48 21N 14 12E
Otterup 73 55 30N 10 22E
Ottery St. Mary 30 50 45N 3 16W
Ottignies 47 50 40N 4 33E
Otto Beit Bridge 127 15 59S 28 56E
Ottosdal 128 26 46S 25 59E
Ottoshoop 128 25 45S 26 58E
Ottsjö 72 63 13N 13 2E
Ottter Ferry 34 56 1N 5 20W
Ottumwa 158 41 0N 92 25W
Otu 121 8 14N 3 22E
Otukpa (Al Owuho) 121 7 9N 7 41E
Oturkpo 121 7 10N 8 15E
Otway, Bahia 176 53 30S 74 0W
Otway, C. 140 38 52S 143 30E
Otwock 54 52 5N 21 20E
Ötz 52 47 13N 10 53E
Ötz, Fl. 52 47 13N 10 53E
Ötz, R. 52 47 14N 10 50E
Ötztaler Alpen 52 46 58N 11 0E
Ou, Neua 100 22 18N 101 48E
Ou, R. 100 20 4N 102 13E
Ouachita Mts. 159 34 50N 94 30W
Ouachita, R. 159 33 0N 92 15W
Ouadane 116 20 50N 11 40W
Ouadda 117 8 15N 22 20E
Ouagadougou 121 12 25N 1 30W
Ouahigouya 120 13 40N 2 25W
Ouahila 118 27 50N 5 0W
Ouahran = Oran 118 35 37N 0 39W
Oualâta 121 17 20N 6 55W
Ouallene 118 24 41N 1 11E
Ouanda Djallé 117 8 55N 22 53E
Ouango 124 4 19N 22 30E
Ouargla 119 31 59N 5 25E
Ouarkziz, Djebel 118 28 50N 8 0W
Ouarzazate 118 30 55N 6 55W
Ouatagouna 121 15 11N 0 43E
Oubangi, R. 124 1 0N 17 50E
Oubarakai, O. 119 27 20N 9 0E
Ouche, R. 43 47 11N 5 10E
Oud-Gastel 47 51 35N 4 28E
Oud Turnhout 47 51 19N 5 0E
Ouddorp 46 51 50N 3 57E
Oude-Pekela 46 53 6N 7 0E
Oude Rijn, R. 46 52 12N 4 24E
Oudega 46 53 8N 6 0E
Oudenaarde 47 50 50N 3 37E
Oudenbosch 47 51 35N 4 32E
Oudenburg 47 51 11N 3 1E
Ouderkerk, Holl. Mérid., Neth. 46 51 56N 4 38E
Ouderkerk, Utrecht, Neth. 46 52 18N 4 55E
Oudeschild 46 53 2N 4 50E
Oudewater 46 52 2N 4 52E
Oudkarspel 46 52 43N 4 49E
Oudon 42 47 22N 1 19W
Oudon, R. 42 47 47N 1 2W
Oudtshoorn 128 33 35S 22 14E
Oued Sbita 118 25 50N 5 2W
Ouellé 120 7 26N 4 1W
Ouessa 120 11 4N 2 47W
Ouessant, Île d' 42 48 28N 5 6W
Ouesso 124 1 37N 16 5E
Ouezzane 118 34 51N 5 42W
Ouffet 47 50 26N 5 28E
Oughter L. 38 54 2N 7 30W
Oughterard 38 53 26N 9 20W
Ougrée 47 50 36N 5 32E
Ouidah 121 6 25N 2 0E
Ouimet 150 48 43N 88 35W
Ouistreham 42 49 17N 0 18W
Ouj, R. 118 51 15N 29 45E
Oujda □ 118 33 18N 1 25W
Oujeft 116 20 2N 13 0W
Oulad Naïl, Mts. des 118 34 30N 3 30E
Ouled Djellal 119 34 28N 5 2E
Oulmès 118 33 17N 6 0W
Oulton 29 52 29N 1 40E
Oulton Broad 29 52 28N 1 43E
Oulu 74 65 1N 25 29E
Oulu □ 74 65 10N 27 20E
Oulujärvi 74 64 25N 27 0E
Oulujoki 74 64 45N 26 30E
Oulun Lääni □ 74 64 36N 27 20E
Oulx 62 45 2N 6 49E
Oum el Bouaghi 119 35 55N 7 6E
Oum el Ksi 118 29 4N 6 59W
Oum-er-Rbia 118 32 30N 6 30W
Oum-er-Rbia, O. 118 32 30N 6 30W
Oumè 120 5 21N 5 27W
Ounane, Dj. 119 25 4N 7 10E
Ounasjoki 74 66 31N 25 44E
Oundle 29 52 28N 0 28W
Ounguati 128 21 54S 15 46E
Ounianga Kébir 117 19 4N 20 29E
Ounlivou 121 7 20N 1 34E
Our, R. 47 49 55N 6 5E
Ouray 161 38 3N 107 48W
Oureg, Oued el 118 32 34N 2 10E
Ourém 170 1 33S 47 6W
Ouricuri 170 7 53S 40 5W
Ourinhos 173 23 0S 49 54W
Ourini 117 16 7N 22 25E
Ourique 57 37 38N 8 16W
Ouro Fino 173 22 16S 46 25W
Ouro Prêto 173 20 20S 43 30W
Ouro Sogui 120 15 36N 13 19W
Oursi 121 14 41N 0 27W
Ourthe, R. 47 50 29N 5 35E
Ouse 138 42 25S 146 42E
Ouse, R., Sussex, U.K. 29 50 58N 0 3E
Ouse, R., Yorks., U.K. 33 54 3N 0 7E
Oust 44 42 52N 1 13E
Oust, R. 42 48 8N 2 49W
Out Skerries, Is. 36 60 25N 0 50W
Outardes, R. 151 50 0N 69 4W
Outer Hebrides, Is. 36 57 30N 7 40W
Outer I. 151 51 10N 58 35W
Outes 56 42 52N 8 55W
Outjo 128 20 5S 16 7E
Outlook, Can. 153 51 30N 107 0W
Outlook, U.S.A. 158 48 53N 104 46W
Outreau 43 50 40N 1 36E
Outwell 29 52 36N 0 14E
Ouyen 140 35 1S 142 22E
Ouzouer-le-Marché 42 47 54N 1 32E
Ovada 62 44 39N 8 40E
Ovalle 172 30 33S 71 18W
Ovamboland = Owambo 128 17 20S 16 30E
Ovar 56 40 51N 8 40W
Ovejas 174 9 32N 75 14W
Ovens 141 36 35S 146 46E
Over Flakkee, I. 47 51 45N 4 5E
Over Wallop 28 51 9N 1 35W
Overbister 37 59 16N 2 33W
Overdinkel 46 52 14N 7 2E
Overflakkee 46 51 44N 4 10E
Overijse 47 50 47N 4 32E
Overijssel 46 50 46N 4 32E
Overijssel □ 46 52 25N 6 35E
Overijsselsch Kanaal 46 52 31N 6 35E
Överkalix 74 66 19N 22 50E
Overpelt 47 51 12N 5 20E
Overstand 29 52 55N 1 20W
Overton, Clwyd, U.K. 31 52 58N 2 56W
Overton, Hants, U.K. 28 51 14N 1 16W
Overton, U.S.A. 161 36 32N 114 31W
Övertorneå 74 66 23N 23 40E
Overum 73 58 0N 16 20E
Ovid, Colo., U.S.A. 158 41 0N 102 17W
Ovid, N.Y., U.S.A. 162 42 41N 76 49W
Ovidiopol 82 46 15N 30 30E
Oviedo 56 43 25N 5 50W
Oviedo □ 56 43 20N 6 0W
Oviken 72 63 0N 14 23E
Oviksfjällen 72 63 0N 13 49E
Övör Hangay □ 106 45 0N 102 30E
Ovoro 121 5 26N 7 16E
Övre Sirdal 71 58 48N 6 43E
Øvre Sirdal 71 58 48N 6 47E
Ovruch 80 51 25N 28 45E
Owaka 143 46 27S 169 40E
Owambo 128 17 20S 16 30E
Owasco L. 162 42 50N 76 31W
Owase 111 34 7N 136 5E
Owatonna 158 44 3N 93 17W
Owego 162 42 6N 76 17W
Owel, L. 38 53 34N 7 24W
Owen 140 34 15S 138 32E

Owen Falls	**126**	0 30N	33 5 E
Owen Mt.	**143**	41 35 S	152 33 E
Owen Sound	**150**	44 35N	80 55W
Owen Stanley Range	**135**	8 30 S	147 0 E
Owendo	**124**	0 17N	9 30 E
Oweniny R.	**38**	54 13N	9 32W
Owenkillew R.	**38**	54 44N	7 15W
Owens L.	**163**	36 20N	118 0W
Owens, R.	**163**	36 32N	117 59W
Owensboro	**156**	37 40N	87 5W
Owensville	**158**	38 20N	91 30W
Owerri	**121**	5 29N	7 0 E
Owhango	**142**	39 51 S	175 20 E
Owl, R.	**153**	57 51N	92 44W
Owo	**121**	7 18N	5 30 E
Owosso	**156**	43 0N	84 10W
Owston Ferry	**33**	53 28N	0 47W
Owyhee	**160**	42 0N	116 3W
Owyhee, R.	**160**	43 10N	117 37W
Owyhee Res.	**160**	43 30N	117 30W
Ox Mts.	**38**	54 6N	9 0W
Oxberg	**72**	61 7N	14 11 E
Oxelösund	**73**	58 43N	17 15 E
Oxford, N.Z.	**143**	43 18 S	172 11 E
Oxford, U.K.	**28**	51 45N	1 15W
Oxford, Mass., U.S.A.	**162**	42 7N	71 52W
Oxford, Miss., U.S.A.	**159**	34 22N	89 30W
Oxford, N.C., U.S.A.	**156**	36 19N	78 36W
Oxford, N.Y., U.S.A.	**162**	42 27N	75 36W
Oxford, Ohio, U.S.A.	**156**	39 30N	84 40W
Oxford, Pa., U.S.A.	**162**	39 47N	75 59W
Oxford □	**28**	51 45N	1 15W
Oxford L.	**153**	54 51N	95 37W
Oxilithos	**69**	38 35N	24 7 E
Oxley	**140**	34 11 S	144 6 E
Oxley Cr.	**108**	27 35 S	153 0 E
Oxnard	**163**	34 10N	119 14W
Oya	**102**	2 55N	111 55 E
Oyabe	**111**	36 47N	136 56 E
Oyama	**111**	36 18N	139 48 E
Oyana	**110**	32 32N	130 18 E
Oyem	**124**	1 42N	11 43 E
Oyen	**153**	51 22N	110 28W
Øyeren	**71**	59 48N	11 14 E
Öyeren	**71**	59 50N	11 15 E
Oykel Bridge	**37**	57 58N	4 45W
Oykell, R.	**37**	57 55N	4 26W
Oymyakon	**77**	63 25N	143 10 E
Oyo	**121**	7 46N	3 56 E
Oyo □	**121**	8 0N	3 30 E
Oyonnax	**45**	46 16N	5 40 E
Oyster B.	**138**	42 15 S	148 5 E
Öystese	**71**	60 22N	6 9 E
Øystese	**71**	60 24N	6 12 E
Oytal	**85**	42 54N	73 17 E
Ozamis (Mizamis)	**103**	8 15N	123 50 E
Ozark, Ala., U.S.A.	**157**	31 29N	85 39W
Ozark, Ark., U.S.A.	**159**	35 30N	93 50W
Ozark, Mo., U.S.A.	**159**	37 0N	93 15W
Ozark Plateau	**159**	37 20N	91 40W
Ozarks, L. of	**158**	38 10N	93 0W
Ózd	**53**	48 14N	20 15 E
Ozerhinsk	**80**	53 40N	27 7 E
Ozërnyy	**84**	51 8N	60 50 E
Ozieri	**64**	40 35N	9 0 E
Ozimek	**54**	50 41N	18 11 E
Ozona	**159**	30 43N	101 11W
Ozorków	**54**	51 57N	19 16 E
Ozren, Mt.	**66**	43 55N	18 29 E
Ozu	**110**	33 30N	132 33 E
Ozu Kumamoto	**110**	32 52N	130 52 E
Ozuluama	**165**	21 40N	97 50W
Ozun	**70**	45 47N	25 50 E

P

Pa	**120**	11 33N	3 19W
Pa-an	**98**	16 45N	97 40 E
Pa Mong Dam	**100**	18 0N	102 22 E
Pa Sak, R.	**101**	15 30N	101 0 E
Paal	**47**	51 2N	5 10 E
Paar, R.	**49**	48 42N	11 27 E
Paarl	**128**	33 45 S	18 56 E
Paatsi, R.	**74**	68 55N	29 0 E
Paauilo	**147**	20 3N	155 22W
Pab Hills	**94**	26 30N	66 45 E
Pabbay I.	**36**	57 46N	7 12W
Pabbay, Sd. of	**36**	57 45N	7 4W
Pabianice	**54**	51 40N	19 20 E
Pabna	**98**	24 1N	89 18 E
Pabo	**126**	2 56N	32 3 E
Pacajá, R.	**170**	1 56 S	50 50W
Pacajus	**170**	4 10 S	38 38W
Pacasmayo	**174**	7 20 S	79 35W
Pacaudière, La	**43**	46 11N	3 52 E
Paceco	**64**	37 59N	12 32 E
Pachhar	**94**	24 40N	77 42 E
Pachino	**65**	36 43N	15 4 E
Pacho	**174**	5 8N	74 10W
Pachora	**96**	20 38N	75 29 E
Pachpadra	**93**	25 58N	72 10 E
Pachuca	**165**	20 10N	98 40W
Pachung	**108**	31 58N	106 40 E
Pacific	**152**	54 48N	128 28W
Pacific Grove	**163**	36 38N	121 58W
Pacific Ocean	**143**	10 0N	140 0W
Pacifica	**163**	37 36N	122 30W
Packsaddle	**140**	30 36 S	141 58 E
Pacoh	**152**	53 0N	132 30W
Pacov	**52**	49 27N	15 0 E
Pacsa	**53**	46 44N	17 2 E
Pacuí, R.	**171**	16 46 S	45 1W
Pacy-sur-Eure	**171**	49 1N	1 23 E
Paczkow	**54**	50 28N	17 0 E
Padaido, Kepulauan	**103**	1 5 S	138 0 E
Padalarang	**103**	7 50 S	107 30 E
Padang	**102**	1 0 S	100 20 E
Padang, I.	**102**	1 0 S	100 10 E
Padangpanjang	**102**	0 30 S	100 20 E
Padangsidimpuan	**102**	1 30N	99 15 E
Padatchuang	**98**	19 41N	96 35 E
Padborg	**73**	54 49N	9 21 E
Paddock Wood	**29**	51 13N	0 24 E
Paddockwood	**153**	53 30N	105 30W
Paderborn	**48**	51 42N	8 44 E
Padesul	**70**	45 40N	22 22 E
Padiham	**32**	53 48N	2 20W
Padina	**70**	44 50N	27 8 E
Padlei	**153**	62 10N	97 5W
Padloping Island	**149**	67 0N	63 0W
Padma, R.	**98**	23 22N	90 32 E
Padmanabhapuram	**97**	8 16N	77 17 E
Pádova	**63**	45 24N	11 52 E
Padra	**94**	22 15N	73 7 E
Padrauna	**95**	26 54N	83 59 E
Padre I.	**159**	27 0N	97 20W
Padrón	**56**	42 41N	8 39W
Padstow	**32**	50 33N	4 57W
Padstow Bay	**30**	50 35N	4 58W
Padua = Pádova	**63**	45 24N	11 52 E
Paducah, Ky., U.S.A.	**156**	37 0N	88 40W
Paducah, Tex., U.S.A.	**159**	34 3N	100 16W
Padul	**57**	37 1N	3 38W
Padula	**65**	40 20N	15 40 E
Padwa	**96**	18 27N	82 37 E
Paekakariki	**142**	40 59 S	174 58 E
Paektu-san	**107**	42 0N	128 3 E
Paengaroa	**142**	37 49 S	176 29 E
Paengnyŏng Do	**107**	37 57N	124 40 E
Paeroa	**142**	37 23 S	175 41 E
Paesana	**62**	44 40N	7 18 E
Pag	**63**	44 27N	15 5 E
Pag, I.	**63**	44 50N	15 0 E
Paga	**121**	11 1N	1 8W
Pagadian	**103**	7 55N	123 30 E
Pagai Selatan, I.	**102**	3 0 S	100 15W
Pagai Utara, I.	**102**	2 35 S	100 0 E
Pagalu, I.	**114**	1 35 S	3 35 E
Pagaralam	**102**	4 0 S	103 17 E
Pagastikós Kólpos	**68**	39 15N	23 12 E
Pagatan	**102**	3 33 S	115 59 E
Page	**158**	47 11N	97 37W
Paglieta	**63**	42 10N	14 30 E
Pagnau	**123**	8 15N	34 7 E
Pagny-sur-Moselle	**43**	48 59N	6 2 E
Pagosa Springs	**161**	37 16N	107 4W
Pagwa River	**150**	50 2N	85 14W
Pahala	**147**	20 25N	156 0W
Pahang □	**101**	3 40N	102 20 E
Pahang, R.	**101**	3 30N	103 9 E
Pahang, st.	**101**	3 30N	103 9 E
Pahiatua	**142**	40 27 S	175 50 E
Pahoa	**147**	19 30N	154 57W
Pahokee	**157**	26 50N	80 30W
Pahrump	**161**	36 15N	116 0W
Pahsien	**106**	39 10N	116 20 E
Pahsientung	**107**	43 11N	120 57 E
Pai	**100**	19 19N	98 27 E
Paia	**147**	20 54N	156 22W
Paible	**36**	57 35N	7 30W
Paich'eng	**105**	45 40N	122 52 E
Paich'i	**109**	28 2N	111 18 E
P'aichou	**109**	30 12N	113 56 E
Paicines	**163**	36 44N	121 17W
Paide	**80**	58 57N	25 31 E
Paignton	**30**	50 26N	3 33W
Paiho, China	**109**	32 49N	110 3 E
Paiho, Taiwan	**109**	23 21N	120 25 E
Paihok'ou	**109**	31 46N	110 13 E
Päijänne	**75**	61 30N	25 30 E
Pailin	**101**	12 46N	102 36 E
Pailolo Chan.	**147**	21 5N	156 42W
Paimbœuf	**42**	47 17N	2 0W
Paimboeuf	**44**	47 17N	2 2W
Paimpol	**42**	48 48N	3 4W
Painan	**102**	1 15 S	100 40 E
Painesville	**156**	41 42N	81 18W
Painiu	**109**	32 51N	112 10 E
Painscastle	**31**	52 7N	3 13W
Painswick	**28**	51 47N	2 11W
Paint l.	**153**	55 28N	97 57W
Painted Desert	**161**	36 40N	112 0W
Paintsville	**156**	37 50N	82 50W
Paipa	**174**	5 47N	73 7W
Paise	**108**	23 55N	106 28 E
Paisha	**106**	34 23N	112 32 E
Paisley, U.K.	**34**	55 51N	4 27W
Paisley, U.S.A.	**160**	42 43N	120 40W
Paita	**174**	5 5 S	81 0W
Paiva, R.	**56**	40 50N	7 55W
Paiyin	**105**	36 45N	104 4 E
Paiyü	**99**	31 12N	98 45 E
Paiyunopo	**106**	41 46N	109 58 E
Pajares	**56**	39 57N	1 48W
Pak Lay	**100**	18 15N	101 27 E
Pak Phanang	**101**	8 21N	100 12 E
Pak Sane	**100**	18 22N	103 39 E
Pak Song	**100**	15 11N	106 14 E
Pak Suong	**100**	19 58N	102 15 E
Pakala	**97**	13 29N	79 8 E
Pakanbaru	**102**	0 30N	101 15 E
Pakaraima, Sierra	**174**	6 0N	60 0W
Pakemba	**127**	13 3 S	29 58 E
Pakenham	**141**	38 6 S	145 30 E
Pakhoi = Peihai	**108**	21 30N	109 5 E
Pakhtakor	**85**	40 2N	65 46 E
Pakistan ■	**93**	30 0N	70 0 E
Pakistan, East = Bangladesh ■	**99**	24 0N	90 0 E
Pakkading	**100**	18 19N	103 59 E
Paknam = Samut Prakan	**100**	13 36N	100 36 E
P'ako	**105**	30 52N	81 19 E
Pakokku	**98**	21 30N	95 0 E
Pakpattan	**94**	30 25N	73 16 E
Pakrac	**66**	45 27N	17 12 E
Paks	**53**	46 38N	18 55 E
Pakse	**100**	15 5N	105 52 E
Paksikori	**107**	42 27N	130 31 E
Paktya □	**93**	33 0N	69 15 E
Pakwach	**126**	2 28N	31 27 E
Pal	**93**	33 45N	79 33 E
Pala, Chad	**117**	9 25N	15 5 E
Pala, U.S.A.	**163**	33 22N	117 5W
Pala, Zaïre	**126**	6 45 S	29 30 E
Palabek	**126**	3 22N	32 33 E
Palacious	**159**	28 44N	96 12W
Palafrugell	**58**	41 55N	3 10 E
Palagiano	**65**	40 35N	17 0 E
Palagonia	**65**	37 20N	14 43 E
Palagruza	**63**	42 24N	16 15 E
Palaiókastron	**69**	35 12N	26 18 E
Palaiokhora	**69**	35 16N	23 39 E
Pálairos	**69**	38 45N	20 51 E
Palais, Le	**42**	47 20N	3 10W
Palakol	**96**	16 31N	81 46 E
Palam	**96**	19 0N	77 0 E
Palamás	**68**	39 26N	22 4 E
Palamós	**58**	41 50N	3 10 E
Palampur	**94**	32 10N	76 30 E
Palana, Austral.	**138**	39 45 S	147 55 E
Palana, U.S.S.R.	**77**	59 10N	160 10 E
Palanan	**103**	17 8N	122 29 E
Palandri	**95**	33 42N	73 40 E
Palanpur	**94**	24 10N	72 25 E
Palapye	**128**	22 30 S	27 7 E
Palar, R.	**97**	12 27N	80 13 E
Palas	**95**	35 4N	73 4 E
Palatka	**157**	29 40N	81 40W
*Palau Is.	**130**	7 30N	134 30 E
Palauig	**103**	15 26N	119 54 E
Palauk	**101**	13 10N	98 40 E
Palavas	**44**	43 32N	3 56 E
Palawan, I.	**102**	10 0N	119 0 E
Palayancottai	**97**	8 45N	77 45 E
Palazzo San Gervásio	**65**	40 53N	15 58 E
Palazzolo Acreide	**65**	37 4N	14 43 E
Paldiski	**80**	59 23N	24 9 E
Pale	**66**	43 50N	18 38 E
Palel	**98**	24 27N	94 2 E
Paleleh	**103**	1 10N	121 50 E
Palembang	**102**	3 0 S	104 50 E
Palencia	**56**	42 1N	4 34W
Palencia □	**56**	42 31N	4 33W
Palermo, Colomb.	**174**	2 54N	75 26W
Palermo, Italy	**64**	38 8N	13 20 E
Palermo, U.S.A.	**160**	39 30N	121 37W
Palestine, Asia	**90**	32 0N	35 0 E
Palestine, U.S.A.	**159**	31 42N	95 35W
Palestrina	**64**	41 50N	12 52 E
Paletwa	**98**	21 30N	92 50 E
Palghat	**97**	10 46N	76 42 E
Palgrave	**29**	52 22N	1 7 E
Palgrave, Mt.	**136**	23 22 S	115 58 E
P'ali	**105**	27 45N	89 10 E
Pali	**94**	25 50N	73 20 E
Palik'un	**105**	43 35N	92 51 E
Palimé	**121**	6 57N	0 37 E
Palintaoch'i	**107**	43 59N	119 20 E
Palinuro, C.	**65**	40 1N	15 14 E
Palinyuch'i (Tapanshang)	**107**	43 40N	118 20 E
Palisade	**158**	40 35N	101 10W
Paliseul	**47**	49 54N	5 8 E
Palitana	**94**	21 32N	71 49 E
Palizada	**165**	18 18N	92 8W
Palizzi	**65**	37 58N	15 59 E
Palk Bay	**97**	9 30N	79 30 E
Palk Strait	**97**	10 0N	80 0 E
Palkonda	**96**	18 36N	83 48 E
Palkonda Ra.	**97**	13 50N	79 20 E
Pallasgreen	**39**	52 35N	8 22W
Pallaskenry	**39**	52 39N	8 53W
Pallasovka	**81**	50 4N	47 0 E
Palleru, R.	**96**	17 30N	79 40 E
Pallinup	**137**	34 0 S	117 55 E
Pallisa	**126**	1 12N	33 43 E
Palliser Bay	**142**	41 26 S	175 5 E
Palliser, C.	**142**	41 37 S	175 14 E
Pallu	**94**	28 59N	74 14 E
Palm Beach	**157**	26 46N	80 0W
Palm Desert	**163**	33 43N	116 22W
Palm Is.	**138**	18 40 S	146 35 E
Palm Springs	**163**	33 51N	116 35W
Palma, Canary Is.	**16**	28 40N	17 50W
Palma, Mozam.	**127**	10 46 S	40 29 E
Palma, Spain	**58**	39 33N	2 39 E
Palma, Bahía de	**59**	39 30N	2 39 E
Palma del Río	**57**	37 43N	5 17W
Palma di Montechiaro	**64**	37 12N	13 46 E
Palma, I.	**116**	28 45N	17 50W
Palma, La, Panama	**166**	8 15N	78 0W
Palma, La, Spain	**57**	37 21N	6 38W
Palma, R.	**171**	10 10N	71 50W
Palma Soriano	**166**	20 15N	76 0W
Palmanova	**63**	45 54N	13 18 E
Palmares	**170**	8 41 S	35 36W
Palmarito	**174**	7 37N	70 10W
Palmarola, I.	**64**	40 57N	12 50 E
Palmas	**173**	26 29 S	52 0W
Palmas, C.	**120**	4 27N	7 46W
Palmas de Monte Alto	**171**	14 16 S	43 10W
Pálmas, G. di	**64**	39 0N	8 30 E
Palmdale	**163**	34 36N	118 7W
Palmeira	**171**	25 25 S	50 0W
Palmeira dos Índios	**170**	9 25 S	36 37W
Palmeirais	**170**	12 31 S	41 34W
Palmeiras, R.	**171**	12 22 S	47 8W
Palmeirinhas, Pta. das	**124**	9 2 S	12 57 E
Palmela	**57**	38 32N	8 57W
Palmelo	**171**	17 20 S	48 27W
Palmer, Alaska, U.S.A.	**147**	61 35N	149 10W
Palmer, Mass., U.S.A.	**162**	42 9N	72 21W
Palmer Arch	**13**	64 15 S	65 0W
Palmer Lake	**158**	39 10N	104 52W
Palmer Pen.	**13**	73 0 S	60 0W
Palmer, R., N. Terr., Austral.	**138**	24 30 S	133 0 E
Palmer, R., Queens., Austral.	**138**	16 5 S	142 43 E
Palmerston	**142**	45 29 S	170 43 E
Palmerston, C.	**133**	21 32 S	149 29 E
Palmerston North	**143**	40 21 S	175 39 E
Palmerton	**162**	40 47N	75 36W
Palmetto	**157**	27 33N	82 33W
Palmi	**65**	38 21N	15 51 E
Palmira, Argent.	**172**	32 59 S	68 25W
Palmira, Colomb.	**174**	3 32N	76 16W
Palmyra, Mo., U.S.A.	**158**	39 45N	91 30W
Palmyra, N.J., U.S.A.	**162**	40 0N	75 1W
Palmyra, Pa., U.S.A.	**162**	40 18N	76 36W
Palmyra = Tadmor	**92**	34 30N	37 55 E
Palni	**97**	10 30N	77 30 E
Palni Hills	**97**	10 14N	77 33 E
Palo Alto	**163**	37 25N	122 8W
Palo del Colle	**65**	41 4N	16 43 E
Paloe	**103**	8 20 S	121 43 E
Paloma, La	**172**	30 35 S	71 0W
Palombara Sabina	**63**	42 4N	12 45 E
Palopo	**103**	3 0 S	120 16 E
Palos, Cabo de	**59**	37 38N	0 40W
Palos Verdes	**163**	33 48N	118 23W
Palos Verdes, Pt.	**163**	33 43N	118 26W
Palouse	**160**	46 59N	117 5W
Palparara	**138**	24 47 S	141 22 E
Pålsboda	**73**	59 3N	15 22 E
Palu, Indon.	**103**	1 0 S	119 59 E
Palu, Turkey	**92**	38 45N	40 0 E
Paluan	**103**	13 35N	120 29 E
Palwal	**94**	28 8N	77 19 E
Pama, China	**108**	24 9N	107 15 E
Pama, Upp. Vol.	**121**	11 19N	0 44 E
Pamanukan	**103**	6 16 S	107 49 E
Pamban I.	**97**	9 24N	79 35 E
Pamekasan	**103**	7 10 S	113 29 E
Pameungpeuk	**103**	7 38 S	107 44 E
Pamiench'eng	**107**	43 13N	124 2 E
Pamiers	**44**	43 7N	1 39 E
Pamir, R.	**85**	37 1N	72 41 E
Pamirs, Ra.	**85**	37 40N	73 0 E
Pamlico, R.	**157**	35 25N	76 40W
Pamlico Sd.	**157**	35 20N	76 0W
Pampa	**159**	35 35N	100 58W
Pampa de las Salinas	**172**	32 1 S	66 58W
Pampa, La □	**172**	36 50 S	66 0W
Pampanua	**103**	4 22 S	120 14 E
Pamparato	**62**	44 16N	7 54 E
Pampas, Argent.	**172**	34 0 S	64 0W
Pampas, Peru	**174**	12 20 S	74 50W
Pamplona, Colomb.	**174**	7 23N	72 39W
Pamplona, Spain	**58**	42 48N	1 38W
Pampoenpoort	**128**	31 3 S	22 40 E
Pamunkey, R.	**162**	37 32N	76 50W
Pana	**158**	39 25N	89 0W
Panaca	**161**	37 51N	114 50W
Panagyurishte	**67**	42 49N	24 15 E
Panaitan, I.	**103**	6 35 S	105 10 E
Panaji (Panjim)	**97**	15 25N	73 50 E
Panamá	**166**	9 0N	79 25W
Panama ■	**166**	8 48N	79 55W
Panama Canal	**166**	9 10N	79 56W
Panama Canal Zone	**166**	9 10N	79 56W
Panama City	**157**	30 10N	85 41W
Panamá, Golfo de	**166**	8 4N	79 20W
Panamint Mts.	**161**	36 15N	117 20W
Panamint Springs	**163**	36 20N	117 28W
Panão	**174**	9 55 S	75 55W
Panare	**101**	6 51N	101 30 E
Panarea, I.	**65**	38 38N	15 3 E
Panaro, R.	**62**	44 48N	11 5 E
Panarukan	**103**	7 40 S	113 52 E
Panay, G.	**103**	11 0N	122 30 E
Panay I.	**103**	11 10N	122 30 E
Pancake Ra.	**161**	38 30N	116 0W
Pančevo	**66**	44 52N	20 41 E
Panciu	**70**	45 54N	27 8 E
Pancorbo, Paso	**58**	42 32N	3 5W
Pandan	**103**	11 45N	122 10 E
Pandangpanjang	**102**	0 40 S	100 20 E
Pandeglang	**103**	6 25 S	106 0 E
Pandharpur	**96**	17 41N	75 20 E
Pandhurna	**96**	21 36N	78 35 E
Pandilla	**58**	41 32N	3 43W
Pando	**173**	34 30 S	56 0W
Pando, L. = Hope L.	**139**	28 24 S	139 18 E
Panevëzys	**80**	55 42N	24 25 E
Panfilov	**76**	44 30N	80 0 E
Panfilovo	**81**	50 25N	42 46 E
Pang-Long	**99**	23 11N	98 45 E
Pang-Yang	**99**	22 7N	98 48 E

*Renamed Belau

Panga **Paulista**

Panga	**126**	1 52N	26 18 E
Pangaíon Óros	**68**	40 50N	24 0 E
Pangalanes, Canal des	**129**	22 48 S	47 50 E
Pangani	**126**	5 25 S	38 58 E
Pangani □	**126**	5 25 S	39 0 E
Pangani, R.	**126**	4 40 S	37 50 E
Pangbourne	**28**	51 28N	1 5W
P'angchiang	**106**	42 50N	113 1 E
Pangfou	**109**	32 55N	117 25 E
Pangi	**126**	3 10 S	26 35 E
Pangkai	**98**	22 40N	97 31 E
Pangkalanberandan	**102**	4 1N	98 20 E
Pangkalansusu	**102**	4 2N	98 42 E
Pangkoh	**102**	3 5 S	114 8 E
Pangnirtung	**149**	66 0N	66 0W
Pangong Tso, L.	**95**	34 0N	78 20 E
Pangrango	**103**	6 46 S	107 1 E
Pangsau Pass	**98**	27 15N	96 10 E
Pangta	**105**	30 14N	97 24 E
Pangtara	**98**	20 57N	96 40 E
Panguitch	**161**	37 52N	112 30W
Pangutaran Group	**103**	6 18N	120 34 E
Panhandle	**159**	35 23N	101 23W
P'anhsien	**108**	25 46N	104 39 E
Pani Mines	**94**	22 29N	73 50 E
Panipat	**94**	29 25N	77 2 E
Panjal Range	**94**	32 30N	76 50 E
Panjgur	**93**	27 0N	64 5 E
Panjim = Panaji	**93**	15 25N	73 50 E
Panjinad Barrage	**93**	29 22N	71 15 E
Panjwai	**94**	31 26N	65 27 E
Pankadjene	**103**	4 46 S	119 34 E
Pankal Pinang	**102**	2 0 S	106 0 E
Pankshin	**121**	9 25N	9 25 E
P'anlung Chiang, R.	**108**	21 18N	105 25 E
Panmunjŏm	**107**	37 59N	126 38 E
Panna	**95**	24 40N	80 15 E
Panna Hills	**95**	24 40N	81 15 E
Pannuru	**97**	16 5N	80 34 E
Panorama	**173**	21 21 S	51 51W
Panruti	**97**	11 46N	79 35 E
P'anshan	**107**	41 12N	122 4 E
P'anshih	**107**	42 55N	126 3 E
Pant'anching	**106**	39 7N	103 52 E
Pantano	**161**	32 0N	110 32W
Pantar, I.	**103**	8 28 S	124 10 E
Pantelleria	**64**	36 52N	12 0 E
Pantelleria, I.	**64**	36 52N	12 0 E
Pantha	**98**	24 7N	94 17 E
Pantin Sakan	**98**	18 38N	97 33 E
Pantjo	**103**	8 42 S	118 40 E
Pantón	**56**	42 31N	7 37W
Pantukan	**103**	7 17N	125 58 E
Panuco	**165**	22 0N	98 25W
Panyam	**121**	9 27N	9 8 E
P'anyü	**109**	23 2N	113 20 E
Pão de AçIcar	**171**	9 45 S	37 26W
Paoan	**109**	22 32N	114 8 E
Paoch'eng	**106**	33 14N	106 56 E
Paochi	**106**	34 25N	107 11 E
Paochiatun	**107**	33 56N	120 12 E
Paoching	**108**	28 41N	109 35 E
Paok'ang	**109**	31 57N	111 20 E
Paokuot'u	**107**	42 20N	120 42 E
Páola	**65**	39 21N	16 2 E
Paola	**158**	38 36N	94 50W
Paonia	**161**	38 56N	107 37W
Paoshan, Shanghai, China	**109**	31 25N	121 29 E
Paoshan, Yunnan, China	**105**	25 7N	99 9 E
Paote	**106**	39 7N	111 13 E
Paoti	**107**	39 44N	117 18 E
Paoting	**106**	38 50N	115 30 E
Paot'ou	**106**	40 35N	110 3 E
Paoua	**117**	7 25N	16 30 E
Paoying	**107**	33 15N	119 20 E
Papá	**53**	47 22N	17 30 E
Papa Sd.	**37**	59 20N	2 56W
Papa, Sd. of	**36**	60 19N	1 40W
Papa Stour I.	**36**	60 20N	1 40W
Papa Stronsay I.	**37**	59 10N	2 37W
Papa Westray I.	**37**	59 20N	2 55W
Papagayo, Golfo de	**166**	10 4N	85 50W
Papagayo, R., Brazil	**164**	12 30 S	58 10W
Papagayo, R., Mexico	**165**	16 36N	99 43W
Papagni R.	**97**	14 10N	78 30 E
Papaikou	**147**	19 47N	155 6W
Papakura	**142**	37 4 S	174 59 E
Papaloapan, R.	**164**	18 2N	96 51W
Papantla	**165**	20 45N	97 21W
Papar	**102**	5 45N	116 0 E
Paparoa	**142**	36 6 S	174 16 E
Paparoa Range	**143**	42 5 S	171 35 E
Pápas, Ákra	**69**	38 13N	21 6 E
Papatoetoe	**142**	36 59 S	174 51 E
Papenburg	**48**	53 7N	7 25 E
Papien Chiang, R. (Da)	**108**	22 56N	101 47 E
Papigochic, R.	**164**	29 9N	109 40W
Paposo	**172**	25 0 S	70 30W
Paps, The, mts.	**39**	52 0N	9 15W
Papua, Gulf of	**135**	9 0 S	144 50 E
Papua New Guinea ■	**135**	8 0 S	145 0 E
PapuCa	**63**	44 22N	15 30 E
Papudo	**172**	32 29 S	71 27W
Papuk, mts.	**66**	45 30N	17 30 E
Papun	**98**	18 0N	97 30 E
Pará = Belém	**170**	1 20 S	48 30W
Pará □	**175**	3 20 S	52 0W
Parábita	**65**	40 3N	18 8 E
Paracatú	**171**	17 10 S	46 50W
Paracatu, R.	**171**	16 30 S	45 4W
Paracel Is.	**102**	16 49N	111 2 E
Parachilna	**140**	31 10 S	138 21 E
Parachinar	**94**	34 0N	70 5 E
Paracombe	**109**	34 51 S	138 47 E
Paracuru	**170**	3 24 S	39 4W
Paradas	**57**	37 18N	5 29W
Paradela	**56**	42 44N	7 37W
Paradip	**95**	20 15N	86 35 E
Paradise	**160**	47 27N	114 54W
Paradise, R.	**151**	53 27N	57 19W
Paradise Valley	**160**	41 30N	117 28W
Parado	**103**	8 42 S	118 30 E
Paradyz	**54**	51 19N	20 2 E
Parafield	**109**	34 47 S	138 38 E
Parafield Airport	**109**	34 48 S	138 38 E
Paragould	**159**	36 5N	90 30W
Paragua, La	**174**	6 50N	63 20W
Paragua, R.	**174**	6 30N	63 30W
Paraguaçu Paulista	**173**	22 22 S	50 35W
Paraguaçu, R.	**171**	12 45 S	38 54W
Paraguai, R.	**174**	16 0 S	57 52W
Paraguaipoa	**174**	11 21N	71 57W
Paraguana, Pen. de	**174**	12 0N	70 0W
Paraguarí	**172**	25 36 S	57 0W
Paraguarí □	**172**	26 0 S	57 10W
Paraguay ■	**172**	23 0 S	57 0W
Paraguay, R.	**172**	27 18 S	58 38W
Paraíba = Joéo Pessoa	**164**	7 10 S	35 0W
Paraiba □	**170**	7 0 S	36 0W
Paraíba do Sul, R.	**173**	21 37 S	41 3W
Paraibano	**171**	6 30 S	44 1W
Parainen	**75**	60 18N	22 18 E
Paraíso	**165**	19 3 S	52 59W
Paraiso	**165**	18 24N	93 14W
Parakhino Paddubye	**80**	58 46N	33 10 E
Parakou	**121**	9 25N	2 40 E
Parakylia	**140**	30 24 S	136 25 E
Paralion-Astrous	**69**	37 25N	22 45 E
Paramagudi	**97**	9 31N	78 39 E
Paramaribo	**175**	5 50N	55 10W
Parambu	**170**	6 13 S	40 43W
Paramillo, Nudo del	**174**	7 4N	75 55W
Paramirim	**171**	13 26 S	42 15W
Paramirim, R.	**171**	11 34 S	43 18W
Paramithiá	**68**	39 30N	20 35 E
Paramushir, Ostrov	**77**	40 24N	156 0 E
Paran, N.	**90**	30 14N	34 48 E
Paraná	**172**	32 0 S	60 30W
Paranã	**171**	12 30 S	47 40W
Paraná □	**173**	24 30 S	51 0W
Paraná, R.	**172**	33 43 S	59 15W
Paranã, R.	**171**	22 25 S	53 1W
Paranaguá	**173**	25 30 S	48 30W
Paranaíba, R.	**171**	18 0 S	49 12W
Paranapanema, R.	**173**	22 40 S	53 9W
Paranapiacaba, Serra do	**173**	24 31 S	48 35W
Paranavaí	**173**	23 4 S	52 28W
Parang, Jolo, Phil.	**103**	5 55N	120 54 E
Parang, Mindanao, Phil.	**103**	7 23N	124 16 E
Parangaba	**170**	3 45 S	38 33W
Paraóin	**66**	43 54N	21 27 E
Paraparanma	**143**	40 57 S	175 3 E
Parapóla, I.	**69**	36 55N	23 27 E
Paraspóri, Ákra	**69**	35 55N	27 15 E
Paratinga	**171**	12 40 S	43 10W
Paratoo	**140**	32 42 S	139 22 E
Parattah	**138**	42 22 S	147 23 E
Paraúna	**171**	17 2 S	50 26W
Paray-le-Monial	**45**	46 27N	4 7 E
Parbati, R.	**94**	25 51N	76 34 E
Parbatipur	**98**	25 39N	88 55 E
Parbhani	**96**	19 8N	76 52 E
Parchim	**48**	53 25N	11 50 E
Parczew	**54**	51 9N	22 52 E
Pardee Res.	**163**	38 16N	120 51W
Pardes Hanna	**90**	32 28N	34 57 E
Pardilla	**56**	41 33N	3 43W
Pardo, R., Bahia, Brazil	**171**	15 40 S	39 0W
Pardo, R., Mato Grosso, Brazil	**171**	21 0 S	53 25W
Pardo, R., Minas Gerais, Brazil	**171**	15 48 S	44 48W
Pardo, R., São Paulo, Brazil	**171**	20 45 S	48 0W
Pardubice	**52**	50 3N	15 45 E
Pare	**103**	7 43 S	112 12 E
Pare □	**126**	4 10 S	38 0 E
Pare Mts.	**126**	4 0 S	37 45 E
Pare Pare	**103**	4 0 S	119 45 E
Parecis, Serra dos	**174**	13 0 S	60 0W
Paredes de Nava	**56**	42 9N	4 42W
Parelhas	**170**	6 41 S	36 39W
Paren	**77**	62 45N	163 0 E
Parengarenga Harbour	**142**	34 31 S	173 0 E
Parent	**150**	47 55N	74 35W
Parent, Lac.	**150**	48 31N	77 1W
Parentis-en-Born	**44**	44 21N	1 4W
Parepare	**103**	4 0 S	119 40 E
Parfino	**80**	57 59N	31 34 E
Parfuri	**129**	22 28 S	31 17 E
Paria, Golfo de	**174**	10 20N	62 0W
Paria, Pen. de	**174**	10 50N	62 30W
Pariaguán	**174**	8 51N	64 43W
Pariaman	**102**	0 47 S	100 11 E
Paricutín, Cerro	**164**	19 28N	102 15W
Parigi	**103**	0 50 S	120 5 E
Parika	**174**	6 50N	58 20W
Parima, Serra	**174**	2 30N	64 0W
Parinari	**174**	4 35 S	74 25W
Parincea	**70**	46 27N	27 9 E
Parîng, mt.	**70**	45 20N	23 37 E
Parintins	**175**	2 40 S	56 50W
Pariparit Kyun	**99**	14 55 S	93 45 E
Paris, Can.	**150**	43 12N	80 25W
Paris, France	**43**	48 50N	2 20 E
Paris, Idaho, U.S.A.	**160**	42 13N	111 30W
Paris, Ky., U.S.A.	**156**	38 12N	84 12W
Paris, Tenn., U.S.A.	**157**	36 20N	88 20W
Paris, Tex., U.S.A.	**159**	33 40N	95 30W
Parish	**162**	43 24N	76 9W
Pariti	**103**	9 55 S	123 30 E
Park City	**160**	40 42N	111 35W
Park Falls	**158**	45 58N	90 27 E
Park Range	**160**	40 0N	106 30W
Park Rapids	**158**	46 56N	95 0W
Park River	**158**	48 25N	97 17W
Park Rynie	**129**	30 25 S	30 35 E
Park View	**161**	36 45N	106 37W
Parkent	**85**	41 18N	69 40 E
Parker, Ariz., U.S.A.	**161**	34 8N	114 16W
Parker, S.D., U.S.A.	**158**	43 25N	97 7W
Parker Dam	**161**	34 13N	114 5W
Parkersburg	**156**	39 18N	81 31W
Parkerview	**153**	51 21N	103 18W
Parkes, A.C.T., Austral.	**133**	35 18 S	149 8 E
Parkes, N.S.W., Austral.	**141**	33 9 S	148 11 E
Parkfield	**163**	35 54N	120 26W
Parkhar	**85**	37 30N	69 34 E
Parknasilla	**39**	51 49N	9 50W
Parkside	**153**	53 10N	106 33W
Parkston	**158**	43 25N	98 0W
Parksville	**152**	49 20N	124 21W
Parkville	**162**	39 23N	76 33W
Parlakimedi	**96**	18 45N	84 5 E
Parma, Italy	**62**	44 50N	10 20 E
Parma, U.S.A.	**160**	43 49N	116 59W
Parna, R.	**62**	44 27N	10 3 E
Parnaguá	**170**	10 10 S	44 10W
Parnaíba, Piauí, Brazil	**170**	3 0 S	41 40W
Parnaíba, São Paulo, Brazil	**170**	19 34 S	51 14W
Parnaíba, R.	**170**	3 35 S	43 0W
Parnamirim	**170**	8 5 S	39 34W
Parnarama	**170**	5 41 S	43 6W
Parnassōs, mt.	**69**	38 17N	21 30 E
Parnassus	**143**	42 42 S	173 23 E
Párnis, mt.	**69**	38 14N	23 45 E
Párnon Óros	**69**	37 15N	22 45 E
Pärnu	**80**	58 12N	24 33 E
Parola	**96**	20 47N	75 7 E
Paroo Chan.	**133**	30 50 S	143 35 E
Paroo, R.	**139**	30 0 S	144 5 E
Paropamisus Range = Fī roz Kohi	**93**	34 45N	63 0 E
Páros	**69**	37 5N	25 9 E
Páros, I.	**69**	37 5N	25 12 E
Parowan	**161**	37 54N	112 56W
Parpaillon, mts.	**45**	44 30N	6 40 E
Parracombe	**30**	51 11N	3 55W
Parral	**172**	36 10 S	72 0W
Parramatta	**141**	33 48 S	151 1 E
Parramore I.	**162**	37 32N	75 39W
Parras	**164**	25 30N	102 20W
Parrett, R.	**28**	51 7N	2 58W
Parris I.	**157**	32 20N	80 30W
Parrsboro	**151**	45 30N	64 10W
Parry	**153**	49 47N	104 41W
Parry, C.	**147**	70 20N	123 38W
Parry Is.	**12**	77 0N	110 0W
Parry Sound	**150**	45 20N	80 0W
Parshall	**158**	47 56N	102 11W
Parsnip, R.	**152**	55 10N	123 2W
Parsons	**159**	37 20N	95 10W
Parsons Ra., Mts.	**138**	13 30 S	135 15 E
Partabpur	**96**	20 0N	80 42 E
Partanna	**64**	37 43N	12 51 E
Partapgarh	**94**	24 2N	74 40 E
Parthenay	**42**	46 38N	0 16W
Partille	**73**	57 48N	12 18 E
Partinico	**64**	38 3N	13 6 E
Partney	**33**	53 12N	0 7 E
Parton	**32**	54 34N	3 35W
Partry Mts.	**38**	53 40N	9 28W
Partur	**96**	19 40N	76 14 E
Paru, R.	**175**	0 20 S	53 30W
Parur	**97**	10 13N	76 14 E
Paruro	**174**	13 45 S	71 50W
Parvatipuram	**96**	18 50N	83 25 E
Parwan □	**93**	35 0N	69 0 E
Påryd	**73**	56 34N	15 55 E
Parys	**128**	26 52 S	27 29 E
Parys, Mt.	**31**	53 23N	4 18W
Pas-de-Calais □	**43**	50 30N	2 30 E
Pasadena, Calif., U.S.A.	**163**	34 5N	118 9W
Pasadena, Tex., U.S.A.	**159**	29 45N	95 14W
Pasaje	**174**	3 10 S	79 40W
Pasaje, R.	**172**	25 35 S	64 57W
Pascagoula	**159**	30 30N	88 30W
Pascagoula, R.	**159**	30 40N	88 35W
Paşcani	**70**	47 14N	26 45 E
Pasco	**160**	46 10N	119 0W
Pasco, Cerro de	**174**	10 45 S	76 10W
Pascoag	**162**	41 57N	71 42W
Pascoe, Mt.	**137**	27 25 S	120 40 E
Pasewalk	**48**	53 30N	14 0 E
Pasfield L.	**153**	58 24N	105 20W
Pasha, R.	**80**	60 20N	33 0 E
Pashiwari	**95**	34 40N	75 10 E
Pashiya	**84**	58 33N	58 26 E
Pashmakli = Smolyan	**67**	41 36N	24 38 E
Pasighat	**98**	28 4N	95 21 E
Pasir Mas	**101**	6 2N	102 8 E
Pasir Puteh	**101**	5 50N	102 24 E
Pasirian	**103**	8 13 S	113 8 E
Pasley, C.	**137**	33 52 S	123 35 E
Pasman I.	**63**	43 58N	15 20 E
Pasmore, R.	**140**	31 5 S	139 49 E
Pasni	**93**	25 15N	63 27 E
Paso de Indios	**176**	43 55 S	69 0W
Paso de los Libres	**172**	29 44 S	57 10W
Paso de los Toros	**172**	32 36 S	56 37W
Paso Robles	**161**	35 40N	120 45W
Paspebiac	**151**	48 3N	65 17W
Pasrur	**94**	32 16N	74 43 E
Passage East	**39**	52 15N	7 0W
Passage West	**39**	51 52N	8 20W
Passaic	**162**	40 50N	74 8W
Passau	**49**	48 34N	13 27 E
Passendale	**47**	50 54N	3 2 E
Passero, C.	**65**	36 42N	15 8 E
Passo Fundo	**173**	28 10 S	52 30W
Passos	**171**	20 45 S	46 37W
Passow	**48**	53 13N	14 3 E
Passwang	**50**	47 22N	7 41 E
Passy	**43**	45 55N	6 41 E
Pastaza, R.	**174**	2 45 S	76 50W
Pastek	**54**	54 3N	19 41 E
Pasto	**174**	1 13N	77 17W
Pasto Zootécnico do Cunene	**128**	16 20 S	15 20 E
Pastos Bons	**170**	6 36 S	44 5W
Pastrana	**58**	40 27N	2 53W
Pasuruan	**103**	7 40 S	112 53 E
Pasym	**54**	53 48N	20 49 E
Pásztó	**53**	47 52N	19 43 E
Patagonia, Argent.	**176**	45 0 S	69 0W
Patagonia, U.S.A.	**161**	31 35N	110 45W
Patan, India	**93**	23 54N	72 14 E
Patan, Gujarat, India	**96**	17 22N	73 48 E
Patan, Maharashtra, India	**94**	23 54N	72 14 E
Patan (Lalitapur)	**99**	27 40N	85 20 E
Pat'ang Szechwan	**105**	30 2N	98 58 E
Patani	**103**	0 20N	128 50 E
Pataohotzu	**107**	43 5N	127 33 E
Patapsco Res.	**162**	39 27N	76 55W
Pataudi	**94**	28 18N	76 48 E
Patay	**43**	48 2N	1 40 E
Patcham	**29**	50 52N	0 9W
Patchewollock	**140**	35 22 S	142 12 E
Patchogue	**162**	40 46N	73 1W
Patea	**142**	39 45 S	174 30 E
Pategi	**121**	8 50N	5 45 E
Pateley Bridge	**33**	54 5N	1 45W
Patensie	**128**	33 46 S	24 49 E
Paternò	**65**	37 34N	14 53 E
Paternoster, Kepulauan	**102**	7 5 S	118 15 E
Pateros	**160**	48 4N	119 58W
Paterson, Austral.	**141**	32 37 S	151 39 E
Paterson, U.S.A.	**162**	40 55N	74 10W
Paterson Inlet	**143**	46 56 S	168 12 E
Paterson Ra.	**136**	21 45 S	122 10 E
Paterswolde	**46**	53 9N	6 34 E
Pathankot	**94**	32 18N	75 45 E
Patharghata	**98**	22 2N	89 58 E
Pathfinder Res.	**160**	42 0N	107 0W
Pathiu	**101**	10 42N	99 19 E
Pathum Thani	**100**	14 1N	100 32 E
Páti	**103**	6 45 S	111 3 E
Patiala	**94**	30 23N	76 26 E
Patine Kouta	**120**	12 45N	13 45W
Patjitan	**103**	8 12 S	111 8 E
Patkai Bum	**98**	27 0N	95 30 E
Pátmos	**69**	37 21N	26 36 E
Pátmos, I.	**69**	37 21N	26 36 E
Patna, India	**95**	25 35N	85 18 E
Patna, U.K.	**34**	55 21N	4 30W
Patonga	**126**	2 45N	33 15 E
Patos	**170**	7 1 S	37 16W
Patos de Minas	**171**	18 35 S	46 32W
Patos, Lag. dos	**173**	31 20 S	51 0 E
Patosi	**68**	40 42N	19 38 E
Patquía	**172**	30 0 S	66 55W
Pátrai	**69**	38 14N	21 47 E
Pátraikos, Kólpos	**69**	38 17N	21 30 E
Patrick	**32**	54 13N	4 41W
Patrocínio	**171**	18 57 S	47 0W
Patta	**126**	2 10 S	41 0 E
Patta, I.	**126**	2 10 S	41 0 E
Pattada	**64**	40 35N	9 7 E
Pattanapuram	**97**	9 6N	76 33 E
Pattani	**101**	6 48N	101 15 E
Patten	**151**	45 59N	68 28W
Patterdale	**32**	54 33N	2 55W
Patterson, Calif., U.S.A.	**163**	37 30N	121 9W
Patterson, La., U.S.A.	**159**	29 44N	91 20W
Patterson, Mt.	**163**	38 29N	119 20W
Patti	**94**	31 17N	74 54 E
Patti Castroreale	**65**	38 8N	14 57 E
Pattoki	**94**	31 5N	73 52 E
Pattukkottai	**97**	10 25N	79 20 E
Patu	**170**	6 6 S	37 38W
Patuakhali	**98**	22 20N	90 25 E
Patuca, Punta	**166**	15 49N	84 14W
Patuca, R.	**166**	15 20N	84 40W
Patung	**109**	31 0N	110 30 E
Pâturages	**47**	50 25N	3 52 E
Patutahi	**142**	38 38 S	177 55 E
Pátzcuaro	**164**	19 30N	101 40W
Pau	**44**	43 19N	0 25W
Pau d' Arco	**170**	7 30 S	49 22W
Pau dos Ferros	**170**	6 7 S	38 10W
Pauillac	**44**	45 11N	0 46W
Pauini, R.	**174**	1 42 S	62 50W
Pauk	**98**	21 55N	94 30 E
Paul I.	**151**	56 30N	61 20W
Paulatuk	**147**	69 25N	124 0W
Paulhan	**44**	43 33N	3 28 E
Paulis = Isiro	**126**	2 53N	27 58 E
Paulista	**170**	7 57 S	34 53W

Paulistana **Perryton**

Paulistana	**170**	8 9S	41 9W
Paull	**33**	53 42N	0 12W
Paullina	**158**	42 55N	95 40W
Paulo Afonso	**170**	9 21S	38 15W
Paulo de Faria	**171**	20 2S	49 24W
Paulpietersburg	**129**	27 23S	30 50E
Paul's Valley	**159**	34 40N	97 17W
Pauma Valley	**163**	33 16N	116 58W
Paungde	**98**	18 29N	95 30E
Pauni	**96**	20 48N	79 40E
Pavelets	**81**	53 49N	39 14E
Pavia	**62**	45 10N	9 10E
Pavlikeni	**67**	43 14N	25 20E
Pavlodar	**76**	52 33N	77 0E
Pavlof Is.	**147**	55 30N	161 30W
Pavlograd	**82**	48 30N	35 52E
Pavlovo, Gorkiy, U.S.S.R.	**81**	55 58N	43 5E
Pavlovo, Yakut A.S.S.R., U.S.S.R.	**77**	63 5N	115 25E
Pavlovsk	**81**	50 26N	40 5E
Pavlovskaya	**83**	46 17N	39 47E
Pavlovskiy Posad	**81**	55 37N	38 42E
Pavullo nel Frignano	**62**	44 20N	10 50E
Pawahku	**98**	26 11N	98 40E
Pawhuska	**159**	36 40N	96 25W
Pawling	**162**	41 35N	73 37W
Pawnee	**159**	36 24N	96 50W
Pawnee City	**158**	40 8N	96 10W
Pawtucket	**162**	41 51N	71 22W
Paximádhia	**69**	35 0N	24 35E
Paxoi, I.	**68**	39 14N	20 12E
Paxton, Ill., U.S.A.	**156**	40 25N	88 0W
Paxton, Nebr., U.S.A.	**158**	41 12N	101 27W
Paya Bakri	**101**	2 3N	102 44E
Payakumbah	**102**	0 20S	100 35E
Payenhaot'e (Alashantsoch'i)	**106**	38 50N	105 32E
Payenk'ala Shan	**105**	34 20N	97 0E
Payerne	**50**	46 49N	6 56E
Payette	**160**	44 0N	117 0W
Paymogo	**57**	37 44N	7 21W
Payne L.	**149**	59 30N	74 30W
Payne, R.	**149**	60 0N	70 0W
Payneham	**109**	34 54S	138 39E
Paynes Find	**137**	29 15S	117 42E
Paynesville, Liberia	**120**	6 20N	10 45W
Paynesville, U.S.A.	**158**	45 21N	94 44W
Paysandú	**172**	32 19S	58 8W
Payson, Ariz., U.S.A.	**161**	34 17N	111 15W
Payson, Utah, U.S.A.	**160**	40 8N	111 41W
Paz, Bahía de la	**164**	24 15N	110 25W
Paz Centro, La	**166**	12 20N	86 41W
Paz, La, Entre Ríos, Argent.	**172**	30 50S	59 45W
Paz, La, San Luis, Argent.	**172**	33 30S	67 20W
Paz, La, Boliv.	**174**	16 20S	68 10W
Paz, La, Hond.	**166**	14 20N	87 47W
Paz, La, Mexico	**164**	24 10N	110 20W
Paz, La, Bahía de	**164**	24 20N	110 40W
Paz, R.	**166**	13 44N	90 10W
Pazar	**92**	41 10N	40 50E
Pazardzhik	**67**	42 12N	24 20E
Pazin	**63**	45 14N	13 56E
Pčinja, R.	**66**	42 0N	21 45E
Pe Ell	**160**	46 30N	123 18W
Peabody	**162**	42 31N	70 56W
Peace Point	**152**	59 7N	112 27W
Peace, R.	**152**	59 0N	111 25W
Peace River	**152**	56 15N	117 18W
Peace River Res.	**152**	55 40N	123 40W
Peacehaven	**29**	50 47N	0 1E
Peach Springs	**161**	35 36N	113 30W
Peak Downs	**138**	22 55S	148 0E
Peak Downs Mine	**138**	22 17S	148 11E
Peak Hill, N.S.W., Austral.	**141**	32 39S	148 11E
Peak Hill, W. A., Austral.	**137**	25 35S	118 43E
Peak Range	**138**	22 50S	148 20E
Peak, The	**32**	53 24N	1 53W
Peake	**140**	35 25S	140 0E
Peake Cr.	**139**	28 2S	136 7E
Peale Mt.	**161**	38 25N	109 12W
Pearblossom	**163**	34 30N	117 55W
Pearce	**161**	31 57N	109 56W
Pearl Banks	**97**	8 45N	79 45E
Pearl City	**147**	2 21N	158 0W
Pearl Harbor	**147**	21 20N	158 0W
Pearl, R.	**159**	31 50N	90 0W
Pearsall	**159**	28 55N	99 8W
Pearse I.	**152**	54 52N	130 14W
Peary Land	**12**	82 40N	33 0W
Pease, R.	**159**	34 18N	100 15W
Peasenhall	**29**	52 17N	1 24E
Pebane	**127**	17 10S	38 8E
Pebas	**174**	3 10S	71 55W
Pebble Beach	**163**	36 34N	121 57W
Peçanha	**171**	18 33S	42 34W
Péccioli	**62**	43 32N	10 43E
Pechea	**70**	45 36N	27 49E
Pechenezhin	**82**	48 30N	24 48E
Pechenga	**78**	69 30N	31 25E
Pechnezhskoye Vdkhr.	**81**	50 0N	36 50E
Pechora, R.	**78**	62 30N	56 30E
Pechorskaya Guba	**78**	68 40N	54 0E
Pechory	**80**	57 48N	27 40E
Pecica	**66**	46 10N	21 3E
Pečka	**66**	44 18N	19 33E
Pécora, C.	**64**	39 28N	8 23E
Pecos	**159**	31 25N	103 35W
Pecos, R.	**159**	31 22N	102 30W
Pecqueuse	**47**	48 39N	2 3E
Pécs	**53**	46 5N	18 15E
Pedasí	**166**	7 32N	80 3W
Peddapalli	**96**	18 40N	79 24E
Peddapuram	**96**	17 6N	82 5E
Peddavagu, R.	**96**	16 33N	79 8E
Pedder, L.	**138**	42 55S	146 10E
Pedernales	**167**	18 2N	71 44W
Pedirka	**139**	26 40S	135 14E
Pedjantan, I.	**102**	0 5S	106 15E
Pedra Azul	**171**	16 2S	41 17W
Pedra Grande, Recifes do	**171**	17 45S	38 58W
Pedras, Pta. de	**171**	7 38S	34 47W
Pedreiras	**170**	4 32S	44 40W
Pedrera, La	**174**	1 18S	69 43W
Pedro Afonso	**170**	9 0S	48 10W
Pedro Antonio Santos	**165**	18 54N	88 15W
Pedro Cays	**166**	17 5N	77 48W
Pedro Chico	**174**	1 4N	70 25W
Pedro de Valdivia	**172**	22 33S	69 38W
Pedro Juan Caballero	**173**	22 30S	55 40W
Pedro Muñoz	**59**	39 25N	2 56W
Pedrógão Grande	**56**	39 55N	8 0W
Peebinga	**140**	34 52S	140 57E
Peebles	**35**	55 40N	3 12W
Peebles (□)	**26**	55 37N	3 4W
Peekshill	**162**	41 18N	73 57W
Peel, Austral.	**139**	33 20S	149 38E
Peel, I. of Man	**32**	54 14N	4 40W
Peel Fell, mt.	**35**	55 17N	2 35W
Peel, R., Austral.	**141**	30 50S	150 29E
Peel, R., Can.	**147**	67 0N	135 0W
Peelwood	**141**	34 7S	149 27E
Peene, R.	**48**	53 53N	13 53E
Peera Peera Poolanna L.	**139**	26 30S	138 0E
Peers	**152**	53 40N	116 0W
Pegasus Bay	**143**	43 20S	173 10E
Peggau	**52**	47 12N	15 21E
Pego	**59**	38 51N	0 8W
Pegswood	**35**	55 12N	1 38W
Pegu	**99**	17 20N	96 29E
Pegu Yoma, mts.	**98**	19 0N	96 0E
Pegwell Bay	**29**	51 18N	1 22E
Pehčevo	**66**	41 41N	22 55E
Pehuajó	**172**	36 0S	62 0W
Pei Chiang, R.	**109**	23 12N	112 45E
Pei Wan	**107**	36 25N	120 45E
Peian	**105**	48 16N	126 36E
Peichen	**107**	41 38N	121 50E
Peichengchen	**107**	44 30N	123 27E
Peichiang	**109**	23 0N	120 0E
Peihai	**108**	21 30N	109 5E
P'eihsien, Kiangsu, China	**106**	34 44N	116 55E
P'eihsien, Kiangsu, China	**107**	34 20N	117 57E
Peiliu	**109**	22 45N	110 20E
Peine, Chile	**172**	23 45S	68 8W
Peine, Ger.	**48**	52 19N	10 12E
Peip'an Chiang, R.	**108**	25 0N	106 11E
Peip'ei	**105**	29 49N	106 27E
Peip'iao	**107**	41 48N	120 44E
Peip'ing	**106**	39 45N	116 25E
Peissenberg	**49**	47 48N	11 4E
Peitz	**48**	51 50N	14 23E
Peixe	**171**	12 0S	48 40W
Peixe, R.	**171**	21 31S	51 58W
Peize	**46**	53 9N	6 30E
Pek, R.	**66**	44 58N	21 55E
Pekalongan	**103**	6 53S	109 40E
Pekan	**101**	3 30N	103 25E
Pekin	**158**	40 35N	89 40W
Peking = Peip'ing	**106**	39 45N	116 25E
Pelabuhan Ratu, Teluk	**103**	7 5S	106 30E
Pelabuhanratu	**103**	7 0S	106 32E
Pélagos, I.	**68**	39 17N	24 4E
Pelagruza, Is.	**63**	42 24N	16 15E
Pelaihari	**102**	3 55S	114 45E
Pełczyce	**54**	53 3N	15 16E
Peleaga, mt.	**70**	45 22N	22 55E
Pelee I.	**150**	41 47N	82 40W
Pelée, Mt.	**167**	14 40N	61 0W
Pelee, Pt.	**150**	41 54N	82 31W
Pelekech, mt.	**126**	3 52N	35 8E
Peleng, I.	**103**	1 20S	123 30E
Pelham	**157**	31 5N	84 6W
Pelhrimov	**52**	49 24N	15 12E
Pelican	**147**	58 12N	136 28W
Pelican L.	**153**	52 28N	100 20W
Pelican Narrows	**153**	55 10N	102 56W
Pelican Portage	**152**	55 51N	113 0W
Pelican Rapids	**153**	52 45N	100 42W
Peligre, L. de	**167**	19 1N	71 58W
Pelkosenniemi	**74**	67 6N	27 28E
Pella	**158**	41 20N	93 0W
Pélla □	**68**	40 52N	22 0E
Pèllaro	**65**	38 1N	15 40E
Pellworm, I.	**48**	54 30N	8 40E
Pelly Bay	**149**	68 0N	89 50W
Pelly L.	**148**	66 0N	102 0W
Pelly, R.	**147**	62 15N	133 30W
Peloponnese = Pelóponnisos	**69**	37 10N	22 0E
Pelopónnisos Kai Dhitiktí Iprotikí Ellas □	**69**	37 10N	22 0E
Peloritani, Monti	**65**	38 2N	15 15E
Peloro, C.	**65**	38 15N	15 40E
Pelorus Sound	**143**	40 59S	173 59E
Pelotas	**173**	31 42S	52 23W
Pelòvo	**67**	43 26N	24 17E
Pelvoux, Massif de	**45**	44 52N	6 20E
Pelym R.	**84**	59 39N	63 6E
Pemalang	**103**	6 53S	109 23E
Pematang Siantar	**102**	2 57N	99 5E
Pemba, Mozam.	**127**	12 58S	40 30E
Pemba, Zambia	**127**	16 30S	27 28E
Pemba Channel	**126**	5 0S	39 37E
Pemba, I.	**126**	5 0S	39 45E
Pemberton, Austral.	**137**	34 30S	116 0E
Pemberton, Can.	**152**	50 25N	122 50W
Pembina	**153**	48 58N	97 15W
Pembina, R.	**153**	49 0N	98 12W
Pembine	**156**	45 38N	87 59W
Pembrey	**31**	51 42N	4 17W
Pembroke, Can.	**150**	45 50N	77 7W
Pembroke, N.Z.	**143**	44 33S	169 9E
Pembroke, U.K.	**31**	51 41N	4 57W
Pembroke, U.S.A.	**157**	32 5N	81 32W
Pembroke (□)	**26**	51 40N	5 0W
Pembroke Dock	**31**	51 41N	4 57W
Pembury	**29**	51 8N	0 20E
Pen-y-Ghent	**32**	54 10N	2 15W
Pen-y-groes, Dyfed, U.K.	**31**	51 48N	4 3W
Pen-y-groes, Gwynedd, U.K.	**31**	53 3N	4 18W
Peñíscola	**58**	40 22N	0 24E
Peña de Francia, Sierra de	**56**	40 32N	6 10W
Peña Roya, mt.	**58**	40 24N	0 40W
Peña, Sierra de la	**58**	42 32N	0 45W
Penafiel	**56**	41 12N	8 17W
Peñafiel	**56**	41 35N	4 7W
Peñaflor	**57**	37 43N	5 21W
Peñalara, Pico	**56**	40 51N	3 57W
Penally	**31**	51 39N	4 44W
Penalva	**170**	3 18S	45 10W
Penamacôr	**56**	40 10N	7 10W
Penang = Pinang	**101**	5 25N	100 15E
Penápolis	**173**	21 30S	50 0W
Peñaranda de Bracamonte	**56**	40 53N	5 13W
Peñarroya-Pueblonuevo	**57**	38 19N	5 16W
Penarth	**31**	51 26N	3 11W
Peñas, C. de	**56**	43 42N	5 52W
Peñas de San Pedro	**59**	38 44N	2 0W
Peñas, G. de	**176**	47 0S	75 0W
Peñas, Pta.	**174**	11 17N	70 28W
Pench'i	**107**	41 20N	123 48E
Pencoed	**31**	51 31N	3 30W
Pend Oreille, L.	**160**	48 0N	116 30W
Pend Oreille, R.	**160**	49 4N	117 37W
Pendálofon	**68**	40 14N	21 12E
Pendeen	**30**	50 11N	5 39W
Pendelikón	**69**	38 5N	23 53E
Pendembu	**120**	9 7N	12 14W
Pendências	**170**	5 15S	36 43W
Pender B.	**136**	16 45S	122 42E
Pendine	**31**	51 44N	4 33W
Pendle Hill	**32**	53 53N	2 18W
Pendleton, Calif., U.S.A.	**163**	33 16N	117 23W
Pendleton, Oreg., U.S.A.	**160**	45 35N	118 50W
Pendzhikent	**85**	39 29N	67 37E
Penedo	**170**	10 15S	36 36W
Penetanguishene	**150**	44 50N	79 55W
Penfield	**109**	34 44S	138 38E
Pengalengan	**103**	7 9S	107 30E
P'engch'i	**108**	30 50N	105 42E
Penge, Kasai, Congo	**126**	5 30S	24 33E
Penge, Kivu, Congo	**126**	4 27S	28 25E
P'enghsien	**108**	30 59N	103 56E
P'enghu Liehtao	**109**	22 30N	119 30E
P'englai	**107**	37 49N	120 47E
P'engshui	**108**	29 19N	108 12E
P'engtse	**109**	29 53N	116 32E
Penguin	**138**	41 8S	146 6E
Penhalonga	**127**	18 52S	32 40E
Peniche	**57**	39 19N	9 22W
Penicuik	**35**	55 50N	3 14W
Penida, I.	**102**	8 45S	115 30E
Penistone	**33**	53 31N	1 38W
Penitentes, Serra dos	**170**	8 45S	46 20W
Penkridge	**28**	52 44N	2 8W
Penmachno	**31**	53 2N	3 47W
Penmaenmawr	**31**	53 16N	3 55W
Penmarch	**42**	47 49N	4 21W
Penmarch, Pte. de	**42**	47 48N	4 22W
Penn Yan	**162**	42 39N	77 7W
Pennabilli	**63**	43 50N	12 17E
Pennant	**153**	50 32N	108 14W
Penne	**63**	42 28N	13 56E
Penner, R.	**97**	14 50N	78 20E
Penneshaw	**140**	35 44S	137 56E
Pennines	**32**	54 50N	2 20W
Pennino, Mte.	**63**	43 6N	12 54E
Pennsburg	**162**	40 23N	75 30W
Pennsville	**162**	39 39N	75 31W
Pennsylvania □	**156**	40 50N	78 0W
Penny	**152**	53 51N	121 48W
Peno	**80**	57 2N	32 33E
Penola	**140**	37 25S	140 47E
Penong	**139**	31 59S	133 5E
Penonomé	**166**	8 31N	80 21W
Penpont	**35**	55 14N	3 49W
Penrhyn Is.	**131**	9 0S	150 30W
Penrith, Austral.	**141**	33 43S	150 38E
Penrith, U.K.	**32**	54 40N	2 45W
Penryn	**30**	50 10N	5 7W
Pensacola	**157**	30 30N	87 10W
Pensacola Mts.	**13**	84 0S	40 0W
Pense	**153**	50 25N	104 59W
Penshurst, Austral.	**140**	37 49S	142 20W
Penshurst, U.K.	**29**	51 10N	0 12E
Pentecoste	**170**	3 48S	37 17W
Penticton	**152**	49 30N	119 30W
Pentire Pt.	**30**	50 35N	4 57W
Pentland	**138**	20 32S	145 25E
Pentland Firth	**37**	58 43N	3 10W
Pentland Hills	**35**	55 48N	3 25W
Pentland Skerries	**37**	58 41N	2 53W
Pentraeth	**31**	53 17N	4 13W
Pentre Foelas	**31**	53 2N	3 41W
Penukonda	**97**	14 5N	77 38E
Penwortham	**32**	53 45N	2 44W
Penybont	**31**	52 17N	3 18W
Penylan L.	**153**	61 50N	106 20W
Penza	**81**	53 15N	45 5E
Penzance	**30**	50 7N	5 32W
Penzberg	**49**	47 46N	11 23E
Penzhinskaya Guba	**77**	61 30N	163 0E
Penzlin	**48**	53 32N	13 6E
Peó	**66**	42 40N	20 17E
Peoria, Ariz., U.S.A.	**161**	33 40N	112 15W
Peoria, Ill., U.S.A.	**158**	40 40N	89 40W
Pepacton Res.	**162**	42 5N	74 58W
Pepingen	**47**	50 46N	4 10E
Pepinster	**47**	50 34N	5 47E
Pepmbridge	**28**	52 13N	2 54W
Pepperwood	**160**	40 23N	124 0W
Peqini	**68**	41 4N	19 44E
Pera Hd.	**138**	12 55S	141 37E
Perabumilih	**102**	3 27S	104 15E
Perakhóra	**69**	38 2N	22 56E
Peraki, R.	**101**	5 10N	101 4E
Perales de Alfambra	**58**	40 38N	1 0W
Perales del Puerto	**56**	40 10N	6 40W
Peralta	**58**	42 21N	1 49W
Pérama	**69**	35 20N	24 22E
Perast	**66**	42 31N	18 47E
Percé	**151**	48 31N	64 13W
Perche	**42**	48 31N	1 1E
Perche, Collines de la	**42**	42 30N	2 5E
Percival Lakes	**136**	21 25S	125 0E
Percy	**42**	48 55N	1 11W
Percy Is.	**138**	21 39S	150 16E
Percyville	**138**	19 2S	143 45E
Perdido, Mte.	**58**	42 40N	0 50E
Pereira	**174**	4 49N	75 43W
Pereira Barreto	**171**	20 38S	51 7W
Pereira de Eóa	**128**	16 48S	15 50E
Perekerten	**140**	34 55S	143 40E
Perenjori	**137**	29 26S	116 16E
Pereslavi-Zelesskiy	**80**	56 45N	38 58E
Pereyaslav-Khmelnitskiy	**80**	50 3N	31 28E
Perez, I.	**165**	22 24N	89 42W
Perg	**52**	48 15N	14 38E
Pergamino	**172**	33 52S	60 30W
Pergine Valsugano	**63**	46 4N	11 15E
Pérgola	**63**	43 35N	12 50E
Perham	**158**	46 36N	95 36W
Perham Down Camp	**28**	51 14N	1 38W
Perhentian, Kepulauan	**101**	5 54N	102 42E
Peri, L.	**140**	30 45S	143 35E
Periam	**66**	46 2N	20 59E
Peribonca, L.	**151**	50 1N	71 10W
Péribonca, R.	**151**	48 45N	72 5W
Perico	**172**	24 20S	65 5W
Pericos	**164**	25 3N	107 42W
Périers	**42**	49 11N	1 25W
Périgord	**44**	45 0N	0 40E
Périgueux	**44**	45 10N	0 42E
Perija, Sierra de	**174**	9 30N	73 3W
Perim, I.	**91**	12 39N	43 25E
Peristera, I.	**69**	39 15N	23 58E
Peritoró	**170**	4 20S	44 18W
Periyakulam	**97**	10 5N	77 30E
Periyar, L.	**97**	9 25N	77 10E
Periyar, R.	**97**	10 15N	78 10E
Perkam, Tg.	**103**	1 35S	137 50E
Perkasie	**162**	40 22N	75 18W
Perkovió	**63**	43 41N	16 10E
Perlas, Arch. de las	**166**	8 41N	79 7W
Perlas, Punta de	**166**	11 30N	83 30W
Perleberg	**48**	53 5N	11 50E
Perlevka	**81**	51 56N	38 57E
Perlez	**66**	45 11N	20 22E
Perlis □	**101**	6 30N	100 15E
Perm (Molotov)	**84**	58 0N	57 10E
Përmeti	**68**	40 15N	20 21E
Pernambuco = Recife	**170**	8 0S	35 0W
Pernambuco □	**170**	8 0S	37 0W
Pernatty Lagoon	**140**	31 30S	137 12E
Peron, C.	**137**	25 30S	113 30E
Peron Is.	**136**	13 9S	130 4E
Peron Pen.	**137**	26 0S	113 10E
Péronne	**43**	49 55N	2 57E
Péronnes	**47**	50 27N	4 9E
Perosa Argentina	**62**	44 57N	7 11E
Perouse Str., La	**86**	45 40N	142 0E
Perow	**152**	54 35N	126 10W
Perpendicular Pt.	**139**	31 37S	152 52E
Perpignan	**44**	42 42N	2 53E
Perranporth	**30**	50 21N	5 9W
Perranzabuloe	**30**	50 18N	5 7W
Perris	**163**	33 47N	117 14W
Perros-Guirec	**42**	48 49N	3 28W
Perry, Fla., U.S.A.	**157**	30 9N	83 10W
Perry, Ga., U.S.A.	**157**	32 25N	83 41W
Perry, Iowa, U.S.A.	**158**	41 48N	94 5W
Perry, Maine, U.S.A.	**157**	44 59N	67 20W
Perry, Okla., U.S.A.	**159**	36 20N	97 20W
Perry, Mt.	**139**	25 12S	151 41E
Perryton	**159**	36 28N	100 48W

Perryville Ping, R

Perryville, Alas., U.S.A. 147 55 54N 159 10W
Perryville, Mo., U.S.A. 159 37 42N 89 50W
Persberg 72 59 47N 14 15 E
Persepolis 93 29 55N 52 50 E
Pershore 28 52 7N 2 4W
Persia = Iran 93 35 0N 50 0 E
Persian Gulf 93 27 0N 50 0 E
Perstorp 73 56 10N 13 25 E
Perth, Austral. 137 31 57 S 115 52 E
Perth, N.B., Can. 150 46 43N 67 42W
Perth, Ont., Can. 150 44 55N 76 15W
Perth, U.K. 35 56 24N 3 27W
Perth (□) 26 56 30N 4 0W
Perth Amboy 162 40 30N 74 25W
Perthus, Le 44 42 30N 2 53 E
Pertuis 45 43 42N 5 30 E
Pertuis Breton 44 46 17N 1 25W
Pertuis d'Antioche 44 46 6N 1 20W
Peru, Ill., U.S.A. 158 41 18N 89 12W
Peru, Ind., U.S.A. 156 40 42N 86 0W
Peru ■ 174 8 0 S 75 0W
Perúgia 63 43 6N 12 24 E
Perušió 63 44 40N 15 22 E
Péruwelz 47 50 31N 3 36 E
Pervomayskiy 81 53 20N 40 10 E
Pervouralsk 84 56 55N 60 0 E
Perwez 47 50 38N 4 48 E
Pésaro 63 43 55N 12 53 E
Pesca, La 165 23 46N 97 47W
Pescadores Is. (P'enghu Liehtao) 109 23 30N 119 30 E
Pescara 63 42 28N 14 13 E
Peschanokopskoye 83 46 14N 41 4 E
Péscia 62 43 54N 10 40 E
Pescina 63 42 0N 13 39 E
Peseux 50 46 59N 6 53 E
Peshawar 94 34 2N 71 37 E
Peshawar □ 94 35 0N 72 50 E
Peshkopia 68 41 41N 20 25 E
Peshovka 84 59 4N 52 22 E
Peshtera 67 42 2N 24 18 E
Peshtigo 156 45 4N 87 46W
Peski 81 51 14N 42 12 E
Peskovka 81 59 9N 52 28 E
Pêso da Régua 56 41 10N 7 47W
Pesqueira 170 8 20 S 36 42W
Pesquieria 164 29 23N 110 54W
Pesquieria, R. 164 25 54N 99 11W
Pessac 44 44 48N 0 37W
Pessoux 47 50 17N 5 11 E
Pest □ 53 47 29N 19 5 E
Pestovo 80 58 33N 35 18 E
Pestravka 81 52 28N 49 57 E
Péta 69 39 10N 21 2 E
Petah Tiqwa 90 32 6N 34 53 E
Petalidhion, Khóra 69 36 57N 21 55 E
Petaling Jaya 101 3 4N 101 42 E
Petaluma 163 38 13N 122 39W
Petange 47 49 33N 5 55 E
Petatlán 164 17 31N 101 16W
Petauke 127 14 14 S 31 12 E
Petawawa 150 45 54N 77 17W
Petegem 47 50 59N 3 32 E
Petén Itza, Lago 166 16 58N 89 50W
Peter 1st, I. 13 69 0 S 91 0W
Peter Pond L. 153 55 55N 108 44W
Peterbell 150 48 36N 83 21W
Peterboro 162 42 55N 71 59W
Peterborough, S. Australia, Austral. 140 32 58 S 138 51 E
Peterborough, Victoria, Austral. 133 38 37 S 142 50 E
Peterborough, U.K. 29 52 35N 0 14W
Peterchurch 28 52 3N 2 57W
Peterculter 37 57 5N 2 18W
Peterhead 37 57 30N 1 49W
Peterlee 33 54 45N 1 18W
Petersburg, Alas., U.S.A. 152 56 50N 133 0W
Petersburg, Ind., U.S.A. 156 38 30N 87 15W
Petersburg, Va., U.S.A. 162 37 17N 77 26W
Petersburg, W. Va., U.S.A. 156 38 59N 79 10W
Petersfield 29 51 0N 0 56W
Peterswell 39 53 7N 8 46W
Petford 138 17 20 S 144 50 E
Petilia Policastro 65 39 7N 16 48 E
Petit Bois I. 157 30 16N 88 25W
Petit Cap 151 48 58N 63 58W
Petit Goâve 167 18 27N 72 51W
Petit-Quevilly, Le 42 49 26N 1 0 E
Petitcodiac 151 45 57N 65 11W
Petite Saguenay 151 47 59N 70 1W
Petitsikapau, L. 151 54 37N 66 25W
Petlad 94 22 30N 72 45 E
Peto 165 20 10N 89 0W
Petone 142 41 13 S 174 53 E
Petoskey 150 45 22N 84 57W
Petra, Jordan 90 30 20N 35 22 E
Petra, Spain 58 39 37N 3 6 E
Petra, Ostrova 12 76 15N 118 30 E
Petralia 65 37 49N 14 4 E
Petrel 59 38 30N 0 46W
Petrich 67 41 24N 23 13 E
Petrijanec 63 46 23N 16 17 E
Petrikov 80 52 11N 28 29 E
Petrila 70 45 29N 23 29 E
Petrinja 63 45 28N 16 18 E
'Petroland', gasfield 19 53 35N 4 15 E
Petrolândia 170 9 5 S 38 20W
Petrolia 150 42 54N 82 9W
Petrolina 170 9 24 S 40 30W
Petropavlovsk 76 55 0N 69 0 E
Petropavlovsk-Kamchatskiy 77 53 16N 159 0 E
Petrópolis 173 22 33 S 43 9W
Petroşeni 70 45 28N 23 20 E
Petrova Gora 63 45 15N 15 45 E
Petrovac 66 42 13N 18 57 E
Petrovaradin 66 45 16N 19 55 E
Petrovsk 81 52 22N 45 19 E
Petrovsk-Zabaykalskiy 77 51 26N 108 30 E
Petrovskoye, R.S.F.S.R., U.S.S.R. 83 45 25N 42 58 E
Petrovskoye, R.S.F.S.R., U.S.S.R. 84 53 37N 56 23 E
Petrozavodsk 78 61 41N 34 20 E
Petrus Steyn 129 27 38 S 28 8 E
Petrusburg 128 29 4 S 25 26 E
Pettigo 38 54 32N 7 49W
Pettitts 141 34 56 S 148 10 E
Petworth 29 50 59N 0 37W
Peumo 172 34 21 S 71 19W
Peureulak 102 4 48N 97 45 E
Pevek 77 69 15N 171 0 E
Pevensey 29 50 49N 0 20 E
Pevensey Levels 29 50 50N 0 20 E
Peveragno 62 44 20N 7 37 E
Pewsey 28 51 20N 1 46W
Pewsey, Vale of 28 51 20N 1 46W
Peyrehorade 44 43 34N 1 7W
Peyruis 45 44 1N 5 56 E
Pézenas 44 43 28N 3 24 E
Pezinok 53 48 17N 17 17 E
Pfaffenhofen 49 48 31N 11 31 E
Pfäffikon 51 47 13N 8 46 E
Pfarrkirchen 49 48 25N 12 57 E
Pforzheim 49 48 53N 8 43 E
Pfungstadt 49 49 47N 8 36 E
Phagwara 93 31 10N 75 40 E
Phala 128 23 45 S 26 50 E
Phalodi 94 27 12N 72 24 E
Phalsbourg 43 48 46N 7 15 E
Phan 100 19 28N 99 43 E
Phan Rang 101 11 40N 109 9 E
Phan Thiet 101 11 1N 108 9 E
Phanat Nikhom 100 13 27N 101 11 E
Phangan, Ko 101 9 45N 100 0 E
Phangnga 101 8 28N 98 30 E
Phanh Bho Ho Chi Minh 101 10 58N 106 40 E
Phanom Dang Raek, mts. 100 14 45N 104 0 E
Phanom Sarakham 100 13 45N 101 21 E
Pharenda 95 27 5N 83 17 E
Phatthalung 101 7 39N 100 6 E
Phayao 100 19 11N 99 55 E
Phelps, N.Y., U.S.A. 162 42 57N 77 5W
Phelps, Wis., U.S.A. 158 46 2N 89 2W
Phelps L. 153 59 15N 103 15W
Phenix City 157 32 30N 85 0W
Phet Buri 100 13 1N 99 55 E
Phetchabun 100 16 25N 101 8 E
Phetchabun, Thiu Khao 100 16 0N 101 20 E
Phetchaburi 101 13 1N 99 55 E
Phi Phi, Ko 101 7 45N 98 46 E
Phiafay 100 14 48N 106 0 E
Phibun Mangsahan 100 15 14N 105 14 E
Phichai 100 17 22N 100 10 E
Phichit 100 16 26N 100 22 E
Philadelphia, Miss., U.S.A. 159 32 47N 89 5W
Philadelphia, Pa., U.S.A. 162 40 0N 75 10W
Philip 158 44 4N 101 42W
Philip Smith Mts. 147 68 0N 146 0W
Philippeville 47 50 12N 4 33 E
Philippi L. 138 24 20 S 138 55 E
Philippines ■ 103 12 0N 123 0 E
Philippolis 128 30 15 S 25 16 E
Philippopolis = Plovdiv 67 42 8N 24 44 E
Philipsburg 160 46 20N 113 21W
Philipstown 128 30 28 S 24 30 E
Phillip, I. 141 38 30 S 145 12 E
Phillips, Texas, U.S.A. 159 35 48N 101 17W
Phillips, Wis., U.S.A. 158 45 41N 90 22W
Phillips Ra. 136 16 53 S 125 50 E
Phillipsburg, Kans., U.S.A. 158 39 48N 99 20W
Phillipsburg, Penn., U.S.A. 162 40 43N 75 12W
Phillott 139 27 53 S 145 50 E
Philmont 162 42 14N 73 37W
Philomath 160 44 28N 123 21W
Phimai 100 15 13N 102 30 E
Phitsanulok 100 16 50N 100 12 E
Phnom Penh 101 11 33N 104 55 E
Phnom Thbeng 101 13 50N 104 56 E
Phoenicia 162 42 5N 74 14W
Phoenix, Ariz., U.S.A. 161 33 30N 112 10W
Phoenix, N.Y., U.S.A. 162 43 13N 76 18W
Phoenix Is. 130 3 30 S 172 0W
Phoenixville 162 40 12N 75 29W
Phon 100 15 49N 102 36 E
Phon Tiou 100 17 53N 104 37 E
Phong, R. 100 16 23N 102 56 E
Phong Saly 100 21 42N 102 9 E
Phong Tho 100 22 32N 103 21 E
Phongdo 99 30 14N 91 14 E
Phonhong 100 18 30N 102 25 E
Phonum 101 8 49N 98 48 E
Photharam 100 13 41N 99 51 E
Phra Chedi Sam Ong 100 15 16N 98 23 E
Phra Nakhon Si Ayutthaya 100 14 25N 100 30 E
Phra Thong, Ko 101 9 5N 98 17 E
Phrae 100 18 7N 100 9 E
Phrao 101 19 23N 99 15 E
Phrom Phiram 100 17 2N 100 12 E
Phu Dien 100 18 58N 105 31 E
Phu Doan 101 21 40N 105 10 E
Phu Loi 100 20 14N 103 14 E
Phu Ly (Ha Nam) 100 20 35N 105 50 E
Phu Qui 100 19 20N 105 20 E
Phu Tho 100 21 24N 105 13 E
Phuc Yen 100 21 16N 105 45 E
Phuket 100 8 0N 98 28 E
Phuket, Ko, I. 101 8 0N 98 22 E
Phulbari 98 21 52N 88 8 E
Phulera (Phalera) 94 26 52N 75 16 E
Phun Phin 101 9 7N 99 12 E
Phuoc Le (Baria) 101 10 39N 107 19 E
Piabia 138 25 12 S 152 45 E
Piacá 170 7 42 S 47 18W
Piacenza 62 45 2N 9 42 E
Piaçubaçu 170 10 24 S 36 25W
Piádena 62 45 8N 10 22 E
Pialba 139 25 20 S 152 45 E
Pian, Cr. 139 30 2 S 148 12 E
Piancó 171 7 12 S 37 57W
Pianella 63 42 24N 14 5 E
Piangil 140 35 5 S 143 20 E
Pianoro 63 44 20N 11 20 E
Pianosa, I., Puglia, Italy 63 42 12N 15 44 E
Pianosa, I., Toscana, Italy 62 42 36N 10 4 E
Piapot 153 49 59N 109 8W
Pias 57 38 1N 7 29W
Piaseczno 54 52 5N 21 2 E
Piassabussu 171 10 24 S 36 25W
Piastow 54 52 12N 20 48 E
Piatá 171 13 9 S 41 48W
Piatra Neamţ 70 46 56N 26 21 E
Piatra Olt 70 43 51N 25 9 E
Piauí □ 170 7 0 S 43 0W
Piaui, R. 170 6 38 S 42 42W
Piave, R. 63 45 50N 13 9 E
Piazza Ármerina 65 37 21N 14 20 E
Pibor Post 123 6 47N 33 3 E
Pibor, R. 123 7 1N 33 0 E
Pica 174 20 35 S 69 25W
Picard, Plaine de 43 50 0N 2 0 E
Picardie 43 50 0N 2 15 E
Picardy = Picardie 43 50 0N 2 15 E
Picayune 159 30 40N 89 40W
Piccadilly, Austral. 109 34 59 S 138 44 E
Piccadilly, Zambia 127 14 0 S 29 30 E
Picerno 65 40 40N 15 37 E
Pichiang 108 26 40N 98 53 E
Pichieh 108 27 20N 105 20 E
Pichilemu 172 34 22 S 72 9W
Pickerel L. 150 48 40N 91 25W
Pickering 33 54 15N 0 46W
Pickering, Vale of 33 54 0N 0 45W
Pickle Lake 150 51 30N 90 12W
Pico 16 38 28N 28 18W
Pico Truncado 176 46 40 S 68 10W
Picos 170 7 5 S 41 28W
Picos Ancares, Sierra de 56 42 51N 6 52W
Picquigny 43 49 56N 2 10 E
Picton, Austral. 141 34 12 S 150 34 E
Picton, Can. 150 44 1N 77 9W
Picton, N.Z. 143 41 18 S 174 3 E
Pictou 151 45 41N 62 42W
Picture Butte 152 49 55N 112 45W
Picuí 170 6 31 S 36 21W
Picún-Leufú 176 39 30 S 69 5W
Pidley 29 52 33N 0 4W
Pidurutalagala, mt. 97 7 10N 80 50 E
Piedad, La 164 20 20N 102 1W
Piedecuesta 174 6 59N 73 3W
Piedicavallo 62 45 41N 7 57 E
Piedmont 157 33 55N 85 39W
Piedmont = Piemonte 62 45 0N 7 30 E
Piedmont Plat. 157 34 0N 81 30W
Piedmonte d'Alife 65 41 22N 14 22 E
Piedra, R. 58 41 10N 1 45W
Piedrabuena 57 39 0N 4 10W
Piedrahita 56 40 28N 5 23W
Piedras Blancas Pt. 161 35 45N 121 18W
Piedras Negras 164 28 35N 100 35W
Piedras, R. de las 174 11 40 S 70 50W
Piemonte 62 45 0N 7 30 E
Piena 45 42 15N 8 34 E
Piensk 54 51 16N 15 2 E
Pier Millan 140 35 14 S 142 40 E
Pierce 160 46 46N 115 53W
Piería □ 68 40 13N 22 25 E
Pierowall 37 59 20N 3 0W
Pierre, France 43 46 54N 5 13 E
Pierre, U.S.A. 158 44 23N 100 20W
Pierrefeu 45 43 8N 6 9 E
Pierrefonds 43 49 20N 3 0 E
Pierrefontaine 43 47 14N 6 32 E
Pierrefort 44 44 55N 2 50 E
Pierrelatte 45 44 23N 4 43 E
Pieštany 155 48 35N 17 50 E
Piesting, R. 53 48 0N 16 19 E
Pieszyce 54 50 43N 16 33 E
Piet Retief 129 27 1 S 30 50 E
Pietarsaari 74 63 41N 22 40 E
Pietermaritzburg 129 29 35 S 30 25 E
Pietersburg 129 23 54 S 29 25 E
Pietraperzia 65 37 26N 14 8 E
Pietrasanta 62 43 57N 10 12 E
Pietrosu 70 47 12N 25 8 E
Pietrosul 70 47 35N 24 43 E
Pieve di Cadore 63 46 25N 12 22 E
Pieve di Teco 62 44 3N 7 54 E
Pievepélago 62 44 12N 10 35 E
Pigadhítsa 68 39 59N 21 23 E
Pigadia 69 35 30N 27 12 E
Pigeon I. 97 14 2N 74 20 E
Pigeon, R. 150 48 1N 89 42W
Piggott 159 36 20N 90 10W
Pigna 62 43 57N 7 40 E
Pigüe 172 37 36 S 62 25W
Pihani 95 27 36N 80 15 E
Pijnacker 46 52 1N 4 26 E
Pikalevo 80 59 37N 34 0 E
Pikes Peak 158 38 50N 105 10W
Pikesville 162 39 23N 76 44W
Piketberg 128 32 55 S 18 40 E
Pikeville 156 37 30N 82 30W
Pik'ochi 106 40 45N 111 17 E
Pikou 106 32 45N 105 22 E
Pikwitonei 153 55 35N 97 9W
Piła 54 53 10N 16 48 E
Piła □ 54 53 0N 17 0 E
Pila, mte. 59 38 16N 1 11W
Pilaia 68 40 32N 22 59 E
Pilani 94 28 22N 75 33 E
Pilão Arcado 170 10 9 S 42 26W
Pilar, Brazil 170 9 36 S 35 56W
Pilar, Parag. 172 26 50 S 58 10W
Pilas, I. 103 6 39N 121 37 E
Pilatus 51 46 59N 8 15 E
Pilbara Cr. 132 21 15 S 118 22 E
Pilbara Mining Centre 136 21 15 S 118 16 E
Pilcomayo, R. 172 25 21 S 57 42W
Píli 69 36 50N 27 15 E
Pilibhit 95 28 40N 79 50 E
Pilion, mt. 68 39 27N 23 7 E
Pilis 53 47 17N 19 35 E
Pilisvörösvár 53 47 38N 18 56 E
Pilkhawa 94 28 43N 77 42 E
Pilling 32 53 55N 2 54W
Pilltown 39 51 59N 7 49W
Pílos 69 36 55N 21 42 E
Pilot Mound 153 49 15N 98 54W
Pilot Point 159 33 26N 97 0W
Pilot Rock 160 45 30N 118 58W
Pilsen = Plzen 52 49 45N 13 22 E
Pilštanj 63 46 8N 15 39 E
Pilton 28 51 0N 2 35W
Piltown 39 52 22N 7 18W
Pilzno 54 50 0N 21 16 E
Pimba 140 31 18 S 136 46 E
Pimenta Bueno 174 11 35 S 61 10W
Pimentel 174 6 45 S 79 55W
Pimuacan, Rés. 151 49 45N 70 30W
Pina 58 41 29N 0 33W
Pinang, I. 101 5 25N 100 15 E
Pinar del Río 166 22 26N 83 40W
Pinawa 149 50 9N 95 50W
Pince C. 151 46 38N 53 45W
Pinchbeck 29 52 48N 0 9W
Pincher Creek 152 49 30N 113 57W
Pinchi L. 152 54 38N 124 30W
Pinch'uan 108 25 51N 100 34 E
Pinckneyville 158 38 5N 89 20W
Pîncota 66 46 20N 21 45 E
Pind Dadan Khan 94 32 35N 73 47 E
Pindar 137 28 30 S 115 47 E
Pindaré Mirim 170 3 37 S 45 21W
Pindaré, R. 170 3 17 S 44 47W
Pindi Gheb 94 33 14N 72 12 E
Pindiga 121 9 58N 10 53 E
Pindobal 170 3 16 S 48 25W
Pindos Óros 68 40 0N 21 0 E
Pindus Mts. = Pindos Óros 68 40 0N 21 0 E
Pine 161 34 27N 111 30W
Pine Bluff 159 34 10N 92 0W
Pine, C. 151 46 37N 53 32W
Pine City 158 45 46N 93 0W
Pine Creek, N.T., Austral. 132 13 50 S 131 49 E
Pine Creek, Queens., Austral. 138 13 13 S 142 47 E
Pine Dock 153 51 38N 96 48W
Pine Falls 153 50 34N 96 11W
Pine Flat Res. 163 36 50N 119 20W
Pine Grove 162 40 33N 76 23W
Pine Hill 138 23 42 S 147 0 E
Pine, La 160 43 53N 80 45W
Pine Pass 152 55 25N 122 42W
Pine Point 152 60 50N 114 28W
Pine, R., Austral. 108 27 18 S 153 2 E
Pine, R., Can. 153 55 20N 107 38W
Pine Ridge, Austral. 141 31 10 S 147 30 E
Pine Ridge, U.S.A. 158 42 2N 102 35W
Pine River, Can. 153 51 45N 100 30W
Pine River, U.S.A. 158 46 40N 94 20W
Pine Valley 163 32 50N 116 32W
Pinecrest 163 38 12N 120 1W
Pinedale, Ariz., U.S.A. 161 34 23N 110 16W
Pinedale, Calif., U.S.A. 163 36 50N 119 48W
Pinega 52 64 45N 43 40 E
Pinega, R. 78 64 20N 43 0 E
Pinehill 138 23 38 S 146 57 E
Pinerolo 62 44 47N 7 21 E
Pineto 63 42 36N 14 4 E
Pinetop 161 34 10N 109 57W
Pinetown 129 29 48 S 30 54 E
Pinetree 158 43 42N 105 52W
Pineville, Ky., U.S.A. 157 36 42N 83 42W
Pineville, La., U.S.A. 159 31 22N 92 30W
Pinewood 153 48 45N 94 10W
Piney, Can. 153 49 5N 96 10W
Piney, France 43 48 22N 4 21 E
Ping, R. 100 15 42N 100 9 E

Pingaring **Polcura**

Pingaring	**137**	32 40 S	118 32 E
P'ingch'ang	**108**	31 33N	107 6 E
P'ingchiang	**109**	28 42N	113 35 E
P'ingch'uan	**107**	41 0N	118 36 E
Pingelly	**137**	32 29 S	116 59 E
P'ingho	**109**	24 18N	117 2 E
P'inghsiang, Kiangsi, China	**109**	27 39N	113 50 E
P'inghsiang, Kwangsi Chuang, China	**108**	22 6N	106 44 E
P'inghu	**109**	30 38N	121 0 E
P'ingi, Shantung, China	**107**	35 30N	117 36 E
P'ingi, Yünnan, China	**108**	25 40N	104 14 E
P'ingkuo	**108**	23 20N	107 34 E
P'ingli	**108**	32 26N	109 22 E
P'ingliang	**105**	35 32N	106 50 E
Pinglo, Kwangsi-Chuang, China	**109**	24 30N	110 45 E
Pinglo, Ningsia Hui, China	**106**	38 58N	106 30 E
P'inglu	**106**	37 32N	112 14 E
P'ingluch'eng	**106**	39 46N	112 6 E
P'ingnan, Fukien, China	**109**	26 56N	119 3 E
P'ingnan, Kwangsi-Chiang, China	**109**	23 33N	110 23 E
P'ingpa	**108**	26 25N	106 15 E
P'ingpien	**108**	22 54N	103 40 E
Pingrup	**137**	33 32 S	118 29 E
P'ingt'an	**109**	25 31N	119 47 E
P'ingt'ang	**108**	25 50N	107 19 E
P'ingting	**106**	37 48N	113 37 E
P'ingt'ingshan	**106**	33 43N	113 28 E
P'ingtu	**107**	36 47N	119 56 E
P'ingtung	**105**	22 38N	120 30 E
Pingwu	**105**	32 27N	104 25 E
P'ingwu	**108**	32 25N	104 36 E
P'ingyang	**109**	27 40N	120 33 E
P'ingyangchen	**107**	45 11N	131 15 E
P'ingyao	**106**	37 12N	112 10 E
P'ingyin	**106**	36 18N	116 26 E
P'ingyüan, Kwangtung, China	**109**	24 34N	115 54 E
P'ingyüan, Ningsia Hui, China	**106**	37 9N	116 25 E
Pinhai	**107**	34 0N	119 50 E
Pinhal	**173**	22 10 S	46 46W
Pinheiro	**170**	2 31 S	45 5W
Pinhel	**56**	40 18N	7 0W
Pinhoe	**30**	50 44N	3 29W
Pinhsien, Heilung Kiang, China	**107**	45 44N	127 27 E
Pinhsien, Shensi, China	**106**	35 10N	108 10 E
Pini, I.	**102**	0 10N	98 40 E
Piniós, R., Ilia, Greece	**69**	37 38N	21 20 E
Piniós, R., Trikkala, Greece	**68**	39 55N	22 10 E
Pinjarra	**137**	32 37 S	115 52 E
Pink, R.	**153**	56 50N	103 50W
Pinkafeld	**53**	47 22N	16 9 E
Pinlebu	**98**	24 5N	95 22 E
Pinnacles, Austral.	**137**	28 12 S	120 26 E
Pinnacles, U.S.A.	**163**	36 33N	121 8W
Pinnaroo	**140**	35 13 S	140 56 E
Pinon Hills	**163**	34 26N	117 39W
Pinos	**164**	22 20N	101 40W
Pinos, I. de	**166**	21 40N	82 40W
Pinos, Mt	**163**	34 49N	119 8W
Pinos Pt.	**161**	36 50N	121 57W
Pinos Puente	**57**	37 15N	3 45W
Pinotepa Nacional	**165**	16 25N	97 55W
Pinrang	**103**	3 46 S	119 34 E
Pinsk	**80**	52 10N	26 8 E
Pintados	**174**	20 35 S	69 40W
Pinto Butte Mt.	**153**	49 22N	107 27W
Pintumba	**137**	31 50 S	132 18 E
Pinwherry	**34**	55 9N	4 50W
Pinyang	**108**	23 17N	108 47 E
Pinyug	**78**	60 5N	48 0 E
Pinzolo	**62**	46 9N	10 45 E
Pio XII	**170**	3 53 S	45 17W
Pioche	**161**	38 0N	114 35W
Piombino	**62**	42 54N	10 30 E
Pioner, I.	**77**	79 50N	92 0 E
Pionki	**54**	51 29N	21 28 E
Piorini, L.	**174**	3 15 S	62 35W
Piotrków Trybunalski	**54**	51 23N	19 43 E
Piotrków Trybunalski □	**54**	51 30N	19 45 E
Piove di Sacco	**63**	45 18N	12 1 E
Pip	**93**	26 45N	60 10 E
Pipar	**94**	26 25N	73 31 E
Pipariya	**96**	22 45N	78 23 E
Piper, oilfield	**19**	58 30N	0 15 E
Pipéri, I.	**68**	39 20N	24 19 E
Pipestone	**158**	44 0N	96 20W
Pipestone Cr.	**153**	53 37N	109 46W
Pipestone, R.	**150**	52 53N	89 23W
Pipinas	**172**	35 30 S	57 19W
Pipiriki	**142**	38 28 S	175 5 E
Pipmuacan Res.	**151**	49 40N	70 25W
Pippingarra	**136**	20 27 S	118 42 E
Pipriac	**42**	47 49N	1 58W
Piqua	**156**	40 10N	84 10W
Piquet Carneiro	**171**	5 48 S	39 25W
Piquiri, R.	**173**	24 3 S	54 14W
Piracanjuba	**171**	17 18 S	49 1W
Piracicaba	**173**	22 45 S	47 30W
Piracuruca	**170**	3 50 S	41 50W
Piræus = Piraiévs	**69**	37 57N	23 42 E
Piraiévs	**69**	37 57N	23 42 E
Piraiévs □	**69**	37 0N	23 30 E
Piráino	**65**	38 10N	14 52 E
Pirajuí	**173**	21 59 S	49 29W
Piran (Pirano)	**63**	45 31N	13 33 E
Pirane	**172**	25 25 S	59 30W
Piranhas	**170**	9 27 S	37 46W
Pirapemas	**170**	3 43 S	44 14W
Pirapora	**171**	17 20 S	44 56W
Piratyin	**80**	50 15N	32 25 E
Pirbright	**29**	51 17N	0 40W
Pirdop	**67**	42 40N	24 10 E
Pires do Rio	**171**	17 18 S	48 17W
Pirganj	**98**	25 51 S	88 24 E
Pirgos, Ilia, Greece	**69**	37 40N	21 27 E
Pirgos, Messinia, Greece	**69**	36 50N	22 16 E
Pirgovo	**67**	43 44N	25 43 E
Piriac-sur-Mer	**42**	47 22N	2 33W
Piribebuy	**172**	25 26 S	57 2W
Pirin Planina	**67**	41 40N	23 30 E
Pirineos, mts.	**58**	42 40N	1 0 E
Piripiri	**170**	4 15 S	41 46W
Piritu	**174**	9 23N	69 12W
Pirmasens	**49**	49 12N	7 30 E
Pirna	**48**	50 57N	13 57 E
Pirojpur	**98**	22 35N	90 1 E
Pirot	**66**	43 9N	22 39 E
Pirsagat, R.	**83**	40 15N	48 45 E
Pirtleville	**161**	31 25N	109 35W
Piru	**163**	34 25N	118 48W
Piryí	**69**	38 13N	25 59 E
Pisa	**62**	43 43N	10 23 E
Pisa Ra.	**143**	44 52 S	169 12 E
Pisagua	**174**	19 40 S	70 15W
Pisarovina	**63**	45 35N	15 50 E
Pisciotta	**65**	40 7N	15 12 E
Pisco	**174**	13 50 S	76 5W
Piscu	**70**	45 30N	27 43 E
Písek	**52**	49 19N	14 10 E
Pisham	**108**	29 37N	106 13 E
P'ishan	**105**	37 38N	78 19 E
Pishin Lora, R.	**94**	30 15N	66 5 E
Pising	**103**	5 8 S	121 53 E
Pismo Beach	**163**	35 9N	120 38W
Pissos	**44**	44 19N	0 49W
Pisticci	**65**	40 24N	16 33 E
Pistoia	**62**	43 57N	10 53 E
Pistol B.	**153**	62 25N	92 37W
Pisuerga, R.	**56**	42 10N	4 15W
Pisz	**54**	53 38N	21 49 E
Pitalito	**174**	1 51N	76 2W
Pitanga	**171**	24 46 S	51 44W
Pitangui	**171**	19 40 S	44 54 E
Pitarpunga, L.	**140**	34 24 S	143 30 E
Pitcairn I.	**131**	25 5 S	130 5W
Pite älv	**74**	65 44N	20 50W
Piteå	**74**	65 20N	21 25 E
Piteşti	**70**	44 52N	24 54 E
Pithapuram	**96**	17 10N	82 15 E
Pithara	**137**	30 20 S	116 35 E
Píthion	**68**	41 24N	26 40W
Pithiviers	**43**	48 10N	2 13 E
Pitigliano	**63**	42 38N	11 40 E
Pitiquito	**164**	30 42N	112 2W
Pitlochry	**37**	56 43N	3 43W
Pitt I.	**152**	53 30N	129 50W
Pittem	**47**	51 1N	3 13 E
Pittenweem	**35**	56 13N	2 43W
Pittsburg, Calif., U.S.A.	**163**	38 1N	121 50W
Pittsburg, Kans., U.S.A.	**159**	37 21N	94 43W
Pittsburg, Tex., U.S.A.	**159**	32 59N	94 58W
Pittsburgh	**156**	40 25N	79 55W
Pittsfield, Ill., U.S.A.	**158**	39 35N	90 46W
Pittsfield, N.H., U.S.A.	**162**	43 17N	71 18W
Pittston	**162**	41 19N	75 50W
Pittsworth	**139**	27 41 S	151 37 E
Pituri, R.	**138**	22 35 S	138 30 E
Pitzewo	**107**	39 28N	122 30 E
Piuí	**171**	20 28 S	45 58W
Pium	**170**	10 27 S	49 11W
Piura	**174**	5 5 S	80 45W
Piva, R.	**66**	43 15N	18 50 E
Pivijay	**174**	10 28N	74 37W
Piwniczna	**54**	49 27N	20 42 E
Pixariá Óros	**69**	38 42N	23 39 E
Pixley	**163**	35 58N	119 18W
Piyai	**68**	39 17N	21 25 E
Piyang	**109**	32 50N	113 30 E
Piz Bernina	**49**	46 23N	9 45 E
Pizarro	**174**	4 58N	77 22W
Pizol	**51**	46 57N	9 23 E
Pizzo	**65**	38 44N	16 10 E
Placentia	**151**	47 20N	54 0W
Placentia B.	**151**	47 0N	54 40W
Placerville	**160**	38 47N	120 51W
Placetas	**166**	22 15N	79 44W
'Placid', gasfield	**19**	53 25N	4 20 E
Plačkovica, mts.	**66**	41 45N	22 30 E
Pladda, I.	**34**	55 25N	5 7W
Plaffein	**50**	46 45N	7 17 E
Plain Dealing	**159**	32 56N	93 41W
Plainfield	**162**	40 37N	74 28W
Plains, Kans., U.S.A.	**159**	37 20N	100 35W
Plains, Mont., U.S.A.	**160**	47 27N	114 57W
Plains, Tex., U.S.A.	**159**	33 11N	102 50W
Plainview, Nebr., U.S.A.	**158**	42 25N	97 48W
Plainview, Tex., U.S.A.	**159**	34 10N	101 40W
Plainville	**158**	39 18N	99 19W
Plainwell	**156**	42 28N	85 40W
Plaisance	**44**	43 36N	0 3 E
Pláka	**68**	36 45N	24 26 E
Plakhino	**76**	67 45N	86 5 E
Planá	**52**	49 50N	12 44 E
Plana Cays	**167**	22 38N	73 30W
Planada	**163**	37 18N	120 19W
Planaltina	**171**	15 30 S	47 45W
Plancoët	**42**	48 32N	2 13W
Plandište	**66**	45 16N	21 10 E
Planeta Rica	**174**	8 25N	75 36W
Planina, Slovenija, Yugo.	**63**	45 47N	14 19 E
Planina, Slovenija, Yugo.	**63**	46 10N	15 12 E
Plankinton	**158**	43 45N	98 27W
Plano	**159**	33 0N	96 45W
Plant City	**157**	28 0N	82 15W
Plant, La	**158**	45 11N	100 40W
Plaquemine	**159**	30 20N	91 15W
Plasencia	**56**	40 3N	6 8W
Plaški	**63**	45 4N	15 22 E
Plassen	**72**	61 9N	12 30 E
Plast	**84**	54 22N	60 50 E
Plaster Rock	**151**	46 53N	67 22W
Plata, La, Argent.	**172**	35 0 S	57 55W
Plata, La, U.S.A.	**162**	38 32N	76 59W
Plata, La, Río de	**172**	35 0 S	56 40W
Platani, R.	**64**	37 28N	13 23 E
Plateau	**13**	70 55 S	40 0 E
Plateau □	**121**	9 0N	9 0 E
Plateau du Coteau du Missouri	**158**	47 9N	101 5W
Platí, Ákra	**68**	40 27N	24 0 E
Platinum	**147**	59 2N	161 50W
Plato	**174**	9 47N	74 47W
Platte	**158**	43 28N	98 50W
Platte, Piz	**51**	46 30N	9 35 E
Platte, R.	**158**	41 0N	98 0W
Platteville	**158**	40 18N	104 47W
Plattling	**49**	48 46N	12 53 E
Plattsburgh	**156**	44 41N	73 30W
Plattsmouth	**158**	41 0N	96 0W
Plau	**48**	53 27N	12 16 E
Plauen	**48**	50 29N	12 9 E
Plav	**66**	42 38N	19 57 E
Plavnica	**66**	42 10N	19 20 E
Plavsk	**81**	53 40N	37 18 E
Playa Azul	**164**	17 59N	102 24W
Playa de Castilla	**57**	41 25N	0 12W
Playgreen L.	**153**	54 0N	98 15W
Pleasant Bay	**151**	46 51N	60 48W
Pleasant Hill	**158**	38 48N	94 14W
Pleasant Hills	**141**	35 28 S	146 50 E
Pleasant Mount	**162**	41 44N	75 26W
Pleasant Pt.	**143**	44 16 S	171 9 E
Pleasanton	**159**	29 0N	98 30W
Pleasantville	**162**	39 25N	74 30W
Pléaux	**44**	45 8N	2 13 E
Pleiku (Gia Lai)	**101**	14 3N	108 0 E
Plélan-le-Grand	**42**	48 0N	2 7W
Plémet	**42**	48 11N	2 36W
Pléneuf-Val-André	**42**	48 35N	2 32W
Pleniţa	**70**	44 14N	23 10 E
Plenty, Bay of	**142**	37 45 S	177 0 E
Plenty, R.	**138**	23 25 S	136 31 E
Plentywood	**158**	48 45N	104 35W
Plesetsk	**78**	62 40N	40 10 E
Plessisville	**151**	46 14N	71 47W
Plestin-les-Grèves	**42**	48 40N	3 39W
Pleszew	**54**	51 53N	17 47 E
Pleternica	**66**	45 17N	17 48 E
Pletipi L.	**151**	51 44N	70 6W
Pleven	**67**	43 26N	24 37 E
Plevlja	**66**	43 21N	19 21 E
Płock	**54**	52 32N	19 40 E
Płock □	**54**	52 30N	19 45 E
Plöcken Passo	**63**	46 37N	12 57 E
Plockton	**36**	57 20N	5 40W
Ploegsteert	**47**	50 44N	2 53 E
Ploëmeur	**42**	47 44N	3 26W
Ploërmel	**42**	47 55N	2 26W
Ploieşti	**70**	44 57N	26 5 E
Plomárion	**69**	38 58N	26 24 E
Plomb du Cantal	**44**	45 2N	2 48 E
Plombières	**43**	47 59N	6 27 E
Plomin	**63**	45 8N	14 10 E
Plön	**48**	54 8N	10 22 E
Plöner See	**48**	53 9N	15 5 E
Plonge, Lac La	**153**	55 8N	107 20W
Płonsk	**54**	52 37N	20 21 E
Płoty	**54**	53 48N	15 18 E
Plouay	**42**	47 55N	3 21W
Ploudalmézeau	**42**	48 34N	4 41W
Plougasnou	**42**	48 42N	3 49W
Plouha	**42**	48 41N	2 57W
Plouhinec	**42**	48 0N	4 29W
Plovdiv	**67**	42 8N	24 44 E
Plum I.	**162**	41 10N	72 12W
Plumbridge	**38**	54 46N	7 15W
Plummer	**160**	47 21N	116 59W
Plumtree	**127**	20 27 S	27 55 E
Plunge	**80**	55 53N	21 51 E
Pluvigner	**42**	47 46N	3 1W
Plymouth, U.K.	**30**	50 23N	4 9W
Plymouth, Calif., U.S.A.	**163**	38 29N	120 51W
Plymouth, Ind., U.S.A.	**156**	41 20N	86 19W
Plymouth, Mass., U.S.A.	**162**	41 58N	70 40W
Plymouth, N.C., U.S.A.	**157**	35 54N	76 55W
Plymouth, N.H., U.S.A.	**162**	43 44N	71 41W
Plymouth, Pa., U.S.A.	**162**	41 17N	76 0W
Plymouth, Wis., U.S.A.	**156**	43 42N	87 58W
Plymouth Sd.	**30**	50 20N	4 10W
Plympton	**30**	50 24N	4 2W
Plymstock	**30**	50 22N	4 6W
Plynlimon = Pumlumon Fawr	**31**	52 29N	3 47W
Plyussa	**80**	47 40N	29 0 E
Plyussa, R.	**80**	58 40N	28 30 E
Plzen	**52**	49 45N	13 22 E
Pniewy	**54**	52 31N	16 16 E
Pô	**121**	11 14N	1 5W
Po Hai	**107**	38 30N	119 0 E
Po, R.	**62**	45 0N	10 45 E
Poai	**106**	35 10N	113 4 E
Pobé	**121**	7 0N	2 38 E
Pobedino	**76**	49 51N	142 49 E
Pobedy Pik	**76**	40 45N	79 58 E
Pobiedziska	**54**	52 29N	17 19 E
Pobla de Lillet, La	**58**	42 16N	1 59 E
Pobla de Segur	**58**	42 15N	0 58 E
Pobladura de Valle	**56**	42 6N	5 44W
Pocahontas, Arkansas, U.S.A.	**159**	37 18N	81 20W
Pocahontas, Iowa, U.S.A.	**158**	42 41N	94 42W
Pocatello	**160**	42 50N	112 25W
Pochep	**80**	52 58N	33 15 E
Pochinki	**81**	54 41N	44 59 E
Pochinok	**80**	54 28N	32 29 E
Pöchlarn	**52**	48 12N	15 12 E
Pochontas	**152**	53 0N	117 51W
Pochutla	**165**	15 50N	96 31W
Pocinhos	**170**	7 4 S	36 3W
Pocita Casas	**164**	28 32N	111 6W
Pocklington	**33**	53 56N	0 48W
Poções	**171**	14 31 S	40 21W
Pocomoke City	**162**	38 4N	75 32W
Pocomoke, R.	**162**	38 5N	75 34W
Poços de Caldas	**173**	21 50 S	46 45W
Pocrane	**171**	19 37 S	41 37W
PoC!tky	**52**	49 15N	15 14 E
Poddebice	**54**	51 54N	18 58 E
Poděbrady	**52**	50 9N	15 8 E
Podensac	**44**	44 40N	0 22W
Podgorica = Titograd	**66**	42 30N	19 19 E
Podkamennaya Tunguska	**77**	61 50N	90 26 E
Podlapac	**63**	44 45N	15 47 E
Podmokly	**52**	50 48N	14 10 E
Podoleni	**70**	46 46N	26 39 E
Podolínec	**53**	49 16N	20 31 E
Podolsk	**81**	55 25N	37 30 E
Podor	**120**	16 40N	14 50W
Podporozhy	**78**	60 55N	34 2 E
Podravska Slatina	**66**	45 42N	17 45 E
Podsreda	**63**	45 42N	15 41 E
Podu Turcului	**70**	46 11N	27 25 E
Podujevo	**66**	42 54N	21 10 E
Poel, I.	**48**	54 0N	11 25 E
Pofadder	**128**	29 10 S	19 22 E
Pogamasing	**150**	46 55N	81 50W
Poggiardo	**65**	40 3N	18 21 E
Poggibonsi	**63**	43 27N	11 8 E
Pogoanele	**70**	44 55N	27 0 E
Pogorzela	**54**	51 50N	17 12 E
Pogradeci	**68**	40 57N	20 48 E
Poh	**103**	0 46 S	122 51 E
Pohang	**107**	36 1N	129 23 E
Pohorelá	**53**	48 50N	20 2 E
Pohorelice	**53**	48 59N	16 31 E
Pohorje, mts.	**63**	46 30N	15 7 E
Poiana Mare	**70**	43 57N	23 5 E
Poiana Ruscâi, Munţii	**70**	45 45N	22 25 E
Pt. Augusta	**140**	32 30 S	137 50 E
Point Baker	**147**	56 20N	133 35W
Point Cloates	**137**	22 40 S	113 45 E
Point Edward	**150**	43 10N	82 30W
Point Fortin	**167**	10 9N	61 46W
Point Hope	**147**	68 20N	166 50W
Point Lay	**147**	69 45N	163 10W
Point Pass	**140**	34 5 S	139 5 E
Point Pedro	**97**	9 50N	80 15 E
Point Pleasant, N.J., U.S.A.	**162**	40 5N	74 4W
Point Pleasant, W. Va., U.S.A.	**156**	38 50N	82 7W
Point Reyes Nat. Seashore	**163**	38 0N	122 58W
Point Rock	**159**	31 30N	99 56W
Pointe-à-la Hache	**159**	29 35N	89 55W
Pointe-à-Pitre	**167**	16 10N	61 30W
Pointe-Noire	**124**	4 48 S	12 0 E
Poirino	**62**	44 55N	7 50 E
Poisonbush Ra.	**136**	22 30 S	121 30 E
Poissy	**43**	48 55N	2 0 E
Poitiers	**42**	46 35N	0 20W
Poitou, Plaines du	**44**	46 30N	0 1W
Poix	**43**	49 47N	2 0 E
Poix-Terron	**43**	49 38N	4 38 E
Pojoaque	**161**	35 55N	106 0W
Pojuca	**171**	12 21 S	38 20W
Pokaran	**93**	27 0N	71 50 E
Pokataroo	**139**	29 30 S	148 34 E
Poko, Sudan	**123**	5 41N	31 55 E
Poko, Zaïre	**126**	3 7N	26 52 E
Pok'ot'u	**105**	48 46N	121 54 E
Pokrovka	**85**	42 20N	78 0 E
Pokrovsk	**77**	61 29N	126 6 E
Pokrovsk-Uralskiy	**84**	60 10N	59 49 E
Pol	**56**	43 9N	7 20W
Pola	**80**	57 30N	32 0 E
Pola de Allande	**56**	43 16N	6 37W
Pola de Gordón, La	**56**	42 51N	5 41W
Pola de Lena	**56**	43 10N	5 49W
Pola de Siero	**56**	43 24N	5 39W
Pola de Somiedo	**56**	43 5N	6 15W
Polacca	**161**	35 52N	110 25W
Polan	**93**	25 30N	61 10 E
Poland ■	**54**	52 0N	20 0 E
Polanów	**54**	54 7N	16 41 E
Polar Bear Prov. Park	**150**	54 30N	83 20W
Polcura	**172**	37 10 S	71 50W

Połcyn Zdrój	54	53 47N	16 5E
Polden Hills	28	51 7N	2 50W
Polegate	29	50 49N	0 15E
Polessk	80	54 50N	21 8E
Polesworth	28	52 37N	1 37W
Polevskoy	84	56 26N	60 11E
Polewali, Sulawesi, Indon.	103	4 8S	119 43E
Polewali, Sulawesi, Indon.	103	3 21S	119 31E
Polgar	53	47 54N	21 6E
Pŏlgyo-ri	107	34 51N	127 21E
Poli	124	8 34N	12 54E
Políaigos, I.	69	36 45N	24 38E
Policastro, Golfo di	65	39 55N	15 35E
Police	54	53 33N	14 33E
Polička	53	49 43N	16 15E
Polignano a Mare	65	41 0N	17 12E
Poligny	43	46 50N	5 42E
Políkhnitas	69	39 4N	26 10E
Polillo I.	103	14 56N	122 0E
Polis	92	35 3N	32 30E
Polístena	65	38 25N	16 4E
Políyiros	68	40 23N	23 25E
Polkowice	54	51 29N	16 3E
Polla	65	40 31N	15 27E
Pollachi	97	10 35N	77 0E
Pollensa	58	39 54N	3 2E
Pollensa, B. de	58	39 55N	3 5E
Póllica	65	40 13N	15 3E
Pollino, Mte.	65	39 54N	16 13E
Pollock	158	45 58N	100 18W
Pollremon	38	53 40N	8 38W
Polna	80	58 31N	28 0E
Polnovat	76	63 50N	66 5E
Polo, Kwangtung, China	109	23 9N	114 17E
Polo, S.-U., China	105	44 59N	81 57E
Polo, U.S.A.	158	42 0N	89 38W
Pologi	82	47 29N	36 15E
Polonnoye	80	50 6N	27 30E
Polossu	108	31 12N	98 36E
Polotsk	82	55 30N	28 50E
Polperro	30	50 19N	4 31W
Polruan	30	50 17N	4 36W
Polski Trmbesh	67	43 20N	25 38E
Polsko Kosovo	67	43 23N	25 38E
Polson	160	47 45N	114 12W
Poltava	82	49 35N	34 35E
Polur	97	12 32N	79 11E
Polyarny	78	69 8N	33 20E
Pomarance	62	43 18N	10 51E
Pomarico	65	40 31N	16 33E
Pomaro	164	18 20N	103 18W
Pombal, Brazil	170	6 55S	37 50W
Pombal, Port.	56	39 55N	8 40W
Pómbia	69	35 0N	24 51E
Pomeroy, U.K.	38	54 36N	6 56W
Pomeroy, Ohio, U.S.A.	156	39 0N	82 0W
Pomeroy, Wash., U.S.A.	160	46 30N	117 33W
Pomio	135	5 32S	151 33E
Pomona	163	34 2N	117 49W
Pomorie	67	42 26N	27 41E
Pompano	157	26 12N	80 6W
Pompei	65	40 45N	14 30E
Pompey	43	48 50N	6 2E
Pompeys Pillar	160	46 0N	108 0W
Ponape I.	130	6 55N	158 10E
Ponask, L.	150	54 0N	92 41W
Ponass L.	153	52 16N	103 58W
Ponca	158	42 38N	96 41W
Ponca City	159	36 40N	97 5W
Ponce	147	18 1N	66 37W
Ponchatoula	159	30 27N	90 25W
Poncheville, L.	150	50 10N	76 55W
Poncin	45	46 6N	5 25E
Pond	163	35 43N	119 20W
Pond Inlet	149	72 30N	75 0W
Pondicherry	97	11 59N	79 50E
Pondoland	129	31 10S	29 30W
Pondooma	140	33 29S	136 59E
Pondrôme	47	50 6N	5 0E
Ponds, I. of	151	53 27N	55 52W
Ponferrada	56	42 32N	6 35W
Pongaroa	142	40 33S	176 15E
Póngo , Ponte de	127	19 0S	34 0E
Pongo, W.	123	8 0N	27 20E
Poniatowa	54	51 11N	22 3E
Poniec	54	51 48N	16 50E
Ponnaiyar, R.	97	11 50N	79 45E
Ponnani	97	10 45N	75 59E
Ponnani, R.	97	10 45N	75 59E
Ponneri	97	13 20N	80 15E
Ponnyadaung	99	22 0N	94 10E
Ponoi	78	67 0N	41 0E
Ponoi, R.	78	67 10N	39 0E
Ponoka	152	52 42N	113 40W
Ponomarevka	84	53 19N	54 8E
Ponorogo	103	7 52S	111 29E
Pons, France	44	45 35N	0 34W
Pons, Spain	58	41 55N	1 12E
Ponsul, R.	57	39 54N	8 45E
Pont-à-Celles	47	50 30N	4 22E
Pont-à-Mousson	43	45 54N	6 1E
Pont Audemer	42	49 21N	0 30E
Pont Aven	42	47 51N	3 47W
Pont Canavese	62	45 24N	7 33E
Pont Château	42	47 26N	2 8W
Pont-de-Roide	43	47 23N	6 45E
Pont-de-Salars	44	44 18N	2 44E
Pont-de-Vaux	43	46 26N	4 56E
Pont-de-Veyle	45	46 17N	4 53E
Pont-l'Abbé	42	47 52N	4 15W
Pont Lafrance	151	47 40N	64 58W
Pont, Le	50	46 41N	6 20E
Pont-l'Eveque	42	49 18N	0 11E
Pont-St.-Esprit	45	44 16N	4 40E
Pont-sur-Yonne	43	48 18N	3 10E
Ponta de Pedras	170	1 23S	48 52W
Ponta Grossa	173	25 0S	50 10W
Ponta Pora	173	22 20S	55 35W
Ponta São Sebastião	129	22 2S	35 25E
Pontacq	44	43 11N	0 8W
Pontailler	43	47 18N	5 24E
Pontal, R.	170	9 8S	40 12W
Pontalina	171	17 31S	49 27W
Pontardawe	31	51 43N	3 51W
Pontardulais	31	51 42N	4 3W
Pontarlier	43	46 54N	6 20E
Pontassieve	63	43 47N	11 25E
Pontaubault	42	48 40N	1 20W
Pontaumur	44	45 52N	2 40E
Pontcharra	45	45 26N	6 1E
Pontchartrain, L.	159	30 12N	90 0W
Pontchâteau	42	47 25N	2 5W
Ponte Alta do Norte	170	10 45S	47 34W
Ponte Alta, Serra do	171	19 42S	47 40W
Ponte da Barca	56	41 48N	8 25W
Ponte de Sor	57	39 17N	7 57W
Ponte dell 'Olio	62	44 52N	9 39E
Ponte di Legno	62	46 15N	10 30E
Ponte do Lima	56	41 46N	8 35W
Ponte do Pungué	127	19 30S	34 33E
Ponte Leccia	45	42 28N	9 13E
Ponte nell' Alpi	63	46 10N	12 18E
Ponte Nova	173	20 25S	42 54W
Ponte San Martino	62	45 36N	7 47E
Ponte San Pietro	62	45 42N	9 35E
Pontebba	63	46 30N	13 17E
Pontecorvo	64	41 28N	13 40E
Pontedera	62	43 40N	10 37E
Pontefract	33	53 42N	1 19W
Ponteix	153	49 46N	107 29W
Ponteland	35	53 3N	1 45W
Pontelandolfo	65	41 17N	14 41E
Pontemacassar Naikliu	103	9 30S	123 58E
Pontevedra	56	42 26N	8 40W
Pontevedra □	56	42 25N	8 39W
Pontevedra, R. de	56	42 22N	8 45W
Pontevico	62	45 16N	10 6E
Ponthierville = Ubundi	126	0 22S	25 30E
Pontiac, Ill., U.S.A.	158	40 50N	88 40W
Pontiac, Mich., U.S.A.	156	42 40N	83 20W
Pontian Kechil	101	1 29N	103 23E
Pontianak	102	0 3S	109 15E
Pontine Is. = Ponziane, Isole	64	40 55N	13 0E
Pontine Mts. = Karadeniz D.	92	41 30N	35 0E
Pontinia	64	41 25N	13 2E
Pontivy	42	48 5N	3 0W
Pontoise	43	49 3N	2 5E
Ponton, R.	152	58 27N	116 11W
Pontorson	42	48 34N	1 30W
Pontrémoli	62	44 22N	9 52E
Pontresina	51	46 29N	9 48E
Pontrhydfendigaid	31	52 17N	3 50W
Pontrieux	28	48 42N	3 10W
Pontrilas	28	51 56N	2 53W
Ponts-de Cé, Les	42	47 25N	0 30W
Pontypool	31	51 42N	3 1W
Pontypridd	31	51 36N	3 21W
Ponza, I.	64	40 55N	12 57E
Ponziane, Isole	64	40 55N	13 0E
Poochera	139	32 43S	134 51E
Poole	28	50 42N	2 2W
Poole Harb.	28	50 41N	2 0W
Poolewe	36	57 45N	5 38W
Pooley Bridge	32	54 37N	2 49W
Pooley I.	152	52 45N	128 15W
Poonamallee	97	13 3N	80 10E
Poona = Pune	96	18 29N	73 57E
Pooncarie	140	33 22S	142 31E
Poonindie	140	34 34S	135 54E
Poopelloe, L.	140	31 40S	144 0E
Poopó, Lago de	174	18 30S	67 35W
Poor Knights Is.	142	35 29S	174 43E
Pooraka	109	34 50S	138 38E
Poorman	147	64 5N	155 48W
Popai	108	22 13N	109 55E
Popak	101	22 15N	109 56E
Popakai, Austral.	170	32 12S	141 46E
Popakai, Surinam	170	3 20N	55 30W
Popanyinning	137	32 40S	117 2E
Popayán	174	2 27N	76 36W
Poperinge	47	50 51N	2 42E
Popigay	77	71 55N	110 47E
Popilta, L.	140	33 10S	141 42E
Popio, L.	140	33 10S	141 52E
Poplar	158	48 3N	105 9W
Poplar Bluff	159	36 45N	90 22W
Poplar, R., Man., Can.	153	53 0N	97 19W
Poplar, R., N.W.T., Can.	152	61 22N	121 52W
Poplarville	159	30 55N	89 30W
Popocatepetl, vol.	165	19 10N	98 40W
Popokabaka	124	5 49S	16 40E
Pópoli	63	42 12N	13 50E
Popondetta	135	8 48S	148 17E
Popovača	63	45 30N	16 41E
Popovo	67	43 21N	26 18E
Poppel	47	51 27N	5 2E
Poprád	53	49 3N	20 18E
Poprád, R.	53	49 15N	20 30E
Poquoson	162	37 7N	76 21W
Poradaha	98	23 51N	89 1E
Porali, R.	94	27 15N	66 24E
Porangahau	142	40 17S	176 37E
Porangatu	171	13 26S	49 10W
Porbandar	94	21 44N	69 43E
Porcher I.	152	53 50N	130 30W
Porcos, R.	171	12 42S	45 7W
Porcuna	57	37 52N	4 11W
Porcupine, R., Can.	153	59 11N	104 46W
Porcupine, R., U.S.A.	147	67 0N	143 0W
Pordenone	63	45 58N	12 40E
Pordim	67	43 23N	24 51E
Pore	174	5 43N	72 0W
Poreč	63	45 14N	13 36E
Porecatu	171	22 43S	51 24W
Poretskoye	81	55 9N	46 21E
Pori	75	61 29N	21 48E
Porirua	142	41 8S	174 52E
Porjus	74	66 57N	19 50E
Porkhov	80	57 45N	29 38E
Porkkala	75	59 59N	24 26E
Porlamar	174	10 57N	63 51W
Porlezza	62	46 2N	9 8E
Porlock	28	51 13N	3 36W
Porlock B.	28	51 14N	3 37W
Porlock Hill	28	51 12N	3 40W
Porma, R.	56	42 45N	5 21W
Pornic	42	47 7N	2 5W
Poronaysk	77	49 20N	143 0E
Póros	69	37 30N	23 30E
Póros, I.	69	37 30N	23 30E
Poroshiri-Dake	112	42 41N	142 52E
Poroszló	53	47 39N	20 40E
Poroto Mts.	127	9 0S	33 30E
Porraburdoo	137	23 15S	117 28E
Porrentruy	50	47 25N	7 6E
Porreras	58	39 29N	3 2E
Porsangen	74	70 40N	25 40E
Porsgrunn	71	59 10N	9 40E
Port	43	47 43N	6 4E
Port Adelaide	140	34 46S	138 30E
Port Alberni	152	49 15N	124 50W
Port Albert	141	38 42S	146 42E
Port Albert Victor	94	21 0N	71 30E
Port Alexander	147	56 13N	134 40W
Port Alfred, Can.	151	48 18N	70 53W
Port Alfred, S. Afr.	125	33 36S	26 55E
Port Alice	152	50 25N	127 25W
Port Allegany	156	41 49N	78 17W
Port Allen	159	30 30N	91 15W
Port Alma	138	23 38S	150 53E
Port Angeles	160	48 7N	123 30W
Port Antonio	166	18 10N	76 30W
Port Aransas	159	27 49N	97 4W
Port Arthur, Austral.	138	43 7S	147 50E
Port Arthur, U.S.A.	159	30 0N	94 0W
Port Arthur = Lüshun	107	38 51N	121 20E
Port Arthur = Thunder Bay	150	48 25N	89 10W
Port Askaig	34	55 51N	6 8W
Port au Port B.	151	48 40N	58 50W
Port-au-Prince	167	18 40N	72 20W
Port Augusta West	140	32 29S	137 47E
Port Austin	150	44 3N	82 59W
Port aux Basques	151	47 32N	59 8W
Port Awanui	142	37 50S	178 29E
Port Bannatyne	34	55 51N	5 4W
Port Bell	126	0 18N	32 35E
Port Bergé Vaovao	129	15 33S	47 40E
Port Blair	101	11 40N	92 30E
Port Blandford	151	48 30N	53 50W
Port Bolivar	159	29 20N	94 40W
Port Bou	58	42 25N	3 9E
Port Bouet	120	5 16N	4 57W
Port Bradshaw	138	12 30S	137 0E
Port Broughton	140	33 37S	137 56E
Port Burwell	150	42 40N	80 48W
Port Campbell	140	35 37S	143 1E
Port Canning	95	22 17N	88 48E
Port Carlisle	32	54 56N	3 12W
Port-Cartier	151	50 10N	66 50W
Port Chalmers	143	45 49S	170 30E
Port Charlotte	34	55 44N	6 22W
Port Chester	162	41 0N	73 41W
Port Clements	152	53 40N	132 10W
Port Clinton	156	41 30N	83 0W
Port Colborne	150	42 50N	79 10W
Port Coquitlam	152	49 20N	122 45W
Port Curtis	138	24 0S	151 34E
Port Darwin, Austral.	136	12 24S	130 45E
Port Darwin, Falk. Is.	176	51 50S	59 0W
Port Davey	138	43 16S	145 55E
Port-de-Bouc	45	43 24N	4 59E
Port de Paix	167	19 50N	72 50W
Port Deposit	162	39 37N	76 5W
Port Dickson	101	2 30N	101 49E
Port Dinorwic	31	53 11N	4 12W
Port Douglas	138	16 30S	145 30E
Port Edward	152	54 12N	130 10W
Port Elgin	150	44 25N	81 25W
Port Elizabeth	128	33 58S	25 40E
Port Ellen	34	55 38N	6 10W
Port Erin	32	54 5N	4 45W
Port Erroll	37	57 25N	1 50W
Port Essington	136	11 15S	132 10E
Port Etienne = Nouadhibou	116	21 0N	17 0W
Port Ewen	162	41 54N	73 59W
Port Fairy	140	38 22S	142 12E
Port Fitzroy	142	36 8S	175 20E
Port Fouâd = Bûr Fuad	122	31 15N	32 20E
Port Francqui	124	4 17S	20 47E
Port-Gentil	124	0 47S	8 40E
Port Gibson	159	31 57N	91 0W
Port Glasgow	34	55 57N	4 40W
Port Gregory	137	27 40S	114 0E
Port Harcourt	121	4 40N	7 10E
Port Hardy	152	50 41N	127 30W
Port Harrison	149	58 25N	78 15W
Port Hawkesbury	151	45 36N	61 22W
Port Hedland	136	20 25S	118 35E
Port Heiden	147	57 0N	158 40W
Port Hood	151	46 0N	61 32W
Port Hope	150	44 0N	78 20W
Port Hueneme	163	34 7N	119 12W
Port Huron	156	43 0N	82 28W
Port Isaac	30	50 35N	4 50W
Port Isaac B.	30	50 36N	4 50W
Port Isabel	159	26 12N	97 9W
Port Jackson	133	33 50S	151 18E
Port Jefferson	162	40 58N	73 5W
Port Jervis	162	41 22N	74 42W
Port Joinville	42	46 45N	2 23W
Port Kaituma	174	8 3N	59 58W
Port Katon	83	46 27N	38 56E
Port Kelang	101	3 0N	101 23E
Port Kembla	141	34 29S	150 56E
Port La Nouvelle	44	43 1N	3 3E
Port Laoise	39	53 2N	7 20W
Port Lavaca	159	28 38N	96 38W
Port Leyden	162	43 35N	75 21W
Port Lincoln	140	34 42S	135 52E
Port Logan	34	54 42N	4 57W
Port Loko	120	8 48N	12 46W
Port Louis	42	47 42N	3 22W
Port Lyautey = Kenitra	118	34 15N	6 40W
Port Lyttelton	143	43 37N	172 50E
Port Macdonnell	140	38 0S	140 39E
Port Macquarie	141	31 25S	152 54E
Port Maitland	151	44 0N	66 2W
Port Maria	166	18 25N	76 55W
Port Mellon	152	49 32N	123 31W
Port Menier	151	49 51N	64 15W
Port Morant	166	17 54N	76 19W
Port Moresby	135	9 24S	147 8E
Port Mouton	151	43 58N	64 50W
Port Musgrave	138	11 55S	141 50E
Port Navalo	42	47 34N	2 54W
Port Nelson	153	57 3N	92 36W
Port Nicholson	142	41 20S	174 52E
Port Nolloth	128	29 17S	16 52E
Port Norris	162	39 15N	75 2W
Port Nouveau-Quebec (George R.)	149	58 30N	65 50W
Port O'Connor	159	28 26N	96 24W
Port of Ness	36	58 29N	6 13W
Port of Spain	167	10 40N	61 20W
Port Orchard	160	47 31N	122 38W
Port Oxford	160	42 45N	124 28W
Port Pegasus	143	47 12S	167 41E
Port Perry	150	44 6N	78 56W
Port Phillip B.	139	38 10S	144 50E
Port Pirie	140	33 10S	137 58E
Port Pólnocny □	54	54 25N	18 42E
Port Radium = Echo Bay	148	66 10N	117 40W
Port Renfrew	152	48 30N	124 20W
Port Roper	138	14 45S	134 47E
Port Rowan	150	42 40N	80 30W
Port Royal	162	38 10N	77 12W
Port Safaga = Bûr Safâga	122	26 43N	33 57E
Port Said = Bûr Sa'îd	122	31 16N	32 18E
Port St. Joe	157	29 49N	85 20W
Port St. Johns = Umzimvubu	129	31 38S	29 33E
Port-St. Louis	45	43 23N	4 50E
Port St. Louis	129	13 7S	48 48E
Port-St.-Louis-du-Rhône	45	43 23N	4 49E
Port St. Mary	32	54 5N	4 45W
Port St. Servain	151	51 21N	58 0W
Port Sanilac	150	43 26N	82 33W
Port Saunders	151	50 40N	57 18W
Port Shepstone	129	30 44S	30 28E
Port Simpson	152	54 30N	130 20W
Port Stanley	150	42 40N	81 10W
Port Sudan = Bûr Sôdân	122	19 32N	37 9E
Port Sunlight	32	53 22N	3 0W
Port Talbot	31	51 35N	3 48W
Port Taufiq = Bûr Taufiq	122	29 54N	32 32E
Port Townsend	160	48 7N	122 50W
Port-Vendres	44	42 32N	3 8E
Port Victoria	140	34 30S	137 29E
Port Wakefield	140	34 12S	138 10E
Port Washington	156	43 25N	87 52W
Port Weld	101	4 50N	100 38E
Port William	34	54 45N	4 35W
Portachuelo	174	17 10S	63 20W
Portacloy	38	54 20N	9 48W
Portadown (Craigavon)	38	54 27N	6 26W
Portaferry	38	54 23N	5 32W
Portage, Can.	151	46 40N	64 5W
Portage, U.S.A.	158	43 31N	89 25W
Portage la Prairie	153	49 58N	98 18W
Portage Mt. Dam	152	56 0N	122 0W
Portageville	159	36 25N	89 40W
Portaguiran	36	58 15N	6 10W
Portalegre	57	39 19N	7 25W
Portalegre □	57	39 20N	7 40W
Portales	159	34 12N	103 25W
Portarlington	39	53 10N	7 10W
Porte, La	156	41 40N	86 40W
Porteirinha	171	15 44S	43 2W
Portel, Brazil	170	1 57S	50 49W

Portel Prochowice

Portel, Port. 57 38 19N 7 41W
Porter L., N.W.T., Can. 153 61 41N 108 5W
Porter L., Sask., Can. 153 56 20N 107 20W
Porterville, S. Afr. 128 33 0S 18 57E
Porterville, U.S.A. 163 36 5N 119 0W
Portet 44 43 34N 0 11W
Porteynon 31 51 33N 4 13W
Portglenone 38 54 53N 6 30W
Portgordon 37 57 40N 3 1W
Porth Neigwl 31 52 48N 4 35W
Porth Neigwl, B. 31 52 48N 4 33W
Porthcawl 31 51 28N 3 42W
Porthill 160 49 0N 116 30W
Porthleven 30 50 5N 5 19W
Porthmadog 31 52 55N 4 13W
Portile de Fier 70 44 42N 22 30E
Portimão 57 37 8N 8 32W
Portishead 28 51 29N 2 46W
Portknockle 37 57 40N 2 52W
Portland, N.S.W., Austral. 141 33 20S 150 0E
Portland, Victoria, Austral. 140 38 20S 141 35E
Portland, Conn., U.S.A. 162 41 34N 72 39W
Portland, Me., U.S.A. 151 43 40N 70 15W
Portland, Mich., U.S.A. 156 42 52N 84 58W
Portland, Oreg., U.S.A. 160 45 35N 122 40W
Portland B. 140 38 15S 141 45E
Portland Bill 28 50 31N 2 27W
Portland, C. 133 40 46S 148 0E
Portland I. 142 39 20S 177 51E
Portland, I. of 28 50 32N 2 25W
Portland, Pa. 162 40 55N 75 6W
Portland Prom. 149 58 40N 78 33W
Portlaw 39 52 18N 7 20W
Portmagee 39 51 53N 10 22W
Portmahomack 37 57 50N 3 50W
Portmarnock 38 53 25N 6 10W
Portnacroish 34 56 34N 5 24W
Portnahaven 34 55 40N 6 30W
Portneuf 151 46 43N 71 55W
Pôrto, Brazil 170 3 54S 42 42W
Pôrto, Port. 56 41 8N 8 40W
Pôrto □ 56 41 8N 8 20W
Pôrto Alegre, Mato Grosso, Brazil 170 21 40S 53 30W
Pôrto Alegre, Rio Grande do Sul, Brazil 173 30 5S 51 3W
Porto Alexandre 128 15 55S 11 55E
Porto Amboim = Gunza 124 10 50S 13 50E
Porto Amelia = Pemba 127 12 58S 40 30E
Porto Argentera 62 44 15N 7 27E
Porto Azzurro 62 42 46N 10 24E
Porto Botte 64 39 3N 8 33E
Pôrto Calvo 171 9 4S 35 24W
Porto Civitanova 63 43 19N 13 44E
Pôrto da Fôlha 170 9 55S 37 17W
Pôrto de Moz 170 1 41S 52 22W
Pôrto de Pedras 170 9 10S 35 17W
Porto Empédocle 64 37 18N 13 30E
Pôrto Esperança 174 19 37S 57 29W
Pôrto Franco 170 6 20S 47 24W
Porto Garibaldi 63 44 41N 12 14E
Porto, G. de 45 42 17N 8 34E
Pórto Lago 68 41 1N 25 6E
Porto Mendes 173 24 30S 54 15W
Porto Murtinho 174 21 45S 57 55W
Pôrto Nacional 170 10 40S 48 30W
Porto Novo, Benin 121 6 23N 2 42E
Porto Novo, India 97 11 30N 79 38E
Porto Recanati 63 43 26N 13 40E
Porto San Giorgio 63 43 11N 13 49E
Porto San Stéfano 68 42 26N 11 6E
Porto Santo, I. 116 33 45N 16 25W
Pôrto São José 173 22 43S 53 10W
Pôrto Seguro 171 16 26S 39 5W
Porto Tolle 63 44 57N 12 20E
Porto Tórres 64 40 50N 8 23E
Pôrto União 173 26 10S 51 10W
Pôrto Válter 174 8 5S 72 40W
Porto-Vecchio 45 41 35N 9 16E
Pôrto Velho 174 8 46S 63 54W
Portobelo 166 9 35N 79 42W
Portoferráio 62 42 50N 10 20E
Portogruaro 63 45 47N 12 50E
Portola 160 39 49N 120 28W
Portomaggiore 63 44 41N 11 47E
Porton Camp 28 51 8N 1 42W
Portoscuso 64 39 12N 8 22E
Portovénere 62 44 2N 9 50E
Portoviejo 174 1 0S 80 20W
Portpatrick 34 54 50N 5 7W
Portree 36 57 25N 6 11W
Portroe 39 52 53N 8 20W
Portrush 38 55 13N 6 40W
Portsall 42 48 37N 4 45W
Portsalon 38 55 12N 7 37W
Portskerra 37 58 35N 3 55W
Portslade 29 50 50N 0 11W
Portsmouth, Domin. 167 15 34N 61 27W
Portsmouth, U.K. 28 50 48N 1 6W
Portsmouth, N.H., U.S.A. 162 43 5N 70 45W
Portsmouth, Ohio, U.S.A. 156 38 45N 83 0W
Portsmouth, R.I., U.S.A. 162 41 35N 71 44W
Portsmouth, Va., U.S.A. 156 36 50N 76 20W
Portsoy 37 57 41N 2 41W
Portstewart 38 55 12N 6 43W
Porttipahta 74 68 5N 26 30E
Portugal ■ 56 40 0N 7 0W
Portugalete 58 43 19N 3 4W
Portuguesa □ 174 9 10N 69 15W
Portuguese Guinea = Guinea Bissau 120 12 0N 15 0W
Portuguese Timor ■ = Timor 103 8 0S 126 30E
Portumna 39 53 5N 8 12W
Porvenir 176 53 10S 70 30W
Porvoo 75 60 24N 25 40E
Porzuna 57 39 9N 4 9W
Posada, R. 64 40 40N 9 35E
Posadas, Argent. 173 27 30S 56 0W
Posadas, Spain 57 37 47N 5 11W
Poschiavo 51 46 19N 10 4E
Posets, mt. 58 42 39N 0 25E
Poshan 107 36 30N 117 50E
Posídhio, Ákra 68 39 57N 23 30E
Poso 103 1 20S 120 55E
Poso Colorado 172 23 30S 58 45W
Poso, D. 103 1 20S 120 55E
Posong 107 34 46N 129 5E
Posse 171 14 4S 46 18W
Possel 124 5 5N 19 10E
Possession I. 13 72 4S 172 0E
Pössneck 48 50 42N 11 34E
Possut'eng Hu 105 42 0N 87 0E
Post 159 33 13N 101 21W
Post Falls 160 47 50N 116 59W
Postavy 80 55 4N 26 58E
Postbridge 30 50 36N 3 54W
Poste-de-la-Baleine 30 50 36N 3 54W
Poste Maurice Cortier (Bidon 5) 118 22 14N 1 2E
Postiljon, Kepulauan 103 6 30S 118 50E
Postmasburg 128 28 18S 23 5E
Postojna 63 45 46N 14 12E
Potamós 69 39 38N 19 53E
Potchefstroom 125 26 41S 27 7E
Potcoava 70 44 30N 24 39E
Poté 171 17 49S 41 49W
Poteau 159 35 5N 94 37W
Poteet 159 29 4N 98 35W
Potelu, Lacul 70 43 44N 24 20E
Potenza 65 40 40N 15 50E
Potenza Picena 63 43 22N 13 37E
Poteriteri, L. 143 46 5S 167 10E
Potes 56 43 15N 4 42W
Potgietersrus 129 24 10S 29 3E
Poti 83 42 10N 41 38E
Potiraguá 171 15 36S 39 53W
Potiskum 121 11 39N 11 2E
Potlogi 70 44 34N 25 34E
Potomac, R. 162 38 0N 76 23W
Potosí 174 19 38S 65 50W
Potosí □ 174 20 31S 67 0W
Pot'ou 106 37 57N 116 39E
Potrerillos 172 26 20S 69 30W
Potros, Cerro del 172 28 32S 69 0W
Potsdam, Ger. 48 52 23N 13 4E
Potsdam, U.S.A. 156 44 40N 74 59W
Potsdam □ 48 52 40N 12 50E
Potter 158 41 15N 103 20W
Potter Heigham 29 52 44N 1 33E
Potterne 28 51 19N 2 0W
Potters Bar 29 51 42N 0 11W
Potterspury 29 52 5N 0 52W
Pottery Hill = Abu Ballas 122 24 26N 27 36E
Pottstown 162 40 17N 75 40W
Pottsville 162 40 39N 76 12W
Pottuvil 93 6 55N 81 50E
P'otzu 109 23 30N 120 25E
Pouancé 42 47 44N 1 10W
Pouce Coupé 152 55 40N 120 10W
Poughkeepsie 162 41 40N 73 57W
Pouilly 43 47 18N 2 57E
Poulaphouca Res. 39 53 8N 6 30W
Pouldu, Le 42 47 41N 3 36W
Poulsbo 160 47 45N 122 39W
Poultney 162 43 31N 73 14W
Poulton le Fylde 32 53 51N 2 59W
Poundstock 30 50 44N 4 34W
Pouso Alegre, Mato Grosso, Brazil 175 11 55S 57 0W
Pouso Alegre, Minas Gerais, Brazil 173 22 14S 45 57W
Pouzages 44 46 40N 0 50W
Povenets 78 62 50N 34 50E
Poverty Bay 142 38 43S 178 2E
Póvoa de Lanhosa 56 41 33N 8 15W
Póvoa de Varzim 56 41 25N 8 46W
Povorino 81 51 12N 42 28E
Powassan 150 46 5N 79 25W
Poway 163 32 58N 117 2W
Powder, R. 158 46 47N 105 12W
Powell 160 44 45N 108 45W
Powell Creek 136 18 6S 133 46E
Powell River 152 49 22N 125 31W
Powers, Mich., U.S.A. 156 45 40N 87 32W
Powers, Oreg., U.S.A. 160 42 53N 124 2W
Powers Lake 158 48 37N 102 38W
Powick 28 52 9N 2 15W
Powis, Vale of 23 52 40N 3 10W
Powys □ 31 52 20N 3 20W
P'oyang 109 29 1N 116 38E
Poyang Hu 109 29 10N 116 10E
Poyarkovo 77 49 36N 128 41E
Poyntzpass 38 54 17N 6 22W
Poysdorf 53 48 40N 16 37E
Poza de la Sal 58 42 35N 3 31W
Poza Rica 165 20 33N 97 27W
Pozarevac 66 44 35N 21 18E
Pozega 66 45 21N 17 41E
Pozhva 84 59 5N 56 5E
Poznan 54 52 25N 17 0E
Pozo 163 35 20N 120 24W
Pozo Alcón 59 37 42N 2 56W
Pozo Almonte 174 20 10S 69 50W
Pozoblanco 57 38 23N 4 51W
Pozzallo 65 36 44N 15 40E
Pra, R. 121 5 30N 1 38W
Prabuty 54 53 47N 19 15E
Prača 66 43 47N 18 43E
Prachatice 52 49 1N 14 0E
Prachin Buri 100 14 0N 101 25E
Prachuap Khiri Khan 101 11 49N 99 48E
Pradelles 44 44 46N 3 52E
Pradera 174 3 25N 76 15W
Prades 44 42 38N 2 23E
Prado 171 17 20S 39 13W
Prado del Rey 57 36 48N 5 33W
Præstø 73 55 8N 12 2E
Pragersko 63 46 27N 15 42E
Prague = Praha 52 50 5N 14 22E
Praha 52 50 5N 14 22E
Prahecq 44 46 19N 0 26W
Prahita, R. 97 19 0N 79 55E
Prahova □ 70 44 50N 25 50E
Prahova, R. 70 44 50N 25 50E
Prahova, Reg. 70 44 50N 25 50E
Prahovo 66 44 18N 22 39E
Praid 70 46 32N 25 10E
Prainha, Amazonas, Brazil 174 7 10S 60 30W
Prainha, Pará, Brazil 175 1 45S 53 30W
Prairie, Queens., Austral. 138 20 50S 144 35E
Prairie, S. Australia, Austral. 109 34 51S 138 49E
Prairie City 160 45 27N 118 44W
Prairie du Chien 158 43 1N 91 9W
Prairie, R. 159 34 45N 101 15W
Praja 102 8 39S 116 27E
Prajeczno 54 51 10N 19 0E
Pramánda 68 39 32N 21 8E
Pran Buri 100 12 23N 99 55E
Prang 121 8 1N 0 56W
Prapat 102 2 41N 98 58E
Praszka 54 51 32N 18 31E
Prata, Minas Gerais, Brazil 171 19 25S 49 0W
Prata, Pará, Brazil 170 1 10S 47 35W
Prática di Mare 64 41 40N 12 26E
Prato 62 43 53N 11 5E
Prátola Peligna 63 42 7N 13 51E
Pratovécchio 63 43 44N 11 43E
Prats-de-Molló 44 42 25N 2 27E
Pratt 159 37 40N 98 45W
Pratteln 50 47 31N 7 41E
Prättigau 51 46 56N 9 44E
Prattville 157 32 30N 86 28W
Pravara, R. 96 19 30N 74 28E
Pravdinsk 81 56 29N 43 28E
Pravia 56 43 30N 6 12W
Prawle Pt. 30 50 13N 3 41W
Pré-en-Pail 42 48 28N 0 12W
Pré St. Didier 62 45 45N 7 0E
Precordillera 172 30 0S 69 1W
Predáppio 63 44 7N 11 58E
Predazzo 63 46 19N 11 37E
Predejane 66 42 51N 22 9E
Preeceville 153 51 57N 102 40W
Prees 32 52 54N 2 40W
Preesall 32 53 55N 2 58W
Préfailles 42 47 9N 2 11W
Pregonero 174 8 1N 71 46W
Pregrada 63 46 11N 15 45E
Preko 63 44 7N 15 14E
Prelate 153 50 51N 109 24W
Prelog 63 46 18N 16 32E
Premier 152 56 4N 129 56W
Premier Downs 137 30 30S 126 30E
Premont 159 27 19N 91 8W
Premuda, I. 63 44 20N 14 36E
Prenj, mt. 66 43 33N 17 53E
Prenjasi 68 41 6N 20 32E
Prentice 158 45 31N 90 19W
Prenzlau 48 53 19N 13 51E
Prepansko Jezero 68 40 45N 21 0E
Preparis I. 99 14 55N 93 45E
Preparis North Channel 101 15 12N 93 40E
Preparis South Channel 101 14 36N 93 40E
Prerov 53 49 28N 17 27E
Prescot 32 53 27N 2 49W
Prescott, Can. 150 44 45N 75 30W
Prescott, Ariz., U.S.A. 161 34 35N 112 30W
Prescott, Ark., U.S.A. 159 33 49N 93 22W
Preservation Inlet 143 46 8S 166 35E
Preševo 66 42 19N 21 39E
Presho 158 43 56N 100 4W
Preshute 28 51 24N 1 45W
Presicce 65 39 53N 18 13E
Presidencia de la Plaza 172 27 0S 60 0W
Presidencia Roque Sáenz Peña 172 26 45S 60 30W
Presidente Dutra 164 5 15S 44 30W
Presidente Epitácio 171 21 46S 52 6W
Presidente Hayes □ 172 24 0S 59 0W
Presidente Hermes 174 11 0S 61 55W
Presidente Prudente 173 22 5S 51 25W
Presidente Rogue Saena Peña 172 34 33S 58 30W
Presidio, Mexico 164 29 29N 104 23W
Presidio, U.S.A. 159 29 30N 104 20W
Preslav 67 43 10N 26 52E
Prespa, L. = Prepansko Jezero 68 40 45N 21 0E
Prespa, mt. 67 41 44N 25 0E
Presque Isle 151 46 40N 68 0W
Prestatyn 31 53 20N 3 24W
Prestea 120 5 22N 2 7W
Presteigne 31 52 17N 3 0W
Preštice 52 49 34N 13 20E
Preston, Borders, U.K. 35 55 48N 2 18W
Preston, Dorset, U.K. 28 50 38N 2 26W
Preston, Lancs., U.K. 32 53 46N 2 42W
Preston, Idaho, U.S.A. 160 42 0N 112 0W
Preston, Minn., U.S.A. 158 43 39N 92 3W
Preston, Nev., U.S.A. 160 38 59N 115 2W
Preston, C. 136 20 51S 116 12E
Prestonpans 35 55 58N 3 0W
Prestwich 32 53 32N 2 18W
Prestwick 34 55 30N 4 38W
Prêto, R., Bahia 170 11 21S 43 52W
Pretoria 129 25 44S 28 12E
Prettyboy Res. 162 39 37N 76 43W
Preuilly-sur-Claise 42 46 51N 0 56E
Préveza 69 38 57N 20 47E
Préveza □ 68 39 20N 20 40E
Prey-Veng 101 11 35N 105 29E
Priazovskoye 82 46 22N 35 28E
Pribilov Is. 12 56 0N 170 0W
Priboj 66 43 35N 19 32E
Pribram 52 49 41N 14 2E
Price 160 39 40N 110 48W
Price I. 152 52 23N 128 41W
Prichalnaya 83 48 57N 44 33E
Priego 58 40 38N 2 21W
Priego de Córdoba 57 37 27N 4 12W
Priekule 80 57 27N 21 45E
Prieska 128 29 40S 22 42E
Priest Gully Cr. 108 27 29S 153 11E
Priest L. 160 48 30N 116 55W
Priest River 160 48 11N 117 0W
Priest Valley 163 36 10N 120 39W
Priestly 152 54 8N 125 20W
Prievidza 53 48 46N 18 36E
Prijedor 63 44 58N 16 41E
Prijepolje 66 43 27N 19 40E
Prilep 66 41 21N 21 37E
Priluki 80 50 30N 32 15E
Prime Seal I. 138 40 3S 147 43E
Primeira Cruz 170 2 30S 43 26W
Primorsko 67 42 15N 27 44E
Primorsko-Akhtarsk 82 46 2N 38 10E
Primrose L. 153 54 55N 109 45W
Prince Albert 153 53 15N 105 50W
Prince Albert Nat. Park 153 54 0N 106 25W
Prince Albert Pen. 148 72 30N 116 0W
Prince Alfred C. 12 74 20N 124 40W
Prince Charles I. 149 67 47N 76 12W
Prince Edward I. □. 151 44 2N 77 20W
Prince Edward Is. 11 45 15S 39 0E
Prince Frederick 162 38 33N 76 35W
Prince George 152 53 50N 122 50W
Prince of Wales, C. 147 65 50N 168 0W
Prince of Wales I. 147 73 0N 99 0W
Prince of Wales, I. 147 53 30N 131 30W
Prince of Wales Is. 135 10 40S 142 10E
Prince Patrick I. 12 77 0N 120 0W
Prince Regent Inlet 12 73 0N 90 0W
Prince Rupert 152 54 20N 130 20W
Prince William Sd. 147 60 20N 146 30W
Princenhage 47 51 9N 4 45E
Princes Risborough 29 51 43N 0 50W
Princesa Isabel 170 7 44S 38 0W
Princess Anne 162 38 12N 75 41W
Princess Charlotte B. 138 14 25S 144 0E
Princess Mary Ranges 136 15 30S 125 30E
Princess Royal I. 152 53 0N 128 40W
Princeton, Can. 152 49 27N 120 30W
Princeton, Ill., U.S.A. 158 41 25N 89 25W
Princeton, Ind., U.S.A. 156 38 20N 87 35W
Princeton, Ky., U.S.A. 156 37 6N 87 55W
Princeton, Mo., U.S.A. 158 40 23N 93 35W
Princeton, N.J., U.S.A. 162 40 18N 74 40W
Princeton, W. Va., U.S.A. 156 37 21N 81 8W
Princetown 30 50 33N 4 0W
Principe Chan. 152 53 28N 130 0W
Principe da Beira 174 12 20S 64 30W
Principe, I. de 114 1 37N 7 27E
Prineville 160 44 17N 120 57W
Prins Albert 128 33 12S 22 2E
Prins Harald Kyst 13 70 0S 35 1E
Prinzapolca 166 13 20N 83 35W
Prior, C. 56 43 34N 8 17W
Pripet Marshes = Polesye 80 52 0N 28 10E
Pripet, R. = Pripyat, R. 80 51 30N 30 0E
Pripyat, R. 80 51 30N 30 0E
Prislop, Pasul 70 47 37N 25 15E
Pristen 81 51 15N 12 40E
Priština 66 42 40N 21 13E
Pritchard 157 30 47N 88 5W
Pritzwalk 48 53 10N 12 11E
Privas 45 44 45N 4 37E
Priverno 64 41 29N 13 10E
Privolzhsk 81 57 9N 14 9E
Privolzhskaya Vozvyshennest 81 51 0N 46 0E
Privolzhskiy 81 51 25N 46 3E
Privolzhye 81 52 52N 48 33E
Privutnoye 83 47 12N 43 30E
Prizren 66 42 13N 20 45E
Prizzi 64 37 44N 13 24E
Prnjavor 66 44 52N 17 43E
Probolinggo 103 7 46S 113 13E
Probus 30 50 17N 4 55W
Prochowice 54 51 17N 16 20E

Procida, I Qattâra, Munkhafed el

Procida, I.	**64**	40 46N	14 0E
Proctor	**162**	43 40N	73 2W
Proddatur	**97**	14 45N	78 30E
Proença-a-Nova	**57**	39 45N	7 54W
Profondeville	**47**	50 23N	4 52E
Progreso	**165**	21 20N	89 40W
Prokhladnyy	**83**	43 50N	44 2E
Prokletije	**68**	42 30N	19 45E
Prokopyevsk	**76**	54 0N	87 3E
Prokuplje	**66**	43 16N	21 36E
Proletarskaya	**83**	46 42N	41 50E
Prome = Pyè	**99**	18 45N	95 30E
Prophet, R.	**152**	58 48N	122 40W
Propriá	**170**	10 13S	36 51W
Propriano	**45**	41 41N	8 52E
Proserpine	**138**	20 21S	148 36E
Prospect, Austral.	**109**	34 53S	138 36E
Prospect, U.S.A.	**162**	43 18N	75 9W
Prosser	**160**	46 11N	119 52W
Prostějov	**53**	49 30N	17 9E
Proston	**139**	26 14S	151 32E
Proszowice	**54**	50 13N	20 16E
Protection	**159**	37 16N	99 30W
Próti, I.	**69**	37 5N	21 32E
Provadija	**67**	43 12N	27 30E
Proven	**47**	50 54N	2 40E
Provence	**45**	43 40N	5 46E
Providence, Ky., U.S.A.	**156**	37 25N	87 46W
Providence, R.I., U.S.A.	**162**	41 41N	71 15W
Providence Bay	**150**	45 41N	82 15W
Providence C.	**143**	45 59S	166 29E
Providence Mts.	**161**	35 0N	115 30W
Providencia	**174**	0 28S	76 28W
Providencia, I. de	**166**	13 25N	81 26W
Provideniya	**77**	64 23N	173 18E
Province Wellesley	**101**	5 15N	100 20E
Provincetown	**162**	42 5N	70 11W
Provins	**43**	48 33N	3 15E
Provo	**160**	40 16N	111 37W
Provost	**153**	52 25N	110 20W
Prozor	**66**	43 50N	17 34E
Prudentópolis	**171**	25 12S	50 57W
Prudhoe	**35**	54 57N	1 52W
Prudhoe Bay, Austral.	**138**	21 30S	149 30W
Prudhoe Bay, U.S.A.	**147**	70 20N	148 20W
Prudhoe I.	**138**	21 23S	149 45E
Prudhoe Land	**12**	78 1N	65 0W
Prud'homme	**153**	52 20N	105 54W
Prudnik	**54**	50 20N	17 38E
Prüm	**49**	50 14N	6 22E
Pruszcz	**54**	54 17N	19 40E
Pruszków	**54**	52 9N	20 49E
Prut, R.	**70**	46 3N	28 10E
Prvič, I.	**63**	44 55N	14 47E
Prvomay	**67**	42 8N	25 17E
Prydz B.	**13**	69 0S	74 0E
Pryor	**159**	36 17N	95 20W
Przasnysz	**54**	53 2N	20 45E
Przedbórz	**54**	51 6N	19 53E
Przedecz	**54**	52 20N	18 53E
Przemyśl	**54**	49 50N	22 45E
Przemyśl □	**54**	80 0N	23 0E
Przeworsk	**54**	50 6N	22 32E
Przewóz	**54**	51 28N	14 57E
Przhevalsk	**85**	42 30N	78 20E
Przysucha	**54**	51 22N	20 38E
Psakhná	**69**	38 34N	23 35E
Psarà, I.	**69**	38 37N	25 38E
Psathoúra, I.	**68**	39 30N	24 12E
Psel, R.	**82**	49 25N	33 50E
Pserimos, I.	**69**	36 56N	27 12E
Pskem, R.	**85**	41 38N	70 1E
Pskemskiy Khrebet	**85**	42 0N	70 45E
Pskent	**85**	40 54N	69 20E
Pskov	**80**	57 50N	28 25E
Psunj, mt.	**66**	45 25N	17 19E
Pszczyna	**54**	49 59N	18 58E
Pteleón	**69**	39 3N	22 57E
Ptich, R.	**80**	52 30N	28 45E
Ptolemais	**68**	40 30N	21 43E
Ptuj	**63**	46 28N	15 50E
Ptujska Gora	**63**	46 23N	15 47E
Pua	**100**	19 11N	100 55E
Puán	**172**	37 30S	63 0W
P'uan	**108**	25 47N	104 57E
Puan	**107**	35 44N	126 7E
Pubnico	**151**	43 47N	65 50W
Pucallpa	**174**	8 25S	74 30W
P'uchen	**107**	37 21N	118 1E
P'uch'eng	**109**	27 45N	118 47E
Pucheni	**70**	45 12N	25 17E
P'uch'i	**109**	29 43N	113 53E
Pucisce	**63**	43 22N	16 43E
Puck	**54**	54 45N	18 23E
Puddletown	**28**	50 45N	2 21W
Pudsey	**33**	53 47N	1 40W
Pudukkottai	**97**	10 28N	78 47E
Puebla	**165**	19 0N	98 10W
Puebla □	**165**	18 30N	98 0W
Puebla de Alcocer	**57**	38 59N	5 14W
Puebla de Don Fadrique	**59**	37 58N	2 25W
Puebla de Don Rodrigo	**57**	39 5N	4 37W
Puebla de Guzmán	**57**	37 37N	7 15W
Puebla de los Infantes, La	**57**	37 47N	5 24W
Puebla de Montalbán, La	**56**	39 52N	4 22W
Puebla de Sanabria	**56**	42 4N	6 38W
Puebla de Trives	**56**	42 20N	7 10W
Puebla del Caramiñal	**56**	42 37N	8 56W
Puebla, La	**58**	39 50N	3 0E
Pueblo	**158**	38 20N	104 40W
Pueblo Bonito	**161**	36 4N	107 57W
Pueblo Hundido	**172**	26 20S	69 30W
Pueblo Nuevo	**174**	8 26N	71 26W
Pueblonuevo	**55**	38 16N	5 16W
Puelches	**172**	38 5S	66 0W
Puelén	**172**	37 32S	67 38W
Puente Alto	**172**	33 32S	70 35W
Puente del Arzobispo	**56**	39 48N	5 10W
Puente Genil	**57**	37 22N	4 47W
Puente la Reina	**58**	42 40N	1 49W
Puentearas	**56**	42 10N	8 28W
Puentedeume	**56**	43 24N	8 10W
Puentes de García Rodríguez	**56**	43 27N	7 51W
Puerco, R.	**161**	35 10N	109 45W
Puerh	**105**	23 11N	100 56E
P'uerh	**108**	23 5N	101 5E
Puerhching	**105**	47 43N	86 53E
Puerta, La	**59**	38 22N	2 45W
Puerto Aisén	**176**	45 10S	73 0W
Puerto Angel	**165**	15 40N	96 29W
Puerto Arista	**165**	15 56N	93 48W
Puerto Armuelles	**166**	8 20N	83 10W
Puerto Ayacucho	**174**	5 40N	67 35W
Puerto Barrios	**166**	15 40N	88 40W
Puerto Bermejo	**172**	26 55S	58 34W
Puerto Bermúdez	**174**	10 20S	75 0W
Puerto Bolívar	**174**	3 10S	79 55W
Puerto Cabello	**174**	10 28N	68 1W
Puerto Cabezas	**166**	14 0N	83 30W
Puerto Cabo Gracias a Dios	**166**	15 0N	83 10W
Puerto Capaz = Jebba	**118**	35 11N	4 43W
Puerto Carreño	**174**	6 12N	67 22W
Puerto Casado	**172**	22 19S	57 56W
Puerto Castilla	**166**	16 0N	86 0W
Puerto Chicama	**174**	7 45S	79 20W
Puerto Coig	**176**	50 54S	69 15W
Puerto Columbia	**174**	10 59N	74 58W
Puerto Cortés, C. Rica	**166**	8 20N	82 20W
Puerto Cortés, Hond.	**166**	15 51N	88 0W
Puerto Cuemani	**174**	0 5N	73 21W
Puerto Cumarebo	**174**	11 29N	69 21W
Puerto de Cabras	**116**	28 40N	13 30W
Puerto de Morelos	**165**	20 49N	86 52W
Puerto de Santa María	**57**	36 36N	6 13W
Puerto Deseado	**176**	47 45S	66 0W
Puerto Heath	**174**	12 25S	68 45W
Puerto Huitoto	**174**	0 18N	74 3W
Puerto Juárez	**165**	21 11N	86 49W
Puerto La Cruz	**174**	10 13N	64 38W
Puerto Leguízamo	**174**	0 12S	74 46W
Puerto Libertad	**164**	29 55N	112 41W
Puerto Limón, Meta, Colomb.	**174**	3 23N	73 30W
Puerto Limón, Putumayo, Colomb.	**174**	1 3N	76 30W
Puerto Lobos	**176**	42 0S	65 3W
Puerto López	**174**	4 5N	72 58W
Puerto Lumbreras	**59**	37 34N	1 48W
Puerto Madryn	**176**	42 48S	65 4W
Puerto Maldonado	**174**	12 30S	69 10W
Puerto Manotí	**166**	21 22N	76 50W
Puerto Mazarrón	**59**	37 34N	1 15W
Puerto Mercedes	**174**	1 11N	72 53W
Puerto Montt	**176**	41 22S	72 40W
Puerto Natales	**176**	51 45S	72 25W
Puerto Nuevo	**174**	5 53N	69 56W
Puerto Ordaz	**174**	8 16N	62 44W
Puerto Padre	**166**	21 13N	76 35W
Puerto Páez	**174**	6 13N	67 28W
Puerto Peñasco	**164**	31 20N	113 33W
Puerto Pinasco	**172**	22 43S	57 50W
Puerto Pirámides	**176**	42 35S	64 20W
Puerto Plata	**167**	19 40N	70 45W
Puerto Princesa	**94**	9 44N	118 44E
Puerto Quellón	**176**	43 7S	73 37W
Puerto Quepos	**166**	9 29N	84 6W
Puerto Real	**57**	36 33N	6 12W
Puerto Rico	**174**	1 54N	75 10W
Puerto Rico ■	**147**	18 15N	66 45W
Puerto Rico Trough	**14**	20 0N	63 0W
Puerto Sastre	**172**	22 25S	57 55W
Puerto Suárez	**174**	18 58S	57 52W
Puerto Tejada	**174**	3 14N	76 24W
Puerto Umbria	**174**	0 52N	76 33W
Puerto Vallarta	**164**	20 26N	105 15W
Puerto Villamizar	**174**	8 25N	72 30W
Puerto Wilches	**174**	7 21N	73 54W
Puertollano	**57**	38 43N	4 7W
Puertomarín	**56**	42 48N	7 37W
Pueyrredón, L.	**176**	47 20S	72 0W
Puffin I., Ireland	**39**	51 50N	10 25W
Puffin I., U.K.	**31**	53 19N	4 1W
Pugachev	**81**	52 0N	48 55E
Puge	**126**	4 45S	33 11E
Puget Sd.	**160**	47 15N	123 30W
Puget-Théniers	**45**	43 58N	6 53E
Púglia	**65**	41 0N	16 30E
Pugŏdong	**107**	42 5N	130 0E
Pugu	**126**	6 55S	39 4E
Puha	**142**	38 30S	177 50E
P'uhsien	**106**	36 25N	110 4E
Puhute Mesa	**163**	37 25N	116 50W
Pui	**70**	45 30N	23 4E
Puieşti	**70**	46 25N	27 33E
Puig Mayor, Mte.	**58**	39 49N	2 47E
Puigcerdá	**58**	42 24N	1 50E
Puigmal, Mt.	**58**	42 23N	2 7E
Puisaye, Collines de	**43**	47 34N	3 28E
Puiseaux	**43**	48 11N	2 30E
Pujon-chosuji	**107**	40 35N	127 35E
Puka	**68**	42 2N	19 53E
Pukaki L.	**143**	44 4S	170 1E
Pukatawagan	**153**	55 45N	101 20W
Pukchin	**107**	40 12N	125 45E
Pukchŏng	**107**	40 14N	128 18E
Pukearuhe	**142**	38 55S	174 31E
Pukekohe	**142**	37 12S	174 55E
Puketeraki Ra.	**143**	42 58S	172 13E
Pukeuri	**143**	45 4S	171 2E
P'uko	**108**	27 27N	102 34E
Pukoo	**147**	21 4N	156 48W
P'uk'ou	**109**	32 7N	118 43E
Pula	**64**	39 0N	9 0E
Pula (Pola)	**63**	44 54N	13 57E
Pulaski, N.Y., U.S.A.	**162**	43 32N	76 9W
Pulaski, Tenn., U.S.A.	**157**	35 10N	87 0W
Pulaski, Va., U.S.A.	**156**	37 4N	80 49W
Pulawy	**54**	51 23N	21 59E
Pulborough	**29**	50 58N	0 30W
Pulgaon	**96**	20 44N	78 21E
Pulham Market	**29**	52 25N	1 15E
Pulham St. Mary	**29**	52 25N	1 14E
Pulicat, L.	**97**	13 40N	80 15E
Puliyangudi	**97**	9 11N	77 24E
Pullabooka	**141**	33 44S	147 46E
Pullen Cr.	**108**	27 33S	152 54E
Pullman	**160**	46 49N	117 10W
Pulmakong	**121**	11 2N	0 2E
Pulog, Mt.	**103**	16 40N	120 50E
Puloraja	**102**	4 55N	95 24E
Pułtusk	**54**	52 43N	21 6E
Pumlumon Fawr	**31**	52 29N	3 47W
Pumpsaint	**31**	52 3N	3 58W
Puna	**174**	19 45S	65 28W
Puna de Atacama	**172**	25 0S	67 0W
Puná, I.	**174**	2 55S	80 5W
Punakha	**98**	27 42N	89 52E
Punalur	**97**	9 0N	76 56E
Punasar	**94**	27 6N	73 6E
Punata	**174**	17 25S	65 50W
Punch	**95**	33 48N	74 4E
Pune	**96**	18 29N	73 57E
Pungsan	**107**	40 50N	128 9E
P'uning	**109**	23 19N	116 9E
Punjab □	**94**	31 0N	76 0E
Punkatawagon	**153**	55 44N	101 20W
Puno	**174**	15 55S	70 3W
Punt, La	**51**	46 35N	9 56E
Punta Alta	**176**	38 53S	62 4W
Punta Arenas	**176**	53 0S	71 0W
Punta de Díaz	**172**	28 0S	70 45W
Punta de Piedras	**174**	10 54N	64 6W
Punta del Lago Viedma	**176**	49 45S	72 0W
Punta Gorda, Belize	**165**	16 10N	88 45W
Punta Gorda, U.S.A.	**157**	26 55N	82 0W
Punta Prieta	**164**	28 58N	114 17W
Puntabie	**139**	32 12S	134 5E
Puntarenas	**166**	10 0N	84 50W
Puntes de García Rodríguez	**56**	43 27N	7 50W
Punto Fijo	**174**	11 42N	70 13W
Punxsutawney	**156**	40 56N	79 0W
P'upei	**108**	22 16N	109 33E
Puquio	**174**	14 45S	74 10W
Pur, R.	**76**	65 30N	77 40E
Purace, vol.	**174**	2 21N	76 23W
Puračió	**66**	44 33N	18 28E
Purari, R.	**135**	7 49S	145 0E
Purbeck, Isle of	**28**	50 40N	2 5W
Purcell	**159**	35 0N	97 25W
Purchena Tetica	**59**	37 21N	2 21W
Purdy Is.	**138**	3 0S	146 0E
Purfleet	**29**	51 29N	0 15E
Puri	**96**	19 50N	85 58E
Purificación	**174**	3 51N	74 55W
Purísima, La	**164**	26 10N	112 4W
Purley	**28**	51 29N	1 4W
Purli	**96**	18 50N	76 35E
Purmerend	**47**	52 30N	4 58E
Purna, R.	**96**	19 55N	76 20E
Purnea	**95**	25 45N	87 31E
Pursat	**101**	12 34N	103 50E
Puruey	**174**	7 35N	64 48W
Purukcahu	**102**	0 35S	114 35E
Purulia	**95**	23 17N	86 33E
Purus, R.	**174**	5 25S	64 0W
Purwakarta	**103**	6 35S	107 29E
Purwodadi, Jawa, Indon.	**103**	7 7S	110 55E
Purwodadi, Jawa, Indon.	**103**	7 51S	110 0E
Purworejo	**103**	7 43S	110 2E
Puryŏng	**107**	42 0N	129 43E
Pus, R.	**96**	19 50N	77 45E
Pusad	**96**	19 56N	77 36E
Pusan	**107**	35 5N	129 0E
Pushchino	**77**	54 20N	158 10E
Pushkin	**80**	59 45N	30 25E
Pushkino	**81**	51 16N	47 9E
Puskitamika L.	**150**	49 20N	76 30W
Püspökladány	**53**	47 19N	21 6E
Pussa	**129**	24 30S	33 55E
Pustoshka	**80**	56 11N	29 30E
Puszczykowo	**54**	52 18N	16 49E
Putahow L.	**153**	59 54N	100 40W
Putao	**98**	27 28N	97 30E
Putaruru	**142**	38 2S	175 50E
Putbus	**48**	54 19N	13 29E
Put'ehach'i	**105**	48 0N	122 43E
Puţeni	**70**	45 49N	27 42E
Puthein Myit, R.	**99**	15 56N	94 18E
P'ut'ien	**109**	25 27N	118 59E
Putignano	**65**	40 50N	17 5E
P'uting	**108**	26 19N	105 45E
Putlitz	**48**	53 15N	12 3E
Putna	**70**	47 50N	25 33E
Putna, R.	**70**	45 42N	27 26E
Putnam	**162**	41 55N	71 55W
Putnok	**53**	48 18N	20 26E
P'ut'o	**109**	29 58N	122 15E
Putorana, Gory	**77**	69 0N	95 0E
Putorino	**142**	39 4S	177 9E
Putta	**47**	51 4N	4 38E
Puttalam	**93**	8 1N	79 55E
Puttalam Lagoon	**97**	8 15N	79 45E
Putte	**47**	51 22N	4 24E
Putten	**46**	52 16N	5 36E
Puttgarden	**48**	54 28N	11 15E
Puttur	**97**	12 46N	75 12E
Putty	**141**	32 57S	150 42E
Putumayo □	**174**	1 30S	70 0W
Putumayo, R.	**174**	1 30S	70 0W
Putussibau, G.	**102**	0 45N	113 50E
Pututahi	**142**	38 39S	177 53E
Puurs	**47**	51 5N	4 17E
Puy-de-Dôme	**44**	45 46N	2 57E
Puy-de-Dôme □	**44**	45 47N	3 0E
Puy-de-Sancy	**44**	45 32N	2 41E
Puy Guillaume	**44**	45 57N	3 28E
Puy, Le	**44**	45 3N	3 52E
Puy l'Evêque	**44**	44 31N	1 9E
Puyallup	**160**	47 10N	122 22W
P'uyang	**106**	35 41N	115 0E
Puylaurens	**44**	43 35N	2 0E
Puyôo	**44**	43 33N	0 56W
Pwalagu	**121**	10 38N	0 50W
Pwani □, Tanz.	**126**	7 0S	39 0E
Pwani □, Tanz.	**126**	7 0S	39 30E
Pweto	**127**	8 25S	28 51E
Pwinbyu	**98**	20 23N	94 40E
Pwllheli	**31**	52 54N	4 26W
Pya Ozero	**78**	66 8N	31 22E
Pyana, R.	**81**	55 30N	45 0E
Pyandzh	**85**	37 14N	69 6E
Pyandzh, R.	**85**	37 6N	68 20E
Pyapon	**98**	16 5N	95 50E
Pyasina, R.	**77**	72 30N	90 30E
Pyatigorsk	**83**	44 2N	43 0E
Pyatikhatki	**82**	48 28N	33 38E
Pyaye	**98**	19 12N	95 10E
Pyè	**98**	18 49N	95 13E
Pyinbauk	**98**	19 10N	95 12E
Pyinmana	**98**	19 45N	96 20E
Pyŏktong	**107**	40 37N	125 26E
Pyŏnggang	**107**	38 24N	127 17E
Pyŏngtaek	**107**	37 1N	127 4E
P'yŏngyang	**107**	39 0N	125 45E
Pyote	**159**	31 34N	103 5W
Pyramid L.	**160**	40 0N	119 30W
Pyramid Pk.	**163**	36 25N	116 37W
Pyramids	**122**	29 58N	31 9E
Pyrenees	**44**	42 45N	0 18E
Pyrénées-Atlantiques □	**44**	43 15N	1 0W
Pyrénées-Orientales □	**44**	42 35N	2 26E
Pyrzyce	**54**	53 10N	14 55E
Pyshchug	**81**	58 57N	45 27E
Pyshma, R.	**84**	57 8N	66 18E
Pytalovo	**80**	57 5N	27 55E
Python	**127**	17 56S	29 10E
Pyttegga	**71**	62 13N	7 42E
Pyu	**98**	18 30N	96 35E
Pyzdry	**54**	52 11N	17 42E

Q

Qaar Zeitun	**122**	29 10N	25 48E
Qabalon	**90**	32 8N	35 17E
Qabatiya	**90**	32 25N	35 16E
Qadam	**93**	32 55N	66 45E
Qadhimah	**92**	22 20N	39 13E
Qadian	**94**	31 51N	74 19E
Qal at Shajwa	**122**	25 2N	38 57E
Qala-i-Jadid (Spin Baldak)	**94**	31 1N	66 25E
Qala-i-Kirta	**93**	32 15N	63 0E
Qala Nau	**93**	35 0N	63 5E
Qala Punja	**93**	37 0N	72 40E
Qala Yangi	**94**	34 20N	66 30E
Qal'at al Akhdhar	**92**	28 0N	37 10E
Qal'at Saura	**122**	26 10N	38 40E
Qal'eh Shaharak	**93**	34 10N	64 20E
Qalqīlya	**90**	32 12N	34 58E
Qalyûb	**122**	30 12N	31 11E
Qam	**90**	32 36N	35 43E
Qamar, Ghubbat al	**91**	16 20N	52 30E
Qamruddin Karez	**94**	31 45N	68 20E
Qana	**90**	33 12N	35 17E
Qâra	**122**	29 38N	26 30E
Qara Qash, R.	**95**	35 45N	78 45E
Qara Tagh La = Kala Shank'ou	**95**	35 42N	78 20E
Qarachuk	**92**	37 0N	42 2E
Qarah	**92**	29 55N	40 3E
Qardud	**123**	10 20N	29 56E
Qarrasa	**123**	14 38N	32 5E
Qarsa	**123**	9 28N	41 48E
Qaşr Bū Hadi	**119**	31 1N	16 45E
Qasr-e-Qand	**93**	26 15N	60 45E
Qasr Farâfra	**122**	27 0N	28 1E
Qastina	**90**	31 44N	34 45E
Qatar ■	**93**	25 30N	51 15E
Qattâra	**122**	30 12N	27 3E
Qattara Depression = Q. Munkhafed el	**122**	29 30N	27 30E
Qattâra, Munkhafed el	**122**	29 30N	27 30E

Qayen **Rancharia**

Qayen	**93**	33 40N	59 10 E
Qazvin	**92**	36 15N	50 0 E
Qena	**122**	26 10N	32 43 E
Qena, Wadi	**122**	26 57N	32 50 E
Qendrevca	**68**	40 20N	19 48 E
Qesari	**90**	32 30N	34 53 E
Qeshm	**93**	26 55N	56 10 E
Qeshm, I.	**93**	26 50N	56 0 E
Qila Safed	**93**	29 0N	61 30 E
Qila Saifulla	**94**	30 45N	68 17 E
Qiryat 'Anivim	**90**	31 49N	35 7 E
Qiryat Bialik	**90**	32 50N	35 5 E
Qiryat 'Eqron	**90**	31 52N	34 49 E
Qiryat Hayyim	**90**	32 49N	35 4 E
Qiryat Shemona	**90**	33 13N	35 35 E
Qiryat Yam	**90**	32 51N	35 4 E
Qishon, R.	**90**	32 42N	35 7 E
Qishran	**122**	20 14N	40 2 E
Qizan	**123**	16 57N	42 34 E
Qom	**93**	34 40N	51 0 E
Quabbin Res.	**162**	42 17N	72 21W
Quabbo	**123**	12 2N	39 56 E
Quackenbrück	**48**	52 40N	7 59 E
Quadring	**33**	52 53N	0 9W
Quainton	**29**	51 51N	0 53W
Quairading	**137**	32 0S	117 21 E
Quakerstown	**162**	40 27N	75 20W
Qualeup	**137**	33 48S	116 48 E
Quambatook	**138**	35 49S	143 34 E
Quambone	**141**	30 57S	147 53 E
Quan Long	**101**	9 7N	105 8 E
Quanan	**159**	34 20N	99 45W
Quandialla	**141**	34 1S	147 47 E
Quang Nam	**101**	15 55N	108 15 E
Quang Ngai	**101**	15 13N	108 58 E
Quang Yen	**100**	21 3N	106 52 E
Quantock Hills, The	**28**	51 8N	3 10W
Quaraí	**172**	30 15S	56 20W
Quarré les Tombes	**43**	47 21N	4 0 E
Quarryville	**162**	39 54N	76 10W
Quartu Sant' Elena	**64**	39 15N	9 10 E
Quartzsite	**161**	33 44N	114 16W
Quatsino	**152**	50 30N	127 40W
Quatsino Sd.	**152**	50 42N	127 58W
Qubab = Mishmar Aiyalon	**90**	31 52N	34 57 E
Qūchān	**93**	37 10N	58 27 E
Que Que	**127**	18 58S	29 48 E
Queanbeyan	**141**	35 17S	149 14 E
Québec	**151**	46 52N	71 13W
Québec □	**151**	50 0N	70 0W
Quedlinburg	**48**	51 47N	11 9 E
Queen Alexandra Ra.	**13**	85 0S	170 0 E
Queen Anne	**162**	38 55N	75 57W
Queen Bess Mt.	**152**	51 13N	124 35W
Queen Charlotte	**152**	53 15N	132 2W
Queen Charlotte Is.	**152**	53 20N	132 10W
Queen Charlotte Sd.	**143**	41 10S	174 15 E
Queen Charlotte Str.	**152**	51 0N	128 0W
Queen Elizabeth Is.	**10**	78 0N	95 0W
Queen Elizabeth Nat. Pk.	**126**	0 0S	30 0 E
Queen Mary Coast	**13**	70 0S	95 0 E
Queen Maud G.	**148**	68 15N	102 30W
Queenborough	**29**	51 24N	0 46 E
Queen's Chan.	**136**	15 0S	129 30 E
Queensbury	**32**	53 46N	1 50W
Queenscliff	**138**	38 16S	144 39 E
Queensferry	**35**	56 0N	3 25W
Queensland □	**138**	15 0S	142 0 E
Queenstown, Austral.	**138**	42 4S	145 35 E
Queenstown, N.Z.	**143**	45 1S	168 40 E
Queenstown, S. Afr.	**125**	31 52S	26 52 E
Queguay Grande, R.	**172**	32 9S	58 9W
Queimadas	**170**	11 0S	39 38W
Quela	**124**	9 10S	16 56 E
Quelimane	**127**	17 53S	36 58 E
Quemado, N. Mex., U.S.A.	**161**	34 17N	108 28W
Quemado, Tex., U.S.A.	**159**	28 58N	100 35W
Quemoy, I. = Chinmen Tao, I.	**109**	24 25N	118 25 E
Quemú-Quemú	**172**	36 3S	63 36W
Quendale, B. of	**36**	59 53N	1 20W
Quequén	**172**	38 30S	58 30W
Querein	**123**	13 30N	34 50 E
Querétaro	**164**	20 40N	100 23W
Querétaro □	**164**	20 30N	100 30W
Querfurt	**48**	51 22N	11 33 E
Quesada	**59**	37 51N	3 4W
Quesnel	**152**	53 5N	122 30W
Quesnel L.	**152**	52 30N	121 20W
Quesnel, R.	**152**	52 58N	122 29W
Quest, Pte.	**151**	49 52N	64 40W
Questa	**161**	36 45N	105 35W
Questembert	**42**	47 40N	2 28W
Quetico	**150**	48 45N	90 55W
Quetico Prov. Park	**150**	48 30N	91 45W
Quetta	**93**	30 15N	66 55 E
Quetta □	**93**	30 15N	66 55 E
Quezaltenango	**166**	14 40N	91 30W
Quezon City	**103**	14 38N	121 0 E
Qui Nhon	**101**	13 40N	109 13 E
Quiaca, La	**172**	22 5S	65 35W
Quibaxi	**124**	8 24S	14 27 E
Quibdó	**174**	5 42N	76 40W
Quiberon	**42**	47 29N	3 9W
Quibor	**174**	9 56N	69 37W
Quick	**152**	54 36N	126 54W
Quickborn	**48**	53 42N	9 52 E
Quiet L.	**152**	61 5N	133 5W
Quiévrain	**47**	50 24N	3 41 E
Quiindy	**172**	25 58S	57 14W
Quila	**164**	24 23N	107 13W
Quilán, C.	**176**	43 15S	74 30W
Quilengues	**125**	14 12S	14 12 E
Quilimarí	**172**	32 5S	70 30W
Quilino	**172**	30 14S	64 29W
Quillabamba	**174**	12 50S	72 50W
Quillagua	**172**	21 40S	69 40W
Quillaicillo	**172**	31 17S	71 40W
Quillan	**44**	42 53N	2 10 E
Quillebeuf	**42**	49 28N	0 30 E
Quillota	**172**	32 54S	71 16W
Quilmes	**172**	34 43S	58 15W
Quilon	**97**	8 50N	76 38 E
Quilpie	**139**	26 35S	144 11 E
Quilpué	**172**	33 5S	71 33W
Quilty	**39**	52 50N	9 27W
Quilua	**127**	16 17S	39 54 E
Quimilí	**172**	27 40S	62 30W
Quimper	**42**	48 0N	4 9W
Quimperlé	**42**	47 53N	3 33W
Quin	**39**	52 50N	8 52W
Quinag	**36**	58 13N	5 5W
Quincy, Calif., U.S.A.	**160**	39 56N	121 0W
Quincy, Fla., U.S.A.	**157**	30 34N	84 34W
Quincy, Ill., U.S.A.	**158**	39 55N	91 20W
Quincy, Mass., U.S.A.	**162**	42 14N	71 0W
Quincy, Wash., U.S.A.	**160**	47 22N	119 56W
Quines	**172**	32 13S	65 48W
Quinga	**127**	15 49S	40 15 E
Quingey	**43**	47 7N	5 52 E
Quinhagak	**147**	59 45N	162 0W
Quintana de la Serena	**57**	38 45N	5 40W
Quintana Roo □	**165**	19 0N	88 0W
Quintanar de la Orden	**58**	39 36N	3 5W
Quintanar de la Sierra	**58**	41 57N	2 55W
Quintanar del Rey	**59**	39 21N	1 56W
Quintero	**172**	32 45S	71 30W
Quintin	**42**	48 26N	2 56W
Quinto	**58**	41 25N	0 32W
Quinyambie	**139**	30 15S	141 0 E
Quipar, R.	**59**	37 58N	2 3W
Quirihue	**172**	36 15S	72 35W
Quirindi	**141**	31 28S	150 40 E
Quiriquire	**174**	9 59N	63 13W
Quiroga	**56**	42 28N	7 18W
Quirpon I.	**151**	51 32N	55 28W
Quisiro	**174**	10 53N	71 17W
Quissac	**45**	43 55N	4 0 E
Quissanga	**127**	12 24S	40 28 E
Quitilipi	**172**	26 50S	60 13W
Quitman, Ga., U.S.A.	**157**	30 49N	83 35W
Quitman, Miss., U.S.A.	**157**	32 2N	88 42W
Quitman, Tex., U.S.A.	**159**	32 48N	95 25W
Quito	**174**	0 15S	78 35W
Quixadá	**170**	4 55S	39 0W
Quixaxe	**127**	15 17S	40 4 E
Quixeramobim	**170**	5 12S	39 17W
Qul'ân, Jazâ'ir	**122**	24 22N	35 31 E
Qumran	**90**	31 43N	35 27 E
Quneitra	**90**	33 7N	35 48 E
Quoich L.	**36**	57 4N	5 20W
Quoile, R.	**38**	54 21N	5 40W
Quoin I.	**136**	14 54S	129 32 E
Quoin Pt., N.Z.	**143**	46 19S	170 11 E
Quoin Pt., S. Afr.	**128**	34 46S	19 37 E
Quondong	**140**	33 6S	140 18 E
Quorn, Austral.	**140**	32 25S	138 0 E
Quorn, Can.	**150**	49 25N	90 55W
Quorndon	**28**	52 45N	1 10W
Qûs	**122**	25 55N	32 50 E
Quseir	**122**	26 7N	34 16 E
Qusra	**90**	32 5N	35 20 E
Quthing	**129**	30 25S	27 36 E
Quynh Nhai	**100**	21 49N	103 33 E
Qytet Stalin (Kuçove)	**68**	40 47N	19 57 E

R

Ra, Ko	**101**	9 13N	98 16 E
Raa.	**73**	56 0N	12 45 E
Råå	**73**	56 0N	12 45 E
Raahana	**90**	32 12N	34 52 E
Raahe	**74**	64 40N	24 28 E
Raalte	**46**	52 23N	6 16 E
Raamsdonksveer	**47**	51 43N	4 52 E
Raasay I.	**36**	57 25N	6 4W
Raasay, Sd. of	**36**	57 30N	6 8W
Rab	**63**	44 45N	14 45 E
Rab, I.	**63**	44 45N	14 45 E
Raba	**103**	8 36S	118 55 E
Rába, R.	**54**	47 38N	17 38 E
Rabaçal, R.	**56**	41 41N	7 15W
Rabah	**121**	13 5N	5 30 E
Rabai	**126**	3 50S	39 31 E
Rabaraba	**135**	9 58S	149 49 E
Rabastens	**44**	43 50N	1 43 E
Rabastens, Hautes Pyrénées	**44**	43 25N	0 10 E
Rabat	**118**	34 2N	6 48W
Rabaul	**135**	4 24S	152 18 E
Rabbalshede	**73**	58 40N	11 27 E
Rabbit L.	**153**	47 0N	79 38W
Rabbit Lake	**153**	53 8N	107 46W
Rabbit, R.	**152**	59 41N	127 12W
Rabbitskin, R.	**152**	61 47N	120 42W
Rabigh	**92**	22 50N	39 5 E
Rabka	**54**	49 37N	19 59 E
Rača	**66**	44 14N	21 0 E
Rácale	**65**	39 57N	18 6 E
Racalmuto	**64**	37 25N	13 41 E
Racconigi	**62**	44 47N	7 41 E
Race, C.	**151**	46 40N	53 5W
Raceview	**108**	27 38S	152 47 E
Rach Gia	**101**	10 5N	105 5 E
Raciaz	**54**	52 46N	20 10 E
Racibórz (Ratibor)	**54**	50 7N	18 18 E
Racine	**156**	42 41N	87 51W
Rackheath	**29**	52 41N	1 22 E
Rackwick	**37**	58 52N	3 23W
Radama, Is.	**129**	14 0S	47 47 E
Radama, Presqu'île d'	**129**	14 16S	47 53 E
Radan, mt.	**66**	42 59N	21 29 E
Radbuza, R.	**52**	49 35N	13 5 E
Radcliffe, Gr. Manch., U.K.	**32**	53 35N	2 19W
Radcliffe, Notts., U.K.	**33**	52 57N	1 3W
Rade	**71**	59 21N	10 53 E
Radeburg	**48**	51 6N	13 45 E
Radeče	**63**	46 5N	15 14 E
Radekhov	**80**	50 25N	24 32 E
Radford	**156**	37 8N	80 32W
Radhanpur	**94**	23 50N	71 38 E
Radika, R.	**66**	41 38N	20 37 E
Radisson	**153**	52 30N	107 20W
Radium Hill	**133**	32 30S	140 42 E
Radium Hot Springs	**152**	50 48N	116 12W
Radkow	**54**	50 30N	16 24 E
Radley	**28**	51 42N	1 14W
Radlin	**54**	50 3N	18 29 E
Radna	**66**	46 7N	21 41 E
Radnevo	**67**	42 17N	25 58 E
Radnice	**52**	49 51N	13 35 E
Radnor (□)	**26**	52 20N	3 20W
Radnor Forest	**31**	52 17N	3 10W
Radom	**54**	51 23N	21 12 E
Radom □	**54**	51 30N	21 0 E
Radomir	**66**	42 37N	23 4 E
Radomsko	**54**	51 5N	19 28 E
Radomyshl	**80**	50 30N	29 12 E
Radomysl Wielki	**54**	50 14N	21 15 E
Radoszyce	**54**	51 4N	20 15 E
Radoviš	**66**	41 38N	22 28 E
Radovljica	**63**	46 22N	14 12 E
Radöy I.	**71**	60 40N	4 55 E
Radstadt	**52**	47 24N	13 28 E
Radstock	**28**	51 17N	2 25W
Radstock, C.	**139**	33 12S	134 20 E
Raduša	**66**	42 7N	21 15 E
Radviliškis	**80**	55 49N	23 33 E
Radville	**153**	49 30N	104 15W
Radymno	**54**	49 59N	22 52 E
Radyr	**31**	51 32N	3 16W
Radzanów	**54**	52 56N	20 8 E
Radziejów	**54**	52 40N	18 30 E
Radzyn Chełminski	**54**	53 23N	18 55 E
Rae	**152**	62 50N	116 3W
Rae Bareli	**95**	26 18N	81 20 E
Rae Isthmus	**149**	66 40N	87 30W
Raeside, L.	**137**	29 20S	122 0 E
Raetihi	**142**	39 25S	175 17 E
Rafaela	**172**	31 10S	61 30W
Rafah	**122**	31 18N	34 14 E
Rafai	**126**	4 59N	23 58 E
Raffadali	**64**	37 23N	13 29 E
Rafhā	**92**	29 35N	43 35 E
Rafid	**90**	32 57N	35 52 E
Rafsanjān	**93**	30 30N	56 5 E
Raft Pt.	**136**	16 4S	124 26 E
Ragag	**123**	10 59N	24 40 E
Ragama	**93**	7 0N	79 50 E
Ragged Mt.	**137**	33 27S	123 25 E
Raglan, Austral.	**138**	23 42S	150 49 E
Raglan, N.Z.	**142**	37 55S	174 55 E
Raglan, U.K.	**31**	51 46N	2 51W
Ragueneau	**151**	49 11N	68 18W
Ragunda	**72**	63 6N	16 23 E
Ragusa	**65**	36 56N	14 42 E
Raha	**103**	8 20S	118 40 E
Rahad el Berdi	**117**	11 20N	23 40 E
Rahad, Nahr er	**123**	12 40N	35 30 E
Rahden	**48**	52 26N	8 36 E
Raheita	**123**	12 46N	43 4 E
Raheng = Tak	**100**	17 5N	99 10 E
Rahimyar Khan	**94**	28 30N	70 25 E
Rahotu	**142**	39 20S	173 49 E
Raichur	**96**	16 10N	77 20 E
Raiganj	**95**	25 37N	88 10 E
Raigarh, Madhya Pradesh, India	**96**	21 56N	83 25 E
Raigarh, Orissa, India	**96**	19 51N	82 6 E
Raiis	**92**	23 33N	38 43 E
Raijua	**103**	10 37S	121 36 E
Railton	**138**	41 25S	146 28 E
Rainbow	**140**	35 55S	142 0 E
Rainbow Lake	**152**	58 30N	119 23W
Rainham	**29**	51 22N	0 36 E
Rainier	**160**	46 4N	123 0W
Rainier, Mt.	**160**	46 50N	121 50W
Rainworth	**33**	53 8N	1 6W
Rainy L.	**153**	48 30N	92 30W
Rainy River	**153**	48 50N	94 30W
Raipur	**96**	21 17N	81 45 E
Raith	**150**	48 50N	90 0W
Raj Nandgaon	**99**	21 0N	81 0 E
Raja Empat, Kepulauan	**103**	0 30S	129 40 E
Raja-Jooseppi	**74**	68 28N	28 29 E
Raja, Ujung	**102**	3 40N	96 25 E
Rajahmundry	**96**	17 1N	81 48 E
Rajang, R.	**102**	2 30N	113 30 E
Rajapalaiyarm	**97**	9 25N	77 35 E
Rajasthan □	**94**	26 45N	73 30 E
Rajasthan Canal	**94**	30 31N	71 0 E
Rajauri	**95**	33 25N	74 21 E
Rajbari	**98**	23 47N	89 41 E
Rajgarh, Mad. P., India	**94**	24 2N	76 45 E
Rajgarh, Raj., India	**94**	28 40N	75 25 E
Rajgród	**54**	53 42N	22 42 E
Rajhenburg	**63**	46 1N	15 29 E
Rajkot	**94**	22 15N	70 56 E
Rajmahal Hills	**95**	24 30N	87 30 E
Rajnandgaon	**96**	21 5N	81 5 E
Rajojooseppi	**74**	68 25N	28 30 E
Rajpipla	**96**	21 50N	73 30 E
Rajpura	**94**	30 32N	76 32 E
Rajshahi	**98**	24 22N	88 39 E
Rajshahi □	**95**	25 0N	89 0 E
Rakaia	**143**	43 45S	172 1 E
Rakaia, R.	**143**	43 26S	171 47 E
Rakan, Ras	**93**	26 10N	51 20 E
Rakaposhi	**95**	36 10N	74 0 E
Rakaposhi, mt.	**93**	36 20N	74 30 E
Rakha	**122**	18 25N	41 30 E
Rakhni	**94**	30 4N	69 56 E
Rakitovo	**67**	41 59N	24 5 E
Rakkestad	**71**	59 25N	11 21 E
Rakoniewice	**54**	52 10N	16 16 E
Rakops	**128**	21 1S	24 28 E
Rákospalota	**53**	47 30N	19 5 E
Rakovica	**63**	44 59N	15 38 E
Rakovník	**52**	50 6N	13 42 E
Rakovski	**67**	42 21N	24 57 E
Raleigh, Can.	**150**	49 30N	92 5W
Raleigh, U.S.A.	**150**	35 46N	78 38W
Raleigh B.	**157**	34 50N	76 15W
Ralja	**66**	44 33N	20 34 E
Ralls	**159**	33 40N	101 20W
Ralston	**162**	41 30N	76 57W
Rām Allāh	**90**	31 55N	35 10 E
Ram Hd.	**141**	37 47S	149 30 E
Ram, R.	**152**	62 1N	123 41W
Rama, Israel	**90**	32 56N	35 21 E
Rama, Nic.	**166**	12 9N	84 15W
Ramacca	**65**	37 24N	14 40 E
Ramachandrapuram	**96**	16 50N	82 4 E
Ramadi	**92**	33 28N	43 15 E
Ramales de la Victoria	**58**	43 15N	3 28W
Ramalho, Serra do	**171**	13 45S	44 0W
Raman	**101**	6 29N	101 18 E
Ramanathapuram	**97**	9 25N	78 55 E
Ramanetaka, B. de	**129**	14 13S	47 52 E
Ramas C.	**97**	15 5N	73 55 E
Ramat Gan	**90**	32 4N	34 48 E
Ramatlhabama	**128**	25 37S	25 33 E
Ramban	**95**	33 14N	75 12 E
Rambervillers	**43**	48 20N	6 38 E
Rambipudji	**103**	8 12S	113 37 E
Rambla, La	**57**	37 37N	4 45W
Rambouillet	**43**	48 40N	1 48 E
Rambre Kyun	**98**	19 0N	94 0 E
Ramdurg	**97**	15 58N	75 22 E
Rame Head	**30**	50 19N	4 14W
Ramechhap	**95**	27 25N	86 10 E
Ramelau, Mte.	**103**	8 55S	126 22 E
Ramenskoye	**81**	55 32N	38 15 E
Ramgarh, Bihar, India	**95**	23 40N	85 35 E
Ramgarh, Rajasthan, India	**94**	27 16N	75 14 E
Ramgarh, Rajasthan, India	**94**	27 30N	70 36 E
Ramhormoz	**92**	31 15N	49 35 E
Ramla	**90**	31 55N	34 52 E
Ramlat Zaltan	**119**	28 30N	19 30 E
Ramlu Mt.	**123**	13 32N	41 40 E
Ramme	**73**	56 30N	8 11 E
Rammun	**90**	31 55N	35 17 E
Ramna Stacks, Is.	**36**	60 40N	1 20W
Ramnad = Ramanathapuram	**97**	9 25N	78 55 E
Ramnagar	**95**	32 47N	75 18 E
Ramnäs	**72**	59 46N	16 12 E
Ramon	**81**	52 8N	39 21 E
Ramona	**163**	33 1N	116 56W
Ramor L.	**38**	53 50N	7 5W
Ramore	**150**	48 30N	80 25W
Ramos Arizpe	**164**	23 35N	100 59W
Ramos, R.	**164**	25 35N	105 3W
Ramoutsa	**128**	24 50S	25 52 E
Rampart	**147**	65 0N	150 15W
Rampside	**32**	54 6N	3 10W
Rampur, H.P., India	**94**	31 26N	77 43 E
Rampur, M.P., India	**94**	23 25N	73 53 E
Rampur, Orissa, India	**96**	21 48N	83 58 E
Rampur, U.P., India	**94**	28 50N	79 5 E
Rampura	**94**	24 30N	75 27 E
Rampurhat	**95**	24 10N	87 50 E
Ramsbottom	**32**	53 36N	2 20W
Ramsbury	**28**	51 26N	1 37W
Ramsel	**47**	51 2N	4 50 E
Ramsele	**74**	63 31N	16 27 E
Ramsey, Can.	**150**	47 25N	82 20W
Ramsey, Cambs., U.K.	**29**	52 27N	0 6W
Ramsey, Essex, U.K.	**29**	51 55N	1 12 E
*Ramsey, I. of M., U.K.	**32**	54 20N	4 21W
Ramsgate	**29**	51 20N	1 25 E
Ramshai	**98**	26 44N	88 51 E
Rämshyttan	**72**	60 17N	15 15 E
Ramsjö	**72**	62 11N	15 37 E
Ramtek	**96**	21 20N	79 15 E
Ramu, R.	**135**	4 0S	144 41 E
Ramvik	**72**	62 49N	17 51 E
Ranaghat	**95**	23 15N	88 35 E
Ranahu	**94**	25 55N	69 45 E
Ranau	**102**	6 2N	116 40 E
Rancagua	**172**	34 10S	70 50W
Rance	**47**	50 9N	4 16 E
Rance, R.	**42**	48 34N	1 59W
Rancharia	**171**	22 15S	50 55W

Rancheria, R Rennell Sd

Rancheria, R. 152 60 13N 129 7W
Ranchester 160 44 57N 107 12W
Ranchi 95 23 19N 85 27 E
Rancu 70 44 32N 24 15 E
Rand 141 35 33 S 146 32 E
Randallstown 162 39 22N 76 48W
Randalstown 38 54 45N 6 20W
Randan 44 46 2N 3 21 E
Randazzo 65 37 53N 14 56 E
Randböl 73 55 43N 9 17 E
Randers 73 56 29N 10 1 E
Randers Fjord 73 56 37N 10 20 E
Randfontein 129 26 8 S 27 45 E
Randolph, Mass., U.S.A. 162 42 10N 71 3W
Randolph, Utah, U.S.A. 160 41 43N 111 10W
Randolph, Vt., U.S.A. 162 43 55N 72 39W
Randsburg 163 35 26N 117 44W
Randsfjord 71 60 15N 10 25 E
Råne älv 74 66 26N 21 10 E
Råneå 74 65 53N 22 18 E
Ranfurly 143 45 7 S 170 6 E
Rangae 101 6 19N 101 44 E
Rangamati 98 22 38 S 92 12 E
Rangataua 142 39 26 S 175 28 E
Rangaunu B. 142 34 51 S 173 15 E
Rångedala 73 57 47N 13 9 E
Rangeley 156 44 58N 70 33W
Rangely 160 40 3N 108 53W
Ranger 159 32 30N 98 42W
Rangia 98 26 15N 91 20 E
Rangiora 143 43 19 S 172 36 E
Rangitaiki 130 38 52 S 176 23 E
Rangitaiki, R. 142 37 54 S 176 49 E
Rangitata, R. 143 43 45 S 171 15 E
Rangitikei, R. 142 40 17 S 175 15 E
Rangitoto Range 142 38 25 S 175 35 E
Rangkasbitung 103 6 22 S 106 16 E
Rangon 99 16 45N 96 20 E
Rangon, R. 99 16 28N 96 40 E
Rangoon 98 16 45N 96 20 E
Rangpur 98 25 42N 89 22 E
Rangsit 100 13 59N 100 37 E
Ranibennur 97 14 35N 75 30 E
Raniganj 95 23 40N 87 15 E
Ranipet 97 12 56N 79 23 E
Raniwara 93 24 50N 72 10 E
Ranken, R. 138 20 31 S 137 36 E
Rankin 159 31 16N 101 56W
Rankin Inlet 148 62 30N 93 0W
Rankin's Springs 141 33 49 S 146 14 E
Rannes 138 24 6 S 150 11 E
Rannoch L. 37 56 41N 4 20W
Rannoch Moor 34 56 38N 4 48W
Rannoch Sta. 37 56 40N 4 32W
Ranobe, B. de 129 23 3 S 43 33 E
Ranohira 129 22 29 S 45 24 E
Ranomafana, Tamatave, Madag. 129 18 57 S 48 50 E
Ranomafana, Tuléar, Madag. 129 24 34 S 47 0 E
Ranong 101 9 56N 98 40 E
Rantau 102 4 15N 98 5 E
Rantauprapat 102 2 15N 99 50 E
Rantemario 103 3 15 S 119 57 E
Rantis 90 32 4N 35 3 E
Rantoul 156 40 18N 88 10W
Ranum 73 56 54N 9 14 E
Ranwanlenau 128 19 37 S 22 49 E
Raon-l' Étape 43 48 24N 6 50 E
Raoui, Erg er 118 29 0N 2 0W
Rapa Iti, I. 131 27 35 S 144 20W
Rapallo 62 44 21N 9 12 E
Rapang 103 3 45 S 119 55 E
Râpch 93 25 40N 59 15 E
Raphoe 38 54 52N 7 36W
Rapid City 158 44 0N 103 0W
Rapid, R. 152 59 15N 129 5W
Rapid River 156 45 55N 87 0W
Rapides des Joachims 150 46 13N 77 43W
Rapla 80 58 88N 24 52 E
Rapness 37 59 15N 2 51W
Raposos 171 19 57 S 43 48W
Rappahannock, R. 162 37 35N 76 17W
Rapperswil 51 47 14N 8 45 E
Raqqa 92 36 0N 38 55 E
Raquete 127 14 8 S 38 13 E
Raquette Lake 162 43 49N 74 40W
Rareagh 38 53 37N 8 37W
Rarotonga, I. 131 21 30 S 160 0W
Ras al Khaima 93 25 50N 56 5 E
Ra's Al-Unūf 119 30 25N 18 15 E
Ra's at Tannurah 92 26 40N 50 10 E
Ras Dashan, mt. 123 13 8N 37 45 E
Ras el Ma 118 34 26N 0 50W
Ras Gharib 122 28 6N 33 18 E
Ras Mallap 122 29 18N 32 50 E
Rasa, Punta 176 40 50 S 62 15W
Rasboda 72 60 8N 16 58 E
Raseiniai 80 55 25N 23 5 E
Rashad 123 11 55N 31 0 E
Rashîd 122 31 21N 30 22 E
Rashîd, Masabb 122 31 22N 30 17 E
Rasht 92 37 20N 49 40 E
Rasi Salai 100 15 20N 104 9 E
Rasipuram 97 11 30N 78 25 E
Raška 66 43 19N 20 39 E
Raso, C. 170 1 50N 50 0W
Rason, L. 137 28 45 S 124 25 E
Raşova 70 44 15N 27 55 E
Rasovo 67 43 42N 23 17 E
Rasra 95 25 50N 83 50 E
Rass el Oued 119 35 57N 5 2 E
Rasskazovo 81 52 35N 41 50 E
Rastatt 49 48 50N 8 12 E
Rastu 70 43 53N 23 16 E
Raszków 54 51 43N 17 40 E
Rat Buri 100 13 30N 99 54 E
Rat, Is. 147 51 50N 178 15 E
Rat, R. 152 56 0N 99 30W
Rat River 152 61 7N 112 36W
Rätan 72 62 27N 14 33 E
Ratangarh 94 28 5N 74 35 E
Rath 95 25 36N 79 37 E
Rath Luirc (Charleville) 39 52 21N 8 40W
Rathangan 39 53 13N 7 0W
Rathconrah 38 53 30N 7 32W
Rathcoole 39 53 17N 6 29W
Rathcormack 39 52 5N 8 19W
Rathdowney 39 52 52N 7 36W
Rathdrum, Ireland 39 52 57N 6 13W
Rathdrum, U.S.A. 160 47 50N 116 58W
Ratheclaung 98 20 29N 92 45 E
Rathen 37 57 38N 1 58W
Rathenow 48 52 38N 12 23 E
Rathfriland 38 54 12N 6 12W
Rathkeale 39 52 32N 8 57W
Rathkenny 38 53 45N 6 39W
Rathlin I. 38 55 18N 6 14W
Rathlin O'Birne I. 38 54 40N 8 50W
Rathmelton 38 55 3N 7 35W
Rathmolyon 38 53 30N 6 49W
Rathmore, Cork, Ireland 39 51 30N 9 21W
Rathmore, Kerry, Ireland 39 52 5N 9 12W
Rathmore, Kildare, Ireland 39 53 13N 6 35W
Rathmullen 38 55 6N 7 32W
Rathnure 39 52 30N 6 47W
Rathvilly 72 52 54N 6 42W
Ratlam 94 23 20N 75 0 E
Ratnagiri 96 16 57N 73 18 E
Ratnapura 97 6 40N 80 20 E
Ratoath 38 53 30N 6 27W
Raton 159 37 0N 104 30W
Rattaphum 101 7 8N 100 16 E
Ratten 52 47 28N 15 44 E
Rattray 37 56 36N 3 20W
Rattray Hd. 37 57 38N 1 50W
Rättvik 72 60 52N 15 7 E
Ratz, Mt. 152 57 23N 132 12W
Ratzeburg 48 53 41N 10 46 E
Raub 101 3 47N 101 52 E
Rauch 172 36 45 S 59 5W
Raufarhöfn 74 66 27N 15 57W
Raufoss 71 60 44N 10 37 E
Raukumara Ra. 142 38 5 S 177 55 E
Raul Soares 171 20 5 S 42 22W
Rauland 71 59 43N 8 0 E
Rauma 75 61 10N 21 30 E
Rauma, R. 71 62 34N 7 43 E
Raundal 71 60 40N 6 37 E
Raunds 29 52 20N 0 32W
Raung, Mt. 103 8 8 S 114 4 E
Raurkela 96 22 14N 84 50 E
Rava Russkaya 80 50 15N 23 42 E
Ravanusa 64 37 16N 13 58 E
Ravar 93 31 20N 56 51 E
Ravels 47 51 22N 5 0 E
Ravena 162 42 28N 73 49W
Ravenglass 32 54 21N 3 25W
Ravenna, Italy 63 44 28N 12 15 E
Ravenna, U.S.A. 158 41 3N 98 58W
Ravensburg 49 47 48N 9 38 E
Ravenshoe 138 17 37 S 145 29 E
Ravenstein 46 51 47N 5 39 E
Ravensthorpe 137 33 35 S 120 2 E
Ravenstonedale 32 54 26N 2 26W
Ravenswood, Austral. 138 20 6 S 146 54 E
Ravenswood, U.S.A. 156 38 58N 81 47W
Ravensworth 141 32 26 S 151 4 E
Raventasón 174 6 10 S 81 0W
Ravi, R. 94 31 0N 73 0 E
Ravna Gora 63 45 24N 14 50 E
Ravna Reka 66 43 59N 21 35 E
Ravnstrup 73 56 27N 9 17 E
Rawa Mazowiecka 54 51 46N 20 12 E
Rawalpindi 94 33 38N 73 8 E
Rawalpindi □ 93 33 10N 72 50 E
Rawāndūz 92 36 40N 44 30 E
Rawang 101 3 20N 101 35 E
Rawdon 150 46 3N 73 40W
Rawene 142 35 25 S 173 32 E
Rawicz 54 51 36N 16 52 E
Rawlinna 137 30 58 S 125 28 E
Rawlins 160 41 50N 107 20W
Rawlinson Range 137 24 40 S 128 30 E
Rawmarsh 33 53 27N 1 20W
Rawson 176 43 15 S 65 0W
Rawtenstall 32 53 42N 2 18W
Rawuya 121 12 10N 6 50 E
Ray, N. Mex., U.S.A. 159 35 57N 104 8W
Ray, N.D., U.S.A. 158 48 21N 103 6W
Ray, C. 151 47 33N 59 15W
Ray Mts. 147 66 0N 152 10W
Rayachoti 97 14 4N 78 50 E
Rayadrug 97 14 40N 76 50 E
Rayagada 96 19 15N 83 20 E
Raychikhinsk 77 49 46N 129 25 E
Rayevskiy 84 54 4N 54 56 E
Rayin 93 29 40N 57 22 E
Rayleigh 29 51 36N 0 38 E
Raymond, Can. 152 49 30N 112 35W
Raymond, Calif., U.S.A. 163 37 13N 119 54W
Raymond, Wash., U.S.A. 160 46 45N 123 48W
Raymond Terrace 141 32 45 S 151 44 E
Raymondville 159 26 30N 97 50W
Raymore 153 51 25N 104 31W
Rayne 159 30 16N 92 16W
Rayón 164 29 43N 110 35W
Rayong 100 12 40N 101 20 E
Rayville 159 32 30N 91 45W
Raz, Pte. du 42 48 2N 4 47W
Razana 66 44 6N 19 55 E
Razanj 66 43 40N 21 31 E
Razdelna 67 43 13N 27 41 E
Razelm, Lacul 70 44 50N 29 0 E
Razgrad 67 43 33N 26 34 E
Razlog 67 41 53N 23 28 E
Razmak 94 32 45N 69 50 E
Razole 96 16 56N 81 48 E
Razor Back Mt. 152 51 32N 125 0W
Ré, Île de 44 46 12N 1 30W
Rea, L. 39 53 10N 8 32W
Reading, U.K. 29 51 27N 0 57W
Reading, U.S.A. 162 40 20N 75 53W
Realicó 172 35 0 S 64 15W
Réalmont 44 43 48N 2 10 E
Ream 101 10 34N 103 39 E
Reata 164 26 8N 101 5W
Reay 37 58 33N 3 48W
Rebais 43 48 50N 3 10 E
Rebecca L. 137 30 0 S 122 30 E
Rebi 103 5 30 S 134 7 E
Rebiana 117 24 12N 22 10 E
Rebun-Tō 112 45 23N 141 2 E
Recanati 63 43 24N 13 32 E
Recaş 66 45 46N 21 30 E
Recess 38 53 29N 9 4W
Recherche, Arch. of the 137 34 15 S 122 50 E
Rechitsa 80 52 13N 30 15 E
Recht 47 50 20N 6 3 E
Recife 170 8 0 S 35 0W
Recklinghausen 48 51 36N 7 10 E
Reconquista 172 29 10 S 59 45W
Recreo 172 29 25 S 65 10W
Reculver 29 51 22N 1 12 E
Recz 54 53 16N 15 31 E
Red B. 38 55 4N 6 2W
Red Bank 162 40 21N 74 4W
Red Bay 151 51 44N 56 25W
Red Bluff 160 40 11N 122 11W
Red Bluff L. 159 31 59N 103 58W
Red Cliffs 140 34 19 S 142 11 E
Red Cloud 158 40 8N 98 33W
Red Creek 162 43 14N 76 45W
Red Deer 152 52 20N 113 50W
Red Deer L. 153 52 55N 101 20W
Red Deer, R. 152 50 58N 110 0W
Red Deer R. 153 52 53N 101 1W
Red Dial 32 54 48N 3 9W
Red Hook 162 41 55N 73 53W
Red Indian L. 151 48 35N 57 0W
Red L. 158 48 0N 95 0W
Red Lake 153 51 1N 94 1W
Red Lake Falls 158 47 54N 96 30W
Red Lion 162 39 54N 76 36W
Red Lodge 160 45 10N 109 10W
Red Mountain 163 35 37N 117 38W
Red Oak 158 41 0N 95 10W
Red Point Rock 137 32 13 S 127 32 E
Red, R., Can. 153 50 24N 96 48W
Red, R., Minn., U.S.A. 158 48 10N 97 0W
Red, R., Tex., U.S.A. 159 33 57N 95 30W
Red, R. = Hong, R. 100 20 17N 106 34 E
Red Rock 150 48 55N 88 15W
Red Rock, L. 158 41 30N 93 15W
Red Sea 91 25 0N 36 0 E
Red Slate Mtn. 163 37 31N 118 52W
Red Sucker L 153 54 9N 93 40W
Red Tower Pass = Turnu Rosu P. 70 45 33N 24 17 E
Red Wharf Bay 31 53 18N 4 10W
Red Wing 158 44 32N 92 35W
Reda 54 54 40N 18 19 E
Rédange 47 49 46N 5 52 E
Redbank 108 27 36 S 152 52 E
Redbridge 29 51 35N 0 7 E
Redcar 33 54 37N 1 4W
Redcliff 153 50 10N 110 50W
Redcliffe 139 27 12 S 153 0 E
Redcliffe, Mt. 137 28 30 S 121 30 E
Redcliffs 139 34 16 S 142 10 E
Reddersburg 128 29 41 S 26 10 E
Redding 160 40 30N 122 25W
Redditch 28 52 18N 1 57W
Rede, R. 35 55 8N 2 12W
Redenção 170 4 13 S 38 43W
Redesmouth 35 55 7N 2 12W
Redfield 158 45 0N 98 30W
Redhill 29 51 14N 0 10W
Redknife, R. 152 61 14N 119 22W
Redland 37 59 6N 3 4W
Redlands 163 34 0N 117 11W
Redlynch 28 50 59N 1 42W
Redmile 33 52 54N 0 48W
Redmire 32 54 19N 1 55W
Redmond, Austral. 137 34 55 S 117 40 E
Redmond, U.S.A. 160 44 19N 121 11W
Redon 42 47 40N 2 6W
Redonda, I. 167 16 58N 62 19W
Redondela 56 42 15N 8 38W
Redondo 57 38 39N 7 37W
Redondo Beach 163 33 52N 118 26W
Redrock Pt. 152 62 11N 115 2W
Redruth 30 50 14N 5 14W
Redvers 153 49 35N 101 40W
Redwater 152 53 55N 113 6W
Redwood City 163 37 30N 122 15W
Redwood Falls 158 44 30N 95 2W
Ree, L. 38 53 35N 8 0W
Reed City 156 43 52N 85 30W
Reed L. 153 54 38N 100 30W
Reed, Mt. 151 52 5N 68 5W
Reeder 158 47 7N 102 52W
Reedham 29 52 34N 1 33 E
Reedley 163 36 36N 119 27W
Reedsburg 158 43 34N 90 5W
Reedsport 160 43 45N 124 4W
Reedy Creek 140 36 58 S 140 2 E
Reef Pt. 142 35 10 S 173 5 E
Reefton, N.S.W., Austral. 141 34 15 S 147 27 E
Reefton, S. Australia, Austral. 109 34 57 S 138 55 E
Reefton, N.Z. 143 42 6 S 171 51 E
Reepham 29 52 46N 1 6 E
Reeth 32 54 23N 1 56W
Refsnes 71 61 9N 7 14 E
Reftele 73 57 11N 13 35 E
Refugio 159 28 18N 97 17W
Rega, R. 54 53 52N 15 16 E
Regalbuto 65 37 40N 14 38 E
Regar 85 38 30N 68 14 E
Regavim 90 32 32N 35 2 E
Regen 49 48 58N 13 9 E
Regeneração 170 6 15 S 42 41W
Regensburg 49 49 1N 12 7 E
Regensdorf 51 47 26N 8 28 E
Réggio di Calábria 65 38 7N 15 38 E
Réggio nell' Emilia 62 44 42N 10 38 E
Regina 153 50 30N 104 35W
Registan □ 93 30 15N 65 0 E
Registro 173 24 29 S 47 49W
Reguengos de Monsaraz 57 38 25N 7 32W
Rehar 95 23 36N 82 52 E
Rehoboth, Damaraland, Namibia 128 23 15 S 17 4 E
Rehoboth, Ovamboland, Namibia 128 17 55 S 15 5 E
Rehoboth Beach 162 38 43N 75 5W
Rehovot 90 31 54N 34 48 E
Reichenbach, Ger. 48 50 36N 12 19 E
Reichenbach, Switz. 50 46 38N 7 42 E
Reid 137 30 49 S 128 26 E
Reid River 138 19 40 S 146 48 E
Reiden 50 47 14N 7 59 E
Reidsville 157 36 21N 79 40W
Reigate 29 51 14N 0 11W
Reillo 58 39 54N 1 53W
Reims 43 49 15N 4 0 E
Reina 90 32 43N 35 18 E
Reina Adelaida, Arch. 176 52 20 S 74 0W
Reinach, Aargau, Switz. 50 47 14N 8 11 E
Reinach, Basel, Switz. 50 47 29N 7 35 E
Reinbeck 158 42 18N 92 40W
Reindeer I. 153 52 30N 98 0W
Reindeer L. 153 57 15N 102 15W
Reindeer, R. 153 55 36N 103 11W
Reine, La 150 48 50N 79 30W
Reinga, C. 142 34 25 S 172 43 E
Reinosa 56 43 2N 4 15W
Reinosa, Paso 56 42 56N 4 10W
Reira 123 15 25N 34 50 E
Reiss 37 58 29N 3 7W
Reisterstown 162 39 28N 76 50W
Reitdiep 46 53 20N 6 20 E
Reitz 129 27 48 S 28 29 E
Reivilo 128 27 36 S 24 8 E
Rejmyra 73 58 50N 15 55 E
Reka, R. 63 45 40N 14 0 E
Rekovac 66 43 51N 21 3 E
Remad, Oued ber 118 33 28N 1 20W
Remanso 170 9 41 S 42 4W
Remarkable, Mt. 140 32 48 S 138 10 E
Rembang 103 6 42 S 111 21 E
Remchi 118 35 2N 1 26W
Remedios, Colomb. 174 7 2N 74 41W
Remedios, Panama 166 8 15N 81 50W
Remeshk 93 26 55N 58 50 E
Remetea 70 46 45N 29 29 E
Remich 47 49 32N 6 22 E
Remiremont 43 48 0N 6 36 E
Remo 123 6 48N 41 20 E
Remontnoye 83 47 44N 43 37 E
Remoulins 45 43 55N 4 35 E
Remscheid 48 51 11N 7 12 E
Remsen 162 43 19N 75 11W
Rena 71 61 8N 11 20 E
Renda 123 14 30N 40 0 E
Rende 65 39 19N 16 11 E
Rendeux 47 50 14N 5 30 E
Rendína 69 39 4N 21 58 E
Rendsburg 48 54 18N 9 41 E
Rene 77 66 2N 179 25W
Renee, oilfield 19 58 4N 0 16 E
Renens 50 46 31N 6 34 E
Renfrew, Can. 150 45 30N 76 40W
Renfrew, U.K. 34 55 52N 4 24W
Renfrew (□) 26 55 50N 4 30W
Rengat 102 0 30 S 102 45 E
Rengo 172 34 24 S 70 50W
Reni 82 45 28N 28 15 E
Renigunta 97 13 38N 79 30 E
Renish Pt. 36 57 44N 6 59W
Renkum 46 51 58N 5 43 E
Renmark 140 34 11 S 140 43 E
Rennell Sd. 152 53 23N 132 35W

Renner Springs Teleg. Off **Riverton**

Renner Springs Teleg. Off. 138 18 20S 133 47E
Rennes 42 48 7N 1 41W
Rennesøy 71 59 6N 5 43E
Reno 160 39 30N 119 50W
Reno, R. 63 44 45N 11 40E
Renovo 156 41 20N 77 47W
Rens 55 54 54N 9 5E
Rensselaer, Ind., U.S.A. 156 41 0N 87 10W
Rensselaer, N.Y., U.S.A. 162 42 38N 73 41W
Rentería 58 43 19N 1 54W
Renton 160 47 30N 122 9W
Renwicktown 143 41 30S 173 51E
Réo 120 12 28N 2 35E
Réole, La 44 44 35N 0 1W
Reotipur 95 25 33N 83 45E
Repalle 97 16 2N 80 45E
Répcelak 53 47 24N 17 1E
Repton 28 52 50N 1 32W
Republic, Mich., U.S.A. 156 46 25N 87 59W
Republic, Wash., U.S.A. 160 48 38N 118 42W
Republican City 158 40 9N 99 20W
Republican, R. 158 40 0N 98 30W
Repulse B., Antarct. 13 64 30S 99 30E
Repulse B., Austral. 133 20 31S 148 45E
Repulse Bay 149 66 30N 86 30W
Requena, Peru 174 5 5S 73 52W
Requena, Spain 59 39 30N 1 4W
Resele 72 63 20N 17 5E
Resen 66 41 5N 21 0E
Reserve, Can. 153 52 28N 102 39W
Reserve, U.S.A. 161 33 50N 108 54W
Resht = Rasht 92 37 20N 49 40E
Resistencia 172 27 30S 59 0W
Reşiţa 66 45 18N 21 53E
Resko 54 53 47N 15 25E
Resolution I., Can. 149 61 30N 65 0W
Resolution I., N.Z. 143 45 40S 166 40E
Resolven 31 51 43N 3 42W
Resplandes 170 6 17S 45 13W
Resplendor 171 19 20S 41 15W
Ressano Garcia 129 25 25S 32 0E
Rest Downs 141 31 48S 146 21E
Reston, Can. 153 49 33N 101 6W
Reston, U.K. 35 55 51N 2 11W
Restrepo 174 4 15N 73 33W
Reszel 54 54 4N 21 10E
Retalhuleu 166 14 33N 91 46W
Reteag 70 47 10N 24 0E
Retem, O. el 119 33 40N 0 40E
Retenue, Lac de 127 11 0S 27 0E
Rethel 43 49 30N 4 20E
Rethem 48 52 47N 9 25E
Réthimnon 69 35 15N 24 40E
Réthimnon □ 69 35 23N 24 28E
Retie 47 51 16N 5 5E
Rétiers 42 47 55N 1 25W
Retiro 172 35 59S 71 47W
Retortillo 56 40 48N 6 21W
Rétság 53 47 58N 19 10E
Reuland 47 50 12N 6 8E
Réunion, Î. 11 22 0S 56 0E
Reus 58 41 10N 1 5E
Reusel 47 51 21N 5 9E
Reuss, R. 51 47 16N 8 24E
Reuterstadt-Stavenhagen 48 53 41N 12 54E
Reutlingen 49 48 28N 9 13E
Reutte 52 47 29N 10 42E
Reuver 47 51 17N 6 5E
Revda 84 56 48N 59 57E
Revel 44 43 28N 2 0E
Revelganj 95 25 50N 84 40E
Revelstoke 152 51 0N 118 0W
Revigny 43 48 50N 5 0E
Revilla Gigedo, Is. de 131 18 40N 112 0W
Revillagigedo I. 152 55 50N 131 20W
Revin 43 49 55N 4 39E
Revolyutsii, Pix 85 38 31N 72 21E
Revuè, R. 127 19 30S 33 35E
Rewa 95 24 33N 81 25E
Rewari 94 28 15N 76 40E
Rex 147 64 10N 149 20W
Rexburg 160 43 45N 111 50W
Rey Bouba 117 8 40N 14 15E
Rey Malabo 121 3 45N 8 50E
Reyes, Pt. 163 37 59N 123 2W
Reykjahlið 74 65 40N 16 55W
Reykjanes 74 63 48N 22 40W
Reykjavík 74 64 10N 21 57E
Reynolds 153 49 40N 95 55W
Reynolds Ra. 136 22 30S 133 0E
Reynosa 165 26 5N 98 18W
•Rezā'iyeh 92 37 40N 45 0E
•Rezā'iyeh, Daryācheh-ye 92 37 30N 45 30E
Rēzekne 80 56 30N 27 17E
Rezh 84 57 23N 61 24E
Rezina 70 47 45N 29 0E
Rezovo 67 42 0N 28 0E
Rgotina 67 44 1N 22 18E
Rhaeadr Ogwen 31 53 8N 4 0W
Rharis, O. 119 26 30N 5 4E
Rhayader 31 52 19N 3 30W
Rheden 46 52 0N 6 3E
Rheidol, R. 31 52 25N 3 57W
Rhein 153 51 25N 102 15W
Rhein, R. 48 51 42N 6 20E
Rheinbach 48 50 38N 6 54E
Rheine 48 52 17N 7 25E
Rheineck 51 47 28N 9 31E

Renamed Orumiyeh

Rheinfelden 50 47 32N 7 47E
Rheinland-Pfalz □ 49 50 50N 7 0E
Rheinsberg 48 53 6N 12 52E
Rheinwaldhorn 51 46 30N 9 3E
Rhenen 46 51 58N 5 33E
Rheydt 48 51 10N 6 24E
Rhin, R. 48 51 42N 6 20E
Rhinau 43 48 19N 7 43E
Rhine, R. = Rhein 47 51 42N 6 20E
Rhinebeck 162 41 56N 73 55W
Rhinelander 158 45 38N 89 29W
Rhino Camp 126 3 0N 31 22E
Rhisnes 47 50 31N 4 48E
Rhiw 31 52 49N 4 37W
Rho 62 45 31N 9 2E
Rhode Island □ 162 41 38N 71 37W
Rhodes = Ródhos 69 36 15N 28 10E
Rhodes' Tomb 127 20 30S 28 30E
Rhodesia = Zimbabwe ■ 127 20 0S 30 0E
Rhodope Mts. = Rhodopi Planina 67 41 40N 24 20E
Rhondda 31 51 39N 3 30W
Rhône □ 45 45 54N 4 35E
Rhône, R. 45 43 28N 4 42E
Rhos-on-Sea 31 53 18N 3 46W
Rhosllanerchrugog 31 53 3N 3 4W
Rhossilli 31 51 34N 4 18W
Rhu Coigach, C. 36 58 6N 5 27W
Rhuddlan 31 53 17N 3 28W
Rhum, I. 36 57 0N 6 20W
Rhyl 31 53 19N 3 29W
Rhymney 31 51 45N 3 17W
Rhynie 37 57 20N 2 50W
Ri-Aba 121 3 28N 8 40E
Riachão 170 7 20S 46 37W
Riachão do Jacuípe 171 11 48S 39 21W
Riacho de Santana 171 13 37S 42 57W
Rialma 171 15 18S 49 34W
Rialto 163 34 6N 117 22W
Riang 98 27 31N 92 56E
Riaño 56 42 59N 5 0W
Rians 45 43 37N 5 44E
Riansares, R. 58 40 0N 3 0W
Riasi 95 33 10N 74 50E
Riau □ 102 0 0 102 35E
Riau, Kepulauan 102 0 30N 104 20E
Riaza 58 41 18N 3 30W
Riaza, R. 58 41 16N 3 29W
Riba de Saelices 58 40 55N 2 18E
Ribadavia 56 42 17N 8 8W
Ribadeo 56 43 35N 7 5W
Ribadesella 56 43 30N 5 7W
Ribamar 170 2 33S 44 3W
Ribas 58 42 19N 2 15E
Ribat 125 29 50N 60 55E
Ribatejo □ 55 39 15N 8 30W
Ribble, R. 32 54 13N 2 20W
Ribe 73 55 19N 8 44E
Ribe Amt □ 73 55 34N 8 30E
Ribeauvillé 43 48 10N 7 20E
Ribécourt 43 49 30N 2 55E
Ribeira 56 42 36N 8 58W
Ribeira do Pombal 170 10 50S 38 32W
Ribeirão Prêto 173 21 10S 47 50W
Ribeiro Gonçalves 170 7 32S 45 14W
Ribémont 43 49 47N 3 27E
Ribera 64 37 30N 13 13E
Ribérac 44 45 15N 0 20E
Riberalta 174 11 0S 66 0W
Ribnica 63 45 45N 14 45E
Ribnitz-Dangarten 48 54 14N 12 24E
Ričany 52 50 0N 14 40E
Riccall 33 53 50N 1 4W
Riccarton 143 43 32S 172 37E
Riccia 65 41 30N 14 50E
Riccione 63 44 0N 12 39E
Rice Lake 158 45 30N 91 42W
Rich 118 32 16N 4 30W
Rich Hill 159 38 5N 94 22W
Richards B. 129 28 48S 32 6E
Richards Deep 15 25 0S 73 0W
Richards L. 153 59 10N 107 10W
Richardson Mts. 143 44 49S 168 34E
Richardson, R. 153 58 25N 111 14W
Richardton 158 46 56N 102 22W
Riche, C. 137 34 36S 118 47E
Richelieu 42 47 0N 0 20E
Richey 158 47 42N 105 5W
Richfield, Idaho, U.S.A. 160 43 2N 114 5W
Richfield, Utah, U.S.A. 161 38 50N 112 0W
Richfield Springs 162 42 51N 74 59W
Richibucto 151 46 42N 64 54W
Richland, Ga., U.S.A. 157 32 7N 84 40W
Richland, Oreg., U.S.A. 160 44 49N 117 9W
Richland, Wash., U.S.A. 160 46 15N 119 15W
Richland Center 158 43 21N 90 22W
Richlands 156 37 7N 81 49W
Richmond, N.S.W., Austral. 141 33 35S 150 42E
Richmond, Queens., Austral. 138 20 43S 143 8E
Richmond, N.Z. 143 41 4S 173 12E
Richmond, S. Afr. 125 29 51S 30 18E
Richmond, N. Yorks., U.K. 33 54 24N 1 43W
Richmond, Surrey, U.K. 29 51 28N 0 18W
Richmond, Calif., U.S.A. 163 38 0N 122 21W
Richmond, Ind., U.S.A. 156 39 50N 84 50W
Richmond, Ky., U.S.A. 156 37 40N 84 20W
Richmond, Mo., U.S.A. 158 39 15N 93 58W
Richmond, Tex., U.S.A. 159 29 32N 95 42W
Richmond, Va., U.S.A. 162 37 33N 77 27W
Richmond Gulf 150 56 20N 75 50W
Richmond, Mt. 143 41 32S 173 22E
Richmond, Ra. 139 29 0S 152 45E
Richmond Ra. 143 41 32S 173 22E
Richterswil 51 47 13N 8 43E
Richton 157 31 23N 88 58W
Richwood 156 38 17N 80 32W
Rickmansworth 29 51 38N 0 28W
Ricla 58 41 31N 1 24W
Riddarhyttan 72 59 49N 15 33E
Ridderkerk 46 51 52N 4 35E
Riddes 50 46 11N 7 14E
Ridgecrest 163 35 38N 117 40W
Ridgedale 153 53 0N 104 10W
Ridgefield 162 41 17N 73 30W
Ridgeland 157 32 30N 80 58W
Ridgelands 138 23 16S 150 17E
Ridgetown 150 42 26N 81 52W
Ridgewood 162 40 59N 74 7W
Ridgway 156 41 25N 78 43W
Riding Mt. Nat. Park 153 50 50N 100 0W
Ridley Mt. 137 33 12S 122 7E
Ridsdale 35 55 9N 2 8W
Ried 52 48 14N 13 30E
Riehen 50 47 35N 7 39E
Riel 47 51 31N 5 1E
Rienne 47 50 0N 4 53E
Rienza, R. 63 46 49N 11 47E
Riesa 48 51 19N 13 19E
Riesi 65 37 16N 14 4E
Rietfontein 128 26 44S 20 1E
Rieti 63 42 23N 12 50E
Rieupeyroux 44 44 19N 2 12E
Rievaulx 33 54 16N 1 7W
Riez 45 43 49N 6 6E
Rifle 160 39 40N 107 50W
Rifstangi 74 66 32N 16 12W
Rift Valley 126 0 20N 36 0E
Rig Rig 117 14 13N 14 25E
Riga 80 56 53N 24 8E
Riga, G. of = Rīgas Jūras Līcis 80 57 40N 23 45E
Rīgas Jūras Līcis 80 57 40N 23 45E
Rigby 160 43 41N 111 58W
Riggins 160 45 29N 116 26W
Rignac 44 44 25N 2 16E
Rigo 138 9 41S 147 31E
Rigolet 151 54 10N 58 23W
Riihimäki 75 60 45N 24 48E
Riiser-Larsen halvøya 13 68 0S 35 0E
Riishiri-Tō 112 45 11N 141 15E
Rijau 121 11 8N 5 17E
Rijeka Crnojevica 66 42 24N 19 1E
Rijeka (Fiume) 63 45 20N 14 21E
Rijen 47 51 35N 4 55E
Rijkevorsel 47 51 21N 4 46E
Rijn, R. 47 52 5N 4 50E
Rijnsberg 46 52 11N 4 27E
Rijsbergen 47 51 31N 4 41E
Rijssen 46 52 19N 6 30E
Rijswijk 46 52 4N 4 22E
Rike 123 10 50N 39 53E
Rikita 123 5 5N 28 29E
Rila 67 42 7N 23 7E
Rila Planina 66 42 10N 23 30E
Rillington 33 54 10N 0 41W
Rilly 43 49 11N 4 3E
Rima 99 28 35N 97 5E
Rima, R. 121 13 15N 5 15E
Rimavská Sobota 53 48 22N 20 2E
Rimbey 152 52 35N 114 15W
Rimbo 72 59 44N 18 21E
Rimforsa 73 58 8N 15 42E
Rimi 121 12 58N 7 43E
Rímini 63 44 3N 12 33E
Rîmna, R. 70 45 36N 27 3E
Rîmnicu Sărat 70 45 26N 27 3E
Rîmnicu Vîlcece 70 45 9N 24 21E
Rimouski 151 48 27N 68 30W
Rinca 103 8 45S 119 35E
Rincón de Romos 164 22 14N 102 18W
Rinconada 172 22 26S 66 10W
Ringarum 73 58 21N 16 26E
Ringe 73 55 13N 10 28E
Ringel Spitz 51 46 53N 9 19E
Ringford 35 54 55N 4 3W
Ringim 121 12 13N 9 10E
Ringkøbing 73 56 5N 8 15E
Ringkøbing Amt □ 73 56 15N 8 30E
Ringling 160 46 16N 110 56W
Ringmer 29 50 53N 0 5E
Ringmoen 71 60 21N 10 6E
Ringsaker 71 60 54N 10 45E
Ringsend 38 55 2N 6 45W
Ringsjön L. 73 55 55N 13 30E
Ringsted 73 55 25N 11 46E
Ringvassøy 74 69 36N 19 15E
Ringville 39 52 3N 7 37W
Ringwood 28 50 50N 1 48W
Rinia, I. 69 37 23N 25 13E
Rinjani 65 8 20S 116 30E
Rinns, The, Reg. 34 54 52N 5 3W
Rintein 48 52 11N 9 3E
Rio Arica 174 1 35S 75 30W
Rio Branco 174 9 58S 67 49W
Rio Branco 173 32 40S 53 40W
Rio Brilhante 173 21 48S 54 33W
Río Chico 174 10 19N 65 59W
Rio Claro, Brazil 173 22 19S 47 35W
Rio Claro, Trin 167 10 20N 61 25W
Río Colorado 176 39 0S 64 0W
Río Cuarto 172 33 10S 64 25W
Rio das Pedras 129 23 8S 35 28E
Rio de Contas 171 13 36S 41 48W
Rio de Janeiro 173 23 0S 43 12W
Rio de Janeiro □ 173 22 50S 43 0W
Rio del Rey 121 4 42N 8 37E
Rio do Prado 171 16 35S 40 34W
Rio do Sul 173 27 95S 49 37W
Río Gallegos 176 51 35S 69 15W
Río Grande 176 53 50S 67 45W
Rio Grande 173 32 0S 52 20W
Río Grande, Mexico 164 23 50N 103 2W
Río Grande, Nic. 166 12 54N 83 33W
Rio Grande City 159 26 30N 91 55W
Rio Grande del Norte, R. 154 26 0N 97 0W
Rio Grande do Norte □ 170 5 40S 36 0W
Rio Grande do Sul □ 173 30 0S 53 0W
Rio Grande, R. 161 37 47N 106 15W
Río Hato 166 8 22N 80 10W
Rio Lagartos 165 21 36N 88 10W
Rio Largo 171 9 28S 35 50W
Rio Maior 57 39 19N 8 57W
Rio Marina 62 42 48N 10 25E
Rio Mulatos 174 19 40S 66 50W
Rio Muni □ = Mbini □ 121 1 30N 10 0E
Rio Negro 173 26 0S 50 0W
Rio Oriente 166 22 17N 81 13W
Rio Pardo, Minas Gerais, Brazil 171 15 55S 42 30W
Rio Pardo, Rio Grande do Sul, Brazil 173 30 0S 52 30W
Rio Prêto, Serra do 171 13 29S 39 55W
Rio, Punta del 59 36 49N 2 24W
Rio Real 171 11 28S 37 56W
Río Segundo 172 31 40S 63 59W
Río Tercero 172 32 15S 64 8W
Rio Tinto, Brazil 170 6 48S 35 5W
Rio Tinto, Port. 56 41 11N 8 34W
Rio Verde 170 17 50S 51 0W
Río Verde 165 21 56N 99 59W
Rio Vista 163 38 11N 121 44W
Ríobamba 174 1 50S 78 45W
Ríohacha 174 11 33N 72 55W
Rioja, La, Argent. 172 29 20S 67 0W
Rioja, La, Spain 58 42 20N 2 20W
Rioja, La □ 172 29 30S 67 0W
Riom 44 45 54N 3 7E
Riom-és-Montagnes 44 45 17N 2 39E
Rion-des-Landes 44 43 55N 0 56W
Rionegro 174 6 9N 75 22W
Rionero in Vúlture 65 40 55N 15 40E
Ríos 56 41 58N 7 16W
Riosucio, Caldas, Colomb. 174 5 30N 75 40W
Riosucio, Choco, Colomb. 174 7 27N 77 7W
Riou L. 153 59 7N 106 25W
Riparia, Dora, R. 62 45 7N 7 24E
Ripatransone 63 43 0N 13 45E
Ripley, Derby, U.K. 33 53 3N 1 24W
Ripley, N. Yorks, U.K. 33 54 3N 1 34W
Ripley, U.S.A. 159 35 43N 89 34W
Ripoll 58 42 15N 2 13E
Ripon, Calif., U.S.A. 163 37 44N 121 7W
Ripon, Wis., U.S.A. 156 43 51N 88 50W
Riposto 65 37 44N 15 12E
Risalpur 94 34 3N 71 59E
Risan 66 42 32N 18 42E
Risca 31 51 36N 3 6W
Riscle 44 43 39N 0 5W
Rishon Le Zion 90 31 58N 34 48E
Rishpon 90 32 12N 34 49E
Rishton 32 53 46N 2 26W
Riska 71 58 56N 5 52E
Risle, R. 42 48 55N 0 41E
Rîsnov 70 45 35N 25 27E
Rison 159 33 57N 92 11W
Risør 71 58 43N 9 13E
Ritchie's Archipelago 101 12 5N 94 0E
Riti 121 7 57N 9 41E
Ritzville 160 47 10N 118 21W
Riu 98 28 19N 95 3E
Riva Bella Ouistreham 42 49 17N 0 18W
Riva del Garda 62 45 53N 10 50E
Rivadavia, Buenos Aires, Argent. 172 35 29S 62 59W
Rivadavia, Mendoza, Argent. 172 33 13S 68 30W
Rivadavia, Salta, Argent. 172 24 5S 63 0W
Rivadavia, Chile 172 29 50S 70 35W
Rivarolo Canavese 62 45 20N 7 42E
Rivas 166 11 30N 85 50W
Rive-de-Gier 45 45 32N 4 37E
River Cess 120 5 30N 9 25W
Rivera 173 31 0S 55 50W
Riverchapel 39 52 38N 6 14W
Riverdale 163 36 26N 119 52W
Riverhead 162 40 53N 72 40W
Riverhurst 153 50 55N 106 50W
Riverina 136 29 45S 120 40E
Riverina, dist. 133 35 30S 145 20E
Rivers 153 50 2N 100 14W
Rivers □ 121 5 0N 6 30E
Rivers Inlet 152 51 40N 127 20W
Rivers, L. of the 153 49 49N 105 44W
Riversdal 128 34 7S 21 15E
Riverside, Calif., U.S.A. 163 34 0N 117 22W
Riverside, Wyo., U.S.A. 160 41 12N 106 57W
Riversleigh 138 19 5S 138 48E
Riverton, Austral. 140 34 10S 138 46E

Riverton | Ross and Cromarty (□)

Riverton, Can. 153 51 5N 97 0W
Riverton, N.Z. 143 46 21S 168 0E
Riverton, U.S.A. 160 43 1N 108 27W
Riverview 108 27 36S 152 51E
Rives 45 45 21N 5 31E
Rivesaltes 44 42 47N 2 50E
Riviera 62 44 0N 8 30E
Rivière à Pierre 151 46 57N 72 12W
Rivière-au-Renard 151 48 59N 64 23W
Rivière Bleue 151 47 26N 69 2W
Rivière-du-Loup 151 47 50N 69 30W
Rivière Pontecôte 151 49 57N 67 1W
Rivoli 62 45 3N 7 31E
Rivoli B. 140 37 32S 140 3E
Rivungo 128 16 9S 21 51E
Riwaka 143 41 5S 172 59E
Rixensart 47 50 43N 4 32E
Riyadh = Ar Riyad 92 24 41N 46 42E
Rize 92 41 0N 40 30E
Rizzuto, C. 65 38 54N 17 5E
Rjukan 71 59 54N 8 33E
Roa, Norway 71 60 17N 10 37E
Roa, Spain 56 41 41N 3 56W
Road Town 167 18 27N 64 37W
Road Weedon 28 52 14N 1 6W
Roade 29 52 10N 0 53W
Roadhead 32 55 4N 2 44W
Roag, L. 36 58 10N 6 55W
Roan Antelope 127 13 2S 28 19E
Roanne 45 46 3N 4 4E
Roanoke, Ala., U.S.A. 157 33 9N 85 23W
Roanoke, Va., U.S.A. 156 37 19N 79 55W
Roanoke I. 157 35 55N 75 40W
Roanoke, R. 157 36 15N 77 20W
Roanoke Rapids 157 36 36N 77 42W
Roaringwater B. 39 51 30N 9 30W
Roatán 166 16 18N 86 35W
Robbins I. 138 40 42S 145 0E
Robe, R., Austral. 136 21 42S 116 15E
Robe, R., Ireland 38 53 38N 9 10W
Röbel 48 53 24N 12 37E
Robert Lee 159 31 55N 100 26W
Robert Pt. 137 32 34S 115 40E
Roberton 35 55 24N 2 53W
Roberts 160 43 44N 112 8W
Robertsganj 95 24 44N 83 12E
Robertson, Austral. 132 34 37S 150 36E
Robertson, S. Afr. 128 33 46S 19 50E
Robertson I. 13 68 0S 75 0W
Robertson Ra. 136 23 15S 121 0E
Robertsport 120 6 45N 11 26W
Robertstown, Austral. 140 33 58S 139 5E
Robertstown, Ireland 39 53 16N 6 50W
Roberval 150 48 32N 72 15W
Robeson Kanal 12 82 0N 61 30W
Robesonia 162 40 21N 76 8W
Robin Hood's B. 33 54 26N 0 31W
Robinson Crusoe I. 143 33 50S 78 30W
Robinson, R. 138 16 3S 137 16E
Robinson Ranges 137 25 40S 118 0E
Robinson River 138 16 45S 136 58E
Robinvale 140 34 40S 142 45E
Robla, La 56 42 50N 5 41W
Roblin 153 51 14N 101 21W
Roboré 174 18 10S 59 45W
Robson, Mt. 152 53 10N 119 10W
Robstown 159 27 47N 97 40W
Roca, C. da 57 38 40N 9 31W
Roca Partida, I. 164 19 1N 112 2W
Roçadas 128 16 45S 15 0E
Rocas, I. 170 4 0S 34 1W
Rocca d'Aspidé 65 40 27N 15 10E
Rocca San Casciano 63 44 3N 11 30E
Roccalbegna 63 42 47N 11 30E
Roccastrada 63 43 0N 11 10E
Rocella Iónica 65 38 20N 16 24E
Rocester 32 52 56N 1 50W
Rocha 173 34 30S 54 25W
Rochdale 32 53 36N 2 10W
Roche 30 50 24N 4 50W
Roche-Bernard, La 42 47 31N 2 19W
Roche-Canillac, La 44 45 12N 1 57E
Roche-en-Ardenne, La 47 50 11N 5 35E
Roche, La, France 45 46 4N 6 19E
Roche, La, Switz. 50 46 42N 7 7E
Roche-sur-Yon, La 42 46 40N 1 25W
Rochechouart 44 45 50N 0 49E
Rochefort, Belg. 47 50 9N 5 12E
Rochefort, France 44 45 56N 0 57W
Rochefort-en-Terre 42 47 42N 2 22W
Rochefoucauld, La 44 45 44N 0 24E
Rochelle 158 41 55N 89 5W
Rochelle, La 44 46 10N 1 9W
Rocher River 152 61 23N 112 44W
Rocherath 47 50 26N 6 18E
Rocheservière 42 46 57N 1 30W
Rochester, Austral. 140 36 22S 144 41E
Rochester, Can. 152 54 22N 113 27W
Rochester, Kent, U.K. 29 51 22N 0 30E
Rochester, Northum., U.K. 35 55 16N 2 16W
Rochester, Ind., U.S.A. 156 41 5N 86 15W
Rochester, Minn., U.S.A. 158 44 1N 92 28W
Rochester, N.H., U.S.A. 162 43 19N 70 57W
Rochester, N.Y., U.S.A. 156 43 10N 77 40W
Rochford 29 51 36N 0 42E
Rochfortbridge 38 53 25N 7 19W
Rociana 57 37 19N 6 35W
Rociu 70 44 43N 25 2E
Rock Flat 141 36 21S 149 13E
Rock Hall 162 39 8N 76 14W
Rock Hill 157 34 55N 81 2W
Rock Island 158 41 30N 90 35W
Rock Lake 158 48 50N 99 13W
Rock, R. 152 60 7N 127 7W
Rock Rapids 158 43 25N 96 10W
Rock River 160 41 49N 106 0W
Rock Sound 166 24 54N 76 12W
Rock Sprs., Ariz., U.S.A. 161 34 2N 112 11W
Rock Sprs., Mont., U.S.A. 160 46 55N 106 11W
Rock Sprs., Tex., U.S.A. 159 30 2N 100 11W
Rock Sprs., Wyo., U.S.A. 160 41 40N 109 10W
Rock Valley 158 43 10N 96 17W
Rockall I. 16 57 37N 13 42W
Rockanje 46 51 52N 4 4E
Rockcliffe 32 54 58N 3 0W
Rockcorry 38 54 7N 7 0W
Rockdale 159 30 40N 97 0W
Rockefeller Plat. 13 84 0S 130 0W
Rockford 158 42 20N 89 0W
Rockglen 153 49 11N 105 57W
Rockhampton 138 23 22S 150 32E
Rockhampton Downs 138 18 57S 135 10E
Rockhill 39 52 25N 8 44W
Rockingham, Austral. 137 32 15S 115 38E
Rockingham, U.K. 29 52 32N 0 43W
Rockingham B. 138 18 5S 146 10E
Rockingham For. 29 52 28N 0 42W
Rockland, Idaho, U.S.A. 160 42 37N 112 57W
Rockland, Me., U.S.A. 151 44 0N 69 0W
Rockland, Mich., U.S.A. 158 46 40N 89 10W
Rockmart 157 34 1N 85 2W
Rockmills 39 52 13N 8 25W
Rockport, Mass., U.S.A. 162 42 39N 70 36W
Rockport, Mo., U.S.A. 158 40 26N 95 30W
Rockport, Tex., U.S.A. 159 28 2N 97 3W
Rockville, Conn., U.S.A. 162 41 51N 72 27W
Rockville, Md., U.S.A. 162 39 7N 77 10W
Rockwall 159 32 55N 96 30W
Rockwell City 158 42 20N 94 35W
Rockwood 157 35 52N 84 40W
Rocky Ford 158 38 7N 103 45W
Rocky Gully 137 34 30S 117 0E
Rocky Lane 152 58 31N 116 22W
Rocky Mount 157 35 55N 77 48W
Rocky Mountain House 152 52 22N 114 55W
Rocky Mts. 152 55 0N 121 0W
Rocky Pt. 137 33 30S 123 57E
Rockyford 152 51 14N 113 10W
Rocroi 43 49 55N 4 30E
Rod 93 28 10N 63 5E
Roda, La, Albacete, Spain 59 39 13N 2 15W
Roda, La, Sevilla, Spain 57 37 12N 4 46W
Rødberg 71 60 17N 8 56E
Rødby 73 54 41N 11 23E
Rødby Havn 73 54 39N 11 22E
Roddickton 151 50 51N 56 8W
Rødding 73 55 23N 9 3E
Rødekro 73 55 4N 9 20E
Rodel 36 57 45N 6 57W
Roden 46 53 8N 6 26E
Rødenes 71 59 35N 11 34E
Rodenkirchen 48 53 24N 8 26E
Roderick I. 152 52 38N 128 22W
Rodez 44 44 21N 2 33E
Rodholívas 68 40 55N 24 0E
Rodhópi □ 68 41 10N 25 30E
Ródhos 69 36 15N 28 10E
Ródhos, I. 69 36 15N 28 10E
Roding R. 29 51 31N 0 7E
Rödjenäs 73 57 33N 14 50E
Rodna 70 47 25N 24 50E
Rodney, C. 142 36 17S 174 50E
Rodniki 81 57 7N 41 37E
Rodriguez, I. 11 20 0S 65 0E
Roe, R. 38 55 0N 6 56W
Roebling 162 40 7N 74 45W
Roebourne 136 20 44S 117 9E
Roebuck B. 136 18 5S 122 20E
Roebuck Plains P.O. 136 17 56S 122 28E
Roelofarendsveen 46 52 12N 4 38E
Roer, R. 47 51 12N 5 59E
Roermond 47 51 12N 6 0E
Roes Welcome Sd. 149 65 0N 87 0W
Roeselare 47 50 57N 3 7E
Rœulx 47 50 31N 4 7E
Rogachev 80 53 8N 30 5E
Rogagua, L. 174 14 0S 66 50W
Rogaland fylke □ 75 59 12N 6 20E
Rogans Seat, Mt. 32 54 25N 2 10W
Rogaóica 66 44 4N 19 40E
Rogaška Slatina 63 46 15N 15 42E
Rogate 29 51 0N 0 51W
Rogatec 63 46 15N 21 46E
Rogatin 80 29 24N 24 36E
Rogers 159 36 20N 94 0W
Rogers City 156 45 25N 83 49W
Rogerson 160 42 10N 114 40W
Rogersville 157 36 27N 83 1W
Roggan River 151 54 25N 79 32W
Roggel 47 51 16N 5 56E
Roggeveldberge 128 32 10S 20 10E
Roggiano Gravina 65 39 37N 16 9E
Rogliano, France 45 42 57N 9 30E
Rogliano, Italy 65 39 11N 16 20E
Rogoaguado, L. 174 13 0S 65 30W
Rogowo 54 52 43N 17 38E
Rogozno 54 52 45N 16 59E
Rogue, R. 160 42 30N 124 0W
Rohan 42 48 4N 2 45W
Rohnert Park 163 38 16N 122 40W
Rohrbach 43 49 3N 7 15E
Rohri 94 27 45N 68 51E
Rohri Canal 94 26 15N 68 27E
Rohtak 94 28 55N 76 43E
Roi Et 100 15 56N 103 40E
Roisel 43 49 58N 3 6E
Rojas 172 34 10S 60 45W
Rojo, C., Mexico 165 21 33N 97 20W
Rojo, C., W. Indies 147 17 56N 67 11W
Rokan, R. 102 1 30N 100 50E
Rokeby 138 13 39S 142 40E
Rokiskis 80 55 55N 25 35E
Rokitnoye 81 50 57N 35 56E
Rokycany 52 49 43N 13 35E
Rolândia 173 23 5S 52 0W
Røldal 71 59 47N 6 50E
Rolde 46 52 59N 6 39E
Rolette 158 48 42N 99 50W
Rolfstorp 73 57 11N 12 27E
Rolla, Kansas, U.S.A. 159 37 10N 101 40W
Rolla, Missouri, U.S.A. 159 38 0N 91 42W
Rolla, N. Dak., U.S.A. 158 48 50N 99 36W
Rollag 71 60 2N 9 18E
Rollands Plains 141 31 17S 152 42E
Rolle 50 46 28N 6 20E
Rolleston, Austral. 138 24 28S 148 35E
Rolleston, N.Z. 143 43 35S 172 24E
Rollingstone 138 19 2S 146 24E
Rom 123 9 54N 32 16E
Roma, Austral. 139 26 32S 148 49E
Roma, Italy 64 41 54N 12 30E
Roma, Sweden 73 57 32N 18 26E
Roman, Bulg. 67 43 8N 23 54E
Roman, Rumania 70 46 57N 26 55E
Romana, La 167 18 27N 68 57W
Romang, I. 103 7 30S 127 20E
Romania ■ 61 46 0N 25 0E
Romanija planina 66 43 50N 18 45E
Romano, Cayo 166 22 0N 77 30W
Romano di Lombardia 62 45 32N 9 45E
Romanovka = Bessarabka 82 46 21N 28 51E
Romans 62 45 3N 5 3E
Romanshorn 51 47 33N 9 22E
Romanzof, C. 147 62 0N 165 50W
Rombo □ 126 3 10S 37 30E
Rome, U.S.A. 162 41 51N 76 21W
Rome, Ga., U.S.A. 157 34 20N 85 0W
Rome, N.Y., U.S.A. 162 43 14N 75 29W
Rome = Roma 64 41 54N 12 30E
Romeleåsen 73 55 34N 13 33E
Romenây 45 46 30N 5 1E
Romeo 151 47 28N 57 4W
Romerike 71 60 7N 11 10E
Romilly 43 48 31N 3 44E
Romîni 70 44 59N 24 11E
Rommani 118 33 31N 6 40W
Romney 156 39 21N 78 45W
Romney Marsh 29 51 0N 1 0E
Romny 80 50 48N 33 28E
Rømø 73 55 10N 8 30E
Romodan 80 50 0N 33 15E
Romodanovo 81 54 26N 45 23E
Romont 50 46 42N 6 54E
Romorantin-Lanthenay 43 47 21N 1 45E
Romsdal, R. 71 62 25N 8 0E
Romsdalen 74 62 25N 7 50E
Romsey 28 51 0N 1 29W
Ron 100 17 53N 106 27E
Rona I. 36 57 33N 6 0W
Ronan 160 47 30N 114 11W
Ronas Hill 36 60 33N 1 25W
Ronay I. 36 57 30N 7 10W
Roncador Cay 166 13 40N 80 4W
Roncador, Serra do 171 12 30S 52 30W
Roncesvalles, Paso 58 43 1N 1 19W
Ronceverte 156 37 45N 80 28W
Ronciglione 63 42 18N 12 12E
Ronco, R. 63 44 26N 12 15E
Ronda 57 36 46N 5 12W
Ronda, Serranía de 57 36 44N 5 3W
Rondane 71 61 57N 9 50E
Rondón 174 6 17N 71 6W
Rondônia □ 174 11 0S 63 0W
Rong, Koh 101 10 45N 103 15E
Ronge, La, Can. 153 55 5N 105 20W
Ronge, La, Sask., Can. 153 55 6N 105 17W
Ronge, Lac La 153 55 10N 105 0W
Rongotea 142 40 19S 175 25E
Rønne 73 55 6N 14 44E
Ronne Land 13 83 0S 70 0W
Ronneby 73 56 12N 15 17E
Ronsard, C. 137 24 46S 113 10E
Ronse 47 50 45N 3 35E
Roodepoort-Maraisburg 125 26 8S 27 52E
Roodeschool 46 53 25N 6 46E
Roof Butte 161 36 29N 109 5W
Roompot 47 51 37N 3 44E
Roorkee 94 29 52N 77 59E
Roosendaal 47 51 32N 4 29E
Roosevelt, Minn., U.S.A. 158 48 51N 95 2W
Roosevelt, Utah, U.S.A. 160 40 19N 110 1W
Roosevelt I. 13 79 0S 161 0W
Roosevelt, Mt. 152 58 20N 125 20W
Roosevelt Res. 161 33 46N 111 0W
Roosky 38 53 50N 7 55W
Ropczyce 54 50 4N 21 38E
Roper, R. 138 14 43S 135 27E
Ropesville 159 33 25N 102 10W
Ropsley 33 52 53N 0 31W
Roque Pérez 172 35 25S 59 24W
Roquefort 44 44 2N 0 20W
Roquefort-sur-Souizon 44 43 58N 2 59E
Roquemaure 45 44 3N 4 48E
Roquetas 58 40 50N 0 30E
Roquevaire 45 43 20N 5 36E
Roraima □ 174 2 0N 61 30W
Roraima, Mt. 174 5 10N 60 40W
Rorketon 153 51 24N 99 35W
Røros 71 62 35N 11 23E
Rorschach 51 47 28N 9 30E
Rørvik 74 64 54N 11 15E
Rosa, U.S.A. 160 38 15N 122 16W
Rosa, Zambia 127 9 33S 31 15E
Rosa Brook 137 33 57S 115 10E
Rosa, C. 119 37 0N 8 16E
Rosa, Monte 50 45 57N 7 53E
Rosal 56 41 57N 8 51W
Rosal de la Frontera 57 37 59N 7 13W
Rosalia 160 47 26N 117 25W
Rosamund 163 34 52N 118 10W
Rosans 45 44 24N 5 29E
Rosario 172 33 0S 60 50W
Rosário, Maran., Brazil 170 3 0S 44 15W
Rosário, Rio Grande do Sul, Brazil 176 30 15S 55 0W
Rosario, Baja California, Mexico 164 30 0N 116 0W
Rosario, Durango, Mexico 164 26 30N 105 35W
Rosario, Sinaloa, Mexico 164 23 0N 106 0W
Rosario, Venez. 174 10 19N 72 19W
Rosario de la Frontera 172 25 50S 65 0W
Rosario de Lerma 172 24 59S 65 35W
Rosario del Tala 172 32 20S 59 10W
Rosário do Sul 173 30 15S 54 55W
Rosarito 164 28 38N 114 4W
Rosarno 65 38 29N 15 59E
Rosas 58 42 19N 3 10E
Rosas, G. de, 55 42 10N 3 15E
Rosburgh 143 45 33S 169 19E
Roscoe 162 41 56N 74 55W
Roscoff 42 48 44N 4 0W
Roscommon, Ireland 38 53 38N 8 11W
Roscommon, U.S.A. 156 44 27N 84 35W
Roscommon □ 38 53 40N 8 15W
Roscrea 39 52 58N 7 50W
Rose Blanche 151 47 38N 58 45W
Rose Harbour 152 52 15N 131 10W
Rose Ness 37 58 52N 2 50W
Rose Pt. 152 54 11N 131 39W
Rose, R. 138 14 16S 135 45E
Rose Valley 153 52 19N 103 49W
Roseau, Domin. 167 15 20N 61 30W
Roseau, U.S.A. 158 48 51N 95 46W
Rosebery 138 41 46S 145 33E
Rosebud, Austral. 141 38 21S 144 54E
Rosebud, U.S.A. 159 31 5N 97 0W
Roseburg 160 43 10N 123 10W
Rosedale, Austral. 138 24 38S 151 53E
Rosedale, U.S.A. 159 33 51N 91 0W
Rosedale Abbey 33 54 22N 0 51W
Rosée 47 50 14N 4 41E
Rosegreen 39 52 28N 7 51W
Rosehall 37 57 59N 4 36W
Rosehearty 37 57 42N 2 8W
Rosemarkie 37 57 35N 4 8W
Rosemary 152 50 46N 112 5W
Rosenallis 39 53 10N 7 25W
Rosenberg 159 29 30N 95 48W
Rosendaël 43 51 3N 2 24E
Rosenheim 49 47 51N 12 9E
Roseto degli Abruzzi 63 42 40N 14 2E
Rosetown 153 51 35N 108 3W
Rosetta = Rashîd 122 31 21N 30 22E
Roseville 160 38 46N 121 17W
Rosewood, N.S.W., Austral. 141 35 38S 147 52E
Rosewood, N.T., Austral. 136 16 28S 128 58E
Rosewood, Queens., Austral. 139 27 38S 152 36E
Rosh Haniqra, Kefar 90 33 5N 35 5E
Rosh Pinna 90 32 58N 35 32E
Rosh Ze'ira 90 31 14N 35 15E
Roshage C. 73 57 7N 8 35E
Rosières 43 48 36N 6 20E
Rosignano Marittimo 62 43 23N 10 28E
Rosignol 174 6 15N 57 30W
Roşiori-de-Vede 70 44 9N 25 0E
Rositsa 67 43 57N 27 57E
Rositsa, R. 67 43 10N 25 30E
Roskeeragh Pt. 38 54 22N 8 40W
Roskhill 36 57 24N 6 31W
Roskilde 73 55 38N 12 3E
Roskilde Amt □ 73 55 35N 12 5E
Roskilde Fjord 73 55 50N 12 2E
Roskill, Mt. 142 36 55S 174 45E
Roslavl 80 53 57N 32 55E
Roslyn 141 34 29S 149 37E
Rosmaninhal 57 39 44N 7 5W
Røsnæs 73 55 44N 10 55E
Rosneath 34 56 1N 4 49W
Rosolini 65 36 49N 14 58E
Rosporden 42 47 57N 3 50W
Ross, Austral. 138 42 2S 147 30E
Ross, N.Z. 143 42 53S 170 49E
Ross, U.K. 28 51 55N 2 34W
Ross and Cromarty (□) 26 57 43N 4 50W

Ross Dependency Sabang, O

Ross Dependency 13 70 0S 170 5W
Ross I. 13 77 30S 168 0E
Ross Ice Shelf 13 80 0S 180 0W
Ross L. 160 48 50N 121 0W
Ross on Wye 28 51 55N 2 34W
Ross River, Austral. 138 19 15S 146 51E
Ross River, Can. 147 62 30N 131 30W
Ross Sea 13 74 0S 178 0E
Rossa 51 46 23N 9 8E
Rossall Pt. 32 53 55N 3 2W
Rossan Pt. 38 54 42N 8 47W
Rossano Cálabro 65 39 36N 16 39E
Rossburn 153 50 40N 100 49W
Rosscahill 38 53 23N 9 15W
Rosscarbery 39 51 39N 9 1W
Rosscarbery B. 39 51 32N 9 0W
Rossel I. 138 11 30S 154 30E
Rosses B. 38 55 2N 8 30W
Rosses Point 38 54 17N 8 34W
Rosses, The 38 55 2N 8 20W
Rossignol, L., N.S., Can. 151 44 12N 65 0W
Rossignol, L., Qué., Can. 150 52 43N 73 40W
Rossing 128 22 30S 14 50E
Rossland 152 49 6N 117 50W
Rosslare 39 52 17N 6 23W
Rosslau 48 51 52N 12 15E
Rosslea 38 54 15N 7 11W
Rosso 120 16 40N 15 45W
Rossosh 83 50 15N 39 20E
Rossport 150 48 50N 87 30W
Rossum 46 51 48N 5 20E
Røssvatnet 74 65 45N 14 5E
Rossville 138 15 48S 145 15E
Rosthern 153 52 40N 106 20W
Rostock 48 54 4N 12 9E
Rostock □ 48 54 10N 12 30E
Rostov, Don, U.S.S.R. 83 47 15N 39 45E
Rostov, Moskva, U.S.S.R. 81 57 14N 39 25E
Rostrenen 42 48 14N 3 21W
Rostrevor 38 54 7N 6 12W
Roswell 159 33 26N 104 32W
Rosyth 35 56 2N 3 26W
Rota 57 36 37N 6 20W
Rotälven 72 61 30N 14 10E
Rotan 159 32 52N 100 30W
Rotem 47 51 3N 5 45E
Rotenburg 48 53 6N 9 24E
Rothbury 35 55 19N 1 55W
Rothbury Forest 35 55 19N 1 50W
Rothenburg 51 47 6N 8 16E
Rothenburg ob der Tauber 49 49 21N 10 11E
Rother, R. 29 50 59N 0 40W
Rotherham 33 53 26N 1 21W
Rothes 37 57 31N 3 12W
Rothesay, Can. 151 45 23N 66 0W
Rothesay, U.K. 34 55 50N 5 3W
Rothhaar G., mts. 50 51 6N 8 10E
Rothienorman 37 57 24N 2 28W
Rothrist 50 47 18N 8 54E
Rothwell, Northants, U.K. 29 52 25N 0 48W
Rothwell, W. Yorks., U.K. 33 53 46N 1 29W
Roti, I. 103 10 50S 123 0E
Rotkop 128 26 44S 15 27E
Roto 141 33 0S 145 30E
Roto Aira L. 142 39 3S 175 55E
Rotoehu L. 142 38 1S 176 32E
Rotoiti L. 142 41 51S 172 49E
Rotoma L. 142 38 2S 176 35E
Rotondella 65 40 10N 16 30E
Rotoroa Lake 143 41 55S 172 39E
Rotorua 142 38 9S 176 16E
Rotorua, L. 142 38 5S 176 18E
Rotselaar 47 50 57N 4 42E
Rottal 37 56 48N 3 1W
Rotten, R. 50 46 18N 7 36E
Rottenburg 49 48 28N 8 56E
Rottenmann 52 47 31N 14 22E
Rotterdam 46 51 55N 4 30E
Rottingdean 29 50 48N 0 3W
Rottnest I. 137 32 0S 115 27E
Rottumeroog 46 53 33N 6 34E
Rottweil 49 48 9N 8 38E
Rotuma, I. 130 12 25S 177 5E
Roubaix 43 50 40N 3 10E
Roudnice 52 50 25N 14 15E
Rouen 42 49 27N 1 4E
Rouergue 45 44 20N 2 20E
Rough, gasfield 19 53 50N 0 27E
Rough Pt. 39 52 19N 10 0W
Rough Ridge 143 45 10S 169 55E
Rouillac 44 45 47N 0 4W
Rouleau 153 50 10N 104 56W
Round Mt. 139 30 26S 152 16E
Round Mountain 163 38 46N 117 3W
Roundstone 38 53 24N 9 55W
Roundup 160 46 25N 108 35W
Roundwood 39 53 4N 6 14W
Rourkela 95 22 14N 84 50E
Rousay, I. 37 59 10N 3 2W
Rousky 38 54 44N 7 10E
Rousse, L'Île 45 43 27N 8 57E
Roussillon 45 45 24N 4 49E
Rouveen 46 52 37N 6 11E
Rouxville 128 30 11S 26 50E
Rouyn 150 48 20N 79 0W
Rovaniemi 74 66 29N 25 41E
Rovato 62 45 34N 10 0E
Rovenki 83 48 5N 39 27E
Rovereto 62 45 53N 11 3E
Rovigo 63 45 4N 11 48E
Rovinari 70 46 56N 23 10E
Rovinj 63 45 18N 13 40E
Rovira 174 4 15N 75 20W
Rovno 80 50 40N 26 10E
Rovnoye 81 50 52N 46 3E
Rovuma, R. 127 11 30S 36 10E
Rowanburn 35 55 5N 2 54W
Rowena 139 29 48S 148 55E
Rowes 141 37 0S 149 6E
Rowley Shoals 136 17 40S 119 20E
Rowood 161 32 18N 112 54W
Rowrah 32 54 34N 3 26W
Roxa 120 11 15N 15 45W
Roxas 103 11 36N 122 49E
Roxboro 157 36 24N 78 59W
Roxborough Downs 138 22 20S 138 45E
Roxburgh, N.Z. 143 45 33S 169 19E
Roxburgh, U.K. 35 55 34N 2 30W
Roxburgh (□) 26 55 30N 2 30W
Roxby 33 53 38N 0 37W
Roxen 73 58 30N 15 40E
Roy 160 47 17N 109 0W
Roy Hill 136 22 37S 119 58E
Roy, Le 159 38 8N 95 35W
Roya, Peña 58 40 25N 0 40W
Royal Canal 38 53 29N 7 0W
Royal Oak 156 42 30N 83 5W
Royalla 141 35 30S 149 9E
Royan 44 45 37N 1 2W
Roybridge 37 56 53N 4 50W
Roye 43 47 40N 6 31E
Røyken 71 59 45N 10 23E
Royston 29 52 3N 0 1W
Royton 32 53 34N 2 7W
Rozaj 66 42 50N 20 15E
Rozan 54 52 52N 21 25E
Rozdol 80 49 30N 24 1E
Rozier, Le 44 44 13N 3 12E
Roznava 53 48 37N 20 35E
Rozoy 43 48 40N 2 56E
Rozoy-sur-Serre 43 49 40N 4 8E
Rozwadów 54 50 37N 22 2E
Rrësheni 68 41 47N 19 49E
Rtanj, mt. 66 43 45N 21 50W
Rtem, Oued el 119 33 40N 5 34E
Rtishchevo 81 52 35N 43 50E
Rúa 56 42 24N 7 6W
Ruacaná 128 17 20S 14 12E
Ruahine Ra. 142 39 55S 176 2E
Ruamahanga, R. 142 41 24S 175 8E
Ruapehu 142 39 17S 175 35E
Ruapuke I. 143 46 46S 168 31E
Ruatoria 142 37 55S 178 20E
Ruãus, W. 119 30 14N 15 0E
Ruawai 142 36 15S 173 59E
Rub 'al Khali 91 21 0N 51 0E
Rubeho, mts. 126 6 50S 36 25E
Rubery 28 52 24N 1 59W
Rubezhnoye 82 49 6N 38 25E
Rubha Ardvule C. 36 57 17N 7 32W
Rubha Hunish, C. 36 57 42N 6 20W
Rubh'an Dunain, C. 36 57 10N 6 20W
Rubiataba 171 15 8S 49 48W
Rubicone, R. 63 44 0N 12 20E
Rubim 171 16 23S 40 32W
Rubinéia 171 20 13S 51 2W
Rubino 120 6 4N 4 18W
Rubio 174 7 43N 72 22W
Rubona 126 0 29N 30 9E
Rubtsovsk 76 51 30N 80 50E
Ruby 147 64 40N 155 35W
Ruby L. 160 40 10N 115 28W
Ruby Mts. 160 40 30N 115 30W
Rubyvale 138 23 25S 147 45E
Rucava 80 56 9N 20 32E
Ruciane-Nida 54 53 40N 21 32E
RûcûSdia 66 44 59N 21 36E
Rud 71 60 1N 10 1E
Ruda 73 57 6N 16 7E
Ruda Slaska 53 50 16N 18 50E
Rudall 140 33 43S 136 17E
Rudbar 93 30 0N 62 30E
Ruden, I. 48 54 13N 13 47E
Rüdersdorf 48 52 28N 13 48E
Rudewa 127 10 7S 34 47E
Rudgwick 29 51 7N 0 54W
Rudkøbing 73 54 56N 10 41E
Rudna 54 51 30N 16 17E
Rudnichnyy 84 59 38N 52 26E
Rudnik, Bulg. 67 42 36N 27 30E
Rudnik, Yugo. 67 44 7N 20 35E
Rudnik, mt. 67 44 7N 20 35E
Rudnogorsk 77 57 15N 103 42E
Rudnya 80 54 55N 31 13E
Rudnyy 84 52 57N 63 7E
Rudo 66 43 41N 19 23E
Rudolstadt 48 50 44N 11 20E
Rudozem 67 41 29N 24 51E
Rudston 33 54 6N 0 19W
Rŭducaneni 70 46 58N 27 54E
Rŭdŭuţi 70 47 50N 25 59E
Rudyard 156 46 14N 84 35E
Rue 43 50 15N 1 40E
Ruelle 44 45 41N 0 14E
Rufa'a 123 14 44N 33 32E
Ruffec Charente 44 46 2N 0 12W
Rufi 123 5 58N 30 18E
Rufiji □ 126 8 0S 38 30E
Rufiji, R. 124 7 50S 38 15E
Rufino 172 34 20S 62 50W
Rufisque 120 14 40N 17 15W
Rufunsa 127 15 4S 29 34E
Rugby, U.K. 28 52 23N 1 16W
Rugby, U.S.A. 158 48 21N 100 0W
Rugeley 28 52 47N 1 56W
Rügen, I. 48 54 22N 13 25E
Rugezi 126 2 6S 33 18E
Rugles 42 48 50N 0 40E
Ruhāma 90 31 31N 34 43E
Ruhea 98 26 10N 88 25E
Ruhengeri 126 1 30S 29 36E
Ruhla 48 50 53N 10 21E
Ruhland 48 51 27N 13 52E
Ruhr, R. 48 51 25N 7 15E
Ruhuhu, R. 127 10 15S 34 55E
Rui Barbosa 171 12 18S 40 27W
Ruidosa 159 29 59N 104 39W
Ruidoso 161 33 19N 105 39W
Ruinen 46 52 46N 6 21E
Ruinen A Kanaal 46 52 54N 7 8E
Ruinerwold 46 52 44N 6 15E
Ruj, mt. 66 42 52N 22 42E
Rujen, mt. 66 42 9N 22 30E
Ruk 94 27 50N 68 42E
Rukwa □, Tanz. 126 7 0S 31 30E
Rukwa □, Tanz. 126 7 0S 31 30E
Rukwa L. 126 7 50S 32 10E
Rulhieres, C. 136 13 56S 127 22E
Rulles 47 49 43N 5 32E
Rully 167 46 52N 4 44E
Rum Jungle 136 13 0S 130 59E
Ruma 66 45 8N 19 50E
Rumah 92 25 35N 47 10E
Rumania ■ 61 46 0N 25 0E
Rumbalara 138 25 20S 134 29E
Rumbek 123 6 54N 29 37E
Rumbeke 47 50 56N 3 10E
Rumburk 52 50 57N 14 32E
Rumelange 47 49 27N 6 2E
Rumford 156 44 30N 70 30W
Rumia 54 54 37N 18 25E
Rumilly 45 45 53N 5 56E
Rumney 31 51 32N 3 7W
Rumoi 112 43 56N 141 39W
Rumonge 126 3 59S 29 26E
Rumsey 152 51 51N 112 48W
Rumson 162 40 23N 74 0W
Rumula 138 16 35S 145 20E
Rumuruti 126 0 17N 36 32E
Runabay Hd. 38 55 10N 6 2W
Runanga 143 42 25S 171 15E
Runaway, C. 142 37 32S 178 2E
Runcorn, Austral. 108 27 36S 153 4E
Runcorn, U.K. 32 53 20N 2 44W
Rungwa 126 6 55S 33 32E
Rungwa, R. 126 7 15S 33 10E
Rungwe 127 9 11S 33 32E
Rungwe □ 127 9 25S 33 32E
Runka 121 12 28N 7 20E
Runn 72 60 30N 15 40E
Rupa 98 27 15N 92 30E
Rupar 94 31 2N 76 38E
Rupat, I. 102 1 45N 101 40E
Rupea 61 46 2N 25 13E
Rupert House = Fort Rupert 150 51 30N 78 40W
Rupert, R. 150 51 29N 78 45W
Rupsa 98 21 44N 87 20E
Rupununi, R. 175 3 30N 59 30W
Ruquka Gie La 99 31 35N 97 55E
Rurrenabaque 174 14 30S 67 32W
Rus, R. 58 39 30N 2 30W
Rusambo 127 16 30S 32 4E
Rusape 125 18 35S 32 8E
Ruschuk = Ruse 67 43 48N 25 59E
Ruse 67 43 48N 25 59E
Rusetu 70 44 57N 27 14E
Rush 38 53 31N 6 7W
Rushden 29 52 17N 0 37W
Rushford 158 43 48N 91 46W
Rushville, Ill., U.S.A. 158 40 6N 90 35W
Rushville, Ind., U.S.A. 156 39 38N 85 22W
Rushville, Nebr., U.S.A. 158 42 43N 102 35W
Rushworth 141 36 32S 145 1E
Rusken 73 57 15N 14 20E
Ruskington 33 53 5N 0 23W
Russas 171 4 56S 38 2W
Russell, Can. 153 50 50N 101 20W
Russell, N.Z. 142 35 16S 174 10E
Russell, U.S.A. 158 38 56N 98 55W
Russell L., Man., Can. 153 56 15N 101 30W
Russell L., N.W.T., Can. 152 63 5N 115 44W
Russellkonda 96 19 57N 84 42E
Russellville, Ala., U.S.A. 157 34 30N 87 44W
Russellville, Ark., U.S.A. 159 35 15N 93 0W
Russellville, Ky., U.S.A. 157 36 50N 86 50W
Russi 63 44 21N 12 1E
Russian Mission 147 61 45N 161 25W
Russian S.F.S.R. □ 77 62 0N 105 0E
Russkoye Ustie 12 71 0N 149 0E
Rust 53 47 49N 16 42E
Rustam 94 34 25N 72 13E
Rustam Shahr 94 26 58N 66 6E
Rustavi 83 40 45N 44 30E
Rustenburg 128 25 41S 27 14E
Ruston 159 32 30N 92 40W
Ruswil 50 47 5N 8 8E
Rutana 126 3 55S 30 0E
Rutba 92 33 4N 40 15E
Rute 57 37 19N 4 29W
Ruteng 103 8 26S 120 30E
Ruth 160 39 15N 115 1W
Ruth, oilfield 19 55 33N 4 55E
Rutherglen, Austral. 141 36 5S 146 29E
Rutherglen, U.K. 34 55 50N 4 11W
Ruthin 31 53 7N 3 20W
Ruthven 37 57 4N 4 2W
Ruthwell 35 55 0N 3 24W
Rüti 51 47 16N 8 51E
Rutigliano 65 41 1N 17 0E
Rutland 162 43 38N 73 0W
Rutland (□) 26 52 38N 0 40W
Rutland I. 101 11 25N 92 40E
Rutland Plains 138 15 38S 141 49E
Rutledge L. 153 61 33N 110 47W
Rutledge, R. 153 61 4N 112 0W
Rutshuru 126 1 13S 29 25E
Ruurlo 46 52 5N 6 24E
Ruvo di Púglia 65 41 7N 16 27E
Ruvu 126 6 49S 38 43E
Ruvu, R. 126 7 25S 38 15E
Ruvuma □ 127 10 20S 36 0E
Ruvuma, R. 127 11 30S 36 10E
Ruwaidha 92 23 40N 44 40E
Ruwandiz 92 36 40N 44 32E
Ruwenzori Mts. 126 0 30N 29 55E
Ruwenzori, mt. 126 0 30N 29 55E
Ruyigi 126 3 29S 30 15E
Ruzayevka 81 54 10N 45 0E
Ruzhevo Konare 67 42 23N 24 46E
Ruzomberok 53 49 3N 19 17E
Rwanda ■ 126 2 0S 30 0E
Ryaberg 73 56 47N 13 15E
Ryakhovo 67 44 0N 26 18E
Ryan, L. 34 55 0N 5 2W
Ryazan 81 54 50N 39 40E
Ryazhsk 81 53 45N 40 3E
Rybache 76 46 40N 81 20E
Rybachi Poluostrov 78 69 43N 32 0E
Rybachye 85 42 26N 76 12E
Rybinsk (Shcherbakov) 81 58 5N 38 50E
Rybinsk Vdkhr. 81 58 30N 38 0E
Rybnik 54 50 6N 18 32E
Rybnitsa 82 47 45N 29 0E
Rychwał 54 52 4N 18 10E
Ryd 73 56 27N 14 42E
Rydal 32 54 28N 2 59W
Ryde 28 50 44N 1 9W
Rydö 73 56 58N 13 10E
Rydsnäs 73 57 47N 15 9E
Rydułtowy 54 50 4N 18 23E
Rydzyna 54 51 47N 16 39E
Rye, Denmark 73 56 5N 9 45E
Rye, U.K. 29 50 57N 0 46E
Rye Patch Res. 160 40 45N 118 20W
Rye, R. 33 54 12N 0 53W
Ryegate 160 46 21N 109 27W
Ryhope 35 54 52N 1 22W
Rylsk 80 51 30N 34 51E
Rylstone 141 32 46S 149 58E
Rymanów 54 49 35N 21 51E
Ryn 54 53 57N 21 34E
Ryningsnäs 73 57 17N 15 58E
Ryōhaku-Sanchi 111 36 0N 136 49E
Rypin 54 53 3N 19 32E
Ryton, Tyne & Wear, U.K. 35 54 58N 1 44W
Ryton, Warwick, U.K. 28 52 23N 1 25W
Ryūgasaki 111 35 54N 140 11E
Ryūkyū Is. = Nansei-Shotō 112 26 0N 128 0E
Rzepin 54 52 20N 14 49E
Rzeszów 54 50 5N 21 58E
Rzeszów □ 54 50 0N 22 0E
Rzhev 80 56 20N 34 20E

S

s'-Hertogenbosch 47 51 42N 5 17E
Sa 100 18 34N 100 45E
Sa. da Canastra 125 19 30S 46 5W
Sa Dec 101 10 20N 105 46E
Sa-Koi 98 19 54N 97 3E
Sa'ad (Muharraga) 90 31 28N 34 33E
Sa'ādatabād 93 30 10N 53 5E
Saale, R. 48 51 25N 11 56E
Saaler Bodden 48 54 20N 12 25E
Saalfelden 70 47 26N 12 51E
Saalfeld 48 50 39N 11 21E
Saane, R. 50 46 23N 7 18E
Saanen 50 46 29N 7 15E
Saar (Sarre), □ 43 49 20N 6 45E
Saarbrücken 49 49 15N 6 58E
Saarburg 49 49 36N 6 32E
Saaremaa 80 58 30N 22 30E
Saariselkä 74 68 16N 28 15E
Saarland □ 131 49 20N 6 45E
Saarlouis 49 49 19N 6 45E
Saas Fee 50 46 7N 7 56E
Saas-Grund 50 46 7N 7 57E
Saba I. 167 17 30N 63 10W
Sabac 66 44 48N 19 42E
Sabadell 58 41 28N 2 7E
Sabae 111 35 57N 136 11E
Sabagalel 102 1 36S 98 40E
Sabah □ 102 6 0N 117 0E
Sabak 100 3 46N 100 58E
Sábana de la Mar 167 19 7N 69 40W
Sábanalarga 174 10 38N 74 55W
Sabang, O. 102 5 50N 95 15E

Name								Name							
Sabará	171	19	55 S	43	55W			Sagone	45	42	7N	8	42 E		
Sabarania	103	2	5 S	138	18 E			Sagone, G. de	45	42	4N	8	40 E		
Sabari, R.	96	18	0N	81	25 E			Sagori	107	35	25N	126	49 E		
Sabastiya	90	32	17N	35	12 E			Sagra, La, Mt.	59	38	0N	2	35W		
Sabaudia	64	41	17N	13	2 E			Sagres	57	37	0N	8	58W		
Sabderat	123	15	26N	36	42 E			Sagu	98	20	13N	94	46 E		
Sabhah	119	27	9N	14	29 E			Sagua la Grande	166	22	50N	80	10W		
Sabie	129	25	4 S	30	48 E			Saguache	161	38	10N	106	4W		
Sabinal, Mexico	164	30	50N	107	25W			Saguenay, R.	151	48	22N	71	0W		
Sabinal, U.S.A.	159	29	20N	99	27W			Sagunto	58	39	42N	0	18W		
Sabinal, Punta del	59	36	43N	2	44W			Sahaba	122	18	57N	30	25 E		
Sabinas	164	27	50N	101	10W			Sahagún, Colomb.	174	8	57N	75	27W		
Sabinas Hidalgo	164	26	40N	100	10W			Sahagún, Spain	56	42	18N	5	2W		
Sabinas, R.	164	27	37N	100	42W			Saham	90	32	42N	35	46 E		
Sabine	159	29	42N	93	54W			Sahara	118	23	0N	5	0W		
Sabine, R.	159	31	30N	93	35W			Saharanpur	94	29	58N	77	33 E		
Sabinópolis	171	18	40 S	43	6W			Saharien Atlas	118	34	9N	3	29 E		
Sabinov	53	49	6N	21	5 E			Sahasinaka	129	21	49 S	47	49 E		
Sabirabad	83	40	0N	48	30 E			Sahaswan	95	28	5N	78	45 E		
Sabkhat Tawurgha	119	31	48N	15	30 E			Sahel, Canal du	120	14	20N	6	0W		
Sablayan	103	12	5N	120	50 E			Sahibganj	95	25	12N	87	55 E		
Sable	42	47	50N	0	21W			Sahiwal	94	30	45N	73	8 E		
Sable, C., Can.	151	43	29N	65	38W			Sahl Arraba	90	37	26N	35	12 E		
Sable, C., U.S.A.	166	25	5N	81	0W			Sahtaneh, R.	152	59	2N	122	28W		
Sable I.	151	44	0N	60	0W			Sahuaripa	164	29	30N	109	0W		
Sablé-sur-Sarthe	42	47	50N	0	20W			Sahuarita	161	31	58N	110	59W		
Sables-D'Olonne, Les	44	46	30N	1	45W			Sahuayo	164	20	4N	102	43W		
Saboeiro	170	6	32 S	39	54W			Sahy	53	48	4N	18	55 E		
Sabor, R.	56	41	16N	7	10W			Sai Buri	101	6	43N	101	39 E		
Sabou	120	12	1N	2	28W			Saibai I.	135	9	25 S	142	40 E		
Sabrātah	119	32	47N	12	29 E			Sa'id Bundas	117	8	24N	24	48 E		
Sabrina Coast	13	67	0 S	120	0 E			Saïda	118	34	50N	0	11 E		
Sabugal	56	40	20N	7	5W			Sa'idabad	93	29	30N	55	45 E		
Sabzevar	93	36	15N	57	40 E			Saidapet	97	13	0N	80	15 E		
Sabzvaran	93	28	45N	57	50 E			Saidor	135	5	40 S	146	29 E		
Sac City	158	42	26N	95	0W			Saidu	95	34	50N	72	15 E		
Sacandaga Res.	162	43	6N	74	16W			Säie	72	59	8N	12	55 E		
Sacedón	58	40	29N	2	41W			Saighan	93	35	10N	67	55 E		
Sachigo, L.	150	53	50N	92	12W			Saignelégier	50	47	15N	7	0 E		
Sachigo, R.	150	55	6N	88	58W			Saignes	44	45	20N	2	31 E		
Sachinbulako	106	43	5N	111	47 E			Saigō	110	36	12N	133	20 E		
Sachkhere	83	42	25N	43	28 E			Saigon = Phanh Bho Ho Chi Minh	101	10	58N	106	40 E		
Sachseln	51	46	52N	8	15 E			Saih-al-Malih	93	23	37N	58	31 E		
Sacile	63	45	58N	16	7 E			Saihut	91	15	12N	51	10 E		
Säckingen	49	47	34N	7	56 E			Saijō, Ehima, Japan	110	33	55N	133	11 E		
Saco, Me., U.S.A.	162	43	30N	70	27W			Saijō, Hiroshima, Japan	110	34	25N	132	45 E		
Saco, Mont., U.S.A.	160	48	28N	107	19W			Saikhoa Ghat	99	27	50N	95	40 E		
Sacquoy Hd.	37	59	12N	3	5W			Saiki	110	32	58N	131	57 E		
Sacramento, Brazil	171	19	53 S	47	27W			Saillans	45	44	42N	5	12 E		
Sacramento, U.S.A.	163	38	39N	121	30 E			Sailolof	103	1	7 S	130	46 E		
Sacramento Mts.	161	32	30N	105	30W			Saima	107	40	59N	124	15 E		
Sacramento, R.	163	38	3N	121	56W			Saimaa, L.	78	61	15N	28	15 E		
Sacratif, Cabo	59	36	42N	3	28W			St. Abbs	35	55	54N	2	7W		
Sacriston	33	54	49N	1	38W			St. Abb's Head	35	55	55N	2	10W		
Sada	56	43	22N	8	15W			St. Aegyd	52	47	52N	15	33 E		
Sada-Misaki-Hantō	110	33	22N	132	1 E			St. Affrique	44	43	57N	2	53 E		
Sadaba	58	2	19N	1	12W			St. Agnes	30	50	18N	5	13W		
Sa'dani	124	5	58 S	38	35 E			St. Agnes Hd.	30	50	19N	5	14W		
Sadao	101	6	38N	100	26 E			St. Agnes I.	30	49	53N	6	20W		
Sadasivpet	96	17	38N	77	50 E			St.-Agrève	45	45	0N	4	23 E		
Sadberge	33	54	32N	1	30W			St.-Aignan	42	47	16N	1	22 E		
Sadd el Aali	122	24	5N	32	54 E			St. Albans, Austral.	138	24	43 S	139	56 E		
Saddell	34	55	31N	5	30W			St. Albans, Can.	151	47	51N	55	50W		
Saddle, Hd.	38	54	0N	10	10W			St. Albans, U.K.	29	51	44N	0	19W		
Saddle, The	36	57	10N	5	27W			St. Albans, Vt., U.S.A.	156	44	49N	73	7W		
Sade	121	11	22N	10	45 E			St. Albans, W. Va., U.S.A.	156	38	21N	81	50W		
Sadiba	128	18	53 S	23	1 E			St. Alban's Head	28	50	34N	2	3W		
Sadimi	127	9	25 S	23	32 E			St. Albert	152	53	37N	113	40W		
Sado	112	38	0N	138	25 E			St. Amand	43	50	25N	3	6 E		
Sado, R.	57	38	10N	8	22W			St.-Amand-en-Puisaye	43	47	32N	3	5 E		
Sadon, Burma	99	25	28N	98	0 E			St.-Amand-Mont-Rond	44	46	43N	2	30 E		
Sadon, U.S.S.R.	83	42	52N	43	58 E			St.-Amarin	43	47	54N	7	0 E		
Sadri	94	24	28N	74	30 E			St.-Amour	45	46	26N	5	21 E		
Saduya	98	27	50N	95	40 E			St. Andrä	52	46	46N	14	50 E		
Sæby	73	57	21N	10	30 E			St. André, C.	129	16	11 S	44	27 E		
Saelices	58	39	55N	2	49W			St.-André-de-Cubzac	44	44	59N	0	26W		
Safāga	122	26	42N	34	0 E			St. André de l'Eure	42	48	54N	1	16 E		
Safaha	122	26	25N	39	0 E			St.-André-les-Alpes	45	43	58N	6	30 E		
Safaniya	92	28	5N	48	42 E			St. Andrews, Can.	151	47	45N	59	15W		
Safárikovo	53	48	25N	20	20 E			St. Andrews, N.Z.	143	44	33 S	171	10 E		
Safed Koh, Mts.	94	34	15N	64	0 E			St. Andrews, U.K.	35	56	20N	2	48W		
Safford	161	32	54N	109	52W			St. Ann B.	151	46	22N	60	25W		
Saffron Walden	29	52	2N	0	15 E			St. Anne	42	49	43N	2	11W		
Safi, Jordan	90	31	2N	35	28 E			St. Anne's	32	53	45N	3	2W		
Safi, Moroc.	118	32	18N	9	14W			St. Ann's	35	55	14N	3	28W		
Safiah	42	31	27N	34	46 E			St. Ann's Bay	166	18	26N	77	15W		
Safonovo	80	65	40N	47	50 E			St. Ann's Hd.	31	51	41N	5	11W		
Safranbolu	82	41	15N	32	34 E			St. Anthony, Can.	151	51	22N	55	35W		
Sag Harbor	162	40	59N	72	17W			St. Anthony, U.S.A.	160	44	0N	111	49W		
Sag Sag	135	5	32 S	148	23 E			St.-Antonin-Noble-Val	44	44	10N	1	45 E		
Saga, Indon.	103	2	40 S	132	55 E			St. Arnaud	140	36	32 S	143	16 E		
Saga, Kōchi, Japan	110	33	5N	133	6 E			St. Arnaud Ra.	143	42	1 S	172	53 E		
Saga, Saga, Japan	110	33	15N	130	16 E			St. Arthur	151	47	47N	67	46W		
Saga-ken □	110	33	15N	130	20 E			St. Asaph	31	53	15N	3	27W		
Sagåg	71	59	46N	5	25 E			St. Astier	44	45	8N	0	31 E		
Sagaing	98	23	30N	95	30 E			St.-Aubin	50	46	54N	6	47 E		
Sagaing □	98	22	0N	95	30 E			St.-Aubin-du-Cormier	42	48	15N	1	26W		
Sagala	120	14	9N	6	38W			St. Augustin	129	23	33 S	43	46 E		
Sagami-Nada	111	34	58N	139	23 E			St.-Augustin-Saguenay	151	51	13N	58	38W		
Sagami-Wan	111	35	15N	139	25 E			St. Augustine	157	29	52N	81	20W		
Sagamihara	111	35	33N	139	25 E			St. Austell	30	50	20N	4	48W		
Saganoseki	110	33	15N	131	53 E			St.-Avold	43	49	6N	6	43 E		
Sagar	93	23	50N	78	50 E			St. Barthélemy, I.	167	17	50N	62	50W		
Sagara, India	97	14	14N	75	6 E			St. Bathans	143	44	53 S	170	0 E		
Sagara, Japan	111	34	41N	138	12 E			St. Bathan's Mt.	143	44	45 S	169	45 E		
Sagara, L.	126	5	20 S	31	0 E			St. Bees	32	54	29N	3	36W		
Sagawa	110	33	28N	133	11 E			St. Bee's Hd.	32	54	30N	3	38 E		
Sågen	72	60	17N	14	10 E			St.-Benoît-du-Sault	44	46	26N	1	24 E		
Sagil	105	50	20N	91	40 E			St. Bernard, Col du Grand	50	45	53N	7	11 E		
Saginaw	156	43	26N	83	55W			St.-Blaise	50	47	1N	6	59 E		
Saginaw B.	150	43	50N	83	40W										
Sagleipie	45	45	25N	7	0 E										
Saglouc (Sugluk)	149	62	30N	74	15W										

Name								Name							
St. Blazey	32	50	22N	4	48W			St.-Germain-Lembron	44	45	27N	3	14 E		
St. Boniface	153	49	50N	97	10W			St.-Germain-de-Calberte	44	44	13N	3	48 E		
St. Bonnet	45	44	40N	6	5 E			St.-Germain-des-Fossés	44	46	12N	3	26 E		
St. Boswells	35	55	34N	2	39W			St.-Germain-du-Plain	43	46	42N	4	58 E		
St.-Brévin-les-Pins	42	47	14N	2	10W			St.-Germain-Laval	45	45	50N	4	1 E		
St. Briavels	28	51	44N	2	39W			St. Germans	30	50	24N	4	19W		
St.-Brice-en-Coglès	42	48	25N	1	22W			St. Gervais, Haute Savoie, France	45	45	53N	6	42 E		
St. Bride's	151	46	56N	54	10W			St. Gervais, Puy de Dôme, France	44	46	4N	2	50 E		
St. Bride's B.	31	51	48N	5	15W			St.-Gervais-les-Bains	45	45	53N	6	41 E		
St.-Brieuc	42	48	30N	2	46W			St.-Gildas, Pte. de	42	47	8N	2	14W		
St. Budeaux	30	50	23N	4	10W			St.-Gilles	45	43	40N	4	26 E		
St. Buryan	30	50	4N	5	34W			St. Gilles Croix-de-Vie	42	46	41N	1	55W		
St.-Calais	42	47	55N	0	45 E			St.-Gingolph	50	46	24N	6	48 E		
St.-Cast	42	48	37N	2	18W			St.-Girons	44	42	59N	1	8 E		
St. Catharines	150	43	10N	79	15W			St. Gla, L.	72	59	35N	12	30 E		
St. Catherine's I.	157	31	35N	81	10W			St. Goar	49	50	31N	7	43 E		
St. Catherine's Pt.	28	50	34N	1	18W			St. Gotthard P. = San Gottardo	51	46	33N	8	33 E		
St.-Céré	44	44	51N	1	54 E			St. Govan's Hd.	31	51	35N	4	56W		
St. Cergue	50	46	27N	6	10 E			St.-Guadens	44	43	6N	0	44 E		
St. Cernin	44	45	5N	2	25 E			St.-Gualtier	42	46	39N	1	26 E		
St.-Chamond	45	45	28N	4	31 E			St.-Guénolé	42	47	49N	4	23W		
St. Charles, Ill., U.S.A.	156	41	55N	88	21W			St. Harmon	31	52	21N	3	29W		
St. Charles, Mo., U.S.A.	158	38	46N	90	30W			St. Heddinge	73	55	9N	12	26 E		
St.-Chély-d'Apcher	44	44	48N	3	17 E			St. Helena	160	38	29N	122	30W		
St.-Chinian	44	43	25N	2	56 E			St. Helena, I.	15	15	55 S	5	44W		
St. Christopher (St. Kitts)	167	17	20N	62	40W			St. Helenabaai	128	32	40 S	18	10 E		
St.-Ciers-sur-Gironde	44	45	17N	0	37W			St. Helens, Austral.	138	41	20 S	148	15 E		
St. Clair	162	40	42N	76	12W			St. Helens, I.o.W., U.K.	28	50	42N	1	6W		
St. Clair, L.	150	42	30N	82	45W			St. Helens, Merseyside, U.K.	32	53	28N	2	44W		
St.-Claud	44	45	54N	0	28 E			St. Helens, U.S.A.	160	45	55N	122	50W		
St. Claude	153	49	40N	98	20W			St. Helier	42	49	11N	2	6W		
St.-Claude	45	46	22N	5	52 E			St. Hilaire	42	48	35N	1	7W		
St. Clears	31	51	48N	4	30W			St. Hippolyte	43	47	20N	6	50 E		
St.-Cloud	42	48	51N	2	12 E			St. Hippolyte-du-Fort	44	43	58N	3	52 E		
St. Cloud, Fla., U.S.A.	157	28	15N	81	15W			St.-Honoré	43	46	54N	3	50 E		
St. Cloud, Minn., U.S.A.	158	45	30N	94	11W			St.-Hubert	47	50	2N	5	23 E		
St. Coeur de Marie	151	48	39N	71	43W			St. Hyacinthe	150	45	40N	72	58W		
St. Columb Major	30	50	26N	4	56W			St. Ignace	156	45	53N	84	43W		
St. Combs	37	57	40N	1	55W			St. Ignace I.	150	48	45N	88	0W		
St. Cricq, C.	137	25	17 S	113	6 E			St. Ignatius	160	47	25N	114	2W		
St. Croix Falls	158	45	18N	92	22W			St.-Imier	50	47	9N	6	58 E		
St. Croix, I.	147	17	45N	64	45W			St. Issey	30	50	30N	4	55W		
St. Croix, R.	158	45	20N	92	50W			St. Ives, Cambs., U.K.	29	52	20N	0	5W		
St. Cyprien	44	42	37N	3	0 E			St. Ives, Cornwall, U.K.	30	50	13N	5	29W		
St.-Cyr	45	43	11N	5	43 E			St. Ives Bay	30	50	15N	5	27W		
St. Cyrus	36	56	47N	2	25W			St.-James	42	48	31N	1	20W		
St. David's, Can.	151	48	12N	58	52W			St. James	158	43	57N	94	40W		
St. David's, U.K.	31	51	54N	5	16W			St. James C.	152	51	55N	131	0W		
St. David's Head	31	51	54N	5	16W			St. Jean	150	45	20N	73	50W		
St.-Denis	43	48	56N	2	22 E			St.-Jean, C.	124	1	5N	9	20 E		
St.-Denis-d'Orques	42	48	2N	0	17W			St.-Jean-de-Maurienne	45	45	16N	6	28 E		
St. Dennis	30	50	23N	4	53W			St.-Jean-de-Luz	44	43	23N	1	39W		
St. Dié	43	48	17N	6	56 E			St.-Jean-de-Monts	42	46	47N	2	4W		
St. Dizier	43	48	40N	5	0 E			St.-Jean-du-Gard	44	44	7N	3	52 E		
St. Dogmaels	31	52	6N	4	42W			St.-Jean-en-Royans	45	45	1N	5	18 E		
St. Dominick	30	50	28N	4	15W			St-Jean, L.	151	48	40N	72	0W		
St. Donats	31	51	23N	3	32W			St.-Jean-Port-Joli	151	47	15N	70	13W		
St.-Egrève	45	45	14N	5	41 E			St.-Jean, R.	151	50	17N	64	20W		
St. Elias, Mt.	147	60	20N	141	59W			St.-Jérôme, Qué., Can.	150	45	47N	74	0W		
St. Elias Mts.	147	59	30N	137	30W			St. Jérôme, Qué., Can.	151	48	26N	71	53W		
St. Eloy	44	46	10N	2	51 E			St. John, Can.	151	45	20N	66	8W		
St. Emilon	44	44	53N	0	9W			St. John, Kans., U.S.A.	159	37	59N	98	45W		
St. Endellion	30	50	33N	4	49W			St. John, N.D., U.S.A.	158	48	58N	99	40W		
St. Enoder	30	50	22N	4	57W			St. John, C.	151	50	0N	55	32W		
St. Erth	30	50	10N	5	26W			St. John, I.	147	18	20N	64	45W		
St. Étienne	45	45	27N	4	22 E			St. John, R.	151	45	15N	66	4W		
St.-Étienne-de-Tinée	45	44	16N	6	56 E			St. Johns	167	17	6N	61	51W		
St. Eustatius I.	167	17	20N	63	0W			St. John's, Can.	151	47	35N	52	40W		
St. Félicien	150	48	40N	72	25W			St. John's, U.K.	32	54	13N	4	38W		
St. Fergus	37	57	33N	1	50W			St. Johns, Ariz., U.S.A.	161	34	31N	109	26W		
St. Fillans	35	56	25N	4	7W			St. Johns, Mich., U.S.A.	156	43	0N	84	38W		
St. Finian's B.	39	51	50N	10	22W			St. Johns Chapel	32	54	43N	2	10W		
St. Fintan's	151	48	10N	58	50W			St. John's Pt., Ireland	38	54	35N	8	26W		
St.-Florent	151	45	42N	9	18 E			St. John's Pt., U.K.	38	54	14N	5	40W		
St.-Florent-sur-Cher	43	46	59N	2	15 E			St. Johns, R.	157	30	20N	81	30W		
St.-Florentin	43	48	0N	3	45 E			St. Johnsbury	156	44	25N	72	1W		
St.-Flour	44	45	2N	3	6 E			St. Johnston	38	54	56N	7	29W		
St.-Fons	45	45	42N	4	52 E			St. Johnsville	162	43	0N	74	43W		
St. Francis	158	39	48N	101	47W			St. Joseph, La., U.S.A.	159	31	55N	91	15W		
St. Francis C.	128	34	14 S	24	49 E			St. Joseph, Mo., U.S.A.	158	39	40N	94	50W		
St. Francis, R.	159	32	25N	90	36W			St. Joseph, I.	150	46	12N	83	58W		
St.-Fulgent	42	46	50N	1	10W			St. Joseph, L.	150	51	10N	90	35W		
St. Gabriel de Brandon	150	46	17N	73	24W			St. Joseph, R.	156	42	7N	86	30W		
St.-Gengoux-le-National	45	46	37N	4	40 E			St. Joseph's	156	42	5N	86	30W		
St.-Geniez-d'Olt	44	44	27N	2	58 E			St. Jovite	150	46	8N	74	38W		
St. George, Austral.	139	28	1 S	148	41 E			St. Juéry	44	43	55N	2	42 E		
St. George, Can.	151	45	11N	66	50W			St. Julien	45	46	8N	6	5 E		
St. George, P.N.G.	135	4	10 S	152	20 E			St. Julien-Chapteuil	45	45	2N	4	4 E		
St. George, S.C., U.S.A.	157	33	13N	80	37W			St. Julien du Sault	43	48	1N	3	17 E		
St. George, Utah, U.S.A.	161	37	10N	113	35W			St.-Junien	44	45	53N	0	55 E		
St. George, C., Can.	151	48	30N	59	16W			St. Just	30	50	7N	5	41W		
St. George, C., P.N.G.	135	4	49 S	152	53 E			St.-Just-en-Chaussée	43	49	30N	2	25 E		
St. George, C., U.S.A.	157	29	36N	85	2W			St.-Just-en-Chevalet	44	45	55N	3	50 E		
St. George Hd.	139	35	11 S	150	45 E			St. Justin	44	43	59N	0	14W		
St. George Ra., Mts.	136	18	40 S	125	0 E			St. Karlsö, I.	73	57	17N	17	58 E		
St. George West	153	50	33N	96	7W			St. Keverne	30	50	3N	5	5W		
St.-Georges	47	50	37N	2	8 E			St. Kew	30	50	34N	4	48W		
St. George's	151	48	26N	58	31W			St. Kilda	143	45	53 S	170	31 E		
St. Georges, Qué., Can.	151	46	8N	70	40W			St. Kilda, I.	23	57	40N	8	50W		
St. Georges, Quebec, Can.	150	46	42N	72	35W			St. Kitts-Nevis ■	167	17	20N	62	40W		
St. Georges, Fr. Gui.	175	4	0N	52	0W			St. Laurent	153	50	25N	97	58W		
St. George's	167	12	5N	61	43W			St. Laurent-du-Pont	45	45	23N	5	45 E		
St. George's B.	151	48	24N	58	53W			St.-Laurent-en-Grandvaux	45	46	35N	5	45 E		
St. George's Channel	147	52	0N	6	0W			St. Lawrence, Austral.	138	22	16 S	149	31 E		
St. Georges-de-Didonne	44	45	36N	1	0W			St. Lawrence, Can.	151	46	54N	55	23W		
St. Georges Head	141	35	12 S	150	42 E										
St.-Gérard	47	50	21N	4	44 E										
St. Germain	43	48	53N	2	5 E										

St. Lawrence, Gulf of

Sam Ngao

St. Lawrence, Gulf of **151** 48 25N 62 0W
St. Lawrence, I. **147** 63 0N 170 0W
St. Lawrence, R. **151** 49 30N 66 0W
St.-Léger **47** 49 37N 5 39 E
St. Leonard **151** 47 12N 67 58W
St.-Léonard-de-Noblat **44** 45 49N 1 29 E
St. Leonards **29** 50 51N 0 34 E
St. Levan **30** 50 3N 5 36W
St Lewis, R. **151** 52 26N 56 11W
St. Lin **150** 45 44N 73 46W
St.-Lô **42** 49 7N 1 5W
St. Louis, Senegal **120** 16 8N 16 27W
St. Louis, Mich., U.S.A. **156** 43 27N 84 38W
St. Louis, Mo., U.S.A. **158** 38 40N 90 12W
St. Louis R. **158** 47 15N 92 45W
St.-Loup-sur-Semouse **43** 47 53N 6 16 E
St. Lucia, C. **129** 28 32 S 32 29 E
St. Lucia Channel **167** 14 15N 61 0W
St. Lucia I. **167** 14 0N 60 50W
St. Lucia, Lake **129** 28 5 S 32 30 E
St. Lunaire-Griquet **151** 51 31N 55 28W
St. Maarten, I. **167** 18 0N 63 5W
St. Mabyn **30** 50 30N 4 45W
St. Magnus B. **36** 60 25N 1 35W
St.-Maixent-l'École **44** 46 24N 0 12W
St.-Malo **42** 48 39N 2 1W
St. Malo, G. de **42** 48 50N 2 30W
St. Mandrier **45** 43 4N 5 56 E
St. Marc **167** 19 10N 72 50W
St.-Marcellin **45** 45 9N 5 20 E
St. Marcouf, Îs. **42** 49 30N 1 10W
St.-Mard **47** 49 2N 2 42 E
St. Margaret's-at-Cliffe **29** 51 10N 1 23 E
St. Margaret's Hope **37** 58 49N 2 58W
St. Maries **160** 47 17N 116 34W
St. Martin **43** 50 42N 1 38 E
St.-Martin, I. **167** 18 0N 63 0W
St. Martin L. **153** 51 40N 98 30W
St. Martin-Tende-Vésubie **45** 44 4N 7 15 E
St. Martins **151** 45 22N 65 25W
St. Martin's I. **30** 49 58N 6 16W
St. Martinsville **159** 30 10N 91 50W
St.-Martory **44** 43 9N 0 56 E
St. Mary B. **151** 46 50N 53 50W
St. Mary Bourne **28** 51 16N 1 24W
St. Mary C. **120** 13 24N 13 10 E
St. Mary Is. **97** 13 20N 74 35 E
St. Mary, Mt. **135** 8 8 S 146 54 E
St. Mary Pk. **140** 31 32 S 138 34 E
St. Marys, N.S.W., Austral. **133** 33 44 S 150 49 E
St. Marys, Tas., Austral. **138** 41 32 S 148 11 E
St. Mary's, Can. **151** 46 56N 53 34W
St. Mary's, U.K. **37** 58 53N 2 55W
St. Mary's, Ohio, U.S.A. **156** 40 33N 84 20W
St. Mary's, Pa., U.S.A. **156** 41 30N 78 33W
St Marys Bay **151** 44 25N 66 10W
St. Mary's, C. **151** 46 50N 54 12W
St. Mary's I. **30** 49 55N 6 17W
St. Mary's Pk. **133** 31 30 S 138 33 E
St. Mary's Sd. **30** 49 53N 6 19W
St. Mathews I. = Zadetkyi Kyun **101** 10 0N 48 25 E
St.-Mathieu, Pte. de **42** 48 20N 4 45W
St. Matthias Grp. **135** 1 30 S 150 0 E
St.-Maur-des-Fosses **43** 48 48N 2 30 E
St. Maurice **50** 46 13N 7 0 E
St. Maurice R. **150** 47 20N 72 50W
St. Mawes **30** 50 10N 5 1W
St.-Médard-de-Guizières **44** 45 1N 0 4W
St.-Méen-le-Grand **42** 48 11N 2 12W
St. Merryn **30** 50 31N 4 58W
St. Michael **147** 63 30N 162 30W
St. Michaels, Arizona, U.S.A. **161** 35 45N 109 5W
St. Michaels, Maryland, U.S.A. **162** 38 47N 76 14W
St. Michael's Mt. **30** 50 7N 5 30W
St. Michel **45** 45 15N 6 29 E
St. Mihiel **43** 48 54N 5 30 E
St. Minver **30** 50 34N 4 52W
St. Monans **35** 56 13N 2 46W
St.-Nazaire **42** 47 17N 2 12W
St. Neots **29** 52 14N 0 16W
St.-Nicholas-de-Port **43** 48 38N 6 18 E
St. Niklaus **50** 46 10N 7 49 E
St. Ninian's, I. **36** 59 59N 1 20W
St. Olaf **73** 55 40N 14 12 E
St.-Omer **43** 50 45N 2 15 E
St. Osyth **29** 51 47N 1 4 E
St. Ouen **43** 48 50N 2 20 E
St. Pacome **151** 47 24N 69 58W
St. Palais **44** 45 40N 1 8W
St. Pamphile **151** 46 58N 69 48W
St.-Pardoux-la-Rivière **44** 45 29N 0 45 E
St. Pascal **151** 47 32N 69 48W
St. Patrickswell **39** 52 36N 8 43W
St. Paul, Can. **152** 54 59N 111 17W
St. Paul, France **44** 43 44N 1 3W
St. Paul, Minn., U.S.A. **158** 44 54N 93 5W
St. Paul, Nebr., U.S.A. **158** 41 15N 98 30W
St. Paul-de-Fenouillet **44** 42 50N 2 28 E
St. Paul, I., Atl. Oc. **14** 0 50N 31 40W
St. Paul, I., Can. **151** 47 12N 60 9W
St. Paul, I., Ind. Oc. **11** 30 40 S 77 34 E
St. Paul's B. **151** 49 48N 57 58W
St.-Peray **45** 44 57N 4 50 E
St.-Père-en-Retz **42** 47 11N 2 2W
St. Peter **158** 44 15N 93 57W
St. Peter Port **42** 49 27N 2 31W
St. Peters, N.S., Can. **151** 45 40N 60 53W
St. Peters, P.E.I., Can. **151** 46 25N 62 35W
St. Petersburg **157** 27 45N 82 40W
St.-Philbert-de-Grand-Lieu **42** 47 2N 1 39W
St Pierre **151** 46 40N 56 '0W
St.-Pierre-d'Oleron **44** 45 57N 1 19W
St.-Pierre-Église **42** 49 40N 1 24W
St.-Pierre-en-Port **42** 49 48N 0 30 E
Saint-Pierre et Miquelon □ **151** 46 55N 56 10W
St-Pierre, L. **150** 46 12N 72 52W
St.-Pierre-le-Moûtier **43** 46 47N 3 7 E
St. Pierre-sur-Dives **42** 49 2N 0 1W
St.-Pieters Leew **47** 50 47N 4 16 E
St. Pol **43** 50 21N 2 20 E
St.-Pol-de-Léon **42** 48 41N 4 0W
St.-Pol-sur-Mer **43** 51 1N 2 20 E
St. Pons **44** 43 30N 2 45 E
St.-Pourçain-sur-Sioule **43** 46 18N 3 18 E
St.-Quay-Portrieux **42** 48 39N 2 51W
St.-Quentin **43** 49 50N 3 16 E
St. Rambert-d'Albon **45** 45 17N 1 35 E
St.-Raphaël **45** 43 25N 6 46 E
St. Regis **160** 47 20N 115 3W
St.-Rémy-de-Provence **45** 43 48N 4 50 E
St.-Renan **42** 48 26N 4 37W
St.-Saëns **42** 49 41N 1 16 E
St.-Sauveur-en-Puisaye **43** 47 37N 3 12 E
St.-Sauveur-le-Vicomte **42** 49 23N 1 32W
St. Savin **44** 46 34N 0 50 E
St.-Savinien **44** 45 53N 0 42W
St. Sebastien, C. **129** 12 26 S 48 44 E
St.-Seine-l'Abbaye **43** 47 26N 4 47 E
St. Sernin **44** 43 54N 2 35 E
St.-Servan-sur-Mer **42** 48 38N 2 0 E
St.-Sever-Calvados **42** 48 50N 1 3W
St. Simeon **151** 47 51N 69 54W
St. Stephen, Can. **151** 45 16N 67 17W
St. Stephen, U.K. **30** 50 20N 4 52W
St.-Sulpice **44** 43 46N 1 41 E
St.-Sulpice-Laurière **44** 46 3N 1 29 E
St. Teath **30** 50 34N 4 45W
St.-Thegonnec **42** 48 31N 3 57W
St. Thomas **150** 42 45N 81 10W
St. Thomas, I. **147** 18 21N 64 55W
St. Tite **150** 46 45N 72 40W
St. Tropez **45** 43 17N 6 38 E
St. Troud **47** 50 48N 5 10 E
St. Tudwal's Is. **31** 52 48N 4 28W
St. Tudy **30** 50 33N 4 45W
St.-Vaast-la-Hougue **42** 49 35N 1 17W
St. Valéry **43** 50 10N 1 38 E
St.-Valéry-en-Caux **42** 49 52N 0 43 E
St.-Vallier **45** 45 11N 4 50 E
St.-Vallier-de-Thiey **45** 43 42N 6 51 E
St.-Varent **42** 46 53N 0 13W
St. Vincent **14** 18 0N 26 1W
St. Vincent C. **125** 21 58 S 43 20 E
St. Vincent, C. = São Vincente **57** 37 0N 9 0W
St. Vincent-de-Tyrosse **44** 43 39N 1 18W
St. Vincent, G. **140** 35 0 S 138 0 E
St. Vincent, I. **167** 13 10N 61 10W
St. Vincent Passage **167** 13 30N 61 0W
St.-Vith **47** 50 17N 6 9 E
St.-Yrieux-la-Perche **44** 45 31N 1 12 E
Ste.-Adresse **42** 49 31N 0 5 E
Ste.-Agathe-des-Monts **150** 46 3N 74 17W
Ste. Anne **167** 14 26N 60 53W
Ste. Anne de Beaupré **151** 47 2N 70 58W
Ste. Anne de Portneuf **151** 48 38N 69 8W
Ste.-Anne-des-Monts **151** 49 8N 66 30W
Ste. Benoîte **43** 49 47N 3 30 E
Ste. Cecile **151** 47 56N 64 34W
Ste.-Croix **43** 46 49N 6 34W
Ste.-Enimie **44** 44 22N 3 26 E
Ste.-Foy-la-Grande **44** 44 50N 0 13 E
Ste. Genevieve **158** 37 59N 90 2W
Ste. Germaine **151** 46 24N 70 24W
Ste.-Hermine **44** 46 32N 1 4W
Ste.-Livrade-sur-Lot **44** 44 24N 0 36 E
Ste. Marguerite, R. **151** 50 9N 66 36W
Ste. Marie **167** 14 48N 61 1W
Ste.-Marie-aux-Mines **43** 48 10N 7 12 E
Ste. Marie, C. **129** 25 36 S 45 8 E
Ste. Marie de la Madeleine **151** 46 26N 71 0W
Ste. Marie, I. **129** 16 50 S 49 55 E
Ste.-Maure-de-Touraine **42** 47 7N 0 37 E
Ste.-Maxime **45** 43 19N 6 39 E
Ste.-Menehould **43** 49 5N 4 54 E
Ste.-Mère-Église **42** 49 24N 1 19W
Ste. Rose **167** 16 20N 61 45W
Ste. Rose du lac **153** 51 41N 99 30W
Ste. Teresa **172** 33 33 S 60 54W
Saintes **44** 45 45N 0 37W
Saintes, I. des **167** 15 50N 61 35W
Saintes-Maries-de-la-Mer **45** 43 26N 4 26 E
Saintes Maries, Les **45** 43 27N 4 25 E
Saintfield **38** 54 28N 5 50W
Saintonge **44** 45 40N 0 50W
Sairang **99** 23 50N 92 45 E
Sairecábur, Cerro **172** 22 43 S 67 54W
Saitama-ken □ **111** 36 25N 137 0 E
Saito **110** 32 3N 131 18 E
Sajama, Nevada **174** 18 0 S 68 55W
Sajan **66** 45 50N 20 58 E
Sajószentpéter **53** 48 12N 20 44 E
Sajum, mt. **95** 33 20N 79 0 E
Saka Ilkalat **93** 27 20N 64 7 E
Sakai **111** 34 30N 135 30 E
Sakaide **110** 34 15N 133 56 E
Sakaiminato **110** 35 38N 133 11 E
Sakaka **92** 30 0N 40 8 E
Sakami, L. **150** 53 15N 76 45W
Sâkâne, 'Erg i-n **118** 20 30N 1 30W
Sakania **127** 12 43 S 28 30 E
Sakar, I. **138** 5 30 S 148 0 E
Sakarya, R. **82** 40 5N 31 0 E
Sakata **112** 36 38N 138 19 E
Sakchu **107** 40 23N 125 2 E
Sakeny, R. **129** 20 0 S 45 25 E
Sakété **121** 6 40N 2 32 E
Sakhalin, Ostrov **77** 51 0N 143 0 E
Sakhi Gopal **96** 19 58N 85 50 E
Sakhnin **90** 32 52N 35 12 E
Saki **82** 45 16N 33 34 E
Sakiai **80** 54 59N 23 0 E
Sakmara **84** 52 0N 55 20 E
Sakmara, R. **84** 51 46N 55 1 E
Sakołow Małopolski **54** 50 10N 22 9 E
Sakon Nakhon **100** 17 10N 104 9 E
Sakrand **94** 26 10N 68 15 E
Sakri **96** 21 2N 74 40 E
Sakskøbing **73** 54 49N 11 39 E
Saku **111** 36 11N 138 31 E
Sakuma **111** 35 3N 137 56 E
Sakurai **111** 34 30N 135 51 E
Sakuru **111** 35 43N 140 14 E
Säkylä **75** 61 4N 22 20 E
Sal, R. **83** 47 25N 42 20 E
Sal'a **53** 48 10N 17 50 E
Sala **72** 59 58N 16 35 E
Sala Consilina **65** 40 23N 15 35 E
Sala-y-Gomez, I. **131** 26 28 S 105 28W
Salaberry-de-Valleyfield **150** 45 15N 74 8W
Salada, La **164** 24 30N 111 30W
Saladas **172** 28 15 S 58 40W
Saladillo **172** 35 40 S 59 55W
Salado, R., Buenos Aires, Argent. **172** 35 40 S 58 10W
Salado, R., Santa Fe, Argent. **172** 27 0 S 63 40W
Salado, R., Mexico **164** 26 52N 99 19W
Salaga **121** 8 31N 0 31W
Salala, Liberia **120** 6 42N 10 7W
Salala, Sudan **122** 21 17N 36 16 E
Salalah **91** 16 56N 53 59 E
Salama **90** 32 3N 34 48 E
Salamanca, Chile **172** 32 0 S 71 25W
Salamanca, Spain **56** 40 58N 5 39W
Salamanca, U.S.A. **156** 42 10N 78 42W
Salamanca □ **56** 40 57N 5 40W
Salamaua **138** 7 10 S 147 0 E
Salamina **174** 5 25N 75 29W
Sałamis **69** 37 56N 23 30 E
Salar de Atacama **176** 23 30 S 68 25W
Salar de Uyuni **174** 20 30 S 67 45W
Salard **70** 47 12N 22 3 E
Salas **56** 43 25N 6 15W
Salas de los Infantes **58** 42 2N 3 17W
Salavat **84** 53 21N 55 55 E
Salaverry **174** 8 15 S 79 0W
Salawe **126** 3 17 S 32 56 E
Salayar, I. **103** 6 15 S 120 30 E
Salazar, R. **58** 42 45N 1 8W
Salbohed **72** 59 55N 16 22 E
Salbris **43** 47 25N 2 3 E
Salcia **70** 43 56N 24 55 E
Salcombe **30** 50 14N 3 47W
Salcombe Regis **30** 50 41N 3 11W
Saldaña **56** 42 32N 4 48W
Saldanha **128** 33 0 S 17 58 E
Saldanhabaai **128** 33 6 S 18 0 E
Saldus **80** 56 45N 22 37 E
Sale **141** 38 6 S 147 6 E
Salé **118** 34 3N 6 48W
Sale **32** 53 26N 2 19W
Saléa-koïra **121** 16 54N 0 46W
Salebabu **103** 3 45N 125 55 E
Salehabad **93** 35 40N 61 2 E
Salekhard **76** 66 30N 66 25 E
Salem, India **97** 11 40N 78 11 E
Salem, Ind., U.S.A. **156** 38 38N 86 16W
Salem, Mass., U.S.A. **162** 42 29N 70 53W
Salem, Mo., U.S.A. **159** 37 40N 91 30W
Salem, N.H., U.S.A. **162** 42 47N 71 12W
Salem, N.J., U.S.A. **162** 39 34N 75 29W
Salem, N.Y., U.S.A. **162** 43 10N 73 20W
Salem, Ohio, U.S.A. **156** 40 52N 80 50W
Salem, Oreg., U.S.A. **160** 45 0N 123 0W
Salem, Va., U.S.A. **156** 37 19N 80 8W
Salembu, Kepulauan **102** 5 35 S 114 30 E
Salemi **64** 37 49N 12 47 E
Salen, Norway **75** 64 41N 11 27 E
Salen, Highland, U.K. **36** 56 42N 5 48W
Salen, Strathclyde, U.K. **34** 56 31N 5 57W
Salernes **45** 43 34N 6 15 E
Salerno **65** 40 40N 14 44 E
Salerno, G. di **65** 40 35N 14 45 E
Salfit **90** 32 5N 35 11 E
Salford **32** 53 30N 2 17W
Salford Priors **28** 52 10N 1 52W
Salgir, R. **82** 45 30N 34 30 E
Salgótarján **53** 48 5N 19 47 E
Salgueiro **170** 8 4 S 39 6W
Salies-de-Béarn **44** 43 28N 0 56W
Salima **125** 13 47 S 34 28 E
Salin **98** 20 35N 94 40 E
Salina **158** 38 50N 97 40W
Salina Cruz **165** 16 10N 95 10W
Salina, I. **65** 38 35N 14 50 E
Salina, La **174** 10 22N 71 27W
Salinas, Brazil **171** 16 20 S 42 10W
Salinas, Chile **172** 23 31 S 69 29W
Salinas, Ecuador **174** 2 10 S 80 50W
Salinas, Mexico **164** 23 37N 106 8W
Salinas, U.S.A. **163** 36 40N 121 31W
Salinas Ambargasta **172** 29 0 S 65 30W
Salinas, B. de **166** 11 4N 85 45W
Salinas, Cabo de **59** 39 16N 3 4 E
Salinas (de Hidalgo) **164** 22 30N 101 40W
Salinas Grandes **172** 30 0 S 65 0W
Salinas, Pampa de las **172** 31 58 S 66 42W
Salinas, R., Mexico **165** 16 28N 90 31W
Salinas, R., U.S.A. **163** 36 45N 121 48W
Saline, R. **158** 39 10N 99 5W
Salines-les-Bains **43** 46 58N 5 52 E
Salinópolis **170** 0 40 S 47 20W
Salir **57** 37 14N 8 2W
Salisbury, Austral. **140** 34 46 S 138 40 E
*Salisbury, Zimb. **127** 17 50 S 31 2 E
Salisbury, U.K. **28** 51 4N 1 48W
Salisbury, Md., U.S.A. **162** 38 20N 75 38W
Salisbury, N.C., U.S.A. **157** 35 42N 80 29W
Salisbury Plain **28** 51 13N 1 50W
Salitre, R. **170** 9 29 S 40 39W
Salka **121** 10 20N 4 58 E
Salle, La **158** 41 20N 89 5W
Sallent **58** 41 49N 1 54 E
Salles-Curan **44** 44 11N 2 48 E
Salling **73** 56 40N 8 55 E
Sallisaw **159** 35 26N 94 45W
Sallom Junc. **122** 19 23N 37 6 E
Sally Gap, Mt. **39** 53 7N 6 18W
Salmerón **58** 40 33N 2 29W
Salmo **152** 49 10N 117 20W
Salmon **160** 45 12N 113 56W
Salmon Arm **152** 50 40N 119 15W
Salmon Falls **160** 42 55N 114 59W
Salmon Gums **137** 32 59 S 121 38 E
Salmon, R., Can. **152** 54 3N 122 40W
Salmon, R., U.S.A. **160** 46 0N 116 30W
Salmon Res. **151** 48 05N 56 00W
Salmon River Mts. **160** 45 0N 114 30W
Salo **75** 60 22N 23 3 E
Salò **62** 45 37N 10 32 E
Salobreña **57** 36 44N 3 35W
Salome **161** 33 51N 113 37W
Salon-de-Provence **45** 43 39N 5 6 E
Salonica = Thessaloníki **68** 40 38N 22 58 E
Salonta **70** 46 49N 21 42 E
Salop □ **28** 52 36N 2 45W
Salor, R. **57** 39 39N 7 3W
Salou, Cabo **58** 41 3N 1 10 E
Salsacate **172** 31 20 S 65 5W
Salsaker **72** 62 59N 18 20 E
Salses **44** 42 50N 2 55 E
Salsette I. **96** 19 5N 72 50 E
Salsk **83** 46 28N 41 30 E
Salso, R. **65** 37 6N 13 55 E
Salsomaggiore **62** 44 48N 9 59 E
Salt **90** 32 2N 35 43 E
Salt Creek **140** 36 8 S 139 38 E
Salt Creek Telegraph Office **139** 36 0 S 139 35 E
Salt Fork R. **159** 37 25N 98 40W
Salt Lake City **160** 40 45N 111 58W
Salt, R., Can. **152** 60 0N 112 25W
Salt, R., U.S.A. **161** 33 50N 110 25W
Salt Range **94** 32 30N 72 25 E
Salta **172** 24 47 S 65 25W
Salta □ **172** 24 48 S 65 30W
Saltash **30** 50 25N 4 13W
Saltburn by Sea **33** 54 35N 0 58W
Saltcoats **34** 55 38N 4 47W
Saltee Is. **39** 52 7N 6 37W
Saltergate **33** 54 20N 0 40W
Saltfjorden **74** 67 15N 14 20 E
Saltfleet **33** 53 25N 0 11 E
Saltfleetby **33** 53 23N 0 10 E
Salthill **39** 53 15N 9 6W
Saltholm **73** 55 38N 12 43 E
Salthólmavík **74** 65 24N 21 57W
Saltillo **164** 25 30N 100 57W
Salto, Argent. **172** 34 20 S 60 15W
Salto, Uruguay **172** 31 20 S 57 59W
Salto □ **172** 31 20 S 57 59W
Salto Augusto, falls **172** 8 30 S 58 0W
Salto da Divisa **171** 16 0 S 39 57W
Salton City **163** 33 21N 115 59W
Salton Sea **163** 33 20N 115 50W
Saltpond **121** 5 15N 1 3W
Saltsjöbaden **73** 59 15N 18 20 E
Saltspring **152** 48 54N 123 37W
Saltwood **29** 51 4N 1 5 E
Saluda **162** 37 36N 76 36W
Salula, R. **157** 34 12N 81 45W
Salûm **122** 31 31N 25 7 E
Salûm, Khâlig el **122** 31 30N 25 9 E
Salur **96** 18 27N 83 18 E
Saluzzo **62** 44 39N 7 29 E
Salvador, Brazil **171** 13 0 S 38 30W
Salvador, Can. **153** 52 10N 109 25W
Salvador ■ **164** 13 50N 89 0W
Salvador, L. **159** 29 46N 90 16W
Salvaterra **170** 0 46 S 48 31W
Salvaterra de Magos **57** 39 1N 8 47W
Sálvora, Isla **56** 42 30N 8 58W
Salwa **93** 24 45N 50 55 E
Salween, R. **98** 16 31N 97 37 E
Salza, R. **52** 47 43N 15 0 E
Salzach, R. **52** 47 15N 12 25 E
Salzburg **52** 47 48N 13 2 E
Salzgitter **48** 52 2N 10 22 E
Salzwedel **48** 52 50N 11 11 E
Sam Neua **100** 20 29N 104 0 E
Sam Ngao **100** 17 18N 99 0 E

*Renamed Harare

Sam Rayburn Res **San Quintín**

Sam Rayburn Res. **159** 31 15N 94 20W
Sam Son **100** 19 44N 105 54 E
Sam Ten **100** 19 59N 104 38 E
Sama **84** 60 12N 60 22 E
Sama de Langreo **56** 43 18N 5 40W
Samales Group **103** 6 0N 122 0 E
Samalkot **96** 17 3N 82 13 E
Samâlût **122** 28 20N 30 42 E
Samana **94** 30 10N 76 13 E
Samana Cay **167** 23 3N 73 45W
Samanco **174** 9 10S 78 30W
Samanga **127** 8 20S 39 13 E
Samangan **93** 36 15N 67 40 E
Samangwa **126** 4 23S 24 10 E
Samani **112** 42 7N 142 56 E
Samar, I. **103** 12 0N 125 0 E
Samara, R. **84** 53 10N 50 4 E
Samaria **135** 10 39S 150 41 E
Samaria = Shomron **90** 32 15N 35 13 E
Samarkand **85** 39 40N 67 0 E
Samarra **92** 34 16N 43 55 E
Samastipur **95** 25 50N 85 50 E
Samatan **44** 43 29N 0 55 E
Samba, Kashmir **95** 32 32N 75 10 E
Samba, Zaïre **126** 4 38S 26 22 E
Sambaíba **170** 7 8S 45 21W
Sambaina **129** 19 37S 47 8 E
Sambaise **65** 38 58N 16 16 E
Sambalpur **96** 21 28N 83 58 E
Sambas, S. **102** 1 20N 109 20 E
Sambava **129** 14 16S 50 10 E
Sambawizi **127** 18 24S 26 13 E
Sambhal **95** 28 35N 78 37 E
Sambhar **94** 26 52N 75 10 E
Sambonifacio **62** 45 24N 11 16 E
Sambor, Camb. **100** 12 46N 106 0 E
Sambor, U.S.S.R. **80** 49 30N 23 10 E
Sambre, R. **47** 50 27N 4 52 E
Sambuca **64** 37 39N 13 6 E
Samburu □ **126** 1 10N 37 0 E
Sambusu **128** 17 55S 19 21 E
Samchök **107** 37 30N 129 10 E
Samchonpo **107** 34 54N 128 6 E
Same **126** 4 2S 37 38 E
Samedan **51** 46 32N 9 52 E
Samer **43** 50 38N 1 44 E
Samfya **127** 11 16S 29 31 E
Sámi **69** 38 15N 20 39 E
Samna **122** 25 12N 37 17 E
Samnager **71** 60 23N 5 39 E
Samnaun **51** 46 57N 10 22 E
Samnu **119** 27 15N 14 55 E
Samo Alto **172** 30 22S 71 0W
Samoan Is. **10** 14 0S 171 0W
Samobor **63** 45 47N 15 44 E
Samoëns **45** 46 5N 6 45 E
Samoorombón, Bahía **172** 36 5S 57 20W
Samorogouan **120** 11 21N 4 57W
Samos **56** 42 44N 7 20W
Samoš **66** 45 13N 20 49 E
Sámos, I. **69** 37 45N 26 50 E
Samosir, P. **102** 2 35N 98 50 E
Samothráki **68** 40 28N 25 38 E
Samothráki, I. **68** 40 25N 25 40 E
Sampa **120** 8 0N 2 36W
Sampacho **172** 33 20S 64 50W
Sampang **103** 7 11S 113 13 E
Samper de Calanda **58** 41 11N 0 42W
Sampford Courtenay **30** 50 47N 3 58W
Sampit **102** 2 20S 113 0 E
Samra **92** 25 35N 41 0 E
Samreboi **120** 5 34N 7 28 E
Samrée **47** 50 13N 5 39 E
Samrong, Camb. **100** 14 15N 103 30 E
Samrong, Thai. **100** 15 10N 100 40 E
Samsø **73** 55 50N 10 35 E
Samsø Bælt **73** 55 45N 10 45 E
Samsonovo **85** 37 53N 65 15 E
Samsun **92** 41 15N 36 15 E
Samsun Daği **69** 37 45N 27 10 E
Samtredia **83** 42 7N 42 24 E
Samui, Ko **101** 9 30N 100 0 E
Samur, R. **83** 41 30N 48 0 E
Samusole **127** 10 2S 24 0 E
Samut Prakan **100** 13 32N 100 40 E
Samut Sakhon **100** 13 31N 100 20 E
Samut Songkhram (Mekong) **100** 13 24N 100 1 E
Samwari **94** 28 5N 66 46 E
Samyo La **99** 29 55N 84 46 E
San **120** 13 15N 4 45W
San Adrián, C. de **56** 43 21N 8 50W
San Adrián, G. de **56** 43 21N 8 50W
San Agustín **174** 1 53N 76 16W
San Agustin, C. **103** 6 20N 126 13 E
San Agustín de Valle Fértil **172** 30 35S 67 30W
San Ambrosio, I. **131** 26 35S 79 30W
San Andreas **163** 38 17N 120 39W
San Andrés, I. de **166** 12 42N 81 46W
San Andres Mts. **161** 33 0N 106 45W
San Andrés Tuxtla **165** 18 30N 95 20W
San Angelo **159** 31 30N 100 30W
San Anselmo **163** 37 49N 122 34W
San Antonio, Belize **165** 16 15N 89 2W
San Antonio, Chile **172** 33 40S 71 40W
San Antonio, N. Mex., U.S.A. **161** 33 58N 106 57W
San Antonio, Tex., U.S.A. **159** 29 30N 98 30W
San Antonio, Venez. **174** 3 30N 66 44W
San Antonio Abad **59** 38 59N 1 19 E
San Antonio, C., Argent. **172** 36 15S 56 40W
San Antonio, C., Cuba **166** 21 50N 84 57W
San Antonio, C. de **59** 38 48N 0 12 E
San Antonio de Caparo **174** 7 35N 71 27W
San Antonio de los Baños **166** 22 54N 82 31W
San Antonio de los Cobres **172** 24 16S 66 2W
San Antonio do Zaire **124** 6 8S 12 11 E
San Antonio, Mt. (Old Baldy Pk.) **163** 34 17N 117 38W
San Antonio Oeste **176** 40 40S 65 0W
San Antonio, R. **159** 28 30N 97 14W
San Ardo **163** 36 1N 120 54W
San Bartolomeo in Galdo **65** 41 23N 15 2 E
San Benedetto **62** 45 2N 10 57 E
San Benedetto del Tronto **63** 42 57N 13 52 E
San Benedicto, I. **164** 19 18N 110 49W
San Benito **159** 26 5N 97 32W
San Benito Mtn. **163** 36 22N 120 37W
San Benito, R. **163** 36 53N 121 50W
San Bernardino **163** 34 7N 117 18W
San Bernardino, Paso del **51** 46 28N 9 11 E
San Bernardo **172** 33 40S 70 50W
San Bernardo, I. de **174** 9 45N 75 50W
San Blas **164** 26 10N 108 40W
San Blas, C. **157** 29 40N 85 25W
San Blas, Cord. de **166** 9 15N 78 30W
San Borja **174** 15 0S 67 12W
San Buenaventura **164** 27 5N 101 32W
San Buenaventura = Ventura **163** 34 17N 119 18W
San Carlos, Argent. **172** 33 50S 69 0W
San Carlos, Mexico **164** 29 0N 101 10W
San Carlos, Nic. **166** 11 12N 84 50W
San Carlos, Phil. **103** 10 29N 123 25 E
San Carlos, Uruguay **173** 34 46S 54 58W
San Carlos, U.S.A. **161** 33 24N 110 27W
San Carlos, Amazonas, Venez. **174** 1 55N 67 4W
San Carlos, Cojedes, Venez. **174** 9 40N 68 36W
San Carlos de Bariloche **176** 41 10S 71 25W
San Carlos de la Rápita **58** 40 37N 0 35 E
San Carlos del Zulia **174** 9 1N 71 55W
San Carlos L. **161** 33 20N 110 10W
San Carlos = Butuku-Luba **121** 3 29N 8 33 E
San Cataldo **64** 37 30N 13 58 E
San Celoni **58** 41 42N 2 30 E
San Clemente, Chile **172** 35 30S 71 39W
San Clemente, Spain **59** 39 24N 2 25W
San Clemente, U.S.A. **163** 33 29N 117 45W
San Clemente I. **163** 32 53N 118 30W
San Constanzo **63** 43 46N 13 5 E
San Cristóbal, Argent. **172** 30 20S 61 10W
San Cristóbal, Dom. Rep. **167** 18 25N 70 6W
San Cristóbal, Venez. **174** 7 46N 72 14W
San Cristóbal de las Casas **165** 16 50N 92 33W
San Damiano d'Asti **62** 44 51N 8 4 E
San Daniel del Friuli **63** 46 10N 13 0 E
San Demétrio Corone **65** 39 34N 16 22 E
San Diego, Calif., U.S.A. **163** 32 43N 117 10W
San Diego, Tex., U.S.A. **159** 27 47N 98 15W
San Diego, C. **176** 54 40S 65 10W
San Diego de la Unión **164** 21 28N 100 52W
San Donà di Piave **63** 45 38N 12 34 E
San Elpídio a Mare **63** 43 16N 13 41 E
San Estanislao **172** 24 39S 56 26W
San Esteban de Gormaz **58** 41 34N 3 13W
San Felice sul Panaro **62** 44 51N 11 9 E
San Felipe, Chile **172** 32 43S 70 50W
San Felipe, Mexico **164** 31 0N 114 52W
San Felipe, Venez. **174** 10 20N 68 44W
San Felipe, R. **163** 33 12N 115 49W
San Feliu de Guixols **58** 41 45N 3 1 E
San Feliu de Llobregat **58** 41 23N 2 2 E
San Félix **174** 8 20N 62 35W
San Felix, I. **131** 26 30S 80 0W
San Fernando, Chile **172** 34 30S 71 0W
San Fernando, Mexico **164** 30 0N 115 10W
San Fernando, Luzon, Phil. **103** 15 5N 120 37 E
San Fernando, Luzon, Phil. **103** 16 40N 120 23 E
San Fernando, Spain **57** 36 22N 6 17W
San Fernando, Trin **167** 10 20N 61 30W
San Fernando, U.S.A. **163** 34 15N 118 29W
San Fernando de Apure **174** 7 54N 67 28W
San Fernando de Atabapo **174** 4 3N 67 42W
San Fernando di Puglia **65** 41 18N 16 5 E
San Fernando, R. **164** 25 0N 99 0W
San Francisco, Córdoba, Argent. **172** 31 30S 62 5W
San Francisco, San Luis, Argent. **172** 32 45S 66 10W
San Francisco, U.S.A. **163** 37 47N 122 30W
San Francisco de Macorís **167** 19 19N 70 15W
San Francisco del Monte de Oro **172** 32 36S 66 8W
San Francisco del Oro **164** 26 52N 105 50W
San Francisco Javier **59** 38 40N 1 25 E
San Francisco, Paso de **172** 35 40S 70 24W
San Francisco, R. **161** 33 30N 109 0W
San Francisco Solano, Pta. **174** 6 18N 77 29W
San Francisville **159** 30 48N 91 22W
San Fratello **65** 38 1N 14 33 E
San Gabriel **174** 0 36N 77 49W
San Gavino Monreale **64** 39 33N 8 47 E
San German **147** 18 5N 67 3W
San Gil **174** 6 33N 73 8W
San Gimignano **62** 43 28N 11 3 E
San Giórgio di Nogaro **63** 45 50N 13 13 E
San Giórgio Iónico **65** 40 27N 17 23 E
San Giovanni Bianco **62** 45 52N 9 40 E
San Giovanni in Fiore **65** 39 16N 16 42 E
San Giovanni in Persiceto **63** 44 39N 11 12 E
San Giovanni Rotondo **65** 41 41N 15 42 E
San Giovanni Valdarno **63** 43 32N 11 30 E
San Giuliano Terme **62** 43 45N 10 26 E
San Gorgonio Mtn. **163** 34 7N 116 51W
San Gottardo, Paso del **51** 46 33N 8 33 E
San Gregorio, Uruguay **173** 32 37S 55 40W
San Gregorio, U.S.A. **163** 37 20N 122 23W
San Guiseppe Iato **64** 37 37N 13 11 E
San Ignacio, Boliv. **174** 16 20S 60 55W
San Ignacio, Mexico **164** 27 27N 112 51W
San Ignacio, Parag. **172** 26 52S 57 3W
San Ignacio, Laguna **164** 26 50N 113 11W
San Ildefonso, C. **103** 16 0N 122 10 E
San Isidro **172** 34 29S 58 31W
San Jacinto, Colomb. **174** 9 50N 75 8W
San Jacinto, U.S.A. **163** 33 47N 116 57W
San Javier, Misiones, Argent. **173** 27 55S 55 5W
San Javier, Santa Fe, Argent. **172** 30 40S 59 55W
San Javier, Boliv. **174** 16 18S 62 30W
San Javier, Chile **172** 35 40S 71 45W
San Javier, Spain **59** 37 49N 0 50W
San Jerónimo, Sa. de **174** 8 0N 75 50W
San Joaquin **163** 36 36N 120 11W
San Joaquín **174** 10 16N 67 47W
San Joaquin R. **163** 38 4N 121 51W
San Joaquin Valley **163** 37 0N 120 30W
San Jorge **172** 31 54S 61 50W
San Jorge, Bahía de **164** 31 20N 113 20W
San Jorge, Golfo de **176** 46 0S 66 0W
San Jorge, G. de **58** 40 50N 0 55W
San José, Boliv. **174** 17 45S 60 50W
San José, C. Rica **166** 10 0N 84 2W
San José, Guat. **164** 14 0N 90 50W
San José, Luzon, Phil. **103** 15 45N 120 55 E
San José, Mindoro, Phil. **103** 10 50N 122 5 E
San José, Spain **59** 38 55N 1 18 E
San Jose, Calif., U.S.A. **163** 37 20N 121 53W
San Jose, N. Mex., U.S.A. **159** 35 26N 105 30W
San José Carpizo **165** 19 26N 90 32W
San José de Feliciano **172** 30 26S 58 46W
San José de Jáchal **172** 30 5S 69 0W
San José de Mayo **172** 34 27S 56 27W
San José de Ocuné **174** 4 15N 70 20W
San José del Cabo **164** 23 0N 109 50W
San José del Guaviare **174** 2 35N 72 38W
San José, I. **164** 25 0N 110 50W
San Juan, Argent. **172** 31 30S 68 30W
San Juan, Antioquía, Colomb. **174** 8 46N 76 32W
San Juan, Meta, Colomb. **174** 3 26N 73 50W
San Juan, Dom. Rep. **147** 18 49N 71 12W
San Juan, Coahuila, Mexico **164** 29 34N 101 53W
San Juan, Jalisco, Mexico **164** 21 20N 102 50W
San Juan, Querétaro, Mexico **164** 20 25N 100 0W
San Juan, Phil. **103** 8 35N 126 20 E
San Juan, Pto Rico **147** 18 28N 66 37W
San Juan □ **172** 31 9S 69 0W
San Juan Bautista, Parag. **172** 26 37S 57 6W
San Juan Bautista, Spain **59** 39 5N 1 31 E
San Juan Bautista, U.S.A. **163** 36 51N 121 32W
San Juan, C. **147** 18 23N 65 37W
San Juan Capistrano **163** 33 29N 117 40W
San Juan de Guadalupe **164** 24 38N 102 44W
San Juan de los Cayos **174** 11 10N 68 25W
San Juan de los Morros **174** 9 55N 67 21W
San Juan de Norte, B. de **166** 11 30N 83 40W
San Juan del Norte **166** 10 58N 83 40W
San Juan del Puerto **57** 37 20N 6 50W
San Juan del Río **165** 24 47N 104 27W
San Juan del Sur **166** 11 20N 86 0W
San Juan Mts. **161** 38 30N 108 30W
San Juan, Presa de **164** 17 45N 95 15W
San Juan, R., Argent. **172** 32 20S 67 25W
San Juan, R., Colomb. **174** 4 0N 77 20W
San Juan, R., Nic. **166** 11 0N 84 30W
San Juan, R., Calif., U.S.A. **163** 36 14N 121 9W
San Juan, R., Utah, U.S.A. **161** 37 20N 110 20W
San Julián **176** 49 15S 68 0W
San Just, Sierra de **58** 40 45N 0 41W
San Justo **172** 30 55S 60 30W
San Kamphaeng **100** 18 45N 99 8 E
San Lázaro, C. **164** 24 50N 112 18W
San Lázaro, Sa. de **164** 23 25N 110 0W
San Leandro **163** 37 40N 122 6W
San Leonardo **58** 41 51N 3 5W
San Lorenzo, Argent. **172** 32 45S 60 45W
San Lorenzo, Ecuador **174** 1 15N 78 50W
San Lorenzo, Parag. **172** 25 20S 57 32W
San Lorenzo, Venez. **174** 9 47N 71 4W
San Lorenzo de la Parilla **58** 39 51N 2 22W
San Lorenzo de Morunys **58** 42 8N 1 35 E
San Lorenzo, I., Mexico **164** 28 35N 112 50W
San Lorenzo, I., Peru **174** 12 20S 77 35W
San Lorenzo, Mt. **176** 47 40S 72 20W
San Lorenzo, R. **164** 24 15N 107 24W
San Lucas, Boliv. **174** 20 5S 65 0W
San Lucas, Baja California S., Mexico **164** 27 10N 112 14W
San Lucas, Baja California S., Mexico **164** 22 53N 109 54W
San Lucas, U.S.A. **163** 36 8N 121 1W
San Lucas, C. de **164** 22 50N 110 0W
San Lucido **65** 39 18N 16 3 E
San Luis, Argent. **172** 33 20S 66 20W
San Luis, Cuba **166** 22 17N 83 46W
San Luis, Guat. **166** 16 14N 89 27W
San Luis, U.S.A. **161** 37 14N 105 26W
San Luis, Venez. **174** 11 7N 69 42W
San Luis □ **172** 34 0S 66 0W
San Luis de la Loma **164** 17 18N 100 55W
San Luis de la Paz **164** 21 19N 100 32W
San Luis de Potosí **164** 22 9N 100 59W
San Luis de Potosí □ **164** 22 10N 101 0W
San Luis, I. **164** 29 58N 114 26W
San Luis Obispo **161** 35 21N 120 38W
San Luis Res. **163** 37 4N 121 5W
San Luis Río Colorado **164** 32 29N 114 48W
San Luis, Sierra de **172** 37 25N 66 10W
San Marco Argentano **65** 39 34N 16 8 E
San Marco dei Cavoti **65** 41 20N 14 50 E
San Marco in Lámis **65** 41 43N 15 38 E
San Marcos, Guat. **166** 14 59N 91 52W
San Marcos, U.S.A. **159** 29 53N 98 0W
San Marcos, I. **164** 27 13N 112 6W
San Marino **63** 43 56N 12 25 E
San Marino ■ **63** 43 56N 12 25 E
San Martín, Argent. **172** 33 5S 68 28W
San Martín, Colomb. **174** 3 42N 73 42W
San Martín de Valdeiglesias **56** 40 21N 4 24W
San Martín, L. **176** 48 50S 72 50W
San Martino de Calvi **62** 45 57N 9 41 E
San Mateo, Spain **58** 40 28N 0 10 E
San Mateo, U.S.A. **163** 37 32N 122 19W
San Matías **174** 16 25S 58 20W
San Matías, Golfo de **176** 41 30S 64 0W
San Miguel, El Sal. **166** 13 30N 88 12W
San Miguel, Panama **166** 8 27N 78 55W
San Miguel, Spain **59** 39 3N 1 26 E
San Miguel, U.S.A. **163** 35 45N 120 42W
San Miguel, Venez. **174** 9 40N 65 11W
San Miguel de Salinas **59** 37 59N 0 47W
San Miguel de Tucumán **172** 26 50S 65 20W
San Miguel del Monte **172** 35 23S 58 50W
San Miguel I. **163** 34 2N 120 23W
San Miguel, R., Boliv. **174** 16 0S 62 45W
San Miguel, R., Ecuador/Ecuador **174** 0 25N 76 30W
San Miniato **62** 43 40N 10 50 E
San Narcisco **103** 15 2N 120 3 E
San Nicolás de los Arroyas **172** 33 17S 60 10W
San Nicolas I. **154** 33 16N 119 30W
San Onafre **163** 33 22N 117 34W
San Onofre **174** 9 44N 75 32W
San Pablo, Boliv. **172** 21 43S 66 38W
San Pablo, Colomb. **174** 5 27N 70 56W
San Paolo di Civitate **65** 41 44N 15 16 E
San Pedro, Buenos Aires, Argent. **173** 33 43S 59 45W
San Pedro, Jujuy, Argent. **172** 24 12S 64 55W
San Pedro, Chile **172** 21 58S 68 30W
San Pedro, Colomb. **174** 4 56N 71 53W
San Pedro, Dom. Rep. **167** 18 30N 69 18W
San Pedro, Ivory C. **120** 4 50N 6 33W
San Pedro, Mexico **164** 23 55N 110 17W
San Pedro □ **172** 24 0S 57 0W
San Pedro Channel **163** 33 35N 118 25W
San Pedro de Arimena **174** 4 37N 71 42W
San Pedro de Atacama **172** 22 55S 68 15W
San Pedro de Jujuy **172** 24 12S 64 55W
San Pedro de las Colonias **164** 25 50N 102 59W
San Pedro de Lloc **174** 7 15S 79 28W
San Pedro del Norte **166** 13 4N 84 33W
San Pedro del Paraná **172** 26 43S 56 13W
San Pedro del Pinatar **59** 37 50N 0 50W
San Pedro Mártir, Sierra **164** 31 0N 115 30W
San Pedro Mixtepec **165** 16 2N 97 0W
San Pedro Ocampo = Melchor Ocampo **164** 24 52N 101 40W
San Pedro, Pta. **172** 25 30S 70 38W
San Pedro, R., Chihuahua, Mexico **164** 28 20N 106 10W
San Pedro, R., Michoacan, Mexico **164** 19 23N 103 51W
San Pedro, R., Nayarit, Mexico **164** 21 45N 105 30W
San Pedro, R., U.S.A. **161** 32 45N 110 35W
San Pedro, Sierra de **57** 39 18N 6 40W
San Pedro Sula **166** 15 30N 88 0W
San Pedro Tututepec **165** 16 9N 97 38W
San Pedro,Pta. **172** 25 30S 70 38W
San Pietro, I. **64** 39 9N 8 17 E
San Pietro Vernotico **65** 40 28N 18 0 E
San Quintín, Mexico **164** 30 29N 115 57W

San Quintín Santiago

San Quintín, Phil. **103** 16 1N 120 56 E
San, R. **54** 50 25N 22 20 E
San Rafael, Argent. **172** 34 40 S 68 30W
San Rafael, Colomb. **174** 6 2N 69 45W
San Rafael, Calif., U.S.A. **163** 38 0N 122 32W
San Rafael, N. Mex., U.S.A. **161** 35 6N 107 58W
San Rafael, Venez. **174** 10 42N 71 46W
San Rafael Mtn. **163** 34 41N 119 52W
San Ramón de la Nueva Orán **172** 23 10 S 64 20W
San Remo **62** 43 48N 7 47 E
San Román, C. **174** 12 12N 70 0W
San Roque, Argent. **172** 28 15 S 58 45W
San Roque, Spain **57** 36 17N 5 21W
San Rosendo **172** 37 10 S 72 50W
San Saba **159** 31 12N 98 45W
San Salvador **166** 13 40N 89 20W
San Salvador de Jujuy **172** 23 30 S 65 40W
San Salvador (Watlings) I. **167** 24 0N 74 40W
San Sebastián, Argent. **176** 53 10 S 68 30W
San Sebastián, Spain **58** 43 17N 1 58W
San Sebastián, Venez. **174** 9 57N 67 11W
San Serverino **63** 43 13N 13 10 E
San Severo **63** 41 41N 15 23 E
San Simeon **163** 35 39N 121 11W
San Simon **161** 32 14N 109 16W
San Stéfano di Cadore **63** 46 34N 12 33 E
San Telmo **164** 30 58N 116 6W
San Tiburcio **164** 24 8N 101 32W
San Valentin, Mte. **176** 46 30 S 73 30W
San Vicente de Alcántara **57** 39 22N 7 8W
San Vicente de la Barquera **56** 43 30N 4 29W
San Vicente del Caguán **174** 2 7N 74 46W
San Vicenzo **93** 43 9N 10 32 E
San Vito al Tagliamento **63** 45 55N 12 50 E
San Vito, C. **64** 38 11N 12 41 E
San Vito Chietino **63** 42 19N 14 27 E
San Vito dei Normanni **65** 40 40N 17 40 E
San Yanaro **174** 2 47N 69 42W
San Ygnacio **159** 27 6N 92 24W
San Ysidro **161** 32 33N 117 5W
San'a **91** 15 27N 44 12 E
Sana, R. **63** 44 40N 16 43 E
Sanaba **120** 12 25N 3 47W
Sanabria, La **56** 42 0N 6 30W
Sanâfir **122** 27 49N 34 37 E
Sanaga, R. **121** 3 35N 9 38 E
Sanak I **147** 53 30N 162 30W
Sanaloa, Presa **164** 24 50N 107 20W
Sanana **103** 2 5 S 125 50 E
Sanand **94** 22 59N 72 25 E
Sanandaj **92** 35 25N 47 7 E
Sanandita **172** 21 40 S 63 35W
Sanary **45** 43 7N 5 48 E
Sanawad **94** 22 11N 76 5 E
Sanbe-San **110** 35 6N 132 38 E
Sancergues **43** 47 10N 2 54 E
Sancerre **43** 47 20N 2 50 E
Sanch'a Ho **108** 26 55N 106 6 E
Sanch'aho **107** 44 59N 126 1 E
Sánchez **167** 19 15N 69 36W
Sanchiang **108** 25 22N 109 26 E
Sanchor **94** 24 52N 71 49 E
Sanco, Pt. **103** 8 15N 126 24 E
Sancoins **43** 46 47N 2 55 E
Sancti-Spíritus **166** 21 52N 79 33W
Sand Lake **150** 47 46N 84 31W
Sand Point **147** 55 20N 160 32W
Sand, R. **129** 22 25 S 30 5 E
Sand Springs **159** 36 12N 96 5W
Sanda **111** 34 53N 135 14 E
Sanda I. **34** 55 17N 5 35W
Sandah **122** 20 35N 39 32 E
Sandakan **102** 5 53N 118 10 E
Sandalwood **140** 34 55 S 140 9 E
Sandan **101** 12 46N 106 0 E
Sandanski **67** 41 35N 23 16 E
Sandaré **120** 14 40N 10 15W
Sanday I. **36** 57 2N 6 30W
Sanday, I. **37** 59 15N 2 30W
Sanday Sd. **37** 59 11N 2 31W
Sandbach **32** 53 9N 2 23W
Sandbank **34** 55 58N 4 57W
Sande, Möre og Romsdal, Norway **71** 62 15N 5 27 E
Sande, Sogn og Fjordane, Norway **71** 61 20N 5 47 E
Sandefjord **71** 59 10N 10 15 E
Sandeid **71** 59 33N 5 52 E
Sanders **161** 35 12N 109 25W
Sanderson **159** 30 5N 102 30W
Sanderston **140** 34 46 S 139 15 E
Sandfell **74** 63 57N 16 48W
Sandfly L. **153** 55 43N 106 6W
Sandgate, Austral. **139** 27 18 S 153 3 E
Sandgate, U.K. **29** 51 5N 1 9 E
Sandhammaren, C. **73** 55 23N 14 14 E
Sandhead **34** 54 48N 4 58W
Sandhurst **29** 51 21N 0 48W
Sandía **174** 14 10 S 69 30W
Sandikli **92** 38 30N 30 20 E
Sandiman, Mt. **137** 24 21 S 115 20 E
Sandnes **71** 58 50N 5 45 E
Sandness **37** 60 18N 1 38W
Sandoa **124** 9 48 S 23 0 E
Sandomierz **54** 50 40N 21 43 E
Sandona **174** 1 17N 77 28W
Sandover, R. **138** 21 43 S 136 32 E
Sandoway **99** 18 20N 94 30 E
Sandown **28** 50 39N 1 9W
Sandpoint **160** 48 20N 116 40W
Sandray, I. **36** 56 53N 7 30W
Sandringham **29** 52 50N 0 30 E
Sandslån **72** 63 2N 17 49 E
Sandspit **152** 53 14N 131 49W
Sandston **162** 37 31N 77 19W
Sandstone **137** 27 59 S 119 16 E
Sandusky, Mich., U.S.A. **150** 43 26N 82 50W
Sandusky, Ohio, U.S.A. **156** 41 25N 82 40W
Sandveld **128** 32 0 S 18 15 E
Sandvig, Denmark **73** 55 18N 14 48 E
Sandvig, Sweden **72** 55 32N 14 47 E
Sandvika **71** 59 54N 10 29 E
Sandviken **72** 60 38N 16 46 E
Sandwich **29** 51 16N 1 21 E
Sandwich B., Can. **151** 53 40N 57 15W
Sandwich B., S. Afr. **128** 23 25 S 14 20 E
Sandwich, C. **138** 18 14 S 146 18 E
Sandwich Group **13** 57 0 S 27 0W
Sandwip Chan. **99** 22 35N 91 35 E
Sandy **29** 53 8N 0 18W
Sandy Bight **137** 33 50 S 123 20 E
Sandy C., Queens., Austral. **139** 24 42 S 153 15 E
Sandy C., Tas., Austral. **138** 41 25 S 144 45 E
Sandy Cay **167** 23 13N 75 18W
Sandy Cr. **160** 42 20N 109 30W
Sandy L. **150** 53 2N 93 0W
Sandy Lake **150** 53 0N 93 15W
Sandy Narrows **153** 55 5N 103 4W
Sanford, Fla., U.S.A. **157** 28 45N 81 20W
Sanford, Me., U.S.A. **162** 43 28N 70 47W
Sanford, N.C., U.S.A. **157** 35 30N 79 10W
Sanford, Mt. **136** 16 58 S 130 32 E
Sanford Mt. **148** 62 30N 143 0W
Sanford, R. **137** 27 22 S 115 53 E
Sang-i-Masha **94** 33 16N 67 5 E
Sanga **127** 12 22 S 35 21 E
Sanga, R. **124** 1 0N 16 30 E
Sanga Tolon **77** 61 50N 149 40 E
Sangamner **96** 19 30N 74 15 E
Sangar, Afghan. **94** 32 56N 65 30 E
Sangar, U.S.S.R. **77** 63 55N 127 31 E
Sangar Sarcai **94** 34 27N 70 35 E
Sangasanga **102** 0 29 S 117 13 E
Sangchen La **99** 31 30N 84 40 E
Sangchih **109** 29 25N 109 30 E
Sange **126** 6 58 S 84 40 E
Sangeang, I. **103** 8 12 S 119 6 E
Sanger **163** 36 47N 119 35W
Sangerhausen **48** 51 28N 11 18 E
Sanggau **102** 0 5N 110 30 E
Sangihe, Kep. **103** 3 0N 126 0 E
Sangihe, P. **103** 3 45N 125 30 E
Sangju **107** 36 25N 128 10 E
Sangkan Ho **106** 40 24N 115 19 E
Sangkapura **102** 5 52 S 112 40 E
Sangkhla **100** 15 7N 98 28 E
Sangli **96** 16 55N 74 33 E
Sangmélina **121** 2 57N 12 1 E
Sangonera, R. **59** 37 39N 2 0W
Sangpang Bum **98** 26 30N 95 50 E
Sangre de Cristo Mts. **159** 37 0N 105 0W
Sangro, R. **63** 42 10N 14 30 E
Sangudo **152** 53 50N 114 54W
Sangüesa **58** 42 37N 1 17W
Sanguinaires, I. **45** 41 51N 8 36 E
Sanhala **120** 10 3N 6 51W
Sanho **107** 39 59N 117 4 E
Sani R. **100** 13 32N 105 57 E
Sanish **158** 48 0N 102 30W
Sanje **126** 0 49 S 31 30 E
Sankaranayinarkovil **97** 9 10N 77 35 E
Sankeshwar **96** 16 23N 74 23 E
Sankosh, R. **98** 26 24N 89 47 E
Sankt Andra **52** 46 46N 14 50 E
Sankt Antönien **51** 46 58N 9 48 E
Sankt Blasien **49** 47 47N 8 7 E
Sankt Gallen **51** 47 26N 9 22 E
Sankt Gallen □ **51** 47 25N 9 22 E
Sankt Ingbert **49** 49 16N 7 6 E
Sankt Johann **52** 47 22N 13 12 E
Sankt Margrethen **51** 47 28N 9 37 E
Sankt Moritz **51** 46 30N 9 50 E
Sankt Olof **73** 55 37N 14 8 E
Sankt Pölten **52** 48 12N 15 38 E
Sankt Valentin **52** 48 11N 14 33 E
Sankt Veit **52** 46 54N 14 22 E
Sankt Wendel **49** 49 27N 7 9 E
Sankt Wolfgang **52** 47 43N 13 27 E
Sankuru, R. **124** 4 17 S 20 25 E
Sanlúcar de Barrameda **57** 37 26N 6 18W
Sanlucár la Mayor **57** 37 26N 6 18W
Sanluri **64** 39 35N 8 55 E
Sanmártin **70** 46 19N 25 58 E
Sanmen **109** 29 5N 121 35 E
Sanmenhsia **106** 34 46N 111 30 E
Sanming **109** 26 13N 117 35 E
Sannan **111** 35 2N 135 1 E
Sannaspos **128** 29 6 S 26 34 E
Sannicandro Gargánico **65** 41 50N 15 34 E
Sânnicolaul-Maré **66** 46 5N 20 39 E
Sannidal **71** 58 55N 9 15 E
Sannieshof **128** 26 30 S 25 47 E
Sano **111** 36 19N 139 35 E
Sanok **54** 49 35N 22 10 E
Sanokwelle **120** 7 19N 8 38W
Sanpa **108** 29 43N 99 33 E
Sanpah **139** 30 32 S 141 12 E
Sanquhar **35** 55 21N 3 56W
Sansanding Dam **120** 13 37N 6 0W
Sansanné-Mango **121** 10 20N 0 30 E
Sansepolcro **63** 43 34N 12 8 E
Sanshui **109** 23 11N 112 53 E
Sanski Most **63** 44 46N 16 40 E
Sansui **108** 26 57N 108 37 E
Sant' Ágata de Gati **65** 41 6N 14 30 E
Sant' Ágata di Militello **65** 38 2N 14 40 E
Santa Ana, Ecuador **174** 1 10 S 80 20W
Santa Ana, El Sal. **166** 14 0N 89 40W
Santa Ana, Mexico **164** 30 31N 111 8W
Santa Ana, U.S.A. **163** 33 48N 117 55W
Santa Ana, El Beni **174** 13 50 S 65 40W
Sant' Ángelo Lodigiano **62** 45 14N 9 25 E
Sant' Antíoco **64** 39 2N 8 30 E
Sant' Antíoco, I. **64** 39 2N 8 30 E
Sant' Arcángelo di Romagna **63** 44 4N 12 26 E
Santa Bárbara, Brazil **171** 16 0 S 59 0W
Santa Bárbara, Colomb. **174** 5 53N 75 35W
Santa Barbara **166** 14 53N 88 14W
Santa Bárbara, Mexico **164** 26 48N 105 50W
Santa Bárbara, Spain **58** 40 42N 0 29 E
Santa Barbara **163** 34 25N 119 40W
Santa Bárbara **174** 7 47N 71 10W
Santa Barbara Channel **163** 34 20N 120 0W
Santa Barbara I. **163** 33 29N 119 2W
Santa Barbara Is. **161** 33 31N 119 0W
Santa Bárbara, Mt. **59** 37 23N 2 50W
Santa Catalina **174** 10 36N 75 17W
Santa Catalina, G. of **163** 33 0N 118 0W
Santa Catalina, I., Mexico **164** 25 40N 110 50W
Santa Catalina, I., U.S.A. **163** 33 20N 118 30W
Santa Catarina □ **173** 27 25 S 48 30W
Santa Catarina, I. de **173** 27 30 S 48 40W
Santa Caterina **65** 37 37N 14 1 E
Santa Cecília **173** 26 56 S 50 27W
Santa Clara, Cuba **166** 22 20N 80 0W
Santa Clara, Calif., U.S.A. **163** 37 21N 122 0W
Santa Clara, Utah, U.S.A. **161** 37 10N 113 38W
Santa Clara de Olimar **173** 32 50 S 54 54W
Santa Clotilde **174** 2 25 S 73 45W
Santa Coloma de Farnés **58** 41 50N 2 39 E
Santa Coloma de Gramanet **58** 41 27N 2 13 E
Santa Comba **56** 43 2N 8 49W
Santa Croce Camerina **65** 36 50N 14 30 E
Santa Cruz, Argent. **176** 50 0 S 68 50W
Santa Cruz, Boliv. **174** 17 43 S 63 10W
Santa Cruz, Brazil **170** 7 57 S 36 12W
Santa Cruz, Canary Is. **116** 28 29N 16 26W
Santa Cruz, Chile **172** 34 38 S 71 27W
Santa Cruz, C. Rica **166** 10 15N 85 41W
Santa Cruz, Phil. **103** 14 20N 121 30 E
Santa Cruz, Calif., U.S.A. **163** 36 55N 122 1W
Santa Cruz, N. Mexico, U.S.A. **161** 35 59N 106 1W
Santa Cruz □ **174** 17 43 S 63 10W
Santa Cruz Cabrália **171** 16 17 S 39 2W
Santa Cruz de Barahona **167** 18 12N 71 6W
Santa Cruz de Mudela **59** 38 39N 3 28W
Santa Cruz de Tenerife □ **72** 28 10N 17 20W
Santa Cruz del Norte **166** 23 9N 81 55W
Santa Cruz del Retamar **56** 40 8N 4 14W
Santa Cruz del Sur **166** 20 50N 78 0W
Santa Cruz do Rio Pardo **173** 22 54 S 49 37W
Santa Cruz do Sul **173** 29 42 S 52 25W
Santa Cruz I. **154** 34 0N 119 45W
Santa Cruz, Is. **130** 10 30 S 166 0 E
Santa Cruz, R. **176** 50 10 S 70 0W
Santa Elena, Argent. **172** 30 58 S 59 47W
Santa Elena, Ecuador **174** 2 16 S 80 52W
Santa Elena C. **167** 10 54N 85 56W
Santa Enimie **44** 44 24N 3 26 E
Sant' Eufémia, Golfo di **65** 38 50N 16 10 E
Santa Eulalia **59** 40 34N 1 20W
Santa Fe, Argent. **172** 31 35 S 60 41W
Santa Fe, Spain **57** 37 11N 3 43W
Santa Fe, U.S.A. **161** 35 40N 106 0W
Santa Fé □ **172** 31 50 S 60 55W
Santa Filomena **170** 9 0 S 45 50W
Santa Genoveva, Mt. **164** 23 18N 109 52W
Santa Groce di Magliano **65** 41 43N 14 59 E
Santa Helena **170** 2 14 S 45 18W
Santa Helena de Goiás **171** 17 43 S 50 35W
Santa Inês **171** 13 17 S 39 48W
Santa Inés, I. **176** 54 0 S 73 0W
Santa Inés, Mt. **57** 38 32N 5 37W
Santa Isabel, Argent. **172** 36 10 S 67 0W
Santa Isabel, Brazil **171** 13 45 S 56 30W
Santa Isabel = Rey Malabo **121** 3 45N 8 50 E
Santa Isabel do Araguaia **170** 6 7 S 48 19W
Santa Isabel, Pico **121** 4 43N 8 49 E
Santa Juliana **171** 19 19 S 47 32W
Santa Lucía, Corrientes, Argent. **172** 28 58 S 59 5W
Santa Lucía, San Juan, Argent. **172** 31 30 S 68 45W
Santa Lucía, Spain **59** 37 35N 0 58W
Santa Lucia **172** 34 27 S 56 24W
Santa Lucia Range **163** 36 0N 121 20W
Santa Luzia **170** 6 53 S 36 56W
Santa Magdalena, I. **164** 24 50N 112 15W
Santa Margarita, Argent. **172** 38 18 S 61 35W
Santa Margarita, U.S.A. **163** 35 23N 120 37W
Santa Margarita, I. **164** 24 30N 112 0W
Santa Margarita, R. **163** 33 13N 117 23W
Santa Margherita **62** 44 20N 9 11 E
Santa María, Argent. **172** 26 40 S 66 0W
Santa Maria, Brazil **173** 29 40 S 53 40W
Santa Maria **65** 41 3N 14 29 E
Santa María **164** 27 40N 114 40W
Santa Maria, Spain **58** 39 39N 2 45 E
Santa Maria, Switz. **51** 46 36N 10 25 E
Santa Maria, U.S.A. **163** 34 58N 120 29W
Santa Maria, Zambia **127** 11 5 S 29 58 E
Santa María, Bahía de **164** 25 10N 108 40W
Santa Maria, Cabo de **57** 36 39N 7 53W
Santa María da Vitória **171** 13 24 S 44 12W
Santa María del Oro **164** 25 30N 105 20W
Santa Maria di Leuca, C. **65** 39 48N 18 20 E
Santa Maria do Suaçuí **171** 18 12 S 42 25W
Santa María la Real de Nieva **56** 41 4N 4 24W
Santa María, R. **164** 31 0N 107 14W
Santa Marta, Colomb. **174** 11 15N 74 13W
Santa Marta, Spain **57** 38 37N 6 39W
Santa Marta Grande, C. **173** 28 43 S 48 50W
Santa Marta, Ría de **56** 43 44N 7 45W
Santa Marta, Sierra Nevada de **147** 10 55N 73 50W
Santa Monica **163** 34 0N 118 30W
Santa Napa **160** 38 28N 122 45W
Santa Olalla, Huelva, Spain **57** 37 54N 6 14W
Santa Olalla, Toledo, Spain **56** 40 2N 4 25W
Sant' Onofrio **65** 38 42N 16 10 E
Santa Paula **163** 34 20N 119 2W
Santa Pola **59** 38 13N 0 35W
Santa Quitéria **170** 4 20 S 40 10W
Santa Rita, U.S.A. **161** 32 50N 108 0W
Santa Rita, Guarico, Venez. **174** 8 8N 66 16W
Santa Rita, Zulia, Venez. **174** 10 32N 71 32W
Santa Rosa, La Pampa, Argent. **172** 36 40 S 64 30W
Santa Rosa, San Luis, Argent. **172** 32 30 S 65 10W
Santa Rosa, Boliv. **174** 10 25 S 67 20W
Santa Rosa, Brazil **173** 27 52 S 54 29W
Santa Rosa, Colomb. **174** 3 32N 69 48W
Santa Rosa, Hond. **164** 14 40N 89 0W
Santa Rosa, Calif., U.S.A. **163** 38 26N 122 43W
Santa Rosa, N. Mexico, U.S.A. **159** 34 58N 104 40W
Santa Rosa, Amazonas, Venez. **174** 1 29N 66 55W
Santa Rosa, Apure, Venez. **174** 6 37N 67 57W
Santa Rosa de Cabal **174** 4 52N 75 38W
Santa Rosa de Copán **166** 14 47N 88 46W
Santa Rosa de Osos **174** 6 39N 75 28W
Santa Rosa de Río Primero **172** 31 8 S 63 20W
Santa Rosa de Viterbo **174** 5 53N 72 59W
Santa Rosa I., Calif., U.S.A. **163** 34 0N 120 6W
Santa Rosa I., Fla., U.S.A. **157** 30 23N 87 0W
Santa Rosa Mts. **160** 41 45N 117 30W
Santa Rosalía **164** 27 20N 112 30W
Santa Sofia **63** 43 57N 11 55 E
Santa Sylvina **172** 27 50 S 61 10W
Santa Tecla = Nueva San Salvador **164** 13 40N 89 25W
Santa Teresa, Argent. **172** 33 25 S 60 47W
Santa Teresa, Brazil **171** 19 55 S 40 36W
Santa Teresa, Mexico **165** 25 17N 97 51W
Santa Teresa, Venez. **174** 4 43N 61 4W
Santa Teresa di Riva **63** 37 58N 15 21 E
Santa Teresa Gallura **64** 41 14N 9 12 E
Santa Teresinha **170** 12 45 S 39 32W
Santa Vitória **171** 18 50 S 50 8W
Santa Vitória do Palmar **173** 33 32 S 53 25W
Santa Ynez **163** 34 37N 120 5W
Santa Ynez, R. **163** 34 37N 120 41W
Santa Ysabel **163** 33 7N 116 40W
Sant'ai **108** 31 5N 105 2 E
Santadi **64** 39 5N 8 42 E
Santahar **98** 24 48N 88 59 E
Santaluz **171** 11 15 S 39 22W
Santana **171** 13 2 S 44 5W
Santana, Coxilha de **173** 30 50 S 55 35W
Santana do Ipanema **170** 9 22 S 37 14W
Santana do Livramento **173** 30 55 S 55 30W
Santander, Colomb. **174** 3 1N 76 28W
Santander, Spain **56** 43 27N 3 51W
Santander □ **56** 43 25N 4 0W
Santander Jiménez **165** 24 11N 98 29W
Santañy **59** 39 20N 3 5 E
Santaquin **160** 40 0N 111 51W
Santarém, Brazil **175** 2 25 S 54 42W
Santarém, Port. **57** 39 12N 8 42W
Santarém □ **57** 39 10N 8 40W
Santaren Channel **166** 24 0N 79 30W
Santèramo in Colle **65** 40 48N 16 45 E
Santerno, R. **63** 44 10N 11 38 E
Santhia **62** 45 20N 8 10 E
Santiago, Brazil **173** 29 11 S 54 52W
Santiago, Chile **172** 33 24 S 70 50W
Santiago, Dom. Rep. **167** 19 30N 70 40W

Santiago Sayville

Santiago, Panama **166** 8 0N 81 0W
Santiago □ **172** 33 30S 70 50W
Santiago de Compostela **56** 42 52N 8 37W
Santiago de Cuba **166** 20 0N 75 49W
Santiago del Estero **172** 27 50S 64 15W
Santiago del Estero □ **172** 27 50S 64 20W
Santiago do Cacém **57** 38 1N 8 42W
Santiago Ixcuintla **164** 21 50N 105 11W
Santiago Papasquiaro **164** 25 0N 105 20W
Santiago, Punta de **121** 3 12N 8 40E
Santiaguillo, L. de **164** 24 50N 104 50W
Santillana del Mar **56** 43 24N 4 6W
Santipur **95** 23 17N 88 25E
Säntis **51** 47 15N 9 22E
Santisteban del Puerto **59** 38 17N 3 15W
Santo Amaro **171** 12 30S 38 50W
Santo Anastácio **173** 21 58S 51 39W
Santo André **173** 23 39S 46 29W
Santo Ângelo **173** 28 15S 54 15W
Santo Antonio **170** 15 50S 56 0W
Santo Antônio de Jesus **171** 12 58S 39 16W
Santo Antonio do Zaire **124** 6 7S 12 20E
Santo Corazón **174** 18 0S 58 45W
Santo Domingo, Dom. Rep. **167** 18 30N 70 0W
Santo Domingo, Baja Calif. N., Mexico **164** 30 43N 115 56W
Santo Domingo, Baja Calif. S., Mexico **164** 25 32N 112 2W
Santo Domingo, Nic. **166** 12 14N 84 59W
Santo Domingo de la Calzada **58** 42 26N 2 27W
Santo Isabel do Morro **171** 11 34S 50 40W
Santo Stéfano di Camastro **65** 38 1N 14 22E
Santo Stino di Livenza **63** 45 45N 12 40E
Santo Tirso **56** 41 29N 8 18W
Santo Tomas **164** 31 33N 116 24W
Santo Tomás **174** 14 34S 72 30W
Santo Tomé **173** 28 40S 56 5W
Santoña **56** 43 29N 3 20W
Santos **173** 24 0S 46 20W
Santos Dumont **173** 22 55S 43 10W
Santos, Sierra de los **57** 38 7N 5 12W
Santport **46** 52 26N 4 39E
Santu **108** 25 59N 107 52E
Sanur **90** 32 22N 35 15E
Sanvignes-les-Mines **43** 46 40N 4 18E
San'yō **110** 34 2N 131 5E
Sanyuki-Sammyaku **110** 34 5N 133 0E
Sanza Pombo **124** 7 18S 15 56E
São Anastacio **173** 22 0S 51 40W
São Bartolomeu de Messines **57** 37 15N 8 17W
São Benedito **170** 4 3S 40 53W
São Bento **170** 2 42S 44 50W
São Bento do Norte **170** 5 4S 36 2W
São Borja **173** 28 45S 56 0W
São Bras d'Alportel **57** 37 8N 7 58W
São Caitano **170** 8 21S 36 6W
São Carlos **173** 22 0S 47 50W
São Cristóvão **170** 11 15S 37 15W
São Domingos, Brazil **171** 13 25S 46 10W
São Domingos, Guin.-Biss. **170** 12 22N 16 8W
São Domingos do Maranhão **170** 5 42S 44 22W
São Félix, Bahia, Brazil **171** 12 38S 38 58W
São Félix, Mato Grosso, Brazil **171** 11 36S 50 39W
Sao Francisco **171** 16 0S 44 50W
São Francisco do Maranhão **170** 6 15S 42 52W
São Francisco do Sul **173** 26 15S 48 36W
São Francisco, R. **170** 10 30S 36 24W
São Gabriel **173** 30 10S 54 30W
São Gabriel da Palha **171** 18 47S 40 59W
São Gonçalo **173** 22 48S 43 5W
São Gotardo **171** 19 19S 46 3W
Sao Hill **127** 8 20S 35 18E
São João da Boa Vista **173** 22 0S 46 52W
São João da Pesqueira **56** 41 8N 7 24W
São João da Ponte **171** 15 56S 44 1W
São João del Rei **173** 21 8S 44 15W
São João do Araguaia **170** 5 23S 48 46W
São João do Paraiso **171** 15 19S 42 1W
São João do Piauí **170** 8 10S 42 15W
São João dos Patos **170** 6 30S 43 42W
São João Evangelista **171** 18 32S 42 45W
São Joaquim da Barra **171** 20 35S 47 53W
São José, B. de **170** 2 38S 44 4W
São José da Laje **170** 9 1S 36 3W
São José de Mipibu **170** 6 5S 35 15W
São José do Peixe **170** 7 24S 42 34W
São José do Rio Prêto **173** 20 50S 49 20W
São José dos Campos **173** 23 7S 45 52W
São Leopoldo **173** 29 50S 51 10W
São Lourenço, Mato Grosso, Brazil **173** 16 30S 55 5W
São Lourenço, Minas Gerais, Brazil **171** 22 7S 45 3W
São Lourenço, R. **175** 16 40S 56 0W
São Luís do Curu **170** 3 40S 39 14W
São Luís Gonzaga **173** 28 25S 55 0W
São Luís (Maranhão) **170** 2 39S 44 15W
Sao Marcelino **174** 1 0N 67 12W
São Marcelino **174** 1 0N 67 12W
São Marcos, B. de **170** 2 0S 44 0W
São Marcos, R. **171** 18 15S 47 37W
São Martinho **56** 39 30N 9 8W
São Mateus **171** 18 44S 39 50W
São Mateus, R. **171** 18 35S 39 44W
São Miguel **16** 37 33N 25 27W
São Miguel do Araguaia **171** 13 19S 50 13W
São Miguel dos Campos **170** 9 47S 36 5W
São Nicolau, R. **170** 5 45S 42 2W
São Paulo **173** 23 40S 46 50W
São Paulo □ **173** 22 0S 49 0W
São Pedro do Piaui **171** 5 56S 42 43W
São Pedro do Sul **56** 40 46N 8 4W
São Rafael **170** 5 47S 36 55W
São Raimundo das Mangabeiras **170** 7 1S 45 29W
São Raimundo Nonato **170** 9 1S 42 42W
São Romão, Amazonas, Brazil **174** 5 53S 67 50W
São Romão, Minas Gerais, Brazil **171** 16 22S 45 4W
São Roque, C. de **170** 5 30S 35 10W
São Sebastião do Paraiso **173** 20 54S 46 59W
São Sebastião, I. **173** 23 50S 45 18W
São Simão **171** 18 56S 50 30W
São Teotónio **57** 37 30N 8 42W
São Tomé **170** 5 58S 36 4W
São Tomé, C. de **173** 22 0S 41 10W
São Tomé, I. **114** 0 10N 7 0E
São Vicente **173** 23 57S 46 23W
São Vicente, Cabo de **57** 37 0N 9 0W
Saona, I. **167** 18 10N 68 40W
Saône-et-Loire □ **43** 46 25N 4 50E
Saône, R. **43** 46 25N 4 50E
Saonek **103** 0 28S 130 47E
Saoura, O. **118** 29 55N 1 50W
Sapai **68** 41 2N 25 43E
Sapão, R. **170** 11 1S 45 32W
Saparua, I. **103** 3 33S 128 40E
Sapé **170** 7 6S 35 13W
Sapele **121** 5 50N 5 40E
Sapelo I. **157** 31 28N 81 15W
Sapiéntza I. **69** 36 33N 21 43E
Sapodnyy Sayan **77** 52 30N 94 0E
Sapone **121** 12 3N 1 35W
Saposoa **174** 6 55S 76 30W
Sapozhok **81** 53 59N 40 51E
Sappemeer **46** 53 10N 6 48E
Sapporo **112** 43 0N 141 15E
Sapri **65** 40 5N 15 37E
Sapudi, I. **103** 7 2S 114 17E
Sapulpa **159** 36 0N 96 40W
Sapur **95** 34 18N 74 27E
Saqota **123** 12 40N 39 1E
Saqqez **92** 36 15N 46 20E
Sar-i-Pul **93** 36 10N 66 0E
Sar Planina **66** 42 10N 21 0E
Sara **120** 11 40N 3 53W
Sara Buri **100** 14 30N 100 55E
Sarab **92** 38 0N 47 30E
Sarada, R. **99** 28 15N 80 30E
Saragossa = Zaragoza **58** 41 39N 0 53W
Saraguro **174** 3 35S 79 16W
Sarai **70** 44 43N 28 10E
Saraipalli **96** 21 20N 82 59E
Sarajevo **66** 43 52N 18 26E
Saraktash **84** 51 47N 56 22E
Saramati **98** 25 44N 95 2E
Saran **122** 19 35N 40 30E
Saran, G. **102** 0 30S 111 25E
Saranac Lake **156** 44 20N 74 10W
Saranda, Alb. **68** 39 59N 19 55E
Saranda, Tanz. **126** 5 45S 34 59E
Sarandí del Yi **173** 33 18S 55 38W
Sarandí Grande **172** 33 20S 55 50W
Sarangani B. **103** 6 0N 125 13E
Sarangani Is. **103** 5 25N 125 25E
Sarangarh **96** 21 30N 82 57E
Saransk **81** 54 10N 45 10E
Sarapul **84** 56 28N 53 48E
Sarasota **157** 27 10N 82 30W
Saratoga, Calif., U.S.A. **163** 37 16N 122 2W
Saratoga, Wyo., U.S.A. **160** 41 30N 106 56W
Saratoga Springs **162** 43 5N 73 47W
Saratok **102** 3 5S 110 50E
Saratov **81** 51 30N 46 2E
Saravane **100** 15 43N 106 25E
Sarawak □ **102** 2 0N 113 0E
Saraya **120** 12 50N 11 45W
Sarbaz **93** 26 38N 61 19E
Sarbisheh **93** 32 30N 59 40E
Sârbogârd **53** 46 55N 18 40E
Sarca, R. **62** 46 5N 10 45E
Sardalas **119** 25 50N 10 54E
Sardarshahr **94** 28 30N 74 29E
Sardegna, I. **64** 39 57N 9 0E
Sardhana **94** 29 9N 77 39E
Sardinata **174** 8 5N 72 48W
Sardinia = Sardegna **64** 39 57N 9 0E
Sardo **123** 11 56N 41 14E
Sarektjåkkå **74** 67 27N 17 43E
Sarengrad **66** 45 14N 19 16E
Saréyamou **120** 16 25N 3 10W
Sargasso Sea **14** 27 0N 72 0W
Sargent **158** 41 42N 99 24W
Sargodha **94** 32 10N 72 40E
Sargodha □ **94** 31 50N 72 0E
Sarh **117** 9 5N 18 23E
Sarhro, Jebel **118** 31 6N 5 0W
Sári **93** 36 30N 53 11E
Sária, I. **69** 35 54N 27 17E
Sarichef C. **147** 54 38N 164 59W
Sarida, R. **90** 32 4N 35 3E
Sarikamiş **92** 40 22N 42 35E
Sarikei **102** 2 8N 111 30E
Sarina **138** 21 22S 149 13E
Sarine, R. **50** 46 32N 7 4E
Sariñena **58** 41 47N 0 10W
Sarír Tibasti **119** 22 50N 18 30E
Sarita **159** 27 14N 90 49W
Sariwŏn **107** 38 31N 125 46E
Sariyer **67** 41 10N 29 3E
Sark, I. **42** 49 25N 2 20W
Sarkad **53** 46 47N 21 17E
Sarlat-la-Canéda **44** 44 54N 1 13E
Sarles **158** 48 58N 98 57W
Sarmi **103** 1 49S 138 38E
Särna **72** 61 41N 12 58E
Sarnano **63** 43 2N 13 17E
Sarnen **50** 46 53N 8 13E
Sarnia **150** 42 58N 82 23W
Sarno **65** 40 48N 14 35E
Sarnowa **54** 51 39N 16 53E
Sarny **80** 51 17N 26 40E
Särö **73** 57 31N 11 57E
Sarolangun **102** 2 30S 102 30E
Saronikós Kólpos **69** 37 45N 23 45E
Saros Körfezi **68** 40 30N 26 15E
Sárospatak **53** 48 18N 21 33E
Sarosul Romanesc **66** 45 34N 21 43E
Sarpsborg **71** 59 16N 11 12E
Sarracín **58** 42 15N 3 45W
Sarralbe **43** 48 55N 7 1E
Sarraz, La **50** 46 38N 6 30E
Sarre, La **150** 48 45N 79 15W
Sarre, R. **43** 48 49N 7 0E
Sarre-Union **43** 48 55N 7 4E
Sarrebourg **43** 48 43N 7 3E
Sarreguemines **43** 49 1N 7 4E
Sarriá **56** 42 41N 7 29W
Sarrión **58** 40 9N 0 49W
Sarro **120** 13 40N 5 5W
Sarstedt **48** 52 13N 9 50E
Sartène **45** 41 38N 9 0E
Sarthe □ **42** 47 58N 0 10E
Sarthe, R. **42** 47 33N 0 31W
Sartilly **42** 48 45N 1 28W
Sartynya **76** 63 30N 62 50E
Sarum **122** 21 11N 39 10E
Sarúr **93** 23 17N 58 4E
Sárvár **53** 47 15N 16 56E
Sarveston **93** 29 20N 53 10E
Särvfjället **72** 62 42N 13 30E
Sárviz, R. **53** 46 40N 18 40E
Sary Ozek **85** 44 22N 77 59E
Sary-Tash **85** 39 44N 73 15E
Saryagach **85** 41 27N 69 9E
Sarych, Mys. **82** 44 25N 33 25E
Sarykolskiy Khrebet **85** 38 30N 74 30E
Sarykopa, Ozero **84** 50 22N 64 6E
Sarymoin, Ozero **84** 51 36N 64 30E
Saryshagan **76** 46 12N 73 48E
Sarzana **70** 44 7N 9 57E
Sarzeau **42** 47 31N 2 48W
Sas van Gent **47** 51 14N 3 48E
Sasa **90** 33 2N 35 23E
Sasabeneh **91** 7 59N 44 43E
Sasaram **95** 24 57N 84 5E
Sasayama **111** 35 4N 135 13E
Sasca Montanŭ **66** 44 41N 21 45E
Sasebo **110** 33 10N 129 43E
Saser Mt. **95** 34 50N 77 50E
Saskatchewan □ **153** 54 40N 106 0W
Saskatchewan, R. **153** 53 12N 99 16W
Saskatoon **153** 52 10N 106 38W
Sasolburg **129** 26 46S 27 49E
Sasovo **81** 54 25N 41 55E
Sassandra **120** 5 0N 6 8W
Sassandra, R. **120** 5 0N 6 8W
Sássari **64** 40 44N 8 33E
Sassenheim **46** 52 14N 4 31E
Sassnitz **48** 54 29N 13 39E
Sasso Marconi **63** 44 22N 11 12E
Sassocorvaro **63** 43 47N 12 30E
Sassoferrato **63** 43 26N 12 51E
Sassuolo **62** 44 31N 10 47E
Sástago **58** 41 19N 0 21W
Sastown **120** 4 45N 8 27W
Sasumua Dam **126** 0 54S 36 46E
Sasyk, Ozero **70** 45 45N 30 0E
Sasykkul **85** 37 41N 73 11E
Sata-Misaki **110** 30 59N 130 40E
Satadougou **120** 12 40N 11 25W
Satanta **159** 37 30N 101 0W
Satara **96** 17 44N 73 58E
Satilla, R. **157** 31 15N 81 50W
Satka **84** 55 3N 59 1E
Satkania **98** 22 4N 92 3E
Satkhira **98** 22 43N 89 8E
Satmala Hills **96** 20 15N 74 40E
Satna **95** 24 35N 80 50E
Sator, mt. **63** 44 11N 16 43E
Sátoraljaújhely **53** 48 25N 21 41E
Satpura Ra. **94** 21 40N 75 0E
Satrup **48** 54 39N 9 38E
Satsuma-Hantō **110** 31 25N 130 25E
Satsuna-Shotō **112** 30 0N 130 0E
Sattahip **100** 12 41N 100 54E
Sattenpalle **96** 16 25N 80 6E
Satu Mare **70** 47 46N 22 55E
Satui **102** 3 50S 115 20E
Satumare □ **70** 47 45N 23 0E
Satun **101** 6 43N 100 2E
Saturnina, R. **174** 12 15S 58 10W
Sauce **172** 30 5S 58 46W
Sauceda **164** 25 46N 101 19W
Saucillo **164** 28 1N 105 17W
Sauda **71** 59 38N 6 21E
Saúde **170** 10 56S 40 24W
Sauðarkrókur **74** 65 45N 19 40W
Saudi Arabia ■ **92** 26 0N 44 0E
Sauerland **48** 51 0N 8 0E
Saugerties **162** 42 4N 73 58W
Saugues **44** 44 58N 3 32E
Sauherad **71** 59 25N 9 15E
Sauid el Amia **118** 25 57N 6 8W
Saujon **44** 45 41N 0 55W
Sauk Center **158** 45 42N 94 56W
Sauk Rapids **158** 45 35N 94 10W
Saulgau **49** 48 4N 9 32E
Saulieu **43** 47 17N 4 14E
Sault **45** 44 6N 5 24E
Sault Ste. Marie, Can. **150** 46 30N 84 20W
Sault Ste. Marie, U.S.A. **156** 46 27N 84 22W
Saumlaki **103** 7 55S 131 20E
Saumur **42** 47 15N 0 5W
Saunders **152** 52 58N 115 40W
Saunders C. **143** 45 53S 170 45E
Saunders I. **13** 57 30S 27 30W
Saunders Point, Mt. **137** 27 52S 125 38E
Saundersfoot **31** 51 43N 4 42W
Saurbær, Borgarfjarðarsýsla, Iceland **74** 64 24N 21 35W
Saurbær, Eyjafjarðarsýsla, Iceland **74** 65 27N 18 13W
Sauri **121** 11 50N 6 44E
Sausalito **163** 37 51N 122 29W
Sautatá **174** 7 50N 77 4W
Sauveterre, B. **44** 43 25N 0 57W
Sauzé-Vaussais **44** 46 8N 0 8E
Savá **166** 15 32N 86 15W
Sava **65** 40 28N 17 32E
Sava, R. **63** 44 40N 19 50E
Savage **158** 47 43N 104 20W
Savalou **121** 7 57N 2 4E
Savanah Downs **138** 19 30S 141 30E
Savane **127** 19 37S 35 8E
Savanna **158** 42 5N 90 10W
Savanna la Mar **166** 18 10N 78 10W
Savannah, Ga., U.S.A. **157** 32 4N 81 4W
Savannah, Mo., U.S.A. **158** 39 55N 94 46W
Savannah, Tenn., U.S.A. **157** 35 12N 88 18W
Savannah Downs **138** 19 28S 141 47E
Savannah, R. **157** 33 0N 81 30W
Savannakhet **100** 16 30N 104 49E
Savant L. **150** 50 14N 90 6W
Savant Lake **150** 50 30N 90 25W
Savantvadi **97** 15 55N 73 54E
Savanur **97** 14 59N 75 28E
Savda **96** 21 9N 75 56E
Savé **121** 8 2N 2 17E
Save R. **125** 21 16S 34 0E
Saveh **92** 35 2N 50 20E
Savelovo **81** 56 51N 37 20E
Savelugu **121** 9 38N 0 54W
Savenay **42** 47 20N 1 55W
Saverdun **44** 43 14N 1 34E
Saverne **43** 48 39N 7 20E
Savièse **50** 46 17N 7 22E
Savigliano **62** 44 39N 7 40E
Savigny-sur-Braye **44** 47 53N 0 49E
Saviñao **56** 42 35N 7 38W
Savio, R. **63** 43 58N 12 10E
Savnik **66** 42 59N 19 10E
Savognin **51** 46 36N 9 37E
Savoie □ **45** 45 26N 6 35E
Savona **62** 44 19N 8 29E
Savonlinna **78** 61 55N 28 55E
Sävsjö **73** 57 20N 14 40E
Sävsjøström **73** 57 1N 15 25E
Sawahlunto **102** 0 52S 100 52E
Sawai **103** 3 0S 129 5E
Sawai Madhopur **94** 26 0N 76 25E
Sawang Daen Din **100** 17 28N 103 28E
Sawankhalok **100** 17 19N 99 50E
Sawara **111** 35 55N 140 30E
Sawatch Mts. **161** 38 30N 106 30W
Sawbridgeworth **29** 51 49N 0 10E
Sawdā, Jabal as **119** 28 51N 15 12E
Sawel, Mt. **38** 54 48N 7 5W
Sawfajjin, W. **119** 31 46N 14 30E
Sawi **101** 10 14N 99 5E
Sawmills **127** 19 30S 28 2E
Sawston **29** 52 7N 0 11E
Sawtry **29** 52 26N 0 17W
Sawu, I. **103** 10 35S 121 50E
Sawu Sea **103** 9 30S 121 50E
Saxby, R. **138** 18 25S 140 53E
Saxilby **33** 53 16N 0 40W
Saxlingham Nethergate **29** 52 33N 1 16E
Saxmundham **29** 52 13N 1 29E
Saxon **50** 46 9N 7 11E
Saxony, Lower = Niedersachsen **48** 52 45N 9 0E
Say **121** 13 8N 2 22E
Saya **121** 9 30N 3 18E
Sayabec **151** 48 35N 67 41W
Sayaboury **100** 19 15N 101 45E
Sayán **174** 11 0S 77 25W
Sayan, Vostochnyy **77** 54 0N 96 0E
Sayan, Zapadnyy **77** 52 30N 94 0E
Sayasan **83** 42 56N 46 15E
Sayda **92** 33 35N 35 25E
Sayhan Ovoo **106** 45 27N 103 54E
Sayhandulaan **106** 44 40N 109 1E
Saynshand **106** 44 55N 110 11E
Sayō **110** 34 50N 134 22E
Sayre, Okla., U.S.A. **159** 35 20N 99 40W
Sayre, Pa., U.S.A. **162** 42 0N 76 30W
Sayula **164** 19 50N 103 40W
Sayville **162** 40 45N 73 7W

Sazan **Semirara Is**

Sazan 68 40 30N 19 20 E
Sazin 95 35 35N 73 30 E
Sazlika, R. 67 42 15N 25 50 E
Sbeïtla 119 35 12N 9 7 E
Scaër 42 48 2N 3 42W
Scalasaig 34 56 4N 6 10W
Scalby 33 54 18N 0 26W
Scalby Ness 33 54 18N 0 25W
Scalea 65 39 49N 15 47 E
Scalloway 36 60 9N 1 16W
Scalpay, I., Inner Hebrides, U.K. 36 57 18N 6 0W
Scalpay, I., Outer Hebrides, U.K. 36 57 51N 6 40W
Scamblesby 33 53 17N 0 5W
Scammon Bay 147 62 0N 165 49W
Scandia 152 50 20N 112 0W
Scandiano 62 44 36N 10 40 E
Scandinavia 16 64 0N 12 0 E
Scansano 63 42 40N 11 20 E
Scapa Flow 37 58 52N 3 6W
Scarastovore 36 57 50N 7 2W
Scarba, I. 34 56 10N 5 42W
Scarborough, Trin 167 11 11N 60 42W
Scarborough, U.K. 33 54 17N 0 24W
Scargill 143 42 56 S 172 58 E
Scariff 39 52 55N 8 32W
Scariff I. 39 51 43N 10 15W
Scarinish 34 56 30N 6 48W
Scarning 29 52 40N 0 53W
Scarp, I. 36 58 1N 7 8W
Scarpe, R. 43 50 31N 3 27 E
Scarsdale 140 37 41 S 143 39 E
Scattery I. 39 52 37N 9 30W
Scavaig, L. 36 57 8N 6 10W
Scebeli, Uebi 91 2 0N 44 0 E
Scédro, I. 63 43 6N 16 43 E
Scenic 158 43 49N 102 32W
Schaal See 48 53 40N 10 57 E
Schaan 51 47 10N 9 31 E
Schaesberg 47 50 54N 6 0 E
Schaffen 47 51 0N 5 5 E
Schaffhausen 51 47 42N 8 39 E
Schaffhausen □ 51 47 42N 8 36 E
Schagen 47 52 49N 4 48 E
Schaghticoke 162 42 54N 73 35W
Schalkhaar 46 52 17N 6 12 E
Schalkwijk 46 52 0N 5 11 E
Schangnau 50 46 50N 7 47 E
Schänis 51 47 10N 9 3 E
Schärding 52 48 27N 13 27 E
Scharhörn, I. 48 53 58N 8 24 E
Scharnitz 52 47 23N 11 15 E
Scheessel 48 53 10N 9 33 E
Schefferville 151 54 48N 66 50W
Scheibbs 52 48 1N 15 9 E
Schelde, R. 47 51 10N 4 20 E
Scheldewindeke 47 50 56N 3 46 E
Schenectady 162 42 50N 73 58W
Schenevus 162 42 33N 74 50W
Scherfede 48 51 32N 9 2 E
Scherpenheuvel 47 50 58N 4 58 E
Scherpenisse 47 51 33N 4 6 E
Scherpenzeel 46 52 5N 5 30 E
Schesaplana 51 47 5N 9 43 E
Scheveningen 46 52 6N 4 16 E
Schichallion, Mt. 37 56 40N 4 6W
Schiedam 46 51 55N 4 25 E
Schiermonnikoog 46 53 29N 6 10 E
Schiermonnikoog, I. 46 53 30N 6 15 E
Schiers 51 47 58N 9 41 E
Schifferstadt 49 49 22N 8 23 E
Schifflange 47 49 30N 6 1 E
Schijndel 47 51 37N 5 27 E
Schiltigheim 43 48 35N 7 45 E
Schio 63 45 42N 11 21 E
Schipbeek 46 52 14N 6 10 E
Schipluiden 46 51 59N 4 19 E
Schirmeck 43 48 29N 7 12 E
Schladming 52 47 23N 13 41 E
Schlei, R. 48 54 45N 9 52 E
Schleiden 48 50 32N 6 26 E
Schleswig 48 54 32N 9 34 E
Schleswig-Holstein □ 48 54 10N 9 40 E
Schlieren 51 47 28N 8 27 E
Schlüchtern 49 50 20N 9 32 E
Schmalkalden 48 50 43N 10 28 E
Schmölin 48 50 54N 12 22 E
Schneeberg, Austria 52 47 53N 15 55 E
Schneeberg, Ger. 48 50 35N 12 39 E
Schoenberg 47 50 17N 6 16 E
Schofield 158 44 54N 89 39W
Schoharie 162 42 40N 74 19W
Schoharie, R. 162 42 56N 74 18W
Schönberg, Rostock, Ger. 48 53 50N 10 55 E
Schönberg, Schleswig-Holstein, Ger. 48 54 23N 10 20 E
Schönebeck 48 52 2N 11 42 E
Schönenwerd 50 47 23N 8 0 E
Schöningen 48 52 8N 10 57 E
Schoondijke 47 51 21N 3 33 E
Schoonebeek 46 52 39N 6 52 E
Schoonebeek, oilfield 19 52 45N 6 50 E
Schoonhoven 46 51 57N 4 51 E
Schoonoord 46 52 51N 6 46 E
Schoorl 46 52 42N 4 42 E
Schors 80 51 48N 31 56 E
Schortens 48 53 37N 7 51 E
Schoten 47 51 16N 4 30 E
Schouten, Kepulauan 103 1 0 S 136 0 E
Schouter I. 138 42 20 S 148 20 E
Schouwen, I. 47 51 43N 3 45 E
Schramberg 49 48 12N 8 24 E
Schrankogl 52 47 3N 11 7 E
Schreckhorn 50 46 36N 8 7 E
Schreiber 150 48 45N 87 20W
Schroon Lake 162 43 47N 73 46W
Schruns 52 47 5N 9 56 E
Schuler 153 50 20N 110 6W
Schuls 51 46 48N 10 18 E
Schumacher 150 48 30N 81 16W
Schüpfen 50 47 2N 7 24 E
Schüpfheim 50 46 57N 8 2 E
Schurz 163 38 57N 118 48W
Schuyler 158 41 30N 97 3W
Schuylerville 162 43 6N 73 35W
Schuylkill Haven 162 40 37N 76 11W
Schuylkill, R. 162 39 53N 75 12W
Schwabach 49 49 19N 11 3 E
Schwäbisch Gmünd 49 48 49N 9 48 E
Schwäbisch Hall 49 49 7N 9 45 E
Schwäbischer Alb 49 48 30N 9 30 E
Schwanden 51 47 1N 9 5 E
Schwarzach, R. 52 50 30N 11 30 E
Schwarzenberg 48 50 31N 12 49 E
Schwarzenburg 50 46 49N 7 20 E
Schwarzwald 49 48 0N 8 0 E
Schwaz 52 47 20N 11 44 E
Schwedt 48 53 4N 14 18 E
Schweinfurt 49 50 3N 10 12 E
Schweizer Mittelland 50 47 0N 7 15 E
Schweizer Reneke 128 27 11 S 25 18 E
Schwerin 48 53 37N 11 22 E
Schwerin □ 48 53 35N 11 20 E
Schweriner See 48 53 45N 11 26 E
Schwetzingen 49 49 22N 8 35 E
Schwyz 51 47 2N 8 39 E
Schwyz □ 51 47 2N 8 39 E
Sciacca 64 37 30N 13 3 E
Scicli 65 36 48N 14 41 E
Scie, La 151 49 57N 55 36W
Scillave 91 6 22N 44 32 E
Scilly, Isles of 30 49 55N 6 15W
Scinawa 54 51 25N 16 26 E
Scioto, R. 156 39 0N 83 0W
Scituate 162 42 12N 70 44W
Sclayn 47 50 29N 5 2 E
Scobey 158 48 47N 105 30W
Scole 29 52 22N 1 10 E
Scone 141 32 0 S 150 52 E
Scopwick 33 53 6N 0 24W
Scórdia 65 37 19N 14 50 E
Score Hd. 36 60 12N 1 5W
Scoresby Sund 12 70 20N 23 0W
Scorno, Punta dello 64 41 7N 8 23 E
Scotia, Calif., U.S.A. 160 40 36N 124 4W
Scotia, N.Y., U.S.A. 162 42 50N 73 58W
Scotia Sea 13 56 5 S 56 0W
Scotland 158 43 10N 97 45W
Scotland □ 51 57 0N 4 0W
Scotland Neck 157 36 6N 77 24W
Scott 13 77 0 S 165 0 E
Scott, C., Antarct. 13 71 30 S 168 0 E
Scott, C., Austral. 136 13 30 S 129 49 E
Scott City 158 38 30N 100 52W
Scott, I. 13 67 0 S 179 0 E
Scott Inlet 149 71 0N 71 0W
Scott Is. 152 50 48N 128 40W
Scott L. 153 59 55N 106 18W
Scott Reef 136 14 0 S 121 50 E
Scottburgh 129 30 15 S 30 47 E
Scottsbluff 158 41 55N 103 35W
Scottsboro 157 34 40N 86 0W
Scottsburg 157 38 40N 85 46W
Scottsdale 138 41 9 S 147 31 E
Scottsville 157 36 48N 86 10W
Scottville, Austral. 138 20 33 S 147 49 E
Scottville, U.S.A. 156 43 57N 86 18W
Scourie 36 58 20N 5 10W
Scousburgh 36 59 58N 1 20W
Scrabby 38 53 53N 7 32W
Scrabster 37 58 36N 3 31W
Scram, gasfield 19 52 55N 2 42 E
Scramoge 38 53 46N 8 4W
Scranton 162 41 22N 75 41W
Screebe Lodge 38 53 23N 9 33W
Screggan 42 53 15N 7 32W
Scremerston 35 55 44N 1 59W
Scridain, L. 34 56 23N 6 7W
Scunthorpe 33 53 35N 0 38W
Scuol 51 46 48N 10 17 E
Scusciuban 91 10 28N 50 5 E
SE Tor, oilfield 19 56 38N 3 27 E
Sea Isle City 162 39 9N 74 42W
Seabra 171 12 25 S 41 46W
Seabrook, L. 137 30 55 S 119 40 E
Seaford, Austral. 141 38 10 S 145 11 E
Seaford, U.K. 29 50 46N 0 8 E
Seaford, U.S.A. 162 38 37N 75 36W
Seaforth 150 43 35N 81 25W
Seaforth, L. 36 57 52N 6 36W
Seagraves 159 32 56N 102 30W
Seaham 35 54 51N 1 20W
Seahouses 35 55 35N 1 39W
Seal Cove 151 49 57N 56 22W
Seal L. 151 54 20N 61 30W
Seal, R. 153 58 50N 97 30W
Sealga, L. na 36 57 50N 5 18W
Sealy 159 29 46N 96 9W
Seamer 33 54 14N 0 27W
Sean, gasfield 19 53 13N 2 50 E
Searchlight 161 35 31N 114 55W
Searcy 159 35 15N 91 45W
Searles, L. 163 35 47N 117 17W
Seascale 32 54 24N 3 29W
Seaside, Calif., U.S.A. 163 36 37N 121 50W
Seaside, Oreg., U.S.A. 160 46 12N 121 55W
Seaside Park 162 39 55N 74 5W
Seaspray 141 38 25 S 147 15 E
Seaton, U.K. 30 50 42N 3 3W
Seaton, U.K. 32 54 40N 3 31W
Seaton Delaval 35 55 5N 1 33W
Seattle 160 47 41N 122 15W
Seaview Ra. 138 18 40 S 145 45 E
Seaward Kaikouras, Mts. 143 42 10 S 173 44 E
Sebago Lake 162 43 50N 70 35W
Sebastián Vizcaino, Bahia 164 28 0N 114 30W
Sebastopol 160 38 24N 122 49W
Sebastopol = Sevastopol 82 44 35N 33 30 E
Sebderat 123 15 26N 36 42 E
Sebdou 118 34 38N 1 19W
Sebeşului, Mţii. 70 45 56N 23 40 E
Sebewaing 156 43 45N 83 27W
Sebezh 80 56 14N 28 22 E
Sebi 120 15 50N 4 12W
Sebinkarahisar 82 40 22N 38 28 E
Sebiş 70 46 23N 22 13 E
Sebkra Azzel Mati 118 26 10N 0 43 E
Sebkra Mekerghene 118 26 21N 1 30 E
Sebou, Oued 118 34 16N 6 40W
Sebring 157 27 36N 81 47W
Sebta = Ceuta 118 35 52N 5 26W
Sebuku, I. 102 3 30 S 116 25 E
Sebuku, Teluk 102 4 0N 118 10 E
Sečanj 66 45 25N 20 47 E
Secchia, R. 62 44 30N 10 40 E
Sechelt 152 49 25N 123 42W
Sechura, Desierto de 174 6 0 S 80 30W
Seclin 43 50 33N 3 2 E
Secondigny 42 46 37N 0 26W
Sečovce 53 48 42N 21 40 E
Secretary I. 143 45 15 S 166 56 E
Secunderabad 96 17 28N 78 30 E
Seda, R. 57 39 6N 7 53W
Sedalia 158 38 40N 93 18W
Sedan, Austral. 140 34 34 S 139 19 E
Sedan, France 43 49 43N 4 57 E
Sedan, U.S.A. 159 37 10N 96 11W
Sedano 58 42 43N 3 49W
Sedbergh 32 54 20N 2 31W
Seddon 143 41 40 S 174 7 E
Seddonville 143 41 33 S 172 1 E
Sede Ya'aqov 90 32 43N 35 7 E
Sederberg, Mt. 128 32 22 S 19 7 E
Sedgefield 33 54 40N 1 27W
Sedgewick 152 52 48N 111 41W
Sedhiou 120 12 50N 15 30W
Sedičany 52 49 40N 14 25 E
Sedico 63 46 8N 12 6 E
Sedinenie 67 42 16N 24 33 E
Sedley 153 50 10N 104 0W
Sedom 90 31 5N 35 20 E
Sedova, Pik 76 73 20N 55 10 E
Sédrata 119 36 7N 7 31 E
Sedro Woolley 160 48 30N 122 15W
Sedrun 51 46 36N 8 47 E
Seduva 80 55 45N 23 45 E
Sedziszów Małapolski 54 50 5N 21 45 E
Seebad Ahlbeck 48 53 56N 14 10 E
Seefeld 52 47 19N 11 13 E
Seehausen 48 52 52N 11 43 E
Seeheim 128 26 32 S 17 52 E
Seekoe, R. 128 30 34 S 24 45 E
Seeland 50 47 0N 7 6 E
Seelaw 48 52 32N 14 22 E
Seend 28 51 20N 2 2W
Sées 42 48 38N 0 10 E
Seesen 48 51 53N 10 10 E
Sefadu 120 8 35N 10 58W
Séfeto 120 14 8N 9 49W
Sefrou 118 33 52N 4 52W
Sefton 143 43 15 S 172 41 E
Sefton Mt. 143 43 40 S 170 5 E
Sefuri-San 110 33 28N 130 18 E
Sefwi Bekwai 120 6 10N 2 25W
Seg-ozero 76 63 0N 33 10 E
Segamat 101 2 30N 102 50 E
Segarcea 70 44 6N 23 43 E
Segbwema 120 8 0N 11 0W
Segeston 31 51 41N 4 48W
Seget 103 1 24 S 130 58 E
Seggueur, O. 118 32 4N 2 4 E
Segid 123 16 55N 42 0 E
Segonzac 44 45 36N 0 14W
Segorbe 58 39 50N 0 30W
Ségou 120 13 30N 6 10W
Segovia 56 40 57N 4 10W
Segovia □ 56 40 55N 4 10W
Segré 42 47 40N 0 52W
Segre, R. 58 41 40N 0 43 E
Seguam 147 52 0N 172 30W
Seguam Pass. 147 53 0N 175 30W
Séguéla 120 7 55N 6 40W
Segula I. 147 52 0N 178 5W
Segundo 159 37 12N 104 50W
Segundo, R. 172 30 53 S 62 44W
Segura, R. 59 38 9N 0 40W
Segura, Sierra de 59 38 5N 2 45W
Sehithwa 125 20 30 S 22 30 E
Sehore 94 23 10N 77 5 E
Sehwan 94 26 28N 67 53 E
Seica Mare 70 46 1N 24 7 E
Seikpyu 98 20 54N 94 48 E
Seil, I. 34 56 17N 5 37W
Seilandsjøkelen 74 70 25N 23 16 E
Seiling 159 36 10N 99 5W
Seille, R. 45 46 31N 4 57 E
Seilles 47 50 30N 5 6 E
Sein, I. de 42 48 2N 4 52W
Seinäjoki 74 62 48N 22 43 E
Seine-Maritime □ 42 49 40N 1 0 E
Seine □ 43 49 0N 3 0 E
Seine-et-Marne □ 43 48 45N 3 0 E
Seine, R. 42 49 28N 0 15 E
Seine-Saint-Denis □ 43 48 58N 2 24 E
Seini 70 47 44N 23 21 E
Seistan 93 30 50N 61 0 E
Seiyala 122 22 57N 32 41 E
Sejal 174 2 45N 68 0W
Sejerby 73 55 54N 11 10 E
Sejerø 73 55 54N 11 15 E
Sejerø Bugt 73 55 53N 11 9 E
Seka 123 8 10N 36 52 E
Sekaju 102 2 58 S 103 58 E
Seke 126 3 20 S 33 31 E
Sekenke 126 4 18 S 34 11 E
Seki 111 35 29N 136 55 E
Sekigahara 111 35 22N 136 28 E
Sekiu 160 48 30N 124 29W
Sekkane, Erg in 118 20 30N 1 30W
Sekondi 120 5 2N 1 48W
Sekondi-Takoradi 120 5 0N 1 48W
Sekuma 128 24 36 S 23 57 E
Sela Dingay 123 9 58N 39 32 E
Selah 160 46 44N 120 30W
Selama 101 5 12N 100 42 E
Selangor □ 101 3 20N 101 30 E
Selargius 64 39 14N 9 14 E
Selaru, I. 103 8 18 S 131 0 E
Selat Bangka 102 2 30 S 105 30 E
Selawik 147 66 55N 160 10W
Selb 49 50 9N 12 9 E
Selborne 29 51 5N 0 55W
Selby, U.K. 33 53 47N 1 5W
Selby, U.S.A. 158 45 34N 99 55W
Selbyville 162 38 28N 75 13W
Selce 63 45 20N 16 50 E
Selden 158 39 24N 100 39W
Seldovia 147 59 30N 151 45W
Sele, R. 65 40 27N 15 0 E
Selenica 68 40 33N 19 39 E
Selenter See 48 54 19N 10 26 E
Selestat 43 48 10N 7 26 E
Selet 72 63 15N 15 45 E
Seletan, Tg. 102 4 10 S 114 40 E
Seletin 70 47 50N 25 12 E
Selevac 66 44 44N 20 52 E
Selfridge 158 46 3N 100 57W
Sélibaby 120 15 20N 12 15W
Seliger, Oz. 80 57 15N 33 0 E
Seligman 161 35 17N 112 56W
Selim, C. Afr. 126 5 31N 23 48 E
Selim, Turkey 83 40 15N 42 58 E
Selîma, El Wâhât el 122 21 28N 29 31 E
Selinda Spillway 128 18 35 S 23 10 E
Selinoûs 69 37 35N 21 37 E
Selinsgrove 162 40 48N 76 52W
Selipuk Gompa 95 31 23N 82 49 E
Selizharovo 80 57 1N 33 17 E
Selje 71 62 3N 5 22 E
Seljord 71 59 30N 8 40 E
Selkirk, Can. 153 50 10N 97 20W
Selkirk, U.K. 35 55 33N 2 50W
Selkirk (□) 26 55 30N 3 0W
Selkirk I. 153 53 20N 99 6W
Selkirk Mts. 152 51 15N 117 40W
Selles-sur-Cher 43 47 16N 1 33 E
Sellières 43 46 50N 5 32 E
Sells 161 31 57N 111 57W
Sellye 53 45 52N 17 51 E
Selma, Ala., U.S.A. 157 32 30N 87 0W
Selma, Calif., U.S.A. 163 36 39N 119 39W
Selma, N.C., U.S.A. 157 35 32N 78 15W
Selmer 157 35 9N 88 36W
Sélo, Óros 68 41 10N 126 0 E
Selongey 43 47 36N 5 10 E
Selowandoma Falls 127 21 15 S 31 50 E
Selpele 103 0 1 S 130 5 E
Selsey 29 50 44N 0 47W
Selsey Bill 29 50 44N 0 47W
Seltz 43 48 48N 8 4 E
Selu, I. 103 7 26 S 130 55 E
Selukwe 127 19 40 S 30 0 E
Sélune, R. 42 48 38N 1 22W
Selva, Argent. 172 29 50 S 62 0W
Selva, Spain 58 41 13N 1 8 E
Selva Beach, La 163 36 56N 121 51W
Selva, La 58 42 0N 2 45 E
Selvas 174 6 30 S 67 0W
Selwyn 133 21 30 S 140 29 E
Selwyn L. 153 60 0N 104 30W
Selwyn Mts. 147 63 0N 130 0W
Selwyn P.O. 138 21 32 S 140 30 E
Selwyn Ra. 138 21 10 S 140 0 E
Semani, R. 68 40 45N 19 50 E
Semarang 103 7 0 S 110 26 E
Sembabule 126 0 4 S 31 25 E
Semeih 123 12 43N 30 53 E
Semenov 81 56 43N 44 30 E
Semenovka 82 49 37N 33 2 E
Semeru, Mt. 103 8 4 S 113 3 E
Sémi 120 15 4N 13 41W
Semiluki 81 51 41N 39 10 E
Seminoe Res. 160 42 0N 107 0W
Seminole, Okla., U.S.A. 159 35 15N 96 45W
Seminole, Tex., U.S.A. 159 32 41N 102 38W
Semiozernoye 84 52 22N 64 8 E
Semipalatinsk 76 50 30N 80 10 E
Semirara Is. 103 12 0N 121 20 E

Semisopochnoi I Shawbost

Semisopochnoi I. 147 52 0N 179 40W
Semitau 102 0 29N 111 57 E
Semiyarskoye 76 50 55N 78 30 E
Semmering Pass. 52 47 41N 15 45 E
Semnan 93 35 55N 53 25 E
Semnan □ 93 36 0N 54 0 E
Semois, R. 47 49 53N 4 44 E
Semporna 103 4 30N 118 33 E
Semuda 102 2 51 S 112 58 E
Semur-en-Auxois 43 47 30N 4 20 E
Sen. R. 101 13 45N 105 12 E
Sena Madureira 174 9 5 S 68 45W
Senador Pompeu 170 5 40 S 39 20W
Senai 101 1 38N 103 38 E
Senaja 102 6 49 S 117 2 E
Senanga 128 16 2 S 23 14 E
Senatobia 159 34 38N 89 57W
Sendafa 123 9 11N 39 3 E
Sendai, Kagoshima, Japan 110 31 50N 130 20 E
Sendai, Miyagi, Japan 112 38 15N 141 0 E
Sendamangalam 97 11 17N 78 17 E
Sendeling's Drift 128 28 12 S 16 52 E
Sendenhorst 48 51 50N 7 49 E
Sendurjana 96 21 32N 78 24 E
Senec 53 48 12N 17 23 E
Seneca, Oreg., U.S.A. 160 44 10N 119 2W
Seneca, S.C., U.S.A. 157 34 43N 82 59W
Seneca Falls 162 42 55N 76 50W
Seneca L. 162 42 40N 76 58W
Seneffe 47 50 32N 4 16 E
Senegal ■ 120 14 30N 14 30W
Senegal, R. 120 16 30N 15 30W
Senekal 129 28 18 S 27 36 E
Senftenberg 48 51 30N 13 51 E
Senga Hill 127 9 19 S 31 11 E
Senge Khambab (Indus), R. 94 28 40N 70 10 E
Sengerema □ 126 2 10 S 32 20 E
Sengiley 81 53 58N 48 54 E
Sengwa, R. 127 17 10 S 28 15 E
Senhor-do-Bonfim 170 10 30 S 40 10W
Senica 53 48 41N 17 25 E
Senigállia 63 43 42N 13 12 E
Seniku 98 25 32N 97 48 E
Senio, R. 63 44 18N 11 47 E
Senj 63 45 0N 14 58 E
Senja 74 69 25N 17 20 E
Senlis 43 49 13N 2 35 E
Senmonorom 100 12 27N 107 12 E
Sennâr 123 13 30N 33 35 E
Senne, R. 47 50 42N 4 13 E
Sennen 30 50 4N 5 42W
Senneterre 150 48 25N 77 15W
Senno 80 54 45N 29 58 E
Sennori 64 40 49N 8 36 E
Senny Bridge 31 51 57N 3 35W
Seno 100 16 41N 105 1 E
Senonches 42 48 34N 1 2 E
Senorbì 64 39 33N 9 8 E
Senozeče 63 45 43N 14 3 E
Sens 43 48 11N 3 15 E
Senta 66 45 55N 20 3 E
Sentein 44 42 53N 0 58 E
Senteny 126 5 17 S 25 42 E
Sentier, Le 51 46 37N 6 15 E
Sentinel 161 32 56N 113 13W
Sento Sé 170 9 40 S 41 18W
Sentolo 103 7 55 S 110 13 E
Senya Beraku 121 5 28N 0 31W
Seo de Urgel 58 42 22N 1 23 E
Seohara 95 29 15N 78 33 E
Seoni 95 22 5N 79 30 E
Seorinayan 96 21 45N 82 34 E
Separation Point 151 53 37N 57 25W
Seph, R. 33 54 17N 1 9W
Sepik, R. 135 3 49 S 144 30 E
Sepólno Krajenskie 54 53 26N 17 30 E
Sepone 100 16 45N 106 13 E
Sepopa 128 18 49 S 22 12 E
Sepopol 54 54 16N 21 2 E
Sepori 107 38 57N 127 25 E
Sept Îles 151 50 13N 66 22W
Septemvri 67 42 13N 24 6 E
Septimus 138 21 13 S 148 47 E
Sepúlveda 56 41 18N 3 45W
Sequeros 56 40 31N 6 2W
Sequim 160 48 3N 123 9W
Sequoia Nat. Park 163 36 30N 118 30W
Serafimovich 83 49 30N 42 50 E
Seraing 47 50 35N 5 32 E
Seraja 101 2 41N 108 35 E
Seram, I. 103 3 10 S 129 0 E
Serampore 95 22 44N 88 30 E
Serang 103 6 8 S 106 10 E
Serasan 101 2 31N 109 2 E
Serasan, I. 102 2 29N 109 4 E
Seravezza 62 43 59N 10 13 E
Serbia = Srbija 66 43 30N 21 0 E
Sercaia 70 45 49N 25 9 E
Serdo 123 11 56N 41 14 E
Serdobsk 81 52 28N 44 10 E
Seredka 80 58 12N 28 3 E
Seregno 62 45 40N 9 12 E
Seremban 101 2 43N 101 53 E
Serena, La, Chile 172 29 55 S 71 10W
Serena, La, Spain 57 38 45N 5 40W
Serengeti □ 126 2 0 S 34 30 E
Serengeti Plain 126 2 40 S 35 0 E
Serenje 125 13 14 S 30 15 E
Sergach 81 55 30N 45 30 E
Serge, R. 58 42 5N 1 21 E
Sergievsk 81 54 0N 51 10 E
Sergipe □ 170 10 30 S 37 30W
Seria 102 4 37N 114 30 E
Serian 102 1 10N 110 40 E
Seriate 62 45 42N 9 43 E
Sérifontaine 43 49 20N 1 45 E
Sérifos, I. 69 37 9N 24 30 E
Sérignan 44 43 17N 3 17 E
Serik 92 36 55N 31 10 E
Seringapatam Reef 136 13 38 S 122 5 E
Sermaize-les-Bains 43 48 47N 4 54 E
Sermata, I. 103 8 15 S 128 50 E
Sérmide 63 45 0N 11 17 E
Sernovdsk 76 61 20N 73 28 E
Sernovodsk 84 53 54N 51 16 E
Sero 120 14 42N 10 59W
Serón 59 37 20N 2 29W
Serós 58 41 27N 0 24 E
Serov 84 59 36N 60 35 E
Serowe 128 22 25 S 26 43 E
Serpa 57 37 57N 7 38 E
Serpeddi, Punta 64 39 19N 9 28 E
Serpentara 64 39 8N 9 38 E
Serpentine 137 32 23 S 115 58 E
Serpentine L. 137 28 30 S 129 10 E
Serpent's Mouth 174 10 0N 61 30W
Serpis, R. 59 38 45N 0 21W
Serpukhov 81 54 55N 37 28 E
Serra 171 20 7 S 40 18W
Serra Capriola 65 41 47N 15 12 E
Serra do Salitre 74 19 6 S 46 41W
Serra Talhada 170 7 59 S 38 18W
Serradilla 56 39 50N 6 9W
Sérrai □ 68 41 5N 23 37 E
Serramanna 64 39 26N 8 56 E
Serranía de Cuenca 58 40 10N 1 50W
Serrat, C. 119 37 14N 9 10 E
Serres 45 44 26N 5 43 E
Serrezuela 172 30 40 S 65 20W
Serrinha 171 11 39 S 39 0W
Serrita 170 7 56 S 39 19W
Serro 171 18 37 S 43 23W
Sersale 65 39 1N 16 44 E
Sertã 56 39 48N 8 6W
Sertânia 170 8 5 S 37 20W
Sertanópolis 173 23 4 S 51 2W
Sertão 170 10 0 S 40 20W
Sertig 51 46 44N 9 52 E
Serua, P. 103 6 18 S 130 1 E
Serui 103 1 45 S 136 10 E
Serule 128 21 57 S 27 11 E
Sérvia 68 40 9N 21 58 E
Sesajap Lama 102 3 32N 117 11 E
Sese Is. 126 0 30 S 32 30 E
Sesepe 103 1 30 S 127 59 E
Sesfontein 128 19 7 S 13 39 E
Sesheke 128 17 29 S 24 13 E
Sesia, R. 62 45 35N 8 23 E
Sesimbra 57 38 28N 9 20W
Seskanore 38 54 31N 7 15W
Sessa Aurunca 64 41 14N 13 55 E
Sestao 58 43 18N 3 0W
Sesto S. Giovanni 62 45 32N 9 14 E
Sestri Levante 62 44 17N 9 22 E
Sestrières 62 44 58N 6 56 E
Sestrunj, I. 63 44 10N 15 0 E
Sestu 64 39 18N 9 6 E
Sesvenna 51 46 42N 10 25 E
Seta 108 32 20N 100 41 E
Setaka 110 33 9N 130 28 E
Setana 112 42 26N 139 51 E
Sète 44 43 25N 3 42 E
Sete Lagoas 171 19 27 S 44 16W
Sétif 119 36 9N 5 26 E
Seto 111 35 14N 137 6 E
Seto Naikai 110 34 20N 133 30 E
Setouchi 112 28 8N 129 19 E
Setsan 98 16 3N 95 23 E
Settat 118 33 0N 7 40W
Setté Cama 124 2 32 S 9 57 E
Séttimo Tor 62 45 9N 7 46 E
Setting L. 153 55 0N 98 38W
Settle 32 54 5N 2 18W
Settlement Pt. 157 26 40N 79 0W
Setto Calende 62 45 44N 8 37 E
Setúbal 57 38 30N 8 58W
Setúbal □ 57 38 25N 8 35W
Setúbal, B. de 57 38 40N 8 56W
Seul L. 150 50 25N 92 30W
Seul Reservoir, Lac 150 50 25N 92 30W
Seulimeum 102 5 27N 95 15 E
Seuzach 51 47 32N 8 49 E
Sevastopol 82 44 35N 33 30 E
Sevelen 51 47 7N 9 30 E
Seven Emu 138 16 20 S 137 8 E
Seven Heads 39 51 35N 8 43W
Seven Hogs, Is. 39 52 20N 10 0W
Seven, R. 33 54 11N 0 51W
Seven Sisters 31 51 46N 3 43W
Seven Sisters, mt 152 54 56N 128 10W
Sevenoaks 29 51 16N 0 11 E
Sevenum 47 51 25N 6 2 E
Sever, R. 57 39 40N 7 32W
Sévérac-le-Chateau 44 44 20N 3 5 E
Severn Beach 28 51 34N 2 39W
Severn L. 150 53 54N 90 48W
Severn, R., Can. 150 56 2N 87 36W
Severn, R., U.K. 28 51 35N 2 38W
Severn Stoke 28 52 5N 2 13W
Severnaya Zemlya 77 79 0N 100 0 E
Severnyye Uvaly 78 58 0N 48 0 E
Severo-Kurilsk 77 50 40N 156 8 E
Severodonetsk 83 48 50N 38 30 E
Severodvinsk 78 64 27N 39 58 E
Severomoravsky □ 53 49 38N 17 40 E
Severouralsk 84 60 9N 59 57 E
Sevier 161 38 39N 112 11W
Sevier L. 160 39 0N 113 20W
Sevier, R. 161 39 10N 112 50W
Sevilla, Colomb. 174 4 16N 75 57W
Sevilla, Spain 57 37 23N 6 0W
Sevilla □ 57 37 0N 6 0W
Seville = Sevilla 57 37 23N 6 0W
Sevnica 63 46 2N 15 19 E
Sevsk 80 52 10N 34 30 E
Seward 147 60 0N 149 40W
Seward Pen. 147 65 0N 164 0W
Sewell 172 34 10 S 70 45W
Sewer 103 5 46 S 134 40 E
Sexbierum 46 53 13N 5 29 E
Sexsmith 152 55 21N 118 47W
Seychelles, Is. 11 5 0 S 56 0 E
Seyðisfjörður 74 65 16N 14 0W
Seym, R. 80 51 45N 35 0 E
Seymchan 77 62 40N 152 30 E
Seymour, Austral. 141 37 0 S 145 10 E
Seymour, Conn., U.S.A. 162 41 23N 73 5W
Seymour, Ind., U.S.A. 156 39 0N 85 50W
Seymour, Tex., U.S.A. 159 33 35N 99 18W
Seymour, Wis., U.S.A. 156 44 30N 88 20W
Seyne 45 44 21N 6 22 E
Seyne-sur-Mer, La 45 43 7N 5 52 E
Sezana 63 45 43N 13 41 E
Sézanne 43 48 40N 3 40 E
Sezze 64 41 30N 13 3 E
Sfântu Gheorghe 70 45 52N 25 48 E
Sfax 119 34 49N 10 48 E
Sgurr Mor 36 57 42N 5 0W
Sgurr na Ciche 36 57 0N 5 29W
Sgurr na Lapaich 36 57 23N 5 5W
Sha Ch'i, R. 109 26 35N 118 8 E
Shaartuz 85 37 16N 68 8 E
Shaba 126 8 0 S 25 0 E
Shaba Gamba 99 32 8N 88 55 E
Shaballe, R. 123 5 0N 44 0 E
Shabani 127 20 17 S 30 2 E
Shabbear 30 50 52N 4 12W
Shabla 67 43 31N 28 32 E
Shabogamo L. 151 48 40N 77 0W
Shabunda 126 2 40 S 27 16 E
Shackleton 13 78 30 S 36 1W
Shackleton Inlet 13 83 0 S 160 0 E
Shaddad 122 21 25N 40 2 E
Shadi 95 33 24N 77 14 E
Shadrinsk 84 56 5N 63 58 E
Shadwân 122 27 30N 34 0 E
Shaffa 121 10 30N 12 6 E
Shafter 163 35 32N 119 14W
Shaftesbury 28 51 0N 2 12W
Shag Pt. 143 45 29 S 170 52 E
Shagamu 121 6 51N 3 39 E
Shagram 95 36 24N 72 20 E
Shah Bunder 94 24 13N 67 50 E
Shahabad, And. P., India 96 17 10N 78 11 E
Shahabad, Punjab, India 94 30 10N 76 55 E
Shahabad, Raj., India 94 25 15N 77 11 E
Shahabad, Uttar Pradesh, India 95 27 36N 79 56 E
Shāhābād 93 37 40N 56 50 E
Shahada 96 21 33N 74 30 E
Shahapur 96 15 50N 74 34 E
Shāhbād 92 34 10N 46 30 E
Shahdād 93 30 30N 57 40 E
Shahdadkot 94 27 50N 67 55 E
Shahddpur 94 25 55N 68 35 E
Shahganj 95 26 3N 82 44 E
Shahgarh 93 27 15N 69 50 E
Shahhat (Cyrene) 117 32 40N 21 35 E
Shāhī 93 36 30N 52 55 E
Shahjahanpur 95 27 54N 79 57 E
Shaho 106 36 31N 114 35 E
Shahpur, Mad. P., India 94 22 12N 77 58 E
Shahpur, Mysore, India 97 16 40N 76 48 E
Shahpur, Iran 92 38 12N 44 45 E
Shahpur, Pak. 94 28 46N 68 27 E
Shahpura 95 23 10N 80 45 E
Shahr-e Babak 93 30 10N 55 20 E
Shahr Kord 93 32 15N 50 55 E
Shahraban 92 34 0N 45 0 E
Shahreza 93 32 0N 51 55 E
Shahrig 94 30 15N 67 40 E
Shahriza 93 32 0N 51 50 E
Shahrud 93 36 30N 55 0 E
Shahrukh 93 33 50N 60 10 E
Shahsavar 93 36 45N 51 12 E
Shahsien 109 26 25N 117 50 E
Shahuk'ou 106 40 20N 112 18 E
Shaibâra 123 25 26N 36 47 E
Shaikhabad 94 34 0N 68 45 E
Shaim 84 60 21N 64 10 E
Shajapur 94 23 20N 76 15 E
Shakargarh 94 32 17N 75 43 E
Shakawe 128 18 28 S 21 49 E
Shakhristan 85 39 47N 68 49 E
Shakhrisyabz 85 39 3N 66 50 E
Shakhty 83 47 40N 40 10 E
Shakhunya 81 57 40N 47 0 E
Shaki 121 8 41N 3 21 E
Shakopee 158 44 45N 93 30W
Shaktolik 147 64 30N 161 15W
Shala Lake 123 7 30N 38 30 E
Shaldon 30 50 32N 3 31W
Shalkar Karashatau, Ozero 84 50 26N 61 12 E
Shalkar Yega Kara, Ozero 84 50 45N 60 54 E
Sham, J. ash 93 23 10N 57 5 E
Shama 121 5 1N 1 42W
Shamâl Dâfû □ 123 15 0N 25 0 E
Shamâl Kordofân □ 123 15 0N 30 0 E
Shamar, Jabal 92 27 40N 41 0 E
Shamattawa 153 55 51N 92 5W
Shamattawa, R. 150 55 1N 85 23W
Shambe 123 7 2N 30 46 E
Shambu 123 9 32N 37 3 E
Shamgong Dzong 98 27 19N 90 35 E
Shamil, India 94 29 32N 77 18 E
Shamil, Iran 93 27 30N 56 55 E
Shamkhor 83 40 56N 46 0 E
Shamo, L. 123 5 45N 37 30 E
Shamokin 162 40 47N 76 33W
Shamrock 159 35 15N 100 15W
Shamva 125 17 20 S 31 32 E
Shan □ 98 21 30N 98 30 E
Shanagolden 39 52 35N 9 6W
Shanan, R. 123 8 0N 40 20 E
Shanch'eng 109 31 45N 115 30 E
Shandon 163 35 39N 120 23W
Shandon Downs 138 17 45 S 134 50 E
Shanga 121 9 1N 5 2 E
Shangalowe 127 10 50 S 26 30 E
Shangani 127 19 1 S 28 51 E
Shangani, R. 127 18 35 S 27 45 E
Shangchih, (Chuho) 107 45 10N 127 59 E
Shangching 106 33 9N 110 2 E
Shangch'iu 105 34 26N 115 40 E
Shangch'uan Shan, I. 109 21 45N 112 45 E
Shanghai 109 31 10N 121 25 E
Shanghang 109 25 5N 116 30 E
Shangho 107 37 19N 117 9 E
Shanghsien 106 33 30N 109 58 E
Shangjao 109 28 25N 117 57 E
Shangkao 109 28 16N 114 50 E
Shanglin 108 23 26N 108 36 E
Shangnan 106 33 35N 110 49 E
Shangpanch'eng 107 40 50N 118 0 E
Shangshui 106 33 42N 114 34 E
Shangssu 108 22 10N 108 0 E
Shangtsai 106 33 15N 114 20 E
Shangtu 106 41 31N 113 35 E
Shangyu 109 25 59N 114 29 E
Shanhaikuan 107 40 2N 119 48 E
Shanhot'un 107 44 42N 127 12 E
Shanhsien 106 34 51N 116 9 E
Shani 121 10 14N 12 2 E
Shaniko 160 45 0N 120 15W
Shanklin 28 50 39N 1 9W
Shannon, Greenl. 12 75 10N 18 30W
Shannon, N.Z. 142 40 33 S 175 25 E
Shannon Airport 39 52 42N 85 7W
Shannon Bridge 39 53 17N 8 2W
Shannon I. 12 75 0N 18 0W
Shannon, Mouth of the 39 52 30N 9 55W
Shannon, R. 39 53 10N 8 10W
Shansi □ 106 37 30N 112 15 E
Shantar, Ostrov Bolshoi 77 55 9N 137 40 E
Shant'ou 109 23 28N 116 40 E
Shantung □ 105 36 0N 117 30 E
Shantung Pantao 107 37 5N 121 0 E
Shanyang 106 33 39N 110 2 E
Shanyin 106 39 34N 112 50 E
Shaohing 109 30 0N 120 32 E
Shaokuan 109 24 50N 113 35 E
Shaowu 109 27 25N 117 30 E
Shaoyang 109 27 10N 111 30 E
Shap 32 54 32N 2 40W
Shap'ing 109 22 46N 112 57 E
Shapinsay, I. 37 59 2N 2 50W
Shapinsay Sd. 37 59 0N 2 51W
Shaqra 92 25 15N 45 16 E
Sharafa (Ogr) 123 11 59N 27 7 E
Sharavati, R. 97 14 32N 74 0 E
Sharhjui 93 32 30N 67 22 E
Shari 92 27 20N 43 45 E
Sharjah 93 25 23N 55 26 E
Shark B., N. Territory, Austral. 132 11 20 S 130 35 E
Shark B., W. Australia, Austral. 137 25 55 S 113 32 E
Sharm el Sheikh 122 27 53N 34 15 E
Sharon, Mass., U.S.A. 162 42 5N 71 11W
Sharon, Pa., U.S.A. 156 41 18N 80 30W
Sharon, Plain of = Hasharon 90 32 12N 34 49 E
Sharon Springs 162 42 48N 74 37W
Sharp Pt. 138 10 58 S 142 43 E
Sharpe, L. 150 54 10N 93 21W
Sharpe L. 153 50 23N 95 30W
Sharpness 28 51 43N 2 28W
Sharya 81 58 12N 45 40 E
Shasha 123 6 29N 35 59 E
Shashemene 123 7 13N 38 33 E
Shashi 125 21 15 S 27 27 E
Shashi, R. 127 21 40 S 28 40 E
Shashih 109 30 19N 112 14 E
Shasta, Mt. 160 41 45N 122 0W
Shasta Res. 160 40 50N 122 15W
Shati 109 26 6N 114 51 E
Shatsk 81 54 0N 41 45 E
Shattuck 159 36 17N 99 55W
Shaumyani 83 41 13N 44 45 E
Shaunavon 153 49 35N 108 25W
Shaver Lake 163 37 9N 119 18W
Shaw I. 138 20 30 S 149 2 E
Shaw, R. 136 20 21 S 119 17 E
Shawan 105 44 21N 85 37 E
Shawangunk Mts. 162 41 40N 74 25W
Shawano 156 44 45N 88 38W
Shawbost 36 58 20N 6 40W

Shawbury **Siddeburen**

Shawbury **28** 52 48N 2 40W
Shawinigan **150** 46 35N 72 50W
Shawnee **159** 35 15N 97 0W
Shaymak **85** 37 33N 74 50 E
Shaziz **99** 33 10N 82 43 E
Shchĕkino **81** 54 1N 37 28 E
Shcherbakov = Rybinsk **81** 58 5N 38 50 E
Shchigri **81** 51 55N 36 58 E
Shchuchinsk **76** 52 56N 70 12 E
Shchuchye **84** 55 12N 62 46 E
Shchurovo **81** 55 0N 38 51 E
Shebekino **81** 50 28N 37 0 E
Shebele, Wabi **123** 2 0N 44 0 E
Sheboygan **156** 43 46N 87 45W
Shechem **90** 32 13N 35 21 E
Shech'i **106** 33 3N 112 57 E
Shediac **151** 46 14N 64 32W
Sheefry Hills **38** 53 40N 9 40W
Sheelin, Lough **38** 53 48N 7 20W
Sheep Haven **38** 55 12N 7 55W
Sheeps Hd. **39** 51 32N 9 50W
Sheerness **29** 51 26N 0 47 E
Sheet Harbour **151** 44 56N 62 31W
Shefar'am **90** 32 48N 35 10 E
Shefeiya **90** 32 35N 34 58 E
Sheffield, U.K. **33** 53 23N 1 28W
Sheffield, Ala., U.S.A. **157** 34 45N 87 42W
Sheffield, Mass., U.S.A. **162** 42 6N 73 23W
Sheffield, Tex., U.S.A. **159** 30 42N 101 49W
Shefford **29** 52 2N 0 20W
Shegaon **96** 20 48N 76 59 E
Sheho **153** 51 35N 103 13W
Shehojele **123** 10 40N 35 27 E
Shehsien, Anhwei, China **109** 29 52N 118 26 E
Shehsien, Hopeh, China **106** 36 33N 113 40 E
Shehung **108** 31 0N 105 12 E
Shehy Mts. **39** 51 47N 9 15W
Sheikhpura **95** 25 9N 85 53 E
Shek Hasan **123** 13 5N 35 58 E
Shekar Dzong **95** 28 45N 87 0 E
Shekhupura **94** 31 42N 73 58 E
Sheki **83** 41 10N 47 5 E
Sheksna, R. **81** 59 30N 38 30 E
Shelburne, N.S., Can. **151** 43 47N 65 20W
Shelburne, Ont., Can. **150** 44 4N 80 15W
Shelburne B. **133** 11 50 S 143 0 E
Shelburne Falls **162** 42 36N 72 45W
Shelby, Mich., U.S.A. **156** 43 34N 86 27W
Shelby, Mont., U.S.A. **160** 48 30N 111 59W
Shelby, N.C., U.S.A. **157** 35 18N 81 34W
Shelbyville, Ill., U.S.A. **158** 39 25N 88 45W
Shelbyville, Ind., U.S.A. **156** 39 30N 85 42W
Shelbyville, Tenn., U.S.A. **157** 35 30N 86 25W
Sheldon **158** 43 6N 95 51W
Sheldon Point **147** 62 30N 165 0W
Sheldrake **151** 50 20N 64 51W
Shelikef, Str. **147** 58 0N 154 0W
Shelikhova, Zaliv **77** 59 30N 157 0 E
Shell, L. **36** 58 0N 6 28W
Shell Lake **153** 53 19N 107 14W
Shell Lakes **137** 29 20 S 127 30 E
Shellbrook **153** 53 13N 106 24W
Shellharbour **141** 34 31 S 150 51 E
Shelon, R. **80** 58 10N 30 30 E
Shelter Bay **151** 50 30N 67 20W
Shelter I **162** 41 5N 72 21W
Shelton, Conn., U.S.A. **162** 41 18N 73 7W
Shelton, Wash., U.S.A. **160** 47 15N 123 6W
Shemakha **83** 40 50N 48 28 E
Shenandoah, Iowa, U.S.A. **158** 40 50N 95 25W
Shenandoah, Pa., U.S.A. **162** 40 49N 76 13W
Shenandoah, Va., U.S.A. **156** 38 30N 78 38W
Shenandoah, R. **156** 38 30N 78 38W
Shencha **105** 30 56N 88 38 E
Shench'ih **106** 39 8N 112 10 E
Shenchingtzu **107** 44 48N 124 32 E
Shench'iu **106** 33 26N 115 2 E
Shencottah **97** 8 59N 77 18 E
Shendam **121** 9 10N 9 30 E
Shendî **123** 16 46N 33 33 E
Shendurni **96** 20 39N 75 36 E
Shenfield **29** 51 39N 0 21 E
Shengfang **106** 39 5N 116 42 E
Shëngjergji **68** 41 2N 20 10 E
Shëngjini **68** 41 50N 19 35 E
Shenmëria **68** 42 7N 20 13 E
Shenmu **106** 38 54N 110 24 E
Shensi □ **106** 34 50N 109 25 E
Shenton, Mt. **137** 27 57 S 123 22 E
Shenyang **107** 42 50N 123 25 E
Sheopur Kalan **93** 25 40N 76 40 E
Shepetovka **80** 50 10N 27 0 E
Shephelah = Hashefela **90** 31 30N 34 43 E
Shepparton **141** 36 23 S 145 26 E
Sheppey, I. of **29** 51 23N 0 50 E
Shepshed **28** 52 47N 1 18W
Shepton Mallet **28** 51 11N 2 31W
Sher Khan Qala **94** 29 55N 66 10 E
Sher Qila **95** 36 7N 74 2 E
Sherada **123** 7 25N 36 30 E
Sherborne **28** 50 56N 2 31W
Sherborne St. John **28** 51 18N 1 7W
Sherbro I. **120** 7 30N 12 40W
Sherbrooke **151** 45 8N 81 57W
Sherburn, N. Yorks., U.K. **33** 54 12N 0 32W
Sherburn, N. Yorks., U.K. **33** 53 47N 1 15W
Sherburne **162** 42 41N 75 30W
Shercock **38** 54 0N 6 54W
Sherda **119** 20 7N 16 46 E
Shere **29** 51 13N 0 28W
Shereik **122** 18 52N 33 40 E
Sherfield English **28** 51 1N 1 35W
Sheridan, Ark., U.S.A. **159** 34 20N 92 25W
Sheridan, Col., U.S.A. **158** 39 44N 105 3W
Sheridan, Wyo., U.S.A. **160** 44 50N 107 0W
Sheriff Hutton **33** 54 5N 1 0W
Sheriff Muir **35** 56 12N 3 53W
Sheringham **29** 52 56N 1 11 E
Sherkin I. **39** 51 38N 9 25W
Sherkot **95** 29 22N 78 35 E
Sherman **159** 33 40N 96 35W
Sherpur **98** 24 41N 89 25 E
Sherridon **153** 55 8N 101 5W
Sherston **28** 51 35N 2 13W
Sherwood, N.D., U.S.A. **158** 48 59N 101 36W
Sherwood, Tex., U.S.A. **159** 31 18N 100 45W
Sherwood For. **33** 53 5N 1 5W
Shesheke **125** 17 14 S 24 22 E
Sheslay **152** 58 17N 131 45W
Sheslay, R. **152** 58 48N 132 5W
Shethanei L. **153** 58 48N 97 50W
Shetland □ **36** 60 30N 1 30W
Shetland Is. **36** 60 30N 1 30W
Shevaroy Hills **97** 11 58N 78 12 E
Shevchenko **83** 44 25N 51 20 E
Shewa □ **123** 9 33N 38 10 E
Sheyenne **159** 47 52N 99 8W
Sheyenne, R. **158** 47 40N 98 15W
Shiant Is. **36** 57 54N 6 20W
Shiant, Sd. of Scot. **36** 57 54N 6 30W
Shibam **91** 16 0N 48 36 E
Shibata **112** 37 57N 139 20 E
Shiberghan □ **93** 35 45N 66 0 E
Shibetsu **112** 44 10N 142 23 E
Shibîn El Kôm **122** 30 31N 30 55 E
Shibogama L. **150** 53 35N 88 15W
Shibukawa **111** 36 29N 139 0 E
Shibushi **110** 31 25N 131 0 E
Shibushi-Wan **110** 31 24N 131 8 E
Shickshinny **162** 41 9N 76 9W
Shido **110** 34 19N 134 10 E
Shiel, L. **36** 56 48N 5 32W
Shield, C. **138** 13 20 S 136 20 E
Shieldaig **36** 57 31N 5 39W
Shifnal **28** 52 40N 2 23W
Shiga-ken □ **111** 35 20N 136 0 E
Shigaib **117** 15 5N 23 35 E
Shigaraki **111** 34 57N 136 2 E
Shihch'eng **109** 26 19N 116 15 E
Shihchiachuangi **106** 38 2N 114 30 E
Shihch'ien **108** 27 30N 108 14 E
Shihchiu Hu **109** 31 28N 118 53 E
Shihchu **108** 30 4N 108 10 E
Shihch'üan **106** 33 3N 108 17 E
Shihhsing **109** 24 57N 114 4 E
Shihku **108** 26 52N 99 56 E
Shihkuaikou **106** 40 42N 110 20 E
Shihlung **109** 23 55N 113 35 E
Shihmen **109** 29 36N 111 23 E
Shihmenchien **109** 29 33N 116 47 E
Shihmien **108** 29 20N 102 28 E
Shihping **108** 27 2N 108 7 E
Shihp'ing **108** 23 43N 102 30 E
Shihshou **109** 29 43N 112 26 E
Shihtai **109** 30 22N 117 57 E
Shihtien **108** 24 44N 99 11 E
Shiht'ouhotzu **107** 44 52N 128 41 E
Shihtsuishan **106** 39 15N 106 50 E
Shihtsung **108** 24 51N 103 59 E
Shiiba **110** 32 29N 131 4 E
Shijaku **68** 41 21N 19 33 E
Shikarpur, India **94** 28 17N 78 7 E
Shikarpur, Pak. **94** 27 57N 68 39 E
Shikine-Jima **111** 34 19N 139 13 E
Shikohabad **93** 27 6N 78 38 E
Shikoku **110** 33 30N 133 30 E
Shikoku □ **110** 33 30N 133 30 E
Shikoku-Sanchi **110** 33 30N 133 30 E
Shilbottle **35** 55 23N 1 42W
Shilda **84** 51 49N 59 47 E
Shildon **33** 54 37N 1 39W
Shilka **77** 52 0N 115 55 E
Shilka, R. **77** 57 30N 93 18 E
Shillelagh **39** 52 46N 6 32W
Shillingstone **28** 50 54N 2 15W
Shillington **162** 40 18N 75 58W
Shillong **98** 25 35N 91 53 E
Shiloh **90** 32 4N 35 10 E
Shilovo **81** 54 25N 40 57 E
Shima-Hantō **111** 34 22N 136 45 E
Shimabara **110** 32 48N 130 20 E
Shimada **111** 34 49N 138 19 E
Shimane-Hantō **110** 35 30N 133 0 E
Shimane-ken □ **110** 35 0N 132 30 E
Shimenovsk **77** 52 15N 127 30 E
Shimizu **111** 35 0N 138 30 E
Shimo-Jima **110** 32 15N 130 7 E
Shimo-Koshiki-Jima **110** 31 40N 129 43 E
Shimoda **111** 34 40N 138 57 E
Shimodate **111** 36 20N 139 55 E
Shimoga **97** 13 57N 75 32 E
Shimoni **126** 4 38 S 39 20 E
Shimonita **111** 36 13N 138 47 E
Shimonoseki **110** 33 58N 131 0 E
Shimotsuma **111** 36 11N 139 58 E
Shimpuru Rapids **128** 17 45 S 19 55 E
Shimsha, R. **97** 13 15N 76 54 E
Shimsk **80** 58 15N 30 50 E
Shin Dand **93** 33 12N 62 8 E
Shin, L. **37** 58 7N 4 30W
Shin, R. **37** 58 0N 4 26W
Shin-Tone-Gawa **111** 35 57N 140 27 E
Shingbwiyang **98** 26 41N 96 13 E
Shingleton **150** 46 33N 86 33W
Shingu **111** 33 40N 135 55 E
Shinji **110** 35 24N 132 54 E
Shinji Ko **110** 35 26N 132 57 E
Shinjō **112** 38 46N 140 18 E
Shinkafe **121** 13 8N 6 29 E
Shinminato **111** 36 47N 137 4 E
Shinonoi **111** 36 35N 138 9 E
Shinrone **39** 53 0N 7 58W
Shinshiro **111** 34 54N 137 30 E
Shinyanga **126** 3 45 S 33 27 E
Shinyanga □ **126** 3 30 S 33 30 E
Shio-no-Misaki **111** 33 25N 135 45 E
Shiogama **112** 38 19N 141 1 E
Shiojiri **111** 36 6N 137 58 E
Ship I. **159** 30 16N 88 55W
Ship Shoal I. **162** 37 10N 75 45W
Shipbourne **29** 51 13N 0 19 E
Shipdham **29** 52 38N 0 53 E
Shipehenski Prokhod **67** 42 39N 25 28 E
Shipki La **93** 31 45N 78 40 E
Shipley **33** 53 50N 1 47W
Shippegan **151** 47 45N 64 45W
Shippensburg **156** 40 4N 77 32W
Shiprock **161** 36 51N 108 45W
Shipston-on-Stour **28** 52 4N 1 38W
Shipton-under-Wychwood **28** 51 51N 1 35W
Shir Kūh **93** 31 45N 53 30 E
Shirabad **85** 37 40N 67 1 E
Shirahama **111** 33 41N 135 20 E
Shirakawa **111** 36 17N 136 56 E
Shirane-San, Gumma, Japan **111** 36 48N 139 22 E
Shirane-San, Yamanashi, Japan **111** 35 34N 138 9 E
Shiraoi **112** 42 33N 141 21 E
Shirati **126** 1 10 S 34 0 E
Shiraz **93** 29 42N 52 30 E
Shire, R. **127** 16 30 S 35 0 E
Shirebrook **33** 53 13N 1 11W
Shiresh **85** 39 58N 70 59 E
Shirinab, R. **94** 29 30N 66 30 E
Shiringushi **81** 42 54N 53 56W
Shiriya-Zaki **112** 41 25N 141 30 E
Shirol **96** 16 47N 74 41 E
Shirpur **96** 21 21N 74 57 E
Shirvan **93** 37 30N 57 50 E
Shirwa L. = Chilwa L. **127** 15 15 S 35 40 E
Shishmanova **67** 42 58N 23 12 E
Shishmaref **147** 66 15N 166 10W
Shivali, (Sirkall) **97** 11 15N 79 41 E
Shivpuri **94** 25 18N 77 42 E
Shivta **90** 30 53N 34 40 E
Shiwele Ferry **127** 11 25 S 28 31 E
Shiyata **122** 29 25N 25 7 E
Shizuoka **111** 35 0N 138 30 E
Shizuoka-ken □ **111** 35 15N 138 40 E
Shklov **80** 54 10N 30 15 E
Shkoder = Shkodra **68** 42 6N 19 20 E
Shkodra **68** 42 6N 19 20 E
Shkodra □ **68** 42 5N 19 20 E
Shkumbini, R. **68** 41 5N 19 50 E
Shmidt, O. **77** 81 0N 91 0 E
Shō Gawa, R. **111** 36 47N 137 4 E
Shoa Ghimirra, (Wota) **123** 7 4N 35 51 E
Shoal, C. **137** 33 52 S 121 10 E
Shoal Lake **153** 50 30N 100 35W
Shōbara **110** 34 51N 133 1 E
Shōdo-Shima **110** 34 30N 134 15 E
Shoeburyness **29** 51 31N 0 49 E
Shokpar **85** 43 49N 74 21 E
Sholapur **96** 17 43N 75 56 E
Shologontsy **77** 66 13N 114 14 E
Shomera **90** 33 4N 35 17 E
Shōmrōn **90** 32 15N 35 13 E
Shona I. **36** 56 48N 5 50W
Shongopovi **161** 35 49N 110 37W
Shoranur **97** 10 46N 76 19 E
Shorapur **96** 16 31N 76 48 E
Shoreham-by-Sea **29** 50 50N 0 17W
Shortland I. **135** 7 0 S 155 45 E
Shoshone, Calif., U.S.A. **163** 35 58N 116 16W
Shoshone, Idaho, U.S.A. **160** 43 0N 114 27W
Shoshone L. **160** 44 0N 111 0W
Shoshone Mts. **160** 39 30N 117 30W
Shoshong **125** 22 56 S 26 31 E
Shoshoni **160** 43 13N 108 5W
Shostka **80** 51 57N 33 32 E
Shotts **35** 55 49N 3 47W
Shouch'ang **109** 29 22N 119 13 E
Shouhsien **109** 32 35N 116 48 E
Shoukuang **107** 36 53N 118 42 E
Shouning **109** 27 26N 119 27 E
Shouyang **106** 37 59N 113 9 E
Show Low **161** 34 16N 110 0W
Shpola **82** 49 1N 31 30 E
Shreveport **159** 32 30N 93 50W
Shrewsbury **28** 52 42N 2 45W
Shrewton **28** 51 11N 1 55W
Shrivardhan **96** 18 10N 73 3 E
Shrivenham **28** 51 36N 1 39W
Shropshire □ **28** 52 36N 2 45W
Shrule **38** 53 32N 9 7W
Shuangch'eng **107** 45 25N 126 20 E
Shuangchiang **108** 23 33N 99 58 E
Shuangfeng **109** 27 26N 112 10 E
Shuangfeng Tao **109** 26 35N 120 8 E
Shuangkou **107** 34 3N 117 34 E
Shuangliao **105** 43 31N 123 30 E
Shuangpai **108** 24 50N 101 36 E
Shuangshantzu **107** 40 21N 119 12 E
Shuangyang **107** 43 32N 125 40 E
Shuangyashan **105** 46 37N 131 22 E
Shuch'eng **109** 31 27N 116 57 E
Shugden Gomba **99** 29 35N 96 55 E
Shuguri Falls **127** 8 33 S 37 22 E
Shuich'eng **108** 26 35N 104 54 E
Shuichi **109** 27 28N 118 21 E
Shuiyeh **106** 36 8N 114 6 E
Shujalpur **94** 23 43N 76 40 E
Shulan **107** 44 27N 126 57 E
Shumagin Is. **147** 55 0N 159 0W
Shumerlya **81** 55 30N 46 10 E
Shumikha **84** 55 10N 63 15 E
Shunan **109** 29 37N 119 0 E
Shunch'ang **109** 26 48N 117 47 E
Shungay **83** 48 30N 46 45 E
Shungnak **147** 66 55N 157 10W
Shunning **99** 24 35N 99 50 E
Shunte **109** 22 48N 113 17 E
Shuohsien **106** 39 19N 112 25 E
Shupka Kunzang **95** 34 22N 78 22 E
Shuqra **91** 13 22N 45 34 E
Shur, R. **93** 28 30N 55 0 E
Shurab **85** 40 3N 70 33 E
Shurchi **85** 37 59N 67 47 E
Shurkhua **98** 22 15N 93 38 E
Shurma **84** 56 58N 50 21 E
Shusf **93** 31 50N 60 5 E
Shūshtar **92** 32 0N 48 50 E
Shuswap L. **152** 50 55N 119 3W
Shuweika **90** 32 20N 35 1 E
Shuya **81** 56 50N 41 28 E
Shuyak I. **147** 58 35N 152 30W
Shuzenji **111** 34 58N 138 56 E
Shwebo **98** 22 30N 95 45 E
Shwegu **98** 18 49N 95 26 E
Shwegun **98** 17 9N 97 39 E
Shweli Myit **99** 23 45N 96 45 E
Shweli, R. **99** 23 45N 96 45 E
Shwenyaung **98** 20 46N 96 57 E
Shyok **95** 34 15N 78 5 E
Shyok, R. **95** 34 30N 78 15 E
Si Chon **101** 9 0N 99 54 E
Si Kiang = Hsi Chiang, R. **39** 22 20N 113 20 E
Si Prachan **100** 14 37N 100 9 E
Si Racha **101** 13 10N 100 56 E
Siah **92** 22 0N 47 0 E
Siahan Range **93** 27 30N 64 40 E
Siaksriinderapura **102** 0 51N 102 0 E
Sialkot **94** 32 32N 74 30 E
Sialsuk **98** 23 24N 92 45 E
Siam **140** 32 35 S 136 41 E
Siam, G. of **101** 11 30N 101 0 E
Siam = Thailand ■ **100** 16 0N 102 0 E
Sian = Hsian **106** 34 17N 109 0 E
Siantan, P. **101** 3 10N 106 15 E
Siareh **93** 28 5N 60 20 E
Siargao, I. **103** 9 52N 126 3 E
Siari **95** 34 55N 76 40 E
Siasi **103** 5 34N 120 50 E
Siassi **135** 5 40 S 147 51 E
Siátista **68** 40 15N 21 33 E
Siau, I. **103** 2 50N 125 25 E
Siauliai **80** 55 56N 23 15 E
Siaya □ **126** 0 0N 34 20 E
Siazan **83** 41 3N 48 7 E
Sibâi, Gebel el **122** 25 45N 34 10 E
Sibari **65** 39 47N 16 27 E
Sibay **84** 52 42N 58 39 E
Sibaya, L. **129** 27 20 S 32 45 E
Sibbald **153** 51 24N 110 10W
Sibenik **63** 43 48N 15 54 E
Siberia **77** 60 0N 100 0 E
Siberut, I. **102** 1 30 S 99 0 E
Sibi **94** 29 30N 67 48 E
Sibil **103** 4 59 S 140 35 E
Sibiti **124** 3 38 S 13 19 E
Sibiu **70** 45 45N 24 9 E
Sibiu □ **70** 45 50N 24 15 E
Sible Hedingham **29** 51 58N 0 37 E
Sibley, Iowa, U.S.A. **158** 43 21N 95 43W
Sibley, La., U.S.A. **159** 32 34N 93 16W
Sibolga **102** 1 50N 98 45 E
Sibret **47** 49 58N 5 38 E
Sibsagar **98** 27 0N 94 36 E
Sibsey **33** 53 3N 0 1 E
Sibuco **103** 7 20N 122 10 E
Sibuguey B. **103** 7 50N 122 45 E
Sibuko **103** 7 20N 122 10 E
Sibut **117** 5 52N 19 10 E
Sibutu, I. **102** 4 45N 119 30 E
Sibutu Passage **103** 4 50N 120 0 E
Sibuyan, I. **103** 12 25N 122 40 E
Sicamous **152** 50 49N 119 0W
Sicapoo **103** 18 9N 121 34 E
Sicasica **154** 17 20 S 67 45W
Siccus, R. **140** 31 43 S 139 25 E
Sicilia, Canale di **64** 37 25N 12 30 E
Sicilia, I. **65** 37 30N 14 30 E
Sicily = Sicilia **65** 37 30N 14 30 E
Sicuani **174** 14 10 S 71 10W
Siculiana **64** 37 20N 13 23 E
Sid **63** 45 6N 19 16 E
Sidamo □ **123** 5 0N 37 50 E
Sidaouet **121** 18 34N 8 3 E
Sidaradougou **120** 10 42N 4 12W
Sidbury **30** 50 43N 3 12W
Siddeburen **46** 53 15N 6 52 E

Siddipet **Skaneateles**

Siddipet	**96**	18 0N	79 0E
Sidensjo	**72**	63 20N	18 20E
Sidéradougou	**120**	10 42N	4 12W
Siderno Marina	**65**	38 16N	16 17E
Sidheros, Ákra	**69**	35 19N	26 19E
Sidhirókastron	**68**	37 20N	21 46E
Sidhpur	**94**	23 56N	71 25E
Sîdi Abd el Rahman	**122**	30 55N	28 41E
Sîdi Barrâni	**122**	31 32N	25 58E
Sidi-Bel-Abbès	**118**	35 13N	0 10W
Sidi Bennour	**118**	32 40N	9 26W
Sidi Haneish	**122**	31 10N	27 35E
Sidi Ifni	**118**	29 29N	10 3W
Sidi Kacem	**118**	34 11N	5 40W
Sīdī Miftāh	**119**	31 8N	16 58E
Sidi Moussa, O.	**118**	33 0N	8 50W
Sidi Omar	**122**	31 24N	24 57E
Sīdī Yahya	**119**	30 55N	16 30E
Sidlaw Hills	**35**	56 32N	3 10W
Sidlesham	**29**	50 46N	0 46W
Sidmouth	**30**	50 40N	3 13W
Sidmouth, C.	**138**	13 25S	143 36E
Sidney, Can.	**152**	48 39N	123 24W
Sidney, Mont., U.S.A.	**158**	47 51N	104 7W
Sidney, N.Y., U.S.A.	**162**	42 18N	75 20W
Sidney, Ohio, U.S.A.	**156**	40 18N	84 6W
Sidoardjo	**103**	7 30S	112 46E
Sidoktaya	**98**	20 27N	94 15E
Sidon, (Saida)	**92**	33 38N	35 28E
Sidra, G. of = Khalīj Surt	**61**	31 40N	18 30E
Siedlce	**54**	52 10N	22 20E
Siedlce □	**54**	52 0N	22 0E
Siegburg	**48**	50 48N	7 12E
Siegen	**48**	50 52N	8 2E
Siem Pang	**100**	14 7N	106 23E
Siem Reap	**100**	13 20N	103 52E
Siena	**63**	43 20N	11 20E
Sieniawa	**54**	50 11N	22 38E
Sieradź	**54**	51 37N	18 41E
Sieradź □	**54**	51 30N	19 0E
Sieraków	**54**	52 39N	16 2E
Sierck-les-Bains	**43**	49 26N	6 20E
Sierpc	**54**	52 55N	19 43E
Sierpe, Bocas de la	**174**	10 0N	61 30W
Sierra Alta	**58**	40 31N	1 30W
Sierra Blanca	**161**	31 11N	105 17W
Sierra Blanca, mt.	**161**	33 20N	105 54W
Sierra City	**160**	39 34N	120 42W
Sierra Colorado	**176**	40 35S	67 50W
Sierra de Gädor	**59**	36 57N	2 45W
Sierra de Yeguas	**57**	37 7N	4 52W
Sierra Gorda	**172**	23 0S	69 15W
Sierra Leone ■	**120**	9 0N	12 0W
Sierra Majada	**164**	27 19N	103 42W
Sierre	**50**	46 17N	7 31E
Sífnos	**69**	37 0N	24 45E
Sifton	**153**	51 21N	100 8W
Sifton Pass	**152**	57 52N	126 15W
Sig	**118**	35 32N	0 12W
Sigaboy	**103**	6 39N	126 10E
Sigdal	**71**	60 4N	9 38E
Sigean	**44**	43 2N	2 58E
Sighetul Marmatiei	**70**	47 57N	23 52E
Sighişoara	**70**	46 12N	24 50E
Sighty Crag	**35**	55 8N	2 37W
Sigli	**102**	5 25N	96 0E
Siglufjörður	**74**	66 12N	18 55W
Sigma	**103**	11 29N	122 40E
Sigmaringen	**49**	48 5N	9 13E
Signakhi	**83**	40 52N	45 57E
Signau	**50**	46 56N	7 45E
Signy I.	**13**	60 45S	46 30W
Signy-l'Abbaye	**43**	49 40N	4 25E
Sigsig	**174**	3 0S	78 50W
Sigtuna	**72**	59 36N	17 44E
Sigüenza	**58**	41 3N	2 40W
Siguiri	**120**	11 31N	9 10W
Sigulda	**80**	57 10N	24 55E
Sigurd	**161**	38 57N	112 0W
Sihanoukville = Kompong Som	**101**	10 40N	103 30E
Si'ir	**90**	31 35N	35 9E
Siirt	**92**	37 57N	41 55E
Sijarira, Ra.	**127**	17 36S	27 45E
Sijsele	**13**	51 12N	3 20E
Sikandarabad	**94**	28 30N	77 39E
Sikandra Rao	**93**	27 43N	78 24E
Sikar	**94**	27 39N	75 10E
Sikasso	**120**	11 7N	5 35W
Sikerete	**128**	19 0S	20 48E
Sikeston	**159**	36 52N	89 35W
Sikhote Alin, Khrebet	**77**	46 0N	136 0E
Sikiá.	**68**	40 2N	23 56E
Sikinos, I.	**69**	36 40N	25 8E
Sikionia	**69**	38 0N	22 44E
Sikkani Chief, R.	**152**	57 47N	122 15W
Sikkim ■	**98**	27 50N	88 50E
Siklós	**53**	45 50N	18 19E
Sikoro	**120**	12 19N	7 8W
Sikqo	**101**	7 34N	99 21E
Sil, R.	**56**	42 23N	7 30W
Sila, La, Mts.	**65**	39 15N	16 35E
Silacayoapán	**165**	17 30N	98 9W
Silandro	**62**	46 38N	10 48E
Silat adh Dhahr	**90**	32 19N	35 11E
Silba	**63**	44 24N	14 41E
Silba, I.	**63**	44 24N	14 41E
Silchar	**98**	24 49N	92 48E
Silcox	**153**	57 12N	94 10W
Silenrieux	**47**	50 14N	4 27E
Siler City	**157**	35 44N	79 30W
Sileru, R.	**96**	18 0N	82 0E
Silesia = Slask	**54**	51 0N	16 30E
Silet	**118**	22 44N	4 37E
Silgarhi Doti	**95**	29 15N	82 0E
Silghat	**98**	26 35N	93 0E
Silifke	**92**	36 22N	33 58E
Siliguri	**98**	26 45N	88 25E
Siliqua	**64**	39 20N	8 49E
Silistra	**67**	44 6N	27 19E
Siljan, L.	**72**	60 55N	14 45E
Silkeborg	**73**	56 10N	9 32E
Sillajhuay, Cordillera	**174**	19 40S	68 40W
Sillé-le Guillaume	**42**	48 10N	0 8W
Silloth	**32**	54 53N	3 25W
Siloam Springs	**159**	36 15N	94 31W
Silogui	**102**	1 10S	98 46E
Silsbee	**159**	30 20N	94 8W
Silsden	**32**	53 55N	1 55W
Silute	**80**	55 21N	21 33E
Silva Porto = Bié	**125**	12 22S	16 55E
Silvaplana	**51**	46 28N	9 48E
Silver City, Calif., U.S.A.	**160**	36 19N	119 44W
Silver City, N. Mex., U.S.A.	**161**	32 50N	108 18W
Silver Cr., R.	**160**	43 30N	119 30W
Silver Creek	**156**	42 33N	79 9W
Silver L.	**163**	38 39N	120 6W
Silver Lake, Calif., U.S.A.	**163**	35 21N	116 7W
Silver Lake, Oreg., U.S.A.	**160**	43 9N	121 4W
Silver Springs	**162**	39 2N	77 3W
Silverhojden	**72**	60 2N	15 0E
Silvermine, Mts.	**39**	52 47N	8 15W
Silvermines	**39**	52 48N	8 15W
Silverpeak, Ra.	**163**	37 35N	117 45W
Silverstone	**28**	52 5N	1 3W
Silverton, Austral.	**140**	31 52S	141 10E
Silverton, U.K.	**30**	50 49N	3 29W
Silverton, Colo., U.S.A.	**161**	37 51N	107 45W
Silverton, Tex., U.S.A.	**159**	34 30N	101 16W
Silves	**57**	37 11N	8 26W
Silvia	**174**	2 37N	76 21W
Silvies, R.	**160**	43 57N	119 5W
Silvolde	**46**	51 55N	6 23E
Silvretta Gruppe	**51**	46 50N	10 6E
Silwa Bahari	**122**	24 45N	32 55E
Silwan	**90**	31 59N	35 15E
Silwani	**93**	23 18N	78 27E
Silz	**52**	47 16N	10 56E
Sim, C.	**118**	31 26N	9 51W
Simanggang	**102**	1 15N	111 25E
Simão Dias	**170**	10 44S	37 49W
Simard, L.	**150**	47 40N	78 40W
Simarun	**93**	31 16N	51 40E
Simba	**126**	1 41S	34 12E
Simbach	**49**	48 16N	13 3E
Simbo	**126**	4 51S	29 41E
Simcoe	**150**	42 50N	80 20W
Simcoe, L.	**150**	44 25N	79 20W
Simenga	**77**	62 50N	107 55E
Simeon	**47**	50 45N	5 36E
Simeulue, I.	**102**	2 45N	95 45E
Simferopol	**82**	44 55N	34 3E
Simi	**69**	36 35N	27 50E
Simi, I.	**69**	36 35N	27 50E
Simi Valley	**163**	34 16N	118 47W
Simikot	**95**	30 0N	81 50E
Simití	**174**	7 58N	73 57W
Simitli	**66**	41 52N	23 7E
Simla	**94**	31 2N	77 15E
Simleu-Silvaniei	**70**	47 17N	22 50E
Simme, R.	**50**	46 38N	7 25E
Simmern	**48**	49 59N	7 32E
Simmie	**153**	49 56N	108 6W
Simmler	**163**	35 21N	119 59W
Simões	**170**	7 30S	40 49W
Simojärvi	**74**	66 5N	27 10E
Simojoki	**74**	65 46N	25 15E
Simojovel	**165**	17 12N	92 38W
Simonette, R.	**152**	55 9N	118 15W
Simonsbath	**28**	51 8N	3 45W
Simonside, Mt.	**35**	55 17N	2 0W
Simonstown	**128**	34 14S	18 26E
Simontornya	**53**	46 45N	18 33E
Simpang	**101**	4 50N	100 40E
Simpleveld	**47**	50 50N	5 58E
Simplício Mendes	**170**	7 51S	41 54W
Simplon	**50**	46 12N	8 4E
Simplon Pass	**50**	46 15N	8 0E
Simplon Tunnel	**50**	46 15N	8 7E
Simpson Des.	**138**	25 0S	137 0E
Simpungdong	**107**	41 56N	129 29E
Simrishamn	**73**	55 33N	14 22E
Simsbury	**162**	41 52N	72 48W
Simunjan	**102**	1 25N	110 45E
Sîmŭrtin	**70**	46 19N	25 58E
Simushir, Ostrov	**77**	46 50N	152 30E
Sina, R.	**97**	18 25N	75 28E
Sinaai	**47**	51 9N	4 2E
Sinabang	**102**	2 30N	46 30E
Sinai = Es Sînâ'	**122**	29 0N	34 0E
Sinai, Mt. = Musa, G.	**122**	28 32N	33 59E
Sinaia	**70**	45 21N	25 38E
Sinaloa	**164**	25 50N	108 20W
Sinaloa □	**164**	25 0N	107 30W
Sinalunga	**63**	43 12N	11 43E
Sinamaica	**174**	11 5N	71 51W
Sînandrei	**70**	45 52N	21 13E
Sināwan	**119**	31 0N	10 30E
Sinbaung we	**98**	19 43N	95 10E
Sinbo	**98**	24 46N	97 3E
Sincé	**174**	9 15N	75 9W
Sincelejo	**174**	9 18N	75 24W
Sinchangni, Kor., N.	**107**	40 7N	128 28E
Sinchangni, Kor., N.	**107**	39 24N	126 8E
Sinclair	**160**	41 47N	107 35W
Sinclair Mills	**152**	54 5N	121 40W
Sinclair's B.	**37**	58 30N	3 0W
Sincorá, Serra do	**171**	13 30S	41 0W
Sind, R.	**95**	34 18N	75 0E
Sind Sagar Doab	**94**	32 0N	71 30E
Sinda	**127**	17 28S	25 51E
Sindal	**73**	57 28N	10 10E
Sindangan	**103**	8 10N	123 5E
Sindangbarang	**103**	7 27S	107 9E
Sindjai	**103**	5 0S	120 20E
Sinelnikovo	**82**	48 25N	35 30E
Sines	**57**	37 56N	8 51W
Sines, Cabo de	**57**	37 58N	8 53W
Sineu	**58**	39 39N	3 0E
Sinewit, Mt.	**135**	4 44S	152 2E
Sinfra	**120**	6 35N	5 56W
Sing Buri	**100**	14 53N	100 25E
Singa	**123**	13 10N	33 57E
Singanallurt	**97**	11 2N	77 1E
Singaparna	**103**	7 23S	108 4E
Singapore ■	**101**	1 17N	103 51E
Singapore, Straits of	**101**	1 15N	104 0E
Singaraja	**102**	8 15S	115 10E
Singen	**49**	47 45N	8 50E
Singida	**126**	4 49S	34 48E
Singida □	**126**	6 0S	34 30E
Singitikós, Kólpos	**68**	40 6N	24 0E
Singkaling Hkamti	**98**	26 0N	95 45E
Singkang	**103**	4 8S	120 1E
Singkawang	**102**	1 0N	109 5E
Singkep, I.	**102**	0 30S	104 20E
Singleton, Austral.	**141**	32 33S	151 10E
Singleton, U.K.	**29**	50 55N	0 45W
Singleton, Mt.	**137**	29 27S	117 15E
Singö	**72**	60 12N	18 45E
Singoli	**94**	25 0N	75 16E
Singora = Songkhla	**101**	7 12N	100 36E
Singosan	**107**	38 52N	127 25E
Sinhailian (Lienyünchiangshih)	**107**	34 31N	118 15E
Sinhung	**107**	40 11N	127 34E
Siniatsikon, Óros	**68**	40 25N	21 35E
Siniscóla	**64**	40 35N	9 40E
Sinj	**63**	43 42N	16 39E
Sinjajevina, Planina	**66**	42 57N	19 22E
Sinjil	**90**	32 3N	35 15E
Sinkat	**122**	18 55N	36 49E
Sinkiang-Uighur □	**105**	42 0N	86 0E
Sinmark	**107**	38 25N	126 14E
Sinnai Sardinia	**64**	39 18N	9 13E
Sinnar	**96**	19 48N	74 0E
Sinni, R.	**65**	40 6N	16 15E
Sînnicolau-Maré	**70**	46 5N	20 39E
Sinnûris	**122**	29 26N	30 31E
Sinoe, L.	**70**	44 35N	28 50E
Sinoia	**127**	17 20S	30 8E
Sinop	**92**	42 1N	35 11E
Sinop, R.	**82**	42 1N	35 2E
Sinpo	**107**	40 0N	128 13E
Sins	**51**	47 12N	8 24E
Sinskoye	**77**	61 8N	126 48E
Sint Annaland	**47**	51 36N	4 6E
Sint Annaparochie	**46**	53 16N	5 40E
Sint-Denijs	**47**	50 45N	3 23E
Sint Eustatius, I.	**167**	17 30N	62 59W
Sint-Genesius-Rode	**47**	50 45N	4 22E
Sint-Gillis-Waas	**47**	51 13N	4 6E
Sint-Huibrechts-Lille	**47**	51 13N	5 29E
Sint-Katelinje-Waver	**47**	51 5N	4 32E
Sint-Kruis	**47**	51 13N	3 15E
Sint-Laureins	**47**	51 14N	3 32E
Sint Maarten, I.	**167**	18 4N	63 4W
Sint-Michiels	**47**	51 11N	3 15E
Sint Nicolaasga	**46**	52 55N	5 45E
Sint Niklaas	**47**	51 10N	4 9E
Sint Oedenrode	**47**	51 35N	5 29E
Sint Pancras	**46**	52 40N	4 48E
Sint-Pauwels	**47**	51 11N	3 57E
Sint Philipsland	**47**	51 37N	4 10E
Sint Truiden	**47**	50 48N	5 12E
Sint Willebroad	**47**	51 33N	4 33E
Sîntana Ano	**70**	46 20N	21 30E
Sintang	**102**	0 5N	111 35E
Sintjohannesga	**46**	52 55N	5 52E
Sinton	**159**	28 1N	97 30W
Sintra	**57**	38 47N	9 25W
Sinŭiju	**107**	40 5N	124 24E
Sinuk	**147**	64 42N	166 22W
Sinyang = Hsinyang	**109**	32 10N	114 6E
Sinyukha, R.	**82**	48 31N	30 31E
Siófok	**53**	46 54N	18 4E
Sióma	**128**	16 25S	23 28E
Sion	**50**	46 14N	7 20E
Sion Mills	**38**	54 47N	7 29W
Sioua, El Wâhât es	**122**	29 10N	25 30E
Sioux City	**158**	42 32N	96 25W
Sioux Falls	**158**	43 35N	96 40W
Sioux Lookout	**150**	50 10N	91 50W
Sip Song Chaw Thai, reg.	**100**	21 30N	103 30E
Sipan	**66**	42 45N	17 52E
Sipera, I.	**102**	2 18S	99 40E
Sipiwesk L.	**153**	55 5N	97 35W
Sipul	**138**	5 50S	148 28E
Siquia, R.	**166**	12 30N	84 30W
Siquijor, I.	**103**	9 12N	123 45E
Siquirres	**166**	10 6N	83 30W
Siquisique	**174**	10 34N	69 42W
Sir Edward Pellew Group	**138**	15 40S	137 10E
Sir Graham Moore Is.	**136**	13 53S	126 34E
Sir Samuel Mt.	**137**	27 45S	120 40E
Sir Thomas, Mt.	**137**	27 10S	129 45E
Sira	**97**	13 41N	76 49E
Sira, R.	**71**	58 43N	6 40E
Siracusa	**65**	37 4N	15 17E
Sirajganj	**95**	24 25N	89 47E
Sirake	**138**	9 1S	141 2E
Sirakoro	**120**	12 41N	9 14W
Sirasso	**120**	9 16N	6 6W
Siret	**70**	47 55N	26 5E
Siret, R.	**70**	47 58N	26 5E
Siria	**66**	46 16N	21 38E
Sirinhaém	**171**	8 35S	35 7W
Sirkall (Shivali)	**97**	11 15N	79 41E
Sírna, I.	**69**	36 22N	26 42E
Sirnach	**51**	47 28N	8 59E
Sirohi	**94**	24 52N	72 53E
Siroki Brijeg	**66**	43 21N	17 36E
Sironj	**94**	24 5N	77 45E
Síros	**69**	37 28N	24 57E
Síros, I.	**69**	37 28N	24 57E
Sirretta Pk.	**163**	35 56N	118 19W
Sirsa	**94**	29 33N	75 4E
Sirsi	**97**	14 40N	74 49E
Siruela	**57**	38 58N	5 3W
Sisak	**63**	45 30N	16 21E
Sisaket	**100**	15 8N	104 23E
Sisante	**59**	39 25N	2 12W
Sisargas, Islas	**56**	43 21N	8 50W
Sishen	**128**	27 55S	22 59E
Sisipuk I.	**153**	55 40N	102 0W
Sisipuk L.	**153**	55 45N	101 50W
Sisophon	**100**	13 31N	102 59E
Sissach	**50**	47 27N	7 48E
Sisseton	**158**	45 43N	97 3W
Sissonne	**43**	49 34N	3 51E
Sistan-Baluchistan □	**93**	27 0N	62 0E
Sistema Central	**56**	40 40N	5 55W
Sistema Ibérico	**58**	41 0N	2 10W
Sisteron	**45**	44 12N	5 57E
Sisters	**160**	44 21N	121 32W
Sitamarhi	**95**	26 37N	85 30E
Sitapur	**95**	27 38N	80 45E
Siteki	**129**	26 32S	31 58E
Sitges	**58**	41 17N	1 47E
Sithoniá	**68**	40 0N	23 45E
Sitia	**69**	35 13N	26 6E
Sítio da Abadia	**171**	14 48S	46 16W
Sitka	**147**	57 9N	134 58W
Sitona	**123**	14 25N	37 23E
Sitoti	**128**	23 15S	23 40E
Sitra	**122**	28 40N	26 53E
Sittang Myit, R.	**99**	18 20N	96 45E
Sittang, R.	**98**	17 10N	96 58E
Sittard	**47**	51 0N	5 52E
Sittaung	**98**	24 10N	94 35E
Sittensen	**48**	53 17N	9 32E
Sittingbourne	**29**	51 20N	0 43E
Sittwe	**99**	20 15N	92 45E
Situbondo	**103**	7 45S	114 0E
Siuch'uan	**109**	26 20N	114 30E
Siuna	**166**	13 37N	84 45W
Sivaganga	**97**	9 50N	78 28E
Sivagiri	**97**	9 16N	77 26E
Sivakasi	**97**	9 24N	77 47E
Sivand	**93**	30 5N	52 55E
Sivas	**92**	39 43N	36 58E
Siverek	**92**	37 50N	39 25E
Sivrihisar	**92**	39 30N	31 35E
Sivry	**47**	50 10N	4 12E
Sîwa	**122**	29 11N	25 31E
Siwalik Range	**95**	28 0N	83 0E
Siwan	**95**	26 13N	84 27E
Sixmile Cross	**38**	54 34N	7 7W
Sixmilebridge	**39**	52 45N	8 46W
Siyâl, Jazâ'ir	**122**	22 49N	36 6E
Siyana	**94**	28 37N	78 6E
Sizewell	**29**	52 13N	1 38E
Sjaelland	**73**	55 30N	11 30E
Sjaellands Odde	**73**	56 0N	11 15E
Själevad	**72**	63 18N	18 36E
Sjarinska Banja	**66**	42 45N	21 38E
Sjenica	**66**	43 16N	20 0E
Sjernaröy	**71**	59 15N	5 50E
Sjoa	**71**	61 41N	9 40E
Sjöbo	**73**	55 37N	13 45E
Sjöholt	**71**	62 27N	6 52E
Sjönsta	**74**	67 10N	16 3E
Sjösa	**73**	58 47N	17 4E
Skadovsk	**82**	46 17N	32 52E
Skælskör	**73**	55 16N	11 18E
Skagafjörður	**74**	65 54N	19 35W
Skagastölstindane, mt.	**75**	61 25N	8 10E
Skagen	**75**	68 37N	14 27E
Skagen, pt.	**73**	57 43N	10 35E
Skagern	**72**	59 0N	14 20E
Skagerrak	**73**	57 30N	9 0E
Skagway	**147**	59 30N	135 20W
Skaidi	**74**	70 26N	24 30E
Skala Podolskaya	**82**	48 50N	26 15E
Skalat	**80**	49 23N	25 55E
Skalbmierz	**54**	56 22N	12 30E
Skalderviken	**73**	56 22N	12 30E
Skalicd	**53**	48 50N	17 15E
Skallingen, Odde	**73**	55 32N	8 13E
Skalni Dol = Kamenyak	**67**	43 24N	26 57E
Skals	**73**	56 34N	9 24E
Skanderborg	**73**	56 2N	9 55E
Skaneateles	**162**	42 57N	76 26W

Skaneateles L **Sollentuna**

Skaneateles L. 162 42 51N 76 22W
Skånevik 71 59 43N 5 53 E
Skanninge 73 58 24N 15 5 E
Skanör 73 55 24N 12 50 E
Skanor 73 55 24N 12 50 E
Skantzoúra I. 69 39 5N 24 6 E
Skara 73 58 25N 13 30 E
Skaraborgs län □ 73 58 20N 13 30 E
Skarblacka 73 58 36N 15 50 E
Skardhö 71 62 30N 8 47 E
Skardu 95 35 20N 75 35 E
Skaresta 73 58 26N 16 22 E
Skarszewy 54 54 4N 18 25 E
Skarvane, Mt. 71 63 18N 11 27 E
Skarzysko Kamienna 54 51 7N 20 52 E
Skatöy 71 50 50N 9 30 E
Skattungbyn 72 61 10N 14 56 E
Skaw (Grenen) 73 57 46N 10 34 E
Skaw Taing 36 60 23N 0 57W
Skebo 72 59 58N 18 37 E
Skebokvarn 72 59 7N 16 45 E
Skeena Mts. 152 56 40N 128 30W
Skeena, R. 152 54 9N 130 5W
Skeggjastadir 74 66 3N 14 50W
Skegness 33 53 9N 0 20 E
Skeldon 174 6 0N 57 20W
Skellefte älv 74 65 30N 18 30 E
Skellefteå 74 64 45N 20 58 E
Skelleftehamn 74 64 41N 21 14 E
Skellig Rocks 39 51 47N 10 32W
Skellingthorpe 33 53 14N 0 37W
Skelmersdale 32 53 34N 2 49W
Skelmorlie 34 55 52N 4 53W
Skelton, Cleveland., U.K. 33 54 33N 0 59W
Skelton, Cumb., U.K. 32 54 42N 2 50W
Skender Vakuf 66 44 29N 17 22 E
Skene 73 57 30N 12 37 E
Skerries, Rks. 38 55 14N 6 40W
Skerries, The 31 53 27N 4 40W
Skhirra, La = Cekhira 119 34 20N 10 5 E
Skhiza, I. 69 36 41N 20 40 E
Skhoinoúsa, I. 69 36 53N 25 31 E
Ski 71 59 43N 10 52 E
Skíathos, I. 69 39 12N 23 30 E
Skibbereen 39 51 33N 9 16W
Skiddaw, Mt. 32 54 39N 3 9W
Skidegate, Inlet 48 53 20N 132 0W
Skien 71 59 12N 9 35 E
Skierniewice 54 51 58N 20 19 E
Skikda 119 36 50N 6 58 E
Skillingaryd 73 57 27N 14 5 E
Skillinge 73 55 30N 14 16 E
Skillingmark 72 59 48N 120 1 E
Skinari, Akra 69 37 56N 20 40 E
Skipness 34 55 46N 5 20W
Skipsea 33 53 58N 0 13W
Skipton, Austral. 140 37 39 S 143 21 E
Skipton, U.K. 32 53 57N 2 1W
Skirild 73 55 58N 8 53 E
Skirmish Pt. 138 11 59 S 134 17 E
Skiropoúla, I. 69 38 50N 24 21 E
Skíros 69 38 55N 24 34 E
Skíros, I. 69 38 55N 24 34 E
Skivarp 73 55 26N 13 34 E
Skive 73 56 33N 9 2 E
Skjåk 71 61 52N 8 22 E
Skjálfandafljót 74 65 15N 17 25W
Skjálfandi 74 66 5N 17 30W
Skjeberg 71 59 12N 11 12 E
Skjern 73 55 57N 8 30 E
Skjönne 71 60 16N 9 1 E
Skoczów 54 49 49N 18 45 E
Skodje 71 62 30N 6 43 E
Skofja Loka 63 46 9N 14 19 E
Skoger 71 59 42N 10 16 E
Skoghall 72 59 20N 13 30 E
Skoghult 73 56 59N 15 55 E
Skokholm, I. 31 51 42N 5 16W
Skoki 54 52 40N 17 11 E
Skole 80 49 3N 23 30 E
Skomer, I. 31 51 44N 5 19W
Skonsberg 72 62 25N 17 21 E
Skópelos 69 39 9N 23 47 E
Skópelos, I. 69 39 9N 23 47 E
Skopin 81 53 55N 39 32 E
Skopje 66 42 1N 21 32 E
Skorcz 54 43 47N 18 30 E
Skorped 72 63 23N 17 55 E
Skotfoss 71 59 12N 9 30 E
Skoudas 80 56 21N 21 45 E
Skövde 75 58 15N 13 59 E
Skovorodino 77 54 0N 125 0 E
Skowhegan 151 44 49N 69 40W
Skowman 153 51 58N 99 35W
Skradin 63 43 52N 15 53 E
Skreanäs 73 56 52N 12 35 E
Skudeneshavn 71 59 10N 5 10 E
Skull 39 51 32N 9 40W
Skultorp 73 58 24N 13 51 E
Skulyany 82 47 19N 27 39 E
Skunk, R. 158 40 42N 91 7W
Skurup 73 55 28N 13 30 E
Skutskär 73 60 37N 17 25 E
Skvira 82 49 44N 29 32 E
Skwaner, Pegunungan 102 1 0 S 112 30 E
Skwierzyna 54 52 46N 15 30 E
Skye, I. 36 57 15N 6 10W
Skykomish 160 47 43N 121 16W
Skyros (Skíros), L. 69 38 52N 24 37 E
Slagelse 73 55 23N 11 19 E
Slagharen 46 52 37N 6 34 E
Slaidburn 32 53 57N 2 28W
Slaley 35 54 55N 2 4W
Slamannon 140 32 1 S 143 41 E
Slamet, G. 102 7 16 S 109 8 E
Slane 38 53 42N 6 32W
Slaney, R. 39 52 52N 6 45W
Slangerup 73 55 50N 12 11 E
Slânic 70 45 14N 25 58 E
Slankamen 66 45 8N 20 15 E
Slano 66 42 48N 17 53 E
Slantsy 80 59 7N 28 5 E
Slany 52 50 13N 14 6 E
Slask 54 51 25N 16 0 E
Slatbaken 73 58 28N 16 30 E
Slate Is. 150 48 40N 87 0W
Slatina 70 44 28N 24 22 E
Slatington 162 40 45N 75 37W
Slaton 159 33 27N 101 38W
Slave Coast 121 6 0N 2 30 E
Slave Lake 152 55 17N 114 50W
Slave Pt. 152 61 11N 114 56W
Slave, R. 152 61 18N 113 39W
Slavgorod 76 53 10N 78 50 E
Slavinja 66 43 14N 22 50 E
Slavkov (Austerlitz) 53 49 10N 16 52 E
Slavnoye 80 54 24N 29 15 E
Slavonski Brod 66 45 11N 18 0 E
Slavonski Pozega 66 45 20N 17 40 E
Slavuta 80 50 15N 27 2 E
Slavyans 82 48 55N 37 30 E
Slavyansk 82 45 15N 38 11 E
Sława 54 51 52N 16 2 E
Sławno 54 54 20N 16 41 E
Sławoborze 54 53 55N 15 42 E
Slea Hd. 39 52 7N 10 30W
Sleaford 33 53 0N 0 22W
Sleaford B. 139 34 55 S 135 45 E
Sleat, Pt. of 36 57 1N 6 0W
Sleat, Sd. of 36 57 5N 5 47W
Sledmere 33 54 4N 0 35W
Sleeper, Is. 149 56 50N 80 30W
Sleepers, The 149 58 30N 81 0W
Sleepy Eye 158 44 15N 94 45W
Sleidinge 47 51 8N 3 41 E
Sleights 33 54 27N 0 40W
Sleipner, gasfield 19 58 30N 1 48 E
Sleman 103 7 40 S 110 20 E
Slemmestad 71 59 47N 10 30 E
Slemon L. 152 63 13N 116 4W
Slesin 54 52 22N 18 14 E
Sletterhage, Kap 73 56 7N 10 31 E
Slide Mt. 162 42 0N 74 23W
Slidell 159 30 20N 89 48W
Sliedrecht 46 51 50N 4 45 E
Slieve Anierin 38 54 5N 7 58W
Slieve Aughty 39 53 4N 8 30W
Slieve Bernagh 39 52 50N 8 30W
Slieve Bloom 39 53 4N 7 40W
Slieve Callan 39 52 51N 9 16W
Slieve Donard 38 54 10N 5 57W
Slieve Felim 39 52 40N 8 20W
Slieve Gamph 38 54 6N 9 0W
Slieve Gullion 38 54 8N 6 26W
Slieve League 38 54 40N 8 42W
Slieve Mish 39 52 12N 9 50W
Slieve Miskish 39 51 40N 10 10W
Slieve More 38 54 1N 10 3W
Slieve Snaght 38 54 59N 8 7W
Slieve Tooey 38 54 46N 8 39W
Slievenamon Mt. 39 52 25N 7 37W
Sligachan 36 57 17N 6 10W
Sligo 38 54 17N 8 28W
Sligo □ 38 54 10N 8 35W
Sligo B. 38 54 20N 8 40W
Slikkerveer 46 51 53N 4 36 E
Slioch, mt. 36 57 40N 5 20W
Slipje 47 51 9N 2 51 E
Slite 75 57 42N 18 48 E
Sliven 67 42 42N 26 19 E
Slivnitsa 66 42 50N 23 0 E
Sljeme, mt. 63 45 57N 15 58 E
Słupsk □ 54 54 15N 17 30 E
Sloansville 162 42 45N 74 22W
Slobodskoy 84 58 40N 50 6 E
Slobozia, Ialomiţa, Rumania 70 44 34N 27 23 E
Slobozia, Valahia, Rumania 70 44 30N 25 14 E
Slocan 152 49 48N 117 28W
Slochteren 46 53 12N 6 48 E
Slochteren-Groningen, gasfield 19 53 10N 6 45 E
Slöinge 73 56 51N 12 42 E
Słomniki 54 50 16N 20 4 E
Slonim 80 53 4N 25 19 E
Slotermeer 46 52 55N 5 38 E
Slough 29 51 30N 0 35W
Sloughhouse 163 38 26N 121 12W
Slovakia □ 53 48 30N 19 0 E
Slovenia = Slovenija 63 45 58N 14 30 E
Slovenija □ 63 45 58N 14 30 E
Slovenska Bistrica 63 46 24N 15 35 E
Slovenske Krusnohorie 53 48 45N 20 0 E
Slovenské Rhudhorie 52 48 45N 19 0 E
Słubice 54 52 22N 14 35 E
Sluis 47 51 18N 3 23 E
Slunchev Bryag 67 42 40N 27 41 E
Slunj 63 45 6N 15 33 E
Słupca 54 52 15N 17 52 E
Słupsk 54 54 30N 17 3 E
Slurry 128 25 49 S 25 42 E
Slyne Hd. 38 53 25N 10 10W
Slyudyanka 77 51 40N 103 30 E
Smål-Taberg 73 57 42N 14 5 E
Smålandsfarvandet 73 55 10N 11 20 E
Smalandsstenar 73 57 9N 13 24 E
Smålandstarvandet 73 55 10N 11 20 E
Smalltree L. 153 61 0N 105 0W
Smallwood Reservoir 151 54 20N 63 10W
Smara 118 26 48N 11 31W
Smarje 63 46 15N 15 34 E
Smart Syndicate Dam 128 30 45 S 23 10 E
Smeaton 153 53 30N 105 49W
Smedberg 73 58 35N 12 0 E
Smederevo 66 44 40N 20 57 E
Smedstorp 73 55 38N 13 58 E
Smela 82 49 30N 32 0 E
Smerwick Harb. 39 52 12N 10 23W
Smethwick 28 52 29N 1 58W
Smidovich 77 48 36N 133 49 E
Smilde 46 52 58N 6 28 E
Smiley 153 51 38N 109 29W
Smilyan 67 41 29N 24 46 E
Smith 152 55 10N 114 0W
Smith Arm 152 66 15N 123 0W
Smith Center 158 39 50N 98 50W
Smith I. 162 38 0N 76 0W
Smith, R. 152 59 34N 126 30W
Smith Sund 12 78 30N 74 0W
Smithborough 38 54 13N 7 8W
Smithburne, R. 138 17 3 S 140 57 E
Smithers 152 54 45N 127 10W
Smithfield, U.K. 32 54 59N 2 51W
Smithfield, U.S.A. 157 35 31N 78 16W
Smith's Falls 150 44 55N 76 0W
Smithton, N.S.W., Austral. 139 31 0 S 152 48 E
Smithton, Tas., Austral. 138 40 53 S 145 6 E
Smithtown 141 30 58 S 152 56 E
Smithville 159 30 2N 97 12W
Smjörfjöll 74 65 30N 15 42W
Smoky Bay 139 32 22 S 133 56 E
Smoky Falls 150 50 4N 82 10W
Smoky Hill, R. 158 38 45N 98 0W
Smoky Lake 152 54 10N 112 30W
Smola 71 63 23N 8 3 E
Smolensk 80 54 45N 32 0 E
Smolikas, Óros 68 40 9N 20 58 E
Smolník 53 48 43N 20 44 E
Smolyan 67 41 36N 24 38 E
Smooth Rock Falls 150 49 17N 81 37W
Smoothstone L. 153 54 40N 106 50W
Smorgon 80 54 28N 26 24 E
Smulţi 70 45 57N 27 44 E
Smyadovo 67 43 2N 27 1 E
Smyrna 162 39 18N 75 36W
Smyrna = Izmir 92 38 25N 27 8 E
Snaefell 30 54 18N 4 26W
Snaefells Jökull 74 64 45N 23 25W
Snainton 33 54 14N 0 33W
Snaith 33 53 42N 1 1W
Snake I. 141 38 47 S 146 33 E
Snake L. 153 55 32N 106 35W
Snake, R. 160 46 31N 118 50W
Snake Ra., Mts. 160 39 0N 114 30W
Snake River Plain 160 43 13N 113 0W
Snap, The 36 60 35N 0 50W
Snape 29 52 11N 1 29 E
Snarum 71 60 1N 9 54 E
Snasahogarha 72 63 10N 12 20 E
Snedsted 73 56 55N 8 32 E
Sneek 46 53 2N 5 40 E
Sneeker-meer 46 53 2N 5 45 E
Sneem 39 51 50N 9 55W
Snejbjerg 73 56 8N 8 54 E
Sněka 52 50 41N 15 50 E
Snelling 163 37 31N 120 26W
Snettisham 29 52 52N 0 30 E
Snezhnoye 83 48 0N 38 58 E
Sneznik, mt. 63 45 36N 14 35 E
Snigirevka 82 47 2N 32 35 E
Snina 53 49 0N 22 9 E
Snizort, L. 36 57 33N 6 28W
Snohetta 71 62 19N 9 16 E
Snohomish 160 47 53N 122 6W
Snonuten 71 59 31N 6 50 E
Snoul 101 12 4N 106 26 E
Snow Hill 162 38 10N 75 21W
Snow L. 153 54 52N 100 3W
Snowbird L. 153 60 45N 103 0W
Snowdon, Mt. 31 53 4N 4 8W
Snowdrift 153 62 24N 110 44W
Snowdrift, R. 153 62 24N 110 44W
Snowflake 161 34 30N 110 4W
Snowshoe 152 53 43N 121 0W
Snowtown 140 33 46 S 138 14 E
Snowville 160 41 59N 112 47W
Snowy Mt. 162 43 45N 74 26W
Snowy Mts. 141 36 30 S 148 20 E
Snowy, R. 141 37 46 S 148 30 E
Snug Corner 167 22 33N 73 52W
Snyder, Okla., U.S.A. 159 34 4N 99 0W
Snyder, Tex., U.S.A. 159 32 45N 100 57W
Soacha 174 4 35N 74 13W
Soahanina 129 18 42 S 44 13 E
Soalala 129 16 6 S 45 20 E
Soan, R. 94 33 20N 72 40 E
Soanierana-Ivongo 129 16 55 S 49 35 E
Soap Lake 160 47 29N 119 31W
Soay, I. 36 57 9N 6 13W
Soay Sd. 36 57 10N 6 15W
Sobat, Nahr 123 8 32N 32 40 E
Soběslav 52 49 16N 14 45 E
Sobhapur 94 22 47N 78 17 E
Sobinka 81 56 0N 40 0 E
Sobo-Yama 110 32 51N 131 16 E
Sobótka 54 50 54N 16 44 E
Sobrado 56 43 2N 8 2W
Sobral 170 3 50 S 40 30W
Sobreira Formosa 57 39 46N 7 51W
Soc Giang 100 22 54N 106 1 E
Soc Trang = Khonh Hung 101 9 37N 105 50 E
Soča, R. 63 46 20N 13 40 E
Socha 174 6 0N 72 41W
Sochaczew 54 52 15N 20 13 E
Soch'e 105 38 24N 77 20 E
Sochi 83 43 35N 39 40 E
Société, Is. de la 131 17 0 S 151 0W
Socompa, Portezuelo de 172 24 27 S 68 18W
Socorro 174 6 29N 73 16W
Socorro, I. 164 18 45N 110 58W
Socotra, I. 91 12 30N 54 0 E
Socúellmos 59 39 16N 2 47W
Soda Creek 152 52 25N 122 10W
Soda L. 161 35 7N 116 2W
Soda Plains 94 35 30N 79 0 E
Soda Springs 160 42 4N 111 40W
Sodankylä 74 67 29N 26 40 E
Söderfjärden 72 62 3N 17 25 E
Söderfors 72 60 23N 17 25 E
Söderhamn 72 61 18N 17 10 E
Söderköping 72 58 31N 16 35 E
Södermanlands län □ 72 59 10N 16 30 E
Södertälje 72 59 12N 17 50 E
Sodium 128 30 15 S 15 45 E
Sodo 123 7 0N 37 57 E
Södra Vi 73 57 45N 15 45 E
Sodrazica 63 45 45N 14 39 E
Sodus 162 43 13N 77 5W
Soekmekaar 129 23 30 S 29 55 E
Soest, Ger. 48 51 34N 8 7 E
Soest, Neth. 46 52 9N 5 19 E
Soestdijk 46 52 11N 5 17 E
Sofádhes 68 39 28N 22 4 E
Sofara 120 13 59N 4 9W
Sofia = Sofiya 67 42 45N 23 20 E
Sofia, R. 129 15 25 S 48 40 E
Sofievka 82 47 58N 34 14 E
Sofikón 69 37 47N 23 3 E
Sofila 67 42 45N 23 20 E
Sofiya 67 42 45N 23 20 E
Sogad 103 10 30N 125 0 E
Sogakofe 121 6 2N 0 39 E
Sogamoso 174 5 43N 72 56W
Sögel 48 52 50N 7 32 E
Sogeri 135 9 26 S 147 35 E
Sogipo 107 33 13N 126 34 E
Sogn og Fjordane fylke □ 71 61 40N 6 0 E
Sogndal 71 58 20N 6 15 E
Sogndalsfjøra 75 61 14N 7 5 E
Sognefjorden 71 61 10N 5 50 E
Sohâg 122 26 27N 31 43 E
Soham 29 52 20N 0 20 E
Sohano 135 5 22 S 154 37 E
Sŏhori 107 40 7N 128 23 E
Soignies 47 50 35N 4 5 E
Soira, Mt. 123 14 45N 39 30 E
Soissons 43 49 25N 3 19 E
Soitava, R. 53 49 30N 16 37 E
Sojat 94 25 55N 73 38 E
Sok, R. 84 53 24N 50 8 E
Sokal 80 50 31N 24 15 E
Söke 69 37 48N 27 28 E
Sokhós 68 40 48N 23 22 E
Sokhta Chinar 93 35 5N 67 35 E
Sokna 71 60 16N 9 50 E
Soknedal 71 62 57N 10 13 E
Soko Banja 66 43 40N 21 51 E
Sokodé 121 9 0N 1 11 E
Sokó'ka 54 53 25N 23 30 E
Sokol 81 59 30N 40 5 E
Sokolo 120 14 42N 6 8W
Sokolov 52 50 12N 12 40 E
Sokoł ó w Matopolski 53 50 11N 22 7 E
Sokoł ó w Podlaski 54 52 25N 22 15 E
Sokoto 121 13 2N 5 16 E
Sokoto □ 121 12 30N 5 0 E
Sokoto, R. 121 12 30N 6 10 E
Sokuluk 85 42 52N 74 18 E
Sol Iletsk 84 51 10N 55 0 E
Sola 71 58 53N 5 36 E
Sola, R. 126 49 38N 19 8 E
Solai 126 0 2N 36 12 E
Solana, La 59 38 59N 3 14W
Solano 103 16 25N 121 15 E
Solares 56 43 23N 3 43W
Solberga 73 57 45N 14 43 E
Solca 70 47 40N 25 50 E
Solec Kujawski 54 53 5N 18 14 E
Soledad, Colomb. 174 10 55N 74 46W
Soledad, U.S.A. 163 36 27N 121 16W
Soledad, Venez. 174 8 10N 63 34W
Solemint 163 34 25N 118 27W
Solent, The 28 50 45N 1 25W
Solenzara 45 41 53N 9 23 E
Solesmes 43 50 10N 3 30 E
Solfonn, Mt. 71 60 2N 6 57 E
Soligalich 81 59 5N 42 10 E
Solihull 28 52 26N 1 47W
Solikamsk 84 59 38N 56 50 E
Solila 129 21 25 S 46 37 E
Soliman 119 36 42N 10 30 E
Solimões, R. 174 2 15 S 66 30W
Solingen 48 51 10N 7 4 E
Sollas 36 57 39N 7 20W
Sollebrunn 73 58 8N 12 32 E
Sollefteå 72 63 12N 17 20 E
Sollentuna 72 59 26N 17 56 E

Name	Map	Lat	Long
Soller	58	39 43N	2 45 E
Sollerön	72	60 54N	14 38 E
Solna	72	59 22N	18 1 E
Solnechnogorsk	81	56 10N	36 57 E
Sölnkletten, Mt.	71	61 55N	10 18 E
Sologne	59	47 40N	2 0 E
Solojärg	73	56 50N	10 8 E
Solok	102	0 55 S	100 40 E
Sololá	166	14 49N	91 10 E
Solomon Is. ■	135	6 0 S	155 0 E
Solomon, N. Fork, R.	158	39 45N	99 0W
Solomon Sea	135	7 0 S	150 0 E
Solomon, S. Fork, R.	158	39 25N	99 12W
Solomon's Pools = Burak Sulayman	90	31 42N	35 7 E
Solon Springs	158	46 19N	91 47W
Solonópole	170	5 44 S	39 1W
Solor, I.	103	8 27 S	123 0 E
Solotcha	81	54 48N	39 53 E
Solothurn	50	47 13N	7 32 E
Solothurn □	50	47 18N	7 40 E
Solotobe	85	44 37N	66 3 E
Solsona	58	42 0N	1 31 E
Solt	53	46 45N	19 1 E
Solta, I.	63	43 24N	16 15 E
Soltanabad	93	36 29N	58 5 E
Soltaniyeh	92	36 20N	48 55 E
Soltau	48	52 59N	9 50 E
Soltsy	80	58 10N	30 10 E
Solun	105	46 40N	120 40 E
Solund	71	61 5N	4 50 E
Solund I.	71	61 7N	4 50 E
Solunska Glava	66	41 44N	21 31 E
Solva	31	51 52N	5 12W
Solvang	163	34 36N	120 8W
Solvay	162	43 5N	76 17W
Solvesborg	73	56 5N	14 35 E
Sölvesborg	73	56 5N	14 35 E
Solway Firth	32	54 45N	3 38W
Solwezi	127	12 20 S	26 21 E
Somali Rep. ■	91	7 0N	47 0 E
Somaliland	123	12 0N	43 0 E
Sombe Dzong	98	27 13N	89 8 E
Sombernon	43	47 20N	4 40 E
Sombor	66	45 46N	19 17 E
Sombrerete	164	23 40N	103 40W
Sombrero I.	167	18 30N	63 30W
Somerby	29	52 42N	0 49W
Someren	47	51 23N	5 42 E
Somers	160	48 4N	114 18W
Somerset, Austral.	138	10 45 S	142 25 E
Somerset, Can.	153	49 25N	98 39W
Somerset, Colo., U.S.A.	161	38 55N	107 30W
Somerset, Ky., U.S.A.	156	37 5N	84 40W
Somerset, Mass., U.S.A.	162	41 45N	71 10W
Somerset □	28	51 9N	3 0W
Somerset East	128	32 42 S	25 35 E
Somerset, I.	148	73 30N	93 0W
Somerset West	128	34 8 S	18 50 E
Somersham	29	52 24N	0 0W
Somersworth	162	43 15N	70 51W
Somerton, U.K.	28	51 3N	2 45W
Somerton, U.S.A.	161	32 41N	114 47W
Somerville	162	40 34N	74 36W
Someş, R.	70	47 15N	23 45 E
Someşul Mare, R.	70	47 18N	24 30 E
Somma Lombardo	62	45 41N	8 42 E
Somma Vesuviana	65	40 52N	14 23 E
Sommariva	139	26 24 S	146 36 E
Sommatino	65	37 20N	14 0 E
Somme □	43	50 0N	2 20 E
Somme, B. de la	42	5 22N	1 30 E
Sommelsdijk	46	51 46N	4 9 E
Sommen	73	58 12N	15 0 E
Sommen, L.	73	58 0N	15 15 E
Sommepy-Tahure	43	49 15N	4 31 E
Sömmerda	48	51 10N	11 8 E
Sommersted	73	55 19N	9 18 E
Sommesous	43	48 44N	4 12 E
Sommières	45	43 47N	4 6 E
Somogy □	53	46 19N	17 30 E
Somogyszob	53	46 18N	17 20 E
Somoto	166	13 28N	86 37W
Sompolno	54	52 26N	18 45 E
Somport, Paso	58	42 48N	0 31W
Somport, Puerto de	58	42 48N	0 31W
Sompting	29	50 51N	0 20W
Son, Neth.	47	51 31N	5 30 E
Son, Norway	71	59 32N	10 42 E
Son, Spain	56	42 43N	8 58W
Son Hoa	100	13 2N	108 58 E
Son La	100	21 20N	103 50 E
Son Ma	100	15 3N	108 34 E
Son Tay	100	21 8N	105 30 E
Soná	166	8 0N	81 10W
Sonamarg	95	34 18N	75 21 E
Sonamukhi	95	23 18N	87 27 E
Sonamura	98	23 29N	91 15 E
Sönchön	107	39 48N	124 55 E
Soncino	62	45 24N	9 52 E
Sondags, R.	128	32 10N	24 40 E
Sóndala	62	46 20N	10 20 E
Sondar	95	33 28N	75 56 E
Sönder Hornum	73	56 32N	9 38 E
Sønder Omme	73	55 50N	8 54 E
Sønderborg	73	54 55N	9 49 E
Sonderhausen	48	51 22N	10 50 E
Sönderjyllands Amt □	73	55 10N	9 10 E
Sondre Höland	71	59 44N	11 34 E
Sondre Land	71	60 44N	10 21 E
Söndre Stromfjord	12	66 30N	50 52W
Sóndrio	62	46 10N	9 53 E
Sone	127	17 23 S	34 55 E
Sonepat	94	29 0N	77 5 E
Sonepur	96	20 55N	83 50 E
Song	100	18 28N	100 11 E
Song Cau	100	13 20N	109 18 E
Songa, R.	71	59 57N	7 30 E
Söngchön	107	39 12N	126 15 E
Songea	127	10 40 S	35 40 E
Songea □	127	10 30 S	36 0 E
Songeons	43	49 32N	1 50 E
Songjin	107	40 40N	129 10 E
Songjöngni	107	35 8N	126 47 E
Songkhla	101	7 13N	100 37 E
Songnim	107	38 45N	125 39 E
Songwe, Malawi	127	9 44 S	33 58 E
Songwe, Zaïre	127	3 20 S	26 16 E
Sonkel, Ozero	85	41 50N	75 12 E
Sonkovo	81	57 50N	37 5 E
Sonmiani	94	25 25N	66 40 E
Sonning	29	51 28N	0 53W
Sonnino	64	41 25N	13 13 E
Sono, R., Goias, Brazil	170	8 58 S	48 11W
Sono, R., Minas Gerais, Brazil	171	17 2 S	45 32W
Sonobe	111	35 6N	135 28 E
Sonogno	51	46 22N	8 47 E
Sonoma	163	38 17N	122 27W
Sonora, Calif., U.S.A.	163	37 59N	120 27W
Sonora, Texas, U.S.A.	159	30 33N	100 37W
Sonora □	164	28 0N	111 0W
Sonora P.	160	38 17N	119 35W
Sonora, R.	164	28 30N	111 33W
Sonoyta	164	31 51N	112 50W
Sönsan	107	36 14N	128 17 E
Sonskyn	128	30 47 S	26 28 E
Sonsonate	166	13 43N	89 44W
Sonthofen	49	47 31N	10 16 E
Soo Junction	156	46 20N	85 14W
Soochow = Suchou	109	31 15N	120 40 E
Söonder Nissum	73	56 19N	8 11 E
Sop Hao	100	20 33N	104 27 E
Sop Prap	100	17 53N	99 20 E
Sopi	103	2 40N	128 28 E
Sopo, Nahr	123	8 40N	26 30 E
Sopot, Poland	54	54 27N	18 31 E
Sopot, Yugo.	66	44 29N	20 30 E
Sopotnica	66	41 23N	21 13 E
Sopron	49	47 41N	16 37 E
Sop's Arm	151	49 46N	56 56W
Sör-Fron	71	61 35N	9 59 E
Sor, R.	57	39 7N	9 52 E
Sör-Rondane	13	72 0 S	25 0 E
Sör Trøndelag fylke □	71	63 0N	11 0 E
Sora	64	41 45N	13 36 E
Sorada	96	19 32N	84 45 E
Sorah	94	27 13N	68 56 E
Söräker	72	62 30N	17 32 E
Sorano	63	42 40N	11 42 E
Sorata	174	15 50 S	68 50W
Sorbas	59	37 6N	2 7W
Sorbie	34	54 46N	4 26W
Sordale	37	58 33N	3 26W
Sordeval	42	48 44N	0 55W
Sorel	150	46 0N	73 10W
Sörenberg	50	46 50N	8 2 E
Soresina	62	45 17N	9 51 E
Sörfold	74	67 5N	14 20 E
Sorgono	64	40 1N	9 6 E
Sorgues	45	44 1N	4 53 E
Soria	58	41 43N	2 32W
Soria □	58	41 46N	2 28W
Soriano	172	33 24 S	58 19W
Soriano □	176	33 30 S	58 0W
Sorisdale	34	56 40N	6 28W
Sorn	34	55 31N	4 18W
Sorø	73	55 26N	11 32 E
Soro	120	10 9N	9 48W
Sorocaba	173	23 31 S	47 35W
Sorochinsk	84	52 26N	53 10 E
Soroki	82	48 8N	28 12 E
Soroksár	53	47 24N	19 9 E
Soron	94	27 55N	78 45 E
Sorong	103	0 55 S	131 15 E
Sororoca	174	0 43N	61 31W
Soroti	126	1 43N	33 35 E
Sorøy Sundet	74	70 25N	23 0 E
Sorøya	74	70 35N	22 45 E
Soroyane	71	62 25N	5 32 E
Sorraia, R.	57	38 55N	8 53 E
Sorrento, Austral.	139	38 22 S	144 47 E
Sorrento, Italy	65	40 38N	14 23 E
Sorris Sorris	128	21 0 S	14 46 E
Sorsele	74	65 31N	17 30 E
Sorso	64	40 50N	8 34 E
Sorsogon	103	13 0N	124 0 E
Sortat	37	58 32N	3 12W
Sortino	65	37 9N	15 1 E
Sos	58	42 30N	1 13W
Sösan	107	36 47N	126 27 E
Soscumica, L.	150	50 15N	77 27W
Sosdala	73	56 2N	13 41 E
Sosna, R.	81	52 30N	38 0 E
Sosnowiec	54	50 20N	19 10 E
Sospel	45	43 52N	7 27 E
Soštanj	63	46 23N	15 4 E
Sösura	107	42 16N	130 36 E
Sosva	84	59 10N	61 50 E
Sosva, R.	84	59 32N	62 20 E
Soto la Marina, R.	165	23 40N	97 40W
Soto y Amío	56	42 46N	5 53W
Sotra I.	71	60 15N	5 5 E
Sotteville	42	49 24N	1 5 E
Souanké	124	2 10N	14 10 E
Souderton	162	40 19N	75 19W
Soufi	120	15 12N	0 55W
Souflíon	68	41 12N	26 18 E
Soufrière, vol.	167	13 51N	61 4W
Soufrière, vol.	167	13 10N	61 10W
Sougne-Remouchamps	47	50 29N	5 42 E
Souillac	44	44 53N	1 29 E
Souk-Ahras	119	36 17N	7 57 E
Souk el Arba du Rharb	118	34 50N	5 59W
Souk el Khemis	119	36 36N	8 58 E
Soukhouma	100	14 38N	105 48 E
Söul	105	37 31N	127 6 E
Soulac-sur-Mer	44	45 30N	1 7W
Soultz	43	48 57N	7 52 E
Soumagne	47	50 37N	5 44 E
Sound, The	75	56 7N	12 30 E
Soúnion, Ákra	69	37 37N	24 1 E
Sour el Ghozlane	119	36 10N	3 45 E
Sources, Mt. aux	129	28 45 S	28 50 E
Sourdeval	42	48 43N	0 55W
Soure, Brazil	170	0 35 S	48 30W
Soure, Port.	56	40 4N	8 38W
Souris, Man., Can.	153	49 40N	100 20W
Souris, P.E.I., Can.	151	46 21N	62 15W
Souris, R.	153	49 40N	99 34W
Soúrpi	69	39 6N	22 54 E
Sous, R.	118	30 31N	9 27W
Sousa	170	6 45 S	38 10W
Sousel, Brazil	170	2 38 S	52 29W
Sousel, Port.	57	38 57N	7 40W
Souss, O.	118	30 23N	8 24W
Sousse	119	35 50N	10 38 E
Soustons	44	43 45N	1 19W
Souterraine, La	44	46 15N	1 30 E
South Africa, Rep. of, ■	125	30 0 S	25 0 E
South Amboy	162	40 29N	74 17W
South America	168	10 0 S	60 0W
South Auckland & Bay of Plenty □	142	38 30N	177 0 E
South Aulatsivik I.	151	56 45N	61 30W
South Australia □	136	32 0 S	139 0 E
South Baldy, Mt.	161	34 6N	107 27W
South Bend, Indiana, U.S.A.	156	41 38N	86 20W
South Bend, Wash., U.S.A.	160	46 44N	123 52W
South Benfleet	29	51 33N	0 34 E
South Blackwater	138	24 00 S	148 35 E
South Boston	157	36 42N	78 58W
South Br. Ashburton, R.	143	43 30N	171 15 E
South Branch, Can.	151	47 55N	59 2W
South Branch, U.S.A.	151	44 30N	83 55W
South Brent	30	50 26N	3 50W
South Brook	151	49 26N	56 5W
South Buganda □	126	0 15 S	31 30 E
South Cape	147	18 58N	155 24 E
South Carolina □	157	33 45N	81 0W
South Cave	33	53 46N	0 37W
South Charleston	156	38 20N	81 40W
South China Sea	101	7 0N	107 0 E
South Dakota □	158	45 0N	100 0W
South Dell	36	58 28N	6 20W
South Dorset Downs	28	50 40N	2 26W
South Downs	29	50 53N	0 10W
South East C.	138	43 40 S	146 50 E
South East Is.	137	34 17 S	123 30 E
South Elkington	33	53 22N	0 5W
South Esk, R.	37	56 44N	3 3W
South Foreland	29	51 7N	1 23 E
S. Fork, American, R.	163	38 45N	121 5W
South Fork, R.	160	47 54N	113 15W
South Gamboa	164	9 4N	79 40W
South Gate	163	33 57N	118 12W
South Georgia	13	54 30 S	37 0W
South Glamorgan □	31	51 30N	3 20W
South Grafton	139	29 41 S	152 47 E
South Harris, district	36	56 51N	3 10W
South Haven	156	42 22N	86 20W
South Hayling	29	50 47N	0 56W
South Henik, L.	153	61 30N	97 30W
South Horr	126	2 12N	36 56 E
South I., Kenya	126	2 35N	36 35 E
South I., N.Z.	143	43 0 S	170 0 E
South Invercargill	143	46 26N	168 23 E
South Kirby	33	53 35N	1 25W
South Knife, R.	153	58 55N	94 37W
S. Kolok	101	6 2N	101 58 E
South Korea ■	107	36 0N	128 0 E
S. Lembing	101	3 55N	103 3 E
South Magnetic Pole	13	66 30 S	139 30 E
South Marsh Is.	162	38 6N	76 1W
South Milwaukee	156	42 50N	87 52W
South Molton	30	51 1N	3 50W
South Nahanni, R.	152	61 3N	123 21W
South Nesting B.	36	60 18N	1 5W
South Orkney Is.	13	63 0 S	45 0W
South Pass	160	42 20N	108 58W
South Passage	137	26 07 S	113 09 E
S. Petani	101	5 37N	100 30 E
South Petherton	28	50 57N	2 49W
South Petherwin	30	50 35N	4 22W
South Pines	157	35 10N	79 25W
South Platte, R.	158	40 50N	102 45W
South Pt.	151	49 6N	62 11W
South Pole	13	90 0 S	0 0 E
South Porcupine	150	48 30N	81 12W
South Portland	162	43 38N	70 15W
South River, Can.	150	45 52N	79 29W
South River, U.S.A.	162	40 27N	74 23W
South Ronaldsay, I.	37	58 46N	2 58W
S. Sandwich Is.	15	57 0 S	27 0W
South Saskatchewan, R.	153	53 15N	105 5W
South Sd.	39	53 4N	9 28W
South Seal, R.	153	58 48N	98 8W
South Sentinel, I.	101	11 1N	92 16 E
South Shetland Is.	13	62 0 S	59 0W
South Shields	35	54 59N	1 26W
South Sioux City	158	42 30N	96 30W
South Taranaki Bight	142	39 40 S	174 5 E
South Tawton	30	50 44N	3 55W
South Thompson, R.	152	50 40N	120 20W
South Twin I.	150	53 7N	79 52W
South Tyne, R.	35	54 46N	2 25W
South Uist, I.	37	57 4N	7 21W
South Ulvön, I.	72	63 0N	18 45 E
South Walls, I.	37	58 45N	3 7W
South West Africa ■ = Namibia	128	22 0 S	18 9 E
South West C.	138	43 34 S	146 3 E
South West Cape	143	47 16 S	167 31 E
South Williamsport	162	41 14N	77 0W
South Yarmouth	162	41 35N	70 10W
South Yemen ■	91	15 0N	48 0 E
South Yorkshire □	33	53 30N	1 20W
Southam	28	52 16N	1 24W
Southampton, Can.	150	44 30N	81 25W
Southampton, U.K.	28	50 54N	1 23W
Southampton, U.S.A.	162	40 54N	72 22W
Southampton I.	149	64 30N	84 0W
Southampton Water	28	50 52N	1 21W
Southborough	29	51 10N	0 15 E
Southbridge, N.Z.	143	43 48 S	172 16 E
Southbridge, U.S.A.	162	42 4N	72 2W
Southeast C.	147	62 55N	169 40W
Southend, Can.	153	56 19N	103 14W
Southend, U.K.	34	55 18N	5 38W
Southend-on-Sea	29	51 32N	0 42 E
Southern □, Malawi	127	15 0 S	35 0 E
Southern □, S. Leone	120	0 8N	12 30 E
Southern □, Uganda	122	0 30 S	30 30 E
Southern □, Zambia	127	16 20 S	26 20 E
Southern Alps	143	43 41 S	170 11 E
Southern Cross	137	31 12 S	119 15 E
Southern Hills	137	32 15 S	122 40 E
Southern Indian L.	153	57 10N	98 30W
Southern Indian Lake	153	57 0N	99 0W
Southern Ocean	13	62 0 S	160 0W
Southern Uplands	35	55 30N	3 3W
Southery	29	52 32N	0 23 E
Southington	162	41 37N	72 53W
Southland □	143	45 51 S	168 13 E
Southminster	29	51 40N	0 51 E
Southold	162	41 4N	72 26W
Southport, Austral.	139	27 58 S	153 25 E
Southport, U.K.	32	53 38N	3 1W
Southport, U.S.A.	157	33 55N	78 0W
Southwark	29	51 29N	0 5W
Southwell	33	53 4N	0 57W
Southwick	29	50 50N	0 14W
Southwold	29	52 19N	1 41 E
Soutpansberge	129	23 0 S	29 30 E
Souvigny	44	46 33N	3 10 E
Sovata	70	46 35N	25 3 E
Sovetsk, Lithuania, U.S.S.R.	80	55 6N	21 50 E
Sovetsk, R.S.F.S.R., U.S.S.R.	81	57 38N	48 53 E
Sovetskaya Gavan	77	48 50N	140 0 E
Sovicille	63	43 16N	11 12 E
Sovra	66	42 44N	17 34 E
Sowerby	33	54 13N	1 19W
Söya-Misaki	112	45 30N	142 0 E
Soyopa	164	28 41N	109 37W
Sozh, R.	80	53 50N	31 50 E
Sozopol	67	42 23N	27 42 E
Spa	47	50 29N	5 53 E
Spain ■	55	40 0N	5 0W
Spakenburg	46	52 15N	5 22 E
Spalding, Austral.	140	33 30 S	138 37 E
Spalding, U.K.	29	52 47N	0 9W
Spalding, U.S.A.	158	41 45N	98 27W
Spandet	73	55 15N	8 54 E
Spånga	72	59 23N	17 55 E
Spångenäs	73	57 36N	16 7 E
Spangereid	71	58 3N	7 9 E
Spaniard's Bay	151	47 38N	53 20W
Spanish	150	46 12N	82 20W
Spanish Fork	160	40 10N	111 37W
Spanish Pt.	39	52 51N	9 27W
Spanish Sahara □ = Western Sahara	116	25 0N	13 0W
Spanish Town	166	18 0N	77 20W
Sparkford	28	51 2N	2 33W
Sparrows Point	162	39 13N	76 29W
Sparta, Ga., U.S.A.	157	33 18N	82 59W
Sparta, N.J., U.S.A.	162	41 2N	74 38W
Sparta, Wis., U.S.A.	158	43 55N	91 10W
Sparta = Spárti	69	37 5N	22 25 E
Spartanburg	157	35 0N	82 0W
Spartel, C.	118	35 47N	5 56W
Spárti	69	37 5N	22 25 E
Spartivento, C., Calabria, Italy	65	37 56N	16 4 E
Spartivento, C., Sard., Italy	65	38 52N	8 50 E
Spas-Demensk	80	54 20N	34 0 E
Spas-Klepiki	81	54 34N	40 2 E
Spassk-Dalniy	77	44 40N	132 40 E
Spassk-Ryazanskiy	81	54 30N	40 25 E
Spatha Akra.	69	35 42N	23 43 E
Spatsizi, R.	152	57 42N	128 7W
Spean Bridge	36	56 53N	4 55W
Spearfish	158	44 32N	103 52W
Spearman	159	36 15N	101 10W
Speculator	162	43 30N	74 25W
Speed	140	35 21 S	142 27 E
Speer	51	47 12N	9 8 E

Speers Stíra

Speers	153	52 43N	107 34W
Speightstown	167	13 15N	59 39W
Speke	32	53 21N	2 51W
Speke Gulf, L. Victoria	126	2 20S	32 50E
Spekholzerheide	47	50 51N	6 2E
Spelve, L.	34	56 22N	5 45W
Spenard	147	61 5N	149 50W
Spencer, Idaho, U.S.A.	160	44 18N	112 8W
Spencer, Iowa, U.S.A.	158	43 5N	95 3W
Spencer, Nebr., U.S.A.	158	42 52N	98 43W
Spencer, N.Y., U.S.A.	162	42 14N	76 30W
Spencer, W. Va., U.S.A.	156	38 47N	81 24W
Spencer B.	128	25 30S	14 47E
Spencer Bay	148	69 32N	93 32W
Spencer, C.	140	35 20S	136 45E
Spencer G.	140	34 0S	137 20E
Spences Bridge	152	50 25N	121 20W
Spennymoor	33	54 43N	1 35W
Spenser Mts.	143	42 15S	172 45E
Sperkhiós, R.	69	38 57N	22 3E
Sperrin Mts.	38	54 50N	7 0W
Spessart	49	50 0N	9 20E
Spetsai	69	37 16N	23 9E
Spétsai, I.	69	37 15N	23 10E
Spey B.	37	57 41N	3 0W
Spey Bay	37	57 39N	3 4W
Spey, R.	37	57 26N	3 25W
Speyer	49	49 19N	8 26E
Speyer, R.	41	49 18N	7 52E
Spezia = La Spézia	62	44 7N	9 49E
Spézia, La	62	44 8N	9 50E
Spezzano Albanese	65	39 41N	16 19E
Spiddal	39	53 14N	9 19W
Spiekeroog, I.	48	53 45N	7 42E
Spielfeld	63	46 43N	15 38E
Spiez	50	46 40N	7 40E
Spijk	46	53 24N	6 50E
Spijkenisse	46	51 51N	4 20E
Spili	69	35 13N	24 31E
Spilimbergo	63	46 7N	12 53E
Spillimacheen	152	51 6N	117 0W
Spilsby	33	53 10N	0 6E
Spin Baldak	93	31 3N	66 16E
Spinazzola	65	40 58N	16 5E
Spincourt	43	49 20N	5 39E
Spind	71	58 6N	6 53E
Spineni	70	44 43N	24 37E
Spirit Lake	160	47 56N	116 56W
Spirit River	152	55 45N	118 50W
Spiritwood	153	53 24N	107 33W
Spišská Nová Ves	53	48 58N	20 34E
Spišské Podhradie	53	49 0N	20 48E
Spit Pt.	136	20 4S	118 59E
Spithead	29	50 43N	0 56W
Spittal	52	46 48N	13 31E
Spitzbergen (Svalbard)	12	78 0N	17 0E
Split	63	43 31N	16 26E
Split L.	153	56 8N	96 15W
Splitski Kan	63	43 31N	16 20E
Splügen	51	46 34N	9 21E
Splügenpass	51	46 30N	9 20E
Spoffard	159	29 10N	100 27W
Spofforth	33	53 57N	1 28W
Spokane	160	47 45N	117 25W
Sponvika	71	59 7N	11 15E
Spooner	158	45 49N	91 51W
Sporádhes	69	37 0N	27 0E
Sporyy Navolok, M.	76	75 50N	68 40E
Spotswood	162	40 23N	74 23W
Spragge	150	46 15N	82 40W
Sprague	160	47 25N	117 59W
Sprague River	160	42 49N	121 31W
Spratly, I.	102	8 20N	112 0E
Spray	160	44 56N	119 46W
Spree, R.	48	52 23N	13 52E
Sprimont	47	50 30N	5 40E
Spring City, Pa., U.S.A.	162	40 11N	75 33W
Spring City, Utah, U.S.A.	160	39 31N	111 28W
Spring Grove	162	39 55N	76 56W
Spring Hill	141	33 23S	149 9E
Spring Mts.	161	36 20N	115 43W
Spring Valley, Minn., U.S.A.	158	43 40N	92 30W
Spring Valley, N.Y., U.S.A.	162	41 7N	74 4W
Springbok	128	29 42S	17 54E
Springburn	143	43 40S	171 32E
Springdale, Can.	151	49 30N	56 6W
Springdale, Ark., U.S.A.	159	36 10N	94 5W
Springdale, Wash., U.S.A.	160	48 1N	117 50W
Springe	48	52 12N	9 35E
Springerville	161	34 10N	109 16W
Springfield, N.Z.	143	43 19S	171 56E
Springfield, Colo., U.S.A.	159	37 26N	102 40W
Springfield, Ill., U.S.A.	158	39 48N	89 40W
Springfield, Mass., U.S.A.	162	42 8N	72 37W
Springfield, Mo., U.S.A.	159	37 15N	93 20W
Springfield, Ohio, U.S.A.	156	39 50N	83 48W
Springfield, Oreg., U.S.A.	160	44 2N	123 0W
Springfield, Tenn., U.S.A.	157	36 35N	86 55W
Springfield, Va., U.S.A.	162	38 45N	77 13W
Springfield, Vt., U.S.A.	162	43 20N	72 30W
Springfontein	128	30 15S	25 40E
Springhill	151	45 40N	64 4W
Springhouse	152	51 56N	122 7W
Springhurst	141	36 10S	146 31E
Springs	129	26 13S	28 25E
Springsure	138	24 8S	148 6E
Springvale, Queens., Austral.	138	23 33S	140 42E
Springvale, W. Australia, Austral.	136	17 48S	127 41E
Springvale, U.S.A.	162	43 28N	70 48W
Springville, Calif., U.S.A.	163	36 8N	118 49W
Springville, N.Y., U.S.A.	156	42 31N	78 41W
Springville, Utah, U.S.A.	160	40 14N	111 35W
Springwater	153	51 58N	108 23W
Sproatley	33	53 46N	0 9W
Spur	159	33 28N	100 50W
Spurn Hd.	33	53 34N	0 8E
Spuz	66	42 32N	19 10E
Spuzzum	152	49 37N	121 23W
Spydeberg	71	59 37N	11 4E
Squam L.	162	43 45N	71 32W
Squamish	152	49 45N	123 10W
Square Islands	151	52 47N	55 47W
Squillace, Golfo di	65	38 43N	16 35E
Squinzano	65	40 27N	18 1E
Squires, Mt.	137	26 14S	127 46E
Sragen	103	7 28S	110 59E
Srbac	66	45 7N	17 30E
Srbija □	66	43 30N	21 0E
Srbobran	66	45 32N	19 48E
Sre Khtum	101	12 10N	106 52E
Sre Umbell	101	11 8N	103 46E
Srebrnica	66	44 10N	19 18E
Sredinyy Khrebet	77	57 0N	160 0E
Središce	63	46 24N	16 17E
Sredna Gora	67	42 40N	25 0E
Sredne Tambovskoye	77	50 55N	137 45E
Srednekolymsk	77	67 20N	154 40E
Srednevilyuysk	77	63 50N	123 5E
Sredni Rodopi	67	41 40N	24 45E
Sredniy Ural, mts.	166	59 0N	59 0E
Srem	54	52 6N	17 2E
Srepok, R.	100	13 33N	106 16E
Sretensk	77	52 10N	117 40E
Sri Lanka ■	97	7 30N	80 50E
Sriharikota, I.	97	13 40N	81 30E
Srikakulam	96	18 14N	84 4E
Srinagar	95	34 12N	74 50E
Sripur	98	24 14N	90 30E
Srirangam	97	10 54N	78 42E
Srirangapatnam	97	12 26N	76 43E
Srivilliputtur	97	9 31N	77 40E
Środa Wlkp.	54	52 15N	17 19E
Srpska Crnja	66	45 38N	20 44E
Srpska Itabej	66	45 35N	20 44E
Ssu Chiao	109	30 43N	122 28E
Ssuhsien	107	33 25N	117 54E
Ssuhui	109	23 20N	112 41E
Ssunan	108	27 56N	108 14E
Ssup'ing	105	43 10N	124 25E
Ssushui, Honan, China	106	34 51N	113 12E
Ssushui, Shantung, China	107	35 39N	117 15E
Ssutzuwangch'i	106	41 30N	111 37E
Staaten, R.	138	16 24S	141 17E
Stabroek	47	51 20N	4 22E
Stack's Mts.	39	52 20N	9 34W
Stad Delden	46	52 16N	6 43E
Stade	48	53 35N	9 31E
Staden	47	50 59N	3 1E
Staðarhólskirkja	74	65 23N	21 58W
Stadil	73	56 12N	8 12E
Städjan	72	61 56N	12 30E
Stadlandet	71	62 10N	5 10E
Stadsforsen	72	63 0N	16 45E
Stadskanaal	46	53 4N	6 48E
Stadthagen	48	52 20N	9 14E
Stadtlohn	48	51 59N	6 52E
Stadtroda	48	50 51N	11 44E
Stäfa	51	47 14N	8 45E
Stafafell	74	64 25N	14 52W
Staffa, I.	34	56 26N	6 21W
Stafford, U.K.	28	52 49N	2 9W
Stafford, Kansas, U.S.A.	159	38 0N	98 35W
Stafford, Va., U.S.A.	162	38 2S	77 30W
Stafford □	28	52 53N	2 10W
Stafford Springs	162	41 58N	72 20W
Stagnone, I.	64	37 50N	12 28E
Staindrop	33	54 35N	1 49W
Staines	29	51 26N	0 30W
Stainforth	33	53 37N	0 59W
Stainmore For.	32	54 29N	2 5W
Stainton	33	53 17N	0 23W
Stainz	52	46 53N	15 17E
Staithes	33	54 33N	0 47W
Stakkroge	73	55 53N	8 51E
Stala	66	43 43N	21 28E
Stalbridge	28	50 57N	2 22W
Stalden	50	46 14N	7 52E
Stalham	29	52 46N	1 31E
Stalingrad = Volgograd	83	48 40N	44 25E
Staliniri = Tskhinvali	83	42 14N	44 1E
Stalino = Donetsky	82	48 0N	37 45E
Stalinogorsk = Novomoskovsk	81	54 5N	38 15E
Stallingborough	33	53 36N	0 11W
Stalowa Wola	54	50 34N	22 3E
Stalybridge	32	53 29N	1 56W
Stamford, Austral.	138	21 15S	143 46E
Stamford, U.K.	29	52 39N	0 29W
Stamford, Conn., U.S.A.	162	41 5N	73 30W
Stamford, N.Y., U.S.A.	162	42 25N	74 37W
Stamford, Tex., U.S.A.	159	32 58N	99 50W
Stamford Bridge	33	53 59N	0 53W
Stamfordham	35	55 3N	1 53W
Stampersgat	47	51 37N	4 26E
Stamps	159	33 22N	93 30W
Stanberry	158	40 12N	94 32W
Standerton	129	26 55S	29 13E
Standish, U.K.	32	53 35N	2 39W
Standish, U.S.A.	156	43 58N	83 57W
Standon	29	51 53N	0 2E
Stanford	160	47 11N	110 10W
Stanford on Teme	28	52 17N	2 26W
Stange Hedmark	71	60 43N	11 11E
Stanger	129	29 18S	31 21E
Stanhope, Austral.	141	36 27S	144 59E
Stanhope, U.K.	32	54 45N	2 0W
Stanišic	53	45 53N	19 12E
Stanislaus, R.	163	37 40N	121 15W
Stanislav = Ivano-Frankovsk	80	49 0N	24 40E
Stanke Dimitrov	66	42 27N	23 9E
Stanley, Austral.	138	40 46S	145 19E
Stanley, N.B., Can.	151	46 20N	66 50W
Stanley, Sask., Can.	153	55 24N	104 22W
Stanley, Falk. Is.	176	51 40S	58 0W
Stanley, Durham, U.K.	33	54 53N	1 42W
Stanley, Tayside, U.K.	35	56 29N	3 28W
Stanley, Idaho, U.S.A.	160	44 10N	114 59W
Stanley, N.D., U.S.A.	158	48 20N	102 23W
Stanley, Wis., U.S.A.	158	44 57N	91 0W
Stanley Res.	97	11 50N	77 40E
Stanleyville = Kisangani	126	0 35N	25 15E
Stanlow	32	53 17N	2 52W
Stann Creek	165	17 0N	88 20W
Stannington	35	55 7N	1 41W
Stanovoy Khrebet	77	55 0N	130 0E
Stans	51	46 58N	8 21E
Stansmore Ra.	136	21 23S	128 33E
Stansted Mountfitchet	29	51 54N	0 13E
Stanthorpe	139	28 36S	151 59E
Stanton, Can.	147	69 45N	128 52W
Stanton, U.S.A.	159	32 8N	101 45W
Stantsiya Karshi	85	38 49N	65 47E
Stanwix	32	54 54N	2 56W
Staphorst	46	52 39N	6 12E
Stapleford	33	52 56N	1 16W
Staplehurst	29	51 9N	0 35E
Stapleton	158	41 30N	100 31W
Staporkow	54	51 9N	20 31E
Star City	153	52 55N	104 20W
Stara-minskaya	83	46 33N	39 0E
Stara Moravica	66	45 50N	19 30E
Stara Pazova	66	45 0N	20 10E
Stara Planina	67	43 15N	23 0E
Stara Zagora	67	42 26N	25 39E
Starachowice-Wierzbnik	54	51 3N	21 2E
Staraya Russa	80	57 58N	31 10E
Starbuck I.	131	5 37S	155 55W
Stargard	48	53 29N	13 19E
Stargard Szczecinski	54	53 20N	15 0E
Stari Bar	66	42 7N	19 13E
Stari Trg.	63	45 29N	15 7E
Staritsa	80	56 33N	35 0E
Starke	157	30 0N	82 10W
Starkville, Colo., U.S.A.	159	37 10N	104 31W
Starkville, Miss., U.S.A.	157	33 26N	88 48W
Starnberg	49	48 0N	11 20E
Starnberger See	49	48 0N	11 0E
Starobelsk	83	49 27N	39 0E
Starodub	80	52 30N	32 50E
Starogard	54	53 55N	18 30E
Start Bay	30	50 15N	3 35W
Start Pt., Devon, U.K.	30	50 13N	3 38W
Start Pt., Orkney, U.K.	37	59 17N	2 25W
Stary Sacz	54	49 33N	30 26E
Staryy Biryuzyak	83	44 46N	46 50E
Staryy Kheydzhan	77	60 0N	144 50E
Staryy Krym	82	44 48N	35 8E
Staryy Oskol	81	51 12N	37 55E
Stassfurt	48	51 51N	11 34E
State College	156	40 47N	77 49W
State Is.	150	48 40N	87 0W
Staten I.	162	40 35N	74 10W
Staten, I. = Los Estados, I. de	176	54 40S	64 0W
Statesboro	157	32 26N	81 46W
Statesville	157	35 48N	80 51W
Statfjord, oilfield	19	61 15N	1 50E
Stathelle	71	59 3N	9 41E
Stauffer	163	34 45N	119 3W
Staunton, U.K.	28	51 58N	2 19W
Staunton, Ill., U.S.A.	158	39 0N	89 49W
Staunton, Va., U.S.A.	156	38 7N	79 4W
Stavanger	71	58 57N	5 40E
Staveley, Cumbria, U.K.	32	54 24N	2 49W
Staveley, Derby, U.K.	33	53 16N	1 20W
Stavelot	47	50 23N	5 55E
Stavenisse	47	51 35N	4 1E
Staveren	46	52 53N	5 22E
Stavern	71	59 0N	10 1E
Stavfjord	71	61 30N	5 0E
Stavre	72	62 51N	15 19E
Stavropol	83	45 5N	42 0E
Stavroúpolis	68	41 12N	24 45E
Stavsjö	73	48 42N	16 30E
Stawell	140	37 5S	142 47E
Stawell, R.	138	20 38S	142 55E
Stawiszyn	54	51 56N	18 4E
Staxigoe	37	58 28N	3 2W
Steamboat Springs	160	40 30N	106 58W
Stebark	54	53 30N	20 10E
Stebleva	68	41 18N	20 33E
Steckborn	51	47 44N	8 59E
Steele	158	46 56N	99 52W
Steelton	162	40 17N	76 50W
Steelville	159	37 57N	91 21W
Steen, R.	152	59 35N	117 10W
Steen River	152	59 40N	117 12W
Steenbergen	47	51 35N	4 19E
Steenvoorde	43	50 48N	2 33E
Steenwijk	46	52 47N	6 7E
Steep Pt.	137	26 08S	113 8E
Steep Rock	153	51 30N	98 48W
Steep Rock Lake	150	48 50N	91 38W
Stefănesti	70	47 44N	27 15E
Stefanie L. = Chew Bahir	123	4 40N	30 50E
Steffisburg	50	46 47N	7 38E
Stefănesti	70	47 44N	27 15E
Stege	73	55 0N	12 18E
Steierdorf Anina	66	45 6N	21 51E
Steiermark □	52	47 26N	15 0E
Steigerwald	49	49 45N	10 30E
Stein, Neth.	47	50 58N	5 45E
Stein, Switz.	51	47 40N	8 50E
Stein, U.K.	36	57 30N	6 35W
Steinbach	153	49 32N	96 40W
Steinfort	47	49 39N	5 55E
Steinheim	48	51 50N	9 6E
Steinkjer	74	63 59N	11 31E
Steinkopf	125	29 15S	17 48E
Stekene	47	51 12N	4 2E
Stella Land	128	26 45S	24 50E
Stellarton	151	45 32N	62 45W
Stellenbosch	128	33 58S	18 50E
Stellendam	46	51 49N	4 1E
Stelvio, Paso dello	51	46 32N	10 27E
Stemshaug	71	63 19N	8 44E
Stendal	48	52 36N	11 50E
Stene	47	51 12N	2 56E
Stenhousemuir	35	56 2N	3 46W
Stenmagle	73	55 49N	11 39E
Stenness, L., of	37	59 0N	3 15W
Stensele	74	65 3N	17 8E
Stenstorp	73	58 17N	13 45E
Stenungsund	73	58 6N	11 50E
Stepanakert	79	40 0N	46 25E
Stephan	158	48 30N	96 53W
Stephens Cr.	140	32 15S	141 55E
Stephens I., Can.	152	54 10N	130 45W
Stephens I., N.Z.	143	40 40S	174 1E
Stephenville, Can.	151	48 31N	58 30W
Stephenville, U.S.A.	159	32 12N	98 12W
Stepnica	54	53 38N	14 36E
Stepnoi = Elista	83	46 25N	44 17E
Stepnoye	84	54 4N	60 26E
Sterkstroom	128	31 32S	26 32E
Sterlego, Mys	12	80 30N	90 0E
Sterling, Colo., U.S.A.	158	40 40N	103 15W
Sterling, Ill., U.S.A.	158	41 45N	89 45W
Sterling, Kans., U.S.A.	158	38 17N	98 13W
Sterling City	159	31 50N	100 59W
Sterlitamak	84	53 40N	56 0E
Sternberg	48	53 42N	11 48E
Sternberk	53	49 45N	17 15E
Stettin = Szczecin	54	53 27N	14 27E
Stettiner Haff	48	53 50N	14 25E
Stettler	152	52 19N	112 40W
Steubenville	156	40 21N	80 39W
Stevenage	29	51 54N	0 11W
Stevens Port	158	44 32N	89 34W
Stevens Village	147	66 0N	149 10W
Stevenson L.	153	53 55N	95 9W
Stevenson, R.	136	46 15S	134 10E
Stevenston	34	55 38N	4 46W
Stevns Klint	73	55 17N	12 28E
Stewart	152	55 56N	129 57W
Stewart, C.	138	11 57S	134 45E
Stewart, I.	176	54 50S	71 30W
Stewart I.	143	46 58S	167 54E
Stewart River	147	63 19N	139 26W
Stewarton	34	55 40N	4 30W
Stewartstown	38	54 35N	6 40W
Stewiacke	151	45 9N	63 22W
Steyning	29	50 54N	0 19W
Steynsburg	128	31 15S	25 49E
Steyr	52	48 3N	14 25E
Steyr, R.	52	48 57N	14 15E
Steytlerville	128	33 17S	24 19E
Stia	63	43 48N	11 41E
Stiens	46	53 16N	5 46E
Stigler	159	35 19N	95 6W
Stigliano	65	40 24N	16 13E
Stigsnæs	73	55 13N	11 18E
Stigtomta	73	58 47N	16 48E
Stikine Mts.	148	59 30N	129 30W
Stikine, R.	147	58 0N	131 12W
Stilfontein	128	26 50S	26 50E
Stilis	69	38 55N	22 37E
Stillington	33	54 7N	1 5W
Stillwater, Minn., U.S.A.	158	45 3N	92 47W
Stillwater, N.Y., U.S.A.	162	42 55N	73 41W
Stillwater, Okla., U.S.A.	159	36 5N	97 3W
Stillwater Mts.	160	39 45N	118 6W
Stilwell	159	35 52N	94 36W
Stimfalias, L.	69	37 51N	22 27E
Stimson	150	48 58N	80 30W
Stinchar, R.	34	55 10N	4 50W
Stingray Pt.	162	37 35N	76 15W
Stip	66	41 42N	22 10E
Stiperstones Mt.	28	52 36N	2 57W
Stíra	69	38 9N	24 14E

Stiring Wendel **Sukkur**

Stiring Wendel	**43**	49 12N	6 57 E
Stirling, Austral.	**138**	17 12 S	141 35 E
Stirling, Can.	**152**	49 30N	112 30W
Stirling, N.Z.	**143**	46 14 S	169 49 E
Stirling, U.K.	**35**	56 17N	3 57W
Stirling (□)	**26**	56 3N	4 10W
Stirling Ra.	**137**	34 0 S	118 0 E
Stjárneborg	**73**	57 53N	14 45 E
Stjarnsfors	**72**	60 2N	13 45 E
Stjördalshalsen	**71**	63 29N	10 51 E
Stobo	**35**	55 38N	3 18W
Stoborough, oilfield	**19**	50 38N	2 8W
Stockaryd	**73**	57 19N	14 36 E
Stockbridge	**28**	51 7N	1 30W
Stockerau	**53**	48 24N	16 12 E
Stockett	**160**	47 23N	111 7W
Stockholm	**72**	59 20N	18 3 E
Stockholms län □	**72**	59 30N	18 20 E
Stockhorn	**50**	46 42N	7 33 E
Stockport	**32**	53 25N	2 11W
Stocksbridge	**33**	53 30N	1 36W
Stockton, Austral.	**141**	32 56 S	151 47 E
Stockton, Calif., U.S.A.	**163**	38 0N	121 20W
Stockton, Kans., U.S.A.	**158**	39 30N	99 20W
Stockton, Mo., U.S.A.	**159**	37 40N	93 48W
Stockton-on-Tees	**33**	54 34N	1 20W
Stockvik	**72**	62 17N	17 23 E
Stoczek Łukowski	**54**	51 58N	22 22 E
Stode	**72**	62 28N	16 35 E
Stoer	**36**	58 12N	5 20W
Stogovo, mts.	**66**	41 31N	20 38 E
Stoke, N.Z.	**143**	41 19N	173 14 E
Stoke, U.K.	**29**	51 26N	0 41 E
Stoke Ferry	**29**	52 34N	0 31 E
Stoke Fleming	**30**	50 19N	3 36W
Stoke Mandeville	**29**	51 46N	0 47W
Stoke Prior	**28**	52 18N	2 5W
Stokenham	**30**	50 15N	3 40W
Stokes Bay	**150**	45 0N	81 22W
Stokes Pt.	**138**	40 10 S	143 56 E
Stokes Ra.	**136**	15 50 S	130 50 E
Stokesley	**33**	54 27N	1 12W
Stokke	**71**	59 13N	10 17 E
Stokkem	**47**	51 1N	5 45 E
Stokken	**71**	58 31N	8 53 E
Stokkseyri	**74**	63 50N	20 58W
Stokksnes	**74**	64 14N	14 58W
Stolac	**66**	43 8N	17 59 E
Stolberg, Germ., E.	**48**	51 33N	11 0 E
Stolberg, Germ., W.	**48**	50 48N	6 13 E
Stolbovaya, R.S.F.S.R., U.S.S.R.	**77**	64 50N	153 50 E
Stolbovaya, R.S.F.S.R., U.S.S.R.	**81**	55 10N	37 32 E
Stolbtsy	**80**	53 22N	26 43 E
Stolin	**80**	51 53N	26 50 E
Stolnici	**70**	44 31N	24 48 E
Stolwijk	**46**	51 59N	4 47 E
Ston	**66**	42 51N	17 43 E
Stone, Bucks., U.K.	**29**	51 48N	0 52W
Stone, Stafford, U.K.	**32**	52 55N	2 10W
Stone Harbor	**162**	39 3N	74 45W
Stonecliffe	**150**	46 13N	77 56W
Stonehaven	**37**	56 58N	2 11W
Stonehenge, Austral.	**138**	24 22 S	143 17 E
Stonehenge, U.K.	**28**	51 9N	1 45W
Stonehouse, Glous., U.K.	**28**	51 45N	2 18W
Stonehouse, Strathclyde, U.K.	**35**	55 42N	4 0W
Stonewall	**153**	50 10N	97 19W
Stongfjord	**71**	61 28N	14 0 E
Stonham Aspall	**29**	52 11N	1 7 E
Stony L.	**153**	58 51N	98 40W
Stony Point	**162**	41 14N	73 59W
Stony Rapids	**153**	59 16N	105 50W
Stony River	**147**	61 48N	156 48W
Stony Stratford	**29**	52 4N	0 51W
Stony Tunguska = Tunguska, Nizhmaya	**77**	64 0N	95 0 E
Stopnica	**54**	50 27N	20 57 E
Stor Elvdal	**71**	61 30N	11 1 E
Stora Borge Fjell, Mt.	**48**	65 12N	14 0 E
Stora Gla	**72**	59 30N	12 30 E
Stora Karlsö	**73**	57 17N	17 59 E
Stora Lulevatten	**74**	67 10N	19 30 E
Stora Sjøfallet	**74**	67 29N	18 40 E
Storavan	**74**	65 45N	18 10 E
Stord Leirvik, I.	**71**	59 48N	5 27 E
Store Bælt	**73**	55 20N	11 0 E
Store Creek	**141**	32 54 S	149 6 E
Store Heddinge	**73**	55 18N	12 23 E
Storen	**71**	63 3N	10 18 E
Storfjorden	**71**	62 25N	6 30 E
Storm B.	**138**	43 10 S	147 30 E
Storm Lake	**158**	42 35N	95 5W
Stormberg	**125**	31 16 S	26 17 E
Stormsrivier	**128**	33 59 S	23 52 E
Stornoway	**36**	58 12N	6 23W
Storozhinets	**82**	48 14 S	25 45 E
Storr, The, mt.	**36**	57 30N	6 12W
Storrs	**162**	41 48N	72 15W
Storsjö	**72**	62 49N	13 5 E
Storsjöen, Hedmark, Norway	**71**	60 20N	11 40 E
Storsjöen, Hedmark, Norway	**71**	61 30N	11 14 E
Storsjön, Gavleborg, Sweden	**72**	60 35N	16 45 E
Storsjön, Jämtland, Sweden	**72**	62 50N	13 8 E
Storstroms Amt □	**73**	49 50N	11 45 E
Stort, R.	**29**	51 50N	0 7 E
Storuman	**74**	65 5N	17 10 E
Storuman, L.	**74**	65 5N	17 10 E
Storvätteshagna, Mt.	**72**	62 6N	12 30 E
Storvik	**72**	60 35N	16 33 E
Stotfold	**29**	52 2N	0 13W
Stoughton	**153**	49 40N	103 0W
Stour, R., Dorset, U.K.	**28**	50 48N	2 7W
Stour, R., Heref. & Worcs., U.K.	**28**	52 25N	2 13W
Stour, R., Kent, U.K.	**29**	51 15N	0 57 E
Stour, R., Suffolk, U.K.	**29**	51 55N	1 5 E
Stourbridge	**28**	52 28N	2 8W
Stourport	**28**	52 21N	2 18W
Stout, L.	**153**	52 0N	94 40W
Stove Pipe Wells Village	**163**	36 35N	117 11W
Stow	**35**	55 41N	2 50W
Stow Bardolph	**29**	52 38N	0 24 E
Stow-on-the-Wold	**28**	51 55N	1 42W
Stowmarket	**29**	52 11N	1 0 E
Stowupland	**29**	52 12N	1 3 E
Strabane	**38**	54 50N	7 28W
Strabane □	**38**	54 45N	7 25W
Strachan	**37**	57 1N	2 31W
Strachur	**34**	56 10N	5 5W
Stracin	**66**	42 13N	22 2 E
Stradbally, Kerry, Ireland	**39**	52 15N	10 4W
Stradbally, Laoighis, Ireland	**39**	53 2N	7 10W
Stradbally, Waterford, Ireland	**39**	52 7N	7 28W
Stradbroke	**29**	52 19N	1 16 E
Strade	**38**	53 56N	9 8W
Stradella	**62**	45 4N	9 20 E
Stradone	**38**	54 0N	7 12W
Strahan	**138**	42 9 S	145 20 E
Straldzha	**67**	42 35N	26 40 E
Stralkonice	**52**	49 15N	13 53 E
Stralsund	**48**	54 17N	13 5 E
Strand, Hedmark, Norway	**71**	61 18N	11 15 E
Strand, Rogaland, Norway	**71**	59 3N	5 56 E
Strand, S. Afr.	**128**	34 9 S	18 48 E
Stranda	**71**	62 19N	6 58 E
Strandby	**73**	56 47N	9 13 E
Strandebarm	**71**	60 17N	6 0 E
Strandhill	**38**	54 16N	8 34W
Strandvik	**71**	60 9N	5 41 E
Strangford	**38**	54 23N	5 34W
Strängnäs	**72**	59 23N	17 8 E
Stranorlar	**38**	54 58N	7 47W
Stranraer	**34**	54 54N	5 0W
Strasbourg, Can.	**153**	51 4N	104 55W
Strasbourg, France	**43**	48 35N	7 42 E
Strasburg, Ger.	**48**	53 30N	13 44 E
Strasburg, U.S.A.	**158**	46 12N	101 9W
Strassen	**47**	49 37N	6 4 E
Stratford, N.S.W., Austral.	**141**	32 7 S	151 55 E
Stratford, Vic., Austral.	**141**	37 59 S	147 7 E
Stratford, Can.	**150**	43 23N	81 0W
Stratford, N.Z.	**142**	39 20 S	174 19 E
Stratford, Calif., U.S.A.	**163**	36 10N	119 49W
Stratford, Conn., U.S.A.	**162**	41 13N	73 8W
Stratford, Tex., U.S.A.	**159**	36 20N	102 3W
Stratford-on-Avon	**28**	52 12N	1 42W
Stratford St. Mary	**29**	51 58N	0 59 E
Strath Avon	**37**	57 19N	3 23W
Strath Dearn	**37**	57 20N	4 0W
Strath Earn	**35**	56 20N	3 50W
Strath Glass	**37**	57 20N	4 40W
Strath Naver	**37**	58 24N	4 12W
Strath Spey	**37**	57 15N	3 40W
Strathalbyn	**140**	35 13 S	138 53 E
Strathaven	**35**	55 40N	4 4W
Strathbogie, Dist.	**37**	57 25N	2 45W
Strathclyde □	**34**	56 0N	4 50W
Strathcona Prov. Park	**152**	49 38N	125 40W
Strathdon	**37**	57 12N	3 4W
Strathkanaird	**36**	57 58N	5 5W
Strathmore, Austral.	**138**	17 50 S	142 35 E
Strathmore, Can.	**152**	51 5N	113 25W
Strathmore, Highland, U.K.	**37**	58 20N	4 40W
Strathmore, Tayside, U.K.	**37**	56 40N	3 4W
Strathmore, U.S.A.	**163**	36 9N	119 4W
Strathnaver	**152**	53 20N	122 33W
Strathpeffer	**37**	57 35N	4 32W
Strathroy	**150**	42 58N	81 38W
Strathy	**37**	58 30N	4 0W
Strathy Pt.	**37**	58 35N	4 0W
Strathyre	**34**	56 14N	4 20W
Stratmiglo Scot.	**35**	56 16N	3 15W
Stratton, U.K.	**30**	50 49N	4 31W
Stratton, U.S.A.	**158**	39 20N	102 36W
Stratton St. Margaret	**28**	51 35N	1 45W
Straubing	**49**	48 53N	12 35 E
Straumnes	**74**	66 26N	23 8W
Straumsnes Åsskard	**71**	63 4N	8 2 E
Strausberg	**48**	52 40N	13 52 E
Strawberry Res.	**160**	40 0N	111 0W
Strawn	**159**	32 36N	98 30W
Stráznice	**53**	48 54N	17 19 E
Streaky B.	**139**	32 51 S	134 18 E
Streaky Bay	**139**	32 48 S	134 13 E
Streatley	**28**	51 31N	1 9W
Streator	**158**	41 9N	88 52W
Stredočeský □	**52**	49 55N	14 30 E
Stredoslovenský □	**53**	48 30N	19 15 E
Streé	**47**	50 17N	4 18 E
Street	**28**	51 7N	2 43W
Strehaia	**70**	44 37N	23 10 E
Strelcha	**67**	42 30N	24 19 E
Strelka	**77**	58 5N	93 10 E
Streng, R.	**100**	13 12N	103 37 E
Strengelvåg	**74**	68 58N	15 11 E
Strensall	**33**	54 3N	1 2W
Stretford	**32**	53 27N	2 19W
Stretton	**32**	53 21N	2 34W
Strezhevoy	**76**	60 42N	77 34 E
Strezhnoye	**76**	57 45N	84 2 E
Stribro	**52**	49 44N	13 0 E
Strichen	**37**	57 35N	2 5W
Strickland, R.	**135**	7 35 S	141 36 E
Strijen	**46**	51 45N	4 33 E
Strimón, R.	**68**	41 0N	23 30 E
Strimonikós Kólpos	**68**	40 33N	24 0 E
Striven, L.	**34**	55 58N	5 9W
Strofadhes, I.	**69**	37 15N	21 0 E
Strokestown	**38**	53 47N	8 6W
Strom	**71**	60 17N	11 44 E
Ström	**72**	61 52N	17 20 E
Stroma, I. of	**37**	58 40N	3 8W
Strombacka	**72**	61 58N	16 44 E
Strómboli, I.	**65**	38 48N	15 12 E
Stromeferry	**36**	57 20N	5 33W
Stromemore	**36**	57 22N	5 33W
Stromness	**37**	58 58N	3 18W
Ströms Vattudal L.	**74**	64 0N	15 30 E
Stromsberg	**72**	60 28N	17 44 E
Strömsnäsbruk	**73**	56 35N	13 45 E
Strömstad	**72**	58 55N	11 15 E
Stromsund	**74**	63 51N	15 35 E
Stronachlachar	**34**	56 15N	4 35W
Strone	**34**	55 59N	4 54W
Strόngoli	**65**	39 16N	17 2 E
Stronsay Firth	**37**	59 4N	2 50W
Stronsay, I.	**37**	59 8N	2 38W
Strontian	**36**	56 42N	5 32W
Strood	**29**	51 23N	0 30 E
Stroove	**38**	55 13N	6 57W
Stropkov	**53**	49 13N	21 39 E
Stroud	**28**	51 44N	2 12W
Stroud Road	**141**	32 18 S	151 57 E
Stroudsberg	**162**	40 59N	75 15W
Struer	**73**	56 30N	8 35 E
Struga	**66**	41 13N	20 44 E
Strugi Krasnye	**80**	58 21N	28 51 E
Struma, R.	**67**	41 50N	23 18 E
Strumble Hd.	**31**	52 3N	5 6W
Strumica	**66**	41 28N	22 41 E
Strumica, R.	**66**	41 26N	27 46 E
Strusshamn	**71**	60 24N	5 10 E
Struthers	**150**	48 41N	85 51W
Struy	**37**	57 25N	4 40W
Stryama	**67**	42 16N	24 54 E
Stryi	**80**	49 16N	23 48 E
Stryker	**152**	48 40N	114 44W
Stryków	**54**	51 55N	19 33 E
Strzegom	**54**	50 58N	16 20 E
Strzelce Krajenskie	**54**	52 52N	15 33 E
Strzelecki Creek	**139**	29 37 S	139 59 E
Strzelin	**54**	50 46N	17 2 E
Strzelno	**54**	52 35N	18 9 E
Strzyzów	**54**	49 52N	21 47 E
Stuart, Fla., U.S.A.	**157**	27 11N	80 12W
Stuart, Nebr., U.S.A.	**158**	42 39N	99 8W
Stuart I.	**147**	63 55N	164 50W
Stuart L.	**152**	54 30N	124 30W
Stuart Mts.	**143**	45 2 S	167 39 E
Stuart, R.	**152**	54 0N	123 35W
Stuart Range	**139**	29 10 S	134 56 E
Stuart's Ra.	**136**	29 10 S	135 0 E
Stubbekøbing	**73**	54 53N	12 9 E
Stuben	**52**	46 58N	10 31 E
Stuberhuk	**48**	54 23N	11 18 E
Studholme Junc.	**143**	44 42 S	171 9 E
Studland	**28**	50 39N	1 58W
Studley	**28**	52 16N	1 54W
Stugsund	**72**	61 16N	17 18 E
Stugun	**72**	63 10N	15 40 E
Stull, L.	**153**	54 24N	92 34W
Stung-Treng	**100**	13 31N	105 58 E
Stupart, R.	**153**	56 0N	93 25W
Stupino	**81**	54 57N	38 2 E
Sturgeon B.	**153**	52 0N	97 50W
Sturgeon Bay	**156**	44 52N	87 20W
Sturgeon Falls	**150**	46 25N	79 57W
Sturgeon L., Alta., Can.	**152**	55 6N	117 32W
Sturgeon L., Ont., Can.	**150**	50 0N	90 45W
Sturgis, Mich., U.S.A.	**156**	41 50N	85 25W
Sturgis, S.D., U.S.A.	**158**	44 25N	103 30W
Sturko, I.	**73**	56 5N	15 42 E
Sturminster Marshall	**28**	50 48N	2 4W
Sturminster Newton	**28**	50 56N	2 18W
Stúrovo	**53**	47 48N	18 41 E
Sturt Cr.	**136**	19 0 S	128 15 E
Sturt Creek	**136**	19 0 S	128 15 E
Sturt, R.	**136**	34 58 S	138 31 E
Sturton	**33**	53 22N	0 39W
Sturts Meadows	**140**	31 18 S	141 42 E
Stutterheim	**128**	32 33 S	27 28 E
Stuttgart, Ger.	**49**	48 46N	9 10 E
Stuttgart, U.S.A.	**159**	34 30N	91 33W
Stuyvesant	**162**	42 23N	73 45W
Stykkishólmur	**74**	65 2N	22 40W
Styr, R.	**80**	51 4N	25 20 E
Styria = Steiermark	**52**	47 26N	15 0 E
Su-no-Saki	**111**	34 58N	139 45 E
Suakin	**122**	19 0N	37 20 E
Suan	**107**	38 42N	126 22 E
Suaqui	**164**	29 12N	109 41W
Suay Rieng	**101**	11 9N	105 45 E
Subang	**103**	7 30 S	107 45 E
Subansiri, R.	**98**	26 48N	93 50 E
Subi	**101**	2 55N	108 50 E
Subi, I.	**102**	2 58N	108 50 E
Subiaco	**63**	41 56N	13 5 E
Subotica	**66**	46 6N	19 29 E
Success	**153**	50 28N	108 6W
Suceava	**70**	47 38N	26 16 E
Suceava □	**70**	47 37N	26 18 E
Suceava, R.	**70**	47 38N	26 16 E
Sucha-Beskidzka	**54**	49 44N	19 35 E
Suchan	**54**	53 18N	15 18 E
Suchedniów	**54**	51 3N	20 49 E
Such'i	**109**	21 23N	110 16 E
Suchien	**107**	33 58N	118 17 E
Suchil	**164**	23 38N	103 55W
Suchitoto	**166**	13 56N	89 0W
Suchou	**109**	31 15N	120 40 E
Süchow = Hsüchou	**107**	34 15N	117 10 E
Suchowola	**54**	53 33N	23 3 E
Sucio, R.	**174**	6 40N	77 0W
Suck, R.	**39**	53 17N	8 10W
Suckling, Mt.	**135**	9 43 S	148 59 E
Sucre, Boliv.	**174**	19 0 S	65 15W
Sucre, Venez.	**174**	10 25N	64 5W
Sucre □, Colomb.	**174**	8 50N	75 40W
Sucre □, Venez.	**174**	10 25N	63 30W
Sŭcueni	**70**	47 20N	22 5 E
Sucunduri, R.	**174**	6 20 S	58 35W
SuCuraj	**63**	43 10N	17 8 E
Sucuriju	**170**	1 39N	49 57W
Sud-Ouest, Pte. du	**151**	49 23N	63 36W
Sud, Pte.	**151**	49 3N	62 14W
Suda, R.	**81**	59 40N	36 30 E
Sudak	**82**	44 51N	34 57 E
Sudan ■	**117**	15 0N	30 0 E
Sudan, The	**114**	11 0N	9 0 E
Suday	**81**	59 0N	43 15 E
Sudbury, Can.	**150**	46 30N	81 0W
Sudbury, Derby, U.K.	**33**	52 53N	1 43W
Sudbury, Suffolk, U.K.	**29**	52 2N	0 44 E
Sûdd	**123**	8 20N	29 30 E
Süderbrarup	**48**	54 38N	9 47 E
Süderlügum	**48**	54 50N	8 46 E
Sudetan Mts. = Sudety	**53**	50 20N	16 45 E
Sudety	**53**	50 20N	16 45 E
Sudi	**127**	10 11 S	39 57 E
Sudirman, Pengunungan	**103**	4 30N	137 0 E
Sudiţi	**70**	44 35N	27 38 E
Sudogda	**81**	55 55N	40 50 E
Sudr	**122**	29 40N	32 42 E
Sudzha	**80**	51 14N	34 25 E
Sueca	**59**	39 12N	0 21W
Sueur, Le	**158**	44 25N	93 52W
Suez = Suweis	**122**	28 40N	33 0 E
Suf	**90**	32 19N	35 49 E
Sufaina	**92**	23 6N	40 44 E
Suffield	**153**	50 12N	111 10W
Suffolk	**156**	36 47N	76 33W
Suffolk □	**29**	52 16N	1 0 E
Suffolk, East, □	**29**	52 16N	1 10 E
Suffolk, West, □	**29**	52 16N	0 45 E
Sufi-Kurgan	**85**	40 2N	73 30 E
Sufuk	**93**	23 50N	51 50 E
Suga no-Sen	**110**	35 25N	134 25 E
Sugag	**70**	45 47N	23 37 E
Sugar City	**158**	38 18N	103 38W
Sugarloaf Pt.	**126**	32 22 S	152 30 E
Sugluk = Sagloue	**149**	62 10N	75 40W
Sugny	**47**	49 49N	4 54 E
Suhaia, L.	**70**	43 45N	25 15 E
Suhâr	**93**	24 20N	56 40 E
Suhbaatar	**105**	46 54N	113 25 E
Suhl	**48**	50 35N	10 40 E
Suhl □	**48**	50 37N	10 43 E
Suhr	**50**	47 22N	8 5 E
Suhsien	**106**	33 40N	117 0 E
Suhum	**121**	6 5N	0 27W
Suian	**109**	29 28N	118 44 E
Suica	**66**	43 52N	17 11 E
Suich'ang	**109**	28 36N	119 16 E
Suichiang	**108**	28 40N	103 58 E
Suifenho	**107**	44 30N	131 2 E
Suihsien	**109**	31 41N	113 20 E
Suihua	**98**	46 37N	127 0 E
Suilu	**108**	22 20N	107 48 E
Suining, Hunan, China	**108**	26 21N	110 0 E
Suining, Kiangsu, China	**107**	33 54N	117 56 E
Suining, Szechwan, China	**108**	30 31N	105 34 E
Suippes	**43**	49 8N	4 30 E
Suir, R.	**39**	52 31N	7 59W
Suita	**111**	34 45N	135 32 E
Suiteh	**106**	37 35N	110 5 E
Suiyang, Heilungkiang, China	**107**	44 26N	130 51 E
Suiyang, Kweichow, China	**108**	27 57N	107 11 E
Sujangarh	**94**	27 42N	47 31 E
Sukabumi	**103**	6 56 S	106 57 E
Sukadana	**102**	1 10 S	110 0 E
Sukandja	**102**	2 28 S	110 25 E
Sukarnapura = Jajapura	**103**	2 28N	140 38 E
Sukarno, G. = Jaja, Puncak	**103**	3 57 S	137 17 E
Sukchŏn	**107**	39 22N	125 35 E
Sukhinichi	**80**	54 8N	35 10 E
Sukhona, R.	**78**	60 30N	45 0 E
Sukhothai	**100**	17 1N	99 49 E
Sukhoy Log	**84**	56 55N	62 1 E
Sukhumi	**83**	43 0N	41 0 E
Sukkur	**94**	27 50N	68 46 E

Sukkur Barrage **Sydra, G. of**

Sukkur Barrage	**93**	27 50N	68 45 E
Sukma	**96**	18 24N	81 37 E
Sukovo	**66**	43 4N	22 37 E
Sukumo	**110**	32 56N	132 44 E
Sukunka, R.	**152**	55 45N	121 15W
Sul, Canal do	**170**	0 10S	48 30W
Sula, Kepulauan	**103**	1 45S	125 0 E
Sula, R.	**80**	50 0N	33 0 E
Sulaco, R.	**166**	15 2N	87 44W
Sulaiman Range	**94**	30 30N	69 50 E
Sulaimanke Headworks	**94**	30 27N	73 55 E
Sŭlaj □	**70**	47 15N	23 0 E
Sulak, R.	**83**	43 20N	47 20 E
Sulam Tsor	**90**	33 4N	35 6 E
Sulawesi □	**103**	2 0S	120 0 E
Sulawesi, I.	**103**	2 0S	120 0 E
Sulby	**32**	54 18N	4 29W
Sulechów	**54**	52 5N	15 40 E
Sulecin	**54**	52 26N	15 10 E
Sulejów	**54**	51 26N	19 53 E
Sulejówek	**54**	52 13N	21 17 E
Sulgen	**51**	47 33N	9 7 E
Sulima	**120**	6 58N	11 32W
Sulina	**70**	45 10N	29 40 E
Sulingen	**48**	52 41N	8 47 E
Sŭlişte	**70**	45 45N	23 56 E
Suliţa	**70**	47 39N	26 59 E
Sulitälma	**74**	67 17N	17 28 E
Sulitjelma	**74**	61 7N	16 8 E
Sułkowice	**54**	49 50N	19 49 E
Sullana	**174**	5 0S	80 45W
Sullivan, Ill., U.S.A.	**158**	39 40N	88 40W
Sullivan, Ind., U.S.A.	**156**	39 5N	87 26W
Sullivan, Mo., U.S.A.	**158**	38 10N	91 10W
Sullivan Bay	**152**	50 55N	126 50W
Sullom Voe	**36**	60 30N	1 20W
Sully-sur-Loire	**43**	47 45N	2 20 E
Sulmierzyce	**57**	51 36N	17 30 E
Sulmona	**63**	42 3N	13 55 E
Sulo	**105**	39 25N	76 6 E
Sulphur, La., U.S.A.	**159**	30 20N	93 22W
Sulphur, Okla., U.S.A.	**159**	34 35N	97 0W
Sulphur Pt.	**152**	60 56N	114 48W
Sulphur Springs	**159**	33 5N	95 30W
Sulphur Springs, Cr.	**159**	32 50N	102 8W
Sultan	**150**	47 36N	82 47W
Sultanpur	**95**	26 18N	82 10 E
Sulu Arch.	**103**	6 0N	121 0 E
Sulu Sea	**103**	8 0N	120 0 E
Sululta	**123**	9 10N	38 43 E
Sulung Shan	**108**	31 30N	99 30 E
Suluq	**119**	31 44N	20 14 E
Sulyukta	**85**	39 56N	69 34 E
Sulzbach-Rosenburg	**49**	49 30N	11 46 E
Sumalata	**103**	1 0N	122 37 E
Sumampa	**172**	29 25S	63 29W
Sumatera, I.	**102**	0 40N	100 20 E
Sumatera Selatan □	**102**	3 30S	104 0 E
Sumatera Tengah □	**102**	1 0S	100 0 E
Sumatera Utara □	**102**	2 0N	99 0 E
Sumatra	**160**	46 45N	107 37W
Sumatra = Sumatera	**102**	0 40N	100 20 E
Sumba, I.	**103**	9 45S	119 35 E
Sumba, Selat	**103**	9 0S	118 40 E
Sumbawa	**102**	8 26S	117 30 E
Sumbawa, I.	**103**	8 34S	117 17 E
Sumbawanga □	**126**	8 0S	31 30 E
Sumbing, mt.	**103**	7 19S	110 3 E
Sumburgh Hd.	**36**	59 52N	1 17W
Sumdo	**95**	35 6N	79 43 E
Sumé	**170**	7 39S	36 55W
Sumedang	**103**	6 49S	107 56 E
Sümeg	**53**	46 59N	17 20 E
Sumenep	**103**	7 3S	113 51 E
Sumgait	**83**	40 34N	49 10 E
Sumisu-Jima	**111**	31 27N	140 3 E
Sumiswald	**50**	47 2N	7 44 E
Summer Is.	**36**	58 0N	5 27W
Summer L.	**160**	42 50N	120 50W
Summerhill	**38**	53 30N	6 44W
Summerland	**152**	49 32N	119 41W
Summerside	**151**	46 24N	63 47W
Summerville, Ga., U.S.A.	**157**	34 30N	85 20W
Summerville, S.C., U.S.A.	**157**	33 2N	80 11W
Summit, Can.	**150**	47 50N	72 20W
Summit, U.S.A.	**147**	63 20N	149 20W
Summit L.	**152**	54 20N	122 40W
Summit Pk.	**161**	37 20N	106 48W
Sumner, N.Z.	**143**	43 35S	172 48 E
Sumner, U.S.A.	**158**	42 49N	92 7W
Sumner L.	**143**	42 42S	172 15 E
Sumoto	**110**	34 21N	134 54 E
Sumperk	**53**	49 59N	17 0 E
Sumprabum	**98**	26 33N	97 4 E
Sumter	**157**	33 55N	80 10W
Sumy	**80**	50 57N	34 50 E
Sun City	**163**	33 41N	117 11W
Suna	**126**	5 23S	34 48 E
Sunan	**107**	39 15N	125 40 E
Sunart, dist.	**36**	56 40N	5 40W
Sunart, L.	**36**	56 42N	5 43W
Sunburst	**160**	48 56N	111 59W
Sunbury, Austral.	**141**	37 35S	144 44 E
Sunbury, U.S.A.	**162**	40 50N	76 46W
Sunchales	**172**	30 58S	61 35W
Suncho Corral	**172**	27 55S	63 14W
Sunchŏn	**107**	34 52N	127 31 E
Suncook	**162**	43 8N	71 27W
Sund	**71**	60 13N	5 10 E
Sunda Ketjil, Kepulauan	**102**	7 30S	117 0 E
Sunda, Selat	**102**	6 20S	105 30 E
Sundalsöra	**71**	62 40N	8 36 E
Sundance	**158**	44 27N	104 27W
Sundarbans, The	**98**	22 0N	89 0 E
Sundargarh	**96**	22 10N	84 5 E
Sunday Str.	**136**	16 25S	123 18 E
Sundays, R.	**128**	32 10S	24 40 E
Sundby	**73**	56 53N	8 40 E
Sundbyberg	**72**	59 22N	17 58 E
Sunderland, U.K.	**35**	54 54N	1 22W
Sunderland, U.S.A.	**162**	42 27N	72 36W
Sundre	**152**	51 49N	114 38W
Sundridge, Can.	**150**	45 45N	79 25W
Sundridge, U.K.	**29**	51 15N	0 10 E
Sunds	**73**	56 13N	9 1 E
Sundsjö	**72**	62 59N	15 9 E
Sundsvall	**72**	62 23N	17 17 E
Sung Hei	**101**	10 20N	106 2 E
Sungaipakning	**102**	1 19N	102 0 E
Sungaipenuh	**102**	2 1S	101 20 E
Sungaitiram	**102**	0 45S	117 8 E
Sungari, R. = Sunghua Chiang	**107**	44 30N	126 20 E
Sungch'i	**109**	27 2N	118 19 E
Sungchiang	**109**	31 2N	121 14 E
Sungei Lembing	**101**	2 53N	103 4 E
Sungei Patani	**101**	5 38N	100 29 E
Sungei Siput	**101**	4 51N	101 6 E
Sungfou	**109**	31 5N	114 42 E
Sungguminasa	**103**	5 17S	119 30 E
Sunghsien	**106**	34 10N	112 10 E
Sunghua Chiang, R.	**105**	47 42N	132 30 E
Sungikai	**123**	12 20N	29 51 E
Sungk'an	**108**	28 33N	106 52 E
Sungming	**108**	25 22N	103 2 E
Sungpan	**105**	32 50N	103 20 E
Sungp'an	**108**	32 36N	103 36 E
Sungt'ao	**108**	28 12N	109 12 E
Sungtzu Hu	**109**	30 10N	111 45 E
Sungü	**129**	21 18S	32 28 E
Sungurlu	**82**	40 12N	34 21 E
Sungyang	**109**	28 16N	119 29 E
Sunja	**63**	45 21N	16 35 E
Sunk Island	**33**	53 38N	0 7W
Sunkar, Gora	**85**	44 15N	73 50 E
Sunnäsbruk	**72**	61 10N	7 12 E
Sunne, Jamtland, Sweden	**72**	63 7N	14 25 E
Sunne, Varmland, Sweden	**72**	59 52N	13 12 E
Sunnfjord	**71**	61 25N	5 18 E
Sunnhordland	**71**	59 50N	5 30 E
Sunninghill	**29**	51 25N	0 40W
Sunnmöre	**71**	62 15N	6 30 E
Sunnyside, Utah, U.S.A.	**160**	39 40N	110 24W
Sunnyside, Wash., U.S.A.	**160**	46 24N	120 2W
Sunnyvale	**163**	37 23N	122 2W
Sunray	**159**	36 1N	101 47W
Sunshine	**141**	37 48S	144 52 E
Sunson	**121**	9 35N	0 2W
Suntar	**77**	62 15N	117 30 E
Sunyani	**120**	7 21N	2 22W
Suō-Nada	**110**	33 50N	131 30 E
Suolahti	**74**	62 34N	25 52 E
Suonenjoki	**74**	62 37N	27 7 E
Supai	**161**	36 14N	112 44W
Supaul	**95**	26 10N	86 40 E
Supe	**123**	8 34N	35 35 E
Superior, Ariz., U.S.A.	**161**	33 19N	111 9W
Superior, Mont., U.S.A.	**160**	47 15N	114 57W
Superior, Nebr., U.S.A.	**158**	40 3N	98 2W
Superior, Wis., U.S.A.	**158**	46 45N	92 0W
Superior, L.	**155**	47 40N	87 0W
Supetar	**63**	43 25N	16 32 E
Suphan Buri	**100**	14 30N	100 10 E
Suprasśl	**54**	53 13N	23 19 E
Suq al Jumah	**119**	32 58N	13 12 E
Sūr, Leb.	**90**	33 19N	35 16 E
Sūr, Oman	**93**	22 34N	59 32 E
Sur, Pt.	**163**	36 18N	121 54W
Sura, R.	**81**	55 30N	46 20 E
Surab	**94**	28 25N	66 15 E
Surabaja = Surabaya	**103**	7 17S	112 45 E
Surabaya	**103**	7 17S	112 45 E
Surahammar	**72**	59 43N	16 13 E
Suraia	**70**	45 40N	27 25 E
Surakarta	**103**	7 35S	110 48 E
Surakhany	**83**	40 13N	50 1 E
Surandai	**97**	8 58N	77 26 E
Surany	**53**	48 6N	18 10 E
Surat, Austral.	**139**	27 10S	149 6 E
Surat, India	**96**	21 12N	72 55 E
Surat, Khalīj	**119**	31 40N	18 30 E
Surat Thani	**101**	9 6N	99 14 E
Suratgarh	**94**	29 18N	73 55 E
Surazh	**80**	53 5N	32 27 E
Surduc	**70**	47 15N	23 25 E
Surduc Pasul	**70**	45 21N	23 23 E
Surdulica	**66**	42 41N	22 11 E
Sûre, R.	**47**	49 51N	6 6 E
Surendranagar	**94**	22 45N	71 40 E
Surf	**163**	34 41N	120 36W
Surf Inlet	**152**	53 8N	128 50W
Surgères	**44**	46 7N	0 47W
Surhuisterveen	**46**	53 11N	6 10 E
Suri	**95**	23 50N	87 34 E
Surianu, mt.	**70**	45 33N	23 31 E
Suriapet	**96**	17 10N	79 40 E
Surif	**90**	31 40N	35 4 E
Surin	**100**	14 50N	103 34 E
Surin Nua, Ko	**101**	9 30N	97 55 E
Surinam ■	**175**	4 0N	56 15W
Suriname, R.	**170**	4 30N	55 30W
Surkhandarya, R.	**85**	37 12N	67 20 E
Sŭrmasu	**70**	46 45N	25 13 E
Sürmene	**83**	41 0N	40 1 E
Surovikino	**83**	48 32N	42 55 E
Surprise L.	**152**	59 40N	133 15W
Surrey □	**29**	51 16N	0 30W
Surry	**162**	37 8N	76 50W
Sursee	**50**	47 11N	8 6 E
Sursk	**81**	53 3N	45 40W
Surt	**119**	31 11N	16 46 E
Surt, Al Hammādah al	**119**	30 0N	17 50 E
Surtsey	**74**	63 20N	20 30W
Surubim	**170**	7 50S	35 45W
Suruga-Wan	**111**	34 45N	138 30 E
Surup	**103**	6 27N	126 17 E
Surur	**93**	23 20N	58 10 E
Susa	**62**	45 8N	7 3 E
Susaa, R.	**73**	55 20N	11 42 E
Sušac, I.	**63**	42 46N	16 30 E
Susak, I.	**63**	44 30N	14 28 E
Susaki	**110**	33 22N	133 17 E
Susamyr	**85**	42 12N	73 58 E
Susamyrtau, Khrebet	**85**	42 8N	73 15 E
Susangerd	**92**	31 35N	48 20 E
Susanino	**77**	52 50N	140 14 E
Susanville	**160**	40 28N	120 40W
Susch	**51**	46 46N	10 5 E
Sušice	**52**	49 17N	13 30 E
Susquehanna Depot	**162**	41 55N	75 36W
Susquehanna, R.	**156**	41 50N	76 20W
Susques	**172**	23 35S	66 25W
Sussex, Can.	**151**	45 45N	65 37W
Sussex, U.S.A.	**162**	41 12N	74 38W
Sussex (□)	**26**	50 55N	0 20W
Sussex, E. □	**29**	51 0N	0 0 E
Sussex, W. □	**29**	51 0N	0 30W
Susten Pass	**51**	46 43N	8 26 E
Susteren	**47**	51 4N	5 51 E
Sustut, R.	**152**	56 20N	127 30W
Susuman	**77**	62 47N	148 10 E
Susuna	**103**	3 20S	133 25 E
Susung	**109**	30 9N	116 6 E
Susz	**54**	53 44N	19 20 E
Suţeşti	**70**	45 13N	27 27 E
Sutherland, Austral.	**141**	34 2S	151 4 E
Sutherland, Can.	**153**	52 15N	106 40W
Sutherland, S. Afr.	**125**	32 33S	20 40 E
Sutherland, U.S.A.	**158**	41 12N	101 11W
Sutherland (□)	**26**	58 10N	4 30W
Sutherland Falls	**143**	44 48S	167 46 E
Sutherland Pt.	**133**	28 15S	153 35 E
Sutherland Ra.	**137**	25 42S	125 21 E
Sutherlin	**160**	43 28N	123 16W
Sutivan	**63**	43 23N	16 30 E
Sutlej, R.	**94**	30 0N	73 0 E
Sutter Creek	**163**	38 24N	120 48W
Sutterton	**33**	52 54N	0 8W
Sutton, N.Z.	**143**	45 34S	170 8 E
Sutton, U.K.	**29**	51 22N	0 13W
Sutton, U.S.A.	**158**	40 40N	97 50W
Sutton Bridge	**29**	52 46N	0 12 E
Sutton Coldfield	**28**	52 33N	1 50W
Sutton Courtenay	**28**	51 39N	1 16W
Sutton-in-Ashfield	**33**	52 8N	1 16W
Sutton-on-Sea	**33**	53 18N	0 18 E
Sutton, R.	**150**	55 15N	83 45W
Sutton Scotney	**28**	51 9N	1 20W
Suttor, R.	**138**	20 36S	147 2 E
Sutwik I.	**147**	56 35N	157 10W
Suva	**143**	17 40S	178 8 E
Suva Gora	**66**	41 45N	21 3 E
Suva Planina	**66**	43 10N	22 5 E
Suva Reka	**66**	42 21N	20 50 E
Suvarov Is.	**131**	13 15S	163 30W
Suvo Rudïste	**66**	43 17N	20 49 E
Suvorovo	**67**	43 20N	27 35 E
Suwa	**111**	36 2N	138 8 E
Suwa-Ko	**111**	36 3N	138 5 E
Suwałki	**54**	54 8N	22 59 E
Suwałki □	**54**	54 0N	22 30 E
Suwannaphum	**100**	15 33N	105 47 E
Suwannee, R.	**157**	30 0N	83 0W
Suwanose-Jima	**112**	29 38N	129 38 E
Suweis, El	**122**	29 58N	32 31 E
Suweis, Khalîg es	**122**	28 40N	33 0 E
Suweis, Qanâl es	**122**	31 0N	32 20 E
Suwŏn	**107**	37 17N	127 1 E
Suykbulak	**84**	50 25N	62 33 E
Suzak	**85**	44 9N	68 27 E
Suzaka	**111**	36 39N	138 19 E
Sŭzava, R.	**52**	49 50N	15 0 E
Suzdal	**81**	56 29N	40 26 E
Suze, La	**42**	47 54N	0 2 E
Suzuka	**111**	34 55N	136 36 E
Suzuka-Sam	**111**	35 5N	136 30 E
Suzzara	**62**	45 0N	10 45 E
Svalbard, Arctica	**12**	78 0N	17 0 E
Svalbard, Iceland	**74**	66 12N	15 43W
Svalöv	**73**	55 57N	13 8 E
Svanå	**72**	59 46N	15 23 E
Svanvik	**74**	69 38N	30 3 E
Svappavaari	**74**	67 40N	21 03 E
Svarstad	**71**	59 27N	9 56 E
Svartisen	**74**	66 40N	14 16 E
Svartvik	**72**	62 19N	17 24 E
Svatovo	**82**	49 35N	38 5 E
Svay Chek	**100**	13 48N	102 58 E
Svay Rieng	**101**	11 5N	105 48 E
Svealand □	**75**	59 55N	15 0 E
Svedala	**73**	55 30N	13 15 E
Sveg	**72**	62 2N	14 21 E
Sveio	**71**	59 33N	5 23 E
Svelvik	**71**	59 37N	10 24 E
Svendborg	**73**	55 4N	10 35 E
Svene	**71**	59 45N	9 31 E
Svenljunga	**73**	57 29N	13 29 E
Svensbro	**73**	58 15N	13 52 E
Svenstavik	**72**	62 45N	14 26 E
Svenstrup	**73**	56 58N	9 50 E
Sverdlovsk	**84**	56 50N	60 30 E
Sverdrup Is.	**12**	79 0N	97 0W
Svetac	**63**	43 3N	15 43 E
Sveti Ivan Zelina	**63**	45 57N	16 16 E
Sveti Jurij	**63**	46 14N	15 24 E
Sveti Lenart	**63**	46 36N	15 48 E
Sveti Nikola	**66**	41 51N	21 56 E
Sveti Trojica	**63**	46 37N	15 33 E
Svetlogorsk	**80**	52 38N	29 46 E
Svetlograd	**83**	45 25N	42 58 E
Svetlovodsk	**80**	49 2N	33 13 E
Svetlyy	**84**	50 48N	60 51 E
Svetozarevo	**66**	44 0N	21 15 E
Svidnik	**53**	49 20N	21 37 E
Svilaja Pl.	**63**	43 49N	16 31 E
Svilajnac	**66**	44 15N	21 11 E
Svilengrad	**67**	41 49N	26 12 E
Svinö	**73**	55 6N	11 44 E
Svir, R.	**78**	61 2N	34 50 E
Svishov	**67**	43 36N	25 23 E
Svisloch	**80**	53 26N	24 2 E
Svitavy	**53**	49 47N	16 28 E
Svobodnyy	**77**	51 20N	128 0 E
Svoge	**67**	42 59N	23 23 E
Svolvær	**74**	68 15N	14 34 E
Svratka, R.	**53**	49 27N	16 12 E
Svrljig	**66**	43 25N	22 6 E
Swa	**98**	19 15N	96 17 E
Swabian Alps	**49**	48 30N	9 30 E
Swadlincote	**28**	52 47N	1 34W
Swaffham	**29**	52 38N	0 42 E
Swain Reefs	**138**	21 45S	152 20 E
Swainsboro	**157**	32 38N	82 22W
Swakopmund	**128**	22 37S	14 30 E
Swale, R.	**34**	54 18N	1 20W
Swallowfield	**29**	51 23N	0 56W
Swalmen	**47**	51 13N	6 2 E
Swan Hill	**140**	35 20S	143 33 E
Swan Hills	**152**	54 42N	115 24W
Swan Islands	**166**	17 22N	83 57W
Swan L.	**153**	52 30N	100 50W
Swan Pt.	**136**	16 22S	123 1 E
Swan, R.	**132**	32 3S	115 35 E
Swan Reach	**140**	34 35S	139 37 E
Swan River	**153**	52 10N	101 16W
Swanage	**28**	50 36N	1 59W
Swanlinbar	**38**	54 11N	7 42W
Swansea, Austral.	**141**	33 3S	151 35 E
Swansea, U.K.	**31**	51 37N	3 57W
Swansea Bay	**31**	51 34N	3 55W
Swar, R.	**95**	35 15N	72 24 E
Swartberg	**128**	30 15S	29 23 E
Swartberge	**128**	33 20S	22 0 E
Swarte Bank, gasfield	**19**	53 27N	2 10 E
Swartruggens	**128**	25 39S	26 42 E
Swarzedz	**54**	52 25N	17 4 E
Swastika	**150**	48 7N	80 6W
Swatow = Shant'ou	**109**	23 28N	116 40 E
Swatragh	**38**	54 55N	6 40W
Swaziland ■	**129**	26 30S	31 30 E
Sweden ■	**74**	67 0N	15 0 E
Swedru	**121**	5 32N	0 41W
Sweet Home	**160**	44 26N	122 38W
Sweetwater, Nev., U.S.A.	**163**	38 27N	119 9W
Sweetwater, Tex., U.S.A.	**159**	32 30N	100 28W
Sweetwater, R.	**160**	42 31N	107 30W
Swellendam	**128**	34 1S	20 26 E
Świdin	**54**	53 47N	15 49 E
Swidnica	**54**	50 50N	16 30 E
Świdnik	**54**	51 13N	22 39 E
Świebodzice	**54**	50 51N	16 20 E
Swiebodzin	**54**	52 15N	15 37 E
Swiecie	**54**	53 25N	18 30 E
Swietorkrzyskie, Góry	**54**	51 0N	20 30 E
Swift Current	**153**	50 20N	107 45W
Swiftcurrent Cr.	**153**	50 38N	107 44W
Swilly L.	**38**	55 12N	7 35W
Swilly, R.	**38**	54 56N	7 50W
Swindle, I.	**152**	52 30N	128 35W
Swindon	**28**	51 33N	1 47W
Swinemünde = Świnoujście	**54**	53 54N	14 16 E
Swineshead	**33**	57 57N	0 9W
Swinford	**38**	53 57N	8 57W
Świnoujście	**54**	53 54N	14 16 E
Swinton, Borders, U.K.	**35**	55 43N	2 14W
Swinton, Gr. Manch., U.K.	**32**	53 31N	2 21W
Swinton, S. Yorks., U.K.	**33**	53 28N	1 20W
Switzerland ■	**49**	46 30N	8 0 E
Swona, I.	**37**	58 30N	3 3W
Swords	**38**	53 27N	6 15W
Syasstroy	**80**	60 5N	32 15 E
Sybil Pt.	**39**	52 12N	10 28W
Sychevka	**80**	55 45N	34 10 E
Syców	**54**	51 19N	17 40 E
Sydney, Austral.	**141**	33 53S	151 10 E
Sydney, Can.	**151**	46 7N	60 7W
Sydney, U.S.A.	**158**	41 12N	103 0W
Sydney Mines	**151**	46 18N	60 15W
Sydproven	**12**	60 30N	45 35W
Sydra, G. of = Surt	**61**	31 40N	18 30 E

Syke **Tambelan, Kepulauan**

Syke	48	52 55N	8 50 E
Syktyvkar	78	61 45N	50 40 E
Sylacauga	157	33 10N	86 15W
Sylarna, Mt.	72	63 2N	12 11 E
Sylhet	98	24 54N	91 52 E
Sylt, I.	48	54 50N	8 20 E
Sylva, R.	84	58 0N	56 54 E
Sylvan Beach	162	43 12N	75 44W
Sylvan Lake	152	52 20N	114 10W
Sylvania	157	32 45N	81 37W
Sylvester	157	31 31N	83 50W
Sym	76	60 20N	87 50 E
Symington	35	55 35N	3 36W
Symón	164	24 42N	102 35W
Symonds Yat	28	51 50N	2 38W
Synnott Ra.	136	16 30S	125 20 E
Syr Darya	76	45 0N	65 0 E
Syracuse, Kans., U.S.A.	159	38 0N	101 40W
Syracuse, N.Y., U.S.A.	162	43 4N	76 11W
Syrdarya	85	40 50N	68 40 E
Syria ■	92	35 0N	38 0 E
Syriam	98	16 44N	96 19 E
Syrian Des.	92	31 30N	40 0 E
Sysert	84	56 29N	60 49 E
Syston	28	52 42N	1 5W
Syuldzhyukyor	77	63 25N	113 40 E
Syutkya, mt.	67	41 50N	24 16 E
Syzran	81	53 12N	48 30 E
Szabolcs-Szatmár □	53	48 2N	21 45 E
Szamocin	54	53 2N	17 7 E
Szamotuły	54	52 35N	16 34 E
Szaraz, R.	53	46 28N	20 44 E
Szazhalombatta	53	47 20N	18 58 E
Szczara, R.	53	53 15N	25 10 E
Szczebrzeszyn	54	50 42N	22 59 E
Szczecin	54	53 27N	14 27 E
Szczecin □	54	53 25N	14 32 E
Szczecinek	54	53 43N	16 41 E
Szczekocimy	54	50 38N	19 48 E
Szczrk	53	49 42N	19 1 E
Szczuczyn	54	53 36N	22 19 E
Szczytno	54	53 33N	21 0 E
Szechwan □	109	30 15N	103 15 E
Szécsény	53	48 7N	19 30 E
Szeged	53	46 16N	20 10 E
Szeghalom	53	47 1N	21 10 E
Székesfehérvár	53	47 15N	18 25 E
Szekszárd	53	46 22N	18 42 E
Szendrö	53	48 24N	20 41 E
Szentendre	53	47 39N	19 4 E
Szentes	53	46 39N	20 21 E
Szentgotthárd	53	46 58N	16 19 E
Szentlőrinc	53	46 3N	18 1 E
Szerencs	53	48 10N	21 12 E
Szeshui	33	34 50N	113 20 E
Szigetvár	53	46 3N	17 46 E
Szlichtyogowa	54	51 42N	16 15 E
Szob	53	47 48N	18 53 E
Szolnok	53	47 10N	20 15 E
Szolnok □	53	47 15N	20 30 E
Szombathely	53	47 14N	16 38 E
Szprotawa	54	51 33N	15 35 E
Sztum	54	53 55N	19 1 E
Sztuto	54	54 20N	19 15 E
Sztutowo	54	54 20N	19 15 E
Szürvas	53	46 50N	20 38 E
Szydłowiec	54	51 15N	20 51 E
Szypliszki	54	54 17N	23 2 E

T

't Harde	46	52 24N	5 54 E
't Zandt	46	53 22N	6 46 E
Ta-erh Po, L.	106	43 15N	116 35 E
Ta Khli Khok	100	15 18N	100 20 E
Ta Lai	101	11 24N	107 23 E
Taalintehdas	74	60 2N	22 30 E
Taan	107	45 30N	124 18 E
Taavetti	75	60 56N	27 32 E
Taba	92	26 55N	42 30 E
Tabacal	172	23 15S	64 15W
Tabaco	103	13 22N	123 44 E
Tabagné	120	7 59N	3 4W
Tabar Is.	135	2 50S	152 0 E
Tabarca, Isla de	59	38 17N	0 30W
Tabarka	119	36 56N	8 46 E
Tabarra	59	38 37N	1 44 E
Tabas, Khorasan, Iran	93	33 35N	56 55 E
Tabas, Khorasan, Iran	93	32 48N	60 12 E
Tabasará, Serranía de	166	8 35N	81 40W
Tabasco □	165	17 45N	93 30W
Tabatinga	174	4 15S	69 58W
Tabatinga, Serra da	170	10 30S	44 0W
Tabayin	98	22 42N	95 20 E
Tabelbala, Kahal de	118	28 47N	2 0W
Taber	152	49 47N	112 8W
Taberg	162	43 18N	75 37W
Tabernas	59	37 4N	2 26W
Tabernas de Valldigna	59	39 5N	0 13W
Tabigha	90	32 53N	35 33 E
Tabira	170	7 35S	37 33W
Tablas, I.	103	12 25N	122 2 E
Table B.	151	53 40N	56 25W
Table Mt.	128	34 0S	18 22 E
Table Top, Mt.	138	23 24S	147 11 E
Tableland	136	17 16S	126 51 E
Tabletop, mt.	137	22 32S	123 50 E
Tábor	52	49 25N	14 39 E
Tabor	90	32 42N	35 24 E
Tabora	126	5 2S	32 57 E
Tabora □	126	5 0S	33 0 E
Tabory	84	58 31N	64 33 E
Tabou	120	4 30N	7 20W
Tabouda	118	34 44N	5 14W
Tabrīz	92	38 7N	46 20 E
Tabūk	92	28 30N	36 25 E
Täby	72	59 29N	18 4 E
Tacámbaro	164	19 14N	101 28W
Tacarigua, L. de	174	11 3N	68 25W
Tach'aitan	105	37 50N	95 18 E
T'ach'eng	105	46 45N	82 57 E
Tach'eng	106	38 35N	116 39 E
Tach'engtzu	107	41 44N	118 52 E
Tach'i	109	24 51N	121 14 E
Tachia	109	24 25N	120 28 E
Tachiai	108	23 44N	103 57 E
Tachibana-Wan	110	32 45N	130 7 E
Tachikawa	111	35 42N	139 25 E
Tach'in Ch'uan, R.	108	31 57N	102 11 E
Tach'ing Shan, mts.	106	40 50N	111 0 E
Tachira	174	8 7N	72 21W
Tachira □	174	8 7N	72 15W
Tachov	52	49 47N	12 39 E
Tachu	108	30 45N	107 13 E
Tacina, R.	65	39 5N	16 51 E
Tacloban	103	11 15N	124 58 E
Tacna	174	18 0S	70 20W
Tacoma	160	47 15N	122 30W
Tacuarembó	173	31 45S	56 0W
Tacumshin L.	39	52 12N	6 28W
Tadcaster	33	53 53N	1 16W
Tademaït, Plateau du	118	28 30N	2 30 E
Tadent, O.	119	22 30N	7 0 E
Tadjerdjert, O.	119	26 0N	8 0W
Tadjerouna	118	33 31N	2 3 E
Tadjettaret, O.	119	22 0N	7 30W
Tadjmout, O.	118	25 37N	3 48 E
Tadjoura	123	11 50N	42 55 E
Tadjoura, Golfe de	123	11 50N	43 0 E
Tadley	28	51 21N	1 8W
Tadmor, N.Z.	143	41 27S	172 45 E
Tadmor, Syria	92	34 30N	37 55 E
Tado	174	5 16N	76 32W
Tadotsu	110	34 16N	133 45 E
Tadoule L	153	58 36N	98 20W
Tadoussac	151	48 11N	69 42W
Tadzhik S.S.R. □	85	35 30N	70 0 E
Taechŏnni	107	36 21N	126 36 E
Taegu	107	35 50N	128 37 E
Taegwandong	107	40 13N	125 12 E
Taejŏn	107	36 20N	127 28 E
Taerhhanmaoming-anlienhoch'i	106	41 50N	110 27 E
Taerhting	105	37 15N	92 36 E
Taf, R.	31	51 55N	4 36W
Tafalla	58	42 30N	1 41W
Tafang	108	27 10N	105 39 E
Tafar	123	6 52N	28 15 E
Tafas	90	32 44N	36 5 E
Tafassasset, O.	119	23 0N	9 11 E
Tafelbaai	128	33 35S	18 25 E
Tafelney, C.	118	31 3N	9 51W
Tafermaar	103	6 47S	134 10 E
Tafí Viejo	172	26 43S	65 17W
Tafiré	120	9 4N	5 10W
Tafnidilt	118	28 47N	10 58W
Tafraout	118	29 50N	8 58W
Taft, Phil.	103	11 57N	125 30 E
Taft, Ala., U.S.A.	163	35 10N	119 28W
Taft, Tex., U.S.A.	159	27 58N	97 23W
Taga Dzong	98	27 5N	90 0 E
Taganrog	83	47 12N	38 50 E
Taganrogskiy Zaliv	82	47 0N	38 30 E
Tagant	120	18 20N	11 0W
Tagap Ga	98	26 56N	96 13 E
Tagbilaran	103	9 39N	123 51 E
Tage	135	6 19S	143 20 E
Tággia	62	43 52N	7 50 E
Taghmon	39	52 19N	6 40W
Taghrifat	119	29 5N	17 26 E
Taghzout	118	33 30N	4 49W
Tagish	152	60 19N	134 16W
Tagish L.	147	60 10N	134 20W
Tagliacozzo	63	42 4N	13 13 E
Tagliamento, R.	63	45 38N	13 5 E
Táglio di Po	63	45 0N	12 12 E
Tagomago, Isla de	59	39 2N	1 39 E
Tagua, La	174	0 3N	74 40W
Taguatinga	171	12 26S	46 26W
Tagula	135	11 22S	153 15 E
Tagula I.	135	11 30S	153 30 E
Tagum (Hijo)	103	7 33N	125 53 E
Tagus = Tajo, R.	55	39 44N	5 50W
Tahahbala, I.	102	0 30S	98 30 E
Tahakopa	143	46 30S	169 23 E
Tahala	118	34 0N	4 28W
Tahan, Gunong	101	4 45N	102 25 E
Tahara	111	34 40N	137 16 E
Tahat Mt.	119	23 18N	5 21 E
Tāherī	93	27 43N	52 20 E
Tahiti, I.	131	17 37S	149 27W
Tahoe	160	39 12N	120 9W
Tahoe, L.	160	39 0N	120 9W
Tahora	142	39 2S	174 49 E
Tahoua	121	14 57N	5 16 E
Tahsien	108	31 17N	107 30 E
Tahsin	108	22 48N	107 23 E
Tahsinganling Shanmo	105	49 0N	122 0 E
Tahsingkou	107	43 23N	129 39 E
Tahsintien	107	37 37N	120 50 E
Tahsüeh Shan, mts.	108	31 15N	101 20 E
Tahta	122	26 44N	31 32 E
Tahulandang, I.	103	2 27N	125 23 E
Tahuna	103	3 45N	125 30 E
Tahung Shan, mts.	109	31 30N	112 50 E
Tai	108	30 41N	103 29 E
Taï	120	5 55N	7 30W
T'ai Hu	105	31 10N	120 0 E
Tai Shan	109	30 17N	122 10 E
T'aian	107	36 12N	117 7 E
T'aichiang	108	26 40N	108 19 E
T'aichou	109	32 22N	119 45 E
T'aichou Liehtao	109	28 30N	121 53 E
T'aichung	105	24 9N	120 37 E
T'aichunghsien	109	24 15N	120 35 E
Taieri, R.	143	46 3S	170 12 E
Taiga Madema	119	23 46N	15 25 E
T'aihang Shan, mts.	106	35 40N	113 20 E
Taihape	142	39 41S	175 48 E
T'aiho, Anhwei, China	109	33 10N	115 36 E
T'aiho, Kiangsi, China	109	26 50N	114 53 E
T'aihsien	109	32 17N	120 10 E
T'aihsing	109	32 10N	120 4 E
Taihu	109	30 30N	116 25 E
T'aik'ang	106	34 4N	114 52 E
Taikkyi	98	17 20N	96 0 E
T'aiku	106	37 23N	112 34 E
Tailem Bend	140	35 12S	139 29 E
Tailfingen	49	48 15N	9 1 E
Taïma	92	27 35N	38 45 E
Taimyr = Taymyr	77	75 0N	100 0 E
Taimyr, Oz.	77	74 20N	102 0 E
Tain	37	57 49N	4 4W
T'ainan	109	23 0N	120 10 E
T'ainanhsien	109	23 21N	120 17 E
Tainaron, Akra	69	36 22N	22 27 E
Tainggya	98	17 49N	94 29 E
T'aining	109	26 55N	117 12 E
Taintignies	47	50 33N	3 22 E
Taiobeiras	171	15 49S	42 14W
T'aipei	109	25 2N	121 30 E
T'aip'ing	109	30 18N	118 6 E
Taiping	101	4 51N	100 44 E
Taipu	170	5 37S	35 36W
T'aip'ussuchi	106	41 55N	115 23 E
Taisha	110	35 24N	132 40 E
T'aishan	109	22 17N	112 43 E
Taishun	109	27 33N	119 43 E
Taita □	126	4 0S	38 30 E
Taita Hills	126	3 25S	38 15 E
Taitao, Pen. de	176	46 30S	75 0W
T'aitung	105	22 43N	121 4 E
Taivalkoski	74	65 33N	28 12 E
Taiwan (Formosa) ■	109	23 30N	121 0 E
Taiwara	93	33 30N	64 24 E
Taïyetos Óros	69	37 0N	22 23 E
Taiyiba, Israel	90	32 36N	35 27 E
Taiyiba, Jordan	90	31 55N	35 17 E
T'aiyüan	106	37 55N	112 40 E
Ta'izz	91	13 43N	44 7 E
Tajapuru, Furo do	170	1 50S	50 25W
Tajarhī	119	24 15N	14 46 E
Tajicaringa	164	23 15N	104 44W
Tajima	112	35 19N	135 8 E
Tajimi	111	35 19N	137 8 E
Tajimi Gifu	55	35 25N	137 5 E
Tajitos	164	30 58N	112 18W
Tajo, R.	57	40 35N	1 52W
Tajumulco, Volcán de	165	15 20N	91 50W
Tājūrā	119	32 51N	13 27 E
Tak	100	16 52N	99 8 E
Takachiho	110	32 42N	131 18 E
Takahashi	110	34 51N	133 39 E
Takaka	143	40 51S	172 50 E
Takamatsu	110	34 20N	134 5 E
Takanabe	110	32 8N	131 30 E
Takaoka	111	36 40N	137 0 E
Takapau	142	40 2S	176 21 E
Takapuna	142	36 47S	174 47 E
Takasago	110	34 45N	134 48 E
Takasaki	111	36 20N	139 0 E
Takase	110	34 7N	133 48 E
Takatsuki	111	34 51N	135 37 E
Takaungu	126	3 38S	39 52 E
Takawa	110	33 47N	130 51 E
Takayama	111	36 18N	137 11 E
Takayama-Bonchi	111	36 0N	137 18 E
Takefu	111	35 50N	136 10 E
Takehara	110	34 21N	132 55 E
Takeley	29	51 52N	0 16 E
Takeo, Camb.	101	10 59N	104 47 E
Takeo, Japan	110	33 12N	130 1 E
Tåkern	73	58 22N	14 45 E
Takestan	92	36 0N	49 50 E
Taketa	110	32 58N	131 24 E
Takh	95	33 6N	77 32 E
Takhman	101	11 29N	104 57 E
Taki	135	6 29S	155 52 E
Takingeun	102	4 45N	96 50 E
Takla L.	152	55 15N	125 45W
Takla Landing	152	55 30N	125 50W
Takla Makan	105	39 0N	83 0 E
Takoradi	120	4 58N	1 55W
Taku, China	107	38 59N	117 41 E
Taku, Japan	110	33 18N	130 3 E
Taku, R.	152	58 30N	133 50W
Takuan	108	27 44N	103 53 E
Takum	121	7 18N	9 36 E
Takuma	110	34 13N	133 40 E
Takushan	107	39 55N	123 30 E
Tal-y-llyn	31	52 40N	3 44W
Tal-y-sarn	31	53 3N	4 12W
Tala, Uruguay	173	34 21S	55 46W
Tala, U.S.S.R.	77	72 40N	113 30 E
Talach'in	106	36 42N	104 54 E
Talagante	172	33 40S	70 50W
Talaint	118	29 37N	9 45W
Talak	121	18 0N	5 0 E
Talamanca, Cordillera de	166	9 20N	83 20W
Talara	174	4 30S	81 10 E
Talas	85	42 45N	72 0 E
Talas, R.	85	44 0N	70 20 E
Talasea	135	5 20S	150 2 E
Talasskiy, Khrebet	85	42 15N	72 0 E
Talata Mafara	121	12 38N	6 4 E
Talaud, Kepulauan	103	4 30N	127 10 E
Talavera de la Reina	56	39 55N	4 46W
Talawana	136	22 51S	121 9 E
Talawgyi	98	25 4N	97 19 E
Talayan	103	6 52N	124 24 E
Talbot, C.	136	13 48S	126 43 E
Talbragar, R.	141	32 5S	149 15 E
Talca	172	35 20S	71 46W
Talca □	172	35 20S	71 46W
Talcahuano	172	36 40S	73 10W
Talcher	96	20 55N	85 3 E
Talcho	121	14 35N	3 22 E
Taldom	81	56 45N	37 29 E
Taldy Kurgan	76	45 10N	78 45 E
Taleqan □	93	36 40N	69 30 E
Talesh, Kūhhā-Ye	92	39 0N	48 30 E
Talfit	90	32 5N	35 17 E
Talga, R.	136	21 2S	119 51 E
Talgar	85	43 19N	77 15 E
Talgar, Pic	85	43 5N	77 20 E
Talgarth	31	51 59N	3 15W
Talguharai	122	18 19N	35 56 E
Talguppa	93	14 10N	74 45 E
Tali, Shensi, China	106	34 48N	109 48 E
Tali, Yunnan, China	108	25 45N	100 5 E
Tali Post	123	5 55N	30 44 E
Taliabu, I.	103	1 45S	125 0 E
Taliang Shan	108	28 0N	103 0 E
Talibong, Ko	101	7 15N	99 23 E
Talihina	159	34 45N	95 1W
Talikoti	96	16 29N	76 17 E
Talimardzhan	85	38 23N	65 37 E
Taling Ho, R.	107	40 54N	121 38 E
Taling Sung	101	15 5N	99 11 E
Talitsa	84	57 0N	63 43 E
Taliwang	102	8 50S	116 55 E
Talkeetna	147	62 20N	150 0W
Talkeetna Mts.	147	62 20N	149 0W
Tall 'Asūr	90	31 59N	35 77 E
Talla	122	28 5N	30 43 E
Talladale	36	57 41N	5 20W
Talladega	157	33 28N	86 2W
Tallahassee	157	30 25N	84 15W
Tallangatta	141	36 15S	147 10 E
Tallarook	141	37 5S	145 6 E
Tallåsen	72	61 52N	16 2 E
Tallawang	141	32 12S	149 28 E
Tällberg	72	60 51N	15 2 E
Tallebung	141	32 42S	146 34 E
Tallering Pk	137	28 6S	115 37 E
Tallinn (Reval)	80	59 29N	24 58 E
Tallow	39	52 6N	8 0W
Tallowbridge	39	52 6N	8 1W
Tallulah	159	32 25N	91 12W
Talluza	90	32 17N	35 18 E
Talmage	153	49 46N	103 40W
Talmest	118	31 48N	9 21W
Talmont	44	46 27N	1 37W
Talnoye	82	48 57N	30 35 E
Taloda	96	21 34N	74 19 E
Talodi	123	10 35N	30 22 E
Talou Shan, mts.	108	28 20N	107 10 E
Talovaya	81	51 13N	40 38 E
Talpa de Allende	164	20 23N	104 51W
Talsarnau	31	52 54N	4 4W
Talsinnt	118	32 33N	3 27W
Taltal	172	25 23S	70 40W
Taltson L.	153	61 30N	110 15W
Taltson R.	152	61 24N	112 46W
Talwood	139	28 29S	149 29 E
Talyawalka Cr.	140	32 28S	142 22 E
Talybont	31	52 29N	3 59W
Tam Chau	101	10 48N	105 12 E
Tam Ky	100	15 34N	108 29 E
Tam Quan	100	14 35N	109 3 E
Tama	158	41 56N	92 37W
Tama Abu, Pegunungan	102	3 10N	115 0 E
Tamala	137	26 35S	113 40 E
Tamalameque	174	8 52N	73 49W
Tamale	121	9 22N	0 50W
Taman	82	45 14N	36 41 E
Tamana	110	32 58N	130 32 E
Tamanar	118	31 1N	9 46W
Tamano	110	34 35N	133 59 E
Tamanrasset	119	22 56N	5 30 E
Tamanrasset, O.	118	22 0N	2 0 E
Tamanthi	98	25 19N	95 17 E
Tamaqua	162	40 46N	75 58W
Tamar, R.	30	50 33N	4 15W
Támara	174	5 50N	72 10W
Tamarang	141	31 27S	150 5 E
Tamarite de Litera	58	41 52N	0 25 E
Tamashima	110	34 32N	133 40 E
Tamási	53	46 40N	18 18 E
Tamaské	121	14 55N	5 55 E
Tamatave	129	18 10S	49 25 E
Tamatave □	129	18 0S	49 0 E
Tamaulipas □	165	24 0N	99 0W
Tamaulipas, Sierra de	165	23 30N	98 20W
Tamazula	164	24 55N	106 58W
Tamazunchale	165	21 16N	98 47W
Tambacounda	120	13 55N	13 45W
Tambai	123	16 32N	37 13 E
Tambelan, Kepulauan	102	1 0N	107 30 E

Tambellup **Taunton**

Tambellup **137** 34 4S 117 37E
Tambo **138** 24 54S 146 14E
Tambo de Mora **174** 13 30S 76 20W
Tambohorano **129** 17 30S 43 58E
Tambora, G. **102** 8 12S 118 5E
Tamboritha, Mt. **141** 37 31S 146 51E
Tambov **81** 52 45N 41 20E
Tambre, R. **56** 42 55N 8 30W
Tambuku, G. **103** 7 8S 113 40E
Tamburâ **123** 5 40N 27 25E
Tamchaket **120** 17 25N 10 40W
Tamchok Khambab (Brahmaputra) **99** 29 25N 88 0E
Tamdybulak **85** 41 46N 64 36E
Tame **174** 6 28N 71 44W
Tame, R. **28** 52 43N 1 45W
Tamega, R. **56** 41 12N 8 5W
Tamelelt **119** 26 30N 6 14E
Tamenglong **98** 25 0N 93 35E
Tamerfors **75** 61 30N 23 50E
Tamerlanovka **85** 42 36N 69 17E
Tamerton Foliot **30** 50 25N 4 10W
Tamerza **119** 34 23N 7 58E
Tamgak, Mts. **121** 19 12N 8 35E
Tamiahua, Laguna de **165** 21 30N 97 30W
Tamil Nadu □ **97** 11 0N 77 0E
Tamines **47** 50 26N 4 36E
Taming **106** 36 20N 115 10E
Tamins **51** 46 50N 9 24E
Tamluk **95** 22 18N 87 58E
Tammisaari (Ekenäs) **75** 60 0N 23 26E
Tammun' **90** 32 18N 35 23E
Tamnaren **72** 60 10N 17 25E
Tamou **121** 12 45N 2 11E
Tampa **157** 27 57N 82 30W
Tampa B. **157** 27 40N 82 40W
Tampere **75** 61 30N 23 50E
Tampico **165** 22 20N 97 50W
Tampin **101** 2 28N 102 13E
Tamri **118** 30 49N 9 50W
Tamrida = Hadibu **91** 12 35N 54 2E
Tamsagbulag **105** 47 14N 117 21E
Tamsagout **118** 24 5N 6 35W
Tamsalu **80** 59 11N 26 8E
Tamsweg **52** 47 7N 13 49E
Tamu **99** 24 13N 94 12E
Tamuja, R. **57** 39 33N 6 8W
Tamworth, Austral. **141** 31 0S 150 58E
Tamworth, U.K. **28** 52 38N 1 41W
Tamyang **107** 35 19N 126 59E
Tan An **101** 10 32N 106 25E
Tana **74** 70 7N 28 5E
Tana Fd. **74** 70 35N 28 30E
Tana, L. **123** 13 5N 37 30E
Tana, R., Kenya **126** 0 50S 39 45E
Tana, R., Norway **48** 69 50N 26 0E
Tanabe **111** 33 44N 135 22E
Tanabi **171** 20 37S 49 37W
Tanacross **147** 63 40N 143 30W
Tanafjorden **74** 70 45N 28 25E
Tanagro, R. **65** 40 35N 15 25E
Tanahdjampea, I. **103** 7 10S 120 35E
Tanahgrogot **102** 1 55S 116 15E
Tanahmasa, I. **102** 0 5S 98 29E
Tanahmerah **103** 6 0S 140 7E
Tanami **136** 19 59S 129 43E
Tanami Des. **136** 18 50S 132 0E
Tanana **147** 65 10N 152 15W
Tanana, R. **147** 64 25N 145 30W
Tananarive **129** 18 55S 47 31E
Tananarive □ **129** 19 0S 47 0E
Tananarive = Antananarivo **125** 18 55S 47 31E
Tananger **71** 58 57N 5 37E
Tanant **118** 31 54N 6 56W
Tánaro, R. **62** 44 9N 7 50E
Tanaunelia **64** 40 42N 9 45E
Tanba-Sanchi **111** 35 7N 135 48E
Tanbar **97** 25 55S 142 0E
Tancarville **42** 49 29N 0 28E
Tanchai **108** 25 58N 107 49E
T'anch'eng **107** 34 38N 118 21E
Tanda, U.P., India **95** 26 33N 82 35E
Tanda, U.P., India **95** 28 57N 78 56E
Tanda, Ivory C. **120** 7 48N 3 10W
Tandag **103** 9 4N 126 9E
Tandala **127** 9 25S 34 15E
Tândârei **70** 44 39N 27 40E
Tandil **172** 37 15S 59 6W
Tandjungpandan **102** 2 43S 107 38E
Tandlianwald **94** 31 3N 73 9E
Tando Adam **94** 25 45N 68 40E
Tandou L. **140** 32 40S 142 5E
Tandragee **38** 54 22N 6 23W
Tandsbyn **72** 63 0N 14 45W
Tandur **96** 19 11N 79 30E
Tane-ga-Shima **112** 30 35N 130 59E
Taneatua **142** 38 4S 177 1E
Tanen Range **101** 19 40N 99 0E
Tanen Tong Dan, Burma **99** 16 30N 98 30E
Tanen Tong Dan, Thai. **100** 19 43N 98 30E
Taneytown **162** 39 40N 77 10W
Tanezrouft **118** 23 9N 0 11E
Tanfeng **106** 33 45N 110 18E
Tang **38** 53 31N 7 49W
Tang, Koh **101** 10 16N 103 7E
Tang Krasang **101** 12 34N 105 3E
Tang La **99** 32 59N 92 17E
Tang Pass **99** 32 59N 92 17E
Tanga **99** 5 5S 39 2E
Tanga □ **126** 5 20S 38 0E
Tanga Is. **135** 3 20S 153 15E
Tangail **98** 24 15N 89 55E
Tanganyika, L. **126** 6 40S 30 0E
T'angch'i **109** 29 3N 119 24E
Tanger **118** 35 50N 5 49W
Tangerang **103** 6 12S 106 39E
Tangerhütte **48** 52 26N 11 50E
Tangermünde **48** 52 32N 11 57E
T'angho **109** 32 10N 112 20E
Tangier **162** 37 49N 75 59W
Tangier = Tanger **118** 35 50N 5 49W
Tangier I. **162** 37 50N 76 0W
Tangier Sd. **162** 38 3N 75 5W
Tangkak **101** 2 18N 102 34E
T'angku **107** 39 4N 117 45E
T'angkula Shanmo **98** 33 0N 92 0E
Tanglha Shan **99** 33 0N 90 0E
Tangorin P.O. **138** 21 47S 144 12E
Tangra Tso **99** 31 25N 85 30E
Tangshan **106** 34 25N 116 24E
T'angshan **107** 39 40N 118 10E
T'angt'ang **108** 26 29N 104 12E
T'angt'ou **107** 35 21N 118 32E
Tangt'u **109** 31 34N 118 29E
Tanguiéta **121** 10 40N 1 21E
Tangyang, Chekiang, China **109** 29 17N 120 14E
Tangyang, Hupeh, China **109** 30 50N 111 45E
Tangyen Ho, R. **108** 28 55N 108 36E
Tanimbar, Kepulauan **103** 7 30S 131 30E
Taning **106** 36 32N 110 47E
Taniyama **110** 31 31N 130 31E
Tanjay **103** 9 30N 123 5E
Tanjore = Thanjavur **97** 10 48N 79 12E
Tanjung **102** 2 10S 115 25E
Tanjung Malim **101** 3 42N 101 31E
Tanjungbalai **102** 2 55N 99 44E
Tanjungbatu **102** 2 23N 118 3E
Tanjungkarang **102** 5 20S 105 10E
Tanjungpinang **102** 1 5N 104 30E
Tanjungpriok **103** 6 8S 106 55E
Tanjungredeb **102** 2 9N 117 29E
Tanjungselor **102** 2 55N 117 25E
Tank **94** 32 14N 70 25E
Tankan Shan **109** 22 3N 114 16E
Tanleng **108** 30 2N 103 33E
Tanndalen **72** 62 33N 12 18E
Tannin **150** 49 40N 91 0W
Tannis B. **73** 57 40N 10 15E
Tano, R. **120** 6 0N 2 30W
Tanoumrout **119** 23 2N 5 31E
Tanout **121** 14 50N 8 55E
Tanquinho **171** 12 42S 39 43W
Tanshui **109** 25 10N 121 28E
Tanta **122** 30 45N 30 57E
Tantan **118** 28 29N 11 1W
Tantoyuca **165** 21 21N 98 10W
Tantung **107** 40 10N 124 23E
Tantura = Dor **90** 32 37N 34 55E
Tanuku **96** 16 45N 81 44E
Tanum **73** 58 42N 11 20E
Tanunda **140** 34 30S 139 0E
Tanur **97** 11 1N 75 46E
Tanus **44** 44 8N 2 19E
Tanworth **28** 52 20N 1 50W
Tanzania ■ **126** 6 40S 34 0E
Tanzawa-Sanchi **111** 35 27N 139 0E
Tanzilla, R. **152** 58 8N 130 43W
T'aoan **107** 45 20N 122 50E
Taoch'eng **108** 29 3N 100 10E
Taoerh Ho **107** 45 42N 124 5E
Taofu **108** 31 0N 101 9E
Taohsien **109** 25 37N 111 24E
T'aohua Tao **109** 29 48N 122 17E
T'aolo **106** 38 45N 106 40E
Taormina **65** 37 52N 15 16E
Taos **161** 36 28N 105 35W
Taoudenni **118** 22 40N 3 55W
Taoudrart, Adrar **118** 24 25N 2 24E
Taounate **118** 34 32N 4 41W
Taourirt, Alg. **118** 26 37N 0 8E
Taourirt, Moroc. **118** 34 20N 2 47W
Taouz **118** 31 2N 4 0W
T'aoyüan, China **109** 28 54N 111 29E
T'aoyüan, Taiwan **109** 25 0N 121 4E
Tapa **80** 59 15N 26 0E
Tapa Shan **108** 31 45N 109 30E
Tapachula **165** 14 54N 92 17W
Tapah **101** 4 12N 101 15E
Tapajós, R. **175** 4 30S 56 10W
Tapaktuan **102** 3 30N 97 10E
Tapanui **143** 45 56S 169 18E
Tapauá **174** 5 40S 64 20W
Tapauá, R. **174** 6 0S 65 40W
Tapeta **120** 6 36N 8 52W
Taphan Hin **100** 16 13N 100 16E
Tapia **56** 43 34N 6 56W
Tapieh Shan, mts. **109** 31 20N 115 30E
T'ap'ingchen **106** 33 42N 111 44E
Tapini **135** 8 19S 147 0E
Tápiószele **53** 47 45N 19 55E
Tapiraí **171** 19 52S 46 1W
Tapirapé, R. **170** 10 41S 50 38W
Tapirapecó, Serra **174** 1 10N 65 0W
Taplan **140** 34 33S 140 52E
Tapolca **53** 46 53N 17 29E
Tappahannock **162** 37 56N 76 50W
Tapsing **99** 30 22N 96 25E
Tapti, R. **96** 21 25N 75 0E
Tapu **109** 24 31N 116 41E
Tapuaenuku, Mt. **143** 41 55S 173 50E
Tapul Group, Is. **103** 5 35N 120 50E
Tapun **98** 18 22N 95 27E
Taquara **173** 29 36N 50 46W
Taquari, R. **173** 18 10S 56 0W
Taquaritinga **171** 21 24S 48 30W
Tara, Austral. **139** 27 17S 150 31E
Tara, Japan **110** 33 2N 130 11E
Tara, U.S.S.R. **76** 56 55N 74 30E
Tara, Zambia **127** 16 58S 26 45E
Tara-Dake **110** 32 58N 130 6E
Tara, R. **66** 43 10N 19 20E
Tarabagatay, Khrebet **77** 48 0N 83 0E
Tarãbulus, Leb. **92** 34 31N 33 52E
Tarãbulus, Libya **119** 32 49N 13 7E
Taradale **142** 39 33S 176 53E
Tarahouahout **119** 22 47N 5 59E
Tarakan **102** 3 20N 117 35E
Tarakit, Mt. **126** 2 2N 35 10E
Taralga **141** 34 26S 149 52E
Taramakau, R. **143** 42 34S 171 8E
Tarana **141** 33 31S 149 52E
Taranagar **94** 28 43N 75 9E
Taranaki □ **142** 39 5S 174 51E
Tarancón **58** 40 1N 3 1W
Taranga **94** 23 56N 72 43E
Taranga Hill **94** 24 0N 72 40E
Taransay, I. **36** 57 54N 7 0W
Taransay, Sd. of **36** 57 52N 7 0W
Táranto **65** 40 30N 17 11E
Táranto, G. di **65** 40 0N 17 15E
Tarapacá **174** 2 56S 69 46W
Tarapacá □ **172** 20 45S 69 30W
Tarare **45** 45 54N 4 26E
Tararua Range **142** 40 45S 175 25E
Tarascon, Ariège, France **44** 42 50N 1 37E
Tarascon, Bouches-du-Rhône, France **45** 43 48N 4 39E
Tarashcha **82** 49 30N 30 31E
Tarat, Bj. **119** 26 4N 9 7E
Tarauacá **174** 8 6S 70 48W
Tarauacá, R. **174** 7 30S 70 30W
Taravo, R. **45** 41 48N 8 52E
Tarawera **142** 39 2S 176 36E
Tarawera L. **142** 38 13S 176 27E
Tarawera Mt. **142** 38 14S 176 32E
Tarazat, Massif de **119** 20 2N 8 30E
Tarazona **58** 41 55N 1 43W
Tarazona de la Mancha **59** 39 16N 1 55W
Tarbat Ness **37** 57 52N 3 48W
Tarbela Dam **94** 34 0N 72 52E
Tarbert, Ireland **39** 52 34N 9 22W
Tarbert, Strathclyde, U.K. **34** 55 55N 5 25W
Tarbert, W. Isles, U.K. **36** 57 54N 6 49W
Tarbert, L. E. **36** 57 50N 6 45W
Tarbert, L. W., Strathclyde, U.K. **34** 55 58N 5 30W
Tarbert, L. W., W. Isles, U.K. **36** 57 55N 6 56W
Tarbes **44** 43 15N 0 3E
Tarbet, Highland, U.K. **36** 56 58N 5 38W
Tarbet, Strathclyde, U.K. **34** 56 13N 4 44W
Tarbolton **34** 55 30N 4 30W
Tarboro **157** 35 55N 77 3W
Tarbrax **138** 21 7S 142 26E
Tarbū **119** 26 0N 15 5E
Tarcento **63** 46 12N 13 12E
Tarcoola **139** 30 44S 134 36E
Tarcoon **139** 30 15S 146 35E
Tarcǔu, Munţii **70** 46 39N 26 7E
Tardets-Sorholus **44** 43 17N 0 52W
Taree **141** 31 50S 152 30E
Tarentaise **45** 45 30N 6 35E
Tarf Shaqq al Abd **122** 26 50N 36 6E
Tarfa, Wadi el **122** 28 16N 31 15E
Tarfaya **116** 27 55N 12 55W
Targon **44** 44 44N 0 16W
Targuist **118** 34 59N 4 14W
Tarhbalt **118** 30 48N 5 10W
Tarhit **118** 30 58N 2 0W
Tarhūnah **119** 32 15N 13 28E
Tari **135** 5 54S 142 59E
Tarib, Wadi **122** 18 30N 43 23E
Táriba **174** 7 49N 72 13W
Tarifa **57** 36 1N 5 36W
Tarija **172** 21 30S 64 40W
Tarija □ **172** 21 30S 63 30W
Tarim, R. **105** 41 5N 86 40E
Tarime □ **126** 1 15S 34 0E
Taringo Downs **141** 32 13S 145 33E
Taritoe, R. **103** 3 0S 138 5E
Tarka, R. **128** 32 10S 26 0E
Tarkastad **128** 32 0S 26 16E
Tarkhankut, Mys **82** 45 25N 32 30E
Tarko Sale **76** 64 55N 77 50E
Tarkwa **120** 5 20N 2 0W
Tarlac **103** 15 29N 120 35E
Tarland **37** 57 8N 2 51W
Tarleton **32** 53 41N 2 50W
Tarlsland **152** 57 03N 111 40W
Tarlton Downs **138** 22 40S 136 45E
Tarm **73** 55 56N 8 31E
Tarma **174** 11 25S 75 45W
Tarn □ **44** 43 49N 2 8E
Tarn-et-Garonne □ **44** 44 8N 1 20E
Tarn, R. **44** 44 5N 1 2E
Tärna **74** 65 45N 15 10E
Tarna, R. **53** 48 0N 20 5E
Tårnby **73** 55 37N 12 36E
Tarnobrzeg □ **54** 50 40N 22 0E
Tarnów **54** 50 3N 21 0E
Tarnów □ **54** 50 0N 21 0E
Tarnowskie Góry **54** 50 27N 18 54E
Táro, R. **62** 44 37N 9 58E
Tarong **139** 26 47S 151 51E
Taroom **139** 25 36S 149 48E
Taroudannt **118** 30 30N 8 52W
Tarp **48** 54 40N 9 25E
Tarpon Springs **157** 28 8N 82 42W
Tarporley **32** 53 10N 2 42W
Tarquínia **63** 42 15N 11 45E
Tarqumiyah **90** 31 35N 35 1E
Tarragona **58** 41 5N 1 17E
Tarragona □ **58** 41 0N 1 0E
Tarrasa **58** 41 26N 2 1E
Tárrega **58** 41 39N 1 9E
Tarrytown **162** 41 5N 73 52W
Tarshiha = Me'ona **90** 33 1N 35 15E
Tarso Emissi **119** 21 27N 18 36E
Tarso Ovrari **119** 21 27N 17 27E
Tarsus **92** 36 58N 34 55E
Tartagal **172** 22 30S 63 50W
Tartan, oilfield **19** 58 22N 0 5E
Tartas **44** 43 50N 0 49W
Tartna Point **140** 32 54S 142 24E
Tartu **80** 58 25N 26 58E
Tartus **92** 34 55N 35 55E
Tarumirim **171** 19 16S 41 59W
Tarumizu **110** 31 29N 130 42E
Tarussa **81** 54 44N 37 10E
Tarutao, Ko **101** 6 33N 99 40E
Tarutung **102** 2 0N 99 0E
Tarves **37** 57 22N 2 13W
Tarvisio **63** 46 31N 13 35E
Tarz Ulli **119** 25 46N 9 44E
Tas-Buget **85** 44 46N 65 33E
Tasahku **98** 27 33N 97 52E
Tasãwah **119** 26 0N 13 37E
Taschereau **150** 48 40N 78 40W
Taseko, R. **152** 52 4N 123 9W
Tasgaon **96** 17 2N 74 39E
Ta'shan **123** 16 31N 42 33E
Tashauz **76** 42 0N 59 20E
Tashet'ai **106** 41 0N 109 21E
Tashi Chho Dzong **98** 27 31N 89 45E
Tashihch'iao (Yingk'ou) **107** 40 38N 122 30E
T'ashihk'uerhkan **85** 37 47N 75 14E
Tashkent **85** 41 20N 69 10E
Tashkumyr **85** 41 40N 72 10E
Tashkurghan **93** 36 45N 67 40E
Tashtagol **76** 52 47N 87 53E
Tasikmalaya **103** 7 18S 108 12E
Tasjön **74** 64 15N 15 45E
Taşköpru **82** 41 30N 34 15E
Tasman Bay **143** 40 59S 173 25E
Tasman Glacier **143** 43 45S 170 20E
Tasman, Mt. **143** 43 34S 170 12E
Tasman Mts. **143** 41 3S 172 25E
Tasman Pen. **138** 43 10S 148 0E
Tasman, R. **143** 43 48S 170 8E
Tasman Sea **142** 36 0S 160 0E
Tasmania, I., □ **138** 49 0S 146 30E
Tassil Tin-Rerhoh **118** 20 5N 3 55E
Tassili n-Ajjer **119** 25 47N 8 1E
Tassili-Oua-Ahaggar **119** 20 41N 5 30E
Tasty **85** 44 47N 69 7E
Tasu Sd. **152** 52 47N 132 2W
Tata, Hung. **53** 47 37N 18 19E
Tata, Moroc. **118** 29 46N 7 50W
Tatabánya **53** 47 32N 18 25E
Tatar A.S.S.R. □ **84** 55 30N 51 30E
Tatarsk **76** 55 20N 75 50E
*Tatarskiy Proliv **77** 54 0N 141 0E
Tatebayashi **111** 36 15N 139 32E
Tateshina-Yama **111** 36 8N 138 11E
Tateyama **111** 35 0N 139 50E
Tathlina L. **152** 60 33N 117 39W
Tathra **141** 36 44S 149 59E
Tat'ien, Fukien, China **109** 25 42N 117 50E
Tat'ien, Szechwan, China **108** 26 18N 101 45E
Tatinnai L. **153** 60 55N 97 40W
Tatlayoka Lake **152** 51 35N 124 24W
Tatnam, C. **153** 57 16N 91 0W
Tato Ho, R. **108** 31 25N 100 42E
Tatra = Tatry **54** 49 20N 20 0E
Tatry **54** 49 20N 20 0E
Tatsu **108** 29 40N 105 45E
Tatsuno **110** 34 52N 134 33E
Tatta **94** 24 42N 67 55E
Tattenhall **32** 53 7N 2 47W
Tatu Ho, R. **108** 29 35N 103 47E
Tatuī **173** 23 25S 48 0W
Tatum **159** 33 16N 103 16W
Tat'ung, Anhwei, China **109** 30 48N 117 44E
Tat'ung, Shansi, China **106** 40 9N 113 19E
Tatura **141** 36 29S 145 16E
Tatvan **92** 37 28N 42 27E
Tauá **170** 6 1S 40 26W
Taubaté **173** 23 5S 45 30W
Tauberbischofsheim **49** 49 37N 9 40E
Taucha **48** 51 22N 12 31E
Tauern, mts. **52** 47 15N 12 40E
Tauern-tunnel **52** 47 0N 13 12E
Taufikia **123** 9 24N 31 37E
Taumarunui **142** 38 53S 175 15E
Taumaturgo **174** 9 0S 73 50W
Taung **128** 27 33S 24 47E
Taungdwingyi **98** 20 1N 95 40E
Taunggyi **98** 20 50N 97 0E
Taungtha **98** 20 45N 94 50E
Taungup **98** 18 51N 94 14E
Taungup Pass **98** 18 40N 94 45E
Taungup Taunggya **99** 18 20N 93 40E
Taunsa Barrage **95** 31 0N 71 0E
Taunton, U.K. **28** 51 1N 3 7W

**Renamed Sakhalinskiy Zalir*

Taunton Tetbury

Taunton, U.S.A. 162 41 54N 71 6W
Taunus 49 50 15N 8 20 E
Taupo 142 38 41 S 176 7 E
Taupo, L. 142 38 46 S 175 55 E
Tauq 92 35 12N 44 29 E
Taurage 80 55 14N 22 28 E
Tauramena 174 5 1N 72 45W
Tauranga 142 37 35 S 176 11 E
Tauranga Harb. 142 37 30 S 176 5 E
Taureau, Lac 150 46 50N 73 40W
Tauri, R. 135 8 8 S 146 8 E
Taurianova 65 38 22N 16 1 E
Taurus Mts. = Toros Dağlari 92 37 0N 35 0 E
Táuste 58 41 58N 1 18W
Tauz 83 41 0N 45 40 E
Tavani 153 62 10N 93 30W
Tavannes 50 47 13N 7 12 E
Tavas 92 37 35N 29 8 E
Tavda 84 58 7N 65 8 E
Tavda, R. 84 59 30N 63 0 E
Taverny 43 49 2N 2 13 E
Taveta 124 3 31N 37 37 E
Taviche 165 16 38N 96 32W
Tavignano, R. 45 42 7N 9 33 E
Tavira 57 37 8N 7 40W
Tavistock 30 50 33N 4 9W
Tavolara, I. 64 40 55N 9 40 E
Távora, R. 56 41 0N 7 30W
Tavoy 101 14 7N 98 18 E
Tavoy, I. = Mali Kyun 99 13 0N 98 20 E
Taw, R. 30 50 58N 3 58W
Tawang 99 27 37N 91 50 E
Tawas City 156 44 16N 83 31W
Tawau 102 4 20N 117 55 E
Tawngche 98 26 34N 95 38 E
Tawnyinah 38 53 55N 8 45W
Tâworgha' 119 32 1N 15 2 E
Taxila 94 33 42N 72 52 E
Tay Bridge 35 56 28N 3 0W
Tay, Firth of 35 56 25N 3 8W
Tay, L., Austral. 137 32 55 S 120 48 E
Tay, L., U.K. 35 56 30N 4 10W
Tay Ninh 101 11 20N 106 5 E
Tay, R. 35 56 37N 3 38W
Tay Strath 37 56 38N 3 40W
Tayabamba 174 8 15 S 77 10W
Tayao 108 25 41N 101 18 E
Tayaparva La 95 31 35N 83 20 E
Tayeh 109 30 5N 114 57 E
Taylor, Can. 152 56 13N 120 40W
Taylor, Alaska, U.S.A. 147 65 40N 164 50W
Taylor, Pa., U.S.A. 162 41 23N 75 43W
Taylor, Tex., U.S.A. 159 30 30N 97 30W
Taylor, Mt. 143 43 30 S 171 20 E
Taylor Mt. 161 35 16N 107 50W
Taylorville 158 39 32N 89 20W
Taymyr, Oz. 77 74 50N 102 0 E
Taymyr, P-ov. 77 75 0N 100 0 E
Taynuilt 34 56 25N 5 15W
Tayport 34 56 27N 2 52W
Tayr Zebna 90 33 14N 35 23 E
Tayshet 77 55 58N 97 25 E
Tayside □ 35 56 25N 3 30W
Taytay 103 10 45N 119 30 E
Tayu 109 25 38N 114 9 E
Tayülo 105 29 13N 98 13 E
Tayung 109 29 8N 110 30 E
Taz, R. 76 65 40N 82 0 E
Taza 118 34 10N 4 0W
Taze 98 22 57N 95 24 E
Tazenakht 118 30 46N 7 3W
Tazin L. 153 59 44N 108 42W
Tazin, R. 153 60 26N 110 45W
Tazoult 119 35 29N 6 11 E
Tazovskiy 76 67 30N 78 30 E
Tbilisi (Tiflis) 83 41 50N 44 50 E
Tchad (Chad) ■ 117 12 30N 17 15 E
Tchad, Lac 117 13 30N 14 30 E
Tchaourou 121 8 58N 2 40 E
Tchentlo L. 152 55 15N 125 0W
Tchibanga 124 2 45 S 11 12 E
Tchin Tabaraden 121 15 58N 5 50 E
Tczew 54 54 8N 18 50 E
Te Anau L. 143 45 15 S 167 45 E
Te Araroa 142 37 39 S 178 25 E
Te Aroha 142 37 32 S 175 44 E
Te Awamutu 142 38 1 S 175 20 E
Te Horo 142 40 48 S 175 6 E
Te Kaha 142 37 44 S 177 44 E
Te Karaka 142 38 26 S 177 53 E
Te Kauwhata 142 37 25 S 175 9 E
Te Kinga 143 42 35 S 171 31 E
Te Kopuru 142 36 2 S 173 56 E
Te Kuiti 142 38 20 S 175 11 E
Te Puke 142 37 46 S 176 22 E
Te Waewae B. 143 46 13 S 167 33 E
Tea Tree 136 22 11 S 133 17 E
Teaca 70 46 55N 24 30 E
Teague 159 31 40N 96 20W
Tean 109 29 21N 115 42 E
Teangue 36 57 7N 5 52W
Teano 65 41 15N 14 1 E
Teapa 165 17 35N 92 56W
Teba 57 36 59N 4 55W
Tebay 32 54 25N 2 35W
Teberda 83 43 30N 43 54 E
Tébessa 119 35 22N 8 8 E
Tebicuary, R. 172 26 36 S 58 16W
Tebing Tinggi 102 3 38 S 102 1 E
Tébourba 119 36 49N 9 51 E
Téboursouk 119 36 29N 9 10 E
Tebulos 83 42 36N 45 25 E
Tecapa 163 35 51N 116 14W
Tecate 164 32 34N 116 38W
Techa, R. 84 56 13N 62 58 E
Tech'ang 108 27 22N 102 10 E
Techiang 108 28 19N 108 5 E
Techiman 120 7 35N 1 58W
Tech'in 108 28 30N 98 52 E
Tech'ing 109 23 8N 111 46 E
Techirghiol 70 44 4N 28 32 E
Techou 106 37 19N 116 19 E
Tecomán 164 18 55N 103 53W
Tecoripa 164 28 37N 109 57W
Tecuci 70 45 51N 27 27 E
Tecumseh 156 42 1N 83 59W
Tedavnet 38 54 19N 7 2W
Tedesa 123 5 10N 37 40 E
Tedzhen 76 37 23N 60 31 E
Tees B. 72 54 37N 1 10W
Tees, R. 33 54 36N 1 25W
Teesdale 32 54 37N 2 10W
Teesside 33 54 37N 1 13W
Tefé 174 3 25 S 64 50W
Tegal 103 6 52 S 109 8 E
Tegelen 47 51 20N 6 9 E
Teggiano 65 40 24N 15 32 E
Teghra 95 25 30N 85 34 E
Tegid, L. 31 52 53N 3 38W
Tegina 121 10 5N 6 11 E
Tegucigalpa 166 14 10N 87 0W
Tehachapi 163 35 11N 118 29W
Tehachapi Mts. 163 35 0N 118 40W
Tehamiyam 122 18 26N 36 45 E
Tehilla 122 17 42N 36 6 E
Tèhini 120 9 39N 3 32W
Tehrãn 93 35 44N 51 30 E
Tehrãn □ 93 35 0N 49 30 E
Tehsing 109 28 54N 117 34 E
Tehua 109 25 30N 118 14 E
Tehuacán 165 18 20N 97 30W
Tehuantepec 165 16 10N 95 19W
Tehuantepec, Golfo de 165 15 50N 95 0W
Tehuantepec, Istmo de 165 17 0N 94 30W
Tehui 107 44 32N 125 42 E
Teich, Le 44 44 38N 0 59W
Teifi, R. 31 52 4N 4 14W
Teign, R. 30 50 41N 3 42W
Teignmouth 30 50 33N 3 30W
Teikovo 81 56 55N 40 30 E
Teil, Le 45 44 33N 4 40 E
Teilleul, Le 42 48 32N 0 53W
Teishyai 80 55 59N 22 14 E
Teiuş 70 46 12N 23 40 E
Teixeira 170 7 13 S 37 15W
Teixeira de Sousa = Luau 124 10 40 S 22 10 E
Teixeira Pinto 120 12 10N 13 55 E
Tejo, R. 57 39 15N 8 35W
Tejon Pass 163 34 49N 118 53W
Tejung 108 28 46N 99 19 E
Tekamah 158 41 48N 96 14W
Tekapo, L. 143 43 53 S 170 33 E
Tekax 165 20 20N 89 30W
Tekeli 85 44 50N 79 0 E
Tekeze, W. 123 13 50N 37 50 E
Tekija 66 44 42N 22 26 E
Tekirdağ 92 40 58N 27 30 E
Tekkali 96 18 43N 84 24 E
Teko 108 31 49N 98 40 E
Tekoa 160 47 19N 117 4W
Tekoulât, O. 118 22 30N 2 20 E
Tel Adashim 90 32 39N 35 17 E
Tel Aviv-Yafo 90 32 4N 34 48 E
Tel Hanan 90 32 47N 35 3 E
Tel Hazor 90 33 2N 35 2 E
Tel Lakhish 90 31 34N 34 51 E
Tel Malhata 90 31 13N 35 2 E
Tel Megiddo 90 32 35N 38 11 E
Tel Mond 90 32 15N 34 56 E
Tela 166 15 40N 87 28W
Tèlagh 118 34 51N 0 32W
Telanaipura = Jambi 102 1 38 S 103 30 E
Telavi 83 42 0N 45 30 E
Telciu 70 47 25N 24 24 E
Telefomin 135 5 10 S 141 40 E
Telega = Doftana 70 45 17N 25 45 E
Telegraph Cr. 152 58 0N 131 10W
Telekhany 80 52 30N 25 46 E
Telemark fylke □ 71 59 25N 8 30 E
Telén 172 36 15 S 65 31W
Teleneshty 70 47 35N 28 24 E
Teleño 56 42 23N 6 22W
Teleorman □ 70 44 0N 25 0 E
Teleorman, R. 70 44 15N 25 20 E
Teles Pires (São Manuel), R. 174 8 40 S 57 0W
Telescope Peak, Mt. 163 36 6N 117 7W
Teletaye 121 16 31N 1 30 E
Telford 28 52 42N 2 31W
Telfs 52 47 19N 11 4 E
Telgte 48 51 59N 7 46 E
Telichie 139 31 45 S 139 59 E
Télimélé 120 10 54N 13 2W
Telkwa 152 54 41N 126 56W
Tell 90 32 12N 35 12 E
Tell City 156 38 0N 86 44W
Teller 147 65 12N 166 24W
Tellicherry 97 11 45N 75 30 E
Tellin 47 50 5N 5 13 E
Telluride 161 37 58N 107 54W
Telok Anson 101 4 3N 101 0 E
Teloloapán 165 18 21N 99 51W
Telom, R. 101 4 20N 101 46 E
Telpos Iz. 78 63 35N 57 30 E
Telsen 176 42 30 S 66 50W
Teltow 48 52 24N 13 15 E
Telukbetung 102 5 29 S 105 17 E
Telukbutun 101 4 5N 108 7 E
Telukdalem 102 0 45N 97 50 E
Tema 121 5 41N 0 0 E
Temagami L. 150 47 0N 80 10W
Temanggung 103 7 18 S 110 10 E
Temapache 165 21 4N 97 38W
Temax 165 21 10N 88 50W
Tembe 126 0 30 S 28 25 E
Tembeling, R. 101 4 20N 102 23 E
Tembleque 58 39 41N 3 30W
Temblor Ra, mts. 163 35 30N 120 0W
Tembuland □ 129 31 35 S 28 0 E
Teme, R. 28 52 23N 2 15W
Temecula 163 33 26N 117 6W
Temelelt 118 31 50N 7 32W
Temerloh 101 3 27N 102 25 E
Temir Tau 76 53 10N 87 20 E
Temirtau 76 50 5N 72 56 E
Témiscaming 150 46 44N 79 5W
Temma 138 41 12 S 144 42 E
Temnikov 81 54 40N 43 11 E
Temo, R. 64 40 20N 8 30 E
Temora 141 34 30 S 147 30 E
Temosachic 164 28 58N 107 50W
Tempe, S. Afr. 161 29 1 S 26 13 E
Tempe, U.S.A. 161 33 26N 111 59W
Tempe Downs 136 24 22 S 132 24 E
Temperanceville 162 37 54N 75 33W
Tempestad 174 1 20 S 74 56W
Tempino 102 1 55 S 103 23 E
Tèmpio Pausania 64 40 53N 9 6 E
Temple 159 31 5N 97 28W
Temple B. 138 12 15 S 143 3 E
Temple Combe 28 51 0N 2 25W
Temple Ewell 29 51 9N 1 16W
Temple Sowerby 30 54 38N 2 33W
Templemore 39 52 48N 7 50W
Templenoe 39 51 52N 9 40W
Templeton, Austral. 138 18 30 S 142 30 E
Templeton, U.K. 31 51 46N 4 45W
Templeton, U.S.A. 163 35 33N 120 42W
Templeton, R. 138 21 0 S 138 40 E
Templeuve 47 50 39N 3 17 E
Templin 48 53 8N 13 31 E
Tempo 38 54 23N 7 28W
Tempoal 165 21 31N 98 23W
Temryuk 82 45 15N 37 11 E
Temse 47 51 7N 4 13 E
Temska, R. 66 43 17N 22 33 E
Temuco 176 38 50 S 72 50W
Temuka 143 44 14 S 171 17 E
Ten Boer 46 53 16N 6 42 E
Tena 174 0 59 S 77 49W
Tenabo 165 20 2N 90 12W
Tenaha 159 31 57N 94 15W
Tenali 96 16 15N 80 35 E
Tenancingo 165 19 0N 99 33W
Tenango 165 19 0N 99 40W
Tenasserim 100 12 6N 99 3 E
Tenasserim □ 100 14 0N 98 30 E
Tenay 45 45 55N 5 30 E
Tenbury 28 52 18N 2 35W
Tenby 31 51 40N 4 42W
Tenda 45 44 5N 7 34 E
Tenda, Col de 45 44 9N 7 32 E
Tendaho 123 11 39N 40 54 E
Tende 45 44 5N 7 35 E
Tendelti 123 13 1N 31 55 E
Tendjedi, Adrar 119 23 41N 7 32 E
Tendrara 118 33 3N 1 58W
Tendre, Mt. 50 46 35N 6 18 E
Teneida 122 25 30N 29 19 E
Ténéré 119 23 2N 16 0 E
Tenerife, I. 116 28 20N 16 40W
Ténès 118 36 31N 1 14 E
T'eng Ch'ung 99 25 9N 98 22 E
Teng, R. 101 20 30N 98 10 E
Tengah □ 103 2 0 S 122 0 E
Tengah Kepulauan 102 7 5 S 118 15 E
Tengchow = P'englai 107 37 49N 120 47 E
Tengch'uan 108 26 0N 100 4 E
Tengch'ung 108 25 2N 98 28 E
Tengfeng 106 34 27N 113 2 E
Tenggara □ 103 3 0 S 122 0 E
Tenggol, P. 101 4 48N 103 41 E
T'enghsien, Honan, China 109 32 41N 112 5 E
T'enghsien, Kwangsi Chuang, China 109 23 23N 110 54 E
T'enghsien, Shantung, China 105 35 8N 117 9 E
Tengiz, Ozero 76 50 30N 69 0 E
Tengko 99 32 30N 98 0 E
Tengk'o 108 32 32N 97 35 E
Tengk'ou 106 40 18N 106 59 E
Tenigerbad 51 46 42N 8 57 E
Tenille 157 32 58N 82 50W
Tenindewa 137 28 30 S 115 20 E
Tenkasi 97 8 55N 77 20 E
Tenke, Congo 127 11 22 S 26 40 E
Tenke, Zaïre 127 10 32 S 26 7 E
Tenkodogo 121 12 0N 0 10W
Tenna, R. 63 43 12N 13 43 E
Tennant Creek 136 19 30 S 134 0 E
'Tenneco', oilfield 19 54 6N 4 42 E
Tennessee □ 155 36 0N 86 30W
Tenneville 47 50 6N 5 32 E
Tennsift, Oued 118 32 3N 9 28W
Tenom 102 5 4N 115 38 E
Tenosique 165 17 30N 91 24W
Tenri 111 34 46N 135 55 E
Tenryū 111 34 52N 137 55 E
Tent L. 153 62 25N 107 54W
Tenterden 29 51 4N 0 42 E
Tenterfield 139 29 0 S 152 0 E
Teófilo Otôni 171 17 50 S 41 30W
Tepa 120 6 57N 2 30W
Tepalcatepec, R. 164 18 35N 101 59W
Tepao 108 23 21N 106 33 E
Tepehuanes 164 25 21N 105 44W
Tepetongo 164 22 28N 103 9W
Tepic 164 21 30N 104 54W
Tepi'ng 107 37 28N 116 67 E
Teploklyuchenka 85 42 30N 78 30 E
Tepoca, C. 164 29 20N 112 25W
Tequila 164 20 54N 103 47W
Ter Apel 46 52 53N 7 5 E
Ter, R. 58 42 0N 2 30 E
Téra 121 14 0N 0 57 E
Tera, R. 56 41 54N 5 44W
Téramo 63 42 40N 13 40 E
Terang 140 38 15 S 142 55 E
Terawhiti, C. 142 41 16 S 174 38 E
Terborg 46 51 56N 6 22 E
Tercan 92 39 50N 40 30 E
Terceira 16 38 43N 27 13W
Tercero, R. 172 32 58 S 61 47W
Terdal 96 16 33N 75 9 E
Terebovlya 80 49 18N 25 44 E
Teregova 70 45 10N 22 16 E
Terek-Say 85 41 30N 71 11 E
Terembone Cr. 139 30 25 S 148 50 E
Terengganu □ 101 4 55N 103 0 E
Tereshka, R. 81 52 0N 46 36 E
Teresina 170 5 2 S 42 45W
Terewah L. 139 29 52 S 147 35 E
Terezinha 174 0 44N 69 27W
Terges, R. 57 37 49N 7 41W
Tergnier 43 49 40N 3 17 E
Terhazza 118 23 45N 4 59W
Terheijden 47 51 38N 4 45 E
Teriang 101 3 15N 102 26 E
Terkezi 117 18 27N 21 40 E
Terlizzi 65 41 8N 16 32 E
Termas de Chillan 172 36 50 S 71 31W
Terme 82 41 11N 37 0 E
Termez 85 37 0N 67 15 E
Términi Imerese 43 37 59N 13 51 E
Términos, Laguna de 165 18 35N 91 30W
Termoli 63 42 0N 15 0 E
Termon 38 55 3N 7 50W
Termonfeckin 38 53 47N 6 15W
Tern, oilfield 19 61 17N 0 55 E
Ternate 103 0 45N 127 25 E
Terneuzen 47 51 20N 3 50 E
Terney 77 45 3N 136 37 E
Terni 63 42 34N 12 38 E
Ternitz 52 47 43N 16 2 E
Ternopol 80 49 30N 25 40 E
Terowie, N.S.W., Austral. 139 32 27 S 147 52 E
Terowie, Vic., Austral. 140 33 10 S 138 50 E
Terra Bella 163 35 58N 119 3W
Terra Nova B. 13 74 50 S 164 40 E
Terrace 152 54 30N 128 35W
Terrace Bay 150 48 47N 87 10W
Terracina 64 41 17N 13 12 E
Terralba 64 39 42N 8 38 E
Terranuova 63 43 38N 11 35 E
Terrasini Favarotta 64 38 10N 13 4 E
Terrasson 44 45 7N 1 19 E
Terrebonne B. 159 29 15N 90 28W
Terrecht 118 20 10N 0 10W
Terrell 159 32 44N 96 19W
Terrenceville 151 47 40N 54 44W
Terrick Terrick 138 24 44 S 145 5 E
Terry 158 46 47N 105 20W
Terryglass 39 53 3N 8 14W
Terryville 162 41 41N 73 1W
Terschelling, I. 46 53 25N 5 20 E
Terskey Alatau, Khrebet 85 41 50N 77 0 E
Terter, R. 83 40 5N 46 15 E
Teruel 58 40 22N 1 8W
Teruel □ 58 40 48N 1 0W
Tervel 67 43 45N 27 28 E
Tervola 74 66 6N 24 49 E
Teryaweyna L. 140 32 18 S 143 22 E
Tešanj 66 44 38N 17 59 E
Teseney 123 15 5N 36 42 E
Tesha, R. 81 55 32N 43 0 E
Teshio 112 44 53N 141 44 E
Teshio-Gawa, R. 112 44 53N 141 45 E
Tešica 66 43 27N 21 45 E
Tesiyn Gol, R. 105 50 28N 93 4 E
Teslin 147 60 10N 132 43W
Teslin L. 152 60 15N 132 57W
Teslin, R. 152 61 34N 134 35W
Teslió 66 44 37N 17 54 E
Teso □ = Eastern □ 126 1 50N 33 45 E
Tessalit 121 20 12N 1 0 E
Tessaoua 121 13 47N 7 56 E
Tessenderlo 47 51 4N 5 5 E
Tessier 153 51 48N 107 26W
Tessin 48 54 2N 12 28 E
Tessit 121 15 13N 0 18 E
Test, R. 28 51 7N 1 30W
Testa del Gargano 65 41 50N 16 10 E
Teste, La 44 44 37N 1 8W
Tét 53 47 30N 17 33 E
Tetachuck L. 152 53 18N 125 55W
Tetas, Pta. 172 23 31 S 70 38W
Tetbury 28 51 37N 2 9W

Tete Tijibadok

Tete 127 16 13 S 33 33 E
Tete □ 127 15 15 S 32 40 E
Teterev, R. 80 50 30N 29 30 E
Teteringen 47 51 37N 4 49 E
Teterow 48 53 45N 12 34 E
Teteven 67 42 58N 24 17 E
Tethull, R. 152 60 35N 112 12W
Tetiyev 82 49 22N 29 38 E
Tetlin 147 63 14N 142 50W
Tetlin Junction 147 63 29N 142 55W
Tetney 33 53 30N 0 1W
Teton, R. 160 47 58N 111 0W
Tétouan 118 35 35N 5 21W
Tetovo 66 42 1N 21 2 E
Tettenhall 28 52 35N 2 7W
Tetuán = Tétouan 118 35 30N 5 25W
Tetyukhe 77 44 45N 135 40 E
Teuco, R. 172 25 30 S 60 25W
Teufen 51 47 24N 9 23 E
Teulada 64 38 59N 8 47 E
Teulon 153 50 23N 97 16W
Tevere, R. 63 42 30N 12 20 E
Teviot, R. 35 55 21N 2 51W
Teviotdale 35 55 25N 2 50W
Teviothead 35 55 19N 2 55W
Tewantin 139 26 27 S 153 3 E
Tewkesbury 28 51 59N 2 8W
Texada I. 152 49 40N 124 25W
Texarkana, Ark., U.S.A. 159 33 25N 94 0W
Texarkana, Tex., U.S.A. 159 33 25N 94 3W
Texas 139 28 49 S 151 15 E
Texas □ 159 31 40N 98 30W
Texas City 159 27 20N 95 20W
Texel, I. 46 53 5N 4 50 E
Texhoma 159 36 32N 101 47W
Texline 159 36 26N 103 0W
Texoma L. 159 34 0N 96 38W
Teyang 108 31 8N 104 24 E
Teykovo 81 56 55N 40 30 E
Teynham 29 51 19N 0 50 E
Teyr Zebna 90 33 14N 35 23 E
Teza, R. 81 56 41N 41 45 E
Tezin 94 34 24N 69 30 E
Teziutlán 165 19 50N 97 30W
Tezpur 98 26 40N 92 45 E
Tezzeron L. 152 54 43N 124 30W
Tha-anne, R. 153 60 31N 94 37W
Tha Deua, Laos 100 17 57N 102 38 E
Tha Deua, Laos 100 19 26N 101 50 E
Tha Nun 101 8 12N 98 17 E
Tha Pia 100 17 48N 100 32 E
Tha Rua 100 14 34N 100 44 E
Tha Sala 101 8 40N 99 56 E
Tha Song Yang 101 17 34N 97 55 E
Thaba Putsoa, mt. 129 29 45 S 28 0 E
Thabana Ntlenyana, Mt. 129 29 30 S 29 9 E
Thabazimbi 129 24 40 S 26 4 E
Thabeikkyin 98 22 53N 95 59 E
Thai Binh 100 20 27N 106 20 E
Thai Muang 101 8 24N 98 16 E
Thai Nguyen 100 21 35N 105 46 E
Thailand (Siam) ■ 100 16 0N 102 0 E
Thakhek 100 17 25N 104 45 E
Thakurgaon 98 26 2N 88 28 E
Thal 94 33 28N 70 33 E
Thal Desert 93 31 0N 71 30 E
Thala 119 35 35N 8 40 E
Thala La 99 28 25N 97 23 E
Thalabarivat 100 13 33N 105 57 E
Thalkirch 51 46 39N 9 17 E
Thallon 139 28 30 S 148 57 E
Thalwil 51 47 17N 8 35 E
Thame 29 51 44N 0 58W
Thame, R. 29 51 52N 0 47W
Thames 142 37 7 S 175 34 E
Thames, Firth of 142 37 0 S 175 25 E
Thames, R., Can. 150 42 20N 82 25W
Thames, R., N.Z. 142 37 32 S 175 45 E
Thames, R., U.K. 28 51 30N 0 35 E
Thames, R., U.S.A. 162 41 18N 72 9W
Thāmit, W. 119 30 51N 16 14 E
Than Uyen 100 22 0N 103 54 E
Thana 96 19 12N 72 59 E
Thanbyuzayat 98 15 58N 97 44 E
Thanesar 94 30 1N 76 52 E
Thanet, I. of 29 51 21N 1 20 E
Thang Binh 101 15 50N 108 20 E
Thangoo P.O. 136 18 10 S 122 22 E
Thangool 138 24 29 S 150 35 E
Thanh Hoa 100 19 48N 105 46 E
Thanh Hung 101 9 55N 105 43 E
Thanh Thuy 100 22 55N 104 51 E
Thanjavur (Tanjore) 97 10 48N 79 12 E
Thanlwin myit, R. 99 20 0N 98 0 E
Thann 43 47 48N 7 5 E
Thaon 43 48 15N 6 25 E
Thap Sakae 101 11 30N 99 37 E
Thap Than 100 15 27N 99 54 E
Thar (Great Indian) Desert 94 28 25N 72 0 E
Tharad 94 24 30N 71 30 E
Thargomindah 139 27 58 S 143 46 E
Tharrawaddy 98 17 38N 95 48 E
Tharrawaw 98 17 41N 95 28 E
Tharthār, Bahr ath 92 34 0N 43 0 E
Thasopoúla, I. 68 40 49N 24 45 E
Thásos 68 40 50N 24 50 E
Thásos, I. 68 40 40N 24 40 E
That Khe 100 22 16N 106 28 E
Thatcham 28 51 24N 1 17W
Thatcher, Ariz., U.S.A. 161 32 54N 109 46W
Thatcher, Colo., U.S.A. 161 37 38N 104 6W
Thaton 98 16 55N 97 22 E
Thau, Étang de 44 43 23N 3 36 E
Thaungdut 98 24 30N 94 40 E
Thaxted 29 51 57N 0 20 E
Thayer 159 36 34N 91 34W
Thayetmyo 98 19 20N 95 18 E
Thayngen 51 47 49N 8 43 E
Thazi 99 21 0N 96 5 E
The Alberga, R. 139 27 6 S 135 33 E
The Bight 167 24 19N 75 24W
The Corrong 139 36 0 S 139 30 E
The Dalles 160 45 40N 121 11W
The Diamantina 139 26 45 S 139 30 E
The English Company's Is. 138 11 50 S 136 32 E
The Entrance 141 33 21 S 151 30 E
The Four Archers 138 15 31 S 135 22 E
The Frome, R. 139 29 8 S 137 54 E
The Granites 136 20 35 S 130 21 E
The Great Divide 141 35 0 S 149 17 E
The Grenadines, Is. 167 12 30N 61 30W
The Hague (s'Gravenhage) 47 52 7N 7 14 E
The Hamilton, R. 139 26 40 S 135 19 E
The Johnston Lakes 137 32 25 S 120 30 E
The Lake 167 21 5N 73 34W
The Loup 38 54 42N 6 32W
The Macumba, R. 139 27 52 S 137 12 E
The Neales, R. 139 28 8 S 136 47 E
The Oaks 141 34 3 S 150 34 E
The Officer, R. 137 27 46 S 129 46 E
The Pas 153 53 45N 101 15W
The Range 127 19 2 S 31 2 E
The Rock 141 35 15 S 147 2 E
The Salt Lake 139 30 6 S 142 8 E
The Stevenson, R. 139 27 6 S 135 33 E
The Thumbs, Mts. 143 43 35 S 170 40 E
The Warburton, R. 139 28 4 S 137 28 E
Theale 28 51 26N 1 5W
Thebes 122 25 40N 32 35 E
Thedford 158 41 59N 100 31W
Theebine 139 25 57 S 152 34 E
Thekulthili L. 153 61 3N 110 0W
Thelma, oilfield 19 58 25N 1 18 E
Thelon, R. 153 62 35N 104 3W
Thénezay 42 46 44N 0 2W
Thenon 44 45 9N 1 4 E
Theodore 138 24 55 S 150 3 E
Thepha 101 6 52N 100 58 E
Thérain, R. 43 49 15N 2 27 E
Thermaïkos Kólpos 68 40 15N 22 45 E
Thermopílai P. 69 38 48N 22 45 E
Thermopolis 160 43 14N 108 10W
Thesprotía □ 68 39 27N 20 22 E
Thessalía □ 68 39 30N 22 0 E
Thessalon 150 46 20N 83 30W
Thessaloníki 68 40 38N 23 0 E
Thessaloníki □ 68 40 45N 23 0 E
Thessaly = Thessalía 68 39 30N 22 0 E
Thetford 29 52 25N 0 44 E
Thetford Mines 151 46 8N 71 18W
Theun, R. 100 18 19N 104 0 E
Theunissen 128 28 26 S 26 43 E
Theux 47 50 32N 5 49 E
Thevenard 139 32 9 S 133 38 E
Thiámis, R. 68 39 34N 20 18 E
Thiberville 42 49 8N 0 27 E
Thicket Portage 153 55 19N 97 42W
Thief River Falls 158 48 15N 96 10W
Thiel 120 14 55N 15 5W
Thiene 63 45 42N 11 29 E
Thierache 43 49 51N 3 45 E
Thiers 44 45 52N 3 33 E
Thies 120 14 50N 16 51W
Thiet 123 7 37N 28 49 E
Thika 126 1 1 S 37 5 E
Thika □ 126 1 1 S 37 5 E
Thille-Boubacar 120 16 31N 15 5W
Thillot, Le 43 47 53N 6 46 E
Thimphu (Tashi Chho Dzong) 98 27 31N 89 45 E
þingvallavatn 74 64 11N 21 9W
Thionville 43 49 20N 6 10 E
Thirá 69 36 23N 25 27 E
Thirasiá, I. 69 36 26N 25 21 E
Thirlmere, L. 32 54 32N 3 4W
Thirsk 33 54 15N 1 20W
Thisted 75 56 58N 8 40 E
Thistle I. 140 35 0 S 136 8 E
Thistle, oilfield 19 61 20N 1 35 E
Thitgy 98 18 15N 96 13 E
Thitpokpin 98 19 24N 96 1 E
Thiu Khao Phetchabun 101 16 20N 100 55 E
Thivai 69 38 19N 23 19 E
Thiviers 44 45 25N 0 54 E
Thizy 45 46 2N 4 18 E
þjorsa 74 63 47N 20 48W
Thlewiaza, R., Man., Can. 153 59 43N 100 5W
Thlewiaza, R., N.W.T., Can. 153 60 29N 94 40W
Thmar Puok 100 13 57N 103 4 E
Tho Vinh 100 19 16N 105 42 E
Thoa, R. 153 60 31N 109 47W
Thoen 100 17 36N 99 12 E
Thoeng 100 19 41N 100 12 E
Thoissey 45 46 12N 4 48 E
Tholdi 95 35 5N 76 6 E
Tholen 47 51 32N 4 13 E
Thomas, Okla., U.S.A. 159 35 48N 98 48W
Thomas, W. Va., U.S.A. 156 39 10N 79 30W
Thomas, L. 139 26 4 S 137 58 E
Thomas Street 38 53 27N 8 15W
Thomastown 39 52 32N 7 10W
Thomasville, Ala., U.S.A. 157 31 55N 87 42W
Thomasville, Fla., U.S.A. 157 30 50N 84 0W
Thomasville, N.C., U.S.A. 157 35 5N 80 4W
Thommen 47 50 14N 6 5 E
Thompson, Can. 153 55 45N 97 52W
Thompson, U.S.A. 162 41 52N 75 31W
Thompson Falls 160 47 37N 115 26W
Thompson Landing 153 62 56N 110 40W
Thompson, R., Can. 152 50 15N 121 24W
Thompson, R., U.S.A. 158 39 46N 93 37W
Thompsons 161 39 0N 109 50W
Thompsonville 162 42 0N 72 37W
Thomson, R. 138 25 11 S 142 53 E
Thomson's Falls = Nyahururu Falls 126 0 2N 36 27 E
Thon Buri 100 13 43N 100 29 E
Thonburi 101 13 50N 100 36 E
Thônes 45 45 54N 6 18 E
Thongwa 98 16 45N 96 33 E
Thonon-les-Bains 45 46 22N 6 29 E
Thonze 98 17 38N 95 47 E
Thorez 83 48 4N 38 34 E
þorlákshöfn 74 63 51N 21 22W
Thornaby on Tees 33 54 36N 1 19W
Thornborough 138 16 54 S 145 2 E
Thornbury, N.Z. 143 46 17 S 168 9 E
Thornbury, U.K. 28 51 36N 2 31W
Thorndon 29 52 16N 1 8 E
Thorne, U.K. 33 53 36N 0 56W
Thorne, U.S.A. 163 38 36N 118 34W
Thorne Glacier 13 87 30N 150 0 E
Thorney 29 52 37N 0 8W
Thornham 29 52 59N 0 35 E
Thornhill 35 55 15N 3 46W
Thornthwaite 32 54 36N 3 13W
Thornton-Beresfield 141 32 50 S 151 40 E
Thornton Celveleys 32 53 52N 3 1W
Thornton Dale 33 54 14N 0 41W
Thorpe 29 52 38N 1 20 E
Thorpe le Soken 29 51 50N 1 11 E
Thouarcé 43 47 17N 0 30W
Thouin, C. 136 20 20 S 118 10 E
Thousand Oakes 163 34 10N 118 50W
Thrace = Thráki 68 41 10N 25 30 E
Thráki 68 41 9N 25 30 E
Thrakikón Pélagos 68 40 30N 25 0 E
Thrapston 29 52 24N 0 32W
Three Bridges 29 51 7N 0 9W
Three Forks 160 45 5N 111 40W
Three Hills 152 51 43N 113 15W
Three Hummock I. 138 40 25 S 144 55 E
Three Kings Is. 142 34 10 S 172 10 E
Three Lakes 158 45 41N 89 10W
Three Pagodas P. 100 15 16N 98 23 E
Three Points, C. 120 4 42N 2 6W
Three Rivers, Austral. 137 25 10 S 119 5 E
Three Rivers, Calif., U.S.A. 163 36 26N 118 54W
Three Rivers, Tex., U.S.A. 159 28 30N 98 10W
Three Sisters, Mt. 160 44 10N 121 52W
Threlkeld 32 54 37N 3 2W
Threshfield 32 54 5N 2 2W
þórisvatn 74 64 50N 19 26W
Throssell, L. 137 27 27 S 124 16 E
Throssell Ra. 136 17 24 S 126 4 E
þórshöfn 74 66 12N 15 20W
Thrumster 37 58 24N 3 8W
Thuan Moa 101 8 58N 105 30 E
Thubun Lakes 153 61 30N 112 0W
Thueyts 45 44 41N 4 9 E
Thuillies 47 50 18N 4 20 E
Thuin 47 50 20N 4 17 E
Thuir 44 42 38N 2 45 E
Thule 12 77 30N 69 0W
Thun 50 46 45N 7 38 E
Thundelarra 137 28 53 S 117 7 E
Thunder B. 156 45 0N 83 20W
Thunder Bay 150 48 20N 89 0W
Thunder River 152 52 13N 119 20W
Thundulda 137 32 15 S 126 3 E
Thunersee 50 46 43N 7 39 E
Thung Song 101 8 10N 99 40 E
Thunkar 98 27 55N 91 0 E
Thuong Tra 100 16 2N 107 42 E
Thur, R. 51 47 32N 9 10 E
Thurgau □ 51 47 34N 9 10 E
Thüringer Wald 48 50 35N 11 0 E
Thurlby 29 52 45N 0 21W
Thurles 39 52 40N 7 53W
Thurloo Downs 139 29 15 S 143 30 E
Thurmaston 28 52 40N 1 8W
Thurmont 162 39 37N 77 25W
Thurn P. 49 47 20N 12 15 E
Thursby 32 54 40N 3 3W
Thursday I. 138 10 30 S 142 3 E
Thurso, Can. 150 45 36N 75 15W
Thurso, U.K. 37 58 34N 3 31W
Thurso, R. 37 58 36N 3 30W
Thurston I. 13 72 0 S 100 0W
Thury-Harcourt 42 49 0N 0 30W
Thusis 51 46 42N 9 26 E
Thutade L. 152 57 0N 126 55W
Thuy, Le 100 17 14N 106 49 E
Thylungra 139 26 4 S 143 28 E
Thyolo 127 16 7 S 35 5 E
Thysville = Mbanza Ngungu 124 5 12 S 14 53 E
Ti-n-Amzi, O. 121 17 35N 4 20 E
Ti-n-Barraouene, O. 121 18 40N 4 5 E
Ti-n-Emensan 118 22 59N 4 45 E
Ti-n-Geloulet 118 25 58N 4 2 E
Ti-n-Medjerdam, O. 118 25 45N 1 30W
Ti-n-Tarabine, O. 119 21 37N 7 11 E
Ti-n-Zaouaténe 118 48 55 S 77 9W
Tia 141 31 10 S 151 50 E
Tiahualilo 164 26 20N 103 30W
Tianguá 170 3 44 S 40 59W
Tiankoura 120 10 47N 3 17W
Tiaret (Tagdent) 118 35 28N 1 21 E
Tiarra 141 32 46 S 145 1 E
Tiassalé 120 5 58N 4 57W
Tibagi 173 24 30 S 50 24W
Tibagi, R. 173 22 47 S 51 1W
Tibari 123 5 2N 31 48 E
Tibati 121 6 22N 12 30 E
Tiber = Tevere, R. 63 42 30N 12 20 E
Tiber Res. 160 48 20N 111 15W
Tiberias 90 32 47N 35 32 E
Tiberias, L. = Kinneret, Yam 90 32 49N 35 36 E
Tibesti 119 21 0N 17 30 E
Tibet 99 32 30N 86 0 E
Tibet □ 105 32 30N 86 0 E
Tibiri 121 13 34N 7 4 E
Tibleş, mt. 70 47 32N 24 15 E
Tibleş, Mţii 70 47 41N 24 6 E
Tibnīn 90 33 12N 35 24 E
Tibooburra 139 29 26 S 142 1 E
Tibro 73 58 28N 14 10 E
Tibugá, Golfo de 174 5 45N 77 20W
Tiburón, I. 164 29 0N 112 30W
Ticehurst 29 51 2N 0 23 E
Tichit 120 18 35N 9 20W
Ticino □ 51 46 20N 8 45 E
Ticino, R. 62 45 23N 8 47 E
Tickhill 33 53 25N 1 8W
Ticonderoga 162 43 50N 73 28W
Ticul 165 20 20N 89 50W
Tidaholm 73 58 12N 13 55 E
Tiddim 98 23 20N 93 45 E
Tideridjaouine, Adrar 118 23 0N 2 15 E
Tideswell 33 53 17N 1 46W
Tidikelt 118 26 58N 1 30 E
Tidjikdja 120 18 4N 11 35W
Tidore 103 0 40N 127 25 E
Tidra, I. 120 19 45N 16 20W
Tiébélé 121 11 6N 0 59W
Tiébissou 120 7 9N 5 18W
Tiéboro 119 21 20N 17 7 E
Tiefencastel 51 46 40N 9 33 E
Tiego 120 12 6N 2 38 E
T'iehling 107 42 17N 123 50 E
Tiel 46 51 53N 5 26 E
Tielt 47 51 0N 3 20 E
Tien Shan 85 42 0N 80 0 E
Tien Yen 100 21 20N 107 24 E
T'iench'ang 107 32 43N 118 59 E
T'ienchen 106 40 30N 114 6 E
Tiench'eng 109 21 31N 111 18 E
T'ienching 107 39 10N 117 15 E
T'ienchu 108 26 55N 109 12 E
T'iench'üan 108 30 4N 102 50 E
T'ienchuangt'ai 107 40 49N 122 6 E
Tienen 47 50 48N 4 57 E
T'ienho 108 24 47N 108 42 E
T'ienhsi 108 24 26N 106 5 E
Tiénigbé 120 8 11N 5 43W
Tienkianghsien 69 30 25N 107 30 E
T'ienlin 108 24 19N 106 15 E
T'ienmen 109 30 37N 113 10 E
T'ieno 108 25 9N 106 57 E
Tienpai 109 21 30N 111 1 E
T'ienshui 105 34 35N 105 15 E
T'ient'ai 109 29 9N 121 2 E
Tientsin = T'ienching 105 39 10N 117 15 E
T'ientung 108 23 39N 107 8 E
T'ienyang 108 23 43N 106 44 E
Tierp 72 60 20N 17 30 E
Tierra Alta 174 8 11N 76 4W
Tierra Amarilla 172 27 28 S 70 18W
Tierra Colorada 165 17 10N 99 35W
Tierra de Barros 57 38 40N 6 30W
Tierra de Campos 56 42 10N 4 50W
Tierra del Fuego, I. Gr. de 176 54 0 S 69 0W
Tiétar, R. 56 39 55N 5 50W
Tieté, R. 171 20 40 S 51 35W
Tieyon 139 26 12 S 133 52 E
Tiffin 156 41 8N 83 10W
Tifi 123 6 12N 36 55 E
Tiflèt 118 33 54N 6 20W
Tiflis = Tbilisi 83 41 50N 44 50 E
Tifrah 90 31 19N 34 42 E
Tifton 157 31 28N 83 32W
Tifu 103 3 39 S 126 18 E
Tigalda I. 147 54 9N 165 0W
Tighnabruaich 34 55 55N 5 13W
Tigil 77 58 0N 158 10 E
Tignish 151 46 58N 64 2W
Tigre □ 123 13 35N 39 15 E
Tigre, R. 174 3 30 S 74 58W
Tigu 99 29 48N 91 38 E
Tiguentourine 119 28 8N 8 58 E
Tiguila 121 14 44N 1 50W
Tigveni 70 45 10N 24 31 E
Tigyaing 98 23 45N 96 10 E
Tih, Gebel el 122 29 32N 33 26 E
Tihodaine, Dunes de 119 25 15N 7 15 E
Tiji 119 32 0N 11 18 E
Tijiamis 103 7 16 S 108 29 E
Tijibadok 103 6 53 S 106 47 E

Tijirit, O Tolox

Tijirit, O. 120 19 30N 6 15W
Tijuana 164 32 30N 117 3W
Tikal 166 17 2N 89 35W
Tikamgarh 95 24 44N 78 57E
Tikan 138 5 58S 149 2E
Tikhoretsk 83 45 56N 40 5E
Tikhvin 80 59 35N 33 30E
Tikkadouine, Adrar 118 24 28N 1 30E
Tiko 121 4 4N 9 20E
Tikrit 92 34 35N 43 37E
Tiksi 77 71 50N 129 0E
Tilamuta 103 0 40N 122 15E
Tilburg 47 51 31N 5 6E
Tilbury, Can. 150 42 17N 84 23W
Tilbury, U.K. 29 51 27N 0 24E
Tilcara 172 23 30S 65 23W
Tilden 158 42 3N 97 45W
Tilemsès 121 15 37N 4 44E
Tilemsi, Vallée du 121 17 42N 0 15E
Tilghman 162 38 42N 76 20W
Tilhar 95 28 0N 79 45E
Tilia, O. 118 27 32N 0 55E
Tilichiki 77 61 0N 166 5E
Tiligul, R. 82 47 35N 30 30E
Tililane 118 27 49N 0 6W
Tilin 98 21 41N 94 6E
Tilissos 69 38 15N 25 0E
Till, R. 35 55 35N 2 3W
Tillabéri 121 14 7N 1 28E
Tillamook 160 45 29N 123 55W
Tillberga 72 59 42N 16 39E
Tilley 152 50 28N 111 38W
Tillia 121 16 8N 4 47E
Tillicoultry 35 56 9N 3 44W
Tillsonburg 150 42 53N 80 44W
Tilmanstone 29 51 13N 1 18E
Tilos, I. 69 36 27N 27 27E
Tilpa 139 30 57S 144 24E
Tilrhemt 118 33 9N 3 22E
Tilsit = Sovetsk 80 55 6N 21 50E
Tilt, R. 37 56 50N 3 50W
Tilton 162 43 25N 71 36W
Timahoe 39 52 59N 7 12W
Timanskiy Kryazh 78 65 58N 50 5E
Timaru 143 44 23S 171 14E
Timashevo 84 53 22N 51 9E
Timashevsk 83 45 35N 39 0E
Timau 126 0 4N 37 15E
Timbákion 69 35 4N 24 45E
Timbaúba 170 7 31S 35 19W
Timbédra 120 16 17N 8 16W
Timber L. 158 45 29N 101 0W
Timber Mtn. 163 37 6N 116 28W
Timbio 174 2 20N 76 40W
Timbiqui 174 2 46N 77 42W
Timboon 140 38 30S 142 58E
Timbuktu =
Tombouctou 120 16 50N 3 0W
Timdjaouine 118 21 47N 4 30E
Timétrine Montagnes 121 19 25N 1 0W
Timfi Óros 68 39 59N 20 45E
Timfristós, Óros 69 38 57N 21 50E
Timhadite 118 33 15N 5 4W
Timimoun 118 29 14N 0 16E
Timimoun, Sebkha de 118 28 50N 0 46E
Timiris, C. 120 19 15N 16 30W
Timiş □ 66 45 40N 21 30E
Timiş, R. 70 45 30N 21 0E
Timişoara 66 45 43N 21 15E
Timmins 150 48 28N 81 25W
Timmoudi 118 29 20N 1 8W
Timok, R. 66 44 10N 22 40E
Timoleague 39 51 40N 8 51W
Timolin 39 52 59N 6 49W
Timon 170 5 8S 42 52W
Timor □ 103 8 0S 126 30E
Timor, I. 103 9 0S 125 0E
Timor Sea 136 10 0S 127 0E
Timur □ 103 9 0S 125 0E
Tin Alkoum 119 24 30N 10 17E
Tin Gornai 121 16 38N 0 38W
Tin Mtn. 163 36 54N 117 28W
Tîna, Khalîg el 122 31 20N 32 42E
Tinaca Pt. 103 5 30N 125 25E
Tinaco 174 9 42N 68 26W
Tinafak, O. 119 27 10N 7 0W
Tinahely 39 52 48N 6 28W
Tinambacan 103 12 5N 124 32E
Tinapagee 139 29 25S 144 15E
Tinaquillo 174 9 55N 68 18W
Tinaroo Falls 138 17 5S 145 4E
Tinca 70 46 46N 21 58E
Tinchebray 42 48 47N 0 45W
Tindivanam 97 12 15N 79 35E
Tindouf 118 27 50N 8 4W
Tindzhe Dzong 95 28 20N 88 8E
Tineo 56 43 21N 6 27W
Tinerhir 118 31 29N 5 31W
Tinfouchi 118 28 58N 5 54W
T'ing Chiang, R. 109 24 24N 116 35E
Tingan 100 19 42N 110 18E
Tingch'u, R. 108 28 20N 99 12E
Tingewick 28 51 59N 1 4W
Tinggi, Pulau, Is. 101 2 18N 104 7E
Tinghai 109 30 0N 122 10E
Tinghsi 106 35 33N 104 32E
Tinghsiang 106 38 32N 112 59E
Tinghsien 106 38 30N 115 0E
Tingkawk Sakun 98 26 4N 96 44E
Tingk'ouchen 106 39 48N 106 36E
Tinglev 73 54 57N 9 13E
Tingnan 109 24 47N 115 2E
Tingo Maria 174 9 10S 76 0W
Tingpien 106 37 36N 107 38E
Tingshan 109 31 16N 119 51E
Tingsryd 73 56 31N 15 0E
Tingt'ao 106 35 4N 115 34E
Tingvalla 73 58 47N 12 2E
Tingyüan 109 32 32N 117 41E
Tinh Bien 101 10 36N 104 57E
Tinharé, I. de 171 13 30S 38 58W
Tinié 121 14 17N 1 30W
Tinioulig, Sebkra 118 22 30N 6 45W
Tinjoub 118 29 45N 5 40W
Tinkurrin 137 32 59S 117 46E
Tinnia 172 27 0S 62 45W
Tinnoset 71 59 45N 9 3E
Tinnsjø 71 59 55N 8 54E
Tinogasta 172 28 0S 67 40W
Tínos 69 37 33N 25 8E
Tiñoso, C. 59 37 32N 1 6W
Tinsukia 98 27 29N 95 26E
Tintagel 30 50 40N 4 45W
Tintagel Hd. 30 50 40N 4 46W
Tintern 31 51 42N 2 41W
Tintern Abbey 39 52 14N 6 50W
Tintigny 47 49 41N 5 31E
Tintina 172 27 2S 62 45W
Tintinara 140 35 48S 140 2E
Tinto, R. 57 37 30N 5 33W
Tinui 142 40 52S 176 5E
Tinwald 143 43 55S 171 43E
Tioga 162 41 54N 77 9W
Tioman, I. 101 2 50N 104 10E
Tioman, Pulau, Is. 101 2 50N 104 10E
Tionaga 150 48 0N 82 0W
Tione di Trento 62 46 3N 10 44E
Tior 123 6 26N 31 11E
Tioulilin 118 27 1N 0 2W
Tipongpani 99 27 20N 95 55E
Tipperary 39 52 28N 8 10W
Tipperary □ 39 52 37N 7 55W
Tipton, U.K. 28 52 32N 2 4W
Tipton, Calif., U.S.A. 163 36 3N 119 19W
Tipton, Ind., U.S.A. 156 40 17N 86 30W
Tipton, Iowa, U.S.A. 158 41 45N 91 12W
Tiptonville 159 36 22N 89 30W
Tiptree 29 51 48N 0 46E
Tiptur 97 13 15N 76 26E
Tira 90 32 14N 34 56E
Tiracambu, Serra do 170 3 15S 46 30W
Tirahart, O. 118 23 55N 2 0W
Tiran 93 32 45N 51 0E
Tirân 122 27 56N 34 35E
Tirana 68 41 18N 19 49E
Tirana-Durrësi □ 68 41 35N 20 0E
Tirano 62 46 13N 10 11E
Tirarer, Mont 121 19 35N 1 10W
Tiraspol 82 46 55N 29 35E
Tirat Carmel 90 32 46N 34 58E
Tirat Tsevi 90 32 26N 35 31E
Tirat Yehuda 90 32 1N 34 56E
Tiratimine 118 25 56N 3 37E
Tirdout 121 16 7N 1 5W
Tire 92 38 5N 27 50E
Tirebolu 92 40 58N 38 45E
Tiree, I. 34 56 31N 6 55W
Tiree, Passage of 34 56 30N 6 30W
Tîrgoviste 70 44 55N 25 27E
Tîrgu Frumos 70 47 12N 27 2E
Tîrgu-Jiu 70 45 5N 23 19E
Tîrgu Mureş 70 46 31N 24 38E
Tîrgu Neamţ 70 47 12N 26 25E
Tîrgu Ocna 70 46 16N 26 39E
Tîrgu Secuiesc 70 46 0N 26 10E
Tirich Mir Mt. 93 36 15N 71 35E
Tiriola 65 38 57N 16 32E
Tiririca, Serra da 171 17 6S 47 6W
Tirlyanskiy 84 54 14N 58 35E
Tirna, R. 96 18 5N 76 30E
Tîrnava = Botoroaga 70 44 8N 25 32E
Tîrnava Mare, R. 70 46 15N 24 30E
Tîrnava Mica, R. 70 46 17N 24 30E
Tírnavos 68 39 45N 22 18E
Tîrnova 70 45 23N 22 1E
Tîrnǔveni 70 46 19N 24 13E
Tirodi 96 21 35N 79 35E
Tirol □ 52 47 3N 10 43E
Tiros 171 19 0S 45 58W
Tirschenreuth 49 49 51N 12 20E
Tirso, L. 64 40 8N 8 56E
Tirso, R. 64 40 33N 9 12E
Tirstrup 73 56 18N 10 42E
Tirua 142 38 25S 174 40E
Tiruchchirappalli 97 10 45N 78 45E
Tiruchendur 97 8 30N 78 11E
Tiruchengodu 97 11 23N 77 56E
Tirumangalam 97 9 49N 77 58E
Tirunelveli (Tinnevelly) 97 8 45N 77 45E
Tirupati 97 13 45N 79 30E
Tiruppattur 97 12 30N 78 30E
Tiruppur 97 11 12N 77 22E
Tiruturaipundi 97 10 32N 79 41E
Tiruvadaimarudur 97 11 2N 79 27E
Tiruvallar 97 13 9N 79 57E
Tiruvannamalai 97 12 10N 79 12E
Tiruvarur (Negapatam) 97 10 46N 79 38E
Tiruvatipuram 97 12 39N 79 33E
Tiruvottiyur 97 13 10N 80 22E
Tisa, R. 66 45 30N 20 20E
Tisdale 153 52 50N 104 0W
Tiseirhatène, Mares de 118 22 51N 9 30W
Tishomingo 159 34 14N 96 38W
Tisjön 72 60 56N 13 0E
Tisnaren 72 58 58N 15 56E
Tisno 63 44 45N 15 41E
Tišnov 53 49 21N 16 25E
Tisovec 53 48 41N 19 56E
Tissemsilt 118 35 35N 1 50E
Tissit, O. 119 27 28N 9 58W
Tissø 73 55 35N 11 18E
Tista, R. 98 25 23N 89 43E
Tisted 73 56 58N 8 40E
Tisza, R. 53 47 38N 20 44E
Tiszaföldvár 53 47 0N 20 14E
Tiszafüred 53 47 38N 20 50E
Tiszalök 53 48 0N 21 10E
Tiszavasvári 53 47 58N 21 18E
Tit, Alg. 118 27 0N 1 37E
Tit, Alg. 119 23 0N 5 10E
Tit-Ary 77 71 50N 126 30E
Titaguas 58 39 53N 1 6W
Titahi Bay 142 41 6S 174 50E
Titai Damer 123 16 43N 37 25E
Titchfield 28 50 51N 1 13W
Titel 66 45 29N 20 18E
Tithwal 95 34 21N 73 50E
Titicaca, L. 174 15 30S 69 30W
Titilagarh 96 20 15N 83 5E
Tititira Head 98 43 38S 169 26E
Titiwa 121 12 14N 12 53E
Titlis 51 46 46N 8 27E
Titograd 66 42 30N 19 19E
Titov Veles 66 41 46N 21 47E
Titova Korenica 63 44 45N 15 41E
Titovo Uzice 66 43 55N 19 50E
Titule 126 3 15N 25 31E
Titumate 174 8 19N 77 5W
Titusville 156 41 35N 79 39W
Tiumpan Hd. 36 58 15N 6 10W
Tivaouane 120 14 56N 16 45W
Tivat 66 42 28N 18 43E
Tiveden 73 58 50N 14 30E
Tiverton 30 50 54N 3 30W
Tivoli 63 41 58N 12 45E
Tiwi 93 22 45N 59 12E
Tiyo 123 14 41N 40 57E
Tizga 118 32 1N 5 9W
Tizi n'Isly 118 32 28N 5 47W
Tizi Ouzou 119 36 42N 4 3E
Tizmín 165 21 0N 88 1W
Tiznados, R. 174 8 50N 67 50W
Tiznit 118 29 48N 9 45W
Tjalang 103 4 30N 95 43E
Tjangkuang, Tg. 102 7 0S 105 0E
Tjareme, G. 103 6 55S 108 27E
Tjeggelvas 74 66 37N 17 45E
Tjepu 103 7 12S 111 31E
Tjeukemeer 46 52 53N 5 48E
Tjiandjur 103 6 51S 107 7E
Tjibatu 103 7 8S 107 59E
Tjikadjang 103 7 25S 107 48E
Tjimahi 103 6 53S 107 33E
Tjirebon = Cirebon 103 6 45S 108 32E
Tjöllong 71 59 6N 10 3E
Tjöme 71 59 8N 10 26E
Tjonger Kanaal 46 52 52N 6 52E
Tjörn 73 58 0N 11 35E
Tjörnes 74 66 12N 17 9W
Tjuls 73 57 30N 18 15E
Tjurup 102 4 26S 102 13E
Tkibuli 83 42 26N 43 0E
Tkvarcheli 83 42 47N, 41 52E
Tlacolula 165 16 57N 96 29W
Tlacotalpán 165 18 37N 95 40W
Tlaquepaque 164 20 39N 103 19W
Tlaxcala 165 19 20N 98 14W
Tlaxcala □ 165 19 30N 98 20W
Tlaxiaco 165 17 10N 97 40W
Tlell 152 53 34N 131 56W
Tlemcen 118 34 52N 1 15W
Tleta di Sidi Bouguedra 118 32 16N 8 58W
Tleta Sidi Bouguedra 118 32 16N 9 59W
Tlumach 80 48 46N 25 0E
Tłuszcz 54 52 25N 21 25E
Tlyarata 83 42 9N 46 26E
Tmassah 119 26 19N 15 51E
Tmisan 119 27 23N 13 30E
To Bong 100 12 45N 109 16E
T'o Chiang, R. 108 28 56N 105 33E
To-Shima 111 34 31N 139 17E
Toad, R. 152 59 25N 124 57W
Toay 172 36 50S 64 30W
Toba 111 34 30N 136 45E
Toba Kakar 94 31 30N 69 0E
Toba, L. 102 2 40N 98 50E
Toba Tek Singh 94 30 55N 72 25E
Tobago, I. 167 11 10N 60 30W
Tobarra 59 38 35N 1 41W
Tobelo 103 1 25N 127 56E
Tobercurry 38 54 3N 8 43W
Tobermore 38 54 49N 6 43W
Tobermorey 138 22 12S 138 0E
Tobermory, Can. 150 45 12N 81 40W
Tobermory, U.K. 34 56 37N 6 4W
Tobin, L. 136 21 45S 125 49E
Tobin L. 153 53 35N 103 30W
Toboali 102 3 0S 106 25E
Tobol 84 52 40N 62 39E
Tobol, R. 84 58 10N 68 12E
Toboli 103 0 38S 120 12E
Tobolsk 84 58 0N 68 10E
Tobruk = Tubruq 117 32 7N 23 55E
Tobyhanna 162 41 10N 75 15W
Tocantínia 170 9 33S 48 22W
Tocantinópolis 170 6 20S 47 25W
Tocantins, R. 170 14 30S 49 0W
Tocca 157 34 6N 83 17W
Toce, R. 62 46 5N 8 29E
Tochigi 111 36 25N 139 45E
Tochigi-ken □ 111 36 45N 139 45E
Tocina 57 37 37N 5 44W
Toconao 172 34 35N 83 19W
Toconhão, Serra do 171 14 30S 47 46W
Tocópero 174 11 30N 69 16W
Tocopilla 172 22 5S 70 10W
Tocumwal 141 35 45S 145 31E
Tocuyo, R. 174 10 50N 69 0W
Todd, R. 138 24 52S 135 48E
Toddington 29 51 57N 0 31W
Todeli 103 1 38S 124 34E
Todenyang 126 4 35N 35 56E
Todi 63 42 47N 12 24E
Tödi 51 46 48N 8 55E
Todjo 103 1 20S 121 15E
Todmorden 32 53 43N 2 7W
Todos os Santos, Baía
de 171 12 48S 38 38W
Todos Santos 164 23 27N 110 13W
Todos Santos, Bahia de 164 31 48N 116 42W
Todtnau 49 47 50N 7 56E
Toe Hd., Ireland 39 51 29N 9 13W
Toe Hd., U.K. 36 57 50N 7 10W
Toecé 121 11 50N 1 16W
Toetoes B. 143 46 42S 168 41E
Tofield 152 53 25N 112 40W
Tofino 152 49 11N 125 55W
Töfsingdalems National
Park 72 62 15N 12 44E
Tofta 73 57 11N 12 20E
Toftlund 73 55 11N 9 2E
Tōgane 111 35 33N 140 22E
Togba 120 17 26N 10 25W
Toggenburg 51 47 16N 9 9E
Togian, Kepulauan 103 0 20S 121 50E
Togliatti 81 53 37N 49 18E
Togo ■ 121 6 15N 1 35E
Toguzak, R. 84 54 3N 62 44E
Tōhoku □ 112 39 50N 141 45E
Toi 111 34 54N 134 47E
Toinya 123 6 17N 29 46E
Toiyabe Dome 163 38 51N 117 22W
Toiyabe, Ra. 163 39 10N 117 10W
Tōjō 110 34 53N 133 16E
Tok, R. 84 52 46N 52 22E
Tokaanu 142 38 58S 175 46E
Tokachi, R. 112 42 44N 143 42E
Tokaj 53 48 8N 21 27E
Tokala, G. 103 1 30S 121 40E
Tokanui 143 46 34S 168 56E
Tokarahi 143 44 56S 170 39E
Tokat 92 40 22N 36 35E
Tŏkchŏn 107 39 45N 126 18E
Tokelau Is. 130 9 0S 172 0W
Toki 111 35 18N 137 8E
Tokmak, Kirgizia,
U.S.S.R. 84 42 55N 75 45E
Tokmak, Ukraine,
U.S.S.R. 82 47 16N 35 42E
Toko Ra. 138 23 5S 138 20E
Tokomaru Bay 142 38 8S 178 22E
Tokombere 121 11 18N 3 30E
Tókomlós 53 46 24N 20 45E
Tokoname 111 34 53N 136 51E
Tokong 101 5 27N 100 23E
Tokoroa 142 38 20S 175 50E
Tokorozawa 111 35 47N 139 28E
T'ok'ot'o 106 40 15N 111 12E
Toktogul 85 41 50N 72 50E
Tokuii 110 34 11N 131 42E
Tokule 123 14 54N 38 26E
Tokunoshima 112 27 56N 128 55E
Tokushima 110 34 4N 134 34E
Tokushima-ken □ 110 35 50N 134 30E
Tokuyama 110 34 0N 131 50E
Tōkyō 111 35 45N 139 45E
Tōkyō-to □ 111 35 40N 139 30E
Tōkyō-Wan 111 35 25N 139 47E
Tolaerh 105 35 8N 81 33E
Tolaga Bay 142 38 21S 178 20E
Tolageak 147 70 2N 162 50W
Tolbukhin 67 43 37N 27 49E
Toledo, Spain 56 39 50N 4 2W
Toledo, Ohio, U.S.A. 156 41 37N 83 33W
Toledo, Oreg., U.S.A. 160 44 40N 123 59W
Toledo, Wash., U.S.A. 160 42 29N 122 58W
Toledo, Montes de 57 39 33N 4 20W
Tolentino 63 43 12N 13 17E
Tolfino 152 49 6N 125 54W
Tolga, Alg. 119 34 46N 5 22E
Tolga, Norway 71 62 26N 11 1E
Tolima □ 174 3 45N 75 15W
Tolima, Vol. 174 4 40N 75 19W
Tolitoli 103 1 5N 120 50E
Tolkamer 46 51 52N 6 6E
Tolkmicko 54 54 19N 19 31E
Tollarp 73 55 55N 13 58E
Tollesbury 29 51 46N 0 51E
Tolleson 161 33 29N 112 10W
Tollhouse 163 37 1N 119 24W
Tolmachevo 80 58 56N 29 57E
Tolmezzo 63 46 23N 13 0E
Tolmino 63 46 11N 13 45E
Tolna 53 46 25N 18 48E
Tolna □ 53 46 30N 18 30E
Tolne 73 57 28N 10 20E
Tolo 124 2 50S 18 40E
Tolo, Teluk 103 2 20S 122 10E
Tolokiwa I. 138 5 30S 147 30E
Tolon 121 9 26N 1 3W
Tolosa 58 43 8N 2 5W
Tolox 57 36 41N 4 54W

Tolsta Hd
Tregnago

Tolsta Hd. 36 58 20N 6 10W
Toluca 165 19 20N 99 50W
Tolun 106 42 22N 116 30E
Tom Burke 129 23 5S 28 4E
Tomahawk 158 45 28N 89 40W
Tomakomai 112 42 38N 141 36E
Tomales 163 38 15N 122 53W
Tomales B. 163 38 15N 123 58W
Tomar 57 39 36N 8 25W
Tómaros Óros 68 39 29N 20 48E
Tomaszów Lubelski 54 50 29N 23 23E
Tomaszów Mazowiecki 54 51 30N 19 57E
Tomatin 37 57 20N 4 0W
Tomatlán 164 19 56N 105 15W
Tombé 123 5 53N 31 40E
Tombigbee, R. 157 32 0N 88 6W
Tombodor, Serra do 171 12 0S 41 30W
Tombouctou 120 16 50N 3 0W
Tombstone 161 31 40N 110 4W
Tomdoun 36 57 4N 5 2W
Tomé 172 36 36S 73 6W
Tomé-Açu 170 2 25S 48 9W
Tomelilla 73 55 33N 13 58E
Tomelloso 59 39 10N 3 2W
Tomingley 141 32 31S 148 16E
Tomini 103 0 30N 120 30E
Tomini, Teluk 103 0 10S 122 0E
Tominian 120 13 17N 4 35W
Tomiño 56 41 59N 8 46W
Tomintoul 37 57 15N 3 22W
Tomioka 111 36 15N 138 54E
Tomkinson Ranges 137 26 11S 129 5E
Tommot 77 58 50N 126 20E
Tomnavoulin 37 57 19N 3 18W
Tomnop Ta Suos 101 11 20N 104 15E
Tomo, Colomb. 174 2 38N 67 32W
Tomo, Japan 110 34 23N 133 23E
Tomobe 111 36 40N 140 41E
Toms Place 163 37 34N 118 41W
Toms River 162 39 59N 74 12W
Tomsk 76 56 30N 85 12E
Tomtabacken 73 57 30N 14 30E
Tonalá 165 16 8N 93 41W
Tonale, Passo del 62 46 15N 10 34E
Tonalea 161 36 17N 110 58W
Tonami 111 36 56N 136 58E
Tonantins 174 2 45S 67 45W
Tonasket 160 48 45N 119 30W
Tonawanda 156 43 0N 78 54W
Tonbridge 29 51 12N 0 18E
Tondano 103 1 35N 124 54E
Tondela 56 40 31N 8 5W
Tønder 73 54 58N 8 50E
Tondi 97 9 45N 79 4E
Tondi Kiwindi 121 14 28N 2 02E
Tondibi 121 16 39N 0 14W
Tone-Gawa, R. 111 35 44N 140 51E
Tone, R. 137 34 23S 116 25E
Tone R. 30 50 59N 3 15W
Tong 28 52 39N 2 18W
Tonga Is. ■ 130 20 0S 173 0W
Tonga Trench 143 18 0S 175 0W
Tongaat 129 29 33S 31 9E
Tongala 141 36 14S 144 56E
Tongaland 129 27 0S 32 0E
Tongareva I 143 9 0S 158 0W
Tongariro, mt. 142 39 7S 175 50E
Tongchŏnni 107 39 50N 127 25E
Tongeren 47 50 47N 5 28E
Tongio 141 37 14S 147 44E
Tongjosŏn Man 107 39 30N 128 0E
Tongking = Bac-Phan 101 21 30N 105 0E
Tongking, G. of 101 20 0N 108 0E
Tongnae 107 35 12N 129 5E
Tongobory 129 23 32S 44 20E
Tongoy 172 30 25S 71 40W
Tongres = Tongeren 47 50 47N 5 28E
Tongsa Dzong 98 27 31N 90 31E
Tongue 37 58 29N 4 25W
Tongue, Kyle of 37 58 30N 4 30W
Tongue, R. 160 48 30N 106 30W
Tongyang 107 39 9N 126 53E
Tonj 123 7 20N 28 44E
Tonk 94 26 6N 75 54E
Tonkawa 159 36 44N 67 22W
Tonkin = Bac-Phan 100 22 0N 105 0E
Tonkin, G. of 100 20 0N 108 0E
Tonlé Sap 100 13 0N 104 0E
Tonnay-Charente 44 45 56N 0 55W
Tonneins 44 44 24N 0 20E
Tonnerre 43 47 51N 3 59E
Tönning 48 54 18N 8 57E
Tonopah 163 38 4N 117 12W
Tonoshō 110 34 29N 134 11E
Tonosí 166 7 20N 80 20W
Tonsberg 71 59 19N 10 25E
Tonstad 71 58 40N 6 45E
Tonto Basin 61 33 58N 111 15W
Tonyrefail 31 51 35N 3 26W
Tonzang 98 23 36N 93 42E
Tonzi 98 24 39N 94 57E
Tooele 160 40 30N 112 20W
Toolonda 140 36 58S 141 5E
Toombeolo 38 53 26N 9 52W
Toomevara 39 52 50N 8 2W
Toompine 139 27 15S 144 19E
Toongi 141 32 28S 148 30E
Toonpan 138 19 28S 146 48E
Toora 141 38 39S 146 23E
Toora-Khem 77 52 28N 96 9E
Toormore 39 51 31N 9 41W
Toowoomba 139 27 32S 151 56E
Top 93 34 15N 68 35E
Top Ozero 78 65 35N 32 0E
Topalu 70 44 31N 28 3E
Topaz 163 38 41N 119 30W
Topeka 158 39 3N 95 40W
Topki 76 55 25N 85 20E
Topla, R. 53 49 0N 21 36E
Topley 152 54 32N 126 5W
Toplica, R. 66 43 15N 21 30E
Toplița 70 46 55N 25 27E
Topocalma, Pta. 172 34 10S 72 2W
Topock 161 34 46N 114 29W
Topola 66 44 17N 20 32E
Topol'čany 53 48 35N 18 12E
Topoli 83 47 59N 51 45E
Topolnitsa, R. 67 42 21N 24 0E
Topolobampo 164 25 40N 109 10W
Topolovgrad 67 42 5N 26 20E
TopolvůT Mare 66 45 46N 21 41E
Toppenish 160 46 27N 120 16W
Topsham 30 50 40N 3 27W
Topusko 63 45 18N 15 59E
Toquima, Ra. 163 39 0N 117 0W
Tor Bay, Austral. 137 35 5S 117 50E
Tor Bay, U.K. 23 50 26N 3 31W
Tor Ness 37 58 47N 3 18W
Tor, oilfield 19 56 40N 3 35E
Torá 58 41 49N 1 25E
Tora Kit 123 11 2N 32 30E
Torata 174 17 3S 70 1W
Torbat-e Heydarīyeh 93 35 15N 59 12E
Torbat-e Jām 93 35 8N 60 35E
Torbay, Can. 151 47 40N 52 42W
Torbay, U.K. 30 50 26N 3 31W
Torchin 80 50 45N 25 0E
Tordal 71 59 10N 8 45E
Tordesillas 56 41 30N 5 0W
Tordoya 56 43 6N 8 36W
Töre 74 65 55N 22 40E
Töreboda 73 58 41N 14 7E
Torfajökull 74 63 54N 19 0W
Torgau 48 51 32N 13 0E
Torgelow 48 53 40N 13 59E
Torhout 47 51 5N 3 7E
Tori 123 7 53N 33 35E
Torigni-sur-Vire 42 49 3N 0 58W
Torija 58 40 44N 3 2W
Torin 164 27 33N 110 5W
Toriñana, C. 56 43 3N 9 17W
Torino 62 45 4N 7 40E
Torit 123 4 20N 32 55E
Torkovichi 80 58 51N 30 30E
Tormac 66 45 30N 21 30E
Tormentine 151 46 6N 63 46W
Tormes, R. 56 41 7N 6 0W
Tornado Mt. 152 49 55N 114 40W
Tornby 73 57 32N 9 56E
Torne älv 74 65 50N 24 12E
Torneå = Tornio 74 65 50N 24 12E
Torness 37 57 18N 4 22W
Torneträsk 74 68 24N 19 15E
Tornio 74 65 50N 24 12E
Tornionjoki 74 65 50N 24 12E
Tornquist 172 38 0S 62 15W
Toro 56 41 35N 5 24W
Torö 73 58 48N 17 50E
Toro, Cerro del 172 29 0S 69 50W
Toro Pk. 163 33 34N 116 24W
Törökszentmjklés 53 47 11N 20 27E
Toronátos Kólpos 68 40 5N 23 30E
Toronto, Austral. 141 33 0S 151 30E
Toronto, Can. 150 43 39N 79 20W
Toronto, U.S.A. 156 40 27N 80 36W
Toronto, L. 164 27 40N 105 30W
Toropets 80 56 30N 31 40E
Tororo 126 0 45N 34 12E
Toros Dağlari 92 37 0N 35 0E
Torphins 37 57 7N 2 37W
Torpoint 30 50 23N 4 12W
Torpshammar 72 62 29N 16 20E
Torquay, Austral. 140 38 20S 144 19E
Torquay, Can. 153 49 9N 103 30W
Torquay, U.K. 30 50 27N 3 31W
Torquemada 56 42 2N 4 19W
Torralba de Calatrava 57 39 1N 3 44W
Torran Rocks 34 56 14N 6 24W
Torrance 163 33 50N 118 19W
Torrão 57 38 16N 8 11W
Torre Annunziata 64 40 45N 14 26E
Tôrre de Moncorvo 56 41 12N 7 8W
Torre del Greco 65 40 47N 14 22E
Torre del Mar 57 36 44N 4 6W
Torre-Pacheco 29 37 44N 0 57W
Torre Pellice 62 44 49N 7 13E
Torreblanca 58 40 14N 0 12E
Torrecampo 57 38 29N 4 41W
Torrecilla en Cameros 58 42 15N 2 38W
Torredembarra 58 41 9N 1 24W
Torredonjimeno 57 37 46N 3 57W
Torrejoncillo 56 39 54N 6 28W
Torrelaguna 58 40 50N 3 38W
Torrelavega 56 43 20N 4 5W
Torremaggiore 65 41 42N 15 17E
Torremolinos 57 36 38N 4 30W
Torrens Cr. 138 22 23S 145 9E
Torrens Creek 138 20 48S 145 3E
Torrens, L. 140 31 0S 137 50E
Torrente 59 39 27N 0 28W
Torrenueva 59 38 38N 3 22W
Torreón 164 25 33N 103 25W
Torreperogil 59 38 2N 3 17W
Torres, Mexico 164 28 46N 110 47W
Torres, Spain 56 41 6N 5 0W
Tôrres Novas 57 39 27N 8 33W
Torres Strait 135 9 50S 142 20E
Torres Vedras 57 39 5N 9 15W
Torrevieja 59 37 59N 0 42W
Torrey 161 38 12N 111 30W
Torridge, R. 30 50 51N 4 10W
Torridon 36 57 33N 5 34W
Torridon, L. 36 57 35N 5 50W
Torrijos 56 39 59N 4 18W
Törring 73 55 52N 9 29E
Torrington, Conn., U.S.A. 162 41 50N 73 9W
Torrington, Wyo., U.S.A. 158 42 5N 104 8W
Torroboll 37 58 0N 4 23W
Torroella de Montgri 58 42 2N 3 8E
Torrox 57 36 46N 3 57W
Torsås 73 56 24N 16 0E
Torsby 72 60 7N 13 0E
Torsjok 72 57 5N 34 55E
Torsö 73 58 48N 13 45E
Torthorwald 35 55 7N 3 30W
Tortola, I. 147 18 19N 65 0W
Tórtoles de Esgueva 56 41 49N 4 2W
Tortona 62 44 53N 8 54E
Tortoreto 63 42 50N 13 55E
Tortorici 65 38 2N 14 48E
Tortosa 58 40 49N 0 31E
Tortosa C. 58 40 41N 0 52E
Tortosendo 56 40 15N 7 31W
Tortue, I. de la 167 20 5N 72 57W
Tortuga, Isla la 167 11 8N 67 2W
Torud 93 35 25N 55 5E
Torugart, Pereval 85 40 32N 75 24E
Torun 54 53 0N 18 39E
Torup 73 56 57N 13 5E
Torvastad 71 59 23N 5 15E
Torver 32 54 20N 3 7W
Tory I. 38 55 17N 8 12W
Torysa, R. 53 48 50N 21 15E
Torzhok 80 57 5N 34 55E
Tosa 110 33 24N 133 23E
Tosa-shimizu 110 32 52N 132 58E
Tosa-Wan 110 33 15N 133 30E
Tosa-yamada 110 33 36N 133 38E
Toscaig 36 57 23N 5 49W
Toscana 62 43 30N 11 5E
Tosno 80 59 30N 30 58E
Töss, R. 51 47 32N 8 39E
Tossa 58 41 43N 2 56E
Tostado 172 29 15S 61 50W
Tostedt 48 53 17N 9 42E
Tosu 110 33 22N 130 31E
Toszek 54 50 27N 18 32E
Totak 71 59 40N 7 45E
Totana 59 37 45N 1 30W
Toten 71 60 37N 10 53E
Toteng 128 20 22S 22 58E
Tôtes 42 49 41N 1 3E
Totland 28 50 41N 1 32W
Totley 33 53 18N 1 32W
Totma 81 60 0N 42 40E
Totnes 30 50 26N 3 41W
Totonicapán 166 14 50N 91 20W
Totskoye 84 52 32N 52 45E
Tottenham 141 32 14S 147 21E
Totton 28 50 55N 1 29W
Tottori 110 35 30N 134 15E
Tottori-ken □ 110 35 30N 134 12E
Touamotou, Archipel des 131 17 0S 144 0W
Touat 118 27 30N 0 30E
Touba 120 8 15N 7 40W
Toubkal, Djebel 118 31 0N 8 0W
Toubouai, Îles 131 25 0S 150 0W
Toucy 43 47 44N 3 15E
Tougan 120 13 11N 2 58W
Touggourt 119 33 10N 6 0E
Tougué 120 11 25N 11 50W
Toukmatine 119 24 49N 7 11E
Toul 43 48 40N 5 53E
Toulepleu 120 6 32N 8 24W
Toulon 45 43 10N 5 55E
Toulouse 44 43 37N 1 27E
Toummo 119 22 45N 14 8E
Toummo Dhoba 119 22 30N 14 31E
Toumodi 120 6 32N 5 4W
Tounan 109 23 41N 120 28E
Tounassine, Hamada 118 28 48N 5 0W
Toungoo 98 19 0N 96 30E
Touques, R. 42 49 22N 0 8E
Touquet, Le 43 50 30N 1 36E
Tour-du-Pin, La 45 45 33N 5 27E
Touraine 42 47 20N 0 30E
Tourane = Da Nang 100 16 4N 108 13E
Tourcoing 43 50 42N 3 10E
Tourcoingbam 121 13 23N 1 33W
Tournai 47 50 35N 3 25E
Tournan-en-Brie 43 48 44N 2 46E
Tournay 44 43 13N 0 13E
Tournon 45 45 4N 4 50E
Tournon-St.-Martin 42 46 45N 0 58E
Tournus 45 46 35N 4 54E
Touros 170 5 12S 35 28W
Tours 42 47 22N 0 40E
Touside, Pic 119 21 1N 16 18E
T'outaokou 107 42 44N 129 12E
Touwsrivier 128 33 20S 20 0E
Tovar 174 8 20N 71 46W
Tovarkovskiy 81 53 40N 38 5E
Tovdal 71 58 47N 8 10E
Tovdalselva 71 58 20N 8 16E
Towamba 141 37 6S 149 43E
Towanda 162 41 46N 76 30W
Towcester 29 52 7N 0 56W
Tower 158 47 49N 92 17W
Towerhill Cr. 138 22 28S 144 35E
Town Yetholm 35 55 33N 2 19W
Towner 158 48 25N 100 26W
Townsend 160 46 25N 111 32W
Townshend, C. 133 22 18S 150 30E
Townshend, I. 138 22 16S 150 31E
Townsville 138 19 15S 146 45E
Towson 162 39 26N 76 34W
Toyah 159 31 20N 103 48W
Toyahvale 159 30 58N 103 45W
Toyama 111 36 40N 137 15E
Toyama-ken □ 111 36 45N 137 30E
Tōyō 110 33 26N 134 16E
Toyohashi 111 34 45N 137 25E
Toyokawa 111 34 48N 137 27E
Toyonaka 111 34 50N 135 28E
Toyooka 110 35 35N 134 55E
Toyota 111 35 3N 137 7E
Toyoura 110 34 6N 130 57E
Toytepa 85 41 3N 69 20E
Tozeur 119 33 56N 8 8E
Tra On 101 9 58N 105 55E
Trabancos, R. 56 41 0N 5 3E
Trabzon 92 41 0N 39 45E
Tracadie 151 47 30N 64 55W
Tracy, Calif., U.S.A. 163 37 46N 121 27W
Tracy, Minn., U.S.A. 158 44 12N 95 3W
Tradate 62 45 43N 8 54E
Trafalgar 141 38 14S 146 12E
Trafalgar, C. 57 36 10N 6 2W
Traghan 119 26 0N 14 30E
Traian 70 45 2N 28 15E
Trail 152 49 5N 117 40W
Trainor L. 152 60 24N 120 17W
Traipu 171 9 58S 37 1W
Tralee 39 52 16N 9 42W
Tralee B. 39 52 17N 9 55W
Tramelan 50 47 13N 7 7E
Tramore 39 52 10N 7 10W
Tramore B. 39 52 9N 7 10W
Tran Ninh, Cao Nguyen 100 19 30N 103 10E
Tranas 73 58 3N 14 59E
Tranås 73 55 37N 13 59E
Trancas 172 26 20S 65 20W
Tranche-sur-Mer, La 42 46 20N 1 27W
Trancoso 56 40 49N 7 21W
Tranebjerg 73 55 51N 10 36E
Tranemo 73 57 30N 13 20E
Tranent 35 55 57N 2 58W
Trang 101 7 33N 99 38E
Trangahy 129 19 7S 44 43E
Trangan, I. 103 6 40S 134 20E
Trangie 141 32 4S 148 0E
Trångsviken 72 63 19N 14 0E
Trani 65 41 17N 16 24E
Tranoroa 129 24 42S 45 4E
Tranquebar 97 11 1N 79 54E
Tranqueras 173 31 8S 56 0W
Trans Nzoia □ 126 1 0N 35 0E
Transcona 153 49 50N 97 0W
Transilvania 70 46 19N 25 0E
Transkei □ 129 32 15S 28 15E
Transtrand 72 61 6N 13 20E
Transvaal □ 128 25 0S 29 0E
Transylvania = Transilvania 70 46 19N 25 0E
Transylvanian Alps 70 45 30N 25 0E
Trápani 64 38 1N 12 30E
Trappe Peak, Mt. 160 45 56N 114 29W
Traqowel 140 35 50S 144 0E
Traralgon 141 38 12S 146 34E
Traryd 73 56 35N 13 45E
Trarza □ 120 17 30N 15 0W
Tras os Montes e Alto-Douro □ 55 41 25N 7 20W
Trasacco 63 41 58N 13 30E
Trasimeno, L. 63 43 10N 12 5E
Träslöv 73 57 8N 12 21E
Trat 101 12 14N 102 33E
Traun 52 48 14N 14 15E
Traun-see 49 47 48N 13 45E
Traunstein 49 47 52N 12 40E
Trävad 73 58 15N 13 5E
Traveller's L. 140 33 20S 142 0E
Travemünde 48 53 58N 10 52E
Travers, Mt. 143 42 1S 172 45E
Traverse City 156 44 45N 85 39W
Traverse I. 13 48 0S 28 0E
Travnik 66 44 17N 17 39E
Trawbreaga B. 38 55 20N 7 25W
Trawsfynydd 31 52 54N 3 55W
Trayning 137 31 7S 117 46E
Traynor 153 52 20N 108 32W
Trazo 56 43 0N 8 30W
Trbovlje 63 46 12N 15 5E
Trebbia, R. 62 44 52N 9 30E
Trebel, R. 48 54 0N 12 50E
Trebinje 66 42 44N 18 22E
Trebisacce 65 39 52N 16 32E
Trebišnica, R. 66 42 47N 18 8E
Trebišov 53 48 38N 21 41E
Trebizat 66 43 15N 17 30E
Třebon 52 48 59N 14 48E
Trebujena 57 36 52N 6 11W
Trecate 62 45 29N 8 42E
Tredegar 31 51 47N 3 16W
Trefeglwys 31 52 31N 3 31W
Trefriw 31 53 9N 3 50W
Tregaron 31 52 14N 3 56W
Trégastel-Plage 42 48 49N 3 31W
Tregnago 63 45 31N 11 10E

Tregrasse Is Tullow

Tregrasse Is.	138	17 41 S	150 43 E
Tréguier	42	48 47N	3 16W
Trégunc	42	47 51N	3 51W
Tregynon	31	52 32N	3 19W
Treharris	31	51 40N	3 17W
Treherne	153	49 38N	98 42W
Trêia	63	43 30N	13 20 E
Treig, L.	37	56 48N	4 42W
Treignac	44	45 32N	1 48 E
Treinta y Tres	173	33 10 S	54 50W
Treis	49	50 9N	7 19 E
Trekveid	128	30 35 S	19 45 E
Trelde Næs	73	55 38N	9 53 E
Trelech	31	51 56N	4 28W
Trelew	176	43 10 S	65 20W
Trélissac	44	45 11N	0 47 E
Trelleborg	73	55 20N	13 10 E
Trélon	43	50 5N	4 6 E
Tremadoc	31	52 57N	4 9W
Tremadoc, Bay	31	52 51N	4 18W
Tremblade, La	44	45 46N	1 8W
Tremelo	47	51 0N	4 42 E
Trementina	159	35 27N	105 30W
Tremiti, I.	63	42 8N	15 30 E
Tremonton	160	41 45N	112 10W
Tremp	58	42 10N	0 52 E
Trenary	156	46 12N	86 59W
Trenčin	53	48 52N	18 4 E
Trenche, R.	150	47 46N	72 53W
Trenggalek	103	8 5 S	111 44 E
Trenque Lauquen	172	36 0 S	62 45W
Trent, R.	33	53 33N	0 44W
Trentham	32	52 59N	2 12W
Trentino-Alto Adige □	62	46 5N	11 0 E
Trento	62	46 5N	11 8 E
Trenton, Can.	150	44 10N	77 40W
Trenton, Mo., U.S.A.	158	40 5N	93 37W
Trenton, Nebr., U.S.A.	158	40 14N	101 4W
Trenton, N.J., U.S.A.	162	40 15N	74 41W
Trenton, Tenn., U.S.A.	159	35 58N	88 57W
Trepassey	151	46 43N	53 25W
Tréport, Le	42	50 3N	1 20 E
Treptow	48	53 42N	13 15 E
Trepuzzi	65	40 26N	18 4 E
Tres Arroyos	172	38 20 S	60 20W
Três Corações	173	21 30 S	45 30W
Três Lagoas	171	20 50 S	51 50W
Tres Marías, Is.	164	21 25N	106 28W
Três Marias, Reprêsa	171	18 12 S	45 15W
Tres Montes, C.	176	47 0 S	75 35W
Tres Pinos	163	36 48N	121 19W
Três Pontas	173	21 23 S	45 29W
Tres Puentes	172	27 50 S	70 15W
Três Puntas, C.	176	47 0 S	66 0W
Tres Rios	173	22 20 S	43 30W
Tres Valles	165	18 15N	96 8W
Tresco I.	30	49 57N	6 20W
Treshnish Is.	34	56 30N	6 25W
Treska, R.	66	41 45N	21 11 E
Treskavika Planina	66	43 40N	18 20 E
Trespaderne	58	42 47N	3 24W
Tretower	31	51 53N	3 11W
Trets	45	43 27N	5 41 E
Treuchtlingen	49	48 58N	10 55 E
Treuddyn	31	53 7N	3 8W
Treuenbrietzen	48	52 6N	12 51 E
Treungen	75	59 1N	8 31 E
Treviglio	62	45 31N	9 35 E
Trevinca, Peña	56	42 15N	6 46W
Treviso	63	45 40N	12 15 E
Trevose Hd.	30	50 33N	5 3W
Trévoux	45	45 57N	4 47 E
Trgovište	66	42 20N	22 10 E
Triabunna	138	42 30 S	147 55 E
Triánda	69	36 25N	28 10 E
Triang	101	3 13N	102 27 E
Triangle	162	38 33N	77 20W
Triaucourt-en-Argonne	43	48 59N	5 2 E
Tribsees	48	54 4N	12 46 E
Tribulation, C.	138	16 5 S	145 29 E
Tribune	158	38 30N	101 45W
Tricárico	65	40 37N	16 9 E
Tricase	65	39 56N	18 20 E
Trichinopoly = Tiruchchirappalli	97	10 45N	78 45 E
Trichur	97	10 30N	76 18 E
Trida	141	33 1 S	145 1 E
Trier	49	49 45N	6 37 E
Trieste	63	45 39N	13 45 E
Trieste, G. di	63	45 37N	13 40 E
Triggiano	65	41 4N	16 58 E
Triglav	63	46 30N	13 45 E
Trigno, R.	63	41 55N	14 37 E
Trigueros	57	37 24N	6 50W
Trikeri	69	39 6N	23 5 E
Trikhonis, Límni	69	38 34N	21 30 E
Tríkkala	68	39 34N	21 47 E
Trikkala □	68	39 41N	21 30 E
Trikora, G.	103	4 11 S	138 0 E
Trilj	63	43 38N	16 42 E
Trillick	38	54 27N	7 30W
Trillo	58	40 42N	2 35W
Trim	38	53 34N	6 48W
Trimdon	33	54 43N	1 23W
Trimley	29	51 59N	1 19 E
Trincomalee	97	8 38N	81 15 E
Trindade	171	16 40 S	49 30W
Trindade, I.	15	20 20 S	29 50W
Trinidad, Boliv.	174	14 54 S	64 50W
Trinidad, Colomb.	174	5 25N	71 40W
Trinidad, Cuba	166	21 40N	80 0W
Trinidad, Uruguay	172	33 30 S	56 50W
Trinidad, U.S.A.	159	37 15N	104 30W
Trinidad & Tobago ■	167	10 30N	61 20W
Trinidad, I., Argent.	176	39 10 S	62 0W
Trinidad, I., S. Amer.	167	10 30N	61 15W
Trinidad, R.	165	17 49N	95 9W
Trinitápoli	65	41 22N	16 5 E
Trinity, Can.	151	48 22N	53 29W
Trinity, U.S.A.	159	30 50N	95 20W
Trinity B., Austral.	133	16 30 S	146 0 E
Trinity B., Can.	151	48 20N	53 10W
Trinity Mts.	159	40 20N	118 50W
Trinity R.	159	30 30N	95 0W
Trino	62	45 10N	8 18 E
Trion	157	34 35N	85 18W
Trionto C.	65	34 38N	16 47 E
Triora	62	44 0N	7 46 E
Tripoli = Tarabulus	92	34 31N	33 52 E
Tripoli = Tarābulus	119	32 49N	13 7 E
Tripolis	69	37 31N	22 25 E
Tripp	158	43 16N	97 58W
Tripura □	98	24 0N	92 0 E
Trischen, I.	48	54 3N	8 32 E
Tristan da Cunha, I.	15	37 6 S	12 20W
Trivandrum	97	8 31N	77 0 E
Trivento	65	41 48N	14 31 E
Trnava	53	48 23N	17 35 E
Trobriand Is.	135	8 30 S	151 0 E
Trochu	152	51 50N	113 13W
Trodely I.	150	52 15N	79 26W
Trogir	63	43 32N	16 15 E
Troglav, mt.	63	43 56N	16 36 E
Trögstad	71	59 37N	11 16 E
Tróia	65	41 22N	15 19 E
Troilus, L.	150	50 50N	74 35W
Troina	65	37 47N	14 34 E
Trois Fourches, Cap des	118	35 26N	2 58W
Trois Pistoles	151	48 5N	69 10W
Trois-Riviéres	150	46 25N	72 40W
Troisvierges	47	50 8N	6 0 E
Troitsk	84	54 10N	61 35 E
Troitskiy	84	55 29N	37 18 E
Troitsko-Pechorsk	78	62 40N	56 10 E
Trölladyngja	74	64 54N	17 15W
Trolladyngja	74	64 49N	17 29W
Trollhättan	73	58 17N	12 20 E
Trollheimen	71	62 46N	9 1 E
Tromöy	71	58 28N	8 53 E
Troms fylke □	74	68 56N	19 0 E
Tromsø	74	69 40N	18 56 E
Trona	163	35 46N	117 23W
Tronador, Mt.	176	41 53 S	71 0W
Tröndelag, N. □	74	65 0N	12 0 E
Tröndelag, S. □	71	62 0N	10 0 E
Trondheim	71	63 25N	10 25 E
Trondheimsfjorden	74	63 35N	10 30 E
Trönninge	73	56 38N	12 59 E
Trönö	72	61 22N	16 54 E
Tronto, R.	63	42 50N	13 46 E
Troodos, mt.	128	34 58N	32 55 E
Troon	34	55 33N	4 40W
Tropea	65	38 40N	15 53 E
Tropic	161	37 44N	112 4W
Tropoja	68	42 23N	20 10 E
Trossachs, The	34	56 14N	4 24W
Trostan Mt.	38	55 4N	6 10W
Trostberg	49	48 2N	12 33 E
Trotternish, dist.	36	57 32N	6 15W
Troup	159	32 10N	95 3W
Troup Hd.	37	57 41N	2 18W
Trout L., N.W. Terr., Can.	152	60 40N	121 40W
Trout L., Ont., Can.	153	51 20N	93 15W
Trout Lake	150	46 10N	85 2W
Trout, R.	152	61 19N	119 51W
Trout River	151	49 29N	58 8W
Trout Run	162	41 23N	77 3W
Trouville	42	49 21N	0 5 E
Trowbridge	28	51 18N	2 12W
Troy, Turkey	92	39 55N	26 20 E
Troy, Alabama, U.S.A.	157	31 50N	85 58W
Troy, Kans., U.S.A.	158	39 47N	95 2W
Troy, Mo., U.S.A.	158	38 56N	90 59W
Trøy, Montana, U.S.A.	160	48 30N	115 58W
Troy, N.Y., U.S.A.	162	42 45N	73 39W
Troy, Ohio, U.S.A.	156	40 0N	84 10W
Troy, Pa., U.S.A.	162	41 47N	76 47W
Troyan	67	42 57N	24 43 E
Troyes	43	48 19N	4 3 E
Trpanj	66	43 1N	17 15 E
Trstena	53	49 21N	19 37 E
Trstenik	66	43 36N	21 0 E
Trubchevsk	80	52 33N	33 47 E
Truc Giang	101	10 14N	106 22 E
Trucial States = Utd. Arab Emirates	93	24 0N	54 30 E
Truckee	160	39 20N	120 11W
Trujillo, Colomb.	174	4 10N	76 19W
Trujillo, Hond.	166	16 0N	86 0W
Trujillo, Peru	174	8 0 S	79 0W
Trujillo, Spain	57	39 28N	5 55W
Trujillo, U.S.A.	159	35 34N	104 44W
Trujillo, Venez.	174	9 22N	70 26W
Truk Is.	131	7 25N	151 46 E
Trull	28	50 58N	3 8W
Trumann	159	35 42N	90 32W
Trumansburg	162	42 33N	76 40W
Trumbull, Mt.	161	36 25N	113 32W
Trumpington	29	52 11N	0 6 E
Trún	66	42 51N	22 38 E
Trun, France	42	48 50N	0 2 E
Trun, Switz.	51	46 45N	8 59 E
Trundle	141	32 53 S	147 42 E
Trung-Phan, reg.	100	16 0N	108 0 E
Truro, Austral.	140	34 24 S	139 9 E
Truro, Can.	151	45 21N	63 14 E
Truro, U.K.	30	50 17N	5 2W
Trûscău, Muntii	70	46 14N	23 14 E
Truskmore, mt.	38	54 23N	8 20W
Truslove	137	33 20 S	121 45 E
Trustrup	73	56 20N	10 46 E
Truth or Consequences	161	33 9N	107 16W
Trutnov	52	50 37N	15 54 E
Truxton	162	42 45N	76 2W
Truyère, R.	44	44 38N	2 34 E
Trwyn Cilan	31	52 47N	4 31W
Tryavna	67	42 54N	25 25 E
Tryon	157	35 15N	82 16W
Trzciarka	54	53 3N	16 25 E
Trzciel	54	52 23N	15 50 E
Trzcinsko-Zdroj	54	52 58N	14 35 E
Trzebiez	54	53 38N	14 31 E
Trzebinia	54	50 11N	19 30 E
Trzeblatów	54	54 3N	15 18 E
Trzebnica	54	51 20N	17 1 E
Trzemeszno	54	52 33N	17 48 E
Trzič	63	46 22N	14 18 E
Tsafriya	90	31 59N	34 51 E
Tsaidam	105	37 0N	95 0 E
Tsak'o	108	31 56N	99 35 E
Tsamandás	68	39 46N	20 21 E
Tsamkong = Chanchiang	109	21 15N	110 20 E
Tsana Dzong	99	28 0N	91 55 E
Tsanga	99	30 43N	100 32 E
Ts'angchi	108	31 48N	105 57 E
Ts'angchou	106	38 10N	116 50 E
Tsangpo	99	29 40N	89 0 E
Ts'angyüan	108	23 9N	99 15 E
Ts'ao Ho, R.	107	40 32N	124 11 E
Tsaochuang	107	34 30N	117 49 E
Tsaochwang	174	35 11N	115 28 E
Ts'aohsien	106	34 50N	115 31 E
Tsaoyang	109	32 8N	112 42 E
Tsaratanana	129	16 47 S	47 39 E
Tsaratanana, Mt. de	129	14 0 S	49 0 E
Tsarevo = Michurin	67	42 9N	27 51 E
Tsaring Nor	99	34 40N	97 20 E
Tsaritsáni	68	39 53N	15 14 E
Tsau	128	20 8 S	22 29 E
Tsaukaib	128	26 37 S	15 39 E
Tsebrikovo	82	47 9N	30 10 E
Ts'ehung	108	25 2N	105 47 E
Tselinograd	76	51 10N	71 30 E
Tsengch'eng	109	23 17N	113 49 E
Ts'enkung	108	27 13N	108 45 E
Tsetserleg	105	47 36N	101 32 E
Tshabong	128	26 2 S	22 29 E
Tshane	125	24 5 S	21 54 E
Tshela	124	5 4 S	13 0 E
Tshesebe	129	20 43 S	27 32 E
Tshhinvali	83	42 14N	44 1 E
Tshibeke	126	2 40 S	28 35 E
Tshibinda	126	2 23 S	28 30 E
Tshikapa	124	6 17 S	21 0 E
Tshilenge	126	6 12 S	23 40 E
Tshinsenda	127	12 15N	28 0 E
Tshofa	124	5 8 S	25 8 E
Tshombe	129	25 18 S	45 29 E
Tshwane	128	22 24 S	22 1 E
Tsigara	128	20 22 S	25 54 E
Tsihombe	125	25 10 S	45 41 E
Tsilmamo	123	6 1N	35 10 E
Tsimlyansk	83	47 45N	42 0 E
Tsimlyanskoye Vdkhr.	83	48 0N	43 0 E
Tsinan = Chinan	106	36 32N	117 0 E
Tsineng	128	27 05 S	23 05 E
Tsinga, mt.	68	41 23N	24 44 E
Tsinghai □	105	36 0N	96 0 E
Tsingtao = Ch'ingtao	107	36 5N	120 25 E
Tsinjomitondraka	129	15 40 S	47 8 E
Tsiroanomandidy	129	18 46 S	46 2 E
Tsivilsk	81	55 50N	47 25 E
Tsivory	129	24 4 S	46 5 E
Tskhinali	79	42 22N	43 52 E
Tso Chiang, R.	108	22 52N	108 5 E
Tso Morari, L.	95	32 50N	78 20 E
Tsochou	108	22 36N	107 36 E
Tsoch'üan	106	37 3N	113 27 E
Tsodilo Hill	128	18 49 S	21 43 E
Tsogttsetsiy	106	43 43N	105 35 E
Tsokung	108	29 55N	97 44 E
Tsona Dzong	99	28 0N	91 55 E
Tsoshui	106	33 40N	109 9 E
Tsouhsien	106	35 24N	116 58 E
Tsu	111	34 45N	136 25 E
Tsu L.	152	60 40N	111 52W
Tsuchiura	111	36 12N	140 15 E
Tsugaru-Kaikyō	112	41 35N	141 0 E
Tsukumi	110	33 4N	131 52 E
Tsukushi-Sanchi	110	33 25N	130 30 E
Tsumeb	128	19 9 S	17 44 E
Tsumis	128	23 39 S	17 29 E
Tsuna	110	34 28N	134 56 E
Ts'ungchiang	108	25 45N	108 54 E
Tsunhua	107	40 12N	117 56 E
Tsuni	108	27 43N	106 52 E
Tsuno-Shima	110	34 21N	130 52 E
Tsuru	111	35 31N	138 57 E
Tsuruga	111	35 45N	136 2 E
Tsuruga-Wan	111	35 50N	136 3 E
Tsurugi	111	36 37N	136 37 E
Tsurugi-San	110	33 51N	134 6 E
Tsurumi-Saki	110	32 56N	132 5 E
Tsuruoka	112	38 44N	139 50 E
Tsurusaki	110	33 14N	131 41 E
Tsushima	111	35 10N	136 43 E
Tsushima, I.	110	34 20N	129 20 E
Tsvetkovo	82	49 15N	31 33 E
Tu, R.	98	22 50N	97 15 E
Tua, R.	57	41 19N	7 15W
Tuai	143	38 47 S	177 15 E
Tuakau	142	37 16 S	174 59 E
Tual	103	5 30 S	132 50 E
Tuam	38	53 30N	8 50W
Tuamarina	143	41 25 S	173 59 E
Tuamgraney	39	52 54N	8 32W
Tuamotu Arch = Touamotou	131	17 0 S	144 0W
Tuan	108	23 59N	108 3 E
T'uanch'i	108	27 28N	107 7 E
T'uanfeng	109	30 38N	114 52 E
Tuao	103	17 47 S	121 30 E
Tuapse	83	44 5N	39 10 E
Tuatapere	143	46 8 S	167 41 E
Tuath, Loch	34	56 30N	6 15W
Tuba City	161	36 8N	111 12W
Tubac	161	31 45N	111 2W
Tubai Is. = Toubouai, Îles	131	25 0 S	150 0W
Tuban	102	6 57 S	112 4 E
Tubarão	173	28 30 S	49 0W
Tubas	90	32 20N	35 22 E
Tubau	102	3 10N	113 40 E
Tubayq, Jabal at	122	29 30N	27 30 E
Tubbergen	46	52 24N	6 48 E
Tübingen	48	48 31N	9 4 E
Tubize	47	50 42N	4 13 E
Tubja, W.	122	25 27N	38 55 E
Tubruq, (Tobruk)	117	32 7N	23 55 E
Tubuai, Îles	131	25 0 S	150 0W
Tuc Trung	101	11 1N	107 12 E
Tucacas	174	10 48N	68 19W
Tucano	170	10 58 S	38 48W
Tuch'ang	109	29 15N	116 13 E
T'uch'ang	109	24 42N	121 25 E
Tuchodi, R.	152	58 17N	123 42W
Tuchola	54	53 33N	17 52 E
Tuchów	54	49 54N	21 1 E
T'uch'üan	107	45 22N	121 41 E
Tuckanarra	137	27 8 S	118 1 E
Tuckernuck I.	162	41 15N	70 17W
Tucson	161	32 14N	110 59W
Tucumán	172	26 50 S	65 20W
Tucumán □	172	26 48 S	66 2W
Tucumcari	159	35 12N	103 45W
Tucupido	174	9 17N	65 47W
Tucupita	174	9 14N	62 3W
Tucuracas	174	11 45N	72 22W
Tucuruí	170	3 42 S	49 27W
Tuczno	54	53 13N	16 10 E
Tudela	58	42 4N	1 39W
Tudela de Duero	56	41 37N	4 39W
Tudor, Lac	151	55 50N	65 25W
Tudora	70	47 31N	26 45 E
Tudweiliog	31	52 54N	4 37W
Tuella, R.	56	41 50N	7 10W
Tuen	139	28 33 S	145 37 E
Tueré, R.	170	2 48 S	50 59W
Tufi	135	9 8 S	149 19 E
Tugidak I.	147	56 30N	154 40W
Tuguegarao	103	17 35N	121 42 E
Tugur	77	53 50N	136 45 E
Tugwa	128	17 27 S	18 33 E
Tukangbesi, Kepulauan	103	6 0 S	124 0 E
Tukarak I.	150	56 15N	78 45W
Tukobo	120	5 1N	2 47W
Tükrah	119	32 30N	20 37 E
Tuku, mt.	123	9 10N	36 43 E
Tukums	80	57 2N	23 3 E
Tukuyu	127	9 17 S	33 35 E
Tukzar	93	35 55N	66 25 E
Tula, Hidalgo, Mexico	165	20 0N	99 20W
Tula, Tamaulipas, Mexico	165	23 0N	99 40W
Tula, Nigeria	121	9 51N	11 27 E
Tula, U.S.S.R.	81	54 13N	37 32 E
Tulak	93	33 55N	63 40 E
Tulancingo	165	20 5N	98 22W
Tulanssu	105	36 52N	98 24 E
Tulare	163	36 15N	119 26W
Tulare Basin	163	36 0N	119 48W
Tulare Lake	161	36 0N	119 53W
Tularosa	161	33 4N	106 1W
Tulbagh	128	33 16 S	19 6 E
Tulcán	174	0 48N	77 43W
Tulcea	70	45 13N	28 46 E
Tulcea □	70	45 0N	29 0 E
Tulchin	82	48 41N	28 55 E
*Tuléar	129	23 21 S	43 40 E
**Tuléar □	129	21 0 S	45 0 E
Tulemalu L.	153	62 58N	99 25W
Tulgheş	70	4 58N	25 45 E
Tuli, Indon.	103	1 24 S	122 26 E
Tuli, Zimb.	127	21 58 S	29 13 E
Tuliuchen	106	39 1N	116 54 E
Tulkarm	90	32 19N	35 10 E
Tulla, Ireland	39	52 53N	8 45W
Tulla, U.S.A.	159	34 35N	101 44W
Tulla, L.	34	56 33N	4 47W
Tullaghoge	38	54 36N	6 43W
Tullaghought	39	52 25N	7 22W
Tullahoma	157	35 23N	86 12W
Tullamore, Austral.	141	32 39 S	147 36 E
Tullamore, Ireland	39	53 17N	7 30W
Tullaroan	39	52 40N	7 27W
Tulle	44	45 16N	0 47 E
Tullibigeal	141	33 25 S	146 44 E
Tullins	45	45 18N	5 29 E
Tulln	52	48 20N	16 4 E
Tullow	39	52 48N	6 45W

*Renamed Toliara
**Renamed Toliara □

Tullus **Uddingston**

Tullus 123 11 7N 24 40 E
Tully, Austral. 138 17 56 S 145 55 E
Tully, Ireland 38 53 44N 8 9W
Tully, U.S.A. 162 42 48N 76 7W
Tully Cross 38 53 35N 9 59W
Tŭlmaciu 70 45 38N 24 19 E
Tulmaythah 117 32 40N 20 55 E
Tulmur 138 22 40 S 142 20 E
Tulnici 70 45 51N 26 38 E
Tulovo 67 42 33N 25 32 E
Tulsa 159 36 10N 96 0W
Tulsequah 152 58 39N 133 35W
Tulsk 38 53 47N 8 15W
Tulu Milki 123 9 55N 38 14 E
Tulu Welel, Mt. 123 8 56N 35 30 E
Tulua 174 4 6N 76 11W
T'ulufan 105 42 56N 89 10 E
Tulun 77 54 40N 100 10 E
Tulungagung 103 8 5 S 111 54 E
Tum 103 3 28 S 130 21 E
Tuma 81 55 10N 40 30 E
Tuma, R. 166 13 18N 84 50W
Tumaco 174 1 50N 78 45W
Tumatumari 174 5 20N 58 55W
Tumba 72 59 12N 17 48 E
Tumba, L. 124 0 50 S 18 0 E
Tumbarumba 141 35 44 S 148 0 E
Tumbaya 172 23 50 S 65 20W
Tumbes 174 3 30 S 80 20W
Tumbwa 127 11 25 S 27 15 E
Tumby B. 140 34 21 S 136 8 E
T'umen 107 42 55N 129 50 E
T'umen Kiang, R. 107 42 18N 130 41 E
Tumeremo 174 7 18N 61 30W
Tumiritinga 171 18 58 S 41 38W
Tumkur 97 13 18N 77 12 E
Tumleberg 73 58 16N 12 52 E
Tummel, L. 37 56 43N 3 55W
Tummel, R. 37 56 42N 4 5W
T'umot'eyuch'i 106 40 42N 111 8 E
Tump 93 26 7N 62 16 E
Tumpat 101 6 11N 102 10 E
Tumsar 96 21 26N 79 45 E
Tumu 120 10 56N 1 56W
Tumucumaque, Serra de 175 2 0N 55 0W
Tumut 141 35 16 S 148 13 E
Tumutuk 84 55 1N 53 19 E
Tumwater 160 47 0N 122 58W
Tuna, Pta. 147 17 59N 65 53W
Tunas de Zaza 166 21 39N 79 34W
Tunbridge Wells 29 51 7N 0 16 E
T'unch'i 105 29 50N 118 26 E
Tuncurry 141 32 9 S 152 29 E
Tunduru 127 11 0 S 37 25 E
Tunduru □ 127 11 5 S 37 22 E
Tundzha, R. 67 42 0N 26 35 E
Tune 71 59 16N 11 2 E
Tung Chiang, R. 109 22 55N 113 35 E
Tung-Pei 77 44 0N 126 0 E
Tunga La 99 29 0N 94 14 E
Tunga Pass 98 29 0N 94 14 E
Tunga, R. 97 13 42N 75 20 E
Tungabhadra Dam 97 15 21N 76 23 E
Tungabhadra, R. 97 15 30N 77 0 E
Tungachen 106 36 15N 165 12 E
Tungan 109 26 24N 111 17 E
T'ungan 109 24 44N 118 9 E
T'ungcheng, Anhwei, China 109 31 3N 116 58 E
T'ungcheng, Hupeh, China 109 29 15N 113 49 E
Tungch'i 108 28 43N 106 42 E
T'ungchiang, Heilungkiang, China 105 47 40N 132 30 E
T'ungchiang, Szechwan, China 108 31 56N 107 15 E
Tungchingch'eng 107 44 9N 129 7 E
Tungchuan 105 35 4N 109 2 E
T'ungch'uan 106 35 95N 109 5 E
Tungch'uan 108 26 9N 103 7 E
Tungfanghsien, (Paso) 100 18 50N 108 33 E
Tungfeng 107 42 40N 125 34 E
T'unghai 108 24 8N 102 43 E
Tunghai Tao 109 21 2N 110 25 E
Tunghsiang 109 28 14N 116 35 E
T'unghsien 105 39 45N 116 43 E
T'unghsin 106 37 9N 106 28 E
T'unghua 107 41 45N 126 0 E
Tungi 98 23 53N 90 24 E
T'ungjen 105 27 43N 109 10 E
Tungkan 108 23 22N 105 9 E
Tungkou 107 39 52N 124 8 E
Tungku 108 31 52N 100 14 E
T'ungku 109 28 32N 114 23 E
Tungkuan 109 23 0N 113 39 E
T'ungkuan 105 34 37N 110 27 E
Tungkuang 106 37 53N 116 32 E
Tungla 166 13 24N 84 15W
Tunglan 108 24 30N 107 23 E
T'ungliang 108 29 52N 106 2 E
T'ungliao 107 43 37N 122 16 E
Tungling 109 31 0N 117 54 E
Tungliu 109 30 13N 116 55 E
T'unglu 109 29 49N 119 40 E
Tungnafellsjökull 74 64 45N 17 55W
T'ungnan 108 30 14N 105 48 E
Tungning 107 44 3N 131 7 E
T'ungpai 109 32 22N 113 24 E
Tungp'ing 106 35 55N 116 18 E
Tungpu 99 31 42N 98 19 E
Tungshan 109 23 40N 117 31 E
Tungshih 109 24 12N 120 43 E
Tungsten, Can. 152 61 57N 128 16W
Tungsten, U.S.A. 160 40 50N 118 10W
Tungt'ai 109 32 50N 120 46 E
T'ungtao 108 26 21N 109 36 E
T'ungtien 108 26 40N 99 32 E
Tungt'ing Hu 109 29 18N 112 45 E
Tungtzu 108 28 8N 106 49 E
Tunguchumuch'inch'i 106 45 33N 116 50 E
Tunguska, Nizhmaya, R. 77 64 0N 95 0 E
Tunguska, Podkammenaya, R. 77 61 0N 98 0 E
T'ungwei 106 35 18N 105 10 E
T'ungyü 107 44 48N 123 6 E
Tunhua 107 43 20N 128 10 E
Tunhuang 105 40 10N 94 50 E
Tuni 96 17 22N 82 43 E
Tunia 174 2 41N 76 31W
Tunica 159 34 43N 90 23W
Tunis 119 36 50N 10 11 E
Tunis, Golfe de 119 37 0N 10 30 E
Tunisia ■ 119 33 30N 9 10 E
Tunja 174 5 40N 73 25W
Tunkhannock 162 41 32N 75 56W
T'unliu 106 36 19N 112 54 E
Tunnsjøen 74 64 45N 13 25 E
Tuno I. 73 55 58N 10 27 E
T'unpuli Shan 105 35 0N 89 30 E
Tunstall 29 52 7N 1 28 E
Tuntatuliag 147 60 20N 162 45W
Tunungayualuk I. 151 56 0N 61 0W
Tunuyán 172 33 55 S 69 0W
Tunuyán, R. 172 33 33 S 67 30W
Tuolumne 163 37 59N 120 16W
Tuolumne, R. 163 37 36N 121 13W
Tuoy-Khaya 77 62 32N 111 18 E
Tupã 173 21 57 S 50 28W
Tupaciguara 171 18 35 S 48 42W
Tuparro, R. 174 5 0N 68 40W
Tupelo 157 34 15N 88 42W
Tupik 77 54 26N 119 57 E
Tupinambaranas, I. 174 3 0 S 58 0W
Tupirama 170 8 58 S 48 12W
Tupiratins 170 8 23 S 48 8W
Tupiza 172 21 30 S 65 40W
Tupman 163 35 18N 119 21W
Tupper 152 55 32N 120 1W
Tupper L. 156 44 18N 74 30W
Tupungato, Cerro 172 33 15 S 69 50W
Tuque, La 150 47 30N 72 50W
Túquerres 174 1 5N 77 37W
Tur 90 31 47N 35 14 E
Tura, India 98 25 30N 90 16 E
Tura, U.S.S.R. 77 64 20N 99 30 E
Tura, R. 84 57 12N 66 56 E
Turaba, W. 122 21 15N 41 32 E
Turagua, Serranía 174 7 20N 64 35W
Turaiyur 97 11 9N 78 38 E
Turakina 142 40 3 S 175 16 E
Turakirae Hd. 142 41 26 S 174 56 E
Tūrān 93 35 45N 56 50 E
Turan 77 51 38N 101 40 E
Turbenthal 51 47 27N 8 51 E
Tureburg 72 59 30N 17 58 E
Turégano 56 41 9N 4 1W
Turek 54 52 3N 18 30 E
Turen 174 9 17N 69 6W
Turfan Depression 105 42 45N 89 0 E
Turgay 84 49 38N 63 30 E
Turgay, R. 84 48 1N 62 45 E
Tŭrgovishte 67 43 17N 26 38 E
Turgutlu 92 38 30N 27 48 E
Turhal 82 40 24N 36 19 E
Turia, R. 58 39 43N 1 0W
Turiaçl 170 1 40 S 45 28W
Turiaçl, R. 170 3 0 S 46 0W
Turigshih 100 18 42N 109 27 E
Turin = Torino 62 45 3N 7 40 E
Turin Taber 152 49 47N 112 24W
Turinsk 84 58 3N 63 42 E
Turkana □ 126 3 0N 35 30 E
Turkana, L. 80 4 10N 32 10 E
Turkestan 76 43 10N 68 10 E
Turkestanskiy, Khrebet 85 39 35N 69 0 E
Túrkeve 53 47 6N 20 44 E
Turkey ■ 92 39 0N 36 0 E
Turkey Creek P.O. 136 17 2 S 128 12 E
Turki 81 52 0N 43 15 E
Turkmen S.S.R. □ 85 39 0N 59 0 E
Turks Is. 167 21 20N 71 20W
Turks Island Passage 167 21 30N 71 20W
Turku (Åbo) 75 60 30N 22 19 E
Turku-Pori □ 75 60 27N 22 15 E
Turkwell, R. 126 2 30N 35 20 E
Turlock 163 37 30N 120 55W
Turnagain, C. 142 40 28 S 176 38 E
Turnagain, R. 152 59 12N 127 35W
Turnberry, Can. 153 53 25N 101 45W
Turnberry, U.K. 34 55 19N 4 50W
Turneffe Is. 165 17 20N 87 50W
Turner 160 48 52N 108 25W
Turner Pt. 138 11 47 S 133 32 E
Turner River 136 17 52 S 128 16 E
Turner Valley 152 50 40N 114 17W
Turners Falls 162 42 36N 72 34W
Turnhout 47 51 19N 4 57 E
Türnitz 52 47 55N 15 29 E
Turnor L. 153 56 35N 108 35W
Turnov 52 50 34N 15 10 E
Turnovo 67 43 5N 25 41 E
Turnovo □ 67 43 4N 25 39 E
Turnu Mǎgurele 70 43 46N 24 56 E
Turnu Roşu Pasul 70 45 33N 24 17 E
Turnu-Severin 70 44 39N 22 41 E
Turö 73 55 2N 10 40 E
Turon 159 37 48N 98 27W
Tuross Head 141 36 3 S 150 8 E
Turriff 37 57 32N 2 28W
Tursha 81 56 50N 47 45 E
Tursi 65 40 15N 16 27 E
Turtle Hd. I. 138 10 50 S 142 37 E
Turtle L., Can. 153 53 36N 108 38W
Turtle L., N.D., U.S.A. 158 47 30N 100 55W
Turtle L., Wis., U.S.A. 158 45 22N 92 10W
Turtleford 153 53 23N 108 57W
Turua 142 37 14 S 175 35 E
Turubah 92 28 20N 43 15 E
Turukhansk 77 65 50N 87 50 E
Turun ja Porin lääni □ 75 60 27N 22 15 E
Turzovka 53 49 25N 18 41 E
Tuscaloosa 157 33 13N 87 31W
Tuscánia 63 42 25N 11 53 E
Tuscany = Toscana 62 43 28N 11 15 E
Tuscola, Ill., U.S.A. 156 39 48N 88 15W
Tuscola, Tex., U.S.A. 159 32 15N 99 48W
Tuscumbia 157 34 42N 87 42W
Tushan 106 25 50N 107 33 E
Tushino 81 55 44N 37 29 E
Tuskar Rock 39 52 12N 6 10W
Tuskegee 157 32 24N 85 39W
Tŭšnad 70 47 30N 22 33 E
Tustna 71 63 10N 8 5 E
Tuszyn 54 51 36N 19 33 E
Tutaryd 73 56 54N 13 59 E
Tutbury 28 52 52N 1 41W
Tutikorin 97 8 50N 78 12 E
Tutin 66 43 0N 20 20 E
Tutóia 170 2 45 S 42 20W
Tutoko Mt. 143 44 35 S 168 1 E
Tutong 102 4 47N 114 34 E
Tutova, R. 70 46 20N 27 30 E
Tutrakan 67 44 2N 26 40 E
Tutshi L. 152 59 56N 134 30W
Tuttlingen 49 47 59N 8 50 E
Tutuaia 103 8 25 S 127 15 E
Tutye 140 35 12 S 141 29 E
Tuva, A.S.S.R. □ 77 51 30N 95 0 E
Tuxford 33 53 14N 0 52W
Tuxpan 165 20 50N 97 30W
Tuxtla Gutiérrez 165 16 50N 93 10W
Tuy 56 42 3N 8 39W
Tuy An 100 13 17N 109 16 E
Tuy Doc 101 12 15N 107 27 E
Tuy Hoa 100 13 5N 109 17 E
Tuy Phong 101 11 14N 108 43 E
Tuya L. 152 59 7N 130 35W
Tuyen Hoa 100 17 50N 106 10 E
Tuyen Quang 100 21 50N 105 10 E
Tuymazy 84 54 36N 53 42 E
Tuyun 108 26 15N 107 32 E
Tuz Gölü 92 38 45N 33 30 E
Tuz Khurmatli 92 34 52N 44 41 E
Tuz Khurmatu 92 34 50N 44 45 E
Tuzkan, Ozero 85 40 35N 67 28 E
Tuzla 66 44 34N 18 41 E
Tuzlov, R. 83 47 28N 39 45 E
Tvåaker 73 57 4N 12 25 E
Tværsted 73 57 36N 10 12 E
Tvarskog 73 56 34N 16 0 E
Tved 73 56 12N 10 25 E
Tvedestrand 71 58 38N 8 58 E
Tveitsund 71 59 2N 8 31 E
Tvelt 71 60 30N 7 11 E
Tvyrditsa 67 42 42N 25 53 E
Twain Harte 163 38 2N 120 14W
Twardogóra 54 51 23N 17 28 E
Twatt 37 59 6N 3 15W
Tweed, R. 35 55 42N 2 10W
Tweede Exploërmond 46 52 55N 6 56 E
Tweedmouth 35 55 46N 2 1W
Tweedshaws 35 55 26N 3 29W
Tweedsmuir Prov. Park 152 52 55N 126 20W
Twello 46 52 14N 6 6 E
Twelve Pins 38 53 32N 9 50W
Twentynine Palms 163 34 10N 116 4W
Twillingate 151 49 42N 54 45W
Twin Bridges 160 45 33N 112 23W
Twin Falls 160 42 30N 114 30W
Twin Valley 158 47 18N 96 15W
Twinnge 98 21 58N 96 23 E
Twisp 160 48 21N 120 5W
Twistringen 48 52 48N 8 38 E
Two Harbors 158 47 1N 91 40W
Two Hills 152 53 43N 111 45W
Two Mile Borris 39 52 41N 7 43W
Two Rivers 156 44 10N 87 31W
Two Thumbs Ra. 143 43 45 S 170 44 E
Two Tree 138 18 25 S 140 3 E
Twofold B. 141 37 8 S 149 59 E
Twong 123 5 18N 28 29 E
Twyford, Berks., U.K. 29 51 29N 0 51W
Twyford, Hants., U.K. 28 51 1N 1 19W
Ty 73 56 27N 8 32 E
Tyborön 73 56 42N 8 12 E
Tychy 54 50 9N 18 59 E
Tyczyn 54 49 58N 22 2 E
Tydd St. Mary 29 52 45N 0 9 E
Tykocin 54 53 13N 22 46 E
Tyldal 71 62 8N 10 48 E
Tyldesley 32 53 31N 2 29W
Tyler, Minn., U.S.A. 158 44 18N 96 15W
Tyler, Tex., U.S.A. 159 44 18N 96 15W
Tylldal 71 62 7N 10 45 E
Tylösand 73 56 33N 12 40 E
Týn nad Vltavou 52 49 13N 14 26 E
Tynagh 39 53 10N 8 22W
Tyndall, Mt. 143 43 15 S 170 55 E
Tyndinskiy 77 55 10N 124 43 E
Tyndrum 34 56 26N 4 41W
Tyne & Wear □ 35 54 55N 1 35W
Tyne, R., Eng., U.K. 35 54 58N 1 28W
Tyne, R., Scot., U.K. 35 55 58N 2 45W
Tynemouth 35 55 1N 1 27W
Tynset 71 62 17N 10 47 E
Tyre = Sūr 90 33 19N 35 16 E
Tyrifjorden 71 60 2N 10 8 E
Tyringe 73 56 9N 13 35 E
Tyristrand 71 60 5N 10 5 E
Tyrnyauz 83 43 21N 42 45 E
Tyrol = Tirol 52 46 50N 11 20 E
Tyrone □ 38 54 40N 7 15W
Tyrone, Co. 38 54 40N 7 15W
Tyrrell Arm 153 62 27N 97 30W
Tyrrell, L. 140 35 20 S 142 50 E
Tyrrell L. 153 63 7N 105 27W
Tyrrell, R. 140 35 26 S 142 51 E
Tyrrhenian Sea 60 40 0N 12 30 E
Tysfjörden 74 68 10N 16 10 E
Tysmenitsa 80 48 58N 24 50 E
Tysnes 71 60 1N 5 30 E
Tyssedal 71 60 7N 6 35 E
Tystberga 73 58 51N 17 15 E
Tyulgan 84 52 22N 56 12 E
Tyumen 84 57 0N 65 18 E
Tyumen-Aryk 85 44 2N 67 1 E
Tyup 85 42 45N 78 20 E
Tyvoll 71 62 43N 11 21 E
Tywardreath 30 50 21N 4 40W
Tywi, R. 31 51 48N 4 20W
Tywyn 31 52 36N 4 5W
Tzaneen 129 23 47 S 30 9 E
Tzefa 90 31 7N 35 12 E
Tzermiadhes Neapolis 69 35 11N 25 29 E
Tzoumérka, Óros 68 39 30N 21 26 E
Tzu Shui, R. 109 29 2N 112 55 E
Tzuch'ang 106 37 12N 109 44 E
Tzuch'eng 107 36 39N 117 56 E
Tzuch'i 109 27 42N 116 58 E
Tz'uch'i 109 29 59N 121 14 E
Tzuchien 99 27 43N 98 34 E
Tzuchin 109 23 38N 115 10 E
Tzuchung 108 29 49N 104 55 E
Tz'uhsien 106 36 22N 114 23 E
Tzuhsing 109 25 58N 113 24 E
Tzukuei 105 31 0N 110 38 E
Tzukung 108 29 20N 104 50 E
Tz'uli 109 29 25N 111 6 E
Tzummarum 46 53 14N 5 32 E
Tzupo 105 36 49N 118 5 E
T'zuyang 108 32 31N 108 32 E
Tzuyang 108 30 7N 104 39 E
Tzuyün 108 25 45N 106 5 E

U

U Taphao 100 12 35N 101 0 E
Uad Erni, O. 118 26 30N 9 30W
Uainambi 174 1 43N 69 51W
Uanda 138 21 37 S 144 55 E
Uarsciek 91 2 28N 45 55 E
Uasadi-jidi, Sierra 174 4 54N 65 18W
Uasin □ 126 0 30N 35 20 E
Uassem 90 32 59N 36 2 E
Uato-Udo 103 4 3 S 126 6 E
Uatumã, R. 174 1 30 S 59 25W
Uauá 170 9 50 S 39 28W
Uaupés 174 0 8 S 67 5W
Uaxactún 166 17 25N 89 29W
Ub 66 44 28N 20 6 E
Ubá 173 21 0 S 43 0W
Ubaitaba 171 14 18 S 39 20W
Ubangi, R. = Oubangi 124 1 0N 17 50 E
Ubaté 174 5 19N 73 49W
Ubauro 94 28 15N 69 45 E
Ube 110 33 56N 131 15 E
Ubeda 59 38 3N 3 23W
Uberaba 171 19 50 S 47 55W
Uberlândia 171 19 0 S 48 20W
Ubiaja 121 6 41N 6 22 E
Ubolratna Phong, L. 100 16 45N 102 30 E
Ubombo 129 27 31 S 32 4 E
Ubon Ratchathani 100 15 15N 104 50 E
Ubondo 126 0 55 S 25 42 E
Ubort, R. 80 51 45N 28 30 E
Ubrique 57 36 41N 5 27W
Ubundi 126 0 22 S 25 30 E
Ucayali, R. 174 6 0 S 75 0W
Uccle 47 50 48N 4 22 E
Uchaly 84 54 19N 59 27 E
Uchi Lake 153 51 10N 92 40W
Uchiko 110 33 33N 132 39 E
Uchiura-Wan 112 42 25N 140 40 E
Uchte 48 52 29N 8 52 E
Uchterek 85 41 45N 73 12 E
Uckerath 48 50 44N 7 22 E
Uckfield 29 50 58N 0 6 E
Ucluelet 152 48 57N 125 32W
Ucolta 107 32 56 S 138 59 E
Ucuriş 70 46 41N 21 58 E
Uda, R. 77 54 42N 135 14 E
Udaipur 94 24 36N 73 44 E
Udaipur Garhi 95 27 0N 86 35 E
Udamalpet 97 10 35N 77 15 E
Udbina 63 44 31N 15 47 E
Uddeholm 72 60 1N 13 38 E
Uddel 46 52 15N 5 48 E
Uddevalla 73 58 21N 11 55 E
Uddingston 35 55 50N 4 3W

Uddjaur Ust Kuyga

Uddjaur **74** 65 55N 17 50 E
Uden **47** 51 40N 5 37 E
Udgir **96** 18 25N 77 5 E
Udhampur **95** 33 0N 75 5 E
Udi **121** 6 23N 7 21 E
Udine **63** 46 5N 13 10 E
Udine □ **63** 46 3N 13 13 E
Udipi **97** 13 25N 74 42 E
Udmurt, A.S.S.R. □ **84** 57 30N 52 30 E
Udon Thani **100** 17 29N 102 46 E
Udubo **121** 11 52N 10 35 E
Udvoj Balken **67** 42 50N 26 50 E
Udzungwa Range **127** 11 15 S 35 10 E
Ueckermünde **48** 53 45N 14 1 E
Ueda **111** 36 24N 138 16 E
Uedineniya, Os. **12** 78 0N 85 0 E
Uele, R. **124** 3 50N 22 40 E
Uelen **77** 66 10N 170 0W
Uelzen **48** 53 0N 10 33 E
Ueno **111** 34 53N 136 14 E
Uere, R. **124** 3 45N 24 45 E
Uetendorf **50** 46 47N 7 34 E
Ufa **84** 54 45N 55 55 E
Ufa, R. **84** 56 30N 58 10 E
Uffculme **30** 50 45N 3 19W
Ufford **29** 52 6N 1 22 E
Ugad R. **125** 20 55 S 14 30 E
Ugalla, R. **126** 6 0 S 32 0 E
Ugamas **128** 28 0 S 19 41 E
Uganda ■ **126** 2 0N 32 0 E
Ugborough **30** 50 22N 3 53W
Ugchelen **46** 52 11N 5 56 E
Ugento **65** 39 55N 18 10 E
Ugep **121** 5 53N 8 2 E
Ugie **129** 31 10 S 28 13 E
Ugijar **59** 36 58N 3 7W
Ugine **45** 45 45N 6 25 E
Ugla **122** 25 40N 37 42 E
Uglich **81** 57 33N 38 13 E
Ugljane **63** 43 35N 16 46 E
Ugra, R. **80** 54 45N 35 30 E
Ugurchin **67** 43 6N 24 26 E
Uh, R. **53** 48 40N 22 0 E
Uherske Hradiště **53** 49 4N 17 30 E
Uhersky Brod **53** 49 1N 17 40 E
Uhrichsville **156** 40 23N 81 22W
Uig, Lewis, U.K. **36** 58 13N 7 1W
Uig, Skye, U.K. **36** 57 35N 6 20W
Uinta Mts. **160** 40 45N 110 30W
Uitenhage **128** 33 40 S 25 28 E
Uitgeest **46** 52 32N 4 43 E
Uithoorn **46** 52 14N 4 50 E
Uithuizen **46** 53 24N 6 41 E
Uitkerke **47** 51 18N 3 9 E
Ujda = Oujda **118** 34 45N 2 0W
Ujfehértó **53** 47 49N 21 41 E
Ujh, R. **95** 32 40N 75 30 E
Ujhani **95** 28 0N 79 6 E
Uji **111** 34 53N 135 48 E
Ujjain **94** 23 9N 75 43 E
Ujpest **53** 47 22N 19 6 E
Ujszász **53** 47 19N 20 7 E
Ujung Pandang **103** 5 10 S 119 20 E
Uka **77** 57 50N 162 0 E
Ukara I. **126** 1 44 S 33 0 E
Ukehe **121** 6 40N 7 24 E
Ukerewe □ **126** 2 0 S 32 30 E
Ukerewe Is. **126** 2 0 S 33 0 E
Ukholovo **81** 54 47N 40 30 E
Ukhrul **98** 25 10N 94 25 E
Ukhta **78** 63 55N 54 0 E
Ukiah **160** 39 10N 123 9W
Ukki Fort **95** 33 28N 76 54 E
Ukmerge **80** 55 15N 24 45 E
Ukraine S.S.R. □ **82** 48 0N 35 0 E
Uksyanskoye **84** 55 57N 63 1 E
Ukwi **128** 23 29 S 20 30 E
Ulaanbaatar **105** 47 55N 106 53 E
Ulaangom **105** 49 58N 92 2 E
Ulak I. **147** 51 24N 178 58W
Ulamambri **141** 31 19 S 149 23 E
Ulamba **127** 9 3 S 23 38 E
Ulan Bator = Ulaanbaatar **105** 47 55N 106 53 E
Ulan Ude **77** 52 0N 107 30 E
Ulanbel **85** 44 50N 71 7 E
Ulanga □ **127** 8 40 S 36 50 E
Ulanów **54** 50 30N 22 16 E
Ulaya, Morogoro, Tanz. **126** 7 3 S 36 55 E
Ulaya, Shinyanga, Tanz. **126** 4 25 S 33 30 E
Ulbster **37** 58 21N 3 9W
Ulceby Cross **33** 53 14N 0 6 E
Ulcinj **66** 41 58N 19 10 E
Ulco **128** 28 21 S 24 15 E
Ulefoss **71** 59 17N 9 16 E
Ulëza **68** 41 46N 19 57 E
Ulfborg **73** 56 16N 8 20 E
Ulft **46** 51 53N 6 23 E
Ulhasnagar **96** 19 15N 73 10 E
Ulinda **141** 31 35 S 149 30 E
Uljma **66** 45 2N 21 10 E
Ulla, R. **56** 42 45N 8 30W
Ulladulla **141** 35 21 S 150 29 E
Ullånger **72** 62 58N 18 16 E
Ullapool **36** 57 54N 5 10W
Ullared **73** 57 8N 12 42 E
Ulldecona **58** 40 36N 0 20 E
Ullswater, L. **32** 54 35N 2 52W
Ullvättern, L. **72** 59 30N 14 21 E
Ulm **49** 48 23N 10 0 E
Ulmarra **139** 29 37 S 153 4 E
Ulmeni **70** 45 4N 46 40 E
Ulricehamn **73** 57 46N 13 26 E
Ulrum **46** 53 22N 6 20 E
Ulsberg **71** 62 45N 9 59 E
Ulsfeinvik **71** 62 21N 5 53 E
Ulster □ **38** 54 45N 6 30W
Ulster Canal **38** 54 15N 7 0W
Ulstrem **67** 42 1N 26 27 E
Ultima **140** 35 22 S 143 18 E
Ulubaria **95** 22 31N 88 4 E
Ulugh Muztagh **99** 36 40N 87 30 E
Uluguru Mts. **126** 7 15 S 37 30 E
Ulva, I. **34** 56 30N 6 12W
Ulvenhout **47** 51 33N 4 48 E
Ulverston **32** 54 13N 3 7W
Ulverstone **138** 41 11 S 146 11 E
Ulvik **71** 60 35N 6 54 E
Ulvo **73** 56 40N 14 37 E
Ulya **77** 59 10N 142 0 E
Ulyanovsk **81** 54 25N 48 25 E
Ulyasutay **105** 47 45N 96 49 E
Ulysses **159** 37 39N 101 25W
Ulzio **62** 45 2N 6 49 E
Um Qeis **90** 32 40N 35 41 E
Umag **63** 45 26N 13 31 E
Umala **174** 17 25 S 68 5W
Uman **82** 48 40N 30 12 E
Umánaé **12** 70 40N 52 10W
Umánaé Fjord **10** 70 40N 52 0W
Umaria **99** 23 35N 80 50 E
Umarkhed **96** 19 37N 77 38 E
Umarkot **93** 25 15N 69 40 E
Umatilla **160** 45 58N 119 17W
Umba **78** 66 50N 34 20 E
Umbertide **63** 43 18N 12 20 E
Umboi I. **135** 5 40 S 148 0 E
Umbrella Mts. **143** 45 35 S 169 5 E
Umbria □ **63** 42 53N 12 30 E
Ume, R. **74** 64 45N 18 30 E
Umeå **74** 63 45N 20 20 E
Umera **103** 0 12 S 129 30 E
Umfuli, R. **127** 17 50 S 29 40 E
Umgusa **127** 19 29 S 27 52 E
Umi **110** 33 34N 130 30 E
Umiat **147** 69 25N 152 20W
Umka **66** 44 40N 20 19 E
Umkomaas **129** 30 13 S 30 48 E
Umm al Aranib **119** 26 10N 14 54 E
Umm al Qaiwain **93** 25 30N 55 35 E
Umm Arda **123** 15 17N 32 31 E
Umm az Zamul **93** 22 35N 55 18 E
Umm Bel **123** 13 35N 28 0 E
Umm Digulgulaya **123** 10 28N 24 58 E
Umm Dubban **123** 15 23N 32 52 E
Umm el Fahm **90** 32 31N 35 9 E
Umm Hagar **123** 14 20N 36 41 E
Umm Koweika **123** 13 10N 32 16 E
Umm Lajj **92** 25 0N 37 23 E
Umm Merwa **122** 18 4N 32 30 E
Umm Qurein **123** 16 3N 28 49 E
Umm Rumah **122** 25 50N 36 30 E
Umm Ruwaba **123** 12 50N 31 10 E
Umm Said **93** 25 0N 51 40 E
Umm Sidr **123** 14 29N 25 10 E
Ummanz I. **48** 54 29N 13 9 E
Umnak. **147** 53 20N 168 20W
Umnak I. **147** 53 0N 168 0W
Umniati, R. **127** 18 0 S 29 0 E
Umpang **101** 16 3N 98 54 E
Umpqua, R. **160** 43 30N 123 30W
Umrer **96** 20 51N 79 18 E
Umreth **94** 22 41N 73 4 E
Umshandige Dam **127** 20 10 S 30 40 E
Umtali **127** 18 58 S 32 38 E
Umtata **129** 31 36 S 28 49 E
Umuahia-Ibeku **121** 5 33N 7 29 E
Umvukwe Ra.. **127** 16 45 S 30 45 E
Umvuma **127** 19 16 S 30 30 E
Umzimvubu, R. **129** 31 38 S 29 33 E
Umzingwane, R. **127** 21 30 S 29 30 E
Umzinto **129** 30 15 S 30 45 E
Una **94** 20 46N 71 8 E
Una, Mt. **143** 42 13 S 172 36 E
Una, R. **63** 44 50N 16 15 E
Unac, R. **63** 44 42N 16 15 E
Unadilla **162** 42 20N 75 17W
Unalanaska I. **147** 54 0N 164 30W
Uncastillo **58** 42 21N 1 8W
Uncia **174** 18 25 S 66 40W
Uncompahgce Pk., Mt. **161** 38 5N 107 32W
Unden **73** 58 45N 14 25 E
Underbool **140** 35 10 S 141 51 E
Undersaker **72** 63 19N 13 21 E
Undersvik **72** 61 36N 16 20 E
Undredal **71** 60 57N 7 6 E
Unecha **80** 52 50N 32 37 E
Ungarie **141** 33 38 S 146 56 E
Ungarra **140** 34 12 S 136 2 E
Ungava B. **149** 59 30N 67 30W
Ungava Pen. **50** 60 0N 75 0W
Ungeny **82** 47 11N 27 51 E
Unggi **105** 42 16N 130 28 E
Ungwatiri **123** 16 52N 36 10 E
Uni **84** 56 44N 51 47 E
União **170** 4 50 S 37 50W
União da Vitória **173** 26 5 S 51 0W
União dos Palamares **170** 9 10 S 36 2W
Uniejów **54** 51 59N 18 46 E
Unije, I. **63** 44 40N 14 15 E
Unimak I. **147** 54 30N 164 30W
Unimak Pass. **148** 53 30N 165 15W
Union, Mo., U.S.A. **158** 38 25N 91 0W
Union, S.C., U.S.A. **157** 34 49N 81 39W
Union City, N.J., U.S.A. **162** 40 47N 74 5W
Union City, Ohio, U.S.A. **156** 40 11N 84 49W
Union City, Pa., U.S.A. **156** 41 53N 79 50W
Union Gap **157** 46 38N 120 29W
Unión, La, Chile **176** 40 10 S 73 0W
Unión, La, Colomb. **174** 1 35N 77 5W
Unión, La, El Sal. **165** 13 20N 87 50W
Unión, La **164** 17 58N 101 49W
Unión, La, Spain **59** 37 38N 0 53W
Unión, La, Venez. **174** 7 28N 67 53W
Union, Mt. **161** 34 34N 112 21W
Union of Soviet Soc. Rep. ■ **77** 47 0N 100 0 E
Union Springs **157** 32 9N 85 44W
Uniondale Road **128** 33 39 S 23 7 E
Uniontown **156** 39 54N 79 45W
Unirea **70** 44 15N 27 35 E
United Arab Emirates ■ **93** 23 50N 54 0 E
United Arab Republic ■ **113** 27 5N 30 0 E
United Kingdom ■ **27** 55 0N 3 0W
United States of America ■ **155** 37 0N 96 0W
Unity **153** 52 30N 109 5W
Unjha **94** 23 46N 72 24 E
Unnao **95** 26 35N 80 30 E
Uno, Ilha **120** 11 15N 16 13W
Unshin, R. **38** 54 8N 8 26W
Unst, I. **36** 60 50N 0 55W
Unstrut, R. **48** 51 16N 11 29 E
Unter-Engadin **51** 46 48N 10 20 E
Unterägeri **51** 47 8N 8 36 E
Unterkulm **50** 47 18N 8 7 E
Unterseen **50** 46 41N 7 50 E
Unterwalden nid dem Wald □ **51** 46 50N 8 25 E
Unterwalden ob dem Wald □ **51** 46 55N 8 15 E
Unterwaldner Alpen **51** 46 55N 8 15 E
Unterwasser **51** 46 32N 8 21 E
Unturán, Sierra de **174** 1 35N 64 40W
Unuk, R. **152** 56 5N 131 3W
Ünye **82** 41 5N 37 15 E
Unzen-Dake **111** 32 45N 130 17 E
Unzha **81** 57 40N 44 8 E
Unzha, R. **81** 58 0N 43 40 E
Uors **51** 46 42N 9 12 E
Uozu **111** 36 48N 137 24 E
Upa, R. **53** 50 45N 16 15 E
Upal **123** 6 56N 34 12 E
Upata **174** 8 1N 62 24W
Upavon **28** 51 17N 1 49W
Upemba, L. **127** 8 30 S 26 20 E
Upernavik **12** 72 49N 56 20W
Upington **128** 28 25 S 21 15 E
Upleta **94** 21 46N 70 16 E
Upolu Pt. **147** 20 16N 155 52W
Upper Alkali Lake **160** 41 47N 120 0W
Upper Arrow L. **152** 50 30N 117 50W
Upper Austria = Oberösterreich **52** 48 15N 14 10 E
Upper Chapel **31** 52 3N 3 26W
Upper Foster L. **153** 56 47N 105 20W
Upper Heyford **28** 51 54N 1 16W
Upper Hutt **142** 41 8 S 175 5 E
Upper Klamath L. **160** 42 16N 121 55W
Upper L. Erne **38** 54 14N 7 22W
Upper Lake **160** 39 10N 122 55W
Upper Manilla **141** 30 38 S 150 40 E
Upper Marlboro **162** 38 49N 76 45W
Upper Musquodoboit **151** 45 10N 62 58W
Upper Sandusky **156** 40 50N 83 17W
Upper Volta ■ **120** 12 0N 0 30W
Upperchurch **39** 52 43N 8 2W
Upphärad **73** 58 9N 12 19 E
Uppingham **29** 52 36N 0 43W
Uppsala **72** 59 53N 17 38 E
Uppsala län □ **72** 60 0N 17 30 E
Upshi **95** 33 48N 77 52 E
Upstart, C. **138** 19 41 S 147 45 E
Upton, U.K. **32** 53 14N 2 52W
Upton, U.S.A. **158** 44 8N 104 35W
Upton-upon-Severn **28** 52 4N 2 12W
Upwey **28** 50 40N 2 29W
Ur **92** 30 55N 46 25 E
Ura-Tyube **85** 39 55N 69 1 E
Urabá, Golfo de **174** 8 25N 76 53W
Uracará **174** 2 20 S 57 50W
Urach **49** 48 29N 9 25 E
Uraga-Suidō **111** 35 13N 139 45 E
Urakawa **112** 42 9N 142 47 E
Ural, Mt. **141** 33 21 S 146 12 E
Ural Mts. = Uralskie Gory **78** 60 0N 59 0 E
Ural, R. **84** 49 0N 52 0W
Uralla **141** 30 37 S 151 29 E
Uralsk **84** 51 20N 51 20 E
Uralskie Gory **78** 60 0N 59 0 E
Urambo **126** 5 4 S 32 47 E
Urambo □ **126** 5 0 S 32 0 E
Urana **141** 35 15 S 146 21 E
Urandangi **138** 21 32 S 138 14 E
Uranium City **153** 59 34N 108 37W
Uraricaá, R. **174** 3 20N 61 56W
Uravakonda **97** 14 57N 77 12 E
Urawa **111** 35 50N 139 40 E
Uray **76** 60 5N 65 15 E
Urbana, Ill., U.S.A. **156** 40 7N 88 12W
Urbana, Ohio, U.S.A. **156** 40 9N 83 44W
Urbana, La **174** 7 8N 66 56W
Urbánia **63** 43 40N 12 31 E
Urbano Santos **170** 3 12 S 43 23W
Urbel, R. **58** 42 30N 3 49W
Urbino **63** 43 43N 12 38 E
Urbión, Picos de **58** 42 1N 2 52W
Urcos **174** 13 30 S 71 30W
Urda, Spain **57** 39 25N 3 43W
Urda, U.S.S.R. **83** 48 52N 47 23 E
Urdinarrain **172** 32 37 S 58 52W
Urdos **44** 42 51N 0 35W
Urdzhar **76** 47 5N 81 38 E
Ure, R. **33** 54 20N 1 25W
Uren **81** 57 35N 45 55 E
Ures **164** 29 30N 110 30W
Ureshino **110** 33 6N 129 59 E
Urfa **92** 37 12N 38 50 E
Urfahr **52** 48 19N 14 17 E
Urgench **76** 41 40N 60 30 E
Urgun **93** 32 55N 69 12 E
Urgut **85** 39 23N 67 15 E
Uri **95** 34 8N 74 2 E
Uri □ **51** 46 43N 8 35 E
Uribante, R. **174** 7 25N 71 50W
Uribe **174** 3 13N 74 24W
Uribia **174** 11 43N 72 16W
Urim **90** 31 18N 34 32 E
Uriondo **172** 21 41 S 64 41W
Urique **164** 27 13N 107 55W
Urique, R. **164** 26 29N 107 58W
Urirotstock **51** 46 52N 8 32 E
Urk **46** 52 39N 5 36 E
Urla **92** 38 20N 26 55 E
Urlati **70** 44 59N 26 15 E
Urlingford **39** 52 43N 7 35W
Urmia, L. **92** 37 30N 45 30 E
Urmia **92** 37 40N 45 0 E
Urmston **32** 53 28N 2 22W
Urner Alpen **51** 46 45N 8 45 E
Uroševac **66** 42 23N 21 10 E
Urrao **174** 6 20N 76 11W
Urshult **73** 56 31N 14 50 E
Urso **123** 9 35N 41 33 E
Ursus **54** 52 21N 20 53 E
Uruaca **171** 15 30 S 49 41W
Uruaçu **171** 14 30 S 49 10W
Uruapán **164** 19 30N 102 0W
Urubamba **174** 13 5 S 72 10W
Urubamba, R. **174** 11 0 S 73 0W
Uruçuca **171** 14 35 S 39 16W
Uruçuí **170** 7 20 S 44 28W
Uruçuí Prêto, R. **170** 7 20 S 44 38W
Uruçuí, Serra do **170** 9 0 S 44 45W
Urucuia, R. **171** 16 8 S 45 5W
Uruguai, R. **173** 24 0 S 53 30W
Uruguaiana **172** 29 50 S 57 0W
Uruguay ■ **172** 32 30 S 55 30W
Uruguay, R. **172** 28 0 S 56 0W
Urumchi = Wulumuchi **105** 43 40N 87 50 E
Urup, I. **77** 43 0N 151 0 E
Urup, R. **83** 44 19N 41 30 E
Urutaí **171** 17 28 S 48 12W
Uruyén **174** 5 41N 62 25W
Uruzgan □ **93** 33 30N 66 0 E
Uryupinsk **81** 50 45N 42 3 E
Urzhum **81** 57 10N 49 56 E
Urziceni **70** 44 46N 26 42 E
Usa **110** 33 31N 131 21 E
Usa, R. **78** 66 20N 56 0 E
Uşak **92** 38 43N 29 28 E
Usakos **128** 22 0 S 15 31 E
Usambara Mts. **126** 4 50 S 38 20 E
Usedom **48** 53 50N 13 55 E
Useko **124** 5 8 S 32 24 E
Usfan **122** 21 58N 39 27 E
Ush-Tobe **76** 45 16N 78 0 E
Ushakova, O. **12** 82 0N 80 0 E
Ushant = Ouessant, Île d' **42** 48 25N 5 5W
Ushashi **126** 1 59 S 33 57 E
Ushat **123** 7 59N 29 28 E
Ushibuka **110** 32 11N 130 1 E
Ushuaia **176** 54 50 S 68 23W
Ushumun **77** 52 47N 126 32 E
Usk **31** 51 42N 2 53W
Usk, R. **31** 51 37N 2 56W
Uskedal **71** 59 56N 5 53 E
Üsküdar **92** 41 0N 29 5 E
Uslar **48** 51 39N 9 39 E
Usman **81** 52 5N 39 48 E
Usoga □ **126** 0 5N 33 30 E
Usoke **126** 5 7 S 32 19 E
Usolye Sibirskoye **77** 52 40N 103 40 E
Usoro **121** 5 33N 6 11 E
Uspallata, P. de **172** 32 30 S 69 28W
Uspenskiy **76** 48 50N 72 55 E
Usquert **46** 53 24N 6 36 E
Ussel **44** 45 32N 2 18 E
Ussuriysk **77** 43 40N 131 50 E
Ust **52** 50 41N 14 2 E
Ust Aldan = Batamay **77** 63 30N 129 15 E
Ust Amginskoye = Khandyga **77** 62 30N 134 50 E
Ust-Bolsheretsk **77** 52 40N 156 30 E
Ust Buzulukskaya **81** 50 8N 42 11 E
Ust Doneckij **83** 47 35N 40 55 E
Ust Donetskiy **83** 47 35N 40 55 E
Ust Ilga **77** 55 5N 104 55 E
Ust Ilimpeya = Yukti **77** 63 20N 105 0 E
Ust-Ilimsk **77** 58 3N 102 39 E
Ust Ishim **76** 57 45N 71 10 E
Ust Kamchatsk **77** 56 10N 162 0 E
Ust Kamenogorsk **76** 50 0N 82 20 E
Ust Karenga **77** 54 40N 116 45 E
Ust Khayryuzova **77** 57 15N 156 55 E
Ust Kut **77** 56 50N 105 10 E
Ust Kuyga **77** 70 1N 135 36 E

Ust Labinsk Vatoloha, Mt

Ust Labinsk	**83**	45 15N	39 50 E
Ust Luga	**80**	59 35N	28 26 E
Ust Maya	**77**	60 30N	134 20 E
Ust Mil	**77**	59 50N	133 0 E
Ust Nera	**77**	64 35N	143 15 E
Ust Olenek	**77**	73 0N	120 10 E
Ust-Omchug	**77**	61 9N	149 38 E
Ust Port	**76**	70 0N	84 10 E
Ust Tsilma	**78**	65 25N	52 0 E
Ust-Tungir	**77**	55 25N	120 15 E
Ust Urt = Ustyurt	**76**	44 0N	55 0 E
Ust Usa	**78**	66 0N	56 30 E
Ust-Uyskoye	**84**	54 16N	63 54 E
Ust Vorkuta	**76**	67 7N	63 35 E
Ustaoset	**71**	60 30N	8 2 E
Ustaritz	**44**	43 24N	1 27W
Uste	**81**	59 35N	39 40 E
Uster	**51**	47 22N	8 43 E
Usti na Orlici	**53**	49 58N	16 38 E
Usti nad Labem	**52**	50 41N	14 3 E
Ustica, I.	**64**	38 42N	13 10 E
Ustka	**54**	54 35N	16 55 E
Ustron	**54**	49 45N	18 48 E
Ustrzyki Dolne	**54**	49 27N	22 40 E
Ustye	**77**	55 30N	97 30 E
Ustyurt, Plato	**76**	44 0N	55 0 E
Ustyuzhna	**81**	58 50N	36 32 E
Ušće	**66**	43 43N	20 39 E
Usuki	**110**	33 8N	131 49 E
Usulután	**166**	13 25N	88 28W
Usumacinta, R.	**165**	17 0N	91 0W
Usva	**84**	58 41N	57 37 E
Uta	**66**	45 24N	21 13 E
Utah □	**160**	39 30N	111 30W
Utah, L.	**160**	40 10N	111 58W
Ute Cr.	**159**	36 5N	103 45W
Utena	**80**	55 27N	25 40 E
Ütersen	**48**	53 40N	9 40 E
Utete	**124**	8 0S	38 45 E
Uthai Thani	**100**	15 22N	100 3 E
Uthal	**94**	25 44N	66 40 E
Uthmaniyah	**92**	25 5N	49 6 E
Utiariti	**174**	13 0S	58 10W
Utica	**162**	43 5N	75 18W
Utiel	**58**	39 37N	1 11W
Utik L.	**153**	55 15N	96 0W
Utikuma L.	**152**	55 50N	115 30W
Utinga	**171**	12 6S	41 5W
Uto	**110**	32 41N	130 40 E
Utrecht, Neth.	**46**	52 3N	5 8 E
Utrecht, S. Afr.	**129**	27 38S	30 20 E
Utrecht □	**46**	52 6N	5 7 E
Utrera	**57**	37 12N	5 48W
Utsjoki	**74**	69 51N	26 59 E
Utsunomiya	**111**	36 30N	139 50 E
Uttar Pradesh □	**95**	27 0N	80 0 E
Uttaradit	**100**	17 36N	100 5 E
Uttersberg	**72**	59 45N	15 39 E
Uttersley	**73**	54 56N	11 11 E
Uttoxeter	**32**	52 53N	1 50W
Utva, R.	**84**	51 28N	52 40 E
Ütze	**48**	52 28N	10 11 E
Uudenmaan lääni □	**75**	60 25N	25 0 E
Uusikaarlepyy	**74**	63 32N	22 31 E
Uusikaupunki	**75**	60 47N	21 25 E
Uva	**84**	56 59N	52 13 E
Uvac, R.	**66**	43 35N	19 40 E
Uvalde	**159**	29 15N	99 48W
Uvarovo	**81**	51 59N	42 14 E
Uvat	**76**	59 5N	68 50 E
Uvelskiy	**84**	54 26N	61 22 E
Uvinza	**126**	5 5S	30 24 E
Uvira	**126**	3 22S	29 3 E
Uvlova, R.	**52**	49 34N	13 20 E
Uvs Nuur, L.	**105**	50 20N	92 45 E
Uwa	**110**	33 22N	132 31 E
Uwainhid	**92**	24 50N	46 0 E
Uwajima	**110**	33 10N	132 35 E
Uxmal	**165**	20 22N	89 46W
Uyeasound	**36**	60 42N	0 55W
Uyo	**121**	5 1N	7 53 E
Uyu, R.	**98**	24 51N	94 57 E
Uyuk	**85**	43 36N	71 16 E
Uyuni	**172**	20 35S	66 55W
Uyuni, Salar de	**172**	20 10S	68 0W
Uzbekistan S.S.R. □	**85**	40 5N	65 0 E
Uzen, Bol.	**81**	50 0N	49 30 E
Uzen, Mal.	**81**	50 0N	48 30 E
Uzerche	**44**	45 25N	1 35 E
Uzès	**45**	44 1N	4 26 E
Uzgen	**85**	40 46N	73 18 E
Uzh, R.	**80**	51 15N	29 45 E
Uzhgorod	**80**	48 36N	22 18 E
Uzlovaya	**81**	54 0N	38 5 E
Uzun-Agach	**85**	43 35N	76 20 E
Uzunköprü	**67**	41 16N	26 43 E
Uzure	**126**	4 40S	34 22 E
Uzwil	**51**	47 26N	9 9 E

V

Vaal, R.	**128**	27 40S	25 30 E
Vaaldam	**129**	27 0S	28 14 E
Vaals	**47**	50 46N	6 1 E
Vaalwater	**129**	24 15S	28 8 E
Vaasa	**74**	63 16N	21 35 E
Vaasan lääni □	**74**	63 2N	22 50 E
Vaassen	**46**	52 17N	5 58 E
Vabre	**44**	43 42N	2 24 E
Vác	**53**	47 49N	19 10 E
Vacaria	**173**	28 31S	50 52W
Vacaville	**163**	38 21N	122 0W
Vach, R.	**76**	60 56N	76 38 E
Vache, I.-à	**167**	18 2N	73 35W
Väddö	**72**	59 55N	18 50 E
Väderum	**73**	57 32N	16 11 E
Vadnagar	**94**	23 47N	72 40 E
Vado Ligure	**62**	44 16N	8 26 E
Vadodara	**94**	22 20N	73 10 E
Vadsø	**74**	70 3N	29 50 E
Vadstena	**73**	58 28N	14 54 E
Vaduz	**51**	47 8N	9 31 E
Vaerøy, Nordland Fylke, Norway	**74**	67 40N	12 40 E
Vaerøy, Sogn og Fjordane, Norway	**71**	61 17N	4 45 E
Vagney	**43**	48 1N	6 43 E
Vagnhärad	**72**	58 57N	17 33 E
Vagos	**56**	40 33N	8 42W
Vagsöy, I.	**71**	62 0N	5 0 E
Váh, R.	**53**	49 10N	18 20 E
Vaigach	**76**	70 10N	59 0 E
Vaigai, R.	**97**	9 47N	78 23 E
Vaiges	**42**	48 2N	0 30W
Vaihingen	**49**	48 44N	8 58 E
Vaihsel B.	**13**	75 0S	35 0W
Vaijapur	**96**	19 58N	74 45 E
Vaikam	**97**	9 45N	76 25 E
Vaila I.	**36**	60 12N	1 34W
Vailly Aisne	**43**	49 25N	3 30 E
Vaippar, R.	**97**	9 0N	78 25 E
Vaison	**45**	44 14N	5 4 E
Vajpur	**96**	21 24N	73 45 E
Vakarel	**67**	42 35N	23 40 E
Vakhsh, R.	**85**	37 6N	68 18 E
Vaksdal	**71**	60 29N	5 45 E
Vál	**53**	47 22N	18 40 E
Val d' Ajol, Le	**43**	47 55N	6 30 E
Val-de-Marne □	**43**	48 45N	2 28 E
Val-d'Oise □	**43**	49 5N	2 0 E
Val d'Or	**150**	48 7N	77 47W
Val Marie	**153**	49 15N	107 45W
Val-St.-Germain	**47**	48 34N	2 4 E
Valadares	**56**	41 5N	8 38W
Valahia	**70**	44 35N	25 0 E
Valais □	**50**	46 12N	7 45 E
Valais, Alpes du	**50**	46 47N	7 30 E
Valandovo	**66**	41 19N	22 34 E
Valasské MeziríU5	**53**	49 29N	17 59 E
Valaxa, I.	**69**	38 50N	24 29 E
Valcheta	**176**	40 40S	66 20W
Valdagno	**63**	45 38N	11 18 E
Valdahon, Le	**43**	47 8N	6 20 E
Valday	**80**	57 58N	31 9 E
Valdayskaya Vozvyshennost	**80**	57 0N	33 40 E
Valdeazogues, R.	**57**	38 45N	4 55W
Valdemarsvik	**73**	58 14N	16 40 E
Valdepeñas, Ciudad Real, Spain	**57**	38 43N	3 25W
Valdepeñas, Jaén, Spain	**57**	37 33N	3 47W
Valderaduey, R.	**56**	42 30N	5 0W
Valderrobres	**58**	40 53N	0 9 E
Valdes Pen.	**176**	42 30S	63 45W
Valdez	**147**	61 14N	146 10W
Valdivia	**176**	39 50S	73 14W
Valdivia □	**176**	40 0S	73 0W
Valdivia, La	**172**	34 43S	72 5W
Valdobbiádene	**63**	45 53N	12 0 E
Valdosta	**157**	30 50N	83 48W
Valdoviño	**56**	43 36N	8 8W
Valdres	**71**	60 55N	9 28 E
Vale, U.S.A.	**160**	44 0N	117 15W
Vale, U.S.S.R.	**83**	41 30N	42 58 E
Valea lui Mihai	**70**	47 32N	22 11 E
Valença, Brazil	**171**	13 20S	39 5W
Valença, Port.	**56**	42 1N	8 34W
Valença do Piauí	**170**	6 20S	41 45W
Valence	**45**	44 57N	4 54 E
Valence-d'Agen	**44**	44 8N	0 54 E
Valencia, Spain	**59**	39 27N	0 23W
Valencia, Venez.	**174**	10 11N	68 0W
Valencia □	**59**	39 20N	0 40W
Valencia, Albufera de	**59**	39 20N	0 27W
Valencia de Alcántara	**57**	39 25N	7 14W
Valencia de Don Juan	**56**	42 17N	5 31W
Valencia des Ventoso	**57**	38 15N	6 29W
Valencia, G. de	**59**	39 30N	0 20 E
Valencia, L. de	**167**	10 13N	67 40W
Valenciennes	**43**	50 20N	3 34 E
Valensole	**45**	43 50N	5 59 E
Valentia Hr.	**39**	51 56N	10 17W
Valentia I.	**39**	51 54N	10 22W
Valentine, Nebr., U.S.A.	**158**	42 50N	100 35W
Valentine, Tex., U.S.A.	**159**	30 36N	104 28W
Valenton	**160**	48 45N	2 28 E
Valenza	**62**	45 2N	8 39 E
Våler	**71**	60 41N	11 50 E
Valera	**174**	9 19N	70 37W
Valguarnera Caropepe	**65**	37 30N	14 22 E
Valhall, oilfield	**19**	56 17N	3 25 E
Valier	**160**	48 15N	112 9W
Valinco, G. de	**45**	41 40N	8 52 E
Valjevo	**66**	44 18N	19 53 E
Valkeakoski	**75**	61 16N	24 2 E
Valkenburg	**47**	50 52N	5 50 E
Valkenswaard	**47**	51 21N	5 29 E
Vall de Uxó	**58**	40 49N	0 15W
Valla	**72**	59 2N	16 20 E
Valladolid, Mexico	**165**	20 30N	88 20W
Valladolid, Spain	**56**	41 38N	4 43W
Valladolid □	**56**	41 38N	4 43W
Vallata	**65**	41 3N	15 16 E
Valldalssæter	**71**	59 56N	6 57 E
Valle	**71**	59 13N	7 33 E
Valle d'Aosta □	**62**	45 45N	7 22 E
Valle de Arán	**58**	42 50N	0 55 E
Valle de Cabuérniga	**56**	43 14N	4 18W
Valle de la Pascua	**174**	9 13N	66 0W
Valle de Santiago	**164**	20 25N	101 15W
Valle de Zaragoza	**164**	27 28N	105 49W
Valle del Cauca □	**174**	3 45N	76 30W
Valle Fértil, Sierra del	**172**	30 20S	68 0W
Valle Hermosa	**165**	25 35N	102 25 E
Valle Nacional	**165**	17 47N	96 19W
Vallecas	**56**	40 23N	3 41W
Valledupar	**174**	10 29N	73 15W
Vallejo	**163**	38 12N	122 15W
Vallenar	**172**	28 30S	70 50W
Valleraugue	**44**	44 6N	3 39 E
Vallet	**42**	47 10N	1 15W
Valletta	**60**	35 54N	14 30 E
Valley	**31**	53 17N	4 31W
Valley Center	**163**	33 13N	117 2W
Valley City	**158**	46 57N	98 0W
Valley Falls	**160**	42 33N	120 8W
Valley Okolona	**159**	34 0N	88 45W
Valley Springs	**163**	38 11N	120 50W
Valley View	**162**	40 39N	76 33W
Valleyfield	**150**	45 15N	74 8W
Valleyview	**152**	55 5N	117 17W
Valli di Comácchio	**63**	44 40N	12 15 E
Vallimanca, Arroyo	**172**	35 40S	59 10W
Vallo della Lucánia	**65**	40 14N	15 16 E
Vallon	**45**	44 25N	4 23 E
Vallorbe	**50**	46 42N	6 20 E
Valls	**58**	41 18N	1 15 E
Vallsta	**72**	61 31N	16 22 E
Valmaseda	**58**	43 11N	3 12W
Valmiera	**80**	57 37N	25 38 E
Valmont	**42**	49 45N	0 30 E
Valmontone	**64**	41 48N	12 55 E
Valmy	**43**	49 5N	4 45 E
Valnera, Mte.	**58**	43 9N	3 40W
Valognes	**42**	49 30N	1 28W
Valona (Vlora)	**68**	40 32N	19 28 E
Valongo	**56**	40 37N	8 27W
Valpaços	**56**	41 36N	7 17W
Valparaíso, Chile	**172**	33 2S	71 40W
Valparaíso, Mexico	**164**	22 50N	103 32W
Valparaiso	**156**	41 27N	87 2W
Valparaiso □	**172**	33 2S	71 40W
Valpovo	**66**	45 39N	18 25 E
Valréas	**45**	44 24N	5 0 E
Vals	**51**	46 39N	10 11 E
Vals-les-Bains	**45**	44 42N	4 24 E
Vals, R.	**128**	27 28S	26 52 E
Vals, Tanjung	**103**	8 32S	137 32 E
Valsbaai	**128**	34 15S	18 40 E
Valskog	**72**	59 27N	15 57 E
Válta	**68**	40 3N	23 25 E
Valtellina	**62**	46 9N	10 2 E
Valverde del Camino	**57**	37 35N	6 47W
Valverde del Fresno	**56**	40 15N	6 51W
Valyiki	**81**	50 10N	38 5 E
Vama	**70**	47 34N	25 42 E
Vambarra Ra.	**136**	15 13S	130 24 E
Vamdrup	**50**	55 26N	9 10 E
Vammala	**75**	61 20N	22 55 E
Vámos	**69**	35 24N	24 13 E
Vamsadhara, R.	**96**	18 22N	84 15 E
Van	**92**	38 30N	43 20 E
Van Alstyne	**159**	33 25N	96 36W
Van Bruyssel	**151**	47 56N	72 9W
Van Buren, Can.	**151**	47 10N	67 55W
Van Buren, Ark., U.S.A.	**159**	35 28N	94 18W
Van Buren, Me., U.S.A.	**157**	47 10N	68 1W
Van Buren, Mo., U.S.A.	**159**	37 0N	91 0W
Van Canh	**100**	13 37N	109 0 E
Van der Kloof Dam	**128**	30 04S	24 40 E
Van Diemen, C., N.T., Austral.	**136**	11 9S	130 24 E
Van Diemen, C., Queens., Austral.	**138**	16 30S	139 46 E
Van Diemen G.	**136**	11 45S	131 50 E
Van Gölü	**92**	38 30N	43 0 E
Van Horn	**161**	31 3N	104 55W
Van Ninn	**100**	12 42N	109 14 E
Van Reenen P.	**129**	28 22S	29 27 E
Van Tassell	**158**	42 40N	104 3W
Van Tivu, I.	**97**	8 51N	78 15 E
Van Wert	**156**	40 52N	84 31W
Van Yen	**100**	21 4N	104 42 E
Vanavara	**77**	60 22N	102 16 E
Vancouver, Can.	**152**	49 20N	123 10W
Vancouver, U.S.A.	**160**	45 44N	122 41W
Vancouver, C.	**137**	35 2S	118 11 E
Vancouver I.	**152**	49 50N	126 0W
Vandalia, Ill., U.S.A.	**158**	38 57N	89 4W
Vandalia, Mo., U.S.A.	**158**	39 18N	91 30W
Vandeloos Bay	**97**	8 0N	81 45 E
Vandenburg	**163**	34 35N	120 44W
Vanderbijlpark	**86**	26 42S	27 54 E
Vanderhoof	**152**	54 0N	124 0W
Vanderlin I.	**138**	15 44S	137 2 E
Vandyke	**138**	24 10S	147 51 E
Vänern	**73**	58 47N	13 30 E
Vänersborg	**73**	58 26N	12 27 E
Vang Vieng	**100**	18 58N	102 32 E
Vanga	**126**	4 35S	39 12 E
Vangaindrano	**129**	23 21S	47 36 E
Vanguard	**153**	49 55N	107 20W
Vanier	**150**	45 27N	75 40W
Vanimo	**135**	2 42S	141 21 E
Vanivilasa Sagara	**97**	13 45N	76 30 E
Vaniyambadi	**97**	12 46N	78 44 E
Vankleek Hill	**150**	45 32N	75 40W
Vanna	**74**	70 6N	19 50 E
Vannas	**74**	63 58N	19 48 E
Vannes	**42**	47 40N	2 47W
Vanoise, Massif de la	**45**	45 25N	6 40 E
Vanrhynsdorp	**128**	31 36S	18 44 E
Vanrook	**138**	16 57S	141 57 E
Vans, Les	**45**	44 25N	4 7 E
Vansbro	**72**	60 32N	14 15 E
Vanse	**71**	58 6N	6 41 E
Vansittart B.	**136**	14 3S	126 17 E
Vanthli	**94**	21 28N	70 25 E
Vanua Levu, I.	**130**	16 33S	178 8 E
Vanwyksvlei	**128**	30 18S	21 49 E
Vanylven	**71**	62 5N	5 33 E
Vapnyarka	**82**	48 32N	28 45 E
Var □	**45**	43 27N	6 18 E
Vara	**73**	58 16N	12 55 E
Varada, R.	**97**	14 46N	75 15 E
Varades	**42**	47 25N	1 1W
Varaita, R.	**62**	44 35N	7 15 E
Varaldsöy	**71**	60 6N	5 59 E
Varallo	**62**	45 50N	8 13 E
Varanasi (Benares)	**95**	25 22N	83 8 E
Varangerfjorden	**74**	70 3N	29 25 E
Varazdin	**63**	46 20N	16 20 E
Varazze	**62**	44 21N	8 36 E
Varberg	**73**	57 17N	12 20 E
Vardar, R.	**66**	41 25N	22 20 E
Varde	**73**	55 38N	8 29 E
Varde Å	**73**	55 35N	8 19 E
Vardø	**74**	70 23N	31 5 E
Varel	**48**	53 23N	8 9 E
Varella, Mui	**100**	12 54N	109 26 E
Varena	**80**	54 12N	24 30 E
Värendseke	**73**	57 4N	15 0 E
Varennes-sur-Allier	**44**	49 12N	5 0 E
Vareš	**66**	44 12N	18 23 E
Varese	**62**	45 49N	8 50 E
Varese Ligure	**62**	44 22N	9 33 E
Vårgårda	**73**	58 2N	12 49 E
Vargem Bonita	**171**	20 20S	46 22W
Vargem Grande	**170**	3 33S	43 56W
Varginha	**173**	21 33S	45 25W
Vargön	**73**	58 22N	12 20 E
Varhaug	**71**	58 37N	5 41 E
Varillas	**172**	24 0S	70 10W
Varing	**73**	58 30N	14 0 E
Värmdö, I.	**72**	59 18N	18 45 E
Värmeln	**72**	59 35N	13 0 E
Värmlands län □	**72**	59 45N	13 20 E
Varmlandssaby	**72**	59 7N	14 15 E
Varna, Bulg.	**67**	43 13N	27 56 E
Varna, U.S.S.R.	**84**	53 24N	60 58 E
Varna, R.	**96**	17 13N	73 50 E
Varnamo	**73**	57 10N	14 3 E
Varnsdorf	**52**	49 56N	14 38 E
Värö	**73**	51 16N	12 15 E
Varpelev	**73**	55 22N	12 17 E
Värsjö	**73**	56 23N	13 27 E
Varsseveld	**46**	51 56N	6 29 E
Varteig	**71**	59 23N	11 12 E
Varto	**92**	39 10N	41 28 E
Vartofta	**73**	58 6N	13 40 E
Vartry Res.	**39**	53 3N	6 12W
Varvarin	**66**	43 43N	21 20 E
Varzaneh	**93**	32 25N	52 40 E
Várzea Alegre	**170**	6 47S	39 17W
Várzea da Palma	**171**	17 36S	44 44W
Varzi	**62**	44 50N	9 12 E
Varzo	**62**	46 12N	8 15 E
Varzy	**43**	47 22N	3 20 E
Vas □	**53**	47 10N	16 55 E
Vasa	**74**	63 6N	21 38 E
Vasa Barris, R.	**170**	11 10S	37 10W
Vásárosnamény	**53**	48 9N	22 19 E
Väsby	**73**	56 13N	12 37 E
Vascâo, R.	**57**	37 44N	8 15W
Vascongadas	**58**	42 50N	2 45W
Vaşcŭu	**70**	46 28N	22 30 E
Väse	**72**	59 23N	13 52 E
Vasht = Khāsh	**93**	28 20N	61 6 E
Vasil Levski	**67**	43 23N	25 26 E
Vasilevichi	**80**	52 15N	29 50 E
Vasilikón	**69**	38 25N	23 40 E
Vasilkov	**80**	50 7N	30 28 E
Vaslui	**70**	46 38N	27 42 E
Vaslui □	**71**	46 30N	27 30 E
Väsman	**72**	60 9N	15 5 E
Vassa	**74**	63 6N	21 38 E
Vassar, Can.	**153**	49 10N	95 55W
Vassar, U.S.A.	**156**	43 23N	83 33W
Vast Silen, L.	**72**	59 15N	12 15 E
Västerås	**73**	59 37N	16 38 E
Västerbottens län □	**74**	64 58N	18 0 E
Västerdalälven	**72**	60 50N	13 25 E
Västernorrlands län □	**72**	63 30N	17 40 E
Västervik	**73**	57 43N	16 43 E
Västmanland □	**72**	59 55N	16 30 E
Vasto	**63**	42 8N	14 40 E
Vasvár	**53**	47 3N	16 47 E
Vatan	**43**	47 4N	1 50 E
Vaternish Pt.	**36**	57 36N	6 40W
Vatersay, I.	**36**	56 55N	7 32W
Vathí	**69**	37 46N	27 1 E
Váthia	**69**	36 29N	22 29 E
Vatican City ■	**63**	41 54N	12 27 E
Vatin	**66**	45 12N	21 20 E
Vatnajökull	**74**	64 30N	16 48W
Vatnås	**71**	59 58N	9 37 E
Vatne	**71**	62 33N	6 38 E
Vatneyri	**74**	65 35N	24 0W
Vatoloha, Mt.	**129**	17 52S	47 48 E

Vatomandry Vijayadurg

Vatomandry 129 19 20S 48 59E
Vatra-Dornei 70 47 22N 25 22E
Vats 71 59 29N 5 45E
Vättern, L. 73 58 25N 14 30E
Vättis 51 46 55N 9 27E
Vaucluse □ 45 44 3N 5 10E
Vaucouleurs 43 48 37N 5 40E
Vaud □ 50 46 35N 6 30E
Vaughan 161 34 37N 105 12W
Vaughn 160 47 37N 111 36W
Vaulruz 50 46 38N 7 0E
Vaupés □ 174 1 0N 71 0W
Vaupés, R. 174 1 0N 71 0W
Vauvert 45 43 42N 4 17E
Vauxhall 152 50 5N 112 9W
Vavincourt 43 48 49N 5 12E
Vavoua 120 7 23N 6 29W
Vaxholm 72 59 25N 18 20E
Växjö 73 56 52N 14 50E
Vaygach, Ostrov 76 70 0N 60 0E
Vaza Barris, R. 171 10 0S 37 30W
Veadeiros 171 14 7S 47 31W
Veagh L. 38 55 3N 7 57W
Vechta 48 52 47N 8 18E
Vechte, R. 46 52 34N 6 6E
Vecilla, La 56 42 51N 5 27W
Vecsés 53 47 26N 19 19E
Vedaraniam 97 10 25N 79 50E
Vedbæk 73 55 50N 12 33E
Veddige 73 57 17N 12 20E
Vedea, R. 70 44 0N 25 20E
Vedelgem 47 51 7N 3 10E
Vedia 172 34 30S 61 31W
Vedra, Isla del 59 38 52N 1 12E
Vedrin 47 50 30N 4 52E
Veendam 46 53 5N 6 52E
Veenendaal 46 52 2N 5 34E
Veenwouden 46 53 14N 6 0E
Veerle 47 51 4N 4 59E
Vefsna 74 65 48N 13 10E
Vega, Norway 74 65 40N 11 55E
Vega, U.S.A. 159 35 18N 102 26W
Vega Baja 147 18 27N 66 23W
Vega Fd. 74 65 37N 12 0E
Vega, I. 74 65 42N 11 50E
Vega, La 167 19 20N 70 30W
Vegadeo 56 43 27N 7 4W
Vegesack 48 53 10N 8 38E
Vegfjorden 74 65 37N 12 0E
Veggerby 73 56 54N 9 39E
Veggli 71 60 3N 9 9E
Veghel 47 51 37N 5 32E
Vegorritis, Limni 68 40 45N 21 45E
Vegreville 152 53 30N 112 5W
Vegusdal 71 58 32N 8 10E
Veii 63 42 0N 12 24E
Veinticino de Mayo 172 38 0S 67 40W
Veitch 140 34 39S 140 31E
Vejen 73 55 30N 9 9E
Vejer de la Frontera 57 36 15N 5 59W
Vejle 73 55 43N 9 30E
Vejle Amt □ 73 55 2N 11 22E
Vejle Fjord 73 55 40N 9 50E
Vejlo 73 55 10N 11 45E
Vela Luka 63 42 59N 16 44E
Velanai I. 97 9 45N 79 45E
Velarde 161 36 11N 106 1W
Velas, C. 166 10 21N 85 52W
Velasco 159 29 0N 95 20W
Velasco, Sierra de. 172 29 20S 67 10W
Velay, Mts. du 44 45 0N 3 40E
Velb 46 52 0N 5 59E
Velddrif 128 32 42S 18 11E
Velden 47 51 25N 6 10E
Veldhoven 47 51 24N 5 25E
Veldwezelt 47 50 52N 5 38E
Velebit Planina 63 44 50N 15 20E
Velebitski Kanal 63 44 45N 14 55E
Veleka, R. 67 42 4N 27 30E
Velenje 63 46 23N 15 8E
Velestínon 68 39 23N 22 43E
Vélez 174 6 1N 73 41W
Velez 66 43 19N 18 2E
Vélez Blanco 57 37 41N 2 5W
Vélez Málaga 57 36 48N 4 5W
Vélez Rubio 59 37 41N 2 5W
Velhas, R. 171 17 13S 44 49W
Velika 66 45 27N 17 40E
Velika Goricá 63 45 44N 16 5E
Velika Kapela 63 45 10N 15 5E
Velika Kladuša 63 45 11N 15 48E
Velika Morava, R. 66 44 30N 21 9E
Velika Plana 66 44 20N 21 1E
Velikaya, R. 80 56 40N 28 40E
Veliké Kapušany 53 48 34N 22 5E
Velike Lašče 63 45 49N 14 45E
Veliki Backa Kanal 68 45 45N 19 15E
Veliki Jastrebac 66 43 25N 21 30E
Veliki Ustyug 78 60 47N 46 20E
Velikiye Luki 80 56 25N 30 32E
Veliko Turnovo 67 43 5N 25 41E
Velikonda Range 97 14 45N 79 10E
Velikoye, Oz. 81 55 15N 40 0E
Velingrad 67 42 4N 23 58E
Velino, Mt. 63 42 10N 13 20E
Velizh 80 55 30N 31 11E
Velké Karlovice 53 49 20N 18 17E
Velke Mezirici 52 49 21N 16 1E
Velký ostrov Zitný 53 48 5N 17 20E
Vellar, R. 97 11 30N 79 36E
Velletri 64 41 43N 12 43E
Velling 73 56 2N 8 20E
Vellinge 73 55 29N 13 0E
Vellir 74 65 55N 18 28W
Vellore 97 12 57N 79 10E
Velsen-Noord 46 52 27N 4 40E
Velsk 78 61 10N 42 5E
Velten 48 52 40N 13 11E
Veluwe Meer 46 52 24N 5 44E
Velva 158 48 6N 100 56W
Velvendós 68 40 15N 22 6E
Vem 73 56 21N 8 21E
Vembanad Lake 97 9 36N 76 15E
Veme 71 60 14N 10 7E
Ven 73 55 55N 12 45E
Vena 73 57 31N 16 0E
Venado 164 22 50N 101 10W
Venado Tuerto 172 33 50S 62 0W
Venafro 65 41 28N 14 3E
Venarey-les-Laumes 43 47 32N 4 26E
Venaria 62 45 12N 7 39E
Venčane 66 44 24N 20 28E
Vence 45 43 43N 7 6E
Vendas Novas 57 38 39N 8 27W
Vendée 42 46 50N 1 35W
Vendée □ 44 46 40N 1 20W
Vendée, Collines de 42 46 35N 0 45W
Vendée, R. 42 46 30N 0 45W
Vendeuvre-sur-Barse 43 48 14N 4 28E
Vendôme 42 47 47N 1 3E
Vendrell 58 41 10N 1 30E
Vendsyssel 73 57 22N 10 0E
Veneta, Laguna 63 45 19N 12 13E
Venetie 147 67 0N 146 30W
Véneto □ 63 45 30N 12 0E
Venev 81 54 22N 38 17E
Venézia 63 45 27N 12 20E
Venézia, Golfo di 63 45 20N 13 0E
Venezuela ■ 174 8 0N 65 0W
Venezuela, Golfo de 174 11 30N 71 0W
Vengurla 97 15 53N 73 45E
Vengurla Rocks 97 15 50N 73 22E
Venice = Venézia 63 45 27N 12 20E
Vénissieux 45 45 43N 4 53E
Venjansjön 72 60 58N 14 2E
Venkatagiri 97 14 0N 79 35E
Venkatapuram 96 18 20N 80 30E
Venlo 47 51 22N 6 11E
Vennesla 71 58 15N 8 0E
Venø, Is. 73 56 33N 8 38E
Venraij 47 51 31N 6 0E
Venta de Cardeña 57 38 16N 4 20W
Venta de San Rafael 56 40 42N 4 12W
Venta, La 165 18 8N 94 3W
Ventana, Punta de la 164 24 4N 109 48W
Ventersburg 128 28 7S 27 9E
Ventimiglia 62 43 50N 7 39E
Ventnor 28 50 35N 1 12W
Ventotene, I. 64 40 48N 13 25E
Ventry 39 52 8N 10 21W
Ventspils 80 57 25N 21 32E
Ventuari, R. 174 5 20N 66 0W
Ventucopa 163 34 50N 119 29W
Ventura 163 34 16N 119 18W
Ventura, La 164 24 38N 100 54W
Venturosa, La 174 6 8N 68 48W
Venus B. 141 38 40S 145 42E
Veoy 71 62 45N 7 30E
Veoy Is. 71 62 45N 7 30E
Vera, Argent. 172 29 30S 60 20W
Vera, Spain 59 37 15N 1 15W
Veracruz 165 19 10N 96 10W
Veracruz □ 165 19 0N 96 15W
Veraval 94 20 53N 70 27E
Verbánia 62 45 50N 8 55E
Verbicaro 65 39 46N 15 54E
Verbier 50 46 6N 7 13E
Vercelli 62 45 19N 8 25E
Verdalsøra 74 63 48N 11 30E
Verde Grande, R. 171 16 13S 43 49W
Verde Pequeno, R. 171 14 48S 43 31W
Verde, R., Argent. 176 41 55S 66 0W
Verde, R., Goiás, Brazil 171 18 1S 50 14W
Verde, R., Goiás, Brazil 171 19 11S 50 44W
Verde, R., Chihuahua, Mexico 164 26 59N 107 58W
Verde, R., Oaxaca, Mexico 164 15 59N 97 50W
Verde, R., Veracruz, Mexico 165 21 10N 102 50W
Verde, R., Parag. 172 23 9S 57 37W
Verden 48 52 58N 9 18E
Verdhikoúsa 68 39 47N 21 59E
Verdigre 158 42 38N 98 0W
Verdon-sur-Mer, Le 44 45 33N 1 4W
Verdun 43 49 12N 5 24E
Verdun-sur-le Doubs 43 46 54N 5 0E
Vereeniging 129 26 38S 27 57E
Vérendrye, Parc Prov. de 150 47 20N 76 40W
Vereshchagino 84 58 5N 54 40E
Verga, C. 120 10 30N 14 10W
Vergara 58 43 9N 2 28W
Vergato 62 44 18N 11 8E
Vergemont 138 23 33S 143 1E
Vergemont Cr. 138 24 16S 143 16E
Vergt 44 45 2N 0 43E
Verín 56 41 57N 7 27W
Veriña 56 43 32N 5 43W
Verkhnedvinsk 80 55 45N 27 58E
Verkhneuralsk 84 53 53N 59 13E
Verkhniy-Avzyan 84 53 32N 57 33E
Verkhniy Baskunchak 83 48 5N 46 50E
Verkhniy Tagil 84 57 22N 59 56E
Verkhniy Ufaley 84 56 4N 60 14E
Verkhniye Kigi 84 55 25N 58 37E
Verkhnyaya Salda 84 58 2N 60 33E
Verkhoturye 84 58 52N 60 48E
Verkhovye 81 52 55N 37 15E
Verkhoyansk 77 67 50N 133 50E
Verkhoyanskiy Khrebet 77 66 0N 129 0E
Verlo 153 50 19N 108 35W
Verma 71 62 21N 8 3E
Vermenton 43 47 40N 3 42E
Vermilion 153 53 20N 110 50W
Vermilion, B. 159 29 45N 91 55W
Vermilion Bay 153 49 50N 93 20W
Vermilion Chutes 152 58 22N 114 51W
Vermilion, R., Alta., Can. 153 53 22N 110 51W
Vermilion, R., Qué., Can. 150 47 38N 72 56W
Vermillion 158 42 50N 96 56W
Vermont □ 156 43 40N 72 50W
Vern, oilfield 19 55 35N 4 45E
Vernal 160 40 28N 109 35W
Vernalis 163 37 36N 121 17W
Vernayez 50 46 8N 7 3E
Verner 150 46 25N 80 8W
Verneuil, Bois de 50 48 59N 1 59E
Verneuil-sur-Avre 42 48 45N 0 55E
Vernier 50 46 13N 6 5E
Vernon, Can. 152 50 20N 119 15W
Vernon, France 42 49 5N 1 30E
Vernon, U.S.A. 159 34 0N 99 15W
Vero Beach 157 27 39N 80 23W
Véroia 68 40 34N 22 18E
Verolanuova 62 45 20N 10 5E
Véroli 64 41 43N 13 24E
Verona 62 45 27N 11 0E
Veropol 77 66 0N 168 0E
Verrieres, Les 50 46 55N 6 28E
Versailles 43 48 48N 2 8E
Versoix 50 46 17N 6 10E
Vert, C. 120 14 45N 17 30W
Vertou 42 47 10N 1 28W
Vertus 43 48 54N 4 0E
Verulam 129 29 38S 31 2E
Verviers 47 50 37N 5 52E
Vervins 43 49 50N 3 53E
Verwood, Can. 153 49 30N 105 40W
Verwood, U.K. 28 50 53N 1 53W
Veryan 30 50 13N 4 56W
Veryan Bay 30 50 12N 4 51W
Verzej 63 46 34N 16 13E
Vesdre, R. 47 50 36N 6 0E
Veselí nad Luznicí 52 49 12N 14 15E
Veselie 67 42 18N 27 38E
Veselovskoye Vdkhr. 83 47 0N 41 0E
Veselyy Res. 83 47 0N 41 0E
Veshenskaya 83 49 35N 41 44E
Vesle, R. 43 49 17N 3 50E
Veslyana, R. 84 60 20N 54 0E
Vesoul 43 60 40N 6 11E
Vessigebro 73 56 58N 12 40E
Vest-Agder fylke □ 71 58 30N 7 15E
Vest Fjorden 71 68 0N 15 0E
Vesta 166 9 43N 83 3W
Vestby 71 59 37N 10 45E
Vester Hassing 73 57 4N 10 8E
Vesterålen 74 68 45N 14 30E
Vestersche Veld 46 52 52N 6 9E
Vestfjorden 74 67 55N 14 0E
Vestfold fylke □ 71 59 15N 10 0E
Vestmannaeyjar 74 63 27N 20 15W
Vestmarka 71 59 56N 11 59E
Vestnes 71 62 39N 7 5E
Vestone 62 45 43N 10 25E
Vestsjaellands Amt □ 73 55 30N 11 20E
Vestspitsbergen 12 78 40N 17 0E
Vestvågøy 74 68 18N 13 50E
Vesuvio 65 40 50N 14 22E
Vesuvius, Mt. = Vesuvio 65 40 50N 14 22E
Veszprém 53 47 8N 17 57E
Veszprém □ 53 47 5N 17 55E
Vésztő 53 46 55N 21 16E
Vetapalam 97 15 47N 80 18E
Vetlanda 73 57 24N 15 3E
Vetluga 81 57 53N 45 45E
Vetluzhskiy 81 57 17N 45 12E
Vetovo 67 43 42N 26 16E
Vetralia 63 42 20N 12 2E
Vetren 67 42 15N 24 3E
Vettore, Mte. 63 44 38N 7 5E
Veurne 47 51 5N 2 40E
Vevey 50 46 28N 6 51E
Vévi 68 40 47N 21 38E
Veys 92 31 30N 49 0E
Vézelise 43 48 30N 6 5E
Vezhen, mt. 67 42 50N 24 20E
Vi Thanh 101 9 42N 105 26E
Viacha 174 16 30S 68 5W
Viadana 62 44 55N 10 30E
Viana, Brazil 170 3 0S 44 40W
Viana, Port. 55 38 20N 8 0W
Viana, Spain 58 42 31N 2 22W
Viana do Castelo 56 41 42N 8 50W
Vianden 47 49 56N 6 12E
Vianen 46 51 59N 5 5E
Vianna do Castelo □ 56 41 50N 8 30W
Vianópolis 171 16 40S 48 35W
Viar, R. 56 37 45N 5 54W
Viaréggio 62 43 52N 10 13E
Vibank 153 50 20N 103 56W
Vibey, R. 56 42 21N 7 15E
Vibo Valéntia 65 38 40N 16 5E
Viborg 73 56 27N 9 23E
Viborg Amt □ 73 56 30N 9 20E
Vic-en-Bigorre 44 43 24N 0 3E
Vic-Fezensac 44 43 45N 0 18E
Vic Fézensac 44 43 47N 0 19E
Vic-sur-Cère 44 44 59N 2 38E
Vic-sur-Seille 43 48 45N 6 33E
Vicarstown 39 53 5N 7 7W
Vicenza 63 45 32N 11 31E
Vich 58 41 58N 2 19E
Vichada □ 174 5 0N 69 30W
Vichuga 81 57 25N 41 55E
Vichy 44 46 9N 3 26E
Vickerstown 32 54 8N 3 17W
Vicksburg, Mich., U.S.A. 156 42 10N 85 30W
Vicksburg, Miss., U.S.A. 159 32 22N 90 56W
Vico, L. di 63 42 20N 12 10E
Viçosa, Min. Ger., Brazil 170 20 45S 42 53W
Viçosa, Pernambuco, Brazil 170 9 28S 36 14W
Viçosa do Ceará 170 3 34S 41 5W
Vicosoprano 51 46 22N 9 38E
Victor 158 38 43N 105 7W
Victor Emanuel Ra. 135 5 20S 142 15E
Victor Harbour 139 35 30S 138 37E
Victoria, Argent. 172 32 40S 60 10W
Victoria, Austral. 138 21 16S 149 3E
*Victoria, Camer. 121 4 1N 9 10E
Victoria, Can. 152 48 30N 123 25W
Victoria, Chile 176 38 13S 72 20W
Victoria, Guin. 120 10 50N 14 32W
Victoria, H. K. 109 22 25N 114 15E
Victoria, Malay. 102 5 20N 115 20E
Victoria, Tex., U.S.A. 159 28 50N 97 0W
Victoria, Va., U.S.A. 158 38 52N 99 8W
Victoria □, Austral. 131 37 0S 144 0E
Victoria □, Zimb. 127 21 0S 31 30E
Victoria Beach 153 50 40N 96 35W
Victoria de las Tunas 166 20 58N 76 59W
Victoria Falls 127 17 58S 25 45E
Victoria, Grand L. 150 47 31N 77 30W
Victoria Harbour 150 44 45N 79 45W
Victoria I. 148 71 0N 111 0W
Victoria, L., N.S.W., Austral. 140 33 57S 141 15E
Victoria, L., Vic., Austral. 139 38 2S 147 34E
Victoria, L., E. Afr. 126 1 0S 33 0E
Victoria, La 174 10 14N 67 20W
Victoria Ld. 13 75 0S 160 0E
Victoria, Mt., Burma 98 21 15N 93 55E
Victoria, Mt., P.N.G. 135 8 55S 147 32E
Victoria Nile R. 126 2 25N 31 50E
Victoria, R. 136 15 10S 129 40E
Victoria R. Downs 136 16 25S 131 0E
Victoria Ra. 143 42 12S 172 7E
Victoria Res. 151 48 20N 57 27W
Victoria Taungdeik 99 21 15N 93 55E
Victoria West 128 31 25S 23 4E
Victoriaville 151 46 4N 71 56W
Victorica 172 36 20S 65 30W
Victorino 174 2 48N 67 50W
Victorville 163 34 32N 117 18W
Vicuña 172 30 0S 70 50W
Vicuña Mackenna 172 33 53S 64 25W
Vidalia 157 32 13N 82 25W
Vidauban 45 43 25N 6 27E
Videlv, R. 71 58 50N 8 32E
Vidigueira 57 38 12N 7 48W
Vidin 66 43 59N 22 28E
Vidio, Cabo 56 43 35N 6 14W
Vidisha (Bhilsa) 94 23 28N 77 53E
Vidöstern 73 57 5N 14 0E
Vidra 70 45 56N 26 55E
Viduša, mts. 66 42 55N 18 21E
Vidzy 80 54 40N 26 37E
Viedma 176 40 50S 63 0W
Viedma, L. 176 49 30S 72 30W
Vieira 56 41 38N 8 8W
Viejo Canal de Bahama 166 22 10N 77 30W
Viella 58 42 43N 0 44E
Vielsalm 47 50 17N 5 54E
Vien Pou Kha 101 20 45N 101 5E
Vienenburg 48 51 57N 10 35E
Vieng Pou Kha 100 20 41N 101 4E
Vienna, Illinois, U.S.A. 159 37 29N 88 54W
Vienna, Va., U.S.A. 162 38 54N 77 16W
Vienna = Wien 53 48 12N 16 22E
Vienne 45 45 31N 4 53E
Vienne □ 44 45 53N 0 42E
Vienne, R. 42 47 5N 0 30E
Vientiane 100 17 58N 102 36E
Vieques, I. 147 18 8N 65 25W
Vierlingsbeek 47 51 36N 6 1E
Viersen 48 51 15N 6 23E
Vierwaldstättersee 51 47 0N 8 30E
Vierzon 43 47 13N 2 5E
Vieux-Boucau-les-Bains 44 43 48N 1 23W
Vif 45 45 5N 5 41E
Vigan 103 17 35N 120 28E
Vigan, Le 44 44 0N 3 36E
Vigevano 62 45 18N 8 50E
Vigia 170 0 50S 48 5W
Vigía Chico 165 19 46N 87 35W
Vignacourt 43 50 1N 2 15E
Vignemale, Pic du 44 42 47N 0 10W
Vigneulles 43 48 59N 5 40E
Vignola 62 44 29N 11 0E
Vigo 56 42 12N 8 41W
Vigo, Ría de 56 42 15N 8 45W
Vihiers 42 47 10N 0 30W
Vijayadurg 96 16 30N 73 25E

*Renamed Limbe

Vijayawada (Bezwada) Voitsberg

Vijayawada (Bezwada)	96	16 31N	80 39 E
Vijfhuizen	46	52 22N	4 41 E
Vikedal	71	59 30N	5 55 E
Viken, L.	73	58 40N	10 2 E
Vikersund	71	59 58N	10 2 E
Viking	152	53 7N	111 50W
Viking, gasfield	19	53 30N	2 20 E
Vikna	74	64 52N	10 57 E
Vikramasingapuram	97	8 40N	76 47 E
Viksjö	72	62 45N	17 26 E
Vikulovo	76	56 50N	70 40 E
Vila Alferes Chamusca	129	24 27S	33 0 E
Vila Arriaga	125	14 35S	13 30 E
Vila Bittencourt	174	1 20S	69 20W
Vila Cabral = Lichinga	127	13 13S	35 11 E
Vila Caldas Xavier	127	14 28S	33 0 E
Vila Coutinho	127	14 37S	34 19 E
Vila da Maganja	127	17 18S	37 30 E
Vila da Ponte	125	14 35S	16 40 E
Vila de Aljustrel	125	13 30S	19 45 E
Vila de João Belo = Xai-Xai	129	25 6S	33 31 E
Vila de Liquica	103	8 40S	125 20 E
Vila de Manica	125	18 58S	32 59 E
Vila de Rei	57	39 41N	8 9W
Vila de Sena = Sena	127	17 25S	35 0 E
Vila do Bispo	57	37 5N	8 53W
Vila do Conde	56	41 21N	8 45W
Vila Fontes	125	17 51S	35 24 E
Vila Fontes Velha	127	17 51S	35 24 E
Vila Franca de Xira	57	38 57N	8 59W
Vila Gamito	127	14 12S	33 0 E
Vila General Machado	125	11 58S	17 22 E
Vila Gomes da Costa	129	24 20S	33 37 E
Vila Henrique de Carvalho = Lunda	124	9 40S	20 12 E
Vila Junqueiro	127	15 25S	36 58 E
Vila Luisa	129	25 45S	32 35 E
Vila Luso = Moxico	125	11 53S	19 55 E
Vila Machado	127	19 15S	34 14 E
Vila Marechal Carmona = Uige	124	7 30S	14 40 E
Vila Mariano Machado	125	13 3S	14 35 E
Vila Moatize	127	16 11S	33 40 E
Vila Mouzinho	127	14 48S	34 25 E
Vila Murtinho	174	10 20S	65 20W
Vila Nova de Fozcôa	56	41 5N	7 9W
Vila Nova de Ourém	57	39 40N	8 35W
Vila Nova do Seles	125	11 35S	14 22 E
Vila Novo de Gaia	56	41 4N	8 40W
Vila Paiva Couceiro	125	14 37S	14 40 E
Vila Paiva de Andrada	127	18 37S	34 2 E
Vila Pery = Chimoio	127	19 4S	33 30 E
Vila Pouca de Aguiar	56	41 30N	7 38W
Vila Real	56	41 17N	7 48W
Vila Real de Santo Antonio	57	37 10N	7 28W
Vila Robert Williams	125	12 46S	15 30 E
Vila Salazar, Angola	124	9 12S	14 48 E
Vila Salazar, Indon.	103	5 25S	123 50 E
Vila Teixeira da Silva	125	12 10S	15 50 E
Vila Vasco da Gama	127	14 54S	32 14 E
Vila Velha	173	20 20S	40 17W
Vila Verissimo Sarmento	124	8 15S	20 50 E
Vila Viçosa	57	38 45N	7 27W
Vilaboa	56	42 21N	8 39W
Vilaine, R.	42	47 35N	2 10W
Vilanculos	129	22 1S	35 17 E
Vilar Formosa	56	40 38N	6 45W
Vilareal □	56	41 36N	7 35W
Vileyka	80	54 30N	27 0 E
Vilhelmina	74	64 35N	16 39 E
Vilhena	174	12 30S	60 0W
Viliga	77	60 2N	156 56 E
Viliya, R.	80	54 57N	24 35 E
Viljandi	80	58 28N	25 30 E
Villa Abecia	172	21 0S	68 18W
Villa Ahumada	164	30 30N	106 40W
Villa Ana	172	28 28S	59 40W
Villa Ángela	172	27 34S	60 45W
Villa Bella	174	10 25S	65 30W
Villa Bens (Tarfaya)	116	27 55N	12 55W
Villa Cañas	172	34 0S	61 35W
Villa Cisneros = Dakhla	116	23 50N	15 53W
Villa Colón	172	31 38S	68 20W
Villa Constitución	172	33 15S	60 20W
Villa de Cura	174	10 2N	67 29W
Villa de María	172	30 0S	63 43W
Villa de Rosario	172	24 30S	57 35W
Villa Dolores	172	31 58S	65 15W
Villa Franca	172	26 14S	58 20W
Villa Frontera	164	26 56N	101 27W
Villa Guillermina	172	28 15S	59 29W
Villa Hayes	172	25 0S	57 20W
Villa Iris	172	38 12S	63 12W
Villa Julia Molina	167	19 5N	69 45W
Villa Madero	164	24 28N	104 10W
Villa María	172	32 20S	63 10W
Villa Mazán	172	28 40S	66 30W
Villa Mentes	172	21 10S	63 30W
Villa Minozzo	62	44 21N	10 30 E
Villa Montes	172	21 10S	63 30W
Villa Ocampo, Argent.	172	28 30S	59 20W
Villa Ocampo, Mexico	164	26 29N	105 30W
Villa Ojo de Agua	172	29 30S	63 44W
Villa San Agustín	172	30 35S	67 30W
Villa San Giovanni	65	38 13N	15 38 E
Villa San José	172	32 12S	58 15W
Villa San Martín	172	28 9S	64 9W
Villa Santina	63	46 25N	12 55 E
Villa Unión	164	23 12N	106 14W
Villablino	56	42 57N	6 19W
Villabruzzi	91	3 3N	45 18 E
Villacampo, Pantano de	56	41 31N	6 0W
Villacañas	58	39 38N	3 20W
Villacarlos	58	39 53N	4 17 E
Villacarriedo	58	43 14N	3 48W
Villacarrillo	59	38 7N	3 3W
Villacastín	56	40 46N	4 25W
Villach	52	46 37N	13 51 E
Villaciaro	64	39 27N	8 45 E
Villada	56	42 15N	4 59W
Villadiego	56	42 31N	4 1W
Villadossóla	62	46 4N	8 16 E
Villafeliche	58	41 10N	1 30W
Villafranca	58	42 17N	1 46W
Villafranca de los Barros	57	38 35N	6 18W
Villafranca de los Caballeros	59	39 26N	3 21W
Villafranca del Bierzo	56	42 38N	6 50W
Villafranca del Cid	58	40 26N	0 16W
Villafranca del Panadés	58	41 21N	1 40 E
Villafranca di Verona	62	45 20N	10 51 E
Villagarcía de Arosa	56	42 34N	8 46W
Villagrán	165	24 29N	99 29W
Villaguay	172	32 0S	58 45W
Villaharta	57	38 9N	4 54W
Villahermosa, Mexico	165	17 45N	92 50W
Villahermosa, Spain	59	38 46N	2 52W
Villaines-la-Juhel	42	48 21N	0 20W
Villajoyosa	59	38 30N	0 12W
Villalba	56	40 36N	3 59W
Villalba de Guardo	56	42 42N	4 49W
Villalón de Campos	56	42 5N	5 4W
Villalpando	56	41 51N	5 25W
Villaluenga	56	40 2N	3 54W
Villamañ!n	56	42 19N	5 35W
Villamartín	56	36 52N	5 38W
Villamayor	58	41 42N	0 43W
Villamblard	44	45 2N	0 32 E
Villanova Monteleone	64	40 30N	8 28 E
Villanueva, Colomb.	174	10 37N	72 59W
Villanueva, U.S.A.	161	35 16N	105 31W
Villanueva de Castellón	59	39 5N	0 31W
Villanueva de Córdoba	57	38 20N	4 38W
Villanueva de la Fuente	59	38 42N	2 42W
Villanueva de la Serena	57	38 59N	5 50W
Villanueva de la Sierra	56	40 12N	6 24W
Villanueva de los Castillejos	57	37 30N	7 15W
Villanueva del Arzobispo	59	38 10N	3 0W
Villanueva del Duque	57	38 20N	4 38W
Villanueva del Fresno	57	38 23N	7 10W
Villanueva y Geltrú	58	41 13N	1 40 E
Villaodrid	56	43 20N	7 11W
Villaputzu	64	39 28N	9 33 E
Villar del Arzobispo	58	39 44N	0 50W
Villar del Rey	57	39 7N	6 50W
Villarcayo	58	42 56N	3 34W
Villard	45	45 4N	5 33 E
Villard-Bonnot	45	45 14N	5 53 E
Villard-de-Lans	45	45 3N	5 33 E
Villarino de los Aires	56	41 18N	6 23W
Villarosa	65	37 36N	14 9 E
Villarramiel	56	42 2N	4 55W
Villarreal	58	39 55N	0 3W
Villarrica, Chile	176	39 15S	72 30W
Villarrica, Parag.	172	25 40S	56 30W
Villarrobledo	59	39 18N	2 36W
Villarroya de la Sierra	58	41 27N	1 46W
Villarrubia de los Ojos	59	39 14N	3 36W
Villars	45	46 0N	5 2 E
Villarta de San Juan	59	39 15N	3 25W
Villasayas	58	41 24N	2 39W
Villaseca de los Gamitos	56	41 2N	6 7W
Villastar	58	40 17N	1 9W
Villatobas	58	39 54N	3 20W
Villavicencio, Argent.	172	32 28S	69 0W
Villavicencio, Colomb.	174	4 9N	73 37W
Villaviciosa	56	43 32N	5 27W
Villazón	172	22 0S	65 35W
Ville de Paris □	43	48 50N	2 20 E
Ville Marie	150	47 20N	79 30W
Ville Platte	159	30 45N	92 17W
Villedieu	42	48 50N	1 12W
Villefort	44	44 28N	3 56 E
Villefranche	43	47 19N	146 0 E
Villefranche-de-Lauragais	44	43 25N	1 44 E
Villefranche-de-Rouergue	44	44 21N	2 2 E
Villefranche-du-Périgord	44	44 38N	1 5 E
Villefranche-sur-Saône	45	45 59N	4 43 E
Villel	58	40 14N	1 12W
Villemaur	43	48 14N	3 40 E
Villemur-sur-Tarn	44	43 51N	1 31 E
Villena	59	38 39N	0 52W
Villenauxe	43	48 36N	3 30 E
Villenave	44	44 46N	0 33W
Villeneuve, France	43	48 42N	2 25 E
Villeneuve, Italy	62	45 40N	7 10 E
Villeneuve, Switz.	50	46 24N	6 56 E
Villeneuve-l'Archevèque	43	48 14N	3 32 E
Villeneuve-lès-Avignon	45	43 57N	4 49 E
Villeneuve-sur-Allier	44	46 40N	3 13 E
Villeneuve-sur-Lot	44	44 24N	0 42 E
Villeréal	44	44 38N	0 45 E
Villers Bocage	42	49 3N	0 40W
Villers Bretonneux	43	49 50N	2 30 E
Villers-Cotterets	43	49 15N	3 4 E
Villers-Farlay	47	47 0N	5 45 E
Villers-le-Bouillet	47	50 34N	5 15 E
Villers-le-Gambon	47	50 11N	4 37 E
Villers-sur-Mer	42	49 21N	0 2W
Villersexel	43	47 33N	6 26 E
Villerslev	73	56 49N	8 29 E
Villerupt	43	49 28N	5 55 E
Villerville	42	49 26N	0 5 E
Villiers	129	27 2S	28 36 E
Villingen = Schwenningen	49	48 3N	8 29 E
Villisca	158	40 55N	94 59W
Villupuram	97	11 59N	79 31 E
Vilna	152	54 7N	111 55W
Vilnius	80	54 38N	25 25 E
Vils	52	47 33N	10 37 E
Vilsbiburg	49	48 27N	12 23 E
Vilslev	73	55 24N	8 42 E
Vilusi	66	42 44N	18 34 E
Vilvoorde	47	50 56N	4 26 E
Vilyuy, R.	77	63 58N	125 0 E
Vilyuysk	77	63 40N	121 20 E
Vimercate	62	45 38N	9 25 E
Vimiosa	56	41 35N	6 13W
Vimmerby	73	57 40N	15 55 E
Vimo	72	60 50N	14 20 E
Vimoutiers	42	48 57N	0 10 E
Vimperk	52	49 3N	13 46 E
Viña del Mar	172	33 0S	71 30W
Vinaroz	58	40 30N	0 27 E
Vincennes	156	38 42N	87 29W
Vincent	163	34 33N	118 11W
Vinchina	172	28 45S	68 15W
Vindel älv	74	64 20N	19 20 E
Vindeln	74	64 12N	19 43 E
Vinderup	73	56 29N	8 45 E
Vindhya Ra.	94	22 50N	77 0 E
Vinegar Hill	39	52 30N	6 28W
Vineland	162	39 30N	75 0W
Vinga	66	46 0N	21 14 E
Vingnes	71	61 7N	10 26 E
Vinh	100	18 45N	105 38 E
Vinh Linh	100	17 4N	107 2 E
Vinh Loi	101	9 20N	104 45 E
Vinh Long	101	10 16N	105 57 E
Vinh Yen	100	21 21N	105 35 E
Vinhais	56	41 50N	7 0W
Vinica	63	45 28N	15 16 E
Vinita	159	36 40N	95 12W
Vinkeveen	46	52 13N	4 56 E
Vinkovci	66	45 19N	18 48 E
Vinnitsa	82	49 15N	28 30 E
Vinstra	71	61 37N	9 44 E
Vinton, Iowa, U.S.A.	158	42 8N	92 1W
Vinton, La., U.S.A.	159	30 13N	93 35W
Vintu de Jos	70	46 0N	23 30 E
Viöl	48	54 32N	9 12 E
Violet Town	141	36 38S	145 42 E
Vipava	63	45 51N	13 38 E
Vipiteno	63	46 55N	11 25 E
Viqueque	103	8 42S	126 30 E
Vir	85	37 45N	72 5 E
Vir, I.	63	44 17N	15 3 E
Virac	103	13 30N	124 20 E
Virachei	100	13 59N	106 49 E
Virago Sd.	152	54 0N	132 42W
Virajpet	97	12 15N	75 50 E
Viramgam	94	23 5N	72 0 E
Virarajendrapet (Virajpet)	97	12 10N	75 50 E
Viravanallur	97	8 40N	79 30 E
Virden	153	49 50N	100 56W
Vire	42	48 50N	0 53W
Virgem da Lapa	171	16 49S	42 21W
Virgenes, C.	176	52 19S	68 21W
Virgin Gorda, I.	147	18 45N	64 26W
Virgin Is.	147	18 40N	64 30W
Virgin, R., Can.	153	57 2N	108 17W
Virgin, R., U.S.A.	161	36 50N	114 10W
Virginia, Ireland	38	53 50N	7 5W
Virginia, S. Afr.	128	28 8S	26 55 E
Virginia, U.S.A.	158	47 30N	92 32W
Virginia □	156	37 45N	78 0W
Virginia Beach	156	36 54N	75 58W
Virginia City, Mont., U.S.A.	160	45 25N	111 58W
Virginia City, Nev., U.S.A.	160	39 19N	119 39W
Virginia Falls	152	61 38N	125 42W
Virginiatown	150	48 9N	79 36W
Virgins, C.	176	52 10S	68 30W
Virieu-le-Grand	45	45 51N	5 39 E
Virje	66	46 4N	16 59 E
Viroqua	158	43 33N	90 57W
Virovitica	66	45 51N	17 21 E
Virpaza, R.	66	42 14N	19 6 E
Virserum	73	57 20N	15 35 E
Virton	47	49 35N	5 32 E
Virtsu	80	58 32N	23 33 E
Virudhunagar	97	9 30N	78 0 E
Vis	63	43 0N	16 10 E
Vis, I.	63	43 0N	16 10 E
Vis Kanal	63	43 4N	16 5 E
Visalia	163	36 25N	119 18W
Visayan Sea	103	11 30N	123 30 E
Visby	73	57 37N	18 18 E
Viscount Melville Sd.	12	74 10N	108 0W
Visé	47	50 44N	5 41 E
Višegrad	66	43 47N	19 17 E
Viseu, Brazil	170	1 10S	46 20W
Viseu, Port.	56	40 40N	7 55W
Vişeu	70	47 45N	24 25 E
Viseu □	56	40 40N	7 55W
Vishakhapatnam	96	17 45N	83 20 E
Vishera, R.	84	59 55N	56 25 E
Vishnupur	95	23 8N	87 20 E
Visikoi I.	13	56 30S	26 40 E
Visingsö	73	58 2N	14 20 E
Viskafors	73	57 37N	12 50 E
Vislanda	73	56 46N	14 30 E
Vislinskil Zaliv (Zalew Wislany)	54	54 20N	19 50 E
Visnagar	94	23 45N	72 32 E
Višnja Gora	63	45 58N	14 45 E
Viso del Marqués	59	38 32N	3 34W
Viso, Mte.	62	44 38N	7 5 E
Visoko	66	43 58N	18 10 E
Visp	50	46 17N	7 52 E
Vispa, R.	50	46 9N	7 48 E
Visselhovde	48	52 59N	9 36 E
Vissoie	50	46 13N	7 36 E
Vista	163	33 12N	117 14W
Vistonis, Limni	68	41 0N	25 7 E
Vistula, R. = Wisła, R.	54	53 38N	18 47 E
Vit, R.	67	43 30N	24 30 E
Vitanje	63	46 40N	15 18 E
Vitebsk	80	55 10N	30 15 E
Viterbo	63	42 25N	12 8 E
Viti Levu, I.	143	17 30S	177 30 E
Vitiaz Str.	135	5 40S	147 10 E
Vitigudino	56	41 1N	6 35W
Vitim	77	59 45N	112 25 E
Vitim, R.	77	58 40N	112 50 E
Vitina	69	37 40N	22 10 E
Vitina	66	43 17N	17 29 E
Vitória	171	20 20S	40 22W
Vitoria	58	42 50N	2 41W
Vitória da Conquista	171	14 51S	40 51W
Vitória de São Antão	170	8 10S	37 20W
Vitorino Friere	170	4 4S	45 10W
Vitré	42	48 8N	1 12W
Vitry-le-François	43	48 43N	4 33 E
Vitsi, Mt.	68	40 40N	21 25 E
Vittangi	74	67 41N	21 40 E
Vitteaux	43	47 24N	4 30 E
Vittel	43	48 12N	5 57 E
Vittória	65	36 58N	14 30 E
Vittório Véneto	63	45 59N	12 18 E
Vitu Is.	135	4 50S	149 25 E
Vivegnis	47	50 42N	5 39 E
Viver	58	39 55N	0 36W
Vivero	56	43 39N	7 38W
Viviers	45	44 30N	4 40 E
Vivonne, Austral.	140	35 59S	137 9 E
Vivonne, France	44	46 36N	0 15 E
Vivonne B.	140	35 59S	137 9 E
Vivsta	72	62 30N	17 18 E
Vizcaíno, Desierto de	164	27 40N	113 50W
Vizcaíno, Sierra	164	27 30N	114 0W
Vizcaya □	58	43 15N	2 45W
Vizianagaram	96	18 6N	83 10 E
Vizille	45	45 5N	5 46 E
Vizinada	63	45 20N	13 46 E
Viziru	70	45 0N	27 43 E
Vizovice	53	49 12N	17 56 E
Vizzini	65	37 9N	14 43 E
Vlaardingen	46	51 55N	4 21 E
Vladicin Han	66	42 42N	22 1 E
Vladimir	81	56 0N	40 30 E
Vladimir Volynskiy	80	50 50N	24 18 E
Vladimirci	66	44 36N	19 45 E
Vladimirovac	66	45 1N	20 53 E
Vladimirovka, U.S.S.R.	83	44 37N	44 41 E
Vladimirovka, U.S.S.R.	83	48 27N	46 5 E
Vladimirovo	67	43 32N	23 22 E
Vladislavovka	82	45 15N	35 15 E
Vladivostok	82	43 10N	131 53 E
Vlamertinge	47	50 51N	2 49 E
Vlaming Head	137	21 48S	114 5 E
Vlasenica	66	44 11N	18 59 E
Vlasim	52	49 40N	14 53 E
Vlasinsko Jezero	66	42 44N	22 37 E
Vlašió, mt.	66	44 19N	17 37 E
Vlasotinci	66	42 59N	22 7 E
Vleuten	46	52 6N	5 1 E
Vlieland, I.	46	53 30N	4 55 E
Vliestroom	46	53 19N	5 8 E
Vlijmen	47	51 42N	5 14 E
Vlissingen	47	51 26N	3 34 E
Vlora	68	40 32N	19 28 E
Vlora □	68	40 12N	20 0 E
Vltava, R.	52	49 35N	14 10 E
Vlădeasa, mt.	70	46 47N	22 50 E
Vo Dat	101	11 9N	107 31 E
Vobarno	62	45 38N	10 30 E
Vočin	66	45 37N	17 33 E
Vodice	63	43 47N	15 47 E
Vodnany	52	49 9N	14 11 E
Vodnjan	63	44 59N	13 52 E
Voe	36	60 21N	1 15W
Voga	121	6 23N	1 30 E
Vogelkop = Doberai, Jazirah	103	1 25S	133 0 E
Vogelsberg	48	50 37N	9 30 E
Voghera	62	44 59N	9 1 E
Vohémar	129	13 25S	50 0 E
Vohipeno	129	22 22S	47 51 E
Voi	126	3 25S	38 32 E
Void	43	48 40N	5 36 E
Voil, L.	34	56 20N	4 25W
Voineşti, Iaşi, Rumania	70	47 5N	27 27 E
Voineşti, Ploeşti, Rumania	70	45 5N	25 14 E
Voiotia □	69	38 20N	23 0 E
Voiron	45	45 22N	5 35 E
Voiseys B.	151	56 15N	61 50W
Voitsberg	52	47 3N	15 9 E

Voiviis Limni, L.	68	39 30N	22 45 E
Vojens	73	55 16N	9 18 E
Vojmsjön	74	64 55N	16 40 E
Vojnió	63	45 19N	15 43 E
Vojvodina, Auton. Pokragina	66	45 20N	20 0 E
Vokhma	81	59 0N	46 45 E
Vokhma, R.	81	59 0N	46 44 E
Vokhtoga	81	58 46N	41 8 E
Volary	52	48 54N	13 52 E
Volborg	158	45 50N	105 44W
Volchansk	81	50 17N	36 58 E
Volchya, R.	82	48 0N	37 0 E
Volda	71	62 9N	6 5 E
Volendam	46	52 30N	5 4 E
Volga	81	57 58N	38 16 E
Volga Hts. = Privolzhskaya V.S.	79	51 0N	46 0 E
Volga, R.	83	52 20N	48 0 E
Volgodonsk	83	47 33N	42 5 E
Volgograd	83	48 40N	44 25 E
Volgogradskoye Vdkhr.	81	50 0N	45 20 E
Volgorechensk	81	57 28N	41 14 E
Volissós	69	38 29N	25 54 E
Volkerak	47	51 39N	4 18 E
Völkermarkt	52	46 39N	14 39 E
Volkhov	80	59 55N	32 15 E
Volkhov, R.	80	59 30N	32 0 E
Völklingen	49	49 15N	6 50 E
Volkovysk	80	53 9N	24 30 E
Volksrust	129	27 24 S	29 53 E
Vollenhove	46	52 40N	5 58 E
Volnovakha	82	47 35N	37 30 E
Volo	140	31 37 S	143 0 E
Volochayevka	77	48 40N	134 30 E
Volodary	81	56 12N	43 15 E
Vologda	81	59 25N	40 0 E
Volokolamsk	81	56 5N	36 0 E
Volokonovka	81	50 33N	37 58 E
Volontirovka	82	46 28N	29 28 E
Vólos	68	39 24N	22 59 E
Volosovo	80	59 27N	29 32 E
Volozhin	80	54 3N	26 30 E
Volsk	81	52 5N	47 28 E
Volstrup	73	57 19N	10 27 E
Volta, L.	121	7 30N	0 15 E
Volta, R.	121	8 0N	0 10W
Volta Redonda	173	22 31 S	44 5W
Voltaire, C.	136	14 16 S	125 35 E
Volterra	62	43 24N	10 50 E
Voltri	62	44 25N	8 43 E
Volturara Áppula	65	41 30N	15 2 E
Volturno, R.	65	41 18N	14 20 E
Volubilis	118	34 2N	5 33W
Vólvi, L.	68	40 40N	23 34 E
Volzhsk	81	55 57N	48 23 E
Volzhskiy	83	48 56N	44 46 E
Vondrozo	129	22 49 S	47 20 E
Vónitsa	69	38 53N	20 58 E
Voorburg	46	52 5N	4 24 E
Voorne Putten	46	51 52N	4 10 E
Voorst	46	52 10N	6 8 E
Voorthuizen	46	52 11N	5 36 E
Vopnafjörður	74	65 45N	14 40W
Vorarlberg □	52	47 20N	10 0 E
Vóras Óros	68	40 57N	21 45 E
Vorbasse	73	55 39N	9 6 E
Vorden	46	52 6N	6 19 E
Vorderrheim, R.	51	46 49N	9 25 E
Vordingborg	73	55 0N	11 54 E
Voreppe	45	45 18N	5 39 E
Voríai Sporádhes	69	39 15N	23 30 E
Vórios Evvoïkós Kólpos	69	38 45N	23 15 E
Vorkuta	78	67 48N	64 20 E
Vorma	71	60 9N	11 27 E
Vorona, R.	81	52 0N	42 20 E
Voronezh, R.S.S.R., U.S.S.R.	81	51 40N	39 10 E
Voronezh, Ukraine, U.S.S.R.	80	51 47N	33 28 E
Voronezh, R.	81	52 30N	39 30 E
Vorontsovo-Aleksandrovskoïe = Zelenokumsk.	83	44 30N	44 1 E
Voroshilovgrad	83	48 38N	39 15 E
Voroshilovsk = Kommunarsk	83	48 3N	38 40 E
Vorovskoye	77	54 30N	155 50 E
Vorselaar	47	51 12N	4 46 E
Vorskla, R.	82	49 30N	34 31 E
Vorukh	85	39 52N	70 35 E
Vorupør	73	56 58N	8 22 E
Vosges	43	48 20N	7 10 E
Vosges □	43	48 12N	6 20 E
Voskopoja	68	40 40N	20 33 E
Voskresensk	81	55 27N	38 31 E
Voskresenskoye	81	56 51N	45 30 E
Voss	71	60 38N	6 26 E
Vosselaar	47	51 19N	4 52 E
Vostok I.	131	10 5 S	152 23W
Vostotnyy Sayan	77	54 0N	96 0 E
Votice	52	49 38N	14 39 E
Votkinsk	84	57 0N	53 55 E
Votkinskoye Vdkhr.	78	57 30N	55 0 E
Vouga, R.	56	40 46N	8 10W
Voulte-sur-Rhône, La	45	44 48N	4 46 E
Vouvry	50	46 21N	6 21 E
Voúxa, Ákra	69	35 37N	20 32 E
Vouzela	56	40 43N	8 7W
Vouziers	43	49 22N	4 40 E
Voves	43	48 15N	1 38 E
Voxna	72	61 20N	15 30 E
Voy	37	59 1N	3 16W
Vozhe Oz.	78	60 45N	39 0 E
Vozhgaly	81	58 24N	50 1 E
Voznesensk	82	47 35N	31 15 E
Voznesenye	78	61 0N	35 45 E
Vráble	53	48 15N	18 16 E
Vrácevšnica	66	44 2N	20 34 E
Vrådal	71	59 20N	8 25 E
Vradiyevka	82	49 56N	30 38 E
Vraka	68	42 8N	19 28 E
Vrakhnéika	69	38 10N	21 40 E
Vrancea □	70	45 50N	26 45 E
Vrancei, Munţi	70	46 0N	26 30 E
Vrangelja, Ostrov	77	71 0N	180 0 E
Vrangtjarn	72	62 14N	16 37 E
Vranica, mt.	66	43 59N	18 0 E
Vranje	66	42 34N	21 54 E
Vranjska Banja	66	42 34N	22 1 E
Vranov	53	48 53N	21 40 E
Vransko	63	46 17N	14 58 E
Vratsa	67	43 13N	23 30 E
Vratsa □	67	43 30N	23 30 E
Vrbas	66	45 0N	17 27 E
Vrbas, R.	66	44 30N	17 10 E
Vrbnik	63	45 4N	14 32 E
Vrboviec	63	45 53N	16 28 E
Vrbovsko	63	45 24N	15 5 E
Vrchlabí	52	49 38N	15 37 E
Vrede	129	27 24 S	29 6 E
Vredefort	128	27 0 S	26 58 E
Vredenburg	128	32 51 S	18 0 E
Vredendal	128	31 41 S	18 35 E
Vreeswijk	46	52 1N	5 6 E
Vrena	73	58 54N	16 41 E
Vrgorac	66	43 12N	17 20 E
Vrhnika	63	45 58N	14 15 E
Vriddhachalam	97	11 30N	79 10 E
Vridi	120	5 15N	4 3W
Vridi Canal	120	5 15N	4 3W
Vries	46	53 5N	6 35 E
Vriezenveen	46	52 25N	6 38 E
Vrindaban	94	27 37N	77 40 E
Vrnograč	63	43 12N	17 20 E
Vrondádhes	69	38 25N	26 7 E
Vroomshoop	46	52 27N	6 34 E
Vrpolje	66	43 42N	16 1 E
Vršac	66	45 8N	21 18 E
Vršački Kanal	66	45 15N	21 0 E
Vrsheto	67	43 15N	23 23 E
Vryburg	128	26 55 S	24 45 E
Vryheid	129	27 54 S	30 47 E
Vsetín	53	49 20N	18 0 E
Vu Liet	100	18 43N	105 23 E
Vŭcha, R.	67	41 53N	24 26 E
Vučitrn	66	42 49N	20 59 E
Vught	47	51 38N	5 20 E
Vuka, R.	66	45 28N	18 30 E
Vukovar	66	45 21N	18 59 E
Vulcan, Can.	152	50 25N	113 15W
Vulcan, Rumania	70	45 23N	23 17 E
Vulcan, U.S.A.	156	45 46N	87 51W
Vŭlcani	66	46 0N	20 26 E
Vulcano, I.	65	38 25N	14 58 E
Vulchedrŭma	67	43 42N	23 16 E
Vulci	63	42 23N	11 37 E
Vŭleni	70	44 15N	24 45 E
Vulkaneshty	82	45 35N	28 30 E
Vunduzi, R.	127	18 0 S	33 45 E
Vung Tau	101	10 21N	107 4 E
Vûrbitsa	67	42 59N	26 40 E
Vutcani	70	46 26N	27 59 E
Vuyyuru	96	16 28N	80 50 E
Vvedenka	84	54 0N	63 53 E
Vyara	96	21 8N	73 28 E
Vyasniki	81	56 10N	42 10 E
Vyatka, R.	84	56 30N	51 0 E
Vyatskiye Polyany	84	56 5N	51 0 E
Vyazemskiy	77	47 32N	134 45 E
Vyazma	80	55 10N	34 15 E
Vyborg	78	60 43N	28 47 E
Vychegda R.	78	61 50N	52 30 E
Vychodné Beskydy	53	49 30N	22 0 E
Východočeský □	52	50 20N	15 45 E
Východoslovenský □	53	48 50N	21 0 E
Vyg-ozero	78	63 30N	34 0 E
Vyja, R.	81	41 53N	24 26 E
Vypin, I.	97	10 10N	76 15 E
Vyrnwy, L.	31	52 48N	3 30W
Vyrnwy, R.	31	52 43N	3 15W
Vyshniy Volochek	80	57 30N	34 30 E
Vyškov	53	49 17N	17 0 E
Vysoké Mýto	53	49 58N	16 23 E
Vysoké Tatry	53	49 30N	20 0 E
Vysokovsk	81	56 22N	36 30 E
Vysotsk	80	51 43N	36 32 E
Vyssi Brod	92	48 36N	14 20 E
Vytegra	52	61 15N	36 40 E

W

Wa	121	10 7N	2 25W
Waal, R.	46	51 59N	4 8 E
Waalwijk	47	51 42N	5 4 E
Waarschoot	47	51 10N	3 36 E
Waasmunster	47	51 6N	4 5 E
Wabag	135	5 32 S	143 53 E
Wabakimi L.	150	50 38N	89 45W
Wabana	151	47 40N	53 0W
Wabasca	152	55 57N	113 45W
Wabash	156	40 48N	85 46W
Wabash, R.	156	39 10N	87 30W
Wabawng	98	25 18N	97 46 E
Wabeno	156	45 25N	88 40W
Wabi Gestro, R.	123	6 0N	41 35 E
Wabi, R.	123	7 35N	40 5 E
Wabi Shaballe, R.	123	8 0N	40 45 E
Wabigoon, L.	153	49 44N	92 34W
Wabowden	153	54 55N	98 38W
Wabrzezno	54	53 16N	18 57 E
Wabuk Pt.	150	55 20N	85 5W
Wabush City	151	52 55N	66 52W
Wabuska	160	39 16N	119 13W
W.A.C. Bennett Dam	152	56 2N	122 6W
Wachapreague	162	37 36N	75 41W
Wachtebeke	47	51 11N	3 52 E
Waco	159	31 33N	97 5W
Waconichi, L.	150	50 8N	74 0W
Wad ar Rimsa	92	26 5N	41 30 E
Wad Ban Naqa	123	16 32N	33 9 E
Wad Banda	123	13 10N	27 50 E
Wad el Haddad	123	13 50N	33 30 E
Wad en Nau	123	14 10N	33 34 E
Wad Hamid	123	16 20N	32 45 E
Wâd Medanî	123	14 28N	33 30 E
Wad Thana	94	27 22N	66 23 E
Wadayama	110	35 19N	134 52 E
Waddān	119	29 9N	16 45 E
Waddān, Jabal	119	29 0N	16 15 E
Waddeneilanden	46	53 25N	5 10 E
Waddenzee	46	53 6N	5 10 E
Wadderin Hill	137	32 0 S	118 25 E
Waddesdon	29	51 50N	0 54W
Waddingham	33	53 28N	0 31W
Waddington	33	53 10N	0 31W
Waddington, Mt.	152	51 23N	125 15W
Waddinxveen	46	52 2N	4 40 E
Waddy Pt.	139	24 58 S	153 21 E
Wadebridge	30	50 31N	4 51W
Wadena, Can.	153	51 57N	103 38W
Wadena, U.S.A.	158	46 25N	95 2W
Wädenswil	51	47 14N	8 30 E
Wadesboro	157	35 2N	80 2W
Wadhams	152	51 30N	127 30W
Wadhurst	29	51 3N	0 21 E
Wadi	121	13 5N	11 40 E
Wādī ash Shāfi'	119	27 30N	15 0 E
Wādī Banī Walīd	119	31 49N	14 0 E
Wadi Gemâl	122	24 35N	35 10 E
Wadi Halfa	122	21 53N	31 19 E
Wadi Masila	91	16 30N	49 0 E
Wadi Sabha	92	23 50N	48 30 E
Wadlew	54	51 31N	19 23 E
Wadowice	54	49 52N	19 30 E
Wadsworth	160	39 44N	119 22W
Waegwan	107	35 59N	128 23 E
Waenfawr	31	53 7N	4 10W
Wafou Hu	109	32 19N	116 56 E
Wafra	92	28 33N	48 3 E
Wagenberg	47	51 40N	4 46 E
Wageningen	46	51 58N	5 40 E
Wager B.	149	65 26N	88 40W
Wager Bay	149	65 56N	90 49W
Wagga Wagga	141	35 7 S	147 24 E
Waghete	103	4 10 S	135 50 E
Wagin, Austral.	137	33 17 S	117 25 E
Wagin, Nigeria	137	12 42N	7 10 E
Wagon Mound	159	36 10N	105 0W
Wagoner	159	36 0N	95 20W
Wagrowiec	54	52 48N	17 19 E
Wah	94	33 45N	72 40 E
Wahai	103	2 48 S	129 35 E
Wahiawa	147	21 30N	158 2W
Wahnai	94	32 40N	65 50 E
Wahoo	158	41 15N	96 35W
Wahpeton	158	46 20N	96 35W
Wahratta	140	31 58 S	141 50 E
Wai	96	17 56N	73 57 E
Wai, Koh	101	9 55N	102 55 E
Waiai, R.	143	45 36 S	167 45 E
Waianae	147	21 25N	158 8W
Waiau	143	42 39 S	173 5 E
Waiau, R.	143	42 47 S	173 22 E
Waiawe Ganga	97	6 15N	81 0 E
Waibeem	103	0 30 S	132 50 E
Waiblingen	49	48 49N	9 20 E
Waidhofen, Niederösterreich, Austria	52	48 49N	15 17 E
Waidhofen, Niederösterreich, Austria	52	47 57N	14 46 E
Waigeo, I.	103	0 20 S	130 40 E
Waihao Downs	143	44 48 S	170 55 E
Waihao, R.	143	44 52 S	171 11 E
Waiheke Islands	142	36 48 S	175 6 E
Waihi	142	37 23 S	175 52 E
Waihola	143	46 1 S	170 8 E
Waihola L.	143	45 59 S	170 8 E
Waihou, R.	143	37 15 S	175 40 E
Waika	126	2 22 S	25 42 E
Waikabubak	103	9 45 S	119 25 E
Waikaka	143	45 55 S	169 1 E
Waikaoti	131	45 36 S	170 41 E
Waikare, L.	142	37 26 S	175 13 E
Waikaremoana	142	38 42 S	177 12 E
Waikaremoana L.	142	38 49 S	177 9 E
Waikari	143	42 58 S	172 41 E
Waikato, R.	142	37 23 S	174 43 E
Waikawa Harbour	143	46 39 S	169 9 E
Waikerie	140	34 9 S	140 0 E
Waikiekie	142	35 57 S	174 16 E
Waikokopu	142	39 3 S	177 52 E
Waikokopu Harb.	142	39 4 S	177 53 E
Waikouaiti	143	45 36 S	170 41 E
Wailuku	147	20 53N	156 26W
Waimakariri, R.	143	42 23 S	172 42 E
Waimangaroa	143	41 43 S	171 46 E
Waimanola	147	21 19N	157 43W
Waimarie	143	41 35 S	171 58 E
Waimarino	143	40 40 S	175 20 E
Waimate	143	44 53 S	171 3 E
Waimea	147	21 57N	159 39W
Waimea Plain	143	45 55 S	168 35 E
Waimes	47	50 25N	6 7 E
Wainfleet All Saints	33	53 7N	0 16 E
Wainganga, R.	96	21 0N	79 45 E
Waingapu	103	9 35 S	120 11 E
Waingmaw	98	25 21N	97 26 E
Wainiha	147	22 9N	159 34W
Wainuiomata	142	41 17 S	174 56 E
Wainwright, Can.	153	52 50N	110 50W
Wainwright, U.S.A.	147	70 39N	160 10W
Waiotapu	142	38 21 S	176 25 E
Waiouru	142	39 28 S	175 41 E
Waipahi	143	46 6 S	169 15 E
Waipahu	147	21 23N	158 1W
Waipapa Pt.	143	46 40 S	168 51 E
Waipara	143	43 3 S	172 46 E
Waipawa	142	39 56 S	176 38 E
Waipiro	142	38 2 S	176 22 E
Waipori	131	45 50 S	169 52 E
Waipu	142	35 59 S	174 29 E
Waipukurau	142	40 1 S	176 33 E
Wairakei	142	38 37 S	176 6 E
Wairarapa I.	142	41 14 S	175 15 E
Wairau, R.	143	41 32 S	174 7 E
Wairio	143	45 59 S	168 3 E
Wairoa	142	39 3 S	177 25 E
Wairoa, R.	142	36 5 S	173 59 E
Waitaki Plains	143	44 22 S	170 0 E
Waitaki, R.	143	44 23 S	169 55 E
Waitara	142	38 59 S	174 15 E
Waitchie	140	35 22 S	143 8 E
Waitoa	142	37 37 S	175 35 E
Waitotara	142	39 49 S	174 44 E
Waitsburg	160	46 15N	118 10W
Waiuku	142	37 15 S	174 45 E
Wajir	126	1 42N	40 20 E
Wajir □	126	1 42N	40 20 E
Wakaia	143	45 44 S	168 51 E
Wakasa	110	35 20N	134 24 E
Wakasa-Wan	111	34 45N	135 30 E
Wakatipu, L.	143	45 5 S	168 33 E
Wakaw	153	52 39N	105 44W
Wakayama	111	34 15N	135 15 E
Wakayama-ken □	111	33 50N	135 30 E
Wake	110	34 48N	134 8 E
Wake Forest	157	35 58N	78 30W
Wake I.	130	19 18N	166 36 E
Wakefield, N.Z.	143	41 24 S	173 5 E
Wakefield, U.K.	33	53 41N	1 31W
Wakefield, Mass., U.S.A.	162	42 30N	71 3W
Wakefield, Mich., U.S.A.	158	46 28N	89 53W
Wakema	98	16 40N	95 18 E
Wakhan □	93	37 0N	73 0 E
Wakkanai	112	45 28N	141 35 E
Wakkerstroom	129	27 24 S	30 10 E
Wako	150	49 50N	91 22W
Wakool	140	35 28 S	144 23 E
Wakool, R.	140	35 5 S	143 33 E
Wakre	103	0 30 S	131 5 E
Waku	135	6 5 S	149 9 E
Wakuach L.	151	55 34N	67 32W
Walachia □	70	44 40N	25 0 E
Walamba	127	13 30 S	28 42 E
Walberswick	29	52 18N	1 39 E
Wałbrzych	54	50 45N	16 18 E
Walbury Hill	28	51 22N	1 28W
Walcha	141	30 55 S	151 31 E
Walcha Road	141	30 55 S	151 24 E
Walcheren, I.	46	51 30N	3 35 E
Walcott	160	41 50N	106 55W
Walcz	54	53 17N	16 27 E
Wald	51	47 17N	8 56 E
Waldbröl	48	50 52N	7 36 E
Waldeck	48	51 12N	9 4 E
Walden, Colo., U.S.A.	160	40 47N	106 20W
Walden, N.Y., U.S.A.	162	41 32N	74 13W
Waldenburg	50	47 23N	7 45 E
Waldorf	162	38 37N	76 54W
Waldport	160	44 30N	124 2W
Waldron, Can.	153	50 53N	102 35W
Waldron, U.K.	29	50 56N	0 13 E
Waldron, U.S.A.	159	34 52N	94 4W
Waldshut	49	47 37N	8 12 E
Waldya	123	11 50N	39 34 E
Walebing	137	30 40 S	116 15 E
Walembele	120	10 30N	1 14W
Walensee	51	47 7N	9 13 E
Walenstadt	51	47 8N	9 19 E
Wales	147	65 38N	168 10W
Walewale	121	10 21N	0 50W
Walgett	133	30 0 S	148 5 E
Walhalla, Austral.	141	37 56 S	146 29 E
Walhalla, U.S.A.	153	48 55N	97 55W
Waliso	123	8 33N	38 1 E
Walkaway	137	28 59 S	114 48 E
Walker	158	47 4N	94 35W
Walker L., Man., Can.	153	54 42N	96 57W
Walker L., Qué., Can.	151	50 20N	67 11W
Walker L., U.S.A.	163	38 56N	118 46W
Walkerston	138	21 11 S	149 8 E
Wall	158	44 0N	102 14W
Walla Walla, Austral.	141	35 45 S	146 54 E
Walla Walla, U.S.A.	160	46 3N	118 25W

Wallabadah **Weaverham**

Wallabadah	**138**	17 57 S	142 15 E
Wallace, Idaho, U.S.A.	**160**	47 30N	116 0W
Wallace, N.C., U.S.A.	**157**	34 50N	77 59W
Wallace, Nebr., U.S.A.	**158**	40 51N	101 12W
Wallaceburg	**150**	42 40N	82 23W
Wallacetown	**143**	46 21 S	168 19 E
Wallachia = Valahia	**70**	44 35N	25 0 E
Wallal	**139**	26 32 S	146 7 E
Wallal Downs	**136**	19 47 S	120 40 E
Wallambin, L.	**137**	30 57 S	117 35 E
Wallaroo	**140**	33 56 S	137 39 E
Wallasey	**32**	53 26N	3 2W
Walldurn	**49**	49 34N	9 23 E
Wallerawang	**141**	33 25 S	150 4 E
Wallhallow	**138**	17 50 S	135 50 E
Wallingford	**162**	43 27N	72 50W
Wallis Arch.	**142**	13 20 S	176 20 E
Wallisellen	**51**	47 25N	8 36 E
Wallowa	**160**	45 40N	117 35W
Wallowa, Mts.	**160**	45 20N	117 30W
Walls	**36**	60 14N	1 32W
Wallsend, Austral.	**141**	32 55 S	151 40 E
Wallsend, U.K.	**35**	54 59N	1 30W
Wallula	**160**	46 3N	118 59W
Wallumbilla	**139**	26 33 S	149 9 E
Walmer, S. Afr.	**128**	33 57 S	25 35 E
Walmer, U.K.	**29**	51 12N	1 23 E
Walmsley, L.	**153**	63 25N	108 36W
Walney, Isle of	**32**	54 5N	3 15W
Walnut Ridge	**159**	36 7N	90 58W
Walpeup	**140**	35 10 S	142 2 E
Walpole	**29**	52 44N	0 13 E
Walsall	**28**	52 36N	1 59W
Walsenburg	**159**	37 42N	104 45W
Walsh, Austral.	**138**	16 40 S	144 0 E
Walsh, U.S.A.	**159**	37 28N	102 15W
Walsh, R.	**138**	16 31 S	143 42 E
Walshoutem	**47**	50 43N	5 4 E
Walsoken	**29**	52 41N	0 12 E
Walsrode	**48**	52 51N	9 37 E
Waltair	**96**	17 44N	83 23 E
Walterboro	**157**	32 53N	80 40W
Walters	**159**	34 25N	98 20W
Waltershausen	**48**	50 53N	10 33 E
Waltham, Can.	**150**	45 57N	76 57W
Waltham, U.K.	**29**	53 32N	0 6W
Waltham, U.S.A.	**34**	42 22N	71 12W
Waltham Abbey	**29**	51 40N	0 1 E
Waltham Forest	**29**	51 37N	0 2 E
Waltham on the Wolds	**29**	52 49N	0 48W
Waltman	**160**	43 8N	107 15W
Walton	**162**	42 12N	75 9W
Walton-le-Dale	**32**	53 45N	2 41W
Walton-on-the-Naze	**29**	51 52N	1 17 E
Walu	**98**	23 54N	96 57 E
Walvis Ridge	**15**	30 0 S	3 0 E
Walvisbaai	**128**	23 0 S	14 28 E
Walwa	**141**	35 59 S	147 44 E
Wamaza	**126**	4 12 S	27 2 E
Wamba, Kenya	**126**	0 58N	37 19 E
Wamba, Nigeria	**126**	8 58N	8 34 E
Wamba, Zaïre	**121**	2 10N	27 57 E
Wamego	**158**	39 14N	96 22W
Wamena	**103**	3 58 S	138 50 E
Wampo	**99**	31 30N	86 38 E
Wamsasi	**103**	3 27 S	126 7 E
Wan Hat	**98**	20 14N	97 53 E
Wan Kinghao	**98**	21 34N	98 17 E
Wan Lai-Kam	**98**	21 21N	98 22 E
Wan Tup	**98**	21 13N	98 42 E
Wana	**94**	32 20N	69 32 E
Wanaaring	**139**	29 38 S	144 0 E
Wanaka L.	**143**	44 33 S	169 7 E
Wanan	**109**	26 25N	114 50 E
Wanapiri	**103**	4 30 S	135 50 E
Wanapitei	**150**	46 30N	80 45W
Wanapitei L.	**150**	46 45N	80 40W
Wanaque	**162**	41 3N	74 17W
Wanbi	**140**	34 46 S	140 17 E
Wanborough	**28**	51 33N	1 40W
Wanch'eng	**108**	22 51N	107 25 E
Wanch'üan	**106**	35 26N	110 50 E
Wanch'uan	**106**	40 50N	114 56 E
Wandanian	**141**	35 6 S	150 30 E
Wanderer	**127**	19 36 S	30 1 E
Wandiwash	**97**	12 30N	79 30 E
Wandoan	**139**	26 5 S	149 55 E
Wandre	**47**	50 40N	5 39 E
Wandsworth	**29**	51 28N	0 15W
Wanfercée-Baulet	**47**	50 28N	4 35 E
Wanfuchuang	**107**	40 10N	122 34 E
Wang Kai (Ghâbat el Arab)	**123**	9 3N	29 23 E
Wang Noi	**100**	14 13N	100 44 E
Wang, R.	**100**	17 8N	99 2 E
Wang Saphung	**100**	17 18N	101 46 E
Wang Thong	**100**	16 50N	100 26 E
Wanga	**126**	2 58N	29 12 E
Wangal	**103**	6 8 S	134 9 E
Wanganella	**141**	35 6 S	144 49 E
Wanganui	**142**	39 35 S	175 3 E
Wanganui, R., N.I., N.Z.	**142**	39 25 S	175 4 E
Wanganui, R., S.I., N.Z.	**143**	43 3 S	170 26 E
Wangaratta	**141**	36 21 S	146 19 E
Wangchiang	**109**	30 7N	116 41 E
Wangch'ing	**107**	43 14N	129 38 E
Wangdu Phodrang	**98**	27 28N	89 54 E
Wangerooge I.	**48**	53 47N	7 52 E
Wangi	**126**	1 58 S	40 58 E
Wangiwangi, I.	**103**	5 22 S	123 37 E
Wangmo	**108**	25 14N	105 59 E
Wangts'ang	**108**	32 12N	106 21 E

Wangtu	**106**	38 42N	115 4 E
Wanhsien, Hopeh, China	**106**	38 49N	115 7 E
Wanhsien, Kansu, China	**105**	36 45N	107 24 E
Wankaner	**94**	22 42N	71 0 E
Wanki Nat. Park	**128**	19 0 S	26 30 E
Wankie	**127**	18 18 S	26 30 E
Wankie □	**127**	18 18 S	26 30 E
Wanless	**153**	54 11N	101 21W
Wanna Lakes	**137**	28 30 S	128 27 E
Wannien	**109**	28 40N	116 55 E
Wanon Niwar	**100**	17 38N	103 46 E
Wanshengch'ang	**108**	28 58N	106 55 E
Wanssum	**47**	51 32N	6 5 E
Wanstead	**143**	40 8 S	176 30 E
Wantage	**28**	51 35N	1 25W
Wantsai	**109**	28 5N	114 22 E
Wanyin	**98**	20 23N	97 15 E
Wanyüan	**108**	32 4N	108 5 E
Wanzarīk	**119**	27 3N	13 30 E
Wanze	**47**	50 32N	5 13 E
Wapakoneta	**156**	40 35N	84 10W
Wapato	**160**	46 30N	120 25W
Wapawekka L.	**153**	54 55N	104 40W
Wapikopa L.	**150**	42 50N	88 10W
Wapiti, R.	**150**	55 5N	118 18W
Wappingers Fs.	**162**	41 35N	73 56W
Wapsipinican, R.	**158**	41 44N	90 19W
Warabi	**111**	35 49N	139 41 E
Warandab	**91**	7 20N	44 2 E
Warangal	**96**	17 58N	79 45 E
Waratah	**138**	41 30 S	145 30 E
Waratah B.	**139**	38 54 S	146 5 E
Warboys	**29**	52 25N	0 5W
Warburg	**48**	51 29N	9 10 E
Warburton	**141**	37 47 S	145 42 E
Warburton, R.	**143**	27 30 S	138 30 E
Warburton Ra.	**137**	25 55 S	126 28 E
Ward, Ireland	**38**	53 25N	6 19W
Ward, N.Z.	**143**	41 49 S	174 11 E
Ward Cove	**152**	55 25N	132 10W
Ward Hunt, C.	**135**	8 2 S	148 10 E
Ward Hunt Str.	**135**	9 30 S	150 0 E
Ward Mtn.	**163**	37 12N	118 54W
Ward, R.	**139**	26 32 S	146 6 E
Warden	**129**	27 50 S	29 0 E
Wardha	**96**	20 45N	78 39 E
Wardha, R.	**93**	19 57N	79 11 E
Wardington	**28**	52 8N	1 17W
Wardle	**32**	53 7N	2 35W
Wardlow	**152**	50 56N	111 31W
Wardoan	**133**	25 59 S	149 59 E
Wards River	**141**	32 11 S	151 56 E
Ward's Stone, mt.	**32**	54 2N	2 39W
Ware, Can.	**152**	57 26N	125 41W
Ware, U.K.	**29**	51 48N	0 2W
Ware, U.S.A.	**162**	42 16N	72 15W
Waregem	**47**	50 53N	3 27 E
Wareham, U.K.	**28**	50 41N	2 8W
Wareham, U.S.A.	**162**	41 45N	70 44W
Wareham, oilfield	**19**	50 40N	2 8W
Waremme	**47**	50 43N	5 15 E
Waren	**48**	53 30N	12 41 E
Warendorf	**48**	51 57N	8 0 E
Warialda	**139**	29 29 S	150 33 E
Wariap	**103**	1 30 S	134 5 E
Warin Chamrap	**100**	15 12N	104 53 E
Wark	**35**	55 5N	2 14W
Warkopi	**103**	1 12 S	134 9 E
Warkworth, N.Z.	**142**	36 24 S	174 41 E
Warkworth, U.K.	**35**	55 22N	1 38W
Warley	**28**	52 30N	2 0W
Warm Springs, Mont., U.S.A.	**160**	46 11N	112 56W
Warm Springs, Nev., U.S.A.	**161**	38 16N	116 32W
Warman	**153**	52 19N	106 30W
Warmbad, Namibia	**128**	19 14 S	13 51 E
Warmbad, Namibia	**128**	28 25 S	18 42 E
Warmbad, S. Afr.	**129**	24 51 S	28 19 E
Warmenhuizen	**46**	52 43N	4 44 E
Warmeriville	**43**	49 20N	4 13 E
Warminster	**28**	51 12N	2 11W
Warmond	**46**	52 12N	4 30 E
Warnambool Downs	**138**	22 48 S	142 52 E
Warnemünde	**48**	54 9N	12 5 E
Warner	**152**	49 17N	112 12W
Warner Range, Mts.	**160**	41 30 S	120 20W
Warner Robins	**157**	32 41N	83 36W
Warneton	**47**	50 45N	2 57 E
Warnow, R.	**48**	54 0N	12 9 E
Warnsveld	**46**	52 8N	6 14 E
Waroona	**137**	32 50 S	115 58 E
Warora	**96**	20 14N	79 1 E
Warracknabeal	**140**	36 9 S	142 26 E
Warragul	**141**	38 10 S	145 58 E
Warrawaqine	**136**	20 51 S	120 42 E
Warrayelu	**123**	10 40N	39 28 E
Warrego, R.	**139**	30 24 S	145 21 E
Warrego Ra.	**138**	25 15 S	146 0 E
Warren, Austral.	**141**	31 42 S	147 51 E
Warren, Ark., U.S.A.	**159**	33 35N	92 3W
Warren, Pa., U.S.A.	**156**	41 52N	79 10W
Warren, R.I., U.S.A.	**156**	41 43N	71 19W
Warrenpoint	**38**	54 7N	6 15W
Warrens Landing	**153**	53 40N	98 0W
Warrensburg	**158**	38 45N	93 45W
Warrenton, S. Afr.	**128**	28 9 S	24 47 E
Warrenton, U.S.A.	**160**	46 11N	123 59W
Warrenville	**139**	25 48 S	147 22 E
Warri	**121**	5 30N	5 41 E
Warrie	**136**	22 12 S	119 40 E

Warrina	**136**	28 12 S	135 50 E
Warrington, N.Z.	**143**	45 43 S	170 35 E
Warrington, U.K.	**32**	53 25N	2 38W
Warrington, U.S.A.	**157**	30 22N	87 16W
Warrnambool	**140**	38 25 S	142 30 E
Warroad	**158**	49 0N	95 20W
Warsaw	**156**	41 14N	85 50W
Warsaw = Warszawa	**54**	52 13N	21 0 E
Warsop	**33**	53 13N	1 9W
Warstein	**48**	51 26N	8 20 E
Warszawa	**54**	52 13N	21 0 E
Warszawa □	**54**	52 30N	17 0 E
Warta	**54**	51 43N	18 38 E
Warta, R.	**54**	52 40N	16 10 E
Waru	**103**	3 30 S	130 36 E
Warud	**96**	21 30N	78 16 E
Warwick, Austral.	**139**	28 10 S	152 1 E
Warwick, U.K.	**28**	52 17N	1 36W
Warwick, N.Y., U.S.A.	**162**	41 16N	74 22W
Warwick, R.I., U.S.A.	**162**	41 43N	71 25W
Warwick □	**28**	52 20N	1 30W
Wasa	**152**	49 45N	115 50W
Wasatch, Mt., Ra.	**160**	40 30N	111 15W
Wasbank	**129**	28 15 S	30 9 E
Wasbister	**37**	59 11N	3 2W
Wasco, Calif., U.S.A.	**163**	35 37N	119 16W
Wasco, Oreg., U.S.A.	**160**	45 45N	120 46W
Waseca	**158**	44 3N	93 31W
Wasekamio L.	**153**	56 45N	108 45W
Wash, The	**33**	52 58N	0 20W
Washburn, N.D., U.S.A.	**158**	47 23N	101 0W
Washburn, Wis., U.S.A.	**158**	46 38N	90 55W
Washford	**28**	51 9N	3 22W
Washington, U.K.	**35**	54 55N	1 30W
Washington, D.C., U.S.A.	**162**	38 52N	77 0W
Washington, Ga., U.S.A.	**157**	33 45N	82 45W
Washington, Ind., U.S.A.	**156**	38 40N	87 8W
Washington, Iowa, U.S.A.	**158**	41 20N	91 45W
Washington, Miss., U.S.A.	**158**	38 35N	91 20W
Washington, N.C., U.S.A.	**157**	35 35N	77 1W
Washington, N.J., U.S.A.	**162**	40 45N	74 59W
Washington, Ohio, U.S.A.	**156**	39 34N	83 26W
Washington, Pa., U.S.A.	**156**	40 10N	80 20W
Washington, Utah, U.S.A.	**161**	37 10N	113 30W
Washington □	**160**	47 45N	120 30W
Washington Court House	**156**	39 34N	83 26W
* Washington I., Pac. Oc.	**131**	4 43N	160 25W
Washington I., U.S.A.	**156**	45 24N	86 54W
Washington Mt.	**156**	44 15N	71 18W
Washir	**93**	32 15N	63 50 E
Wasian	**103**	1 47 S	133 19 E
Wasilków	**54**	53 12N	23 13 E
Wasior	**103**	2 43 S	134 30 E
Waskaiowaka, L.	**153**	56 33N	96 23W
Waskesiu Lake	**153**	53 55N	106 5W
Wasm	**122**	18 2N	41 32 E
Waspik	**47**	51 41N	4 57 E
Wassen	**51**	46 42N	8 36 E
Wassenaar	**46**	52 8N	4 24 E
Wasserburg	**49**	48 4N	12 15 E
Wassy	**43**	48 30N	4 58 E
Wast Water, L.	**32**	54 26N	3 18W
Waswanipi	**150**	49 40N	75 59W
Waswanipi, L.	**150**	49 35N	76 40W
Watangpone	**103**	4 29 S	120 25 E
Wataroa	**143**	43 18 S	170 24 E
Wataroa, R.	**143**	43 7 S	170 16 E
Watawaha, P.	**103**	6 30 S	122 20 E
Watchet	**28**	51 10N	3 20W
Water Park Pt.	**138**	22 56 S	150 47 E
Water Valley	**159**	34 9N	89 38W
Waterberg, Namibia	**128**	20 30 S	17 18 E
Waterberg, S. Afr.	**129**	24 14 S	28 0 E
Waterberg, mt.	**128**	20 26 S	17 13 E
Waterbury	**162**	41 32N	73 0W
Waterbury L.	**153**	58 10N	104 22W
Waterford, Ireland	**39**	52 16N	7 8W
Waterford, S. Afr.	**128**	33 6 S	25 0 E
Waterford, U.S.A.	**163**	37 38N	120 46W
Waterford □	**39**	51 10N	7 40W
Waterford Harb.	**39**	52 10N	6 58W
Watergate Bay	**30**	50 26N	5 4W
Watergrasshill	**39**	52 1N	8 20W
Waterhen L., Man., Can.	**153**	52 10N	99 40W
Waterhen L., Sask., Can.	**153**	54 28N	108 25W
Wateringen	**46**	52 2N	4 16 E
Waterloo, Belg.	**47**	50 43N	4 25 E
Waterloo, Can.	**150**	43 30N	80 32W
Waterloo, S. Leone	**120**	8 26N	13 8W
Waterloo, U.K.	**32**	53 29N	3 2W
Waterloo, Ill., U.S.A.	**158**	38 22N	90 6W
Waterloo, Iowa, U.S.A.	**158**	42 27N	92 20W
Waterloo, N.Y., U.S.A.	**162**	42 54N	76 53W
Watermeal-Boitsford	**47**	50 48N	4 25 E
Watermeet	**158**	46 15N	89 12W
Waternish	**36**	57 32N	6 35W
Waterton Lakes Nat. Park	**152**	49 5N	114 15W
Watertown, Conn., U.S.A.	**162**	41 36N	73 7W

**Renamed Teraina*

Watertown, N.Y., U.S.A.	**162**	43 58N	75 57W
Watertown, S.D., U.S.A.	**158**	44 57N	97 5W
Watertown, Wis., U.S.A.	**158**	43 15N	88 45W
Waterval-Boven	**129**	25 40 S	30 18 E
Waterville, Ireland	**39**	51 49N	10 10W
Waterville, Me., U.S.A.	**151**	44 35N	69 40W
Waterville, N.Y., U.S.A.	**162**	42 56N	75 23W
Waterville, Wash., U.S.A.	**160**	47 45N	120 1W
Watervliet, Belg.	**47**	51 17N	3 38 E
Watervliet, U.S.A.	**162**	42 46N	73 43W
Wates	**103**	7 53 S	110 6 E
Watford	**29**	51 38N	0 23W
Watford City	**158**	47 50N	103 23W
Wath	**33**	53 29N	1 20W
Wathaman, R.	**153**	57 16N	102 59W
Watheroo	**137**	30 15 S	116 0W
Watien	**109**	32 45N	112 30 E
Wat'ing	**106**	35 25N	106 46 E
Watkins Glen	**162**	42 25N	76 55W
Watlings I.	**167**	24 0N	74 35W
Watlington, Norfolk, U.K.	**29**	52 40N	0 24 E
Watlington, Oxford, U.K.	**29**	51 38N	1 0W
Watonga	**159**	35 51N	98 24W
Watou	**47**	50 51N	2 38 E
Watraba	**139**	31 58 S	133 13 E
Watrous, Can.	**153**	51 40N	105 25W
Watrous, U.S.A.	**159**	35 50N	104 55W
Watsa	**126**	3 4N	29 30 E
Watseka	**156**	40 45N	87 45W
Watson, Austral.	**137**	30 29 S	131 31 E
Watson, Can.	**153**	52 10N	104 30W
Watson Lake	**147**	60 6N	128 49W
Watsontown	**162**	41 5N	76 52W
Watsonville	**163**	36 55N	121 49W
Watten	**37**	21 1 S	144 3 E
Wattenwil	**50**	46 46N	7 30 E
Wattiwarriganna Cr.	**139**	28 57 S	136 10 E
Watton	**29**	52 35N	0 50 E
Wattwil	**51**	47 18N	9 6 E
Watubela, Kepulauan	**103**	4 28 S	131 54 E
Wau	**135**	7 21 S	146 47 E
Waubach	**47**	50 55N	6 3 E
Waubay	**158**	45 42N	97 17W
Waubra	**140**	37 21 S	143 39 E
Wauchope	**141**	31 28 S	152 45 E
Wauchula	**157**	27 35N	81 50W
Waugh	**153**	49 40N	95 20W
Waukegan	**156**	42 22N	87 54W
Waukesha	**156**	43 0N	88 15W
Waukon	**158**	43 14N	91 33W
Wauneta	**158**	40 27N	101 25W
Waupaca	**158**	44 22N	89 8W
Waupun	**158**	43 38N	88 44W
Waurika	**159**	34 12N	98 0W
Wausau	**158**	44 57N	89 40W
Wautoma	**158**	44 3N	89 20W
Wauwatosa	**156**	43 6N	87 59W
Wave Hill	**136**	17 32N	131 0 E
Waveney, R.	**29**	52 24N	1 20 E
Waver R.	**32**	54 50N	3 15W
Waverley	**142**	39 46 S	174 37 E
Waverly, Iowa, U.S.A.	**158**	42 40N	92 30W
Waverly, N.Y., U.S.A.	**162**	42 0N	76 33W
Wavre	**47**	50 43N	4 38 E
Wavreille	**47**	50 7N	5 15 E
Wâw	**123**	7 45N	28 1 E
Waw an Namus	**119**	24 24N	18 11 E
Wawa, Can.	**150**	47 59N	84 47W
Wawa, Nigeria	**121**	9 54N	4 27 E
Wawa, Sudan	**122**	20 30N	30 22 E
Wawanesa	**153**	49 36N	99 40W
Wawoi, R.	**135**	7 48 S	143 16 E
Wawona	**163**	37 32N	119 39W
Waxahachie	**159**	32 22N	96 53W
Waxweiler	**49**	50 6N	6 22 E
Way, L.	**137**	26 45 S	120 16 E
Wayabula Rau	**103**	2 29N	128 17 E
Wayatinah	**138**	42 19 S	146 27 E
Waycross	**157**	31 12N	82 25W
Wayi	**123**	5 8N	30 10 E
Wayne, Nebr., U.S.A.	**158**	42 16N	97 0W
Wayne, W. Va., U.S.A.	**156**	38 15N	82 27W
Waynesboro, Miss., U.S.A.	**157**	31 40N	88 39W
Waynesboro, Pa., U.S.A.	**156**	39 46N	77 32W
Waynesboro, Va., U.S.A.	**156**	38 4N	78 57W
Waynesburg	**156**	39 54N	80 12W
Waynesville	**157**	35 31N	83 0W
Waynoka	**159**	36 38N	98 53W
Waza	**94**	33 22N	69 22 E
Wāzin	**119**	31 58N	10 51 E
Wazirabad, Afghan.	**93**	36 44N	66 47 E
Wazirabad, Pak.	**94**	32 30N	74 8 E
We	**102**	6 3N	95 56 E
Weald, The	**29**	51 7N	0 9 E
Wear, R.	**35**	54 55N	1 22W
Weardale	**32**	54 44N	2 5W
Wearhead	**32**	54 45N	2 14W
Weatherford, Okla., U.S.A.	**159**	35 30N	98 45W
Weatherford, Tex., U.S.A.	**159**	32 45N	97 48W
Weaver, R.	**32**	53 17N	2 35W
Weaverham	**32**	53 15N	2 30W

Webb City Whitby

Webb City 159 37 9N 94 30W
Weber 142 40 24S 176 20E
Webera, Bale, Ethiopia 123 6 29N 40 33E
Webera, Shewa, Ethiopia 123 9 40N 39 0E
Webster, Mass., U.S.A. 162 42 4N 71 54W
Webster, S.D., U.S.A. 158 45 24N 97 33W
Webster, Wis., U.S.A. 158 45 53N 92 25W
Webster City 158 42 30N 93 50W
Webster Green 158 38 38N 90 20W
Webster Springs 156 38 30N 80 25W
Wecliniec 54 51 18N 15 10E
Weda 103 0 30N 127 50E
Weda, Teluk 103 0 30N 127 50E
Weddell I. 176 51 50S 61 0W
Weddell Sea 13 72 30S 40 0W
Wedderburn 140 36 20S 143 33E
Wedge I. 132 30 50S 115 11E
Wedgeport 151 43 44N 65 59W
Wedmore 28 51 14N 2 50W
Wednesbury 28 52 33N 2 1W
Wednesfield 28 52 36N 2 3W
Wedza 127 18 40S 31 33E
Wee Elwah 141 32 2S 145 14E
Wee Waa 139 30 11S 149 26E
Weed 160 41 29N 122 22W
Weedsport 162 43 3N 76 35W
Weemelah 139 29 2S 149 7E
Weenen 129 28 48S 30 7E
Weener 48 53 10N 7 23E
Weert 47 51 15N 5 43E
Weesen 51 47 7N 9 4E
Weesp 46 52 18N 5 2E
Weggis 51 47 2N 8 26E
Wegierska-Gorka 54 49 36N 19 7E
Wegorzewo 54 54 13N 21 43E
Wegrów 54 52 24N 22 0E
Wehl 46 51 58N 6 13E
Wei Ho, R., Honan, China 106 34 58N 113 32E
Wei Ho, R., Shensi, China 106 34 38N 110 20E
Wei-si 99 27 18N 99 18E
Weich'ang 107 41 56N 117 34E
Weichou Tao 108 21 3N 109 2E
Weich'uan 106 34 19N 114 0E
Weida 48 50 47N 12 3E
Weiden 49 49 40N 12 10E
Weifang 107 36 47N 119 10E
Weihai 107 37 30N 122 10E
Weihsi 108 27 18N 99 18E
Weihsin 108 27 48N 105 5E
Weilburg 48 50 28N 8 17E
Weilheim 49 47 50N 11 9E
Weimar 48 51 0N 11 20E
Weinan 106 34 30N 109 35E
Weinfelden 51 47 34N 9 6E
Weingarten 49 47 49N 9 39E
Weinheim 49 49 33N 8 40E
Weining 108 26 50N 104 19E
Weipa 138 12 24S 141 50E
Weir, R., Austral. 139 28 20S 149 50E
Weir, R., Can. 153 56 54N 93 21W
Weir River 153 56 49N 94 6W
Weisen 51 46 42N 9 43E
Weiser 160 44 10N 117 0W
Weishan, Shantung, China 107 34 49N 47 6E
Weishan, Yunnan, China 108 25 16N 100 21E
Weissenburg 49 49 2N 10 58E
Weissenfels 48 51 11N 11 58E
Weisshorn 50 46 7N 7 43E
Weissmies 50 46 8N 8 1E
Weisstannen 51 46 59N 9 22E
Weisswasser 48 51 30N 14 36E
Weiswampach 47 50 8N 6 5E
Wéitra 52 48 41N 14 54E
Weiyüan 106 35 6N 104 14E
Weiyuan 106 35 10N 104 20E
Weiz 52 47 13N 15 39E
Wejherowo 54 54 35N 18 12E
Wekusko 153 54 45N 99 45W
Wekusko L. 153 54 40N 99 50W
Welbourn Hill 139 27 21S 134 6E
Welby 153 50 33N 101 29W
Welch 156 37 29N 81 36W
Welcome 138 15 20S 144 40E
Weldon 35 55 16N 1 46W
Welega □ 123 9 25N 34 20E
Welford, Berks., U.K. 28 51 28N 1 24W
Welford, Northampton, U.K. 28 52 26N 1 5W
Welkenraedt 47 50 39N 5 58E
Welkite 123 8 15N 37 42E
Welkom 128 28 0S 26 50E
Welland 150 43 0N 79 10W
Welland, R. 29 52 43N 0 10W
Wellen 47 50 50N 5 21E
Wellesley Is. 138 17 20S 139 30E
Wellin 47 50 5N 5 6E
Wellingborough 29 52 18N 0 41W
Wellington, Austral. 141 32 35S 148 59E
Wellington, Can. 150 43 57N 77 20W
Wellington, N.Z. 142 41 19S 174 46E
Wellington, S. Afr. 128 33 38S 18 57E
Wellington, U.K. 28 50 58N 3 13W
Wellington, Col., U.S.A. 158 40 43N 105 0W
Wellington, Kans., U.S.A. 159 37 15N 97 25W
Wellington, Nev., U.S.A. 163 38 47N 119 28W
Wellington, Okla., U.S.A. 159 34 55N 100 13W
Wellington □ 143 40 8S 175 36E
Wellington Bridge 39 52 15N 6 45W
Wellington, I. 176 49 30S 75 0W
Wellington, L. 141 38 6S 147 20E
Wellington, Mt. 142 36 55S 174 52E
Wellington (Telford) 28 52 42N 2 31W
Wello, L. 137 26 43S 123 10E
Wellow 28 51 20N 2 22W
Wells, Norfolk, U.K. 29 52 57N 0 51E
Wells, Somerset, U.K. 28 51 12N 2 39W
Wells, Me., U.S.A. 162 43 18N 70 35W
Wells, Minn., U.S.A. 158 43 44N 93 45W
Wells, Nev., U.S.A. 160 41 8N 115 0W
Wells, N.Y., U.S.A. 162 43 24N 74 17W
Wells Gray Prov. Park 152 52 30N 120 15W
Wells L. 137 26 44S 123 15E
Wellsboro 156 41 46N 77 20W
Wellsford 142 36 16S 174 32E
Wellsville, Mo., U.S.A. 158 39 4N 91 30W
Wellsville, N.Y., U.S.A. 156 42 9N 77 53W
Wellsville, Ohio, U.S.A. 156 40 36N 80 40W
Wellsville, Utah, U.S.A. 160 41 35N 111 59W
Wellton 161 32 46N 114 6W
Welmel, W. 123 6 0N 40 20E
Welney 29 52 31N 0 15E
Welo □ 123 11 50N 39 48E
Wels 52 48 9N 14 1E
Welshpool 31 52 40N 3 9W
Welton 33 53 19N 0 29W
Welwel 91 7 5N 45 25E
Welwitschia 128 20 16S 14 59E
Welwyn 153 50 20N 101 30W
Welwyn Garden City 29 51 49N 0 11W
Wem 28 52 52N 2 45W
Wembere, R. 126 4 45S 34 0E
Wembury 30 50 19N 4 6W
Wemmel 47 50 55N 4 18E
Wemyss Bay 34 55 52N 4 54W
Wenatchee 160 47 30N 120 17W
Wench'ang 100 19 38N 110 42E
Wencheng 109 27 48N 120 5E
Wenchi 120 7 46N 2 8W
Wenchiang 108 30 43N 103 56E
Wenchou 109 28 1N 120 39E
Wench'uan 108 31 28N 103 35E
Wendell 160 42 50N 114 51W
Wendesi 103 2 30S 134 10E
Wendo 123 6 40N 38 27E
Wendover, U.K. 29 51 46N 0 45W
Wendover, U.S.A. 160 40 49N 114 1W
Wenduine 47 51 18N 3 5E
Wengan 108 27 0N 107 32E
Wengch'eng 109 24 22N 113 50E
Wenge 126 0 3N 24 0E
Wengen 50 46 37N 7 55E
Wengniut'ech'i 107 42 59N 118 48E
Wengpu 108 32 55N 98 30E
Wengyüan 109 24 21N 114 7E
Wenhsi 106 35 23N 111 8E
Wenhsiang 106 34 36N 110 34E
Wenhsien, Honan, China 106 34 56N 113 4E
Wenhsien, Kansu, China 106 58 0N 104 39E
Wenling 109 28 22N 121 18E
Wenlock 138 13 6S 142 58E
Wenlock Edge 23 52 30N 2 43W
Wenlock, R. 133 12 2S 141 55E
Wenshan 108 23 22N 104 13E
Wenshang 106 35 37N 116 33E
Wenshui, Kweichow, China 108 28 27N 106 31E
Wenshui, Shansi, China 106 37 25N 112 1E
Wensleydale 32 54 18N 2 0W
Wensu 105 41 15N 80 14E
Wenteng 107 37 10N 122 0E
Wentworth 140 34 2S 141 54E
Wentworth, Mt. 138 24 12S 147 1E
Wenut 103 3 11S 133 19E
Weobley 28 52 9N 2 52W
Weott 160 40 19N 123 56W
Wepener 128 29 42S 27 3E
Werbomont 47 50 23N 5 41E
Werda 128 25 24S 23 15E
Werdau 48 50 45N 12 20E
Werder, Ethiopia 91 6 58N 45 1E
Werder, Ger. 48 52 23N 12 56E
Werdohl 48 51 15N 7 47E
Weri 103 3 10S 132 30E
Werkendam 46 51 50N 4 53E
Werne 48 51 38N 7 38E
Wernigerode 48 51 49N 0 45E
Werribee 140 37 54S 144 40E
Werrimull 140 34 25S 141 38E
Werrington 30 50 31N 4 22W
Werris Creek 141 31 18S 150 38E
Wersar 103 1 30S 131 55E
Wertheim 49 49 44N 9 32E
Wervershoof 46 52 44N 5 10E
Wervik 47 50 47N 3 3E
Wesel 48 51 39N 6 34E
Weser, R. 48 53 33N 8 30E
Wesiri 103 7 30S 126 30E
Wesleyville 151 49 8N 53 36W
Wessel, C. 138 10 59S 136 46E
Wessel Is. 138 11 10S 136 45E
Wesselburen 48 54 11N 8 53E
Wessem 47 51 11N 5 49E
Wessington 158 44 30N 98 40W
Wessington Springs 158 44 10N 98 35W
West 159 31 50N 97 5W
West Auckland 33 54 38N 1 42W
West B. 151 45 53N 82 8W
West, B. 159 29 5N 89 27W
West Baines, R. 136 15 36S 129 58E
West Bend 156 43 25N 88 10W
West Bengal □ 95 25 0N 90 0E
West Branch 156 44 16N 84 13W
West Bridgford 33 52 56N 1 8W
West Bromwich 28 52 32N 2 1W
West Burra, I. 36 60 5N 1 21W
West Calder 35 55 51N 3 34W
West Canada Cr. 162 43 1N 74 58W
West Cape Howe 137 35 8S 117 36E
West Chester 162 39 58N 75 36W
West Coker 28 50 55N 2 40W
West Columbia 159 29 10N 95 38W
West Covina 163 34 4N 117 54W
West Derry 162 42 55N 71 19W
West Des Moines 158 41 30N 93 45W
West End 166 26 41N 78 58W
West Falkland Island 176 51 30S 60 0W
West Fen 33 53 5N 0 5W
West Frankfort 158 37 56N 89 0W
West Glamorgan □ 31 51 40N 3 55W
West Grinstead 29 50 58N 0 19W
West Haddon 28 52 21N 1 5W
West Harbour 131 45 51S 170 33E
West Hartford 162 41 45N 72 45W
West Haven 162 41 18N 72 57W
West Hazleton 162 40 58N 76 0W
West Helena 159 34 30N 90 40W
West Hurley 162 41 59N 74 7W
West Indies 158 15 0N 70 0W
West Kilbride 34 55 41N 4 50W
West Kirby 32 53 22N 3 11W
West Lavington 28 51 16N 1 59W
West Linton 35 55 45N 3 24W
West Looe 30 50 21N 4 29W
West Lulworth 28 50 37N 2 14W
West Lunga, R. 127 12 35S 24 45E
West Magpie R. 151 51 2N 64 42W
West Malling 29 51 16N 0 25E
West Memphis 159 35 5N 90 3W
West Meon 28 51 2N 1 3W
West Mersea 29 51 46N 0 55E
West Midlands □ 28 52 30N 1 55W
West Milton 162 41 1N 76 50W
West Monroe 159 32 32N 92 7W
West Nicholson 127 21 2S 29 20E
West Pakistan = Pakistan 93 27 0N 67 0W
West Palm Beach 157 26 44N 80 3W
West Paris 101 44 18N 70 30W
West Parley 28 50 46N 1 52W
West Plains 159 36 45N 91 50W
West Pt. 140 35 1S 135 56E
West Point, Can. 151 49 55N 64 30W
West Point, Jamaica 166 18 14N 78 30W
West Point, Ga., U.S.A. 157 32 54N 85 10W
West Point, Miss., U.S.A. 157 33 36N 88 38W
West Point, Nebr., U.S.A. 158 41 50N 96 43W
West Point, Va., U.S.A. 162 37 35N 76 47W
West Pokot □ 126 1 30N 35 40E
West, R. 162 42 52N 72 33W
West Rasen 33 53 23N 0 23W
West Reading 162 40 20N 75 57W
West Riding (□) 26 53 50N 1 30W
West Road R. 152 53 18N 122 53W
West Rutland 162 43 36N 73 3W
West Schelde = Westerschelde 47 51 23N 3 50E
West Sole, gasfield 19 53 40N 1 15E
West Spitsbergen 12 78 40N 17 0E
West Sussex □ 29 50 55N 0 30W
West-Terschelling 46 53 22N 5 13E
West Virginia □ 156 39 0N 18 0W
West-Vlaanderen □ 47 51 0N 3 0E
West Walker, R. 163 38 54N 119 9W
West Wittering 29 50 44N 0 53W
West Wyalong 141 33 56S 147 10E
West Yellowstone 160 44 47N 111 4W
West York 162 39 57N 76 46W
West Yorkshire □ 33 53 45N 1 40W
Westall 139 32 55S 134 4E
Westbank 152 49 50N 119 25W
Westbourne 29 50 53N 0 55W
Westbrook, Maine, U.S.A. 162 43 40N 70 22W
Westbrook, Tex., U.S.A. 159 32 25N 101 0W
Westbury, Austral. 138 41 30S 146 51E
Westbury, Salop, U.K. 28 52 40N 2 57W
Westbury, Wilts., U.K. 28 51 16N 2 11W
Westbury-on-Severn 28 51 49N 2 24W
Westby 158 48 52N 104 3W
Westend 163 35 42N 117 24W
Wester Ross, dist. 36 57 37N 5 0W
Westerbork 46 52 51N 6 37E
Westerham 29 51 16N 0 5E
Westerland 48 54 51N 8 20E
Western □, Kenya 126 0 30N 34 30E
Western □, Uganda 126 1 45N 31 30E
Western □, Zambia 127 13 15N 27 30E
Western Australia □ 137 25 0S 118 0E
Western Bay 151 46 50N 52 30W
Western Germany ■ 48 50 0N 8 0E
Western Ghats 97 15 30N 74 30E
Western Is. □ 36 57 40N 7 0W
Western River 140 35 42S 136 56E
Western Samoa ■ 130 14 0S 172 0W
Westernport 156 30 30N 79 5W
Westerschelde, R. 47 51 25N 4 0E
Westerstede 48 51 15N 7 55E
Westervoort 46 51 58N 5 59E
Westerwald, mts. 48 50 39N 8 0E
Westfield, U.K. 29 50 53N 0 30E
Westfield, U.S.A. 162 42 9N 72 49W
Westgat 47 51 39N 3 44E
Westhope 158 48 55N 101 0W
Westhoughton 32 53 34N 2 30W
Westkapelle, Belg. 47 51 19N 3 19E
Westkapelle, Neth. 47 51 31N 3 28E
Westland □ 143 43 33S 169 59E
Westland Bight 143 42 55S 170 5E
Westlock 152 54 9N 113 55W
Westmalle 47 51 18N 4 42E
Westmeath □ 38 53 30N 7 30W
Westmine 137 29 2S 116 8E
Westminster 162 39 34S 77 1W
Westmorland 161 33 2N 115 42W
Westmorland (□) 26 54 28N 2 40W
Weston, Malay. 102 5 10N 115 35E
Weston, U.K. 28 52 51N 2 2W
Weston, Oreg., U.S.A. 160 45 50N 118 30W
Weston, W. Va., U.S.A. 156 39 3N 80 29W
Weston I. 150 52 33N 79 36W
Weston-super-Mare 28 51 20N 2 59W
Westport, Ireland 38 53 44N 9 31W
Westport, N.Z. 143 41 46S 171 37E
Westport, U.S.A. 160 46 48N 124 4W
Westport B. 38 53 48N 9 38W
Westray 153 53 36N 101 24W
Westray Firth 37 59 15N 3 0W
Westray, I. 37 59 18N 3 0W
Westree 150 47 26N 81 34W
Westruther 35 55 45N 2 34W
Westview 152 49 50N 124 31W
Westville, Ill., U.S.A. 156 40 3N 87 36W
Westville, Okla., U.S.A. 159 36 0N 94 33W
Westward Ho 30 51 2N 4 16W
Westwood 160 40 26N 121 0W
Wetar, I. 103 7 30S 126 30E
Wetaskiwin 152 52 55N 113 24W
Wetherby 33 53 56N 1 23W
Wethersfield 162 41 43N 72 40W
Wetlet 98 21 13N 95 53E
Wettingen 51 47 28N 8 20E
Wetwang 33 54 2N 0 35W
Wetzikon 51 47 19N 8 48E
Wetzlar 48 50 33N 8 30E
Wevelgem 47 50 49N 3 12E
Wewak 135 3 38S 143 41E
Wewaka 159 35 10N 96 35W
Wexford 39 52 20N 6 28W
Wexford □ 39 52 20N 6 25W
Wexford Harb. 39 52 20N 6 25W
Wey, R. 29 51 19N 0 29W
Weybourne 29 52 57N 1 9E
Weybridge 29 51 22N 0 28W
Weyburn 153 49 40N 103 50W
Weyburn L. 152 63 0N 117 59W
Weyer 52 47 51N 14 40E
Weymouth, Can. 151 44 30N 66 1W
Weymouth, U.K. 28 50 36N 2 28W
Weymouth, U.S.A. 162 42 13N 70 53W
Weymouth, C. 133 12 37S 143 27E
Wezep 46 52 28N 6 0E
Whakamaru 142 38 23S 175 63E
Whakatane 142 37 57S 177 1E
Whale Cove 148 62 11N 92 36W
Whale Firth 36 60 40N 1 10W
Whale, R. 151 58 15N 67 40W
Whales 13 78 0S 165 0W
Whaley Bridge 32 53 20N 2 0W
Whalley 32 53 49N 2 25W
Whalsay, I. 36 60 22N 1 0W
Whalton 35 55 7N 1 46W
Whangamomona 142 39 8S 174 44E
Whangarei 142 35 43S 174 21E
Whangarei Harbour 142 35 45S 174 28E
Whangaroa 142 35 4S 173 46E
Whangumata 142 37 12S 175 53E
Whaplode 29 52 42N 0 3W
Wharanui 143 41 55S 174 6E
Wharfe, R. 33 53 55N 1 30W
Wharfedale 31 54 7N 2 4W
Wharton, N.J., U.S.A. 162 40 53N 74 36W
Wharton, Tex., U.S.A. 159 29 20N 96 6W
Whauphill 34 54 48N 4 31W
Whayjonta 139 29 40S 142 35E
Wheatland 158 42 4N 105 58W
Wheatley Hill 33 54 45N 1 23W
Wheaton, Md., U.S.A. 162 39 3N 77 3W
Wheaton, Minn., U.S.A. 158 45 50N 96 29W
Wheeler, Oreg., U.S.A. 160 45 45N 123 57W
Wheeler, Tex., U.S.A. 159 35 29N 100 15W
Wheeler Peak, Mt. 160 38 57N 114 15W
Wheeler, R. 153 57 34N 104 15W
Wheeler Ridge 163 35 0N 118 57W
Wheeling 156 40 2N 80 41W
Whichham 32 54 14N 3 22W
Whidbey I. 152 48 15N 122 40W
Whidbey Is. 136 34 30S 135 3E
Whiddy, I. 39 51 41N 9 30W
Whimple 30 50 46N 3 21W
Whipsnade 29 51 51N 0 32W
Whiskey Gap 152 49 0N 113 3W
Whiskey Jack L. 153 58 23N 101 55W
Whissendine 29 52 43N 0 46W
Whistleduck Cr. 138 20 15S 135 18E
Whistler 157 30 50N 88 10W
Whiston 32 53 25N 2 45W
Whitburn 35 55 52N 3 41W
Whitby 33 54 29N 0 37W

Whitchurch **Winterberg**

Whitchurch, U.K. 31 51 32N 3 15W
Whitchurch, Devon, U.K. 30 50 31N 4 7W
Whitchurch, Hants., U.K. 28 51 14N 1 20W
Whitchurch, Here., U.K. 28 51 51N 2 41W
Whitchurch, Salop, U.K. 32 52 58N 2 42W
Whitcombe, Mt. 131 43 12 S 171 0 E
Whitcombe, P. 131 43 12 S 171 0 E
White B. 151 50 0N 56 35W
White Bear Res. 151 48 10N 57 05W
White Bird 160 45 46N 116 21W
White Bridge 35 57 11N 4 32W
White Butte 156 46 23N 103 25W
White City 158 38 50N 96 45W
White Cliffs, Austral. 140 30 50 S 143 10 E
White Cliffs, N.Z. 143 43 26 S 171 55 E
White Deer 159 35 30N 101 8W
White Esk, R. 35 55 14N 3 11W
White Hall 158 39 25N 90 27W
White Haven 162 41 3N 75 47W
White Horse Hill 28 51 35N 1 35W
White I. 142 37 30 S 177 13 E
White L., Austral. 136 24 43 S 121 44 E
White L., U.S.A. 159 29 45N 92 30W
White Mts. 163 37 30N 118 15W
White Nile = Nîl el Abyad, Bahr 123 9 30N 31 40 E
White Nile Dam 123 15 24N 32 30 E
White Otter L. 150 49 5N 91 55W
White Pass 147 59 40N 135 3W
White Plains, Liberia 120 6 28N 10 40W
White Plains, U.S.A. 162 41 2N 73 44W
White, R., Ark., U.S.A. 159 36 28N 93 55W
White, R., Colo., U.S.A. 160 40 8N 108 52W
White, R., Ind., U.S.A. 156 39 25N 86 30W
White, R., S.D., U.S.A. 158 43 10N 102 52W
White River, Can. 150 48 35N 85 20W
White River, S. Afr. 129 25 20 S 31 00 E
White River, U.S.A. 158 43 48N 100 5W
White River Junc. 162 43 38N 72 20W
White Russia = Byelorussia, SSR 80 53 30N 27 0 E
White Sea = Beloye More 78 66 30N 38 0 E
White Sulphur Springs, Mont., U.S.A. 160 46 35N 111 0W
White Sulphur Springs, W. Va., U.S.A. 160 37 50N 80 16W
White Volta, R., (Volta Blanche) 121 10 0N 1 0W
White Well 137 31 25 S 131 3 E
Whiteadder Water, R. 35 55 47N 2 20W
Whitecourt 152 54 10N 115 45W
Whiteface 159 33 35N 102 40W
Whitefish 160 48 25N 114 22W
Whitefish L. 153 62 41N 106 48W
Whitefish Pt. 156 46 45N 85 0W
Whitegate, Clare, Ireland 39 52 58N 8 24W
Whitegate, Cork, Ireland 39 51 49N 8 15W
Whitegull, L. 151 55 27N 64 17W
Whitehall, Ireland 39 52 42N 7 2W
Whitehall, U.K. 37 59 9N 2 36W
Whitehall, Mich., U.S.A. 156 43 21N 86 20W
Whitehall, Mont., U.S.A. 160 45 52N 112 4W
Whitehall, N.Y., U.S.A. 162 43 32N 73 28W
Whitehall, Wis., U.S.A. 158 44 20N 91 19W
Whitehaven 32 54 33N 3 35W
Whitehead 38 54 45N 5 42W
Whitehorse 147 60 43N 135 3W
Whitehorse, Vale of 28 51 37N 1 30W
Whitekirk 35 56 2N 2 36W
Whiteman Ra. 135 5 55 S 150 0 E
Whitemark 138 40 7 S 148 3 E
Whitemouth 153 49 57N 95 58W
Whiten Hd. 37 58 34N 4 35W
Whitesail, L. 152 53 35N 127 45W
Whitesand B. 30 50 18N 4 20W
Whitesboro, N.Y., U.S.A. 162 43 8N 75 20W
Whitesboro, Tex., U.S.A. 159 33 40N 96 58W
Whiteshell Prov. Park 153 50 0N 95 40W
Whitetail 158 48 54N 105 15W
Whiteville 157 34 20N 78 40W
Whitewater 156 42 50N 88 45W
Whitewater Baldy, Mt. 161 33 20N 108 44W
Whitewater L. 150 50 50N 89 10W
Whitewood, Austral. 138 21 28 S 143 30 E
Whitewood, Can. 153 50 20N 102 20W
Whitfield 141 36 42 S 146 24 E
Whithorn 162 54 55N 4 25W
Whitianga 142 36 47 S 175 41 E
Whitland 31 51 49N 4 38W
Whitley Bay 35 55 4N 1 28W
Whitman 162 42 4N 70 55W
Whitmire 157 34 33N 81 40W
Whitney 150 45 31N 78 14W
Whitney, Mt. 163 36 35N 118 14W
Whitney Pt. 162 42 19N 75 59W
Whitstable 29 51 21N 1 2 E
Whitsunday I. 138 20 15 S 149 4 E
Whittier 147 60 46N 148 48W
Whittington, Derby, U.K. 33 53 17N 1 26W
Whittington, Salop, U.K. 28 52 53N 3 0W
Whittle, C. 151 50 11N 60 8W
Whittlesea 141 37 27 S 145 9 E
Whittlesey 29 52 34N 0 8W
Whittlesford 29 52 6N 0 9 E
Whitton 33 53 42N 0 39W
Whitwell, Derby, U.K. 33 53 16N 1 11W
Whitwell, Isle of Wight, U.K. 28 50 35N 1 19W
Whitwell, U.S.A. 157 35 15N 85 30W
Whitwick 28 52 45N 1 23W
Whitworth 32 53 40N 2 11W
Whixley 33 54 2N 1 19W
Wholdaia L. 153 60 43N 104 20W
Whyalla 140 33 2 S 137 30 E
Whyjonta 139 29 41 S 142 28 E
Whyte Yarcowie 107 33 13 S 138 54 E
Wiarton 150 44 50N 81 10W
Wiawso 120 6 10N 2 25W
Wiay I. 36 57 24N 7 12W
Wiazow 54 50 50N 17 10 E
Wibaux 158 47 0N 104 13W
Wichian Buri 100 15 39N 101 7 E
Wichita 159 37 40N 97 29W
Wichita Falls 159 33 57N 98 30W
Wick, Scot., U.K. 37 58 26N 3 5W
Wick, Wales, U.K. 31 51 24N 3 32W
Wick R. 37 58 28N 3 14W
Wickenburg 161 33 58N 112 45W
Wickepin 137 32 50 S 117 30 E
Wickett 159 31 37N 102 58W
Wickford 29 51 37N 0 31 E
Wickham 28 50 54N 1 11W
Wickham, C. 138 39 35 S 143 57 E
Wickham Market 29 52 9N 1 21 E
Wicklow 39 53 0N 6 2W
Wicklow □ 39 52 59N 6 25W
Wicklow Gap 39 53 3N 6 23W
Wicklow Hd. 39 52 59N 6 3W
Wicklow Mts. 39 53 0N 6 30W
Wickwar 28 51 35N 2 23W
Widawa 54 51 27N 18 51 E
Widdrington 35 55 15N 1 35W
Wide B. 138 4 52 S 152 0 E
Wide Firth 37 59 2N 3 0W
Widecombe 30 50 34N 3 48W
Widemouth 30 50 45N 4 34W
Widgiemooltha 137 31 30 S 121 34 E
Widnes 32 53 22N 2 44W
Wiek 48 54 37N 13 17 E
Wielbark 54 53 24N 20 55 E
Wielén 54 52 53N 16 9 E
Wieliczka 54 50 0N 20 5 E
Wielun 54 51 15N 18 40 E
Wien 53 48 12N 16 22 E
Wiener Neustadt 53 47 49N 16 16 E
Wieprz, R., Koszalin, Poland 54 54 26N 16 35 E
Wieprz, R., Lublin, Poland 54 51 15N 22 50 E
Wierden 46 52 22N 6 35 E
Wiers 47 50 30N 3 32 E
Wieruszów 54 51 19N 18 9 E
Wiesbaden 49 50 7N 8 17 E
Wiesental 49 49 15N 8 30 E
Wigan 32 53 33N 2 38W
Wiggins, Colo., U.S.A. 158 40 16N 104 3W
Wiggins, Miss., U.S.A. 159 30 53N 89 9W
Wight, I. of 28 50 40N 1 20W
Wigmore 28 52 19N 2 51W
Wigston 28 52 35N 1 6W
Wigton 32 54 50N 3 9W
Wigtown 34 54 52N 4 27W
Wigtown (□) 26 54 53N 4 45W
Wigtown B. 34 54 46N 4 15W
Wihéries 47 50 23N 3 45 E
Wijangala 139 33 57 S 148 59 E
Wijchen 46 51 48N 5 44 E
Wijhe 46 52 23N 6 8 E
Wijk bij Duurstede 46 51 59N 5 21 E
Wil 51 47 28N 9 3 E
Wilamowice 53 49 55N 19 9 E
Wilangee 140 31 28 S 141 20 E
Wilber 158 40 34N 96 59W
Wilburton 159 34 55N 95 15W
Wilcannia 140 31 30 S 143 26 E
Wildbad 49 48 44N 8 32 E
Wildervank 46 53 5N 6 52 E
Wildeshausen 48 52 54N 8 25 E
Wildhorn 50 46 22N 7 21 E
Wildon 52 46 52N 15 31 E
Wildrose, Calif., U.S.A. 163 36 14N 117 11W
Wildrose, N. Dak., U.S.A. 158 48 36N 103 17W
Wildspitze 52 46 53N 10 53 E
Wildstrubel 50 46 24N 7 32 E
Wildwood 162 38 59N 74 46W
Wilgaroon 141 30 52 S 145 42 E
Wilhelm II Coast 13 67 0 S 90 0 E
Wilhelm Mt. 135 5 50 S 145 1 E
Wilhelm-Pieck-Stadt Guben 48 51 59N 14 48 E
Wilhelmina Kanaal 47 51 36N 5 6 E
Wilhelmina, Mt. 175 3 50N 56 30W
Wilhelmsburg, Austria 52 48 6N 15 36 E
Wilhelmsburg, Ger. 48 53 28N 10 1 E
Wilhelmshaven 48 53 30N 8 9 E
Wilhelmstal 128 21 58 S 16 21 E
Wilkes-Barre 162 41 15N 75 52W
Wilkes Land 13 69 0 S 120 0 E
Wilkesboro 157 36 10N 81 9W
Wilkie 153 52 27N 108 42W
Wilkinson Lakes 137 29 40 S 132 39 E
Willamina 160 45 9N 123 32W
Willamulka 140 33 55 S 137 52 E
Willandra Billabong Creek 140 33 22 S 145 52 E
Willapa, B. 160 46 44N 124 0W
Willard, N. Mex., U.S.A. 161 34 35N 106 1W
Willard, N.Y., U.S.A. 162 42 40N 76 50W
Willard, Utah, U.S.A. 160 41 28N 112 1W
Willaumez Pen. 138 5 3 S 150 3 E
Willaura 140 37 31 S 142 45 E
Willberforce, C. 138 11 54 S 136 35 E
Willbriggie 141 34 28 S 146 2 E
Willcox 161 32 13N 109 53W
Willebroek 47 51 4N 4 22 E
Willemstad 167 12 5N 69 0W
Willenhall 28 52 36N 2 3W
Willeroo 136 15 14 S 131 37 E
Willesborough 29 51 8N 0 55 E
Willet 162 42 28N 75 55W
William Cr. 139 28 58 S 136 22 E
William, Mt. 140 37 17 S 142 35 E
William, R. 153 59 8N 109 19W
Williambury 137 23 45 S 115 12 E
Williams, Austral. 137 33 2 S 116 52 E
Williams, U.S.A. 161 35 16N 112 11W
Williams Lake 152 52 2N 122 10W
Williamsburg, Ky., U.S.A. 157 36 45N 84 10W
Williamsburg, Va., U.S.A. 162 37 17N 76 44W
Williamsburg, Va., U.S.A. 162 37 16N 79 43W
Williamson 156 37 46N 82 17W
Williamsport 162 41 18N 77 1W
Williamston 157 35 50N 77 5W
Williamstown, Austral. 141 37 51 S 144 52 E
Williamstown, Ireland 38 53 41N 8 34W
Williamstown, Mass., U.S.A. 162 42 43N 73 12W
Williamstown, N.Y., U.S.A. 162 43 25N 75 53W
Williamstown, N.Y., U.S.A. 162 43 25N 75 54W
Williamsville 159 37 0N 90 33W
Willimantic 162 41 45N 72 12W
Willingdon 29 50 47N 0 17 E
Willis Group 138 16 18 S 150 0 E
Willisau 50 47 7N 8 0 E
Williston, S. Afr. 128 31 20 S 20 53 E
Williston, Fla, U.S.A. 157 29 25N 82 28W
Williston, N.D., U.S.A. 158 48 10N 103 35W
Williston L. 152 56 0N 124 0W
Williton 28 51 9N 3 20W
Willits 160 39 28N 123 17W
Willmar 158 45 5N 95 0W
Willoughby 33 53 14N 0 12 E
Willow Bunch 153 49 20N 105 35W
Willow L. 152 62 10N 119 8W
Willow Lake 158 44 40N 97 40W
Willow River 152 54 6N 122 28W
Willow Springs 159 37 0N 92 0W
Willow Tree 141 31 40 S 150 45 E
Willow Wall 107 41 30N 120 40 E
Willowlake, R. 152 62 42N 123 8W
Willowmore 128 33 15 S 23 30 E
Willows, Austral. 138 23 45 S 147 25 E
Willows, U.S.A. 160 39 30N 122 10W
Wills Cr. 138 22 43 S 140 2 E
Wills, L. 136 21 25 S 128 51 E
Wills Pt. 159 32 42N 95 57W
Willunga 140 35 15 S 138 30 E
Wilmeta 156 42 6N 87 44W
Wilmington, Austral. 140 32 39 S 138 7 E
Wilmington, U.K. 30 50 46N 3 8W
Wilmington, Del., U.S.A. 162 39 45N 75 32W
Wilmington, Ill., U.S.A. 156 41 19N 88 10W
Wilmington, N.C., U.S.A. 157 34 14N 77 54W
Wilmington, Ohio, U.S.A. 156 39 29N 83 46W
Wilmington, Vt., U.S.A. 162 42 52N 72 52W
Wilmslow 32 53 19N 2 14W
Wilnecote 28 52 36N 1 40W
Wilpena Cr. 140 31 25 S 139 29 E
Wilrijk 47 51 9N 4 22 E
Wilsall 160 45 59N 110 4W
Wilson, U.S.A. 162 40 41N 75 15W
Wilson, N.C., U.S.A. 157 35 44N 77 54W
Wilson Bluff 137 31 41 S 129 0 E
Wilson Inlet 137 35 0 S 117 20 E
Wilson, Mt. 161 37 55N 105 3W
Wilson, R., Queens., Austral. 139 27 38 S 141 24 E
Wilson, R., W. Australia, Austral. 136 16 48 S 128 16 E
Wilson's Promontory 141 38 55 S 146 25 E
Wilster 48 53 55N 9 23 E
Wilton, U.K. 28 51 5N 1 52W
Wilton, U.S.A. 158 47 12N 100 53W
Wilton, R. 138 14 45 S 134 33 E
Wiltshire □ 28 51 20N 2 0W
Wiltz 47 49 57N 5 55 E
Wiluna 137 26 36 S 120 14 E
Wimblington 29 52 31N 0 5 E
Wimborne Minster 28 50 48N 2 0W
Wimereux 43 50 45N 1 37 E
Wimmera 133 36 30 S 142 0 E
Wimmera, R. 140 36 8 S 141 56 E
Winam G. 126 0 20 S 34 15 E
Winburg 128 28 30 S 27 2 E
Wincanton 28 51 3N 2 24W
Winchelsea, Austral. 140 38 10 S 144 1 E
Winchelsea, U.K. 29 50 55N 0 43 E
Winchendon 162 42 40N 72 3W
Winchester, N.Z. 143 44 11 S 171 17 E
Winchester, U.K. 28 51 4N 1 19W
Winchester, Conn., U.S.A. 162 41 53N 73 9W
Winchester, Conn., U.S.A. 162 41 55N 73 8W
Winchester, Idaho, U.S.A. 160 46 11N 116 32W
Winchester, Ind., U.S.A. 156 40 10N 84 56W
Winchester, Ky., U.S.A. 156 38 0N 84 8W
Winchester, Mass., U.S.A. 162 42 28N 71 10W
Winchester, N.H., U.S.A. 162 42 47N 72 22W
Winchester, Tenn., U.S.A. 157 35 11N 86 8W
Winchester, Va., U.S.A. 156 39 14N 78 8W
Wind, R. 160 43 30N 109 30W
Wind River Range, Mts. 160 43 0N 109 30W
Windber 156 40 14N 78 50W
Winder 157 34 0N 83 40W
Windera 139 26 17 S 151 51 E
Windermere 32 54 24N 2 56W
Windermere, L. 32 54 20N 2 57W
Windfall 152 54 12N 116 13W
Windflower L. 152 62 52N 118 30W
Windhoek 128 22 35 S 17 4 E
Windischgarsten 52 47 42N 14 21 E
Windmill Pt. 162 37 35N 76 17W
Windom 158 43 48N 95 3W
Windorah 138 25 24 S 142 36 E
Window Rock 161 35 47N 109 4W
Windrush, R. 28 51 48N 1 35W
Windsor, Austral. 141 33 37 S 150 50 E
Windsor, Newf., Can. 151 48 57N 55 40W
Windsor, N.S., Can. 151 44 59N 64 5W
Windsor, Ont., Can. 150 42 18N 83 82W
Windsor, N.Z. 143 44 59 S 170 49 E
Windsor, U.K. 29 51 28N 0 36W
Windsor, Col., U.S.A. 158 40 33N 104 55W
Windsor, Conn., U.S.A. 162 41 50N 72 40W
Windsor, Miss., U.S.A. 158 38 32N 93 31W
Windsor, N.Y., U.S.A. 162 42 5N 75 37W
Windsor, Vt., U.S.A. 162 43 30N 72 25W
Windsorton 128 28 16 S 24 44 E
Windward Is. 167 13 0N 63 0W
Windward Passage 167 20 0N 74 0W
Windy L. 153 60 20N 100 2W
Windygap 39 52 28N 7 24W
Windygates 35 56 12N 3 1W
Winefred L. 153 55 30N 110 30W
Winejok 123 9 1N 27 30 E
Winfield 159 37 15N 97 0W
Wing 29 51 54N 0 41W
Wingate Mts. 136 14 25 S 130 40 E
Wingen 141 31 54 S 150 54 E
Wingene 47 51 3N 3 17 E
Wingham, Austral. 141 31 48 S 152 22 E
Wingham, Can. 150 43 55N 81 20W
Wingham, U.K. 29 51 16N 1 12 E
Winifred 160 47 30N 109 28W
Winisk 150 55 20N 85 15W
Winisk L. 150 52 55N 87 22W
Winisk, R. 150 55 17N 85 5W
Wink 159 31 49N 103 9W
Winkleigh 30 50 49N 3 57W
Winkler 153 49 15N 97 56W
Winklern 52 46 52N 12 52 E
Winneba 121 5 25N 0 36W
Winnebago 158 43 43N 94 8W
Winnebago L. 156 44 0N 88 20W
Winnecke Cr. 136 18 35 S 131 34 E
Winnemucca 160 41 0N 117 45W
Winnemucca, L. 160 40 25N 19 21W
Winner 158 43 23N 99 52W
Winnetka 156 42 8N 87 46W
Winnett 160 47 2N 108 28W
Winnfield 159 31 57N 92 38W
Winnibigoshish L. 158 47 25N 94 12W
Winning Pool 136 23 9 S 114 30 E
Winnipeg 153 49 50N 97 9W
Winnipeg Beach 153 50 30N 96 58W
Winnipeg, L. 153 52 0N 97 0W
Winnipeg, R. 153 50 38N 96 19W
Winnipegosis 153 51 39N 99 55W
Winnipegosis L. 153 52 30N 100 0W
Winnipesaukee, L. 162 43 38N 71 21W
Winnisquam L. 162 43 33N 71 30W
Winnsboro, Lou, U.S.A. 159 32 10N 91 41W
Winnsboro, S.C., U.S.A. 157 34 23N 81 5W
Winnsboro, Tex., U.S.A. 158 32 56N 95 15W
Winokapau, L. 151 53 15N 62 50W
Winona, Miss., U.S.A. 159 33 30N 89 42W
Winona, Wis., U.S.A. 158 44 2N 91 45W
Winooski 156 44 31N 73 11W
Winschoten 46 53 9N 7 3 E
Winsen 48 53 21N 10 11 E
Winsford 32 53 12N 2 31W
Winslow, U.K. 29 51 57N 0 52W
Winslow, U.S.A. 161 35 2N 110 41W
Winstead 162 41 55N 73 5W
Winster 33 53 9N 1 42W
Winston-Salem 157 36 7N 80 15W
Winsum 46 53 20N 6 32 E
Winter Garden 157 28 33N 81 35W
Winter Haven 157 28 0N 81 42W
Winter Park 157 28 34N 81 19W
Winterberg 48 51 12N 8 30 E

Winterborne Abbas Yaapeet

Winterborne Abbas **28** 50 43N 2 30W
Winters **159** 31 58N 99 58W
Winterset **158** 41 18N 94 0W
Winterswijk **46** 51 58N 6 43 E
Winterthur **51** 47 30N 8 44 E
Winterton, Humberside, U.K. **33** 53 39N 0 37W
Winterton, Norfolk, U.K. **29** 52 43N 1 43 E
Winthrop, Minn., U.S.A. **158** 44 31N 94 25W
Winthrop, Wash., U.S.A. **160** 48 27N 120 6W
Winton, Austral. **138** 22 24 S 143 3 E
Winton, N.Z. **143** 46 8 S 168 20 E
Winton, U.S.A. **157** 36 25N 76 58W
Wirksworth **33** 53 5N 1 34W
Wirral **23** 53 25N 3 0W
Wirraminna **140** 31 12 S 136 13 E
Wirrulla **139** 32 24 S 134 31 E
Wisbech **29** 52 39N 0 10 E
Wisborough Green **29** 51 2N 0 30W
Wisconsin □ **158** 44 30N 90 0W
Wisconsin Dells **158** 43 38N 89 45W
Wisconsin, R. **158** 45 25N 89 45W
Wisconsin Rapids **158** 44 25N 89 50W
Wisdom **147** 45 36N 113 1W
Wiserman **147** 67 25N 150 15W
Wishaw **35** 55 46N 3 55W
Wishek **158** 46 20N 99 35W
Wiske, R. **33** 54 26N 1 27W
Wisła **53** 49 38N 18 53 E
Wisła, R. **54** 53 38N 18 47 E
Wisłok, R. **53** 50 7N 22 25 E
Wisłoka, R. **53** 49 50N 21 28 E
Wismar **48** 53 53N 11 23 E
Wismar B. **48** 54 0N 11 15 E
Wisner **158** 42 0N 96 46W
Wissant **43** 50 52N 1 40 E
Wissembourg **43** 48 57N 7 57 E
Wissenkerke **47** 51 35N 3 45 E
Wistoka, R. **54** 49 50N 21 28 E
Witbank **129** 25 51 S 29 14 E
Witchita **159** 37 40N 97 22W
Witchyburn **37** 57 37N 2 37W
Witdraai **128** 26 58 S 20 48 E
Witham **29** 51 48N 0 39 E
Witham, R. **33** 53 3N 0 8W
Withern **33** 53 19N 0 9 E
Withernsea **33** 53 43N 0 2W
Witkowo **54** 52 26N 17 45 E
Witley **29** 51 9N 0 39W
Witmarsum **46** 53 6N 5 28 E
Witney **28** 51 47N 1 29W
Witnossob, R. **128** 23 0 S 18 40 E
Wittdün **48** 54 38N 8 23 E
Witten **48** 51 26N 7 19 E
Wittenberg **48** 51 51N 12 39 E
Wittenberge **48** 53 0N 11 44 E
Wittenburg **48** 53 30N 11 4 E
Wittenoom, W. Australia, Austral. **132** 22 15 S 118 20 E
Wittenoom, W. Australia, Austral. **136** 18 34 S 128 51 E
Wittersham **29** 51 1N 0 42 E
Wittingen **48** 52 43N 10 43 E
Wittlich **49** 50 0N 6 54 E
Wittmund **48** 53 39N 7 35 E
Wittow **48** 54 37N 13 21 E
Wittstock **48** 53 10N 12 30 E
Witzenhausen **48** 51 20N 9 50 E
Wiveliscombe **28** 51 2N 3 20W
Wivenhoe **29** 51 51N 0 59 E
Wiyeb, W. **123** 7 15N 40 15 E
Władysławowo **54** 52 6N 18 28 E
Wlen **160** 51 0N 15 39 E
Wlingi **103** 8 5 S 112 25 E
Włocławek **54** 52 40N 19 3 E
Włodawa **54** 51 33N 23 31 E
Włoszczowa **54** 50 50N 19 55 E
Woburn, U.K. **29** 51 59N 0 37W
Woburn, U.S.A. **162** 42 31N 71 7W
Woburn Sands **29** 51 1N 0 38W
Wodonga **141** 36 5 S 146 50 E
Wodzisław Sl. **54** 50 1N 18 26 E
Woerden **46** 52 5N 4 54 E
Woerht'ukou **106** 42 35N 112 19 E
Woerth **43** 48 57N 7 45 E
Woevre **43** 49 15N 5 45 E
Wognum **46** 52 40N 5 1 E
Wohlen **51** 47 21N 8 17 E
Wokam, I. **103** 5 45 S 134 28 E
Wokha **98** 26 6N 94 16 E
Woking, Can. **152** 55 35N 118 50W
Woking, U.K. **29** 51 18N 0 33W
Wokingham **29** 51 25N 0 50W
Wolbrom **54** 50 24N 19 45 E
Woldegk **48** 53 27N 13 35 E
Wolf Creek **160** 47 1N 112 2W
Wolf L. **152** 60 24N 133 42W
Wolf Point **158** 48 6N 105 40W
Wolf, R. **152** 60 17N 132 33W
Wolf Rock **30** 49 56N 5 50W
Wolfe I. **150** 44 7N 76 20W
Wolfeboro **162** 43 35N 71 12W
Wolfenbüttel **48** 52 10N 10 33 E
Wolfenden **152** 52 0N 119 25W
Wolfheze **46** 52 0N 5 48 E
Wolfram **138** 17 6 S 145 0 E
Wolf's Castle **31** 51 53N 4 57W
Wolfsberg **52** 46 50N 14 52 E
Wolfsburg **48** 52 27N 10 49 E
Wolgast **48** 54 3N 13 46 E
Wolhusen **50** 47 4N 8 4 E
Wolin **54** 53 40N 14 37 E
Wollaston, Islas **176** 55 40 S 67 30W
Wollaston L. **153** 58 7N 103 10W
Wollaston Pen. **148** 69 30N 115 0W
Wollogorang **138** 17 13 S 137 57 E
Wollongong **141** 34 25 S 150 54 E
Wolmaransstad **128** 27 12 S 26 13 E
Wolmirstedt **48** 52 15N 11 35 E
Wołomin **54** 52 19N 21 15 E
Wołow **54** 51 20N 16 38 E
Wolseley, Austral. **140** 36 23 S 140 54 E
Wolseley, Can. **153** 50 25N 103 15W
Wolseley, S. Afr. **128** 33 26 S 19 7 E
Wolsingham **32** 54 44N 1 52W
Wolstenholme Sound **12** 74 30N 75 0W
Wolsztyn **54** 52 8N 16 5 E
Wolvega **46** 52 52N 6 0 E
Wolverhampton **28** 52 35N 2 6W
Wolverton **29** 52 3N 0 48W
Wolviston **33** 54 39N 1 25W
Wombera **123** 10 45N 35 49 E
Wombwell **33** 53 31N 1 23W
Wommels **46** 53 6N 5 36 E
Wonarah P.O. **138** 19 55 S 136 20 E
Wonboyn **141** 37 15 S 149 55 E
Wonck **47** 50 46N 5 38 E
Wondai **139** 26 20 S 151 49 E
Wondelgem **47** 51 5N 3 44 E
Wonder Gorge **127** 14 40 S 29 0 E
Wongalarroo L. **140** 31 32 S 144 0 E
Wongan **137** 30 51 S 116 37 E
Wongan Hills **137** 30 53 S 116 42 E
Wongawal **137** 25 5 S 121 55 E
Wonosari **103** 7 38 S 110 36 E
Wŏnsan **107** 39 11N 127 27 E
Wonston **28** 51 9N 1 18W
Wonthaggi **141** 38 37 S 145 37 E
Wonyulgunna Hill, Mt. **137** 24 52 S 119 44 E
Woocalla **140** 31 42 S 137 12 E
Wood Buffalo Nat. Park **152** 56 28N 113 41W
Wood Green **138** 22 26 S 134 12 E
Wood Is. **136** 16 24 S 123 19 E
Wood L. **153** 55 17N 103 17W
Wood Lake **158** 42 38N 100 14W
Wood Mt. **153** 49 14N 106 30W
Woodah I. **138** 13 27 S 136 10 E
Woodanilling **137** 33 31 S 117 24 E
Woodbine **162** 39 14N 74 49W
Woodbourne **162** 41 46N 74 35W
Woodbridge **29** 52 6N 1 19 E
Woodburn **139** 29 6 S 153 23 E
Woodbury, U.K. **30** 50 40N 3 24W
Woodbury, U.S.A. **162** 39 50N 75 9W
Woodchopper **147** 65 25N 143 30W
Wooden Bridge **39** 52 50N 6 13W
Woodend **140** 37 20N 144 33 E
Woodford **39** 53 3N 8 23W
Woodfords **163** 38 47N 119 50W
Woodhall Spa. **33** 53 10N 0 12W
Woodham Ferrers **29** 51 40N 0 37 E
Woodlake **163** 36 25N 119 6W
Woodland **160** 38 40N 121 50W
Woodlands **137** 24 46 S 118 8 E
Woodlark I. **135** 9 10 S 152 50 E
Woodley **29** 51 26N 0 54W
Woodpecker **152** 53 30N 122 40W
Woodplumpton **32** 53 47N 2 46W
Woodridge **153** 49 20N 96 9W
Woodroffe, Mt. **137** 26 20 S 131 45 E
Woodruff, Ariz., U.S.A. **161** 34 51N 110 1W
Woodruff, Utah, U.S.A. **160** 41 30N 111 4W
Woods, L., Austral. **138** 17 50 S 133 30 E
Woods, L., Can. **151** 54 30N 65 13W
Woods, Lake of the **153** 49 30N 94 30W
Woodside, S. Australia, Austral. **140** 34 58 S 138 52 E
Woodside, Victoria, Austral. **141** 38 31 S 146 52 E
Woodstock, N.S.W., Austral. **141** 33 45 S 148 53 E
Woodstock, Queens., Austral. **138** 19 35 S 146 50 E
Woodstock, W.A., Austral. **136** 21 41 S 118 57 E
Woodstock, N.B., Can. **151** 46 11N 67 37W
Woodstock, Ont., Can. **150** 43 10N 80 45W
Woodstock, U.K. **28** 51 51N 1 20W
Woodstock, Ill., U.S.A. **158** 42 17N 88 30W
Woodstock, Vt., U.S.A. **162** 43 37N 72 31W
Woodstown **162** 39 39N 75 20W
Woodville, N.Z. **142** 40 20 S 175 53 E
Woodville, U.S.A. **159** 30 45N 94 25W
Woodward **159** 36 24N 99 28W
Woodward, Mt. **137** 26 0 S 131 0 E
Woody **163** 35 42N 118 50W
Wookey **28** 51 13N 2 41W
Wookey Hole **28** 51 13N 2 41W
Wool **28** 50 41N 2 13W
Woolacombe **30** 51 10N 4 12W
Woolamai, C. **141** 38 30 S 145 23 E
Wooler **35** 55 33N 2 0W
Woolgangie **137** 31 12 S 120 35 E
Woolyeenyer, Mt. **137** 32 16 S 121 47 E
Woombye **139** 26 40 S 152 55 E
Woomera **140** 31 11 S 136 47 E
Woonona **141** 34 21 S 150 54 E
Woonsocket **162** 42 0N 71 30W
Woonsockett **158** 44 5N 98 15W
Wooramel **137** 25 45 S 114 40 E
Wooramel, R. **137** 25 30 S 114 30 E
Wooroloo **137** 31 48 S 116 18 E
Wooroorooka **139** 29 0 S 145 41 E
Wooster **156** 40 38N 81 55W
Wootton Bassett **28** 51 32N 1 55W
Wootton Wawen **28** 52 16N 1 47W
Worb **50** 46 56N 7 33 E
Worcester, S. Afr. **125** 33 39 S 19 27 E
Worcester, U.K. **28** 52 12N 2 12W
Worcester, Mass., U.S.A. **162** 42 14N 71 49W
Worcester, N.Y., U.S.A. **162** 42 35N 74 45W
Worcestershire (□) **26** 52 13N 2 10W
Worfield **28** 52 34N 2 22W
Wörgl **52** 47 29N 12 3 E
Worikambo **121** 10 43N 0 11W
Workington **32** 54 39N 3 34W
Worksop **33** 53 19N 1 9W
Workum **46** 52 59N 5 26 E
Worland **160** 44 0N 107 59W
Wormerveer **46** 52 30N 4 46 E
Wormhoudt **43** 50 52N 2 28 E
Wormit **35** 56 26N 2 59W
Worms **49** 49 37N 8 21 E
Worms Head **29** 51 33N 4 19W
Worplesdon **29** 51 16N 0 36W
Worsley **137** 33 15 S 116 2 E
Wortham, U.K. **29** 52 22N 1 3 E
Wortham, U.S.A. **159** 31 48N 96 27W
Wörther See **52** 46 37N 14 19 E
Worthing **29** 50 49N 0 21W
Worthington **158** 43 35N 95 30W
Wosi **103** 0 15 S 128 0 E
Wota (Shoa Ghimirra) **123** 7 4N 35 51 E
Wotton-under-Edge **28** 51 37N 2 20W
Woubrugge **46** 52 10N 4 39 E
Woudenberg **46** 52 5N 5 25 E
Woudsend **46** 52 56N 5 38 E
Wour **119** 21 14N 16 0 E
Wouw **47** 51 31N 4 23 E
Wowoni, I. **103** 4 5 S 123 5 E
Woy Woy **141** 33 30 S 151 19 E
Wragby **33** 53 17N 0 18W
Wrangell **147** 56 30N 132 25W
Wrangell, I. **152** 56 20N 132 10W
Wrangell Mts. **147** 61 40N 143 30W
Wrangle **33** 53 3N 0 9 E
Wrath, C. **36** 58 38N 5 0W
Wray **158** 40 8N 102 18W
Wreck I. **162** 37 12N 75 48W
Wrekin, The, Mt. **28** 52 41N 2 35W
Wrens **157** 33 13N 82 23W
Wrentham **29** 52 24N 1 39 E
Wrexham **31** 53 5N 3 0W
Wriezen **48** 52 43N 14 9 E
Wright, Can. **152** 51 52N 121 40W
Wright, Phil. **103** 11 42N 125 2 E
Wright, Mt. **151** 52 40N 67 25W
Wrightlington **28** 51 18N 2 16W
Wrightson, Mt. **161** 31 49N 110 56W
Wrightsville **162** 40 2N 76 32W
Wrightwood **163** 34 21N 117 38W
Wrigley **148** 63 16N 123 27W
Writtle **29** 51 44N 0 27 E
Wrocław **54** 51 5N 17 5 E
Wrocław □ **54** 51 0N 17 0 E
Wronki **54** 52 41N 16 21 E
Wrotham **29** 51 18N 0 20 E
Wroughton **28** 51 31N 1 47W
Wroxham **29** 52 42N 1 23 E
Września **54** 52 21N 17 36 E
Wschowa **54** 51 48N 16 20 E
Wu Chiang, R. **108** 29 42N 107 20 E
Wu Shui, R. **109** 27 7N 109 57 E
Wuan **106** 36 45N 114 2 E
Wubin **137** 30 6 S 116 37 E
Wuch'ang, Heilungkiang, China **107** 44 55N 127 10 E
Wuch'ang, Hupeh, China **109** 30 30N 114 15 E
Wuch'eng **108** 30 48N 98 46 E
Wuch'i **108** 31 28N 109 36 E
Wuchiang **109** 31 10N 120 37 E
Wuchih Shan, mts. **100** 18 45N 109 45 E
Wuch'ing **107** 39 25N 117 7 E
Wuchou **105** 23 33N 111 18 E
Wuch'uan, Inner Mong., China **106** 41 8N 111 24 E
Wuch'uan, Kwangsi-Chuang, China **109** 21 29N 110 49 E
Wuch'uan, Kweichow, China **108** 28 30N 107 58 E
Wuchung **106** 38 4N 106 12 E
Wufeng **109** 30 12N 110 36 E
Wuhan **109** 30 35N 114 15 E
Wuho **107** 33 9N 117 53 E
Wuhsi **105** 31 30N 120 20 E
Wuhsiang **106** 36 50N 112 52 E
Wuhsing **109** 30 49N 120 5 E
Wuhsüan **108** 23 36N 109 39 E
Wuhu **105** 31 18N 118 20 E
Wuhu (Wou-tou) **109** 31 21N 118 30 E
Wui, Anhwei, China **109** 28 53N 119 48 E
Wui, Hopeh, China **106** 37 49N 115 54 E
Wui Shan, mts. **105** 27 30N 117 30 E
Wukang **109** 26 50N 110 15 E
Wukari **121** 7 57N 9 42 E
Wulachieh **107** 44 5N 126 27 E
Wulanhaot'e **105** 46 5N 122 5 E
Wulanpulang **106** 41 8N 110 56 E
Wulehe **121** 3 42N 0 0 E
Wuliang Shan, mts. **108** 24 0N 100 55 E
Wuliaru, I. **103** 7 10 S 131 0 E
Wulien **107** 35 45N 119 12 E
Wuluk'omushih Ling **105** 36 25N 87 25 E
Wulumuchi **105** 43 40N 87 50 E
Wulunku Ho, R. **105** 46 58N 87 28 E
Wum **121** 6 40N 10 2 E
Wuming **108** 23 11N 108 12 E
Wuneba **123** 4 49N 30 22 E
Wuning **109** 29 16N 115 0 E
Wunnummin L. **150** 52 55N 89 10W
Wunsiedel **49** 50 2N 12 0 E
Wunstorf **48** 52 26N 9 29 E
Wuntho, Burma **98** 21 44N 96 2 E
Wuntho, Burma **99** 23 55N 95 45 E
Wupao **106** 37 35N 110 45 E
Wup'ing **109** 25 9N 116 5 E
Wuppertal, Ger. **48** 51 15N 7 8 E
Wuppertal, S. Afr. **128** 32 13 S 19 12 E
Wurarga **137** 28 25 S 116 15 E
Würenlingen **51** 47 32N 8 16 E
Wurung **138** 19 13 S 140 38 E
Würzburg **49** 49 46N 9 55 E
Wurzen **48** 51 21N 12 45 E
Wushan, Kansu, China **106** 34 42N 104 58 E
Wushan, Szechwan, China **108** 31 3N 109 57 E
Wushench'i **106** 38 57N 109 15 E
Wustrow **48** 54 4N 11 33 E
Wusu **105** 44 27N 84 37 E
Wutai **106** 38 44N 113 18 E
Wuti **107** 37 46N 117 39 E
Wuting **108** 25 33N 102 26 E
Wuting = Huimin **107** 37 32N 117 33 E
Wuting Ho, R. **106** 37 8N 110 25 E
Wut'ungch'iao **108** 29 24N 104 0 E
Wutunghaolan **107** 42 49N 120 11 E
Wuustwezel **47** 51 23N 4 36 E
Wuwei, Anhwei, China **109** 31 22N 117 55 E
Wuwei, Kansu, China **105** 37 55N 102 48 E
Wuyang **106** 33 25N 113 36 E
Wuyo **121** 10 23N 11 50 E
Wuyüan, Inner Mong., China **106** 41 6N 108 16 E
Wuyüan, Kiangsi, China **109** 29 17N 117 54 E
Wuyün **105** 49 17N 129 40 E
Wyaaba Cr. **138** 16 27 S 141 35 E
Wyalkatchem **137** 31 8 S 117 22 E
Wyalong **139** 33 54 S 147 16 E
Wyalusing **162** 41 40N 76 16W
Wyandotte **156** 42 14N 83 13W
Wyandra **139** 27 12 S 145 56 E
Wyangala Res. **141** 33 54 S 149 0 E
Wyara, L. **139** 28 42 S 144 14 E
Wych Farm, oilfield **19** 50 38N 2 2W
Wycheproof **140** 36 0N 143 17 E
Wye **29** 51 11N 0 56 E
Wye, R. **28** 52 0N 2 36W
Wyemandoo, Mt. **137** 28 28 S 118 29 E
Wyk **48** 54 41N 8 33 E
Wylfa Hd. **31** 53 25N 4 28W
Wylye, R. **28** 51 8N 1 53W
Wymondham, Leicester, U.K. **29** 52 45N 0 42W
Wymondham, Norfolk, U.K. **29** 52 34N 1 7 E
Wymore **158** 40 10N 97 8W
Wynberg **128** 34 2 S 18 28 E
Wynbring **139** 30 33 S 133 32 E
Wyndham, Austral. **136** 15 33 S 128 3 E
Wyndham, N.Z. **143** 46 20 S 168 51 E
Wynne **159** 35 15N 90 50W
Wynnstay **31** 52 36N 3 33W
Wynnum **139** 27 27 S 153 9 E
Wynyard **153** 51 45N 104 10W
Wyola, L. **137** 29 8 S 130 17 E
Wyoming □ **154** 42 48N 109 0W
Wyong **141** 33 14 S 151 24 E
Wyre Forest **28** 52 24N 2 24W
Wyre, I. **37** 59 7N 2 58W
Wyre, R. **37** 53 52N 2 57W
Wyrzysk **54** 53 10N 17 17 E
Wysoka **54** 53 13N 17 2 E
Wyszków **54** 52 36N 21 25 E
Wyszogród **54** 52 23N 20 9 E
Wytheville **156** 37 0N 81 3W

X

Xai-Xai **129** 25 6 S 33 31 E
Xambioá **170** 6 25 S 48 40W
Xanten **48** 51 40N 6 27 E
Xanthí **68** 41 10N 24 58 E
Xanthí □ **68** 41 10N 24 58 E
Xapuri **174** 10 35 S 68 35W
Xau **128** 21 15 S 24 44 E
Xavantina **173** 21 15 S 52 48W
Xenia **156** 39 42N 83 57W
Xieng Khouang **100** 19 17N 103 25 E
Xilókastron **69** 38 4N 22 43 E
Xinavane **129** 25 2 S 32 47 E
Xingu, R. **175** 2 25 S 52 35W
Xiniás, L. **69** 39 2N 22 12 E
Xique-Xique **170** 10 50 S 42 40W
Xuan Loc **101** 10 56N 107 14 E
Xuyen Moc **101** 10 34N 107 25 E

Y

Ya 'Bud **90** 32 27N 35 10 E
Yaamba **138** 23 8 S 150 22 E
Yaan **108** 30 0N 102 59 E
Yaapeet **140** 35 45 S 142 3 E

CIB

Yabassi Yorktown

Yabassi 121 4 30N 9 57 E
Yabba North 141 36 13 S 145 42 E
Yabelo 123 4 57N 38 8 E
Yablanitsa 67 43 2N 24 5 E
Yablonovyy Khrebet 77 53 0N 114 0 E
Yabrīn 92 23 7N 48 52 E
Yach'i 108 27 35N 106 40 E
Yachiang 108 30 4N 101 7 E
Yacuiba 172 22 0 S 63 25W
Yadgir 96 16 45N 77 5 E
Yadkin, R. 157 36 15N 81 0W
Yadrin 81 55 57N 46 6 E
Yaeyama-Shotō 112 24 25N 124 0 E
Yagaba 121 10 14N 1 20W
Yagoua 124 10 20N 14 58 E
Yagur 90 32 45N 35 4 E
Yaha 101 6 29N 101 8 E
Yahk 152 49 6N 116 10W
Yahuma 124 1 0N 22 5 E
Yaihsien 100 18 14N 109 29 E
Yaizu 111 34 52N 138 20 E
Yajua 121 11 27N 12 49 E
Yakage 110 34 37N 133 35 E
Yakataga 147 60 5N 142 32W
Yakiang 99 30 4N 101 15 E
Yakima 160 46 42N 120 30W
Yakima, R. 160 47 0N 120 30W
Yako 120 12 59N 2 15W
Yakoruda 67 42 1N 23 29 E
Yakshur Bodya 84 57 11N 53 7 E
Yaku-Jima 112 30 20N 130 30 E
Yakut A.S.S.R. □ 77 62 0N 130 0 E
Yakutat 147 59 50N 139 44W
Yakutsk 77 62 5N 129 40 E
Yala 101 6 33N 101 18 E
Yalabusha, R. 159 33 53N 89 50W
Yalbalgo 137 25 10 S 114 45 E
Yalboroo 138 20 50 S 148 40 E
Yalgoo 137 28 16 S 116 39 E
Yalikavak 69 37 6N 27 18 E
Yalinga 117 6 20N 23 10 E
Yalkubul, Punta 165 21 32N 88 37W
Y'allaq, G. 122 30 21N 33 31 E
Yalleroi 138 24 3 S 145 42 E
Yallourn 141 38 10 S 146 18 E
Yalpukh, Oz. 70 45 30N 28 41 E
Yalta 82 44 30N 34 10 E
Yalu Chiang, R. 107 39 45N 124 20 E
Yalung Chiang, R. 105 26 35N 101 45 E
Yalutorovsk 76 56 30N 65 40 E
Yam Kinneret 90 32 49N 35 36 E
Yamada 110 33 43N 130 49 E
Yamaga 110 33 1N 130 41 E
Yamagata 112 38 15N 140 15 E
Yamagata-ken □ 112 38 30N 140 0 E
Yamagawa 110 31 12N 130 39 E
Yamaguchi 110 34 10N 131 32 E
Yamaguchi-ken □ 110 34 20N 131 40 E
Yamal, Poluostrov 76 71 0N 70 0 E
Yamana 92 24 5N 47 30 E
Yamanaka 111 36 15N 136 22 E
Yamanashi-ken □ 111 35 40N 138 40 E
Yamankhalinka 83 47 43N 49 21 E
Yamantau 78 54 20N 57 40 E
Yamantau, Gora 84 54 15N 58 6 E
Yamato 111 35 27N 139 25 E
Yamatotakada 111 34 31N 135 45 E
Yamazaki 110 35 0N 134 32 E
Yamba, N.S.W., Austral. 139 29 26 S 153 23 E
Yamba, S. Australia, Austral. 140 34 10 S 140 52 E
Yambah 138 23 10 S 133 50 E
Yâmbiô 123 4 35N 28 16 E
Yambol 67 42 30N 26 36 E
Yamdena 103 7 45 S 131 20 E
Yame 110 33 13N 130 35 E
Yamethin 98 20 29N 96 18 E
Yamil 121 12 53N 8 4 E
Yamma-Yamma L. 139 26 16 S 141 20 E
Yampa, R. 160 40 37N 108 0W
Yampi Sd. 136 16 8 S 123 38 E
Yampol 82 48 15N 28 15 E
Yamrat 121 10 11N 9 55 E
Yamrukohal, Mt. 67 42 44N 24 52 E
Yamun 90 32 29N 35 14 E
Yamuna (Jumna), R. 94 27 0N 78 30 E
Yan 121 10 5N 12 11 E
Yan Oya 97 9 0N 81 10 E
Yana, R. 77 69 0N 134 0 E
Yanac 140 36 8 S 141 25 E
Yanagawa 110 33 10N 130 24 E
Yanahara 110 34 58N 134 2 E
Yanam 96 16 47N 82 15 E
Yanaul 84 56 25N 55 0 E
Yanbu 'al Bahr 92 24 0N 38 5 E
Yancannia 139 30 12 S 142 35 E
Yanchep 137 31 30 S 115 45 E
Yanco 141 34 38 S 146 27 E
Yanco Cr. 141 35 14 S 145 35 E
Yandabome 138 7 1 S 145 46 E
Yandal 137 27 35 S 121 10 E
Yandanooka 137 29 18 S 115 29 E
Yandaran 138 24 43 S 152 6 E
Yandil 137 26 20 S 119 50 E
Yandoon 98 17 0N 95 40 E
Yanfolila 120 11 11N 8 9W
Yangambi 126 0 47N 24 20 E
Yangch'angtzukou 106 41 31N 109 1 E
Yangch'eng 106 35 32N 112 26 E
Yangchiang 109 21 55N 111 55 E
Yangchiaoch'iao 109 29 45N 112 45 E
Yangchiapa 106 42 6N 113 46 E
Yangchou 109 32 24N 119 26 E
Yangchoyung Hu 105 29 0N 90 40 E
Yangch'ü = T'aiyüan 106 37 55N 112 40 E
Yangch'üan 106 37 54N 113 36 E
Yangch'un 109 22 10N 111 47 E
Yanghsien 106 33 20N 107 30 E
Yanghsin 109 29 53N 115 10 E
Yangi-Yer 76 40 17N 68 48 E
Yangibazar 85 41 40N 70 53 E
Yangikishlak 85 40 25N 67 10 E
Yangiyul 85 41 0N 69 3 E
Yangku 106 36 8N 115 48 E
Yangliuch'ing 107 39 11N 117 9 E
Yangp'i 108 25 40N 100 0 E
Yangp'ing 109 31 13N 111 33 E
Yangp'ingkuan 106 33 2N 105 56 E
Yangshan 109 24 28N 112 38 E
Yangshuo 109 24 45N 110 24 E
Yangtze (Ch'ang Chiang) 109 1 48N 121 53 E
Yangyang 107 38 4N 128 38 E
Yangyüan 106 40 5N 114 12 E
Yanhee Res. 101 17 30N 98 45 E
Yanko Cr. 139 35 17 S 145 15 E
Yankton 158 42 55N 97 25W
Yanna 139 26 58 S 146 0 E
Yanonge 126 0 35N 24 38 E
Yantabulla 139 29 21 S 145 0 E
Yantra, R. 67 43 35N 25 37 E
Yany Kurgan 85 43 55N 67 15 E
Yao, Chad 117 12 56N 17 33 E
Yao, Japan 111 34 32N 135 36 E
Yao Yai, Ko 101 8 0N 98 35 E
Yaoan 108 25 32N 101 12 E
Yaoundé 121 3 50N 11 35 E
Yaowan 107 34 10N 118 3 E
Yap Is. 103 9 30N 138 10 E
Yapen 103 1 50 S 136 0 E
Yapen, Selat 103 1 20 S 136 10 E
Yapo, R. 174 0 30 S 77 0W
Yappar, R. 138 18 22 S 141 16 E
Yaqui, R. 164 28 28N 109 30W
Yar 84 58 14N 52 5 E
Yar-Sale 76 66 50N 70 50 E
Yaracuy □ 174 10 20N 68 45W
Yaraka 138 24 53 S 144 3 E
Yaransk 81 57 13N 47 56 E
Yaratishky 80 54 3N 25 52 E
Yarcombe 30 50 51N 3 6W
Yarda 117 18 35N 19 0 E
Yardea P.O. 139 32 23 S 135 32 E
Yare, R. 29 52 36N 1 28 E
Yarensk 78 61 10N 49 8 E
Yarfa 122 24 40N 38 35 E
Yari, R. 174 1 0N 73 40W
Yaringa North 137 25 53 S 114 30 E
Yaringa South 137 26 0 S 114 28 E
Yarkand = Soch'e 105 38 24N 77 20 E
Yarkhun, R. 95 36 30N 72 45 E
Yarm 33 54 31N 1 21W
Yarmouth, Can. 151 43 53N 65 45W
Yarmouth, U.K. 28 50 42N 1 29W
Yaroslavl 81 57 35N 39 55 E
Yarra Yarra Lakes 137 29 40 S 115 45 E
Yarraden 138 14 28 S 143 15 E
Yarraloola 136 21 33 S 115 52 E
Yarram 141 38 29 S 146 40 E
Yarraman 139 26 50 S 152 0 E
Yarraman Cr. 139 26 46 S 152 1 E
Yarranvale 139 26 50 S 145 20 E
Yarras 141 31 25 S 152 20 E
Yarrawonga 141 36 0 S 146 0 E
Yarrow 35 55 32N 3 0W
Yarrowee, R. 140 38 18 S 144 30 E
Yarto 140 35 28 S 142 16 E
Yartsevo 77 60 20N 90 0 E
Yarumal 174 6 58N 75 24W
Yaselda, R. 80 52 26N 25 30 E
Yashi 121 12 23N 7 54 E
Yashiro-Jima 110 33 55N 132 15 E
Yasin 95 36 24N 73 15 E
Yasinovataya 82 48 7N 37 57 E
Yasinski, L. 150 53 16N 77 35W
Yasnogorsk 81 54 32N 37 38 E
Yasothon 100 15 50N 104 10 E
Yass 141 34 49 S 148 54 E
Yasugi 110 35 26N 133 15 E
Yas'ur 90 32 54N 35 10 E
Yatagan 69 37 20N 28 10 E
Yate 28 51 32N 2 26W
Yates Center 159 37 53N 95 45W
Yates Pt. 143 44 29 S 167 49 E
Yathkyed L. 153 62 40N 98 0W
Yathong 141 32 37 S 145 33 E
Yatsuo 111 36 34N 137 8 E
Yatsushiro 110 32 30N 130 40 E
Yatsushiro-Kai 110 32 30N 130 25 E
Yatta 90 31 27N 35 6 E
Yatta Plat. 126 2 0 S 38 0 E
Yattah 90 31 27N 35 6 E
Yatton 28 51 23N 2 50W
Yauyos 174 12 10 S 75 50W
Yaval 96 21 10N 75 42 E
Yavan 85 38 19N 69 2 E
Yavari R. 174 4 50 S 72 0W
Yavorov 80 49 55N 23 20 E
Yawatahama 110 33 27N 132 24 E
Yawri B. 120 8 22N 13 0W
Yaxley 29 52 31N 0 14W
Yazagyo 98 23 30N 94 6 E
Yazd (Yezd) 93 31 55N 54 27 E
Yazdan 93 33 30N 60 50 E
Yazoo City 159 32 48N 90 28W
Yazoo, R. 159 32 35N 90 50W
Ybbs 52 48 12N 15 4 E
Yding Skovhøj 75 55 59N 9 46 E
Yea 141 37 14 S 145 26 E
Yealering 137 32 36 S 117 36 E
Yealmpton 30 50 21N 4 0W
Yearinan 141 31 10 S 149 11 E
Yebbi-Souma 119 21 7N 17 54 E
Yebbigué 119 22 30N 17 30 E
Yebel Jarris Tighzert, O. 118 28 10N 9 37W
Yebyu 99 14 15N 98 13 E
Yechŏn 107 36 39N 128 27 E
Yecla 59 38 35N 1 5W
Yécora 164 28 20N 108 58W
Yedashe 98 17 24N 95 50 E
Yeddou 118 28 5N 9 2W
Yeeda River 136 17 31 S 123 38 E
Yeelanna 139 34 9 S 135 45 E
Yefremov 81 53 15N 38 3 E
Yegorlyk, R. 83 46 15N 41 30 E
Yegorlykskaya 83 46 5N 40 35 E
Yegoryevsk 81 55 27N 38 55 E
Yegros 172 26 20 S 56 25W
Yehchih 108 27 39N 99 0 E
Yehsien 106 33 37N 113 20 E
Yehud 90 32 3N 34 53 E
Yehuda, Midbar 90 31 35N 34 57 E
Yei 123 4 3N 30 40 E
Yei, Nahr 123 5 50N 30 20 E
Yelan 81 50 55N 43 43 E
Yelan Kolenovski 81 51 16N 40 45 E
Yelandur 97 12 6N 77 0 E
Yelanskoye 77 61 25N 128 0 E
Yelarbon 139 28 33 S 150 49 E
Yelatma 81 55 0N 41 52 E
Yelets 81 52 40N 38 30 E
Yelimané 120 15 9N 22 49 E
Yell, I. 36 60 35N 1 5W
Yell Sd. 36 60 33N 1 15W
Yellamanchilli (Elamanchili) 96 17 26N 82 50 E
Yellow Sea 105 35 0N 123 0 E
Yellowdine 137 31 17 S 119 40 E
Yellowhead P. 152 52 53N 118 25W
Yellowknife 152 62 27N 114 21W
Yellowknife, R. 152 62 31N 114 19W
Yellowstone L. 160 44 30N 110 20W
Yellowstone National Park 160 44 35N 110 0W
Yellowstone, R. 158 46 35N 105 45W
Yelnya 80 54 35N 33 15 E
Yelsk 80 51 50N 29 3 E
Yelvertoft 138 20 13 S 138 53 E
Yelwa 122 10 49N 8 41 E
Yemanzhelinsk 84 54 58N 61 18 E
Yemen ■ 91 15 0N 44 0 E
Yemen, South ■ 91 15 0N 48 0 E
Yen Bai 100 21 42N 104 52 E
Yenakiyevo 82 48 15N 38 5 E
Yenan 106 36 42N 109 25 E
Yenangyaung 98 20 30N 95 0 E
Yenanma 98 19 46N 96 48 E
Yenchang 106 36 44N 110 2 E
Yench'eng, Honan, China 106 33 37N 114 0 E
Yench'eng, Kiangsu, China 107 33 24N 120 10 E
Yench'i 105 42 4N 86 34 E
Yenchi 107 42 53N 129 31 E
Yench'ih 106 37 47N 107 24 E
Yenchihsien 107 42 46N 129 24 E
Yenchin 108 28 4N 104 14 E
Yench'ing 106 40 28N 115 58 E
Yenching 108 29 7N 98 33 E
Yenchou 105 35 40N 116 50 E
Yench'uan 106 36 52N 110 11 E
Yenda 141 34 13 S 146 14 E
Yendéré 120 10 12N 4 59W
Yendi 121 9 29N 0 1W
Yenfeng 108 25 52N 101 5 E
Yenho 108 28 35N 108 28 E
Yenhsing 108 25 22N 101 44 E
Yenisaia 68 41 1N 24 57 E
Yenisey, R. 76 68 0N 86 30 E
Yeniseysk 77 58 39N 92 4 E
Yeniseyskiy Zaliv 76 72 20N 81 0 E
Yenne 45 45 43N 5 44 E
Yenotyevka 83 47 15N 47 0 E
Yenpien 108 26 54N 101 34 E
Yenshan, Hopeh, China 107 38 3N 117 12 E
Yenshan, Yunnan, China 108 23 40N 104 22 E
Yenshou 107 45 27N 128 19 E
Yent'ai 107 37 35N 121 25 E
Yent'ing 108 31 19N 105 20 E
Yenyüan 108 27 25N 101 33 E
Yenyuka 77 58 20N 121 30 E
Yeo, L. 137 28 0 S 124 30 E
Yeo, R. 28 51 1N 2 46W
Yeola 96 20 0N 74 30 E
Yeotmal 96 20 20N 78 15 E
Yeoval 141 32 41 S 148 39 E
Yeovil 28 50 57N 2 38W
Yepes 56 39 55N 3 39W
Yeppoon 138 23 5 S 150 47 E
Yeráki 69 37 0N 22 42 E
Yerbogachen 77 61 16N 108 0 E
Yerevan 83 40 10N 44 20 E
Yerilla 137 29 24 S 121 47 E
Yerington 163 38 59N 119 10W
Yerla, R. 96 17 35N 74 30 E
Yermakovo 77 52 35N 126 20 E
Yermo 163 34 58N 116 50W
Yermolayevo 78 52 58N 56 12 E
Yerofey Pavlovich 77 54 0N 122 0 E
Yerseke 47 51 29N 4 3 E
Yershov 81 51 15N 48 27 E
Yerūshalayim 90 31 47N 35 10 E
Yerville 42 49 40N 0 53 E
Yes Tor, Mt. 30 50 41N 3 59W
Yesagyo 98 21 38N 95 14 E
Yesan 107 36 41N 126 51 E
Yeşilirmak 82 41 0N 36 40 E
Yeso 159 34 29N 104 87W
Yessentuki 83 44 0N 42 45 E
Yeste 59 38 22N 2 19W
Yeu, I. d' 42 46 42N 2 20W
Yevlakh 83 40 39N 47 7 E
Yevpatoriya 82 45 15N 33 20 E
Yevstratovskiy 81 50 11N 39 2 E
Yeya, R. 83 46 40N 39 0 E
Yeysk Staro 82 46 40N 38 12 E
Yhati 172 25 45 S 56 35W
Yhú 173 25 0 S 56 0W
Yi, R. 172 33 7 S 57 8W
Yialí, I. 69 36 41N 27 11 E
Yiáltra 69 38 51N 22 59 E
Yiânisádhes, I. 69 35 20N 26 10 E
Yiannitsa 68 40 46N 22 24 E
Yibal 91 22 10N 56 8 E
Yidhá 68 40 35N 22 53 E
Yinchiang 108 27 58N 108 20 E
Yinch'uan 105 38 30N 106 20 E
Yindarlgooda, L. 137 30 40 S 121 52 E
Ying Ho, R. 109 32 30N 116 32 E
Yingch'eng 109 30 55N 113 33 E
Yingchiang 108 24 48N 98 5 E
Yinghsien 106 39 36N 113 12 E
Yingk'ou 107 40 38N 122 30 E
Yingp'an, Chiang, G. 108 21 20N 109 30 E
Yingp'anshan 108 27 56N 105 34 E
Yingshan, Hupeh, China 109 31 37N 113 46 E
Yingshan, Hupeh, China 109 30 50N 115 45 E
Yingshan, Szechwan, China 108 31 6N 106 35 E
Yingshang 109 32 36N 116 16 E
Yingtan 105 28 12N 117 0 E
Yingte 109 24 10N 113 24 E
Yinkanie 140 34 22 S 140 17 E
Yinmabin 99 22 10N 94 55 E
Yinnietharra 137 24 39 S 116 12 E
Yioúra, I. 68 39 23N 24 10 E
Yipang 101 22 15N 101 26 E
Yirga Alem 124 6 34N 38 29 E
Yithion 69 36 46N 22 34 E
Yizre'el 90 32 34N 35 19 E
Ylitornio 74 66 19N 23 39 E
Ylivieska 74 64 4N 24 28 E
Yngaren 73 58 50N 16 35 E
Ynykchanskiy 77 60 15N 137 43 E
Yoakum 159 29 20N 97 10W
Yobuko 110 33 32N 129 54 E
Yog Pt. 103 13 55N 124 20 E
Yogyakarta 103 7 49 S 110 22 E
Yoho Nat. Park 152 51 25N 116 30W
Yojoa, L. de 166 14 53N 88 0W
Yŏju 107 37 20N 127 35 E
Yokadouma 124 3 35N 14 50 E
Yōkaichi 111 35 6N 136 12 E
Yōkaichiba 111 35 42N 140 33 E
Yokkaichi 111 35 0N 136 30 E
Yoko 121 5 50N 12 20 E
Yokohama 111 35 27N 139 39 E
Yokosuka 111 35 20N 139 40 E
Yokote 112 39 20N 140 30 E
Yola 121 9 10N 12 29 E
Yolaina, Cordillera de 166 11 30N 84 0W
Yom Mae Nam 101 15 15N 100 20 E
Yonago 110 35 25N 133 19 E
Yŏnan 107 37 55N 126 11 E
Yonezawa 112 37 57N 140 4 E
Yong Peng 101 2 0N 103 3 E
Yong Sata 101 7 8N 99 41 E
Yongampo 107 39 56N 124 23 E
Yŏngchon 107 35 58N 128 56 E
Yŏngdŏk 107 36 24N 129 22 E
Yŏngdŭngpo 107 37 31N 126 54 E
Yŏnghŭng 107 39 31N 127 18 E
Yŏngju 107 36 50N 128 40 E
Yŏngwŏl 107 37 11N 128 28 E
Yonibana 120 8 30N 12 19W
Yonker 153 52 40N 109 40W
Yonkers 162 40 57N 73 51W
Yonne □ 43 47 50N 3 40 E
Yonne, R. 43 48 23N 2 58 E
Yonov 121 7 33N 8 42 E
Yoqueam 90 32 40N 35 6 E
York, Austral. 137 31 52 S 116 47 E
York, U.K. 33 53 58N 1 7W
York, Ala., U.S.A. 157 32 30N 88 18W
York, Nebr., U.S.A. 158 40 55N 97 35W
York, Pa., U.S.A. 162 39 57N 76 43W
York, C. 138 10 42 S 142 31 E
York Factory 153 57 0N 92 18W
York Haven 162 40 7N 76 46W
York, Kap 12 75 55N 66 25W
York, R. 162 37 15N 76 23W
York Sd. 136 14 50 S 125 5 E
York, Vale of 23 54 15N 1 25W
Yorke Pen. 140 34 50 S 137 40 E
Yorkshire Wolds 33 54 0N 0 30W
Yorkton 153 51 11N 102 28W
Yorktown, Tex., U.S.A. 159 29 0N 97 29W

Yorktown Zell

Yorktown, Va., U.S.A.	162	37 14N	76 30W
Yornup	137	34 2S	116 10E
Yoro	166	15 9N	87 7W
Yosemite National Park	163	38 0N	119 30W
Yosemite Village	163	37 45N	119 35W
Yoshii	110	33 16N	129 46E
Yoshimatsu	110	32 0N	130 47E
Yoshkar Ola	81	56 49N	47 10E
Yŏsu	107	34 47N	127 45E
Youanmi	137	28 37S	118 49E
Youbou	152	48 53N	124 13W
Youghal	39	51 58N	7 51W
Youghal B.	39	51 55N	7 50W
Youkounkoun	120	12 35N	13 11W
Young, Austral.	141	34 19S	148 18E
Young, Can.	153	51 47N	105 45W
Young, Uruguay	172	32 44S	57 36W
Young, U.S.A.	161	34 9N	110 56W
Young Ra.	143	44 10S	169 30E
Younghusband, L.	140	30 50S	136 5E
Younghusband Pen.	140	36 0S	139 25E
Youngstown, Can.	153	51 35N	111 10W
Youngstown, U.S.A.	156	41 7N	80 41W
Youssoufia	118	32 16N	8 31W
Yoweragabbie	137	28 14S	117 39E
Yowrie	141	36 17S	149 46E
Yoxall	28	52 45N	1 49W
Yoxford	29	52 16N	1 30E
Yozgat	92	39 51N	34 47E
Ypané, R.	172	23 29S	57 19W
Yport	42	49 45N	0 15E
Ypres	47	50 50N	2 52E
Ypsilanti	156	42 18N	83 40W
Yreka	160	41 44N	122 40W
Ysabel Chan.	135	2 0S	150 0E
Ysbyty Ystwyth	31	52 20N	3 50W
Ysleta	161	31 45N	106 24W
Yssingeaux	45	45 9N	4 8E
Ystad	73	55 26N	13 50E
Ystalyfera	31	51 46N	3 48W
Ystradgynlais	31	51 47N	3 45W
Ystwyth, R.	31	52 24N	4 2W
Ythan, R.	37	57 26N	2 12W
Ytre Adal	71	60 15N	10 14E
Ytterhogdal	72	62 12N	14 56E
Ytyk-Kel	77	62 20N	133 28E
Yü Chiang, R., China	105	22 50N	108 6E
Yü Chiang, R., China	108	22 50N	108 6E
Yu Shui, R.	108	28 37N	110 23E
Yüan Chiang, R.	109	29 0N	111 50E
Yüan Chiang, R (Hong.)	108	29 12N	111 43E
Yüanan	109	31 3N	111 34E
Yüanchiang, Hünan, China	109	28 50N	112 23E
Yüanchiang, Yunnan, China	108	23 40N	102 0E
Yüanch'ü	106	35 18N	111 41E
Yüanli	109	24 27N	120 39E
Yüanlin	109	23 45N	120 30E
Yuanling	109	28 30N	110 5E
Yüanmou	108	25 42N	101 32E
Yuanyang	108	23 10N	102 58E
Yüanyang	108	35 3N	113 57E
Yuat, R.	135	4 10S	143 52E
Yuba City	160	39 12N	121 37W
Yübari	112	43 4N	141 59E
Yübetsu	112	43 13N	144 5E
Yucatán □	165	21 30N	86 30W
Yucatán Basin	14	20 0N	84 0W
Yucatán Channel	166	22 0N	86 30W
Yucca	161	34 56N	114 6W
Yucca Valley	163	34 8N	116 30W
Yücha	108	26 55N	101 24E
Yucheng	106	36 55N	116 40E
Yüch'i	108	24 25N	102 35E
Yuch'i	109	26 10N	118 11E
Yüchiang	109	28 24N	116 53E
Yüch'ien	109	30 12N	119 24E
Yüch'ing	108	27 13N	107 54E
Yudino	76	55 10N	67 55E
Yüehhsi, Anhwei, China	109	30 54N	116 22E
Yüehhsi, Szechwan, China	108	28 36N	102 35E
Yüehyang	109	29 20N	113 7E
Yuendumu	136	22 16S	131 49E
Yufu-Dake	110	33 17N	131 33E
Yugoslavia ■	66	44 0N	20 0E
Yühsien	106	34 10N	113 30E
Yuhsien, Hunan, China	109	27 2N	113 20E
Yuhsien, Shansi, China	106	38 5N	113 24E
Yühuan Tao, I.	109	28 5N	121 15E
Yukan	109	28 43N	116 35E
Yukhnov	80	54 44N	35 15E
Yüki	111	36 18N	139 53E
Yukon □	147	63 0N	135 0W
Yukon, R.	147	65 30N	150 0W
Yukti	77	63 20N	105 0E
Yukuhashi	110	33 44N	130 59E
Yule, R.	136	20 24S	118 12E
Yuli	122	9 44N	10 12E
Yülin	100	18 10N	109 31E
Yulin, Guangdong, China	109	22 36N	110 7E
Yulin, Shensi, China	105	38 15N	109 30E
Yuma, Ariz., U.S.A.	161	32 45N	114 37W
Yuma, Colo., U.S.A.	158	40 10N	102 43W
Yuma, B. de	167	18 20N	68 35W
Yumali	140	35 32S	139 45E
Yumbe	126	3 28N	31 15E
Yumbi	126	1 12S	26 15E
Yumbo	174	3 35N	76 28W
Yümenhsien	105	40 17N	97 12E
Yün Ho	107	33 16N	118 45E
Yun Ho	109	35 0N	117 0E
Yuna	137	28 20S	115 0E
Yünan	109	23 14N	111 31E
Yunaska I.	147	52 40N	170 40W
Yünch'eng, Shansi, China	106	35 1N	110 59E
Yünch'eng, Shantung, China	106	35 35N	115 56E
Yunfou	109	22 56N	112 2E
Yungan	109	25 50N	117 25E
Yungas	174	17 0S	66 0W
Yungay	172	37 10S	72 5W
Yungch'eng	106	33 56N	116 22E
Yungchi	106	34 52N	110 26E
Yungch'ing	106	39 19N	116 29E
Yungch'uan	108	20 22N	105 52E
Yungch'un	109	25 19N	118 17E
Yungfeng	109	27 20N	115 27E
Yungfu	109	24 59N	109 59E
Yungho	106	36 44N	110 39E
Yunghsin	109	16 55N	114 18E
Yunghsing	109	26 8N	113 6E
Yunghsiu	109	29 8N	115 42E
Yungjen	108	26 4N	101 42E
Yungk'ang, Chekiang, China	109	28 53N	120 2E
Yungk'ang, Kwangsi Chuang Aut. Region, China	108	22 48N	107 51E
Yungnien	106	36 49N	114 33E
Yungning, Kwangsi Chuang A. R., China	108	22 45N	108 29E
Yungning, Ningsia Hui A. R., China	106	38 18N	106 18E
Yungning, Yunnan, China	108	27 50N	100 40E
Yungningchai	106	36 35N	108 51E
Yungp'ing	108	25 25N	99 36E
Yungshan	108	28 11N	103 35E
Yungsheng	108	26 42N	100 45E
Yungshun, Hunan, China	108	29 3N	109 50E
Yungshun, Kwangsi Chuang, China	108	22 48N	108 55E
Yungt'ai	109	25 52N	118 55E
Yungteng	106	36 44N	103 24E
Yungting	109	24 49N	116 46E
Yunho = Lishui	109	28 6N	119 34E
Yünhsi	109	33 0N	110 22E
Yünhsiao	109	24 1N	117 15E
Yünhsien, Hupeh, China	105	32 50N	110 53E
Yünhsien, Yunnan, China	108	24 25N	100 6E
Yünlin	109	23 42N	120 31E
Yunling Shan, mts.	108	28 30N	98 50E
Yunlung	99	25 50N	99 25E
Yünmeng	109	31 1N	113 39E
Yunnan □	108	25 0N	102 30E
Yunndaga	137	29 45S	121 0E
Yunomae	110	32 12N	130 59E
Yunotso	110	35 5N	132 21E
Yunquera de Henares	58	40 47N	3 11W
Yunta	140	32 34S	139 36E
Yünyang	108	30 55N	108 56E
Yüp'ing	108	27 14N	108 54E
Yupyongdong	107	41 49N	128 53E
Yur	77	59 52N	137 49E
Yurga	76	55 42N	84 51E
Yuria	84	59 22N	54 10E
Yuribei	76	71 20N	76 30E
Yurimaguas	174	5 55S	76 0W
Yurya	81	59 1N	49 13E
Yuryev Polskiy	81	56 30N	59 47E
Yuryevets	81	57 25N	43 2E
Yuryuzan	84	54 27N	58 28E
Yuscarán	166	13 58N	86 51W
Yusha, Jebel	90	32 4N	35 41E
Yüshan	109	28 40N	118 15E
Yüshanchen	108	29 31N	108 25E
Yushe	106	37 4N	112 58E
Yüshu	105	33 1N	96 44E
Yushu	107	44 46N	126 34E
Yüt'ai	106	35 2N	116 40E
Yüt'ien	107	39 53N	117 45E
Yütu	109	26 0N	115 24E
Yütz'u	106	37 42N	112 44E
Yüwang	106	37 9N	106 28E
Yuyang	108	28 44N	108 46E
Yüyang	109	30 12N	119 56E
Yüyao	109	30 3N	121 9E
Yuyao	109	30 0N	121 20E
Yuyu	105	40 20N	112 30E
Yuyü	106	40 10N	112 25E
Yüyuan	109	28 9N	121 11E
Yuzha	81	56 40N	42 10E
Yuzhno-Sakhalinsk	77	47 5N	142 5E
Yuzhno-Surkhanskoye Vodokhranilishehe	85	37 53N	67 42E
Yuzhno-Uralsk	84	54 26N	61 15E
Yuzhnyy Ural, mts.	84	53 0N	58 0E
Yvelines □	43	48 40N	1 45E
Yverdon	50	46 47N	6 39E
Yvetot	42	49 37N	0 44E
Yvonand	50	46 48N	6 44E

Z

Za, O.	118	34 5N	2 30W
Zaalayskiy Khrebet	85	39 20N	73 0E
Zaamslag	47	51 19N	3 55E
Zaan, R.	46	52 25N	4 52E
Zaandam	47	52 26N	4 49E
Zab, Monts du	119	34 55N	5 0E
Zabalj, Yugo.	66	45 21N	20 5E
Zabalj, Yugo.	66	45 23N	20 5E
Zabari	66	44 22N	21 15E
Zabarjad	122	23 40N	36 12E
Zabaykalskiy	77	49 40N	117 10E
Zabkowice Slaskie	54	50 22N	19 17E
Zabljak	66	42 19N	19 10E
Zabludow	54	53 0N	23 19E
Zabno	54	50 9N	20 53E
Zăbol	93	31 0N	61 25E
Zăbolī	93	27 10N	61 35E
Zabré	121	11 12N	0 36W
Zabrze	54	50 24N	18 50E
Zacapa	166	14 59N	89 31W
Zacapu	164	19 50N	101 43W
Zacatecas	164	22 49N	102 34W
Zacatecas □	164	23 30N	103 0W
Zacatecolua	166	13 29N	88 51W
Zacaultipán	165	20 39N	98 36W
Zacoalco	164	20 10N	103 40W
Zadar	63	44 8N	15 8E
Zadawa	121	11 33N	10 19E
Zadetkyi Kyun	101	10 0N	98 25E
Zadonsk	81	52 25N	38 56E
Zafed	90	32 58N	35 29E
Zafora, I.	69	36 5N	26 24E
Zafra	57	38 26N	6 30W
Zagan	54	51 39N	15 22E
Zagazig	122	30 40N	31 12E
Zaghouan	119	36 23N	10 10E
Zaglivérion	68	40 36N	23 15E
Zaglou	118	27 17N	0 3W
Zagnanado	121	7 18N	2 28E
Zagorá	68	39 27N	23 6E
Zagora	118	30 14N	5 51W
Zagórów	54	52 10N	17 54E
Zagorsk	81	56 20N	38 10E
Zagórz	54	49 30N	22 14E
Zagreb	63	45 50N	16 0E
Zāgros, Kudha-ye	93	33 45N	47 0E
Zagubica	66	44 15N	21 47E
Zaguinaso	120	10 1N	6 14W
Zāhedān	93	29 30N	60 50E
Zahirabad	96	17 43N	77 37E
Zahlah	92	33 52N	35 50E
Zahna	48	51 54N	12 47E
Zahrez Chergui	118	35 0N	3 30E
Zahrez Rharbi	118	34 50N	2 55E
Zailiyskiy Alatau, Khrebet	85	43 5N	77 0E
Zainsk	84	55 18N	52 4E
Zaïr	118	29 47N	5 51W
Zaïre, R.	124	1 30N	28 0E
Zaïre, Rep. of ■	124	3 0S	23 0E
Zaječar	66	43 53N	22 18E
Zakamensk	77	50 23N	103 17E
Zakariya	90	31 43N	34 57E
Zakataly	83	41 38N	46 35E
Zakavkazye	83	42 0N	44 0E
Zakhu	92	37 10N	42 50E
Zákinthos	69	37 47N	20 54E
Zákinthos, I.	69	37 45N	27 45E
Zakopane	54	49 18N	19 57E
Zala □	53	46 42N	16 50E
Zala, R.	53	46 53N	17 6E
Zalaegerszeg	53	46 53N	16 47E
Zalakomár	53	46 33N	17 10E
Zalalövö	53	46 51N	16 35E
Zalamea de la Serena	57	38 40N	5 38W
Zalamea la Real	57	37 41N	6 38W
Zalau	121	10 30N	8 58E
Zalazna	84	58 39N	52 31E
Zalec	63	46 16N	15 10E
Zaleshchiki	82	48 45N	25 45E
Zalewo	54	53 55N	19 41E
Zalingei	117	13 5N	23 10E
Zaltan, Jabal	119	28 46N	19 45E
Zaltbommel	46	51 48N	5 15E
Zalů	121	47 12N	23 5E
Zambeke	126	2 8N	25 17E
Zambèze, R.	127	18 46S	36 16E
Zambezi, R.	127	18 46S	36 16E
Zambezia □	127	16 15S	37 30E
Zambia ■	125	15 0S	28 0E
Zamboanga	103	6 59N	122 3E
Zambrano	174	9 45N	74 49W
Zametchino	81	53 30N	42 30E
Zamora, Mexico	164	20 0N	102 21W
Zamora, Spain	56	41 30N	5 45W
Zamora □	56	41 30N	5 46W
Zamość	54	50 50N	23 22E
Zamuro, Sierra del	174	4 0N	62 30W
Zamzam, W.	119	31 0N	14 30E
Zan	121	9 26N	0 17W
Zanaga	124	2 48S	13 48E
Záncara, R.	58	39 20N	3 0W
Zandvoort	46	52 22N	4 32E
Zanesville	156	39 56N	82 2W
Zangue, R.	127	18 5S	35 10E
Zanjan	92	36 40N	48 35E
Zannone, I.	64	40 38N	13 2E
Zante = Zákinthos	69	37 47N	20 54E
Zanthus	137	31 2S	123 34E
Zanzibar	126	6 12S	39 12E
Zanzibar I.	126	6 12S	39 12E
Zanzūr	119	32 55N	13 1E
Zaouatalaz	119	24 57N	8 16E
*Zaouiet El Kahla	119	27 10N	6 40E
Zaouiet Reggane	118	26 32N	0 3E
Zapadna Morava, R.	66	43 50N	20 15E
Zapadnaya Dvina	80	56 15N	32 3E
Západné Beskydy	54	49 30N	19 0E
Zapadočesky □	52	49 35N	13 0E
Západoslovenský □	53	48 30N	17 30E
Zapala	176	39 0S	70 5W
Zapaleri, Cerro	172	22 49S	67 11W
Zapata	159	26 56N	92 17W
Zapatón, R.	57	39 0N	6 49W
Zaporozhye	82	47 50N	35 10E
Zapponeta	65	41 27N	15 57E
Zara	92	39 58N	37 43E
Zaragoza, Colomb.	174	7 30N	74 52W
Zaragoza, Coahuila, Mexico	164	28 30N	101 0W
Zaragoza, Nuevo León, Mexico	165	24 0N	99 36W
Zaragoza, Spain	58	41 39N	0 53W
Zaragoza □	58	41 35N	1 0W
Zarand	93	30 46N	56 34E
Zarasai	80	55 40N	26 12E
Zarate	172	34 7S	59 0W
Zaraysk	81	54 48N	38 53E
Zaraza	174	9 21N	65 19W
Zarembo I.	152	56 20N	132 50W
Zari	73	13 8N	12 37E
Zaria	121	11 0N	7 40E
Zarisberge	128	24 30S	16 15E
Zarki	54	50 38N	19 21E
Zarnów	54	51 16N	20 9E
Zarnuqa	90	31 53N	34 47E
Zarów	54	50 56N	16 29E
Zarqa, R.	90	32 10N	35 37E
Zaruma	174	3 40S	79 30W
Zary	54	51 37N	15 10E
Zarza de Alange	57	38 49N	6 13W
Zarza de Granadilla	56	40 14N	6 3W
Zarza, La	57	37 42N	6 51W
Zarzaïtine	119	28 32N	9 5E
Zarzal	174	4 24N	76 4W
Zarzis	119	33 31N	11 2E
Zas	56	43 4N	8 53W
Zashiversk	77	67 25N	142 40E
Zaskar Mountains	95	33 15N	77 30E
Zaskar, R.	95	33 55N	77 2E
Zastron	128	30 18S	27 7E
Zatec	52	50 20N	13 32E
Zator	54	49 59N	19 28E
Zavala	66	42 50N	17 59E
Zavareh	93	33 35N	52 28E
Zaventem	47	50 53N	4 28E
Zavetnoye	83	47 13N	43 50E
Zavidovići	66	44 27N	18 13E
Zavitinsk	77	50 10N	129 20E
Zavodoski, I.	13	56 0S	27 45W
Zavolzhye	81	56 37N	43 18E
Zawadzkie	54	50 37N	18 28E
Zawidów	54	51 1N	15 1E
Zawiercie	54	50 30N	19 13E
Zâwyet Shammâs	122	31 30N	26 37E
Zâwyet Um el Rakham	122	31 18N	27 1E
Zâwyet Ungeila	122	31 23N	26 42E
Zayandeh, R.	93	32 35N	32 0E
Zayarsk	77	56 20N	102 55E
Zaysan	76	47 28N	84 52E
Zaysan, Oz.	76	48 0N	83 0E
Zâzamt, W.	119	30 29N	14 30E
Zazir, O.	119	22 0N	5 40E
Zázrivá	53	49 16N	19 7E
Zbarazh	80	49 43N	25 44E
Zbaszyn	54	52 14N	15 56E
Zbaszynek	54	52 16N	15 51E
Zblewo	54	53 56N	18 19E
Zdandijk	46	52 82N	4 49E
Zdolbunov	80	50 30N	26 15E
Zdrelo	66	44 16N	21 28E
Zdunska Wola	54	51 37N	18 59E
Zduny	54	51 39N	17 21E
Zeballos	152	49 59N	126 50W
Zebediela	129	24 20S	29 17E
Zedelgem	47	51 8N	3 8E
Zeebrugge	47	51 19N	3 12E
Zeehan	138	41 52S	145 25E
Zeeland	47	51 41N	5 40E
Zeeland □	47	51 30N	3 50E
Ze'elim	90	31 13N	34 32E
Zeelst	47	51 25N	5 25E
Zeerust	128	25 31S	26 4E
Zefat	90	32 58N	35 29E
Zegdou	118	29 51N	4 53W
Zege	123	11 43N	37 18E
Zegelsem	47	50 49N	3 43E
Zegoua	120	10 32N	5 35W
Zehdenick	48	52 59N	13 20E
Zeil, Mt.	136	23 24S	132 23E
Zeila	91	11 15N	43 30E
Zeist	46	52 5N	5 15E
Zeita	90	32 23N	35 2E
Zeitz	48	51 3N	12 9E
Zele	47	51 4N	4 2E
Zelendolsk	81	55 55N	48 30E
Zelengora, mts.	66	43 22N	18 30E
Zelenika	66	42 27N	18 37E
Zelenogradsk	80	54 53N	20 29E
Zelenokumsk	83	44 30N	44 1E
Zelenovski	83	48 6N	50 45E
Zelhem	47	52 0N	6 21E
Zell	49	47 42N	7 50E

*Renamed Bordj Omar Driss

Place	Pg	Lat		N/S	Long		E/W
Zell am See	52	47	19	N	12	47	E
Zella Mehlis	48	50	40	N	10	41	E
Zelouane	86	35	1	N	2	58	W
Zelzate	47	51	13	N	3	47	E
Zémio	126	5	2	N	25	5	E
Zemmora	118	35	44	N	0	51	E
Zemora, I.	119	37	5	N	10	56	E
Zemoul, W.	118	29	15	N	7	30	W
Zemst	47	50	59	N	4	28	E
Zemun	66	44	51	N	20	25	E
Zenica	66	44	10	N	17	57	E
Zenina	118	34	30	N	2	37	E
Zentsüji	110	34	14	N	133	47	E
Zepce	66	44	28	N	18	2	E
Zeravshan	85	39	10	N	68	39	E
Zeravshan, R.	85	39	32	N	63	45	E
Zeravshanskiy, Khrebet	85	39	20	N	69	0	E
Zerbst	48	51	59	N	12	8	E
Zerhamra	118	29	58	N	2	30	W
Zerków	54	52	4	N	17	32	E
Zermatt	50	46	2	N	7	46	E
Zernez	51	46	42	N	10	7	E
Zernograd	83	46	52	N	40	11	E
Zeroud, O.	119	35	30	N	9	30	E
Zerqani	68	41	30	N	20	20	E
Zestafoni	83	42	6	N	43	0	E
Zetel	48	53	33	N	7	57	E
Zetland (□)	26	60	30	N	0	15	W
Zetten	46	51	56	N	5	44	E
Zeulenroda	48	50	39	N	12	0	E
Zeven	48	53	17	N	9	19	E
Zevenaar	46	51	56	N	6	5	E
Zevenbergen	47	51	38	N	4	37	E
Zévio	62	45	23	N	11	10	E
Zeya	77	54	2	N	127	20	E
Zeya, R.	77	53	30	N	127	0	E
Zeyse	123	5	44	N	37	23	W
Zeytin	92	37	53	N	36	53	E
Zézere, R.	56	40	0	N	7	55	W
Zgierz	54	51	45	N	19	27	E
Zgorzelec	54	51	10	N	15	0	E
Zhabinka	80	52	13	N	24	2	E
Zhailma	84	51	30	N	61	50	E
Zhalanash	85	43	3	N	78	38	E
Zhamensk	80	54	37	N	21	17	E
Zhanadarya	85	44	45	N	64	40	E
Zhanatas	76	43	11	N	81	18	E
Zharkol	84	49	57	N	64	5	E
Zharkovskiy	80	55	56	N	32	19	E
Zhashkov	82	49	15	N	30	5	E
Zhdanov	82	47	5	N	37	31	E
Zheleznogorsk-Ilimskiy	77	56	34	N	104	8	E
Zherdevka	81	51	56	N	41	21	E
Zhetykol, Ozero	84	51	2	N	60	54	E
Zhigansk	77	66	35	N	124	10	E
Zhigulevsk	81	53	28	N	49	45	E
Zhirhovsk	81	50	57	N	44	49	E
Zhitomir	80	50	20	N	28	40	E
Zhizdra	80	53	45	N	34	40	E
Zhlobin	80	52	55	N	30	0	E
Zhmerinka	82	49	2	N	28	10	E
Zhodino	80	54	5	N	28	17	E
Zhovtnevoye	82	47	54	N	32	2	E
Zhuantobe	85	43	43	N	78	18	E
Zhukovka	80	53	35	N	33	50	E
Zhupanovo	77	51	59	N	15	9	E
Ziarat	94	30	25	N	67	30	E
Zichem	47	51	2	N	4	59	E
Ziebice	54	50	37	N	17	2	E
Ziel, Mt.	136	23	20	S	132	30	E
Zielona Góra	54	51	57	N	15	31	E
Zielona Góra □	54	51	57	N	15	30	E
Zierikzee	47	51	40	N	3	55	E
Ziesar	48	52	16	N	12	19	E
Zifta	122	30	43	N	31	14	E
Zigazinskiy	84	53	50	N	57	20	E
Zigey	117	14	50	N	15	50	E
Ziguinchor	120	12	25	N	16	20	W
Zihuatanejo	164	17	38	N	101	33	W
Zikhron Ya'Aqov	90	32	34	N	34	56	E
Zile	92	40	15	N	36	0	E
Zilfi	92	26	12	N	44	52	E
Zilina	53	49	12	N	18	42	E
Zillah	119	28	40	N	17	41	E
Zillertaler Alpen	52	47	6	N	11	45	E
Zima	77	54	0	N	102	5	E
Zimane, Adrar in	118	22	10	N	4	30	E
Zimapán	165	20	40	N	99	20	W
Zimba	127	17	20	S	26	25	E
Zimbabwe ■	127	20	16	S	31	0	E
Zimovniki	83	47	10	N	42	25	E
Zinal	50	46	8	N	7	38	E
Zinder	121	13	48	N	9	0	E
Zinga	127	9	16	S	38	41	E
Zingem	47	50	54	N	3	40	E
Zingst	48	54	24	N	12	45	E
Zini, Yebel	118	28	0	N	11	0	W
Ziniaré	121	12	44	N	1	10	W
Zinjibar	91	13	5	N	46	0	E
Zinkgruvan	73	58	50	N	15	6	E
Zinnowitz	48	54	5	N	13	54	E
Zion Nat. Park	161	37	25	N	112	50	W
Zipaquirá	174	5	0	N	74	0	W
Zippori	90	32	64	N	35	16	E
Zirc	53	47	17	N	17	42	E
Ziri	63	47	17	N	11	14	E
Zirje, I.	63	43	39	N	15	42	E
Zirl	52	47	17	N	11	14	E
Zisterdorf	53	48	33	N	16	45	E
Zitácuaro	164	19	20	N	100	30	W
Zitava, R.	53	48	14	N	18	21	E
Zitiste	66	45	30	N	2	32	E
Zitsa	68	39	47	N	20	40	E
Zittau	48	50	54	N	14	47	E
Zitundo	129	26	48	S	32	47	E
Zivinice	66	44	27	N	18	36	E
Ziway, L.	123	8	0	N	38	50	E
Ziz, Oued	118	31	40	N	4	15	W
Zizip	92	37	5	N	37	50	E
Zlarin	63	43	42	N	15	49	E
Zlatar	63	46	5	N	16	3	E
Zlataritsa	67	43	2	N	24	55	E
Zlatibor	66	43	45	N	19	43	E
Zlatista	67	42	41	N	24	7	E
Zlatna	70	46	8	N	23	11	E
Zlatograd	67	41	22	N	25	7	E
Zlatoust	78	55	10	N	59	40	E
Zletovo	66	41	59	N	22	17	E
Zlitan	119	32	25	N	14	35	E
Złocieniec	54	53	30	N	16	1	E
Złoczew	54	51	24	N	18	35	E
Zlot	66	44	1	N	22	0	E
Złotoryja	54	51	8	N	15	55	E
Złotów	54	53	22	N	17	2	E
Złoty Stok	54	50	27	N	16	53	E
Zmeinogorsk	76	51	10	N	82	13	E
Zmigród	54	51	28	N	16	53	E
Zmiyev	82	49	45	N	36	27	E
Znamenka	82	48	45	N	32	30	E
Znin	54	52	51	N	17	44	E
Znojmo	52	48	50	N	16	2	E
Zoar	128	33	30	S	21	26	E
Zobia	126	3	0	N	25	50	E
Zoetermeer	46	52	3	N	4	30	E
Zofingen	50	47	17	N	7	56	E
Zogno	62	45	49	N	9	41	E
Zolder	47	51	1	N	5	19	E
Zollikofen	50	47	0	N	7	28	E
Zollikon	51	47	21	N	8	34	E
Zolochev	80	49	45	N	24	58	E
Zolotonosha	82	49	45	N	32	5	E
Zomba	127	15	30	S	35	19	E
Zombi	126	3	35	N	29	10	E
Zomergem	47	51	7	N	3	33	E
Zongo	124	4	12	N	18	0	E
Zonguldak	82	41	28	N	31	50	E
Zonhoven	47	50	59	N	5	23	E
Zorgo	121	12	22	N	0	35	W
Zorita	57	39	17	N	5	39	W
Zorleni	70	46	14	N	27	44	E
Zornitsa	67	42	23	N	26	58	E
Zorritos	174	3	50	S	80	40	W
Zory	54	50	3	N	18	44	E
Zorzor	120	7	46	N	9	28	W
Zossen	48	52	13	N	13	28	E
Zottegam	47	50	52	N	3	48	E
Zouar	119	20	30	N	16	32	E
Zouérabe	116	22	35	N	12	30	W
Zousfana, O.	118	31	51	N	1	30	W
Zoutkamp	46	53	20	N	6	18	E
Zqorzelec	54	51	9	N	15	0	E
Zrenjanin	66	45	22	N	20	23	E
Zuarungu	121	10	49	N	0	52	W
Zuba	121	9	11	N	7	12	E
Zubair, Jazâir	123	15	0	N	42	10	E
Zubia	57	37	8	N	3	33	W
Zubtsov	80	56	10	N	34	34	E
Zueitina	119	30	58	N	20	7	E
Zuénoula	120	7	34	N	6	3	W
Zuera	58	41	51	N	0	49	W
Zug	51	47	10	N	8	31	E
Zug □	51	47	9	N	8	35	E
Zugar	123	14	0	N	42	40	E
Zugdidi	83	42	30	N	41	48	E
Zugersee	51	47	7	N	8	35	E
Zugspitze	49	47	25	N	10	59	E
Zuid-Holland □	46	52	0	N	4	35	E
Zuid-horn	46	53	15	N	6	23	E
Zuidbeveland	47	51	30	N	3	50	E
Zuidbroek	46	53	10	N	6	52	E
Zuidelijk-Flevoland	46	52	22	N	5	22	E
Zuidlaarder meer	46	53	8	N	6	42	E
Zuidland	46	51	49	N	4	15	E
Zuidlaren	46	53	6	N	6	42	E
Zuidwolde	46	52	40	N	6	26	E
Zújar	59	37	34	N	2	50	W
Zújar, Pantano del	57	38	55	N	5	35	W
Zújar, R.	59	38	30	N	5	30	E
Zula	123	15	17	N	39	40	E
Zulia □	174	10	0	N	72	10	W
Zülpich	48	50	41	N	6	38	E
Zululand	129	43	19	N	2	15	W
Zumaya	58	43	19	N	2	15	W
Zumbo	127	15	35	S	30	26	E
Zummo	121	9	51	N	12	59	E
Zumpango	165	19	48	N	99	6	W
Zundert	47	51	28	N	4	39	E
Zungeru	121	9	48	N	6	8	E
Zuni	161	35	7	N	108	57	W
Zupania	66	45	4	N	18	43	E
Zur	66	42	13	N	20	34	E
Zura	84	57	36	N	53	24	E
Zūrandului	70	46	14	N	22	7	E
Zürich	51	47	22	N	8	32	E
Zürich □	51	47	26	N	8	40	E
Zürichsee	51	47	18	N	8	40	E
Zuromin	54	53	4	N	19	57	E
Zuru	121	11	27	N	5	4	E
Zurzach	51	47	35	N	8	18	E
Zut, I.	63	43	52	N	15	17	E
Zutendaal	47	50	56	N	5	35	E
Zutphen	46	52	9	N	6	12	E
Zuwárrah	119	32	58	N	12	1	E
Zuyevka	84	58	27	N	51	10	E
Zuzemberk	63	45	52	N	14	56	E
Zvenigorodka	82	49	4	N	30	56	E
Zverinogolovskoye	84	55	0	N	62	30	E
Zvezdets	67	42	6	N	27	26	E
Zvolen	53	48	33	N	19	10	E
Zvonce	66	42	57	N	22	34	E
Zvornik	66	44	26	N	19	7	E
Zwaag	46	52	40	N	5	4	E
Zwanenburg	46	52	23	N	4	45	E
Zwarte Meer	46	52	38	N	5	57	E
Zwarte Waler	46	52	39	N	6	1	E
Zwartemeer	46	52	43	N	7	2	E
Zwartsluis	46	52	39	N	6	4	E
Zwedru (Tchien)	120	5	59	N	8	15	W
Zweibrücken	49	49	15	N	7	20	E
Zwenkau	48	51	13	N	12	19	E
Zwetti	52	48	35	N	15	9	E
Zwickau	48	50	43	N	12	30	E
Zwijnaarde	47	51	0	N	3	43	E
Zwijndrecht, Belg.	47	51	13	N	4	20	E
Zwijndrecht, Neth.	46	51	50	N	4	39	E
Zwolle	46	52	31	N	6	6	E
Zymoelz, R.	152	54	33	N	128	31	W
Zyrardów	54	52	3	N	20	35	E
Zywiec	54	44	42	N	19	12	E

Recent Place-Name Changes

The following place-name changes have recently occurred in Angola, Iran, Madagascar, Mozambique, Vietnam and Zimbabwe. The new names are given on the maps but the former names are in the index.

Angola

Former Name	New name
Ambrizete	Nzeto
Artur de Paiva	Capelongo
Bié	Kuito
Cassinga	Kassinga
Dundo	Luachimo
General Machado	Camacupa
João de Almeida	Chibia
Macedo do Cavaleiros	Andulo
Mariano Machado	Ganda
Moçâmedes	Namibe
Nova Redondo	Ngunza
Ongiva	Ngiva
Paiva Couceiro	Gambos
Robert Williams	Caála
Roçadas	Xangongo
San António do Zaïre	Soyo
Teixeira da Silva	Bailundo
Vila Ariaga	Bibala
Vila Marechal Carmona	Uíge

Iran

Former name	New name
Bandar-e Pahlavi	Bandar-e Anzalī
Bandar-e Shah	Bandar-e Torkeman
Bandar-e Shahpur	Bandar-e Khomeynī
Dehkhvareqan	Āzar Shahr
Dezh Shahpur	Marīvan
Kermanshah	Qahremānshahr
Khorramshahr	Khorramshahr (Khūnīnshahr)
Naft Shah	Naftshahr
Reza'iyeh	Orūmīyeh
Reza'iyeh, Daryacheh-ye	Orūmīyeh, Daryācheh-ye
Sar Eskand Khan	Āzarān
Shāhābād	Eslāmābād-e Gharb
Shāhī	Qā'emshahr
Shahpur	Salmās
Shahreza	Qomsheh
Shāhrud	Emāmrūd
Shahsavar	Tunekābon
Soltaniyeh	Sa'īdīyeh

Madagascar

Former name	New name
Ambre, C. de	Bobaomby, Tanjon' i
Ambre, Mt. d'	Ambohitra
Brickaville	Vohibinany
Chesterfield I.	Vestale, Toraka
Diégo Suarez	Antsirañana
Fénérive	Fenoarivo Atsinanana
Fort-Dauphin	Faradofay
Majunga	Mahajanga
Midongy du Sud	Midongy Atsimo
Ste. Marie, C.	Vohimena, T.' i
Ste. Marie, I.	Boraha, Nosy
Tamatave	Toamasina
Tuléar	Toliara

Mozambique

Former name	New name
Augusto Cardosa	Metangula
Entre Rios	Malema
Malvérnia	Chicualacuala
Mau-é-ele	Marão
Olivença	Lupilichi
Vila Alferes Chamusca	Guijá
Vila Caldas Xavier	Muende
Vila Coutinho	Ulonguè
Vila Fontes	Caia
Vila de Junqueiro	Gurué
Vila Luísa	Marracuene
Vila Paiva de Andrada	Gorongoza

Vietnam

Former name	New name
An Loc	Hon Quan
An Tuc	An Khe
Chau Phu	Chau Doc
Dien Bien Phu	Dien Bien
Hau Bon	Cheo Reo
Khanh Hung	Soc Trang
Kien Hung	Go Quao
Phuoc Le	Ba Ria
Quan Long	Ca Mau
Truc Giang	Ben Tre

Zimbabwe

Former name	New name
Balla Balla	Mbalabala
Belingwe	Mberengwa
Chipinga	Chipinge
Dett	Dete
Enkeldoorn	Chivhu
Essexvale	Esigodini
Fort Victoria	Masvingo
Gwelo	Gweru
Hartley	Chegutu
Gatooma	Kadoma
Inyazura	Nyazura
Marandellas	Marondera
Mashaba	Mashava
Melsetter	Chimanimani
Mrewa	Murewa
Mtoko	Mutoko
Nuanetsi	Mwenezi
Que Que	Kwekwe
Salisbury	Harare
Selukwe	Shurugwi
Shabani	Zvishavane
Sinoia	Chinhoyi
Somabula	Somabhula
Tjolotjo	Tsholotsho
Umvuma	Mvuma
Umtali	Mutare
Wankie	Hwange

Chinese Place-Names

The following list gives the Pin Yin nameform and the modified Wade-Giles nameform for the principal places in China. Pin Yin is officially approved by the Chinese and is gaining in use throughout the world. Wade-Giles is the transcription selected for the maps and index in this atlas and is still extensively used in the West.

Pin Yin	Wade-Giles	Pin Yin	Wade-Giles	Pin Yin	Wade-Giles
Anhui	Anhwei	Jiangxi	Kiangsi	Taizhou	T'aichou
Anqing	Anch'ing	Jiaxing	Chiahsing	Tandong	T'antung
Baoding	Paoting	Jilin	Chilin	Tanggula Shan	T'angkula Shanmo
Baoji	Paochi	Jinan	Chinan	Tian Shan	Tien Shan
Baotou	Paot'ou	Jingdezhen	Chingtechen	Tianjin	T'ienching
Bei'an	Peian	Jinhua	Chinhua	Tianshui	Tienshui
Beihai	Peihai	Jining	Chining	Tongchuan	Tungchwan
Beijing	Peip'ing	Jinxi	Chinhsi	Tonghua	T'unghua
Bengbu	Pangfou	Jinxian	Chinhsien	Tongling	Tungling
Benxi	Pench'i	Jinzhou	Chinchou	Ürümqi	Wulumuchi
Boshan	Poshan	Jiujiang	Chiuchiang	Wanxian	Wanhsien
Cangzhou	Ts'angchou	Jixi	Chihsi	Wenzhou	Wenchou
Changchi	Ch'angchih	Junggur Pendi	Dzungaria	Wutongqiao	Wut'ungchi'ao
Changchun	Ch'angch'un	Kashi	Kashgar	Wuxi	Wuhsi
Changde	Changt'e	Lanzhou	Lanchou	Wuzhou	Wuchou
Changsha	Ch'angsha	Lianyungan	Lienyünchiangshih	Xiaguan	Hsiakuan
Changshu	Ch'angshu	Liuzhou	Liuchou	Xiamen	Hsiamen
Changzhou	Ch'angchou	Lüda	Lüta	Xi'an	Hsian
Chengde	Ch'engte	Luoshan	Loshan	Xiangfan	Hsiangfan
Chengdu	Ch'engtu	Luoyang	Loyang	Xiangtan	Hsiangt'an
Chongqing	Ch'ungch'ing	Luzhou	Luchou	Xianyang	Hsienyang
Da Hinggan Ling	Tahsinganling Shanmo	Manzhouli	Manchouli	Xiao Hinggan Ling	Hsiaohsinganling Shanmo
Datong	Tat'ung	Meixian	Meihsien	Xingtai	Hsingt'ai
Dezhou	Techou	Mudanjiang	Mutanchiang	Xining	Hsinging
Dongchuan	Tungch'uan	Nanchong	Nanch'ung	Xinjiang Uygur Zizhiqu	Singkiang-Uigur
Duyun	Tuyün	Nanjing	Nanching	Xinjin	Hsinchin
Fujian	Fukien	Nantong	Nant'ung	Xinxiang	Hsinhsiang
Fuxin	Fouhsinshin	Nanzhang	Nanch'ang	Xuanhua	Hsüanhua
Fuzhou	Fuchou	Neijiang	Neichiang	Xuchang	Hsüch'ang
Gansu	Kansu	Ningbo	Ningpo	Xuzhou	Hsüchou
Ganzhou	Kanchou	Ningxia Huizu Zizhiqu	Ningsia Hui	Yangquan	Yangch'üan
Gejiu	Kochiu	Pingdingshan	P'ingt'ingshan	Yangzhou	Yangchou
Guangdong	Kwangtung	Pingxiang	P'inghsiang	Yanji	Yenchi
Guangxi Zhuangzu Zizhiqu	Kwangsi-Chuang	Qaidam Pendi	Tsaidam	Yanjin	Yench'eng
Guangzhou	Kuangchou	Qingdao	Ch'ingtao	Yantai	Yent'ai
Guilin	Kueilin	Qinghai	Tsinghai	Yibin	Ipin
Guiyang	Kueiyang	Qingjiang	Ch'ingchiang	Yichang	Ich'ang
Guizhou	Kweichow	Qinhuangdao	Ch'inhuangtao	Yingchuan	Yinch'uan
Hangzhou	Hangchou	Qiqihar	Ch'ich'ihaerh	Yining	Ining
Harbin	Haerhpin	Quanzhou	Ch'üanchou	Yiyang	Iyang
Hebei	Hopei	Rugao	Jukao	Yuci	Yutz'ü
Hebi	Haopi	Sanmenxia	Sanmenhsia	Zaozhuang	Tsaochuang
Hechuan	Hoch'uan	Shaanxi	Shensi	Zhangjiakou	Changchiak'ou
Hefei	Hofei	Shandong	Shantung	Zhangjiang	Chanchiang
Hegang	Haokang	Shangqiu	Shangch'iu	Zhangzhou	Changchou
Heilong Jiang	Heilungkiang	Shangrao	Shangjao	Zhao'an	Ch'aoan
Henan	Honan	Shanxi	Shansi	Zhejiang	Chekiang
Hohhot	Huhohaot'e	Shaoguan	Shaokuan	Zhengzhou	Chengchou
Huaide	Huaite	Shaoxing	Shaohsing	Zhenjiang	Chenchiang
Huangshi	Huangshih	Shijiazhuang	Shihchiachuangi	Zhuhai	Chuhai
Hubei	Hupei	Shizuishan	Shihtsuishan	Zhuzhou	Chuchou
Jiamusi	Chiamussu	Shunde	Shunte	Zigong	Tzukung
Ji'an	Chian	Sichuan	Szechwan	Zunyi	Tsuni
Jiangmen	Chiangmen	Siping	Ssup'ing		
Jiangsu	Kiangsu	Suxian	Suhsien		
		Suzhou	Suchou		

Geographical Terms

This is a list of some of the geographical words from foreign languages which are found in the place names on the maps and in the index. Each is followed by the language and the English meaning.

Afr. afrikaans
Alb. albanian
Amh. amharic
Ar. arabic
Ber. berber
Bulg. bulgarian
Bur. burmese

Chin. chinese
Cz. czechoslovakian
Dan. danish
Dut. dutch
Fin. finnish
Flem. flemish
Fr. french

Gae. gaelic
Ger. german
Gr. greek
Heb. hebrew
Hin. hindi
I.-C. indo-chinese
Ice. icelandic

It. italian
Jap. japanese
Kor. korean
Lapp. lappish
Lith. lithuanian
Mal. malay
Mong. mongolian

Nor. norwegian
Pash. pashto
Pers. persian
Pol. polish
Port. portuguese
Rum. rumanian
Russ. russian

Ser.-Cr. serbo-croat
Siam. siamese
Sin. sinhalese
Som. somali
Span. spanish
Swed. swedish
Tib. tibetan
Turk. turkish

A. (Ain) *Ar.* spring
–á *Ice.* river
a *Dan., Nor., Swed.* stream
–abad *Pers., Russ.* town
Abyad *Ar.* white
Ad. (Adrar) *Ar., Ber.* mountain
Ada, Adasi *Tur.* island
Addis *Amh.* new
Adrar *Ar., Ber.* mountain
Ain *Ar.* spring
Ákra *Gr.* cape
Akrotíri *Gr.* cape
Alb *Ger.* mountains
Albufera *Span.* lagoon
–ålen *Nor.* islands
Alpen *Ger.* mountain pastures
Alpes *Fr.* mountains
Alpi *It.* mountains
Alto *Port.* high
–älv, –älven *Swed.* stream, river
Amt *Dan.* first-order administrative division
Appennino *It.* mountain range
Arch. (Archipiélago) *Span.* archipelago
Arcipelago *It.* archipelago
Arq. (Arquipélago) *Port.* archipelago
Arr. (Arroyo) *Span.* stream
–Ås, –åsen *Nor., Swed.* hill
Autonomna Oblast *Ser.-Cr.* autonomous region
Ayios *Gr.* island
Ayn *Ar.* well, waterhole

B(a). (Baía) *Port.* bay
B. (Baie) *Fr.* bay
B. (Bahía) *Span.* bay
B. (Ben) *Gae.* mountain
B. (Bir) *Ar.* well
B. (Bucht) *Ger.* bay
B. (Bugt.) *Dan.* bay
Baai, –baai *Afr.* bay
Bâb *Ar.* gate
Bäck, –bäcken *Swed.* stream
Back, backen, *Swed.* hill
Bad, –baden *Ger.* spa
Bādiya, –t *Ar.* desert
Baek *Dan.* stream
Baelt *Dan.* strait
Bahía *Span.* bay
Bahr *Ar.* sea, river
Bahra *Ar.* lake
Baía *Port.* bay
Baie *Fr.* bay
Bajo, –a, *Span.* lower
Bakke *Nor.* hill
Bala *Pers.* upper
Baltä *Rum.* marsh, lake
Banc *Fr.* bank
Bander *Ar., Mal.* port
Bandar *Pers.* bay
Banja *Ser. Cr.* spa resort
Barat *Mal.* western
Barr. (Barrage) *Fr.* dam
Barracão *Port.* dam, waterfall
Bassin *Fr.* bay
Bayt *Heb.* house, village
Bazar *Hin.* market, bazaar
Be'er *Heb.* well
Beit *Heb.* village
Belo-, Belyy, Belaya,

Beloye, *Russ.* white
Ben *Gae.* mountain
Bender *Somal.* harbour
Berg,(e) –berg(e) *Afr.* mountain(s)
Berg, –berg *Ger.* mountain
–berg, –et *Nor., Swed.* hill, mountain, rock
Bet *Heb.* house, village
Bir, Bîr *Ar.* well
Birket *Ar.* lake, bay, marsh
Bj. (Bordj) *Ar.* port
–bjerg *Dan.* hill, point
Boca *Span.* river mouth
Bodden *Ger.* bay, inlet
Bogaz, Boğaz, –ı *Tur.* strait
Boka *Ser.-Cr.* gulf, inlet
Bol. (Bolshoi) *Russ.* great, large
Bordj *Ar.* fort
–borg *Dan., Nor., Swed.* castle, fort
–botn *Nor.* valley floor
bouche(s) *Fr.* mouth
Br. (Burnu) *Tur.* cape
Bratul *Rum.* distributary stream
–breen *Nor.* glacier
–bruck *Ger.* bridge
–brunn *Swed.* well, spring
Bucht *Ger.* bay
Bugt, –bugt *Dan.* bay
Buheirat *Ar.* lake
Bukit *Mal.* hill
Bukten *Swed.* bay
–bulag *Mong.* spring
Bûr *Ar.* port
Burg. *Ar.* fort
Burg, –burg *Ger.* castle
Burnu *Tur.* cape
Burun *Tur.* cape
Butt *Gae.* promontory
–by *Dan., Nor., Swed.* town
–byen *Nor., Swed.* town

C. (Cabo) *Port., Span.* headland, cape
C. (Cap) *Fr.* cape
C. (Capo) *It.* cape
Cabeza *Span.* peak, hill
Camp *Port., Span.* land, field
Campo *Span.* plain
Campos *Span.* upland
Can. (Canal) *Fr., Span.* canal
Canale *It.* canal
Canalul *Ser.-Cr.* canal
Cao Nguyên *Thai.* plateau, tableland
Cap *Fr.* cape
Capo *It.* cape
Cataracta *Sp.* cataract
Cauce *Span.* intermittent stream
Causse *Fr.* upland (limestone)
Cayi *Tur.* river
Cayo(s) *Span.* rock(s), islet(s)
Cerro *Span.* hill, peak
Ch. (Chaîne(s)) *Fr.* mountain range(s)
Ch. (Chott) *Ar.* salt lake
Chaco *Span.* jungle
Chaîne(s) *Fr.* mountain range(s)
Chap. (Chapada) *Port.* hills, upland

Chapa *Span.* hills, upland
Chapada *Port.* hills, upland
Chaung *Bur.* stream, river
Chen *Chin.* market town
Ch'eng *Chin.* town
Chiang *Chin.* river
Ch'ih *Chin.* pool
Ch'ŏn *Kor.* river
–chŏsuji *Kor.* reservoir
Chott *Ar.* salt lake, swamp
Chou *Chin.* district
Chu *Tib.* river
Chung *Chin.* middle
Chute *Fr.* waterfall
Co. (Cerro) *Span.* hill, peak
Coch. (Cochilla) *Port.* hills
Col *Fr., It.* Pass
Colline(s) *Fr.* hill(s)
Conca *It.* plain, basin
Cord. (Cordillera) *Span.* mountain chain
Costa *It., Span.* coast
Côte *Fr.* coast, slope, hill
Cuchillas *Spain* hills
Cu-Lao *I.-C.* island

D. (Dolok) *Mal.* mountain
Dágh *Pers.* mountain
Dağ(ı) *Tur.* mountain(s)
Dağları *Tur.* mountain range
Dake *Jap.* mountain
–dal *Nor.* valley
–dal, –e *Dan., Nor.* valley
–dal, –en *Swed.* valley, stream
Dalay *Mong.* sea, large lake
–dalir *Ice.* valley
–dalur *Ice.* valley
–damm, –en *Swed.* lake
Danau *Mal.* lake
Dao *I.-O.* island
Dar *Ar.* region
Darya *Russ.* river
Daryācheh *Pers.* marshy lake, lake
Dasht *Pers.* desert, steppe
Daung *Bur.* mountain, hill
Dayr *Ar.* depression, hill
Debre *Amh.* hill
Deli *Ser.-Cr.* mountain(s)
Denizi *Tur.* sea
Dépt. (Département) *Fr.* first-order administrative division
Desierto *Span.* desert
Dhar *Ar.* region, mountain chain
Dj. (Djebel) *Ar.* mountain
Dō *Jap., Kor.* island
Dong *Kor.* village, town
Dong *Bur.* jungle region
–dorf *Ger.* village
–dorp *Afr.* village
–drif *Afr.* ford
–dybet *Dan.* marine channel
Dzong *Tib.* town, settlement

Eil.-eiland(en) *Afr., Dut.* island(s)
–elv *Nor.* river
'emeq *Heb.* plain, valley
'erg *Ar.* desert with dunes
Estrecho *Span.* strait
Estuario *Span.* estuary

Étang *Fr.* lagoon
–ey(jar) *Ice.* island(s)

F. (Fiume) *It.* river
F. Folyó *Hung.* river
Fd. (Fjord) *Nor.* Inlet of sea
–feld *Ger.* field
–fell *Ice.* mountain, hill
–feng *Chin.* mountain
Fiume *It.* river
Fj. (–fjell) *Nor.* mountain
–fjall *Ice.* mountain(s), hill(s)
–fjäll(et) *Swed.* hill(s), mountain(s), ridge
–fjällen *Swed.* mountains
–fjard(en) *Swed.* fjord, bay, lake
Fjeld *Dan.* mountain
–fjell *Nor.* mountain, rock
–fjord(en) *Nor.* inlet of sea
–fjorden *Dan.* bay, marine channel
–fjörður *Ice.* fjord
Fl. (Fleuve) *Fr.* river
Fl. (Fluss) *Ger.* river
–flói *Ice.* bay, marshy country
Fluss *Ger.* river
foce, –i *It.* mouth(s)
Folyó *Hung.* river
–fontein *Afr.* fountain, spring
–fors, –en, *Swed.* rapids, waterfall
Foss *Ice., Nor.* waterfall
–furt *Ger.* ford
Fylke *Nor.* first-order administrative division

G. (Gebel) *Ar.* mountain
G. (Gebirge) *Ger.* hills, mountains
G. (Golfe) *Fr.* gulf
G. (Golfo) *It.* gulf
G. (Gora) *Bulg., Russ., Ser.-Cr.* mountain
G. (Gunong) *Mal.* mountain
–gang *Kor.* river
Ganga *Hin., Sin.* river
–gat *Dan.* sound
–gau *Ger.* district
Gave *Fr.* stream
–gawa *Jap.* river
Geb. (Gebirge) *Ger.* hills, mountains
Gebel *Ar.* mountain
Geziret *Ar.* island
Ghat *Hin.* range of hills
Ghiol *Rum.* lake
Ghubbat *Ar.* bay, inlet
Gji *Alb.* bay
Gjol *Alb.* lagoon, lake
Gl. (Glava) *Ser.-Cr.* mountain, peak
Glen. *Gae.* valley
Gletscher *Ger.* glacier
Gobi *Mong.* desert
Gol *Mong.* river
Golfe *Fr.* gulf
Golfo *It., Span.* gulf
Gomba *Tib.* settlement
Gora *Bulg., Russ., Ser.-Cr.* mountain(s)
Góry *Pol., Russ.* mountain
Gölü *Tur.* lake
–gorod *Russ.* small town
Grad *Bulg., Russ., Ser-Cr.* town, city

Grada *Russ.* mountain range
Guba *Russ.* bay
–Guntō *Jap.* island group
Gunong *Mal.* mountain
Gură *Rum.* passage

H. Hadabat *Ar.* plateau
–hafen *Ger.* harbour, port
Haff *Ger.* bay
Hai *Chin.* sea
Haihsia *Chin.* strait
–hale *Dan.* spit, peninsula
Hals *Dan., Nor.* peninsula, isthmus
Halvø *Dan.* peninsula
Halvøya *Nor.* peninsula
Hāmad, Hamada, Hammādah *Ar.* stony desert, plain
–hamn *Swed., Nor.* harbour, anchorage
Hāmūn *Ar.* plain
Hāmūn *Pers.* low-lying marshy area
–Hantō *Jap.* peninsula
Harju *Fin.* hill
Hassi *Ar.* well
–haug *Nor.* hill
Hav *Swed.* gulf
Havet *Nor.* sea
–havn *Dan., Nor.* harbour
Hegyseg *Hung.* forest
Heide *Ger.* heath
Hi. (hassi) *Ar.* well
Ho *Chin.* river
–hø *Nor.* peak
Hochland *Afr.* highland
Hoek, –hoek *Afr., Dut.* cape
Höfn *Ice.* harbour, port
–hög, –en, –högar, –högarna *Swed.* hill(s), peak, mountain
Höhe *Ger.* hills
Holm *Dan.* island
–holm, –holme, –holzen, *Swed.* island
Hon *I.-C.* island
Hora *Cz.* mountain
–horn *Nor.* peak
Hory *Cz.* mountain range, forest
–hoved *Dan.* point, headland, peninsula
Hráun *Ice.* lava
–hsi *Chin.* mountain, stream
–hsiang *Chin.* village
–hsien *Chin.* district
Hu *Chin.* lake
Huk *Dan., Ger.* point
Huken *Nor.* head

I. (Île) *Fr.* island
I. (Ilha) *Port.* island
I. (Insel) *Ger.* island
I. (Isla) *Span.* island
I. (Isola) *It.* island
Idehan *Ar., Ber.* sandy plain
Île(s) *Fr.* island(s)
Ilha *Port.* island
Insel(n) *Ger.* island(s)
Irmak *Tur.* river
Is. (Inseln) *Ger.* islands
Is. (Islas) *Span.* islands
Is. (Isola) *It.* island
Isola, –e *It.* island(s)
Istmo *Span.* isthmus

J. (Jabal) *Ar.* mountain
J. (Jazīra) *Ar.* island
J. (Jebel) *Ar.* mountain
J. (Jeziora) *Pol.* lake
Jabal *Ar.* mountain, range
–jaur *Swed.* lake
Jasovir *Bulg.* reservoir
Jazā'ir *Ar.* islands
Jazira *Ar.* island
Jazireh *Pers.* island
Jebel *Ar.* mountain
Jezero *Ser.-Cr.* lake
Jezioro *Pol.* lake
–Jima *Jap.* island
Jøkelen *Nor.* glacier
–joki *Fin.* stream
–jökull *Ice.* glacier
Jūras Līcis *Lat.* bay, gulf

K. (Kap) *Dan.* cape
K (Khalig) *Ar.* gulf
K. (Kiang) *Chin.* river
K. (Kuala) *Mal.* confluence, estuary
Kaap *Afr.* cape
Kai *Jap.* sea
Kaikyō *Jap.* strait
Kamennyy *Russ.* stony
Kampong *Mal.* village
Kan. (Kanal) *Ser.-Cr.* channel, canal
Kanaal *Dut., Flem.* canal
Kanal *Dan.* channel, gulf
Kanal *Ger., Swed.* canal, stream
kanal *Ser.-Cr.* channel, canal
Kang *Kor.* river, bay
Kangri *Tib.* mountain glacier
Kap *Dan., Ger.* cape
Kapp *Nor.* cape
Kas *I.-C.* island
–kaupstaður *Ice.* market town
–kaupunki *Fin.* town
Kavīr *Pers.* salt desert
Kébir *Ar.* great
Kéfar *Heb.* village, hamlet
–ken *Jap.* first-order administrative division
Kep *Alb.* cape
Kepulauan *Mal.* archipelago
Ketjil *Mal.* lesser, little
Khalīg, Khalij *Ar.* gulf
khamba, –idg *Tib.* source, spring
Khawr *Ar.* wadi
Khirbat *Ar.* ruins
Kho Khot *Thai.* isthmus
Khōr *Pers.* creek, estuary
Khrebet *Russ.* mountain range
Kiang *Chin.* river
–klint *Dan.* cliff
–Klintar *Swed.* hills
Kloof *Afr.* gorge
Knude *Dan.* point
Ko *Jap.* lake
Ko *Thai.* island *I*
Kohi *Pash.* mountains
Kol *Russ.* lake
Kolymskoye *Russ.* mountain range
Kólpos *Gr., Tur.* gulf, bay
Kompong *Mal.* landing place
–kop *Afr.* hill

-köping Swed. market town
Körfezi Tur. gulf
Kosa Russ. spit
-koski Fin. cataract, rapids
-kraal Afr. native village
Krasnyy Russ. red
Kryash Russ. ridge, hills
Kuala Mal. confluence, estuary
kuan Chin. pass
Kuh –hha Pers. mountains
Kul Russ. lake
Kulle Swed. hill, shoal
Kum Russ. sandy desert
Kumpu Fin. hill
Kurgan Russ. mound
Kwe Bur. bay, gulf
Kyst Dan. coast
Kyun, –zu, –umya Bur. island(s)

L. (Lac) Fr. lake
L. (Lacul) Rum. lake
L. (Lago) It., Span. lake, lagoon
L. (Lagoa) Port. lagoon
L. (Límni) Gr. lake
L. (Loch) Gae. (lake, inlet)
L. (Lough) Gae. (lake, inlet)
La Tib. pass
La (Lagoa) Port. lagoon
-laagte Afr. watercourse
Läani Fin. first-order administrative division
Län Swed. first-order administrative division
Lac Fr. lake
Lacul Rum. lake, lagoon
Lago It., Span. lake, lagoon
Lagoa Port. lagoon
Laguna It., Span. lagoon, intermittent lake
Lagune Fr. lake
Lahti Fin. bay, gulf, cove
Lakhti Russ. bay, gulf
Lampi Fin. lake
Land Ger. first-order administrative division
-land Dan. region
-land Afr., Nor. land, province
Lido It. beach, shore
Liehtao Chin. islands
Lilla Swed. small
Límni Gr. lake
Ling Chin. mountain range, ice
Linna Fin. historical fort
Llano Span. prairie, plain
Loch Gae. (lake)
Lough Gae. (lake)
Lum Alb. river
Lund Dan. forest
-lund, -en Swed. wood(s)

M. (Maj, Mai) Alb. mountain, peak
M. (Mont) Fr. mountain peak
M. (Mys) Russ. cape
Madīna(h) Ar. town, city
Madiq Ar. strait
Maj Alb. peak
Mäki Fin. hill, hillside
Mal Alb. mountain
Mal Russ. little, small
Mal/a, -i, -o Ser.-Cr. small, little
Man Kor. bay
Mar Span. lagoon, sea
Mare Rum. great
Marisma Span. marsh
-mark Dan., Nor. land
Marsā Ar. anchorage, bay, inlet
Masabb Ar. river mouth
Massif Fr. upland, plateau
Mato Port. forest
Mazar Pers. shrine, tomb
Meer Afr., Dut., Ger. lake sea

Mi., Mti. (Monti) It. mountains
Miao Chin. temple, shrine
Midbar Heb. wilderness
Mif. (Massif) Fr. upland, plateau
Misaki Jap. cape, point
-mo Nor., Swed. heath, island
-mon Swed. heath
Mong Bur. town
Mont Fr. hill, mountain
Montagna It. mountain
Montagne Fr. hill, mountain
Montaña Span. mountain
Monte It., Port., Span. mountain
Monti It. mountains
More Russ. sea
Mörön Hung. river
Mt. (Mont) Fr. mountain
Mt. (Monti) It. mountain
Mt. (Montaña) Span. mountain range
Mte. (Monte) It., Port., Span. mountain
Mți. (Munți) Rum. mountain
Mts. (Monts) Fr. mountains
Muang Mal. town
Mui Ar., I.-C. cape
Mull Gae. (promontory)
Mund, –mund Afr. mouth
Munkhafed Ar. depression
Munte Rum. mount
Munți(i) Rum. mountain(s)
Muong Mal. village
Myit Bur. river
Myitwanya Bur. mouths of river
–mýri Ice. bog
Mys Russ. cape

N. (Nahal) Heb. river
Naes Dan. point, cape
Nafūd Ar. sandy desert
Nahal Heb. river
Nahr Ar. river, stream
Najd Ar. plateau, pass
Nakhon Thai. town
Nam I.-C. river
-nam Kor. south
-näs Swed. cape
-nes Ice., Nor. cape
Ness, –ness Gae. promontory, cape
Nez Fr. cape
-niemi Fin. cape, point, peninsula, island
Nizhne, –iy Russ. lower
Nizmennost Russ. plain, lowland
Nísos, Nísoi Gr. island(s)
Nor Chin. lake
Nor Tib. peak
Nos Bulg., Russ. cape, point
Nudo Span. mountain
Nuruu Mong. mountain range
Nuur Mong. lake

O. (Ostrov) Russ. island
O (Ouâdî, Oued) Ar. wadi
-ö Swed. island, peninsula, point
-öar, (-na) Swed. islands
Oblast Russ. administrative division
Öbor Mong. inner
Occidental Fr., Span. western
Odde Dan., Nor. point, peninsula, cape
Oji Alb. bay
Ojo Span. spring
Oki Jap. bay
-ön Swed. island peninsula
Ondör Mong. high, tall

-ör Swed. island, peninsula, point
Orașul Rum. city
Ord Gae. point
Óri Gr. mountains
Oriental Span. eastern
Órmos Gr. bay
Óros Gr. mountain
Ort Ger. point, cape
Ostrov(a) Russ. island(s)
Otok(-i) Ser.-Cr. island(s)
Ouadi, –edi Ar. dry watercourse, wadi
Ouzan Pers. river
Ova (–si) Tur. plains, lowlands
-øy, (-a) Nor. island(s)
Oya Hin. point
Oya Sin. river
Oz. (Ozero, a) Russ. lake(s)

P. (Passo) It. pass
P. (Pasul) Rum. pass
P. (Pico) Span. peak
P. (Prokhod) Bulg. pass
-pää Fin. hill(s), mountain
Pahta Lapp. hill
Pampa, –s Span. plain(s) salt flat(s)
Pan. (Pantano) Span. Reservoir
Pantao Chin. peninsula
Parbat Urdu mountain
Pas Fr. gap
Paso Span. pass, marine channel
Pass Ger. pass
Passo It. pass
Pasul Rum. pass
Patam Hin. small village
Patna, –patnam Hin. small village
Pegunungan Mal. mountain, range
Pei, –pei Chin. north
Pélagos Gr. sea
Pen. (Península) Span. peninsula
Peña Span. rock, peak
Península Span. peninsula
Per. (Pereval) Russ. pass
Pertuis Fr. channel
Peski Russ. desert, sands
Phanom I.-C., Thai. mountain
Phnom I.-C. mountain
Phu I.-C. mountain
Pic Fr. peak
Pico(s) Span. peak(s)
Pik Russ. peak
Piz., pizzo It. peak
Pl. (Planina) Ser.-Cr. mountain, range
Plage Fr. beach
Plaine Fr. plain
Planalto Span. plateau
Planina Bulg., Ser.-Cr. mountain, range
Plat. (Plateau) Fr. level upland
Plato Russ. plateau
Playa Span. beach
P-ov. (Poluostrov) Russ. peninsula
Pointe Fr. point, cape
Pojezierze Pol. lakes plateau
Polder Dut. reclaimed farmland
-pólis Gr. city, town
Poluostrov Russ. peninsula
Połwysep Pol. peninsula
Pont Fr. bridge
Ponta Port. point, cape
Ponte It. bridge
Poort Afr. passage, gate
-poort Dut. port
Porta Port. pass
Porțil, -e Rum. gate
Portillo Span. pass
Porto It. port
Porto Port., Span. port

Pot. (Potámi, Potamós) Gr. river
Poulo I.-C. island
Pr. (Průsmyk) Cz. pass
Pradesh Hin. state
Presa Span. reservoir
Presqu'île Fr. peninsula
Prokhod Bulg. pass
Proliv Russ. strait
Prusmyk Cz. pass
Pso. (Passo) It. pass
Pta. (Ponta) Port. point, cape
Pta. (Punta) It., Span. point, cape, peak
Pte. (Pointe) Fr. point cape
Puerto Span. port, pass
Puig Cat. peak
Pulau Mal. island
Puna Span. desert plateau
Punta It., Span. point, peak
Puy Fr. hill

Qal'at Ar. fort
Qanal Ar. canal
Qasr Ar. fort
Qiryat Heb. town
Qolleh Pers. mountain

Ramla Ar. sand
Rann Hin. swampy region
Rao I.-C. river
Ras Amh. cape, headland
Rãs Ar. cape, headland
Recife(s) Port. reef(s)
Reka Bulg., Cz., Russ. river
Repede Rum. rapids
Represa Port. dam
Reshteh Pers. mountain range
-Rettō Jap. group of islands
Ría Span. estuary, bay
Ribeirão Port. river
Rijeka Ser.-Cr. river
Rio Port. river
Río Span. river
Riv. (Riviera) It. coastal plain, coast, river
Riviera It. coast
Rivière Fr. river
Roche Fr. rock
Rog Russ. horn
-rück Ger. ridge
Rüd Pers. stream, river
Rudohorie Cz. ore mountains
Rzeka Pol. river

S. (Sungei) Mal. river
Sa. (Serra) It., Port. range of hills
Sa. (Sierra) Span. range of hills
-saari Fin. island
Sadd Ar. dam
Sagar, –ara Hin., Urdu lake
Saharā Ar. desert
Sahrã Ar. desert
Sa'id Ar. highland
Sakar Fin. mountain
-Saki Jap. point
Sal. (Salar) Span. salt pan
Salina(s) Span. salt flat(s)
-salmi Fin. strait, sound, lake, channel
Saltsjöbad Swed. resort
Sammyaku Jap. mountain, range
Samut Thai. gulf
-San Jap. hill, mountain
Sap. (Sapadno) Russ. west
Sasso It. mountain
Se, Sé I.-C. river
Sebkha, –kra Ar. salt flats
See Ger. lake
-see Ger. sea
-şehir Turk. town
Selat Mal. strait
-selkä Fin. bay, lake, sound, ridge, hills

Selva Span. forest, wood
Seno Span. bay, sound
Serír Ar. desert of small stones
Serra It., Port. range of hills
Serranía Span. mountains
Sev. (Severo) Russ. north
-shahr Pers. city, town
Shan Chin. hills, mountains, pass
Shan-mo Chin. mountain range
Shatt Ar. river
-Shima Jap. island
Shimāli Ar. northern
-Shotō Jap. group of islands
Shuik'u Chin. reservoir
Sierra Span. hill, range
Sjö, sjön Swed. lake, bay, sea
Sjøen Dan. sea
Skär Swed. island, rock, cape
Skog Nor. forest
-skog, –skogen Swed. wood(s)
-skov Dan. forest
Slieve Gae. range of hills
-sø Dan., Nor. lake
Sør Nor. south, southern
Solonchak Russ. salt lake, marsh
Souk Ar. market
Spitze Ger. peak, mountain
-spruit Afr. stream
-stad Afr., Nor., Swed. town
-stadt Ger. town
Staður Ice. town
Stausee Ger. reservoir
Stenón Gr. strait, pass
Step Russ. plain
Str. (Stretto) It. strait
-strand Dan., Nor. beach
-strede Nor. straits
-strete Nor. straits
Stretto It. strait
Stroedet Dan. strait
-ström, –strömmen Swed. stream(s)
-stroom Afr. large river
Suidō Jap. strait, channel
Sûn Bur. cape
Sund Dan. sound
-sund, –sundet Swed. sound, estuary, inlet
-sund(et) Nor. sound
Sungai, –ei Mal. river
Sungei Mal. river
Sur Span. south, southern
Sveti Bulg. pass
Syd Dan., Swed. south

Tai –tai Chin. tower
Tal Mong. plain, steppe
-tal Ger. valley
Tall Ar. hills, hummocks
Tandjung Mal. cape, headland
Tao Chin. island
Tassili Ar. rocky plateau
Tau Russ. mountain, range
Taung Bur. mountain, south
Taunggya Bur. pass
Tělok I.-C., Mal. bay bight
Teluk Mal. bay, gulf
Tg. (Tandjung) Mal. cape, headland
-thal Ger. valley
Thok Tib. town
Tierra Span. land, country
-tind Nor. peak
Tjärn, –en, –et Swed. lake
Tong Nor. village, town
Tong Bur., Thai. mountain range
Tonle I.-C. large river, lake
-träsk Swed. bog, swamp
Tsangpo Tib. large river
Tso Tib. lake

Tsu Jap. entrance, bay
Tulur Ar. hill
T'un Chin. village
Tung Chin. east
Tunnel Fr. tunnel
Tunturi Fin. hill(s), mountain(s), ridge

Uad Ar. dry watercourse, wadi
Udjung Mal. cape
Udd, udde, udden Swed. point, peninsula
Uebi Somal. river
Us Mong. water
Ust Russ. river mouth
Uul Mong., Russ. mountain, range

V. (Volcán) Span. volcano
-vaara Fin. hill, mountain, ridge, peak
-våg Nor. bay
Val Fr., It. valley
Valea Rum. valley
-vall, –vallen Swed. mountain
Valle Span. valley
Vallée Fr. valley
Valli It. lake, lagoon
Väst Swed. west
-vatn Ice., Nor. lake
Vatten Swed. lake
Vdkhr. (Vodokhranilishche) Russ. reservoir
-ved, –veden Swed. range, hills
Veld, –veld Afr. field
Velik/a, -e, -i, -o Ser.Cr. large
-vesi Fin. water, lake, bay sound, strait
Vest Dan., Nor. west
Vf. (vîrful) Rum. peak, mountain
-vidda Nor. plateau
Vig Dan. bay, inlet, cove, lagoon, lake, bight
-vik, –vika, –viken Nor., Swed. bay, cove, gulf, inlet, lake
Vila Port. small town
Villa Span. town
Ville Fr. town
Vinh I.-C. bay
Vîrful Rum. peak, mountain
-vlei Afr. pond, pool
Vodokhranilishche Russ. reservoir
Vol. (Volcán) Span. volcano, mountain
Vorota Russ. gate
Vostochnyy Russ. eastern
Vozyshennost Russ. heights, uplands
Vrata Bulg. gate, pass
Vrchovina Cz. mountainous country
Vrchy Cz. mountain range
Vung I.-C. gulf
-vuori Fin. mountain, hill

W. (Wādī) Ar. dry watercourse
Wāhât Ar. oasis
Wald Ger. wood, forest
Wan Chin., Jap. bay
Webi Amh. river
Woestyn Afr. desert

Yam Heb. sea
Yang Chin. ocean
Yazovir Bulg. reservoir
Yoma Bur. mountain range
-yüan Chin. spring

-Zaki Jap. peninsula
Zalew Pol. lagoon, swamp
Zaliv Russ. bay
Zan Jap. mountain
Zatoka Pol. bay
Zee Dut. sea
Zemlya Russ. land, island(s)

The *Marley & Me* Collection

About the Author

John Grogan grew up in Orchard Lake, Michigan, outside Detroit, and earned degrees from Central Michigan and Ohio State universities. He spent more than twenty years as an award-winning newspaper journalist in Michigan, Florida, and Pennsylvania, most recently as metropolitan columnist for the *Philadelphia Inquirer*. He also is the former editor of Rodale's *Organic Gardening* magazine. His first book, *Marley & Me*, was a number one international bestseller, and is now a major motion picture. John lives in a two-hundred-year-old stone farmhouse in eastern Pennsylvania with his wife and three children.

The *Marley &
Me* Collection

A Special Two-Book Omnibus

JOHN GROGAN

HODDER &
STOUGHTON

First published in Great Britain in 2006 & 2008 by Hodder & Stoughton
An Hachette UK company

1

A CIP catalogue record for this title is available from the British Library

Hardback ISBN 978 1 473 69582 5

Typeset in Garamond Book by Hewer Text UK Ltd, Edinburgh
Printed and bound by CPI Group (UK) Ltd, Croydon, CR0 4YY

Hodder & Stoughton policy is to use papers that are natural, renewable
and recyclable products and made from wood grown in sustainable
forests. The logging and manufacturing processes are expected to
conform to the environmental regulations of the country of origin.

Hodder & Stoughton Ltd
Carmelite House
50 Victoria Embankment
London EC4Y 0DZ

www.hodder.co.uk

Contents

Marley & Me

Dear Reader,

When I sat down to write *Marley & Me*, I had no idea what lay ahead. I knew only that there was a story inside me burning to get out, a story I needed to tell. It was the story of my wife, Jenny, and me starting our life together and the big, nutty, incorrigible, lovable dog that changed it all. Changed us, changed our children, changed the family we would become. The first step in that odyssey was a column I wrote in the *Philadelphia Inquirer* on January 6, 2004, saying good-bye to that dog, Marley, a Labrador retriever like no other. That column, which is included at the end of this special edition of *Marley & Me*, drew such an overwhelming response, I knew I had touched on something bigger, the story not just of a dog, not just of a family with a dog, but of the journey humans and animals take together—the ups, the downs; the laughter, the tears; the joys and the heartbreaks. A journey worth taking.

For nine months I wrote in solitude, mostly in the pre-dawn darkness, not quite believing anyone would want to read an entire book about my very ordinary life. Then an amazing thing happened. My book was published in the

United States and soon after in many countries: the United Kingdom, Australia, New Zealand, Ireland (especially pleasing) and South Africa — and I was alone no more.

From Los Angeles to London, from the Catskills to the Cotswolds—and eventually the globe—the letters and e-mails and phone calls began arriving. They came from retirees and newlyweds, from police officers and firefighters, from college students and construction workers. They came from soldiers in Iraq and Afghanistan and from children in elementary schools. They came in a daily torrent and many of them said nearly the same thing: "It was like you were describing my life." They, too, had made the journey worth taking. in the very ordinariness of our lives, I had somehow managed to find the universal.

Many of these readers have become like friends, making me laugh out loud and, occasionally, pause to bite my life. They've embraced me like a member of their own families. One painted a beautiful portrait of Marley in oils and mailed it to me; another sent me songs she composed after the loss of her dog; several baked gourmet treats for our new lab, Gracie. A K-9 officer in Los Angeles gave me an elaborate framed dog-obedience diploma, complete with a gold paw-print stamp, because the real one had proved so elusive. Many blessed me with their sense of humor, such as the young woman who sent me a photograph with the provocative subject line: "Hot bedroom action." I opened the image to find her under the covers reading *Marley & Me*—with her pet boxer snoozing on top of her, the covers pulled to his chin.

Marleyandme.com has evolved into a sort of boisterous town square populated by thousands of dog lovers and book aficionados sharing stories and photos and advice and consolation. Friendships have been forged, phone numbers exchanged, invitations issued. Some are planning to meet in person. Yet another gift my never-do-well Marley has bestowed upon those he has touched—the gift of community.

Jenny and I have a new dog now, and, yes, it's another yellow Labrador retriever. Her name is Gracie, and she is the anti-Marley—sweet, calm, sedate, focused. Every day I tell her, "Gracie, you're a great dog but don't expect a book about you. You're *too* good." And that makes me smile at the memory of the eternally mischievous Marley who filled our lives with so much joyous havoc. It amuses me to no end to think he has become a household name to millions.

Dogs are great. Bad dogs, if we can really call them that, are perhaps the greatest of them all.

—John Grogan
October 2006

In memory of my father, Richard Frank Grogan,
whose gentle spirit infuses every page of this book

✣

Contents

Preface

The Perfect Dog

✻

I n the summer of 1967, when I was ten years old, my father caved in to my persistent pleas and took me to get my own dog. Together we drove in the family station wagon far into the Michigan countryside to a farm run by a rough-hewn woman and her ancient mother. The farm produced just one commodity—dogs. Dogs of every imaginable size and shape and age and temperament. They had only two things in common: each was a mongrel of unknown and indistinct ancestry, and each was free to a good home. We were at a mutt ranch.

"Now, take your time, son," Dad said. "Your decision today is going to be with you for many years to come."

I quickly decided the older dogs were somebody else's charity case. I immediately raced to the puppy cage. "You want to pick one that's not timid," my father coached. "Try rattling the cage and see which ones aren't afraid."

I grabbed the chain-link gate and yanked on it with a loud clang. The dozen or so puppies reeled backward, collapsing on top of one another in a squiggling heap of fur. Just one remained. He was gold with a white blaze on his chest, and he charged the gate, yapping fearlessly. He jumped up and excitedly licked my fingers through the fencing. It was love at first sight.

I brought him home in a cardboard box and named him Shaun. He was one of those dogs that give dogs a good name. He effortlessly mastered every command I taught him and was naturally well behaved. I could drop a crust on the floor and he would not touch it until I gave the okay. He came when I called him and stayed when I told him to. We could let him out alone at night, knowing he would be back after making his rounds. Not that we often did, but we could leave him alone in the house for hours, confident he wouldn't have an accident or disturb a thing. He raced cars without chasing them and walked beside me without a leash. He could dive to the bottom of our lake and emerge with rocks so big they sometimes got stuck in his jaws. He loved nothing more than riding in the car and would sit quietly in the backseat beside me on family road trips, content to spend hours gazing out the window at the passing world. Perhaps best of all, I trained him to pull me through the neighborhood dog-sled-style as I sat on my bicycle, making me the hands-down envy of my friends. Never once did he lead me into hazard.

He was with me when I smoked my first cigarette (and my last) and when I kissed my first girl. He was right there beside me in the front seat when I snuck out my older brother's Corvair for my first joyride.

Shaun was spirited but controlled, affectionate but calm. He even had the dignified good manners to back himself modestly into the bushes before squatting to do his duty, only his head peering out. Thanks to this tidy habit, our lawn was safe for bare feet.

Relatives would visit for the weekend and return home determined to buy a dog of their own, so impressed were they with Shaun—or "Saint Shaun," as I came to call him. It was a family joke, the saint business, but one we could almost believe. Born with the curse of uncertain lineage, he was one of the tens of thousands of unwanted dogs in America. Yet by some stroke of almost providential good fortune, he became wanted. He came into my life and I into his—and in the process, he gave me the childhood every kid deserves.

The love affair lasted fourteen years, and by the time he died I was no longer the little boy who had brought him home on that summer day. I was a man, out of college and working across the state in my first real job. Saint Shaun had stayed behind when I moved on. It was where he belonged. My parents, by then retired, called to break the news to me. My mother would later tell me, "In fifty years of marriage, I've only seen your father cry twice. The first time was when we lost Mary Ann"—my sister, who was stillborn. "The second time was the day Shaun died."

Saint Shaun of my childhood. He was a perfect dog. At least that's how I will always remember him. It was Shaun who set the standard by which I would judge all other dogs to come.

CHAPTER 1

And Puppy Makes Three

❋

W
e were young. We were in love. We were rollicking in those sublime early days of marriage
when life seems about as good as life can get.
We could not leave well enough alone.

And so on a January evening in 1991, my wife of fifteen
months and I ate a quick dinner together and headed off to
answer a classified ad in the *Palm Beach Post*.

Why we were doing this, I wasn't quite sure. A few weeks
earlier I had awoken just after dawn to find the bed beside
me empty. I got up and found Jenny sitting in her bathrobe
at the glass table on the screened porch of our little
bungalow, bent over the newspaper with a pen in her hand.

There was nothing unusual about the scene. Not only was
the *Palm Beach Post* our local paper, it was also the source
of half of our household income. We were a two-newspaper-
career couple. Jenny worked as a feature writer in the *Post*'s
"Accent" section; I was a news reporter at the competing
paper in the area, the South Florida *Sun-Sentinel*, based an
hour south in Fort Lauderdale. We began every morning

poring over the newspapers, seeing how our stories were played and how they stacked up to the competition. We circled, underlined, and clipped with abandon.

But on this morning, Jenny's nose was not in the news pages but in the classified section. When I stepped closer, I saw she was feverishly circling beneath the heading "Pets—Dogs."

"Uh," I said in that new-husband, still-treading-gently voice. "Is there something I should know?"

She did not answer.

"Jen-Jen?"

"It's the plant," she finally said, her voice carrying a slight edge of desperation.

"The plant?" I asked.

"That dumb plant," she said. "The one we killed."

The one *we* killed? I wasn't about to press the point, but for the record it was the plant that *I* bought and *she* killed. I had surprised her with it one night, a lovely large dieffenbachia with emerald-and-cream variegated leaves. "What's the occasion?" she'd asked. But there was none. I'd given it to her for no reason other than to say, "Damn, isn't married life great?"

She had adored both the gesture and the plant and thanked me by throwing her arms around my neck and kissing me on the lips. Then she promptly went on to kill my gift to her with an assassin's coldhearted efficiency. Not that she was trying to; if anything, she nurtured the poor thing to death. Jenny didn't exactly have a green thumb. Working on the assumption that all living things require water, but apparently forgetting that they also need air, she began flooding the dieffenbachia on a daily basis.

"Be careful not to overwater it," I had warned.

"Okay," she had replied, and then dumped on another gallon.

The sicker the plant got, the more she doused it, until finally it just kind of melted into an oozing heap. I looked at its limp skeleton in the pot by the window and thought, *Man, someone who believes in omens could have a field day with this one.*

Now here she was, somehow making the cosmic leap of logic from dead flora in a pot to living fauna in the pet classifieds. *Kill a plant, buy a puppy.* Well, of course it made perfect sense.

I looked more closely at the newspaper in front of her and saw that one ad in particular seemed to have caught her fancy. She had drawn three fat red stars beside it. It read: "Lab puppies, yellow. AKC purebred. All shots. Parents on premises."

"So," I said, "can you run this plant-pet thing by me one more time?"

"You know," she said, looking up. "I tried so hard and look what happened. I can't even keep a stupid houseplant alive. I mean, how hard is *that*? All you need to do is water the damn thing."

Then she got to the real issue: "If I can't even keep a plant alive, how am I ever going to keep a baby alive?" She looked like she might start crying.

The BabyThing, as I called it, had become a constant in Jenny's life and was getting bigger by the day. When we had first met, at a small newspaper in western Michigan, she was just a few months out of college, and serious adulthood still seemed a far distant concept. For both of us, it was our first professional job out of school. We ate a lot of pizza, drank a lot of beer, and gave exactly zero thought to the possibility of someday being anything other than young, single, unfettered consumers of pizza and beer.

But years passed. We had barely begun dating when various job opportunities—and a one-year postgraduate program for me—pulled us in different directions across the eastern United States. At first we were one hour's drive apart. Then we were three hours apart. Then eight, then twenty-four. By the time we both landed together in South Florida and tied the knot, she was nearly thirty. Her friends were having babies. Her body was sending her strange messages. That once seemingly eternal window of procreative opportunity was slowly lowering.

I leaned over her from behind, wrapped my arms around her shoulders, and kissed the top of her head. "It's okay," I said. But I had to admit, she raised a good question. Neither of us had ever really nurtured a thing in our lives. Sure, we'd had pets growing up, but they didn't really count. We always knew our parents would keep them alive and well. We both knew we wanted to one day have children, but was either of us really up for the job? Children were so . . . so . . . scary. They were helpless and fragile and looked like they would break easily if dropped.

A little smile broke out on Jenny's face. "I thought maybe a dog would be good practice," she said.

As we drove through the darkness, heading northwest out of town where the suburbs of West Palm Beach fade into

sprawling country properties, I thought through our decision to bring home a dog. It was a huge responsibility,
especially for two people with full-time jobs. Yet we knew
what we were in for. We'd both grown up with dogs and
loved them immensely. I'd had Saint Shaun and Jenny had
had Saint Winnie, her family's beloved English setter. Our
happiest childhood memories almost all included those
dogs. Hiking with them, swimming with them, playing
with them, getting in trouble with them. If Jenny really
only wanted a dog to hone her parenting skills, I would
have tried to talk her in off the ledge and maybe placate
her with a goldfish. But just as we knew we wanted
children someday, we knew with equal certainty that
our family home would not be complete without a dog
sprawled at our feet. When we were dating, long before
children ever came on our radar, we spent hours discussing our childhood pets, how much we missed them and
how we longed someday—once we had a house to call
our own and some stability in our lives—to own a dog
again.

Now we had both. We were together in a place we did
not plan to leave anytime soon. And we had a house to call
our very own.

It was a perfect little house on a perfect little quarter-acre
fenced lot just right for a dog. And the location was just
right, too, a funky city neighborhood one and a half blocks
off the Intracoastal Waterway separating West Palm Beach
from the rarified mansions of Palm Beach. At the foot of our
street, Churchill Road, a linear green park and paved trail
stretched for miles along the waterfront. It was ideal for

jogging and bicycling and Rollerblading. And, more than anything, for walking a dog.

The house was built in the 1950s and had an Old Florida charm—a fireplace, rough plaster walls, big airy windows, and French doors leading to our favorite space of all, the screened back porch. The yard was a little tropical haven, filled with palms and bromeliads and avocado trees and brightly colored coleus plants. Dominating the property was a towering mango tree; each summer it dropped its heavy fruit with loud thuds that sounded, somewhat grotesquely, like bodies being thrown off the roof. We would lie awake in bed and listen: *Thud! Thud! Thud!*

We bought the two-bedroom, one-bath bungalow a few months after we returned from our honeymoon and immediately set about refurbishing it. The prior owners, a retired postal clerk and his wife, loved the color green. The exterior stucco was green. The interior walls were green. The curtains were green. The shutters were green. The front door was green. The carpet, which they had just purchased to help sell the house, was green. Not a cheery kelly green or a cool emerald green or even a daring lime green but a puke-your-guts-out-after-split-pea-soup green accented with khaki trim. The place had the feel of an army field barracks.

On our first night in the house, we ripped up every square inch of the new green carpeting and dragged it to the curb. Where the carpet had been, we discovered a pristine oak plank floor that, as best we could tell, had never suffered the scuff of a single shoe. We painstakingly sanded and varnished it to a high sheen. Then we went out and blew the better part of two weeks' pay for a handwoven Persian rug,

which we unfurled in the living room in front of the fireplace. Over the months, we repainted every green surface
and replaced every green accessory. The postal clerk's
house was slowly becoming our own.

Once we got the joint just right, of course, it only made
sense that we bring home a large, four-legged roommate
with sharp toenails, large teeth, and exceedingly limited
English-language skills to start tearing it apart again.

"Slow down, dingo, or you're going to miss it," Jenny
scolded. "It should be coming up any second." We were
driving through inky blackness across what had once been
swampland, drained after World War II for farming and later
colonized by suburbanites seeking a country lifestyle.

As Jenny predicted, our headlights soon illuminated a
mailbox marked with the address we were looking for. I
turned up a gravel drive that led into a large wooded
property with a pond in front of the house and a small
barn out back. At the door, a middle-aged woman named
Lori greeted us, a big, placid yellow Labrador retriever by
her side.

"This is Lily, the proud mama," Lori said after we
introduced ourselves. We could see that five weeks after
birth Lily's stomach was still swollen and her teats pronounced. We both got on our knees, and she happily
accepted our affection. She was just what we pictured a
Lab would be—sweet-natured, affectionate, calm, and
breathtakingly beautiful.

"Where's the father?" I asked.

"Oh," the woman said, hesitating for just a fraction of a second. "Sammy Boy? He's around here somewhere." She quickly added, "I imagine you're dying to see the puppies."

She led us through the kitchen out to a utility room that had been drafted into service as a nursery. Newspapers covered the floor, and in one corner was a low box lined with old beach towels. But we hardly noticed any of that. How could we with nine tiny yellow puppies stumbling all over one another as they clamored to check out the latest strangers to drop by? Jenny gasped. "Oh my," she said. "I don't think I've ever seen anything so cute in my life."

We sat on the floor and let the puppies climb all over us as Lily happily bounced around, tail wagging and nose poking each of her offspring to make sure all was well. The deal I had struck with Jenny when I agreed to come here was that we would check the pups out, ask some questions, and keep an open mind as to whether we were ready to bring home a dog. "This is the first ad we're answering," I had said. "Let's not make any snap decisions." But thirty seconds into it, I could see I had already lost the battle. There was no question that before the night was through one of these puppies would be ours.

Lori was what is known as a backyard breeder. When it came to buying a purebred dog, we were pure novices, but we had read enough to know to steer clear of the so-called puppy mills, those commercial breeding operations that churn out purebreds like Ford churns out Tauruses. Unlike mass-produced cars, however, mass-produced pedigree puppies can come with serious hereditary problems, running the gamut from hip dysplasia to early blindness, brought on by multigenerational inbreeding.

Lori, on the other hand, was a hobbyist, motivated more by love of the breed than by profit. She owned just one female and one male. They had come from distinct bloodlines, and she had the paper trail to prove it. This would be Lily's second and final litter before she retired to the good life of a countrified family pet. With both parents on the premises, the buyer could see firsthand the lineage—although in our case, the father apparently was outside and out of pocket.

The litter consisted of five females, all but one of which already had deposits on them, and four males. Lori was asking $400 for the remaining female and $375 for the males. One of the males seemed particularly smitten with us. He was the goofiest of the group and charged into us, somersaulting into our laps and clawing his way up our shirts to lick our faces. He gnawed on our fingers with surprisingly sharp baby teeth and stomped clumsy circles around us on giant tawny paws that were way out of proportion to the rest of his body. "That one there you can have for three-fifty," the owner said.

Jenny is a rabid bargain hunter who has been known to drag home all sorts of things we neither want nor need simply because they were priced too attractively to pass up. "I know you don't golf," she said to me one day as she pulled a set of used clubs out of the car. "But you wouldn't believe the deal I got on these." Now I saw her eyes brighten. "Aw, honey," she cooed. "The little guy's on clearance!"

I had to admit he was pretty darn adorable. Frisky, too. Before I realized what he was up to, the rascal had half my watchband chewed off.

"We have to do the scare test," I said. Many times before I had recounted for Jenny the story of picking out Saint Shaun when I was a boy, and my father teaching me to make a sudden move or loud noise to separate the timid from the self-assured. Sitting in this heap of pups, she gave me that roll of the eyes that she reserved for odd Grogan-family behavior. "Seriously," I said. "It works."

I stood up, turned away from the puppies, then swung quickly back around, taking a sudden, exaggerated step toward them. I stomped my foot and barked out, "Hey!" None seemed too concerned by this stranger's contortions. But only one plunged forward to meet the assault head-on. It was Clearance Dog. He plowed full steam into me, throwing a cross-body block across my ankles and pouncing at my shoelaces as though convinced they were dangerous enemies that needed to be destroyed.

"I think it's fate," Jenny said.

"Ya think?" I said, scooping him up and holding him in one hand in front of my face, studying his mug. He looked at me with heart-melting brown eyes and then nibbled my nose. I plopped him into Jenny's arms, where he did the same to her. "He certainly seems to like us," I said.

And so it came to be. We wrote Lori a check for $350, and she told us we could return to take Clearance Dog home with us in three weeks when he was eight weeks old and weaned. We thanked her, gave Lily one last pat, and said good-bye.

Walking to the car, I threw my arm around Jenny's shoulder and pulled her tight to me. "Can you believe it?" I said. "We actually got our dog!"

"I can't wait to bring him home," she said.

Just as we were reaching the car, we heard a commotion coming from the woods. Something was crashing through the brush—and breathing very heavily. It sounded like what you might hear in a slasher film. And it was coming our way. We froze, staring into the darkness. The sound grew louder and closer. Then in a flash the thing burst into the clearing and came charging in our direction, a yellow blur. A very *big* yellow blur. As it galloped past, not stopping, not even seeming to notice us, we could see it was a large Labrador retriever. But it was nothing like the sweet Lily we had just cuddled with inside. This one was soaking wet and covered up to its belly in mud and burrs. Its tongue hung out wildly to one side, and froth flew off its jowls as it barreled past.

In the split-second glimpse I got, I detected an odd, slightly crazed, yet somehow joyous gaze in its eyes. It was as though this animal had just seen a ghost—and couldn't possibly be more tickled about it.

Then, with the roar of a stampeding herd of buffalo, it was gone, around the back of the house and out of sight. Jenny let out a little gasp.

"I think," I said, a slight queasiness rising in my gut, "we just met Dad."

Running with the Blue Bloods

✳

Our first official act as dog owners was to have a fight. It began on the drive home from the breeder's and continued in fits and snippets through the next week. We could not agree on what to name our Clearance Dog. Jenny shot down my suggestions, and I shot down hers. The battle culminated one morning before we left for work.

"*Chelsea?*" I said. "That is *such* a chick name. No boy dog would be caught dead with the name Chelsea."

"Like he'll really know," Jenny said.

"Hunter," I said. "Hunter is perfect."

"*Hunter?* You're kidding, right? What are you, on some macho, sportsman trip? Way too masculine. Besides, you've never hunted a day in your life."

"He's a male," I said, seething. "*He's supposed to be masculine.* Don't turn this into one of your feminist screeds."

This was not going well. I had just taken off the gloves. As Jenny wound up to counterpunch, I quickly tried to return the deliberations to my leading candidate. "What's wrong with Louie?"

"Nothing, if you're a gas-station attendant," she snapped.

"Hey! Watch it! That's my grandfather's name. I suppose we should name him after your grandfather? 'Good dog, *Bill*!' "

As we fought, Jenny absently walked to the stereo and pushed the play button on the tape deck. It was one of her marital combat strategies. When in doubt, drown out your opponent. The lilting reggae strains of Bob Marley began to pulse through the speakers, having an almost instant mellowing effect on us both.

We had only discovered the late Jamaican singer when we moved to South Florida from Michigan. In the white-bread backwaters of the Upper Midwest, we'd been fed a steady diet of Bob Seger and John Cougar Mellencamp. But here in the pulsing ethnic stew that was South Florida, Bob Marley's music, even a decade after his death, was everywhere. We heard it on the car radio as we drove down Biscayne Boulevard. We heard it as we sipped *cafés cubanos* in Little Havana and ate Jamaican jerk chicken in little holes-in-the-wall in the dreary immigrant neighborhoods west of Fort Lauderdale. We heard it as we sampled our first conch fritters at the Bahamian Goombay Festival in Miami's Coconut Grove section and as we shopped for Haitian art in Key West.

The more we explored, the more we fell in love, both with South Florida and with each other. And always in the background, it seemed, was Bob Marley. He was there as we baked on the beach, as we painted over the dingy green

walls of our house, as we awoke at dawn to the screech of
wild parrots and made love in the first light filtering through
the Brazilian pepper tree outside our window. We fell in
love with his music for what it was, but also for what it
defined, which was that moment in our lives when we
ceased being two and became one. Bob Marley was the
soundtrack for our new life together in this strange, exotic,
rough-and-tumble place that was so unlike anywhere we had
lived before.

And now through the speakers came our favorite song of
all, because it was so achingly beautiful and because it spoke
so clearly to us. Marley's voice filled the room, repeating the
chorus over and over: "Is this love that I'm feeling?" And at
the exact same moment, in perfect unison, as if we had
rehearsed it for weeks, we both shouted, "Marley!"

"That's it!" I exclaimed. "That's our name." Jenny was
smiling, a good sign. I tried it on for size. "Marley, come!" I
commanded. "Marley, stay! Good boy, Marley!"

Jenny chimed in, "You're a cutie-wootie-woo, Marley!"

"Hey, I think it works," I said. Jenny did, too. Our fight
was over. We had our new puppy's name.

The next night after dinner I came into the bedroom where
Jenny was reading and said, "I think we need to spice the
name up a little."

"What are you talking about?" she asked. "We both love it."

I had been reading the registration papers from the
American Kennel Club. As a purebred Labrador retriever
with both parents properly registered, Marley was entitled

to AKC registration as well. This was only really needed if you planned to show or breed your dog, in which case there was no more important piece of paper. For a house pet, however, it was superfluous. But I had big plans for our Marley. This was my first time rubbing shoulders with anything resembling high breeding, my own family included. Like Saint Shaun, the dog of my childhood, I was a mutt of indistinct and undistinguished ancestry. My lineage represented more nations than the European Union. This dog was the closest to blue blood I would ever get, and I wasn't about to pass up whatever opportunities it offered. I admit I was a little starstruck.

"Let's say we want to enter him in competitions," I said. "Have you ever seen a champion dog with just one name? They always have big long titles, like Sir Dartworth of Cheltenham."

"And his master, Sir Dorkshire of West Palm Beach," Jenny said.

"I'm serious," I said. "We could make money studding him out. Do you know what people pay for top stud dogs? They all have fancy names."

"Whatever floats your boat, honey," Jenny said, and returned to her book.

The next morning, after a late night of brainstorming, I cornered her at the bathroom sink and said, "I came up with the perfect name."

She looked at me skeptically. "Hit me," she said.

"Okay. Are you ready? Here goes." I let each word fall slowly from my lips: "Grogan's . . . Majestic . . . Marley . . . of . . . Churchill." *Man,* I thought, *does that sound regal.*

"Man," Jenny said, "does that sound dumb."

I didn't care. I was the one handling the paperwork, and I had already written in the name. In ink. Jenny could smirk all she wanted; when Grogan's Majestic Marley of Churchill took top honors at the Westminster Kennel Club Dog Show in a few years, and I gloriously trotted him around the ring before an adoring international television audience, we'd see who would be laughing.

"Come on, my dorky duke," Jenny said. "Let's have breakfast."

CHAPTER 3

Homeward Bound

❊

W hile we counted down the days until we could bring Marley home, I belatedly began reading up on Labrador retrievers. I say *belatedly* because virtually everything I read gave the same strong advice: *Before* buying a dog, make sure you thoroughly research the breed so you know what you're getting into. Oops.

An apartment dweller, for instance, probably wouldn't do well with a Saint Bernard. A family with young children might want to avoid the sometimes unpredictable chow chow. A couch potato looking for a lapdog to idle the hours away in front of the television would likely be driven insane by a border collie, which needs to run and work to be happy.

I was embarrassed to admit that Jenny and I had done almost no research before settling on a Labrador retriever. We chose the breed on one criterion alone: curb appeal. We often had admired them with their owners down on the Intracoastal Waterway bike trail—big, dopey, playful galumphs that seemed to love life with a passion not often seen in this world. Even more embarrassing, our decision was influenced not by *The Complete Dog Book*, the bible of dog breeds published by the American Kennel Club, or by any other reputable guide. It was influenced by that other heavyweight of canine literature, "The Far Side" by Gary Larson. We were huge fans of the cartoon. Larson filled his panels with witty, urbane Labs doing and saying the darnedest things. Yes, they talked! What wasn't to like? Labs were immensely amusing animals—at least in Larson's hands. And who couldn't use a little more amusement in life? We were sold.

Now, as I pored through more serious works on the Labrador retriever, I was relieved to learn that our choice, however ill informed, was not too wildly off the mark. The literature was filled with glowing testimonials about the Labrador retriever's loving, even-keeled personality, its gentleness with children, its lack of aggression, and its desire to please. Their intelligence and malleability had made them a leading choice for search-and-rescue training and as guide dogs for the blind and handicapped. All this boded well for a pet in a home that would sooner or later likely include children.

One guide gushed: "The Labrador retriever is known for its intelligence, warm affection for man, field dexterity and undying devotion to any task." Another marveled at the breed's immense loyalty. All these qualities had pushed the Labrador retriever from a specialty sporting dog, favored by bird hunters because of its skill at fetching downed pheasants and ducks from frigid waters, into America's favorite family pet. Just the year before, in 1990, the Labrador retriever had knocked the cocker spaniel out of the top spot on the American Kennel Club registry as the nation's most popular breed. No other breed has come close to overtaking the Lab since. In 2004 it took its fifteenth straight year as the AKC's top dog, with 146,692 Labs registered. Coming in a distant second were golden retrievers, with 52,550, and, in third place, German shepherds, with 46,046.

Quite by accident, we had stumbled upon a breed America could not get enough of. All those happy dog owners couldn't be wrong, could they? We had chosen a proven winner. And yet the literature was filled with ominous caveats.

Labs were bred as working dogs and tended to have boundless energy. They were highly social and did not do well left alone for long periods. They could be thick-skulled and difficult to train. They needed rigorous daily exercise or they could become destructive. Some were wildly excitable and hard for even experienced dog handlers to control. They had what could seem like eternal puppyhoods, stretching three years or more. The long, exuberant adolescence required extra patience from owners.

They were muscular and bred over the centuries to be inured to pain, qualities that served them well as they dove into the icy waters of the North Atlantic to assist fishermen. But in a home setting, those same qualities also meant they could be like the proverbial bull in the china closet. They were big, strong, barrel-chested animals that did not always realize their own strength. One owner would later tell me she once tied her male Lab to the frame of her garage door so he could be nearby while she washed the car in the driveway. The dog spotted a squirrel and lunged, pulling the large steel doorframe right out of the wall.

And then I came across a sentence that struck fear in my heart. "The parents may be one of the best indications of the future temperament of your new puppy. A surprising amount of behavior is inherited." My mind flashed back to the frothing, mud-caked banshee that came charging out of the woods, the night we picked out our puppy. *Oh my,* I thought. The book counseled to insist, whenever possible, on seeing both the dam and the sire. My mind flashed back again, this time to the breeder's ever-so slight hesitation when I asked where the father was. *Oh . . . he's around here somewhere.* And then the way she quickly changed the topic. It was all making sense. Dog buyers in the know would have demanded to meet the father. And what would they have found? A manic dervish tearing blindly through the night as if demons were close on his tail. I said a silent prayer that Marley had inherited his mother's disposition.

Individual genetics aside, purebred Labs all share certain predictable characteristics. The American Kennel Club sets standards for the qualities Labrador retrievers should possess. Physically, they are stocky and muscular, with short, dense, weather-resistant coats. Their fur can be black, chocolate brown, or a range of yellows, from light cream to a rich fox red. One of the Labrador retriever's main distinguishing characteristics is its thick, powerful tail, which resembles that of an otter and can clear a coffee table in one quick swipe. The head is large and blocky, with powerful jaws and high-set, floppy ears. Most Labs are about two feet tall in the withers, or top of the shoulders, and the typical male weighs sixty-five to eighty pounds, though some can weigh considerably more.

But looks, according to the AKC, are not all that make a Lab a Lab. The club's breed standard states: "True Labrador retriever temperament is as much a hallmark of the breed as the 'otter' tail. The ideal disposition is one of a kindly, outgoing, tractable nature, eager to please and non-aggressive towards man or animal. The Labrador has much that appeals to people. His gentle ways, intelligence and adaptability make him an ideal dog."

An ideal dog! Endorsements did not come much more glowing than that. The more I read, the better I felt about our decision. Even the caveats didn't scare me much. Jenny and I would naturally throw ourselves into our new dog, showering him with attention and affection. We were dedicated to taking as long as needed to properly train him in obedience and social skills. We were both enthusiastic walkers, hitting the waterfront trail nearly every evening after work, and many mornings, too. It would be just natural to bring our new dog along with us on our power walks. We'd tire the little rascal out. Jenny's office was only a mile away, and she came home every day for lunch, at which time she could toss balls to him in the backyard to let him burn off even more of this boundless energy we were warned about.

A week before we were to bring our dog home, Jenny's sister, Susan, called from Boston. She, her husband, and their two children planned to be at Disney World the following week; would Jenny like to drive up and spend a few days with them? A doting aunt who looked for any opportunity to bond with her niece and nephew, Jenny was dying to go. But she was torn. "I won't be here to bring little Marley home," she said.

"You go," I told her. "I'll get the dog and have him all settled in and waiting for you when you get back."

I tried to sound nonchalant, but secretly I was overjoyed at the prospect of having the new puppy all to myself for a few days of uninterrupted male bonding. He was to be our joint project, both of ours equally. But I never believed a dog could answer to two masters, and if there could be only one alpha leader in the household hierarchy, I wanted it to be me. This little three-day run would give me a head start.

A week later Jenny left for Orlando—a three-and-a-half-hour drive away. That evening after work, a Friday, I returned to the breeder's house to fetch the new addition to our lives. When Lori brought my new dog out from the back of the house, I gasped audibly. The tiny, fuzzy puppy we had picked out three weeks earlier had more than doubled in size. He came barreling at me and ran headfirst into my ankles, collapsing in a pile at my feet and rolling onto his back, paws in the air, in what I could only hope was a sign of supplication. Lori must have sensed my shock. "He's a growing boy, isn't he?" she said cheerily. "You should see him pack away the puppy chow!"

I leaned down, rubbed his belly, and said, "Ready to go home, Marley?" It was my first time using his new name for real, and it felt right.

In the car, I used beach towels to fashion a cozy nest for him on the passenger seat and set him down in it. But I was barely out of the driveway when he began squirming and wiggling his way out of the towels. He belly-crawled in my direction across the seat, whimpering as he advanced. At the center console, Marley met the first of the countless predicaments he would find himself in over the course of his life. There he was, hind legs hanging over the passenger side of the console and front legs hanging over the driver's side. In the middle, his stomach was firmly beached on the emergency brake. His little legs were going in all directions, clawing at the air. He wiggled and rocked and swayed, but he was grounded like a freighter on a sandbar. I reached over and ran my hand down his back, which only excited him more and brought on a new flurry of squiggling. His hind paws desperately sought purchase on the carpeted hump between the two seats. Slowly, he began working his hind quarters into the air, his butt rising up, up, up, tail furiously going, until the law of gravity finally kicked in. He slalomed headfirst down the other side of the console, somersaulting onto the floor at my feet and flipping onto his back. From there it was a quick, easy scramble up into my lap.

Man, was he happy—desperately happy. He quaked with joy as he burrowed his head into my stomach and nibbled the buttons of my shirt, his tail slapping the steering wheel like the needle on a metronome.

I quickly discovered I could affect the tempo of his wagging by simply touching him. When I had both hands on the wheel, the beat came at a steady three thumps per second. *Thump. Thump. Thump.* But all I needed to do was press one finger against the top of his head and the rhythm jumped from a waltz to a bossa nova. *Thump-thump-thump-thump-thump-thump!* Two fingers and it jumped up to a mambo. *Thump-thumpa-thump-thump-thumpa-thump!* And when I cupped my entire hand over his head and massaged my fingers into his scalp, the beat exploded into a machine-gun, rapid-fire samba. *Thumpthumpthumpthumpthumpthumpthumpthump!*

"Wow! You've got rhythm!" I told him. "You really are a reggae dog."

When we got home, I led him inside and unhooked his leash. He began sniffing and didn't stop until he had sniffed every square inch of the place. Then he sat back on his haunches and looked up at me with cocked head as if to say, *Great digs, but where are my brothers and sisters?*

The reality of his new life did not fully set in until bedtime. Before leaving to get him, I had set up his sleeping quarters in the one-car garage attached to the side of the house. We never parked there, using it more as a storage and utility room. The washer and dryer were out there, along with our ironing board. The room was dry and comfortable and had a rear door that led out into the fenced backyard. And with its concrete floor and walls, it was virtually indestructible. "Marley," I said cheerfully, leading him out there, "this is your room."

I had scattered chew toys around, laid newspapers down in the middle of the floor, filled a bowl with water, and made a bed out of a cardboard box lined with an old bedspread. "And here is where you'll be sleeping," I said, and lowered him into the box. He was used to such accommodations but had always shared them with his siblings. Now he paced the perimeter of the box and looked forlornly up at me. As a test, I stepped back into the house and closed the door. I stood and listened. At first nothing. Then a slight, barely audible whimper. And then full-fledged crying. It sounded like someone was in there torturing him.

I opened the door, and as soon as he saw me he stopped. I reached in and pet him for a couple of minutes, then left again. Standing on the other side of the door, I began to count. One, two, three . . . He made it seven seconds before the yips and cries began again. We repeated the exercise several times, all with the same result. I was tired and decided it was time for him to cry himself to sleep. I left the garage light on for him, closed the door, walked to the opposite side of the house, and crawled into bed. The concrete walls did little to muffle his pitiful cries. I lay there, trying to ignore them, figuring any minute now he would give up and go to sleep. The crying continued. Even after I wrapped my pillow around my head, I could still hear it. I thought of him out there alone for the first time in his life, in this strange environment without a single dog scent to be had anywhere. His mother was missing in action, and so were all his siblings. The poor little thing. How would I like it?

I hung on for another half hour before getting up and going to him. As soon as he spotted me, his face brightened and his tail began to beat the side of the box. It was as if he were saying, *Come on, hop in; there's plenty of room.*

Instead, I lifted the box with him in it and carried it into my bedroom, where I placed it on the floor tight against the side of the bed. I lay down on the very edge of the mattress, my arm dangling into the box. There, my hand resting on his side, feeling his rib cage rise and fall with his every breath, we both drifted off to sleep.

CHAPTER 4

Mr. Wiggles

❖

For the next three days I threw myself with abandon into our new puppy. I lay on the floor with him and let him scamper all over me. I wrestled with him. I used an old hand towel to play tug-of-war with him—and was surprised at how strong he already was. He followed me everywhere—and tried to gnaw on anything he could get his teeth around. It took him just one day to discover the best thing about his new home: toilet paper. He disappeared into the bathroom and, five seconds later, came racing back out, the end of the toilet-paper roll clenched in his teeth, a paper ribbon unrolling behind him as he sprinted across the house. The place looked like it had been decorated for Halloween.

Every half hour or so I would lead him into the backyard to relieve himself. When he had accidents in the house, I scolded him. When he peed outside, I placed my cheek against his and praised him in my sweetest voice. And when he pooped outside, I carried on as though he had just delivered the winning Florida Lotto ticket.

When Jenny returned from Disney World, she threw herself into him with the same utter abandon. It was an amazing thing to behold. As the days unfolded I saw in my young wife a calm, gentle, nurturing side I had not known existed. She held him; she caressed him; she played with him; she fussed over him. She combed through every strand of his fur in search of fleas and ticks. She rose every couple of hours through the night—night after night—to take him outside for bathroom breaks. That more than anything was responsible for him becoming fully housebroken in just a few short weeks.

Mostly, she fed him.

Following the instructions on the bag, we gave Marley three large bowls of puppy chow a day. He wolfed down every morsel in a matter of seconds. What went in came out, of course, and soon our backyard was as inviting as a minefield. We didn't dare venture out into it without eyes sharply peeled. If Marley's appetite was huge, his droppings were huger still, giant mounds that looked virtually unchanged from what had earlier gone in the other end. Was he even digesting this stuff?

Apparently he was. Marley was growing at a furious pace. Like one of those amazing jungle vines that can cover a house in hours, he was expanding exponentially in all directions. Each day he was a little longer, a little wider, a little taller, a little heavier. He was twenty-one pounds when I brought him home and within weeks was up to fifty. His cute little puppy head that I so easily cradled in one hand as I drove him home that first night had rapidly morphed into something resembling the shape and heft of a blacksmith's anvil. His paws were enormous, his flanks already rippled with muscle, and his chest almost as broad as a bulldozer. Just as the books promised, his slip of a puppy tail was becoming as thick and powerful as an otter's.

What a tail it was. Every last object in our house that was at knee level or below was knocked asunder by Marley's wildly wagging weapon. He cleared coffee tables, scattered magazines, knocked framed photographs off shelves, sent beer bottles and wineglasses flying. He even cracked a pane in the French door. Gradually every item that was not bolted down migrated to higher ground safely above the sweep of his swinging mallet. Our friends with children would visit and marvel, "Your house is already baby-proofed!"

Marley didn't actually wag his tail. He more wagged his whole body, starting with the front shoulders and working backward. He was like the canine version of a Slinky. We swore there were no bones inside him, just one big, elastic muscle. Jenny began calling him Mr. Wiggles.

And at no time did he wiggle more than when he had something in his mouth. His reaction to any situation was the same: grab the nearest shoe or pillow or pencil—really, any item would do—and run with it. Some little voice in his head seemed to be whispering to him, "Go ahead! Pick it up! Drool all over it! Run!"

Some of the objects he grabbed were small enough to conceal, and this especially pleased him—he seemed to think he was getting away with something. But Marley would never have made it as a poker player. When he had something to hide, he could not mask his glee. He was always on the rambunctious side, but then there were those moments when he would explode into a manic sort of hyperdrive, as if some invisible prankster had just goosed him. His body would quiver, his head would bob from side to side, and his entire rear end would swing in a sort of spastic dance. We called it the Marley Mambo.

"All right, what have you got this time?" I'd say, and as I approached he would begin evasive action, waggling his way around the room, hips sashaying, head flailing up and down like a whinnying filly's, so overjoyed with his forbidden prize he could not contain himself. When I would finally get him cornered and pry open his jaws, I never came up empty-handed. Always there was something he had plucked out of the trash or off the floor or, as he got taller, right off the dining room table. Paper towels, wadded Kleenex, grocery receipts, wine corks, paper clips, chess pieces, bottle caps—it was like a salvage yard in there. One day I pried open his jaws and peered in to find my paycheck plastered to the roof of his mouth.

Within weeks, we had a hard time remembering what life had been like without our new boarder. Quickly, we fell into a routine. I started each morning, before the first cup of coffee, by taking him for a brisk walk down to the water and back. After breakfast and before my shower, I patrolled the backyard with a shovel, burying his land mines in the sand at the back of the lot. Jenny left for work before nine, and I seldom left the house before ten, first locking Marley out in the concrete bunker with a fresh bowl of water, a host of toys, and my cheery directive to "be a good boy, Marley." By twelve-thirty, Jenny was home on her lunch break, when she would give Marley his midday meal and throw him a ball in the backyard until he was tuckered out. In the early weeks, she also made a quick trip home in the middle of the afternoon to let him out. After dinner most evenings we walked together with him back down to the waterfront, where we would stroll along the Intracoastal as the yachts from Palm Beach idled by in the glow of the sunset.

Stroll is probably the wrong word. Marley strolled like a runaway locomotive strolls. He surged ahead, straining against his leash with everything he had, choking himself hoarse in the process. We yanked him back; he yanked us forward. We tugged; he pulled, coughing like a chain smoker from the collar strangling him. He veered left and right, darting to every mailbox and shrub, sniffing, panting, and peeing without fully stopping, usually getting more pee on himself than the intended target. He circled behind us, wrapping the leash around our ankles before lurching forward again, nearly tripping us. When someone approached with another dog, Marley would bolt at them joyously, rearing up on his hind legs when he reached the end of his leash, dying to make friends. "He sure seems to love life," one dog owner commented, and that about said it all.

He was still small enough that we could win these leash tug-of-wars, but with each week the balance of power was shifting. He was growing bigger and stronger. It was obvious that before long he would be more powerful than either of us. We knew we would need to rein him in and teach him to heel properly before he dragged us to humiliating deaths beneath the wheels of a passing car. Our friends who were veteran dog owners told us not to rush the obedience regimen. "It's too early," one of them advised. "Enjoy his puppyhood while you can. It'll be gone soon enough, and then you can get serious about training him."

That is what we did, which is not to say that we let him totally have his way. We set rules and tried to enforce them consistently. Beds and furniture were off-limits. Drinking from the toilet, sniffing crotches, and chewing chair legs were actionable offenses, though apparently worth suffering a scolding for. *No* became our favorite word. We worked with him on the basic commands—come, stay, sit, down— with limited success. Marley was young and wired, with the attention span of algae and the volatility of nitroglycerine. He was so excitable, any interaction at all would send him into a tizzy of bounce-off-the-walls, triple-espresso exuberance. We wouldn't realize it until years later, but he showed early signs of that condition that would later be coined to describe the behavior of thousands of hard-to-control, ants-in-their-pants schoolchildren. Our puppy had a textbook case of attention deficit hyperactivity disorder.

Still, for all his juvenile antics, Marley was serving an important role in our home and our relationship. Through his very helplessness, he was showing Jenny she could handle this maternal nurturing thing. He had been in her care for several weeks, and she hadn't killed him yet. Quite to the contrary, he was thriving. We joked that maybe we should start withholding food to stunt his growth and suppress his energy levels.

Jenny's transformation from coldhearted plant killer to

nurturing dog mom continued to amaze me. I think she amazed herself a little. She was a natural. One day Marley began gagging violently. Before I even fully registered that he was in trouble, Jenny was on her feet. She swooped in, pried his jaws open with one hand, and reached deep into his gullet with the other, pulling out a large, saliva-coated wad of cellophane. All in a day's work. Marley let out one last cough, banged his tail against the wall, and looked up at her with an expression that said, *Can we do it again?*

As we grew more comfortable with the new member of our family, we became more comfortable talking about expanding our family in other ways. Within weeks of bringing Marley home, we decided to stop using birth control. That's not to say we decided to get pregnant, which would have been way too bold a gesture for two people who had dedicated their lives to being as indecisive as possible. Rather, we backed into it, merely deciding to stop trying *not* to get pregnant. The logic was convoluted, we realized, but it somehow made us both feel better. No pressure. None at all. We weren't trying for a baby; we were just going to let whatever happened happen. Let nature take its course. *Que será, será* and all that.

Frankly, we were terrified. We had several sets of friends who had tried for months, years even, to conceive without luck and who had gradually taken their pitiful desperation public. At dinner parties they would talk obsessively about doctor's visits, sperm counts, and timed menstrual cycles, much to the discomfort of everyone else at the table. I mean, what were you supposed to say? "I think your sperm counts sound just fine!" It was almost too painful to bear. We were scared to death we would end up joining them.

Jenny had suffered several severe bouts of endometriosis before we were married and had undergone laparoscopic surgery to remove excess scar tissue from her fallopian tubes, none of which boded well for her fertility. Even more troubling was a little secret from our past. In those blindly passionate early days of our relationship, when desire had a stranglehold on anything resembling common sense, we had thrown caution into the corner with our clothes and had sex with reckless abandon, using no birth control whatsoever. Not just once but many times. It was incredibly dumb, and, looking back on it several years later, we should have been kissing the ground in gratitude for miraculously escaping an unwanted pregnancy. Instead, all either of us could think was, *What's wrong with us? No normal couple could possibly have done all that unprotected fornicating and gotten away with it.* We were both convinced conceiving was going to be no easy task.

So as our friends announced their plans to try to get pregnant, we remained silent. Jenny was simply going to stash her birth-control prescription away in the medicine cabinet and forget about it. If she ended up pregnant, fantastic. If she didn't, well, we weren't actually trying anyway, now, were we?

Winter in West Palm Beach is a glorious time of year, marked by crisp nights and warm, dry, sunny days. After the insufferably long, torpid summer, most of it spent in air-conditioning or hopping from one shade tree to the next in an attempt to dodge the blistering sun, winter was our time to celebrate the gentle side of the subtropics. We ate all our meals on the back porch, squeezed fresh orange juice from the fruit of the backyard tree each morning, tended a tiny herb garden and a few tomato plants along the side of the house, and picked saucer-sized hibiscus blooms to float in little bowls of water on the dining room table. At night we slept beneath open windows, the gardenia-scented air wafting in over us.

On one of those gorgeous days in late March, Jenny invited a friend from work to bring her basset hound, Buddy, over for a dog playdate. Buddy was a rescued pound dog with the saddest face I had ever seen. We let the two dogs loose in the backyard, and off they bounded. Old Buddy wasn't quite sure what to make of this hyperenergized yellow juvenile who raced and streaked and ran tight circles around him. But he took it in good humor, and the two of them romped and played together for more than an hour before they both collapsed in the shade of the mango tree, exhausted.

A few days later Marley started scratching and wouldn't stop. He was clawing so hard at himself, we were afraid he might draw blood. Jenny dropped to her knees and began one of her routine inspections, working her fingers through his coat, parting his fur as she went to see his skin below. After just a few seconds, she called out, "Damn it! Look at this." I peered over her shoulder at where she had parted Marley's fur just in time to see a small black dot dart back under cover. We laid him flat on the floor and began going through every inch of his fur. Marley was thrilled with the two-on-one attention and panted happily, his tail thumping the floor. Everywhere we looked we found them. Fleas! Swarms of them. They were between his toes and under his collar and burrowed inside his floppy ears. Even if they were slow enough to catch, which they were not, there were simply too many of them to even begin picking off.

We had heard about Florida's legendary flea and tick problems. With no hard freezes, not even any frosts, the bug populations were never knocked back, and they flourished in the warm, moist environment. This was a place where even the millionaires' mansions along the ocean in Palm Beach had cockroaches. Jenny was freaked out; her puppy was crawling with vermin. Of course, we blamed Buddy without having any solid proof. Jenny had images of not only the dog being infested but our entire home, too. She grabbed her car keys and ran out the door.

A half hour later she was back with a bag filled with enough chemicals to create our own Superfund site. There were flea baths and flea powders and flea sprays and flea foams and flea dips. There was a pesticide for the lawn, which the guy at the store told her we had to spray if we were to have any hope of bringing the little bastards to their knees. There was a special comb designed to remove insect eggs.

I reached into the bag and pulled out the receipt. "Jesus Christ, honey," I said. "We could have rented our own crop duster for this much."

My wife didn't care. She was back in assassin mode—this

time to protect her loved ones—and she meant business. She threw herself into the task with a vengeance. She scrubbed Marley in the laundry tub, using special soaps. She then mixed up the dip, which contained the same chemical, I noted, as the lawn insecticide, and poured it over him until every inch of him was saturated. As he was drying in the garage, smelling like a miniature Dow Chemical plant, Jenny vacuumed furiously—floors, walls, carpets, curtains, upholstery. And then she sprayed. And while she doused the inside with flea killer, I doused the outside with it. "You think we nailed the little buggers?" I asked when we were finally finished.

"I think we did," she said.

Our multipronged attack on the flea population of 345 Churchill Road was a roaring success. We checked Marley daily, peering between his toes, under his ears, beneath his tail, along his belly, and everywhere else we could reach. We could find no sign of a flea anywhere. We checked the carpets, the couches, the bottoms of the curtains, the grass—nothing. We had annihilated the enemy.

CHAPTER 5

The Test Strip

✳

A few weeks later we were lying in bed reading when Jenny closed her book and said, "It's probably nothing."

"What's probably nothing," I said absently, not looking up from my book.

"My period's late."

She had my attention. "Your period? It is?" I turned to face her.

"That happens sometimes. But it's been over a week. And I've been feeling weird, too."

"Weird how?"

"Like I have a low-level stomach flu or something. I had one sip of wine at dinner the other night, and I thought I was going to throw up."

"That's not like you."

"Just the thought of alcohol makes me nauseous."

I wasn't going to mention it, but she also had been rather cranky lately.

"Do you think—" I began to ask.

"I don't know. Do you?"

"How am I supposed to know?"

"I almost didn't say anything," Jenny said. "Just in case—you know. I don't want to jinx us."

That's when I realized just how important this was to her— and to me, too. Somehow parenthood had snuck up on us; we were ready for a baby. We lay there side by side for a long while, saying nothing, looking straight ahead.

"We're never going to fall asleep," I finally said.

"The suspense is killing me," she admitted.

"Come on, get dressed," I said. "Let's go to the drugstore and get a home test kit."

We threw on shorts and T-shirts and opened the front door, Marley bounding out ahead of us, overjoyed at the prospect of a late-night car ride. He pranced on his hind legs by our tiny Toyota Tercel, hopping up and down, shaking, flinging saliva off his jowls, panting, absolutely beside himself with anticipation of the big moment when I would open the back door. "Geez, you'd think he was the father," I said. When I opened the door, he leaped into the backseat with such gusto that he sailed clear to the other side without touching down, not stopping until he cracked his head loudly, but apparently with no ill effect, against the far window.

The pharmacy was open till midnight, and I waited in the car with Marley while Jenny ran in. There are some things guys just are not meant to shop for, and home pregnancy tests come pretty close to the top of the list. The dog paced in the backseat, whining, his eyes locked on the front door of the pharmacy. As was his nature whenever he was excited, which was nearly every waking moment, he was panting, salivating heavily.

"Oh for God's sake, settle down," I told him. "What do you think she's going to do? Sneak out the back door on us?" He responded by shaking himself off in a great flurry, showering me in a spray of dog drool and loose hair. We had become used to Marley's car etiquette and always kept an emergency bath towel on the front seat, which I used to wipe down myself and the interior of the car. "Hang tight," I said. "I'm pretty sure she plans to return."

Five minutes later Jenny was back, a small bag in her hand. As we pulled out of the parking lot, Marley wedged his shoulders between the bucket seats of our tiny hatchback, balancing his front paws on the center console, his nose touching the rearview mirror. Every turn we made sent him crashing down, chest first, against the emergency brake. And after each spill, unfazed and happier than ever, he would teeter back up on his perch.

A few minutes later we were back home in the bathroom with the $8.99 kit spread out on the side of the sink. I read the directions aloud. "Okay," I said. "It says it's accurate ninety-nine percent of the time. First thing you have to do is pee in this cup." The next step was to dip a skinny plastic test strip into the urine and then into a small vial of a solution that came with the kit. "Wait five minutes," I said. "Then we put it in the second solution for fifteen minutes. If it turns blue, you're officially knocked up, baby!"

We timed off the first five minutes. Then Jenny dropped the strip into the second vial and said, "I can't stand here watching it."

We went out into the living room and made small talk, pretending we were waiting for something of no more significance than the tea kettle to boil. "So how about them Dolphins," I quipped. But my heart was pounding wildly, and a feeling of nervous dread was rising from my stomach. If the test came back positive, whoa, our lives were about to change forever. If it came back negative, Jenny would be crushed. It was beginning to dawn on me that I might be, too. An eternity later, the timer rang. "Here we go," I said. "Either way, you know I love you."

I went to the bathroom and fished the test strip out of the vial. No doubt about it, it was blue. As blue as the deepest ocean. A dark, rich, navy-blazer blue. A blue that could be confused with no other shade. "Congratulations, honey," I said.

"Oh my God" is all she could answer, and she threw herself into my arms.

As we stood there by the sink, arms around each other, eyes closed, I gradually became aware of a commotion at our feet. I looked down and there was Marley, wiggling, head bobbing, tail banging the linen-closet door so hard I thought he might dent it. When I reached down to pet him, he dodged away. Uh-oh. It was the Marley Mambo, and that could mean just one thing.

"What do you have this time?" I said, and began chasing him. He loped into the living room, weaving just out of my reach. When I finally cornered him and pried open his jaws, at first I saw nothing. Then far back on his tongue, on the brink of no return, ready to slip down the hatch, I spotted something. It was skinny and long and flat. And as blue as the deepest ocean. I reached in and pulled out our positive test strip. "Sorry to disappoint you, pal," I said, "but this is going in the scrapbook."

Jenny and I started laughing and kept laughing for a long time. We had great fun speculating on what was going through that big blocky head of his. *Hmmm, if I destroy the evidence, maybe they'll forget all about this unfortunate episode, and I won't have to share my castle with an interloper after all.*

Then Jenny grabbed Marley by the front paws, lifted him up on his hind legs and danced around the room with him. "You're going to be an uncle!" she sang. Marley responded in his trademark way—by lunging up and planting a big wet tongue squarely on her mouth.

The next day Jenny called me at work. Her voice was bubbling. She had just returned from the doctor, who had officially confirmed the results of our home test. "He says all systems are go," she said.

The night before, we had counted back on the calendar, trying to pinpoint the date of conception. She was worried that she had already been pregnant when we went on our hysterical flea-eradication spree a few weeks earlier. Exposing herself to all those pesticides couldn't be good, could it? She raised her concerns with the doctor, and he told her it was probably not an issue. Just don't use them anymore, he advised. He gave her a prescription for prenatal vitamins and told her he'd see her back in his office in three weeks for a sonogram, an electronic-imaging process that would give us our first glimpse of the tiny fetus growing inside Jenny's belly.

"He wants us to make sure we bring a videotape," she said, "so we can save our own copy for posterity."

On my desk calendar, I made a note of it.

CHAPTER 6

Matters of the Heart

❉

The natives will tell you South Florida has four seasons. Subtle ones, they admit, but four distinct seasons nonetheless. Do not believe them. There are only two—the warm, dry season and the hot, wet one. It was about the time of this overnight return to tropical swelter when we awoke one day to realize our puppy was a puppy no more. As rapidly as winter had morphed into summer, it seemed, Marley had morphed into a gangly adolescent. At five months old, his body had filled out the baggy wrinkles in its oversized yellow fur coat. His enormous paws no longer looked so comically out of proportion. His needle-sharp baby teeth had given way to imposing fangs that could destroy a Frisbee—or a brand-new leather shoe—in a few quick chomps. The timbre of his bark had deepened to an intimidating boom. When he stood on his hindlegs, which he did often, tottering around like a dancing Russian circus bear, he could rest his front paws on my shoulders and look me straight in the eye.

The first time the veterinarian saw him, he let out a soft

whistle and said, "You're going to have a big boy on your hands."

And that we did. He had grown into a handsome specimen, and I felt obliged to point out to the doubting Miss Jenny that my formal name for him was not so far off the mark. Grogan's Majestic Marley of Churchill, besides residing on Churchill Road, was the very definition of majestic. When he stopped chasing his tail, anyway. Sometimes, after he ran every last ounce of nervous energy out of himself, he would lie on the Persian rug in the living room, basking in the sun slanting through the blinds. His head up, nose glistening, paws crossed before him, he reminded us of an Egyptian sphinx.

We were not the only ones to notice the transformation. We could tell from the wide berth strangers gave him and the way they recoiled when he bounded their way that they no longer viewed him as a harmless puppy. To them he had grown into something to be feared.

Our front door had a small oblong window at eye level, four inches wide by eight inches long. Marley lived for company, and whenever someone rang the bell, he would streak across the house, going into a full skid as he approached the foyer, careening across the wood floors, tossing up throw rugs as he slid and not stopping until he crashed into the door with a loud thud. He then would hop up on his hind legs, yelping wildly, his big head filling the tiny window to stare straight into the face of whoever was on the other side. For Marley, who considered himself the resident Welcome Wagon, it was a joyous overture. For door-to-door sales people, postal carriers, and anyone else who didn't know him, though, it was as if Cujo had just jumped out of the Stephen King novel and the only thing that stood between them and a merciless mauling was our wooden door. More than one stranger, after ringing the doorbell and seeing Marley's barking face peering out at them, beat a quick retreat to the middle of the driveway, where they stood waiting for one of us to answer.

This, we found, was not necessarily a bad thing.

Ours was what urban planners call a changing neighborhood. Built in the 1940s and '50s and initially populated by snowbirds and retirees, it began to take on a gritty edge as the original homeowners died off and were replaced by a motley group of renters and working-class families. By the time we moved in, the neighborhood was again in transition, this time being gentrified by gays, artists, and young professionals drawn to its location near the water and its funky, Deco-style architecture.

Our block served as a buffer between hard-bitten South Dixie Highway and the posh estate homes along the water. Dixie Highway was the original U.S. 1 that ran along Florida's eastern coast and served as the main route to Miami before the arrival of the interstate. It was five lanes of sun-baked pavement, two in each direction with a shared left-turn lane, and it was lined with a slightly decayed and unseemly assortment of thrift stores, gas stations, fruit stands, consignment shops, diners, and mom-and-pop motels from a bygone era.

On the four corners of South Dixie Highway and Churchill Road stood a liquor store, a twenty-four-hour convenience mart, an import shop with heavy bars on the window, and an open-air coin laundry where people hung out all night, often leaving bottles in brown bags behind. Our house was in the middle of the block, eight doors down from the action.

The neighborhood seemed safe to us, but there were telltales of its rough edge. Tools left out in the yard disappeared, and during a rare cold spell, someone stole every stick of firewood I had stacked along the side of the house. One Sunday we were eating breakfast at our favorite diner, sitting at the table we always sat at, right in the front window, when Jenny pointed to a bullet hole in the plate glass just above our heads and noted dryly, "That definitely wasn't there last time we were here."

One morning as I was pulling out of our block to drive to work, I spotted a man lying in the gutter, his hands and face bloody. I parked and ran up to him, thinking he had been hit by a car. But when I squatted down beside him, a strong stench of alcohol and urine hit me, and when he began to talk, it was clear he was inebriated. I called an ambulance and waited with him, but when the crew arrived he refused treatment. As the paramedics and I stood watching, he staggered away in the direction of the liquor store.

And there was the night a man with a slightly desperate air about him came to my door and told me he was visiting a house in the next block and had run out of gas for his car. Could I lend him five dollars? He'd pay me back first thing in the morning. *Sure you will, pal,* I thought. When I offered to call the police for him instead, he mumbled a lame excuse and disappeared.

Most unsettling of all was what we learned about the small

house kitty-corner from ours. A murder had taken place there just a few months before we moved in. And not just a run-of-the-mill murder, but a horribly gruesome one involving an invalid widow and a chain saw. The case had been all over the news, and before we moved in we were well familiar with its details—everything, that is, except the location. And now here we were living across the street from the crime scene.

The victim was a retired school teacher named Ruth Ann Nedermier, who had lived in the house alone and was one of the original settlers of the neighborhood. After hip-replacement surgery, she had hired a day nurse to help care for her, which was a fatal decision. The nurse, police later ascertained, had been stealing checks out of Mrs. Nedermier's checkbook and forging her signature.

The old woman had been frail but mentally sharp, and she confronted the nurse about the missing checks and the unexplained charges to her bank account. The panicked nurse bludgeoned the poor woman to death, then called her boyfriend, who arrived with a chain saw and helped her dismember the body in the bathtub. Together they packed the body parts in a large trunk, rinsed the woman's blood down the drain, and drove away.

For several days, Mrs. Nedermier's disappearance remained a mystery, our neighbors later told us. The mystery was solved when a man called the police to report a horrible stench coming from his garage. Officers discovered the trunk and its ghastly contents. When they asked the homeowner how it got there, he told them the truth: his daughter had asked if she could store it there for safekeeping.

Although the grisly murder of Mrs. Nedermier was the most-talked-about event in the history of our block, no one had mentioned a word about it to us as we prepared to buy the house. Not the real estate agent, not the owners, not the inspector, not the surveyor. Our first week in the house, the neighbors came over with cookies and a casserole and broke the news to us. As we lay in our bed at night, it was hard not to think that just a hundred feet from our bedroom window a defenseless widow had been sawn into pieces. It was an inside job, we told ourselves, something that would never happen to us. Yet we couldn't walk by the place or even look out our front window without thinking about what had happened there.

Somehow, having Marley aboard with us, and seeing how strangers eyed him so warily, gave us a sense of peace we might not have had otherwise. He was a big, loving dope of a dog whose defense strategy against intruders would surely have been to lick them to death. But the prowlers and predators out there didn't need to know that. To them he was big, he was powerful, and he was unpredictably crazy. And that is how we liked it.

Pregnancy suited Jenny well. She began rising at dawn to exercise and walk Marley. She prepared wholesome, healthy meals, loaded with fresh vegetables and fruits. She swore off caffeine and diet sodas and, of course, all alcohol, not even allowing me to stir a tablespoon of cooking sherry into the pot.

We had sworn to keep the pregnancy a secret until we

were confident the fetus was viable and beyond the risk of miscarriage, but on this front neither of us did well. We were so excited that we dribbled out our news to one confidant after another, swearing each to silence, until our secret was no longer a secret at all. First we told our parents, then our siblings, then our closest friends, then our office mates, then our neighbors. Jenny's stomach, at ten weeks, was just starting to round slightly. It was beginning to seem real. Why not share our joy with the world? By the time the day arrived for Jenny's examination and sonogram, we might as well have plastered it on a billboard: John and Jenny are expecting.

I took off work the morning of the doctor's appointment and, as instructed, brought a blank videotape so I could capture the first grainy images of our baby. The appointment was to be part checkup, part informational meeting. We would be assigned to a nurse-midwife who could answer all our questions, measure Jenny's stomach, listen for the baby's heartbeat, and, of course, show us its tiny form inside of her.

We arrived at 9:00 A.M., brimming with anticipation. The nurse-midwife, a gentle middle-aged woman with a British accent, led us into a small exam room and immediately asked: "Would you like to hear your baby's heartbeat?" Would we ever, we told her. We listened intently as she ran a sort of microphone hooked to a speaker over Jenny's abdomen. We sat in silence, smiles frozen on our faces, straining to hear the tiny heartbeat, but only static came through the speaker.

The nurse said that was not unusual. "It depends on how

the baby is lying. Sometimes you can't hear anything. It might still be a little early." She offered to go right to the sonogram. "Let's have a look at your baby," she said breezily.

"Our first glimpse of baby Grogie," Jenny said, beaming at me. The nurse-midwife led us into the sonogram room and had Jenny lie back on a table with a monitor screen beside it.

"I brought a tape," I said, waving it in front of her.

"Just hold on to it for now," the nurse said as she pulled up Jenny's shirt and began running an instrument the size and shape of a hockey puck over her stomach. We peered at the computer monitor at a gray mass without definition. "Hmm, this one doesn't seem to be picking anything up," she said in a completely neutral voice. "We'll try a vaginal sonogram. You get much more detail that way."

She left the room and returned moments later with another nurse, a tall bleached blonde with a monogram on her fingernail. Her name was Essie, and she asked Jenny to remove her panties, then inserted a latex-covered probe into her vagina. The nurse was right: the resolution was far superior to that of the other sonogram. She zoomed in on what looked like a tiny sac in the middle of the sea of gray and, with the click of a mouse, magnified it, then magnified it again. And again. But despite the great detail, the sac just looked like an empty, shapeless sock to us. Where were the little arms and legs the pregnancy books said would be formed by ten weeks? Where was the tiny head? Where was the beating heart? Jenny, her neck craned sideways to see the screen, was still brimming with anticipation and asked the nurses with a little nervous laugh, "Is there anything in there?"

I looked up to catch Essie's face, and I knew the answer was the one we did not want to hear. Suddenly I realized why she hadn't been saying anything as she kept clicking up the magnification. She answered Jenny in a controlled voice: "Not what you'd expect to see at ten weeks." I put my hand on Jenny's knee. We both continued staring at the blob on the screen, as though we could will it to life.

"Jenny, I think we have a problem here," Essie said. "Let me get Dr. Sherman."

As we waited in silence, I learned what people mean when they describe the swarm of locusts that descends just before they faint. I felt the blood rushing out of my head and heard buzzing in my ears. *If I don't sit down,* I thought, *I'm going to collapse.* How embarrassing would that be? My strong wife bearing the news stoically as her husband lay unconscious on the floor, the nurses trying to revive him with smelling salts. I half sat on the edge of the examining bench, holding Jenny's hand with one of mine and stroking her neck with the other. Tears welled in her eyes, but she didn't cry.

Dr. Sherman, a tall, distinguished-looking man with a gruff but affable demeanor, confirmed that the fetus was dead. "We'd be able to see a heartbeat, no question," he said. He gently told us what we already knew from the books we had been reading. That one in six pregnancies ends in miscarriage. That this was nature's way of sorting out the weak, the retarded, the grossly deformed. Apparently remembering Jenny's worry about the flea sprays, he told us it was nothing we did or did not do. He placed his hand on Jenny's cheek and leaned in close as if to kiss her. "I'm sorry," he said. "You can try again in a couple of months."

We both just sat there in silence. The blank videotape sitting on the bench beside us suddenly seemed like an incredible embarrassment, a sharp reminder of our blind, naïve optimism. I wanted to throw it away. I wanted to hide it. I asked the doctor: "Where do we go from here?"

"We have to remove the placenta," he said. "Years ago, you wouldn't have even known you had miscarried yet, and you would have waited until you started hemorrhaging."

He gave us the option of waiting over the weekend and returning on Monday for the procedure, which was the same as an abortion, with the fetus and placenta being vacuumed from the uterus. But Jenny wanted to get it behind her, and so did I. "The sooner the better," she said.

"Okay then," Dr. Sherman said. He gave her something to force her to dilate and was gone. Down the hall we could hear him enter another exam room and boisterously greet an expectant mother with jolly banter.

Alone in the room, Jenny and I fell heavily into each other's arms and stayed that way until a light knock came at the door. It was an older woman we had never seen before. She carried a sheaf of papers. "I'm sorry, sweetie," she said to Jenny. "I'm so sorry." And then she showed her where to sign the waiver acknowledging the risks of uterine suction.

When Dr. Sherman returned he was all business. He injected Jenny first with Valium and then Demerol, and the procedure was quick if not painless. He was finished before the drugs seemed to fully kick in. When it was over, she lay nearly unconscious as the sedatives took their full effect. "Just make sure she doesn't stop breathing," the doctor said, and he walked out of the room. I couldn't believe it. Wasn't it his job to make sure she didn't stop breathing? The waiver she signed never said "Patient could stop breathing at any time due to overdose of barbiturates." I did as I was told, talking to her in a loud voice, rubbing her arm, lightly slapping her cheek, saying things like, "Hey, Jenny! What's my name?" She was dead to the world.

After several minutes Essie stuck her head in to check on us. She caught one glimpse of Jenny's gray face and wheeled out of the room and back in again a moment later with a wet washcloth and smelling salts, which she held under Jenny's nose for what seemed forever before Jenny began to stir, and then only briefly. I kept talking to her in a loud voice, telling her to breathe deeply so I could feel it on my hand. Her skin was ashen; I found her pulse: sixty beats per minute. I nervously dabbed the wet cloth across her forehead, cheeks, and neck. Eventually, she came around, though she was still extremely groggy. "You had me worried," I said. She just looked blankly at me as if trying to ascertain why I might be worried. Then she drifted off again.

A half hour later the nurse helped dress her, and I walked her out of the office with these orders: for the next two weeks, no baths, no swimming, no douches, no tampons, no sex.

In the car, Jenny maintained a detached silence, pressing herself against the passenger door, gazing out the window. Her eyes were red but she would not cry. I searched for comforting words without success. Really, what could be said? We had lost our baby. Yes, I could tell her we could try again. I could tell her that many couples go through the same thing. But she didn't want to hear it, and I didn't want to say it. Someday we would be able to see it all in perspective. But not today.

I took the scenic route home, winding along Flagler Drive, which hugs West Palm Beach's waterfront from the north end of town, where the doctor's office was, to the south end, where we lived. The sun glinted off the water; the palm trees swayed gently beneath the cloudless blue sky. It was a day meant for joy, not for us. We drove home in silence.

When we arrived at the house, I helped Jenny inside and onto the couch, then went into the garage where Marley, as always, awaited our return with breathless anticipation. As soon as he saw me, he dove for his oversized rawhide bone and proudly paraded it around the room, his body wagging, tail whacking the washing machine like a mallet on a kettledrum. He begged me to try to snatch it from him.

"Not today, pal," I said, and let him out the back door into the yard. He took a long pee against the loquat tree and then came barreling back inside, took a deep drink from his bowl, water sloshing everywhere, and careened down the hall, searching for Jenny. It took me just a few seconds to lock the back door, mop up the water he had spilled, and follow him into the living room.

When I turned the corner, I stopped short. I would have bet a week's pay that what I was looking at couldn't possibly happen. Our rambunctious, wired dog stood with his shoulders between Jenny's knees, his big, blocky head resting quietly in her lap. His tail hung flat between his legs, the first time I could remember it not wagging whenever he was touching one of us. His eyes were turned up at her, and he whimpered softly. She stroked his head a few times and then, with no warning, buried her face in the thick fur of his neck and began sobbing. Hard, unrestrained, from-the-gut sobbing.

They stayed like that for a long time, Marley statue-still, Jenny clutching him to her like an oversized doll. I stood off to the side feeling like a voyeur intruding on this private moment, not quite knowing what to do with myself. And then, without lifting her face, she raised one arm up toward me, and I joined her on the couch and wrapped my arms around her. There the three of us stayed, locked in our embrace of shared grief.

CHAPTER 7

Master and Beast

❖

The next morning, a Saturday, I awoke at dawn to find Jenny lying on her side with her back to me, weeping softly. Marley was awake, too, his chin resting on the mattress, once again commiserating with his mistress. I got up and made coffee, squeezed fresh orange juice, brought in the newspaper, made toast. When Jenny came out in her robe several minutes later, her eyes were dry and she gave me a brave smile as if to say she was okay now.

After breakfast, we decided to get out of the house and walk Marley down to the water for a swim. A large concrete breakwater and mounds of boulders lined the shore in our neighborhood, making the water inaccessible. But if you walked a half dozen blocks to the south, the breakwater curved inland, exposing a small white sand beach littered with driftwood—a perfect place for a dog to frolic. When we reached the little beach, I wagged a stick in front of Marley's face and unleashed him. He stared at the stick as a starving man would stare at a loaf of bread, his eyes never leaving the prize. "Go get it!" I shouted, and hurled the stick as far out into the water as I could. He cleared the concrete wall in one spectacular leap, galloped down the beach and out into the shallow water, sending up plumes of spray around him. This is what Labrador retrievers were born to do. It was in their genes and in their job description.

No one is certain where Labrador retrievers originated, but this much is known for sure: it was not in Labrador. These muscular, short-haired water dogs first surfaced in the 1600s a few hundred miles to the south of Labrador, in Newfoundland. There, early diarists observed, the local fishermen took the dogs to sea with them in their dories, putting them to good use hauling in lines and nets and fetching fish that came off the hooks. The dogs' dense, oily coats made them impervious to the icy waters, and their swimming prowess, boundless energy, and ability to cradle fish gently in their jaws without damaging the flesh made them ideal work dogs for the tough North Atlantic conditions.

How the dogs came to be in Newfoundland is anyone's guess. They were not indigenous to the island, and there is no evidence that early Eskimos who first settled the area brought dogs with them. The best theory is that early ancestors of the retrievers were brought to Newfoundland by fishermen from Europe and Britain, many of whom jumped ship and settled on the coast, establishing communities. From there, what is now known as the Labrador retriever may have evolved through unintentional, willy-nilly cross-breeding. It likely shares common ancestry with the larger and shaggier Newfoundland breed.

However they came to be, the amazing retrievers soon were pressed into duty by island hunters to fetch game birds and waterfowl. In 1662, a native of St. John's, Newfoundland, named W. E. Cormack journeyed on foot across the island and noted the abundance of the local water dogs, which he found to be "admirably trained as retrievers in fowling and . . . otherwise useful." The British gentry eventually took notice and by the early nineteenth century were importing the dogs to England for use by sportsmen in pursuit of pheasant, grouse, and partridges.

According to the Labrador Retriever Club, a national hobbyist group formed in 1931 and dedicated to preserving the integrity of the breed, the name Labrador retriever came about quite inadvertently sometime in the 1830s when the apparently geographically challenged third earl of Malmesbury wrote to the sixth duke of Buccleuch to gush about his fine line of sporting retrievers. "We always call mine Labrador dogs," he wrote. From that point forward, the name stuck. The good earl noted that he went to great lengths to keep "the breed as pure as I could from the first." But others were less religious about genetics, freely crossing Labradors with other retrievers in hopes that their excellent qualities would transfer. The Labrador genes proved indomitable, and the Labrador retriever line remained distinct, winning recognition by the Kennel Club of England as a breed all its own on July 7, 1903.

B. W. Ziessow, an enthusiast and longtime breeder, wrote for the Labrador Retriever Club: "The American sportsmen adopted the breed from England and subsequently developed and trained the dog to fulfill the hunting needs of this country. Today, as in the past, the Labrador will eagerly enter ice cold water in Minnesota to retrieve a shot bird; he'll work all day hunting doves in the heat of the Southwest—his only reward is a pat for a job well done."

This was Marley's proud heritage, and it appeared he had inherited at least half of the instinct. He was a master at pursuing his prey. It was the concept of returning it that he did not seem to quite grasp. His general attitude seemed to be, *If you want the stick back that bad, YOU jump in the water for it.*

He came charging back up onto the beach with his prize in his teeth. "Bring it here!" I yelled, slapping my hands together. "C'mon, boy, give it to me!" He pranced over, his whole body wagging with excitement, and promptly shook water and sand all over me. Then to my surprise he dropped the stick at my feet. *Wow,* I thought. *How's that for service?* I looked back at Jenny, sitting on a bench beneath an Australian pine, and gave her a thumbs-up. But when I reached down to pick up the stick, Marley was ready. He dove in, grabbed it, and raced across the beach in crazy figure-eights. He swerved back, nearly colliding with me, taunting me to chase him. I made a few lunges at him, but it was clear he had both speed and agility on his side. "You're supposed to be a Labrador retriever!" I shouted. "Not a Labrador evader!"

But what I had that my dog didn't was an evolved brain that at least slightly exceeded my brawn. I grabbed a second stick and made a tremendous fuss over it. I held it over my head and tossed it from hand to hand. I swung it from side to side. I could see Marley's resolve softening. Suddenly, the stick in his mouth, just moments earlier the most prized possession he could imagine on earth, had lost its cachet. My stick drew him in like a temptress. He crept closer and closer until he was just inches in front of me. "Oh, a sucker is born every day, isn't he, Marley?" I cackled, rubbing the stick across his snout and watching as he went cross-eyed trying to keep it in his sights.

I could see the little cogs going in his head as he tried to figure out how he could grab the new stick without relinquishing the old one. His upper lip quivered as he tested the concept of making a quick two-for-one grab. Soon I had my free hand firmly around the end of the stick in his mouth. I tugged and he tugged back, growling. I pressed the second stick against his nostrils. "You know you want it," I whispered. And did he ever; the temptation was too much to bear. I could feel his grip loosening. And then he made his move. He opened his jaws to try to grab the second stick without losing the first. In a heartbeat, I whipped both sticks high above my head. He leaped in the air, barking and spinning, obviously at a loss as to how such a carefully laid battle strategy could have gone so badly awry. "This is why I am the master and you are the beast," I told him. And with that he shook more water and sand in my face.

I threw one of the sticks out into the water and he raced after it, yelping madly as he went. He returned a new, wiser opponent. This time he was cautious and refused to come anywhere near me. He stood about ten yards away, stick in mouth, eying the new object of his desire, which just happened to be the old object of his desire, his first stick, now perched high above my head. I could see the cogs moving again. He was thinking, *This time I'll just wait right here until he throws it, and then he'll have no sticks and I'll have both sticks.* "You think I'm really dumb, don't you, dog," I said. I heaved back and with a great, exaggerated groan hurled the stick with all my might. Sure enough, Marley roared into the water with his stick still locked in his teeth. The only thing was, I hadn't let go of mine. Do you think Marley figured that out? He swam halfway to Palm Beach before catching on that the stick was still in my hand.

"You're cruel!" Jenny yelled down from her bench, and I looked back to see she was laughing.

When Marley finally got back onshore, he plopped down in the sand, exhausted but not about to give up his stick. I showed him mine, reminding him how far superior it was to his, and ordered, "Drop it!" I cocked my arm back as if to throw, and the dummy bolted back to his feet and began heading for the water again. "Drop it!" I repeated when he returned. It took several tries, but finally he did just that. And the instant his stick hit the sand, I launched mine into the air for him. We did it over and over, and each time he seemed to understand the concept a little more clearly. Slowly the lesson was sinking into that thick skull of his. If he returned his stick to me, I would throw a new one for him. "It's like an office gift exchange," I told him. "You've got to give to get." He leaped up and smashed his sandy mouth against mine, which I took to be an acknowledgment of a lesson learned.

As Jenny and I walked home, the tuckered Marley for once did not strain against his leash. I beamed with pride at what we had accomplished. For weeks Jenny and I had been working to teach him some basic social skills and manners, but progress had been painfully slow. It was like we were living with a wild stallion—and trying to teach it to sip tea from fine porcelain. Some days I felt like Anne Sullivan to Marley's Helen Keller. I thought back to Saint Shaun and how quickly I, a mere ten-year-old boy, had been able to teach him all he needed to know to be a great dog. I wondered what I was doing wrong this time.

But our little fetching exercise offered a glimmer of hope. "You know," I said to Jenny, "I really think he's starting to get it."

She looked down at him, plodding along beside us. He was soaking wet and coated in sand, spittle foaming on his lips, his hard-won stick still clenched in his jaws. "I wouldn't be so sure of that," she said.

The next morning I again awoke before dawn to the sounds of Jenny softly sobbing beside me. "Hey," I said, and wrapped my arms around her. She nestled her face against my chest, and I could feel her tears soaking through my T-shirt.

"I'm fine," she said. "Really. I'm just—you know."

I did know. I was trying to be the brave soldier, but I felt it, too, the dull sense of loss and failure. It was odd. Less than forty-eight hours earlier we had been bubbling with anticipation over our new baby. And now it was as if there had never been a pregnancy at all. As if the whole episode was just a dream from which we were having trouble waking.

Later that day I took Marley with me in the car to pick up a few groceries and some things Jenny needed at the pharmacy. On the way back, I stopped at a florist shop and bought a giant bouquet of spring flowers arranged in a vase, hoping they would cheer her up. I strapped them into the seat belt in the backseat beside Marley so they wouldn't spill. As we passed the pet shop, I made the split-second decision that Marley deserved a pick-me-up, too. After all, he had done a better job than I at comforting the inconsolable woman in our lives. "Be a good boy!" I said. "I'll be right back." I ran into the store just long enough to buy an oversized rawhide chew for him.

When we got home a few minutes later, Jenny came out to meet us, and Marley tumbled out of the car to greet her. "We have a little surprise for you," I said. But when I reached in the backseat for the flowers, the surprise was on me. The bouquet was a mix of white daisies, yellow mums, assorted lilies, and bright red carnations. Now, however, the carnations were nowhere to be found. I looked more closely and found the decapitated stems that minutes earlier had held blossoms. Nothing else in the bouquet was disturbed. I glared at Marley and he was dancing around like he was auditioning for *Soul Train*. "Get over here!" I yelled, and when I finally caught him and pried open his jaws, I found the incontrovertible evidence of his guilt. Deep in his cavernous mouth, tucked up in one jowl like a wad of chewing tobacco, was a single red carnation. The others presumably were already down the hatch. I was ready to murder him.

I looked up at Jenny and tears were streaming down her cheeks. But this time, they were tears of laughter. She could not have been more amused had I flown in a mariachi band for a private serenade. There was nothing left for me to do but laugh, too.

"That dog," I muttered.

"I've never been crazy about carnations anyway," she said.

Marley was so thrilled to see everyone happy and laughing again that he jumped up on his hind legs and did a break dance for us.

The next morning, I awoke to bright sun dappling through the branches of the Brazilian pepper tree and across the bed. I glanced at the clock; it was nearly eight. I looked over at my wife sleeping peacefully, her chest rising and falling with long, slow breaths. I kissed her hair, draped an arm across her waist, and closed my eyes again.

CHAPTER 8

A Battle of Wills

❆

When Marley was not quite six months old, we signed him up for obedience classes. God knew he needed it. Despite his stick-fetching breakthrough on the beach that day, he was proving himself a challenging student, dense, wild, constantly distracted, a victim of his boundless nervous energy. We were beginning to figure out that he wasn't like other dogs. As my father put it shortly after Marley attempted marital relations with his knee, "That dog's got a screw loose." We needed professional help.

Our veterinarian told us about a local dog-training club that offered basic obedience classes on Tuesday nights in the parking lot behind the armory. The teachers were unpaid volunteers from the club, serious amateurs who presumably had already taken their own dogs to the heights of advanced behavior modification. The course ran eight lessons and cost fifty dollars, which we thought was a bargain, especially considering that Marley could destroy fifty dollars' worth of shoes in thirty seconds. And the club all but guaranteed we'd be marching home after graduation with the next great Lassie. At registration we met the woman who would be teaching our class. She was a stern, no-nonsense dog trainer who subscribed to the theory that there are no incorrigible dogs, just weak-willed and hapless owners.

The first lesson seemed to prove her point. Before we were fully out of the car, Marley spotted the other dogs gathering with their owners across the tarmac. A party! He leaped over us and out of the car and was off in a tear, his leash dragging behind him. He darted from one dog to the next, sniffing private parts, dribbling pee, and flinging huge wads of spit through the air. For Marley it was a festival of smells—so many genitals, so little time—and he was seizing the moment, being careful to stay just ahead of me as I raced after him. Each time I was nearly upon him, he would scoot a few feet farther away. I finally got within striking distance and took a giant leap, landing hard with both feet on his leash. This brought him to a jolting halt so abrupt that for a moment I thought I might have broken his neck. He jerked backward, landed on his back, flipped around, and gazed up at me with the serene expression of a heroin addict who had just gotten his fix.

Meanwhile, the instructor was staring at us with a look that could not have been more withering had I decided to throw off my clothes and dance naked right there on the blacktop. "Take your place, please," she said curtly, and when she saw both Jenny and me tugging Marley into position, she added: "You are going to have to decide which of you is going to be trainer." I started to explain that we both wanted to participate so each of us could work with him at home, but she cut me off. "A dog," she said definitively, "can only answer to one master." I began to protest, but she silenced me with that glare of hers—I suppose the same glare she used to intimidate her dogs into submission—and I slinked off to the sidelines with my tail between my legs, leaving Master Jenny in command.

This was probably a mistake. Marley was already considerably stronger than Jenny and knew it. Miss Dominatrix was only a few sentences into her introduction on the importance of establishing dominance over our pets when Marley decided the standard poodle on the opposite side of the class deserved a closer look. He lunged off with Jenny in tow.

All the other dogs were sitting placidly beside their masters at tidy ten-foot intervals, awaiting further instructions. Jenny was fighting valiantly to plant her feet and bring Marley to a halt, but he lumbered on unimpeded, tugging her across the parking lot in pursuit of hot-poodle butt-sniffing action. My wife looked amazingly like a water-skier being towed behind a powerboat. Everyone stared. Some snickered. I covered my eyes.

Marley wasn't one for formal introductions. He crashed into the poodle and immediately crammed his nose between her legs. I imagined it was the canine male's way of asking, "So, do you come here often?"

After Marley had given the poodle a full gynecological examination, Jenny was able to drag him back into place. Miss Dominatrix announced calmly, "That, class, is an example of a dog that has been allowed to think he is the alpha male of his pack. Right now, he's in charge." As if to drive home the point, Marley attacked his tail, spinning wildly, his jaws snapping at thin air, and in the process he wrapped the leash around Jenny's ankles until she was fully immobilized. I winced for her, and gave thanks that it wasn't me out there.

The instructor began running the class through the sit and down commands. Jenny would firmly order, "Sit!" And Marley would jump up on her and put his paws on her shoulders. She would press his butt to the ground, and he would roll over for a belly rub. She would try to tug him into place, and he would grab the leash in his teeth, shaking his head from side to side as if he were wrestling a python. It was too painful to watch. At one point I opened my eyes to see Jenny lying on the pavement face down and Marley standing over her, panting happily. Later she told me she was trying to show him the down command.

As class ended and Jenny and Marley rejoined me, Miss Dominatrix intercepted us. "You really need to get control over that animal," she said with a sneer. *Well, thank you for that valuable advice. And to think we had signed up simply to provide comic relief for the rest of the class.* Neither of us breathed a word. We just retreated to the car in humiliation and drove home in silence, the only sound Marley's loud panting as he tried to come down from the high of his first structured classroom experience. Finally I said, "One thing you can say for him, he sure loves school."

The next week Marley and I were back, this time without Jenny. When I suggested to her that I was probably the closest thing to an alpha dog we were going to find in our home, she gladly relinquished her brief title as master and commander and vowed to never show her face in public again. Before leaving the house, I flipped Marley over on his back, towered over him, and growled in my most intimidating voice, "I'm the boss! You're not the boss! I'm the boss! Got it, Alpha Dog?" He thumped his tail on the floor and tried to gnaw on my wrists.

The night's lesson was walking on heel, one I was especially keen on mastering. I was tired of fighting Marley every step of every walk. He already had yanked Jenny off her feet once when he took off after a cat, leaving her with bloody knees. It was time he learned to trot placidly along by our sides. I wrestled him to our spot on the tarmac, yanking him back from every dog we passed along the way. Miss Dominatrix handed each of us a short length of chain with a steel ring welded to each end. These, she told us, were choker collars and would be our secret weapons for teaching our dogs to heel effortlessly at our sides. The choker chain was brilliantly simple in design. When the dog behaved and walked beside its master as it was supposed to, with slack in its lead, the chain hung limply around its neck. But if the dog lunged forward or veered off course, the chain tightened like a noose, choking the errant hound into gasping submission. It didn't take long, our instructor promised, before dogs learned to submit or die of asphyxia. *Wickedly delicious,* I thought.

I started to slip the choker chain over Marley's head, but he saw it coming and grabbed it in his teeth. I pried his jaw open to pull it out and tried again. He grabbed it again. All the other dogs had their chains on; everyone was waiting. I grabbed his muzzle with one hand and with the other tried to lasso the chain over his snout. He was pulling backward, trying to get his mouth open so he could attack the mysterious coiled silver snake again. I finally forced the chain over his head, and he dropped to the ground, thrashing and snapping, his paws in the air, his head jerking from side to side, until he managed to get the chain in his teeth again. I looked up at the teacher. "He likes it," I said.

As instructed, I got Marley to his feet and got the chain out of his mouth. Then, as instructed, I pushed his butt down into a sit position and stood beside him, my left leg brushing his right shoulder. On the count of three, I was to say, "Marley, heel!" and step off with my left—never my right—foot. If he began to wander off course, a series of minor corrections—sharp little tugs on the leash—would bring him back into line. "Class, on the count of three," Miss Dominatrix called out. Marley was quivering with excitement. The shiny foreign object around his neck had him in a complete lather. "One . . . two . . . three."

"Marley, heel!" I commanded. As soon as I took my first step, he took off like a fighter jet from an aircraft carrier. I yanked back hard on the leash and he made an awful coughing gasp as the chain tightened around his airway. He sprang back for an instant, but as soon as the chain loosened, the momentary choking was behind him, ancient history in that tiny compartment of his brain dedicated to life lessons learned. He lunged forward again. I yanked back and he gasped once more. We continued like this the entire length of the parking lot, Marley yanking ahead, me yanking back, each time with increasing vigor. He was coughing and panting; I was grunting and sweating.

"Rein that dog in!" Miss Dominatrix yelled. I tried to with all my might, but the lesson wasn't sinking in, and I considered that Marley just might strangle himself before he figured it out. Meanwhile, the other dogs were prancing along at their owners' sides, responding to minor corrections just as Miss Dominatrix said they would. "For God's sake, Marley," I whispered. "Our family pride is on the line."

The instructor had the class queue up and try it again. Once again, Marley lurched his way manically across the blacktop, eyes bulging, strangling himself as he went. At the other end, Miss Dominatrix held Marley and me up to the class as an example of how not to heel a dog. "Here," she said impatiently, holding out her hand. "Let me show you." I handed the leash to her, and she efficiently tugged Marley around into position, pulling up on the choker as she ordered him to sit. Sure enough, he sank back on his haunches, eagerly looking up at her. *Damn.*

With a smart yank of the lead, Miss Dominatrix set off with him. But almost instantly he barreled ahead as if he were pulling the lead sled in the Iditarod. The instructor corrected hard, pulling him off balance; he stumbled, wheezed, then lunged forward again. It looked like he was going to pull her arm out of its socket. I should have been embarrassed, but I felt an odd sort of satisfaction that often comes with vindication. She wasn't having any more success than I was. My classmates snickered, and I beamed with perverse pride. *See, my dog is awful for everyone, not just me!*

. Now that I wasn't the one being made the fool, I had to admit, the scene was pretty hilarious. The two of them, having reached the end of the parking lot, turned and came lurching back toward us in fits and starts, Miss Dominatrix scowling with what clearly was apoplectic rage, Marley joyous beyond words. She yanked furiously at the leash, and Marley, frothing at the mouth, yanked back harder still, clearly enjoying this excellent new tug-of-war game his teacher had called on him to demonstrate. When he caught sight of me, he hit the gas. With a near-supernatural burst of adrenaline, he made a dash for me, forcing Miss Dominatrix to break into a sprint to keep from being pulled off her feet. Marley didn't stop until he slammed into me with his usual joie de vivre. Miss Dominatrix shot me a look that told me I had crossed some invisible line and there would be no crossing back. Marley had made a mockery of everything she preached about dogs and discipline; he had publicly humiliated her. She handed the leash back to me and, turning to the class as if this unfortunate little episode had never occurred, said, "Okay, class, on the count of three . . ."

When the lesson was over, she asked if I could stay after for a minute. I waited with Marley as she patiently fielded questions from other students in the class. When the last one had left, she turned to me and, in a newly conciliatory voice, said, "I think your dog is still a little young for structured obedience training."

"He's a handful, isn't he?" I said, feeling a new camaraderie with her now that we'd shared the same humiliating experience.

"He's simply not ready for this," she said. "He has some growing up to do."

It was beginning to dawn on me what she was getting at. "Are you trying to tell me—"

"He's a distraction to the other dogs."

"—that you're—"

"He's just too excitable."

"—kicking us out of class?"

"You can always bring him back in another six or eight months."

"So you're kicking us out?"

"I'll happily give you a full refund."

"You're kicking us out."

"Yes," she finally said. "I'm kicking you out."

Marley, as if on cue, lifted his leg and let loose a raging stream of urine, missing his beloved instructor's foot by mere centimeters.

Sometimes a man needs to get angry to get serious. Miss Dominatrix had made me angry. I owned a beautiful, pure-bred Labrador retriever, a proud member of the breed famous for its ability to guide the blind, rescue disaster victims, assist hunters, and pluck fish from roiling ocean swells, all with calm intelligence. How dare she write him off after just two lessons? So he was a bit on the spirited side; he was filled with nothing but good intentions. I was going to prove to that insufferable stuffed shirt that Grogan's Majestic Marley of Churchill was no quitter. We'd see her at Westminster.

First thing the next morning, I had Marley out in the backyard with me. "Nobody kicks the Grogan boys out of obedience school," I told him. "Untrainable? We'll see who's untrainable. Right?" He bounced up and down. "Can we do it, Marley?" He wiggled. "I can't hear you! Can we do it?" He yelped. "That's better. Now let's get to work."

We started with the sit command, which I had been practicing with him since he was a small puppy and which he already was quite good at. I towered over him, gave him my best alpha-dog scowl, and in a firm but calm voice ordered him to sit. He sat. I praised. We repeated the exercise several times. Next we moved to the down command, another one I had been practicing with him. He stared intently into my eyes, neck straining forward, anticipating my directive. I slowly raised my hand in the air and held it there as he waited for the word. With a sharp downward motion, I snapped my fingers, pointed at the ground and said, "Down!" Marley collapsed in a heap, hitting the ground with a thud. He could not possibly have gone down with more gusto had a mortar shell just exploded behind him. Jenny, sitting on the porch with her coffee, noticed it, too, and yelled out, "Incoming!"

After several rounds of hit-the-deck, I decided to move up to the next challenge: come on command. This was a tough one for Marley. The coming part was not the problem; it was waiting in place until we summoned him that he could not get. Our attention-deficit dog was so anxious to be plastered against us he could not sit still while we walked away from him.

I put him in the sit position facing me and fixed my eyes on his. As we stared at each other, I raised my palm, holding it out in front of me like a crossing guard. "Stay," I said, and took a step backward. He froze, staring anxiously, waiting for the slightest sign that he could join me. On my fourth step backward, he could take it no longer and broke free, racing up and tumbling against me. I admonished him and tried it again. And again and again. Each time he allowed me to get a little farther away before charging. Eventually, I stood fifty feet across the yard, my palm out toward him. I waited. He sat, locked in position, his entire body quaking with anticipation. I could see the nervous energy building in him; he was like a volcano ready to blow. But he held fast. I counted to ten. He did not budge. His eyes froze on me; his muscles bulged. *Okay, enough torture,* I thought. I dropped my hand and yelled, "Marley, come!"

As he catapulted forward, I squatted and clapped my hands to encourage him. I thought he might go racing willy-nilly across the yard, but he made a beeline for me. *Perfect!* I thought. "C'mon, boy!" I coached. "C'mon!" And come he did. He was barreling right at me. "Slow it down, boy," I said. He just kept coming. "Slow down!" He had this vacant, crazed look on his face, and in the instant before impact I realized the pilot had left the wheelhouse. It was a one-dog stampede. I had time for one final command. "STOP!" I screamed. *Blam!* He plowed into me without breaking stride and I pitched backward, slamming hard to the ground. When I opened my eyes a few seconds later, he was straddling me with all four paws, lying on my chest and desperately licking my face. *How did I do, boss?* Technically speaking, he had followed orders exactly. After all, I had failed to mention anything about stopping once he got to me.

"Mission accomplished," I said with a groan.

Jenny peered out the kitchen window at us and shouted, "I'm off to work. When you two are done making out, don't forget to close the windows. It's supposed to rain this afternoon." I gave Linebacker Dog a snack, then showered and headed off to work myself.

When I arrived home that night, Jenny was waiting for me at the front door, and I could tell she was upset. "Go look in the garage," she said.

I opened the door into the garage and the first thing I spotted was Marley, lying on his carpet, looking dejected. In that instant snapshot image, I could see that his snout and front paws were not right. They were dark brown, not their usual light yellow, caked in dried blood. Then my focus zoomed out and I sucked in my breath. The garage—our indestructible bunker—was a shambles. Throw rugs were shredded, paint was clawed off the concrete walls, and the ironing board was tipped over, its fabric cover hanging in ribbons. Worst of all, the doorway in which I stood looked like it had been attacked with a chipper-shredder. Bits of wood were sprayed in a ten-foot semicircle around the door, which was gouged halfway through to the other side. The bottom three feet of the doorjamb were missing entirely and nowhere to be found. Blood streaked the walls from where Marley had shredded his paws and muzzle. "Damn," I said, more in awe than anger. My mind flashed to poor Mrs. Nedermier and the chainsaw murder across the street. I felt like I was standing in the middle of a crime scene.

Jenny's voice came from behind me. "When I came home for lunch, everything was fine," she said. "But I could tell it was getting ready to rain." After she was back at work, an intense storm moved through, bringing with it sheets of rain, dazzling flashes of lightning, and thunder so powerful you could almost feel it thump against your chest.

When she arrived home a couple of hours later, Marley, standing amid the carnage of his desperate escape attempt, was in a complete, panic-stricken lather. He was so pathetic she couldn't bring herself to yell at him. Besides, the incident was over; he would have no idea what he was being punished for. Yet she was so heartsick about the wanton attack on our new house, the house we had worked so hard on, that she could not bear to deal with it or him. "Wait till your father gets home!" she had threatened, and closed the door on him.

Over dinner, we tried to put what we were now calling "the wilding" in perspective. All we could figure was that, alone and terrified as the storm descended on the neighborhood, Marley decided his best chance at survival was to begin digging his way into the house. He was probably listening to some ancient denning instinct handed down from his ancestor, the wolf. And he pursued his goal with a zealous efficiency I wouldn't have thought possible without the aid of heavy machinery.

When the dishes were done, Jenny and I went out into the garage where Marley, back to his old self, grabbed a chew toy and bounced around us, looking for a little tug-of-war action. I held him still while Jenny sponged the blood off his fur. Then he watched us, tail wagging, as we cleaned up his handiwork. We threw out the rugs and ironing-board cover, swept up the shredded remains of our door, mopped his blood off the walls, and made a list of materials we would need from the hardware store to repair the damage—the first of countless such repairs I would end up making over the course of his life. Marley seemed positively ebullient to have us out there, lending a hand with his remodeling efforts. "You don't have to look so happy about it," I scowled, and brought him inside for the night.

CHAPTER 9

The Stuff Males Are Made Of

❊

Every dog needs a good veterinarian, a trained professional who can keep it healthy and strong and immunized against disease. Every new dog owner needs one, too, mostly for the advice and reassurance and free counsel veterinarians find themselves spending inordinate amounts of their time dispensing. We had a few false starts finding a keeper. One was so elusive we only ever saw his high-school-aged helper; another was so old I was convinced he could no longer tell a Chihuahua from a cat. A third clearly was catering to Palm Beach heiresses and their palm-sized accessory dogs. Then we stumbled upon the doctor of our dreams. His name was Jay Butan—Dr. Jay to all who knew him—and he was young, smart, hip, and extraordinarily kind. Dr. Jay understood dogs like the best mechanics understand cars, intuitively. He clearly adored animals yet maintained a healthy sensibility about their role in the human world. In those early months, we kept him on speed dial and consulted him about the most inane concerns. When Marley began to develop rough scaly patches on his elbows, I feared he was developing some rare and, for all we knew, contagious skin ailment. Relax, Dr. Jay told me, those were just calluses from lying on the floor. One day Marley yawned wide and I spotted an odd purple discoloration on the back of his tongue. *Oh my God,* I thought. *He has cancer.* Kaposi's sarcoma of the mouth. Relax, Dr. Jay advised, it was just a birthmark.

Now, on this afternoon, Jenny and I stood in an exam room with him, discussing Marley's deepening neurosis over thunderstorms. We had hoped the chipper-shredder incident in the garage was an isolated aberration, but it turned out to be just the beginning of what would become a lifelong pattern of phobic, irrational behavior. Despite Labs' reputation as excellent gun dogs, we had ended up with one who was mortally terrified of anything louder than a popping champagne cork. Firecrackers, backfiring engines, and gunshots all terrified him. Thunder was a house of horrors all its own. Even the hint of a storm would throw Marley into a meltdown. If we were home, he would press against us, shaking and drooling uncontrollably, his eyes darting nervously, ears folded back, tail tucked between his legs. When he was alone, he turned destructive, gouging away at whatever stood between him and perceived safety. One day Jenny arrived home as clouds gathered to find a wild-eyed Marley standing on top of the washing machine, dancing a desperate jig, his nails clicking on the enamel top. How he got up there and why he felt the urge in the first place, we never determined. People could be certifiably nuts, and as best as we could figure, so could dogs.

Dr. Jay pressed a vial of small yellow pills into my hand

and said, "Don't hesitate to use these." They were sedatives that would, as he put it, "take the edge off Marley's anxiety." The hope, he said, was that, aided by the calming effects of the drug, Marley would be able to more rationally cope with storms and eventually realize they were nothing but a lot of harmless noise. Thunder anxiety was not unusual in dogs, he told us, especially in Florida, where huge boomers rolled across the peninsula nearly every afternoon during the torpid summer months. Marley nosed the vial in my hands, apparently eager to get started on a life of drug dependency.

Dr. Jay scruffed Marley's neck and began working his lips as though he had something important to say but wasn't quite sure how to say it. "And," he said, pausing, "you probably want to start thinking seriously about having him neutered."

"Neutered?" I repeated. "You mean, as in . . ." I looked down at the enormous set of testicles—comically huge orbs—swinging between Marley's hind legs.

Dr. Jay gazed down at them, too, and nodded. I must have winced, maybe even grabbed myself, because he quickly added: "It's painless, really, and he'll be a lot more comfortable." Dr. Jay knew all about the challenges Marley presented. He was our sounding board on all things Marley and knew about the disastrous obedience training, the numbskull antics, the destructiveness, the hyperactivity. And lately Marley, who was seven months old, had begun humping anything that moved, including our dinner guests. "It'll just remove all that nervous sexual energy and make him a happier, calmer dog," he said. He promised it wouldn't dampen Marley's sunny exuberance.

"God, I don't know," I said. "It just seems so . . . so final."

Jenny, on the other hand, was having no such compunctions. "Let's snip those suckers off!" she said.

"But what about siring a litter?" I asked. "What about carrying on his bloodline?" All those lucrative stud fees flashed before my eyes.

Again Dr. Jay seemed to be choosing his words carefully. "I think you need to be realistic about that," he said. "Marley's a great family pet, but I'm not sure he's got the credentials he would need to be in demand for stud." He was being as diplomatic as possible, but the expression on his face gave him away. It almost screamed out, *Good God, man! For the sake of future generations, we must contain this genetic mistake at all costs!*

I told him we would think about it, and with our new supply of mood-altering drugs in hand, we headed home.

It was at this same time, as we debated slicing away Marley's manhood, that Jenny was placing unprecedented demands on mine. Dr. Sherman had cleared her to try to get pregnant again. She accepted the challenge with the single-mindedness of an Olympic athlete. The days of simply putting away the birth control pills and letting whatever might happen happen were behind us. In the insemination wars, Jenny was going on the offensive. For that, she needed me, a key ally who controlled the flow of ammunition. Like most males, I had spent every waking moment from the age of fifteen trying to convince the opposite sex that I was a worthy mating partner. Finally, I had found someone who agreed. I should have been thrilled. For the first time in my life, a woman wanted me more than I wanted her. This was guy heaven. No more begging, no more groveling. Like the best stud dogs, I was at last in demand. I should have been ecstatic. But suddenly it all just seemed like work, and stressful work at that. It was not a rollicking good romp that Jenny craved from me; it was a baby. And that meant I had a job to perform. This was serious business. That most joyous of acts overnight became a clinical drill involving basal-temperature checks, menstrual calendars, and ovulation charts. I felt like I was in service to the queen.

It was all about as arousing as a tax audit. Jenny was used to me being game to go at the slightest hint of an invitation, and she assumed the old rules still applied. I would be, let's say, fixing the garbage disposal and she would walk in with her calendar in hand and say, "I had my last period on the seventeenth, which means"—and she would pause to count ahead from that date—"that we need to do it—NOW!"

The Grogan men have never handled pressure well, and I was no exception. It was only a matter of time before I suffered the ultimate male humiliation: performance failure. And once that happened, the game was over. My confidence was shot, my nerve gone. If it happened once, I knew it could happen again. Failure evolved into a self-fulfilling prophecy. The more I worried about performing my husbandly duty, the less I was able to relax and do what had always come naturally. I quashed all signs of physical affection lest I put ideas in Jenny's head. I began to live in mortal fear that my wife would, God forbid, ask me to rip her clothes off and have my way with her. I began thinking that perhaps a life of celibacy in a remote monastery wouldn't be such a bad future after all.

Jenny was not about to give up so easily. She was the hunter; I was the prey. One morning when I was working in my newspaper's West Palm Beach bureau, just ten minutes from home, Jenny called from work. Did I want to meet her at home for lunch? *You mean alone? Without a chaperone?*

"Or we could meet at a restaurant somewhere," I countered. A very crowded restaurant. Preferably with several of our coworkers along. And both mothers-in-law.

"Oh, c'mon," she said. "It'll be fun." Then her voice lowered to a whisper and she added, "Today's a good day. I . . . think . . . I'm . . . ovulating." A wave of dread washed over me. *Oh God, no. Not the O word.* The pressure was on. It was time to perform or perish. To, quite literally, rise or fall. *Please don't make me,* I wanted to plead into the phone. Instead I said as coolly as I could, "Sure. Does twelve-thirty work?"

When I opened the front door, Marley, as always, was there to greet me, but Jenny was nowhere to be found. I called out to her. "In the bathroom," she answered. "Out in a sec." I sorted through the mail, killing time, a general sense of doom hovering over me, the way I imagined it hovered over people waiting for their biopsy results. "Hey there, sailor," a voice behind me said, and when I turned around, Jenny was standing there in a little silky two-piece thing. Her flat stomach peeked out from below the top, which hung precariously from her shoulders by two impossibly thin straps. Her legs had never looked longer. "How do I look?" she said, holding her hands out at her sides. She looked incredible, that's how she looked. When it comes to sleep-wear, Jenny is squarely in the baggy T-shirt camp, and I could tell she felt silly in this seductive getup. But it was having the intended effect.

She scampered into the bedroom with me in pursuit. Soon we were on top of the sheets in each other's arms. I closed my eyes and could feel that old lost friend of mine stirring. The magic was returning. *You can do this, John.* I tried to conjure up the most impure thoughts I could. *This was going to work!* My fingers fumbled for those flimsy shoulder straps. *Roll with it, John. No pressure.* I could feel her breath now, hot and moist on my face. And heavy. Hot, moist, heavy breath. *Mmmm, sexy.*

But wait. What was that smell? Something on her breath. Something at once familiar and foreign, not exactly unplea-sant but not quite enticing, either. I knew that smell, but I couldn't place it. I hesitated. *What are you doing, you idiot? Forget the smell. Focus, man. Focus!* But that smell—I could not get it out of my head. *You're getting distracted, John. Don't get distracted.* What was it? *Stay the course!* My curiosity was getting the better of me. *Let it go, guy. Let it go!* I began sniffing the air. A food; yes, that was it. But what food? Not crackers. Not chips. Not tuna fish. I almost had it. It was . . . Milk-Bones?

Milk-Bones! That was it! She had Milk-Bone breath. *But why?* I wondered—and I actually heard a little voice ask the question in my head—*Why has Jenny been eating Milk-Bones?* And besides, I could feel her lips on my neck . . .

How could she be kissing my neck and breathing in my face all at once? It didn't make any—

Oh . . . my . . . God.

I opened my eyes. There, inches from my face, filling my entire frame of vision, loomed Marley's huge head. His chin rested on the mattress, and he was panting up a storm, drool soaking into the sheets. His eyes were half closed—and he looked entirely too in love. "Bad dog!" I shrieked, recoiling across the bed. "No! No! Go to bed!" I frantically ordered. "Go to bed! Go lie down!" But it was too late. The magic was gone. The monastery was back.

At ease, soldier.

The next morning I made an appointment to take Marley in to have his balls cut off. I figured if I wasn't going to have sex for the rest of my life, he wasn't either. Dr. Jay said we could drop Marley off before we went to work and pick him up on our way home. A week later, that's just what we did.

As Jenny and I got ready, Marley caromed happily off the walls, sensing an impending outing. For Marley, any trip was a good trip; it didn't matter where we were going or for how long. Take out the trash? *No problem!* Walk to the corner for a gallon of milk? *Count me in!* I began to feel pangs of guilt. The poor guy had no idea what lay in store for him. He trusted us to do the right thing, and here we were secretly plotting to emasculate him. Did betrayal get any more treacherous than this?

"Come here," I said, and wrestled him to the floor where I gave him a vigorous belly scratch. "It won't be so bad.

You'll see. Sex is highly overrated." Not even I, still re-bounding from my bad run of luck the last couple of weeks, believed that. Who was I fooling? Sex was great. Sex was incredible. The poor dog was going to miss out on life's single greatest pleasure. The poor bastard. I felt horrible.

And I felt even worse when I whistled for him and he bounded out the door and into the car with utter blind faith that I would not steer him wrong. He was revved up and ready to go on whatever excellent adventure I saw fit. Jenny drove and I sat in the passenger seat. As was his habit, Marley balanced his front paws on the center console, his nose touching the rearview mirror. Every time Jenny touched the brakes, he went crashing into the windshield, but Marley didn't care. He was riding shotgun with his two best friends. Did life get any better than this?

I cracked my window, and Marley began listing to star-board, leaning against me, trying to catch a whiff of the outdoor smells. Soon he had squirmed his way fully onto my lap and pressed his nose so firmly into the narrow crack of the window that he snorted each time he tried to inhale. *Oh, why not?* I thought. This was his last ride as a fully equipped member of the male gender; the least I could do was give him a little fresh air. I opened the window wide enough for him to stick his snout out. He was enjoying the sensation so much, I opened it farther, and soon his entire head was out the window. His ears flapped behind him in the wind, and his tongue hung out like he was drunk on the ether of the city. God, was he happy.

As we drove down Dixie Highway, I told Jenny how bad I felt about what we were about to put him through. She was beginning to say something no doubt totally dismissive of my qualms when I noticed, more with curiosity than alarm, that Marley had hooked both of his front paws over the edge of the half-open window. And now his neck and upper shoulders were hanging out of the car, too. He just needed a pair of goggles and a silk scarf to look like one of those World War I flying aces.

"John, he's making me nervous," Jenny said.

"He's fine," I answered. "He just wants a little fresh—"

At that instant he slid his front legs out the window until his armpits were resting on the edge of the glass.

"John, grab him! Grab him!"

Before I could do anything, Marley was off my lap and scrambling out the window of our moving car. His butt was up in the air, his hind legs clawing for a foothold. He was making his break. As his body slithered past me, I lunged for him and managed to grab the end of his tail with my left hand. Jenny was braking hard in heavy traffic. Marley dangled fully outside the moving car, suspended upside down by his tail, which I had by the most tenuous of grips. My body was twisted around in a position that didn't allow me to get my other hand on him. Marley was frantically trotting along with his front paws on the pavement.

Jenny got the car stopped in the outside lane with cars lining up behind us, horns blaring. "Now what?" I yelled. I was stuck. I couldn't pull him back in the window. I couldn't open the door. I couldn't get my other arm out. And I didn't dare let go of him or he would surely dash in the path of one of the angry drivers swerving around us. I held on for dear life, my face, as it were, scrunched against the glass just inches from his giant flapping scrotum.

Jenny put the flashers on and ran around to my side, where she grabbed him and held him by the collar until I could get out and help her wrestle him back into the car. Our little drama had unfolded directly in front of a gas station, and as Jenny got the car back into gear I looked over to see that all the mechanics had come out to take in the show. I thought they were going to wet themselves, they were laughing so hard. "Thanks, guys!" I called out. "Glad we could brighten your morning."

When we got to the clinic, I walked Marley in on a tight leash just in case he tried any more smart moves. My guilt was gone, my resolve hardened. "You're not getting out of this one, Eunuch Boy," I told him. He was huffing and puffing, straining against his leash to sniff all the other animal smells. In the waiting area he was able to terrorize a couple of cats and tip over a stand filled with pamphlets. I turned him over to Dr. Jay's assistant and said, "Give him the works."

That night when I picked him up, Marley was a changed dog. He was sore from the surgery and moved gingerly. His eyes were bloodshot and droopy from the anesthesia, and he was still groggy. And where those magnificent crown jewels of his had swung so proudly, there was . . . nothing. Just a small, shriveled flap of skin. The irrepressible Marley bloodline had officially and forever come to an end.

CHAPTER 10

The Luck of the Irish

❋

O ur lives increasingly were being defined by work.
Work at the newspapers. Work on the house.
Work around the yard. Work trying to get preg-
nant. And, nearly a full-time vocation in itself, work raising
Marley. In many ways, he was like a child, requiring the time
and attention a child requires, and we were getting a taste of
the responsibility that lay ahead of us if we ever did have a
family. But only to a degree. Even as clueless as we were about
parenting, we were pretty sure we couldn't lock the kids in
the garage with a bowl of water when we went out for the day.

We hadn't even reached our second wedding anniversary
and already we were feeling the grind of responsible, grown-
up, married life. We needed to get away. We needed a vacation,
just the two of us, far from the obligations of our daily lives. I
surprised Jenny one evening with two tickets to Ireland. We
would be gone for three weeks. There would be no itineraries,
no guided tours, no must-see destinations. Only a rental car, a
road map, and a guide to bed-and-breakfast inns along the way.
Just having the tickets in hand lifted a yoke from our shoulders.

First we had a few duties to dole out, and at the top of the list was Marley. We quickly ruled out a boarding kennel. He was too young, too wired, too rambunctious to be cooped up in a pen twenty-three hours a day. As Dr. Jay had predicted, neutering had not diminished Marley's exuberance one bit. It did not affect his energy level or loony behavior, either. Except for the fact that he no longer showed an interest in mounting inanimate objects, he was the same crazed beast. He was way too wild— and too unpredictably destructive when panic set in—to pawn off at a friend's house. Or even at an enemy's house, for that matter. What we needed was a live-in dog-sitter. Obviously, not just anyone would do, especially given the challenges Marley presented. We needed someone who was responsible, trustworthy, *very* patient, and strong enough to reel in seventy pounds of runaway Labrador retriever.

We made a list of every friend, neighbor, and coworker we could think of, then one by one crossed off names. Total party boy. *Scratch.* Too absentminded. *Scratch.* Averse to dog drool. *Scratch.* Too mousy to control a dachshund let alone a Lab. *Scratch.* Allergic. *Scratch.* Unwilling to pick up dog droppings. *Scratch.* Eventually, we were left with just one name. Kathy worked in my office and was single and unattached. She grew up in the rural Midwest, loved animals, and longed to someday trade in her small apartment for a house with a yard. She was athletic and liked to walk. True, she was shy and a little on the meek side, which could make it hard for her to impose her will on alpha Marley, but otherwise she would be perfect. Best of all, she said yes.

The list of instructions I prepared for her couldn't have been more painstakingly detailed were we leaving a criti-

cally ill infant in her care. The Marley Memo ran six full
pages single-spaced and read in part:

FEEDING: Marley eats three times a day, one two-
cup measure at each meal. The measuring cup is
inside the bag. Please feed him when you get up in
the morning and when you get home from work.
The neighbors will come in to feed him midafternoon. This totals six cups of food a day, but if
he's acting famished please give him an extra cup or
so. As you're aware, all that food has to go
somewhere. See POOP PATROL below.
VITAMINS: Each morning, we give Marley one Pet
Tab vitamin. The best way to give it to him is to
simply drop it on the floor and pretend he's not
supposed to have it. If he thinks it's forbidden, he
will wolf it down. If for some reason that doesn't
work, you can try disguising it in a snack.
WATER: In hot weather, it's important to keep
plenty of fresh water on hand. We change the water
next to his food bowl once a day and top it off if it's
running low. A word of caution: Marley likes to
submerge his snout in the water bowl and play
submarine. This makes quite a mess. Also his jowls
hold a surprising amount of water, which runs out
as he walks away from the bowl. If you let him, he'll
wipe his mouth on your clothes and the couches.
One last thing: He usually shakes after taking a big
drink, and his saliva will fly onto walls, lampshades,
etc. We try to wipe this up before it dries, at which

time it becomes almost impossible to remove.

FLEAS AND TICKS: If you notice these on him, you can spray him with the flea and tick sprays we have left. We've also left an insecticide that you can spray on the rugs, etc., if you think a problem is starting. Fleas are tiny and fast, and hard to catch, but they seldom bite humans, we've found, so I wouldn't be too concerned. Ticks are larger and slow and we do occasionally see these on him. If you spot one on him and have the stomach for it, just pick it off and either crush it in a tissue (you may need to use your fingernails; they're amazingly tough) or wash it down the sink or toilet (the best option if the tick is engorged with blood). You've probably read about ticks spreading Lyme disease to humans and all the long-term health problems that can cause, but several vets have assured us that there is very little danger of contracting Lyme disease here in Florida. Just to make sure, wash your hands well after removing a tick. The best way to pick a tick off Marley is to give him a toy to hold in his mouth to keep him occupied, and then pinch his skin together with one hand while you use your fingernails of the other hand as pincers to pull the tick off. Speaking of which, if he gets too smelly, and you're feeling brave, you can give him a bath in the kiddie pool we have in the backyard (for just that purpose), but wear a bathing suit. You'll get wet!

EARS: Marley tends to get a lot of wax buildup in his ears, which if left untreated can lead to infections. Once or twice while we're gone, please use cotton balls and the blue ear-cleaning solution to clean as much gunk out of his ears as you can. It's pretty nasty stuff so make sure you're wearing old clothes.

WALKS: Without his morning walk, Marley tends to get into mischief in the garage. For your own sanity, you may also want to give him a quick jaunt before bed, but that's optional. You will want to use the choker chain to walk him, but never leave it on him when he's unattended. He could strangle himself, and knowing Marley he probably would.

BASIC COMMANDS: Walking him is much easier if you can get him to heel. Always begin with him in a sitting position at your left, then give the command "Marley, heel!" and step off on your left foot. If he tries to lunge ahead, give him a sharp jerk on the leash. That usually works for us. (He's been to obedience school!) If he's off the leash, he usually is pretty good about coming to you with the command "Marley, come!" Note: It's best if you're standing and not crouched down when you call him.

THUNDERSTORMS: Marley tends to get a little freaked-out during storms or even light showers. We keep his sedatives (the yellow pills) in the cupboard with the vitamins. One pill thirty minutes before the storm arrives (you'll be a weather forecaster before you know it!) should do the trick. Getting Marley to swallow pills is a bit of an art form. He won't eat them like he does his vitamins, even if you drop them on the floor and pretend he shouldn't have them. The best technique is to straddle him and pry his jaws open with one hand. With the other, you push the pill as far down his throat as you can get it. It needs to be past the point of no return or he will cough it back up. Then stroke his throat until he swallows it. Obviously, you'll want to wash up afterward.

POOP PATROL: I have a shovel back under the mango tree that I use for picking up Marley's messes. Feel free to clean up after him as much or as little as you like, depending on how much you plan to walk around the backyard. Watch your step!

OFF-LIMITS: We do NOT allow Marley to:

* Get up on any piece of furniture.
* Chew on furniture, shoes, pillows, etc.
* Drink out of the toilet. (Best to keep lid down at all times, though beware: He's figured out how to flip it up with his nose.)
* Dig in the yard or uproot plants and flowers. He usually does this when he feels he's not getting enough attention.
* Go in any trash can. (You may have to keep it on top of the counter.)
* Jump on people, sniff crotches, or indulge in any other socially unacceptable behavior. We've especially been trying to cure him of arm chewing, which, as you can imagine, not a lot of people appreciate. He still has a way to go. Feel free to give him a swat on the rump and a stern "No!"

* Beg at the table.
* Push against the front screen door or the porch
  screens. (You'll see several have already been
  replaced.)

Thanks again for doing all this for us, Kathy. This is a
giant favor. I'm not quite sure how we could have
managed otherwise. Hope you and Marley become
good pals and you are as entertained by him as we are.

I brought the instructions in to Jenny and asked if there
was anything I had forgotten. She took several minutes to
read them and then looked up and said, "What are you
thinking? You can't show her this." She was waving them at
me. "You show her this and you can forget about Ireland.
She's the only person we could find willing to do this. If she
reads this, that's it. She'll start running and won't stop until
she hits Key West." Just in case I had missed it the first time
around, she repeated: "What on earth were you thinking?"
  "So you think it's too much?" I asked.
  But I've always believed in full disclosure, and show it to
her I did. Kathy did flinch noticeably a few times, especially
as we went over tick-removal techniques, but she kept any
misgivings to herself. Looking daunted and just a little green,
but far too kind to renege on a promise, she held fast. "Have
a great trip," she said. "We'll be fine."

Ireland was everything we dreamed it would be. Beautiful,
bucolic, lazy. The weather was gloriously clear and sunny

most days, leading the locals to fret darkly about the possibility of drought. As we had promised ourselves, we kept no schedules and set no itineraries. We simply wandered, bumping our way along the coast, stopping to stroll or shop or hike or quaff Guinness or simply gaze out at the ocean. We stopped the car to talk to farmers bringing in their hay and to photograph ourselves with sheep standing in the road. If we saw an interesting lane, we turned down it. It was impossible to get lost because we had no place we needed to be. All of our duties and obligations back home were just distant memories.

As evening approached each day, we would begin looking for a place to spend the night. Invariably, these were rooms in private homes run by sweet Irish widows who doted on us, served us tea, turned down our sheets, and always seemed to ask us the same question, "So, would you two be planning to start a family soon?" And then they would leave us in our room, flashing back knowing, oddly suggestive smiles as they closed the door behind them.

Jenny and I became convinced there was a national law in Ireland that required all guest beds to face a large, wall-mounted-likeness of either the pope or the Virgin Mary. Some places provided both. One even included an oversized set of rosary beads that dangled from the headboard. The Irish Celibate Traveler Law also dictated that all guest beds be extremely creaky, sounding a rousing alarm every time one of its occupants so much as rolled over.

It all conspired to create a setting that was about as conducive to amorous relations as a convent. We were in someone else's home—someone else's *very Catholic* home—with thin walls and a loud bed and statues of saints and virgins, and a nosy hostess who, for all we knew, was hovering on the other side of the door. It was the last place you would think to initiate sex. Which, of course, made me crave my wife in new and powerful ways.

We would turn off the lights and crawl into bed, the springs groaning under our weight, and immediately I would slip my hand beneath Jenny's top and onto her stomach.

"No way!" she would whisper.

"Why not?" I would whisper back.

"Are you nuts? Mrs. O'Flaherty is right on the other side of that wall."

"So what?"

"We can't!"

"Sure we can."

"She'll hear everything."

"We'll be quiet."

"Oh, *right*!"

"Promise. We'll barely move."

"Well, go put a T-shirt or something over the pope first," she would finally say, relenting. "I'm not doing anything with him staring at us."

Suddenly, sex seemed so . . . so . . . illicit. It was like I was in high school again, sneaking around under my mother's suspicious gaze. To risk sex in these surroundings was to risk shameful humiliation at the communal breakfast table the next morning. It was to risk Mrs. O'Flaherty's raised eyebrow as she served up eggs and fried tomatoes, asking with a leering grin, "So, was the bed comfortable for you?"

Ireland was a coast-to-coast No Sex Zone. And that was all the invitation I needed. We spent the trip bopping like bunnies.

Still, Jenny couldn't stop fretting about her big baby back home.

Every few days she would feed a fistful of coins into a pay phone and call home for a progress report from Kathy. I would stand outside the booth and listen to Jenny's end of the conversation.

"He did? . . . Seriously? . . . Right into traffic? . . . You weren't hurt, were you? . . . Thank God . . . I would have screamed, too . . . What? Your shoes? . . . Oh no! *And* your purse? . . . We'll certainly pay for repairs . . . Nothing left at all? . . . Of course, we insist on replacing them . . . And he what? . . . Wet cement, you say? What's the chance of that happening?"

And so it would go. Each call was a litany of transgressions, one worse than the next, many of which surprised even us, hardened survivors of the puppy wars. Marley was the incorrigible student and Kathy the hapless substitute teacher. He was having a field day.

When we arrived home, Marley raced outside to greet us. Kathy stood in the doorway, looking tired and strained. She had the faraway gaze of a shell-shocked soldier after a particularly unrelenting battle. Her bag was packed and sitting on the front porch, ready to go. She held her car key in her hand as if she could not wait to escape. We gave her gifts, thanked her profusely, and told her not to worry about the ripped-out screens and other damage. She excused herself politely and was gone.

As best as we could figure, Kathy had been unable to exert any authority at all over Marley, and even less control. With each victory, he grew bolder. He forgot all about heeling, dragging her behind him wherever he wished to go. He refused to come to her. He grabbed whatever suited him— shoes, purses, pillows—and would not let go. He stole food off her plate. He rifled through the garbage. He even tried taking over her bed. He had decided he was in charge while the parents were away, and he was not going to let some mild-mannered roommate pull rank and put the kibosh on his fun.

"Poor Kathy," Jenny said. "She looked kind of broken, don't you think?"

"Shattered is more like it."

"We probably shouldn't ask her to dog-sit for us again."

"No," I answered. "That probably wouldn't be a good idea."

Turning to Marley, I said, "The honeymoon's over, Chief. Starting tomorrow, you're back in training."

The next morning Jenny and I both started back to work. But first I slipped the choker chain around Marley's neck and took him for a walk. He immediately lunged forward, not even pretending to try to heel. "A little rusty, are we?" I asked, and heaved with all my might on his leash, knocking him off his paws. He righted himself, coughed, and looked up at me with a wounded expression as if to say, *You don't have to get rough about it. Kathy didn't mind me pulling.*

"Get used to it," I said, and placed him in a sit position. I adjusted the choke chain so it rode high on his neck, where experience had taught me it had the most effect. "Okay, let's try this again," I said. He looked at me with cool skepticism.

"Marley, heel!" I ordered, and stepped briskly off on my left foot with his leash so short my left hand was actually gripping the end of his choke chain. He lurched and I tugged sharply, tightening the stranglehold without mercy. "Taking advantage of a poor woman like that," I mumbled. "You ought to be ashamed of yourself." By the end of the walk, my grip on the leash so tight that my knuckles had turned white, I finally managed to convince him I wasn't fooling around. This was no game but rather a real-life lesson in actions and consequences. If he wanted to lurch, I would choke him. Every time, without exception. If he wanted to cooperate and walk by my side, I would loosen my grip and he would barely feel the chain around his neck. Lurch, choke; heel, breathe. It was simple enough for even Marley to grasp. Over and over and over again we repeated the sequence as we marched up and down the bike path. Lurch, choke; heel, breathe. Slowly it was dawning on him that I was the master and he was the pet, and that was the way it was going to stay. As we turned in to the driveway, my recalcitrant dog trotted along beside me, not perfectly but respectably. For the first time in his life he was actually heeling, or at least attempting a close proximity of it. I would take it as a victory. "Oh, yes," I sang joyously. "The boss is back."

Several days later Jenny called me at the office. She had just been to see Dr. Sherman. "Luck of the Irish," she said. "Here we go again."

CHAPTER 11

The Things He Ate

❊

This pregnancy was different. Our miscarriage had taught us some important lessons, and this time we had no intention of repeating our mistakes. Most important, we kept our news the most closely guarded secret since D-day. Except for Jenny's doctors and nurses, no one, not even our parents, was brought into our confidence. When we had friends over, Jenny sipped grape juice from a wineglass so as not to raise suspicions. In addition to the secrecy, we were simply more measured in our excitement, even when we were alone. We began sentences with conditional clauses, such as "If everything works out . . ." and "Assuming all goes well." It was as though we could jinx the pregnancy simply by gushing about it. We didn't dare let our joy out of check lest it turn and bite us.

We locked away all the chemical cleaners and pesticides. We weren't going down that road again. Jenny became a convert to the natural cleaning powers of vinegar, which was up to even the ultimate challenge of dissolving Marley's dried saliva off the walls. We found that boric acid, a white powder lethal to bugs and harmless to humans, worked pretty well at keeping Marley and his bedding flea-free. And if he needed an occasional flea dip, we would leave it to professionals.

Jenny rose at dawn each morning and took Marley for a brisk walk along the water. I would just be waking up when they returned, smelling of briny ocean air. My wife was the picture of robust health in all ways but one. She spent most days, all day long, on the verge of throwing up. But she wasn't complaining; she greeted each wave of nausea with what can only be described as gleeful acceptance, for it was a sign that the tiny experiment inside her was chugging along just fine.

Indeed it was. This time around, Essie took my videotape and recorded the first faint, grainy images of our baby. We could hear the heart beating, see its four tiny chambers pulsing. We could trace the outline of the head and count all four limbs. Dr. Sherman popped his head into the sonogram room to pronounce everything perfect, and then looked at Jenny and said in that booming voice of his, "What are you crying for, kid? You're supposed to be happy." Essie whacked him with her clipboard and scolded, "You go away and leave her alone," then rolled her eyes at Jenny as if to say, "Men! They are so clueless."

When it came to dealing with pregnant wives, clueless would describe me. I gave Jenny her space, sympathized with her in her nausea and pain, and tried not to grimace noticeably when she insisted on reading her *What to Expect When You're Expecting* book aloud to me. I complimented her figure as her belly swelled, saying things like "You look great. Really. You look like a svelte little shoplifter who just slipped a basketball under her shirt." I even tried my best to indulge her increasingly bizarre and irrational behavior. I was soon on a first-name basis with the overnight clerk at the twenty-four-hour market as I stopped in at all hours for ice cream or apples or celery or chewing gum in flavors I never knew existed. "Are you sure this is clove?" I would ask him. "She says it has to be clove."

One night when Jenny was about five months pregnant she got it in her head that we needed baby socks. Well, sure we did, I agreed, and of course we would lay in a full complement before the baby arrived. But she didn't mean we would need them eventually; she meant we needed them right now. "We won't have anything to put on the baby's feet when we come home from the hospital," she said in a quavering voice.

Never mind that the due date was still four months away. Never mind that by then the outside temperature would be a frosty ninety-six degrees. Never mind that even a clueless guy like me knew a baby would be bundled head to toe in a receiving blanket when released from the maternity ward.

"Honey, c'mon," I said. "Be reasonable. It's eight o'clock on Sunday night. Where am I supposed to find baby socks?"

"We need socks," she repeated.

"We have weeks to get socks," I countered. "Months to get socks."

"I just see those little tiny toes," she whimpered.

It was no use. I drove around grumbling until I found a Kmart that was open and picked out a festive selection of socks that were so ridiculously minuscule they looked like matching thumb warmers. When I got home and poured them out of the bag, Jenny was finally satisfied. At last we had socks. And thank God we had managed to grab up the last few available pair before the national supply ran dry, which could have happened at any moment without warning. Our baby's fragile little digits were now safe. We could go to bed and sleep in peace.

As the pregnancy progressed, so did Marley's training. I worked with him every day, and now I was able to entertain our friends by yelling, "Incoming!" and watching him crash to the floor, all four limbs splayed. He came consistently on command (unless there was something riveting his attention, such as another dog, cat, squirrel, butterfly, mailman, or floating weed seed); he sat consistently (unless he felt strongly like standing); and heeled reliably (unless there was something so tempting it was worth strangling himself over—see dogs, cats, squirrels, etc., above). He was coming along, but that's not to say he was mellowing into a calm, well-behaved dog. If I towered over him and barked stern orders, he would obey, sometimes even eagerly. But his default setting was stuck on eternal incorrigibility.

He also had an insatiable appetite for mangoes, which fell by the dozens in the backyard. Each weighed a pound or more and was so sweet it could make your teeth ache. Marley would stretch out in the grass, anchor a ripe mango between his front paws, and go about surgically removing every speck of flesh from the skin. He would hold the large pits in his mouth like lozenges, and when he finally spit them out they looked like they had been cleaned in an acid bath. Some days he would be out there for hours, noshing away in a fruit-and-fiber frenzy.

As with anyone who eats too much fruit, his constitution began to change. Soon our backyard was littered with large piles of loose, festively colored dog droppings. The one advantage to this was that you would have to be legally blind to accidentally step in a heap of his poop, which in mango season took on the radiant fluorescence of orange traffic cones.

He ate other things as well. And these, too, did pass. I saw the evidence each morning as I shoveled up his piles. Here a toy plastic soldier, there a rubber band. In one load a mangled soda-bottle top. In another the gnawed cap to a ballpoint pen. "So that's where my comb went!" I exclaimed one morning.

He ate bath towels, sponges, socks, used Kleenex. Handi Wipes were a particular favorite, and when they eventually came out the other end, they looked like little blue flags marking each fluorescent orange mountain.

Not everything went down easily, and Marley vomited with the ease and regularity of a hard-core bulimic. We would hear him let out a loud *gaaaaack!* in the next room, and by the time we rushed in, there would be another household item, sitting in a puddle of half-digested mangoes and dog chow. Being considerate, Marley never puked on the hardwood floors or even the kitchen linoleum if he could help it. He always aimed for the Persian rug.

Jenny and I had the foolish notion that it would be nice to have a dog we could trust to be alone in the house for short periods. Locking him in the bunker every time we stepped out was becoming tedious, and as Jenny said, "What's the point of having a dog if he can't greet you at the door when you get home?" We knew full well we didn't dare leave him in the house unaccompanied if there was any possibility of a rainstorm. Even with his doggie downers, he still proved himself capable of digging quite energetically for China. When the weather was clear, though, we didn't want to have to lock him in the garage every time we stepped out for a few minutes.

We began leaving him briefly while we ran to the store or dropped by a neighbor's house. Sometimes he did just fine and we would return to find the house unscathed. On these days, we would spot his black nose pushed through the miniblinds as he stared out the living room window waiting for us. Other days he didn't do quite so well, and we usually knew trouble awaited us before we even opened the door because he was not at the window but off hiding some-where.

In Jenny's sixth month of pregnancy, we returned after being away for less than an hour to find Marley under the bed—at his size, he really had to work to get under there—looking like he'd just murdered the mailman. Guilt radiated off him. The house seemed fine, but we knew he was hiding some dark secret, and we walked from room to room, trying to ascertain just what he had done wrong. Then I noticed that the foam cover to one of the stereo speakers was missing. We looked everywhere for it. Gone without a trace.

Marley just might have gotten away with it had I not found incontrovertible evidence of his guilt when I went on poop patrol the next morning. Remnants of the speaker cover surfaced for days.

During our next outing, Marley surgically removed the woofer cone from the same speaker. The speaker wasn't knocked over or in any way amiss; the paper cone was simply gone, as if someone had sliced it out with a razor blade. Eventually he got around to doing the same to the other speaker. Another time, we came home to find that our four-legged footstool was now three-legged, and there was no sign whatsoever—not a single splinter—of the missing limb.

We swore it could never snow in South Florida, but one day we opened the front door to find a full blizzard in the living room. The air was filled with soft white fluff floating down. Through the near whiteout conditions we spotted Marley in front of the fireplace, half buried in a snowdrift, violently shaking a large feather pillow from side to side as though he had just bagged an ostrich.

For the most part we were philosophical about the damage. In every dog owner's life a few cherished family heirlooms must fall. Only once was I ready to slice him open to retrieve what was rightfully mine.

For her birthday I bought Jenny an eighteen-karat gold necklace, a delicate chain with a tiny clasp, and she immediately put it on. But a few hours later she pressed her hand to her throat and screamed, "My necklace! It's gone." The clasp must have given out or never been fully secured.

"Don't panic," I told her. "We haven't left the house. It's

got to be right here somewhere." We began scouring the house, room by room. As we searched, I gradually became aware that Marley was more rambunctious than usual. I straightened up and looked at him. He was squirming like a centipede. When he noticed I had him in my sights, he began evasive action. *Oh, no,* I thought—the Marley Mambo. It could mean only one thing.

"What's that," Jenny asked, panic rising in her voice, "hanging out of his mouth?"

It was thin and delicate. And gold. "Oh, shit!" I said.

"No sudden moves," she ordered, her voice dropping to a whisper. We both froze.

"Okay, boy, it's all right," I coaxed like a hostage negotiator on a SWAT team. "We're not mad at you. Come on now. We just want the necklace back." Instinctively, Jenny and I began to circle him from opposite directions, moving with glacial slowness. It was as if he were wired with high explosives and one false move could set him off.

"Easy, Marley," Jenny said in her calmest voice. "Easy now. Drop the necklace and no one gets hurt."

Marley eyed us suspiciously, his head darting back and forth between us. We had him cornered, but he knew he had something we wanted. I could see him weighing his options, a ransom demand, perhaps. *Leave two hundred unmarked Milk-Bones in a plain paper bag or you'll never see your precious little necklace again.*

"Drop it, Marley," I whispered, taking another small step forward. His whole body began to wag. I crept forward by degrees. Almost imperceptibly, Jenny closed in on his flank. We were within striking distance. We glanced at each other and knew, without speaking, what to do. We had been through the Property Recovery Drill countless times before. She would lunge for the hindquarters, pinning his back legs to prevent escape. I would lunge for the head, prying open his jaws and nabbing the contraband. With any luck, we'd be in and out in a matter of seconds. That was the plan, and Marley saw it coming.

We were less than two feet away from him. I nodded to Jenny and silently mouthed, "On three." But before we could make our move, he threw his head back and made a loud smacking sound. The tail end of the chain, which had been dangling out of his mouth, disappeared. "He's eating it!" Jenny screamed. Together we dove at him, Jenny tackling him by the hind legs as I gripped him in a headlock. I forced his jaws open and pushed my whole hand into his mouth and down his throat. I probed every flap and crevice and came up empty. "It's too late," I said. "He swallowed it." Jenny began slapping him on the back, yelling, "Cough it up, damn it!" But it was no use. The best she got out of him was a loud, satisfied burp.

Marley may have won the battle, but we knew it was just a matter of time before we won the war. Nature's call was on our side. Sooner or later, what went in had to come out. As disgusting as the thought was, I knew if I poked through his excrement long enough, I would find it. Had it been, say, a silver chain, or a gold-plated chain, something of any less value, my queasiness might have won out. But this chain was solid gold and had set me back a decent chunk of pay. Grossed out or not, I was going in.

And so I prepared Marley his favorite laxative—a giant

bowl of dead-ripe sliced mangoes—and settled in for the long wait. For three days I followed him around every time I let him out, eagerly waiting to swoop in with my shovel. Instead of tossing his piles over the fence, I carefully placed each on a wide board in the grass and poked it with a tree branch while I sprayed with a garden hose, gradually washing the digested material away into the grass and leaving behind any foreign objects. I felt like a gold miner working a sluice and coming up with a treasure trove of swallowed junk, from shoelaces to guitar picks. But no necklace. Where the hell was it? Shouldn't it have come out by now? I began wondering if I had missed it, accidentally washing it into the grass, where it would remain lost forever. But how could I miss a twenty-inch gold chain? Jenny was following my recovery operation from the porch with keen interest and even came up with a new nickname for me. "Hey, Scat Man Doo, any luck yet?" she called out.

On the fourth day, my perseverance paid off. I scooped up Marley's latest deposit, repeating what had become my daily refrain—"I can't believe I'm doing this"—and began poking and spraying. As the poop melted away, I searched for any sign of the necklace. Nothing. I was about to give up when I spotted something odd: a small brown lump, about the size of a lima bean. It wasn't even close to being large enough to be the missing jewelry, yet clearly it did not seem to belong there. I pinned it down with my probing branch, which I had officially christened the Shit Stick, and gave the object a strong blast from the hose nozzle. As the water washed it clean, I got a glimmer of something exceptionally bright and shiny. Eureka! I had struck gold.

The necklace was impossibly compressed, many times smaller than I would have guessed possible. It was as though some unknown alien power, a black hole perhaps, had sucked it into a mysterious dimension of space and time before spitting it out again. And, actually, that wasn't too far from the truth. The strong stream of water began to loosen the hard wad, and gradually the lump of gold unraveled back to its original shape, untangled and unmangled. Good as new. No, actually better than new. I took it inside to show Jenny, who was ecstatic to have it back, despite its dubious passage. We both marveled at how blindingly bright it was now—far more dazzling than when it had gone in. Marley's stomach acids had done an amazing job. It was the most brilliant gold I had ever seen. "Man," I said with a whistle. "We should open a jewelry-cleaning business."

"We could make a killing with the dowagers in Palm Beach," Jenny agreed.

"Yes, ladies," I parroted in my best slick-salesman voice, "our secret patented process is not available at any store! The proprietary Marley Method will restore your treasured valuables to a blinding brilliance you never thought possible."

"It's got possibilities, Grogan," Jenny said, and went off to disinfect her recovered birthday present. She wore that gold chain for years, and every time I looked at it I had the same vivid flashback to my brief and ultimately successful career in gold speculation. Scat Man Doo and his trusty Shit Stick had gone where no man had ever gone before. And none should ever go again.

CHAPTER 12

Welcome to the Indigent Ward

❄

You don't give birth to your first child every day, and so, when St. Mary's Hospital in West Palm Beach offered us the option of paying extra for a luxury birthing suite, we jumped at the chance. The suites looked like upper-end hotel rooms, spacious, bright, and well appointed with wood-grained furniture, floral wallpaper, curtains, a whirlpool bath, and, just for Dad, a comfy couch that folded out into a bed. Instead of standard-issue hospital food, "guests" were offered a choice of gourmet dinners. You could even order a bottle of champagne, though this was mostly for the fathers to chug on their own, as breast-feeding mothers were discouraged from having more than a celebratory sip.

"Man, it's just like being on vacation!" I exclaimed, bouncing on the Dad Couch as we took a tour several weeks before Jenny's due date.

The suites catered to the yuppie set and were a big source of profits for the hospital, bringing in hard cash from couples with money to blow above the standard insurance allotment for deliveries. A bit of an indulgence, we agreed, but why not?

When Jenny's big day came and we arrived at the hospital, overnight bag in hand, we were told there was a little problem.

"A problem?" I asked.

"It must be a good day for having babies," the receptionist said cheerfully. "All the birthing suites are already taken."

Taken? This was the most important day of our lives. What about the comfy couch and romantic dinner for two and champagne toast? "Now, wait a second," I complained. "We made our reservation weeks ago."

"I'm sorry," the woman said with a noticeable lack of sympathy. "We don't exactly have a lot of control over when mothers go into labor."

She made a valid point. It wasn't like she could hurry someone along. She directed us to another floor, where we would be issued a standard hospital room. But when we arrived in the maternity ward, the nurse at the counter had more bad news. "Would you believe every last room is filled?" she said. No, we couldn't. Jenny seemed to take it in stride, but I was getting testy now. "What do you suggest, the parking lot?" I snapped.

The nurse smiled calmly at me, apparently well familiar with the antics of nervous fathers-to-be, and said, "Don't you worry. We'll find a spot for you."

After a flurry of phone calls, she sent us down a long hallway and through a set of double doors, where we found ourselves in a mirror image of the maternity ward we had just left except for one obvious difference—the patients were definitely not the buttoned-down, disposable-income yuppies we had gone through Lamaze class with. We could hear the nurses talking in Spanish to patients, and standing in the hallway outside the rooms, brown-skinned men holding straw hats in rugged hands waited nervously.

Palm Beach County is known as a playground for the obscenely rich, but what is less widely known is that it also is home to huge farms that stretch across drained Everglades swamp for miles west of town. Thousands of migrant workers, mostly from Mexico and Central America, migrate into South Florida each growing season to pick the peppers, tomatoes, lettuce, and celery that supply much of the East Coast's winter vegetable needs. It seems we had discovered where the migrant workers came to have their babies. Periodically, a woman's anguished scream would pierce the air, followed by awful moans and calls of *"Mi madre!"* The place sounded like a house of horrors. Jenny was white as a ghost.

The nurse led us into a small cubicle containing one bed, one chair, and a bank of electronic monitors and handed Jenny a gown to change into. "Welcome to the indigent ward!" Dr. Sherman said brightly when he breezed in a few minutes later. "Don't be fooled by the bare-bones rooms," he said. They were outfitted with some of the most sophisticated medical equipment in the hospital, and the nurses were some of the best trained. Because poor women often lacked access to prenatal care, theirs were some of the highest-risk pregnancies. We were in good hands, he assured us as he broke Jenny's water. Then, as quickly as he had appeared, he was gone.

Indeed, as the morning progressed and Jenny fought her way through ferocious contractions, we discovered we were in very good hands. The nurses were seasoned professionals who exuded confidence and warmth, attentively hovering over her, checking the baby's heartbeat and coaching Jenny along. I stood helplessly by, trying my best to be supportive, but it wasn't working. At one point Jenny snarled at me through gritted teeth, "If you ask me one more time how I'm doing, I'm going to RIP YOUR FACE OFF!" I must have looked wounded because one of the nurses walked around to my side of the bed, squeezed my shoulders sympathetically, and said, "Welcome to childbirth, Dad. It's all part of the experience."

I began slipping out of the room to join the other men waiting in the hallway. Each of us leaned against the wall beside our respective doors as our wives screamed and moaned away. I felt a little ridiculous, dressed in my polo shirt, khakis, and Top-Siders, but the farmworkers didn't seem to hold it against me. Soon we were smiling and nodding knowingly to one another. They couldn't speak English and I couldn't speak Spanish, but that didn't matter. We were in this together.

Or almost together. I learned that day that in America pain relief is a luxury, not a necessity. For those who could afford it—or whose insurance covered it, as ours did—the hospital provided epidurals, which delivered pain-blocking oblivion directly into the central nervous system. About four hours into Jenny's labor, an anesthesiologist arrived and slipped a long needle through the skin along her spine and attached it to an intravenous drip. Within minutes, Jenny was numb from the waist down and resting comfortably. The Mexican women nearby were not so lucky. They were left to tough it out the old-fashioned way, and their shrieks continued to puncture the air.

The hours passed. Jenny pushed. I coached. As night fell I stepped out into the hall bearing a tiny swaddled football. I lifted my newborn son above my head for my new friends to see and called out, *"Es el niño!"* The other dads flashed big smiles and held up their thumbs in the international sign of approval. Unlike our heated struggle to name our dog, we would easily and almost instantly settle on a name for our firstborn son. He would be named Patrick for the first of my line of Grogans to arrive in the United States from County Limerick, Ireland. A nurse came into our cubicle and told us a birthing suite was now available. It seemed rather beside the point to change rooms now, but she helped Jenny into a wheelchair, placed our son in her arms, and whisked us away. The gourmet dinner wasn't all it was cracked up to be.

During the weeks leading up to her due date, Jenny and I had had long strategy talks about how best to acclimate Marley to the new arrival who would instantly knock him off his until-now undisputed perch as Most Favored Dependent. We wanted to let him down gently. We had heard stories of dogs becoming terribly jealous of infants and acting out in unacceptable ways—everything from urinating on prized possessions to knocking over bassinets to outright attacks— that usually resulted in a one-way ticket to the pound. As we converted the spare bedroom into a nursery, we gave Marley full access to the crib and bedding and all the various accoutrements of infancy. He sniffed and drooled and licked until his curiosity was satisfied. In the thirty-six hours that Jenny remained hospitalized recuperating after the birth, I made frequent trips home to visit Marley, armed with receiving blankets and anything else that carried the baby's scent. On one of my visits, I even brought home a tiny used disposable diaper, which Marley sniffed with such vigor I feared he might suck it up his nostril, requiring more costly medical intervention.

When I finally brought mother and child home, Marley was oblivious. Jenny placed baby Patrick, asleep in his car carrier, in the middle of our bed and then joined me in greeting Marley out in the garage, where we had an uproarious reunion. When Marley had settled down from frantically wild to merely desperately happy, we brought him into the house with us. Our plan was to just go about our business, not pointing the baby out to him. We would hover nearby and let him gradually discover the presence of the newcomer on his own.

Marley followed Jenny into the bedroom, jamming his nose deep into her overnight bag as she unpacked. He clearly had no idea there was a living thing sitting on our bed. Then Patrick stirred and let out a small, birdlike chirp. Marley's ears pulled up and he froze. *Where did that come from?* Patrick chirped again, and Marley lifted one paw in the air, pointing like a bird dog. My God, he was *pointing* at our baby boy like a hunting dog would point at . . . *prey*. In that instant, I thought of the feather pillow he had attacked with such ferocity. He wasn't so dense as to mistake a baby for a pheasant, was he?

Then he lunged. It was not a ferocious "kill the enemy" lunge; there were no bared teeth or growls. But it wasn't a "welcome to the neighborhood, little buddy" lunge, either. His chest hit the mattress with such force that the entire bed jolted across the floor. Patrick was wide awake now, eyes wide. Marley recoiled and lunged again, this time bringing his mouth within inches of our newborn's toes. Jenny dove for the baby and I dove for the dog, pulling him back by the collar with both hands. Marley was beside himself, straining to get at this new creature that somehow had snuck into our inner sanctum. He reared on his hind legs and I pulled back on his collar, feeling like the Lone Ranger with Silver. "Well, that went well," I said.

Jenny unbuckled Patrick from his car seat; I pinned Marley between my legs and held him tightly by the collar with both fists. Even Jenny could see Marley meant no harm. He was panting with that dopey grin of his; his eyes were bright and his tail was wagging. As I held tight, she gradually came closer, allowing Marley to sniff first the baby's toes, then his feet and calves and thighs. The poor kid was only a day and a half old, and he was already under attack by a Shop-Vac. When Marley reached the diaper, he seemed to enter an altered state of consciousness, a sort of Pampers-induced trance. He had reached the holy land. The dog looked positively euphoric.

"One false move, Marley, and you're toast," Jenny warned, and she meant it. If he had shown even the slightest aggression toward the baby, that would have been it. But he never did. We soon learned our problem was not keeping Marley from hurting our precious baby boy. Our problem was keeping him out of the diaper pail.

As the days turned into weeks and the weeks into months, Marley came to accept Patrick as his new best friend. One night early on, as I was turning off the lights to go to bed, I couldn't find Marley anywhere. Finally I thought to look in the nursery, and there he was, stretched out on the floor beside Patrick's crib, the two of them snoring away in stereophonic fraternal bliss. Marley, our wild crashing bronco, was different around Patrick. He seemed to understand that this was a fragile, defenseless little human, and he moved gingerly whenever he was near him, licking his face and ears delicately. As Patrick began crawling, Marley would lie quietly on the floor and let the baby scale him like a mountain, tugging on his ears, poking his eyes, and pulling out little fistfuls of fur. None of it fazed him. Marley just sat like a statue. He was a gentle giant around Patrick, and he accepted his second-fiddle status with bonhomie and good-natured resignation.

Not everyone approved of the blind faith we placed in our dog. They saw a wild, unpredictable, and powerful beast—he was approaching a hundred pounds by now—and thought us foolhardy to trust him around a defenseless infant. My mother was firmly in this camp and not shy about letting us know it. It pained her to watch Marley lick her grandson. "Do you know where that tongue has been?" she would ask rhetorically. She warned us darkly that we should never leave a dog and a baby alone in the same room. The ancient predatory instinct could surface without warning. If it were up to her, a concrete wall would separate Marley and Patrick at all times.

One day while she was visiting from Michigan, she let out a shriek from the living room. "John, quick!" she screamed. "The dog's biting the baby!" I raced out of the bedroom, half dressed, only to find Patrick swinging happily in his wind-up swing, Marley lying beneath him. Indeed, the dog was snapping at the baby, but it was not as my panicky mother had feared. Marley had positioned himself directly in Patrick's flight path with his head right where Patrick's bottom, strapped in a fabric sling, stopped at the peak of each arc before swinging back in the opposite direction. Each time Patrick's diapered butt came within striking distance, Marley would snap playfully at it, goosing him in the process. Patrick squealed with delight. "Aw, Ma, that's nothing," I said. "Marley just has a thing for his diapers."

Jenny and I settled into a routine. At nighttime she would get up with Patrick every few hours to nurse him, and I would take the 6:00 A.M. feeding so she could sleep in. Half asleep, I would pluck him from his crib, change his diaper, and make a bottle of formula for him. Then the payoff: I would sit on the back porch with his tiny, warm body nestled against my stomach as he sucked on the bottle. Sometimes I would let my face rest against the top of his head and doze off as he ate lustily. Sometimes I would listen to National Public Radio and watch the dawn sky turn from purple to pink to blue. When he was fed and I had gotten a good burp out of him, I would get us both dressed, whistle for Marley, and take a morning walk along the water. We invested in a jogging stroller with three large bicycle tires that allowed it to go pretty much anywhere, including through sand and over curbs. The three of us must have made quite a sight each morning, Marley out in front leading the charge like a mush dog, me in the rear holding us back for dear life, and Patrick in the middle, gleefully waving his arms in the air like a traffic cop. By the time we arrived home, Jenny would be up and have coffee on. We would strap Patrick into his high chair and sprinkle Cheerios on the tray for him, which Marley would snitch the instant we turned away, laying his head sideways on the tray and using his tongue to scoop them into his mouth. *Stealing food from a baby,* we thought; *how low will he stoop?* But Patrick seemed immensely amused by the whole routine, and pretty soon he learned how to push his Cheerios over the side so he could watch Marley scramble around, eating them off the floor. He also discovered that if he dropped Cheerios into his lap, Marley would poke his head up under the tray and jab Patrick in the stomach as he went for the errant cereal, sending him into peals of laughter.

Parenthood, we found, suited us well. We settled into its rhythms, celebrated its simple joys, and grinned our way through its frustrations, knowing even the bad days soon enough would be cherished memories. We had everything we could ask for. We had our precious baby. We had our numbskull dog. We had our little house by the water. Of course, we also had each other. That November, my news-paper promoted me to columnist, a coveted position that gave me my own space on the section front three times a week to spout off about whatever I wanted. Life was good. When Patrick was nine months old, Jenny wondered aloud when we might want to start thinking about having another baby.

"Oh, gee, I don't know," I said. We always knew we wanted more than one, but I hadn't really thought about a time frame. Repeating everything we had just gone through seemed like something best not rushed into. "I guess we could just go back off birth control again and see what happens," I suggested.

"Ah," Jenny said knowingly. "The old *Que será, será* school of family planning."

"Hey, don't knock it," I said. "It worked before."

So that is what we did. We figured if we conceived anytime in the next year, the timing would be about right. As Jenny did the math, she said, "Let's say six months to get pregnant and then nine more months to deliver. That would put two full years between them."

It sounded good to me. Two years was a long way off. Two years was next to an eternity. Two years was almost not real. Now that I had proved myself capable of the manly duty of insemination, the pressure was off. No worries, no stress. Whatever would be would be.

A week later, Jenny was knocked up.

CHAPTER 13

A Scream in the Night

⁕

With another baby growing inside her, Jenny's odd, late-night food cravings returned. One night it was root beer, the next grapefruit. "Do we have any Snickers bars?" she asked once a little before midnight. It looked like I was in for another jaunt down to the all-night convenience store. I whistled for Marley, hooked him to his leash, and set off for the corner. In the parking lot, a young woman with teased blond hair, bright lavender lips, and some of the highest heels I had ever seen engaged us. "Oh, he's so cute!" she gushed. "Hi, puppy. What's your name, cutie?" Marley, of course, was more than happy to strike up a friendship, and I pulled him tight against me so he wouldn't slobber on her purple miniskirt and white tank top. "You just want to kiss me, poochie, don't you?" she said, and made smooching noises with her lips.

As we chatted, I wondered what this attractive woman was doing out in a parking lot along Dixie Highway alone at this hour. She did not appear to have a car. She did not appear to be on her way into or out of the store. She was just there, a parking-lot ambassador cheerfully greeting strangers and their dogs as they approached as though she were our neighborhood's answer to the Wal-Mart greeters. Why was she so immensely friendly? Beautiful women were never friendly, at least not to strange men in parking lots at midnight. A car pulled up, and an older man rolled down his window. "Are you Heather?" he asked. She shot me a bemused smile as if to say, *You do what you have to do to pay the rent.* "Gotta run," she said, hopping into the car. "Bye, puppy."

"Don't fall too in love, Marley," I said as they drove off. "You can't afford her."

A few weeks later, at ten o'clock on a Sunday morning, I walked Marley to the same store to buy a *Miami Herald,* and again we were approached, this time by two young women, teenagers really, who both looked strung out and nervous. Unlike the first woman we had met, they were not terribly attractive and had taken no efforts to make themselves more so. They both looked desperate for their next hit off a crack pipe. "Harold?" one of them asked me. "Nope," I said, but what I was thinking was, *Do you really think some guy would show up for anonymous sex and bring his Labrador retriever along?* How twisted did these two think I was? As I pulled a newspaper out of the box in front of the store, a car arrived—Harold, I presumed—and the girls drove off with him.

I wasn't the only one witnessing the burgeoning prostitution trade along Dixie Highway. On a visit, my older sister, dressed as modestly as a nun, went for a midday walk and was propositioned twice by would-be johns trolling by in cars. Another guest arrived at our house to report that a woman had just exposed her breasts to him as he drove past, not that he particularly minded.

In response to complaints from residents, the mayor promised to publicly embarrass men arrested for soliciting, and the police began running stings, positioning undercover women officers on the corner and waiting for would-be customers to take the bait.

The decoy cops were the homeliest hookers I had ever seen— think J. Edgar Hoover in drag—but that didn't stop men from seeking their services. One bust went down on the curb directly in front of our house—with a television news crew in tow.

If it had been just the hookers and their customers, we could have made our separate peace, but the criminal activity didn't stop there. Our neighborhood seemed to grow dicier each day. On one of our walks along the water, Jenny, suffering a particularly debilitating bout of pregnancy-related nausea, decided to head home alone while I continued on with Patrick and Marley. As she walked along a side street, she heard a car idling behind her. Her first thought was that it was a neighbor pulling up to say hello or someone needing directions. When she turned to look into the car, the driver sat fully exposed and masturbating. After he got the expected response, he sped in reverse down the street so as to hide his license tag.

When Patrick was not quite a year old, murder again came to our block. Like Mrs. Nedermier, the victim was an elderly woman who lived alone. Hers was the first house as you turned onto Churchill Road off Dixie Highway, directly behind the all-night, open-air Laundromat, and I only knew her to wave to as I passed. Unlike Mrs. Nedermier's murder, this crime did not afford us the tidy self-denial of an inside job. The victim was chosen at random, and the attacker was a stranger who snuck into her house while she was in the backyard hanging her laundry on a Saturday afternoon. When she returned, he bound her wrists with telephone cord and shoved her beneath a mattress as he ransacked the house for money. He fled with his plunder as my frail neighbor slowly suffocated beneath the weight of the mattress. Police quickly arrested a drifter who had been seen hanging around the coin laundry; when they emptied his pockets they found his total haul had been sixteen dollars and change. The price of a human life.

The crime swirling around us made us grateful for Marley's bigger-than-life presence in our house. So what if he was an avowed pacifist whose most aggressive attack strategy was known as the Slobber Offensive? Who cared if his immediate response to the arrival of any stranger was to grab a tennis ball in the hope of having someone new to play catch with? The intruders didn't need to know that. When strangers came to our door, we no longer locked Marley away before answering. We stopped assuring them how harmless he was. Instead we now let drop vaguely ominous warnings, such as "He's getting so unpredictable lately," and "I don't know how many more of his lunges this screen door can take."

We had a baby now and another on the way. We were no longer so cheerfully cavalier about personal safety. Jenny and I often speculated about just what, if anything, Marley would do if someone ever tried to hurt the baby or us. I tended to think he would merely grow frantic, yapping and panting. Jenny placed more faith in him. She was convinced his special loyalty to us, especially to his new Cheerios pusher, Patrick, would translate in a crisis to a fierce primal protectiveness that would rise up from deep within him. "No way," I said. "He'd ram his nose into the bad guy's crotch and call it a day." Either way, we agreed, he scared the hell out of people. That was just fine with us. His presence made the difference between us feeling vulnerable or secure in our own home. Even as we continued to debate his effectiveness as a protector, we slept easily in bed knowing he was beside us. Then one night he settled the dispute once and for all.

It was October and the weather still had not turned. The night was sweltering, and we had the air-conditioning on and windows shut. After the eleven o'clock news I let Marley out to pee, checked Patrick in his crib, turned off the lights, and crawled into bed beside Jenny, already fast asleep. Marley, as he always did, collapsed in a heap on the floor beside me, releasing an exaggerated sigh. I was just drifting off when I heard it—a shrill, sustained, piercing noise. I was instantly wide awake, and Marley was, too. He stood frozen beside the bed in the dark, ears cocked. It came again, penetrating the sealed windows, rising above the hum of the air conditioner. A scream. A woman's scream, loud and unmistakable. My first thought was teenagers clowning around in the street, not an unusual occurrence. But this was not a happy, stop-tickling-me scream. There was desperation in it, real terror, and it was dawning on me that someone was in terrible trouble.

"Come on, boy," I whispered, slipping out of bed.

"Don't go out there." Jenny's voice came from beside me in the dark. I hadn't realized she was awake and listening.

"Call the police," I told her. "I'll be careful."

Holding Marley by the end of his choker chain, I stepped out onto the front porch in my boxer shorts just in time to glimpse a figure sprinting down the street toward the water. The scream came again, from the opposite direction. Outside, without the walls and glass to buffet it, the woman's voice filled the night air with an amazing, piercing velocity, the likes of which I had heard only in horror movies. Other porch lights were flicking on. The two young men who shared a rental house across the street from me burst outside, wearing nothing but cutoffs, and ran toward the screams. I followed cautiously at a distance, Marley tight by my side. I saw them run up on a lawn a few houses away and then, seconds later, come dashing back toward me.

"Go to the girl!" one of them shouted, pointing. "She's been stabbed."

"We're going after him!" the other yelled, and they sprinted off barefoot down the street in the direction the figure had fled. My neighbor Barry, a fearless single woman who had bought and rehabilitated a rundown bungalow next to the Nedermier house, jumped into her car and joined the chase.

I let go of Marley's collar and ran toward the scream. Three doors down I found my seventeen-year-old neighbor standing alone in her driveway, bent over, sobbing in jagged raspy gasps. She clasped her ribs, and beneath her hands I could see a circle of blood spreading across her blouse. She was a thin, pretty girl with sand-colored hair that fell over her shoulders. She lived in the house with her divorced mother, a pleasant woman who worked as a night nurse. I had chatted a few times with the mother, but I only knew her daughter to wave to. I didn't even know her name.

"He said not to scream or he'd stab me," she said, sobbing; her words gushed out in heaving, hyperventilated gulps. "But I screamed. I screamed, and he stabbed me." As if I might not believe her, she lifted her shirt to show me the puckered wound that had punctured her rib cage. "I was sitting in my car with the radio on. He just came out of nowhere." I put my hand on her arm to calm her, and as I did I saw her knees buckling. She collapsed into my arms, her legs folding fawnlike beneath her. I eased her down to the pavement and sat cradling her. Her words came softer, calmer now, and she fought to keep her eyes open. "He told me not to scream," she kept saying. "He put his hand on my mouth and told me not to scream."

"You did the right thing," I said. "You scared him away."

It occurred to me that she was going into shock, and I had not the first idea what to do about it. *Come on, ambulance. Where are you?* I comforted her in the only way I knew how, as I would comfort my own child, stroking her hair, holding my palm against her cheek, wiping her tears away. As she grew weaker, I kept telling her to hang on, help was on the way. "You're going to be okay," I said, but I wasn't sure I believed it. Her skin was ashen. We sat alone on the pavement like that for what seemed hours but was in actuality, the police report later showed, about three minutes. Only gradually did I think to check on what had become of Marley. When I looked up, there he stood, ten feet from us, facing the street, in a determined, bull-like crouch I had never seen before. It was a fighter's stance. His muscles bulged at the neck; his jaw was clenched; the fur between his shoulder blades bristled. He was intensely focused on the street and appeared poised to lunge. I realized in that instant that Jenny had been right. If the armed assailant returned, he would have to get past my dog first. At that moment I knew—I absolutely knew without doubt—that Marley would fight him to the death before he would let him at us. I was emotional anyway as I held this young girl, wondering if she was dying in my arms. The sight of Marley so uncharacteristically guarding us like that, so majestically fierce, brought tears to my eyes. Man's best friend? Damn straight he was.

"I've got you," I told the girl, but what I meant to say, what I should have said, was that *we* had her. Marley and me. "The police are coming," I said. "Hold on. Please, just hold on."

Before she closed her eyes, she whispered, "My name is Lisa."

"I'm John," I said. It seemed ridiculous, introducing ourselves in these circumstances as though we were at a neighborhood potluck. I almost laughed at the absurdity of it. Instead, I tucked a strand of her hair behind her ear and said, "You're safe now, Lisa."

Like an archangel sent from heaven, a police officer came charging up the sidewalk. I whistled to Marley and called,

"It's okay, boy. He's okay." And it was as if, with that whistle, I had broken some kind of trance. My goofy, good-natured pal was back, trotting in circles, panting, trying to sniff us. Whatever ancient instinct had welled up from the recesses of his ancestral psyche was back in its bottle again. Then more officers swarmed around us, and soon an ambulance crew arrived with a stretcher and wads of sterile gauze. I stepped out of the way, told the police what I could, and walked home, Marley loping ahead of me.

Jenny met me at the door and together we stood in the front window watching the drama unfold on the street. Our neighborhood looked like the set from a police television drama. Red strobe lights splashed through the windows. A police helicopter hovered overhead, shining its spotlight down on backyards and alleys. Cops set up roadblocks and combed the neighborhood on foot. Their efforts would be in vain; a suspect was never apprehended and a motive never determined. My neighbors who gave chase later told me they had not even caught a glimpse of him. Jenny and I eventually returned to bed, where we both lay awake for a long time.

"You would have been proud of Marley," I told her. "It was so strange. Somehow he knew how serious this was. He just knew. He felt the danger, and he was like a completely different dog."

"I told you so," she said. And she had.

As the helicopter thumped the air above us, Jenny rolled onto her side and, before drifting off, said, "Just another ho-hum night in the neighborhood." I reached down and felt in the dark for Marley, lying beside me.

"You did all right tonight, big guy," I whispered, scratching his ears. "You earned your dog chow." My hand on his back, I drifted off to sleep.

It said something about South Florida's numbness to crime that the stabbing of a teenage girl as she sat in her car in front of her home would merit just six sentences in the morning newspaper. The *Sun-Sentinel*'s account of the crime ran in the briefs column on page 3B beneath the headline "Man Attacks Girl."

The story made no mention of me or Marley or the guys across the street who set out half naked after the assailant. It didn't mention Barry, who gave chase in her car. Or all the neighbors up and down the block who turned on porch lights and dialed 911. In South Florida's seamy world of violent crime, our neighborhood's drama was just a minor hiccup. No deaths, no hostages, no big deal.

The knife had punctured Lisa's lung, and she spent five days in the hospital and several weeks recuperating at home. Her mother kept the neighbors apprised of her recovery, but the girl remained inside and out of sight. I worried about the emotional wounds the attack might leave. Would she ever again be comfortable leaving the safety of her home? Our lives had come together for just three minutes, but I felt invested in her as a brother might be in a kid sister. I wanted to respect her privacy, but I also wanted to see her, to prove to myself she was going to be all right.

Then as I washed the cars in the driveway on a Saturday, Marley chained up beside me, I looked up and there she stood. Prettier than I had remembered. Tanned, strong, athletic—looking whole again. She smiled and asked, "Remember me?"

"Let's see," I said, feigning puzzlement. "You look vaguely familiar. Weren't you the one in front of me at the Tom Petty concert who wouldn't sit down?"

She laughed, and I asked, "So how are you doing, Lisa?"

"I'm good," she said. "Just about back to normal."

"You look great," I told her. "A little better than the last time I saw you."

"Yeah, well," she said, and looked down at her feet. "What a night."

"What a night," I repeated.

That was all we said about it. She told me about the hospital, the doctors, the detective who interviewed her, the endless fruit baskets, the boredom of sitting at home as she healed. But she steered clear of the attack, and so did I. Some things were best left behind.

Lisa stayed a long time that afternoon, following me around the yard as I did chores, playing with Marley, making small talk. I sensed there was something she wanted to say but could not bring herself to. She was seventeen; I didn't expect her to find the words. Our lives had collided without plan or warning, two strangers thrown together by a burst of inexplicable violence. There had been no time for the usual proprieties that exist between neighbors; no time to establish boundaries. In a heartbeat, there we were, intimately locked together in crisis, a dad in boxer shorts and a teenage girl in a blood-soaked blouse, clinging to each other and to hope. There was a closeness there now. How could there

not be? There was also awkwardness, a slight embarrassment, for in that moment we had caught each other with
our guards down. Words were not necessary. I knew she
was grateful that I had come to her; I knew she appreciated
my efforts to comfort her, however lame. She knew I cared
deeply and was in her corner. We had shared something that
night on the pavement— one of those brief, fleeting moments of clarity that define all the others in a life—that
neither of us would soon forget.

"I'm glad you stopped by," I said.

"I'm glad I did, too," Lisa answered.

By the time she left, I had a good feeling about this girl.
She was strong. She was tough. She would move forward.
And indeed I found out years later, when I learned she had
built a career for herself as a television broadcaster, that she
had.

CHAPTER 14

An Early Arrival

❖

"John."

Through the fog of sleep, I gradually registered my name being called. "John. John, wake up." It was Jenny; she was shaking me. "John, I think the baby might be coming."

I propped myself up on an elbow and rubbed my eyes. Jenny was lying on her side, knees pulled to her chest. "The baby what?"

"I'm having bad cramps," she said. "I've been lying here timing them. We need to call Dr. Sherman."

I was wide awake now. *The baby was coming?* I was wild with anticipation for the birth of our second child—another boy, we already knew from the sonogram. The timing, though, was wrong, terribly wrong. Jenny was twenty-one weeks into the pregnancy, barely halfway through the forty-week gestation period. Among her motherhood books was a collection of high-definition in utero photographs showing a fetus at each week of development. Just days earlier we had sat with the book, studying the photos taken at twenty-one weeks and marveling at how our baby was coming along. At twenty-one weeks a fetus can fit in the palm of a hand. It weighs less than a pound. Its eyes are fused shut, its fingers like fragile little twigs, its lungs not yet developed enough to distill oxygen from air. At twenty-one weeks, a baby is barely viable. The chance of surviving outside the womb is small, and the chance of surviving without serious, long-term health problems smaller yet. There's a reason nature keeps babies in the womb for nine long months. At twenty-one weeks, the odds are exceptionally long.

"It's probably nothing," I said. But I could feel my heart pounding as I speed-dialed the ob-gyn answering service. Two minutes later Dr. Sherman called back, sounding groggy himself. "It might just be gas," he said, "but we better have a look." He told me to get Jenny to the hospital immediately. I raced around the house, throwing items into an overnight bag for her, making baby bottles, packing the diaper bag. Jenny called her friend and coworker Sandy, another new mom who lived a few blocks away, and asked if we could drop Patrick off. Marley was up now, too, stretching, yawning, shaking. *Late-night road trip!* "Sorry, Mar," I told him as I led him out to the garage, grave disappointment on his face. "You've got to hold down the fort." I scooped Patrick out of his crib, buckled him into his car seat without waking him, and into the night we went.

At St. Mary's neonatal intensive care unit, the nurses quickly went to work. They got Jenny into a hospital gown and hooked her to a monitor that measured contractions and the baby's heartbeat. Sure enough, Jenny was having a contraction every six minutes. This was definitely not gas. "Your baby wants to come out," one of the nurses said. "We're going to do everything we can to make sure he doesn't just yet."

Over the phone Dr. Sherman asked them to check whether she was dilating. A nurse inserted a gloved finger and reported that Jenny was dilated one centimeter. Even I knew this was not good. At ten centimeters the cervix is fully dilated, the point at which, in a normal delivery, the mother begins to push. With each painful cramp, Jenny's body was pushing her one step closer to the point of no return.

Dr. Sherman ordered an intravenous saline drip and an injection of the labor inhibitor Brethine. The contractions leveled out, but less than two hours later they were back again with a fury, requiring a second shot, then a third.

For the next twelve days Jenny remained hospitalized, poked and prodded by a parade of perinatalogists and tethered to monitors and intravenous drips. I took vacation time and played single parent to Patrick, doing my best to hold everything together— the laundry, the feedings, meals, bills, housework, the yard. Oh, yes, and that other living creature in our home. Poor Marley's status dropped precipitously from second fiddle to not even in the orchestra. Even as I ignored him, he kept up his end of the relationship, never letting me out of his sight. He faithfully followed me as I careened through the house with Patrick in one arm, vacuuming or toting laundry or fixing a meal with the other. I would stop in the kitchen to toss a few dirty plates into the dishwasher, and Marley would plod in after me, circle around a half dozen times trying to pinpoint the exact perfect location, and then drop to the floor. No sooner had he settled in than I would dart to the laundry room to move the clothes from the washing machine to the dryer. He would follow after me, circle around, paw at the throw rugs until they were arranged to his liking, and plop down again, only to have me head for the living room to pick up the newspapers. So it would go. If he was lucky, I would pause in my mad dash to give him a quick pat.

One night after I finally got Patrick to sleep, I fell back on the couch, exhausted. Marley pranced over and dropped his rope tug toy in my lap and looked up at me with those giant brown eyes of his. "Aw, Marley," I said. "I'm beat." He put his snout under the rope toy and flicked it up in the air, waiting for me to try to grab it, ready to beat me to the draw. "Sorry, pal," I said. "Not tonight." He crinkled his brow and cocked his head. Suddenly, his comfortable daily routine was in tatters. His mistress was mysteriously absent, his master no fun, and nothing the same. He let out a little whine, and I could see he was trying to figure it out. *Why doesn't John want to play anymore? What happened to the morning walks? Why no more wrestling on the floor? And where exactly is Jenny, anyway? She hasn't run off with that Dalmatian in the next block, has she?*

Life wasn't completely bleak for Marley. On the bright side, I had quickly reverted to my premarriage (read: slovenly) lifestyle. By the power vested in me as the only adult in the house, I suspended the Married Couple Domesticity Act and proclaimed the once banished Bachelor Rules to be the law of the land. While Jenny was in the hospital, shirts would be worn twice, even three times, barring obvious mustard stains, between washes; milk could be drunk directly from the carton, and toilet seats would remain in the upright position unless being sat on. Much to Marley's delight, I instituted a 24/7 open-door policy for the bathroom. After all, it was just us guys. This gave Marley yet a new opportunity for closeness in a confined space. From there, it only made sense to let him start drinking from the bathtub tap. Jenny would have been appalled, but the way I saw it, it sure beat the toilet. Now that the Seat-Up Policy was firmly in place (and thus, by definition, the Lid-Up Policy, too), I needed to offer Marley a viable alternative to that attractive porcelain pool of water just begging him to play submarine with his snout.

I got into the habit of turning the bathtub faucet on at a trickle while I was in the bathroom so Marley could lap up some cool, fresh water. The dog could not have been more thrilled had I built him an exact replica of Splash Mountain. He would twist his head up under the faucet and lap away, tail banging the sink behind him. His thirst had no bounds, and I became convinced he had been a camel in an earlier life. I soon realized I had created a bathtub monster; pretty soon Marley began going into the bathroom alone without me and standing there, staring forlornly at the faucet, licking at it for any lingering drop, flicking the drain knob with his nose until I couldn't stand it any longer and would come in and turn it on for him. Suddenly the water in his bowl was somehow beneath him.

The next step on our descent into barbarity came when I was showering. Marley figured out he could shove his head past the shower curtain and get not just a trickle but a whole waterfall. I'd be lathering up and without warning his big tawny head would pop in and he'd begin lapping at the shower spray. "Just don't tell Mom," I said.

I tried to fool Jenny into thinking I had everything effortlessly under control. "Oh, we're totally fine," I told her, and then, turning to Patrick, I would add, "aren't we, partner?" To which he would give his standard reply: "Dada!" and then, pointing at the ceiling fan: "Fannnnn!" She knew better. One day when I arrived with Patrick for our daily visit, she stared at us in disbelief and asked, "What in God's name did you do to him?"

"What do you mean, what did I do to him?" I replied. "He's great. You're great, aren't you?"

"Dada! Fannnn!"

"His outfit," she said. "How on earth—"

Only then did I see. Something was amiss with Patrick's snap-on one-piece, or "onesie" as we manly dads like to call it. His chubby thighs, I now realized, were squeezed into the armholes, which were so tight they must have been cutting off his circulation. The collared neck hung between his legs like an udder. Up top, Patrick's head stuck out through the unsnapped crotch, and his arms were lost somewhere in the billowing pant legs. It was quite a look.

"You goof," she said. "You've got it on him upside down."

"That's your opinion," I said.

But the game was up. Jenny began working the phone from her hospital bed, and a couple of days later my sweet, dear aunt Anita, a retired nurse who had come to America from Ireland as a teenager and now lived across the state from us, magically appeared, suitcase in hand, and cheerfully went about restoring order. The Bachelor Rules were history.

When her doctors finally let Jenny come home, it was with the strictest of orders. If she wanted to deliver a healthy baby, she was to remain in bed, as still as possible. The only time she was allowed on her feet was to go to the bathroom. She could take one quick shower a day, then back into bed. No cooking, no changing diapers, no walking out for the mail, no lifting anything heavier than a toothbrush—and that meant her baby, a stipulation that nearly killed her. Complete bed rest, no cheating. Jenny's doctors had successfully shut down the early labor; their goal now was to keep it shut down for the next twelve weeks minimum. By then the baby would be thirty-five weeks along, still a little puny but fully developed and able to meet the outside world on its own terms. That meant keeping Jenny as still as a glacier. Aunt Anita, bless her charitable soul, settled in for the long haul. Marley was tickled to have a new playmate. Pretty soon he had Aunt Anita trained, too, to turn on the bathtub faucet for him.

A hospital technician came to our home and inserted a catheter into Jenny's thigh; this she attached to a small battery-powered pump that strapped to Jenny's leg and delivered a continuous trickle of labor-inhibiting drugs into her bloodstream. As if that weren't enough, she rigged Jenny with a monitoring system that looked like a torture device—

an oversized suction cup attached to a tangle of wires that hooked into the telephone. The suction cup attached to Jenny's belly with an elastic band and registered the baby's heartbeat and any contractions, sending them via phone line three times a day to a nurse who watched for the first hint of trouble. I ran down to the bookstore and returned with a small fortune in reading materials, which Jenny devoured in the first three days. She was trying to keep her spirits up, but the boredom, the tedium, the hourly uncertainty about the health of her unborn child, were conspiring to drag her down. Worst of all, she was a mother with a fifteen-month-old son whom she was not allowed to lift, to run to, to feed when he was hungry, to bathe when he was dirty, to scoop up and kiss when he was sad. I would drop him on top of her on the bed, where he would pull her hair and stick his fingers into her mouth. He'd point to the whirling paddles above the bed, and say, "Mama! Fannnnn!" It made her smile, but it wasn't the same. She was slowly going stir-crazy.

Her constant companion through it all, of course, was Marley. He set up camp on the floor beside her, surrounding himself with a wide assortment of chew toys and rawhide bones just in case Jenny changed her mind and decided to jump out of bed and engage in a little spur-of-the-moment tug-of-war. There he held vigil, day and night. I would come home from work and find Aunt Anita in the kitchen cooking dinner, Patrick in his bouncy seat beside her. Then I would walk into the bedroom to find Marley standing beside the bed, chin on the mattress, tail wagging, nose nuzzled into Jenny's neck as she read or snoozed or merely stared at the

ceiling, her arm draped over his back. I marked off each day
on the calendar to help her track her progress, but it only
served as a reminder of how slowly each minute, each hour,
passed. Some people are content to spend their lives in idle
recline; Jenny was not one of them. She was born to bustle,
and the forced idleness dragged her down by imperceptible
degrees, a little more each day. She was like a sailor caught
in the doldrums, waiting with increasing desperation for the
faintest hint of a breeze to fill the sails and let the journey
continue. I tried to be encouraging, saying things like "A
year from now we're going to look back on this and laugh,"
but I could tell part of her was slipping from me. Some days
her eyes were very far away.

When Jenny had a full month of bed rest still to go, Aunt
Anita packed her suitcase and kissed us good-bye. She had
stayed as long as she could, in fact extending her visit several
times, but she had a husband at home who she only half
jokingly fretted was quite possibly turning feral as he survived alone on TV dinners and ESPN. Once again, we were
on our own.

I did my best to keep the ship afloat, rising at dawn to
bathe and dress Patrick, feed him oatmeal and puréed
carrots, and take him and Marley for at least a short walk.
Then I would drop Patrick at Sandy's house for the day while
I worked, picking him up again in the evening. I would
come home on my lunch hour to make Jenny her lunch,
bring her the mail—the highlight of her day—throw sticks
to Marley, and straighten up the house, which was slowly

taking on a patina of neglect. The grass went uncut, the laundry unwashed, and the screen on the back porch remained unrepaired after Marley crashed through it, cartoon-style, in pursuit of a squirrel. For weeks the shredded screen flapped in the breeze, becoming a de facto doggie door that allowed Marley to come and go as he pleased between the backyard and house during the long hours home alone with the bedridden Jenny. "I'm going to fix it," I promised her. "It's on the list." But I could see dismay in her eyes. It took all of her self-control not to jump out of bed and whip her home back into shape. I grocery-shopped after Patrick was asleep for the night, sometimes walking the aisles at midnight. We survived on carry-outs, Cheerios, and pots of pasta. The journal I had faithfully kept for years abruptly went silent.

There was simply no time and less energy. In the last brief entry, I wrote only: "Life is a little overwhelming right now."

Then one day, as we approached Jenny's thirty-fifth week of pregnancy, the hospital technician arrived at our door and said, "Congratulations, girl, you've made it. You're free again." She unhooked the medicine pump, removed the catheter, packed up the fetal monitor, and went over the doctor's written orders. Jenny was free to return to her regular lifestyle. No restrictions. No more medications. We could even have sex again. The baby was fully viable now. Labor would come when it would come. "Have fun," she said. "You deserve it."

Jenny tossed Patrick over her head, romped with Marley in the backyard, tore into the housework. That night we celebrated by going out for Indian food and catching a show at a local comedy club. The next day the three of us continued the festivities by having lunch at a Greek restaurant. Before the gyros ever made it to our table, however, Jenny was in full-blown labor. The cramps had begun the night before as she ate curried lamb, but she had ignored them. She wasn't going to let a few contractions interrupt her hard-earned night on the town. Now each contraction nearly doubled her over. We raced home, where Sandy was on standby to take Patrick and keep an eye on Marley. Jenny waited in the car, puffing her way through the pain with sharp, shallow breaths as I grabbed her overnight bag. By the time we got to the hospital and checked into a room, Jenny was dilated to seven centimeters. Less than an hour later, I held our new son in my arms. Jenny counted his fingers and toes. His eyes were open and alert, his cheeks blushed.

"You did it," Dr. Sherman declared. "He's perfect."

Conor Richard Grogan, five pounds and thirteen ounces, was born October 10, 1993. I was so happy I barely gave a second thought to the cruel irony that for this pregnancy we had rated one of the luxury suites but had hardly a moment to enjoy it. If the delivery had been any quicker, Jenny would have given birth in the parking lot of the Texaco station. I hadn't even had time to stretch out on the Dad Couch.

Considering what we had been through to bring him safely into this world, we thought the birth of our son was big news—but not so big that the local news media would turn out for it. Below our window, though, a crush of television news trucks gathered in the parking lot, their satellite dishes poking into the sky. I could see reporters with microphones doing their stand-ups in front of the cameras. "Hey, honey," I said, "the paparazzi have turned out for you."

A nurse, who was in the room attending to the baby, said, "Can you believe it? Donald Trump is right down the hall."

"Donald Trump?" Jenny asked. "I didn't know he was pregnant."

The real estate tycoon had caused quite a stir when he moved to Palm Beach several years earlier, setting up house in the sprawling former mansion of Marjorie Merriweather Post, the late cereal heiress. The estate was named Mar-a-Lago, meaning "Sea to Lake," and as the name implied, the property stretched for seventeen acres from the Atlantic Ocean to the Intracoastal Waterway and included a nine-hole golf course. From the foot of our street we could look across the water and see the fifty-eight-bedroom mansion's Moorish-influenced spires rising above the palm trees. The Trumps and the Grogans were practically neighbors.

I flicked on the TV and learned that The Donald and girlfriend Marla Maples were the proud parents of a girl, appropriately named Tiffany, who was born not long after Jenny delivered Conor. "We'll have to invite them over for a playdate," Jenny said.

We watched from the window as the television crews swarmed in to catch the Trumps leaving the hospital with their new baby to return to their estate. Marla smiled demurely as she held her newborn for the cameras to capture; Donald waved and gave a jaunty wink. "I feel great!" he told the cameras. Then they were off in a chauffeured limousine.

The next morning when our turn came to leave for home, a pleasant retiree who volunteered at the hospital guided Jenny and baby Conor through the lobby in a wheelchair and out the automatic doors into the sunshine. There were no camera crews, no satellite trucks, no sound bites, no live reports. It was just us and our senior volunteer. Not that anyone was asking, but I felt great, too. Donald Trump was not the only one bursting with pride over his progeny.

The volunteer waited with Jenny and the baby while I pulled the car up to the curb. Before buckling my newborn son into his car seat, I lifted him high above my head for the whole world to see, had anyone been looking, and said, "Conor Grogan, you are every bit as special as Tiffany Trump, and don't you ever forget it."

CHAPTER 15

A Postpartum Ultimatum

❄

These should have been the happiest days of our lives, and in many ways they were. We had two sons now, a toddler and a newborn, just seventeen months apart. The joy they brought us was profound. Yet the darkness that had descended over Jenny while she was on forced bed rest persisted. Some weeks she was fine, cheerfully tackling the challenges of being responsible for two lives completely dependent on her for every need. Other weeks, without warning, she would turn glum and defeated, locked in a blue fog that sometimes would not lift for days. We were both exhausted and sleep deprived. Patrick was still waking us at least once in the night, and Conor was up several more times, crying to be nursed or changed. Seldom did we get more than two hours of uninterrupted sleep at a stretch. Some nights we were like zombies, moving silently past each other with glazed eyes, Jenny to one baby and I to the other. We were up at midnight and at two and at three-thirty and again at five. Then the sun would rise and with it another day, bringing renewed hope and a bone-aching weariness as we began the cycle over again. From down the hall would come Patrick's sweet, cheery, wide-awake voice—"Mama! Dada! Fannnn!"—and as much as we tried to will it otherwise, we knew sleep, what there had been of it, was behind us for another day. I began making the coffee stronger and showing up at work with shirts wrinkled and baby spit-up on my ties. One morning in my newsroom, I caught the young, attractive editorial assistant staring intently at me. Flattered, I smiled at her. *Hey, I might be a dad twice over now, but the women still notice me.* Then she said, "Do you know you have a Barney sticker in your hair?"

Complicating the sleep-deprived chaos that was our lives, our new baby had us terribly worried. Already underweight, Conor was unable to keep nourishment down. Jenny was on a single-minded quest to nurse him to robust health, and he seemed equally intent on foiling her. She would offer him her breast, and he would oblige her, suckling hungrily. Then, in one quick heave, he would throw it all up. She would nurse him again; he would eat ravenously, then empty his stomach yet again. Projectile vomiting became an hourly occurrence in our lives. Over and over the routine repeated itself, each time Jenny becoming more frantic. The doctors diagnosed reflux and referred us to a specialist, who sedated our baby boy and snaked a scope down his throat to scrutinize his insides. Conor eventually would outgrow the condition and catch up on his weight, but for four long months we were consumed with worry over him. Jenny was a basket case of fear and stress and frustration, all exacerbated by lack of sleep, as she nursed him nearly nonstop and then watched helpless as he tossed her milk back at her. "I feel so inadequate," she

would say. "Moms are supposed to be able to give their babies everything they need." Her fuse was as short as I had seen it, and the smallest infractions—a cupboard door left open, crumbs on the counter—would set her off.

The good news was that Jenny never once took out her anxiety on either baby. In fact, she nurtured both of them with almost obsessive care and patience. She poured every ounce of herself into them. The bad news was that she directed her frustration and anger at me and even more at Marley. She had lost all patience with him. He was squarely in her crosshairs and could do no right. Each transgression—and there continued to be many—pushed Jenny a little closer to the edge. Oblivious, Marley stayed the course with his antics and misdeeds and boundless ebullience. I bought a flowering shrub and planted it in the garden to commemorate Conor's birth; Marley pulled it out by the roots the same day and chewed it into mulch. I finally got around to replacing the ripped porch screen, and Marley, by now quite accustomed to his self-made doggie door, promptly dove through it again. He escaped one day and when he finally returned, he had a pair of women's panties in his teeth. I didn't want to know.

Despite the prescription tranquilizers, which Jenny was feeding him with increasing frequency, more for her sake than for his, Marley's thunder phobia grew more intense and irrational each day. By now a soft shower would send him into a panic. If we were home, he would merely glom on to us and salivate nervously all over our clothes. If we weren't home, he sought safety in the same warped way, by digging and gouging through doors and plaster and linoleum. The more I repaired, the more he destroyed. I could not keep up with him. I should have been furious, but Jenny was angry enough for both of us. Instead, I started covering for him. If I found a chewed shoe or book or pillow, I hid the evidence before she could find it. When he crashed through our small home, the bull in our china closet, I followed behind him, straightening throw rugs, righting coffee tables, and wiping up the spittle he flung on the walls. Before Jenny discovered them, I would race to vacuum up the wood chips in the garage where he had gouged the door once again. I stayed up late into the night patching and sanding so by morning when Jenny awoke the latest damage would be covered over. "For God's sake, Marley, do you have a death wish?" I said to him one night as he stood at my side, tail wagging, licking my ear as I knelt and repaired the most recent destruction. "You've got to stop this."

It was into this volatile environment that I walked one evening. I opened the front door to find Jenny beating Marley with her fists. She was crying uncontrollably and flailing wildly at him, more like she was pounding a kettledrum than imposing a beating, landing glancing blows on his back and shoulders and neck. "Why? Why do you do this?" she screamed at him. "Why do you wreck everything?" In that instant I saw what he had done. The couch cushion was gouged open, the fabric shredded and the stuffing pulled out. Marley stood with head down and legs splayed as though leaning into a hurricane. He didn't try to flee or dodge the blows; he just stood there and took each one without whimper or complaint.

"Hey! Hey! Hey!" I shouted, grabbing her wrists. "Come on. Stop. Stop!" She was sobbing and gasping for breath. "Stop," I repeated.

I stepped between her and Marley and shoved my face directly in front of hers. It was like a stranger was staring back at me. I did not recognize the look in her eyes. "Get him out of here," she said, her voice flat and tinged with a quiet burn. "Get him out of here now."

"Okay, I'll take him out," I said, "but you settle down."

"Get him out of here and keep him out of here," she said in an unsettling monotone.

I opened the front door and he bounded outside, and when I turned back to grab his leash off the table, Jenny said, "I mean it. I want him gone. I want him out of here for good."

"Come on," I said. "You don't mean that."

"I mean it," she said. "I'm done with that dog. You find him a new home, or I will."

She couldn't mean it. She loved this dog. She adored him despite his laundry list of shortcomings. She was upset; she was stressed to the breaking point. She would reconsider. For the moment I thought it was best to give her time to cool down. I walked out the door without another word. In the front yard, Marley raced around, jumping into the air and snapping his jaws, trying to bite the leash out of my hand. He was his old jolly self, apparently no worse for the pummeling. I knew she hadn't hurt him. In all honesty, I routinely whacked him much harder when I played rough with him, and he loved it, always bounding back for more. As was a hallmark of his breed, he was immune to pain, an unstoppable machine of muscle and sinew. Once when I was in the driveway washing the car, he jammed his head into the bucket of soapy water and galloped blindly off across the front lawns with the bucket firmly stuck over his head, not stopping until he crashed full force into a concrete wall. It didn't seem to faze him. But slap him lightly on the rump with an open palm in anger, or even just speak to him with a stern voice, and he acted deeply wounded. For the big dense oaf that he was, Marley had an incredibly sensitive streak. Jenny hadn't hurt him physically, not even close, but she had crushed his feelings, at least for the moment. Jenny was everything to him, one of his two best pals in the whole world, and she had just turned on him. She was his mistress and he her faithful companion. If she saw fit to strike him, he saw fit to suck it up and take it. As far as dogs went, he was not good at much; but he was unquestionably loyal. It was my job now to repair the damage and make things right again.

Out in the street, I hooked him to his leash and ordered, "Sit!" He sat. I pulled the choker chain up high on his throat in preparation for our walk. Before I stepped off I ran my hand over his head and massaged his neck. He flipped his nose in the air and looked up at me, his tongue hanging halfway down his neck. The incident with Jenny appeared to be behind him; now I hoped it would be behind her, as well. "What am I going to do with you, you big dope?" I asked him. He leaped straight up, as though outfitted with springs, and smashed his tongue against my lips.

Marley and I walked for miles that evening, and when I finally opened the front door, he was exhausted and ready to collapse quietly in the corner. Jenny was feeding Patrick a jar of baby food as she cradled Conor in her lap. She was calm and appeared back to her old self. I unleashed Marley and he took a huge drink, lapping lustily at the water, sloshing little tidal waves over the side of his bowl. I toweled up the floor and stole a glance in

Jenny's direction; she appeared unperturbed. Maybe the horrible moment had passed. Maybe she had reconsidered. Maybe she felt sheepish about her outburst and was searching for the words to apologize. As I walked past her, Marley close at my heels, she said in a calm, quiet voice without looking at me, "I'm dead serious. I want him out of here."

Over the next several days she repeated the ultimatum enough times that I finally accepted that this was not an idle threat. She wasn't just blowing off steam, and the issue was not going away. I was sick about it. As pathetic as it sounds, Marley had become my male-bonding soul mate, my near-constant companion, my friend. He was the undisciplined, recalcitrant, nonconformist, politically incorrect free spirit I had always wanted to be, had I been brave enough, and I took vicarious joy in his unbridled verve. No matter how complicated life became, he reminded me of its simple joys. No matter how many demands were placed on me, he never let me forget that willful disobedience is sometimes worth the price. In a world full of bosses, he was his own master. The thought of giving him up seared my soul. But I had two children to worry about now and a wife whom we needed. Our household was being held together by the most tenuous of threads. If losing Marley made the difference between meltdown and stability, how could I not honor Jenny's wishes?

I began putting out feelers, discreetly asking friends and coworkers if they might be interested in taking on a lovable and lively two-year-old Labrador retriever. Through word of mouth, I learned of a neighbor who adored dogs and couldn't refuse a canine in need. Even he said no. Unfortunately, Marley's reputation preceded him.

Each morning I opened the newspaper to the classifieds as if I might find some miracle ad: "Seeking wildly energetic, out-of-control Labrador retriever with multiple phobias. Destructive qualities a plus. Will pay top dollar." What I found instead was a booming trade in young adult dogs that, for whatever reason, had not worked out. Many were purebreds that their owners had spent several hundred dollars for just months earlier. Now they were being offered for a pittance or even for free. An alarming number of the unwanted dogs were male Labs.

The ads were in almost every day, and were at once heartbreaking and hilarious. From my insider's vantage point, I recognized the attempts to gloss over the real reasons these dogs were back on the market. The ads were full of sunny euphemisms for the types of behavior I knew all too well. "Lively . . . loves people . . . needs big yard . . . needs room to run . . . energetic . . . spirited . . . powerful . . . one of a kind." It all added up to the same thing: a dog its master could not control. A dog that had become a liability. A dog its owner had given up on.

Part of me laughed knowingly; the ads were comical in their deception. When I read "fiercely loyal" I knew the seller really meant "known to bite." "Constant companion" meant "suffers separation anxiety," and "good watchdog" translated to "incessant barker." And when I saw "best offer," I knew too well that the desperate owner really was asking, "How much do I need to pay you to take this thing off my hands?" Part of me ached with sadness. I was not a quitter; I did not believe Jenny was a quitter, either. We were not the kind of people who pawned off our problems in the classifieds. Marley was undeniably a handful. He was nothing like the stately dogs both of us had grown up with. He had a host of bad habits and behaviors. Guilty as charged. He also had come a great distance from the spastic puppy we had brought home two years earlier. In his own flawed way, he was trying. Part of our journey as his owners was to mold him to our needs, but part also was to accept him for what he was. Not just to accept him, but to celebrate him and his indomitable canine spirit. We had brought into our home a living, breathing being, not a fashion accessory to prop in the corner. For better or worse, he was our dog. He was a part of our family, and, for all his flaws, he had returned our affection one hundredfold. Devotion such as his could not be bought for any price.

I was not ready to give up on him.

Even as I continued to make halfhearted inquiries about finding Marley a new home, I began working with him in earnest. My own private Mission: Impossible was to rehabilitate this dog and prove to Jenny he was worthy. Interrupted sleep be damned, I began rising at dawn, buckling Patrick into the jogging stroller, and heading down to the water to put Marley through the paces. Sit. Stay. Down. Heel. Over and over we practiced. There was a desperation to my mission, and Marley seemed to sense it. The stakes were different now; this was for real. In case he didn't fully understand that, I spelled it out for him more than once without mincing words: "We're not screwing around here, Marley. This is it. Let's go." And I would put him through the commands again, with my helper Patrick clapping and calling to his big yellow friend, "Waddy! Hee-O!"

By the time I reenrolled Marley in obedience school, he was a different dog from the juvenile delinquent I had first shown up with. Yes, still as wild as a boar, but this time he knew I was the boss and he was the underling. This time there would be no lunges toward other dogs (or at least not many), no out-of-control surges across the tarmac, no crashing into strangers' crotches. Through eight weekly sessions, I marched him through the commands on a tight leash, and he was happy—make that overjoyed—to cooperate. At our final meeting, the trainer—a relaxed woman who was the antithesis of Miss Dominatrix—called us forward. "Okay," she said, "show us what you've got."

I ordered Marley into a sit position, and he dropped neatly to his haunches. I raised the choker chain high around his throat and with a crisp tug of the lead ordered him to heel. We trotted across the parking lot and back, Marley at my side, his shoulder brushing my calf, just as the book said it should. I ordered him to sit again, and I stood directly in front of him and pointed my finger at his forehead. "Stay," I said calmly, and with the other hand I dropped his leash. I stepped backward several paces. His big brown eyes fixed on me, waiting for any small sign from me to release him, but he remained anchored. I walked in a 360-degree circle around him. He quivered with excitement and tried to rotate his head, Linda Blair–style, to watch me, but he did not budge. When I was back in front of him, just for kicks, I snapped my fingers and yelled, "Incoming!" He hit the deck like he was storming Iwo Jima. The teacher burst out laughing, a good sign. I turned my back on him and walked thirty feet away. I could feel his eyes burning into my back, but he held fast. He was quaking violently by the time I turned around to face him. The volcano was getting ready to blow. Then, spreading my feet into a wide boxer's stance in anticipation of what was coming, I said, "Marley . . ." I let his name hang in the air for a few seconds. "Come!" He shot at me with everything he had, and I braced for impact. At the last instant I deftly sidestepped him with a bullfighter's grace, and he blasted past me, then circled back and goosed me from behind with his nose.

"Good boy, Marley," I gushed, dropping to my knees. "Good, good, good boy! You a good boy!" He danced around me like we had just conquered Mount Everest together.

At the end of the evening, the instructor called us up and handed us our diploma. Marley had passed basic obedience training, ranking seventh in the class. So what if it was a class of eight and the eighth dog was a psychopathic pit bull that seemed intent on taking a human life at the first opportunity? I would take it. Marley, my incorrigible, untrainable, undisciplined dog, had passed. I was so proud I could have cried, and in fact I actually might have had Marley not leapt up and promptly eaten his diploma.

On the way home, I sang "We Are the Champions" at the top of my lungs. Marley, sensing my joy and pride, stuck his tongue in my ear. For once, I didn't even mind.

There was still one piece of unfinished business between Marley and me. I needed to break him of his worst habit of all: jumping on people. It didn't matter if it was a friend or a stranger, a child or an adult, the meter reader or the UPS driver. Marley greeted them the same way—by charging at them full speed, sliding across the floor, leaping up, and planting his two front paws on the person's chest or shoulders as he licked their face. What had been cute when he was a cuddly puppy had turned obnoxious, even terrifying for some recipients of his uninvited advances. He had knocked over children, startled guests, dirtied our friends' dress shirts and blouses, and nearly taken down my frail mother. No one appreciated it. I had tried without success to break him of jumping up, using standard dog-obedience techniques. The message was not getting through. Then a veteran dog owner I respected said, "You want to break him of that, give him a swift knee in the chest next time he jumps up on you."

"I don't want to hurt him," I said.

"You won't hurt him. A few good jabs with your knee, and I guarantee you he'll be done jumping."

It was tough-love time. Marley had to reform or relocate. The next night when I arrived home from work, I stepped in the front door and yelled, "I'm home!" As usual, Marley came barreling across the wood floors to greet me. He slid the last ten feet as though on ice, then lifted off to smash his paws into my chest and slurp at my face. Just as his paws made contact with me, I gave one swift pump of my knee, connecting in the soft spot just below his rib cage. He gasped slightly and slid down to the floor, looking up at me with a wounded expression, trying to figure out what had gotten into me. He had been jumping on me his whole life; what was with the sudden sneak attack?

The next night I repeated the punishment. He leapt, I

kneed, he dropped to the floor, coughing. I felt a little cruel, but if I were going to save him from the classifieds, I knew I had to drive home the point. "Sorry, guy," I said, leaning down so he could lick me with all four paws on the ground. "It's for your own good."

The third night when I walked in, he came charging around the corner, going into his typical high-speed skid as he approached. This time, however, he altered the routine. Instead of leaping, he kept his paws on the ground and crashed headfirst into my knees, nearly knocking me over. I'd take that as a victory. "You did it, Marley! You did it! Good boy! You didn't jump up." And I got on my knees so he could slobber me without risking a sucker punch. I was impressed. Marley had bent to the power of persuasion.

The problem was not exactly solved, however. He may have been cured of jumping on me, but he was not cured of jumping on anyone else. The dog was smart enough to figure out that only I posed a threat, and he could still jump on the rest of the human race with impunity. I needed to widen my offensive, and to do that I recruited a good friend of mine from work, a reporter named Jim Tolpin. Jim was a mild-mannered, bookish sort, balding, bespectacled, and of slight build. If there was anyone Marley thought he could jump up on without consequence, it was Jim. At the office one day I laid out the plan. He was to come to the house after work, ring the doorbell, and then walk in. When Marley jumped up to kiss him, he was to give him all he had. "Don't be shy about it," I coached. "Subtlety is lost on Marley."

That night Jim rang the bell and walked in the door. Sure enough, Marley took the bait and raced at him, ears flying back. When Marley left the ground to leap up on him, Jim took my advice to heart. Apparently worried he would be too timid, he dealt a withering blow with his knee to Marley's solar plexus, knocking the wind out of him. The thud was audible across the room. Marley let out a loud moan, went bug-eyed, and sprawled on the floor.

"Jesus, Jim," I said. "Have you been studying kung fu?"

"You told me to make him feel it," he answered.

He had. Marley got to his feet, caught his breath, and greeted Jim the way a dog should—on all four paws. If he could have talked, I swear he would have cried uncle. Marley never again jumped up on anyone, at least not in my presence, and no one ever kneed him in the chest or anywhere else again.

One morning, not long after Marley abandoned his jumping habit, I woke up and my wife was back. My Jenny, the woman I loved who had disappeared into that unyielding blue fog, had returned to me. As suddenly as the postpartum depression had swept over her, it swept away again. It was as if she had been exorcised of her demons. They were gone. Blessedly gone. She was strong, she was upbeat, she was not only coping as a young mother of two, but thriving. Marley was back in her good graces, safely on solid ground. With a baby in each arm, she leaned to kiss him. She threw him sticks and made him gravy from hamburger drippings. She danced him around the room when a good song came on the stereo. Sometimes at night when he was calm, I would find her lying on the floor with him, her head resting on his neck. Jenny was back. Thank God, she was back.

CHAPTER 16

The Audition

✳

S ome things in life are just too bizarre to be anything but true, so when Jenny called me at the office to tell me Marley was getting a film audition, I knew she couldn't be making it up. Still, I was in disbelief. "A what?" I asked.

"A film audition."

"Like for a movie?"

"Yes, like for a movie, dumbo," she said. "A feature-length movie."

"Marley? A feature-length movie?"

We went on like this for some time as I tried to reconcile the image of our lug-head chewer of ironing boards with the image of a proud successor to Rin Tin Tin leaping across the silver screen, pulling helpless children from burning buildings.

"Our Marley?" I asked one more time, just to be sure.

It was true. A week earlier, Jenny's supervisor at the *Palm Beach Post* called and said she had a friend who needed to ask a favor of us. The friend was a local photographer named

Colleen McGarr who had been hired by a New York City film-production company called the Shooting Gallery to help with a movie they planned to make in Lake Worth, the town just south of us. Colleen's job was to find a "quintessential South Florida household" and photograph it top to bottom—the bookshelves, the refrigerator magnets, the closets, you name it—to help the directors bring realism to the film.

"The whole set crew is gay," Jenny's boss told her. "They're trying to figure out how married couples with kids live around here."

"Sort of like an anthropological case study," Jenny said.

"Exactly."

"Sure," Jenny agreed, "as long as I don't have to clean first."

Colleen came over and started photographing, not just our possessions but us, too. The way we dressed, the way we wore our hair, the way we slouched on the couch. She photographed toothbrushes on the sink. She photographed the babies in their cribs. She photographed the quintessentially heterosexual couple's eunuch dog, too. Or at least what she could catch of him on film. As she observed, "He's a bit of a blur."

Marley could not have been more thrilled to participate. Ever since babies had invaded, Marley took his affection where he could find it. Colleen could have jabbed him with a cattle prod; as long as he was getting some attention, he was okay with it. Colleen, being a lover of large animals and not intimidated by saliva showers, gave him plenty, dropping to her knees to wrestle with him.

As Colleen clicked away, I couldn't help thinking of the

possibilities. Not only were we supplying raw anthropological data to the filmmakers, we were essentially being given
our own personal casting call. I had heard that most of the
secondary actors and all of the extras for this film would be
hired locally. What if the director spotted a natural star amid
the kitchen magnets and poster art? Stranger things had
happened.

I could just picture the director, who in my fantasy
looked a lot like Steven Spielberg, bent over a large table
scattered with hundreds of photographs. He flips impatiently through them, muttering, "Garbage! Garbage! This
just won't do." Then he freezes over a single snapshot. In
it a rugged yet sensitive, quintessentially heterosexual male
goes about his family-man business. The director stubs his
finger heavily into the photo and shouts to his assistants,
"Get me this man! I must have him for my film!" When
they finally track me down, I at first humbly demur before
finally agreeing to take the starring role. After all, the show
must go on.

Colleen thanked us for opening our home to her and left.
She gave us no reason to believe she or anyone else
associated with the movie would be calling back. Our duty
was now fulfilled. But a few days later when Jenny called me
at work to say, "I just got off the phone with Colleen
McGarr, and you are NOT going to believe it," I had no
doubt whatsoever that I had just been discovered. My heart
leapt. "Go on," I said.

"She says the director wants Marley to try out."

"Marley?" I asked, certain I had misheard. She didn't seem
to notice the dismay in my voice.

"Apparently, he's looking for a big, dumb, loopy dog to play the role of the family pet, and Marley caught his eye."

"Loopy?" I asked.

"That's what Colleen says he wants. Big, dumb, and loopy."

Well, he had certainly come to the right place. "Did Colleen mention if he said anything about me?" I asked.

"No," Jenny said. "Why would he?"

Colleen picked Marley up the next day. Knowing the importance of a good entrance, he came racing through the living room to greet her at full bore, pausing only long enough to grab the nearest pillow in his teeth because you never knew when a busy film director might need a quick nap, and if he did, Marley wanted to be ready.

When he hit the wood floor, he flew into a full skid, which did not stop until he hit the coffee table, went airborne, crashed into a chair, landed on his back, rolled, righted himself, and collided head-on with Colleen's legs. At least he didn't jump up, I noted.

"Are you sure you don't want us to sedate him?" Jenny asked.

The director would want to see him in his unbridled, unmedicated state, Colleen insisted, and off she went with our desperately happy dog beside her in her red pickup truck.

Two hours later Colleen and Company were back and the verdict was in: Marley had passed the audition. "Oh, shut up!" Jenny shrieked. "No way!" Our elation was not dampened a bit when Colleen told us Marley was the only one up for the part. Nor when she broke the news that his would be the only nonpaying role in the movie.

I asked her how the audition went.

"I got Marley in the car and it was like driving in a Jacuzzi," she said. "He was slobbering on everything. By the time I got him there, I was drenched." When they arrived at production headquarters at the GulfStream Hotel, a faded tourist landmark from an earlier era overlooking the Intracoastal Waterway, Marley immediately impressed the crew by jumping out of the truck and tearing around the parking lot in random patterns as if expecting the aerial bombing to commence at any moment. "He was just berserk," she recounted, "completely mental."

"Yeah, he gets a little excited," I said.

At one point, she said, Marley grabbed the checkbook out of a crew member's hand and raced away, running a series of tight figure-eights to nowhere, apparently determined this was one way to guarantee a paycheck.

"We call him our Labrador evader," Jenny apologized with the kind of smile only a proud mother can give.

Marley eventually calmed down enough to convince everyone he could do the part, which was basically to just play himself. The movie was called *The Last Home Run,* a baseball fantasy in which a seventy-nine-year-old nursing home resident becomes a twelve-year-old for five days to live his dream of playing Little League ball. Marley was cast as the hyperactive family dog of the Little League coach, played by retired major-league catcher Gary Carter.

"They really want him to be in their movie?" I asked, still incredulous.

"Everyone loved him," Colleen said. "He's perfect."

In the days leading up to shooting, we noticed a certain

subtle change in Marley's bearing. A strange calm had come
over him. It was as if passing the audition had given him new
confidence. He was almost regal. "Maybe he just needed
someone to believe in him," I told Jenny.

If anyone believed, it was her, Stage Mom Extraordinaire.
As the first day of filming approached, she bathed him. She
brushed him. She clipped his nails and swabbed out his ears.

On the morning shooting was to begin, I walked out of
the bedroom to find Jenny and Marley tangled together as if
locked in mortal combat, bouncing across the room. She
was straddling him with her knees tightly hugging his ribs
and one hand grasping the end of his choker chain as he
bucked and lurched. It was like having a rodeo right in my
own living room. "What in God's name are you doing?" I
asked.

"What's it look like?" she shot back. "Brushing his teeth!"

Sure enough, she had a toothbrush in the other hand and
was doing her best to scrub his big white ivories as Marley,
frothing prodigiously at the mouth, did his best to eat the
toothbrush. He looked positively rabid.

"Are you using toothpaste?" I asked, which of course
begged the bigger question, "And how exactly do you
propose getting him to spit it out?"

"Baking soda," she answered.

"Thank God," I said. "So it's *not* rabies?"

An hour later we left for the GulfStream Hotel, the boys in
their car seats and Marley between them, panting away with
uncharacteristically fresh breath. Our instructions were to
arrive by 9:00 A.M., but a block away, traffic came to a
standstill. Up ahead the road was barricaded and a police

officer was diverting traffic away from the hotel. The filming had been covered at length in the newspapers—the biggest event to hit sleepy Lake Worth since *Body Heat* was filmed there fifteen years earlier—and a crowd of spectators had turned out to gawk. The police were keeping everyone away. We inched forward in traffic, and when we finally got up to the officer I leaned out the window and said, "We need to get through."

"No one gets through," he said. "Keep moving. Let's go."

"We're with the cast," I said.

He eyed us skeptically, a couple in a minivan with two toddlers and family pet in tow. "I said move it!" he barked.

"Our dog is in the film," I said.

Suddenly he looked at me with new respect. "You have the dog?" he asked. The dog was on his checklist.

"I have the dog," I said. "Marley the dog."

"Playing himself," Jenny chimed in.

He turned around and blew his whistle with great fanfare. "He's got the dog!" he shouted to a cop a half block down. "Marley the Dog!"

And that cop in turn yelled to someone else, "He's got the dog! Marley the Dog's here!"

"Let 'em through!" a third officer shouted from the distance.

"Let 'em through!" the second cop echoed.

The officer moved the barricade and waved us through. "Right this way," he said politely. I felt like royalty. As we rolled past him he said once again, as if he couldn't quite believe it, "He's got the dog."

In the parking lot outside the hotel, the film crew was ready for action. Cables crisscrossed the pavement; camera tripods and microphone booms were set up. Lights hung from scaffolding. Trailers held racks of costumes. Two large tables of food and drinks were set up in the shade for cast and crew. Important-looking people in sunglasses bustled about. Director Bob Gosse greeted us and gave us a quick rundown of the scene to come. It was simple enough. A minivan pulls up to the curb, Marley's make-believe owner, played by the actress Liza Harris, is at the wheel. Her daughter, played by a cute teenager named Danielle from the local performing-arts school, and son, another local budding actor not older than nine, are in the back with their family dog, played by Marley. The daughter opens the sliding door and hops out; her brother follows with Marley on a leash. They walk off camera. End of scene.

"Easy enough," I told the director. "He should be able to handle that, no problem." I pulled Marley off to the side to wait for his cue to get into the van.

"Okay, people, listen up," Gosse told the crew. "The dog's a little nutty, all right? But unless he completely hijacks the scene, we're going to keep rolling." He explained his thinking: Marley was the real thing—a typical family dog— and the goal was to capture him behaving as a typical family dog would behave on a typical family outing. No acting or coaching; pure cinema verité. "Just let him do his thing," he coached, "and work around him."

When everyone was set to go, I loaded Marley into the van and handed his nylon leash to the little boy, who looked terrified of him. "He's friendly," I told him. "He'll just want to lick you. See?" I stuck my wrist into Marley's mouth to demonstrate.

Take one: The van pulls to the curb. The instant the daughter slides open the side door, a yellow streak shoots out like a giant fur ball being fired from a cannon and blurs past the cameras trailing a red leash.

"Cut!"

I chased Marley down in the parking lot and hauled him back.

"Okay, folks, we're going to try that again," Gosse said. Then to the boy he coached gently, "The dog's pretty wild. Try to hold on tighter this time."

Take two. The van pulls to the curb. The door slides open. The daughter is just beginning to exit when Marley huffs into view and leaps out past her, this time dragging the white-knuckled and white-faced boy behind him.

"Cut!"

Take three. The van pulls up. The door slides open. The daughter exits. The boy exits, holding the leash. As he steps away from the van the leash pulls taut, stretching back inside, but no dog follows. The boy begins to tug, heave, and pull. He leans into it and gives it everything he has. Not a budge. Long, painfully empty seconds pass. The boy grimaces and looks back at the camera.

"Cut!"

I peered into the van to find Marley bent over licking himself where no male was ever meant to lick. He looked up at me as if to say, *Can't you see I'm busy?*

Take four: I load Marley into the back of the van with the boy and shut the door. Before Gosse calls "Action!" he breaks for a few minutes to confer with his assistants. Finally, the scene rolls. The van pulls to the curb. The door slides open. The daughter steps out. The boy steps out, but with a bewildered look on his face. He peers directly into the camera and holds up his hand. Dangling from it is half the leash, its end jagged and wet with saliva.

"Cut! Cut! Cut!"

The boy explained that as he waited in the van, Marley began gnawing on the leash and wouldn't stop. The crew and cast were staring at the severed leash in disbelief, a mix of awe and horror on their faces as though they had just witnessed some great and mysterious force of nature. I, on the other hand, was not surprised in the least. Marley had sent more leashes and ropes to their graves than I could count; he even managed to chew his way through a rubber-coated steel cable that was advertised "as used in the airline industry." Shortly after Conor was born, Jenny came home with a new product, a doggie travel harness that allowed her to buckle Marley into a car seat belt so he couldn't wander around the moving vehicle. In the first ninety seconds using the new device, he managed to chew through not only the heavy harness itself but the shoulder strap of our brand-new minivan.

"Okay, everybody, let's take a break!" Gosse called out. Turning to me, he asked—in an amazingly calm voice— "How quickly can you find a new leash?" He didn't have to tell me how much each lost minute cost him as his union-scale actors and crew sat idle.

"There's a pet store a half mile from here," I said. "I can be back in fifteen minutes."

"And this time get something he can't chew through," he said.

I returned with a heavy chain leash that looked like something a lion trainer might use, and the filming continued, take after failed take. Each scene was worse than the one before. At one point, Danielle the teenage actress let out a desperate shriek mid-scene and screamed with true horror in her voice, "Oh my God! His thing is out!"

"Cut!"

In another scene, Marley was panting so loudly at Danielle's feet as she spoke on the telephone to her love interest that the sound engineer flipped off his headphones in disgust and complained loudly, "I can't hear a word she's saying. All I hear is heavy breathing. It sounds like a porn flick."

"Cut!"

So went day 1 of shooting. Marley was a disaster, unmitigated and without redemption. Part of me was defensive—*Well, what did they expect for free? Benji?*—and part was mortified. I self-consciously stole glances at the cast and crew and could see it plainly on their faces: *Where did this animal come from, and how can we send him back?* At the end of the day one of the assistants, clipboard in hand, told us the shooting lineup was still undecided for the next morning. "Don't bother coming in tomorrow," he said. "We'll call if we need Marley." And to ensure there was no confusion, he repeated: "So unless you hear from us, don't show up. Got it?" Yeah, I got it, loud and clear. Gosse had sent his underling to do the dirty work. Marley's fledgling acting career was over. Not that I could blame them.

With the possible exception of that scene in *The Ten Commandments* where Charlton Heston parts the Red Sea, Marley had presented the biggest logistical nightmare in the history of cinema. He had caused who knows how many thousands of dollars in needless delays and wasted film. He had slimed countless costumes, raided the snack table, and nearly toppled a thirty-thousand-dollar camera. They were cutting their losses, writing us out. It was the old "Don't call us, we'll call you" routine.

"Marley," I said when we got home, "your big chance and you really blew it."

The next morning I was still fretting over our dashed dreams of stardom when the phone rang. It was the assistant, telling us to get Marley to the hotel as soon as possible. "You mean you want him back?" I asked.

"Right away," he said. "Bob wants him in the next scene."

I arrived thirty minutes later, not quite believing they had invited us back. Gosse was ebullient. He had watched the raw footage from the day before and couldn't have been happier. "The dog was hysterical!" he gushed. "Just hilarious. Pure madcap genius!" I could feel myself standing taller, chest puffing out.

"We always knew he was a natural," Jenny said.

Shooting continued around Lake Worth for several more days, and Marley continued to rise to the occasion. We hovered in the wings with the other stage parents and hangers-on, chatting, socializing, and then falling abruptly silent whenever the stagehand yelled, "Ready on set!" When the word "Cut!" rang out, the party continued. Jenny even managed to get Gary Carter and Dave Winfield, the Baseball Hall of Fame all-star who was making a cameo in the movie, to sign baseballs for each of the boys.

Marley was lapping up stardom. The crew, especially the women, fawned over him. The weather was brutally hot, and one assistant was assigned the exclusive duty of following Marley around with a bowl and a bottle of spring water, pouring him drinks at will. Everyone, it seemed, was feeding him snacks off the buffet table. I left him with the crew for a couple of hours while I checked in at work, and when I returned I found him sprawled out like King Tut, paws in the air, accepting a leisurely belly rub from the strikingly gorgeous makeup artist. "He's such a lover!" she cooed.

Stardom was starting to go to my head, too. I began introducing myself as "Marley the Dog's handler" and dropping lines such as "For his next movie, we're hoping for a barking part." During one break in the shooting, I walked into the hotel lobby to use the pay phone. Marley was off his leash and sniffing around the furniture several feet away. A concierge, apparently mistaking my star for a stray, intercepted him and tried to hustle him out a side door. "Go home!" he scolded. "Shoo!"

"Excuse me?" I said, cupping my hand over the mouthpiece of the phone and leveling the concierge with my most withering stare. "Do you have any idea who you're talking to?"

We remained on the set for four straight days, and by the time we were told Marley's scenes were all completed and his services no longer needed, Jenny and I both felt we were part of the Shooting Gallery family. Granted, the only unpaid members of the family, but members nonetheless. "We love you guys!" Jenny blurted out to all within earshot as we herded Marley into the minivan. "Can't wait to see the final cut!"

But wait we did. One of the producers told us to give them eight months and then call and they'd mail us an advance copy. After eight months when I called, however, a front-desk person put me on hold and returned several minutes later to say, "Why don't you try in another couple months?" I waited and tried, waited and tried, but each time was put off. I started feeling like a stalker, and I could imagine the receptionist, hand cupped over the phone, whispering to Gosse at the editing table, "It's that crazy dog guy again. What do you want me to tell him this time?"

Eventually I stopped calling, resigned that we would never see *The Last Home Run,* convinced that no one ever would, that the project had been abandoned on the editing-room floor on account of the overwhelming challenges of trying to edit that damn dog out of every scene. It would be two full years later before I would finally get my chance to see Marley's acting skills.

I was in Blockbuster when on a whim I asked the clerk if he knew anything about a movie called *The Last Home Run.* Not only did he know about it; he had it in stock. In fact, as luck would have it, not a single copy was checked out.

Only later would I learn the whole sad story. Unable to attract a national distributor, the Shooting Gallery had no choice but to relegate Marley's movie debut to that most ignoble of celluloid fates. *The Last Home Run* had gone straight to video. I didn't care. I raced home with a copy and yelled to Jenny and the kids to gather round the VCR. All told, Marley was on-screen for less than two minutes, but I had to say they were two of the livelier minutes in the film. We laughed! We cried! We cheered!

"Waddy, that you!" Conor screamed.

"We're famous!" Patrick yelled.

Marley, never one to get hung up on pretenses, seemed unimpressed. He yawned and crawled beneath the coffee table. By the time the end credits rolled, he was sound asleep. We waited with breath held as the names of all the actors of the two-legged variety had scrolled by. For a minute, I thought our dog was not going to merit a credit. But then there it was, listed in big letters across the screen for all to see: "Marley the Dog . . . As Himself."

CHAPTER 17

In the Land of Bocahontas

❈

O ne month after filming ended for *The Last Home Run,* we said good-bye to West Palm Beach and all the memories it held. There had been two more murders within a block of our home, but in the end it was clutter, not crime, that drove us from our little bungalow on Churchill Road. With two children and all the accoutrements that went with them, we were packed, quite literally, to the rafters. The house had taken on the pallid sheen of a Toys "R" Us factory outlet. Marley was ninety-seven pounds, and he could not turn around without knocking something over. Ours was a two-bedroom house, and we foolishly thought the boys could share the second room. But when they kept waking each other up, doubling our nocturnal adventures, we moved Conor out to a narrow space between the kitchen and the garage. Officially, it was my "home office," where I played guitar and paid bills. To anyone who saw it, though, there was really no sugarcoating it: We had moved our baby out into the breezeway. It sounded horrible. A breezeway was just a half step up from a garage, which, in turn, was nearly synonymous with a barn. And what kind of parents would raise their boy in a barn? A breezeway had a certain unsecured sound to it: a place open to the wind—and anything else that might blow in. Dirt, allergens, stinging insects, bats, criminals, perverts. A breezeway was where you would expect to find the garbage cans and wet tennis shoes. And in fact it was the place where we kept Marley's food and water bowls, even after Conor took up residence there, not because it was a space fit only for an animal but simply because that's where Marley had come to expect them.

Our breezeway-cum-nursery sounded Dickensian, but it really wasn't that bad; it was almost charming. Originally, it was built as a covered, open-air pass-through between the house and garage, and the previous owners had closed it in years earlier. Before declaring it a nursery, I replaced the old leaky jalousies with modern, tight-fitting windows. I hung new blinds and applied a fresh coat of paint. Jenny covered the floor with soft rugs, hung cheerful drawings, and dangled whimsical mobiles from the ceiling. Still, how did it look? Our son was sleeping in the breezeway while the dog had full run of the master bedroom.

Besides, Jenny was now working half-time for the *Post*'s feature section, and mostly from home, as she attempted to juggle children and career. It only made sense for us to relocate closer to my office. We agreed it was time to move.

Life is full of little ironies, and one of them was the fact that, after months of searching, we settled on a house in the one South Florida city I took the greatest glee in publicly ridiculing. That place was Boca Raton, which, translated from the Spanish, means literally "Mouth of the Rat." And what a mouth it was.

Boca Raton was a wealthy Republican bastion largely populated with recent arrivals from New Jersey and New York. Most of the money in town was new money, and most of those who had it didn't know how to enjoy it without making fools of themselves. Boca Raton was a land of luxury sedans, red sports cars, pink stucco mansions crammed onto postage-stamp lots, and balkanized walled developments with guards at the gates. The men favored linen pants and Italian loafers sans socks and spent inordinate amounts of time making important-sounding cellphone calls to one another. The women were tanned to the consistency of the Gucci leather bags they favored, their burnished skin set off by hair dyed alarming shades of silver and platinum.

The city crawled with plastic surgeons, and they had the biggest homes and most radiant smiles of all. For Boca's well-preserved women, breast implants were a virtual requirement of residency. The younger women all had magnificent boob jobs; the older women all had magnificent boob jobs *and* face-lifts. Butt sculpting, nose jobs, tummy tucks, and tattooed mascara rounded out the cosmetic lineup, giving the city's female population the odd appearance of being foot soldiers in an army of anatomically correct inflatable dolls. As I once sang in a song I wrote for a press skit, "Liposuction and silicone, a girl's best friends in Boca Raton."

In my column I had been poking fun at the Boca lifestyle, starting with the name itself. Residents of Boca Raton never actually called their city Boca Raton. They simply referred to it by the familiar "Boca." And they did not pronounce it as the dictionary said they should, with a long *O, BO-kuh*. Rather they gave it a soft, nasal, Jersey-tinged inflection. It was *BOHW-kuh!* as in, "Oh, the manicured shrubbery is *bew-tee-ful* here in *BOHW-kuh!*"

The Disney movie *Pocahontas* was in the theaters then, and I launched a running spoof on the Indian-princess theme, which I titled "Bocahontas." My gold-draped protagonist was an indigenous suburban princess who drove a pink BMW, her rock-hard, surgically enhanced breasts jutting into the steering wheel, allowing her to drive hands-free, talking on her cell phone and teasing her frosted hair in the rearview mirror as she raced to the tanning salon. Bocahontas lived in a pastel designer wigwam, worked out each morning at the tribal gym—but only if she could find parking within ten feet of the front door—and spent her afternoons stalking wild furs, trusty AmEx card in hand, at the ceremonial hunting grounds known as Town Center Mall.

"Bury my Visa at Mizner Park," Bocahontas intones solemnly in one of my columns, a reference to the city's toniest shopping strip. In another, she adjusts her buckskin Wonderbra and campaigns to make cosmetic surgery tax-deductible.

My characterization was cruel. It was uncharitable. It was only slightly exaggerated. Boca's real-life Bocahontases were the biggest fans of those columns, trying to figure out which of them had inspired my fictional heroine. (I'll never tell.) I was frequently invited to speak before social and community groups and invariably someone would stand up and ask,

"Why do you hate *BOHW-kuh* so much?" It wasn't that I hated Boca, I told them; it was just that I loved high farce. No place on earth delivered it quite like the pretty-in-pink Mouth of the Rat.

So it only made sense that when Jenny and I finally settled on a house, it was located at ground zero of the Boca experience, midway between the waterfront estates of east Boca Raton and the snooty gated communities of west Boca Raton (which, I relished pointing out to the very zip-code-conscious residents, fell outside the city limits in unincorporated Palm Beach County). Our new neighborhood was in one of the few middle-class sections in the city, and its residents liked to joke with a certain reverse snobbery that they were on the wrong side of both sets of tracks. Sure enough, there were two sets of railroad tracks, one defining the eastern boundary of the neighborhood and one the western. At night you could lie in bed and listen to the freight trains moving through on their way to and from Miami.

"Are you crazy?" I said to Jenny. "We can't move to Boca! I'll be run out of town on a rail. They'll serve my head up on a bed of organic mesclun greens."

"Oh, come on," she said. "You're exaggerating again."

My paper, the *Sun-Sentinel,* was the dominant newspaper in Boca Raton, far outpacing the *Miami Herald,* the *Palm Beach Post,* or even the local *Boca Raton News* in circulation. My work was widely read in the city and its western developments, and because my photograph appeared above my column, I was frequently recognized. I didn't think I was exaggerating. "They'll skin me alive and hang my carcass in front of Tiffany's," I said.

But we had been looking for months, and this was the first house that met all our criteria. It was the right size at the right price and in the right place, strategically located between the two offices where I split my time. The public schools were about as good as public schools got in South Florida, and for all its superficialities, Boca Raton had an excellent park system, including some of the most pristine ocean beaches in the Miami–Palm Beach metropolitan area. With more than a little trepidation, I agreed to go forward with the purchase. I felt like a not-so-secret agent infiltrating the enemy's encampment. The barbarian was about to slip inside the gate, an unapologetic Boca-basher crashing the Boca garden party. Who could blame them for not wanting me?

When we first arrived, I slinked around town self-consciously, convinced all eyes were on me. My ears burned, imagining people were whispering as I passed. After I wrote a column welcoming myself to the neighborhood (and eating a fair amount of crow in the process), I received a number of letters saying things like "You trash our city and now you want to live here? What a shameless hypocrite!" I had to admit, they made a point. An ardent city booster I knew from work couldn't wait to confront me. "So," he said gleefully, "you decided tacky Boca isn't such a bad place after all, huh? The parks and the tax rate and the schools and beaches and zoning, all that's not so bad when it comes time to buy a house, is it?" All I could do was roll over and cry uncle.

I soon discovered, however, that most of my neighbors here on the wrong side of both sets of tracks were sympathetic to my written assaults on what one of them called "the gauche and vulgar among us." Pretty soon I felt right at home.

Our house was a 1970s-vintage four-bedroom ranch with twice the square footage of our first home and none of the charm. The place had potential, though, and gradually we put our mark on it. We ripped up the wall-to-wall shag carpeting and installed oak floors in the living room and Italian tile everywhere else. We replaced the ugly sliding glass doors with varnished French doors, and I slowly turned the bereft front yard into a tropical garden teeming with gingers and heliconias and passion vines that butterflies and passersby alike stopped to drink in.

The two best features of our new home had nothing to do with the house itself. Visible from our living room window was a small city park filled with playground equipment beneath towering pines. The children adored it. And in the backyard, right off the new French doors, was an in-ground swimming pool. We hadn't wanted a pool, worrying about the risk to our two toddlers, and Jenny made our Realtor blanch when she suggested filling it in. Our first act on the day we moved in was to surround the pool with a four-foot-high fence worthy of a maximum-security prison. The boys—Patrick had just turned three and Conor eighteen months when we arrived—took to the water like a pair of dolphins. The park became an extension of our backyard and the pool an extension of the mild season we so cherished. A swimming pool in Florida, we soon learned, made the difference between barely enduring the withering summer months and actually enjoying them.

No one loved the backyard pool more than our water dog, that proud descendant of fishermen's retrievers plying the ocean swells off the coast of Newfoundland. If the pool gate was open, Marley would charge for the water, getting a running start from the family room, going airborne out the open French doors and, with one bounce off the brick patio, landing in the pool on his belly with a giant flop that sent a geyser into the air and waves over the edge. Swimming with Marley was a potentially life-threatening adventure, a little like swimming with an ocean liner. He would come at you full speed ahead, his paws flailing out in front of him. You'd expect him to veer away at the last minute, but he would simply crash into you and try to climb aboard. If you were over your head, he pushed you beneath the surface. "What do I look like, a dock?" I would say, and cradle him in my arms to let him catch his breath, his front paws still paddling away on autopilot as he licked the water off my face.

One thing our new house did not have was a Marley-proof bunker. At our old house, the concrete one-car garage was pretty much indestructible, and it had two windows, which kept it tolerably comfortable even in the dead of summer. Our Boca house had a two-car garage, but it was unsuitable for housing Marley or any other life-form that could not survive temperatures above 150 degrees. The garage had no windows and was stiflingly hot. Besides, it was finished in drywall, not concrete, which Marley had already proved himself quite adept at pulverizing. His thunder-induced panic attacks were only getting worse, despite the tranquilizers.

The first time we left him alone in our new house, we shut him in the laundry room, just off the kitchen, with a blanket and a big bowl of water. When we returned a few hours later, he had scratched up the door. The damage was minor, but we had just mortgaged our lives for the next thirty years to buy this house, and we knew it didn't bode well. "Maybe he's just getting used to his new surroundings," I offered.

"There's not even a cloud in the sky," Jenny observed skeptically. "What's going to happen the first time a storm hits?"

The next time we left him alone, we found out. As thunderheads rolled in, we cut our outing short and hurried home, but it was too late. Jenny was a few steps ahead of me, and when she opened the laundry-room door she stopped short and uttered, "Oh my God." She said it the way you would if you had just discovered a body hanging from the chandelier. Again: "Oh . . . My . . . God." I peeked in over her shoulder, and it was uglier than I had feared. Marley was standing there, panting frantically, his paws and mouth bleeding. Loose fur was everywhere, as though the thunder had scared the hair right out of his coat. The damage was worse than anything he had done before, and that was saying a lot. An entire wall was gouged open, obliterated clear down to the studs. Plaster and wood chips and bent nails were everywhere. Electric wiring lay exposed. Blood smeared the floor and the walls. It looked, literally, like the scene of a shotgun homicide.

"Oh my God," Jenny said a third time.

"Oh my God," I repeated. It was all either of us could say.

After several seconds of just standing there mute, staring at the carnage, I finally said, "Okay, we can handle this. It's all fixable." Jenny shot me her look; she had seen my repairs. "I'll call a drywall guy and have it professionally repaired," I said. "I won't even try to do this one myself." I slipped Marley one of his tranquilizers and worried silently that this latest destructive jag might just throw Jenny back into the funk she had sunk into after Conor's birth. Those blues, however, seemed to be long behind her. She was surprisingly philosophical about it.

"A few hundred bucks and we'll be good as new," she chirped.

"That's what I'm thinking, too," I said. "I'll give a few extra speeches to bring in some cash. That'll pay for it."

Within a few minutes, Marley was beginning to mellow. His eyelids grew heavy and his eyes deeply bloodshot, as they always did when he was doped up. He looked like he belonged at a Grateful Dead concert. I hated to see him this way, I always hated it, and always resisted sedating him. But the pills helped him move past the terror, past the deadly threat that existed only in his mind. If he were human, I would call him certifiably psychotic. He was delusional, paranoid, convinced a dark, evil force was coming from the heavens to take him. He curled up on the rug in front of the kitchen sink and let out a deep sigh. I knelt beside him and stroked his blood-caked fur. "Geez, dog," I said. "What are we going to do with you?" Without lifting his head, he looked up at me with those bloodshot stoner eyes of his, the saddest, most mournful, eyes I have ever seen, and just gazed at me. It was as if he were trying to tell me something,

something important he needed me to understand. "I know," I said. "I know you can't help it."

The next day Jenny and I took the boys with us to the pet store and bought a giant cage. They came in all different sizes, and when I described Marley to the clerk he led us to the largest of them all. It was enormous, big enough for a lion to stand up and turn around in. Made out of heavy steel grating, it had two bolt-action barrel locks to hold the door securely shut and a heavy steel pan for a floor. This was our answer, our own portable Alcatraz. Conor and Patrick both crawled inside and I slid the bolts shut, locking them in for a moment. "What do you guys think?" I asked. "Will this hold our Superdog?"

Conor teetered at the cage door, his fingers through the bars like a veteran inmate, and said, "Me in jail."

"Waddy's going to be our prisoner!" Patrick chimed in, delighted at the prospect.

Back home, we set up the crate next to the washing machine. Portable Alcatraz took up nearly half the laundry room. "Come here, Marley!" I called when it was fully assembled. I tossed a Milk-Bone in and he happily pranced in after it. I closed and bolted the door behind him, and he stood there chewing his treat, unfazed by the new life experience he was about to enter, the one known in mental-health circles as "involuntary commitment."

"This is going to be your new home when we're away," I said cheerfully. Marley stood there panting contentedly, not a trace of concern on his face, and then he lay down and let out a sigh. "A good sign," I said to Jenny. "A very good sign."

That evening we decided to give the maximum-security

dog-containment unit a test run. This time I didn't even need a Milk-Bone to lure Marley in. I simply opened the gate, gave a whistle, and in he walked, tail banging the metal sides. "Be a good boy, Marley," I said. As we loaded the boys into the minivan to go out to dinner, Jenny said, "You know something?"

"What?" I asked.

"This is the first time since we got him that I don't have a pit in my stomach leaving Marley alone in the house," she said. "I never even realized how much it put me on edge until now."

"I know what you mean," I said. "It was always a guessing game: 'What will our dog destroy this time?' "

"Like, 'How much will this little night out at the movies cost us?' "

"It was like Russian roulette."

"I think that crate is going to be the best money we ever spent," she said.

"We should have done this a long time ago," I agreed. "You can't put a price on peace of mind."

We had a great dinner out, followed by a sunset stroll on the beach. The boys splashed in the surf, chased seagulls, threw fistfuls of sand in the water. Jenny was uncharacteristically relaxed. Just knowing Marley was safely secured inside Alcatraz, unable to hurt himself or anything else, was a balm. "What a nice outing this has been," she said as we walked up the front sidewalk to our house.

I was about to agree with her when I noticed something in my peripheral vision, something up ahead that wasn't quite right. I turned my head and stared at the window beside the front door. The miniblinds were shut, as they always were when we left the house. But about a foot up from the bottom of the window the metal slats were bent apart and something was sticking through them.

Something black. And wet. And pressed up against the glass. "What the—?" I said. "How could . . . Marley?"

When I opened the front door, sure enough, there was our one-dog welcoming committee, wiggling all over the foyer, pleased as punch to have us home again. We fanned out across the house, checking every room and closet for telltales of Marley's unsupervised adventure. The house was fine, untouched. We converged on the laundry room. The crate's door stood wide open, swung back like the stone to Jesus' tomb on Easter morning. It was as if some secret accomplice had snuck in and sprung our inmate. I squatted down beside the cage to have a closer look. The two bolt-action barrel locks were slid back in the open position, and—a significant clue—they were dripping with saliva. "It looks like an inside job," I said. "Somehow Houdini here licked his way out of the Big House."

"I can't believe it," Jenny said. Then she uttered a word I was glad the children were not close enough to hear.

We always fancied Marley to be as dumb as algae, but he had been clever enough to figure out how to use his long, strong tongue through the bars to slowly work the barrels free from their slots. He had licked his way to freedom, and he proved over the coming weeks that he was able to easily repeat the trick whenever he wanted. Our maximum-security prison had in fact turned out to be a halfway house. Some days we would return to find him resting peacefully in the cage; other days he'd be waiting at the front window. Involuntary commitment was not a concept Marley was going to take lying down.

We took to wiring both locks in place with heavy electrical cable. That worked for a while, but one day, with distant rumbles on the horizon, we came home to find that the bottom corner of the cage's gate had been peeled back as though with a giant can opener, and a panicky Marley, his paws again bloodied, was firmly stuck around the rib cage, half in and half out of the tight opening. I bent the steel gate back in place as best I could, and we began wiring not only the slide bolts in place but all four corners of the door as well. Pretty soon we were reinforcing the corners of the cage itself as Marley continued to put his brawn into busting out. Within three months the gleaming steel cage we had thought so impregnable looked like it had taken a direct hit from a howitzer. The bars were twisted and bent, the frame pried apart, the door an ill-fitting mess, the sides bulging outward. I continued to reinforce it as best I could, and it continued to hold tenuously against Marley's full-bodied assaults. Whatever false sense of security the contraption had once offered us was gone. Each time we left, even for a half hour, we wondered whether this would be the time that our manic inmate would bust out and go on another couch-shredding, wall-gouging, door-eating rampage. So much for peace of mind.

CHAPTER 18

Alfresco Dining

❊

arley didn't fit into the Boca Raton scene any better than I did. Boca had (and surely still has) a disproportionate share of the world's smallest, yappiest, most pampered dogs, the kind of pets that the Bocahontas set favored as fashion accessories. They were precious little things, often with bows in their fur and cologne spritzed on their necks, some even with painted toenails, and you would spot them in the most unlikely of places—peeking out of a designer handbag at you as you waited in line at the bagel shop; snoozing on their mistresses' towels at the beach; leading the charge on a rhinestone-studded leash into a pricey antiques store. Mostly, you could find them cruising around town in Lexuses, Mercedes-Benzes, and Jaguars, perched aristocratically behind the steering wheels on their owners' laps. They were to Marley what Grace Kelly was to Gomer Pyle. They were petite, sophisticated, and of discriminating taste. Marley was big, clunky, and a sniffer of genitalia. He wanted so much to have them invite him into their circle; they so much were not about to.

With his recently digested obedience certificate under his belt, Marley was fairly manageable on walks, but if he saw something he liked, he still wouldn't hesitate to lunge for it, threat of strangulation be damned. When we took strolls around town, the high-rent pooches were always worth getting all choked up over. Each time he spotted one, he would break into a gallop, barreling up to it, dragging Jenny or me behind him at the end of the leash, the noose tightening around his throat, making him gasp and cough. Each time Marley would be roundly snubbed, not only by the Boca minidog but by the Boca minidog's owner, who would snatch up young Fifi or Suzi or Cheri as if rescuing her from the jaws of an alligator. Marley didn't seem to mind. The next minidog to come into sight, he would do it all over again, undeterred by his previous jilting. As a guy who was never very good at the rejection part of dating, I admired his perseverance.

Outside dining was a big part of the Boca experience, and many restaurants in town offered alfresco seating beneath palm trees whose trunks and fronds were studded with strings of tiny white lights. These were places to see and be seen, to sip caffè lattes and jabber into cell phones as your companion stared vacantly at the sky. The Boca minidog was an important part of the alfresco ambience. Couples brought their dogs with them and hooked their leashes to the wrought-iron tables where the dogs would contentedly curl up at their feet or sometimes even sit up at the table beside their masters, holding their heads high in an imperious manner as if miffed by the waiters' inattentiveness.

One Sunday afternoon Jenny and I thought it would be fun to take the whole family for an outside meal at one of the popular meeting places. "When in Boca, do as the Boca-lites," I said. We loaded the boys and the dog into the minivan and headed to Mizner Park, the downtown shopping plaza modeled after an Italian piazza with wide sidewalks and endless dining possibilities. We parked and strolled up one side of the three-block strip and down the other, seeing and being seen—and what a sight we must have made. Jenny had the boys strapped into a double stroller that could have been mistaken for a maintenance cart, loaded up in the back with all manner of toddler paraphernalia, from applesauce to wet wipes. I walked beside her, Marley, on full Boca minidog alert, barely contained at my side. He was even wilder than usual, beside himself at the possibility of getting near one of the little purebreds prancing about, and I gripped hard on his leash. His tongue hung out and he panted like a locomotive.

We settled on a restaurant with one of the more affordable menus on the strip and hovered nearby until a sidewalk table opened up. The table was perfect—shaded, with a view of the piazza's central fountain, and heavy enough, we were sure, to secure an excitable hundred-pound Lab. I hooked the end of Marley's leash to one of the legs, and we ordered drinks all around, two beers and two apple juices.

"To a beautiful day with my beautiful family," Jenny said, holding up her glass for a toast. We clicked our beer bottles; the boys smashed their sippy cups together. That's when it happened. So fast, in fact, that we didn't even realize it had happened. All we knew was that one instant we were sitting at a lovely outdoor table toasting the beautiful day, and the next our table was on the move, crashing its way through the sea of other tables, banging into innocent bystanders, and making a horrible, ear-piercing, industrial-grade shriek as it scraped over the concrete pavers. In that first split second, before either of us realized exactly what bad fate had befallen us, it seemed distinctly possible that our table was possessed, fleeing our family of unwashed Boca invaders, which most certainly did not belong here. In the next split second, I saw that it wasn't our table that was haunted, but our dog. Marley was out in front, chugging forward with every ounce of rippling muscle he had, the leash stretched tight as piano wire.

In the fraction of a second after that, I saw just where Marley was heading, table in tow. Fifty feet down the sidewalk, a delicate French poodle lingered at her owner's side, nose in the air. *Damn,* I remember thinking, *what is his thing for poodles?* Jenny and I both sat there for a moment longer, drinks in hand, the boys between us in their stroller, our perfect little Sunday afternoon unblemished except for the fact that our table was now motoring its way through the crowd. An instant later we were on our feet, screaming, running, apologizing to the customers around us as we went. I was the first to reach the runaway table as it surged and scraped down the piazza. I grabbed on, planted my feet, and leaned back with everything I had. Soon Jenny was beside me, pulling back, too. I felt like we were action heroes in a western, giving our all to rein in the runaway train before it jumped the tracks and plunged over a cliff. In the middle of all the bedlam, Jenny actually turned and called over her shoulder, "Be right back, boys!" *Be right back?* She made it sound so ordinary, so expected, so planned, as if we often did this sort of thing, deciding on the spur of the moment that, oh, why not, it might just be fun to let Marley lead us on a little table stroll around town, maybe doing a bit of window-shopping along the way, before we circled back in time for appetizers.

When we finally got the table stopped and Marley reeled in, just feet from the poodle and her mortified owner, I turned back to check on the boys, and that's when I got my first good look at the faces of my fellow alfresco diners. It was like a scene out of one of those E. F. Hutton commercials where an entire bustling crowd freezes in silence, waiting to hear a whispered word of investment advice. Men stopped in midconversation, cell phones in their hands. Women stared with opened mouths. The Bocalites were aghast. It was finally Conor who broke the silence. "Waddy go walk!" he screamed with delight.

A waiter rushed up and helped me drag the table back into place as Jenny held Marley, still fixated on the object of his desire, in a death grip. "Let me get some new place settings," the waiter said.

"That won't be necessary," Jenny said nonchalantly. "We'll just be paying for our drinks and going."

It wasn't long after our excellent excursion into the Boca alfresco-dining scene that I found a book in the library titled *No Bad Dogs* by the acclaimed British dog trainer Barbara Woodhouse. As the title implied, *No Bad Dogs* advanced the same belief that Marley's first instructor, Miss Dominatrix, held so dear—that the only thing standing between an incorrigible canine and greatness was a befuddled, indecisive, weak-willed human master. Dogs weren't the problem,

Woodhouse held; people were. That said, the book went on to describe, chapter after chapter, some of the most egregious canine behaviors imaginable. There were dogs that howled incessantly, dug incessantly, fought incessantly, humped incessantly, and bit incessantly. There were dogs that hated all men and dogs that hated all women; dogs that stole from their masters and dogs that jealously attacked defenseless infants. There were even dogs that ate their own feces. *Thank God,* I thought, *at least he doesn't eat his own feces.*

As I read, I began to feel better about our flawed retriever. We had gradually come to the firm conclusion that Marley was indeed the world's worst dog. Now I was buoyed to read that there were all sorts of horrid behaviors he did *not* have. He didn't have a mean bone in his body. He wasn't much of a barker. Didn't bite. Didn't assault other dogs, except in the pursuit of love. Considered everyone his best friend. Best of all, he didn't eat or roll in scat. Besides, I told myself, there are no bad dogs, only inept, clueless owners like Jenny and me. It was our fault Marley turned out the way he had.

Then I got to chapter 24, "Living with the Mentally Unstable Dog." As I read, I swallowed loudly. Woodhouse was describing Marley with an understanding so intimate I could swear she had been bunking with him in his battered crate. She addressed the manic, bizarre behavior patterns, the destructiveness when left alone, the gouged floors and chewed rugs. She described the attempts by owners of such beasts "to make some place either in the house or yard dogproof." She even addressed the use of tranquilizers as a desperate (and largely ineffective) last measure to try to return these mentally broken mutts to the land of the sane.

"Some are born unstable, some are made unstable by their living conditions, but the result is the same: the dogs, instead of being a joy to their owners, are a worry, an expense, and often bring complete despair to an entire family," Woodhouse wrote. I looked down at Marley snoozing at my feet and said, "Sound familiar?"

In a subsequent chapter, titled "Abnormal Dogs," Woodhouse wrote with a sense of resignation: "I cannot stress often enough that if you wish to keep a dog that is not normal, you must face up to living a slightly restricted existence." *You mean like living in mortal fear of going out for a gallon of milk?* "Although *you* may love a subnormal dog," she continued, "other people must not be inconvenienced by it." *Other people such as, hypothetically speaking, Sunday diners at a sidewalk café in Boca Raton, Florida?*

Woodhouse had nailed our dog and our pathetic, codependent existence. We had it all: the hapless, weak-willed masters; the mentally unstable, out-of-control dog; the trail of destroyed property; the annoyed and inconvenienced strangers and neighbors. We were a textbook case. "Congratulations, Marley," I said to him. "You qualify as subnormal." He opened his eyes at the sound of his name, stretched, and rolled onto his back, paws in the air.

I was expecting Woodhouse to offer a cheery solution for the owners of such defective merchandise, a few helpful tips that, when properly executed, could turn even the most manic of pets into Westminster-worthy show dogs. But she ended her book on a much darker note: "Only the owners of unbalanced dogs can really know where the line can be drawn between a dog that is sane and one that is mentally unsound. No one can make up the owner's mind as to what to do with the last kind. I, as a great dog lover, feel it is kinder to put them to sleep."

Put them to sleep? Gulp. In case she wasn't making herself clear, she added, "Surely, when all training and veterinary help has been exhausted and there is no hope that the dog will ever live a reasonably normal existence, it is kinder to pet and owner to put the dog to sleep."

Even Barbara Woodhouse, lover of animals, successful trainer of thousands of dogs their owners had deemed hopeless, was conceding that some dogs were simply beyond help. If it were up to her, they would be humanely dispatched to that great canine insane asylum in the sky.

"Don't worry, big guy," I said, leaning down to scratch Marley's belly. "The only sleep we're going to be doing around this house is the kind you get to wake up from."

He sighed dramatically and drifted back to his dreams of French poodles in heat.

It was around this same time that we also learned not all Labs are created equal. The breed actually has two distinct subgroups: English and American. The English line tends to be smaller and stockier than the American line, with blockier heads and gentle, calm dispositions. They are the favored line for showing. Labs belonging to the American line are noticeably larger and stronger, with sleeker, less squat features. They are known for their endless energy and high spirits and favored for use in the field as hunting and sports dogs. The same qualities that make the American line of Labs so unstoppably superb in the woods makes them challenges in the family home. Their exuberant energy level, the literature warned, should not be underestimated.

As the brochure for a Pennsylvania retriever breeder, Endless Mountain Labradors, explains it: "So many people ask us, 'What's the difference between the English and the American (field) Labs?' There is such a big difference that the AKC is considering splitting the breed. There is a difference in build, as well as temperament. If you are looking for strictly a field dog for field trial competition, go for the American field dog. They are athletic, tall, lanky, thin, but have VERY hyper, highstrung personalities, which do not lend themselves to being the best 'family dogs.' On the other hand, the English Labs are very blocky, stocky, shorter in their build. Very sweet, quiet, mellow, lovely dogs."

It didn't take me long to figure out which line Marley belonged to. It was all beginning to make sense. We had blindly picked out a type of Lab best suited to stampeding across the open wilderness all day. If that weren't enough, our specific choice just happened to be mentally unbalanced, unwound, and beyond the reach of training, tranquilizers, or canine psychiatry. The kind of subnormal specimen an experienced dog trainer like Barbara Woodhouse might just consider better off dead. *Great,* I thought. *Now we find out.*

Not long after Woodhouse's book opened our eyes to Marley's crazed mind, a neighbor asked us to take in their cat for a week while they were on vacation. Sure, we said, bring him over. Compared with a dog, cats were easy. Cats ran on autopilot, and this cat in particular was shy and elusive, especially around Marley. He could be counted on to hide beneath the couch all day and only come out after we were asleep to eat his food, kept high out of Marley's reach, and use the kitty-litter box, which we tucked away in a discreet corner of the screened patio that enclosed the pool. There was nothing to it, really. Marley was totally unaware the cat was even in the house.

Midway through the cat's stay with us, I awoke at dawn to a loud, driving beat resonating through the mattress. It was Marley, quivering with excitement beside the bed, his tail slapping the mattress at a furious rate. *Whomp! Whomp! Whomp!* I reached out to pet him, and that sent him into evasive maneuvers. He was prancing and dancing beside the bed. The Marley Mambo. "Okay, what do you have?" I asked him, eyes still shut. As if to answer, Marley proudly plopped his prize onto the crisp sheets, just inches from my face. In my groggy state, it took me a minute to process what exactly it was. The object was small, dark, of indefinable shape, and coated in a coarse, gritty sand. Then the smell reached my nostrils. An acrid, pungent, putrid smell. I bolted upright and pushed backward against Jenny, waking her up. I pointed at Marley's gift to us, glistening on the sheets.

"That's not . . ." Jenny began, revulsion in her voice.

"Yes, it is," I said. "He raided the kitty-litter box."

Marley couldn't have looked more proud had he just presented us with the Hope diamond. As Barbara Wood-house had so sagely predicted, our mentally unstable, abnormal mutt had entered the feces-eating stage of his life.

CHAPTER 19

Lightning Strikes

�ֵ

fter Conor's arrival, everyone we knew—with the exception of my very Catholic parents who were praying for dozens of little Grogans—assumed we were done having children. In the two-income, professional crowd in which we ran, one child was the norm, two were considered a bit of an extravagance, and three were simply unheard-of. Especially given the difficult pregnancy we had gone through with Conor, no one could understand why we might want to subject ourselves to the messy process all over again. But we had come a long way since our newly-wed days of killing houseplants. Parenthood became us. Our two boys brought us more joy than we ever thought anyone or anything possibly could. They defined our life now, and while parts of us missed the leisurely vacations, lazy Saturdays reading novels, and romantic dinners that lingered late into the night, we had come to find our pleasures in new ways—in spilled applesauce and tiny nose prints on windowpanes and the soft symphony of bare feet padding down the hallway at dawn. Even on the worst days, we usually managed to find something to smile over, knowing by now what every parent sooner or later figures out, that these wondrous days of early parenthood—of diapered bottoms and first teeth and incomprehensible jabber—are but a brilliant, brief flash in the vastness of an otherwise ordinary lifetime.

We both rolled our eyes when my old-school mother clucked at us, "Enjoy them while you can because they'll be grown up before you know it." Now, even just a few years into it, we were realizing she was right. Hers was a well-worn cliché but one we could already see was steeped in truth. The boys *were* growing up fast, and each week ended another little chapter that could never again be revisited. One week Patrick was sucking his thumb, the next he had weaned himself of it forever. One week Conor was our baby in a crib; the next he was a little boy using a toddler bed for a trampoline. Patrick was unable to pronounce the L sound, and when women would coo over him, as they often did, he would put his fists on his hips, stick out his lip, and say, "Dos yadies are yaughing at me." I always meant to get it on videotape, but one day the L's came out perfectly, and that was that. For months we could not get Conor out of his Superman pajamas. He would race through the house, cape flapping behind him, yelling, "Me Stupe Man!" And then it was over, another missed video moment.

Children serve as impossible-to-ignore, in-your-face time-pieces, marking the relentless march of one's life through what otherwise might seem an infinite sea of minutes, hours, days, and years. Our babies were growing up faster than either of us wanted, which partially explains why, about a year after moving to our new house in Boca, we began trying for our third. As I said to Jenny, "Hey, we've got four bedrooms now; why not?" Two tries was all it took. Neither of us would admit we wanted a girl, but of course we did, desperately so, despite our many pronouncements during the pregnancy that having three boys would be just great.

When a sonogram finally confirmed our secret hope, Jenny draped her arms over my shoulders and whispered, "I'm so happy I could give you a little girl." I was so happy, too.

Not all our friends shared our enthusiasm. Most met news of our pregnancy with the same blunt question: "Did you mean to?" They just could not believe a third pregnancy could be anything other than an accident. If indeed it was not, as we insisted, then they had to question our judgment. One acquaintance went so far as to chastise Jenny for allowing me to knock her up again, asking, in a tone best reserved for someone who had just signed over all her worldly possessions to a cult in Guyana: "What *were* you thinking?"

We didn't care. On January 9, 1997, Jenny gave me a belated Christmas present: a pink-cheeked, seven-pound baby girl, whom we named Colleen. Our family only now felt like it was complete. If the pregnancy for Conor had been a litany of stress and worry, this pregnancy was text-book perfect, and delivering at Boca Raton Community Hospital introduced us to a whole new level of pampered customer satisfaction. Just down the hall from our room was a lounge with a free, all-you-can-drink cappuccino station—

so very *Boca.* By the time the baby finally came, I was so jacked up on frothy caffeine, I could barely hold my hands still to snip the umbilical cord.

When Colleen was one week old, Jenny brought her outside for the first time. The day was crisp and beautiful, and the boys and I were in the front yard, planting flowers. Marley was chained to a tree nearby, happy to lie in the shade and watch the world go by. Jenny sat in the grass beside him and placed the sleeping Colleen in a portable bassinet on the ground between them. After several minutes, the boys beckoned for Mom to come closer to see their handiwork, and they led Jenny and me around the garden beds as Colleen napped in the shade beside Marley. We wandered behind some large shrubbery from where we could still see the baby but passersby on the street could not see us. As we turned back, I stopped and motioned for Jenny to look out through the shrubs. Out on the street, an older couple walking by had stopped and were gawking at the scene in our front yard with bewildered expressions. At first, I wasn't sure what had made them stop and stare. Then it hit me: from their vantage point, all they could see was a fragile newborn alone with a large yellow dog, who appeared to be babysitting single-handedly.

We lingered in silence, stifling giggles. There was Marley, looking like an Egyptian sphinx, lying with his front paws crossed, head up, panting contentedly, every few seconds pushing his snout over to sniff the baby's head. The poor couple must have thought they had stumbled on a case of felony child neglect. No doubt the parents were out drinking at a bar somewhere, having left the infant alone in the care of the neighborhood Labrador retriever, who just might attempt to nurse the infant at any second. As if he were in on the ruse, Marley without prompting shifted positions and rested his chin across the baby's stomach, his head bigger than her whole body, and let out a long sigh as if he were saying, *When are those two going to get home?* He appeared to be protecting her, and maybe he was, though I'm pretty sure he was just drinking in the scent of her diaper.

Jenny and I stood there in the bushes and exchanged grins. The thought of Marley as an infant caregiver—Doggie Day Care— was just too good to let go. I was tempted to wait there and see how the scene would play out, but then it occurred to me that one scenario might involve a 911 call to the police. We had gotten away with storing Conor out in the breezeway, but how would we explain this one? ("Well, I know how it must look, Officer, but he's actually surprisingly responsible . . .") We stepped out of the bushes and waved to the couple—and watched the relief wash over their faces. Thank God, that baby hadn't been thrown to the dogs after all.

"You must really trust your dog," the woman said somewhat cautiously, betraying a belief that dogs were fierce and unpredictable and had no place that close to a defenseless newborn.

"He hasn't eaten one yet," I said.

❖

Two months after Colleen arrived home I celebrated my
fortieth birthday in a most inauspicious manner, namely,
by myself. The Big Four-O is supposed to be a major
turning point, the place in life where you bid restless
youth farewell and embrace the predictable comforts of
middle age. If any birthday merited a blowout celebration,
it was the fortieth, but not for me. We were now responsible parents with three children; Jenny had a new baby
pressed to her breast. There were more important things
to worry about. I arrived home from work, and Jenny was
tired and worn down. After a quick meal of leftovers, I
bathed the boys and put them to bed while Jenny nursed
Colleen. By eight-thirty, all three children were asleep, and
so was my wife. I popped a beer and sat out on the patio,
staring into the iridescent blue water of the lit swimming
pool. As always, Marley was faithfully at my side, and as I
scratched his ears, it occurred to me that he was at about
the same turning point in life. We had brought him home
six years earlier. In dog years, that would put him somewhere in his early forties now. He had crossed unnoticed
into middle age but still acted every bit the puppy. Except
for a string of stubborn ear infections that required Dr.
Jay's repeated intervention, he was healthy. He showed no
signs whatsoever of growing up or winding down. I had
never thought of Marley as any kind of role model, but
sitting there sipping my beer, I was aware that maybe he
held the secret for a good life. Never slow down, never
look back, live each day with adolescent verve and spunk
and curiosity and playfulness. If you think you're still a
young pup, then maybe you are, no matter what the

calendar says. Not a bad philosophy for life, though I'd take a pass on the part that involved vandalizing couches and laundry rooms.

"Well, big guy," I said, pressing my beer bottle against his cheek in a kind of interspecies toast. "It's just you and me tonight. Here's to forty. Here's to middle age. Here's to running with the big dogs right up until the end." And then he, too, curled up and went to sleep.

I was still moping about my solitary birthday a few days later when Jim Tolpin, my old colleague who had broken Marley of his jumping habit, called unexpectedly and asked if I wanted to grab a beer the next night, a Saturday. Jim had left the newspaper business to pursue a law degree at about the same time we moved to Boca Raton, and we hadn't spoken in months. "Sure," I said, not stopping to wonder why. Jim picked me up at six and took me to an English pub, where we quaffed Bass ale and caught up on each other's lives. We were having a grand old time until the bartender called out, "Is there a John Grogan here? Phone for John Grogan."

It was Jenny, and she sounded very upset and stressed-out. "The baby's crying, the boys are out of control, and I just ripped my contact lens!" she wailed into the phone. "Can you come home right away?"

"Try to calm down," I said. "Sit tight. I'll be right home." I hung up, and the bartender gave me a you-poor-sorry-hen-pecked-bastard kind of a nod and simply said, "My sympathies, mate."

"Come on," Jim said. "I'll drive you home."

When we turned onto my block, both sides of the

street were lined with cars. "Somebody's having a party," I said.

"Looks like it," Jim answered.

"For God's sakes," I said when we reached the house. "Look at that! Someone even parked in my driveway. If that isn't nerve."

We blocked the offender in, and I invited Jim inside. I was still griping about the inconsiderate jerk who parked in my driveway when the front door swung open. It was Jenny with Colleen in her arms. She didn't look upset at all. In fact, she had a big grin on her face. Behind her stood a bagpipe player in kilts. *Good God! What have I walked in on?* Then I looked beyond the bagpipe player and saw that someone had taken down the kiddy fence around the pool and launched floating candles on the water. The deck was crammed with several dozen of my friends, neighbors, and coworkers. Just as I was making the connection that all those cars on the street belonged to all these people in my house, they shouted in unison, "HAPPY BIRTHDAY, OLD MAN!"

My wife had not forgotten after all.

When I was finally able to snap my jaw shut, I took Jenny in my arms, kissed her on the cheek, and whispered in her ear, "I'll get you later for this."

Someone opened the laundry-room door looking for the trash can, and out bounded Marley in prime party mode. He swept through the crowd, stole a mozzarella-and-basil appetizer off a tray, lifted a couple of women's miniskirts with his snout, and made a break for the unfenced swimming pool. I tackled him just as he was launching into his signature running belly flop and dragged him back to solitary confinement. "Don't worry," I said. "I'll save you the leftovers."

It wasn't long after the surprise party—a party whose success was marked by the arrival of the police at midnight to tell us to pipe down—that Marley finally was able to find validation for his intense fear of thunder. I was in the backyard on a Sunday afternoon under brooding, darkening skies, digging up a rectangle of grass to plant yet another vegetable garden. Gardening was becoming a serious hobby for me, and the better I got at it, the more I wanted to grow. Slowly I was taking over the entire backyard. As I worked, Marley paced nervously around me, his internal barometer sensing an impending storm. I sensed it, too, but I wanted to get the project done and figured I would work until I felt the first drops of rain. As I dug, I kept glancing at the sky, watching an ominous black thunderhead forming several miles to the east, out over the ocean. Marley was whining softly, beckoning me to put down the shovel and head inside. "Relax," I told him. "It's still miles away."

The words had barely left my lips when I felt a previously unknown sensation, a kind of quivering tingle on the back of my neck. The sky had turned an odd shade of olive gray, and the air seemed to go suddenly dead as though some heavenly force had grabbed the winds and frozen them in its grip. *Weird,* I thought as I paused, leaning on my shovel to study the sky. That's when I heard it: a buzzing, popping, crackling surge of energy, similar to what you sometimes can hear standing beneath high-tension power lines. A sort of *pffffffffffft* sound filled the air around me, followed by a brief instant of utter silence. In that instant, I knew trouble was coming, but I had no time to react. In the next fraction of a second, the sky went pure, blindingly white, and an explosion, the likes of which I had never heard before, not in any storm, at any fireworks display, at any demolition site, boomed in my ears. A wall of energy hit me in the chest like an invisible linebacker. When I opened my eyes who knows how many seconds later, I was lying facedown on the ground, sand in my mouth, my shovel ten feet away, rain pelting me. Marley was down, too, in his hit-the-deck stance, and when he saw me raise my head he wiggled desperately toward me on his belly like a soldier trying to slide beneath barbed wire. When he reached me he climbed right on my back and buried his snout in my neck, frantically licking me. I looked around for just a second, trying to get my bearings, and I could see where the lightning had struck the power-line pole in the corner of the yard and followed the wire down to the house about twenty feet from where I had been standing. The electrical meter on the wall was in charred ruins.

"Come on!" I yelled, and then Marley and I were on our feet, sprinting through the downpour toward the back door as new bolts of lightning flashed around us. We did not stop until we were safely inside. I knelt on the floor, soaking wet, catching my breath, and Marley clambered on me, licking my face, nibbling my ears, flinging spit and loose fur all over everything. He was beside himself with fear, shaking uncontrollably, drool hanging off his chin. I hugged him, tried to calm him down. "Jesus, that was close!" I said, and realized that I was shaking, too. He looked up at me with those big empathetic eyes that I swore could almost talk. I was sure I knew what he was trying to tell me. *I've been trying to warn you for years that this stuff can kill you. But would anyone listen? Now will you take me seriously?*

The dog had a point. Maybe his fear of thunder had not been so irrational after all. Maybe his panic attacks at the first distant rumblings had been his way of telling us that Florida's violent thunderstorms, the deadliest in the country, were not to be dismissed with a shrug. Maybe all those destroyed walls and gouged doors and shredded carpets had been his way of trying to build a lightning-proof den we could all fit into snugly. And how had we rewarded him? With scoldings and tranquilizers.

Our house was dark, the air-conditioning, ceiling fans, televisions, and several appliances all blown out. The circuit breaker was fused into a melted mess. We were about to make some electrician a very happy man. But I was alive and so was my trusty sidekick. Jenny and the kids, tucked safely away in the family room, didn't even know the house had been hit. We were all present and accounted for. What else mattered? I pulled Marley into my lap, all ninety-seven nervous pounds of him, and made him a promise right then and there: Never again would I dismiss his fear of this deadly force of nature.

CHAPTER 20

Dog Beach

✳

A s a newspaper columnist, I was always looking for interesting and quirky stories I could grab on to. I wrote three columns each week, which meant that one of the biggest challenges of the job was coming up with a constant stream of fresh topics. Each morning I began my day by scouring the four South Florida daily newspapers, circling and clipping anything that might be worth weighing in on. Then it was a matter of finding an approach or angle that would be mine. My very first column had come directly from the headlines. A speeding car crammed with eight teenagers had flipped into a canal along the edge of the Everglades. Only the sixteen-year-old driver, her twin sister, and a third girl had escaped the submerged car. It was a huge story that I knew I wanted to come in on, but what was the fresh angle I could call my own? I drove out to the lonely crash sight hoping for inspiration, and before I even stopped the car I had found it. The classmates of the five dead children had transformed the pavement into a tapestry of spray-painted eulogies. The blacktop was covered shoulder-

to-shoulder for more than a half mile, and the raw emotion
of the outpouring was palpable. Notebook in hand, I began
copying the words down. "Wasted youth," said one message, accompanied by a painted arrow pointing off the road
and into the water. Then, there in the middle of the communal catharsis, I found it: a public apology from the young
driver, Jamie Bardol. She wrote in big, loopy letters, a child's
scrawl: "I wish it would have been me. I'm sorry." I had
found my column.

Not all topics were so dark. When a retiree received an
eviction notice from her condo because her pudgy pooch
exceeded the weight limit for pets, I swooped in to meet the
offending heavyweight. When a confused senior citizen
crashed her car into a store while trying to park, fortunately
hurting no one, I was close behind, speaking to witnesses.
The job would take me to a migrant camp one day, a
millionaire's mansion the next, and an inner-city street
corner the day after that. I loved the variety; I loved the
people I met; and more than anything I loved the near-total
freedom I was afforded to go wherever I wanted whenever I
wanted in pursuit of whatever topic tickled my curiosity.

What my bosses did not know was that behind my
journalistic wanderings was a secret agenda: to use my
position as a columnist to engineer as many shamelessly
transparent "working holidays" as I possibly could. My
motto was "When the columnist has fun, the reader has
fun." Why attend a deadening tax-adjustment hearing in
pursuit of column fodder when you could be sitting, say, at
an outdoor bar in Key West, large alcoholic beverage in
hand? Someone had to do the dirty work of telling the story

of the lost shakers of salt in Margaritaville; it might as well be me. I lived for any excuse to spend a day goofing around, preferably in shorts and T-shirt, sampling various leisurely and recreational pursuits that I convinced myself the public needed someone to fully investigate. Every profession has its tools of the trade, and mine included a reporter's notebook, a bundle of pens, and a beach towel. I began carrying sunscreen and a bathing suit in my car as a matter of routine.

I spent one day blasting through the Everglades on an airboat and another hiking along the rim of Lake Okeechobee. I spent a day bicycling scenic State Road A1A along the Atlantic Ocean so I could report firsthand on the harrowing proposition of sharing the pavement with confused blueheads and distracted tourists. I spent a day snorkeling above the endangered reefs off Key Largo and another firing off clips of ammunition at a shooting range with a two-time robbery victim who swore he would never be victimized again. I spent a day lolling about on a commercial fishing boat and a day jamming with a band of aging rock musicians. One day I simply climbed a tree and sat for hours enjoying the solitude; a developer planned to bulldoze the grove in which I sat to make way for a high-end housing development, and I figured the least I could do was give this last remnant of nature amid the concrete jungle a proper funeral. My biggest coup of all was when I talked my editors into sending me to the Bahamas so I could be on the forward edge of a brewing hurricane that was making its way toward South Florida. The hurricane veered harmlessly out to sea, and I spent three days beachside at a luxury hotel, sipping piña coladas beneath blue skies.

It was in this vein of journalistic inquiry that I got the idea to take Marley for a day at the beach. Up and down South Florida's heavily used shoreline, various municipalities had banned pets, and for good reason. The last thing beachgoers wanted was a wet, sandy dog pooping and peeing and shaking all over them as they worked on their tans. NO PETS signs bristled along nearly every stretch of sand.

There was one place, though, one small, little-known sliver of beach, where there were no signs, no restrictions, no bans on four-legged water lovers. The beach was tucked away in an unincorporated pocket of Palm Beach County about halfway between West Palm Beach and Boca Raton, stretching for a few hundred yards and hidden behind a grassy dune at the end of a dead-end street. There was no parking, no restroom, no lifeguard, just an unspoiled stretch of unregulated white sand meeting endless water. Over the years, its reputation spread by word of mouth among pet owners as one of South Florida's last safe havens for dogs to come and frolic in the surf without risking a fine. The place had no official name; unofficially, everyone knew it as Dog Beach.

Dog Beach operated on its own set of unwritten rules that had evolved over time, put in place by consensus of the dog owners who frequented it, and enforced by peer pressure and a sort of silent moral code. The dog owners policed themselves so others would not be tempted to, punishing violators with withering stares and, if needed, a few choice words. The rules were simple and few: Aggressive dogs had to stay leashed; all others could run free. Owners were to bring plastic bags with them to pick up any droppings their animal might deposit. All trash, including bagged dog waste, was to be carted out. Each dog should arrive with a supply of fresh drinking water. Above all else, there would be absolutely no fouling of the water. The etiquette called for owners, upon arriving, to walk their dogs along the dune line, far from the ocean's edge, until their pets relieved themselves. Then they could bag the waste and safely proceed to the water.

I had heard about Dog Beach but had never visited. Now I had my excuse. This forgotten vestige of the rapidly disappearing Old Florida, the one that existed before the arrival of waterfront condo towers, metered beach parking, and soaring real estate values, was in the news. A pro-development county commissioner had begun squawking about this unregulated stretch of beach and asking why the same rules that applied to other county beaches should not apply here. She made her intent clear: outlaw the furry critters, improve public access, and open this valuable resource to the masses.

I immediately locked in on the story for what it was: a perfect excuse to spend a day at the beach on company time. On a drop-dead-perfect June morning, I traded my tie and briefcase for swimsuit and flip-flops and headed with Marley across the Intracoastal Waterway. I filled the car with as many beach towels as I could find—and that was just for the drive over. As always, Marley's tongue was hanging out, spit flying everywhere. I felt like I was on a road trip with Old Faithful. My only regret was that the windshield wipers weren't on the inside.

Following Dog Beach protocol, I parked several blocks away, where I wouldn't get a ticket, and began the long hike in through a sleepy neighborhood of sixties-vintage bungalows, Marley leading the charge. About halfway there, a gruff voice called out, "Hey, Dog Guy!" I froze, convinced I was about to be busted by an angry neighbor who wanted me to keep my damn dog the hell off his beach. But the voice belonged to another pet owner, who approached me with his own large dog on a leash and handed me a petition to sign urging county commissioners to let Dog Beach stand. Speaking of standing, we would have stood and chatted, but the way Marley and the other dog were circling each other, I knew it was just a matter of seconds before they either (a) lunged at each other in mortal combat or (b) began a family. I yanked Marley away and continued on. Just as we reached the path to the beach, Marley squatted in the weeds and emptied his bowels. Perfect. At least that little social nicety was out of the way. I bagged up the evidence and said, "To the beach!"

When we crested the dune, I was surprised to see several people wading in the shallows with their dogs securely tethered to leashes. What was this all about? I expected the dogs to be running free in unbridled, communal harmony. "A sheriff's deputy was just here," one glum dog owner explained to me. "He said from now on they're enforcing the county leash ordinance and we'll be fined if our dogs are loose." It appeared I had arrived too late to fully enjoy the simple pleasures of Dog Beach. The police, no doubt at the urging of the politically connected anti–Dog Beach forces, were tightening the noose. I obediently walked Marley along the water's edge with the other dog owners, feeling more like I was in a prison exercise yard than on South Florida's last unregulated spit of sand.

I returned with him to my towel and was just pouring Marley a bowl of water from the canteen I had lugged along when over the dune came a shirtless tattooed man in cutoff blue jeans and work boots, a muscular and fierce-looking pit bull terrier on a heavy chain at his side. Pit bulls are known for their aggression, and they were especially notorious during this time in South Florida. They were the dog breed of choice for gang members, thugs, and toughs, and often trained to be vicious. The newspapers were filled with accounts of unprovoked pit bull attacks, sometimes fatal, against both animals and humans. The owner must have noticed me recoiling because he called out, "Don't you worry. Killer's friendly. He don't never fight other dogs." I was just beginning to exhale with relief when he added with obvious pride, "But you should see him rip open a wild hog! I'll tell you, he can get it down and gutted in about fifteen seconds."

Marley and Killer the Pig-Slaying Pit Bull strained at their leashes, circling, sniffing furiously at each other. Marley had never been in a fight in his life and was so much bigger than most other dogs that he had never been intimidated by a challenge, either. Even when a dog attempted to pick a fight, he didn't take the hint. He would merely pounce into a playful stance, butt up, tail wagging, a dumb, happy grin on his face. But he had never before been confronted by a trained killer, a gutter of wild game. I pictured Killer lunging without warning for Marley's throat and not letting go.

Killer's owner was unconcerned. "Unless you're a wild hog, he'll just lick you to death," he said.

I told him the cops had just been here and were going to ticket people who didn't obey the leash ordinance. "I guess they're cracking down," I said.

"That's bullshit!" he yelled, and spit into the sand. "I've been bringing my dogs to this beach for years. You don't need no leash at Dog Beach. Bullshit!" With that he unclipped the heavy chain, and Killer galloped across the sand and into the water. Marley reared back on his hind legs, bouncing up and down. He looked at Killer and then up at me. He looked back at Killer and back at me. His paws padded nervously on the sand, and he let out a soft, sustained whimper. If he could talk, I knew what he would have asked. I scanned the dune line; no cops anywhere in sight. I looked at Marley. *Please! Please! Pretty please! I'll be good. I promise.*

"Go ahead, let him loose," Killer's owner said. "A dog ain't meant to spend his life on the end of a rope."

"Oh, what the hell," I said, and unsnapped the leash. Marley dashed for the water, kicking sand all over us as he blasted off. He crashed into the surf just as a breaker rolled in, tossing him under the water. A second later his head reappeared, and the instant he regained his footing he threw a cross-body block at Killer the Pig-Slaying Pit Bull, knocking both of them off their feet. Together they rolled beneath a wave, and I held my breath, wondering if Marley had just crossed the line that would throw Killer into a homicidal, Lab-butchering fury. But when they popped back up again, their tails were wagging, their mouths grinning. Killer jumped on Marley's back and Marley on Killer's, their jaws clamping playfully around each other's throats. They chased each other up the waterline and back again, sending plumes of spray flying on either side of them. They pranced, they danced, they wrestled, they dove. I don't think I had ever before, or have ever since, witnessed such unadulterated joy.

The other dog owners took our cue, and pretty soon all the dogs, about a dozen in total, were running free. The dogs all got along splendidly; the owners all followed the rules. It was Dog Beach as it was meant to be. This was the real Florida, unblemished and unchecked, the Florida of a forgotten, simpler time and place, immune to the march of progress.

There was only one small problem. As the morning progressed, Marley kept lapping up salt water. I followed behind him with the bowl of fresh water, but he was too distracted to drink. Several times I led him right up to the bowl and stuck his nose into it, but he spurned the fresh water as if it were vinegar, wanting only to return to his new best friend, Killer, and the other dogs.

Out in the shallows, he paused from his play to lap up even more salt water. "Stop that, you dummy!" I yelled at him. "You're going to make yourself . . ." Before I could finish my thought, it happened. A strange glaze settled over his eyes and a horrible churning sound began to erupt from his gut. He arched his back high and opened and shut his mouth several times, as if trying to clear something from his craw. His shoulders heaved; his abdomen contorted. I hurried to finish my sentence: ". . . sick."

The instant the word left my lips, Marley fulfilled the prophecy, committing the ultimate Dog Beach heresy. *GAAAAAAAAACK!*

I raced to pull him out of the water, but it was too late. Everything was coming up. *GAAAAAAAAACK!* I could see last night's dog chow floating on the water's surface, looking surprisingly like it had before it went in. Bobbing among the nuggets were undigested corn kernels he had swiped off the kids' plates, a milk-jug cap, and the severed head of a tiny plastic soldier. The entire evacuation took no more than three seconds, and the instant his stomach was emptied he looked up brightly, apparently fully recovered with no lingering aftereffects, as if to say, *Now that I've got that taken care of, who wants to bodysurf?* I glanced nervously around, but no one had seemed to notice. The other dog owners were occupied with their own dogs farther down the beach, a mother not far away was focused on helping her toddler make a sandcastle, and the few sunbathers scattered about were lying flat on their backs, eyes closed. *Thank God!* I thought, as I waded into Marley's puke zone, roiling the water with my feet as nonchalantly as I could to disperse the evidence. *How embarrassing would that have been?* At any rate, I told myself, despite the technical violation of the No. 1 Dog Beach Rule, we had caused no real harm. After all, it was just undigested food; the fish would be thankful for the meal, wouldn't they? I even picked out the milk-jug cap and soldier's head and put them in my pocket so as not to litter.

"Listen, you," I said sternly, grabbing Marley around the snout and forcing him to look me in the eye. "Stop drinking salt water. What kind of a dog doesn't know enough to not drink salt water?" I considered yanking him off the beach and cutting our adventure short, but he seemed fine now. There couldn't possibly be anything left in his stomach. The damage was done, and we had gotten away with it unde- tected. I released him and he streaked down the beach to rejoin Killer.

What I had failed to consider was that, while Marley's stomach may have been completely emptied, his bowels were not. The sun was reflecting blindingly off the water, and I squinted to see Marley frolicking among the other dogs. As I watched, he abruptly disengaged from the play and began turning in tight circles in the shallow water. I knew the circling maneuver well. It was what he did every morning in the backyard as he prepared to defecate. It was a ritual for him, as though not just any spot would do for the gift he was about to bestow on the world. Sometimes the circling could go on for a minute or more as he sought just the perfect patch of earth. And now he was circling in the shallows of Dog Beach, on that brave frontier where no dog had dared to poop before. He was entering his squatting position. And this time, he had an audience. Killer's dad and several other dog owners were standing within a few yards of him. The mother and her daughter had turned from their sandcastle to gaze out to sea. A couple approached, walking hand in hand along the water's edge. "No," I whispered. "Please, God, no."

"Hey!" someone yelled out. "Get your dog!"

"Stop him!" someone else shouted.

As alarmed voices cried out, the sunbathers propped themselves up to see what all the commotion was about.

I burst into a full sprint, racing to get to him before it was too late. If I could just reach him and yank him out of his squat before his bowels began to move, I might be able to interrupt the whole awful humiliation, at least long enough to get him safely up on the dune. As I raced toward him, I had what can only be described as an out-of-body experience. Even as I ran, I was looking down from above, the scene unfolding one frozen frame at a time. Each step seemed to last an eternity. Each foot hit the sand with a dull thud. My arms swung through the air; my face contorted in a sort of agonized grimace. As I ran, I absorbed the slow-mo frames around me: a young woman sunbather, holding her top in place over her breasts with one hand, her other hand plastered over her mouth; the mother scooping up her child and retreating from the water's edge; the dog owners, their faces twisted with disgust, pointing; Killer's dad, his leathery neck bulging, yelling. Marley was done circling now and in full squat position, looking up to the heavens as if saying a little prayer. And I heard my own voice rising above the din and uncoiling in an oddly guttural, distorted, drawn-out scream: *"Noooooooooooooooo!"*

I was almost there, just feet from him. "Marley, no!" I screamed. "No, Marley, no! No! No! No!" It was no use. Just as I reached him, he exploded in a burst of watery diarrhea. Everyone was jumping back now, recoiling, fleeing to higher ground. Owners were grabbing their dogs. Sunbathers scooped up their towels. Then it was over. Marley trotted out of the water onto the beach, shook off with gusto, and turned to look at me, panting happily. I pulled a plastic bag out of my pocket and held it helplessly in the air. I could see immediately it would do no good. The waves crashed in, spreading Marley's mess across the water and up onto the beach.

"Dude," Killer's dad said in a voice that made me appreciate how the wild hogs must feel at the instant of Killer's final, fatal lunge. "That was not cool."

No, it wasn't cool at all. Marley and I had violated the sacred rule of Dog Beach. We had fouled the water, not once but twice, and ruined the morning for everyone. It was time to beat a quick retreat.

"Sorry," I mumbled to Killer's owner as I snapped the leash on Marley. "He swallowed a bunch of seawater."

Back at the car, I threw a towel over Marley and vigorously rubbed him down. The more I rubbed, the more he shook, and soon I was covered in sand and spray and fur. I wanted to be mad at him. I wanted to strangle him. But it was too late now. Besides, who wouldn't get sick drinking a half gallon of salt water? As with so many of his misdeeds, this one was not malicious or premeditated. It wasn't as though he had disobeyed a command or set out to intentionally humiliate me. He simply had to go and he went. True, at the wrong place and the wrong time and in front of all the wrong people. I knew he was a victim of his own diminished mental capacity. He was the only beast on the whole beach dumb enough to guzzle seawater. The dog was defective. How could I hold that against him?

"You don't have to look so pleased with yourself," I said as I loaded him into the backseat. But pleased he was. He could not have looked happier had I bought him his own Caribbean island. What he did not know was that this would be his last time setting a paw in any body of salt water. His days—or rather, hours—as a beach bum were behind him. "Well, Salty Dog," I said on the drive home, "you've done it this time. If dogs are banned from Dog Beach, we'll know why." It would take several more years, but in the end that's exactly what happened.

CHAPTER 21

A Northbound Plane

❊

S hortly after Colleen turned two, I inadvertently set off a fateful series of events that would lead us to leave Florida. And I did it with the click of a mouse. I had wrapped up my column early for the day and found myself with a half hour to kill as I waited for my editor. On a whim I decided to check out the website of a magazine I had been subscribing to since not long after we bought our West Palm Beach house. The magazine was *Organic Gardening*, which was launched in 1942 by the eccentric J. I. Rodale and went on to become the bible of the back-to-the-earth movement that blossomed in the 1960s and 1970s.

Rodale had been a New York City businessman specializing in electrical switches when his health began to fail. Instead of turning to modern medicine to solve his problems, he moved from the city to a small farm outside the tiny borough of Emmaus, Pennsylvania, and began playing in the dirt. He had a deep distrust of technology and believed the modern farming and gardening methods sweeping the country, nearly all of them relying on chemical pesticides and fertilizers, were not the saviors of American agriculture they purported to be. Rodale's theory was that the chemicals were gradually poisoning the earth and all of its inhabitants. He began experimenting with farming techniques that mimicked nature. On his farm, he built huge compost piles of decaying plant matter, which, once the material had turned to rich black humus, he used as fertilizer and a natural soil builder. He covered the dirt in his garden rows with a thick carpet of straw to suppress weeds and retain moisture. He planted cover crops of clover and alfalfa and then plowed them under to return nutrients to the soil. Instead of spraying for insects, he unleashed thousands of ladybugs and other beneficial insects that devoured the destructive ones. He was a bit of a kook, but his theories proved themselves. His garden flourished and so did his health, and he trumpeted his successes in the pages of his magazine.

By the time I started reading *Organic Gardening*, J. I. Rodale was long dead and so was his son, Robert, who had built his father's business, Rodale Press, into a multimillion-dollar publishing company. The magazine was not very well written or edited; reading it, you got the impression it was put out by a group of dedicated but amateurish devotees of J. I.'s philosophy, serious gardeners with no professional training as journalists; later I would learn this was exactly the case. Regardless, the organic philosophy increasingly made sense to me, especially after Jenny's miscarriage and our suspicion that it might have had something to do with the pesticides we had used. By the time Colleen was born, our yard was a little organic oasis in a suburban sea of chemical weed-and-feed applications and pesticides. Passersby often stopped to admire our thriving front garden, which I tended with increasing passion, and they almost always asked the same question: "What do you put on it to make it look so good?" When I answered, "I don't," they looked at me uncomfortably, as though they had just stumbled upon something unspeakably subversive going on in well-ordered, homogeneous, conformist Boca Raton.

That afternoon in my office, I clicked through the screens at *organicgardening.com* and eventually found my way to a button that said "Career Opportunities." I clicked on it, why I'm still not sure. I loved my job as a columnist; loved the daily interaction I had with readers; loved the freedom to pick my own topics and be as serious or as flippant as I wanted to be. I loved the newsroom and the quirky, brainy, neurotic, idealistic people it attracted. I loved being in the middle of the biggest story of the day. I had no desire to leave newspapers for a sleepy publishing company in the middle of nowhere. Still, I began scrolling through the Rodale job postings, more idly curious than anything, but midway down the list I stopped cold. *Organic Gardening*, the company's flagship magazine, was seeking a new managing editor. My heart skipped a beat. I had often daydreamed about the huge difference a decent journalist could make at the magazine, and now here was my chance. It was crazy; it was ridiculous. A career editing stories about cauliflower and compost? Why would I want to do that?

That night I told Jenny about the opening, fully expecting her to tell me I was insane for even considering it. Instead she surprised me by encouraging me to send a résumé. The idea of leaving the heat and humidity and congestion and crime of South Florida for a simpler life in the country appealed to her. She missed four seasons and hills. She missed falling leaves and spring daffodils. She missed icicles and apple cider. She wanted our kids and, as ridiculous as it sounds, our dog to experience the wonders of a winter blizzard. "Marley's never even chased a snowball," she said, stroking his fur with her bare foot.

"Now, there's a good reason for changing careers," I said.

"You should do it just to satisfy your curiosity," she said. "See what happens. If they offer it to you, you can always turn them down."

I had to admit I shared her dream about moving north again.

As much as I enjoyed our dozen years in South Florida, I was a northern native who had never learned to stop missing three things: rolling hills, changing seasons, and open land. Even as I grew to love Florida with its mild winters, spicy food, and comically irascible mix of people, I did not stop dreaming of someday escaping to my own private paradise—not a postage-stamp-sized lot in the heart of hyperprecious Boca Raton but a real piece of land where I could dig in the dirt, chop my own firewood, and tromp through the forest, my dog at my side.

I applied, fully convincing myself it was just a lark. Two weeks later the phone rang and it was J. I. Rodale's granddaughter, Maria Rodale. I had sent my letter to "Dear Human Resources" and was so surprised to be hearing from the owner of the company that I asked her to repeat her last name. Maria had taken a personal interest in the magazine

her grandfather had founded, and she was intent on returning it to its former glory. She was convinced she needed a
professional journalist, not another earnest organic gardener, to do that, and she wanted to take on more challenging
and important stories about the environment, genetic engineering, factory farming, and the burgeoning organic
movement.

I arrived for the job interview fully intending to play hard
to get, but I was hooked the moment I drove out of the
airport and onto the first curving, two-lane country road. At
every turn was another postcard: a stone farmhouse here, a
covered bridge there. Icy brooks gurgled down hillsides,
and furrowed farmland stretched to the horizon like God's
own golden robes. It didn't help that it was spring and every
last tree in the Lehigh Valley was in full, glorious bloom. At a
lonely country stop sign, I stepped out of my rental car and
stood in the middle of the pavement. For as far as I could see
in any direction, there was nothing but woods and meadows. Not a car, not a person, not a building. At the first pay
phone I could find, I called Jenny. "You're not going to
believe this place," I said.

Two months later the movers had the entire contents of our
Boca house loaded into a gigantic truck. An auto carrier
arrived to haul off our car and minivan. We turned the house
keys over to the new owners and spent our last night in
Florida sleeping on the floor of a neighbor's home, Marley
sprawled out in the middle of us. "Indoor camping!" Patrick
shrieked.

The next morning I arose early and took Marley for what would be his last walk on Florida soil. He sniffed and tugged and pranced as we circled the block, stopping to lift his leg on every shrub and mailbox we came to, happily oblivious to the abrupt change I was about to foist on him. I had bought a sturdy plastic travel crate to carry him on the airplane, and following Dr. Jay's advice, I clamped open Marley's jaws after our walk and slipped a double dose of tranquilizers down his throat. By the time our neighbor dropped us off at Palm Beach International Airport, Marley was red-eyed and exceptionally mellow. We could have strapped him to a rocket and he wouldn't have minded.

In the terminal, the Grogan clan cut a fine form: two wildly excited little boys racing around in circles, a hungry baby in a stroller, two stressed-out parents, and one very stoned dog. Rounding out the lineup was the rest of our menagerie: two frogs, three goldfish, a hermit crab, a snail named Sluggy, and a box of live crickets for feeding the frogs. As we waited in line at check-in, I assembled the plastic pet carrier. It was the biggest one I could find, but when we reached the counter, a woman in uniform looked at Marley, looked at the crate, looked back at Marley, and said, "We can't allow that dog aboard in that container. He's too big for it."

"The pet store said this was the 'large dog' size," I pleaded.

"FAA regulations require that the dog can freely stand up inside and turn fully around," she explained, adding skeptically, "Go ahead, give it a try."

I opened the gate and called Marley, but he was not about

to voluntarily walk into this mobile jail cell. I pushed and prodded, coaxed and cajoled; he wasn't budging. Where were the dog biscuits when I needed them? I searched my pockets for something to bribe him with, finally fishing out a tin of breath mints. This was as good as it was going to get. I took one out and held it in front of his nose. "Want a mint, Marley? Go get the mint!" and I tossed it into the crate. Sure enough, he took the bait and blithely entered the box.

The lady was right; he didn't quite fit. He had to scrunch down so his head wouldn't hit the ceiling; even with his nose touching the back wall, his butt stuck out the open door. I scrunched his tail down and closed the gate, nudging his rear inside. "What did I tell you?" I said, hoping she would consider it a comfortable fit.

"He's got to be able to turn around," she said.

"Turn around, boy," I beckoned to him, giving a little whistle. "Come on, turn around." He shot a glance over his shoulder at me with those doper eyes, his head scraping the ceiling, as if awaiting instructions on just how to accomplish such a feat.

If he could not turn around, the airline was not letting him aboard the flight. I checked my watch. We had twelve minutes left to get through security, down the concourse, and onto the plane. "Come here, Marley!" I said more desperately. "Come on!" I snapped my fingers, rattled the metal gate, made kissy-kissy sounds. "Come on," I pleaded. "Turn around." I was about to drop to my knees and beg when I heard a crash, followed almost immediately by Patrick's voice.

"Oops," he said.

"The frogs are loose!" Jenny screamed, jumping into action.

"Froggy! Croaky! Come back!" the boys yelled in unison.

My wife was on all fours now, racing around the terminal as the frogs cannily stayed one hop ahead of her. Passersby began to stop and stare. From a distance you could not see the frogs at all, just the crazy lady with the diaper bag hanging from her neck, crawling around like she had started the morning off with a little too much moonshine. From their expressions, I could tell they fully expected her to start howling at any moment.

"Excuse me a second," I said as calmly as I could to the airline worker, then joined Jenny on my hands and knees.

After doing our part to entertain the early-morning travel crowd, we finally captured Froggy and Croaky just as they were ready to make their final leap for freedom out the automatic doors. As we turned back, I heard a mighty ruckus coming from the dog crate. The entire box shivered and lurched across the floor, and when I peered in I saw that Marley had somehow gotten himself turned around. "See?" I said to the baggage supervisor. "He can turn around, no problem."

"Okay," she said with a frown. "But you're really pushing it."

Two workers lifted Marley and his crate onto a dolly and wheeled him away. The rest of us raced for our plane, arriving at the gate just as the flight attendants were closing the hatch. It occurred to me that if we missed the flight, Marley would be arriving alone in Pennsylvania, a scene of potential pandemonium I did not even want to contemplate. "Wait! We're here!" I shouted, pushing Colleen ahead of me, the boys and Jenny trailing by fifty feet.

As we settled into our seats, I finally allowed myself to exhale. We had gotten Marley squared away. We had captured the frogs. We had made the flight. Next stop, Allentown, Pennsylvania. I could relax now. Through the window I watched as a tram pulled up with the dog crate sitting on it. "Look," I said to the kids. "There's Marley." They waved out the window and called, "Hi, Waddy!"

As the engines revved and the flight attendant went over the safety precautions, I pulled out a magazine. That's when I noticed Jenny freeze in the row in front of me. Then I heard it, too. From below our feet, deep in the bowels of the plane, came a sound, muffled but undeniable. It was pitifully mournful sound, a sort of primal call that started low and rose as it went. *Oh, dear Jesus, he's down there howling.* For the record, Labrador retrievers do not howl. Beagles howl. Wolves howl. Labs do not howl, at least not well. Marley had attempted to howl twice before, both times in answer to a passing police siren, tossing back his head, forming his mouth into an *O* shape, and letting loose the most pathetic sound I have ever heard, more like he was gargling than answering the call of the wild. But now, no question about it, he was howling.

The passengers began to look up from their newspapers and novels. A flight attendant handing out pillows paused and cocked her head quizzically. A woman across the aisle from us looked at her husband and asked: "Listen. Do you hear that? I think it's a dog." Jenny stared straight ahead. I stared into my magazine. If anyone asked, we were denying ownership.

"Waddy's sad," Patrick said.

No, son, I wanted to correct him, *some strange dog we have never seen before and have no knowledge of is sad.* But I just pulled my magazine higher over my face, following the advice of the immortal Richard Milhous Nixon: plausible deniability. The jet engines whined and the plane taxied down the runway, drowning out Marley's dirge. I pictured him down below in the dark hold, alone, scared, confused, stoned, not even able to fully stand up. I imagined the roaring engines, which in Marley's warped mind might be just another thunderous assault by random lightning bolts determined to take him out. The poor guy. I wasn't willing to admit he was mine, but I knew I would be spending the whole flight worrying about him.

The airplane was barely off the ground when I heard another little crash, and this time it was Conor who said, "Oops." I looked down and then, once again, stared straight into my magazine. *Plausible deniability.* After several seconds, I furtively glanced around. When I was pretty sure no one was staring, I leaned forward and whispered into Jenny's ear: "Don't look now, but the crickets are loose."

CHAPTER 22

In the Land of Pencils

❄

We settled into a rambling house on two acres perched on the side of a steep hill. Or perhaps it was a small mountain; the locals seemed to disagree on this point. Our property had a meadow where we could pick wild raspberries, a woods where I could chop logs to my heart's content, and a small, spring-fed creek where the kids and Marley soon found they could get exceptionally muddy. There was a fireplace and endless garden possibilities and a white-steepled church on the next hill, visible from our kitchen window when the leaves dropped in the fall.

Our new home even came with a neighbor right out of Central Casting, an orange-bearded bear of a man who lived in a 1790s stone farmhouse and on Sundays enjoyed sitting on his back porch and shooting his rifle into the woods just for fun, much to Marley's unnerved dismay. On our first day in our new house, he walked over with a bottle of home-made wild-cherry wine and a basket of the biggest blackberries I had ever seen. He introduced himself as Digger. As we surmised from the nickname, Digger made his living as an excavator. If we had any holes we needed dug or earth we wanted moved, he instructed, we were to just give a shout and he'd swing by with one of his big machines. "And if you hit a deer with your car, come get me," he said with a wink. "We'll butcher it up and split the meat before the game officer knows a thing." No doubt about it, we weren't in Boca anymore.

There was only one thing missing from our new bucolic existence. Minutes after we pulled into the driveway of our new house, Conor looked up at me, big tears rolling out of his eyes, and declared: "I thought there were going to be pencils in Pencilvania." For our boys, now ages seven and five, this was a near deal breaker. Given the name of the state we were adopting, both of them arrived fully expecting to see bright yellow writing implements hanging like berries from every tree and shrub, there for the plucking. They were crushed to learn otherwise.

What our property lacked in school supplies, it made up for in skunks, opossums, woodchucks, and poison ivy, which flourished along the edge of our woods and snaked up the trees, giving me hives just to look at it. One morning I glanced out the kitchen window as I fumbled with the coffeemaker and there staring back at me was a magnificent eight-point buck. Another morning a family of wild turkeys gobbled its way across the backyard. As Marley and I walked through the woods down the hill from our house one Saturday, we came upon a mink trapper laying snares. A mink trapper! Almost in my backyard! What the Bocahontas set would have given for that connection.

Living in the country was at once peaceful, charming—and just a little lonely. The Pennsylvania Dutch were polite but cautious of outsiders. And we were definitely outsiders. After South Florida's legion crowds and lines, I should have been ecstatic about the solitude. Instead, at least in the early months, I found myself darkly ruminating over our decision to move to a place where so few others apparently wanted to live.

Marley, on the other hand, had no such misgivings. Except for the crack of Digger's gun going off, the new country lifestyle fit him splendidly. For a dog with more energy than sense, what wasn't to like? He raced across the lawn, crashed through the brambles, splashed through the creek. His life's mission was to catch one of the countless rabbits that considered my garden their own personal salad bar. He would spot a rabbit munching the lettuce and barrel off down the hill in hot pursuit, ears flapping behind him, paws pounding the ground, his bark filling the air. He was about as stealthy as a marching band and never got closer than a dozen feet before his intended prey scampered off into the woods to safety. True to his trademark, he remained eternally optimistic that success waited just around the bend. He would loop back, tail wagging, not discouraged in the least, and five minutes later do it all over again. Fortunately, he was no better at sneaking up on the skunks.

Autumn came and with it a whole new mischievous game: Attack the Leaf Pile. In Florida, trees did not shed their leaves in the fall, and Marley was positively convinced the foliage drifting down from the skies now was a gift meant just for him. As I raked the orange and yellow leaves into giant heaps, Marley would sit and watch patiently, biding his time, waiting until just the right moment to strike. Only after I had gathered a mighty towering pile would he slink forward, crouched low. Every few steps, he would stop, front paw raised, to sniff the air like a lion on the Serengeti stalking an unsuspecting gazelle. Then, just as I leaned on my rake to admire my handiwork, he would lunge, charging across the lawn in a series of bounding leaps, flying for the last several feet and landing in a giant belly flop in the middle of the pile, where he growled and rolled and flailed and scratched and snapped, and, for reasons not clear to me, fiercely chased his tail, not stopping until my neat leaf pile was scattered across the lawn again. Then he would sit up amid *his* handiwork, the shredded remains of leaves clinging to his fur, and give me a self-satisfied look, as if his contribution were an integral part of the leaf-gathering process.

Our first Christmas in Pennsylvania was supposed to be white. Jenny and I had had to do a sales job on Patrick and Conor to convince them that leaving their home and friends in Florida was for the best, and one of the big selling points was the promise of snow. Not just any kind of snow, but deep, fluffy, made-for-postcards snow, the kind that fell from the sky in big silent flakes, piled into drifts, and was of just the right consistency for shaping into snowmen. And snow for Christmas Day, well, that was best of all, the Holy Grail of northern winter experiences. We wantonly spun a Currier and Ives image for them of waking up on Christmas morning to a starkly white landscape, unblemished except for the solitary tracks of Santa's sleigh outside our front door.

In the week leading up to the big day, the three of them sat in the window together for hours, their eyes glued on the leaden sky as if they could will it to open and discharge its load. "Come on, snow!" the kids chanted. They had never seen it; Jenny and I hadn't seen it for the last quarter of our lives. We wanted snow, but the clouds would not give it up. A few days before Christmas, the whole family piled into the minivan and drove to a farm a half mile away where we cut a spruce tree and enjoyed a free hayride and hot apple cider around a bonfire. It was the kind of classic northern holiday moment we had missed in Florida, but one thing was absent. Where was the damn snow? Jenny and I were beginning to regret how recklessly we had hyped the inevitable first snowfall. As we hauled our fresh-cut tree home, the sweet scent of its sap filling the van, the kids complained about getting gypped. First no pencils, now no snow; what else had their parents lied to them about?

Christmas morning found a brand-new toboggan beneath the tree and enough snow gear to outfit an excursion to Antarctica, but the view out our windows remained all bare branches, dormant lawns, and brown cornfields. I built a cheery fire in the fireplace and told the children to be patient. The snow would come when the snow would come.

New Year's arrived and still it did not come. Even Marley seemed antsy, pacing and gazing out the windows, whimpering softly, as if he too felt he had been sold a bill of goods. The kids returned to school after the holiday, and still nothing. At the breakfast table they gazed sullenly at me, the father who had betrayed them. I began making lame excuses, saying things like "Maybe little boys and girls in some other place need the snow more than we do."

"Yeah, right, Dad," Patrick said.

Three weeks into the new year, the snow finally rescued me from my purgatory of guilt. It came during the night after everyone was asleep, and Patrick was the first to sound the alarm, running into our bedroom at dawn and yanking open the blinds. "Look! Look!" he squealed. "It's here!" Jenny and I sat up in bed to behold our vindication. A white blanket covered the hillsides and cornfields and pine trees and rooftops, stretching to the horizon. "Of course, it's here," I answered nonchalantly. "What did I tell you?"

The snow was nearly a foot deep and still coming down. Soon Conor and Colleen came chugging down the hall, thumbs in mouths, blankies trailing behind them. Marley was up and stretching, banging his tail into everything, sensing the excitement. I turned to Jenny and said, "I guess going back to sleep isn't an option," and when she confirmed it was not, I turned to the kids and shouted, "Okay, snow bunnies, let's suit up!"

For the next half hour we wrestled with zippers and leggings and buckles and hoods and gloves. By the time we were done, the kids looked like mummies and our kitchen like the staging area for the Winter Olympics. And competing in the Goof on Ice Downhill Competition, Large Canine Division, was . . . Marley the Dog. I opened the front door and before anyone else could step out, Marley blasted past us, knocking the well-bundled Colleen over in the process.

The instant his paws hit the strange white stuff—*Ah, wet! Ah, cold!*—he had second thoughts and attempted an abrupt about-face. As anyone who has ever driven a car in snow knows, sudden braking coupled with tight U-turns is never a good idea.

Marley went into a full skid, his rear end spinning out in front of him. He dropped down on one flank briefly before bouncing upright again just in time to somersault down the front porch steps and headfirst into a snowdrift. When he popped back up a second later, he looked like a giant powdered doughnut. Except for a black nose and two brown eyes, he was completely dusted in white. The Abominable Snowdog. Marley did not know what to make of this foreign substance. He jammed his nose deep into it and let loose a violent sneeze. He snapped at it and rubbed his face in it. Then, as if an invisible hand reached down from the heavens and jabbed him with a giant shot of adrenaline, he took off at full throttle, racing around the yard in a series of giant, loping leaps interrupted every several feet by a random somersault or nosedive. Snow was almost as much fun as raiding the neighbors' trash.

To follow Marley's tracks in the snow was to begin to understand his warped mind. His path was filled with abrupt twists and turns and about-faces, with erratic loops and figure-eights, with corkscrews and triple lutzes, as though he were following some bizarre algorithm that only he could understand. Soon the kids were taking his lead, spinning and rolling and frolicking, snow packing into every crease and crevice of their outerwear. Jenny came out with buttered toast, mugs of hot cocoa, and an announcement: school was canceled. I knew there was no way I was getting my little two-wheel-drive Nissan out the driveway anytime soon, let alone up and down the unplowed mountain roads, and I declared an official snow day for me, too.

I scraped the snow away from the stone circle I had built that fall for backyard campfires and soon had a crackling blaze going. The kids glided screaming down the hill in the toboggan, past the campfire and to the edge of the woods, Marley chasing behind them. I looked at Jenny and asked, "If someone had told you a year ago that your kids would be sledding right out their back door, would you have believed them?"

"Not a chance," she said, then wound up and unleashed a snowball that thumped me in the chest. The snow was in her hair, a blush in her cheeks, her breath rising in a cloud above her.

"Come here and kiss me," I said.

Later, as the kids warmed themselves by the fire, I decided to try a run on the toboggan, something I hadn't done since I was a teenager. "Care to join me?" I asked Jenny.

"Sorry, Jean Claude, you're on your own," she said.

I positioned the toboggan at the top of the hill and lay back on it, propped up on my elbows, my feet tucked inside its nose. I began rocking to get moving. Not often did Marley have the opportunity to look down at me, and having me prone like that was tantamount to an invitation. He sidled up to me and sniffed my face. "What do you want?" I asked, and that was all the welcome he needed. He clambered aboard, straddling me and dropping onto my chest. "Get off me, you big lug!" I screamed. But it was too late. We were already creeping forward, gathering speed as we began our descent.

"Bon voyage!" Jenny yelled behind us.

Off we went, snow flying, Marley plastered on top of me, licking me lustily all over my face as we careered down the slope. With our combined weight, we had considerably more momentum than the kids had, and we barreled past the point where their tracks petered out. "Hold on, Marley!" I screamed. "We're going into the woods!"

We shot past a large walnut tree, then between two wild cherry trees, miraculously avoiding all unyielding objects as we crashed through the underbrush, brambles tearing at us. It suddenly occurred to me that just up ahead was the bank leading down several feet to the creek, still unfrozen. I tried to kick my feet out to use as brakes, but they were stuck. The bank was steep, nearly a sheer drop-off, and we were going over. I had time only to wrap my arms around Marley, squeeze my eyes shut, and yell, "Whoaaaaaa!"

Our toboggan shot over the bank and dropped out from beneath us. I felt like I was in one of those classic cartoon moments, suspended in midair for an endless second before falling to ruinous injury. Only in this cartoon I was welded to a madly salivating Labrador retriever. We clung to each other as we crash-landed into a snowbank with a soft *poof* and, hanging half off the toboggan, slid to the water's edge. I opened my eyes and took stock of my condition. I could wiggle my toes and fingers and rotate my neck; nothing was broken. Marley was up and prancing around me, eager to do it all over again. I stood up with a groan and, brushing myself off, said, "I'm getting too old for this stuff." In the months

ahead it would become increasingly obvious that Marley
was, too.

Sometime toward the end of that first winter in Pennsylvania
I began to notice Marley had moved quietly out of middle
age and into retirement. He had turned nine that December,
and ever so slightly he was slowing down. He still had his
bursts of unbridled, adrenaline-pumped energy, as he did on
the day of the first snowfall, but they were briefer now and
farther apart. He was content to snooze most of the day, and
on walks he tired before I did, a first in our relationship. One
late-winter day, the temperature above freezing and the
scent of spring thaw in the air, I walked him down our hill
and up the next one, even steeper than ours, where the
white church perched on the crest beside an old cemetery
filled with Civil War veterans. It was a walk I took often and
one that even the previous fall Marley had made without
visible effort, despite the angle of the climb, which always
got us both panting. This time, though, he was falling
behind. I coaxed him along, calling out words of encouragement, but it was like watching a toy slowly wind down as
its battery went dead. Marley just did not have the oomph
needed to make it to the top. I stopped to let him rest before
continuing, something I had never had to do before. "You're
not going soft on me, are you?" I asked, leaning over and
stroking his face with my gloved hands. He looked up at me,
his eyes bright, his nose wet, not at all concerned about his
flagging energy. He had a contented but tuckered-out look
on his face, as though life got no better than this, sitting

along the side of a country road on a crisp late-winter's day
with your master at your side. "If you think I'm carrying
you," I said, "forget it."

The sun bathed over him, and I noticed just how much
gray had crept into his tawny face. Because his fur was so
light, the effect was subtle but undeniable. His whole
muzzle and a good part of his brow had turned from buff
to white. Without us quite realizing it, our eternal puppy had
become a senior citizen.

That's not to say he was any better behaved. Marley was
still up to all his old antics, simply at a more leisurely pace.
He still stole food off the children's plates. He still flipped
open the lid of the kitchen trash can with his nose and
rummaged inside. He still strained at his leash. Still swallowed a wide assortment of household objects. Still drank
out of the bathtub and trailed water from his gullet. And
when the skies darkened and thunder rumbled, he still
panicked and, if alone, turned destructive. One day we
arrived home to find Marley in a lather and Conor's mattress
splayed open down to the coils.

Over the years, we had become philosophical about the
damage, which had become much less frequent now that
we were away from Florida's daily storm patterns. In a dog's
life, some plaster would fall, some cushions would open,
some rugs would shred. Like any relationship, this one had
its costs. They were costs we came to accept and balance
against the joy and amusement and protection and companionship he gave us. We could have bought a small yacht
with what we spent on our dog and all the things he
destroyed. Then again, how many yachts wait by the door

all day for your return? How many live for the moment they can climb in your lap or ride down the hill with you on a toboggan, licking your face?

Marley had earned his place in our family. Like a quirky but beloved uncle, he was what he was. He would never be Lassie or Benji or Old Yeller; he would never reach Westminster or even the county fair. We knew that now. We accepted him for the dog he was, and loved him all the more for it.

"You old geezer," I said to him on the side of the road that late-winter day, scruffing his neck. Our goal, the cemetery, was still a steep climb ahead. But just as in life, I was figuring out, the destination was less important than the journey. I dropped to one knee, running my hands down his sides, and said, "Let's just sit here for a while." When he was ready, we turned back down the hill and poked our way home.

CHAPTER 23

Poultry on Parade

✳

That spring we decided to try our hand at animal husbandry. We owned two acres in the country now; it only seemed right to share it with a farm animal or two. Besides, I was editor of *Organic Gardening*, a magazine that had long celebrated the incorporation of animals—and their manure—into a healthy, well-balanced garden. "A cow would be fun," Jenny suggested.

"A cow?" I asked. "Are you crazy? We don't even have a barn; how can we have a cow? Where do you suggest we keep it, in the garage next to the minivan?"

"How about sheep?" she said. "Sheep are cute." I shot her my well-practiced you're-not-being-practical look.

"A goat? Goats are adorable."

In the end we settled on poultry. For any gardener who has sworn off chemical pesticides and fertilizers, chickens made a lot of sense. They were inexpensive and relatively low-maintenance. They needed only a small coop and a few cups of cracked corn each morning to be happy. Not only did they provide fresh eggs, but, when let loose to roam, they spent their days studiously scouring the property, eating bugs and grubs, devouring ticks, scratching up the soil like efficient little rototillers, and fertilizing with their high-nitrogen droppings as they went. Each evening at dusk they returned to their coop on their own. What wasn't to like? A chicken was an organic gardener's best friend. Chickens made perfect sense. Besides, as Jenny pointed out, they passed the cuteness test.

Chickens it was. Jenny had become friendly with a mom from school who lived on a farm and said she'd be happy to give us some chicks from the next clutch of eggs to hatch. I told Digger about our plans, and he agreed a few hens around the place made sense. Digger had a large coop of his own in which he kept a flock of chickens for both eggs and meat.

"Just one word of warning," he said, folding his meaty arms across his chest. "Whatever you do, don't let the kids name them. Once you name 'em, they're no longer poultry, they're pets."

"Right," I said. Chicken farming, I knew, had no room for sentimentality. Hens could live fifteen years or more but only produced eggs in their first couple of years. When they stopped laying, it was time for the stewing pot. That was just part of managing a flock.

Digger looked hard at me, as if divining what I was up against, and added, "Once you name them, it's all over."

"Absolutely," I agreed. "No names."

The next evening I pulled into the driveway from work, and the three kids raced out of the house to greet me, each cradling a newborn chick. Jenny was behind them with a fourth in her hands. Her friend, Donna, had brought the baby birds over that afternoon. They were barely a day old and peered up at me with cocked heads as if to ask, "Are you my mama?"

Patrick was the first to break the news. "I named mine Feathers!" he proclaimed.

"Mine is Tweety," said Conor.

"My wicka Wuffy," Colleen chimed in.

I shot Jenny a quizzical look.

"Fluffy," Jenny said. "She named her chicken Fluffy."

"Jenny," I protested. "What did Digger tell us? These are farm animals, not pets."

"Oh, get real, Farmer John," she said. "You know as well as I do that you could never hurt one of these. Just look at how cute they are."

"Jenny," I said, the frustration rising in my voice.

"By the way," she said, holding up the fourth chick in her hands, "meet Shirley."

Feathers, Tweety, Fluffy, and Shirley took up residence in a box on the kitchen counter, a lightbulb dangling above them for warmth. They ate and they pooped and they ate some more—and grew at a breathtaking pace. Several weeks after we brought the birds home, something jolted me awake before dawn. I sat up in bed and listened. From downstairs came a weak, sickly call. It was croaky and hoarse, more like a tubercular cough than a proclamation of dominance. It sounded again: *Cock-a-doodle-do!* A few seconds ticked past and then came an equally sickly, but distinct, reply: *Rook-ru-rook-ru-roo!*

I shook Jenny and, when she opened her eyes, asked:

"When Donna brought the chicks over, you did ask her to check to make sure they were hens, right?"

"You mean you can do that?" she asked, and rolled back over, sound asleep.

It's called sexing. Farmers who know what they are doing can inspect a newborn chicken and determine, with about 80 percent accuracy, whether it is male or female. At the farm store, sexed chicks command a premium price. The cheaper option is to buy "straight run" birds of unknown gender. You take your chances with straight run, the idea being that the males will be slaughtered young for meat and the hens will be kept to lay eggs. Playing the straight-run gamble, of course, assumes you have what it takes to kill, gut, and pluck any excess males you might end up with. As anyone who has ever raised chickens knows, two roosters in a flock is one rooster too many.

As it turned out, Donna had not attempted to sex our four chicks, and three of our four "laying hens" were males. We had on our kitchen counter the poultry equivalent of Boys Town U.S.A. The thing about roosters is they're never content to play second chair to any other rooster. If you had equal numbers of roosters and hens, you might think they would pair off into happy little Ozzie and Harriet–style couples. But you would be wrong. The males will fight endlessly, bloodying one another gruesomely, to determine who will dominate the roost. Winner takes all.

As they grew into adolescents, our three roosters took to posturing and pecking and, most distressing considering they were still in our kitchen as I raced to finish their coop in the backyard, crowing their testosterone-pumped hearts out. Shirley, our one poor, overtaxed female, was getting way more attention than even the most lusty of women could want.

I had thought the constant crowing of our roosters would drive Marley insane. In his younger years, the sweet chirp of a single tiny songbird in the yard would set him off on a frenetic barking jag as he raced from one window to the next, hopping up and down on his hind legs. Three crowing roosters a few steps from his food bowl, however, had no effect on him at all. He didn't seem to even know they were there. Each day the crowing grew louder and stronger, rising up from the kitchen to echo through the house at five in the morning. *Cock-a-doodle-dooooo!* Marley slept right through the racket. That's when it first occurred to me that maybe he wasn't just ignoring the crowing; maybe he couldn't hear it. I walked up behind him one afternoon as he snoozed in the kitchen and said, "Marley?" Nothing. I said it louder: "Marley!" Nothing. I clapped my hands and shouted, "MARLEY!" He lifted his head and looked blankly around, his ears up, trying to figure out what it was his radar had detected. I did it again, clapping loudly and shouting his name. This time he turned his head enough to catch a glimpse of me standing behind him. *Oh, it's you!* He bounced up, tail wagging, happy—and clearly surprised— to see me. He bumped up against my legs in greeting and gave me a sheepish look as if to ask, *What's the idea sneaking up on me like that?* My dog, it seemed, was going deaf.

It all made sense. In recent months Marley seemed to simply ignore me in a way he never had before. I would call for him and he would not so much as glance my way. I would take him outside before turning in for the night, and he would sniff his way across the yard, oblivious to my whistles and calls to get him to turn back. He would be asleep at my feet in the family room when someone would ring the doorbell—and he would not so much as open an eye.

Marley's ears had caused him problems from an early age. Like many Labrador retrievers, he was predisposed to ear infections, and we had spent a small fortune on antibiotics, ointments, cleansers, drops, and veterinarian visits. He even underwent surgery to shorten his ear canals in an attempt to correct the problem. It had not occurred to me until after we brought the impossible-to-ignore roosters into our house that all those years of problems had taken their toll and our dog had gradually slipped into a muffled world of faraway whispers.

Not that he seemed to mind. Retirement suited Marley just fine, and his hearing problems didn't seem to impinge on his leisurely country lifestyle. If anything, deafness proved fortuitous for him, finally giving him a doctor-certified excuse for disobeying. After all, how could he heed a command that he could not hear? As thick-skulled as I always insisted he was, I swear he figured out how to use his deafness to his advantage. Drop a piece of steak into his bowl, and he would come trotting in from the next room. He still had the ability to detect the dull, satisfying thud of meat on metal. But yell for him to come when he had somewhere else he'd rather be going, and he'd stroll blithely away from you, not even glancing guiltily over his shoulder as he once would have.

"I think the dog's scamming us," I told Jenny. She agreed his hearing problems seemed selective, but every time we tested him, sneaking up, clapping our hands, shouting his name, he would not respond. And every time we dropped food into his bowl, he would come running. He appeared to be deaf to all sounds except the one that was dearest to his heart or, more accurately, his stomach: the sound of dinner.

Marley went through life insatiably hungry. Not only did we give him four big scoops of dog chow a day—enough food to sustain an entire family of Chihuahuas for a week—but we began freely supplementing his diet with table scraps, against the better advice of every dog guide we had ever read. Table scraps, we knew, simply programmed dogs to prefer human food to dog chow (and given the choice between a half-eaten hamburger and dry kibble, who could blame them?). Table scraps were a recipe for canine obesity. Labs, in particular, were prone to chubbiness, especially as they moved into middle age and beyond. Some Labs, especially those of the English variety, were so rotund by adulthood, they looked like they'd been inflated with an air hose and were ready to float down Fifth Avenue in the Macy's Thanksgiving Day Parade.

Not our dog. Marley had many problems, but obesity was not among them. No matter how many calories he devoured, he always burned more. All that unbridled high-strung exuberance consumed vast amounts of energy. He was like a high-kilowatt electric plant that instantly converted every ounce of available fuel into pure, raw power. Marley was an amazing physical specimen, the kind of dog passersby stopped to admire. He was huge for a Labrador

retriever, considerably bigger than the average male of his
breed, which runs sixty-five to eighty pounds. Even as he
aged, the bulk of his mass was pure muscle—ninety-seven
pounds of rippled, sinewy brawn with nary an ounce of fat
anywhere on him. His rib cage was the size of a small beer
keg, but the ribs themselves stretched just beneath his fur
with no spare padding. We were not worried about obesity;
exactly the opposite. On our many visits to Dr. Jay before
leaving Florida, Jenny and I would voice the same concerns:
We were feeding him tremendous amounts of food, but still
he was so much thinner than most Labs, and he always
appeared famished, even immediately after wolfing down a
bucket of kibble that looked like it was meant for a draft
horse. Were we slowly starving him? Dr. Jay always responded the same way. He would run his hands down
Marley's sleek sides, setting him off on a desperately happy
Labrador evader journey around the cramped exam room,
and tell us that, as far as physical attributes went, Marley was
just about perfect. "Just keep doing what you're doing," Dr.
Jay would say. Then, as Marley lunged between his legs or
snarfed a cotton ball off the counter, Dr. Jay would add:
"Obviously, I don't need to tell you that Marley burns a lot of
nervous energy."

Each evening after we finished dinner, when it came time
to give Marley his meal, I would fill his bowl with chow and
then freely toss in any tasty leftovers or scraps I could find.
With three young children at the table, half-eaten food was
something we had in plentiful supply. Bread crusts, steak
trimmings, pan drippings, chicken skins, gravy, rice, carrots,
puréed prunes, sandwiches, three-day-old pasta—into the

bowl it went. Our pet may have behaved like the court jester, but he ate like the Prince of Wales. The only foods we kept from him were those we knew to be unhealthy for dogs, such as dairy products, sweets, potatoes, and choco-late. I have a problem with people who buy human food for their pets, but larding Marley's meals with scraps that would otherwise be thrown out made me feel thrifty—waste not, want not—and charitable. I was giving always-appreciative Marley a break from the endless monotony of dog-chow hell.

When Marley wasn't acting as our household garbage disposal, he was on duty as the family's emergency spill-response team. No mess was too big a job for our dog. One of the kids would flip a full bowl of spaghetti and meatballs on the floor, and we'd simply whistle and stand back while Old Wet Vac sucked up every last noodle and then licked the floor until it gleamed. Errant peas, dropped celery, runaway rigatoni, spilled applesauce, it didn't matter what it was. If it hit the floor, it was history. To the amazement of our friends, he even wolfed down salad greens.

Not that food had to make it to the ground before it ended up in Marley's stomach. He was a skilled and unremorseful thief, preying mostly on unsuspecting children and always after checking to make sure neither Jenny nor I was watch-ing. Birthday parties were bonanzas for him. He would make his way through the crowd of five-year-olds, shamelessly snatching hot dogs right out of their little hands. During one party, we estimated he ended up getting two-thirds of the birthday cake, nabbing piece after piece off the paper plates the children held on their laps.

It didn't matter how much food he devoured, either

through legitimate means or illicit activities. He always wanted more. When deafness came, we weren't completely surprised that the only sound he could still hear was the sweet, soft thud of falling food.

One day I arrived home from work to find the house empty. Jenny and the kids were out somewhere, and I called for Marley but got no response. I walked upstairs, where he sometimes snoozed when left alone, but he was nowhere in sight. After I changed my clothes, I returned downstairs and found him in the kitchen up to no good. His back to me, he was standing on his hind legs, his front paws and chest resting on the kitchen table as he gobbled down the remains of a grilled cheese sandwich. My first reaction was to loudly scold him. Instead I decided to see how close I could get before he realized he had company. I tiptoed up behind him until I was close enough to touch him. As he chewed the crusts, he kept glancing at the door that led into the garage, knowing that was where Jenny and the kids would enter upon their return. The instant the door opened, he would be on the floor under the table, feigning sleep. Apparently it had not occurred to him that Dad would be arriving home, too, and just might sneak in through the front door.

"Oh, Marley?" I asked in a normal voice. "What do you think you're doing?" He just kept gulping the sandwich down, clueless to my presence. His tail was wagging languidly, a sign he thought he was alone and getting away with a major food heist. Clearly he was pleased with himself.

I cleared my throat loudly, and he still didn't hear me. I made kissy noises with my mouth. Nothing. He polished off one sandwich, nosed the plate out of the way, and stretched forward to reach the crusts left on a second plate. "You are such a bad dog," I said as he chewed away. I snapped my fingers twice and he froze midbite, staring at the back door. *What was that? Did I hear a car door slam?* After a moment, he convinced himself that whatever he heard was nothing and went back to his purloined snack.

That's when I reached out and tapped him once on the butt. I might as well have lit a stick of dynamite. The old dog nearly jumped out of his fur coat. He rocketed backward off the table and, as soon as he saw me, dropped onto the floor, rolling over to expose his belly to me in surrender. "Busted!" I told him. "You are so busted." But I didn't have it in me to scold him. He was old; he was deaf; he was beyond reform. I wasn't going to change him. Sneaking up on him had been great fun, and I laughed out loud when he jumped. Now as he lay at my feet begging for forgiveness I just found it a little sad. I guess secretly I had hoped he'd been faking all along.

I finished the chicken coop, an A-frame plywood affair with a drawbridge-style gangplank that could be raised at night to keep out predators. Donna kindly took back two of our three roosters and exchanged them for hens from her flock. We now had three girls and one testosterone-pumped guy bird that spent every waking minute doing one of three things: pursuing sex, having sex, or crowing boastfully about the sex he had just scored. Jenny observed that roosters are what men would be if left to their own devices, with no social conventions to rein in their baser instincts, and I couldn't disagree. I had to admit, I kind of admired the lucky bastard.

We let the chickens out each morning to roam the yard, and Marley made a few gallant runs at them, charging ahead barking for a dozen paces or so before losing steam and giving up. It was as though some genetic coding deep inside him was sending an urgent message: "You're a retriever; they are birds. Don't you think it might be a good idea to chase them?" He just did not have his heart in it. Soon the birds learned the lumbering yellow beast was no threat whatsoever, more a minor annoyance than anything else, and Marley learned to share the yard with these new, feathered interlopers. One day I looked up from weeding in the garden to see Marley and the four chickens making their way down the row toward me as if in formation, the birds pecking and Marley sniffing as they went. It was like old friends out for a Sunday stroll. "What kind of self-respecting hunting dog are you?" I chastised him. Marley lifted his leg and peed on a tomato plant before hurrying to rejoin his new pals.

CHAPTER 24

The Potty Room

✻

A person can learn a few things from an old dog. As the months slipped by and his infirmities mounted, Marley taught us mostly about life's uncompromising finiteness. Jenny and I were not quite middle-aged. Our children were young, our health good, and our retirement years still an unfathomable distance off on the horizon. It would have been easy to deny the inevitable creep of age, to pretend it might somehow pass us by. Marley would not afford us the luxury of such denial. As we watched him grow gray and deaf and creaky, there was no ignoring his mortality—or ours. Age sneaks up on us all, but it sneaks up on a dog with a swiftness that is both breathtaking and sobering. In the brief span of twelve years, Marley had gone from bubbly puppy to awkward adolescent to muscular adult to doddering senior citizen. He aged roughly seven years for every one of ours, putting him, in human years, on the downward slope to ninety.

His once sparkling white teeth had gradually worn down to brown nubs. Three of his four front fangs were missing, broken off one by one during crazed panic attacks as he tried to chew his way to safety. His breath, always a bit on the fishy side, had taken on the bouquet of a sun-baked Dumpster. The fact that he had acquired a taste for that little appreciated delicacy known as chicken manure didn't help, either. To our complete revulsion, he gobbled the stuff up like it was caviar.

His digestion was not what it once had been, and he became as gassy as a methane plant. There were days I swore that if I lit a match, the whole house would go up. Marley was able to clear an entire room with his silent, deadly flatulence, which seemed to increase in direct correlation to the number of dinner guests we had in our home. "Marley! Not again!" the children would scream in unison, and lead the retreat. Sometimes he drove even himself away. He would be sleeping peacefully when the smell would reach his nostrils; his eyes would pop open and he'd furl his brow as if asking, *"Good God! Who dealt it?"* And he would stand up and nonchalantly move into the next room.

When he wasn't farting, he was outside pooping. Or at least thinking about it. His choosiness about where he squatted to defecate had grown to the point of compulsive obsession. Each time I let him out, he took longer and longer to decide on the perfect spot. Back and forth he would promenade; round and round he went, sniffing, pausing, scratching, circling, moving on, the whole while sporting a ridiculous grin on his face. As he combed the grounds in search of squatting nirvana, I stood outside, sometimes in the rain, sometimes in the snow, sometimes in the dark of night, often barefoot, occasionally just in my boxer shorts, knowing from experience that I didn't dare leave him unsupervised lest he decide to meander up the hill to visit the dogs on the next street.

Sneaking away became a sport for him. If the opportunity presented itself and he thought he could get away with it, he would bolt for the property line. Well, not exactly bolt. He would more sniff and shuffle his way from one bush to the next until he was out of sight. Late one night I let him out the front door for his final walk before bed. Freezing rain was forming an icy slush on the ground, and I turned around to grab a slicker out of the front closet. When I walked out onto the sidewalk less than a minute later, he was nowhere to be found. I walked out into the yard, whistling and clapping, knowing he couldn't hear me, though pretty sure all the neighbors could. For twenty minutes I prowled through our neighbors' yards in the rain, making quite the fashion statement dressed in boots, raincoat, and boxer shorts. I prayed no porch lights would come on. The more I hunted, the angrier I got. *Where the hell did he mosey off to this time?* But as the minutes passed, my anger turned to worry. I thought of those old men you read about in the newspaper who wander away from nursing homes and are found frozen in the snow three days later. I returned home, walked upstairs, and woke up Jenny. "Marley's disappeared," I said. "I can't find him anywhere. He's out there in the freezing rain." She was on her feet instantly, pulling on jeans, slipping into a sweater and boots. Together we broadened the search. I could hear her way up the side of the hill, whistling and clucking for him as I crashed through the woods in the dark, half expecting to find him lying unconscious in a creek bed.

Eventually our paths met up. "Anything?" I asked.

"Nothing," Jenny said.

We were soaked from the rain, and my bare legs were stinging from the cold. "Come on," I said. "Let's go home and get warm and I'll come back out with the car." We walked down the hill and up the driveway. That's when we saw him, standing beneath the overhang out of the rain and overjoyed to have us back. I could have killed him. Instead, I brought him inside and toweled him off, the unmistakable smell of wet dog filling the kitchen. Exhausted from his late-night jaunt, Marley conked out and did not budge till nearly noon the next day.

Marley's eyesight had grown fuzzy, and bunnies could now scamper past a dozen feet in front of him without him noticing. He was shedding his fur in vast quantities, forcing Jenny to vacuum every day—and still she couldn't keep up with it. Dog hair insinuated itself into every crevice of our home, every piece of our wardrobe, and more than a few of our meals. He had always been a shedder, but what had once been light flurries had grown into full-fledged blizzards. He would shake and a cloud of loose fur would rise around him, drifting down onto every surface. One night as I watched television, I dangled my leg off the couch and absently stroked his hip with my bare foot. At the commercial break, I looked down to see a sphere of fur the size of a grapefruit near where I had been rubbing. His hairballs rolled across the wood floors like tumbleweeds on a windblown plain.

Most worrisome of all were his hips, which had mostly forsaken him. Arthritis had snuck into his joints, weakening them and making them ache. The same dog that once could ride me bronco-style on his back, the dog that could lift the entire dining room table on his shoulders and bounce it around the room, could now barely pull himself up. He groaned in pain when he lay down, and groaned again when he struggled to his feet. I did not realize just how weak his hips had become until one day when I gave his rump a light pat and his hindquarters collapsed beneath him as though he had just received a cross-body block. Down he went. It was painful to watch.

Climbing the stairs to the second floor was becoming increasingly difficult for him, but he wouldn't think of sleeping alone on the main floor, even after we put a dog bed at the foot of the stairs for him. Marley loved people, loved being underfoot, loved resting his chin on the mattress and panting in our faces as we slept, loved jamming his head through the shower curtain for a drink as we bathed, and he wasn't about to stop now. Each night when Jenny and I retired to our bedroom, he would fret at the foot of the stairs, whining, yipping, pacing, tentatively testing the first step with his front paw as he mustered his courage for the ascent that not long before had been effortless. From the top of the stairs, I would beckon, "Come on, boy. You can do it." After several minutes of this, he would disappear around the corner in order to get a running start and then come charging up, his front shoulders bearing most of his weight. Sometimes he made it; sometimes he stalled midflight and had to return to the bottom and try again. On his most pitiful attempts he would lose his footing entirely and slide ingloriously backward down the steps on his belly. He was too big for me to carry, but increasingly I found myself following him up the stairs, lifting his rear end up each step as he hopped forward on his front paws.

Because of the difficulty stairs now posed for him, I assumed Marley would try to limit the number of trips he made up and down. That would be giving him far too much credit for common sense. No matter how much trouble he had getting up the stairs, if I returned downstairs, say to grab a book or turn off the lights, he would be right on my heels, clomping heavily down behind me. Then, seconds later, he would have to repeat the torturous climb. Jenny and I both took to sneaking around behind his back once he was upstairs for the night so he would not be tempted to follow us back down. We assumed sneaking downstairs without his knowledge would be easy now that his hearing was shot and he was sleeping longer and more heavily than ever. But he always seemed to know when we had stolen away. I would be reading in bed and he would be asleep on the floor beside me, snoring heavily. Stealthily, I would pull back the covers, slide out of bed, and tiptoe past him out of the room, turning back to make sure I hadn't disturbed him. I would be downstairs for only a few minutes when I would hear his heavy steps on the stairs, coming in search of me. He might be deaf and half blind, but his radar apparently was still in good working order.

This went on not only at night but all day long, too. I would be reading the newspaper at the kitchen table with Marley curled up at my feet when I would get up for a refill from the coffeepot across the room. Even though I was within sight and would be coming right back, he would lumber with difficulty to his feet and trudge over to be with me. No sooner had he gotten comfortable at my feet by the coffeepot than I would return to the table, where he would again drag himself and settle in. A few minutes later I would walk into the family room to turn on the stereo, and up again he would struggle, following me in, circling around and collapsing with a moan beside me just as I was ready to walk away. So it would go, not only with me but with Jenny and the kids, too.

As age took its toll, Marley had good days and bad days. He had good minutes and bad minutes, too, sandwiched so close together sometimes it was hard to believe it was the same dog.

One evening in the spring of 2002, I took Marley out for a short walk around the yard. The night was cool, in the high forties, and windy. Invigorated by the crisp air, I started to run, and Marley, feeling frisky himself, galloped along beside me just like in the old days. I even said out loud to him, "See, Marl, you still have some of the puppy in you." We trotted together back to the front door, his tongue out as he panted happily, his eyes alert. At the porch stoop, Marley gamely tried to leap up the two steps—but his rear hips collapsed on him as he pushed off, and he found himself awkwardly stuck, his front paws on the stoop, his belly resting on the steps and his butt collapsed flat on the sidewalk. There he sat, looking up at me like he didn't know what had caused such an embarrassing display. I whistled and slapped my hands on my thighs, and he flailed his front legs valiantly, trying to get up, but it was no use. He could not lift his rear off the ground. "Come on, Marley!" I called, but he was immobilized. Finally, I grabbed him under the front shoulders and turned him sideways so he could get all four legs on the ground. Then, after a few failed tries, he was able to stand. He backed up, looked apprehensively at the stairs for a few seconds, and loped up and into the house. From that day on, his confidence as a champion stair climber was shot; he never attempted those two small steps again without first stopping and fretting.

No doubt about it, getting old was a bitch. And an undignified one at that.

Marley reminded me of life's brevity, of its fleeting joys and missed opportunities. He reminded me that each of us gets just one shot at the gold, with no replays. One day you're swimming halfway out into the ocean convinced this is the day you will catch that seagull; the next you're barely able to bend down to drink out of your water bowl. Like Patrick Henry and everyone else, I had but one life to live. I kept coming back to the same question: What in God's name was I doing spending it at a gardening magazine? It wasn't that my new job did not have its rewards. I was proud of what I had done with the magazine. But I missed newspapers desperately. I missed the people who read them and the people who write them. I missed being part of the big story of the day, and the feeling that I was in my own small way helping to make a difference. I missed the adrenaline surge of writing on deadline and the satisfaction of waking up the next morning to find my in-box filled with e-mails responding to my words. Mostly, I missed telling stories. I wondered why I had ever walked away from a gig that so perfectly fit my disposition to wade into the treacherous waters of magazine management with its bare-bones budgets, relentless advertising pressures, staffing headaches, and thankless behind-the-scenes editing chores.

When a former colleague of mine mentioned in passing that the *Philadelphia Inquirer* was seeking a metropolitan columnist, I leapt without a second's hesitation. Columnist positions are extremely hard to come by, even at smaller papers, and when a position does open up it's almost always filled internally, a plum handed to veteran staffers who've proved themselves as reporters. The *Inquirer* was well respected, winner of seventeen Pulitzer Prizes over the years and one of the country's great newspapers. I was a fan, and now the *Inquirer*'s editors were asking to meet me. I wouldn't even have to relocate my family to take the job. The office I would be working in was just forty-five minutes down the Pennsylvania Turnpike, a tolerable commute. I don't put much stock in miracles, but it all seemed too good to be true, like an act of divine intervention.

In November 2002, I traded in my gardening togs for a *Philadelphia Inquirer* press badge. It quite possibly was the happiest day of my life. I was back where I belonged, in a newsroom as a columnist once again.

I had only been in the new job for a few months when the first big snowstorm of 2003 hit. The flakes began to fall on a Sunday night, and by the time they stopped the next day, a blanket two feet deep covered the ground. The children were off school for three days as our community slowly dug out, and I filed my columns from home. With a snowblower I borrowed from my neighbor, I cleared the driveway and opened a narrow canyon to the front door. Knowing Marley could never climb the sheer walls to get out into the yard, let alone negotiate the deep drifts once he was off the path, I cleared him his own "potty room," as the kids dubbed it—a small plowed space off the front walkway where he could do his business. When I called him outside to try out the new facilities, though, he just stood in the clearing and sniffed the snow suspiciously. He had very particular notions about what constituted a suitable place to answer nature's call, and this clearly was not what he had in mind. He was willing to lift his leg and pee, but that's where he drew the line. *Poop right here? Smack in front of the picture window? You can't be serious.* He turned and, with a mighty heave to climb up the slippery porch steps, went back inside.

That night after dinner I brought him out again, and this time Marley no longer could afford the luxury of waiting. He had to go. He nervously paced up and down the cleared walkway, into the potty room and out onto the driveway, sniffing the snow, pawing at the frozen ground. *No, this just won't do.* Before I could stop him, he somehow clambered up and over the sheer snow wall the snowblower had cut and began making his way across the yard toward a stand of white pines fifty feet away. I couldn't believe it; my arthritic, geriatric dog was off on an alpine trek. Every couple of steps his back hips collapsed on him and he sank down into the snow, where he rested on his belly for a few seconds before struggling back to his feet and pushing on. Slowly, painfully, he made his way through the deep snow, using his still-strong front shoulders to pull his body forward. I stood in the driveway, wondering how I was going to rescue him when he finally got stuck and could go no farther. But he trudged on and finally made it to the closest pine tree. Suddenly I saw what he was up to. The dog had a plan. Beneath the dense branches of the pine, the snow was just a few inches deep. The tree acted like an umbrella, and once underneath it Marley was free to move about and squat comfortably to relieve himself. I had to admit, it was pretty brilliant. He circled and sniffed and scratched in his customary way, trying to locate a worthy shrine for his daily offering. Then, to my amazement, he abandoned the cozy shelter and lunged back into the deep snow en route to the next pine tree. The first spot looked perfect to me, but clearly it was just not up to his sterling standards.

With difficulty he reached the second tree, but again, after considerable circling, found the area beneath its branches unsuitable. So he set off to the third tree, and then the fourth and the fifth, each time getting farther from the driveway. I tried calling him back, though I knew he couldn't hear me. "Marley, you're going to get stuck, you dumbo!" I yelled. He just plowed ahead with single-minded determination. The dog was on a quest. Finally, he reached the last tree on our property, a big spruce with a dense canopy of branches out near where the kids waited for the school bus. It was here he found the frozen piece of ground he had been looking for, private and barely dusted with snow. He circled a few times and creakily squatted down on his old, shot, arthritis-riddled haunches. There he finally found relief. Eureka!

With mission accomplished, he set off on the long journey home. As he struggled through the snow, I waved my arms and clapped my hands to encourage him. "Keep coming, boy! You can make it!" But I could see him tiring, and he still had a long way to go. "Don't stop now!" I yelled. A dozen yards from the driveway, that's just what he did. He was done. He stopped and lay down in the snow, exhausted. Marley did not exactly look distressed, but he didn't look at ease, either. He shot me a worried look. *Now what do we do, boss?* I had no idea. I could wade through the snow to him, but then what? He was too heavy for me to pick up and carry. For several minutes I stood there, calling and cajoling, but Marley wouldn't budge.

"Hang on," I said. "Let me get my boots on and I'll come get you." It had dawned on me that I could wrestle him up onto the toboggan and pull him back to the house. As soon as he saw me approaching with the toboggan, my plan became moot. He jumped up, reenergized. The only thing I could think was that he remembered our infamous ride into the woods and over the creek bank and was hoping for a repeat. He lurched forward toward me like a dinosaur in a tar pit. I waded out into the snow, stomping down a path for him as I went, and he inched ahead. Finally we scrambled over the snowbank and onto the driveway together. He shook the snow off and banged his tail against my knees, prancing about, all frisky and cocky, flush with the bravado of an adventurer just back from a jaunt through uncharted wilderness. To think, I had doubted he could do it.

The next morning I shoveled a narrow path out to the far spruce tree on the corner of the property for him, and Marley adopted the space as his own personal powder room for the duration of the winter. The crisis had been averted, but bigger questions loomed. How much longer could he continue like this? And at what point would the aches and indignities of old age outstrip the simple contentment he found in each sleepy, lazy day?

CHAPTER 25

Beating the Odds

✻

W hen school let out for the summer, Jenny packed the kids into the minivan and headed to Boston for a week to visit her sister. I stayed behind to work. That left Marley with no one at home to keep him company and let him out. Of the many little embarrassments old age inflicted on him, the one that seemed to bother him most was the diminished control he had over his bowels. For all Marley's bad behavior over the years, his bathroom habits had always been surefire. It was the one Marley feature we could brag about. From just a few months of age, he never, ever, had accidents in the house, even when left alone for ten or twelve hours. We joked that his bladder was made of steel and his bowels of stone.

That had changed in recent months. He no longer could go more than a few hours between pit stops. When the urge called, he had to go, and if we were not home to let him out, he had no choice but to go inside. It killed him to do it, and we always knew the second we walked into the house when he had had an accident. Instead of greeting us at the door in his exuberant manner, he would be standing far back in the room, his head hanging nearly to the floor, his tail flat between his legs, the shame radiating off him. We never punished him for it. How could we? He was nearly thirteen, about as old as Labs got. We knew he couldn't help it, and he seemed to know it, too. I was sure if he could talk, he would profess his humiliation and assure us that he had tried, really tried, to hold it in.

Jenny bought a steam cleaner for the carpet, and we began arranging our schedules to make sure we were not away from the house for more than a few hours at a time. Jenny would rush home from school, where she volunteered, to let Marley out. I would leave dinner parties between the main course and dessert to give him a walk, which, of course, Marley dragged out as long as possible, sniffing and circling his way around the yard. Our friends teasingly wondered aloud who was the real master over at the Grogan house.

With Jenny and the kids away, I knew I would be putting in long days. This was my chance to stay out after work, wandering around the region and exploring the towns and neighborhoods I was now writing about. With my long commute, I would be away from home ten to twelve hours a day. There was no question Marley couldn't be alone that long, or even half that long. We decided to board him at the local kennel we used every summer when we went on vacation. The kennel was attached to a large veterinarian practice that offered professional care if not the most personal service. Each time we went there, it seemed, we saw a different doctor who knew nothing about Marley except what was printed in his chart. We never even learned their names. Unlike our beloved Dr. Jay in Florida, who knew Marley almost as well as we did and who truly had become a family friend by the time we left, these were strangers—competent strangers but strangers nonetheless. Marley didn't seem to mind.

"Waddy go doggie camp!" Colleen screeched, and he perked up as though the idea had possibilities. We joked about the activities the kennel staff would have for him: hole digging from 9:00 to 10:00; pillow shredding from 10:15 to 11:00; garbage raiding from 11:05 to noon, and so on. I dropped him off on a Sunday evening and left my cell phone number with the front desk. Marley never seemed to fully relax when he was boarded, even in the familiar surroundings of Dr. Jay's office, and I always worried a little about him. After each visit, he returned looking gaunter, his snout often rubbed raw from where he had fretted it against the grating of his cage, and when he got home he would collapse in the corner and sleep heavily for hours, as if he had spent the entire time away pacing his cage with insomnia.

That Tuesday morning, I was near Independence Hall in downtown Philadelphia when my cell phone rang. "Could you please hold for Dr. So-and-so?" the woman from the kennel asked. It was yet another veterinarian whose name I had never heard before. A few seconds later the vet came on the phone. "We have an emergency with Marley," she said.

My heart rose in my chest. "An emergency?"

The vet said Marley's stomach had bloated with food, water, and air and then, stretched and distended, had flipped over on itself, twisting and trapping its contents. With nowhere for the gas and other contents to escape, his stomach had swelled painfully in a life-threatening condition known as gastric dilatation-volvulus. It almost always required surgery to correct, she said, and if left untreated could result in death within a few hours.

She said she had inserted a tube down his throat and released much of the gas that had built up in his stomach, which relieved the swelling. By manipulating the tube in his stomach, she had worked the twist out of it, or as she put it, "unflipped it," and he was now sedated and resting comfortably.

"That's a good thing, right?" I asked cautiously.

"But only temporary," the doctor said. "We got him through the immediate crisis, but once their stomachs twist like that, they almost always will twist again."

"Like how almost always?" I asked.

"I would say he has a one percent chance that it won't flip again," she said. *One percent? For God's sake*, I thought, *he has better odds of getting into Harvard.*

"One percent? That's it?"

"I'm sorry," she said. "It's very grave."

If his stomach did flip again—and she was telling me it was a virtual certainty—we had two choices. The first was to operate on him. She said she would open him up and attach the stomach to the cavity wall with sutures to prevent it from flipping again. "The operation will cost about two thousand dollars," she said. I gulped. "And I have to tell you, it's very invasive. It will be tough going for a dog his age." The recovery would be long and difficult, assuming he made it through the operation at all. Sometimes older dogs like him did not survive the trauma of the surgery, she explained.

"If he was four or five years old, I would be saying by all means let's operate," the vet said. "But at his age, you have to ask yourself if you really want to put him through that."

"Not if we can help it," I said. "What's the second option?"

"The second option," she said, hesitating only slightly, "would be putting him to sleep."

"Oh," I said.

I was having trouble processing it all. Five minutes ago I was walking to the Liberty Bell, assuming Marley was happily relaxing in his kennel run. Now I was being asked to decide whether he should live or die. I had never even heard of the condition she described. Only later would I learn that bloat was fairly common in some breeds of dogs, especially those, such as Marley, with deep barrel chests. Dogs who scarfed down their entire meal in a few quick gulps—Marley, once again—also seemed to be at higher risk. Some dog owners suspected the stress of being in a kennel could trigger bloat, but I later would see a professor of veterinarian medicine quoted as saying his research showed no connection between kennel stress and bloat. The vet on the phone acknowledged Marley's excitement around the other dogs in the kennel could have brought on the attack. He had gulped down his food as usual and was panting and salivating heavily, worked up by all the other dogs around him. She thought he might have swallowed so much air and saliva that his stomach began to dilate on its long axis, making it vulnerable to twisting. "Can't we just wait and see how he does?" I asked. "Maybe it won't twist again."

"That's what we're doing right now," she said, "waiting and watching." She repeated the one percent odds and added, "If his stomach flips again, I'll need you to make a quick decision. We can't let him suffer."

"I need to speak with my wife," I told her. "I'll call you back."

When Jenny answered her cell phone she was on a crowded tour boat with the kids in the middle of Boston Harbor. I could hear the boat's engine chugging and the guide's voice booming through a loudspeaker in the background. We had a choppy, awkward conversation over a bad connection. Neither of us could hear the other well. I shouted to try to communicate what we were up against. She was only getting snippets. Marley . . . emergency . . . stomach . . . surgery . . . put to sleep.

There was silence on the other end. "Hello?" I said. "Are you still there?"

"I'm here," Jenny said, then went quiet again. We both knew this day would come eventually; we just did not think it would be today. Not with her and the kids out of town where they couldn't even have their good-byes; not with me ninety minutes away in downtown Philadelphia with work commitments. By the end of the conversation, through shouts and blurts and pregnant pauses, we decided there was really no decision at all. The vet was right. Marley was fading on all fronts. It would be cruel to put him through a traumatic surgery to simply try to stave off the inevitable.

We could not ignore the high cost, either. It seemed obscene, almost immoral, to spend that kind of money on an old dog at the end of his life when there were unwanted dogs put down every day for lack of a home, and more important, children not getting proper medical attention for lack of financial resources. If this was Marley's time, then it was his time, and we would see to it he went out with dignity and without suffering. We knew it was the right thing, yet neither of us was ready to lose him.

I called the veterinarian back and told her our decision. "His teeth are rotted away, he's stone-deaf, and his hips have gotten so bad he can barely get up the porch stoop anymore," I told her as if she needed convincing. "He's having trouble squatting to have a bowel movement."

The vet, whom I now knew as Dr. Hopkinson, made it easy on me. "I think it's time," she said.

"I guess so," I answered, but I didn't want her to put him down without calling me first. I wanted to be there with him if possible. "And," I reminded her, "I'm still holding out for that one percent miracle."

"Let's talk in an hour," she said.

An hour later Dr. Hopkinson sounded slightly more optimistic. Marley was still holding his own, resting with an intravenous drip in his front leg. She raised his odds to five percent. "I don't want you to get your hopes up," she said. "He's a very sick dog."

The next morning the doctor sounded brighter still. "He had a good night," she said. When I called back at noon, she had removed the IV from his paw and started him on a slurry of rice and meat. "He's famished," she reported. By the next call, he was up on his feet. "Good news," she said. "One of our techs just took him outside and he pooped and peed." I cheered into the phone as though he had just taken Best in Show. Then she added: "He must be feeling better. He just gave me a big sloppy kiss on the lips." Yep, that was our Marley.

"I wouldn't have thought it possible yesterday," the doc said, "but I think you'll be able to take him home tomorrow." The following evening after work, that's just what I did. He looked terrible—weak and skeletal, his eyes milky and crusted with mucus, as if he had been to the other side of death and back, which in a sense I guess he had. I must have looked a little ill myself after paying the eight-hundred-dollar bill. When I thanked the doctor for her good work, she replied, "The whole staff loves Marley. Everyone was rooting for him."

I walked him out to the car, my ninety-nine-to-one-odds miracle dog, and said, "Let's get you home where you belong." He just stood there looking woefully into the backseat, knowing it was as unattainable as Mount Olympus. He didn't even try to hop in. I called to one of the kennel workers, who helped me gingerly lift him into the car, and I drove him home with a box of medicines and strict instructions. Marley would never again gulp a huge meal in one sitting, or slurp unlimited amounts of water. His days of playing submarine with his snout in the water bowl were over. From now on, he was to receive four small meals a day and only limited rations of water—a half cup or so in his bowl at a time. In this way, the doctor hoped, his stomach would stay calm and not bloat and twist again. He also was never again to be boarded in a large kennel surrounded by barking, pacing dogs. I was convinced, and Dr. Hopkinson seemed to be, too, that that had been the precipitating factor in his close call with death.

That night, after I got him home and inside, I spread a sleeping bag on the floor in the family room beside him. He was not up to climbing the stairs to the bedroom, and I didn't have the heart to leave him alone and helpless. I knew he would fret all night if he was not at my side. "We're having a sleepover, Marley!" I proclaimed, and lay down next to him. I stroked him head to tail until huge clouds of fur rolled off his back. I wiped the mucus from the corners of his eyes and scratched his ears until he moaned with pleasure. Jenny and the kids would be home in the morning; she would pamper him with frequent minimeals of boiled hamburger and rice. It had taken him thirteen years, but Marley had finally merited people food, not leftovers but a stovetop meal made just for him. The children would throw their arms around him, unaware of how close they had come to never seeing him again.

Tomorrow the house would be loud and boisterous and full of life again. For tonight, it was just the two of us, Marley and me. Lying there with him, his smelly breath in my face, I couldn't help thinking of our first night together all those years ago after I brought him home from the breeder, a tiny puppy whimpering for his mother. I remembered how I dragged his box into the bedroom and the way we had fallen asleep together, my arm dangling over the side of the bed to comfort him. Thirteen years later, here we were, still inseparable. I thought about his puppyhood and adolescence, about the shredded couches and eaten mattresses, about the wild walks along the Intracoastal and the cheek-to-jowl dances with the stereo blaring. I thought about the swallowed objects and purloined paychecks and sweet moments of canine-human empathy. Mostly I thought about what a good and loyal companion he had been all these years. What a trip it had been.

"You really scared me, old man," I whispered as he stretched out beside me and slid his snout beneath my arm to encourage me to keep petting him. "It's good to have you home."

We fell asleep together, side by side on the floor, his rump half on my sleeping bag, my arm draped across his back. He woke me once in the night, his shoulders flinching, his paws twitching, little baby barks coming from deep in his throat, more like coughs than anything else. He was dreaming. Dreaming, I imagined, that he was young and strong again. And running like there was no tomorrow.

CHAPTER 26

Borrowed Time

❄

Over the next several weeks, Marley bounced back from the edge of death. The mischievous sparkle returned to his eyes, the cool wetness to his nose, and a little meat to his bones. For all he'd been through, he seemed none the worse off. He was content to snooze his days away, favoring a spot in front of the glass door in the family room where the sun flooded in and baked his fur. On his new low-bulk diet of petite meals, he was perpetually ravenous and was begging and thieving food more shamelessly than ever. One evening I caught him alone in the kitchen up on his hind legs with his front paws on the kitchen counter, stealing Rice Krispies Treats from a platter. How he got up there on his frail hips, I'll never know. Infirmities be damned; when the will called, Marley's body answered. I wanted to hug him, I was so happy at the surprise display of strength.

The scare of that summer should have snapped Jenny and me out of our denial about Marley's advancing age, but we quickly returned to the comfortable assumption that the crisis was a one time fluke, and his eternal march into the sunset could resume once again. Part of us wanted to believe he could chug on forever. Despite all his frailties, he was still the same happy-go-lucky dog. Each morning after his breakfast, he trotted into the family room to use the couch as a giant napkin, walking along its length, rubbing his snout and mouth against the fabric as he went and flipping up the cushions in the process. Then he would turn around and come back in the opposite direction so he could wipe the other side. From there he would drop to the floor and roll onto his back, wiggling from side to side to give himself a back rub. He liked to sit and lick the carpeting with lust, as if it had been larded with the most delectable gravy he had ever tasted. His daily routine included barking at the mailman, visiting the chickens, staring at the bird feeder, and making the rounds of the bathtub faucets to check for any drips of water he could lap up. Several times a day he flipped the lid up on the kitchen trash can to see what goodies he could scavenge. On a daily basis, he launched into Labrador evader mode, banging around the house, tail thumping the walls and furniture, and on a daily basis I continued to pry open his jaws and extract from the roof of his mouth all sorts of flotsam from our daily lives—potato skins and muffin wrappers, discarded Kleenex and dental floss. Even in old age, some things did not change.

As September 11, 2003, approached, I drove across the state to the tiny mining town of Shanksville, Pennsylvania, where United Flight 93 had crashed into an empty field on that infamous morning two years earlier amid a passenger uprising. The hijackers who had seized the flight were believed to be heading for Washington, D.C. , to crash the plane into the White House or the Capitol, and the passengers who rushed the cockpit almost certainly saved countless lives on the ground. To mark the second anniversary of the attacks, my editors wanted me to visit the site and take my best shot at capturing that sacrifice and the lasting effect it had on the American psyche.

I spent the entire day at the crash site, lingering at the impromptu memorial that had risen there. I talked to the steady stream of visitors who showed up to pay their respects, interviewed locals who remembered the force of the explosion, sat with a woman who had lost her daughter in a car accident and who came to the crash site to find solace in communal grief. I documented the many mementoes and notes that filled the gravel parking lot. Still I was not feeling the column. What could I say about this immense tragedy that had not been said already? I went to dinner in town and pored over my notes. Writing a newspaper column is a lot like building a tower out of blocks; each nugget of information, each quote and captured moment, is a block. You start by building a broad foundation, strong enough to support your premise, then work your way up toward the pinnacle. My notebook was full of solid building blocks, but I was missing the mortar to hold them all together. I had no idea what to do with them.

After I finished my meat loaf and iced tea, I headed back to the hotel to try to write. Halfway there, on an impulse, I pulled a U-turn and drove back out to the crash site, several miles outside town, arriving just as the sun was slipping behind the hillside and the last few visitors were pulling away. I sat out there alone for a long time, as sunset turned to dusk and dusk to night. A sharp wind blew down off the hills, and I pulled my Windbreaker tight around me. Towering overhead, a giant American flag snapped in the breeze, its colors glowing almost iridescent in the last smoldering light. Only then did the emotion of this sacred place envelop me and the magnitude of what happened in the sky above this lonely field begin to sink in. I looked out on the spot where the plane hit the earth and then up at the flag, and I felt tears stinging my eyes. For the first time in my life, I took the time to count the stripes. Seven red and six white. I counted the stars, fifty of them on a field of blue. It meant more to us now, this American flag. To a new generation, it stood once again for valor and sacrifice. I knew what I needed to write.

I shoved my hands into my pockets and walked out to the edge of the gravel lot, where I stared into the growing blackness. Standing out there in the dark, I felt many different things. One of them was pride in my fellow Americans, ordinary people who rose to the moment, knowing it was their last. One was humility, for I was alive and untouched by the horrors of that day, free to continue my happy life as a husband and father and writer. In the lonely blackness, I could almost taste the finiteness of life and thus its preciousness. We take it for granted, but it is fragile, precarious, uncertain, able to cease at any instant without notice. I was reminded of what should be obvious but too often is not, that each day, each hour and minute, is worth cherishing.

I felt something else, as well—an amazement at the boundless capacity of the human heart, at once big enough to absorb a tragedy of this magnitude yet still find room for the little moments of personal pain and heartache that are part of any life. In my case, one of those little moments was my failing dog. With a tinge of shame, I realized that even amid the colossus of human heartbreak that was Flight 93, I could still feel the sharp pang of the loss I knew was coming.

Marley was living on borrowed time; that much was clear. Another health crisis could come any day, and when it did, I would not fight the inevitable. Any invasive medical procedure at this stage in his life would be cruel, something Jenny and I would be doing more for our sake than his. We loved that crazy old dog, loved him despite everything—or perhaps *because* of everything. But I could see now the time was near for us to let him go. I got back in the car and returned to my hotel room.

The next morning, my column filed, I called home from the hotel. Jenny said, "I just want you to know that Marley really misses you."

"Marley?" I asked. "How about the rest of you?"

"Of course we miss you, dingo," she said. "But I mean Marley really, really misses you. He's driving us all bonkers."

The night before, unable to find me, Marley had paced and sniffed the entire house over and over, she said, poking through every room, looking behind doors and in closets. He struggled to get upstairs and, not finding me there, came back down and began his search all over again. "He was really out of sorts," she said.

He even braved the steep descent into the basement,

where, until the slippery wooden stairs put it off-limits to him, Marley had happily kept me company for long hours in my workshop, snoozing at my feet as I built things, the sawdust floating down and covering his fur like a soft snowfall. Once down there, he couldn't get back up the stairs, and he stood yipping and whining until Jenny and the kids came to his rescue, holding him beneath the shoulders and hips and boosting him up step by step.

At bedtime, instead of sleeping beside our bed as he normally did, Marley camped out on the landing at the top of the stairs where he could keep watch on all the bedrooms and the front door directly at the bottom of the stairs in case I either (1) came out of hiding; or (2) arrived home during the night, on the chance I had snuck out without telling him. That's where he was the next morning when Jenny went downstairs to make breakfast. A couple of hours passed before it dawned on her that Marley still had not shown his face, which was highly unusual; he almost always was the first one down the steps each morning, charging ahead of us and banging his tail against the front door to go out. She found him sleeping soundly on the floor tight against my side of the bed. Then she saw why. When she had gotten up, she had inadvertently pushed her pillows—she sleeps with three of them— over to my side of the bed, beneath the covers, forming a large lump where I usually slept. With his Mr. Magoo eyesight, Marley could be forgiven for mistaking a pile of feathers for his master. "He absolutely thought you were in there," she said. "I could just tell he did. He was convinced you were sleeping in!"

We laughed together on the phone, and then Jenny said, "You've got to give him points for loyalty." That I did. Devotion had always come easily to our dog.

I had been back from Shanksville for only a week when the crisis we knew could come at any time arrived. I was in the bedroom getting dressed for work when I heard a terrible clatter followed by Conor's scream: "Help! Marley fell down the stairs!" I came running and found him in a heap at the bottom of the long staircase, struggling to get to his feet. Jenny and I raced to him and ran our hands over his body, gently squeezing his limbs, pressing his ribs, massaging his spine. Nothing seemed to be broken. With a groan, Marley made it to his feet, shook off, and walked away without so much as a limp. Conor had witnessed the fall. He said Marley had started down the stairs but, after just two steps, realized everyone was still upstairs and attempted an about-face. As he tried to turn around, his hips dropped out from beneath him and he tumbled in a free fall down the entire length of the stairs.

"Wow, was he lucky," I said. "A fall like that could have killed him."

"I can't believe he didn't get hurt," Jenny said. "He's like a cat with nine lives."

But he had gotten hurt. Within minutes he was stiffening up, and by the time I arrived home from work that night, Marley was completely incapacitated, unable to move. He seemed to be sore everywhere, as though he had been worked over by thugs. What really had him laid up, though, was his front left leg; he was unable to put any weight at all on it. I could squeeze it without him yelping, and I suspected he had pulled a tendon. When he saw me, he tried to struggle to his feet to greet me, but it was no use. His left front paw was useless, and with his weak back legs, he just had no power to do anything. Marley was down to one good limb, lousy odds for any four-legged beast. He finally made it up and tried to hop on three paws to get to me, but his back legs caved in and he collapsed back to the floor. Jenny gave him an aspirin and held a bag of ice to his front leg. Marley, playful even under duress, kept trying to eat the ice cubes.

By ten-thirty that night, he was no better, and he hadn't been outside to empty his bladder since one o'clock that afternoon. He had been holding his urine for nearly ten hours. I had no idea how to get him outside and back in again so he could relieve himself. Straddling him and clasping my hands beneath his chest, I lifted him to his feet. Together we waddled our way to the front door, with me holding him up as he hopped along. But out on the porch stoop he froze. A steady rain was falling, and the porch steps, his nemesis, loomed slick and wet before him. He looked unnerved. "Come on," I said. "Just a quick pee and we'll go right back inside." He would have no part of it. I wished I could have persuaded him to just go right on the porch and be done with it, but there was no teaching this old dog that new trick. He hopped back inside and stared morosely up at me as if apologizing for what he knew was coming. "We'll try again later," I said. As if hearing his cue, he half squatted on his three remaining legs and emptied his full bladder on the foyer floor, a puddle spreading out around him. It was the first time since he was a tiny puppy that Marley had urinated in the house.

The next morning Marley was better, though still hobbling about like an invalid. We got him outside, where he urinated and defecated without a problem. On the count of three, Jenny and I together lifted him up the porch stairs to get him back inside. "I have a feeling," I told her, "that Marley will never see the upstairs of this house again." It was apparent he had climbed his last staircase. From now on, he would have to get used to living and sleeping on the ground floor.

I worked from home that day and was upstairs in the bedroom, writing a column on my laptop computer, when I heard a commotion on the stairs. I stopped typing and listened. The sound was instantly familiar, a sort of loud clomping noise as if a shod horse were galloping up a gangplank. I looked at the bedroom doorway and held my breath. A few seconds later, Marley popped his head around the corner and came sauntering into the room. His eyes brightened when he spotted me. *So there you are!* He smashed his head into my lap, begging for an ear rub, which I figured he had earned.

"Marley, you made it!" I exclaimed. "You old hound! I can't believe you're up here!"

Later, as I sat on the floor with him and scruffed his neck, he twisted his head around and gamely gummed my wrist in his jaws. It was a good sign, a telltale of the playful puppy still in him. The day he sat still and let me pet him without trying to engage me would be the day I knew he had had enough. The previous night he had seemed on death's door, and I again had braced myself for the worst. Today he was panting and pawing and trying to slime my hands off. Just when I thought his long, lucky run was over, he was back.

I pulled his head up and made him look me in the eyes. "You're going to tell me when it's time, right?" I said, more a statement than a question. I didn't want to have to make the decision on my own. "You'll let me know, won't you?"

CHAPTER 27

The Big Meadow

❄

Winter arrived early that year, and as the days grew short and the winds howled through the frozen branches, we cocooned into our snug home. I chopped and split a winter's worth of firewood and stacked it by the back door. Jenny made hearty soups and homemade breads, and the children once again sat in the window and waited for the snow to arrive. I anticipated the first snowfall, too, but with a quiet sense of dread, wondering how Marley could possibly make it through another tough winter. The previous one had been hard enough on him, and he had weakened markedly, dramatically, in the ensuing year. I wasn't sure how he would navigate ice-glazed sidewalks, slippery stairs, and a snow-covered landscape. It was dawning on me why the elderly retired to Florida and Arizona.

On a blustery Sunday night in mid-December, when the children had finished their homework and practiced their musical instruments, Jenny started the popcorn on the stove and declared a family movie night. The kids raced to pick out a video, and I whistled for Marley, taking him outside with me to fetch a basket of maple logs off the woodpile. He poked around in the frozen grass as I loaded up the wood, standing with his face into the wind, wet nose sniffing the icy air as if divining winter's descent. I clapped my hands and waved my arms to get his attention, and he followed me inside, hesitating at the front porch steps before summoning his courage and lurching forward, dragging his back legs up behind him.

Inside, I got the fire humming as the kids queued up the movie. The flames leapt and the heat radiated into the room, prompting Marley, as was his habit, to claim the best spot for himself, directly in front of the hearth. I lay down on the floor a few feet from him and propped my head on a pillow, more watching the fire than the movie. Marley didn't want to lose his warm spot, but he couldn't resist this opportunity. His favorite human was at ground level in the prone position, utterly defenseless. Who was the alpha male now? His tail began pounding the floor. Then he started wiggling his way in my direction. He sashayed from side to side on his belly, his rear legs stretched out behind him, and soon he was pressed up against me, grinding his head into my ribs. The minute I reached out to pet him, it was all over. He pushed himself up on his paws, shook hard, showering me in loose fur, and stared down at me, his billowing jowls hanging immediately over my face. When I started to laugh, he took this as a green light to advance, and before I quite knew what was happening, he had straddled my chest with his front paws and, in one big free fall, collapsed on top of me in a heap. "Ugh!" I screamed under his weight. "Full-frontal Lab attack!" The kids squealed. Marley could not believe his good fortune. I wasn't even trying to get him off me. He squirmed, he drooled, he licked me all over the face and nuzzled my neck. I could barely breathe under his weight, and after a few minutes I slid him half off me, where he remained through most of the movie, his head, shoulder, and one paw resting on my chest, the rest of him pressed against my side.

I didn't say so to anyone in the room, but I found myself clinging to the moment, knowing there would not be too many more like it. Marley was in the quiet dusk of a long and eventful life. Looking back on it later, I would recognize that night in front of the fire for what it was, our farewell party. I stroked his head until he fell asleep, and then I stroked it some more.

Four days later, we packed the minivan in preparation for a family vacation to Disney World in Florida. It would be the children's first Christmas away from home, and they were wild with excitement. That evening, in preparation for an early-morning departure, Jenny delivered Marley to the veterinarian's office, where she had arranged for him to spend our week away in the intensive care unit where the doctors and workers could keep their eyes on him around the clock and where he would not be riled by the other dogs. After his close call on their watch the previous summer, they were happy to give him the Cadillac digs and extra attention at no extra cost.

That night as we finished packing, both Jenny and I commented on how strange it felt to be in a dog-free zone. There was no oversized canine constantly underfoot, shadowing our every move, trying to sneak out the door with us each time we carried a bag to the garage. The freedom was liberating, but the house seemed cavernous and empty, even with the kids bouncing off the walls.

The next morning before the sun was over the tree line, we piled into the minivan and headed south. Ridiculing the whole Disney experience is a favorite sport in the circle of parents I run with. I've lost track of how many times I've said, "We could take the whole family to Paris for the same amount of money." But the whole family had a wonderful time, even naysayer Dad. Of the many potential pitfalls— sickness, fatigue-induced tantrums, lost tickets, lost children, sibling fistfights—we escaped them all. It was a great family vacation, and we spent much of the long drive back north recounting the pros and cons of each ride, each meal, each swim, each moment. When we were halfway through Maryland, just four hours from home, my cell phone rang. It was one of the workers from the veterinarian's office. Marley was acting lethargic, she said, and his hips had begun to droop worse than usual. He seemed to be in discomfort. She said the vet wanted our permission to give him a steroid shot and pain medication. Sure, I said. Keep him comfortable, and we'd be there to pick him up the next day.

When Jenny arrived to take him home the following afternoon, December 29, Marley looked tired and a little out of sorts but not visibly ill. As we had been warned, his hips were weaker than ever. The doctor talked to her about putting him on a regimen of arthritis medications, and a worker helped Jenny lift him into the minivan. But within a half hour of getting him home, he was retching, trying to clear thick mucus from his throat. Jenny let him out into the front yard, and he simply lay on the frozen ground and could not or would not budge. She called me at work in a panic. "I can't get him back inside," she said. "He's lying out there in the cold, and he won't get up." I left immediately, and by the time I arrived home forty-five minutes later, she had managed to get him to his feet and back into the house. I found him sprawled on the dining room floor, clearly distressed and clearly not himself.

In thirteen years I had not been able to walk into the house without him bounding to his feet, stretching, shaking, panting, banging his tail into everything, greeting me like I'd just returned from the Hundred Years' War. Not on this day. His eyes followed me as I walked into the room, but he did not move his head. I knelt down beside him and rubbed his snout. No reaction. He did not try to gum my wrist, did not want to play, did not even lift his head. His eyes were far away, and his tail lay limp on the floor.

Jenny had left two messages at the animal hospital and was waiting for a vet to call back, but it was becoming obvious this was turning into an emergency. I put a third call in. After several minutes, Marley slowly stood up on shaky legs and tried to retch again, but nothing would come out. That's when I noticed his stomach; it looked bigger than usual, and it was hard to the touch. My heart sank; I knew what this meant. I called back the veterinarian's office, and this time I described Marley's bloated stomach. The receptionist put me on hold for a moment, then came back and said, "The doctor says to bring him right in."

Jenny and I did not have to say a word to each other; we both understood that the moment had arrived. We braced the kids, telling them Marley had to go to the hospital and the doctors were going to try to make him better, but that he was very sick. As I was getting ready to go, I looked in, and Jenny and the kids were huddled around him as he lay on the floor so clearly in distress, making their good-byes. They each got to pet him and have a few last moments with him. The children remained bullishly optimistic that this dog who had been a constant part of their lives would soon be back, good as new. "Get all better, Marley," Colleen said in her little voice.

With Jenny's help, I got him into the back of my car. She gave him a last quick hug, and I drove off with him, promising to call as soon as I learned something. He lay on the floor in the backseat with his head resting on the center hump, and I drove with one hand on the wheel and the other stretched behind me so I could stroke his head and shoulders. "Oh, Marley," I just kept saying.

In the parking lot of the animal hospital, I helped him out of the car, and he stopped to sniff a tree where the other dogs all pee—still curious despite how ill he felt. I gave him a minute, knowing this might be his last time in his beloved outdoors, then tugged gently at his choker chain and led him into the lobby. Just inside the front door, he decided he had gone far enough and gingerly let himself down on the tile floor. When the techs and I were unable to get him back to his feet, they brought out a stretcher, slid him onto it, and disappeared with him behind the counter, heading for the examining area.

A few minutes later, the vet, a young woman I had never met before, came out and led me into an exam room where she put a pair of X-ray films up on a light board. She showed me how his stomach had bloated to twice its normal size. On the film, near where the stomach meets the intestines, she traced two fist-sized dark spots, which she said indicated a twist. Just as with the last time, she said she would sedate him and insert a tube into his stomach to release the gas causing the bloating. She would then use the tube to manually feel for the back of the stomach. "It's a long shot," she said, "but I'm going to try to use the tube to massage his stomach back into place." It was exactly the same one percent gamble Dr. Hopkinson had given over the summer. It had worked once, it could work again. I remained silently optimistic.

"Okay," I said. "Please give it your best shot."

A half hour later she emerged with a grim face. She had tried three times and was unable to open the blockage. She had given him more sedatives in the hope they might relax his stomach muscles. When none of that worked, she had inserted a catheter through his ribs, a last-ditch attempt to clear the blockage, also without luck. "At this point," she said, "our only real option is to go into surgery." She paused, as if gauging whether I was ready to talk about the inevitable, and then said, "Or the most humane thing might be to put him to sleep."

Jenny and I had been through this decision five months earlier and had already made the hard choice. My visit to Shanksville had only solidified my resolve not to subject Marley to any more suffering. Yet standing in the waiting room, the hour upon me once again, I stood frozen. The doctor sensed my agony and discussed the complications that could likely be expected in operating on a dog of Marley's age. Another thing troubling her, she said, was a bloody residue that had come out on the catheter, indicating problems with the stomach wall. "Who knows what we might find when we get in there," she said.

I told her I wanted to step outside to call my wife. On the cell phone in the parking lot, I told Jenny that they had tried everything short of surgery to no avail. We sat silently on the phone for a long moment before she said, "I love you, John."

"I love you, too, Jenny," I said.

I walked back inside and asked the doctor if I could have a couple of minutes alone with him. She warned me that he was heavily sedated. "Take all the time you need," she said. I found him unconscious on the stretcher on the floor, an IV shunt in his forearm. I got down on my knees and ran my fingers through his fur, the way he liked. I ran my hand down his back. I lifted each floppy ear in my hands—those crazy ears that had caused him so many problems over the years and cost us a king's ransom—and felt their weight. I pulled his lip up and looked at his lousy, worn-out teeth. I picked up a front paw and cupped it in my hand. Then I dropped my forehead against his and sat there for a long time, as if I could telegraph a message through our two skulls, from my brain to his. I wanted to make him understand some things.

"You know all that stuff we've always said about you?" I whispered. "What a total pain you are? Don't believe it.

Don't believe it for a minute, Marley." He needed to know that, and something more, too. There was something I had never told him, that no one ever had. I wanted him to hear it before he went.

"Marley," I said. "You are a *great* dog."

I found the doctor waiting at the front counter. "I'm ready," I said. My voice was cracking, which surprised me because I had really believed I'd braced myself months earlier for this moment. I knew if I said another word, I would break down, and so I just nodded and signed as she handed me release forms. When the paperwork was completed, I followed her back to the unconscious Marley, and I knelt in front of him again, my hands cradling his head as she prepared a syringe and inserted it into the shunt. "Are you okay?" she asked. I nodded, and she pushed the plunger. His jaw shuddered ever so slightly. She listened to his heart and said it had slowed way down but not stopped. He was a big dog. She prepared a second syringe and again pushed the plunger. A minute later, she listened again and said, "He's gone." She left me alone with him, and I gently lifted one of his eyelids. She was right; Marley was gone.

I walked out to the front desk and paid the bill. She discussed "group cremation" for $75 or individual cremation, with the ashes returned, for $170. No, I said; I would be taking him home. A few minutes later, she and an assistant wheeled out a cart with a large black bag on it and helped me lift it into the backseat. The doctor shook my hand, told me how sorry she was. She had done her best, she said. It was his time, I said, then thanked her and drove away.

In the car on the way home, I started to cry, something I almost never do, not even at funerals. It only lasted a few minutes. By the time I pulled into the driveway, I was dry-eyed again. I left Marley in the car and went inside where Jenny was sitting up, waiting. The children were all in bed asleep; we would tell them in the morning. We fell into each other's arms and both started weeping. I tried to describe it to her, to assure her he was already deeply asleep when the end came, that there was no panic, no trauma, no pain. But I couldn't find the words. So we simply rocked in each other's arms. Later, we went outside and together lifted the heavy black bag out of the car and into the garden cart, which I rolled into the garage for the night.

CHAPTER 28

Beneath the Cherry Trees

✳

S leep came fitfully that night, and an hour before
dawn I slid out of bed and dressed quietly so as not to
wake Jenny. In the kitchen I drank a glass of water—
coffee could wait—and walked out into a light, slushy
drizzle. I grabbed a shovel and pickax and walked to the
pea patch, which hugged the white pines where Marley had
sought potty refuge the previous winter. It was here I had
decided to lay him to rest.

The temperature was in the mid-thirties and the ground
blessedly unfrozen. In the half dark, I began to dig. Once I
was through a thin layer of topsoil, I hit heavy, dense clay
studded with rocks—the backfill from the excavation of
our basement—and the going was slow and arduous. After
fifteen minutes I peeled off my coat and paused to catch
my breath. After thirty minutes I was in a sweat and not yet
down two feet. At the forty-five-minute mark, I struck
water. The hole began to fill. And fill. Soon a foot of
muddy cold water covered the bottom. I fetched a bucket
and tried to bail it, but more water just seeped in. There

was no way I could lay Marley down in that icy swamp. No way.

Despite the work I had invested in it—my heart was pounding like I had just run a marathon—I abandoned the location and scouted the yard, stopping where the lawn meets the woods at the bottom of the hill. Between two big native cherry trees, their branches arching above me in the gray light of dawn like an open-air cathedral, I sunk my shovel. These were the same trees Marley and I had narrowly missed on our wild toboggan ride, and I said out loud, "This feels right." The spot was beyond where the bulldozers had spread the shale substrata, and the native soil was light and well drained, a gardener's dream. Digging went easily, and I soon had an oval hole roughly two by three feet around and four feet deep. I went inside and found all three kids up, sniffling quietly. Jenny had just told them.

Seeing them grieving—their first up-close experience with death—deeply affected me. Yes, it was only a dog, and dogs come and go in the course of a human life, sometimes simply because they become an inconvenience. It was only a dog, and yet every time I tried to talk about Marley to them, tears welled in my eyes. I told them it was okay to cry, and that owning a dog always ended with this sadness because dogs just don't live as long as people do. I told them how Marley was sleeping when they gave him the shot and that he didn't feel a thing. He just drifted off and was gone. Colleen was upset that she didn't have a chance to say a real good-bye to him; she thought he would be coming home. I told her I had said good-bye for all of us. Conor, our budding author, showed me something he had made for Marley, to go in the grave with him. It was a drawing of a big red heart beneath which he had written: "To Marley, I hope you know how much I loved you all of my life. You were always there when I needed you. Through life or death, I will always love you. Your brother, Conor Richard Grogan." Then Colleen drew a picture of a girl with a big yellow dog and beneath it, with spelling help from her brother, she wrote, "P. S.—I will never forget you."

I went out alone and wheeled Marley's body down the hill, where I cut an armful of soft pine boughs that I laid on the floor of the hole. I lifted the heavy body bag off the cart and down into the hole as gently as I could, though there was really no graceful way to do it. I got into the hole, opened the bag to see him one last time, and positioned him in a comfortable, natural way—just as he might be lying in front of the fireplace, curled up, head tucked around to his side. "Okay, big guy, this is it," I said. I closed the bag up and returned to the house to get Jenny and the kids.

As a family, we walked down to the grave. Conor and Colleen had sealed their notes back-to-back in a plastic bag, and I placed it right beside Marley's head. Patrick used his jackknife to cut five pine boughs, one for each of us. One by one, we dropped them in the hole, their scent rising around us. We paused for a moment, then all together, as if we had rehearsed it, said, "Marley, we love you." I picked up the shovel and tossed the first scoop of dirt in. It slapped heavily on the plastic, making an ugly sound, and Jenny began to weep. I kept shoveling. The kids stood watching in silence.

When the hole was half filled, I took a break and we all walked up to the house, where we sat around the kitchen table and told funny Marley stories. One minute tears were welling in our eyes, the next we were laughing. Jenny told the story of Marley going bonkers during the filming of *The Last Home Run* when a stranger picked up baby Conor. I told about all the leashes he had severed and the time he peed on our neighbor's ankle. We described all the things he had destroyed and the thousands of dollars he had cost us. We could laugh about it now. To make the kids feel better, I told them something I did not quite believe. "Marley's spirit is up in dog heaven now," I said. "He's in a giant golden meadow, running free. And his hips are good again. And his hearing is back, and his eyesight is sharp, and he has all his teeth. He's back in his prime—chasing rabbits all day long."

Jenny added, "And having endless screen doors to crash through." The image of him barging his way oafishly through heaven got a laugh out of everyone.

The morning was slipping away, and I still needed to go to work. I went back down to his grave alone and finished filling the hole, gently, respectfully, using my boot to tamp down the loose earth. When the hole was flush with the ground, I placed two large rocks from the woods on top of it, then went inside, took a hot shower, and drove to the office.

In the days immediately after we buried Marley, the whole family went silent. The animal that was the amusing target of so many hours of conversation and stories over the years had become a taboo topic. We were trying to return our lives to normal, and speaking of him only made it harder. Colleen in particular could not bear to hear his name or see his photo. Tears would well in her eyes and she would clench her fists and say angrily, "I don't want to talk about him!"

I resumed my schedule, driving to work, writing my column, coming home again. Every night for thirteen years he had waited for me at the door. Walking in now at the end of the day was the most painful part of all. The house seemed silent, empty, not quite a home anymore. Jenny vacuumed like a fiend, determined to get up the bucketsful of Marley fur that had been falling out in massive clumps for the past couple of years, insinuating itself into every crevice and fold. Slowly, the signs of the old dog were being erased. One morning I went to put my shoes on, and inside them, covering the insoles, lay a carpet of Marley fur, picked up by my socks from walking on the floors and gradually deposited inside the shoes. I just sat and looked at it—actually petted it with two fingers—and smiled. I held it up to show Jenny and said, "We're not getting rid of him that easy." She laughed, but that evening in our bedroom, Jenny—who had not said much all week— blurted out: "I miss him. I mean I really, *really* miss him. I ache-inside miss him."

"I know," I said. "I do, too."

I wanted to write a farewell column to Marley, but I was afraid all my emotion would pour out into a gushy, maudlin piece of self-indulgence that would only humiliate me. So I stuck with topics less dear to my heart. I did, however, carry a tape recorder with me, and when a thought came to me, I would get it down. I knew I wanted to portray him as he was and not as some impossibly perfect reincarnation of Old Yeller or Rin Tin Tin, as if there were any danger of that. So many people remake their pets in death, turning them into supernatural, noble beasts that in life did everything for their masters except fry eggs for breakfast. I wanted to be honest. Marley was a funny, bigger-than-life pain in the ass who never quite got the hang of the whole chain-of-command thing. Honestly, he might well have been the world's worst-behaved dog. Yet he intuitively grasped from the start what it meant to be man's best friend.

During the week after his death, I walked down the hill several times to stand by his grave. Partly, I wanted to make sure no wild animals were coming around at night. The grave remained undisturbed, but already I could see that in the spring I would need to add a couple of wheelbarrows of soil to fill the depression where it was settling. Mostly I just wanted to commune with him. Standing there, I found myself replaying random snippets from his life. I was embarrassed by how deep my grief went for this dog, deeper than for some humans I had known. It's not that I equated a dog's life with a human's, but outside my immediate family few people had given themselves so selflessly to me. Secretly, I brought Marley's choker chain in from the car, where it had sat since his final ride to the hospital, and stashed it beneath the underwear in my dresser, where each morning I could reach down and touch it.

I walked around all week with a dull ache inside. It was actually physical, not unlike a stomach virus. I was lethargic, unmotivated. I couldn't even muster the energy to indulge my hobbies—playing guitar, woodworking, reading. I felt out of sorts, not sure what to do with myself. I ended up going to bed early most nights, at nine-thirty, ten o'clock.

On New Year's Eve we were invited to a neighbor's house for a party. Friends quietly expressed their condolences, but we all tried to keep the conversation light and moving. This was, after all, New Year's Eve. At dinner, Sara and Dave Pandl, a pair of landscape architects who had moved back to Pennsylvania from California to turn an old stone barn into their home, and who had become our dear friends, sat at one corner of the table with me, and we talked at length about dogs and love and loss. Dave and Sara had put down their cherished Nelly, an Australian shepherd, five years earlier and buried her on the hill beside their farmhouse. Dave is one of the most unsentimental people I have ever met, a quiet stoic cut from taciturn Pennsylvania Dutch stock. But when it came to Nelly, he, too, struggled with a deep inner grief. He told me how he combed the rocky woods behind his home for days until he found the perfect stone for her grave. It was naturally shaped like a heart, and he took it to a stone carver who inscribed "Nelly" into its surface. All these years later, the death of that dog still touched them profoundly. Their eyes misted up as they told me about her. As Sara said, blinking back her tears, sometimes a dog comes along that really touches your life, and you can never forget her.

That weekend I took a long walk through the woods, and by the time I arrived at work on Monday, I knew what I wanted to say about the dog that touched my life, the one I would never forget.

I began the column by describing my walk down the hill with the shovel at dawn and how odd it was to be outdoors without Marley, who for thirteen years had made it his business to be at my side for any excursion. "And now here I was alone," I wrote, "digging him this hole."

I quoted my father who, when I told him I had to put the old guy down, gave the closest thing to a compliment my dog had ever received: "There will never be another dog like Marley."

I gave a lot of thought to how I should describe him, and this is what I settled on: "No one ever called him a great dog—or even a good dog. He was as wild as a banshee and as strong as a bull. He crashed joyously through life with a gusto most often associated with natural disasters. He's the only dog I've ever known to get expelled from obedience school." I continued: "Marley was a chewer of couches, a slasher of screens, a slinger of drool, a tipper of trash cans. As for brains, let me just say he chased his tail till the day he died, apparently convinced he was on the verge of a major canine breakthrough." There was more to him than that, however, and I described his intuition and empathy, his gentleness with children, his pure heart.

What I really wanted to say was how this animal had touched our souls and taught us some of the most important lessons of our lives. "A person can learn a lot from a dog, even a loopy one like ours," I wrote. "Marley taught me about living each day with unbridled exuberance and joy, about seizing the moment and following your heart. He taught me to appreciate the simple things—a walk in the woods, a fresh snowfall, a nap in a shaft of winter sunlight. And as he grew old and achy, he taught me about optimism in the face of adversity. Mostly, he taught me about friendship and self-lessness and, above all else, unwavering loyalty."

It was an amazing concept that I was only now, in the wake of his death, fully absorbing: Marley as mentor. As teacher and role model. Was it possible for a dog—any dog, but especially a nutty, wildly uncontrollable one like ours— to point humans to the things that really mattered in life? I believed it was. Loyalty. Courage. Devotion. Simplicity. Joy. And the things that did not matter, too. A dog has no use for fancy cars or big homes or designer clothes. Status symbols mean nothing to him. A waterlogged stick will do just fine. A dog judges others not by their color or creed or class but by who they are inside. A dog doesn't care if you are rich or poor, educated or illiterate, clever or dull. Give him your heart and he will give you his. It was really quite simple, and yet we humans, so much wiser and more sophisticated, have always had trouble figuring out what really counts and what does not. As I wrote that farewell column to Marley, I realized it was all right there in front of us, if only we opened our eyes. Sometimes it took a dog with bad breath, worse manners, and pure intentions to help us see.

I finished my column, turned it in to my editor, and drove home for the night, feeling somehow lighter, almost buoyant, as though a weight I did not even know I had been carrying was lifted from me.

CHAPTER 29

The Bad Dog Club

✳

W hen I arrived at work the next morning, the red message light on my telephone was blinking. I punched in my access code and received a recorded warning I had never heard before. "Your mailbox is full," the voice said. "Please delete all unneeded messages."

I logged on to my computer and opened my e-mail. Same story. The opening screen was filled with new messages, and so was the next screen, and the one after that, and after that, too. The morning e-mail was a ritual for me, a visceral, if inexact, barometer of the impact that day's column had made. Some columns brought as few as five or ten responses, and on those days I knew I had not connected. Others brought several dozen, a good day. A few brought even more. But this morning there were hundreds, far more than anything I had received before. The headers at the top of the e-mails said things like "Deepest condolences," "About your loss," or simply "Marley."

Animal lovers are a special breed of human, generous of

spirit, full of empathy, perhaps a little prone to sentimentality, and with hearts as big as a cloudless sky. Most who wrote and called simply wanted to express their sympathies, to tell me they, too, had been down this road and knew what my family was going through. Others had dogs whose lives were drawing to their inevitable ends; they dreaded what they knew was coming, just as we had dreaded it, too.

One couple wrote, "We fully understand and we mourn for your loss of Marley, and for our loss of Rusty. They'll always be missed, never truly replaced." A reader named Joyce wrote, "Thanks for reminding us of Duncan, who lies buried in our own backyard." A suburbanite named Debi added: "Our family understands how you feel. This past Labor Day we had to put our golden retriever Chewy to sleep. He was thirteen and had many of the same afflictions you named with your dog. When he couldn't even get up to go outside to relieve himself that last day, we knew we couldn't let him keep suffering. We, too, had a burial in our backyard, under a red maple that will always be his memorial."

An employment recruiter named Monica, owner of Katie the Lab, wrote: "My condolences and tears to you. My girl Katie is only two and I always think, 'Monica, why did you go and let this wonderful creature steal your heart like this?'" From Carmela: "Marley must have been a great dog to have a family that loved him so much. Only dog owners can understand the unconditional love they give and the tremendous heartache when they are gone." From Elaine: "Such short little lives our pets have to spend with us, and they spend most of it waiting for us to come home each day. It is amazing how much love and laughter they bring into our lives and even how much closer we become with each other because of them." From Nancy: "Dogs are one of the wonders of life and add so very much to ours." From MaryPat: "To this day I miss the sound of Max's tags jingling as he padded through the house checking things out; that silence will drive you nuts for a while, especially at night." From Connie: "It's just the most amazing thing to love a dog, isn't it? It makes our relationships with people seem as boring as a bowl of oatmeal."

When the messages finally stopped coming several days later, I counted them up. Nearly eight hundred people, animal lovers all, had been moved to contact me. It was an incredible outpouring, and what a catharsis it was for me. By the time I had plowed through them all—and answered as many as I could—I felt better, as though I was part of a giant cyber-support group. My private mourning had become a public therapy session, and in this crowd there was no shame in admitting a real, piercing grief for something as seemingly inconsequential as an old, smelly dog.

My correspondents wrote and called for another reason, too. They wanted to dispute the central premise of my report, the part in which I insisted Marley was the world's worst-behaved animal. "Excuse me," the typical response went, "but yours couldn't have been the world's worst dog—because mine was." To make their case, they regaled me with detailed accounts of their pets' woeful behavior. I heard about shredded curtains, stolen lingerie, devoured birthday cakes, trashed auto interiors, great escapes, even a swallowed diamond engagement ring, which made Marley's taste for gold chains seem positively lowbrow by comparison. My in-box resembled a television talk show, *Bad Dogs and the People Who Love Them*, with the willing victims lining up to proudly brag, not about how wonderful their dogs were but about just how awful. Oddly enough, most of the horror stories involved large loopy retrievers just like mine. We weren't alone after all.

A woman named Elyssa described how her Lab Mo always broke out of the house when left alone, usually by crashing through window screens. Elyssa and her husband thought they had foiled Mo's wandering ways by closing and locking all the ground-floor windows. It hadn't occurred to them to close the upstairs windows, as well. "One day my husband came home and saw the second-floor screen hanging loose. He was scared to death to look for him," she wrote. Just as her husband began to fear the worst, "Mo all of a sudden came around the corner of the house with his head down. He knew he was in trouble, but we were amazed he was not hurt. He had flown through the window and landed on a sturdy bush that broke his fall."

Larry the Lab swallowed his mistress's bra and then burped it up in one piece ten days later. Gypsy, another Lab with adventurous tastes, devoured a jalousie window. Jason, a retriever–Irish setter mix, downed a five-foot vacuum cleaner hose, "interior reinforcing wire and all," his owner, Mike, reported. "Jason also ate a two-by-three-foot hole in a plaster wall and backhoed a three-foot-long trench in the carpet, stretching back from his favorite spot by the window," Mike wrote, adding, "but I loved that beast."

Phoebe, a Lab mix, was kicked out of two different boarding kennels and told never to return, owner Aimee wrote. "It seems she was the gang leader in breaking out of not only her cage but doing the favor for two other dogs, too. They then helped themselves to all kinds of snacks during the overnight hours." Hayden, a hundred-pound Lab, ate just about anything he could get his jaws around, owner Carolyn reported, including a whole box of fish food, a pair of suede loafers, and a tube of superglue, "not in the same sitting." She added: "His finest hour, though, was when he tore the garage-door frame out of the wall because I had foolishly attached his leash to it so he could lie in the sunshine."

Tim reported his yellow Lab Ralph was every bit as much a food thief as Marley, only smarter. One day before going out, Tim placed a large chocolate centerpiece on top of the refrigerator where it would be safely out of Ralph's reach. The dog, his owner reported, pawed open the cupboard drawers, then used them as stairs to climb onto the counter, where he could balance on his hind legs and reach the chocolate, which was gone without a trace when his master returned home. Despite the chocolate overdose, Ralph showed no ill effects. "Another time," Tim wrote, "Ralph opened the refrigerator and emptied its contents, including things in jars."

Nancy clipped my column to save because Marley reminded her so much of her retriever Gracie. "I left the article on the kitchen table and turned to put away the scissors," Nancy wrote. "When I turned back, sure enough, Gracie had eaten the column."

Wow, I was feeling better by the minute. Marley no longer sounded all that terrible. If nothing else, he certainly had plenty of company in the Bad Dog Club. I brought several of the messages home to share with Jenny, who laughed for the first time since Marley's death. My new friends in the Secret Brotherhood of Dysfunctional Dog Owners had helped us more than they ever would know.

The days turned into weeks and winter melted into spring. Daffodils pushed up through the earth and bloomed around Marley's grave, and delicate white cherry blossoms floated down to rest on it. Gradually, life without our dog became more comfortable. Days would float by without me even thinking of him, and then some little cue—one of his hairs on my sweater, the rattle of his choker chain as I reached into my drawer for a pair of socks— would bring him abruptly back. As time passed, the recollections were more pleasant than painful. Long-forgotten moments flashed in my head with vivid clarity like clips being rerun from old home videos: The way Lisa the stabbing victim had leaned over and kissed Marley on the snout after she got out of the hospital. The way the crew on the movie set fawned over him. The way the mail lady slipped him a treat each day at the front door. The way he held mangoes in his front paws as he nibbled out the flesh. The way he snapped at the babies' diapers with that look of narcotic bliss on his face, and the way he begged for his tranquilizers like they were steak bits. Little moments hardly worth remembering, and yet here they were, randomly playing out on my mental movie screen at the least likely times and places. Most of them made me smile; a few made me bite my lip and pause.

I was in a staff meeting at the office when this one came to me: It was back in West Palm Beach when Marley was still a puppy and Jenny and I were still dreamy-eyed newlyweds. We were strolling along the Intracoastal Waterway on a crisp winter's day, holding hands, Marley out in front, tugging us along. I let him hop up on the concrete breakwater, which was about two feet wide and three feet above the water's surface. "John," Jenny protested. "He could fall in." I looked at her dubiously. "How dumb do you think he is?" I asked. "What do you think he'll do? Just walk right off the edge into thin air?" Ten seconds later, that's exactly what he did, landing in the water with a huge splash and requiring a complicated rescue operation on our part to get him back up the wall and onto land again.

A few days later I was driving to an interview when out of nowhere came another early scene from our marriage: a romantic getaway weekend to a beachfront cottage on Sanibel Island before children arrived. The bride, the groom—and Marley. I had completely forgotten about that weekend, and here it was again, replaying in living color: driving across the state with him wedged between us, his nose occasionally bumping the gearshift lever into neutral.

Bathing him in the tub of our rental place after a day on the beach, suds and water and sand flying everywhere. And later, Jenny and I making love beneath the cool cotton sheets, an ocean breeze wafting over us, Marley's otter tail thumping against the mattress.

He was a central player in some of the happiest chapters of our lives. Chapters of young love and new beginnings, of budding careers and tiny babies. Of heady successes and crushing disappointments; of discovery and freedom and self-realization. He came into our lives just as we were trying to figure out what they would become. He joined us as we grappled with what every couple must eventually confront, the sometimes painful process of forging from two distinct pasts one shared future. He became part of our melded fabric, a tightly woven and inseparable strand in the weave that was us. Just as we had helped shape him into the family pet he would become, he helped to shape us, as well—as a couple, as parents, as animal lovers, as adults. Despite everything, all the disappointments and unmet expectations, Marley had given us a gift, at once priceless and free. He taught us the art of unqualified love. How to give it, how to accept it. Where there is that, most of the other pieces fall into place.

The summer after his death we installed a swimming pool, and I could not help thinking how much Marley, our tireless water dog, would have loved it, loved it more than any of us possibly could, even as he gouged the liner with his claws and clogged the filter with his fur. Jenny marveled at how easy it was to keep the house clean without a dog shedding and drooling and tracking in dirt. I admitted how nice it was to walk barefoot in the grass without watching where I stepped. The garden was definitely better off without a big, heavy-pawed rabbit chaser crashing through it. No doubt about it, life without a dog was easier and immensely simpler. We could take a weekend jaunt without arranging boarding. We could go out to dinner without worrying what family heirloom was in jeopardy. The kids could eat without having to guard their plates. The trash can didn't have to go up on the kitchen counter when we left. Once again we could sit back and enjoy in peace the wondrous show of a good lightning storm. I especially liked the freedom of moving around the house without a giant yellow magnet glued to my heels.

Still, as a family, we were not quite whole.

One morning in late summer I came down for breakfast, and Jenny handed me a section of the newspaper folded over to expose an inside page. "You're not going to believe this," she said.

Once a week, our local paper featured a dog from a rescue shelter that needed a home. The profile always featured a photograph of the dog, its name, and a brief description, written as if the dog were speaking in the first person, making its own best case. It was a gimmick the shelter people used to make the animals seem charming and adorable. We always found the doggie résumés amusing, if for no other reason than the effort made to put the best shine on unwanted animals that had already struck out at least once.

On this day, staring up from the page at me was a face I instantly recognized. Our Marley. Or at least a dog that could have been his identical twin. He was a big male yellow Lab with an anvil head, furrowed brow, and floppy ears cocked back at a comical angle. He stared directly into the camera lens with a quivering intensity that made you just know that seconds after the picture was snapped he had knocked the photographer to the ground and tried to swallow the camera. Beneath the photo was the name: Lucky. I read his sales pitch aloud. This is what Lucky had to say about himself: "Full of zip! I would do well in a home that is quiet while I am learning how to control my energy level. I have not had an easy life so my new family will need to be patient with me and continue to teach me my doggie manners."

"My God," I exclaimed. "It's him. He's back from the dead."

"Reincarnation," Jenny said.

It was uncanny how much Lucky looked like Marley and how much the description fit him, too. Full of zip? Problem controlling energy? Working on doggie manners? Patience required? We were well familiar with those euphemisms, having used them ourselves. Our mentally unbalanced dog was back, young and strong again, and wilder than ever. We both stood there, staring at the newspaper, not saying anything.

"I guess we could go look at him," I finally said.

"Just for the fun of it," Jenny added.

"Right. Just out of curiosity."

"What's the harm of looking?"

"No harm at all," I agreed.

"Well then," she said, "why not?"

"What do we have to lose?"

The following column appeared in the the
Philadelphia Inquirer, *January 6, 2004*

SAYING FAREWELL TO A FAITHFUL PAL
John Grogan, *Inquirer* columnist

I n the gray of dawn, I found the shovel in the garage and walked down the hill to where the lawn meets the woods. There, beneath a wild cherry tree, I began to dig. The earth was loose and blessedly unfrozen, and the work went fast. It was odd being out in the backyard without Marley, the Labrador retriever who for 13 years made it his business to be tight by my side for every excursion out the door, whether to pick a tomato, pull a weed, or fetch the mail. And now here I was alone, digging him this hole.

"There will never be another dog like Marley," my father said when I told him the news, that I finally had to put the old guy down. It was as close to a compliment as our pet ever received.

No one ever called him a great dog—or even a good dog. He was as wild as a banshee and as strong as a bull. He crashed joyously through life with a gusto most often associated with natural disasters.

He's the only dog I've ever known to get expelled from obedience school.

Marley was a chewer of couches, a slasher of screens, a slinger of drool, a tipper of trash cans. He was so big he could eat off the kitchen table with all four paws planted on the floor—and did so whenever we weren't looking.

Marley shredded more mattresses and dug through more drywall than I care to remember, almost always out of sheer terror brought on by his mortal enemy, thunder.

CUTE BUT DUMB

He was a majestic animal, nearly 100 pounds of quivering muscle wrapped in a luxurious fur coat the color of straw. As for brains, let me just say he chased his tail till the day he died, apparently convinced he was on the verge of a major canine breakthrough.

That tail could clear a coffee table in one swipe. We lost track of the things he swallowed, including my wife's gold necklace, which we eventually recovered, shinier than ever. We took him with us once to a chi-chi outdoor cafe and tied him to the heavy wrought-iron table. Big mistake. Marley spotted a cute poodle and off he bounded, table in tow.

But his heart was pure.

When I brought my wife home from the doctor after our first pregnancy ended in a miscarriage, that wild beast gently rested his blocky head in her lap and just whimpered. And when babies finally arrived, he somehow understood they were something special and let them climb all over him, tugging his ears and pulling out little fistfuls of fur. One day when a stranger tried to hold one of the children, our jolly giant showed a ferocity we never imagined was inside him.

As the years passed, Marley mellowed, and sleeping

became his favorite pastime. By the end, his hearing was shot, his teeth were gone, his hips so riddled with arthritis he barely could stand. Despite the infirmities, he greeted each day with the mischievous glee that was his hallmark. Just days before his death, I caught him with his head stuck in the garbage pail.

LIFE LESSONS LEARNED

A person can learn a lot from a dog, even a loopy one like ours.

Marley taught me about living each day with unbridled exuberance and joy, about seizing the moment and following your heart. He taught me to appreciate the simple things—a walk in the woods, a fresh snowfall, a nap in a shaft of winter sunlight. And as he grew old and achy, he taught me about optimism in the face of adversity.

Mostly, he taught me about friendship and selflessness and, above all else, unwavering loyalty.

When his time came last week, I knelt beside him on the floor of the animal hospital, rubbing his gray snout as the veterinarian discussed cremation with me. No, I told her, I would be taking him home with me.

The next morning, our family would stand over the hole I had dug and say goodbye. The kids would tuck drawings in beside him. My wife would speak for us all when she'd say: "God, I'm going to miss that big, dumb lug."

But now I had a few minutes with him before the doctor returned. I thought back over his 13 years—the destroyed furniture and goofy antics; the sloppy kisses and utter devotion. All in all, not a bad run.

I didn't want him to leave this world believing all his bad press. I rested my forehead against his and said: Marley, you are a great dog.''

Acknowledgments

No man is an island, authors included, and I would like to thank the many people whose support helped me bring this book to fruition. At the top of the list, let me start by expressing my deep appreciation to my agent, the talented and indefatigable Laurie Abkemeier of DeFiore and Company, who believed in this story and my ability to tell it even before I fully did myself. I am convinced that without her unflagging enthusiasm and coaching, this book would still be locked in my head. Thank you, Laurie, for being my confidante, my advocate, my friend.

My heartfelt thanks to my wonderful editor, Mauro Di-Preta, whose judicious and intelligent editing made this a better book, and to the always cheerful Joelle Yudin, who kept track of all the details. Thanks also to Michael Morrison, Lisa Gallagher, Seale Ballenger, Ana Maria Allessi, Christine Tanigawa, Richard Aquan, and everyone in the HarperCollins group for falling in love with Marley and his story, and making my dream a reality.

I owe a debt to my editors at the *Philadelphia Inquirer* for rescuing me from my self-imposed exile from the newspaper business that I love so much, and for giving me the priceless gift of my own column in one of America's greatest newspapers.

I am beyond grateful to Anna Quindlen whose early enthusiasm and encouragement meant more to me than she will ever know.

A hearty thank-you to Jon Katz, who gave me valuable advice and feedback, and whose books, especially *A Dog Year: Twelve Months, Four Dogs, and Me*, inspired me.

To Jim Tolpin, a busy lawyer who always found the time to give me free and sage advice. To Pete and Maureen Kelly, whose companionship—and cottage overlooking Lake Huron—was the tonic I needed. To Ray and JoAnn Smith for being there when I needed them most, and to Timothy R. Smith for the beautiful music that made me cry. To Digger Dan for the steady supply of smoked meats, and to my siblings, Marijo, Timothy, and Michael Grogan, for the cheerleading. To Maria Rodale for trusting me with a beloved family heirloom and helping me find my balance. To all those friends and colleagues too numerous to mention for their kindness, support, and good wishes . . . thank you all.

I could not have even contemplated this project without my mother, Ruth Marie Howard Grogan, who taught me early on the joy of a good tale well told and shared her gift for storytelling with me. With sadness, I remember and honor my biggest fan of all, my father Richard Frank Grogan, who died on December 23, 2004, as this book was going into production. He did not get the chance to read it, but I was able to sit with him one night as his health failed and read the few opening chapters aloud, even making him laugh. That smile, I will remember forever.

I owe a huge debt to my lovely and patient wife, Jenny, and my children, Patrick, Conor, and Colleen, for allowing me to trot them out into the public spotlight, sharing the most intimate of details. You guys are good sports, and I love you beyond words.

Finally (yes, last once again), I need to thank that pain-in-the-ass four-legged friend of mine, without whom there would be no *Marley & Me*. He'd be happy to know that his debt for all the shredded mattresses, gouged drywall, and swallowed valuables is now officially satisfied in full.

The Longest Trip Home

To J.R., R.S., and D.P.,
who taught me early on the meaning of friendship

Contents

Preface

❉

The call came on a school night in the autumn of 2002. Jenny was out, and I was fixing dinner for our three children, who were already at the table. I grabbed the phone on the third ring.

"John!" My father's voice boomed through the earpiece. He sounded exceptionally buoyant. At eighty-six, Dad was quite the physical specimen. Just as when he was a young man, he began each morning with calisthenics, including forty push-ups. He always loved the outdoors and still cut his own acre of grass, gardened, shoveled snow, and climbed on the roof to clean the gutters. Dad bustled up and down the stairs of his home with a teenager's vigor and routinely got by on six hours of sleep. His handwriting was as neat and controlled as on the day he went to work as a draftsman for General Motors in 1940, and he honed his mind each night by breezing through the crossword puzzle in the newspaper as he ate peanuts in his trademark way—with chopsticks so he wouldn't get his fingers greasy.

There was never enough time in each day for everything he wanted to get done, and fourteen years shy of becoming a centenarian, he joked that someday when life settled down, he would get to all that leisure reading on his list. "When I retire," he'd say.

"Hey, Dad," I said. "What's up?"

"Just checking in," he said. "How's everyone there?" I gave him quick updates on the kids, told him we were all fine. We chatted aimlessly for a few minutes as I carried the pasta and sauce to the table.

I placed my hand over the mouthpiece. "It's Grandpa," I whispered to the children and motioned to them to dig in.

"Everyone says hi," I told him.

"Say," he said, pausing just a little too long, "I need to talk to you about something."

"Is Mom okay?" I asked.

It was my mother we all worried about. Over the years she had grown weak and fragile. Her hips and lower back had deteriorated, rendering her all but immobile. And in recent years her memory had begun to slip. Dad had become her full-time caregiver, helping her bathe and dress, and doling out a daily regimen of medications that was comical in its quantity and complexity. Always the engineer, he kept track of them all with a meticulous flowchart. There were pills for her heart, for her diabetes, for her arthritis, for her aches, for what doctors said were the early stages of Alzheimer's disease. Despite Dad's characteristically upbeat tone, with every phone call I wondered if this would be the one with the bad news.

"Mom's fine," Dad said. "Mom's doing all right. It's me. I got a little bad news today."

"You did?" I asked, stepping out of the kitchen and away from the kids.

"It's the darnedest thing," he said. "I've been feeling a little run-down lately, but nothing worth mentioning. Just kind of tired."

"You have a lot on your plate, taking care of Mom and the house and everything."

"That's all I thought it was. But a few days ago I took Mother in to Dr. Bober for her regular checkup. The doctor took one look at me and asked, 'Are you feeling okay? You look washed out.' I told her I was a little worn down but otherwise fine, and she said, 'Well, let's get you tested just to make sure you're not anemic.'"

"And?"

"And the results came back, and sure enough, I'm anemic."

"So they give you iron or something, right?"

"They can treat the anemia, but there's more to it. The anemia is just a symptom of something a little more serious."

He hesitated a moment, and I could tell he was choosing his words carefully. "After my blood work came back, Dr. Bober said she wanted to rule out some other things and sent me in for more tests." He paused. "They show I have a kind of leukemia, and—"

"Leukemia?"

"Not the bad kind," he said quickly. "There's acute leukemia, which is what you think of when you say leukemia—the kind that can kill so quickly. I don't have that. I have something called chronic lymphocytic leukemia. It's just lying there in my bloodstream not doing anything. The doctors say it could sit there dormant for years."

"How many years?" I asked.

"Anywhere from a couple to ten or twenty," Dad said.

My mind raced to process everything I was hearing. "So that's good, right?" I asked. "It may just sit there for the rest of your life."

"That's what the doctor said: 'Go about your life, Richard, and forget about it.' I should try not to worry and they'd treat any symptoms, like the anemia, and monitor my blood every four months."

"How are you doing on the 'try not to worry' front?" I asked.

"So far pretty good," he said. "I just want to stay healthy so I can take care of Mother for as long as she needs me."

Standing phone to ear from three states away, I felt a swell of optimism. Dad always bounced back. He had bounced back from the heart attack he suffered shortly after retiring from General Motors and from prostate cancer after I was married. Dad, a man who greeted adversity with stoic determination, would bounce back from this, too. The sleeping cancer would simply be something to monitor as my father marched vigorously into his nineties, holding together the strands of the life he and my mother had spent more than a half century building together.

"It's really nothing," Dad assured me. "I'm going to follow doctors' orders and try to forget about it."

That's when I asked: "Dad, what can I do?"

"Not a thing," he insisted. "I'm fine. Really."

"Are you sure?" I asked.

"Absolutely," he said and then added the one request that was so deeply important to him, the one thing that seemed so simple and effortless, and yet the one I had such difficulty delivering to him.

"Just keep me in your prayers," he said.

PART ONE

❋

Growing Up

CHAPTER 1

✼

Wake up, little sleepyheads."

The voice drifted through the ether. "Wake up, wake up, boys. Today we leave on vacation." I opened one eye to see my mother leaning over my oldest brother's bed across the room. In her hand was the dreaded feather. "Time to get up, Timmy," she coaxed and danced the feather tip beneath his nostrils. Tim batted it away and tried to bury his face in the pillow, but this did nothing to deter Mom, who relished finding innovative ways to wake us each morning.

She sat on the edge of the bed and fell back on an old favorite. "Now, if you don't like Mary Kathleen McGurny just a little bit, keep a straight face," she chirped cheerily. I could see my brother, eyes still shut, lock his lips together, determined not to let her get the best of him this time. "Just a tiny bit? An eeny teeny bit?" she coaxed, and as she did she brushed the feather across his neck. He clamped his lips tight and squeezed his eyes shut. "Do I see a little smile? Oops, I think I see just a little one. You like her just a tiny bit, don't you?" Tim was twelve and loathed Mary Kathleen McGurny as only a twelve-year-old boy could loathe a girl known for picking her nose so aggressively on the playground it would bleed, which was exactly why my mother had chosen her for the morning wake-up ritual. "Just a little?" she teased, flicking the feather across his cheek and into his ear until he could take it no more. Tim scrunched his face into a tortured grimace and then exploded in laughter. Not that he was amused. He jumped out of bed and stomped off to the bathroom.

One victory behind her, my mother and her feather moved to the next bed and my brother Michael, who was nine and equally repelled by a girl in his class. "Now, Mikey, if you don't like Alice Treewater just a smidgen, keep a straight face for me . . ." She kept at it until she broke his resolve. My sister, Marijo, the oldest of us four, no doubt had received the same treatment in her room before Mom had started on us boys. She always went oldest to youngest.

Then it was my turn. "Oh, Johnny boy," she called and danced the feather over my face. "Who do you like? Let me think, could it be Cindy Ann Selahowski?" I grimaced and burrowed my face into the mattress. "Keep a straight face for me if it isn't Cindy Ann Selahowski." Cindy Ann lived next door, and although I was only six and she five, she had already proposed marriage numerous times. My chin trembled as I fought to stay serious. "Is it Cindy Ann? I think it just might be," she said, darting the feather over my nostrils until I dissolved into involuntary giggles.

"Mom!" I protested as I jumped out of bed and into the cool dewy air wafting through the open window, carrying on it the scent of lilacs and fresh-cut grass.

"Get dressed and grab your beer cartons, boys," Mom announced. "We're going to Sainte Anne de Beaupré's today!" My beer carton sat at the foot of my bed, covered in leftover wallpaper, the poor man's version of a footlocker. Not that we were poor, but my parents could not resist the lure of a nickel saved. Each kid had one, and whenever we traveled, our sturdy cardboard cartons doubled as suitcases. Dad liked the way they stacked neatly in the back of the Chevrolet station wagon. Both of them loved that they were completely and utterly free.

Even in our very Catholic neighborhood, all the other families took normal summer vacations, visiting national monuments or amusement parks. Our family traveled to holy miracle sites. We visited shrines and chapels and monasteries. We lit candles and kneeled and prayed at the scenes of alleged divine interventions. The Basilica of Sainte-Anne-de-Beaupré, located on the Saint Lawrence River near Quebec, was one of the grandest miracle sites in all of North America, and it was just a seven-hour drive from our home outside Detroit. For weeks, Mom and Dad had regaled us with tales of the many miracles of healing that had happened there over the centuries, beginning in 1658 when a peasant working on the original church reported a complete cure of his rheumatism as he laid stones in the foundation. "The Lord works in mysterious ways," Dad liked to say.

When I got downstairs with my packed beer carton, Dad already had the tent trailer, in which we would sleep on our expedition, hooked to the back of the station wagon. Mom had sandwiches made, and soon we were off. Sainte-Anne-de-Beaupré did not disappoint. Carved of white stone and sporting twin spires that soared to the heavens, the basilica was the most graceful, imposing building I had ever seen. And inside was better yet: the walls of the main entrance were covered with crutches, canes, leg braces, bandages, and various other implements of infirmity too numerous to count that had been cast off by those Sainte Anne had chosen to cure.

All around us were disabled pilgrims who had come to pray for their own miracles. We lit candles, and then Mom and Dad led us into a pew, where we dropped to our knees and prayed to Sainte Anne, even though none of us had anything that needed fixing. "You need to ask to receive," Mom whispered, and I bowed my head and asked Sainte Anne to let me walk again if I ever lost the use of my legs. Outside, we climbed the hillside to make the Stations of the Cross, pausing to pray at each of the fourteen stops depicting an event in Jesus' final hours. The highlight of the visit was our climb up the twenty-eight steps that were said to be an exact replica of the steps Christ climbed to face Pontius Pilate before his crucifixion. But we didn't just climb the steps. We climbed them on our knees, pausing on each one to say half a Hail Mary aloud. We went in pairs, Mom and Dad first, followed by Marijo and Tim, and behind them, Michael and me. Step One: "Hail Mary, full of grace, the Lord is with thee; blessed art thou amongst women and blessed is the fruit of thy womb, Jesus." As we uttered the name of Jesus, we bowed our heads deeply. Step Two: "Holy Mary, mother of God, pray for us sinners, now and at the hour of our death, amen." Then we moved to the next step and started again. Over and over we recited the prayer as we slowly made our way to the top, Michael and I jabbing each other and crossing our eyes to see who could make the other laugh first.

On our way to the parking lot, we visited the gift shop, where I picked out a snow globe with Sainte Anne inside. Mom filled a bottle from a spigot behind the cathedral, figuring it had to be as holy as the water from Lourdes and other miracle sites. The parish priest would later bless it for her, and she would keep it in the linen closet and bring it out whenever we were sick with a particularly stubborn fever or sore throat or earache, touching the water to our foreheads or throats or ears and tracing a sign of the cross.

On the way home, Mom and Dad played the honeymoon game, which always delighted us kids no end. "Get down low, children, out of sight!" Mom coached and slid over in the seat up close to my father, resting her head on his shoulder and planting little kisses on his neck and cheek as he drove, both hands on the wheel and a quiet grin on his face. Dad wasn't one for displays of affection—he sent each of us off to bed at night not with a hug or a kiss but with a firm handshake—yet he seemed to enjoy the honeymoon game as much as the rest of us.

"Smooch smooch, Richie," Mom cooed.

We four kids lay in a heap on the backseat, looking up at them in lovebird mode and squealing at our clever subterfuge. Every passing motorist surely thought our parents were newlyweds on their honeymoon. Little did any of them know that the smooching couple already had four children hiding in the backseat and giggling with abandon. "Here comes another car," we'd scream in unison. "Kiss him again! Kiss him again!" And Mom would gladly comply.

Another successful family miracle trip was coming to an end. We had camped out in the crisp Canadian air, thrown rocks in Lake Ontario, eaten my mother's famous pork and beans cooked over an open fire, and prayed our way up twenty-eight steps on our knees. Life was safe and warm and good. I had parents who loved God and each other and us. I had two brothers and a sister to play and run and fight with. I had a house and toys and my own beer carton in which I could carry anything I wanted. Best of all, I had the comforting knowledge that if anything ever did go wrong, there was always Sainte Anne de Beaupré just a day's drive away, ready to use her miraculous healing powers to make everything right again. It was a dreamy, wondrous time.

CHAPTER 2

✳

My parents met in 1947, shortly after my father returned from four years on an aircraft carrier in the South Pacific. A year to the day later, they were married, and just weeks after that, expecting their first child.

Before they set off on the road to parenthood, though, they made a pact that each of their offspring would be named after either the Virgin Mary or her husband, Saint Joseph, who had selflessly taken on all the responsibility of fatherhood without any of the fun of procreation. Immaculate conception was a given in our household, with no room for debate. The Holy Spirit had miraculously planted the seed of God's only begotten son into the Virgin Mary's womb. Uncomplaining Saint Joseph took it from there. Even as a little boy, I thought this terribly unfair.

My sister, the eldest, got the Daily Double of Catholic names. My parents baptized her Mary Josephine, later shortened to Marijo. Next came Timothy Joseph and Michael Joseph.

But before the boys there was another girl, one who didn't make it. My parents baptized her Mary Ann, even though she never took a single breath. The only one ever to see her, and then only for a few moments, was my father, who described her as perfect in every way, like a flawless porcelain doll. Hospitals administered anesthesia to women delivering in those days, and when my mother finally awoke, my father was waiting at her bedside searching for the words to tell her. He would never forget the look on her face in the instant she opened her eyes. She was radiant, a smile spreading on her lips, her eyes widening with joyous expectation. Then he squeezed her hand and said, "Ruthie, our baby's with the Lord now."

They cried and prayed and told themselves this was God's plan and there had to be a reason she was in heaven already before she ever had a chance to experience life on earth. Then they arranged for a Catholic burial, her tiny casket resting to this day between my grandparents' graves in Ann Arbor.

I came along in 1957. John Joseph. Mom and Dad were hoping I would be a Saint Patrick's Day baby. When I missed that date, they rooted for Saint Joseph's Day, which would have been fitting, given all our middle names. Late again. When I finally arrived on March 20, I had other bragging rights. I came into the world on the first day of spring.

Mom called me her little daffodil.

Right from the start, Mom's little daffodil was no wallflower. Maybe it was the Cap'n Crunch cereal I devoured in vast quantities each morning, so sugary it made my teeth tingle. Maybe it was simply being the youngest of four and doing what was necessary to hog as much of my parents' attention as possible. Whatever the reason, I was born with abundant energy and few tools for containing it. My earliest memories are of racing through the house like a miniature tornado, shrieking joyously at the top of my lungs. Sometimes Dad would simply swoop me off my feet and hold me off the ground, legs still pumping, until I calmed down enough that I wouldn't hurt myself. On one of my runabouts through the house, I grabbed Mom's broom and held it over my head like a knight with a lance. "Stop! Now!" Mom ordered. I did, but only after the broom struck the large glass globe hanging from the foyer ceiling, sending it showering down on me in a thousand shards.

That night at dinner, Dad pulled out his stopwatch and said, "Johnny, we're going to try a little test. I want you to sit perfectly still for one full minute."

"Not a word, not a wiggle," Mom added. It was clear they were convinced I could not do it.

The first try, I lasted twelve seconds. Then thirty. Eventually I made it to sixty seconds, sitting there, grinning and twisting my face up, thinking this new game was great fun. The instant Dad clicked off the stopwatch and said, "Why, I'll be doggoned, he did it," I shot out of my chair like a Saturn space rocket and orbited the living room several times, pinging off the furniture.

In kindergarten the teacher noted my need to practice self-restraint and helped by frequently sending me to the corner to sit alone. She called Mom to come get me only on special occasions, such as the day I used two of my fingers like a fork to poke a classmate in the eyes, just like Moe did to Curly in my favorite show of all time, *The Three Stooges*.

When we got home after that incident, Mom said to me as she did after so many of them: "Johnny, go get George."

Mom was a firm believer in the power of spankings to modify behavior, and George was her enforcer. Before George had a name, he was simply the laundry stick, a thin board about eighteen inches long and two inches wide that Mom used to poke the clothes down into the suds in the washing machine. "Johnny, go get the laundry stick," Mom would say, and I knew what was coming, a crack across the backside.

Then one evening, my father treated us to dinner at a fancy restaurant, and all four of us kids, giddy with excitement, would not settle down. Mom was too embarrassed to let the other diners overhear her threatening her children with a spanking, so from thin air she pulled two names. Looking at Marijo, she asked matter-of-factly, as if issuing pleasantries: "Would you like a little visit from Suzie when we get home?" And from her tone and the look in her eye, Marijo figured out right away that a visit from this Suzie person would not be pleasant.

Then she leveled her calm gaze at my brothers and me. "And boys, how would you like to meet my friend George?" Subtlety being lost on me, I screamed out, "Sure!" Then Mom added: "You remember George, don't you? My friend who lives in the laundry room?" Suddenly I didn't want to meet George anymore.

When we got home, she wrote the words on the stick in permanent marker where they remained for years, even as the soapy wash water faded them to gray: *George* on one side, *Suzie* on the other. From that day forward, the George-

and-Suzie Spanking Stick was an effective part of Mom's arsenal. Usually a mere threat of a visit from George or Suzie was all that was needed to pull us back into line, but when punishment was required, Marijo always got her spanking on the Suzie side and the boys on the George side. The stick struck fear in the hearts of all four of us, even though Mom's whacks—and they always came from Mom, Dad not having the stomach for any type of corporal punishment— weren't much harder than love taps. That didn't stop me, however, from stuffing my pants with multiple copies of *National Geographic* to cushion the blow. I thought I was being outstandingly clever, but whenever Mom spotted a bulky load in my britches, she simply lowered her aim, to the back of my thighs.

Our neighborhood was known as Harbor Hills, though it really had neither. What it did have was a pair of gentle slopes on my street and a small man-made boat basin carved out by bulldozers between the two not-quite-hills.

The boat basin fed through a channel into Cass Lake, one of the largest inland bodies of water in metropolitan Detroit and unquestionably the biggest selling point of Harbor Hills, which consisted of three streets arranged in a sort of caste system in relation to the water. Only those fortunate enough to have waterfront lots could actually see the lake from their homes. These homes were large and glorious beyond description, and the people who lived in them were doctors and lawyers and business owners. Elsewhere in the neighborhood, on the landlocked lots, the dads tended to work in more middle-income professions. They were draftsmen and insurance agents and plumbers, and of course, automobile workers. Many, many of them, my father included, were gainfully employed by one of Detroit's Big Three—General Motors, Ford, or Chrysler. The farther away from the water you got in the neighborhood, the more modest the houses became.

But there was a great equalizer in Harbor Hills, and that was The Outlot.

The Outlot was a sort of grassy public space—not quite a park but more than a mowed field—covering a few acres right on the water. It surrounded the boat basin and was set aside by the developer for the exclusive use of the neighborhood. No matter how far back in the neighborhood you lived, you still had a piece of lake frontage to use as your own. There were big shade trees and picnic tables and, best of all, a small, stony beach with a raft and roped-off swimming area, where every kid in the neighborhood spent virtually every waking moment between Memorial Day and Labor Day. It was nothing fancy, but it was a beach, and that's all that mattered. The boat basin, universally known as The Lagoon, was lined with rickety wooden docks, and every house in the neighborhood was assigned one side of a dock. When you bought in Harbor Hills, you were getting more than just a suburban home on three-quarters of an acre. You were getting a waterfront lifestyle without the cost of a waterfront home—a place to swim and sunbathe and water-ski and picnic with the cool lake breezes in your face. My parents never experienced anything close to this growing up during the Great Depression, and like all good parents, they wanted more for their kids. They saved for years to move us out of the city to this Shangri-la on the shore. When you were lounging by the water on a perfect summer's day, it was hard to believe the gray, belching auto plants of Pontiac were just a ten-minute drive away.

In the summer, we swam and swam and swam. My brothers and sister and I were soon true amphibians, as comfortable in the water as out. This was a point of immense pride for my father, a landlocked city kid who only learned to swim, and then not well, when he joined the navy after Pearl Harbor. For my mother, who never learned to swim at all, it was simply a mystery. But summer wasn't the only season when we gathered in The Outlot. In the winter, we shoveled the snow off The Lagoon and skated until our legs ached and our toes were numb. We skated in the daylight, and we skated at night, the ice illuminated by the glow of rudimentary floodlights rigged to a nearby power pole. Sometimes one of the dads would build a warming fire next to the ice, and we would huddle around it, all runny noses and rosy cheeks, our breath rising in steamy clouds. In the spring and fall, the kids of the neighborhood—and there were dozens of us—were again down at the water, hanging out, goofing off, soaking our shoes, throwing sand at each other, and skipping stones. Every Easter there was a neighborhood egg hunt, and every Labor Day the annual Harbor Hills picnic, the highlight of which was the decorated bike parade. There were games and hot dogs and root beer on tap and, best of all, coal-roasted corn on the cob dipped in melted butter. The dads roasted the corn and ran the games; the moms anchored the potluck and dessert tables.

But Cass Lake was only half of what lured my parents to Harbor Hills. The other half, an even more powerful draw for them, was Our Lady of Refuge. They believed fervently in their duty to raise their children as devout Catholics. That meant not only Mass every Sunday—a nonnegotiable—but Mass on as many weekdays as possible, too. It meant receiving the holy sacraments of confession and communion and confirmation. It meant evening rosaries and Stations of the Cross, altar-boy training and staying up for Midnight Mass on Christmas. It meant smudged foreheads on Ash Wednesday and a Catholic education from the knuckle-rapping, hair-tugging, ear-twisting Sisters of Saint Felix in their brown habits and starched white face boards. The nuns, Mom and Dad assured us, were building our character.

Our house was three doors from Our Lady of Refuge, and my mother could stand at the living-room window and watch us march across the backyards, not losing sight of us until we entered the back door of the school. They had worked hard and saved relentlessly to move here, but they never regretted a dime of the cost. This, they were convinced, was the perfect place to raise a family. Many of our neighbors were just like my parents, practicing Catholics drawn to the neighborhood's twin attractions.

The beach and the church were the two poles of our universe. All life, all activity seemed to gravitate around one or the other. We were either at the beach or at Our Lady of Refuge—in school or in church or waiting for confession or playing soccer or hardball on the athletic fields. Either that or we were on our bicycles riding between the two.

To say my parents were devout Catholics is like saying the sun runs a little hot. It defined who they were. They were Catholics first, and then Americans and spouses and parents. Right from the start, their relationship was forged in their mutual devotion to Jesus and the Blessed Mother. One of their earliest dates was Mass followed by a rosary. As a kid hearing my mother tell the story for the umpteenth time, I could only sit, mouth agape in something approaching mortification, thinking, *Oh my God, I have the squarest parents in the universe.*

For fun, my siblings and I would sometimes count the Virgin Marys in the house; at one point we were up to forty-two. They filled every room, and they were not alone. Commingling with them were various likenesses of Jesus, Joseph, John the Baptist, Francis of Assisi, and an assortment of other saints and angels. There were crucifixes everywhere you turned in our house, the anguished, dying son of God staring down at us from the cross as we ate breakfast, brushed our teeth, and watched television. There were priest-blessed candles and holy water and palm fronds. Rosaries were scattered about in ashtrays and candy bowls. It was like living in a religious supply store. We even had an emergency Holy Communion kit, consisting of an aged oak box lined in purple velvet containing a silver chalice, a silver platter to hold communion wafers, two candleholders, and a cross. I had no idea where it came from, but it looked official and could be pressed into service by visiting priests who might want to say Mass at our dining room table. This happened more often than one might think.

My mother was constantly inviting priests to the house, and once she got them there, inviting them to give a group blessing or lead a prayer or say Mass. The priests, knowing a home-cooked meal would follow, seldom refused. She was a gifted cook, and her promise of good food even managed to lure a couple of bishops. We kids treated them like rock stars, taking turns dropping to our knees and kissing the big rings on their hands. It helped that two of Mom's brothers were priests. Father Joe and Father Vin, as we all knew them, visited often and, especially in the summer months, brought priest friends along to relax and enjoy the beach. It seemed we had clergy in our house more days than not, and they became a natural part of our family dynamic. Having Father O'Flaherty or Brother McGhee or even Bishop Schuster at the dinner table with us was just the way it was.

Our family was many things, but first we were Catholics. Of all my parents' dreams for their four children, only one was immutable: that we grow up imbued with the faith—devout, lifelong, practicing Catholics.

✼

CHAPTER 3

D espite my parents' best efforts, you could say my life as a good Catholic boy got off to a rocky start.

In the spring of 1964, I was preparing to celebrate First Holy Confession. Or at least that's how the nuns put it—*celebrate*—as though we would be having a party with cake and balloons. To a Catholic school second grader, this was a watershed event, and the sisters at Our Lady of Refuge had been preparing my classmates and me for the holy sacrament for months. We had all been baptized as infants; that was our first holy sacrament, and thank God for that because, as Sister and my parents pointed out repeatedly and very matter-of-factly, baptized Catholics were the only ones getting into heaven. The Protestants, Jews, Muslims, and everybody else were heading straight for limbo, certainly better than hell but basically just an eternal waiting room outside heaven's gate.

Holy Confession was our second sacrament, and its importance could not be overstated. This was the Lord's gift to us, our chance to purge the sins from our second-grade souls, to confess our transgressions—the pilfered candy and whispered swear words, the cruel taunts and creative lies—and seek God's forgiveness. It was a beautiful thing, the nuns assured us. We would receive our penance from the priest, who was just a breath shy of God himself and had his full authority to forgive. A few Hail Marys, a few Our Fathers—maybe even a half dozen of each if we had some doozies on our list—and all would be bygones. We would walk out of the dark confession box with a spring in our step and a lightness to our shoulders because we would no longer be carrying the burden of sin. At least not our own sins. We were all stuck with Original Sin, thanks to Adam and Eve and the way they caved in to temptation and ate the apple, but there wasn't anything we could do about that. It was kind of like being born with a genetic defect; you just had to deal with it. We could wipe out our own transgressions, though, and start over fresh. As with the bath Mom made my brothers and me take every Saturday night, lined up in a row in the tub, the old grime washed down the drain, leaving us clean and ready to start getting dirty all over again.

There was another important reason for the sacrament of confession. It was a necessary precursor to the even more important sacrament of Holy Communion, in which the priest—who, did I mention, was just a breath shy of God himself?—would take an ordinary piece of bread and through a miracle turn it into the body of Christ. Not a symbol of the body of Christ, but an actual piece of his flesh. We'd be eating Jesus! And not only that, but we would get to dress up like we were getting married as we did it, the girls in lacy white dresses with veils and pearl-beaded gloves, the boys in navy-blue suits and ties just like our dads wore. The

miracle, the nuns told us, was called *transubstantiation*—
the changing of bread and wine into the body and blood
of Christ. We would know it was real the instant we
swallowed a little piece of Jesus because we would feel his
presence in us. He would fill us with a warm glow, a joy a
thousand times greater than the joy of an ice cream sundae
on a hot August day or the Detroit Tigers making it to the
World Series (something that would actually happen a few
years later and which we all considered a miracle in its own
right). But first we had to scour the impurities from our tot-
size temples to make way for the Lord.

Sins were broken down into two groups. There were the
run-of-the-mill venial sins—swearing, tattling, disobeying,
coveting thy neighbor's oxen. Then there were the biggies,
the mortal sins. This would include, for instance, slaying
your brother like Cain did to Abel or worshipping false idols
over the Lord thy God. The nuns assured us that the priests
were very experienced and had heard every sin imaginable,
even the mortals, and we shouldn't feel ashamed to tell
them anything. Besides, they assured us, it was totally
confidential. The priests took a vow never to divulge your
sins, even if you were a famous murderer the police were
looking for. Not only was it confidential; the whole affair
was completely anonymous. We got to kneel in a dark box
and talk through a screen to the priest on the other side.
We could see him, but he couldn't see us. It was brilliant.
He wouldn't know who we were even if he did want to tell
the police or, worse, our parents.

Confession would be great, the first important step on the
road to being lifelong Catholics and our ticket to salvation.

It was the key to unlock our temples so that when we ate Jesus' body and sipped his blood he'd feel right at home inside us.

There was only one problem. My little temple carried a dark, shameful secret—two of them, actually—and I knew God would not wipe them clean with a few recited prayers or even a few hundred.

The first had to do with Mrs. Selahowski next door, whose daughter Cindy Ann Selahowski was not shy about letting me know she intended to marry me someday. It was a prospect that made my blood run cold, which is why Mom loved to tease me about her. Mrs. Selahowski, on the other hand, held an entirely different allure. Young, thin, and blond, she was my first love. It began when I was a preschooler. I played at their house nearly every day, and whenever Mrs. S. would walk into their rumpus room, I would gaze in adoration. When I was still napping in the afternoons, my mother would often lie beside me and doze off herself. I remember watching her as she slept, her face just inches from mine, and thinking she was the most beautiful woman in the whole world. After Mrs. Selahowski came on my radar, I revised my assessment.

Fueling my desire was Mrs. Selahowski's obsession with having the deepest tan in all of Michigan. Every single day, beginning in late spring, she would be out in her backyard, stretched on a chaise longue worshipping the sun. She would bake out there for hours in a tiny two-piece bathing suit, her blond hair piled loosely atop her head, rhinestone-encrusted sunglasses shading her eyes, baby oil slathered over her golden body. When she would lie on her stomach, she often reached back and unfastened her bathing suit top, which I found wildly provocative. One false move, and her bosom—I pronounced the word *ba-zooms*—would be fully exposed. From my second-story bedroom window, I had the perfect vantage point, and I prayed fervently for the lawn sprinklers to come on and shock her onto her feet. For my birthday, I asked for a telescope. "Our little Galileo," I heard Mom tell Dad.

A schoolboy crush would have been one thing, but by the time second grade had rolled around I had clearly moved into the sinful land of lust. I was coveting my neighbor's wife—poor Mr. Selahowski, he was such a nice man—and wife coveting was on the list not just of mortal sins but of *grave* mortal sins. That alone made me terrified of the confessional and the wrath I knew awaited me. But it got worse.

Sister Mary Lawrence was my second-grade teacher. She was stern and no-nonsense, a tiny woman who, as best as I could tell, was barely into her twenties. She wore the somber brown, scratchy wool habit of her order. A veil covered her hair, and stiffly starched linen boxed in her forehead, ears, and neck so that only the center of her face showed. Obviously she was no Mrs. Selahowski, but still kind of pretty. At least what I could see of her.

One day I was sitting in class lost in my thoughts, gazing at Sister in front of the chalkboard as she called on various students to stand and read aloud. The floor-length brown robes fascinated me, and I couldn't help wondering what she wore under them. Did she wear a bra and girdle like Mom? Or more of a flowing white nightgown getup like Florence Nightingale? Or frilly petticoats like Miss Kitty on *Gunsmoke*? Pretty soon, without meaning to, I was undressing her. Not to be dirty, but just to see what was underneath. I pictured her alone in her room at the convent, tired at the end of the day, pulling off her veil, her hair tumbling down, then slipping out of the habit, letting it drop to the floor. Sure enough, underneath was a flowing white gown that at once managed to be both impossibly modest and revealing. From there, it was just a small hop on the Mortal Sin Express to get her out of her undergarments. I was lost in the moment, totally enjoying Sister's nakedness, the droning voices of my classmates miles away.

That's when I heard my name.

My eyes moved from Sister's milky, naked torso to her face. She was fully clothed again, her face sandwiched between the mortarboards, and she was staring right at me.

"Well?" she asked. "Come on now. We haven't got all day."

"Uh," I responded.

"Begin where Michael left off."

I knew the drill. I was to stand beside my desk and read in a loud clear voice from my Catholic Reader until Sister said, "Thank you, take your seat." The only problem was, at that exact moment I happened to be sporting a full-blown, raging, miniature . . . situation. I still was not sure what to call that thing that sometimes visited when I least expected it. I looked down at my lap and my navy-blue uniform pants were poking up like a pup tent. I still believed in the literal power of prayer then, and I pulled out every big gun I could think of. *Please, dear Jesus, dear God the Father, dear*

Holy Spirit, please make it go away. The tent pole held its ground. *All the angels and saints in heaven, please. Please! Don't make me stand up. Dear Blessed Mother, make her call someone else.*

"Uhhh," I said. I was stalling for time. *Please, Saint Christopher, Saint Francis, Saint Joseph the Carpenter.*

"Mr. Grogan, we are all waiting."

I lifted my book off my desk and fidgeted with the pages, pretending to find my place. *Dear Saints Peter and Paul, Saint Matthew, Saint Monica, please, please. All the poor souls in purgatory. Help!*

"Now, Mr. Grogan," Sister said in a voice that told me there would be no more stalling.

I took a deep breath and stood up, giving a sort of salute as I did. In an ill-conceived attempt to hide the evidence, I held the book as low as I could, my arms fully extended at belt level. But this served only to highlight my predicament. It looked like I was using the bulge in my trousers as a book rest. A couple of kids began to giggle. I soldiered on. "Soon they saw an animal jump out of the snow," I read aloud. "It was a gray rabbit. Hop hop, it went to the big tree." I held the book away from me to steal a glance at my crotch. Still standing tall. I searched my brain for anyone who might rescue me from this humiliation. *Please, dear Saint Aloysius. Saint John the Baptist. Saint Thomas? Please, saint . . . saint . . . Saint Someone. Saint Anyone! Make it go away.*

Then I remembered Sainte Anne de Beaupré. Of course! Sainte Anne! My old friend! Surely she would remember me from my pilgrimage. The Stations of the Cross, the holy water, all those stairs I climbed on my knees. Mom had said that if I asked, she would hear me. Besides, malfunctioning body parts were her specialty. *Dear Sainte Anne, please fix this. Fix it now. Fix it like you fixed all those broken people. Please, Sainte Anne, if you can make cripples walk and blind men see, I know you can make this thing go away.*

Not even she could help. "Soon an old mother rabbit and five baby rabbits came to eat," I read. More kids snickered. If Sister noticed my aroused state, she gave no sign. Finally she released me from my torture. "Take your seat, please," she said and called the next student. I sat, and when I looked down, it was gone.

In the weeks that followed, Sister continued to drill us about our sins and how we were to confess them. Over and over again we reviewed the protocol—pulling back the curtain and walking into the dark box, kneeling in front of the screen and waiting for Father to open the little door between us. Then we were to begin, "Forgive me, Father, for I have sinned . . ." Boy, had I ever. I had fantasized the most salacious thoughts imaginable. I had coveted not only Mr. Selahowski's wife, but Jesus' wife, too. We were taught the nuns were the brides of Christ, and they wore the wedding bands to prove it. I had gazed upon a dedicated servant of the Church, wife of Jesus, and stripped her bare with my eyes. I was in serious trouble. I steeled myself to tell the truth. As Sister had made clear, the worst sin of all would be to lie in the confessional because you would really be lying to God, and no one got away with that. I approached First Confession with all the joy of a condemned inmate making that last lonely walk to the gallows.

Our Lady of Refuge was a young parish, being built in phases. There were three buildings: a large, ominous brick convent where the nuns lived, a friendlier-looking rectory where the priests lived, and the school, serving first through eighth grades. The real church was still years off, eventually to be built on the soccer field. In the meantime, church was held in that part of the school designed to become the gymnasium. It was an austere cinder-block structure with industrial glass-block windows and a linoleum floor. In front was a rudimentary sanctuary, still in cinder block but with thick red carpeting to give it a regal air, and a marble altar bedecked in starched linens beneath a towering crucifix. Separating the sanctuary from the pews was a varnished oak railing fitted with red-velvet kneelers where the faithful lined up to receive Jesus' body and, on special occasions, a sip of his blood, too. Our house of worship was to the great cathedrals of Europe, and even to the just mildly magnificent churches of America, what a White Castle is to Morton's steak house. But to me it was grand, mysterious, and enticing beyond words, permeated with the smells of incense and beeswax.

This gym-turned-house-of-worship was where my first confession would take place. The church had a confessional built into each of the four corners, wired with red and green lights activated by weight-sensitive switches on the kneeler inside to let you know if it was empty or occupied by a confessing sinner. Because we had seventy children in the two second-grade classes, plus the public-school kids from the parish, the pastor had asked priests from the Catholic seminary across the road to help out.

Four showed up to help Father handle about a hundred kids. Every one of the priests had been to our house for dinner; every one of them knew me by name. To accommodate the fifth priest, a portable confessional was set up in a cloakroom off the vestibule. It was basically a folding divider with a grate to speak through, a kneeler on one side for the penitent and a chair on the other for the priest. The children were divided into five groups and assigned confessionals. I was in the group assigned to the portable unit. No problem. Through the open door of the cloakroom, I could see it was just as private as the permanent booths. Unless Father recognized my voice, he would never guess that the sex-crazed nun coveter on the other side of the screen was actually the son of Ruth and Richard Grogan, loyal and devout parishioners and two of his most energetic volunteers.

I was about twelfth in line. Each child ahead of me walked into the cloakroom, closed the door behind him, and emerged a few minutes later with a penance to say. As I waited my turn, I practiced my lines. *Forgive me, Father, for I have sinned. This is my first confession.* Breakfast roiled in my stomach. How could I admit what I had done? "Impure thoughts" did not begin to cover it. *Please, Saint Dominic Savio, childhood saint, don't let Father recognize my voice.*

I had hardened myself to the task at hand. I would march in and lay it all out so I could purify my temple for Jesus and start anew. No more lusting, no more leering, no more stiffies.

A chubby classmate named James Coombs was immediately ahead of me, and when he came out from his confession, he did something none of the other children had done. He closed the door to the cloakroom behind him. *Click.*

My turn. I walked up and tried the knob. I turned it back and forth. I rattled it. Nothing. *Dear God the Father, dear Jesus, dear Holy Spirit, all the angels and saints in heaven, please don't let it be locked.* I shook the door again, this time more forcefully. I shot Coombs a dirty look, and he shrugged his shoulders as if to say, *I didn't know.* Fear rose in my throat. Father was in there waiting, wondering what had become of the next penitent. I knocked the door against its frame. I hit it with my shoulder. Then it opened. There stood Father Schroeder, the pastor, looking down at me. "Ah, Johnny Grogan, come in, my son. We'll have to do something about that lock, won't we?"

Oh, dear God, let me die now.

He took his place behind the partition, and I knelt, seeing his silhouette through the screen, smelling his aftershave mixed with the churchy mustiness of the room. I briefly weighed the two options before me: eternal damnation or immediate shame and humiliation. There was only one thing to do.

"Forgive me, Father, for I have sinned," I said. "This is my first confession."

Then I lied my ass off.

Father Schroeder had a positive ID on me; he was friends with my parents and over at our house practically every week for dinner or lunch or just to say hello. I could tell the truth, confessing the shameful secret that at the ripe age of seven I was already a sexual deviant. I could come clean and face what seemed near-certain condemnation, humiliation, and excoriation by my parents, the nuns, and the principal, all of whom Father would surely tell after he was done screaming at me in the confessional so that all my classmates would hear, too. Or I could simply . . . fudge a little. Actually, it would not be so much a lie as a small sin of omission. I would just leave a few things out.

"I fought with my brothers twelve times," I confessed through the screen. "I disobeyed my parents six times. I lied to Sister about my homework two times."

"Anything else, my son."

"Not really, Father."

"Go ahead," he coaxed. "There must be something more."

Oh God, he knew. He knew I was holding back. I had to give him something, anything. Anything but the truth. I started making things up.

"Well, I stole a radio."

"A radio, you say?"

"Yes, Father."

"You must return it, my son."

"I can't, Father."

"But you must."

"I threw it in the lake, Father."

"Good Lord, Johnny, what possessed you?"

"I didn't want anyone to know. And I . . ." My mind raced for a transgression that would at once be salacious enough to satisfy him without humiliating me. "I looked at naked ladies in *National Geographic*." I could see his silhouette nod as though he had heard this one before. I searched for a number. "Sixty-seven times."

"Sixty-seven?" Father asked. "Did you say sixty-seven?"

"Maybe sixty-eight, Father. I kind of lost count."

I filled out my list with age-appropriate misdeeds. "I lied to my parents ten times; used the Lord's name in vain nine times; read my sister's journal three times." Finally, the priest seemed satisfied.

"Anything else, my son?"

"That about does it, Father."

He mumbled absolution, blessed me, and gave me my penance—three Hail Marys and three Our Fathers. I bounded from the cloakroom with a mix of relief and dread.

My first confession. My chance to scrub my soul clean and return to the good graces of the Lord. And I had lied. Lied to Father and lied to God. What was worse, I knew there would be no going back now. I would have to lie in confession for the rest of my life. Because how could I ever confess to lying in my First Holy Confession? There was no choice now but to take these sins to the grave with me, and I knew what that meant.

I was seven years old and already doomed to an eternity in hell. Even the Protestants and Jews and Muslims would fare better than that.

CHAPTER 4

✳

G rowing up in Harbor Hills, I had two nearby playmates, but I never considered them friends. Next door was Cindy Ann Selahowski, the girl who was blind to my crush on her mother. In the house behind us was a crusty-eyed boy named Lawrence who was still calling for his mother to wipe his behind when he was seven years old. As casual playmates, they were fine. What I did not have was a best friend.

Then in 1966, when I was nine, a new family moved in on the next street. A family the likes of which I had never before known. The parents spoke in clipped brogues and constantly walked around with mugs of milky tea in their hands. The father, who worked at one of the General Motors factories, had immigrated to the United States from Wales as a young man; the mother was from Ireland. Their accents were as strong as the day they stepped onto American soil. They were the Cullens, Bevan and Claire, colorful and opinionated—and blessed, if you could call it that, with six sons. The second oldest, Tommy, was my age.

Shortly after they moved in, I wandered over to check out the new kid and found him and his five brothers working in the yard with wheelbarrows, shovels, and rakes. In the driveway were towering piles of wood chips, dumped there for free by the power company. One wheelbarrow at a time, the Cullen boys were spreading the mulch around the one-acre property. Their home had gone up on a lot that was nearly pure sand, and Mr. Cullen was nothing if not thrifty and inventive. With six mouths to feed on a blue-collar paycheck, he did not have disposable income to pay a landscaping company to lay down topsoil and sod. And so he struck a deal with the workers who trimmed tree branches away from the electric lines. They agreed to drop their trimmings for free at his house; it saved them the longer drive to the dump and tipping fees. You could call Mr. Cullen a pioneer organic gardener. From the old country, he brought the generational wisdom that plant matter—branches, leaves, bark, grass clippings—would eventually break down into humus, the foundation of rich soil and a healthy lawn. What he lacked in money, he made up for in time and energy—and free child labor. He was a tightly wound bundle of muscles with enough confidence to fill a stadium, and his plan was to cover the entire sandy property with six inches of mulch, give it a year to break down into loam, till it under, and plant his grass seed.

Truck after truck pulled up that summer with huge steaming piles of debris. On that first visit, I said a few words to Tommy, then just stood watching as he hurried back to work before he got scolded. Mr. Cullen, working beside his boys, eventually noticed me. He paused, wiped the sweat from his brow, and shouted out in his heavy brogue, "Well, what are you waitin' for, mon? Get your hands out of your pockets and grab a shovel!"

It was, I would learn over the years, Mr. Cullen's pet peeve and signature command. Hands in pockets could do no work; they were idle and useless, the sign of a slouch. On an almost hourly basis, he would yell out at someone—a son, a neighborhood kid, the scouts he would oversee as scoutmaster—"Get your hands out of your pockets, mon!"

On that first day, not knowing what else to do and unwilling to turn my back on his commanding presence, I did just what he ordered. I pulled my hands out of my pockets, grabbed a shovel, and began slinging mulch. There was something satisfying about the work, even if blisters quickly rose on my soft palms, and I returned day after day to help. Soon I was eating peanut butter sandwiches with the other boys at the long table in the Cullen kitchen. And soon Tommy and I were fast friends, as our parents would become, as well. The Cullens, like most of the families in the neighborhood, were Catholic and active in the parish. Like the Grogan kids, all six Cullen boys were enrolled at Refuge.

Tommy and I sweated together making the Cullen lawn, but mostly we played. That first summer, Mr. Cullen and my dad took us out and let us choose our first bicycles. Tommy and I settled on the identical model, the Schwinn Typhoon. It was big and heavy, with fat balloon tires and handlebars solid enough to carry a passenger. Tommy picked out a metallic red Typhoon. I went with metallic blue. We had our wheels, we had our freedom. Harbor Hills, every square inch of it, was our turf.

Tommy and I bombed up and down the neighborhood streets, coasted no-hands down the little not-quite-hills, and stood on our pedals to huff up the other side. We rode to the school to shoot baskets. Rode through people's backyards.

We had only one restriction on our summer wanderings: no leaving the neighborhood. Despite the ironclad edict, soon after Tommy and I brought home our Typhoons we did just that. The bikes gave us mobility we had not known, and the temptation was too great. I felt like Adam with the apple. About a half mile from our house, along busy Orchard Lake Road, was a small shopping plaza with a supermarket, a pharmacy, a pizza parlor, a chicken take-out place, and knickknack shops. Our first trip to the plaza seemed terribly daring. Our hearts pounding, we peered at every passing car, fearing one of the neighbors would spot us and call our parents. But no one did, and soon the plaza became our second home. We would hang out there for hours, buying candy bars and sodas with the money we had made by cashing in returnable bottles we found along the way. A small order of fries was 32 cents with tax at the chicken joint, and we would each cough up 16 cents to split an order, which we would drown in ketchup and eat sitting on the sidewalk.

We swiped books of matches from the pizza parlor and would have wars in the parking lot, flicking lit matches at each other. We hung out at the record store and were soon hooked on Paul Revere and the Raiders, the Rolling Stones, the Beach Boys, and most of all, the Beatles.

Mostly, though, we rode to The Outlot to swim and hang out. Mr. Cullen brought a no-nonsense, tough-love sensibility to his sons. Girls might need warm water to wash up in the morning, but cold water worked just fine for men.

Suntan lotion was for softies. So were beach towels. Real men air-dried, and that's what Tommy did every day after we swam, goose bumps rising on his skin. Soon I stopped bringing my towel, too.

It was at The Outlot, when we pulled off our shirts to jump in the water, that the one big difference between us became obvious. I was chubby, pale, and bespectacled, with a blubbery spare tire hanging over my suit and little breasts that actually had a sag to them. Tommy was just the opposite, lean and muscular, not an inch of spare flesh to pinch. The sun turned his skin a deep bronze and his blond hair to a silvery white. I envied his Adonis looks.

One day Tommy and I swam out to the wooden raft anchored in our swim area where a group of neighborhood girls our age sunbathed. In an attempt to show off, I took a running leap and dove into the water. When I climbed back on the raft, the girls encouraged me to dive again. I obliged them, and they asked again. And again. They were tanned and skinny, all legs and giggles, and they seemed fascinated by my running dive. I was basking in their attention until Tommy finally dove in after me and bobbed up, his face inches from mine. "Don't dive anymore," he whispered. "They're all just laughing at you."

That night after I took off my glasses and climbed into bed, I prayed to all the saints and angels in heaven, to God the Father, God the Son, and God the Holy Spirit, to make me less fat and more tan. Less clumsy and more athletic. More like Tommy, a boy the girls admired rather than ridiculed.

*   *   *

Near the end of fourth grade, as spring was poised to burst into summer, Dad and Mr. Cullen drove Tommy and me far out into the country to a farm where each of us could pick out a free puppy. For months I had been pestering my parents for a dog, promising to feed and care for it, insisting I would not shun my responsibilities once the novelty wore off. Our family had always had cats, first Lulu and later Felix. Cats were fine, but I wanted a dog. After months of deflecting me, Mom and Dad gave in. I think it was mostly Dad convincing Mom that a boy and a dog were meant to go together. As a child, Dad had had Fritz the German shepherd, who was his loyal companion into adulthood, bringing laughter and joy into a childhood that wasn't always easy. At the farm, the fathers told us to take our time and choose carefully because these pups would most likely be with us for the rest of our boyhoods.

Tommy chose a black-and-tan mutt he named Toffee, and I brought home Shaun, a golden, long-haired dog of unknown ancestry with a white blaze on his chest. I thought he was the most beautiful creature I had ever seen. Tommy and I sat side by side in the backseat of the station wagon, holding our puppies on our laps, letting them clamber over us and lick our faces. Soon they were tagging along with us everywhere we went. Within weeks, Toffee was struck and killed by a car, but Shaun would be at my side through the rest of my childhood—and I kept my end of the promise, feeding and caring for him every day until I left home for college.

It was 1967. While Tommy and I began another endless summer, my parents' comfortable world was exploding around them. The Vietnam War was escalating, and my cousins Joey and Vince had both shipped out to fight, while my other cousins joined thousands of students in antiwar protests on the campus of the University of Michigan, my father's alma mater. The Apollo space program, which hoped to put the first man on the moon, was reeling from a launchpad fire earlier that year that killed three astronauts, and America's cities were tinderboxes of racial tension, ready to erupt in even deadlier flames.

My sister, Marijo, had abandoned her pleated skirts and sweater sets for muslin smocks, bell-bottoms, and round wire-framed glasses, and began bringing home college boys with long hair, flowing beards, and names like Strike and Freedom, whom my parents greeted at the door with nervous smiles and awkward small talk. Tim, sixteen and enrolled at an all-boy Catholic high school, was lashing out against my parents' orderly world. He would sit silently simmering through Sunday Mass, refusing to participate. He was fighting hard to grow his own hair out that summer, and my parents were fighting back with everything they had, convinced that long hair was a stepping-stone on the path to drugs, sex, and this new, loud, and radically unnerving music they did not understand. The strain began to show on my parents' faces.

One afternoon I walked in from the beach to find Mom sobbing inconsolably in the living room. My swimming suit was still dripping as I put my arm around her.

"What's the matter, Mom?" I asked.

"It's Tim," she blurted out. "I've lost him."

"No you didn't," I insisted. "He's not lost. I just saw him. He's down at the beach. I just saw him there."

She bawled all the harder. "You don't understand. I've lost him, I've lost him." I rubbed her back a little, finally realizing it was his heart and soul she felt slipping from her. "It's gonna be okay, Mom," I said.

She dried her eyes on her apron and gave me a brave smile. "That's what I keep asking our Lord for," she said. "Now go get out of that wet suit, and I'll make you a snack."

That year the Animals released "When I Was Young," a song that Tommy and I adopted as our anthem. One verse in particular captured our ten-year-old preoccupations. It began: "I smoked my first cigarette at ten, and for girls I had a bad yen." School had been out for just a few days when Tommy and I decided it was time to fulfill the prophecy. I don't recall whose idea it was, but together we hatched a plot to buy our first pack of cigarettes.

We had been fascinated by the idea of smoking for months. The teenagers down at the beach, at least the cool ones, all smoked when no parents were around. It was clear that the short path to acceptance was to have a cigarette hanging from your lips. My uncle Father Joe was a devout priest. He also loved his Scotch, his Lucky Strikes, and the horse races, habits my parents tolerated but did not share. Mom and Dad knew that most smokers got hooked as teens, as Father Joe had, and told me they would buy me a gold watch for my twenty-first birthday if I stayed away from cigarettes until then. But the promise of gold could not compete with the promise of coolness. After one of Father Joe's weekly visits, I snitched a snubbed-out, half-smoked Lucky from the ashtray, and Tommy and I raced into the woods on the edge of the neighborhood to try it out. He held the match to it while I puffed. Then I handed it to him and he puffed. Our eyes watered, our noses ran, and we coughed uncontrollably. Two puffs each and we had had enough. But rather than be deterred, we settled on a simple truth: filterless Lucky Strikes might work for Father Joe, but we needed to get our hands on something smoother, something with a filter. The older kids all seemed to gravitate toward Marlboros, and they never seemed to cough or wheeze. That's what we needed, a pack of Marlboros.

The plan was hatched. The shopping plaza where we hung out had cigarettes, but only over the counter. We needed a vending machine safe from prying eyes, and we both knew what that meant: a road trip to Sylvan Lanes bowling alley. It was a good five miles away, but we knew it had a cigarette machine in the outer lobby, separated from the bowling lanes by glass doors. We set out on a hot June morning, pedaling through the back streets of the neighboring town of Keego Harbor until we got to the next village beyond that. We parked our bikes around the corner from the bowling alley, out of sight, and approached the door. We knew from the older kids that a pack of cigarettes cost 35 cents, and Tommy had brought a quarter and I a dime.

"I'll keep a lookout," I volunteered.

"Why do you get to be the lookout?" he asked.

Because I was petrified, that's why. I just said, "You're faster than I am," and Tommy seemed to see my logic because he grasped the coins in his fist and boldly strolled down the sidewalk and through the smoked-glass doors. He was in there forever, and I tried to look nonchalant as I kept my eye on the parking lot for grown-ups. It was early and all was quiet. Finally he burst out of the doors and came sprinting toward me. That was all the signal I needed to take off at full throttle. By the time Tommy caught me, I was around the corner and swinging my leg over the bar of my Typhoon.

"Stop! Stop!" he hissed. "I don't have them." He held up the dime. "I got the quarter in, but then one of the workers spotted me." Tommy had spent all that time in there studying the league schedules on the wall, trying to summon the nerve to drop in the dime and pull the lever. "Here," he said, pressing the coin in my palm. "Your turn."

My pride trumped my fear. I couldn't refuse the assignment without unmasking myself as a total jelly ball of cowardice. Inside, I perused the bulletin boards and gumball machine, all the while sneaking glances through the interior doors at the workers. When they seemed suitably distracted, I sidled over to the cigarette machine and yawned with great effect, stretching lazily and patting my mouth. *Look at me! See how relaxed and at home I am here in the outer lobby of Sylvan Lanes. Just another ho-hum day. Not nervous at all. Bored, actually.* Directly in front of me loomed the money slot. All I needed to do was reach out, slip in the dime, and pull the Marlboro lever. I rubbed the dime in my fingers, summoning my nerve. That's when I heard a metallic clink and watched helplessly as the coin rolled across the floor. I was on my hands and knees, butt up in the air, peering under the machine when I heard the door swing open. I looked up, and there stood a man. In uniform. A very large man in uniform. My heart stopped. *Dear Jesus, Dear Holy Spirit, Dear God the Father . . .* A full second passed, and I could see him trying to process why a child would be sprawled on the floor beneath the vending machine. I smiled weakly. Then I realized his was the uniform of a deliveryman. He pushed a dolly loaded with beer past me and disappeared inside. What if he reported me to the manager? I wasn't about to stick around to find out.

Back outside, I explained our dilemma to Tommy, and we spent the better part of a half hour strategizing about what to do next. Twenty-five cents of our money sat in the machine and ten cents beneath it. The only prospect worse than getting caught would be someone coming along to buy cigarettes and getting our quarter. There was no turning back now. This time we would go in together. Tommy volunteered to dive for the dime; I would watch the doors and stand ready to pull the lever once he got the coin in the slot.

Inside, the plan went like clockwork. Tommy quickly located the dime deep beneath the machine, scrambled to his feet, and without looking back, shoved it in the slot. "Pull! Pull!" he ordered.

I froze with fear. "Pull!" he yelled.

I lunged in the general direction of the Marlboro lever and pulled. With a loud, happy burp, the machine dropped a pack of cigarettes down the chute and into the tray. I grabbed the pack and was about to dash out the door when

I saw my mistake. Tommy saw it, too. "Oh no," he said as if he had just witnessed a horrible accident.

I wasn't holding the manly red-and-white packaging of Marlboro. I had accidentally pulled the lever for a low-tar, low-nicotine cigarette recently put on the market to address health concerns. Tommy could not have looked more mortified had a decomposing body part spilled out at us.

"True Blues?" he gasped. "True Blues! Oh God, girl ciggies." It was a fate of unspeakable shame. I stared at them as if, through the sheer force of concentration, I might be able to transform them into Marlboros, like the priests transformed bread into the body of Christ. We both stood there for a moment longer before the precariousness of our situation sank in. We were standing in a public lobby holding evidence of criminal wrongdoing.

"Crotch 'em!" Tommy barked, and I shoved them down the front of my shorts inside my underwear. We bolted out the doors and sprinted to our getaway vehicles. "Don't run! Don't run!" I insisted even as I raced as fast as my legs would carry me. We grabbed our bikes, got a running start, then hopped aboard with one foot as we swung the other leg over the seat. It was our well-practiced power takeoff, and it was the quickest way to go from zero to a full-throttle fifteen miles per hour. We pedaled off in a standing position, pumping furiously with everything we had. When we finally looked over our shoulders several blocks later, no one was following. We had pulled it off. So what if I had chosen the most unapologetically wimpy cigarette known to mankind? We had our smokes, our entrance to cool-kid, grown-up behavior. Tommy and I settled back on our seats and rode through the neighborhoods side by side, no hands, whooping and laughing as we went. Ours were the joyful cries of victory. "True Blues," he said, still in disbelief but now with more amusement than disdain. "Fucking True Blues."

"Fucking yeah," I said. And we laughed some more.

Across Erie Drive from my house was a vacant lot covered in high weeds. At the back of the lot, a rickety wooden stairway led down the steep bank to Cass Lake and a narrow sand beach. Someday, another fancy doctor's house would rise there, but for now it was an absentee landowner's investment—and Tommy's and my personal clubhouse. It was totally private and totally ours. Right near the water's edge was a large tree with a hollow in the trunk, perfect for stashing all sorts of boyhood contraband. Over the years, that hollow would safely and dryly hide copies of girlie magazines, purloined adult beverages, and bags of marijuana. On this day, it became the tabernacle for our first pack of cigarettes.

Tommy and I rode directly there from the bowling alley, ditched our bikes out of sight in the weeds, and made our way down to the water's edge. There we ripped off the cellophane, tore open the foil, and each placed one of the long, skinny cigarettes between our lips. Tommy lit his own and then held out the match and lit mine. We puffed and coughed, puffed and coughed. Our eyes watered, our heads spun. Honestly, it wasn't much better than Father Joe's half-smoked Lucky Strike, but we persevered in the pursuit of cool. We each finished one cigarette, then passed a third between us.

The moment was so heady, it seemed only natural to try out the new vocabulary we had learned that school year.

"Fuck!" Tommy shouted at the top of his lungs. "Fuuuuuck!"

"Shit!" I shouted. "Shiiiiit!"

"Goddamn!" he yelled.

"Motherfucker!" I added.

"Son of a bitch!"

"Bastard!"

We went on like this, passing the cigarette between us and happily screaming out every filthy word we could think of, our voices carrying over the water to nowhere. Part of us wanted to get them out of us, flush them from our souls, because we knew they were bad and wrong and sins to be confessed. Part of us thrilled at the rebelliousness of it. It was our way of letting the Sisters of Saint Felix, the priests of Our Lady of Refuge, and our very Catholic parents know they had not won the indoctrination battle quite yet. Not by a long shot.

After we had buried the butts, we rubbed cedar boughs between our hands to mask the smell. Crossing the street to my house, we marched single file through the kitchen, right past my mother at her primary battle station, the kitchen sink, proceeded up the stairs past the matching statues of Saint Joseph and the Virgin Mary and into the bathroom. There we locked the door and squeezed gobs of toothpaste into our mouths, squishing and laughing and jabbing each other. We emerged moments later, reeking of nicotine, cedar, and Crest, and marched right past Mom again. If she noticed anything suspicious, she never let on.

⁜

CHAPTER 5

A few weeks later, in July of 1967, we awoke to a pall of smoke hanging over the horizon. The city of Detroit was on fire. All three television networks were covering the riots live, and my family and I circled the television, mesmerized. The scenes were shocking. It was a war zone, just like in the movies, except this was real and it was taking place just thirty minutes down the John Lodge Expressway, in the city where I was born. Entire blocks were ablaze, burned-out cars smoldered, firefighters were taking gunfire from snipers on rooftops, the police were pinned down in their precinct houses. Terrified residents scrambled for cover, and angry mobs looted and torched store after store. Soon National Guard soldiers in armored vehicles would rumble down Cass Avenue, and eventually troops from the 82nd Airborne, too. Detroit had long been a tinderbox of inequality and racial animosity, and the night before, a single spark—a police raid on an after-hours drinking club—had set it off.

As we watched the mayhem unfold, the telephone rang. It was Father Vin, my mother's younger brother, who was the pastor of Saint Catherine's, an inner-city parish once proud home to Polish and Italian immigrants arriving in this country to work in the auto plants but now steeply in decline. He needed help. He had thirty-five people, mostly women and children, crammed into the rectory with him. When the rioting erupted the night before, they began streaming to his front door in search of safety. He and his parishioners had spent the night huddled on the floor with the lights off, crawling from room to room on hands and knees, afraid a stray bullet could pierce a window at any moment. He was now working the phones, seeking places for the families to ride out the storm.

Mom hung up and said to us, "We're going to have some company for a few days, kids." This did not surprise any of us. My parents were nothing if not do-gooders. Part of their Catholic faith was to help others less fortunate, and they threw themselves into various acts of charity with the zealousness of missionaries. Mom, it seemed, was always baking casseroles or collecting used clothing for families down on their luck, and Dad was constantly dragging us kids along to visit shut-ins and the like. One of my earliest memories was of accompanying my father to a tuberculosis sanitarium to deliver magazines to the patients, something he did once a month every month for years.

On more than one occasion, my parents took in sick or convalescing people who had no one else to look after them. One of them was a parish priest who lived with us for weeks, commandeering my sister's bedroom as he recovered from back surgery. They both volunteered for every imaginable duty at Our Lady of Refuge, from changing the altar linens to leading rosary groups, and my father gave gallons of his blood to the Red Cross. "When you're at the end of your life," Dad liked to say, "it won't be what you received that matters, but what you gave." Father Vin knew that if he asked, they would say yes.

An hour later, his black Chevrolet pulled into our driveway, crammed with children. The effect was almost comical, with heads and limbs and torsos poking out in all directions. How he fit them all in there, I didn't know, but one by one they untangled themselves and stepped out, seven of them, ranging in age from eight to fifteen, each grasping a paper sack containing meager belongings. They stood silently in the driveway, staring at us like we were aliens, and in a sense I suppose we were to them. Even before their neighborhood began to burn, they could only imagine a place like this, with its big, sprawling houses and parklike lawns, towering shade trees, and a lake and beach just down the street. Marijo, Tim, Mike, and I stared back with the same puzzled, slightly suspicious looks. We could not have been more dumbfounded had a flying saucer landed in our driveway and deposited a band of Martians. The children came from two families. They were clearly very poor and very dirty, dressed in ill-fitting hand-me-downs. The new arrivals had a streetwise, mess-with-me-at-your-own-peril toughness about them, even the younger ones. With our cigarettes and swear words, Tommy Cullen and I thought we were tough. In that instant I grasped the undeniable truth. We weren't tough at all. We were sheltered suburban kids trying to act tough. These kids were the real thing. Until that day I'd had only the vaguest notion that places like Detroit, with its festering poverty and hopelessness, existed. My whole world was Harbor Hills, with its summer schedule of swimming and horseback-riding lessons and stolen puffs on cigarettes. We considered ourselves solidly middle class—just one car and an antiquated black-and-white television, after all—but I could tell from these kids' faces that they saw us as impossibly privileged. It was as though they had just parachuted into the Land of Oz.

My mother broke the silence. "All right, everyone into swimsuits and down to the lake. It's too hot not to be swimming!" She directed all the boys into the garage to change, and all the girls upstairs. Only later did I learn her hidden agenda: she wanted the opportunity to launder their clothing and underwear without embarrassing them.

Down at the beach, the city kids eyed the water warily. Suddenly they didn't look so tough. They looked afraid. What to me was a source of endless, effortless fun, to them was a deadly threat. Not one of them knew how to swim. Fortunately, our stretch of Cass Lake had a gradual drop-off. You could wade for yards and still not be up to your armpits, and even in the deepest part of the swim area the water was barely over a ten-year-old's head. Soon we were all frolicking in the shallows, splashing each other, whooping and laughing. Shaun pranced among us, jumping and barking. In the water, the sun glistening on our wet skin, the differences of class and privilege washed away and we were all just kids on a hot summer day.

Ours was a three-bedroom house, with my sister having the smallest bedroom to herself and my brothers and I sharing a larger room. When we got back from the beach, my mother had turned the boys' bedroom into a dormitory for the visiting girls. That evening, when my father arrived home from work, he set up the tent trailer we used for summer camping trips in the backyard, and this became the boys' domain.

For five days and nights, as the riot raged unabated, eventually claiming forty-three lives, the children stayed with us, and gradually, cautiously, we became friends. One boy, Leo, was my age, and we took to each other. We swam and rode bikes and sneaked down to the shopping plaza to hang out. Tommy and I led him to the hollow tree where we stashed our True Blues. Leo knew all about smoking, including how to inhale. He showed us how to suck the smoke deep into our lungs, hold it for a few seconds, and then exhale it through our nostrils. Not only did this give us something unfathomably cool to show off in front of the older kids at the beach, but the head-spinning, stomach-churning rush was like nothing I had experienced before.

Leo, it turned out, had another talent I could only dream of. The kid could draw like no one I had ever met. Right before my eyes, he cranked out amazingly accurate renderings of any comic book or cartoon character I would toss at him. Superman, Batman, Flash Gordon, Captain America—he could do them all. From the Sunday comics, he would copy exact replicas of Nancy and Beetle Bailey and Dagwood. I, on the other hand, could barely make stick figures, and I swooned over his talent, especially after learning he had nurtured it on his own, with no help from any adult. I became his loyal groupie and he my artistic mentor. "It's easy," I remember him saying. "You just look at the lines and do the same thing." With his tutoring, I managed to produce rudimentary versions of the Peanuts characters, and Leo was kind enough to say things like "See, I told you. You just need to look at the lines."

While we were swimming, smoking, and sketching, Mom was working. She went into full dorm-mother overdrive that week, reeling out towering platters of tuna-salad sandwiches for lunch and oversize trays of lasagna and hot dog casserole for dinner.

Each meal, of course, began as all meals in our house did, with a prayer. Dad if he was home (Mom if he wasn't) would ask for quiet and then bless himself, touching his fingertips to his forehead, then his chest, then each shoulder as he said, "In the name of the Father, the Son, and the Holy Spirit." We did the same, dropping our eyes to the empty plates before us and mumbling along with the prayer hammered into us from earliest memory: "Bless us, O Lord, and these thy gifts, which we are about to receive from thy bounty through Christ, our Lord, amen." I had no idea what those words meant, and no curiosity to learn, either, but I happily rattled them off, knowing that no food would reach my plate until I did. It was just what we did in our home, one of the small prices of admission. Some kids had to take off their shoes at the front door; we had to pray before the first bite.

I passed most meal prayers with a singular mission: to make my brothers laugh. In one of my proudest moments, I caught Michael's eye just after he had sneaked a big swig of milk. When the prayer began, he froze, holding the milk in his mouth. I made my most moronic face, crossing my eyes, and just as we reached the words "and these thy gifts," Michael exploded in hysterics, milk spraying from both nostrils. And he, not I, was the one who got in trouble. Life didn't get any better than that.

One of my favorite parts of our house was the screened-in porch just off the kitchen. We did not have air-conditioning, and all summer our family pretty much lived out there, eating our meals at a glass table and sitting around late into the night in the dark listening to Mom spin stories about growing up as one of nine children being raised by a widow in the Great Depression. Her stories were tapestries filled with colorful characters—Uncle Bert the bootlegger and Aunt Lulu with the enormous bosom and the aged Mrs. Fink next door who was the target of endless childhood pranks. In one of Mom's favorite stories, she described how she once called Mrs. Fink and pretended to be from the phone company. "We're going to be blowing the dust out of your phone lines," she said in her most grown-up voice. "You're going to want to spread newspapers on the floor because they haven't been cleaned in quite some time and it could cause quite a mess." And then she and her brothers and sisters watched through the window with delight as poor Mrs. Fink did just that.

My mom never lost that juvenile sense of humor. Every day was an opportunity for another prank, and I came to believe that one of her primary reasons for having children was to have a steady supply of subjects to torture. She would hold a pin in her lips and then pucker up for a kiss, pricking whichever one of us took the bait. She told us she could do magic, and if we would look up the sleeve of an old winter coat she had, we would see all the stars in the universe. When she finally coaxed a victim to put his head inside the coat and peer up the sleeve, she'd mumble some made-up magic incantation and then ask, "Do you see the stars yet?" When the victim, from under the coat, said no, still no stars, she'd add, "How about now?" and pour a glass of water down the sleeve and into the person's face. This delighted her no end. Of course, it worked only once per victim, and soon we were in on the conspiracy, luring various friends, classmates, and neighbors into her lair. My quiet father would just nod his head and smile patiently at his wife's antics.

With the seven Detroit kids in our house, my mother was delighted to have a new audience to subject to her tales and tricks, and she held court each evening after dinner. Before the week was over, every kid got a face full of water down the sleeve of that old coat, and every kid got a pinprick kiss. At first they didn't know what to make of this nutty woman, but soon they were all calling her Aunt Ruthie and treating her like their own mother.

Some nights, as darkness fell, we roasted marshmallows over dying coals in the backyard and lay in the dewy grass, staring up at the stars that our visitors had not even known existed, so obliterated were they by the city lights where they lived. And then Aunt Ruthie would bark the order for bath time—the girls one night, the boys the next—not letting anyone escape until she had inspected their feet and necks to make sure they had been properly scoured.

By the end of the week, when Father Vin returned in his Chevrolet to collect the children and return them to the smoldering ruins of their neighborhood, we were all tight friends. More than that, really. We had become like cousins. Everyone hugged and promised to stay in touch. Leo presented me with a full-color portfolio of action heroes. I gave him my lucky rabbit's foot, which I figured he needed more than I did.

"Everybody in the car," Father Vin ordered, and my mother handed each of them a paper grocery bag filled with clean, folded clothes she'd collected for them, and gave each of them a long hug and a kiss, this time without any pins. Father Vin's good deed had an unintended cruel edge to it. He had dropped these seven children of the inner city into the magical Land of Oz, a place of lakes and parks and star-studded skies, and allowed them to stay just long enough to realize what wonders lay beyond their grasp. They saw my life—they had to—as a fairy tale, a tantalizing dream from which they would soon awaken. The greater lesson was mine to take. Despite our differences of place and privilege, we were all just kids. Kids who loved goofing off and hated wearing shoes. Kids who forgot manners and found mischief. We said the same prayers to the same God, yet God had not blessed us the same. Even then, I found it unfair. What I learned in school, about all men being created equal, might be true. But I had discovered that all children did not grow up equal. Never again could I pretend the playing field was level, that all kids got the same shot at life's boundless possibilities.

"Thanks for teaching me to dog-paddle," Leo shouted out the window as Father Vin backed down the driveway.

"Thanks for the drawings," I shouted back.

I waved as the car disappeared down Erie Drive, the children's happy faces peering back through the rear window. For a year or so, we kept our promise to stay in touch. And then, after Father Vin's transfer to another parish in another city, we lost track of each other forever.

✳

M y parents had a lot of dreams for their four children, but none so all-consuming as the dream that one of us might someday heed the call to a religious vocation. If they could choose between having one of us become, say, a Nobel Prize–winning scientist or a parish priest, there was no question they'd pick the priest every time. As Dad frequently reminded us, a priest was God's embodiment on earth. Priests did his work and were endowed with his infallible moral judgment. My mother held the same belief and was indescribably proud to have two brothers who wore the Roman collar. She herself came close to entering the convent after high school before realizing her true calling was as a mother and baker of the world's most outrageously moist oatmeal cookies.

Growing up, my brother Michael came closest to fulfilling their dream. While other kids were playing cowboys and Indians or astronauts and race-car drivers, Mike was down in the basement playing priest. Mom sewed him vestments out of scraps of corduroy and satin, and hemmed and starched old sheets to serve as altar linens. An antique dresser from her childhood was drafted into service as an altar. Covered in Mom's linens and other churchly accoutrements, it looked impressively official, and Mike behaved accordingly. With great solemnity, he donned his vestments and proffered blessings to any who would stand still for them. He said Mass—reciting the entire liturgy verbatim in Latin—and gave long, impassioned sermons. He consecrated cubes of bread and glasses of grape juice and sometimes drafted me into the role of altar boy as he distributed pretend Holy Communion.

Michael led rosaries and wafted incense through the air. He made himself available to hear confessions, though as far as I know got no takers. When we brought home Dickie Bird and Lady Bird, a pair of parakeets, Michael bestowed on them the sacrament of marriage. After all, we were hoping they would start a family. And when Dickie turned up dead on the floor of the cage one morning, the young priest in training invited the neighbors in for what turned into a two-hour high funeral Mass, including a forty-minute eulogy. Dickie was one great parakeet, and yes, we all loved him dearly, but even I was impressed that anyone could find forty minutes' worth of things to say about a bird. I spent the whole service admiring the tanned shoulders of Mrs. Selahowski in her sleeveless sundress.

What some parents might have found alarming, Mom and Dad found boundlessly endearing, and they nurtured my brother's budding vocation with enthusiasm. Mom armed him with candlesticks, hymnals, a crucifix, and an old pewter goblet to hold the grape juice. Dad faithfully captured my brother's priestly reenactments on 8-millimeter home movies. Their son might have been only twelve, but he was already on the road to the priesthood. It was everything they'd ever dreamed.

I was another story. While Michael was saying Mass in the basement, I had found a different calling. My father was a longtime photo buff, and he subscribed to *Popular Photography*. The magazine itself was quite boring, made even more so by the fact that Dad tore off and discarded the covers because they often featured pouty-lipped models sporting come-hither looks. But the tiny classified advertisements in the back grabbed my attention. One after another featured ads for photography courses. The ads promised that you, too, could lead the exciting life of a professional model photographer. And to illustrate just how exciting that life could be, many of the ads featured tiny thumbnail photos of that most exciting possibility of all: topless women. Topless women smiling into the camera, pouting into the camera, ignoring the camera. Some frolicked in the surf; some lounged on park benches or reclined in convertibles. Some were in bikini bottoms, others in nighties that had mysteriously slipped off their shoulders and fallen around their waists. One, I remember, was dressed for a horseback ride. She wore knee-high boots, riding pants, and a hat; she even carried a crop. The only things missing were her blouse and bra. It was impossibly provocative, this concept that women might set out on any given day having breezily forgotten a few essential items of clothing, leaving their wondrous milky bazooms fully, gloriously exposed. I holed up next to the furnace for hours with those magazines, studying the various pairs of breasts with the intensity of an anatomist. My God, it was better than the underwear section of the Sears catalog. Better even than *National Geographic.*

While my brother was memorizing the Eucharistic prayer, I was memorizing as many breasts as I could fix my eyes on. Once Tommy Cullen moved into the neighborhood, he joined me at the Altar of the Voluptuous Bosom. We both worshipped with the fervor of new converts and passed countless lazy afternoons discussing the relative merits of various boob sizes and shapes. We debated large and droopy versus small and pert. We became discerning connoisseurs of the female nipple and areola. We noted the effects a swim in chilly water could have on them and the way they could glow iridescent in candlelight. Breasts became our business. If ogling them was a sin—and I knew it surely was—it certainly did not feel like one. I conveniently purged it from my confession list along with all the others.

Perhaps it was because Dad's photo magazine collection was becoming a little too thumb worn, or because Michael was showing an interest in photography and beginning to read some of the articles, but one day Mom and Dad called the two of us into the kitchen. On the table were a few issues of *Popular Photography,* the covers duly removed.

"This is a great magazine with a lot of informative articles about photography," Dad began. "But sometimes it runs photos that we do not approve of. Photos of ladies without many clothes on." I gazed up at him with the biggest doe eyes I could muster as if the thought of half-naked women had never occurred to me and, now that he had brought it up, was truly horrifying. "We would be very disappointed if we found out either of you were looking at them," he said.

"It's natural for boys to be curious about the opposite sex," Mom chimed in. "Do you have any questions? Is there anything you want to ask us?"

I did have one burning question. I knew girls did not have penises like boys, but from there, things got murky. One boy at school had told me, quite knowingly, that they had miniature versions of wieners. Another that they had tunnels. A third said he had seen his sister and could swear on the Bible there was nothing there at all. I was ten years old and still anatomically clueless. I wanted an up close, personal view of female parts, but I wasn't about to ask Mom for it.

"Any questions at all?" Mom beckoned. Michael and I both shook our heads furiously no.

"These doggone advertisers," Dad lamented. "Why do they have to go and spoil a perfectly good magazine?"

"We don't want you to think there's anything dirty about the human body," Mom interjected. "There's not. The human body is beautiful. It's God's creation, and it is truly a thing of beauty." I must have nodded my agreement with a bit too much enthusiasm because she quickly added: "But promise me you won't ever look at those pictures."

"I promise," Michael said, and from the way he said the words, I knew the young priest in training meant them.

"I promise, too," I repeated.

Beneath the table, inside my PF Flyers, my toes remained firmly crossed.

In the autumn after Detroit went up in flames, Tommy and I signed up to be altar boys. In both our houses, all the sons were expected to serve at Mass, no questions asked. It was not an elective like soccer or karate. My sister, on the other hand, was off the hook because girls weren't allowed. At first I considered this terribly unfair, not because I was a budding feminist outraged that the Church would treat my sister and any other girl as somehow unworthy to grace the altar, but because she got a free pass and I didn't. My outrage disappeared the instant I learned of one of the great secret perks of altar service: free booze. Tommy and I had heard the rumors, supported by credible eyewitness accounts, that altar boys got to sneak swigs of the leftover sacramental wine. Our parents were ecstatic at our decision to join the altar corps, and now, with the promise of daily morning cocktails, so were we.

The rumors proved true. On our first Mass as servers, Tommy and I were paired with two older boys who knew the ropes. They helped us select our outfits from a closet in a room off the sanctuary. The altar-boy uniform consisted of two parts: a floor-length black cassock that buttoned down the front; and a short white linen gown of sorts, called a surplice, that slipped over the cassock and gave altar boys their classic black-and-white look. So dressed, we resembled miniature priests, although close up you could see that the cassocks and surplices had a lot of miles on them. Most were covered in wax spills, and nearly every garment had at least one burn hole from a misadventure with a candle or incense ember.

Tommy quickly located a cassock that fit him perfectly. For me, the job was more challenging. The cassocks that were the correct length were too tight around the middle.

When I found one that buttoned comfortably around my stomach, it bunched around my feet and dragged on the floor, an accident waiting to happen. Finally I found one I could live with—a little tight at the waist but also just a few inches long at my feet. It would have to do.

The older boys walked us through our duties, which began with lighting the altar candles. Then they led us into a small closet in the sacristy where Father donned his vestments. Inside were shelves lined with crystal cruets, a sink, and a refrigerator filled with jugs of altar wine. Our job was to fill one cruet with wine and a second with water—the essential ingredients for the priest to perform the miracle of transubstantiation. We placed both on the altar. At the appropriate time, the priest would motion for two of us to approach with the cruets. As he recited the Eucharistic prayers, he would reach over for the wine and pour some into his chalice, then for the water, which he would add to the wine in proportions that said a lot about the priest's tolerance for an alcoholic drink first thing in the morning. A teetotaler priest would use mostly water with a splash of wine, but most would use nearly all wine with just a drop or two of water.

As we filled the cruets in the closet under the older boys' direction, we got our first hint of the rewards to come. "We're lucky this morning, boys," one of the veteran servers said. "We've got Father Donohue. Two-Drop Donohue. He barely touches the wine." Tommy and I looked at each other, trying to figure out what Father Donohue's altar-wine habits had to do with us. Then the other boy said with a wink, "The less for Father, the more for us."

My first Mass as an altar boy was uneventful. The older boys handled the important duties, and Tommy and I mostly concentrated on trying to look solemn. I genuflected a lot, mumbled through the prayers I never quite memorized, and got to ring a brass bell when Father raised the communion wafer toward heaven, and again when he lifted his chalice of wine. There was an art to bell ringing, and somehow I made both events sound like five-alarm fires.

Our mentors were right. Father Donohue placed barely a drop of wine in his chalice. After communion, he wrapped up the service with the words "The Mass is over. Go in peace to love and serve the Lord," and we formed a procession down the center aisle. One of the older boys led the way, carrying a large crucifix. The next followed with the Bible. Then came Tommy and me, immediately in front of Father, each brandishing a large beeswax candle on a floor-length brass holder. This was a challenging maneuver. The candles on their stands resembled flaming javelins and were nearly as tall as we were. The tip of each candle was fitted with a brass ring that created a reservoir, preventing the hot liquid wax from running down the sides. The trick was to make it down the aisle without spilling any of the pooled wax. Tommy and I gripped our candles with sweaty palms and crept down the aisle as if we were wired with explosives. Both of us made it without incident, and I said a little prayer of thanksgiving for not having tripped on my too-long gown.

Back in the sacristy behind the altar, Father hung up his vestments and departed for the rectory, leaving us boys to finish up. We blew out the candles, straightened the linens, and returned the pair of cruets to the closet where they were to be emptied, rinsed, and dried. One of the older boys immediately uncorked the wine cruet and took a swig, then handed it to his friend, who took another swig. "Here's to Two-Drop Donohue," he toasted as he handed the cruet to me. I held it in my hands, knowing this had to be a major-league mortal sin, chugging the same holy wine Father turned into the blood of Christ.

"Go ahead," one of the boys said. "They don't care. Honest."

Who was I to argue? We were just emptying the cruets as instructed, weren't we? And to waste was a sin. I placed the cruet to my lips and poured in a mouthful. It was sticky and sweet and musky. When I swallowed, I felt an unpleasant burn, followed by an odd, comforting warmth that spread through my body. I handed the cruet to Tommy as I stifled a cough. We went one more round, and then the cruet was empty. I dutifully rinsed and dried it and replaced it on the shelf, my feet and fingertips tingling. As I hung my cassock and surplice up, I noticed that my eye-hand coordination was just slightly off.

Outside the church, my parents waited, their faces beaming. They had sat in the front pew for their youngest son's debut as an altar boy. "We're very proud of you, son," Dad said. "You're doing the Lord's work."

I smiled glassily and turned my head to divert my breath from him.

"Just next time," he counseled, "go a little easier on the bells."

✳

Besides being zealous Catholics, my parents were famously frugal. They never did manage to shake the imprint of growing up hand to mouth during the Depression, and even though they now lived in a spacious new house in a desirable subdivision on a lake, they carried with them the habits they grew up with. Mom cut paper napkins in half. She made her cup of tea in the morning and set the tea bag by the stove to dry for another use. Dad hung paper towels over the edge of the sink to dry for a second and sometimes third use. He had it down to an art form: the first use would involve a task that required a fresh towel, such as wiping a dish; the next use would be less critical, such as cleaning up a spill on the floor; from there the multitasking towel would move to the garage where Dad would use it to check the oil dipstick on the car.

His desire to find maximum utility applied to all things. He used oversize junk-mail envelopes to organize his important papers, each meticulously labeled in his draftsman's hand. After washing the car, he would shout through the house, "I've got a nice bucket of sudsy water down here! Anyone need some good sudsy water? Perfectly good still!" As far as I know, Dad never got a single taker for his slightly used soapy water, but that didn't discourage him from going through the same ritual the next time. "Who needs soapy water? Got a nice clean bucket down here!"

Neither of them could bring themselves to throw anything out. If a lamp or appliance broke, Dad would store it away in the basement as a potential source of parts for a future repair. In the kitchen, we had what surely remains the world's largest collection of washed-out mayonnaise jars and margarine tubs. My mother came home one day, immensely pleased with herself for scoring an unbelievable price on a set of nesting dessert bowls. Then I saw why they were such a bargain: each was emblazoned with the Delta Airlines logo. "See," Mom said proudly, "they don't quite nestle. The airline wouldn't take them." For years, I ate my ice cream while dreaming of flying Delta to far-off places.

Instead of replacing our broken toaster, Dad figured out all it needed was a sturdy piece of masking tape to hold down the lever. When the bread was fully toasted, the unit would make a horrible grating sound and begin vibrating frantically across the counter as it strained against the tape to pop up. That was our clue to leap for the toaster and rip off the tape before smoke started pouring out. More times than not, we were too late, but Dad always had the same response, even as he scraped the carbon off the toast's surface: "I like it on the dark side." We kept that old toaster for years, and the only maintenance it required was a new piece of tape every month or two.

One of the more visible signs of my parents' frugality was our lawn mower. In Harbor Hills, the yards were large and required a substantial machine to keep them manicured. Most of the wealthier neighbors with lake frontage hired lawn services; the rest of us cut our own grass. The first thing nearly every home owner did upon moving to Harbor Hills was to purchase a gleaming new riding mower with a padded seat. Dad would not even consider such an extravagance; instead he found a used walk-behind mower that was already an antique. By the time I was in grade school, the Gravely had taken on the rusty sheen of a museum piece with its old-fashioned round mowing deck, jutting oak handgrips, and faded red paint. The muffler was barely functioning, and the engine's roar drowned out all other sounds within a hundred yards. Occasionally it would backfire with the velocity of a shotgun, and I could watch the neighbors flinch as if taking sniper fire. The Gravely looked and sounded like it belonged in a scene from *The Grapes of Wrath,* before the Okies leave the Dust Bowl for California. But Dad pronounced it "perfectly adequate for our needs" and scoffed at the modern riding mowers, which he pointed out no man could ride without resembling a circus clown. Besides, he claimed to enjoy the workout he got trotting along behind the Gravely as it roared across our acre of grass in a cloud of blue smoke. For all its faded glory, it ran reliably, and Dad, an adept engine tinkerer, ensured that it stayed that way, repacking bearings and rebuilding the carburetor as needed.

Grass-cutting was a weekly father-son event. As Dad cut with the Gravely, my older brother Tim trimmed with a push mower, and Mike and I coiled hoses, picked up sticks, and raked clippings. More than my brothers, I gravitated toward yard work, and I tagged along with Dad as he completed various chores, whether it was planting marigolds or fertilizing the rhododendrons or trimming the hedges, something he did using a complex system of stakes and strings to assure symmetrical perfection. I was his helper, his tool fetcher, his grunt laborer, and I loved being out there with him.

If Mom was the family talker and storyteller, Dad was the listener. He was introspective bordering on taciturn and not much for aimless chitchat. But there was something about physical labor that brought out his talkative side. Working side by side, our hands in the dirt, he would freely share tips and techniques with me, always looking for opportunities to teach a little lesson, the lessons I imagine his father had taught him. At the workbench, it might be the importance of sanding with the grain or measuring twice before making a cut. In the garden, he would point out the complex social structure of an ant colony and the nifty way nature turned old grass clippings and leaves into rich plant food. It was on one of these work excursions that Dad finally worked up his courage to deliver my one and only sex-education lesson.

We were finished mowing and had just planted petunias around the oak tree. He directed me to drag a hose over to water them, but when the hose proved too short, he asked me to bring another length from the garage. Then it was time to connect the two hoses.

"John, hand me the female end, will you?" Dad said.

I stared dumbfounded at the two ends of the hose. I had no idea what he was talking about. "The what?" I asked.

"The female end," he said, a hint of exasperation in his voice, as if to add: *You're not going to make me explain how male and female parts go together, are you?*

I picked up both ends and stared at them. By this stage of my life—age twelve—I had moved on from the tiny boob shots of *Popular Photography* to the flawless women of *Playboy,* compliments of Marty Wolkoff, a classmate who lived one neighborhood over and whose father subscribed. I even got brief glimpses during a Boy Scout campout of Pat Wendell's big brother's "library," which was a worn leather satchel containing a well-thumbed collection of pornography showing men in a fully aroused state and women positioned as if posing for a gynecologists' convention. Thanks to these visual aids, I finally had a clear concept of male and female anatomy (though I was still unclear how exactly they went together). But looking at the ends of the garden hose, I could see no correlation whatsoever to anything I had seen in those magazines. I stood there gripping the hose ends with a look on my face that I suppose was not unlike the look my dog Shaun might have struck if given the task of figuring out an algebraic equation.

"Here," my father said with a weary sigh, grabbing each hose end away from me. "This is the male end," and he held up the end with the brass threads showing. "And this is the female." He jammed the male into the female and began twisting the threads together. "The male screws into the female like this," he said, then paused before adding: "Just like in nature."

Suddenly I saw what he was getting at. Just like in nature . . . *Ewwwww.*

"Got it?" he said.

I nodded up and down, my mouth agape. If I appeared awestruck, it was not over this anatomical breakthrough but over my father's choice of props. It occurred to me that never before had any father pressed into service a garden hose to demonstrate the act of sexual intercourse. Not birds and bees. Not mating wolves. Not oak trees and acorns. The two ends of a rubber hose. Only my dad.

"I got it," I said.

"Good. Now let's get back to work."

With that, my sexual education was officially over. Dad had fulfilled his fatherly duty, one he no doubt had fretted over for months before delivering. He never came anywhere near the topic with me again.

Other kids, especially those with older brothers, were more than happy to fill in the details. With the help of the Playboy Advisor and Penthouse Forum, and the wildly candid *The Happy Hooker*, which Tommy and I pooled our money to buy, and which featured among its many colorful stories a memorable encounter with a German shepherd, I was slowly piecing together the nuts and bolts of sex. I saw how the parts fit together, and why. It was all nature's way of assuring that the human race would carry on.

What puzzled me, though, was why, if sex was so natural and so necessary, it was also so bad. If God was the creator of all things, and God was infallible and could do no wrong, then why did the priests and the nuns and my parents and Tommy's parents and every other adult I knew treat this aspect of God's handiwork as unspeakably embarrassing? It didn't make sense. My mother could look at a rosebush in bloom and say, "See, Johnny, that rose is proof of our Lord. There is no other possible explanation for something so perfect and beautiful." But when it came to swelling penises, lubricating vaginas, and mating urges so intense they could blind both men and women to even the need for food, God's perfect handiwork seemed a little, well, less perfect. I suppose that's why the Blessed Virgin Mother got a special pass from all the heavy breathing and unpleasantries of coitus.

For Lent that year, Mom and Dad urged each of us kids to give up something special, something that would be a true hardship and honor the ultimate sacrifice Christ made when he died on the cross to save our souls. Lent began in late winter with one of my favorite holy days, Ash Wednesday, during which we got to walk around all day with a sooty smudge on our foreheads that made us look like junior firefighters. It continued for six weeks and was intended to be a time of personal reflection leading up to Easter. My parents told us to give it some thought and find a meaningful act. For instance, giving up creamed spinach wouldn't be much of a sacrifice, nor would giving up something so specific you probably wouldn't encounter it anyway. You couldn't give up, say, lemon meringue pie and simply switch to apple or pumpkin. Likewise, on the charitable acts front, you couldn't promise to do something you were supposed to do anyway, like take out the trash or complete homework. You couldn't vow to brush your teeth every morning. It had to be a real sacrifice, something that took effort. Something that was a struggle to fulfill.

I thought and thought before landing on the perfect Lenten sacrifice. It would be the ultimate challenge for a twelve-year-old boy who had recently discovered that uniquely satisfying, solitary pleasure one could enjoy while locked in the bathroom with a copy of *Popular Photography* or *The Happy Hooker*.

I would give up that one thing I had recently come to enjoy most in life, the thing that at once was a source of profound pleasure and profound guilt because I knew it was a sin, and a sin I committed on a daily, sometimes hourly, basis.

My sacrifice was not a joke; it was not a lark. I was deadly serious. On the bookshelf in my parents' bedroom I had found a Catholic primer on human sexuality and read all about the sin of masturbation, or "self-pollution," as the book called it. Self-pollution was a depraved sin, a weakness of the flesh. It was a surrender to lust and a selfish act, too, because every time one self-polluted was a time he was not sharing the sacred seed with the sacred womb, as God intended. For the record, I was primed and ready to share every last sacred seed in my arsenal with whatever womb waggled my way. I was dying to share. But I was not so delusional as to pretend it was going to happen any time soon, if ever.

Tommy and I both had girlfriends now. His was Karen Mc-Kinney, a sandy blonde who always seemed to sport a sunburned nose, even in winter. Mine was Barbie Barlow, who had bright brown eyes that actually twinkled when she smiled, and budding hints of breasts beneath her plaid school jumper. The only thing was, Karen and Barbie didn't have the slightest clue they were our girlfriends. We jostled with them on the playground, pulled evil pranks on them, and pretended we more or less detested them. But each afternoon down at the beach with our cigarettes, Tommy and I would gush at length about their many virtues and what we would do with our goddesses if we ever, hypothetically, got up the nerve to let them know we liked them.

No, I wasn't too worried about the selfish part of my sin. I would happily share my seed if I could. In the meantime, I figured, there were plenty more where they came from. I was self-polluting at a furious pace, despite the Catholic remorse that followed each explosive release. I had allowed myself to become a virtual landfill of self-pollution. My temple was so dirtied by my actions, the Lord would never choose to fill it with his spirit. I was convinced what I was doing was horribly wrong, a serious transgression against God that would only increase the already near-certain likelihood that I would spend eternity burning. When Mom and Dad asked what I had decided to give up for Lent, I told them it was private. They were always respectful of their children's privacy, and this was no exception. They asked no questions. "Just try your hardest," Dad said. "If you do that, and in your heart you know you did the very best you could do, then that's all we ask. That's good enough for us."

The first day of Lent went quite well. In anticipation of my cold turkey abstinence plan, I had gone on a self-pollution bender the previous evening. I passed Day One with only a few passing impure thoughts. Day Two was not so easy.

I had caught a glimpse of Barbie Barlow's underpants on the playground as she climbed the monkey bars—so close, so out of reach—and recounting the glorious moment in exquisite detail later for Tommy only heightened the tension. Barbie Barlow in pink panties; I could think of nothing else. By the time I got home from school on Day Three, I was crazed with hormonal lust. *Please, dear Jesus, dear God the Father, dear Holy Spirit, give me strength.* I really wanted to keep my promise, but not even they could infuse me with the necessary willpower. Less than thirty-six hours into my six-week vow of abstinence, I caved in to desire. I wasn't proud of myself. *A onetime lapse,* I promised, and marked the calendar above my bed with a small *X* to mark my fall. I vowed not to let it happen again. But as the weeks progressed, I marked *X* after *X*. My calendar became a minefield of *X*s, littering the days of the week and providing a shameful road map of my sinful secret life.

"How are you doing with your Lenten resolution?" Dad asked a couple of weeks into it.

"I'm sure trying," I said with a jauntiness I hoped would leave room for optimistic interpretation.

"That's all we ask, son," he answered and left it at that.

CHAPTER 8

⁜

The seven days leading up to Easter are known as Holy Week, and it was the year's most sacred and important time in our Catholic household, bigger even than Christmas. This was the week, we were taught, when Jesus laid down his life for our sins. In the words we recited each Sunday at Mass, it was the week when "he suffered under Pontius Pilate, was crucified, died, and was buried. He descended into hell, and on the third day he arose again, in fulfillment of the scriptures, and ascended into heaven to sit at the right hand of the Father." It's not every day someone covers so much ground in a single week, and our family celebrated each step of the way. It began with Palm Sunday, the day Jesus and his disciples had arrived in Jerusalem nearly two thousand years earlier, and wrapped up a week later with Easter Sunday, marking the day when Christians believe Jesus rose to heaven. In the middle was Holy Thursday, marking Jesus' last supper with his disciples, and Good Friday, which I always thought was egregiously misnamed considering that the only begotten son of God was hanged from a cross to die that day.

For some reason, my mother got it into her head that our family should celebrate Holy Thursday the way the

Lord celebrated it nearly two thousand years earlier—with a traditional Jewish Passover dinner. Mom didn't know much about Judaism other than it wasn't Catholicism and that meant it was not the one true faith. But she knew Jesus had been a Jew and had spent his final meal on earth celebrating Passover. If it was good enough for Jesus, it was good enough for the Grogans.

Our neighborhood was so Catholic it could have qualified as an official outpost of the Vatican. There were a few Protestant families, and then there were the Kabcenells, who lived down the street from us, right across from the convent. To my knowledge, they were the only Jews for miles around. Mom and Mrs. Kabcenell were neighborly but danced around the topic of their faiths. They both seemed to think some things were best left unexplored.

But this Lent Mom went on a Passover crusade, and she wanted to get it just right. She laid out her plan to Mrs. Kabcenell, who was more than happy to sign on as Mom's Seder mentor. The two of them were on the phone for hours, Mom furiously jotting down Passover pointers and Kabcenell family recipes for matzo ball soup and *charoset,* a salad of spiced apples and chopped nuts. Naturally, the more they spoke, the less mysterious the other's religion seemed.

When Mom announced at dinner one day that we'd be celebrating Passover on Holy Thursday, I was thrilled. "We get to drink wine! We get to drink wine!" I squealed. The Kabcenells had a son my age. I had told him all about the fringe drinking benefits of being an altar boy, and he had told me all about the intoxicating virtues of Mogen David and Manischewitz.

On that Thursday before Easter, Mom called us to the table, and we found it laid out with an assortment of unfamiliar dishes. Dad took his seat at the head of the table. As the youngest child, I had the honor of asking the question to start things off.

"What is the meaning of this night, Father?" I read off a card my mother had handed me, being careful not to glance at my brothers. I knew they would be wanting payback for all the times I had made them laugh when they were supposed to be solemn.

Dad took his cue and read from a borrowed Haggadah, a Jewish prayer book that told the story of the Israelites' flight from slavery in Egypt. We ate unleavened matzo, and Dad explained how the Jews, in their haste, did not have time to let their bread rise. We dipped parsley in salt water, and sampled horseradish, which he said symbolized suffering and tears. My mouth stuffed with sawdust-dry crumbs and my eyes watering from the horseradish, I decided those Catholic fish sticks we ate every Friday during Lent weren't so bad after all.

We ate hard-boiled eggs, which he told us stood for spring and renewal. The apple mixture was a reminder of the mortar the Jewish slaves used to build pyramids, and I had to admit Mom's version had the consistency of concrete. The wine was the highlight, even if it did remind me of grape cough syrup. The Catholics, I decided, definitely had an edge when it came to the quaffability of their sacramental alcoholic beverages.

"Sip, don't gulp," my father admonished. He had no idea that my training as an altar boy had taught me otherwise.

The Seder behind us, Mom brought out a roasted shank of lamb, a reminder of the first Passover sacrifice. "Hey, this is just like our Catholic lamb!" I said. It was dawning on me that Catholics and Jews were not that different after all. Something else was dawning on me as well. I am certain it wasn't the message my mother hoped I would take from our Passover celebration, but sitting there as my parents tried to connect the Judeo and Christian traditions, I suddenly realized: there was no one true faith and no one chosen people. Not us, not the Kabcenells, not anyone. Heaven was not a paradise reserved for the exclusive use of any one religion. The Lord could not be that unfair. There could be either one God who loved everybody the same, or no God at all.

Whatever Mom's motivation, she succeeded in bridging at least one gap: she and Mrs. Kabcenell remained close friends for years to come, and the Passover Seder became an annual event in our house.

If there was one day out of the year on which even the most wayward Catholic dragged himself into church, it was Easter Sunday. The services were always packed, and Father added extra Masses to handle the crowds. Every altar boy was pressed into duty, and I was assigned the eleven o'clock Mass. It was a mob scene. Every pew was crammed. People stood three deep along the side and rear walls. The choir loft overflowed and so did the glass-encased cry room, filled with mothers and noisy babies. Dozens of white lilies lined the altar, filling the church with an overpowering, nearly narcotic fragrance. All the mothers and daughters came decked out in their new spring dresses, and there was real excitement in the air. I felt like I was at a rock concert—and I was onstage with the main act.

During communion, the congregants filed forward, pew by pew, to the altar rail. My job was to stand next to the priest and balance a gold plate beneath each chin as Father pressed a host on the parishioner's tongue. Just in case Father fumbled the host, which happened at least once per Mass, I was there to catch it. Or at least try. If I was lucky and caught it on the plate, Father could simply pick it up and carry on. But more times than not, it missed and fell to the ground, in which case Father would have to bend down, retrieve it, and swallow it himself.

Some priests were so skilled they could deftly pop a host on the tongue without making any flesh-to-flesh contact and almost never fumbling. But most of them, in their caution not to drop Christ's body and risk a sacrilege, ended up touching the recipient's lip or tongue, then doing it again for the next person in line, and the next. Standing beside him, I could actually see Father's thumb and fingertips wet with saliva. The number of germs spread in communion lines should have triggered a four-alarm public-health alert, but no one seemed to mind. What was a little shared spit among true believers who were all going to heaven anyway? Besides, it was hard to imagine the son of God would come into your body and then let you catch a disease simply because Father's host-dispensing skills weren't up to par. If Jesus could multiply fishes and loaves and raise the dead, he could certainly make sure no one contracted strep throat from the communion line.

I was holding the gold plate for Father when my eyes wandered down the altar rail. There, making her way toward me, was the lovely, budding-breasted Barbie Barlow. She was in a wispy pastel dress with a matching ribbon in her hair. It was the first time I had seen her in anything other than her blue plaid school uniform, which resembled something that would be issued at a women's penitentiary. I nearly gasped out loud. She looked beautiful, ethereal, as if it were Barbie who was meant to ascend to heaven on that spring day. She seemed to float toward me in the communion line, and soon she would be kneeling right before me. I sucked in my stomach and stood taller. So what if my cassock pinched around the middle and bunched at my feet; I never felt prouder to be in the uniform of the altar corps. When it was her turn, Barbie knelt in front of the priest and lowered her eyes. I slipped the gold plate beneath her chin and watched, mesmerized, as her lips parted and her tongue slipped out to accept the host. She swallowed, blessed herself, and just as she was stepping away, glanced at me and smiled. It was only a little grin—the kind one classmate might slip another in recognition—but her eyes had that twinkle, and I felt my heart stutter. The ascension-worthy Barbie Barlow had bestowed her beatific smile upon me. My eyes followed her as she returned to her pew and knelt again, still grinning my way. I nearly dropped the gold plate.

As Mass concluded, the other altar boys and I formed our usual procession. I carefully lifted one of the big floor-length candles from its stand and took my place behind the boy carrying the Bible. Father proclaimed the Mass over, blessed everyone, and told them to go in peace to love and serve the Lord. That was the cue for the organist, who launched into the recessional hymn, and the congregation began to sing. It was the big finale of the biggest service of the year, and Father joined us in line for our grand parade down the center aisle. I scanned the crowd, and there was Barbie holding a hymnal, looking right at me with those twinkling eyes. I sneaked a small smile back and gripped my giant candle in its long brass holder, wielding it like a knight with a lance. Father gave a sign, and we stepped forward, down the steps. As we marched toward the rear of church, I stared straight ahead with my manliest expression. How could she *not* be impressed? I stole another quick glance. She was still looking, still twinkling.

That's when it happened. It started with a barely noticeable tug on my cassock. In the next instant, the tug became a pull and the pull a sharp yank. The toe of my shoe had gotten tangled in the hem dragging on the floor. I steadied the candle in front of me, the flame flickering inches from my face, and tried to free my foot. A little shake would do it, I was sure. The trapped foot was in midstep; I just needed to kick the material clear before my foot hit the ground and all would be well. I was confident I could recover without so much as a misstep. But as my foot made contact with the floor, I could feel the cassock heaving down hard at my shoulders. It felt like someone had reached up from a hole in the floor and grabbed ahold. I heard my voice rise above the organ music: "Whoaaaa!"

I made one last, valiant maneuver, shooting out my other foot to regain my balance. In that split second, I paused to marvel at my ability to keep my oversize candle with its voluminous pool of hot liquid wax stable through my crisis. I stumbled forward on the pinned fabric, and my free foot did the only thing it could do. It made a giant, graceful arc as if kicking a football. What it kicked, though, was the bottom of the brass candlestick. My hands gripped the stick in the middle, making an efficient fulcrum point. As the bottom flew forward, the top jerked back. Simple physics.

Scalding wax showered down on me, coating my hair and forehead, searing my skin. Wax ran over my eyebrows and into my lashes. It felt like someone had pressed a hot iron to my face. I heard my scream, as if from outside myself: *Yeow!* But the worst part, the very worst part, even worse than the scorching pain of bubbling wax on my skin, was my glasses. I was blind without them, and they were doused in wax, rendering them opaque. With a rip of fabric, I felt my foot break free, and I quickly regained my balance. But now I could not see a thing. I began to weave and swerve blindly down the aisle, caroming off the other altar boys and the ends of the pews. I heard Father's whispered voice behind me: "For the love of God!" I peered desperately into the opaqueness of my lenses and found a small break in the coating through which I could see. It was like looking through a keyhole stuffed with spiderwebs. The first thing I did was get my bearings. I was back on track, heading straight down the aisle. The next thing I did was find Barbie in the crowd. Maybe her head had been down as she prayed.

Maybe she had her nose in her songbook. Maybe she hadn't noticed a thing.

When I finally located her, right there beside her parents, she was staring directly at me. The sweet, twinkly smile from a few moments earlier was gone, replaced by a big, openmouthed grin. Barbie was laughing. The whole congregation, it seemed, was laughing. The other altar boys were laughing. I think even Father was laughing. Who could blame them? I looked like a blind escapee from the wax museum.

I peered through my waxy glasses at the shoulders of the boy in front of me and plowed ahead, past Barbie, past my parents, who were not laughing but grimacing, past everyone, and out the rear doors. Later, back in the sacristy, I ran hot water over my glasses and combed as much wax out of my hair and eyebrows as I could. The other altar boys chortled at my public humiliation but in the end took pity and let me have the entire cruet of wine to myself. I accepted gratefully.

CHAPTER 9

※

The Detroit riots had scared everyone and cracked the resolve of many families living in the city, pushing them to sell their homes at fire-sale prices and flee to the suburbs. One of those families moved into a new contractor house kitty-corner to ours on June 6, 1968—the day after Senator Robert Kennedy was shot and killed at the Ambassador Hotel in Los Angeles. My family sat glued to the television that day, but I mostly looked out the living-room window at the moving van across the backyards, depositing the new family in our midst. Even from a distance, I could see there were five children, and the oldest looked just about my age.

His name was Ronald, and he was the world's biggest Detroit Tigers fan, wearing his team letter jacket everywhere and usually carrying a souvenir program in his back pocket. On his first day in the neighborhood, as everyone else in the nation reeled in shock over the second Kennedy assassination in five years, Tommy and I wandered over to give the new kid our Harbor Hills Welcome Wagon treatment.

The boy barely came up to my shoulder and was skinny and pale with freckles all over his face; his toes pointed inward like a pigeon's and his knees knocked together. Tommy walked right up to him and without saying a word slammed him hard in the chest with both palms, knocking him to the ground. Then we ridiculed his Tigers jacket and stomped on his souvenir program. I felt a little bad about it, but Tommy was convinced it was important to establish the neighborhood pecking order right up front. When Ronald did not cry or run away, we decided he was worthy.

Tommy, who exhibited an early knack for ironic observation, quickly rechristened him Rock. Of course, Rock looked more like a twig than anything so unyielding as stone, which made the nickname all the more delicious. It stuck, and we welcomed him into our Secret Society of Smokers, Swearers, and Sacramental Wine Swiggers. Soon our constant twosome was a threesome.

The following summer, the Sacorellis moved in directly behind the Cullens. Mr. and Mrs. Sacorelli had arrived from Italy as teenagers and brought a lot of the old country with them. He spoke in fulsomely accented English that reminded me of the man in the spaghetti-sauce commercials. Mrs. Sacorelli spoke no English at all, did not drive, and seldom ventured farther than ten feet from her kitchen stove. She lived to cook, and amazing smells of tomatoes, garlic, and veal filled the house and wafted across the neighborhood day and night. The Sacorellis made their own pasta, rolling the dough out on the kitchen table with floured hands. They stuffed their own sausages and hung them from the rafters in the basement to cure. They pressed grapes in a hand-cranked contraption that looked like a torture device, and kept oak casks of homemade wine below the hanging meats. Unlike the rest of us kids in the neighborhood, the six Sacorelli kids did not have to filch their booze. Before each meal, one of them was dispatched to the basement to pour a pitcher for the table and the whole family to share.

Right in the middle of the Sacorelli pack was Anthony, a rosy-cheeked cherub our age whose giant brown eyes brought every girl in the neighborhood to her knees. Tommy, Rock, and I did a quick assessment—let's see, magnet for the opposite sex, check; a mom who would feed us vast quantities of delicious food but couldn't understand anything we said, double check; *and* an unlimited source of free, untraceable booze. "You're in, Sack," Tommy proclaimed, and then we were four.

Actually, we were five if you counted Shaun, my dog, who accompanied us everywhere—to The Outlot and the basketball courts, to the smoking tree and each other's houses. He was so naturally well behaved, the whole family nicknamed him Saint Shaun. He tagged along without a leash, came whenever I whistled, and happily pulled me through the neighborhood on my bike. Some school days he showed up unannounced at the playground during recess and joined our soccer games. He spent hours at the beach with us, diving off the dock and reemerging with giant rocks in his mouth. He even raced along as we rode our bikes down to the shopping plaza for candy and French fries, waiting patiently outside for us to reemerge, his eyes fixed on whatever door I had entered.

Shaun was a fixture in the neighborhood and was mostly well received. Those were more tolerant days, and the neighbors hardly seemed to notice that a dog, especially one as well mannered as he, was running unleashed through their yards and across the community beach. Only one person complained, and that was Old Man Pemberton. He had been retired for as long as anyone could remember and was as ancient as the Great Pyramid at Giza. Mr. Pemberton's property abutted The Outlot and looked out over The Lagoon, and he spent hours every day fussing about, hand-pulling dandelions from his grass, sculpting his hedges, watering flower baskets, and touching up the trim on his house. He scrubbed his driveway with soapy water and used a blowtorch to incinerate weeds that dared show their heads above the white pebbles surrounding his mailbox. The place, with its giant picture windows looking out over the boat basin and the lake beyond, belonged in a magazine. It was perfect in all ways but one: it shared an unfenced property line with The Outlot. His emerald lawn blended seamlessly into the common property, and this drove Mr. Pemberton insane. As families walked through The Outlot to their boats or the beach, they invariably cut across the lower corner of his yard, causing him to glare and sputter. If the offenders were kids, he would shout out, "You're on private property!" Eventually he painted a sign with a giant arrow and drove it into the ground on his property line, directing trespassers to stay on the other side. Every kid in the neighborhood promptly and gleefully ignored it. So did Shaun.

Mr. Pemberton appointed himself the enforcer of neighborhood rules and was constantly scolding children for every imaginable infraction. "This isn't a playground," he'd yell. "No shouting! No jumping on the docks! No throwing sand! No glass containers allowed!" If teenagers were down at the beach after dark—and there was no better place to take a girl and a six-pack than the beach late at night—he would turn on the powerful spotlights mounted to the eaves of his house and dial the police. My free-running dog was a particular irritant to him. "Pets must be leashed at all times!" he would bark. "No dogs allowed on the beach!" "Yes, Mr. Pemberton," I would mumble, and the next day Shaun would be right back there beside me, swimming and sniffing and diving.

Of course, when Tommy, Rock, Sack, and I got together and felt the collective itch for wrongdoing that boys of a certain age are powerless to resist, Mr. Pemberton was almost always our target of choice. With four houses among us, our parents seldom knew exactly where we were. We could be howling around the neighborhood till midnight, and the Cullens would think we were all at the Sacorellis', the Sacorellis would be sure we were at the Grogans', and so on. It was a beautiful arrangement. Some nights we camped out in a tent in one of our backyards, and these nights were best of all, especially if we knew neighborhood girls were also sleeping out. All four of our houses were roughly in a row—mine backed up to Rock's, Tommy's was across the street from Rock's, and Sack's was behind Tommy's—and we could watch as each house went dark for the night. That was our cue to get up and wander around. Our top destination was the party store on the corner where we could buy loads of candy and where Tommy perfected the art of walking out with bottles of Boone's Farm shoved down the crotch of his shorts. He did this while the rest of us created a diversion at the cash register, usually involving fumbled change or fizzing sodas. How he got away with it, I never understood, the theft was so obvious. The bottle filled the front of his shorts with a lusty exuberance that gave him the look of the most generously endowed thirteen-year-old on earth. With cocktails secured, we would lie on our backs in a field of tall grass, safely hidden from headlights, puffing our Marlboros and passing the bottle of wine. About halfway through the bottle, one of us would usually seize on yet another brilliant scheme to pimp Old Man Pemberton.

We put dog feces in his mailbox and poured motor oil on his driveway. We collected trash from houses up and down the street and spread it across his front yard. One of our better schemes was to tiptoe to the side of his house where he stored his canoe and hoist it into the branches of a nearby tree.

There were so many kids in the neighborhood, all of them avowed antagonists of the Pembertons, that the old man didn't know where to begin. We were all suspects, and the older teens, who had the most reason to despise him, were the biggest suspects of all.

Dad had his own vague suspicions, even if he couldn't prove them. "Go easy on Mr. Pemberton," he would counsel. "Show respect and give him his space. Someday you'll be old and you'll understand." Dad was big on the Golden Rule and recited it often. "Remember, John, do unto others as you'd have them do unto you."

Mr. Cullen was less diplomatic. One afternoon he lined us up in the driveway, pushed his face up to ours, and said, "Get your hands outta your pockets, mon, and listen up. If

I ever find out you've been messing with Mr. Pemberton or anyone else in this neighborhood, I'm going to ride your bloody ass to Singapore and back. Do you understand me, boys?" We looked at the ground and nodded. We understood perfectly.

But then came the Fourth of July and the big fireworks celebration at Pine Lake Country Club.

It was a private, pricey club with a spectacular golf course nestled along Pine Lake, the next lake over from ours and an easy bike ride away. Like many kids in the neighborhood, Tommy, Sack, and I worked as caddies there, schlepping golf bags on our shoulders and handing nine irons and drivers to the golfers. (Rock, if I recall, tried it once and never went back.) We earned four dollars for eighteen holes, and usually got a 50-cent tip. Sometimes we could squeeze in two rounds a day—sweaty, tiring work but not bad money when you could buy a loaded eight-inch pizza at the Village Inn for $1.79. Being a caddy had other privileges. If you didn't mind dodging sprinklers and lawn mowers, you could golf for free on Mondays. You could always bum a cigarette and hear obscene jokes at the caddy shack. And every July Fourth, caddies were allowed to hang out in the employee parking lot of the country club for an up close view of the fireworks display. A very up close view. The club members were in their lounge chairs on the fairways where they could watch the pyrotechnics explode over the water. But we got to watch from a vantage point just yards from the launchpad, in a roped-off corner of the parking lot. The workers would drop a charge, mortar-style, into a steel tube, light the fuse, and jump back. *Boom!* Up it would streak into the sky above the water, blossoming into a rainbow of screaming colors and whistling streamers. Two other boys from our class at Refuge were caddies, too, and they joined up with us. One we called Doggie on account of the woebegone expression perpetually engraved on his face, even when he was laughing. Doggie looked like he had basset hound in his gene line. The other boy we all knew as Poison for his ability to traipse through poison ivy without getting so much as an itch. He was an adopted kid with a wild streak that made Tommy and the rest of us look like angels. Poison kept count of the number of bottles of Boone's Farm he stole from local stores, and one day proudly proclaimed himself an ace, having surpassed one hundred.

The six of us crowded around the launch site with the other caddies, mouths agape as the pyrotechnic rockets soared skyward yards from our faces. It was like being ringside at Cape Canaveral for a space launch. That's when we noticed the open crates of fireworks sitting just inside the rope line, unguarded.

Over and over, workers filed over to the crates, grabbed a rocket or two, and filed back to the launchpad a dozen yards away. I'm not sure how we got the idea, or if we even discussed it. I can't even remember which of us bent over the rope and reached into the crate. I just know it wasn't me. And I know I thought it was a *very* bad idea. If an M-80 could blow off Kevin McConnell's thumb and two fingers, as one with a faulty fuse had done a few years earlier, what could one of these babies do? But in the next instant there we were, scurrying along the edge of the parking lot in the dark, cutting in and out of the pine trees—in possession of a four-foot-long, ready-to-fire missile. "Jesus Christ! Jesus Christ!" I hissed as I raced to keep up. "Oh my God! Jesus Christ!" We cut through the back of the golf course, jumped fences, and made our way through a series of backyards and woods, avoiding all roads. The rocket was heavy and we took turns carrying it in teams of two. When we got to the field of tall grass where we liked to drink wine, we lay down out of sight with our prize and caught our breath. No one was following us; apparently no one had even noticed. As our fear of capture ebbed, we became drunk on the endless possibilities for our newly acquired arsenal. Just holding it in our hands was a narcotic. You could almost feel the pent-up power pulsing beneath its skin, ready to be unleashed at the place and time of our choosing. We hashed out several scenarios but in the end all agreed there was no time like the present, and no audience more fitting, more deserving, and certainly more likely to respond in a memorable way than Old Man Pemberton.

The plot was brilliant, pure genius. It would be hilarious, spectacular, epic. The prank to end all pranks. The escapade of a lifetime. After this caper, we could retire as mischief-makers, knowing our world-class reputations would be secure. We were going to launch a one-rocket fireworks show in Mr. Pemberton's front yard. Directly in front of those big picture windows. The ones we knew he sat behind in the dark, watching for teenage miscreants sneaking down to the water's edge with their beer and blankets. He wanted something to see? We'd give him something to see.

We had studied the workers at the country club. Launching looked simple. You dropped the rocket in a tube, lit the fuse, and stood back. Virtually foolproof. We hoisted our contraband and made our way through the fields and across Commerce Road to Harbor Hills, stopping on the way to pick out a length of clay sewer pipe, about six inches across and three feet long, from a construction site. It would make a perfect launch tube.

A few minutes later, we lay on our stomachs beneath a gnarly apple tree in The Outlot. From this vantage point we could study the Pemberton house, all dark and quiet. Our destination was a clump of shrubs in the Pembertons' front yard, behind which we could hide as we prepared our missile for launch. Two by two, we made the dash. No lights came on.

Doggie and Tommy began kicking up the sod with their heels, digging a shallow hole, and Poison ground the sewer pipe into it, working it down into the dirt until it stood upright on its own. We checked the alignment and pronounced it just about perfect, with just enough arc to get the firework directly over the house before it exploded, its display showering down directly in front of the picture windows. Sack and I slid the rocket into the tube. Then we all looked at each other. Who was going to light the fuse? Who was willing to take responsibility for this stunt of the century? It wasn't going to be me. I was happy to be the coward and was the first to back away. So did Sack and Rock and Doggie. Finally, Tommy grabbed the matches out of Poison's hand. "I'll do it," he said.

His hand was trembling as he lit the match and held it to the fuse, which protruded from just below the missile's nose. For a second nothing happened, and I thought, with some relief, that we had a dud. I was just starting to exhale when the fuse caught, just like a sparkler, and began burning toward the rocket. Tommy jumped back with the rest of us, but as he did, he bumped the tube. Now it was no longer pointing skyward with just the perfect arc to bring the light show directly overhead. Now it was pointing directly at the Pembertons' roof.

"Holy shit!" Tommy cried.

"Holy shit!" we all echoed.

Without another word, Tommy dashed forward, grabbed the clay tube in both hands, the sparkling fuse lighting his face, and tugged it back into position. The fuse was two-thirds gone. He let go and the tube again slumped down. There were just a few seconds left. Tommy straightened it again and this time pushed it down into the dirt with all his strength. Then he dove back with us and lay on his stomach. That's when we saw that Tommy's best had not been good enough. The tube had again shifted, this time pointing even lower than before. It was pointing so low, in fact, that it looked like the rocket might plow into the lawn a few yards ahead of us.

We held our ears. I said a prayer. With a deafening boom and blinding flash, the firework screamed off in a near horizontal position. It skimmed over Mr. Pemberton's perfect lawn and nipped a shrub, gaining elevation as it went. We stared frozen, holding our breath as it zeroed in on the front of the house, spiraling directly toward those giant plate-glass windows. The rocket's total journey could not have lasted more than a second or two, but it unfolded before us in slow motion. I could picture Mr. Pemberton lurching back in his chair in the window. I could see the terror on his face, the dawning realization that he was going to die. *Dear God, what have we done?* I thought.

Blam! The firework slammed into the brick wall, right between the two windows. Another three feet in either direction and it would have crashed through the glass and into the house. It disintegrated into the bricks with a loud blast, followed by a series of shrieking, burning streamers flying in all directions. Bursts of multicolored sparks sprayed outward, catching the grass on fire. The explosions kept coming. In plumes of green and red and blue and blinding white. Whirling, whistling flares corkscrewed out and skipped across the lawn. Glowing balls of fire catapulted in all directions.

And then it was over. We all lay there for a moment, staring at the pall of smoke hanging a few feet above the ground. "Fuck!" someone whispered. Then Poison was on his feet and sprinting toward the beach like I had never seen anyone run before. The rest of us bolted after him.

"Holy shit! Holy shit!" Tommy kept saying.

Dear Jesus, dear God the Father, dear Holy Spirit, I prayed silently. *Don't let us have killed Mr. Pemberton. Don't let his house burn down. Please, don't let him die. Please, don't let us get caught.*

We waded into the lake and, hugging the shoreline, made our way up the beach, not stopping until we reached the vacant lot where the smoking tree stood. No doubt the police were in the neighborhood by now. We crept up the bluff and peered over the edge at the street. All dark and quiet. Silently we crawled through the empty field and were almost to my street when we heard a car engine. "Down!" Tommy hissed, and we lay flat in the weeds, our breath ragged and nervous, so loud I was certain it would give us away. First a pair of headlights swept over us, then a spotlight. The police cruiser continued down the street, raking each lawn with its powerful beam. After it was out of sight, we scurried across the street and divided up without a word, each heading to his own home.

Inside, Dad was still up.

"How were the fireworks?" he asked.

"Great," I said. "Incredible."

"Well, good," he said. And with that, I walked upstairs, washed my face and hands, and turned in for the night.

The next morning I paced nervously around the house, acting as nonchalant as possible but dying to find out just how much damage we had done. I watched my parents carefully, but they showed no signs of knowing anything. Each time the phone rang I jumped, but they were all false alarms. Finally I put on my trunks and announced I was heading down for a swim.

"Okay, honey," Mom said. "I'll have lunch ready when you get back."

Down at The Outlot I concentrated on not staring over at the Pembertons' house. Only a guilty man would show up the next morning to gawk. I could not stare. I must not gaze. The briefest momentary glance was all I dare risk. After all, I just happened to be strolling by on my way for a refreshing morning dip. I looked up at the trees, marveled at the blue sky, paused to admire the water. Then, as subtly as I knew how, I let my head drift in the direction of the Pemberton property, and that's when I saw it. The brick wall where the firework hit was charred black. The hedge below was burned lifeless. The eves and awnings were scorched, and the lawn was marred with trails of blackened, seared grass. There in the midst of the carnage was Mr. Pemberton, raking up the debris as best he could. Just as I looked at him he looked at me, and what I saw staring back was not steely defiance or suspicious accusation, but defeat. He was a broken man. In his watery eyes, I saw only a question: "Why? Why would you kids do this to us?" I didn't have an answer. I looked away and continued down to the beach, being careful to stay on the outside of Mr. Pemberton's arrow sign. I wanted to turn back and apologize, to tell him we never meant for it to turn out this way. Instead, I kept walking and did not look back.

After my swim, I cut through the neighbors' yards so I wouldn't have to face the old man again. By the time I arrived home, Dad knew about the fireworks at the Pembertons. He had heard from Mr. Cullen, who had heard from Mr. Sacorelli, who had heard from another neighbor. The news was all over Harbor Hills.

"Do you know anything about this?" Dad asked.

"No, Dad."

"You don't know anything about this?" he said.

"Not a thing, Dad."

He studied my face. "I better not find out that you did, do you understand?"

"You won't, Dad," I promised.

That night I lay on top of the sheets in the July heat, the crickets' symphony drifting through the screened windows, and squeezed my eyes shut. "Dear Jesus, dear God the Father, dear Holy Spirit," I whispered. "Tell Mr. Pemberton I'm sorry. Tell him we didn't mean it. Tell him it wasn't as cruel as it seems. It was just a dumb idea. And thanks for not letting it turn out any worse."

CHAPTER 10

T
he nuns at Our Lady of Refuge were renowned for their cruelty. With the relish of medieval torture masters, they imposed a strict discipline that relied on physical pain and the constant threat that it could be visited on anyone at any moment for any reason. Corporal punishment was an important part of the Catholic education experience, and the tool of choice was the twelve-inch steel-lined ruler, which every nun carried at all times like every police officer carries a gun. Small and compact, it allowed Sister to make her way among our desks, delivering welt-raising blows without warning other than the brief shrill whistling sound the ruler made as it rushed through the air in the instant before impact. The knuckles were a favorite target, followed by the forearms, kneecaps, thighs, and occasionally the back of the head. Passing notes? *Whack!* Chewing gum? *Whack!* Staring absently out the window? *Whack!* Holding your pencil wrong? *Whack, whack, whack!*

For the bigger discipline jobs, the nuns brought out the heavy armaments—stout wooden yardsticks and the even more deadly rubber-tipped pointers. Punishment was styled after the public flogging of old and involved both pain and humiliation. The guilty student was ordered to the front of the class to assume the position: back to the class, feet spread, palms pressed on the blackboard. He—I can't remember a girl ever being up there—would be forced to wait while Sister fetched her yardstick. She always took her time. The waiting was torture. One sharp, withering whack across the back of the thighs, and it was over. But the worst part was yet to come—the public humiliation of turning to face the class. Some boys cried, some merely blinked back tears; the strongest managed to stay dry-eyed or even smirk defiantly. But there was one thing no one could hide, and that was the wet, clammy palm prints left behind on the blackboard. They served as a sort of corporal-punishment fear detector. You might be able to fake a brave face, but the sweaty palm prints told the truth. The class would roar with laughter, and Sister would chortle with approval. *Look how smart the smart aleck looks now, class.*

The nuns had other tricks, too. Over the years, I had my ears twisted, hair yanked, and face slapped. One nun, with a major leaguer's accuracy, wound up and hurled a chalk eraser across the room, nailing a student on the forehead. In seventh grade, I spent hours decorating an old cigar box to hold my pencils and pens. I was working at my desk with it open beside me when the perpetually angry Sister Mary Edward, for reasons I never determined, slapped it to the floor, sending the contents flying. "Now pick it up," she sneered and walked away, leaving me to crawl on my hands and knees among the desks as my classmates snickered. This kind of treatment was nothing new. My mother remembered—with great humor, for some reason—a nun at her Catholic school forcing her younger brother to eat a dead fly he had been caught playing with. Forcing an insect carcass down the throat of a second grader—now, there's the Christian spirit! Nuns and abuse just seemed to go hand in hand.

The only thing was, none of us considered it abuse, least of all our parents, who had the same basic response to every reported atrocity: "Well, if Sister decided you deserved to be hung by your thumbs while she flogged you with a cat-o'-nine-tails, then Sister must have had a good reason." The nuns were not quite as infallible as priests, but they were close. If they chose to smack or ridicule us, we obviously got what was coming to us.

I became convinced that the only real joy in the nuns' austere, lonely lives was the terrified yelps of small children. There was one exception at Our Lady of Refuge, and that was Sister Nancy Marie. She was young, mid- to late twenties, and plain but with a beatific smile and shiny complexion that combined to give her a preternatural glow. Unlike the older, more conservative nuns with their scratchy habits and starched face boards, she dressed in a knee-length skirt with a blouse and jacket. Except for a crucifix around her neck and a small veil on her head, which allowed a shock of hair to tumble onto her forehead, she barely even looked like a nun.

All the students loved Sister Nancy Marie. She was one of the original "What Would Jesus Do?" disciples, and took seriously her vows to act like Christ. No matter how serious your transgression—forgotten homework, chatting in class, playground fisticuffs—she would never strike, never scold, never even raise her voice. Her response to almost any situation was to fix those earnest brown eyes on you, clasp her hands together, and say, "Now, let's see how we can resolve this." In her vocation, she was a lamb among embittered wolves.

I suppose we should have gone easy on her.

Sister Nancy Marie was the religious-education instructor, and it was her job to infuse us with the wonders of our faith. It was in her nature to win our hearts with sweetness, and she sometimes managed to make religion seem fun. One of her innovations was to let us choose popular songs by our favorite bands to play during Mass. We would bring in our record albums and listen to the lyrics of Simon and Garfunkel or Bob Dylan or The Doors, discussing any themes that might apply. Most of the songs were complete stretches, but she gave us latitude. I remember playing The Beatles' "A Day in the Life," from *Sgt. Pepper's Lonely Hearts Club Band,* at one student Mass. At another, I suggested "Tired of Waiting for You" by The Kinks, and Sister approved it. What this song of boy-girl longing had to do with religion, I didn't know, but Sister Nancy Marie was game. She was always looking for ways to blur the line between the secular and the spiritual, to demonstrate that God could and should be integrated into every part of our lives. It would be up to Tommy, with wholehearted encouragement from me, to determine Sister Nancy Marie's limits.

We had no cafeteria at Refuge and ate lunch at our desks. One day in seventh grade, Sister Nancy Marie announced a new idea: Record Day, at which we could bring in albums to play during the lunch hour. When Record Day arrived, she rolled in the record player on its cart, plugged it in, and invited us to take turns playing our favorite songs while we ate our sandwiches. "Listen carefully to the lyrics," she beckoned. "Contemplate what the artist is saying. What is his message? How does it touch your lives?" And then she left the room. Sister Nancy Marie operated on trust. No need to stand over her students with a club. Treat them like adults, and they will act like adults. One girl stepped forward and put on "Where Have All the Flowers Gone?" Another dropped the needle on Peter, Paul, and Mary's version of "Blowin' in the Wind." A third offered The Byrds' rendition of "Mr. Tambourine Man." Then Tommy stood up. He, too, had brought a favorite album, carried inconspicuously into school between his books. The album was by The Fugs— and The Fugs definitely were not what Sister Nancy Marie had in mind for contemplative lunchtime listening.

They were the raunchiest, most indecent band I had ever heard. Some critics would later hail them as the original punk band, bravely paving the way for the Ramones and the Sex Pistols and all the others to follow. But on this day, they were just one thing to Tommy and me: the biggest Catholic-school no-no we could imagine. One song opened in a yodeling voice, sustaining an obscenity. Another had the catchy title "Boobs A Lot." A third sang the praises of marijuana and cunnilingus.

But the coup de grâce, the album's pièce de résistance, was track three, a song called "Supergirl." Unlike relationship songs by the Beatles or Monkees or Stones, this one did not waste time on holding hands or gazing dreamily into eyes or even spending the night together. It got right to the point in the opening line.

I'm not sure whose idea it was to play "Supergirl" in class. My memory is that it began as an abstract hypothetical. *Just imagine the look on old Nancy Marie's face if "Supergirl" ever came on.* From there, it was elevated to an idea. *What if we sneaked Supergirl on? My God, how hilarious would that be?* And from an idea it graduated to a dare. And if there was one thing I already knew about Tommy, it was never to challenge him to do anything you did not want to see him try.

Tommy carried his record to the front of the room and peeked out the door into the empty hallway. All clear. He pulled the vinyl disk from its cardboard sleeve and placed it on the spinning turntable. As always, I was rapidly losing my nerve. *Don't do it, Tommy,* I telegraphed. *It's not too late. Don't do it.* Leaning over for a better view, he balanced the needle over the vinyl.

"Now, boys and girls," he called out in a high voice that was his imitation of Sister Nancy Marie. "I want you to contemplate what the artist is saying. Listen to the words. How do they touch your lives?" He hesitated for a moment, then expertly dropped the needle onto the empty band between tracks two and three.

Tommy reached for the volume knob and cranked it as high as it would go. Amplified pops, hisses, and crackles filled the classroom. He raced back to his seat, and the song began, first with clashing guitar chords and then with the opening lyrics. At full volume, the music was badly distorted.

But the words remained perfectly understandable. They boomed through the room and out the open door. And this is what they said:

"I want a girl who can fuck like an angel."

The F-word stood above the rest, and screamed down the hallway like a fireball, filling every corner, crack, nook, and cranny of Our Lady of Refuge. It was so loud, I wondered if Mom could hear it back home in our kitchen four doors away. *"I want a girl who can FUUUUUUCK like an angel."*

The second verse began: "I want a girl who can—" The class never found out what. Sister Nancy Marie, her face as red as I have ever seen a human face, sprinted into the room. She was running so fast her veil actually flew out straight behind her, like a flag in a stiff wind. She dove at the record player, arced her arm like a tennis pro executing a perfect backstroke, swung it around, and smacked the needle with all her strength. It skidded across the vinyl with the sound of ripping fabric. Then the room went silent. She picked up the album in both hands, raised it over her head, not unlike the way the priest raised the host to heaven during the consecration, and brought it down hard on the side of the cart. The Fugs shattered into a hundred pieces. She threw the chunk still in her hands to the floor and stomped on it. She was screaming and shaking, her face now a deep crimson. The crucifix had flung around her neck and somehow ended up behind her, hanging between her shoulders. She stopped, bowed her head, and stood there silently for a few seconds, eyes closed, breathing heavily. Then she reached around and retrieved her crucifix, raising it to her lips and kissing it as she blessed herself. Her voice was calm again. "No one is leaving this classroom until I know who did this," she said. "This . . . this . . ."—and her voice rose again—"this . . . disgusting . . . filth."

I glanced over at Tommy; he was as white as chalk. Then I saw why. On the desk in front of him in plain view sat the Fugs album cover. It was the one part of our brilliant plan we had overlooked. There was no hiding it now. He folded his hands over it, and we both stared straight ahead. Within seconds, Tommy was busted. Sister ordered him to the principal's office. Not long after, I was summoned, too. As a co-conspirator with advanced knowledge of the crime, I was in nearly as much trouble.

The principal, Sister Mary Noel, segregated us, Tommy in her office and me in the tiny nurse's station across the hall. She dealt with him first, as I waited with clammy palms. Finally the door opened and in she walked. I was expecting her to be angry, but she mostly looked sad.

"Mr. Grogan, tell me this," she began, and I braced for an interrogation on the Fugs conspiracy. But her questions had nothing to do with it. "What are you going to be in this life?" she asked. "Are you going to be a tree that spreads its roots deep and reaches proudly to the sky? Or are you going to be a weed that bends in any breeze and never grows to its full potential?" I stared blankly at her. *What in God's name is she talking about?*

"You come from solid stock, John Grogan. Your parents planted an acorn that has the potential to grow into a mighty oak. But you choose to mingle in the weeds instead of growing strong. You could be a leader in the forest, standing tall above all the other trees. The weeds never amount to anything. They don't take root and are quickly overshadowed by the other trees. Is that what you want?"

Sister Noel pushed her face close to mine. "What are you going to be? A solid oak? Or a common weed wallowing in the ditch?" I sat silently. Frankly, I didn't want to be either. I liked being a boy just fine. And if being an oak tree meant turning my back on Tommy—and it was dawning on me that that was what Sister was getting at—I'd take my chances as a weed. Tommy was my best friend; we'd grow together side by side.

"An oak or a weed?" Sister repeated. "Only you can decide." She told me she was going to let me sit there to think about the choice before me, and on her way out the door she turned back and said it one more time: "An oak or a weed?"

Our parents were called, and that night at home I tried to put the best spin on the day's events. The incident confirmed my parents' opinion of rock music as an evil, perverted influence on their children's lives. A couple of years earlier, I had pranced through the house singing the words to the Rolling Stones song "Let's Spend the Night Together," and my shocked mother confiscated the album, saying, "The sacred union of a man and a woman should never be trivialized. Our Lord blesses it only within the sacrament of marriage."

The Fugs made those lyrics seem quaint by comparison. I feigned innocence, telling them it was Tommy's idea and I had no clue what was on that album or that he planned to put it on and turn up the volume. I had been wrongly ensnared, I insisted, because he was my best friend, a case of guilt by association. I felt a little bad blaming it all on him, but I knew my parents would never confront Mr. and Mrs. Cullen about it. And besides, I was pretty sure that at that exact moment he was blaming it all on me. We had covered for each other this way before. That's what best friends were for. My parents looked at me skeptically and said what they always said, that they believed me and that I deserved whatever punishment the good sisters saw fit to impose.

Tommy and I spent the next week reporting to the convent each day after school. For bringing The Fugs and the F-word into the halls of Our Lady of Refuge, there would be no beatings or knuckle-raps or twisted ears. For this offense, we were ordered to do something we had never heard of any other student being ordered to do—enter the private, mysterious residence of the Sisters of Saint Felix to work on our hands and knees.

The convent was made of brick, large and imposing, and inside it was dark and smelled of fried food and floor wax. There was a chapel lit only by votive candles in red glass canisters where the nuns prayed, and small, cell-like rooms where they slept. Tommy and I were put to work scrubbing the baseboards and washing walls on all three floors. It really wasn't so bad, and when we were done each evening, the sisters led us into the kitchen and gave us each a glass of milk and a dish of whatever they were having for dinner. I remember lots of boiled meats and vegetables.

One afternoon as we scooted along the second-floor hallway on our knees with our buckets and scrub brushes, Tommy and I heard the soft click of a latch. A door opened in front of us, and out stepped one of the ancient nuns. But something was not right, and soon I saw what: her habit and headdress were missing, replaced by a floral housecoat and slippers. What shocked us most was to see her without her veil and face boards. She had cropped gray hair. Her face was wrinkled and saggy, fuller and softer than it looked wedged into her headgear. We stared up at her. She was no longer the harsh, humorless authority figure from school, but simply an old and tired lady. It took her a moment to notice us, and when she did, she hurried past without a word and disappeared down the hall.

"Whoa! Did you see that?" Tommy asked.

"Whoa!" I said.

As we worked, Tommy and I snooped around, peering into closets and down staircases and listening to the smothering silence. A favorite rumor around school was that the nuns maintained a secret tunnel beneath the playground connecting the convent to the rectory, allowing late-night liaisons with the priests. Tommy and I set out to prove its existence once and for all, but what we discovered instead was a place so oppressive, it felt like a black hole from which not even sunlight could escape. There were no sounds in there. No laughter or music or chatting voices. Only the hushed whispers of prayer and the creaks of rubber-soled shoes on linoleum.

It hardly seemed equitable. Across the soccer field, the priests lived in a house much like any in the neighborhood, large and breezy and comfortable. They had a housekeeper and cook, a color television and stereo, thick woven rugs, a regulation pool table, a wine cellar, and a well-stocked bar from which they could enjoy a cocktail at the end of the day.

But here in the convent, there were none of those comforts. The sisters had taken vows of poverty, and they lived in utter austerity. Their only recreation, as far as I could see, were the evening walks they took in pairs around the neighborhood. No wonder they were always so grim. My stint scrubbing the convent had opened my eyes to these alien creatures in brown wool who ruled their students without mercy. They weren't beasts or ogres. They were women. Women who had given their lives to God and the Church. From what I could tell, many of them were lonely and isolated and demoralized. Even then I had to ask, If God is really up there calling the shots, and if he is all great and all merciful as we were taught, why would he treat these women who had sacrificed their lives in his service so harshly? Why would he treat his male servants so much better? To my parents, this was just the way it was. Men and women answered God's call in different ways. To them, the priests deserved adulation and creature comforts, and the nuns were happy in their simple lives of deprivation. I wasn't buying it. The nuns, I decided, needed their own advocate, their own patron saint, someone like Saint Joan of Arc not afraid to fight for what she believed. But then look what happened to that strong woman. We learned all about her in school. Burned at the stake as a heretic.

Sister Nancy Marie, as we knew she would, eventually forgave us our trespasses. Just as Jesus would have done, she returned to her cheery ways and earnest looks. Neither Tommy nor I ever did replace that Fugs album. The truth was, the only thing it had going for it were the dirty words. We liked to think we sacrificed it for the greater glory of our cause—to let the nuns know the battle was not over, and we would grow into whatever kind of trees we wanted. We were pretty sure The Fugs, if they ever found out, would have approved.

CHAPTER 11

✳

My parents were the trusting sort, even when I gave them every reason not to be. The evidence against me could be overwhelming, as it was in the Fugs incident, but if I pleaded my innocence earnestly enough they usually bought the story, no matter how far-fetched. Or at least they pretended to. When, on a scout campout, Dad caught a group of us inside a tent smoking, I told him an unnamed older boy from a neighboring campsite had given us two cigarettes to try, and "a few of us"—the clear inference being that I was not one of them—had lit them up. It was a transparent lie. All he had to do was smell my breath or fingers to catch me. But Dad accepted my account. Just as he had accepted the story that the *Penthouse* he found hidden in the culvert under our driveway must have been stashed there by unknown neighbor kids. Dad wasn't dumb; he wasn't naive. He wanted to believe what he wanted to believe—that his son, a good Catholic boy who received Holy Communion every Sunday and confessed his sins once a month, would not let him down. He and Mom always seemed to give me the benefit of the doubt.

Usually I did not deserve their blind trust, but there was one time I ended up wrongly accused, and from that day forward I never again took their faith in me for granted.

The smoking tree down by the water, in addition to being my gang's gathering spot for cigarettes, swearing, and stolen Boone's Farm, was a place I went often by myself. On these solo trips, I did nothing more delinquent than sit and stare across the water and daydream. Early on, my father had instilled in me a deep love of nature and the outdoors, and I could sit for hours in the woods fantasizing about wilderness survival. When I was in Boy Scouts, Dad regularly took me into the woods, where he taught me how to use the sun as a compass, fashion a lean-to from pine boughs, and forage edible plants from the forest floor. I read everything I could find on the topic and knew how to splint a broken leg with a tree branch, weave vines into rope, and brew tea from staghorn sumac. Fire-making was a particular point of pride for me. I learned how to find dry kindling even in the soggiest conditions, arrange sticks so the air could wick through them, and nurse the feeblest flame to life. I practiced until I never needed more than one match. I built my fires responsibly, always careful to fully extinguish them before leaving.

On a chilly fall day after school at the start of eighth grade, I whistled for Shaun and the two of us headed down to the smoking tree. Shaun chased ducks into the water and fetched rocks off the bottom, and I decided to build a small fire. I peeled a few shavings of papery bark off a white birch for my tinder, gathered a variety of kindling and dry sticks, positioned them into a tepee, and lit the bark. One match and a few soft puffs on the flame, and I had a cheery little blaze to sit beside as I dreamed of surviving in the Yukon with nothing but a jackknife and flint and steel. As the sun set over the lake, I let the little fire die, then stirred the embers into the sand. Twenty feet away was a neighbor's wood dock, out of the water and piled in sections against the bluff for the winter. Beneath it were some charred driftwood and a mess of spent matches from what looked like a long-ago attempt at a campfire. I thought nothing of it other than to disdain whoever needed to use so many matches to start one blaze.

I whistled for Shaun and then, just for the sheer joy of being a boy outdoors with his dog on a crisp fall evening, began to run. I raced up the bluff and sprinted across the field back home as if a bear were on my tail. It was the running that must have caught Mr. Simpson's eye. He lived next to the vacant lot, and he was second only to Old Man Pemberton as the grouchiest grown-up in the neighborhood. He had shooed my friends and me off the vacant lot more than once.

I was home only a few minutes, washing up for dinner, when the doorbell rang. I opened the door, and it was Mr. Simpson. He asked to speak to my father. Dad came and invited him inside, but something I could not make out was mumbled, and Dad stepped out on the porch and shut the door behind him. The two men stood in the cold talking for several minutes, and when Dad came in he had a look that told me there was a problem.

"Were you down at the water across the street just now?" he asked.

"Yes," I told him. "I took Shaun for a swim."

"Were you messing around with matches?"

Dad knew my skill as a one-match fire-maker. I was surprised at his choice of words. I told him about making the little fire and sitting beside it before burying it in sand and heading home.

"Did you run away for some reason?" he asked.

I began to see where the questions were leading. How do you explain sprinting wildly from a fire for no reason other than to feel the wind in your face and your heart beat against your ribs? "I just felt like running," I said.

Then he came out with it: "Mr. Simpson thinks you tried to set his dock on fire. He saw you running away, and when he went down, he found combustibles piled up and burned matches, and warm coals nearby. You were the only one down there."

"Dad," I said.

"This is serious, John. He wants to call the police."

"Dad, I didn't do it. I saw those matches, too. It wasn't me."

It sounded as lame as all my other lies. Yes, I was down there with matches. Yes, I had lit a fire. Yes, there were dying coals in the sand nearby. Yes, I had sprinted manically from the scene. But no, I had nothing to do with it. "Dad, honest, I didn't—"

He stopped me in midsentence. "I know you didn't," he said. "I'll talk to him." Then he added the words that meant so much: "I believe you."

Over the years I had given him so many reasons not to believe. Now for the first time I needed him to, and he did. He had taken my version over the version of a grown-up.

I wanted to throw myself in his arms, to hug him, and to reassure him that this time his faith was not misplaced. But being a Grogan man, I did as Grogan men were expected to do. And Grogan men didn't hug, they didn't kiss, and they never said, "I love you." I jabbed my hand toward him, and he grasped it in his and shook it vigorously. The robust Grogan handshake.

"Now, let's go eat," Dad said.

Eighth grade drifted by, and as graduation approached, every one of my friends gushed about heading to the state-of-the-art public high school recently built a few miles down Orchard Lake Road. It had a swimming pool, tennis courts, a groomed running track, a sunny courtyard, and an acoustically tuned performing arts auditorium. Our tax dollars at work, and everyone was going. Tommy and Rock and Sack and Doggie and all the cute girls from the neighborhood. Everyone, that is, except me.

My parents enrolled me at Brother Rice, an all-boys Catholic high school in Birmingham, a half-hour drive away in one of Detroit's wealthiest suburbs. The kids who attended Brother Rice were the same kids whose parents owned memberships at the country club where I caddied. Tim and Mike had gone there, and both told hair-raising stories of the sadistic disciplinary techniques of the Irish Christian Brothers who ran the place, tactics that made those of the Sisters of Saint Felix sound quaint by comparison. Tim hated all four of his years there; he bristled at the authority, at the wealth and hypocrisy, at the religious doctrine crammed down his throat. Michael, who years earlier had abandoned his priestly aspirations but still loved everything Catholic, felt at home there. As for me, I didn't want to be separated from my friends, but I accepted Brother Rice as a given. It was where the Grogan sons were meant to go, just as the Grogan daughter was meant to attend Marian, the all-girls Catholic high school separated from the boys' school by a drainage moat. Marijo and Tim were now both attending Catholic colleges, and Mike was on his way to one in the fall. We were preordained for Catholic education. It was the one thing on which my frugal parents did not mind spending their savings.

Shortly after dousing myself in hot wax, I had hung up my cassock for good and retired from the altar-boy corps. That did not mean I had a choice about attending Mass. In our home, Mass fell in the same category as breathing. Each Sunday morning began the same way: Mom waking us with that feather of hers and saying, "Get up, lazybones, time for Mass."

Nearly every Sunday, Dad served on the altar beside the priest. He was a lay minister, which meant that he read scripture and intentions for the sick, announced hymns, and led the congregation in liturgical responses. He even got to distribute communion from the altar rail, right alongside the priest. Dad took his duties seriously, and he genuflected reverentially every time he passed in front of the Blessed Sacrament. He bowed his head deeply in prayer and sang at the top of his lungs. Unlike Mom, who couldn't hold a tune if the Pope himself requested it, Dad had a good voice and wasn't shy about using it. He sang and recited prayers with his eyes closed, something he could do because he had every hymn lyric and every prayer fully committed to memory. When the priest raised the communion host skyward at the moment of consecration, Dad would bow deeply and press a fist to his heart as if he had just witnessed something so magnificent it was blinding. It's hard to describe his bearing on the altar without making him sound sanctimonious. And some thought he was, including one condescending priest who, it came back to us, had sneeringly dubbed him Holy Richard. But he wasn't; he was merely caught up in the rapture of his faith. He was the exact same way when no one was watching. Dad was a nighthawk, always the last to bed, and sometimes I would get up late at night to use the bathroom and peek into my parents' bedroom to find him on his knees lost in silent prayer, his head buried in the covers of the bed inches from his sleeping wife. His devotion was no act.

Neither was my mother's. She was physically incapable of receiving Holy Communion without bursting into tears. I don't mean tearing up a little; I mean bawling. It was as predictable as the sunrise. She would file up to the altar rail, hands folded, eyes respectfully down, but looking just fine. If she recognized someone in line, she would smile, even wink. Then she would swallow the host, and by the time she was back in the pew and on her knees, the tears would be streaming down her cheeks like she had just been informed her entire family was lost at sea. Everyone knelt after communion; that was expected. But Mom knelt in a pose of utter surrender, her face buried in her hands resting on the back of the pew in front of her, fat tears falling to the floor. The Lord was inside her now; she was helpless to resist.

Communion would end, and the priest would work through his ritualistic chalice cleaning as the congregation continued to kneel. When he was finished, he would announce, "Let us stand." And everyone would stand. Everyone except Mom, who would remain in her kneeling position, head down, face buried, snorting and sniffling away, lost in her communion with Christ. When I was little, I found great amusement in Mom's boo-hooing, but as I grew older the last thing I wanted was to stand out in a crowd. I just wanted her to get up when everyone else got up, and to try to keep the waterworks to a minimum. Sometimes she stayed there with her head down right through the recessional hymn, and even as the church emptied around her. It was an amazing thing to watch. She was totally swept away, oblivious to anything around her. I marveled at how something so simple—swallowing a small wheat wafer— could bring such an emotional reaction. I tried to share it. I would swallow the host and squeeze my eyes shut and try to feel Christ inside me. But I felt nothing, nothing but a low burn in my stomach, the host's reminder that I had fasted and was hungry for breakfast. Why, I wondered, was I not able to experience the same blissful magic? Maybe I was doing something wrong. I concentrated with all my might, burying my head in my hands like she did and beckoning the Lord into my soul. Still nothing. If he ever visited, he certainly was stealthy about it. I didn't waste any energy worrying about it, and soon I learned the art of daydreaming while appearing to be deep in prayer.

When Tim was home from college, it never occurred to me why he always chose to attend a service other than the one my parents attended. Then one Sunday shortly after I graduated from Our Lady of Refuge I tagged along with him and found out. As we walked over, he asked, "Are you going in or coming with me?" At first I didn't know what he meant, and then it struck me: He wasn't going to Mass. He never went to Mass. Tim, I found out that day, had stopped attending years earlier, at least whenever he could get away with it, carefully covering his tracks to keep it from our parents. He knew it would crush them.

Part of his cover was to swing by the church and peer in the doors just as the service was starting. He had learned that Dad always asked what priest was on the altar, not as a way of checking up on his kids but because he was genuinely curious. He followed the priests like a gambler follows racehorses. By getting a positive ID, Tim could nonchalantly answer, "Father Schroeder," or whoever it happened to be.

"We need to spot the priest, then we've got an hour to kill," Tim said. "I usually go over to Saint Mary's and walk around."

Saint Mary's was a Catholic prep school, college, and seminary directly across Commerce Road from our neighborhood. Its primary purpose was to train future priests. It might sound counterintuitive, skipping Mass to hang around a Catholic seminary, but the grounds of Saint Mary's were breathtaking; it was one of the most serene

places on the planet. Situated on a bluff overlooking
Orchard Lake, a smaller, more bucolic twin to Cass Lake,
the campus long ago had housed a military academy and
was studded with castlelike brick buildings and oak trees
that had stood there since before the Civil War. Tim and
I strolled the shady paths and sat in the grass looking out
over the water. With his slightly longish hair and quirky
taste in clothes, Tim was impossibly cool in my estimation,
and I was honored that he had trusted me with his secret.
Getting caught skipping Mass, we both knew, would be
tantamount to an act of family treason.

It was one of those perfect summer days that made
all the lousy Michigan weather worth it. The marvels of
nature were everywhere—in the sun on our faces, the
breeze in our hair, the birds surrounding us with song. Tim
squinted across the water, its rippled surface dazzled with
a million shards of sunlight, and said, "Now this is my kind
of religious experience." His words took me aback. It had
not before occurred to me that there could be any religious
experience other than the one drilled into us at home and
church and school. I thought about that for a few seconds
and decided it was my kind, too. From that day forward,
whenever he was home from college, Tim and I sneaked off
each Sunday morning to spend an hour communing with
nature—and each other. Brother to brother. We jokingly
christened our new faith the Church of Tim and John. I
didn't realize it at the time, but that summer was a turning
point for me—the point at which I stopped trying to feel
the same religious fervor as my parents. I rarely skipped
Mass without my brother, but from then on I attended in

body only, reciting the words from memory while my mind roamed to the far corners of the planet.

That September, Tommy and all the others started at West Bloomfield, and I headed off to Brother Rice. My friends were now free to wear jeans and T-shirts and grow out their hair; I reported to school each morning in dress shirt, navy slacks, tie, and loafers.

I settled into my new routine without complaint, going from class to class and sitting quietly during study hall, staying beneath the brothers' radar. I became friendly with a few boys, but it wasn't the same as with Tommy, Rock, or Sack. My new classmates had all grown up together at Saint Regis, the Catholic elementary school next to Brother Rice. They were clubby, and I was a stranger peering in from the periphery.

In the opening weeks of the school year, the old gang would still convene each afternoon down at the beach or at the smoking tree or behind the football field at Saint Mary's. They told me all about their new world and the cast of characters that inhabited it—the desirable girls and cool older kids and druggies who showed up high every day. In great detail, they described various romantic pursuits and failures. And I told them what I could about my new world. Honestly, there wasn't much to tell. The only bright spot was that Barbie Barlow's parents had sent her to Marian next door, but she might as well have been at the Sorbonne. Sometimes I would catch a glimpse of her in the distance across the moat, playing soccer or waiting for her ride, but

I never got any closer. She was like a mirage, shimmering in the distance.

One day after school, Tommy pulled a cigarette from his pocket and ran it beneath his nostrils. It was different from other cigarettes I had seen, fat in the middle with twisted ends. "Time to smoke a doobie," he said brightly and lit up. The joint worked its way around the circle, and when it came to me I hesitated only briefly before sucking in a mouthful of smoke. I had no desire to try marijuana—it scared me—but I was more afraid of losing my friends. Somehow they had all graduated to pot without me even knowing it. I held the smoke in my mouth, acrid and musky, and consciously tried not to inhale it into my lungs. I believed what the Christian Brothers told us in health class, that a single puff of marijuana could lead in short order to ever more dangerous drugs. In no time you would be a desperate heroin junkie breaking into homes.

Tommy caught me. "Don't just hold it in your mouth," he chided. "Inhale it."

"I am," I lied.

As the leaves fell and autumn surrendered to winter, my old friends slipped away from me. There was no drama or confrontation. They merely forgot about me by degrees. They had new friends now and new social ladders to climb. Gradually they stopped calling, stopped dropping by, stopped inviting me to tag along on Friday nights. I spent most of the rest of that year alone. Alone at school. Alone at the Our Lady of Refuge rectory each evening, where I earned a dollar an hour as the office boy who answered the phones. Mostly I spent it alone in the basement with the headphones on, listening over and over to Bob Dylan sing "Sad-Eyed Lady of the Lowlands" and "Desolation Row." Mom and Dad noticed.

"How's everything at school?" they would ask at dinner. By now it was just the three of us.

"Fine," I would say. And I meant it. Things weren't bad; they weren't good. They were just . . . *flat*.

"So, anything new?" they would prod. I had always been the chatterbox of the dinner hour, regaling my family with rapid-fire tales of every aspect of my day, even my misdeeds, at least those I thought would draw a laugh.

"Not really," I would say.

In the spring of that year, 1972, Mom and Dad sat me down. Mom did the talking, as usual, with Dad nodding silently beside her. "We've been thinking, honey," she said. "If you want to go to West Bloomfield next year, you can. We're good with that. It's your decision."

Dad chimed in: "Whatever you choose, we'll support."

I could hardly believe my ears. I knew how important a Catholic education was to them, how much they believed it was the ticket to building character and strong faith. Yet they had also watched Brother Rice turn Tim inside himself, like a turtle retracting into its shell to seal out the world. Now they saw me withdrawing, too. The joy had gone out of my life; my spirit was nearly suffocated. In the end, their fear of losing me as they had lost Tim seemed to outweigh their fervor for a religious education.

Now the decision to leave was mine. Brother Rice was not without its merits. Even as a fourteen-year-old, I recognized its academic excellence. Two teachers in particular had found a way to connect with me. There was Mr. Stark, the track coach, who taught Freshman Math for Dummies. That's not what they called it, but that's what it was. For the first time in my life, I experienced the thrill of conquering an algebraic equation.

Then there was Brother McKenna, my English composition teacher, who had all the warmth of an Arctic winter. Students loathed him. His standards were ridiculously high and inflexible. We had to write a personal essay every week, and if it had one misspelling, we would receive zero credit. A scratched-out word or sloppy handwriting would cut the grade in half. He drilled into us the seriousness of our craft and the need to edit our words, to take pride in them, to polish them like gemstones, not presenting them to the world until they were as perfect as humanly possible. Writing had always come fairly effortlessly to me, but I was sloppy and undisciplined. He returned paper after paper marked with failing or near-failing grades. Then midway through the school year, he handed back a paper marked with an A. Not a single word of encouragement, just the letter. It was all I needed. For the first time in my life, I saw there was something I could do as well or better than the other, smarter kids.

Yet the choice to leave was ridiculously easy. After thinking it over for a couple of days, I told Mom and Dad my decision. True to their word, they held their tongues and arranged my transfer.

The school year wound down, and I said good-bye to Mr. Stark and Brother McKenna, who encouraged me to keep writing with these measured words: "When you're willing to work at it, there's actually something there." The last day of school was dedicated to cleaning out lockers and turning in textbooks, and then I was free. The next day would mark the start of vacation and a lazy summer of swimming, sunbathing, and hanging out. It would also mark an event that would make my parents rethink the decision to let me transfer to public school before I even arrived.

CHAPTER 12

⁜

D odge Park was located directly across Cass Lake from Harbor Hills, about a mile away as the crow flies. From The Outlot we could see its large sandy public beaches bristling with lifeguard towers, and the acres of parked cars glimmering in the sun beyond. Dodge Park covered several hundred wooded acres crisscrossed by hiking trails, but its beaches were by far the park's most popular feature. Teenagers flocked from every school district around to spend summer days there. It was more than just a place to swim and sunbathe; it was a scene. And a huge part of that scene revolved around illegal drug use. Every sunny summer day, Dodge Park took on the feel of a mini-Woodstock. The beaches and sidewalks and picnic areas were crammed with thousands of sunburned teenagers and young adults, most in cutoff blue jeans, the boys bare-chested, the girls in halters or bikini tops. Amateur musicians formed knots, strumming on guitars and banging out rhythms on congas and bongos. Marijuana smoke and the smell of patchouli oil hung in the air, and dealers openly plied their wares. Kids tripping on LSD and hallucinogenic mushrooms, or merely stoned on pot and hashish, lay on their backs staring up at the sky. The newspapers had begun writing about the park's growing drug problem; some arrests had been made, and there were community calls to crack down more forcefully so parents could again feel comfortable bringing their children to swim.

Even though Harbor Hills had its own beach, every kid in my neighborhood considered Dodge Park the destination of choice. In stiflingly boring southeastern Michigan, it was like having our own Haight-Ashbury right across the water. I had managed to make it over there a couple of times the previous summer before Dad caught wind of the mushrooming drug culture and forbade me to enter the park. I tried to argue the point, but he was firm. "I don't care if all your friends are going," he said. "You are not. We have a perfectly good beach right down the street."

Now it was the first full day of summer vacation, and everyone who was anyone was heading to Dodge Park. I had run into Tommy the previous day after arriving home from Brother Rice for the last time, and he predicted, "It's going to be the party to end all parties." They were all getting a ride there with Doggie's older brother. "You should come with us," he said. It was the first invitation I'd gotten from him in months, and I wanted desperately to go. "Nah," I said. "My dad won't go for it."

The next morning I instead headed down to The Lagoon. Four years earlier, when I was ten, Dad had surprised us with a sailboat. Although he was a landlubber at heart, he decided a boat would be the perfect vehicle for summer family togetherness. Besides, our house came with dock privileges. It seemed a shame not to use them.

The boat was a sleek little sloop of British design with oiled teak floorboards and varnished mahogany benches that comfortably seated five. He and Mom (who never once set foot on it) had christened it *Mary Ann* after my stillborn sister, and Dad jumped into the learning curve of sailing the same way he jumped into any other life challenge—with nose-to-grindstone determination. He read books and manuals, scoured magazine articles, and attended workshops. Dad somehow managed to turn even the leisurely pursuit of sailing into an awful lot of hard work. Marijo and Michael never really took to the sailboat, but Tim and I did with gusto and in a way my father never could—with seat-of-the-pants confidence. We did no reading or studying; we simply felt the wind and let it carry us. Soon Tim and I were taking it out on our own, often with Tommy or Rock or Sack along for the ride. Tim would skipper and we would crew, trimming the jib and hiking out over the high side to provide human ballast. By the time I was in ninth grade, I had honed my sailing skills to the point where not only could I skipper the boat, but I could skipper it singlehandedly. On that first day of vacation, knowing everyone was gathering at Dodge Park, I grabbed the sails and headed out for a solo cruise.

I didn't set out to disobey my father; this I can say truthfully. But I was only on the water a few minutes when I began rationalizing my way across the lake in the direction of the party to end all parties. *He didn't say anything about going near the park,* I reasoned. *What's the harm in sailing past for a closer look?* And then, once I was skimming by just outside the swim-area buoys, I took another tack: *Maybe I'll pull up on shore for a few minutes, just to stretch my*

legs. That's not actually in *the park, just on the edge of it.* I
spotted a muddy flat off to the side of the beach and headed
for it. Once my bow hit the shore, I figured: *A quick walk
up the beach and back, and I'm outta here. He'll never
even know. How could he ever know?* I dropped the sails
and headed off into the sea of hippie humanity. It was not
even noon and already marijuana smoke hovered thick in
the air.

The wide sand beach was on a man-made island
separated from the rest of Dodge Park by a stagnant canal.
Visitors parked on the mainland and walked across a wide
pedestrian bridge to the beach. I had landed the boat on the
mainland side of the canal. As I began to cross the bridge
I realized I was wading into a giant, bustling drug bazaar.
Dealers lined each railing, nearly shoulder to shoulder,
rattling off their offerings in singsongy stage whispers: *pot,
hash, Quaaludes, mescaline.* Money and packets were
changing hands in plain sight. Marijuana no longer scared
me, but harder drugs did, and I had no intention of buying
anything, even if I had thought to bring money. But the
walk was so thrilling, so forbidden, that when I reached the
other side I turned around and headed back across again.
Back and forth I strolled, absorbing the scene.

I made my way across the crowded beach and when I
didn't see Tommy or any of the old Refuge gang, I decided
to head back to the drug bridge for one last pass. I was
lingering in the middle of the bridge—*chocolate acid,
blotter acid, rainbow acid*—when I noticed a large covered
maintenance truck rumble up to one entrance of the bridge,
then a second identical truck pull to the other end. I was

marveling at how tightly synchronized the trash pickups were when the canvas flaps flew back and from each truck streamed a dozen armed and helmeted riot police, wielding wooden batons. They sealed off the bridge, and suddenly dozens of plastic bags and pill bottles were flying through the air and raining down into the water. It was like the Bible story, except it wasn't manna falling from heaven but marijuana and mescaline.

The cops were pointing and shouting, and one was taking photographs. It was clear they had been watching the dealings for some time and knew who they were after. I fought my way through the pandemonium and tried to squeeze my way off the bridge. "No one on or off," a cop barked, pushing his baton into my chest. I turned and made my way to the other end where I met the same blue wall. "I was just on my way to the snack shack," I pleaded to an officer, so scared my voice quavered. "I got caught in the middle." The cop looked at me, this cloddish kid in glasses and a Catholic-school haircut. "Go on, get out of here," he said and pushed me past.

I was off the bridge, but I was on the island side, separated from my boat by the murky green canal. Besides, now that I wasn't in danger of arrest, I wanted to stick around and watch the drama unfold. A huge throng of kids began to crowd around the bridge. They were pouring off the beaches, surging forward. Soon a few started shouting, hurling insults and swear words.

"Fuck you, pig!" someone shouted. The crowd began to oink and snort. The cops pushed forward with their batons.

"Back! Back!" they shouted.

"Fuck you! Fuck you!"

"Oink! Oink! Oink! Oink!"

From behind me, a bottle flew through the sky, smashing on the pavement among the police officers. Then a second bottle. Then a fusillade of bottles. Soon everything that could fly flew: cans, cups, tubes of suntan oil, half-eaten hot dogs. Some of the officers had moved onto the bridge and were handcuffing and hauling off the drug suspects. The others turned their backs to us, and when they turned back, they were wearing gas masks. A few seconds later, the first canister came lobbing into our midst, sending up a plume of thick smoke. A boy ran forward, holding his shirt over his face, and heaved it back. More canisters arrived to replace it.

The standoff lasted for the better part of two hours before the police arrested everyone they planned to arrest and slowly extricated themselves. The crowd began to dissipate. I knew I had been on the island way too long. I needed to get back across the lake. I crossed the bridge, found the boat undisturbed, raised the sails, and set off.

The local paper was the *Oakland Press,* which my father had hand-delivered as a boy back when it was the *Pontiac Press.* Back when Pontiac was something other than a dying factory town no one wanted their business named after. It was an afternoon paper, arriving on front stoops by 4 P.M.

I was home only a half hour when the phone rang. It was Rock, and he was breathless.

"Jesus Christ! Do you know about the paper?"

"Know what about it?"

"You're on the front page! Your photo. On the front fucking page! Right next to some kid throwing a bottle."

"Hold on," I said and ran to the front porch where the paper lay. I unrolled it, and there, filling the top half of page one, was a photo of a teenager with an angry sneer on his face and his arm cocked back ready to launch a one-quart beer bottle. Several feet behind the youth was a gaggle of other kids. And off to the side of them, standing alone, was a pudgy kid in black-rimmed glasses and baggy shorts. "Holy shit," I cried. "It's me." In the photo, my eyes were on the boy with the bottle and my mouth hung open in sheer dumbfounded amazement. I looked like I had just been delivered to the drug bust by turnip truck.

"Holy shit!" I said again. It was time for evasive action.

I hung up on Rock, made sure Mom was nowhere in sight, and carried the front section of the paper under my T-shirt upstairs, where I stashed it between my mattress and box spring. I raced back downstairs and scattered the other sections of the paper around on the table in what I thought would appear a natural way. Then I summoned Tim and Michael upstairs to our bedroom.

"This better be good," Tim said impatiently. I pulled out the newspaper and handed it to him.

"Holy shit!" Tim said.

"Your ass is grass," Michael said.

"What am I going to do?" I asked.

"We can't let Dad see it," Tim said.

"Must keep it hidden at all costs," Michael said.

"You guys have to cover for me," I begged. "Dad always reads the paper when he gets home." They agreed they would do what they could.

Sure enough, right after dinner, as was his routine, Dad settled into his favorite chair in the living room with the paper. I sat upstairs, silently counting the seconds. *One thousand one, one thousand two, one thousand . . .*

"Who's got the front page?" his voice boomed out.

No answer.

"Has anyone seen the front page?" Silence. "Tim? Mike?" he shouted up the stairs.

"Haven't seen it, Dad," they called back in unison.

"John? Are you up there? Did you take the front page?"

"Not me, Dad," I said.

"Doggone it all, anyway. Who's always taking the paper before I've had a chance to read it?" It was a pet peeve of his.

"Ruth!" he yelled into the kitchen. "Did you throw out the front page already?"

"No, dear," she called back.

I lay on my bed, holding my breath, praying he'd let it go. He huffed around a little while longer, threw around some doggones and son-of-a-guns, and then settled for the latest issue of *National Geographic*. "Doggone it," I heard him mumble to himself. "I pay for a subscription to the paper and then it disappears before I can even see it."

I looked over at my brothers and held up both thumbs. "Close one," I mouthed silently.

The next morning I lay awake in bed, my brothers asleep beside me, thinking about the previous day's events. What was the chance, I thought, that of all those people at the park, I'd be one of a handful to end up on the front page? At least I wasn't the kid throwing the bottle, I thought. Think of the trouble he's in. I began to grin. Now that it was over, it was pretty funny. And what a great story I'd have to tell the old gang. This would show them that a year at an all-boys Catholic school hadn't whipped me. I wouldn't even have to embellish; I had photographic proof of my role, front and center in the bust and subsequent riot. It even involved *tear gas*. Did it get any better than that? No one could deny me my glory. It was a new day, and Dad would be on to the next edition of the paper when he got home. The matter, as far as I was concerned, was officially closed.

As I lay there congratulating myself, the doorbell rang. I heard my mother's voice, "Oh, Father Dan! So nice to see you. Come in, please. How about a cup of coffee?" It was Father Dan O'Sullivan, a young assistant pastor who had joined the parish several years earlier and who oversaw my duties as office boy at the rectory. He was also the priest who, shortly after arriving at the parish, had put an end to the altar-boy wine-pilfering scam once and for all.

Father Dan had become a family friend, and it wasn't unusual for him to stop in unannounced, coincidentally usually at mealtime. Mom would always offer to set another place at the table, and he would always accept. His mooching tactics were transparent, but Mom didn't mind. To have a priest at her table was a great honor, and she was proud that her meals seemed the most mooch-worthy of any in the parish. But on this day, Father Dan wasn't there to eat.

"Did you see yesterday's paper?" he asked. "Did you see John?" His voice was positively buoyant, like he had just discovered I'd made valedictorian.

"John? My John?" Mom said, sounding a bit awestruck herself. "In the paper?"

"Right on the front page!" Father Dan boasted. "Look at this!" He had brought his copy along just in case we wanted an extra. *Oh God.*

Tim looked over at me with one of those you-poor-sorry-bastard looks on his face. I began to count again. *One thousand one. One thous—*

"John Joseph Grogan, you get down here right this instant."

I climbed out of bed and pulled on a pair of shorts. "I mean *now!*" she shouted. Mom stood only five feet even, but when she wanted to, she could be pretty intimidating. Behind her back, my brothers and I had nicknamed her Little Napoleon.

Downstairs, she laid into me. What was I thinking, and who gave me the right, and didn't I know better, and hadn't they raised me to be smarter than that? Even after Father Dan excused himself, she wouldn't let it go. Why did I do these things, and wasn't it a shame, and oh, mother of mercy, and glory be to the Father and the Son and the Holy Spirit, and how does this reflect on the family, did I ever stop to consider that, and won't everyone be talking about the Grogans now? She was like a boxer with her opponent on the ropes, and she just kept pummeling. "I knew we should never have let you switch to West Bloomfield," she said. "I knew it was a mistake. Should we march you straight back to Brother Rice? Is that what you want, mister?"

I spent the whole day in my room, and when Dad got home that evening, I got it even worse. He was the angriest

I had ever seen him. So angry I half expected him to strike me across the face, which is saying a lot, because my father, the man who captured houseflies in his hand like a kung-fu master and released them outdoors unhurt, never hit anyone. All the spanking was left up to Mom.

Not only had I disobeyed him, but I had willingly mingled with drug users and dealers. Worse, I had joined the crowd of rioters instead of retreating. By my very presence, I had fueled a mob and had disrespected and endangered the police officers whose job it was to uphold the laws of this country. Dad was big on respecting authority.

"But I didn't—"

"Shut up," he snapped. Dad never said "shut up." "I don't want your excuses. You listen to me. If I ever—*ever!*—catch you being disrespectful to a police officer, I will kick your ass from one end of this house to the other," he yelled. "Do you understand me?"

It was the first time I had ever heard him use the A-word, and the last time, too. I knew he meant business.

"Yes, Dad," I said and slunk off to begin a long grounding that kept me chained to our yard or my job at the rectory for a good portion of the summer.

On the bright side, I knew every kid at West Bloomfield High would learn, in advance of my arrival, all about the new kid who had ended up on the front page, caught in the middle of the infamous Dodge Park drug riot. Being grounded was no fun, and I felt bad about upsetting Mom and Dad, but it seemed a modest price to pay for such notoriety. Life, I was learning, was full of trade-offs.

❋

As the days of summer whiled by, Mom and Dad gradually calmed down. They stopped threatening to send me back to Brother Rice and stopped wondering aloud where they had gone wrong. By degrees, they loosened the grip on my grounding until I was at last fully free again to sail and swim and hang out at the beach trying, mostly in vain, to catch the attention of the golden, leggy girls stretched out on their terry-cloth towels. I stayed away from Dodge Park; after the bust, I heard it wasn't the same anyway.

Five nights a week I worked until 9:00 at the rectory. Summer nights were deathly quiet there, and some would pass without a single phone call or doorbell ring. The priests were rarely there, and I would pass my three hours reading J. R. R. Tolkien and shooting pool down in the basement. By 9:03 I would be home and back in cutoffs and a T-shirt. Often by 9:10 a knock would come at the door and there would be Tommy, usually with Rock and Sack in tow, asking if I wanted to "take a walk around the neighborhood." A walk around the neighborhood was code for coming out to smoke a joint and then head to the party store for munchies. By the summer before tenth grade,

Tommy had established himself as an enthusiastic devotee of marijuana. He was the hardest worker of all of us, cutting lawns all over the neighborhood, and much of his earnings went to keep him stocked in pot. He always carried a bag, and his generosity was legendary. Tommy didn't care if the rest of us seldom reciprocated. To him, pot smoking was an inherently social act, never meant to be enjoyed alone. He was always happy to share his stash.

Tommy's love of *cannabis sativa* was obvious on first sight. His eyes seemed to have grown permanently bloodshot and his eyelids took on a perpetual droop. To better see, he would tilt his head back to peer through his slits, often with his mouth slightly open in a congenial half grin. He adopted a word that summer that he found fitting for nearly all occasions: *dubious.* In Tommy's hands, the word had multiple meanings, ranging from doubtful to excellent. Often it was simply a statement of agreement.

"Dubious, man," he would say, nodding. "Definitely dubious." Or sometimes: "Indubitably. Most indubitably." In the hierarchy of high-school cliques, Tommy was a poster boy for the one known as the Stoners.

Rock and Sack were less enthusiastic. They would never refuse the pass of a joint, but they seldom bought pot of their own. I was even more ambivalent, and I still tried to fake the deep inhales, worried about getting too high and waking up one day a desperate heroin addict. That's not to say I did not enjoy the effects of marijuana. We would pass a joint and suddenly everything about this world and our place in it seemed hilarious. Simple observations became impossibly profound. Indubitably so. One night we talked at length about the poses in *Playboy,* and Tommy made an impassioned case against rear shots. They were simply, he argued, a waste of ink. "If I want to see a butt, I'll look in the mirror," he said, and I remember thinking, *Wow, exactly, man.* It was a moment of insight like few I'd ever had.

After each one of our late-night "walks," I'd parade back into the house and promptly set about making myself a snack of immense proportions, usually involving multiple pieces of toast plastered in swaths of peanut butter and jelly. Mom and Dad often commented on my late-night cravings.

"Good Lord, John," Dad would say. "Didn't anyone feed you today?"

Mom would add, "I swear that boy has a hollow leg."

But if they ever tied my munchies to marijuana, they never let on. Slightly stoned and happily full, I'd say good night, give Dad the Grogan handshake, and stumble off to bed.

I had inherited my parents' frugality, and I was way too cheap to spend ten hard-earned dollars on a small packet of marijuana, what was known as a dime bag. At my meager pay scale, that was more than three nights of work. Besides, there was little motivation to buy my own when Tommy was constantly offering to share his. I had, however, inherited Dad's passion for plants, and the previous summer I had tended a small vegetable garden in the backyard, raising tomatoes, peppers, eggplants, and green beans. That summer after ninth grade, I added one more crop to my plot: a single bushy marijuana plant.

My fascination with cultivating cannabis had begun a few months earlier, before school let out, when Tommy complained about the large number of seeds in his latest purchase. I was serious enough about my gardening that I started my vegetable plants from seed indoors to get a jump on the growing season. At that very moment, my bedroom windowsills were lined with seedlings, which I nurtured with loving attention. Suddenly I had one of those lightbulb-over-the-head bursts of brilliance: Tommy had extra seeds; I had extra windowsill space. Eureka! Just like Jesus with the miracle of the loaves and fishes, I would transform those tiny, unwanted seeds into a bounty of homegrown marijuana. I picked out a handful of the plumpest seeds and germinated them in paper cups of peat moss. Mixed in with the tomatoes and marigolds, the baby marijuana plants were inconspicuous. Besides, my parents knew next to nothing about illicit substances, despite Dad's recent purchase of a book called something like *Knowing What Your Children Know about Drugs*. I was convinced they wouldn't recognize a marijuana plant if it knocked on the door and introduced itself.

The plants were still quite tiny when Dad came into my bedroom one day and paused to admire my sturdy seedlings. The classic notched five-leaf clusters of the cannabis family smiled up at him. I remained calm. *Dad wouldn't know a marijuana leaf if it bit him in the ass.*

"What are these here?" he asked.

"Those?" I said. "What, the marigolds?"

"No, not the marigolds," he said. "These right here."

"Oh, the eggplants."

"No, not the eggplants. These."

"Oh, *those,*" I exclaimed, as if finally clearing up some lifelong misunderstanding. "Those. Um, those were from a project for science class. We, um, had to grow examples of monocotyledons and dicotyledons. Brother Fallon told us we could take them home if we wanted." Dad stared at me with a look of deep skepticism. "Those are the dicotyledons," I added.

"Dicotyledons?" he asked.

"Yep, the dicotyledons." I was pretty sure I had satisfied his curiosity, and was feeling pleased at the swift-footed agility with which I had done so.

"Dicotyledons," he said one more time.

"Dicotyledons," I repeated.

He hesitated a second, took two steps toward the door, then said, "Well, get rid of them, or we can meet with your science teacher and ask all about them."

Busted. Dad apparently knew more than I had given him credit for. As with so many things involving his children, I could tell he knew but didn't want to know. I imagine it was like the cigarettes he had caught us with in the tent years earlier. He just wanted them to go away so he could return to a state of plausible denial.

I did get rid of the plants, all but one of them. The stockiest one I could not bear to kill. I hid it among the weeds in the vacant lot across the street, protected from the chill air beneath a cloche made from a plastic milk carton whose bottom I had sliced off. And when the weather warmed suitably to plant my garden, I nestled it among the tomato plants, where I was again convinced it would go unnoticed. My sturdy little pot plant prospered there among the Big Boys and Brandywines and indeed went unnoticed for several weeks, through my post–Dodge Park grounding, until its growth began to outpace that of the plants around it. Soon it protruded a foot above the surrounding camouflage. Why I did not realize the folly of this situation, I cannot say, other than to attribute it to the unique qualities of the fifteen-year-old mind. A bushy marijuana plant towering above the tomatoes right in front of the living-room window? Why would anyone notice that?

Then one Saturday, not long after Dad had been out cutting grass, I checked my garden and the plant was gone. A hole stood in the soil where it had been extracted, roots and all. Nearby, on the compost pile, I found its wilted remains. Just to make sure Grogan's Home Grown never found its way back into the earth, Dad had snipped the roots from the stem.

What he didn't consider was that his son just might pick the corpse off the pile and dry the leaves to smoke. When I was done, I had enough dried leaves to roll several joints. One day Rock and I were walking to the shopping plaza, and I lit one up. We both coughed and wheezed. It was the harshest thing I had ever tried inhaling, worse even than Father Joe's old, stubbed-out Lucky Strikes. And as far as any mind-altering effects, we might as well have been smoking pencil shavings. All Grogan's Home Grown gave either of us was a headache. Despite that, I continued to carry a couple of joints with me whenever I went out. Like any farmer, I was proud of my harvest. I knew it wasn't worth smoking, but having my own private stash in my pocket somehow made me feel more street-worthy—and less of a mooch when Tommy broke out his own supply. I could say things like "Or we could smoke one of mine," knowing that no one would ever take me up on the offer.

The last day of summer vacation arrived and with it a bittersweet edge. Every kid in the neighborhood was at the beach, soaking up every possible ray of sunshine, knowing it was our last hoorah before jumping into the new school year. I breathed in the beach's unique fragrance of Coppertone, algae, and cigarette smoke, and captured mental photographs of the girls with their oiled stomachs and legs, fixing them in my mind for another season.

That night, Tommy and Sack showed up at the door. Rock had passed; he was the most academically inclined of us, and his parents didn't want him out the night before the first day of school. "I'm going out for a walk," I called to Dad and headed out the door.

"Don't stay out too late," he called after me. "School tomorrow."

All three of us were in high spirits. The next morning I would be tasting public education for the first time, and Tommy and Sack were talking up the experience, telling me how great it would be. They made West Bloomfield sound a lot like an indoor version of Dodge Park, filled with slinky girls, wild boys, and barely disguised drug abuse. As they portrayed it, no one actually attended classes. Everyone just hung out all day in the parking lot and designated smoking areas, chatting, flirting, and smoking. Our laughter filled the night as we walked down Erie Drive toward The Outlot, steering playfully into each other like bumper cars.

We were right in front of Old Man Pemberton's place when from behind us, out of nowhere, appeared a car that had crept up, lights off. First I heard the squawk of a radio transmission, then the low rumble of an idling engine. I was just turning to see the words TO SERVE AND PROTECT on the door when a spotlight blinded us. Tommy instinctively veered off and began walking across the Pembertons' lawn, his back to the light.

"Right there!" one officer shouted. "The blond kid just dropped something." They were out of the car, rushing toward him, yelling for him to stop, which he did. "Don't move!" they yelled back at Sack and me.

As they descended on Tommy, I reached into my shirt pocket, pulled out the two joints of Grogan's Home Grown, and let them fall in the grass. Then I sauntered toward them.

"All right, up against the car, Cullen." The cops knew Tommy by name. One searched him, finding rolling papers and a small pipe, as the other retrieved the plastic bag Tommy had dropped. They placed him in the backseat and closed the door, then turned to Sack and me. I recognized the older cop as Sergeant Glover, a fixture around town, and the younger one as Officer Reisler, who had lived next door to us when he was a teenager.

"Do you two have anything on you?" Glover asked. "Don't lie to me. What are you carrying?"

"Nothing," we insisted in chorus.

"We were just out for a walk," I said.

The cops stared at us. They looked almost ready to buy it. Tommy was the one who had been on their radar for months.

"Honest, we don't have anything," Sack said, those giant brown eyes of his growing as big and liquid as puddles.

To help make the case, I added: "You can search us if you want." The words were not even out of my mouth before I knew I had made a horrible mistake. I could see it on Sack's face, which went instantly gray.

"Let's just do that," Sergeant Glover said, and they pushed both of us up against the squad car and began patting us down. Sack looked over at me the way I imagine Jesus looked at Judas at the moment of betrayal. "Nothing, huh?" Sergeant Glover said as he pulled a brass hash pipe from Sack's front pants pocket. I had forgotten about his pipe. "You just earned yourself a free ride to the station," he said and put Sack in the backseat with Tommy.

I came up clean, as I knew I would, and they never spotted the two joints in the grass. Officer Reisler led me around to the back of the car and got close to my face.

"Do you remember me? Do you remember me from next door when you were a little kid?" I told him I did. "Do you know what this would do to your father? Do you have any idea how this would crush him?" I shrugged. "Your father is a great man. Do you realize that? Do you know how outstanding your father is? He doesn't deserve this. This would kill him. You want to put your father in the grave?"

I thought he was being a little dramatic, but I just nodded and looked at my feet.

"All right, what else are you into?" he asked. "Acid? Speed? Downers? Don't bullshit me. What else?" I swore I hadn't tried any of those things, and I hadn't. "Just pot once in a while," I said, and he seemed to take me at my word.

"You want me to take you down to the station with your pals and have your dad come pick you up? Is that what you want? You want your dad to see you in the lockup?" I said I didn't. Then he started back in on what it would do to my great father, the sudden death by broken heart. "If it wasn't for how much I respect your father, I'd haul your ass in. I don't give a shit about you. But your father I care about." I nodded that I understood.

"This is what I'm going to do," Officer Reisler said. "I'm going to let you turn around and walk home. You're going to go straight home, and you're going to keep your nose clean, understand? I'm going to be watching you. I am going to be watching every step you take. Got it?"

"Yes, sir," I said. He walked around the car and got in front with Sergeant Glover. The car pulled away, and as it did, Tommy and Sack both turned and looked out the rear window at me. They didn't look angry, not even betrayed. Just scared. Scared and small and fragile. Part of me wanted to be in there with them.

I waited until the car disappeared around the curve, then I turned and ran. Ran as fast as I could. But I didn't run straight home as Officer Reisler had ordered. I cut through a neighbor's side yard and jumped a fence, then another and another, weaving through the backyards until I was at Rock's door. He answered and instantly knew something was wrong.

"What happened?" he whispered.

"Just get out here," I said.

He pulled the door shut and followed me into the dark and behind a row of shrubs where we could lie in the grass unseen. I was convinced the squad car was going to make another pass at any second to make sure I had not disobeyed. My breath came out in jagged gasps, and I could feel my hands shaking. Rock listened intently as I recounted the entire event. When I was done, he thought for a moment and I waited for him to say something reassuring. "You mean you *told* them to search you?" he asked. It was, I would learn, the main takeaway point of the whole tangled story. I had not simply stood by and *allowed* the police to pat down my best friend. I had *invited* them to. Offered it up like a party favor. *You can search us if you want.*

Rock and I lay out in the wet grass, watching the Cullen and Sacorelli houses from behind the bushes. Fifteen minutes passed before we saw Mr. Cullen start his pickup truck and drive off, his headlights sweeping briefly over us as he pulled out of his driveway. A few minutes later, Mr. Sacorelli followed. We waited out there until both vehicles returned and both fathers marched their sons silently inside.

Two of my three best friends had been arrested, and I had not. The third was trying to understand why I would have suggested a police search. In the morning, I would land for the first time in that unknown, intimidating world known as public high school. I had a bad feeling about the welcome I would receive. A very bad feeling.

After the lights went off in the Cullen and Sacorelli homes, I said good-bye to Rock and cut through the backyards to my house, where I found Dad in his chair, reading and eating peanuts with chopsticks.

"No snack tonight?" he asked.

"Not very hungry," I said. "I'm just going to bed." We shook hands, and I headed upstairs.

In the weeks and months that followed, Officer Reisler stayed true to his word, pulling his squad car to the curb in front of our house whenever he passed by. If I was outside, he would stare at me through his windshield. Sometimes he would sit there for an hour, doing his paperwork. If Dad was in the yard with me, cutting grass or raking leaves, Reisler would look me in the eyes, then look across the yard at my oblivious father trotting along behind the Gravely. He'd look back at me, and I could almost hear his words: *Do you have any idea what this would do to him?*

For the life of him, Dad couldn't figure out why the police kept pulling up directly in front of our house to idle their cars and fill out their reports. He didn't notice it was always the same officer. "There they are again," he would say, marveling as if he were witnessing a great mystery of nature. "That's the darnedest thing. They have the entire town to patrol, and every doggone Saturday they pull up here and just sit. It's almost like clockwork."

"No idea, Dad," I would say.

"Huh. Me, either." And he'd scratch his head and return to his work.

I lived in dread that one day his curiosity would get the better of him and he'd walk up to the squad car, knock on the glass, and inquire. But he never did, and Officer Reisler never divulged my secret.

It was Tommy's dad who nearly exposed me. A couple of weeks after retrieving their son from the police station, Mr. and Mrs. Cullen were passing by on their evening walk. I watched helplessly from the next room as Mom spotted them and opened the front door. "Hello there, Bevan! Hi, Claire!" she called out. *No, Mom, don't do this.* Mr. Cullen was the last person I wanted to face. *Please, Mom. Please don't . . .* "How about a nice cup of tea?" *Oh, Mom.* They turned up the driveway, and I raced to the top of the stairs, just out of sight. Mr. Cullen ran hot in the best of circumstances and was never one to mince words. Once, when a teenage driver flipped Mr. Cullen the middle finger over some traffic dispute, Mr. Cullen chased him for miles in the family van with his wife and all six children aboard, finally catching the kid at a traffic light, jumping out, and pounding on his windshield. My chest tightened and I felt my stomach twist.

At first the conversation was filled with pleasant small talk. Mom poured tea for Mrs. Cullen and herself; Dad brought out two beers. That's when the conversation turned to children.

"Don't get me started about the children in this neighborhood," Mr. Cullen said. "They're all angels, aren't they? All perfect, bloody little angels. All of them except my sons."

I heard my mother clear her throat nervously.

"If there's marijuana, it's gotta be the Cullen boys. If there's drinkin' goin' on, well, certainly it must be the

Cullen boys. If anything happens in the neighborhood, haul in the Cullen boys. They're never alone when it happens, but they always are when the blame comes down." Then he changed his voice to mimic a spoiled schoolboy. " 'Oh, it wasn't me, Mum; it wasn't me, Pop. It was all the Cullen boys. I told 'em not to, Mum. I ran the other way, Pop.' It's always the Cullen boys, and let me tell you"—and he paused for emphasis—"I'm bloody goddamn sick of it." I knew how he looked when he got worked up, the way the veins popped out on his temples and his forehead went crimson. I knew that's how he looked right now. "What the bloody hell, mon? I'm not making excuses for my boys. I know they're not perfect. Boys are gonna do what boys will do. I did it, too. But the parents around here need to get their bloody heads out of the sand and open their eyes."

From my parents' polite, awkward responses I could tell they were trying to figure out exactly what he was telling them—and at the same time not wanting to know. It was a comfortable pattern in our family: the less known and the less said, the better. Mom and Dad never asked Mr. Cullen to elaborate, and they never asked me to, either. For that, I was grateful.

❖

I f life at Brother Rice had been isolated and hollow, at West Bloomfield High it was something altogether lonelier. At least at Brother Rice I was physically removed from those I cared about and could pretend they still cared about me. At the new school my old friends swirled around me, already comfortably ensconced in their social circles, and I hung awkwardly on the edge like a man clinging to a cliff, waiting in vain for a hand up. The bad feeling in my gut the night of Tommy's and Sack's arrest turned out to be well founded. I was the Catholic schoolkid no one wanted to be seen with, the one who had gotten his best friend busted. Some of my old Refuge pals openly shunned me. Doggie, so concerned about currying favor with the cool crowd, would walk right past me in the hallway without so much as a nod.

Tommy and Sack were more gracious. They both managed to forgive me for that night and held no grudges, but they had their own friends now. Tommy was surrounded by stoners and dopers who went through each day in a mind-altered stupor. Sack was constantly trailed by a harem of boy-crazy girls in hip-hugger bell-bottoms about whom he was too shy to do anything but blush. Rock had found his own niche, too, in the music and drama cliques. Then there was me, a clique of one.

Now that I was free from the dress and grooming codes of Brother Rice, my uniform became bell-bottoms and flannel shirts, and I began to grow my hair out. But unlike Sack's hair, a satiny black mane that fell straight to his shoulders, mine was as ornery as a Brillo pad. For every inch it grew in length, it expanded two inches sideways. By the time it reached my shoulders, my exploding jungle of kinky curls gave me the look of an active volcano. Adding to my look were my new glasses, which were an oversize aviator design in tortoiseshell frames. What might have looked hip on Peter Fonda in *Easy Rider,* on me, with my thick, soda-bottle prescription, had quite a different effect. The first time she saw me in them, Mom cried out, "What were you thinking? You look like a raccoon!" She later apologized, but moms are usually right, and this time so was mine.

Mom was right about something else, too. That fall I began dropping weight at a rapid clip without trying, and I was convinced there was only one possible explanation: I had cancer. What else could it be? I was dying, it was obvious, and what a tragedy it was, given my tender years. After weeks of working myself into a panic, I went to Mom and confided my all-but-certain terminal illness. Mom didn't miss a beat. She threw her head back and had a good laugh. "Cancer? Honey, you don't have cancer," she said, wiping a tear from her eye. "You're just losing your baby fat."

Tommy and Sack and Rock tried to include me in their social groups, and we all sat together at lunch, but somehow something had changed. I stumbled through that first year at West Bloomfield in a fog, putting one foot in front of the other, marching dutifully from class to class, but not feeling fully there. My grades reflected it.

In the course of one semester, I went from As and Bs at Brother Rice to mostly Ds. Algebra II was particularly vexing for me. Unlike at the Catholic school, there was no Math for Dummies track; the whiz kids and the struggling students were all clumped together. It didn't take me long to become hopelessly lost. The teacher was an attractive woman a few years out of college with bright eyes and long blond hair. She was funny and sweet, and I wanted to impress her. At first I raised my hand when she asked if there were questions, but after the third or fourth explanation that only bewildered me more, I stopped raising my hand. There were only so many times I could say, "I still don't get it." She gave up on me, and I gave up on algebra. I simply started taking my best wild guesses, with disastrous results.

When Mom and Dad saw my report card, I thought they would blow double gaskets. I braced myself for the "We should never have let you transfer to public school" speech, but they surprised me. I can only guess they somehow understood what a rocky transition I was having. They said what they always said when I underperformed: "All we ask is that you try your hardest. Your best is good enough for us." I nodded along, but I knew in my heart I wasn't even doing that.

The biggest difference between parochial and public education, I learned that year, had nothing to do with uniforms or prayers at the start and close of each school day. The biggest difference was that teachers in Catholic schools did not allow you to fail. If they had to ride you every day of the school year, they would. If they had to beat the knowledge into you, they would. At West Bloomfield, the teachers offered learning the way waiters offer canapés at a cocktail party. You could help yourself or wave them away. If I wanted to learn, they would teach me; if I chose not to, they were happy to ignore me. After nine years of Catholic education, where the nuns and brothers forced performance, often by threat of physical pain, I was free to fail.

Complicating my academic prospects was the way I chose to commute to school each morning. Rock faithfully took the bus or caught a ride with his father on the way to work, but Tommy declared school buses the ultimate in uncool and began hitchhiking the four-mile route. Soon Sack and I were joining him. In rain, in sleet, through two feet of snow, and most of the year in the dark before dawn, we would trudge the half mile to the corner across from the party store and stick out our thumbs. Often on the way Tommy would light a joint to pass. Depending on the difficulty we had getting a ride—not just anyone would stop for three teenage boys—I would arrive at school not only late but stoned as well. My first class was French—another course in which I was tanking—and one morning the teacher asked me to stand and tell the class something about myself. All I could think to say was *"Je m'appelle Jean. Je suis très fatigué."* Very tired and very fried.

There was only one class in which I excelled, and that was American literature. The teacher, Christine Shotwell, was just out of college and, unlike my algebra teacher, not the stuff of teenage crushes. She sported sensible eyeglasses and a no-fuss haircut. For some reason, she took an interest in me, and I read everything she threw at me: *The Crucible, The Scarlet Letter, Of Mice and Men, The Old Man and the Sea*. I fell in love with Steinbeck and Hemingway and the worlds they portrayed, so far removed from my own. Then I discovered J. D. Salinger and *The Catcher in the Rye*. In Holden Caulfield I found a teenager every bit as bewildered and awkward as I was. On every page I recognized a little piece of myself. In Holden, I found a soul mate.

One day after class, Mrs. Shotwell stopped me on my way out the door. "I was wondering," she said, "have you ever thought about keeping a journal?" I dabbled in little satires and attempts at humor, but a diary of my own thoughts and feelings had never occurred to me. "I think you ought to try it," she said. "Who knows what might spill out?" I took her advice, and soon I was hooked. I kept the journal for myself but also for her, an adult who for the first time seemed to care what was locked inside me. The more I shared with her, the more her feedback—wise and heartfelt and never patronizing or judgmental—fueled my desire to write.

Shortly after school let out for the summer, Tommy called with exciting news. Saint Mary's was hosting a large casino-night fund-raiser for its most generous benefactors. It would be a men's night of eating, drinking, gambling, and smoking cigars, and the college was recruiting neighborhood kids for a variety of jobs, working for tips.

"It's gonna be easy money," Tommy promised.

"Count me in," I said. As luck would have it, Tommy and I, and several of our friends, were assigned to the bar service. Not only were the drinkers rumored to be the best tippers of all, but our jobs allowed us to easily swipe a few extra beers for ourselves.

At the end of the night, our pockets stuffed with tips and our stomachs with leftover food, we retrieved our purloined beers from the ditch where we had stashed them, and made our way across Commerce Road and through the dark neighborhood to the smoking tree, which over the years had become more of a toking-and-drinking tree.

"Beautiful!" Tommy exclaimed, cracking open a lukewarm brew. "Is this fucking beautiful or what?"

"It's fucking beautiful," I agreed, and we all toasted with a clink of bottles. "Indubitably so."

And beautiful it was. I was back with my friends, back in the fold, accepted once again. Sitting shoulder to shoulder on the beach, feet in the water, we laughed and ribbed and prodded each other just like old times. Only one thing was different. Tommy lit a joint to share, and when it came to me I passed it along without lifting it to my lips and without feeling the need to. I had survived tenth grade without self-destructing and picked up some valuable pointers along the way. One of them was that if you had to impress your friends to keep them, they weren't really friends in the first place. I was figuring out that life was too short and brilliant to spend it suspended in a marijuana cloud. However my life was meant to turn out, it was mine alone to seize or squander. No one else was going to do it for me.

Tommy let out a whoop, and so did I. We had made it to another endless summer. I took a swig of beer and let my body sink into the cool damp sand. Indubitably beautiful, indeed.

⁂

Not long into junior year, I found my niche at West Bloomfield—in the grungy, cramped office of the student newspaper.

The *Spectrum* drew a motley assemblage of students, most of whom did not fit in anywhere else. Tommy was solidly off on the tech-ed track by now, but Sack, Rock, and I, sensing an easy elective, signed on as staff writers. The paper was appallingly bad, even by high-school standards; so bad, in fact, that nearly everyone around school, students and teachers alike, referred to it as the *Rectum*. The paper offered the obligatory news on sports and extracurricular activities, uncritical reviews of school musicals, and predictable editorials (cafeteria food bad; student rights good). But mostly it contained rambling diatribes about whatever topic tickled an individual staffer's fancy: women's rights, Elton John's latest tour, the environment, acupuncture. After buying a pair of Earth Shoes, the negative-heel Danish footwear that was all the rage then, Sack was inspired to write a two-page celebration of their many virtues. Rock gushed at length about Bob Dylan's newly released *Blood on the Tracks*. For reasons I'm still not sure of, I weighed in on

Transcendental Meditation, which I had never tried and knew almost nothing about.

Our student adviser, an easygoing teacher named Ms. Pappas, provided abundant freedom but little structure or guidance and almost no quality standards. She let us get away with sloppy, lazy work, and our copy went into print riddled with spelling and grammatical errors. Where was the exacting Brother McKenna when we needed him? I did my part to help the *Rectum* maintain its reputation for mediocrity, cranking out whatever drivel required the least amount of time and energy.

There were a few students attempting serious journalism, and one of them penned a piece titled "Fact and Fiction about Gay Life." It was a thoughtful, intelligent essay that was well researched. Ms. Pappas cleared it for publication and sent the issue off to the printer. But when the *Spectrum* came off the presses and we opened it to page 24, a prominent chunk of the text was missing, replaced by an empty white rectangle. There was only one possible culprit: Mr. Cavin. Our principal insisted on reviewing every galley before releasing it to the printer.

He had held up publication in the past to demand we remove or rewrite stories he found too controversial or provocative, but this was the first time he had censored an article without informing our adviser in advance. He had simply papered over the section he did not like. It was an act that would galvanize us as young journalists. My fellow *Spectrum* staffers and I were outraged. Where were our constitutional rights? Where was our freedom of expression? Did the First Amendment not apply to us? The *Spectrum* received no money from the school district, surviving entirely on its own meager revenues from advertisements and the 25-cent cover price. Didn't that make us quasi-independent? Ms. Pappas tried to calm us, but we could tell she was upset, too, and felt just as violated.

I reacted by marching to the public library and checking out a book I had browsed through before—a book on the radical underground press. It was a topic that had fascinated me for several years, ever since visiting Marijo at the University of Michigan at the height of the antiwar movement. In my bedroom, I read through the case studies of various underground newspapers, many of which sprang to life during the counterculture movement of the late 1960s. They were to mainstream papers what espresso was to instant coffee; I found them impossibly romantic and edgy. I was especially smitten by the *Fifth Estate,* an underground paper started in Detroit several years earlier by a seventeen-year-old in his parents' basement. It had grown into one of the country's most prominent and longest-running alternative voices, providing a platform for the likes of Michigan's homegrown radical John Sinclair, head of the White Panther Party. If that kid could do it, why couldn't I?

I began to dream in earnest. What if I launched my very own underground paper at West Bloomfield High? What if we wrote whatever we wanted in it, and distributed it without anyone's permission? What if we used words as weapons to challenge the school administration? My mind raced, and I pulled out a notebook and began capturing ideas. For several days, I could barely sleep. By the end

of the week I had a mission statement, several possible
names, and a list of potential story topics. I laid out my
plan to Rock and Sack, and they immediately signed on
as my coeditors. Together, we recruited a small army of
students eager to participate. Others sought us out and
asked to join. Everyone, it seemed, wanted to stick it to
The Man.

Most of the volunteers were boys, but among them
were three girls in my grade whom I had seen around
school but did not know well. They had impressed me
the previous year, however, by smiling sympathetically
at me in the hallway at a time when it seemed every
other student had ostracized me. In the stratified world
of West Bloomfield cliques, Lori, Sue, and Anna were
solidly in the one known as the Hippie Chicks. They
eschewed makeup and favored muslin peasant smocks
and beads. Sue was tiny with a freckled face surrounded
by a crown of ringlets that reminded me of Little Orphan
Annie. Lori was tall and lanky with long sand-colored hair
into which she was always braiding whatever she had at
hand: flowers, beads, yarn, ribbon. Anna was the most
exotic of the three with a deep mocha complexion and a
jungle of dark, frizzy hair even wilder than mine. In the
summer, when her skin was especially dark, strangers
occasionally mistook her for black. The three of them
were constantly together, so much so that it had become
a joke around school. People called out to them as if to
a single entity: *Lorisueanna.* I sensed I was just enough
of an outcast at school to make me vaguely interesting
to them. I found them interesting, too, if a little earnest,

and though I wouldn't dare admit it even to my best friends, cute. Girls were alien goddesses I admired from afar but could seldom summon the courage to approach. Now I would be working side by side with these three, a prospect I found exhilarating.

We named our nascent publication *Innervisions,* inspired by (some would charge ripped off from) the Stevie Wonder album of the same name that had come out the previous summer. Beneath it we added the tagline "West Bloomfield's Independent Student Press." The newly assembled staff began gathering after school to write, edit, and lay out pages. Our only publishing tools were a pair of electric typewriters, which meant that the only way to typeset our copy was to hand-type our stories into narrow columns, starting over every time we made a mistake. It was tedious, infuriating work, but we stuck with it, day after day. When the copy was finally all in columns, we cut them out with scissors and pasted them onto page dummies, where we added rub-on headlines, photographs, and simple line drawings. Sack's piece, titled "What the Hell's Profanity?" made a spirited defense of foul language by using as much of it as he could work in. Rock delivered a screed about the school's ban on students leaving the campus for lunch. I busted on my drafting teacher for giving students extra credit for buying tickets to the basketball games he coached. I also penned the front-page essay explaining the mission of *Innervisions*. "This paper does not kiss ass to the parents and other adults of the community by printing only what they want to hear in order to feel more secure," I wrote in grand fashion.

Yet for all my bluster, I toiled for hours on this labor of love without daring to breathe a word about it to my own parents. *Innervisions* was filled with foul language, drug humor, and disrespectful portrayals of authority figures. One cartoon showed the vice principal with a tag on his ankle labeling him "Grade A Bullshit." Another was a drug-addled spoof of the Peanuts comic strip showing "Loosie" and a goateed Charlie Brown smoking catnip in Snoopy's doghouse. Before Dad found and ripped out my marijuana plant growing among the tomatoes, I proudly photographed it, and that picture made its way onto page 3 to illustrate an irreverent—some would say sacrilegious—biblical parody titled "The Parable of the Lids and the Busches." In it, a rock star named Messiah, surrounded by his twelve faithful roadies, multiplied two bags of pot and four beers into enough mind-altering substances to inebriate a stadium filled with five thousand concertgoers. I knew Mom and Dad would definitely not see the humor in any of it.

I was pouring my soul into something I believed in, something I was proud of, something that for the first time in my life gave me the thrill of accomplishment. Yet I could not bring myself to share it with them. I knew they would disapprove. I could see the hurt on their faces and hear the dismay in their voices. In truth, much of the content that I knew would offend them also bothered me. Nearly all the drug humor came from a single student, a senior by the name of Justin Jorgenson, who had signed on as the fourth coeditor and who funneled his considerable creative talent into juvenile humor. He and I argued bitterly over creative control. I pushed for hard-hitting social commentary; he for off-color parody with shock value. I wanted the *Fifth Estate* meets the *Village Voice;* Justin wanted *Mad* magazine meets *High Times*. In the end, I kept the worst of it out, but only the worst.

On the morning of April 7, 1974, my cohorts and I arrived on campus with 900 copies of the eight-page debut issue of *Innervisions*, printed on mint-green paper, under our arms. We fanned out through the hallways, bathrooms, and courtyard, quietly peddling them for a dime each. Curiosity ran high, and sales were brisk. Teachers were our best customers of all, often buying multiple copies. Several of them slipped us five- and ten-dollar bills to help defray our printing costs. The whole school was buzzing about "the new underground paper," and by third hour, we had sold 750 copies, covering our seventy-five-dollar printing tab in full. With the donations from teachers, we were already in the black with 150 copies still to sell. Life as an underground newspaper editor seemed every bit as romantic as I had imagined it would be.

The next period, all four editors—we had brashly listed our names on the masthead—were summoned out of class to Principal Cavin's office. He invited us to have seats and opened on a congenial note, telling us how surprised he was to see our "little newsletter" and complimenting us on our initiative. "Quite frankly," he observed, "I didn't think you four had it in you."

As principal, he said, he always liked to encourage students to pursue their passions, even if ours were misguided and immature. "I hardly know where to begin," he said and slid a copy of the paper in front of us. He went right to the catnip cartoon, then flipped the page and tapped his finger ominously on the photo of my marijuana plant. "Pro-drug messages," he said with a heavy voice. "And this," he said, slapping his palm down on the Messiah parable. "You find this amusing? Not only does it glorify drug abuse, it offends religious belief." He went through the issue page by page, pointing out the many transgressions that made *Innervisions* totally inappropriate for distribution on campus.

"And this," he said, pointing to the cartoon of the vice principal labeled as "Grade A Bullshit." "This defames Mr. Coe's character."

"That's impossible," Justin, the lippiest among us, shot back. "Mr. Coe has no character to defame."

"Zip it," Cavin ordered.

What seemed to rankle him most was the letter we printed in full from our beloved and highly respected humanities teacher. Linda Miller Atkinson had turned me on to Greek architecture and Roman sculpture. She helped me see the beauty in the dribbles of a Pollock abstract and the blurry watercolors of a Monet. She began each class by turning off the lights and playing Stravinsky's *Rite of Spring*. Now she was leaving in frustration and disgust—and she had slipped us a copy of her scathing resignation letter. *Innervisions* had an exclusive.

"You had no right to print this," Cavin said, his voice tensing in a way that let me know our goal of wounding the enemy with well-aimed words had worked. "This is privileged workplace correspondence." He then began rattling off a long list of school district policies we had violated: unsanctioned activities on campus, soliciting funds without authorization, use of profanity, promotion of illegal activities, defamation of character, and the catchall "portraying students and faculty in ways not in the best interest of the school district." He ordered us to cease and desist immediately and to turn over all unsold copies.

If we wanted to produce future issues of our publication, that was fine with him, Cavin said, but with two stipulations. We would have to give it away for free. And every word would have to be preapproved by the administration.

"So more censorship," I said.

"You know, boys, freedom of speech is a big, big responsibility," he said. "Bigger than you understand. You've shown you're not capable of grasping that responsibility."

He warned us that if we didn't comply we would face serious disciplinary action. "I won't have this crap in my school, do you understand?" he said. Then, pausing to look each of us in the eye: "And I will be calling your parents."

The heady experience of a free press had lasted exactly four hours. We handed over the remaining copies we had on us and filed out. We quickly found out, however, that being hauled to the principal's office for a stern upbraiding was not without its rewards. Throngs of kids—including girls who had never before deigned to acknowledge our existence—gathered around us, asking for every detail. We gladly obliged, embellishing with abandon our martyrdom on the altar of an unfettered press. For the first time since arriving at West Bloomfield, I was at the center of attention. I had rattled the establishment; I had made waves. I had gotten people talking and thinking. Right then and there, I decided my future calling. I was going to be a journalist.

When Dad arrived home that evening, I greeted him at the door with our customary handshake, then handed him a copy of *Innervisions*. I handed one to Mom, too. Cavin had not called yet; I figured I was better off breaking the news to them myself. Besides, the community weekly newspaper had interviewed us for a story it was running on the new unauthorized student publication, and I knew from experience that there was no hiding the paper from Dad.

"What's this?" he asked.

"Just something I've been working on the last couple months," I said. "I'd like you to read it."

He and Mom sat at the kitchen table and began reading in silence, and I stood in the next room, waiting for what seemed forever. When they called me in, they didn't yell or threaten to send me back to Brother Rice. They asked a lot of questions, and I told them the whole story, starting with the principal censoring our student paper.

"You came up with this all on your own?" Dad asked.

"Yeah," I said.

"And no one helped you put this together?"

"Just us."

He paged through it once more. "I don't agree with everything you say in here," he said. "Not by a long shot. But I respect what you've done. You stood up for what you believe. That's important."

That's when I saw it on his face, a look I had seen before but not often. A look that told me what he couldn't bring himself to say, not without undermining the principal's authority, yet his expression was as clear to me as the written word: a parent's pride. My conservative, buttoned-down, play-by-the-rules father was proud of his son for breaking rules and speaking out against a perceived injustice. He was proud of me, I imagined, for finally finding the gumption to undertake something, anything, that required focus and discipline. Probably more than anything, he was proud of me for believing strongly enough in a cause to fight for it, even if it was not the cause he had hoped for.

"If you ask me, that principal got what he had coming," Mom said. "Covering over that girl's story without even telling anyone. Why, the nerve of him!"

"Can we eat dinner now?" I asked.

"Heavens, yes," Mom said. "Go wash your hands."

If *Innervisions* was all the buzz at West Bloomfield that week, Pete Grunwald's big party was the only topic on anyone's tongue when classes resumed after the weekend. Pete was a charter member of the Stoners and Potheads and never passed up an opportunity to party. When his parents decided to head off to a heating-and-cooling convention and leave Pete alone for the weekend, he went into high gear.

By the time Tommy, Sack, Rock, and I arrived, cars lined both sides of the street for blocks in either direction. The yard was filled with teens, many of whom I did not recognize, smoking and drinking beer from plastic cups. Inside, the place was a sardine can of sweating, shoulder-to-shoulder humanity. Marijuana and cigarette smoke choked the air, and Led Zeppelin blasted from the stereo. The legal drinking age in Michigan was eighteen then, and Pete had enlisted a group of seniors to buy kegs of beer, which sat on ice in the laundry room.

The house was trashed. How he was going to hide this from his parents when they returned, I couldn't imagine. But when I finally bumped into him in the crowd, he looked up from taking a long hit off a joint and smiled beatifically like he had not a care in the world.

I made it to the keg and poured a beer, and when I turned around I saw I had lost Tommy, Rock, and Sack. I also noticed couples peeling off and heading upstairs. Despite a nonstop series of crushes and infatuations, I still had not so much as kissed a girl. Until recently, I had been able to find consolation in the knowledge that no one else in my inner circle had, either, but over spring vacation, Sack had finally overcome his shyness enough to have his first make-out session—and the girl was a year older, which made his good fortune all the more enviable. I watched the couplings at the party with a combination of envy and heartache.

"Hey, Mr. Editor Man," I heard in my ear, and when I turned around, there stood Lori, Sue, and Anna, as always clustered so tightly together as to appear singular. They had worked hard on *Innervisions,* uncomplainingly taking on many of the most tedious tasks. I was grateful to them, and had grown close to all three of them.

"Lorisueanna! Hi," I said. We tried talking over the blaring music, but it was nearly impossible.

"Let's get out of here," Anna shouted, and we squeezed our way toward the door. Pete's house overlooked a large pond lined with cattails, and we walked down to the water's edge where a couple of dozen others had gathered. A kid who had taken it upon himself to play host wandered through the yard, filling beer glasses from a pitcher. We stood and drank and talked. Then, as if by some mysterious, preordained signal, Anna and Sue disappeared. One instant they were there, the next they had simply vanished. It was the first time I could remember the three of them not being together, and I half expected Lori to fly into a panic, but when I looked at her, she didn't seem concerned at all.

A canoe lay overturned at the water's edge, and we sat on it and looked up at the stars. In the moonlight, I had to admit she looked lovely. As we made small talk, I studied her upturned nose, delicate neck, and round cheeks. The magnitude of the moment was not lost on me. Here was a girl sitting right beside me in the dark—with her coterie dismissed. And she was acting like there was no place on earth she would rather be. I reached up and touched her hair spilling like a waterfall down her back. She leaned slightly into me and let out a purr. I moved my arm behind her until I had it around her waist. *Holy Christ,* I thought, *this is it!* In slow motion, our faces inched closer until our cheeks brushed; then we turned our heads and let our lips touch. I kissed her once gently, like you might kiss your grandmother. Twice. On the third peck, Lori wedged my head in her hands and shoved her tongue into my mouth. I had spent the last five years imagining what French kissing would be like, but I never imagined it could come on so abruptly. I always thought it was something you worked up to, over weeks and months. Lori's tongue was a fearsome thing, lashing and licking and darting about. Her teeth were more fearsome yet. They gnashed and clacked and nipped at my lips and tongue. This wouldn't have been an issue except that Lori was an orthodontist's early retirement dream; she had enough metal in her mouth to clad Old Ironsides with plenty left over for the *Monitor* and the *Merrimack*. French kissing with Lori was a little like French kissing with a power tool. I spent half the time marveling at my amazing luck and the other half trying to prevent serious injury.

Lori was a lioness. We smashed our mouths together, clacked our teeth, and banged noses. Our hands roamed freely over each other. But as the night stretched on, I found myself feeling increasingly . . . restless. Restless and trapped. I found myself opening one eye to peer over her shoulder, looking for an excuse to break away.

Finally I got my break. Tommy's voice boomed down the hill. "Hey, Grogie," he yelled. "If you're coming with us, get your ass up here." I hastily excused myself from Lori, gave her a few just-for-Grandma parting lip pecks, and raced off to rejoin my friends, who grilled me for details the whole way home. I was giddy at my conquest, even if it was not exactly the earth-moving experience I had dreamed of.

The next morning I awoke late. When I walked downstairs, Mom and Dad were already home from Mass, drinking coffee and chatting at the kitchen table. The instant they saw me they went silent. They stared not into my eyes but at a spot slightly above and to the right of my upper lip.

"What?" I asked.

"Nothing," Dad replied.

Then Mom, in her don't-ask-don't-tell voice: "So how was the party last night?"

"Pretty good," I said.

"You had a nice time?"

"Okay," I said. "Nothing special."

"Did people dance?"

"No, Mom, no one danced."

"Then what did everyone do all night?"

"Just stood around and talked," I said.

They continued to gaze at the spot above my lip, their heads cocked quizzically.

I excused myself and headed to the bathroom. In the mirror, I saw what had so intrigued them. Just above my upper lip, my skin was missing. Lioness Lori had gnawed a nickel-size piece of my face off. The wound was a brilliant red and oozed a clear liquid. I was certain it was visible from outer space and could tell it would take weeks to disappear. There was no mistaking the injury. I had been mauled either by a rabid raccoon or by an overzealous make-out partner with braces. Mom and Dad knew better than to ask. My parents would spend the next three weeks dutifully pretending they did not notice the giant scab above my mouth. My real dread was returning to school the next day. The only one who would be more humiliated than I was the girl whose dangerous teeth had inflicted such injury. The one every boy in our class would henceforth know affectionately as Ole Razorblades.

Mom tapped on the door. "Honey, hurry it up or you'll miss the eleven o'clock and have to wait till the twelve-thirty."

Oh shit. Sunday. Mass.

"Be right out, Ma," I called. At least there would be no one to see me where I was heading, across Commerce Road to the shores of Orchard Lake and the Church of Tim and John.

❖

My upper lip eventually healed, and Lori and I survived the taunts of our classmates. They could tease us all they wanted; what they couldn't do was take away the notoriety we now enjoyed as one of the school's hot make-out couples. "They're just jealous," Lori said to me one day in the cafeteria, and I was quick to believe it. Still, she didn't seem any more impressed with my kissing prowess than I was with hers. Neither of us initiated a repeat engagement. But I wore my lip scab with pride until the day it finally fell off—proof positive that the awkward kid with the big hair and big glasses had finally been kissed.

As the school year wound down, my cohorts and I managed to put out a second issue of *Innervisions,* but it wasn't the same. The excitement and passion of the first issue were gone, replaced by a sort of dull, dutiful tedium. We toiled away with all the joy of taxpayers preparing for an audit. Our main motivation was pride. We didn't want Cavin and the school board to think they had bullied us into submission. More important, we didn't want the teachers and our fellow students to think it.

Work on the second and, as it would turn out, final issue was marked by apathy and bitter infighting. Many of our contributors drifted away, and those who remained turned in lazy ramblings not much edgier than the dross running in the *Spectrum*. The only one still cranking out copy at a furious pace was Justin, and it was more juvenile and offensive than ever. I hated all of it, but with the dearth of copy from anyone else, nearly all of it made it in. Mom and Dad were vaguely aware we were working on a second issue, but I knew they weren't expecting this.

We couldn't buckle to Cavin's demands, not if we were to retain a shred of credibility, but we also knew we couldn't openly defy him. He was watching now, and he would swoop in and seize all our copies within minutes of us carrying them onto school property. In the end, we decided to produce and sell the paper completely off school grounds, safely beyond his reach. The big gamble was whether the students and teachers would leave campus to buy a copy at one of several locations nearby where we would have hawkers waiting. In a front-page editorial describing Cavin's demands and our decision to move off campus, I wrote, "Please don't allow this inconvenience to prevent you from going out and buying a copy. It's a small hassle for a large amount of information and entertainment." But very few made the effort.

By midmorning, we had sold barely 200 of the 1,000 copies printed, and most of those were in the half hour before school started. Once classes were in session, sales dropped to a trickle. If we didn't come up with a new strategy soon, we faced a humiliating defeat and a big financial loss. We huddled and debated, and by late morning we abandoned the off-site selling locations and sneaked the unsold copies onto campus, where we quietly began peddling them in lavatories and locker wells. Sales by this method were slow, painstaking, and risky. Hundreds of unsold copies remained.

Over lunch, Justin came up with an idea even I had to admit was brilliant. The *Spectrum* was also on sale that day, and each of us on staff was expected to walk the halls hawking it. "We're out there selling the *Spectrum* in plain sight, right?" Justin said over lunch. "Is anyone thinking what I'm thinking?" A few minutes later we were back in the *Spectrum* office surrounded by piles of the approved paper and piles of *Innervisions*. "Start stuffing," Justin said.

We spread out across school peddling the *Spectrum* with newfound zeal. "Get your *Spectrum*! Come on, people, support your student newspaper! *Spectrum*! Get your *Spectrum*! Only a quarter!" At one point Mr. Cavin passed me and, sounding sincerely impressed, said, "Now that's the spirit, Mr. Grogan." What he did not know was that each time one of us snagged a customer, we would quietly ask, "Interested in a copy of *Innervisions* with that?" If the buyer was, he would add a dime to the purchase price and receive a copy off the bottom of the stack—with *Innervisions* tucked inside.

We felt like drug dealers pushing our dope under the noses of administrators, but the plan was working. At least until the president of the school board, a humorless man named Robert Carter, arrived on campus and stopped to buy a copy of the *Spectrum* on his way in. I watched from across the courtyard as he approached one of our double agents, an underclassman who had no idea our school district even had a president, let alone what he looked like. *No, please God, no,* I whispered. Carter reached into his pocket for a quarter. I held my breath as the unsuspecting volunteer accepted the change. *Off the top of the stack,* I prayed. *Take it off the top.* I could see the kid's lips moving and knew what he must be saying. Then I watched as the board president reached in his pocket and produced another coin. *Oh no, oh no, oh no.* From the bottom of the stack, the student handed him a paper.

Fifteen minutes later all four editors were back in Mr. Cavin's office, and this time Cavin sat quietly while Mr. Carter did the talking. He could barely contain his anger. Little flecks of saliva hit my face as he spat out a string of threats. But they were mostly hollow. We had only a few days left of school. Suspending us for the rest of the year was meaningless. They knew it and we knew it. The president tore up his copy of *Innervisions* and threw it at us, green paper fluttering down like confetti. "You're done. This is over now. Do I make myself clear?" he asked.

"Yes, sir," we mumbled and filed out of the office past Cavin, who gave us a look that said, *See what you've done? Now I'm in trouble, too.* Quite honestly, we *were* done. We did not have any more fight in us. We were tired; we were worn down; we just wanted to join everyone else out in the courtyard soaking up the sun and signing yearbooks. A free press, I was learning, involved nine-tenths thankless tedium and one-tenth glory, and then only on a good day. As ordered, we delivered the 500 unsold copies of *Innervisions* to the principal's office to be destroyed.

On the way out of school at the end of the day, I bumped into Mrs. Atkinson, our rebellious heroine, who was within days of leaving to become a lawyer. She asked me how sales had gone. When I told her what had happened, she asked how much money we had lost.

"We had a little surplus left over from the first issue," I said. "I guess about twenty-five dollars."

She opened her purse and pressed a twenty- and a five-dollar bill into my hand. "Now you're even," she said.

I wanted to throw my arms around her. I wanted to tell her how great she was, what an amazing teacher; what an inspiration and role model. I wanted to say I would never forget her and what she had taught me, not only about Greek columns and prehistoric pottery but about questioning the status quo and challenging authority. What I said was "Gee, Mrs. A., thanks."

"Keep 'em sweating," she said with a smile. "And don't ever think you haven't made a difference."

Perhaps Mrs. Atkinson was onto something. The next fall when I returned to West Bloomfield as a senior, *Innervisions* was just a distant memory. But in the offices of the *Spectrum* something was distinctly different. The staff seemed to have more confidence, our adviser more interest in challenging us, and the stories more heft. We pushed the envelope more often and more aggressively. Despite that, Mr. Cavin backed off. He deferred to our adviser's judgment and no longer took it upon himself to impose his will on our content. Staff members published articles on birth control, teacher contract negotiations, and other hot-button topics without so much as a peep from the administration. I may have been flattering myself, but it seemed Cavin and the school board didn't want to inflame any more passions among the student journalists. Why risk waking that sleeping bear again?

That fall marked another change at West Bloomfield, one involving the inseparable trinity known as *Lorisueanna*. When the first day of school arrived, the threesome was a twosome. Just *Lorisue*. During the summer, Anna's family had moved out of state. In the halls, Lori and Sue now walked in tandem, a hole between them where Anna had once stood. They seemed somehow not quite complete without their friend. I had grown closer to all three of them, and I, too, was sad to see her gone. Anna had a quiet intelligence and independence I admired, and I liked her crazy hair and shy smile.

One day after the leaves had fallen, Lori found me in the hall. She was beaming. "Guess what," she said, grabbing my arm. "Anna's coming back to visit! She'll be here for three days over Thanksgiving." Anna had been so miserable in her new town and school that her parents had sprung for an airline ticket back to Michigan, where she would spend the holiday weekend at Lori's house. Sue would be sleeping over, too. The threesome, however briefly, would be reunited.

"It's going to be so great!" Lori gushed. "And it gets better. My parents are going to be out of town on the last night. We'll have the house to ourselves. You *must* come over." Her braces had come off over the summer and she flashed me her newly perfect smile.

"I must, huh?" I said coyly.

"You must." More dazzling smile.

"Well, then, I'll be there," I said.

And I was. Unlike Pete Grunwald's bash, Lori's was small and discreet—a party of four. Months earlier, I had discovered a store where I could buy beer without being asked to show identification, and I arrived with a couple of six-packs. Lori made omelets. The four of us sat around, talking and listening to Arlo Guthrie records. Sue was the first to drift off, waking just long enough to head upstairs to bed sometime after midnight. Lori was next, growing quiet and finally falling into a heavy sleep on the couch a few feet from where Anna and I sat side by side on the floor, talking and looking at album covers. She smiled at me. "Guess we're the last two standing," she said.

And then her hand was on my knee, and my hand was in her incorrigible hair, brushing it back from her face. She closed her eyes. I took a moment to study her face and realized how pretty she was—prettier than I had allowed myself to notice. I kissed her cheek, then her nose. Our lips found each other, tentatively at first and then without reservation. Almost instantly I knew I was experiencing something very different from that night the previous spring on the overturned canoe. As her mouth opened to mine, I paused momentarily to marvel, *So this is how a kiss is supposed to feel.* My heart raced and breath came in short, anxious jags. I forgot about everything but Anna.

About the lights that were far too bright, about my already blown curfew, even about Lori softly snoring an arm's length away.

"You're shivering," Anna whispered.

"I know," I said and folded her onto her back on the floor and rolled on top of her. She slid a hand inside my T-shirt. As I kissed her, I began to fumble with the buttons of her blouse and eventually her jeans.

By the time we heard the yawn, we were in a fully compromised position. Anna's shirt was wide open; her jeans were unzipped, panties peeking out. My shirt was up around my shoulder blades. From behind us, Lori yawned again, this time louder and with a dramatic effect that reminded me of how the Cowardly Lion yawned in *The Wizard of Oz*. Anna and I froze, our mouths still sealed together, our hands locked in place where they had been roaming. It was as though we had been playing musical make-out chairs and the music had just stopped. Anna's eyes were wide open now, and I knew she was wondering the same thing I was: how long had Lori been awake, trying to figure out how to extricate herself? I pictured her lying on the couch for the past hour debating her options. Should she attempt to sneak out silently and hope we didn't notice? Feign sleep until we eventually left for a bedroom? Let out a big, casual yawn as if, ho-hum, she woke to these types of surprises every night? I heard Lori rustle on the couch and then her footsteps as she stepped over us and walked out of the room and up the stairs, pausing on her way to switch off the lights.

"Oh, God," I whispered.

"Oh well," Anna whispered back and playfully nipped at my lower lip.

We continued where we had left off. In the vernacular of teenage boys everywhere, I was rounding third base and making the final sprint toward home plate when Anna pulled back almost imperceptibly and kissed me on the bridge of my nose.

"John," she whispered, "I'm not ready to go all the way."

We were both virgins, both feeling our way for the first time. Even as I explored her breasts and tugged at her underwear, I had been worrying, too. Maybe it was everything the nuns and brothers had preached about mortal sins and our bodies as temples of Christ. Or Mom and Dad's constant ranting about the sanctity of what they called "marital relations." Or the fears they all planted of unwanted pregnancies, dashed dreams, and ruined lives. I would never admit it, but I wasn't ready, either.

"It's just . . . ," Anna began. "We're just going so fast. Can we slow down a little?"

"I can respect that," I said, feigning a worldliness I could only dream of, as if I bedded girls on a nightly basis and this once was willing to make a special exception. Secretly I was relieved beyond words.

We lay together on the floor, half naked, kissing and touching and giggling, until I thought to check my watch and was shocked to see it was 3 A.M. "I've got to go," I said. "I was supposed to be home hours ago." I didn't mention it, but it was also now officially Sunday morning, and Mom would be waking me in a few hours to get ready for Mass. We pulled our clothes together and Anna walked me to the door.

"Come over in the morning for a late breakfast?" she asked.

"That sounds good," I said.

On the drive home, I plotted my strategy for sneaking upstairs and into bed without waking Mom or Dad. The trick was to make sure Shaun didn't bark. He was a smart dog and could usually tell my approach from a stranger's.

I pulled Dad's big Monte Carlo into the garage and before opening the door to the laundry room let out a soft whistle, the whistle I had used with Shaun since he was a puppy. Then I silently turned the knob and stepped inside. Shaun was right there to greet me, stretching and shaking, his tags clinking. I knelt down and scratched his ears. "Hey, boy," I whispered. "You miss me?" I slipped out of my shoes and tiptoed through the kitchen in the dark. As I silently passed the living room, feeling for the handrail to the stairs, Little Napoleon's voice came out of the blackness.

"Where have you been?"

"Oh—hi, Mom."

"Don't 'hi, Mom' me. Do you know what time it is? Do you know how long I've been sitting up? Do you have any idea how worried I've been?" In the dark, I could hear her rosary beads clinking.

I spun a tale about watching a late-night movie with my friends and all four of us dozing off and next thing we knew, gee, look at the time, and wow, can you believe how late it is, and oh man, where did the night go? In her nightgown and slippers, she stepped closer and peered up at me. I could tell she was trying to sniff my breath for booze or other illicit substances, and on that front I was safe. My last beer had been hours earlier. "Really, Ma, it was just the four of us hanging out all night."

"For all I knew, you were lying dead on the side of the road," she scolded. Then, as if a whole new sordid scenario had just dawned on her: "Were her parents home?"

"Mr. and Mrs. Sheldon? The Sheldons? Oh, sure. Of course. Where else would they be? Mrs. Sheldon made really great popcorn. For the movie. Really buttery. Delicious."

Mom stared at me, trying to divine where the truth lay. At least there were no visible gnaw marks on me this time. "I just don't know what these parents are thinking letting boys and girls sit up half the night together," she said. "It's a recipe for trouble."

"They were right there the whole time, Mom," I said. "That Mr. S., what a night owl. Loves the Civil War. Sits up all night reading about the Civil War."

"I was worried half to death," she scolded. "Not even a phone number to call. Not even a last name."

"I should have called, Ma," I said. "But you know, we all fell asleep." I could tell from the way her voice was softening that she once again would choose to believe me, or at least pretend to.

"Now up to bed," she said, "before I blister you. You're still not too big to turn over my knee, you know."

I gave her a quick peck on the cheek and headed upstairs, my head swimming with the events of the night. *Anna, Anna, my God, Anna.* I repeated her name in my head like a mantra as I drifted off into a deep, happy sleep.

* * *

The next morning—or rather, several hours later that same morning—I dragged myself to the 9 A.M. with my parents, then headed back to Lori's house for what I pictured would be a boisterous group breakfast around the kitchen table, all four of us jabbering away like the good friends we were. But when I arrived, Anna answered the door alone. Lori and Sue were nowhere in sight. It was obvious they had cleared out to give us time alone. Anna beamed at me, all swoony like, and I knew something had changed, something major. Somehow, over the course of a few hours, everything was different. We were no longer four pals, and Anna and I, without anyone asking my thoughts on the matter, had become a couple. I resisted a creeping sense of panic.

Anna made eggs and toast, and then I took her to one of my favorite places, a rambling, decrepit greenhouse on a remote country road where Dad used to take us when we were younger. Walking in from the cold was like walking into a tropical rain forest. The air was so heavy with moisture it condensed on the glass and dripped onto our heads.

We walked through the rows of greenery, hand in hand, pausing occasionally to kiss or merely hug. At one point we caught our reflection in a steamy pane of glass and both burst out laughing. Our hair had ballooned with the humidity, doubling in volume.

"Lotta freaks," Anna said, mimicking Arlo Guthrie from his performance at Woodstock, and she reached up and smoothed my hair into a bulky ponytail, which she held in her hands briefly before releasing it to spring back over my shoulders. She was flying home later that afternoon, and we both knew we would not see each other, at best, for many months. Out in the parking lot, I leaned against Dad's Monte Carlo, and she slipped her arms around me and rested her head on my shoulder. Neither of us wanted to say good-bye. I was not sure what real love was supposed to feel like, but I knew what I felt in my chest at that moment had to be close. I pressed my face into her hair and breathed her in. *Anna, Anna, my God, Anna.*

"I'll write," she said.

"I'll write, too," I promised.

❉

As senior year progressed, Anna and I wrote less and less often. At first our letters were twice a week, then weekly, then monthly, and finally, as we both prepared to graduate from our respective schools, not at all. I had a new circle of friends in addition to the old regulars; she had forged bonds at her new school.

Then, a week before commencement, a new distraction came into my life. She was a sophomore whom I had met late in the year through Rock, who was in the school play with her. Becky had inherited her father's olive complexion and her mother's almond eyes. She was a talented stage performer with a beautiful singing voice, a high soprano, polished by years of professional training her blue-collar parents really could not afford. But she wasn't known for her acting prowess or her ability to hit high C on command. She was universally known, around school and town, and everywhere she went, for just one thing. Two, actually.

Becky had the largest, fullest, most magnificent breasts of any girl ever to walk the halls of West Bloomfield High School. They began just south of her collarbone and protruded more or less straight outward in open defiance of Sir Isaac Newton for what seemed, at least to the adolescent male eye, miles before curving gently earthward again. This normally would be considered a desirable characteristic, the type of chest some women spend thousands of dollars to achieve surgically. And it would have been for Becky, too, if only she had the body to accommodate it. If only she were a little taller. But Becky was just five feet one. The effect those expansive, gravity-defying breasts had on that compact frame was overwhelming. It was like cramming the Grand Tetons into Rhode Island. No matter what Becky did or said, how well she acted or sang or competed in softball, she was recognized only as "the girl with the big knockers."

No matter what she wore—the baggiest sweaters, the most demure blouses, her father's oversize blazers—she stood out in any crowd. Men of all ages would literally gasp aloud from fifty feet away as if they had just glimpsed Haley's comet at close range. Women always noticed, too, and a surprising number of them were quick to deliver commentary beneath their breath.

Three days before classes let out for summer, Becky arrived at school with an armful of carnations, which she distributed to friends and favorite teachers. As I walked between classes she stopped me in the hall and held out a stem. "This is for you, John Grogan."

I was surprised. I had met her only a few weeks earlier and then just to chat in the hall. I was one of the few boys in school who hadn't thought to stare at her chest, at least not in an obvious way, or make lewd comments, and perhaps that helped me make her short list of flower recipients. I accepted the carnation and thanked her.

Becky stood there in the crowded hall, beaming up at me as if waiting for a receipt. I had no gift to give her, not even a yearbook to ask her to sign. Until that moment, she had barely registered as a blip on my radar. It seemed only gracious to make a gesture of appreciation. I leaned over to give her a thank-you peck. But as my lips touched her cheek she turned her head so our mouths banged together. The next thing I knew, Becky's lips were locked over mine. I always despised those exhibitionist types who made out in the hallway at school. Couldn't they wait till they were alone? But I would be lying if I said I didn't kiss back. By the time we finally broke apart, I was late for class, and my carnation looked like it had been run over by a steamroller.

"Call me?" she said, holding an invisible phone to her ear.

"Absolutely," I answered and rushed off.

I graduated with a C-plus grade point average, exactly in the middle of my class. I had joined no clubs, played no sports, performed no community service. Undistinguished with a capital *U*. With that kind of academic record, I was not getting into the University of Michigan, where my father and sister went, or even into sprawling Michigan State University, which Rock was off to in the fall along with scores of other classmates. But I did get accepted into Central Michigan University, located three hours north of my home, in the middle of the Chippewa Indian reservation. Central was the kind of college willing to take a chance on a student with mediocre grades, so-so SAT scores, and scant evidence of ambition. The admissions officer seemed to like me, especially my gumption in starting *Innervisions*. And he seemed to understand and sympathize with the difficulty I had transitioning from nine years of regimented Catholic education into a laissez-faire public school.

At commencement, I did have bragging rights to one claim: I had the longest hair of any boy in the West Bloomfield class of 1975, with three or four inches to spare. My parents had learned something from their bitter and ultimately futile battles with Tim over the length of his hair. By the time I was in high school they had mellowed considerably, and on more than one occasion I overheard Mom on the phone to another parent say, "As long as he stays out of trouble and keeps his grades up, what does that big mop of hair really matter?" They sat in the bleachers as I filed up for my diploma, big colorful bow tie around my neck, frizzy curls streaming out from under my mortarboard and over my gown. They couldn't have looked prouder.

I invited Becky to attend the school-sponsored graduation party with me, where we ended up making out so furiously next to the punch bowl that parent chaperones twice pulled us apart to tell us to cool it. Finally we abandoned the party and continued our mutual exploration outside in Dad's Monte Carlo. By night's end, it was official: without even meaning to, I had a steady girlfriend. Becky was playful, flirty, curious, eager to please. Becky was on fire. Becky was exactly the kind of girl Mom wanted to keep as far away from her sons as possible. She was convinced Becky was like girls she had known growing up; they were the ones who seduced boys, got pregnant, and forced them into dead-end marriages. Besides, Becky was a Protestant, another mark against her in my mother's mind.

Never mind that Becky was two years behind me in school and, because of a late birthday, nearly three years younger. In Mom's eyes, she was the calculating predator and I the innocent prey.

Like everyone else, Mom couldn't help noticing Becky's impressive breasts and the intoxicating effect they had on males. In one famous family encounter, my long-divorced uncle Artie was at our house for a Sunday cookout and hit it off so well with Becky that I asked them to pose for a photo. Uncle Artie gladly obliged, slinging his arm around Becky's shoulder and pulling her close to him. He pressed his face to hers and they both beamed into the lens. "Okay, big smiles," I coached. Through the lens, it looked like the perfect shot, and when the prints came back, the shot indeed was almost perfect. There they were, looking like best pals, my sixty-year-old uncle and fifteen-year-old girlfriend. Only one small thing was amiss, and that was Uncle Artie's eyes. Specifically, where they were aiming. The photo showed Becky and Uncle Artie smiling directly into the camera, but with my uncle's eyes rolled sideways and down, nearly popping from their sockets—eyebrows forced upward into a salacious arch—staring directly into Becky's cleavage.

My brothers and I found the photo hilarious, and even Becky had to laugh. She was used to such odd male behavior and didn't seem to mind the attention. Mom, on the other hand, was not amused. The snapshot only reinforced her perception of Becky as a seductress who could use her physical attributes to short-circuit the brains of otherwise levelheaded males, forcing them to forget every last lesson their mothers had taught them. Whenever I brought Becky around the house, Mom was careful to be pleasant, but I could tell what she was thinking. To Mom, Becky's breasts were powerful man-seeking missiles in the arms race to conquer her youngest son's moral character. She had nothing in her arsenal of rosary beads and holy water that could begin to compete. Mom's singular mission in life became to keep the two of us from having any unsupervised time together. This, too, proved a losing battle.

Dad, on the other hand, was completely unfazed by Becky's breasts. He seemed oblivious to their existence. He was kind and fatherly to her, and if he in any way disapproved of her, he never gave a hint. Becky loved him for it.

That summer we saw each other nearly every night and often during the day, too. We would go to movies, go to the beach, shoot pool. I'd tag along with her on babysitting jobs. Wherever we ended up, whatever the activity, it always concluded the same way, with us mashing and groping and working each other into nervous powerhouses of barely contained, unconsummated sexual energy.

One day we took the sailboat out and made it only a quarter mile offshore before I succumbed to Becky in her bikini. I dropped the tiller, pulled her into my arms, and slid down onto the floorboards with her as the sails flapped and the boat turned in lazy circles. When we got back to the dock, Dad was standing there, looking puzzled. He often walked to the beach to watch me sail, studying my form on the water and then critiquing it after I returned to shore. Usually he had nothing but praise. Today, though, he was perplexed.

"What the heck happened out there?" he asked, genuinely baffled. "It looked like you were clipping along just fine and all of a sudden everything went haywire. I could see the sails luffing and the boat turning."

Becky and I sneaked grins at each other. "That? Oh, *that*. We were just goofing around," I said. "I let go of the tiller for kicks, just to see what would happen."

Dad appeared to buy my story. If Mom detected a potential pregnancy-inducing liaison in every unchaperoned moment, Dad seemed blissfully unaware that sex before marriage was even possible. The fact that Becky and I would choose to interrupt a perfectly good sailing tack for no reason other than "kicks" simply reinforced his conviction that teens were strange and inexplicable life-forms best given a wide berth.

Mom, meanwhile, was praying fervently each night to the Virgin Mother to keep me chaste. Much to my chagrin, her prayers seemed to be working. For all our hot and heavy foreplay, Becky and I still had not had sex. More times than I cared to count, we came tantalizingly close, but never all the way. My hot-blooded girlfriend had mastered the art of seduction but was less sure about surrendering the goods. And how could I blame her? She was still a virgin, and even more confused than I was. Night after night she would accompany me to the brink of intimacy before backing off.

Summer was winding down, I would soon be off to college, and I remained a virgin. A crazed and highly frustrated virgin.

Still, I wanted to be prepared just in case. One morning when I knew it would be quiet, I headed to Dandy Drugs and—after lurking in the aisles for what seemed hours, pretending to read the labels on Pepto-Bismol and Old Spice bottles—summoned the nerve to buy a three-pack of condoms. After eighteen years without the need for a single prophylactic, I could not fathom ever requiring more than three. Three condoms seemed wildly optimistic. Three condoms, I was convinced, would last the rest of my life. I slid one into my wallet and hid the other two above a basement ceiling panel where I knew Mom and Dad wouldn't find them. I was ready when Becky was.

Then the unexpected happened. One week before I was to leave for college, the doorbell rang, and on the front porch stood Anna. Her skin was the color of cocoa from a summer of sun, her hair a shimmer of tight, frizzy curls. She wore shorts and flip-flops and a loose muslin smock, a small silver Star of David around her neck. The instant I saw her, all the feelings from the previous autumn came rushing back. *Anna, Anna, my God, Anna.*

"Hi," she said with a smile that told me the feelings had not left her, either.

"Hi," I answered.

Then we were walking through the dark, hand in hand. We walked down Erie Drive, across The Outlot to the beach, stopping along the way to fetch a blanket from the boat. Neither of us needed to say a word; we both knew where the night would take us. I led her to a grassy place beneath one of the giant oak trees, and together we spread the blanket and sank down on it.

"I missed you," I whispered. It had been eight months since our last kiss, but the transition was seamless. Here we were again, our lips and torsos and limbs pressed together as if no time at all had passed. The humid night air surrounded us and distant lightning flashed silently in the sky. I pulled my face back far enough to look into her eyes.

"You're sure?" I asked.

"I'm sure," Anna said and pulled my face back to hers.

That's when I felt a wet, cold jab on the back of my neck. I jolted upright and turned. Shaun lunged forward and began licking my face. He was wildly happy to have found us, and was panting and prancing about. "Aww, puppy," Anna cooed and reached up to pet him.

"No! No, wait," I said. "Quick! Button your shirt! Sit up!" If Shaun was here, that could mean just one thing.

I stood up, pulled my shirt down, and looked around. From the direction we had just come danced a flashlight beam, growing brighter and bigger as it drew closer. I waited until it was nearly upon us.

"Hi, Dad," I said. "Over here."

The beam fell on us briefly and then went dark.

"You remember Anna," I continued. "My friend from New Jersey? She's back visiting."

Dad said hello to her, then turned back to me. "Your mother's concerned," he said. "She sent me down to check on you." I paused to marvel at my mother's ability to sniff out possible hanky-panky from hundreds of yards away. As far as I knew, she hadn't even seen Anna come to the door. From the pained tone of Dad's voice, I could tell this was the last thing he wanted to be doing on his Saturday night. He had been ordered here against his will, Little Napoleon's foot soldier. I could tell he was embarrassed to be caught in the middle.

"We're just talking, Dad. Catching up."

"Why don't you catch up at the house. That would probably be better."

"Sure, good idea," I said. "We'll be right up."

"How right up?"

"Twenty minutes?"

He hesitated in the dark. I could picture his face, and I imagined it grimacing. I could see him weighing what he would tell his wife when he returned alone. "Twenty minutes," he said.

"Twenty minutes. Promise."

"Okay then," he said and flicked on his flashlight and walked away.

We both sat frozen until the flashlight beam disappeared on the other side of The Lagoon. Then I was on my feet, pulling her up onto hers.

"Come on, quick," I said. "We don't have much time."

"John," she said. "We can't. What if he comes back?"

"I have a place," I said. "A secret place we used to go as kids."

I threw the blanket over my shoulder and led her down into the water. "Watch the rocks," I warned as we waded knee-deep along the shoreline. Ahead of us, a small peninsula jutted out into the lake, thick with underbrush. I led Anna around the little spit of land, which separated the neighborhood beach from a private home. On the other side, a steep stairway led up the embankment to the house, but first, on the edge of the water, was a tiny secluded beach. Just big enough for two people on a blanket. Tommy and I had discovered it years earlier.

"What do you think?" I asked.

"I think it's perfect," she said.

Within seconds we were out of our clothes. She lay down on the blanket and pulled me on top of her. The sensation of our bare flesh pressed together was like nothing I had ever imagined. I was delirious with desire.

"My condom!" I nearly shouted. "I have a condom."

I fumbled for my wallet, and she helped me put it on. I sank back on top of her, felt our skin make contact again, her breasts against my chest, her stomach flat against mine. It was as if our bodies had always been meant to fit together. I was so excited. So incredibly excited.

Too excited. My orgasm came in a matter of seconds. It came with no warning. It came before I was even fully inside her.

"It was still wonderful," she said.

But I knew it wasn't. I lay motionless on top of her. She traced her fingertips along my spine and whispered in my ear. I don't remember what she said, but whatever it was, it gave me all the encouragement I needed. Seconds later I was ready for her again and she for me.

"Grab another condom," she whispered.

I froze. "Another condom?"

"Yeah. Hurry."

"Um. I don't have another one."

"You only brought one?" The disappointment in her voice bordered on annoyance.

"I didn't know."

From the way Anna recoiled on the blanket, I knew what she wanted to say: What kind of an idiot would carry only one lousy condom? What she said was: "Just hold me, okay?"

I racked my brain. "We could try to use it over again," I offered.

"No," she said, clearly appalled at the idea. "That won't work."

In the end, we did what high school kids for eons have done, and that was to err on the side of recklessness. We made love with no protection at all. Afterward, we lay together and I cradled her face in my hands. "You are so beautiful," I said.

We were late. It was time to go before Mom sent Dad in search of us again. At the house, I called inside, "Back!" I saw Dad in the living room check his watch. Anna and I sat on the porch and talked, then I walked her to her car.

"I'm glad you came back," I said.

"I am, too."

She unclasped the Star of David from her neck and put it around mine. For my birthday that year, Marijo had given me a silver cross with the word *Alleluia* stamped on it, and I removed it from my neck. Anna held her hair up for me, and I fumbled to clasp it around hers. We both started laughing.

"This will drive the parents insane," Anna said.

"Yours and mine both," I said.

We stood in the dark, rocking gently in each other's arms, our foreheads pressed together. The first hint of autumn drifted on the breeze, and with it an awareness that my life had reached a juncture. Everything was soon about to change—or perhaps was already changing. I was leaving home in a week, leaving my parents' nest and the childhood they had given me. I was leaving without my virginity and with no concept of the irrevocability of life's chapters.

I kissed Anna on the lips. Once, twice, three times. And then she was gone. Back to New Jersey, to college in Boston, to a life that, as it turned out, would remain fully separate and apart from my own.

PART TWO

*

Breaking Away

CHAPTER 18

✳

By 1982 I was three years out of Central Michigan University, where I had finally gotten serious about academics and graduated cum laude with twin majors in journalism and English. I was working as a reporter at a small newspaper in the far southwest corner of the state, covering murders, robberies, rapes, and lesser crimes. I lived alone in an apartment carved out of the second story of a turn-of-the-century house perched on a bluff above Lake Michigan. And I was still dating Becky. Or perhaps more accurately, Becky was still dating me.

Just as she had instigated that first kiss in the hallway of West Bloomfield High seven years earlier, Becky continued to be the driving force that kept us hanging on as a couple. I followed the course of least resistance, going along for the ride—and for the sex, which finally came to pass in my dorm room at Central Michigan after Becky went on the Pill and persuaded her mother to drive her the two hours to campus to spend the weekend.

That visit marked a watershed in my struggle for candor with my parents. I had never grown comfortable with the lies and deceit, and once in college I was determined to be more forthcoming. But my parents seldom rewarded my attempts at honesty. I learned that over and over, but never as much as I did during that Homecoming weekend when Mom called while Becky was in the room with me, waiting for her mother to arrive to take her home.

"So what's new?" Mom asked.

"Oh, not much," I said.

"Nothing at all?"

"Not really."

"Surely you must have something to report," she said, not accusatorily but with enough zeal to make me think, *Oh God, she knows*.

"Well," I said, "Becky's here for the weekend."

Long pause.

"Becky? There with you?" Mom asked.

"Yes. Her mom brought her up for Homecoming."

"For the day?"

"No, for the weekend." I glanced over at Becky and could tell from her expression that I was making a grave mistake. But my pride was on the line. I wasn't going to lie to my mother in front of my girlfriend and roommates. Besides, I was an adult now, old enough to vote, and figured it was time to be my own man. "She's actually here right now."

"She is? Where did she stay last night?" Mom asked.

"Here at the dorm."

"Where at the dorm?"

"Here in my room."

"Your room? Then where did you stay?"

Now it was my turn to pause. It was the moment of truth. I could easily lie and tell her I bunked across the hall, or I could be a man and tell it straight. "Here in my room, Mom."

A drawn breath, and then: "John, what are you trying to tell me?"

Before I could answer, she started in about the sanctity of marriage, and the need for God's blessing of sexual relations, and the repercussions of one irresponsible act. It was time to abandon ship. The SS *Honesty* was going down.

"Mom," I interrupted. "Nothing happened. Nothing at all, okay? She slept in my bed and I slept on the beanbag. We just slept, that's all."

"Do you expect me to—?"

"Not a thing, Mom. Not a thing happened."

I quickly got off the line before the grilling could resume, but the fallout from that moment of candor continued for weeks, with Mom lamenting the decision to send me to public schools and Dad threatening to make me live at home while attending a local Catholic college.

On my next visit home, I sat with them in the living room, looked into their eyes, and repeated my lie with straight-faced sincerity: "Honest, nothing happened." I repeated the words over and over, like a hypnotist.

They finally seemed to buy it. "We believe you, dear," Mom said as Dad nodded silently in agreement, "but it was very foolish of you to put yourself in such a situation of temptation. Your guardian angel can only do so much. You were just asking for trouble."

"I can see that now," I said and promised them I would not make the same mistake again. Silently I told myself that, at least when it came to my parents, the truth was not always the best course. From that day forward, I simply told them what I knew they wanted to hear—or at least refrained from telling them what they did not. The decision was a simple one that allowed me to continue down the path of least resistance with them. The only trade-off was with my pride and integrity. It was a swap I was willing to make.

I became one of those underclassmen with a girlfriend back home, and I would see Becky whenever I returned for holidays or long weekends, during which we slinked around behind the backs of my parents, who were still hoping against all circumstantial evidence that their youngest son's virginity was intact and would remain so until marriage. Fortunately, we had allies in Becky's permissive parents, who understood our need to have alone time in Becky's bedroom with the door locked.

After graduating from high school, Becky followed me to Central, even though I had not encouraged her. It was the only college she applied to. By then I was living off campus in a coed house, and she was in a dormitory. My journalism classes were on the other side of campus from her music courses. We saw each other when we could, and I enjoyed having her there, but I continued to treat her like a part-time girlfriend. Becky, always the accommodating one, allowed me to.

Then I got out of college and moved halfway across the state, and our relationship returned to long-distance status, with weekend visits a couple of times a month. By 1982 she was out of college, too—and looking to begin a life together. She pushed to move in with me, and I resisted. I liked Becky and cared about her; we had natural chemistry and many good times together. But I could not imagine spending my life with her. The joke among my male friends was that my idea of commitment would be to invite Becky to move to Grand Rapids, sixty miles to the north, so she'd be only an hour's drive away, not three. That wasn't far from the mark. The truth was, the status quo suited me fine. I got to have a fun-loving girlfriend and lover without all the baggage of a full-time relationship. Our twice-monthly visits together, most of which were spent in bed, were just about the right amount of Becky for me. She hung on, hoping for more, even as my lackluster commitment became increasingly impossible to ignore. The relationship lapsed into a tired stasis, becoming more and more strained.

Every Sunday afternoon like clockwork my parents called to catch up, and every Sunday I perpetuated a freewheeling fiction about the life I was leading. Actually, just two aspects of it: church and Becky. In our weekly chat, one of the first questions always out of their mouths was "How was Mass this morning?" I had grown adept at hiding from them the fact that, except during visits home, I had not gone to church since the day I left for college six years earlier. "Oh, pretty good," I would say, and I'm sure it had been for those in attendance. Mom and Dad knew better than to ask too many questions, and I knew better than to offer too many details. Over the years I had perfected the art of obfuscating without exactly lying outright. I would drop little nuggets of hope into our weekly phone conversations like a sailor might drop life preservers to men overboard. I wanted to give them something to cling to. I would say things like "Saint Bart's just put a beautiful addition onto the back of the church." I was careful not to say I had actually set foot inside Saint Bart's, but that's the impression I hoped to leave.

Sometimes my efforts returned to haunt me. I prepared for my parents' first weekend visit to my new apartment by looking up the nearest Catholic church in the phone book. I found the intersection on a map and memorized the route. I called ahead and got the Mass times so I could breezily let drop, as if I did this every Sunday, "Should we shoot for the nine-fifteen, the eleven o'clock, or the twelve-thirty?" I thought I had covered all my bases. But when we arrived at the intersection where the church was located, there wasn't one church but three. I had no idea which one was for Catholics and knew I had only a few seconds to figure it out. My eyes searched for any sign of Catholicism: a statue of the Virgin Mary, a crucifix, anything. Finally I spotted a plain cross, swallowed hard, and pulled into the parking lot—of a Lutheran church. "I think we want to be over there," Dad said, pointing across the street. Then from the backseat, more playful than scolding, Mom chimed in: "Oh, Johnny boy."

When it came to Becky, my duplicity was even more creative. Each phone call they would inquire, "So, have you seen Becky lately?" They would ask it in a breezy, chatty way, just like they asked about Mass. But as with Mass, I knew they were probing for information. I was careful to give away no usable intelligence. As far as my parents knew, Becky had never once stayed at my apartment. When I visited her at the university, my tale went, I stayed with male friends, and when she visited me in Saint Joseph, I arranged to have her stay with a married couple I knew from work, who were gracious enough to open their spare bedroom to her. I gave my parents the same things my siblings had learned to give them: plausible deniability and enough leeway to allow them to believe they were succeeding in their lifelong mission to raise their children as devout and chaste practicing Catholics. None of us wanted to disappoint them.

My paper was called the *Herald-Palladium* and it served the racially divided cities of Saint Joseph and Benton Harbor, though not equally, with daily doses of crime news, ribbon cuttings, and small-town gossip. Crimes committed by blacks against whites received especially sensational play. A favorite feature was the weekly photo gallery of deadbeat dads who had not paid their child support. It was truly an awful newspaper and an awful place to work, run by a former World War II submarine commander who barked orders and threats like he was still operating under martial law. With the exception of four grandmotherly ladies who ran the women's page, the staff consisted entirely of white men, nearly all of whom smoked. An inky cloud of cigarette, cigar, and pipe smoke clung to the ceiling of the newsroom at all hours of the day.

Into this morass one snowy winter's day marched a young woman. I noticed her right away. How could I not? She arrived fresh out of Michigan State University to begin her journalism career as the *Herald-Palladium*'s first-ever woman news reporter. The whole staff had anticipated the arrival of "the girl reporter" for weeks. And now here she was, standing in the newsroom, tall and slender, with a refined bearing and sandy blond hair that fell to her shoulders. Instantly, I was smitten. When I finally got a chance to introduce myself, she cut me off and insisted she had already met me during an earlier whirlwind of introductions.

"Um, no, you didn't," I corrected her.

"Yes I did."

"Nope. You're confusing me with someone else," I said and wanted to add, *You're the first woman under fifty to set foot in this newsroom and easily the most beautiful. Believe me, if I'd met you, I'd remember.*

"I'm sure I met you."

"Not me. Wrong guy."

We continued back and forth like this until it became so awkward that the only course left was to walk away. I never did get the chance to properly introduce myself. Was I really that forgettable? To me and every other man on staff, she was the biggest event to hit the paper in years: a young, pretty, single woman breaking the gender barrier. To her, I was just one of the many faceless males, married and unmarried, who hovered around her, fawning and jockeying for her attention. Before walking off, she cheerfully dropped into the conversation what she had told all the rest, that she had taken the job primarily to be near her steady boyfriend, who was a graduate student at Notre Dame University, a half hour down the road.

"That's great," I said. "Makes perfect sense."

I had just met this woman and already I was experiencing a piercing pang of heartsickness the likes of which I had seldom felt during seven years of dating Becky. Maybe it was because Becky tried so hard and this new woman, Jenny, showed no interest in trying at all. She was already taken and, even if she had not been, could not have cared less about me. She couldn't even tell me apart from the next guy in line. Her indifference made me want her all the more.

As winter stretched into spring, Jenny and I gradually became pals. We shot messages back and forth on our computers and gossiped in the lunchroom. We began going out after work for pizza and beer and took weekend hikes in the wooded dunes along Lake Michigan. She told me all about her boyfriend; I told her about my girlfriend, making the relationship sound stronger than it was. I didn't want to sound too eager.

That spring I bought an aging but seaworthy twenty-eight-foot sailboat with a cabin that slept four, and she volunteered to meet me down at the marina to help work on it. Together, we scrubbed and painted the bottom, sanded and oiled the teak trim, waxed the decks, monkeyed with the engine. We often worked until dusk and then found ourselves in the cockpit as the sun set over the water, drinking wine or splitting carryouts. Jenny had become my closest friend, and although I steadfastly pretended otherwise, so much more. At long last I had a view of what love really was, and I was falling headfirst into it at a dizzying speed. I felt like a spider cascading over Niagara Falls, powerless to do anything but be swept away. I didn't realize it at the time, but Jenny felt that way, too. Over Memorial Day weekend we had dinner together, at which we both confessed how hollow our respective relationships had grown. At the end of the evening, back at her apartment, I leaned over and kissed her. It was a kiss that would forever change our lives. The next weekend Jenny summoned the Notre Dame boyfriend to a restaurant and broke up with him. Shortly after that, I did the same with Becky. She acted almost relieved to at last get a clear decision from me.

The relationship advanced at a breathless pace, a pace I had never dreamed possible. Every day Jenny and I seemed to fall more in love. I found everything about her intriguing, including her sharp tongue and stinging wit. Even when we had fights I swooned over her. She called me Yogi Grogie, and I called her Jen-Jen. She was always doing things to steal my heart. After buying her first microwave oven, she invited me over for an all-microwave dinner, and the pork chops came out so thoroughly overdone they had turned translucent, as hard and brittle as petrified wood. "I'm so humiliated!" she wailed, but I found her disastrous cooking skills, so unlike my mother's, irresistibly endearing. One autumn night she slept over at my apartment. The next morning when we walked outside, I saw she had camouflaged her bright orange Chevy Vega with a thick layer of fallen leaves to disguise its presence in front of my place. She was concerned for her reputation, and I found it adorable beyond words.

In phone calls home, I gushed to Mom and Dad about this new girl in my life. They sounded elated, truly thrilled. I suspect the real reason was that Becky was finally out of the picture.

"Is she a Catholic?" Mom and Dad asked in chorus.

"Um, no," I said. "She's Presbyterian." From the silence on the line, I could hear their disappointment. I knew just how Mom would break the news to the church ladies when she announced John's new girlfriend: "Well, she's not a Catholic, but if they're really in love, I suppose that's what matters most."

"Yep, Presbyterian," I repeated. But even that was a stretch. Jenny was raised marginally Presbyterian, but no one in her family was religious, least of all her. "We're a bunch of heathens," she liked to quip, and I prayed silently she would never use the line in front of my parents. It was bad enough for them to know that Jenny was not Catholic; to know she was nothing at all would be heresy.

"Presbyterians are actually quite a bit like Catholics," I offered. "Lots of similarities."

"Some major differences, too," Dad shot back. "The Protestants won't even acknowledge our Blessed Virgin Mother or the Immaculate Conception. They deny the core tenets of Catholicism." Then he recited, as he had so many times before, why Catholicism was the one true faith. I didn't even try to argue.

"She can convert!" Mom exclaimed with a eureka-moment brightness in her voice. "Lots of people convert before marrying a Catholic."

"Ma, stop it!" I said. "Let's not get carried away. We just started dating." What I could have said, though, with absolute certainty, was that Jenny would never, ever convert. Not for me, not for any man. Not for all the love or money in the world. If I wanted her, I would have to take her just the way she was, and that was fine with me.

"It's just something to think about as you two get more serious," Mom said.

When they finally met her, during a weekend visit to my apartment, Mom and Dad seemed nearly as smitten by Jenny as I was. She was elegant and charming and clearly crazy about their son. She impressed Dad with her homemade apple pie and Mom with her spotless apartment. Mostly, she impressed them by not being Becky. In fact, she was nearly the antithesis of Becky. She had no mountainous missiles to scramble men's minds. She radiated girl-next-door wholesomeness and clearly looked forward to marriage and motherhood. Jenny seemed to like my parents a lot, too. Their budding relationship, I noted, was off to a very promising start.

CHAPTER 19

❉

A small-town newspaper like the *Herald-Palladium* was a career destination for only two kinds of journalists: those with ties to the area who were willing to make professional sacrifices to put down roots, and those without the talent or ambition to move on. For everyone else it was a humble first career rung until something better came along. My break came about a year after meeting Jenny when I was hired by the *Kalamazoo Gazette* to write about politics. Kalamazoo was a college town an hour's drive due east of Saint Joseph, and Jenny helped me move into my new apartment. Several months later Jenny got her break, too, moving to the *Muskegon Chronicle* to cover education. With her move, we were now more than two hours apart, driving to see each other every weekend and occasionally midweek, as well. The long-distance commute was far from ideal, but it was bearable, and our shared hope was that the next career jump would bring us into the same city again.

Then I received a letter that was like winning the lottery, only better. I had been accepted into a midcareer fellowship program at Ohio State University. The opportunity was amazing, a full ride covering tuition and living expenses for a year of study, culminating in a master's degree in journalism. The program accepted only ten journalists a year from dozens of applications nationwide. I knew it could be my ticket out of small-town newspaper jobs. I couldn't pass it up. But Columbus was nine hours from Muskegon, and I knew Jenny would be crushed. This was a part of the dream she had not counted on, a part that did not include her. I thought about it overnight, then accepted without telling her.

It was cowardly of me and in bad form. When I finally broke the news to her, what made her angriest of all was that I had not included her in the decision. We were a couple planning a future together, and I had thrust a unilateral edict upon her. I think she just wanted to be asked, even if she knew the only answer she could give was "Yes, go."

We survived the year but not without some calluses to our souls. Even though we spoke every night on the phone, it was impossible not to grow apart with the distance. Jenny was working undercover in the local high school, posing as a student for a series of investigative articles. I was deep into my graduate studies. We were on separate planets whose orbits no longer quite aligned. Then it got worse.

From Ohio State, I was accepted into a second journalism fellowship program, this one in Saint Petersburg, Florida. Jenny and I were now twenty-six hours apart. And when the three-month program ended, I was hired as a reporter at the South Florida *Sun-Sentinel,* across the state in Fort Lauderdale. My dream of landing at a metropolitan paper had been realized, but at the expense of reuniting with Jenny. Our future looked bleak. How long could a couple go on like this, barely seeing each other, getting by with phone calls and letters? We were both ready to give up.

Always the good girlfriend, Jenny offered to help me move my belongings to Florida and set up my new apartment—a fact I kept hidden from my parents because I could think of no plausible way to explain where she might sleep other than with me. While in town, she walked unannounced into the newsroom of the *Palm Beach Post* and handed her résumé and writing samples to the editors. They were especially impressed with her undercover high-school work. Two weeks later she had the job, and a month after that I helped her move into an apartment just a fifteen-minute drive from my own. Our dream had taken a few major detours but ultimately landed us where we had always hoped. Mom and Dad congratulated us heartily—especially after I made clear we had separate apartments.

Six months into Jenny's one-year lease, I said, "This is crazy. I love you. You love me. We spend all our time together anyway. Why don't we just move in together?"

Jenny blinked hard, and I thought she was going to cry. Then she threw her arms around my neck and said, "I accept."

We found a funky neighborhood we liked in West Palm Beach, just a couple of blocks from the Intracoastal Waterway, and soon stumbled upon a squat white bungalow with a front yard consisting entirely of weeds. It was the first house in the block off the main drag, Dixie Highway, and the most modest, too. In front of it was a sign that read FOR RENT.

As moving day neared, we discussed how we would break the news to our parents. Jenny was concerned that her mother and father would react badly. I, on the other hand, insisted to Jenny that my parents would have no problems at all. After all, they adored Jenny and knew how much we loved each other. They just wanted us to be happy, right? And this move was making us more than happy; we were giddy with excitement. So much so that we talked the landlord into giving us the key early so we could strip and polish the hardwood floors.

"I don't know, John," Jenny said. "Your parents are pretty conservative."

"They'll be fine," I assured her. "You just worry about your folks."

But secretly, deep inside, I was a nervous puddle. I was thirty years old and embarrassed to admit it but terrified to tell them something so simple as "Jenny and I have decided to live together." Part of me knew I was being ridiculous. I was an adult living on my own. What could they do? Encumber my allowance? Part of me struggled with wave after wave of dread. All my years of filtering the truth, of little deceits and outright lies, made it all the worse. With my help, they had allowed themselves to be deluded.

The previous Sunday, Mom and Dad had called for their weekly chat, only earlier than normal. Jenny had slept over, and we were just making coffee. As she always did, Mom asked me if I had gone to Mass yet that morning. No, I said, not yet. She then asked if I planned to see Jenny later in the day.

"Actually, I'm heading over to her place right after Mass," I said, managing to work two lies into one sentence. Jenny pretended not to overhear, and I knew she was embarrassed for me, a thirty-year-old still lying to his mother. I considered myself moral, ethical, even a little boring, with nothing to be ashamed of. Yet I dreaded the news I had to break to them, and my biggest fear was that when I did, Mom and Dad would blame Jenny. "He was such a good Catholic boy until he met . . . *that woman*!"

On the morning of our move, I pulled the rental truck up to Jenny's apartment, but before we began loading she called her parents. When she hung up a few minutes later, she said, "Wow, that was easier than I thought it would be. They really sounded pleased for us. My dad said his only regret was that he couldn't be here to help us move."

"He said that?"

"Yep. 'I just wish I could be there to help you move.' "

"Great," I said. "One down, one to go. My parents will be a breeze."

I put off calling them until all our possessions were in the moving van ready to be delivered to our new house. I wanted the move to be past the point of no return before breaking it to them.

I dialed their number and Mom picked up.

"Hi, Mom," I said. "Can you get Dad on the other line? I have some news to share with you both."

A few seconds later she was back with Dad. We made small talk for a minute and then Dad asked, "So what's this big news Mother tells me you have?"

"Well," I said. "Are you sitting down?" A nervous laugh escaped my lips. I knew they would have reservations, but I hoped they could, if not embrace, at least respect our decision. I wanted to believe they'd react as I knew they would if I announced we were engaged to be married. In my mind, this day was tantamount to that, the first step in our shared life together.

"Jenny and I have decided to move in together," I said.

Long pause, then Dad's voice: "I'm sorry? You what?"

"Decided to move in together."

Silence.

"We found a cute little house, and it seemed crazy paying two rents, and it's really convenient to both our offices. Right down by the water. And . . . we're moving in together."

Several seconds passed. I asked: "Are you still there?"

"We're here," Dad said.

"Today, actually. We're moving today. I have the truck loaded and ready to go."

Mom spoke next, and once she started there was no stopping her. "This is a big mistake—John, don't do this—do you hear me? Don't do it. Do you know how big a mistake this is? You'll be tarnishing your relationship forever. You don't want to do this—you can never take it back—you'll always regret it." Her words sprayed out like machine-gun fire.

Then Dad brought out the howitzers: "Sure, it's fine for you. It's fine for the man. But what about Jenny? What about the woman? What's that tell the world about her and your respect for her? Have you thought about her reputation? What happens to her when you get tired of this?" His message was clear: from this point forward she would be a marked woman—stained, used, unsuitable for marriage.

"Dad," I said, an edge of pleading in my voice, "that's so old-fashioned. Things have changed. People don't think that way anymore."

"Morals don't go in and out of style," he snapped. "That's what's wrong with this age, the moral relativism. 'If it feels good, do it.' Well, you know what? Right and wrong are right and wrong. They don't change. And living together out of wedlock is wrong. It's plain wrong."

Then he got to his main point. "You'll be living in a state of sin. Is that what you want? To live with the pall of sin over you?"

Mom broke in: "This will ruin the marriage. The Lord won't bless this union. You're dooming your future." She begged me to reconsider.

"Mom, c'mon," I pleaded.

"Your marriage will be damned before it ever starts," she said.

"Ma . . ."

"Have you thought about pregnancy? About birth control? What if Jenny gets pregnant? What then? Do you want a baby born out of wedlock? That child will carry this shame for his entire life. Is that what you want?"

My God, I thought. *They really still believe I'm a virgin. I'm thirty years old and they're afraid I'll accidentally get Jenny knocked up. They think Jenny and I have never had sex. Unbelievable. How were they able to delude themselves for so long?* Until that moment, I never quite believed they had bought into all my deceit. Mom's voice rattled on like a Gatling gun, laying down a withering cross fire of recrimination. She worked every angle to dissuade me. I was barely hearing her words. Finally I shouted over her.

"Stop! Look, the moving truck is in the driveway. Our apartments are both empty. Everything's in the truck. We're not reconsidering. It's too late. This is happening."

A long, long silence. Then Dad's voice: "You understand our position and I think we understand yours. We should let you go now." In the background, I could tell Mom was crying.

"Okay, then," I said.

"John?" Dad said. A long silence filled the phone line. "John, you will always be our son."

"I know, Dad," I said and hung up.

"Well, that went well," I said, and Jenny slipped her arms around me from behind and said, "I could tell."

"Let's not let it ruin the day," I said. "We're moving in together!" I kissed her on the lips, then gave her a slap on the backside and said, "We've got work to do."

As we carried our combined furnishings and possessions into our new rental house, I tried hard to seal away the phone call. But the more I tried, the more it filled my head. The whole thing was really my fault, I told myself. Had I been more honest and up-front with them all along, starting years earlier, my announcement would not have hit them so hard. Part of me felt pain for disappointing them; part of me, self-loathing for lacking the character to stand tall and be myself around them; part of me, anger at them for being so rigid. I continued to worry about Jenny and what this incident would do to her relationship with my parents. How could she not harbor resentment toward them now?

They made it clear what they thought of our arrangement, and by extension what they thought of us. If I was the sinner, what did that make her?

We were crazy about our two-bedroom house with the weedy yard and drippy faucets. There were orange and avocado trees out back loaded with fruit and a little patio where we could sit beneath the palms with our coffee and newspapers in the morning. There was a washer with a clothesline instead of a dryer, which we found impossibly romantic. Off the laundry was a one-car garage Jenny would spend an entire weekend repainting to convert into a studio for me. There was even a fireplace to take the chill off winter nights. We were like kids with a new toy, and we raced from one room to the next, then made the circuit all over again.

And yet, a quiet pall hung over the day. As we carried in the last boxes, mingling our two lives at last into one, an image flashed before my eyes. An image of my parents. They were sitting together in the living room, holding their rosaries, having just prayed for my soul. They were big on praying for lost souls. Mom was weeping and red-eyed, Dad shaking his head, deep worry on his face. Both of them were wondering aloud where they had gone wrong.

CHAPTER 20

✳

One week into our new life together, a letter arrived. I recognized the handwriting right away as belonging to Mom. I had not spoken with her or Dad since moving day. Now that she'd had time to calm down, maybe she was seeing things more clearly. Maybe she was writing to apologize. I tore open the envelope.

"Dear John," her letter opened, "I write this with a heavy heart." It was not the opening I had hoped for, and I could feel my chest tighten. "I have been numb since our telephone conversation. Strange that so few words could affect one so much. I just realized that this is the very first time I have had to shed tears over you. For thirty years you have given us nothing but joy and pride. I don't need to say how disappointed both Dad and I are at your decision. Somehow we thought we had instilled higher ethics and morals in you. We didn't think we had to preach; we thought we were teaching you by example." And then the razor-edged saber to the heart: "I'm sorry I have failed you."

Just like in the phone conversation with me, her words poured out in bursts: "Honestly, I can't understand what your problem is . . . If you love someone enough to sleep with them, it just seems to me that you would want to have your relationship blessed . . . Without doubt, this is the biggest decision you have had to make; I hope you are prepared to meet the responsibilities that go with it . . . Have you thought of the children that could result? Are you ready to cope with birth control and abortion?"

The problem, she noted, was that we had tried to make this important life decision on our own without spiritual guidance. "This is the time for both of you to turn to prayer. God is the only one who knows what the future holds. It is He, and He alone, who can guide you during this most important time of your lives. Don't be so proud as to think you can make your own decisions without His help . . . We were made to love and serve God. He is our Creator. We can't say we believe this and yet go about doing what He has asked us not to do. I am asking you to please take the time to converse with God. Tell Him how you feel, what your doubts are, your fears. Then listen! Think about making a retreat. Talk to a priest. Explore every avenue. It is your life—your future happiness."

She concluded this way: "We have loved you for the past thirty years and we are not about to stop now. No matter what your decision. Parents don't stop loving just because they are disappointed in their children. Of course, it would be much nicer loving with joy in our hearts rather than being laden with this heavy burden. But you are a man; only you can make the final decision. I think we know you well enough that you will do what you feel is right in your heart. But sometimes we are deceived by our own desires, so try to think straight . . . We will keep both of you in our prayers. We want you to find complete happiness—not just for a few months but for a lifetime."

The letter, three pages single-spaced, was classic Mom, a combination of heartfelt concern and overwrought emotions with a few well-aimed jabs of Catholic guilt skillfully slipped in. *Of course, it would be much nicer loving with joy in our hearts rather than being laden with this heavy burden . . .* When she felt strongly about something, she was incapable of self-censoring. When it came to influencing her children's lives, she had no on-off switch. It all came pouring out. What outsiders might see as meddling, I saw in a more positive light: a well-intentioned, if misguided and somewhat heavy-handed, effort to steer her brood down the right path.

I assumed Jenny would see it in the same light, which prompted me to make what in retrospect was one of the bigger mistakes of my life: I showed her the letter.

I did so without thinking. I did so assuming she would find it an amusing window into my mother's personality: the tenacious Little Napoleon in prime fighting form, grasping at every weapon in her arsenal to win this battle for her son's soul. I knew the letter was fueled by the best of intentions, but that did not soften my mother's judgmental tone. Before Jenny even said a word, I knew what a mistake I had made. I could see it in her face, at once wounded and angry.

"It's just my mom being my mom," I said, wishing I could push back the clock three minutes and bury the letter forever.

"What we share is beautiful, but to her it's just dirty. Dirty and wrong," Jenny said.

"Oh, c'mon," I pleaded. "She's just upset. It's a Catholic mother thing. They all do it. Don't take it personally."

A few days later, another letter arrived, this one bearing the crisp draftsman's lettering of my father.

"Dear John," it began. "By this time you have received Mother's letter. I want to add a few of my personal thoughts while the iron is hot. Mother did enough 'preaching' for both of us so all I want to say is that I agree with and support all she said. One of our big worries is that this may be the first step in your drifting away from the Church and losing your faith—so keep praying and don't stop going to Mass on Sunday. Your faith is precious. Please understand that we are concerned so much because we want only the best of everything for you. Now that we have said all this, we will not bring it up again. You are a grown man and it is your life."

He closed the letter: "One last thought, John. Don't do, or not do, anything because you think it is what *we* want. That would be a mistake. Do what you know is best for *you*. Whatever your decision, Mother and I will always stand by you and be your loving and caring parents. Give our love to Jenny. None of this has changed our feelings of affection toward her."

He signed it, "Sincerely, Dad."

I returned the letter to its envelope and slipped it into the bottom of my sock drawer, beside Mom's. Even though his words were more conciliatory than Mom's, they still carried the unmistakable mark of disapproval. I decided it would be best not to show his letter to Jenny. My life of filtering and parsing the truth was entering a new chapter. No longer did I need only to protect my parents from my own reality; now I had to shelter my girlfriend from theirs, as well.

That evening at dinner, I said, "I heard from my dad today."

"Oh, yeah?" Jenny said.

"He sent their love to you, and said none of this has changed how they feel about you."

"Oh, I'm sure it hasn't," she said.

"Sarcasm duly noted," I replied.

It was several weeks before I responded to either letter. I kept it breezy, telling them about work and our neighborhood and the routine we had fallen into. But I did want them to know that their doom-and-gloom predictions were not coming true. "After two months Jenny and I are very happy in our new home," I wrote. "We both agree we are the most content we've ever been. The strain of constantly commuting was proving to be a real test of our relationship. It was not a healthy way to live, and it was not a smart way to try to maintain a vital relationship. I know you disapprove of our decision, and maybe in a perfect world where we weren't thrown into a strange, sometimes hostile, culture hundreds of miles from our family and friends, things would have been different. But so far we have no regrets."

We had no regrets at all. We bought bikes and took long rides around Palm Beach. We strolled along the Intracoastal Waterway most evenings and spent weekends in Key West and Sanibel. We sipped café cubanos in Little Havana and began every morning by squeezing fresh orange juice from our tree. We planted tomatoes on our patio and coaxed grass to grow in the weedy front yard.

The night before Jenny's birthday, I stayed up late making a homemade card, which I put on the bedstand for her to find when she awoke. Inside it read:

He was an unreformed rock-and-roll animal
In love with a lanky gorgeous blonde
Who had wit, style and grace.
She even laughed at his bad jokes
And made him feel more handsome than he really
     was.
He never much said it, being the (not so) strong,
     silent type,
but he knew he was the luckiest guy around.
They lived happily ever after.
The End.

Our lives felt full, complete, contented, despite my parents' disapproval and the strain it had caused. Eleven months after moving in together, I took Jenny to pick out a new stereo to replace the assemblage of college-vintage components we had each brought into the relationship. It sounded magnificent and was by far our biggest joint purchase. After we got it home and hooked up, I popped in an Anita Baker CD and danced Jenny around the living room.

When the song ended, I said, "Okay, sit down, right here on the couch. I have something for you." I pulled a tiny box from my pocket and handed it to her. Inside was a diamond engagement ring.

CHAPTER 21

✳

J enny began planning in earnest for our wedding, and I began lobbying just as earnestly to make it a Catholic ceremony. I did it for the exact reason my father had warned against—to make him and Mom happy. To fix the damage and heal the wounds. I thought a Catholic wedding would make everything right again. And not just a Catholic exchange of vows, but the whole shebang: a full Catholic wedding Mass complete with the consecration of the bread and wine followed by Holy Communion. Just like they had had.

Jenny knew how important it was to me and agreed, even though it would involve weeks of instruction from a Catholic priest. For her, it was just another of the many chores that went into preparing for a wedding—find a caterer, pick a menu, buy a dress, submit to weeks of rigorous Catholic indoctrination. We agreed to get married back at Our Lady of Refuge, and I asked my two uncles, Father Vin and Father Joe, now both in retirement, to officiate. All they needed, they told us, was the official document showing we had successfully completed our religious training back in our home parish in Florida. I had no idea what or where my home parish was, having never bothered to look up a church near our rental house, but I wasn't going to tell my elderly uncles that. I found our parish, and together we signed up for instruction. We were assigned to an assistant pastor named Father David.

When he showed up at our house one evening for the first meeting, we were both surprised to see a young man dressed in shorts, T-shirt, and sandals. He had a bushy mop of hair and a day's growth of beard; he looked more like he had arrived to teach surfing than religious instruction. Father David did not seem at all perturbed that we were living together. If he was judging us, he did not show it. Jenny instantly liked him, and by the end of the evening we were joking and laughing over wine like old friends.

The Catholic orthodoxy requires both parents, even one who is not a Catholic, to solemnly vow to raise the children in the Catholic faith, promising that they will attend Mass regularly and receive the sacraments. To Jenny, this was akin to forcing a Frenchman to pledge allegiance to Great Britain. Why, she asked, should she be required to raise her children in a religion she neither practiced nor believed in? The conciliatory Father David seemed to understand that he could not push too hard without risking losing us entirely to a justice of the peace. He proposed a compromise: that she agree only to *consider* raising our children Catholic when the time came. Sure, she would agree to consider it, she said, adding, "John's the Catholic. If he wants the kids raised in his faith, then he's going to have to be the one to do it." She agreed that she wouldn't block my efforts, and Father David seemed satisfied. We signed the pledge.

"What a nice guy!" Jenny said after he left. "He's really great. Very reasonable. He's nothing like those holier-than-thou stuffed shirts at your parents' parish." I smiled at our good fortune in finding a young, moderate priest flexible enough to bend his way around some of the Church's more rigid rules. If there was a God, then Father David was God's gift to us, the perfect priest to help me navigate the treacherous waters between my fiancée's and my parents' sensibilities.

But before our next weekly meeting, a distraught Father David called with bad news. His superiors had abruptly re-assigned him to a job that would allow him no contact with parishioners. "They seem to think I'm a bit too much of a maverick," he said.

"Can't you finish up with us?" I asked.

"No," he said. "I'd like to but I can't. I'm sorry."

The parish reassigned us to another priest, a rotund little man with oily skin and close-set eyes that had a slightly leering quality about them. Unlike Father David, he issued edicts in absolute terms, telling us not only how we would be married but how we would live our married life. He seemed to especially enjoy talking to the young couples in our group about sex. The priest dedicated the entire final session to the joys of human sexuality. The more he talked, the more animated he became.

Father Beady Eyes wanted us to know that once we were married we could forget everything we had been told about sex being bad and sinful. "Ignore all that," he said. "Starting on your wedding night, none of that applies." Sex between a married man and woman was a natural thing, a beautiful thing, even a holy and sacred thing. We were to pursue it without hesitation or guilt, with gusto even. "Enjoy it, embrace it, celebrate it!" he said, voice rising in both pitch and volume. His eyes darted from one couple to the next, as though picturing each of us on our wedding night locked in blissful, naked, steamy coitus.

I leaned over and whispered into Jenny's ear: "I think he's enjoying this topic just a little too much."

"Way too much," she whispered back. "He's creeping me out."

The irony of the afternoon was not lost on either of us. Here was this single, celibate man who in all likelihood had never even held hands with a member of the opposite sex standing before a room full of couples offering sage sex advice. It was like hiring a blind man to teach sharpshooting.

But his lack of credibility did not slow Father down. He was even more animated as he gave his blessing to various forms of sexual foreplay. "There's nothing at all wrong with keeping things fun and interesting," he counseled. "Feel free to spice things up." There was only one restriction on our free, unfettered Catholic lovemaking, Father warned, and that was that the penis always, always, always must end up in the vagina. "You must do nothing to keep the sperm from the egg. You must do nothing to subvert God's plan."

This led Father into a detailed description of the only form of birth control we were allowed to practice: the rhythm method. The beauty of this form of birth control was that couples simply stopped having sex during those periods of the month deemed most fertile. The rhythm method was not a sin in the eyes of God, Father explained, because it simply entailed the absence of sex, not the enjoyment of it for some reason other than procreation. And Father insisted it could be highly effective. I knew this to be the case, as evidenced by all those families I'd grown up with back at Our Lady of Refuge with ten, twelve, even fourteen children. My own mother was one of nine, and she swore by the rhythm method. One thing we could all agree on: it worked with 100 percent effectiveness as long as you weren't having sex.

I could sense Jenny nearing her boiling point. At any second she might leap to her feet and tell Father Beady Eyes what she really thought of him and his advice. And I knew she would want to throw in something about his salacious leer as well. "We're almost through," I whispered, as I might if she were undergoing a root canal. "Just sit tight. Nearly over." I offered her my hand to squeeze.

Father left us with one final thought: "When you and your spouse are engaged in sexual union, remember you are not making love with each other. You are making love with our Lord Jesus Christ." We then all bowed our heads as Father led us in prayer that Jesus would bless our wedding-night union with his presence.

Father Beady Eyes handed us the official document showing we had successfully completed religious marriage instruction, and we bolted through the doors and into the sunshine. When we reached the car, I pushed Jenny against the door and kissed her. "Making love with Jesus!" I exclaimed. "A threesome! Now *that* I did not expect to hear."

She burst into laughter, and I could feel her relax in my arms. I knew I definitely owed her big-time for this one.

We set our wedding date for Labor Day weekend, but first came Rock's wedding. Of all my old friends from the neighborhood, Rock was the one with whom I had stayed closest. Even as college and careers took us in opposite directions, we remained best friends, traveling together, camping, and double-dating. I had largely lost track of Tommy and Sack and the others, but not Rock. Now he was getting married in Chicago, just three months before our planned date, and I wouldn't think of missing it. Only after booking our flights did I learn that the guest list included my parents, to whom Rock was almost like a fourth son after years as a regular presence in our home. Other parents from the neighborhood would be attending as well, and we were all staying in the same hotel. It would be my first time seeing them since Jenny and I had moved in together, and I feared that the sight of their son and future daughter-in-law sharing a room before marriage would be painful for them—not only on moral grounds, but social, as well. They no doubt had kept our cohabitation a secret; now it would be obvious to all their friends and neighbors attending the wedding. More salt in their already raw wounds.

And yet I kept telling myself, "You have nothing to hide. You have nothing to be ashamed of. This is their problem, not yours." In preparation for marriage, and feeling our Catholic instruction had fallen somewhat short, Jenny and I had signed up for premarriage counseling with a therapist.

The sessions were designed to help couples understand and address the challenges of marriage in advance and to teach relationship skills, including how to resolve conflicts without leaving lasting scars. In the first session, I immediately launched into a lengthy description of the tension with my parents over our cohabitation. I fully expected the therapist, an affable and warm man named John Adams, to take my side and chastise Jenny for not being more sympathetic to my dilemma. I wanted him to tell her she really needed to be more accommodating of my parents' sensibilities.

But Dr. Adams seemed bewildered by my concerns. "You're how old again?" he asked. I told him, and he continued, "Do you live at home with your parents?"

"No."

"Do you rely on them to support you?"

"No."

"Do you owe them money?"

"No."

"College loans?"

"No."

"Do they pay your car insurance? Your grocery bill? Your utilities?"

By now I was getting the point. He raised his hands in the air. "So why do you let them control your life? What will they do to you?"

"Well, you see, it's just that . . ."

"You don't want to disappoint them," he said, finishing my sentence. "I understand that. But there's a way to be respectful of your parents and their mores without letting them run your life."

Dr. Adams dedicated a lot of our premarriage counseling to helping me find a way to break free of their gravitational pull. I was overdue to live my own life without worrying how they would judge it. I needed to be myself without apology, he counseled, and then it would be up to them to accept me or not. With his advice in mind, I arrived in Chicago, determined to enjoy the weekend with my live-in girlfriend just as I would if they weren't there. I braced for the fallout.

But when we met my parents in the hotel lobby, all was breezily pleasant. They treated us to lunch, and we had an easy, comfortable conversation. Not a heavy word was uttered. We exchanged small gifts, and Jenny briefed my mother on the wedding preparations. Mom, for the umpteenth time, regaled us with the funny story of her own wedding day, how nervous Dad was and how Father Joe overslept and almost missed the ceremony. Dad sat and smiled, nodding his head as he always did when his wife held court.

That evening we sat with them at the wedding Mass, and Mom and Dad smiled up at me as I read a scripture passage from the altar, at Rock's request. They seemed to enjoy the reception. Only the next morning, as we prepared to check out of the hotel, did I finally see what simmered just below the surface. I left Jenny in our hotel room while I went two doors down to visit my parents. I was barely inside the door when they let loose. They had their son to themselves for a moment; this was their chance to speak candidly.

"John, we have something important we want to talk to you about," Dad said.

And then, immediately, Mom: "We don't think you should have a Mass at your wedding."

At first I misunderstood their intent. I thought they were trying to spare Jenny and me the longer ceremony if it wasn't what we really wanted. I figured they knew we were acting more for their sake than our own. "No, really, we don't mind," I said. "The full Mass is fine with both of us."

"You don't understand," Dad said. "We don't think it's a good idea."

"You don't?"

"We don't think it's right given how you're living."

"How I'm living?"

"Living in sin," Mom said. "John, you are living in a state of sin. And you're flaunting it. Look at you, staying together in this hotel in front of everyone."

"You'd be making a mockery of the Mass," Dad continued.

"Oh," I said.

"Jenny's not a Catholic. From what we can tell, you aren't a practicing Catholic anymore," he said. "It would be hypocritical. The Mass should not be window dressing."

The message was slowly sinking in, and I reeled from their words. I was no longer worthy. No longer fit to participate in that singularly most important, transforming experience of their lives, the Eucharist.

"Okay," I said. "We don't have to have a Mass."

"It seems to us you've lost all your faith," Dad said. Just two weeks earlier they had returned from a pilgrimage to the tiny village of Medjugorje in Bosnia-Herzegovina where believers claim the Virgin Mary had repeatedly appeared.

Their breathless, unquestioning description of the alleged miracles had made me wince. Dad said he could tell from my muted response that I no longer shared their beliefs.

"Dad," I said. "Faith is a gift. You can't force it on someone. It's always come so effortlessly to you."

"Tell us the truth," Mom interjected. "Do you still go to church?"

I looked at her for a long moment. Studied her face, the face I had lied to so many times over so many years. "No," I said. "Not for a long, long time."

My mother acted as if she had taken a hit to the chest, knocking the wind out of her. She rested one hand on the chair back and stared out the window as if studying something far off on the interstate. "Oh," she said. "I didn't know that."

"It's not Jenny," I quickly added. "Don't think it's Jenny. I stopped going long before I ever met her. Long before."

We stood in a circle, saying nothing. "Look, I need to get going," I said. I was opening the door when Dad's voice boomed after me.

"John!"

I froze, then turned back. As I did he threw himself against me and buried his face in my shoulder, locking me in a grip so tight it was as if he would never let go. I felt him shaking, his chest lurching against me. Then I felt a warm wetness on my neck and heard his sobs, his jagged gasps. The man I had never seen shed a tear, my Rock of Gibraltar, was crying in my arms.

Soon Mom joined us, wrapping her arms around both Dad and me and crying uncontrollably. I imagine the sight of her husband weeping was too much to bear. I looked down at her face and it was filled with so much anguish I thought of Michelangelo's *Pietà,* showing the sorrowful Virgin Mary holding Jesus' body. I stood dry-eyed, sandwiched between them, rocking gently, awkwardly. "I'm sorry," I murmured, unsure if it was loud enough for them to hear. I was sorry, not for my actions, not for loving Jenny and wanting to be with her, not for failing to embrace those beliefs my parents embraced. But sorry for how much pain I had caused them. Sorry for the years of deception and now for the sucker punch of revelations that so quickly shredded, like shrapnel to the heart, all they had allowed themselves to believe for so long. Sorry for the gaping rift our religious differences had torn in the fabric of an otherwise loving family.

"I'm sorry," I said again, louder.

Finally Dad raised his head and wiped his face. His composure fully back, he said in a voice as strong as ever, "You're going to be late."

Back in my room, I found Jenny packing. "How'd it go with your parents?" she asked.

"Fine," I said. "We just chatted."

"Good. No more heavy stuff?"

"Nope. Not at all."

The next weekend, the phone rang and it was Dad. He sounded sheepish.

"Listen," he said. "I want you to try to forget everything we said in the hotel room in Chicago. We were out of place.

It's your wedding, John. If you want a Mass, you should have a Mass."

"Thanks, Dad," I said. "I appreciate that. Jenny and I talked it over. We won't be having the Mass."

✳

Mom nearly succeeded in sabotaging the wedding. Not that she was consciously trying to. I would never accuse her of that. But how else to explain the sandwich she made for me a mere ninety minutes before I was to walk down the aisle to meet my bride?

On September 2, 1989, I awoke before dawn on the foldout couch in my parents' basement. Jenny was staying with friends across town, and as tradition dictated, we were not to see or speak to each other until we met at the altar later that day. My stomach churned away like a washing machine, and my bowels rumbled. My nerves were on high alert. The previous night at the rehearsal dinner it all still seemed pretend. But now in the gray light before sunrise there was no more denying reality. My gut, quite literally, was telling me so. This was really happening. At the age of thirty-two, I was at last kissing my bachelorhood good-bye. In seven hours I would be a married man, and I was not too proud to admit the prospect terrified me. I pulled myself out of bed, slipped into my running shoes, and took a jog around Harbor Hills and Saint Mary's College. Then I picked up my tuxedo, stopped for a haircut and beard trim, and set up tables in the backyard for a champagne toast and receiving line that would take place between the wedding and reception.

It was just about time to shower and dress when Mom said, "You really should eat something. If there's any day you need to keep up your strength, it's today. Let me make you a sandwich." I had no appetite, but I knew she was right. I wouldn't make it through the long day ahead without nourishment.

A few minutes later, she brought out a sandwich on toast and I took a bite. "What is this?" I asked.

"Liverwurst and onions," she said.

It occurred to me that eating liverwurst and onions just before kissing my bride for the first time as man and wife might not be the wisest move.

"Do you think this is a good idea, Mom?" I asked.

"Why wouldn't it be? You love liverwurst and onions."

I pulled back the bread and studied the interior. Fat, thick rings of white onion, raw and pungent, towered above the liver spread. They were so strong, my eyes watered just looking at them. The sandwich might as well have had the words DEATH BREATH branded across it. Why I didn't push it aside or at least remove the onions, I can't say. Instead I took bite after bite, washing it down with a glass of milk.

Only after my plate was empty did the slow, odorous burn begin to pulsate through my mouth. As I showered, it radiated off my tongue and lips like a radioactive experiment gone wrong. I brushed my teeth, once, twice, three times, then gargled with mouthwash. None of it made a dent. I ran to the kitchen and made a poultice of white bread soaked in milk, plastering it between my tongue and the roof of my mouth. I brushed some more, swished another swig of Listerine, then puffed into my cupped hands. My eyes blinked hard. I didn't just reek. I was toxic.

By the time I was huddled in the back of the church with my brothers, who were serving as co-best men, it was obvious that moms are not always right, and that two hundred guests were all too soon going to realize that as well. Tim and Mike, standing about four feet from me, sniffed in unison. It was Tim who spoke. "Don't tell me you let Mom feed you one of those liverwurst sandwiches," he said.

"What makes you say that?" I asked and popped another breath mint.

Jenny later told me my liver-and-onion breath hit her when she was still several feet down the aisle. Her father, on whose arm she walked, confirmed that she was not exaggerating. I wouldn't have blamed her had she turned and run for the parking lot.

Despite the vapors rising off me, Jenny answered "I do" to all the salient questions. When it was my turn, I did my best to repeat my vows without once exhaling. It was really quite a feat, even if it did make me sound remarkably like Darth Vader. *Jenny . . . I . . . am . . . your . . . husband.*

And then it was over. A full wedding Mass would have stretched an hour or more, but we were in and out in fifteen minutes. I silently thanked Mom and Dad for that. Before we exchanged vows, Father Vin gave a short homily in which he reminded us that we weren't really marrying each other; we were both marrying our Lord Jesus Christ. He left out the part about the wedding night.

Late that night after the band had packed up and all the guests had gone home, Jenny and I checked into a Holiday Inn a few miles from Harbor Hills. With the exception of my onion breath, which, with the help of a barrage of gum and mints, had dissipated about halfway through the receiving line, the entire day had gone off without a hitch. I could laugh now at Little Napoleon's sandwich choice and the idea that, whether consciously or not, she was making one final attempt to derail a marriage she was convinced was doomed by virtue of its sinful prelude. Both she and my father had been perfect hosts, graciously greeting guests, welcoming Jenny's family, and opening their home for both the rehearsal dinner the previous night and the champagne reception. They gave no hint to anyone of the pain that preceded the day.

The hotel room was unspectacular, but it was ours and ours alone. Just us and Jesus.

"We did it," Jenny said as she let her wedding dress fall to the floor.

"You're stuck with me now," I said, and we collapsed on the bed together, at once exhausted and exhilarated, and made love for the first time as husband and wife.

The next morning, Jenny and I boarded an express train to Toronto, where we spent a blissful week honeymooning. Our plan was to return to my parents' house, spend the night, then leave early the next morning for the long drive back to South Florida. This would be our first time staying at the house as a married couple and, now that we sported wedding bands, the first time Mom and Dad would no longer insist we sleep in separate rooms. I assumed we would commandeer the foldout couch in the basement, but when we arrived home at the end of the week, Mom had other plans.

"I'm putting you in our room," she announced.

"Oh, we couldn't do that, Ruth," Jenny said. "The couch will be just great."

"Nonsense," she replied. "You'll be much more comfortable."

"That's so nice, Ruth," Jenny said. "But the couch is great."

"I won't hear of it," Mom said. "This way you'll have your privacy." And from the way my mother said it—a slight, barely noticeable rise of the eyebrows—I could tell what she was thinking—and it was grandchildren. I glanced at Jenny and knew her skin had begun to crawl.

"Thank you, Ruth, it's very kind, but really," Jenny said in her firmest, no-nonsense voice, "I'd prefer the basement."

"Absolutely not," Mom shot back. "The room's all set for you."

"No, really, I insist," Jenny said.

"No," Mom said in a way that made clear she had no intention of backing down, "*I* insist."

Dad and I locked eyes, and I could tell we were both thinking the same thing: this was between the two women, and only a fool would get between them. It would be their first battle of wills as mother-in-law and daughter-in-law. The first of many to come.

"Ruth," Jenny said, her voice tensing as she carefully

enunciated each word, "I do not want to sleep in your room."

"I have it all set up for you," Mom retorted. "Let me show it to you."

And then we were upstairs standing in their bedroom, and I understood why my mother had been so adamant. She had been busy converting it into a romantic honeymoon suite. Fresh flowers stood in a vase on the bedstand. Two sets of her best towels waited on the bed. The covers were turned down, exposing floral sheets she had taken the time to iron. And on the pillow sat two foil-wrapped chocolates. It was just like what Father Beady Eyes had said. Now that we were married, my mother had abandoned her crusade against sexual relations and was now anxious to help facilitate a pregnancy. I could see the color running out of Jenny's face. Her fight-or-flight instinct was kicking in and I sensed she was looking for the nearest door to bolt through.

"This bed has always been," Mom began, and I contemplated leaping across the room, knocking her to the floor, and cupping my hand over her mouth—*No, Mom, don't say it. Please, Mom, don't*—"very lucky for your father and me."

Oh no, she said it. Jenny was now beyond gray. She looked like she'd entered a catatonic state. I imagined she was repeating in her head, *This is not happening to me. This cannot be happening.* She stood perfectly still, not saying a word.

"Great, Mom, thanks," I said. "Fantastic. This will be terrific. We'll get unpacked now." I nudged her out of the room and closed the door. Then I looked around. In Mom's effort to create a romantic boudoir, she had failed to consider the many religious artifacts in the room and the effect they might have on the libidos of others less devout. On one wall was a framed portrait of the Pope staring benevolently at the bed. On another was a wooden crucifix showing Christ in the agony of death, blood trickling down his face and side. I counted three statues of the Virgin Mary, one of them nearly life-size, and another of Saint Francis. A bottle of mail-order holy water was on the windowsill. My mother's Bible sat on one bedstand, my father's prayer book on the other. And hanging from the headboard was the pièce de résistance—an oversize rosary that looked like it had been special ordered for Paul Bunyan. It was a good four feet long, and each wooden bead was the size of a walnut, strung together on a heavy chain. I plopped down on the bed, and the giant beads clanked loudly against the frame.

"It's not so bad," I said to Jenny. She just stood in silence. "It's only for one night. C'mon, honey, it's fine. Isn't it fine?" And then: "She means well. She's trying." I didn't have the heart to tell her that Father Vin would also be spending the night, and would be in my old room, immediately on the other side of the wall, his headboard inches from our own. Nor that Mom and Dad would be on the sleeper sofa immediately below us.

"We'll just have to be quiet," I offered helpfully.

Jenny at last spoke: "Don't touch me tonight."

"Oh, come on. Relax. It's just a room." And for me, it was. I had grown up with these Catholic adornments and barely noticed them.

"I mean it," she said. "You will not touch me."

That night after dinner when we retired for the night, Jenny still had not relaxed. Sex had become such a powder-keg issue between her and my parents, I guess I couldn't blame her. Before marriage, sex had been our downfall, our dirty little secret that had brought shame to the family name. Now we were supposed to embrace it with vigor in their bed with the saints and angels and Pope watching—and my uncle the priest inches away on the other side of the wall. She slid into the king-size bed and hugged the edge of the mattress as though she were expecting six or seven others to join us. I crawled in from the other side and slid up against her, draping one leg over hers. "Do not touch me," she repeated in a way that told me not to push my luck.

Despite that, I thought a little levity could only help ease the tension. I sat up on my side of the bed and began to rock. Slowly at first, then with increasing vigor. Pretty soon the bed frame was creaking, the springs squeaking. Then the giant rosary beads began to knock against the headboard. *Clank, clank, clank.* Even Jenny would have to admit this was funny. Here we were, freshly minted newlyweds in my parents' very Catholic bed, not having sex but making noises that would make it sound like we were. Hilarious! At any moment I fully expected Jenny to burst out laughing.

Suffice it to say, Jenny did not burst out laughing. She did not grin or smile or even nod. What she did was leap out of bed so quickly I thought for a moment that my mother might have left hot coals in the sheets. I then spent the next hour trying to convince my bride that walking back to Florida in the middle of the night was not practical. I eventually coaxed her back into my parents' bed, where we slept with four feet of empty mattress between us and nary a squeak or creak heard all night.

The next morning, after hurried good-byes, we began our trip south, the backseat and trunk filled with wedding gifts. We were nearly to Georgia before Jenny found it in her heart to forgive me, not only for the simulated sex sounds but, more important, for failing to take her side against my mother. I promised her then and there that she would never again have to sleep in my parents' bed.

✳

We were barely back in Florida as husband and wife when we began shopping for a house to call our own. Our rental place had its charm, but something felt different now, and we ached to put down roots. With marriage came a sense of security and permanence we both found reassuring. Jenny and I had insisted we did not need a marriage certificate to be fully committed to each other, that the wedding was just a formality, but we were both surprised at how much marriage changed our dynamic. For the first time since meeting, we each knew the other wasn't going anywhere. No one would be running off alone for the next job opportunity or fellowship. This was our life now, a life together. The prospect of cosigning away thirty years of it to a bank mortgage no longer felt terrifying.

Just one block away on a much prettier street, we found a small bungalow for sale. Unlike our rental house, it was meticulously kept, with a lush lawn surrounded by exotic tropical plantings. Jenny gasped aloud when we spotted it on our evening walk. "It's perfect," she said before even getting a peek inside. "The green paint has to go, but otherwise it's just right."

Several weeks later, we walked out of a bank office with the deed and the keys to the front door—and headed straight to our new address: 345 Churchill Road. As soon as we were in the driveway, Jenny jumped out of the car and bolted for the door, key in hand.

"No, no! Wait! Don't go in! Wait for me!" I shouted after her. I wanted to do this right. I caught up with her on the porch, took the key from her, turned it in the lock, and swung the door open. Then, without a word of warning, I scooped Jenny into my arms and lifted her off her feet. She let out a surprised, joyful whoop.

"You goof!" she said, throwing her arms around my neck. "What are you doing?"

"Here we go," I announced. "Our first step into our very own home. Our new life." And with that I carried her across the threshold. We paused there for a moment just inside the entrance, silently reveling.

"Now put me down," Jenny said, "before you hurt yourself."

As the months passed, we turned the little bungalow into our own, repainting the walls, hanging Haitian artwork, and lifting the shag carpeting to discover burnished oak floors beneath. We planted a garden and brought home a behaviorally challenged Labrador retriever puppy we named Marley, who quickly wiggled his way into our hearts despite causing all sorts of havoc on a daily basis. Outside our bedroom window were a gardenia bush and a giant Brazilian pepper tree where wild parrots roosted, and each morning we awoke to the flowers' scent and the birds' chatter. Life seemed about as good as life could get.

Yet the strain with my parents remained. I had assumed all the bad blood that had preceded the marriage would wash away with the Catholic ceremony, but the wounds ran deep. Jenny had not gotten over how judgmental they had been, especially my mother's emotional prediction that our marriage was doomed to failure. In their moral certitude, she saw smugness and superiority and an implicit belief that she was somehow inferior, not quite the good Catholic wife they had prayed for their son to find. She was convinced they blamed her for pulling me away from the faith. "In their eyes, I'm your downfall," she said more than once.

My parents were hurt, too. Hurt by my belated honesty. Hurt by our rejection of their values. Hurt by Jenny's barely concealed contempt for everything they believed and by my acquiescence in that contempt. My parents' medieval interpretation of Catholicism, with its literal belief in guardian angels hovering over our shoulders to protect us from the dark agents of Satan, struck both of us as almost comically superstitious. The difference was that I had grown up with it and took it all in stride. Jenny, on the other hand, was unable to hide how bizarre she found it all. To her it was all hocus-pocus, no different from tossing salt over one's shoulder for good luck. She met their various expressions of faith with a sort of bemused bewilderment, usually accompanied by a grimacing cringe, which I knew my parents interpreted as mocking. In their eyes, her discomfort was disrespect.

On one of Jenny's first visits to my parents' house, shortly after we began dating, Mom cornered her in the kitchen and pulled from her apron pocket a small glass bottle with a hand-printed label. *Oh no,* I thought, *she's got the holy water.* I watched as she uncorked the bottle and moved closer to Jenny. *Put it away, Mom. Put it back in your apron. You barely know this girl yet.* Without a word of explanation, Mom wetted her thumb with the contents and made the sign of the cross on Jenny's forehead as she murmured, "In the name of the Father and of the Son and of the Holy Spirit." Dad looked on approvingly. As with most things they did, the act was well-intentioned. They wanted to bless this potential new member of our family and ensure that the Lord smiled on our new relationship. Jenny could not have looked more shocked had my mother clicked her heels and flown off on a broomstick. "It's just something old-fashioned Catholics do," I told her later, but that moment set the tone for many more to come.

Those days were far behind us now. With the help of my strong-willed wife, I had finally broken free from my parents' influence. I no longer felt the need to lie or obfuscate. I was unapologetically my own person now, officially in the category known as "nonpracticing Catholic." But this freedom came at a cost. It was as though a wall of bulletproof glass had risen between my parents and me. I could still see and hear them through it, but it wasn't the same. We avoided religion, politics, and social issues such as abortion and gay rights—any hot-button topic that would expose the gaping rift in our values. They didn't ask; I didn't tell. They no longer gushed about the latest prayer hour they had organized at church, or inquired of me about Sunday Mass. Their faith and my lack of it had become our taboo topic.

As it hovered over us, suffocating the relationship, we all pretended it did not exist.

More than anything, I think they realized they had met their match in Jenny and needed to clam up or risk losing me entirely. If my mother was Little Napoleon, then Jenny was her Waterloo. Mom seemed to understand she would not win this fight—not without losing her son as a casualty of war.

Soon enough there was another prize on the horizon that my parents did not want to risk losing a part of. Jenny was pregnant. The prospect of a grandchild excited them beyond words, and when the first pregnancy ended in a miscarriage, my parents grieved with us, even as they attributed the loss to God's mysterious plan. Soon enough we were expecting again, and in May 1992, we brought Patrick Joseph Grogan home from the hospital. We chose his middle name after Jenny's father, but I was happy to let my parents believe I was carrying on their Mary-and-Joseph tradition. A week later, Jenny's parents arrived to spend ten days with us, and the visit was comfortable and easy. Her mother took over the cooking and cleaning, and each day as I worked, Jenny and the baby would join her parents on an outing—to the mall, the Japanese gardens, even the beach, where Jenny could sit in the shade and nurse her newborn son.

Two days after Jenny's parents left, mine called from a campground outside Atlanta where they had arrived the previous day in their motor home. They were on their way to see us and their first grandson, but the trip had another purpose: to make a pilgrimage to a farm in Conyers,

Georgia, east of Atlanta, where apparitions of the Virgin Mary had been reported by the farm's owner. The Catholic Church refused to endorse the alleged sightings, but the farm woman's word was good enough for Mom and Dad.

"Our Blessed Mother says we all need to pray if we are to have any hope," Mom said. Then she put Dad on the phone, and their pilgrimage to the latest alleged miracle site made more sense to me. He had news to share. On the day Patrick was born, Dad's doctor had found a cancerous tumor on his prostate, and he was scheduled to begin radiation as soon as he returned from our place. He assured me the doctors were confident they could knock it into remission.

"Why didn't you tell me sooner?" I asked.

"You were having your first baby," he said. "I didn't want to put a damper on your joy."

"I never want to be kept in the dark, Dad," I said. "Whatever the news, and whenever you get it, I want you to share it with me, okay?"

"Fair enough," Dad said.

When they pulled up in their recreational vehicle the next evening, they both looked older and more fragile than I had remembered from just a few months earlier. For the previous dozen years, they had happily tooled all over the country and Mexico in their rolling home on a Chevrolet truck chassis, sightseeing, visiting relatives, and making pilgrimages to various shrines and holy sites. But now I could see the strain on their faces, the weariness in their shoulders. At seventy-six, they were slowing down, and the rigors of long-distance road travel were clearly becoming too much for them. I realized with a tinge of sadness that this chapter of their lives would soon be coming to a close.

This was their first time visiting us since before we had decided to live together two years earlier, and I wanted it to go well. But they were barely in the door when I sensed Jenny's stress levels rising. As my mother cradled the baby, cooing over him, Jenny hovered nearby, clearly anxious. After dinner, she pulled me aside in the kitchen.

"Look," she whispered. "I don't want your mother trying one of her secret home baptisms on our baby." I dismissed her concerns as ridiculous, but they were not without foundation. When my mother was a schoolgirl, she would secretly baptize the non-Catholic children she babysat. Even as an adult, she saw nothing wrong with this and told the story with great affection. She had been taught that lay Catholics could perform an emergency baptism in certain circumstances. In her eyes, she was rescuing her young charges from an eternity in limbo, that perpetual waiting room between heaven and hell that the nuns taught us was the final destination for the world's millions of pagan babies. Jenny had heard the story, too, and now that she had her own child, she was unnerved by the possibility of her mother-in-law performing mysterious religious rituals over him without her knowledge.

"No one's performing any secret baptisms," I assured her, but I could see she wasn't convinced. She would not let Patrick out of her sight.

On the surface, my parents' visit was comfortable enough. Mom took over most of the cooking, and Dad puttered around the yard. We made easy small talk, sticking to our unspoken list of safe topics. We sat down to meals, and they made no attempt to pray over the food. They were in our home and clearly playing by our rules. Yet as their stay progressed, my mother increasingly picked up on Jenny's discomfort. At one point when she had me alone for a moment, she said, "Jenny acts like I've never held a baby before. What, does she think I'm going to drop him or something?"

"Chalk it up to new-mom jitters," I told her. "Don't take it personally, Mom."

From my father's glances, I knew he was offering her similar counsel when they were alone in their RV parked in the driveway. While I was at work, they wanted to free Jenny up so she could run errands or catch up on her sleep without having to worry about the baby. But Jenny deflected their offers, taking him wherever she went, whether it was to the store or into the bedroom for a nap. They couldn't help but feel snubbed.

Despite Jenny's worries, my parents had no intention of attempting an emergency baptism on their grandson, but that did not mean they had forgotten about the promise we had made when we married in the Catholic faith. One evening I returned home from work to find them alone in the living room. Jenny had taken the baby and gone shopping. "She didn't say when she'd be back," Mom said with a wounded look.

I had barely kicked my shoes off when they jumped at the opportunity to speak to me privately. "Say, we've been meaning to ask you," Dad began, and I braced for what I knew was coming. "Have you set a date for the baptism?"

"We're talking about it," I said. And we had been.

"The baptism is important," Dad said. "Without it, Patrick cannot have eternal salvation."

"It's something we're working on," I said.

"What's to work on?" Mom snapped. "He's already almost a month old. I don't know what you're waiting for."

"We plan to get to it," I said.

Her face grew grave. "You do know that if something, God forbid, were to happen to him, he couldn't go to heaven. He would be barred forever from entering our Lord's kingdom."

"I'm not too worried about that," I said.

"Well, you should be."

I felt the blood rising in my cheeks. "Do you really think God would cast aside an innocent infant just because his parents didn't get around to having him baptized?" I could not resist adding: "And do you really think a Catholic baby is somehow more sacred in God's eyes than a Jewish baby or a Muslim baby—or a baby that's nothing at all?" The Catholic belief that it was the "one true faith" had stuck in my craw for years.

"We're all born with original sin," Dad said. "By baptizing him, you'll wash that sin away and let Patrick become a child of God."

I held my tongue and stared at the floor.

"Let's all pray together," Mom suggested, and before I could protest, she grabbed my hand in one of hers and Dad's hand in the other. Dad closed the circle by gripping my free hand with his.

"Let us bow our heads and pray," he began. "In the name of the Father, and of the Son, and of the Holy Spirit."

I bowed my head as we recited the Lord's Prayer, but all I could think was that if Jenny walked in the door, her worst fears would be confirmed: secret incantations going on behind her back. I strained to listen for the sound of a car door slamming. Of the thousands of Our Fathers I had recited aloud, this one was the longest. When it finally ended, I said, "You really don't need to worry about it. Patrick will be baptized. We just need to do it at our own pace." Then I excused myself and went to the bathroom to splash water on my face.

The next morning, on the sixth day of what was to have been a ten-day visit, my parents announced they had decided to cut their visit short and leave the following day for home. The official reason was that South Florida's steamy weather was too uncomfortable for them, which I knew to be true. Mom especially wilted in even moderate heat and humidity. They were also worried about Dad's prostate cancer and the radiation regimen that awaited him. "I have to admit I'm not looking forward to what's coming," he said. "I might as well get back home and get it over with." But I knew the strain with Jenny had something to do with it as well.

Oddly, that evening was the most relaxed of the visit. Jenny and my mother were both noticeably at ease. They chatted amiably, and we all laughed as Mom told funny stories from her childhood and mine. I asked more about the cancer, and the planned bone scan that would tell him whether it had spread beyond his prostate. Dad said, "It's in God's hands. Whatever the Lord chooses for me, that's what it will be."

Mom chimed in: "We have dedicated our lives to spreading our Blessed Mother's message, and we still have a lot of work to do. I can't do it without your dad, so I know the Lord is going to give him many more healthy years with me."

"We still have too much work to do," Dad agreed. I knew they were not just putting on brave faces. This was what they believed. I marveled at their complete and unshakable faith.

The next morning Jenny packed them a picnic lunch and I helped load the motor home. Everything stayed upbeat until Dad leaned over to say good-bye to his grandson. As he stroked the back of his hand on Patrick's cheek, Mom began to weep. Her bullish confidence seemed to have vanished overnight. I imagined she was wondering if her husband would live long enough to see his grandson again.

The juxtaposition of my son's life just beginning and my father's in jeopardy was not lost on me, either. I wanted to say something profound to Dad, but the words did not come. Instead, I gave Mom a long hug and Dad the famous Grogan handshake, squeezing his hand in mine a little longer than I might have otherwise. I told them how much it meant to me that they had made the trip. As I watched them lumber off in the motor home, a pain seared my heart like an electric shock. Even though inside the house waited a wife who loved me and a beautiful son who would be my joy for the rest of my years, I could not help feeling oddly alone. Standing on the curb watching as they turned the corner, I saw it clearly: one family just beginning on life's voyage, another approaching journey's end.

*　　*　　*

In September, when Patrick was four months old, Jenny and I brought him to Michigan to be baptized in the sanctuary of Our Lady of Refuge. True to her word to Father David, Jenny said she would not stand in the way if that was what I wanted. And even though I no longer even pretended to be a practicing Catholic (when asked, my stock response was "I was *raised* Catholic"), it was what I wanted. I was hard-pressed to explain why. I was no longer a spiritual Catholic, and maybe I never had been, but I still considered myself Catholic. It was part of who I was and part of what I wanted my children to become. I knew that my parents—Dad in particular—considered this the exact wrong reason to baptize a child. The words *cultural Catholic*, with their embrace of the nostalgia of the faith without the faith itself, were anathema to him. Yet I could not deny that the term fit me.

Whatever my reasons, Mom and Dad rejoiced at the news of our decision. When I called home to tell them we would have him baptized at Refuge, they both immediately began planning the guest list.

"Um, Jenny and I were thinking we'd keep it small," I interrupted. "You know, just immediate family."

"Nonsense," Mom said. "We need to invite the neighbors. And the relatives. And the prayer group. I'll host the reception afterward."

"Mom," I said, the exasperation rising in my voice.

"What? You want to show off your baby, don't you? Besides, if you don't, people will start to wonder if there's something wrong with him."

"Wrong? Like he's the Hunchback of West Palm Beach?" I said.

"People talk," she said. "My grandson is perfect in every way, and I want to show him off."

More important, I suspected, she wanted to show off the fact that her grandson would no longer be a godless pagan baby. I diplomatically tried to temper her enthusiasm, telling her we needed to be respectful of Jenny's sensibilities as the mother. "You don't want to spook her, Mom," I said.

"Why on earth would this spook anyone?" she responded. "By the way, now that you've started a family, don't you think it's time you think about returning to Mass again?"

In the end, I won a few concessions, but Mom largely got what she wanted. Jenny repeated that this was my event, and she was going to stay out of it, which mostly she did.

Father Joe's lifelong love of Lucky Strikes had finally caught up with him, and he had died of cancer the previous year, slipping away peacefully in Marijo's former bedroom, where my parents had nursed him around the clock in his final months. But Father Vin remained healthy and vital, living in a log cabin in the Michigan woods, and he happily agreed to come out of retirement to officiate.

We asked Rock and his wife to be the godparents, and they drove in from Chicago for the big day. As they held Patrick in their arms, Father Vin launched into the rites of baptism, a surprisingly large part of which involved driving the devil from our baby's tarnished soul.

I knew it was going to be hard on Jenny when Father Vin announced to the thirty or so people gathered in the sanctuary that he was going to start off with "a prayer of exorcism."

"Almighty Father," Father Vin prayed, "you sent your holy son into the world to cast out the power of Satan, prince of evil, and to rescue man from the kingdom of darkness. We pray for this child to set him free from original sin and make him a temple for your whole spirit to dwell within him." From the side of my eye I could see Jenny's mouth tighten.

"Do you reject sin?" Father Vin asked in a clear voice, beckoning us to answer on Patrick's behalf and our own.

As a group, we responded, "I do." Jenny sat motionless, a look of quiet distress spreading across her face.

"Do you reject the glamour of evil?"

"I do."

"Do you reject Satan, father of sin, prince of darkness?" Jenny's hands, resting on the pew, tightened into ashen fists. The thought of an exorcism being held over her precious infant was too much for her. I imagined she was waiting for Patrick's head to start spinning on its neck like Linda Blair's did in *The Exorcist,* and I could tell she was fighting the urge to grab her baby and bolt for the exit.

I leaned in close until my lips rested against her ear. "Lamaze breathing," I whispered. "Quick, shallow breaths. Blow it away." I made little puffing sounds. "We're almost done."

Three times, Father Vin splashed water over Patrick's head as he chanted, "I baptize you in the name of the Father, and of the Son, and of the Holy Spirit." He used his thumb to rub sacred oils onto our son's forehead, chest, and back in the sign of a cross and placed a starched linen bib on him to signify his purification from original sin.

"Patrick Joseph, you have become a new creation," my uncle pronounced. "I claim you for Christ our savior by the sign of the cross."

Then it was over. The neighbors and relatives crowded around to coo over Patrick. Father Vin playfully hoisted his great-nephew in the air and congratulated him for uttering barely a squawk during the ceremony. "You're a Christian now," he said. "All baptized."

Off to the side, I slipped my arm around Jenny and rubbed her back.

"That Satan is so far out of here, he's halfway to Pluto by now," I said, trying to make her laugh. "Father Vin kicked Satan's ass! If Patrick takes the wrong path in life, we won't have the devil to blame."

She gave me a little smile.

"You okay?" I asked.

"I'm okay," she said. "Definitely ready for a beer."

"Me, too," I agreed. "Maybe a couple." And on the way home for Mom's punch-and-cookie reception, I made a quick detour to the party store on the corner where Tommy and I used to loiter and bought a twelve-pack.

❖

Thirteen months after Patrick's baptism, Jenny and I welcomed another member into our family. We baptized him Conor Richard, but this time we did it on our own turf, at the local parish in West Palm Beach where Father Beady Eyes had coached us on the rhythm method. It was a group ceremony, with several babies being baptized together, and the priest was more subdued than my uncle about exorcising Satan from the souls of the innocent. Because of the distance and my parents' advancing age, they did not attend, and that simplified matters, too. Jenny and I were both surprisingly relaxed, and later I sent photos to my parents so they would have proof their second grandchild, too, had been accepted into God's embrace.

Then came our daughter, Colleen Ruth, and our family was officially complete. We were five now, and it felt right. As with Conor, we had her baptized in a group ceremony at the church near our new home in Boca Raton. This time there wasn't even a priest present; a married deacon handled the duties. My aging parents could rest easy at last, knowing their grandchildren were no longer destined to spend eternity in God's waiting room. I felt I had done my duty and could relax.

The Lord apparently still had more work for Dad to do, as Mom had predicted, because he banished Dad's prostate cancer with the same vigor Father Vin had used to banish Satan. After several rounds of radiation therapy, his doctors pronounced the cancer obliterated and told him, "You'll die of something else before this ever comes back." He attributed his good fortune to the power of prayer and returned to his robust ways.

The Lord must have had more work for Mom, too. The year after Colleen's birth, Mom's cardiologist determined that her arteries were almost completely blocked. She was just one overexertion away from a stroke or heart attack. At the hospital, doctors tried to open the passages with shunts, but ended up rushing her into emergency open-heart surgery, from which she emerged, after a lengthy recovery, feeling better than she had in years. She no longer had to stop to catch her breath or pop nitroglycerin pills to control palpitations. There was only one adverse side effect of the quadruple bypass surgery, and it was a major one. Doctors warned us that Mom might seem forgetful and mentally adrift for several weeks because of the amount of time she spent on an external heart pump during surgery, and they were right. What they had not predicted was that Mom's mind would never quite fully return, never quite be as sharp again. The day of her surgery marked the beginning of a long, gradual descent, barely noticeable at first, into memory loss.

She also struggled with debilitating arthritis, and as my mother grew more frail, Dad took on more and more of the household responsibilities—vacuuming, grocery shopping, even expanding his cooking repertoire. He still cut his own grass, shoveled his own driveway, trimmed his own hedges, and found time to regularly weed and water the flower beds around the church.

As a couple, my parents retreated more and more into their faith. Their friends were dropping around them on what seemed a near-weekly basis, and their own close calls had given them a deeper sense of their mortality. I had not thought it possible, but with each year they became even more fundamentalist. With the exception of the evening news, they no longer watched anything on television except for EWTN, the Eternal Word Television Network, founded by a scowling, scolding nun named Mother Angelica, whom they adored for her conservative screeds against the depravity of society. In a modern world from which they increasingly felt estranged, Mother Angelica played to their sensibilities. With her black-and-white reduction of life's complexities, she was the comforting anchor to their past. When Pope John Paul II came to America, my parents sat glued to EWTN for days, videotaping his every appearance and motorcade.

As our lives moved in their separate orbits, we fell into a rhythm. My parents and I spoke on the phone every week or two and exchanged cards on birthdays and anniversaries. Every winter they would fly to South Florida to spend a week with us, and every summer Jenny and I would load the kids in the minivan and drive the thirty hours to spend a week with them. Unlike those earlier visits, they did not push any agenda, did not even try to pray aloud before meals in our presence. Each morning they would arise and slip out the door for Mass, not inviting us or even telling us where they were going. Jenny and I would be careful not to comment on their devotion to EWTN or the growing number of Virgin Marys populating the house. Jenny and my mother had arrived at their own separate peace, finding a common bond in the kids; nearly all their discussions stuck to that neutral ground. Dad and I, too, hammered out a safe zone, talking of careers, home repairs, and our shared love of gardening. I would help Dad with yard chores and take the kids to the playground at Our Lady of Refuge and to The Lagoon to fish for bluegills or the Harbor Hills beach to swim where Tommy, Rock, Sack, and I had spent so many hours.

As we sat down for dinner on the screened porch one summer evening, Colleen in a high chair, the boys kneeling on their wrought-iron seats so their chins would clear the glass tabletop, I asked without warning or forethought, "Grandpa, are you going to lead us in a prayer?" I'm not sure what brought the words to my lips, but I knew I wanted my children to at least experience a taste of that safe, ordered world I enjoyed at their age. And I wanted to give my parents permission to be themselves around their grandchildren. My father looked up at me and blinked a couple of times. It wasn't easy to surprise the old man, but I had managed. He missed just one beat, then raised his fingertips to his forehead in preparation of making the sign of the cross, and began, "In the name of the Father, and of the Son, and of the Holy Spirit." The boys followed his lead and did their best to bless themselves. "Bless us, oh Lord, and these thy gifts . . ." At the end, he ad-libbed, "And thank you, God, for blessing us with John and Jenny and our three beautiful grandchildren, and for bringing them safely home to see us." The kids joined their grandparents with a loud "Amen."

With the kids young, it was easy to pretend the question of their religious upbringing was settled. But soon enough Patrick arrived in second grade and at the age where he should have been preparing for his first confession and First Holy Communion. My parents waited in anxious silence for an announcement, but that was not going to happen. Not for him or for his younger brother or sister. In the years since Patrick's birth, Jenny and I had settled into a life wholly our own. Something about the heady responsibility of having three tiny lives in my hands helped me put my relationship with my own parents in perspective. My priorities were with Jenny and our children now, and I embraced my new role as husband, father, and home owner. I was who I was, and as Dr. Adams the marriage therapist had counseled me several years earlier, it was now up to my parents to accept their son, or not, for the man he had become. I could tell they were trying their best to do that.

I gradually grew more comfortable in my skin as a nonpracticing Catholic, one with no particular animosity for the religion but also one who disagreed with enough of its teachings to know I did not belong. For as long as I could remember, one of Dad's favorite targets of antipathy was that certain kind of Catholic who chose Church rulings to obey or ignore as if they were options on a menu. There were few people on earth Dad held in more contempt than these cafeteria Catholics. "Doggone it all anyway," he would carp. "These people pick and choose what they want to believe like they are at the drive-thru window at McDonald's."

For all our disagreements over religion, on this we were in accord. So many of my contemporaries called themselves practicing Catholics when in actuality they were practicing only what they wanted. They embraced the feel-good aspects while conveniently disregarding whichever of the Church's hierarchical edicts they did not like. They might practice birth control, support abortion rights, roll their eyes at the Church's condemnation of homosexuality, and question why women were banned from the priesthood, and yet they still called themselves Catholics. I knew Mom and Dad were deeply disappointed in my choices, but at least they couldn't accuse me of picking and choosing off the Catholic prix fixe menu.

The clergy child sex abuse scandal that would rock the foundations of the Catholic Church was just beginning to come to light as my boys were entering grade school, and this vaporized what little was left of my crumbling faith. The actions of the pedophile priests against the most vulnerable and defenseless members of their flocks were sickening enough, but even more so were the calculated efforts of their superiors to silence the victims and bury the truth. I knew that for every predatory priest and every amoral bishop protecting him there were hundreds practicing their vocation with Christlike piety. Priests like my two uncles. Yet the blossoming scandal screamed of the highest order of hypocrisy. The molesters and their protectors perpetrated their evil while holding themselves up each Sunday in their snowy white vestments as the embodiment of Christ. They were the ultimate cafeteria Catholics, but I would never say that to my father. I could only imagine how devastated he was by the spreading scandal, though he would eventually chalk it up to "a few bad apples" corrupted by liberal elements within the Church and the depraved culture of modern society. I could only bite my tongue. As I put it in one late-night phone call to Tim, who unlike me had fallen away from the Church with a great deal of lingering anger, "It's a good time to take a break from being a Catholic."

On our own, Jenny and I set out to do our best to raise our children as moral and ethical beings, to instill in them goodness and compassion and generosity. We would not be seeking the help of any organized religion.

Mom and Dad breathed not a word. They dared not. As each child reached and missed Catholic benchmarks—first confession, first communion, confirmation—they kept their lips sealed. Jenny had made it clear that she would not tolerate any more meddling, and there had been enough flare-ups and power struggles that they knew she was not bluffing. They had gradually accepted that I shared her resolve. They weren't going to jeopardize access to their son and grandchildren by opening their mouths again.

Instead, they began to mail us things. First came a giant, heavyweight family Bible with gold-edged pages and a note encouraging us to make it a central part of our lives. Next came a wall-size crucifix and a note suggesting we display it prominently in our home. Then came a statue of the Virgin Mary and a thick treatise explaining the Catholic catechism.

There were children's prayer books and Bible stories, and birthday gifts of rosaries.

Finally, a copy of *Catholic Parenting* magazine arrived with a handwritten letter from Dad saying he had bought us a one-year subscription. "Hopefully you and Jenny will find a few things in each issue that will be helpful," he wrote.

We had been silent on the subject for too long, and I knew I owed him my thoughts. Just because my parents no longer badgered me didn't mean they had stopped worrying. In a letter thanking him for the subscription, I wrote, "I know we're not raising the kids quite the way you would like, but I want you to know that we put a lot of thought and energy into the spiritual side of their upbringing. We are working hard, and to the very best of our ability, to raise them as moral, principled people. We're doing it our own way, but our end goal, I think, is the same as yours."

A few months earlier, I had joined the *Philadelphia Inquirer* as a metropolitan columnist, giving my unvarnished opinions on a variety of topics. It was the same basic job I'd had in my last several years at the Fort Lauderdale paper, but with one big difference: the columns were now posted online. Mom and Dad were able to read each one the same day it was published, and Dad especially followed my work with zeal. I was past the point of trying to shelter him from my views, which in my column included harsh indictments of the Catholic Church over the child abuse cover-up. Still, I felt the need to explain.

"As you may have gathered from my columns, I'm a bit jaded about the institutions of men—the political, judicial, corporate, and, yes, religious," I wrote to him. "But that doesn't mean I'm jaded about what the institutions represent—democracy, justice, enterprise, faith. We humans are frail and flawed, and it goes against my grain to have one group of flawed humans trying to tell another group of flawed humans how to live. Besides, you know I'm not much of a joiner. So I'm picking my way delicately through the minefield of parenthood on my own, trying to steer the right path, making course corrections along the way. All I can promise is that I will keep an open mind."

I concluded: "I'm sorry for the pain I know I've caused you and Mom, but I know you respect that each of us must follow our own moral compass. Please, try not to worry too much, which I know is easier said than done. You have been a great father to me. I'm trying hard to be the same to my kids. Thanks for teaching by example."

Dad did not respond for two months. When he did, he apologized for the delay and explained that caring for Mom, who was becoming increasingly dependent on him for even the most basic needs, "is becoming more and more of a full-time job." He added, "I am not complaining. I thank the good Lord that I am able to take care of Ruthie, and I pray that I will always be able to do so."

Then he turned his pen to what I had written.

"I was pleased and comforted to hear that you and Jenny are working hard on giving the children day-to-day guidance in spiritual matters so that Christian principles will be the foundation of their value system as they grow up." He said he understood our desire to try to do it without the help of organized religion. "However, I sincerely hope that, when the time is right," he added, "you will introduce them to the beauty of their Catholic heritage."

"I haven't given up on the Church, but I do feel the need to proceed with caution regarding it," I responded. "I know you're praying for Jenny, the kids, and me, and I really do appreciate that. We can use all the help we can get."

And I meant it.

PART THREE

❊

Coming Home

❊

That winter, a cherished life came to a crashing end back home in Harbor Hills. The giant maple tree that for decades had dominated the backyard of my parents' house had fallen in a blizzard. Dad called to break the news as if we had lost a family member. The tree had self-seeded there when I was a toddler and grown tall and magnificent over the years, shading many a cookout and giving us kids sturdy branches to climb.

"The end of an era," Dad said and called a tree service to come remove it, stump, roots, and all.

As spring neared, Dad looked out the living-room window, and where once he had seen loss he now saw possibility. "Say," he said in one of our weekly chats, "I'm thinking now that the maple tree is gone and the sun can get through again, that maybe that spot would be a nice place for a little flower garden. Something Mother could sit and look out on."

For all its magnificence, the maple had been a flora bully, hogging water and nutrients and blocking life-giving sunlight from reaching the soil, creating an inhospitable zone where only a few tough clumps of grass and wild mint could hang on. With its demise, the patch of earth was again available for a new generation of plant life. "I thought maybe you could give me some ideas," Dad said.

When Jenny and I moved with the children to Pennsylvania in 1999, it was so I could try my hand as a gardening editor. I spent three years as editor of *Organic Gardening* magazine before realizing daily newspapers were where my heart lay and taking the job at the *Philadelphia Inquirer*. Dad was an accomplished gardener in his own right, but he mostly stuck to marigolds, petunias, and other tried-and-true annual flowers from the garden center, and he hoped I could steer him toward more interesting varieties.

I was thrilled to be able to help. My father was so self-sufficient, even at eighty-seven, that he did not give me many opportunities. Over the next several weeks, we discussed at length the merits of different plants, the strategy of mixing perennials with annuals for season-long color, and of choosing varieties of differing heights to give the garden three-dimensional breadth. I was enjoying the process enormously, partly because I loved gardening, but more, I realized, because it gave us a shared father-son project over which to bond, just like in my childhood with science fairs and home improvements.

One evening, after the snow had melted and the ground thawed, I grabbed my spade and a bushel basket and headed into my yard. At one garden bed, I stooped over and rooted around until I found the tiny spears of a dormant hosta poking through the mulch. With my shovel, I dug the plate-size root clump out and quartered it into four equal chunks. One I replaced in the hole, and the remaining three I wrapped in newspaper and placed in the basket. I moved on to the purple coneflower and repeated the process. Then to the brown-eyed Susans and bee balm, the phlox and daisies, the fragrant anise hyssop and the lustily prolific daylilies. Soon my basket overflowed with a variety of perennials Dad could pop into the ground and watch take root. One of a gardener's greatest joys is the joy of giving. It is an easy, painless act of generosity because of the garden's endless bounty, which reminded me of the miracle of the loaves and fishes we learned about in school: the more you shared, the more there was to share. Putting together this care package from my garden to Dad's pleased me greatly. I worked with a smile on my face.

A few days later when the box showed up on my parents' porch, Dad wasted no time in calling me. "Holy smokes!" he said. "What's all this? It's like Christmas in March!" It was the most excited I had heard him in a long time. I had not sent him anything he could not have ordered from a nursery, but he acted as though I had shared exotic riches from a far distant land. "This is fantastic!"

"That'll get your garden started," I said. "You can fill it in with some annuals later."

And that is what my father did, hoeing up the circle where the maple had stood, working compost and leaf mulch into the soil, and tamping in the dormant plant divisions. My father's exercise was a vote of confidence in the future. From the lifeless brown clumps of roots would sprout new life. And Dad would eventually realize his sweet and selfless wish: that the woman to whom he was so deeply devoted could sit on the porch in the fresh air, her daydreams adrift on the breeze, and soak in the garden's soothing presence. The garden would rise and flower and stand as a modest testament to nature's exquisite exuberance and sweeping rhythms, and to its unsentimental resilience. For forty years, the old tree had graced our yard, and now in its absence a new generation was about to take root, one that would not have been possible had the towering giant remained. Seasons change, trees fall, seeds sprout. From death and decay spring new wonders. Life moves irrevocably forward.

Like garden plants, the four Grogan children had taken root in various ways and places. Marijo had become a social worker outside Ann Arbor and spent her days helping hard-luck families piece together broken lives. Tim was an economist working for a business magazine in New York City. After earning an MBA and working for a time as a financial analyst, Michael had become incapacitated with a bevy of ill-defined and energy-sapping symptoms that doctors eventually diagnosed as chronic fatigue syndrome. He quit his job in Southern California and moved back in with Mom and Dad to begin a long, slow recuperation.

I was the only one of the four to have married. Marijo, like me, had drawn our parents' disapproval when she moved in with her longtime partner and soul mate, a British psychologist named Kent, forgoing marriage and instead opting for an informal commitment ceremony in the woods behind their home. Tim, too, had lived with a woman for several years before the relationship soured. He and Michael remained unattached, and the four of us joked about the amount of prayer energy Mom and Dad burned imploring God to find them good Catholic girls to settle down with.

The chasm religion had cleaved between my parents and me brought competing emotions: the heady feeling of liberation tempered by the dull, aching sadness—sometimes palpable, sometimes barely registered, but present every day—of knowing I had caused my parents so much heartache. In their own ways, I suspected, Marijo, Tim, and Michael had each struggled with a similar conflict, but it was something none of us talked much about. Our parents' expectations were difficult to meet, and we all knew how much it meant to them that we follow in their very Catholic footsteps.

As I moved through my forties and watched my children grow from toddlers into lanky preteens, life seemed to finally find its equilibrium. Mom had survived open-heart surgery and a hip replacement. Dad had beaten prostate cancer, and appeared to have struck a truce with the leukemia discovered lurking in his bloodstream the previous year. Every four months he submitted a blood sample, and every four months the doctors returned the same report: status quo. My parents chugged on, day to day, finding comfort and joy in their faith and learning to accept that their children, to varying degrees, had not and would not. We were all thankful that Mom, with her memory and physical vigor waning, had Dad to care for her, which allowed them to stay in their home, living the independent life they so cherished. Neither of them could bear to consider a retirement community or, worse, assisted-living facility. With his abundant energy and sharp mind, Dad continued to astound all of us. Despite the sleeping leukemia within him, his only apparent concession to age was half an aspirin and a thirty-minute nap each afternoon.

In addition to all his other duties, he took on one other
role that had traditionally been my mother's—the family's
worrier-in-chief. As Mom's mind gradually let go, drifting like
clouds across a wind-whipped sky, so did her matriarchal
willpower and seemingly superhuman capacity for fretting
about those she loved. That job was now Dad's alone.

Our lives, connected by blood yet now so clearly separate
and distinct, marched on. Some days, the good ones, I could
believe they would continue this way forever.

CHAPTER 26

⁂

Not long after Dad got his new garden planted, he called, but it was not to talk about plants. "Say, John," he began, "I wanted to give you a little update on my leukemia."

I could hear something in his voice, buried beneath the calm and confidence. Something that sounded like fear.

"Everything's still holding steady, right?" I asked.

"That's just it," Dad said. "The last blood test has the doctor concerned. My platelets seem to be dropping. Just a little, but he doesn't want to see that."

I had only the vaguest notion of platelets, and he explained to me what the oncologist had explained to him, that they were the blood's clotting agents, produced in vast quantities by cells in the bone marrow. Platelets coursed through the blood like microscopic masons with buckets of cement, ready to rush to the site of any injury and quickly mortar the wound. They are what save all of us from bleeding to death. In a healthy adult, 150,000 to 450,000 platelets swim in a tiny microliter of blood. If those levels drop to 20,000 or below, the patient is at serious risk of bleeding uncontrollably from even a minor bruise or cut.

"But I'm not anywhere near that," Dad said. "I'm just a little on the low side of normal." He said the doctor wanted to see him every two months instead of every four. "He just wants to watch it more closely, that's all."

We danced around the topic a little more, both advancing the fiction that the dropping platelets were really no cause for alarm. Dad wasn't even going to tell Mom. He was fiercely protective of her, and with her mind drifting as it was, he was afraid she would have a hard time grasping anything but the word *cancer*. One thing she knew from experience—from her father, several siblings, and countless friends—was that cancer seldom carried a happy ending. He didn't want to worry her.

That's when I asked, "Dad, do you want me to come home?"

"Oh heavens no," he answered without hesitation, as if I had just proposed sending him on a transatlantic cruise or some other indulgence of mind-boggling extravagance. "You have your own family to worry about, and your job. You've got your hands full. Jenny needs you there. Besides, there's nothing to do here. I feel fine. I'm keeping up on everything. We're just going to watch this thing a little more closely."

"Okay," I said. "But you'll call me if you need me, right?"

He assured me he would.

"You'll be in all of our thoughts, Dad," I said, groping for the right words.

"John?"

A moment of silence hung on the phone line.

"And maybe your prayers, too?"

"My thoughts and prayers, Dad," I said. "My thoughts and prayers."

For the next six months, Dad maintained his routine, even as his platelet counts trickled in the wrong direction with each new blood test. His oncologist told him about a newly approved chemotherapy regimen that had shown some early promise against Dad's form of leukemia. He asked my father to consider the treatment as a preemptive move while the leukemia was still largely inactive, but when the doctor described the debilitating side effects and told my father he would be laid up for several weeks, too weak to take care of himself or my mother, Dad recoiled. The decision to submit to the treatment was a huge one because it would mean crossing the line for the first time from independent living to a life totally reliant on others. For Dad, that would be like voluntarily stepping off a cliff.

"I think it makes more sense to just keep watching it," he said. "As long as it's still in check, I don't see the sense in trying anything that drastic."

Then on October 25, 2004, a Sunday morning, came another phone call. This time it was my brother Michael. "I'm calling from the hospital," he said. "It's Dad."

With his training as a financial analyst, Michael tended to see the world as numbers guys do—in binary code, absolutes without shadings of gray. He had been living at home for more than a decade as he slowly recovered from his maddening case of chronic fatigue syndrome, my parents nursing him for years just as they did when he was their baby. Now he was stronger, though still easily fatigued, and it was his turn to be there for them. Michael's nature was to get right to the point.

"Dad's been admitted," he said. "They're afraid if they send him home he could bleed to death."

Bleed to death? I struggled to process the words. "Start at the beginning," I said.

The night before, Michael had come home from a play to find my father in the bathroom hemorrhaging blood from his rectum. "Buckets of blood," my brother said. Dad had packed towels around himself to try to stanch the gush, but the towels just became sodden. The blood kept coming. At the emergency room, a test showed that my father's platelet count had nose-dived. I remembered the magic number of 20,000. Anything below that and you were at risk of spontaneously erupting into uncontrolled, potentially fatal bleeding. My father's count, Michael reported, was down to 1,500.

"Fifteen thousand, you mean," I corrected.

"No," Michael said. "Fifteen hundred."

The bleeding had erupted at the site of an old injury—a tissue burn caused by the radiation Dad received to treat his prostate cancer a decade earlier. "The doctors cauterized it and got the bleeding to stop," Michael said. "But they can't let him go home. If the bleeding starts again, they're afraid we couldn't get him back here in time."

"So they'll give him more platelets, right?" I asked.

"That's the plan," he said. "Until they get the platelet count up to twenty thousand, he's not coming home."

My mind bounced from one thought to the next, the consequences, immediate and distant, cascading around me. Dad's alarming drop of platelets meant he could begin hemorrhaging at any moment. But equally grave, it also meant the sleeping dragon that was his leukemia was awake now. Even if doctors pumped him up with a steady transfusion of platelets, wouldn't these new recruits, too, eventually meet the same fate? I felt a slow, sickening hollow spread through my stomach.

And then there was Mom. Mom, who could no longer care for herself. Mom with medications so complex they required an engineer's flowchart. Mom, who would forget to eat without my father gently badgering her. Mom, who was utterly helpless without him.

"So, Mike," I asked, "has Dad said anything about Mom?"

"Not yet," he said. "We haven't had a chance to talk."

Michael, as it turned out, had dropped my father at the emergency room and, at Dad's insistence, returned home to be with Mom. My father did not like to leave her alone in the house for even a half hour, worried that she could tumble down the stairs or fall in the bathroom or turn on a stove burner and walk away. My brother was now doing his best to shuttle between house and hospital, trying to take care of my mother and be there for my father. It had only been a few hours, and already it was clear how impossible it would be for him to sustain.

Thanks to my father's stamina, my parents had managed to live independently into their late eighties, still in the same house. Now, that independent lifestyle was in jeopardy. I had known for years that all it would take to bring their house of cards crashing down was one small mishap—a broken hip, a chronic illness, even a bum knee that would knock my father out of commission. It appeared that day had arrived. And yet I am an optimist by nature, and denial, in the face of a harsh reality, can be a sweet narcotic. I kept telling myself that the platelet transfusions would stick, that the dragon would return to hibernation, that in a best-case scenario, Dad could return to normal and hold things together for another year. Another year might be all he needed.

On my last visit home, I had found a card on my mother's bed table from the previous Christmas. Inside it was my father's handwriting. "Dearest Ruth," it read. "I thank the Lord every day for giving you to me, and for watching over us all these years. My prayer now is that He will bless you with peace, happiness, and healing, and that I will always be able to take care of you. I love you, Ruthie. Richard."

As a child, I thought my father was invincible, a sort of humble superhero whom nothing could hurt and no one could take from me. I grew up convinced he would live forever. That fantasy was long past, but I wanted him to have a shot at his last wish. I wanted him to be able to be there for the only true love of his life as long as she needed him. Like Dad, I didn't want her to have to experience a life without him.

Michael and I stayed in touch throughout the day, and by midafternoon my father had been admitted to a private room in a brand-new wing of the hospital. The switchboard patched me through, and Dad picked up.

"Hey there," I said. "What's the big idea getting sick on us?"

Dad laughed. "I guess I didn't have enough on my plate," he said. "I needed something else to keep life interesting."

"Well, you sure did that," I said.

His voice sounded as strong as ever, and he assured me he was feeling fine, no worse at all for the tremendous blood loss of the previous sixteen hours. He felt so good, in fact, he said it was like he was on vacation. "You should see the room," he gushed. "I feel like I'm at a resort! It's just like a hotel. The docs just want to keep an eye on me. This will be my excuse to get a good rest and catch up on my reading."

He didn't want me to worry. He never wanted any of us to worry. In his eyes, it was the father's job to worry, not to be worried over. "I really couldn't feel better," he repeated. "I almost feel guilty taking up this big, beautiful room when there are so many sick people who could really use it."

"Dad," I said, feeling my way carefully, "I'm thinking maybe I'll come home for a few days."

"Oh, you don't need to do that," he said. "Heck, I hope to be back home in a couple days. Mike said he'll keep an eye on Mom until I get back, and until then I'm just going to lie here and relax. We've got everything under control. You don't need to come home for me. Really."

"Okay, but you'll let me know, won't you?" I said. "You'll let me know when you need me there."

The next day on the phone, Dad told me his leukemia specialist had visited him and planned to start him on the newly approved chemotherapy course that Dad had earlier rejected. The time for procrastinating was over. The treatments would last for six weeks and would be coupled with a strong course of steroids, which he said would help his platelets rebuild. "The doctor says it'll knock me back a good bit," Dad said, "but he's hoping it will send the leukemia into remission so I can get out of here."

The chance for a preemptive attack on the sleeping monster had passed. Now it was awake and on its feet—and ready for a good fight.

CHAPTER 27

❋

My father's stay in the tastefully decorated private room at Saint Joseph Mercy Hospital in Pontiac would not be quite the luxury getaway he had at first imagined. He had been in the room only a day when his specialist, an oncology hematologist named Dr. Franklin, ordered a spinal tap, a procedure Dad described in his understated way as "not the most pleasant experience of my life." The purpose of the procedure was to extract a sample of bone marrow to better learn how aggressively the leukemia was advancing. The marrow was where the leukemia's secrets lurked. The worst part was not the tap itself, but what came after: the waiting. Dr. Franklin promised he would be back in touch by midafternoon, and Dad lay in his room alone, watching the clock, summoning the emotional strength to receive whatever prognosis awaited him. I called midafternoon, and he told me, "I'm just sitting here waiting to hear back. Now they're saying it won't be till the end of the day."

Dad regrouped and braced himself for the dinner hour. But his meal arrived and with it a message that Dr. Franklin had gone home for the night. A nurse assured him the doctor would drop by on his rounds first thing in the morning, and

Dad spent a mostly sleepless night waiting for the sun to rise. Dawn came, but not the doctor. Another nervous day of waiting. The string of delays for a man whose life was on the line came close to feeling like criminal torture, the kind of psychological abuse banned by civilized societies. With each phone call Dad sounded slightly more desperate. "They're not telling me anything," he said. "I'm just sitting here." He was hoping the results would show the leukemia holding steady and the steroids and transfusions working together to boost his platelet count so he could go home. "I'm ready to get out of here," he said.

When Dr. Franklin finally showed up, it was not with the report my father had hoped. First he delivered the brighter news: Dad's platelet counts were indeed creeping up, from 1,500 to 4,000, still dangerously low but moving in the right direction. No longer was the doctor setting a specific threshold before he would release my father; now he simply said he wanted to see "continued significant improvement" before he'd consider letting Dad out of the hospital. The second half of his report, we later learned, was what had caused the delays. Dr. Franklin had sought a second opinion to be certain of his findings: the leukemia was spreading aggressively, rampaging unchallenged through my father's bloodstream. That new chemotherapy regimen, the one he had broached with my father months earlier, was still Dad's best shot at bringing the disease to its knees, he said, and they would begin immediately. Later that day, as Dad described it to me on the phone, we both agreed it sounded straightforward enough. Six quick, painless treatments one week apart. And if his platelet count continued to rise, he could go home and receive them as an outpatient. Other than that, he just needed to rest and let the powerful meds do their job. The chemo, the doctor had explained, would have a cumulative effect and each week would grow more powerful in its counterattacks on the cancer cells. The side effects would also increase exponentially, the doctor warned, but that was the cost of admission. "I guess I'm not going to be feeling too great for a while," Dad said. But six weeks and it would be behind him.

"Let's talk about something else," he said.

"Well, I have some news," I said, pausing to consider how to transition from life-threatening disease to a development that was the highlight of my career. "You know that book I've been working on?" I asked.

"The one about you and Marley?" he said.

"Well, guess what? I sold it over the weekend. To a publisher in New York."

"No kidding," Dad said, his voice brightening. "Give me all the details."

Over the months, I had sketched out the basic premise for him in our weekly phone calls. *Marley & Me* was my own story, the story of starting out with Jenny as newlyweds and the incorrigible Labrador retriever that crashed into our lives and changed the family we would become.

Almost from the first day we brought him home, Marley had proved himself to be unlike any pet we had ever owned. He lived life in a big way, with verve and insouciance and a boundless joy seldom seen in this world. Quite early on, I discovered he was a good source of story fodder. At dinner parties or around the watercooler at work, and later in my newspaper column, I began recounting Marley's over-the-top antics and misdeeds, and I found they made people laugh. But Marley was more than just a punch line; he had grown to become an important member of our family, shaping us even as we tried to bend him to our will. Like most journalists, I had dreamed for years of one day writing a book, but I always searched for a topic from other people's lives—something suitably important to merit a book-length examination. Only gradually did I begin to realize that the book I was meant to write was quite literally lying at my feet. And so, in early 2004, not long after saying good-bye to Marley for the last time, I sat down and began to write.

While I was working on the book in the early morning hours before my regular job, my conviction at times faltered. Some days I honestly could not imagine anyone other than friends and family wanting to read it. Dad's confidence, however, had never waned. He was always my biggest cheerleader.

"Six publishing houses bid on it, Dad," I said.

"I'll be doggoned," he said.

How ironic, I thought, that I would receive some of the most exciting news of my life within hours of my father receiving some of the worst of his. My insides were a scramble of mixed emotions.

"That's great, John," he said before signing off. "That's really, really great."

We talked by phone every day. I filled him in on the most recent book developments and he gave me the latest medical update. The first round of chemo, he reported, had gone fine and he was feeling no side effects. "It was no big deal," he said. The steroids, on the other hand, were making him agitated, animated—and uninhibited in sharing his opinions. He spent his days in his hospital room reading the papers, watching CNN, and growing more and more worked up about the impending presidential election. As far as I knew, Dad never voted for a Democrat in his life, but he mostly kept his political views to himself. This election was different. He loathed his fellow Catholic John Kerry, seeing him as the manifestation of secular godlessness and liberalism that was ruining this country. Dad began firing off emotional letters to all four of his kids. He knew we all leaned liberal and that we considered George W. Bush's first term a disastrous mix of mind-boggling incompetence and blustery hubris. But the election, he had convinced himself, was not about ideology or competence but rather good and evil, faith and cynicism. In a letter dated October 26, he wrote, "This is a fight for the soul of America! Morality and spiritual values versus our decadent culture. If Kerry wins, our nation will be following the path of the Roman Empire to destruction."

He asked Michael to mail copies to each of us. My brother added a note of his own: "He's been sitting in his hospital bed with nothing to do but watch the news, and his blood has been boiling. I think it's quite a good sign that he has summoned the energy to write this note that expresses the passion of his convictions—all while waiting for news on his personal fate. Please take these comments in that light." I did, and so did Marijo and Tim.

As children we grew up with our parents' conservative views as a given, the uncompromising fixed prism through which we viewed the world. Abortion was murder; birth control insulted God's will; sexuality was a sacred procreative duty reserved solely for the sacrament of marriage; homosexuality was an abomination. As adults, each of us, to varying degrees, had rejected those tenets. The terrain was so emotionally fraught that we had learned years earlier to simply dance around it. If Dad needed to vent about the election, that was fine with us. It all seemed so immaterial to what really mattered in our family. Bush or Kerry, who cared? We just wanted our father to get better and get home.

When Dad was not raving about politics and the decline of Western civilization, he was working through a checklist of personal business that had suddenly taken on new importance. From his hospital bed, he talked to his lawyer, updated his will, and named Michael the executor of his estate and his medical guardian in case he became incapacitated and could no longer make his own decisions. He also filed a document with the hospital giving clear instructions about the topic none of us was prepared to discuss: end-of-life decisions. True to his Catholic faith, he wanted nothing that would unnaturally shorten his life. But he was also clear that when his time came, when all hope was gone, he did not want heroic or extraordinary measures to keep him alive. He would fight this thing with all he had, but nothing more. He was certain in his conviction of heaven and hell, and he had done his best to lead a good and moral life. When the call came to leave this life for an eternity in heaven, he was not about to say, "Sorry, Lord, not quite ready yet."

There was one last piece of unfinished business: Ruthie. Dad was figuring out that even if he were allowed to return home, he would be in no shape to care for himself, let alone his wife. After less than a week in the hospital, he could already see Michael becoming overwhelmed as Mom's full-time caregiver. It was just too much for him—the pills, the meals, the linen changes, and pull-up diapers. That was one aspect of my mother's care he just could not bring himself to do: help with her bathroom needs. In the past, she had stubbornly rejected the idea of visits from nursing aides. Her mind might be drifting, but her modesty was firmly intact, and she was not going to allow a stranger to see her naked. Marijo, who lived more than an hour away, was driving out regularly around her job as a social worker to take care of Mom's hygiene needs. It was not sustainable. Dad knew this; we all did.

From his hospital bed, Dad finally did the one thing he had fiercely resisted for so many years as Mom declined: he requested an application to Lourdes Nursing Home. It was a lovely nursing home, or as lovely as these places get, run by Catholic nuns and situated on a bluff overlooking Watkins Lake outside Pontiac, less than a mile from the original homestead where the first of our Grogans had settled after arriving from County Limerick, Ireland, in 1850. Lourdes was where his mother had spent her last few years, and Dad was so grateful for the respectful care she received that he became a generous donor of both his money and time.

The truth was my mother should have been in a nursing home, or at least an assisted-living facility, five years earlier, as her mind and vigor and continence left her. And no doubt she would have been if not for my father's energetic outpouring of care. He feared nursing homes like a deer fears fire. They were the last stop on life's trolley line, an admission that you were ready to relinquish all you had worked to build. Now he was seeing his options running out, at least for the short term. Independent living, that thing he cherished most, had been predicated on his ability to stay healthy and vigorous, able to mind all the details. He was the knight guarding the queen's castle, and now the invaders had robbed him of his sword and shield.

While he recovered from the debilitations of chemotherapy, he would need a place with full-time nursing care, not just for himself but for Mom, too. Lourdes, he told me, had one suite designed for married couples. It consisted of two small bedrooms, a sitting room, and a bathroom. A retired priest celebrated Mass in the chapel down the hall two mornings a week. "That would be ideal," he said. He portrayed it as a short-term solution until they could move back home. "Just until I'm back on my feet again," he said, but there was something in his voice that told me he knew what I knew: that nursing homes are rarely short-term.

A nursing home might be the solution, but admission could take months. Michael, still struggling with his chronic fatigue symptoms, clearly needed help with Mom. Tim was in New York, and I in Pennsylvania, both holding down full-time jobs. Marijo was self-employed with a full roster of clients. We exchanged nervous phone calls and e-mails, all with the same underlying question: what about Mom?

Over the years, from adolescence into adulthood, Tim was always more my friend than my brother. We traveled and camped together, hung out at each other's homes, played clunker rock 'n' roll together on our electric guitars, swigged beer, confided in each other about most everything, and over the years helped each other out of various scrapes. Even when he was a teenager trying desperately to assume the mantle of cool, he let me, the chubby, bespectacled brother six years his junior, tag along with him and his friends. My very first trip away from home without my parents was with him. I was a freshman in high school, he was a college student—and our favorite band of all time, The Kinks, was coming to Toronto. It was a five-hour drive, but we didn't care. We jumped in the family's green Chevrolet Nova and set off despite Dad's protests: "Doggone it all anyway! You can't just go driving halfway around the country to see a rock concert." We bought tickets from a scalper on the street and after the concert joined the surging scene on Yonge Street. That night, Tim secured us beds at the YMCA, and when an old man with a creepy glint in his eye began hovering around me, Tim swooped in and that was the last I saw of him.

I always assumed my brother would be a lifelong bachelor. After a couple of long relationships that had not worked out, he had settled into the single life in New York City, working long hours at his magazine and living in a series of small apartments. He marched through much of his forties and into his fifties alone. But the year before Dad got sick, Tim found himself seated on a commuter train beside a young woman from the Philippines en route to her job as a nanny. They struck up a conversation, then met the next day for coffee at Penn Station. A romance bloomed, and when Dad learned that Elizabeth had somehow convinced Tim to attend Easter Sunday Mass with her at Saint Patrick's Cathedral, he knew his prayers had been answered.

In August 2004, two months before he was hospitalized, Dad walked Elizabeth down the aisle of Our Lady of Refuge and gave her hand in matrimony to his eldest son. Father Vin officiated, and Michael and I shared best-man duties. Marijo was Elizabeth's maid of honor. Mom was in the front row, beaming, alongside Jenny and our kids. It was a happy day. Our whole family was together, something that had become a rarity as the years passed. Tim, the perennial bachelor, the one the family worried most about, had found a good woman, and they were off on their new life together.

My father adored Elizabeth. Unlike his own children, she was an unquestioning Catholic who accepted the Church's teachings and edicts just as he did, without reservation or parsing. Her traditional values were in lockstep with his, and he was convinced that God had brought her into his fallen-away Catholic son's life for a purpose. "This is no coincidence," he said after the first time he met her.

Now with him hospitalized and the question of Mom's care looming larger by the hour, it was Elizabeth who stepped forward. On November 3, 2004, less than three months after her wedding day and two weeks after Dad was admitted to the hospital, Elizabeth flew to Detroit to take over Mom's care. We were all grateful, but Dad saw it as more than simply the generous act of a good-hearted person. The Lord, he was convinced, had sent a guardian angel not only into Tim's life, but into his as well.

CHAPTER 28

Jenny had watched my hand-wringing mostly from the sidelines. This was my father, not hers, and she didn't want to interfere, but I could tell she was growing impatient with my dithering. Dad was entering his third week in the hospital, and still I procrastinated about flying home to see him. I kept waiting for the right opportunity, the best window. Maybe late November would be good. Maybe right after Christmas; wouldn't that cheer him up? Maybe after the New Year once we had the holidays behind us. Jenny couldn't hide her frustration. It was obvious what she would do if it were her father—she would have been on a plane weeks earlier.

Finally, one morning over coffee, she spilled out, "Will you wake up? What are you waiting for? Do you want to put it off until he's gone and then spend the rest of your life with regrets? God, open your eyes, John." Her voice softened. "Look, I know you're hoping he beats this. We all are. But c'mon. What if he can't?"

She was right. I had lulled myself into believing my father would live forever. He always managed to beat back adversity. I had convinced myself he'd pull through this crisis, too. But she raised a legitimate question: What *was* I waiting for? A bedside visit did not constitute an admission of defeat, did it?

I left for work and spent the drive into Philadelphia mulling over the question, when suddenly I remembered a moment from long ago, in the winter of 1987. I was still single then and had just arrived in Florida to begin my new job at the newspaper in Fort Lauderdale. Jenny would land her own job in the area and follow a few weeks later, but for that moment I was alone and had no idea what our future held. It was my first time living so far from home, and I knew no one. Always the loyal parents, Mom and Dad soon arrived in their recreational vehicle. They had driven hundreds of miles to help their youngest son—the one Mom reminded me had been so hopelessly homesick during his first year at sleepaway camp—get settled. For two weeks they stayed, camping at an RV park a few miles from my new apartment. Every evening after work I would drive directly there to sit in the dinette of their motor home with them, eating Mom's meatloaf and telling them every detail of my new job. I had been hired to cover the world's most boring beat: transportation. But they hung on every word as if I'd just arrived from a fascinating adventure abroad. Mom pasted each of my articles in a scrapbook, and Dad read and reread every one, peppering me with questions about the inner workings of road construction, toll structures, and traffic flow in Palm Beach County.

It would be our last great visit, the final one in which they could claim me as all their own. For those two weeks, I was still their youngest son, faithfully caught in the orbit of their gravity and happy to be their satellite. Soon enough,

Jenny and I would be living together, and then married and parents, and everything would change forever. I missed the parents I had then as I knew they missed that son.

When I arrived home from work that evening, I said, "So I was thinking of flying to Detroit and spending a few days."

"I think that would be good," Jenny said.

The chemotherapy was doing a job on Dad. In our daily phone calls, he continued to keep up a good game. The hospital room was like a resort, the nurses were spoiling him, the food really wasn't too bad. But I could hear it in his voice, which had grown somehow smaller and weaker, slightly higher and reedier. The booming confidence was gone. He told me the treatments were not making him too nauseated, but they had sapped his strength. His limbs felt like deadweights, and sometimes the simple act of reading exhausted him. One day he confessed to being so enervated he couldn't pull himself out of bed to walk to the bathroom. He had to ring for a nurse to help him up. Never in his life had he felt so helpless.

When I told him I had booked my ticket, his voice brightened. "I'm glad you're coming home, John," he said.

"I'm glad, too, Dad."

A week before I was scheduled to arrive, Dad received a happy surprise. He was getting discharged. His platelet counts were still not great, but with the chemotherapy, transfusions, and steroids, they had steadily risen, and Dr. Franklin was satisfied Dad could rest just as well at home as in the hospital. Any bleeding at all and he was to return immediately. And he was to avoid public places and contact with strangers. The chemo had compromised his immune system, and Dr. Franklin did not want him exposed to germs he might not be able to fight off. Once a week for the remaining three weeks he would come to the hospital for his chemo treatment and blood work. Other than that, he was home free. Elizabeth had efficiently taken control of the household chores, meals, and Mom's care. She had let him know she would be honored to nurse him as well. He was too weak to be proud and had gratefully accepted.

"I might as well be lying in my own bed as here," he said. "Of course, I'll have to take it easy."

"Oh, you mean no heavy lifting?" I asked. "You won't be out climbing on the roof and cleaning gutters?"

"Not right away," he said.

"You better take it easy, mister," I admonished, "or when I get home, you'll have me to contend with."

I could feel his smile through the phone line.

CHAPTER 29

*

I flew into Detroit Metropolitan Airport on the morning after Thanksgiving. Michael met me in baggage claim.

"How is Dad doing?" I asked as we drove home through a steady drizzle.

"Status quo," Mike said in that infuriatingly opaque way of his.

"What's that mean?" I asked.

"Holding steady," he said. "Of course, the chemo is taking its toll."

"How?"

He hesitated as if considering where to begin, then simply said, "Well, you'll see."

As I walked in from the garage to the laundry room, I plucked from the recesses of my memory one of the corny family expressions I had grown up hearing whenever a close friend or relative arrived. "Hey, hey," I called out. "Look what the dog dragged in!"

"Ruth! He's home!" I heard my father's voice from the next room. After a long moment, longer than I had expected, he came around the corner, and I sucked in my breath. I barely recognized him. Dressed in pajamas and a robe, he leaned heavily on a cane as he shuffled gingerly toward me, his slippered feet not lifting off the linoleum. My always ramrod-straight, speed-walking, up-with-the-sun father was stooped over as he inched forward in a manner that can only be described as doddering. What was most shocking, though, was his face. It was as round and puffy as a beach ball, his skin stretched tight as if ready to pop. He had told me the daily steroid treatments had caused him to retain fluids and swell, but I wasn't expecting this. I noticed his wrists and hands were just as swollen.

"John! You're home!" he said jovially but in a voice weaker than I had known. I took his hand in both of mine and gave it the vigorous Grogan shake.

"I'm home, Dad," I said. "It's good to see you."

"Well, I'm not much to look at right now," he said, "but I'm getting along. Come on in and say hello to your mother."

I followed behind him as he inched his way into the living room, where she sat in front of the window, her own cane across her knees. "Look who's here, Ruthie," he announced.

"Hi, Mom," I said, dropping to one knee in front of her so we could be eye to eye. "It's John."

"Who'd you think I thought it would be," she shot back, "the milkman?" I saw a little of the old glimmer in her eye and smiled. "Come here and give your old ma a kiss," she said, and I smacked my lips against her forehead and then her cheek.

"Where are Jenny and the kids?"

"Remember, Ma? I came alone this time," I said. "You've got your baby all to yourself for a change." For effect, I draped my arm over her shoulder and pretended to sit in her lap, putting no weight on her.

"Oh, what a darling baby you were," she marveled and patted my leg.

"And it's a good thing," I said, "or you would have sent me back."

"You were my little pistol," she said.

We made small talk about my flight and the house and all the leaves that still needed raking.

"We're in crisis mode around here," Dad announced. "With this darn cancer and the hospital and everything, I've given up on all my fall chores. I'm just letting everything go."

"Don't worry about that, Dad," I said. "Reinforcements have arrived."

My mother now slept most of the day, as many as eighteen hours out of every twenty-four, and since returning from the hospital, Dad was quickly exhausted and taking extended naps, too. I planned to fill the quiet hours working around the place. Elizabeth, in addition to caring for both her new parents-in-law, had the inside of the house looking the best it had in years, but outside awaited a long backlog of jobs.

"There's a new yardman in town," I said, "and I hear he works cheap."

Mom looked up at me with clear, green, faraway eyes and asked, "Are Jenny and the kids here?"

One missed beat. My eyes met Dad's. "Not this time, Mom," I said as I would another half-dozen times throughout the day.

Dad eased himself down into the chair next to me, and I asked about his swollen face and hands. He pulled up his pajama pant legs to reveal ankles that looked like something out of a circus sideshow. They were the size of clubs, with large sores and cracks marbling the skin. "It gets stretched so tight, it splits right open," he said. Michael had been cleaning them for him and wrapping his legs in gauze. The pain was impossible to ignore, but he did his best, offering it up, as he had with all hardships over the years, for the poor souls in purgatory.

"The worst part is my mouth," Dad said. "It's so dry I can hardly swallow. Everything I try to eat tastes like sawdust." He opened his lips to expose a swollen, cracked tongue that looked like it should belong to a tortoise. The chemo, as Michael had hinted, was wreaking havoc on him.

A few days earlier he had been inching his way down the stairs when he fell backward on his butt. He wasn't hurt, but he was stuck on the step, unable to pull himself back to his feet. He had to call for help, and it took both Michael and Elizabeth to haul him up. My dad, the man who as recently as a few months earlier had started each morning with sets of jumping jacks and push-ups, had lost nearly all his strength.

"I'm weak as a kitten," he confessed.

"But just think, Dad," I said, searching for a bright spot. "You've only got three more weeks to go. You're halfway through."

"I just hope it works," he said.

"If you weren't getting better, the doctors wouldn't have let you come home," I offered, and he nodded as if that made sense.

After lunch, both Mom and Dad went upstairs to sleep, and I headed into the yard under a leaden sky to rake leaves.

When all the trash cans were filled, I climbed on the roof to clean the gutters. Dad had been fretting about his clogged gutters for weeks. The older he got, the more obsessive he had become about the little details of his daily life, especially those that interfered with his routine. If he discovered a new box of cereal opened before the old one was finished, he would shout through the house, "Who opened the new cereal?" and continue to grumble until the old box was finally used up. While visiting him the previous summer, I had volunteered to cut the grass, and drove him crazy by circling the yard in a counterclockwise pattern when he had always—for forty-five years—gone clockwise. At least now he could stop worrying about the gutters. I saved the mucky, soggy leaves to show him all that had come out.

After a few hours of work, I ducked my head inside, but they were both still asleep, so I decided to take a walk—to the first of the twin attractions that had brought my family to Harbor Hills. I followed the same path I had taken every school day for eight years, from our back door to the side door of Our Lady of Refuge. The school had a large addition now, and the new church covered the soccer field, but the original buildings looked the same. The door was locked. I walked around to the front of the school, past the football field where I had played offensive guard for the Refuge Ravens, past the convent where Tommy and I had scrubbed floors, and pulled on the door. It swung open. School was out for the holiday, and the place was silent. But that smell, the permeating aroma of floor wax, chalk, and overripe bananas, with a slight undertone of stale vomit, was just as I remembered it. I walked into the classroom where Tommy had played the Fugs song and sat in a desk approximately where mine had been. I peered through the locked door into the principal's office where we had been sent for punishment. I found my second-grade classroom, where I had embarrassed myself while fantasizing about Sister Mary Lawrence. On the teacher's desk was a wooden ruler, and I gave it a practice swing through the air. It whistled just like I remembered them whistling in the instant before contact.

"Wow," I said aloud to the empty room. "Forty years."

Back home, Dad was awake and looking more rested. When I announced that I would be cooking dinner, he volunteered to keep me company. The one positive side effect of the steroids was that they made my reserved father unusually chatty and animated. He leaned against the counter and talked my ear off as I sautéed onions and garlic. He especially enjoyed describing the cooking skills he had found late in life. When we were kids and Mom was not around to cook, Dad had only two items in his culinary repertoire: Campbell's tomato soup, into which he would melt cubes of Swiss cheese, and fried bologna sandwiches. We kids found both indescribably delicious, which always amused my mother, whose gourmet gifts her well-fed brood mostly took for granted. Since she had given up on cooking, Dad had taught himself to make stew, chili, various casseroles, and his specialty, chicken vegetable soup.

"You've become a regular Galloping Gourmet," I said, and I could tell he liked the comparison even if he knew I was teasing.

"As they say, necessity is the mother of invention."

*   *   *

My second day home went much like the first. We lingered at the kitchen table over breakfast, talking about everything and nothing in particular. I told Dad about my work at the newspaper and in my garden; I brought him up to date on the kids and their hobbies. He talked about projects he wanted to get to around the house and gave me updates on various neighbors I had known growing up. The Selahowskis from next door were living in Florida now and Cindy Ann, the girl who had showered me with unrequited love at the age of six, was working as a music teacher. Tommy's parents were also in Florida where they had been enjoying an active and healthy retirement until Mr. Cullen was diagnosed with stomach cancer, which he was fighting as only Mr. Cullen could. Tommy, Dad had heard, was divorced and living in Phoenix, where he managed commercial properties. There were funerals to report on and moves to nursing homes. My parents were at that stage of life. For many years now, the obituaries were the section of the paper they turned to first.

When Dad went upstairs to join Mom for a nap, Michael and I put up storm windows. Then I took another walk. This time I headed to the other pole of my Harbor Hills childhood: The Outlot. In front of the Pemberton house, which long ago had changed hands after the old man died, I paused. Right here, I thought, was where the police car had rolled up behind us. I walked a few steps onto the lawn. And here was where I dropped those two pathetic homegrown joints of mine. I looked down into the grass, half expecting to find them still hiding there.

I walked on, past where we had the Labor Day picnics and bike parades, and down to The Lagoon where the *Mary*

Ann had spent fourteen consecutive summers before being retired. As I stood on the wobbly boat dock, it came back to me, an event that even in that long-ago moment I had understood was a turning point: the final voyage on the *Mary Ann*. It was the last time Dad and I would ever sail together.

In 1981 I was two years out of college and working across the state at the *Herald-Palladium*. Even though I lived three hours away, I came home that spring, put a fresh coat of wax on the sailboat, and launched it for the season. Dad was retired by then, and I thought that if the boat were in the water he might use it. Even in retirement, he worked too hard; I wanted him to have a leisurely pursuit. But when I returned home in August for a weekend visit, I learned he had not been out once. Honestly, he had been making excuses not to sail ever since I was old enough to take the boat out alone.

"I'm going for a sail, Dad," I said. "Want to join me?"

"No, you go ahead," he said. "I've got so much to do around here."

"Aw, c'mon," I beckoned. "Come with me. For old times' sake. Just a short one." I persisted until he agreed.

The day was blustery but nothing we hadn't handled before in our sturdy day sailer. I started out at the helm, steering the boat through whitecaps and spilling wind from the sails when gusts hit. *Mary Ann* heeled up playfully and plunged forward. Across the lake, I offered the tiller and mainsheet to Dad, who accepted them reluctantly. He had not sailed much at all for many years, and I could see he was nervous. But the old magic quickly came back to him, and I caught him grinning as he peered up into the rigging, checking his sail trim.

"We've had a lot of good sails on this baby," I said, and he nodded in agreement. "Remember how you used to tell me that life was like skippering a sailboat? How you needed to pick a dot on the horizon and be careful not to veer off course?" Dad smiled at his attempt to find a life lesson in the everyday.

"Small corrections," he said. "I think that's what I used to tell you. Life is all about small, continuous corrections."

"At least if you don't want to run aground," I said.

He was opening his mouth to say something else when the big gust hit. I felt it on the back of my neck first, and then, a fraction of a second later, in the sails. All experienced sailors know what to do when a big gust hits: nose into the wind and release the sails to spill their load. Dad knew this, too, and had done it countless times. Instead, he just gripped tighter to the tiller and rope controlling the mainsail. I let the jib fly and scrambled onto the high side of the boat. Dad sat frozen, staring at the water pouring in.

Another second and he shouted: "John, take it!"

I lunged toward him.

"John! Help!" In his voice was something I had never heard before: panic.

Dad had always been the cool, collected one in our household. When I was still in preschool, Mom knocked a can of paint off a ladder in the living room, sending it splashing over the curtains, couch, and carpet. She sank to her knees and wept. But Dad instantly leaped to the rescue, barking calm orders to each of us—"Marijo, towels! Tim, a bucket of cold water! Michael, sponges!"—and got most of it up before it stained. Dad was always at his best in a crisis. He had always been the shepherd of his flock, the one we all relied on to fix any problem, right any wrong.

Not on this day. As the boat tipped beyond the point of no return, I realized our roles had finally reversed. He was the lamb now, and I the protector. Suddenly his heart attack from a few years earlier loomed large before me, as did two of the doctor's stern warnings: avoid stressful situations and avoid shocks to the body, such as a sudden plunge into cold water. An electrifying surge of adrenaline coursed through me.

I grabbed the tiller, but it was too late. *Mary Ann* was already dropping onto her side, her cockpit filling, her mast and sails settling onto the lake's surface. We both flopped into the water. Terror flashed in my father's eyes.

"It's okay, Dad," I said. "We're okay. See, everything's okay." I got him into a life jacket and helped him straddle the gunwale sticking out of the water. Then I swam around the boat, gathering up paddles and seat cushions.

"We'll have this puppy back up in no time," I called to him. In fourteen years of sailing, it was the first time either of us had capsized. "We're fine, Dad. Just a little wet."

And within a few moments, he was fine again, his calm, steady demeanor back. "Guess I'm a little rusty," he said sheepishly.

"That was one big gust," I said. "I didn't see it coming, either." And with that, I stood on the centerboard, gripped the gunwale, and rocked backward until the boat pulled upright again. Dad clung to the side as I bailed, and soon enough we had drifted onto a sandbar where we could stand and Dad could easily climb back in.

"Way to go, Pops, breaking our perfect record," I ribbed him as we tied up to the dock.

"Quite a day," Dad said.

"Quite a day," I agreed. And it was. As I pulled down the sails, I realized that my father would never again step aboard the *Mary Ann*, and I would never again share those shoulder-to-shoulder afternoons on the water with him, the closest thing to intimacy we ever had. There are moments in life that fade from memory so quickly they are gone almost before they are over. Then there are those that stick, the ones we carry with us through the years like precious parcels of clarity stitched close to our hearts, becoming part of who we are. Standing together there, soaking wet, I already understood that this was one of those moments.

I saw the paths of our lives crossing like jet contrails in an empty sky. Mine was rising toward adulthood and future's bright promise. His had begun the gradual descent toward life's inescapable conclusion.

A pair of ducks landed on the surface of The Lagoon, snapping me back to the present. Twenty-three years had passed since that last sail. Twenty-three years, and how far our opposing trajectories had carried us.

❅

CHAPTER 30

Johhn, do me a favor, will you?" Dad asked. We were sitting in Marijo's old bedroom, converted years earlier into a television room, where we had just finished watching the six o'clock news. From downstairs I could hear Elizabeth bustling about in the kitchen and smell the ginger and garlic drifting up as she prepared her specialty for dinner, an Asian noodle dish filled with chicken, shrimp, and vegetables.

"Sure, Dad," I said.

"Go into my room, next to my bed, and bring me the box you made me."

I walked across the hall and found it on the bed table, beside his flashlight and alarm clock. It was my first time seeing it since eleven months earlier when I mailed it to him for his eighty-eighth birthday. I was never quite sure what to call it. It wasn't fancy enough to be a jewelry box, and besides, Dad had no jewelry except for a couple of pairs of cuff links and his wedding band, which had not left his finger in fifty-six years. It wasn't really a keepsake box. It was just a box, handmade by me from hardwoods I had salvaged from the forest behind my house in Pennsylvania. Squat and solid, it had a drawer in the bottom and a lid on top that swung open.

Woodworking had always been a hobby for me, though one for which I had no particular gift. Over the years, I had made picture frames and cutting boards and toy cars for the kids. In recent years I had begun scouring the woods for fallen logs of particularly beautiful varieties—red oak, black walnut, black cherry—sawing them into planks, and planing the planks into boards. Dad's box was more than a year in the planning and making. My whole life I had given him predictable gifts: aftershave and neckties and fat biographies of dead presidents. But he wasn't getting any younger, and there was no denying we had grown apart in the years since I had married. It was our lifelong cross to bear together, the burden of our religious differences. Dad was blessed with the gift of faith; I was born with the curse of skepticism. He was hardwired to believe, I to doubt. Making the box, just like planning the garden, had been my attempt to pole-vault the chasm, to let him know I still cared.

I picked up the box, which was heavier than I remembered, and stroked the satiny, hand-rubbed finish. Mom was asleep on her side in the bed, her legs tucked up in a half curl, childlike. I didn't want to wake her, not that there was much danger of that. I tiptoed out with the box and set it on Dad's knees.

"I thought you'd like to see what I'm using it for," he said and lifted the lid.

Inside was a trove of family treasures, many of which I never knew existed. He pulled them out one by one and gave me a brief rundown on each: his grandfather's silver and ebony rosary; his father's wire-framed eyeglasses; his mother's driver's license; both parents' wedding bands. From a small manila envelope, he poured out a pile of military insignias and bars he had earned in the navy. "We used to call this fruit salad," he said.

He opened the little bottom drawer and pulled out the gold watch his father received from the Rapid Vehicle Motor Company in 1909 for being on the first expedition to reach the summit of Pikes Peak in Colorado in a motorized vehicle, and the lucky rabbit's foot my grandfather had carried with him. In a small pouch was a collection of General Motors service pins, each with a small diamond, marking various milestones in his forty-year career. Dad described each item to me. So I would know. So someday when I rummaged through the box with my children or grandchildren, or they with theirs, these objects would mean something, would be something more than faded bric-a-brac. Each had a story to tell, the story of our family. Each was a strand connecting us to our past. I could tell that Dad did not want them to slip into oblivion.

From the very bottom of the drawer he removed a folded sheet of paper that I recognized as the note I had slipped into the box before shipping it to him. Now he held it in front of us and read aloud the words I had written almost one year earlier. My note described the process of building the box, from selecting the logs to rubbing on a final coat of wax. It described how I beveled the lid and chiseled out recesses to fit the hinges. I confessed how many mistakes I had made along the way, and the resulting compromises

I was forced to accept in what had begun as a quest for perfection. The box was a lot like life in that way, I suppose.

I ended the note this way:

> *The kids watched the box slowly take shape, and that was good. They knew it was for their grandfather, which made it all the more special for them. Colleen, in particular, took an interest and built a simple pine box of her own, with my help, beside me. It was a good opportunity for one-on-one father-daughter time and reminded me of the hours you and I spent together at the workbench in the basement. I learned a lot from you down there.*
>
> *That is the story of your box, Dad, built with humble hands and an open heart. I have no idea what you possibly will use it for, and I bet you don't, either. But I hope you will place it where you will see it in the morning, or perhaps late at night. And each time you see it, I want you to know how much I appreciate all you have been—and continue to be—to me. You're all any boy could ever ask for in a father.*

Dad refolded the note and returned it to the bottom of the box. "It means a lot to me, John," he said.

Then Elizabeth called from downstairs that dinner was ready, and I said, "I guess it's time to eat."

After dinner, while Michael and Elizabeth did the dishes, I gingerly broached a topic I had been rehearsing for days. In my suitcase was a video camera that I had packed with the intention of interviewing Dad on tape for posterity. Mom was the family chronicler, a natural-born storyteller. Her tales were burned into all her children's memories. But Dad rarely offered glimpses into his past, not because he was secretive but simply so modest he couldn't fathom anyone wanting to hear about his life. I wanted to capture his story in his own words before it was too late, but therein lay the awkwardness: *before it was too late.* Once the chemotherapy kicked in, I fully expected Dad to beat his leukemia, but how could I ask him for this interview as he battled a potentially fatal disease, without sounding like I had already given up? I might as well be asking him to record his last will and testament. No matter how you dressed it, the request was what it was. Children ask their parents for these things only when they know time is running out. I stammered around before finally spitting it out.

"Say, Dad, I was thinking," I said. "I'd like to interview you about your life. I brought my video camera."

"That's fine," he said, not missing a beat. "I'd be happy to."

I set up the camera on a tripod, framed him in the viewfinder, and pushed the record button.

"Where should we start?" I asked.

"You're the interviewer," Dad said.

"Okay, how about at the beginning. When and where were you born?"

"December 10, 1915. On the Franklin Road in Pontiac, Michigan. Two-forty-one Franklin."

"Were you born in a hospital or at home?"

"At home. A doctor would come to the house back in those days."

"Let's back up. Who was the first of our Grogans to come from Ireland?"

"James. My great-uncle James was the first. He came over right after the Civil War and bought a small farm on Scott Lake Road, just about ten minutes from here. A few years after he got the farm, James sent for his younger brother Patrick," Dad continued. "Patrick was my great-grandfather." Dad loved that I had named my firstborn after the family forefather.

"What's your first memory?" I asked.

"That's easy," Dad said and told me a story I had not heard since childhood. When my father was still a toddler, his mother contracted tuberculosis and was shipped off to a sanitarium in Ohio to recover. Dad was sent to live with his grandmother while his father stayed behind to work. His mother—my grandmother Edna—was gone for two years, and Dad knew her only from the letters she wrote home. Then one afternoon he awoke from his nap to find a stranger leaning over him.

"I opened my eyes and there was this kind-looking lady gazing down at me. She was smiling at me, and I knew it was Mom. I knew right away. I don't know how but I did."

His voice cracked, and he forced a small laugh to shake off the emotion. "I get choked up, even now, when I think about it," he said. "That was my first memory."

I continued to lead him chronologically through the steps of his life: his childhood as a Catholic schoolboy;

the births of his sister and brother; his father's heyday as a sought-after crackerjack mechanic in the nascent days of the automobile, followed by his long, discouraging struggle to rebuild his career after the Depression hit. He described the family moves to Cleveland, New York, Philadelphia, and back to New York as his father chased short-lived jobs, and the string of apartments, neighborhoods, and schools that came with the family's itinerant lifestyle. I was amazed at the detail of his memory. He recalled the street addresses of every place he had lived, some for as little as a few months, and the names of teachers he had not seen in eighty years.

When Dad was halfway through his junior year in high school, in the Germantown section of Philadelphia, his father lost yet another job, and this time had run out of options. The family moved back to reclaim the homestead on Franklin Road in Pontiac after its new owner defaulted on a land-contract loan. They arrived to find the house of my father's birth being used as a brothel. My grandfather chased off the prostitutes, plowed up the lawn for a vegetable garden, and took a job as a field hand, fixing cars in his driveway at night for extra money.

Dad's plan was to graduate from Pontiac High School and try for a job in one of the auto factories to help support the family. "College wasn't even a dream," he said. "We didn't have any money." But as the school year drew to a close, an amazing thing happened. As Dad liked to point out, it illustrated the life-altering impact a single kind act by one individual can make.

"My French teacher, Miss Blanche Avery, bless her soul," Dad began, and then paused for several seconds before continuing. "She called me up after class one day and asked, 'What are you going to do after you graduate?' I said, 'I don't know; try to get a job, I guess.' She said, 'You really ought to go to college.' I told her, 'Well, I don't have any money or anything.' That's when she offered to—" He stopped in midsentence and I could tell he was fighting to maintain his composure. "She offered to pay my tuition out of her own pocket." His voice broke again, the magnitude of this teacher's generosity still overwhelming him all these decades later. "I said, 'No, no. No, I couldn't. My father would never allow that.' Then she started talking to me about scholarships. She said, 'Let me talk to the principal.' It turns out the principal was friends with the personnel manager over at Pontiac Motors, and the next thing I knew they were talking about me being a good fit for GMI."

"General Motors Institute in Flint," I said.

"Yes. It was a cooperative. You worked one month, went to school one month, and earned your way as you went. You had to be sponsored by a GM plant or division." Pontiac Motors sponsored my father, and he spent the next four years alternating between classes in Flint and working in various automobile jobs in Pontiac. "I made fifty-five cents an hour, and my tuition was thirty-five dollars a month, plus room and board," Dad said. "If you were careful, you could even save a little."

GMI was not accredited to offer academic degrees, but Dad was able to transfer the credits he earned there to the University of Michigan, where he graduated with honors from the College of Engineering in 1939, making him the first of our line of Grogans to receive a college degree. I asked how his father had reacted to such a point of pride.

"Dad wasn't much for showing his emotions," my father recalled. "He wasn't what you'd call gushy or demonstrative. But I think he was proud. I'm sure he was proud of me."

With his newly minted degree, my father returned to Pontiac Motors as a junior draftsman, living at home and helping to support his family. Not long after, his father succumbed to prostate cancer, dying at the age of fifty-six, a broken man. "We were all right there around his bed with him when he drew his last breath," Dad said.

My father settled in as the sole breadwinner for his mother and younger brother and sister. Then came December 7, 1941, and the Japanese attack on Pearl Harbor. My father could easily have ridden out the war in safety and without even losing face. He had ironclad double deferments. Not only was he supporting a widow and two dependents, but his plant had rapidly retooled to serve the war effort, and he was put to work designing large armaments. He was needed on the home front, by both his family and his country. He enlisted anyway.

"Why did you do that?" I asked.

Dad ran his fingers along the tablecloth and thought for a moment. "It just seemed like the right thing," he said.

"How are you doing?" I asked. "Getting tired?"

"Mouth's a little dry."

I got him a glass of water and changed videotapes, then asked, "Tell me about meeting Mom." A slight smile spread across his face, and I could see how in love with her he still was. I had heard her version of their courtship many times, but I wanted to hear it from him.

After the war, Dad returned to Pontiac, reclaimed his old job at Pontiac Motors, and moved back in with his mother and younger sister and brother. As was his habit, he resumed attending Mass each morning before work, where the associate pastor, the Reverend Joseph Howard, befriended him. Part of the reason Dad caught the young priest's eye, no doubt, was my father's generosity. Dad always believed in sharing whatever money he had with the Church. The entire time he was in the South Pacific, he kept track of the weekly offerings he was missing back home. Upon his return, he dropped a check for the accumulated lump sum in the collection basket. Not long after, Father Howard invited the newly returned navy lieutenant to the Howard family home in Ann Arbor for Sunday dinner and to meet his mother. What the priest failed to mention was that his younger sister, Ruth, would also be there. She had spent the war working at the Willow Run fighter-plane factory outside Ann Arbor and at age thirty was still single and living at home. My uncle Father Joe was playing matchmaker.

As Mom countless times told the story, she was not at all interested in the quiet, bookish man. She was pretty and confident and too proud to swoon over the first eligible bachelor her older brother dragged home on that August day in 1946. My father, on the other hand, was smitten by the petite brunette with the slightly off-kilter sense of humor. She had a natural way of filling his awkward silences with her laughter and endless banter. He felt comfortable around her. In his methodical, bashful way, Dad began courting her and eventually won her heart. (Mom's version always included a hilarious account of her shy suitor's weeks-long attempt to summon the courage to kiss her for the first time.) They married a year to the day after that first dinner, on August 16, 1947, with Father Joe and Father Vin officiating. Eleven months later they brought Marijo home from the hospital.

For two hours Dad talked as I recorded. He described the early blissful years of their marriage in a one-bedroom apartment in Detroit with a cardboard box for a dining-room table. He described their first house, on Pembroke Street in Detroit, and how he built a sandbox in the tiny backyard. He described the heartbreak of losing Mary Ann, and the promise of moving to Harbor Hills when I was one year old, where his children would enjoy the advantages he never experienced. He filled me in on everything he could think of that came before the point where my own memories began. Then he said, "I'm feeling a little tired now," and I turned off the camera and watched him, cane in hand, slowly climb the stairs to his bedroom.

Before dawn the next morning, the whole house was awake and bustling. Elizabeth fried eggs; Michael warmed up the car and scraped frost from the windshield. I would soon be leaving for the airport. It was time to return to my own family. Even Mom managed to crawl out of bed and come downstairs in her bathrobe to see me off. She sat at the kitchen table nursing a cup of instant coffee, and I kissed her on the cheek and said, "I'll try to get home in the spring, okay?"

"That would be nice, dear," she said.

Dad was in his pajamas and bathrobe, too, but he insisted on walking me out to the car. I loaded my bag in the trunk and turned back to him, standing in the garage, looking fragile. I walked over, extending my hand for the customary Grogan handshake. As I did, he hooked his cane over his wrist and extended both arms to me. I hesitated for a moment, then stepped into them. I felt them wrap around me, and mine around him.

"Aw, Dad," I said, "this has been great."

"Thanks for coming, John," he said. "I know it's not easy to get away."

As we stood there embracing, I remembered the last thing Jenny had said to me as she dropped me at the airport three days earlier. Her words rang in my head: "If there's anything you've been wanting to say to him, you probably should say it this trip." Now here I was leaving and I had not said the one thing I knew was long overdue. I drew a breath and summoned my courage.

"I love you, Dad," I said.

His words came back so quickly, so instantaneously, they seemed almost an echo of my own. They burst from him like water bursts from a broken pipe. It was as if they had been poised there for decades, hovering just inside his lips awaiting permission to be released.

"I love you, too, Johnny," he said.

Johnny. He had not called me that since I was a little boy. *Johnny*.

I clung to him for a moment longer, then got into the car with Michael. "Keep getting better!" I called out the window as we backed down the driveway. He waved one last time, and we were gone.

❋

CHAPTER 31

Whu en I returned home, Jenny asked, "Just how depressing was it?"

"A little sad," I said. "Just a little. The clock's definitely ticking. Even if Dad makes a full recovery, he's so weak now. I don't know how he can keep taking care of Mom and the house and everything. On the brighter side, Mom seems to be holding her own, and Dad was tired but in good spirits. He's still got a lot of fight left in him." I told her about the toll the chemotherapy had taken and the mementos he had pulled out of his box to share with me. I described my walks around the neighborhood and the taped interview with him on my last night home. "Whatever happens, I'm so glad I did that," I said.

"It's good that you went," Jenny said. "At their age, you just don't know."

As if to prove her point, two weeks later the phone rang. My father was back in the hospital. On December 12, a nurse came to the house to check on him. She took one look at his cracked and oozing ankles and ordered him immediately to the emergency room, fearing they were infected. But it wasn't his swollen extremities that kept him there. The doctor who saw him put a stethoscope to his chest and did not like what he heard: the faintest hint of congestion. Infection was the biggest risk of the chemotherapy regimen my father was on. Not only were the powerful drugs that coursed through his bloodstream attacking every cancer cell they encountered, they were attacking every white blood cell as well. And those white blood cells protected him from opportunistic invaders. Without them he was defenseless.

An X-ray confirmed the doctor's concern. A tiny spot of pneumonia had taken root in one lung. "You can barely see it," Dad said on the phone from his hospital bed. "But they don't want to take any chances. So I'm back in again. They've got me on an antibiotic IV to nip it in the bud."

The nurse had been wrong about my father's ankles, but had she not ordered him to the hospital, the spot of pneumonia could have gone undetected for weeks as it grew silently, filling his lungs with oxygen-robbing mucus. We both agreed her overreaction had been a blessing and saved him from a serious setback. "My guardian angel was looking out for me," Dad said.

With just one treatment remaining, the doctors suspended his chemotherapy, saying they needed to hold off on the final dose until the lung infection was under control. The chemotherapy was working better than hoped, sending his platelet count to near-normal levels. But the side effects had increased exponentially with each week, rendering him helpless. Two days before entering the hospital, on December 10, my father had celebrated his eighty-ninth birthday in bed, too enervated and nauseated to make it downstairs to eat the salmon dinner Michael had prepared for him, knowing it was a favorite. And now the drugs had compromised his immune system as well. I marveled at how a medication intended to save a life could go so far toward destroying it.

Unlike his earlier hospital stay, this time there was no private room that reminded him of a swanky resort. He was in a bare-bones cubicle with a loud, complaining roommate and inattentive nursing staff. When I called the next day, he sounded frazzled, nearly desperate. He was too weak to sit up and feed himself, but the orderlies simply left the food on a tray beside the bed. "I can't get the food to my mouth," he said. "I can't take a sip of water."

"Sit tight, Dad," I said. "We're going to fix this." And we did, browbeating the staff to give him the attention he needed and urging them to assign him the next available private room. Michael began to advocate for him more aggressively. In hospitals as elsewhere in life, we were learning, the old bromide proved true: the squeaky wheels really did get the grease. I tried to monitor him as best I could from afar by phone. Each report was more discouraging than the last. The doctors were having no success stamping out the pneumonia. They tried different antibiotics in different combinations without luck. He was now breathing with the help of an oxygen mask to compensate for his lungs' decreased capacity. During one visit, Michael overheard an attending physician in the hallway tell a colleague, "This thing is mushrooming. Nothing we throw at it is touching it."

My father's immune system was shot, allowing the pneumonia to rampage with impunity. I began to think of it as a violent predator on the loose in a small town where the populace had no sheriff, no posse, not even any pitchforks with which to defend themselves. Dr. Bober, my parents' longtime family physician, was our liaison with the hospital staff. She briefed Michael, who in turn briefed the rest of us. Dad's case was proving a medical conundrum, she said. His doctors needed to suspend the chemotherapy if they were to have any hope of reining in the potentially deadly pneumonia. But with the cancer-fighting drugs stopped, his platelet levels had resumed their perilous plummet, erasing most of the progress he had made. The leukemia was back on its feet, stronger than ever. Now there were two predators on the loose, both intent on taking him. To treat one served only to enable the other.

"Hang in there, Dad," I said on his third day of hospitalization. "They've got a new antibiotic they're going to try tomorrow. We just need it to kick in. Once the pneumonia is tackled, we can go after the leukemia again."

"I don't have any choice but to hang in there," he said.

On the fourth day, I called from my cell phone as I shopped for Christmas presents. The phone rang a dozen times before my father picked up.

"Hi, Dad," I said. "Is this an okay time?"

"No, it's not," he said, his voice distraught. "It's not good at all. I need to go now." He hung up, and a wave of dread washed over me. Only later would I learn that a priest was at his side at that moment, administering the Last Rites, the Catholic sacrament for the dying. That's why he couldn't talk. Dad was not done fighting; he hadn't given up. But he realized the growing gravity of his situation and wanted to be prepared. I was focused on his physical well-being; he was thinking of his spiritual.

As I drove home, I did something I had not done for many, many years. I prayed. I began just as I had started my prayers each night as a young boy. "Dear Jesus, dear God the Father, dear Holy Spirit, all the saints and angels in heaven," I said aloud. "Let the new antibiotic work. Please. Let the chemo work. Let Dad get better. Let him get over this hump so he can have another couple years. Or one. That's all I'm asking. One year. Mom needs him. We all still need him. Amen."

I made the sign of the cross just as the nuns had taught me to four decades earlier, touching the fingertips of my right hand to my forehead, chest, and each shoulder. Even alone in the car, I felt embarrassed. I had stopped believing in the literal power of prayer many years earlier and came to think of it as a strictly contemplative act whose value lay in self-examination and revelation. How many Jews had prayed in the concentration camps? How many murder victims had prayed in the instant before the trigger was pulled? How many sick and dying had sought God's intervention in vain? And yet here I was. I no longer knew if I believed in the miracle of prayer. At this moment, my father's life in the balance, I knew with certainty I wanted to.

Later that day, we finally got some good news. A private room had come available. At 4 P.M. Dad was wheeled into his new quarters, and almost instantly he sounded better, more tranquil and at peace. I felt a surge of optimism. Here he could get the rest he needed, build his strength, fight back. The new antibiotic held promise, and the chemotherapy regimen had already proved its efficacy, if only he could get well enough to tolerate it again. But the new accommodations were short-lived. His doctors had been monitoring both his respiration—the number of breaths he took each minute—and the oxygen in his blood as indicators of how efficiently his lungs were working. The numbers had been gradually slipping all week even as the doctors enriched the oxygen mixture coming through his breathing mask. A healthy adult averages twelve breaths per minute, but Dad was taking as many as thirty. Even as he gasped, the oxygen levels in his blood could not keep up. The numbers had passed a threshold that triggered a hospital protocol: my father was being transferred to the intensive care unit.

"I don't want to go to the ICU," he pleaded to Michael. "The ICU is Death Row. People don't come out of there." Michael assured him that it was where he could get the best, most advanced treatment. Regardless, there was no choice. At 10 P.M. a team of orderlies wheeled Dad out of his private room and into the ICU.

The next morning I called Tim at his office in New York City. "We need to get home," I told him. Tim completely agreed. With Elizabeth still there, he had been planning to drive home to spend Christmas, anyway. Before leaving he just needed to wrap up an assignment or two at his magazine, he said, and take care of a few other work duties. Then he should be clear to head to Michigan, maybe as early as the middle of the following week, which would get him there for Christmas Eve. It was my brother's turn to deny reality.

"Next week?" I interrupted. "Tim, don't you see? We might not have until next week. We need to go now."

There was a pause on the line, then my brother said, "I'll be at your place at eight tomorrow morning. We'll drive in together. We can get there by dark."

"I'll be ready," I said.

❖

CHAPTER 32

The next morning, Jenny drove me to an exit along Interstate 78 to rendezvous with Tim as he headed west from New York City. We shared the same sense of urgency now, and the half hour saved was a half hour sooner we would be at our father's side. As I slipped into the passenger seat of my brother's car, Jenny handed me a bag of sandwiches. "This way you won't have to stop to eat," she said. I kissed her good-bye and said, "I'll keep you posted."

Tim and I were only a few miles down the road when the stories began. I'm not sure which of us started them, but once we started we went on for hours. Funny stories, embarrassing stories, painful stories. The time-polished gems my mother told at the kitchen table; the tales she had no idea existed. Family stories had always been the thread that stitched together the tapestry of our lives. They amused us in good times and soothed us in bad. They filled the awkward silences when things were not right and fueled the warmth when they were. Mostly they provided the context that made us something more than six people related by blood—the context that made us that messy, imperfect, spectacularly infuriating and confounding and essential entity, a family.

"Remember the time we snuck down to the lake on the way home from church in our Sunday-best dress shoes, and you fell in?" I asked.

"You little shit," Tim said, grinning. He had sworn me to secrecy that day, knowing that a spanking with the George-and-Suzie Stick awaited him if Mom found out. Ruining his shoes was bad enough, but sneaking to the lake without permission—and dragging his baby brother along—were the graver offenses. His plan was to hide the shoes under his bed until they dried, and Mom would never be the wiser. But as we tiptoed through the kitchen, the euphoria of having my older brother's fate in my hands was too much to bear. "Mom! Mom!" I exploded. "Timmy fell in the water in his brand-new church shoes!"

"You whopped my ass pretty good for that one," I said.

"You deserved it," he answered, and I couldn't disagree.

I was a tireless troublemaker. One Easter when I was about six, I was hunting for my basket and opened the door to the clothes dryer to find Michael's basket hidden inside, his name printed in big block letters on a card stuck in the colored grass. I quietly closed the door, looked both ways, and turned on the dryer. It made a horrible racket as the eggs and chocolates and jelly beans tumbled in the steel drum. I thought it was the funniest prank I had ever pulled—until Mom led Michael to my basket, plucked out my name card, and replaced it with his. She opened the dryer, tossed in my tag among the broken eggs, linty jelly beans, and melted chocolates and said calmly, "This one's yours now, Johnny." Suddenly I was no longer laughing.

"You've got to admit," Tim said, "she had a good sense of justice."

We recounted the family camping trips to Michigan's Upper Peninsula, the frigid winds howling in off Lake Superior forcing us all to wear winter coats in July.

"Do you remember Mom's pork and beans over the camp stove?" Tim asked.

"Oh God, yes," I said. "Nothing has ever tasted so delicious."

We laughed about our elaborate schemes for skipping Sunday Mass, and the pranks we played on the nuns. One of my finest moments was the day in sixth grade when the ancient and decrepit Sister Mary Clementia screamed over our voices that she wanted to hear a pin drop. She pulled a large stickpin from her veil, held it in the air, and yelled, "Silence! I'm going to count to three, and I better hear this." As she began her countdown, I folded over the lid to my milk carton, placed it on the floor, and poised my heel above it. "One . . . two . . . three." Just as she released the pin, I stomped on the empty carton with everything I had. It exploded with a boom that nearly sent Sister through the ceiling. I had to stay after school every day for a week, writing over and over "I shall not misbehave in school," but it was worth every minute for that one instant of Hitchcock-worthy terror on her face.

Tim said he could beat that. At Brother Rice, there was the equally ancient and decrepit Brother O'Hara, who each morning like clockwork would enter the classroom and stomp his foot in the trash can to compress the litter. One day Tim and his classmates filled the can with water and sprinkled a layer of crumpled papers across the surface. In came Brother O'Hara and plunged his leg knee-deep in water.

We recounted the family vacations to miracle sites, the Thanksgiving morning family hikes through the woods as the turkey roasted in the oven, and the way Shaun loved to leap into snowdrifts. There were Mom's aniseed cookies and homemade eggnog at Christmas and Dad's dramatic manger scene beneath the giant twinkling star he suspended in the upstairs bathroom window with strings of white lights stretching down to the ground.

"Remember the Christmas Dad was in the hospital after his heart attack?" I asked. "And the two of us trying to put up the tree without him?"

"What a disaster," Tim said. We were adults by then, and the task was simple enough—we simply needed to drill a hole in the bottom of the trunk to accept the spike in the stand—but together Tim and I broke one drill bit after another, growing more and more hysterical as we did. What made it all the funnier to us at the time was the contrast between our ineptness and Dad's effortless competence. He had done the same procedure for years without once breaking a bit.

"Dad always made everything look so easy," I said.

That made me think of a story Tim had not heard: Shortly after I got my driver's license, Michael called from a party asking for a ride home. I jumped to volunteer, anxious for a chance to drive alone. Mom and Dad were cautious with teens and cars—forbidding their children to drive without a parent for a full year after becoming licensed—but they agreed to this trip. It was about twenty minutes away, and I'd have my brother with me for the drive home. Dad gave me directions. I whistled for Shaun to join me and set out into the night. Soon I was hopelessly lost, driving up and down back roads without streetlights, drifting deeper into the gritty neighborhoods surrounding Pontiac's factories. Panic rising in my chest, I pulled into the driveway of a darkened house to turn around, and as I pulled out, I cut the wheel too hard and the back tire of the family Monte Carlo dropped into the ditch. I gunned the engine again and again but the car would not budge. Outside, I dropped to my knees and could see the axle resting on the ground. Shaun must have sensed my anxiety because he began to yip. The front door of the house opened, and a woman in a bathrobe appeared in the beams of my headlights. Someone who would help, I thought.

"Turn those goddamn headlights off!" she barked. "And get off my property. We're trying to sleep."

"But—" I began.

"And shut that dog up!"

"May I use your phone?"

"Off my property or I'm calling the cops!" she yelled and slammed the door. I was now unhinged. I locked Shaun in the car, still barking wildly, and ran down the dark road until I came to a house with lights on. I knocked on the door and begged the man who answered to let me call my father. He sized me up, then told me to wait outside while he called for me. Fifteen minutes later, Dad pulled up. I had never been so happy to see one of my parents. He could see my distress. "Everything's going to be fine," he said.

"These things happen." I warned him about the angry lady threatening to call the police, and he was not at all ruffled. "We'll be out of her hair in a few minutes," he said.

My can-do father pulled a jack and a large piece of lumber from the trunk of his company car, hoisted the Monte Carlo up until the axle was clear, wedged the wood under the tire, and expertly backed it out of the ditch. He could have criticized me or ridiculed my incompetence. He could have grumbled about having to come out at midnight to rescue me. Instead he put his arm around my shoulder and simply said, "Driving's like anything else; you'll get better with practice. Now let's go fetch your brother before he thinks we forgot about him."

"Dad got us out of a lot of jams over the years," Tim said as we drove through the mountains of central Pennsylvania.

I couldn't talk about Dad and cars without telling the story of the time I walked into the house during a weekend visit home from college and breathlessly described the beautiful woman I had encountered minutes earlier: "So I pull up to the red light and in the car next to me is this total fox."

"A fox?" my guileless father said in astonishment. "A fox? Right there in the car? Alive? A live fox?" Somehow he had managed to turn my moment of roadside lust into a *Wild Kingdom* episode.

Not even Mom was that clueless. "Oh, Richard," she scolded, shaking her head.

Just as the sun set, we pulled onto Erie Drive. Elizabeth and Michael greeted us at the door, and we all ate dinner with

Mom, who seemed listless and detached despite our best efforts to keep the conversation upbeat. She appeared only marginally aware that her husband was hospitalized, and even less aware for what reason, but she was definitely not herself, and I wondered if she missed him on a more primal level. The man she had spent the past fifty-seven years with was suddenly not in her bed at night, not at the breakfast table in the morning. The man who had cared for her every need over the past decade had disappeared.

After dinner, Mike volunteered to do the dishes, and Elizabeth, Tim, and I headed to Saint Joseph Mercy Hospital for the 8:30 to 10 P.M. visiting hours—one of three times during the day family members were allowed in. When we arrived in the ICU, a nurse directed us to place masks over our mouths and noses. Dad was in a respiratory infectious containment room, and the masks were to protect him from our germs and us from his. Once we were masked, she opened the door to his room, and there he lay amid a warren of machines, pumps, wires, tubes, and monitors. A heavy plastic mask with a rubber gasket was clamped over his nose and mouth, connected by a hose to an external respirator that rhythmically pumped powerful bursts of oxygen into his lungs. Needles and tubes poked into his bruised, puffy arms. I swallowed hard.

"Hi, Dad," I said and squeezed his knee through the blanket.

"Hey, Dad," Tim said and touched his shoulder.

He smiled apologetically through the mask, and I could tell he was embarrassed by all the fuss being made over him. I knew what this eternally humble man was thinking:

wouldn't all these fancy machines and medicines and experts be better used on someone who really needed them?

"How was the trip?" His voice came muffled through the heavy mask in between breaths, and it was difficult to hear him over the whir of the machines. "The trip," he repeated. "How was it?"

Tim and I filled the room with happy chatter, telling him about the drive, the gasoline prices, the weather, and our disdain for the Ohio Turnpike. I filled him in on the kids and work and the antics of our new dog, Gracie. We talked about anything we could think of to keep the conversation afloat. Each burst of monologue was followed by an awkward silence. We made vague, optimistic comments about Dad's prognosis and the high hopes for the latest antibiotic cocktail. "Once that kicks in, we're going to see a big difference, I bet," I volunteered.

Dad seemed distracted, like he was not quite paying attention. Then he blurted out what was on his mind. Through the mask, muffled and cottony, came the words "What do you think we should do about Mother?"

Tim and I exchanged glances. "Mom?" I asked.

Dad through the mask, each phrase separated by a deep forced breath: "If I get out of here . . . it's going to take months . . . to get back on my feet . . . Elizabeth can't stay forever . . . she needs to be home with her husband . . . Mike can't handle it alone." He waited for a breath to pass and added: "We need to talk about Mom. What's best."

"Lourdes," I said. I knew it was where he wanted her to end up if the day came when he could no longer care for her. "They'd take good care of her. And you, too, as you recover and get your strength back."

"Lourdes," Dad said, pausing to summon his most emphatic voice, "is the *best*." It was an important declaration for Tim and Elizabeth to hear. In the Philippines, where Elizabeth grew up, sending an aged parent to a nursing home was unheard of, and Elizabeth was lobbying to bring Mom back to New Jersey to stay with them, even though they lived up a steep staircase with no elevator and had only one small bedroom. Marijo, too, was trying to figure out how she could care for Mom around her job as a social worker. I even considered our house, despite knowing that the strain on our marriage would be devastating.

My father seemed intent on heading off all these well-intentioned, misguided plans. He knew firsthand the hours and level of commitment her care required. "She belongs at Lourdes," he said. "She won't like it at first. She'll be angry, but she'll get over it. She'll forget and be okay. Lourdes is the best."

Tim and I looked at each other and nodded. We promised to make an appointment to talk to the administrator about getting them both in there after Dad was released from the hospital. Dad nodded his approval, and with the topic settled he visibly relaxed. Even here in the ICU, my father was mentally running through his to-do list, taking care of business. He always was a detail man. He reminded us that the lawn mower and snowblower needed to be winterized and the hoses drained before they froze.

The conversation dwindled, and eventually we sat in silence by his side, listening to the breathing machine do its work. The nurse ducked her head in the door and gave us the five-minute warning.

"I guess it's time to go, Dad," I said.

"We'll be back in the morning, okay?" Tim added.

Dad nodded and we began to slip into our coats. That's when Elizabeth, in her broken English, offered, "Daddy, you like we say prayer?"

His eyes brightened and he nodded up and down.

We all bowed our heads and began the Lord's Prayer together. "Our Father who art in heaven . . ." But there was a problem. Tim and I no longer remembered the words that had been drilled into us thousands of times. It had been years since we had recited the prayer on our own, and whenever we were in a family gathering, we simply took our cues from Dad, mumbling along and blending in. But on this night, Dad's voice was buried inside the breathing mask, nearly impossible to understand. Elizabeth's English was too broken to help. We were adrift and couldn't even fake it: ". . . hallowed be thy name; thy *blah-blah blah*, thy *blah* be *blah-blah* . . . On *blub-blub* as it *blah-blah mumble*."

The prayer stretched on forever as we stumbled along. We might as well have been trying to recite *Beowulf* from memory. There was no hiding our rustiness. I looked at Dad and his eyes were closed as he prayed aloud. Then I made the mistake of looking at Tim. As soon as our eyes met, he let out the slightest giggle. That triggered my urge to giggle, too. I felt a laugh pushing its way up from my chest and took a gulp to try to hold it in. My shoulders began to shake. The situation was awful; beyond awkward. But something about it was unbearably funny, too. Little honks of air escaped from my nose. Tears welled in my eyes. I stared hard at my knees, trying to think unfunny thoughts. The more I tried to be serious, the worse it got—exactly like when Father Stanislaw, the old Polish priest from the seminary, would sing off-key at the solemn Good Friday service when we were kids. The more you knew you should not laugh, the more hilarious everything seemed.

From across the bed, I heard a piglike snort and glanced up to see Tim shaking, his eyes squeezed shut, as he plowed blindly ahead: ". . . give us *blah blub*, our *blah-blah blub* . . ." I joined back in: "and de-*blah-blah* us from *mumble*, for-*blah-blub* and *blub-blah*. Amen." We both said the "Amen" in loud, ringing voices. We had that part down. Tim and I wiped our eyes and tried to pretend the prayer had gone off like clockwork. Dad just looked at us with tired, resigned eyes.

In the doorway, with Tim and Elizabeth already down the hall, I turned back to look at him. He was staring up at the ceiling, each forced breath pushing his chin up and his head back into the pillow. The doctors had told him to work at inhaling deeply; the oxygen infusion into his lungs was part of the cure. Breath was life, and he concentrated on pulling each one deep inside him. "Good night, Dad," I whispered and raised two fingers to my lips, throwing him a kiss.

CHAPTER 33

⁂

A s the days to Christmas ticked down, we settled into a routine. I took the morning visitation, Tim and Elizabeth took the afternoon slot, and Mike and I returned together for the final visit of the night. Marijo shuttled back and forth from her home and office an hour away to join us whenever she could. When we weren't with Dad, we mostly sat with Mom, telling old stories, massaging her shoulders, keeping her company.

That afternoon, as a gray, dreary dusk fell, I sat alone in the living room with Mom. Tim and Elizabeth were at the hospital; Mike was out running errands. Elizabeth had draped a few strings of holiday lights over the long-silent piano and through the houseplants on the windowsill in a valiant effort to give the place a hint of holiday cheer. But the decorations just made the house seem all the more forlorn, a vestige of its former holiday self, when the fireplace had roared and the air was filled with children's joyous shrieks and the scent of pine boughs. Sitting there, I could not resist the lure of memories from long ago when my parents were in their prime and committed to sinking endless energy into making Christmas magical.

Every other family I knew as a kid simply went to the store and bought Christmas lights for their trees. Not ours. Dad spent hours hand-wiring his own lights of a special design, guaranteed to never cause a spark because they ran in series on a single wire. What that meant was that if one bulb went out, they all went out. Part of our family ritual every year was unscrewing bulb after bulb and testing each one to find the culprit. Some years we would work late into Christmas Eve trying to get those crazy lights figured out. Then we'd all race out into the cold to make it to Our Lady of Refuge for midnight Mass, which, with its giant nativity scene, banks of red poinsettias, and curfew-busting mystique, seemed magical indeed.

The house had never seemed so silent.

"Just you and me, Ruthie," I said as we sat in the growing gloom.

"Just me and my number three son," she said.

"Are you hungry? Can I make you something?"

"Maybe a little, sure," she said. I helped her to the kitchen table, my hands under her armpits in case she stumbled, and warmed a plate of leftovers in the microwave.

"You were hungry!" I exclaimed when she finished. "You cleaned your plate." I felt the familiar swell of satisfaction as when my own kids ate everything put before them. She was more like them now than I would ever have imagined. My mother had come full circle. She had stopped worrying about her children, stopped fretting about our life choices and spiritual well-being, stopped trying to bend us to her will. All the flashpoints that had seemed so important and consumed so much of her emotional energy had washed away like flotsam on an outgoing tide. We had to hide candy from her now, pester her to eat her vegetables and drink enough water, remind her to brush her teeth, and bribe her with treats to take her medicines.

Back in the living room, I steered her to her favorite chair, and we sat in the glow of the colored lights, the house so quiet I could hear the whisper of air rising from the heating vents.

"Just five days till Christmas, Ma," I said.

"Will Dad be home for Christmas?" she asked.

"I don't know, Mom," I said. "I don't think so."

We sat for a long time, listening to the heat.

"No snow yet," she said eventually, looking out into the twilight.

"Maybe by Christmas," I said.

That's when she began to sing. Soft and reedy, her weak voice carrying a certain warble, as if coming from a tiny bird or a little girl.

"I'm dreaming of a white Christmas . . ."

I marveled at my mother's mind. From what part of her faraway memory had the song surfaced? I had not heard her sing "White Christmas" in decades.

My choices were to sit and listen to that plaintively lonely voice, or join in. Together we sang through the verse, conjuring images of snowcapped evergreens and children awaiting Santa's arrival.

Neither of us knew more than the first verse, and so we sang it over again. Over and over. When she had sung all she wanted, she stopped and sighed.

"That Bing Crosby, heavens how he could sing," she

said, and then she was asleep in her chair, the silence again enveloping us.

The next morning, Tuesday, I arrived at the hospital at 10 A.M. to find Dad propped up and breathing comfortably through a light plastic mask that rested loosely over his nose and mouth. The big suction mask with the forced air pressure sat idle in the corner. "My blood oxygen has been pretty good," he said, "so they thought they'd give me a break." Through the light mask, I could hear him perfectly.

"That's great, Dad," I said. "You're making progress."

"I'm not so sure, John," he said. "I don't know anymore." He looked searchingly at me. "What do you think? Do you think I can beat this?"

On this matter of utmost significance, he had not before asked my opinion. I hesitated. My honest response was that my optimism soared and plunged on an hourly basis. One moment I saw the possibility of a full recovery and a continuation of the lifestyle for which my parents had worked so hard. The next moment I realized their days of independence were over. Even in a best-case scenario, my parents would need to live in a facility with nursing care. There would be no more driving or lawn cutting or grocery shopping. And the moment after that I was all but certain Dad's worst fear would come true, and he would never be leaving the ICU. The doctors were running out of options. The pneumonia and leukemia were in a race to the finish, and neither showed signs of slowing. I had no clue whether he could beat this thing. With each day it seemed less likely. I was trying to be realistic. I didn't want to patronize him.

"I don't know, Dad," I said. "We just need to keep fighting. We need to keep pushing."

"And praying," he added.

"And praying, Dad. You can't give up."

He nodded in agreement. "I just want to get better so I can be there for Mother," he said. "I want to take care of her for however long she has left." He remained hopelessly devoted to her. She was his everything, and it seemed his only wish was to outlive her by one day. I lifted the mask up and held the straw from his water glass to his lips so he could sip.

"One day at a time, Dad," I said.

"You know I've been fretting about Christmas."

"You mean you haven't gotten out to buy my gift yet?" I deadpanned.

"I don't want to spoil Christmas for everyone."

"Oh, Dad, you're not."

"You should be home with Jenny and the kids," he said. "We both know that."

"I'm playing it by ear," I said. "I may fly home on Christmas Eve. We'll see."

I had already spoken with Jenny about the possibility of missing the holiday, and she had told me she and the kids would be fine. "You need to be there right now," she had said.

I changed topics. "Mike and I went to Lourdes yesterday and talked to the administrator," I said. "She was great. Told us how much they all admire you and appreciate all you've done for them over the years."

Dad's eyes widened with expectation. "And?"

"And they have a long waiting list, but she said they'll do whatever it takes to find a spot for you and Mom," I said. "We got to peek at the suite near the chapel, the one for a couple. It has two bedrooms and a sitting room; it would be perfect for you and Mom. The paperwork's done."

"That's good," Dad said. "It's good you took care of that."

I didn't tell him the suite would soon be available, nor why: the current occupant, an aged priest, was days from death. Nursing homes were a lot like the ICU that way, the last station on the stagecoach ride of life.

We sat quietly for a few minutes.

"Say," he began, and I could tell from the way he was wetting his lips that he was about to say something he had been rehearsing. "This is a good time to talk to you about something." He held out his hand for me to take. I slipped my fingers through his and sat beside him on the bed.

"Sure," I said.

"What are you doing about the kids' religion?"

My heart sank. Our taboo topic was back on the table. We both knew the answer to his question, and it was *nothing*. "Dad," I said in almost a whisper, letting his name hang on the air. "I'm doing my best. I know it's not how you did it, or how you want me to do it, but I'm trying to raise them right."

"You are raising them right, John," he said, and he squeezed my hand. "You're a good father. I just worry about them growing up without religion and prayer in their lives. Prayer, especially, is so important."

I wanted to give him assurances, to tell him what I knew he longed to hear, that his grandchildren would receive the sacraments and attend Mass every week and be raised as good Catholics. I knew I couldn't say that and be true to myself—or honest to him. I owed him my honesty. I respected him too much to give him any less. Besides, he was an intelligent man; over the years, I had gradually come to realize that all my sugarcoated half-truths had not fooled him for a moment. Mom maybe, but not Dad.

He must have sensed my discomfort. "I know you have issues with the Church," he said.

"Yeah, I do," I said. "But I haven't given up on it just yet. I'm not done trying to figure it out." And that much was true: I hadn't, and I wasn't.

"That's all I can ask," he said.

Lunch arrived, and I pulled up his mask and fed him his soup and yogurt one spoonful at a time.

That evening Michael and I arrived for the 8:30 visit and again we found Dad breathing comfortably through the lighter mask. I was figuring out that the nurses switched masks when they knew family members were expected so he could talk and be heard more easily. After we left, they would switch back to the heavy ventilator mask. All the ICU nurses were caring, but one, a woman about my age named Michelle, was particularly kind and was Dad's favorite. She seemed sincerely fond of him and always had a cheerful word. Michelle routinely let us stay past visiting hours and sometimes slipped us sodas and snacks. It was just like her to think to switch masks so her patient could have more meaningful time with his children.

Dad had good color in his face and was relaxed and resting comfortably. Michael and I had a pleasant visit with him. We told him more about our trip to Lourdes and the suite it had on standby. We gave him the daily update on Mom, assuring him she missed him but otherwise was doing fine.

The ICU staff had begun timing meal deliveries to our visits because Dad was too weak to feed himself, and they were too busy to do it for him. Another bowl of pureed soup—one of the few things he could swallow with his swollen mouth—arrived and I again fed it to him by the spoonful, just as I did with my children before they were old enough to feed themselves.

"I'm helpless as a baby," Dad apologized between bites.

"You've been through the wringer," I said. "Now open up; here comes another bite."

On the drive home that night, I told Michael I had made a decision. I would fly home that Thursday and return three days later, the day after Christmas. "Dad's holding his own," I said. "He's eating well. He's breathing comfortably, even on the lighter mask. I can't imagine anything changing too dramatically in the next few days."

"It should be pretty much status quo through the holiday, I'd think," Michael agreed.

"I'll dash home for Christmas and be back the next day."

That was the plan.

CHAPTER 34

❊

I awoke early the next morning and booked a flight home for Christmas, then called Jenny.

"Are you sure you should be leaving?" she asked.

I assured her my father was stable and in for the long haul. "Last night he actually looked the best he has all week," I said. "Whichever way this goes, it's going to be a long, slow process."

I showered, ate a bowl of cereal, and headed to the hospital for my regular ten-to-noon shift. When I arrived, I knew right away something was wrong. The door to Dad's room was wide open, a crash cart in the doorway. Michelle intercepted me in the hallway, her face drawn and white. "I'm so glad you're here. Your dad's had a very rough morning," she said. "Twice his blood oxygen crashed. We had the respiratory team in here. They really had to work on him to get him out of danger. It was touch and go." The goal was to keep his blood oxygen saturation as close to 100 percent as possible. All week it had been hovering in the 90s, which was good. At an oxygen saturation level of 86 percent, alarms are triggered. On this morning, the alarms rang at 8 A.M. and again ninety minutes later, and both times the levels plunged, bottoming out below 70 percent even as he gasped 40 breaths per minute. Blood oxygen levels that low for more than a few minutes could result in stroke or damage to his brain and other vital organs, Michelle said.

"He's resting now," she said, "but this is a threshold day for your family." I remember thinking how odd a word choice that was, *threshold*. It was as if she knew our family would soon be stepping through a doorway, crossing from one chapter of life into another, never to return again. "We need clear direction on what you want us to do," she said. "If it happens again—and it will, it's just a matter of when—we'll need to intubate him and put him on a ventilator." She hesitated. "If that's what the family wants." She didn't have to tell me the ramifications of being ventilated, or what the alternative meant. I looked through the doorway at Dad. The big suction mask was again clamped over his face, pushing his head back into the pillow with each forced breath. His mouth was agape, struggling to accept each gust. His eyes were shut, his body still. There was now even more equipment surrounding him.

The respiratory therapist who had worked on him joined us. "If we intubate him, he likely will never come off," she said. "At this stage, it's nearly impossible to wean them off the vent again. You need to know that. I've been doing this for sixteen years, and I haven't seen anyone in your father's condition come off it yet."

"I see," I said. But I didn't see at all. The words were pinging off the inside of my skull like pinballs. I felt blindsided by the surprise attack of information. I had arrived planning to tell him about the flight I had just booked; he was going to assure me he'd be fine until I returned. That was how our visit was supposed to go. Now all I could think was that I would not be able to feed him his lunch.

"Dr. Bober's expecting your call," Michelle said and she led me to the nurses' station and dialed. The doctor confirmed everything the others had just told me. The pneumonia was winning; Dad's lungs were shutting down. A ventilator would breathe indefinitely for him, but that was not a blessing. He could linger for months as the leukemia slowly ravaged him.

"Nature's trying to take its course," she said. "Pneumonia is sometimes known as 'the merciful death' because it takes terminal patients quickly." The doctor knew my father's wishes as well as I did. He had made it clear he wanted to fight with everything he had as long as any chance of meaningful recovery remained. But if not, he wanted no heroic measures to keep him alive. In his religious paradigm, that would be defying God's will.

"I think today is your dad's day," the doctor said in a voice that was so gentle and so kind I nearly began to cry. "Call your brothers and sister. I'll meet you all there in an hour, okay?"

I did as I was told, then walked into Dad's room and stood at his side. He appeared to be unconscious. The whir of the machine filled the room. I could see his breath fog the mask as he exhaled and disappear as another massive gust of oxygen pushed in. Michelle came in and said, "He's been through a lot this morning. He's exhausted." She shook his shoulder vigorously and spoke in a loud voice:

"Mr. Grogan, can you hear me? Mr. Grogan, wake up. Do you need anything? Mr. Grogan, your son is here."

Gradually Dad returned from his deep sleep. I touched his arm and put my lips close to his ear. "Dad, it's John," I said. "I'm here. I'm right here." He didn't open his eyes but nodded his head up and down in small, quick movements. He began to move his mouth inside the mask and was trying to lift his head and claw his hand out from beneath the blanket.

"Do you need something, Mr. Grogan?" Michelle asked in a loud voice. "Are you thirsty?" He shook his head no. "Are your lips dry?" No. "Is the mask too tight?" No. "Are you too warm?" Finally: "Are you trying to say something?" My father's head nodded vigorously in the affirmative, his eyes still closed. She unstrapped the mask and pulled it aside.

"What is it, Dad?" I asked.

"Are the kids all here?" he asked.

"It's John, Dad. The others will be here in a few minutes."

He lay there for a moment as if summoning from deep within the strength to speak. His eyes fluttered open momentarily, and he said, "I'm tired." And then, each word coming out like its own sentence: "I. Don't. Want. To. Fight. This. Anymore."

I looked at Michelle. She nodded her head that it was okay, and I looked back at my father.

"You don't need to fight anymore, Dad," I said. "You gave it everything you had. You can stop. You can just relax now." I told him what Dr. Bober had told me, that she could make sure he did not suffer. "You've been so brave, Dad," I said. "So brave. You can let go now."

Michelle replaced his mask, and he drifted back into his deep retreat. I waited in the hallway until Marijo, Tim, and Michael arrived. Their eyes were red, and I could tell they had been crying in the car on the way over. "There's something you all need to hear," I said and called Michelle over. "We took the mask off Dad and he said a few words. Michelle, I just want to make sure you heard what I heard."

"He said he was tired and didn't want to fight anymore," she said. I was so grateful for her testimony. I did not want his last words, his final wish, to rest on my shoulders alone. "Those were his words," she repeated, " 'I don't want to fight this anymore.' "

By the time Dr. Bober arrived we were all in agreement that there would be no more medical intervention. Dad was ready; we had to be, too. In the ICU lounge, the doctor walked us through how the day would go. A palliative care team would take over from here, she said, and would administer adequate morphine and muscle relaxants to override his breathing impulse and eliminate any gasping reflex as his blood oxygen levels dropped. "His lungs are so compromised," the doctor said, "I don't think it will take very long."

The four of us had agreed that Mom would want to say good-bye to her husband, but when we told Dr. Bober we planned to bring her up to his bedside for a few minutes, she looked appalled. "Don't do that to your mother," she pleaded. "Please, don't. She won't be able to process all this. It will only traumatize her. Let her remember him the way he was." It was the best advice anyone could have given.

Dr. Bober said she wanted to say good-bye to the man who had been her patient and friend for twenty years. When she came out of his room a few minutes later, she was crying.

A few minutes later, a woman arrived and introduced herself as Peg Nelson. She was a nurse practitioner on the palliative care team and would be managing Dad's last hours. I instantly liked her. She was matter-of-fact without seeming blasé, sympathetic without being maudlin. She gave us a reasoned and full explanation of what the next few hours would hold. When we were ready, she would inject Dad with the morphine and muscle relaxant, then remove his breathing mask. "He will deeply relax and slip into unconsciousness and not feel any discomfort."

Like Dr. Bober, she said, "It should come very quickly."

Awkwardly, we asked about the logistics of death: When should we say our good-byes? Would he be able to hear us? She said we should say what we wanted him to hear before the injections, and that he would still be semiaware for several minutes after.

I asked when all of this was going to happen. Part of me hoped she would say we could come back tomorrow. "We can start anytime," she said. "You should eat something first. Why don't we meet back here in an hour, after you've had a chance to get some lunch." An hour. My siblings and I looked at each other. The moment was slowly sinking in. We were scheduling our father's death like we might schedule a dentist appointment. Two-thirty would work. Right after we'd had time to grab a bite to eat.

"My God," Marijo said and placed a hand over her mouth.

In the cafeteria, we picked at our food. I managed to choke down half a turkey sandwich. I knew without doubt that we were making the right decision, the decision Dad wanted, the one that Dr. Bober assured us was inevitable. He would finally be free from the pain and exhaustion and debilitation of fighting this losing battle. It was the right thing. Why then did it not feel that way?

After lunch, we stopped in the hospital chapel, and I knelt in front of the miniature altar and tried to pray. "Please take him quickly," I whispered into my hands. "Without trauma or pain. Don't let him be afraid. Let him go without doubting his beliefs." I took comfort in his certainty that eternal salvation awaited him on the other side, and that his beloved wife would join him in heaven soon enough. Before I stood up, I whispered, "Help me live my life half as well as he has lived his."

I found Tim and Mike sitting on a bench just outside the chapel. Marijo was still inside, deep in her own moment of contemplation. "I'm going to go up and sit with Dad," I said. "See you up there in a few minutes."

In his room, I found him as we had left him, eyes closed, body still, the whir of the breathing machine filling the air. I rested one hand on his shoulder and the other on his wrist beneath the blanket. "Dad, it's John," I said, and he opened his eyes. I could see he was alert and aware, though terribly weak. He began to mumble something beneath the mask, his words lost in the whirlwind of oxygen. I hushed him.

"Dad," I said, my voice quaking, "Jesus is going to take you home today. In just a little while, he's going to take you." Dad's eyes were closed again. He moved his head up and down in short, jerky motions, and I knew he understood. Whatever I had to say, now was the time. I drew in a breath.

"Dad, you know how much I love you. I love you so much." He began urgently working his mouth inside the mask, desperately trying to communicate something. "Don't try to talk. It's okay. I know. I know you love me, too. I know that. I know you'd say it if you could. You love me." His head jerked up and down. "And I know you're proud of me, Dad. I never doubted that. Don't think I ever did." More little head jerks. I told him not to worry about Mother; we'd take good care of her. I repeated the words he had said to me a few days earlier: "Mom's going to be okay." More nods.

From earlier conversations, I knew he worried that the family might crumble after he and my mother were gone, that without their glue, the four of us kids would drift apart. I assured him we would not. "We're going to look out for each other, Dad. We'll keep the family together."

There was one more thing I wanted to tell him, something I had been rehearsing for the past several days even as I denied that the time was near to say them. "Dad, can you hear me?" I asked, my lips close to his ear. He nodded. I paused to steady my voice. "Dad, it has been an honor to be your son. I am so honored and so proud." I swallowed hard, fighting to maintain composure. "An honor."

I glanced over my shoulder, and there was Tim in the doorway. "Okay, Dad," I whispered. "Tim's here now." I ran my palm once over his sandpapery stubble, just as I liked to do when I was a little boy sitting in his lap. As then, I found the touch of it oddly soothing, at once rough and warm. One more time I told him I loved him, then kissed his temple and walked out of the room.

⚜

CHAPTER 35

When the others had each had their private good-byes with him, we gathered in the hallway and told Peg we were ready. The one thing we knew Dad would want was a priest to give him final absolution. Not that any of us thought he needed it. "If this man's not getting into heaven," Tim said, only half joking, "then no one is." Michael earlier had called Father Vin to ask if he would drive to the hospital from his home, more than an hour away. We thought it fitting that the priest who had married our parents and baptized all their children be there to see the first of them off, but a blizzard was threatening to sweep in off the Great Lakes, and our uncle was afraid to be caught on the interstate. We couldn't blame him. He, too, was an old man now. Michelle said she would track down the hospital chaplain.

In the room, we surrounded the bed, Marijo and I on Dad's right, Tim and Mike on his left. We each laid claim to a part of our father, a forearm or knee or shoulder, and placed our hands on him. Four children, eight hands. "We're all here, Daddy," Marijo said.

Peg was standing by with two syringes. "Are we ready?" she asked in that gentle, calm way of hers. We nodded, and she gave the injections. Almost instantly we could feel his limbs going slack beneath our hands. "We're going to let him relax for a few minutes," she said and looked at the clock. It was 2:50 P.M.

At just before 3:00, Peg removed the mask and flicked off the respirator. Without the rattling whir of the machine, the room went suddenly silent. It felt nearly serene. The four of us, and Peg and Michelle, too, kept our eyes fixed on the monitor that read Dad's blood oxygen levels. They were at 96 percent when the mask came off and began slipping almost immediately: 93 . . . 89 . . . 74. As Peg had promised, our father showed no sign of discomfort or anxiety. "We love you, Dad," the four of us said in unison.

The chaplain, a priest from Nigeria, arrived and in a clear, lilting voice administered the Last Rites, my father's second time receiving the sacrament in as many weeks. The priest dabbed sacred oil on my father's forehead and palms, using his thumb to smear it in the sign of a cross. "May the Lord who frees you from sin save you and raise you up," he prayed aloud. Then, with brief condolences to us, he was gone. Marijo suggested that Dad would find comfort in hearing us say a decade of the rosary: one Our Father and ten Hail Marys followed by a short prayer I grew up knowing only as the Glory Be to the Father. None of us had a rosary, and we used our fingers to count off each Hail Mary. With my sister and Michael leading the way, Tim and I this time were able to keep up without stumbling.

As we finished the prayers, I looked out the window and saw the first snowflakes dancing from the sky. The front edge of the storm pushing in from Canada had arrived.

That's when we heard the angels sing. The voices came from far down the hall, growing louder as they neared us. A group of hospital volunteers was strolling the halls of this saddest of all wings, where battles are surrendered and life meets its inevitable end, pausing at each door to sing a Christmas carol.

Outside Dad's room, they sang "Silent Night," their soothing voices surrounding us like an embrace. I liked the idea of Dad drifting off to something so peaceful. "All is calm, all is bright . . ." We thanked them; then Tim asked, "Do you know Ave Maria? Our father was very devoted to the Blessed Mother. It would mean a lot." The lead caroler apologized; they had not rehearsed it. We thanked them again and turned back to Dad. The carolers must have reconsidered because from behind us came their voices once more, as warm and burnished as polished mahogany. As the first snowstorm of the winter swirled outside, dusting the world in white, they sang the song our father loved most. It was hard not to smile, and not to cry a little, too.

As the afternoon slipped away, the life-giving oxygen in my father's bloodstream slipped away with it. The numbers on the monitor continued to fall. 64 . . . 57 . . . 45. At 40, Peg broke the silence to say, "They don't get much lower than this." His heart, however, beat steadily on, and his blood pressure remained strong. Even in unconsciousness, he continued to draw slow, even breaths. My father was defying the predictions of a quick death.

At 6 P.M., we made a group decision. Tim and Marijo would go home and tell Mom. It was something we all dreaded, but in the end she would prove herself once again the tough old bird, accepting the news stoically. I suspect she knew before any of us that her husband would not be coming home. Mike and I would stay behind and sit with Dad. Even though he was in a deep coma now, we would not risk him dying alone. For the next two hours, the two of us sat there mostly in silence, watching Dad breathe. Finally I said, "Why don't you go home and get some rest. I'll call if anything changes." I wanted to give my brother a break; he looked exhausted. But mostly I wanted to sit alone with my father for a little while longer. Mike agreed to my offer, but first I walked to the cafeteria, ordered a bowl of soup, and called Jenny to bring her and the children up to date.

After I was done eating, I returned to the room and sent Michael home. Standing beside the bed, I let my eyes travel from my father's face to the snow outside. Now that there was no turning back, I no longer felt so helpless or inconsolable, nor did death seem so terrifying. Just the opposite. If anything, it felt peaceful. Peaceful and almost . . . beautiful. As natural a part of life's rhythm as a baby's first breath or a butterfly's inaugural ascent from the cocoon. Standing there, I thought about spring's glide into summer, and summer's march to autumn, and the reliable promise of dawn in every setting sun. I thought about the old maple tree that fell in the yard and the young garden that flourished in its footprint. Mostly I thought about Dad and the exemplary life he had led—and, for all our differences, the indelible mark he had left on me.

Michelle stuck her head in the door to say she was going home for the night. "I'm going to miss your dad," she said.

"He thought the world of you," I told her, and she hugged me.

Her replacement on the night shift was a young, extraordinarily gentle man named James. He had black hair, brown skin, a white smile, and an almost beatific presence. "Is there anything I can bring you?" he asked.

"No," I said, then reconsidered. "Actually, yes. Could I borrow a pen and a pad of paper?"

"Our father was many things," I wrote as I sat on the bed beside him, my leg touching his. Then I began to list them: son, brother, husband, father, grandfather. Engineer, mathematician, war veteran, scout leader, volunteer. Stamp collector, gardener, sailor, classical music buff. Faithful Catholic. I looked up at him lying peacefully in the netherworld between life and death, and wrote, "Mostly he was a good guy. A good and sensitive and gentle man." Without intending to, I had begun to write the eulogy I would deliver at his funeral the next week.

I scribbled it all down on the pad, describing his itinerant childhood and the French teacher who helped him find his way to college and a future he had never dreamed possible. I mentioned his double deferment after Pearl Harbor and his decision to enlist anyway. I wrote how he returned from the war with four years of Sunday church collections in his pocket and how that serendipitously led him to my mother. I joked about his engineer's sense of precision and his quirky affection for chopsticks.

I told the story of Dad's Rube Goldberg invention for storing the *Mary Ann* during the winter, designing and building a series of braces and pulleys to haul it up into the rafters above where he parked his car. Just before the inaugural test of his boat-lifting invention, he looked over at me, his junior assistant and tool fetcher, and said brightly, "One decimal point off, Johnny boy, and there goes the Buick." He knew he had the decimal point right, but he wanted me to know that even small, innocent mistakes can lead to major consequences.

I wrote until I was out of things to say, then I folded the pages and pushed them into my pocket. "Well, Dad," I said, brushing my fingers through his white fringe of hair. "It's been quite an adventure." I let my fingers trace over his eyebrows and down the slope of his nose. "I'm going to miss you."

At eleven o'clock, Tim returned with Elizabeth, and I retreated to the lounge down the hall with a blanket and pillow. The next thing I knew Elizabeth was shaking me. "Come quick," she said. "Daddy's eyes open."

When I got to the room, his eyes were indeed open, but they were vacant. His heart rate was dropping and his breathing, which had been slow and steady all night, now came in short gasps separated by eternally long silences. Tim and I squeezed his arms and talked to him even though we knew he could not hear. He exhaled one final deep breath, and Tim and I both looked at the monitor. The green line made one last bump and then traveled flat across the screen. James the nurse must have been watching the same line from his station down the hall because he appeared behind us and said in the gentlest voice, "He's gone." A few minutes later, a doctor I had never seen before arrived and listened with a stethoscope. Time of death: 1:16 A.M., Thursday, December 23, 2004.

We walked out of the hospital and into an undisturbed snowscape that managed to make even grimy Pontiac— the city where my father was born and where, eighty-nine years and two weeks later, he had died—appear impossibly beautiful. Three inches of virgin snow covered everything, glistening in the streetlights. There were not even any tire tracks. Somehow it felt perfect, as if the heavens had conspired to wrap my father and all that he had touched in a shroud of purity and goodness and grace.

In Dad's Buick, I pulled out onto Woodward Avenue and led the way through the still-falling snow, Tim and Elizabeth following behind. I took it slow, peering through the beating wiper blades to follow the road beneath its unmarred white blanket. It was 3 A.M. when I slid beneath a comforter on the couch in the basement and fell into a deep and dream-filled sleep.

*

CHAPTER 36

I awoke before dawn and tiptoed into the kitchen, closing the door behind me so as not to disturb the others. I made coffee and called the airline to try to change my flight, which was scheduled to leave in a few hours. It was hard to believe that I had been so bullishly confident Dad would be fine while I skipped out for a few days. The last eighteen hours did not quite seem real, and I paused to remind myself I had not simply dreamed them. Now here I was, holding on the line, hoping to get some kind of bereavement consideration. I wanted to push the flight back one day, flying home on Christmas Eve. When the customer service agent finally came on, I explained my circumstances. "My father died five hours ago," I said. "I need to help plan his funeral today." She told me she was sorry for my loss but she couldn't rebook my flight without charging a penalty. The Christmas Eve flights were running nine hundred dollars a ticket. Supply and demand. I felt what little spirit that was left in me drain away.

Then she said: "What city are you flying out of again?"

"Detroit," I said.

"You're in luck," she told me. "That airport has declared a ground snow emergency, which means we don't expect people to make it there. I can rebook you tomorrow at the same price, no penalty."

My heart leaped, and only then did I realize how badly I missed Jenny and the kids and needed to get back to them. I looked out the window at the uninterrupted snowscape emerging in the gray light and had to smile. I did not believe in miracles, not in the literal way my parents did, but I couldn't resist the idea that my father had performed his first. I snickered at the thought that his very first order of business upon arriving at heaven's gate was to dial in a snowstorm so John could change his flight without a penalty and get home to his family for Christmas. My famously frugal father would have just hated to see a perfectly good airline ticket go to waste.

When Mom awoke, she asked, "Did Dad die?"

"Yes, Mom," I said, wrapping my arms around her. "About one-fifteen this morning."

"Oh," she said.

After breakfast, Marijo and I went into his closet and picked out a gray suit, light blue shirt, and striped tie. From the box I had made him, I pulled out his General Motors forty-year service pin with the tiny diamond and attached it to the lapel of the jacket. Marijo retrieved his grandfather's rosary, which we agreed belonged in his hands. Then with Michael we drove to the funeral home, picked out a casket that we thought fit his personality—modest but of solid hardwood—and planned the service.

Later that afternoon, we sat with Mom and paged through old photo albums for a slide show that would run at his viewing. It was therapeutic for all of us, and Mom enjoyed looking through the snapshots of their life together. I feared they might make her sad, a reminder of all that had been and was now gone, but her eyes brightened and she launched into her chestnuts. "Oh, there's Irene O'Brien. Did I tell you about the time we fell into the river?" She had, many times, but we sat and listened intently as if it were the first telling. Then we reached the photos of us as kids and teenagers, and we managed to laugh at our bad haircuts and cringe-worthy fashion statements from the sixties and seventies.

We picked out a representative selection, starting with a photo of Dad as a toddler, then as a young boy, teen, college student, navy lieutenant, bachelor, newlywed, new father, retiree. It ended with a photo of him walking Elizabeth down the aisle at Our Lady of Refuge that summer. We marveled at how handsome he looked in his twenty-fifth-anniversary GM portrait, the young executive with the pinnacle of his career still ahead of him. And at how beautiful Mom was in her early twenties with her lustrous hair parted on the side and swept back behind one ear. As we sorted through a lifetime of memories, the passage of time was palpable. My parents' chapter was all but closed now, collapsing into the dust of memory.

Dad had wanted me to spend Christmas with my own family, and the next day that is what I did, flying home to Pennsylvania in time for Christmas Eve dinner. He had been right; it was where I belonged, and it never felt so good to be back. The day after Christmas, just as the sun was peeking over the white pines, Jenny and I packed the kids, the dog, and our best clothes into the minivan and left on the same ten-hour drive Tim and I had made not quite two weeks earlier.

Six priests and a bishop concelebrated the funeral Mass, with Father Vin giving the homily, portraying Dad in saintly terms that surely would have embarrassed him. Mom sat stoically in the front row, weeping only once. Tim read two passages from the Bible, Marijo announced a list of intentions, and Michael gave a brief history of Dad's life. Then it was my turn and I stood on the altar and gave the eulogy I had written in the hospital room. As I spoke, I looked out and saw the faces from my childhood. Old neighbors and classmates and long-forgotten acquaintances. Rock was there, and Sack, and Tommy's mother, Mrs. Cullen, herself a widow of just two months. Afterward, she told me Tommy sent his best from Arizona.

There was another group at the funeral I had not known about. A group of men, most of them about my age, who belonged to a men's prayer group my father had started. Once a month they got together for prayer and fellowship. Thirty of them had shown up in matching dark suits to serve as pallbearers, and it was instantly obvious my father had meant a great deal to them. The sight of them lined up two abreast to escort my father's casket down the center aisle to the altar was moving. For me, it was also painful, for in them I saw the son he surely wished I could have been—the kind who embraced and shared his reverence and devotion. As one by one they filed past me in the receiving line, shaking my hand and telling me how much they admired my father and what a spiritual inspiration he had been to them, I could not help feeling my failings. With each of them, he enjoyed the relationship he could only dream of with me, one that did not need to be censored or sanitized or danced around. One he could embrace openly without fear of a son's squirming rejection. Long ago, he had stopped sharing that part of himself with me, and I had been grateful that he had. We had both come to realize that religion, that grand unifying force that should have been the healing, binding balm that cemented our family, was the single most painful strain on it. When I looked at these men of certitude and shared belief, I could not help seeing the adult son my father had finally, after years of struggle, conceded I would never be.

After the funeral, and the lunch hosted by the women's altar society, and the drive to Ann Arbor to lower my father's casket into the earth beside the grave of his long-departed infant daughter, Tim and I decided to fire up the snowblower. Our longtime neighbor, Les Schoonover, had shown up unannounced the morning of Dad's death to plow out the driveway, one of countless small acts of kindness that touched us as a family and made me realize the greatest comfort to the grieving comes not from words but from actions. But more snow was threatening, and from his hospital bed Dad had urged us to start up the snowblower and make sure it was ready for the coming winter.

In the garage, we checked the oil, topped off the gasoline, and set the choke. Michael would be taking over Dad's snowblowing duties now, but he was perhaps the least mechanical person on the planet, and Tim and I knew we needed to show him how to run it. When it came time to start it, we were stumped. Somewhere was an electric ignition button, but it eluded us. We searched and searched and finally paused to scratch our heads.

"Hold on," I blurted out. "Let me go ask—" I stopped short, catching myself. We stood looking at each other, our breath vaporizing in the cold air.

"Dad," Tim said, finishing the sentence for me. "That was my first thought, too. Ask Dad."

"He's really gone," I said. "It's just now sinking in."

Tim and I had both lived independently for years, but always in the back of our minds we had known our father was there if we needed him. For a loan or career advice or handyman tips or life guidance or a place to move back to if all else failed. No longer. The paternal safety net was officially and permanently cut away. It was our turn now.

"Come on," Tim said, "we can figure this out." And we eventually did, locating the button in a hiding place beneath the carburetor. The snowblower roared to life, ready for another season.

CHAPTER 37

✳

The months passed. Winter's snows surrendered to spring's trumpet call. The forsythia bloomed with exceptional vigor that year, followed by the cherry trees and azaleas and redbuds. Our backyard hens hatched out a clutch of chicks, and the wild rabbits emerged from the woods with their babies to stage nightly raids on the vegetable garden. The Canada geese again flew north in V-formation. Like I knew it would, life marched on.

Three days after my father's death, as we prepared to bury him, a human tragedy of unimaginable proportions struck halfway around the world. A tsunami off the coast of Sumatra sent a giant wall of water cascading across the Indian Ocean at the speed of a jet plane, claiming an estimated 150,000 lives and displacing millions. And yet my siblings and I barely registered it at the time. Enmeshed in our own grief and personal loss, we somehow did not even notice this indiscriminate extinction of human life. Now, months later, it offered a valuable contrast to our own experience. People die every minute of every day; sometimes they die in vast numbers without warning, sometimes in horrific and terrifying ways, sometimes decades before their time. My father had lived a long and healthy life. He had remained vital and physically strong until the final few months, and mentally sharp until the end. As deaths go, his was a gentle and peaceful one, surrounded by his children. He had had time to put his affairs in order without too much time to linger, and he left this world believing it was just the warm-up act, that the true journey, the real reward, still awaited him. Not such a bad way to exit a full and worthy life.

In the months following my father's death, a new friend came unexpectedly onto my horizon. His name was Michael Murray, and he was a regular reader of my newspaper column who one day took the time to send an e-mail commenting on one of my pieces. His words reflected an intelligence and sensitivity I admired. I wrote back, and soon we were corresponding. I liked him right away. He was smart and thoughtful; funny and self-deprecating; direct and plainspoken. Only gradually did I figure out that my new e-mail pal was a Roman Catholic priest. He did not hide his religious faith, but he did not wear it on his sleeve, either. He insisted I skip the "Father" business and just call him Michael. I was so comfortable being candid with him that sometimes I had to remind myself I was talking with a clergyman.

He was a fan of what I did for a living, of using words to reach out to the larger community. As he put it in one e-mail, "Just remember: Jesus's favorite and most frequent way of teaching was telling stories. Is it any surprise that as things have come and gone with the passage of time, storytelling remains? It is part and parcel of what makes us human—and puts us in touch with our humanity." He called writing my "ministry" and added, "In your own way, John, you are doing God's work."

One day in May we met at a pub near my office for bratwursts and beer. Michael was my age, broad-shouldered and bearded, a guy's guy who looked more likely to be running a lumber mill than a retreat center. His father had died six years earlier, and his mother now lived alone on the family homestead. He was trying to balance his vocation with his care for her. Trying to be a good son but feeling guilty that his best was not quite enough. We had a lot to talk about.

As I drove home afterward, I had to laugh. Was Dad meddling again? It seemed oddly coincidental that this likeable, nonjudgmental, wise priest had just happened to pop into my life. I enjoyed the image of Dad somewhere in a cloud-ensconced heaven, white robes flowing just like in the cartoons, hard at work to find the perfect moral adviser to parachute into my life. I could almost hear him ruminating: "That John's a piece of work. Whoever I send can't be too conservative; can't be preachy; can't be overly dogmatic or holier than thou; can't come on too strong. Has to be a regular kind of guy. Someone who can curse a little and enjoy beer. Should be about his age, too. Hmmm, let's see. Ah, what do we have here? Father Michael Murray at the Oblates of Saint Francis de Sales down in Wilmington. A little liberal for my taste, but John would like that. This looks like a good fit." I found something comforting in the fantasy of my father busy at the switch, minding the details, like the Wizard of Oz furiously working the levers behind the giant curtain.

*   *   *

Summer turned to fall and fall to winter. As Christmas neared, I brought home a tree and strung lights. But mostly I thought about how to mark the first anniversary of my father's death. I couldn't visit his grave; it was three states away. I couldn't get together with my siblings or my mother; we were scattered across an even wider swath of geography. I didn't want to drag Jenny and the kids through some kind of schmaltzy family ceremony. Maybe I would just take a hike in the woods, like I did so often with him as a kid.

On December 22, I wrote Father Michael a brief e-mail: "Tomorrow's the anniversary of my dad's death. I'd appreciate you keeping him in your prayers." Over his lifetime, Dad had spent a fortune making prayer offerings for others; I knew if anyone would appreciate having a priest say a prayer for him, it was Dad. A few minutes later came Michael's response: "I'll do your dad one better. I'll say Mass for him. And for you. Merry Christmas, John." Why this meant so much to me I still do not know. I had spent a lifetime avoiding Mass, ridiculing it, daydreaming through it, trying to get out of it at every turn. Yet Michael's gesture touched me deeply. In my reply, I thanked him and added this postscript: "Who knows, this prodigal son just might get up a little early tomorrow and stop by a church on the way to work."

The next morning I did exactly that. Saint Joseph's Catholic Church was just down the hill from my house, but in five years I had never once walked through its doors. I arrived as the nuns were shepherding in scores of exuberant students from the parish elementary school, positioning them in the pews with a full arm's length between each child to discourage horseplay. It was the last day of school before their Christmas break, and the kids bubbled with excitement. The girls wore blue plaid jumpers with knee socks and the boys dress shirts with navy ties and slacks, just as we had back at Our Lady of Refuge. Some things did not change. The altar was decorated with a life-size crèche scene and scores of potted poinsettias, another throwback to my past, and the altar servers wore the same ill-fitting, wax-spattered cassocks. I slipped into the empty back row, not quite sure why I had come or whether I would stay. Out of habit, I knelt and crossed myself. As kids, we were taught to say a silent prayer as we waited for the Mass to start, but no prayers came to me, and I spent the time watching the children fidgeting in the pews, thinking it was an experience my own children had never known.

The organist launched into a hymn, signaling us that the priest and altar servers—boys *and* girls now—had begun their way up the center aisle. Father was a tall, graying man with a folksy manner. He was good with the kids, and geared the liturgy to them. During his sermon, he walked up and down the aisle, talking to them about the true meaning of Christmas and coaxing them into a dialogue. During the Offertory, a boy and girl nervously carried the vessels of wine and communion wafers down the aisle, and I remembered the thrill of being picked for that special task—the excitement tinged with terror over the imminent possibility of stumbling and sending the sacraments flying.

After the priest consecrated the hosts and wine, it was time for the kiss of peace, that part of the Mass where congregants are encouraged to turn to those around them and offer a greeting. I had always dreaded the stilted handshakes and forced pleasantries with strangers, and I was grateful that I was sitting alone in the last row. I watched as the children exchanged gleeful greetings, their one opportunity to bridge the dead zones between them and touch. Three pews in front of me, a freckle-faced girl about nine greeted the children on either side of her. Then she turned around and smiled at me. I nodded at her, and she knelt on the seat and stretched far over the back of the pew, so far I thought she might tumble into the empty row behind her. She extended her arm out to me. It took me a second to realize she wanted to shake my hand. I reached forward over the empty pew in front of me and met her halfway, letting her hand slip into mine. "Peace of the Lord be with you," I mumbled woodenly, the words that had been drilled into me decades earlier.

"Merry Christmas, mister," the little girl said. And her face and voice and bright eyes were filled with such innocence, such beauty and wonderment and unbridled joy, I could not help but feel a rush of holiday warmth. For just a moment I wanted to scoop her up and hug her.

"Merry Christmas," I said.

The children filed to the altar for Holy Communion, and when it was my turn I filed up behind them. Except for the wafer I had accepted at my father's funeral Mass, it was the first time I had received the sacrament in many, many years. I knew I was no doubt violating some ironclad Church rule—I had not been to confession in decades—but I didn't care. It was the anniversary of my father's death and something I wanted to do, for reasons I could not quite pinpoint. As I made my way back to the pew, the organist began "Silent Night," and all the children sang along in their squeaky sweet voices. I flashed back to my father's deathbed and the hospital carolers who had gathered in the doorway. In my pew, I knelt and rested my face in my cupped hands. I closed my eyes and let the music carry me to a serene and safe place.

"Hey, Dad," I whispered. "Bet you didn't think you'd find me here, huh?" It had been a year; there was much to catch him up on. I told him about the kids and how fast they were growing up. "You should hear Patrick on the trumpet," I said. "He's really getting the hang of it. And Conor's quite the little writer now. The teacher asks for ten sentences; he turns in ten pages. You wouldn't even recognize Colleen; she's a foot taller than when you saw her last and reading chapter books now."

I told him about my own book, the one he had known about but never gotten the chance to read. "It's on the bestseller list, Dad, and each week it moves a little higher. I know how proud you'd be." I told him how Mom was doing and how Michael was getting along alone at the house. "You're not going to believe this, but he's mastered both the lawn mower *and* the snowblower." I assured him the Buick was still going strong, and we'd gotten the gutters cleaned out before the first freeze. I told him how much everyone missed him. "I can't believe a whole year has gone by," I said.

From somewhere far outside our private conversation I heard the priest's voice boom out: "The Mass is over. Now go in peace to love and serve the Lord." Then everyone was singing "Joy to the World," and I could hear the squealing, happy children filing out past me. That's when I realized I was crying. I was not sure for how long or why. Maybe it was the children's sweet angel voices or the season's celebration of birth and how for me it would now always be tinged with loss as well. Maybe it was the girl who offered me her hand, and with it a reminder of all life's promises and broken dreams. I had fought back tears at the hospital a year earlier and again at the funeral, but nothing like this. I was a mess, a snot-nosed, blubbering mess. I kept my head down and let the tears soak my sweater sleeve. "For Christ's sake, John," I whispered. "You're acting like Mom." Now I could see more clearly why she cried her eyes out each time she received the Eucharist. Part of it, no doubt, was her belief that she quite literally was taking Christ's body into her own, but maybe another part was that it helped her feel closer to those she had loved and lost. Maybe it was her portal into a place where she could commune with her parents and lost siblings and the infant daughter she would never hold. I thought of the lay definition of communion: the sharing or exchanging of intimate thoughts and feelings, especially on a mental or spiritual level. Maybe that was what all her tears were about.

When I looked up, the church was empty and silent again. I wiped my face on my sleeve and told Dad to take it easy and not worry too much about the rest of us left behind. "We're going to be okay, Dad," I said, and I knew we would. I knew I would. It was my life, for better or worse. He had laid the groundwork; the rest was up to me. The only expectations I had to meet now were my own.

I walked out into the wan December sunlight, the cold morning air a welcome slap to my face. Rummaging through my pockets, I found a tissue and gave my nose a good blow. Then I started the car and drove off to begin a new day.

Epilogue

❋

At the front desk I signed in, then made my way down the polished linoleum floors to the last door on the right. To the corner suite we had briefly, hopefully, considered the place where my mother and father could live out their days together, and where Mom now stayed alone. Peering in the door, I spotted her cane against the couch, but her wheelchair was gone and so was she.

At the nurses' station, I said, "I'm Ruth Grogan's son. Is she around?" It was a ridiculous question. This was a nursing home. Of course she was around. All the patients were always around.

"Ruth's at Mass right now," the nurse said and pointed toward the chapel.

I walked down the hall past a row of wizened women lined up along one wall in their wheelchairs. A few looked up at me; most stared at the floor. One called out, "Take me with you."

At the chapel entrance, I peered through the glass doors to see an ancient priest, himself a resident, saying Mass before a handful of nuns and about three dozen women in wheelchairs. From behind, the residents all looked alike—crowns of fine white hair bowed between slumped shoulders. At first I thought their heads were lowered in prayer but quickly realized every one of them was sound asleep. Among them, I spotted Mom, a sweater over her shoulders, her chin resting on her chest, eyes closed.

"Wake up, Ruthie," I whispered, sidling up beside her and kissing her on top of the head. "It's your number three son."

Her eyes opened and she smiled up at me with wonderment as if she were seeing me for the first time, even though I had visited the previous evening with Jenny and the children. After a few seconds, a glimmer of recognition spread across her face. "Oh, hi, John," she whispered.

I sank down on one knee and rubbed her shoulders, looking up at Father as he soldiered through the profession of faith for the sleeping residents. When I looked back, Mom's eyes were closed again, too. At communion, the priest walked down the rows of wheelchairs, waking each resident long enough to press a wheat wafer on her tongue. Mom opened her mouth without opening her eyes and murmered, "Amen." The instant the host was inside her, she pressed a fist to her heart and began moving her lips in silent prayer, even though she still appeared asleep. Some things were not easily lost.

After Mass, I wheeled her into the courtyard, where she tilted her head toward the sun and smiled. Deep furrows crossed her face now, and her hair was as snowy as an egret, but it was a child's face basking in the warmth, lost in innocence. She began to hum and then sing, her fingers dancing on an imaginary keyboard. It was a song I had never heard before, a children's ditty about a brash child swallowed by an alligator she thought she could tame. Mom had no idea what she had eaten for breakfast that morning or why I had miraculously materialized beside her at Mass, but she reeled effortlessly through the stanzas, not missing a beat.

"Where did you learn that?" I asked.

"Girl Scouts," she said.

"Girl Scouts?" I exclaimed with a laugh. "That was eighty years ago! It's about time you got around to singing it to me."

That was all the invitation she needed to sing it all over again.

I wheeled her back to her room and positioned her in front of the window where she could look out on the lawn and gardens. "I'll be back this evening with Jenny and the kids," I told her. "We're here all week."

"I'll count on it, dear," she said, but I knew better.

"Love you, Mom," I said, pressing my lips to her temple.

"Love you, too, sweetheart," Mom said. Then she added something I was not expecting.

"Once they leave home, that's it," she said. "They come back to visit, but it's never the same."

I wanted to protest, but she was right. It never is. It never was.

Outside on the sidewalk, I glanced back through the window where I had left her. She was gazing up at something far away as if her eyes had locked on an airplane or flock of geese in the distant sky. I waved and caught her eye, and she flashed me the same startled look of pleasant surprise she had given me in the chapel.

"Aw, Mom," I whispered.

She blew me a kiss, and I blew her one, too.

Acknowledgments

�֍

Writing is a solitary act, and yet a book like this one cannot happen without the help and support of many people.

I would like to start by thanking my literary agent, Laurie Abkemeier, for the indispensable role she played in developing this story from a seed of an idea to a finished manuscript. She served as my sounding board, brainstorming partner, cheerleader, therapist, and first line reader and editor, and her suggestions proved invaluable. I owe a big debt of gratitude to my entire publishing team at William Morrow for believing in this book and making it a reality, including Michael Morrison, Lisa Gallagher, Lynn Grady, Seale Ballenger, Michael Brennan, Jennifer Schulkind, Ben Bruton, and especially my editor, Mauro DiPreta.

I want to thank Anna Quindlen, Doris Kearns Goodwin, Brian DeFiore, Jim Tolpin, Dan Sullivan, JoAnn Burke, Susan and Peter Brown, and Sara and Dave Pandl for their listening ears, encouraging words, and wise counsel. Ray Albertson took a dilapidated shack and turned it into a beautiful writing studio for me that exceeded my wildest dreams. Nice work, Ray! Thanks also are due to Lehigh University in Bethlehem, Pennsylvania, in whose elegant

Linderman Library I wrote much of this book while my studio was under construction.

My siblings, Marijo Grogan, Timothy Grogan, and Michael Grogan, trusted me to tell this story accurately, honestly, and sensitively, even while recognizing that each of us sees our shared past through a unique prism; I appreciate the faith they put in me. My siblings also helped me reconstruct many of the scenes in this book, sharing their own insights and memories, and Michael dedicated hours to helping me find and catalog a half century of family photographs, movies, memorabilia, and documents. My mother, Ruth Marie Howard Grogan, even in advanced age, continues to inspire me with her wit, spirit, and boundless sense of humor, and her lifelong gift of storytelling is reflected in these pages. My late father, Richard, remains a strong presence in my life, guiding me by his past example, and I often find myself asking the W.W.D.D. question—what would Dad do? My eternal debt of gratitude to both my parents for a happy childhood, and for a love so deep and unconditional it defines the word.

Finally, a big affectionate thank-you to my loving wife, Jenny, and children, Patrick, Conor, and Colleen, for once again allowing me to mine our family experience and their lives for my inspiration. Thank you for your support and understanding and for always being there for me at the start and end of each day. This book is about family, and I am so grateful for mine. I love each of you beyond words.